CQ's Politics in America 2004

THE 108TH CONGRESS

By Congressional Quarterly's Staff
David Hawkings and Brian Nutting, Editors

★

Congressional Profiles

Contact Information

District Data

Key Votes

★

CQ

Robert W. Merry, President and Publisher
David Rapp, Editor and Senior Vice President
Keith A. White, General Manager and Senior Vice President
John A. Jenkins, General Manager and Senior Vice President, CQ Press

Published by Congressional Quarterly Inc.
Andrew Barnes, Chairman
Andrew P. Corty, Vice Chairman
Nelson Poynter (1903–1978), Founder

CQ Press
1255 22nd Street, N.W., Suite 400
Washington, D.C. 20037
202-729-1900; toll-free, 1-866-4CQ-PRESS (1-866-427-7737)
www.cqpress.com

The paper used in this publication exceeds the requirements of the American National Standard for Information Sciences–Permanence of Paper for Printed Library Materials, ANSI Z39.48-1992.

Printed and bound in the United States of America

07 06 05 04 03 5 4 3 2 1

ISBN 1-56802-813-X (cloth) ISBN 1-56802-814-8 (paper)

ISSN 1064-6809

The Library of Congress catalogued an earlier edition of this title as follows:

Congressional Quarterly's Politics in America: 1994, the 103rd Congress / by CQ's political staff: Phil Duncan, Editor

p. cm.

Includes index.

1. United States. Congress — Biography. 2. United States. Congress — Committees. 3. United States. Congress — Election districts — Handbooks, manuals, etc. I. Duncan, Phil. II. Congressional Quarterly Inc. III. Title: Politics in America.
JK1010.C67 1993 328.73'073'45'0202

Politics in America 2004

THE 108TH CONGRESS

Politics in America

THE 12TH EDITION

There are a million stories in the U.S. Congress, Washington's peculiar version of the Naked City. There are those "stories of a lifetime," political sea changes that mark the beginning of one era of American politics and the end of another. Since the first version of this book was published in 1981, we have lived through the Reagan revolution, the end of the Cold War, the Persian Gulf War, the Republican takeover of the House, the impeachment of President Clinton, the disputed 2000 presidential election, the terrorist attacks of Sept. 11, 2001, and a second war against Iraq.

Then there are those individual stories — smaller in scope and national impact, perhaps, but often just as significant to the lives and fortunes of the American polity. These are the stories that form the sum and substance of the 12th edition of this biennial series, "Politics in America," a compendium of profiles of the 535 members and five delegates who make up the 108th Congress, which convened on Jan. 7, 2003.

The men and women who now occupy seats in the Senate and the House of Representatives developed their perspectives, their partisan ideologies and their very careers in the shadow of the momentous events of the past quarter-century. They have responded to those events in similar and dissimilar ways. The object of this book is to examine each elected representative in the context of his or her own experience — be it personal, communal or driven by political expedience.

At Congressional Quarterly, which has been reporting on Congress since the end of World War II, we have long known that each member, from the most famous to the most obscure, has an interesting story to tell. We have organized this reference work so that each "chapter" — a profile of the lawmaker and the district or state that sent that person to Washington — is given comparable length and weight. We have sought to make every member understood as a political actor, a public policymaker and a personality.

Moreover, our approach is to evaluate each member by his or her own standards. We do not try to decide where a politician ought to stand on a controversial issue; our interest has been to assess how they go about expressing their views and how effective they are at achieving their self-proclaimed goals.

The journalistic rationale for this approach remains true to the nature of politics. Who these members are, as human beings and as political operators, changes much more slowly than the provisions of their latest legislative initiatives. And where they stand — both philosophically and in the context of the battle for political control — changes much more slowly than the latest pitch and yaw of current events.

The CQ staff of reporters, editors and researchers follows both the events and players on Capitol Hill on a weekly, daily and even hourly basis. Their coverage appears in print and online in the CQ Weekly, a news magazine widely regarded as the "bible" of Congress; CQ Today, a legislative news-daily covering all important action on Capitol Hill; and CQ.com, the online legislative tracking service that combines stories, votes, bills and exhaustive archives along with Web-powered searching capability.

The CQ staff, widely recognized on Capitol Hill as the resident experts on Congress and its members, are the authors of this book. Under the direction of editors David Hawkings and Brian Nutting, and managing editor H. Amy Stern, who bring more than 50 years of experience to the enterprise, they provide the most authoritative, insightful and objective view into this Naked City as can be found anywhere.

David Rapp
Editor and Senior Vice President
Congressional Quarterly Inc.

Congress' Unique Composition

The political interplay along Pennsylvania Avenue should prove particularly complex and intense.

As the 108th Congress starts finding its rhythm this spring, American troops are in Baghdad, their military campaign concluded but the shape of the postwar occupation and reconstruction effort not yet defined. A stagnant economy, a deepening federal budget deficit, and the long-term costs of the Iraq war and its aftermath cast doubt on the future of federal fiscal policy. So, as in the past, uncertainty is a constant while lawmakers — individually and collectively — chart their course toward the next election in 2004.

The personality of this Congress and the motivations for each member's behavior will be shaped as much by national and international events as by the political and institutional dynamics of the House and Senate. These forces — both external and intramural — are always in flux, guaranteeing that the heady mix of political and personal intrigue, ambition, talent and venality in the Capitol never stops bubbling.

Four years ago, U.S. involvement in Kosovo loomed as a potentially all-consuming issue that would shape the congressional agenda. That proved not to be the case, as the Serbian regime collapsed, and the 106th Congress devolved into a place of grudging compromise and unfinished business.

Two years ago, Washington began the year debating how to apportion a budget in surplus with both the executive and legislative branches of government barely under unified Republican control for the first time since 1954. But the core dynamics of the 107th Congress started changing soon thereafter. Vermont's disaffected James M. Jeffords quit the GOP and delivered Senate control to the Democrats; the terrorist attacks of Sept. 11, 2001, transformed the legislative agenda; the surplus disappeared — and lawmakers were compelled to set up offices on the sidewalk or in makeshift quarters when the Capitol and their offices were evacuated after an anthrax attack.

And just before the 108th began, the sudden fall of Sen. Trent Lott illustrated anew the unpredictable nature of congressional fates, individual as well as institutional. At lunchtime on Dec. 5, 2002, the Mississippian was the unchallenged leader of the Senate Republicans, as he had been for 6½ years, and he was a month away from reclaiming the majority leader's mantle. By the end of that snowy afternoon, his off-the-cuff endorsement of Strom Thurmond's segregationist 1948 presidential campaign had sealed his fate — he just did not know it for another two weeks. In those intervening days, the agendas of the Republican Party and President Bush also were modified to include revisiting the party's approach to civil rights.

As at the start of the 107th Congress in 2001, the White House and the Capitol are entirely under Republican control, although this time there appears to be no doubt that the party will hold on to that combined power at least until the 2004 election. Still, with at least six incumbent members of Congress seeking the Democratic nomination to oppose Bush's presumed bid for re-election, the political interplay along Pennsylvania Avenue should prove particularly complex and intense.

The margins of control in Congress remain narrow by historical standards: 51 Republicans, 48 Democrats and an independent in the Senate; 229 Republicans, 205 Democrats and an independent in the House. That means GOP leaders have just one more vote at their nominal disposal than they need to form a party-line majority in the Senate. When the GOP musters its troops in the House, it has only 11 members more than it needs to guarantee a majority. One consequence is that there will be occasions in the 108th Congress where all members, not only the leaders and committee

Members' Occupations

108th Congress

	House			Senate			Congress
	Democrat	Republican	Total	Democrat	Republican	Total	Total
Actor/Entertainer		2	2				2
Aeronautics		2	2				2
Agriculture	8	17	25		5	5	30
Artistic/Creative		1	2*				2*
Business	55	107	162	10	17	27	189
Clergy	1	1	2				2
Education	50	39	90*	7	6	13	103*
Engineering	1	5	6		1	1	7
Health Care	4	2	6				6
Homemaker/Domestic	2	2	4				4
Journalism	4	8	13*	1	6	7	20*
Labor/Blue Collar	5	2	7	1	2	3	10
Law	86	75	161	28	30	59†	220†
Law Enforcement	6	3	9		1	1	10
Medicine/Doctor	4	10	14		3	3	17
Military		4	4		1	1	5
Professional Sports	1	1	2		1	1	3
Public Service/Politics	85	70	155	18	14	32	187
Real Estate	3	31	34	2	1	3	37
Science	2	3	5				5
Secretarial/Clerical		2	2				2
Technical/Skilled Labor	1	2	3				3
Miscellaneous	1	3	4				4

* Total includes Independent Bernard Sanders of Vermont; † Total includes Independent James M. Jeffords of Vermont.
Note: Some members have had more than one occupation.

Members' Religious Affiliations

108th Congress

	House			Senate			Congress
	Democrat	Republican	Total	Democrat	Republican	Total	Total
African Methodist Episcopal	4		4				4
Baptist	32	33	65	1	5	6	71
Christian Church	3		3				3
Christian Reformed Church		2	2				2
Christian Scientist		5	5				5
Disciples of Christ	1		1				1
Eastern Orthodox		5	5	1	1	2	7
Episcopalian	10	24	34	3	7	10	44
Jewish	24	1	26*	9	2	11	37*
Lutheran	9	10	19	3	1	4	23
Methodist	16	33	49	7	5	12	61
Mormon	3	9	12	1	4	5	17
Pentecostal		4	4				4
Presbyterian	11	26	37	3	10	13	50
Protestant — Unspecified	12	22	34	2	2	4	38
Roman Catholic	71	53	124	14	11	25	149
Seventh-day Adventist	1	1	2				2
Unitarian	1	1	2	1		1	3
United Church of Christ/ Congregationalist		2	2	3	2	6†	8†
Unspecified, other	7		7		1	1	8

* Total includes Independent Bernard Sanders of Vermont; † Total includes Independent James M. Jeffords of Vermont.

chairmen, will have opportunities to be at the center of issues of import to their colleagues and the country. That is what makes it worthwhile to understand each lawmaker.

The fact is, they have many ways to go about doing the work of Congress. Some members aspire more than anything to shape and influence legislation on the great issues of the day. After his first two years as chairman of the House Ways and Means Committee, Bill Thomas has become universally acknowledged as an expert on the broad array of health care policies as well as on nuances of the complex tax code. He is nobody's lackey.

Some members believe, above all else, that they must adhere to certain core principles, and that compromise on those matters is unthinkable. Rep. Barbara Lee has earned a footnote in history as the only lawmaker to vote against authorizing a military response to the attacks of Sept. 11. Others say pragmatism must rule in such a diverse legislative body: John B. Breaux has made himself indispensible, on both sides of the aisle in the Senate, as a consummate dealmaker.

Many of the "true believers" of the legendary GOP Class of 1994 now say years of hard experience have made them much more amenable to compromise. Roger Wicker, the president of that class in its freshman term, is now a happy laborer on the House Appropriations Committee, where collegial accommodation is the coin of the realm. But others of that famously combative class, such as John Shadegg, maintain that too much concession of core conservative principles led to the steady shrinking of the GOP margin of control that continued until the 2002 election.

Some lawmakers, particularly those whose ideology is far from that of the congressional majority in Congress, have concluded that they stand little chance of influencing legislation, so they take to the airwaves to trumpet their message. Liberal Democrat Peter A. DeFazio is much better known to viewers of the House on C-SPAN than to the organizers of legislative conference committees. (Then again, being an accomplished rhetorical warrior can pay dividends over the long term: That approach propelled a back-bencher by the name of Newt Gingrich into the leadership of the 1994 Republican takeover of Congress.)

Still others emphasize constituent service — from finding lost federal benefits checks to winning big-ticket parochial earmarks in spending bills — to such an extent that their constituents don't care a bit that their representative seldom introduces a bill or speaks on the floor. The paltry name recognition in Washington for Democrat Robert A. Brady or Republican Pat Tiberi does not reflect the depth of those House members' involvements in the workings of Philadelphia and Columbus, Ohio.

And there is the age-old argument about whether lawmakers should be expected to represent the majority view of their constituents on every matter, or whether they have been entrusted by the voters to exercise their best judgment: Is a member who gauges hometown opinion before casting a vote a true representative of constituents' views, or a political chameleon?

Finally, in an era where congressional leaders are roundly criticized for their inability to lead, surely there is something to be said for lawmakers who see their role as loyal follower. If nothing else, they can use their accrued political capital to occasionally benefit their constituents.

WHERE THEY STAND

So in each of this book's profiles we have attempted to identify where members stand in the institution — and not only in which of the above-mentioned congressional niches they may fit. Our aim is to signal as well each lawmaker's place on the ideological spectrum, how each voted on the key

About the Editors

David Hawkings, the senior editor for legislative affairs at Congressional Quarterly, directs the company's coverage of the political and legislative workings of the congressional leadership. He was previously the CQ Weekly's economic policy editor, where he directed coverage of taxes, appropriations, the budget and trade. For two years before that he was managing editor of the CQ Daily Monitor, the forerunner of CQ Today. A native of New York and a graduate of Bucknell University, before coming to CQ in 1995 he was a Washington correspondent for Thomson Newspapers and a reporter, columnist and editor at The San Antonio Light. He lives in Washington with his wife, Betsy, and their sons, Harry and Charlie.

Brian Nutting came to Congressional Quarterly in 1982, joining the staff of the CQ Weekly magazine. He moved to the CQ Daily Monitor in 1984 as a reporter and later became managing editor. He began working on Politics in America in 1997. Born in Greeley, Colo., he earned bachelor's and master's degrees from the University of Utah. He worked for the Salt Lake Tribune for 11 years before joining CQ. He lives in Rockville, Md. He and his wife Suzanne have two daughters, Meredith and Christina.

issues of the day, and also where each of them is positioned on Capitol Hill: how a committee assignment, a personality trait or a work philosophy makes the lawmaker a player or a force to be reckoned with.

The shorthanded label of a member's home state and political party — Katherine Harris, *R-Fla.* — provides only initial clues about political philosophy and legislative priorities. It signals nothing close to the whole story: There are Florida Republicans who trend further to the left than some Florida Democrats. And a lawmaker from the Gulf Coast retirement centers has many different priorities than a member from Miami. In the back of this book are membership rosters for influential ideological caucuses. There are also lists of those lawmakers who backed their party, and the president, most often and least often in the 107th Congress.

Education, career and public service background, hobbies, personal friendships and countless experiences also shape each lawmaker's public persona. To know that Rep. Pete Sessions is the father of a child with Down syndrome helps explain why he breaks from his solid GOP conservatism and reaches across the aisle to work on such issues as education and health care for disadvantaged and special-needs children. The fact that Sen. Orrin G. Hatch is an accomplished songwriter helps explain his views in the Judiciary Committee on intellectual property rights issues. That Rep. Kevin Brady's father was murdered in a South Dakota courtroom helps explain why he breaks from many Texans to oppose legislation that permits carrying concealed weapons.

It is also true that each senator and House member is a datapoint in a fascinating demographic portrait of our federal legislature, which the Framers of the late 18th century assumed would reflect the nation as a whole. And the 108th Congress fulfills this prediction. The children of the post-World War II generation have taken the reins of leadership more clearly than ever before, and for the first time they compose a majority of the membership of Congress. These Baby Boomers, defined by demographers as those born between the start of 1946 and the end of 1964, hold 54 percent of all the seats — 246 in the House, 41 in the Senate.

The gain in influence of the postwar generation has been fastest in the Senate. A decade ago, there were only eight such senators; in 2003, both the majority leader and minority leader of the Senate were Boomers. But only in the House has the arrival of the *next* generation begun. As the 108th began, there were 18 members (4 percent of the total) born in Generation X, meaning since 1965.

The number of lawyers continues its decline: 41 percent of the membership in 2003, down from 58 percent in 1969. So, too, does the number of military veterans: 29 percent of the membership in 2003, down from 73 percent between 1969 and 1974. But the number of lawmakers with prior experience in a state legislature has grown steadily — to 51 percent in the 108th, up from 32 percent a decade before.

The continued growth in the ranks of younger lawmakers means, of course, that the older generation is steadily departing, suggesting that the notion of a static, "permanent Congress" is readily refutable. It is true that, by the end of the 108th Congress, 11 lawmakers will have spent more than half their lives at work in the Capitol, and that four of the top 10 longest-serving senators in history are currently in office. But it is also true that only 40 percent of House Republicans served in the minority in Congress (before 1995), and only 47 percent of House Democrats have enough tenure to recall their party running the show.

David Hawkings and Brian Nutting
April 2003

Table of Contents

FLORIDA

GEORGIA

HAWAII

IDAHO

ILLINOIS

INDIANA

IOWA

KANSAS

NEBRASKA

NEVADA

NEW HAMPSHIRE

NEW JERSEY

NEW MEXICO

NEW YORK

NORTH CAROLINA

NORTH DAKOTA

OHIO

Explanation of Statistics

State Profiles

State profile pages contains information on governors, compositions of state legislatures and information about major cities. Information on state legislatures reflects their status as of April 2003. Details about the makeup of the state legislatures, salaries of members, the legislative schedule, registered voters and state term limits were obtained from state officials.

POPULATION AND URBAN STATISTICS

Demographic information for each state and congressional district was obtained from the Census Bureau and the Bureau of Economic Analysis, both within the Department of Commerce.

Violent crime rates are from 2000. The poverty rate is from 1999. The numbers of federal workers and military personnel are from 2001.

DISTRICT STATISTICS

The tables include the popular vote for the major candidates for president in 2000 in each congressional district. The totals have been calculated to reflect the results within the House district lines in effect for the 2002 election (for the 108th Congress) — as redrawn in most states subsequent to the 2000 election to reflect results of the 2000 census. Gregory L. Giroux of Congressional Quarterly calculated the election results for 16 states. Figures generated by state legislatures or election officials as part of the redistricting process are used for 12 states. Calculations by the National Committee for an Effective Congress, a public interest group based in Washington, D.C., were used for 14 states. (Maine did not redistrict before the 2002 election; the remaining seven states have only one House seat.)

In most cases, the votes for George W. Bush, Al Gore and Ralph Nader are given. In some cases, however, the district-by-district breakdown for votes received by Nader is not available. In some instances, only the vote for Bush and Gore is available; in other cases, all third-party candidates are tallied together under the Nader listing.

The figures for racial composition, Hispanic origin, median household income, types of employment, age, education, urban vs. rural residence and size of each congressional district are from the Census Bureau. The racial composition figures reflect census respondents who described themselves as of one race. The white population figure is for non-Hispanic whites. The median household income figure is for 1999. The occupational breakdown combines figures from the Census Bureau's management, professional and relations occupations category and its sales and office occupations category to comprise the white-collar category we have presented. The blue-collar category includes three Census Bureau categories: farming, fishing and forestry; construction, extraction and maintenance; and production, transportation and material moving occupations. The college education table shows the percentage of people, age 25 and older, who have completed at least a bachelor's degree. The district's area is presented in square miles of land area.

Presidential Vote by District

CQ used three sources to determine the 2000 presidential vote in each House district:

Congressional Quarterly: Alabama, Arkansas, Connecticut, Hawaii, Iowa, Kansas, Kentucky, Louisiana, Maryland, Massachusetts, Mississippi, Nebraska, New Hampshire, Tennessee, Virginia, West Virginia

National Committee for an Effective Congress: Arizona, Idaho, Illinois, Missouri, New Jersey, New Mexico, New York, North Carolina, Oregon, Oklahoma, Rhode Island, South Carolina, Utah, Washington

State legislatures or state election officials: California, Colorado, Florida, Georgia, Indiana, Michigan, Minnesota, Nevada, Ohio, Pennsylvania, Texas, Wisconsin

Maine did not begin redrawing its House district lines until spring 2003. The other seven states have only one House seat: Alaska, Delaware, Montana, North Dakota, South Dakota, Vermont and Wyoming.

Member Profiles

Committees

Standing and select committee assignments as of April 2003 are listed for Senate and House members, as are assignments to major joint committees. Full committee and subcommittee chairmanships are noted.

A complete roster of committee and subcommittee assignments is in the back of the book.

Key to Party Abbreviations

21ST	21st Century
AC	American Constitution
AF	America First
AFE	Anti Federalist
AKI	Alaskan Independence
AMH	American Heritage
AMI	American Independent
C	Conservative
CA	Constitutional American
CC	Concerned Citizens
CFC	Conscience for Congress
CITFIRST	Citizens First
CMO	Cool Moose
CNSTP	Constitution
CONSTL	Constitutional
COPP	Concerns of People
D	Democratic
DCSTATE	D.C. Statehood
EF	Earth Federation
FDM	Freedom
FE	Free Energy
GI	Green Independent
GR	Grassroots
GREEN	Green
HHD	Honesty, Humanity, Duty
HUM	Human Rights
I	Independent
IA	Independent American
ICM	Independent Citizens Movement
INDC	Independence
IP	Independent Party
L	Liberal
LAWR	LaRouche Was Right
LIBERT	Libertarian
LMN	Legal Marijuana Now
LMP	Legalize Marijuana
LTI	Lower Tax Independent
LU	Liberty Union
MML	Make Marijuana Legal
MNTAX	Minnesota Taxpayers
MOD	Republican Moderate
MOUNT	Mountain
MRF	Marijuana Reform
NEB	Nebraska
NJC	New Jersey Conservative

continued on next page

Career and Political Highlights

The member's principal occupations before becoming a full-time public official are given, with the most recent occupation listed first. Often, the political offices listed were part-time jobs and the member continued working at his or her "career" job. Where available, the member's college major is given. Political highlights listed include elected positions in government, high party posts, posts requiring legislative confirmation and unsuccessful candidacies for public office. Dates given cover years of service, not election dates.

Elections

General-election returns for 2000 and 2002 are listed for House members, with primary results for 2002 as well. For senators and governors, their most recent election results are listed in detail. Returns do not include candidates who received less than 1 percent of the vote. Because percentages have been rounded and some minor candidates have been excluded, election results do not always add up to 100 percent.

Earlier election victories are noted for members of the House and Senate, with the member's percentage of the vote given. If no percentage is given for a year, the member either did not run or lost the election.

For special elections and primaries where a candidate would have won outright if he or she had received a majority of the votes, two election tallies are given, one for the initial election and one for the subsequent runoff.

PRIMARY ELECTIONS

Primary-election procedures in two states deserve special note. Washington has a blanket, or open, primary, in which candidates of all parties appear on the same ballot; the candidate in each party with the most votes advances to the general election. Louisiana holds its primary on Election Day. It is an open primary, with candidates from all parties on the ballot. Any candidate who receives more than half the votes, or who is unopposed, is elected. If no candidate receives an outright majority, the top two vote-getters, regardless of party, advance to a runoff election later.

Key Votes

Profiles of members who served in the 107th Congress are accompanied by a selection of key votes in 2001 and 2002, as chosen by CQ's editors. These captions give the bill number, a brief description of the matter being voted upon, a breakdown of the vote, the date of the vote and President Bush's position on that particular vote.

Senate Key Votes

2002

Pass farm bill reversing crop subsidy limits: Passage of the measure (HR 2646) to reauthorize federal agriculture programs for five years and re-establish programs to supply payments to farmers when commodity prices fall below a specified level. Passed 58-40: R 9-38; D 48-2 (ND 40-1, SD 8-1); I 1-0. Feb. 13, 2002.

Postpone tougher automobile fuel efficiency standards: Levin, D-Mich., amendment to the bill (S 517) to direct the National Highway Traffic Safety Administration to set a new Corporate Average Fuel Economy (CAFE) standard in 15 months. Congress would be permitted to raise the standard if NHTSA did not act within the 15-month time period. Adopted 62-38: R 43-6; D 19-31 (ND 14-27, SD 5-4); I 0-1. March 13, 2002.

Overhaul campaign finance law; ban "soft money" and restrict advocacy advertising: Passage of the bill (HR 2356) to outlaw "soft money" donations to national political parties but allow up to $10,000 in soft-money donations to state and local parties for voter registration and get-out-the-vote activity. The bill would prevent issue ads from targeting specific candidates within 60 days of a general election or 30 days of a primary. The bill also would increase the individual contribution limit from $1,000 to $2,000 per election for House and Senate candidates, both of which would be indexed for inflation. Passed (thus cleared for the president) 60-40: R 11-38; D 48-2 (ND 40-1, SD 8-1); I 1-0. March 20, 2002.

Set federal election standards: Passage of the bill (S 565) to impose voting-procedure requirements on states. It would require states to let voters verify their votes before casting a ballot, allow voters to change their ballots before submitting their vote, give voters replacement ballots if they make a mistake and notify voters if they vote for more than one candidate for an office. Passed 99-1: R 48-1; D 50-0 (ND 41-0, SD 9-0); I 1-0. April 11, 2002.

Support oil drilling in Arctic National Wildlife Refuge: Motion to invoke cloture (thus limiting debate) on the Murkowski, R-Alaska, amendment to the energy bill (S 517). The Murkowski amendment would allow for oil and gas development in a portion of the Arctic National Wildlife Refuge. It would designate an additional 1.5 million acres as wilderness in exchange for opening to drilling approximately 1.5 million acres of non-wilderness in the coastal plain region of the refuge. Three-fifths of the total Senate (60) is required to invoke cloture. Motion rejected 46-54: R 41-8; D 5-45 (ND 2-39, SD 3-6); I 0-1. April 18, 2002.

Revive fast-track procedures for trade agreements: Passage of the bill (HR 3009) that would allow special trade promotion authority for congressional consideration of trade agreements reached before June 1, 2005; extend duty-free status to certain products from Bolivia, Colombia, Ecuador and Peru; and reauthorize and expand a program to provide retraining and relocation assistance to U.S. workers hurt by trade agreements. Passed 66-30: R 41-5; D 24-25 (ND 16-24, SD 8-1); I 1-0. A "yea" was a vote in support of the president's position. May 23, 2002.

Create federal insurance coverage for catastrophic terrorist losses: Passage of the bill (S 2600) that would require the federal government to reimburse insurance companies for 90 percent of catastrophic losses related to terrorism between $10 billion and $100 billion in 2002, with an option to renew the program the following year to cover 90 percent of claims between $15 billion and $100 billion. Passed 84-14: R 34-14; D 49-0 (ND 40-0, SD 9-0); I 1-0. June 18, 2002

Tighten federal accounting and corporate governance regulation: Passage of the bill (S 2673) that would require more complete disclosure of corporate finances and overhaul regulation of the accounting industry. The bill would establish a new oversight board to police accounting firms, and forbid firms from providing investment banking, management consulting and other services for publicly traded companies. It would create new criminal penalties for shareholder fraud and obstruction of justice involving document shredding and require corporate executives to attest to the accuracy of financial statements. Passed 97-0: R 46-0; D 50-0 (ND 41-0, SD 9-0); I 1-0. July 15, 2002.

Advance bipartisan Medicare prescription drug plan: Graham, D-Fla., motion to waive the Budget Act with respect to the Frist, R-Tenn., point of order against the Graham amendment to a bill (S 812). The Graham amendment would provide prescription drug coverage for Medicare recipients with incomes of up to 200 percent of the poverty level. It also would provide catastrophic coverage for drug costs over $3,300 per year for an annual payment of $25 per year. Three-fifths of the total Senate (60) is required to waive the Budget Act. (Subsequently, the chair upheld the point of order, and the amendment fell.) Motion rejected 49-50: R 4-44;

Key to Party Abbreviations

continued from previous page

NJI	New Jersey Independents
NL	Natural Law
NNT	No New Taxes
NON	Non-Partisan
NP	New Progressive
PAC	Politicians Are Crooks
PACIFIC	Pacific
PAT	Patriot
PCH	The People's Champion
PFP	Peace and Freedom
PLC	Pro Life Conservative
PLP	Pro Life
POPDEM	Popular Democratic
PPD	Popular Democratic
PRI	Puerto Rican Independence
PRO	Progressive
R	Republican
REF	Reform
RJF	Restore Justice Freedom
RTL	Right to Life
S	Socialist
SSS	Save Social Security
SW	Socialist Workers
TAX	Taxpayers
TLC	Term Limits Candidate
UC	United Citizens
USP	U.S. Pacifist
USTAX	U.S. Taxpayers
VG	Vermont Grassroots
WFM	Working Families
WG	Wisconsin Greens
X	Not applicable

Key Votes

CQ editors selected key votes from roll-call votes taken during the 107th Congress. The following symbols are used:

Y	voted for (yea)
N	voted against (nay)
#	paired for
+	announced for
X	paired against
–	announced against
P	voted "present"
C	voted "present" to avoid possible conflict of interest
?	did not vote or otherwise make a position known.
I	ineligible
S	Speaker exercised his discretion to not vote

D 45-5 (ND 38-3, SD 7-2); I 0-1. July 31, 2002.

Create independent Sept. 11 commission: Lieberman, D-Conn., amendment to a bill (HR 5005) to establish a National Commission on Terrorist Attacks Upon the United States to investigate the facts and circumstances relating to the Sept. 11, 2001, attacks. The panel would be required to report its initial findings and recommendations to the president and to Congress within six months of its first meeting, followed by a second report in one year. Adopted 90-8: R 41-8; D 48-0 (ND 39-0, SD 9-0); I 1-0. Sept. 24, 2002.

Back Democratic Homeland Security Department proposal: Motion to invoke cloture (thus limiting debate) on the Lieberman, D-Conn., substitute amendment to a bill (HR 5005) to create a Cabinet-level Homeland Security Department charged with protecting domestic security. Motion rejected 50-49: R 1-48; D 48-1 (ND 41-0, SD 7-1); I 1-0. Three-fifths of the total Senate (60) is required to invoke cloture. Sept. 26, 2002.

Authorize war against Iraq: Passage of the joint resolution (H J Res 114) to authorize use of force against Iraq and require the administration to report to Congress that diplomatic options have been exhausted before, or within 48 hours after, military action has begun. The president would be required to submit a progress report to Congress every 60 days. Passed (thus cleared for the president) 77-23: R 48-1; D 29-21 (ND 21-20, SD 8-1); I 0-1. A "yea" was a vote in support of the president's position. Oct. 11, 2002.

2001

Confirm John Ashcroft as attorney general: Confirmation of President Bush's nomination of former Sen. John Ashcroft of Missouri to be attorney general. Confirmed 58-42: R 50-0; D 8-42 (ND 6-35, SD 2-7). A "yea" was a vote in support of the president's position. Feb. 1, 2001.

Nullify Clinton Labor Department ergonomics rule: Passage of the joint resolution (S J Res 6) that would provide for congressional disapproval of the ergonomics rule submitted by the Labor Department during the Clinton administration, stating the rule would have no force or effect. Passed 56-44: R 50-0; D 6-44 (ND 1-40, SD 5-4). March 6, 2001.

Cut taxes by $1.35 trillion through fiscal 2011: Adoption of the conference report on the reconciliation bill (HR 1836) that would reduce taxes by $1.35 trillion through fiscal 2011 through income tax rate cuts, relief of the "marriage penalty," a phaseout of the federal estate tax, doubling the child tax credit, and providing incentives for retirement savings. The bill's provisions would expire Dec. 31, 2010. Adopted (thus cleared for the president) 58-33: R 46-2; D 12-31 (ND 7-27, SD 5-4). A "yea" was a vote in support of the president's position. May 26, 2001. *(NOTE: This is not the key tax vote chosen by CQ editors in 2001.)*

Pass Democratic bill to bolster rights of patients in managed-care plans: Passage of the bill (S 1052) to provide federal protections, such as access to specialty and emergency room care, and allow patients to appeal a health plan organization's decision on coverage and treatment. It also would allow patients to sue health insurers in state courts over quality-of-care claims and at the federal level over administrative or non-medical coverage disputes. Federal-level economic and non-economic damages would not be capped; punitive damages would be capped at $5 million. Passed 59-36: R 9-35; D 50-0 (ND 41-0, SD 9-0); I 0-1. A "nay" was a vote in support of the president's position. June 29, 2001.

Permit a new round of military base closings: Warner, R-Va., motion to table (kill) the Bunning, R-Ky., amendment that would strike a provision in the defense authorization bill (S 1438) to authorize an additional round of base realignment and closures in 2003. Motion agreed to 53-47:

R 21-28; D 31-19 (ND 25-16, SD 6-3); I 1-0. Sept. 25, 2001.

Expand law enforcement power to investigate suspected terrorists: Passage of the bill (HR 3162) to allow disclosure of wiretap information among certain government officials, authorize disclosure of secret grand jury information to certain government officials, and allow the detention of foreigners suspected of having ties to terrorism. It also would make it easier for law enforcement to track voice and Internet communications using surveillance techniques and would strengthen laws to combat money laundering. Most of the intelligence-gathering provisions would sunset after four years. Passed (thus cleared for the president) 98-1: R 49-0; D 48-1 (ND 40-1, SD 8-0); I 1-0. A "yea" was a vote in support of the president's position. Oct. 25, 2001.

House Key Votes

2002

Overhaul campaign finance law; ban "soft money" and restrict advocacy advertising: Passage of the bill (HR 2356) to outlaw "soft money" donations to national political parties but allow up to $10,000 in soft-money donations to state and local parties for voter registration and get-out-the-vote activity. The bill would prevent issue ads from targeting specific candidates within 60 days of a general election or 30 days of a primary. The bill also would increase the individual contribution limit from $1,000 to $2,000 per election, indexed for inflation. Passed 240-189: R 41-176; D 198-12 (ND 150-6, SD 48-6); I 1-1. Feb. 14, 2002.

Back Bush's defense budget increase: Passage of the bill (HR 4546) that would authorize $383.4 billion for defense programs for fiscal 2003. It would include the president's request of $7.8 billion for missile defense systems and $7.3 billion for counterterrorism programs. It would provide $475 million for the Crusader artillery system. The bill also would exempt military activities from certain environmental regulations and include an average 4.7 percent pay increase for military personnel. Passed 359-58: R 212-1; D 146-56 (ND 100-51, SD 46-5); I 1-1. May 10, 2002.

Extend 1996 welfare law: Passage of the bill (HR 4737) that would authorize $16.5 billion to renew the Temporary Assistance for Needy Families block grant program through fiscal 2007 and require new welfare aid conditions. The bill would require individuals to work 40 hours per week to be eligible for assistance and require states to have 70 percent or more of their families working by 2007. It would authorize additional funding for child care and marriage promotion activities. Passed 229-197: R 214-4; D 14-192 (ND 7-147, SD 7-45); I 1-1. A "yea" was a vote in support of the president's position. May 10, 2002.

Adopt Bush's discretionary spending limit: Adoption of the rule (H Res 428) providing for House floor consideration of a bill (HR 4775) that would provide $28.8 billion in supplemental appropriations for fiscal 2002, more than half of which would go toward military operations. Adopted 216-209: R 214-3; D 1-205 (ND 1-153, SD 0-52); I 1-1. May 22, 2002.

Pass GOP Medicare prescription drug plan: Passage of the bill (HR 4954) that would allow Medicare recipients to cover prescription drug costs through private insurance policies beginning in 2005. The bill would cost $350 billion over 10 years. Subsidies would be given to reduce premiums and co-payments for low-income patients. The bill would include subsidies for insurers. It also would increase Medicare payments to health care providers at a 10-year cost of $34.5 billion. Passed 221-208: R 212-8; D 8-199 (ND 6-148, SD 2-51); I 1-1. June 28, 2002.

Create independent Sept. 11 commission: Roemer, D-Ind., amendment to an intelligence authorization bill (HR 4628) to establish a Nation-

Key Votes

CQ editors selected key votes from roll-call votes taken during the 107th Congress. The following symbols are used:

Y	voted for (yea)
N	voted against (nay)
#	paired for
+	announced for
X	paired against
–	announced against
P	voted "present"
C	voted "present" to avoid possible conflict of interest
?	did not vote or otherwise make a position known.
I	ineligible
S	Speaker exercised his discretion to not vote
ND	Northern Democrats
SD	Southern Democrats (Ala., Ark., Fla., Ga., Ky., La., Miss., N.C., Okla., S.C., Tenn., Texas, Va.)

Key Votes

CQ editors selected key votes from roll-call votes taken during the 107th Congress. The following symbols are used:

- Y voted for (yea)
- N voted against (nay)
- # paired for
- + announced for
- X paired against
- – announced against
- P voted "present"
- C voted "present" to avoid possible conflict of interest
- ? did not vote or otherwise make a position known.
- I ineligible
- S Speaker exercised his discretion to not vote

al Commission on Terrorist Attacks Upon the United States. The commission would examine and report on the facts and circumstances relating to the 2001 terrorist attacks. Its scope would include federal government intelligence activities, law enforcement, diplomacy, immigration, border security, commercial aviation, and the flow of assets to terrorist organizations. Adopted 219-188: R 25-183; D 193-4 (ND 145-1, SD 48-3); I 1-1. A "nay" was a vote in support of the president's position. July 25, 2002.

Extend union protections to Homeland Security Department employees: Morella, R-Md., amendment to the Homeland Security Department creation bill (HR 5005) to give federal employees who transfer into the new department the right to join a union if they were under union protection before the transfer. The president could exempt employees from union membership when duties are directly related to the war on terrorism. Rejected 208-222: R 5-214; D 202-7 (ND 153-2, SD 49-5); I 1-1. A "nay" was a vote in support of the president's position. July 26, 2002.

Revive fast-track procedures for trade agreements: Adoption of the conference report on the bill (HR 3009) that would allow special trade promotion authority for congressional consideration of trade agreements reached prior to June 1, 2005; provide benefits for workers displaced or financially harmed by increased imports; and extend duty-free status to certain products from Bolivia, Colombia, Ecuador and Peru. Adopted (thus sent to the Senate) 215-212: R 190-27; D 25-183 (ND 11-143, SD 14-40); I 0-2. A "yea" was a vote in support of the president's position. July 27, 2002.

Authorize war against Iraq: Passage of the joint resolution (H J Res 114) that would authorize President Bush to use the U.S. military as he deems necessary and appropriate to defend U.S. national security against Iraq and enforce U.N. Security Council resolutions regarding Iraq. The president would be required to report to Congress, no later than 48 hours after using force, his determination that diplomacy or other peaceful means would not ensure U.S. national security. The president also would be required to report to Congress every 60 days on actions relevant to the resolution. Passed 296-133: R 215-6; D 81-126 (ND 49-105, SD 32-21); I 0-1. A "yea" was a vote in support of the president's position. Oct. 10, 2002.

Advance bankruptcy overhaul opposed by abortion opponents: Adoption of the rule (H Res 606) to provide for House floor consideration of the conference report on the bill (HR 333) that would require debtors able to repay $10,000 or 25 percent of their debts over five years to file under Chapter 13, which requires a reorganization of debts under a repayment plan, instead of seeking to discharge their debts under Chapter 7. It also would block abortion and other protesters from declaring bankruptcy to avoid paying court-ordered fines and judgments. Rejected 172-243: R 124-87; D 48-155 (ND 24-127, SD 24-28); I 0-1. Nov. 14, 2002.

2001

Nullify Clinton Labor Department ergonomics rule: Passage of the joint resolution (S J Res 6) stating congressional disapproval of the ergonomics rule submitted by the Labor Department during the Clinton administration, stating the rule would have no force or effect. Passed 223-206: R 206-13; D 16-192 (ND 2-152, SD 14-40); I 1-1. March 7, 2001.

Cut taxes by $1.35 trillion through fiscal 2011: Adoption of the conference report on the reconciliation bill (HR 1836) that would reduce taxes by $1.35 trillion through fiscal 2011, through income tax rate cuts, relief of the "marriage penalty," a phaseout of the federal estate tax, doubling the child tax credit, and providing incentives for retirement savings. The bill's provisions would expire Dec. 31, 2010. Adopted (thus sent to the Senate)

240-154: R 211-0; D 28-153 (ND 17-118, SD 11-35); I 1-1. May 26, 2001. A "yea" was a vote in support of the president's position. *(NOTE: This is not the key tax vote chosen by CQ editors in 2001.)*

Maintain ban on oil drilling in Arctic National Wildlife Refuge: Markey, D-Mass., amendment to an energy bill (HR 4) that would maintain the current prohibition on oil drilling in the Arctic National Wildlife Refuge by striking language opening the reserve up to development. Rejected 206-223: R 34-186; D 171-36 (ND 141-13, SD 30-23); I 1-1. A "nay" was a vote in support of the president's position. Aug 1, 2001.

Approve Bush proposal to limit managed care plan liability for coverage decisions: Norwood, R-Ga., amendment to a patients' rights bill (HR 2563) to allow patients alleging harm because of denial of care to sue a health maintenance organization in state court — but federal, not state, law would govern. It would limit non-economic damages to $1.5 million. Punitive damages would be limited to the same amount. Adopted 218-213: R 214-6; D 3-206 (ND 2-153, SD 1-53); I 1-1. A "yea" was a vote in support of the president's position. Aug. 2, 2001.

Divert money from crop subsidy payments to land conservation: Boehlert, R-N.Y., amendment to the farm bill (HR 2646) that would shift $1.9 billion from fixed and countercyclical payments to farm and undeveloped land conservation programs, including the Farmland and Ranchland Protection Program and the Wildlife Habitat Incentives Program. Rejected 200-226: R 54-161; D 145-64 (ND 132-23, SD 13-41); I 1-1. Oct. 4, 2001.

Expand law enforcement power to investigate suspected terrorists: Passage of a bill (HR 3162) to allow disclosure of wiretap information among certain government officials, authorize disclosure of secret grand jury information to certain government officials, and allow the detention of foreigners suspected of having ties to terrorism. It also would make it easier for law enforcement to track voice and Internet communications using surveillance techniques and would strengthen laws to combat money laundering. Most of the intelligence-gathering provisions would sunset after four years. Passed 357-66: R 211-3; D 145-62 (ND 103-50, SD 42-12); I 1-1. A "yea" was a vote in support of the president's position. Oct. 24, 2001.

Voting Studies

Each year, Congressional Quarterly studies the frequency with which each member of Congress supports or opposes a given position. For example, a score of 25 percent under the support column in the presidential support study would indicate that the member supported the president 25 percent of the time on the votes that were used in the study. An explanation of each of the voting studies follows.

PARTY UNITY

Party unity votes are defined as votes in the Senate and House that split the parties, a majority of voting Democrats opposing a majority of voting Republicans. Votes on which the parties agree, or on which either party divides evenly, are excluded. Party unity scores represent the percentage of party unity votes on which a member voted "yea" or "nay" in agreement with a majority of the member's party. Opposition-to-party scores represent the percentage of party unity votes on which a member voted "yea" or "nay" in disagreement with a majority of the member's party. The score is based only on votes cast; failure to vote did not alter a member's score.

PRESIDENTIAL SUPPORT

CQ tries to determine what the president personally, as distinct from other administration officials, does and does not want in the way of legislative action. This is done by analyzing his messages to Congress, news

Congress by its Numbers

A new Congress is elected in each even-numbered year and convenes at the start of each odd-numbered year. As a shorthand, this book frequently refers to the actions of a particular Congress by its number. (The sequence began with the 1st Congress, which was elected in 1788.)

	ELECTED:	MET IN:
98th Congress	1982	1983 and 1984
99th Congress	1984	1985 and 1986
100th Congress	1986	1987 and 1988
101st Congress	1988	1989 and 1990
102nd Congress	1990	1991 and 1992
103rd Congress	1992	1993 and 1994
104th Congress	1994	1995 and 1996
105th Congress	1996	1997 and 1998
106th Congress	1998	1999 and 2000
107th Congress	2000	2001 and 2002
108th Congress	2002	2003 and 2004

conference remarks and other public statements and documents.

Occasionally, important measures are so extensively amended that it is impossible to characterize final passage as a victory or a defeat for the president. These votes have been excluded from the study. Votes on motions to recommit, to reconsider or to table (kill) often are key tests that govern the outcome. Such votes are included in the presidential support tabulations.

The score is based only on votes cast; failure to vote did not lower a member's score. All votes have equal statistical weight in the analysis.

Interest Group Ratings

Ratings for members of Congress by four advocacy groups are chosen to represent liberal, conservative, business and labor viewpoints. Following is a description of each group in the order they appear.

AMERICAN FEDERATION OF LABOR-CONGRESS OF INDUSTRIAL ORGANIZATIONS (AFL-CIO)

The AFL-CIO was formed when the American Federation of Labor and the Congress of Industrial Organizations merged in 1955. With affiliates claiming more than 13 million members, the AFL-CIO accounts for about three-fourths of national union membership. For senators, the ratings are based on eight votes in 1998, nine votes in 1999, eight votes in 2000, 16 votes in 2001 and 13 votes in 2002. For members of the House, the ratings are based on 10 votes in 1998, nine votes in 1999, 10 votes in 2000, 12 votes in 2001 and nine votes in 2002. (www.aflcio.org)

AMERICANS FOR DEMOCRATIC ACTION (ADA)

Americans for Democratic Action was founded in 1947 by a group of liberal Democrats that included Minnesota Sen. Hubert H. Humphrey and Eleanor Roosevelt. In each of the last five years, the ADA ratings are based on 20 votes in each chamber of Congress. (www.adaction.org)

CHAMBER OF COMMERCE OF THE UNITED STATES (CCUS)

The Chamber of Commerce of the United States represents local, regional and state chambers as well as trade and professional organizations. It was founded in 1912 to be "a voice for organized business." For senators, the ratings are based on 18 votes in 1998, 17 votes in 1999, 15 votes in 2000, 14 votes in 2001 and 20 votes in 2002. For members of the House, the ratings are based on 18 votes in 1998, 25 votes in 1999, 21 votes in 2000, 22 votes in 2001 and 20 votes in 2002. (www.uschamber.org)

AMERICAN CONSERVATIVE UNION (ACU)

The American Conservative Union was founded in 1964 "to mobilize resources of responsible conservative thought across the country and further the general cause of conservatism." The organization intends to provide education in political activity, "prejudice in the press," foreign and military policy, domestic economic policy, the arts, professions and sciences. For senators, the ratings are based on 25 votes in 1998, 25 votes in 1999, 25 votes in 2000, 24 votes in 2001 and 20 votes in 2002. For members of the House, the ratings are based on 25 votes each year. (www.conservative.org)

District Descriptions

Congressional district lines were redrawn in 2001 or 2002 (with the exception of Maine, which plans to do so in 2003) to reflect reapportionment and changes in population patterns revealed in the 2000 census. The description briefly sets forth the economic, sociological, demographic and political forces that are the keys to elections and which influence the legislative agenda of the district's member of Congress. Some city population figures are from the Census Bureau; other data come from Congressional Staff Directories, compiled in partnership with Capitol Technology Group.

Redistricting Increases Polarization

Lawmakers are feeling less compelled to appeal to a broad spectrum of views.

Deepening partisanship will be a likely result, and the situation may be locked in place for a decade.

It remains an article of faith among members of Congress that they "vote their districts." That is, they view and portray themselves more than anything as stewards for their constituents' interests rather than as acolytes for their party leaders.

In the 108th Congress, however, the difference between voting one's district and voting one's party can be difficult to detect, particularly in the House. Most of its 435 districts — as redrawn for this decade in 2001 and 2002 in response to the results of the census taken as the decade began — have been configured to strongly favor one of the two major political parties. So the overwhelming majority of the House members in office in 2003 and 2004 will be from the same party as most of their constituents.

The consequences on the south side of the Capitol are already becoming clear: More lawmakers are feeling less compelled than in the past to appeal to a broad spectrum of views — because their constituents are, in great measure, ideologically just like they are. Deepening partisanship in the House will be a likely result, and the situation may be locked in place until the next congressional maps are drawn after the 2010 census.

This latest political-demographic trend is most readily ascertained by comparing the party that holds a House seat with the party whose presidential candidate carried the district in the 2000 election. Looking at the districts as they were previously drawn — which were in effect on Election Day 2000 — there were 86 (one out of every five) in which voters elected a House candidate of one party but preferred the presidential nominee of the opposite party. By artfully redrawing congressional district lines for this decade in a number of states, mapmakers reduced by 28 percent, to 62, the list of ticket-splitting districts in 2002. That means that, in only one out of every seven House seats, voters elected a congressional candidate from a party different from what their presidential choice would have been in 2000.

That level of ticket-splitting is the lowest since at least 1952, the earliest election year for which complete presidential-vote-by-district data is available. It is far lower than the 110 split districts (25 percent of the total) after the re-election of both Democratic President Bill Clinton and an all-Republican Congress in 1996, and it pales by comparison with the 192 split districts (44 percent) in the 1972 election that re-elected not only Republican President Richard M. Nixon but also a solidly Democratic Congress.

This might seem at odds with the macro-level perception of the United States as a nation whose partisan loyalties are divided nearly evenly. This impression was strengthened by the razor's-edge outcome of the 2000 presidential election — in which George W. Bush narrowly won in the Electoral College while narrowly losing the popular vote — as well as by the relatively small margins by which Republicans control the House and Senate in the Congress that convened in January 2003.

But that near-even national split is the sum total of states and districts that increasingly have hardened into "red" or "blue" strongholds on the political map for either the Republicans or the Democrats. The strength of a district's political leanings is a good indicator of how faithfully its representative will toe the party line. This is particularly true in the House. Far from spurring greater electoral participation and competition, the redistricting that followed the 2000 census and preceded the 2002 elections mainly benefited incumbents and narrowed the field of competitive races.

REDISTRICTING CHANGES THE CROWD

One part of the country that joined the trend toward partisan fidelity in 2002, with a big assist from redistricting, is essentially on Congress'

Narrow GOP Wins In Gore Districts

These five Republicans won by fewer than 10 percentage points in 2002 in House districts whose voters preferred Al Gore for president in 2000:

Member	Percentage Point Victory Margin
Bob Beauprez, Colo. (7)	0.1
Jim Gerlach, Pa. (6)	2.7
Anne M. Northup, Ky. (3)	3.2
Jim Leach, Iowa (2)	6.5
Rob Simmons, Conn. (2)	8.2

Narrow Democratic Wins In Bush Districts

These 12 Democrats won by fewer than 10 percentage points in 2002 in House districts whose voters preferred George W. Bush for president in 2000:

Member	Percentage Point Victory Margin
Rodney Alexander, La. (5)	0.6
Jim Matheson, Utah (2)	0.7
Jim Marshall, Ga. (3)	1.0
Tim Holden, Pa. (17)	2.8
Dennis Moore, Kan. (3)	3.3
Ken Lucas, Ky. (4)	3.6
Charles W. Stenholm, Texas (17)	4.0
Chet Edwards, Texas (11)	4.4
Earl Pomeroy, N.D. (AL)	4.8
Baron P. Hill, Ind. (9)	5.0
Lincoln Davis, Tenn. (4)	5.6
Darlene Hooley, Ore. (5)	9.6

doorstep: Maryland's reliably Democratic 8th District, which takes in the suburbs just north of Washington, chose Democratic state Sen. Chris Van Hollen over Constance A. Morella, a moderate Republican who had held the seat for 16 years. Far above average in affluence and education, 8th District residents had long pointed to their support of Morella to deflect suggestions that they were automatic Democratic votes. Morella, in turn, maintained her popularity with a legislative voting record that often was the most liberal among House Republicans.

But Democrats completely controlled Maryland's redistricting process in 2002 and fashioned a map that made the 8th District even more reflexively Democratic — and more attractive to prospective challengers. An activist legislator popular among the Democrats' liberal base, Van Hollen won by 4 percentage points.

The partisan impact was immediate. As moderate as Morella was, she still joined with most Democratic members against most of her Republican colleagues on only 41 percent of mostly party-line votes in her final term. In the first three months of 2003, Van Hollen voted with the majority Democratic position on every such "party unity" vote.

The redistricting of California ended the political career of Republican Steve Horn, another leading GOP moderate during his decade in the House. His Democratic-leaning district in Los Angeles County was redrawn with an even more strongly liberal slant, and he chose to retire. Much of the territory Horn represented is now held by Democrat Linda T. Sánchez, who is expected to vote solidly with her party's leadership.

The 2002 elections also thinned the Democratic Party of some of its leading centrists. Ronnie Shows of Mississippi had departed from the national Democratic orthodoxy on issues such as abortion and gun control during his two House terms. He was nonetheless defeated after a court-imposed redistricting plan compelled him to seek re-election against Republican Charles W. "Chip" Pickering Jr. in Mississippi's heavily Republican district. And David Phelps, another socially conservative Democrat first elected in 1998, lost a redistricting-induced matchup with Republican John Shimkus in Illinois.

A handful of members have managed to survive against the partisan tides in their districts. They include conservative Democrats such as Kentucky's Ken Lucas and Texans Charles W. Stenholm and Ralph M. Hall. But these members' districts are otherwise so strongly Republican — all favored Bush by lopsided margins in 2000 — that their successors are likely, if not certain, to be conservative Republicans.

ONE-PARTY DISTRICTS, LOPSIDED VOTING

The increasing number of one-party districts could be elevating the importance of primaries, which in politically one-sided districts essentially foreordain election to Congress. In 2002, eight House members were defeated in primary elections, and eight more in the general election: That was the first time as many had lost in a primary as in November since at least 1946, the first year for which complete statistics are available.

While primary challenges do increase competition, they also may have the effect of reinforcing the high-pitched partisanship that has marked congressional affairs for years now. Primaries in strongly Republican districts tend to be dominated by the most conservative voters, and primaries in strongly Democratic districts often are dominated by the most liberal voters. It can be difficult in either case for a centrist candidate to prevail.

The Club for Growth, a conservative organization that backs candidates who support tax and spending cuts, has served notice that it will vigorously support primary challengers to Republican members who do not adhere to its principles. One beneficiary of the Club's largess in 2002 was Scott Garrett, a conservative state assemblyman who was elected to New Jersey's Republican-leaning 5th District to succeed Marge Roukema, who retired. The Club previously had backed Garrett in his narrowly unsuccessful 2000 primary challenge to Roukema, a leading Republican moderate who supported abortion rights and gun control measures.

The net result of the hardening of party lines at the local level is a House that is more polarized than ever. In 2002, congressional Republicans had an average party unity score of 89 percent, compared with an average of 64 percent three decades earlier. Congressional Democrats had an average party unity score of 86; in 1972, it was 57 percent.

In the first three months of 2003, there were 33 party unity votes, meaning a majority of House Republicans voted against a majority of House Democrats. The GOP voted unanimously on 16 of those votes, or nearly half the time. Just one or two Republicans voted with the majority Democratic position on nine other votes. Democrats voted unanimously eight times; just one or two Democrats voted with most Republicans on nine occasions.

While these numbers will not necessarily extrapolate over the course of the 108th, they suggest an uptick in the party-line trend. In 2002, Republicans voted unanimously on just 54 of the 209 party unity votes, or one-quarter of them. Democrats voted unanimously on 37 of those votes, or less than one-fifth of them.

INCUMBENT SECURITY

The degree of partisan unity parallels the measure of incumbent security that has been abetted by redistricting. Of the 398 House members in 2002 who sought re-election, 382 were successful — a 96 percent success rate. It was the third-consecutive election in which fewer than 10 House members were defeated in November; that phenomenon had occurred in only three of the 26 previous House elections since World War II.

A big reason for incumbents' outstanding success rate in 2002 was that the district lines were tailored to their overwhelming advantage. Members of Congress in many states forged bipartisan compromises with their legislatures to protect or even strengthen their House districts' partisan leanings — in some cases choosing collective incumbent protection over maps that might have given opportunities to both parties to gain additional seats. Even in states that redistricted under the direction of nonpartisan commissions and judicial panels, which might be expected to treat House incumbents less favorably than legislators, tended to view seniority positively and drew congressional maps that shielded incumbents from political danger.

And redistricting often locks in a party's advantage in a district for an entire decade. Of the 435 House districts, 324 (75 percent) stayed in the same party's hands through the five elections from 1992 through 2000 — even though that period included the "revolutionary" 1994 election in which Republicans won control of Congress for the first time in four decades. A consequence of the most recent redistricting process is that there will be another decade-long partisan lock on most House districts.

Nowhere was pro-incumbent redistricting more consequential than in California. By far the nation's most populous state, it gained one seat in the 2000 reapportionment, bringing its delegation to an all-time record of 53 — meaning one out of every eight seats in the House is held by a Californian.

With Democrat Gray Davis as governor and the Democratic Party solidly in control of the California Legislature, some national Democratic strategists argued for drawing a congressional map that would have augmented the party's already considerable 12-seat advantage in the state's

Narrow GOP Wins In Bush Districts

These 12 Republicans won by fewer than 10 percentage points in 2002 in House districts whose voters preferred George W. Bush for president in 2000:

Member	Percentage Point Victory Margin
Ginny Brown-Waite, Fla. (5)	1.7
Mike D. Rogers, Ala. (3)	2.1
Phil Gingrey, Ga. (11)	3.3
Rick Renzi, Ariz. (1)	3.6
Henry Bonilla, Texas (23)	4.3
Chris Chocola, Ind. (2)	4.7
John Hostettler, Ind. (8)	5.3
Tom Cole, Okla. (4)	7.7
Bill Janklow, S.D. (AL)	7.8
Robin Hayes, N.C. (8)	9.0
Katherine Harris, Fla. (13)	9.6
John Shimkus, Ill. (19)	9.6

Narrow Democratic Wins In Gore Districts

These nine Democrats won by fewer than 10 percentage points in 2002 in House districts whose voters preferred Al Gore for president in 2000:

Member	Percentage Point Victory Margin
Timothy H. Bishop, N.Y. (1)	1.6
Joseph M. Hoeffel, Pa. (13)	3.6
Michael H. Michaud, Maine (2)	4.0
Chris Van Hollen, Md. (8)	4.2
Rick Larsen, Wash. (2)	4.3
Dennis Cardoza, Calif. (18)	7.9
Leonard L. Boswell, Iowa (3)	8.4
C.A. Dutch Ruppersberger, Md. (2)	8.6
Julia Carson, Ind. (7)	9.0

House delegation as the decade began. But this view was not shared by the seven California Democratic House members who were elected or re-elected in 2000 with 55 percent of the vote or less — or by their colleagues. They felt their party had reached a high-water mark in the 2000 election, when it gained four House seats in California for a total of 32.

Rather than spreading Democratic voters more widely in hopes of undercutting some Republican incumbents, the Democratic members wanted their own political security shored up. And Republicans, who have fared terribly in recent California elections, were eager for a deal that they hoped would arrest their precipitous political decline in the state.

The outcome was a bargain under which the lines were shifted to add Democratic voters to districts held by Democratic members and Republican voters to districts held by Republicans.

With redistricting assuring Democrats of the state's new seat, 33 California Democrats won in 2002 with an average of 68 percent of the vote; just four were elected or re-elected with less than 60 percent. The 20 victorious Republicans won with an average of 67 percent, and all of them won at least 60 percent.

The remap brought a radical improvement in political fortune for Democrat Jane Harman, for example. In a politically marginal suburban Los Angeles district, starting in 1992 she won her first three House terms with 48 percent, 48 percent and 52 percent of the vote. After giving her seat up for a 1998 bid for governor that failed, two years later Harman narrowly won her seat back — again with 48 percent. But for this decade, Harman's district was redrawn with a more solidly Democratic orientation, and she prevailed in 2002 by 26 percentage points.

There were a few states in which a dominant party played redistricting for keeps, resulting in gains for their party. But in some cases, they did so by creating "safe" districts not only for their own party, but for the opposition as well.

Michigan, for example, lost one seat in reapportionment, but the Republicans used their control of the legislature and governorship to draw a map that produced a House delegation of nine Republicans and six Democrats in the 108th — more than reversing the Democrats' 9-7 advantage in the 107th. The main beneficiary of the plan was Republican Mike Rogers, a freshman who had won by 111 votes in the closest House race of 2000. To strengthen his fortunes and those of other Republican candidates, GOP mapmakers pulled GOP voters from Democratic-held districts, while at the same time packing Democratic voters into districts that Democratic candidates would then be strongly favored to win. The result was that serious Democratic opposition was scared off. Rogers won by 85,605 votes — and became a top lieutenant in the GOP whip organization in 2003.

To be sure, there were isolated exceptions to this decade's pattern of redistricting benefiting incumbents. In Iowa, for example, all four House incumbents were placed in some measure of political jeopardy in 2002, because the state's new political map had been configured by a nonpartisan agency that was required to disregard political registration data, election results or even incumbents' home addresses. But even then, all three Republicans and the Democrat managed to leverage the other benefits of incumbency and win re-election in November.

Gregory L. Giroux

Hispanic Districts

Congressional districts with the largest percentage of Hispanics. (Hispanics may be of any race):

District	Hispanic	Member
Texas 15	78.3%	Hinojosa, D
Texas 16	77.7%	Reyes, D
California 34	77.2%	Roybal-Allard, D
Illinois 4	74.5%	Gutierrez, D
Texas 27	71.6%	Ortiz, D
California 38	70.6%	Napolitano, D
California 31	70.2%	Becerra, D
Florida 21	69.7%	L. Diaz-Balart, R
Texas 28	69.6%	Rodriguez, D
Texas 20	68.2%	Gonzalez, D

Black Districts

Congressional districts with the largest percentage of African-Americans:

District	Black	Member
Illinois 1	65.2%	Rush, D
Louisiana 2	63.7%	Jefferson, D
Mississippi 2	63.2%	Thompson, D
Illinois 2	62.0%	Jackson, D
Alabama 7	61.7%	Davis, D
Illinois 7	61.6%	Davis, D
Michigan 14	61.1%	Conyers, D
Pennsylvania 2	60.8%	Fattah, D
Michigan 13	60.5%	Kilpatrick, D
New York 10	60.2%	Towns, D

Asian Districts

Congressional districts with the largest percentage of Asians:

District	Asian	Member
Hawaii 1	53.6%	Abercrombie, D
California 15	29.2%	Honda, D
California 8	28.7%	Pelosi, D
California 12	28.5%	Lantos, D
California 13	28.2%	Stark, D
Hawaii 2	28.0%	Case, D
New York 5	24.5%	Ackerman, D
California 29	23.7%	Schiff, D
California 16	23.4%	Lofgren, D
California 32	18.4%	Solis, D

American Indian Districts

Congressional districts with the largest percentage of American Indians:

District	Indian	Member
Arizona 1	22.1%	Renzi, R
New Mexico 3	18.9%	Udall, D
Oklahoma 2	16.8%	Carson, D
Alaska AL	15.4%	Young, R
North Carolina 7	8.5%	McIntyre, D
South Dakota AL	8.1%	Janklow, R
Montana AL	6.0%	Rehberg, R
Oklahoma 3	6.0%	Lucas, R
Oklahoma 1	5.8%	Sullivan, R
Oklahoma 4	5.5%	Cole, R

Oldest Districts

Congressional districts with the highest median age:

District	Median Age	Member
Florida 13	47.4	Harris, R
Florida 14	47.4	Goss, R
Florida 5	45.5	Brown-Waite, R
Florida 19	45.1	Wexler, D
Florida 16	44.5	Foley, R
Florida 10	43.9	Young, R
Florida 22	43.0	Shaw, R
Florida 9	41.1	Bilirakis, R
Florida 15	41.0	Weldon, R
Pennsylvania 18	41.0	Murphy, R

Youngest Districts

Congressional districts with the lowest median age:

District	Median Age	Member
Utah 3	24.5	Cannon, R
California 43	26.7	Baca, D
California 20	26.9	Dooley, D
Arizona 4	27.1	Pastor, D
Illinois 4	27.2	Gutierrez, D
Texas 29	27.4	Green, D
New York 16	27.5	Serrano, D
California 47	27.6	Loretta Sanchez, D
Utah 1	27.6	Bishop, R
California 34	27.9	Roybal-Allard, D

Richest Districts

Congressional districts with the highest median household income in 1999:

District	Income	Member
Virginia 11	$80,397	Davis, R
New Jersey 11	$79,009	Frelinghuysen, R
California 14	$77,985	Eshoo, D
Georgia 6	$75,611	Isakson, R
California 15	$74,947	Honda, D
New Jersey 7	$74,823	Ferguson, R
Colorado 6	$73,393	Tancredo, R
New Jersey 5	$72,781	Garrett, R
Illinois 13	$71,686	Biggert, R
Illinois 10	$71,663	Kirk, R

Poorest Districts

Congressional districts with the lowest median household income in 1999:

District	Income	Member
New York 16	$19,311	Serrano, D
Kentucky 5	$21,915	Rogers, R
West Virgina 3	$25,630	Rahall, D
California 31	$26,093	Becerra, D
Alabama 7	$26,672	Davis, D
California 20	$26,800	Dooley, D
Mississippi 2	$26,894	Thompson, D
Louisiana 5	$27,453	Alexander, D
Louisiana 2	$27,514	Jefferson, D
Texas 15	$27,530	Hinojosa, D

Most Government Workers

Congressional districts with the largest percentage of workers employed by local, state, federal or international government organizations:

District	Workers	Member
Maryland 4	29.0%	Wynn, D
Maryland 5	28.8%	Hoyer, D
Florida 2	28.5%	Boyd, D
Alaska AL	26.8%	Young, R
New Mexico 3	25.8%	Udall, D
California 5	24.8%	Matsui, D
New York 10	24.6%	Towns, D
Arizona 1	24.4%	Renzi, R
Maryland 7	24.3%	Cummings, D
Virginia 11	24.2%	Davis, R

Most Educated

Congressional districts with the largest percentage of people, aged 25 and older, with at least a bachelor's degree:

District	Degree	Member
New York 14	56.9%	Maloney, D
Virginia 8	53.8%	Moran, D
Maryland 8	53.7%	Van Hollen, D
California 30	53.5%	Waxman, D
California 14	52.2%	Eshoo, D
Georgia 6	50.7%	Isakson, R
Virginia 11	48.9%	Davis, R
North Carolina 4	48.0%	Price, D
New York 8	47.8%	Nadler, D
Illinois 10	47.5%	Kirk, R

Least Educated

Congressional districts with the largest percentage of people, 25 and older, without a high school diploma:

District	No Diploma	Member
California 34	53.7%	Roybal-Allard, D
California 31	52.5%	Becerra, D
California 20	49.8%	Dooley, D
California 47	49.6%	Loretta Sanchez, D
New York 16	49.5%	Serrano, D
Illinois 4	48.3%	Gutierrez, D
Texas 29	47.7%	Green, D
New York 12	43.6%	Velázquez, D
Texas 15	41.9%	Hinojosa, D
California 38	41.6%	Napolitano, D

Foreign Born

Congressional districts with the largest percentage of residents born outside the United States (native Americans born abroad are not included):

District	Foreign Born	Member
Florida 21	56.6%	L. Diaz-Balart, R
California 31	56.2%	Becerra, D
Florida 18	54.0%	Ros-Lehtinen, R
California 47	50.7%	Loretta Sanchez, D
California 34	47.2%	Roybal-Allard, D
Florida 25	46.6%	M. Diaz-Balart, R
New York 5	45.6%	Ackerman, D
California 28	44.0%	Berman, D
California 29	43.8%	Schiff, D
California 32	41.7%	Solis, D

ALABAMA

Gov. Bob Riley (R)

First elected: 2002
Length of term: 4 years
Term expires: 1/07
Salary: $101,433
Phone: (334) 242-7100
Hometown: Ashland
Born: Oct. 3, 1944; Ashland, Ala.
Religion: Baptist
Family: Wife, Patsy Riley; four children (one deceased)
Education: U. of Alabama, B.A. 1965 (business administration)
Career: Auto dealer; trucking company executive; farmer
Political highlights: Ashland City Council, 1972-76; candidate for mayor of Ashland, 1976; U.S. House, 1997-2003
Election results:

2002 GENERAL		
Bob Riley (R)	672,225	49.2%
Donald Siegelman (D)	669,105	49.0%
John Sophocleus (LIBERT)	23,272	1.7%

Lt. Gov. Lucy Baxley (D)

First elected: 2002
Length of term: 4 years
Term expires: 1/07
Salary: $48,620
Phone: (334) 242-7900

STATE LEGISLATURE

Legislature: Meets annually, limited to 30 legislative days within 105 calendar days
House: 105 members, 4-year terms
2003 breakdown: 42R, 63D; 98 men, 7 women
Salary: $10/day; $50 for each 3-day week; $2,280/month expenses
Phone: (334) 242-7600
Senate: 35 senators, 4-year terms
2003 breakdown: 10R, 25D; 32 men, 3 women
Salary: $10/day; $50 for each 3-day week; $2,280/month expenses
Phone: (334) 242-7800

STATE TERM LIMITS

Governor: 2 consecutive terms
Senate: No
House: No

URBAN STATISTICS

CITY	POPULATION
Birmingham	242,820
Montgomery	201,568
Mobile	198,915
Huntsville	158,216
Tuscaloosa	77,906

REGISTERED VOTERS

Voters do not register by party.

POPULATION

2002 population (est.)	4,486,508
2000 population	4,447,100
1990 population	4,040,587
Percent change (1990-2000)	+10.1%
Rank among states (2002)	22
Median age	35.8
Born in state	73.4%
Foreign born	2%
Violent crime rate	486/100,000
Poverty level	16.1%
Federal workers	50,081
Military	38,706

REDISTRICTING

Alabama retained its seven House seats in reapportionment. The state legislature drew a new map, which the governor signed on Jan. 31, 2002.

MISCELLANEOUS

Web: www.state.al.us
Capital: Montgomery
STATE ELECTION OFFICIAL
(334) 242-7210
DEMOCRATIC HEADQUARTERS
(334) 262-2221
REPUBLICAN HEADQUARTERS
(205) 978-2500

District Statistics

DIST.	2000 VOTE FOR PRESIDENT BUSH	GORE	NADER	WHITE	BLACK	ASIAN	HISP	MEDIAN INCOME	WHITE COLLAR	BLUE COLLAR	SERVICE INDUSTRY	OVER 64	UNDER 18	COLLEGE EDUCATION	RURAL	SQ. MILES
1	60%	37%	1%	68%	28%	1%	1%	$34,739	55%	31%	15%	13%	27%	19%	36%	6,317
2	61	38	1	67	29	1	2	$32,460	55	31	14	13	26	18	50	10,502
3	52	47	1	65	32	1	1	$30,806	52	34	14	13	25	17	47	7,834
4	61	37	1	90	5	0	3	$31,344	46	42	12	15	24	11	73	8,372
5	54	44	1	78	17	1	2	$38,054	57	30	13	12	25	24	41	4,486
6	74	25	0	89	8	1	2	$46,946	68	22	10	12	24	30	38	4,564
7	34	65	0	36	62	1	1	$26,672	53	29	17	13	26	15	28	8,669
STATE	56	42	1	70	26	1	2	$34,135	55	31	13	13	25	19	45	50,744
U.S.	47.9	48.4	3	69	12	4	13	$41,994	60	25	15	12	26	24	21	3,537,438

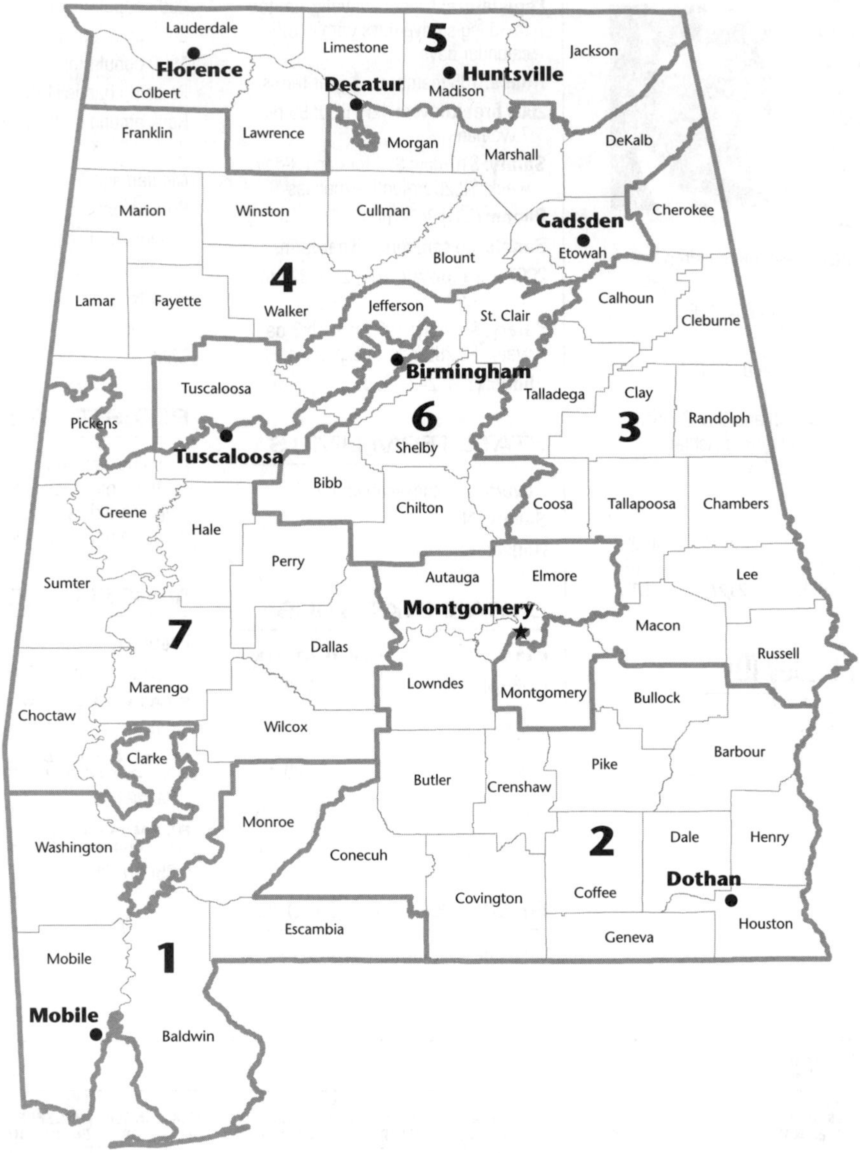
5
4
6
3
7
2
1
Lauderdale
Limestone
Jackson
Florence
Huntsville
Decatur
Madison
Colbert
Franklin
Lawrence
Morgan
Marshall
DeKalb
Marion
Winston
Cullman
Gadsden
Cherokee
Etowah
Blount
Lamar
Fayette
Walker
Jefferson
St. Clair
Calhoun
Cleburne
Birmingham
Tuscaloosa
Talladega
Clay
Pickens
Randolph
Shelby
Tuscaloosa
Bibb
Greene
Chilton
Coosa
Tallapoosa
Chambers
Hale
Perry
Sumter
Autauga
Elmore
Lee
Montgomery
Macon
Dallas
Russell
Marengo
Lowndes
Montgomery
Bullock
Choctaw
Wilcox
Clarke
Barbour
Pike
Butler
Crenshaw
Monroe
Washington
Dale
Henry
Conecuh
Dothan
Covington
Coffee
Houston
Escambia
Geneva
Mobile
Mobile
Baldwin

Sen. Richard C. Shelby (R)

CAPITOL OFFICE
224-5744
senator@shelby.senate.gov
shelby.senate.gov
110 Hart 20510-0103; fax 224-3416

COMMITTEES
Appropriations
(Transportation, Treasury & General Government - chairman)
Banking, Housing & Urban Affairs - chairman
Governmental Affairs
Special Aging

HOMETOWN
Tuscaloosa

BORN
May 6, 1934, Birmingham, Ala.

RELIGION
Presbyterian

FAMILY
Wife, Annette Nevin Shelby; two children

EDUCATION
U. of Alabama, A.B. 1957, LL.B. 1963

CAREER
Lawyer; city prosecutor

POLITICAL HIGHLIGHTS
Ala. Senate, 1971-79 (served as a Democrat); U.S. House, 1979-87 (served as a Democrat)

ELECTION RESULTS

1998 GENERAL

Richard C. Shelby (R)	817,973	63.2%
Clayton Suddith (D)	474,568	36.7%

1998 PRIMARY

Richard C. Shelby (R)	unopposed

PREVIOUS WINNING PERCENTAGES
1992 (65%); 1986 (50%); 1984 House Election (97%); 1982 House Election (97%); 1980 House Election (73%); 1978 House Election (94%)
*Elected as a Democrat 1978-92

Elected 1986; 3rd term

Thirteen years before becoming a Republican, Shelby was courted to make the jump by the most prominent Democratic apostate of them all, President Reagan. Then a House member from Tuscaloosa, Shelby demurred, saying he preferred to work on changing his party from within.

"This was not something done on a whim, this was years in the making," Shelby said in 2002 when asked to recall when he finally gave up his lifelong party affiliation in 1994 — the very day after Republicans won control of Congress. "Where I philosophically belong is in the Republican Party."

That assertion aside, Shelby remains something of an anomaly within the ranks of his adopted party. Pegged as a fiscal and social conservative largely because of his well-publicized political journey — which has made him a poster boy for the rise of the GOP across the South — Shelby's record is more complex than that. In the 107th Congress, only 10 Republicans broke from their party on Senate party-line votes more often than Shelby did. And only six GOP senators voted against President Bush's wishes more often than Shelby.

His departures from the Republican mainstream come most notably on consumer protection matters, where he evinces a strong populist bent on questions about privacy, predatory lending and stock market regulation. As the new chairman in the 108th Congress of the Banking, Housing and Urban Affairs Committee, Shelby has served notice that he will champion what he views as the public's interest, rather than the interest of corporate America.

In his first term as chairman, he was planning to push legislation to roll back the 1995 law that curbed shareholder lawsuits. And his decidedly un-Republican hard line on consumer privacy is a stance that worries business lobbyists. The main issue in the 108th will be whether to allow affiliated banking, securities and insurance concerns broad latitude to exchange information about their customers — which Shelby ardently opposes.

In his first high-profile act as chairman, Shelby lectured William H. Donaldson during his confirmation hearings in 2003 to head the Securities and Exchange Commission on the need to inspire fear on Wall Street — and to remember the SEC chairman has "an obligation to the American people, period."

Shelby was similarly blunt-spoken in the 107th Congress, when his most visible role was as the top Republican, and vice chairman, of the Intelligence Committee. He said that "an intelligence failure of unprecedented magnitude" had preceded the Sept. 11, 2001, terrorist attacks. In particular, he singled out what he said were shortcomings by the Central Intelligence Agency, which he has criticized for relying too much on technological tools and not enough on the work of its agents.

Shelby was at the forefront of the congressional probe into the inability of the various U.S. intelligence agencies to foresee the attacks. He also pushed for the provisions in the law creating the Department of Homeland Security that allow intelligence information to be shared more readily among federal agencies. He left the panel at the start of the 108th, none too soon for his legion of critics in the spy agencies.

Generally seen as one of the most genial, least excitable and lowest-profile senators, Shelby advocates a limited role for the federal government in economic affairs, except when the actions of malefactors endanger the free-market system. His vision for government is that it should "try first to do no harm, except where people are doing harm to the marketplace. We have to root those people out."

His immersion in the privacy issue dates back to the 106th Congress, when he learned that some states were providing information from driver's licenses to marketing firms without motorists' knowledge. Shelby was a co-founder of the Congressional Privacy Caucus in 1999 and that year won enactment of a law requiring states to obtain permission before sharing personal data, such as Social Security numbers and driver's license information.

But he does take some pro-business stands. He favors doing away with a raft of what he says are unnecessary federal regulations governing banks, credit unions and thrifts, saying that there have been "a lot of laws put on the books in the last 50 years that make no sense today."

Another venue from which Shelby asserts influence is the Appropriations Committee. A seat on that panel had been denied him by the Democrats during his first eight years as a senator. But when Shelby switched parties, he was rewarded not only with an Appropriations assignment but also with the gavel of the Treasury, Postal Service and General Government Subcommittee.

He chaired the Transportation Appropriations Subcommittee in the 106th and 107th Congresses and heads the new Transportation and Treasury panel in the 108th.

On Appropriations, Shelby looks out for federal installations in his home state. He has been of special service to Huntsville, seeking to leverage his chairmanship to direct more commercial airline service there and to protect the booming space and defense economy. In 1999, the Richard C. Shelby Center for Missile Intelligence, a 200,000-square foot scientific and technical center with a $33 million price tag, opened at the Army's Redstone Arsenal in Huntsville.

But Shelby downplays his influence, at least publicly. "I tell my people back home that the only reason you will survive is if you're part of the national purpose," he says.

Shelby's party switch in 1994 struck many as opportunistic. But he said he made the move because of what he saw as the demise of the pro-defense, conservative wing of the Democratic Party. "I grew up a Southern Democrat," Shelby said, adding that many of his brethren were Democrats "because of the Civil War, not because of ideology."

Shelby spent most of the 1960s as a municipal prosecutor in Tuscaloosa, and he sometimes cites his law enforcement background in justifying his political flexibility. He entered electoral politics by serving eight years in the state Senate, where he often was at odds with Gov. George C. Wallace. Although Shelby initially was interested in the lieutenant governorship in 1978, more than a dozen other Democrats had the same idea. But one of his former law partners, Democrat Walter Flowers, gave up his House seat that year to run for the Senate, and Shelby was easily persuaded to change course and run for Congress.

For eight years, Shelby worked largely behind the scenes in the House, devoting his time to bringing federal projects to his district. But he also became an increasingly reliable ally of the Republicans on the Energy and Commerce Committee. Ironically enough, his election to the Senate as a Democrat in 1986 was a 1 percentage point victory over one-term incumbent Jeremiah Denton, who had been the first Republican elected to statewide office in Alabama since Reconstruction.

Shelby has had less trouble running for re-election to the Senate since then, thanks to the inability of either party to recruit top-tier opponents against him and the senator's prodigious skill at raising money.

KEY VOTES

2002

- Yes Pass farm bill reversing crop subsidy limits
- Yes Postpone tougher automobile fuel efficiency standards
- No Overhaul campaign finance law; ban "soft money" and restrict advocacy advertising
- Yes Set federal election standards
- Yes Support oil drilling in Arctic National Wildlife Refuge
- ? Revive fast-track procedures for trade agreements
- Yes Create federal insurance coverage for catastrophic terrorist losses
- Yes Tighten federal accounting and corporate governance regulation
- No Advance bipartisan Medicare prescription drug plan
- Yes Create independent Sept. 11 commission
- No Back Democratic Homeland Security Department proposal
- Yes Authorize war against Iraq

2001

- Yes Confirm John Ashcroft as attorney general
- Yes Nullify Clinton Labor Department ergonomics rule
- Yes Cut taxes by $1.35 trillion through fiscal 2011
- No Pass Democratic bill to bolster rights of patients in managed-care plans
- No Permit a new round of military base closings
- Yes Expand law enforcement power to investigate suspected terrorists

CQ VOTE STUDIES

	PARTY UNITY		PRESIDENTIAL SUPPORT	
	Support	Oppose	Support	Oppose
2002	80%	20%	87%	13%
2001	88%	12%	97%	3%
2000	97%	3%	45%	55%
1999	89%	11%	38%	62%
1998	91%	9%	34%	66%
1997	93%	7%	57%	43%
1996	94%	6%	33%	67%
1995	90%	10%	30%	70%
1994	50%	50%	67%	33%
1993	37%	63%	46%	54%

INTEREST GROUPS

	AFL-CIO	ADA	CCUS	ACU
2002	38%	10%	85%	80%
2001	19%	5%	93%	100%
2000	0%	0%	93%	100%
1999	22%	10%	71%	84%
1998	0%	5%	78%	92%
1997	14%	5%	90%	92%
1996	0%	5%	77%	90%
1995	0%	5%	89%	91%
1994	83%	30%	50%	55%
1993	73%	35%	82%	64%

Sen. Jeff Sessions (R)

CAPITOL OFFICE
224-4124
senator@sessions.senate.gov
sessions.senate.gov
493 Russell 20510-0104; fax 224-3149

COMMITTEES
Armed Services
(Airland - chairman)
Budget
Health, Education, Labor & Pensions
Judiciary
(Administrative Oversight & the Courts - chairman)
Joint Economic

HOMETOWN
Mobile

BORN
Dec. 24, 1946, Hybart, Ala.

RELIGION
Methodist

FAMILY
Wife, Mary Blackshear Sessions; three children

EDUCATION
Huntingdon College, B.A. 1969 (history); U. of Alabama, J.D. 1973

MILITARY SERVICE
Army Reserve, 1973-86

CAREER
Lawyer; teacher

POLITICAL HIGHLIGHTS
Assistant U.S. attorney, 1975-77; U.S. attorney, 1981-93; Ala. attorney general, 1995-97

ELECTION RESULTS

2002 GENERAL		
Jeff Sessions (R)	792,561	58.6%
Susan Parker (D)	538,878	39.8%
Jeff Allen (LIBERT)	20,234	1.5%
2002 PRIMARY		
Jeff Sessions (R)		unopposed

PREVIOUS WINNING PERCENTAGES
1996 (52%)

Elected 1996; 2nd term

A low-key and steadfast conservative, Sessions played an important role during his first Senate term — often behind the scenes — on diverse topics, including bankruptcy, missile defense, domestic preparedness and education. On his desk is a small plaque with a quote from Ronald Reagan: "There is no limit to what a man can do or where he can go if he doesn't mind who gets the credit."

But throughout his time in Washington, Sessions has been most closely associated with the issue of the Senate's role in confirming judges, a subject on which he has a unique perspective.

Sessions was well-known by many senators before he joined their ranks in 1997. In 1986, his nomination to the federal bench was rejected by the Senate Judiciary Committee. He was only the second judicial nominee in 48 years whose nomination was killed by the committee.

Sessions' opponents accused him of "gross insensitivity" on racial issues. After voting 8-10 against his confirmation, the panel refused, 9-9, to send the nomination to the floor for a vote. (The nays included the man Sessions replaced in the Senate, Democrat Howell Heflin.)

Sessions was serving as chief prosecutor for the Southern District of Alabama and making a name for himself through his prosecution of drug dealers when President Reagan nominated him to be a federal judge. But according to sworn statements by Justice Department lawyers, Sessions called the NAACP and the American Civil Liberties Union "communist-inspired" and said they tried to "force civil rights down the throats of people." Sessions said his words were in jest or misrepresented.

Now a member of the Judiciary Committee, he allows that his presence alongside several of the members who voted against his confirmation — Republican Arlen Specter and Democrats Joseph R. Biden Jr., Robert C. Byrd, Edward M. Kennedy and Patrick J. Leahy — is a "great irony." But he has been welcomed even by his political opponents.

In the 107th Congress, Sessions complained that the Democratic-run Senate seemed to be changing the ground rules — placing the burden on a judicial nominee to prove his fitness, rather than putting the onus on the Senate to justify rejecting the president's choice. In a hearing in the Administrative Oversight and the Courts Subcommittee called the "Ghosts of Nominations Past," Sessions said the process for confirming judges had been perverted.

"I remember [them] well," he said, referring to the hotly contested and partisan nomination hearings of Robert Bork in 1987 and Clarence Thomas in 1991 and his own nomination hearing. "We were 'Borked' before they had given it a name," he said. He chairs the courts subcommittee, which has jurisdiction over judicial appointments, in the 108th.

On Judiciary, Sessions has also been involved in legislation focusing on the forfeiture of assets of convicted criminals, negotiating changes in bankruptcy law and increasing funding for overburdened crime labs.

Sessions also sits on the Armed Services Committee, where he urges increased budgets for the Pentagon and seeks to protect Alabama military bases and the interests of defense contractors, although he was willing in 2001 to support another round of military base closings. He is an advocate of the missile defense system. In the 107th, he wrote legislation to give tax breaks to military personnel serving at hardship posts.

Sessions, whose voting record is consistently conservative, chairs the

Republican Steering Committee, an unofficial group of about 30 mostly conservative senators who meet periodically to discuss policy issues.

During his first term, Sessions fought hard for money to fund the Center for Domestic Preparedness (CDP) and Noble Hospital Training Center, located at the old Ft. McClellan at Anniston. The CDP trains fire, police and medical personnel on how to react to biological, chemical or nuclear attacks. Noble trains hospital personnel on how to deal with mass casualties stemming from such attacks. Long before the Sept. 11, 2001, terrorist attacks on the United States, Sessions was warning that it was not a question of if, but when, terrorists would strike.

Sessions is a believer in the benefits of nuclear power. In the 107th, he offered a bill to give a tax credit for construction and upgrades of nuclear power plants, arguing that it made sense from an environmental standpoint and would reduce the nation's dependence on imported fossil fuels. He was cheered when the Tennessee Valley Authority announced plans in 2002 to restart a nuclear plant at Browns Ferry in northern Alabama that had been shut since 1985.

Sessions and his wife both taught school long ago, and he lists education as a top priority. On the Health, Education, Labor and Pensions Committee, he has sought changes in the federal program that supports the education of disabled children, saying he was responding to complaints from teachers. The Individuals with Disabilities Act should be amended to give schools greater leeway in dealing with disruptive students, Sessions argues. The tax cut legislation enacted in 2001 included provisions he wrote to make college tuition savings plans 100 percent tax-free.

Sessions grew up in the tiny towns of Hybart and Camden, southwest of Montgomery. His father owned a general store and then a farm equipment dealership, and Sessions worked around the stores and lived what he describes as an idyllic childhood. A high school teacher introduced him to the National Review magazine, which he says "helped me to appreciate the United States and to develop a political philosophy that respected hard work, faith and country."

His parents were not active politically but urged him to take an interest in government, which he did, as a history and political science student in college. He was active in the Young Republicans and student body president at Huntingdon College in Alabama. After earning his law degree, Sessions was a lawyer for a firm in Russellville, Ala., becoming assistant U.S. attorney in 1975. He was named U.S. attorney for the Southern District of Alabama in 1981 and eventually won the notice of the Reagan White House and the nomination to a federal judgeship.

After the Senate turned back his nomination, Sessions returned to his work as a federal prosecutor. In 1994, he ran for state attorney general, and with a corruption scandal raging in Montgomery, he rode to victory on a vow to clean up the ethics mess.

Two years later, Sessions was on the move again, lured into the Senate race by Democrat Howell Heflin's retirement after 18 years in Washington. Six other Republicans joined Sessions in the party primary, and he emerged the winner in a runoff.

In the general election, Sessions faced Roger Bedford, chairman of the state Senate Judiciary Committee. He appealed to Alabama's conservative Christian activists with his advocacy of a constitutional amendment permitting school prayer. In the end, Sessions prevailed over Bedford with 52 percent, giving Alabama two Republican senators for the first time since Reconstruction.

In 2002, he cruised past Democrat Susan Parker, the state auditor, by 19 percentage points.

KEY VOTES

2002

Yes Pass farm bill reversing crop subsidy limits
Yes Postpone tougher automobile fuel efficiency standards
No Overhaul campaign finance law; ban "soft money" and restrict advocacy advertising
Yes Set federal election standards
Yes Support oil drilling in Arctic National Wildlife Refuge
No Revive fast-track procedures for trade agreements
No Create federal insurance coverage for catastrophic terrorist losses
Yes Tighten federal accounting and corporate governance regulation
No Advance bipartisan Medicare prescription drug plan
Yes Create independent Sept. 11 commission
No Back Democratic Homeland Security Department proposal
Yes Authorize war against Iraq

2001

Yes Confirm John Ashcroft as attorney general
Yes Nullify Clinton Labor Department ergonomics rule
Yes Cut taxes by $1.35 trillion through fiscal 2011
No Pass Democratic bill to bolster rights of patients in managed-care plans
Yes Permit a new round of military base closings
Yes Expand law enforcement power to investigate suspected terrorists

CQ VOTE STUDIES

	PARTY UNITY		PRESIDENTIAL SUPPORT	
	Support	Oppose	Support	Oppose
2002	87%	13%	88%	12%
2001	95%	5%	97%	3%
2000	97%	3%	42%	58%
1999	94%	6%	24%	76%
1998	98%	2%	28%	72%
1997	99%	1%	56%	44%

INTEREST GROUPS

	AFL-CIO	ADA	CCUS	ACU
2002	25%	10%	84%	90%
2001	20%	5%	86%	96%
2000	0%	0%	86%	100%
1999	11%	0%	88%	100%
1998	0%	0%	89%	100%
1997	0%	0%	70%	100%

Rep. Jo Bonner (R)

CAPITOL OFFICE
225-4931
www.house.gov/bonner
315 Cannon 20515-0101; fax 225-0562

COMMITTEES
Agriculture
Budget
Science

HOMETOWN
Mobile

BORN
Nov. 19, 1959, Selma, Ala.

RELIGION
Episcopalian

FAMILY
Wife, Janee Bonner; two children

EDUCATION
U. of Alabama, B.A. 1982 (journalism), attended 1998 (law)

CAREER
Congressional chief of staff; congressional aide; campaign aide

POLITICAL HIGHLIGHTS
No previous office

ELECTION RESULTS

2002 GENERAL		
Jo Bonner (R)	108,102	60.5%
Judy McCain Belk (D)	67,507	37.8%
Richard M. Coffee (LIBERT)	2,957	1.7%
2002 PRIMARY RUNOFF		
Jo Bonner (R)	32,421	62.4%
Tom Young (R)	19,501	37.6%
2002 PRIMARY		
Jo Bonner (R)	29,857	40.3%
Tom Young (R)	15,087	20.3%
David Whetstone (R)	10,997	14.8%
Albert Lipscomb (R)	7,429	10.0%
Chris Pringle (R)	6,001	8.1%
Rusty Glover (R)	4,374	5.9%

Elected 2002; 1st term

If there is one aspect of House membership at which Bonner can be expected to excel as a freshman, it is constituent service.

Bonner won Alabama's 1st District seat after almost 16 years as an aide to nine-term Republican predecessor Sonny Callahan, including more than a decade as Callahan's chief of staff. But unlike many top assistants who work on Capitol Hill and seldom see the home district, Bonner relocated back to his native South Alabama several years ago. The move gave him the opportunity to work directly with constituents.

"I love politics and I love people," Bonner said. "Government service is a people-driven job if you're in it for the right reason."

Bonner, who received assignments to the Agriculture, Budget and Science committees, had declined to identify his preference early on, saying he wanted to be a "team player." He will get plenty of opportunity to do that, too: Shortly after his election, he was appointed as an assistant majority whip, a role in which he will be asked to round up votes for the House Republican leadership.

When Callahan announced in March 2002 that he would not seek re-election to a seat that had been in Republican hands since 1965, Bonner jumped into the race. He won the most votes in a seven-way June primary but fell short of a majority, forcing a runoff.

First District voters' familiarity with Bonner carried him past his well-funded runoff opponent, Tom Young, who had left his job on Alabama Republican Sen. Richard C. Shelby's staff to seek the seat. Bonner won that contest with 62 percent before cruising past Democrat Judy McCain Belk, a businesswoman, in the November election.

Like many of his colleagues, Bonner has said that creating a prescription-drug benefit for seniors is near the top of his agenda. He also has said improving the economy is a priority in a district that includes the city of Mobile and has lost timber and textile jobs. His admiration for Callahan is evident, and his voting pattern is expected to be similarly conservative.

ALABAMA 1

Southwest – Mobile

Crop fields and pine forests merge with Alabama's shoreline to form the 1st. Although the city of Mobile is the anchor of the state's only Gulf Coast district, a symbiotic relationship between the industrial and rural areas balances the district's economy.

Forestry feeds the district's timber mills and shipping companies, though a deep recession in the Southeast Asian market in the mid- to late-1990s forced cutbacks in the local timber industry. Mobile's State Docks, one of the nation's largest commercial shipping centers, supports a shipbuilding industry that has stagnated in recent years. South Alabama still relies on its rich soil for the staple products — trees, cotton and soybeans — that have given the region strength for decades.

But the overall contraction of timber, ship-related industries and a once-thriving textile industry forced the district to diversify. Tourism, based around the Gulf Coast, has been the most immediate remedy. Retail outlets spur employment and chemical and aerospace companies help broaden the district's economy.

The shift to GOP voting seen in much of the South took root early here. Republicans have held the House seat since 1965, and the district overwhelmingly favored GOP presidential candidates in the 1990s and 2000. Mobile residents lean Republican, though Democrats long have had a foothold in rural parts of the district. Local elections can become battles over issues such as farm subsidies and trade.

MAJOR INDUSTRY
Commercial shipping, timber, textiles

CITIES
Mobile, 198,915; Prichard, 28,633

NOTABLE
Gulf Shores' National Shrimp Festival draws more than 200,000 visitors each October; Mobile annually hosts America's Junior Miss competition and college football's Senior Bowl.

Rep. Terry Everett (R)

CAPITOL OFFICE
225-2901
terry.everett@mail.house.gov
www.house.gov/everett
2312 Rayburn 20515-0102; fax 225-8913

COMMITTEES
Agriculture
Armed Services
(Strategic Forces - chairman)
Veterans' Affairs
Select Intelligence

HOMETOWN
Enterprise

BORN
Feb. 15, 1937, Dothan, Ala.

RELIGION
Baptist

FAMILY
Wife, Barbara Everett

EDUCATION
Dale County H.S., graduated 1955

MILITARY SERVICE
Air Force, 1955-59

CAREER
Newspaper executive; construction company owner; farm owner; real estate developer; newspaper reporter

POLITICAL HIGHLIGHTS
No previous office

ELECTION RESULTS

2002 GENERAL		
Terry Everett (R)	129,233	68.8%
Charles Woods (D)	55,495	29.5%
Floyd Shackelford (LIBERT)	2,948	1.6%
2002 PRIMARY		
Terry Everett (R)		unopposed
2000 GENERAL		
Terry Everett (R)	151,830	68.2%
Charles Woods (D)	64,958	29.2%
Wallace McGahan (LIBERT)	4,111	1.9%

PREVIOUS WINNING PERCENTAGES
1998 (69%); 1996 (63%); 1994 (74%); 1992 (49%)

Elected 1992; 6th term

Everett is a self-made millionaire who started out as a farm reporter for southeastern Alabama's Dothan Eagle and later built a chain of newspapers. He has owned a home building company and served as chairman of the board of a local bank.

But as the son of a sharecropper and railroad worker, Everett, who owns a farm that produces peanuts and other crops, is still more comfortable wearing boots than wingtips and being known as a regular guy from southeast Alabama than as a member of Congress.

The district's farm and military interests and Everett's own experience in farming and the Air Force have made him a good match for his long roster of committee assignments: Agriculture, Armed Services, Veterans' Affairs and Intelligence. An Air Force intelligence analyst in the 1950s, Everett won a seat on the Intelligence panel in 2002, as the war on terrorism took center stage in Congress.

In the 108th Congress, he sought the chairmanship of the Agriculture Committee but lost out to Virginian Robert W. Goodlatte. Instead, Everett got the chairmanship of the Armed Services panel's Strategic Forces Subcommittee, which has jurisdiction over missile defense, military space activities and Department of Energy defense programs.

Armed Services is the third panel on which he has chaired a subcommittee. In the 107th Congress, he was an Agriculture subcommittee chairman, and in the 104th through the 106th, he ran a Veterans' Affairs subcommittee.

Everett's seniority and committee assignments have allowed him to serve his region vigorously, most notably in helping to revamp the government's peanut subsidy program and save it from extinction. During the rewrite of the farm bill in the 107th, he argued that maintaining government help for peanut growers was vital to national security — a view that played well back home but earned him some tart criticism elsewhere.

Southeastern Alabama has been among the nation's leading peanut producers since the boll weevil wiped out most of the cotton crop a century ago. When the Republicans took over in the 104th Congress and began talking about ending many of the subsidy programs in place since the New Deal, Everett — then in only his second term — was a key player in the campaign that retained the price supports for peanut farmers in the 1996 farm bill.

The next time the farm bill was rewritten, Everett was better positioned to protect peanut farmers for the long haul. As chairman of the Agriculture Subcommittee on Specialty Crops in the 107th, Everett led the effort that ended the Depression-era peanut program — which had kept prices high by effectively limiting who may grow peanuts to those who held a government quota. Instead, peanuts were placed under the same system that is used for other major crops such as corn and grains.

The peanut issue has brought him national attention before. Everett and other lawmakers from peanut-growing districts blocked a plan by the Department of Transportation in 1998 to create peanut-free buffer zones on commercial airliners to protect passengers with allergies to the legume. He said the proposal was "precisely this kind of dumb bureaucratic decision-making which rightly causes Americans to be distrustful of their government."

On Armed Services, Everett looks out for his district's numerous defense contractors and its two major military bases, Maxwell Air Force

Base and Fort Rucker, where Army and Air Force helicopter crews train.

Everett has had a seat on Veterans' Affairs since he arrived in Washington in 1993. From 1997 through 2000, he chaired the panel's Oversight and Investigations Subcommittee, and he aggressively investigated reported problems within the Department of Veterans Affairs (VA). His probes of favoritism in burial policies, delays in payment of disability claims, complaints about substandard medical care, and the VA's problem-riddled computer modernization program put Everett in the news nationally.

Everett's oversight of the VA first made news in 1997 when his subcommittee began looking into allegations that the Clinton administration had traded scarce burial plots in Arlington National Cemetery for political donations. Everett ultimately turned up no evidence of presidential wrongdoing, but the inquiry led to House passage in the 106th of legislation he cosponsored to tighten requirements for interment at the cemetery.

He investigated reports of sexual harassment and serious mismanagement at veterans hospitals. His subcommittee also looked into allegations that the VA was harassing whistleblower employees and it investigated the quality of care in VA hospitals.

Everett's parents died when he was a youth in Midland City, just north of Dothan, and he was largely responsible for his younger siblings when he returned from a four-year hitch in the Air Force. He became a wealthy man when he sold most of his small weekly and daily newspapers in the late 1980s. He also was a home builder for a while and headed a savings and loan in his birthplace of Dothan. He lives in Enterprise, home of a giant statue to the boll weevil.

He was 55 years old in 1992 and virtually unknown in political circles when Republican Bill Dickinson decided to retire after 14 terms. An insurgent within his own party, Everett claimed the GOP nomination by defeating a state senator who was the choice of the party establishment.

In the fall campaign against state Treasurer George C. Wallace Jr., son of the former governor, Everett proved to have a winning combination of message and means. He spent hundreds of thousands of dollars of his own money blanketing the district in billboards and radio and TV ads blaring: "Send a message, not a politician." Everett won with a bare plurality of 49 percent that year but has had no trouble winning re-election five times since.

The political landscape of his territory was minimally altered by redistricting, and in 2002 he won with 69 percent against businessman Charles Woods, similar to his showing against Woods two years earlier.

KEY VOTES

2002

- No Overhaul campaign finance law; ban "soft money" and restrict advocacy advertising
- Yes Back Bush's defense budget increase
- Yes Extend 1996 welfare law
- Yes Adopt Bush's discretionary spending limit
- Yes Pass GOP Medicare prescription drug plan
- No Create independent Sept. 11 commission
- No Extend union protections to Homeland Security Department employees
- Yes Revive fast-track procedures for trade agreements
- Yes Authorize war against Iraq
- No Advance bankruptcy overhaul opposed by abortion opponents

2001

- Yes Nullify Clinton Labor Department ergonomics rule
- Yes Cut taxes by $1.35 trillion through fiscal 2011
- No Maintain ban on oil drilling in Arctic National Wildlife Refuge
- Yes Approve Bush proposal to limit managed-care plan liability for coverage decisions
- No Divert money from crop subsidy payments to land conservation
- Yes Expand law enforcement power to investigate suspected terrorists

CQ VOTE STUDIES

	PARTY UNITY		PRESIDENTIAL SUPPORT	
	Support	Oppose	Support	Oppose
2002	99%	1%	85%	15%
2001	97%	3%	93%	7%
2000	97%	3%	14%	86%
1999	95%	5%	15%	85%
1998	94%	6%	20%	80%

INTEREST GROUPS

	AFL-CIO	ADA	CCUS	ACU
2002	0%	0%	84%	100%
2001	8%	5%	87%	100%
2000	0%	0%	78%	90%
1999	33%	5%	80%	91%
1998	11%	5%	89%	100%

ALABAMA 2
Southeast — part of Montgomery, Dothan

Besides Dothan and part of the state capital, Montgomery, the 2nd consists of scattered small towns. The district is probably best known for its peanut farms, but poultry, cotton and tree farming are also important. The local economy has suffered in recent years from hurricanes, floods, droughts and ice storms. Farther south, around Dothan, high-tech and auto parts plants have replaced textile mills that moved overseas.

Defense and state government provide steady employment. Maxwell Air Force Base and its Gunter Annex are responsible for most of the Air Force's computer systems. A Hyundai plant scheduled to open in 2005 in the neighboring 3rd District is expected to employ about 2,000 people.

Tourism also contributes to the economy, particularly in Montgomery, though many historic sites of the Civil Rights movement are in the 3rd. The Robert Trent Jones Golf Trail, large antebellum homes in Eufaula and fishing at Lake Eufaula attract visitors to the area.

Redistricting following the 2000 census shuffled the population of Montgomery: The 2nd now shares the city with the 3rd, and the 7th was completely removed from the city. A large military retiree population underscores a conservative constituency that usually votes Republican. On the local level, the 2nd usually sends Democrats to the state legislature.

MAJOR INDUSTRY

Agriculture, military, manufacturing

MILITARY BASES

Fort Rucker (Army), 5,112 military, 6,480 civilian; Maxwell Air Force Base, 5,791 military, 16,080 civilian (2002)

CITIES

Montgomery (pt.), 127,986; Dothan, 57,737; Prattville, 24,303; Enterprise, 21,178; Ozark, 15,119; Troy, 13,935; Eufaula, 13,908

NOTABLE

Dothan hosts a national peanut festival annually; The Hank Williams Sr. museum is in Georgiana; The Boll Weevil Monument in Enterprise is a tribute to the insect, whose destruction of the cotton crop persuaded farmers to switch to peanuts.

Rep. Mike D. Rogers (R)

CAPITOL OFFICE
225-3261
www.house.gov/mike-rogers
514 Cannon 20515-0103; fax 226-8485

COMMITTEES
Agriculture
Armed Services

HOMETOWN
Anniston

BORN
July 16, 1958, Hammond, Ind.

RELIGION
Baptist

FAMILY
Wife, Donna Elizabeth "Beth" Rogers; three children

EDUCATION
Jacksonville State U., B.A. 1981 (political science & psychology), M.P.A. 1985; Birmingham School of Law, J.D. 1991

CAREER
Lawyer; laid-off worker assistance program director; psychiatric counselor

POLITICAL HIGHLIGHTS
Calhoun County Commission, 1987-91; candidate for Ala. House, 1990; Ala. House, 1995-2002 (minority leader, 1998-2000)

ELECTION RESULTS

2002 GENERAL		
Mike D. Rogers (R)	91,169	50.3%
Joe Turnham (D)	87,351	48.2%
George Crispin (LIBERT)	2,565	1.4%
2002 PRIMARY		
Mike D. Rogers (R)	28,113	76.1%
Jason Dial (R)	4,681	12.7%
Jeff Fink (R)	4,134	11.2%

Elected 2002; 1st term

Freshman Rogers figures to be a reliable vote for President Bush on a variety of issues. Like many Republicans, he campaigned on his support for the tax cut package enacted with Bush's backing in 2001 and for the administration's efforts to ensure homeland security.

But there is at least one issue on which the president will have an uphill battle in enlisting Rogers' support: Social Security. Rogers opposes creation of personal accounts within Social Security, a concept that Bush supports, and he sent out campaign literature highlighting that position.

Rogers' split from conservative orthodoxy on that and some other issues highlights the diverse interests in Alabama's politically competitive 3rd District, which his Republican predecessor, Bob Riley, had left open to stage a successful 2002 bid for governor.

Another example is Rogers' expression of environmental concerns. He lives in what is known as the "pink zone," the area around the Anniston Army Depot that would be most affected should an accident occur while the government is burning a stockpile of chemical weapons there.

With the depot in Anniston, Maxwell Air Force Base in an adjoining district and the Army's Fort Benning just across the state line in Georgia, the military is a major employer in the 3rd. And Speaker J. Dennis Hastert has made good on a promise that Rogers would get a seat on the Armed Services Committee.

Rogers, a lawyer and state legislator, set his sights on the 3rd District seat in early 2001, relinquishing a leadership role in the state House so he could concentrate on a congressional campaign if Riley sought the governorship. Riley did so and Rogers easily captured the party's nomination. The Democratic nominee, former state party chairman Joe Turnham, made a vigorous bid, but Rogers benefited from a superior fundraising operation and the support of national GOP leaders, prevailing by a slim, 2-point margin.

Rogers and his staff have experienced the expected confusion that comes with the fact that he is not the only Mike Rogers in the House; Michigan's Mike Rogers, also a Republican, has served since 2001.

ALABAMA 3

East — part of Montgomery, Auburn, Anniston

With agriculture, industry, universities and part of the capital city of Montgomery, the 3rd can claim to be a microcosm of the state. Revised during 2002 redistricting to decrease its Republican strength, the 3rd now has many socially conservative Democrats who favor GOP presidential candidates, as well as blacks, who make up one-third of the population, and small pockets of university liberals who support Democrats on all levels.

Anniston relies heavily on the federal government. The Army left Fort McClellan in 1999, but the base has been turned into a training facility for first respondents to chemical, biological and nuclear terrorist attacks. There is a Honda plant in Lincoln, and Hyundai's first U.S. facility is scheduled to open in 2005 south of Montgomery.

Auburn University is one of the state's largest employers and a leading agricultural research center. Construction of a chemical weapons incinerator at the Anniston Army Depot has raised environmental concerns.

Redistricting removed some western territory, while adding many Montgomery attractions, including the state Capitol and the Dexter Avenue Baptist Church, where the 1955 bus boycott was launched.

MAJOR INDUSTRY
Higher education, agriculture, textiles

MILITARY BASES
Anniston Army Depot, 2,647 civilian (2002)

CITIES
Montgomery (pt.), 73,582; Auburn, 42,987; Phenix City, 28,265; Anniston, 24,276

NOTABLE
Tuskegee University, founded in 1881, was one of the nation's first black colleges; Talladega Superspeedway.

Rep. Robert B. Aderholt (R)

CAPITOL OFFICE
225-4876
robert@mail.house.gov
www.house.gov/aderholt
1433 Longworth 20515-0104; fax 225-5587

COMMITTEES
Appropriations

HOMETOWN
Haleyville

BORN
July 22, 1965, Haleyville, Ala.

RELIGION
Congregationalist Baptist

FAMILY
Wife, Caroline Aderholt; one child

EDUCATION
Birmingham Southern U., B.A. 1987 (history & political science); Samford U., J.D. 1990

CAREER
Lawyer; gubernatorial aide

POLITICAL HIGHLIGHTS
Republican nominee for Ala. House, 1990; Haleyville municipal judge, 1992-96

ELECTION RESULTS

2002 GENERAL		
Robert B. Aderholt (R)	139,705	86.7%
Tony McLendon (LIBERT)	20,858	13.0%
2002 PRIMARY		
Robert B. Aderholt (R)		unopposed
2000 GENERAL		
Robert B. Aderholt (R)	140,009	60.6%
Marsha Folsom (D)	86,400	37.4%
Craig Goodrich (LIBERT)	3,519	1.5%

PREVIOUS WINNING PERCENTAGES
1998 (56%); 1996 (50%)

Elected 1996; 4th term

Aderholt's dueling priorities in Congress were highlighted by a trip he took with President Bush aboard Air Force One in June 2001. Aderholt is best known for his efforts to bring religious values into the public sphere, and part of the trip's agenda was a meeting with Alabama ministers to promote the president's "faith-based" initiative to channel federally funded social services through churches.

But in his news release touting his face time with Bush, Aderholt (ADD-ur-holt) emphasized that he also had lobbied the chief executive on behalf of local concerns.

The vigorous advocacy of traditional values in a congenial and soft-spoken manner is the hallmark of Aderholt's legislative career. His most publicized cause in Washington has been to permit public displays of the Ten Commandments, a mission he embraced soon after he arrived in 1997, when a federal judge, citing the First Amendment, ordered a judge in Aderholt's district to remove a copy of the commandments from his courtroom wall.

Aderholt's promotion of the Ten Commandments is his attempt to counter what he sees as the unnecessary exclusion of religion from public life. The House in 1997 adopted his resolution endorsing the public display of the commandments. Aderholt, however, has changed his tack by seeking legislation leaving it up to each state to decide whether to allow displays of the commandments in public offices and courtrooms. "Discrimination against religion under the guise of separation of church and state needs to end," he says.

As a member of the U.S. Helsinki Commission monitoring human rights in Europe and the former Soviet Union, Aderholt has extended his campaign for freedom of religious expression overseas, demanding greater respect for religious freedom from the governments of Georgia and Turkmenistan.

On other social policy issues, he is an unstinting conservative. He favors constitutional amendments to outlaw all abortions except to save the life of the woman, and to allow prayer on public property and in public schools. He also opposes human cloning and embryonic stem-cell research.

Aderholt assiduously attends to the economic needs of his constituents, who often are as economically strapped as they are socially conservative. Ever since GOP leaders awarded him a prized appointment to the Appropriations Committee in 1997, Aderholt has quietly steered federal dollars toward northern Alabama.

He has waged more combative — though unsuccessful — efforts to protect the regionally important steel and textile industries that have been clobbered by foreign competition. After a Gulf States Steel plant in Gadsden closed in 2000, eliminating 1,700 jobs, Aderholt backed legislation to provide loan guarantees for steel companies hurt by foreign imports, part of an effort to attract a buyer to reopen the plant.

The next year, when VF Corp., manufacturer of Lee and Wrangler jeans, closed four factories in and around the 4th District, Aderholt voted against granting the president fast-track authority to negotiate trade deals. Seven months later he voted for the final version of the bill, reversing course after House leaders promised to fight against lifting tariffs on socks made in the Caribbean — an issue of parochial importance because Fort Payne in Aderholt's district is the self-proclaimed "Sock Capital of the World."

Aderholt was one of only two GOP freshmen to receive an appointment to the Appropriations Committee in the 105th Congress — the Republican leadership sought to help the newcomer solidify his hold on the historically Democratic 4th District.

Aderholt is a believer in the GOP appropriator's creed: The federal government should tax and spend less, but one's constituents should get at least their fair share of whatever flows from the federal spigot. He has been particularly energetic in funding the continued construction of an interstate-grade highway from Birmingham to Memphis.

His office also releases a steady stream of announcements on more modest projects — $2.3 million to upgrade a National Guard facility in Gadsden and $2 million for a mine-clearing system under development in Cullman, to cite two projects from 2002. In the 108th, he is seeking help to upgrade highways in Etowah County, where expansion of the Honda plant has greatly increased traffic.

The son of a judge who also was a Baptist pastor, Aderholt's own judicious and strait-laced demeanor was nurtured not only in his home but also all around it. Northern Alabama has been one of the most religiously conservative areas of the nation, where the permissiveness of the 1960s and 1970s mostly did not infiltrate.

Aderholt grew up with politics. When he was about 5, he wrote a campaign letter touting his father in a local election, and he recalls meeting Bob Dole when he was about 11. A month after his law school graduation, Aderholt was nominated for a state House seat, but he lost the general election. Appointed to a municipal court judgeship in 1992, he went to work for Republican Gov. Fob James Jr. in 1995.

When Tom Bevill retired in 1996 after 15 terms, Aderholt said, he was encouraged to try for the seat because he felt it shared demographic and political characteristics with the neighboring 1st District of Mississippi, a longtime Democratic bastion that Roger Wicker had won for the Republican Party two years before. In the GOP primary, Aderholt took 49 percent against four rivals and got the nomination when the second-place finisher declined to demand a runoff. Democrats put up a strong candidate in former state Sen. Robert T. "Bob" Wilson Jr., who was nearly as conservative as Aderholt on social issues. Dole carried the 4th District by 5 percentage points over Bill Clinton that year, while Aderholt prevailed by 2 points.

Aderholt strengthened his hold on the district in his next two elections, though he faced Democrats with strong name recognition: Donald Bevill, son of the longtime congressman, in 1998; and Marsha Folsom, wife of former Gov. Jim Folsom Jr., in 2000. But in 2002, with Aderholt's constituency minimally altered by redistricting, the Democrats did not field an opponent.

KEY VOTES

2002

No Overhaul campaign finance law; ban "soft money" and restrict advocacy advertising
Yes Back Bush's defense budget increase
Yes Extend 1996 welfare law
Yes Adopt Bush's discretionary spending limit
Yes Pass GOP Medicare prescription drug plan
No Create independent Sept. 11 commission
No Extend union protections to Homeland Security Department employees
Yes Revive fast-track procedures for trade agreements
Yes Authorize war against Iraq
No Advance bankruptcy overhaul opposed by abortion opponents

2001

Yes Nullify Clinton Labor Department ergonomics rule
Yes Cut taxes by $1.35 trillion through fiscal 2011
No Maintain ban on oil drilling in Arctic National Wildlife Refuge
Yes Approve Bush proposal to limit managed-care plan liability for coverage decisions
No Divert money from crop subsidy payments to land conservation
Yes Expand law enforcement power to investigate suspected terrorists

CQ VOTE STUDIES

	PARTY UNITY		PRESIDENTIAL SUPPORT	
	Support	Oppose	Support	Oppose
2002	96%	4%	82%	18%
2001	96%	4%	85%	15%
2000	91%	9%	20%	80%
1999	95%	5%	14%	86%
1998	91%	9%	21%	79%

INTEREST GROUPS

	AFL-CIO	ADA	CCUS	ACU
2002	11%	0%	90%	92%
2001	17%	10%	87%	91%
2000	30%	15%	71%	88%
1999	33%	5%	80%	84%
1998	30%	10%	83%	96%

ALABAMA 4

North central – Gadsden, part of Decatur

Encompassing mountains, foothills, flatlands and large waterways, the 4th stretches the width of the state, bordering Georgia and Mississippi. A small black population and the absence of a major city distinguish it from the rest of Alabama.

One of the state's poorest districts, the 4th has suffered through textile companies moving overseas and a decline in coal mining, with some relief from an underlying agricultural economy. Rubber and steel plants in Gadsden, the district's only sizable city, have downsized as a result of strikes and foreign competition.

Efforts by local officials to attract new, moderate-size businesses may be helped by "Corridor X," a road project that locals hope will become an interstate. Many residents work in surrounding metropolitan areas — such as Huntsville in the 5th, and Birmingham, which is split between the 6th and 7th districts. Mobile home manufacturing plants fuel Marshall County's economy. Cullman County's agricultural industry includes everything from cotton and soybeans to chickens and cattle. DeKalb County, a mountainous region in the northeastern part of the state, includes some of the region's natural sights and tourist destinations.

The rural 4th's population is socially conservative, especially on gun control and religious issues. The district originally adhered to Democratic populism, but has voted Republican on recent presidential ballots. In 1996, voters sent a Republican to Congress for just the second time since Reconstruction, and have re-elected him since.

MAJOR INDUSTRY

Agriculture, manufacturing, mining

CITIES

Gadsden, 38,978; Albertville, 17,247; Jasper, 14,052; Cullman, 13,995

NOTABLE

Fort Payne and surrounding DeKalb County, billed as the "sock capital of the world," have more than 100 mills that employ more than 6,000 workers; Winston County briefly became the "free state of Winston" when Alabama seceded from the union; The world's longest yard sale, which starts in Gadsden and ends 450 miles later in Covington, Ky., attracts 400,000 bargain shoppers for one weekend in August.

Rep. Robert E. 'Bud' Cramer (D)

CAPITOL OFFICE
225-4801
budmail@mail.house.gov
www.house.gov/cramer
2368 Rayburn 20515-0105; fax 225-4392

COMMITTEES
Appropriations
Select Intelligence

HOMETOWN
Huntsville

BORN
Aug. 22, 1947, Huntsville, Ala.

RELIGION
Methodist

FAMILY
Widowed; one child

EDUCATION
U. of Alabama, B.A. 1969 (English), J.D. 1972

MILITARY SERVICE
Army, 1972; Army Reserve, 1976-78

CAREER
Lawyer

POLITICAL HIGHLIGHTS
Madison County district attorney, 1981-91

ELECTION RESULTS

2002 GENERAL		
Robert E. "Bud" Cramer (D)	143,029	73.3%
Stephen P. Engel (R)	48,226	24.7%
Alan Barksdale (LIBERT)	3,772	1.9%
2002 PRIMARY		
Robert E. "Bud" Cramer (D)		unopposed
2000 GENERAL		
Robert E. "Bud" Cramer (D)	186,059	88.8%
Alan Barksdale (LIBERT)	22,110	10.6%

PREVIOUS WINNING PERCENTAGES
1998 (70%); 1996 (56%); 1994 (50%); 1992 (66%); 1990 (67%)

Elected 1990; 7th term

The word "Democrat" is nowhere to be found in Cramer's official biography on his House Web site, where the descriptive word about Cramer's politics is "conservative."

That is appropriate, as Cramer's voting record since 1995 has marked him as one of the most conservative House Democrats in the 108th Congress. But his support of conservative causes is a necessity for political survival in the 5th District; Jimmy Carter was the last Democratic presidential candidate to carry Alabama's northernmost district.

After a surge of Republican voting nearly ousted him in 1994, Cramer — never a liberal — reacted by further distancing himself from Democratic party stances, and he redoubled his work on district needs. But this was not a new role for him. Since his first term, Cramer has taken the socially as well as fiscally conservative stand on many issues, opposing gun control proposals, for instance, and supporting a constitutional amendment to mandate federal balanced budgets.

During the Democratic-controlled 103rd Congress, Cramer backed his party's leadership and President Clinton more than three-fourths of the time. But since 1994, when his party lost the House majority and he nearly lost his seat, Cramer has voted with his fellow Democrats only slightly more than half the time.

In the 107th Congress, he voted against his party 45 percent of the time on votes that split the parties, third-most among Democrats, while backing President Bush 64 percent of the time, again, third among Democrats who served the entire Congress.

Most notably, Cramer was among the 28 Democrats who broke with their party to support Bush's tax cut plan. He also voted with the GOP on building a missile defense system and drilling for oil in the Arctic National Wildlife Refuge. And he sided with Republicans on a measure to limit the rights of patients to sue their health plans and on an aviation security bill that would have given the president discretion over whether security personnel should be private or government workers.

An approachable and pragmatic man, Cramer is a founding member of the "Blue Dogs," the coalition of conservative House Democrats, and he was co-chairman of its political action committee during the 2002 election cycle.

Cramer is often the target of entreaties from Republicans to switch parties. Early in 2002, shortly after it was reported the GOP was dangling an assignment to the Intelligence Committee as an inducement, Democrats arranged for Cramer to get a seat on the panel.

He stayed with the Democrats in the 107th Congress on legislation to overhaul campaign finance law. He also opposed Bush's request for fast-track authority to negotiate trade agreements that Congress cannot amend and a proposal to provide vouchers for students to attend private schools.

Cramer says one of his proudest achievements in the 107th was to get the Commerce Department to reverse its plans to close a weather station in his tornado-prone district. He argued that doing so would put thousands of lives at risk because the next closest radar would be too far away to provide timely warnings. A new state-of-the-art station was built. The deal was set in motion in 2000, when Cramer voted for an administration-backed measure permanently granting China normal trading status — but only after Commerce agreed to reconsider the weather station's fate.

Cramer serves on the Appropriations subcommittee that funds the departments of Housing and Veterans Affairs and many independent agencies, including NASA. His fiscal conservatism is tempered by his support for NASA and the Pentagon, both of which have a major presence in the 5th District. Huntsville is home to NASA's Marshall Space Flight Center and the Army's Redstone Arsenal.

Cramer also looks out for programs run by the Tennessee Valley Authority, the massive public works project created to provide low-cost energy, flood control and economic development in a multistate region. He was cheered in 2002 when the TVA board decided to restart a nuclear plant at Browns Ferry in northern Alabama that had been shut since 1985.

Economic development is one of Cramer's priorities. He says he likes to "knock on the doors of businesses" to tout North Alabama as an attractive place to do business. In 2001, he traveled to an international auto show in Detroit to pitch a proposal for Toyota to put a V-8 engine manufacturing plant in the region. Toyota agreed and ground was broken later that year. In the 1990s, he helped persuade McDonnell-Douglas (since merged with Boeing Corp.) to build a $450 million, 500-job rocket booster plant in Decatur.

Although conservative on social issues, Cramer supports abortion rights in general. As his late wife battled cancer (she died in 1987), she needed an abortion to prolong her life. He does, however, favor a ban on a procedure its opponents call "partial birth" abortion.

For a decade before coming to Congress, Cramer was the district attorney in Huntsville, where he founded the Children's Advocacy Center to shelter and counsel abused children. (In Congress, he was responsible for legislation in 1992 to provide federal assistance to a growing national network of centers modeled on the Huntsville program.)

His work on behalf of children, coupled with programs his office instituted to prosecute bad-check cases and spousal abuse, earned Cramer a reputation as a champion of the victim; he was honored by President Reagan in a 1987 White House ceremony.

When Democrat Ronnie G. Flippo left the district open in 1990 to run for governor, Cramer won his seat with two-thirds of the vote. But in the GOP landslide four years later — which swept out a cadre of other white Southern Democrats in the House — Cramer won by just 1,770 votes over well-funded and well-connected Wayne Parker, son-in-law of Texas GOP Rep. Bill Archer, later the Ways and Means Committee chairman.

Since then Cramer has won by comfortable margins; in a district minimally changed by redistricting, he took 73 percent in 2002.

KEY VOTES

2002

Yes Overhaul campaign finance law; ban "soft money" and restrict advocacy advertising
Yes Back Bush's defense budget increase
Yes Extend 1996 welfare law
No Adopt Bush's discretionary spending limit
No Pass GOP Medicare prescription drug plan
Yes Create independent Sept. 11 commission
Yes Extend union protections to Homeland Security Department employees
No Revive fast-track procedures for trade agreements
Yes Authorize war against Iraq
Yes Advance bankruptcy overhaul opposed by abortion opponents

2001

Yes Nullify Clinton Labor Department ergonomics rule
Yes Cut taxes by $1.35 trillion through fiscal 2011
No Maintain ban on oil drilling in Arctic National Wildlife Refuge
No Approve Bush proposal to limit managed-care plan liability for coverage decisions
No Divert money from crop subsidy payments to land conservation
Yes Expand law enforcement power to investigate suspected terrorists

CQ VOTE STUDIES

	PARTY UNITY		PRESIDENTIAL SUPPORT	
	Support	Oppose	Support	Oppose
2002	61%	39%	62%	38%
2001	50%	50%	67%	33%
2000	66%	34%	49%	51%
1999	53%	47%	54%	46%
1998	60%	40%	54%	46%

INTEREST GROUPS

	AFL-CIO	ADA	CCUS	ACU
2002	44%	45%	80%	56%
2001	50%	45%	82%	65%
2000	40%	35%	80%	40%
1999	78%	55%	72%	41%
1998	70%	65%	78%	44%

ALABAMA 5
North – Huntsville

A large section of the Tennessee River winds through the 5th, a strip of land across the northern tier of Alabama that borders Georgia, Mississippi and Tennessee.

Reliant on agriculture before World War II, the district now owes its economic well-being to the federal government. Huntsville is best known for hosting the NASA Marshall Space Flight Center, but defense has contributed more to its economy.

Redstone Arsenal benefited from base closures in the 1990s, incorporating Army aviation duties into its missile command center and increasing its personnel. Redstone has attracted several high-tech plants, and Cummings Research Park in Huntsville, with more than 200 tenants and a work force of more than 20,000, boasts that it is the second-largest research park in the United States.

Tennessee Valley Authority facilities line the river's shores throughout the 5th. Boeing built a satellite rocket booster plant in Decatur in 1999, which aided the local economy. Toyota began building its first V-8 engine plant outside of Japan in Huntsville in 2001.

Voters in the 5th have never sent a Republican to Congress, but GOP presidential candidates have enjoyed a slight edge recently. The district generally claims a socially conservative constituency.

MAJOR INDUSTRY
Defense, government, technology

MILITARY BASES
Redstone Arsenal (Army), 2,225 military, 9,164 civilian (2002)

CITIES
Huntsville, 158,216; Decatur (pt.), 44,655; Florence, 36,264; Madison, 29,329; Athens, 18,967

NOTABLE
"Muscle Shoals Sound" originated at Fame Recording Studios, where Aretha Franklin, Otis Redding and Wilson Pickett recorded hit songs; Helen Keller was born in Tuscumbia.

Rep. Spencer Bachus (R)

CAPITOL OFFICE
225-4921
www.house.gov/bachus
442 Cannon 20515-0106; fax 225-2082

COMMITTEES
Financial Services
(Financial Institutions & Consumer Credit - chairman)
Judiciary
Transportation & Infrastructure

HOMETOWN
Birmingham

BORN
Dec. 28, 1947, Birmingham, Ala.

RELIGION
Baptist

FAMILY
Wife, Linda Bachus; three children, two stepchildren

EDUCATION
Auburn U., B.A. 1969; U. of Alabama, J.D. 1972

MILITARY SERVICE
Ala. National Guard, 1969-71

CAREER
Lawyer; manufacturer

POLITICAL HIGHLIGHTS
Ala. Senate, 1983; Ala. House, 1983-87; Ala. Board of Education, 1987-91; candidate for Ala. attorney general, 1990; Ala. Republican Party chairman, 1991-92

ELECTION RESULTS

2002 GENERAL		
Spencer Bachus (R)	178,171	89.8%
J. McAllister (LIBERT)	19,639	9.9%
2002 PRIMARY		
Spencer Bachus (R)	79,509	87.8%
Terry Reagin Sr. (R)	11,042	12.2%
2000 GENERAL		
Spencer Bachus (R)	212,751	88.0%
Terry Reagin Sr. (LIBERT)	28,129	11.6%

PREVIOUS WINNING PERCENTAGES
1998 (72%); 1996 (71%); 1994 (79%); 1992 (52%)

Elected 1992; 6th term

A steadfast conservative with strong religious views, Bachus casts a dependable Republican vote on issues such as tax cuts, abortion and illegal immigration. He was often an outspoken critic of President Clinton.

But that's not the complete picture: Bachus (BACK-us) surprises many of his colleagues by venturing outside that mold in his active support of Third World debt relief.

A devout Baptist, Bachus views debt relief in religious terms. His interest in helping the world's poorest nations was sparked by a meeting he attended at a Birmingham church where he heard a presentation on the Bread for the World relief organization. He argues that Americans have a moral obligation to help the less fortunate in poor countries. "We have so much and these countries have so little," he told The Washington Post. "We're all members of the human race, you know."

In a White House ceremony in late 2000 honoring key participants in legislation to write off hundreds of millions of dollars in debt owed to the United States by Third World countries, Clinton joked that the praise might cause Bachus political difficulties at home. The president said that Bachus, who "had absolutely nothing to gain by doing this," had joined the cause "because he thought it was the right thing to do."

In 2001 Bachus also sought to impose economic sanctions on Sudan in hopes of halting what he characterized as genocide against Christians in southern Sudan. In so doing, he bucked the Bush administration on a foreign policy issue that offered no political payoff and seemingly had no direct relevance to his constituents.

Bachus, who said he knew several Alabamians who had done missionary work in Sudan, said the sanctions were aimed at drying up the country's oil revenue, "which is blood money, which is resulting in the death of millions of people" when it is used to buy military equipment. "It is immoral to finance a war machine you know is wrong," Bachus told the New York Daily News. The House approved Bachus' proposal, 422-2, but the Bush administration, saying it preferred negotiations to sanctions, was able to water it down substantially.

Although Bachus has gained praise from many of his political opponents for his foreign policy stands, Bachus does not portray himself as a rebel; he seems content to highlight his efforts on the home front. He says his accomplishments include directing more highway funds to Alabama from his seat on the Transportation Committee, creating a wildlife refuge along a stretch of the Cahaba River, helping make college more affordable, and increasing health care benefits for the elderly under Medicare.

In 2002, he was an early proponent of making permanent the temporary $1.35 trillion package of tax cuts enacted the year before. The tax law contained measures, akin to those proposed by Bachus, to double the adoption tax credit and to eliminate federal taxes on state-sponsored college tuition savings plans. Also in the 107th, Bachus opposed legislation providing amnesty for illegal immigrants and cosponsored a bill to make it a crime to circumvent state parental consent law to take a minor to another state for an abortion.

Bachus is plain-spoken and earnest, reflecting the old maxim that "what you see is what you get." But he can also lash out with an acerbic wit. In 2002, he jumped into a dispute between bank and credit union officials at a hearing he chaired, saying, "Ever been in a food fight?" They "get you in trouble when you're in school. They're usually not that constructive." His colleagues can also be on the receiving end of his sharp tongue. Once he sarcastically asked aloud for the services of an audiologist when he thought that Banking Committee Chairman Jim Leach of Iowa had called the vote wrong.

Bachus chairs the Financial Services Subcommittee on Financial Institutions and Credit, and in the 107th Congress he wrote legislation to substantially increase federal deposit insurance coverage levels. He acknowledged that his bill gave the Federal Reserve and the Treasury "a lot of heartburn."

Also in the 107th, he supported an amendment by liberal Democrat Maxine Waters of California that encouraged banks to offer basic "lifeline" accounts to make banking more accessible to poor people. The House passed the bill overwhelmingly in 2002, but the Senate never took it up in the face of opposition from GOP senators and the Bush administration. Bachus reintroduced the measure early in the 108th.

He also has badgered federal regulators to analyze the lending guidelines of so-called payday lenders, who make short-term, high-interest loans to people who need money before they get their next paycheck.

Bachus operates more quietly on the Transportation Committee, where he devotes his energy to the time-honored pursuit of bringing home the bacon. He was able to get money for a new control tower at the Birmingham airport and worked for federal funds for the Corridor X project — an upgrade of U.S. 78, the highway between Birmingham and Memphis. In the 107th and again in the 108th, he also proposed legislation to help cities and counties build tornado shelters in modular home communities.

Bachus, who once owned a sawmill and was a practicing criminal trial lawyer for two decades, began his career in elective office in 1983. He served in the state legislature, on the state board of education and as chairman of the Alabama GOP.

In his first House election bid, Bachus benefited handsomely from the post-1990 census remapping of Alabama's congressional districts, which eviscerated the district held for five terms by Democratic Rep. Ben Erdreich and transformed it into a solidly Republican bastion. Bachus won a 52 percent victory in 1992 and has been re-elected with at least 70 percent of the vote since.

In redistricting for the 2002 election, Bachus' district became even more securely Republican.

KEY VOTES

2002

- No Overhaul campaign finance law; ban "soft money" and restrict advocacy advertising
- Yes Back Bush's defense budget increase
- Yes Extend 1996 welfare law
- Yes Adopt Bush's discretionary spending limit
- Yes Pass GOP Medicare prescription drug plan
- No Create independent Sept. 11 commission
- No Extend union protections to Homeland Security Department employees
- Yes Revive fast-track procedures for trade agreements
- Yes Authorize war against Iraq
- Yes Advance bankruptcy overhaul opposed by abortion opponents

2001

- Yes Nullify Clinton Labor Department ergonomics rule
- Yes Cut taxes by $1.35 trillion through fiscal 2011
- No Maintain ban on oil drilling in Arctic National Wildlife Refuge
- Yes Approve Bush proposal to limit managed-care plan liability for coverage decisions
- No Divert money from crop subsidy payments to land conservation
- Yes Expand law enforcement power to investigate suspected terrorists

CQ VOTE STUDIES

	PARTY UNITY		PRESIDENTIAL SUPPORT	
	Support	Oppose	Support	Oppose
2002	98%	2%	89%	11%
2001	96%	4%	97%	3%
2000	89%	11%	24%	76%
1999	90%	10%	17%	83%
1998	89%	11%	20%	80%

INTEREST GROUPS

	AFL-CIO	ADA	CCUS	ACU
2002	11%	0%	100%	100%
2001	8%	0%	95%	96%
2000	10%	5%	85%	88%
1999	33%	20%	76%	84%
1998	10%	5%	89%	84%

ALABAMA 6

Central – suburban Birmingham and Tuscaloosa

Alabama's most prosperous district, the 6th is a combination of the whiter and wealthier portions of Birmingham and Tuscaloosa and their suburbs. Rural life still dots the district, but fields and forests are steadily turning into shopping malls.

Birmingham's success beginning in the 1980s started with a shift from steel to white-collar business. Banks and medical facilities have made the city a hub for the deep South. Though most of Birmingham's population is in the neighboring 7th, commuters from suburbs in the 6th enjoy the bulk of the city's wealth. Jefferson County's well-to-do, almost exclusively white bedroom communities such as Homewood, Mountain Brook and Hoover are home to people who work in Birmingham's business district.

The 6th takes in a small portion of Tuscaloosa, a medium-size city that is starting to feel the effects of Birmingham's expansion. A nearby Mercedes-Benz plant (in the 7th District) joins the city's chemical and rubber manufacturers and adds to the district's employment base. But the area's signature undoubtedly is University of Alabama football, which attracts fanatics statewide to watch the "Crimson Tide." The campus falls just outside of the 6th's borders.

The Republican 6th moved further into the GOP column after redistricting in 2002. GOP-leaning areas in Bibb, Chilton, Coosa and St. Clair counties were added from the 3rd District, where Democrats hoped to gain an advantage. More Birmingham- and Tuscaloosa-area voters were shifted from the 6th into the overwhelmingly Democratic, black-majority 7th. The contrast between the 6th and 7th can lead to conflict, particularly when funds for infrastructure are at stake. Universities in Birmingham and Tuscaloosa account for the 7th's few Democratic votes.

MAJOR INDUSTRY

Banking, manufacturing, higher education

CITIES

Hoover, 62,742; Birmingham (pt.), 26,723; Vestavia Hills, 24,476; Alabaster, 22,619; Mountain Brook, 20,604

NOTABLE

A 55-foot cast-iron statue in Birmingham of Vulcan, the Roman god of fire and metalworking, is one of the world's largest iron figures.

Rep. Artur Davis (D)

CAPITOL OFFICE
225-2665
www.house.gov/arturdavis
208 Cannon 20515-0107; fax 226-9567

COMMITTEES
Budget
Financial Services

HOMETOWN
Birmingham

BORN
Oct. 9, 1967, Montgomery, Ala.

RELIGION
Lutheran

FAMILY
Single

EDUCATION
Harvard U., A.B. 1990 (government), J.D. 1993

CAREER
Lawyer

POLITICAL HIGHLIGHTS
Assistant U.S. attorney, 1994-98; sought Democratic nomination for U.S. House, 2000

ELECTION RESULTS

2002 GENERAL		
Artur Davis (D)	153,735	92.4%
Lauren Orth McCay (LIBERT)	12,100	7.3%
2002 PRIMARY RUNOFF		
Artur Davis (D)	52,394	56.0%
Earl F. Hilliard (D)	41,162	44.0%
2002 PRIMARY		
Earl F. Hilliard (D)	46,224	45.7%
Artur Davis (D)	43,519	43.1%
Sam Wiggins III (D)	11,315	11.2%

Elected 2002; 1st term

Economic development tops Davis' agenda in his first term. If his campaign was any indication, he should have some ideas about bringing funds from Washington to Alabama's black-majority 7th District, one of the nation's poorest constituencies.

Davis grabbed headlines during his successful bid to oust five-term Rep. Earl F. Hilliard in the June 2002 Democratic primary. The challenger received contributions from a nationwide network of pro-Israel donors who saw Hilliard's views as pro-Arab.

But Davis — who had held Hilliard to 58 percent of the vote in an underfunded 2000 primary bid — did not make Middle East issues the focus of his campaign. Rather, he made the case that Hilliard had done little to lift up the economically disadvantaged of West Alabama's "Black Belt."

Davis envisions using his newfound influence to help constituents on "bread and butter" issues. He wants to aggressively court private-public partnerships as the means to a better economic outlook.

Raised by his mother and grandmother after his parents divorced, Davis worked his way to Harvard University, where he earned two degrees. He was an intern at the Southern Poverty Law Center and a clerk to a federal judge. Later, he was a federal prosecutor, then worked in private practice.

Davis says he plans to reach out to well-placed colleagues in the House Republican majority. "You can choose to take people at face value or take time to get to know their concerns," Davis told The Associated Press shortly after his election. "I think my predecessor looked at them as a bunch of conservatives who didn't share his agenda, and I think you have to look deeper than that."

Hilliard fell short of the majority he needed in the three-candidate primary to avoid a runoff. Davis, who finished second in the first-round contest, then blew past Hilliard to win the runoff with 56 percent.

Davis' general election victory was a foregone conclusion: The GOP did not field a candidate in the overwhelmingly Democratic district.

ALABAMA 7

West central – parts of Birmingham and Tuscaloosa

The 7th combines large portions of Birmingham and Tuscaloosa with poor, rural communities in west-central Alabama. In contrast to its white, well-to-do neighbor, the Republican 6th District, the 7th's residents tend to be lower- to middle-class blacks who vote overwhelmingly Democratic. The 7th lost its portion of Montgomery to the 3rd during 2002 redistricting, while it gained parts of Jefferson and Tuscaloosa counties.

The 7th's part of Birmingham, the densely populated downtown area, has lagged behind the rest of the city. Still, there are signs of revitalization: old buildings are being restored into high-rent apartments.

Several steel plants and communications firms have kept district unemployment down. Near Tuscaloosa, a Mercedes-Benz plant in Vance now tops an industrial sector that complements small- to medium-size businesses. One of the district's best known employers is the University of Alabama in Tuscaloosa.

The Black Belt, named for the traditionally rich soil in rural Alabama, accounts for the rest of the district. This poverty-filled area has not known prosperity since before the Civil War, when cotton plantation owners made fortunes from slave labor.

Power struggles between the region's existing black political machine and a new generation of black leaders have made for interesting primaries here in recent years.

MAJOR INDUSTRY
Agriculture, higher education, manufacturing

CITIES
Birmingham (pt.), 216,097; Tuscaloosa (pt.), 68,928; Bessemer (pt.), 27,599; Selma, 20,512

NOTABLE
Edmund Pettus Bridge in Selma was the site of "Bloody Sunday," when Alabama state troopers beat and gassed peaceful civil rights marchers on their way from Selma to Montgomery in 1965.

ALASKA

Gov. Frank H. Murkowski (R)

First elected: 2002
Length of term: 4 years
Term expires: 12/06
Salary: $85,776
Phone: (907) 465-3500
Hometown: Fairbanks
Born: March 28, 1933; Seattle, Wash.
Religion: Roman Catholic
Family: Wife, Nancy Gore; six children
Education: Santa Clara U., attended 1951-53; Seattle U., B.A. 1955 (economics)
Military Service: Coast Guard, 1955-56
Career: Banker
Political highlights: Alaska commissioner of economic development, 1966-70; Republican nominee for U.S. House, 1970; U.S. Senate, 1981-2002
Election results:

2002 GENERAL		
Frank H. Murkowski (R)	129,279	55.9%
Fran Ulmer (D)	94,216	40.7%
Diane E. Benson (GREEN)	2,926	1.3%

Lt. Gov. Loren Leman (R)

First elected: 2002
Length of term: 4 years
Term expires: 12/06
Salary: $80,000
Phone: (907) 465-3520

STATE LEGISLATURE

Legislature: Meets from January-May, with a limit of 121 calendar days
House: 40 members, 2-year terms
2003 breakdown: 27R, 13D; 32 men, 8 women
Salary: $24,012
Phone: (907) 465-3725
Senate: 20 members, 4-year terms
2003 breakdown: 12R, 8D; 16 men, 4 women
Salary: $24,012
Phone: (907) 465-3701

STATE TERM LIMITS

Governor: 2 consecutive terms
Senate: No
House: No

URBAN STATISTICS

CITY	POPULATION
Anchorage	260,283
Juneau	30,711
Fairbanks	30,224
Sitka	8,835
Ketchikan	7,922

REGISTERED VOTERS

Undeclared	37%
Republican	26%
Democrat	16%

POPULATION

2002 population (est.)	643,786
2000 population	626,932
1990 population	550,043
Percent change (1990-2000)	+14%
Rank among states (2002)	47
Median age	32.4
Born in state	38.1%
Foreign born	5.9%
Violent crime rate	567/100,000
Poverty level	9.4%
Federal workers	16,363
Military	22,786

REDISTRICTING

Alaska retained its one House seat in reapportionment.

MISCELLANEOUS

Web: www.state.ak.us
Capital: Juneau
STATE ELECTION OFFICIAL
(907) 465-4611
DEMOCRATIC HEADQUARTERS
(907) 258-3050
REPUBLICAN HEADQUARTERS
(907) 276-4467

District Statistics

DIST.	2000 VOTE FOR PRESIDENT BUSH	GORE	NADER	WHITE	BLACK	ASIAN	HISP	MEDIAN INCOME	WHITE COLLAR	BLUE COLLAR	SERVICE INDUSTRY	OVER 64	UNDER 18	COLLEGE EDUCATION	RURAL	SQ. MILES
AL	59%	28%	10%	68%	3%	4%	4%	$51,571	61%	24%	16%	6%	30%	25%	34%	571,951
STATE	59	28	10	68	3	4	4	$51,571	61	24	16	6	30	25	34	571,951
U.S.	47.9	48.4	3	69	12	4	13	$41,994	60	25	15	12	26	24	21	3,537,438

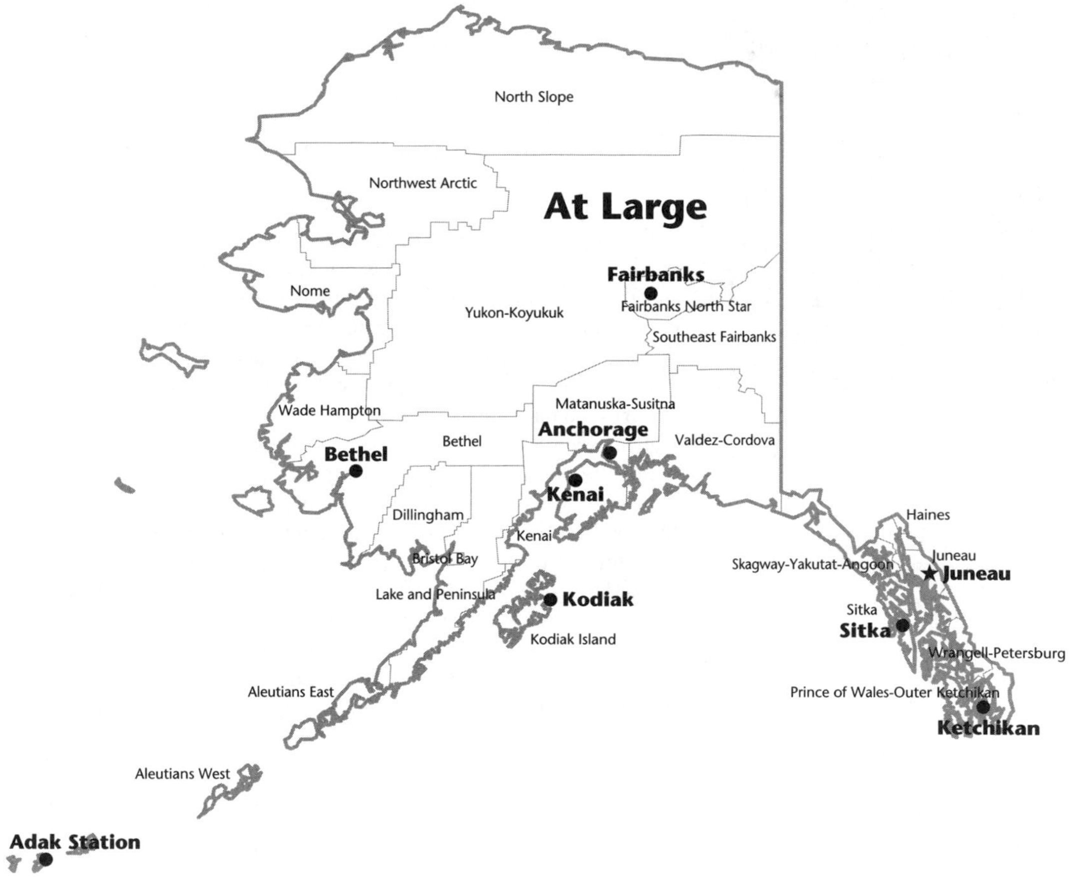
North Slope
Northwest Arctic
At Large
Fairbanks
Nome
Yukon-Koyukuk
Fairbanks North Star
Southeast Fairbanks
Matanuska-Susitna
Wade Hampton
Anchorage
Bethel
Bethel
Valdez-Cordova
Kenai
Dillingham
Kenai
Haines
Bristol Bay
Skagway-Yakutat-Angoon
Juneau
Juneau
Lake and Peninsula
Kodiak
Sitka
Sitka
Kodiak Island
Wrangell-Petersburg
Aleutians East
Prince of Wales-Outer Ketchikan
Ketchikan
Aleutians West
Adak Station

Sen. Ted Stevens (R)

CAPITOL OFFICE
224-3004
stevens.senate.gov
522 Hart 20510-0201; fax 224-2354

COMMITTEES
Appropriations - chairman
(Defense - chairman)
Commerce, Science & Transportation
Governmental Affairs
Rules & Administration
Special Aging
Joint Library - chairman

HOMETOWN
Girdwood

BORN
Nov. 18, 1923, Indianapolis, Ind.

RELIGION
Episcopalian

FAMILY
Wife, Catherine Stevens; six children

EDUCATION
U. of California, Los Angeles, B.A. 1947 (political science); Harvard U., LL.B. 1950

MILITARY SERVICE
Army Air Corps, 1943-46

CAREER
Lawyer

POLITICAL HIGHLIGHTS
U.S. attorney, 1953-56; Republican nominee for U.S. Senate, 1962; Alaska House, 1965-68 (majority leader and Speaker pro tempore, 1967-68); sought Republican nomination for U.S. Senate, 1968

ELECTION RESULTS

2002 GENERAL		
Ted Stevens (R)	179,438	78.2%
Frank Vondersaar (D)	24,133	10.5%
Jim Sykes (GREEN)	16,608	7.2%
Jim Dore (AKI)	6,724	2.9%
Leonard Karpinski (LIBERT)	2,354	1.0%
2002 PRIMARY		
Ted Stevens (R)	64,315	88.9%
Mike Aubrey (R)	7,997	11.1%

PREVIOUS WINNING PERCENTAGES
1996 (77%); 1990 (66%); 1984 (71%); 1978 (76%); 1972 (77%); 1970 Special Election (60%)

Elected 1970; 6th full term

Appointed December 1968

Tenacious, tough and unabashedly old school, Stevens is well into his fourth decade of blazing his own trail in the Senate.

His longevity brought with it revived power as well as new stature in the 108th Congress. With Republicans back in control, and with 47-year veteran Strom Thurmond of South Carolina having retired, Stevens is the most senior member of the majority party in the Senate. As such he has become the chamber's president pro tempore — a mostly symbolic job that, under the Constitution, places him third in the line of presidential succession after the vice president and the Speaker of the House.

Of more regular import, Stevens also reclaimed the chairmanship of the Senate Appropriations Committee, placing him in position to shape the spending priorities of a president of his own party. But there is little expectation of sweet budgetary collegiality between Stevens and the Bush White House. Stevens' mind set has been slow to adapt to the reality, and the political strength, of a Republican president determined to compel a Republican Congress to hold down the growth of spending.

As a result Stevens knocked heads frequently with the administration during the 107th Congress, when for the final 18 months he was the Appropriations panel's ranking minority party member. Stevens and Robert C. Byrd of West Virginia, the panel's like-minded top Democrat, won a few and lost a few. Their collaborative victories included defending congressional earmarks despite a White House campaign against them; their shared setbacks came as the president repeatedly used veto threats to keep appropriators from exceeding White House limits.

Asked in 2001 what White House Budget Director Mitchell E. Daniels Jr. could do to repair his uneasy relations with Congress, Stevens growled: "Go home to Indiana."

In the first two years of the Bush administration, Stevens supported Byrd's campaign to breach the discretionary spending ceiling decreed by the president. They succeeded in adding about $6 billion in 2001 — bolstered by the spirit of bipartisanship and the lack of interest in cutting homeland defense corners after the Sept. 11, 2001, terrorist attacks. But Bush took a harder line in 2002 and, after he helped Hill Republicans to important congressional gains in the midterm election, GOP appropriators quickly fell into line. Stevens cut about $10 billion from Byrd-drafted bills when he assembled a mammoth package to wrap up, almost half a year behind schedule, spending deliberations for the budget year that began October 2002.

Soon after taking over the chairmanship of Appropriations in 1997, Stevens warned colleagues that he was "a mean, miserable SOB." During his tenure — which will end after the 108th because of GOP-imposed term limits — he has ruled the appropriations process in customary curmudgeonly fashion. Often when working through a difficult jam, he will don a necktie bearing the likenesses of legendary cartoon tough guys like the Incredible Hulk and the Tasmanian Devil.

As the neckwear suggests, Stevens' bark can be worse than his bite. His frequent explosions are usually short-lived, and offense is rarely taken. Longtime Stevens watchers say they have often seen him throw a fit and then exit the room with a wink. "I believe in using my emotions, not losing my emotions," he says.

For all his bluster, Stevens remains a throwback to the clubby pragmatism that once permeated the Senate and its spending committee. His work with Byrd and other Democrats is essential to driving 13 appropriations bills through a political and legislative battleground each year. Still, Stevens and Byrd experienced some strains in their relationship as control of the panel shifted to Byrd in the middle of 2001 and then back to Stevens in 2003. Stevens complained privately that Byrd was too heavy-handed in running the committee; and during deliberations on the wrap-up spending bill early in the 108th, Stevens kept Byrd frozen out of the talks.

Stevens is just as likely to combat fellow Republicans in Congress as he is Democrats or the president. Especially since he took the gavel at Appropriations, Stevens has routinely butted heads with GOP conservatives, who have more sway over writing the annual congressional budget than in producing the bills to put that budget into practice. So while he has lost some battles, in the end Stevens generally has gotten his way.

And Alaska has always fared well. Stevens' attention to the state's parochial needs is legendary, and he has brought federal funds to virtually every remote region of the state. In 1998, he created the Denali Commission, which distributes grants for rural health clinics, energy projects and community clothes-washing centers in those parts of Alaska without running water. It has received more than $200 million in federal funds. In 2000, a grateful state legislature named the Anchorage International Airport for Stevens.

Away from Appropriations, Stevens is known as an ardent promoter of timber cutting and oil drilling in parts of his state that environmentalists are eager to preserve. He also was a principal author of the 1978 law that gave rise to the modern U.S. Olympic Committee.

Stevens once dreamed of becoming majority leader. In 1984, after eight years as Republican whip, he ran a strong race for the top Senate leadership post, losing to Bob Dole of Kansas by only three votes.

When Dole's successor as GOP leader, Trent Lott, was forced from the leadership at the end of 2002 after making racially insensitive remarks, Stevens was among Lott's few steadfast defenders.

With his typical concern for the Senate as an institution, in 1999 Stevens helped broker a bipartisan agreement on how to conduct the impeachment trial of President Clinton in a way that avoided the partisanship that marked the House proceedings and outraged much of the public. As the trial proceeded, he urged the House prosecutors of the case to avoid a lengthy trial and not to call witnesses. In the end, he was among the 10 Republicans voting to acquit Clinton of perjury in attempting to conceal his relationship with former White House intern Monica Lewinsky. (He did, however, vote to convict the president on obstruction-of-justice charges.)

After flying C-46 transports throughout China during World War II and earning the Distinguished Flying Cross, Stevens earned a law degree and became a federal prosecutor for three years in the mid-1950s. He began his pursuit of a Senate seat not long after Alaska became a state in 1959. He got the party's nomination for the job in 1962 but managed just 41 percent against Democrat Ernest J. Gruening that fall.

Stevens, who went on to serve in the Alaska House, including a stint as majority leader, tried for the Senate again in 1968 but was defeated in the GOP primary. Later that year, however, Democratic Sen. E.L. Bartlett died, and Stevens was appointed to the seat by GOP Gov. Walter J. Hickel. In the 1970 contest to serve the final two years of Bartlett's term, Stevens defeated liberal Democrat Wendell P. Kay with 60 percent of the vote.

Stevens has cruised to re-election ever since, including in 1978, when he suffered injuries in the plane crash that took the life of his first wife. His narrowest victory, in 1990, was with 66 percent against Democratic gadfly Michael Beasley. His best showing, in 2002, was with 78 percent against Democratic lawyer and engineer Frank Vondersaar.

KEY VOTES

2002

- No Pass farm bill reversing crop subsidy limits
- Yes Postpone tougher automobile fuel efficiency standards
- No Overhaul campaign finance law; ban "soft money" and restrict advocacy advertising
- Yes Set federal election standards
- Yes Support oil drilling in Arctic National Wildlife Refuge
- Yes Revive fast-track procedures for trade agreements
- Yes Create federal insurance coverage for catastrophic terrorist losses
- Yes Tighten federal accounting and corporate governance regulation
- No Advance bipartisan Medicare prescription drug plan
- Yes Create independent Sept. 11 commission
- No Back Democratic Homeland Security Department proposal
- Yes Authorize war against Iraq

2001

- Yes Confirm John Ashcroft as attorney general
- Yes Nullify Clinton Labor Department ergonomics rule
- Yes Cut taxes by $1.35 trillion through fiscal 2011
- No Pass Democratic bill to bolster rights of patients in managed-care plans
- No Permit a new round of military base closings
- Yes Expand law enforcement power to investigate suspected terrorists

CQ VOTE STUDIES

	PARTY UNITY		PRESIDENTIAL SUPPORT	
	Support	Oppose	Support	Oppose
2002	89%	11%	95%	5%
2001	88%	12%	97%	3%
2000	92%	8%	56%	44%
1999	90%	10%	36%	64%
1998	82%	18%	54%	46%
1997	79%	21%	71%	29%
1996	90%	10%	45%	55%
1995	89%	11%	32%	68%
1994	73%	27%	52%	48%
1993	82%	18%	33%	67%

INTEREST GROUPS

	AFL-CIO	ADA	CCUS	ACU
2002	23%	10%	100%	83%
2001	25%	20%	86%	92%
2000	0%	5%	100%	92%
1999	33%	10%	88%	84%
1998	25%	20%	94%	56%
1997	14%	30%	80%	58%
1996	29%	20%	85%	80%
1995	8%	5%	94%	73%
1994	43%	25%	67%	77%
1993	55%	25%	91%	80%

Sen. Lisa Murkowski (R)

CAPITOL OFFICE
224-6665
murkowski.senate.gov
322 Hart 20510-0202; fax 224-5301

COMMITTEES
Energy & Natural Resources
(Water & Power - chairwoman)
Environment & Public Works
Indian Affairs
Veterans' Affairs

HOMETOWN
Anchorage

BORN
May 22, 1957, Ketchikan, Alaska

RELIGION
Roman Catholic

FAMILY
Husband, Verne Martell; two children

EDUCATION
Willamette U., attended 1975-77; Georgetown U., B.A. 1980 (economics); Willamette U., J.D. 1985

CAREER
Lawyer; state legislative aide

POLITICAL HIGHLIGHTS
Anchorage District Attorney, 1987-89; Alaska House, 1999-2002

Appointed December 2002; 1st term

During her relatively brief tenure as a state legislator, Murkowski built a reputation as a risk taker and tough advocate for her constituents — terms that have been used more than once to describe her father. Republican Frank H. Murkowski served 22 years in the Senate before winning election as governor of Alaska in 2002 and appointing his daughter to fill the remaining two years of his Senate term.

The younger Murkowski, however, is ideologically different enough from her father that his decision to name her as his replacement took many by surprise. Murkowski was known in Alaska as a moderate — a label never applied to her father, a conservative stalwart during his years in Washington. "Every time we give, we lose," he once said. In contrast, during her four years in the state House, Lisa Murkowski earned a reputation as a problem solver by trying to build consensus.

One difference that has brought attention concerns abortion. While her father opposed abortion rights, Murkowski believes that a woman has a right to an abortion, but with some restrictions, such as a ban on most late-term abortions. Yet Murkowski contends that she is as far to the right as her paternal predecessor on most issues and suggests that she might be viewed as a moderate only by the strictly conservative standards of her state.

"I think you have to keep in mind that my label came from the Alaska Legislature," she said. "If you look at the body I am in now and the colleagues that I now have, I think it is probably too soon to label me."

Her arrival is unique in senatorial history. Five other children of former senators are in the Senate in the 108th Congress. On four previous occasions a senator's son succeeded to his father's seat. And twice before governors have named members of their immediate families — their wives — to fill Senate vacancies. However, in addition to bringing the roster of women in the Senate to 14, a record, Lisa Murkowski is also the first senator's daughter ever in the Senate, and she is also the first person ever appointed to the Senate by a parent.

As a consequence, her appointment sparked fervent accusations of nepotism, even by many political commentators and legislators in Alaska who viewed her as fully qualified for the job. "So I've got a lot of work to do — I don't deny that," Murkowski says. "I've got to establish to my constituents that I truly am the best choice to represent them."

After only four years in the state House, Murkowski had been elected by her Republican colleagues as majority leader just before her December 2002 appointment to the Senate. Her peers attributed her fast rise to her studious nature and her willingness to research issues and develop proposals to address them. When Murkowski and other legislators became frustrated with the legislature's inaction in solving state budget problems, they formed a caucus that suggested the possibility of raising taxes — a rather daring stand in Alaska — to offset projected shortfalls of close to $1 billion.

Nearly everyone, including Frank Murkowski, eventually got behind a "dime a drink" alcoholic beverage tax that Lisa Murkowski introduced. But the political risk of that stance — and her opposition to a bill to limit state funding for abortions for poor women — was borne out in August 2002: A more conservative challenger held Murkowski to 53 percent of the vote in the Republican primary for her state House seat.

Murkowski said early in 2003 that she was unsure whether she would have to alter her legislative style as a freshman senator. "In the state legislature, you have the ability to sometimes be a lightning rod to shake things up for the better," she said. "Here in the Senate you're tied to a tradition. . . . But does that mean that you just docilely walk in line? I don't think so. I certainly hope not."

Murkowski inherited her father's Hart Senate Office Building suite. And she was able to win a seat on the Energy and Natural Resources Committee, which deals with issues crucial to Alaska's economy — and on which her father was the top Republican for the final eight years of his Senate career. She was one of two freshmen to win subcommittee gavels on the panel; she chairs the Water and Power Subcommittee.

She also took seats previously held by her father on the Indian Affairs and Veterans' Affairs committees, as well as an assignment to the Environment and Public Works Committee, which deals with many Alaska-centric issues.

Murkowski is cognizant that, without the seniority that her father had accrued, her work to influence legislation and deliver for her constituents will be slow going during the 108th Congress — after which she will stand for election on her own in a state that has come to expect the three members of its congressional delegation to wield clout disproportionate to their number.

But she said she would work "hand in glove" with the state's senior senator, Republican Ted Stevens, who has plenty of sway as the chairman of the Appropriations Committee. And Alaska's lone representative, Republican Don Young, who chairs the House Transportation and Infrastructure Committee, is also in a position to help Murkowski produce tangible results for the state.

Murkowski's legislative priorities are in line with those of her father, as well as Stevens and Young. It has surprised no one in Washington that Murkowski strongly favors opening Alaska's Arctic National Wildlife Refuge to oil and gas exploration, a stand for which her father was best-known. She also backs construction of a natural gas pipeline in Alaska.

Although Murkowski says national defense and security are valid reasons to run a budget deficit, she plans to look closely for ways to get the country out of the red as soon as possible. "It concerns me that we have gone from a situation where we had a surplus to, in very short order, looking at a deficit," she says.

After an internship in Stevens' office as a high school senior, Murkowski began college in Seattle but came East to earn her degree at Georgetown. After moving to Juneau and working as a state legislative aide, she earned a law degree, then worked as an attorney in the state court system. She was active in Anchorage GOP circles before running for the state House in 1998.

Murkowski says that her upbringing stressed civic duty. Although her father was a banker who did not run for the Senate until she had graduated from college, she says her family was always active on local issues. Growing up a Murkowski, she says, meant "knowing that you were a part of a family that was involved in shaping the state of Alaska." Nonetheless, she says, "politics was not necessarily dinner conversation. We did have good family conversations about what was happening, but didn't sit around and talk about the merits of Goldwater vs. Kennedy."

As her service in the Senate began, Murkowski was relatively confident that her Democratic opponent in 2004 would be Tony Knowles, who remained popular even when his maximum two terms as governor came to an end in 2002. She plans to make the long flight home frequently, not only to campaign but also to visit with her husband and two young sons.

Rep. Don Young (R)

CAPITOL OFFICE
225-5765
www.house.gov/donyoung
2111 Rayburn 20515-0201; fax 225-0425

COMMITTEES
Resources
Select Homeland Security
Transportation & Infrastructure - chairman

HOMETOWN
Fort Yukon

BORN
June 9, 1933, Meridian, Calif.

RELIGION
Episcopalian

FAMILY
Wife, Lula Young; two children

EDUCATION
Yuba Junior College, A.A. 1952; California State U., Chico, B.A. 1958

MILITARY SERVICE
Army, 1955-57

CAREER
Elementary school teacher; riverboat captain

POLITICAL HIGHLIGHTS
Fort Yukon City Council, 1960-64; mayor of Fort Yukon, 1964-68; Alaska House, 1967-70; Alaska Senate, 1971-73; Republican nominee for U.S. House, 1972

ELECTION RESULTS

2002 GENERAL		
Don Young (R)	169,685	74.5%
Clifford Mark Greene (D)	39,357	17.3%
Russell deForest (GREEN)	14,435	6.3%
2002 PRIMARY		
Don Young (R)		unopposed
2000 GENERAL		
Don Young (R)	190,862	69.6%
Clifford Mark Greene (D)	45,372	16.5%
Anna C. Young (GREEN)	22,440	8.2%
Jim Dore (AKI)	10,085	3.7%

PREVIOUS WINNING PERCENTAGES
1998 (63%); 1996 (59%); 1994 (57%); 1992 (47%); 1990 (52%); 1988 (63%); 1986 (56%); 1984 (55%); 1982 (71%); 1980 (74%); 1978 (55%); 1976 (71%); 1974 (54%); 1973 Special Election (51%)

Elected March 1973; 15th full term

Young is starting his fourth decade representing the nation's largest state with one of the House's most outsize personalities. His disposition is that of the rugged, even cantankerous individualist. And he has sought to capitalize on his bombastic style — short on temper, long on red-meat rhetoric, never afraid to make his point louder than anyone else — to leverage respect for his ambitious ideas about the deregulation of natural resources and the promotion of public works.

The 108th Congress is Young's second as chairman of the Transportation and Infrastructure Committee, which simultaneously had on the agenda its two biggest recurring tasks: updating federal highway and mass transit programs and renewing aviation programs. As debate on the surface transportation bill began, Young was characteristically bold in his proposal to raise the federal tax on motor fuels — and to dedicate the increase entirely to public works for the first time since 1983 — in order to finance a 40 percent increase on road and bridge spending during the next six years.

In that debate, as in others, Young can be expected to brush past those holding different opinions with an abrupt dismissiveness.

Whether the economic benefits of drilling for oil in the Arctic National Wildlife Refuge outweigh the environmental risks is one of the most intensely debated, and exhaustively researched, national policy questions of the day. And yet for Young the answer seems without nuance. "It is right for this nation and for the people," Young declared on the House floor in 2001, as the House debated whether to make drilling in the refuge part of an energy policy overhaul. "It is right for my people in the state of Alaska. It is the best thing we have going, and how dare members talk about something when they have never been there. Shame on them."

In his first term as Transportation chairman, Young was a central player in moving several major laws enacted by the 107th Congress in response to the Sept. 11, 2001, terrorist attacks. Principal among them was the aviation security law that federalized airport screeners and mandated the inspection of all checked baggage. Young was an advocate, along with President Bush, of giving the administration the option of hiring either government employees or private contract workers. But the Democratic Senate insisted that the screeners be federal employees, and Bush yielded to their view in order to secure a quick victory.

Young also helped shape another law, signed less than two weeks after the attacks, that provided up to $15 billion in financial assistance to the airline industry. Enactment was delayed over the question of whether to include aid for out-of-work aviation workers; the final deal did not, but Young suggested that he would revisit the issue in the 108th. He also was an influential champion of three more laws enacted in 2002: to arm and train airline passenger pilots; to improve the safety and security of the underground pipeline system; and to bolster security at seaports. In the 108th, he serves on the new Homeland Security Committee.

For the six years before taking the Transportation gavel, Young chaired the House panel with jurisdiction over public lands and the environment — the first Republican to do so in 40 years. Under the Democrats the committee had been most recently called Natural Resources; under Young it was renamed, simply, Resources. Like many Western Republicans, Young is an eager ally of energy, mining and timber interests and a vigorous advocate of the rights of private property holders. His zeal for loosening the government's grip on federal lands puts him squarely at odds with environmentalists, who deride him as a blatant exploiter of the nation's most precious resources. Young, in turn, has likened the environmentalists to communists.

And yet, in the 106th Congress Young surprised both his environmentalist enemies and his property rights friends. He joined his frequent nemesis on the committee, ranking Democrat George Miller of California, on a plan to guarantee $45 billion in conservation spending over 15 years by dedicating a portion of federal oil and gas drilling revenues to the effort. When appropriators and the Clinton administration reached agreement on a smaller amount and made it subject to annual renewal, Young brayed that he had been rolled by his colleagues. "The natives are getting restless, buddy," he growled to an opponent on the House floor.

A staunch opponent of gun control and an avid sportsman — a huge Kodiak bear skin is mounted on the wall of his Washington office — Young is also a determined guardian of the economic interests of his state. His Web site offers an exhaustive list of the more than $2 billion in special appropriations he "helped to secure" for Alaska in the 107th.

He did so despite missing 18 percent of the House's recorded votes, one of the 10 worst lawmaker participation rates of the 107th. In December 2001, he flew home to Alaska because, he said, he was frustrated with the Senate's slow pace of moving legislation that might have brought the session to a close. No excuse, the Fairbanks Daily News-Miner said in a critical editorial: "Representing the people of Alaska — primarily through votes in Congress — is Young's job."

Born in California, Young moved to Alaska to teach, then became a licensed riverboat captain and a member of the Dog Mushers Association. The only election he has ever lost was his first, in 1972. His opponent, freshman Democrat Nick Begich, disappeared without a trace along with House Majority Leader Hale Boggs during an October airplane flight from Anchorage to Juneau. Begich still beat Young by almost 12,000 votes.

When Begich's seat was declared vacant a few weeks later, Young edged out Emil Notti, the former state Democratic chairman, in a 1973 special election. Young weathered a vigorous challenge in the post-Watergate election of 1974, then enjoyed relatively comfortable re-election margins until 1990. That year and in 1992, he barely survived challenges from John E. Devens, the former Democratic mayor of Valdez. Young conceded in advertisements that he was "abrasive" and "arrogant," but a worthy fighter for Alaska's interests. He has not been seriously challenged since.

KEY VOTES

2002

No Overhaul campaign finance law; ban "soft money" and restrict advocacy advertising
Yes Back Bush's defense budget increase
Yes Extend 1996 welfare law
Yes Adopt Bush's discretionary spending limit
Yes Pass GOP Medicare prescription drug plan
? Create independent Sept. 11 commission
No Extend union protections to Homeland Security Department employees
No Revive fast-track procedures for trade agreements
Yes Authorize war against Iraq
Yes Advance bankruptcy overhaul opposed by abortion opponents

2001

Yes Nullify Clinton Labor Department ergonomics rule
Yes Cut taxes by $1.35 trillion through fiscal 2011
No Maintain ban on oil drilling in Arctic National Wildlife Refuge
Yes Approve Bush proposal to limit managed-care plan liability for coverage decisions
No Divert money from crop subsidy payments to land conservation
? Expand law enforcement power to investigate suspected terrorists

CQ VOTE STUDIES

	PARTY UNITY		PRESIDENTIAL SUPPORT	
	Support	Oppose	Support	Oppose
2002	94%	6%	86%	14%
2001	98%	2%	86%	14%
2000	86%	14%	21%	79%
1999	91%	9%	16%	84%
1998	89%	11%	28%	72%

INTEREST GROUPS

	AFL-CIO	ADA	CCUS	ACU
2002	13%	10%	90%	86%
2001	13%	5%	89%	91%
2000	22%	10%	78%	73%
1999	33%	10%	88%	86%
1998	44%	20%	78%	84%

ALASKA

At large

Alaska's remoteness belies its dependence on Washington, D.C. The state's proximity to Russia and the Far East makes it a military stronghold; the federal government is Alaska's largest employer. Other economic boosters — oil, minerals and timber — lie mostly on federally owned land.

A never-ending battle for control over the local economy has made voters here hostile to Washington and led them to vote overwhelmingly Republican in national elections. Alaska has not elected a Democrat to Congress since 1974. Its congressional delegation vigorously opposed a Clinton administration rule banning road building and most logging in the Tongass National Forest, and the lawmakers have been the most outspoken advocates of opening land to oil and gas exploration.

The state has tried to build a privatized economy through tourism, a sometimes booming industry hurt by the nation's post-Sept. 11 economic downturn. But most Alaskans view oil exploration as the best way to independence and heavily favor drilling in the Arctic National Wildlife Refuge. The state was able to scrap its sales and income taxes and provide residents with annual royalties when it struck black gold near Prudhoe Bay in the 1970s.

Alaska's partisan vote is majority Republican, but voters in a few cities, the panhandle and the sparsely populated tundra vote more Democratic. Third parties proliferate in this cold, conservative frontier state, where most voters register as either independent or nonpartisan.

MAJOR INDUSTRY

Oil, defense, tourism, fishing, timber, mining

MILITARY BASES

Elmendorf Air Force Base, 6,458 military, 2,013 civilian; Fort Wainwright (Army), 4,000 military, 650 civilian; Eielson Air Force Base, 3,000 military, 1,000 civilian; Fort Richardson (Army), 2,000 military, 800 civilian; Clear Air Force Station, 100 military, 52 civilian; Fort Greely (Army), 13 military, 85 civilian (2001)

CITIES

Anchorage, 260,283; Juneau, 30,711; Fairbanks, 30,224

NOTABLE

Mt. McKinley is the highest point in North America, at 20,320 feet.

ARIZONA

Gov. Janet Napolitano (D)

First elected: 2002
Length of term: 4 years
Term expires: 1/07
Salary: $95,000
Phone: (602) 542-4331
Hometown: Phoenix
Born: Nov. 29, 1957; Manhattan, N.Y.
Religion: Methodist
Family: Single
Education: Santa Clara U., B.S. 1979 (political science); U. of Virginia, J.D. 1983
Career: Lawyer
Political highlights: U.S. attorney, 1993-97; Ariz. attorney general, 1999-2003
Election results:

2002 GENERAL		
Janet Napolitano (D)	566,284	46.2%
Matt Salmon (R)	554,465	45.2%
Richard Mahoney (I)	84,947	6.9%
Barry Hess (LIBERT)	20,356	1.7%

Secretary of State Jan Brewer (R)

(no lieutenant governor)
First elected: 2002
Length of term: 4 years
Term expires: 1/07
Salary: $70,000
Phone: (602) 542-4285

STATE LEGISLATURE

Legislature: Meets 100 days, January-April
House: 60 members, 2-year terms
2003 breakdown: 39R, 21D; 44 men, 16 women
Salary: $24,000
Phone: (602) 542-3032
Senate: 30 members, 2-year terms
2003 breakdown: 17R, 13D; 22 men, 8 women
Salary: $24,000
Phone: (602) 542-3559

STATE TERM LIMITS

Governor: 2 consecutive terms
Senate: 4 consecutive terms
House: 4 consecutive terms

URBAN STATISTICS

CITY	POPULATION
Phoenix	1,321,045
Tucson	486,699
Mesa	396,375
Glendale	218,812
Scottsdale	202,705

REGISTERED VOTERS

Republican	42%
Democrat	36%
Other	22%

POPULATION

2002 population (est.)	5,456,453
2000 population	5,130,632
1990 population	3,665,228
Percent change (1990-2000)	+40%
Rank among states (2002)	19
Median age	34.2
Born in state	34.7%
Foreign born	12.8%
Violent crime rate	532/100,000
Poverty level	13.9%
Federal workers	46,967
Military	33,485

REDISTRICTING

Arizona gained two House seats in reapportionment. The Arizona Independent Redistricting Commission adopted a new, eight-district map on Oct. 12, 2001.

MISCELLANEOUS

Web: www.state.az.us
Capital: Phoenix

STATE ELECTION OFFICIAL
(602) 542-8683

DEMOCRATIC HEADQUARTERS
(602) 298-4200

REPUBLICAN HEADQUARTERS
(602) 957-7770

District Statistics

DIST.	2000 VOTE FOR PRESIDENT BUSH	GORE	NADER	WHITE	BLACK	ASIAN	HISP	MEDIAN INCOME	WHITE COLLAR	BLUE COLLAR	SERVICE INDUSTRY	OVER 64	UNDER 18	COLLEGE EDUCATION	RURAL	SQ. MILES
1	50%	45%	4%	58%	1%	1%	16%	$32,979	53%	27%	20%	14%	28%	18%	45%	58,608
2	56	41	2	78	2	2	14	$42,432	60	23	17	20	24	19	11	20,220
3	54	42	3	79	2	2	14	$48,108	68	18	14	10	25	30	4	598
4	34	62	3	29	7	1	58	$30,624	44	36	20	7	33	10	0	199
5	53	43	3	77	3	3	13	$51,780	73	14	13	10	23	40	3	1,406
6	60	37	2	77	2	2	17	$47,976	63	23	14	14	28	24	3	724
7	39	56	4	39	3	1	51	$30,828	51	29	20	11	30	13	16	22,873
8	49	47	4	74	3	2	18	$40,656	67	17	16	17	23	31	13	9,007
STATE	51	45	3	64	3	2	25	$40,558	61	23	16	13	27	24	12	113,635
U.S.	47.9	48.4	3	69	12	4	13	$41,994	60	25	15	12	26	24	21	3,537,438

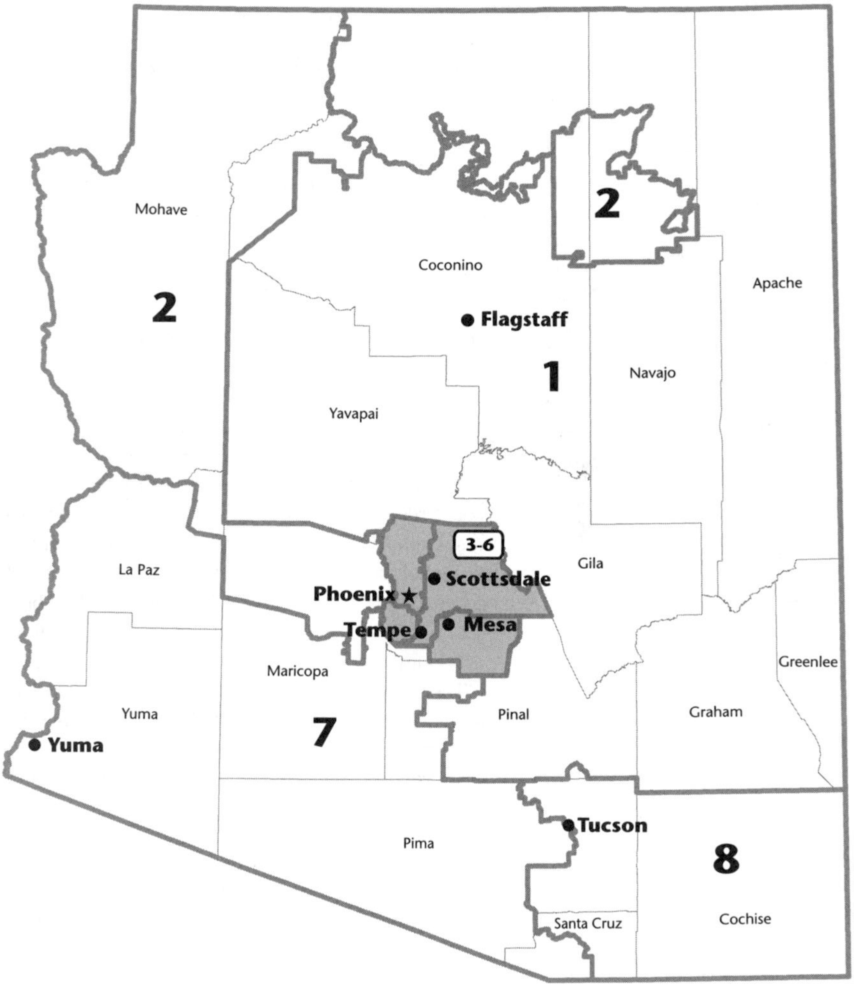
Mohave
2
Coconino
2
Apache
Flagstaff
1
Navajo
Yavapai
3-6
Gila
Scottsdale
La Paz
Phoenix
Tempe
Mesa
Maricopa
Greenlee
Yuma
Pinal
Graham
7
Yuma
Tucson
Pima
8
Santa Cruz
Cochise

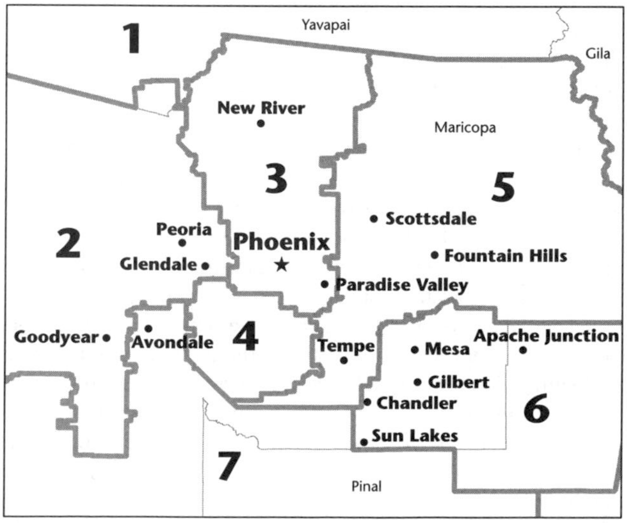
1
Yavapai
Gila
New River
Maricopa
3
5
Scottsdale
2
Peoria
Phoenix
Fountain Hills
Glendale
Paradise Valley
Goodyear
Avondale
4
Tempe
Mesa
Apache Junction
Gilbert
Chandler
6
Sun Lakes
7
Pinal

Sen. John McCain (R)

CAPITOL OFFICE
224-2235
john_mccain@mccain.senate.gov
mccain.senate.gov
241 Russell 20510-0303; fax 228-2862

COMMITTEES
Armed Services
Commerce, Science & Transportation - chairman
Indian Affairs

HOMETOWN
Phoenix

BORN
Aug. 29, 1936, Panama Canal Zone, Panama

RELIGION
Episcopalian

FAMILY
Wife, Cindy McCain; seven children

EDUCATION
U.S. Naval Academy, B.S. 1958; National War College, attended 1973-74

MILITARY SERVICE
Navy, 1958-81

CAREER
Navy officer; Senate Navy liaison; beer distributor

POLITICAL HIGHLIGHTS
U.S. House, 1983-87; sought Republican nomination for president, 2000

ELECTION RESULTS

1998 GENERAL

John McCain (R)	696,577	68.7%
Ed Ranger (D)	275,224	27.2%
John C. Zajac (LIBERT)	23,004	2.3%
Robert "Bob" Park (REF)	18,288	1.8%

1998 PRIMARY

John McCain (R)	unopposed

PREVIOUS WINNING PERCENTAGES
1992 (56%); 1986 (61%); 1984 House Election (78%); 1982 House Election (66%)

Elected 1986; 3rd term

His failed bid for the White House has paradoxically increased McCain's clout during the administration of George W. Bush, the man to whom McCain lost the 2000 Republican nomination. His potential popularity with independent voters undiminished, McCain was able to leverage his standing as the Senate's most nationally recognized maverick to advance a range of his causes in the 107th Congress.

Since running for president — and especially since the enactment in 2002 of the campaign finance overhaul law that is the legislative high point of his two decades in Congress — McCain increasingly has positioned himself near the center, and frequently to the left, of his party's national ideological spectrum on the defining domestic issues of the day, including health care, the environment and the economy. And he has shown no tendency to shy away from disagreements with President Bush.

As a result, in the 107th he voted with most Senate Republicans against most Democrats only 72 percent of the time, and he backed Bush only 91 percent of the time. Only the four most moderate GOP senators had lower scores. Before his presidential bid, McCain had been a reliable Republican vote. From the GOP takeover of the Senate in 1995 through 2000, his party-unity score was 88 percent.

"I've always had this streak, but I would argue that the presidential campaign did make me more of a populist," McCain said in the summer of 2002 in describing his political evolution.

His repositioning, especially when it has come at the expense of the party's agenda in the closely divided Senate, has brought grumbled accusations from GOP colleagues that McCain is grandstanding. His boosters say it is more complicated, that McCain is seeking to stoke a rebirth of dormant progressivism in the GOP and thereby attract the pivotal portion of the electorate that remains dissatisfied with both major political parties.

McCain's turn to the center has fostered speculation that he might make another run at the presidency. He demurs every time he is asked — which is quite often — while setting an aggressive agenda for himself in the 108th Congress, including making preparations to seek a fourth term.

Nowhere did McCain stray more publicly, or with more success, in the 107th than on campaign finance. After a seven-year battle against Republican filibusters, McCain and Wisconsin Democrat Russell D. Feingold finally won enactment of their bill to ban unregulated "soft money" donations to federal candidates and restrict issue advocacy advertising. Bush reluctantly signed the measure, hoping to get McCain off his back and out of the limelight. While the new law headed toward the Supreme Court for review, however, McCain continued to make the administration uncomfortable by pursuing a populist legislative course.

He joined with Democrats to push against the White House's wishes for an independent commission to investigate the Sept. 11, 2001, terrorist attacks, a tough patients' bill of rights, lower prices for generic prescription drugs, new gun control measures and stricter fuel efficiency standards. He also voted with Democrats in opposing Bush's $1.35 trillion tax cut, the president's plan for oil drilling in the Arctic National Wildlife Refuge, and provisions in the bill to create the Homeland Security Department that would have protected vaccine makers from lawsuits and insulated corporations that avoid U.S. taxes by moving their headquarters overseas.

McCain single-handedly stalled confirmation of Bush's nominations for a month in the summer of 2002 in an effort to get Democrat Ellen Weintraub appointed to the Federal Election Commission. McCain and Feingold were upset by the FEC's interpretation of the new law, saying the commission was intentionally undermining their efforts to reduce the influence of money in politics. McCain relented only after Bush promised to appoint Weintraub eventually; he did so in December, after the FEC had finished work on the most important regulations to implement the statute.

McCain further incensed Republicans in 2002 by calling on Security and Exchange Commission Chairman Harvey Pitt to resign after a rash of corporate scandals. His declaration that Pitt had been "slow and tepid" in responding to corporate abuses marked the first time an influential Republican had joined the chorus of critics of the SEC chairman. The tide soon turned in favor of strict regulations to promote corporate accountability. Bush signed such a package in July, and Pitt resigned three months later.

McCain's votes do not perturb his colleagues nearly as much as his attitude. In a chamber where members of the club are expected to treat one another with deference, McCain comes off as too eager to use sharp elbows, too quick to discard customary courtesies and entirely too self-righteous. He angers GOP leaders, appropriators and individual senators alike by frequently attempting to eliminate spending projects for their states that he labels "pork."

After a year and a half as top-ranking Republican, the party's 2002 midterm election wins allowed McCain to reclaim the gavel at the Commerce Committee. He signaled he would use the panel's broad jurisdiction to take a leading role in congressional oversight of U.S. industry, especially transportation and telecommunications. McCain will continue to promote ideas and prod big companies — from automobile makers to Hollywood studios — into, in his view, acting responsibly and dealing fairly with consumers.

Six-year GOP term limits will force McCain out of the Commerce chairmanship after 2004, but he is in line to eventually take over the gavel of the Armed Services Committee. As a member of that panel, he has pushed to increase military salaries. Although he argues against deploying troops unless vital national interests are at stake, he defends the president's prerogative to guide military policy. He ardently backed Bush's quest to force Iraq to comply with United Nations weapons inspections at the end of 2002.

A key part of McCain's political appeal lies in his personal story. The scion of the first father-and-son admirals in U.S. Navy history, McCain earned his reputation as a rebel by finishing fifth from the bottom in the class of 1958 at Annapolis. But his countervailing reputation as a hero was cemented nine years later, when his plane was shot down in Vietnam and he spent five and a half years enduring torture and solitary confinement as a prisoner of war. His experiences were recounted in a best-selling memoir, "Faith of My Fathers."

McCain first ran for Congress in 1982, winning the seat of retiring House Minority Leader John J. Rhodes by convincing voters that his post-Vietnam job as the Navy's Senate liaison gave him a knowledge of "how Washington works." After two House terms, McCain drew 61 percent of the vote to succeed retiring GOP Sen. Barry Goldwater in 1986. During his first Senate term, McCain was one of five senators accused of interceding with federal regulators on behalf of wealthy savings and loan operator Charles H. Keating Jr. A protracted Ethics Committee investigation ended with McCain receiving a mild rebuke in 1991. While that black mark lowered his 1992 re-election margin to 56 percent, it had no lasting impact. In 1998, he won a third term with nearly 69 percent of the vote. And two years later, 5 million voters, including a majority of New Hampshire's first-in-the-nation voters, chose McCain over Bush in the GOP primaries.

KEY VOTES

2002

No Pass farm bill reversing crop subsidy limits
No Postpone tougher automobile fuel efficiency standards
Yes Overhaul campaign finance law; ban "soft money" and restrict advocacy advertising
Yes Set federal election standards
No Support oil drilling in Arctic National Wildlife Refuge
Yes Revive fast-track procedures for trade agreements
Yes Create federal insurance coverage for catastrophic terrorist losses
Yes Tighten federal accounting and corporate governance regulation
No Advance bipartisan Medicare prescription drug plan
Yes Create independent Sept. 11 commission
No Back Democratic Homeland Security Department proposal
Yes Authorize war against Iraq

2001

Yes Confirm John Ashcroft as attorney general
Yes Nullify Clinton Labor Department ergonomics rule
No Cut taxes by $1.35 trillion through fiscal 2011
Yes Pass Democratic bill to bolster rights of patients in managed-care plans
Yes Permit a new round of military base closings
Yes Expand law enforcement power to investigate suspected terrorists

CQ VOTE STUDIES

	PARTY UNITY		PRESIDENTIAL SUPPORT	
	Support	Oppose	Support	Oppose
2002	80%	20%	90%	10%
2001	67%	33%	91%	9%
2000	83%	17%	38%	62%
1999	90%	10%	38%	62%
1998	84%	16%	49%	51%
1997	84%	16%	70%	30%
1996	95%	5%	32%	68%
1995	90%	10%	36%	64%
1994	91%	9%	44%	56%
1993	91%	9%	28%	72%

INTEREST GROUPS

	AFL-CIO	ADA	CCUS	ACU
2002	33%	20%	79%	78%
2001	27%	40%	50%	68%
2000	14%	5%	75%	81%
1999	0%	5%	75%	77%
1998	29%	20%	76%	68%
1997	14%	5%	100%	80%
1996	0%	0%	100%	95%
1995	8%	0%	100%	91%
1994	0%	10%	80%	96%
1993	18%	15%	82%	83%

Sen. Jon Kyl (R)

CAPITOL OFFICE
224-4521
info@kyl.senate.gov
kyl.senate.gov
730 Hart 20510-0304; fax 224-2207

COMMITTEES
Energy & Natural Resources
Finance
(Health Care - chairman)
Judiciary
(Terrorism, Technology & Homeland Security - chairman)

HOMETOWN
Phoenix

BORN
April 25, 1942, Oakland, Neb.

RELIGION
Presbyterian

FAMILY
Wife, Caryll Kyl; two children

EDUCATION
U. of Arizona, B.A. 1964 (political science), LL.B. 1966

CAREER
Lawyer

POLITICAL HIGHLIGHTS
U.S. House, 1987-95

ELECTION RESULTS

2000 GENERAL		
Jon Kyl (R)	1,108,196	79.3%
William Toel (I)	109,230	7.8%
Vance Hansen (GREEN)	108,926	7.8%
Barry Hess (LIBERT)	70,724	5.1%
2000 PRIMARY		
Jon Kyl (R)		unopposed

PREVIOUS WINNING PERCENTAGES
1994 (54%); 1992 House Election (59%); 1990 House Election (61%); 1988 House Election (87%); 1986 House Election (65%)

Elected 1994; 2nd term

Kyl has built a reputation as a studious workhorse, patient enough to spend years pursuing his unambiguously conservative goals. Particularly during his second term, which reaches its midpoint in the 108th Congress, he has seen his labors pay off with a steady rise in prominence — both among Senate Republicans and nationally on issues of national security and defense.

He has proved particularly well-positioned to play an influential role in a Congress at war. As the new chairman of the GOP Policy Committee, the No. 4 spot in the Senate Republican hierarchy, his main job is to help shape the party's message and agenda. And, with the departure of several of the Senate's most prominent spokesmen for conservative causes at the end of the 107th Congress, many of the advocacy groups on the right mention Kyl when asked who might emerge in that role.

On the Finance Committee, Kyl (KILE) has promised to make "supply-side" tax relief one of his top priorities. He is one of his party's pre-eminent advocates for the creation of a national missile defense system and for a robust national security posture overall. As a member of the Intelligence Committee in the 107th, he also had an interest in anti-terrorism long before the attacks of Sept. 11, 2001; just a month earlier he had visited Pakistan, which would be a crucial U.S. ally for the campaign in Afghanistan.

On the Judiciary Subcommittee on Technology, Terrorism and Government Information, Kyl has led the effort to rewrite wiretapping laws and other statutes to make it easier for law enforcement to track and capture terrorists. Ideas he long advocated — such as allowing investigators to use "roving wiretaps" to follow suspects using multiple cell phones — were included in the anti-terrorism law enacted soon after the 2001 attacks.

The son of a former House member, Kyl has an appreciation for the institutional rhythms and traditions of Congress, and that has led to some of his joint ventures with Democrats. After Sept. 11, he continued a longstanding collaboration with California liberal Dianne Feinstein on legislation to improve the tracking and monitoring of foreigners seeking entry into the United States. With liberal Democrat Charles E. Schumer of New York, he has cosponsored a measure to expand the FBI's authority for surveillance of non-citizens suspected of planning terrorist attacks.

At the same time, Kyl has earned a reputation as one of the clearest voices among the Senate's ultra-conservatives, working most often behind the scenes with like-minded colleagues to push an agenda aimed at reducing the role of the federal government. In the 107th Congress he chaired the Senate Steering Committee, a caucus of Republican conservatives. His voting record makes him one of the most reliable votes for Bush and the GOP leadership. He backed the president 98 percent of the time in the 107th Congress and sided with his party 97 percent of the time when it squared off against the Democrats.

Kyl can frequently be seen racing through the Capitol — often to and from the offices of other top leaders — never choosing a casual stroll.

He has played a key role on important GOP issues, including the reorganization of the chamber and judicial nominations, and he is trusted and liked by his Republican colleagues. No one opposed Kyl for the Policy Committee job in the 108th, which was open because of a term limit on Larry E. Craig of Idaho.

Kyl kept a fairly low profile during his first six years in the Senate, but in the opening weeks of the Bush presidency, he played a visible and central role in the battle for confirmation of John Ashcroft as attorney general. Kyl and Missouri's Ashcroft had forged a close friendship after both arrived in the Senate in 1995 and joined the Judiciary Committee. Almost as soon as he was tapped as attorney general, Ashcroft asked Kyl to serve as his spokesman to counter the anticipated barrage of criticism from liberal interest groups; Kyl took on the task with enthusiasm. During Judiciary Committee confirmation hearings, he methodically rebutted attacks by Massachusetts Democrat Edward M. Kennedy that Kyl said "had the effect of distorting Sen. Ashcroft's record."

National security is the one policy sphere in which Kyl consistently has taken a leading role. Since his time in the House, where he was a member of the Armed Services panel, he has been a main advocate of a national missile defense system. He strongly supported Bush's decision in 2002 to withdraw from the 1972 Anti-Ballistic Missile Treaty, which banned nationwide anti-missile defense. Kyl pushed to include $7.4 billion for missile defenses in that year's defense spending law — a major victory for the administration on the most politically contentious military issue of the past two decades.

Kyl favors unilateral steps over negotiated agreements to neutralize emerging military threats; as a general proposition, he contends, the United States should rely on its own military means to guarantee its national security rather than on diplomatic agreements.

His refusal to go along with what he sees as excessive federal spending sometimes has led Kyl to cast the only "no" vote on an appropriations bill. He also is among those pushing hardest to permanently extend all or parts of the 2001 tax cut, a Bush priority. On the other hand, he was able to use a seat on the Appropriations Committee in the 106th Congress to help his state, including securing funds for border patrol and customs personnel and other drug enforcement initiatives.

In the 107th, Kyl left Appropriations and picked up two committees that he said would help him better serve Arizona. Finance has jurisdiction over Social Security and Medicare, the entitlement programs so vital to the state's large retired population. Energy enables him to focus on local resources issues. One priority for Kyl is ensuring Arizona's access to electric power supplies in the face of the energy crisis that gripped neighboring California. He also has been working to shepherd through Congress an agreement that would settle the disputed allocation of water from the Gila River among native Indian tribes, farmers and cities.

Raised in a political family, Kyl was active in Republican Party affairs long before his first House run in 1986. His father, John H. Kyl, represented Iowa for 11 years in the 1960s and 1970s, and helped prepare the younger Kyl for a life in politics by coaching him in public speaking.

A business-oriented lawyer and former president of the Phoenix Chamber of Commerce, the younger Kyl was able to garner strong support from the business community to win a primary over John Conlon, a former House member trying for a comeback. Kyl then easily won the general election in the traditionally Republican 4th District, from which GOP Rep. Eldon Rudd was retiring after a decade.

Kyl won three easy re-elections to the House and launched a Senate bid in 1994 even before incumbent Democrat Dennis DeConcini announced his retirement. He breezed through to the GOP nomination while first-term Rep. Sam Coppersmith struggled through a three-way battle to secure the Democratic nomination. Voters in Arizona were in a mood to hear the themes Kyl had always stressed — too much government, too much taxation and too much regulation. He prevailed over Coppersmith by 14 percentage points. Six years later, the Democrats did not field a candidate.

KEY VOTES

2002

No Pass farm bill reversing crop subsidy limits
Yes Postpone tougher automobile fuel efficiency standards
No Overhaul campaign finance law; ban "soft money" and restrict advocacy advertising
Yes Set federal election standards
Yes Support oil drilling in Arctic National Wildlife Refuge
Yes Revive fast-track procedures for trade agreements
No Create federal insurance coverage for catastrophic terrorist losses
Yes Tighten federal accounting and corporate governance regulation
No Advance bipartisan Medicare prescription drug plan
Yes Create independent Sept. 11 commission
No Back Democratic Homeland Security Department proposal
Yes Authorize war against Iraq

2001

Yes Confirm John Ashcroft as attorney general
Yes Nullify Clinton Labor Department ergonomics rule
Yes Cut taxes by $1.35 trillion through fiscal 2011
No Pass Democratic bill to bolster rights of patients in managed-care plans
Yes Permit a new round of military base closings
Yes Expand law enforcement power to investigate suspected terrorists

CQ VOTE STUDIES

	PARTY UNITY		PRESIDENTIAL SUPPORT	
	Support	Oppose	Support	Oppose
2002	96%	4%	96%	4%
2001	98%	2%	99%	1%
2000	99%	1%	41%	59%
1999	97%	3%	34%	66%
1998	96%	4%	33%	67%
1997	99%	1%	57%	43%
1996	98%	2%	23%	77%
1995	98%	2%	21%	79%
House Service:				
1994	96%	4%	44%	56%
1993	97%	3%	31%	69%

INTEREST GROUPS

	AFL-CIO	ADA	CCUS	ACU
2002	15%	0%	90%	100%
2001	6%	5%	100%	100%
2000	0%	0%	85%	100%
1999	0%	0%	82%	100%
1998	0%	0%	76%	96%
1997	0%	0%	70%	96%
1996	0%	5%	100%	100%
1995	0%	0%	100%	100%
House Service:				
1994	0%	5%	83%	90%
1993	0%	5%	100%	96%

Rep. Rick Renzi (R)

Elected 2002; 1st term

Renzi, the father of 12 children — the most of any member of Congress — is a social and fiscal conservative. He is against abortion and vows to oppose any attempts to raise income taxes.

A former contractor for the Defense Department who gained security clearance a decade ago, Renzi ambitiously hoped for placement on the Intelligence Committee — one of the highest-profile House panels since the Sept. 11, 2001, terrorist attacks. But given his freshman status, he had to settle for other assignments.

He did win a seat on the Resources Committee, which he had sought as well. Elected to represent Arizona's sprawling 1st District, which is made up mainly of wilderness and desert, Renzi campaigned on a promise to improve the management of national forest lands.

Another priority is bringing about changes that would make rural health care more efficient and attainable — an issue that affects many people in the 1st District.

The son of an Army general, Renzi started successful Arizona businesses in the fields of real estate investing and insurance. He is no stranger to the Washington area: In addition to his stint with the Defense Department, he attended law school at Catholic University and interned for Arizona Republican Sen. Jon Kyl while in school.

Running in one of the nation's largest districts — it is bigger in area than the state of Illinois — Renzi had to win over voters the old-fashioned way: by traveling thousands of miles and enlisting local volunteers to get the word out. His victory in 2002 also required a little help from his partisan friends. GOP leaders, including President Bush and Vice President Dick Cheney, went westward to stump and raise money for the political newcomer.

Renzi also was able to draw on his personal wealth to help him prevail over five opponents in the Republican primary and narrowly defeat the Democratic nominee, businessman George Cordova, in a district that appears to provide neither party with a definitive advantage.

CAPITOL OFFICE
225-2315
rick.renzi@mail.house.gov
www.house.gov/renzi
418 Cannon 20515-0301; fax 226-9739

COMMITTEES
Financial Services
Resources
Veterans' Affairs

HOMETOWN
Flagstaff

BORN
June 11, 1958, Fort Monmouth, N.J.

RELIGION
Roman Catholic

FAMILY
Wife, Roberta Renzi; 12 children

EDUCATION
Northern Arizona U., B.S. 1980 (criminal justice); Catholic U. of America, J.D. 2002

CAREER
Insurance company owner; Defense Department counter-intelligence contractor; real estate agent

POLITICAL HIGHLIGHTS
No previous office

ELECTION RESULTS

2002 GENERAL		
Rick Renzi (R)	85,967	49.2%
George Cordova (D)	79,730	45.6%
Edwin Porr (LIBERT)	8,990	5.2%
2002 PRIMARY		
Rick Renzi (R)	11,379	24.4%
Lewis Noble Tenney (R)	9,569	20.5%
Sydney Ann Hay (R)	9,550	20.5%
Alan Everett (R)	7,321	15.7%
Bruce Whiting (R)	6,872	14.8%
David Stafford (R)	1,894	4.1%

ARIZONA 1

North and east — Flagstaff, Prescott, Navajo reservation

A mix of rural conservatives, artistic liberals and dependably Democratic Navajo voters makes for unpredictable elections in the immense 1st, but that does not mean the residents have nothing in common.

Tired of being represented by politicians in Phoenix and Mesa, the eight counties of the 1st pushed hard for a district of their own when the state was awarded two new House seats following the 2000 census. Neither party has a distinct voter registration advantage in the 58,608-square-mile swath of Arizona, larger than 30 states, but nearly all locals call themselves environmentalists in a district that includes both sides of the Grand Canyon.

The district, which mostly follows county lines, is missing a chunk of land in its northern section to avoid placing the Hopi Nation in the same district as the Navajo Nation. The two tribes have historical land disputes. To connect the Hopi land with the the western Arizona-based 2nd District, mapmakers sliced the Colorado River from the 1st where it cuts through the Grand Canyon. The district has the largest American Indian population (23 percent) in the nation.

The 1st, home to great natural beauty, tribal lands and the city of Sedona, felt its tourist economy suffer during the recession that began in the late-1990s. The 1st also faced drought and then forest fires in 2002, wounding the logging industry and straining the resources of local governments in the north.

MAJOR INDUSTRY
Tourism, copper mining, logging

CITIES
Flagstaff, 52,894; Prescott, 33,938

NOTABLE
Arizona's most significant Civil War battle took place at Picacho Peak; Lowell Observatory, in Flagstaff, is where Clyde Tombaugh discovered Pluto in 1930.

Rep. Trent Franks (R)

CAPITOL OFFICE
225-4576
www.house.gov/franks
1237 Longworth 20515-0302; fax 225-6328

COMMITTEES
Armed Services
Budget
Small Business

HOMETOWN
Glendale

BORN
June 19, 1957, Uravan, Colo.

RELIGION
Baptist

FAMILY
Wife, Josephine Franks

EDUCATION
Ottawa U. (Ariz.), attended 1989-90

CAREER
Oil company executive; conservative think tank president; state children's programs director

POLITICAL HIGHLIGHTS
Ariz. House, 1985-87; defeated for re-election to Ariz. House, 1986; sought Republican nomination for U.S. House, 1994

ELECTION RESULTS

2002 GENERAL		
Trent Franks (R)	100,359	59.9%
Randy Camacho (D)	61,217	36.6%
Edward R. Carlson (LIBERT)	5,919	3.5%
2002 PRIMARY		
Trent Franks (R)	14,749	27.7%
Lisa Atkins (R)	13,952	26.2%
John Keegan (R)	10,560	19.8%
Scott Bundgaard (R)	8,701	16.3%
Dusko Jovicic (R)	3,805	7.1%
Mike Schaefer (R)	933	1.8%
Dick Hensley (R)	618	1.2%

Elected 2002; 1st term

Before his 2002 election to Congress, Franks' only previous legislative experience was as a one-term state representative from 1985 to 1987. Yet the conservative oilman never quite left his state's political arena. His ongoing work as an activist on social issues, including strong opposition to abortion, made him well-known to local Republican figures, who describe him as a behind-the-scenes dealmaker.

Friends and colleagues call Franks a gentle giant when he works to influence legislation, using soft-spoken persistence to gain allies.

He has made policy related to education and families something of a specialty. He drew up state legislation, enacted in 1997, that established a tax credit for donations to nonprofit organizations that help state residents pay for private school tuition. The plan has been copied in at least two other states.

Franks sits on the Armed Services Committee — an assignment he sought — where he will look out for the interests of Luke Air Force Base in preparation for the next round of base closings. He also got posts on the Budget and Small Business panels.

If his campaign to succeed retired Republican Rep. Bob Stump is any indication, Franks can make things happen without attracting a lot of attention.

His 2002 primary victory — which virtually guaranteed his election in Arizona's strongly Republican 2nd District — was a shock to the many who expected the seat to be filled by Lisa Atkins, Stump's former chief of staff. Franks edged past Atkins by just 797 votes in a seven-way GOP primary, then handily defeated the Democratic candidate, high school history teacher Randy Camacho.

Franks lost his first attempt at a U.S. House seat to a Republican primary rival with whom he now serves in the Arizona delegation. That 1994 race for the open 4th District seat went to John Shadegg, who won that November and was elected to a fifth term in 2002.

ARIZONA 2

Northwest and central – most of Glendale, Peoria, Lake Havasu City; Hopi reservation

Although the 2nd spans the northwestern corner of Arizona, Republicans living in the fast-growing Phoenix suburbs in the district's southeast dominate its politics. This area, which includes a small portion of the city itself, takes in suburbs such as Peoria, most of Glendale and the retirement community of Sun City. It is home to the vast majority of the 2nd's voters.

Most of the district's land is in Mohave County, where Lake Havasu City, Bullhead City and Kingman are located. Democrats maintain isolated areas of influence among American Indians in the northwest, where younger, lower-income and larger minority populations live. Overall, the district is almost 80 percent white and gave Republican George W. Bush 56 percent of the vote in the 2000 presidential election.

The 2nd also includes the Hopi reservation, an appendage separated from the surrounding Navajo reservation (located in the 1st). To reach the Hopi land, the 2nd follows the Colorado River through the Grand Canyon, though both sides of the canyon are in the 1st.

The district's economy, once grounded in agriculture, has diversified to include manufacturing jobs in the aerospace, electronics, communications and chemical industries. Diversification helped soften the blow of the early-2000s recession.

MAJOR INDUSTRY
Retail, manufacturing, tourism

MILITARY BASES
Luke Air Force Base, 6,485 military, 2,112 civilian (2001)

CITIES
Glendale (pt.), 146,483; Peoria, 108,364; Phoenix (pt.), 47,199

NOTABLE
Lake Havasu City has been home to the old London Bridge since 1971; The Phoenix Coyotes hockey team was scheduled to move into a new arena in Glendale in 2003.

Rep. John Shadegg (R)

CAPITOL OFFICE
225-3361
j.shadegg@mail.house.gov
www.house.gov/shadegg
306 Cannon 20515-0303; fax 225-3462

COMMITTEES
Energy & Commerce
Financial Services
Select Homeland Security
(Emergency Preparedness & Response - chairman)

HOMETOWN
Phoenix

BORN
Oct. 22, 1949, Phoenix, Ariz.

RELIGION
Episcopalian

FAMILY
Wife, Shirley Shadegg; two children

EDUCATION
U. of Arizona, B.A. 1972, J.D. 1975

MILITARY SERVICE
Ariz. Air National Guard, 1969-75

CAREER
State prosecutor; lawyer

POLITICAL HIGHLIGHTS
No previous office

ELECTION RESULTS

2002 GENERAL		
John Shadegg (R)	104,847	67.3%
Charles Hill (D)	47,173	30.3%
Mark J. Yannone (LIBERT)	3,731	2.4%
2002 PRIMARY		
John Shadegg (R)		unopposed
2000 GENERAL		
John Shadegg (R)	140,396	64.0%
Ben Jankowski (D)	71,803	32.7%
Ernest Hancock (LIBERT)	7,298	3.3%

PREVIOUS WINNING PERCENTAGES
1998 (65%); 1996 (67%); 1994 (60%)

Elected 1994; 5th term

Shadegg is one of the most unwaveringly conservative voices on Capitol Hill. A member of the "revolutionary" House GOP class of 1994, he arrived in Congress as a disciple of Speaker Newt Gingrich, not only in his small-government philosophy but also in his confrontational political style. And he has retained the take-no-prisoners attitude to a degree that many of his fifth-term colleagues have not. Shadegg is now a leader of the conservative stalwarts who are unafraid to make their own leadership uncomfortable.

In the 107th Congress, it was the intransigence of Shadegg (SHAD-egg) and other conservatives that forced Congress in 2002 to live within President Bush's declared limit on federal spending. When the conservatives refused to cast votes to support the strategy of GOP appropriators — which, the conservatives concluded, was designed to force a breach of the president's ceiling — the House Republican leadership had to abandon work on spending bills until after the election. Early in 2003, Bush got his way.

Citizens Against Government Waste, a group that seeks to hold down what it considers excessive federal spending, lists Shadegg as one of only four "taxpayer superheros" in the House.

Shadegg is energetic, informed about the issues and amicable. He also is extraordinarily stubborn — with one of the "strongest backbones" in the House, according to a 2002 Washingtonian magazine survey of congressional aides

Shadegg's approach — he says he would prefer to lose on principles rather than win on politics — led to his chairmanship from 2000 to 2002 of the caucus of about 60 Republicans who aim to reduce the role of the federal government and are not inclined toward compromise. (The group was known through the 106th Congress as the Conservative Action Team, or CATs, but has changed its name to the Republican Study Committee.) In 1995 Shadegg succeeded Newt Gingrich of Georgia as chairman of GOPAC, the political action committee Gingrich created to help engineer his party's takeover. Shadegg ran that group until 1998.

But Shadegg, who colleagues say has ambitions to rise in the House leadership, also has been helpful to his leadership. In the 106th, when a band of GOP mavericks threatened to join Democrats to defeat the Republican health care agenda, Shadegg helped stave off an embarrassing defeat for the leaders by drafting a plan designed to find a middle ground on managed-care regulation. His proposal soared above two other Republican alternatives and came nearest to toppling the largely Democratic measure the House ultimately passed.

Speaker J. Dennis Hastert tapped Shadegg as one of his representatives to negotiate with Senate leaders on the managed-care issue. Those talks came to naught in 2000. But Shadegg secured a reputation as an eloquent spokesman for the GOP view that, with health care costs rising, any move to increase the legal rights of managed-care patients must not lead to a flood of new lawsuits, which ultimately would increase insurance prices.

Shadegg's health care proposals are market-oriented. He champions a range of initiatives aimed at employing private insurance to shrink the ranks of the uninsured. He advocates medical savings accounts, tax credits to help people buy insurance, full tax deductibility for the self-employed, and the creation of new insurance risk pools for small-business workers and others.

A strong advocate of a limited government, Shadegg was one of a relative handful of House members who voted against the overhaul of federal education policy that Bush pushed to enactment in 2002; Shadegg said the law will expand the federal authority too much.

A skilled lawyer who appears to relish the details of the legislative process, Shadegg has served since 1999 on the Energy and Commerce Committee, a consolation prize when he was denied his request for assignment to Ways and Means. In the 107th, when the GOP gave some of Energy and Commerce's jurisdiction to a reconstituted Financial Services Committee, Shadegg was one of four members permitted to sit on both panels. In the 108th Congress, Shadegg was on the House GOP's Steering Committee, which makes committee assignments, and he won kudos for his success in getting good assignments for both of Arizona's GOP freshmen — Rick Renzi and Trent Franks. Shadegg himself got an added seat on the new Homeland Security panel.

Shadegg's family name is well-known in Arizona GOP circles. His late father, Stephen, was a longtime political adviser to Barry Goldwater, the five-term Arizona senator and 1964 Republican presidential nominee. The younger Shadegg developed his own political connections, working in the state attorney general's office and then serving as counsel to the House Republican Caucus in the Arizona Legislature.

The election law expertise he gained in Phoenix came in handy when he wrote a position paper for House Republican leaders on the application of law in the disputed 2000 presidential contest. He went to Florida, the locus of the dispute, and was a prominent public spokesman for George W. Bush's position.

A ferocious critic of President Clinton, Shadegg boycotted the 1999 State of the Union address, contending that the embattled president should have postponed his speech until his Senate impeachment trial was over.

But Shadegg is an equal-opportunity critic, taking aim at his own leaders when he thinks they have strayed too far from conservative policies. One reason Hastert paid such close attention to Shadegg's budgetary concerns in 2002 was because Shadegg had earlier accused Gingrich of selling out conservative Republicans with some of his own budget deals.

Shadegg took 60 percent of the vote in 1994 to win the House seat vacated when Republican Jon Kyl won election to the Senate. He has won about two-thirds of the vote in each of his four subsequent re-election races; his seat — which was called the 4th District in the 1990s — was kept reliably Republican under redistricting for this decade.

KEY VOTES

2002

No Overhaul campaign finance law; ban "soft money" and restrict advocacy advertising
Yes Back Bush's defense budget increase
Yes Extend 1996 welfare law
Yes Adopt Bush's discretionary spending limit
Yes Pass GOP Medicare prescription drug plan
No Create independent Sept. 11 commission
No Extend union protections to Homeland Security Department employees
Yes Revive fast-track procedures for trade agreements
Yes Authorize war against Iraq
No Advance bankruptcy overhaul opposed by abortion opponents

2001

Yes Nullify Clinton Labor Department ergonomics rule
Yes Cut taxes by $1.35 trillion through fiscal 2011
No Maintain ban on oil drilling in Arctic National Wildlife Refuge
Yes Approve Bush proposal to limit managed-care plan liability for coverage decisions
No Divert money from crop subsidy payments to land conservation
Yes Expand law enforcement power to investigate suspected terrorists

CQ VOTE STUDIES

	PARTY UNITY		PRESIDENTIAL SUPPORT	
	Support	Oppose	Support	Oppose
2002	98%	2%	87%	13%
2001	96%	4%	84%	16%
2000	96%	4%	22%	78%
1999	95%	5%	15%	85%
1998	97%	3%	22%	78%

INTEREST GROUPS

	AFL-CIO	ADA	CCUS	ACU
2002	11%	0%	90%	100%
2001	0%	5%	96%	96%
2000	0%	5%	80%	96%
1999	0%	0%	79%	96%
1998	0%	0%	89%	100%

ARIZONA 3
Northern Phoenix; Paradise Valley

Encompassing a large northern chunk of Phoenix and the hills and suburbs north of the city, the 3rd is Arizona's least minority-influenced district — 79 percent of its residents are white. Still, the district is changing with the rest of the state as the number of Hispanics increases.

Nearly half of the district's voters are registered Republicans who consistently support economically and socially conservative candidates at the local and federal levels. The district, numbered the 4th until redistricting following the 2000 census, supported GOP candidates in presidential contests in the 1990s and 2000, with George W. Bush capturing 54 percent of the vote in 2000.

Democrats are concentrated in the southern part of the 3rd, where the district extends to downtown Phoenix. Seeds of liberalism also are developing in the more rural sections north of Phoenix, as young professionals move into planned communities such as New River.

The entire Phoenix area experienced explosive growth during the 1990s. The city itself (divided among five congressional districts) grew by almost one-third, and even small Cave Creek north of the city grew by more than one-fourth. The area is home to many manufacturing companies, including producers of semiconductors, electronics and aerospace equipment. Aerospace manufacturer Honeywell has a division headquarters in the 3rd.

Many of the state's most affluent and politically active residents live east of Phoenix in the posh community of Paradise Valley, where the median household income is more than $150,000. The town is exclusively zoned for single-family residential use and collects no property taxes.

MAJOR INDUSTRY

Technology, manufacturing, electronics

CITIES

Phoenix (pt.), 603,604; Paradise Valley, 13,664; New River, 10,740

NOTABLE

Locally brewed Cave Creek Chili Beer has a pepper in every bottle; Carefree is home to a giant sundial that locals call the third-largest working sundial in the Western Hemisphere.

Rep. Ed Pastor (D)

CAPITOL OFFICE
225-4065
www.house.gov/pastor
2465 Rayburn 20515-0304; fax 225-1655

COMMITTEES
Appropriations

HOMETOWN
Phoenix

BORN
June 28, 1943, Claypool, Ariz.

RELIGION
Roman Catholic

FAMILY
Wife, Verma Mendez Pastor; two children

EDUCATION
Arizona State U., B.A. 1966 (chemistry), J.D. 1974

CAREER
Teacher; gubernatorial aide; public policy consultant

POLITICAL HIGHLIGHTS
Maricopa County Board of Supervisors, 1977-91

ELECTION RESULTS

2002 GENERAL		
Ed Pastor (D)	44,517	67.4%
Jonathan Barnert (R)	18,381	27.8%
Amy Gibbons (LIBERT)	3,167	4.8%
2002 PRIMARY		
Ed Pastor (D)		unopposed
2000 GENERAL		
Ed Pastor (D)	84,034	68.5%
Bill Barenholtz (R)	32,990	26.9%
Geoffrey Weber (LIBERT)	3,169	2.6%
Barbara Shelor (NL)	2,412	2.0%

PREVIOUS WINNING PERCENTAGES
1998 (68%); 1996 (65%); 1994 (62%); 1992 (66%); 1991 Special Election (56%)

Elected September 1991; 6th full term

Pastor has two qualities — patience and pragmatism — that have helped him succeed politically. Now into his second decade in the House, he is one of the highest ranking Hispanic lawmakers in Washington.

He enjoys a prominent spot in the House Democratic leadership. He has been one of his party's chief deputy whips since 1999 and he sits on the Appropriations Committee.

The leadership also relies on his calm judgment. In 2002, Pastor was asked to serve on the special ethics panel that recommended the expulsion of Ohio Democrat James A. Traficant Jr., after he was convicted on corruption charges.

Pastor (pass-TOR) entered the House after waiting patiently for the venerable Democrat Morris K. Udall to step down. Udall suffered from Parkinson's disease for more than a decade, but he stayed on until May 1991, when his health finally forced his resignation soon after celebrating his 30th year in the House.

Pastor learned to be pragmatic after spending years in the minority in local government positions back home in Phoenix. As the first Hispanic congressman from Arizona, Pastor quickly set about becoming an insider. He was helped in this quest by the Democratic Party's desire to promote promising minority members.

He received a seat on Appropriations in 1993, after election to his first full term. His posts on the Transportation (now Transportation/Treasury) and Energy and Water Development subcommittees have enabled him to keep a steady flow of grants and federal building contracts headed toward his district. He understands the chemistry of the legislative process as well as chemistry itself: He has a degree in that field and taught it in high school for a time.

Pastor gets high ratings from labor and education organizations. He also calls attention to his approving scores from environmental organizations — including an early endorsement for 2002 from the Sierra Club. But it is the issue of immigration that commands much of his attention.

In September 2001, Pastor gave his party's weekly radio address following the Washington visit of Mexican President Vicente Fox. Pastor emphasized his party's support for revamped immigration policies, including loosened restrictions on immigrants from Mexico and Canada. "There are millions of resident undocumented immigrants in this country," Pastor said. "This is their home, and they are not going anywhere."

His speech came just three days before the Sept. 11 attacks, which caused many lawmakers to insist that immigration and border restrictions be tightened. But Pastor did not agree. "Fear and suspicion lead to discrimination and racial profiling," he wrote in an op-ed piece in the Arizona Republic. "Attacks on freedom, in the name of terrorism or in the name of security, are attacks on our way of life." Later, Pastor introduced amnesty legislation that would allow illegal entrants who had been in the United States since before Jan. 1, 2000, to apply to be legal residents. Those who had lived in the United States for at least five years could apply for permanent residency.

Pastor was chairman of the Congressional Hispanic Caucus in 1995-96, and he was a leader in the fight against GOP efforts to clamp down on illegal immigration and to bar government services and benefits from being provided to legal immigrants. He also has opposed occasional Republican efforts to make English the official language of the federal government.

Such a law would be unconstitutional, Pastor argues, and also would not have the unifying impact that Republicans say they intend. "Language minorities want to learn English and participate in American institutions," he says. "But this legislation will further isolate non-native speakers of English and discourage them from fully integrating themselves into society." Pastor's wife, Verma, was the longtime director of bilingual programs for the Arizona Department of Education.

The oldest son of a copper miner, Pastor grew up in a working class household about 85 miles east of Phoenix. He was the first member of his family to attend college. After his time teaching high school, he earned a law degree and ended up as an aide to Democratic Gov. Raul Castro.

Pastor was elected to the Maricopa County Board of Supervisors in 1976. During his years there — often as the only Democrat — he generally got along with the GOP majority and was able to achieve much of his legislative agenda. "I said I would never attack them personally," he told the Arizona Daily Star. "In return, I expected them to respect my positions and to listen when I made my pitch." He said his minority-party status on the board of supervisors taught him patience and sharpened his negotiating skills.

Pastor had been eyeing a run for the 2nd District, which during the 1980s and 1990s stretched from Phoenix to Tucson and west to Yuma on the California border, ever since it was drawn in 1982 as the state's most Hispanic district. He quit his post on the Board of Supervisors two days after Udall's resignation to mount a full-time quest to win the subsequent special election. He was the establishment's choice, having built up a healthy war chest and high name recognition as a supervisor, and in the five-person special primary he prevailed by 5 percentage points over Tucson Mayor Tom Volgy. His 11-point victory in the special election over Republican Pat Conner, a Yuma County supervisor, remains his closest House election.

Pastor told supporters during his initial House campaign, according to the Arizona Daily Star, that when he was growing up, "No one would even dream that one day a Hispanic, born into a blue-collar mining family, would ever stand a chance to serve their nation in the Congress of the United States."

Reapportionment for this decade gave Arizona two additional House seats, and Pastor chose to run in the newly drawn 4th District nestled in the suburbs of Phoenix. Its population was 58 percent Hispanic at the time of the census, slightly less than the 62 percent in the territory of his old 2nd District seat. But that caused him no electoral difficulty; in 2002, he won re-election with 67 percent of the vote.

KEY VOTES

2002

- Yes Overhaul campaign finance law; ban "soft money" and restrict advocacy advertising
- Yes Back Bush's defense budget increase
- No Extend 1996 welfare law
- No Adopt Bush's discretionary spending limit
- No Pass GOP Medicare prescription drug plan
- Yes Create independent Sept. 11 commission
- Yes Extend union protections to Homeland Security Department employees
- No Revive fast-track procedures for trade agreements
- No Authorize war against Iraq
- No Advance bankruptcy overhaul opposed by abortion opponents

2001

- No Nullify Clinton Labor Department ergonomics rule
- No Cut taxes by $1.35 trillion through fiscal 2011
- Yes Maintain ban on oil drilling in Arctic National Wildlife Refuge
- No Approve Bush proposal to limit managed-care plan liability for coverage decisions
- Yes Divert money from crop subsidy payments to land conservation
- No Expand law enforcement power to investigate suspected terrorists

CQ VOTE STUDIES

	PARTY UNITY		PRESIDENTIAL SUPPORT	
	Support	Oppose	Support	Oppose
2002	92%	8%	28%	72%
2001	89%	11%	21%	79%
2000	90%	10%	81%	19%
1999	91%	9%	83%	17%
1998	91%	9%	82%	18%

INTEREST GROUPS

	AFL-CIO	ADA	CCUS	ACU
2002	100%	95%	40%	0%
2001	92%	100%	39%	8%
2000	100%	90%	52%	8%
1999	89%	100%	24%	0%
1998	100%	100%	39%	4%

ARIZONA 4

Downtown and south Phoenix; part of Glendale

Centered around Phoenix in Arizona's rapidly growing "Valley of the Sun," the Hispanic-majority 4th remains a Democratic stronghold in a generally Republican state.

The district is dominated by lower-income neighborhoods in downtown Phoenix that tend to elect Democrats. These areas have been undergoing a slow economic change in the last few years as more white-collar workers buy up housing, but the influx has yet to shake the 4th's solidly liberal base.

The 4th's portion of the city includes the Phoenix airport (one of the nation's busiest), the state Capitol, the Heard Museum of American Indian art and culture, Mystery Castle and shopping complexes, including Arizona Center and Desert Sky Mall. Bank One Ballpark and America West Arena, home to most of the Phoenix sports teams, are here, and health care jobs also aid the economy.

Glendale — shared with the 2nd District — is a conservative, prosperous community that nearly doubled its population during the 1990s. A few agricultural or undeveloped areas remain in the southwestern edge of the district, but they probably will be overtaken in the coming years as the city continues to sprawl outward.

Arizona's Hispanic voters tend to break from the Democratic Party on some social issues, opposing abortion rights and favoring some traditionally Republican "family values"-type legislation. The 4th has the state's highest percentage of Hispanic residents (58 percent) and its highest percentage of blacks (7 percent).

MAJOR INDUSTRY

Retail, government, manufacturing

CITIES

Phoenix (pt.) 558,408; Glendale (pt.), 72,329; Guadalupe, 5,228

NOTABLE

In the late 1800s, residents chose the name "Phoenix" to reflect that the town would rise from the ashes of a once-thriving Indian civilization.

Rep. J.D. Hayworth (R)

CAPITOL OFFICE
225-2190
jdhayworth@mail.house.gov
www.house.gov/hayworth
2434 Rayburn 20515-0305; fax 225-3263

COMMITTEES
Resources
Ways & Means

HOMETOWN
Scottsdale

BORN
July 12, 1958, High Point, N.C.

RELIGION
Baptist

FAMILY
Wife, Mary Hayworth; three children

EDUCATION
North Carolina State U., B.A. 1980 (speech communications & political science)

CAREER
Radio commentator; sports broadcaster; public relations consultant; insurance agent

POLITICAL HIGHLIGHTS
No previous office

ELECTION RESULTS

2002 GENERAL		
J.D. Hayworth (R)	103,870	61.2%
Craig Columbus (D)	61,559	36.3%
Warren Severin (LIBERT)	4,383	2.6%
2002 PRIMARY		
J.D. Hayworth (R)		unopposed
2000 GENERAL		
J.D. Hayworth (R)	186,687	61.4%
Larry Nelson (D)	108,317	35.6%
Rick Duncan (LIBERT)	9,000	3.0%

PREVIOUS WINNING PERCENTAGES
1998 (53%); 1996 (48%); 1994 (55%)

Elected 1994; 5th term

For a man who loves the verbal battles of politics as much as Hayworth, it was only natural he would run for House Republican Conference chairman in the 108th Congress. The job is all about selling the GOP message, a natural fit for the former sports anchor and radio commentator who thrives on deflating Democrats and scoring points in ideological debates. His lopsided loss to Deborah Pryce of Ohio was a disappointment, but even without an official leadership position, one can expect Hayworth to continue to speak out as a proud and enthusiastic spokesman for his party.

Hayworth has a natural advantage: He is never in danger of getting lost in the crowd. A big and burly college football player, he also has a booming voice that instantly reminds his audience of his broadcasting background. He never lacks confidence or seeks a low profile. Always affable and cheerful in person, Hayworth wears loud, colorful suits — the kind that stand out vividly on television — and makes frequent appearances on radio talk shows and cable television shows such as "Crossfire" to serve up his best intellectual ammunition for Republican policies.

Hayworth has cultivated a reputation as one of the most loyal soldiers in the House GOP. He voted with his party 98 percent of the time in the 107th Congress and frequently travels throughout the country to raise money for Republican candidates. But it was his communications background that formed the basis of his campaign for GOP Conference chairman when J.C. Watts of Oklahoma retired. "I understand the principles of the effective marketing of ideas and have had an opportunity to build a good working relationship with the news media and with our Republican activists," he said.

More to the point, however, Hayworth relishes the fight with liberals. He is a devoted fan of conservative radio personality Rush Limbaugh, and one does not have to look far to find similarities in the two men's combative debating styles. "While facts are stubborn things," Hayworth said during one floor speech, "we would simply point out to my friends on the left that throughout their time and the last time they were in control of this House they spent all of the Social Security surplus, they gave us the largest tax increase in American history, and they sunk us deeper into debt." In the eyes of his supporters, that fighting spirit is his greatest strength.

"When the Democrats 'push,' our conference needs someone who, in the words of the pollsters, can 'push back' and do so effectively. That's J.D.," says Rep. Howard Coble. (The lawmakers share more than political views: Coble represents High Point, N.C., where Hayworth was born.)

Hayworth has not achieved the same kind of prominence in the legislative arena, but he is starting to make his mark. In 2002, the House passed a bill, which he had pushed from his Ways and Means Committee seat, to encourage low- and moderate-income people to buy long-term care insurance by creating a new tax deduction for the premiums. In addition, he has promoted legislation to help his district's substantial population of American Indians. Hayworth, who co-chairs the Congressional Native American Caucus, killed an attempt to limit an inquiry into the Interior Department's alleged mismanagement of thousands of trust fund accounts for the benefit of American Indians.

Mostly, however, Hayworth favors legislation to promote conservative causes, such as a constitutional amendment he cosponsored in the 107th to permit voluntary prayer in schools. He also wants to give the legislative branch more control over the federal bureaucracy. Hayworth sponsors a bill every Congress to require both congressional and presidential approval of all future regulations issued by government agencies.

Occasionally, Hayworth has landed in hot water through a poor choice of words. During the 2002 debate on the campaign finance overhaul bill, he spoke in favor of an amendment to bar legal immigrants from contributing to political campaigns — an issue of extreme sensitivity among Hispanics, a group President Bush was trying to court. Hayworth did not help that cause with his speech, which ended: "Yes, I guess it is poisonous to disallow enemies of this state access to our political system."

Hayworth said he was not talking about legal immigrants in general, but about a notorious 1996 fundraiser at a Buddhist temple attended by Vice President Al Gore. But he was pummeled by Democrats who thought he was calling all legal residents enemies of this state.

Hayworth also drew fire in Arizona when he sent out a fundraising letter in July 1998 that called President Clinton an "unprincipled, philandering president" and claimed Clinton had presided over "the most corrupt administration in U.S. history." Local Democrats accused Hayworth of lowering himself to mean-spirited name-calling and claimed he had abused his congressional privilege to send mail at public expense.

Hayworth, never one to be plagued by self-doubt or second thoughts, takes his critics in stride. He says he was prepared for people to have lower expectations of him when he entered politics because of his reputation as a "somewhat irreverent, gregarious" TV personality.

After attending North Carolina State University on a football scholarship, Hayworth held sports broadcasting jobs in Cincinnati and Greenville, S.C., before landing in Phoenix. He moved into political commentary, an outgrowth of his longstanding interest in government. A political history buff — he is an aficionado of the presidency of Dwight D. Eisenhower — he can readily recount anecdotes from Arizona's colorful past.

Though Hayworth's 1994 6th District House bid was his first political campaign, he was already a familiar and well-liked figure to voters thanks to his seven years on Phoenix's CBS affiliate and his work with area charitable events off the air. In the GOP sweep, he defeated freshman Democrat Karan English by 14 percentage points. But, in a district that narrowly backed George Bush in 1992 and then Bill Clinton in 1996, Democrats mounted aggressive challenges to Hayworth in each of the next three elections. Redistricting, however, made the renumbered 5th District more reliably Republican — with more suburbs and less American Indian reservation territory. In 2002, Hayworth cruised to a fifth term with 61 percent.

KEY VOTES

2002

No Overhaul campaign finance law; ban "soft money" and restrict advocacy advertising
Yes Back Bush's defense budget increase
Yes Extend 1996 welfare law
Yes Adopt Bush's discretionary spending limit
Yes Pass GOP Medicare prescription drug plan
No Create independent Sept. 11 commission
No Extend union protections to Homeland Security Department employees
Yes Revive fast-track procedures for trade agreements
Yes Authorize war against Iraq
No Advance bankruptcy overhaul opposed by abortion opponents

2001

Yes Nullify Clinton Labor Department ergonomics rule
Yes Cut taxes by $1.35 trillion through fiscal 2011
No Maintain ban on oil drilling in Arctic National Wildlife Refuge
Yes Approve Bush proposal to limit managed-care plan liability for coverage decisions
No Divert money from crop subsidy payments to land conservation
Yes Expand law enforcement power to investigate suspected terrorists

CQ VOTE STUDIES

	PARTY UNITY		PRESIDENTIAL SUPPORT	
	Support	Oppose	Support	Oppose
2002	98%	2%	85%	15%
2001	98%	2%	91%	9%
2000	96%	4%	20%	80%
1999	96%	4%	15%	85%
1998	94%	6%	23%	77%

INTEREST GROUPS

	AFL-CIO	ADA	CCUS	ACU
2002	11%	0%	85%	100%
2001	8%	5%	87%	100%
2000	11%	5%	84%	100%
1999	11%	10%	80%	100%
1998	0%	0%	89%	100%

ARIZONA 5
Scottsdale; Tempe; part of Phoenix and Mesa

Wealth, beautiful sunsets and conservative politics abound in the 5th, which takes in a sliver of Phoenix and then spreads east to Tempe, Scottsdale and the western parts of Chandler and Mesa.

Scottsdale, known for its golf courses and tournaments, and Fountain Hills to the east draw retirees and their bank accounts — the 2000 census showed both communities had higher incomes and median ages than the state and nation.

Farther south, Tempe bucks the trend. The home of Arizona State University, its median age is under 30. Its more liberal voters slightly offset but do not heavily endanger the district's GOP bent. Overall, Republicans hold an 18-point voter registration advantage, and George W. Bush carried the district by 10 points in the 2000 presidential election.

Tourism props up much of the area's economy, with resorts, parks, golf courses, rugged scenery and spring training baseball to convince travelers that the area is the right place for an upscale retreat. The district's small portion of Phoenix includes the city's zoo and the Desert Botanical Garden.

The Salt River and Fort McDowell Indian reservations are attracting guests of their own, and not just for the casinos. The Scottsdale Pavillions shopping mall, just inside the Salt River border, and the Out of Africa Wildlife Park in Fort McDowell are examples of reservations working with private businesses to develop their land.

MAJOR INDUSTRY
Tourism, education, health care

CITIES
Scottsdale, 202,705; Tempe, 158,625; Mesa (pt.), 96,622; Phoenix (pt.), 85,765; Chandler (pt.), 66,823; Fountain Hills, 20,235

NOTABLE
Fender, the guitar-maker, is based on the Salt River reservation; The fountain at Fountain Hills shoots a stream of water 560 feet into the air, which makes the Guinness World Records as "tallest fountain;" Frank Lloyd Wright's Taliesin West in Scottsdale was the architect's winter home; Taliesin Architects, based in Scottsdale, seeks to continue Wright's practices.

Rep. Jeff Flake (R)

CAPITOL OFFICE
225-2635
jeff.flake@mail.house.gov
www.house.gov/flake
424 Cannon 20515-0306; fax 226-4386

COMMITTEES
International Relations
Judiciary
Resources

HOMETOWN
Mesa

BORN
Dec. 31, 1962, Snowflake, Ariz.

RELIGION
Mormon

FAMILY
Wife, Cheryl Flake; five children

EDUCATION
Brigham Young U., B.A. 1986 (international relations), M.A. 1987 (political science)

CAREER
Public policy institute director; African business trade representative; lobbyist

POLITICAL HIGHLIGHTS
No previous office

ELECTION RESULTS

2002 GENERAL		
Jeff Flake (R)	103,094	65.9%
Deborah Thomas (D)	49,355	31.6%
Andy Wagner (LIBERT)	3,888	2.5%
2002 PRIMARY		
Jeff Flake (R)		unopposed
2000 GENERAL		
Jeff Flake (R)	123,289	53.6%
David Mendoza (D)	97,455	42.4%
Jon Burroughs (LIBERT)	9,227	4.0%

Elected 2000; 2nd term

In his first term in the House, Flake voted against the rewrite of federal education law, the new farm bill, the federal bailout of the airline industry, the creation of a Homeland Security Department, a law tightening corporate accounting standards, a measure to overhaul election procedures, and most of the annual appropriations bills.

Flake's rationale? The federal government is too big. It taxes and spends too much and is involved in matters better left to the states and individuals.

On each of those votes, he was among the small minority of Republicans who opposed the GOP-drafted measures. If Texas GOP Rep. Ron Paul is the famous "Dr. No" — casting lonely no votes on spending bills and many other measures that enjoy widespread support, even from his Republican colleagues — then Flake is rapidly becoming known as his junior associate.

In the 107th Congress, Flake voted against every one of the regular 13 spending bills that came up for a vote, with the exception of the defense and military construction measures.

In 2002, Flake was one of only eight Republicans who voted against a GOP prescription drug plan, even though it was cheaper than the Democrats' version. He argued that it would become an out-of-control entitlement. "I didn't come here to expand government like that," Flake said. "It will be a middle-class entitlement that will run away from us."

Flake does not worry that his naysaying will cost him, either among his colleagues on Capitol Hill or with voters back home in Mesa. He has already said that he will serve no more than three terms in the House — following the lead of his predecessor, Republican Matt Salmon.

The fact that he is not trying to win support down the road for a top committee assignment or a place in the inner councils of leadership has freed him to take tough stands, Flake says. He affiliates with the Republican Study Committee, a group of several dozen of the most conservative House Republicans, who share his views of limited government.

At the top of Flake's legislative agenda is reducing federal taxes. He backed an even larger tax cut than the one sought by President Bush in 2001, and he has worked to make those tax cuts, due to expire in 2011, permanent.

Also high on Flake's agenda in the 107th was an overhaul of the Immigration and Naturalization Service and an end to the four-decade-old ban on travel to Cuba. Flake says the two matters are related. The same government agency that should be watching for foreigners who are national security risks has been wasting valuable resources, Flake argues, in tracking down American tourists who have gone to Cuba illegally. He says that the best way to bring down the Castro regime is to increase contact between Americans and Cubans. In both 2001 and 2002 he authored an amendment, opposed by the Bush administration and GOP leaders, to lift the Cuba travel ban.

Flake also wants an end to the United States' economic embargo on Cuba. Castro "is not a man who has missed too many meals because of the embargo," Flake told the Wall Street Journal. "After 40 years, it's time to try something else."

And though the INS was restructured with the creation of the new Homeland Security Department, Flake believes the federal government must do more to help states cope with border security problems.

Although he is not afraid to go it alone, Flake is easygoing and personable. He spends his free time in the House gym playing basketball, and he was one of the stars of the Republicans' 2002 win over the Democrats in their annual charity baseball game.

Flake and his nine siblings grew up on the family ranch near Snowflake, about 100 miles northeast of Phoenix. The town is named after Erastus Snow and William Flake (Flake's great-great-grandfather), Mormon settlers who founded the town in 1878.

He went on a two-year Mormon Church mission to Zimbabwe and South Africa in 1982 — an experience that he says has shaped his life. He majored in international relations at Brigham Young University. In 1989, Flake, as director of the Foundation for Democracy, moved to Namibia — then recently separated from South Africa — to develop its constitution and help the nation's leaders move toward independence.

Flake returned to Arizona in 1992 to take the helm of the Goldwater Institute, a conservative think tank named for the late GOP Sen. Barry Goldwater, the 1964 Republican presidential nominee. A major focus of the institute is education, Flake says. It has worked to create charter schools and a tax credit plan that helps fund private school scholarships.

Despite this background, Flake says he has no interest in serving on the Education and the Workforce Committee in that he does not see a large federal role in education. The job of the government, he says, is to fulfill its promise to fund the education of disabled students so that states can spend their money on other important educational needs.

When Salmon stepped down after three terms in 2000, Flake entered the race to replace him. He told Reason magazine that during his tenure at the Goldwater Institute, "I enjoyed immensely the ability to gripe, complain and moan about public policy" without being held accountable. "I felt it was time to stand up and see what I could do about it," Flake said.

Flake's main challenge in his 2000 campaign was winning the crowded primary in the dependably Republican 1st District. Salmon's endorsement gave him an important boost over his four primary opponents, and his 32 percent of the tally was enough to capture the nomination.

In November, buoyed by significant financial support from the Club for Growth, a group of fiscally conservative Republicans that favors lower taxes, free trade and smaller government, Flake bested Democratic labor lobbyist David Mendoza, who also was the Democrats' nominee against Salmon in 1998.

Redistricting after the 2000 census gave the GOP a tailor-made district (now numbered the 6th) in the eastern Phoenix suburbs. In the 2002 election, Flake cruised past Democrat Deborah Thomas, a retired state employee, by 34 percentage points.

KEY VOTES

2002

No Overhaul campaign finance law; ban "soft money" and restrict advocacy advertising
Yes Back Bush's defense budget increase
Yes Extend 1996 welfare law
Yes Adopt Bush's discretionary spending limit
No Pass GOP Medicare prescription drug plan
No Create independent Sept. 11 commission
No Extend union protections to Homeland Security Department employees
Yes Revive fast-track procedures for trade agreements
Yes Authorize war against Iraq
No Advance bankruptcy overhaul opposed by abortion opponents

2001

Yes Nullify Clinton Labor Department ergonomics rule
Yes Cut taxes by $1.35 trillion through fiscal 2011
No Maintain ban on oil drilling in Arctic National Wildlife Refuge
Yes Approve Bush proposal to limit managed-care plan liability for coverage decisions
No Divert money from crop subsidy payments to land conservation
Yes Expand law enforcement power to investigate suspected terrorists

CQ VOTE STUDIES

	PARTY UNITY		PRESIDENTIAL SUPPORT	
	Support	Oppose	Support	Oppose
2002	89%	11%	70%	30%
2001	90%	10%	77%	23%

INTEREST GROUPS

	AFL-CIO	ADA	CCUS	ACU
2002	22%	5%	65%	96%
2001	0%	5%	74%	92%

ARIZONA 6

Southeast Phoenix suburbs – most of Mesa and Chandler, Gilbert, Apache Junction

Rooted in the conservative leanings of an affluent, historically Mormon population, the suburban 6th favors Republican candidates. The district still has a significant population of Mormons, as well as a mix of young couples who commute to Phoenix. The area's warm sunny days have helped draw an established population of retirees from other states.

The district begins east of Phoenix, where it takes in all but the westernmost segments of Mesa and Chandler, both of which have experienced tremendous population growth over the past 20 years. Manufacturing aids the economy in Mesa, the state's third-largest city and now within the nation's top 50 in population.

Chandler, not as dependent on tourism as its neighbors, fuels its economy through retail business while attempting to attract biotechnology firms. Between the two cities is Gilbert, which has several construction-related businesses.

Redistricting following the 2000 census made the 6th — previously numbered the 1st — more conservative by slicing off the Democratic university town of Tempe and the district's portion of Phoenix. The district expanded east to take in part of largely agricultural Pinal County, including Apache Junction on the county's northern border.

Republicans now hold an almost 25-point edge in party registration, and the redrawn district gave George W. Bush 60 percent of the vote in the 2000 presidential election. More than 75 percent white, the 6th has more white residents and fewer minorities than the state average.

MAJOR INDUSTRY
Manufacturing, high-tech, retail

CITIES
Mesa (pt.), 299,753; Chandler (pt.), 109,758; Gilbert, 109,697; Apache Junction, 31,814

NOTABLE
Chandler's Ostrich Festival, held each March, features ostrich races and a parade; Mesa is the spring training home of the Chicago Cubs baseball team, which has led the Arizona Cactus League in attendance for many of the past 20 years; Mesa was founded by Mormons.

Rep. Raúl M. Grijalva (D)

CAPITOL OFFICE
225-2435
raul.grijalva@mail.house.gov
www.house.gov/grijalva
1440 Longworth 20515-0307; fax 226-6846

COMMITTEES
Education & Workforce
Resources

HOMETOWN
Tucson

BORN
Feb. 19, 1948, Tucson, Ariz.

RELIGION
Roman Catholic

FAMILY
Wife, Ramona F. Grijalva; three children

EDUCATION
U. of Arizona, B.A. 1986 (sociology)

CAREER
University dean; community center director

POLITICAL HIGHLIGHTS
Tucson Unified School District Governing Board, 1974-86; Pima County Board of Supervisors, 1989-2002

ELECTION RESULTS

2002 GENERAL		
Raúl M. Grijalva (D)	61,256	59.0%
Ross Hieb (R)	38,474	37.1%
John L. Nemeth (LIBERT)	4,088	3.9%
2002 PRIMARY		
Raúl M. Grijalva (D)	14,835	40.9%
Elaine Richardson (D)	7,589	20.9%
Jaime P. Gutierrez (D)	5,401	14.9%
Lisa Otondo (D)	2,302	6.3%
Luis Armando Gonzales (D)	2,105	5.8%
Mark Fleisher (D)	2,022	5.6%
Sherry Smith (D)	1,058	2.9%
Jesus Romo (D)	1,008	2.8%

Elected 2002; 1st term

Grijalva (raa-OOL gree-HAHL-va), whose father was a Mexican immigrant ranch hand, says he brings a real-world perspective to the issue of immigration. His district covers about two-thirds of Arizona's border with Mexico, and the economy is significantly supported by seasonal immigrant workers.

He plans to push for several changes to improve the lot of immigrants, but he opposes guest-worker programs that would allow foreigners to work legally in the United States without easing the path to permanent residency. He calls the concept "a piecemeal gesture."

A seat on the Education and the Workforce panel will enable him to work on one of his top issues. New Mexico is plagued by high dropout rates and below-average academic performance; Grijalva favors higher federal funding to address these and other school problems. He spent 12 years on the Tucson School Board and had the Grijalva Elementary School in Tucson named in his honor. His wife is a librarian.

He wants to help empower his American Indian constituents by working with tribal governments to find ways to diversify the Indian communities' historically depressed economies.

Grijalva earned a reputation for advocating environmental protection over land development during his 13 years on the Pima County Board of Supervisors. In a county with a booming population, it was a fight that did not always go his way. He will be able to continue that fight on the Resources Committee.

As an elected official in Tucson, Grijalva seldom wore a tie, but he has quietly acquiesced to the congressional dress code. After his election a number of constituents, realizing his paucity of neckwear, donated ties to his rapidly growing selection.

Grijalva's grass-roots approach and his years in local office enabled him to emerge from a crowded field in the 2002 Democratic primary for the new 7th District seat. That win was tantamount to a general-election victory in the heavily Democratic, Hispanic-majority district, and Grijalva easily bested Republican Ross Hieb, a farmer and forester, by 22 percentage points.

ARIZONA 7

Southwest – part of Tucson, Yuma, Avondale

Stretching mainly south and west from Phoenix, the Hispanic-majority 7th crosses large reservations and rural areas to take in Yuma, downtown Tucson and most of Arizona's border with Mexico. The district, most of which was in the 2nd until redistricting following the 2000 census, is a Democratic stronghold.

The 7th includes the University of Arizona in Tucson, southern Arizona's top employer, and the Mexican border town of Nogales. It also climbs the California border, taking in most of La Paz and all of Yuma counties. The economy is supported by seasonal immigrant workers, who buttress the agriculture and service industries but boost poverty statistics. The 7th has more blue-collar workers and fewer college graduates than other Arizona districts.

Some conservative ranching communities exist in Yuma County and elsewhere in the district, but their political impact is largely offset by a Democratic-voting American Indian presence. The Tohono O'odham and Gila River reservations are the 7th's largest, and American Indians make up 6 percent of the district's population. Overall, Democrats have an almost 2-to-1 advantage over Republicans.

MAJOR INDUSTRY
Agriculture, tourism, education

MILITARY BASES
Marine Corps Air Station Yuma, 4,825 military, 174 civilian; Yuma Proving Ground (Army), 127 military, 622 civilian (2002)

CITIES
Tucson (pt.), 230,164; Yuma, 77,515; Avondale, 35,883; Phoenix (pt.), 26,069

NOTABLE
Yuma Territorial Prison was turned into a high school, then a shelter for railroad vagrants, and now is a state historic park.

Rep. Jim Kolbe (R)

CAPITOL OFFICE
225-2542
www.house.gov/kolbe
2266 Rayburn 20515-0308; fax 225-0378

COMMITTEES
Appropriations
(Foreign Operations & Export Financing - chairman)

HOMETOWN
Tucson

BORN
June 28, 1942, Evanston, Ill.

RELIGION
Methodist

FAMILY
Divorced

EDUCATION
Northwestern U., B.A. 1965 (political science); Stanford U., M.B.A. 1967 (economics)

MILITARY SERVICE
Navy, 1965-69; Naval Reserve, 1970-77

CAREER
Land planning firm executive; gubernatorial aide

POLITICAL HIGHLIGHTS
Ariz. Senate, 1977-83; Republican nominee for U.S. House, 1982

ELECTION RESULTS

2002 GENERAL		
Jim Kolbe (R)	126,930	63.3%
Mary Judge Ryan (D)	67,328	33.6%
Joe Duarte (LIBERT)	6,142	3.1%
2002 PRIMARY		
Jim Kolbe (R)	35,546	72.5%
James "Jim" Behnke (R)	13,502	27.5%
2000 GENERAL		
Jim Kolbe (R)	172,986	60.2%
George Cunningham (D)	101,564	35.3%
Michael Jay Green (GR)	9,010	3.1%
Aage Nost (LIBERT)	4,049	1.4%

PREVIOUS WINNING PERCENTAGES
1998 (52%); 1996 (69%); 1994 (68%); 1992 (67%); 1990 (65%); 1988 (68%); 1986 (65%); 1984 (51%)

Elected 1984; 10th term

President Bush's bid to win international backing for his war on terrorism has an important ally in Kolbe, who is well-positioned to dole out foreign aid to, and shepherd trade agreements with, allies in the effort.

Kolbe (COAL-bee) had been at the helm of the Appropriations Subcommittee on Foreign Operations — which writes an annual measure that sets levels of direct foreign aid, contributions to international financial institutions and military sales financing — for less than a year when the Sept. 11, 2001, attacks forced the United States to reassess its international priorities. But in preparation for the new assignment, Kolbe had embarked on a frenzied schedule of travel to the Middle East, South America and Asia to study foreign aid programs and their effectiveness.

And Kolbe already had some recent experience that was particularly relevant right after Sept. 11, when Afghanistan's Taliban regime turned into enemy No. 1 and Pakistan became a vital if somewhat shaky ally. Kolbe had visited a squalid Pakistani refugee camp in May 2001 that was home to 60,000 displaced Afghan refugees. After the attacks and the decision to send forces to Afghanistan, his panel took the lead in providing humanitarian assistance to innocent victims of the battle against terrorism. "We will do something extraordinary that hadn't ever been done before," Kolbe said. "We will fight war, and we will feed people at the same time."

Kolbe's internationalist bent stretches back four decades, to a college year abroad. With a small group of students, he crisscrossed the globe, spending time in dozens of cities, living with families and attending classes. "I just look at the world, I think, differently today as a result of that experience," he said. "I've always been fascinated with world affairs and international issues, and I think that really turned me truly into an internationalist."

Kolbe has routinely channeled this experience into activism for trade liberalization. In the 107th Congress he was a leader in the successful campaign to grant Bush fast-track authority to negotiate trade deals that cannot be amended by Congress. He earlier helped round up votes when Congress granted China status as a permanent normal trading partner of the United States in 2000 and when it ratified the North American Free Trade Agreement in 1993.

Kolbe breaks with the party on social issues, supporting abortion rights and some gun control. It was for this reason that he lost badly when he sought the chairmanship of the Republican Policy Committee after the GOP won control of the House in 1994. In his Foreign Operations chairmanship, he has tried to walk a moderate line on international aid for family planning and threw up his arms in frustration in 2002 when a dispute over that aid deadlocked his bill. Unable to broker a compromise with conservative Republicans, who wanted to deny aid to Chinese government operatives suspected of forcing women to have abortions, Kolbe handed the problem to Speaker J. Dennis Hastert to solve.

Before moving to Foreign Operations, Kolbe spent four years as chairman of the Appropriations Subcommittee on the Treasury, Postal Service and General Government. In that post, he developed a reputation of trying to work in the classic role of an appropriations "cardinal" by trying to assemble a bill each year that was a string of bipartisan compromises. He became known as a cool-headed broker who works well with lawmakers of both parties and will occasionally resort to humor to smooth the way for an agreement. At one committee meeting in 2000, he produced a chihuahua doll singing "La Bamba" to ease tension.

In 1996, Kolbe's personal life became an issue when he acknowledged his homosexuality after criticism from gay rights activists unhappy with his vote for legislation opposing same-sex marriage. He made his declaration after learning that a magazine was about to break the news. "The fact that I am this way has never, nor will it ever, change my commitment to represent all the people of Arizona's 5th District," Kolbe said. "I am the same person." He said he backed the measure on same-sex marriage because it allowed states to define marriage.

Since then, Kolbe has pushed for legislation to ban hate crimes based on sexual orientation. In 2002, he won adoption of an amendment to the District of Columbia appropriations bill that would permit city employee health plans to provide benefits to unmarried domestic partners.

To many outside Washington, Kolbe is best known as the lawmaker who wants to eliminate the penny. He gained some notoriety when the NBC television show "The West Wing" used his bill as the basis for a plot line.

Kolbe has been a prominent advocate of partial privatization of Social Security. He has teamed up with Democrats on several occasions to recommend allowing individuals to invest a small percentage of their Social Security payroll taxes in government-picked investment funds and to gradually raise the retirement age to 70.

A former real estate consultant with an MBA from Stanford University, Kolbe first came to Washington as a Senate page sponsored by Arizona Republican Barry Goldwater. He later served two years as a Navy lieutenant on patrol boats in Vietnam. After six years in the state Senate, he won his first House victory in 1984, avenging a loss he had suffered two years earlier at the hands of Democrat James F. McNulty Jr. Kolbe rode a horse in his commercials and reminded voters that he spent much of his youth on a cattle ranch near Sonoita — while McNulty was born and raised in Boston.

Kolbe's status as the only openly gay Republican in Congress has had little lasting impact on his political career. He was held to 52 percent of the vote in 1998 by former Tucson Mayor Tom Volgy. And at the 2000 Republican National Convention, members of the Texas delegation doffed their cowboy hats and prayed when Kolbe gave a speech. But he has won his last two elections handily. In 2002 he defeated Tucson attorney Mary Judge Ryan by 30 percentage points in a redrawn portion of southeastern Arizona — renamed the 8th District because of the state's gains from reapportionment, and an area with demographics that could make it a potential partisan battleground.

KEY VOTES

2002

- No Overhaul campaign finance law; ban "soft money" and restrict advocacy advertising
- Yes Back Bush's defense budget increase
- Yes Extend 1996 welfare law
- No Adopt Bush's discretionary spending limit
- Yes Pass GOP Medicare prescription drug plan
- No Create independent Sept. 11 commission
- No Extend union protections to Homeland Security Department employees
- Yes Revive fast-track procedures for trade agreements
- Yes Authorize war against Iraq
- Yes Advance bankruptcy overhaul opposed by abortion opponents

2001

- Yes Nullify Clinton Labor Department ergonomics rule
- Yes Cut taxes by $1.35 trillion through fiscal 2011
- No Maintain ban on oil drilling in Arctic National Wildlife Refuge
- Yes Approve Bush proposal to limit managed-care plan liability for coverage decisions
- Yes Divert money from crop subsidy payments to land conservation
- Yes Expand law enforcement power to investigate suspected terrorists

CQ VOTE STUDIES

	PARTY UNITY		PRESIDENTIAL SUPPORT	
	Support	Oppose	Support	Oppose
2002	88%	12%	82%	18%
2001	91%	9%	84%	16%
2000	85%	15%	39%	61%
1999	80%	20%	40%	60%
1998	81%	19%	40%	60%

INTEREST GROUPS

	AFL-CIO	ADA	CCUS	ACU
2002	0%	20%	100%	80%
2001	0%	20%	96%	60%
2000	0%	20%	80%	68%
1999	0%	20%	91%	70%
1998	10%	15%	89%	72%

ARIZONA 8

Southeast – part of Tucson and northern suburbs

Located in the state's southeastern corner bordering New Mexico and Mexico, the 8th contains many swing voters and independents who often favor moderates in national elections. Most residents live in Pima County, primarily in the Tucson metropolitan area, although Cochise County makes up most of the district geographically. Both urban and rural areas grew by about 20 percent during the 1990s.

Tucson is surrounded by mountain ranges, but the majestic Santa Catalinas just north of the city are the local landmark. Population growth is heavy here as residents literally "head for the hills" and the wealthy, unincorporated areas of Casas Adobes and Catalina Foothills. These and other northern suburban communities are home to affluent, retired and military residents who moved to the area from other states in recent years and add to the district's GOP lean. Central areas of Tucson, including the University of Arizona, are in the neighboring 7th.

Democrats hold the majority in Santa Cruz and Cochise counties, which have large Hispanic populations, but Republicans lead in overall voter registration by about 5 percentage points. George W. Bush won the 2000 presidential vote here by 2 percent.

The various military jets that fly past Tucson on their way to or from Davis-Monthan Air Force Base reveal two of the area's economic engines: military and manufacturing. The city has a number of high-tech defense contractors and aerospace firms, including Raytheon Missile Systems, but the district is increasingly dependent on service industries, including tourism, to support its economic base. Tucson's growing suburbs have made construction an economic force as well.

MAJOR INDUSTRY
Service, manufacturing, military, aerospace, tourism, agriculture

MILITARY BASES
Davis-Monthan Air Force Base, 6,097 military, 1,219 civilian; Fort Huachuca (Army), 4,176 military, 1,984 civilian (1999)

CITIES
Tucson (pt.), 256,535; Casas Adobes (unincorporated), 54,011; Catalina Foothills (unincorporated), 53,794; Sierra Vista, 37,775

NOTABLE
Tombstone, "the town too tough to die," was notorious for its boomtown lawlessness in the late 1800s.

ARKANSAS

Gov. Mike Huckabee (R)

First elected: Succeeded Jim Guy Tucker on July 15, 1996; elected 1998
Length of term: 4 years
Term expires: 1/07
Salary: $73,603
Phone: (501) 682-2345
Hometown: Little Rock
Born: Aug. 24, 1955; Hope, Ark.
Religion: Baptist
Family: Wife, Janet Huckabee; three children
Education: Ouachita Baptist U., B.A. 1976; Southwestern Baptist Theological Seminary, attended 1976-77
Career: Television talk show host; television documentary producer; pastor
Political highlights: Lieutenant governor, 1993-96
Election results:

2002 GENERAL		
Mike Huckabee (R)	427,189	53.0%
Jimmie Lou Fisher (D)	378,303	46.9%

Lt. Gov. Winthrop P. Rockefeller (R)

First elected: 1996
Length of term: 4 years
Term expires: 1/07
Salary: $35,574
Phone: (501) 682-2144

STATE LEGISLATURE

General Assembly: Meets 60 calendar days, January-March, in odd-numbered years
House: 100 members, 2-year terms
2003 breakdown: 30R, 70D; 85 men, 15 women
Salary: $13,442
Phone: (501) 682-7771
Senate: 35 members, 4-year terms (effective 2004)
2003 breakdown: 8R, 27D; 28 men, 7 women
Salary: $13,442
Phone: (501) 682-6107

STATE TERM LIMITS

Governor: 2 terms
Senate: 2 terms
House: 3 terms

URBAN STATISTICS

CITY	POPULATION
Little Rock	183,133
Fort Smith	80,268
North Little Rock	60,433
Fayetteville	58,047
Jonesboro	55,515

REGISTERED VOTERS

Voters do not register by party.

POPULATION

2002 population (est.)	2,710,079
2000 population	2,673,400
1990 population	2,350,725
Percent change (1990-2000)	+13.7%
Rank among states (2002)	33
Median age	36
Born in state	63.9%
Foreign born	2.8%
Violent crime rate	445/100,000
Poverty level	15.8%
Federal workers	20,543
Military	18,894

REDISTRICTING

Arkansas retained its four House seats in reapportionment. The state legislature drew a new map, which the governor allowed to become law without his signature on April 20, 2001.

MISCELLANEOUS

Web: www.state.ar.us
Capital: Little Rock

STATE ELECTION OFFICIAL
(501) 682-5070

DEMOCRATIC HEADQUARTERS
(501) 374-2361

REPUBLICAN HEADQUARTERS
(501) 372-7301

District Statistics

DIST.	2000 VOTE FOR PRESIDENT BUSH	GORE	NADER	WHITE	BLACK	ASIAN	HISP	MEDIAN INCOME	WHITE COLLAR	BLUE COLLAR	SERVICE INDUSTRY	OVER 64	UNDER 18	COLLEGE EDUCATION	RURAL	SQ. MILES
1	48%	50%	1%	80%	17%	0%	2%	$28,940	49%	37%	14%	15%	26%	12%	56%	17,151
2	49	48	1	76	19	1	2	$37,221	60	26	14	12	25	23	34	5,922
3	60	37	2	87	2	1	6	$33,915	53	33	14	13	26	18	46	8,490
4	48	49	1	71	24	0	3	$29,675	48	37	15	16	25	13	55	20,505
STATE	51	46	1	79	16	1	3	$32,182	53	33	14	14	25	17	47	52,068
U.S.	47.9	48.4	3	69	12	4	13	$41,994	60	25	15	12	26	24	21	3,537,438

Benton
Springdale
Fayetteville
Washington
Carroll
Boone
Marion
Baxter
Fulton
Randolph
Clay
Madison
Newton
Searcy
Izard
Sharp
Lawrence
Greene
Stone
Independence
Craighead
Jonesboro
Mississippi
3
1
Crawford
Fort Smith
Franklin
Johnson
Pope
Van Buren
Cleburne
Jackson
Poinsett
Sebastian
Logan
Conway
Faulkner
White
Cross
Crittenden
West Memphis
Woodruff
2
Yell
Perry
St. Francis
Scott
Pulaski
Jacksonville
Lee
Saline
Lonoke
Prairie
Monroe
Little Rock
Montgomery
Garland
Polk
Hot Springs
Phillips
Grant
Jefferson
Arkansas
Hot Spring
Pine Bluff
Howard
Pike
Clark
Sevier
4
Dallas
Cleveland
Lincoln
Desha
Little River
Hempstead
Nevada
Ouachita
Calhoun
Drew
Bradley
Miller
Columbia
Union
Ashley
Chicot
Lafayette

Sen. Blanche Lincoln (D)

CAPITOL OFFICE
224-4843
blanche_lincoln@lincoln.senate.gov
lincoln.senate.gov
355 Dirksen 20510-0404; fax 228-1371

COMMITTEES
Agriculture, Nutrition & Forestry
Finance
Select Ethics
Special Aging

HOMETOWN
Little Rock

BORN
Sept. 30, 1960, Helena, Ark.

RELIGION
Episcopalian

FAMILY
Husband, Steve Lincoln; two children

EDUCATION
Randolph-Macon Woman's College, B.A. 1982 (biology)

CAREER
Lobbyist; congressional aide

POLITICAL HIGHLIGHTS
U.S. House, 1993-97

ELECTION RESULTS

1998 GENERAL		
Blanche Lincoln (D)	385,878	55.1%
Fay Boozman (R)	292,906	41.8%
Charley E. Heffley (REF)	21,860	3.1%
1998 PRIMARY RUNOFF		
Blanche Lincoln (D)	134,203	62.4%
Winston Bryant (D)	80,889	37.6%
1998 PRIMARY		
Blanche Lincoln (D)	145,009	45.5%
Winston Bryant (D)	87,183	27.4%
Scott Ferguson (D)	44,761	14.0%
Nate Coulter (D)	41,848	13.1%

PREVIOUS WINNING PERCENTAGES
1994 House Election (53%); 1992 House Election (70%)

Elected 1998; 1st term

Lincoln came to the Senate in 1999 vowing not to let the demands of the job overwhelm her commitment to her young twin boys. In a chamber filled with workaholics, Lincoln was determined to balance her public and private responsibilities, which meant limiting weekend business trips and Senate breakfasts on weekdays and keeping free as many of her nights as possible.

Now with her boys in school and four years' experience in balancing competing demands, Lincoln is eager to become a player in the 108th Congress on issues such as taxes, welfare and agriculture. She is the state's senior senator, as fellow Democrat Mark Pryor unseated Republican Tim Hutchinson in 2002.

Lincoln still says her family comes first, but she is now more often seen at the early morning meetings and evening gatherings that are part of a senator's job description. Yet she remains grounded in reality. As she said in "Nine and Counting," a collaborative book written by the nine women who served in the Senate in the 106th Congress, "It's hard to be high and mighty when you've got peanut butter on your sleeve."

Lincoln told Working Mother magazine late in 2000 that her mother's example of "organizing education programs at the church, volunteering for the PTA, keeping the books for our farm, and raising four children" showed her how to find a balance.

A farmer's daughter whose Arkansas roots go back seven generations, Lincoln is a founding member of the moderate Senate New Democrats as well as the bipartisan Centrist Coalition, which works across party lines in search of compromises on key issues. In the 107th Congress, for example, she developed a welfare bill with the "tripartisan" backing of Democrats, Republicans and independent James M. Jeffords of Vermont.

Lincoln is savvy and polished and knows how to make deals. She breaks from her party now and then, as she did on the 2001 tax cut offered by President Bush, which she supported only after it was altered to her liking. She waited until the measure included a provision to make a child tax credit partially refundable. She also backed a repeal of a number of Clinton administration ergonomics rules for the workplace and supported an increase in automobile fuel efficiency standards. Later, she offered a bill to permanently repeal the estate tax for family-owned businesses and farms.

She has taken advantage of rare one-on-one opportunities with the president to get her points across. During a trip on Air Force One in 2001, when Bush lobbied her to support his tax cut, she handed him two letters spelling out her requests for expedited disaster relief for Arkansas farmers and increased anti-poverty efforts in the Mississippi Delta region. She had a similar encounter with fellow Arkansan Bill Clinton when he was in the White House. Lincoln pressed her agenda during a social gathering. "It just made sense that if you're going to spend a couple of hours with the president, you might as well take advantage of the proximity," she later wrote.

Lincoln's "people skills" win her plaudits among Capitol Hill aides: In its annual survey of staff attitudes about lawmakers, Washingtonian magazine said she ranked high in the "just plain nice" category.

Lincoln says the Senate's even partisan split in the 107th Congress offered good opportunities for members in the center. She landed a key assignment in the 107th on the powerful Finance Committee along with a seat on Ethics, both of which bode well for movement up the Democratic ranks.

Lincoln also serves on the Agriculture panel, where she looks out for home state farming interests. "Agriculture is really my base, not only for my state's economy but also my heritage," she says. In the 107th, she eventually backed a big farm bill that expanded the federal government's stake in agriculture, but only after she worked to raise the Senate's initial cap on annual payments to individual farmers. She specifically looks to protect Arkansas producers of catfish and soybeans. She wrote a measure in the 107th to provide a tax credit to promote the production of biodiesel, which is made from soybeans. Lincoln also supports lifting the embargo on agricultural trade with Cuba.

She brings a rural perspective to many issues in Congress. Lincoln says that rural areas have unique problems that cannot be fixed with a "one size fits all" approach. She is proud of her work in the 106th Congress to win authorization and an initial $30 million start-up appropriation for an eight-state Delta Regional Authority, modeled after the larger Appalachian Regional Commission, to foster economic development in the South.

In the 108th, she will work to secure a key role for the Pine Bluff Arsenal in the production of vaccines to combat bioterrorism.

One year out of college, Blanche Lambert got her start on Capitol Hill in 1983 as a receptionist for Arkansas Democratic Rep. Bill Alexander. She left after two years for a series of research positions with lobbying firms and then decided in late 1991 to head home to organize her first campaign for Congress — a challenge to Alexander's renomination. As she wrote in "Nine and Counting," "Daddy always said, 'I don't want to hear you whining about things you're not willing to do something about.' He'd tell us, 'Either stop griping, or get out there and change it.' "

Her 1992 run attracted little notice until news broke that Alexander was among the top 10 abusers in the House bank overdraft scandal. She took 61 percent in the primary and coasted to victory in November. She married Steve Lincoln, an obstetrician and gynecologist who specializes in fertility, in 1993 and won re-election the following year.

Lincoln's outgoing personality and ability to relate to her constituents — duck hunting is among her leisure pursuits — have made her a popular politician in Arkansas. Seen as a rising star among Arkansas Democrats, Lincoln put it all aside when she decided not to seek a third House term in 1996 after becoming pregnant with her twins.

But her career interruption did not last long: When Democrat Dale Bumpers announced that he would not seek a fifth Senate term in 1998, Lincoln jumped at the opportunity to return to politics.

She benefited from an embarrassing stumble by state Sen. Fay Boozman, who reportedly said that a woman was unlikely to become pregnant when she is raped because of hormonal responses in her body he referred to as "God's little protective shield." Lincoln accused Boozman of being insensitive. He later apologized, but the damage was done; she won by 13 points.

After her election, Lincoln said the voters in Arkansas knew what they were getting when they sent her to Washington. She says she let her constituents know early on "that I'm moving my family with me because I want to watch my family grow up. I want to see their school plays. We'll be back here every holiday and every chance I get, but I'm not going to sacrifice my family for this job."

Arkansas was the first state to send a popularly elected woman to the Senate — Hattie Caraway in 1932. Lincoln carried a quote from Caraway's campaign with her when she ran in 1998: "If I can hold on to my sense of humor and a modicum of dignity, I shall have a wonderful time running for office whether I get there or not."

When she won, Lincoln became the youngest woman ever elected to the Senate. She often refers to lessons she has learned from Caraway's career and displays a portrait of Caraway in her office.

KEY VOTES

2002

- No Pass farm bill reversing crop subsidy limits
- Yes Postpone tougher automobile fuel efficiency standards
- Yes Overhaul campaign finance law; ban "soft money" and restrict advocacy advertising
- Yes Set federal election standards
- No Support oil drilling in Arctic National Wildlife Refuge
- Yes Revive fast-track procedures for trade agreements
- Yes Create federal insurance coverage for catastrophic terrorist losses
- Yes Tighten federal accounting and corporate governance regulation
- Yes Advance bipartisan Medicare prescription drug plan
- Yes Create independent Sept. 11 commission
- Yes Back Democratic Homeland Security Department proposal
- Yes Authorize war against Iraq

2001

- No Confirm John Ashcroft as attorney general
- Yes Nullify Clinton Labor Department ergonomics rule
- Yes Cut taxes by $1.35 trillion through fiscal 2011
- Yes Pass Democratic bill to bolster rights of patients in managed-care plans
- Yes Permit a new round of military base closings
- Yes Expand law enforcement power to investigate suspected terrorists

CQ VOTE STUDIES

	PARTY UNITY		PRESIDENTIAL SUPPORT	
	Support	Oppose	Support	Oppose
2002	61%	39%	89%	11%
2001	79%	21%	71%	29%
2000	80%	20%	84%	16%
1999	83%	17%	80%	20%
House Service:				
1996	66%	34%	63%	37%
1995	64%	36%	63%	37%
1994	79%	21%	73%	27%
1993	87%	13%	72%	28%

INTEREST GROUPS

	AFL-CIO	ADA	CCUS	ACU
2002	77%	70%	75%	40%
2001	88%	85%	79%	28%
2000	50%	70%	86%	20%
1999	89%	95%	65%	12%
House Service:				
1996	57%	30%	64%	36%
1995	58%	60%	63%	20%
1994	33%	60%	83%	10%
1993	75%	65%	45%	25%

Sen. Mark Pryor (D)

CAPITOL OFFICE
224-2353
mark_pryor@pryor.senate.gov
217 Russell 20510-0403; fax 228-3973

COMMITTEES
Armed Services
Governmental Affairs
Small Business & Entrepreneurship

HOMETOWN
Little Rock

BORN
Jan. 10, 1963, Fayetteville, Ark.

RELIGION
Christian

FAMILY
Wife, Jill Pryor; two children

EDUCATION
U. of Arkansas, B.A. 1985 (history), J.D. 1988

CAREER
Lawyer

POLITICAL HIGHLIGHTS
Ark. House, 1991-95; sought Democratic nomination for Ark. attorney general, 1994; Ark. attorney general, 1999-2003

ELECTION RESULTS

2002 GENERAL		
Mark Pryor (D)	433,386	53.9%
Tim Hutchinson (R)	370,735	46.1%
2002 PRIMARY		
Mark Pryor (D)		unopposed

Elected 2002; 1st term

With his strong political bloodlines, Pryor hardly surprised Arkansans when he was elected to the state House at age 27, when he was chosen state attorney general at 35 and when, four years later, he was the only Democrat in 2002 to take over a Republican-held Senate seat.

In defeating one-term Republican incumbent Tim Hutchinson, Pryor benefited from the fondness voters still feel for his father. David Pryor, also a Democrat, held the same Senate seat for 18 years ending in 1997 and had previously been governor for four years. One of the new senator's grandmothers, Susie Newton Pryor, was among the first women to seek public office in Arkansas after women won the right to vote.

Pryor was the nation's youngest attorney general when he was elected in 1998. He celebrated his 40th birthday four days after he was sworn in to the Senate, making him the second-youngest senator in the 108th Congress, after freshman Republican John H. Sununu of New Hampshire, who is 20 months Pryor's junior.

Running in a conservative-leaning state, Pryor emphasized his conservative views on social policy and religion. He positioned himself as an ideological heir to the "New Democrat" centrism popularized by another successful Arkansan, President Clinton. Pryor said his role model as a senator would be his father, who was known as an affable, politically moderate statesman who relied on friendships to build coalitions.

"People probably see a lot of my dad in me, and that's okay," he told USA Today during the campaign. As he settled into his office in the Hart Building, he placed an "Arkansas Comes First" plaque on his desk, a hand-me-down from his father's Senate desk set.

During the campaign, Pryor portrayed Hutchinson — the only Republican ever elected to the Senate from Arkansas — as overly partisan for siding 95 percent of the time with the GOP on party-line votes. (As he campaigned for re-election, Hutchinson during the 107th Congress actually brought that party unity score down to 88 percent.) Pryor's own platform indicated that there would be issues on which he would be happy to work with President Bush and Senate Republicans, and others on which he would support traditional Democratic stands.

For example, he favored granting Bush the authority to launch a military campaign against Iraq. He supports the rights of gun owners — he is one himself — and endorses tough sentences for criminals. But, in opposition to Bush and many Republicans, he opposes oil drilling in the Arctic, advocates raising the minimum wage by at least $1 and would spend more generously on federal education aid. And, from his seat on the Armed Services Committee, Pryor will separate himself from the administration over its efforts to deploy a missile defense system. He says he has never been convinced that such a system would work and calls funding it "unwise."

Pryor has said he is personally against abortion but refuses to identify himself as "pro-choice" or "pro-life" because, he says, the issue of abortion rights is much more complex than those labels. He said a woman should be able to choose abortion to end a pregnancy started by rape or incest or when there is a risk to her life; he also voted to ban a procedure its opponents call "partial birth" abortion.

He holds conservative views on some fiscal matters. He has called for the permanent repeal of estate taxes because in his view the taxes do inappropriate harm to small businesses and family farms. From his seat on the

Small Business Committee, he wants to promote tax cuts for small businesses and tax credits for businesses that help pay for their employees' health coverage.

Pryor calls himself a "deficit hawk." He has said he wants to "get the deficit under control and get our debt eradicated," which he contends will boost economic growth by keeping interest rates low.

But Pryor should not be mistaken for a Republican. He opposes proposals to cut the corporate alternative minimum tax. He opposes the partial privatization of Social Security. And he supports the Democratic version of a patients' bill of rights, including patients' right to sue their insurers when they are harmed by denial of coverage.

In January 2003, Pryor allied himself with eight Democrats and six Republicans who were looking for alternatives to the tax cuts Bush proposed as an economic stimulus, the centerpiece of which was sharply reduced taxation of stock dividends.

Along with his other two assignments, Pryor was pleased to obtain a seat on Governmental Affairs — in part because his father served on the committee, but also because it oversees the Homeland Security Department. He says the new department's organizational structure raises questions about its efficiency. He also wants to protect some local interests in that organization. Along with Arkansas' other senator, Democrat Blanche Lincoln, he has aggressively pushed for Pine Bluff Arsenal in southeastern Arkansas to be the site for a national vaccine production facility.

He has said he will also use his spot on Armed Services — the panel assignment Pryor said he most coveted, during his Senate campaign — to look after the arsenal and Little Rock Air Force Base.

Pryor began the 108th Congress affiliating with a bloc of Southern Democrats who often provide the Senate's swing vote. Protecting the interests of coal-burning plants in his home state, he voted in favor of a Bush administration plan to allow industrial plants to upgrade their facilities without improving air pollution controls. He also supported a Republican drought relief amendment that was opposed by most Democrats but favored by the rice and soybean farmers of his state.

Pryor started in politics early. When his family moved to the Washington area after his father's election to the Senate in 1978, Pryor became class president at Walt Whitman High School in suburban Bethesda, Md. As his father had been three decades earlier, he was a congressional page in 1982. He then headed to his hometown, Fayetteville, to earn undergraduate and law degrees at the University of Arkansas.

Elected to the state House two years out of law school, his budding career was set back when he lost the Democratic primary for attorney general in 1994. Shortly thereafter, he was diagnosed with sarcoma, a rare form of cancer that left him unable to walk unassisted for more than a year after surgery. But the disease went into remission and has not returned. This enabled Pryor to restart his political career. Elected attorney general in 1998, he sued tobacco companies for smoking-related health care costs and made it possible for Arkansans to block telemarketing calls.

His Senate bid turned out to be the Democrats' one big recruiting success in 2002. While Pryor had strengths in his familiar name and centrist profile, Hutchinson entered as a wounded incumbent. In 1999, Hutchinson divorced his wife of 29 years and married a former Senate staff aide — leading some constituents in socially conservative Arkansas to question the "family values" platform on which Hutchinson, a Baptist minister, ran in 1996. Pryor never talked about the divorce, but he frequently touted his own religious and family values. He not only won, but did so by a comfortable 8 percentage point margin.

Rep. Marion Berry (D)

CAPITOL OFFICE
225-4076
www.house.gov/berry
1113 Longworth 20515-0401; fax 225-5602

COMMITTEES
Appropriations

HOMETOWN
Gillett

BORN
Aug. 27, 1942, Stuttgart, Ark.

RELIGION
Methodist

FAMILY
Wife, Carolyn Berry; two children

EDUCATION
U. of Arkansas, attended 1960-62 (pre-pharmacy);
U. of Arkansas, Little Rock, B.S. 1965 (pharmacy)

CAREER
Farmer; White House aide; pharmacist

POLITICAL HIGHLIGHTS
Gillett City Council, 1976-80; Ark. Soil and Water Conservation Commission, 1986-94 (chairman, 1992)

ELECTION RESULTS

2002 GENERAL		
Marion Berry (D)	129,701	66.8%
Tommy F. Robinson (R)	64,357	33.2%
2002 PRIMARY		
Marion Berry (D)		unopposed
2000 GENERAL		
Marion Berry (D)	120,266	60.2%
Susan Myshka (R)	79,437	39.7%

PREVIOUS WINNING PERCENTAGES
1998 (100%); 1996 (53%)

Elected 1996; 4th term

Although Berry's main focus for the past three decades has been farming, his brief career as a pharmacist helped to put him in the middle of the health care debates during his early years in the House. Democratic leaders have tapped him to represent the rural and more conservative factions of their caucus on managed-care and prescription drug issues.

With an easygoing manner and a slow, Southern drawl, Berry makes a point of playing up his rural background. He once described himself to an audience back home as nothing more than a "farmer who got more involved in politics than maybe I should have."

Berry's involvement in agriculture has been varied — running the family farm in southeast Arkansas, holding posts in the state and federal agriculture bureaucracy and serving for six years on the House Agriculture Committee.

In the 108th Congress, Berry got a sought-after seat on the Appropriations Committee, forcing him to give up his assignments to the Agriculture and Transportation panels.

Berry still looks out for the soybean, cotton and rice farmers of the Mississippi River Delta, but since the start of his second term much of his time has been taken up with health care. Trained as a pharmacist in the 1960s, he worked as one in Little Rock for two years after college. He has not practiced pharmacy since, though he has retained his license. (He is the only registered pharmacist in Congress.)

A co-chairman of the Democratic Caucus Health and Medicare Task Force, he was also one of three co-chairmen of a group of Democrats who sought to develop a plan to deal with the high cost of prescription drugs. Berry makes it clear that the local pharmacist is not to blame for the high cost of drugs for the elderly, most of whom do not have insurance coverage to help pay for their prescriptions. Drug manufacturers are the bad guys, according to Berry. "The American people pay two to three times more for medication than anywhere else in the world," he said in 2002. "We would consider other countries evil if they did that."

Arkansas is particularly affected by high drug costs as the state has a large percentage of elderly people living in poverty. Berry has worked on legislation that would permit pharmacies to import drugs from Canada and other countries where prices are lower.

As a member of the "Blue Dogs," a coalition of conservative Democrats, Berry was sought out by the group because of his pharmacy background to co-chair its health task force. When Democratic leaders went about fashioning their patients' rights bill in the 106th Congress, they made sure that the views of the Blue Dogs — a key bloc of votes — were considered. Berry worked closely with Democrat John D. Dingell of Michigan and Republicans Charlie Norwood of Georgia and Greg Ganske of Iowa on the patients' rights measure. In the 107th, when the Bush White House cut a separate deal with Norwood, Democrats chose Berry to deliver their weekly radio address to complain about the resulting bill.

In his voting record, Berry strays from the Democratic Party position about a third of the time on issues such as gun control and constitutional amendments mandating a balanced budget, requiring a two-thirds majority vote to raise taxes, and permitting prayer in schools. In the 107th, he backed President Bush 41 percent of the time.

Although Berry is no fan of big government, he is quick to herald federal spending that benefits his constituents. His office churns out news releases announcing federal funding for local road-building projects and the award of grants to local schools and law enforcement agencies. The 1st District is the poorest House district in one of the poorest states in the nation. Berry's interests include economic development such as improving rural and children's health care (including championing a visa program that brings foreign doctors to underserved areas), making education more affordable and keeping Medicare premiums low.

Even with his focus on health care, Berry has not ignored agriculture issues. He has urged increased export opportunities and removal of sanctions that bar farm exports to nations such as Cuba. And he pressed the interests of his farmers, who were hurt by low prices, in the writing of the new farm bill in the 107th.

Berry also joined with other lawmakers in the region to complain about imports from Vietnam of fish that were labeled catfish. Berry and his colleagues said the fish were improperly labeled and were undermining the business of domestic catfish producers.

After his stint in the pharmacy, Berry managed the family's soybean, rice, corn and wheat farm in Gillett. He recalls going with his father to the general store, where the men gathered to talk about current events and politics. Though his father and grandfather never held elective office, Berry says their involvement in civic affairs set an example for him.

He began his political career in 1976, when he was elected to the Gillett City Council. In 1982, he became Bill Clinton's gubernatorial campaign coordinator in Arkansas County, a post he also held in 1986 and 1990.

As governor, Clinton in 1986 named Berry to the state Soil and Water Conservation Commission; he served for eight years and chaired the panel in 1992. He moved to Washington when Clinton appointed him special assistant to the president for agricultural trade and food assistance issues.

When Democrat Blanche Lincoln became pregnant with twins and decided to leave the House in 1996, Berry won a close contest to fill her seat against Republican Warren Dupwe, who had held Lincoln to 53 percent in 1994.

In a district that has not elected a Republican since Reconstruction, Berry easily sailed through two re-election campaigns. In 2002, after brushing aside talk that he should run for the Senate, he took 67 percent against Tommy Robinson, who was seeking a political comeback a dozen years after switching to the Republican Party, giving up a seat in the House after three terms and then losing the 1990 GOP gubernatorial primary.

KEY VOTES

2002

- Yes Overhaul campaign finance law; ban "soft money" and restrict advocacy advertising
- Yes Back Bush's defense budget increase
- No Extend 1996 welfare law
- No Adopt Bush's discretionary spending limit
- No Pass GOP Medicare prescription drug plan
- Yes Create independent Sept. 11 commission
- Yes Extend union protections to Homeland Security Department employees
- No Revive fast-track procedures for trade agreements
- Yes Authorize war against Iraq
- Yes Advance bankruptcy overhaul opposed by abortion opponents

2001

- No Nullify Clinton Labor Department ergonomics rule
- No Cut taxes by $1.35 trillion through fiscal 2011
- No Maintain ban on oil drilling in Arctic National Wildlife Refuge
- No Approve Bush proposal to limit managed-care plan liability for coverage decisions
- No Divert money from crop subsidy payments to land conservation
- Yes Expand law enforcement power to investigate suspected terrorists

CQ VOTE STUDIES

	PARTY UNITY		PRESIDENTIAL SUPPORT	
	Support	Oppose	Support	Oppose
2002	79%	21%	42%	58%
2001	65%	35%	40%	60%
2000	67%	33%	55%	45%
1999	67%	33%	60%	40%
1998	70%	30%	63%	37%

INTEREST GROUPS

	AFL-CIO	ADA	CCUS	ACU
2002	78%	70%	50%	32%
2001	92%	60%	43%	52%
2000	60%	35%	76%	48%
1999	78%	60%	58%	29%
1998	80%	70%	67%	28%

ARKANSAS 1

Northeast – Jonesboro, West Memphis

One of the nation's poorest districts, the 1st stretches across Arkansas' northeastern third, reaching from the Mississippi Delta through fertile plains and into the hilly north, where the Ozark Mountains begin.

Poverty is most notably present within the largely white, older populations in the northwest and the former sharecropping communities in the Democratic Delta. In the mid-1990s, the predominantly black Delta communities began working with Arkansas State University in Jonesboro to attract tourism and manufacturing, but have made little headway. The area receives government support in the form of the Delta Regional Authority, which seeks to increase economic development in the areas along the Mississippi River.

Some of the nation's largest rice and cotton producers farm the Delta and house their corporate headquarters in the 1st. Cattle and poultry businesses are prosperous in the north. Manufacturing is strong in several cities, including Stuttgart, Batesville and Jonesboro. One of the nation's largest steel production plants bolsters Blytheville, where the population and economy sagged after Eaker Air Force Base closed in 1992.

The 1st elects few Republicans at the state or federal level. A Republican has not represented the district since 1875, and Democratic presidential candidates carried the area in the 1990s and 2000, although Al Gore took the 1st with just under 50 percent in 2000. Western Lonoke County — home to Little Rock suburbanites and some military personnel — leans Republican, as do some of the 1st's northwestern counties. The heavily Christian district is socially conservative in many areas.

MAJOR INDUSTRY

Agriculture, steel production, manufacturing

CITIES

Jonesboro, 55,515; West Memphis, 27,666; Paragould, 22,017; Blytheville, 18,272; Cabot, 15,261; Forrest City, 14,774

NOTABLE

Author John Grisham was born in Jonesboro; The world duck calling championship is held annually in Stuttgart.

Rep. Vic Snyder (D)

CAPITOL OFFICE
225-2506
snyder.congress@mail.house.gov
www.house.gov/snyder
1330 Longworth 20515-0402; fax 225-5903

COMMITTEES
Armed Services
Veterans' Affairs

HOMETOWN
Little Rock

BORN
Sept. 27, 1947, Medford, Ore.

RELIGION
Presbyterian

FAMILY
Single

EDUCATION
Willamette U., B.A. 1975 (chemistry); U. of Oregon, M.D. 1979; U. of Arkansas, Little Rock, J.D. 1988

MILITARY SERVICE
Marine Corps, 1967-69

CAREER
Physician; lawyer

POLITICAL HIGHLIGHTS
Ark. Senate, 1991-96

ELECTION RESULTS

2002 GENERAL		
Vic Snyder (D)	142,752	92.9%
Ed Garner (write-in)	10,874	7.1%
2002 PRIMARY		
Vic Snyder (D)	55,098	72.4%
Jim B. Baker (D)	21,033	27.6%
2000 GENERAL		
Vic Snyder (D)	126,957	57.5%
Bob Thomas (R)	93,692	42.5%

PREVIOUS WINNING PERCENTAGES
1998 (58%); 1996 (52%)

Elected 1996; 4th term

Snyder's 15 years as a family physician and his emergence as a thoughtful voice on the Armed Services Committee position him to be a key player in the battles over health care and national security that loom so large on the congressional agenda. But rather than introducing bills and making speeches on the House floor, Snyder's long suit is working behind the scenes.

To be sure, Snyder pulls his weight in the Democrats' effort to broaden health care for senior citizens, lacing his remarks on prescription drug coverage for seniors or patients' problems with their health maintenance organizations with references to his personal experience. But he typically focuses on more detailed issues within those broader debates.

Snyder counts as a major achievement his role in overturning a Medicare regulation that halted coverage for immunosuppressive drugs after less than four years. When some organ transplant recipients stopped taking the drugs because they found they could not pay for them, it sometimes led to organ rejection and the need for another costly transplant — which Medicare covered. Snyder rounded up cosponsors for a bill in the 106th Congress that changed the regulation.

A member of the centrist New Democrat Coalition, Snyder's priorities have included balancing the budget while ensuring a strong federal role in education, health care and national defense. But he also has begun digging into foreign policy issues, partly because of his travels abroad.

After repeatedly being told by U.S. ambassadors that their embassies were short of experienced Foreign Service officers, Snyder asked the General Accounting Office, Congress' watchdog agency, to examine the situation. The agency found that, because of staffing shortfalls in hardship posts, relatively junior diplomats were in jobs for which they lacked the experience and expertise, including fluency in the local language. "If you're understaffed and you don't speak the language, you're at a disadvantage," he said.

Snyder is an active participant in the Cuba Working Group, a bipartisan coalition of more than 40 House members trying to end the 40-year-old economic embargo against Cuba. The group includes all four House members from Arkansas, which likely would do a booming business selling poultry, rice and soybeans to the island nation if trade were resumed. Snyder contends that U.S. credibility is undermined by the glaring inconsistency of trading with communist-led China and Vietnam while trying to isolate Cuba. "All it has done is hurt the Cuban people and hurt the ability of the American people to trade with Cuba," he said of the embargo.

A Vietnam War veteran (he dropped out of college to join the Marines, without telling his mother beforehand), Snyder holds seats on the Armed Services and Veterans' Affairs committees and devotes much of his attention in the House to the work of those panels. Early on, he and the rest of the state delegation turned back a proposal to move some of the training done at Little Rock Air Force Base to other locations — a shift that might have made the Arkansas facility more vulnerable to future base closure rounds. In the 108th, he and other Arkansas lawmakers are pressing for Pine Bluff Arsenal, in the neighboring 4th District, to be given a key role as a producer of vaccines to protect against bioterrorism.

In 2001, he was one of the few members of Armed Services to support President Bush's demand for another base-closing round, citing the repeated contentions by senior military and Pentagon civilian leaders that they were spending scarce money keeping up more bases than they needed. The same year, Snyder was named to the top Democratic slot on the Armed Services personnel subcommittee, known as Total Force in the 108th.

On the Veterans' Affairs Subcommittee on Health, he pressured the Defense and Veterans Affairs departments to do more to address the problems of Gulf War syndrome, a mysterious range of ailments reported by veterans of the 1991 military campaign in the Persian Gulf.

Snyder also has been persistent in his efforts to get veterans tested and treated for a serious type of hepatitis, a liver disease that affects about one-tenth of all veterans in central Arkansas, according to a Department of Veterans Affairs study. On that issue, he has a personal as well as a professional perspective — the husband of a 1998 campaign adviser died of the disease.

Born and raised in Oregon, Snyder as a young man spent much of his time in libraries — he has degrees in both medicine and law, though he has never practiced the latter discipline. After earning his medical degree at the University of Oregon, he came to Arkansas in 1979 to do his medical residency. He remained in his adoptive state, working as a family doctor.

Snyder served six years in the state Senate, where his priorities included support for small business, increased jail time for violent criminals, a crackdown on underage drinking, and a repeal of the state sales tax on food.

When Democratic incumbent Ray Thornton announced his retirement in 1996, Snyder entered the 2nd District race as an underdog, facing two tough opponents in the primary — prosecuting attorney Mark Stodola and John Edwards, a former aide to retiring U.S. Sen. David Pryor. Snyder finished second to Stodola in the primary but surged in the runoff campaign to narrowly edge out his foe.

Snyder embraced the national Democratic themes in the fall campaign, pledging to oppose GOP initiatives on Medicare, education and the environment. He posted a 52 percent to 48 percent victory over Republican Bud Cummins, a businessman and lawyer, while President Clinton carried the 2nd District by 18 percentage points.

In his re-election campaigns, Snyder won by 16 percentage points in 1998 and by 15 points in 2000, before rolling to a easy victory in 2002 against only a write-in opponent. In all four of his House campaigns, Snyder has refused to begin fundraising until much later than is traditional. His rule, he says, is to begin three months before the primary. He acknowledges that his approach can be risky — particularly in his first campaign, where he was the underdog, and in his second campaign, where he was coming off a narrow victory. But he told the Arkansas Democrat-Gazette: "If it helps shorten the campaign . . . that's an improvement."

KEY VOTES

2002

- Yes Overhaul campaign finance law; ban "soft money" and restrict advocacy advertising
- Yes Back Bush's defense budget increase
- No Extend 1996 welfare law
- No Adopt Bush's discretionary spending limit
- No Pass GOP Medicare prescription drug plan
- Yes Create independent Sept. 11 commission
- Yes Extend union protections to Homeland Security Department employees
- Yes Revive fast-track procedures for trade agreements
- No Authorize war against Iraq
- Yes Advance bankruptcy overhaul opposed by abortion opponents

2001

- No Nullify Clinton Labor Department ergonomics rule
- No Cut taxes by $1.35 trillion through fiscal 2011
- Yes Maintain ban on oil drilling in Arctic National Wildlife Refuge
- No Approve Bush proposal to limit managed-care plan liability for coverage decisions
- No Divert money from crop subsidy payments to land conservation
- Yes Expand law enforcement power to investigate suspected terrorists

CQ VOTE STUDIES

	PARTY UNITY		PRESIDENTIAL SUPPORT	
	Support	Oppose	Support	Oppose
2002	85%	15%	41%	59%
2001	75%	25%	33%	67%
2000	89%	11%	90%	10%
1999	84%	16%	78%	22%
1998	80%	20%	81%	19%

INTEREST GROUPS

	AFL-CIO	ADA	CCUS	ACU
2002	67%	80%	60%	12%
2001	83%	85%	38%	13%
2000	90%	70%	55%	4%
1999	78%	85%	29%	4%
1998	90%	85%	61%	16%

ARKANSAS 2

Central — Little Rock

Encompassing Little Rock, eight surrounding counties and part of a ninth, the 2nd is Arkansas' axis of government activity. More than half of the district's population is focused in the Little Rock area, where strong black, union and university populations offer solid support to Democrats in most elections.

The district includes the state's largest white-collar population and has the highest median income. While the district supported Arkansas' former governor, Bill Clinton, heavily in the 1992 and 1996 presidential elections, George W. Bush narrowly carried the 2nd in 2000.

Democratic support is concentrated in poor and working-class neighborhoods in east Little Rock, which is heavily black. Rural agriculture and mining communities in outlying areas also tend to support Democrats, although social conservatism is more common.

Affluent neighborhoods in north and west Little Rock are more likely to vote for Republicans. The GOP has gained popularity within rapidly growing suburbs in Faulkner, Saline and Pulaski counties, which are fed by affluent whites leaving Little Rock. Republicans also fare well in White County, where Church of Christ-affiliated Harding University is located.

MAJOR INDUSTRY

Government, higher education, military

MILITARY BASES

Little Rock Air Force Base, 4,942 military, 852 civilian (2000)

CITIES

Little Rock, 183,133; North Little Rock, 60,433; Conway, 43,167; Jacksonville, 29,916; Benton, 21,906; Sherwood, 21,511; Searcy, 18,928

NOTABLE

The William J. Clinton Presidential Center will be located along the south bank of the Arkansas River in Little Rock; Little Rock Air Force Base has the largest C-130 training and airlift facility in the world; The Arkansas state Capitol, completed in 1915, was built on the site of the state penitentiary, partially using prison labor; Gen. Douglas MacArthur was born in Little Rock; North Little Rock's "Old Mill" was seen in the opening credits of "Gone with the Wind."

Rep. John Boozman (R)

Elected November 2001; 1st full term

CAPITOL OFFICE
225-4301
www.house.gov/boozman
1708 Longworth 20515-0403; fax 225-5713

COMMITTEES
Transportation & Infrastructure
Veterans' Affairs

HOMETOWN
Rogers

BORN
Dec. 10, 1950, Shreveport, La.

RELIGION
Baptist

FAMILY
Wife, Cathy Boozman; three children

EDUCATION
U. of Arkansas, attended 1969-72; Southern College of Optometry, O.D. 1977

CAREER
Optometrist; cattle farm owner

POLITICAL HIGHLIGHTS
Rogers Public Schools Board of Education, 1994-2001

ELECTION RESULTS

2002 GENERAL		
John Boozman (R)	141,478	98.9%
George N. Lyne (write-in)	1,577	1.1%
2002 PRIMARY		
John Boozman (R)		unopposed
2001 SPECIAL		
John Boozman (R)	53,308	55.7%
Mike Hathorn (D)	40,237	42.0%
Sarah Marsh (GREEN)	1,779	1.9%

Boozman's arrival on Capitol Hill late in 2001 added another lawmaker with a health care background to the Razorback State's roster. A doctor of optometry, Boozman (BOZE-man)and his brother founded an eye clinic that became well-known throughout northwest Arkansas.

Boozman won a special election to replace Republican Asa Hutchinson, who left to become head of the Drug Enforcement Administration, joining the House in time for the last three weeks of the 2001 session.

Initially, Boozman made little use of his health background, largely because he joined Congress mid-stream. In the 107th Congress, he focused on issues of particular importance locally, including the district's transportation and water infrastructure needs and trade policies. He has sought to open up overseas markets for Arkansas exports, notably rice and poultry. His work on health issues was confined to membership in a Republican group that did background work on a bill to provide Medicare prescription drug coverage.

In the 108th Congress, Boozman says, he expects to broaden his agenda to include health care and education, topics he has a strong interest in as an optometrist of more than 20 years and as a nearly seven-year veteran of the local school board.

In the 107th, he broke with the Bush administration and joined a growing number of lawmakers who favor dropping the longstanding trade embargo against Cuba. Arkansas farmers and corporations view Cuba as an untapped market for the state's rice and poultry exports. Boozman reasoned that if the U.S. government favors liberalized trade with China as a way of affecting internal change there, the same rationale could be applied to Cuba. "Not only are you exporting and importing products, but you export and import ideas," he told a group of businessmen in Springdale, reported the Arkansas Democrat-Gazette.

Boozman's district includes the headquarters of retailer Wal-Mart and food giant Tysons Foods, Inc., and he was one of the first lawmakers to speak out against the labor strife at West Coast ports that threatened to shut down trade with the Pacific Rim in 2002.

As a member of the Transportation Committee, Boozman's priority in the 107th was to secure funding for Interstate 49, which promises to make a significant improvement in north-south highway traffic through western Arkansas. He also has worked to provide better air service in the 3rd District, including pressing for more passenger service to Fort Smith and for federal grants to improve a number of the district's airports.

Boozman teamed up with Republican Roy Blunt on water quality issues, including seeking Environmental Protection Agency grants. Blunt represents the district just north of the 3rd across the border in Missouri. Boozman also worked with Oklahoma lawmakers from districts to the west.

He casts a dependably conservative vote. His political leanings are characterized by his affiliation with the Republican Study Committee, a group of several dozen of the most conservative House Republicans. Boozman regards himself as a "nuts and bolts type of guy," saying he is not that interested in appearing on television or introducing dozens of bills that have no chance of advancing. In the 107th Congress, for example, he introduced only two bills, both of which were to name post offices. Both measures passed the House and one became law.

Boozman was an offensive lineman for two years at the University of

Arkansas before leaving to attend optometry school in Memphis. (The congressman is more optometrist than lineman, however, in his soft-spoken demeanor.) In 1977 he set up the eye clinic in his hometown of Rogers.

Snyder's only previous political office was the seat he held for almost seven years on the school board in Rogers. He is politically well-connected, however.

His brother Fay, an ophthalmologist who was a partner in the eye clinic and who is now state health director, lost to Democrat Blanche Lincoln as the GOP nominee in the 1998 open-seat Senate race. That well-publicized contest raised public recognition of the Boozman name.

Boozman's choices for his first-year congressional staff paid homage to two well-known Arkansas Republican families. They included the son of GOP Gov. Mike Huckabee, whose endorsement helped Boozman in his 2000 special-election primary race, and the ex-wife of Republican Sen. Tim Hutchinson.

When Asa Hutchinson (Tim's brother) left the House to head up the DEA, Boozman entered the four-candidate GOP field seeking Hutchinson's seat. He finished first in the primary but was forced into a runoff race by conservative state Sen. Gunner DeLay, a distant cousin of House Republican leader Tom DeLay of Texas. Boozman, who was endorsed by Huckabee, won the runoff with 57 percent.

Boozman's image as the more "moderate" Republican helped him in the general-election contest against Democratic state Rep. Mike Hathorn. The 50-year-old Boozman campaigned on his "life experience," his trump card against the 28-year-old Hathorn's experience in the state legislature. Boozman and Hathorn each took conservative stands on social issues, such as abortion and gun control.

Boozman was conservative enough to satisfy the district's Republican voters, who usually hold sway. (George W. Bush took 59 percent in the district in 2000.) But because he was careful not to appear doctrinaire, he was able to win support from Democrats and independents and cruised to a 14 percentage point victory.

The 3rd District is by far the most Republican of Arkansas' four districts — the GOP has won every congressional election there since 1966. For almost two-thirds of those years, the GOP lawmaker from the 3rd was the only Republican in the Arkansas House delegation.

Redistricting left the 3rd's partisan makeup unchanged, and in 2002 Democrats did not even bother to field a candidate. Boozman captured 99 percent of the vote against a write-in candidate.

KEY VOTES

2002

- No Overhaul campaign finance law; ban "soft money" and restrict advocacy advertising
- Yes Back Bush's defense budget increase
- Yes Extend 1996 welfare law
- Yes Adopt Bush's discretionary spending limit
- Yes Pass GOP Medicare prescription drug plan
- No Create independent Sept. 11 commission
- No Extend union protections to Homeland Security Department employees
- Yes Revive fast-track procedures for trade agreements
- Yes Authorize war against Iraq
- No Advance bankruptcy overhaul opposed by abortion opponents

CQ VOTE STUDIES

	PARTY UNITY		PRESIDENTIAL SUPPORT	
	Support	Oppose	Support	Oppose
2002	95%	5%	85%	15%
2001	100%	0%	100%	0%

INTEREST GROUPS

	AFL-CIO	ADA	CCUS	ACU
2002	11%	0%	95%	96%
2001	25%	—	100%	100%

ARKANSAS 3

Northwest – Fort Smith, Fayetteville

Arkansas' hilly northwest subscribes to a rugged conservatism unique in this heavily Democratic state, and its Republican bent remains despite an influx of newcomers. It voted heavily in favor of George W. Bush in 2000 and was the state's only district to withhold hearty support from native son Bill Clinton in 1996. The 3rd has sent a Republican to Congress since the 1966 election.

Median household income, low in much of Arkansas, ranks in the bottom third of congressional districts nationwide, reflecting the 3rd's population of poor whites who live in the Ozark hills and farming communities. Residents in the Ozark mountains tend to be self-reliant and favor limited government, voting most often for Republicans.

Fayetteville, Springdale, Bentonville and Rogers in the state's northwest corner represent a wealthier part of the district, where history, religious tradition and an influx of retirees have created a solid Republican base. The 2000 census rated this northwestern corridor one of the 10 fastest-growing metropolitan areas in the country, with 48 percent growth over the 1990s.

Though the northwest sets the political tone, the rest of the 3rd — particularly farming communities and the city of Fort Smith — is more open to electing Democrats at the state level. Fayetteville and Springdale also have some liberal-leaning areas.

Hometown giants Tyson Foods in Springdale and Wal-Mart in Bentonville sustain the 3rd's economy, as does the University of Arkansas in Fayetteville. The closure of Fort Chaffee Army Base, near Fort Smith, in the late 1990s hit the district hard, but the military has recently made attempts to redevelop the land.

MAJOR INDUSTRY

Agriculture, livestock, retail

CITIES

Fort Smith, 80,268; Fayetteville, 58,047; Springdale, 45,798; Rogers, 38,829; Russellville, 23,682; Bentonville, 19,730

NOTABLE

Sen. J. William Fulbright, who established the Fulbright fellowships, lived in Fayetteville; The seven-story Christ of the Ozarks Statue in Eureka Springs was completed in 1966.

Rep. Mike Ross (D)

CAPITOL OFFICE
225-3772
www.house.gov/ross
314 Cannon 20515-0404; fax 225-1314

COMMITTEES
Agriculture
Financial Services

HOMETOWN
Prescott

BORN
Aug. 2, 1961, Texarkana, Ark.

RELIGION
Methodist

FAMILY
Wife, Holly Ross; two children

EDUCATION
U. of Arkansas, Little Rock, B.A. 1987 (political science)

CAREER
Pharmacy owner; wholesale drug and medical supply company field representative; aide to lieutenant governor

POLITICAL HIGHLIGHTS
Nevada County Quorum Court, 1983-85; Ark. Senate, 1991-2001

ELECTION RESULTS

2002 GENERAL		
Mike Ross (D)	119,723	60.6%
Jay Dickey (R)	77,972	39.4%
2002 PRIMARY		
Mike Ross (D)		unopposed
2000 GENERAL		
Mike Ross (D)	108,143	51.0%
Jay Dickey (R)	104,017	49.0%

Elected 2000; 2nd term

A graduate of Hope High School, Ross' early involvement in politics linked him to another, more well-known man from Hope. As a 21-year-old, Ross drove Bill Clinton around the state as Clinton campaigned for governor. At the same time, Ross waged his own campaign for a term on Nevada County's legislative body, the Quorum Court. Clinton and Ross both won their elections that year and continued their climb up the political ladder.

Ross has always been interested in politics, he told the Arkansas Democrat-Gazette, dating back to when he was 10 years old and he met Democratic Gov. Dale Bumpers at a highway dedication ceremony. Ross went on to spend two decades in Arkansas politics while gaining business experience as the owner of a pharmacy in the small town of Prescott, about a dozen miles up the road from Hope.

Like Clinton, Ross is a New Democrat. In the 107th Congress, he joined the New Democrat Coalition, which is made up of several dozen centrist, pro-business House Democrats. One of his first bills was a measure calling for a study to decide whether Clinton's birthplace in Hope should be made a national historic site.

Ross is also a member of the "Blue Dogs," an alliance of conservative Democrats in the House. In the 107th, he bucked the Democratic Party on 28 percent of the votes in which the two parties took opposing sides.

The 4th District is socially conservative, and Ross says he plans to walk a centrist path as its representative. He at times breaks with Democrats on abortion and denounces gun control legislation, although he supports laws designed to keep weapons out of schools. In 2002, he was endorsed by the National Rifle Association.

He backed President Bush when Congress voted late in 2002 to authorize the president to wage war against Iraq, and he supports the Bush administration's efforts to lift the prohibition on oil drilling in Alaska's Arctic National Wildlife Refuge. Yet unlike a number of New Democrats, Ross voted against a bill giving the president fast-track authority to negotiate trade agreements that Congress cannot amend. Ross complained that unfair foreign trade practices have cost his district jobs.

In the 108th Congress, Ross was named to the Democratic Steering Committee, which makes Democratic committee assignments, and he played a role in the appointment of home-state colleague Marion Berry to the Appropriations Committee.

Saying he plans to be Arkansas' "economic ambassador," Ross speaks of attracting new industries to his economically lagging district and watching out for the existing job base at the Army's Pine Bluff Arsenal, which deals with chemical and biological weapons and has become important in homeland security efforts.

He also wants funding for two interstate highway projects that will traverse his district, improving transportation for the area's farmers and loggers. The highways — I-49, running roughly from Texarkana north to Bentonville, and I-69, arcing northeastward across the southeastern part of the district — have been authorized, but their progress depends on annual funding.

Ross serves on the Agriculture Committee, where he watches out for his state's peanut growers and stands up for the area's catfish farmers, who are faced with what Ross says is unfair competition from imported fish from

Vietnam. The fish are labeled — improperly, Ross says — as catfish. He has worked to extend Chapter 12 bankruptcy protections for farmers. Ross also sits on the Financial Services panel.

Ross was a radio announcer in college, and the Democrats have already made use of his deep "radio voice" in delivering their response to Bush's weekly radio speech. Ross' energetic efforts to communicate with his constituents includes not only a weekly radio show, but weekly e-mail newsletters and a steady stream of press releases, often as many as 20 a month. Some Arkansas observers have described Ross as stiff and robotic in formal settings, but in a one-on-one conversation he comes across as informed and affable.

Ross says he will refuse the annual cost-of-living pay raise for lawmakers until the minimum wage is increased. In the meantime, he directs the pay raise to a scholarship fund for two 4th District college students.

Both of Ross' parents were schoolteachers. He went to junior college in Texarkana for a while, combining that with a job at the radio station in Hope, where he started working when he was 15.

He earned his degree in political science at 25 while working as a top aide to Arkansas' lieutenant governor, Winston Bryant. He took time off in 1988 to serve as a regional coordinator for Democrat Michael S. Dukakis' presidential campaign.

After winning election to the state Senate in 1990, Ross made a living as a field representative for a wholesale drug and medical supply company. He and his wife, Holly, bought a pharmacy (Holly's Health Mart) in Prescott. His wife is the pharmacist.

In 2000, Ross entered the 4th District race, challenging four-term Republican Rep. Jay Dickey. Ross' status as the widely regarded front-runner for the Democratic nomination made him the target of attacks by his three opponents in the party's bitter primary — two of his primary foes later endorsed Dickey. He then endured a hard-fought campaign against Dickey, whose folksy manner had previously kept him popular despite the 4th's traditional Democratic leanings. Ross' narrow win was the Democrats' only victory over an incumbent outside California in November 2000.

Ross knew that his 2 percentage point victory left him vulnerable for 2002, and he quickly set about raising a large campaign war chest. Dickey was back for a rematch, and many political observers expected the race to be close once again. But Ross eventually won handily, with 61 percent of the vote.

KEY VOTES

2002

- Yes Overhaul campaign finance law; ban "soft money" and restrict advocacy advertising
- Yes Back Bush's defense budget increase
- No Extend 1996 welfare law
- No Adopt Bush's discretionary spending limit
- No Pass GOP Medicare prescription drug plan
- Yes Create independent Sept. 11 commission
- Yes Extend union protections to Homeland Security Department employees
- No Revive fast-track procedures for trade agreements
- Yes Authorize war against Iraq
- No Advance bankruptcy overhaul opposed by abortion opponents

2001

- No Nullify Clinton Labor Department ergonomics rule
- Yes Cut taxes by $1.35 trillion through fiscal 2011
- No Maintain ban on oil drilling in Arctic National Wildlife Refuge
- No Approve Bush proposal to limit managed-care plan liability for coverage decisions
- No Divert money from crop subsidy payments to land conservation
- Yes Expand law enforcement power to investigate suspected terrorists

CQ VOTE STUDIES

	PARTY UNITY		PRESIDENTIAL SUPPORT	
	Support	Oppose	Support	Oppose
2002	73%	27%	50%	50%
2001	70%	30%	37%	63%

INTEREST GROUPS

	AFL-CIO	ADA	CCUS	ACU
2002	78%	65%	55%	32%
2001	92%	65%	48%	36%

ARKANSAS 4
South — Pine Bluff, Hot Springs

Covering much of Arkansas' southern half, from the Mississippi River to the Texas and Oklahoma borders, the 4th is a socially conservative but Democratic district that took a Republican swing in the 1990s.

The district narrowly elected its first GOP representative of the 20th century in 1992, but overwhelmingly supported Hope-born and Hot Springs-raised Bill Clinton in both his presidential bids. In 2000, the 4th not only supported Al Gore in the presidential race, but also elected a Democrat to the House. State legislators in the 4th are almost exclusively Democrats.

Rice, soybeans, cotton and rural poverty characterize the eastern edge of the 4th, where many Mississippi River communities have black-majority populations. Democrats receive their most faithful support from these areas and from blue-collar and minority populations in Little River and Lafayette counties to the west. Republicans fare better in oil- and chemical-producing southern cities such as El Dorado, as well as in military and white-collar areas near Pine Bluff and Hot Springs. The timber industry here discourages pro-environment candidates.

The Pine Bluff Arsenal, which once produced the nation's supply of biological weapons, is home to an emergency preparedness center and a center for toxicological research. A chemical weapons disposal facility is under construction at the arsenal, and the base hopes to house the nation's first government-owned vaccine production plant to guard against bioterrorism. A decision was expected in 2003.

MAJOR INDUSTRY
Timber, agriculture, livestock

MILITARY BASES
Pine Bluff Arsenal (Army), 409 military, 982 civilian (1999)

CITIES
Pine Bluff, 55,085; Hot Springs, 35,750; Texarkana, 26,448; El Dorado, 21,530; Camden, 13,154

NOTABLE
Author Maya Angelou was raised in Stamps; Country singer Johnny Cash was born in Kingsland; Hot Springs, the state's premier tourist attraction, was a getaway for mobsters such as Charles "Lucky" Luciano and Al Capone in the 1930s.

CALIFORNIA

Gov. Gray Davis (D)

First elected: 1998
Length of term: 4 years
Term expires: 1/07
Salary: $175,000
Phone: (916) 445-2841
Hometown: Los Angeles
Born: Dec. 26, 1942; Bronx, N.Y.
Religion: Roman Catholic
Family: Wife, Sharon Davis
Education: Stanford U., A.B. 1964; Columbia U., J.D. 1967
Military Service: Army, 1967-69
Career: Lawyer
Political highlights: Candidate for Calif. treasurer, 1974; Calif. governor's chief of staff, 1975-81; Calif. Assembly, 1983-87; Calif. controller, 1987-95; sought Democratic nomination for U.S. Senate, 1992; lieutenant governor, 1995-99
Election results:

2002 GENERAL		
Gray Davis (D)	3,533,490	47.3%
Bill Simon (R)	3,169,801	42.4%
Peter Miguel Camejo (GR)	393,036	5.3%
Gary D. Copeland (LIBERT)	161,203	2.2%
Reinhold Gulke (AMI)	128,035	1.7%
Iris Adam (NL)	88,415	1.2%

Lt. Gov. Cruz M. Bustamante (D)

First elected: 1998
Length of term: 4 years
Term expires: 1/07
Salary: $123,744
Phone: (916) 445-8994

STATE LEGISLATURE

Legislature: Meets year-round, with recess
Assembly: 80 members, 2-year terms
2003 breakdown: 32R, 48D; 55 men, 25 women
Salary: $99,000
Phone: (916) 445-3614
Senate: 40 members, 4-year terms
2003 breakdown: 15R, 25D; 30 men, 10 women
Salary: $99,000
Phone: (916) 445-4251

STATE TERM LIMITS

Governor: 2 terms
Senate: 2 terms
Assembly: 3 terms

URBAN STATISTICS

CITY	POPULATION
Los Angeles	3,694,820
San Diego	1,223,400
San Jose	894,943
San Francisco	776,733
Long Beach	461,522

REGISTERED VOTERS

Democrat	44%
Republican	35%
Unaffiliated	15%
Other	5%

POPULATION

2002 population (est.)	35,116,033
2000 population	33,871,648
1990 population	29,760,021
Percent change (1990-2000)	+13.8%
Rank among states (2002)	1
Median age	33.3
Born in state	50.2%
Foreign born	26.2%
Violent crime rate	622/100,000
Poverty level	14.2%
Federal workers	246,152
Military	228,903

REDISTRICTING

California gained one House seat in reapportionment. The state legislature drew a new 53-district map, which the governor signed on Sept. 26, 2001.

MISCELLANEOUS

Web: www.state.ca.us
Capital: Sacramento
STATE ELECTION OFFICIAL
(916) 657-2166
DEMOCRATIC HEADQUARTERS
(916) 442-5707
REPUBLICAN HEADQUARTERS
(818) 841-5210

District Statistics

DIST.	2000 VOTE FOR PRESIDENT BUSH	GORE	NADER	WHITE	BLACK	ASIAN	HISP	MEDIAN INCOME	WHITE COLLAR	BLUE COLLAR	SERVICE INDUSTRY	OVER 64	UNDER 18	COLLEGE EDUCATION	RURAL	SQ. MILES
1	38%	51%	n/a	71%	1%	4%	18%	$38,918	58%	24%	18%	13%	25%	25%	24%	11,006
2	60	33	n/a	76	1	4	14	$33,559	55	27	18	15	26	17	32	21,758
3	54	40	n/a	74	4	6	11	$51,313	68	19	13	12	26	27	14	3,374
4	58	36	n/a	84	1	2	9	$49,387	63	20	16	14	26	25	33	16,453
5	34	58	n/a	43	14	15	21	$36,719	63	20	17	11	28	21	0	147
6	30	62	n/a	76	2	4	15	$59,115	68	18	14	13	23	38	10	1,625
7	30	65	n/a	43	17	13	21	$52,778	60	23	17	10	27	22	1	349
8	14	76	n/a	43	9	29	16	$52,322	73	12	15	13	14	44	0	35
9	13	77	n/a	35	26	15	19	$44,314	69	17	14	11	23	37	0	132
10	40	54	n/a	65	6	9	15	$65,245	69	18	13	12	27	36	3	1,013
11	52	44	n/a	64	3	9	20	$61,996	68	21	11	10	29	29	10	2,277
12	28	66	n/a	48	3	29	16	$70,307	73	15	12	14	21	41	0	117
13	29	65	n/a	38	6	28	21	$62,415	67	22	11	10	25	32	1	221
14	34	59	n/a	60	3	16	18	$77,985	77	13	10	12	22	52	6	826
15	36	58	n/a	47	2	29	17	$74,947	74	17	9	10	24	42	1	286

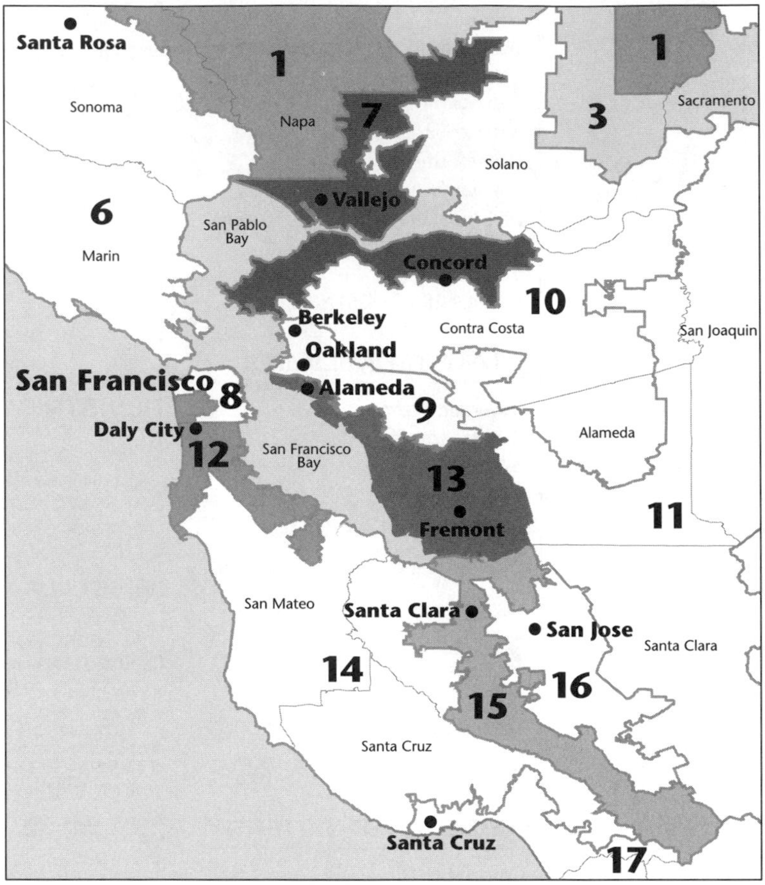

District Statistics

DIST.	2000 VOTE FOR PRESIDENT BUSH	GORE	NADER	WHITE	BLACK	ASIAN	HISP	MEDIAN INCOME	WHITE COLLAR	BLUE COLLAR	SERVICE INDUSTRY	OVER 64	UNDER 18	COLLEGE EDUCATION	RURAL	SQ. MILES
16	32%	62%	n/a	32%	3%	23%	38%	$67,689	61%	25%	14%	8%	27%	27%	1%	230
17	32	59	n/a	46	3	5	43	$49,234	55	28	16	10	27	25	10	4,820
18	43	52	n/a	39	6	9	42	$34,211	46	37	17	10	34	10	9	3,052
19	57	38	n/a	60	3	4	28	$41,225	59	25	15	12	28	20	19	6,692
20	42	53	n/a	21	7	6	63	$26,800	38	43	19	7	35	6	9	4,982
21	59	37	n/a	46	2	5	43	$36,047	53	31	16	10	32	15	20	8,026
22	63	33	n/a	67	6	3	21	$41,801	58	25	17	11	29	18	18	10,417
23	39	53	n/a	49	2	5	42	$44,874	57	26	17	12	25	26	2	1,042
24	53	42	n/a	69	2	4	22	$61,453	68	19	14	11	28	30	6	3,883
25	54	40	n/a	57	8	4	27	$49,002	60	24	16	8	32	19	12	21,484
26	52	42	n/a	53	4	15	24	$58,968	71	17	12	11	27	32	1	752
27	35	58	n/a	45	4	11	36	$46,781	66	20	14	11	26	26	0	151
28	23	70	n/a	31	4	6	56	$40,439	58	26	16	9	29	24	0	77

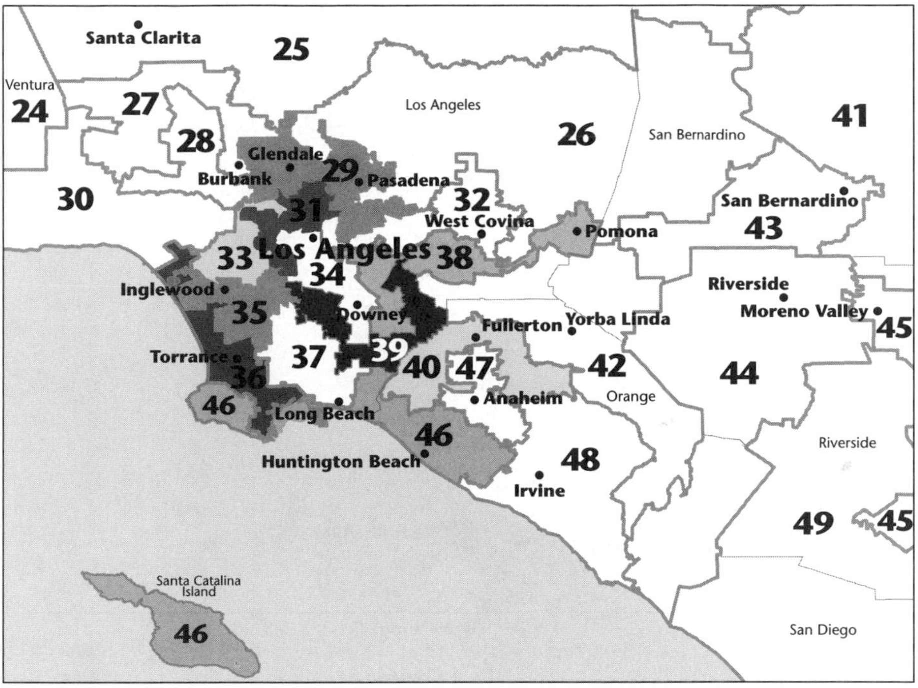

District Statistics

DIST.	2000 VOTE FOR PRESIDENT BUSH	GORE	NADER	WHITE	BLACK	ASIAN	HISP	MEDIAN INCOME	WHITE COLLAR	BLUE COLLAR	SERVICE INDUSTRY	OVER 64	UNDER 18	COLLEGE EDUCATION	RURAL	SQ. MILES
29	37%	56%	n/a	39%	6%	24%	26%	$43,895	70%	16%	14%	13%	23%	33%	1%	101
30	27	66	n/a	76	3	9	8	$60,713	84	7	9	15	17	54	2	286
31	18	73	n/a	10	4	14	70	$26,093	44	34	22	7	30	14	0	39
32	30	64	n/a	15	3	18	62	$41,394	51	33	16	9	31	14	0	92
33	13	80	n/a	20	30	12	35	$31,655	64	18	18	10	24	27	0	48
34	25	69	n/a	11	4	5	77	$29,863	44	40	16	8	32	9	0	58
35	16	78	n/a	10	34	6	47	$32,156	53	28	19	8	33	13	0	55
36	37	55	n/a	48	4	13	30	$51,633	71	16	13	10	23	37	0	75
37	21	72	n/a	17	25	11	43	$34,006	54	29	17	8	33	15	0	75
38	27	67	n/a	14	4	10	71	$42,488	51	34	15	9	32	13	0	104
39	34	60	n/a	21	6	10	61	$45,307	55	31	14	8	33	15	0	65
40	55	40	n/a	49	2	16	30	$54,356	65	22	13	11	27	26	0	100
41	54	40	n/a	64	5	4	23	$38,721	57	25	17	14	28	18	11	13,314

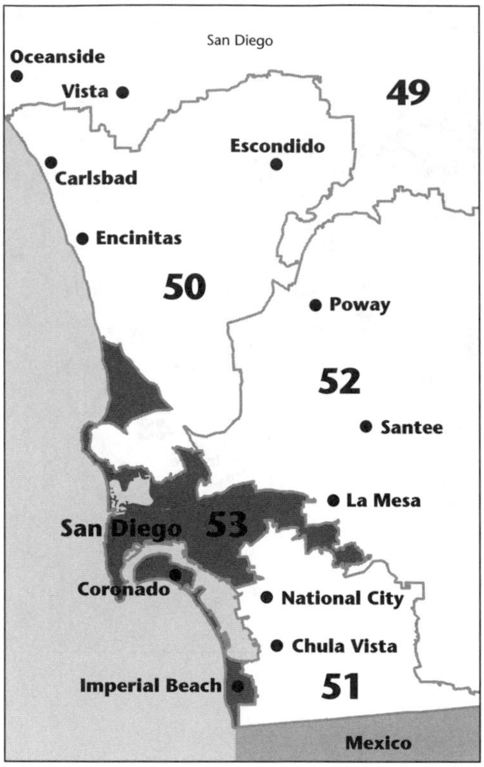

District Statistics

DIST.	2000 VOTE FOR PRESIDENT BUSH	GORE	NADER	WHITE	BLACK	ASIAN	HISP	MEDIAN INCOME	WHITE COLLAR	BLUE COLLAR	SERVICE INDUSTRY	OVER 64	UNDER 18	COLLEGE EDUCATION	RURAL	SQ. MILES
42	58%	38%	n/a	54%	3%	16%	24%	$70,463	74%	15%	11%	8%	28%	35%	1%	314
43	33	61	n/a	23	12	3	58	$37,390	46	37	17	6	37	9	1	191
44	52	44	n/a	51	5	5	35	$51,578	59	27	14	8	31	21	2	522
45	50	46	n/a	50	6	3	38	$40,468	53	26	21	16	29	17	10	5,980
46	53	41	n/a	63	1	15	17	$61,567	73	16	12	13	22	36	0	264
47	40	55	n/a	17	1	14	65	$41,618	41	39	20	6	33	10	0	55
48	57	39	n/a	68	1	13	15	$69,663	80	10	10	12	23	47	0	212
49	57	38	n/a	58	5	3	30	$46,445	58	26	16	13	29	21	10	1,690
50	52	41	n/a	66	2	10	19	$59,813	71	16	13	12	25	40	2	300
51	38	56	n/a	21	9	12	53	$39,243	55	26	20	10	31	15	4	4,582
52	56	38	n/a	73	4	5	14	$52,940	68	18	14	11	27	29	6	2,113
53	36	56	n/a	51	7	8	29	$36,637	65	17	19	10	21	32	0	95
STATE	42	53	4	47	6	11	32	$47,493	63	22	15	11	27	27	6	155,959
U.S.	47.9	48.4	3	69	12	4	13	$41,994	60	25	15	12	26	24	21	3,537,438

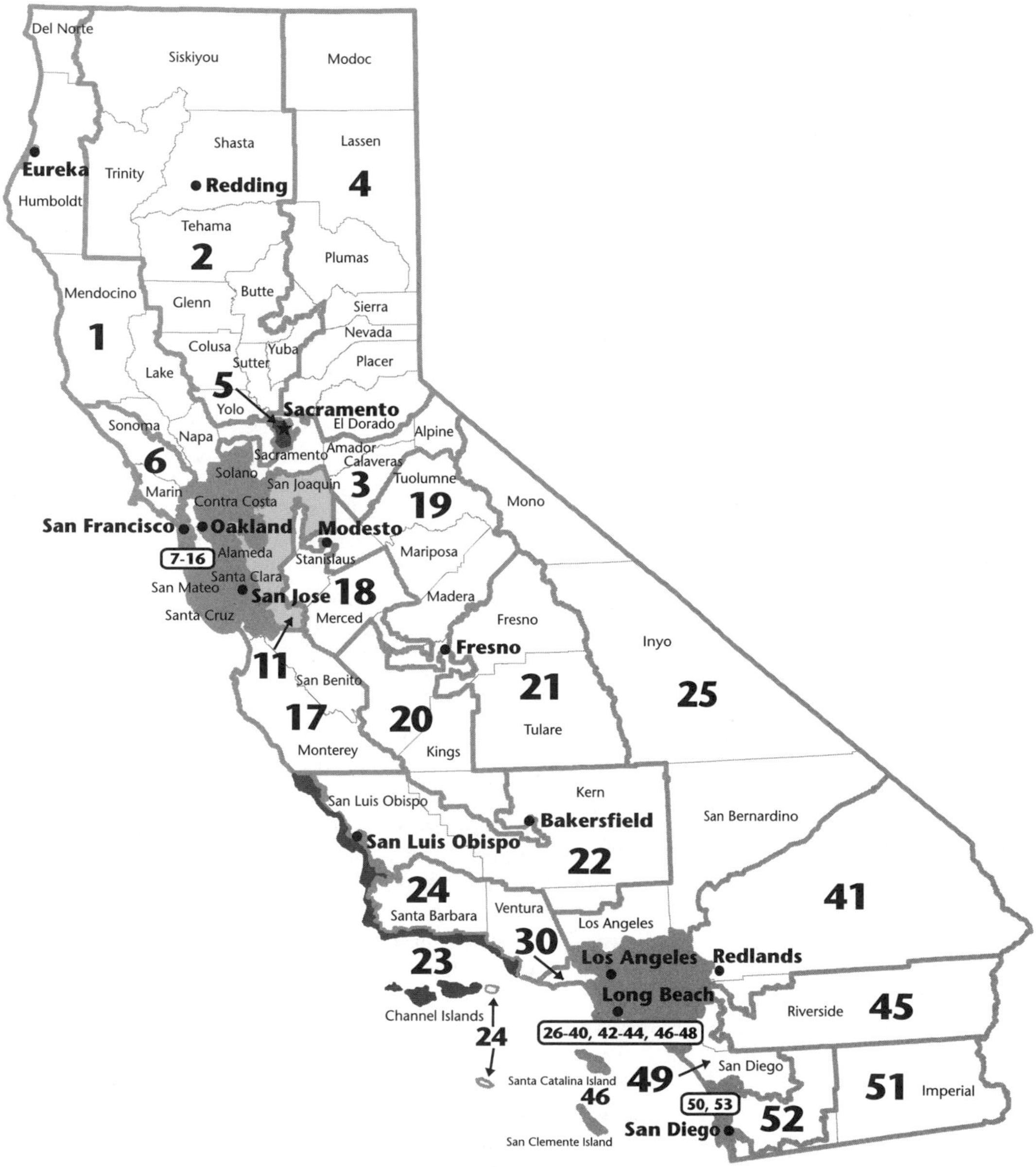
Del Norte
Siskiyou
Modoc
Shasta
Lassen
Eureka
Trinity
Redding
4
Humboldt
Tehama
2
Plumas
Mendocino
Glenn
Butte
Sierra
1
Nevada
Colusa
Yuba
Placer
Sutter
Lake
5
Yolo
Sacramento
El Dorado
Sonoma
Napa
Alpine
Sacramento
Amador
6
Calaveras
Solano
Tuolumne
San Joaquin
3
Marin
Contra Costa
19
Mono
San Francisco
Oakland
Modesto
7-16
Alameda
Stanislaus
Mariposa
Santa Clara
San Mateo
San Jose
18
Madera
Santa Cruz
Merced
Fresno
11
Fresno
Inyo
San Benito
21
25
17
20
Tulare
Monterey
Kings
Kern
San Luis Obispo
Bakersfield
San Bernardino
San Luis Obispo
22
24
41
Santa Barbara
Ventura
Los Angeles
30
23
Los Angeles
Redlands
Long Beach
Channel Islands
Riverside
45
24
26-40, 42-44, 46-48
San Diego
Santa Catalina Island
49
46
50, 53
51
Imperial
52
San Diego
San Clemente Island

Sen. Dianne Feinstein (D)

CAPITOL OFFICE
224-3841
feinstein.senate.gov
331 Hart 20510-0504; fax 228-3954

COMMITTEES
Appropriations
Energy & Natural Resources
Judiciary
Rules & Administration
Select Intelligence

HOMETOWN
San Francisco

BORN
June 22, 1933, San Francisco, Calif.

RELIGION
Jewish

FAMILY
Husband, Richard Blum; one child, three stepchildren

EDUCATION
Stanford U., A.B. 1955 (history)

CAREER
Public official

POLITICAL HIGHLIGHTS
San Francisco Board of Supervisors, 1970-78 (president, 1970-71, 1974-75, 1978); mayor of San Francisco, 1978-89; Democratic nominee for governor, 1990

ELECTION RESULTS

2000 GENERAL		
Dianne Feinstein (D)	5,932,522	55.8%
Tom Campbell (R)	3,886,853	36.6%
Medea Benjamin (GREEN)	326,828	3.1%
Gail Lightfoot (LIBERT)	187,718	1.8%
Diane Beall Templin (AMI)	134,598	1.3%
2000 PRIMARY (OPEN)		
Dianne Feinstein (D)	3,759,560	51.2%
Tom Campbell (R)	1,697,208	23.1%
Ray Haynes (R)	679,034	9.2%
Bill Horn (R)	453,630	6.2%
Michael Schmier (D)	181,104	2.5%
Gail Lightfoot (LIBERT)	120,622	1.6%

PREVIOUS WINNING PERCENTAGES
1994 (47%); 1992 Special Election (54%)

Elected 1992; 2nd full term

Feinstein knows how to straddle the ideological divide between the two parties without seeming indecisive. That has been key to her success on a broad range of issues, from campaign finance to human cloning to the Israeli-Palestinian conflict.

She rose to national prominence as San Francisco's mayor from 1978 to 1989 but has never fit the stereotype of the softhearted "San Francisco liberal." She is tough on crime and frequently votes pro-business, and her annual support scores from the U.S. Chamber of Commerce are typically higher than the average Senate Democrat's.

Feinstein (FINE-stine) says she developed her political mantra — "govern from the center" — while serving as mayor and trying to work out solutions that satisfied the diverse political forces in her city. Her moderation, personal appeal and high name recognition have made her one of California's most enduring political figures.

A member of the moderate Senate New Democrats and the Centrist Coalition, she is popular in the Senate; unlike her home state Democratic colleague, Barbara Boxer, Feinstein largely avoids alienating Republicans with stinging verbal assaults. In fact, it seems many of her battles are with Democrats. In 2001, she was visibly angry in a confrontation with Judiciary Chairman Patrick J. Leahy, a Vermont Democrat, over the need for more federal judges in California. And in 2002, she complained when Majority Leader Tom Daschle excluded her from negotiations involving ethanol, noting, "It's hard to have this kind of thing done by somebody you thought was a friend."

Feinstein has an impact on a diverse portfolio of issues, in part because California is so important electorally but also because of her ability to unemotionally conduct business in the enemy camp. When both parties were on the verge of throwing in the towel on the overhaul of campaign finance law, she teamed up with Republican Fred Thompson of Tennessee in 2001 on a compromise amendment that rescued the bill.

Likewise, Feinstein joined with Republican Mitch McConnell of Kentucky in 2002 on a Senate proposal to sever U.S. ties with the Palestine Liberation Organization after the peace process in the Middle East broke down amid a series of suicide bombings against Israeli citizens. The proposal was shelved when the Bush White House pleaded for time to try to halt the violence, but the plan sent a signal worldwide of the dismay in Congress with Yasser Arafat and the Palestinians.

Feinstein also tried to find the center in the human cloning debate, which was as thorny as any abortion dispute of recent decades. In the 107th Congress, she cosponsored with moderate Senate Republican Arlen Specter of Pennsylvania an alternative to an outright ban on human cloning being pushed by conservatives. Their compromise would have permitted cloning only to extract human cells for biomedical research, not to re-create a person. The Senate ultimately postponed the issue.

Feinstein is among the political moderates who are critical to the outcome of any fight in the closely divided Senate. She was one of 12 Senate Democrats who gave President Bush a big victory early on by voting for his sweeping cuts in tax rates.

She can be just as potent when working against the White House. During the 2001 fight over John Ashcroft's nomination as attorney general, Feinstein was not among the most vocal critics of Ashcroft's conservative positions. But her pointed appraisal — "It's very hard to change your stripes or change your spots" — was duly noted by her colleagues.

Feinstein is a senior member of the Intelligence Committee and a key player on Judiciary, which has given her a voice in shaping the many anti-terrorism policies born of the Sept. 11, 2001, terrorist attacks. Because of California's chronic energy shortages, she is also a player on energy legislation. In the 107th, she negotiated with Republicans to clamp down on energy market trading after revelations that Enron Corp. may have manipulated those markets.

She attempts to put a human face on the issue of the day. Whatever the topic under debate, Feinstein tries to find the story of someone who is affected personally as a vehicle for illustrating her points.

One issue on which Feinstein takes a strong stand is gun control. "I've lived a life that has been impacted by weapons," she wrote in "Nine and Counting," a book by the nine female senators serving in 2000. "So this is not an esoteric, academic exercise for me. Nor is it a political exercise."

In November 1978, while serving on the San Francisco Board of Supervisors, Feinstein discovered the body of Mayor George Moscone after he and Harvey Milk, the city's first openly gay supervisor, were shot to death in City Hall by former Supervisor Dan White. Feinstein succeeded Moscone and won plaudits for the dignified manner in which she held the city together in the wake of the killings.

Feinstein's role, recalled in the documentary "The Life and Times of Harvey Milk," has given her credibility in the gun debate. When GOP Sen. Larry E. Craig of Idaho, a National Rifle Association board member, once hinted that Feinstein did not have much weapons knowledge, she recounted how she had tried to find Milk's pulse after he was shot.

Feinstein has fought hard on various women's issues. She was a prominent skeptic during the Rules Committee's investigation of a GOP challenge to Louisiana Democrat Mary L. Landrieu's narrow 1996 Senate victory. "Hell hath no fury like a man beaten by a woman," Feinstein said. "Women have to fight our way in this process all the way up. No one hands us anything."

Certainly no one handed her the Senate seat, which she first won in a special election in 1992 against Republican John Seymour, who had been appointed after Republican Sen. Pete Wilson was elected governor in 1990. Boxer was also running in 1992, and the pair — despite their differences in personality and philosophy — campaigned as "Thelma and Louise," the leading ladies of politics' much-ballyhooed "Year of the Woman."

In 1994, Feinstein faced a tough challenge from millionaire GOP Rep. Michael Huffington, who outspent her by slightly more than a 2-to-1 ratio in what was at the time the most expensive Senate contest ever. Not until she and other Democrats turned attack ads against him — and it was revealed that Huffington had hired an illegal immigrant as a household employee — did Feinstein begin pulling ahead.

Her Republican opponent six years later, former Rep. Tom Campbell, had trouble raising money and did little to inspire his party's conservatives, offering centrist views and even calling Feinstein an effective senator at one point in the campaign. Seen as a pragmatist with a consensus-building approach to politics, Feinstein cruised to re-election.

The larger question in 2000 was whether Vice President Al Gore would tap her as his running mate. In the end, Connecticut Sen. Joseph I. Lieberman, not Feinstein, became the first Jewish vice-presidential candidate from a major political party. In 1984, Democratic nominee Walter F. Mondale had given Feinstein strong consideration before selecting Rep. Geraldine Ferraro of New York to be the first female vice-presidential candidate from a major party.

KEY VOTES

2002

Yes Pass farm bill reversing crop subsidy limits
No Postpone tougher automobile fuel efficiency standards
Yes Overhaul campaign finance law; ban "soft money" and restrict advocacy advertising
Yes Set federal election standards
No Support oil drilling in Arctic National Wildlife Refuge
Yes Revive fast-track procedures for trade agreements
Yes Create federal insurance coverage for catastrophic terrorist losses
Yes Tighten federal accounting and corporate governance regulation
Yes Advance bipartisan Medicare prescription drug plan
Yes Create independent Sept. 11 commission
Yes Back Democratic Homeland Security Department proposal
Yes Authorize war against Iraq

2001

No Confirm John Ashcroft as attorney general
No Nullify Clinton Labor Department ergonomics rule
Yes Cut taxes by $1.35 trillion through fiscal 2011
Yes Pass Democratic bill to bolster rights of patients in managed-care plans
No Permit a new round of military base closings
Yes Expand law enforcement power to investigate suspected terrorists

CQ VOTE STUDIES

	PARTY UNITY		PRESIDENTIAL SUPPORT	
	Support	Oppose	Support	Oppose
2002	83%	17%	76%	24%
2001	85%	15%	71%	29%
2000	88%	12%	84%	16%
1999	91%	9%	87%	13%
1998	87%	13%	88%	12%
1997	86%	14%	89%	11%
1996	81%	19%	90%	10%
1995	80%	20%	84%	16%
1994	89%	11%	92%	8%
1993	90%	10%	92%	8%

INTEREST GROUPS

	AFL-CIO	ADA	CCUS	ACU
2002	92%	80%	55%	20%
2001	94%	85%	71%	12%
2000	50%	70%	54%	28%
1999	78%	100%	53%	4%
1998	88%	90%	61%	4%
1997	57%	85%	50%	4%
1996	86%	95%	38%	20%
1995	100%	95%	37%	13%
1994	63%	70%	40%	8%
1993	100%	85%	9%	13%

Sen. Barbara Boxer (D)

CAPITOL OFFICE
224-3553
boxer.senate.gov
112 Hart 20510-0505; fax 228-1338

COMMITTEES
Commerce, Science & Transportation
Environment & Public Works
Foreign Relations

HOMETOWN
Greenbrae

BORN
Nov. 11, 1940, Brooklyn, N.Y.

RELIGION
Jewish

FAMILY
Husband, Stewart Boxer; two children

EDUCATION
Brooklyn College, B.A. 1962 (economics)

CAREER
Congressional aide; journalist; stockbroker

POLITICAL HIGHLIGHTS
Candidate for Marin County Board of Supervisors, 1972; Marin County Board of Supervisors, 1977-83 (president, 1980); U.S. House, 1983-93

ELECTION RESULTS

1998 GENERAL		
Barbara Boxer (D)	4,410,056	53.1%
Matt Fong (R)	3,575,078	43.0%
Ted Brown (LIBERT)	93,926	1.1%
1998 PRIMARY (OPEN)		
Barbara Boxer (D)	2,574,284	43.9%
Matt Fong (R)	1,292,662	22.1%
Darrell Issa (R)	1,143,107	19.5%
Frank Riggs (R)	295,886	5.0%
John Pinkerton (D)	219,250	3.7%
Ted Brown (LIBERT)	67,408	1.2%

PREVIOUS WINNING PERCENTAGES
1992 (48%); 1990 House Election (68%); 1988 House Election (73%); 1986 House Election (74%); 1984 House Election (68%); 1982 House Election (52%)

Elected 1992; 2nd term

An ardent feminist, a defender of environmental regulation and an enemy of the National Rifle Association, Boxer offers no apologies for her partisan passions or her bold style. "My political style is to be extremely candid and straight from the shoulders, and not to be mealy-mouthed or waffle," she says. "When I believe in something, I believe in it strongly."

That aggressive approach often brings her to the Senate floor for impassioned speeches and legislative efforts that can be more symbolic than effective. Her press clippings are many, her ceremonial bill-signing pens few. Unlike fellow California Sen. Dianne Feinstein, also a Democrat, Boxer has little appetite for the philosophical trade-offs necessary to get things done in a Senate narrowly divided between the two parties.

In the 107th Congress, Senate Democratic leaders sought to capitalize on Boxer's nimbleness with a sound bite by giving her the newly created post of chief deputy for strategic outreach. She's become a regular on news shows and at press conferences — with the help of her "Boxer Box," a portable platform that gets her to mike level.

Unhappy with President Bush's response to revelations of massive corporate accounting fraud in 2002, Boxer said: "We heard he was going to have a Teddy Roosevelt moment, but when you really cut to the substance, he had a teddy bear moment."

But the same traits that make her so effective as a spokeswoman for Democratic ideals have also made her a top target in 2004, when she faces re-election. Republicans count Boxer among the most vulnerable incumbents as the GOP strives to build on its slim majority. The only factor arguing against an all-out assault on her seat is the enormous expense of mounting a statewide campaign in California.

But Boxer isn't likely to drift to the center as election time nears. While some politicians pride themselves on their ability to horse-trade and compromise in pursuit of legislation, Boxer usually operates as an unremitting activist, offering proposals that have no chance of adoption just to make a point about how things ought to be. "I'm very consistent on the issues," Boxer says. "I'm not the type of person that changes views based on polls or . . . the way the wind is blowing."

On the wall of her Capitol Hill office hangs a picture of Boxer as a House member, leading six other female representatives up the steps of the Senate in 1991 to demand public hearings on law professor Anita Hill's allegations of sexual harassment against Supreme Court nominee Clarence Thomas. Today she believes that that attention-grabbing stunt helped spark a voter backlash against the overwhelmingly white, male makeup of the Senate, which ultimately led to the 1992 elections being termed the "Year of the Woman." Boxer, who had represented California's 6th House District for 10 years, was elected to the Senate that year along with Feinstein, Patty Murray of Washington and Carol Moseley-Braun of Illinois.

"Women saw what happened and realized they still weren't receiving anything approaching a full measure of representation," Boxer wrote in "Nine and Counting," a book she co-authored in 2000 with the eight other women senators of the 106th Congress.

In her first and difficult re-election campaign in 1998 against conservative GOP State Treasurer Matt Fong, The Sacramento Bee described Boxer as "a high-profile, high-energy politician with a bent for partisanship and self-promotion." Former Senate Majority Leader Bob Dole once called her "the most partisan senator I've ever known." Her voting record puts her to the left of such well-known liberals as Edward M. Kennedy of Massachusetts and Tom Harkin of Iowa.

If Boxer's absolutism raises the profile of her top issues — women's health, the environment, corporate fraud and the oppression of Afghan women — it can also hurt her chances of success. Her unfashionable adherence to liberal tenets often doesn't play well in the clubby Senate. Many times she doesn't get the backing she needs to get her proposals written into law, and her hard-line amendments win little support from Republicans and sometimes even other Democrats.

One of her major efforts in 2001 was a proposal to protect workers' 401(k) plans by capping concentrations of company stocks in each employee's investment portfolio. The bill out of Kennedy's Health, Education, Labor and Pensions Committee ultimately limited stock accumulations but did not cap them.

As a member of the Environment Committee, she was a leader in 2001 in efforts to clean up abandoned industrial sites known as brownfields. She has pushed since the 1990s for a ban on the gasoline additive MTBE, a suspected carcinogen. And she is one of the Bush administration's harshest critics on the environment, condemning its proposed rollbacks of clean air regulations, new rules allowing more logging in national forests and its interpretation of "dolphin-safe" tuna fishing regulations.

Nor is Boxer a friend of big oil companies. In the 106th Congress, she fought an attempt by oil-state senators to delay new Interior Department rules that effectively increased oil royalties. While her efforts — including a filibuster — were ultimately unsuccessful, she gave oil-state senators the battle of their lives. "It was one of the hardest fights I've had," said Texas Republican Kay Bailey Hutchison.

One of 11 Jewish senators and a member of the Foreign Relations Committee, Boxer is quick to defend Israel in its conflicts with its Arab neighbors. After a series of terrorist attacks on Israeli citizens in 2002, Boxer cosponsored legislation sanctioning Syria.

Drawn into politics in the 1960s as a young Vietnam War protester, Boxer voted against both the 1991 Persian Gulf resolution sought by the senior George Bush and the younger Bush's 2002 use-of-force request against Iraq.

She has been a major impediment to the administration's conservative nominees for judgeships. Casting aside the usual courtesies among home-state lawmakers, Boxer's well-known opposition stopped GOP Rep. Christopher Cox from being appointed to the 9th U.S. Circuit Court of Appeals.

Boxer occasionally partners with more moderate Republicans on lower-profile issues, such as efforts with Arlen Specter of Pennsylvania to increase health research funding. In the sweeping federal education bill passed in 2001, she won $1.5 billion for after-school programs.

Boxer is a stockbroker by training. But she is a child of immigrant parents and attended public schools in Brooklyn, and so sees herself as a defender of the middle class. "You can't hand anybody anything; it doesn't work that way. But you can give them a chance," Boxer says.

After six years on the Marin County Board of Supervisors, Boxer was elected to the House in 1982 as the beneficiary of one of the decade's more creative acts of district line-drawing. She ran for the Senate with encouragement from women senators including Maryland Democrat Barbara A. Mikulski. And she got a boost from the dynamism of her pairing with Feinstein, who was seeking California's other Senate seat.

Boxer beat out fellow House Democrat Mel Levine and Lt. Gov. Leo T. McCarthy in the primary. In November, she held off the GOP nominee, conservative TV commentator Bruce Herschensohn, by 5 percentage points.

KEY VOTES

2002

Yes Pass farm bill reversing crop subsidy limits
No Postpone tougher automobile fuel efficiency standards
Yes Overhaul campaign finance law; ban "soft money" and restrict advocacy advertising
Yes Set federal election standards
No Support oil drilling in Arctic National Wildlife Refuge
No Revive fast-track procedures for trade agreements
Yes Create federal insurance coverage for catastrophic terrorist losses
Yes Tighten federal accounting and corporate governance regulation
Yes Advance bipartisan Medicare prescription drug plan
Yes Create independent Sept. 11 commission
Yes Back Democratic Homeland Security Department proposal
No Authorize war against Iraq

2001

No Confirm John Ashcroft as attorney general
No Nullify Clinton Labor Department ergonomics rule
– Cut taxes by $1.35 trillion through fiscal 2011
Yes Pass Democratic bill to bolster rights of patients in managed-care plans
No Permit a new round of military base closings
Yes Expand law enforcement power to investigate suspected terrorists

CQ VOTE STUDIES

	PARTY UNITY		PRESIDENTIAL SUPPORT	
	Support	Oppose	Support	Oppose
2002	95%	5%	65%	35%
2001	98%	2%	64%	36%
2000	100%	0%	92%	8%
1999	97%	3%	84%	16%
1998	90%	10%	90%	10%
1997	97%	3%	89%	11%
1996	94%	6%	90%	10%
1995	95%	5%	90%	10%
1994	92%	8%	87%	13%
1993	95%	5%	91%	9%

INTEREST GROUPS

	AFL-CIO	ADA	CCUS	ACU
2002	100%	90%	40%	5%
2001	100%	95%	42%	0%
2000	67%	85%	41%	4%
1999	100%	100%	47%	4%
1998	88%	95%	59%	4%
1997	86%	100%	50%	0%
1996	100%	100%	23%	5%
1995	100%	100%	26%	0%
1994	88%	95%	20%	0%
1993	91%	90%	9%	8%

Rep. Mike Thompson (D)

CAPITOL OFFICE
225-3311
www.house.gov/mthompson
119 Cannon 20515-0501; fax 225-4335

COMMITTEES
Agriculture
Budget
Transportation & Infrastructure

HOMETOWN
St. Helena

BORN
Jan. 24, 1951, St. Helena, Calif.

RELIGION
Roman Catholic

FAMILY
Wife, Janet Thompson; two children

EDUCATION
California State U., Chico, B.A. 1982 (political science), M.A. 1996 (public administration)

MILITARY SERVICE
Army, 1969-73

CAREER
Vintner; winery maintenance supervisor; state legislative aide; college instructor

POLITICAL HIGHLIGHTS
Calif. Senate, 1990-98

ELECTION RESULTS

2002 GENERAL		
Mike Thompson (D)	118,669	64.1%
Lawrence Wiesner (R)	60,013	32.4%
Kevin Bastian (LIBERT)	6,534	3.5%
2002 PRIMARY		
Mike Thompson (D)		unopposed
2000 GENERAL		
Mike Thompson (D)	155,638	65.0%
Russell J. "Jim" Chase (R)	66,987	28.0%
Cheryl Kreier (NL)	7,173	3.0%
Emil Rossi (LIBERT)	6,376	2.7%
Pamela Elizondo (REF)	3,161	1.3%

PREVIOUS WINNING PERCENTAGES
1998 (62%)

Elected 1998; 3rd term

Thompson's controversial visit to Baghdad in 2002, just before the vote in Congress authorizing the use of force against Iraq, ultimately did not hurt his re-election chances or his status within the party.

Six weeks after the trip, Thompson was re-elected by a 2-to-1 margin. And when lawmakers convened for the 108th Congress, he got two plum committee assignments — Budget and Transportation.

The Baghdad fact-finding trip with fellow Democrats Jim McDermott of Washington and David E. Bonior of Michigan drew intense criticism, particularly when McDermott spoke out against President Bush's motives in considering a war with Iraq.

But Thompson, a Vietnam War veteran, said little publicly, and many of his Democratic colleagues and constituents thought he had been unfairly tarred. "Mike went there for all the right reasons and just got caught up in something he doesn't agree with," said Democrat Chris John of Louisiana.

Thompson's new committee assignments were due, in some measure, to his close relationship with new Democratic leader Nancy Pelosi and his selection by his California colleagues as their representative on the Democratic Steering Committee, which makes committee assignments.

Thompson played a role in Californian Pelosi's successful bid for Democratic whip in 2001, helping to attract the more conservative Democrats to Pelosi's side in her race against Steny H. Hoyer.

To take the Budget and Transportation seats, he had to relinquish the assignment on Armed Services he had in his first two terms. Thompson had made a name for himself before his arrival on Capitol Hill as the chairman of the California Senate Budget Committee.

While working his way up the ladder in Washington, Thompson has devoted much of his attention to helping California's wine industry. A former vintner, he has pressed hard for federal dollars to fight insect-borne crop diseases and worked to expand trade markets for California wine and produce. He has made several trips to Cuba since he was first elected in 1998, seeking to open that nation to California's wines and rice.

Along with California Republican George P. Radanovich, Thompson is a co-founder of the Congressional Wine Caucus, which hosts speakers and tasting events for members and nearly anyone else Thompson can invite. The group now includes lawmakers from California to New York.

During his first term, Thompson focused largely on issues of parochial concern, such as a local zip code dispute and flood control efforts. He often teamed with a neighboring Democrat, liberal Lynn Woolsey, to secure funding for area projects, such as the repair of the Golden Gate Bridge.

He continued his local efforts in his second term, sponsoring legislation to provide $600 million for Pacific salmon recovery programs in five Western states.

His highest-profile measure may be the Congressional Gold Medal he and fellow Californian, Democratic Sen. Dianne Feinstein, won for "Peanuts" creator Charles Schulz, a longtime resident of Santa Rosa.

On national issues, Thompson shares the same priorities as most House Democrats: education, health care and the environment. He sounds like an old-fashioned Democrat when he says, "I really believe in public service and I really believe in government." He told a Healdsburg town hall meeting in 1999 that Social Security "is without question the most important government program we have. In addition to that, it's probably the most successful government program we've got."

But Thompson is no rubber stamp for big government programs; as a member of the conservative House "Blue Dog" coalition, he is friendly toward business and defines leadership as "finding what people can live with."

Thompson became interested in public service as a young man working as a maintenance supervisor at the Beringer Vineyard in Napa Valley. "I was the guy the Hispanic field laborer would come to with their problems," he says. Seeking to intervene on behalf of one Hispanic worker who had been cheated by a mechanic, Thompson recalls, "The guy in the repair shop said: 'What do you care — the guy's just a Mexican.' "

Outraged, Thompson said he realized that to be able to help people effectively, he would have to complete his education. He had dropped out of high school and joined the Army, serving as a staff sergeant and platoon leader with the 173rd Airborne Brigade in Vietnam, where he was wounded and received a Purple Heart. In his late 20s and early 30s, he got his high school diploma and earned a college degree.

A political science professor suggested that he apply for a fellowship working with the state legislature, which led to a second career as a staff member. Thompson ran for elective office himself in 1990, winning a seat in the state Senate.

During his tenure in the California Senate, Thompson built coalitions across party lines on budget and other matters. In tandem with a Republican state senator, he sponsored a welfare overhaul bill that provided recipients with child care aid, job training and education to move them off the public assistance rolls. He also won passage of a measure that cut the salaries of some state officials and another that required health insurance companies to cover preventive health care for children.

Because of California's legislative term limits, Thompson gained increasing seniority quickly in Sacramento. But those same limits meant that he would be out of a job after the 1998 elections, so he set his sights on Congress. The prospect of facing the popular Thompson, it was widely speculated, was the reason Republican Rep. Frank Riggs abandoned his seat in favor of a quixotic, late bid for the Senate.

Riggs had represented the 1st District for two of the previous three terms; his turnstile career was emblematic of the district, which had sent four different men to Congress since 1988. But Thompson's easy re-election in 2002, in a district redrawn to be more favorable to Democrats, make him more confident that he can hold onto the seat for the foreseeable future.

KEY VOTES

2002

Yes Overhaul campaign finance law; ban "soft money" and restrict advocacy advertising
Yes Back Bush's defense budget increase
No Extend 1996 welfare law
No Adopt Bush's discretionary spending limit
No Pass GOP Medicare prescription drug plan
Yes Create independent Sept. 11 commission
Yes Extend union protections to Homeland Security Department employees
No Revive fast-track procedures for trade agreements
No Authorize war against Iraq
Yes Advance bankruptcy overhaul opposed by abortion opponents

2001

No Nullify Clinton Labor Department ergonomics rule
No Cut taxes by $1.35 trillion through fiscal 2011
Yes Maintain ban on oil drilling in Arctic National Wildlife Refuge
No Approve Bush proposal to limit managed-care plan liability for coverage decisions
Yes Divert money from crop subsidy payments to land conservation
Yes Expand law enforcement power to investigate suspected terrorists

CQ VOTE STUDIES

	PARTY UNITY		PRESIDENTIAL SUPPORT	
	Support	Oppose	Support	Oppose
2002	93%	7%	26%	74%
2001	88%	12%	31%	69%
2000	89%	11%	81%	19%
1999	85%	15%	76%	24%

INTEREST GROUPS

	AFL-CIO	ADA	CCUS	ACU
2002	100%	90%	53%	8%
2001	92%	95%	50%	8%
2000	70%	75%	66%	8%
1999	78%	95%	44%	4%

CALIFORNIA 1

Northern Coast – Eureka; Napa, Davis

It takes about nine hours to travel the length of the 1st, a journey that starts in Yolo County, across the river from Sacramento, and ends at the Oregon border in Del Norte County, one of the district's three coastal counties. In between are wineries and majestic redwoods, for which the Northern Coast is famous.

The 1st is notable for its breadth and diversity. Even the weather patterns vary across the district, with a rainy north and arid farmland in the south. Apart from wine and timber, other dominant industries include commercial fishing in Crescent City, Eureka and Fort Bragg, and tourism. The University of California, Davis, in Yolo County is another major employer.

To the north, Mendocino, Humboldt and Del Norte counties long have been a battleground for environmentalists and the timber industry. Tensions reached a peak in the summer of 1990 with "Redwood Summer" demonstrations over the proposed logging of the Headwaters Forest, one of last stands of virgin redwood trees. Isolated protests still occur, but have not reached the same degree of intensity.

East of Mendocino, Lake County's economy is a mix of ranching, farming and tourism, centered on Clearlake. Its relatively low cost of living, relative to Bay Area cities, makes this a retirees' haven. South of Mendocino, the 1st takes in part of wine-producing Sonoma County and all of Napa County. Half of the state's wineries are in the district.

Environmental issues, including offshore drilling, continue to make the 1st volatile, despite a Democratic voter registration advantage and the district's backing of Democratic presidential candidates in the 1990s and 2000. Ralph Nader received 15 percent of the 2000 presidential vote in Mendocino County and 13 percent in Humboldt County. Del Norte was the only county in the 1st to support George W. Bush.

MAJOR INDUSTRY

Timber, agriculture, tourism

CITIES

Napa, 72,585; Davis, 60,308; Woodland (pt.), 39,455

NOTABLE

Niebaum-Coppola is the winery owned by film director Francis Ford Coppola.

Rep. Wally Herger (R)

CAPITOL OFFICE
225-3076
www.house.gov/herger
2268 Rayburn 20515-0502; fax 225-1740

COMMITTEES
Ways & Means
(Human Resources - chairman)

HOMETOWN
Marysville

BORN
May 20, 1945, Sutter County, Calif.

RELIGION
Mormon

FAMILY
Wife, Pamela Herger; nine children (one deceased)

EDUCATION
American River College, A.A. 1967; California State U., Sacramento, attended 1969

CAREER
Rancher; gas company executive

POLITICAL HIGHLIGHTS
Calif. Assembly, 1980-86

ELECTION RESULTS

2002 GENERAL		
Wally Herger (R)	117,747	65.8%
Mike Johnson (D)	52,455	29.3%
Patrice Thiessen (NL)	4,860	2.7%
Charles Martin (LIBERT)	3,923	2.2%
2002 PRIMARY		
Wally Herger (R)	71,028	88.8%
Walter Thompson (R)	6,616	8.3%
Bob Todd (R)	2,370	3.0%
2000 GENERAL		
Wally Herger (R)	168,172	65.7%
Stan Morgan (D)	72,075	28.2%
John McDermott (NL)	8,910	3.5%
Charles Martin (LIBERT)	6,699	2.6%

PREVIOUS WINNING PERCENTAGES
1998 (63%); 1996 (61%); 1994 (64%); 1992 (65%); 1990 (64%); 1988 (59%); 1986 (58%)

Elected 1986; 9th term

Although he has been on the Ways and Means Committee since 1993, Herger is most visible on Western land issues.

Even in the 107th Congress, when Herger took the gavel of the Ways and Means panel's Human Resources Subcommittee as it assessed the workings of the nation's welfare system, Herger continued to devote a considerable portion of his time and effort to matters such as irrigation in the Klamath River Basin, development limitations imposed by the Endangered Species Act and timber harvesting in national forests.

He grew up on his family's 200-acre cattle ranch and plum farm in the Northern California town of Rio Oso. He also worked in the family's oil and gas business. Well-to-do financially, he draws heavily on his small-business and ranching background in his work on Capitol Hill.

Herger's conservative views on Western land use sit well with his Republican constituency, many of whom believe the entire federal government should be less obtrusive.

As his Ways and Means panel reviewed the welfare law, which Congress had drastically overhauled in 1996 and which was up for renewal in 2002, most of the witnesses Herger called argued that big changes were not warranted. Herger said the revised welfare system had lifted more than 2 million children out of poverty. "The 1996 welfare reforms are working and working well. I am wary of changes that would undermine that progress," he said.

The House passed legislation based in part on Herger's subcommittee's work, calling for welfare recipients to work 40 hours a week and providing incentives to promote marriage and teenage sexual abstinence. The legislation stalled in the Senate. Herger and his subcommittee will try again in the 108th.

On Ways and Means, his only committee assignment, Herger has placed a high priority on building and preserving a solid family structure — a key aspect of the effort to reduce the welfare rolls, he says. "Obviously, we cannot mandate a successful marriage, but it behooves us to look into ways to promote the positives of marriage," he said. In 2001, he was the chief sponsor of legislation, which became law, to increase funding for adoption, foster care and post-adoption services.

One of Herger's contributions to the sweeping 1996 welfare overhaul was to authorize payments of as much as $400 to state and local prisons when they reported an inmate who fraudulently received Supplemental Security Income payments. His legislation was inspired by a sheriff in his district who noted that prisoners had extra money around the first of the month to spend at the prison commissary. Regulations already outlawed prisoners from receiving such payments, but there was little enforcement.

In 1999, Herger was able to expand on his earlier provision by cutting down on Social Security payments to prisoners in state and local jails. "Taxpayers already pay for inmates' food, clothing and shelter," Herger said. "It's unacceptable that prisoners have also been receiving fraudulent benefit checks as bonuses every month."

Herger has been equally concerned about government meddling in land- and water-use issues. One of Herger's main missions in Congress is to prevent environmentalists from encroaching on the rights of loggers, ranchers and private property owners in his district.

Although he is usually low-key, approachable and friendly, Herger chafes over what he views as extreme environmental policies. In the 107th Congress, he directed his outrage at the "government-caused disaster" in the Klamath River basin of northern California and southern Oregon, in which water needed by farmers for irrigation was withheld in order to protect two species of fish. "As a result, the economy of an entire community of 70,000 people is being bankrupted," he complained. Herger questioned the benefits to endangered species of withholding the irrigation water.

The Klamath basin matter was, in Herger's view, only the latest in a long string of outrages by local environmentalists. In 1997, after major flooding, Herger argued that levee repairs on the Feather River north of Sacramento had been deferred to protect the habitat of the threatened elderberry beetle. "We're literally wasting millions of dollars in terms of environmental hoops we're jumping through," he said.

Herger has been happier with the decision-making process of the Air Force regarding its Northern California bases. The Air Force in 2002 began basing the Global Hawk unmanned aerial reconnaissance plane at Beale Air Force Base in Northern California. More than 1,600 jobs are expected to be added to Beale, which currently hosts the U-2 and SR-71 spy planes, once the entire contingent of planes arrives.

There is little suspense when Herger approaches the electronic voting device on the House floor. His voting record is solidly in the conservative camp of House Republicans, as his membership in the conservative Republican Study Committee would suggest. He supports the GOP position about 97 percent of the time.

Herger won election to the state Assembly in 1980 and was in his third term there when GOP Rep. Gene Chappie announced his retirement from the House in 1986. Linking himself to President Reagan and California's Republican governor, George Deukmejian, Herger won the general election with 58 percent. He has had little electoral difficulty since then. Redistricting in 2001 shifted his district to the west — it looks much the same as it did during the 1980s — but left him with his two major population centers, Redding and Chico, and presented him with no re-election worries.

Legislative work aside, Herger scored a personal best in Washington in 1997. He delivered a game-tying double in the last inning of the annual congressional baseball game. The GOP won the game, and Herger told a reporter for Roll Call newspaper: "That was one of the best feelings I've had in my life. It doesn't get any sweeter than that." But the annual baseball game can be humbling as well. In the 1999 game, Herger was best remembered for a face-planting tumble between home plate and first base as he tried to leg out a hit.

KEY VOTES

2002

No Overhaul campaign finance law; ban "soft money" and restrict advocacy advertising
Yes Back Bush's defense budget increase
Yes Extend 1996 welfare law
Yes Adopt Bush's discretionary spending limit
Yes Pass GOP Medicare prescription drug plan
No Create independent Sept. 11 commission
No Extend union protections to Homeland Security Department employees
Yes Revive fast-track procedures for trade agreements
Yes Authorize war against Iraq
Yes Advance bankruptcy overhaul opposed by abortion opponents

2001

Yes Nullify Clinton Labor Department ergonomics rule
Yes Cut taxes by $1.35 trillion through fiscal 2011
No Maintain ban on oil drilling in Arctic National Wildlife Refuge
Yes Approve Bush proposal to limit managed-care plan liability for coverage decisions
No Divert money from crop subsidy payments to land conservation
Yes Expand law enforcement power to investigate suspected terrorists

CQ VOTE STUDIES

	PARTY UNITY		PRESIDENTIAL SUPPORT	
	Support	Oppose	Support	Oppose
2002	98%	2%	82%	18%
2001	97%	3%	90%	10%
2000	96%	4%	21%	79%
1999	97%	3%	22%	78%
1998	96%	4%	23%	77%

INTEREST GROUPS

	AFL-CIO	ADA	CCUS	ACU
2002	11%	0%	100%	100%
2001	0%	0%	96%	96%
2000	0%	0%	85%	95%
1999	0%	5%	88%	92%
1998	0%	0%	88%	100%

CALIFORNIA 2
North central – Redding, Chico

Previously abutting most of the state's border with Nevada north of Lake Tahoe, the mountainous 2nd was reshaped during redistricting following the 2000 census to form a north-south strip down the center of the state, from the Oregon border to just north of Sacramento. It includes the Sutter-Buttes mountain range.

Agriculture dominates the 2nd, which gained five farming counties — Sutter, Colusa, Glenn, Tehama and part of Yolo — through redistricting. The district is rural, with rice farms and orchards producing walnuts, olives and peaches. Much of its economic activity is centered in Shasta County, home to mining and forestry interests. Shasta Lake, the state's largest man-made reservoir, attracts tourism. Redding, the 2nd's largest city, is about 160 miles north of Sacramento in Shasta County. Both the city and county experienced strong growth through the 1980s and 1990s.

The 2nd has had to fight to save its agriculture industry from harsh weather — much of it was declared a disaster area after flooding in 1997. Wildfires account for at least one major fire every summer, especially in the northernmost counties of Shasta, Trinity and Siskiyou. Water also is a perennial issue: Two-thirds of the state's supply comes from the upper third of the state. The timber industry has steadily declined since the 1990s, in the process diminishing some of the tension between environmental interests and the industry.

The district retains its overwhelmingly white and Republican character, but there has been a steady influx of Sikhs in the Yuba City area, as well as an infusion of Democratic-leaning Hispanic farm workers.

MAJOR INDUSTRY
Agriculture, timber, tourism, health care

MILITARY BASES
Beale Air Force Base, 3,442 military, 1,029 civilian (2000)

CITIES
Redding, 80,865; Chico, 59,954; Yuba City, 36,758

NOTABLE
The dormant Mount Shasta volcano in Siskiyou County is near the southern end of the Cascade Mountains; The Sierra Nevada Brewing Co. is in Chico; GOP presidential nominee Bob Dole fell from a stage at a rally in Chico in 1996, saying later that he had "fallen for Chico."

Rep. Doug Ose (R)

CAPITOL OFFICE
225-5716
www.house.gov/ose
236 Cannon 20515-0503; fax 226-1298

COMMITTEES
Agriculture
Financial Services
Government Reform
(Energy Policy, Natural Resources & Regulatory Affairs - chairman)

HOMETOWN
Sacramento

BORN
June 27, 1955, Sacramento, Calif.

RELIGION
Lutheran

FAMILY
Wife, Lynnda Ose; two children

EDUCATION
U. of California, Berkeley, B.S. 1977 (business administration)

CAREER
Storage company founder; real estate developer

POLITICAL HIGHLIGHTS
No previous office

ELECTION RESULTS

2002 GENERAL		
Doug Ose (R)	121,732	62.5%
Howard Beeman (D)	67,136	34.4%
Douglas Tuma (LIBERT)	6,050	3.1%
2002 PRIMARY		
Doug Ose (R)		unopposed
2000 GENERAL		
Doug Ose (R)	129,254	56.2%
Bob Kent (D)	93,067	40.4%
Douglas Tuma (LIBERT)	5,227	2.3%
Channing Jones (NL)	2,634	1.1%

PREVIOUS WINNING PERCENTAGES
1998 (52%)

Elected 1998; 3rd term

A pro-business, moderate Republican, Ose got a prime perch in his second term from which to advance the GOP's goal of reducing government regulation of business: the chairmanship of a Government Reform subcommittee that oversees the regulatory process.

Ever since the Republican Party took control of the House in 1995, the leaders of the Government Reform Committee have given a number of junior members chairmanships from which to challenge the scope and implementation of federal regulations. Ose (OH-see), who became wealthy in the commercial real estate and self-storage businesses, uses his background to argue for a less intrusive government presence.

In the 107th Congress his Energy Policy, Natural Resources and Regulatory Affairs Subcommittee conducted an ambitious and wide-ranging slate of hearings; the first one examined the appropriateness of a slew of regulations issued in the final days of the Clinton administration.

He then broadened that inquiry, working with the Bush administration's regulatory czar, John D. Graham, to focus on what he considers overly burdensome regulations. But Ose also chastised the Bush administration's Office of Management and Budget for what he described as its "non-compliance with statutory requirements" in reporting to Congress on the costs and benefits of federal regulations and paperwork.

His panel also conducted hearings on the gifts that the Clintons took with them when they left the White House. Ose said the detailed investigation, which Democrats denounced as partisan, was aimed at determining the need for legislation to standardize presidential gift rules. Long before the hearing, Ose had introduced a bill to make the National Archives responsible for keeping an inventory of White House gifts.

Yet Ose's top priority as subcommittee chairman has been California's energy policies. He held hearings on the state's energy crisis, which has included power outages and price increases. He complained that a state agency had received preferential treatment in buying power, costing other customers millions of dollars. He introduced legislation to give the Federal Energy Regulatory Commission power to investigate and avert price gouging in the energy market. He also urged state officials to increase energy production, including from such alternative sources as biomass.

The plain-spoken Ose has a laid-back style and says his approach is one of consensus building. A soccer ball given to him by friends carries a stress-relieving suggestion: "Something to kick when things get tough." Ose plays soccer recreationally, along with basketball.

Ose also has played a central role in negotiations among Northern California lawmakers over how to protect the Sacramento area from flooding. Ose took a neutral stance initially and encouraged the negotiations to continue. "I wanted to make sure everyone kept communicating. We needed to settle this," he said. In 2001 Ose endorsed raising the height of the Folsom Dam on the American River, while still favoring the construction of another, more expensive dam upriver at Auburn.

On fiscal matters, he follows the mainstream of his party by backing proposals to reduce government waste and cut taxes. In the 107th Congress, he offered legislation requiring the president and lawmakers to forfeit their pay when the annual spending bills are not passed on time.

Ose is a member of the Republican Main Street Partnership, which seeks to promote centrist policymaking. He established a California chapter, which he chairs. Like many of his Main Street colleagues, Ose sometimes strays from the more conservative GOP line on social policy issues. He supports abortion rights and some gun control, including child safety locks and instant background checks.

Ose has taken moderate stands on environmental issues, backing bills to restrict mining, preserve waterways and bar clear-cutting unless new trees are planted. He was one of 41 House Republicans to vote to enact the campaign finance law in 2002.

Citing his experience in real estate, Ose stresses the importance of increased federal spending on programs aimed at nurturing economic development. He says he understands the relationship between banks and local businesses and builders. From his seat on the Financial Services Committee, he is a staunch advocate of policies designed to ensure the availability of credit for small businesses and consumers. He also has supported efforts to provide block grants to help middle-class families buy homes.

Ose entered politics after a long career as a builder. He gained experience in residential housing projects while working for his family's development business, and he started his own company in 1985 specializing in storage warehouse development. Before coming to Congress, he was active in civic affairs as a member of the Citrus Heights Chamber of Commerce and the Sacramento Housing and Redevelopment Commission. He was a leader in the lengthy battle over Citrus Heights' incorporation, which took place in 1997.

When 10-term Democratic Rep. Vic Fazio announced plans to retire, Ose jumped at the chance to succeed him. He upset a socially conservative GOP state legislator in the 1998 primary and defeated Democratic lawyer Sandie Dunn by 7 percentage points in the general election. Ose spent $2.1 million, including $1.4 million of his own money. In 2000, he cruised to victory, taking 56 percent against Democrat Bob Kent, a local businessman.

Although Democrats controlled the redistricting process in 2001, the new California maps generally protected incumbents, and the new 3rd District map was no exception — with the GOP gaining strength. The new district, heading east from the population base around Sacramento instead of north, as it did in the 1990s, presents Ose with a considerable number of new constituents, but he cruised to a 28-point victory in 2002.

Ose's name is among those mentioned as a possible GOP Senate candidate in 2004, particularly because he has said he would serve no more than three House terms.

KEY VOTES

2002

Yes Overhaul campaign finance law; ban "soft money" and restrict advocacy advertising
\+ Back Bush's defense budget increase
Yes Extend 1996 welfare law
Yes Adopt Bush's discretionary spending limit
Yes Pass GOP Medicare prescription drug plan
No Create independent Sept. 11 commission
No Extend union protections to Homeland Security Department employees
Yes Revive fast-track procedures for trade agreements
Yes Authorize war against Iraq
Yes Advance bankruptcy overhaul opposed by abortion opponents

2001

Yes Nullify Clinton Labor Department ergonomics rule
Yes Cut taxes by $1.35 trillion through fiscal 2011
No Maintain ban on oil drilling in Arctic National Wildlife Refuge
Yes Approve Bush proposal to limit managed-care plan liability for coverage decisions
No Divert money from crop subsidy payments to land conservation
Yes Expand law enforcement power to investigate suspected terrorists

CQ VOTE STUDIES

	PARTY UNITY		PRESIDENTIAL SUPPORT	
	Support	Oppose	Support	Oppose
2002	86%	14%	84%	16%
2001	90%	10%	81%	19%
2000	89%	11%	33%	67%
1999	78%	22%	37%	63%

INTEREST GROUPS

	AFL-CIO	ADA	CCUS	ACU
2002	11%	20%	89%	84%
2001	17%	20%	100%	64%
2000	0%	15%	85%	76%
1999	0%	30%	92%	68%

CALIFORNIA 3

Central – Sacramento suburbs

Redistricting following the 2000 census radically changed the 3rd from a north Central Valley district to one that stretches east to west, from Alpine County on the Nevada border to Solano County. The redrawn district is more Republican and more white.

The new 3rd used to be Mother Lode country, which drew gold seekers and now attracts those who want to leave the state's crowded cities while still working in a burgeoning high-tech economy. It gets most of its population — about 85 percent — from a chunk of Sacramento County that includes the affluent Sacramento suburbs of Citrus Heights and Rio Linda.

Wineries and agriculture dominate the 3rd's economy, especially grape, almond and prune production, except in the forestry-heavy eastern county of Alpine, where mountains and skiing are prevalent. The closure of McClellan Air Force Base in 2001 dealt a blow to the area's economy, but it has been mitigated by the base's conversion into a business park (shared with the 5th), which has sought to attract high-tech and defense microelectronics activity.

Sacramento County, whose residents tend to work in state government or the high-tech industries that attract transplants from San Francisco, is the politically competitive heart of the district. Its surrounding areas are largely rural and Republican, and the district as a whole gave GOP presidential nominee George W. Bush 54 percent of the vote in 2000.

Water and flood control are important local issues. The Sacramento valley is prone to flooding from the Sacramento and American rivers, and while the last major floods occurred in 1995 and 1997, minor flooding happens more often.

MAJOR INDUSTRY

Agriculture, timber, technology

CITIES

Citrus Heights, 85,071; Arden-Arcade (unincorporated) (pt.), 53,597; Folsom, 51,884; Carmichael, 49,742

NOTABLE

Angels Camp in Calaveras County hosts the annual jumping frog contest made famous by Mark Twain.

Rep. John T. Doolittle (R)

CAPITOL OFFICE
225-2511
www.house.gov/doolittle
2410 Rayburn 20515-0504; fax 225-5444

COMMITTEES
Appropriations
House Administration
Joint Printing

HOMETOWN
Rocklin

BORN
Oct. 30, 1950, Glendale, Calif.

RELIGION
Mormon

FAMILY
Wife, Julia Doolittle; two children

EDUCATION
U. of California, Santa Cruz, B.A. 1972 (history); U. of the Pacific, J.D. 1978

CAREER
Lawyer; state legislative aide

POLITICAL HIGHLIGHTS
Calif. Senate, 1980-90

ELECTION RESULTS

2002 GENERAL		
John T. Doolittle (R)	147,997	64.8%
Mark Norberg (D)	72,860	31.9%
Allen M. Roberts (LIBERT)	7,247	3.2%
2002 PRIMARY		
John T. Doolittle (R)	79,575	77.5%
Bill Kirby (R)	23,083	22.5%
2000 GENERAL		
John T. Doolittle (R)	197,503	63.4%
Mark Norberg (D)	97,974	31.5%
William Frey (LIBERT)	9,494	3.1%
Robert Ray (NL)	6,452	2.1%

PREVIOUS WINNING PERCENTAGES
1998 (63%); 1996 (60%); 1994 (61%); 1992 (50%); 1990 (51%)

Elected 1990; 7th term

Doolittle is something of an elder statesman among the impassioned and partisan conservatives of the House. He had been in Congress for four years by 1994, when so many other likeminded Republicans were elected that the party was able to take over the Capitol. Eight years later, after winning election to his seventh term, Doolittle was unopposed at the end of 2002 for election as secretary of the Republican Conference, the sixth-ranking post on the House GOP's official leadership ladder.

He spent the 107th Congress as a leader of the effort to thwart a revamping of the ways that campaigns are financed, principally by barring the unregulated donations to the political parties known as "soft money." Doolittle argued that the law enacted in 2002 was overtly unconstitutional. He also viewed the new restrictions as "disastrous" for the GOP's fundraising future.

Forty-one Republicans ultimately voted for the bill in the House. But Doolittle's displeasure was directed mostly at the 20 Republicans who had signed a discharge petition to force the measure to the floor against the wishes of the GOP leadership. "I don't intend to let bygones be bygones," he said afterward. "I can guarantee there will be consequences in the long term."

Doolittle always has pushed zealously for a diminished federal role in people's lives. He viewed the campaign finance bill as just another example of federal interference. He decries what he sees as threats to personal freedom — sometimes even by members of his own party — in the name of a well-meaning public policy goal. "Our freedom is at stake, and too many people are willing to give it away," Doolittle warns.

He is enough of an old hand now to understand that things happen slowly in Washington. But that doesn't mean Doolittle likes it or is willing to adopt less ambitious goals. He says he believes that conservatives should be aggressive in advancing their principles rather than passively playing defense against the barrage of "big government" proposals offered up by liberals.

In 1997, Doolittle was one of a band of conservative Republicans who felt that top party leaders were giving in too readily to President Clinton, forsaking bedrock conservative principles instead of continuing to press aggressively for the GOP's "Contract With America" legislative agenda. In an effort to hold his party's leadership to a firm conservative line on economic and social policy issues, he co-founded the Conservative Action Team (the CATs), now known as the Republican Study Committee.

In the 106th Congress, Doolittle gained clout when he was named as a deputy whip. In the 107th, he won a seat on Appropriations.

Doolittle approaches his congressional work with the same serious-minded zeal that he evinced as a Mormon missionary in Argentina just after college, and he does not mind if he ruffles a few feathers.

After serving his first two terms in the minority, Doolittle brought an ambitious agenda to the GOP-controlled 104th Congress. As chairman of the Resources Committee's Water and Power Subcommittee, he promoted a pro-development agenda that often put him at loggerheads with advocates of environmental protection. Despite his subcommittee gavel, he was unable to garner enough GOP support to achieve a sell-off of federal power agencies or to tilt the allocation of water in the vast Sacramento Valley away from environmental purposes and toward agriculture. Doolittle long has supported completing the huge Auburn Dam in his district, which has been at the center of a bruising battle over federal water development policy.

Doolittle also has been a proponent of giving lawmakers per diem payments for each day the House is in session, but the proposal has been scuttled by the leadership. More popular was his bill, enacted in 2001, to give local elected officials the authority to order that the U.S. flag be flown at half-staff. Before his bill, only the president and governors had the authority to order the flag lowered.

Raised in a conservative household in Southern California, Doolittle was 13 when he became intrigued by Barry Goldwater, the 1964 GOP presidential nominee. But his family had moved to the Northern part of the state by then, and Doolittle remembers being perhaps "the only Goldwater supporter in my freshman class" at Cupertino High School.

For college, Doolittle chose the Santa Cruz campus of the University of California over Brigham Young University. Doolittle's politics would have fit in nicely at BYU. But he says he is glad he went to Santa Cruz, even though the liberal campus was in tune with the "free love, lawlessness and drugs" of the era. Doolittle was one of only 15 Young Republicans at Santa Cruz, which he says taught him to take independent stances and think for himself. "It was a fabulous experience," he says.

Goldwater had inspired in Doolittle the desire to seek office, and, after a two-year church mission to Argentina and law school, Doolittle took his résumé to Sacramento in search of a job with the state legislature.

He worked for state Sen. H.L. Richardson, who not only was an influential conservative lawmaker but also a mentor and adviser when Doolittle launched his own bid for the state Senate in 1980. Richardson persuaded Doolittle to run against an entrenched Democratic incumbent. With California favorite son Ronald Reagan heading the GOP ticket that year, Doolittle won a narrow upset. He quickly made himself known in Sacramento, particularly as a dogged proponent of expanded testing for AIDS.

In 1990, Doolittle inherited what had been a safe district from his retiring six-term predecessor, Republican Norman D. Shumway, who also had positioned himself on the GOP's right flank. Doolittle narrowly beat Democrat Patricia Malberg in 1990 and 1992 in what was then the 14th District.

Aided by a 1992 remapping that made the district, renumbered the 4th, more Republican, he coasted to re-election through the 1990s.

Redistricting after the 2000 census restored the northern counties that he had represented in his first two terms, but it did little to alter the GOP orientation of the district. In 2002, Doolittle easily beat back a GOP primary challenge from a political novice who argued that Doolittle's politics were too conservative and went on in November to win by a 2-to-1 ratio.

KEY VOTES

2002

- No Overhaul campaign finance law; ban "soft money" and restrict advocacy advertising
- Yes Back Bush's defense budget increase
- Yes Extend 1996 welfare law
- Yes Adopt Bush's discretionary spending limit
- Yes Pass GOP Medicare prescription drug plan
- No Create independent Sept. 11 commission
- No Extend union protections to Homeland Security Department employees
- Yes Revive fast-track procedures for trade agreements
- Yes Authorize war against Iraq
- ? Advance bankruptcy overhaul opposed by abortion opponents

2001

- Yes Nullify Clinton Labor Department ergonomics rule
- Yes Cut taxes by $1.35 trillion through fiscal 2011
- No Maintain ban on oil drilling in Arctic National Wildlife Refuge
- Yes Approve Bush proposal to limit managed-care plan liability for coverage decisions
- No Divert money from crop subsidy payments to land conservation
- Yes Expand law enforcement power to investigate suspected terrorists

CQ VOTE STUDIES

	PARTY UNITY		PRESIDENTIAL SUPPORT	
	Support	Oppose	Support	Oppose
2002	98%	2%	84%	16%
2001	97%	3%	91%	9%
2000	96%	4%	23%	77%
1999	93%	7%	17%	83%
1998	94%	6%	17%	83%

INTEREST GROUPS

	AFL-CIO	ADA	CCUS	ACU
2002	13%	5%	84%	91%
2001	17%	0%	91%	100%
2000	0%	5%	76%	88%
1999	11%	5%	80%	91%
1998	10%	5%	89%	100%

CALIFORNIA 4

Northeast – Roseville, Rocklin

Redistricting following the 2000 census brought major changes to the 4th. Where it previously occupied California's northeast-central belt, moving from Sacramento to Lake Tahoe and then south, the district now heads north after reaching Lake Tahoe, along the Nevada border up to Oregon in the state's northeastern corner.

Laden with rivers, lakes and the mountain ranges that give their names to Sierra and Nevada counties, the 4th's new district lines have added timber and agriculture to the economic mainstays of mining and technology.

The mining counties of Placer and El Dorado lend the 4th its Gold Rush feel, though technology drives one of the fastest growth rates in the state. Placer, El Dorado and Nevada counties are home to facilities of big technology names like Hewlett-Packard and Oracle. These three counties, which along with a sliver of Sacramento County make up the southern part of the district, account for more than three-fourths of its population and continue to draw those who want to leave the state's crowded cities but still work in the high-tech economy.

The 4th is a popular vacation destination, with numerous ski resorts dotting the Sierra Nevada mountain range, as well as Lake Tahoe in eastern El Dorado and Placer counties. Placer, with cheap property and abundant natural beauty, is rapidly becoming a draw for retirees. Whites make up 84 percent of the population, which gives the district the highest percentage in the state.

This is safe Republican territory. George W. Bush took 58 percent of the vote in the 2000 presidential election, and Republicans hold a 13-point edge in party registration.

MAJOR INDUSTRY
Computers, agriculture, mining, tourism

MILITARY BASES
Sierra Army Depot, 1 military, 602 civilian (2001)

CITIES
Roseville, 79,921; Rocklin, 36,330; Orangevale (unincorporated), 26,705

NOTABLE
Squaw Valley, near Lake Tahoe, hosted the 1960 Winter Olympics.

Rep. Robert T. Matsui (D)

CAPITOL OFFICE
225-7163
www.house.gov/matsui
2310 Rayburn 20515-0505; fax 225-0566

COMMITTEES
Ways & Means

HOMETOWN
Sacramento

BORN
Sept. 17, 1941, Sacramento, Calif.

RELIGION
Methodist

FAMILY
Wife, Doris Matsui; one child

EDUCATION
U. of California, Berkeley, A.B. 1963; U. of California, Hastings College of the Law, J.D. 1966

CAREER
Lawyer

POLITICAL HIGHLIGHTS
Sacramento City Council, 1971-78 (vice mayor, 1977)

ELECTION RESULTS

2002 GENERAL		
Robert T. Matsui (D)	92,726	70.5%
Richard Frankhuizen (R)	34,749	26.4%
Timothy E. Roloff (LIBERT)	4,103	3.1%
2002 PRIMARY		
Robert T. Matsui (D)		unopposed
2000 GENERAL		
Robert T. Matsui (D)	147,025	68.7%
Ken Payne (R)	55,945	26.1%
Ken Adams (GREEN)	6,195	2.9%
Cullene Lang (LIBERT)	2,919	1.4%

PREVIOUS WINNING PERCENTAGES
1998 (72%); 1996 (70%); 1994 (68%); 1992 (69%); 1990 (60%); 1988 (71%); 1986 (76%); 1984 (100%); 1982 (90%); 1980 (71%); 1978 (53%)

Elected 1978; 13th term

From the moment President Bush took office, Matsui's work in the 107th Congress had a single focus: all Social Security, all the time. Facing a president who had proposed letting people invest some of their mandatory contributions to the government's retirement income program into private savings accounts instead, Matsui became the point man for House Democrats in their fight against the plan.

In the 108th, Matsui will battle the GOP on another front as well: He is the chairman of the Democratic Congressional Campaign Committee, the House Democrats' candidate recruitment and fundraising arm. His appointment, by his California ally Nancy Pelosi, angered some black Democrats, who had pushed hard for Louisiana's William J. Jefferson. Matsui and Pelosi met in 1978, when she appeared at his first congressional fundraiser. They have been friends ever since and have collaborated frequently in the House.

A soft-spoken lawmaker who comes across as knowledgeable without seeming like a know-it-all, Matsui's previous leading role was as the most prominent pro-trade Democrat in the House, a member who works in friendly fashion with business interests as well as Republicans. But the Social Security debate may be a better fit for his profile as one of the most socially liberal members of Congress.

As the top-ranking member of the Ways and Means Subcommittee on Social Security since 1999, Matsui is perfectly positioned to lead the supercharged rhetorical fight against private savings accounts in the 108th Congress, although it may not turn into a legislative battle unless President Bush wins re-election in 2004 and makes it a priority of his second term.

Matsui is one of the few lawmakers in either party with a deep understanding of the complexities of the program. To his critics, including Republicans and some centrist Democrats, Matsui has been putting his expertise to poor use — giving credibility to partisan Democratic attacks that ultimately will make it harder to find a bipartisan solution to Social Security's long-term solvency problems. Matsui, however, argues he is fighting against a plan that would make Social Security's finances worse, not better.

To make his case, Matsui points to the recommendations issued in 2001 by a 16-member bipartisan commission appointed by Bush. It endorsed the president's central argument: that private accounts would allow Americans to "build substantial wealth." But it acknowledged that none of its three personal retirement account plans would solve Social Security's financial problems, that some combination of benefit reductions and tax increases would still be needed, and that there would be substantial startup costs in creating the accounts. In addition, Matsui says the stock market decline of 2001 and 2002, and the corporate scandals that may have helped cause them, should be a powerful argument against Bush's plan.

Matsui was similarly a thorn in the side of the previous president on one of his most prominent social policy initiatives — fellow Democrat Bill Clinton's proposed overhaul of the welfare system. During a 1994 subcommittee hearing on Clinton's plan, which predated the more sweeping Republican plan Clinton signed into law in 1996, the normally diplomatic Matsui angrily lashed out at Clinton's proposal to end cash welfare benefits after two years. "Can you discuss this in a way that I'll be confident that these people will not be screwed?" he asked a Department of Health and Human Services official.

In 2002, Matsui took a position that seemed at odds with his pro-trade record: He voted against the law reviving fast-track procedures for congressional action on presidential trade deals. For Matsui, the issue was not the merits of free trade, but the danger that Congress would be giving up the authority to protect U.S. laws on environmental protection, antitrust issues and food safety. Bush, Matsui said before the final House vote, "can negotiate without giving this major delegation of authority by the United States Congress to the president of the United States."

By contrast, Matsui was the White House's point person in 2000 on the law that granted permanent normal trade status to China, perhaps the most important foreign policy bill in the 106th Congress. It was a role he accepted with some reluctance. Matsui had headed the effort to deliver to Clinton the Democratic votes he needed to enact the 1993 law approving the North American Free Trade Agreement. After that, he voted against a Clinton bid to revive fast-track, saying later he did not want his vote on trade — or any other issue — to become predictable, which he thought would weaken his hand in bargaining on any future legislation.

Matsui says his sense of social justice stems from his incarceration as a child. At 5 months old, he and his family were sent to an internment camp with other Americans of Japanese ancestry during World War II; he lived there more than three years. His father was forced to give up his wholesale produce business, and his mother had nightmares about the camp until she died in 1984. At a 1998 news conference, Matsui recalled how deeply the experience was burned in his memory. When, as a child, he was asked by a schoolteacher whether he had been interned, he had denied it. "The mere fact that I was incarcerated would've raised the specter that . . . perhaps I was a spy, that I was an enemy alien," Matsui said. "That still lives with me."

Matsui's mother did not live to see the enactment, in the 100th Congress, of a law to provide federal redress to the surviving Japanese-Americans who were interned. Matsui called the measure "one of the most monumental legislative feats that has occurred" in recent decades.

Matsui had planned to become an architect. But he says he felt summoned to a life of public service by President Kennedy's appeal at the outset of the 1960s for a new generation of leaders. He established his political career locally, winning two elections to the Sacramento City Council. In 1972, he chaired Rep. John E. Moss Jr.'s re-election campaign. Six years later, Matsui was preparing to run for the county Board of Supervisors when Moss announced his retirement. Two other prominent Democrats filed for the seat, but Matsui's campaign war chest gave him a clear advantage.

The 5th District has grown more liberal as it has shrunk geographically during his tenure, and Matsui consistently draws about 70 percent of the vote.

KEY VOTES

2002

- Yes Overhaul campaign finance law; ban "soft money" and restrict advocacy advertising
- Yes Back Bush's defense budget increase
- No Extend 1996 welfare law
- No Adopt Bush's discretionary spending limit
- No Pass GOP Medicare prescription drug plan
- Yes Create independent Sept. 11 commission
- Yes Extend union protections to Homeland Security Department employees
- No Revive fast-track procedures for trade agreements
- No Authorize war against Iraq
- No Advance bankruptcy overhaul opposed by abortion opponents

2001

- No Nullify Clinton Labor Department ergonomics rule
- No Cut taxes by $1.35 trillion through fiscal 2011
- Yes Maintain ban on oil drilling in Arctic National Wildlife Refuge
- No Approve Bush proposal to limit managed-care plan liability for coverage decisions
- Yes Divert money from crop subsidy payments to land conservation
- Yes Expand law enforcement power to investigate suspected terrorists

CQ VOTE STUDIES

	PARTY UNITY		PRESIDENTIAL SUPPORT	
	Support	Oppose	Support	Oppose
2002	97%	3%	24%	76%
2001	92%	8%	28%	72%
2000	97%	3%	91%	9%
1999	94%	6%	88%	12%
1998	92%	8%	82%	18%

INTEREST GROUPS

	AFL-CIO	ADA	CCUS	ACU
2002	100%	100%	35%	0%
2001	91%	95%	35%	0%
2000	90%	85%	47%	4%
1999	78%	100%	29%	0%
1998	90%	95%	39%	4%

CALIFORNIA 5
Sacramento

Two things tend to dominate the 5th — state politics and triple-digit temperatures that send air conditioners into overdrive. Located in California's hot Central Valley, the 5th is home to the state capital, Sacramento, and reaches east and south to include a few upper-middle-class suburbs such as Arden-Arcade and Elk Grove (both of which are shared with the 3rd District).

Sacramento first attracted fortune seekers as the starting point of the Gold Rush of 1849. State government now provides the lion's share of employment, although other sectors are increasing in importance.

The city's economy has improved since a statewide recession in the early 1990s, with real estate value and population numbers growing against turn-of-the-century state and national economic trends. Several big-name technology companies are major employers in the 5th.

Overall, Democrats hold a substantial edge in voter registration. Sacramento used to be a swing district, supporting Ronald Reagan and George Bush in the presidential elections of the 1980s and Republican Pete Wilson in the 1990 gubernatorial race. But Democrats gained strength in the 1992 redistricting, when some of the more affluent, GOP-leaning suburbs were stripped. This trend continued in redistricting following the 2000 census, as mapmakers added suburbs such as Rancho Cordova and North Highlands (both shared with the 3rd). Al Gore captured 58 percent of the 5th's vote in the 2000 presidential election.

The city itself is slightly more diverse than neighboring communities, but whites, Hispanics, Asians and blacks each account for at least 14 percent of the district's residents.

MAJOR INDUSTRY
State government, technology

CITIES
Sacramento, 407,018; Arden-Arcade (unincorporated) (pt.), 42,428; Parkway-South Sacramento (unincorporated), 36,468

NOTABLE
The California State Railroad Museum is one of North America's largest railroad museums; Sacramento is California's oldest incorporated city.

Rep. Lynn Woolsey (D)

CAPITOL OFFICE
225-5161
www.house.gov/woolsey
2263 Rayburn 20515-0506; fax 225-5163

COMMITTEES
Education & Workforce
Science

HOMETOWN
Petaluma

BORN
Nov. 3, 1937, Seattle, Wash.

RELIGION
Presbyterian

FAMILY
Divorced; four children

EDUCATION
U. of Washington, attended 1955-57 (business); U. of San Francisco, B.S. 1980 (human resources & organization)

CAREER
Personnel service owner

POLITICAL HIGHLIGHTS
Petaluma City Council, 1985-93

ELECTION RESULTS

2002 GENERAL		
Lynn Woolsey (D)	139,750	66.7%
Paul L. Erickson (R)	62,052	29.6%
Richard Barton (LIBERT)	4,936	2.4%
Jeff Rainforth (REF)	2,825	1.4%
2002 PRIMARY		
Lynn Woolsey (D)	69,158	80.5%
Michael F. Martini (D)	16,770	19.5%
2000 GENERAL		
Lynn Woolsey (D)	182,116	64.3%
Ken McAuliffe (R)	80,169	28.3%
Justin Moscoso (GREEN)	13,248	4.7%
Richard Barton (LIBERT)	4,691	1.7%
Alan Barreca (NL)	2,894	1.0%

PREVIOUS WINNING PERCENTAGES
1998 (68%); 1996 (62%); 1994 (58%); 1992 (65%)

Elected 1992; 6th term

In a Congress where political moderates and deal-cutting pragmatists often hold sway, Woolsey revels in her unambiguous liberalism.

She offers proposals that have no chance of adoption; amid President Bush's soaring wartime popularity after Sept. 11, Woolsey pressed in 2001 for a vote on a resolution condemning his nuclear arms policy. She stages spectacles that make other lawmakers uneasy: While protesting inaction on a sexual non-discrimination treaty in 1999, Woolsey and nine other placard-toting congresswomen were removed from a Senate Foreign Relations Committee hearing by the Capitol police. She takes on widely popular organizations: After the Boy Scouts of America banned avowed homosexuals from membership, Woolsey offered a measure in 2000 to revoke their charter. It garnered just 12 votes.

To her detractors, Woolsey has been an ineffective back bencher, neither influential in shaping national legislation nor successful in bringing big federal money to her home in the north San Francisco Bay area. To her admirers, she represents a rare voice of conscience in Congress, speaking out against war in Iraq and in support of racial minorities, women, children, the elderly and those in need.

Woolsey was elected to Congress from the Petaluma City Council in 1992, the "Year of the Woman," in which a record 26 women were sent to Capitol Hill for the first time. Her seat was opened when fellow Democratic liberal Barbara Boxer gave it up to run successfully for the Senate, and Woolsey's gender was an important asset as she won the nomination in an upset against eight other candidates. Woolsey was the underdog in the general election, too, until her Republican opponent, Bill Filante, known as the most liberal Republican in the state Assembly, fell ill with brain cancer and suspended his campaign a few weeks before the election.

She has since won re-election with ease. In this decade's redistricting, her territory remains largely the same as in the 1990s: a progressive redoubt that takes in all of Marin and much of Sonoma counties. Many of her constituents are affluent former hippies who have retained their youthful idealism, the sort for whom the moniker "brie and chardonnay liberals" was coined. She faced a primary challenge in 2002 from Santa Rosa Mayor Mike Martini, who argued that she was too liberal and out of touch with business and farm interests. She beat him by 61 points.

Woolsey has a perspective on the federal safety net that is unique in Congress, where she is the only lawmaker who was once a single parent on welfare. At age 29, she divorced her stockbroker husband, which wrenched her from what she has described as a "Leave It To Beaver" suburban life in 1960s Marin County. To support her children — they were 1, 3 and 5 at the time — she sold her house and returned a new station wagon. To land a job as a secretary she admits she lied about her personal circumstances. Public assistance supplemented her wages until she remarried three years later. Woolsey eventually went back to college to get her degree, at age 42, and started her own human resources consulting company.

Knowing firsthand about buying groceries with food stamps and finding doctors who accepted Medi-Cal, California's Medicaid program, Woolsey arrived in Congress opposing efforts to cut people off from a system that she considers to have been her economic salvation. She was an unswerving opponent of the welfare law enacted in 1996, which set lifetime limits on benefits, and she played an active role in the debate during the 107th

Congress on rewriting that statute. That debate continues in the 108th.

"Someone will get up and talk about their humble beginnings, and how they lifted themselves up by their bootstraps," Woolsey said of the debate. "But, the very next minute, they'll be crusading to rip the safety net out from under children, families and seniors."

Woolsey wants to expand child care services for welfare recipients, and to permit welfare recipients to receive work credit while they are studying to complete their high school and college degrees.

Education has been a main legislative focus for Woolsey, who holds seats on both the Science and Education panels. She has twice introduced her "Go Girl" legislation to encourage girls to study science and math, but the measure got nowhere in either the 106th or 107th Congresses.

She has been angling for a seat on the Appropriations panel, and was among a number of Democrats who said they had been promised slots on the panel in the 108th — contingent upon Democrats regaining control of the House.

After the Sept. 11, 2001, attacks, Woolsey was among the 66 House members who opposed the law that greatly extended the federal government's police powers to combat terrorism. "I'm afraid the Bill of Rights could be the next victim of terrorism," Woolsey says.

Occasionally, Woolsey has been able to line up some GOP backing for her proposals, such as a school breakfast program that became law in the 105th Congress. In the 104th, she collaborated with Illinois Republican Henry J. Hyde, the Judiciary chairman, in proposing legislation to enlist the IRS in efforts to track down parents who fail to pay child support. She has sided with California Republicans on local issues, such as increasing funds for Highway 101, protecting the Golden Gate Bridge from earthquake damage, and getting federal support for California agricultural products, such as wine.

But Woolsey is better known for her clashes with conservatives, in which she has occasionally proved herself adept at crafting a witty sound bite. Protesting House GOP efforts to bar the District of Columbia from providing intravenous drug users with clean needles to cut down on the spread of infectious diseases, she said in 1999: "Some on the Republican side treat D.C. like their own conservative petri dish." The mother of a gay man, she has criticized what she calls a "shameful discriminatory policy toward gays in the military" promoted by Republicans in the 1990s. And after House Speaker Newt Gingrich once complained about being disrespected by President Clinton with his poor seat assignment aboard Air Force One, she asked: "Why doesn't the crybaby Speaker cry about real babies?"

KEY VOTES

2002

Yes Overhaul campaign finance law; ban "soft money" and restrict advocacy advertising
No Back Bush's defense budget increase
No Extend 1996 welfare law
No Adopt Bush's discretionary spending limit
No Pass GOP Medicare prescription drug plan
Yes Create independent Sept. 11 commission
Yes Extend union protections to Homeland Security Department employees
No Revive fast-track procedures for trade agreements
No Authorize war against Iraq
No Advance bankruptcy overhaul opposed by abortion opponents

2001

No Nullify Clinton Labor Department ergonomics rule
No Cut taxes by $1.35 trillion through fiscal 2011
Yes Maintain ban on oil drilling in Arctic National Wildlife Refuge
No Approve Bush proposal to limit managed-care plan liability for coverage decisions
Yes Divert money from crop subsidy payments to land conservation
No Expand law enforcement power to investigate suspected terrorists

CQ VOTE STUDIES

	PARTY UNITY		PRESIDENTIAL SUPPORT	
	Support	Oppose	Support	Oppose
2002	99%	1%	25%	75%
2001	98%	2%	14%	86%
2000	98%	2%	79%	21%
1999	97%	3%	78%	22%
1998	95%	5%	85%	15%

INTEREST GROUPS

	AFL-CIO	ADA	CCUS	ACU
2002	100%	95%	35%	0%
2001	100%	100%	26%	0%
2000	100%	100%	40%	8%
1999	100%	95%	12%	4%
1998	100%	100%	28%	8%

CALIFORNIA 6

Northern Bay Area – Sonoma and Marin counties

Travel north across the Golden Gate Bridge and the scenery changes from the cityscape of San Francisco to the Pacific coastline and inland hills that make up the 6th. This area north of the city is home to upper-middle-class suburbanites who commute to San Francisco and the "Telecom Valley," which extends north from San Rafael to Santa Rosa.

The 6th includes all of Marin County and most of Sonoma County. The area has grown significantly since the bridge opened in 1937 and continues to prosper. In recent years, migration from the city has created a tight housing market. As of 2002, the median house price for Marin County was $700,000, while Sonoma County's was $375,000.

Marin is home to San Quentin State Prison, San Rafael (the largest city in the county) and popular getaway spots such as Point Reyes National Seashore, Sausalito and Muir Woods. To the north, Sonoma County is home to a California State University campus and Santa Rosa, the largest city in the district. Wine and dairy ranching dominate the economy here, although high-tech companies have made inroads. Petaluma, with Victorian architecture left untouched by the 1906 earthquake, is near the Sonoma-Marin county line.

The district's affluent residents think of themselves as progressive and tolerant of diverse views. The 6th is one of the most liberal in the Democrat-dominated Golden State. After flirting with Republicanism in the late 1970s and early 1980s, it turned solidly Democratic, giving Democrat Al Gore 62 percent to George W. Bush's 30 percent in the 2000 presidential election. Democrats outnumber Republicans 2-to-1 in voter registration.

MAJOR INDUSTRY
Telecommunications, agriculture, tourism

CITIES
Santa Rosa, 147,595; San Rafael, 56,063; Petaluma, 54,548

NOTABLE
San Rafael is home to film producer and director George Lucas' companies, Industrial Light & Magic, Lucasfilm Ltd. and Skywalker Sound; Sen. Barbara Boxer, D, represented the 6th from 1983 to 1993.

Rep. George Miller (D)

CAPITOL OFFICE
225-2095
george.miller@mail.house.gov
www.house.gov/georgemiller
2205 Rayburn 20515-0507; fax 225-5609

COMMITTEES
Education & Workforce - ranking member
Resources

HOMETOWN
Martinez

BORN
May 17, 1945, Richmond, Calif.

RELIGION
Roman Catholic

FAMILY
Wife, Cynthia Miller; two children

EDUCATION
San Francisco State U., B.A. 1968; U. of California, Davis, J.D. 1972

CAREER
Lawyer; state legislative aide

POLITICAL HIGHLIGHTS
Democratic nominee for Calif. Senate, 1969

ELECTION RESULTS

2002 GENERAL		
George Miller (D)	97,849	70.7%
Charles R. Hargrave (R)	36,584	26.4%
Scott A. Wilson (LIBERT)	3,943	2.9%
2002 PRIMARY		
George Miller (D)		unopposed
2000 GENERAL		
George Miller (D)	159,692	76.5%
Christopher Hoffman (R)	44,154	21.2%
Martin Sproul (NL)	4,943	2.4%

PREVIOUS WINNING PERCENTAGES
1998 (77%); 1996 (72%); 1994 (70%); 1992 (70%); 1990 (61%); 1988 (68%); 1986 (67%); 1984 (66%); 1982 (67%); 1980 (63%); 1978 (63%); 1976 (75%); 1974 (56%)

Elected 1974; 15th term

A liberal firebrand who came of political age during the Watergate scandal, Miller is the bane of corporate interests and an advocate of government programs for the underprivileged. An ally of Minority Leader Nancy Pelosi, a fellow Californian from a district just across the San Francisco Bay, he is also an increasingly powerful voice on education and the environment.

He often grabs attention with vitriolic floor speeches against the Republican majority. He voted with Democrats 99 percent of the time on key votes in 2002. But Miller, a founding member of the Progressive Caucus, also can be tough on his own party when, in his judgment, it drifts too far to the center. "There just can't be two Republican Parties," he is fond of saying.

Miller was an early backer of Pelosi, whom he encouraged to run first for whip, then minority leader. He didn't much care for the inclusive leadership style of Pelosi's predecessor, Richard A. Gephardt, saying the party had a weaker message as a result. With Gephardt's retirement from the leadership team, Miller is a constant pressure on the new leaders to stay true to liberal beliefs.

He has been around long enough, however, to know that if he wants to influence policy, there are times to set speeches aside and strike deals. Miller was one of four authors of the landmark education overhaul of 2001, a bipartisan undertaking that gave President Bush many of the elements of his "Leave No Child Behind" schools initiative.

In early meetings on the legislation, Bush took to calling him "Big George" — an acknowledgement of his importance to House passage. And while willing to help the GOP pass its bill, Miller was just as quick to assail Bush afterward for setting aside too few dollars to pay for commitments in the legislation to measuring the progress of minority and low-income children in public schools.

Miller is ideally situated, at least for a member of the House minority, to promote his views. He is the senior Democrat on the Education and the Workforce Committee. And although he is no longer the top-ranking Democrat on the Resources Committee — a role he gave up for the top spot on the Education panel — he continues to be deeply involved in environmental issues.

He is a favorite of environmental groups — the Sierra Club once dubbed him a "green giant" — and he annually wins high marks for his voting record from groups such as the League of Conservation Voters.

If GOP control of the House means Miller can't write bills his way, he makes up for it with high-profile policy brawls. For six years, he did battle with the similarly blustery and sharp-elbowed Resources chairman, Don Young of Alaska, his ideological opposite.

When Young stepped down as chairman at the end of 2000, Miller paid tribute: "Under that grizzly-bear exterior is a very, very caring individual." But he was quick to add, "It's been a real pain in the rear because of your outlook on some of these issues."

Miller was the chief critic of Young's attempts to scale back the Endangered Species Act, limit creation of wilderness areas, and accelerate timber harvests in national forests. He even blocked some of Young's non-controversial proposals, just to show he was not to be easily shut out of the process. In subsequent years, after the polarizing effects of the GOP takeover eased, Miller sometimes found it more productive to work with his nemesis.

He joined Young in the 106th Congress to push the Conservation and Reinvestment Act, which would have guaranteed that $45 billion in oil royalties be spent over 15 years for land conservation. The legislation ultimately stalled, but the efforts of the bipartisan coalition Miller helped assemble weren't in vain. The bill ultimately was replaced by a $12 billion, six-year conservation plan hatched by the White House and congressional appropriators.

Miller frequently clashes with the opposing party on the labor issues close to his heart. In 2000, Republicans tried to stop the Clinton administration from issuing ergonomics rules, which sought to regulate workplace conditions to avoid repetitive-stress injuries. That brought a typical response from Miller. "Maybe the Republicans would recognize ergonomics injuries if we applied them to tennis and golf," he said.

His sometimes hot-tempered personality earned him a place in House lore in 1995 when he and Virginia Democrat James P. Moran got into a shoving match with California Republicans Robert K. Dornan and Randy "Duke" Cunningham over a bill to bar the use of funds for deploying troops in Bosnia without prior congressional approval.

Miller also has waged a long war against federal funding for sugar price supports. He calls the $400 million-a-year program "corporate welfare, pure and simple." His phase-out bill in 2001 failed, a disappointment for both the lawmaker and C&H Sugar Co., a major refinery in his district that stood to benefit if the subsidies disappeared and cheap sugar imports flooded the market.

He is the third George Miller in his family to earn a living in government. His grandfather, George Miller Sr., was the assistant civil engineer in Richmond. His father, George Jr., was a state senator for 20 years. Miller, who is named George Miller III, was a law student in 1969 when his father died. He won the Democratic nomination to succeed his father in the state Senate but lost the election.

He went to work as a legislative aide to state Sen. George Moscone, the Democratic floor leader and one-time mayor of San Francisco. In 1974, when Democratic Rep. Jerome Waldie decided to run for governor, Miller sought his seat in Congress.

He won a tough, three-way Democratic primary. In the general election, he exploited the Watergate scandal, which was fresh in voters' minds, disclosing his campaign finances twice a month and chiding his opponent for not doing the same. He took 56 percent of the vote and has since won re-election easily.

KEY VOTES

2002

- Yes Overhaul campaign finance law; ban "soft money" and restrict advocacy advertising
- No Back Bush's defense budget increase
- No Extend 1996 welfare law
- No Adopt Bush's discretionary spending limit
- No Pass GOP Medicare prescription drug plan
- Yes Create independent Sept. 11 commission
- Yes Extend union protections to Homeland Security Department employees
- No Revive fast-track procedures for trade agreements
- No Authorize war against Iraq
- No Advance bankruptcy overhaul opposed by abortion opponents

2001

- No Nullify Clinton Labor Department ergonomics rule
- No Cut taxes by $1.35 trillion through fiscal 2011
- Yes Maintain ban on oil drilling in Arctic National Wildlife Refuge
- No Approve Bush proposal to limit managed-care plan liability for coverage decisions
- Yes Divert money from crop subsidy payments to land conservation
- No Expand law enforcement power to investigate suspected terrorists

CQ VOTE STUDIES

	PARTY UNITY		PRESIDENTIAL SUPPORT	
	Support	Oppose	Support	Oppose
2002	97%	3%	22%	78%
2001	98%	2%	23%	77%
2000	96%	4%	76%	24%
1999	93%	7%	74%	26%
1998	97%	3%	84%	16%

INTEREST GROUPS

	AFL-CIO	ADA	CCUS	ACU
2002	100%	100%	30%	4%
2001	100%	100%	27%	0%
2000	100%	95%	38%	12%
1999	89%	100%	4%	8%
1998	100%	100%	19%	8%

CALIFORNIA 7

Northeastern Bay Area — Vallejo, Richmond

Situated along the San Pablo Bay and home to marshes and wetlands where the Sacramento and San Joaquin deltas feed into the bay, the 7th combines industrial and suburban areas of north Contra Costa County with the western end of more rural Solano County.

In Contra Costa County, the district takes in residential Concord (shared with the 10th) and the industrial cities of Richmond and Martinez along San Pablo Bay, home to oil, steel and biotechnology. Richmond, which has a black plurality, was home to one of the largest World War II shipbuilding operations.

Vallejo, the largest city in the district, was the site of Mare Island Naval Shipyard, which closed in 1996 after more than 140 years of operation. The city converted the island to a private commercial-residential property, which is still in development.

Vallejo and other traditionally Democratic Solano County communities — including Green Valley and Vacaville, which were added to the northern part of the 7th in redistricting following the 2000 census — are home to farm-support services.

Redistricting also shaved off Democratic-voting areas like Suisun City, Fairfield, Cordelia and Kensington to shore up the neighboring 10th District for Democrats, but the 7th is still a safe Democratic seat.

MAJOR INDUSTRY

Petrochemicals, steel, biotechnology, agriculture, health care

MILITARY BASES

Naval Weapons Station Seal Beach, Detachment Concord, 200 military, 500 civilian (2001)

CITIES

Vallejo, 116,760; Richmond, 99,216; Vacaville, 88,625; Pittsburg, 56,769

NOTABLE

The forerunner to the martini, the "Martinez Special," became popular in the city of Martinez during the Gold Rush; Actor Tom Hanks was born in Concord; Vallejo (twice) and Benicia both served as the state capital in the 1850s.

Rep. Nancy Pelosi (D)

CAPITOL OFFICE
225-4965
sf.nancy@mail.house.gov
www.house.gov/pelosi
2371 Rayburn 20515-0508; fax 225-8259

COMMITTEES
Minority Leader – no committee assignments

HOMETOWN
San Francisco

BORN
March 26, 1940, Baltimore, Md.

RELIGION
Roman Catholic

FAMILY
Husband, Paul Pelosi; five children

EDUCATION
Trinity College (D.C.), A.B. 1962

CAREER
Public relations consultant; senatorial campaign committee finance chairwoman; homemaker

POLITICAL HIGHLIGHTS
Calif. Democratic Party chairwoman, 1981-83

ELECTION RESULTS

2002 GENERAL		
Nancy Pelosi (D)	127,684	79.6%
G. Michael German (R)	20,063	12.5%
Jay Pond (GREEN)	10,033	6.3%
Ira Spivack (LIBERT)	2,659	1.7%
2002 PRIMARY		
Nancy Pelosi (D)	65,949	93.1%
Paul Gregory McConnell (D)	4,898	6.9%
2000 GENERAL		
Nancy Pelosi (D)	181,847	84.4%
Adam Sparks (R)	25,298	11.7%
Erik Bauman (LIBERT)	5,645	2.6%
David Smithstein (NL)	2,638	1.2%

PREVIOUS WINNING PERCENTAGES
1998 (86%); 1996 (84%); 1994 (82%); 1992 (82%); 1990 (77%); 1988 (76%); 1987 Special Runoff Election (63%); 1987 Special Election (36%)

Elected June 1987; 8th full term

As the new House minority leader, Pelosi is the first woman ever to head a political party in Congress and the most liberal Democratic leader in modern times.

Elected to the House in 1987, the San Francisco Democrat is a relatively junior member compared with some of her long-serving colleagues. She got the job of leader through a combination of political acumen, motivational skill and fundraising prowess. The fact that she is a woman was a big plus. In 2002, having suffered their worst election in eight years, Democrats were looking for a new face and a new direction.

Her ascent was a repudiation of the centrist politics that had prevailed since the Clinton administration. Pelosi (pah-LO-see) overcame a strong contender with more seniority, Martin Frost of Texas, who had promised leadership from the center. Many moderate-to-conservative lawmakers were willing to overlook Pelosi's ideology and support her in the closed balloting, banking on her leadership skills to help lead them to majority status. Pelosi says, "I'm a non-menacing progressive Democrat."

Nevertheless, she seemed ready to shake things up in the 108th Congress. She pressed several senior Democrats to part with coveted assignments in 2003 as part of her campaign to boost the representation of junior members and conservatives, in particular, but also Hispanics and blacks. As party leader, Pelosi holds no committee seats.

Majority Republicans know that behind Pelosi's ready smile and studied graciousness is a tough opponent. They are certain to try to stymie her first two years as leader by portraying her as a throwback to discredited liberal policies of the 1960s and 1970s. Pelosi has a 95 percent lifetime support score from Americans for Democratic Action, a leading liberal advocacy group, and a similar career-spanning score from the AFL-CIO. Both figures are above the average for House Democrats.

She is willing to take positions unpopular with, or ignored by, other Democrats and is a relentless fighter for her causes. Given San Francisco's large Chinese-American population, she has battled in vain through three administrations to sanction China for its human rights record. She is also a strong defender of civil rights for homosexuals, another important constituency in the city.

She has been a persistent critic of the Bush administration. She sided with the White House only 26 percent of the time in the 107th Congress. She is at odds with Republicans on most legislation dealing with abortion rights, gun control and environmental protection and voted against the president's $1.35 trillion tax cut in 2001.

But Pelosi has shown some willingness to be pragmatic on high-profile issues. As top Democrat on a special panel charged with writing the bill to create the Homeland Security Department in 2002, for example, she opposed the House measure out of concern it would limit civil liberties. But she joined the minority of House Democrats who voted for the bill in final form.

Her zeal in fundraising is well-known. She gave more than $1 million to congressional candidates in 2002, more than any other House Democrat. She stumped for candidates and helped raise several million dollars for the Democratic Congressional Campaign Committee. She even offers to drum up donations for candidates who do not seek her out.

Pelosi succeeds Richard A. Gephardt, the minority leader since Democrats lost the majority in 1995. He stepped aside after the party's losses in the 2002 election. Frost was Pelosi's principal competition but bowed out a week before the leadership elections after concluding he could not win. Pelosi was chosen 177-29 over Harold E. Ford Jr. of Tennessee, a late entrant who made an appeal to conservatives but was never expected to win. Pelosi also was helped by support from the California Democratic delegation, the largest in the House.

Her election capped a remarkably fast rise. In 2001 she was elected Democratic whip, 118-95, over Steny H. Hoyer of Maryland, who courted moderates and conservatives. As whip, Pelosi became the highest-ranking woman in Congress' history, eclipsing Maine's Margaret Chase Smith, who chaired the Senate Republican Conference from 1967 to 1972.

In the 107th, Pelosi was the top Democrat on the Intelligence Committee, and she used her leverage as whip to press for an independent commission with broad authority to investigate government lapses before the Sept. 11, 2001, terrorist attacks.

As the senior Democrat on the Foreign Operations Appropriations Subcommittee in the 105th and 106th Congresses, she worked to increase debt forgiveness for poor countries, secure more money to fight AIDS globally, and preserve aid to international family planning groups. On Appropriations she also promoted funding for breast cancer research, government housing for AIDS victims and an expansion of the Bay Area's subway system to the San Francisco airport.

Politics is in Pelosi's blood. Her father, Thomas J. D'Alesandro Jr., was a freshman Democratic congressman from Baltimore when she was born in 1940. After serving four terms, he went on to become that city's mayor for 12 years. (Her brother, Thomas, also was Baltimore's mayor, from 1967 to 1971.)

After college, Pelosi moved to San Francisco, married, raised five children and became a Democratic Party activist. As chairman of the California Democratic Party, she helped attract the party's 1984 national convention to her hometown. She lost her bid for the chairmanship of the Democratic National Committee the next year but was named finance chairman of the Democratic Senatorial Campaign Committee in the run-up to the 1986 election.

All this made her more familiar to national party activists than to San Francisco voters in 1987, when the city's principal House seat came open with the death of Democrat Sala Burton. But Pelosi used her insider's contacts and captured the nomination, which was tantamount to election in one of the nation's most solidly Democratic districts. She won in 2002 with 80 percent, her smallest share of the vote in a dozen years.

KEY VOTES

2002

- Yes Overhaul campaign finance law; ban "soft money" and restrict advocacy advertising
- Yes Back Bush's defense budget increase
- No Extend 1996 welfare law
- No Adopt Bush's discretionary spending limit
- No Pass GOP Medicare prescription drug plan
- Yes Create independent Sept. 11 commission
- Yes Extend union protections to Homeland Security Department employees
- No Revive fast-track procedures for trade agreements
- No Authorize war against Iraq
- No Advance bankruptcy overhaul opposed by abortion opponents

2001

- No Nullify Clinton Labor Department ergonomics rule
- No Cut taxes by $1.35 trillion through fiscal 2011
- Yes Maintain ban on oil drilling in Arctic National Wildlife Refuge
- No Approve Bush proposal to limit managed-care plan liability for coverage decisions
- Yes Divert money from crop subsidy payments to land conservation
- Yes Expand law enforcement power to investigate suspected terrorists

CQ VOTE STUDIES

	PARTY UNITY		PRESIDENTIAL SUPPORT	
	Support	Oppose	Support	Oppose
2002	99%	1%	23%	77%
2001	97%	3%	28%	72%
2000	96%	4%	79%	21%
1999	96%	4%	81%	19%
1998	97%	3%	84%	16%

INTEREST GROUPS

	AFL-CIO	ADA	CCUS	ACU
2002	100%	100%	37%	0%
2001	100%	100%	35%	0%
2000	100%	100%	42%	8%
1999	88%	95%	12%	0%
1998	100%	95%	33%	12%

CALIFORNIA 8

Most of San Francisco

Since the Gold Rush in the mid-19th century, San Francisco has attracted visitors, new residents and fortune seekers from around the globe. "The City," as it is known to natives, is famous for its landmarks, food and a diverse collection of neighborhoods, from the Italian and Hispanic centers of North Beach and the Mission District to spots such as Chinatown, hippie haven Haight-Ashbury and the gay mecca of Castro.

More than 80 percent of the city's residents live in the 8th, which forms a backward C-shape. The 12th District to the west and south takes in neighborhoods just south of Golden Gate Park and west of Twin Peaks. Whites make up 43 percent of the 8th, followed by Asians, at 29 percent.

A center for protest during the Vietnam War, the city also barred police from arresting illegal immigrants fleeing Central American bloodshed in the 1980s, in opposition to federal immigration officials. More recently, the city has helped fund the largest needle exchange program in the nation and in 2002 approved an initiative to study whether to grow and distribute medical marijuana to seriously ill patients. The city also chose, however, to cut its once-bountiful direct payments to the homeless and shift that money to create more housing and services. The 8th is safe Democratic territory. Democrat Al Gore won the 2000 presidential vote here by 62 percentage points.

MAJOR INDUSTRY

Tourism, financial services, health care

CITIES

San Francisco (pt.), 639,088

NOTABLE

San Francisco was home to the nation's only declared monarch, Norton I, who named himself Emperor of the United States and Protector of Mexico in 1859; Throughout his "reign," Norton issued various proclamations, including orders to bar Congress from meeting in Washington and to construct a bridge between San Francisco and Oakland — more than 60 years before construction of the Bay Bridge; Alcatraz Island, home to the first West Coast fort and lighthouse and used as a federal maximum-security prison from 1934 to 1963, was occupied in protest by American Indians from 1969 to 1971.

Rep. Barbara Lee (D)

CAPITOL OFFICE
225-2661
barbara.lee@mail.house.gov
www.house.gov/lee
1724 Longworth 20515-0509; fax 225-9817

COMMITTEES
Financial Services
International Relations

HOMETOWN
Oakland

BORN
July 16, 1946, El Paso, Texas

RELIGION
Baptist

FAMILY
Husband, Michael Millben; two children

EDUCATION
Mills College, B.A. 1973 (psychology); U. of California, Berkeley, M.S.W. 1975

CAREER
Congressional aide

POLITICAL HIGHLIGHTS
Calif. Assembly, 1990-96; Calif. Senate, 1996-98

ELECTION RESULTS

2002 GENERAL		
Barbara Lee (D)	135,893	81.4%
Jerald Udinsky (R)	25,333	15.2%
James M. Eyer (LIBERT)	5,685	3.4%
2002 PRIMARY		
Barbara Lee (D)	68,550	84.8%
Kevin A. Greene (D)	12,257	15.2%
2000 GENERAL		
Barbara Lee (D)	182,352	85.0%
Arneze Washington (R)	21,033	9.8%
Fred Foldvary (LIBERT)	7,051	3.3%
Ellen Jefferds (NL)	4,214	2.0%

PREVIOUS WINNING PERCENTAGES
1998 (83%); 1998 Special Election (67%)

Elected April 1998; 3rd full term

No matter what accomplishments Lee achieves during her congressional career, she may well be remembered most for her lone "no" vote in Congress on Sept. 14, 2001, against a resolution authorizing President Bush to use "all necessary and appropriate force" to retaliate against the terrorist attacks that had occurred three days earlier.

Lee agonized over her vote, and did not make up her mind until she attended a memorial service at the Washington National Cathedral earlier in the day. She decided on her course after hearing an invocation by the Rev. Nathan D. Baxter, the cathedral dean, who prayed that "despite our grief we may not become the evil we deplore." Lee's vote brought in sacks of hate mail and death threats that at one point necessitated police protection. But she has never second-guessed herself.

"That was the right vote then and it's the right vote today," Lee said more than a year later. "The resolution gave the president very broad authority to use military force. I don't believe the rush to judgment during an emotional, fearful time is the best decision."

Her solitary stance made Lee an instant hero of the American peace movement, and so her office was a rallying point later in the 107th Congress for those opposed to a war to oust Saddam Hussein from power in Iraq. Lee said that a pre-emptive invasion, which Congress authorized in 2002, would set "a dangerous precedent." She offered an amendment to the war resolution that called on the United States to work through the United Nations to ensure that Iraq was not developing weapons of mass destruction. The House rejected it by a 5-to-1 ratio.

Lee's overall voting record shows her to be one of the most liberal members of the House, and her priorities mesh with the economic, health care and education needs of her racially diverse constituency. Some of the needs are urgent, she argues, such as recognizing the devastating effect of AIDS on the African-American community. She also has struggled to change a longstanding U.S. policy that forbids aid to private family planning organizations that either perform abortions or offer abortion counseling services abroad.

Employing a straightforward, conversational style, she argues for affirmative action and needle-exchange programs, as well as child care and economic development in poor neighborhoods. She is the co-chairman of the Progressive Caucus, the most liberal faction of House Democrats.

Lee says that confrontational tactics are sometimes called for, such as when she joined her female House colleagues in barging into a 1999 Senate Foreign Relations Committee hearing to demand action on an international treaty against sexual discrimination. "My paradigm is to blend confrontational tactics to confront injustice head-on and to use legislation whenever possible to solve the less-pressing problems," she said.

Lee serves on the Financial Services and International Relations committees, and she focuses much of her efforts on matters of interest to those panels. In the 107th Congress, she successfully sponsored an amendment to a housing bill that would allow domestic violence victims to remain in public housing, rather than be evicted along with their attackers.

Even before her vote against using armed forces against al Qaeda, Lee's credentials as a leading congressional pacifist were strong. She was one of the original sponsors of a bill in the 107th to establish a Cabinet-level Department of Peace. In 1999, she cast another sole "no" vote in the House against a resolution of support for U.S. troops conducting air strikes in Yugoslavia.

Lee urged Alameda County officials to declare a state of emergency in the battle against AIDS, and she wrote legislation to greatly increase U.S. support for combating the disease. She also wants to increase U.S. trade with Africa, an issue she has been working on since her days in the California Assembly. In 2000, however, she was one of only five black lawmakers to oppose enactment of a law to expand trade with sub-Saharan Africa, arguing that the measure did not go far enough in dealing with long-range solutions to African economic development and did not address such issues as workers' rights and the environment.

Lee's politics are shaped by early-life recollections of discrimination. Her mother initially was refused treatment at an El Paso hospital when in labor with her. She attended a segregated school and later, she says, a riot was touched off when she was chosen the first black cheerleader at her high school in Southern California. She says many of her experiences with discrimination "are relatively common with the general experiences of blacks of my generation" and "have fueled my disdain for injustices."

Lee had never even registered to vote when she was faced with a course requirement at Oakland's Mills College to work for a political campaign during the presidential election year of 1972. She signed on with Democratic Rep. Shirley Chisholm of New York, the nation's first notable black candidate for president. Lee rose quickly through the ranks, eventually running Chisholm's Northern California campaign and, as she proudly recalled a quarter-century later, receiving an "A" in the course.

While earning a master's in social work, Lee helped start a community health center in Berkeley before going to work for Democrat Ronald V. Dellums, her predecessor in the House, in 1975. She worked for him in both California and Washington before running for the state legislature, where she served six years in the Assembly and one year in the Senate. When Dellums revealed his plans to resign from the House in early 1998, he endorsed Lee to succeed him and she easily won the special election.

Lee's stand against the 2001 war resolution inevitably invites comparisons to Jeanette Rankin, the Montana Republican who was the only member of Congress to vote against the U.S. entry into both world wars. But while Rankin left the House one year after each of those votes — she lost a Senate bid in 1918, and she did not run for re-election in 1942 — Lee's vote did nothing to weaken her political standing. She won her third full term in 2002 with four-fifths of the vote.

KEY VOTES

2002

Yes Overhaul campaign finance law; ban "soft money" and restrict advocacy advertising
No Back Bush's defense budget increase
No Extend 1996 welfare law
No Adopt Bush's discretionary spending limit
No Pass GOP Medicare prescription drug plan
Yes Create independent Sept. 11 commission
Yes Extend union protections to Homeland Security Department employees
No Revive fast-track procedures for trade agreements
No Authorize war against Iraq
No Advance bankruptcy overhaul opposed by abortion opponents

2001

No Nullify Clinton Labor Department ergonomics rule
No Cut taxes by $1.35 trillion through fiscal 2011
Yes Maintain ban on oil drilling in Arctic National Wildlife Refuge
No Approve Bush proposal to limit managed-care plan liability for coverage decisions
Yes Divert money from crop subsidy payments to land conservation
No Expand law enforcement power to investigate suspected terrorists

CQ VOTE STUDIES

	PARTY UNITY		PRESIDENTIAL SUPPORT	
	Support	Oppose	Support	Oppose
2002	99%	1%	25%	75%
2001	97%	3%	12%	88%
2000	97%	3%	82%	18%
1999	94%	6%	76%	24%
1998	99%	1%	85%	15%

INTEREST GROUPS

	AFL-CIO	ADA	CCUS	ACU
2002	100%	90%	30%	0%
2001	100%	95%	22%	0%
2000	100%	90%	33%	4%
1999	100%	100%	16%	8%
1998	100%	75%	14%	5%

CALIFORNIA 9

Northwest Alameda County — Oakland, Berkeley

Across the bay from San Francisco, the 9th is anchored by Oakland and Berkeley, two racially diverse and liberal communities that gained national attention for their political activism in the 1960s.

More than 60 percent of district residents live in Oakland, which is 38 percent black. The city's unemployment rate is slightly above the national average, but revitalization efforts have kept the area in good health, despite the closing of several military facilities. In the city's eastern hills, the neighborhoods tend to be wealthy and less diverse. Tension between blacks and police gave birth to the Black Panther Party in 1966.

Just north of Oakland, Berkeley is home to the flagship campus of the University of California system and looks out over the bay from the Berkeley Hills. Home to student protests in the 1960s, Berkeley still looks much the way it did then. The remainder of the district includes smaller communities such as Albany, a suburb at the north end of the district; Piedmont, a residential "suburb in the city" in Oakland's hills; and several additions from redistricting following the 2000 census: Ashland, Castro Valley, Cherryland and Fairview, which are unincorporated sections of Alameda County southeast of Oakland.

The 9th also includes the fast-growing bayside city of Emeryville, home to biotechnology firms, high-tech companies and headquarters of animation studio Pixar ("Toy Story," "Monsters, Inc.").

With a core constituency in the left-leaning cities of Oakland and Berkeley, the 9th is a Democratic stronghold. Republicans account for only 12 percent of registered voters.

MAJOR INDUSTRY
Biotechnology, shipping

CITIES
Oakland, 399,484; Berkeley, 102,743; Castro Valley (unincorporated) (pt.), 57,224

NOTABLE
Since 1970, Jack London Square in Oakland has featured the relocated cabin where the author, who ran for Oakland mayor twice, lived during the Yukon Gold Rush of 1897; West Oakland was a terminus for the transcontinental railroad.

Rep. Ellen O. Tauscher (D)

CAPITOL OFFICE
225-1880
www.house.gov/tauscher
1034 Longworth 20515-0510; fax 225-5914

COMMITTEES
Armed Services
Transportation & Infrastructure

HOMETOWN
Alamo

BORN
Nov. 15, 1951, Newark, N.J.

RELIGION
Roman Catholic

FAMILY
Divorced; one child

EDUCATION
Seton Hall U., B.A. 1974 (early childhood education)

CAREER
Child care screening executive; marketing executive; investment banker

POLITICAL HIGHLIGHTS
No previous office

ELECTION RESULTS

2002 GENERAL		
Ellen O. Tauscher (D)	126,390	75.6%
Sonia Harden (LIBERT)	40,807	24.4%
2002 PRIMARY		
Ellen O. Tauscher (D)	496,121	83.4%
Kurt Rasmussen (D)	9,867	16.6%
2000 GENERAL		
Ellen O. Tauscher (D)	160,429	52.6%
Claude B. Hutchison Jr. (R)	134,863	44.2%
Valerie Janlois (NL)	9,527	3.1%

PREVIOUS WINNING PERCENTAGES
1998 (53%); 1996 (49%)

Elected 1996; 4th term

A serious player on defense issues and a pro-business Democrat who is not afraid to go her own way, Tauscher is seen as someone to watch on Capitol Hill.

Early in 2001, Tauscher (rhymes with HOW-sher) was elected vice chairman of the Democratic Leadership Council, an organization of centrist Democrats. Later that year, she was chosen as vice chairman of a Democratic task force on homeland security, adding to a résumé that led Washingtonian magazine to call her one of the 100 most powerful women in Washington.

Her centrist politics — the San Francisco Chronicle has described her as "about the closest thing the Bay Area has to a Republican" — led to some intraparty friction late in 2001 when she was the only California Democrat to back Maryland's Steny H. Hoyer in the campaign for party whip against San Francisco's Nancy Pelosi. It was not personal, Tauscher says, explaining she believes House Democrats must move toward centrist, pro-business positions and that Hoyer better fit that bill.

For a time, there was some talk that Pelosi supporters in the California Legislature would punish Tauscher when they drew new congressional district lines, but the district ended up much to her liking. The GOP did not even field a candidate against her in 2002, and she defeated a Libertarian candidate by a 3-to-1 ratio. After the election, when House Democrats chose a new leader when Richard A. Gephardt stepped down, Tauscher backed Pelosi, noting her "incredible political acumen, but also her boundless energy and devotion to friends and family."

Tauscher's committee assignments are Armed Services and Transportation. She touts the hundreds of millions of federal dollars that have gone to the Bay Area during her tenure. She is not averse to complaining about "bureaucratic foot-dragging" by the Environmental Protection Agency that has delayed some needed area transportation projects.

She sought the Armed Services post in order to watch out for the interests of the Lawrence Livermore and Sandia California national laboratories in her district, which both conduct defense-related research. Tauscher has developed an expertise in non-proliferation efforts that aim to combat the spread of nuclear, biological and chemical weapons.

Tauscher's other expertise is more domestic. In 1992, faced with difficulties in securing child care for her daughter, she founded a business that screens prospective child care workers. When looking for a caregiver for her daughter, "I started meeting tax fugitives and 300-pound people with no teeth," she told The Record, the newspaper that covers her childhood area of northern New Jersey. She also published a child care reference guidebook.

The child care screening venture was her second business career. Tauscher also worked on Wall Street for 14 years as a stockbroker and investment banker. She was one of the first women to hold a seat on the New York Stock Exchange. She told the San Francisco Examiner that she once confronted her boss to demand pay equal to a male colleague's and got it. "Because of prominence and reputation, they couldn't diddle with me like they could a lot of women," she said.

"Because of my business background, I understand the art of the deal," she says. "Compromise is not a dirty word." Her business-oriented philosophy and her interest in defense issues have won her campaign endorsements from the Chamber of Commerce and Veterans of Foreign Wars. In Congress, she has been given higher rankings by the Chamber than by the AFL-CIO several times in annual analyses of members' votes.

She favors expanded foreign trade and was quick to caution labor that her vote in late 2001 against reviving presidential fast-track trade negotiating authority was an anomaly. She said she objected to the timing of the vote, coming with the economy in a recession. She argued that dealing with joblessness at home should be a higher priority. In 2002, when the House voted on the final version of the bill, she voted "aye."

On most social policy issues, Tauscher is a traditional Democrat. She favors abortion rights, robust environmental protections, federal arts funding and an active federal role in improving education.

In addition to her New Democrat affiliation, Tauscher has joined the "Blue Dogs," a coalition of Democrats who favor conservative fiscal policies.

Tauscher cosponsored a balanced-budget constitutional amendment and is a strong advocate of cutting taxes, particularly capital gains taxes and the estate tax. In 2001, she was one of the 28 House Democrats who voted for the final version of the $1.35 trillion, 10-year tax cut that was the signature domestic achievement of President Bush's first year. She also argued, unsuccessfully, for a "trigger" that would permit the rate cuts to continue from year to year if the budget continued in the black.

The eldest daughter of an Irish Catholic family, Tauscher was the first person in her family to attend college, majoring in early childhood education. From Seton Hall University, she watched the World Trade Center's twin towers being built across the Hudson River. After graduating and finding it difficult to land a teaching job, she looked across the river at Wall Street and asked, "Why not?"

She married computer executive Bill Tauscher (they have since divorced) and moved to Northern California in 1989. She became active in local politics, helping Dianne Feinstein in her 1992 special-election and 1994 Senate campaigns before acquiescing to last-minute cajoling from Feinstein and others and launching her own quest for Congress in 1996.

The 10th District had been represented by Republican Bill Baker since 1993. But by 1996, he had taken a hard enough line against abortion and in favor of gun owners' rights that he had alienated a portion of district voters. While using $1.7 million of her own money and outspending Baker by almost 2-to-1, Tauscher won by fewer than 2 percentage points.

In 1998, she easily outdistanced political novice Charles Ball. She won another competitive race in 2000, fending off an aggressive challenge from GOP banker Claude B. Hutchison Jr. Now, she is often mentioned as a possible candidate for higher office in either 2004 or 2006.

KEY VOTES

2002

- Yes Overhaul campaign finance law; ban "soft money" and restrict advocacy advertising
- Yes Back Bush's defense budget increase
- No Extend 1996 welfare law
- No Adopt Bush's discretionary spending limit
- No Pass GOP Medicare prescription drug plan
- Yes Create independent Sept. 11 commission
- Yes Extend union protections to Homeland Security Department employees
- Yes Revive fast-track procedures for trade agreements
- Yes Authorize war against Iraq
- Yes Advance bankruptcy overhaul opposed by abortion opponents

2001

- No Nullify Clinton Labor Department ergonomics rule
- Yes Cut taxes by $1.35 trillion through fiscal 2011
- Yes Maintain ban on oil drilling in Arctic National Wildlife Refuge
- No Approve Bush proposal to limit managed-care plan liability for coverage decisions
- Yes Divert money from crop subsidy payments to land conservation
- Yes Expand law enforcement power to investigate suspected terrorists

CQ VOTE STUDIES

	PARTY UNITY		PRESIDENTIAL SUPPORT	
	Support	Oppose	Support	Oppose
2002	86%	14%	35%	65%
2001	84%	16%	40%	60%
2000	85%	15%	78%	22%
1999	84%	16%	77%	23%
1998	81%	19%	77%	23%

INTEREST GROUPS

	AFL-CIO	ADA	CCUS	ACU
2002	78%	85%	65%	8%
2001	83%	85%	48%	4%
2000	50%	70%	71%	20%
1999	67%	100%	68%	8%
1998	60%	75%	72%	12%

CALIFORNIA 10

East Bay suburbs — Fairfield, Antioch, Livermore

Anyone driving through the Caldecott Tunnel across the Alameda-Contra Costa county line or on Interstate 680 during rush hour probably will be surrounded by 10th District residents on their way to and from work in San Francisco or San Jose. Separated from the rest of the Bay Area by the hills east of Oakland, the 10th's residents are mainly well-educated, well-paid professionals who work outside the district.

The 10th's residents have managed to fend off overdevelopment from their hills and hidden valleys while keeping pace with the rest of the area economically, giving the district a different feel from its more urban neighbors to the west. Almost two-thirds of residents live in the 10th's portion of Contra Costa County, including Antioch and most of Concord (shared with the 7th District).

Some of the residents here represent white flight from Oakland that is now generations old. But many newer commuters are younger and identify with San Francisco or Berkeley. The district retains a moderate political character — residents tend to be conscious of pocketbook issues but also share their Bay Area neighbors' views on the environment and other quality-of-life issues.

The district's Solano County portion is a growing but still largely agricultural area where commuters may head south to the Bay Area or north to Sacramento. Added along with a sliver of Sacramento County during redistricting following the 2000 census, these areas made the previously competitive district more Democratic. Residents here are more working-class than their "new Democrat" suburban district-mates. Growth will soon make these areas a part of the suburbs.

MAJOR INDUSTRY

Research, health care, agriculture, service

MILITARY BASES

Travis Air Force Base, 10,570 military, 1,121 civilian (2001)

CITIES

Fairfield, 96,178; Antioch, 90,532; Livermore, 73,345; Concord (pt.), 72,540

NOTABLE

Lawrence Livermore National Laboratory is one of the country's leading centers of experimental physics research and defense analysis; Fairfield is home to the Jelly Belly jellybean factory.

Rep. Richard W. Pombo (R)

CAPITOL OFFICE
225-1947
rpombo@mail.house.gov
www.house.gov/pombo
2411 Rayburn 20515-0511; fax 226-0861

COMMITTEES
Agriculture
Resources - chairman

HOMETOWN
Tracy

BORN
Jan. 8, 1961, Tracy, Calif.

RELIGION
Roman Catholic

FAMILY
Wife, Annette Pombo; three children

EDUCATION
California State Polytechnic U., Pomona, attended 1979-81 (agriculture & business)

CAREER
Rancher

POLITICAL HIGHLIGHTS
Tracy City Council, 1990-92

ELECTION RESULTS

2002 GENERAL		
Richard W. Pombo (R)	104,921	60.3%
Elaine Dugger Shaw (D)	69,035	39.7%
2002 PRIMARY		
Richard W. Pombo (R)	53,525	87.0%
Thomas A. Benigno (R)	7,982	13.0%
2000 GENERAL		
Richard W. Pombo (R)	120,635	57.8%
Tom Santos (D)	79,539	38.1%
Kathryn Russow (LIBERT)	5,036	2.4%
Jon Kurey (NL)	3,397	1.6%

PREVIOUS WINNING PERCENTAGES
1998 (61%); 1996 (59%); 1994 (62%); 1992 (48%)

Elected 1992; 6th term

Of all the nicknames that President Bush has given people, calling Pombo "Marlboro Man" may be the most on target. Pombo is a straight-talking, conservative Western rancher, most comfortable in his cowboy boots and cowboy hat.

In Congress, Pombo's agenda is just what the Marlboro Man would be pushing if he was not off mending fences or rounding up strays — preserving the rights of property owners and reducing the role of the federal government across the board, including fewer regulations and lower taxes.

A fourth generation member of a large Central Valley family that raises dairy and beef cattle and is involved in trucking and real estate, Pombo still lives on the family spread in Tracy where he grew up. He cultivates an image as a straightforward man who stakes out a position and sticks with it. Even his political foes say he is a nice guy, although they criticize his conservative views and his unwillingness to compromise.

In the 108th Congress, Pombo leapfrogged over several more-senior GOP colleagues to win election as chairman of the Resources Committee, where he will wield considerable influence over natural resources policy, his bread-and-butter issue during his decade in Congress.

Pombo's ascension did not sit well with environmentalists, or even some of his GOP colleagues. Colorado's Joel Hefley, one of the Republicans with more seniority on the panel, groused that Pombo's victory was due to his fundraising prowess and that seniority should not have been ignored. Hefley quit the committee shortly thereafter.

Pombo made his feelings about the environmental movement clear when, in 1996, he co-authored "This Land Is Our Land," a book that warned of an "eco-federal coalition" of government regulators and environmental groups with an agenda that "owes more to communism than to any other philosophy." He says he sees better prospects for a decrease in government regulations with a Republican president directing the federal regulatory agencies.

In the 107th, Pombo was chairman of the Western Caucus, a group of several dozen Republican lawmakers (not all of whom are from the West), whose goal is to ensure the preservation of private property rights, access to public lands and local land control. Pombo said he wants to do a better job of educating his congressional colleagues about Western interests. He also was a co-founder of the San Joaquin County Citizen's Land Alliance, a group advancing the interests of property owners.

In both the 106th and 107th Congresses, Pombo opposed a plan to spend billions of dollars for land conservation programs, including the purchase of private land. "I believe the federal government already owns too much land and should not come out West and buy more," he argued in 2001.

Pombo is best-known for his efforts on Resources, where he long has been an important player in the Republican effort to overhaul major environmental statutes, including the 1973 Endangered Species Act. Pombo says the law puts preservation of plants and animals ahead of the well-being of people and treads on the rights of private property owners. "Sound science — not political science" is his rallying cry when discussing endangered species legislation.

When the Republicans took control of the House in 1995, Pombo, even though he had just two years' experience, was given a key role in their efforts to cut back federal environmental regulations. Successes were few and far between; contributing to the difficulty was the fact that Pombo and fellow Republican Sherwood Boehlert of New York — the co-chairmen of a GOP environmental task force — clashed often and were unable to bridge the gap between the environmental views of Western and Eastern Republicans. Since then, Pombo has continued to scuffle periodically with Eastern Republicans on environmental issues, although he has scaled back some of his proposals. He likes to point out that he has sponsored a bill to ban the use of the MTBE additive in gasoline, which reduces harmful emissions but contaminates groundwater.

Pombo also serves on the Agriculture Committee, a key position for his heavily agricultural Central Valley district. For six years, he chaired the Livestock Subcommittee, which put him at the center of regional battles over dairy subsidies. In the 106th Congress, Pombo took the lead in efforts to slow the Environmental Protection Agency's move to ban the use of some common pesticides.

In the 107th he served on the Transportation panel, working for continued funding for the Altamont Commuter Express train between Stockton and San Jose, championing development of high-speed rail in California, and seeking funding for local highway projects in the Central Valley.

Pombo is the grandson of a Portuguese immigrant who came to the Central Valley early in the 20th century. The huge Pombo clan is well-known in the area, and one longtime neighbor told the San Francisco Examiner that he remembers young Richard as a "clean-cut young man from a strict family." He attended college in Southern California for a few years, while working in a slaughterhouse. Pombo did not finish school; instead, he headed back to Tracy and became partners with his father and brothers.

Pombo had served only two years on the Tracy City Council when he was convinced to run for the House in 1992 in the newly drawn 11th District. He was a clear underdog in the primary against Sacramento County Supervisor Sandra Smoley. He won by branding her a liberal, then fended off negative ads in the general election by saying he was a rancher out to defend his neighbors rather than an ambitious politician. Pombo prevailed by 2 percentage points and has since won re-election comfortably.

In 2002, redistricting also gave him substantial chunks of Alameda and Contra Costa counties, and Pombo's re-election campaign centered around whether he fit in with the new constituents who live closer to the San Francisco-Oakland-Berkeley urban areas. But Pombo pointed out that traffic congestion and an array of other suburban issues had already come to San Joaquin County, and that the basic concerns before the voters were the same. He won by more than 20 points.

KEY VOTES

2002

No Overhaul campaign finance law; ban "soft money" and restrict advocacy advertising
Yes Back Bush's defense budget increase
? Extend 1996 welfare law
Yes Adopt Bush's discretionary spending limit
Yes Pass GOP Medicare prescription drug plan
No Create independent Sept. 11 commission
No Extend union protections to Homeland Security Department employees
Yes Revive fast-track procedures for trade agreements
Yes Authorize war against Iraq
No Advance bankruptcy overhaul opposed by abortion opponents

2001

Yes Nullify Clinton Labor Department ergonomics rule
Yes Cut taxes by $1.35 trillion through fiscal 2011
No Maintain ban on oil drilling in Arctic National Wildlife Refuge
Yes Approve Bush proposal to limit managed-care plan liability for coverage decisions
No Divert money from crop subsidy payments to land conservation
Yes Expand law enforcement power to investigate suspected terrorists

CQ VOTE STUDIES

	PARTY UNITY		PRESIDENTIAL SUPPORT	
	Support	Oppose	Support	Oppose
2002	96%	4%	84%	16%
2001	96%	4%	84%	16%
2000	95%	5%	19%	81%
1999	93%	7%	12%	88%
1998	93%	7%	23%	77%

INTEREST GROUPS

	AFL-CIO	ADA	CCUS	ACU
2002	11%	5%	85%	96%
2001	25%	10%	87%	96%
2000	10%	5%	76%	100%
1999	22%	5%	88%	100%
1998	10%	10%	89%	96%

CALIFORNIA 11

San Joaquin Valley; inland East Bay; part of Stockton

A mix of bedroom communities along commuter corridors east of San Francisco Bay and inland developing agricultural country, the 11th has one common thread: conservative tendencies in the voting booth. The district is wrench-shaped, with the handle running along Interstate 680 and south past San Jose, while the northern end surrounds Stockton on three sides (central Stockton is in the 18th District).

The district includes more than 40 percent of Stockton's residents and almost all of surrounding San Joaquin County's area, where farmland is giving way to high-end residential development. Hourlong drives to San Francisco or San Jose can more than double during rush hour. The technology boom has pushed some Bay Area commuters to Stockton, and easing the gridlock is a top concern. The diverse city leans Democratic, but the 11th's portion leans Republican.

Dairy and wine grapes make up the district's biggest agricultural exports. Interstate 205 breaks off from Interstate 5 to head west to San Francisco, making it a key transportation hub. Lodi and Tracy are two main trucking centers through which the district's agricultural products travel. Woodbridge and Lodi produce 40 percent of the state's premium wine grapes — many of which are shipped to the Napa Valley for bottling. Stockton's location as a port city on the San Joaquin River makes it a transportation hub as well.

Residents in the rural, agricultural valley areas are sometimes at odds with their hillier suburban neighbors over water use and the smog that drifts east into the valley.

MAJOR INDUSTRY
Agriculture, technology, service

MILITARY BASES
Defense Distribution Depot San Joaquin, 3 military, 1,644 civilian (2001)

CITIES
Stockton (pt.), 104,409; Pleasanton (pt.), 58,432; Lodi, 56,999; Tracy, 56,929

NOTABLE
Stockton, named for Robert F. Stockton — who proclaimed California as U.S. territory — was the first community in California to have an American name, all others being of Spanish or Native American origin.

Rep. Tom Lantos (D)

CAPITOL OFFICE
225-3531
www.house.gov/lantos
2413 Rayburn 20515-0512; fax 226-9789

COMMITTEES
Government Reform
International Relations - ranking member

HOMETOWN
San Mateo

BORN
Feb. 1, 1928, Budapest, Hungary

RELIGION
Jewish

FAMILY
Wife, Annette Tillemann Lantos; two children

EDUCATION
U. of Washington, B.A. 1949, M.A. 1950; U. of California, Berkeley, Ph.D. 1953 (economics)

CAREER
Professor; congressional aide

POLITICAL HIGHLIGHTS
Millbrae School District Board of Trustees, 1959-66 (president, 1960-61, 1965-66)

ELECTION RESULTS

2002 GENERAL		
Tom Lantos (D)	105,597	68.1%
Michael Moloney (R)	38,381	24.8%
M. Abu-Ghazalah (LIBERT)	11,006	7.1%
2002 PRIMARY		
Tom Lantos (D)		unopposed
2000 GENERAL		
Tom Lantos (D)	158,404	74.5%
Mike Garza (R)	44,162	20.8%
Barbara Less (LIBERT)	6,431	3.0%
Rifkin Young (NL)	3,559	1.7%

PREVIOUS WINNING PERCENTAGES
1998 (74%); 1996 (72%); 1994 (67%); 1992 (69%); 1990 (66%); 1988 (71%); 1986 (74%); 1984 (70%); 1982 (57%); 1980 (46%)

Elected 1980; 12th term

Lantos has become an unexpected and valuable ally of President Bush and House Majority Leader Tom DeLay on foreign policy issues, particularly those affecting the Middle East.

Their alliance is both personal and philosophical. Bush's national security adviser, Condoleezza Rice, befriended Lantos during her time as provost at Stanford University, so now he has ready access to a key administration policymaker.

At the same time, Lantos, DeLay and many of Bush's foreign policy advisers share a muscular view of foreign policy in which they seek to employ unquestioned military dominance and perceived moral authority to right global wrongs. In Lantos' case, this view is rooted in personal experience: The top Democrat on the International Relations Committee is a Hungarian-born Holocaust survivor who was a fighter in the Nazi resistance in Budapest.

The GOP-Lantos alliance has had the most impact on U.S. policy toward the Middle East. Like Republican neoconservatives, Lantos believes that a strong assertion of U.S. power can transform the region in the U.S. interest. Perhaps the House's most influential Jewish lawmaker, he pushed early for military action against Saddam Hussein, backs a tough Israeli stand against the Palestinian Authority, has sharply criticized Saudi Arabia for financing terrorism and has backed new sanctions on Iran and Libya. Lantos has criticized some elements of the proposed "Marshall Plan" for the Middle East written by his committee chairman, Republican Henry J. Hyde of Illinois, as too timid in its attempts to bring democracy to the region.

After becoming top-ranking panel Democrat in the 107th Congress, Lantos played an important behind-the-scenes role in helping Minority Leader Richard A. Gephardt and the White House write the 2002 resolution authorizing a war against Iraq. Then, Lantos joined with Hyde to ensure the measure would sail through the panel and the House with sufficient Democratic support. "Had the United States and its allies confronted Hitler earlier, had we acted sooner to stymie his evil designs, the 51 million lives needlessly lost during that war could have been saved," he said.

Indeed, it is Lantos, not Hyde, who often plays the driving role in setting the committee's agenda and thus the House's foreign policy stance. Hyde learned a painful lesson about Lantos' power soon after taking the International Relations gavel in the 107th. At Lantos' urging, the committee defied Hyde by approving a State Department authorization bill that overturned anti-abortion restrictions on family planning assistance that Hyde had championed. Since then, Hyde has rarely moved legislation without Lantos' support, and he often advances Lantos' proposals.

In working with Republicans on the Middle East, Lantos has broken from the views of his fellow Bay Area lawmakers and many of his constituents. On other issues, Lantos' expansive world view fits better with liberal orthodoxy. He has long been one of Congress' most vigorous defenders of human rights overseas. In the 107th, he shepherded through Congress legislation to improve rule-of-law programs in Russia and attempted to cut off imports from Myanmar to force its military dictatorship toward democracy. He also tried unsuccessfully to block China from hosting the Olympics in 2008 because of its human rights record.

Bush recognized Lantos' interest in human rights when he asked the Californian in the 107th to lead an effort to repeal Cold War trade restrictions on Russia that had been imposed to encourage the Soviet government to allow Jewish emigration. Lantos also led a successful effort to have the United States rejoin the United Nations Educational, Scientific, and Cultural Organization, which it had left two decades earlier amid disputes over UNESCO's alleged anti-American and anti-Israel bias.

Lantos is eloquent and intellectual — some say haughty — with the courtly air of a man bred in prewar Central Europe. There is no desk in his congressional office, only settees and chairs, and visitors are offered tea. His wife, Annette, is a regular presence in the office.

Resolute and self-assured, Lantos is determined to defeat his opponents. And the Republican-controlled House has given him plenty of opportunity to practice his verbal warfare. As the No. 2 Democrat on the Government Reform Committee in the 105th Congress, Lantos was irked by the GOP conduct of an investigation of the fundraising practices of President Clinton's 1996 re-election campaign. He took aim at Independent Counsel Donald C. Smaltz for neglecting to declare his GOP affiliation. The congressman compared Smaltz to U.N. Secretary General Kurt Waldheim, who, Lantos said, "conveniently forgot several years when he was a Nazi."

In 1997, GOP Rep. Tom Coburn of Oklahoma said that when NBC had broadcast the Holocaust film "Schindler's List," it had reached "an all-time low with full frontal nudity, violence and profanity." Lantos, who labored in a Nazi work camp in 1944 and then escaped, held a news conference in rebuttal. "I find it far less discouraging that some child may have learned a four-letter word," he said. "I am more concerned about the 1.5 million children killed in the Holocaust." Coburn apologized the next day.

Lantos was working as a consultant to the Senate Foreign Relations Committee when Republican Bill Royer won a 1979 special House election to replace Democrat Leo J. Ryan, who had been assassinated the year before in Jonestown, Guyana. Well-known within loyal Democratic circles, Lantos left his job right after Royer's victory and began preparing for a challenge in 1980. The one-time economics professor at San Francisco State University had held elective office only as a suburban school board president, but he took advantage of the incumbent's overconfidence and won by 3 percentage points. Lantos put down Royer's comeback attempt by 17 points in 1982, and he has topped 65 percent in every election since.

Lantos served from 1991 through 1994 with his son-in-law, Dick Swett, a New Hampshire Democrat. In 2002, he put much of his personal energies and fundraising muscle behind electing his daughter Katrina Swett to Congress. But she lost to Republican Charles Bass, just as her husband had.

KEY VOTES

2002

Yes Overhaul campaign finance law; ban "soft money" and restrict advocacy advertising
Yes Back Bush's defense budget increase
No Extend 1996 welfare law
No Adopt Bush's discretionary spending limit
No Pass GOP Medicare prescription drug plan
Yes Create independent Sept. 11 commission
Yes Extend union protections to Homeland Security Department employees
No Revive fast-track procedures for trade agreements
Yes Authorize war against Iraq
No Advance bankruptcy overhaul opposed by abortion opponents

2001

No Nullify Clinton Labor Department ergonomics rule
No Cut taxes by $1.35 trillion through fiscal 2011
Yes Maintain ban on oil drilling in Arctic National Wildlife Refuge
No Approve Bush proposal to limit managed-care plan liability for coverage decisions
Yes Divert money from crop subsidy payments to land conservation
Yes Expand law enforcement power to investigate suspected terrorists

CQ VOTE STUDIES

	PARTY UNITY		PRESIDENTIAL SUPPORT	
	Support	Oppose	Support	Oppose
2002	94%	6%	20%	80%
2001	96%	4%	26%	74%
2000	98%	2%	87%	13%
1999	96%	4%	83%	17%
1998	95%	5%	81%	19%

INTEREST GROUPS

	AFL-CIO	ADA	CCUS	ACU
2002	100%	95%	30%	4%
2001	100%	95%	30%	8%
2000	100%	85%	47%	4%
1999	100%	85%	14%	0%
1998	100%	100%	33%	8%

CALIFORNIA 12

Part of San Mateo County; most of western San Francisco

A mix of scenic coastal mountains and bayside commuter traffic jams, the 12th lies between its two well-known neighbors of San Francisco and the Silicon Valley.

The district includes a western section of San Francisco, but most residents live in heavily populated San Mateo County suburbs, either in Daly City or between two main commuter routes — the Junipero Serra Freeway (Interstate 280) and Bayshore Freeway (U.S. Highway 101). The 12th also covers a portion of Pacific coastline from the Great Highway in San Francisco through Pacifica to Moss Beach, and the district stretches southeast to San Carlos and part of Redwood City, about halfway to San Jose.

Despite a downturn in the 12th's high-tech economy and in Silicon Valley to the south, real estate prices have continued to rise in one of the highest-demand retail markets in the country. The district's largest employer remains San Francisco International Airport, though a number of biotechnology firms have set up shop in the South San Francisco area, making biotechnology one of the area's leading industries. Almost 30 percent of the district's residents are Asian, with Daly City home to the district's highest concentration. The Farallon Islands, a national wildlife refuge about 30 miles west of San Francisco, also belong to the district.

District residents cover a wide range of the political spectrum, but Democrats hold a strong edge in voter registration. At the southern end of the district, residents of the affluent communities of Burlingame and Hillsborough are more conservative, while voters in the San Francisco area are more Democratic.

MAJOR INDUSTRY

Biotechnology, airport, software

CITIES

San Francisco (pt.), 137,645; Daly City, 103,621; San Mateo, 92,482

NOTABLE

The Museum of Pez Memorabilia is in Burlingame; Daly City has the largest concentration of Filipinos outside of the Philippines; Software firm Oracle's corporate headquarters are in Redwood Shores.

Rep. Pete Stark (D)

CAPITOL OFFICE
225-5065
www.house.gov/stark
239 Cannon 20515-0513; fax 226-3805

COMMITTEES
Ways & Means
Joint Economic - ranking member
Joint Taxation

HOMETOWN
Hayward

BORN
Nov. 11, 1931, Milwaukee, Wis.

RELIGION
Unitarian

FAMILY
Wife, Deborah Roderick Stark; seven children

EDUCATION
Massachusetts Institute of Technology, B.S. 1953 (engineering); U. of California, Berkeley, M.B.A. 1960

MILITARY SERVICE
Air Force, 1955-57

CAREER
Banker

POLITICAL HIGHLIGHTS
Sought Democratic nomination for Calif. Senate, 1969

ELECTION RESULTS

2002 GENERAL		
Pete Stark (D)	86,495	71.1%
Syed R. Mahmood (R)	26,852	22.1%
Mark W. Stroberg (LIBERT)	3,703	3.0%
Don Grundmann (AMI)	2,772	2.3%
John J. Bambey (REF)	1,901	1.6%
2002 PRIMARY		
Pete Stark (D)		unopposed
2000 GENERAL		
Pete Stark (D)	129,012	70.4%
James Goetz (R)	44,499	24.3%
Howard Mora (LIBERT)	4,623	2.5%

PREVIOUS WINNING PERCENTAGES
1998 (71%); 1996 (65%); 1994 (65%); 1992 (60%); 1990 (58%); 1988 (73%); 1986 (70%); 1984 (70%); 1982 (61%); 1980 (55%); 1978 (65%); 1976 (71%); 1974 (71%); 1972 (53%)

Elected 1972; 16th term

During three decades in Congress, Stark has built a reputation as one of Congress' premier experts on health policy, pushing a liberal agenda calling for health insurance for all Americans and a prescription drug benefit for Medicare recipients.

While he gets results, Stark's efforts sometimes are undercut by an abrasive and confrontational personality. His sharp tongue makes even fellow Democrats squirm at times. When the party fared poorly in the 2002 congressional elections, Stark urged House Minority Leader Richard A. Gephardt and Senate Democratic leader Tom Daschle to resign. "Gephardt in particular has done a lousy job of running the [Democratic] caucus," he said.

With a liberal's faith in the ability of government to improve the lot of the underprivileged, Stark is a leader of Democratic efforts to add prescription drug coverage to Medicare and to give patients more power over their managed-care plans. He is the second-ranking Democrat on the powerful Ways and Means panel, and the top Democrat on its Health Subcommittee.

Stark has no use for GOP proposals in recent years to have insurance companies develop and sell prescription drug policies to the more than 40 million senior citizens and disabled people on Medicare. He advocates letting the federal government develop a plan on its own, at significantly higher cost to taxpayers. Stark likes to say that you can't create a meaningful prescription drug benefit "on the cheap."

He speaks from hard experience. In 1988, Stark and Ways and Means Chairman Dan Rostenkowski of Illinois reached what should have been a milestone in their careers with passage of the Catastrophic Health Care Act, which created broad new benefits under Medicare. But senior citizens across the country rose up in protest — a group of them even chased Rostenkowski's car — complaining about the new out-of-pocket costs of the program. The next year, the law was ignominiously repealed.

In the 107th Congress, Stark pushed a plan by a bipartisan coalition to give patients new powers to sue their health insurers in disputes over the delivery or denial of care. Republican leaders argued that the legislation would escalate health care costs and cause millions of workers to lose their insurance. The bill eventually stalled.

Stark is sometimes willing to hold his nose and work with Republicans. Since 1995, when the GOP gained the majority, he has helped win new preventative care benefits for Medicare beneficiaries and pushed Congress to reduce out-of-pocket costs for hospital outpatient services. And he won passage of a bill requiring medical facilities to use safer blood-drawing devices. But he failed to block more funding for Medicare HMOs, which he said were poorly managed.

Stark may be best-known for two laws enacted in 1989 and 1993, known as "Stark I" and "Stark II." They strictly regulate physician referrals of Medicare patients to medical facilities in which the doctors have a financial interest, such as laboratories and physical therapy clinics.

Success on that front was quickly followed by disappointment. In 1994, Stark worked with President Clinton to promote universal health care. Although he wasn't entirely happy with the legislation that emerged from his panel, it was at least movement toward his vision of making health care universally available. The bill narrowly got through committee but was ultimately rejected by Congress as too complex and too far-reaching.

On other key issues, Stark toes the Democratic line. He sided with his party 99 percent of the time in 2002 on votes that pitted the two parties against each other. In the 107th, he was one of three lawmakers who declined to condemn a controversial court decision declaring the words "under God" in the Pledge of Allegiance unconstitutional. In 2002, Stark opposed the measure allowing the use of force against Iraq and called President Bush "an inexperienced, desperate young man."

Stark, whose blue-collar district is becoming increasingly more dependent on the high-tech economy, is blunt in his criticisms of that industry. In 1998, he voted against an industry-backed bill to boost the number of visas for temporary foreign workers. "High-tech has been among the selfish and least helpful corporations in the country," Stark told the San Francisco Chronicle. "All they've ever done is come to us and ask for tax breaks and free trade. They're all take and no give."

Though he speaks his mind, Stark also has learned the hard way to tone down his comments. In 1995, he lashed out at Republican Nancy L. Johnson, calling the widely respected Connecticut lawmaker a "whore for the insurance industry." He issued an apology after 32 women lawmakers demanded one.

Stark grew up in Wisconsin and graduated from the Massachusetts Institute of Technology. After serving in the Air Force in the 1950s, he moved West and got a master's degree in business from the University of California at Berkeley. Though he chose a traditional line of work — at age 31 he had already founded two banks — he became a rabid opponent of the war in Vietnam. He even raised a huge neon peace symbol over one of his banks in suburban Walnut Creek.

In 1969, he made his first bid for public office, losing a primary race for a state legislative seat to George Miller, then a young law school student and now a House colleague. Three years later, Stark decided to take on another George Miller, this one an old-school conservative who had represented Oakland in Congress as a Democrat for 28 years.

Stark spent his money generously and made Miller's support of the Vietnam War a major issue on the way to a primary win. The November election was competitive, but Stark managed 53 percent.

Only once since then has Stark had a close call. Lulled by years of easy re-elections, he made only a token effort in the 1980 election. Conservative Republican William J. Kennedy, a tireless campaigner, galvanized a host of volunteers in the midst of Ronald Reagan's first presidential landslide and held Stark to 55 percent.

KEY VOTES

2002

Yes Overhaul campaign finance law; ban "soft money" and restrict advocacy advertising
No Back Bush's defense budget increase
No Extend 1996 welfare law
No Adopt Bush's discretionary spending limit
No Pass GOP Medicare prescription drug plan
Yes Create independent Sept. 11 commission
Yes Extend union protections to Homeland Security Department employees
No Revive fast-track procedures for trade agreements
No Authorize war against Iraq
No Advance bankruptcy overhaul opposed by abortion opponents

2001

No Nullify Clinton Labor Department ergonomics rule
No Cut taxes by $1.35 trillion through fiscal 2011
? Maintain ban on oil drilling in Arctic National Wildlife Refuge
No Approve Bush proposal to limit managed-care plan liability for coverage decisions
Yes Divert money from crop subsidy payments to land conservation
No Expand law enforcement power to investigate suspected terrorists

CQ VOTE STUDIES

	PARTY UNITY		PRESIDENTIAL SUPPORT	
	Support	Oppose	Support	Oppose
2002	99%	1%	23%	77%
2001	97%	3%	19%	81%
2000	96%	4%	81%	19%
1999	95%	5%	75%	25%
1998	98%	2%	87%	13%

INTEREST GROUPS

	AFL-CIO	ADA	CCUS	ACU
2002	100%	100%	26%	0%
2001	100%	95%	26%	0%
2000	100%	95%	25%	4%
1999	100%	85%	8%	8%
1998	100%	90%	6%	8%

CALIFORNIA 13

East Bay — Fremont, Hayward, Alameda

Bordered by San Francisco Bay to the west, Silicon Valley to the south and Oakland to the north, the 13th is an industrially and culturally diverse suburban area. The district is dotted with many working-class communities and often is described as the less glamorous side of the bay, but its large Hispanic and Asian populations — including immigrants from India, China, Afghanistan and the Philippines — have flourished culturally. The area's blue-collar industry historically has given Democrats a solid base of support.

Fremont and Hayward are the two largest cities in the district. Hayward is home to a campus of the California State University system; Fremont's General Motors-Toyota joint auto plant employs more than 5,000. Both cities have become more oriented toward technology industries as Silicon Valley has extended its influence to the East Bay. The population of the Tri-City area — Newark, Fremont and Union City — has grown by nearly 120,000 since 1980 and the region's high-tech industry has grown beside it. Computer manufacturers, including Hewlett-Packard and Sun Microsystems, have offices there. San Leandro, just south of Oakland, is home to a Coca-Cola plant, as well as Otis Spunkmeyer's cookie empire and The North Face, which produces outdoor equipment.

Alameda's closed Naval Air Station in the north is being converted into homes and recreational facilities. The island city features 100-year-old Victorian homes and hosts a museum aboard the USS Hornet, a World War II aircraft carrier. Oakland International Airport falls within the 13th's boundaries, though Oakland itself is located in the neighboring 9th.

MAJOR INDUSTRY

Electronics, industrial machinery, food product processing

CITIES

Fremont, 203,413; Hayward, 140,030; San Leandro, 79,452

NOTABLE

Ghirardelli Chocolate, the nation's longest continuously operating chocolate manufacturer, has headquarters in San Leandro; Fremont is home to Mission San Jose, which was founded by Father Fermin Lasuen in 1797.

Rep. Anna G. Eshoo (D)

CAPITOL OFFICE
225-8104
annagram@mail.house.gov
www.house.gov/eshoo
205 Cannon 20515-0514; fax 225-8890

COMMITTEES
Energy & Commerce
Select Intelligence

HOMETOWN
Atherton

BORN
Dec. 13, 1942, New Britain, Conn.

RELIGION
Roman Catholic

FAMILY
Divorced; two children

EDUCATION
Canada College, A.A. 1975 (English)

CAREER
State legislative aide

POLITICAL HIGHLIGHTS
Candidate for San Mateo County Community College District Board of Trustees, 1977; Democratic National Committee, 1980-92; San Mateo County Board of Supervisors, 1982-92 (president, 1986); Democratic nominee for U.S. House, 1988

ELECTION RESULTS

2002 GENERAL		
Anna G. Eshoo (D)	117,055	68.2%
Joseph H. Nixon (R)	48,346	28.2%
Andrew B. Carver (LIBERT)	6,277	3.7%
2002 PRIMARY		
Anna G. Eshoo (D)		unopposed
2000 GENERAL		
Anna G. Eshoo (D)	161,720	70.2%
Bill Quraishi (R)	59,338	25.8%
Joseph W. Dehn III (LIBERT)	4,715	2.1%
John H. Black (NL)	4,489	2.0%

PREVIOUS WINNING PERCENTAGES
1998 (69%); 1996 (65%); 1994 (61%); 1992 (57%)

Elected 1992; 6th term

The daughter of immigrants who instilled in her a deep appreciation of the privileges of living in the United States, after a decade in the House Eshoo has developed a means to move smoothly between her two main roles: On the Energy and Commerce Committee, she is a consensus builder with pro-business leanings on technology and health care matters. And she is a close friend and confidante of Democratic leader Nancy Pelosi, a fellow Northern Californian. In the 108th Congress, Pelosi named Eshoo to the Intelligence Committee.

Her childhood was preparation for her adult life in public office, although she did not take that route until she was well into her 30s. "In our prayers at dinner, we thanked God for the food and also thanked God for this country," she says in recalling her childhood. "My parents very much shaped a sense of obligation to give and to do." She was a civic activist, even as a full-time homemaker and mother of young children, and then moved into the realm of electoral politics as her children got older.

That career path is similar to Pelosi's, and by operating in similar Democratic circles the two have been acquainted for more than 30 years. Their shared passion for politics now blossoms during shared late-night dinners of Vietnamese noodle soup and ice cream in Georgetown. "I like vanilla with chocolate chips. Nancy is a total chocoholic. In a way, that's the basic difference between us," Eshoo said.

Now in her sixth term representing Silicon Valley, Eshoo (EH-shoo) is a New Democrat centrist — liberal on many issues but a firm believer in business development and risk-taking entrepreneurship. After the Sept. 11, 2001, terrorist attacks, Eshoo helped the high-tech industry that is at the core of her district's economy adjust its legislative priorities to fit growing concerns about national security and privacy. Eshoo backed efforts to limit the sharing among federal agencies of information collected from borrowers, farmers and taxpayers. She remained a champion of looser export rules for computer hardware and encryption software, on grounds that overseas buyers could get similar products from foreign manufacturers so the national security was not so much at risk.

Eshoo said that the economic downturn of 2001 influenced her decision to vote that December and again the next July against a bill to give the president fast-track authority to negotiate agreements that Congress cannot amend. She had voted for a similar bill in 1997, for the North American Free Trade Agreement in 1993, for the creation of the World Trade Organization the next year and for the establishment of permanent normal trade relations with China in 2000.

While trying to pressure Republicans to support more aid for displaced workers, Eshoo continued in the 107th Congress to burnish her reputation as a dealmaker on health care and technology issues. She and Pennsylvania Republican James C. Greenwood worked out an agreement on a measure to streamline Food and Drug Administration approval procedures for complex medical devices — language that went beyond the terms of a 1997 law Eshoo had helped write. She reached another compromise with Republicans to extend a law that gives pharmaceutical companies an extra six months on expiring drug patents to tailor and test treatment plans for children.

In the 106th Congress, Eshoo solidified a reputation for mastery of details in technology-related legislation. She championed enactment of a law to authorize the use of "electronic signatures" to seal some contracts. Her work on the measure had begun in the 105th.

On social issues and the environment, Eshoo has a reputation as a reliable liberal. She supports abortion rights and favors gun control.

Eshoo's pro-business stands have at times put her at odds with Democratic leaders. In 1995, she helped override President Clinton's veto of a measure to limit lawsuits by disgruntled investors — one of only two laws enacted over a Clinton veto. And in the 106th Congress, Eshoo initially joined with Republicans in voting to end the estate tax, but she rejoined the party fold later in voting to sustain Clinton's veto of the measure. She also voted consistently in the 107th against the various components of Bush's signature tax cut.

Eshoo has sought to require insurance companies to pay for reconstructive breast surgery if they pay for cancer-related mastectomies. And she pushed for Medicaid coverage for treatment of breast and cervical cancers detected in Medicaid-covered screening programs.

The daughter of immigrants from Armenia and modern-day Iran, Eshoo was drawn to Democratic politics in her native New Britain, Conn. Her father, a jeweler and watchmaker, took the family to political rallies and hung portraits of Franklin D. Roosevelt and Harry S Truman in their home. One day, as she was walking home from grade school, a man in a big car drove by with a police escort, stopped and offered her a ride. Eshoo accepted the lift — from President Truman. As a high school senior, she organized more than 800 students to work for John F. Kennedy. "Back then, I really thought that I was the one who put him over the top."

The family moved to California, and Eshoo married young and devoted herself mostly to raising two children. She was active in the PTA and civic groups such as the League of Women Voters, earned a two-year associate's degree in English literature, and then, at 34, lost a race for the local community college board of trustees.

Eshoo got an internship with Leo McCarthy, speaker of the California Assembly, and eventually became his chief of staff. Active in local party politics, she won appointment to the Democratic National Committee. In 1982, McCarthy urged her to run for the San Mateo County Board of Supervisors. That post, which she held for a decade, shaped her pragmatic philosophy.

In 1988, Eshoo ran unsuccessfully for the House against Republican Tom Campbell, taking a solid 46 percent. Four years later, she tried again and won, boosted by a redrawn district map that added more Democratic voters and by Campbell's decision to run for the Senate. With her high-tech interests and her energy, she has co-opted business support from the GOP, and her subsequent elections have come without major difficulty.

KEY VOTES

2002

Yes Overhaul campaign finance law; ban "soft money" and restrict advocacy advertising
No Back Bush's defense budget increase
No Extend 1996 welfare law
No Adopt Bush's discretionary spending limit
No Pass GOP Medicare prescription drug plan
Yes Create independent Sept. 11 commission
Yes Extend union protections to Homeland Security Department employees
No Revive fast-track procedures for trade agreements
No Authorize war against Iraq
No Advance bankruptcy overhaul opposed by abortion opponents

2001

No Nullify Clinton Labor Department ergonomics rule
No Cut taxes by $1.35 trillion through fiscal 2011
Yes Maintain ban on oil drilling in Arctic National Wildlife Refuge
No Approve Bush proposal to limit managed-care plan liability for coverage decisions
Yes Divert money from crop subsidy payments to land conservation
Yes Expand law enforcement power to investigate suspected terrorists

CQ VOTE STUDIES

	PARTY UNITY		PRESIDENTIAL SUPPORT	
	Support	Oppose	Support	Oppose
2002	95%	5%	24%	76%
2001	90%	10%	33%	67%
2000	89%	11%	82%	18%
1999	90%	10%	85%	15%
1998	95%	5%	90%	10%

INTEREST GROUPS

	AFL-CIO	ADA	CCUS	ACU
2002	100%	100%	42%	0%
2001	100%	95%	39%	0%
2000	70%	75%	55%	8%
1999	56%	95%	28%	4%
1998	89%	90%	39%	0%

CALIFORNIA 14

Southern San Mateo and northwestern Santa Clara counties; most of Santa Cruz County

The 14th's economic center is Palo Alto, home to Stanford University and tech giants such as Hewlett-Packard. This Silicon Valley stronghold known for innovation has undergone tremendous economic growth since the 1980s. The orchards surrounding Stanford have given way to some of the nation's most expensive housing, even after the technology bubble burst.

The district borders the bay and the Pacific, creeping north toward the San Francisco suburbs and south into Santa Cruz County, almost to the Monterey County line. Most residents live in cities along the bay between San Francisco and San Jose, including Sunnyvale, Mountain View and Redwood City. Labor from large numbers of Asians and Hispanics aided the tech boom. Soaring housing prices, though stable in the past few years, and traffic snarls were the major results.

The 14th's innovation-minded voters are liberal on many social issues but prefer a laissez faire government that does not impede change. Environmental consciousness is high, particularly in Santa Cruz County. Conservative pockets do exist in wealthy areas such as Saratoga and Monte Sereno in Santa Clara County, but Democrats hold a 15 percentage point edge in voter registration and the district gave Democrat Al Gore 59 percent of the vote in the 2000 presidential election.

MAJOR INDUSTRY

Computers, biotechnology, defense, agriculture

MILITARY BASES

Onizuka Air Force Station, 125 military, 165 civilian (2002)

CITIES

Sunnyvale, 131,760; Mountain View, 70,708; Palo Alto, 58,598; Redwood City (pt.), 52,873

NOTABLE

A water tower painted as a Libby's fruit cocktail can stands where the cannery operated in Sunnyvale; Hangar One at Moffett Federal Airfield (now a NASA research station) housed a blimp for the Navy; Hewlett-Packard was founded in 1939 in a Palo Alto garage, which is now a tourist attraction; Half Moon Bay holds an annual pumpkin festival.

Rep. Michael M. Honda (D)

CAPITOL OFFICE
225-2631
mike.honda@mail.house.gov
www.house.gov/honda
1713 Longworth 20515-0515; fax 225-2699

COMMITTEES
Science
Transportation & Infrastructure

HOMETOWN
San Jose

BORN
June 27, 1941, Stockton, Calif.

RELIGION
Protestant

FAMILY
Wife, Jeanne Honda; two children

EDUCATION
San Jose State U., B.S. 1969 (biological sciences), B.A. 1970 (Spanish), M.A. 1973 (education)

CAREER
Teacher; principal; Peace Corps volunteer

POLITICAL HIGHLIGHTS
San Jose School Board, 1981-90; Santa Clara County Board of Supervisors, 1990-96; Calif. Assembly, 1996-2000

ELECTION RESULTS

2002 GENERAL		
Michael M. Honda (D)	87,482	65.8%
Linda Rae Hermann (R)	41,251	31.0%
Jeff Landauer (LIBERT)	4,289	3.2%
2002 PRIMARY		
Michael M. Honda (D)		unopposed
2000 GENERAL		
Michael M. Honda (D)	128,545	54.3%
Jim Cunneen (R)	99,866	42.2%
Ed Wimmers (LIBERT)	4,820	2.0%
Douglas Gorney (NL)	3,591	1.5%

Elected 2000; 2nd term

Born to nisei farm workers in what is now called Silicon Valley, Honda was just a few months old when the Japanese launched a surprise attack on Pearl Harbor. He and his family were shipped off to an internment camp in Colorado, where they spent about two and a half years before they were able to move to Chicago when his dad joined Navy intelligence.

Sixty years later, when terrorists carried out the Sept. 11, 2001, attacks against the United States, Honda was one of the most outspoken members of the House in working to ensure that other Americans were not treated like his family in 1941 only because "we looked like the enemy."

Honda wrote President Bush expressing concern about "government-sanctioned racial profiling." And he joined with fellow California Democrat Robert T. Matsui, whose family was also interned during World War II, in speaking out against reports of harassment and attacks on Arab-Americans, Muslims and members of other ethnic groups.

"We can seek out the perpetrators without victimizing our citizens," Honda told the Oakland Tribune. "Targeting people because they have the same religion or ethnic background, that's not the American way, even if it has been a part of American history," he said. He and Matsui felt "a particular responsibility based upon a unique experience," he told The Associated Press.

Representing a district that includes a healthy slice of California's Silicon Valley, Honda has a congressional agenda that is appropriately centered on the high-technology industry. He formed a bipartisan Mobile Commerce Task Force to discuss issues facing the development of wireless technology. He favors the repeal of export controls on high-performance computers and permanent renewal of the research and development tax credit. In the 108th he introduced a bill calling for a beefed-up federal effort in research into nanotechnology, the manipulation of matter at the level of a single atom. Reflecting the attention he pays to technology issues, Honda's congressional Web site was named one of the best on Capitol Hill by the independent Congressional Management Foundation.

Yet his focus is not solely on the business side of technology development. Honda also advocates for better computer education, which he says will help train the next generation of high-tech workers. He supports expanding the "e-rate" program that provides federal money to help wire schools and libraries to the Internet. He sees advantages for Silicon Valley companies in increased federal funding for training adults in technology skills. He was involved in the drafting of cyber-security legislation to safeguard private and government computers. And he cosponsored legislation that responded to the Sept. 11 attacks to require cutting-edge technology, such as retinal scanning, at certain airports to improve security.

Honda also wants to find regional solutions and federal funding to deal with the downside of his district's recent economic boom, including traffic congestion and high housing costs. "Because this is the economic engine of the country, if we don't solve the problems here, the efficiency of the economy will come down," he said.

In the 107th Congress, Honda worked with local officials to build support for an extension of the Bay Area Rapid Transit system (BART) to San Jose, and he used his seat on the Transportation and Infrastructure Committee to press for federal funds for the mass transit system.

Honda remembers little of his internment. He was too young, and he said his parents were reluctant to talk about it afterward. But Honda was a key participant in the Japanese-American community in the effort that resulted in the 1988 law providing a formal apology and compensation to Japanese-Americans who were interned during World War II. That effort inspired Honda, once he reached Congress, to work for reparations for Americans who were prisoners of the Japanese during the war. In 2001, he and California GOP Rep. Dana Rohrabacher cosponsored a bill to reopen the peace treaty with Japan to demand that Japanese companies pay slave-labor compensation to former POWs.

Honda said his parents were always civic-minded despite their internment experience. The family moved back to California in 1953 and his parents became strawberry sharecroppers. Honda took janitorial and delivery jobs to pay his way through San Jose State University. He was one credit shy of graduation when, unsure of what to do next, he joined the new overseas volunteer effort, called the Peace Corps.

After a two-year stint in El Salvador, where he built schools and medical clinics, he returned to California to finish college. He took a job as a science teacher and later served as a principal.

Fluent in Spanish from his years in El Salvador, Honda developed strong ties to San Jose's Hispanic community. He went to Norman Y. Mineta, then a city councilman, to volunteer his services to the city. When Mineta was elected mayor, Honda received an appointment to the city planning commission. Mineta, who went on to serve in Congress and as a member of the Cabinet in both the Clinton and George W. Bush administrations, has remained Honda's friend and mentor.

Honda's 1971 appointment to the planning commission led to elected posts at the local school board, the county board of supervisors and in 1996, election to the California Assembly.

When moderate Republican Rep. Tom Campbell left the 15th District open in 2000 to run for the Senate, Democrats viewed it as a prime opportunity. But it took a phone call from President Clinton just before the candidate filing deadline to persuade Honda to make the race. Honda wanted to make sure the national party would provide necessary backing for his bid. The campaign against GOP state Rep. Jim Cunneen, a Campbell protégé, was hard-fought, but Honda wound up winning in the Democratic-leaning district by 12 percentage points.

In 2002, bolstered by redistricting and his ties to the Asian and Hispanic communities in a district where almost half the residents are from those constituencies, Honda cruised to re-election by a better than 2-to-1 ratio.

KEY VOTES

2002

Yes Overhaul campaign finance law; ban "soft money" and restrict advocacy advertising
No Back Bush's defense budget increase
No Extend 1996 welfare law
No Adopt Bush's discretionary spending limit
No Pass GOP Medicare prescription drug plan
Yes Create independent Sept. 11 commission
Yes Extend union protections to Homeland Security Department employees
No Revive fast-track procedures for trade agreements
No Authorize war against Iraq
No Advance bankruptcy overhaul opposed by abortion opponents

2001

No Nullify Clinton Labor Department ergonomics rule
– Cut taxes by $1.35 trillion through fiscal 2011
Yes Maintain ban on oil drilling in Arctic National Wildlife Refuge
No Approve Bush proposal to limit managed-care plan liability for coverage decisions
Yes Divert money from crop subsidy payments to land conservation
No Expand law enforcement power to investigate suspected terrorists

CQ VOTE STUDIES

	PARTY UNITY		PRESIDENTIAL SUPPORT	
	Support	Oppose	Support	Oppose
2002	99%	1%	21%	79%
2001	95%	5%	24%	76%

INTEREST GROUPS

	AFL-CIO	ADA	CCUS	ACU
2002	100%	95%	30%	0%
2001	100%	95%	39%	0%

CALIFORNIA 15

Santa Clara County — part of San Jose

Home to one-third of San Jose's residents, the 15th touches the southern end of San Francisco Bay in the north, then descends inland through Silicon Valley to still-rural but fast-growing farm towns.

The district has a diverse population that includes one of the nation's heaviest concentrations of Asian-Americans outside of Hawaii. Slightly less than 30 percent of residents are Asian, the highest percentage in any California district. Vietnamese, Chinese and Filipino Americans have flocked to the north to take white- and blue-collar jobs, while Hispanics, 17 percent of the 15th's population, make up a big part of the labor force in the south. Immigration is the top issue caseworkers face.

West of San Jose, the district includes Santa Clara, a Spanish mission in the late 1700s, and other more affluent suburbs including Campbell, Cupertino and Los Gatos. These areas house high-tech companies that boomed in the 1990s but have suffered higher unemployment since the tech bubble burst. Housing — stable but still quite expensive — and transit troubles plague the area. The economy remains technology-based, however, and Sun Microsystems is based in Santa Clara.

To the south, Gilroy's famous garlic farms anchor a more traditionally Democratic agricultural community. But open land is quickly being snatched up as the San Jose suburbs continue to bulge southward.

The district gave 58 percent to Democrat Al Gore in the 2000 presidential election, though if any political trend is apparent here it is an increase in independent voters who seek moderation. Generally liberal on environmental and social issues, voters also favor less government regulation of business.

MAJOR INDUSTRY

Computers, biotechnology, health care, agriculture

CITIES

San Jose (pt.), 295,018; Santa Clara, 102,361; Milpitas, 62,698

NOTABLE

Santa Clara University, founded in 1851, is California's oldest institution of higher learning; Winchester Mystery House in San Jose is a 160-room Victorian mansion famous for oddities such as staircases that lead nowhere; Apple Computer was founded in Cupertino; Gilroy is known as the "Garlic Capital of the World."

Rep. Zoe Lofgren (D)

CAPITOL OFFICE
225-3072
zoe.lofgren@mail.house.gov
www.house.gov/lofgren
102 Cannon 20515-0516; fax 225-3336

COMMITTEES
Judiciary
Science
Select Homeland Security

HOMETOWN
San Jose

BORN
Dec. 21, 1947, San Mateo, Calif.

RELIGION
Unspecified

FAMILY
Husband, John Marshall Collins; two children

EDUCATION
Stanford U., A.B. 1970 (political science); Santa Clara U., J.D. 1975

CAREER
Lawyer; nonprofit housing development director; professor; congressional aide

POLITICAL HIGHLIGHTS
San Jose-Evergreen Community College District Board of Trustees, 1979-81; Santa Clara County Board of Supervisors, 1981-95

ELECTION RESULTS

2002 GENERAL		
Zoe Lofgren (D)	72,370	67.0%
Douglas Adams McNea (R)	32,182	29.8%
Dennis Umphress (LIBERT)	3,434	3.2%
2002 PRIMARY		
Zoe Lofgren (D)		unopposed
2000 GENERAL		
Zoe Lofgren (D)	115,118	72.1%
Horace Thayn (R)	37,213	23.3%
Dennis Umphress (LIBERT)	4,742	3.0%
Edward Klein (NL)	2,673	1.7%

PREVIOUS WINNING PERCENTAGES
1998 (73%); 1996 (66%); 1994 (65%)

Elected 1994; 5th term

Impelled by her district's high-technology-driven economy, Lofgren often focuses on issues connected to e-commerce and the nation's move toward instant, round-the-clock communications.

Silicon Valley is just to the west of Lofgren's 16th District, and many of her constituents work in the high-technology sector. Lofgren (her first name is pronounced ZO) does not pretend to be an expert in computer technology — she was a political science major in college — but she says that representing a high-tech district requires elected officials to be knowledgeable about the industry.

Although most lawmakers are now technology-savvy — from personal experience and as a matter of public policy — Lofgren still sees one of her roles as assisting in the high-tech education of decision-makers. She sometimes sees value in a go-slow approach on Capitol Hill, particularly on high-tech matters, and she says that some decisions have been made without full appreciation of the new technology or the implications of those decisions.

Lofgren has a solid record of favoring liberalized foreign trade, not surprising for a lawmaker from a heavily high-tech district. But in the 107th Congress, like many other pro-trade Democrats, she voted against a bill to give the president fast-track authority to negotiate trade agreements that Congress cannot amend. She and her colleagues argued that the timing of the vote, with the economy reeling from the Sept. 11, 2001, terrorist attacks and the bankruptcy of many dot-com companies, was wrong.

On social issues, Lofgren is a strong supporter of the Democratic line, and she occasionally shows her frustration with the GOP majority, particularly during debate on issues before the Judiciary Committee, on which she sits.

In 2001, when the committee approved a bill to ban human cloning, Lofgren argued that it also imposed unjustified restrictions on stem cell research. "Since when did outlawing research to cure awful diseases become the 'morally correct' position?" Lofgren asked.

But her social views do not prevent Lofgren from working in a quieter way to influence the content of bills that Republicans are pushing. She has sought common ground with the GOP, especially in the technology arena.

She waged a long struggle with the Clinton administration to convince policymakers that restrictions on the export of state-of-the-art forms of encryption technology did not keep it out of the hands of foreign terrorists or crooks — they could simply obtain it elsewhere. And, she said, the restrictions placed U.S. makers of encryption software, which allows digital information to be scrambled, at a competitive disadvantage.

Immigration law was Lofgren's specialty as a lawyer early in her career, and she served on the House Democrats' immigration task force in the 107th. She criticized the Immigration and Naturalization Service's handling of requests for citizenship, calling it "dismal," and sought improvements in the treatment of unaccompanied children applying for asylum.

As the mother of two children, Lofgren takes a strong interest in education. She says that her primary focus as a public official is to see that all children "at least have the same opportunity that I had — and right now not all of them do." She introduced legislation in the 106th Congress and again in the 107th urging high school officials to consider starting school later in the day, citing studies that teenagers are not fully alert early in the morning.

The nation's technology industry was particularly hard hit by big declines in stock prices in 2001. Lofgren introduced legislation to ease the tax burden for many workers who exercised stock purchase options offered by their employers. A quirk in the tax code based tax liability on the value of the stock when the purchase option was exercised, not when the stock was sold. That left many people with the double whammy of huge tax bills and virtually worthless stock.

In the 108th, she ran for Democratic Caucus vice chairman, but withdrew before balloting was complete when it was apparent that James E. Clyburn of South Carolina had the race wrapped up.

Lofgren grew up in a blue-collar neighborhood in south Palo Alto. Her father was a truck driver and her mother was a secretary and later a school cafeteria cook. "I didn't meet a Republican until I went to junior high school," she recalls. While other mothers went door-to-door collecting money for the March of Dimes, Lofgren's mother went after "dollars for Democrats." Lofgren would spend long hours talking politics with her Swedish immigrant grandfather, and she recalls that, instead of dating or going to dances, she and her friends went to political rallies.

Lofgren went to Stanford on a scholarship and then headed to Washington, D.C., landing an internship with Democratic Rep. Don Edwards. Convinced that she needed to go to law school when the House's legislative counsel "ripped to shreds — and for good reason" a draft of a bill she had written, she returned to California and got a law degree.

She served as the first executive director of San Jose's Community Housing Developers, a nonprofit involved in creating low-income housing. In 1979, a colleague urged her to run for the local community college board of trustees. She did and won. A year later, she was elected to the Santa Clara County Board of Supervisors, where she served 14 years. She was often in conflict with San Jose's Democratic mayor, Tom McEnery, who pushed downtown redevelopment. Lofgren argued that the money would have been better spent on education and human services.

When Edwards retired after 32 years, the Democratic primary saw a face-off between Lofgren and McEnery, who was no longer mayor. Lofgren launched her campaign while standing on a kitchen breadbox in the living room of her house in San Jose. She benefited from an uproar that ensued when state election officials barred her from describing herself as "county supervisor/mother" on the ballot. The flap drew national attention to Lofgren's candidacy, and she went on to upset McEnery. She won handily that November and has coasted to re-election since.

KEY VOTES

2002

- Yes Overhaul campaign finance law; ban "soft money" and restrict advocacy advertising
- No Back Bush's defense budget increase
- No Extend 1996 welfare law
- No Adopt Bush's discretionary spending limit
- No Pass GOP Medicare prescription drug plan
- Yes Create independent Sept. 11 commission
- Yes Extend union protections to Homeland Security Department employees
- No Revive fast-track procedures for trade agreements
- No Authorize war against Iraq
- No Advance bankruptcy overhaul opposed by abortion opponents

2001

- No Nullify Clinton Labor Department ergonomics rule
- No Cut taxes by $1.35 trillion through fiscal 2011
- Yes Maintain ban on oil drilling in Arctic National Wildlife Refuge
- No Approve Bush proposal to limit managed-care plan liability for coverage decisions
- Yes Divert money from crop subsidy payments to land conservation
- Yes Expand law enforcement power to investigate suspected terrorists

CQ VOTE STUDIES

	PARTY UNITY		PRESIDENTIAL SUPPORT	
	Support	Oppose	Support	Oppose
2002	94%	6%	15%	85%
2001	87%	13%	30%	70%
2000	90%	10%	82%	18%
1999	87%	13%	84%	16%
1998	92%	8%	88%	12%

INTEREST GROUPS

	AFL-CIO	ADA	CCUS	ACU
2002	100%	100%	26%	0%
2001	100%	90%	35%	0%
2000	80%	85%	52%	4%
1999	67%	95%	29%	4%
1998	90%	95%	47%	0%

CALIFORNIA 16

Most of San Jose

The high-tech boom of the 1990s has propelled San Jose out of San Francisco's shadow and earned it a reputation as "the capital of Silicon Valley." A metropolitan area unto itself, San Jose is now home to the Bay Area's NBC affiliate and a professional hockey franchise.

The district includes two-thirds of San Jose and almost 40 percent of Santa Clara County's population, but all but 8 percent of the 16th's residents live in San Jose — the only city in the district and the third largest in the state. Silicon Valley's tremendous growth has rubbed off on the city, creating a white-collar work force and helping to establish it as a leading exporter of high-tech goods. An economic downturn has sent unemployment, once as low as 2 percent, soaring past 8 percent, but housing prices have remained high. The county has the area's highest median income and highest rate of charitable giving.

The 16th is one of the most ethnically diverse districts in the Bay Area. Its Asian population includes the nation's second-largest Vietnamese community, but Hispanics represent the district's largest group at 38 percent. Whites make up 32 percent of the population.

Redistricting after the 2000 census concentrated the 16th more around San Jose, removing hilly areas east of the city and southern areas including Morgan Hill (now in the 11th) and Gilroy (now in the 15th).

The 16th has been solidly liberal and Democratic for many years, and an influx of Hispanics has helped continue that trend. However, white-collar workers are becoming more common and could begin to shift the district's politics to the right. Al Gore took 62 percent of the district's vote in the 2000 presidential election.

MAJOR INDUSTRY

Technology, health care, finance

CITIES

San Jose (pt.), 590,306; Alum Rock (unincorporated), 13,479

NOTABLE

San Jose served as the state capital for a short time after California's annexation by the United States; In 1777, San Jose became the state's first civilian settlement under Spanish rule; Norman Y. Mineta San Jose International Airport is named for former Rep. and Transportation Secretary Mineta.

Rep. Sam Farr (D)

CAPITOL OFFICE
225-2861
samfarr@mail.house.gov
www.house.gov/farr
1221 Longworth 20515-0517; fax 225-6791

COMMITTEES
Appropriations

HOMETOWN
Carmel

BORN
July 4, 1941, San Francisco, Calif.

RELIGION
Episcopalian

FAMILY
Wife, Shary Baldwin Farr; one child

EDUCATION
Willamette U., B.S. 1963 (biology)

CAREER
State legislative aide; Peace Corps volunteer

POLITICAL HIGHLIGHTS
Monterey County Board of Supervisors, 1975-80; Calif. Assembly, 1980-93

ELECTION RESULTS

2002 GENERAL		
Sam Farr (D)	101,632	68.1%
Clint Engler (R)	40,334	27.0%
R. Glock-Grueneich (GREEN)	4,885	3.3%
Jascha Lee (LIBERT)	2,418	1.6%
2002 PRIMARY		
Sam Farr (D)	51,251	91.1%
Art Dunn (D)	5,008	8.9%
2000 GENERAL		
Sam Farr (D)	143,219	68.6%
Clint Engler (R)	51,557	24.7%
E. Craig Coffin (GREEN)	8,215	3.9%
Rick Garrett (LIBERT)	2,510	1.2%
Lawrence Fenton (REF)	2,263	1.1%

PREVIOUS WINNING PERCENTAGES
1998 (65%); 1996 (59%); 1994 (52%); 1993 Special Runoff Election (54%); 1993 Special Election (26%)

Elected June 1993; 5th full term

Farr has two principal passions in representing his Central Coast territory: advocacy for military facilities in his district and careful stewardship of the region's natural resources.

While pro-military and pro-environment obligations might seem a contradictory mix for a liberal Democrat, Farr does not see it that way. "The military has been very good stewards of their land out there," Farr said.

His district is not a big producer of military hardware, but rather hosts a collection of generally personnel-oriented facilities, allowing Farr to advocate for his military constituency while focusing on traditional Democratic issues such as education and housing. The Defense Language Institute Foreign Language Center in Monterey will almost certainly grow in importance during the war on terrorism that began in 2001. The Naval Postgraduate School, also in Monterey, is a center for computer research in such areas as war games and intelligence gathering.

Farr, a member of the Appropriations Committee, complained that President Bush's initial 2002 budget proposed a 14 percent cut in military construction spending. "I think the president is big on military hardware and soft on quality-of-life issues," said Farr, who is a member of the Military Construction and Agriculture subcommittees.

The 17th was dealt a blow in 1994 when Fort Ord was ordered closed. Farr has worked to ease the base's transition to civilian use, helping secure $51 million to open the Monterey Bay campus of California State University there. The base also houses a Defense Department Finance Center, a veterans clinic and an environmental research center for the University of California at Santa Cruz. During the 107th, Farr pressed hard for development of low-income housing on the property.

Farr, a biology major in college, is eager to preserve the natural beauty of his district, which boasts rich soil, bountiful fisheries and some of the most beautiful vistas in the world. "I'm trying to make eco-tourism and education the economic engines for the Big Sur region, rather than economic exploitation," he said. In 2002, Farr's bill to protect 55,000 acres near the Big Sur coast won approval.

Across the spectrum of issues, Farr is generally a dependable vote for the Democratic leadership. Normally, confrontation is not a significant part of his style. He prefers to work unobtrusively, concentrating on his roster of priority matters. However, some GOP positions on environmental issues can elicit a sharp retort, such as when he said at a Resources Committee hearing, "There is 100 percent agreement in this room that we all love forests. The difficulty is that 50 percent of them love it vertical, and 50 percent of them love [forests] horizontal."

Farr was the elected chairman of the California Democratic delegation in the 106th Congress, a post he used to build consensus among members of the huge, often fractious group. Farr proudly notes that it is the largest and most diverse delegation in Congress, both racially and in gender.

The 17th includes fertile inland regions, with Salinas serving as a marketing center for such produce as lettuce, avocados and artichokes from surrounding farms in the nation's "salad bowl." In the 105th, Farr looked out for those farming interests from a seat on the Agriculture Committee, which he gave up to join Appropriations in 1999.

In the 105th, Farr also served on the Resources Committee, where he worked on ocean issues, urging Congress and the administration to initiate a comprehensive review of the nation's policies on maritime and coastal matters. He has continued to work on those issues even after leaving the committee. Though Republicans had blocked his legislation to expand environmental protections for California offshore islands that are home to seabirds and marine mammals and to expand the Pinnacles National Monument in the coastal range, Farr was able to achieve these goals in 2000 when President Clinton used Farr's bill as the basis for an executive order creating new national monuments.

Farr's keen interest in environmental issues was manifest in 1998 when, frustrated with the lackluster recycling effort in congressional offices, he got the House to dictate that $100,000 be set aside for implementation of an aggressive recycling program on Capitol Hill. Farr said he was not trying to "fulfill some sort of ecowarrior's dream to save trees," but rather aiming to earn money, reduce landfill costs and "make the House a good corporate citizen." That goal may be a while in coming; in the 107th Congress, Farr observed that the recycling effort still suffered from half-hearted participation. Taking a jab at GOP leaders in Congress, Farr said, "I don't think it will fully work until you have a leadership that is committed to it."

Farr's father was a longtime California state legislator who played a key role in the highway beautification effort of Lady Bird Johnson. Now, the younger Farr is active with the Oceans Caucus and House Sustainable Development Caucus, which weighs in on a range of issues with environmental implications, including electricity deregulation, fisheries regulation and the development of alternative fuels.

Farr, who was born on July 4, is proud of his work on the 1996 immigration law to encourage mass naturalization ceremonies around the country on that date. He makes a habit of participating in such a ceremony on each of his birthdays.

After spending what he calls two "character-forming" years with the Peace Corps in Colombia following his graduation from college, Farr returned home and went to work as a staffer in the California Assembly. He later won election to the Monterey County Board of Supervisors. After five years there, he was elected to the state legislature and served the next 12 1/2 years in Sacramento.

In 1993, he won a House special election to replace Democrat Leon E. Panetta, who had become Clinton's first White House budget director, winning by 9 percentage points over Republican Bill McCampbell. After winning a 1994 rematch by 8 points, Farr has won succeeding elections by wide margins.

KEY VOTES

2002

Yes Overhaul campaign finance law; ban "soft money" and restrict advocacy advertising
No Back Bush's defense budget increase
No Extend 1996 welfare law
No Adopt Bush's discretionary spending limit
No Pass GOP Medicare prescription drug plan
Yes Create independent Sept. 11 commission
Yes Extend union protections to Homeland Security Department employees
No Revive fast-track procedures for trade agreements
No Authorize war against Iraq
No Advance bankruptcy overhaul opposed by abortion opponents

2001

No Nullify Clinton Labor Department ergonomics rule
No Cut taxes by $1.35 trillion through fiscal 2011
Yes Maintain ban on oil drilling in Arctic National Wildlife Refuge
No Approve Bush proposal to limit managed-care plan liability for coverage decisions
Yes Divert money from crop subsidy payments to land conservation
No Expand law enforcement power to investigate suspected terrorists

CQ VOTE STUDIES

	PARTY UNITY		PRESIDENTIAL SUPPORT	
	Support	Oppose	Support	Oppose
2002	99%	1%	25%	75%
2001	96%	4%	24%	76%
2000	95%	5%	82%	18%
1999	96%	4%	85%	15%
1998	95%	5%	87%	13%

INTEREST GROUPS

	AFL-CIO	ADA	CCUS	ACU
2002	100%	95%	35%	0%
2001	100%	95%	43%	0%
2000	90%	95%	45%	8%
1999	78%	100%	17%	0%
1998	100%	100%	44%	0%

CALIFORNIA 17

Monterey, San Benito and Santa Cruz counties — Salinas, Santa Cruz

The 17th includes the most populated part of upscale Santa Cruz County, with its namesake city and several sizable seaside communities. Farther south, in Monterey County, Monterey attracts tourists, and exclusive Pebble Beach is home to celebrities and Silicon Valley executives. While Santa Cruz County is a Democratic stronghold, Republican-leaning farmers and retirees in Monterey and San Benito counties can pull the Democratic district to the right.

South of Santa Cruz County, agriculture drives the economy. Major wineries and vineyards also dot the landscape. Salinas, the seat of Monterey County and the district's largest city, is known as the nation's "salad bowl" for its fresh vegetables. The district's 43 percent Hispanic population is concentrated in the Salinas Valley, where Hispanics are beginning to win local offices. More than 60 percent of district residents live in Monterey County.

Residents in the 17th expected to suffer economically when they lost Fort Ord in 1994. But California State University Monterey Bay has since opened on a portion of the site, and the influx of students and related jobs is expected to help replace 17,000 military jobs. The region also has developed as a center for marine sciences, with more than a dozen major research institutions located around the Monterey Bay coastline.

MAJOR INDUSTRY

Agriculture, tourism, higher education

MILITARY BASES

Defense Language Institute Foreign Language Center/Presidio of Monterey (Army), 3,992 military, 1,646 civilian (2002); Naval Postgraduate School, 1,783 military, 1,769 civilian (2002); Fleet Numerical Meteorology and Oceanography Center, 94 military, 162 civilian (1999); Fort Hunter Liggett (Army), 15 military, 175 civilian (2002)

CITIES

Salinas, 151,060; Santa Cruz, 54,593; Watsonville, 44,265; Hollister, 34,413

NOTABLE

Clint Eastwood was mayor of Carmel-by-the-Sea; The Monterey Bay National Marine Sanctuary is the nation's largest marine sanctuary.

Rep. Dennis Cardoza (D)

CAPITOL OFFICE
225-6131
www.house.gov/cardoza
503 Cannon 20515-0518; fax 225-0819

COMMITTEES
Agriculture
Resources
Science

HOMETOWN
Atwater

BORN
March 31, 1959, Merced, Calif.

RELIGION
Roman Catholic

FAMILY
Wife, Kathleen McLoughlin; three children

EDUCATION
U. of Maryland, B.A. 1982 (government & politics)

CAREER
Bowling alley executive; realtor; state legislative aide

POLITICAL HIGHLIGHTS
Atwater City Council, 1984-87; Merced City Council, 1994-95; Calif. Assembly, 1996-2002

ELECTION RESULTS

2002 GENERAL

Dennis Cardoza (D)	56,181	51.3%
Dick Monteith (R)	47,528	43.4%
Kevin H. Cripe (AMI)	3,641	3.3%
Linda M. DeGroat (LIBERT)	2,194	2.0%

2002 PRIMARY

Dennis Cardoza (D)	22,879	53.2%
Gary A. Condit (D)	16,618	38.7%
Ralph L. White (D)	1,344	3.1%
Sukhmander Singh (D)	963	2.2%
Joseph Martin (D)	740	1.7%
Elvis Pringle (D)	440	1.0%

Elected 2002; 1st term

A self-described "raging moderate" and "policy wonk," Cardoza rose to prominence during his six years in the California Assembly through compromise and hard work — a pattern he is poised to repeat as a freshman in the 108th Congress. "I'm a guy who hates campaigns, but I love doing legislative work," he says.

Cardoza, who was elected by his colleagues as a regional whip, hopes he ultimately will be better-known for his policy prowess than as the man who won a March 2002 primary to oust scandal-plagued Democratic Rep. Gary A. Condit, for whom Cardoza once worked.

As a power player in the state legislature's Democratic leadership — he chaired the Rules Committee — Cardoza made his biggest mark with a measure to combat pollution affecting his constituency in California's Central Valley. On Capitol Hill, his Agriculture and Resources committee assignments give him a platform to continue his work on resources issues.

Cardoza also led efforts to improve HMO service in rural areas and to secure law enforcement funds to fight methamphetamine abuse. He promises to keep working on the federal level to fund the Merced branch of the University of California, which is scheduled to open in 2004.

Liberal on most social issues, Cardoza says he is a moderate when it comes to business regulation. His priorities include economic development and infrastructure improvements for his district, where unemployment is high and education levels below average. A Portuguese-American, Cardoza is a member of the Congressional Hispanic Caucus.

Cardoza once regarded Condit as a political mentor but challenged him for the 18th District seat after the 2001 disappearance of Washington intern Chandra Levy resulted in revelations of a relationship she had with the married congressman. Though Condit denied any connection to Levy's disappearance and was never declared a suspect, his political support evaporated. Cardoza easily won the primary, then prevailed over GOP state Sen. Dick Monteith by a comfortable 8 points in the general election.

CALIFORNIA 18

Central Valley – Merced, part of Stockton and Modesto

While the location of the Central Valley-based 18th remained largely intact, redistricting after the 2000 census pushed the district's political lean sharply left. Fearing that the scandal surrounding then-Rep. Gary A. Condit could move the seat into the GOP column, the Democratic-controlled state legislature redrew it from a highly competitive seat into one with a 17-point Democratic registration edge. Though still dominated by agriculture, the district now includes the central portion of the diverse and Democratic city of Stockton.

Central California's Merced County, along with half of Stanislaus County, make up the district's agricultural base. Modesto, the Stanislaus County seat, has its own canning and food-processing industry, as well as the Gallo Winery, which accounts for about one-fourth of domestic wine sales. The city has grown substantially over the years, spurred by businesses fleeing California's congested coastal cities and by the Central Valley's successful agriculture industry.

The port city of Stockton (shared with the 11th), on the San Joaquin River, is a transportation hub that some Bay Area commuters call home. Almost 60 percent of the city's residents — Stockton's most Democratic ground — live in the 18th. Whites and Hispanics each make up about 40 percent of the district's overall population.

Local issues tend to revolve around water availability and the preservation of farmland. The seasonal economy has contributed to higher unemployment rates than in other parts of California.

MAJOR INDUSTRY
Agriculture, wine, food processing

CITIES
Stockton (pt.), 139,362; Modesto (pt.), 133,975; Merced, 63,893

NOTABLE
Stockton has the largest Sikh population in the United States.

Rep. George P. Radanovich (R)

Elected 1994; 5th term

CAPITOL OFFICE
225-4540
www.house.gov/radanovich
438 Cannon 20515-0519; fax 225-3402

COMMITTEES
Energy & Commerce
Resources
(National Parks, Recreation & Public Lands - chairman)

HOMETOWN
Mariposa

BORN
June 20, 1955, Mariposa, Calif.

RELIGION
Roman Catholic

FAMILY
Wife, Ethie Radanovich; one child

EDUCATION
California Polytechnic State U., San Luis Obispo, B.S. 1978 (agriculture business management)

CAREER
Vintner; bank manager; carpenter

POLITICAL HIGHLIGHTS
Mariposa County Board of Supervisors, 1989-92 (chairman, 1991); sought Republican nomination for U.S. House, 1992

ELECTION RESULTS

2002 GENERAL		
George P. Radanovich (R)	106,209	67.3%
John Veen (D)	47,403	30.0%
Patrick McHargue (LIBERT)	4,190	2.7%
2002 PRIMARY		
George P. Radanovich (R)		unopposed
2000 GENERAL		
George P. Radanovich (R)	144,517	64.9%
Daniel Rosenberg (D)	70,578	31.7%
Elizabeth Taylor (LIBERT)	4,264	1.9%

PREVIOUS WINNING PERCENTAGES
1998 (79%); 1996 (67%); 1994 (57%)

Radanovich has long argued that the size of the federal government is out of control. He not only wants a smaller federal role in the nation but also an increased reliance on the private sector. He used to make his case by carting around a misshapen chair, with one leg — representing government — much longer than the other three legs, representing family, business, and religious and civic organizations.

Radanovich (ruh-DON-o-vitch) doesn't use his prop much anymore, but he now has another symbol to drive home his point – sludge. As the new chairman of the Resources Committee's National Parks, Recreation and Public Lands Subcommittee, Radanovich in the 107th Congress quickly grabbed onto a juicy story. The Army Corps of Engineers, with a permit from the Environmental Protection Agency, was regularly discharging sludge containing toxic chemicals into the Potomac River, which is the habitat of the endangered short-nosed sturgeon.

The discovery gave weight to his long-held assertion that the government was selectively enforcing clean water and endangered species laws — ignoring violations in the nation's capital area while strictly enforcing the laws in the West. Radanovich held hearings, appeared in television and radio interviews, and hammered away at the issue for months. Late in 2002, the EPA withdrew the permit.

Earlier, in 2000, he argued that the federal government was also disregarding the Endangered Species Act by failing to protect the bald eagle and sturgeon during work to replace the Wilson Bridge across the Potomac River just south of Washington. "It is intolerable to have one set of standards for Washington, D.C., and another for the rest of the country," Radanovich said.

Radanovich is now in his fifth term in the House, and his agenda is still driven by the same basic tenets that the large GOP Class of 1994 made their mantra — reduce the size and scope of government, shift authority from the federal government to state and local levels, eliminate regulations that stifle business, and emphasize personal responsibility. Specifically, Radanovich wants these principles applied to the West. He and other Western Republicans argue that Easterners (and particularly government bureaucrats) do not understand the unique issues facing the West, where the federal government owns huge tracts of land and where access to water is crucial.

Radanovich has tried to advance the agenda advocated by the Western Caucus, which he chaired in the 106th Congress. The group espouses a "new environmentalism," which holds that private property owners and local governments should be given incentives and authority to ensure that land and water are well cared for and efficiently used.

In the 107th, as Congress worked on legislation to reauthorize the massive federal-state water project in California known as CALFED, Radanovich made it clear that he viewed agricultural and urban water requirements to be a higher priority than environmental and endangered species needs. "I say don't give them money until they get reality," he argued.

The 19th District contains Yosemite National Park, and Radanovich is wary of proposals to address park overcrowding that might hurt tourist-dependent towns and businesses near the park. He opposed portions of a master plan to reduce crowding and restore the park after devastating 1997 floods, saying the plan called for less parking and fewer campsites. "They [environmentalists] want to make the park so hard to get into that people just won't come," he said.

Radanovich's party loyalty, including his work on behalf of other Republican candidates, won him a prized post on the Energy and Commerce Committee in the 107th.

Radanovich and fellow California lawmaker (and former vineyard owner) Mike Thompson formed the Congressional Wine Caucus to educate colleagues about wine and to join on legislative and regulatory matters pertaining to wine. In the 107th, they urged repeal of a "special occupational tax" on businesses that make, distribute, sell or deliver alcoholic products. And they opposed efforts to ban Internet sales of wine, which they said were driven by wine wholesalers trying to maintain their distribution monopoly.

One of eight children of a Croatian immigrant who owned and operated a clothing store in Mariposa, Radanovich spent much of his teenage years on the family's small ranch just outside of town. He earned a college degree in agricultural business management, and after working a few years as a banker, a carpenter and a substitute teacher, Radanovich pursued his first love, farming. The wines for which California is famous are produced primarily in the valleys of Napa, Sonoma and Santa Clara. But Radanovich's dream, inspired by memories of his grandfather making wine in the cellar, was to establish a winery in the Mariposa County foothills of the Sierra Nevada — an area where livestock grazing generally takes precedence over farming. He persisted, and Radanovich Winery now ships about 6,000 cases annually of sauvignon blanc, merlot and other wines.

In building his business, the vintner gained firsthand familiarity with the issues of water allocation, farm labor, taxes and regulation. That led him to a seat on the Mariposa County Board of Supervisors in 1989. In 1992, he made his first bid for Congress. Mariposa is far from the district's population center in Fresno County, where he was largely unknown, but Radanovich acquitted himself well that year, losing a close race to eventual GOP nominee Tal Cloud. Two years later, Cloud decided not to run, and Radanovich took advantage of the GOP tilt in the district caused by the post-1990 census remapping. He cruised to victory over incumbent Democratic Rep. Richard H. Lehman and has racked up formidable margins of victory since then.

In 2002, redistricting shifted the boundaries of his district to the north, but its electorate was no less friendly, and Radanovich cruised to a 37-point win.

Radanovich, who had said he would limit himself to five terms in the House, has backed down somewhat from that pledge. And late in 2002 he began mulling a bid for the Senate in 2004.

KEY VOTES

2002

- No Overhaul campaign finance law; ban "soft money" and restrict advocacy advertising
- Yes Back Bush's defense budget increase
- Yes Extend 1996 welfare law
- Yes Adopt Bush's discretionary spending limit
- Yes Pass GOP Medicare prescription drug plan
- No Create independent Sept. 11 commission
- No Extend union protections to Homeland Security Department employees
- Yes Revive fast-track procedures for trade agreements
- Yes Authorize war against Iraq
- Yes Advance bankruptcy overhaul opposed by abortion opponents

2001

- Yes Nullify Clinton Labor Department ergonomics rule
- Yes Cut taxes by $1.35 trillion through fiscal 2011
- No Maintain ban on oil drilling in Arctic National Wildlife Refuge
- Yes Approve Bush proposal to limit managed-care plan liability for coverage decisions
- No Divert money from crop subsidy payments to land conservation
- Yes Expand law enforcement power to investigate suspected terrorists

CQ VOTE STUDIES

	PARTY UNITY		PRESIDENTIAL SUPPORT	
	Support	Oppose	Support	Oppose
2002	96%	4%	89%	11%
2001	96%	4%	93%	7%
2000	96%	4%	22%	78%
1999	95%	5%	18%	82%
1998	96%	4%	20%	80%

INTEREST GROUPS

	AFL-CIO	ADA	CCUS	ACU
2002	11%	5%	95%	88%
2001	0%	5%	95%	92%
2000	0%	5%	90%	100%
1999	0%	5%	96%	88%
1998	0%	0%	94%	100%

CALIFORNIA 19

Central Valley — part of Fresno and Modesto, Turlock, Madera

A fertile farm district, the 19th includes the heart of Central California's San Joaquin Valley. It takes in almost all of Madera County and part of the city of Fresno, home to large numbers of Hispanics, Hmong and Armenians. All of Mariposa and Tuolumne counties are in the district, along with about half of Stanislaus County.

The 19th is rural and Republican. The district has had a Republican in Congress since 1995 and supported GOP presidential candidates in 1992, 1996 and in 2000, when it gave 57 percent of the vote to George W. Bush. Farmers and senior citizens, leery of government regulations and environmental protection laws, tend to be moderate conservatives. Farming and water issues are perpetual hot topics and are becoming more significant as population growth means less water for agricultural use.

The district's portion of Stanislaus County includes less than a third of Modesto's population and the growing city of Turlock. Tuolumne and Mariposa counties, which along with Madera County to the south are home to Yosemite National Park, are sparsely populated areas that account for only one-tenth of the district's population. They feature Sierra Nevada mountains, skiing and forests in the east and former Gold Rush towns such as Jamestown, Sonora and Mariposa in the west.

Tourism at Yosemite helps keep the 19th's economy afloat, though the district suffers from high unemployment because of the seasonal nature of its driving industries. The district picked up all of Yosemite, which was only partially in the old 19th, in redistricting following the 2000 census. Hispanics make up 28 percent of residents.

MAJOR INDUSTRY
Agriculture, dairy, tourism

CITIES
Fresno (pt.), 189,836; Turlock, 55,810; Modesto (pt.), 54,881; Madera, 43,207

NOTABLE
The Yosemite Valley was deeded to California in 1864 as a public trust, and Yosemite National Park was created in 1890.

Rep. Cal Dooley (D)

CAPITOL OFFICE
225-3341
dooley.house.gov
1201 Longworth 20515-0520; fax 225-9308

COMMITTEES
Agriculture
Resources

HOMETOWN
Visalia

BORN
Jan. 11, 1954, Visalia, Calif.

RELIGION
Protestant

FAMILY
Wife, Linda Phillips Dooley; two children

EDUCATION
U. of California, Davis, B.S. 1977 (agricultural economics); Stanford U., M.A. 1987 (management)

CAREER
Farmer; state legislative aide

POLITICAL HIGHLIGHTS
No previous office

ELECTION RESULTS

2002 GENERAL		
Cal Dooley (D)	47,627	63.7%
Andre Minuth (R)	25,628	34.3%
Varrin Swearingen (LIBERT)	1,515	2.0%
2002 PRIMARY		
Cal Dooley (D)		unopposed
2000 GENERAL		
Cal Dooley (D)	66,235	52.4%
Rich Rodriguez (R)	57,563	45.5%
Walter Ruehlig (NL)	1,416	1.1%
Arnold Kriegbaum (LIBERT)	1,320	1.0%

PREVIOUS WINNING PERCENTAGES
1998 (61%); 1996 (57%); 1994 (57%); 1992 (65%); 1990 (55%)

Elected 1990; 7th term

As a co-founder of the House New Democrat Coalition, a growing group of moderate, pro-business lawmakers who say they seek bipartisan solutions, Dooley is just the kind of person that Republicans look to team up with on issues such as trade and education. And, as a fourth generation farmer from California's Central Valley, he can be expected to weigh in on the side of agriculture — and against many of his Democratic colleagues from urban areas — in the tussle over precious water resources in the West.

Even though he may waver from the party line — he went against the grain about 30 percent of the time in the 107th Congress — Dooley is a loyal Democrat, more apt to reach out to like-minded Republicans on trade or natural resources issues than to openly defy his party's leadership. Dooley's appeal to both sides of the aisle is necessary in a district with a large Hispanic population that was trending Republican through the 1990s.

Those expectations have been borne out throughout his career; in the 107th Congress Dooley's interests aligned with the GOP's desire to develop bipartisan support for an education overhaul bill and for legislation to give the president fast-track authority to negotiate trade agreements that Congress cannot amend.

It is a measure of Dooley's reputation as a leader of centrist Democrats — he co-founded the New Democrat Coalition in 1997 along with Virginia's James P. Moran and former Indiana Rep. Tim Roemer — that his name was floated, during the disputed 2000 presidential election, as a potential appointee to either a Bush or a Gore administration.

After a tough 2000 re-election campaign, and taken aback by some constituent complaints that he had grown out of touch with their needs, Dooley took pains in the 107th to let voters know what he was doing on their behalf. He drafted a Valley Action Plan that highlighted a legislative agenda attuned to local needs, including funds for infrastructure, crime, agriculture, education, health care and economic development. His voting record leaned a little more toward the Republican side than it already had.

In House votes in the 107th Dooley supported President Bush more often than any other Western Democrat. And Dooley's news releases often start with these words: "Dooley hails Bush . . ." In 2002, at his urging, the Bush administration convened a special intra-agency task force dedicated to studying economic development in the Central Valley. He also worked with Republicans on a measure to reauthorize CALFED — the multibillion-dollar California water management system — in terms more favorable to agriculture than the previous 1992 law.

A top Democrat on both the Resources and Agriculture panels, Dooley's views on water issues have always put him at odds with fellow Californian George Miller, who for almost a decade was the top Democrat on Resources. Miller's urbanized district's residential and industrial demands for water compete with the agriculture-rich Central Valley's thirst for irrigation water.

Dooley helped negotiate the final version of the massive 2002 farm bill, but voted against it, saying it was bad for Central Valley farmers and dairymen, who do not benefit greatly from many government subsidy programs.

In the 107th Congress, Dooley's interests aligned with the GOP's in an effort to develop bipartisan support for the education overhaul law enacted in 2002. During debate on the education measure, Dooley and a number of his New Democrat colleagues were able to win inclusion of several elements of their own education plan, which demanded more accountability from local schools, in the package that became law.

In 2001, Dooley teamed with GOP Ways and Means Chairman Bill Thomas of California and fellow Democrats William J. Jefferson of Louisiana and John Tanner of Tennessee to draft fast-track legislation (the Bush administration calls it trade promotion authority) that addressed traditional Democratic desires, among them that U.S. negotiators must insist that the trade pacts include labor and environmental protections. Dooley tried to round up Democratic support for the bill. Ultimately, only 21 Democrats backed it, although a number of other pro-trade Democrats said their opposition was directed toward the timing of the vote, which came as the country was reeling from the Sept. 11, 2001, terrorist attacks. When the bill came up again in 2002, Dooley was one of 25 Democratic "ayes."

Dooley has sided with the GOP on other issues. In 2001, for example, he joined Republicans to overturn workplace ergonomic regulations and backed drilling in the Arctic National Wildlife Refuge. He occasionally will back Republicans on budget issues, such as a 2000 vote to cut estate taxes and a 1993 vote against President Clinton's budget plan.

For a century Dooley's family has tried to coax from the ground a range of crops that includes cotton, alfalfa and walnuts. President of the California Future Farmers of America at age 18, Dooley went on to earn a degree in agriculture economics at the University of California-Davis and a master's in management from Stanford University — all good preparation for a supervisory role in the family's San Joaquin Valley business, Dooley Farms.

Dooley was drawn early into not only his family's farming concern but also into politics, another field in which his family had some expertise: His brother and sister-in-law were senior aides to former Gov. Edmund G. "Jerry" Brown Jr. In 1987, Dooley went to work for state Sen. Rose Ann Vuich, a legendary Fresno Democrat. Dooley's association with Vuich helped him temper the more-liberal flavor of his relatives' politics.

In 1990, Dooley won the 20th District seat with 55 percent, toppling six-term GOP Rep. Charles "Chip" Pashayan Jr., who was tainted by the 1989 savings and loan scandal. After an easy victory in 1992, Dooley's winning margin slipped a bit in the big GOP year of 1994, leading Republicans to keep him in their sights in future races. In 2000, even though he had endorsements from such traditionally GOP-leaning groups as the U.S. Chamber of Commerce and the Business Roundtable, Dooley struggled to a 7-point victory over former television anchorman Rich Rodriguez. Given a more friendly constituency in redistricting, in the 2002 election Dooley won an easy, 29 percentage point victory over physician Andre Minuth, a first-time candidate.

KEY VOTES

2002

Yes Overhaul campaign finance law; ban "soft money" and restrict advocacy advertising
Yes Back Bush's defense budget increase
No Extend 1996 welfare law
No Adopt Bush's discretionary spending limit
No Pass GOP Medicare prescription drug plan
Yes Create independent Sept. 11 commission
No Extend union protections to Homeland Security Department employees
Yes Revive fast-track procedures for trade agreements
Yes Authorize war against Iraq
Yes Advance bankruptcy overhaul opposed by abortion opponents

2001

Yes Nullify Clinton Labor Department ergonomics rule
Yes Cut taxes by $1.35 trillion through fiscal 2011
No Maintain ban on oil drilling in Arctic National Wildlife Refuge
No Approve Bush proposal to limit managed-care plan liability for coverage decisions
No Divert money from crop subsidy payments to land conservation
Yes Expand law enforcement power to investigate suspected terrorists

CQ VOTE STUDIES

	PARTY UNITY		PRESIDENTIAL SUPPORT	
	Support	Oppose	Support	Oppose
2002	72%	28%	51%	49%
2001	67%	33%	53%	47%
2000	82%	18%	71%	29%
1999	77%	23%	72%	28%
1998	80%	20%	80%	20%

INTEREST GROUPS

	AFL-CIO	ADA	CCUS	ACU
2002	67%	65%	85%	24%
2001	50%	65%	77%	32%
2000	60%	70%	90%	20%
1999	44%	80%	80%	8%
1998	80%	85%	67%	4%

CALIFORNIA 20

Central Valley — Kings County, parts of Fresno and Bakersfield

The Hispanic-majority 20th reaches from Fresno to Bakersfield, through rural portions of Fresno, Kings and Kern counties. A swing district until being redrawn following the 2000 census, Democrats were left with a 20-point voter registration edge once state lawmakers completed the remap.

The 20th still bears much of the burden of the San Joaquin Valley's urban and rural poor, and is beset by crime and high unemployment. It also is one of California's most rural districts, and has some of the nation's poorest and least-educated residents, many of whom are Hispanic and Hmong immigrants who work in the district's farming community.

The district includes the area known as the Westlands. Here, federal water projects have spawned vast farms with battalions of workers. Motorists on Interstate 5 see nary a town while they pass fields filled with a wide variety of products, including alfalfa, cotton, fruits, sugar beets, wheat and nuts.

Roughly 40 percent of Fresno — the city is split between the 19th, 20th and 21st districts — is in the 20th, which takes in much of downtown and Hispanic areas in the southern section of the city. The downtown portion includes a multipurpose stadium, which opened in 2002 and is home to a minor league baseball team, that local leaders hope will give an economic boost to the city once known for its proliferation of car thefts. In recent years, the 20th also has attracted many state and privately run prisons that assist the area's shaky economy.

MAJOR INDUSTRY

Agriculture, dairy, prisons

MILITARY BASES

Naval Air Station Lemoore, 5,500 military, 1,300 civilian (2001)

CITIES

Fresno (pt.), 154,998; Bakersfield (pt.), 43,284; Hanford, 41,686; Delano, 38,824

NOTABLE

Fresno resident Mike Reynolds, whose daughter was murdered, was the catalyst behind California's "three strikes" ballot initiative.

Rep. Devin Nunes (R)

CAPITOL OFFICE
225-2523
nunes.house.gov
1017 Longworth 20515-0521; fax 225-3404

COMMITTEES
Agriculture
Resources

HOMETOWN
Tulare

BORN
Oct. 1, 1973, Tulare, Calif.

RELIGION
Roman Catholic

FAMILY
Single

EDUCATION
College of the Sequoias, A.A. 1993; California Polytechnic State U., San Luis Obispo, B.S. 1995 (agricultural business), M.S. 1996 (agriculture)

CAREER
Farmer

POLITICAL HIGHLIGHTS
College of the Sequoias Board of Trustees, 1996-2002; sought Republican nomination for U.S. House, 1998

ELECTION RESULTS

2002 GENERAL		
Devin Nunes (R)	87,544	70.5%
David G. LaPere (D)	32,584	26.2%
Jonathan Richter (LIBERT)	4,070	3.3%
2002 PRIMARY		
Devin Nunes (R)	21,438	37.0%
Jim Patterson (R)	19,099	33.0%
Mike Briggs (R)	14,864	25.7%
Tom Wright (R)	1,413	2.4%

Elected 2002; 1st term

His election in 2002 at age 29 made Nunes the youngest member of his class and the second-youngest member in the House (after Florida Republican Adam H. Putnam).

Nunes (NOO-ness) came to Washington with political connections that could give him clout beyond his years. The help he received from Ways and Means Committee Chairman Bill Thomas — the powerful Republican who represents a neighboring California district — boosted him to victory over tough competition in his March 2002 primary. Earlier, President Bush had appointed Nunes as an Agriculture Department official in California on Thomas' recommendation.

Yet Nunes may not be the easiest vote for the Republican leadership to count on. After he won the 21st District seat, Nunes signed on with the Republican Main Street Partnership, a group of party moderates.

Nunes' district in California's Central Valley is largely agricultural, and he sought and won seats on the Agriculture and Resources panels. He touts his background as a third-generation dairy farmer and his plan to build new dams to increase water storage in the area. On his second day in office, Nunes introduced a bill to study the feasibility of building a dam on the San Joaquin River.

His strategies to combat his district's high unemployment and below-average education levels reflect his conservative leanings. He advocates tax cuts that he says could help farmers, including a reduction in the marginal tax rate and elimination of the alternative minimum and capital gains taxes. He also wants to ease environmental regulations.

Nunes used his endorsements, a fundraising advantage and his status as the only candidate from the rural part of the district to beat state Rep. Mike Briggs and former Fresno Mayor Jim Patterson in the GOP primary and then cruised to victory in the general election.

Nunes' connections could not aid him in one respect: He drew the last number in the House lottery for office space.

CALIFORNIA 21

Central Valley — Tulare County, part of Fresno

The agriculture-dominated 21st is home to all of Tulare and part of Fresno counties, which vie each year for the title of top farm goods-producing county in the nation. Tulare was the winner in 2001, with more than $3.5 billion in agricultural commodities. In addition to about 20 percent of Fresno, the district takes in some of the mountains and forests of the Sierra Nevada chain on its eastern edge.

Tulare County is the world's largest dairy producing area, with more than $1 billion in dairy goods in 2001. But the county produces more than 250 other agricultural goods, including oranges, cattle, grapes, cotton and nuts. It is no surprise that farming and water issues are perpetual hot topics and are becoming more significant as population growth means less water for agricultural use. Unlike other areas, where supply and transportation is a concern, the big problem here is water storage. The district also faces high unemployment and below-average education rates.

The district includes the eastern, conservative portion of Fresno, including Fresno Yosemite International Airport and the Fresno branch of California State University. It also holds the cities of Visalia and Clovis, agricultural towns that have become cities in their own right. Clovis calls itself the gateway to the Sierra Nevadas.

During redistricting following the 2000 census, the 21st was created as an open seat, merging rural, conservative areas likely to elect a Republican. The district gave George W. Bush 59 percent of the vote in the 2000 presidential election, and GOP candidates should dominate for the foreseeable future.

MAJOR INDUSTRY
Agriculture, transportation, tourism

CITIES
Visalia, 91,565; Fresno (pt.), 82,818; Clovis, 68,468; Tulare, 43,994; Porterville, 39,615

NOTABLE
Mount Whitney, at 14,494 feet, is the tallest point in the lower 48 states.

Rep. Bill Thomas (R)

CAPITOL OFFICE
225-2915
bill.thomas@mail.house.gov
www.house.gov/billthomas
2208 Rayburn 20515-0522; fax 225-8798

COMMITTEES
Ways & Means - chairman
Joint Taxation - chairman

HOMETOWN
Bakersfield

BORN
Dec. 6, 1941, Wallace, Idaho

RELIGION
Baptist

FAMILY
Wife, Sharon Thomas; two children

EDUCATION
Santa Ana Community College, A.A. 1961; San Francisco State U., B.A. 1963, M.A. 1965

CAREER
Professor

POLITICAL HIGHLIGHTS
Calif. Assembly, 1974-78

ELECTION RESULTS

2002 GENERAL		
Bill Thomas (R)	120,473	73.3%
Jaime A. Corvera (D)	38,988	23.7%
Frank Coates (LIBERT)	4,824	2.9%
2002 PRIMARY		
Bill Thomas (R)		unopposed
2000 GENERAL		
Bill Thomas (R)	142,539	71.6%
Pedro Martinez (D)	49,318	24.8%
James Manion (LIBERT)	7,243	3.6%

PREVIOUS WINNING PERCENTAGES
1998 (79%); 1996 (66%); 1994 (68%); 1992 (65%); 1990 (60%); 1988 (71%); 1986 (73%); 1984 (71%); 1982 (68%); 1980 (71%); 1978 (59%)

Elected 1978; 13th term

In just two years at the helm of the Ways and Means Committee, Thomas has proven to be the most effective tax legislator in years.

Part policy wonk, part party strategist and part self-described head case, he writes tax bills nearly single-handedly. The former political science professor wades into the arcana of the IRS code with zeal. He functions on just a few hours of sleep, driving fellow lawmakers to distraction in post-midnight negotiations on legislation.

Thomas' peers consider him to be one of the most personally difficult members of Congress to deal with. He lectures, insults and cuts off colleagues. But even his critics admit the guy is good.

He has a major hand in tax, trade, Medicare and Social Security legislation. In the 107th Congress Thomas guided nine bills to passage. They were some of the most significant laws enacted in that two-year period, including President Bush's $1.35 trillion tax cut, the trade law that gave the president fast-track trade negotiating authority and the $42 billion economic stimulus package of 2002.

Thomas' success stems from his close coordination with the GOP whip; he keeps tabs on where members stand and whether he has the votes to pass a bill. He rarely wins many Democratic votes, but that hardly matters to him. His approach goes hand-in-glove with the president's, which is to pass the most conservative bills possible in the House as a way of improving the White House bargaining position with Senate Democrats.

Thomas has remade himself from a health care specialist — he chaired the Ways and Means Health Subcommittee for six years — into a tax expert. He is driven, he once told an interviewer, by "a very big inferiority complex."

Even as it churns out bill after bill, Ways and Means in Thomas' grip is a land of fierce partisanship and resentment among fellow Republicans. He knows he sometimes rubs people the wrong way. "People get mad because you work so hard it shows them up a little bit," he said.

For all his detractors, Thomas has some loyal admirers. A few aides have been with him for more than a decade. GOP Rep. Jim McCrery of Louisiana is his right hand on Ways and Means. Republican Nancy Johnson of Connecticut is a fan, though Thomas rarely pays attention to her moderate views or allows her much power as chairman of the Health Subcommittee. "He doesn't pussy foot around," she says. "If you've got a dumb idea, he'll tell you that you've got a dumb idea."

In a 2002 survey of congressional aides by Washingtonian magazine, Thomas was judged to be the meanest lawmaker in the House; he ranked third for "Biggest Windbag" but also placed third for "Brainiest."

Unlike many lawmakers, Thomas is willing to take on thankless, unpopular tasks. When U.S. Trade Representative Robert Zoellick asked Thomas to help on a foreign tax problem he was having with Europe, Thomas rewrote the forcign tax code to stave off $4 billion in trade sanctions.

Thomas shies away from articulating a tax philosophy. He is neither a supply-sider nor an anti-deficit hard-liner. He calls himself a "pragmatic conservative." While he's unlikely to launch a major tax simplification or reform project, he does enjoy slipping in significant tax changes when no one is looking. In the foreign tax bill, for example, he tucked in modifications to the foreign tax credit system to help U.S.-based multinationals that are increasingly making their products in China and abroad.

Thomas became Ways and Means chairman in 2001 after the retirement of Republican Bill Archer of Texas, who had the job since the first days of the GOP majority in 1995. Thomas bested Philip M. Crane of Illinois, who had 10 years more seniority but was viewed as less energetic a legislator, though not as abrasive a leader, as Thomas.

Thomas had made a name for himself as the top Republican on the Health Subcommittee. He immersed himself in health policy, rising at 4 a.m. for six months to read background material. "Basically I got a medical degree," he said. He eventually could discuss the politics of health policy as well as the intricacies of Medicare reimbursements at the county level.

He was unable to advance his proposal to move consumers away from the employer-based health insurance system to one based on tax credits that individuals could spend as they wished. And his prescription drug plan in 2000, which created a public-private program, was rejected after private insurers called it completely unworkable. He did succeed with legislation in 1997 making significant changes to Medicare, the federal program providing health insurance to 40 million senior citizens and disabled people.

In 1998 and 1999, Thomas served on the 17-member commission studying long-term changes to ensure Medicare's survival when the baby boom generation retires. However, the panel could not settle on a plan that could muster the 11 votes needed to send it to Congress.

Thomas' detail-oriented approach was useful when he was chairman of the House Administration Committee from 1995 to 2000. He dealt with the new majority's housekeeping tasks and also helped retool Capitol security measures after two U.S. Capitol Police officers were fatally shot in 1998.

Thomas oversaw the privatization of several House services and slashed committee staffing by a third. He also presided over the first-ever outside audit of House finances, which gave Republicans evidence to back their claims that under Democratic rule, the House was a financial mess. Funds were poorly accounted for and frequently overspent, and lawmakers were sometimes the culprits. A 1999 audit gave the House a clean bill of health for the first time, a victory for the chairman.

Thomas was first elected to the California Assembly in 1974 as a conservative. Four years later, when GOP Rep. William Ketchum died after the 1978 primary, Thomas positioned himself as the moderate GOP alternative. It took him seven ballots at a nominating convention to beat two conservative opponents. He went on to easily defeat Democrat Bob Sogge, a former state Senate aide. While he has faced some primary challenges through the years, his seat in his heavily GOP district is secure.

KEY VOTES

2002

No Overhaul campaign finance law; ban "soft money" and restrict advocacy advertising
Yes Back Bush's defense budget increase
Yes Extend 1996 welfare law
Yes Adopt Bush's discretionary spending limit
Yes Pass GOP Medicare prescription drug plan
No Create independent Sept. 11 commission
No Extend union protections to Homeland Security Department employees
Yes Revive fast-track procedures for trade agreements
Yes Authorize war against Iraq
Yes Advance bankruptcy overhaul opposed by abortion opponents

2001

Yes Nullify Clinton Labor Department ergonomics rule
Yes Cut taxes by $1.35 trillion through fiscal 2011
No Maintain ban on oil drilling in Arctic National Wildlife Refuge
Yes Approve Bush proposal to limit managed-care plan liability for coverage decisions
No Divert money from crop subsidy payments to land conservation
Yes Expand law enforcement power to investigate suspected terrorists

CQ VOTE STUDIES

	PARTY UNITY		PRESIDENTIAL SUPPORT	
	Support	Oppose	Support	Oppose
2002	91%	9%	90%	10%
2001	95%	5%	90%	10%
2000	92%	8%	32%	68%
1999	89%	11%	31%	69%
1998	89%	11%	28%	72%

INTEREST GROUPS

	AFL-CIO	ADA	CCUS	ACU
2002	0%	10%	100%	80%
2001	8%	15%	100%	68%
2000	0%	10%	90%	80%
1999	0%	10%	96%	66%
1998	10%	0%	100%	92%

CALIFORNIA 22

Kern and San Luis Obispo counties — Bakersfield

The 22nd stretches from San Luis Obispo County near the coast inland to Ridgecrest in Kern County, dipping south into northwestern Los Angeles County. The district, previously numbered the 21st, lost its portion of Tulare County in redistricting following the 2000 census, though it remains consistently Republican. More than two-thirds of its residents live in Kern County.

Kern is known for oil production and has a strong agricultural industry. Along with the farm-oriented San Luis Obispo area (the city itself is in the coastal 23rd District), the counties produce billions of dollars each year in crops such as grapes, citrus, cotton and nuts. San Luis Obispo nurtures vineyards and cattle.

Bakersfield, some of which falls in the 20th District, is Kern County's largest city and sits in the southern end of the San Joaquin Valley. Along with Lancaster in Los Angeles County, it continues to see the most growth. Here, oil and agriculture dominate the economy, although the city is trying to diversify by promoting its growing telecommunications, financial and light manufacturing sectors.

San Luis Obispo County trends conservative, with many conservative Democrats in the northern part. Agricultural and military aviation issues remain dominant concerns for residents.

MAJOR INDUSTRY
Agriculture, oil, military

MILITARY BASES
Naval Air Warfare Center Weapons Division, China Lake, 1,164 military, 880 civilian (2002) (shared with the 25th); Edwards Air Force Base, 3,633 military, 7,903 civilian (2002) (shared with the 25th)

CITIES
Bakersfield (pt.), 203,773; Lancaster (pt.), 65,976; Oildale, 27,885

NOTABLE
Bakersfield was known as the country music capital of the West; Country music star Buck Owens has his Crystal Palace museum and theater in Bakersfield; The nation's first jet- and rocket-powered flights took off from Edwards Air Force Base; The world's largest novelty ice cream plant, for Nestle Ice Cream Co., is in Bakersfield.

Rep. Lois Capps (D)

CAPITOL OFFICE
225-3601
www.house.gov/capps
1707 Longworth 20515-0523; fax 225-5632

COMMITTEES
Budget
Energy & Commerce

HOMETOWN
Santa Barbara

BORN
Jan. 10, 1938, Ladysmith, Wis.

RELIGION
Lutheran

FAMILY
Widowed; three children (one deceased)

EDUCATION
Pacific Lutheran U., B.S. 1959 (nursing); Yale U., M.A. 1964 (religion); U. of California, Santa Barbara, M.A. 1990 (education)

CAREER
Elementary school nurse; college instructor

POLITICAL HIGHLIGHTS
No previous office

ELECTION RESULTS

2002 GENERAL		
Lois Capps (D)	95,752	59.0%
Beth Rogers (R)	62,604	38.6%
James E. Hill (LIBERT)	3,866	2.4%
2002 PRIMARY		
Lois Capps (D)		unopposed
2000 GENERAL		
Lois Capps (D)	135,538	53.1%
Mike Stoker (R)	113,094	44.3%

PREVIOUS WINNING PERCENTAGES
1998 (55%); 1998 Special Runoff Election (53%); 1998 Special Election (45%)

Elected March 1998; 3rd full term

Brought to Congress by tragic personal circumstances, Capps has evolved from a politically inexperienced widow who claimed her late husband's seat to a seasoned lawmaker serving her third term in the House.

Her unusual history, coupled with a district that until recently had many Republican voters, makes Democrat Capps a political wild card at times. She is passionate about more government spending for health care but has supported GOP-inspired tax cuts.

Capps went into the 108th Congress with a distinctly more Democratic district as a result of redistricting. That is certain to affect her political evolution, just as it has influenced her thinking on her term-limit pledge. When she was elected in 1998, Capps said she would stay just three terms, her service ending in 2004. But in early 2003, Capps said she would run again in 2004. She said she had made the pledge while still recovering from her husband's death, but "I see things a little differently now."

Walter Capps was elected in 1996, becoming the first Democrat to win the coastal California district in a half century. He suffered a fatal heart attack less than a year later. Lois Capps replaced him in a nationally watched special election early in 1998.

Tragedy followed Capps to Washington. In 2000, she lost her daughter, a psychology professor at the University of California at Berkeley, to lung cancer at age 35. Since then, Capps has grown close to Republican Rep. Deborah Pryce of Ohio, who also lost a daughter to cancer.

Those personal events, and Capps' professional background as a registered nurse, explain her focus on health care policy. She sits on the Energy and Commerce Committee, and its Health Subcommittee. She also co-chairs the House Democratic Task Force on Health, which develops the party's position on the overhaul of Medicare and a prescription drug benefit for senior citizens.

Capps said her proudest moment in the 107th Congress was passage in 2002 of her bill to provide federal training, grants and scholarships to address the national nursing shortage. She also has sponsored measures to increase funding for cancer research and stroke prevention. She joined a bipartisan effort on a bill allowing states to use Medicaid funds for screening, assessment and treatment of victims of domestic violence.

Also in 2001, she secured $50,000 for a local program to remove tattoos from ex-gang members, which drew ridicule from conservative radio host Rush Limbaugh and a few newspaper editorial writers.

Capps often breaks with her party on the issue of tax cuts. During the Clinton administration, she voted to override the Democratic president's veto of Republican bills that slashed estate taxes and eliminated the marriage penalty in the tax code. In 2001, she was one of only 28 House Democrats to vote for President Bush's sweeping $1.35 trillion tax cut.

Capps is more pro-business than other liberal Democrats, a reflection of a district dominated by small businesses, family farms and the large estates of Hollywood stars who live in Santa Barbara County. She voted to normalize trade with China, despite the opposition of organized labor. The U.S. Chamber of Commerce in 2002 gave Capps its "Spirit of Enterprise" award for voting with business on 15 of 20 issues scored by the chamber.

Capps' support for business does not extend to big oil companies that want to drill in California waters. Her district, among the most naturally beautiful in the country, takes in Santa Barbara and other well-heeled communities opposed to the drilling. In the 107th Congress, Capps won House passage of an Interior spending bill amendment blocking drilling off the coast, but her provision was scaled back in conference.

On the biggest foreign policy issue of the 107th, Capps opposed the resolution authorizing the use of force against Iraq. She said invading Iraq was inconsistent with longstanding U.S. foreign policy requiring "specific provocation." Capps' late husband, a popular religious studies professor at the University of California in Santa Barbara, taught courses on peace studies and the Vietnam War.

The daughter and granddaughter of Lutheran ministers, Capps grew up in small towns in Wisconsin and Montana. She has a master's degree in religion from Yale. She worked as a nurse for many years in the Santa Barbara School District and also headed the county's teenage pregnancy counseling project.

In Washington, she is well-liked by colleagues and staff. In 2002, Washingtonian magazine gave her the top spot in its "Just Plain Nice" category, based on a survey of congressional aides.

The 22nd District had been a competitive one, split between Democrats and Republicans, when Walter Capps won election. Lois Capps helped her husband by standing in for him at campaign events in 1996 while he recovered from injuries from a car accident caused by a drunken driver. (Capps also was in the car.)

In her election in 1998, she benefited from her late husband's political organization and disunity among Republicans. A contest on the GOP side between conservative state Rep. Tom Bordonaro and moderate state Rep. Brooks Firestone became a bitter and symbolic struggle of what the party was undergoing nationally. Speaker Newt Gingrich backed Firestone while conservative firebrands like Whip Tom DeLay supported Bordonaro.

Capps stayed focused on local issues and stressed Democratic themes of protecting the environment and improving education and health care. She won by 9 percentage points over Bordonaro, becoming the 35th widow to win a House seat after the death of a husband.

Capps won re-election in November 1998 to a full term, again besting Bordonaro, this time by 12 points. In 2000, Republicans targeted her district, but she turned back Republican Mike Stoker, a former Santa Barbara County supervisor. In 2002, redistricting gave Democrats a 45 percent to 33 percent registration edge over Republicans. Capps overwhelmingly beat Beth Rogers, from a wealthy fourth-generation Ventura County farming family.

KEY VOTES

2002

Yes Overhaul campaign finance law; ban "soft money" and restrict advocacy advertising
Yes Back Bush's defense budget increase
No Extend 1996 welfare law
No Adopt Bush's discretionary spending limit
No Pass GOP Medicare prescription drug plan
Yes Create independent Sept. 11 commission
Yes Extend union protections to Homeland Security Department employees
No Revive fast-track procedures for trade agreements
No Authorize war against Iraq
No Advance bankruptcy overhaul opposed by abortion opponents

2001

No Nullify Clinton Labor Department ergonomics rule
Yes Cut taxes by $1.35 trillion through fiscal 2011
Yes Maintain ban on oil drilling in Arctic National Wildlife Refuge
No Approve Bush proposal to limit managed-care plan liability for coverage decisions
Yes Divert money from crop subsidy payments to land conservation
Yes Expand law enforcement power to investigate suspected terrorists

CQ VOTE STUDIES

	PARTY UNITY		PRESIDENTIAL SUPPORT	
	Support	Oppose	Support	Oppose
2002	93%	7%	32%	68%
2001	92%	8%	36%	64%
2000	89%	11%	73%	27%
1999	90%	10%	80%	20%
1998	91%	9%	73%	27%

INTEREST GROUPS

	AFL-CIO	ADA	CCUS	ACU
2002	89%	90%	45%	12%
2001	92%	85%	43%	4%
2000	70%	70%	75%	16%
1999	78%	100%	44%	8%
1998	78%	85%	71%	18%

CALIFORNIA 23

Central Coast – Oxnard, Santa Barbara, Santa Maria, San Luis Obispo

The 23rd is a sliver of coastline stretching from north of San Luis Obispo into Ventura County, which lies northwest of Los Angeles. Three main cities — Oxnard, Santa Barbara and San Luis Obispo — register high numbers of Democrats, especially Oxnard, which has a significant blue-collar Hispanic population. Like much of California's coast, the district is liberal on social issues.

The district's other major city, Santa Maria, is the most Republican, but wealthy members of Hollywood's elite in Santa Barbara County and students at California Polytechnic State University in San Luis Obispo and the University of California, Santa Barbara tilt the 23rd to the left.

Agriculture is a mainstay in the San Luis Obispo area, as well as in Santa Maria, which also is known for manufacturing. Oxnard is home to large biotech companies and the Port of Hueneme, the only international port on the central coast, which imports and exports the majority of cars in the state. Tourism also helps this beach-front district's economy, and universities contribute to the wealth of the 23rd.

Redistricting following the 2000 census gave the district, previously numbered the 22nd, its coastal shape — at one point it narrows to the width of a strip of shoreline — and its Democratic lean. The new district gave Democrat Al Gore 53 percent of the vote in the 2000 presidential election. Hispanics make up two-fifths of the population.

MAJOR INDUSTRY

Agriculture, military, tourism

MILITARY BASES

Vandenberg Air Force Base, 3,297 military, 1,021 civilian (2002) (shared with the 24th); Naval Base Ventura County, 4,024 military, 329 civilian (2001) (shared with the 24th)

CITIES

Oxnard, 170,358; Santa Barbara, 92,325; Santa Maria, 77,423; Goleta (unincorporated), 55,204

NOTABLE

Santa Barbara was the birthplace of the Egg McMuffin; Hearst Castle, a historic house museum at San Simeon, was home to William Randolph Hearst; Channel Islands National Park.

Rep. Elton Gallegly (R)

CAPITOL OFFICE
225-5811
www.house.gov/gallegly
2427 Rayburn 20515-0524; fax 225-1100

COMMITTEES
International Relations
(International Terrorism, Nonproliferation & Human Rights - chairman)
Judiciary
Resources
Select Intelligence

HOMETOWN
Simi Valley

BORN
March 7, 1944, Huntington Park, Calif.

RELIGION
Protestant

FAMILY
Wife, Janice Gallegly; four children

EDUCATION
California State U., Los Angeles, attended 1962-63

CAREER
Real estate broker

POLITICAL HIGHLIGHTS
Simi Valley City Council, 1979-86; mayor of Simi Valley, 1980-86

ELECTION RESULTS

2002 GENERAL		
Elton Gallegly (R)	120,585	65.2%
Fern Rudin (D)	58,755	31.8%
Gary Harber (LIBERT)	5,666	3.1%
2002 PRIMARY		
Elton Gallegly (R)		unopposed
2000 GENERAL		
Elton Gallegly (R)	119,479	54.1%
Michael Case (D)	89,918	40.7%
Cary Savitch (REF)	6,473	2.9%
Roger Peebles (LIBERT)	3,708	1.7%

PREVIOUS WINNING PERCENTAGES
1998 (60%); 1996 (60%); 1994 (66%); 1992 (54%); 1990 (58%); 1988 (69%); 1986 (68%)

Elected 1986; 9th term

Gallegly is among the lawmakers whose profile should rise in the 108th Congress. As chairman of the newly created International Relations Subcommittee on International Terrorism, he has oversight duties that include monitoring al Qaeda and similar organizations. His new posting to the Intelligence Committee adds to his involvement in the issue.

When Chairman Henry J. Hyde picked him for the subcommittee chairmanship, the Illinois Republican cited Gallegly's "wealth of experience" on both the International Relations and Judiciary committees. For his part Gallegly (GAL-uh-glee), who previously chaired the International Relations panel's Subcommittee on Europe, said the job was the most important assignment he has had since arriving in Congress in 1987.

That may be true. But it certainly was not his first choice.

Gallegly waged an aggressive campaign to become chairman of the Resources Committee in the 108th upon the retirement of Utah's James V. Hansen. While careful to pay homage to the seniority of H. James Saxton of New Jersey, the highest-ranking Republican on the committee with an interest in the chairmanship, Gallegly — who ranks just below Saxton in GOP committee seniority — promoted himself as a Westerner more in tune with the property rights views of Republican leaders.

But the GOP leadership skipped over Gallegly, Saxton and three other more-senior Republicans vying for the post in order to elevate to the chairmanship Richard W. Pombo of California, a protégé of new Majority Leader Tom DeLay. On Resources, Gallegly has looked after his state's water interests and helped those landowners who are struggling to develop property in compliance with federal environmental protection laws. "Endangered species and property rights are not mutually exclusive, although they would be separate bills," Gallegly said. He promotes what he has termed "common sense environmentalism."

His highest-profile initiative in that area came out of the Judiciary Committee in the 105th Congress. Gallegly's legislation was designed to give landowners and business developers more clout in challenging local zoning laws that prevent them from building on their property. The measure, pushed by property rights advocates, drew opposition from environmentalists, historic preservationists, governors and local officials. It passed in the House but died in the Senate.

Gallegly — who is among a handful of members to hold four committee assignments — is one of Judiciary's few non-lawyers. He has gained a reputation for adopting a hard line against illegal immigrants, and with federal officials keeping a closer eye on U.S. borders to stop terrorists, Gallegly hopes to draw more attention to that cause.

Despite his focus on such hot-button issues, Gallegly has an easygoing demeanor with a touch of self-deprecation. "You have to work with leadership and sub-chairs and members to make law," he said. "Just throwing something up against the wall to see if it sticks is not my style."

While building a conservative voting record overall, Gallegly occasionally casts his lot with Democrats, such as backing tighter regulation of health maintenance organizations. As the former mayor of Simi Valley, a community close enough to Los Angeles that many of its residents are concerned about the spread of urban crime, Gallegly voted for the 1993 law creating a five-day waiting period for handgun purchases. He was one of 42 Republicans who voted for the 1994 crime bill sought by President Clinton, which included a ban on certain semiautomatic assault-style weapons.

Gallegly is remembered for his unsuccessful 1996 effort to allow local school districts to decide whether to provide a public school education to the children of illegal immigrants. He argued that states such as California could not afford to educate such children and that the promise of free schooling was a magnet drawing illegal immigrants into the country.

Gallegly has made a special cause of war veterans. In the 107th Congress, he won passage of a bill that directs the Pentagon to award the Korea Defense Service Medal to military personnel who have served there since the war ended in 1954. In the 106th, Gallegly won enactment of a law authorizing a plaque at the Vietnam Veterans Memorial honoring veterans who died after their service in Vietnam but as a result of injuries from the war.

When he was growing up, Gallegly followed the political persuasions of his father, a lifelong Democrat. But he described his father to the Los Angeles Times as "an FDR Democrat, and they're much different from the Democrats of today. He believed in government helping people who couldn't help themselves, but not those who could."

In high school, the younger Gallegly's Democratic views earned him the nickname "Walter Reuther" — a reference to the long-tenured president of the United Auto Workers union. But, after dropping out of college for financial reasons, Gallegly went into the real estate business (with an initial investment of $45) and built a successful brokerage. Frustrated in his dealings with local government, he decided to run for office himself in 1979, urged on by his business colleagues.

Gallegly won a seat on the Simi Valley City Council and served concurrently as mayor for six years before running for Congress in 1986. His path to Washington was opened when GOP Rep. Bobbi Fiedler gave up her House seat after three terms to run, unsuccessfully, for the Senate. Touting his record as mayor of Simi Valley, where he was well-known for having boosted economic development, Gallegly defeated Tony Hope, the comedian's son, in the GOP primary and then won the general election by 40 points.

The area Gallegly represented in the 1990s was much more competitive politically; in 2000 it was carried by Al Gore and Gallegly was held to 54.1 percent of the vote, his lowest share ever, by real estate lawyer Michael Case. But the House map was redrawn for this decade with incumbent protection in mind, and Gallegly's home was situated in a district — relabeled the 24th — that was more reliably Republican. In his 2002 re-election he took 65 percent against Democrat Fern Rudin, a former paralegal and self-employed public relations consultant from Thousand Oaks.

KEY VOTES

2002

No Overhaul campaign finance law; ban "soft money" and restrict advocacy advertising
Yes Back Bush's defense budget increase
Yes Extend 1996 welfare law
Yes Adopt Bush's discretionary spending limit
Yes Pass GOP Medicare prescription drug plan
No Create independent Sept. 11 commission
No Extend union protections to Homeland Security Department employees
Yes Revive fast-track procedures for trade agreements
Yes Authorize war against Iraq
Yes Advance bankruptcy overhaul opposed by abortion opponents

2001

Yes Nullify Clinton Labor Department ergonomics rule
Yes Cut taxes by $1.35 trillion through fiscal 2011
No Maintain ban on oil drilling in Arctic National Wildlife Refuge
Yes Approve Bush proposal to limit managed-care plan liability for coverage decisions
No Divert money from crop subsidy payments to land conservation
Yes Expand law enforcement power to investigate suspected terrorists

CQ VOTE STUDIES

	PARTY UNITY		PRESIDENTIAL SUPPORT	
	Support	Oppose	Support	Oppose
2002	94%	6%	82%	18%
2001	96%	4%	91%	9%
2000	85%	15%	35%	65%
1999	88%	12%	24%	76%
1998	90%	10%	21%	79%

INTEREST GROUPS

	AFL-CIO	ADA	CCUS	ACU
2002	11%	5%	95%	100%
2001	17%	0%	100%	88%
2000	0%	5%	85%	72%
1999	33%	25%	84%	79%
1998	20%	15%	83%	76%

CALIFORNIA 24

Ventura and Santa Barbara counties – Thousand Oaks, Simi Valley

Located north and west of the close-in Los Angeles suburbs, the 24th includes nearly all of Ventura County and inland Santa Barbara County.

Ventura County, where more than four-fifths of district residents live, is a mix of lower-income farming communities and more-upscale residential neighborhoods, such as Moorpark, one of district's fastest-growing cities. The county passed a slow-growth ballot initiative in 1998 in an effort to stave off urban sprawl. After absorbing some destruction from the 1994 Northridge earthquake, Ventura County now has growing electronics, finance and insurance sectors. Industries ranging from agriculture to biotechnology to construction have contributed to the county's recovery.

Because Ventura borders Los Angeles County to the south and east, it often is identified with its urban neighbor. The central and western portions of the district — mainly in Santa Barbara County — are more agricultural, producing grapes, broccoli and strawberries, and including most of the Los Padres National Forest. Many residents are employed by hospitals and universities. San Nicolas Island and the Anacapa Islands also fall within the 24th's boundaries.

The district's reliable Republicanism comes from interior Santa Barbara — the neighboring 23rd contains the more Democratic coast. Vandenberg Air Force Base and south Ventura County cities such as Simi Valley and Thousand Oaks also contribute to the GOP base.

MAJOR INDUSTRY
Biotechnology, aerospace, service

MILITARY BASES
Vandenberg Air Force Base, 3,297 military, 1,021 civilian (2002) (shared with the 23rd); Naval Base Ventura County, 4,024 military, 329 civilian (2001) (shared with the 23rd)

CITIES
Thousand Oaks, 117,005; Simi Valley, 111,351; Ventura (pt.), 79,416

NOTABLE
The Ronald Reagan Presidential Library is in Simi Valley; An all-white Simi Valley jury acquitted three police officers accused of beating motorist Rodney King, touching off Los Angeles riots in 1992.

Rep. Howard P. 'Buck' McKeon (R)

CAPITOL OFFICE
225-1956
tellbuck@mail.house.gov
www.house.gov/mckeon
2351 Rayburn 20515-0525; fax 226-0683

COMMITTEES
Armed Services
Education & Workforce
(21st Century Competitiveness - chairman)

HOMETOWN
Santa Clarita

BORN
Sept. 9, 1939, Los Angeles, Calif.

RELIGION
Mormon

FAMILY
Wife, Patricia McKeon; six children

EDUCATION
Brigham Young U., B.S. 1985

CAREER
Clothing store owner

POLITICAL HIGHLIGHTS
William S. Hart School Board, 1978-87; Santa Clarita City Council, 1987-92 (mayor, 1987-88)

ELECTION RESULTS

2002 GENERAL		
Howard "Buck" McKeon (R)	80,775	65.0%
Robert "Bob" Conaway (D)	38,674	31.1%
Frank M. Consolo Jr. (LIBERT)	4,887	3.9%
2002 PRIMARY		
Howard "Buck" McKeon (R)	37,000	84.5%
James O. Aldrich (R)	6,810	15.5%
2000 GENERAL		
Howard "Buck" McKeon (R)	138,628	62.2%
Sid Gold (D)	73,921	33.2%
Bruce Acker (LIBERT)	7,219	3.2%
Mews Small (NL)	3,010	1.4%

PREVIOUS WINNING PERCENTAGES
1998 (75%); 1996 (62%); 1994 (65%); 1992 (52%)

Elected 1992; 6th term

Now in his sixth term, McKeon has carved out a niche of influence on education matters and looks out for his district's defense and aerospace contractors while demonstrating his willingness to work across party lines.

While he is one of the most reliably conservative votes in the House, the soft-spoken, genial McKeon works quietly and in a nonconfrontational manner to advance his agenda. McKeon has had experience being in the minority: He arrived in Congress when House Republicans had no real power and minimal input into legislation. Perhaps that is one reason he has been able to work well with Democrats on two hotly contested and partisan issues, education and job training, which were under his purview as chairman of the Education panel's Postsecondary Education, Training and Life-Long Learning Subcommittee for six years.

In the 107th Congress, forced by GOP-imposed term limits to give up the Postsecondary Education gavel, McKeon took on the chairmanship of Education's Subcommittee on 21st Century Competitiveness.

McKeon was a conferee in the 107th on a bill that revamped federal education programs, and he drafted the provisions on teacher training and technology in education. He also worked on legislation he called FEDUP — an initiative to streamline the higher education bureaucracy.

McKeon acknowledges that education is a difficult area politically for many Republicans. "Our base does not want us to do anything because it's not a federal role. So, if we do something, it makes the base mad," he said. McKeon is eager to compromise on education: "We get beat up by Democrats who want 100,000 teachers, hate-crime language and gun control. And we have Republicans who want vouchers and who consider testing obtrusive."

In the 107th, he was the leading sponsor of a bipartisan bill that sought to remove a financial disincentive for private sector workers to leave their jobs and become public school teachers. Rules governing Social Security benefits penalized such workers by reducing their private sector retirement benefits. "Becoming a teacher is hard enough. I think we should do all we can to encourage teaching as a second career," McKeon said. He is also a supporter of increased funding for historically black colleges.

He has won friends in the education community; he was honored in 2002 by the National Association of Independent Colleges and Universities, whose president said, "No one in Congress has done more to keep higher education accessible and affordable for millions of students of all backgrounds."

In the 105th Congress, McKeon worked with his panel's ranking Democrat, Dale E. Kildee of Michigan, on legislation to keep banks in the business of making loans to college students. McKeon also was the force behind the creation of a commission to study the matter of rapidly increasing college tuition. Earlier in McKeon's congressional career, he showed his perseverance in the four-year effort to overhaul and consolidate federal job training and adult education programs, legislation that eventually became law in 1998. And in 2000, he helped win reauthorization of the Older Americans Act, the program that supports nutrition and job programs for the elderly. In both cases, McKeon had to overcome opposition from some conservatives who preferred more local control over the spending.

McKeon once observed that in his constituency, "most people would just as soon the government went away." But even in the conservative-dominated 25th District, there are federal expenditures locals embrace — particularly for military projects. Early in his congressional tenure, McKeon had to plead with fiscal conservatives in his own party to approve an activist federal role in helping Southern California rebuild after the 1994 Northridge earthquake — the epicenter of which was in what was then his district.

With many aerospace plants in his district, McKeon continually pushes for increased defense spending from his perch on the Armed Services Committee. The 25th District hosts a Lockheed Martin plant and a NASA facility that prepares space shuttles for flights. He champions the development of the next generation of space vehicle, the X-33; the next generation of fighter, the Joint Strike Fighter; and the Global Hawk reconnaissance plane. Manufacturers in his district have thousands of jobs at stake on the projects.

McKeon in the 107th sought to revive an issue that had been debated throughout the 1990s — whether to build more B-2 bombers, which he said had proved their worth in Kosovo and Afghanistan. "It's a no-brainer," McKeon argued. "If we go to places like Iraq, we're going to need these planes." Northrop Grumman's Palmdale plant was the final assembly plant for the B-2.

Upon arriving in Washington, McKeon, a millionaire owner of a chain of Western-wear stores (since sold), organized the Congressional Boot Caucus, where footwear aficionados from both sides of the aisle could meet, talk boots and hear presentations from manufacturers on new boot fashions.

McKeon's initial political involvement was with his local school board; and he was the first mayor of Santa Clarita after it incorporated in 1987. He says he came to Congress to get off the Santa Clarita City Council: He had been a member of the council for two terms and was only reluctantly gearing up to run for a third in 1991 when redistricting created a new House seat around his Santa Clarita base.

McKeon jumped at the chance to run for something else and was the surprise GOP primary winner over Phillip D. Wyman, a 14-year state Assembly veteran. The victory largely determined the outcome in November in the heavily Republican 25th District. McKeon had a sizable spending advantage and defeated Democratic lawyer and rancher James H. "Gil" Gilmartin by 19 points. Since then, he has won re-election with even more ease.

In the 108th, McKeon has a much more far-flung constituency. His district now stretches about 300 miles north to Mono County, almost to Lake Tahoe, adding four military installations and five Indian tribes. As a result, McKeon's concerns have expanded to such issues as grazing rights, wilderness protection and tourism. The two northernmost counties have only about 30,000 people, and the population base remains in the Santa Clarita-Palmdale area. The district has become slightly more Republican.

KEY VOTES

2002

- No Overhaul campaign finance law; ban "soft money" and restrict advocacy advertising
- Yes Back Bush's defense budget increase
- Yes Extend 1996 welfare law
- Yes Adopt Bush's discretionary spending limit
- Yes Pass GOP Medicare prescription drug plan
- No Create independent Sept. 11 commission
- No Extend union protections to Homeland Security Department employees
- Yes Revive fast-track procedures for trade agreements
- Yes Authorize war against Iraq
- No Advance bankruptcy overhaul opposed by abortion opponents

2001

- Yes Nullify Clinton Labor Department ergonomics rule
- Yes Cut taxes by $1.35 trillion through fiscal 2011
- No Maintain ban on oil drilling in Arctic National Wildlife Refuge
- Yes Approve Bush proposal to limit managed-care plan liability for coverage decisions
- No Divert money from crop subsidy payments to land conservation
- Yes Expand law enforcement power to investigate suspected terrorists

CQ VOTE STUDIES

	PARTY UNITY		PRESIDENTIAL SUPPORT	
	Support	Oppose	Support	Oppose
2002	95%	5%	90%	10%
2001	99%	1%	98%	2%
2000	95%	5%	30%	70%
1999	93%	7%	22%	78%
1998	95%	5%	24%	76%

INTEREST GROUPS

	AFL-CIO	ADA	CCUS	ACU
2002	11%	5%	90%	88%
2001	8%	0%	100%	88%
2000	0%	5%	85%	92%
1999	0%	5%	96%	79%
1998	0%	5%	100%	96%

CALIFORNIA 25

Northern Los Angeles and San Bernardino counties; Inyo and Mono counties

The vast 25th stretches from east-central California on the Nevada border south along the mountains and through Death Valley before crossing the Mojave Desert and San Bernardino County into northern Los Angeles County, where it takes in the tip of the city.

Nearly three-fourths of residents live in Los Angeles County, though only 5 percent of the county's overall populace is in the district. The 25th's suburbs and desert are solidly Republican, including a mix of upper-middle-class residents and more-conservative working-class whites. More than one-fourth of the district is Hispanic, however.

Most of the land in Mono and Inyo counties, added during redistricting following the 2000 census, is government-owned, and a few bedroom communities' economies rely on tourism, mining and agriculture. Santa Clarita Valley is suburban, but attracts manufacturing that cannot afford to locate in Los Angeles proper. The 25th's fastest-growing area is the Antelope Valley desert due north of LA, home to Lancaster and Palmdale.

Economically, the 25th has suffered more from the dwindling aerospace industry than from the 1994 earthquake that collapsed buildings and a freeway. It now faces the challenges of managing and irrigating vast tracts of desert, much of it federally owned, and spurring its economy by attracting more industry and manufacturing jobs.

MAJOR INDUSTRY

Tourism, manufacturing, construction, aerospace, military

MILITARY BASES

Fort Irwin (Army), 4,914 military, 3,781 civilian (2002); Edwards Air Force Base, 3,633 military, 7,903 civilian (2002) (shared with the 22nd); Naval Air Warfare Center Weapons Division, China Lake, 1,164 military, 880 civilian (2002) (shared with the 22nd); Marine Corps Logistics Base Barstow, 301 military, 1,456 civilian (2002)

CITIES

Santa Clarita, 151,088; Palmdale, 116,670; Victorville, 64,029; Lancaster (pt.), 52,742; Los Angeles (pt.), 22,882

NOTABLE

Badwater in Death Valley is the lowest point in the United States at 282 feet below sea level; Baker has a 134-foot-high thermometer.

Rep. David Dreier (R)

CAPITOL OFFICE
225-2305
www.house.gov/dreier
237 Cannon 20515-0526; fax 225-7018

COMMITTEES
Rules - chairman
Select Homeland Security

HOMETOWN
San Dimas

BORN
July 5, 1952, Kansas City, Mo.

RELIGION
Christian Scientist

FAMILY
Single

EDUCATION
Claremont Men's College, B.A. 1975 (political science); Claremont Graduate U., M.A. 1976 (American government)

CAREER
Real estate developer; university fundraiser

POLITICAL HIGHLIGHTS
Republican nominee for U.S. House, 1978

ELECTION RESULTS

2002 GENERAL		
David Dreier (R)	95,360	63.8%
Marjorie Musser Mikels (D)	50,081	33.5%
Randall Weissbuch (LIBERT)	4,089	2.7%
2002 PRIMARY		
David Dreier (R)		unopposed
2000 GENERAL		
David Dreier (R)	116,557	56.8%
Janice M. Nelson (D)	81,804	39.9%
Randall Weissbuch (LIBERT)	2,823	1.4%
M. Lawrence Allison (NL)	2,083	1.0%

PREVIOUS WINNING PERCENTAGES
1998 (58%); 1996 (61%); 1994 (67%); 1992 (58%); 1990 (64%); 1988 (69%); 1986 (72%); 1984 (71%); 1982 (65%); 1980 (52%)

Elected 1980; 12th term

The 108th Congress will carry Dreier to the end of his tenure as chairman of the Rules Committee, where since 1999 his role has been to set the procedural levers on the House floor in ways that steer the outcome in the Republican leadership's favor. To the task he has brought a firm hand — outstretched, generally with a warm smile, from the sleeve of an impeccably pressed suit jacket.

In the 107th Congress, Dreier used his legislative skills and his charm to help shape what was arguably the most important domestic legislation of the second session, to create the Department of Homeland Security and carry out the biggest reordering of the federal bureaucracy in five decades. Dreier's main objective was to see that state and local governments, not Washington, gain much of the control over the law enforcement and public safety spending. In the 108th, he also serves on the new Homeland Security panel that oversees the new department.

But the Rules chairmanship places Dreier in the middle of every consequential legislative fight. His responsibility is to ensure that the ground rules for floor debate — what amendments may be offered, and by whom — are fair enough to quell significant complaints about fairness, but not so fair as to hand procedural advantage to the Democrats. "My first priority is to move our agenda," he says.

But in so doing, he remains polite and composed. He almost always identifies colleagues on the floor and in committee not only by their home state but also by their hometown, even when he is preparing to tell them their amendment will never be discussed on the House floor.

To that stressful task Dreier brings an energy level noticeable even in the workaholic world of the Capitol. The son of a Marine Corps drill sergeant, his day often begins at dawn with a brisk run. And it often ends long after dark, quite literally in a cigar-smoke-filled room hashing details of a GOP-blessed script for the next day's proceedings.

"The difference between the House and the Senate," he once said in describing his lack of interest in higher office, "is that on the floor of the Senate, it's like you're in a living room; and the floor of the House of Representatives is like an arena — it's intense."

Dreier continues to play a leading role on trade liberalization, technology and other economic development issues important to southern California. During the 107th, he helped orchestrate the two razor-thin victories in the House that were essential to enacting the 2002 law reviving fast-track procedures for congressional action on trade deals negotiated by the president. In the 108th, a top aim is to enact tax cuts that might stimulate business expansion.

Dreier's role as a political operative and fundraiser has recently become less obvious. In 2000 he was California co-chairman for George W. Bush's presidential campaign, served as parliamentarian for the Republican National Convention in Philadelphia and chaired GOPAC, the Republican Party's political action committee for state and local candidates. But he has since relinquished the chairmanship of GOPAC and has scaled back his involvement with the organization. Instead, Dreier has used his political action committee, the American Success PAC, to direct more than $800,000 before the last two elections to candidates sharing his view that globalization is in the national interest.

A quarter-century after entering public life, Dreier still describes himself as a Reagan Republican who believes in the primacy of the free market and wants government to stay out of the way of private enterprise. So his public face is that of the quintessential college Republican all grown up. Still, he does not look as if he has aged much since he first ran for Congress at age 26 from a room at his alma mater, Claremont Men's College (now Claremont McKenna), where he was a public relations official after obtaining undergraduate and graduate degrees. He lost that 1978 race, but prevailed two years later in a rematch.

Dreier sees himself as a reformer within the House. In 1993 he was co-vice chairman of a bipartisan, bicameral commission that recommended a number of operational changes to Congress. After Republicans took over in 1995, they instituted a number of the panel's proposals — slashing committee staff by one-third, subjecting Congress to federal anti-discrimination and workplace safety laws, eliminating proxy voting in all House committees and imposing six-year term limits for committee chairmen.

Dreier has an abiding interest in the history and well-being of the House. He says that a relative, Richard Bland Lee of Virginia, served on the first Rules panel near the end of the 18th century. But Dreier is by no means stuck in the past. In 1996, he spearheaded the "21st Century Congress" project, which sought to promote new technologies to enliven the political process. He has since planned online and fully interactive congressional hearings, using e-mail, video conferencing, television and the Internet to create a virtual hearing room for witnesses across the country.

The telegenic Dreier is at his best when playing to an audience, whether on the talk-show circuit, in the well of the House, or kibitzing in the press gallery with radio and television crews. But though he is often in the limelight, Dreier also has been known to disappear into his private hideaway in the Capitol for a quick game of pinball on his vintage "Voltan Woman" machine.

Dreier is a native of Kansas City, Mo., and remains active in his family's real estate investment firm there. In his first, underfinanced campaign in 1978, Dreier came within 12,000 votes of defeating Democratic incumbent James F. Lloyd. Two years later, he swamped Lloyd in fundraising and won by 12,000 votes, aided by that year's Reagan presidential landslide. His subsequent re-elections have been by comfortable, if not lopsided, margins.

California's incumbent-protection congressional redistricting plan for this decade made Dreier's territory — known as the 28th District in the last decade, when it twice voted Democratic for president — more predictably Republican. In 2002 he won by 30 percentage points.

KEY VOTES

2002

No Overhaul campaign finance law; ban "soft money" and restrict advocacy advertising
Yes Back Bush's defense budget increase
Yes Extend 1996 welfare law
Yes Adopt Bush's discretionary spending limit
Yes Pass GOP Medicare prescription drug plan
No Create independent Sept. 11 commission
No Extend union protections to Homeland Security Department employees
Yes Revive fast-track procedures for trade agreements
Yes Authorize war against Iraq
Yes Advance bankruptcy overhaul opposed by abortion opponents

2001

Yes Nullify Clinton Labor Department ergonomics rule
Yes Cut taxes by $1.35 trillion through fiscal 2011
No Maintain ban on oil drilling in Arctic National Wildlife Refuge
Yes Approve Bush proposal to limit managed-care plan liability for coverage decisions
No Divert money from crop subsidy payments to land conservation
Yes Expand law enforcement power to investigate suspected terrorists

CQ VOTE STUDIES

	PARTY UNITY		PRESIDENTIAL SUPPORT	
	Support	Oppose	Support	Oppose
2002	93%	7%	92%	8%
2001	97%	3%	100%	0%
2000	94%	6%	30%	70%
1999	91%	9%	30%	70%
1998	91%	9%	26%	74%

INTEREST GROUPS

	AFL-CIO	ADA	CCUS	ACU
2002	11%	5%	100%	84%
2001	8%	10%	100%	84%
2000	0%	5%	90%	92%
1999	0%	10%	96%	80%
1998	10%	0%	100%	92%

CALIFORNIA 26

Northeastern Los Angeles suburbs

Set in the foothills of the San Gabriel Mountains, the 26th is a mix of Los Angeles bedroom communities and the mountainous Angeles National Forest, which comprises its northern half. The commuter-heavy district takes in middle- to upper-class suburbs, many of which have retained their own identities and quaint downtowns.

The district includes wealthy, Republican communities surrounding Pasadena, such as La Cañada Flintridge and San Marino, and other Los Angeles County cities such as Arcadia, Glendora, Monrovia and San Dimas. Outside La Cañada Flintridge is NASA's Jet Propulsion Laboratory, which contributes to the area's high-tech flavor along with the California Institute of Technology in Pasadena (in the 29th District) and engineering firms in Monrovia. Many of the 26th's residents commute to work in downtown Los Angeles or have high-tech manufacturing jobs just outside the district.

In its chunk of San Bernardino County, where orchard country has given way to rapidly developing suburbs, the district includes the Inland Valley suburbs of Rancho Cucamonga, Upland and Montclair. Rapid development has brought young, wealthy fiscally minded Republicans to town — not unlike Orange County to the south. The valley is populated by service employers such as corporate call centers and technology groups. Most other industry is confined to small defense subcontractors and service industries, though the area has seen some growth in trade-related import and export businesses.

Like many Los Angeles suburbanites, residents here tend to be socially moderate and economically conservative. The district went for George W. Bush in the 2000 presidential contest by nearly 10 points. While not as diverse as most of its neighbors, the district is one-fourth Hispanic.

MAJOR INDUSTRY

Service, manufacturing, health care, biotechnology

CITIES

Rancho Cucamonga, 127,743; Upland, 68,393; Arcadia, 53,054; Glendora, 49,415

NOTABLE

Santa Anita Park thoroughbred racetrack is in Arcadia; The Huntington Library, a museum and garden in San Marino, has in its collection Thomas Gainsborough's painting, The Blue Boy, and a Gutenberg Bible.

Rep. Brad Sherman (D)

CAPITOL OFFICE
225-5911
brad.sherman@mail.house.gov
www.house.gov/sherman
1030 Longworth 20515-0527; fax 225-5879

COMMITTEES
Financial Services
International Relations
Science

HOMETOWN
Sherman Oaks

BORN
Oct. 24, 1954, Los Angeles, Calif.

RELIGION
Jewish

FAMILY
Single

EDUCATION
U. of California, Los Angeles, B.A. 1974; Harvard U., J.D. 1979

CAREER
Accountant; lawyer

POLITICAL HIGHLIGHTS
Calif. State Board of Equalization, 1991-97 (chairman, 1991-95)

ELECTION RESULTS

2002 GENERAL		
Brad Sherman (D)	79,815	62.0%
Robert M. Levy (R)	48,996	38.0%
2002 PRIMARY		
Brad Sherman (D)		unopposed
2000 GENERAL		
Brad Sherman (D)	155,398	66.0%
Jerry Doyle (R)	70,169	29.8%
Juan Ros (LIBERT)	6,966	3.0%
Michael Cuddehe (NL)	2,911	1.2%

PREVIOUS WINNING PERCENTAGES
1998 (57%); 1996 (50%)

Elected 1996; 4th term

A traditional Democrat on social and environmental issues, Sherman is a hawk on foreign policy, particularly when it comes to terrorism. Smart and funny, he describes himself as a "recovering nerd." He used to say that he only sought jobs held in the lowest possible public esteem, which was why his career evolved from certified public accountant to lawyer to tax collector. But in the wake of the accounting scandal that erupted after the collapse of Enron Corp. in 2001, Sherman joked that being a CPA no longer belonged at the top of his list.

Sherman voted in late 2002 to authorize the use of force against Iraq and, from his seat on the International Relations Committee, called for an expanded investigative role for the CIA and a renewed debate on whether the U.S. government should sponsor assassinations.

On immigration issues, Sherman has joined conservative Republicans from California in support of tamper-proof worker identification cards as well as legislation to tighten restrictions on government benefits for illegal aliens and to track down illegal immigrants. But Sherman is quick to point out that he is generally a "mainstream Democrat" on immigration policy. He supported reinstating a provision of the Immigration and Naturalization Act that allowed illegal immigrants to apply for Green Cards without having to leave the United States. Sherman has also steadfastly voted against allowing the military to patrol the U.S. border with Mexico.

But after the September 2001 terrorist attacks, Sherman issued a tough call to arms that was tempered only by an admonition to respect ethnic diversity. "We must wage war against all of the well-organized and well-financed groups who have dedicated themselves to killing Americans," he wrote in an op-ed piece published shortly after Sept. 11."We should seek United Nations approval for our actions, but we must be prepared to act alone."

Active on environmental issues, Sherman has cosponsored legislation to protect endangered species, restrict commercial logging and limit arsenic in drinking water. Sherman responded to an energy crisis in his home state at the start of the decade by calling for temporary price controls on electricity. He also introduced bills to allow Western states to extend daylight-saving time to two hours between May and September and to consider year-round daylight-saving time.

Sherman criticized a decision by President Bush in 2001 to back federal funding for stem cell research but only for 60 existing cell lines. "He went as far as he could while still maintaining most of his right-wing support, and we get only as much science as the far right will allow," Sherman said.

Drawing on his accounting background, Sherman repeatedly has urged Congress to authorize permanently a popular tax credit for corporate research and development, instead of renewing the credit for one year at a time and allowing it to expire periodically. He also sponsored a bill in the 107th Congress that would have required the Securities and Exchange Commission to review the annual reports of the non-governmental entities that set accounting standards.

A hard-liner on balanced budgeting — he had a seat on the Budget Committee in his first term — Sherman's initial campaign for Congress was based in part on the premise that the "lower interest rates we can achieve from balancing the federal budget will do more for economic growth than any Republican proposal and more for the low-income working families than any Democratic program." He backed the 1997 budget-balancing package (although he refused to support it until President Clinton won concessions from the GOP). And he has supported a constitutional amendment to require a two-thirds majority vote of Congress to raise taxes (although he switched his position and voted against the idea in 2002).

Sherman scored a significant victory in his first term by shepherding to enactment a $700 million proposal to buy environmentally sensitive lands. The funding was part of the initial 1997 budget deal between Clinton and the bipartisan congressional leadership, but it took an amendment by Sherman in the Budget Committee to ensure that the money was appropriated.

Included was money to buy property to augment the Santa Monica Mountains National Recreation Area, part of $16 million that Sherman steered to the area in his first three terms. The recreation area is no longer in his House district, which was renumbered and shifted to the east in 2001. Still, Sherman has vowed to stay involved in issues related to the mountains — development and combating natural disasters — because his new constituents use them frequently, as did his previous ones.

One of Sherman's pet projects is altering the order of presidential succession. His legislation would ensure that the presidency remained in the hands of the same political party by allowing the president to designate either the Speaker of the House or the House minority leader as second in line after the vice president, followed by either the majority or minority leader of the Senate, rather than the Senate president pro tempore.

Sherman got his start in politics as a child, stuffing envelopes for Democratic Rep. George E. Brown Jr., a longtime family friend. He was elected to the five-member California Board of Equalization in 1990 and re-elected in 1994.

Before his initial campaign, Sherman sewed up the backing of most area Democrats, first among them Anthony C. Beilenson, who was retiring after holding the House seat for 10 terms. He won the nomination with 54 percent against six other candidates and the general election by 6 percentage points; since then his victory margins have ranged from 19 to 37 points.

Sherman fought hard against a drastic redrawing of his district by the California Legislature in 2001, arguing that he should have "a continuity with the constituents." But critics said that Sherman opposed the new map because it added tens of thousands of Latino voters to his constituency, leaving him more vulnerable to a primary challenge from a Hispanic candidate. Sherman's ultimately unsuccessful effort did not endear him to California Democrats. Don Perata, who chaired the state Senate Reapportionment Committee, said he "wanted to Fed-Ex Brad Sherman to another galaxy."

KEY VOTES

2002

Yes Overhaul campaign finance law; ban "soft money" and restrict advocacy advertising
Yes Back Bush's defense budget increase
No Extend 1996 welfare law
No Adopt Bush's discretionary spending limit
No Pass GOP Medicare prescription drug plan
Yes Create independent Sept. 11 commission
Yes Extend union protections to Homeland Security Department employees
No Revive fast-track procedures for trade agreements
Yes Authorize war against Iraq
No Advance bankruptcy overhaul opposed by abortion opponents

2001

No Nullify Clinton Labor Department ergonomics rule
No Cut taxes by $1.35 trillion through fiscal 2011
Yes Maintain ban on oil drilling in Arctic National Wildlife Refuge
No Approve Bush proposal to limit managed-care plan liability for coverage decisions
Yes Divert money from crop subsidy payments to land conservation
Yes Expand law enforcement power to investigate suspected terrorists

CQ VOTE STUDIES

	PARTY UNITY		PRESIDENTIAL SUPPORT	
	Support	Oppose	Support	Oppose
2002	95%	5%	28%	72%
2001	92%	8%	33%	67%
2000	93%	7%	83%	17%
1999	87%	13%	78%	22%
1998	83%	17%	72%	28%

INTEREST GROUPS

	AFL-CIO	ADA	CCUS	ACU
2002	89%	100%	35%	4%
2001	92%	95%	39%	12%
2000	100%	90%	47%	20%
1999	89%	95%	32%	8%
1998	80%	95%	61%	20%

CALIFORNIA 27

Part of the San Fernando Valley; part of Burbank

While most of the 27th is in Los Angeles, few of the district's residents identify themselves as "Angelenos." Instead, they see themselves as part of the region's fast-growing communities: the Van Nuys, Encino and Sherman Oaks areas of Los Angeles in the San Fernando Valley north of the central city.

The Valley — primarily the 27th and 28th districts — was behind a failed ballot measure in 2002 to secede from the rest of the city amid complaints that too much of its taxes went over the mountains to city services in central Los Angeles. Though the measure was initiated by the Valley's traditional white, middle- to upper-class voters, the 27th's suburban havens have been transformed by immigrants and no longer are dominated by that group. Forty-five percent white and 36 percent Hispanic, the district also has seen an explosion of Asian immigrants, particularly from India and Pakistan, who have added to the district's working-class flavor.

The flat, gridlike streets of the 27th hold the Burbank and Van Nuys airports, as well as several colleges, including California State University Northridge. Reservoirs in the northwest corner provide water to more than 10 million Los Angeles residents.

While many San Fernando Valley residents worry about traffic congestion on their commutes to downtown or west Los Angeles, quality-of-life issues including health care and air quality are major concerns as well. Immigration is one among several factors that have made the district solidly Democratic — it gave Democrat Al Gore 58 percent of the vote in the 2000 presidential election.

MAJOR INDUSTRY
Biotechnology, service

CITIES
Los Angeles (pt.), 591,573; Burbank (pt.), 45,436

NOTABLE
The San Fernando Valley is known as the pornography capital of the world.

Rep. Howard L. Berman (D)

CAPITOL OFFICE
225-4695
howard.berman@mail.house.gov
www.house.gov/berman
2221 Rayburn 20515-0528; fax 225-3196

COMMITTEES
International Relations
Judiciary

HOMETOWN
North Hollywood

BORN
April 15, 1941, Los Angeles, Calif.

RELIGION
Jewish

FAMILY
Wife, Janis Berman; one child, one stepchild

EDUCATION
U. of California, Los Angeles, B.A. 1962 (international relations), LL.B. 1965

CAREER
Lawyer

POLITICAL HIGHLIGHTS
Calif. Assembly, 1972-82

ELECTION RESULTS

2002 GENERAL		
Howard L. Berman (D)	73,771	71.4%
David R. Hernandez Jr. (R)	23,926	23.2%
Kelley L. Ross (LIBERT)	5,629	5.5%
2002 PRIMARY		
Howard L. Berman (D)		unopposed
2000 GENERAL		
Howard L. Berman (D)	96,500	84.1%
Bill Farley (LIBERT)	13,052	11.4%
David Cossak (NL)	5,229	4.6%

PREVIOUS WINNING PERCENTAGES
1998 (82%); 1996 (66%); 1994 (63%); 1992 (61%); 1990 (61%); 1988 (70%); 1986 (65%); 1984 (63%); 1982 (60%)

Elected 1982; 11th term

A low-key liberal who does not seek out the spotlight, Berman has built a solid reputation as an institutionalist and a serious-minded legislator who can work across party lines.

The bulk of his legislative work takes place in the Judiciary and International Relations committees, where in the 108th Congress he is the second-ranking Democrat on both panels. In recent years, he has focused his efforts primarily on intellectual property rights, the movie industry, immigration, and U.S. relations with hostile nations such as Libya and Iran.

The Judiciary Committee is known as one of the most partisan House panels and, populated as it is by lawyers, it is well-known for loud, raucous and often entertaining debate over social policy. But the Subcommittee on the Courts, the Internet and Intellectual Property, where Berman has been the top Democrat since the 106th Congress, does not fit that mold. Disagreements do not often occur over political issues; rather, the panel's members must delve deep into the details of arcane law as well as familiarize themselves with rapidly developing new technologies.

Berman seems to enjoy tackling complicated technology questions as the panel wrestles with a range of issues — including privacy, copyright and patent protection, and business practices — that have emerged with the advent of the Internet and wireless communication.

Berman's seniority on the subcommittee is important to Southern California's many writers, composers and other artists with a stake in guarding copyrights. He works to protect copyright owners from the piracy of their works, an increasing threat as Internet use has grown. Berman says the long-term interest of Internet users is best served by providing incentives for people to continue to create, whether it be books, movies, music, computer software, a business method or an invention.

A longtime advocate for migrant farm laborers, Berman also uses his Judiciary seat to champion legislation to improve the working conditions and immigrant status of farm workers and to permit the children of illegal immigrants to remain in the United States as long as they are in school.

After the Sept. 11, 2001, terrorist attacks, Berman pushed legislation to tighten immigration controls; improve monitoring of foreign nationals, particularly students, already in the country; and boost the use of technology to screen entrants at the border. He also favored applying asset seizure penalties that had been aimed at drug kingpins to convicted terrorists. But he objected to language in the anti-terrorism law enacted in 2001 that permits federal authorities to detain immigrants indefinitely.

While much of Berman's work on Judiciary centers on immigration, he also must be concerned about emigration of a particular sort: movie industry jobs moving to Canada and other foreign locations. Such "runaway production" — where movie producers are enticed by tax breaks and other cost-saving offers to do business abroad — costs the Southern California economy billions of dollars, Berman says.

On International Relations, he is a strong supporter of Israel and a leader in efforts to halt the international spread of weapons. In 1996 he played a key role in the passage of legislation imposing sanctions on foreign companies that did business with Libya and Iran — nations closely linked with international terrorism. In the 107th, he worked to renew that sanctions law for five more years.

After serving a six-year stint as the top-ranking Democrat on the Committee on Standards of Official Conduct, Berman rotated off the ethics committee in the 108th. In the 107th, he was the top Democrat on an adjudicatory subcommittee of the panel that recommended unanimously to expel Ohio Democrat James A. Traficant Jr., who had been convicted on 10 felony counts. During his tenure, the ethics panel implemented sweeping changes in its procedures to make it more difficult to lodge ethics complaints to simply aid political campaigns. Serving on the committee is a thankless task that generally falls to non-confrontational soldiers such as Berman.

He credits his interest in public affairs to a favorite high school teacher. "My parents weren't political, so she was the person who moved me to challenge assumptions and to debate issues," he told the Los Angeles Daily News.

As a legislative intern while at UCLA law school, Berman worked on labor issues with Cesar Chavez's United Farm workers. "From then on, I was hooked," he told the Daily News. He succeeded Henry A. Waxman as president of the school's Federation of Young Democrats, and in 1968 he helped his friend Waxman win a seat in the state Assembly. This marked the start of the Berman-Waxman political organization, a network of like-minded politicians and activists who pooled resources to back candidates with money and organizational assistance, thereby influencing western Los Angeles County politics for years.

After graduating from college, Berman spent a year as a VISTA volunteer before practicing labor relations law in Los Angeles. In 1972, after working behind the scenes to help other Democrats win elections, it was Berman's turn to run, and he won a seat in the California Assembly. A consummate facilitator and tactician with a relaxed style, Berman soon rose to majority leader but lost a bid to become speaker.

He won his seat in Congress in 1982 after state House Speaker Willie L. Brown Jr. helped draw a congressional redistricting plan that included a perfect district for Berman. Since then, he has won re-election easily.

In California redistricting for the current decade, the Golden State's House Democratic delegation hired Berman's brother, Michael, as a consultant to draft a revised map. The district lines that were eventually approved protected most incumbents, angering Southern California Hispanics who had clamored for a map that would favor election of another Hispanic. The district, which had been numbered the 26th, saw a decrease in its Hispanic population from about 65 percent to about 56 percent. In 2002, Berman defeated Republican David R. Hernandez Jr., by better than a 3-to-1 ratio.

KEY VOTES

2002

- Yes Overhaul campaign finance law; ban "soft money" and restrict advocacy advertising
- Yes Back Bush's defense budget increase
- No Extend 1996 welfare law
- No Adopt Bush's discretionary spending limit
- No Pass GOP Medicare prescription drug plan
- Yes Create independent Sept. 11 commission
- Yes Extend union protections to Homeland Security Department employees
- No Revive fast-track procedures for trade agreements
- Yes Authorize war against Iraq
- No Advance bankruptcy overhaul opposed by abortion opponents

2001

- No Nullify Clinton Labor Department ergonomics rule
- No Cut taxes by $1.35 trillion through fiscal 2011
- Yes Maintain ban on oil drilling in Arctic National Wildlife Refuge
- No Approve Bush proposal to limit managed-care plan liability for coverage decisions
- Yes Divert money from crop subsidy payments to land conservation
- Yes Expand law enforcement power to investigate suspected terrorists

CQ VOTE STUDIES

	PARTY UNITY		PRESIDENTIAL SUPPORT	
	Support	Oppose	Support	Oppose
2002	96%	4%	24%	76%
2001	92%	8%	38%	62%
2000	96%	4%	94%	6%
1999	94%	6%	90%	10%
1998	95%	5%	85%	15%

INTEREST GROUPS

	AFL-CIO	ADA	CCUS	ACU
2002	100%	90%	37%	10%
2001	100%	95%	36%	4%
2000	100%	100%	50%	4%
1999	67%	95%	26%	0%
1998	100%	90%	36%	5%

CALIFORNIA 28
Part of the San Fernando Valley

The 28th starts in the San Fernando Valley north of Los Angeles, where it takes in the small city of San Fernando and includes the Los Angeles communities of Pacoima, Arleta, Panorama City, Van Nuys and North Hollywood. The southern border follows in part famed Mulholland Drive, taking in Encino, Sherman Oaks and Studio City in the Hollywood Hills north of Beverly Hills.

Once composed of predominately white, suburban Los Angeles communities, the area has attracted large numbers of Hispanics, who now make up 56 percent of the district's population. That majority is a major contributor to the Democratic voting tendency in the district, which gave Democrat Al Gore 70 percent of the vote in the 2000 presidential election.

The 28th's thriving commercial district, centered on financial services, is just south of Route 101, along Ventura Boulevard, where bank branch offices in office towers compete with miles of fast-food outlets, trendy restaurants and strip malls. It passes by the Sherman Oaks Galleria, home of the Valley Girl and recently renovated with businesses and upscale restaurants. A number of movies and TV shows have been filmed at the CBS Studio Center in Studio City, including "Hill Street Blues," "Roseanne" and "Seinfeld."

Defense industry closures and the 1994 Northridge earthquake hit the district hard. It has stayed afloat, however, fueled by the technology and entertainment industries and the growth of service industries that are increasingly driven by new immigrants. The district has some manufacturing plants, but Van Nuys, which lost a General Motors plant in 1992, got a boost from a new retail center and industrial park that opened on the old GM site in 2000.

MAJOR INDUSTRY
Service, entertainment, manufacturing, health care

CITIES
Los Angeles (pt.), 615,523; San Fernando, 23,564

NOTABLE
The Academy of Television Arts and Sciences, which presents the annual Emmy Awards, is based in North Hollywood; Actors Robert Redford and Marilyn Monroe attended Van Nuys High School; Rock & Roll Hall of Famer Ritchie Valens ("La Bamba") is a native of Pacoima.

Rep. Adam B. Schiff (D)

CAPITOL OFFICE
225-4176
www.house.gov/schiff
326 Cannon 20515-0529; fax 225-5828

COMMITTEES
International Relations
Judiciary

HOMETOWN
Burbank

BORN
June 22, 1960, Framingham, Mass.

RELIGION
Jewish

FAMILY
Wife, Eve Schiff; two children

EDUCATION
Stanford U., A.B. 1982 (political science & pre-med); Harvard U., J.D. 1985

CAREER
Federal prosecutor; lawyer

POLITICAL HIGHLIGHTS
Assistant U.S. attorney, 1987-93; Democratic nominee for Calif. Assembly (special election), 1994; Democratic nominee for Calif. Assembly, 1994; Calif. Senate, 1996-2000

ELECTION RESULTS

2002 GENERAL		
Adam B. Schiff (D)	76,036	62.6%
Jim Scileppi (R)	40,616	33.4%
Ted Brown (LIBERT)	4,889	4.0%
2002 PRIMARY		
Adam B. Schiff (D)		unopposed
2000 GENERAL		
Adam B. Schiff (D)	113,708	52.7%
James E. Rogan (R)	94,518	43.8%
Miriam Hospodar (NL)	3,873	1.8%
Ted Brown (LIBERT)	3,675	1.7%

Elected 2000; 2nd term

A former federal prosecutor, Schiff found himself in the middle of the biggest issues of the 107th Congress — homeland security and U.S. relations with nations of the Middle East and South Asia — by virtue of his assignments to the Judiciary and International Relations committees.

Although his style is hardly flashy, Schiff came to Congress as something of a celebrity. His 2000 campaign for the 27th District against two-term GOP Rep. James E. Rogan, one of the most hotly contested races in the country, drew even more attention and campaign money than many of the year's Senate races. Rogan had made himself a Democratic target because of his high-profile involvement in the impeachment of President Clinton.

Schiff, then a state senator, and Rogan raised in all more than $10 million between them — a House race record. Outside groups spent millions more on television ads that sought to influence the outcome. After being sworn in, Schiff announced that campaign finance overhaul would be a top priority. He joined with GOP freshman Mark Steven Kirk of Illinois, another victor of an expensive race, to form "Freshmen for Reform."

In the California Legislature, Schiff was known as "tenacious but thoughtful." In his first House term, he aligned himself with the conservative Democratic "Blue Dog" coalition and the slightly less conservative New Democrat Coalition. His parents, although not active politically, had opposing political views. Schiff says that his father is a Democrat and his mother is a Republican, and "maybe that's why I'm a moderate."

Schiff backed President Bush 36 percent of the time in the 107th Congress, more often than the average Democrat. He was one of 28 Democrats who voted to enact the Bush tax cut in 2001, and he argues that fiscal discipline is important in Washington "in good times and bad times." Nevertheless, his party ties remained strong enough that he was elected president of the Democratic freshman class for the first half of 2002.

Schiff's seat on the Judiciary Committee is a nice fit for the one-time assistant U.S. attorney, who made fighting juvenile crime a centerpiece of his early political career. He had also served as chairman of the California Senate Judiciary Committee.

He played an active role during House Judiciary deliberations on the counterterrorism law that was written in the months after the Sept. 11, 2001, attacks. He says his experience as a prosecutor made him more comfortable than some of his colleagues with certain elements of the package. Even though he backed the measure, a vital factor in his support was that some of the more controversial new law enforcement powers were to be suspended after four years.

A central goal of his political agenda is the promotion of early childhood education, from preschool through third grade. A larger investment in helping preschool children has been proven to reduce crime, Schiff says. A big supporter of the early learning program Head Start, Schiff believes that preschools should have the best teachers. Schiff also was involved in the Big Brother program in the late 1980s, and he still has a close relationship with his "little brother," who went on to graduate from Yale.

Although much of the attention in his 2000 campaign was on his opponent's role in Clinton's impeachment, Schiff also focused on local issues, including transportation, protection of open space in the San Gabriel foothills and water quality. In the 107th Congress, Schiff and Democratic Sen. Barbara Boxer of California were able to obtain federal grants for a water treatment plant for Glendale, whose city drinking water wells have long been tainted by chromium 6 and other toxic metals.

Schiff, whose district has a large Armenian population, immediately joined in the longstanding legislative effort to call on the president to formally recognize as genocide the deaths of millions of Armenians that began in 1915 at the hands of the Ottoman Empire, in what is now Turkey. As a state senator, Schiff helped secure state funds for a documentary on Armenia.

Schiff's diplomatic skills will be called on in the 108th Congress, as an important local issue is certain to divide his district. The decades-long battle over whether the 710 freeway should be extended has pitted the northeast Los Angeles communities against each other. Because of redistricting, one district — Schiff's 29th — contains both of the leading protagonists: South Pasadena and Alhambra.

Schiff was born in Massachusetts. His father was a traveling salesman in the clothing business and was transferred to California when Schiff was nine. When he entered Stanford, Schiff could not decide between medicine and law and so majored in both pre-med and political science. He was accepted to both medical school and law school. Although his parents urged him to become a doctor, Schiff chose law school, deciding that it afforded broader opportunities for public service.

After getting his law degree at Harvard, he returned to California and clerked for a federal judge; his fascination with the cases that federal prosecutors presented, he says, led him eventually to his six years of work in the U.S. Attorney's office.

One of his colleagues, Tom Umberg, who was elected to the California Assembly, was the inspiration for Schiff's move into politics. "I wanted to deal with the root causes of the problems I was dealing with as a U.S. attorney," Schiff explains. He was unsuccessful at first, losing to Rogan in 1994, in both a special- and a general-election Assembly race. He rebounded in 1996, winning a state Senate district that included the old 27th Congressional District.

Schiff in 2000 again faced Rogan, who had moved up to the U.S. House in 1996. In one of the marquee House races of the year, Schiff captured a 9 percentage point victory in a 27th District that was trending more Democratic. In 2002, now running in the newly drawn 29th, which tilts even more Democratic, Schiff cruised to a 29-point victory.

Schiff's wife is named Eve, and he is amused by the attention that the Adam and Eve pairing gets. His wife is less amused, and they have steadfastly resisted the expected suggestions for their children's names, opting instead for Alexa and Elijah.

KEY VOTES

2002

Yes Overhaul campaign finance law; ban "soft money" and restrict advocacy advertising
Yes Back Bush's defense budget increase
No Extend 1996 welfare law
No Adopt Bush's discretionary spending limit
No Pass GOP Medicare prescription drug plan
Yes Create independent Sept. 11 commission
Yes Extend union protections to Homeland Security Department employees
No Revive fast-track procedures for trade agreements
Yes Authorize war against Iraq
No Advance bankruptcy overhaul opposed by abortion opponents

2001

No Nullify Clinton Labor Department ergonomics rule
Yes Cut taxes by $1.35 trillion through fiscal 2011
Yes Maintain ban on oil drilling in Arctic National Wildlife Refuge
No Approve Bush proposal to limit managed-care plan liability for coverage decisions
Yes Divert money from crop subsidy payments to land conservation
Yes Expand law enforcement power to investigate suspected terrorists

CQ VOTE STUDIES

	PARTY UNITY		PRESIDENTIAL SUPPORT	
	Support	Oppose	Support	Oppose
2002	92%	8%	32%	68%
2001	83%	17%	40%	60%

INTEREST GROUPS

	AFL-CIO	ADA	CCUS	ACU
2002	88%	95%	45%	8%
2001	83%	85%	39%	13%

CALIFORNIA 29

Glendale; Pasadena; Alhambra; part of Burbank

Set in the foothills of the San Gabriel Mountains, the 29th includes the Los Angeles suburbs of Glendale, Pasadena, Alhambra and part of Burbank. Over the years, immigration and the growing nearby Hollywood economy have transformed once-WASPish neighborhoods, giving the district a Democratic lean.

The 29th is home to few movie stars, but many of those whose names appear farther down in movie credits live here. While a high-tech community has sprung up around the California Institute of Technology and a number of colleges, the district is primarily residential.

The area includes a wide mix of ethnicities. Monterey Park (shared with the 32nd) is upper-middle-class and known as "Little Taipei" for its Taiwanese and other Asian immigrants. Glendale is home to about 75,000 Armenians, the largest such community outside of Armenia. Alhambra is heavily Hispanic and Asian, and upscale San Gabriel has a strong Italian community. Overall the district is about one-fourth Asian and one-fourth Hispanic. About 60 different languages are spoken in Glendale's public schools.

Though in the Los Angeles area, Glendale and Pasadena, a lush former resort town, have their own downtowns. Television and movie production studios drive the economy in Burbank. Redeveloping landfills is a challenge in Monterey Park, while residents of South Pasadena and Alhambra argue over whether to extend Interstate 710 through their cities.

MAJOR INDUSTRY
Entertainment, technology, engineering

CITIES
Glendale, 194,973; Pasadena, 133,936; Alhambra, 85,804; Burbank (pt.), 54,880

NOTABLE
The Rose Bowl is in Pasadena, which hosts the Tournament of Roses Parade; Burbank is home to the studios of Warner Bros., Disney and NBC; The Norton Simon Museum of Art in Pasadena holds etchings by Rembrandt and a collection of Picasso graphics; Griffith Park is one of the nation's largest municipal parks.

Rep. Henry A. Waxman (D)

CAPITOL OFFICE
225-3976
www.house.gov/waxman
2204 Rayburn 20515-0530; fax 225-4099

COMMITTEES
Energy & Commerce
Government Reform - ranking member

HOMETOWN
Los Angeles

BORN
Sept. 12, 1939, Los Angeles, Calif.

RELIGION
Jewish

FAMILY
Wife, Janet Waxman; two children

EDUCATION
U. of California, Los Angeles, B.A. 1961 (political science), J.D. 1964

CAREER
Lawyer

POLITICAL HIGHLIGHTS
Calif. Assembly, 1968-74

ELECTION RESULTS

2002 GENERAL		
Henry A. Waxman (D)	130,604	70.4%
Tony Goss (R)	54,989	29.6%
2002 PRIMARY		
Henry A. Waxman (D)	52,785	89.6%
Kevin Feldman (D)	6,146	10.4%
2000 GENERAL		
Henry A. Waxman (D)	180,295	75.7%
Jim Scileppi (R)	45,784	19.2%
J. C. Anderson (LIBERT)	7,944	3.3%
Bruce Currivan (NL)	4,178	1.8%

PREVIOUS WINNING PERCENTAGES
1998 (74%); 1996 (68%); 1994 (68%); 1992 (61%); 1990 (69%); 1988 (72%); 1986 (88%); 1984 (63%); 1982 (65%); 1980 (64%); 1978 (63%); 1976 (68%); 1974 (64%)

Elected 1974; 15th term

A persistent nature, paired with masteries of detail and process gained during almost three decades in the House, has enabled Waxman to enhance energy conservation, expand access to health care and bolster environmental protection — even when his party controls neither the White House nor Congress.

Waxman is among the House's most adroit political practitioners. While he brings his extensive knowledge on a broad policy portfolio into behind-the-scenes negotiations, he can be a forceful partisan combatant in front of the television cameras. He is patient and willing to cut deals with Republicans when necessary. Compromise, Waxman says, "can further your ideas and even help you improve your ideas."

As his party's senior member of the Government Reform Committee, Waxman has emerged as a Democratic ethics watchdog who has focused public attention on the Bush administration's ties to business lobbyists.

As the second-ranking Democrat on the Energy and Commerce Committee, he employs techniques similar to those of John D. Dingell of Michigan, the panel's most-senior Democrat. Both are precise questioners during oversight hearings and force agencies to provide extensive information. Waxman is aggressive but employs humor and is usually controlled, a style that can bedevil his adversaries.

During the 107th Congress, Waxman accused the Bush administration of favoritism toward energy companies and suggested that the stock holdings of Karl Rove, the president's political adviser, posed potential conflicts of interest. It was this crusade that led Waxman to unwittingly place in some jeopardy the ability of Congress to oversee the workings of the executive branch. Knowing they could not get requisite Republican backing for subpoenas, Waxman and Dingell asked the General Accounting Office in 2001 to probe the involvement of energy companies in the formulation of administration energy policy. The GAO ended up filing an unprecedented lawsuit in 2002 seeking to compel Vice President Dick Cheney to release records of his energy task force. In early 2003, the GAO decided not to appeal a federal judge's ruling that the congressional agency lacked the legal standing to bring such a suit — which Waxman called "a tremendous setback for open government."

Waxman's aggressive approach to the White House may be a response to the Government Reform probe of Democratic fundraising before the 1996 election. Waxman has labeled that inquiry as "the most partisan, unfair and abusive investigation since the McCarthy hearings in the 1950s."

Waxman has criticized some of the broad powers detailed to the new Department of Homeland Security. He said the department was assigned too many duties, would treat its employees as "second-class citizens" and had "no effective mechanism" to coordinate with the FBI and CIA.

Waxman's main base of operations has been Energy and Commerce, where he chaired the Health and the Environment Subcommittee for the 16 years before the GOP became the majority in 1995. He has won many of his victories by maneuvering persistently to secure one small objective at a time, rather than making a broad frontal assault.

On occasion, Waxman has looked to cut deals with Energy and Commerce Republicans. In 2002, he supported a compromise with Chairman Billy Tauzin of Louisiana to increase funding for the Food and Drug Administration, accelerate medical device approvals and allow private parties to inspect factories. But Waxman opposed Tauzin on other issues in the 107th, including an energy overhaul that he called a "lost opportunity" to conserve energy.

One of Waxman's most significant accomplishments was the 1990 Clean Air Act. For nearly a decade, he fought with Dingell and the Reagan administration to secure tougher measures to control acid rain and smog. As chairman, Dingell stoutly defended the auto industry and the interests of Midwestern states that rely on coal-burning power plants. But Waxman skillfully built coalitions on motor vehicle pollution controls against Dingell's will. The measure ultimately enacted was more stringent than the GOP administration had proposed.

A one-time smoker, Waxman now is the leading congressional crusader against the tobacco industry. He convened the 1994 hearing during which the chief executives of the nation's seven largest tobacco companies testified under oath that they did not believe nicotine was addictive. And Waxman's tough views on tobacco were part of a platform that helped him, after only his second term, defeat Richardson Preyer of North Carolina for a subcommittee gavel in 1978.

Waxman grew up in an apartment above the Los Angeles grocery store run by his father, who was the son of Russian immigrants and who instilled in his son an appreciation of the New Deal ideals. Waxman's political career began at UCLA in the 1960s, when he and fellow student Howard L. Berman became active in California's Federation of Young Democrats. In 1968, after a term as chairman of the state federation, Waxman, with Berman's support, challenged Democratic state Assemblyman Lester McMillan in a primary. McMillan had been in office 26 years and was nearing retirement. Waxman beat him with 64 percent of the vote.

It was the beginning of the so-called Waxman-Berman machine, an informal network of like-minded politicians who pooled their resources to back candidates with money, organization and political savvy. The "machine" was functioning so smoothly in 1974 that Waxman had little trouble winning a new House seat created with him in mind. Berman waltzed into his own House seat eight years later.

Waxman's constituents in Beverly Hills and part of Hollywood are not only politically involved, but many are also wealthy. They have been generous with their donations to Waxman's political action committee, and in turn its contributions to other House members have broadened Waxman's influence among his colleagues. His own campaigns are formalities; he has never won re-election with less than 61 percent of the vote.

KEY VOTES

2002

- Yes Overhaul campaign finance law; ban "soft money" and restrict advocacy advertising
- ? Back Bush's defense budget increase
- No Extend 1996 welfare law
- No Adopt Bush's discretionary spending limit
- No Pass GOP Medicare prescription drug plan
- Yes Create independent Sept. 11 commission
- Yes Extend union protections to Homeland Security Department employees
- No Revive fast-track procedures for trade agreements
- Yes Authorize war against Iraq
- No Advance bankruptcy overhaul opposed by abortion opponents

2001

- No Nullify Clinton Labor Department ergonomics rule
- ? Cut taxes by $1.35 trillion through fiscal 2011
- Yes Maintain ban on oil drilling in Arctic National Wildlife Refuge
- No Approve Bush proposal to limit managed-care plan liability for coverage decisions
- Yes Divert money from crop subsidy payments to land conservation
- Yes Expand law enforcement power to investigate suspected terrorists

CQ VOTE STUDIES

	PARTY UNITY		PRESIDENTIAL SUPPORT	
	Support	Oppose	Support	Oppose
2002	98%	2%	25%	75%
2001	95%	5%	32%	68%
2000	98%	2%	87%	13%
1999	96%	4%	86%	14%
1998	97%	3%	85%	15%

INTEREST GROUPS

	AFL-CIO	ADA	CCUS	ACU
2002	100%	80%	33%	5%
2001	100%	90%	36%	0%
2000	89%	90%	45%	4%
1999	88%	95%	17%	0%
1998	100%	100%	18%	4%

CALIFORNIA 30

West Los Angeles County — Santa Monica, West Hollywood

Boasting such glamorous locales as Beverly Hills, Malibu, Bel Air and Pacific Palisades, there are few places in the 30th that have not been immortalized by a television show or movie. The district is home to a large Jewish population, the University of California, Los Angeles, and the activist gay community of West Hollywood.

Eclectic, wealthy and Democratic describe many of the district's residents. Members of England's royal family have stayed at the Regent Beverly Wilshire hotel at the southern end of the exclusive Rodeo Drive shopping strip, and thousands annually crowd the streets of West Hollywood to witness the gay and lesbian pride parade. The district votes overwhelmingly Democratic in elections at all levels.

The district stretches north from the Santa Monica and Malibu beaches across the Santa Monica Mountains to Calabasas and Hidden Hills on the north side of the range.

The 30th is about three-fourths white and the economy is overwhelmingly white-collar. Entertainment executives lunch with financial advisers and real estate developers, and tourism brings in large amounts of money. Thousands flock annually to the legendary Grauman's Chinese Theater, where they can compare their handprints and footprints to those of the stars, or see Whoopi Goldberg's braids, preserved in cement. The area's seven medical centers make health care an important economic engine.

MAJOR INDUSTRY

Entertainment, higher education, health care

CITIES

Los Angeles (pt.), 399,622; Santa Monica, 84,084; West Hollywood, 35,716

NOTABLE

Hugh Hefner's Playboy Mansion is where prominent Democrats, including presidential candidates Gary Hart, Jerry Brown and Jesse Jackson, have held fundraisers; Santa Monica Pier, an amusement park that stretches out into the ocean, was built in 1909 and features an antique carousel.

Rep. Xavier Becerra (D)

CAPITOL OFFICE
225-6235
www.house.gov/becerra
1119 Longworth 20515-0531; fax 225-2202

COMMITTEES
Ways & Means

HOMETOWN
Los Angeles

BORN
Jan. 26, 1958, Sacramento, Calif.

RELIGION
Roman Catholic

FAMILY
Wife, Carolina Reyes; three children

EDUCATION
Stanford U., A.B. 1980 (economics), J.D. 1984

CAREER
State prosecutor; state legislative aide; lawyer

POLITICAL HIGHLIGHTS
Calif. Assembly, 1990-92; candidate for mayor of Los Angeles, 2001

ELECTION RESULTS

2002 GENERAL		
Xavier Becerra (D)	54,569	81.2%
Luis Vega (R)	12,674	18.9%
2002 PRIMARY		
Xavier Becerra (D)		unopposed
2000 GENERAL		
Xavier Becerra (D)	83,223	83.3%
Tony Goss (R)	11,788	11.8%
Jason Heath (LIBERT)	2,858	2.9%
Gary Hearne (NL)	2,051	2.1%

PREVIOUS WINNING PERCENTAGES
1998 (81%); 1996 (72%); 1994 (66%); 1992 (58%)

Elected 1992; 6th term

A rising Latino political star, Becerra suffered a career setback in 2001, but since then, he has turned his attention to his work in the House with renewed determination. The Stanford-educated Becerra is the first Hispanic lawmaker to sit on Ways and Means. And, until the 2001 Los Angeles mayoral race, he had never lost an election.

Becerra (his full name is pronounced HAH-vee-air beh-SEH-ra) waged an uphill struggle in 2001 to become the first Latino mayor in the modern history of Los Angeles. Hampered by low name recognition, he failed to make it past the April 10 primary in a 14-candidate field, capturing just 6 percent of the vote.

He returned to Washington full time after the primary and remained active on Ways and Means, focusing on trade and Social Security issues and matters of import to the movie and television business. He also weighed in on homeland security measures, seeking to improve airport baggage screening procedures while protecting individual civil liberties.

A member of the Progressive Caucus — the organization of the most liberal Democrats in the House — Becerra voted in the 107th Congress to enact the sweeping anti-terrorism law that most members of the caucus said went too far in restricting civil liberties. But Becerra said that "extraordinary times call for extraordinary measures." He later complained, however, about a requirement in the aviation security law enacted in 2001 that airport passenger and baggage screeners be U.S. citizens.

Becerra has joined with other Hispanic and African-American lawmakers in pressing television network executives to increase the number of minorities on television shows. On Ways and Means, Becerra also has championed legislation to give the film industry incentives to stay in the United States to shoot their movies rather than choosing cheaper locations abroad.

Becerra continues to focus on immigration matters — an issue that dominated his first six years in Congress. In his first two terms, Becerra's seat on the Judiciary Committee gave him an outlet to advance his views on immigration policy. He left Judiciary for Ways and Means in his third term, a switch that concerned many Hispanic leaders who believed they were losing an effective advocate on immigration matters. But Becerra then was elected chairman of the Congressional Hispanic Caucus, which made immigration policy a top priority. He served as caucus chairman from 1997 to 1998.

Becerra's district, although 70 percent Hispanic, also is home to a large Asian population, including much of the neighborhood known as Koreatown. In the 107th Congress, Becerra sponsored a measure in support of efforts by Korean Americans to hold reunions with relatives who live in North Korea.

Becerra can count a number of successes on behalf of his immigrant constituents. The rewrite of federal education policy enacted in 2002 included his proposal to make community libraries eligible for federal after-school funds. In 1997, he played a lead role in negotiations that restored to many elderly and disabled legal immigrants Social Security benefits that had been eliminated in the 1996 welfare overhaul law.

Becerra's interest in immigration matters is personal as well as political. His father was born in the United States, but he spent much of his early life in Mexico, moving back and forth across the border. Becerra's mother was born in Mexico. The congressman says he wears his father's wedding ring to remind himself of his modest beginnings.

Becerra applied to Stanford, he says, after coming across an application to the school in a trash can. He worked his way through college while majoring in economics; he was the first member of his family to earn a college degree. After graduation, he took a fellowship with the California Senate. His interest in community advocacy work led him to Stanford law school. Becerra's first job as a lawyer was with a legal services office in Worcester, Mass., helping mentally ill clients. When he returned to California, Becerra worked briefly for state Sen. Art Torres and then for the state attorney general's office.

The congressman says he never envisioned a life in electoral politics. But in 1990, urged on by friends and colleagues, he waged and won a campaign for the California Assembly. Becerra had not yet completed his first term in Sacramento when he was recruited in 1992 for the newly drawn, overwhelmingly Hispanic 30th District seat. He outdistanced nine other candidates in the primary and easily won in November, with 58 percent of the vote, against Republican Morry Waksberg and three minor-party candidates.

His subsequent re-elections came with steadily increasing shares of the vote — 66 percent, 72 percent, 81 percent and 83 percent in 2000.

Despite facing no real challenge in his bid for a fifth House term in 2000, Becerra spent hundreds of thousands of dollars, an investment in reinforcing his political base with an eye on the coming mayoral race. He spent another $1.7 million on that campaign, but found that was insufficient in the expensive Los Angeles media market. He finished fifth in the primary.

Later it was discovered that his campaign was responsible for anonymous telephone calls attacking one of his main rivals, Antonio Villaraigosa. Becerra apologized, saying he felt "betrayed" by his campaign staff. Villaraigosa, who advanced to a runoff election before losing to James Hahn, briefly considered mounting a challenge to Becerra's House seat in 2002.

Becerra's poor showing in the mayoral race, the phone call flap, and the revelation that he had joined in urging President Clinton to consider a pardon for convicted drug trafficker Carlos Vignali tarnished Becerra's clean-cut image. Vignali's father had contributed to Becerra's campaign, and the son's sentence was commuted during the final days of the Clinton administration.

In 2002, Becerra won re-election to the House with 81 percent of the vote.

KEY VOTES

2002

Yes Overhaul campaign finance law; ban "soft money" and restrict advocacy advertising
No Back Bush's defense budget increase
No Extend 1996 welfare law
No Adopt Bush's discretionary spending limit
No Pass GOP Medicare prescription drug plan
Yes Create independent Sept. 11 commission
Yes Extend union protections to Homeland Security Department employees
No Revive fast-track procedures for trade agreements
No Authorize war against Iraq
No Advance bankruptcy overhaul opposed by abortion opponents

2001

– Nullify Clinton Labor Department ergonomics rule
– Cut taxes by $1.35 trillion through fiscal 2011
Yes Maintain ban on oil drilling in Arctic National Wildlife Refuge
No Approve Bush proposal to limit managed-care plan liability for coverage decisions
Yes Divert money from crop subsidy payments to land conservation
Yes Expand law enforcement power to investigate suspected terrorists

CQ VOTE STUDIES

	PARTY UNITY		PRESIDENTIAL SUPPORT	
	Support	Oppose	Support	Oppose
2002	100%	0%	23%	77%
2001	97%	3%	27%	73%
2000	95%	5%	92%	8%
1999	96%	4%	85%	15%
1998	99%	1%	88%	12%

INTEREST GROUPS

	AFL-CIO	ADA	CCUS	ACU
2002	88%	100%	32%	0%
2001	100%	95%	40%	0%
2000	90%	90%	45%	8%
1999	78%	100%	22%	0%
1998	100%	90%	35%	0%

CALIFORNIA 31

Northeast and south central Los Angeles

The only district completely contained within the city of Los Angeles, the 31st is densely populated, heavily Hispanic and staunchly Democratic. It starts west of downtown Los Angeles and stretches south into south central L.A. and northeast toward Pasadena. Hispanics (70 percent) and Asians (14 percent) outnumber whites (10 percent). Voter turnout is usually low.

Rapid immigration is changing many of the district's already diverse communities. Asians, Armenians, Russians and Hispanics have been moving to the 31st, with many settling in the district's western side. This area, which includes part of East Hollywood, the mid-Wilshire area and Koreatown, was hit hard by the 1992 riots. Pico Union and Westlake are dominated by Central American immigrants. Other heavily Hispanic communities include Highland Park, Cypress Park and Glassell Park.

Directly west of Elysian Park, where Dodger Stadium is located, is the artsy and gentrifying Echo Park. A nearby area was recognized as Filipinotown in 2002. To the northeast sits Eagle Rock, a hilly, middle-class pocket of relative affluence that votes Democratic but leans more toward the political center than other parts of the 31st. The eastern side leads to Lincoln Heights and El Sereno — heavily Hispanic, blue-collar areas with a significant Mexican immigrant presence. The district also has part of south central Los Angeles east of the University of Southern California.

While poor, the 31st is not as economically troubled as some of its southern neighbors. It falls mostly outside federal empowerment zone lines drawn after the riots. Entertainment studios and a slew of hospitals contribute to the local economy, as do white-collar businesses along Wilshire Boulevard, a central business corridor.

MAJOR INDUSTRY

Service, entertainment, tourism, health care

CITIES

Los Angeles (pt.), 639,088

NOTABLE

Paramount Pictures is the only major motion picture studio still based in Hollywood.

Rep. Hilda L. Solis (D)

CAPITOL OFFICE
225-5464
solis.house.gov
1725 Longworth 20515-0532; fax 225-5467

COMMITTEES
Energy & Commerce

HOMETOWN
El Monte

BORN
Oct. 20, 1957, Los Angeles, Calif.

RELIGION
Roman Catholic

FAMILY
Husband, Sam H. Sayyad

EDUCATION
California State Polytechnic U., Pomona, B.A. 1979; U. of Southern California, M.P.A. 1981

CAREER
State college preparation program director; White House aide

POLITICAL HIGHLIGHTS
Rio Hondo Community College Board of Trustees, 1985-92; Los Angeles County Insurance Commission, 1991-93; Calif. Assembly, 1992-94; Calif. Senate, 1994-2000

ELECTION RESULTS

2002 GENERAL		
Hilda L. Solis (D)	58,530	68.8%
Emma E. Fischbeck (R)	23,366	27.5%
Michael McGuire (LIBERT)	3,183	3.7%
2002 PRIMARY		
Hilda L. Solis (D)		unopposed
2000 GENERAL		
Hilda L. Solis (D)	89,600	79.4%
K. Lieberg-Wong (GREEN)	10,294	9.1%
Michael McGuire (LIBERT)	7,138	6.3%
Richard Griffin (NL)	5,882	5.2%

Elected 2000; 2nd term

The daughter of immigrant parents, Solis is one of the most liberal members of the House. Energetic and unafraid to take on entrenched opposition, she spent her first term demonstrating her commitment to labor, immigration and environmental issues.

She came to the House the hard way, taking on Democratic incumbent Matthew G. Martinez in the March 2000 primary. Calling on grass-roots support from labor and capitalizing on discontent with Martinez's attention to local issues, Solis soundly defeated him. She was the only member of the Class of 2000 who unseated a member of her own party.

"I had butterflies," she told the Los Angeles Times of her decision to challenge Martinez. It took several months for her to commit: "I'm a very cautious person," she told the Times.

Solis may be alone in characterizing herself as "cautious." While in the California Legislature she overcame strong opposition from GOP Gov. Pete Wilson and the California business community to win passage of environmental protections for minority communities. The "environmental justice" legislation, which Wilson vetoed and Democratic Gov. Gray Davis later signed, was aimed at countering what Solis believes are a disproportionate number of waste sites and polluting factories in poor neighborhoods. Solis said she saw many examples of these dumps in her neighborhood while growing up.

She earned the John F. Kennedy Profile in Courage Award from the Kennedy Library in 2000 for her work promoting environmental justice. Securing such legislation on a national level is one of her priorities in the House, and in the 108th Congress she not only won a coveted seat on the Energy and Commerce Committee, but she was named the top Democrat on the panel's Environment and Hazardous Materials Subcommittee.

Solis had to give up seats on the Resources and Education panels. On the latter, in the 107th she continued the work on labor issues that she had begun in the California Legislature. During her eight years there, she was a force behind the effort to increase the state's minimum wage — again overcoming a Wilson veto.

She is a member of the Progressive Caucus; her lifetime rating from the liberal Americans for Democratic Action is 100 percent. In the 107th Congress, she was the second-most loyal House Democrat on votes that pitted Democrats against Republicans.

With personal experience in immigration issues, Solis has pressured the Immigration and Naturalization Service to speed up its processing of citizenship applications. When Congress moved to strengthen aviation security in the aftermath of the Sept. 11, 2001, terrorist attacks, she urged her colleagues to permit legal immigrants to continue to serve as airport screeners. When that failed, she tried to expedite the naturalization process for non-citizen screeners.

Joining with members of the Congressional Hispanic and Black caucuses, Solis has pushed legislation to improve health care access for low-income people. She also championed a measure to assist victims of domestic abuse.

Solis is one of seven children of immigrant parents who met in a U.S. citizenship class. Her mother is from Nicaragua and her father is from Mexico. Her father held a number of blue-collar jobs and helped the Teamsters union organize at the battery recycling plant where he was employed. This plant was one of the polluters that Solis recalls from her childhood.

The first member of her family to go to college, Solis said she was inspired by a high school counselor, who came to her home to help her fill out college and financial aid applications. She said her parents' work ethic set an example and convinced her to set her own high goals.

Solis worked her way through school, earning a bachelor's degree in political science and a graduate degree in public administration. Required to arrange her own internship as part of her graduate studies, Solis wrote dozens of letters and landed a dream assignment as the editor of a newsletter for the Carter administration's White House Office of Hispanic Affairs. She stayed on in Washington, working at the Office of Management and Budget's civil rights division during the early months of the Reagan administration. After returning to California, Solis took a job as director of a state program that helped disadvantaged students prepare for college.

Her first taste of elective office came in 1985, when she won election to the Rio Hondo Community College's board of trustees. After a brief stint as an appointed member of the Los Angeles County Insurance Commission, Solis was elected to the California Assembly in 1992. She moved up to the Senate in 1994, becoming its youngest member and first Hispanic woman. While in Sacramento, she benefited by networking with other leading California Hispanics, including Dolores Huerta, co-founder of the United Farm Workers union, and Gloria Molina, a trailblazing Latina in Southern California politics.

Legislative term limits would have forced Solis out of the state Senate in 2002, and so she began talking to local Democratic officials in late 1998 about taking on Martinez. The congressman was getting criticism for being inattentive to local concerns, and his politics on issues such as abortion and gun control were considerably more conservative than Solis'. She won a few key early endorsements from organized labor and women's groups. She also earned the support of Sen. Barbara Boxer and former Rep. Esteban E. Torres, but only one House Democratic member — Loretta Sanchez — backed her in the primary.

Solis had high name recognition as her 24th District Senate seat encompassed most of Martinez's congressional district. Her dynamic personality contrasted markedly with Martinez's low-key manner, and she outspent him by a considerable margin. Solis cruised to a 62 percent to 29 percent victory in the March 7 primary.

The Republicans failed to field a candidate for the fall election. Solis won easily in the eastern Los Angeles County Hispanic-majority district, a Democratic stronghold, capturing 79 percent against three minor-party candidates. In 2002, redistricting did nothing to alter the Democratic and Hispanic bent of the district, now numbered the 32nd, and she won by 41 points.

KEY VOTES

2002

Yes Overhaul campaign finance law; ban "soft money" and restrict advocacy advertising
Yes Back Bush's defense budget increase
No Extend 1996 welfare law
No Adopt Bush's discretionary spending limit
No Pass GOP Medicare prescription drug plan
Yes Create independent Sept. 11 commission
Yes Extend union protections to Homeland Security Department employees
No Revive fast-track procedures for trade agreements
No Authorize war against Iraq
No Advance bankruptcy overhaul opposed by abortion opponents

2001

No Nullify Clinton Labor Department ergonomics rule
No Cut taxes by $1.35 trillion through fiscal 2011
Yes Maintain ban on oil drilling in Arctic National Wildlife Refuge
No Approve Bush proposal to limit managed-care plan liability for coverage decisions
Yes Divert money from crop subsidy payments to land conservation
Yes Expand law enforcement power to investigate suspected terrorists

CQ VOTE STUDIES

	PARTY UNITY		PRESIDENTIAL SUPPORT	
	Support	Oppose	Support	Oppose
2002	100%	0%	18%	82%
2001	99%	1%	17%	83%

INTEREST GROUPS

	AFL-CIO	ADA	CCUS	ACU
2002	100%	100%	28%	0%
2001	100%	100%	30%	0%

CALIFORNIA 32
East Los Angeles; El Monte; West Covina

The 32nd sits just east of the city of Los Angeles. It takes in the southern and central San Gabriel Valley and stretches northeast to Azusa, with several good-size cities in between. Once a largely white community, the 32nd has acquired a Hispanic majority from city residents moving to the suburbs. As a result, once-Republican enclaves have become solid Democratic domains.

The district's shrinking pockets of Republican and older white voters are in Azusa. El Monte, in the heart of the San Gabriel Valley, and Baldwin Park to the east are middle-income, blue-collar cities and the 32nd's Democratic base. El Monte also has some older white voters, mostly Democrats, and the city has a substantial new immigrant population. Monterey Park (shared with the 29th) is upper-middle class — the district's richest area — and is known as "Little Taipei" for its Taiwanese and other Asian immigrants. Another large Asian population lives in wealthy, liberal-leaning West Covina. The district has several daily Chinese-language papers.

The 32nd lacks a dominant industry, and the San Gabriel Valley has suffered from higher unemployment rates than the rest of the nation. Most residents commute outside the district to work. Once a small farming town, El Monte became home to some small aerospace factories. It is now a light manufacturing area with a huge retail auto complex. Irwindale is among the district's industrial centers.

MAJOR INDUSTRY

Service, light manufacturing

CITIES

El Monte, 115,965; West Covina, 105,080; Baldwin Park, 75,837; Rosemead, 53,505

NOTABLE

MGM's trademark roaring lion came from Gay's Lion Farm in El Monte, where animal trainer Charles Gay kept African lions until 1942; El Monte's original settlers were drawn by the California Gold Rush; The Los Angeles County Sheriff's Department is based in Monterey Park; City of Hope National Medical Center in Duarte is a research hospital specializing in cancer and other life-threatening diseases.

Rep. Diane Watson (D)

CAPITOL OFFICE
225-7084
www.house.gov/watson
125 Cannon 20515-0533; fax 225-2422

COMMITTEES
Government Reform
International Relations

HOMETOWN
Los Angeles

BORN
Nov. 12, 1933, Los Angeles, Calif.

RELIGION
Roman Catholic

FAMILY
Single

EDUCATION
U. of California, Los Angeles, B.A. 1954 (education); California State U., Los Angeles, M.S. 1968 (school psychology); Harvard U., attended 1981-82; Claremont Graduate School, Ph.D. 1987 (educational administration)

CAREER
School administrator; state education department official; teacher; school psychologist

POLITICAL HIGHLIGHTS
Los Angeles County Board of Education, 1975-78; Calif. Senate, 1978-98; candidate for Los Angeles County Board of Supervisors, 1992; U.S. ambassador to the Federal States of Micronesia, 1999-2001

ELECTION RESULTS

2002 GENERAL		
Diane Watson (D)	97,779	82.6%
Andrew Kim (R)	16,699	14.1%
Charles Tate (LIBERT)	3,971	3.4%
2002 PRIMARY		
Diane Watson (D)		unopposed
2001 SPECIAL RUNOFF		
Diane Watson (D)	75,584	74.8%
Noel Irwin Hentschel (R)	20,088	19.9%
Donna J. Warren (GREEN)	3,792	3.8%
Ezola Foster (REF)	1,557	1.5%

Elected June 2001; 1st full term

Watson has held elective office for about a quarter of a century, but she describes herself as a community activist rather than a politician. She says she is a problem solver and agitator for constituencies with no voice.

Watson arrived on Capitol Hill in June 2001 to succeed Democrat Julian C. Dixon, who died in December 2000, one month after winning a 12th term. She quickly established herself as an outspoken liberal, while proposing a legislative agenda that focused on housing, health care, education and economic development in her district. She is a member of the Progressive Caucus, a group of the most liberal House Democrats. In the 107th Congress, she opposed President Bush more often than all but five of her House colleagues.

Yvonne Braithwaite Burke, who had defeated Watson in a bruising 1992 campaign for Los Angeles County supervisor, told the Capitol Hill newspaper Roll Call after Watson's election to Congress that the new congresswoman was "an aggressive personality. . . . Diane is not a woman who sits back and waits for anything."

After arriving in the House, Watson issued press releases assailing the Republican budget plan as a "recipe for disaster," complaining about the GOP "raiding Medicare," and warning of the Bush administration's "power grab" in usurping civil liberties in the name of homeland security. Attending the United Nations World Conference Against Racism along with other members of the Congressional Black Caucus, Watson told the delegates: "America is a racist state."

Despite her fiery rhetoric, Watson's appearance in her first term on the International Relations and Government Reform committees was generally low-key and politic. That was also the persona of her predecessor Dixon, who was known for his diplomatic and soft-spoken manner. The two had known each other for years as they had attended Dorsey High School together.

On Government Reform, Watson continued an effort, begun while she was in the state Senate, to get rid of mercury amalgam in dental fillings, saying it caused health risks. Fighting against opponents who labeled the entire effort junk science, she found a powerful ally in Washington — Republican Dan Burton of Indiana, chairman of Government Reform in the 107th Congress. Although the two see eye-to-eye on little else, they both agree on the dangers of mercury. (Burton believes his grandson developed autism after receiving doses of mercury contained in the nine vaccines he got in one day.)

Watson was rebuffed in her bid to join the House Entertainment Industry Task Force because it was a Republican group, so she formed the Democrat Entertainment Caucus. She hopes the caucus will focus lawmakers' attention on such issues as intellectual property rights, film piracy and the film industry's growing practice of shooting at cheaper locations abroad. Watson's district hosts a number of movie studios, and thousands of her constituents are involved in the entertainment industry. She had hoped to move to the Judiciary panel in the 108th Congress to work on intellectual property issues but failed to win assignment to the committee.

Watson's father was a police officer and her mother was a postal worker. She says she put in time at the local post office, sorting Christmas mail for seven seasons. But Watson's career choice was education.

She earned bachelor's and master's degrees and a Ph.D. in a variety of education-related disciplines, and she was a teacher and administrator in the Los Angeles school system for more than a decade. She taught college classes while working on health issues for the state Department of Education.

She entered politics in 1975, winning election to the Los Angeles County school board — the first black woman ever elected to the post. Three years later she achieved another first, becoming the first black woman elected to the state Senate.

Watson shook things up in the Senate, described by the California Political Almanac as a "club heretofore made up primarily of old white men set in their ways." Watson, the Almanac wrote, "seemed to specialize in crashing the party and opening the windows."

Watson chaired the Senate's Health and Human Services Committee for 17 years, and she was the first non-lawyer to serve on the Judiciary Committee. She was credited with helping rebuild her community after the 1992 riots sparked by the acquittal of police officers charged with beating motorist Rodney King. She also worked to blunt the effects of the 1996 welfare overhaul law on California's poor and to help people suffering with HIV/AIDS.

While she was in the state Senate, her use of campaign funds came under scrutiny. She agreed to pay a penalty of $21,075, according to the California Political Almanac.

After state term limits ended her Senate career in 1998, President Clinton named her ambassador to Micronesia, a federation of more than 600 islands in the Pacific.

When Dixon died, Watson says she was urged by many of Dixon's constituents to come home and run for the seat. In her special-election bid, Watson put her lifetime of political activism among Los Angeles' African-American population to good use. She took 33 percent of the vote, defeating 10 other Democrats in the April primary. State Sen. Kevin Murray, who had the backing of U.S. Rep. Maxine Waters, finished second with 27 percent.

The primary win virtually guaranteed victory in the overwhelmingly Democratic 32nd District. In the June general election, Watson took 75 percent of the vote, besting Republican tour company owner Noel Irwin Hentschel. At 67, she was the oldest freshman in the 107th Congress.

Redistricting shifted the boundaries of Watson's district (re-numbered the 33rd) slightly east and north, but its essential Democratic character was unchanged. She cruised to an easy re-election in 2002, winning with 83 percent of the vote.

KEY VOTES

2002

- Yes Overhaul campaign finance law; ban "soft money" and restrict advocacy advertising
- ? Back Bush's defense budget increase
- No Extend 1996 welfare law
- No Adopt Bush's discretionary spending limit
- No Pass GOP Medicare prescription drug plan
- Yes Create independent Sept. 11 commission
- Yes Extend union protections to Homeland Security Department employees
- No Revive fast-track procedures for trade agreements
- No Authorize war against Iraq
- No Advance bankruptcy overhaul opposed by abortion opponents

2001

- Yes Maintain ban on oil drilling in Arctic National Wildlife Refuge
- No Approve Bush proposal to limit managed-care plan liability for coverage decisions
- Yes Divert money from crop subsidy payments to land conservation
- No Expand law enforcement power to investigate suspected terrorists

CQ VOTE STUDIES

	PARTY UNITY		PRESIDENTIAL SUPPORT	
	Support	Oppose	Support	Oppose
2002	98%	2%	16%	84%
2001	95%	5%	17%	83%

INTEREST GROUPS

	AFL-CIO	ADA	CCUS	ACU
2002	100%	85%	26%	0%
2001	100%	50%	25%	0%

CALIFORNIA 33
West Los Angeles; Culver City

The 33rd is an ethnically diverse, Democratic district that begins about a mile inland from Venice Beach, runs east through Culver City and ends up in south central Los Angeles. From there it runs north through Koreatown, the "Miracle Mile" district and Hollywood.

Blacks, Hispanics and Asians account for more than three-fourths of the population, but the 33rd has no single racial majority. Nearly 70 percent of the district's registered voters are Democrats. Several major demographic shifts have dramatically changed the makeup. The first was in the 1960s when the district's Jewish population migrated to the area's now more upscale northwest end and the district's center became predominantly black. Since the 1990s, there has been an influx of Hispanic immigrants, who now account for the largest part of the population, at almost 35 percent.

The 33rd has a solid middle class, as well as some sharply contrasting areas such as wealthy Hancock Park — where the mayor's official residence is located — and poor south central Los Angeles, which witnessed intense racial strife during the 1992 riots.

The largest business sector is the service industry, with health care also providing employment for many. Though the 33rd is no longer the film production hub it used to be, it is home to the real Tinseltown — Hollywood — and entertainment continues to be a factor in its overall economy.

For recreation, residents and tourists flock to Exposition Park in downtown Los Angeles. In addition to the Los Angeles County Natural History Museum and the California Science Center, the park boasts the Los Angeles Memorial Coliseum, which has hosted two Olympiads.

MAJOR INDUSTRY
Service, entertainment, health care

CITIES
Los Angeles (pt.), 582,746; Culver City, 38,816; View Park-Windsor Hills (unincorporated), 10,958

NOTABLE
The University of Southern California; MGM Studios (now part of Sony Picture Studios); The Academy Awards ceremony moved to the Kodak Theatre in 2002.

Rep. Lucille Roybal-Allard (D)

CAPITOL OFFICE
225-1766
www.house.gov/roybal-allard
2330 Rayburn 20515-0534; fax 226-0350

COMMITTEES
Appropriations
Standards of Official Conduct

HOMETOWN
East Los Angeles

BORN
June 12, 1941, Boyle Heights, Calif.

RELIGION
Roman Catholic

FAMILY
Husband, Edward T. Allard III; two children, two stepchildren

EDUCATION
California State U., Los Angeles, B.A. 1965 (speech)

CAREER
Nonprofit worker

POLITICAL HIGHLIGHTS
Calif. Assembly, 1986-92

ELECTION RESULTS

2002 GENERAL		
Lucille Roybal-Allard (D)	48,734	74.0%
Wayne Miller (R)	17,090	26.0%
2002 PRIMARY		
Lucille Roybal-Allard (D)		unopposed
2000 GENERAL		
Lucille Roybal-Allard (D)	60,510	84.6%
Wayne Miller (R)	8,260	11.5%
Nathan Craddock (LIBERT)	1,601	2.2%
William Harpur (NL)	1,200	1.7%

PREVIOUS WINNING PERCENTAGES
1998 (87%); 1996 (82%); 1994 (81%); 1992 (63%)

Elected 1992; 6th term

Roybal-Allard is the first Mexican-American woman ever elected to Congress. Her father was Edward R. Roybal, one of only three Hispanic members of the House when he arrived in 1963. For 30 years in Congress, he fought to win greater political clout for Hispanics in his Southern California district — a battle that shaped the political ambitions of his daughter.

Despite her political pedigree, Roybal-Allard grew up facing discrimination and discouragement. She recalls being punished as a child for speaking Spanish in school. She also remembers how her family would be stopped and questioned when they tried to enter hotels. Even her own family tried to dampen her efforts to rise above her station. Her father's relatives ridiculed him for sending his daughters to college, saying all that was expected of them was marriage and children. Later, her own siblings discouraged her from entering politics, citing the difficulties their father faced.

Overcoming such obstacles, Roybal-Allard became a pioneer for Latinas. She was the first woman to head the Congressional Hispanic Caucus and the first Hispanic woman appointed to the Appropriations Committee, posts she achieved in the 106th Congress.

Today, she realizes that she has become a role model for young Hispanic women. "We really have to succeed," she says. "We're evaluated more harshly than men. . . . We have to show that we're capable of doing the job."

She says the discrimination she faced as a youth has also made her particularly sensitive to the problems of immigrants to the United States. During the 107th Congress, Roybal-Allard fought hard but unsuccessfully to make permanent the part of the federal immigration code, known as Section 245 (i), that permits immigrants whose visas have expired to remain in the United States while their applications are processed.

Also in the 107th, during debate on legislation to abolish the Immigration and Naturalization Service, Roybal-Allard successfully won addition of an amendment to create a new Office of Immigration Statistics to compile information on decisions to deny applications for citizenship and other immigration benefits, tracking who is denied and why.

Before entering politics, Roybal-Allard worked for the United Way and then served as an assistant director on the Alcoholism Council of East Los Angeles. In Congress, she has focused much of her legislative energy on fighting underage drinking. In the 107th, she introduced legislation directing the secretary of Health and Human Services (HHS) to launch a national media campaign to discourage teenagers from using alcohol. "While we have an extensive campaign to combat illegal drug use, the fact remains that alcohol kills more teens than all other drugs combined," she said.

In 2001, she successfully won a $1 million earmark for HHS to develop new programs to curb underage drinking. A year later, Roybal-Allard became a vocal critic of the NBC television network after it announced it would start airing liquor ads. The network eventually reversed its decision.

On local issues, Roybal-Allard drew plaudits in the 105th Congress for her role in awakening the power of the California House delegation, which had been divided and ineffective. As the first elected chairman of the California Democratic delegation, she worked with her Republican counterpart, Jerry Lewis, to find issues on which the majority of the delegation could agree.

Her membership on the Treasury, Postal Service Appropriations Subcommittee in the 106th had particular meaning for her; her father had been its chairman for 12 years. In the 108th, she serves on the new Homeland Security Subcommittee as well as the panel with jurisdiction over the departments of Labor, Health and Human Services and Education.

Drawing on her experience in Sacramento, another of her legislative priorities has been to improve the lot of women victimized by domestic violence. As a Budget Committee member in the 104th Congress, she inserted language into a 1996 budget resolution to ensure that changes in the welfare system would not exacerbate domestic violence problems faced by low-income women, who might have to choose between staying with an abusive husband for economic support or facing homelessness and hunger.

Also in the 104th, as in every Congress since, Roybal-Allard has offered legislation to give unemployment insurance benefits to women forced to leave jobs because of domestic violence. The measure also calls on employers to provide domestic violence victims with leave to seek medical help, counseling and legal assistance, and to make court appearances.

In her legislative work, Roybal-Allard tries to balance the related but not always overlapping needs of the two chief components of her constituency: the minority "underclass" mired in chronic poverty and a substantial Latino working class of laborers and shop owners. In recent years, Roybal-Allard and other community leaders have been working hard to encourage citizenship applications and to speed the process.

Roybal-Allard generally has been a dependable supporter of Democratic Party positions and often has won 100 percent favorable ratings from the AFL-CIO. But after considerable soul-searching, she opposed her allies in organized labor in the 103rd Congress to support the North American Free Trade Agreement and creation of the World Trade Organization. Since then, however, she has voted against two of the principal trade measures opposed by organized labor: to make China a permanent normal trade partner of the United States in the 106th, and to revive fast-track procedures for congressional action on trade deals in the 107th.

Roybal-Allard served six years in the California state Assembly before winning election to succeed her father in 1992. She jumped at the chance to run for her father's seat, drawing insubstantial opposition in the Democratic primary and winning in November by a 2-to-1 margin. She has won with no less than 74 percent of the vote in each re-election since. (During her first decade in Washington, the area of Los Angeles she represented was, at 86 percent after the 2000 census, the most Hispanic congressional district in the nation. Her newly redrawn district's Latino population is 77 percent.)

KEY VOTES

2002

- Yes Overhaul campaign finance law; ban "soft money" and restrict advocacy advertising
- Yes Back Bush's defense budget increase
- No Extend 1996 welfare law
- No Adopt Bush's discretionary spending limit
- No Pass GOP Medicare prescription drug plan
- Yes Create independent Sept. 11 commission
- Yes Extend union protections to Homeland Security Department employees
- No Revive fast-track procedures for trade agreements
- No Authorize war against Iraq
- No Advance bankruptcy overhaul opposed by abortion opponents

2001

- No Nullify Clinton Labor Department ergonomics rule
- No Cut taxes by $1.35 trillion through fiscal 2011
- Yes Maintain ban on oil drilling in Arctic National Wildlife Refuge
- No Approve Bush proposal to limit managed-care plan liability for coverage decisions
- Yes Divert money from crop subsidy payments to land conservation
- Yes Expand law enforcement power to investigate suspected terrorists

CQ VOTE STUDIES

	PARTY UNITY		PRESIDENTIAL SUPPORT	
	Support	Oppose	Support	Oppose
2002	99%	1%	22%	78%
2001	95%	5%	24%	76%
2000	98%	2%	90%	10%
1999	97%	3%	86%	14%
1998	99%	1%	86%	14%

INTEREST GROUPS

	AFL-CIO	ADA	CCUS	ACU
2002	100%	100%	35%	0%
2001	100%	100%	30%	0%
2000	100%	90%	35%	8%
1999	89%	95%	16%	0%
1998	100%	100%	29%	0%

CALIFORNIA 34

East central Los Angeles; Downey; Bellflower

The Democratic 34th takes in the heart and southeastern part of Los Angeles and has an overwhelming Hispanic majority. At 77 percent, the district has the largest concentration of Hispanics in California.

The local economy revolves around businesses in the revitalizing downtown area and nearby light manufacturing centers such as Vernon and Commerce. Downtown businesses include toy, jewelry and garment manufacturers and retailers. Some spaces downtown are being transformed into lofts. Many of Los Angeles' civic buildings, including city hall, courthouses and the county prison, are in the 34th.

Vernon's population, according to the 2000 census, is a mere 91 people, but during the day it jumps to more than 50,000 as workers stream into its food-processing and furniture plants. The district also is attracting new "green" industries, such as recycling companies.

One of California's poorest and least-educated districts, the 34th had among the lowest voter turnouts of any district in the nation in 2000. Al Gore won the 2000 presidential vote with 69 percent of the vote — despite the district's inclusion of slightly more suburban and conservative Downey and Bellflower, located to the south where there are fewer Hispanics. Other areas include Little Tokyo and part of Pico Union and Chinatown. Despite redevelopment and many small businesses, the area has seen a rise in crime rates.

Brighter spots include the Walt Disney Concert Hall, which was scheduled to open in 2003 and become the Los Angeles Philharmonic's new home. Transportation hub Union Station and the end of the 20-mile Alameda Corridor rail link connecting L.A. and the ports of Los Angeles and Long Beach are in the district, as is the Staples Center, home to basketball's Lakers and Clippers and hockey's Kings.

MAJOR INDUSTRY

Government, manufacturing, service, retail

CITIES

Los Angeles (pt.), 188,018; Downey, 107,323; Bellflower, 72,878

NOTABLE

The 2000 Democratic National Convention was held at the Staples Center; Downtown's El Pueblo de Los Angeles Historic Monument, including Olvera Street, is the oldest section of Los Angeles.

Rep. Maxine Waters (D)

CAPITOL OFFICE
225-2201
www.house.gov/waters
2344 Rayburn 20515-0535; fax 225-7854

COMMITTEES
Financial Services
Judiciary

HOMETOWN
Los Angeles

BORN
Aug. 15, 1938, St. Louis, Mo.

RELIGION
Christian

FAMILY
Husband, Sidney Williams; two children

EDUCATION
California State U., Los Angeles, B.A. 1970

CAREER
Head Start official

POLITICAL HIGHLIGHTS
Calif. Assembly, 1976-90

ELECTION RESULTS

2002 GENERAL		
Maxine Waters (D)	72,401	77.5%
Ross Moen (R)	18,094	19.4%
Gordon Michael Mego (AMI)	2,912	3.1%
2002 PRIMARY		
Maxine Waters (D)		unopposed
2000 GENERAL		
Maxine Waters (D)	100,569	86.5%
Carl McGill (R)	12,582	10.8%
Gordon Michael Mego (AMI)	1,911	1.6%

PREVIOUS WINNING PERCENTAGES
1998 (89%); 1996 (86%); 1994 (78%); 1992 (83%); 1990 (79%)

Elected 1990; 7th term

A combative liberal, Waters is outspoken and fearless in defending the interests of her poor, minority-dominated district in south-central Los Angeles. When she is upset about something — a not uncommon situation, with Republicans running the House — she has been known to target withering blasts at her political opponents and sometimes even her allies.

George W. Bush is a favorite target. Waters protested vehemently when the Supreme Court ruled he had won Florida's electoral votes and therefore the presidency. Later, she told a Nation of Islam rally that Bush had overstepped the wartime authority Congress had given him after the Sept. 11, 2001, terrorist attacks on the United States. Earlier in the 107th Congress, she led the rhetorical opposition when Bush picked John Ashcroft to be attorney general. Her news release headlines often are filled with such phrases as "expresses outrage," "denounces," "condemns," and "assails."

The California Political Almanac, observing her 14 years in the state Assembly as well as her tenure in Washington, once described her as "a brassy bundle of energy" and described her strident espousal of her views as approaching most issues "with a firmly closed mind."

Whether Waters' highly charged rhetoric dilutes her influence is arguable, however, as her high-profile involvement in such issues as economic and political developments in Africa and Cuba and the battle against AIDS have ensured those matters are not ignored.

Since the 106th Congress, she has been a chief deputy whip and a member of the Democratic Steering Committee, which makes committee assignments. She had hoped to win a seat on the Appropriations Committee in the 108th, particularly with the retirement of black Democrat Carrie P. Meek of Florida. But there were few openings, and Waters did not get the post.

In the aftermath of the contested presidential election, Democratic leaders named Waters to head a task force on the election process. Charging that "many citizens are being denied their right to fully participate in our election process," she characterized the matter as "the first major civil rights issue of the 21st century." Waters' Democrats-only panel held a series of hearings and made recommendations. Throughout the 107th Congress, although generally not directly involved in the negotiations, the group played an important role in keeping up pressure for eventual congressional action.

With Republicans in the majority, Waters seldom finds sympathy for her repeated pleas for assistance to the inner cities, but she is at her rhetorical best as an insurgent. "Being in the minority means you don't get your legislation heard, you don't get to chair a committee, and you don't influence policies in other parts of the world," she says.

On the Judiciary Committee, Waters offers her two cents' worth in the often boisterous discussions in what may be the most partisan committee on Capitol Hill. She was one of President Clinton's staunchest supporters during the panel's impeachment proceedings. In the 107th Congress, to everyone's surprise, the committee fashioned a post-Sept. 11 bipartisan antiterrorism bill that won her support. But the final version was not to her liking: It "is a faulty and irresponsible piece of legislation that undermines our civil liberties and disregards the Constitution," she argued.

Waters brings her advocacy for minorities and the poor to the Financial Services panel, where she works to stop banks from charging transaction fees to small depositors and to stop engaging in "predatory" lending practices, in which customers in low-income communities pay higher interest rates and fees. She wants to reinstate the income tax deduction for interest on personal loans, in hopes of reducing the use of home equity loans, which is often the only viable borrowing option for many low-income people.

Over the years, Waters has won a few battles to obtain job training and community development funding for her district and for the fight against AIDS, which she argues has become an epidemic in Los Angeles County, particularly among blacks.

A virtual lock for re-election in her 90 percent minority district — largely left alone in the most recent redistricting — Waters is under no electoral pressure to trim her liberal sails or to heed the calls for civility and cooperation in the House. During a quarrel, she has been known to tell a colleague to "shut up." No one doubts the depth and sincerity of Waters' feelings, but many lawmakers — in both parties — are put off by her temper and by her unrelenting sense of the rightness of her decidedly liberal opinions. Waters says that if she softens her stance and engages in the give-and-take typical of Washington politics, her constituents will feel let down.

Born in St. Louis as one of 13 children in a welfare family, Waters was raised in public housing projects. As a teenager, she bused tables in a segregated restaurant. Married just after high school, she moved in 1961 with her first husband and two children to Los Angeles, where she worked in a clothing factory and for the telephone company.

Waters' public career began in 1966, when she volunteered as an assistant teacher in the new Head Start program while attending college. From Head Start, she got into community-organizing activities and then politics. After working as a volunteer and a consultant to several candidates, she won an upset 1976 victory for a seat in the state Assembly representing many of the same neighborhoods she now serves in Congress.

Waters got her chance to run for Congress in 1990, when Democrat Augustus F. Hawkins retired after his 14th term. She had been preparing for the move for years. During redistricting debates in the legislature in 1982, Waters maneuvered to remove from Hawkins' district a blue-collar, mainly white suburb she saw as unfriendly territory. Her 1990 election to the House was never in doubt, and she has won handily since.

Waters is on the board of the St. Louis (formerly Los Angeles) Rams, as is Rep. Richard A. Gephardt. Her rooting interest in the Rams gave her something in common with former GOP Majority Leader Dick Armey of Texas, whose brother is the Rams' general manager. Proving that sports can minimize ideological differences, when caught up in the excitement of a Rams score at the 2002 Super Bowl, Waters and Armey hugged.

KEY VOTES

2002

Yes Overhaul campaign finance law; ban "soft money" and restrict advocacy advertising
Yes Back Bush's defense budget increase
No Extend 1996 welfare law
No Adopt Bush's discretionary spending limit
No Pass GOP Medicare prescription drug plan
Yes Create independent Sept. 11 commission
Yes Extend union protections to Homeland Security Department employees
No Revive fast-track procedures for trade agreements
No Authorize war against Iraq
No Advance bankruptcy overhaul opposed by abortion opponents

2001

No Nullify Clinton Labor Department ergonomics rule
? Cut taxes by $1.35 trillion through fiscal 2011
Yes Maintain ban on oil drilling in Arctic National Wildlife Refuge
No Approve Bush proposal to limit managed-care plan liability for coverage decisions
Yes Divert money from crop subsidy payments to land conservation
No Expand law enforcement power to investigate suspected terrorists

CQ VOTE STUDIES

	PARTY UNITY		PRESIDENTIAL SUPPORT	
	Support	Oppose	Support	Oppose
2002	97%	3%	21%	79%
2001	96%	4%	12%	88%
2000	96%	4%	85%	15%
1999	97%	3%	87%	13%
1998	94%	6%	85%	15%

INTEREST GROUPS

	AFL-CIO	ADA	CCUS	ACU
2002	100%	95%	22%	0%
2001	100%	95%	23%	0%
2000	100%	85%	26%	0%
1999	100%	100%	12%	0%
1998	100%	80%	21%	0%

CALIFORNIA 35

South central Los Angeles; Inglewood

South central Los Angeles' 35th is one of the most secure Democratic districts in the state. Almost 70 percent of its voters register as Democrats, and Al Gore captured 78 percent of the vote here in the 2000 presidential election. Once predominantly black, the district is seeing a huge influx of Hispanics. It still has the state's highest concentration of African-Americans at 34 percent, but Hispanics are the district's racial plurality, comprising 47 percent of the population. Gardena has a large and politically influential Japanese community.

Riots put the 35th in the headlines in 1992 in the wake of a verdict acquitting white police officers accused of beating black motorist Rodney King. Issues of poverty, joblessness and lack of basic human services remain. Police-community relations, public safety and economic development are central public policy concerns.

The district is set between downtown Los Angeles to the north, beaches to the west, Torrance to the south and the industrial Alameda Corridor to the east. Redistricting following the 2000 census added Los Angeles International Airport, the region's largest employer. The 35th is mostly poor, but there are middle-class areas in Inglewood and the South Bay cities of Gardena and Hawthorne. Efforts to lure businesses have met with some success. In 1994, the area became part of a federal empowerment zone set up to help areas affected by the riots.

Gardena receives a strong revenue stream as one of the only cities in Los Angeles County that allows poker parlors, which account for a chunk of the city's budget. In 1999, the Los Angeles Lakers and Kings moved from the Great Western Forum in Inglewood to the new Staples Center in the nearby 34th, a disappointment for the 35th.

MAJOR INDUSTRY

Aerospace, service, manufacturing

CITIES

Los Angeles (pt.), 280,597; Inglewood, 112,580; Hawthorne, 84,112

NOTABLE

Hollywood Park racetrack is in Inglewood; Hawthorne was the birthplace of the Beach Boys and Northrop Corp., before it became aerospace giant Northrop Grumman Corp.; Central Avenue, on the district's eastern edge, was the West Coast hub of African-American entertainment during the jazz age.

Rep. Jane Harman (D)

CAPITOL OFFICE
225-8220
jane.harman@mail.house.gov
www.house.gov/harman
2400 Rayburn 20515-0536; fax 226-7290

COMMITTEES
Select Homeland Security
Select Intelligence - ranking member

HOMETOWN
Venice

BORN
June 28, 1945, Queens, N.Y.

RELIGION
Jewish

FAMILY
Husband, Sidney Harman; four children

EDUCATION
Smith College, B.A. 1966 (government); Harvard U., J.D. 1969

CAREER
Lawyer; White House aide; congressional aide

POLITICAL HIGHLIGHTS
U.S. House, 1993-99; sought Democratic nomination for governor, 1998

ELECTION RESULTS

2002 GENERAL		
Jane Harman (D)	88,198	61.4%
Stuart Johnson (R)	50,328	35.0%
Mark McSpadden (LIBERT)	5,225	3.6%
2002 PRIMARY		
Jane Harman (D)		unopposed
2000 GENERAL		
Jane Harman (D)	115,651	48.4%
Steven T. Kuykendall (R)	111,199	46.6%
Daniel Sherman (LIBERT)	6,073	2.5%
John Konopka (REF)	3,549	1.5%

PREVIOUS WINNING PERCENTAGES
1996 (52%); 1994 (48%); 1992 (48%)

Elected 1992; 5th term

Did not serve 1999-2001

The only member of the House Class of 2000 who had been in Congress before, Harman quickly involved herself in the central issue before the 107th Congress — the battle against international terrorism. And, as the top Democrat on the Intelligence Committee and a member of the new Homeland Security panel in the 108th, she remains in the thick of that action.

One might argue that she is better prepared for those responsibilities than she would have been had she been in Congress in 1999 and 2000.

Harman, who represented the 36th District for six years before giving up the seat to wage an unsuccessful 1998 run for governor, spent much of her two-year hiatus as one of 10 members of the congressionally mandated National Council on Terrorism. The panel issued a report in 2000 warning that the terrorist threat to the United States had increased and that "today's terrorists seek to inflict mass casualties." The commission recommended keeping better track of foreign students and advocated a greater role for the Defense Department in responding to major terrorist attacks on U.S. soil.

Harman had been on the Intelligence and National Security (now Armed Services) panels and, when Democratic political operatives pleaded with her to run for the 36th District seat again in 2000, she exacted a promise that she would be returned to the Intelligence panel if she won.

She did get a seat on the committee, and was the top Democrat on the panel's new Terrorism and Homeland Security Subcommittee. She was ahead of the White House in calling for the appointment of a homeland security adviser, and she was also one of the earliest congressional advocates of the creation of a new Department of Homeland Security — doing so months before President Bush made the idea his own.

Harman's approach to budget issues is similar to that of other moderate Democrats, including those in the fiscally conservative "Blue Dog" coalition, of which she is a member. She also affiliates with the business-oriented New Democrat Coalition, and in 2002 she was elected president of the coalition's new executive council.

Harman appeals to the swing voters in her upscale, suburban Los Angeles district with her moderate fiscal stands and liberal social views, such as support for abortion rights. At the same time, she breaks with most Democrats and votes for liberalized trade opportunities and is a strong proponent of a healthy defense budget. The 36th District is home to a number of defense contractors and the Los Angeles Air Force Base in El Segundo. Harman has called her district "the aerospace center of the universe."

Although homeland security issues led her agenda in the 107th Congress, the self-described middle-aged mother of four has a number of domestic priorities as well. Harman was the only freshman to win a spot on the Energy and Commerce panel, and before the Sept. 11, 2001, terrorist attacks, one of her most time-consuming issues was the California energy crisis.

On the local debate over whether to expand Los Angeles International Airport, Harman has weighed in on the side of those who favor a regional solution. She would prefer to see greater use of other area airports rather than expanding LAX. She also supported a local effort to keep the Harbor-UCLA Medical Center open in the face of funding shortfalls. Harman backed a ballot measure to increase property taxes to fund county trauma centers and said that Harbor-UCLA, the closest trauma center to the ports and the airport, is vital to homeland security. The initiative was approved by a nearly 3-to-1 margin.

Harman's father fled Nazi Germany, then emigrated to the United States. She was born in New York City, but when she was 4, she and her family moved to Southern California, where her father, a doctor, had relocated his practice. She grew up in West Los Angeles.

Harman was an intern in Washington in 1964 when she was attending Smith College, and as she told the Los Angeles Times, "Somehow the seeds were planted." After earning a law degree from Harvard, she returned to Washington to work for Democratic Sen. John Tunney of California and the Senate Judiciary Committee. In 1977, she went to work in the Carter White House as deputy secretary to the Cabinet, and then she moved to the Pentagon, serving as a special counsel.

She did not return to California until 1991. She and her second husband, millionaire audio equipment manufacturer Sidney Harman, settled in the 36th District, where incumbent Democrat Mel Levine was relinquishing his House seat to run, unsuccessfully, for the Senate.

Her recent return to California was an issue in her bid to succeed Levine, but a larger factor was the anti-abortion position of the Republican candidate, Joan Milke Flores. Harman made abortion rights a centerpiece of her campaign. She spent a considerable amount of her own money and emerged with a 6 percentage point victory.

The 36th was a swing district throughout the 1990s, and her re-elections in 1994 and 1996 were hard-fought affairs. When she opted to run for governor instead in 1998 — she fell short in a tight three-way primary to Lt. Gov. Gray Davis, who went on to victory that November — Steven T. Kuykendall picked up the seat for the GOP by 2.3 percentage points.

In 2000, Harman won back the seat by 1.8 points. Assured by House Democratic leaders that she would regain her past seniority, Harman agreed to run just two days before the filing deadline. Both candidates focused on issues and avoided mudslinging, and the contest was close, largely because they agreed on many major issues — Kuykendall, too, touted his support for abortion rights and defense spending.

Remapping before the 2002 election gave the 36th a much more Democratic tilt — in part by removing affluent areas such as Harman's former home in Rolling Hills on the Palos Verdes Peninsula, which is now in the 46th District. Harman won her most lopsided victory yet, taking three-fifths of the vote against attorney Stuart Johnson, who described himself as the only Indian-American nominee for federal office in 2002.

KEY VOTES

2002

Yes Overhaul campaign finance law; ban "soft money" and restrict advocacy advertising
Yes Back Bush's defense budget increase
No Extend 1996 welfare law
No Adopt Bush's discretionary spending limit
No Pass GOP Medicare prescription drug plan
Yes Create independent Sept. 11 commission
Yes Extend union protections to Homeland Security Department employees
Yes Revive fast-track procedures for trade agreements
Yes Authorize war against Iraq
No Advance bankruptcy overhaul opposed by abortion opponents

2001

No Nullify Clinton Labor Department ergonomics rule
No Cut taxes by $1.35 trillion through fiscal 2011
Yes Maintain ban on oil drilling in Arctic National Wildlife Refuge
No Approve Bush proposal to limit managed-care plan liability for coverage decisions
Yes Divert money from crop subsidy payments to land conservation
Yes Expand law enforcement power to investigate suspected terrorists

CQ VOTE STUDIES

	PARTY UNITY		PRESIDENTIAL SUPPORT	
	Support	Oppose	Support	Oppose
2002	83%	17%	42%	58%
2001	84%	16%	40%	60%
1998	83%	17%	78%	22%
1997	83%	17%	72%	28%
1996	75%	25%	67%	33%

INTEREST GROUPS

	AFL-CIO	ADA	CCUS	ACU
2002	50%	60%	65%	36%
2001	83%	90%	52%	20%
1998	63%	80%	83%	15%
1997	63%	60%	80%	25%
1996	64%	60%	60%	26%

CALIFORNIA 36

Southwest Los Angeles County — Torrance, Redondo Beach, Manhattan Beach

The 36th is home to some of Los Angeles' most famous beaches — and biggest aerospace firms. It hugs the Pacific coast south from Venice through El Segundo to Manhattan, Hermosa and Redondo beaches. Redistricting following the 2000 census removed the Republican Palos Verdes Peninsula to give the district a Democratic lean. Presidential candidate Al Gore took 55 percent of the vote here in 2000 and Democrats hold a 13-point voter registration edge.

Venice's eclectic beaches are considered the state's most liberal havens outside of Berkeley. Manhattan Beach and Marina del Rey, with its huge private marina, are ritzier. Torrance, the district's largest whole city, is split politically. It is wealthier toward the coast, but inland sections include middle- and working-class areas that have conservative and labor-heavy pockets. New immigrants and poorer residents live just west of Interstate 110.

A number of major companies maintain headquarters in the 36th, and aerospace firms in El Segundo and Redondo Beach drive the economy. The district has some of the state's most-educated residents. Some had trouble finding work as defense and aerospace spending shrank, but many employers, such as Hughes Electronics Corp. and Northrop Grumman, have successfully converted to non-defense projects. Such efforts to diversify the economy and encourage dual-use technology resulted in an economic boost.

MAJOR INDUSTRY
Aerospace, high-tech, manufacturing

MILITARY BASES
Los Angeles Air Force Base, 13,034 military, 1,000 civilian (1999)

CITIES
Los Angeles (pt.), 295,808; Torrance, 137,946; Redondo Beach, 63,261; Manhattan Beach, 33,582

NOTABLE
The Hyperion sewage treatment plant in Playa del Rey, the subject of a multiple-decade environmental lawsuit, is now one of cleanest plants in the Los Angeles area; Hughes and subsidiary DirecTV are based in El Segundo.

Rep. Juanita Millender-McDonald (D)

CAPITOL OFFICE
225-7924
millender.mcdonald@mail.house.gov
www.house.gov/millender-mcdonald
1514 Longworth 20515-0537; fax 225-7926

COMMITTEES
House Administration
Small Business
Transportation & Infrastructure
Joint Library

HOMETOWN
Carson

BORN
Sept. 7, 1938, Birmingham, Ala.

RELIGION
Baptist

FAMILY
Husband, James McDonald Jr.; five children

EDUCATION
U. of Redlands, B.S. 1981 (business administration); California State U., Los Angeles, M.A. 1988 (educational administration); U. of Southern California, attending (public administration)

CAREER
Teacher; school program administrator

POLITICAL HIGHLIGHTS
Carson City Council, 1990-92 (mayor pro tempore, 1991-92); Calif. Assembly, 1992-96

ELECTION RESULTS

2002 GENERAL		
J. Millender-McDonald (D)	63,445	72.9%
Oscar A. Velasco (R)	20,154	23.2%
Herb Peters (LIBERT)	3,413	3.9%
2002 PRIMARY		
J. Millender-McDonald (D)	25,302	77.7%
Peter Mathews (D)	7,269	22.3%
2000 GENERAL		
J. Millender-McDonald (D)	93,269	82.3%
Vernon Van (R)	12,762	11.3%
Margaret Glazer (NL)	4,094	3.6%
Herb Peters (LIBERT)	3,150	2.8%

PREVIOUS WINNING PERCENTAGES
1998 (85%); 1996 (85%); 1996 Special Election (27%)

Elected March 1996; 4th full term

A dependable Democratic vote who at times has been a critic of the Bush administration, Millender-McDonald is nevertheless willing to work with Republicans if she thinks it will help her constituents in one of California's poorest districts.

Her interests range across the domestic and social policy spectra, from local transportation projects to industrial development and job training, child care to illegal drug use, education to women's issues at home and abroad. Her rhetoric can take a hard edge when it serves her purpose and particularly when she detects what she views as GOP indifference toward the plight of the poor.

First elected to Congress in 1996, Millender-McDonald is in her third career, and she draws liberally from all of her previous experiences.

She is the daughter of a minister, who taught her the importance of self-respect and a good education. She married early and had five children by the time she was 26. At the age of 42, with her children older, she got her college degree and embarked on a career as a math and English teacher, and then as an administrator, in the Los Angeles school system.

She was active in local Democratic Party politics, serving as a delegate at the 1984 and 1988 Democratic National Conventions. Then, at age 51, she entered elective politics, winning a city council seat in Carson, a low-income city between Los Angeles and Long Beach.

At each step in her professional life, Millender-McDonald's forceful self-confidence has enabled her to become a powerful and noticeable presence. She has a host of ideas that she thinks would make the world a better place, and she persists, although many of them are a tough sell in a conservative-run House. "I am here for the fight and the long haul to ensure . . . fairness to my constituents," she said in a floor speech a few months after she arrived.

Millender-McDonald described those she worried most about during debate on an economic stimulus bill in 2001: "Large numbers of our constituents, particularly women, are employed in the service economy. They hold part-time or low-paying jobs. Many also have been the first to lose employment due to the layoffs and to the impact of the September 11th terrorist attacks. . . . This situation is highly notable in minority communities across the major urban areas of America. What is being viewed as a recession in much of the country could be termed a depression in these already disadvantaged communities."

Millender-McDonald is by any measure a liberal, but not an inflexible one. If cooperating with Republicans offers a chance of boosting the 37th District's struggling economy, she'll do it. As a member of the Transportation Committee, she joined GOP Chairman Don Young of Alaska in 2002 in challenging a proposed huge reduction in funding for highway projects, which threatened to cut California highway funds by $618 million. In 2002, she cheered the opening of the Alameda Corridor rail project from area ports to the railyards. She played a key role in getting funds for the project.

In the 107th Congress, her top transportation priorities included supporting the federal government's takeover of airport baggage and passenger screening. Having the federal government assume that responsibility, she said, would bring travelers back and ultimately protect the jobs of airport workers. She also sought to ensure that private screeners could apply for the same jobs in the newly created Transportation Security Administration.

Millender-McDonald was involved in the effort to keep aircraft manufacturer Boeing Inc. from closing its plant in Long Beach, which builds the C-17 military transport jet. Congress ultimately ordered the Air Force to buy 180 of the planes from Boeing.

A former director of gender equity programs with the Los Angeles Unified School District, some of Millender-McDonald's legislative efforts focus specifically on discrimination against women. She has called for specific assurances that women will receive a fair share of federal vocational education training dollars. And from her seat on Transportation's Aviation Subcommittee, she pressed for hearings on the alleged sexual harassment of female air-traffic controllers. In the 107th, she was co-chairman of the Congressional Caucus for Women's Issues.

In the areas of women's health, job training, child care and other social issues, Millender-McDonald has been a critic of the Bush administration's record, saying that Bush's stance on women's issues was "very dismal."

Millender-McDonald also sits on the Small Business Committee, where she has risen rapidly to rank second in Democratic seniority. In the 108th Congress, she added a seat on the House Administration panel.

A critic of tuition vouchers and other education ideas advanced by conservatives, Millender-McDonald has said the GOP first should recognize the "deplorable" physical condition of many public schools and commit billions of federal dollars to repairs and renovations. Nevertheless, she voted for a Bush proposal in 2001 to require annual reading and mathematics tests as part of a reauthorization of federal education funding.

In 1999, Millender-McDonald had a post office in Compton, Calif., named for Democratic Rep. Mervyn M. Dymally, who represented much of what is now the 37th District between 1981 and 1993, and helped her get elected to the Carson City Council in 1990 and the state Assembly two years later. She captured her House seat in a March 1996 special election after Democratic Rep. Walter R. Tucker III resigned; he had been convicted of federal extortion and tax evasion charges stemming from actions he took as mayor of Compton, before his election to Congress.

In each of her re-elections, Millender-McDonald has captured more than 70 percent of the vote. Changing demographics in the Los Angeles area threatened to jeopardize her career after the 2000 census, when the Hispanic population in her district surged to 57 percent. But the Democratic legislature drew a new district that reduced the Hispanic share of her constituency to 43 percent. The new 37th takes in much of Long Beach and other areas that in the 1990s were in the neighboring 38th District, a move that prompted its representative, moderate Republican Steve Horn, to retire in 2002.

KEY VOTES

2002

Yes Overhaul campaign finance law; ban "soft money" and restrict advocacy advertising
? Back Bush's defense budget increase
No Extend 1996 welfare law
No Adopt Bush's discretionary spending limit
No Pass GOP Medicare prescription drug plan
Yes Create independent Sept. 11 commission
Yes Extend union protections to Homeland Security Department employees
No Revive fast-track procedures for trade agreements
No Authorize war against Iraq
No Advance bankruptcy overhaul opposed by abortion opponents

2001

No Nullify Clinton Labor Department ergonomics rule
? Cut taxes by $1.35 trillion through fiscal 2011
Yes Maintain ban on oil drilling in Arctic National Wildlife Refuge
No Approve Bush proposal to limit managed-care plan liability for coverage decisions
Yes Divert money from crop subsidy payments to land conservation
Yes Expand law enforcement power to investigate suspected terrorists

CQ VOTE STUDIES

	PARTY UNITY		PRESIDENTIAL SUPPORT	
	Support	Oppose	Support	Oppose
2002	96%	4%	27%	73%
2001	95%	5%	26%	74%
2000	98%	2%	91%	9%
1999	97%	3%	88%	12%
1998	96%	4%	84%	16%

INTEREST GROUPS

	AFL-CIO	ADA	CCUS	ACU
2002	100%	85%	44%	0%
2001	100%	90%	35%	4%
2000	100%	90%	50%	8%
1999	78%	100%	30%	0%
1998	100%	95%	31%	4%

CALIFORNIA 37

Southern Los Angeles County – most of Long Beach, Compton, Carson

The 37th combines some of the state's poorest and most Democratic communities with a large chunk of middle-class Long Beach. Minorities make up almost 85 percent of the population, with Hispanics as the dominant group, totalling 43 percent of residents. The district is one-fourth black and more than one-tenth Asian.

Many residents are concentrated in the lower- and middle-class cities of Compton and Carson south of Los Angeles; the district also contains a tiny sliver of Los Angeles itself. These communities boost Democratic presidential candidates to high margins of victory in the 37th. Al Gore captured 72 percent of the vote here in 2000.

The district's south end contains the non-coastal portion of Long Beach (the port is in the 46th), which holds a more suburban, politically mixed community. It has a sizable Cambodian population, and more than four dozen languages are spoken in the schools.

The 37th's troubled economy suffered in the 1992 riots when fires ravaged parts of Compton. Despite redevelopment, Compton still has blocks-long stretches of abandoned buildings and vacant lots, and gang problems persist.

There are some bright spots, however. Several national retailers and fast-food chains have moved into communities once considered undevelopable, and home sales have increased. The multibillion-dollar Alameda Corridor project, which links the ports of Long Beach and Los Angeles south of the 27th to distribution areas in Los Angeles north of the district, created construction jobs for the area, and local leaders hope it will continue to provide an economic boost.

MAJOR INDUSTRY

Service, manufacturing, oil

CITIES

Long Beach (pt.), 368,591; Compton, 93,493; Carson, 89,730; Los Angeles (pt.), 33,808

NOTABLE

Toyota, which operates a manufacturing plant in Long Beach, is the title sponsor of the Grand Prix of Long Beach auto race.

Rep. Grace F. Napolitano (D)

Elected 1998; 3rd term

CAPITOL OFFICE
225-5256
grace@mail.house.gov
www.house.gov/napolitano
1609 Longworth 20515-0538; fax 225-0027

COMMITTEES
International Relations
Resources
Small Business

HOMETOWN
Norwalk

BORN
Dec. 4, 1936, Brownsville, Texas

RELIGION
Roman Catholic

FAMILY
Husband, Frank Napolitano; five children

EDUCATION
Brownsville H.S., graduated 1954

CAREER
Regional transportation claims agent

POLITICAL HIGHLIGHTS
Norwalk City Council, 1986-92 (mayor, 1989-90); Calif. Assembly, 1992-98

ELECTION RESULTS

2002 GENERAL		
Grace F. Napolitano (D)	62,600	71.1%
Alex A. Burrola (R)	23,126	26.3%
Al Cuperus (LIBERT)	2,301	2.6%
2002 PRIMARY		
Grace F. Napolitano (D)	21,815	65.0%
Gregory Salcido (D)	11,755	35.0%
2000 GENERAL		
Grace F. Napolitano (D)	105,980	71.3%
Robert Canales (R)	33,445	22.5%
Julia F. Simon (NL)	9,262	6.2%

PREVIOUS WINNING PERCENTAGES
1998 (68%)

Representing the suburbs and bedroom communities east of Los Angeles, first in the state Assembly and now in the House, has been a second calling for Napolitano.

Her first began early. Married at age 18, Napolitano had five children by age 23; attending to their needs, while also working at the Ford Motor Co., was her focus for decades. With her children now grown — and the parents to 14 children of their own — Napolitano directs her attention to Congress, where she is in her third term. There, she has often used the same manner with which she once tended to her family to address the needs of her constituents and colleagues alike.

She has looked out for the well-being of her mostly Hispanic constituency, laboring to win funds to address the mental health problems of teenage Latinas, focusing in particular on their high suicide rates. And she has developed a strong interest in environmental issues, successfully pressuring President Bush to support the cleanup of a uranium slag heap whose runoff threatened the water supplies in her district.

At the Capitol, she has tried to win over her political opponents in much the way she and her husband, Frank, won customers to their Italian restaurant — through their stomachs. While in Sacramento, Napolitano's contribution to bipartisan civility was to feed her colleagues at the state House. Napolitano has kept up her ways of culinary wooing in Congress. She prides herself on catering her own fundraisers with homemade Mexican molés, guacamole and other dishes. She says such personal involvement is the best way to express her thanks to her supporters. "I treat them like I would my family," she says.

Napolitano grew up in Brownsville, Texas, the daughter of a Mexican immigrant who raised her two children on a shoestring budget. Napolitano has cultivated a strong connection to her mother's homeland as a public official. As chairman of the state legislature's International Trade and Development Committee, she traveled to Mexico many times and traveled again with President Clinton in 1999. In the 107th Congress, she added the International Relations Committee to her portfolio.

Napolitano had been deeply immersed in the details of the 1993 North American Free Trade Agreement among the United States, Canada and Mexico, and she describes herself as a believer in the value of open commerce. Still, she represented a district with double-digit unemployment and a prevailing sense that it was left behind in the economic boom of the 1990s.

Those conflicting pressures have placed her in a difficult situation on the key trade votes of her tenure. Considered one of the last of the undecided lawmakers in 2000 — when Clinton and big businesses pushed to grant China permanent normal trade status over the objections of labor unions and environmentalists — she eventually voted against the bill. "I know trade is good," she said afterward. "I know it's where we are going, but it's not good for the district." She was much less publicly conflicted the next year, however, signaling all along that she would oppose the legislation Bush sought to revive presidential fast-track trade negotiating powers.

All the while, though, Napolitano has focused much of her energy on her other committee assignments, particularly the Resources panel.

Her biggest triumph was persuading Bush to follow through on ensuring that the Energy Department clean up more than 10 million tons of waste left over from 30 years of uranium mining. The waste pile, near Moab, Utah, is said to be leaking thousands of gallons of radioactive uranium and other toxins daily into the Colorado River, which provides much of the West's drinking water. Bush did not include cleanup funds in his initial budget in 2001. Napolitano joined with a bipartisan coalition of lawmakers from Utah and California to successfully pressure Bush, and then Congress, to support the program.

Napolitano also was one of several Los Angeles-area legislators who garnered $25 million for the cleanup of two aquifers that provide drinking water for millions of people in the region.

In 2001, she joined with other Southern Californians to oppose legislation that would authorize nearly $3 billion for a program designed to restore the Sacramento-San Joaquin delta. She and other foes objected to the bill's bias in favor of farmers in California's Central Valley, which they said would come at the expense of drinking water in their area. But she showed a more pragmatic streak than some of her colleagues, winning support for an amendment to allow more than one-quarter of the money to be spent on water recycling projects in California.

Napolitano's grandmotherly image, enhanced by her silvery hair, can be deceptive. She can be a fierce political fighter and had to overcome a number of political hurdles and slights to make it to Washington.

In her first run for political office, Napolitano challenged the Norwalk establishment and won a seat on the city council by 28 votes. She capitalized on outrage over an expensive city council trip to Palm Springs and campaigned with $35,000 she borrowed using her home as collateral. Napolitano had caught the political bug years earlier as a volunteer in Norwalk's efforts to cultivate a sister-city relationship with Hermosillo, Mexico. She first joined the group to show her children and "other youngsters on this side how lucky they were" compared to Mexican children, but became enmeshed in the efforts and managed the organization's budget.

Napolitano served in the state legislature for six years and was mayor and councilwoman in Norwalk — her district's second-largest municipality — during the six years before that. Nonetheless, she was overlooked when Democrat Esteban E. Torres announced his retirement in 1997. Torres threw his support to his top aide and son-in-law, James Casso. But Napolitano won by 618 votes in the primary, then won two-thirds of the vote in November. She increased her winning percentage to 71 percent in both 2000 and 2002. Redistricting shifted the district eastward to pick up Pomona; its Hispanic population in 2000 was 70 percent.

KEY VOTES

2002

Yes Overhaul campaign finance law; ban "soft money" and restrict advocacy advertising
Yes Back Bush's defense budget increase
No Extend 1996 welfare law
No Adopt Bush's discretionary spending limit
No Pass GOP Medicare prescription drug plan
Yes Create independent Sept. 11 commission
Yes Extend union protections to Homeland Security Department employees
No Revive fast-track procedures for trade agreements
No Authorize war against Iraq
No Advance bankruptcy overhaul opposed by abortion opponents

2001

No Nullify Clinton Labor Department ergonomics rule
No Cut taxes by $1.35 trillion through fiscal 2011
Yes Maintain ban on oil drilling in Arctic National Wildlife Refuge
No Approve Bush proposal to limit managed-care plan liability for coverage decisions
Yes Divert money from crop subsidy payments to land conservation
Yes Expand law enforcement power to investigate suspected terrorists

CQ VOTE STUDIES

	PARTY UNITY		PRESIDENTIAL SUPPORT	
	Support	Oppose	Support	Oppose
2002	98%	2%	21%	79%
2001	96%	4%	24%	76%
2000	95%	5%	94%	6%
1999	92%	8%	77%	23%

INTEREST GROUPS

	AFL-CIO	ADA	CCUS	ACU
2002	89%	100%	40%	0%
2001	100%	90%	35%	4%
2000	100%	95%	47%	4%
1999	89%	90%	45%	0%

CALIFORNIA 38
East Los Angeles County – Pomona, Norwalk

The Democratic 38th, once a predominantly white area, has become a middle- and working-class Hispanic-majority district. A sideways "L" shape, it takes in the southeast Los Angeles County city of Norwalk, then stretches north along Interstate 5 to include nearly half of East Los Angeles. It then runs east through Montebello and Pico Rivera, goes north a bit to La Puente and then extends a thin arm parallel to the 60 Freeway into the Inland Valley to take in Pomona, the district's largest city, at the county's eastern edge.

Though mostly blue-collar, the district contains some affluent and conservative areas such as Hacienda Heights, Rowland Heights (shared with the 42nd) and a narrow sliver of Whittier.

Small businesses dominate the 38th, which contains the heart of East Los Angeles' business district. Stores generally are owned or operated by Hispanics. These near-in suburbs are in places populated by what used to be called Muppies — Mexican yuppies who have moved in and fixed up old homes.

Montebello is an upper-middle-class Hispanic area, with a lot of home-grown residents. Pico Rivera has been called a pure Middle American working community, Hispanic-style. The city received a major blow in 2000 with the closure of a Northrop Grumman B-2 plant. Norwalk, the district's second-largest city, is a bedroom community. Santa Fe Springs is an industrial area with light manufacturing and oil wells.

The district's workers and seniors ensure that it is reliably Democratic on all levels as voters focus on health care and small-business support issues. Democratic presidential candidate Al Gore received 67 percent of the vote here in 2000. California State Polytechnic University, Pomona and Cerritos College add students to the Democratic mix.

MAJOR INDUSTRY
Manufacturing, oil

CITIES
Pomona, 149,473; Norwalk, 103,298; Pico Rivera, 63,428; Montebello, 62,150

NOTABLE
The Pomona Swap Meet and Car Show is billed as the largest collection of antique cars, parts and accessories on the West Coast.

Rep. Linda T. Sánchez (D)

CAPITOL OFFICE
225-6676
www.house.gov/lindasanchez
1007 Longworth 20515-0539; fax 226-1012

COMMITTEES
Government Reform
Judiciary
Small Business

HOMETOWN
Lakewood

BORN
Jan. 28, 1969, Orange, Calif.

RELIGION
Roman Catholic

FAMILY
Husband, Mark G. Valentine

EDUCATION
U. of California, Berkeley, B.A. 1991 (Spanish literature); U. of California, Los Angeles, J.D. 1995

CAREER
Union official; campaign aide; lawyer

POLITICAL HIGHLIGHTS
No previous office

ELECTION RESULTS

2002 GENERAL		
Linda T. Sánchez (D)	52,256	54.8%
Tim Escobar (R)	38,925	40.8%
Richard Newhouse (LIBERT)	4,165	4.4%
2002 PRIMARY		
Linda T. Sánchez (D)	10,804	33.5%
Hector De La Torre (D)	9,450	29.3%
Sally M. Havice (D)	6,223	19.3%
Helen M. Rahder (D)	2,698	8.4%
Ken Graham (D)	1,879	5.8%
A. R. "Cecy" Groom (D)	1,230	3.8%

Elected 2002; 1st term

With her victory in California's 39th District, Linda Sánchez joins her older sibling in Congress, Democrat Loretta Sanchez of the 47th, making them the first sisters to serve together.

Linda is the sixth of seven children of Mexican immigrant parents. Though she and Loretta share an American success story, Linda took a different path to Congress and promises to be no clone.

Linda went to UCLA Law School and has been practicing civil rights and employment law since she passed the bar in 1995; Loretta got an M.B.A. from American University in Washington and became a financial adviser. Linda has worked on labor issues for several unions and strikes a more liberal posture than her sister, who is a member of the conservative Democratic coalition known as the "Blue Dogs."

"Having worked with laws in the courtroom, I've really seen how legislation impacts people," she says. In the 108th Congress, she won a seat on the Judiciary panel — the only Democratic freshman to do so. She wants to help her district's blue-collar constituents rebound from the recent economic downturn. Jobs that pay a living wage and provide health care benefits are necessary, she says. She also cites as priorities easing school overcrowding and providing prescription drug coverage for senior citizens.

Linda and Loretta share a town house on Capitol Hill and like to discuss their differences: Linda, who is nine years younger, is a night owl; Loretta an early riser. Linda is messy, Loretta neat. They even spell their last name differently: Linda uses an accent.

The younger Sánchez jumped into the race for Congress after Republican Rep. Steve Horn's district was carved up during redistricting, spurring Horn to retire. The new 39th was configured to elect a Hispanic Democrat. Sánchez's more politically experienced primary opponents groused about the high-profile help her sister provided, but to no avail. Sánchez won the six-person contest with 34 percent of the vote. After her primary victory, she was a shoo-in in the general election.

CALIFORNIA 39

Southeast Los Angeles County — South Gate, Lakewood

The 39th is a product of the post-2000 census redistricting cycle: State legislators carved the area out as an open seat designed to elect a Hispanic Democrat from Los Angeles County south of downtown. It is 61 percent Hispanic and registered Democrats outnumber Republicans almost 2-to-1. Despite their external similarities, most of these communities have little interaction with one another.

The district has a strong organized-labor movement. Towns like Whittier (shared with the 42nd) and Lakewood have a number of industrial centers, and most residents work in the district or nearby rather than commuting to downtown Los Angeles, Orange County or Long Beach.

Whittier and South Whittier, on the U-shaped district's northeastern tip, are home to many second- and third-generation Latino families, and pockets of wealth exist there. La Mirada and the Asian-American-heavy Cerritos, on the eastern arm of the U, are slightly more conservative communities that resemble cities in neighboring, richer Orange County — former farm areas now dependent on aerospace and technology jobs. Lakewood, on the southern arc of the U, is more blue-collar, while South Gate, Lynwood and Paramount, farther west, are heavily working class and include many new immigrants.

MAJOR INDUSTRY
Manufacturing, aerospace

CITIES
South Gate, 96,375; Lakewood, 79,345; Lynwood, 69,845; Whittier (pt.), 56,918

NOTABLE
Whittier, where Richard M. Nixon lived and attended college, was the epicenter of L.A.'s 1987 earthquake; Paramount is home to Zamboni, maker of the ice resurfacing machines used at skating and hockey rinks; The home of the last Mexican governor of California is in Pio Pico Historical Park.

Rep. Ed Royce (R)

CAPITOL OFFICE
225-4111
www.house.gov/royce
2202 Rayburn 20515-0540; fax 226-0335

COMMITTEES
Financial Services
International Relations
(Africa - chairman)

HOMETOWN
Fullerton

BORN
Oct. 12, 1951, Los Angeles, Calif.

RELIGION
Roman Catholic

FAMILY
Wife, Marie Royce

EDUCATION
California State U., Fullerton, B.A. 1977 (accounting & finance)

CAREER
Tax manager

POLITICAL HIGHLIGHTS
Calif. Senate, 1982-92

ELECTION RESULTS

2002 GENERAL		
Ed Royce (R)	92,422	67.6%
Christina Avalos (D)	40,265	29.5%
Charles McGlawn (LIBERT)	3,955	2.9%
2002 PRIMARY		
Ed Royce (R)		unopposed
2000 GENERAL		
Ed Royce (R)	129,294	62.7%
Gill G. Kanel (D)	64,938	31.5%
Ron Jevning (NL)	6,597	3.2%
Keith Gann (LIBERT)	5,275	2.6%

PREVIOUS WINNING PERCENTAGES
1998 (63%); 1996 (63%); 1994 (66%); 1992 (57%)

Elected 1992; 6th term

Royce won notice during his early terms in the House by crusading against federal programs that he considered wasteful and by attacking funding for projects in other lawmakers' districts. But his more successful legislative efforts have had their impact far from U.S. shores.

After terrorists attacked the Pentagon and World Trade Center in 2001, Royce resurrected a bill to establish Radio Free Afghanistan to beam news into that war-ravaged country. Royce had promoted the idea unsuccessfully for five years, but after the attacks Congress quickly embraced the plan and appropriated $19 million for the initial effort.

The new focus on combating terrorism interrupted Royce's focus on expanding U.S. trade ties with sub-Saharan Africa. In 2000, he helped win enactment of legislation reducing tariffs and quotas on imports from that region. That law, which also expanded the U.S. trade relationship with Caribbean nations, broke a six-year impasse on trade legislation.

As chairman of the House International Relations Subcommittee on Africa, Royce won House passage in the 107th Congress of a bill that would gradually permit increased imports of African-made fabric and yarn.

The sub-Saharan bills grew out of Royce's view that trade is an effective way to help lift nations out of poverty and keep totalitarian regimes out of power. "For too long our African policy has been based on foreign aid," Royce said in 1998. "The United States needs to encourage African nations to move toward the free market and steer them in the direction of self-sufficiency. Markets work and subsidies don't."

In the 108th Congress, Royce is serving his fourth term as chairman of the Africa Subcommittee; he was given a special waiver to remain beyond the GOP's three-term limit.

International relations issues are important in Royce's Orange County district, which is home to an array of Asian-American nationalities and one of the nation's largest concentrations of Vietnamese-Americans.

Royce travels occasionally to Africa and Asia, sometimes stirring controversy along the way. He drew criticism in early in 2001, when he was part of a congressional delegation to India but left the group when it traveled to Pakistan. Critics said he bent to the will of Indian-American groups that raised funds for his election campaigns, but Royce said he did not want to legitimize President Pervez Musharraf, who had come to power in a coup. A year earlier, Royce was scolded by the government of Vietnam when he departed from his official itinerary to meet with a monk living under house arrest for resisting government efforts to establish an official Communist Buddhist church.

Royce and Washington Democratic Rep. Jim McDermott have been leaders in the Congressional Caucus on India and Indian-American Affairs. Royce also is active in the U.S.-Korean interparliamentary exchange.

Royce's commitment to international cooperation and free trade reflects the conservative economic viewpoint he developed as a youth while growing up in a blue-collar, Democratic household.

In high school, he became intrigued by the free-market message in the book "Economics in One Lesson" by Henry Hazlitt. The author challenged prevailing economic thinking that gave government a central role, and that spurred Royce to read similar books on economic theory. Growing more convinced his views were on solid ground, Royce found himself defending the unorthodox viewpoints to fellow students and to teachers. He said he is glad he was drawn to unconventional economic views. "The real advantage was that people would argue with me," he said, which gave him plenty of practice articulating his positions.

In Congress, Royce attacked government largess, riling some members of his own party. His zeal has not faded, but his activism as the longtime co-chairman of the Congressional Porkbusters Coalition and a member of the Stop Corporate Welfare Coalition has subsided.

Royce acknowledges that his cause lost momentum when budget deficits temporarily gave way to surpluses and balancing the budget could no longer be used as a battle cry. And with a Republican now in the White House, the congressional GOP tends to let President Bush lead the fight against spending increases beyond those proposed by his administration.

California lawmakers say Royce played a key role in maintaining GOP power in their state when the political map was redrawn based on the 2000 census. Royce joined California Republican Rep. David Dreier and House GOP campaign committee chairman Thomas M. Davis III of Virginia to promote a plan intended to protect the 20 seats held by Republicans.

Royce spent 10 years in the California Senate, where he wrote the nation's first law making it a felony to stalk or threaten someone with injury — giving the police recourse when a stalker has not yet attacked an intended victim. He also was the guiding force behind a 1990 ballot proposition, approved by voters, setting forth rights for victims of crimes. In the 107th and 108th Congresses, Royce has introduced a victim's rights amendment to the Constitution.

In Washington, Royce has continued his anti-stalking campaign, winning enactment of a measure similar to the one he sponsored in California. The federal law, signed in 1996, made it a crime to cross state lines with the intent to stalk or harass. In 1999, Royce and other lawmakers won enactment of a bill expanding the behavior that constitutes stalking.

After 10 years in Sacramento, Royce jumped at the chance to run for the House in 1992 when iconoclastic Republican William E. Dannemeyer gave up his seat to run for the Senate. Royce had represented a sizable slice of the House district in the state Senate, and he drew no primary opposition. His Democratic opponent, Molly McClanahan, proved too liberal for conservative Republican Orange County and Royce prevailed by almost 20 percentage points. He has had no trouble winning re-election.

In 2002, redistricting, which removed the Los Angeles County portion of Royce's old 39th District and renumbered it the 40th, gave Royce no electoral headaches; he won by 38 points.

KEY VOTES

2002

- No Overhaul campaign finance law; ban "soft money" and restrict advocacy advertising
- Yes Back Bush's defense budget increase
- Yes Extend 1996 welfare law
- Yes Adopt Bush's discretionary spending limit
- Yes Pass GOP Medicare prescription drug plan
- No Create independent Sept. 11 commission
- No Extend union protections to Homeland Security Department employees
- Yes Revive fast-track procedures for trade agreements
- Yes Authorize war against Iraq
- Yes Advance bankruptcy overhaul opposed by abortion opponents

2001

- Yes Nullify Clinton Labor Department ergonomics rule
- Yes Cut taxes by $1.35 trillion through fiscal 2011
- No Maintain ban on oil drilling in Arctic National Wildlife Refuge
- Yes Approve Bush proposal to limit managed-care plan liability for coverage decisions
- No Divert money from crop subsidy payments to land conservation
- Yes Expand law enforcement power to investigate suspected terrorists

CQ VOTE STUDIES

	PARTY UNITY		PRESIDENTIAL SUPPORT	
	Support	Oppose	Support	Oppose
2002	97%	3%	82%	18%
2001	93%	7%	84%	16%
2000	93%	7%	25%	75%
1999	92%	8%	16%	84%
1998	90%	10%	21%	79%

INTEREST GROUPS

	AFL-CIO	ADA	CCUS	ACU
2002	11%	0%	85%	100%
2001	8%	5%	74%	100%
2000	0%	0%	80%	100%
1999	11%	5%	76%	96%
1998	13%	5%	71%	100%

CALIFORNIA 40

North central Orange County — Orange, Fullerton

Like most of Orange County, the 40th is largely affluent and Republican, though these inland areas are less affluent than the coast. The district forms a half circle, extending north from Los Alamitos on the Los Angeles County border to take in most of Fullerton before turning southeast to reach Orange and Villa Park. It wraps around Anaheim and Garden Grove, taking in small chunks of each.

Orange, the solidly suburban district's largest city, and Fullerton are both upper middle class, while Stanton and Cypress are the district's more blue-collar communities. The median home price in the district is about $275,000, median income is high and unemployment is low. Whites make up about half of the district's population, which is seeing an influx of wealthier Hispanics. Several cities are nearly half Hispanic, while the district overall is 30 percent Hispanic and 16 percent Asian. In the 2000 presidential race, George W. Bush defeated Al Gore here 55 percent to 40 percent.

Before massive growth in the 1960s and 1970s, Orange County consisted largely of orange and lemon groves, and many cities were dairy farm communities. Now the economy centers on aerospace and defense, and new high-tech firms have sprung up in the district. The 40th also has a sizable senior population.

Fullerton is home to a Raytheon facility and a Kimberly-Clark paper mill, as well as a California State University campus that is the city's major employer. Adams Rite Aerospace in Fullerton makes airplane cockpit security doors, which Congress mandated after the Sept. 11 terrorist attacks. Orange is a health care center, and the district is home to four major hospitals.

MAJOR INDUSTRY

Aerospace, defense, manufacturing, health care

CITIES

Orange, 128,821; Fullerton (pt.), 108,151; Anaheim (pt.), 87,082; Buena Park, 78,282

NOTABLE

Beach Boulevard in Buena Park features attractions such as Knott's Berry Farm — the first theme park in the United States, the Movieland Wax Museum, Ripley's Believe It or Not, Wild Bill's Wild West Dinner Extravaganza and the Medieval Times dinner and tournament.

Rep. Jerry Lewis (R)

CAPITOL OFFICE
225-5861
www.house.gov/jerrylewis
2112 Rayburn 20515-0541; fax 225-6498

COMMITTEES
Appropriations
(Defense - chairman)

HOMETOWN
Redlands

BORN
Oct. 21, 1934, Seattle, Wash.

RELIGION
Presbyterian

FAMILY
Wife, Arlene Lewis; four children, three stepchildren

EDUCATION
U. of California, Los Angeles, B.A. 1956 (government)

CAREER
Insurance executive

POLITICAL HIGHLIGHTS
San Bernardino School Board, 1965-68; Calif. Assembly, 1968-78; Republican nominee for Calif. Senate, 1973

ELECTION RESULTS

2002 GENERAL		
Jerry Lewis (R)	91,326	67.4%
Keith A. Johnson (D)	40,155	29.6%
Kevin Craig (LIBERT)	4,052	3.0%
2002 PRIMARY		
Jerry Lewis (R)		unopposed
2000 GENERAL		
Jerry Lewis (R)	151,069	79.9%
Frank Schmit (NL)	19,029	10.1%
Jay Lindberg (LIBERT)	18,924	10.0%

PREVIOUS WINNING PERCENTAGES
1998 (65%); 1996 (65%); 1994 (71%); 1992 (63%); 1990 (61%); 1988 (70%); 1986 (77%); 1984 (85%); 1982 (68%); 1980 (72%); 1978 (61%)

Elected 1978; 13th term

With his gleaming smile and affable manner, Lewis has the demeanor of a successful insurance salesman — which he once was — and not that of a legislative bomb-thrower. But throughout his tenure as chairman of the Defense Appropriations Subcommittee, which is scheduled to come to its term-limited conclusion after the 108th Congress, his geniality has not prevented Lewis from openly challenging Pentagon priorities.

Lewis' confrontational approach is all the more striking because he is a denizen of the most collegial and accommodating of all congressional institutions: the Appropriations Committee.

The subcommittee over which Lewis presides writes the first draft of the annual bill that allocates more discretionary federal spending than any other measure — $355 billion in the 2003 budget year. As soon as he took the gavel in 1999, Lewis raised the most serious legislative challenge to a major weapons program in years when he tried to deny $1.8 billion requested to begin producing the Lockheed Martin F-22 jet fighter, the Air Force's premier modernization effort.

The program was chronically over-budget and a symbol for a whole family of big-ticket programs that had been designed to fight the now-defunct Soviet Union, Lewis argued. So it was an ideal issue on which to lay down a marker: He would use his chairmanship to goad the Pentagon to budget realistically. And he would press the services less to upgrade Cold War weapons to fight conventional wars and more to develop and field "smart" weapons and more agile forces that could deal with non-traditional threats.

Ultimately, a lobbying tsunami by the Air Force and the plane's contractors persuaded Congress to approve the money. But all the services got the message that Lewis would use his clout to make them keep program costs under control and adapt to the new military requirements of the post-Cold War world.

Three years later, Lewis warned Defense Secretary Donald H. Rumsfeld that the Bush administration's budget did not live up to Rumsfeld's own call for "transformation" of U.S. forces. "Hard decisions and trade-offs have not been made," he said. "It is imperative that budgetary priority be assigned to those systems that will enable our efforts to eradicate terrorism and transform the military to succeed, rather than funding programs that have nothing but bureaucratic inertia behind them."

Still, Lewis is willing to accommodate other members' requests for usually modest add-ons to administration budgets, and he is no slouch at steering funds to his own sprawling desert district. For example, the final defense spending law written in the 107th Congress dictated that $13 million be spent to continue Army-sponsored research at Loma Linda University on the use of proton beams to treat cancer, and $3 million go to the the University of Redlands to map the habitat for the endangered desert tortoise around the Army's Fort Irwin. And Lewis' interest in promising new military technology meshes nicely with his constituents' interests. He was an early and avid supporter of the Predator remotely piloted drone airplane — assembled by Lewis' constituents — that proved useful in the campaign in Afghanistan that started in 2001.

His aptitude for compromise sidetracked Lewis' rise in the leadership ranks. In 1992, Dick Armey of Texas elbowed him out of his job as the third-ranking Republican in the House, making Lewis a casualty of conservatives' demand for a more confrontational approach to the long-established Democratic majority. After Republicans took control of the House in 1995, Lewis strained his relations with Democratic appropriators by dutifully enforcing the new regime's fiscal austerity as chairman of the Appropriations subcommittee that funds veterans, housing, space and environmental programs.

When Lewis moved to the defense panel four years later, he had boned up well in advance, consulting with a wide network of informal advisers within the Pentagon and at think tanks. He concluded that the long-range defense budgets could not accommodate all the services' modernization plans and that some of those plans were being overtaken by radical changes in the international environment and in technology. He got to test his theses early on, by writing a midyear spending bill in 1999 to pay for the U.S.-led air war against Yugoslavia — which he called "firehose learning" in what the Pentagon lacked.

Lewis' effort against the F-22 was only his opening gambit. The next year, he roughly doubled the amount Clinton sought for an Army plan to develop a combat unit that could be deployed much more quickly. In 2001, he threatened to cancel a missile-tracking satellite program that had serious technical and cost problems. In 2002, the F-22 was back in the bulls-eye, with Lewis' panel urging the Air Force to slow production until more of the lagging flight test program was completed. And he lambasted top Pentagon civilians for being too dismissive of congressional defense specialists who could offer the administration useful advice and vital political support.

Lewis dates his interest in government to a trip he made to Washington in 1955. Some of his fellow UCLA students were forced to ride on a separate tourist boat on the Potomac because they were black, and this planted in Lewis the idea that he would have to participate actively in public service if he expected to effect changes in the country. Today he speaks of using his post to make the world safer and more peaceful for his grandchildren.

He left the insurance business to enter GOP politics in the early 1960s, winning a seat on the San Bernardino School Board. After three years there, he won a state Assembly seat that he held for a decade. Lewis is a safe bet for election in the House. His San Bernardino County-based district, now numbered the 41st, has given him at least 61 percent of the vote in 13 elections, no matter the precise boundaries. The redistricting of California in 2001 to add an additional House seat removed the huge but sparsely populated Inyo County from the territory Lewis represents, and his district was relabeled the 41st — but nothing was done to alter its essential GOP character.

KEY VOTES

2002

No Overhaul campaign finance law; ban "soft money" and restrict advocacy advertising
Yes Back Bush's defense budget increase
Yes Extend 1996 welfare law
Yes Adopt Bush's discretionary spending limit
Yes Pass GOP Medicare prescription drug plan
No Create independent Sept. 11 commission
No Extend union protections to Homeland Security Department employees
Yes Revive fast-track procedures for trade agreements
Yes Authorize war against Iraq
No Advance bankruptcy overhaul opposed by abortion opponents

2001

Yes Nullify Clinton Labor Department ergonomics rule
Yes Cut taxes by $1.35 trillion through fiscal 2011
No Maintain ban on oil drilling in Arctic National Wildlife Refuge
Yes Approve Bush proposal to limit managed-care plan liability for coverage decisions
No Divert money from crop subsidy payments to land conservation
Yes Expand law enforcement power to investigate suspected terrorists

CQ VOTE STUDIES

	PARTY UNITY		PRESIDENTIAL SUPPORT	
	Support	Oppose	Support	Oppose
2002	92%	8%	87%	13%
2001	97%	3%	97%	3%
2000	87%	13%	36%	64%
1999	85%	15%	33%	67%
1998	88%	12%	33%	67%

INTEREST GROUPS

	AFL-CIO	ADA	CCUS	ACU
2002	11%	10%	84%	88%
2001	8%	5%	100%	80%
2000	0%	0%	80%	64%
1999	11%	20%	92%	73%
1998	22%	10%	100%	75%

CALIFORNIA 41
Most of San Bernardino County — Redlands

The 41st includes vast desert and mountain stretches and most of the nation's largest county, San Bernardino, but is home to less than one-third of county residents. The district takes in some eastern Inland Valley communities and a northwest sliver of Riverside County before crossing the San Bernardino Mountains and part of the Mojave Desert to reach the mountains along the Nevada and Arizona borders. Republicans enjoy a 10-point edge in voter registration.

Nearly everyone lives in the western quarter of the 41st, where the district's Inland Empire, Victor Valley and Riverside County areas are located. Redlands, Highland, Yucaipa and a portion of the city of San Bernardino are nestled south of the San Bernardino Mountains.

The Victor Valley high-desert cities of Hesperia and Apple Valley to the north have seen rapid growth. Affordable land and housing have made the area a magnet for Los Angeles and Orange County workers since the 1990s. The Riverside County portion of the 41st takes in the San Jacinto Valley and the areas of Banning, San Jacinto, Beaumont and Calimesa.

As the 41st heads northeast, bordered by Interstate 15 on the north and the San Bernardino-Riverside county line on the south, towns become scarce and desert, mountains and dry lakes dominate. Exits off Interstate 15 lead mostly to dirt roads. Much of the land here is arid or mountainous, making development difficult. Local hospitals and the government remain the largest employers.

MAJOR INDUSTRY
Service, manufacturing, military

MILITARY BASES
Marine Corps Air Ground Combat Center, Twentynine Palms, 9,147 military, 1,397 civilian (2001)

CITIES
Redlands, 63,591; Hesperia, 62,582; San Bernardino (pt.), 54,789; Apple Valley, 54,239

NOTABLE
The Mojave National Preserve, designated in 1994, features the Devil's Playground dunes and the Kelso railroad depot, which was built in 1924; Roy Rogers' former ranch was in Apple Valley.

Rep. Gary G. Miller (R)

CAPITOL OFFICE
225-3201
PublicCA41@mail.house.gov
www.house.gov/garymiller
1037 Longworth 20515-0542; fax 226-6962

COMMITTEES
Financial Services
Transportation & Infrastructure

HOMETOWN
Diamond Bar

BORN
Oct. 16, 1948, Huntsville, Ark.

RELIGION
Protestant

FAMILY
Wife, Cathy Miller; four children

EDUCATION
Mt. San Antonio Community College, attended 1968-70

MILITARY SERVICE
Army, 1967-68

CAREER
Real estate developer

POLITICAL HIGHLIGHTS
Diamond Bar Municipal Advisory Council, 1988-89; Diamond Bar City Council, 1989-90; sought Republican nomination for Calif. Senate, 1990; Diamond Bar City Council, 1991-95 (mayor, 1993-94); sought Republican nomination for Calif. Senate (special election), 1994; Calif. Assembly, 1995-98

ELECTION RESULTS

2002 GENERAL		
Gary G. Miller (R)	98,476	67.8%
Richard Waldron (D)	42,090	29.0%
Donald Yee (LIBERT)	4,680	3.2%
2002 PRIMARY		
Gary G. Miller (R)		unopposed
2000 GENERAL		
Gary G. Miller (R)	104,695	58.9%
Rudy Favila (D)	66,361	37.4%
David F. Kramer (NL)	6,560	3.7%

PREVIOUS WINNING PERCENTAGES
1998 (53%)

Elected 1998; 3rd term

A self-made millionaire in the housing and real estate development business, Miller's work in Congress is aimed, to a large degree, at making it possible for others to follow in his footsteps.

He works to reduce environmental and business regulations that hinder business, advocates government spending for infrastructure projects — highways, aviation, drinking water and wastewater treatment plants, and school construction — and backs tax cuts, apprenticeship programs and cleanups of polluted industrial sites that help the building and construction industry, which Miller says is larger than the automotive and steel industries combined.

Miller's frustrations in working with government regulations in his development business led to his own involvement in public life.

In 2001, Miller founded the Building a Better America Caucus, to increase awareness of housing and construction issues, particularly involving compliance with government regulations, worker training and affordable housing issues.

Miller considers himself a fiscal and social conservative, and his first foray into public life was as the board member of a Christian school. He subscribes to Republican tenets of shrinking the federal government, overhauling the tax code and advancing a pro-family agenda.

That, coupled with Miller's pro-business inclinations, give him a voting record in Congress that is solidly Republican. In the 107th Congress, he backed the GOP position 99 percent of the time on votes that pitted the two parties against each other, ranking him as the fifth-most-loyal Republican.

Miller, who had left his post on the Transportation panel in the 107th, returned in the 108th, dropping seats on Science and Budget.

Despite his clear ideological preferences, Miller does not evince a partisan demeanor, perhaps in part because he began his legislative service in a closely divided California Assembly. He makes friends readily and draws kudos from Democrats for his efforts to cooperate with them. A Democrat who served with him in the Assembly told the Orange County Register, "He has an ideology that's fairly conservative, but it's without inflammatory overtones. Miller doesn't like partisan bickering."

Republican Whip Tom DeLay, after watching the GOP freshman Class of 1998 during orientation sessions, tapped Miller to be an assistant whip, telling the Register he was looking for people who "have an ability to create relationships quickly, and he was obviously a guy who could do that."

In the 107th Congress, Miller's legislative priorities included a bill to encourage small communities to clean up contaminated industrial sites known as brownfields. Miller's bill, which passed the House, would have given cities more flexibility in spending community development grant money to clean up these contaminated sites.

Miller has pushed for more federal money to treat and recycle water in California's Inland Empire. He also tried, on a number of fronts, to make home ownership in his district more affordable. Miller calls it the crisis of the "new homeless" — middle-class families whose incomes are still far below what is needed to buy a home in the district. He advocates negotiations with Canada to do away with a steep tariff on softwood lumber that Miller says adds about $1,500 to the cost of an average home.

A Civil War history buff, Miller in 2002 won enactment of his bill to provide federal grants to help state and local governments preserve battle sites.

When he first came to Congress, Miller called for the repeal of the Endangered Species Act. Softening that stance since the Bush administration came to power, he says his priority is for the act to be properly implemented. Miller says there is now more federal cooperation on environmental issues with local officials and private businessmen.

Miller's other priorities include getting the federal government to increase its financial support for the education of disabled students, something he says the government has required local school districts to provide. He also wants continued federal funding for the Alameda Corridor East project to improve rail traffic from Southern California ports eastward through his district.

Miller was raised by his mother and grandparents. At an early age, his family moved from Arkansas, where he was born, to Whittier, east of Los Angeles; many poor families from Oklahoma and Arkansas had settled there.

He attended community college for a while, but decided that college was not right for him. In the California Legislature and now in Congress, Miller has been an advocate for job training and apprenticeship programs.

After leaving school, he started a fledgling partnership with an experienced contractor, and they bid on home improvement contracts with the Department of Housing and Urban Development. He says he learned on the job, and moved on to building single-family homes and eventually to developing planned communities.

Miller began his political career on the Diamond Bar Municipal Advisory Council and then as a member of Diamond Bar's first city council after the city was incorporated in 1989. He became mayor in 1993.

He has made a habit of challenging fellow Republicans. He lost state Senate primary bids in 1990 and 1994, the latter in a special election. Early in 1995, when voters forced a recall election of state Assemblyman Paul Horcher, who left the Republican Party and backed the liberal Democrat Willie Brown as speaker, Miller ran to replace Horcher and won.

In 1998, Miller was convinced that his Diamond Bar neighbor Jay C. Kim had to be replaced in the House after his conviction on campaign finance illegalities. Miller challenged the three-term lawmaker in the GOP primary. He won by almost 4,000 votes, with Kim coming in third. In all of his races, Miller bankrolled his campaign with large infusions of his own money.

He was the only challenger to defeat an incumbent in a primary that year. The Republican-leaning 41st District then handed Miller a 13-point general-election victory. In 2000, his margin of victory increased to 22 percentage points, and in 2002, with the district shifted to the south and west and renumbered the 42nd in remapping, he won by 39 points.

KEY VOTES

2002

- No Overhaul campaign finance law; ban "soft money" and restrict advocacy advertising
- Yes Back Bush's defense budget increase
- Yes Extend 1996 welfare law
- Yes Adopt Bush's discretionary spending limit
- Yes Pass GOP Medicare prescription drug plan
- No Create independent Sept. 11 commission
- No Extend union protections to Homeland Security Department employees
- Yes Revive fast-track procedures for trade agreements
- Yes Authorize war against Iraq
- No Advance bankruptcy overhaul opposed by abortion opponents

2001

- Yes Nullify Clinton Labor Department ergonomics rule
- Yes Cut taxes by $1.35 trillion through fiscal 2011
- No Maintain ban on oil drilling in Arctic National Wildlife Refuge
- Yes Approve Bush proposal to limit managed-care plan liability for coverage decisions
- No Divert money from crop subsidy payments to land conservation
- Yes Expand law enforcement power to investigate suspected terrorists

CQ VOTE STUDIES

	PARTY UNITY		PRESIDENTIAL SUPPORT	
	Support	Oppose	Support	Oppose
2002	99%	1%	90%	10%
2001	99%	1%	100%	0%
2000	97%	3%	25%	75%
1999	96%	4%	21%	79%

INTEREST GROUPS

	AFL-CIO	ADA	CCUS	ACU
2002	0%	0%	95%	100%
2001	8%	0%	100%	100%
2000	0%	0%	95%	100%
1999	0%	5%	96%	88%

CALIFORNIA 42

Parts of Orange, Los Angeles and San Bernardino counties — Mission Viejo, Chino

Though most of its population lives in Orange County, the Republican 42nd is centered around the area where Orange, Los Angeles and San Bernardino counties come together east of Los Angeles proper.

From there, the 42nd has a long arm that stretches southeast and then southwest farther into Orange County to Mission Viejo. Its southeasternmost city, Rancho Santa Margarita, is also its newest; its population of 47,000 incorporated in 2000. A chunk of eastern Anaheim also falls within the district's borders.

Chino and Chino Hills in San Bernardino County have an agricultural heritage, but dairy production is giving way to manufacturing and service industries. Diamond Bar, Whittier (shared with the 39th) and Rowland Heights (shared with the 38th) in Los Angeles County have large Asian populations. Hispanics and Asians also are found in the northern Orange County cities of Brea (one of the fastest-growing in the county), La Habra and Placentia (shared with the 40th), though this Orange County segment is predominantly white-collar and white. Conservatism persists even among non-whites, and Republicans hold a 20 percentage point voter registration edge in the 42nd.

Overall, the district is predominantly middle- and upper-class and is about 24 percent Hispanic and 16 percent Asian. It is home to many married couples and families but has a low percentage of senior citizens. Unemployment is low and housing prices, particularly in Orange County, are above average. Many of the residential communities' commuters travel to work in Los Angeles or nearby Irvine (which is located in the 48th).

MAJOR INDUSTRY

Service, manufacturing, dairy

CITIES

Mission Viejo, 93,102; Chino, 67,168; Chino Hills, 66,787; La Habra, 58,974; Yorba Linda, 58,918; Diamond Bar, 56,287; Anaheim (pt.), 55,395

NOTABLE

Yorba Linda, the birthplace and burial site of President Richard M. Nixon, is the home of the Nixon Library.

Rep. Joe Baca (D)

CAPITOL OFFICE
225-6161
www.house.gov/baca
328 Cannon 20515-0543; fax 225-8671

COMMITTEES
Agriculture
Financial Services
Resources

HOMETOWN
San Bernardino

BORN
Jan. 23, 1947, Belen, N.M.

RELIGION
Roman Catholic

FAMILY
Wife, Barbara Baca; four children

EDUCATION
California State U., Los Angeles, B.A. 1971 (sociology)

MILITARY SERVICE
Army, 1966-68

CAREER
Travel agency owner; corporate community relations executive

POLITICAL HIGHLIGHTS
San Bernardino Valley College District trustee, 1979-93; sought Democratic nomination for Calif. Assembly, 1988, 1990; Calif. Assembly, 1992-98 (Speaker pro tempore, 1995); Calif. Senate, 1998-99

ELECTION RESULTS

2002 GENERAL		
Joe Baca (D)	45,374	66.4%
Wendy C. Neighbor (R)	20,821	30.5%
Ethel M. Mohler (LIBERT)	2,145	3.1%
2002 PRIMARY		
Joe Baca (D)		unopposed
2000 GENERAL		
Joe Baca (D)	90,585	59.8%
Elia Pirozzi (R)	53,239	35.1%
John Ballard (LIBERT)	4,059	2.7%
Gwyn Hartley (NL)	3,694	2.4%

PREVIOUS WINNING PERCENTAGES
1999 Special Runoff Election (51%); 1999 Special Election (32%)

Elected November 1999; 2nd full term

With single-minded ambition, Baca has catapulted himself from shoeshine boy to congressman, and now he is aggressively and unabashedly seeking to move up the House Democratic leadership ladder. Baca is the first to acknowledge he is aggressive: "I'm a fighter because I know what it's like to struggle," he says.

He is the first Hispanic congressman from the part of Southern California known as the Inland Empire, anchored by the city of San Bernardino.

Baca has made no secret of the fact that he would like a seat on the Rules Committee, or perhaps even the Transportation panel. So far, he has not been successful, although in the 108th Congress he traded a seat on the Science Committee for one on Financial Services, to go with the Agriculture panel assignment he has had since his arrival late in 1999, when he won the seat of the late George E. Brown Jr.

Baca's interests generally lie outside his committees, however. Only one of the 48 bills he introduced in his first three-plus years in the House was referred to the committees on which he sat.

Baca fared better outside the committee shuffle: In the 107th he was named to the Democratic Steering Committee, which makes committee assignments; and he was chosen as a regional whip in both the 107th and 108th. In the 108th, he is second vice chairman of the Hispanic Caucus.

Baca's ambition and drive can rub people the wrong way. He has ruffled more than a few feathers during his political ascent. Some colleagues say he is pushy and will take the lion's share of credit for joint projects.

The congressman refers to himself as "working Joe Baca," a reference not only to his reputation for hard work, but also to his strong support for organized labor. He has counted on the backing of unions in all of his elections, and campaign help from union members played an important role in his narrow special-election Democratic primary win over Brown's widow, Marta Macias Brown. His election night victory rally was at a local Teamsters hall.

He remains mindful of the needs of his working-class constituents and his union supporters. In the 107th, Baca voted, along with most Democrats, against giving the president fast-track trade negotiating authority, which most unions oppose. But he broke with his party in backing oil drilling in Alaska's Arctic National Wildlife Refuge, aligning himself with the Teamsters, who valued the jobs the oil drilling would create.

Baca's politics tend to be more conservative than those of his predecessor, and his support for gun owners' rights was a major issue in his race against Marta Brown. He affiliates himself with the "Blue Dogs," a coalition of conservative House Democrats.

Baca's wife and two of his children are teachers, and he was pleased with provisions in the education policy overhaul enacted in 2002 that expanded bilingual education and teacher training, directed more funds to migrant education and established a dropout prevention program of particular importance to Hispanic students.

An Army paratrooper, Baca was the chief sponsor of legislation — which received considerable attention — to require that Congressional Medals of Honor be made of 90 percent gold. Baca's bill, first introduced in 2000, caused a stir when he noted the medal is now made of brass and costs as little as $30. The Congressional Gold Medal, which is given to dignitaries and requires no heroic action, is made of gold, at a cost of as much as $30,000. Baca estimated the gold Medal of Honor would cost about $2,300.

For all his focused determination, Baca sometimes reveals a more humorous, self-deprecating side. When he made his first remarks to the House after being sworn in and the microphone had to be lowered for him, Baca joked, "I used to be 6-foot-5 as a paratrooper, but I made a lot of jumps; that is why I am only 5-foot-6."

He is a spark plug on the Democrats' baseball team. In the 2000 charity game against the GOP team, third baseman Baca's glasses were smashed in a collision with Republican Steve Buyer of Indiana. The glasses were taped together, and Baca stayed in the game. The next year, he aggravated an elbow problem and had to have minor surgery.

Baca was born in tiny Belen, N.M., just south of Albuquerque. The son of a railroad laborer and the youngest of 15 children in a house where little English was spoken, Baca as a boy moved with his family to Barstow, Calif. He shined shoes starting at age 10, delivered newspapers and worked as a janitor; he labored for the Santa Fe Railroad between his high school graduation and the arrival of his draft notice in 1966. After leaving the Army and earning a degree in sociology, Baca entered the white-collar world as a community affairs representative for a local phone company.

His political career began in 1979 with election to the San Bernardino Community College District Board, where he served 14 years. After unsuccessful attempts to oust Democratic state Rep. Jerry Eaves in the 1988 and 1990 primaries, he easily won the Assembly seat when Eaves departed.

He coasted to re-election twice, then trounced his GOP opponent to win a state Senate seat in 1998. But returning to Sacramento was not Baca's preferred goal for 1998; he threatened to challenge Brown in the Democratic primary and boasted he could beat the incumbent in every precinct. Although in the end he did not run, his aggressiveness was taken as an affront by some party stalwarts.

When Brown died midway through his 18th term, Baca immediately jumped into the special-election race — offending the congressman's widow and her supporters, who said it was inappropriate for him to enter the race such a short time after the party had helped him win an expensive contest for the state Senate.

After his victory in the November special-election primary, Baca's well-organized political apparatus and the Democratic leaning district enabled him to post a 6-point win over GOP businessman Elia Pirozzi. In 2000, Pirozzi was back for a rematch, but Baca crushed him by 25 points. In 2002, running in a newly drawn district that is more Democratic and more Hispanic, Baca took two-thirds of the vote.

KEY VOTES

2002

- Yes Overhaul campaign finance law; ban "soft money" and restrict advocacy advertising
- Yes Back Bush's defense budget increase
- No Extend 1996 welfare law
- No Adopt Bush's discretionary spending limit
- No Pass GOP Medicare prescription drug plan
- Yes Create independent Sept. 11 commission
- Yes Extend union protections to Homeland Security Department employees
- No Revive fast-track procedures for trade agreements
- No Authorize war against Iraq
- No Advance bankruptcy overhaul opposed by abortion opponents

2001

- No Nullify Clinton Labor Department ergonomics rule
- ? Cut taxes by $1.35 trillion through fiscal 2011
- No Maintain ban on oil drilling in Arctic National Wildlife Refuge
- No Approve Bush proposal to limit managed-care plan liability for coverage decisions
- No Divert money from crop subsidy payments to land conservation
- Yes Expand law enforcement power to investigate suspected terrorists

CQ VOTE STUDIES

	PARTY UNITY		PRESIDENTIAL SUPPORT	
	Support	Oppose	Support	Oppose
2002	91%	9%	28%	72%
2001	89%	11%	31%	69%
2000	83%	17%	75%	25%
1999	100%	0%	100%	0%

INTEREST GROUPS

	AFL-CIO	ADA	CCUS	ACU
2002	89%	95%	42%	13%
2001	100%	85%	48%	24%
2000	100%	80%	44%	16%

CALIFORNIA 43

Southwest San Bernardino County — Ontario, Fontana, most of San Bernardino

The cities of San Bernardino, Fontana and Ontario form the base of the 43rd, which is located in the heart of the Inland Valley east of Los Angeles in San Bernardino County.

The district is part of California's fastest-growing region. Some residents commute into Los Angeles along the Pomona and San Bernardino freeways. The Ontario airport, a recently expanded transportation hub, and the sprawling Ontario Mills mall are here. Fontana and Rialto, farther east, also have seen explosive growth.

The 43rd is almost 60 percent Hispanic, and registered Democrats outnumber Republicans almost 2-to-1. Even as some neighboring suburbs have trended wealthier and more conservative, ethnically diverse San Bernardino and Colton (both of which are shared with the 41st) consistently vote Democratic. The district favors Democrats on all levels and gave Al Gore a 28-point margin of victory in the 2000 presidential contest.

This area was a fruit-packing center in the 1930s. Today, its citrus industry shares space with electronics and aerospace firms. A steel mill bankruptcy in the 1980s and the 1994 closing of nearby Norton Air Force Base hurt the district's employment rolls, but new government jobs and growing high-tech and manufacturing industries prove the economy is recovering.

Though it has prospered like its neighbors in Orange and Los Angeles counties, the district retains a diverse and working-class feel. Local leaders work on efforts to combine economic growth and smart development.

MAJOR INDUSTRY
Manufacturing, electronics, construction

CITIES
Ontario, 158,007; San Bernardino (pt.), 130,612; Fontana, 128,929; Rialto, 91,873; Colton (pt.), 43,349

NOTABLE
Wyatt Earp's brother, Virgil, was the first marshal of Colton; Fontana is the birthplace of the Hell's Angels.

Rep. Ken Calvert (R)

CAPITOL OFFICE
225-1986
www.house.gov/calvert
2201 Rayburn 20515-0544; fax 225-2004

COMMITTEES
Armed Services
Resources
(Water & Power - chairman)
Science

HOMETOWN
Riverside

BORN
June 8, 1953, Corona, Calif.

RELIGION
Protestant

FAMILY
Divorced

EDUCATION
Chaffey College, A.A. 1973 (business); San Diego State U., B.A. 1975 (economics)

CAREER
Real estate executive; restaurant executive

POLITICAL HIGHLIGHTS
Sought Republican nomination for U.S. House, 1982; Riverside County Republican Party chairman, 1984-88

ELECTION RESULTS

2002 GENERAL		
Ken Calvert (R)	76,686	63.7%
Louis Vandenberg (D)	38,021	31.6%
Phill Courtney (GREEN)	5,756	4.8%
2002 PRIMARY		
Ken Calvert (R)	30,967	70.1%
Martin Collen (R)	11,106	25.2%
Khalid Jafri (R)	2,087	4.7%
2000 GENERAL		
Ken Calvert (R)	140,201	73.7%
Bill Reed (LIBERT)	29,755	15.6%
Nathaniel Adam (NL)	20,376	10.7%

PREVIOUS WINNING PERCENTAGES
1998 (56%); 1996 (55%); 1994 (55%); 1992 (47%)

Elected 1992; 6th term

Now entering his second decade in Congress, Calvert has been a reliable vote for the House Republican leadership and a champion of "a smaller, less invasive government." Where he has sought to have his greatest impact, and where he has reached out most prominently to Democrats, has been on trying to involve the federal government in one of his state's most intractable problems.

A former businessman, and since 2001 the chairman of the Resources Committee's Water and Power Subcommittee, Calvert is an ardent promoter of legislation to reauthorize and restructure Calfed, the California Federal Bay-Delta Program, which aims to enhance the state's water supply, reliability and quality. In the 108th Congress, as in the 107th, the issue will be at the top of Calvert's legislative agenda.

The Calfed project stretches over the enormous delta that begins in the San Francisco Bay area, and extends from the Sacramento Valley in the north to the San Joaquin Valley in the south — providing irrigation and drinking water for two-thirds of the state's population. Calvert is working to rewrite the law in a way that bridges differences among farmers, homeowners and environmentalists. "I enjoy working water," Calvert said. "I work this bill every single day."

Calvert sought the chairmanship of the full Resources panel in the 108th, along with six other Republicans. Fellow Californian Richard W. Pombo got the nod, leapfrogging over Calvert and four other more-senior aspirants.

Calvert represents an area with a diverse economy, where agriculture, manufacturing, the military and tourism interests sometimes clash with environmental advocates who raise issues of land use and urban sprawl. From his seats on three committees — Armed Services and Science are the others — Calvert has a hand in policies that shape these conflicts. Although he dropped his seat on the Agriculture panel after the 106th Congress to join Armed Services, he still keeps an eye on legislation that would have an impact on avocado and citrus farmers in the region.

Calvert is a member of more than two dozen informal congressional organizations that reflect the varied concerns of his constituents, ranging from the Manufactured Housing Caucus (an industry leader, Fleetwood Enterprises, is headquartered in his district) to the Real Estate Caucus (Calvert's occupation before coming to Congress) to the Native American Caucus (he is one-eighth Cherokee).

Calvert's conservative view of government makes him wary of tougher environmental regulations. He says enforcement of the Endangered Species Act must be tempered with common sense. When Democrats ran the House, he once lamented, "Rats, bugs and even weeds were more important than people. Certain bureaucrats have become so eager to list new species as endangered, they have lost sight of the intent of the Endangered Species Act and ignored human concerns."

While keeping an eye on water issues from his subcommittee chairman's perch, Calvert joins other Western lawmakers who say the federal government tramples on landowners' rights in the name of environmental preservation, and he advocates legislation to protect private property owners. He is skeptical of environmentalists who warn that pollution contributes to global warming. Although he has not moderated his views, Calvert said he is trying to pick his battles more carefully.

Starting in 1997 Calvert sought to require candidates to raise at least 50 percent of their campaign contributions from within their home districts, but the idea was never seriously considered as part of the campaign finance law enacted in 2002.

Calvert is a native son of the area he now represents — not all that common in the rapidly growing region that is now part of the Los Angeles megalopolis. He was born in Corona, just west of Riverside. His family was in the restaurant business. Later, his father, who had changed parties to become a Republican in the mid-1960s, turned to politics, winning election to the city council and then as Corona's mayor. The younger Calvert remembers working on Richard M. Nixon's 1968 presidential campaign and as a college student, he interned in the Capitol Hill office of GOP Rep. Victor Veysey.

After graduation, Calvert used his economics degree and interest in business to try his hand at the family business. He handled the business side of the Jolly Fox restaurant in Corona, while his brother was the chef. He expanded into other ventures — a motel, a bowling alley, other restaurants — before going into real estate.

At age 28, with "lots of time and not much money," Calvert in 1982 jumped into an open-seat race for Congress, in the old 37th District, which contained most of Riverside County. Relying on door-to-door campaigning, he did surprisingly well against a large field headed by Riverside County Supervisor Al McCandless, losing the GOP nomination by just 868 votes.

Calvert stayed active in local party affairs, significantly increasing GOP registration in Riverside County and helping run the gubernatorial campaigns of Republicans George Deukmejian and Pete Wilson. When reapportionment created a new 43rd District for the western part of Riverside County in 1992, Calvert was positioned to run again; he emerged the winner of a tough GOP primary and took a hard-fought victory in November.

Calvert's congressional tenure got off to a rough start. In his first term, a tryst with a prostitute drew widespread notice. He said his "inappropriate" behavior stemmed from depression over his recent divorce and his father's suicide.

Following the negative publicity, Calvert won the 1994 GOP primary by just 2 percentage points, but the national surge that delivered the House to the GOP carried him to a 55 percent victory. Since then, Calvert's toughest challenges have come from his own party. In 2000 he won the nomination with 58 percent. In 2002, in redistricted territory, now numbered the 44th but politically similar to his previous constituency, Calvert took 70 percent in a three-way primary and cruised to a sixth term in November.

KEY VOTES

2002

No Overhaul campaign finance law; ban "soft money" and restrict advocacy advertising
Yes Back Bush's defense budget increase
Yes Extend 1996 welfare law
Yes Adopt Bush's discretionary spending limit
Yes Pass GOP Medicare prescription drug plan
No Create independent Sept. 11 commission
No Extend union protections to Homeland Security Department employees
Yes Revive fast-track procedures for trade agreements
Yes Authorize war against Iraq
Yes Advance bankruptcy overhaul opposed by abortion opponents

2001

Yes Nullify Clinton Labor Department ergonomics rule
Yes Cut taxes by $1.35 trillion through fiscal 2011
No Maintain ban on oil drilling in Arctic National Wildlife Refuge
Yes Approve Bush proposal to limit managed-care plan liability for coverage decisions
No Divert money from crop subsidy payments to land conservation
Yes Expand law enforcement power to investigate suspected terrorists

CQ VOTE STUDIES

	PARTY UNITY		PRESIDENTIAL SUPPORT	
	Support	Oppose	Support	Oppose
2002	96%	4%	89%	11%
2001	98%	2%	93%	7%
2000	94%	6%	31%	69%
1999	92%	8%	30%	70%
1998	94%	6%	24%	76%

INTEREST GROUPS

	AFL-CIO	ADA	CCUS	ACU
2002	11%	0%	100%	92%
2001	17%	0%	100%	91%
2000	0%	0%	80%	84%
1999	0%	5%	96%	80%
1998	0%	0%	100%	92%

CALIFORNIA 44

Northwestern Riverside County – Riverside, Corona

The 44th is a fast-growing residential district that lies east of Los Angeles and north of San Diego. It contains about one-third of Riverside County's residents and the southeastern portion of Orange County that borders San Diego County. Registered Republicans outnumber Democrats about 50 percent to 35 percent, and George W. Bush won the 2000 presidential vote here with 52 percent.

The district includes the city of Riverside and the rest of the burgeoning northwestern edge of Riverside County. Riverside began growing navel oranges — still one of the area's major crops — in the 19th century. While the 44th has become increasingly Republican overall, the more blue-collar Riverside communities and the areas around the University of California, Riverside lean Democratic.

The district is undergoing major growth as young, white-collar families move into its cities. The trend is especially true in Norco and Corona, where low real estate prices have produced attractive bedroom communities for commuters into Orange and Los Angeles counties. Despite the influx, manufacturing and agriculture (including dairy, citrus, grapes, dates and avocados) contribute to the economy, though they are being driven farther east and out of the district as the Los Angeles area continues to expand. Orange County areas include the coastal city of San Clemente, San Juan Capistrano (shared with the 48th) and Santa Ana Mountain forests.

Local officials are trying to halt illegal drug production in the Inland Empire, dubbed by some as the methamphetamine capital of the world.

MAJOR INDUSTRY
Manufacturing, agriculture, health care

MILITARY BASES
Naval Surface Warfare Center, Corona Division, 1,761 military, 831 civilian (2001)

CITIES
Riverside, 255,166; Corona, 124,966; San Clemente, 49,936

NOTABLE
Riverside's Mission Inn was where Richard and Pat Nixon were married and Ronald and Nancy Reagan stopped on their honeymoon.

Rep. Mary Bono (R)

CAPITOL OFFICE
225-5330
www.house.gov/bono
404 Cannon 20515-0545; fax 225-2961

COMMITTEES
Energy & Commerce

HOMETOWN
Palm Springs

BORN
Oct. 24, 1961, Cleveland, Ohio

RELIGION
Protestant

FAMILY
Husband, Glenn Baxley; two children

EDUCATION
U. of Southern California, B.F.A. 1984 (art history)

CAREER
Homemaker; restaurateur

POLITICAL HIGHLIGHTS
No previous office

ELECTION RESULTS

2002 GENERAL		
Mary Bono (R)	87,101	65.2%
Elle K. Kurpiewski (D)	43,692	32.7%
Rod Miller-Boyer (LIBERT)	2,740	2.1%
2002 PRIMARY		
Mary Bono (R)		unopposed
2000 GENERAL		
Mary Bono (R)	123,738	59.2%
Ron Oden (D)	79,302	37.9%
Gene Smith (REF)	4,135	2.0%

PREVIOUS WINNING PERCENTAGES
1998 (60%); 1998 Special Election (64%)

Elected April 1998; 3rd full term

Now in her third full term in the House, Bono is now regarded more as a lawmaker than a celebrity. The passage of time has diminished the novelty factor of her successful campaign to succeed her husband, entertainer-turned-politician Sonny Bono.

She is nevertheless one of the most sought-after guests on the campaign fundraising circuit and makes public appearances across the country on behalf of GOP colleagues, who take advantage of her popular appeal. "She has a freshness and common-sense approach that is rather unusual in people like us," Majority Leader Tom DeLay of Texas told Gannett News Service. She says she accommodates as many requests as she can, while making sure she has time at home in Palm Springs with her two children.

Bono's years as a celebrity spouse prepared her, to some extent, for the level of attention she received after her election. (CBS's "Entertainment Tonight" had covered her announcement that she would run to succeed her husband.) She shares Sonny's self-deprecating manner and says she understands that the public can be overly fascinated with such matters as the hair and shoe styles of powerful women, while men in such roles are not similarly scrutinized.

On Capitol Hill, she has cultivated the image of an average person, plain-speaking, unpretentious and interested in rolling up her sleeves and mastering the details of her job. Bono focuses on the day-to-day issues facing her Inland Empire constituents, such as high energy bills, the availability of low-income housing, access to water, and resolution of a longstanding Indian land claim. She also seeks to direct federal defense spending to the contractors in her district.

Bono came to the House with little political preparation and in the middle of the session, without benefit of the orientation meetings that freshmen normally get. Nevertheless, she says she brought an appreciation for the challenges faced by a working single mother. She also had small-business experience as the manager of a restaurant she and Sonny owned.

When Bono first arrived in Congress, her goal was to continue her husband's work, notably saving the Salton Sea, a Southern California man-made lake that is threatened by increasing salinity and pollution from agricultural and industrial runoff. By the end of 1998, Congress had agreed to fund a study to determine the extent of the problem and to begin the lake's rehabilitation. Bono also helped shepherd through the House a copyright extension bill, initially championed by and eventually named after Sonny.

At first, she was given Sonny's committees, including a seat on the Judiciary Committee. At times during the panel's consideration of President Clinton's impeachment she seemed a bit disengaged, bypassing turns to ask questions, but she later won praise for her efforts to cut through the legalese and ask the questions that were uppermost in people's minds.

In the 107th Congress, boosted by the goodwill she built through her campaign efforts for her GOP colleagues, Bono won a coveted seat on the Energy and Commerce Committee. She was also named to a GOP task force focusing on the cost of prescription drugs.

During the 2001 California energy crisis, Bono focused on the difficulties low-income people were having in paying their bills. She held town meetings to get out the word about federal assistance, and she was able to win added funding for the Low Income Home Energy Assistance Program. She also pushed the federal government to reduce its energy consumption.

She won passage of legislation in 2000 ratifying the settlement of an agreement to compensate the Torres Martinez Desert Cahuilla Indian tribe, which lost land when the Salton Sea was created early in the 20th century. In the 107th Congress, she secured funds for the settlement.

Bono has continued her work on saving the Salton Sea, expending considerable energy in the 107th on negotiations over allocation of Colorado River water. A mandated reduction in California's share of the river water, and internal fights within the state over which localities should get the water, ended up posing a severe threat to the Salton Sea — by lowering the water level significantly. That issue remains for the 108th to deal with.

Bono also keeps a watchful eye on California vineyards' battle against Pierce's disease, which is spread by a small flying insect known as the glassy-winged sharpshooter.

Bono will stray from conservative Republican philosophy on occasion, particularly on the issues of cloning and abortion. "I am neither pro-choice nor pro-life, and I am also both pro-choice and pro-life," she told the California Riverside Press-Enterprise. "I believe that's the way most Americans truly are." She also joined Democrats in voting for a campaign finance overhaul measure in 2002.

Bono, whose father was a surgeon and whose mother was a chemist, grew up in South Pasadena, Calif. She worked her way through college, majoring in art history, and was celebrating her graduation at Sonny Bono's restaurant when she met the owner. They hit it off and married two years later, in 1986.

At the beginning of 1998, she was a stay-at-home mom in Washington, D.C., driving her children to school and working on her martial arts skills while Sonny went off to Capitol Hill every morning. After Sonny's January 1998 death in a skiing accident, she was urged to run for her husband's seat by GOP leaders who worried that the seat might fall into Democratic hands.

Bono won a special election in April with almost two-thirds of the vote. She has not been seriously threatened in her re-election bids, and redistricting in 2001 increased the GOP tilt of the newly numbered 45th District, permitting her to post a 2-to-1 re-election victory in 2002. Some California political analysts have mentioned her as a potential Senate candidate in 2004, citing her moderate image, wide name recognition and plain-spoken manner.

Bono was linked romantically for a while with a country music drummer, providing fodder for the tabloids; but in late 2001 she married Wyoming businessman Glenn Baxley, the founder of a company that designs Western and resort clothing.

KEY VOTES

2002

- Yes Overhaul campaign finance law; ban "soft money" and restrict advocacy advertising
- Yes Back Bush's defense budget increase
- Yes Extend 1996 welfare law
- Yes Adopt Bush's discretionary spending limit
- Yes Pass GOP Medicare prescription drug plan
- No Create independent Sept. 11 commission
- No Extend union protections to Homeland Security Department employees
- Yes Revive fast-track procedures for trade agreements
- Yes Authorize war against Iraq
- Yes Advance bankruptcy overhaul opposed by abortion opponents

2001

- Yes Nullify Clinton Labor Department ergonomics rule
- Yes Cut taxes by $1.35 trillion through fiscal 2011
- No Maintain ban on oil drilling in Arctic National Wildlife Refuge
- Yes Approve Bush proposal to limit managed-care plan liability for coverage decisions
- No Divert money from crop subsidy payments to land conservation
- Yes Expand law enforcement power to investigate suspected terrorists

CQ VOTE STUDIES

	PARTY UNITY		PRESIDENTIAL SUPPORT	
	Support	Oppose	Support	Oppose
2002	89%	11%	84%	16%
2001	92%	8%	84%	16%
2000	86%	14%	30%	70%
1999	85%	15%	25%	75%
1998	92%	8%	23%	77%

INTEREST GROUPS

	AFL-CIO	ADA	CCUS	ACU
2002	11%	10%	95%	71%
2001	17%	15%	100%	68%
2000	0%	5%	100%	68%
1999	22%	15%	79%	76%
1998	29%	0%	93%	95%

CALIFORNIA 45
Riverside County — Moreno Valley, Palm Springs

Ritzy desert resorts, a booming service industry and large, irrigated farms fuel the economy of the 45th, whose residents largely reside in one of two Riverside County areas: rapidly growing Inland Empire communities — such as Moreno Valley, Hemet and Murrieta in the west — or upscale, resort-filled Coachella Valley cities farther east.

The Palm Springs area, including Cathedral City, Indian Wells, La Quinta and Indio, attracts visitors to its numerous golf courses. Once known as playgrounds for the rich and retired, the resort cities have seen an influx of younger, middle-class families. Still, the 45th has the highest percentage of senior citizens in California.

Although the district leans Republican, pockets in Rancho Mirage and Palm Springs tend to vote Democratic. Overall, the district gave George W. Bush 50 percent of its vote in the 2000 presidential election, and Republicans hold an 8-point voter registration advantage.

The 45th has grown into a diverse community that is home to some of the richest and poorest areas in the state, with Palm Springs on one end of the economic spectrum and some of the district's Indian reservations on the other. Many poor residents work as migrant farm laborers, in the growing gaming industry and at tourist shops. Health care service providers and small educational institutions have begun to settle in the district, spurring an increase in professionals.

The Salton Sea — located mainly in the 51st District — attracted attention in the 1990s as one of the nation's most polluted bodies of water. Congress voted in 1998 to fund a cleanup effort in honor of the late GOP Rep. Sonny Bono, who represented the Riverside district (at the time numbered the 44th) from 1995 until his death in January 1998.

MAJOR INDUSTRY

Services, tourism, agriculture, manufacturing

CITIES

Moreno Valley, 142,381; Hemet, 58,812; Indio, 49,116; Murrieta, 44,282

NOTABLE

Palm Springs is known as the golf capital of the world; President Gerald R. Ford retired to Rancho Mirage; Joshua Tree National Park (shared with the 41st) boasts an abundance of the namesake yuccas and other desert plants and animals.

Rep. Dana Rohrabacher (R)

CAPITOL OFFICE
225-2415
dana@mail.house.gov
www.house.gov/rohrabacher
2338 Rayburn 20515-0546; fax 225-0145

COMMITTEES
International Relations
Science
(Space & Aeronautics - chairman)

HOMETOWN
Huntington Beach

BORN
June 21, 1947, Coronado, Calif.

RELIGION
Baptist

FAMILY
Wife, Rhonda Rohrabacher

EDUCATION
Los Angeles Harbor College, attended 1965-67; California State U., Long Beach, B.A. 1969 (history); U. of Southern California, M.A. 1971 (American studies)

CAREER
White House speechwriter; journalist

POLITICAL HIGHLIGHTS
No previous office

ELECTION RESULTS

2002 GENERAL		
Dana Rohrabacher (R)	108,807	61.8%
Gerrie Schipske (D)	60,890	34.6%
Keith Gann (LIBERT)	6,488	3.7%
2002 PRIMARY		
Dana Rohrabacher (R)		unopposed
2000 GENERAL		
Dana Rohrabacher (R)	136,275	62.1%
Ted Crisell (D)	71,066	32.4%
Don Hull (LIBERT)	8,409	3.8%
Constance Betton (NL)	3,635	1.7%

PREVIOUS WINNING PERCENTAGES
1998 (59%); 1996 (61%); 1994 (69%); 1992 (55%); 1990 (59%); 1988 (64%)

Elected 1988; 8th term

With a long-held interest in Central Asia, Rohrabacher is one of a few members of Congress who, after the nightmare of Sept. 11, 2001, could accurately declare "I told you so" about the dangers emanating from the region.

On the day of the terrorist attacks, Rohrabacher (ROAR-ah-bah-kur) had been scheduled to meet with National Security Council officials at the White House to warn them to expect a possible terrorist attack from Osama bin Laden and the ruling Taliban regime of Afghanistan.

When Congress reconvened a few days later, he took to the House floor and described his many trips to Central Asia, including an undercover sojourn to Afghanistan just before he was sworn into Congress in 1989. He recounted the sad history of Afghanistan over the previous two decades, and took the Clinton administration to task for what Rohrabacher characterized as its disinterest in capturing bin Laden when it had the chance.

Rohrabacher has always had a particular interest in foreign affairs, and from his seat on the International Relations Committee he has made a name for himself as an outspoken conservative voice. He is one of the few public figures in Washington who still refers to the People's Republic of China as "Red China," and he promotes an "America first" brand of foreign policy, which includes arguing for stricter immigration controls.

He is hardly a conventional right-winger, however. Rohrabacher's congressional Web site features a photo of him surfing in a black wetsuit, with the caption, "Fighting for Freedom . . . and Having Fun." (He represents Huntington Beach, a surfing community in coastal Southern California.) He counts writers, artists and musicians such as heavy metal vocalist Sammy Hagar, folk singer Joan Baez and rock-and-roll guitarist "Skunk" Baxter among his friends. Rohrabacher's relationship with Baxter led to the latter's involvement as a respected unofficial adviser to the House GOP on missile defense issues.

Rohrabacher makes it clear he has no use for the United Nations, once calling it "a collection of tin-pot dictatorships and corrupt regimes." And he derides the effort to impose controls on the emission of greenhouse gases, referring to reports of global warming as "global baloney."

Rohrabacher has been a critic of U.S. policy toward China throughout his congressional tenure — no matter whether the administration has been Republican or Democratic. He was a vigorous opponent of the law, enacted in 2000, permanently permitting Chinese goods to enter the United States under the same low tariffs afforded most countries. In 2002, he voted against a bill to give the president fast-track authority to negotiate trade agreements that Congress cannot amend, saying he did not want to diminish congressional authority. But Rohrabacher generally favors expanded foreign trade, as long as it is "free trade amongst free people."

Rohrabacher argues that there are many things the federal government should not spend any money on, including the United Nations and public services for illegal immigrants.

But on the Science Committee, Rohrabacher usually eschews liberal-bashing and urges Congress to open its checkbook for policies and projects important to aerospace interests that have a big economic impact in his district. Boeing Co., a prime contractor on NASA's space station, is a major employer in the 46th.

In the 108th Congress, although he had expressed interest in becoming chairman of the International Relations panel's Asia Subcommittee, Rohrabacher instead continues to chair the Science Committee's Space and Aeronautics Subcommittee, after receiving a special waiver to exceed the GOP's three-term limit on chairmanships. As investigations were getting under way to determine the cause of the February 2003 in-flight destruction of the space shuttle Columbia, Rohrabacher expressed continuing support for space exploration.

During his younger days, Rohrabacher was a hard-drinking, banjo-playing wanderer who worked as a house-painter. He later found steady work as a reporter and editorial writer for the conservative Orange County Register. He served as assistant press secretary for Ronald Reagan's 1976 and 1980 presidential campaigns, then became a White House speechwriter for President Reagan.

Rohrabacher once said he patterned his life on that of Ernest Hemingway, a "man's man." The congressman, who says John Wayne taught him how to drink tequila, has mellowed in recent years. In 1997, he married his former campaign manager, Rhonda Carmony. In a 1999 interview with the semiweekly Washington newspaper The Hill, Rohrabacher gushed about his new and toned-down lifestyle — but that is a relative term. As California political scientist Jack Pitney told The Associated Press, "even a toned-down Dana Rohrabacher is more vivid than most members."

In his first bid for elective office, in 1988, Rohrabacher ran for the House seat being vacated by GOP Rep. Dan Lungren, who ran instead for state treasurer. The contenders in the primary included an Orange County supervisor who had Lungren's support and California State University-Long Beach President Steve Horn (who would run and win in a neighboring House district in 1992, serving for 10 years). But Rohrabacher found a way to win.

A campaign fundraiser featuring retired Marine Lt. Col. Oliver L. North of Iran-contra fame — who had worked just a few doors down from Rohrabacher at the White House — raised Rohrabacher's standing among conservatives while adding $100,000 to his coffers. He ended up with 35 percent of the primary vote, well ahead of his nearest rival. Rohrabacher has encountered little difficulty in his general-election contests, though he and Carmony were fined for campaign finance irregularities in connection with their 1995 effort to replace Assemblywoman Doris Allen.

In the 108th Congress, Rohrabacher's newly drawn district once again includes the port of Long Beach, as it did in his first two terms before redistricting in the early 1990s; but the new constituency caused him no distress at the polls in 2002, as he easily defeated Democrat Gerrie Schipske (who had lost to Horn in the 38th District in 2000).

KEY VOTES

2002

- No Overhaul campaign finance law; ban "soft money" and restrict advocacy advertising
- Yes Back Bush's defense budget increase
- Yes Extend 1996 welfare law
- Yes Adopt Bush's discretionary spending limit
- Yes Pass GOP Medicare prescription drug plan
- Yes Create independent Sept. 11 commission
- No Extend union protections to Homeland Security Department employees
- No Revive fast-track procedures for trade agreements
- Yes Authorize war against Iraq
- Yes Advance bankruptcy overhaul opposed by abortion opponents

2001

- Yes Nullify Clinton Labor Department ergonomics rule
- Yes Cut taxes by $1.35 trillion through fiscal 2011
- No Maintain ban on oil drilling in Arctic National Wildlife Refuge
- Yes Approve Bush proposal to limit managed-care plan liability for coverage decisions
- Yes Divert money from crop subsidy payments to land conservation
- Yes Expand law enforcement power to investigate suspected terrorists

CQ VOTE STUDIES

	PARTY UNITY		PRESIDENTIAL SUPPORT	
	Support	Oppose	Support	Oppose
2002	94%	6%	77%	23%
2001	93%	7%	86%	14%
2000	94%	6%	16%	84%
1999	94%	6%	12%	88%
1998	90%	10%	26%	74%

INTEREST GROUPS

	AFL-CIO	ADA	CCUS	ACU
2002	22%	5%	85%	96%
2001	0%	10%	78%	96%
2000	10%	10%	61%	96%
1999	22%	5%	76%	96%
1998	20%	5%	67%	100%

CALIFORNIA 46

Coastal Los Angeles and Orange counties — Huntington Beach, Costa Mesa

The 46th is a comfortably conservative district that runs along the coast south of Los Angeles. An eclectic mix of residents, including senior citizens, surfers and aerospace workers, live in several communities. In the northwest is an ultra-wealthy, mountainous peninsula containing Rancho Palos Verdes, Palos Verdes Estates and Rolling Hills Estates. In the center is a more blue-collar area around Long Beach Harbor. The district continues southeast into the wealthier Orange County communities of Huntington Beach and Costa Mesa.

At Seal Beach, just over the line into Orange County, two-thirds of the city's residents are 65 or older and roughly one-third live in Leisure World, a seniors community. Huntington Beach is a hub for both surfers and aerospace workers, many of whom work at the Boeing plant that is a prime design and manufacturing facility for the space station and Delta rocket.

Generally speaking, the coastal areas are more Republican and the inland areas slightly more Democratic. Despite its proximity to Los Angeles, the district is more than 60 percent white. The 46th's interior, which includes Costa Mesa, Fountain Valley and part of Westminster and Santa Ana, tends to be less affluent than the coastal cities. These towns are solidly middle-class residential areas. Many of the area's blue-collar workers are employed by aerospace companies within the district or in Anaheim, Torrance or Long Beach.

MAJOR INDUSTRY

Aerospace, high-tech, manufacturing

MILITARY BASES

Naval Weapons Station Seal Beach, 200 military, 600 civilian (2002)

CITIES

Huntington Beach, 189,594; Costa Mesa, 108,724; Long Beach (pt.), 83,666; Westminster (pt.), 60,399

NOTABLE

Huntington Beach hosts major surfing tournaments and is home to the International Surfing Museum; Catalina Island, a tourist destination, and San Clemente Island, which is owned by the Navy, are included in the 46th; Seal Beach is known for its seals and sea lions.

Rep. Loretta Sanchez (D)

Elected 1996; 4th term

CAPITOL OFFICE
225-2965
loretta@mail.house.gov
www.house.gov/sanchez
1230 Longworth 20515-0547; fax 225-5859

COMMITTEES
Armed Services
Select Homeland Security

HOMETOWN
Anaheim

BORN
Jan. 7, 1960, Lynwood, Calif.

RELIGION
Roman Catholic

FAMILY
Husband, Stephen Simmons Brixey III

EDUCATION
Chapman U., B.S. 1982 (economics); American U., M.B.A. 1984 (finance)

CAREER
Financial adviser; strategic management associate

POLITICAL HIGHLIGHTS
Candidate for Anaheim City Council, 1994

ELECTION RESULTS

2002 GENERAL		
Loretta Sanchez (D)	42,501	60.9%
Jeff Chavez (R)	24,346	34.9%
Paul Marsden (LIBERT)	2,944	4.2%
2002 PRIMARY		
Loretta Sanchez (D)		unopposed
2000 GENERAL		
Loretta Sanchez (D)	70,381	60.2%
Gloria Matta Tuchman (R)	40,928	35.0%
Richard Boddie (LIBERT)	3,159	2.7%
Larry G. Engwall (NL)	2,440	2.1%

PREVIOUS WINNING PERCENTAGES
1998 (56%); 1996 (47%)

In some ways, Sanchez is a study in contradictions. A daughter of working-class Mexican immigrants, she describes herself as growing up a "shy, quiet girl" who did not speak English. But as an adult she evolved into a brassy politician who became a national Democratic heroine in 1996 by upsetting Rep. Robert K. Dornan, a fiery conservative Republican.

She can be fiercely partisan; a former co-chairman of the Democratic National Committee, she was among nine House members voting "present" on a 2001 resolution honoring Ronald Reagan's 90th birthday. Yet she is willing to allow her partisanship to take a back seat to parochialism: In 2001 she worked vigorously for Senate confirmation of two of President Bush's more controversial nominees — George L. Argyros to be ambassador to Spain and Gaddi H. Vasquez to run the Peace Corps. They were from heavily Republican Orange County, the heart of her district.

Though viewed as media-savvy and an energetic symbol of the rising political influence of both women and Hispanic-Americans, Sanchez has made headlines for stubbornly doing or saying things that go against the conventional grain. In 2000, for instance, she embarrassed fellow Democrats on the eve of their national convention in Los Angeles by refusing to cancel a fundraiser at the Playboy mansion. Though she changed the venue at the last minute, she seemed to relish the controversy. The next year, her office's pet goldfish was named "Hef" after Playboy founder Hugh Hefner.

In 2001, Sanchez offered The Washington Post this account of what she told Bush about education policy: "If you really feel what you're telling me, then get off your butt and get this sold."

Her outspokenness notwithstanding, Sanchez is mastering the art of politics. She has become a supreme party fundraiser. She also was an early ally of fellow Californian Nancy Pelosi, the party leader for the 108th Congress; and she has effectively used her committee assignments — Armed Services and Education and the Workforce in the 107th — to address the needs of her largely minority, low-income district. In the 108th, she won a seat on the Homeland Security panel and gave up her post on Education.

In 2002, she drew on her political capital, including Pelosi's aid, to help her younger sister Linda Sánchez, a civil rights and labor lawyer, win election in the newly designed 39th District in nearby Los Angeles County. They are the first sisters to serve together in Congress, and as the two sisters were sworn in, on Loretta's 43rd birthday, the "bossy" big sister happily deflected the attention. The sisters point out that they have significantly different personalities (and some political differences as well), which makes rooming together in Washington an interesting experience.

Loretta Sanchez traces her ambitions to first-grade catechism class. A nun asked her what she wanted to be when she grew up. "I answered, 'The pope. He's the head of everyone, the one making the rules,' " Sanchez told the Orange County Register.

Sanchez's childhood reticence was so complete that her mother took her to doctors for advice. Her father forced her to take speech and drama classes in school. Acutely aware of her parents' limited income, she worked her way through college and earned a master's degree in business administration. Feeling isolated as a Hispanic woman in the investment world, she made her first foray into politics in 1994, losing a race for an Anaheim City Council seat.

Two years later, she brazenly took on the 46th District's Dornan, a controversial conservative icon. After winning a four-way primary with 35 percent of the vote, she drew attention from liberal groups who played a hunch that their archenemy might not have his guard up. Thanks to the increasing number of Hispanics in the district and backlash against a ballot initiative to end most state affirmative action programs, Sanchez appeared to score a stunning 984-vote upset.

Dornan claimed he lost to illegal voting by non-citizens. A three-member House task force later said it found such instances, but not enough of them to prove they could have affected the outcome. In a 1998 rematch, Sanchez defeated a better-financed Dornan by 17 percentage points. Her re-elections since have been by larger margins, and redistricting in 2001 (the district is now the 47th) did not harm her electoral prospects.

Sanchez credits government with much of her success. "I am a Head Start child, a public school kid, a Pell Grant recipient," she once said in a House speech. "I think some federal programs do work for our children."

As a member of the Education panel, Sanchez says that conservative Republicans are not committed to improving public education. When Bush's 2003 budget proposal threatened to cut education grants, including one for low-income children in her district, she responded, "If he can run deficits for the military, then he can run deficits to educate our children."

The daughter of a unionized machinist father and a secretary mother who worked to organize plant workers into a union, Sanchez joined the United Food and Commercial Workers when she scooped ice cream in high school, and she had a union scholarship to college. Given such ties, she generally votes labor's way. In the 107th, she voted against reviving fast-track procedures for congressional action on trade deals. And, coming from a district with one of the largest Vietnamese communities outside Vietnam, she voted against a trade agreement with Vietnam, saying that political and human rights conditions in that country needed improvement.

On Armed Services, Sanchez has reservations about some military spending, but she has backed continued production of fighter planes, such as the F-22, that are important to the California economy. An abortion rights supporter, Sanchez has failed in her annual efforts to overturn a ban on overseas military abortions.

Though Sanchez is allied with the Democratic left on most social issues, she follows a center-right course on fiscal policy, as a member of the Democratic "Blue Dogs." She also has sided with conservatives on such issues as amending the Constitution to outlaw flag desecration and encouraging states to prosecute violent juvenile offenders as adults.

KEY VOTES

2002

- Yes Overhaul campaign finance law; ban "soft money" and restrict advocacy advertising
- Yes Back Bush's defense budget increase
- No Extend 1996 welfare law
- No Adopt Bush's discretionary spending limit
- No Pass GOP Medicare prescription drug plan
- Yes Create independent Sept. 11 commission
- Yes Extend union protections to Homeland Security Department employees
- No Revive fast-track procedures for trade agreements
- No Authorize war against Iraq
- No Advance bankruptcy overhaul opposed by abortion opponents

2001

- No Nullify Clinton Labor Department ergonomics rule
- No Cut taxes by $1.35 trillion through fiscal 2011
- Yes Maintain ban on oil drilling in Arctic National Wildlife Refuge
- No Approve Bush proposal to limit managed-care plan liability for coverage decisions
- Yes Divert money from crop subsidy payments to land conservation
- No Expand law enforcement power to investigate suspected terrorists

CQ VOTE STUDIES

	PARTY UNITY		PRESIDENTIAL SUPPORT	
	Support	Oppose	Support	Oppose
2002	96%	4%	21%	79%
2001	88%	12%	24%	76%
2000	94%	6%	75%	25%
1999	90%	10%	75%	25%
1998	90%	10%	78%	22%

INTEREST GROUPS

	AFL-CIO	ADA	CCUS	ACU
2002	100%	100%	32%	4%
2001	92%	90%	32%	12%
2000	89%	65%	63%	17%
1999	89%	95%	36%	4%
1998	100%	95%	44%	8%

CALIFORNIA 47

Orange County — most of Santa Ana, Anaheim and Garden Grove

A blue-collar inland strip full of older suburban homes and younger families, the majority-Hispanic 47th is unlike its mostly affluent, Republican neighbors in Orange County. Located about 30 miles southeast of Los Angeles, it takes in part of four cities: Santa Ana, Anaheim, Garden Grove and Fullerton, where a growing number of Hispanics and other ethnic minorities are changing its demographics and creating a strong Democratic voter base.

Almost half the district's population is in Santa Ana — the Orange County seat — which has higher unemployment and more blue-collar jobs than surrounding areas. The city is one of only three in the county in which registered Democrats outnumber Republicans.

Three-fourths of diverse and growing Garden Grove's residents live in the 47th, which has the center (a mix of Vietnamese, Koreans and Hispanics) and the eastern (heavily Hispanic) sections. An influx of Southeast Asian refugees has spurred a conservative backlash from some residents who worry that increased social services will lead to higher taxes. But the Asian community, some of which is heavily Christian, has a conservative side of its own.

Anaheim, Orange County's second-largest city after Santa Ana, has a large tourism industry and the 47th has some of its most Democratic areas. The small chunk of Fullerton in the district's northern end is heavily Hispanic, though that city leans Republican overall.

Apart from Disneyland, no single employer drives the area's economy. Defense subcontractors and small businesses are scattered throughout the district.

MAJOR INDUSTRY
Small business, service, defense, tourism

CITIES
Santa Ana (pt.), 299,552; Anaheim (pt.), 185,537; Garden Grove (pt.), 125,336; Fullerton (pt.), 17,852

NOTABLE
The 47th's part of Anaheim is home to Disneyland, the 2002 World Series champion Angels and the Mighty Ducks hockey team.

Rep. Christopher Cox (R)

CAPITOL OFFICE
225-5611
christopher.cox@mail.house.gov
www.house.gov/chriscox
2402 Rayburn 20515-0548; fax 225-9177

COMMITTEES
Energy & Commerce
Select Homeland Security - chairman

HOMETOWN
Newport Beach

BORN
Oct. 16, 1952, St. Paul, Minn.

RELIGION
Roman Catholic

FAMILY
Wife, Rebecca Cox; three children

EDUCATION
U. of Southern California, B.A. 1973; Harvard U., M.B.A. 1977, J.D. 1977

CAREER
White House counsel; lawyer; professor

POLITICAL HIGHLIGHTS
No previous office

ELECTION RESULTS

2002 GENERAL		
Christopher Cox (R)	122,884	68.4%
John L. Graham (D)	51,058	28.4%
Joe Cobb (LIBERT)	5,607	3.1%
2002 PRIMARY		
Christopher Cox (R)	84,229	89.4%
David Cobert (R)	6,367	6.8%
Dave Forman (R)	3,654	3.9%
2000 GENERAL		
Christopher Cox (R)	181,365	65.6%
John L. Graham (D)	83,186	30.1%
David Nolan (LIBERT)	8,081	2.9%
Iris Adam (NL)	3,769	1.4%

PREVIOUS WINNING PERCENTAGES
1998 (68%); 1996 (66%); 1994 (72%); 1992 (65%); 1990 (68%); 1988 (67%)

Elected 1988; 8th term

Cool intellect and a golden political pedigree have marked Cox as a rising star — through seven terms in the House. His unmet challenge has been to convince colleagues he can adapt his low-key and methodical style to the highest leadership jobs, which require more overt passion and chummy charisma.

Instead, in the 108th Congress, Cox was pressed to take on a high-profile role as chairman of the Homeland Security Committee, which oversees the new federal department merging all or part of 22 federal agencies. He said his select committee would work to "simplify the oversight burden" spread among the many standing committees that have jurisdiction over some aspect of the far-flung department.

Cox got the Homeland Security post after he lost out to Thomas M. Davis III of Virginia in a bid to become chairman of the Government Reform Committee, replacing Indiana's Dan Burton, who was forced by GOP term limits to step aside in 2003. Although both Cox and Connecticut's Christopher Shays had more seniority on the panel, GOP leaders decided to reward Davis for his work as chairman of the party's 2002 campaign committee. Cox retained his chairmanship of the Republican Policy Committee, which he first got in 1995.

Erudite and well-read, and with law and graduate business degrees from Harvard, Cox has a breadth of interests — ranging from fiscal to foreign policy — that also reflect his background as a former aide to President Reagan, a securities lawyer and a Russologist. His wife, Rebecca, an airline lobbyist, says that her husband reads mathematics texts for fun. But Cox is no mere policy wonk. His reasoned arguments have led to bipartisan triumphs, such as extending the Internet tax moratorium in the 107th Congress and enacting limits on securities fraud lawsuits over President Clinton's veto in the 104th Congress. In the 107th, Cox was one of four Republicans who joined Chairman Michael G. Oxley of Ohio on the new Financial Services Committee while keeping a seat on the Energy and Commerce Committee.

After the collapse of Enron Corp., Cox voted for the corporate accountability law of 2002, but he refused to back down from attacks on business regulation and securities lawsuits. He compared trial lawyers with rogue corporate executives "whose motive was greed."

A trademark of Cox's style has been his steady work on issues vital to both parties. He co-chaired a bipartisan panel in the 107th that devised a plan to ensure continuity of Congress after a terrorist attack. Its central recommendation was for quick state elections to replace lawmakers who were casualties. In the 106th he chaired another bipartisan panel, which examined China's alleged theft of U.S. nuclear and military technology.

Cox's skills as a broker and expertise in intelligence made him a player on homeland security after the Sept. 11, 2001, attacks. Cox was meeting with Defense Secretary Donald H. Rumsfeld when the planes hit the World Trade Center, and he had just left the Pentagon when it was struck by other al Qaeda hijackers. The experience reinforced his support for a missile defense system and new military strategies. The war against terrorism, he said, will not be "governed by the outdated rules of the Cold War."

A staunch conservative, Cox once left a hospital bed after an appendectomy in 1997 so he could vote for a tax cut measure. He is a champion for lower taxes, including permanent repeal of the estate tax. He backed fast-track trade negotiating authority for Bush, and is a reliable conservative on most social issues.

Intensely ambitious, Cox twice considered running for Speaker when the post came up for grabs late in 1998 — after the resignations of Speaker Newt Gingrich and the man the GOP had picked to succeed him, Robert L. Livingston — but he backed away quickly when it was clear he lacked support. The only question for Cox has long been whether he would stay in Congress or take a job in the Bush administration or the federal bench. His shot at a vacancy in 2001 on the 9th U.S. Circuit Court of Appeals in the 107th was blocked by a home state senator, Democrat Barbara Boxer.

On the GOP leadership ladder, Cox has at times disdained the back-slapping style required to win the Speaker's gavel but has shown loyalty by deferring to leadership on key votes. A longtime critic of proposals to upgrade trade relations with China, Cox joined President Clinton and GOP leaders in 2000 in supporting permanent normal trading status for Beijing, after working for inclusion of language requiring annual reviews of China's record on human rights. On the subject of relations with China, he and Democratic leader Nancy Pelosi have worked harmoniously for years.

In 1997, he was one of just 26 Republicans who opposed a balanced-budget deal between congressional Republicans and Clinton. But he eventually voted for the spending and tax bills to implement the deal.

Cox is a determined advocate of smaller government and changing the federal budget process to boost fiscal discipline. He voted against the massive transportation bill in 1998, contending that California did not get a fair share of highway and mass transit funding. Cox said he preferred that states be permitted to keep gas tax receipts and deal with their own transportation needs.

At Harvard, Cox was a law school classmate of Massachusetts Democratic Rep. Barney Frank, and finished business school two years after Bush. After graduating, Cox clerked with judges on federal appeals courts in San Francisco and Honolulu, practiced law with a Newport Beach firm, and published with his father an English version of the former official Soviet newspaper Pravda.

He became a senior associate counsel in the Reagan White House in 1986 and stayed until 1988, when Republican Robert E. Badham announced plans to retire from his Orange County House seat. In a crowded primary field, Cox separated himself by using his Washington connections. He distributed literature picturing him with Reagan and Vice President George Bush in the White House. He took 67 percent of the vote in the general election and has won with similar ease since.

KEY VOTES

2002

No	Overhaul campaign finance law; ban "soft money" and restrict advocacy advertising
Yes	Back Bush's defense budget increase
Yes	Extend 1996 welfare law
Yes	Adopt Bush's discretionary spending limit
Yes	Pass GOP Medicare prescription drug plan
?	Create independent Sept. 11 commission
No	Extend union protections to Homeland Security Department employees
Yes	Revive fast-track procedures for trade agreements
Yes	Authorize war against Iraq
Yes	Advance bankruptcy overhaul opposed by abortion opponents

2001

Yes	Nullify Clinton Labor Department ergonomics rule
Yes	Cut taxes by $1.35 trillion through fiscal 2011
No	Maintain ban on oil drilling in Arctic National Wildlife Refuge
Yes	Approve Bush proposal to limit managed-care plan liability for coverage decisions
No	Divert money from crop subsidy payments to land conservation
Yes	Expand law enforcement power to investigate suspected terrorists

CQ VOTE STUDIES

	PARTY UNITY		PRESIDENTIAL SUPPORT	
	Support	Oppose	Support	Oppose
2002	95%	5%	86%	14%
2001	96%	4%	93%	7%
2000	95%	5%	19%	81%
1999	93%	7%	18%	82%
1998	92%	8%	27%	73%

INTEREST GROUPS

	AFL-CIO	ADA	CCUS	ACU
2002	11%	0%	89%	96%
2001	0%	5%	91%	96%
2000	0%	0%	80%	100%
1999	11%	0%	75%	95%
1998	10%	0%	89%	100%

CALIFORNIA 48

Southern Orange County – Irvine, Newport Beach

The 48th covers the Orange County coast from Newport Beach south through Laguna Beach to Dana Point, and it takes in a chunk of the inland county from the coast through Irvine to the foothills of the Santa Ana mountains. Registered Republicans outnumber Democrats nearly 2-to-1 here, and the district is distinguished by its large white-collar labor force and its high household income.

Newport Beach is a wealthy enclave noted for its beautiful sandy beaches, luxurious housing and solid Republicanism. Many workers commute from the north or east, where living is cheaper. Laguna Beach attracts more scuba divers than swimmers and is a more liberal enclave known as "the arts colony." Inland is Laguna Woods, home to a significant number of senior citizens, Laguna Niguel and Laguna Hills. Nearly 70 percent of district residents are white.

Smog, crime and other problems endemic to Los Angeles do not affect these areas. Transportation troubles are among the toughest problems on the horizon, as traffic backs up and increases the risk of air and water pollution. Toll roads in the area have helped, but residents generally oppose a new commuter train.

While Republicans dominate the 48th, pockets of Democratic strength can be found in the district's inland sections and in the more liberal-leaning community surrounding the University of California, Irvine. The university's engineering and biomedical research programs have attracted a large number of thriving high-tech and biotechnology firms to the area, which is beginning to rival Silicon Valley.

The late-1990s closure of the El Toro and Tustin Marine Corps Air stations did not have a huge impact on the economy, but the El Toro closure did touch off a fierce battle over whether to turn it into a commercial airport. After numerous referenda, the 4,700-acre parcel is set to become a park.

MAJOR INDUSTRY

High-tech, biomedical, tourism

CITIES

Irvine, 143,072; Newport Beach, 70,032; Tustin, 67,504; Laguna Niguel, 61,891

NOTABLE

The El Toro "Y," where Interstates 5 and 405 split, is in Irvine.

Rep. Darrell Issa (R)

CAPITOL OFFICE
225-3906
www.house.gov/issa
211 Cannon 20515-0549; fax 225-3303

COMMITTEES
Energy & Commerce

HOMETOWN
Vista

BORN
Nov. 1, 1953, Cleveland, Ohio

RELIGION
Antioch Orthodox Christian Church

FAMILY
Wife, Kathy Issa; one child

EDUCATION
Kent State U., A.A. 1976 (general studies); Siena Heights College, B.A. 1976 (business)

MILITARY SERVICE
Army, 1970-72, 1976-80; Army Reserve, 1980-88

CAREER
Car alarm company owner; electronics manufacturing company executive

POLITICAL HIGHLIGHTS
Sought Republican nomination for U.S. Senate, 1998

ELECTION RESULTS

2002 GENERAL		
Darrell Issa (R)	94,594	77.2%
Karl W. Dietrich (LIBERT)	26,891	22.0%
2002 PRIMARY		
Darrell Issa (R)		unopposed
2000 GENERAL		
Darrell Issa (R)	160,627	61.4%
Peter Kouvelis (D)	74,073	28.3%
Eddie Rose (REF)	11,240	4.3%
Sharon K. Miles (NL)	8,269	3.2%
Joe Cobb (LIBERT)	7,269	2.8%

Elected 2000; 2nd term

A conservative voice on both economic and social issues, Issa is a man willing to take a risk. Having made his fortune in the car-alarm business, he volunteered in 1996 to be the front man for business in a controversial campaign to overturn racial and gender preferences in California state contracting and college admissions.

The authors of Proposition 209, the "California Civil Rights Initiative," were having trouble finding a prominent businessman to take the lead on an issue that might get him branded a racist, but Issa (EYE-sah) said he was "willing to stick my head out" — neither the first nor the last time he has sought out confrontation. The initiative to end racial and gender preferences in state government decisions passed narrowly.

The grandson of Lebanese immigrants, Issa has found himself subjected to other risks. Three weeks after the Sept. 11, 2001, terrorist attacks on the United States, he was barred from boarding an Air France plane on the first leg of an official trip to the Middle East. Issa said that while Democratic Rep. Robert Wexler of Florida was permitted to board, he was stopped because, "I had an Arab surname and a one-way ticket to Saudi Arabia." Issa started the trip the next day.

Two months later, two men affiliated with the Jewish Defense League were charged with plotting to bomb Issa's San Clemente district office. Authorities believe that an erroneous quote attributed to Issa during his Middle East visit may have sparked a retaliatory plot. One of the suspects died in what authorities said was a suicide; the other entered a guilty plea.

Issa in the 108th Congress won a seat on the Energy and Commerce Committee, campaigning for the job by distributing a computer CD touting his qualifications to members of the panel that makes assignments. Issa had been eager to join the panel in the middle of the 107th Congress when a vacancy arose, but he was passed over for a GOP colleague in a more politically competitive House district.

To take the Energy post, Issa had to give up his posts on the Small Business, International Relations and Judiciary panels.

In the 107th, Issa made more than a half dozen trips abroad, mostly to the Middle East, during his first year in Congress. He has also served as president of the American Task Force for Lebanon, which advocates a role for that nation in the Middle East peace process.

After leaving the Army, Issa used his $7,000 in life savings to invest in a small Cleveland car-alarm business. He and his wife, Kathy, eventually took control of the business and moved it in 1985 to Vista, about 30 miles north of San Diego. He immersed himself in industry activities, and in 1999 and 2000 he was chairman of the board of the Consumer Electronics Association, an industry trade group. Issa holds a number of patents, most of them related to vehicle security, with titles such as "advanced embedded code hopping system."

When he was asked if he could hold his own on the Judiciary Committee without a law degree, Issa replied: "How many of those lawyers can say they've won $16 million in judgments against patent infringements?"

In keeping with his interest in new technologies, Issa has supported a number of congressional initiatives aimed at increasing use of alternative fuels, including incentives for driving gasoline-electric hybrid vehicles. His state has been coping since the start of the decade with severe energy shortages as a result of inconsistent electricity supplies.

As a freshman, Issa was elected by his California GOP colleagues to the 46-member Republican Policy Committee, the party's chief forum for policy discussions, a post he retained in the 108th Congress.

Issa was born into a working-class family in Cleveland, where his father worked two jobs — as a salesman and an X-ray technician. His father and uncles had all served in World War II, and "we grew up wearing left-over Eisenhower jackets," Issa said.

On his 17th birthday, just two months into his high school senior year, Issa quit school and joined the Army. "It happened at a time when folks either ran toward or away from stuff like this," he said about his decision to join the military during the Vietnam War. After he had served two years, including a stint in a bomb disposal unit, the Army paid for Issa's college education with the understanding that he would return to active duty upon graduation. He earned a degree in business administration and returned to the Army. He left again after four years, and returned to Cleveland with plans to start a business.

After moving his company to the San Diego area, Issa was involved behind the scenes in local GOP politics — as the San Francisco Chronicle put it, "writing checks and attending chicken dinners." He briefly considered challenging 49th District Democratic Rep. Lynn Schenk in 1994, but polls showed Brian P. Bilbray would be a strong candidate — he ended up winning the seat by 5,000 votes in the Republican takeover election — and Issa remained on the sidelines.

His 1996 experience with the ballot initiative, along with his work to recruit thousands of volunteers to help San Diego host the 1996 Republican convention, drew Issa further into local politics. He spent $11 million on a failed bid for the 1998 GOP nomination to challenge Democratic Sen. Barbara Boxer, losing in a close GOP primary contest to state Treasurer Matt Fong. (Issa is considering whether he wants to seek a rematch in 2004.)

Undeterred, Issa was back two years later when Republican Ron Packard announced his retirement from the 48th District after 18 years in the House. In the reliably Republican district, which was home to President Nixon, Issa weathered a nine-candidate primary.

Issa's wealth may have provided him the essential edge: He sank $2 million into his primary campaign. The general election was routine by comparison, with Issa taking 61 percent to defeat Democrat Peter Kouvelis, a retired Marine officer, who spent only about $20,000. In 2002, Democrats did not field a candidate and Issa took 77 percent against a Libertarian and a write-in candidate.

KEY VOTES

2002

No Overhaul campaign finance law; ban "soft money" and restrict advocacy advertising
Yes Back Bush's defense budget increase
Yes Extend 1996 welfare law
Yes Adopt Bush's discretionary spending limit
Yes Pass GOP Medicare prescription drug plan
? Create independent Sept. 11 commission
No Extend union protections to Homeland Security Department employees
Yes Revive fast-track procedures for trade agreements
Yes Authorize war against Iraq
Yes Advance bankruptcy overhaul opposed by abortion opponents

2001

Yes Nullify Clinton Labor Department ergonomics rule
Yes Cut taxes by $1.35 trillion through fiscal 2011
No Maintain ban on oil drilling in Arctic National Wildlife Refuge
Yes Approve Bush proposal to limit managed-care plan liability for coverage decisions
No Divert money from crop subsidy payments to land conservation
Yes Expand law enforcement power to investigate suspected terrorists

CQ VOTE STUDIES

	PARTY UNITY		PRESIDENTIAL SUPPORT	
	Support	Oppose	Support	Oppose
2002	94%	6%	85%	15%
2001	96%	4%	88%	12%

INTEREST GROUPS

	AFL-CIO	ADA	CCUS	ACU
2002	13%	0%	100%	96%
2001	17%	10%	100%	84%

CALIFORNIA 49
North San Diego County; West Riverside County

One of the fastest-growing areas in California, the heavily residential 49th in northwestern San Diego County and western Riverside County is home to many rapidly changing bedroom communities.

Commuters travel to jobs in San Diego (a sliver of which falls in the 49th) and, to a lesser extent, Orange County, while tourists visit the wineries in Riverside County. Almost 60 percent white and solidly conservative, the district gave George W. Bush 57 percent of the vote in the 2000 presidential election.

The 1990s saw areas like Lake Elsinore, Canyon Lake and Sun City in Riverside County turn from retirement communities into family-oriented commuter towns. Perris, which largely remains a retirement community, is the district's only city in which Democrats hold an edge.

Massive Camp Pendleton Marine Corps Base sits on the district's coast, but the local economy relies less on military contracts than its Orange County and San Diego neighbors. Sony has a plant in Rancho Bernardo (in northeast San Diego) that makes laptop computers, among other electronics. Beach visitors to Oceanside and the Pacific Coast also boost the local economy.

Though most residents live in San Diego County, growth has been prodigious in Temecula, the heart of the district's wine industry, in Riverside County. Ballooning and skydiving are among the tourist attractions in the more-rural northern parts of the district.

MAJOR INDUSTRY
Medical devices, services, manufacturing, tourism, defense

MILITARY BASES
Camp Pendleton Marine Corps Base, Air Station and Naval Hospital, 32,000 military, 7,000 civilians (2002); Naval Weapons Station Seal Beach, Detachment Fallbrook, 100 military, 300 civilian (2003)

CITIES
Oceanside, 161,029; Vista, 89,857; Temecula, 57,716; Perris, 36,189; Fallbrook (unincorporated), 29,100; Lake Elsinore, 28,928

NOTABLE
Fallbrook is a leader in avocado production; Julian produces 10,000 apple pies a week each fall; The San Onofre nuclear power plant is on the Pacific Coast next to Camp Pendleton.

Rep. Randy 'Duke' Cunningham (R)

CAPITOL OFFICE
225-5452
www.house.gov/cunningham
2350 Rayburn 20515-0550; fax 225-2558

COMMITTEES
Appropriations
Select Intelligence

HOMETOWN
San Diego

BORN
Dec. 8, 1941, Los Angeles, Calif.

RELIGION
Christian

FAMILY
Wife, Nancy Cunningham; three children

EDUCATION
U. of Missouri, B.A. 1964 (education), M.A. 1965 (education); National U., M.B.A. 1985

MILITARY SERVICE
Navy, 1966-87

CAREER
Computer software executive; Top Gun flight school instructor; teacher and coach

POLITICAL HIGHLIGHTS
No previous office

ELECTION RESULTS

2002 GENERAL

Randy "Duke" Cunningham (R)	111,095	64.3%
Del G. Stewart (D)	55,855	32.3%
Richard M. Fontanesi (LIBERT)	5,751	3.3%

2002 PRIMARY

Randy "Duke" Cunningham (R)	54,491	86.7%
James B. Hart (R)	8,354	13.3%

2000 GENERAL

Randy "Duke" Cunningham (R)	172,291	64.3%
George "Jorge" Barraza (D)	81,408	30.4%
Daniel L. Muhe (LIBERT)	7,159	2.7%
Eric Hunter Bourdette (NL)	6,941	2.6%

PREVIOUS WINNING PERCENTAGES
1998 (61%); 1996 (65%); 1994 (67%); 1992 (56%); 1990 (46%)

Elected 1990; 7th term

Cunningham is a gruff and straight-talking man, ready reminders of his 20-year Navy career as a Vietnam War "ace" and "Top Gun" flight instructor. Committed to conservative causes, he remains a stout defender of the military, a favorite of the National Rifle Association — and a perennial proponent of legislation to protect the flag from desecration.

Cunningham disdains what he calls "politically correct" views, and he sometimes finds himself in hot water for his verbal and physical outbursts. He once intimated that opponents of the F-22 fighter jet were all liberals and socialists, and chided the acting secretary of the Army for what he termed a "B.S." statement. Discarding the usual House floor decorum, Cunningham once told Vermont lawmaker Bernard Sanders, "sit down, you socialist."

But in his seventh term in the House, Cunningham may be mellowing. Lately he seems to have toned down the verbal barrages. His hometown newspaper, the San Diego Union-Tribune, noted in 2001 that Cunningham's temper had not made front page news for quite some time and dared to ask whether the Navy pilot was "going soft."

Cunningham told the newspaper, "I found out being a gentleman politician — with passion — sometimes gets the job done better." Democratic Rep. James P. Moran, who once engaged in a shoving match with Cunningham, told the newspaper that Cunningham can intimidate but is not a backstabber. "He's a stand-up guy," the paper quoted Moran as saying.

But as for the extent of Cunningham's mellowing, Moran is not convinced. Asked later about the Union-Tribune's thesis, Moran said, "it's all relative. . . . I would not call him a low-key or milquetoast personality."

And some evidence of his straight-talking style continues. Cunningham late in 2001 blasted Judiciary Committee Chairman F. James Sensenbrenner Jr., a fellow Republican, for "heavy-handed behavior [that] is unbecoming a chairman of a major committee." Cunningham was upset that Sensenbrenner had canceled, at the last minute, a hearing on Cunningham's legislation to permit off-duty and retired law enforcement officers to carry concealed weapons. Cunningham went so far as to file a discharge petition to try to circumvent Sensenbrenner's committee and bring the bill directly to the House floor.

Despite his aggressive talk, Cunningham has a sensitive side. He appeared to fight back tears in 1999 when urging his colleagues to support a constitutional amendment outlawing flag desecration. "This is not a matter of freedom of speech," he said. "There is nothing in this amendment that prevents someone from speaking or writing or doing any of the other things, but just the radical burning of the symbol that we hold dear." He continues to offer flag protection amendments in every Congress.

Cunningham has said "my passions are national security and education," but his legislative agenda includes other issues as well. He supports the continued moratorium on offshore drilling off the coast of California. In the 105th, Cunningham was a prime advocate of an international agreement to protect dolphins from inadvertent catch by tuna fishermen. (The "dolphin-safe" bill, which did not have universal approval from environmental groups, was important to the San Diego tuna fishing industry because fishermen could then use more efficient methods.)

Cunningham also is a proponent of health research. After prostate cancer surgery in 1998, he urged his colleagues to boost prostate cancer research funding. In both the 106th and 107th, hoping to raise awareness about health issues that men frequently ignore, Cunningham introduced legislation to establish an Office of Men's Health at the Health and Human Services Department. In the 107th, splitting from many conservatives, Cunningham urged President Bush to allow some continued stem cell research.

A former chairman of an Education subcommittee, he pressed to give local school boards more authority over federal education dollars. Cunningham long has argued that billions of dollars in such federal spending are wasted by bureaucrats and never make it down to the "zip code," where he says teachers and administrators can use the money wisely. Cunningham's wife was a school administrator and former principal in the San Diego area before taking a job in the Bush administration in 2002 as a special assistant to the secretary of Education.

As a member of the Appropriations Committee, Cunningham in the 107th worked to increase impact aid, which helps communities with substantial federal facilities such as military bases to support their schools — an important funding source in San Diego. Cunningham won his Appropriations seat in the 105th Congress, his fourth term. As a member of the Defense Subcommittee, he strongly supports efforts to raise military spending. He is a proponent of the Global hawk and Predator unmanned reconnaissance planes. He has used his own Navy training to advance military spending. In 1998, he test flew a new version of the F-18 Navy fighter that had faced some criticism and declared it "head and shoulders above other aircraft I've tested and flown."

Cunningham began his career as an Illinois high school teacher and swim coach, training two athletes to Olympic medals. He joined the Navy at 25 and became the first ace — a combat pilot who shoots down five enemy planes — of the Vietnam War, at one point narrowly avoiding capture after his F-4 fighter was shot down over North Vietnam. After winning a passel of medals, including the Navy Cross, he returned to the United States to train pilots at Miramar Naval Air Station north of San Diego.

After he left the military for a business career, his background caught the eye of southern California's Republican Rep. Duncan Hunter. Cunningham agreed to leave his beach home in exclusive Del Mar and move to the older, middle-class suburb of Chula Vista to challenge Democratic Rep. Jim Bates in 1990 in the old 44th District. Targeting evangelical Christians and conservative Democrats, Cunningham eked out a narrow victory.

After redistricting in 1992, he ran in the solidly Republican 51st and was re-elected by comfortable margins. Redistricting for 2002 did not hurt him either. His new district, numbered the 50th, still contains a healthy Republican majority, and Cunningham cruised to a 2-to-1 victory.

KEY VOTES

2002

- No Overhaul campaign finance law; ban "soft money" and restrict advocacy advertising
- Yes Back Bush's defense budget increase
- Yes Extend 1996 welfare law
- Yes Adopt Bush's discretionary spending limit
- Yes Pass GOP Medicare prescription drug plan
- No Create independent Sept. 11 commission
- No Extend union protections to Homeland Security Department employees
- Yes Revive fast-track procedures for trade agreements
- Yes Authorize war against Iraq
- No Advance bankruptcy overhaul opposed by abortion opponents

2001

- Yes Nullify Clinton Labor Department ergonomics rule
- Yes Cut taxes by $1.35 trillion through fiscal 2011
- No Maintain ban on oil drilling in Arctic National Wildlife Refuge
- Yes Approve Bush proposal to limit managed-care plan liability for coverage decisions
- No Divert money from crop subsidy payments to land conservation
- Yes Expand law enforcement power to investigate suspected terrorists

CQ VOTE STUDIES

	PARTY UNITY		PRESIDENTIAL SUPPORT	
	Support	Oppose	Support	Oppose
2002	97%	3%	86%	14%
2001	96%	4%	95%	5%
2000	94%	6%	26%	74%
1999	95%	5%	20%	80%
1998	93%	7%	25%	75%

INTEREST GROUPS

	AFL-CIO	ADA	CCUS	ACU
2002	11%	0%	89%	96%
2001	17%	5%	96%	96%
2000	0%	5%	95%	92%
1999	0%	10%	92%	88%
1998	0%	0%	100%	100%

CALIFORNIA 50

North San Diego; Escondido; Carlsbad

With its beautiful beach communities and upper-middle-class suburbs, the San Diego-area 50th is a steadily growing GOP stronghold.

The area's wealth is a testament to a booming technology industry north of San Diego that has been likened to a mini-Silicon Valley. The growth of cellular technology companies and computer firms has contributed to the area's image. Military firms and defense contractors have diversified the boom. Construction of opulent homes continues apace, and locals and tourists compete for time at a plethora of golf courses.

The 50th's conservative corridor, which runs north and south through the district along Interstate 15, includes the Marine Corps base in Miramar (shared with the 52nd), which until 1996 was home to the Navy's famed "Top Gun" fighter school. As part of downsizing, the Naval Air Station moved to Nevada, and Marines from the closing El Toro and Tustin bases moved to Miramar.

Unlike San Diego's south side, the 50th is two-thirds white and heavily Republican. Coastal cities such as Del Mar, Carlsbad and Encinitas, where beach replenishment and the environment are issues, add some liberals to the district, but they are outweighed by inland voters in well-off San Diego communities and Escondido, which is north of the city on Interstate 15. Republicans have a voter registration advantage of more than 15 points.

MAJOR INDUSTRY

Technology, defense, manufacturing

MILITARY BASES

Marine Corps Air Station Miramar, 10,000 military, 1,500 civilian (2000) (shared with the 52nd)

CITIES

San Diego (pt.), 262,523; Escondido, 133,559; Carlsbad, 78,247; Encinitas, 58,014; San Marcos, 54,977

NOTABLE

Carlsbad grows and distributes most of the West Coast's fresh-cut flowers and is home to several major golf equipment manufacturers, as well as the Legoland theme park; Rancho Santa Fe was the home of the Heaven's Gate cult when members committed mass suicide in 1997; The Ecke Ranch produces 80 percent of the world's poinsettias.

Rep. Bob Filner (D)

CAPITOL OFFICE
225-8045
www.house.gov/filner
2428 Rayburn 20515-0551; fax 225-9073

COMMITTEES
Transportation & Infrastructure
Veterans' Affairs

HOMETOWN
San Diego

BORN
Sept. 4, 1942, Pittsburgh, Pa.

RELIGION
Jewish

FAMILY
Wife, Jane Merrill Filner; two children

EDUCATION
Cornell U., B.A. 1963 (chemistry); U. of Delaware, M.A. 1969 (history); Cornell U., Ph.D. 1973 (history of science)

CAREER
Public official; college professor

POLITICAL HIGHLIGHTS
San Diego School Board, 1979-83 (president, 1982); candidate for San Diego City Council, 1983; San Diego City Council, 1987-92 (deputy mayor, 1991)

ELECTION RESULTS

2002 GENERAL		
Bob Filner (D)	59,541	57.9%
Maria Guadalupe Garcia (R)	40,430	39.3%
Jeffrey S. Keup (LIBERT)	2,816	2.7%
2002 PRIMARY		
Bob Filner (D)	25,179	70.4%
Daniel C. Ramirez (D)	10,584	29.6%
2000 GENERAL		
Bob Filner (D)	95,191	68.3%
Bob Divine (R)	38,526	27.6%
David Willoughby (LIBERT)	3,472	2.5%
Leeann Kendall (NL)	2,283	1.6%

PREVIOUS WINNING PERCENTAGES
1998 (99%); 1996 (62%); 1994 (57%); 1992 (57%)

Elected 1992; 6th term

An irrepressible liberal, Filner often finds himself frustrated by what he considers the esoteric political tactics of the Democratic leadership in the House. But the one-time aide to progressive icon Hubert H. Humphrey, the former senator and vice president, still finds ways to create a splash on issues he cares about.

Drawing on his background as a grass-roots organizer and 1960s civil rights activist, Filner argues that Democratic leaders should organize more publicity stunts and fewer parliamentary maneuvers to get the party's message out to the public.

"We're stuck in this Beltway stuff. . . . They do motions to recommit. Who cares, besides us?" Filner said of the procedural maneuvers that allow the House minority to make political points by trying to send legislation they view as objectionable back to committee.

Indeed, Filner unabashedly claims to use political stunts as "organizing tools" to whip up the public's interest in policy.

In 2003, criticizing the Bush administration's proposed spending on veterans' benefits, Filner suggested that veterans groups ought to stage a march on Washington.

During California's electricity crisis at the start of the decade, which hit Filner's hometown of San Diego hard, he was so angered that he filed motions in court alleging the utility companies were guilty of murder, extortion and grand larceny. As a result of the electricity debacle, Filner began working with local leaders to create a municipal utility in the San Diego area.

Before that crisis, Filner surprised members of the Congressional Black Caucus by joining their parliamentary attempt at a January 2001 joint session to prevent Congress from certifying the Electoral College's 2000 presidential results, which formally resolved the contested election in favor of George W. Bush. Filner was so incensed by the Supreme Court ruling the previous month, which effectively decided the election, that he briefly considered introducing a resolution of impeachment in the House against some of the justices, he said.

Filner ruffled GOP feathers when he showed up at the 1996 Republican National Convention in San Diego and set up a makeshift booth labeled "The Democrat Is In," modeled after the one used by Lucy in the comic strip "Peanuts."

Despite his appetite for political theater, Filner has a serious side, which is often apparent in his advocacy of veterans' interests. He is second in seniority among Democrats on the Veterans Affairs Committee. As top-ranking Democrat on the subcommittee on Benefits in the 105th and 106th Congresses, Filner worked to improve aid to homeless veterans and sponsored legislation to guarantee veterans the right to reclaim state government jobs after their military service. In the 107th Congress, he was the top Democrat on the subcommittee on Health.

Filner has made repeated bids to win benefits for Filipino veterans who served with U.S. forces in World War II. His efforts, inspired by the large Filipino community in his district, won him the gratitude of the Philippine government, particularly when he was arrested with Filipino-American protesters who had chained themselves to the White House fence in 1997.

Filner also sits on the Transportation Committee, where he has worked with other Californians to get as much money as possible for local projects as Congress reauthorized federal surface transportation programs. Of particular importance to Filner is funding for projects along the Mexican border. Facilities there were strained by increased trade traffic under the North American Free Trade Agreement, which he opposed. And the terrorist attacks of Sept. 11, 2001, brought even more congestion as border security increased. Filner expressed satisfaction with a Bush administration increase in border security personnel but continued to press for additional funding and border gates south of San Diego.

On other issues, Filner is unafraid to buck his party when he thinks his colleagues are giving political victories to their foes. He was among the minority of Democrats who opposed the education law enacted at the end of Bush's first year in office. "Why should we give [Bush] a political victory for something that's not really going to be implemented? I don't know why the Democrats voted for it," Filner said after the president proposed less spending for education in fiscal 2003 than the law permitted.

Filner has championed environmental protection back home. He has pushed legislation to reduce the effect of sewage from Mexico on the California coast and has said he will work to save the polluted Salton Sea, most of which is in his district. Filner also is at home arranging small-business workshops and publicizing sources of microloans and other government help for entrepreneurs in the low-income quarters of the district.

A native Pennsylvanian, Filner's dedication to the civil rights movement led him to leave college and join the Freedom Rides in 1961. Arrested during a sit-in at a Mississippi lunch counter with John Lewis, now a House colleague from Georgia, Filner spent several months in prison. After his release, he finished college and later earned a doctorate in the history of science.

Filner taught history at San Diego State University in the 1970s. After working for Humphrey and Rep. Don Fraser, both Minnesota Democrats, he spent four years on the San Diego School Board and five more on the city council before running for a newly created 50th District House seat in 1992. His single-minded devotion to fundraising and tireless campaigning helped him overcome five Democratic primary foes, and the nomination led him to a string of relatively easy general-election victories.

When the California Legislature took up redistricting for this decade, state Rep. Juan Vargas tried to include more Hispanic neighborhoods in the new 51st to benefit his potential candidacy. The entire California-Mexico border as well as low-income portions of rural Imperial County were added, but Vargas' plan was not altogether embraced and he declined to run, sparing Filner his first serious primary fight in a decade. Nevertheless, Filner's 58 percent was his lowest share of the vote since 1994.

KEY VOTES

2002

- Yes Overhaul campaign finance law; ban "soft money" and restrict advocacy advertising
- No Back Bush's defense budget increase
- No Extend 1996 welfare law
- No Adopt Bush's discretionary spending limit
- No Pass GOP Medicare prescription drug plan
- Yes Create independent Sept. 11 commission
- Yes Extend union protections to Homeland Security Department employees
- No Revive fast-track procedures for trade agreements
- No Authorize war against Iraq
- No Advance bankruptcy overhaul opposed by abortion opponents

2001

- No Nullify Clinton Labor Department ergonomics rule
- No Cut taxes by $1.35 trillion through fiscal 2011
- Yes Maintain ban on oil drilling in Arctic National Wildlife Refuge
- No Approve Bush proposal to limit managed-care plan liability for coverage decisions
- Yes Divert money from crop subsidy payments to land conservation
- No Expand law enforcement power to investigate suspected terrorists

CQ VOTE STUDIES

	PARTY UNITY		PRESIDENTIAL SUPPORT	
	Support	Oppose	Support	Oppose
2002	99%	1%	22%	78%
2001	99%	1%	12%	88%
2000	99%	1%	88%	12%
1999	98%	2%	85%	15%
1998	97%	3%	85%	15%

INTEREST GROUPS

	AFL-CIO	ADA	CCUS	ACU
2002	89%	100%	25%	0%
2001	100%	95%	22%	0%
2000	100%	95%	27%	0%
1999	89%	100%	20%	0%
1998	100%	100%	22%	4%

CALIFORNIA 51

Central and southern San Diego; Imperial County

The part-urban, part-rural 51st runs the entire length of California's border with Mexico except for the western tip at the Pacific Ocean. It includes part of central San Diego and all of Imperial County, which is sometimes at odds with the city constituency. The Democratic district, previously an urban stronghold numbered the 50th, increased its original area tremendously through post-census 2000 redistricting.

The district's San Diego portion, which begins south and east of downtown, is working class and heavily Hispanic, and has some of the worst of the city's problems. Much of the growth that has boosted areas north of San Diego has left the 51st behind. NAFTA and the Sept. 11 attacks have slowed the border traffic-dependent economy — Mexican shoppers spend more than $3 billion a year at area malls. A sizable military and veteran population has produced a more even party split in the booming residential suburb of Chula Vista.

Imperial County is heavily agricultural, with an annual crop yield of about $1 billion, and about 70 percent Hispanic. Unemployment runs as high as 30 percent in some areas. Voters here are more conservative than their city cousins but still lean Democratic.

Border issues, particularly illegal immigration — which fills agricultural labor jobs — illegal drugs and wastewater treatment, are important in the Hispanic-majority 51st, which gave 56 percent to presidential nominee Al Gore in 2000. Its areas compete for water and are under pressure to reduce dependency on the Colorado River. Environmentalists object to one proposed solution — the Salton Sea (shared with the 45th) — which they say is key to the local ecosystem and to migratory birds.

MAJOR INDUSTRY

Service, manufacturing, agriculture, retail

MILITARY BASES

Naval Station San Diego (shared with the 53rd), 43,160 military, 5,400 civilian (2000); El Centro Naval Air Facility, 297 military, 103 civilian (2001)

CITIES

San Diego (pt.), 239,457; Chula Vista, 173,556; National City, 54,260

NOTABLE

San Diego-Tijuana border crossing at San Ysidro is the world's busiest; Otay Mesa is known as the television capital of the world for its consumer electronics manufacturing.

Rep. Duncan Hunter (R)

CAPITOL OFFICE
225-5672
www.house.gov/hunter
2265 Rayburn 20515-0552; fax 225-0235

COMMITTEES
Armed Services - chairman
Select Homeland Security

HOMETOWN
El Cajon

BORN
May 31, 1948, Riverside, Calif.

RELIGION
Baptist

FAMILY
Wife, Lynne Hunter; two children

EDUCATION
U. of Montana, attended 1966-67; U. of California, Santa Barbara, attended 1967-68; Western State U., B.S.L. 1976, J.D. 1976

MILITARY SERVICE
Army, 1969-71

CAREER
Lawyer

POLITICAL HIGHLIGHTS
No previous office

ELECTION RESULTS

2002 GENERAL		
Duncan Hunter (R)	118,561	70.2%
Peter Moore-Kochlacs (D)	43,526	25.8%
Michael Benoit (LIBERT)	6,923	4.1%
2002 PRIMARY		
Duncan Hunter (R)		unopposed
2000 GENERAL		
Duncan Hunter (R)	131,345	64.7%
Craig B. Barkacs (D)	63,537	31.3%
Michael Benoit (LIBERT)	5,995	3.0%
Robert Sherman (NL)	2,117	1.0%

PREVIOUS WINNING PERCENTAGES
1998 (76%); 1996 (65%); 1994 (64%); 1992 (53%); 1990 (73%); 1988 (74%); 1986 (77%); 1984 (75%); 1982 (69%); 1980 (53%)

Elected 1980; 12th term

As the new chairman of the Armed Services Committee in the 108th Congress, the blunt-speaking but affable Hunter has become one of Capitol Hill's most prominent Republican voices on defense issues.

A decorated Vietnam War veteran representing a solidly Republican district with a large military presence, Hunter remains the epitome of the congressional defense hawk. He was a steadfast supporter of President Reagan's military buildup in the 1980s. And he was also among the harshest critics of President Clinton for requesting defense budgets that Hunter deemed dangerously anemic. But in his single-minded pursuit of a more robust military budget — which his allies call principled and his critics call bullheaded — Hunter also has clashed with the Bush White House and the House Republican leadership when their budget-cutting priorities have reined in Pentagon spending plans.

For instance, when Defense Secretary Donald H. Rumsfeld moved to successfully spike the Crusader mobile cannon project in 2002 so that the Army could afford to develop more-advanced weapons, Hunter contended that the administration was forcing an unwise choice between two important projects. "What we have to do is try to work with the administration and get a budget that is not going to require us to fight between good systems," he said.

On the other hand, Hunter's self-confidence sometimes makes him an uncomfortable ally for the defense establishment. He sounds out independent experts on some issues and, on occasion, has been willing to challenge the armed services on both technical and organizational issues.

In the early 1990s, for instance, he battled for years to make the Navy explore more-novel designs and missions for nuclear-powered submarines. More recently, he has pushed for a pilot program to let small companies bid to take over ongoing weapons programs, despite warnings from industry and the Pentagon that this would produce chaos.

A member of the defense panel since he was elected to the House at the age of 32, Hunter is relatively young for one of his legislative seniority. His sometimes boisterous informality contrasts starkly with the courtly gravitas of his counterpart, Senate Armed Services Committee Chairman John W. Warner of Virginia. But Hunter matches the fervor of his support for a strong military with a solid grasp of the arguments and a forceful style of presentation. When GOP congressional defense mavens lobbied President Bush in January 2002 for a larger than anticipated increase in Pentagon spending, it was Hunter — not the soft-spoken Bob Stump of Arizona, who was then Armed Services chairman — who made the pitch, using an array of poster-size briefing charts replete with Pentagon statistics and quotes from top-ranking military officers.

When Stump announced the following April that he would not seek reelection because of illness, Curt Weldon, another hawk concerned with drumming up support for defense, contemplated challenging Hunter for the panel's top Republican slot. But after a few weeks, he deferred to Hunter, who was next in line by seniority. Hunter promises to take on a more ambitious and activist agenda than Stump.

On fiscal and social issues, Hunter casts a reliably conservative vote. A leader of the Conservative Opportunity Society, founded by Newt Gingrich in the early 1980s, Hunter began working his way up the House GOP leadership ladder, winning the chair of the Republican Research

Committee in 1989, the same year Gingrich became minority whip. But in 1994, he lost a bid for chairman of the Republican Conference to Ohio's John A. Boehner, who came to Congress 10 years after Hunter. Since then, he has focused on his Armed Services work.

On trade and border security issues, Hunter's views blend conservative populism with a concern for keeping U.S.-developed technology out of hostile hands. When the House voted in 2000 to grant China permanent normal trade status, Hunter led a band of Republicans who warned that the vote would help Beijing rebuild its military to threaten the United States. In 2002, he warned that Iraq would benefit from legislation — which ultimately never made it to the House floor — that would have liberalized restrictions on the export of powerful computers and other militarily relevant technologies. "The bill would loosen export controls over sensitive, dual-use items that Saddam Hussein is trying to acquire illicitly to develop weapons of mass destruction," he wrote to colleagues.

Hunter opposed the 1993 North American Free Trade Agreement and was against aid to Mexico after the devaluation of the peso in 1994. He also has worked to upgrade fences along the Mexican border and to hire more Border Patrol agents to reduce the flow of illegal immigrants from that country. In both the 107th and 108th Congresses, he introduced bills to bar the export of natural gas to fuel pollution-causing electric Mexican plants just across the border from the 52nd District.

These positions have prompted some San Diego business executives to question whether he is attuned to the needs of the area's growing economy, which has expanded beyond defense into high technology and telecommunications and now seeks greater cooperation with Mexico. But Hunter has encountered no significant political downside to his views.

For three years in the late 1970s, Hunter ran a storefront legal office in San Diego's Hispanic district, often giving free legal advice to poor people. His work in the usually Democratic inner city and his tireless campaigning helped produce his 1980 upset victory over nine-term Democrat Lionel Van Deerlin. Hunter, who won a Bronze Star for participating in 25 helicopter combat assaults in Vietnam, blasted Van Deerlin as "anti-defense" and promised a pro-Pentagon stance would keep jobs in the San Diego area, which boasts the nation's largest naval base and numerous defense industries. The message helped propel Hunter to a 53 percent majority.

He secured his hold on the district in subsequent campaigns, except in 1992. Redistricting, plus Hunter's record of overdrafts at the House bank, held him to 53 percent. But since then, he has coasted to re-election.

KEY VOTES

2002

- No Overhaul campaign finance law; ban "soft money" and restrict advocacy advertising
- Yes Back Bush's defense budget increase
- Yes Extend 1996 welfare law
- Yes Adopt Bush's discretionary spending limit
- Yes Pass GOP Medicare prescription drug plan
- No Create independent Sept. 11 commission
- Yes Extend union protections to Homeland Security Department employees
- No Revive fast-track procedures for trade agreements
- Yes Authorize war against Iraq
- No Advance bankruptcy overhaul opposed by abortion opponents

2001

- Yes Nullify Clinton Labor Department ergonomics rule
- Yes Cut taxes by $1.35 trillion through fiscal 2011
- No Maintain ban on oil drilling in Arctic National Wildlife Refuge
- Yes Approve Bush proposal to limit managed-care plan liability for coverage decisions
- No Divert money from crop subsidy payments to land conservation
- Yes Expand law enforcement power to investigate suspected terrorists

CQ VOTE STUDIES

	PARTY UNITY		PRESIDENTIAL SUPPORT	
	Support	Oppose	Support	Oppose
2002	94%	6%	78%	22%
2001	95%	5%	88%	12%
2000	94%	6%	19%	81%
1999	91%	9%	21%	79%
1998	93%	7%	20%	80%

INTEREST GROUPS

	AFL-CIO	ADA	CCUS	ACU
2002	33%	10%	75%	88%
2001	17%	5%	91%	100%
2000	10%	10%	71%	76%
1999	44%	15%	70%	84%
1998	11%	5%	71%	100%

CALIFORNIA 52

Eastern San Diego; inland San Diego County

The 52nd, which wraps around the east side of San Diego from Poway in the north to east of Otay Mesa in the south, is predominantly made up of wealthy, conservative suburbs. It contains about 15 percent of San Diego's residents and is solidly Republican ground, complemented by growing, rich suburbs.

After years of slow economic growth, the late 1990s marked a turnaround, particularly in El Cajon, where property values and home sales rose dramatically. San Diego's large military and defense-related work force contributes to the district's conservative personality and robust economy. Though most of the area's military bases are in the 53rd, many residents commute to nearby defense and military contracting jobs. Blue- and white-collar employees alike tend to vote Republican in the almost three-fourths white district.

Poway has a more wealthy, rural feel to it than the surrounding suburban sprawl, where growth is becoming a hot issue. Just outside of Poway is an expanse of evenly developed suburbs that includes Rancho Bernardo (shared with the 49th) and Scripps Ranch, areas within San Diego's city limits that have attracted retirees and young families alike.

The district also stretches about 100 miles east and north through mountains and protected desert parks to the San Diego County borders. Until redistricting following the 2000 census, the 52nd also had much of California's border with Mexico and all of rural Imperial County to the east. But those areas were moved into the 51st, making this district more conservative and dominated by suburban interests.

MAJOR INDUSTRY

Technology, manufacturing

MILITARY BASES

Marine Corps Air Station Miramar, 10,000 military, 1,500 civilian (2000) (shared with the 50th)

CITIES

San Diego (pt.), 164,554; El Cajon, 94,869; La Mesa, 54,749; Santee, 52,975; Poway, 48,044

NOTABLE

The Unarius society, based in El Cajon, believes UFOs will bring "a new beginning for planet earth."

Rep. Susan A. Davis (D)

CAPITOL OFFICE
225-2040
susan.davis@mail.house.gov
www.house.gov/susandavis
1224 Longworth 20515-0553; fax 225-2948

COMMITTEES
Armed Services
Education & Workforce
Veterans' Affairs

HOMETOWN
San Diego

BORN
April 13, 1944, Cambridge, Mass.

RELIGION
Jewish

FAMILY
Husband, Steve Davis; two children

EDUCATION
U. of California, Berkeley, B.A. 1965 (sociology); U. of North Carolina, M.A. 1968 (social work)

CAREER
High school leadership program director; public television producer; social worker

POLITICAL HIGHLIGHTS
San Diego Board of Education, 1983-92 (president, 1989-92); Calif. Assembly, 1994-2000

ELECTION RESULTS

2002 GENERAL		
Susan A. Davis (D)	72,252	62.2%
Bill VanDeWeghe (R)	43,891	37.8%
2002 PRIMARY		
Susan A. Davis (D)		unopposed
2000 GENERAL		
Susan A. Davis (D)	113,400	49.6%
Brian P. Bilbray (R)	105,515	46.2%
Doris Ball (LIBERT)	6,526	2.9%
Tahir Bhatti (NL)	3,048	1.3%

Elected 2000; 2nd term

The debate on how best to direct the federal government's attention and resources often boils down to basic disputes between defense and education, and Davis is one of the few lawmakers who is situated in both camps: A former school board member who says she believes education should be the nation's top priority, Davis also backs extra funding for certain defense programs. Representing a district with a substantial military presence, including defense plants, thousands of active military personnel and thousands more veterans, Davis cannot afford to simply choose books over barracks, and she wants the government to find money for both.

Davis is the daughter of a pediatrician and the wife of a psychiatrist. She was a military wife, accompanying her husband to Japan while he served as an Air Force doctor. She has sociology and social work degrees. She served on a school board for nine years and in the California Legislature for six.

In both the 107th and 108th Congresses, Davis was one of only three House Democrats to serve on both the Armed Services and Education and the Workforce committees.

On Armed Services, she has been active in efforts to improve military housing, and in 2001 she worked to ensure that children of low-income military personnel remained eligible for free or reduced-cost school lunches even when housing allowances were increased to meet higher costs, such as in the San Diego area.

Another priority for Davis is to fully fund federal impact aid, which helps school systems in communities that have a significant federal presence, such as military bases on which no property taxes are paid. Over the years, the impact aid program has not received full funding, and in the debate in the 107th Davis was a leader in the drive to increase it.

Midway through her first term, Davis added a seat on Veterans' Affairs and late in 2001, she helped in the search for a shelter for homeless veterans in San Diego to replace a facility that was no longer available.

Having affiliated herself in her first term with the moderate New Democrat Coalition, she supported President Bush on issues such as expanded foreign trade and annual reading and math testing in elementary and middle schools — both issues were ones on which she broke ranks with the majority of her Democratic colleagues in the 107th.

Davis took great pains to explain her vote in 2001 in favor of giving the president authority to negotiate trade agreements that would receive fast-track consideration by Congress. Several of her pro-trade New Democrat colleagues voted against the legislation, arguing that the timing was wrong. But Davis was among only 21 members of her party — and one of only two from California — voting "yes." She argued that on balance the bill would benefit her district. Still, she called it the "most agonizing vote of my first year in Washington." In 2002, she again voted "aye" on the bill.

Trained in social work, Davis places great importance on mentoring, which was a key component of a fellowship program she ran in the 1990s designed to teach multi-ethnic high school students leadership and citizenship skills. In Congress, she often pays tribute to other mentors in San Diego with a "mentor of the month" proclamation.

Davis also is concerned about diet supplements. Continuing an interest that began in her days in the California Assembly when she chaired the Consumer Protection subcommittee, Davis wrote bills to restrict sales of supplements containing ephedrine and to give the Food and Drug Administration more authority over supplements. An ephedrine labeling bill written by Davis had passed the state legislature, only to be vetoed by Democratic Gov. Gray Davis, who said the issue was a federal matter.

Davis was in graduate school in North Carolina when she met Steve Davis, who was studying to be a psychiatrist. After they married, they spent two years in Japan while he served in the Air Force.

When the family returned stateside and eventually settled in San Diego, Davis became active in community activities. She volunteered at her son's pre-school and soon became its principal. She joined the League of Women Voters, serving as the president of the San Diego chapter. Davis also worked at the local public television station.

In 1983, when Bob Filner (who now represents the neighboring 51st District) left the San Diego City School Board to run for the city council, Davis won the election to replace him. While still on the school board, she also helped start a local fellowship program for pre-teens and teenagers to learn about how business and government works and to gain leadership skills. She did not seek re-election to the school board in 1992 and became the fellowship program's first executive director.

Two years later she was back on the ballot, winning the first of three terms to the California Assembly. In addition to her work to regulate diet supplements, Davis focused her efforts in Sacramento on reducing class sizes, rewarding top teachers and improving patient access to medical care. She worked on the state law that allows women to directly access an obstetrician-gynecologist, rather than having to first obtain a referral. In the 107th Congress, she introduced similar legislation at the federal level.

A California term-limit law barred Davis from running again for the Assembly in 2000. Democrat Nancy Pelosi urged her to run for Congress instead. Pelosi invited Davis to shadow her for a day at the Capitol and provided fundraising contacts, giving Davis her own experience with mentoring.

The political vulnerability of the 49th District's GOP incumbent, Brian P. Bilbray — he had twice won with less than 50 percent of the vote — provided Davis with a window of opportunity, and she took full advantage of it in 2000, capturing a narrow, 3 percentage point victory.

Davis' vote in favor of the fast-track trade legislation cost her the support of the AFL-CIO, which had pumped almost a quarter of a million dollars into the 2000 campaign. But she benefited from the newly drawn district lines that transformed her previously marginal district into a safer Democratic seat. In 2002, she won her second term in the renumbered 53rd District with 62 percent over Republican Bill Van DeWeghe, a business lawyer.

KEY VOTES

2002

- Yes Overhaul campaign finance law; ban "soft money" and restrict advocacy advertising
- Yes Back Bush's defense budget increase
- No Extend 1996 welfare law
- No Adopt Bush's discretionary spending limit
- No Pass GOP Medicare prescription drug plan
- Yes Create independent Sept. 11 commission
- Yes Extend union protections to Homeland Security Department employees
- Yes Revive fast-track procedures for trade agreements
- No Authorize war against Iraq
- No Advance bankruptcy overhaul opposed by abortion opponents

2001

- No Nullify Clinton Labor Department ergonomics rule
- No Cut taxes by $1.35 trillion through fiscal 2011
- Yes Maintain ban on oil drilling in Arctic National Wildlife Refuge
- No Approve Bush proposal to limit managed-care plan liability for coverage decisions
- Yes Divert money from crop subsidy payments to land conservation
- Yes Expand law enforcement power to investigate suspected terrorists

CQ VOTE STUDIES

	PARTY UNITY		PRESIDENTIAL SUPPORT	
	Support	Oppose	Support	Oppose
2002	92%	8%	35%	65%
2001	89%	11%	40%	60%

INTEREST GROUPS

	AFL-CIO	ADA	CCUS	ACU
2002	89%	90%	50%	8%
2001	83%	90%	48%	12%

CALIFORNIA 53

Downtown San Diego; Imperial Beach

The coastal 53rd is the economic engine that drives surrounding districts. It includes San Diego's downtown, large employers, coastline and most of its military bases. Redistricting following the 2000 census scooped away wealthy and Republican-leaning communities such as La Jolla and Clairemont from the north end, making the district, previously numbered the 49th, much more Democratic.

The 53rd now includes Hispanic Democratic areas east of the city such as Lemon Grove as well as a big chunk of central San Diego. It still contains some Reagan Democrats but also includes blue-collar, central city areas like North Park, City Heights, Barrio Logan and Hillcrest, one of the area's most liberal and Democratic places and the center of the city's gay community. The result is a 29 percent Hispanic district that favored Democrat Al Gore over Republican George W. Bush by 56 percent to 36 percent in the 2000 presidential election.

Higher education in the district includes the University of California, San Diego on its northern tip, San Diego State University and the University of San Diego. Private companies have formed biomedical research partnerships with the schools. The 53rd's economy has benefited from a presence of biotech and telecommunications firms, but the downtown area and military presence have kept it diverse enough to avoid downturns.

MAJOR INDUSTRY

Telecommunications, defense, biotechnology

MILITARY BASES

Naval Station San Diego (shared with the 51st), 43,160 military, 5,400 civilian; Naval Air Station North Island/Naval Amphibious Base Coronado, 17,968 military, 9,211 civilian; Naval Base Point Loma, 3,500 military, 5,500 civilian (2000); Naval Medical Center San Diego, 3,071 military, 1,290 civilian; Marine Corps Recruit Depot San Diego, 1,725 military, 906 civilian (2002)

CITIES

San Diego (pt.), 542,356; Imperial Beach, 26,992; Lemon Grove, 24,918

NOTABLE

SeaWorld, the San Diego Zoo and Balboa Park, the city's cultural center, are major tourist attractions; Qualcomm Stadium, home to baseball's Padres and football's Chargers, hosted the 2003 Super Bowl.

COLORADO

Gov. Bill Owens (R)

First elected: 1998
Length of term: 4 years
Term expires: 1/07
Salary: $90,000
Phone: (303) 866-2471
Hometown: Denver
Born: Oct. 22, 1950; Fort Worth, Texas
Religion: Roman Catholic
Family: Wife, Frances Owens; three children
Education: Stephen F. Austin State U., B.S. 1973; U. of Texas, M.P.A. 1975
Career: Management consultant; petroleum association director
Political highlights: Colo. House, 1983-89; Colo. Senate, 1989-95; Colo. treasurer, 1995-99
Election results:

2002 GENERAL		
Bill Owens (R)	884,583	62.6%
Rollie Heath (D)	475,372	33.6%
Ron Forthofer (GREEN)	32,099	2.3%
Ralph Shnelvar (LIBERT)	20,547	1.5%

Lt. Gov. Jane E. Norton (R)

First elected: 2002
Length of term: 4 years
Term expires: 1/07
Salary: $77,184
Phone: (303) 866-2087

STATE LEGISLATURE

General Assembly: Meets 120 days, January-May
House: 65 members, 2-year terms
2003 breakdown: 37R, 28D; 41 men, 24 women
Salary: $30,000
Phone: (303) 866-2904
Senate: 35 members, 4-year terms
2003 breakdown: 18R, 17D; 27 men, 8 women
Salary: $30,000
Phone: (303) 866-2316

STATE TERM LIMITS

Governor: 2 terms
Senate: 2 consecutive terms
House: 4 consecutive terms

URBAN STATISTICS

CITY	POPULATION
Denver	554,636
Colorado Springs	360,890
Aurora	276,393
Lakewood	144,126
Fort Collins	118,652

REGISTERED VOTERS

Republican	37%
Unaffiliated	32%
Democrat	30%

POPULATION

2002 population (est.)	4,506,542
2000 population	4,301,261
1990 population	3,294,394
Percent change (1990-2000)	+30.6%
Rank among states (2002)	24
Median age	34.3
Born in state	41.1%
Foreign born	8.6%
Violent crime rate	334/100,000
Poverty level	9.3%
Federal workers	51,455
Military	42,802

REDISTRICTING

Colorado gained one House seat in reapportionment. The state legislature failed to agree on a plan and a state district court judge adopted a new, seven-district map on Jan. 25, 2002.

MISCELLANEOUS

Web: www.state.co.us
Capital: Denver
STATE ELECTION OFFICIAL
(303) 894-2680
DEMOCRATIC HEADQUARTERS
(303) 830-8989
REPUBLICAN HEADQUARTERS
(303) 758-3333

District Statistics

DIST.	2000 VOTE FOR PRESIDENT BUSH	GORE	NADER	WHITE	BLACK	ASIAN	HISP	MEDIAN INCOME	WHITE COLLAR	BLUE COLLAR	SERVICE INDUSTRY	OVER 64	UNDER 18	COLLEGE EDUCATION	RURAL	SQ. MILES
1	35%	65%	n/a	54%	10%	3%	30%	$39,658	64%	21%	15%	11%	22%	34%	0%	171
2	45	55	n/a	79	1	3	15	$55,204	66	21	13	7	25	39	13	5,615
3	58	42	n/a	75	1	0	21	$35,970	56	26	17	13	25	24	39	53,963
4	61	39	n/a	79	1	1	17	$43,389	60	26	14	10	26	29	25	30,898
5	67	33	n/a	77	6	2	11	$45,454	63	21	15	9	27	30	14	7,708
6	62	38	n/a	88	2	3	6	$73,393	77	13	9	7	29	47	15	4,104
7	49.5	50.5	n/a	69	6	3	20	$46,149	63	24	13	10	25	26	2	1,258
STATE	51	42	5	74	4	2	17	$47,203	65	22	14	10	26	33	16	103,718
U.S.	47.9	48.4	3	69	12	4	13	$41,994	60	25	15	12	26	24	21	3,537,438

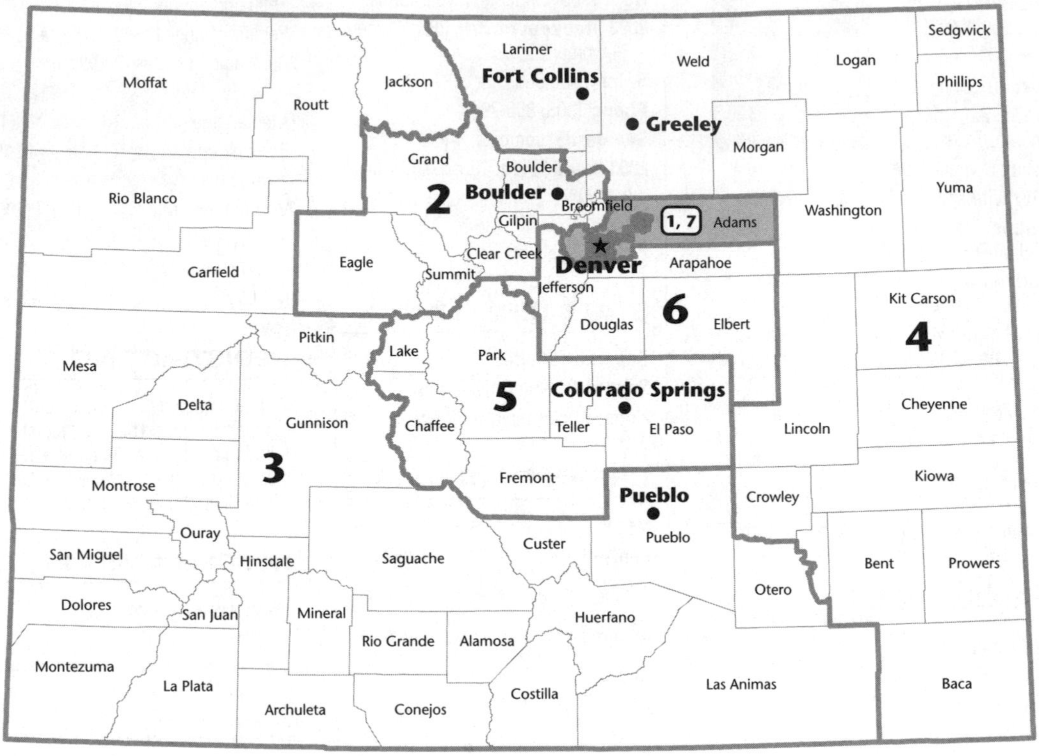

Moffat
Routt
Jackson
Larimer
Fort Collins
Weld
Logan
Sedgwick
Phillips
Greeley
Morgan
Grand
Boulder
2
Boulder
Broomfield
Gilpin
1, 7
Adams
Washington
Yuma
Rio Blanco
Garfield
Eagle
Summit
Clear Creek
Denver
Arapahoe
Jefferson
6
Douglas
Elbert
Kit Carson
4
Mesa
Pitkin
Lake
Park
Delta
5
Colorado Springs
Gunnison
Chaffee
Teller
El Paso
Lincoln
Cheyenne
3
Montrose
Fremont
Pueblo
Pueblo
Crowley
Kiowa
Ouray
San Miguel
Hinsdale
Saguache
Custer
Bent
Prowers
Dolores
San Juan
Mineral
Otero
Huerfano
Rio Grande
Alamosa
Montezuma
La Plata
Costilla
Las Animas
Baca
Archuleta
Conejos

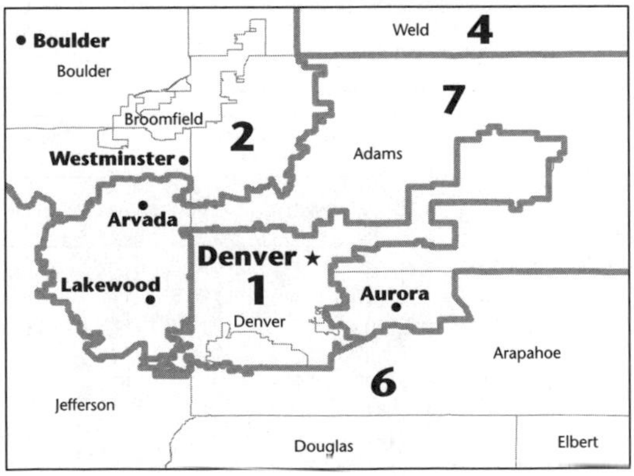

Boulder
Boulder
Weld
4
Broomfield
2
7
Westminster
Adams
Arvada
Denver
1
Lakewood
Aurora
Denver
Arapahoe
6
Jefferson
Douglas
Elbert

Sen. Ben Nighthorse Campbell (R)

CAPITOL OFFICE
224-5852
campbell.senate.gov
380 Russell 20510-0605; fax 224-1933

COMMITTEES
Appropriations
(Legislative - chairman)
Energy & Natural Resources
Indian Affairs - chairman
Veterans' Affairs

HOMETOWN
Ignacio

BORN
April 13, 1933, Auburn, Calif.

RELIGION
Unspecified

FAMILY
Wife, Linda Campbell; two children

EDUCATION
San Jose State U., B.A. 1957 (physical education & fine arts); Meiji U. (Tokyo, Japan), attended 1960-64 (Japanese culture)

MILITARY SERVICE
Air Force, 1951-53

CAREER
Jewelry designer; rancher; horse trainer; police officer; teacher

POLITICAL HIGHLIGHTS
Colo. House, 1983-87 (served as a Democrat); U.S. House, 1987-93 (served as a Democrat)

ELECTION RESULTS

1998 GENERAL		
Ben Nighthorse Campbell (R)	829,370	62.5%
Dottie Lamm (D)	464,754	35.0%
David S. Segal (LIBERT)	14,024	1.1%
1998 PRIMARY		
Ben Nighthorse Campbell (R)	154,702	70.6%
William Eggert (R)	64,347	29.4%

PREVIOUS WINNING PERCENTAGES
1992 (52%); 1990 House Election (70%); 1988 House Election (78%); 1986 House Election (52%)
*Elected as a Democrat 1986-92

Elected 1992; 2nd term

Unlike the legions of lawmakers who carefully plotted their entries into political life, Campbell came to public service entirely by accident.

When bad weather forced him to abandon a 1983 jewelry-selling trip to the West Coast in his single-engine airplane, Campbell instead attended a meeting of Colorado Democrats who happened to be looking for a state House seat candidate. He agreed to be drafted, won that election and — in just 10 years — climbed the legislative ladder from the statehouse to the House of Representatives and on to the Senate.

Campbell has a reputation as an iconoclast who shuns many of the conventions of the Senate while focusing on American Indian and environmental issues. He presents himself as overtly irascible and does not hide his mixed feelings about his life in Congress. "These are not easy jobs," he has said. "Anybody who thinks you're going to have a normal life is naive. The return for me is to be able to get things done."

His ponytail, jeans and cowboy boots make him instantly recognizable on the Senate floor and earned him a spot on Washingtonian magazine's "fashion victim" list for the 107th Congress.

"I don't see why, just 'cause you get elected, you have to drop your whole lifestyle and suddenly buy into this Potomac look," Campbell, who designs and makes his own Southwestern jewelry, told The Denver Post in 2000. "To heck with it." Campbell says that he favors bolo ties, rather than the traditional four-in-hand, because of a windpipe injury sustained while training for captain of the 1964 U.S. Olympic judo team.

Campbell's politics have drifted to the right since his switch from the Democratic to the Republican Party in 1995, halfway through his initial Senate term, and he backs such conservative causes as cutting taxes and regulations and barring desecration of the American flag. Campbell publicly opposed a 2002 federal appellate court decision that found that requiring schoolchildren to recite the pledge of allegiance was unconstitutional because it includes the phrase "one nation, under God."

Although other Republican senators eagerly queued up to watch the inauguration of President Bush in 2001, Campbell gave up a prime seat in the viewing stand so that he could ride in the inaugural parade down Pennsylvania Avenue on a motorcycle featuring a Stars and Stripes design. Eight years earlier, Campbell donned a Cheyenne headdress and rode a horse in President Clinton's 1993 inaugural parade.

But he is hardly in lock step with Senate conservatives. Instead, Campbell, who is a Northern Cheyenne tribal chief, tends to look out for the interests of his home state as well as for American Indians. "I kind of inherited a national constituency when I got elected," he said. "I try to be a conduit for them." With the GOP takeover of the Senate in the 108th Congress, Campbell chairs the Indian Affairs Committee.

In the 106th, Campbell won enactment of legislation creating a national historic site at Sand Creek in Colorado, where more than 150 Cheyennes and Arapahos were massacred in 1864. He also has worked to improve medical care for Indians, establish an office within the Department of Agriculture to help Indians market products overseas, and streamline the system under which Indians bequeath land to their heirs. He also sponsored a law enacted in the 107th that expanded the statute of limitations for fraud claims related to tribal trust fund management.

Campbell has clashed with environmentalists more often than not, opposing Clinton's plans during the 106th to restrict development on federal lands and assailing a bipartisan proposal to spend billions of dollars to preserve open space, saying it "reeks of socialism." His conservative views and support for private property rights helped make him a leading candidate to be Bush's initial Interior secretary, but the job ultimately went to another Coloradan, Gale A. Norton.

On the Appropriations Committee, Campbell has snagged tens of millions of dollars in federal funding for Colorado programs ranging from antidrug initiatives to military base projects to national parks.

The Coloradan is not shy about reminding his colleagues of his heritage when fighting for a share of the federal pie. In 1997, he defended a $6 million appropriation for the controversial Animas-La Plata water project in Southwestern Colorado, despite opposition from fiscal conservatives worried about wasting money and environmentalists concerned about ecological damage. The project was backed by the Ute Indians, who saw it as the fulfillment of a century-old government promise to ensure water supplies to the Southern Ute Reservation.

"We do not intentionally kill Indians with bullets or disease anymore," he said on the floor. "But it seems clear that some of our brothers want to kill their livelihood, kill their opportunity, kill their future, kill their culture and kill the natural resources that we promised them in every one of the 472 treaties that we then broke as an arm of the U.S. government."

But true to his general doubts about government, Campbell wants to encourage Indians to gradually wean themselves of their reliance on Washington. For that to happen, Campbell says, "we've got to make sure that the federal government works with them, not against them."

Campbell had a moment in the national limelight when he announced his decision to join the GOP in March 1995, shortly after Republicans took over Congress. His statement came the day after he voted for a balanced-budget constitutional amendment that failed to win Senate passage; he decided he no longer was comfortable calling himself a Democrat.

The switch infuriated Democrats. But on announcing his new party affiliation, Campbell underscored that he would continue on an independent course. "I have always been considered a moderate, much to the consternation of the Democratic Party," Campbell said. "My moderacy will now be to the consternation of the right wing of the Republican Party."

Raised by an alcoholic father and a mother with tuberculosis, Campbell was a high school dropout and a gang member before turning his life around. He served in the Air Force and worked his way through college driving a truck before finding success as an Olympian. Campbell has also been a teacher, a prison counselor and a policeman. In 1986, he prevailed over Republican incumbent Mike Strang to win a House seat covering the western half of the state, and he won easy re-election twice before making his move for the Senate.

He won by 9 points in 1992 over GOP businessman and former state Sen. Terry Considine, even though Campbell had to correct a statement in his campaign literature that said he had been trapped behind enemy lines in Korea for five weeks. He acknowledged that such an incident never happened while he served in Korea with the Air Force police. In 1998, he cruised to victory by a 27-point margin over Democrat Dottie Lamm.

Publicly ambivalent about staying in the Senate, Campbell said he was delaying until 2003 a decision on whether to run for a third term. Stock market losses in 2001 drained tens of thousands of dollars out of his campaign fund. But he signaled his intentions when he bought a 50-foot tractor trailer, dubbed "Nighthorse One," and outfitted it as a "rolling campaign headquarters." Democrats viewed Campbell as one of their top targets for 2004.

KEY VOTES

2002

No Pass farm bill reversing crop subsidy limits
Yes Postpone tougher automobile fuel efficiency standards
No Overhaul campaign finance law; ban "soft money" and restrict advocacy advertising
Yes Set federal election standards
Yes Support oil drilling in Arctic National Wildlife Refuge
No Revive fast-track procedures for trade agreements
No Create federal insurance coverage for catastrophic terrorist losses
Yes Tighten federal accounting and corporate governance regulation
No Advance bipartisan Medicare prescription drug plan
Yes Create independent Sept. 11 commission
No Back Democratic Homeland Security Department proposal
Yes Authorize war against Iraq

2001

Yes Confirm John Ashcroft as attorney general
Yes Nullify Clinton Labor Department ergonomics rule
Yes Cut taxes by $1.35 trillion through fiscal 2011
? Pass Democratic bill to bolster rights of patients in managed-care plans
No Permit a new round of military base closings
Yes Expand law enforcement power to investigate suspected terrorists

CQ VOTE STUDIES

	PARTY UNITY		PRESIDENTIAL SUPPORT	
	Support	Oppose	Support	Oppose
2002	82%	18%	91%	9%
2001	89%	11%	96%	4%
2000	97%	3%	50%	50%
1999	88%	12%	32%	68%
1998	82%	18%	47%	53%
1997	83%	17%	66%	34%
1996	82%	18%	48%	52%
1995	80%	20%	38%	62%
1994	78%	22%	83%	17%
1993	80%	20%	83%	17%

INTEREST GROUPS

	AFL-CIO	ADA	CCUS	ACU
2002	38%	30%	85%	88%
2001	40%	15%	85%	92%
2000	14%	5%	84%	96%
1999	22%	15%	94%	88%
1998	38%	25%	83%	76%
1997	29%	25%	60%	72%
1996	80%	45%	82%	78%
1995	22%	30%	94%	59%
1994	88%	55%	50%	25%
1993	80%	75%	18%	12%

Sen. Wayne Allard (R)

Elected 1996; 2nd term

CAPITOL OFFICE
224-5941
allard.senate.gov
525 Dirksen 20510-0606; fax 224-6471

COMMITTEES
Armed Services
(Strategic Forces - chariman)
Banking, Housing & Urban Affairs
(Housing & Transportation - chairman)
Budget
Environment & Public Works

HOMETOWN
Loveland

BORN
Dec. 2, 1943, Fort Collins, Colo.

RELIGION
Protestant

FAMILY
Wife, Joan Allard; two children

EDUCATION
Colorado State U., D.V.M. 1968

CAREER
Veterinarian

POLITICAL HIGHLIGHTS
Colo. Senate, 1983-91; U.S. House, 1991-97

ELECTION RESULTS

2002 GENERAL		
Wayne Allard (R)	717,892	50.7%
Tom Strickland (D)	648,129	45.8%
Douglas Campbell (AC)	21,547	1.5%
Rick Stanley (LIBERT)	20,776	1.5%
2002 PRIMARY		
Wayne Allard (R)		unopposed

PREVIOUS WINNING PERCENTAGES
1996 (51%); 1994 House Election (72%); 1992 House Election (58%); 1990 House Election (54%)

Allard is a product of the new century politics of Colorado and much of the modern West. He is a states' rights-loving conservative with an innate skepticism of the federal government. But he sometimes is confoundingly pro-environment, to the distraction of his liberal critics who derisively describe him as "environmental lite." All in all, he appeals to the emerging class of independent-minded, conservative voter that increasingly dominates the state's politics.

A fifth-generation Coloradan raised on a ranch in one of the state's most isolated areas, Allard (AL-ard) is an amiable man with a plodding speaking style whose resolve often is underestimated by his political foes. He was labeled one of the most vulnerable Senate freshmen seeking re-election in 2002, but he surprised the pundits when he beat former U.S. attorney Tom Strickland by 5 percentage points.

Allard's anti-tax and anti-regulatory positions are among the most politically conservative in the Senate. It defies conventional wisdom then that the most eye-catching photograph in his Senate office depicts him holding a wounded eagle at a Colorado wildlife refuge established by legislation he helped write. Allard reflects the preferences of a state that has grown increasingly conservative with the influx of high-tech entrepreneurs and suburbanites in the 1990s, but that has retained a soft spot for the federal government when it comes to preserving the natural splendor of Colorado.

Still, he remains an enemy of national environmental groups, who don't like his anti-regulatory stands on clean water mandates and endangered species. In the 108th Congress, Allard's appointment to the Environment and Public Works Committee — he dropped Agriculture — displeased some environmental groups, including the League of Conservation Voters, which had labeled Allard one of its "dirty dozen" and supported Strickland in the 2002 election.

Allard says he tries to strike a balance between economic development and protection of the environment. "You have to be sensitive to the environment but also protect private property rights and Colorado's water rights as well," he says. "That's where I get crosswise with the environmental groups in Washington."

He is most proud of his legislative handiwork establishing the Great Sand Dunes National Park and converting the radioactivity-tainted Rocky Flats, a former nuclear weapons facility outside Denver, to a national wildlife refuge.

As the chairman of the Senate Renewable Energy and Energy Efficiency Caucus, he sponsored a bill in 2001 creating a 15 percent tax break for solar heating and electrical systems in homes. In 2000, he supported a permanent ban on commercial flights over Rocky Mountain National Park.

Allard likes to say he is party-blind when it comes to working with Colorado Democrats for the state's interests. But there is a limit to the warm feelings between him and the state's Democrats. When Allard ran television ads in the campaign featuring a picture of Democratic Rep. Mark Udall, who had worked with Allard on the Rocky Flats bill, Udall demanded the senator stop airing his image. Allard refused.

Allard is well-positioned to push his agenda of smaller government and a strong military. A member of the Budget Committee, he supported President Bush's massive tax cut in 2001. Before that, he pressed for eliminating the national debt over two decades by using large amounts of the budget surplus. His bill was soundly defeated in the Senate in the 106th Congress and became moot when the surplus dried up in the 107th.

Allard chairs the Armed Services' Strategic Forces Subcommittee, where he is a key congressional promoter of a missile defense system that would repel missiles launched against the United States. In the 107th Congress, he helped forge a compromise after Democrats objected to a Bush administration proposal to loosen Pentagon and congressional oversight of technologically dicey elements of the program. He is unswayed by critics who have long contended the system is technically infeasible.

"If you can make offensive weapons obsolete with effective defense systems, you eliminate the arms race," he says. "We have to push the limits, and that means we're going to have a few failures."

Allard also chairs the Banking Subcommittee on Housing and Transportation. In 2000, he floated a plan to transfer most federal funds for housing and homeless programs to the states, and to place more congressional controls on the Department of Housing and Urban Development.

In his three terms in the House, Allard also compiled a solidly conservative record. He advocated eliminating the Education, Energy and Commerce departments and supported a constitutional amendment banning abortion. In the mid-1990s, Allard tried unsuccessfully to eliminate funding for the National Biological Survey, a field census of threatened species, because he feared that the survey would expand the scope of the Endangered Species Act.

The lawmaker subscribes to the concept of the citizen-politician. He grew up on his family's ranch, rising at dawn and working until sunset baling hay. His great-great-grandfather, a trapper and explorer, was among the first permanent settlers of northern Colorado.

Allard wanted to be a veterinarian since grade school. So after getting his degree in veterinary medicine from Colorado State University, he and his wife, Joan, a microbiologist, opened their own small-animal practice in Loveland, northwest of Denver.

Allard's first government job was as Loveland's part-time health officer. Later, he divided his time between the Colorado Senate and his veterinary practice for eight years. In 1990, Republican Hank Brown, then the 4th District representative, decided to run for the Senate, and Allard successfully sought Brown's seat.

Brown gave Allard another opening by retiring from the Senate after just one term. The 1996 GOP primary became a showdown between Allard and state Attorney General Gale A. Norton. Norton had better statewide name recognition, but Allard had better fundraising.

Both touted their conservative views. Norton hoped to attract moderates with her support for abortion rights. Allard portrayed himself as a down-to-earth, common-sense lawmaker who kept his political career in perspective, maintaining his veterinary license even though he had sold the practice in the early 1990s. Allard easily won the primary. (Norton went on to become secretary of the interior in 2001.)

Allard created a stir in the 1996 general election when, during a televised debate with Democratic nominee Strickland, he responded affirmatively to a hypothetical question about whether he would support public hanging to deter crime. Allard drew vigorous opposition from environmentalists but won strong support from conservative Christian groups, and he went on to win by 5 percentage points.

In a 2002 rematch, Strickland tried to make the environment an issue again. Allard fought back with a campaign that summed up the election as a choice between a "lawyer lobbyist or a veterinarian who loves animals."

KEY VOTES

2002

No Pass farm bill reversing crop subsidy limits
Yes Postpone tougher automobile fuel efficiency standards
No Overhaul campaign finance law; ban "soft money" and restrict advocacy advertising
Yes Set federal election standards
Yes Support oil drilling in Arctic National Wildlife Refuge
Yes Revive fast-track procedures for trade agreements
Yes Create federal insurance coverage for catastrophic terrorist losses
Yes Tighten federal accounting and corporate governance regulation
No Advance bipartisan Medicare prescription drug plan
Yes Create independent Sept. 11 commission
No Back Democratic Homeland Security Department proposal
Yes Authorize war against Iraq

2001

Yes Confirm John Ashcroft as attorney general
Yes Nullify Clinton Labor Department ergonomics rule
Yes Cut taxes by $1.35 trillion through fiscal 2011
No Pass Democratic bill to bolster rights of patients in managed-care plans
Yes Permit a new round of military base closings
Yes Expand law enforcement power to investigate suspected terrorists

CQ VOTE STUDIES

	PARTY UNITY		PRESIDENTIAL SUPPORT	
	Support	Oppose	Support	Oppose
2002	91%	9%	96%	4%
2001	98%	2%	97%	3%
2000	98%	2%	35%	65%
1999	97%	3%	23%	77%
1998	97%	3%	28%	72%
1997	98%	2%	48%	52%
House Service:				
1996	94%	6%	36%	64%
1995	95%	5%	20%	80%
1994	97%	3%	40%	60%
1993	93%	7%	20%	80%

INTEREST GROUPS

	AFL-CIO	ADA	CCUS	ACU
2002	17%	5%	100%	100%
2001	6%	5%	100%	100%
2000	0%	0%	93%	100%
1999	0%	0%	100%	95%
1998	0%	5%	83%	100%
1997	0%	0%	80%	100%
House Service:				
1996	9%	10%	100%	100%
1995	0%	0%	96%	88%
1994	0%	5%	83%	95%
1993	0%	15%	91%	96%

Rep. Diana DeGette (D)

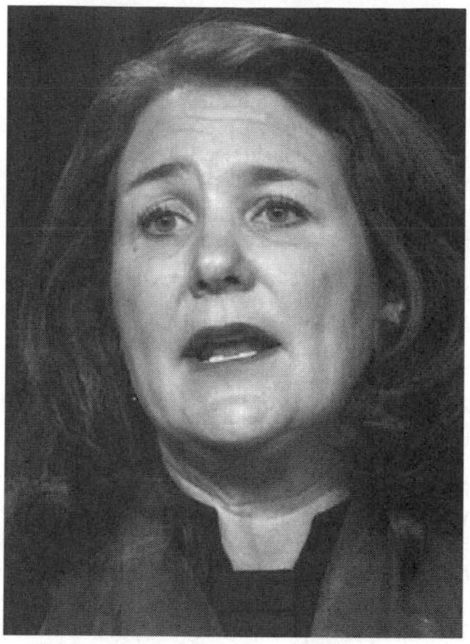

CAPITOL OFFICE
225-4431
degette@mail.house.gov
www.house.gov/degette
1530 Longworth 20515-0601; fax 225-5657

COMMITTEES
Energy & Commerce

HOMETOWN
Denver

BORN
July 29, 1957, Tachikawa, Japan

RELIGION
Presbyterian

FAMILY
Husband, Lino Lipinsky; two children

EDUCATION
Colorado College, B.A. 1979 (political science); New York U., J.D. 1982

CAREER
Lawyer; state public defender

POLITICAL HIGHLIGHTS
Colo. House, 1993-96

ELECTION RESULTS

2002 GENERAL		
Diana DeGette (D)	111,718	66.3%
Ken Chlouber (R)	49,884	29.6%
Ken Seaman (GREEN)	3,209	1.9%
Kent Leonard (LIBERT)	2,584	1.5%
2002 PRIMARY		
Diana DeGette (D)	24,526	73.5%
Ramona Martinez (D)	8,853	26.5%
2000 GENERAL		
Diana DeGette (D)	141,831	68.7%
Jesse L. Thomas (R)	56,291	27.3%
Richard Combs (LIBERT)	5,852	2.8%
Lyle L. Nasser (REF)	2,452	1.2%

PREVIOUS WINNING PERCENTAGES
1998 (67%); 1996 (57%)

Elected 1996; 4th term

With a temperament alternating between affable and fiery, DeGette has shown a deft legislative touch while at the same time proving herself a dependable liberal ally of her party's leadership. In the 108th Congress, she was rewarded with a Democratic leadership post of her own — the newly created position of floor whip, where she will be Whip Steny H. Hoyer's lieutenant in helping corral House Democrats' votes and keeping the legion of other deputy whips on task.

As a member of the Energy and Commerce Committee, in the 107th Congress DeGette (duh-GET) was particularly fierce on corporate responsibility issues as the panel launched its investigations of business scandals, beginning with the bankruptcy of the energy behemoth Enron Corp. She found herself facing one of the 1st District's biggest employers — the regional telephone giant Qwest Communications International Inc. — under the bright lights of the panel in 2001.

Some lawmakers would have tried to defend the hometown company; Degette used Qwest as a punching bag for exercising her pro-consumer views. "In the waning days of the go-go Internet boom, a group of cowboys by the name of Qwest came riding into town and they acquired U S West.," she said. "Their bad business decisions have had a significant impact on our local economy, the local workforce and the community as a whole."

DeGette made an auspicious arrival on Capitol Hill in 1997 with her appointment to what is now called Energy and Commerce; she was the only freshman Democrat named to an exclusive House panel in the 105th Congress. Using that assignment — and her status as the successor to Patricia Schroeder, a legendarily tart-tongued and peripatetic lawmaker — Degette soon made her presence felt on a broad array of topics: the budget, public housing, abortion rights, gun control, health care and tobacco regulation. (The tobacco industry is a frequent target of DeGette's. Her mother, who started smoking at age 16, died of lung cancer 38 years later.)

In the 108th, DeGette's subcommittee assignments are a shorthand for the continued breadth of her interests: Health; Environment and Hazardous Materials; Commerce, Trade and Consumer Protection.

DeGette bitterly opposed legislation in the 107th that would limit medical malpractice damages and plaintiff attorneys' fees, a proposal that the GOP was putting near the top of its priorities again in the 108th.

DeGette has devoted much of her attention to children's needs, determining that few other lawmakers were focusing on those issues or could bring to the task her personal perspective as a parent of two young daughters. One of them has diabetes, and in the 107th DeGette won enactment of a law to require that medical devices that would be used on children be reviewed by pediatric experts before they are put on the market. She has also pushed to give children priority on organ transplant lists.

She laments what she views as a double standard for assessing women politicians. No one asks a male politician with young children how he copes with the dual roles of career and parenting, DeGette observes.

Her advocacy on behalf of children is one reason for her long-time support of gun control, which intensified after 15 people died in the 1999 rampage at Columbine High School, just outside her district. In the 107th she fought legislation that moved through Energy and Commerce to shield gun manufacturers from lawsuits. In the 106th her language to ban the import of large-capacity ammunition clips was part of a gun control bill that passed the House but died in negotiations with the Senate.

DeGette offers an amendment annually to lift a ban on federal funding for abortions for women in federal prisons. She also is a vocal critic of the drive to ban the late-term procedure described by its critics as "partial birth" abortion. "To assume that any woman would choose this tragic procedure after carrying a healthy fetus for 8 or 9 months is offensive to the women who are facing this gruesome decision," she has said. "And it is offensive to all women."

In 2002, she won enactment of a law making the Violence Against Women Office independent within the Justice Department.

Although she posts a reliably liberal and partisan voting record — she stood with the Democrats on 97 percent of party unity votes in the 107th, and she backed President Bush less than one-quarter of the time — she insists she is ready to seek out bipartisan cooperation as circumstances warrant.

Her most notable departure from party orthodoxy may have come in 2000: She was among a small cluster of elected Democrats in the nation who endorsed former Sen. Bill Bradley for president instead of Al Gore.

DeGette's father was serving in the Air Force and stationed in Japan when she was born, but most of her childhood was spent in the Denver area. When her parents divorced, DeGette, the eldest of five children, took some after-school jobs to help pay the bills. She recalls being profoundly affected, at age 10, by the news coverage of the assassination of the Rev. Dr. Martin Luther King Jr., which broadened her horizons and instilled in her an interest in the civil rights movement.

After earning her law degree at New York University, she was a public defender in Denver before going into private law practice, where she specialized in cases of discrimination based on disability, sex and age.

She was active in local party politics and won a seat in the Colorado House in 1992. As a freshman, DeGette won enactment of a law — upheld by the Supreme Court in 2000 — requiring protesters to stay 8 feet away from anyone within 100 feet of the entrance to a clinic where abortions are performed. She made it to the party leadership but early in 1996 resigned from the legislature to concentrate on her bid to succeed Schroeder.

DeGette won a highly publicized battle with Joe Rogers, a lawyer and former aide to Colorado GOP Sen. Hank Brown. Rogers, who is black, got the endorsement of a group of black ministers, but DeGette was backed by Denver Mayor Wellington Webb, a black Democrat. Spending twice as much as her opponent, she won by 17 percentage points. She has won her subsequent three races with two-thirds of the vote.

KEY VOTES

2002

- Yes Overhaul campaign finance law; ban "soft money" and restrict advocacy advertising
- No Back Bush's defense budget increase
- No Extend 1996 welfare law
- No Adopt Bush's discretionary spending limit
- No Pass GOP Medicare prescription drug plan
- Yes Create independent Sept. 11 commission
- Yes Extend union protections to Homeland Security Department employees
- No Revive fast-track procedures for trade agreements
- No Authorize war against Iraq
- No Advance bankruptcy overhaul opposed by abortion opponents

2001

- No Nullify Clinton Labor Department ergonomics rule
- No Cut taxes by $1.35 trillion through fiscal 2011
- Yes Maintain ban on oil drilling in Arctic National Wildlife Refuge
- No Approve Bush proposal to limit managed-care plan liability for coverage decisions
- Yes Divert money from crop subsidy payments to land conservation
- No Expand law enforcement power to investigate suspected terrorists

CQ VOTE STUDIES

	PARTY UNITY		PRESIDENTIAL SUPPORT	
	Support	Oppose	Support	Oppose
2002	98%	2%	25%	75%
2001	96%	4%	23%	77%
2000	93%	7%	88%	12%
1999	95%	5%	84%	16%
1998	97%	3%	86%	14%

INTEREST GROUPS

	AFL-CIO	ADA	CCUS	ACU
2002	100%	95%	35%	0%
2001	100%	95%	39%	0%
2000	90%	75%	47%	8%
1999	78%	100%	24%	0%
1998	100%	95%	22%	4%

COLORADO 1
Denver

Mostly within the capital city of Denver, the 1st is a bastion of liberalism in a conservative-leaning state. A Republican last won Denver's House seat in 1970, and Ronald Reagan, in 1980, was the last Republican to carry Denver for president.

Denver's diversity — the fast-growing Hispanic community makes up nearly a third of the city's population while blacks make up more than a tenth — is reflected by residents' electoral decisions. Mayor Wellington Webb, an African-American elected in 1991, succeeded Federico Peña, a Hispanic who later served in President Clinton's Cabinet. City officials are using the $5 billion Denver International Airport, which opened in 1995 and has become one of the nation's 10 busiest, to increase exports and lure European and Asian companies to locate or expand their business here.

Dependent on the region's oil and gas industries, Denver suffered during the oil bust of the 1980s, but the city boomed in the 1990s. The economy became more diversified as technology and telecommunications industries revitalized downtown and surrounding areas. The former Lowry Air Force Base is now an education center; the former Fitzsimons Army Medical Center is home to the University of Colorado medical school and a bioscience research park.

Area sports fans have had a lot to cheer about in recent years, as football's Broncos won two Super Bowls and hockey's Colorado Avalanche won two Stanley Cups. New baseball (1995) and football (2001) stadiums, as well as a new arena (1999), opened in the city.

Ninety percent of the 1st District's residents live in Denver. The rest live just south of the city, in well-off communities such as Englewood and Cherry Hills Village.

MAJOR INDUSTRY

Telecommunications, computers, health care, government

CITIES

Denver, 554,636; Englewood, 31,727

NOTABLE

The Great American Beer Festival is the nation's largest and oldest annual brewing competition; U.S. Mint coin production facility.

Rep. Mark Udall (D)

CAPITOL OFFICE
225-2161
www.house.gov/markudall
115 Cannon 20515-0602; fax 226-7840

COMMITTEES
Agriculture
Resources
Science

HOMETOWN
Boulder

BORN
July 18, 1950, Tucson, Ariz.

RELIGION
Unspecified

FAMILY
Wife, Maggie Fox; two children

EDUCATION
Williams College, B.A. 1972 (American civilization)

CAREER
Colo. Outward Bound School executive director

POLITICAL HIGHLIGHTS
Colo. House, 1997-99

ELECTION RESULTS

2002 GENERAL		
Mark Udall (D)	123,504	60.1%
Sandy Hume (R)	75,564	36.8%
Norm Olsen (LIBERT)	3,579	1.7%
2002 PRIMARY		
Mark Udall (D)		unopposed
2000 GENERAL		
Mark Udall (D)	155,725	55.0%
Carolyn Cox (R)	109,338	38.6%
Ron Forthofer (GREEN)	12,398	4.4%
David Baker (LIBERT)	5,655	2.0%

PREVIOUS WINNING PERCENTAGES
1998 (50%)

Elected 1998; 3rd term

An accomplished mountaineer who has climbed within a few thousand feet of Mount Everest's summit, Udall epitomizes the outdoorsy, can-do, granola-munching spirit of Boulder, his hometown and the political heart of the 2nd District. But he also has deep and emotional ties to Congress. He was 10 when his father, the legendarily witty and energetic liberal Morris K. Udall, first won election to the House from Arizona in 1961.

In his own congressional office four decades later, Udall keeps a pair of his father's size 15, white high-top sneakers, a joking reminder that he has big congressional shoes to fill.

Udall and his New Mexico cousin Tom — whose father, Stewart, represented Arizona in the late 1950s — achieved a rare double feat by winning a pair of House seats in 1998 and resurrecting a congressional dynasty. Mark Udall pledged to follow his father's example as a staunch environmentalist and Democratic loyalist — a vow that became more poignant when the elder Udall died a month after his son's election, following a battle with Parkinson's disease that had compelled his resignation from Congress in 1991.

In addressing issues such as urban sprawl and prescription drug pricing, Mark Udall also has built a following among the independents clustered in the suburbs northwest of Denver. Courting the political center will be more important for Udall in this decade. Redistricting has added three Republican-leaning mountain counties to the 2nd. And Udall has signaled that he has aspirations to be a senator and might run as soon as 2004 for the seat Republican Ben Nighthorse Campbell has held since 1993. Udall briefly considered mounting a challenge in 2002 to Colorado's other Republican senator, Wayne Allard.

Udall plays up his experience as a mountain climber and former executive director of the Colorado Outward Bound School, saying people have to take risks and believe in causes to be true leaders. When wildfires scorched large sections of Colorado in 2002, Udall was skeptical of a Bush administration plan to ease some environmental regulations to allow more cutting of small trees and underbrush that can help fuel blazes. He said he feared such rollbacks ultimately would open the door to larger and less environmentally sensitive logging.

Udall also voted against the 2002 law authorizing President Bush to go to war against Iraq, saying that he feared a large-scale conflict could result in hundreds or thousands of U.S. casualties.

On domestic policy, Udall has stuck close to the Democratic line; in the 107th Congress he sided with his party 94 percent of the time. But he has shown an independent streak on foreign policy: He broke with Democrats, for example, to support a bill that would have required President Clinton to seek congressional approval before ordering ground troops into Kosovo.

Despite his outspokenness and liberal-leaning record, the tall, telegenic lawmaker is popular with colleagues from both parties and regarded as thoughtful, principled and deliberative. He frequently works with Allard and Colorado Republicans in the House on conservation measures, such as a 2002 law that designated more than 30,000 acres in the James Peak area as wilderness or protected areas, restricting development. He also teamed with Republican Rep. Tom Tancredo to seek highway funds for improvements to the Boulder Turnpike. Udall regularly has breakfast with Republican Sen. John McCain, who as a freshman House member from Arizona two decades ago recalls regularly receiving sage advice from Udall's father.

In the 108th Congress, drawing on his reputation as one of the fittest members of Congress, Udall joined with Republican House colleague Zach Wamp of Tennessee to form the Congressional Fitness Caucus as a forum to encourage lawmakers to get more exercise.

No issue strikes such a chord with Udall as the environment. His father and his uncle Stewart — who was Interior secretary in the Kennedy and Johnson administrations — were instrumental in writing land preservation policy in the West; his wife, Maggie Fox, is a lawyer with the Sierra Club in Colorado. From his seat on the Resources Committee, Udall can see a portrait of his father, who chaired the panel from 1977 to 1991.

During his two years in the Republican-controlled state House, which preceded his election to Congress, Udall wrote an anti-poaching bill that increased fines for bagging trophy-size wildlife — and then won over reluctant GOP lawmakers, who had viewed the measure as anti-hunting.

On the Science Committee, Udall has expressed frustration at what he views as the Bush administration's unwillingness to detail its climate-change policy. He and his cousin have promoted legislation to create a program to encourage volunteers to help federal agencies preserve parks, forests and other sensitive tracts. Udall also has a plan to keep undeveloped a 6,000-acre buffer zone around the contaminated and decommissioned Rocky Flats nuclear weapons plant in his district. In the 107th Congress, he took the lead in legislation to make information gathered from satellites available to local communities for land-use and environmental planning.

Udall has been a vocal advocate of gun control, particularly in the wake of the 1999 massacre at Columbine High School in a neighboring congressional district. On the first anniversary of the shootings, he declined an invitation from Clinton to fly on Air Force One to Denver for a gun control rally, saying it was more important to him to cast a symbolic vote in the House in favor of jumpstarting negotiations on a gun control bill.

Udall can be an aggressive campaigner. In his first House race — for the seat Democrat David E. Skaggs relinquished after a dozen years — Udall hammered hard when his GOP opponent, former Boulder Mayor Bob Greenlee, questioned the scientific validity of global warming. Udall also spent hours campaigning door-to-door in an effort, he said, to prove he was a "legitimate Coloradan" and not just trying to capitalize on a famous name. In one of the more expensive House races that year, Udall prevailed by just 5,500 votes, less than 3 percent. His margin of victory grew to 16 percentage points in 2000 and 23 points in 2002.

KEY VOTES

2002

Yes Overhaul campaign finance law; ban "soft money" and restrict advocacy advertising
No Back Bush's defense budget increase
No Extend 1996 welfare law
No Adopt Bush's discretionary spending limit
No Pass GOP Medicare prescription drug plan
Yes Create independent Sept. 11 commission
Yes Extend union protections to Homeland Security Department employees
No Revive fast-track procedures for trade agreements
No Authorize war against Iraq
No Advance bankruptcy overhaul opposed by abortion opponents

2001

No Nullify Clinton Labor Department ergonomics rule
No Cut taxes by $1.35 trillion through fiscal 2011
Yes Maintain ban on oil drilling in Arctic National Wildlife Refuge
No Approve Bush proposal to limit managed-care plan liability for coverage decisions
Yes Divert money from crop subsidy payments to land conservation
No Expand law enforcement power to investigate suspected terrorists

CQ VOTE STUDIES

	PARTY UNITY		PRESIDENTIAL SUPPORT	
	Support	Oppose	Support	Oppose
2002	93%	7%	33%	67%
2001	96%	4%	30%	70%
2000	93%	7%	77%	23%
1999	93%	7%	80%	20%

INTEREST GROUPS

	AFL-CIO	ADA	CCUS	ACU
2002	89%	95%	40%	4%
2001	100%	100%	35%	0%
2000	90%	85%	47%	12%
1999	100%	100%	28%	4%

COLORADO 2
Northwest Denver suburbs; Boulder

The liberal "granola" culture of Boulder — home to the University of Colorado and a committed corps of environmentalists — permeates much of the 2nd. But the district is mostly moderate in its political tone, exhibiting a slight but hardly overwhelming Democratic lean.

After a decade of strong growth, redistricting following the 2000 census redrew the 2nd to include more of Adams County, which is adjacent to Denver and has a blue-collar tone, and less of Boulder County, which had been entirely within the district. The 2nd also shed most of its share of fast-growing suburban Jefferson County.

Although they contain only a fraction of the 2nd's voters, Eagle, Grand and Summit counties, which were added during redistricting, form an overwhelming majority of the district's land area. Skiing is king in these mountain counties on the district's western border; the resort city of Vail is in Eagle County. The 2nd also includes some communities north of Denver in southwestern Weld County.

Environmental issues still play heavily here, and because Boulder has been one of the fastest-growing cities in the state, urban sprawl has gained some attention. Another concern is the Rocky Flats facility, a former plutonium plant located near the Boulder-Jefferson county line, which is now an environmental cleanup site.

Education is a high priority in the 2nd, site of the state's flagship university and several federal research labs. The liberal strain in the academic community helped Green Party presidential nominee Ralph Nader garner 12 percent of the Boulder County vote in 2000, well above his statewide total of 5 percent. But newcomers — who can overcome Boulder's slow-growth regulations and afford a home in the resulting high-priced real estate market — tend to be more fiscally conservative than voters past.

MAJOR INDUSTRY
Information technology, government laboratories, higher education

CITIES
Westminster (pt.), 100,850; Boulder, 94,673; Thornton (pt.), 82,378

NOTABLE
The atomic clock at the National Institute of Standards and Technology in Boulder is the nation's official timekeeper.

Rep. Scott McInnis (R)

CAPITOL OFFICE
225-4761
www.house.gov/mcinnis
320 Cannon 20515-0603; fax 226-0622

COMMITTEES
Resources
(Forests & Forest Health - chairman)
Ways & Means

HOMETOWN
Grand Junction

BORN
May 9, 1953, Glenwood Springs, Colo.

RELIGION
Roman Catholic

FAMILY
Wife, Lori McInnis; three children

EDUCATION
Fort Lewis College, B.A. 1975 (business administration); St. Mary's U. (Texas), J.D. 1980

CAREER
Lawyer; police officer; firefighter

POLITICAL HIGHLIGHTS
Colo. House, 1983-93 (majority leader, 1991-93)

ELECTION RESULTS

2002 GENERAL		
Scott McInnis (R)	143,431	65.8%
Denis Berckefeldt (D)	68,110	31.3%
J. Brent Shroyer (LIBERT)	4,370	2.0%
2002 PRIMARY		
Scott McInnis (R)		unopposed
2000 GENERAL		
Scott McInnis (R)	199,204	65.8%
Curtis Imrie (D)	87,921	29.1%
Drew Sakson (LIBERT)	9,982	3.3%
Victor A. Good (REF)	5,433	1.8%

PREVIOUS WINNING PERCENTAGES
1998 (66%); 1996 (69%); 1994 (70%); 1992 (55%)

Elected 1992; 6th term

When he first came to Washington, McInnis made no secret of his intention not to stick around too long: He said he would serve no more than four terms. And, to avoid becoming too comfortable in the nation's capital, he decided to sleep in his office.

A decade later, Capitol Hill seems to have grown on McInnis. He announced in 1998 that he had changed his mind about the term limits pledge, and in 2002 he let it be known that he would be interested in chairing the Resources Committee in the 108th Congress — despite his low seniority on the panel. McInnis did not get the post — Californian Richard W. Pombo, with even less seniority, got the job. But McInnis retained his chairmanship of the Forests and Forest Health Subcommittee and his seat on the powerful tax-writing Ways and Means Committee.

House GOP leaders have had a hand in McInnis' change of heart: They have been good to him over the years, handing him a seat on the powerful Rules Committee in just his second term, beseeching him to stay in the House and forgo a run for the Senate in 1998, swapping his Rules seat for a spot on Ways and Means when he decided to stay. The leadership also put him on the Resources panel, despite the fact that a post on Ways and Means usually precludes any other committee assignment.

That is not to say he has decided to become a lifer in the House. For one thing, he still sleeps in his office, showering in the House gym after an early morning workout.

If he leaves the House, it will likely be in pursuit of a higher office. In 1998, McInnis geared up for a Senate run believing that Colorado GOP Sen. Ben Nighthorse Campbell would step down. But Campbell decided to run again. Exchanging barbs, McInnis contended Campbell had reneged on a promise, while Campbell said McInnis should "stop whining." McInnis eventually sought re-election to the House and the two have reconciled. McInnis still thinks of running for the Senate or for governor sometime down the road.

Perhaps because he bunks down in his office and the House chamber is so convenient, McInnis has become a recognizable face on C-SPAN, as he makes frequent late night "special order" speeches. He likes to tout the virtues of common sense, which he says he finds missing in many aspects of government and modern-day life. That is a recurring theme of his speeches, whether the topic is profiling airline passengers or dealing with America's energy problems.

McInnis makes good use of his two committee posts. As chairman of Resources' Forests and Forest Health Subcommittee, he has worked for a reduced federal role in land-use policy, particularly as it affected Colorado's wide-open Western Slope. He favors multiple uses for much of the land, including development and recreation as well as preservation.

In the 107th, McInnis pressured federal agencies to develop a unified plan for dealing with chronic wasting disease, related to mad cow disease, which presented a serious health problem for the nation's deer and elk populations. McInnis drafted a bill to address the problem but told the agencies he would hold off if they came up with an interagency plan. Early in the 108th, he filed another bill, saying the agencies had failed.

McInnis also blasted government researchers for planting fake lynx fur in a Western forest. If a survey had determined that there were lynx, which is a threatened species, in the national forest, timber harvesting and winter sports might have been restricted in the area. "They planted evidence, just like a bad cop goes into a house and plants drugs," he said.

From his seat on Ways and Means, McInnis offered legislation to halt so-called corporate inversions, in which U.S. companies can avoid taxes by relocating their headquarters oversees. "I smell a skunk," he said.

McInnis is a former firefighter. In 2002, as fires blackened hundreds of thousands of acres of Western lands, he worked to secure added federal money to battle the blazes. He also wrote a bill to address insurance concerns that had prevented Australian firefighters from joining the fight. McInnis, whose parents' home in Glenwood Springs was threatened by the fires (just as in 1994), urged the Bush administration to create a national fire czar post to coordinate the nation's firefighting and fire prevention policy.

McInnis was honored in 2000 by his hometown newspaper, the Glenwood Post, as "Person of the Decade." The Post acknowledged that McInnis isn't universally liked and that his hard-edged views do not make him a favorite with Democrats or environmentalists, but the editors wrote: "Yet, love McInnis or hate him, there's no denying the power he has come to wield in Washington."

McInnis returns the favor by making a point of paying tribute to his constituents. His staff pores through local newspapers and other sources in search of reports of ordinary people who have done something of value in their community. McInnis then places a tribute to them in the Congressional Record, sometimes as many as 20 a week.

It was a Democrat who sparked McInnis' interest in politics. He was in grade school when he met the legendary Rep. Wayne Aspinall, the longtime chairman of the House Interior Committee, at the dedication of a tree farm. "I didn't know what a congressman was. I knew it was something important, I guess," he says. Aspinall gave McInnis a donkey pin from his lapel.

As a young man, McInnis worked as a police officer, a volunteer firefighter and a lawyer before winning a seat in the Colorado House at age 29. He moved through the ranks, and at age 37, became majority leader.

In 1992, when Campbell, then a Democrat, left the 3rd District to run for the Senate, McInnis was ready to make a bid for Congress. Touting his 10 years of legislative experience, McInnis scored a solid 11-point victory over Democratic Lt. Gov. Mike Callihan. He has since won easily, with more than 65 percent of the vote, proving that most voters had little concern about his term limits turnabout. Redistricting after the 2000 census cost McInnis several Western Slope counties, but it also added a couple of agricultural counties in the southeast portion of the state. The district remained GOP-friendly, and McInnis cruised to a 2-to-1 victory in 2002.

KEY VOTES

2002

- No Overhaul campaign finance law; ban "soft money" and restrict advocacy advertising
- Yes Back Bush's defense budget increase
- Yes Extend 1996 welfare law
- Yes Adopt Bush's discretionary spending limit
- Yes Pass GOP Medicare prescription drug plan
- No Create independent Sept. 11 commission
- No Extend union protections to Homeland Security Department employees
- Yes Revive fast-track procedures for trade agreements
- Yes Authorize war against Iraq
- Yes Advance bankruptcy overhaul opposed by abortion opponents

2001

- Yes Nullify Clinton Labor Department ergonomics rule
- Yes Cut taxes by $1.35 trillion through fiscal 2011
- No Maintain ban on oil drilling in Arctic National Wildlife Refuge
- Yes Approve Bush proposal to limit managed-care plan liability for coverage decisions
- No Divert money from crop subsidy payments to land conservation
- Yes Expand law enforcement power to investigate suspected terrorists

CQ VOTE STUDIES

	PARTY UNITY		PRESIDENTIAL SUPPORT	
	Support	Oppose	Support	Oppose
2002	96%	4%	89%	11%
2001	95%	5%	98%	2%
2000	93%	7%	25%	75%
1999	93%	7%	20%	80%
1998	92%	8%	26%	74%

INTEREST GROUPS

	AFL-CIO	ADA	CCUS	ACU
2002	13%	0%	95%	100%
2001	8%	0%	83%	86%
2000	0%	10%	84%	95%
1999	13%	20%	88%	92%
1998	0%	5%	100%	96%

COLORADO 3
Western Slope; Pueblo

The expansive 3rd, which captures Colorado's entire western border and all but one county on its southern edge, displays some of the abundant variety found outside the state's urban centers: the rural poor, the resort rich, the old steel mill town and the isolated Hispanic counties. Redistricting following the 2000 census kept the 3rd's character intact while moving the borders farther from Denver.

Residential growth and a substantial agricultural constituency have made water and land two of the 3rd's hottest issues. Most of the state's rivers flow down the Western Slope to Nevada and California. Farmers here would like to see more of that water stored for local use. Meanwhile, residential development has driven up property values.

A century of boom-and-bust mineral speculation — in gold, silver, uranium and shale oil — has left the Western Slope dotted with small, struggling towns. The San Luis Valley and rural areas west of Interstate 25 have been hardest hit. Profits also have shrunk in the 3rd's other economic mainstays, namely cattle ranching in the west and steel production in Pueblo. But with plenty of national parks and ski resorts, tourism has quickly filled the void.

Residential Colorado has spilled over the Continental Divide onto the Western Slope. The newcomers, many of whom migrated to the area to build rustic retirement homes, tend to vote Republican. But Pueblo County, the district's most populous, is heavily unionized, more than one-third Hispanic and voted decisively for Al Gore in 2000. Some heavily Hispanic, sparsely populated counties border New Mexico.

There is a liberal strain in some southwestern Colorado communities. Green Party presidential nominee Ralph Nader's top four counties in Colorado were in the 3rd District, topped by San Miguel County (17.2 percent), which includes Telluride. Farther north, Pitkin County, which takes in the Aspen ski resort, gave Nader 13 percent of the vote.

MAJOR INDUSTRY
Tourism, skiing, agriculture

CITIES
Pueblo, 102,121; Grand Junction, 41,986; Clifton, 17,345

NOTABLE
The U.S. Government Consumer Information Center is in Pueblo.

Rep. Marilyn Musgrave (R)

CAPITOL OFFICE
225-4676
rep.musgrave@mail.house.gov
www.house.gov/musgrave
1208 Longworth 20515-0604; fax 225-5870

COMMITTEES
Agriculture
Education & Workforce
Small Business

HOMETOWN
Fort Morgan

BORN
Jan. 27, 1949, Greeley, Colo.

RELIGION
Assemblies of God

FAMILY
Husband, Steve Musgrave; four children

EDUCATION
Colorado State U., B.A. 1972 (social studies)

CAREER
Homemaker; teacher

POLITICAL HIGHLIGHTS
Morgan County School Board, 1990-94; Colo. House, 1995-99; Colo. Senate, 1999-2003

ELECTION RESULTS

2002 GENERAL		
Marilyn Musgrave (R)	115,359	55.0%
Stan Matsunaka (D)	87,499	41.7%
John Volz (LIBERT)	7,097	3.4%
2002 PRIMARY		
Marilyn Musgrave (R)	28,683	64.6%
Jeff Bedingfield (R)	15,743	35.4%

Elected 2002; 1st term

A self-described social and fiscal conservative, Musgrave tenaciously pursued her right-of-center views during her tenure in the state Senate. Among her stands, she opposed abortion and supported cutting taxes, allowing law-abiding gun owners to carry concealed weapons and defining marriage exclusively as a union between a man and a woman.

The winner of an open-seat 2002 race to succeed retiring Republican Rep. Bob Schaffer in Colorado's 4th District, Musgrave said she planned to continue pressing her conservative views in a "friendly but firm" manner.

An advocate of making permanent the tax cuts President Bush signed into law in 2001, Musgrave fought in the state Senate to pass a 5 percent tax cut, eliminate the state's "marriage penalty" tax, and exempt farm and ranch equipment and agricultural repair parts from sales taxes.

She chaired the state Senate's Transportation Committee for two years and in Washington initially hoped for assignment to the Transportation panel, but then decided to seek seats on the Agriculture and Education committees, which she received.

Musgrave, who began her political career on the Morgan County school board, says she supports the rights of parents to direct the education of their children, whether it be in public, private or religious schools, or in home schooling.

Schaffer's decision to abide by a pledge he made to limit his House service to three terms created an opening for Musgrave, who easily defeated a more moderate opponent in the Republican primary.

Democratic strategists touted their candidate, state Senate President Stan Matsunaka, as a moderate who had a history of winning in Republican-leaning areas. But Musgrave benefited from her strong political skills and a robust Republican voter turnout effort that also helped re-elect Sen. Wayne Allard (who formerly represented the 4th District). Musgrave prevailed with 55 percent of the vote. Her victory continued a Republican winning streak in the district dating to 1972.

COLORADO 4

North and east – Fort Collins

The 4th, which covers Colorado's eastern plains and touches five other states, looks more like Kansas than Colorado. Intensive irrigation has turned these prairies where buffalo roamed into productive wheat and corn fields. Cattle production in the eastern counties ranks among the highest in the nation. But as demand for beef has fallen and wheat prices have declined, ranchers and farmers have faced hard times.

Fort Collins — the district's most populous city and home to Colorado State University — sits more than 50 miles from Boulder and Denver, but it has been able to cash in on the recent economic boom in the Front Range. Some high-tech industry has moved into the city, and the relatively low cost of living has attracted new residents.

The 4th has a long history of supporting GOP House members, and most of the district includes rural Republican territory. Several counties here gave George W. Bush more than two-thirds of their votes in the 2000 presidential election, with Cheyenne County awarding Bush a statewide high of 79 percent and Washington County giving him his second-highest total. Fort Collins is an exception to the district's strong GOP tilt and tends to support Democrats in local elections.

Redistricting following the 2000 census stripped the fast-growing 4th of several counties in the northwestern (Adams, Arapahoe and Elbert) and southwestern (Las Animas, most of Otero) parts of the district. The Republican-leaning northeastern portion of Boulder County, including the city of Longmont, was added.

MAJOR INDUSTRY
Agriculture, meatpacking, higher education

CITIES
Fort Collins, 118,652; Greeley, 76,930; Longmont, 71,093; Loveland, 50,608

NOTABLE
The Greeley Independence Stampede is a rodeo and country music festival held annually during the week of July 4th; The Kit Carson County Carousel is in Burlington.

Rep. Joel Hefley (R)

CAPITOL OFFICE
225-4422
www.house.gov/hefley
2372 Rayburn 20515-0605; fax 225-1942

COMMITTEES
Armed Services
(Readiness - chairman)
Standards of Official Conduct - chairman

HOMETOWN
Colorado Springs

BORN
April 18, 1935, Ardmore, Okla.

RELIGION
Presbyterian

FAMILY
Wife, Lynn Hefley; three children

EDUCATION
Oklahoma Baptist U., B.A. 1957; Oklahoma State U., M.S. 1962

CAREER
Community planner; management consultant

POLITICAL HIGHLIGHTS
Colo. House, 1977-79; Colo. Senate, 1979-87 (assistant majority leader, 1981-86)

ELECTION RESULTS

2002 GENERAL		
Joel Hefley (R)	128,118	69.4%
Curtis Imrie (D)	45,587	24.7%
Biff Baker (LIBERT)	10,972	5.9%
2002 PRIMARY		
Joel Hefley (R)		unopposed
2000 GENERAL		
Joel Hefley (R)	253,330	82.7%
Kerry Kantor (LIBERT)	37,719	12.3%
Randy MacKenzie (NL)	15,260	5.0%

PREVIOUS WINNING PERCENTAGES
1998 (73%); 1996 (72%); 1994 (100%); 1992 (71%); 1990 (66%); 1988 (75%); 1986 (70%)

Elected 1986; 9th term

"I fit this district very, very well," Hefley told a reporter in the fall of 2002. "My specialty has been defense; I think it's the main role for the federal government, and I represent a highly defense-oriented district."

Indeed, defense spending accounts for a good share of the economic activity in the 5th District — home of Northern Command, which is charged with protecting the U.S. homeland; the Air Force Academy; and Fort Carson and other installations at which more than 25,000 active-duty personnel are stationed. The district's large population of military retirees contributes to its rock-ribbed conservative political personality. So Hefley's pro-Pentagon voting record, fiscal tight-fistedness, and opposition both to gay rights and abortion rights all go down well with his constituents.

For years, Hefley's only disconnect with his voters was electronic: Although his constituents work for a raft of high-tech companies, he was one of the last House members to establish a Web site. He finally created a home page at the start of the 107th Congress, but without an e-mail link to his office. Hefley said he wanted to protect his staff from being swamped by junk e-mail. But he also may have been trying to hold on to the laid-back, homespun style that — along with his conservatism — has made him seemingly unbeatable in the district.

As chairman of the Armed Services Subcommittee on Military Installations during the Clinton administration, Hefley regularly berated the White House for proposing inadequate budgets, then won more for defense facilities and family housing than the administration requested. He also bitterly opposed Clinton's requests to close unneeded bases. Unlike some other Republicans, Hefley agreed that the Pentagon had more facilities than it needed. But he contended that Clinton could not be trusted to manage further cutbacks because he had manipulated the 1995 round of base closings to help his re-election prospects.

In 2001, when President Bush and Defense Secretary Donald H. Rumsfeld demanded another base-closing round, Hefley urged them to identify from the outset uniquely important bases at no risk of closure, in order to spare some communities uncertainty. His idea was not adopted.

As chairman of the Subcommittee on Readiness since 2002, Hefley has backed the Pentagon's request for limited exemptions from the Endangered Species Act and other environmental laws, which the department says interfere with realistic training. His favorite argument for the proposed changes has been the Marine Corps' sprawling Camp Pendleton on the California coast where, after storming ashore in a mock landing, troops are bused to another part of the base — so as not to harm the endangered California gnatcatcher, a small songbird that likes that beach. "We want to train people the way they're going to fight," he says.

Hefley shares with most other Western Republicans a skepticism toward federal restrictions on land use. But his concern is practical as well as principled. From his senior seat on the Resources Committee he argued that Congress has been too eager to designate new national parks while failing to maintain existing facilities. Accordingly, he secured creation of a process to review proposed additions to the parks system — a move he said would save more money for "crown jewel" parks such as Yosemite and Yellowstone. Over Hefley's vigorous objection, Speaker J. Dennis Hastert pushed a bill in 2001 that waived the review process in order to designate President Reagan's boyhood home in Hastert's home state of Illinois a national monument.

Hefley expressed his displeasure with GOP leaders early in the 108th Congress when Californian Richard W. Pombo was picked to chair the Resources panel over four more-senior members who wanted the job — Hefley among them. Hefley criticized the GOP leadership for rewarding Pombo's fundraising prowess over the seniority system. Shortly thereafter, Hefley left the Resources panel, citing ongoing scheduling conflicts with his Armed Services subcommittee.

It was not the only time as the 108th began that Hefley was overlooked by the party hierarchy. As chairman of the Committee on Standards of Official Conduct, he tried to stop or at least minimize two changes to the House's ethics rules before they were pushed though by GOP leaders. One allowed charities to give lawmakers free trips; the other permitted lobbyists to cater meals in congressional offices. Hefley lamented, "Part of our job is to make sure, not only that people not do evil, but that it not appear evil."

As ethics chairman, it fell to Hefley to run the proceedings in 2002 that led to only the second expulsion of a House member since the Civil War. Democrat James A. Traficant Jr. of Ohio had been convicted of federal bribery, tax evasion and racketeering charges that year, but he maintained that he was the victim of a government vendetta and behaved with his customarily ribald flamboyance during the hearings before Hefley's committee. "It's the most difficult week I've ever had in politics," the chairman later said.

A former community planner and management consultant, Hefley boasts an unusual set of hobbies. The Oklahoma native acquired roping skills and participated in rodeos as a youth, and he still counts calf-roping as one of his pastimes. Hefley also is an accomplished, if decidedly partisan, political cartoonist and says that he plans to assemble a book of his favorite caricatures someday.

Hefley had served a decade in the Colorado General Assembly when Republican Ken Kramer vacated the 5th District seat to run for the Senate in 1986. Hefley and a colleague from the legislature sought to avoid a primary by flipping a coin to determine who would make the House bid. Hefley won the toss, but he drew a primary challenge anyway from millionaire Harold A. Krause, who viewed Hefley as too moderate. After surviving the primary, Hefley took 70 percent against Democratic businessman Bill Story.

Since then Hefley has been held below that mark only twice. The most recent time was in 2002, after Colorado was awarded a new House seat in reapportionment and the 5th District was significantly reshaped. It was kept reliably Republican, however, and Hefley won with 69 percent against Democrat Curtis Imrie, a self-styled subsistence rancher and burro breeder.

KEY VOTES

2002

? Overhaul campaign finance law; ban "soft money" and restrict advocacy advertising
Yes Back Bush's defense budget increase
Yes Extend 1996 welfare law
Yes Adopt Bush's discretionary spending limit
Yes Pass GOP Medicare prescription drug plan
No Create independent Sept. 11 commission
No Extend union protections to Homeland Security Department employees
Yes Revive fast-track procedures for trade agreements
Yes Authorize war against Iraq
No Advance bankruptcy overhaul opposed by abortion opponents

2001

Yes Nullify Clinton Labor Department ergonomics rule
Yes Cut taxes by $1.35 trillion through fiscal 2011
No Maintain ban on oil drilling in Arctic National Wildlife Refuge
Yes Approve Bush proposal to limit managed-care plan liability for coverage decisions
No Divert money from crop subsidy payments to land conservation
Yes Expand law enforcement power to investigate suspected terrorists

CQ VOTE STUDIES

	PARTY UNITY		PRESIDENTIAL SUPPORT	
	Support	Oppose	Support	Oppose
2002	92%	8%	85%	15%
2001	92%	8%	81%	19%
2000	93%	7%	15%	85%
1999	90%	10%	17%	83%
1998	92%	8%	21%	79%

INTEREST GROUPS

	AFL-CIO	ADA	CCUS	ACU
2002	13%	0%	78%	100%
2001	18%	5%	74%	96%
2000	10%	10%	84%	100%
1999	38%	20%	79%	100%
1998	0%	0%	75%	100%

COLORADO 5
South central — Colorado Springs

God and country dominate the 5th, an overwhelmingly conservative district where registered Republicans outnumber Democrats by a 2-to-1 ratio. Military installations employ tens of thousands of people in the Colorado Springs area. The popular resort town is a prime destination for retired military personnel, who come to enjoy the scenery and find like-minded neighbors. James Dobson's Focus on the Family and other evangelical organizations are based in the 5th.

Defense cutbacks threatened the district in the early 1990s when Congress tried but failed to put Fort Carson on its list of closures. Since then, the district has made itself an indispensable arm of the modern military. Colorado Springs houses the U.S. Space Command, the North American Aerospace Defense Command and a good portion of the country's satellite defense research.

The city also has broadened its economic base: Direct and indirect military expenditures account for about 40 percent of the economy, down from 60 percent a decade ago. But much of the new industry, including superconductor and computer development, depends on the defense industry. Like much of Colorado's Front Range, the city attracts lots of money from tourists, many of whom come to make the 14,110-foot ascent up Pikes Peak.

More than 80 percent of district residents live in El Paso County (Colorado Springs), which has topped 500,000 residents. Redistricting in 2002 removed the district's portions of Douglas and Arapahoe counties near Denver and added three counties farther west.

MAJOR INDUSTRY
Military, tourism, semiconductors

MILITARY BASES
Fort Carson (Army), 15,773 military, 1,839 civilian; Peterson Air Force Base, 4,559 military, 1,495 civilian; U.S. Air Force Academy, 1,987 military, 1,905 civilian; Schriever Air Force Base, 2,151 military, 458 civilian; Cheyenne Mountain Air Force Station, 977 military, 111 civilian (1999)

CITIES
Colorado Springs, 360,890; Security-Widefield (unincorporated), 29,845

NOTABLE
The U.S. Olympic Headquarters is in Colorado Springs.

Rep. Tom Tancredo (R)

CAPITOL OFFICE
225-7882
tom.tancredo@mail.house.gov
www.house.gov/tancredo
1130 Longworth 20515-0606; fax 226-4623

COMMITTEES
Budget
International Relations
Resources

HOMETOWN
Littleton

BORN
Dec. 20, 1945, North Denver, Colo.

RELIGION
Presbyterian

FAMILY
Wife, Jackie Tancredo; two children

EDUCATION
U. of North Colorado, B.A. 1968

CAREER
Think tank president; teacher

POLITICAL HIGHLIGHTS
Colo. House, 1977-81; U.S. Education Department regional representative, 1981-93

ELECTION RESULTS

2002 GENERAL		
Tom Tancredo (R)	158,851	66.9%
Lance Wright (D)	71,327	30.0%
Adam D. Katz (LIBERT)	7,323	3.1%
2002 PRIMARY		
Tom Tancredo (R)		unopposed
2000 GENERAL		
Tom Tancredo (R)	141,410	53.9%
Ken Toltz (D)	110,568	42.1%
Adam D. Katz (LIBERT)	6,885	2.6%
John Heckman (COPP)	3,614	1.4%

PREVIOUS WINNING PERCENTAGES
1998 (56%)

Elected 1998; 3rd term

Tancredo is a stalwart advocate of conservative causes, speaking out for school vouchers, gun owners' rights, tax cuts, and, in the 107th Congress, a wholesale toughening of the nation's immigration policy.

In his first term, he signed a California group's pledge to eliminate all public schools, saying that "separation of school and state is essential to restore parental responsibility." Tancredo (tan-CRAY-doe) told the Denver Post that he aimed "to push the envelope of debate."

In his third term, what he pushed against was the nation's policy on immigration. He posted a series of "Unbelievable But True Immigration Stories" on his official Web site. "When I got here, somebody told me, 'There's only one way to get something done — talk about it constantly.' I remember saying, 'I can do that,' " he told the Post.

His campaign against immigration and in favor of tighter border controls came at the same time the GOP was working hard to woo Hispanic voters, and it angered the Bush White House. Tancredo was given a warning in 2002 from top Bush aide Karl Rove: "Do not darken the door of the White House."

Undeterred, Tancredo gave an interview to the Washington Times in which he again blasted the administration's immigration policy. He said he did not relish the public dispute with the president, but he told the Denver Post: "If the issue didn't demand it, I wouldn't do it." House Speaker J. Dennis Hastert met with Tancredo to ask him not to pursue an effort to make it harder for legal immigrants to collect food stamps, an issue that threatened to make many Republicans uncomfortable. Tancredo acquiesced, grudgingly.

The Sept. 11, 2001, terrorist attacks against the United States brought immigration and border security issues to the top of the congressional agenda. The membership of the Immigration Reform Caucus, which Tancredo chairs, jumped from 15 to 64.

He says his interest in immigration began in the 1970s when increasing numbers of immigrants to Colorado forced the state to implement bilingual education programs. He says he wants to impose a national moratorium on immigration because of its cost to the nation. Under his plan, the number of legal immigrants would be reduced from the current 1.2 million or so annually to about 300,000, approximately the same number of people who emigrate from the United States each year.

Tancredo's grandparents came to the United States from Italy, but he says they always regarded themselves as Americans and not as Italian-Americans.

Tancredo is conservative on fiscal matters as well. He wants to make the 2001 tax cuts permanent and supports efforts to scrap the current income tax system and replace it with a national sales tax or a flat tax. On his office wall, Tancredo displays a pair of boxing gloves presented to him by a local business group to honor his tax-fighting efforts.

A former public school teacher and regional official in President Reagan's Education Department, Tancredo once advocated doing away with the Department of Education, but he now presses the federal government to make good on its promises to fund special education for disabled students. He also favors school vouchers and opposes bilingual education.

Tancredo's association with staunchly conservative causes was tested by the events of April 20, 1999, the day two students went on a shooting rampage at Columbine High School — just blocks from his suburban Denver home — killing 12 classmates and a teacher before turning their guns on themselves. In an interview with the Capitol Hill newspaper The Hill, the evangelical Presbyterian and self-proclaimed Second Amendment advocate attributed the killings to Satan.

Tancredo later endorsed some gun controls, including a Colorado ballot initiative that required background checks for all firearms sales at gun shows. By doing so, he prompted protests from some gun owners groups but largely inoculated himself against charges from Colorado Democrats that he was on the political fringe and out of touch with his constituents.

From his seat on the International Relations Committee, Tancredo has been a leading player in the effort by congressional conservatives to bring pressure on Sudan to end its 20 years of civil war. The war pits Sudan's Muslim-dominated government against predominantly Christian rebels. Tancredo, who says he heard about the conflict in his church, and his allies have considered offering legislation to provide arms to the Christian rebels.

The son of a truck driver and a department store clerk, Tancredo grew up in a working-class part of Denver. He became a social studies teacher, enticed by a program that paid half of his student loans if he agreed to teach for five years.

His political career began with a challenge to the junior high school class he was teaching in the 1970s: He told his 32 students that he would run for public office if each of them volunteered with a campaign. To his surprise, all of them called his bluff. The class then decided that Tancredo should run for the Colorado House.

During his four years in the state legislature, Tancredo was one of the conservatives dubbed the "House crazies" by the press and Democratic Gov. Richard Lamm for their efforts to overhaul the state's tax system.

In 1981, Tancredo began a 12-year tenure as the Education Department's regional representative. He advocated dismantling the department and downsized his own regional staff by 75 percent. He then served as president of the Libertarian Independence Institute think tank during 1993-98.

Though he had not held elective office since 1981, Tancredo edged out four other Republicans in the 1998 primary and then breezed to victory in November to succeed retiring GOP Rep. Dan Schaefer. In 2000, he fought off a spirited challenge from dry cleaning executive Ken Toltz, capturing 54 percent of the vote. In 2002, redistricting made the 6th District more friendly to the GOP and Tancredo captured two-thirds of the vote.

He initially pledged to serve no more than six years, which would make the 108th Congress his last. But in 2002, he acknowledged he was having second thoughts about the pledge.

KEY VOTES

2002

- No Overhaul campaign finance law; ban "soft money" and restrict advocacy advertising
- Yes Back Bush's defense budget increase
- Yes Extend 1996 welfare law
- Yes Adopt Bush's discretionary spending limit
- Yes Pass GOP Medicare prescription drug plan
- Yes Create independent Sept. 11 commission
- No Extend union protections to Homeland Security Department employees
- Yes Revive fast-track procedures for trade agreements
- Yes Authorize war against Iraq
- No Advance bankruptcy overhaul opposed by abortion opponents

2001

- Yes Nullify Clinton Labor Department ergonomics rule
- Yes Cut taxes by $1.35 trillion through fiscal 2011
- No Maintain ban on oil drilling in Arctic National Wildlife Refuge
- Yes Approve Bush proposal to limit managed-care plan liability for coverage decisions
- No Divert money from crop subsidy payments to land conservation
- Yes Expand law enforcement power to investigate suspected terrorists

CQ VOTE STUDIES

	PARTY UNITY		PRESIDENTIAL SUPPORT	
	Support	Oppose	Support	Oppose
2002	96%	4%	76%	24%
2001	94%	6%	77%	23%
2000	93%	7%	17%	83%
1999	94%	6%	18%	82%

INTEREST GROUPS

	AFL-CIO	ADA	CCUS	ACU
2002	11%	5%	79%	100%
2001	8%	5%	70%	100%
2000	10%	5%	71%	96%
1999	11%	10%	88%	100%

COLORADO 6
Denver suburbs — part of Aurora; Douglas County

Managing growth is a top priority for the affluent, white-collar suburbs that lie south of Denver and comprise the 6th. Highway congestion has become a serious problem as commuters living in suburban bedroom communities head into Denver every morning.

Steep housing prices on the West Coast have resulted in an influx of Californians, especially to Douglas County, which increased its population by 191 percent in the 1990s, the fastest clip in the country.

The 6th was redrawn following the 2000 census to include Douglas, which accounts for 30 percent of the district's population and solidifies it as a Republican stronghold. Douglas supported George W. Bush by a 2-to-1 ratio in 2000. The county is quickly filling up with young, well-educated professionals with families, and it has the state's highest median income. Technology sector growth in the suburbs has made the 6th one of the most highly educated districts.

Contrasts are evident in Arapahoe County, where a plurality of district residents reside even though the county is overwhelmingly rural. The urban, western portion of Arapahoe, which includes the county seat of Littleton just south of Denver, has many residential and retail areas. Nearly one-third of Aurora, Colorado's third most-populous city, is in the district. Columbine High School, site of a 1999 shooting that left 15 dead, is in Littleton, which makes gun control an emotional issue in the 6th.

The district's Hispanic population (slightly less than 6 percent) is the lowest percentage in the state. Minorities total 12 percent of residents, making the 6th the only district in Colorado where minorities represent less than 20 percent of the population.

MAJOR INDUSTRY
Manufacturing

CITIES
Aurora (pt.), 78,878; Highlands Ranch, 70,931; Southglenn (unincorporated), 43,520; Littleton, 40,340

NOTABLE
The "Buffalo Bill" Cody grave and museum is near Golden; The Comanche Crossing Railroad Site near Strasburg marks the place where the last spike was driven in 1870 to create the first continuous transcontinental railroad.

Rep. Bob Beauprez (R)

CAPITOL OFFICE
225-2645
www.house.gov/beauprez
511 Cannon 20515-0607; fax 225-5278

COMMITTEES
Small Business
Transportation & Infrastructure
Veterans' Affairs

HOMETOWN
Arvada

BORN
Sept. 22, 1948, Lafayette, Colo.

RELIGION
Roman Catholic

FAMILY
Wife, Claudia Beauprez; four children

EDUCATION
U. of Colorado, B.S. 1970 (education)

CAREER
Bank owner; dairy farmer

POLITICAL HIGHLIGHTS
Colo. Republican Party chairman, 1999-2002

ELECTION RESULTS

2002 GENERAL		
Bob Beauprez (R)	81,789	47.3%
Mike Feeley (D)	81,667	47.2%
Dave Chandler (GREEN)	3,274	1.9%
Victor A. Good (REF)	3,133	1.8%
G. T. "Bud" Martin (LIBERT)	2,906	1.7%
2002 PRIMARY		
Bob Beauprez (R)	10,172	38.2%
Rick O'Donnell (R)	8,213	30.8%
Sam Zakhem (R)	4,848	18.2%
Joe Rogers (R)	3,430	12.9%

Elected 2002; 1st term

Beauprez's biography reads like a classic American success story. A grandson of immigrants, Beauprez married his high school sweetheart, worked on the family farm, then opened his own business. He cherishes the ideal of America as the "land of opportunity."

The winner of 2002's closest election — in a new suburban Denver district drawn to be a partisan battleground — Beauprez (bo-PRAY) says he wants to use his seat in Congress to provide others with the same opportunities that allowed his family to flourish. The key, he says, is improved education, a stronger economy and lower taxes.

Beauprez models much of his platform after the political philosophy of President Bush, who made two campaign stops for him. Beauprez says his first priority in Congress is to make permanent the tax cuts Bush pushed to enactment in 2001. But the steel tariffs the president imposed in 2002 run counter to Beauprez's free-trade stance.

Beauprez angled for and won a seat on the Transportation Committee. With the Denver suburbs notorious for traffic congestion and water shortages, he said a slot on that panel would yield tangible benefits for his constituents. Beauprez was named the freshman class representative on the Republican Policy Committee and also won an appointment to the bottom rung of the GOP whip ladder.

Beauprez was state Republican chairman when he was recruited by party leaders to run in the 7th, the new district fast-growing Colorado had earned in reapportionment following the 2000 census. His strong party ties enabled him to survive a tough primary contest in which Rick O'Donnell, a top aide to Republican Gov. Bill Owens, was his main competitor.

Even tougher was Beauprez's general-election race with Democratic former state Sen. Mike Feeley, who actually outran Beauprez among voters who cast ballots on Election Day. But a strong Republican absentee-ballot drive propelled Beauprez to victory by a 121-vote margin — an outcome that was not officially decided until the results of a recount were announced five weeks after the election.

COLORADO 7

Denver suburbs — Lakewood, parts of Aurora and Arvada

Awarded to fast-growing Colorado following the 2000 census, the new 7th is a middle-class suburban area that surrounds Denver (and the 1st District) from the west, north and east before extending east to take in the remainder of Adams County.

The bulk of the district's population is in Jefferson County, where more than half of residents live and which forms its western edge. The 7th takes in Lakewood, a middle-class area that abuts Denver to the west; Golden, which includes the Coors Brewing Co.; and nearly all of Arvada.

Minorities represent nearly a third of residents, giving the 7th the second-highest total in the state. Commerce City, a Hispanic-majority, lower-middle-class area just north of Denver, and most of the city of Aurora (shared with the 6th) are in the 7th. Aurora has the largest African-American percentage (13 percent) in Colorado.

Buckley Air Force Base is a link in the Air Force Space Command satellite tracking system and has attracted aerospace firms to the area. The Rocky Mountain Arsenal, which once produced chemical weapons, is expected to be rid of pollutants by 2011.

The 7th is Colorado's most competitive district. Al Gore narrowly carried the area in 2000, and the two major parties are equal in voter registration. The slight Democratic lean of Adams and Arapahoe counties is largely offset by the GOP lean in Jefferson.

MAJOR INDUSTRY
Communications, aerospace, manufacturing

MILITARY BASES
Buckley Air Force Base, 1,935 military, 306 civilian (1999)

CITIES
Aurora (pt.), 197,515; Lakewood, 144,126; Arvada (pt.), 98,941; Wheat Ridge, 32,913

NOTABLE
Dinosaur Ridge is near Morrison.

CONNECTICUT

Gov. John G. Rowland (R)

First elected: 1994
Term expires: 1/07
Salary: $150,000
Phone: (860) 566-4840
Hometown: Waterbury
Born: May 24, 1957; Waterbury, Conn.
Religion: Roman Catholic
Family: Wife, Patricia Rowland; five children
Education: Villanova U., B.S. 1979 (business administration)
Career: Insurance broker; business consultant
Political highlights: Conn. House, 1981-85; U.S. House, 1985-91; Republican nominee for governor, 1990
Election results:

2002 GENERAL		
John G. Rowland (R)	573,958	56.1%
Bill Curry (D)	448,984	43.9%

Lt. Gov. M. Jodi Rell (R)

First elected: 1994
Length of term: 4 years
Term expires: 1/07
Salary: $110,000
Phone: (860) 524-7384

STATE LEGISLATURE

General Assembly: Meets January-June in odd-numbered years; February-May in even-numbered years
House: 151 members, 2-year terms
2003 breakdown: 57R, 94D; 104 men, 47 women
Salary: $32,500
Phone: (860) 240-0400
Senate: 36 members, 2-year terms
2003 breakdown: 15R, 21D; 28 men, 8 women
Salary: $33,500
Phone: (860) 240-0500

STATE TERM LIMITS

Governor: No
Senate: No
House: No

URBAN STATISTICS

CITY	POPULATION
Bridgeport	139,529
New Haven	123,626
Hartford	121,578
Stamford	117,083

REGISTERED VOTERS

Unaffiliated	42%
Democrat	34%
Republican	23%

POPULATION

2002 population (est.)	3,460,503
2000 population	3,405,565
1990 population	3,287,116
Percent change (1990-2000)	+3.6%
Rank among states (2002)	29
Median age	37.4
Born in state	57%
Foreign born	10.9%
Violent crime rate	325/100,000
Poverty level	7.9%
Federal workers	21,296
Military	16,675

REDISTRICTING

Connecticut lost one House seat in reapportionment. The Connecticut Reapportionment Commission adopted a new, five-district map on Dec. 21, 2001.

MISCELLANEOUS

Web: www.state.ct.us
Capital: Hartford

STATE ELECTION OFFICIAL
(860) 509-6100

DEMOCRATIC HEADQUARTERS
(860) 296-1775

REPUBLICAN HEADQUARTERS
(860) 547-0589

District Statistics

DIST.	2000 VOTE FOR PRESIDENT BUSH	GORE	NADER	WHITE	BLACK	ASIAN	HISP	MEDIAN INCOME	WHITE COLLAR	BLUE COLLAR	SERVICE INDUSTRY	OVER 64	UNDER 18	COLLEGE EDUCATION	RURAL	SQ. MILES
1	33%	61%	4%	72%	13%	2%	11%	$50,227	66%	20%	14%	15%	24%	28%	7%	653
2	40	54	6	89	3	2	4	$54,498	63	21	16	12	24	29	33	2,028
3	34	60	5	76	11	3	8	$49,752	65	21	14	15	24	28	3	459
4	43	53	3	71	11	3	13	$66,598	72	16	13	13	26	42	4	457
5	43	52	4	80	5	2	11	$53,118	63	23	14	14	25	30	14	1,248
STATE	38	56	4	77	9	2	9	$53,935	66	20	14	14	25	31	12	4,845
U.S.	47.9	48.4	3	69	12	4	13	$41,994	60	25	15	12	26	24	21	3,537,438

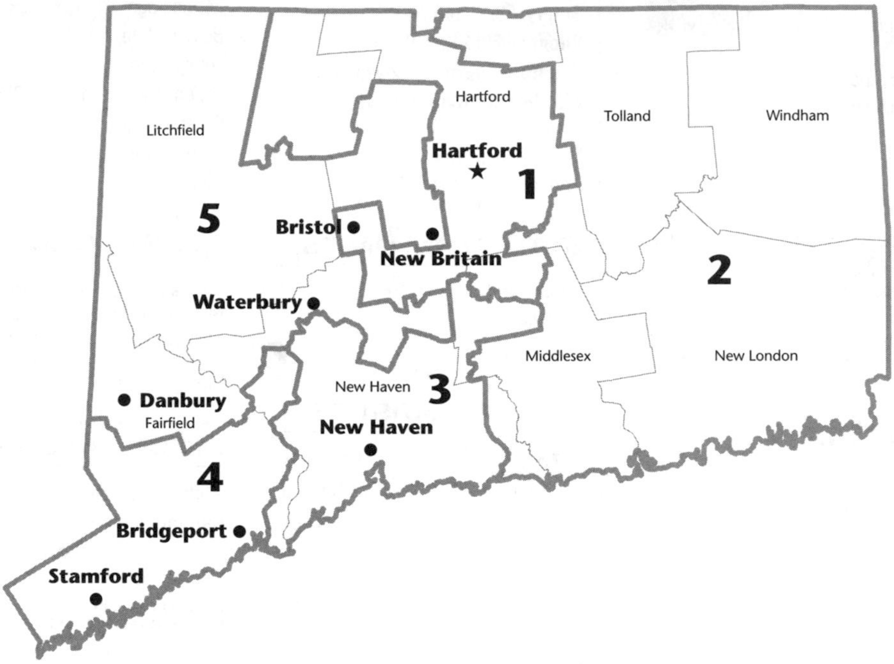
Hartford
Litchfield
Tolland
Windham
Hartford
1
5
Bristol
New Britain
2
Waterbury
Middlesex
New London
New Haven
3
Danbury
Fairfield
New Haven
4
Bridgeport
Stamford

Sen. Christopher J. Dodd (D)

CAPITOL OFFICE
224-2823
senator@dodd.senate.gov
dodd.senate.gov
448 Russell 20510-0702; fax 224-1083

COMMITTEES
Banking, Housing & Urban Affairs
Foreign Relations
Health, Education, Labor & Pensions
Rules & Administration - ranking member
Joint Library

HOMETOWN
East Haddam

BORN
May 27, 1944, Willimantic, Conn.

RELIGION
Roman Catholic

FAMILY
Wife, Jackie Marie Clegg; one child

EDUCATION
Providence College, B.A. 1966; U. of Louisville, J.D. 1972

MILITARY SERVICE
Army Reserve, 1969-75

CAREER
Lawyer; Peace Corps volunteer

POLITICAL HIGHLIGHTS
U.S. House, 1975-81

ELECTION RESULTS

1998 GENERAL

Christopher J. Dodd (D)	628,306	65.2%
Gary Franks (R)	312,177	32.4%
William Kozak (CC)	12,261	1.3%

1998 PRIMARY

Christopher J. Dodd (D)	unopposed

PREVIOUS WINNING PERCENTAGES
1992 (59%); 1986 (65%); 1980 (56%); 1978 House Election (70%); 1976 House Election (65%); 1974 House Election (59%)

Elected 1980; 4th term

Like his best buddy in the Senate, fellow Democrat Edward M. Kennedy, Dodd is the white-maned patriarch of a prominent Irish-American political family from New England, and he has spent decades in Congress combining liberal ideological instincts with a talent for cutting legislative deals. But unlike Kennedy, Dodd still openly harbors aspirations for higher office.

In 1994, he lost by one vote to Tom Daschle in an election for Senate Democratic leader. Eight years later, when Daschle contemplated relinquishing the leader's job to run for president, Dodd set about assessing support for another run. And as the 108th Congress began, he considered seeking the Democratic presidential nomination for himself in 2004. He decided against a bid in March 2003, saying he believed he could have more of an impact by staying in the Senate.

Dodd remains a study in contrasts. He thrives on waging partisan rhetorical battles — and did so as chairman of the Democratic National Committee at the height of the Republican "revolution" in the 104th Congress — but he positions himself as a pragmatist in legislative clinches. He is a liberal who often sides with business interests. And he was a leader on children's issues long before his first child, Grace, was born when he was 56, in the same week as the terrorist attacks of September 2001.

In the halls of the Senate, Dodd still comes off as something akin to the class clown. A quip ever ready on his lips, he can be seen joking with everyone from fellow senators to reporters to the Capitol elevator operators. Dodd's comfort level in part derives from his standing as a child of the Senate. His father, Thomas J. Dodd, was a Democratic senator from Connecticut for two terms, although his career declined after his censure in 1967 for misusing political contributions.

To this day, the senator views his father's colleagues as having wrongly spurned him, and so Dodd has cast two memorable votes to signal his preference for senatorial reciprocity over partisan victory. He was among just eight Democrats who joined the majority to confirm John Ashcroft, a former GOP senator from Missouri, as attorney general in 2003. And he was among just three Democrats to join the minority backing confirmation of John Tower, a former GOP senator from Texas, as defense secretary in 1989.

In the 107th Congress, Dodd directed much of his partisan energies at Otto J. Reich, President Bush's nominee to serve as assistant secretary of state for the Western Hemisphere. Dodd had tangled with Reich, a prominent Cuban-American conservative, for decades over issues ranging from aid to the Nicaraguan rebels in the 1980s to the U.S. embargo on Cuba today. So when Dodd gained the chairmanship of the Foreign Relations Committee's Western Hemisphere subcommittee, he made it a priority to keep Reich away from the State Department, refusing to even hold a hearing on his nomination. In the end, however, Bush prevailed for a short while, bringing Reich on board temporarily with recess appointments.

Dodd also was a driving force behind the 2002 law that imposed new disclosure and conflict-of-interest rules on accounting firms that audit publicly traded companies and increased criminal penalties for securities fraud. Bolstered by a wave of public outcry over accounting scandals at companies such as Enron Corp. and WorldCom Inc., Dodd and other Democrats were able to force the White House to swallow their bill rather than the weaker version the administration initially preferred.

But these fights were more the exception than the rule for Dodd, whose penchant for compromise has made him capable of forging coalitions with members of both parties.

As chairman of Rules and Administration for most of the 107th, Dodd worked with Republicans Mitch McConnell of Kentucky and Christopher S. Bond of Missouri to write the compromise language at the heart of a law, enacted in 2002, designed to prevent a repeat of the disputed 2000 presidential contest. The measure set the first federal standards for the conduct of elections and authorized $3.9 billion in federal aid over three years to meet those standards.

Much of Dodd's recent work on Foreign Relations has been bipartisan. He joined with Secretary of State Colin L. Powell to alter a program of certifying the cooperation of other countries with U.S. anti-drug efforts that had angered many U.S. allies, such as Mexico. And with the exception of Reich, Dodd has tended to back controversial nominees, saying "presidents, by and large, should get the nominees they want."

On another issue, though, Dodd's family loyalty put him on a collision course with the White House. For months, while the GOP tried to block cooperation with a new global court set up to try those accused of genocide and other crimes, Dodd stonewalled — recalling his father's days as a lead prosecutor at the Nuremberg trials of Nazi war criminals after World War II.

Dodd's tendency toward compromise partly reflects his need to walk a tightrope between his own liberal leanings and the needs of industries vital to Connecticut's economy. An ardent advocate on the Banking Committee for the state's insurance industries, he helped broker a deal with the White House in 2002 on a law creating a federal program to insure commercial property and casualty firms that sell terrorism insurance.

Dodd has long been a strong advocate on issues affecting children. In the 107th, he argued passionately that Bush's education bill should include more money for schools in poor areas. A prime sponsor of the 1993 law requiring businesses to grant workers time to address their family or medical needs, Dodd pushed legislation in the 106th Congress to improve child care safety and quality, and to make it more affordable. He also has been a leader in the effort to require safety locks on handguns.

For many years, Dodd's interest in family issues seemed odd, given the widespread Washington chatter about his personal life, including a period of well-publicized carousing in the 1980s with Kennedy. (Both senators were divorced at the time.) But after a decade-long courtship, Dodd married Jackie Marie Clegg, an Export-Import Bank official, in 1999. One of his Senate friends, Republican Orrin G. Hatch of Utah, had long urged the Roman Catholic Dodd to marry Clegg, who, like Hatch, is a Mormon.

While the senator learned to be a parent in 2002, he stumped for lawmakers in 23 states, including key early presidential primary states Iowa, New Hampshire and South Carolina. And he raised substantial funds for a 2004 Senate run that could have been diverted to a presidential campaign.

Despite the cloud over the senior Dodd's congressional career, the family name still resonated with voters when Christopher Dodd, at age 30, won an open House seat, which had been held by a Republican, in the post-Watergate election of 1974.

When Democrat Abraham Ribicoff retired six years later, Dodd became the youngest person ever elected to the Senate from Connecticut. He took 56 percent against former Sen. James L. Buckley of New York, who carried the standard of the newly resurgent conservative wing of the state GOP and whose family homestead is in Connecticut.

Dodd has won his subsequent elections more easily, taking almost two-thirds of the vote in 1998 against Gary A. Franks, who had lost re-election to the House two years before.

KEY VOTES

2002

Yes Pass farm bill reversing crop subsidy limits
No Postpone tougher automobile fuel efficiency standards
Yes Overhaul campaign finance law; ban "soft money" and restrict advocacy advertising
Yes Set federal election standards
No Support oil drilling in Arctic National Wildlife Refuge
No Revive fast-track procedures for trade agreements
Yes Create federal insurance coverage for catastrophic terrorist losses
Yes Tighten federal accounting and corporate governance regulation
Yes Advance bipartisan Medicare prescription drug plan
Yes Create independent Sept. 11 commission
Yes Back Democratic Homeland Security Department proposal
Yes Authorize war against Iraq

2001

Yes Confirm John Ashcroft as attorney general
No Nullify Clinton Labor Department ergonomics rule
No Cut taxes by $1.35 trillion through fiscal 2011
Yes Pass Democratic bill to bolster rights of patients in managed-care plans
Yes Permit a new round of military base closings
Yes Expand law enforcement power to investigate suspected terrorists

CQ VOTE STUDIES

	PARTY UNITY		PRESIDENTIAL SUPPORT	
	Support	Oppose	Support	Oppose
2002	94%	6%	68%	32%
2001	98%	2%	66%	34%
2000	95%	5%	98%	2%
1999	90%	10%	86%	14%
1998	91%	9%	93%	7%
1997	87%	13%	94%	6%
1996	89%	11%	81%	19%
1995	87%	13%	92%	8%
1994	90%	10%	95%	5%
1993	92%	8%	98%	2%

INTEREST GROUPS

	AFL-CIO	ADA	CCUS	ACU
2002	100%	80%	40%	5%
2001	94%	95%	36%	16%
2000	75%	95%	53%	13%
1999	88%	95%	53%	0%
1998	88%	95%	61%	4%
1997	57%	90%	50%	4%
1996	100%	85%	38%	10%
1995	92%	95%	32%	4%
1994	75%	80%	38%	0%
1993	82%	75%	36%	12%

Sen. Joseph I. Lieberman (D)

CAPITOL OFFICE
224-4041
lieberman.senate.gov
706 Hart 20510-0703; fax 224-9750

COMMITTEES
Armed Services
Environment & Public Works
Governmental Affairs - ranking member
Small Business & Entrepreneurship

HOMETOWN
New Haven

BORN
Feb. 24, 1942, Stamford, Conn.

RELIGION
Jewish

FAMILY
Wife, Hadassah Lieberman; four children

EDUCATION
Yale U., B.A. 1964 (politics & economics), LL.B. 1967

CAREER
Lawyer

POLITICAL HIGHLIGHTS
Conn. Senate, 1971-80 (majority leader, 1975-80); Democratic nominee for U.S. House, 1980; Conn. attorney general, 1983-89; Democratic nominee for vice president, 2000

ELECTION RESULTS

2000 GENERAL

Joseph I. Lieberman (D)	828,902	63.2%
Philip A. Giordano (R)	448,077	34.2%
William Kozak (CC)	25,509	2.0%

2000 PRIMARY

Joseph I. Lieberman (D)	unopposed

PREVIOUS WINNING PERCENTAGES
1994 (67%); 1988 (50%)

Elected 1988; 3rd term

When Al Gore decided not to run for president in 2004, he paved the way for Lieberman to plunge into a campaign that he had reluctantly promised to forego had his former ticket-mate tried again. Lieberman started with one important edge: Having been the Democratic nominee for vice president in 2000, he began the 108th Congress as the only member who had ever appeared on every ballot in the nation.

Whether or not Lieberman leverages that stature into the next presidential nomination, his standing as a nationally known figure seemed sure to help him advance his views on the entire panoply of public policy issues in a Senate filled with similarly robust egos — and a handful of presidential rivals, too. Lieberman's role as top Democrat on the Governmental Affairs Committee, which has oversight of much of the government workings, afforded him his most prominent legislative forum.

Lieberman has shed much of his persona as the engaging neophyte of the 2000 presidential campaign trail, when he charmed voters with a broad smile and gee-whiz attitude that made him appear constantly surprised and grateful that he was on the ticket, the first Jew ever to reach such a position. Instead, the combativeness and ambition that have always undergirded his political career have emerged more regularly from behind his warm and low-key public face.

In the 107th, Lieberman used his new prominence to push for a Department of Homeland Security long before President Bush accepted the idea. As chairman of Governmental Affairs between June 2001 and the end of 2002, Lieberman and his panel left a stamp on some of the biggest debates during the start of the Bush administration. The committee investigated the high-profile bankruptcies at Enron Corp. and other companies, which set the stage for enactment of the most far-reaching corporate regulatory law since the New Deal. The panel wrote the law consolidating 22 federal agencies in the biggest government reorganization since World War II. And Lieberman compelled Bush to accept the creation of an independent probe with wide latitude to investigate government failures that might have precipitated the terrorist attacks of Sept. 11, 2001.

In the 108th, Lieberman also will continue his longstanding efforts to infuse public life with religious faith. Most notably, he is still working to write a compromise version of Bush's proposal to give faith-based organizations federal funds to provide social services. During the 2000 campaign, the observant Orthodox Jew refused to campaign on the Sabbath. And he brushed aside questions about whether the country was ready for a Jewish president or vice president. "While my faith was the focus of the earliest reactions to my candidacy, it was not even mentioned at the end of the campaign," he told the Senate. "That is good news for all Americans."

But Republican critics contended that as Gore's running mate Lieberman seriously tarnished his image as a principled centrist and bipartisan bridge-builder by knuckling under to powerful liberal interest groups and backing away from some of his positions. They said he had abandoned his support for school vouchers and for some privatization of Social Security and soft-pedaled his frequent condemnations of the entertainment industry in order to help Democrats raise money from Hollywood.

On the Armed Services Committee, Lieberman looks out for Connecticut's defense-related industries and is more supportive of a robust military budget than many Democrats. He is among the minority of committee

Democrats who support moving ahead with a national missile defense system as soon as technologically feasible. In 1996, he was a leading proponent of a blue-ribbon panel to review long-range defense plans. He became a staunch proponent of large-scale war games to test novel ways of organizing U.S. forces to address post-Soviet threats.

Despite all that, Lieberman usually sticks to party positions. He is solidly in favor of abortion rights and gun control and consistently supported President Clinton on budget and tax issues. He has longstanding good relations with labor, gay rights advocates and environmentalists. And in the battles over homeland security, Lieberman has stood squarely with Democratic leaders fighting to protect union contracts and representation for federal workers.

Lieberman's centrist reputation stems from his stand on such issues as education. In 2000, he was one of nine Senate Democrats supporting a bill to create tax-deferred education savings accounts that parents could use for tutoring, supplies or private school tuition — a backdoor approach, in the view of liberal Democrats, to the GOP idea of creating vouchers that would drain money from the public schools. Lieberman also sided with some Republicans against trial lawyers, another Democratic constituency, in a 1996 vote for a bill to limit damages in product liability cases. The measure was strongly backed by insurance companies — a major industry in Connecticut.

Lieberman had spoken in favor of the idea of partially "privatizing" Social Security — a concept roundly opposed by Clinton and Gore under which individuals could invest a portion of their Social Security payroll tax in the securities markets. Gore and many other leading Democrats said such a plan could undermine the financial structure of Social Security. After his vice presidential nomination was announced, Lieberman reversed course, and his office distributed a previously unpublished essay titled, "My Private Journey Away From Privatization," in which he said "the promises and the numbers" of privatization advocates "don't add up."

Before the 2000 campaign, Lieberman was perhaps best-known to the nation for a September 1998 speech that criticized Clinton's behavior in the Monica Lewinsky scandal as "not just inappropriate. It is immoral. And it is harmful, for it sends a message of what is acceptable behavior to the larger American family — particularly to our children." The senator never called for the president's resignation, nor did he advocate the lesser penalty of censure. By condemning Clinton's behavior but also declaring "that talk of impeachment and resignation now is unwise," he may have bucked up the prospects of the very person he was so publicly upbraiding. Like all other Senate Democrats, he voted against convicting Clinton during the 1999 impeachment trial.

Lieberman always has been politically ambitious. He won a state Senate seat in 1970 — helped by a 24-year-old campaign aide named Bill Clinton, who was then at Yale Law School — and soon rose to majority leader. He lost a race for the U.S. House in the Reagan landslide of 1980, but rebounded in 1982 to become Connecticut attorney general.

Six years later, Lieberman mounted a tough and sometimes negative campaign for the Senate and won a narrow upset victory over Lowell P. Weicker Jr., a three-term liberal Republican. To win, he had to carry off the rare feat of rallying core, generally liberal Democratic supporters while at the same time running to the right of Weicker on school prayer and foreign policy. Bucking the Republican tide in 1994, Lieberman rolled up 67 percent of the vote against former GOP state Sen. Jerry Labriola. In 2000, the Gore-Lieberman ticket carried Connecticut with 56 percent of the vote — but Lieberman cruised to a third term in the Senate with 63 percent against Philip A. Giordano, the Republican mayor of Waterbury.

KEY VOTES

2002

Yes Pass farm bill reversing crop subsidy limits
No Postpone tougher automobile fuel efficiency standards
Yes Overhaul campaign finance law; ban "soft money" and restrict advocacy advertising
Yes Set federal election standards
No Support oil drilling in Arctic National Wildlife Refuge
Yes Revive fast-track procedures for trade agreements
Yes Create federal insurance coverage for catastrophic terrorist losses
Yes Tighten federal accounting and corporate governance regulation
Yes Advance bipartisan Medicare prescription drug plan
Yes Create independent Sept. 11 commission
Yes Back Democratic Homeland Security Department proposal
Yes Authorize war against Iraq

2001

No Confirm John Ashcroft as attorney general
No Nullify Clinton Labor Department ergonomics rule
No Cut taxes by $1.35 trillion through fiscal 2011
Yes Pass Democratic bill to bolster rights of patients in managed-care plans
Yes Permit a new round of military base closings
Yes Expand law enforcement power to investigate suspected terrorists

CQ VOTE STUDIES

	PARTY UNITY		PRESIDENTIAL SUPPORT	
	Support	Oppose	Support	Oppose
2002	85%	15%	77%	23%
2001	93%	7%	69%	31%
2000	88%	12%	94%	6%
1999	87%	13%	89%	11%
1998	80%	20%	83%	17%
1997	77%	23%	93%	7%
1996	76%	24%	90%	10%
1995	72%	28%	82%	18%
1994	76%	24%	88%	12%
1993	83%	17%	95%	5%

INTEREST GROUPS

	AFL-CIO	ADA	CCUS	ACU
2002	92%	85%	60%	20%
2001	93%	95%	43%	28%
2000	80%	75%	33%	20%
1999	78%	95%	47%	0%
1998	75%	80%	56%	16%
1997	29%	75%	60%	20%
1996	86%	75%	54%	35%
1995	100%	95%	33%	10%
1994	71%	65%	30%	8%
1993	82%	65%	45%	20%

Rep. John B. Larson (D)

CAPITOL OFFICE
225-2265
www.house.gov/larson
1005 Longworth 20515-0701; fax 225-1031

COMMITTEES
Armed Services
House Administration - ranking member
Science
Joint Library
Joint Printing

HOMETOWN
East Hartford

BORN
July 22, 1948, Hartford, Conn.

RELIGION
Roman Catholic

FAMILY
Wife, Leslie Larson; three children

EDUCATION
Central Connecticut State U., B.S. 1971 (history)

CAREER
Insurance company owner; high school teacher

POLITICAL HIGHLIGHTS
East Hartford Board of Education, 1978-79; East Hartford Town Council, 1979-83; Conn. Senate, 1983-95 (president pro tempore, 1987-95); sought Democratic nomination for governor, 1994

ELECTION RESULTS

2002 GENERAL		
John B. Larson (D)	134,698	66.8%
Phil Steele (R)	66,968	33.2%
2002 PRIMARY		
John B. Larson (D)		unopposed
2000 GENERAL		
John B. Larson (D)	151,932	71.9%
Bob Backlund (R)	59,331	28.1%

PREVIOUS WINNING PERCENTAGES
1998 (58%)

Elected 1998; 3rd term

Larson's dedication to public service and his determined support of his hometown's biggest employer are both rooted in his upbringing.

Pratt & Whitney put food on Larson's table during his childhood, and now Larson is doing his best to return the favor as a member of the Armed Services Committee. Larson's father worked for the engine manufacturer headquartered in East Hartford, and Larson grew up with seven siblings in Hartford's Mayberry Village, a public housing project where many Pratt & Whitney employees lived.

His mother, who worked at the state Capitol in Hartford and served on the East Hartford Town Council, encouraged her children to involve themselves in public life. Larson's younger brother, Timothy, is now mayor of East Hartford.

Affable and gregarious, Larson says he also was inspired to enter public service by the example of President Kennedy, another Catholic from a large New England family. Yet he remains more fixed in the middle of the Democratic Party than Kennedy was. Larson affiliates with the New Democrat Coalition, a group of several dozen centrist Democrats.

In the 108th Congress, New Democratic leader Nancy Pelosi made Larson the top-ranking Democrat on the House Administration panel and appointed him to the Democratic Steering Committee, which makes committee assignments, two indications that his star is on the rise within Democratic ranks.

He casts a dependable Democratic vote on most matters, including voting "no" on measures to expand overseas trade that organized labor opposes. In 2000, Larson voted against permanently granting China normal trade status, explaining he was keeping a campaign promise he had made to labor interests in his heavily Democratic district. Larson acknowledged, however, that the legislation likely would help Connecticut exports. And in both 2001 and 2002, he voted against a bill to give the president fast-track authority to negotiate trade agreements that Congress cannot amend.

From his seat on the Armed Services Committee, Larson looks out for Pratt & Whitney, which makes the engines for such military aircraft as the F-22 jet fighter, the Joint Strike Fighter and the C-17. He also is a co-founder of the Tactical Air Caucus, which supports the funding of new fighters. In his first year in Congress, Larson strenuously, and ultimately successfully, fought proposed cuts to the F-22, which critics said was draining money from other important Pentagon projects. "It's a matter of being eternally vigilant," he explained.

Larson also has a seat on the Science Committee, where he shows his support for the aerospace industry. He has championed legislation to increase funding for aerospace research and development and for the development of fuel cell technology. He advocates increased emphasis on science and technology education.

One of his first successes on Capitol Hill came in his first term when he sponsored legislation directing the librarian of Congress to prepare a history of the House. He headed off potential partisan bickering by signing on both Speaker J. Dennis Hastert and Minority Leader Richard A. Gephardt as cosponsors.

A former high school football coach, Larson often emphasizes the importance of teamwork, particularly in the partisan atmosphere of the House. "There will always be rugged individualists, and we will always praise them. . . . But what gets the job done is teamwork," he once told the Southern Connecticut Business Journal.

After graduating from Central Connecticut State University, Larson taught high school history and coached for about five years. He then went into the insurance business. Stints on the local school board and town council were followed by his election in 1982 to the state Senate.

When Republicans took control of the state Senate in 1984, Larson was the only Democrat allowed to chair a committee, the Energy and Technology panel. Two years later, when the Democrats won back a majority, he was named Senate president pro tem, the state's third-highest office. He served in that post for the next eight years — making him the longest-serving president pro tem in state history.

Larson wrote Connecticut's Family and Medical Leave Act — the first such law enacted in the country. He also pushed for "family resource centers," public school buildings that are used to offer child care and family support services.

He waged an unsuccessful bid for governor in 1994, gaining the endorsements of his party leaders but losing the primary to state Comptroller Bill Curry.

Out of public office for the first time in 15 years, Larson returned to the insurance business. In 1996 he led a statewide volunteer drive, "ConneCT '96," that aimed to wire all the state's schools and libraries to the Internet. His interest in that issue continues in Congress, where he has chaired the Digital Divide Caucus, which works to make technology available to all Americans, regardless of geography or socioeconomic circumstances.

When veteran 1st District Democratic Rep. Barbara B. Kennelly announced late in 1997 that she was running for governor in 1998, Larson was the first Democrat to file for her seat. He edged past Miles S. Rapoport, the Connecticut secretary of state, in the primary and then cruised to a 17 percentage point victory in November.

In 2000, he pinned a 44-point defeat on Republican Bob Backlund, a charismatic former professional wrestler with no prior political experience. Larson refrained from negative campaigning, saying only that his opponent did not seem to have a full grasp of the issues. He was not hurt by the fact that the 1st is so solidly liberal that it was once described by the Hartford Courant as a district in which "a Democrat could probably take a two-year nap and be re-elected."

In 2002, with the 1st left largely intact by redistricting, Larson again won easily by a 2-to-1 ratio.

KEY VOTES

2002

Yes Overhaul campaign finance law; ban "soft money" and restrict advocacy advertising
Yes Back Bush's defense budget increase
No Extend 1996 welfare law
No Adopt Bush's discretionary spending limit
No Pass GOP Medicare prescription drug plan
Yes Create independent Sept. 11 commission
Yes Extend union protections to Homeland Security Department employees
No Revive fast-track procedures for trade agreements
No Authorize war against Iraq
No Advance bankruptcy overhaul opposed by abortion opponents

2001

No Nullify Clinton Labor Department ergonomics rule
No Cut taxes by $1.35 trillion through fiscal 2011
Yes Maintain ban on oil drilling in Arctic National Wildlife Refuge
No Approve Bush proposal to limit managed-care plan liability for coverage decisions
Yes Divert money from crop subsidy payments to land conservation
Yes Expand law enforcement power to investigate suspected terrorists

CQ VOTE STUDIES

	PARTY UNITY		PRESIDENTIAL SUPPORT	
	Support	Oppose	Support	Oppose
2002	95%	5%	30%	70%
2001	88%	12%	22%	78%
2000	93%	7%	85%	15%
1999	93%	7%	83%	17%

INTEREST GROUPS

	AFL-CIO	ADA	CCUS	ACU
2002	100%	95%	50%	0%
2001	92%	90%	45%	8%
2000	90%	95%	57%	12%
1999	78%	100%	38%	4%

CONNECTICUT 1
Central – Hartford, Bristol

Situated midway between Boston and New York – roughly 100 miles from each – the 1st is an attractive commercial center for businesses straddling the Northeast Corridor. Insurance companies, banks and state government are the lifeblood of Hartford and its well-off suburbs.

Hartford saw a renewal in the 1990s, cleaning up its downtown and attracting several high-tech manufacturing firms. But challenges remain: While Hartford remains the most populous city in the 1st District, it experienced a 13 percent population decline in the 1990s. West Hartford, the next most populous city, grew by 6 percent.

Hartford is overwhelmingly minority and staunchly Democratic. The city gave Al Gore 80 percent of the vote in the 2000 presidential election, more than any other city or town in the state. Democrats outnumber Republicans in the 1st by more than a 2-to-1 ratio. The district gave Gore his largest vote margin in Connecticut, and a Republican has not represented Hartford in the House since 1959.

Hispanics comprise 40 percent of Hartford residents; most of them are Puerto Rican. City voters in November 2001 elected Hartford's first Hispanic mayor.

In the 1990s, the 1st was relatively compact in shape. Connecticut lost one seat in the 2000 reapportionment, and the 1st now resembles a backward "C." The new district takes in some sparsely populated towns in northwestern Connecticut and part of Middletown, where Wesleyan University is located. The district also includes Democratic-leaning Bristol, where ESPN has its headquarters.

MAJOR INDUSTRY

Insurance, banking, defense, government

CITIES

Hartford, 121,578; West Hartford (unincorporated), 63,589; Bristol, 60,062; East Hartford (unincorporated), 49,575; Central Manchester (unincorporated), 30,595; Newington (unincorporated), 29,306

NOTABLE

The Hartford Courant (founded in 1764) is the nation's oldest newspaper in continuous circulation; Noah Webster, author of the first American dictionary, was born in West Hartford; Hartford's Wadsworth Atheneum is the nation's oldest public art museum.

Rep. Rob Simmons (R)

CAPITOL OFFICE
225-2076
www.house.gov/simmons
215 Cannon 20515-0702; fax 225-4977

COMMITTEES
Armed Services
Transportation & Infrastructure
Veterans' Affairs
(Health - chairman)

HOMETOWN
Stonington

BORN
Feb. 11, 1943, Manhattan, N.Y.

RELIGION
Episcopalian

FAMILY
Wife, Heidi Simmons; two children

EDUCATION
Haverford College, B.A. 1965 (English literature); Harvard U., M.P.A. 1979; U. of Connecticut, attended 1988-91 (political science)

MILITARY SERVICE
Army, 1965-68; Army Reserve, 1970-2000

CAREER
Professor; congressional aide; CIA agent

POLITICAL HIGHLIGHTS
Candidate for Stonington Board of Selectmen, 1985; Stonington Republican Town Committee, 1986-92 (chairman, 1988-92); Conn. House, 1991-2001

ELECTION RESULTS

2002 GENERAL		
Rob Simmons (R)	117,434	54.1%
Joseph D. Courtney (D)	99,674	45.9%
2002 PRIMARY		
Rob Simmons (R)		unopposed
2000 GENERAL		
Rob Simmons (R)	114,380	50.6%
Sam Gejdenson (D)	111,520	49.4%

Elected 2000; 2nd term

Simmons' service as an Army intelligence officer in Vietnam and his decade as a CIA operations officer gave him instant credibility among his colleagues after the Sept. 11, 2001, terrorist attacks as someone who would understand the nature of international terrorism. A former staff director of the Senate Intelligence Committee, he was lifted almost immediately from the relative obscurity that most freshman House members face.

"The minute he says, 'When I was in the CIA,' all ears are focused on what's the next thing he's going to say," said fellow Class of 2000 Republican Mark Steven Kirk of Illinois.

Simmons' opinion was often sought during congressional inquiries on how the terrorist attacks were carried out. And when the House debated whether to authorize a military attack on Iraq, his words of caution and his support for a Democratic-drafted alternative that called for the president to work with the United Nations were surprising to some in his party.

Although he does not serve on the Intelligence Committee, Simmons worked closely with panel members after Sept. 11. He was able to include in the 2001 intelligence authorization bill a section that requires the CIA to pay full liability insurance for its agents, instead of just half. "We need to treat them like heroes instead of scoundrels," he said, arguing that success in the war against terrorism depends in large measure on keeping experienced agents in the fold.

Simmons said he lost one of his best friends, a man he worked with in Vietnam, when a suicide bomber blew up the U.S. embassy in Beirut in 1983. His friend and a number of other CIA agents were killed. "That was the day the war on terrorism began for me," Simmons told Roll Call, a Capitol Hill newspaper.

Simmons' military background — he still wears his Army dog tags — helped him land seats on the Armed Services and Veterans' Affairs committees. He has taken a special interest in submarine projects at General Dynamics' Electric Boat Corp., which is headquartered in the 2nd District and is one of the largest employers in southern New England. He also won a seat on the Transportation and Infrastructure Committee, where he worked to obtain funding to complete Route 11 from Salem to Waterford.

Simmons says he often tells people he regards himself as a fiscal conservative, "because it's your money," and a social moderate, "because it's your life." He aligns himself with the moderate Republican Main Street Partnership, which says it is "committed to building America's principled but pragmatic center." Simmons says he has always wanted to lead a life of public service and adds that he is not ashamed of being a politician, which he calls "a citizen in action."

Simmons represents a swing district, which was happy with a Democrat for 20 years, so he will buck the GOP leadership on occasion. In his first term, in fact, he strayed from the party line more than any other GOP freshman. He voted against a bill to enhance presidential trade negotiating authority, which was opposed by organized labor, and he backed enactment of the law to overhaul campaign financing. In both instances, Simmons was among a small minority of Republicans.

Endorsed in 2002 by the League of Conservation Voters and the Friends of the Earth, Simmons won approval in the 107th of a bill to study whether Eightmile River should be designated as a wild and scenic river. He also was one of only 34 House Republicans who voted in 2001 to continue the prohibition on drilling in the Alaska National Wildlife Refuge.

A top priority for Simmons is to involve local authorities in the process of deciding whether to grant American Indian tribes federal recognition, and with it the right to operate gambling casinos. There are already two huge Indian-run casinos in his district, and Simmons is concerned that the tribal recognition process — he calls it the "black hole of recognition" — will lead to more, without any local input.

Simmons says he was greatly influenced by his maternal grandfather, Robert Ruhl, for whom he is named. Ruhl was editor and publisher of Oregon's Medford Mail Tribune and during his tenure, the newspaper won the 1934 Pulitzer Prize for public service for its campaign against unscrupulous local politicians. Simmons worked for the paper during summer breaks and envisioned a life in public service, intending to become a journalist as well. But the Vietnam War was under way when he graduated from college, so he enlisted rather than be drafted. He spent 19 months in Vietnam as an Army intelligence officer, winning two bronze stars. He then joined the CIA, working as an operations officer for a decade, including five years on assignment in East Asia. He left the agency in 1979 after hundreds of agents were dismissed as part of a post-Vietnam downsizing.

After earning a master's degree in public administration from Harvard, Simmons worked for two years as a legislative assistant to Rhode Island GOP Sen. John H. Chafee. Two years later, in 1981, he went to work for the Senate Intelligence Committee, where he found himself facing off against top CIA officials over what became the Iran-Contra scandal. He left the staff in 1985 and returned to his native Connecticut.

During five terms in the Connecticut House, he worked on transportation and education issues. After receiving 73 percent of the vote in a district that was just one-quarter Republican in 1998, Simmons began to explore a return to Washington as an elected official. Though Democrat Sam Gejdenson had been elected to a 10th term with 61 percent of the vote that year, he had had closer calls in his three previous races — winning by just 21 votes in 1994.

Simmons decided to take on Gejdenson in 2000 by tapping into local issues and contending that the incumbent's voting record was too liberal for the district. He won one of the year's biggest upsets by 2,860 votes.

In 2002, redistricting did little to alter the 2nd District's politically competitive nature, and Simmons' bid for a second term was on the shortlist of races to watch nationwide. Both national party organizations targeted the race for special attention, and in the end Simmons was held to 54 percent of the vote by the Democratic candidate, former state Rep. Joseph D. Courtney.

KEY VOTES

2002

Yes Overhaul campaign finance law; ban "soft money" and restrict advocacy advertising
Yes Back Bush's defense budget increase
Yes Extend 1996 welfare law
Yes Adopt Bush's discretionary spending limit
Yes Pass GOP Medicare prescription drug plan
No Create independent Sept. 11 commission
Yes Extend union protections to Homeland Security Department employees
No Revive fast-track procedures for trade agreements
Yes Authorize war against Iraq
Yes Advance bankruptcy overhaul opposed by abortion opponents

2001

Yes Nullify Clinton Labor Department ergonomics rule
Yes Cut taxes by $1.35 trillion through fiscal 2011
Yes Maintain ban on oil drilling in Arctic National Wildlife Refuge
Yes Approve Bush proposal to limit managed-care plan liability for coverage decisions
Yes Divert money from crop subsidy payments to land conservation
Yes Expand law enforcement power to investigate suspected terrorists

CQ VOTE STUDIES

	PARTY UNITY		PRESIDENTIAL SUPPORT	
	Support	Oppose	Support	Oppose
2002	78%	22%	78%	22%
2001	83%	17%	77%	23%

INTEREST GROUPS

	AFL-CIO	ADA	CCUS	ACU
2002	22%	35%	90%	68%
2001	25%	35%	91%	44%

CONNECTICUT 2

East – Norwich, New London, Storrs

The state's largest and most working-class district, the 2nd runs from the waterfront of Middlesex and New London counties north to the Massachusetts border through small towns and the main campus of the University of Connecticut in Storrs.

The defense industry continues to be the district's major economic force, but it now shares some of that responsibility with the American Indian-owned Foxwoods and Mohegan Sun casinos. The economic shift started in the early 1990s, when some of the submarine contracts in New London and Groton were sent to Newport News, Va., just as Foxwoods, and later Mohegan Sun, began attracting visitors.

Defense and casino matters sit atop the district's list of political issues. The stream of gamblers and casino employees traveling through the district has strained the 2nd's highways, making transportation an election-year issue. In addition, the casinos and surrounding towns have quarreled over which regulations should apply to reservation land.

Despite a series of close elections throughout the 1980s and 1990s, Democrats were able to maintain their lock on the 2nd until 2000, when Rob Simmons became the first Republican elected since 1972. The district became slightly less Democratic in redistricting following the 2000 census, as liberal-leaning Middletown was excised from the 2nd and split up between the 1st and 3rd districts.

MAJOR INDUSTRY
Gambling, defense, health care

MILITARY BASES
New London Naval Submarine Base, 7,441 military, 1,534 civilian (2002)

CITIES
Norwich, 36,117; New London, 25,671; Willimantic (unincorporated), 15,823; Storrs (unincorporated), 10,996

NOTABLE
Foxwoods Resort and Casino, owned by the Mashantucket Pequot Tribal Nation, is the largest resort casino in the world, with annual revenue of $1 billion; New London is home to the U.S. Coast Guard Academy; The Mystic Seaport maritime museum is in Mystic.

Rep. Rosa DeLauro (D)

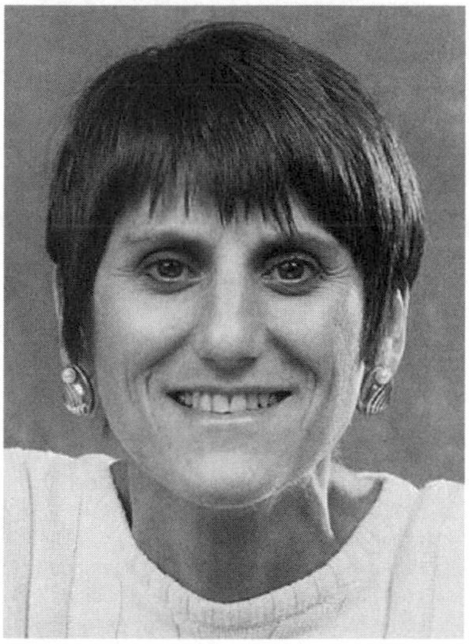

CAPITOL OFFICE
225-3661
www.house.gov/delauro
2262 Rayburn 20515-0703; fax 225-4890

COMMITTEES
Appropriations
Budget

HOMETOWN
New Haven

BORN
March 2, 1943, New Haven, Conn.

RELIGION
Roman Catholic

FAMILY
Husband, Stanley Greenberg; three stepchildren

EDUCATION
London School of Economics, attended 1962-63; Marymount College, B.A. 1964; Columbia U., M.A. 1966 (international politics)

CAREER
Political activist; congressional and mayoral aide

POLITICAL HIGHLIGHTS
No previous office

ELECTION RESULTS

2002 GENERAL		
Rosa DeLauro (D)	121,557	65.6%
Richter Elser (R)	54,757	29.5%
Charlie Pillsbury (GREEN)	9,050	4.9%
2002 PRIMARY		
Rosa DeLauro (D)		unopposed
2000 GENERAL		
Rosa DeLauro (D)	156,910	71.9%
June Gold (R)	60,037	27.5%

PREVIOUS WINNING PERCENTAGES
1998 (71%); 1996 (71%); 1994 (63%); 1992 (66%); 1990 (52%)

Elected 1990; 7th term

DeLauro is one of her party's fiercest liberal champions and a sharp critic of the Republican leadership in Congress. In more than a dozen years in the House, this outspoken daughter of Italian immigrants has broken gender barriers to climb the Democratic leadership ladder, eventually running the party's communications arm as Minority Leader Richard A. Gephardt's handpicked assistant in the 107th Congress.

In recent years, her rise has been slowed by two significant setbacks. As the 108th Congress organized, she lost a race for Democratic Caucus chairman to Robert Menendez of New Jersey, by a lone vote, 104-103. DeLauro's appeal as a woman in leadership could not overcome Menendez's as a Hispanic, especially since Democrats already had a woman, Nancy Pelosi, in the top leadership post.

The loss marked the second time DeLauro was defeated for the position. In her first race for caucus chairman in 1998, she lost to Martin Frost of Texas. Though she is among the most influential Democrats in the House, all of her leadership roles so far have been appointive.

Providing some consolation in the 108th, DeLauro got a seat on the Budget Committee, and Pelosi made her the co-chairman of the Democratic Steering Committee, which makes committee assignments.

DeLauro is easily one of the most recognizable faces in the House. Her finger-in-the-eye floor speeches ooze partisanship and are often accompanied by copious podium-pounding. Her trademark daywear — bright colors, bold prints and chunky jewelry — lands her on the occasional magazine worst-dressed list.

There is no mistaking though that DeLauro is as crafty a politician as there is. She has been a voice for the party on national issues such as abortion rights and women's health parity. But she also tends to business at home. She is uncharacteristically hawkish on federal funding for the Black Hawk and Comanche helicopters, both products of the Stratford, Conn.-based Sikorsky Aircraft Corp.

In the minority, she has been less able to shape policy than to define what it is Democrats don't like about GOP proposals. As one of four chief deputy whips after her party lost the majority in 1995, she was one of the creators of its "Rapid Response" operation, designed to speed the party's message to the media. Such techniques are now a staple of national politics.

Ridiculing Republicans' resistance to a Clinton administration school construction program, DeLauro said: "Let them visit kids sitting in trailers and explain why they hung them out to dry."

DeLauro works to ensure that her party does not take for granted the women voters who are one of its strongest constituencies. In the 106th Congress, she successfully pushed a bill requiring insurers to pay for 48 hours of hospital care after a mastectomy — ending a practice commonly known as "drive-through mastectomies." Her interest in women's health issues stems in part from her own battle with ovarian cancer several years ago. DeLauro has said she felt she was handed a "second chance at life" and that all women deserve the same.

She also has sponsored legislation to make child care more readily available and has advocated toughening penalties against employers who do not pay women and men equally for the same work. A staunch proponent of abortion rights, DeLauro has tried to change the law excluding abortion from the list of covered procedures in the medical policies of federal workers.

All of the significant figures in DeLauro's life are passionately political. Her parents were both blue-collar activists on the New Haven City Council, and her husband is Stanley Greenberg, a prominent Democratic pollster and former adviser to President Clinton.

DeLauro developed her liberal views and political smarts growing up in Wooster Square, a tight-knit Italian neighborhood in New Haven. Her father, Ted, was an immigrant who became a New Haven alderman, and her mother, Luisa, was a factory worker who got her high school diploma studying at night. Her mother also became a city alderman.

Her parents' home was the hub of neighborhood meetings about happenings in the schools, the availability of jobs, and hassles with immigration officials. When her father decided to run for the city council, he kept a file box filled with voters' names and their concerns, then walked door-to-door to seek their votes.

As part of the first college-educated generation in her family, DeLauro graduated with honors from Marymount College in Tarrytown, N.Y., and got a master's degree in international politics from Columbia University.

In the 1960s, she became a community organizer in President Johnson's War on Poverty, then worked for the mayor of New Haven. She eventually proved her mettle running Democrat Chris Dodd's first campaign for the Senate. When he won, she became his chief of staff for seven years. She expanded her political network by taking the helm of Emily's List, the powerful fundraising group promoting women's candidacies for higher office.

In 1990, when Democratic Rep. Bruce Morrison gave up his 3rd District seat to run for governor of Connecticut, DeLauro was ready to step out of supporting roles and become a candidate herself. Her political contacts enabled her to raise money quickly and shoo away intraparty competition.

Republicans put up state Sen. Thomas Scott, an energetic conservative opposed to gun control and abortion rights. He made some headway portraying DeLauro as a far-left radical, but her coalition of activist liberals and blue-collar voters gave her a 4 percentage point victory.

Scott came back for a rematch in 1992, but DeLauro was ready with a healthy campaign war chest. She won with 66 percent of the vote and has been easily re-elected since then.

DeLauro seems destined to carry on the legacy of her mother, a woman ahead of her time who once exhorted other women to speak up for themselves in the political arena. In an old newsletter clipping that DeLauro has saved, her mother is quoted as saying, "Come on, girls. Let's make ourselves heard."

KEY VOTES

2002

- Yes Overhaul campaign finance law; ban "soft money" and restrict advocacy advertising
- Yes Back Bush's defense budget increase
- No Extend 1996 welfare law
- No Adopt Bush's discretionary spending limit
- No Pass GOP Medicare prescription drug plan
- Yes Create independent Sept. 11 commission
- Yes Extend union protections to Homeland Security Department employees
- No Revive fast-track procedures for trade agreements
- No Authorize war against Iraq
- No Advance bankruptcy overhaul opposed by abortion opponents

2001

- No Nullify Clinton Labor Department ergonomics rule
- No Cut taxes by $1.35 trillion through fiscal 2011
- Yes Maintain ban on oil drilling in Arctic National Wildlife Refuge
- No Approve Bush proposal to limit managed-care plan liability for coverage decisions
- Yes Divert money from crop subsidy payments to land conservation
- Yes Expand law enforcement power to investigate suspected terrorists

CQ VOTE STUDIES

	PARTY UNITY		PRESIDENTIAL SUPPORT	
	Support	Oppose	Support	Oppose
2002	96%	4%	22%	78%
2001	95%	5%	26%	74%
2000	97%	3%	87%	13%
1999	97%	3%	82%	18%
1998	97%	3%	82%	18%

INTEREST GROUPS

	AFL-CIO	ADA	CCUS	ACU
2002	100%	100%	35%	0%
2001	100%	95%	35%	0%
2000	100%	90%	42%	8%
1999	100%	100%	16%	0%
1998	100%	100%	28%	8%

CONNECTICUT 3

South – New Haven, Milford

Working-class, bedrock constituents of the Democratic Party mix with the liberal ivory tower elite in the 3rd. Situated on the state's southern coast, it encompasses both the working-class elements of New Haven, a busy blue-collar port, and prestigious Yale University. Yale might be the city's largest employer, but labor issues have sometimes caused tension between the university and the city's blue-collar workers. All this stands in contrast to the surrounding towns, where professionals who commute throughout Connecticut and as far as New York City reside. New Haven, like most Connecticut cities, is far poorer than its surrounding suburbs.

The district is solidly Democratic, with the outlying towns leaning to the right of New Haven. The district picked up most of Democratic stronghold Middletown during redistricting following the 2000 census. The 3rd is home to many minority groups, most living in New Haven, that traditionally support Democrats. New Haven has a high percentage of Hispanics and blacks. The district also is home to many Italian-Americans, who have increasingly moved to the suburbs.

The defense industry plays a large role in the 3rd. Sikorsky Aircraft, a helicopter manufacturer based in Stratford, depends on the military for survival, and Pratt & Whitney has a plant in North Haven. The 3rd was dealt a blow when Stratford Army Engine Plant was shut down in 1995, and the district has had trouble attracting new industries. New Haven has tried to lure tourists to its waterfront and business groups to its convention centers, with mild success.

MAJOR INDUSTRY

Trade, manufacturing, defense

CITIES

New Haven, 123,626; West Haven, 52,360; Milford, 52,305; Stratford (unincorporated), 49,976; Middletown (pt.), 34,329; Naugatuck, 30,989

NOTABLE

The frisbee was invented at Yale University in 1920 when students discovered that empty pie plates from the Frisbee Baking Co. of nearby Bridgeport were fun to toss around on New Haven Green; Milford is home to the headquarters of the Subway sandwich shop chain; Polls conducted by Quinnipiac University in Hamden are frequently cited by national news organizations.

Rep. Christopher Shays (R)

CAPITOL OFFICE
225-5541
rep.shays@mail.house.gov
www.house.gov/shays
1126 Longworth 20515-0704; fax 225-9629

COMMITTEES
Budget
Financial Services
Government Reform
(National Security, Emerging Threats & International Relations - chairman)
Select Homeland Security

HOMETOWN
Bridgeport

BORN
Oct. 18, 1945, Darien, Conn.

RELIGION
Christian Scientist

FAMILY
Wife, Betsi deRaismes Shays; one child

EDUCATION
Principia College, B.A. 1968 (American history & political science); New York U., M.B.A. 1974 (urban affairs & economics), M.P.A. 1978

CAREER
Real estate broker; public official; Peace Corps volunteer

POLITICAL HIGHLIGHTS
Conn. House, 1975-87; Republican candidate for mayor of Stamford, 1983

ELECTION RESULTS

2002 GENERAL		
Christopher Shays (R)	113,197	64.4%
Stephanie Sanchez (D)	62,491	35.6%
2002 PRIMARY		
Christopher Shays (R)		unopposed
2000 GENERAL		
Christopher Shays (R)	119,155	57.6%
Stephanie Sanchez (D)	84,472	40.9%

PREVIOUS WINNING PERCENTAGES
1998 (69%); 1996 (60%); 1994 (74%); 1992 (67%); 1990 (77%); 1988 (72%); 1987 Special Election (57%)

Elected August 1987; 8th full term

Shays capped his 15th year in the House with the legislative coup of his career — enactment in 2002 of new limits on the flow of money into federal campaigns, a cause he had long championed in vain. But victory came with a price. Shays was denied the chairmanship of the Government Reform Committee as a result of his open defiance of the House GOP leadership, which strongly opposed his campaign finance bill.

He did manage to secure the second-ranking Republican seat on the Budget Committee, where he had been a deficit warrior in the 1990s. And he was appointed to the new Homeland Security Committee, which will be a hub of anti-terrorism efforts in the aftermath of the Sept. 11, 2001, attacks. Shays also retained the gavel of the Government Reform Subcommittee on National Security, where he has been a critic of the government's response to terrorist threats.

But he didn't get what he wanted most, the gavel of the full Government Reform Committee. Because of his seniority, Shays was in line to replace Indiana's Dan Burton in the 108th Congress, when Burton's six-year term expired. The Republican leadership instead gave the post to Thomas M. Davis III of Virginia. Davis had endeared himself to the party hierarchy by engineering the well-financed campaign organization that brought the GOP six additional House seats in 2002. Meanwhile, Shays bucked the leaders in grand fashion — not only by pushing his campaign finance bill but also by rebelling at key moments when they demanded party loyalty. "I am a maverick," Shays said. "I realize that there are consequences."

As he had in earlier attempts in the late 1990s, Shays teamed with Democrat Martin T. Meehan of Massachusetts in 2001 to try to get a bill to the floor. Their legislation clamped down on "soft money" contributions, large donations from individuals and corporations that were flowing to the major parties despite widespread criticism that the money was a corrupting influence in politics. When the leadership proposed ground rules for debate that Shays thought unfairly handicapped his bill, he fought back by defeating those rules on the floor — a major breach of party discipline.

Early the next year, the accounting scandal centered on the politically well-connected Enron Corp. provided a new opportunity for Shays and Meehan. With public attention once again focused on the issue of influence buying in Washington, they resurrected their legislation, this time using more-aggressive tactics. Shays got 19 Republicans to join Democrats on a "discharge petition" to compel a floor vote despite the stated desires of GOP leaders to avoid one.

With momentum in their favor, Shays and Meehan pushed the bill through, working with Republican John McCain of Arizona and Democrat Russell D. Feingold of Wisconsin on a companion Senate measure. The legislation was enacted, marking the first time since 1960 that the use of a discharge petition had resulted so quickly in a major change in federal law.

As a moderate among the predominantly conservative House Republicans, Shays touts a long list of issues on which he routinely goes against the grain. In the 107th Congress, he sided with the Democrats on party-line votes 22 percent of the time, more often than all but four other House Republicans. And he voted against President Bush's wishes 26 percent of the time, more often than nine House GOP colleagues. His contrarian views, sometimes delivered with pained sincerity, leave colleagues grumbling that he is more interested in publicity than issues.

But many of Shays' positions flow naturally from the Rockefeller Republicanism that, while dying elsewhere in the country, still sustains dinner party conversations on the East Coast, including in the tony suburbs of the 4th District. They also appeal to Shay's other big constituency, the struggling residents of the city of Bridgeport, the state's biggest city.

Shays supports gun control and abortion rights, and he has opposed efforts to eliminate family planning funds from spending bills. He was one of only four House Republicans who opposed all of the articles of impeachment against President Clinton. He has bucked his leadership to support raising the minimum wage and banning job discrimination against gay people. After more than 60 of his constituents died on Sept. 11, he sought, against Bush's wishes, a broad independent inquiry into government lapses in tracking terrorists.

He is particularly proud of his environmental positions. "That's what really defines me as a moderate," he says. "I believe we're not going to have a world to live in if we neglect it."

Still, Shays can be a team player. He was touting the virtues of the GOP tax cuts and spending reductions as the 108th began. During debate on the 2002 law creating the Homeland Security Department, Shays offered a key amendment on the rights of federal unionized workers, an issue that divided Republicans. His measure gave GOP moderates the chance to vote for something that seemed to favor labor, but which essentially preserved the expanded management authority the White House sought.

Shays was a conscientious objector during the Vietnam War. After marrying right out of college, he and Betsi Shays spent two years in the Fiji Islands as Peace Corps volunteers; she now holds a senior job at the agency.

At age 29 Shays was elected to the state House in a rare Republican victory in the post-Watergate election of 1974. During his 13 years in Hartford, he developed his anti-establishment reputation. In 1985, he served several days in jail on a contempt citation after attempting to make a courtroom statement accusing a judge of going easy on an attorney charged with misconduct.

The name recognition from that incident helped propel him to the House two years later, when veteran Republican Stewart B. McKinney died. With an extensive grass-roots network and tireless campaigning, Shays defeated the anointed GOP candidate in the primary and then won the special election with 57 percent against Democrat Christine M. Niedermeier. He has not faced a substantial electoral challenge since. The 4th District was made slightly more Republican in 2001 redistricting.

KEY VOTES

2002

- Yes Overhaul campaign finance law; ban "soft money" and restrict advocacy advertising
- Yes Back Bush's defense budget increase
- Yes Extend 1996 welfare law
- Yes Adopt Bush's discretionary spending limit
- Yes Pass GOP Medicare prescription drug plan
- No Create independent Sept. 11 commission
- No Extend union protections to Homeland Security Department employees
- Yes Revive fast-track procedures for trade agreements
- Yes Authorize war against Iraq
- Yes Advance bankruptcy overhaul opposed by abortion opponents

2001

- Yes Nullify Clinton Labor Department ergonomics rule
- Yes Cut taxes by $1.35 trillion through fiscal 2011
- Yes Maintain ban on oil drilling in Arctic National Wildlife Refuge
- Yes Approve Bush proposal to limit managed-care plan liability for coverage decisions
- Yes Divert money from crop subsidy payments to land conservation
- Yes Expand law enforcement power to investigate suspected terrorists

CQ VOTE STUDIES

	PARTY UNITY		PRESIDENTIAL SUPPORT	
	Support	Oppose	Support	Oppose
2002	80%	20%	82%	18%
2001	75%	25%	65%	35%
2000	71%	29%	49%	51%
1999	66%	34%	48%	52%
1998	58%	42%	57%	43%

INTEREST GROUPS

	AFL-CIO	ADA	CCUS	ACU
2002	11%	20%	95%	76%
2001	17%	35%	83%	32%
2000	30%	40%	76%	60%
1999	11%	55%	60%	44%
1998	40%	45%	56%	40%

CONNECTICUT 4

Southwest — Bridgeport, Stamford

The 4th runs along Connecticut's sparkling "Gold Coast," bordering Long Island Sound, from the outskirts of New York City to Bridgeport on the district's southeast border. The contrast between working-class Bridgeport and the district's widespread wealth creates a complex world for politicians to navigate, as polo clubs rub elbows with the decayed city.

Many residents travel to jobs in New York City and Stamford, causing severe traffic problems on Interstate 95, already a congested route. Traffic issues permeate the public debate. Welfare-to-work programs also have become an issue. Having failed to place welfare recipients in good jobs in Bridgeport, the state's largest city, the local government began making moves to find employment for low-income residents in the affluent suburbs.

The 4th's political landscape is driven by the suburban elite, giving the district more registered Republicans than any other in Connecticut. Still, the 4th gave the edge to the Democratic presidential candidate in 1996 and 2000. A majority of the population in the poor, urban areas votes Democratic. Darien and New Canaan were the only two Connecticut jurisdictions to give George W. Bush more than 60 percent of the vote in 2000, while Al Gore's 73 percent showing in Bridgeport was among his highest in the state.

Republican mayors long dominated local politics. But Democrats made big inroads in 2001 when a Democrat won the race for first selectman in Greenwich and Norwalk's incumbent GOP mayor lost a re-election bid.

MAJOR INDUSTRY

Manufacturing, banking, medical

CITIES

Bridgeport, 139,529; Stamford, 117,083; Norwalk, 82,951; Trumbull (unincorporated), 34,243; Shelton (pt.), 28,192

NOTABLE

Republican Sen. Prescott Bush (1952-63), the father of the 41st president and a grandfather of the 43rd president, reared his family in Greenwich; General Electric's corporate headquarters are in Fairfield; P.T. Barnum, founder of the Ringling Bros., Barnum & Bailey Circus, made his home in Bridgeport; Bridgeport was the largest producer of ammunition for the Allied forces during both world wars.

Rep. Nancy L. Johnson (R)

CAPITOL OFFICE
225-4476
www.house.gov/nancyjohnson
2113 Rayburn 20515-0705; fax 225-4488

COMMITTEES
Ways & Means
(Health - chairwoman)

HOMETOWN
New Britain

BORN
Jan. 5, 1935, Chicago, Ill.

RELIGION
Unitarian

FAMILY
Husband, Ted Johnson; three children

EDUCATION
Radcliffe College, B.A. 1957; U. of London, attended 1957-58

CAREER
Civic leader

POLITICAL HIGHLIGHTS
Republican candidate for New Britain Common Council, 1975; Conn. Senate, 1977-83

ELECTION RESULTS

2002 GENERAL		
Nancy L. Johnson (R)	113,626	54.3%
Jim Maloney (D)	90,616	43.3%
Joseph A. Zdonczyk (CC)	3,709	1.8%
2002 PRIMARY		
Nancy L. Johnson (R)		unopposed
2000 GENERAL		
Nancy L. Johnson (R)	143,698	62.6%
Paul Vincent Valenti (D)	75,471	32.9%
Audrey A. Cole (GREEN)	7,303	3.2%
Timothy A. Knibbs (CC)	3,071	1.3%

PREVIOUS WINNING PERCENTAGES
1998 (58%); 1996 (50%); 1994 (64%); 1992 (70%); 1990 (74%); 1988 (66%); 1986 (64%); 1984 (64%); 1982 (52%)

Elected 1982; 11th term

As one of the House GOP's small cadre of moderates, Johnson is invariably overruled by the more conservative Republican leadership on matters such as government spending and abortion rights. But she perseveres and attempts to influence the debate.

"Legislation isn't something that any one voice can develop. It has to be developed through a process that we all participate in," she says.

Again in the 107th Congress, Johnson made no headway on three of her priorities: aid for those without health insurance, a prescription drug benefit for seniors on Medicare, and federally backed bonds for school construction.

The prescription drug issue showed two sides of Johnson: the rebellious Republican willing to challenge the party line and the cautious lawmaker careful not to isolate herself within her party. Initially, Johnson pressed colleagues to make prescription drug coverage a priority and provide assistance to all seniors, not just the poorest. But when other Republicans countered with a more limited $350 billion proposal, Johnson jumped aboard. She then adopted the party line, calling an $800 billion-plus Democratic plan "breathtakingly irresponsible."

The process began anew, when early in the 108th Congress Johnson expressed wariness about Bush administration plans for tax cuts that would leave no room in the budget for a Medicare prescription drug benefit.

Johnson said she is not tempted to switch parties. Keeping her in the GOP fold are her free-trade views and her seniority. In the 108th she is tied for 20th in longevity among House Republicans; she is also chairwoman of the powerful Ways and Means panel's Health Subcommittee.

"The Republicans have a far greater respect for the value and importance of local power and individual responsibility to the success of our democracy than do the Democrats. Democrats, on the other hand, have a better understanding of the power of national consistency, that standards be set nationally," Johnson says. She adds that the value placed on local government and personal responsibility gives the United States the strength it has, and that since the Sept. 11, 2001, terrorist attacks, she feels more strongly about her participation in the Republican Party than she ever has.

She enjoys a congenial relationship with the more conservative Ways and Means Chairman, California Republican Bill Thomas. The two often can be seen talking on the House floor. "We're both policy maniacs," she says.

Although it is not clear how much of what Johnson has to say makes its way into the chairman's draft bills, Thomas included in two 2002 tax bills provisions she sought to crack down on companies that move their headquarters to Bermuda or other offshore tax havens. Tool and hardware maker Stanley Works, based in Johnson's district, canceled such a move in the face of a political outcry. She says Thomas "had a lot of reservations about that legislation but . . . he knew how important it was with me to address the issue."

In the 108th, Johnson plans to take another crack at a prescription drug benefit and in the process will try to rein in Medicare's runaway expenses. "That system has many problems. I don't think that you can do prescription drugs in a vacuum," she says.

The congresswoman is used to being squeezed from both sides. During her first three House terms, Johnson's pursuit of a prestigious committee assignment was thwarted by GOP conservatives, who took a dim view of her support for abortion rights and her calls for more diversity in the

Republican Party. She landed a Ways and Means Committee seat in 1989, but she was soundly beaten in a bid for a low-level leadership post three years later.

Johnson's closest allies in the House are other moderate Republicans, but she is unwilling to stray as far as some of them do from the party line. The Connecticut lawmaker must, for example, look out for the insurance companies that are a major presence in her state — making it difficult for her to support any significant regulation of health insurers.

She voted against the bipartisan managed-care overhaul bill passed by the House in 1999 and backed a more-limited alternative endorsed by the GOP leadership. Johnson's Ways and Means colleague, Democrat Pete Stark of California, once called her "a whore for the insurance industry." He later apologized.

Johnson was chairwoman of the House ethics committee during the 104th Congress, and events during that tenure almost ended her House career. The marquee case before the panel involved the fundraising activities of Speaker Newt Gingrich, and her handling of the matter displeased lawmakers and constituents in both parties. Democrats accused her of dragging the case out to help the Republican Speaker; Republicans said her actions played into the Democrats' hands. She won her eighth term in 1996 by only 1,587 votes.

A Chicago native, Johnson came East to go to college, married, raised three children and got involved in community affairs in New Britain. Her civic activism led Republicans to recruit her into politics. After losing a city council election in 1975, she won a state Senate seat the next year, waging a door-to-door campaign to defeat a Democratic incumbent by 150 votes. By 1980, her winning share was up to 62 percent.

When Democratic Rep. Toby Moffett announced he was giving up the 6th District seat to run for the Senate in 1982, Johnson moved to take his place. She captured the backing of the Republican Party establishment, and she overwhelmed a conservative opponent in the primary. In November, she defeated the badly underfunded Democrat, state Sen. Bill Curry, by 4 percentage points.

Johnson's district teeters between moderate Republican and Democratic leanings. After the close call in 1996, she pushed her percentage of the vote up to 63 in 2000. But Johnson faced another stiff test in 2002, when Connecticut lost a House seat in reapportionment and her district was combined with that of Democratic Rep. Jim Maloney. In the incumbent vs. incumbent matchup, she won re-election by 11 points.

KEY VOTES

2002

Yes Overhaul campaign finance law; ban "soft money" and restrict advocacy advertising
Yes Back Bush's defense budget increase
Yes Extend 1996 welfare law
Yes Adopt Bush's discretionary spending limit
Yes Pass GOP Medicare prescription drug plan
Yes Create independent Sept. 11 commission
No Extend union protections to Homeland Security Department employees
Yes Revive fast-track procedures for trade agreements
Yes Authorize war against Iraq
Yes Advance bankruptcy overhaul opposed by abortion opponents

2001

Yes Nullify Clinton Labor Department ergonomics rule
Yes Cut taxes by $1.35 trillion through fiscal 2011
Yes Maintain ban on oil drilling in Arctic National Wildlife Refuge
Yes Approve Bush proposal to limit managed-care plan liability for coverage decisions
Yes Divert money from crop subsidy payments to land conservation
Yes Expand law enforcement power to investigate suspected terrorists

CQ VOTE STUDIES

	PARTY UNITY		PRESIDENTIAL SUPPORT	
	Support	Oppose	Support	Oppose
2002	75%	25%	75%	25%
2001	76%	24%	70%	30%
2000	71%	29%	51%	49%
1999	67%	33%	54%	46%
1998	62%	38%	57%	43%

INTEREST GROUPS

	AFL-CIO	ADA	CCUS	ACU
2002	11%	30%	90%	56%
2001	17%	30%	87%	32%
2000	10%	35%	90%	56%
1999	22%	55%	83%	36%
1998	50%	55%	83%	16%

CONNECTICUT 5

West – Danbury, New Britain, most of Waterbury

Based in the western part of the state, the 5th is a mix of bucolic farmland and mid-size industrial cities that includes nearly equal parts of the old 5th and 6th districts. The two were largely combined following the 2000 census when slow-growing Connecticut lost one House seat in reapportionment.

Waterbury is the 5th's most populous city, with about four of five city residents living in the district (the rest live in the 3rd District). The city is middle-class and racially diverse, with blacks and Hispanics together totaling 40 percent of the population. East of Waterbury, in the 5th's eastern edge, is Cheshire, an upper-income, Republican-leaning area, and Meriden, a Democratic-voting area with a large (21 percent) Hispanic population and a sizable Polish-American constituency.

North and east of Waterbury the district branches off to take in New Britain, where in 2002 directors of the toolmaking company Stanley Works voted — before reversing themselves — to reincorporate in Bermuda. New Britain, which lost population in the 1990s, has an ample Hispanic community and votes Democratic.

Danbury, located in the southwestern corner of the district, grew by 14 percent in the 1990s and has attracted immigrants from South America, the Caribbean and southeast Asia.

The 5th is a politically competitive district. Al Gore and Sen. Joseph I. Lieberman won the redrawn area in the 2000 presidential contest by 9 percentage points, their smallest margin in the state. The GOP runs well in the medium-size and small towns in the district's center. George W. Bush carried several towns north and east of Danbury, including burgeoning New Milford and Newtown, in 2000.

MAJOR INDUSTRY

Manufacturing, health care, insurance, defense

CITIES

Waterbury (pt.), 88,624; Danbury, 74,848; New Britain, 71,538; Meriden, 58,244; Torrington (pt.), 20,202

NOTABLE

Cheshire was designated the "Bedding Plant Capital of Connecticut" by the state legislature.

DELAWARE

Gov. Ruth Ann Minner (D)

First elected: 2000
Length of term: 4 years
Term expires: 1/05
Salary: $114,000
Phone: (302) 739-4101
Hometown: Milford
Born: Jan. 17, 1935; Milford, Del.
Religion: Methodist
Family: Widowed; three children
Education: Delaware Technical and Community College, G.E.D. 1968
Career: Towing company owner; state legislative aide
Political highlights: Del. House, 1975-83; Del. Senate, 1983-93; lieutenant governor, 1993-2001
Election results:

2000 GENERAL		
Ruth Ann Minner (D)	191,695	59.2%
John Burris (R)	128,603	39.8%
Floyd E. McDowell Sr. (IP)	3,271	1.0%

Lt. Gov. John Carney (D)

First elected: 2000
Length of term: 4 years
Term expires: 1/05
Salary: $61,200
Phone: (302) 739-4151

STATE LEGISLATURE

General Assembly: Meets January-June
House: 41 members, two-year terms
2003 breakdown: 29R, 12D; 30 men, 11 women
Salary: $34,800
Phone: (302) 739-4087
Senate: 21 members, 4-year terms
2003 breakdown: 8R, 13D; 13 men, 8 women
Salary: $34,800
Phone: (302) 739-4129

STATE TERM LIMITS

Governor: 2 terms
Senate: No
House: No

URBAN STATISTICS

CITY	POPULATION
Wilmington	72,664
Dover	32,135
Newark	28,547
Milford	6,732
Seaford	6,699

REGISTERED VOTERS

Democrat	43%
Republican	34%
Other	23%

POPULATION

2002 population (est.)	807,385
2000 population	783,600
1990 population	666,168
Percent change (1990-2000)	+17.6%
Rank among states (2002)	45
Median age	36
Born in state	48.3%
Foreign born	5.7%
Violent crime rate	684/100,000
Poverty level	9.2%
Federal workers	5,438
Military	8,799

REDISTRICTING

Delaware retained its one House seat in reapportionment.

MISCELLANEOUS

Web: www.state.de.us
Capital: Dover

STATE ELECTION OFFICIAL
(302) 739-4277

DEMOCRATIC HEADQUARTERS
(302) 996-9458

REPUBLICAN HEADQUARTERS
(302) 651-0260

District Statistics

DIST.	2000 VOTE FOR PRESIDENT BUSH	GORE	NADER	WHITE	BLACK	ASIAN	HISP	MEDIAN INCOME	WHITE COLLAR	BLUE COLLAR	SERVICE INDUSTRY	OVER 64	UNDER 18	COLLEGE EDUCATION	RURAL	SQ. MILES
AL	42%	55%	3%	72%	19%	2%	5%	$47,381	63%	23%	15%	13%	25%	25%	20%	1,954
STATE	42	55	3	72	19	2	5	$47,381	63	23	15	13	25	25	20	1,954
U.S.	47.9	48.4	3	69	12	4	13	$41,994	60	25	15	12	26	24	21	3,537,438

Wilmington
Newark
New Castle
Dover
Kent
At Large
Sussex

Sen. Joseph R. Biden Jr. (D)

CAPITOL OFFICE
224-5042
senator@biden.senate.gov
biden.senate.gov
221 Russell 20510-0802; fax 224-0139

COMMITTEES
Foreign Relations - ranking member
Judiciary

HOMETOWN
Wilmington

BORN
Nov. 20, 1942, Scranton, Pa.

RELIGION
Roman Catholic

FAMILY
Wife, Jill Biden; four children (one deceased)

EDUCATION
U. of Delaware, B.A. 1965 (history & political science); Syracuse U., J.D. 1968

CAREER
Lawyer

POLITICAL HIGHLIGHTS
New Castle County Council, 1970-72

ELECTION RESULTS

2002 GENERAL

Joseph R. Biden Jr. (D)	135,253	58.2%
Raymond J. Clatworthy (R)	94,793	40.8%

2002 PRIMARY

Joseph R. Biden Jr. (D)	unopposed

PREVIOUS WINNING PERCENTAGES
1996 (60%); 1990 (63%); 1984 (60%); 1978 (58%); 1972 (50%)

Elected 1972; 6th term

As his sixth term began in the 108th Congress, Biden had just celebrated his 60th birthday, and on Feb. 16, 2003, he had served in the Senate for exactly half his life. Such a distinction belongs to only three other current senators — fellow Democrats Robert C. Byrd of West Virginia, Daniel K. Inouye of Hawaii and Edward M. Kennedy of Massachusetts — and it suggests that a lawmaker has developed into something of an institution, not only at home and in the Capitol but also in the national consciousness.

Biden fits the bill, although in ways he may not always appreciate. He has won six statewide victories but has drawn more than three-fifths of the vote only once, and in 2002 he actually fared slightly worse than he did against the same low-profile opponent of six years before. To the American public, which knows him mostly as a frequent, smirking guest on the Sunday television talk shows, he is perceived as both extraordinarily eloquent — and unusually long-winded, even for politician.

In the Senate, that same loquaciousness has lubricated a long roster of legislative deal-cutting on both social and domestic policy, and it has helped him develop for the Democrats a rapport with Secretary of State Colin L. Powell, national security adviser Condoleezza Rice and other Bush administration officials. At the same time, his tendency to talk without thinking continues to be Biden's political Achilles' heel. His rhetorical flourishes have harmed as much as helped his aspirations for a greater national political role, from his failed 1988 presidential run to his tenure as chairman of the Foreign Relations Committee in the 107th Congress.

Biden chaired that panel during a signature moment in the history of American foreign policy — the aftermath of the Sept. 11, 2001, terrorist attacks — and he was well-prepared for that task. Not only did he have decades of experience in foreign policy, but as a former chairman of the Judiciary Committee he brought together many strands of knowledge important to the war on terrorism. Indeed, on the day before the attacks, Biden warned in a National Press Club speech that the United States faced a grave threat from a terrorist attack.

So it was no surprise that Biden's colleagues looked to him to help draft the resolution that gave Bush authority to wage war against al Qaeda and the Taliban regime in Afghanistan. Biden steered a careful course between giving Bush sufficient authority to prosecute terrorists and surrendering congressional oversight over foreign policy. After the successful overthrow of the Taliban, Biden continued to press the administration to provide a large, international peacekeeping force for Afghanistan, warning that without foreign troops that country could return to chaos.

Biden had mixed results from his other high-profile endeavor of the 107th: slowing Bush's rush to war with Iraq. Biden insisted that any action required both congressional and United Nations approval, and he took credit when Bush chose to follow that path. But the president also rebuffed an attempt by Biden to pass legislation requiring a go-slow approach. Instead, Bush bypassed the panel entirely, cutting a separate deal with House Democratic Leader Richard A. Gephardt of Missouri.

As chairman, Biden also pushed to enactment a law allowing the United States to forgive former Soviet debt if the funds were applied to non-proliferation programs in the former Soviet states, and a law authorizing State Department activities and paying off the third and final installment of close to $1 billion in U.S. debts to the United Nations. Still, Biden drew repeated criticism from his House counterpart, International Relations Chairman Henry J. Hyde, that he was more interested in making speeches than laws.

And Biden's tongue also tripped him up on more than one occasion. He drew barbs from Republicans, for example, when he said that Bush had to be willing to deploy ground forces to go "mano a mano" with the Afghans. As a critical New Republic profile put it, Biden is "legendary for speaking impulsively and leaving others to clean up the mess. . . . Not exactly the person you want out front when the country is at war."

Biden's occasional carelessness had plagued him before. Hoping to win the 1988 Democratic presidential nomination, he withdrew six months before the first primary, amid reports that he had plagiarized passages in speeches and a 1965 law school paper and had exaggerated his résumé.

Biden's stewardship at Judiciary from 1987 to 1995 will probably be best-remembered for his handling of the 1991 nomination of Clarence Thomas for the Supreme Court. The nationally televised committee hearings at which professor Anita F. Hill accused Thomas of sexual harassment were an acute embarrassment to Biden, whose committee had not conducted more than a cursory investigation of Hill's charges until after they were leaked to the media. But Biden also compiled a substantial legislative record wielding that gavel, including a comprehensive anti-crime law in 1994 and an anti-terrorism law in 1996. Indeed, Biden is quick to point out that six years before the Sept. 11 attacks, he had proposed many of the provisions included in the anti-terrorism law enacted subsequently, but that those suggestions had been derailed by civil libertarians.

When Democrats regained control of the Senate in June 2001, upon the defection of Vermont's James M. Jeffords from the GOP, Biden had his pick of the Foreign Relations or Judiciary gavels. After a period of carefully calculated public indecision, Biden took the Foreign Relations panel but forced the new Judiciary chairman, Democrat Patrick J. Leahy of Vermont, to name him chairman of the Crime and Drugs Subcommittee. That has allowed Biden to pursue his long-term interest in anti-narcotics efforts.

And for the rest of the 107th, Biden was the Judiciary Democrat most likely to support Bush nominees, repeatedly warning that his party was setting itself up for a round of GOP reprisals whenever it next controls the White House.

The son of a Scranton, Pa., automobile dealer, Biden — who overcame a childhood stutter — often speaks with a self-deprecation that is part of his charm. But part of what has made the senator such a compelling political figure are the tragedies and dramas of his private life. He was the underdog when, as a 29-year-old county councilman, he summoned his celebrated brashness to challenge Republican Sen. J. Caleb Boggs in 1972. Running on a dovish Vietnam platform and accusing the incumbent of being a do-nothing, he won by 3,162 votes.

Five weeks later, Biden's wife, Neilia, and their infant daughter, Amy, were killed and their two sons seriously injured in an automobile accident. Biden said at first that he did not want to take the job he had just won. Persuaded by Majority Leader Mike Mansfield to assume his seat, Biden was sworn in at the bedside of one of his sons.

After 15 years building his Senate credentials and rebuilding his life — he remarried and commutes by train from Wilmington every day — Biden made his short presidential bid. In 1988, a brain aneurysm nearly killed him. By early 1989, he was back in action but looked potentially vulnerable to a GOP challenge in 1990. Conservatives were eager to avenge the Senate's 1987 rejection, during Biden's Judiciary chairmanship, of Robert H. Bork for the Supreme Court. But Biden's return to good health bolstered Delaware's affections and he won with 63 percent, his personal best.

KEY VOTES

2002

- Yes Pass farm bill reversing crop subsidy limits
- No Postpone tougher automobile fuel efficiency standards
- Yes Overhaul campaign finance law; ban "soft money" and restrict advocacy advertising
- Yes Set federal election standards
- No Support oil drilling in Arctic National Wildlife Refuge
- Yes Revive fast-track procedures for trade agreements
- Yes Create federal insurance coverage for catastrophic terrorist losses
- Yes Tighten federal accounting and corporate governance regulation
- Yes Advance bipartisan Medicare prescription drug plan
- Yes Create independent Sept. 11 commission
- Yes Back Democratic Homeland Security Department proposal
- Yes Authorize war against Iraq

2001

- No Confirm John Ashcroft as attorney general
- No Nullify Clinton Labor Department ergonomics rule
- No Cut taxes by $1.35 trillion through fiscal 2011
- Yes Pass Democratic bill to bolster rights of patients in managed-care plans
- Yes Permit a new round of military base closings
- Yes Expand law enforcement power to investigate suspected terrorists

CQ VOTE STUDIES

	PARTY UNITY		PRESIDENTIAL SUPPORT	
	Support	Oppose	Support	Oppose
2002	89%	11%	77%	23%
2001	94%	6%	65%	35%
2000	88%	12%	91%	9%
1999	93%	7%	89%	11%
1998	87%	13%	91%	9%
1997	82%	18%	84%	16%
1996	79%	21%	92%	8%
1995	87%	13%	85%	15%
1994	92%	8%	89%	11%
1993	92%	8%	97%	3%

INTEREST GROUPS

	AFL-CIO	ADA	CCUS	ACU
2002	100%	80%	50%	10%
2001	100%	100%	38%	12%
2000	63%	80%	60%	16%
1999	89%	95%	47%	4%
1998	88%	85%	56%	4%
1997	57%	70%	70%	16%
1996	86%	80%	46%	20%
1995	92%	95%	37%	17%
1994	86%	80%	20%	0%
1993	91%	80%	33%	21%

Sen. Thomas R. Carper (D)

CAPITOL OFFICE
224-2441
carper.senate.gov
513 Hart 20510-0803; fax 228-2190

COMMITTEES
Banking, Housing & Urban Affairs
Environment & Public Works
Governmental Affairs
Special Aging

HOMETOWN
Wilmington

BORN
Jan. 23, 1947, Beckley, W.Va.

RELIGION
Presbyterian

FAMILY
Wife, Martha Carper; two children

EDUCATION
Ohio State U., B.A. 1968 (economics); U. of Delaware, M.B.A. 1975

MILITARY SERVICE
Navy, 1968-73; Naval Reserve, 1973-92

CAREER
State economic development official

POLITICAL HIGHLIGHTS
Del. treasurer, 1977-83; U.S. House, 1983-93; governor, 1993-2001

ELECTION RESULTS

2000 GENERAL

Thomas R. Carper (D)	181,566	55.5%
William V. Roth Jr. (R)	142,891	43.7%

2000 PRIMARY

Thomas R. Carper (D)	unopposed

PREVIOUS WINNING PERCENTAGES
1990 House Election (66%); 1988 House Election (68%); 1986 House Election (66%); 1984 House Election (58%); 1982 House Election (52%)

Elected 2000; 1st term

Carper is a centrist, pro-business Democrat, a posture that has helped him win 11 races in a state that generally eschews ideological politics. And, in the Senate, he says, "when you're a centrist, you're in on every play."

"I was a New Democrat before it was fashionable," says Carper. "I really think that we need more people in Congress who think like governors — who are results-oriented, who are not so ideologically driven, people who are impatient with gridlock, and maybe a little less partisan."

Carper was a governor himself. He has held an elected position in Delaware since he was 29, when he was state treasurer. He went on to serve 10 years in the House as the state's sole congressman, was elected governor in 1993, and in 2000 ran for the Senate, beating popular five-term Republican Sen. William V. Roth Jr.

Carper applies his experience as a governor to his work in the Senate. Every couple of months, he organizes gatherings of the former governors in the Senate — there were 12 in the 107th Congress — to discuss how proposals they implemented in the statehouse might work in Congress. In 2002, Carper was named chairman of the Democratic Leadership Council's "best practices" committee, which scours the country for successful local programs that might work in other parts of the nation. The DLC is the national organization of the New Democrat movement.

He is more at home in the closely divided Senate than he was in the House, where he says he often found himself at odds with his party's leaders because of his fiscally conservative views. In the 1980s, the Democrats controlled the House, and the moderate and conservative wings of the party had little clout.

Carper observes that much has changed since his days in the House — "there were times when I felt like an interloper in my own party." When he returned to Capitol Hill in 2001, he found that moderate and conservative Democrats had gained considerable power.

The Senate in the 107th Congress included about 20 moderates among the 50 Democrats, and Carper noted, "Given the strength of those numbers, our caucus has little choice but to welcome us warmly." In fact, in the 108th Congress, he was named to a newly formed four-member executive committee to advise Democratic leader Tom Daschle on coordinating the party's strategy and message.

Carper's voting record proves his middle-of-the-road tendencies. In the 107th, he supported President Bush just over 75 percent of the time, the seventh-highest record among Senate Democrats. He strayed from the party line on 22 percent of the votes in which the two parties were in opposition, more often than all but seven of his Democratic colleagues.

Consensus is a key word in Carper's vocabulary. He told the Wilmington News Journal that he believed his job as a centrist was to help develop consensus, adding that with the GOP takeover of the Senate, "I'll have plenty of opportunity now to see how good I am at it."

For his part, he says his consensus-building skills were sharpened in his work with the National Governors' Association, where he and Michigan's Republican Gov. John Engler worked together to develop welfare overhaul plans that formed the basis for the federal welfare law of 1996. In 1998-99, he chaired the governors association.

Carper favors increasing federal aid for education, but he believes local authorities must show results in order to continue receiving the money. In December 2000, two soon-to-be ex-governors — Carper and George W. Bush — met at Bush's Texas ranch to discuss education reform.

The first bill Carper introduced in the Senate was a measure to increase the number of public charter schools in the country and to encourage local school districts to offer parents a choice of which public school their child attends. He worked with former New Hampshire Gov. Judd Gregg, a Republican, on this legislation, which was eventually included in the big education authorization bill that became law in 2001.

In the 108th Congress, Carper says his legislative priorities include reorganizing the postal service, providing affordable housing and making it tougher in class action lawsuits to go "venue shopping."

Carper is a strong supporter of Amtrak, the federally subsidized passenger railroad. Both Carper and Democrat Joseph R. Biden Jr., the senior Delaware senator, spend every night at home in Wilmington and then commute to Washington on Amtrak. In 2002, Carper helped lead an effort to provide $1.2 billion to upgrade security at the railroad and to include funds needed to subsidize its continued operations.

Carper was born in West Virginia and raised in southern Virginia. His family moved to Columbus, Ohio, when he was in high school. He went to Ohio State University on an ROTC scholarship. Years later, he told the Columbus Dispatch that, until he became governor, the best job he ever had was washing dishes at an Ohio State sorority house during his college days.

Carper told the newspaper that while he was in the ROTC and preparing to serve in the military, he was undergoing a political transformation. In 1964, he had campaigned for Republican presidential candidate Barry Goldwater. But by the time he was a college senior, he was volunteering in the anti-Vietnam War presidential campaign of Democratic Sen. Eugene McCarthy. Yet Carper says he wore his Navy uniform to graduation. He served in the Navy for five years, including wartime service in reconnaissance planes in Southeast Asia.

After he was discharged, Carper came to the University of Delaware in 1973 to earn a master's in business administration. He remained to work for the state's economic development department. He has said he had no master plan for politics — that he decided to enter the arena when he was lying on a beach in 1976 and heard a radio report that Democrats could not find a candidate for state treasurer. He entered the race and beat a strongly favored Republican.

In 1982, again after Democrats had trouble recruiting a candidate, he made a late decision to challenge GOP Rep. Thomas B. Evans. Carper's burgeoning campaign, aided by the state's economic problems and Evans' romantic involvement with lobbyist Paula Parkinson, returned the state's House seat to Democratic control for the first time since 1966, via a slim, 11,000-vote margin.

After a decade in the House, he won the governorship, and after eight years in the governor's mansion, Carper in 2000 sought a return to Washington in a "battle-of-the-titans" challenge to Roth, Delaware's popular Republican senator.

The ambition, energy and hard work that have been Carper trademarks throughout his career were evident in his win over Roth, the Senate Finance Committee chairman who was the architect of the Roth IRA retirement plan. Carper found ways to distinguish himself from Roth, on health care and in other policy areas. Although he did not directly make a point of it, age was also a factor: He was 53, Roth was 79.

Voters gave Carper a surprisingly large 12 percentage point victory.

KEY VOTES

2002

Yes Pass farm bill reversing crop subsidy limits
Yes Postpone tougher automobile fuel efficiency standards
Yes Overhaul campaign finance law; ban "soft money" and restrict advocacy advertising
Yes Set federal election standards
No Support oil drilling in Arctic National Wildlife Refuge
Yes Revive fast-track procedures for trade agreements
Yes Create federal insurance coverage for catastrophic terrorist losses
Yes Tighten federal accounting and corporate governance regulation
Yes Advance bipartisan Medicare prescription drug plan
Yes Create independent Sept. 11 commission
Yes Back Democratic Homeland Security Department proposal
Yes Authorize war against Iraq

2001

No Confirm John Ashcroft as attorney general
No Nullify Clinton Labor Department ergonomics rule
No Cut taxes by $1.35 trillion through fiscal 2011
Yes Pass Democratic bill to bolster rights of patients in managed-care plans
Yes Permit a new round of military base closings
Yes Expand law enforcement power to investigate suspected terrorists

CQ VOTE STUDIES

	PARTY UNITY		PRESIDENTIAL SUPPORT	
	Support	Oppose	Support	Oppose
2002	74%	26%	79%	21%
2001	80%	20%	72%	28%
House Service:				
1992	76%	24%	32%	68%
1991	76%	24%	37%	63%
1990	89%	11%	23%	77%
1989	85%	15%	41%	59%
1988	87%	13%	30%	70%
1987	77%	23%	32%	68%

INTEREST GROUPS

	AFL-CIO	ADA	CCUS	ACU
2002	85%	80%	50%	25%
2001	93%	90%	58%	24%
House Service:				
1992	67%	75%	63%	40%
1991	92%	55%	40%	20%
1990	92%	78%	21%	17%
1989	83%	80%	50%	21%
1988	77%	75%	64%	24%
1987	75%	72%	53%	9%
1986	86%	55%	50%	27%
1985	71%	55%	50%	24%

Rep. Michael N. Castle (R)

CAPITOL OFFICE
225-4165
delaware@mail.house.gov
www.house.gov/castle
1233 Longworth 20515-0801; fax 225-2291

COMMITTEES
Education & Workforce
(Education Reform - chairman)
Financial Services

HOMETOWN
Wilmington

BORN
July 2, 1939, Wilmington, Del.

RELIGION
Roman Catholic

FAMILY
Wife, Jane Castle

EDUCATION
Hamilton College, B.A. 1961 (economics); Georgetown U., LL.B. 1964

CAREER
Lawyer; state prosecutor

POLITICAL HIGHLIGHTS
Del. House, 1967-69; Del. Senate, 1969-77 (minority leader, 1976-77); lieutenant governor, 1981-85; governor, 1985-93

ELECTION RESULTS

2002 GENERAL		
Michael N. Castle (R)	164,605	72.1%
Micheal C. Miller Sr. (D)	61,011	26.7%
Brad C. Thomas (LIBERT)	2,789	1.2%
2002 PRIMARY		
Michael N. Castle (R)		unopposed
2000 GENERAL		
Michael N. Castle (R)	211,797	67.6%
Micheal C. Miller Sr. (D)	96,488	30.8%

PREVIOUS WINNING PERCENTAGES
1998 (66%); 1996 (70%); 1994 (71%); 1992 (55%)

Elected 1992; 6th term

For Castle, being a moderate Republican does not always mean having to yield to the wishes of his far more powerful conservative brethren.

In the second half of the 107th Congress, for example, Castle led a group of likeminded GOP House members into a battle for increased spending at the departments of Labor, Health and Human Services and Education. Despite significant pressure from the leadership to accept the level sought by President Bush, Castle refused to budge. The ensuing standoff led to an impasse that kept the 2002 budget debate going into 2003, but Castle's crew gained at least some measure of what they were after.

Castle can often be found just off the House floor, expanding on the news of the day to a clutch of reporters. He frequently is the lawmaker that journalists approach for the details whenever the word spreads that the moderates are planning a maverick stand.

To be sure, Castle does join the Republican mainstream on most bellwether votes. But in the 107th he bucked President Bush's wishes 28 percent of the time and broke from the party fold on 21 percent of party-line floor votes — among the top 10 House GOP strays on both counts. He breaks ranks most often on polarizing domestic policy issues such as gun control, campaign finance and environmental policy. He labels himself a "pragmatist," believing that being a social moderate with fiscally conservative views is the only way to get things done in Congress. His middle-of-the-road positioning, combined with the political acumen he brought to the House from eight years in the governor's mansion, have landed Castle in the middle of some of the most contentious debates on Capitol Hill. In the 108th Congress, he is a leader of three centrist coalitions: the Tuesday Group of moderate Republicans, the Republican Main Street Partnership and the bipartisan House Centrist Coalition, formed in 2000. On major issues, Castle often carries a substantial bloc of moderate votes behind his positions.

Amiable and relatively quiet, Castle is nonetheless forceful in his opinions and sometimes bold about confronting the GOP leadership when he feels it is pursuing an overly conservative course. In 2000, Castle enraged Majority Whip Tom DeLay by yielding speaking time on the House floor to Democrat Harold E. Ford Jr. of Tennessee, who went on to excoriate the GOP leadership for threatening to draw out budget battles with President Clinton.

Castle was among the dozen GOP lawmakers who voted against three of the four articles of impeachment against President Clinton in 1998. The next year, he successfully defied conservatives on raising the minimum wage, winning adoption of language that ensured states would not be able to opt out of the new compensation level ordered that year. Also in 1999, he was one of six Republicans who signed a petition to force Speaker J. Dennis Hastert to bring campaign finance legislation to the House floor, and he did the same thing in 2001.

Castle nonetheless counts himself an ally of the Speaker, who consults with him regularly. In 1998, Castle promoted Hastert as a candidate for majority leader against conservative Texan Dick Armey. Armey kept his job, but a month later — when Republicans were scrambling to fill the gap left by the abrupt exit of Speaker-designate Robert L. Livingston — the consensus-building qualities Castle had praised in Hastert made him the party's unanimous choice for the top job.

As chairman of the Education and the Workforce panel's Education Reform Subcommittee, Castle is considered an authority on education issues, even though some conservatives, fearing his moderate bent, have sought to prevent major legislation, such as the sweeping education policy overhaul of the 107th, from going through his panel.

Although his social policy stances are to the left of most Republicans, Castle also advocates fiscal views that often call for more frugality than some Republicans might like. In the 106th, he cast one of only three GOP votes against his party's $792 billion tax cut, which he said was "going too far, too fast" to return a big portion of the newly forecast surplus; more of the revenue should be put to work drawing down the federal debt instead, he said. Still, in the 107th he joined the united House GOP in backing Bush's tax cut of nearly twice that size.

Castle's seat on the Financial Services Committee is important to Delaware's large corporate constituency. From that post, he has sought to raise federal revenues by overhauling the commemorative coin program. In the 105th, he was a principal author of the law — which he estimated would raise $3.4 billion for the government — ordering that images commemorating each of the 50 states be placed on the reverse sides of new quarters. The coins are being minted in the order each state entered the Union, which made Delaware's first out of the gate.

Castle combined his desire for fiscal restraint with his support for pro-environment initiatives in 1999 when he released a "dirty dozen" list of wasteful federal programs that also pose a risk to the environment. The move recalled his unsuccessful attempt in 1998 to cut about $9 billion in member-specific projects from a mammoth, $218 billion transportation bill that he said was fiscally irresponsible. He may try again in the 108th, when that highway law is up for renewal.

The 6-foot, 4-inch Castle was a basketball star in high school. But he caught the political bug as an adult. He got a law degree from Georgetown University in 1964; the following year, at age 26, he became Delaware's deputy attorney general. Two years later, he began a 10-year career in the General Assembly and went on to serve as lieutenant governor and then governor for eight years.

With his gubernatorial term ending, Castle decided to try for the state's at-large congressional seat in 1992. He won a tough, four-way GOP primary and in November managed 55 percent against a former lieutenant governor, Democrat S.B. Woo. (Castle swapped jobs with Democrat Thomas R. Carper, who left the House for the governorship that year and is now Delaware's junior senator.) With at least two-thirds of voters backing him every two years, Castle has coasted to re-election.

KEY VOTES

2002

Yes Overhaul campaign finance law; ban "soft money" and restrict advocacy advertising
Yes Back Bush's defense budget increase
Yes Extend 1996 welfare law
Yes Adopt Bush's discretionary spending limit
Yes Pass GOP Medicare prescription drug plan
No Create independent Sept. 11 commission
No Extend union protections to Homeland Security Department employees
Yes Revive fast-track procedures for trade agreements
Yes Authorize war against Iraq
Yes Advance bankruptcy overhaul opposed by abortion opponents

2001

Yes Nullify Clinton Labor Department ergonomics rule
Yes Cut taxes by $1.35 trillion through fiscal 2011
Yes Maintain ban on oil drilling in Arctic National Wildlife Refuge
Yes Approve Bush proposal to limit managed-care plan liability for coverage decisions
Yes Divert money from crop subsidy payments to land conservation
Yes Expand law enforcement power to investigate suspected terrorists

CQ VOTE STUDIES

	PARTY UNITY		PRESIDENTIAL SUPPORT	
	Support	Oppose	Support	Oppose
2002	79%	21%	78%	22%
2001	79%	21%	67%	33%
2000	74%	26%	49%	51%
1999	69%	31%	49%	51%
1998	63%	37%	51%	49%

INTEREST GROUPS

	AFL-CIO	ADA	CCUS	ACU
2002	11%	25%	95%	76%
2001	25%	30%	83%	48%
2000	20%	30%	80%	68%
1999	33%	55%	72%	44%
1998	40%	30%	67%	42%

DELAWARE

At large

Long considered a bellwether in national elections, Delaware went for Al Gore in 2000, ending the state's 12-election streak of supporting the winning presidential ticket. Voters pursue ticket-splitting with rare relish at all levels, but the state is generally incumbent-friendly and has embraced Republican Rep. Michael N. Castle with large majorities.

Democrats are strong in Wilmington, the state's largest city. Fifty years ago, almost half the state's residents lived here, but the city's 73,000 residents now cast only about 10 percent of Delaware's vote, largely because of migration to the booming suburbs. The capital, Dover, set in the state's midsection in Kent County, also has a Democratic constituency.

The GOP's strength lies in Wilmington's suburbs and south of the Chesapeake and Delaware canal, in the poultry farms and coastal marshes of the Delmarva Peninsula. A string of beach resorts in the southeast corner draws hundreds of thousands of tourists each year. The growing number of retirees in these beach communities has made rural Sussex County one of the state's fastest-growing areas and increased its conservative tenor.

Delaware enjoys relatively low unemployment, and its favorable tax rates attract the headquarters of many financial services companies, especially credit card firms. Thanks to liberal incorporation rules, Delaware is the on-paper home to 60 percent of the Fortune 500, which keeps the state's specialized business court busy. Wilmington is the very real home to the DuPont Company, one of Delaware's largest private employers.

MAJOR INDUSTRY
Financial services, manufacturing, tourism

MILITARY BASES
Dover Air Force Base, 3,927 military, 1,990 civilian (2001)

CITIES
Wilmington, 72,664; Dover, 32,135; Newark, 28,547

NOTABLE
Ralph Nader's report, "The Company State" (1971), described the du Pont family's influence on Delaware — the family once owned the newspaper and held the governor's mansion; In 1787, Delaware was the first state to ratify the Constitution.

FLORIDA

Gov. Jeb Bush (R)

First elected: 1998
Length of term: 4 years
Term expires: 1/07
Salary: $123,175
Phone: (850) 488-4441
Hometown: Coral Gables
Born: Feb. 11, 1953; Midland, Texas
Religion: Roman Catholic
Family: Wife, Columba Bush; three children
Education: U. of Texas, B.A. 1973 (Latin American studies)
Career: Real estate developer; nonprofit chairman
Political highlights: Fla. secretary of commerce, 1987-89; Republican nominee for governor, 1994
Election results:

2002 GENERAL		
Jeb Bush (R)	2,856,845	56.0%
Bill McBride (D)	2,201,427	43.2%

Lt. Gov. Frank T. Brogan (R)

First elected: 1998
Length of term: 4 years
Term expires: 1/07
Salary: $118,000
Phone: (850) 488-4711

STATE LEGISLATURE

General Assembly: Meets 60 days March-May; session often extended
House: 120 members; 2-year terms
2003 breakdown: 81R, 39D; 93 men, 27 women
Salary: $29,328
Phone: (850) 488-1157
Senate: 40 members; 4-year terms
2003 breakdown: 26R, 14D; 31 men, 9 women
Salary: $29,328
Phone: (850) 487-5270

STATE TERM LIMITS

Governor: 2 terms
Senate: 2 terms
House: 4 terms

URBAN STATISTICS

CITY	POPULATION
Jacksonville	735,617
Miami	362,470
Tampa	303,447
St. Petersburg	248,232
Hialeah	226,419

REGISTERED VOTERS

Democrat	44%
Republican	40%
No party	17%

POPULATION

2002 population (est.)	16,713,149
2000 population	15,982,378
1990 population	12,937,926
Percent change (1990-2000)	+23.5%
Rank among states (2002)	4
Median age	38.7
Born in state	32.7%
Foreign born	16.7%
Violent crime rate	812/100,000
Poverty level	12.5%
Federal workers	118,600
Military	106,092

REDISTRICTING

Florida gained two House seats in reapportionment. The state legislature drew a new, 25-district map, which the governor signed on March 27, 2002.

MISCELLANEOUS

Web: www.state.fl.us
Capital: Tallahassee

STATE ELECTION OFFICIAL
(850) 488-7690

DEMOCRATIC HEADQUARTERS
(850) 222-3411

REPUBLICAN HEADQUARTERS
(850) 222-7920

District Statistics

DIST.	2000 VOTE FOR PRESIDENT BUSH	GORE	NADER	WHITE	BLACK	ASIAN	HISP	MEDIAN INCOME	WHITE COLLAR	BLUE COLLAR	SERVICE INDUSTRY	OVER 64	UNDER 18	COLLEGE EDUCATION	RURAL	SQ. MILES
1	67%	30%	1%	78%	14%	2%	3%	$36,738	57%	25%	18%	13%	24%	20%	23%	4,642
2	51	46	2	72	22	1	3	$34,718	62	21	18	12	23	24	38	9,425
3	34	64	1	38	49	2	8	$29,785	52	27	21	11	28	13	10	1,796
4	64	33	1	78	14	2	4	$43,947	65	21	14	11	24	24	22	4,118
5	52	45	2	88	5	1	6	$34,815	55	27	17	26	20	14	36	4,044
6	57	41	2	79	12	2	5	$36,846	61	23	16	15	23	21	31	2,912
7	53	45	2	81	9	1	7	$40,525	63	21	16	18	22	25	13	1,797
8	53	45	2	70	7	3	18	$41,568	64	20	17	14	23	26	8	987
9	53	45	2	85	4	2	8	$40,742	68	18	14	20	22	25	6	634
10	47	49	3	88	4	2	4	$37,168	65	20	15	23	18	23	0	175
11	38	59	2	48	27	2	20	$33,559	61	22	17	12	25	21	0	244
12	54	44	1	72	13	1	12	$37,769	56	28	16	17	25	17	16	1,956
13	53	44	2	86	4	1	8	$40,187	59	24	18	29	18	24	11	2,599
14	60	38	2	84	5	1	9	$42,541	60	22	19	27	18	24	9	1,057
15	52	45	2	78	7	2	11	$39,397	58	22	19	20	22	22	10	2,545

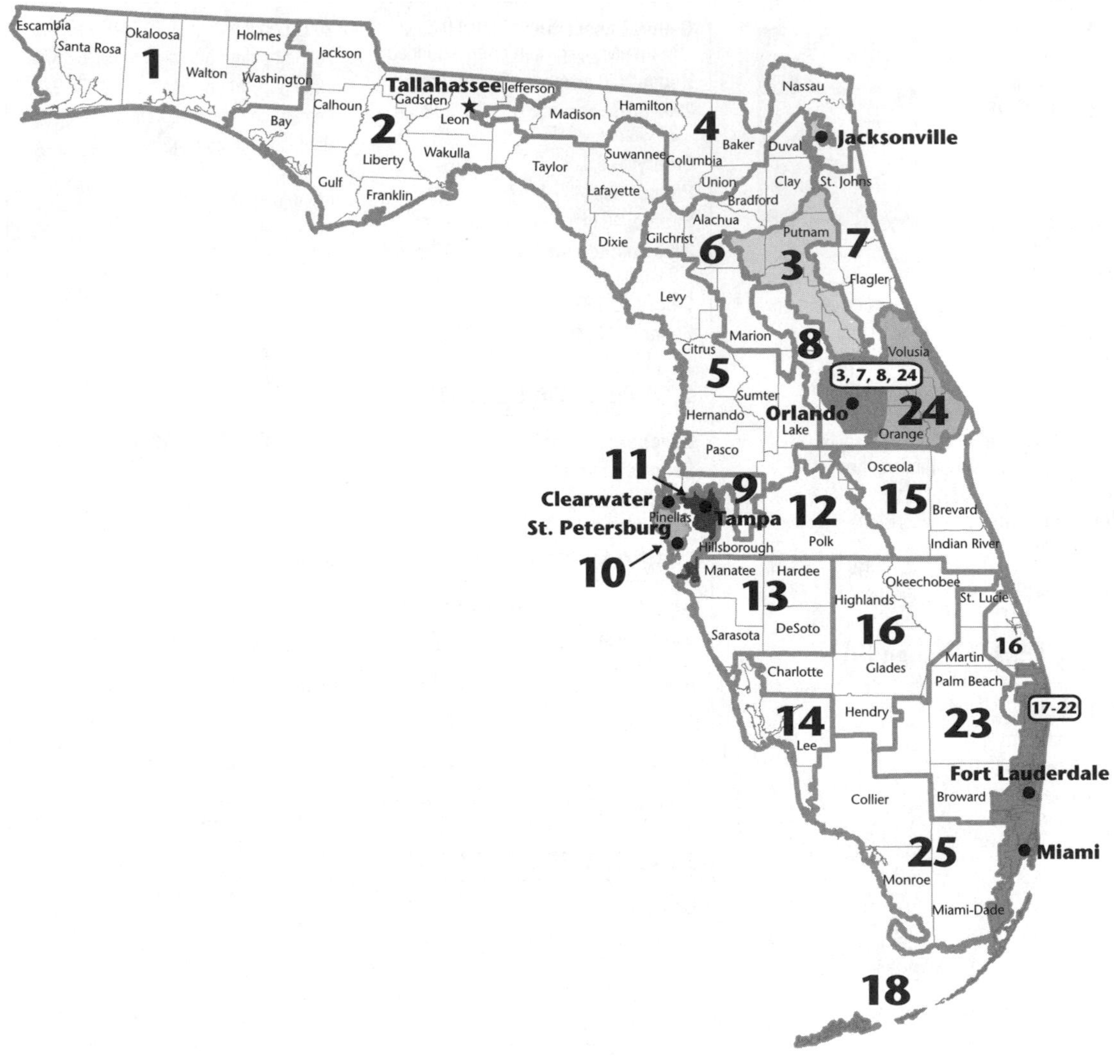

District Statistics

DIST.	2000 VOTE FOR PRESIDENT BUSH	GORE	NADER	WHITE	BLACK	ASIAN	HISP	MEDIAN INCOME	WHITE COLLAR	BLUE COLLAR	SERVICE INDUSTRY	OVER 64	UNDER 18	COLLEGE EDUCATION	RURAL	SQ. MILES
16	52%	46%	2%	82%	6%	1%	10%	$39,408	58%	25%	17%	25%	21%	20%	15%	4,538
17	15	84	1	18	55	2	21	$30,426	52	24	23	11	29	14	0	97
18	56	42	1	30	6	1	63	$32,298	60	21	18	18	19	26	1	355
19	27	71	1	77	6	2	13	$42,237	67	17	15	30	19	26	0	231
20	30	68	1	67	8	2	21	$44,034	69	16	14	17	21	30	0	160
21	57	42	1	21	7	2	70	$41,426	64	23	14	13	24	23	0	135
22	46	51	2	82	4	2	11	$51,200	69	16	14	21	19	34	1	268
23	20	79	1	29	51	1	14	$31,309	48	28	24	12	28	13	2	3,362
24	52	46	2	80	6	2	10	$43,954	65	20	15	15	23	26	9	1,583
25	54	44	1	24	10	2	62	$44,489	62	23	15	9	29	20	6	4,268
STATE	48.9	48.84	2	65	14	2	17	$38,819	61	22	17	18	23	22	11	53,927
U.S.	47.9	48.4	3	69	12	4	13	$41,994	60	25	15	12	26	24	21	3,537,438

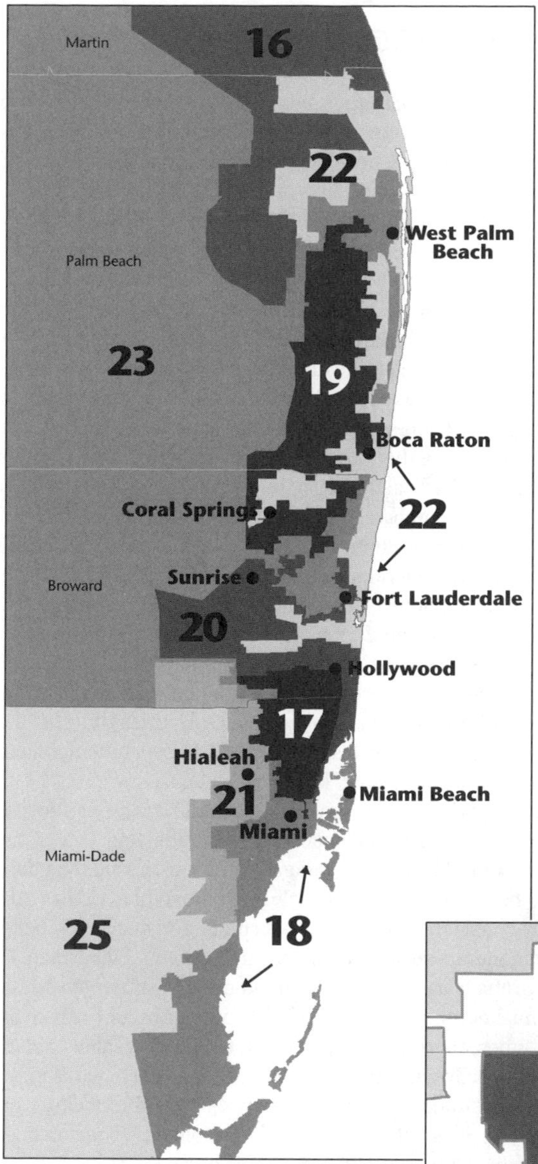
Martin
16
22
West Palm Beach
Palm Beach
23
19
Boca Raton
22
Coral Springs
Sunrise
Broward
Fort Lauderdale
20
Hollywood
17
Hialeah
21
Miami Beach
Miami
Miami-Dade
18
25

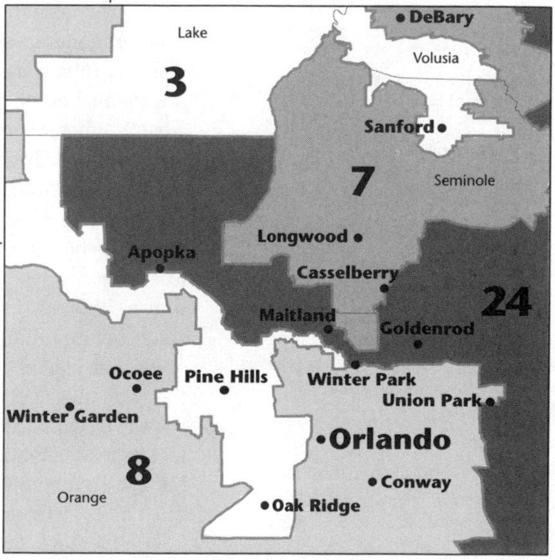
DeBary
Lake
Volusia
3
Sanford
7
Seminole
Longwood
Apopka
Casselberry
24
Maitland
Goldenrod
Ocoee
Pine Hills
Winter Park
Union Park
Winter Garden
Orlando
8
Conway
Orange
Oak Ridge

Sen. Bob Graham (D)

CAPITOL OFFICE
224-3041
bob_graham@graham.senate.gov
graham.senate.gov
524 Hart 20510-0903; fax 224-2237

COMMITTEES
Energy & Natural Resources
Environment & Public Works
Finance
Veterans' Affairs - ranking member

HOMETOWN
Miami Lakes

BORN
Nov. 9, 1936, Miami Lakes, Fla.

RELIGION
United Church of Christ

FAMILY
Wife, Adele Khoury Graham; four children

EDUCATION
U. of Florida, B.A. 1959 (political science & economics); Harvard U., LL.B. 1962

CAREER
Real estate developer; lawyer

POLITICAL HIGHLIGHTS
Fla. House, 1967-71; Fla. Senate, 1971-79; governor, 1979-87

ELECTION RESULTS

1998 GENERAL		
Bob Graham (D)	2,436,407	62.5%
Charlie Crist (R)	1,463,755	37.5%
1998 PRIMARY		
Bob Graham (D)		unopposed

PREVIOUS WINNING PERCENTAGES
1992 (65%); 1986 (55%)

Elected 1986; 3rd term

Well-liked by his colleagues, pragmatic and ever so slightly quirky, Graham has built a long record of accomplishment as a leading moderate on national security issues, health care and other matters. He considered that record solid enough to add his name to the list of Democrats looking to challenge President Bush's re-election.

"We're facing unprecedented problems in terms of our domestic economy, in terms of our international relations, particularly the war on terrorism and Iraq," Graham said at the end of 2002, when he surprised most party operatives by declaring himself interested in a presidential candidacy. "I'm not satisfied with the direction we are being led today."

A former Intelligence Committee chairman, Graham planned to make his credentials as an aggressive hawk in the war against terrorism a central part of his campaign. In the 107th Congress, he voted against the resolution authorizing military action against Iraq because he considered it "too timid." During the debate, the Senate rejected his amendment that would also have authorized Bush to use force against Hezbollah and other terrorist groups, which Graham predicted would strike if Iraq were attacked.

Graham also planned to emphasize his eight years as governor, predicting that voters would gravitate to a presidential aspirant with "some executive ability." And he noted that his home state's problems of growth, immigration and environmental hazards were instructive in dealing with the nation as a whole. "Florida has been living America's future," he said.

His preliminary plans to seek the 2004 Democratic nomination hit an early and unexpected snag, however. In February 2003, he underwent heart surgery. His physicians pronounced the surgery a success, but Graham delayed an official announcement of candidacy.

While it would be his first national campaign, it would be the third time Graham has come somewhere close to the White House. Al Gore had seriously considered Graham as his running mate in 2000 before picking another moderate senator, Connecticut's Joseph I. Lieberman. Eight years before, Graham was on Bill Clinton's final list of six contenders for the vice presidential nomination; reportedly, it came down to Graham and Gore.

Both times, there were reports that Graham's zealous habit of writing down every daily detail of his life in small spiral notebooks may have hurt his chances. Graham has saved nearly 4,000 of the books, which he has called "my greatest attempt at staying disciplined." The notebooks remain one of the best-known oddities about his behavior, along with his decision to almost always wear a solid navy or maroon necktie dotted with his state's silhouette in white. (He planned to buy ties paying homage to other states before hitting the campaign trail.)

As chairman of the Intelligence Committee, Graham was propelled onto the national stage as never before by the attacks of Sept. 11, 2001. Under normal circumstances, he would not have been on the panel at all, much less its leader. Senate rules called for his eight-year tenure to end in 2000, but the Democrats permitted him to stay on because the panel had lost most of its Democratic members before the start of the 107th Congress.

Graham took the gavel just three months before the al Qaeda attacks, when Vermont's James M. Jeffords quit the GOP and tipped the Senate's balance of power. Graham put a premium on working closely with Republicans, readily agreeing to follow the lead of fellow Floridian Porter J. Goss, the House Intelligence Committee's chairman, in writing the annual measure setting policy and spending levels for the intelligence community.

Later, Graham and Goss led an unprecedented bipartisan effort to have their committees join forces to investigate why the CIA and other intelligence agencies did not foresee the attacks. The 10-month joint inquiry faced several difficulties, including the resignation of the original staff director and news leaks that incurred the wrath of the White House. It produced a report finding no "smoking gun" that could have averted the attacks but criticized the lack of coordination among spy agencies. "What our intelligence community needs is the equivalent of an admiral of the fleet," Graham said when the inquiry released its findings. "Each agency or ship has a captain, but someone needs to command the entire fleet."

Graham left Intelligence in the 108th Congress to take over as the top-ranking Democrat on the Veterans' Affairs Committee. He continued to serve on the Finance, Environment and Public Works and Energy and Natural Resources panels.

A quiet man, Graham can sometimes come across as curt or detached. He has never emerged as a spokesman for his party on the Sunday morning talk shows, perhaps because he hews to the center. (In the 107th he backed Bush 73 percent of the time, almost square in the middle of Senate Democrats' presidential support.) "What I think I'm best at is bringing people together around an honorable and reasonable position," he told The Tampa Tribune. "My approach to getting things done in the Senate is that you start at the 50-yard line and you begin to build out in each direction until you get a majority. Very few things happen, get accomplished, when you start in the end zone."

Graham has coupled his interest with bridging partisan divides with a dogged devotion to his state's most parochial concerns — an approach that has won him legions of supporters back home. Since 1974, when he was a state senator, he has logged hundreds of "work days," sampling avocations from firefighter to teacher; he says that the jobs help him stay in touch with the needs of ordinary people. "Graham is a hard-working, level-headed grown-up. How many of those will you find in Congress?" The Palm Beach Post asked in endorsing his 1998 re-election.

While more conservative than many Democrats, Graham is not viewed as a maverick. He is a strong supporter of environmental safeguards. He has voted to raise the minimum wage and to uphold President Clinton's veto of a ban on a procedure its opponents call "partial birth" abortion. But he also has backed the death penalty and constitutional amendments outlawing flag burning. And while he voted to ban job discrimination based on sexual orientation, he also voted to allow states to ignore same-sex marriages. Mindful of his large elderly constituency, Graham has helped lead efforts to expand Medicare benefits to cover prescription drugs.

Graham's father, a wealthy dairy farmer, was a state senator in the 1930s and 1940s and a candidate for governor in 1944. After graduating from Harvard Law School, the younger Graham joined his father in the real estate business and amassed a fortune with projects that included the development of Miami Lakes. He was eased into politics by his half-brother Phil, publisher of The Washington Post. Before his suicide in 1963, Phil Graham introduced Bob to many influential Democrats, including Lyndon B. Johnson, for whom Bob Graham worked at the 1960 Democratic National Convention.

Graham's record at the ballot box is undefeated. Elected to the state House in 1966, he moved to the state Senate in 1970, succeeded Democrat Reubin Askew as governor in 1978 and then, his two terms over, trounced one-term Republican incumbent Paula Hawkins by 10 percentage points in 1986. His two subsequent re-elections have been more lopsided.

KEY VOTES

2002

Yes Pass farm bill reversing crop subsidy limits
No Postpone tougher automobile fuel efficiency standards
Yes Overhaul campaign finance law; ban "soft money" and restrict advocacy advertising
Yes Set federal election standards
No Support oil drilling in Arctic National Wildlife Refuge
Yes Revive fast-track procedures for trade agreements
Yes Create federal insurance coverage for catastrophic terrorist losses
Yes Tighten federal accounting and corporate governance regulation
Yes Advance bipartisan Medicare prescription drug plan
Yes Create independent Sept. 11 commission
Yes Back Democratic Homeland Security Department proposal
No Authorize war against Iraq

2001

No Confirm John Ashcroft as attorney general
No Nullify Clinton Labor Department ergonomics rule
No Cut taxes by $1.35 trillion through fiscal 2011
Yes Pass Democratic bill to bolster rights of patients in managed-care plans
Yes Permit a new round of military base closings
Yes Expand law enforcement power to investigate suspected terrorists

CQ VOTE STUDIES

	PARTY UNITY		PRESIDENTIAL SUPPORT	
	Support	Oppose	Support	Oppose
2002	77%	23%	79%	21%
2001	94%	6%	67%	33%
2000	91%	9%	95%	5%
1999	88%	12%	93%	7%
1998	85%	15%	83%	17%
1997	71%	29%	84%	16%
1996	81%	19%	86%	14%
1995	80%	20%	84%	16%
1994	85%	15%	92%	8%
1993	85%	15%	90%	10%

INTEREST GROUPS

	AFL-CIO	ADA	CCUS	ACU
2002	85%	75%	60%	20%
2001	94%	100%	36%	16%
2000	75%	80%	60%	16%
1999	78%	100%	35%	4%
1998	50%	85%	61%	4%
1997	29%	60%	80%	8%
1996	71%	85%	46%	15%
1995	92%	95%	47%	13%
1994	75%	75%	30%	8%
1993	82%	65%	36%	16%

Sen. Bill Nelson (D)

CAPITOL OFFICE
224-5274
billnelson.senate.gov
716 Hart 20510-0905; fax 228-2183

COMMITTEES
Armed Services
Budget
Commerce, Science & Transportation
Foreign Relations

HOMETOWN
Tallahassee

BORN
Sept. 29, 1942, Miami, Fla.

RELIGION
Episcopalian

FAMILY
Wife, Grace H. Nelson; two children

EDUCATION
Yale U., B.A. 1965; U. of Virginia, J.D. 1968

MILITARY SERVICE
Army, 1968-70; Army Reserve, 1965-71

CAREER
Lawyer

POLITICAL HIGHLIGHTS
Fla. House, 1973-79; U.S. House, 1979-91; sought Democratic nomination for governor, 1990; Fla. treasurer and insurance commissioner, 1995-2001

ELECTION RESULTS

2000 GENERAL		
Bill Nelson (D)	2,989,487	51.0%
Bill McCollum (R)	2,705,348	46.2%
Willie Logan (I)	80,830	1.4%
2000 PRIMARY		
Bill Nelson (D)	692,147	77.5%
Newall Daughtrey (D)	105,650	11.8%
David B. Higginbottom (D)	95,492	10.7%

PREVIOUS WINNING PERCENTAGES
1988 House Election (61%); 1986 House Election (73%); 1984 House Election (61%); 1982 House Election (71%); 1980 House Election (70%); 1978 House Election (61%)

Elected 2000; 1st term

The furor over the 2000 presidential vote in Florida overshadowed the outcome of the state's Senate race that year, in which Nelson scored a signal victory for an otherwise beleaguered Florida Democratic Party. Almost always deployed behind the scenes since then, the political skills Nelson applied to that campaign have been put to use by the party's Senate leadership. In the 108th Congress, he was named one of a handful of deputy whips; in the 107th, he was vice chairman of the Democratic Senatorial Campaign Committee.

As he moves through the midpoint of his first term, Nelson is positioning himself squarely in the ideological center of the Senate, a place that makes political sense for a senator representing such a closely divided constituency. As a member of the centrist New Democrats, he has often deviated from the more liberal party line. In his first two years in office, he backed President Bush three-quarters of the time, more often than all but 10 other Democrats.

It was not until his third year as a senator, however, that Nelson took a clear opening to make a high-profile legislative name for himself. As the only member of the 108th Congress who has traveled in space, Nelson was uniquely positioned to shape congressional response to the loss of the space shuttle Columbia in 2003.

While chairing the House Science Committee's Space Subcommittee, Nelson was as a payload specialist on a 1986 mission of Columbia, and later that year he played a central role in the probe of the space shuttle Challenger disaster. Long before Columbia broke apart, Nelson had used his seat on the Senate Commerce Subcommittee on Science, Technology and Space to denounce what he views as persistent underfunding of NASA and to warn of the danger of delaying upgrades to the shuttles. He has pressed to accelerate development of a reusable space plane to ferry astronauts to and from the International Space Station as a supplement to the shuttles; in the longer term, he says NASA should look at replacing the shuttle with a new craft for astronauts and cargo.

For Nelson, his 1986 ride on Columbia offered evidence of his political savvy and his commitment to meeting the needs of his constituents: at the time the congressional district he represented included the Kennedy Space Center at Cape Canaveral. His office is still filled with posters, books, models and other memorabilia of space travel. But to his critics, the voyage highlighted Nelson's preference for style over substance and brought into sharp relief his lack of legislative accomplishment. A Florida business magazine once labeled him an "empty suit" on its cover.

Nelson is often overshadowed by his state's senior senator, Bob Graham. A fellow Democrat and former chairman of the Intelligence Committee, Graham is a star performer in Florida politics and a leader on many of the national security issues that Nelson is also called upon to confront as a member of the Foreign Relations and Armed Services committees.

On those panels, and in the Senate as a whole, Nelson has focused mainly on those issues of particular concern to Floridians and on maximizing his skill as a fundraiser. His vice chairmanship of the party's Senate campaign arm has given Nelson a seat in Senate leadership meetings. And in 2002, he created his own political action committee — Moving America Forward — to channel more money to Democratic candidates.

On Foreign Relations in the 107th, he won Senate approval of a resolution expressing support for the Varela Project, a petition drive by Cuban democracy activists to trigger a referendum in Cuba to push for expansion of civil liberties. Florida's influential Cuban-American community warmly endorsed that effort. On Armed Services, he pushed through legislation requiring the Bush administration to investigate more fully the fate of Scott Speicher, a Jacksonville Navy pilot shot down over Iraq during the Persian Gulf War. Nelson's intervention came after a CIA report concluded that Speicher probably survived the crash and was captured.

Nelson has taken a keen interest in efforts to unearth the legacy of dangerous weapons tests during the Cold War. In the 107th, he advanced legislation to determine whether U.S. sailors were harmed in the 1960s when the Navy spread biological and chemical weapons on ships in the Pacific. He also won hearings on revelations that servicemen and civilians may have been exposed to harmful toxins during biological weapons tests at a former Air Force base in Boca Raton in the 1950s.

Responding to reports in several Florida newspapers, Nelson pressed the EPA to phase out the use of arsenic-treated wood — most commonly used in playgrounds, waterfront decks, picnic tables and fences — which has been linked to cancer.

A former state insurance commissioner, Nelson has tried to turn that experience to his advantage on Capitol Hill. After the Sept. 11, 2001, terrorist attacks, he attempted to play a pivotal role in legislation to establish a federal backstop for commercial property and casualty insurers in cases of terrorism. But while he was initially regarded as an expert, the Senate ultimately brushed off Nelson's suggestions.

Appealing to Florida's large and politically powerful senior citizen population, Nelson has demonstrated an interest in consumer protection and privacy issues. He introduced a bill to keep insurance companies, banks and other financial institutions that merge from sharing medical and financial information about customers without their explicit consent. And he sought to block pharmaceutical manufacturers from striking deals with drugstores under which they agree to persuade customers to buy alternative drugs different from those recommended by their doctors.

Nelson is a fifth-generation Floridian: his great-great-grandfather came to the Panhandle from Denmark in 1829. Nelson represented Brevard County in the state legislature, then ran for an open House seat in 1978 at age 36, taking conservative stands on economic issues and advocating more military spending. In the House, he was an early member of the moderate Democratic Leadership Council, and his voting record confirmed his self-description as a "New Democrat." Yet despite the glowing publicity attending his adventure as an astronaut, Nelson lost in the 1990 Democratic primary for governor — his only electoral defeat.

He was elected the insurance commissioner four years later, a high-profile position that gave him a launching pad for his Senate race. Nelson dealt with the aftermath of Hurricane Andrew, which ravaged South Florida and the state's insurance market in 1992. He also helped obtain a $206 million settlement for African-Americans who had been overcharged for life insurance and burial policies, bolstering his image as a consumer watchdog and his appeal among black voters.

From the time he announced his intention to run, Nelson was the front-runner for the seat that Republican Connie Mack was vacating after two terms. Nelson benefited from Democratic anger at his opponent, Bill McCollum, a 10-term congressman. McCollum's conservatism on social issues and his role in President Clinton's impeachment enabled Nelson to portray him as too far to the right for most Floridians. Nelson's 5 percentage point win stemmed a political tide in the state that had given the GOP control of the governorship, the legislature and most of Florida's U.S. House seats.

KEY VOTES

2002

Yes Pass farm bill reversing crop subsidy limits
No Postpone tougher automobile fuel efficiency standards
Yes Overhaul campaign finance law; ban "soft money" and restrict advocacy advertising
Yes Set federal election standards
No Support oil drilling in Arctic National Wildlife Refuge
Yes Revive fast-track procedures for trade agreements
Yes Create federal insurance coverage for catastrophic terrorist losses
Yes Tighten federal accounting and corporate governance regulation
Yes Advance bipartisan Medicare prescription drug plan
Yes Create independent Sept. 11 commission
Yes Back Democratic Homeland Security Department proposal
Yes Authorize war against Iraq

2001

No Confirm John Ashcroft as attorney general
No Nullify Clinton Labor Department ergonomics rule
No Cut taxes by $1.35 trillion through fiscal 2011
Yes Pass Democratic bill to bolster rights of patients in managed-care plans
Yes Permit a new round of military base closings
Yes Expand law enforcement power to investigate suspected terrorists

CQ VOTE STUDIES

	PARTY UNITY		PRESIDENTIAL SUPPORT	
	Support	Oppose	Support	Oppose
2002	77%	23%	78%	22%
2001	92%	8%	70%	30%
House Service:				
1990	77%	23%	40%	60%
1989	80%	20%	47%	53%
1988	72%	28%	46%	54%
1987	76%	24%	42%	58%

INTEREST GROUPS

	AFL-CIO	ADA	CCUS	ACU
2002	85%	70%	70%	30%
2001	100%	95%	43%	16%
House Service:				
1990	86%	50%	0%	27%
1989	91%	60%	50%	31%
1988	71%	45%	43%	56%
1987	63%	52%	53%	35%
1986	43%	15%	61%	77%
1985	47%	30%	54%	71%
1984	15%	20%	57%	59%
1983	47%	40%	55%	57%

Rep. Jeff Miller (R)

CAPITOL OFFICE
225-4136
jeff.miller@mail.house.gov
www.house.gov/jeffmiller
331 Cannon 20515-0901; fax 225-3414

COMMITTEES
Armed Services
Veterans' Affairs

HOMETOWN
Chumuckla

BORN
June 27, 1959, St. Petersburg, Fla.

RELIGION
Methodist

FAMILY
Wife, Vicki Miller; two children

EDUCATION
U. of Florida, B.A. 1984 (journalism)

CAREER
Real estate broker; state agriculture department official

POLITICAL HIGHLIGHTS
Fla. House, 1998-2001

ELECTION RESULTS

2002 GENERAL		
Jeff Miller (R)	152,635	74.6%
Bert Oram (D)	51,972	25.4%
2002 PRIMARY		
Jeff Miller (R)	41,990	64.5%
Michael C. Francisco (R)	23,164	35.6%
2001 SPECIAL		
Jeff Miller (R)	53,247	65.7%
Steve Briese (D)	22,695	28.0%
John G. Ralls Jr. (X)	5,115	6.3%

Elected October 2001; 1st full term

Miller may be an ideological twin to his predecessor, Joe Scarborough, but his personal style could not be more different.

Both Republicans are deeply conservative. They are anti-abortion, pro-gun, pro-tax cut and pro-military — assets in this staunchly Republican district. But while Scarborough was an aggressive activist who enjoyed the spotlight and did not mind the label of "rebel," Miller has served more quietly as a consensus-builder who works with his party's leaders. Miller is friendly and approachable, but unlike his outspoken and telegenic predecessor, he often flies beneath the media's radar.

Miller won a special election in October 2001 after Scarborough resigned from the House to spend more time with his children. The former real estate broker and political aide arrived with an eclectic résumé. In earlier periods of his life, he worked in a sheriff's office, as a stock car racer and as a part-time auctioneer. When he was in high school, he was a deejay for the local radio station.

To the applause of many in the largely conservative small towns near Pensacola and Fort Walton Beach, Miller embraces what he calls "traditional values." An active church member who is strongly anti-abortion, Miller would support a constitutional amendment to ban abortion. Although he is not one of the dozen or so lawmakers who are known for their activism in fighting abortion, Miller has nudged House leaders during personal conversations to take stronger positions against the practice.

His highest legislative priorities are protecting the numerous military installations in the Pensacola area, including Pensacola Naval Air Station and Eglin Air Force Base, and serving the veterans of his district. His positions as a member of the Armed Services and Veterans' Affairs committees are critically important to his constituents. On Armed Services, Miller is a stout defender of increased Pentagon spending to support military readiness. Many of the bills that he cosponsored during the 107th Congress addressed military or veterans' issues.

Miller opposes drilling for oil and gas off the Florida coast, not only because of the potential detrimental environmental impact on beaches, but also to maintain the areas used for training exercises by pilots from Eglin Air Force Base.

Miller was bitten by the politics bug fairly early. As a journalism major at the University of Florida, he was elected president of college fraternities for Southeast Florida. This distinction came after he had become the president of the university's agriculture fraternity, Alpha Gamma Rho, and then the president of the school's fraternity system. He remains an enthusiastic supporter of the Florida Gators football team, a passion he shares with his two grown sons.

Fresh out of college, Miller joined the staff of Florida Agriculture Commissioner Doyle Connor. He later served as a state representative for the north Florida district that he now represents in Congress. During his stint in the Florida House, Miller chaired a committee on utilities and telecommunications. On a more personal note, he expressed his interest in stock car racing by sponsoring legislation that restricted public access to autopsy photos after the death of NASCAR driver Dale Earnhardt Sr.

Miller's colleagues say that as a sixth-generation Floridian whose parents sold real estate and operated a cattle ranch near Clearwater, he instinctively understands the needs of his district, which is dotted with rural farm towns, such as his hometown, Chumuckla. His aides like to say that he is just as comfortable in cowboy boots as he is in a business suit.

A member of the Republican Study Group, the group formerly known as the Conservative Action Team, Miller hopes that by working within the system to influence the direction of the party, he will be effective in winning more support for his conservative philosophy. With Republicans controlling the House, Senate and White House, Miller is pursuing more-limited federal government, lower taxes, fewer regulations and support for more-traditional social values.

His first legislative act in the 108th Congress was to offer a bill to rescind the 3.1 percent cost of living pay increase that members of Congress accepted for 2003. Miller was frustrated that President Bush allowed only a 3.1 percent pay raise for federal civilian employees, including those working for the Central Intelligence Agency, Department of Defense and Department of Transportation, rather than a 4.1 percent increase such as was approved for the military. "Many of our federal employees are on the front lines of the war on terrorism. The last thing we need to do is to take away the pay raise they deserve," Miller said. "Let's start with cutting the pay of members of Congress."

In January 2003, Miller was one of just four House members to vote against an extension of unemployment benefits that had expired Dec. 28, 2002. "At what point do we quit providing a check to someone without a job?" asked Miller. "I'm afraid that extending these benefits will diminish the desire to go out and find a job," he said, according to the Associated Press.

One of two members first elected to Congress in special elections soon after the terrorist attacks of Sept. 11, 2001, Miller has said that although national security quickly became the focus of voters' concerns, those issues do not erase the kitchen-table fears of everyday life. "They want to know that their congressman will work to help fix the sagging economy," said Miller, adding that tax reduction is a key piece of his agenda.

He wants to make permanent the 10-year tax cut package of 2001 and enact new reductions, particularly for small companies. As a former small-business owner, Miller is close to the business leaders in his community.

Miller ran in a district with strong Republican tendencies. He won the 2001 special election to replace Scarborough by 66 percent to 28 percent over Democrat Steve Briese. In his 2002 re-election, Miller captured almost three-fourths of the ballots cast, beating Democrat Bert Oram by more than 100,000 votes.

KEY VOTES

2002

- No Overhaul campaign finance law; ban "soft money" and restrict advocacy advertising
- Yes Back Bush's defense budget increase
- Yes Extend 1996 welfare law
- Yes Adopt Bush's discretionary spending limit
- Yes Pass GOP Medicare prescription drug plan
- No Create independent Sept. 11 commission
- No Extend union protections to Homeland Security Department employees
- Yes Revive fast-track procedures for trade agreements
- Yes Authorize war against Iraq
- No Advance bankruptcy overhaul opposed by abortion opponents

2001

- Yes Expand law enforcement power to investigate suspected terrorists

CQ VOTE STUDIES

	PARTY UNITY		PRESIDENTIAL SUPPORT	
	Support	Oppose	Support	Oppose
2002	98%	2%	85%	15%
2001	100%	0%	100%	0%

INTEREST GROUPS

	AFL-CIO	ADA	CCUS	ACU
2002	0%	0%	84%	100%
2001	17%	—	78%	100%

FLORIDA 1

Panhandle — Pensacola, Fort Walton Beach

Some residents of the 1st refer to the area as "Lower Alabama," and in spirit the area is much closer to the Old South than the state's big metropolitan areas. The district, which stretches from north of Panama City to Pensacola, has several large military bases and a mostly white population. Its Gulf Coast beaches and open spaces attract both tourists and residents seeking a small-town feel. Walton and Oklaloosa counties (part of which are in the 2nd) increased their populations by more than 40 percent in the 1990s.

Tourism, health care and retirement communities helped boost an economy slowed by manufacturing losses in the 1980s and early 1990s. Growth here is slower than in Florida's southern regions, but St. Joe, a paper company turned real estate giant, is planning to develop largely rural northwestern Florida. Interstate 10 slips between the Blackwater River State Forest, which borders Alabama, and Eglin Air Force Base, connecting the western tip and Pensacola to the rest of the state.

The 1st is more staunchly conservative than its slight GOP registration advantage indicates. The district's Democrats are more "Dixiecrats" than liberals, and several local and state officials from the area have switched to the GOP after decades as Democrats. The military presence also plays a significant role in politics; a large segment of the Okaloosa population is military employees. Republican Gov. Jeb Bush took 77 percent in Okaloosa and 75 percent in Santa Rosa in the 2002 election, his second- and third-best showings in the state.

MAJOR INDUSTRY
Defense, health care, tourism

MILITARY BASES
Naval Air Station Pensacola, 9,206 military, 4,374 civilian (2002); Eglin Air Force Base, 7,244 military, 3,301 civilian (2001); Hurlburt Field (Air Force), 7,322 military, 853 civilian (2000); Naval Air Station Whiting Field, 1,676 military, 443 civilian (2003); Naval Technical Training Center Corry Station, 2,030 military, 268 civilian (1999)

CITIES
Pensacola, 56,255; Ferry Pass, 27,176; Brent, 22,257

NOTABLE
The "Blue Angels" flight group is housed at Naval Air Station Pensacola; Much of "The Truman Show" movie was filmed in the town of Seaside.

Rep. Allen Boyd (D)

CAPITOL OFFICE
225-5235
www.house.gov/boyd
107 Cannon 20515-0902; fax 225-5615

COMMITTEES
Appropriations

HOMETOWN
Monticello

BORN
June 6, 1945, Valdosta, Ga.

RELIGION
Methodist

FAMILY
Wife, Stephanie A. Boyd; three children

EDUCATION
North Florida Junior College, A.A. 1966; Florida State U., B.S. 1969 (accounting)

MILITARY SERVICE
Army, 1969-71

CAREER
Farmer

POLITICAL HIGHLIGHTS
Sought Democratic nomination for Jefferson County Board of County Commissioners, 1972; Fla. House, 1989-97

ELECTION RESULTS

2002 GENERAL		
Allen Boyd (D)	152,164	66.9%
Tom McGurk (R)	75,275	33.1%
2002 PRIMARY		
Allen Boyd (D)		unopposed
2000 GENERAL		
Allen Boyd (D)	185,579	72.1%
Doug Dodd (R)	71,754	27.9%

PREVIOUS WINNING PERCENTAGES
1998 (95%); 1996 (59%)

Elected 1996; 4th term

Boyd is a fifth-generation farmer in the mostly rural Florida Panhandle, and his conservatism on a broad array of fiscal and social issues has enabled him to entrench himself in the 2nd District while many similar Southern districts have elected Republicans in recent years.

He is a member of the "Blue Dogs," the coalition of fiscally conservative House Democrats who try to exert a center-right pull on the party. Boyd, who founded a similar group when he was in the Florida Legislature, was co-chairman for communication and outreach for the congressional group in the 107th Congress.

Boyd favors paying down the national debt rather than approving major tax reductions. When the nation returned to deficit spending in 2002, he said the $1.35 trillion, 10-year tax cut enacted the year before (without his vote) should be reconsidered. "Congress and the president need to make tough choices to address the changes in the budget outlook," he said. "We must sit down in a bipartisan manner and develop realistic tax and spending levels that will put us back on the glide path to a balanced budget."

As the 108th Congress began, Boyd spoke out against a second round of deep tax cuts proposed by Bush. While they were tempting in the name of economic stimulus, he said, Democrats should be unwilling to go along without offsets to prevent a deepening of the deficit.

Although Boyd has called for restraint on the spending side of the ledger, he is not shy about pushing for government cash when the interests of his district are at stake. He increased his leverage to do so at the start of his second term, in 1999, when he was awarded a coveted spot on the Appropriations Committee; he has since used his assignment to the Military Construction Subcommittee to look out for the 2nd District's Tyndall Air Force Base. Boyd has worked to speed runway upgrades and other improvements at Tyndall in preparation for the arrival there of the F-22, the Air Force's premier air-to-air combat plane. Boyd also has pushed for an $8.1 million physical fitness center at the Panama City-area installation.

Having been a junior infantry officer in Vietnam, Boyd puts a high priority on ways to retain U.S. air superiority over potential military foes. At a subcommittee hearing, he once reflected on his ground combat duty, recalling the morale boost of getting support from U.S. aircraft: "One of the greatest moments in an infantryman's life," he said, was "when he saw those fast movers coming across."

Boyd in the 108th is co-chairman of the bipartisan Congressional Rural Caucus and retains a seat on the Agriculture Appropriations Subcommittee, where he has fought for farmers hurt by the citrus canker. His fiscal conservatism did not prevent him from voting for the 2002 farm law, which calls for an $83 billion increase in commodity subsidies over 10 years. Boyd said the previous statute, which had replaced New Deal-era crop payments with a system more reflective of free-market principles, failed because it was not coupled with sufficient trade expansion and looser federal regulation. Boyd's own record on trade liberalization is mixed: He voted for the 2000 law making permanent the normal U.S.-China trade relationship, but he voted against the 2002 law giving the president the latitude to negotiate trade deals that Congress must vote on without alteration.

In the 107th he backed President Bush's position almost half the time, and he strayed from his party on three out of every 10 mostly party-line votes.

Boyd's conservative side has been evident on a range of domestic issues.

In the 107th, he was the only Florida Democrat who voted to repeal government rules, issued by President Clinton and strongly opposed by business interests, requiring employers to set up a wide range of programs to prevent repetitive stress injuries. He also backed legislation to prevent the EPA from banning certain pesticides unless it could prove that the decision was based on thorough scientific study.

In 1997, he was one of only six Democrats voting to eliminate the National Endowment for the Arts, and in 2000 he was one of just five Democrats who voted against legislation to increase the minimum wage. He supports a constitutional amendment to ban flag desecration and favors banning the procedure labeled "partial birth" abortion by its opponents.

A lifelong hunter, Boyd opposes gun control legislation. He and his sister-in-law, Janegale Boyd, who succeeded him in the state House, have hosted annual charity fundraising dove hunts and dinners, which have been criticized by animal rights protesters and some who object to the fact that lobbyists help pay the food and drink tab.

A product of rural Jefferson County, just east of Tallahassee, Boyd was reared on the family farm. He went to Florida State University just down the road, spent two years in the Army, and then returned home to help his relatives raise cattle, cotton, sod and peanuts. He became involved in a variety of agricultural organizations and civic groups.

A failed bid in 1972 for an open county commission seat seemed to have rid Boyd of whatever inclination he had for elective office, but more than a decade later, another open seat beckoned him. He won a 1989 special election to the state House and served eight years, cultivating good relations with the business community.

He first won his 2nd District seat in 1996 after the retirement of three-term Democrat Pete Peterson. Boyd demonstrated that he could hold together the 2nd's traditional Democratic coalition: Tallahassee-area voters with jobs in state and local government and higher education; blacks; and the portion of the white electorate still clinging to an inherited aversion to the GOP, which in that region was the party of the enemy in the Civil War.

He has not been seriously challenged since, enabling him to focus on fundraising activities aimed at electing more conservative Democrats to augment the rolls of the Blue Dog coalition. The 2nd District, which had been politically competitive throughout the 1990s, was tilted slightly toward the GOP for this decade in post-census redistricting. Still, Boyd won two-thirds of the vote in 2002 against Republican Tom McGurk, a former head of the Florida Department of Management Services.

KEY VOTES

2002

Yes Overhaul campaign finance law; ban "soft money" and restrict advocacy advertising
Yes Back Bush's defense budget increase
Yes Extend 1996 welfare law
No Adopt Bush's discretionary spending limit
No Pass GOP Medicare prescription drug plan
No Create independent Sept. 11 commission
No Extend union protections to Homeland Security Department employees
No Revive fast-track procedures for trade agreements
Yes Authorize war against Iraq
? Advance bankruptcy overhaul opposed by abortion opponents

2001

Yes Nullify Clinton Labor Department ergonomics rule
? Cut taxes by $1.35 trillion through fiscal 2011
No Maintain ban on oil drilling in Arctic National Wildlife Refuge
No Approve Bush proposal to limit managed-care plan liability for coverage decisions
No Divert money from crop subsidy payments to land conservation
Yes Expand law enforcement power to investigate suspected terrorists

CQ VOTE STUDIES

	PARTY UNITY		PRESIDENTIAL SUPPORT	
	Support	Oppose	Support	Oppose
2002	71%	29%	50%	50%
2001	70%	30%	44%	56%
2000	68%	32%	57%	43%
1999	70%	30%	67%	33%
1998	69%	31%	62%	38%

INTEREST GROUPS

	AFL-CIO	ADA	CCUS	ACU
2002	75%	70%	58%	40%
2001	82%	70%	52%	32%
2000	30%	50%	80%	40%
1999	67%	70%	68%	20%
1998	89%	65%	65%	32%

FLORIDA 2
Panhandle – part of Tallahassee, Panama City

The 2nd stretches around Florida's Big Bend, joining the Panhandle with the state capital of Tallahassee (a small part of which is in the 4th District) and the north-central part of the state. Taking in all or part of 16 counties, the district features tobacco and peanut farms, forests and uncongested towns. While safely Democratic, the 2nd is not as liberal as districts in southeast Florida.

Democrats outnumber Republicans more than 2-to-1, but many have conservative views on fiscal and social issues. The exception is the Tallahassee area (Leon County), home to Florida State University and Florida A&M University, where a more liberal sentiment exists. Panama City has a stronger conservative element, as do the smaller communities that ring the Gulf Coast. Black residents — the majority of whom live in the Tallahassee area or in neighboring Gadsden County — make up about one-fifth of the district's voting-age population. Bill McBride, the 2002 Democratic gubernatorial nominee, took at least 60 percent of the vote in Gadsden, Leon, Jefferson and Liberty counties.

The 2nd's economy is driven by its land — from the Gulf Coast beaches where oysters are harvested to farms stocked with soybeans and peanuts. Agriculture has struggled occasionally because of bad weather and low prices, but a steady base of government employees buffers any long-term economic effects. Florida's forestry industry has suffered some setbacks but maintains a strong presence. Panama City relies on tourism and the economic benefits of the military community around Tyndall Air Force Base.

MAJOR INDUSTRY
Agriculture, government, manufacturing

MILITARY BASES
Tyndall Air Force Base, 3,621 military, 680 civilian (2001)

CITIES
Tallahassee (pt.), 147,167; Panama City, 36,417; Callaway, 14,233

NOTABLE
The Suwannee River was made famous by Stephen Foster's song, "Old Folks at Home"; Liberty County has the fewest registered Republicans of any county in the state — 206 as of October 2002.

Rep. Corrine Brown (D)

CAPITOL OFFICE
225-0123
www.house.gov/corrinebrown
2444 Rayburn 20515-0903; fax 225-2256

COMMITTEES
Transportation & Infrastructure
Veterans' Affairs

HOMETOWN
Jacksonville

BORN
Nov. 11, 1946, Jacksonville, Fla.

RELIGION
Baptist

FAMILY
Divorced; one child

EDUCATION
Florida A&M U., B.S. 1969 (sociology), M.A. 1971 (education); U. of Florida, Ed.S. 1974

CAREER
College guidance counselor; travel agency owner

POLITICAL HIGHLIGHTS
Candidate for Fla. House, 1980; Fla. House, 1983-93

ELECTION RESULTS

2002 GENERAL		
Corrine Brown (D)	88,462	59.3%
Jennifer Carroll (R)	60,747	40.7%
2002 PRIMARY		
Corrine Brown (D)	unopposed	
2000 GENERAL		
Corrine Brown (D)	102,143	57.6%
Jennifer Carroll (R)	75,228	42.4%

PREVIOUS WINNING PERCENTAGES
1998 (55%); 1996 (61%); 1994 (58%); 1992 (59%)

Elected 1992; 6th term

Staunchly partisan and unwaveringly liberal, Brown is an emphatic advocate for most Democratic policies and a voluble critic of Republican initiatives. As often as not, however, her exhortations and lamentations come from the sidelines.

She has been particularly outspoken against President Bush, saying his budget priorities have "dangerous flaws" that sacrifice a commitment to the poor and elderly in favor of defense and tax cuts. And she was an early skeptic of the president's conduct of foreign policy, in particular his commitment to removing Saddam Hussein from power. "I remain unconvinced the administration has adequately laid out its case for a war against Iraq," she said in February 2003.

But as Brown enters her second decade in the House, she has built up sufficient seniority to do more than just speak out against proposals she dislikes. In the 108th Congress she assumed the top Democratic post on the Transportation and Infrastructure panel's Railroads Subcommittee, affording her an opportunity to shape legislation to reauthorize Amtrak, the financially troubled federally subsidized passenger rail system.

In the 107th, she used her position as the top-ranking Democrat on the Coast Guard and Maritime Subcommittee to press for greater security at her hometown Port of Jacksonville and other seaports around the country. She helped shape the port security law enacted in 2002.

From her seat on Transportation she has been able to direct a good share of federal funding to her district and state. During the 1998 reauthorization of federal transportation programs, Florida received a 57 percent increase. Brown also won airport and light-rail funding for Orlando and its suburbs, as well as money for a new courthouse and a new bridge in Jacksonville.

There are several military installations near the 3rd District, including the Jacksonville Naval Air Station. Jacksonville is also home to many retired military personnel, and Brown keeps an eye on their needs as a member of the Veterans' Affairs Committee. Brown would like to see more emphasis placed on the military's human resources, such as increasing training. She sees the military as a place where families, particularly poor families, can find opportunities and learn self-discipline.

As the second-vice chairman of the Congressional Black Caucus, she speaks out on improving access to health care for minorities and low-income people, and she has worked to make minority hiring a priority at the Transportation Security Administration since its creation in 2001.

Brown is a vocal defender of affirmative action. In 2000, she led protests against Florida GOP Gov. Jeb Bush's decision to end the practice in state government jobs and at state universities. Brown said that under the governor's executive order, "Many minority children will not get the breaks they need to get a college education." But she also stresses self-reliance, telling an audience at a black heritage festival, "We are responsible for everything that has happened to us" politically in recent years.

After the 2000 election controversy in Florida — when voters, including many minorities, were turned away from some polling places and thousands of ballots were miscast or uncounted — Brown joined the volley of criticism and began working to overhaul the election process. She backed the election standards law enacted in 2002, unlike several colleagues in the Black Caucus who felt the measure did not do enough.

Brown has a long history of fending off allegations of ethical lapses. Her 1992 primary opponent, former state Rep. Andrew E. Johnson, filed charges with the Florida Commission on Ethics claiming that Brown received illegal campaign donations and made a staff member from her state representative's office work in her travel agency.

In 1998, The St. Petersburg Times published a story saying Brown had benefited from a $10,000 check she received from the Rev. Henry J. Lyons, president of the National Baptist Convention USA Inc. Lyons had been charged in federal and state court with crimes including extortion, theft and conspiracy. Brown denied the allegation.

Also in 1998, the Committee on Standards of Official Conduct began investigating her financial dealings with a West African businessman. Just before the 2000 election, the panel ruled that Brown had "demonstrated, at the least, poor judgment." The panel decided not to take disciplinary action in large measure because key witnesses "were beyond the reach of the committee's subpoena power."

Brown was steered into politics by one of her sorority sisters at Florida A&M University, Gwendolyn Sawyer Cherry, who went on to become the first black Florida state representative. Although Brown lost her first state House race in 1980, Cherry kept after her to try again, and Brown won a seat in 1982. She served in the state House for a decade.

After a black-majority 3rd District was created by redistricting for the 1990s, Brown was one of four candidates in the district's bitter Democratic primary. She had to overcome ethics charges brought against her by one of her Democratic opponents, but emerged from a runoff with a 64 percent victory; latent acrimony helped hold her share of the vote to 59 percent in November 1992 against Republican Don Weidner.

The district has been redrawn twice since then, and for this decade African-Americans make up slightly less than half the population.

Brown has had to work for each of her general-election victories. She has garnered more than three-fifths of the vote — a traditional threshold for being seen as having a safe seat — in only one of her six races, when she got a lift from President Clinton's re-election coattails in 1996.

Republicans have run a black candidate against Brown in three of her re-election campaigns, seeking to eliminate race as a factor. Most recently, in 2000 and 2002, their nominee was Jennifer Carroll, a retired Navy lieutenant who had made a name for herself as a Jacksonville-area community activist. Carroll spent $1 million to get 42 percent of the vote in 2000; in her second attempt she spent only one-third as much and took 41 percent.

KEY VOTES

2002

- Yes Overhaul campaign finance law; ban "soft money" and restrict advocacy advertising
- Yes Back Bush's defense budget increase
- No Extend 1996 welfare law
- No Adopt Bush's discretionary spending limit
- No Pass GOP Medicare prescription drug plan
- Yes Create independent Sept. 11 commission
- Yes Extend union protections to Homeland Security Department employees
- No Revive fast-track procedures for trade agreements
- No Authorize war against Iraq
- No Advance bankruptcy overhaul opposed by abortion opponents

2001

- No Nullify Clinton Labor Department ergonomics rule
- No Cut taxes by $1.35 trillion through fiscal 2011
- Yes Maintain ban on oil drilling in Arctic National Wildlife Refuge
- No Approve Bush proposal to limit managed-care plan liability for coverage decisions
- Yes Divert money from crop subsidy payments to land conservation
- Yes Expand law enforcement power to investigate suspected terrorists

CQ VOTE STUDIES

	PARTY UNITY		PRESIDENTIAL SUPPORT	
	Support	Oppose	Support	Oppose
2002	95%	5%	29%	71%
2001	92%	8%	24%	76%
2000	92%	8%	82%	18%
1999	93%	7%	83%	17%
1998	95%	5%	84%	16%

INTEREST GROUPS

	AFL-CIO	ADA	CCUS	ACU
2002	100%	95%	42%	0%
2001	100%	95%	43%	8%
2000	100%	80%	50%	9%
1999	89%	100%	28%	0%
1998	100%	95%	31%	4%

FLORIDA 3

North – parts of Jacksonville, Orlando and Gainesville

The 3rd, which bounces among three of Florida's northern cities, includes both heavily urban areas and long stretches of swamps and lakes along the St. Johns River. The racial and political demographics of the black-dominated 3rd were hardly changed during redistricting following the 2000 census, though the district no longer includes the Daytona Beach area, and it now extends west from its poles of Jacksonville and Orlando to pick up voters in Gainesville, home to the University of Florida (though the university itself is in the 6th District).

Democrats dominate the 3rd — they make up almost 65 percent of registered voters. Some rural areas are home to Republicans and old-line conservative Democrats, but not enough to counter the district's strong proclivity toward Democratic candidates for federal office. Al Gore won the 2000 presidential vote here by 30 percentage points.

The 3rd includes a large portion of Putnam County. Often referred to as the Bass Fishing Capital of the World, Putnam is a blue-collar region. The 3rd does contain some tinges of conservatism, particularly in Clay County and in the Palatka area (shared with the 7th) on the St. Johns River.

Mostly blue-collar, the district relies on Naval Air Station Jacksonville (in the 4th District) and other area government facilities for jobs. CSX Corp. also is based in Jacksonville. The city's emergence as a financial center has helped the district's economic outlook, while Orlando residents work in tourism jobs at locations such as Walt Disney World (in the 8th District). Most of the areas in between have agricultural land and lack major private employers, contributing to the 3rd's poor overall economic profile.

MAJOR INDUSTRY

Defense, government, higher education, transportation

CITIES

Jacksonville (pt.), 251,892; Orlando (pt.), 61,906; Pine Hills, 41,764; Gainesville (pt.), 35,540; Oak Ridge, 22,349; Sanford (pt.), 21,786

NOTABLE

Eatonville was the hometown of Harlem Renaissance author Zora Neale Hurston.

Rep. Ander Crenshaw (R)

CAPITOL OFFICE
225-2501
www.house.gov/crenshaw
127 Cannon 20515-0904; fax 225-2504

COMMITTEES
Appropriations
Budget

HOMETOWN
Jacksonville

BORN
Sept. 1, 1944, Jacksonville, Fla.

RELIGION
Episcopalian

FAMILY
Wife, Kitty Crenshaw; two children

EDUCATION
U. of Georgia, A.B. 1966 (political science); U. of Florida, J.D. 1969

CAREER
Investment bank executive; lawyer

POLITICAL HIGHLIGHTS
Fla. House, 1972-78; candidate for Fla. secretary of state, 1978; sought Republican nomination for U.S. Senate, 1980; Fla. Senate, 1986-94 (president, 1993); sought Republican nomination for governor, 1994

ELECTION RESULTS

2002 GENERAL		
Ander Crenshaw (R)		unopposed
2002 PRIMARY		
Ander Crenshaw (R)	39,303	89.7%
Deborah Katz Pueschel (R)	4,509	10.3%
2000 GENERAL		
Ander Crenshaw (R)	203,090	67.0%
Tom Sullivan (D)	94,587	31.2%
Deborah Katz Pueschel (I)	5,609	1.9%

Elected 2000; 2nd term

Crenshaw has drawn on his easygoing charm and the valuable experience he gained as the leader of an evenly divided Florida Senate to make a favorable impression early in his career on Capitol Hill.

As a freshman in the 107th Congress, he was chosen by his colleagues in the GOP Class of 2000 as their representative to the leadership. He also was named to the GOP Policy Committee, the Republican prescription drug task force and the party's whip team.

He won assignment to the Appropriations Committee in the 108th Congress, and he says the preparation and teamwork skills he learned as a basketball player for the University of Georgia helped him gain the appointment. He also was tapped to be a deputy whip.

Crenshaw says he did his "pre-game homework" in lobbying for the Appropriations post, lining up support among Sunshine State colleagues and letting the GOP leadership know that it could count on him. He was willing to subjugate his commitment to helping his district's military bases when, as the freshman class liaison to the leadership, he urged the Armed Services Committee to support a leadership-drafted budget plan that called for less defense spending than the committee had wanted.

Although Crenshaw had been out of politics for six years before winning the 4th District seat, his résumé was of great interest to GOP leaders preparing to deal with a slim margin of control in the 107th Congress.

Crenshaw had been in a similar situation before. In 1993, he was the first Republican to preside over the Florida Senate in 118 years, leading a chamber split evenly between Republicans and Democrats. His reputation as a straight shooter and someone who would seek consensus kept the power-sharing agreement from descending into chaos and acrimony. Although he often disagreed with Democratic Gov. Lawton Chiles, particularly over taxes, almost everyone had positive things to say about Crenshaw when the session ended. "What I tried to do was involve everybody in the process," he says.

It has been the same on Capitol Hill, where he set out to learn the issues on his committees, build relationships with his colleagues and cement his reputation as a team player. Many comments about Crenshaw include the observation that "he's a nice guy."

Crenshaw is conservative across the board on both fiscal and social issues. He told the Orlando Sentinel, "On balance, I'd start with the proposition that government doesn't solve problems very well." But he tends to focus on finding pragmatic solutions rather than taking ideological stands. He is most interested in military and transportation issues: Northeast Florida is home to several military bases and a constituency, centered in Jacksonville, faced with sprawl and clogged roadways.

From his seat on Armed Services in the 107th, Crenshaw gained funding for a number of Florida bases and defense contractors. He also bragged about winning transportation funding for parochial projects including a bicycle route, bus facilities and a ferry terminal. As part of the aviation security measure enacted in 2001, Crenshaw won inclusion of language to require background checks for flight students; some of the al Qaeda hijackers in the Sept. 11, 2001, terrorist attacks had learned to fly at Florida flight schools.

Although he is not usually outspoken on social issues, Crenshaw emphasized in many of his campaigns a decline in moral values that he has called "problems of the soul." He won House approval of a resolution recognizing the importance of young people to America's future and encouraged participation in an annual American Youth Day, to be held on a Saturday near the beginning of the school year.

Crenshaw's family has been in the Jacksonville area since 1901. A lanky 6-foot-4, he went to Georgia on a basketball scholarship. He was the third member of his family, following his father and brother, to win a letter for the Bulldogs. After graduating with a degree in political science, Crenshaw earned a law degree and practiced law for a while, but he soon switched to investment banking, working for several national firms.

Politics was not on his radar screen until he started dating Kitty Kirk, the daughter of Florida Gov. Claude R. Kirk Jr., the first Republican to hold that post since Reconstruction. Before then, he told the Orlando Sentinel, "I was absolutely apolitical. I just didn't pay attention to all that stuff."

Crenshaw entered politics himself in 1972, winning election to the state House, where he served for six years. He was elected to the state Senate in 1986. Many of his Senate colleagues commented that he maintained a laid-back attitude toward his job. But that same relaxed manner enabled him to build a base of trust among lawmakers of both parties that served him well when he was elected Senate president in 1993.

Though Jacksonville-area voters have elected him three times to the state House, three times to the state Senate (once in a special election) and twice to Congress, he has lost three statewide elections. He lost a bid for secretary of state in 1978, came in third in the Republican Senate primary in 1980 and finished fourth in the GOP primary for governor in 1994.

In the seven-year interim between his service in the state House and his special-election victory to the Senate, Crenshaw's career as an investment banker made him a wealthy man. After leaving the state Senate in 1995, he had given little thought to returning to politics until 2000, when Republican Rep. Tillie Fowler decided to abide by her term-limit pledge. His entry into the race chased off several would-be candidates, and his easy primary win guaranteed victory in the solidly Republican 4th District.

In redistricting for this decade, Crenshaw's previously compact Duval and Nassau County district was altered. It now stretches from the Atlantic Ocean beaches of Duval and Nassau more than 150 miles west to the Leon County outskirts of Tallahassee. The new borders did not endanger Crenshaw's electoral prospects. He easily dispatched a GOP primary foe in 2002 and had no Democratic opponent in his bid for a second term.

The first name he uses, Ander, is a shortened version of his given name Alexander; it was coined by his older brother.

KEY VOTES

2002

- No Overhaul campaign finance law; ban "soft money" and restrict advocacy advertising
- Yes Back Bush's defense budget increase
- Yes Extend 1996 welfare law
- Yes Adopt Bush's discretionary spending limit
- Yes Pass GOP Medicare prescription drug plan
- No Create independent Sept. 11 commission
- No Extend union protections to Homeland Security Department employees
- Yes Revive fast-track procedures for trade agreements
- Yes Authorize war against Iraq
- Yes Advance bankruptcy overhaul opposed by abortion opponents

2001

- Yes Nullify Clinton Labor Department ergonomics rule
- Yes Cut taxes by $1.35 trillion through fiscal 2011
- No Maintain ban on oil drilling in Arctic National Wildlife Refuge
- Yes Approve Bush proposal to limit managed-care plan liability for coverage decisions
- No Divert money from crop subsidy payments to land conservation
- Yes Expand law enforcement power to investigate suspected terrorists

CQ VOTE STUDIES

	PARTY UNITY		PRESIDENTIAL SUPPORT	
	Support	Oppose	Support	Oppose
2002	98%	2%	90%	10%
2001	97%	3%	91%	9%

INTEREST GROUPS

	AFL-CIO	ADA	CCUS	ACU
2002	11%	0%	100%	96%
2001	17%	0%	100%	92%

FLORIDA 4

North – part of Jacksonville, sliver of Tallahassee

The solidly Republican 4th is anchored in Jacksonville and the surrounding beach communities of Duval County. It wraps around the northeast corner of the state and then runs across the northern border counties as far west as Leon County, where it narrows to a finger to take in a small eastern part of Tallahassee, the state capital.

Overall, Democrats outnumber Republicans, who are clustered in Duval County. But many Democrats in the more rural areas of the district are old-line conservatives who now vote Republican. One such example is Baker County, where Democrats hold a 6-to-1 registration advantage but Republican Jeb Bush won 69 percent of the vote in the 2002 gubernatorial election. Overall, the 4th gave George W. Bush 64 percent of the vote in the 2000 presidential election.

The Jacksonville-based 4th was once a thin strip along the East Coast, but redistricting in 2002 gave it an east-west cast that alters the set of issues important to voters. Agriculture and inland water are now vital in a district once dominated by coastal issues. Much of the 4th shadows Interstate 10, a highway that bridges the 150 miles of rural territory between Jacksonville and Tallahassee.

Jacksonville is a major center for the financial services industry, which provides many of the jobs not associated with the Navy's strong presence in the district along the St. Johns River.

MAJOR INDUSTRY

Defense, financial services, tourism

MILITARY BASES

Naval Station Mayport, 12,254 military, 1,260 civilian (1999); Naval Air Station Jacksonville, 10,086 military, 7,261 civilian (1999)

CITIES

Jacksonville (pt.), 396,879; Jacksonville Beach, 20,990; Atlantic Beach, 13,368; Fernandina Beach, 10,549; Lake City, 9,980

NOTABLE

Fernandina Beach is the only part of the current United States to have existed under eight flags: France, Spain (twice), England, "Patriot," "Green Cross of Florida," Mexico, Confederate and U.S.

Rep. Ginny Brown-Waite (R)

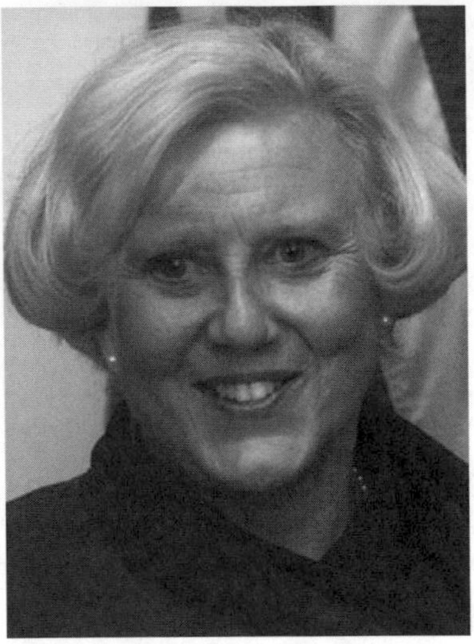

CAPITOL OFFICE
225-1002
www.house.gov/brown-waite
1516 Longworth 20515-0905; fax 226-6559

COMMITTEES
Budget
Financial Services
Veterans' Affairs

HOMETOWN
Brooksville

BORN
Oct. 5, 1943, Albany, N.Y.

RELIGION
Roman Catholic

FAMILY
Husband, Harvey Waite; three children

EDUCATION
State U. of New York, Albany, B.S. 1976; Russell Sage College, M.A. 1984 (public administration)

CAREER
Health care consultant; state legislative aide

POLITICAL HIGHLIGHTS
Hernando County Board of Commissioners, 1991-93; Fla. Senate, 1992-2002 (president pro tempore, 2001-2002)

ELECTION RESULTS

2002 GENERAL		
Ginny Brown-Waite (R)	121,998	47.9%
Karen L. Thurman (D)	117,758	46.2%
Jack "Thro" Gargan (I)	8,639	3.4%
Brian Moore (I)	6,223	2.4%
2002 PRIMARY		
Ginny Brown-Waite (R)	31,242	57.6%
Don Gessner (R)	23,008	42.4%

Elected 2002; 1st term

A veteran of legislative battles in two states — as a policy aide in the New York Legislature and as a state senator in Florida — Brown-Waite has a hands-on approach to solving problems. The onetime owner of a Mr. Donut franchise went to school and learned how to make the doughnuts. "In case the baker doesn't show up, you know how to do it," Brown-Waite said. "It makes you appreciate the baker a whole lot."

Health care, veterans and transportation issues promise to be at the top of her congressional agenda. She represents a growing, mostly suburban population with a large number of retirees.

Brown-Waite calls herself a conservative, eschewing the label of moderate. Yet her 10-year career in the Florida Senate was notable for her ability to rise within the Republican ranks while bucking party orthodoxy on some issues.

Brown-Waite, who had lost relatives to smoking-related illnesses, supported efforts by past Democratic Gov. Lawton Chiles to sue tobacco companies on behalf of Florida. She received high marks from the League of Conservation Voters as a state legislator and is proud of her oversight of HMOs while serving as chairman of the Florida Senate's Health Committee.

Her independent streak seems to fit the former part-time college professor, who cruises down Florida's Gulf Coast in a classic 1959 MG automobile. She has not always ingratiated herself with colleagues: Her fierce style has drawn criticism in the past, particularly when she served as a Hernando County commissioner.

Brown-Waite's narrow 2002 victory in Florida's 5th District was a coup for state Republican leaders, who had engineered a redistricting plan aimed at ousting five-term Democratic Rep. Karen L. Thurman.

After easily winning the GOP primary, Brown-Waite overcame a determined effort by the moderate Thurman to keep her seat. Brown-Waite won by a margin of less than 2 percentage points.

FLORIDA 5

Northern west coast — Pasco, Hernando counties

Located north of Tampa on Florida's west coast, the 5th includes Hernando, Citrus and part of Pasco counties and portions of five other counties. Its eastern part, in Lake County, extends to the greater Orlando area.

During redistricting following the 2000 census, the legislature swapped Democratic strongholds for GOP bailiwicks in an effort to elect a Republican to the House. The resulting electorate is almost evenly divided between Republicans and Democrats, with about 17 percent of voters registered as independents. Two of the most notable changes were the exclusion of Alachua County — which includes the Democratic-leaning Gainesville voters around the University of Florida — and the Pasco County coast. Mapmakers instead added more-conservative areas of Pasco.

Social Security, prescription drugs and veterans affairs are the dominant political issues in the 5th, where more than one-fourth of residents are 65 or older. Although its populace often has fought development, the district's communities have been filling up more rapidly in recent decades as additional retirees move into the area.

Tougher economic times have hit parts of the 5th, but many communities are thriving anyway. Businesses continue to buy up land in Pasco County, and industrial parks in Pasco and Hernando counties are havens for small manufacturing companies.

MAJOR INDUSTRY
Manufacturing, service, health care

CITIES
Spring Hill, 69,078; Land O' Lakes, 20,971; Homosassa Springs, 12,458

NOTABLE
Brooksville was named for Rep. Preston Brooks of South Carolina, who in 1856 bludgeoned Sen. Charles Sumner, Mass., with a cane after Sumner gave an anti-slavery speech in which he denounced a senator who was a relative of Brooks.

Rep. Cliff Stearns (R)

CAPITOL OFFICE
225-5744
www.house.gov/stearns
2370 Rayburn 20515-0906; fax 225-3973

COMMITTEES
Energy & Commerce
(Commerce, Trade & Consumer Protection - chairman)
Veterans' Affairs

HOMETOWN
Ocala

BORN
April 16, 1941, Washington, D.C.

RELIGION
Presbyterian

FAMILY
Wife, Joan Stearns; three children

EDUCATION
George Washington U., B.S. 1963 (electrical engineering)

MILITARY SERVICE
Air Force, 1963-67

CAREER
Hotel and restaurant executive; advertising account executive

POLITICAL HIGHLIGHTS
No previous office

ELECTION RESULTS

2002 GENERAL		
Cliff Stearns (R)	141,570	65.4%
David E. Bruderly (D)	75,046	34.6%
2002 PRIMARY		
Cliff Stearns (R)		unopposed
2000 GENERAL		
Cliff Stearns (R)		unopposed

PREVIOUS WINNING PERCENTAGES
1998 (100%); 1996 (67%); 1994 (99%); 1992 (65%); 1990 (59%); 1988 (53%)

Elected 1988; 8th term

After 14 years in the House, Stearns spends less time talking about conservative causes than he used to and more time shaping legislation. When he first joined Congress, Stearns was known mostly for spearheading battles against abortion rights and funding for the National Endowment for the Arts.

But he has risen through the ranks over the years to assume a leadership role on two subcommittees. First, he chaired the Veterans' Affairs Subcommittee on Health, where he was a vocal advocate for veterans. He helped expand health care for veterans and pressed for more federal attention to Gulf War syndrome, a mysterious group of health problems that afflicted some Persian Gulf veterans. Although he was no longer a Veterans' Affairs subcommittee chairman in the 107th Congress, Stearns continued to work on veterans issues, introducing a bill to authorize a veterans' cemetery in the Jacksonville area.

As chairman of the Energy and Commerce Subcommittee on Commerce, Trade and Consumer Protection in the 107th, Stearns led his panel in developing legislation to protect the privacy of consumers who shop via the Internet and to overhaul accounting standards in the wake of a series of corporate accounting scandals. He also wrote legislation to shield gun manufacturers and sellers from liability lawsuits for civil damages based on a gun owner's illegal use of a firearm.

His subcommittee held hearings on such topics as sports agents' relationships with college athletes, online travel services and business ethics. Stearns co-chaired a noteworthy hearing in 2001 at which the chairmen of Ford Motor Co. and Bridgestone/Firestone Inc. exchanged accusations about which company was at fault for a series of fatal car crashes.

Stearns also serves on Energy and Commerce's Oversight Subcommittee, where he had tough words for executives of Enron Corp. and Arthur Andersen LLP, Enron's accountants, after Enron filed for bankruptcy, admitting it had presented substantially false financial reports. "This is human greed," Stearns said.

But Stearns continues to champion conservative causes. He was a forerunner of the tough-talking fiscal and social conservatives who came to Congress in droves in the 1990s. Many of his speeches and votes on the floor reflect his strong support for what he calls "traditional values," and he does not mince words in making his points.

In debate on a constitutional amendment that would have banned flag desecration, he said, "Burning the flag is not a method of speech or expression. It is . . . a clear measure of hatred for our country."

In the 107th Congress, he continued to oppose the National Endowment for the Arts, offering an amendment to cut $10 million from the NEA's budget and direct it to energy conservation programs. He also tried to take $12 million from the Corporation for Public Broadcasting and give it to the Centers for Disease Control. And he signed a letter to the Public Broadcasting Service expressing concern about the possible addition of an HIV-positive character to the children's show "Sesame Street"; plans for such a character had been announced on the South African version of the show.

Analyses of his voting record by the American Conservative Union and the liberal Americans for Democratic Action are good indicators of where Stearns fits on the political spectrum. His lifetime score from the ACU is 95; his ADA score is 8.

Republican leaders called on Stearns' party loyalty in 2001 when a bill giving the president fast-track authority to negotiate trade agreements that Congress cannot amend came up for a vote. Over the years, Stearns had opposed such legislation, which he feared could harm his district's citrus growers.

But late in 2001, President Bush gave Stearns a ride on Air Force One and extracted a promise that he would support the bill if his vote were needed. It was, and Stearns voted "aye," saying that supporting the president in a time of war was more important than his district's concerns. The final tally was 215-214.

A few months later, when the House-Senate conference version of the bill came to a vote, Stearns' support was not needed. He returned to his usual "no" vote.

Stearns was born and raised in Washington, D.C., where his father worked as a Justice Department lawyer. During his college days at The George Washington University, where he majored in electrical engineering, Stearns was part of the Air Force ROTC. He served four years in the Air Force as a specialist in aerospace engineering and satellite reconnaissance. (On Capitol Hill, Stearns co-chairs the Air Force Caucus.)

After his stint in the Air Force, Stearns worked in advertising before going into business for himself. He took over a dilapidated motel in Massachusetts; later, spotting what he viewed as an undervalued Howard Johnson's for sale in north central Florida, Stearns moved to the Sunshine State in the mid-1970s. He built a thriving motel and restaurant management business and involved himself in local affairs in Ocala.

He became director of the Chamber of Commerce, served on the board of a major local hospital, and joined church and civic groups. In 1988 Stearns ran for an open House seat and, through his local alliances and political savvy, was able to beat two better-connected candidates for the Republican nomination.

Although he was a heavy underdog in the general election against Democratic state House Speaker Jon Mills, Stearns' limited political background gave him a salient, populist theme: He said the time had come for "a citizen congressman." Stearns went on to out-hustle an overconfident Mills for the seat.

His last competitive race was in 1990. Democrats didn't even field a candidate against him in 1998 or 2000. Redistricting in 2002 did him no political harm. Democrats ran engineer David E. Bruderly, a political novice, but Stearns cruised to victory with 65 percent of the vote.

KEY VOTES

2002

- No Overhaul campaign finance law; ban "soft money" and restrict advocacy advertising
- Yes Back Bush's defense budget increase
- Yes Extend 1996 welfare law
- Yes Adopt Bush's discretionary spending limit
- Yes Pass GOP Medicare prescription drug plan
- – Create independent Sept. 11 commission
- No Extend union protections to Homeland Security Department employees
- No Revive fast-track procedures for trade agreements
- Yes Authorize war against Iraq
- No Advance bankruptcy overhaul opposed by abortion opponents

2001

- Yes Nullify Clinton Labor Department ergonomics rule
- Yes Cut taxes by $1.35 trillion through fiscal 2011
- No Maintain ban on oil drilling in Arctic National Wildlife Refuge
- Yes Approve Bush proposal to limit managed-care plan liability for coverage decisions
- No Divert money from crop subsidy payments to land conservation
- Yes Expand law enforcement power to investigate suspected terrorists

CQ VOTE STUDIES

	PARTY UNITY		PRESIDENTIAL SUPPORT	
	Support	Oppose	Support	Oppose
2002	96%	4%	82%	18%
2001	93%	7%	83%	17%
2000	96%	4%	17%	83%
1999	93%	7%	18%	82%
1998	92%	8%	18%	82%

INTEREST GROUPS

	AFL-CIO	ADA	CCUS	ACU
2002	22%	5%	82%	96%
2001	18%	5%	91%	96%
2000	10%	5%	80%	100%
1999	33%	10%	72%	92%
1998	10%	5%	83%	96%

FLORIDA 6

North central – parts of Jacksonville, Gainesville and Ocala

The boomerang-shaped 6th takes in large swaths of rural territory, as well as western Duval County, western Gainesville and part of Ocala. The southern tip is in Leesburg, which is within Orlando's sphere in the center of the state.

Despite a slight Democratic registration advantage, the GOP has a clear edge in most federal races. But voters are willing to support conservative candidates from either major party. Fifty-seven percent of voters favored George W. Bush in the 2000 presidential election.

The district contains three regions with distinct interests. The northern end is centered in Jacksonville (shared with the 3rd and 4th districts), which is heavily influenced by the military. Gainesville, shared with the 3rd in the middle of the district, is home to the University of Florida and a major veterans hospital, while the southern area is a haven for retirees.

The district includes all of two small counties — Gilchrist and Bradford — and parts of six others, including Alachua and Marion, each of which contains about one-quarter of the 6th's population. Alachua, which includes Gainesville, is the biggest Democratic outpost in the district, while Republicans have their strongest registration edge in the Clay County Jacksonville suburbs and exurbs west of the St. Johns River. Republican Gov. Jeb Bush took more than 77 percent of the Clay vote in the 2002 governor's race, his best showing in the state.

MAJOR INDUSTRY

Higher education, health care, agriculture, forestry, defense

CITIES

Jacksonville (pt.), 86,846; Gainesville (pt.), 59,907; Lakeside, 30,927; Ocala (pt.), 29,559

NOTABLE

The Florida Museum of Natural History is located on the campus of the University of Florida in Gainesville; Camp Blanding, in Clay County, is a 73,000-acre Florida Army National Guard training center that was used for multiple purposes by the Army during World War II— including serving as a prisoner-of-war camp.

Rep. John L. Mica (R)

CAPITOL OFFICE
225-4035
john.mica@mail.house.gov
www.house.gov/mica
2445 Rayburn 20515-0907; fax 226-0821

COMMITTEES
Government Reform
House Administration
Transportation & Infrastructure
(Aviation - chairman)

HOMETOWN
Winter Park

BORN
Jan. 27, 1943, Binghamton, N.Y.

RELIGION
Episcopalian

FAMILY
Wife, Pat Mica; two children

EDUCATION
Miami-Dade Community College, A.A. 1965; U. of Florida, B.A. 1967 (political science & education)

CAREER
Cellular telephone company executive; government consultant; real estate investor; congressional aide

POLITICAL HIGHLIGHTS
Fla. House, 1977-81; Republican nominee for Fla. Senate, 1980

ELECTION RESULTS

2002 GENERAL		
John L. Mica (R)	142,147	59.6%
Wayne Hogan (D)	96,444	40.4%
2002 PRIMARY		
John L. Mica (R)		unopposed
2000 GENERAL		
John L. Mica (R)	171,018	63.2%
Daniel Vaughen (D)	99,531	36.8%

PREVIOUS WINNING PERCENTAGES
1998 (100%); 1996 (62%); 1994 (73%); 1992 (56%)

Elected 1992; 6th term

Mica emerged as a legislative leader in the 107th Congress with his adept handling of aviation security issues after the Sept. 11, 2001, terrorist attacks. He himself will admit that he has mellowed from his earlier incendiary days when his legislative tactics were sometimes likened to those of Attila the Hun.

Chairman of the Transportation panel's Aviation Subcommittee, Mica successfully shepherded an aid and security package for the financially vulnerable airline industry that was brought before his panel. By the end of 2001, his subcommittee had established a new agency to oversee transportation security and provided federal assistance in installing improved baggage screening machines. Before Sept. 11, the subcommittee focused mostly on flight delays, consumer complaints, proposed airline mergers and congestion in the aviation network.

Within 10 days after the terrorist attacks, Mica's panel had arranged for congressional hearings on aviation security and the future of the aviation industry. After the initial airline financial aid package in 2001 and the formation of the new Transportation Security Administration, Mica continued to press for long-range action to help the struggling airline industry, saying that the new security requirements had imposed additional financial burdens on carriers. He was also a proponent of the effort to authorize pilots to carry weapons and to train them in their proper use.

In the last five Congresses, Mica has chaired three different subcommittees, which have been concerned with such disparate subjects as the federal civil service and the war against drugs as well as the aviation industry. When he took over the chairmanship of the Government Reform Committee's Civil Service Subcommittee in the 104th Congress, his eagerness to downsize the government, overhaul federal regulations and change federal employee policies led to a scathing denunciation from the president of a federal employees union, who called Mica "the most dangerous man in history to chair" the subcommittee.

But by the end of his tenure, the animosity between Mica and government employees groups had eased somewhat. In the 105th, for example, Mica worked to increase federal workers' choices in life insurance and health coverage.

In the 106th Congress, Mica became the chairman of Government Reform's Criminal Justice Subcommittee, where he sought bipartisan cooperation, even taking his panel to the districts of Democratic members for field hearings. His priority was the battle against illegal drugs, and he coined the phrase "Drugs Destroy Lives."

Mica once said that he had "the inclination of Newt Gingrich" — referring to the former Speaker of the House, who was a confrontational agitator when the GOP was in the minority — "but I hope I have the political wisdom of Bob Michel," a pragmatist who was the House GOP leader from 1981 to 1995. "You want to get things done, but sometimes you need to throw bombs," Mica says. In recent years, the Bob Michel side of Mica's personality has been gaining the edge. "I've tempered a bit," he acknowledges.

Mica's mellowing has not altered his political views. He remains a dependable vote for the GOP leadership, with a strong pro-business rating for his votes in Congress. One area in which Mica departs from many of his GOP colleagues is his concern for environmental protection. He fights for restoration of the Florida Everglades and the preservation of lands and waters in central and northern Florida.

Although Mica's national focus has shifted to reflect his committee responsibilities, his local agenda has remained constant. From his seat on the Transportation Committee, he has been a longtime champion of commuter rail service for his district in the Orlando suburbs. He first proposed a 52-mile light rail system that failed to attract much local support, and then he aimed for a commuter rail service using existing rail lines. At the same time, Mica secured money for expanded bus service and a new highway that would bypass a particularly congested stretch of Interstate 4.

A critic of Amtrak, in the 107th he proposed splitting off the profitable Northeast Corridor and Virginia-to-Florida Auto Train routes for management by an interstate compact of states or a private company. His bill was silent, however, on what to do with the remainder of Amtrak's system.

A history buff, Mica has long pushed for approval of a visitors center at the U.S. Capitol. The shooting incident in 1998 that left two police officers dead provided new impetus for the visitors center, which is being built, largely underground, just east of the Capitol. Mica sits on the Capitol Preservation Commission, which is overseeing the project.

Mica is the older brother of Daniel A. Mica, a Democrat who represented Florida in Congress from 1979 to 1989. Another Mica brother was an aide to Democratic Gov. Lawton Chiles. John Mica became a Republican in high school, however, when he was a member of Youth for Nixon.

Mica served in the state legislature from 1977 to 1981 and was chief of staff and administrative assistant for Florida GOP Sen. Paula Hawkins from 1981 to 1985. He then turned to private business ventures, including international trade consulting and the cellular telephone business, and subsequently became a millionaire.

Redistricting and a retirement gave Mica an opening to run for Congress in 1992. GOP Rep. Craig T. James decided not to seek a third House term, and the new Florida map for the 1990s gave the 7th District a clear Republican tilt. Mica won by 13 percentage points, and he has been re-elected with ease since.

In redistricting after the 2000 census, much of Mica's district went to the new 24th, just to the south, while the 7th shifted to the north into St. Johns and Flagler counties. While Mica worked to introduce himself to new voters, Democrat Wayne Hogan, an attorney, spent millions of dollars of his own money, in an effort to shape the new constituents' views. Hogan seemed to be making headway, but the final tally gave Mica a 19-point victory.

KEY VOTES

2002

No Overhaul campaign finance law; ban "soft money" and restrict advocacy advertising
Yes Back Bush's defense budget increase
Yes Extend 1996 welfare law
Yes Adopt Bush's discretionary spending limit
Yes Pass GOP Medicare prescription drug plan
No Create independent Sept. 11 commission
No Extend union protections to Homeland Security Department employees
Yes Revive fast-track procedures for trade agreements
Yes Authorize war against Iraq
No Advance bankruptcy overhaul opposed by abortion opponents

2001

Yes Nullify Clinton Labor Department ergonomics rule
Yes Cut taxes by $1.35 trillion through fiscal 2011
No Maintain ban on oil drilling in Arctic National Wildlife Refuge
Yes Approve Bush proposal to limit managed-care plan liability for coverage decisions
No Divert money from crop subsidy payments to land conservation
Yes Expand law enforcement power to investigate suspected terrorists

CQ VOTE STUDIES

	PARTY UNITY		PRESIDENTIAL SUPPORT	
	Support	Oppose	Support	Oppose
2002	96%	4%	90%	10%
2001	98%	2%	95%	5%
2000	96%	4%	19%	81%
1999	91%	9%	18%	82%
1998	92%	8%	23%	77%

INTEREST GROUPS

	AFL-CIO	ADA	CCUS	ACU
2002	0%	0%	95%	96%
2001	17%	0%	96%	92%
2000	10%	5%	80%	88%
1999	22%	10%	88%	80%
1998	10%	10%	89%	92%

FLORIDA 7

East – St. John's County, Daytona Beach

The 7th follows Interstate 95 from southeast of Jacksonville to northern Daytona Beach, where it turns to follow Interstate 4 west into the Orlando area. It includes all of fast-growing Flagler and St. Johns counties, as well as most of Volusia County, parts of Putnam and Seminole counties and a tiny sliver of Orange County. Two-fifths of the district's population lives in Volusia, mostly on the strip of coast stretching from Ormond Beach to Daytona Beach.

Once a major agricultural area, Seminole County now serves as the suburban home to middle- and upper-class Orlando commuters and their families. But inland portions of the district maintain some agrarian heritage, especially in Flagler County. Daytona Beach continues to attract college students, bikers and race car fans with its beaches and sporting events, including the Daytona 500 stock car race, which is in the nearby 24th District.

The steady influx of people has meant a sustained economic boom, but also has pushed growth-management issues to the top of the local agenda. Retirees have flocked to once-small towns closer to the ocean, drawing retail shops but not as many larger employers. The base is broadened by a growing aerospace industry near Daytona Beach, helped by Embry-Riddle Aeronautical University.

Republicans hold a slim party registration edge and won the 1992, 1996 and 2000 presidential elections in the 7th, which was significantly altered in redistricting following the 2000 census to allow for the creation of the new 24th. Republicans George W. Bush and Bill McCollum won 53 percent and 51 percent, respectively, here in their 2000 races. But some moderate Democrats also have had success among the 7th's voters.

MAJOR INDUSTRY

Tourism, aerospace, service

CITIES

Daytona Beach, 53,629; Deltona, 47,033; Ormond Beach, 36,301; Palm Coast, 32,732; Wekiwa Springs, 23,169; Palm Valley, 19,860

NOTABLE

St. Augustine is the oldest continuously inhabited city in the United States; Jackie Robinson Stadium — named for Major League Baseball's first African-American player — is in Daytona Beach, where Robinson was the first black player in a spring training game.

Rep. Ric Keller (R)

CAPITOL OFFICE
225-2176
www.house.gov/keller
419 Cannon 20515-0908; fax 225-0999

COMMITTEES
Education & Workforce
Judiciary

HOMETOWN
Orlando

BORN
Sept. 5, 1964, Johnson City, Tenn.

RELIGION
Methodist

FAMILY
Wife, Cathy Keller; two children

EDUCATION
East Tennessee State U., B.S. 1986 (speech communications); Vanderbilt U., J.D. 1992

CAREER
Lawyer

POLITICAL HIGHLIGHTS
No previous office

ELECTION RESULTS

2002 GENERAL		
Ric Keller (R)	123,497	65.1%
Eddie Diaz (D)	66,099	34.9%
2002 PRIMARY		
Ric Keller (R)		unopposed
2000 GENERAL		
Ric Keller (R)	125,253	50.8%
Linda Chapin (D)	121,295	49.2%

Elected 2000; 2nd term

Keller arrived in Congress in 2001 ready to pursue the seemingly disparate goals of reducing the role of government while at the same time supporting increases for government programs aimed at helping disadvantaged children.

His agenda generally calls for less regulation so that businesses can create jobs and generate prosperity as well as large tax cuts. But he sees a role for the federal government in making sure the less fortunate have the opportunity to succeed.

Described by the Orlando Sentinel as a "bootstrap conservative," Keller's political philosophy can be traced to his childhood. He was raised by a single mother earning a modest secretary's salary in a one-bedroom house that they shared with his two siblings and his grandmother. "I have a bias in favor of poor kids," Keller says. "The best way to help other poor folks is to help businesses and individuals create jobs," he told the Sentinel.

Though Keller had never held elective office before coming to the House, he was quick out of the starting blocks when he got to Congress. He was the first member of the Class of 2000 to introduce a bill and a resolution. Both measures sought to increase funding for Pell Grants, which provide federal aid to college students.

Keller says Pell Grants made his own college education possible. He told the Orlando Sentinel that "an education is a child's passport out of poverty." He believes the federal government has a key role to play, including providing the funds for Pell Grants and also helping with money to build more classrooms.

In his first term, Keller formed a Pell Grant Caucus, and as its chairman worked to increase the maximum grant from $3,750 to $4,000. Keller says he will push for another, more substantial increase in the 108th Congress.

Keller also is a firm believer in mentoring programs. He works with a number of Orlando area organizations that help troubled young people, serving on the board of directors of the Orlando/Orange County COMPACT Program, which mentors students at risk of dropping out of high school. He has been a mentor to several high school students as well.

In Congress, he proposed legislation to give tax credits to businesses that let employees spend company time mentoring at-risk kids. From his seat on the Education and Workforce Committee, he worked with Nebraska GOP Rep. Tom Osborne on legislation to authorize federal education funds for grants to local mentoring programs. The measure became law as part of the large 2001 education authorization bill.

Keller also has a seat on the Judiciary Committee, where he pushed a bill to prohibit federal prison officials from using tax dollars to provide cable television for inmates. He said the money would be better directed to schools that are unable to afford computers, permanent classrooms and basic equipment. But the measure did not make it through the House.

Keller did win House approval of an amendment to require the attorneys for plaintiffs in class action suits to disclose their fees when a case is settled or the plaintiffs win in court. He cited one class action suit in which the lawyers received $2 million while each of the plaintiffs got a coupon for a box of cereal.

Keller describes himself as the ideological heir to the man he replaced, 10-term conservative Republican Bill McCollum. But the folksy, informal Keller is quite different from the more buttoned-down McCollum.

Keller can laugh at himself. He said he hated it when a New York newspaper columnist described him in 2000 as a "ferocious cherub." He went on a crash diet when he arrived in Washington, losing more than 30 pounds and joking that he would only eat dessert when the Orlando Sentinel wrote nice things about him. Keller wrote jokes for Florida Gov. Jeb Bush during his unsuccessful 1994 gubernatorial campaign.

As a private lawyer in Orlando, Keller helped write two state constitutional amendments concerning cleanup of the Florida Everglades. One, dubbed "Polluter Pays" and passed by a wide margin in 1996, held that sugar companies should contribute to Everglades restoration. In Congress, Keller was among the minority of Florida lawmakers who voted to reduce the sugar subsidy. He has said he favors outright elimination of federal subsidies to U.S. sugar companies.

Keller had just made partner at his Orlando law firm when he jumped into the 8th District House race to replace McCollum, who waged an unsuccessful bid for Senate. The precipitating factor, Keller says, was his outrage over a House vote on the sugar program, in which several lawmakers changed their positions on the heavily lobbied issue at the last minute. It was Keller's first foray into politics, and his candidacy was lightly regarded. In the three-way GOP primary Keller's vigorous style and conservative politics earned him attention. He finished second and then came from behind to win an October runoff against veteran state Rep. Bill Sublette.

Democrats made a strong bid to capture the normally Republican 8th District seat by running a well-known local figure, former Orange County Commission Chairwoman Linda Chapin. But Chapin saw her once-comfortable lead in the polls shrink in the face of Keller's campaign sprint, which was bolstered by support from Republican strategists striving to keep the seat in GOP hands. Keller was backed by the Club for Growth, a group of fiscally conservative Republicans, who poured more than $400,000 into the campaign.

Keller won by fewer than 4,000 votes. He immediately set to work to shore himself up for re-election, raising a considerable amount of money in his first few months in the House.

Most observers believed his 2002 re-election bid would present another tough challenge. But Keller amassed a large campaign war chest and redistricting gave him a favorable new constituency. Keller's Democratic foe, Eddie Diaz, was unable to gain any traction. Keller breezed to victory, with 65 percent of the vote.

He has pledged to serve no more than eight years in the House.

KEY VOTES

2002

- No Overhaul campaign finance law; ban "soft money" and restrict advocacy advertising
- Yes Back Bush's defense budget increase
- Yes Extend 1996 welfare law
- Yes Adopt Bush's discretionary spending limit
- Yes Pass GOP Medicare prescription drug plan
- No Create independent Sept. 11 commission
- No Extend union protections to Homeland Security Department employees
- Yes Revive fast-track procedures for trade agreements
- Yes Authorize war against Iraq
- Yes Advance bankruptcy overhaul opposed by abortion opponents

2001

- Yes Nullify Clinton Labor Department ergonomics rule
- Yes Cut taxes by $1.35 trillion through fiscal 2011
- No Maintain ban on oil drilling in Arctic National Wildlife Refuge
- Yes Approve Bush proposal to limit managed-care plan liability for coverage decisions
- No Divert money from crop subsidy payments to land conservation
- Yes Expand law enforcement power to investigate suspected terrorists

CQ VOTE STUDIES

	PARTY UNITY		PRESIDENTIAL SUPPORT	
	Support	Oppose	Support	Oppose
2002	99%	1%	87%	13%
2001	97%	3%	95%	5%

INTEREST GROUPS

	AFL-CIO	ADA	CCUS	ACU
2002	11%	0%	100%	100%
2001	9%	0%	100%	96%

FLORIDA 8
Central – most of Orlando

The 8th surrounds western Orlando and includes upscale parts of the region, a large chunk of the city, including much of the downtown area, and the Walt Disney World complex. It then pushes north to take in parts of Lake and Marion counties, giving it a rural element.

One of Florida's few landlocked districts, the 8th is thriving nonetheless, powered by the presence of Walt Disney World and the tourism industry in the Orlando area, the world's top vacation destination. Redistricting in 2002 removed territory in eastern Orange County and near Kissimmee.

Residents of Orlando's suburbs — from middle-class areas near the city to well-heeled Winter Park and Windermere — support conservative Republicans on social and economic issues. The population is younger, wealthier and more educated than most Florida districts. While conservative Democrats were once competitive here, Republicans now mostly prevail in Orange County elections. But the county's surging Hispanic population, which spurred its 28 percent growth in the 1990s, has put Orange within political reach of Democratic statewide candidates. Unlike Miami-area Hispanics who are of Cuban descent and vote Republican, many Orlando-area Hispanics are of Puerto Rican stock and vote Democratic. Al Gore in 2000 was the first Democratic presidential nominee to carry Orange County since Franklin D. Roosevelt in 1944.

Although tourism leads the economy, the district also relies on a growing technology sector headed by defense and aerospace contractor Lockheed Martin and Oracle Corp. Technology and research have replaced the dwindling military presence — Orlando's Naval Training Center was shut down in 1999, costing about 4,000 full-time jobs. The research park of the University of Central Florida's Institute for Simulation and Training is an economic engine.

MAJOR INDUSTRY
Tourism, aerospace, TV production

CITIES
Orlando (pt.), 123,842; Ocoee (pt.), 23,591; Ocala (pt.), 16,384; Eustis, 15,106

NOTABLE
Dozens of well-known professional athletes — including golf's Tiger Woods and baseball's Ken Griffey Jr. — live in the 8th; Costumed Disney World employees are members of the Teamsters Union.

Rep. Michael Bilirakis (R)

CAPITOL OFFICE
225-5755
www.house.gov/bilirakis
2269 Rayburn 20515-0909; fax 225-4085

COMMITTEES
Energy & Commerce
(Health - chairman)
Veterans' Affairs

HOMETOWN
Palm Harbor

BORN
July 16, 1930, Tarpon Springs, Fla.

RELIGION
Greek Orthodox

FAMILY
Wife, Evelyn Bilirakis; two children

EDUCATION
U. of Pittsburgh, B.S. 1959 (engineering); George Washington U., attended 1959-60; U. of Florida, J.D. 1963

MILITARY SERVICE
Air Force, 1951-55

CAREER
Lawyer; county judge; restaurateur; engineer

POLITICAL HIGHLIGHTS
No previous office

ELECTION RESULTS

2002 GENERAL		
Michael Bilirakis (R)	169,369	71.5%
Chuck Kalogianis (D)	67,623	28.5%
2002 PRIMARY		
Michael Bilirakis (R)	unopposed	
2000 GENERAL		
Michael Bilirakis (R)	210,318	81.9%
Jon Scott Duffey (REF)	46,474	18.1%

PREVIOUS WINNING PERCENTAGES
1998 (100%); 1996 (69%); 1994 (100%); 1992 (59%); 1990 (58%); 1988 (100%); 1986 (71%); 1984 (79%); 1982 (51%)

Elected 1982; 11th term

Bilirakis' willingness to follow has made the Republican leadership more amenable to giving him a chance to lead. He is now in his fifth consecutive term as chairman of the Energy and Commerce subcommittee that has jurisdiction over health legislation.

In that role, Bilirakis (bih-la-RACK-us) has been involved in much of the important medical legislation debated on Capitol Hill over the last decade and, in an era of GOP-imposed term limits on committee and subcommittee chairmanships, he occupies an unusual position. While House Republican rules require chairmen to relinquish their gavels after three terms, Bilirakis was able to take advantage of a restructuring of the Energy and Commerce Committee at the beginning of the 107th Congress that altered the jurisdiction of his Health and Environment subcommittee.

By removing environmental matters from the panel's jurisdiction, Energy and Commerce Chairman Billy Tauzin of Louisiana was able to create a new subcommittee for Bilirakis, thus resetting the term-limit clock. The new Health Subcommittee addresses Medicaid and the regulation of health insurance, food and drugs.

Since health care has been such a hot political topic on Capitol Hill in recent years, many decisions on legislation and legislative strategy have been made by the party leadership. And Republican leaders have often formed separate task forces — on patients' rights and prescription drugs, for example — rather than rely on the traditional committee structure to develop legislation. But, while major health legislation stalled in the 107th Congress, Bilirakis was able to win approval of a bill to establish a federal scholarship program to help alleviate the national nursing shortage.

Bilirakis also took the lead in 2002 on a bill to assure doctors and hospitals that they cannot be threatened with losing federal funding if they refuse to perform abortions. The measure, which Bilirakis said merely clarified an existing "conscience clause," nevertheless sparked a partisan debate. It passed the House, but died in the Senate.

Friendly and diligent, Bilirakis prides himself on being a party loyalist, but he will also team up with Democrats. In the 107th, he and Democrat Sherrod Brown of Ohio led an effort to scale back a 5.4 percent reduction in Medicare and Medicaid payments to doctors, which, Bilirakis argued, threatened senior citizens' access to medical care if doctors limited their participation in the federal programs.

A pragmatist, Bilirakis has pushed for bipartisan agreement on contentious legislation since his days as top-ranking minority member of the Health and the Environment Subcommittee. He has continued that practice as subcommittee chairman, sometimes to the consternation of more-combative conservative members of his own party. Yet his moderate reputation has proved beneficial to the GOP on occasion. For example, with Bilirakis as chairman, Republican leaders in the 104th Congress had a useful symbol for their argument that the party's plan to rein in the cost of Medicaid and Medicare would save the programs, not hurt older people. Why else, they asked, would Bilirakis agree to lead the charge? From late 1997 to early 1999, Bilirakis was a member of the 17-member commission to study long-term changes to ensure the solvency of Medicare.

Periodically, he is criticized by GOP colleagues for being too willing to work with Democrats — particularly when GOP efforts to restrain government spending run counter to Bilirakis' sense of obligation to watch out for the interests of the many elderly residents of his district, who are wary of any tampering with their health care or retirement benefits.

Bilirakis is known for being accessible to his constituents, and he is particularly attentive to the needs of senior citizens, who make up almost a quarter of the 9th District's population — one of the highest percentages of any district.

On the Veterans' Affairs Committee, Bilirakis has worked to increase benefits for widows of veterans and pressed for hearings to probe allegations of sexual harassment, mismanagement and poor care at Department of Veterans Affairs medical facilities. He sought the chairmanship in 2001 but lost out to the more-senior Christopher H. Smith of New Jersey. Nevertheless, in the 107th he was the point man in the effort to allow veterans to receive both their full retirement as well as disability benefits.

A champion of Greek causes, Bilirakis often delivers floor speeches commemorating special events in Greece. He does not lose an opportunity to criticize the Turks, who continue to control northern Cyprus. He and his wife share the same ancestry, and her homemade Greek food is a big hit at community gatherings and at an annual party in Washington for family, friends, constituents and dignitaries, including the Greek ambassador.

The son of immigrants, Bilirakis moved from the Tampa Bay area to western Pennsylvania soon after he was born. He turned down college scholarships and instead went to work in the Pittsburgh steel mills to help the family finances. He spent four years in the Air Force, and later earned an engineering degree. After working for the Federal Power Commission in Washington, he returned to Florida for law school and stayed, working in the aerospace industry and then opening a law practice a few miles from his birthplace. He became involved in several small businesses, taught at area community colleges and served stints as an appointed local judge.

A Democrat until 1970, Bilirakis was intermittently involved in local GOP campaigns, but never considered running for office himself until 1982, when he entered the race for the newly drawn 9th. Asked what had triggered his interest, Bilirakis replied, "I found myself out of challenges." In a three-way primary, the favorite, state House GOP leader Curt Kiser, made the mistake of taking his nomination for granted, while Bilirakis blanketed the district with signs saying that his was "a hard name to spell but an easy one to remember." After an upset victory, Bilirakis narrowly edged Democratic state Rep. George Sheldon by espousing conservative positions but mostly by convincing voters that he was a nice guy. He has won re-election since then by comfortable margins and has been unopposed in three elections.

KEY VOTES

2002

- No Overhaul campaign finance law; ban "soft money" and restrict advocacy advertising
- Yes Back Bush's defense budget increase
- Yes Extend 1996 welfare law
- Yes Adopt Bush's discretionary spending limit
- Yes Pass GOP Medicare prescription drug plan
- No Create independent Sept. 11 commission
- No Extend union protections to Homeland Security Department employees
- Yes Revive fast-track procedures for trade agreements
- Yes Authorize war against Iraq
- No Advance bankruptcy overhaul opposed by abortion opponents

2001

- Yes Nullify Clinton Labor Department ergonomics rule
- Yes Cut taxes by $1.35 trillion through fiscal 2011
- No Maintain ban on oil drilling in Arctic National Wildlife Refuge
- Yes Approve Bush proposal to limit managed-care plan liability for coverage decisions
- Yes Divert money from crop subsidy payments to land conservation
- ? Expand law enforcement power to investigate suspected terrorists

CQ VOTE STUDIES

	PARTY UNITY		PRESIDENTIAL SUPPORT	
	Support	Oppose	Support	Oppose
2002	98%	2%	87%	13%
2001	91%	9%	86%	14%
2000	91%	9%	24%	76%
1999	90%	10%	17%	83%
1998	91%	9%	20%	80%

INTEREST GROUPS

	AFL-CIO	ADA	CCUS	ACU
2002	11%	0%	89%	100%
2001	25%	10%	91%	84%
2000	10%	5%	71%	80%
1999	38%	20%	88%	84%
1998	10%	5%	89%	92%

FLORIDA 9

West – suburbs north of Tampa

Suburban and rural areas north of Tampa and St. Petersburg form the bulk of the 9th, which encompasses coastal areas of Pinellas and Pasco counties as well as a large chunk of Hillsborough County.

The 9th is mostly residential, and more than one-fifth of the population is 65 or older. Clearwater, the largest city, is known as a beach resort and as the "spiritual headquarters" of the Church of Scientology, which has a large community in the city. Palm Harbor and Tarpon Springs have many Greek Orthodox residents, descendants of the area's earliest settlers.

The 9th's economy is driven by tourism, and many residents commute to Tampa and St. Petersburg. Service-oriented industries add to the mix, but the predominance of shopping centers and strip malls has created growth problems in the coastal areas. The 9th's economy has grown along with its population, though its northeast portions have lagged behind the Clearwater area. Hillsborough County is mostly suburban; Pasco County, which is bisected by Interstate 75, lacks major industry, though it has several sources of spring water.

The 9th long has been a home for mostly Republican retirees, and the GOP retains a slight edge in the district because of its dominance in Hillsborough. Many of the county's most heavily Republican precincts are in the 9th, in towns like Bloomingdale and Valrico east of I-75 and in the upscale Westchase area in western Hillsborough. The parts of Pinellas that are in the 9th also are decidedly Republican. Democrats hold their own in the 9th's share of Pasco County, where Democrats and Republicans are even in voter registration.

MAJOR INDUSTRY

Tourism, health care, technology

CITIES

Clearwater (pt.), 79,189; Palm Harbor (pt.), 30,806; East Lake, 29,394; Bayonet Point, 23,577; Plant City (pt.), 22,445; Holiday, 21,904

NOTABLE

Tarpon Springs' waters were a major source of sea sponges before they were killed off in the 1940s by toxic blooms of algae known as red tides; Jack Eckerd, founder of the Eckerd chain of drug stores that originated in Clearwater, was the Republican gubernatorial nominee in 1978, losing to Democrat Bob Graham.

Rep. C.W. Bill Young (R)

CAPITOL OFFICE
225-5961
bill.young@mail.house.gov
www.house.gov/young
2407 Rayburn 20515-0910; fax 225-9764

COMMITTEES
Appropriations - chairman
Select Homeland Security

HOMETOWN
Indian Rocks Beach

BORN
Dec. 16, 1930, Harmarville, Pa.

RELIGION
Methodist

FAMILY
Wife, Beverly Young; three children

EDUCATION
Pennsylvania public schools, attended

MILITARY SERVICE
Fla. National Guard, 1948-57

CAREER
Insurance executive; public official

POLITICAL HIGHLIGHTS
Fla. Senate, 1961-71 (minority leader, 1967-71)

ELECTION RESULTS

2002 GENERAL		
C.W. Bill Young (R)		unopposed
2002 PRIMARY		
C.W. Bill Young (R)		unopposed
2000 GENERAL		
C.W. Bill Young (R)	146,799	75.7%
Josette Green (NL)	26,908	13.9%
Randy Heine (NP)	20,296	10.5%

PREVIOUS WINNING PERCENTAGES
1998 (100%); 1996 (67%); 1994 (100%); 1992 (57%); 1990 (100%); 1988 (73%); 1986 (100%); 1984 (80%); 1982 (100%); 1980 (100%); 1978 (79%); 1976 (65%); 1974 (76%); 1972 (76%); 1970 (67%)

Elected 1970; 17th term

During his rocky tenure as chairman of the Appropriations Committee, Young has repeatedly found himself caught between his loyalties to the committee, on the one hand, and to the House leadership and President Bush, on the other. Young is a consummate team player, however, invariably deferring to the GOP leaders and the president — even as the standing of his committee eroded. That pattern is likely to continue in the 108th Congress, Young's final term at the Appropriations helm.

Throughout the 107th Congress, Young was a voice in the GOP ranks for additional spending at the very time that a new president of his own party was vowing to defeat Congress' annual drive in that direction. In 2001, in the aftermath of the Sept. 11 attacks, Young and the appropriators prevailed upon Bush to permit additional funding for domestic programs such as education. In 2002, however, Bush served notice of his spending ceiling early on and then refused to relent.

Young hoped to extract himself from the squeeze by falling into a familiar pattern. He pushed through smaller, less controversial spending bills with increases above Bush's request, while "starving" the more expensive — and politically problematic — bills in the expectation that all sides would ultimately conclude it was in their self-interest to add more money. When Republican conservatives caught on and refused to go along, all the domestic appropriations bills were put on hold until after the midterm election.

At that point, Young met with the president but was rebuffed when he asked Bush to support about $9 billion more in spending (about 1 percent of the year's grand total), which the chairman argued was a small but necessary price for winning enough votes to pass the bills.

As the 108th Congress began, Young signaled that he was prepared to adapt to the reality of a tough-on-spending Republican president. The first lesson came as Congress belatedly enacted a wrapup spending package that met Bush's bottom line — refuting Young's claim that it could not be done.

With Congress and the White House completely in GOP hands, Young can no longer count on Democratic leverage to force additional domestic discretionary spending. Republican domination of the appropriations process also will threaten the bipartisan, get-the-bills-done mindset that has characterized Young's leadership of the committee. His non-confrontational style personifies the go-along, get-along culture of Appropriations. But it is also a product of a legislative attitude forged during 24 years in what seemed like a permanent House GOP minority, when working with Democrats was a prerequisite for accomplishing anything.

Because they were considered too accommodating of more spending, Speaker Newt Gingrich skipped over Young and two other more-senior members in 1994 in picking the first Republican chairman of House Appropriations in 40 years. Instead, Young spent four years chairing the panel's Defense Subcommittee, a choice consolation prize that gave him great influence in a policy arena that long had been a prime focus of his attention. Young has been an unwavering advocate of steady growth in military spending.

When Young took over the full committee in 1999, he fell into a pattern of allowing conservatives to dominate the early stages of appropriations negotiations until legislative reality — the need to gain President Clinton's signature — tilted the playing field in the appropriators' favor. Time and again, Young's efforts to write bipartisan bills were overruled by GOP leaders, especially Majority Whip Tom DeLay, who insisted that the bills more closely reflect the priorities of GOP conservatives. Young protested, correctly as it turned out, that a partisan appropriations process would only ensure a year-end showdown that would maximize Clinton's leverage.

As is natural for a senior appropriator, Young has done much for his district, where construction has begun on a $45 million National Guard readiness center, the largest such project in more than a half-century. But the legislative initiative that seems closest to Young's heart is one that is not targeted at the western coast of Florida: research on bone marrow transplants and for a federally sponsored bone marrow donor registry funded through the defense budget. Young became interested in the issue in the 1980s after he met a 10-year-old constituent for whom bone marrow donors could not be found. After adopting the cause, Young learned in 1990 that his eldest daughter had a leukemia treatable only through such a transplant. She received bone marrow that restored her health.

In the 108th, Young reorganized the Appropriations subcommittee structure to create a new panel to fund only the new Homeland Security Department. His unilateral approach to the reorganization miffed his Senate Appropriations counterpart, Republican Ted Stevens of Alaska.

On some issues, Young shows a moderate streak. He has broken from the party line to support a minimum wage increase, for example, and a ban on semiautomatic assault-style weapons. And he approaches environmental issues from the perspective of a district that places a premium on the condition of its coastal waters. He has worked to prevent offshore oil and gas drilling, and he also has used his Appropriations position to fund efforts to replenish the sand on shrinking beaches in his district.

Young was born into hardscrabble poverty in Pennsylvania's coal country during the Depression. His father, an alcoholic, abandoned his family when Young was a boy, and after his mother became ill, the family stayed with relatives in St. Petersburg. Young worked his way to success in the insurance business before going into politics in 1960, when he was elected as the sole Republican in the Florida Senate. By 1967, there were 20 others, and Young was minority leader.

In 1970, he inherited Florida's most dependable Republican House seat from William C. Cramer, who ran for the Senate. The 10th District has tilted Democratic, but more often than not, Young has been re-elected with ease. Since 1982, Democrats have fielded a candidate only in alternate elections. Following that pattern, Young was unopposed in 2002.

KEY VOTES

2002

No Overhaul campaign finance law; ban "soft money" and restrict advocacy advertising
Yes Back Bush's defense budget increase
Yes Extend 1996 welfare law
Yes Adopt Bush's discretionary spending limit
Yes Pass GOP Medicare prescription drug plan
No Create independent Sept. 11 commission
No Extend union protections to Homeland Security Department employees
Yes Revive fast-track procedures for trade agreements
Yes Authorize war against Iraq
No Advance bankruptcy overhaul opposed by abortion opponents

2001

Yes Nullify Clinton Labor Department ergonomics rule
Yes Cut taxes by $1.35 trillion through fiscal 2011
No Maintain ban on oil drilling in Arctic National Wildlife Refuge
Yes Approve Bush proposal to limit managed-care plan liability for coverage decisions
No Divert money from crop subsidy payments to land conservation
Yes Expand law enforcement power to investigate suspected terrorists

CQ VOTE STUDIES

	PARTY UNITY		PRESIDENTIAL SUPPORT	
	Support	Oppose	Support	Oppose
2002	94%	6%	88%	12%
2001	96%	4%	91%	9%
2000	90%	10%	33%	67%
1999	89%	11%	31%	69%
1998	92%	8%	24%	76%

INTEREST GROUPS

	AFL-CIO	ADA	CCUS	ACU
2002	13%	0%	85%	96%
2001	17%	5%	91%	80%
2000	11%	5%	84%	72%
1999	38%	20%	86%	73%
1998	0%	0%	93%	90%

FLORIDA 10

West – most of Pinellas County, St. Petersburg

The 10th takes in about 70 percent of Pinellas County, including most of St. Petersburg and its upscale beachfront communities. From the southern portion of Pinellas, it excludes Clearwater in the central part of the county and captures Dunedin and Palm Harbor.

One of Florida's first Republican areas, the district had become increasingly Democratic over the years. But unlike many areas in Florida, the 10th did not see its population boom in the 1990s, a result of the already crowded conditions in most of the district. During redistricting in 2002, it was reshaped to help Republicans stave off a Democratic trend. A significant piece of St. Petersburg — including Pinellas County's southern tip — was ceded to the neighboring, Democratic-held 11th District, and a piece north of Clearwater was added in.

Now Democrats and Republicans appear fairly evenly matched here, though Rep. Young wins by large margins. Democratic nominee Al Gore won the 2000 presidential race among the voters of the reconfigured 10th by fewer than 5,000 votes. Bill Clinton won here in 1996 and voters favored George Bush in 1992.

Nearly one-fourth of the district's residents are 65 or older, and many retirees reside in Largo and the Gulf Coast towns. Younger residents tend to live in Pinellas Park and St. Petersburg, closer to major employers and Tampa. Tourism has been an economic mainstay for the district, accounting for about $2 billion a year from area hotels and attractions, and the district includes two airports — though the future of the field that serves smaller aircraft is uncertain. High-tech manufacturers and financial services companies have helped to diversify the district's economy.

MAJOR INDUSTRY
Tourism, health care, retail

CITIES
St. Petersburg (pt.), 179,087; Largo, 69,371; Pinellas Park, 45,658

NOTABLE
Greyhounds have raced at St. Petersburg's Derby Lane, one of several area dog tracks, since the 1920s; The Salvador Dalí Museum in St. Petersburg houses a comprehensive collection of works by the Spanish surrealist painter.

Rep. Jim Davis (D)

CAPITOL OFFICE
225-3376
www.house.gov/jimdavis
409 Cannon 20515-0911; fax 225-5652

COMMITTEES
Energy & Commerce

HOMETOWN
Tampa

BORN
Oct. 11, 1957, Tampa, Fla.

RELIGION
Episcopalian

FAMILY
Wife, Peggy Bessent Davis; two children

EDUCATION
Washington and Lee U., B.A. 1979; U. of Florida, J.D. 1982

CAREER
Lawyer

POLITICAL HIGHLIGHTS
Fla. House, 1988-97 (majority leader, 1994-97)

ELECTION RESULTS

2002 GENERAL		
Jim Davis (D)		unopposed
2002 PRIMARY		
Jim Davis (D)		unopposed
2000 GENERAL		
Jim Davis (D)	149,465	84.6%
Charlie Westlake (LIBERT)	27,197	15.4%

PREVIOUS WINNING PERCENTAGES
1998 (65%); 1996 (58%)

Elected 1996; 4th term

A moderate who sees himself as "a problem-solver and a peacemaker" in the legislative arena, Davis has been a quiet but respected voice on contentious matters since coming to Washington in 1997. Calm and deliberative in manner, he honed his conciliation skills during eight years in the Florida House, the final two as majority leader.

In the 108th Congress, Davis holds three important posts — a seat on the Energy and Commerce Committee, co-chairmanship of the New Democrat Coalition, and membership on the House Democrats' Steering Committee, which sets tone and strategy on legislative and political matters. His moderate New Democrat colleagues had lobbied hard to put Davis on the Energy and Commerce Committee in the 107th Congress, and he finally got the assignment in the 108th.

Davis' New Democrat label and experience lent weight to his consideration of a gubernatorial bid in 2002, but he opted not to wade into a competitive Democratic primary. Instead, he continued his concentration on fiscal and education issues in Washington, although his name continues to surface as a potential statewide candidate.

A longtime fiscal conservative, Davis annually ranks high on the Concord Coalition's "tough choices" scorecard. The coalition is a nonpartisan, grassroots organization that advocates fiscal responsibility.

Davis voted against enacting the politically popular 1998 surface transportation law — which authorized significant increases in funding for highway and transit programs — because it called for more spending than envisioned under a budget-balancing agreement of the previous year. And he voted against five appropriations bills at the end of 1999, arguing, "There's a lot of indefensible pork in here. It sets a bad precedent." For the same reason, he opposed a $13 billion supplemental spending bill in 2000.

But Davis is equally critical of tax cuts that he says lead to long-term deficits. In 2003, as President Bush proposed a new round of tax cuts centered around a plan to eliminate taxes on most stock dividends to help grow the economy, Davis shunned the idea. "I will support economic stimulus, but any plan that's enacted cannot compromise our ability to fund homeland security improvements or mortgage our children's futures by driving up the deficit." He also voted in 2001 against Bush's signature $1.35 trillion, 10-year tax cut package.

In his first term, Davis said his priority was "finding a way to balance the budget while protecting our seniors" — always a concern of Florida politicians because of the state's large contingent of elderly voters. He attempted to pursue both goals in 2002 by joining other New Democrats in backing a compromise Medicare prescription drug proposal that would have helped seniors with low incomes or unusually high annual drug costs.

On the House Administration Committee in the 107th, Davis had a hand in shaping the voting procedure law enacted in response to the problem-riddled 2000 presidential election in Florida.

To take the Energy and Commerce post, Davis had to relinquish his other assignments, which included International Relations, where he was a strong advocate for trade liberalization. Although he is generally a supporter of organized labor, Davis broke ranks with the unions to vote for the 2002 law reviving fast-track procedures for congressional action on trade treaties and for the 2000 law permanently granting normal trade status to China — the Port of Tampa's largest trading partner.

In 2002, as the International Relations panel debated the resolution supporting military strikes against Iraq, Davis failed to win approval of his amendment that would have tightened requirements on the president to exhaust all diplomatic efforts before going to war. Still, he voted for the final resolution on the House floor.

Education is a major concern for the congressman, and in the 106th Congress he proposed solving chronic teacher shortages by providing mid-career professionals with up to $5,000 in grants to pay for teacher training. The plan won backing in 2000 from the Clinton White House, which included $25 million in the budget for it.

An opponent of school vouchers, Davis argues that the government instead should boost spending on charter schools. Charter schools, he says, are public schools that are open to everyone, whereas vouchers help parents send their children to private schools.

Although he generally takes a liberal stance on social policy issues, Davis was one of just two Florida House Democrats voting in 1997 to ban a procedure its opponents call "partial birth" abortion. Also, he backed a constitutional amendment to ban desecration of the U.S. flag.

Like Florida's senior senator, Democrat Bob Graham, the detail-oriented Davis uses small, colored notebooks to scribble both personal and business reminders to himself.

Davis was born into a Tampa family active in local politics: His father was a judge, his grandfather a mayor. Davis followed in the family tradition in 1988 when, as a lawyer and civic activist, he won the first of four terms in the state House.

When veteran Democratic Rep. Sam M. Gibbons announced plans to retire from the House in 1996, Davis was the least known of four Democrats who campaigned to succeed him. But with prolific fundraising, he was able to buy television advertising for the primary — the only Democrat to do so — and he played up his endorsements from local teacher, police and firefighter unions.

After beating former Tampa Mayor Sandy Warshaw Freedman in a runoff, Davis turned his attention to Republican Mark Sharpe, who was making his third try for the 11th District after losing to Gibbons in 1992 and 1994. Buoyed by a treasury that topped $935,000 for the entire campaign and by an easy Bill Clinton victory in the district's presidential voting, Davis won by 16 percentage points.

He has continued to post comfortable victories, and in 2002 he was unopposed.

KEY VOTES

2002

Yes Overhaul campaign finance law; ban "soft money" and restrict advocacy advertising
Yes Back Bush's defense budget increase
No Extend 1996 welfare law
No Adopt Bush's discretionary spending limit
No Pass GOP Medicare prescription drug plan
Yes Create independent Sept. 11 commission
Yes Extend union protections to Homeland Security Department employees
Yes Revive fast-track procedures for trade agreements
Yes Authorize war against Iraq
Yes Advance bankruptcy overhaul opposed by abortion opponents

2001

No Nullify Clinton Labor Department ergonomics rule
No Cut taxes by $1.35 trillion through fiscal 2011
Yes Maintain ban on oil drilling in Arctic National Wildlife Refuge
No Approve Bush proposal to limit managed-care plan liability for coverage decisions
Yes Divert money from crop subsidy payments to land conservation
Yes Expand law enforcement power to investigate suspected terrorists

CQ VOTE STUDIES

	PARTY UNITY		PRESIDENTIAL SUPPORT	
	Support	Oppose	Support	Oppose
2002	85%	15%	48%	52%
2001	79%	21%	42%	58%
2000	85%	15%	82%	18%
1999	81%	19%	79%	21%
1998	81%	19%	74%	26%

INTEREST GROUPS

	AFL-CIO	ADA	CCUS	ACU
2002	89%	75%	65%	24%
2001	83%	80%	48%	12%
2000	70%	75%	57%	16%
1999	56%	80%	44%	12%
1998	80%	85%	67%	16%

FLORIDA 11

West — Tampa, south St. Petersburg

The 11th ranges from Tampa to south St. Petersburg and part of Bradenton. One of the younger and more racially diverse districts in the state, the 11th combines what is left of a traditional blue-collar manufacturing base with the newer high-tech and service industries that have transformed Tampa into a major Southern city. The Tampa-St. Petersburg area was a finalist to host the 2004 Republican convention, which was awarded to New York City.

The district was reconfigured in 2002 to take in some of the Democrats in the St. Petersburg area who presented a threat to the GOP's security in the neighboring Pinellas County-based 10th. Blacks and Hispanics together comprise about half of the 11th's population, with heavy concentrations of blacks in south St. Petersburg, east Tampa and parts of Bradenton, and Hispanics in west Tampa and the Egypt Lake-Leto and Town 'n' Country areas just northwest of the city. It is a heavily Democratic district that gave Al Gore 59 percent of the vote in 2000.

As its economy continues to evolve, the Tampa area has attracted professional sports arenas and a steady military presence at MacDill Air Force Base. Tampa's airport and seaport make it a major shipping and transportation hub, while its traditional cigar industry is attempting a comeback from harder years. The University of South Florida, one of the state's largest schools, is on the city's northern end.

The influence of Cuban and Spanish culture is most pronounced in Ybor City, a downtown Tampa neighborhood named after the man who brought the first cigar factory to Tampa. The neighborhood's success in reinventing itself as a nighttime hot spot has given the area new life.

MAJOR INDUSTRY
Retail, health care, finance

MILITARY BASES
MacDill Air Force Base, 3,975 military, 820 civilian (1999)

CITIES
Tampa (pt.), 284,199; Town 'n' Country, 72,523; St. Petersburg (pt.), 69,145

NOTABLE
Pirate Jose Gaspar, better known as Gasparilla, had a hideout in Tampa; Native tribes named the area Tampa, which means "sticks of fire"; The U.S. Central Command, responsible for U.S. military interests in the Middle East, is based at MacDill Air Force Base.

Rep. Adam H. Putnam (R)

CAPITOL OFFICE
225-1252
www.house.gov/putnam
506 Cannon 20515-0912; fax 226-0585

COMMITTEES
Agriculture
Budget
Government Reform
(Technology, Information Policy, Intergovernmental Relations & the Census - chairman)
Resources
Joint Economic

HOMETOWN
Bartow

BORN
July 31, 1974, Bartow, Fla.

RELIGION
Episcopalian

FAMILY
Wife, Melissa Putnam; two children

EDUCATION
U. of Florida, B.S. 1995 (economics)

CAREER
State legislator; citrus and cattle rancher

POLITICAL HIGHLIGHTS
Fla. House, 1997-2000

ELECTION RESULTS

2002 GENERAL		
Adam H. Putnam (R)		unopposed
2002 PRIMARY		
Adam H. Putnam (R)		unopposed
2000 GENERAL		
Adam H. Putnam (R)	125,224	57.0%
Michael Stedem (D)	94,395	43.0%

Elected 2000; 2nd term

Youthful ambition is nothing new to Putnam: When he was 11 years old he told his grandfather that he would run for governor some day. He was only 26 when he was elected to Congress, yet his résumé already included four years of legislative experience. Elected to the Florida Legislature in 1996, a year out of college, Putnam chaired the state House Agriculture Committee before coming to Washington.

The novelty of being one of the youngest congressmen ever has worn off for Putnam — aides stopped using the phrase "the youngest member of Congress" in his news releases before his first term ended — but the label is not likely to go away immediately: In the 108th Congress, he remains the youngest member.

Another continuing theme is his role of defending Florida citrus, a task that Putnam embraces but does not want to define his political career. Hailing from a prominent Central Florida citrus and cattle ranching family, he continues to advocate for the state's orange growers.

During his first term, Putnam's support for citrus thrust him into the spotlight on both of the House votes on legislation limiting Congress to casting only an up-or-down vote on trade agreements. President Bush, during one closed-door meeting of House Republicans as part of his campaign for that "fast-track" legislation, urged those who did not favor the measure to reconsider. "I'm talking about you, Red," the president told the red-haired congressman. Putnam then withstood a furious last-minute pitch by House GOP leaders. "I feel like I'm going to throw up," he said after voting "no."

The bill narrowly passed anyway, but House leaders brought a slightly different version back the next year, hoping to gain broader support. After negotiations stalled with Putnam and another Florida Republican, Mark Foley, House GOP leaders signaled they were prepared to find the votes to pass the measure without support from the citrus industry. That motivated Putnam, who met with administration officials and secured a few changes to enhance the industry's standing in the final text, which he voted for. "By the time the second vote came around, I had learned there's a fine line between raising an issue and being marginalized," Putnam said. "We came pretty close to being marginalized."

To track any trade deals that could affect the citrus industry, Putnam established a panel of state growers and producers, and he has hosted meetings with officials including U.S. Trade Representative Robert B. Zoellick. Putnam also was one of 15 House members invited by the Pentagon in June 2002 to witness a war game that simulated the effects of an "agri-terrorism" attack on the nation's beef supply.

Putnam has at times expressed frustration about serving on the Agriculture panel, which is dominated by lawmakers from the midwestern states that grow the bulk of the subsidized crops: corn, soybeans and wheat. But as Florida's lone representative on the panel, he is unlikely to give up his seat.

In his first term on the Budget Committee, Putnam pressed hard for language to bolster the long-term solvency of Social Security — an issue of paramount importance to Generation X members, but also of profound political complexity to the GOP. At one point in the writing of the annual budget resolution, Chairman Jim Nussle, a fellow Republican of Iowa, tartly urged Putnam to back down. "I think you may want to reconsider this one, sport," the chairman said.

In the 108th Congress, Putnam became chairman of the Government

Reform panel's subcommittee on Technology, Information Policy Intergovernmental Relations and the Census — the youngest chairman in at least a half-century. He has highlighted the need to secure the nation's deep-water seaports, of which Florida has several. He and allies were able to place some language in a House-passed measure creating a Department of Homeland Security to address seaport security. As vice chairman of the panel's National Security Subcommittee, Putnam was able to weigh in on the impact of the Sept. 11, 2001, terrorist attacks and the war against terrorism. (On the morning of the attacks, Putnam was one of several congressmen accompanying President Bush on a Florida visit. He rode on Air Force One briefly during the day before returning to Florida and posted a description of the experience on his House Web site.)

While Putnam says he likes Government Reform's focus on long-range issues and problems, he also tries to find solutions to immediate federal problems. When Bush announced that practice bombing runs would cease on the island of Vieques, off Puerto Rico, Putnam had several lawmakers and military officials tour Avon Park Air Force Range in the 12th District to assess its suitability for training runs using non-live ordnance.

While in Tallahassee, Putnam was a frequent participant in legislative debates. That has not been true in Washington, however. Unaccustomed to the structure of House debates, Putnam also shuns the one-minute speeches that other junior lawmakers often give on the floor.

A fifth-generation Floridian, Putnam is not typical of many of his generation. Once described by a Republican colleague as "26 going on 50," Putnam does not shy away from serious situations. At the height of a 2001 crisis over China's detention of a Navy plane, Putnam dispatched a letter to the Chinese ambassador sternly warning the government to return the plane and its crew, one of whom was a Putnam constituent.

When he ran for Congress, Putnam declined MTV's request to follow him on the campaign trail, saying he didn't want any "purple-hair yahoo" asking whether he wore "boxers or briefs."

During college, Putnam served as a student ambassador for his school and interned in the Washington office of Republican Rep. Charles T. Canady. He remains an avid University of Florida sports fan.

Canady made way for Putnam in 2000 when he observed a pledge to limit his service to four terms. Putnam easily defeated Democratic auto dealer Michael Stedem, who tried to make Putnam's youth an issue. Barring a statewide run, Putnam is likely to be able to hold the seat for the foreseeable future; in 2002, he was unopposed for re-election.

KEY VOTES

2002

- No Overhaul campaign finance law; ban "soft money" and restrict advocacy advertising
- Yes Back Bush's defense budget increase
- Yes Extend 1996 welfare law
- Yes Adopt Bush's discretionary spending limit
- Yes Pass GOP Medicare prescription drug plan
- No Create independent Sept. 11 commission
- No Extend union protections to Homeland Security Department employees
- Yes Revive fast-track procedures for trade agreements
- Yes Authorize war against Iraq
- No Advance bankruptcy overhaul opposed by abortion opponents

2001

- Yes Nullify Clinton Labor Department ergonomics rule
- Yes Cut taxes by $1.35 trillion through fiscal 2011
- No Maintain ban on oil drilling in Arctic National Wildlife Refuge
- Yes Approve Bush proposal to limit managed-care plan liability for coverage decisions
- No Divert money from crop subsidy payments to land conservation
- Yes Expand law enforcement power to investigate suspected terrorists

CQ VOTE STUDIES

	PARTY UNITY		PRESIDENTIAL SUPPORT	
	Support	Oppose	Support	Oppose
2002	98%	2%	88%	12%
2001	98%	2%	90%	10%

INTEREST GROUPS

	AFL-CIO	ADA	CCUS	ACU
2002	0%	0%	95%	96%
2001	18%	5%	96%	88%

FLORIDA 12

West central – Polk and Hillsborough counties

Florida's 12th has plenty of land but much of it is covered by citrus groves and more than 500 natural lakes, not beaches and developments. Centered east of Tampa and southwest of Orlando, it includes almost all of Polk County, suburban and exurban portions of southern and eastern Hillsborough County, and a small slice of western Osceola County.

A Democratic registration advantage belies the social and economic conservatism of most residents. The GOP has the edge in the third of the district located in Hillsborough County, and the 12th backed Republican presidential candidates in 1992, 1996 and 2000. Traditional Southern Democrats probably could make state and local elections more competitive, but Republicans have had much better success recruiting top-quality candidates for important offices recently.

The 12th's economy is driven by Polk County's agricultural prowess. Polk is the state's top producer of citrus and is Florida's leader in overall farmland. Tomatoes and strawberries are cultivated in the Hillsborough County portion of the district.

The 12th's economy grew steadily during the 1990s, despite some weather-related dips among citrus crops. Florida's phosphate mining industry has its home around Bartow and Mulberry, while Publix Supermarkets is headquartered in Lakeland. These industries provide consistent economic support, while citrus crops are more prone to ups and downs.

Retirees are attracted to the district's significant retirement communities — including Sun City Center — while baseball fans enjoy spring training games at many stadiums in the area.

MAJOR INDUSTRY
Agriculture, mining, utilities

CITIES
Brandon (pt.), 72,878; Lakeland (pt.), 71,079; Winter Haven, 26,487

NOTABLE
Spook Hill, in Lake Wales, is a local oddity where cars parked in neutral at the base of the hill will roll up, defying gravity; Cypress Gardens, Florida's first theme park, is in Winter Haven.

Rep. Katherine Harris (R)

CAPITOL OFFICE
225-5015
katherine.harris@mail.house.gov
www.house.gov/harris
116 Cannon 20515-0913; fax 226-0828

COMMITTEES
Financial Services
International Relations

HOMETOWN
Sarasota

BORN
April 5, 1957, Key West, Fla.

RELIGION
Presbyterian

FAMILY
Husband, Anders Ebbeson; one child

EDUCATION
Agnes Scott College, B.A. 1979 (history); Harvard U., M.P.A. 1996

CAREER
Computer company marketing executive; real estate firm executive

POLITICAL HIGHLIGHTS
Fla. Senate, 1994-98; Fla. secretary of state, 1999-2002

ELECTION RESULTS

2002 GENERAL		
Katherine Harris (R)	139,048	54.8%
Jan Schneider (D)	114,739	45.2%
2002 PRIMARY		
Katherine Harris (R)	47,761	68.3%
John C. Hill (R)	22,144	31.7%

Elected 2002; 1st term

No other freshman of the 108th Congress has anything remotely akin to Harris' standing as a nationally polarizing political figure.

As Florida's secretary of state, Harris oversaw the counting of the state's thousands of disputed ballots in 2000, and her strict interpretation of election law helped seal the presidential victory for George W. Bush. To Republicans, her steadfastness made her an unalloyed hero. To Democrats, she merited all the vituperative and personal ridicule she endured.

Upon her arrival on Capitol Hill, Harris expressed a desire to avoid the limelight, telling the Sarasota Herald-Tribune, "I like the anonymity" of being just one of 435 members. Even political foes, such as Democratic Rep. Robert Wexler, who served with her in the state Senate, described Harris as "a very persuasive and gracious person" and held out hope that she could "use her notoriety to benefit Florida." At the same time, however, Harris was still pointing back to her time on the world stage by promoting her autobiography, "Center of the Storm," which combined her memories of the 2000 election with a welter of advice about morality and management.

Harris always was a heavy favorite to win the seat that Republican Dan Miller, abiding by a term-limits pledge, gave up after five terms. She breezed past her GOP primary opposition, raised a total of $3 million and campaigned with the confidence of an incumbent. But the election indicated that Harris remained as unpopular as ever among Democrats, at least in Florida. Challenged by little-known Jan Schneider — a law school classmate of Bill Clinton and Hillary Rodham at Yale — Harris won with a modest 55 percent. Nevertheless, early in her term she was thinking about a 2004 Senate bid.

The GOP leadership made her an assistant whip and gave her seats on the Financial Services and International Relations panels, good fits with her background. The granddaughter of Florida land tycoon Ben Hill Griffin, she spent four years as secretary of state — where expanding trade was a big part of her job — after four years in the state Senate. There, she chaired the Commerce Committee, putting her in the legislature's pro-business leadership.

FLORIDA 13

Southwest – Sarasota, most of Bradenton

Midwestern retirees flock to the Gulf Coast cities of Sarasota and Bradenton, making the 13th a reliably Republican district. Sarasota and Manatee counties have nearly 90 percent of the district's population; the more affluent tend to live near Sarasota while middle-class residents are more prevalent around Bradenton.

Most residents live near the coast, while farmland and citrus groves are inland. Sarasota County cultivates a refined image with its art museums, theater and symphony performances. It generally draws a more highly educated and wealthier class of retirees than most other west coast communities in Florida.

The 13th shares Bradenton, the county seat and retail center of Manatee County, with the 11th District. Bradenton has a more noticeable mix of incomes and ethnic groups. The 13th has the nation's highest median age, and its proportion of people 65 years and older (29 percent) makes it a popular home for older part-time residents.

Service industries, including investment companies, and trade make up much of the labor force. The district's proximity to Gulf beaches, barrier islands and a large state park makes the environment a bipartisan concern, with residents attuned to the problems of beach erosion and the effects of rapid population growth.

Republicans outnumber Democrats by nearly 50 percent in registration, and voters overwhelmingly favor GOP candidates in statewide races. Republican nominees won the district in the 1992, 1996 and 2000 presidential elections.

MAJOR INDUSTRY
Health care, financial services

CITIES
Sarasota, 52,715; Bradenton (pt.), 39,385; North Port, 22,797

NOTABLE
Former circus owner John Ringling brought his circus to the Sarasota area each winter.

Rep. Porter J. Goss (R)

CAPITOL OFFICE
225-2536
porter.goss@mail.house.gov
www.house.gov/goss
108 Cannon 20515-0914; fax 225-6820

COMMITTEES
Rules
Select Homeland Security
Select Intelligence - chairman

HOMETOWN
Sanibel

BORN
Nov. 26, 1938, Waterbury, Conn.

RELIGION
Presbyterian

FAMILY
Wife, Mariel Goss; four children

EDUCATION
Yale U., B.A. 1960 (classics & Greek)

MILITARY SERVICE
Army, 1960-62

CAREER
Newspaper founder; CIA agent

POLITICAL HIGHLIGHTS
Sanibel City Council, 1974-82 (mayor, 1975-77, 1982); Lee County Commission, 1983-88 (chairman, 1985-86)

ELECTION RESULTS

2002 GENERAL		
Porter J. Goss (R)		unopposed
2002 PRIMARY		
Porter J. Goss (R)		unopposed
2000 GENERAL		
Porter J. Goss (R)	242,614	85.2%
Sam Farling (NL)	41,988	14.8%

PREVIOUS WINNING PERCENTAGES
1998 (100%); 1996 (73%); 1994 (100%); 1992 (82%); 1990 (100%); 1988 (71%)

Elected 1988; 8th term

Pleas by President Bush and Vice President Dick Cheney, combined with a waiver of House rules to allow him to retain his Intelligence Committee chairmanship, helped persuade Goss to postpone his announced retirement and remain at the Capitol in the 108th Congress.

His decision to stay through the end of an eighth term in 2004 was greeted with enthusiasm and relief by many of his constituents and colleagues, a testament to the respect Goss engenders. A decade as a CIA clandestine services officer before entering politics gave Goss experience that has proved invaluable as Congress seeks to address its recent vulnerabilities to terrorism, though that same background has led to occasional criticism that Goss is too close to the agencies his panel oversees.

Goss normally shuns the spotlight and was not well-known outside of Congress before the al Qaeda attacks of Sept. 11, 2001. But he was a vital resource to his colleagues well before then. Indeed, when congressional leaders were evacuated to a secure facility in the hours following the attacks, Goss was taken with them. In the 108th, he also serves on the new Homeland Security panel that oversees the newly established Cabinet department.

Speaker J. Dennis Hastert arranged for a waiver of House rules to permit Goss to remain on Intelligence beyond the usual term limit and to retain his chairmanship as well. Under normal circumstances, no lawmaker can serve on Intelligence in more than four of any six Congresses. Goss has been a member since 1995 and chairman since 1997. And he has been a hands-on leader, organizing and leading briefings for non-committee members who want to keep abreast of international developments. He said that has helped instill confidence in his judgment.

"I do a lot of advocacy work for the intelligence community," he said. "Primarily it's because we're dealing almost totally with classified information. When I go to my colleagues on the House floor and say, 'Look, I can't tell you how much it is,' or 'These terms, I can't tell you what they are, but trust me, it's okay,' that's asking a lot."

Approachable, straight-talking and pragmatic, Goss has worked on a bipartisan basis on a range of issues. His mediation was viewed as essential to the 2002 law creating an independent commission to investigate government lapses in advance of the Sept. 11 attacks. Before he took the reins of the Intelligence Committee, Goss served in 1996 as chairman of an ethics subcommittee that studied charges of alleged improprieties in the political fundraising activities of Speaker Newt Gingrich.

On the Rules Committee, which sets the terms for floor debate, Goss is well-positioned to effect legislative and institutional change. It was Goss who persuaded Hastert to take a working group on terrorism and make it an Intelligence subcommittee, even though that rankled some other committee and subcommittee chairmen with jurisdiction over the issue.

A comfortable victor in eight House elections, Goss seems well-suited for his Gulf Coast district in southwest Florida. He won his first bid for Congress with 71 percent of the vote in 1988. As a term-limits supporter, he considered leaving after winning re-election in 1998 but concluded he still could play a useful role on national security issues — the same tug that pulled him into a re-election campaign in 2002.

Goss often was mentioned as a potential director of the Central Intelligence Agency after George W. Bush won the presidency. Although he said he was interested in the job, Goss denied actively seeking it. He encouraged Bush to take his time in finding a director and backed President Clinton's director, George J. Tenet, who kept the position. "If George is looking over his shoulder, he knows he's not looking at me," Goss said.

Goss is solidly conservative on social and economic issues but follows an independent course. He notes that he did not come to politics through the traditional party ranks. After leaving the CIA and moving to Florida in 1971, he helped found a weekly newspaper, amassed a fortune — in 2001 he listed assets of at least $15 million — and became immersed in civic issues. "I was a citizen-activist upset about zoning," he recalled. "I was so appalled by the arrogance and contrariness of the local government."

After Democratic Gov. Bob Graham named him to the Lee County Commission, Goss — tagged as the commission's environmentalist — got involved in debates about managing growth countywide. He easily won a full term, which set him up to compete for the House seat that Republican Rep. Connie Mack vacated to run for the Senate in 1988.

Goss has continued to stray from GOP orthodoxy on the environment, an important issue for his tourist-dependent Gulf Coast constituency. He strongly opposes oil and gas development on the continental shelf off Florida, and he voted for a Democratic amendment that prohibited spending for oil and gas development off Florida's Panhandle. He also introduced a bill to halt drilling while a federal-state task force develops a permanent policy.

Goss' background as a community activist also led him to become a strong advocate of congressional reforms. He has supported term limits and joined the fight to enact changes in lobbying and gift-giving rules. And, because of his number of retiree constituents, Goss has been active on Social Security and health issues. He served on the 1994 congressional entitlements commission as well as on several GOP health task forces. And he sponsored the 1998 law creating a $750 million fund to compensate hemophiliacs who contract the AIDS virus via contaminated blood products.

One of his most satisfying accomplishments as a lawmaker, he says, was helping secure more than $1 billion for intelligence activities in 1998 — money to help address some of the weaknesses identified by an independent panel that investigated the CIA's inability to warn of India's nuclear tests that year. But Goss says that more needs to be spent on intelligence agencies, and that they need better oversight. He wants the government to recruit more spies. He also advocates a greater focus on data analysis, increased investment in cutting-edge technologies and stepping up covert activity.

KEY VOTES

2002

No Overhaul campaign finance law; ban "soft money" and restrict advocacy advertising
Yes Back Bush's defense budget increase
Yes Extend 1996 welfare law
Yes Adopt Bush's discretionary spending limit
Yes Pass GOP Medicare prescription drug plan
No Create independent Sept. 11 commission
No Extend union protections to Homeland Security Department employees
Yes Revive fast-track procedures for trade agreements
Yes Authorize war against Iraq
Yes Advance bankruptcy overhaul opposed by abortion opponents

2001

Yes Nullify Clinton Labor Department ergonomics rule
Yes Cut taxes by $1.35 trillion through fiscal 2011
No Maintain ban on oil drilling in Arctic National Wildlife Refuge
Yes Approve Bush proposal to limit managed-care plan liability for coverage decisions
Yes Divert money from crop subsidy payments to land conservation
Yes Expand law enforcement power to investigate suspected terrorists

CQ VOTE STUDIES

	PARTY UNITY		PRESIDENTIAL SUPPORT	
	Support	Oppose	Support	Oppose
2002	95%	5%	92%	8%
2001	97%	3%	95%	5%
2000	95%	5%	26%	74%
1999	91%	9%	28%	72%
1998	93%	7%	32%	68%

INTEREST GROUPS

	AFL-CIO	ADA	CCUS	ACU
2002	11%	0%	100%	84%
2001	8%	0%	100%	80%
2000	0%	0%	80%	96%
1999	0%	10%	92%	80%
1998	13%	5%	86%	91%

FLORIDA 14
Southwest — Cape Coral, Fort Myers, Naples

A haven for retirees and tourists, the solidly Republican 14th features Gulf Coast beaches and a rapidly expanding population centered in Lee County. It also takes in the coastal edge of Collier County and a small slice of Charlotte County. Most residents live near the coast, between the shore and Interstate 75, which runs through the entire district before turning eastward into the Everglades.

The population of Collier County grew by more than 65 percent during the 1990s, while neighboring Lee expanded by almost a third. The increase in Lee County was pushed by Cape Coral, where the population has swelled in recent years. Originally a retirement community, Cape Coral has been attracting young professionals, service industries and land developers. Wealthier retirees live around Naples, where golf courses and high-rise condominiums are plentiful and new construction helps put the area among the top 10 in the state in taxable property value.

Florida Gulf Coast University, which opened in Lee County in 1997, and the nearby Everglades help promote a bustling eco-tourism industry and marine biology. The barrier islands act as a magnet for tourists — Sanibel Island is renowned for the seashells that wash up on its beaches from the Gulf of Mexico.

Small Democratic pockets exist within the district's cities, like Fort Myers and Cape Coral, but the 14th has the largest Republican registration edge in the state and regularly gives GOP candidates high vote percentages. In 2002, GOP Gov. Jeb Bush took 67 percent of the Lee County vote, winning 168 of 175 precincts.

MAJOR INDUSTRY

Tourism, health care, agriculture

CITIES

Cape Coral, 102,286; Fort Myers, 48,208; North Fort Myers, 40,214; Lehigh Acres, 33,430; Bonita Springs, 32,797; Naples, 20,976

NOTABLE

Collier County was created as a favor to land baron and streetcar advertising mogul Baron G. Collier, who helped build the Tamiami Trail, which stretches from Tampa to Miami; Lee County includes the spring training homes of two major league baseball teams — the Boston Red Sox and the Minnesota Twins; The J.N. "Ding" Darling Wildlife Refuge is on Sanibel Island.

Rep. Dave Weldon (R)

CAPITOL OFFICE
225-3671
www.house.gov/weldon
2347 Rayburn 20515-0915; fax 225-3516

COMMITTEES
Appropriations

HOMETOWN
Palm Bay

BORN
Aug. 31, 1953, Amityville, N.Y.

RELIGION
Christian

FAMILY
Wife, Nancy Weldon; two children

EDUCATION
State U. of New York, Stony Brook, B.S. 1978 (biochemistry); State U. of New York, Buffalo, M.D. 1981

MILITARY SERVICE
Army Medical Corps, 1981-87; Army Reserve, 1987-92

CAREER
Physician

POLITICAL HIGHLIGHTS
No previous office

ELECTION RESULTS

2002 GENERAL		
Dave Weldon (R)	146,414	63.2%
Jim Tso (D)	85,433	36.9%
2002 PRIMARY		
Dave Weldon (R)	46,086	83.5%
Gerry Newby (R)	9,126	16.5%
2000 GENERAL		
Dave Weldon (R)	176,189	58.8%
Patsy Kurth (D)	117,511	39.2%
Gerry Newby (I)	5,744	1.9%

PREVIOUS WINNING PERCENTAGES
1998 (63%); 1996 (51%); 1994 (54%)

Elected 1994; 5th term

A strong-willed, blunt-talking conservative, Weldon arrived in Washington as part of the revolutionary GOP Class of 1994, and he takes a back seat to no one in his defense of conservative social values. He began his involvement in politics in the late 1980s as the co-founder of a conservative group, the Space Coast Family Forum, that endorsed candidates based on their stances on abortion, sex education and other social issues.

He has continued along that path in Washington, as a member of a group known as the Values Action Team, which urges GOP leaders to advance conservative, pro-family policies. He was among the lawmakers, for example, who pledged to post a copy of the Ten Commandments in their offices to show support for such displays in schools and other public places.

But the issue that has brought Weldon the most attention in recent years is his effort with Michigan Democrat Bart Stupak to ban the cloning of human embryos for any purpose, including medical research. The House passed the bill in 2002, but it stalled in the Democratic-controlled Senate.

In early 2003, as a corporation established by a religious sect claimed that it had cloned the first human infant, the two lawmakers reintroduced their legislation. "Any attempt at human cloning, for whatever purpose, is a gross form of human experimentation that the American people oppose," Weldon said.

Weldon has another legislative passion: space. Until redistricting in 2002, his "Space Coast" district included the Kennedy Space Center, and the area economy depends greatly on NASA and private companies attracted there by space-related work. In the 108th Congress, House GOP leaders awarded Weldon a coveted seat on the Appropriations Committee; he vowed to use his influence to help fund NASA projects, including the shuttle program and the International Space Station. He called the two programs "essential to our nation's continued international leadership in space."

A physician who specializes in internal medicine, Weldon cites the scientific potential offered by a permanent outpost in space. It would give researchers "a fundamentally new tool to explore fields such as medicine, materials sciences, biology and astronomy," Weldon said in a letter to his House colleagues. Immediately after the space shuttle Columbia disaster in February 2003, he insisted that NASA press ahead once officials determined the cause of the accident. "We should never retreat from our progress in space exploration."

Weldon has made homeland security another of his priorities. He introduced a bill in the 107th Congress to establish a temporary moratorium on issuing immigrant visas to anyone from a country named as a sponsor of terrorism. His measure specifically cited Iran, Iraq and North Korea as well as U.S. allies such as Saudi Arabia and Egypt.

Locally, Weldon has tried to look out for the military veterans who populate his district. He supported building a new veterans hospital but lowered his sights when prospects for that appeared uncertain. Instead, he won approval for a $25 million outpatient clinic and for a pilot project that permits the Department of Veterans Affairs to contract with local hospitals for inpatient care for veterans.

In the social policy arena, Weldon prescribes remedies that sit well with the culturally conservative voters whose influence is growing along central Florida's East Coast. He has been a passionate proponent of congressional efforts to ban a procedure its opponents call "partial birth" abortion. He says he became a staunch abortion foe after he and his wife, unable to have children of their own, decided to adopt.

Religion plays an important part in Weldon's life. He says he tries to read the Bible and pray every day, and he lists among his political influences his "idol . . . Jesus Christ."

In the 106th Congress, Weldon authored a bill, which passed the House, to force those formally accused of rape to submit to a test for the HIV virus — even before going to trial. He argued that time is of the essence in beginning treatment to lower the risk of contracting AIDS.

Weldon casts every bit as conservative a vote as those within the brash element of the GOP Class of 1994, but in the 104th Congress he was more reserved in his public pronouncements than some of his classmates who said Speaker Newt Gingrich and other party leaders were too willing to compromise.

Like many Floridians, Weldon is a transplant from the North. He grew up on Long Island, the son of a postal clerk. He worked his way through his undergraduate days as an X-ray technician, and the Army paid his way through medical school. After a three-year stint as an Army doctor, he moved to Florida in 1987 and joined an internal medicine group.

Other than his involvement in the Space Coast Family Forum, Weldon's only taste of political life until his run for Congress came when he was president of his local homeowners association. But when two-term Democratic Rep. Jim Bacchus unexpectedly decided to retire in 1994, Weldon entered the race, overcoming criticism that he was too conservative for the district. Weldon's Family Forum ties gave him a ready-made base of support among conservatives, and he won the GOP nomination, capturing 54 percent of the vote in a runoff.

That year found the district's voters in a conservative mood, and Weldon emphasized his support for mainstream GOP fare: tax cuts, welfare reform and other aspects of the House Republicans' "Contract With America." Aided by an extensive get-out-the-vote effort conducted by groups such as the Christian Coalition, Weldon defeated Democrat Sue Munsey, a former head of the Cocoa Beach Area Chamber of Commerce, with 54 percent.

In 2000, Weldon dealt House Democratic leader Richard A. Gephardt a double defeat: Not only did Weldon win re-election to a seat Democrats had a slim hope of grabbing; his unexpectedly large 20 percentage point victory came over Gephardt's cousin, state Sen. Patsy Kurth. And in 2002, Weldon coasted to an even larger victory over Democratic challenger Jim Tso, a management and investment adviser.

KEY VOTES

2002

- No Overhaul campaign finance law; ban "soft money" and restrict advocacy advertising
- Yes Back Bush's defense budget increase
- Yes Extend 1996 welfare law
- Yes Adopt Bush's discretionary spending limit
- Yes Pass GOP Medicare prescription drug plan
- No Create independent Sept. 11 commission
- No Extend union protections to Homeland Security Department employees
- Yes Revive fast-track procedures for trade agreements
- Yes Authorize war against Iraq
- No Advance bankruptcy overhaul opposed by abortion opponents

2001

- Yes Nullify Clinton Labor Department ergonomics rule
- Yes Cut taxes by $1.35 trillion through fiscal 2011
- No Maintain ban on oil drilling in Arctic National Wildlife Refuge
- Yes Approve Bush proposal to limit managed-care plan liability for coverage decisions
- No Divert money from crop subsidy payments to land conservation
- Yes Expand law enforcement power to investigate suspected terrorists

CQ VOTE STUDIES

	PARTY UNITY		PRESIDENTIAL SUPPORT	
	Support	Oppose	Support	Oppose
2002	98%	2%	85%	15%
2001	95%	5%	77%	23%
2000	96%	4%	19%	81%
1999	95%	5%	16%	84%
1998	94%	6%	16%	84%

INTEREST GROUPS

	AFL-CIO	ADA	CCUS	ACU
2002	11%	0%	90%	100%
2001	8%	5%	87%	92%
2000	10%	5%	76%	92%
1999	22%	10%	88%	92%
1998	0%	0%	89%	92%

FLORIDA 15

Central coast — Indian River County; parts of Brevard, Osceola and Polk counties

Most people in the GOP-tilting 15th live along the Atlantic Coast in Brevard and Indian River counties, primarily between the conservative strongholds of Merritt Island and Vero Beach. In addition to all of Indian River County and three-quarters of Brevard County, the 15th contains most of Osceola County and a sliver of Polk County. It is home to the Cape Canaveral Air Force Station, though redistricting in 2002 placed Kennedy Space Center, often associated with Cape Canaveral, in the new, neighboring 24th District. The Air Force Station, Patrick Air Force Base — just a few miles south — and the Kennedy Space Center are the region's economic engine, pushing a thriving technology industry and helping to insulate it from downturns.

Melbourne and Palm Bay in the northeastern portion of the district combine to form a major population center. Most cities in the 15th have seen steady growth, and a Disney complex near Vero Beach is helping to change that sleepy town into a high-profile resort.

Fast-growing Kissimmee, a heavily Hispanic city in the district's portion of Osceola County, depends on the industry built up around Walt Disney World and other nearby tourist destinations. Democrats hold a slight registration edge in Osceola, and conservative Democrats can compete throughout the district. But the GOP holds a significant registration edge in the 15th, and voters here favored the Republican presidential candidate in 1992, 1996 and 2000 — including giving George W. Bush a 7 percentage point cushion over Democrat Al Gore.

MAJOR INDUSTRY

Technology, defense, tourism

MILITARY BASES

Patrick Air Force Base, 2,312 military, 942 civilian (1999)

CITIES

Palm Bay, 79,413; Melbourne, 71,382; Kissimmee, 47,814; Merritt Island (pt.), 27,291; Yeehaw Junction, 21,778; Vero Beach South, 20,362

NOTABLE

Kissimmee used to be known as the "cow capital of Florida"; Vero Beach is best-known as the spring training home of baseball's Los Angeles Dodgers.

Rep. Mark Foley (R)

CAPITOL OFFICE
225-5792
www.house.gov/foley
104 Cannon 20515-0916; fax 225-3132

COMMITTEES
Ways & Means

HOMETOWN
West Palm Beach

BORN
Sept. 8, 1954, Newton, Mass.

RELIGION
Roman Catholic

FAMILY
Single

EDUCATION
Palm Beach Community College, attended 1973-75

CAREER
Catering company founder; real estate broker; restaurant chain owner

POLITICAL HIGHLIGHTS
Lake Worth City Council, 1977-79; sought Democratic nomination for Fla. House, 1980; Lake Worth city commissioner, 1982-84; sought Democratic nomination for Palm Beach County Commission, 1984; Republican nominee for Fla. House, 1986; Fla. House, 1991-93; Fla. Senate, 1993-95

ELECTION RESULTS

2002 GENERAL		
Mark Foley (R)	176,171	78.9%
Jack McLain (CNSTP)	47,169	21.1%
2002 PRIMARY		
Mark Foley (R)		unopposed
2000 GENERAL		
Mark Foley (R)	176,153	60.2%
Jean Elliott Brown (D)	108,782	37.2%
John Michael McGuire (REF)	7,556	2.6%

PREVIOUS WINNING PERCENTAGES
1998 (100%); 1996 (64%); 1994 (58%)

Elected 1994; 5th term

Thanks to his approachable demeanor and his acquisition of several totems of power on Capitol Hill, Foley is one of the more visible figures in Congress. Whether the issue is taxes or trade, homeland security or corporate responsibility, internal congressional political machinations or the pleadings of the entertainment industry before Congress, Foley is there with a comment — and what he says is routinely quotable.

Foley also has a wealth of political experience and know-how. He served in two local and two state offices before coming to Congress, where he has a seat on the Ways and Means Committee.

As the 108th Congress began, Foley was giving serious consideration to mounting a campaign for the Senate in 2004.

His legislative background sets him a bit apart from the ideological conservatives elected with him in the GOP sweep of 1994. He comes across as more patient and less dogmatic, and he is willing to go against his party's line from time to time. Those qualities — combined with a mastery of tactical legislative thinking and proven fundraising skills — have earned him increasingly frequent mention as a statewide candidate.

On most issues Foley is a reliable conservative vote, although he has tendencies that mark him as a moderate among his Southern Republican peers, most notably on the environment and abortion. When he feels he must, Foley will lock horns with the GOP leadership. In the 107th Congress he initially opposed legislation to revive fast-track procedures for congressional action on trade deals, a top priority for President Bush; but ultimately he reversed course and voted for the final version once language was added to protect citrus and sugar growers, both important to his district. He also pushed House Republicans to strike a quick compromise with the Senate on legislation to crack down on corporate fraud. And he was one of 41 Republicans who bucked their leadership to join Democrats in voting for the sweeping campaign finance law enacted in 2002.

In the 107th, Foley won approval of a bill to increase research on drugs and medical devices that aid in treating relatively rare diseases.

His other priorities in the 107th included legislation that would give prescription drug coverage to Medicare beneficiaries and a bid to abolish the Immigration and Naturalization Service, which Foley called "the most bumbling, stumbling agency in all the land." In an effort to help the tourism industry recover after the Sept. 11, 2001, terrorist attacks, Foley also sponsored a bill to authorize the Department of Commerce to provide $100 million in grants to states for tourism-related advertising.

Walt Disney Co. and Universal Studios are powerful economic players in his state, and Miami is to Latin music what Nashville is to country music. Foley's work on Capitol Hill includes the chairmanship of the Entertainment Industry Task Force, which lets him look out for those interests, as well as hobnob with celebrities and seek their political contributions. As a leading GOP emissary to Hollywood, he has worked to assure the industry that the GOP shares many of their concerns. He has sought to protect intellectual property rights and to stop the exodus of movie production to cheaper locations abroad.

Foley's first brush with the entertainment business came in 1980 when the makers of the film "Body Heat" set up shop in Lake Worth, Fla., where he ran a restaurant called the Lettuce Patch. He got a walk-on part — most of his frames ended up on the cutting room floor, he laments — but he remembers what a boost the movie crew's business gave to the local economy. (He also snagged a bit part in a 2000 movie, "The Librarians.")

Foley, who is fiscally frugal, has played a leading role in fights to eliminate some big-ticket federal expenditures that he deemed wasteful, such as the Pentagon's B-2 bomber and a host of energy research and water projects. But he has also pushed for some tax breaks, such as a proposal for a five-year extension of the credit for electricity produced from wind. And he was a chief proponent of the provisions lowering the taxes on estates and gifts in the 2001 tax cut law.

For several years a major Foley priority has been legislation to require people to give businesses 90 days' notice before suing them over non-compliance with accessibility standards in the Americans with Disabilities Act. Foley said that in many cases, businesses would comply with the law if given a chance. "All we're saying is, let's not start active litigation until they've been notified of the problem," he said.

Foley also has been active in helping Holocaust survivors. In the 105th Congress, he worked on behalf of the more than 5,000 Floridians who were survivors, supporting their effort to recover as many of their lost assets as possible. In the 106th, he followed up with seminars to help the survivors with the nuts-and-bolts of filing insurance claims for benefits long denied them. In the 107th, he introduced legislation intended to secure survivors' assets from foreign insurance companies.

Born into an Irish Catholic family on the outskirts of Boston, Foley moved to Florida as a child and says he began his political career at age 5, distributing fliers for a local candidate. In 1975, he opened the Lettuce Patch with his mother and later became a real estate broker. He won a seat on the Lake Worth City Council two years later, at 22. After some failed bids to move up the political ladder, his career began lurching forward with his election to the state House in 1990. He moved to the state Senate two years later — where he chaired the Agriculture committee — and just two years after that he was elected to Congress to succeed Republican Tom Lewis, who retired. Foley's image as a moderate generated some opposition from conservatives in the GOP primary. But his fundraising apparatus was impressive, and he won easily.

His re-election contests have been uneventful and might be that way for the coming decade, because redistricting for the 2000s improved GOP prospects in the 16th District. But Foley takes fundraising seriously. He formed a political action committee and has made substantial contributions to other GOP candidates in the past three elections.

KEY VOTES

2002

- Yes Overhaul campaign finance law; ban "soft money" and restrict advocacy advertising
- Yes Back Bush's defense budget increase
- Yes Extend 1996 welfare law
- Yes Adopt Bush's discretionary spending limit
- Yes Pass GOP Medicare prescription drug plan
- No Create independent Sept. 11 commission
- No Extend union protections to Homeland Security Department employees
- Yes Revive fast-track procedures for trade agreements
- Yes Authorize war against Iraq
- Yes Advance bankruptcy overhaul opposed by abortion opponents

2001

- Yes Nullify Clinton Labor Department ergonomics rule
- Yes Cut taxes by $1.35 trillion through fiscal 2011
- Yes Maintain ban on oil drilling in Arctic National Wildlife Refuge
- Yes Approve Bush proposal to limit managed-care plan liability for coverage decisions
- No Divert money from crop subsidy payments to land conservation
- Yes Expand law enforcement power to investigate suspected terrorists

CQ VOTE STUDIES

	PARTY UNITY		PRESIDENTIAL SUPPORT	
	Support	Oppose	Support	Oppose
2002	90%	10%	90%	10%
2001	89%	11%	81%	19%
2000	81%	19%	39%	61%
1999	78%	22%	32%	68%
1998	84%	16%	38%	62%

INTEREST GROUPS

	AFL-CIO	ADA	CCUS	ACU
2002	11%	15%	95%	92%
2001	25%	30%	91%	64%
2000	0%	20%	80%	68%
1999	11%	35%	72%	64%
1998	20%	20%	100%	80%

FLORIDA 16

South central – Port St. Lucie, parts of Port Charlotte and Wellington

The 16th sprawls across south-central Florida, connecting wealthy east coast communities with Charlotte Harbor on the west coast. In between, rural Floridians raise cattle and grow sugar cane, particularly around Lake Okeechobee. The district surrounds the western side of the lake and includes most of St. Lucie County's white population near the Atlantic Ocean, from the southern part of the Fort Pierce area to Port St. Lucie. With the lake and beaches, environmental issues play a significant role in local politics.

St. Lucie County is the most populous jurisdiction in the 16th, accounting for about one-fourth of the district population. It has a slight Republican lean: in 2002, GOP Gov. Jeb Bush took 55 percent of the vote in the 16th's share of St. Lucie, which includes all of Port St. Lucie and most of Fort Pierce and Lakewood Park. Martin County, which is older and even more solidly Republican, includes wealthy Jupiter Island.

Robust population growth required the 16th to shed 120,000 people in 2002 redistricting to meet the population equality requirement. Mapmakers accomplished this by excising 240,000 Palm Beach County residents and adding others in Republican-leaning Charlotte County on the state's west coast. The 16th's remaining share of Palm Beach County includes parts of Jupiter and Palm Beach Gardens, as well as most of Wellington, a growing, wealthy subdivision southwest of West Palm Beach.

The 16th had a slight Democratic tilt in the 1990s, but changes in redistricting gave it a slight Republican edge. George W. Bush and Republican former Rep. Bill McCollum each won 52 percent of the vote here in the 2000 presidential and senatorial races, respectively.

MAJOR INDUSTRY

Agriculture, government, health care

CITIES

Port St. Lucie, 88,769; Port Charlotte (pt.), 39,610; Wellington (pt.), 35,797; Palm City, 20,097

NOTABLE

LaBelle, on the shores of the Caloosahatchee River, hosts the annual Swamp Cabbage Festival, held at the end of February.

Rep. Kendrick B. Meek (D)

Elected 2002; 1st term

Meek drew neither surprise nor opposition in 2002, when he followed in the footsteps of his trailblazing mother, Democratic Rep. Carrie P. Meek, who retired after five terms in the House.

Kendrick Meek said watching his mother's service on the Appropriations Committee strengthened his understanding of the relationship between money and policy. "I believe the way we appropriate sets the priorities for America . . . and this world," Meek said. "That's where all our principles and all our values start, where we put our money."

After graduating from Florida A&M University in 1989, Meek served five years as a state trooper — guarding Democratic Lt. Gov. Buddy McKay for a time — before entering politics. He was elected twice to the Florida House and once to the state Senate by Miami-area voters, and his tenure earned him a reputation as a lawmaker whose interest in policy extended outside the state capital of Tallahassee.

The father of two says his motivation in politics is that of a parent interested in how policy affects his children. As a state senator, Meek formed the Coalition to Reduce Class Size when the legislature did not act.

Meek lists health care — including fighting HIV/AIDS — and immigration as issues of great importance to his constituents.

His committee assignments on Armed Services and Homeland Security broaden the focus of his attentions.

Meek was long regarded as the heir apparent to his mother's House seat. When she announced just days before the candidate filing deadline that she would not seek re-election, Kendrick Meek was the only candidate who entered the contest to succeed her. He is the first son to directly succeed his mother since West Virginia Democrat James Kee entered the House in 1965.

Meek spent most of the 2002 campaign season working on his education coalition's successful drive to pass a state ballot initiative to reduce school class size — overcoming opposition by Republican Gov. Jeb Bush. The two political foes had crossed paths earlier, when Meek staged a sit-in at the governor's office to oppose Bush's affirmative action policies.

CAPITOL OFFICE
225-4506
www.house.gov/kenmeek
1039 Longworth 20515-0917; fax 226-0777

COMMITTEES
Armed Services
Select Homeland Security

HOMETOWN
Miami

BORN
Sept. 6, 1966, Miami, Fla.

RELIGION
Baptist

FAMILY
Wife, Leslie Dixon Meek; two children

EDUCATION
Florida A&M U., B.S. 1989 (criminal justice)

CAREER
Security firm business development aide; state trooper

POLITICAL HIGHLIGHTS
Fla. House, 1994-98; Fla. Senate, 1998-2002

ELECTION RESULTS

2002 GENERAL	
Kendrick B. Meek (D)	unopposed
2002 PRIMARY	
Kendrick B. Meek (D)	unopposed

FLORIDA 17

Southeast – parts of Miami and Hollywood

The black-majority 17th, once a long strip running from the Broward County border through Miami to points south, became more compact during redistricting following the 2000 census. The new district takes in some well-to-do areas and some of the region's most destitute, but is confined to northeast Miami-Dade County and southeast Broward County.

Overtown, once the hub of African-American wealth in the region, spent decades in decline. But that area, along with others in the district, is part of Miami-Dade's federal empowerment zone, and revitalization efforts are under way. Officials are encouraging public-private partnerships as a means to rebuild communities.

Infrastructure is a big part of the picture in the 17th: Miami International Airport is located just outside the district, and another airport in Opa-Locka serves as a base for civilian pilots. Interstate 95 and Route 1 wind through the district. Health concerns are a major topic for residents, many of whom are uninsured. In addition, the HIV/AIDS epidemic has hit the 17th hard, particularly in the black community.

Democrats are a lock at all levels in the 17th, where Republican candidates in statewide races often get less than 25 percent of the vote. Al Gore won 84 percent here in the 2000 presidential race — his best showing in the state.

MAJOR INDUSTRY
Transportation, service, entertainment

CITIES
Miami (pt.), 81,688; Hollywood (pt.), 57,267; North Miami (pt.), 50,514; Miramar (pt.), 41,272; Carol City (pt.), 35,858

NOTABLE
Overtown's Lyric Theater, which for decades hosted eminent black entertainers, has been restored.

Rep. Ileana Ros-Lehtinen (R)

CAPITOL OFFICE
225-3931
www.house.gov/ros-lehtinen
2160 Rayburn 20515-0918; fax 225-5620

COMMITTEES
Government Reform
International Relations
(Middle East & Central Asia - chairwoman)

HOMETOWN
Miami

BORN
July 15, 1952, Havana, Cuba

RELIGION
Roman Catholic

FAMILY
Husband, Dexter Lehtinen; two children, two stepchildren

EDUCATION
Miami-Dade Community College, A.A. 1972; Florida International U., B.A. 1975 (English & education), M.S. 1976-86 (education); U. of Miami, attending

CAREER
Teacher; private school administrator

POLITICAL HIGHLIGHTS
Fla. House, 1983-87; Fla. Senate, 1987-89

ELECTION RESULTS

2002 GENERAL		
Ileana Ros-Lehtinen (R)	103,512	69.1%
Ray Chote (D)	42,852	28.6%
Orin Opperman (I)	3,423	2.3%
2002 PRIMARY		
Ileana Ros-Lehtinen (R)	38,885	88.0%
May Chote (R)	5,327	12.1%
2000 GENERAL		
Ileana Ros-Lehtinen (R)		unopposed

PREVIOUS WINNING PERCENTAGES
1998 (100%); 1996 (100%); 1994 (100%); 1992 (67%); 1990 (60%); 1989 Special Election (53%)

Elected August 1989; 7th full term

The first Cuban-American and the first Hispanic woman elected to Congress, Ros-Lehtinen has long preached the wisdom of keeping Cuba isolated as long as President Fidel Castro wields power. But divisions within the Republican Party on the issue in recent years have forced a change in Ros-Lehtinen's arguments, if not her combative style. They also have broadened her interests beyond the Florida Straits.

Upon assuming the chairmanship of the International Relations Subcommittee on International Operations and Human Rights in the 107th Congress, Ros-Lehtinen (pronounced il-ee-AH-na ross-LAY-tin-nen) continued to press Cuba on its treatment of political dissidents and those practicing religion. But she also used her subcommittee to highlight the plight of dissidents in countries as far-flung as Pakistan, Northern Ireland and the Congo, drawing praise from some human rights lobbyists. In the 108th, she chairs the panel's Middle East and Central Asia Subcommittee.

Cuban issues, however, remain a major focus of her work, especially since Congress has moved toward softening restrictions on U.S. dealings with the island nation. She has seen some successes: At the end of 2001, the Russian government closed an intelligence facility in Cuba that she had long targeted. She had introduced several bills that would have blocked a rescheduling or forgiveness of Russian debts until the facility was closed.

But after a broad majority of the House voted in 2002 to lift the 42-year-old ban on travel by U.S. citizens to Cuba, Ros-Lehtinen and her allies declared that they had "lost the moral high ground" in their campaign to keep in place the economic embargo against the island nation. So Ros-Lehtinen switched arguments, claiming that doing business with Castro's Cuba is bad for U.S. firms, which have few legal protections when doing so.

Even so, she and her allies face an uphill battle: Grain and fruit producers are among the most eager to sell their products to Cuba, and they wield significant clout in Congress. And some of her Republican colleagues no longer see the embargo in the old Cold War terms of containing a Communist foe.

Ros-Lehtinen's prominent role in the Elián González episode in 1999-2000 also upset some in the GOP. Elián's U.S. relatives sought Ros-Lehtinen's help in keeping the boy in this country after the 5-year-old was rescued from the ocean as he and his mother tried to reach U.S. shores. (Elián's mother drowned in the attempt.) Ros-Lehtinen not only spoke out on behalf of Elián's U.S. relatives, she also visited the boy several times, even attending his birthday party and bringing him a monster truck for Christmas.

Her efforts received the ultimate accolade for a Cuban-American legislator: a direct personal attack from Cuba's state-run newspaper, Granma, which called her a "ferocious wolf disguised as a woman." She was so proud that she had "loba feroz" (shortened to "loba frz") stamped on a vanity license plate. Some social conservatives, however, looked askance at her role, agreeing that Elián should be returned to his father in Cuba.

At home, Ros-Lehtinen has played a role on another important South Florida issue. After the Army Corps of Engineers developed a plan to restore the natural water flow of the Everglades, Ros-Lehtinen was instrumental in blocking an attempt to condemn land on the Everglades' eastern edge that contained about 300 homes.

Ros-Lehtinen has clashed with some in her party who have tried to push restrictive immigration policies. She opposed measures to overhaul the welfare system, curb illegal immigration and designate English as the official U.S. language.

Ros-Lehtinen and fellow Floridian Lincoln Diaz-Balart were the only Republicans voting against the final version of a welfare overhaul bill in 1996, warning of an "anti-immigrant sentiment." The pair were so unhappy with the welfare and immigration bills passed in the 104th that in March 1996 they rejoined the Congressional Hispanic Caucus, led by House Democrats, as a show of unity against anti-immigrant feelings. The two Republicans had left the caucus at the start of the 104th to comply with the spirit of a GOP move to do away with such organizations. They again left the group in early 1997 after caucus Chairman Xavier Becerra, a California Democrat, took a trip to Cuba in December 1996.

Ros-Lehtinen often has been cold to lowering trade barriers, voting in 1995 against granting President Clinton the power to negotiate expedited trade agreements and in 2000 against permanently granting China normal trade status. But she reversed course in the 107th Congress, supporting fast-track trade negotiating authority for President Bush.

Educated in Miami, Ros-Lehtinen became a teacher and ran a bilingual private school in South Florida. In 1982, at age 30, she was the first Hispanic elected to the state legislature. Although not a major power broker in Tallahassee, she was an articulate campaigner and leading member of South Florida's Cuban-American community.

In a 1989 special-election race to replace the late Democratic Rep. Claude Pepper, Ros-Lehtinen easily defeated three other candidates for the Republican nomination. With generous support from the national Republican Party, she beat Democrat Gerald Richman, a Jewish Miami Beach lawyer with limited political experience. Stressing her support for Israel, she traveled there during the campaign, but the race was close and Ros-Lehtinen's victory margin was less than expected.

Richman's showing led some to believe Ros-Lehtinen's re-election was uncertain. But she prepared well, and several formidable Democrats skipped the 1990 race; she won with 60 percent that year and by a 2-to-1 ratio in a new, overwhelmingly Hispanic district in 1992. That was her closest election; four times she has run unopposed.

Reapportionment in 2002 gave her a more demographically diverse district that includes the Florida Keys, a prime tourist attraction. Ros-Lehtinen had sought the territory in part because it is also a common destination for Cuban refugees seeking asylum in the United States.

KEY VOTES

2002

- Yes Overhaul campaign finance law; ban "soft money" and restrict advocacy advertising
- Yes Back Bush's defense budget increase
- Yes Extend 1996 welfare law
- Yes Adopt Bush's discretionary spending limit
- Yes Pass GOP Medicare prescription drug plan
- No Create independent Sept. 11 commission
- No Extend union protections to Homeland Security Department employees
- Yes Revive fast-track procedures for trade agreements
- Yes Authorize war against Iraq
- No Advance bankruptcy overhaul opposed by abortion opponents

2001

- Yes Nullify Clinton Labor Department ergonomics rule
- Yes Cut taxes by $1.35 trillion through fiscal 2011
- No Maintain ban on oil drilling in Arctic National Wildlife Refuge
- Yes Approve Bush proposal to limit managed-care plan liability for coverage decisions
- No Divert money from crop subsidy payments to land conservation
- Yes Expand law enforcement power to investigate suspected terrorists

CQ VOTE STUDIES

	PARTY UNITY		PRESIDENTIAL SUPPORT	
	Support	Oppose	Support	Oppose
2002	93%	7%	85%	15%
2001	94%	6%	87%	13%
2000	86%	14%	30%	70%
1999	83%	17%	27%	73%
1998	81%	19%	29%	71%

INTEREST GROUPS

	AFL-CIO	ADA	CCUS	ACU
2002	11%	10%	75%	88%
2001	17%	10%	86%	71%
2000	30%	15%	71%	64%
1999	33%	25%	71%	73%
1998	67%	15%	67%	80%

FLORIDA 18
Southeast – most of Miami; Florida Keys

The 18th features the glitz of downtown Miami and the southern part of Miami Beach, but its political base comes from the Latin-dominated areas west of downtown — though it gave up some Hispanic suburbs when a third GOP-leaning, Hispanic-majority South Florida district was drawn during redistricting in 2002. From Miami, the 18th winds its way south along the coast and then follows U.S. 1 through the Florida Keys. More than three-fifths of the district's residents are of Hispanic origin and many are stridently anti-Castro.

The district has a wide mix of areas, from the downtrodden sections of Little Havana to wealthy Coral Gables (home to the University of Miami), Key Biscayne and Fisher Island. Residents tend to be conservative on foreign policy issues but more in line with Democrats on welfare and other social issues. A strong economy that does not rely solely on tourism has translated into little opposition for incumbents, including Rep. Ros-Lehtinen, who has had no active opposition in recent elections.

The Keys, particularly Key West, have a significant gay and lesbian population in addition to older natives who adhere to the independence and environmentalism of the "Conch Republic." The Port of Miami and Miami International Airport, which is in the 21st District, are major transportation centers that feed thriving trade and tourism industries.

In 2000, the district was the center of national attention when federal agents seized Cuban refugee Elián Gonzalez, then 6 years old, from the Little Havana home of his relatives.

MAJOR INDUSTRY
Trade, transportation, tourism

CITIES
Miami (pt.), 270,214; Miami Beach (pt.), 75,172; Coral Gables, 42,249; Westchester, 30,271; Key West, 25,478; Coral Terrace, 24,380

NOTABLE
Little Havana dominoes players gather at "Domino Park" — actually named Maximo Gomez Park, after a Cuban revolutionary; A giant sculpted hand stretches out toward the sky at the Holocaust Memorial in Miami Beach; Richard M. Nixon vacationed regularly on Key Biscayne.

Rep. Robert Wexler (D)

CAPITOL OFFICE
225-3001
www.house.gov/wexler
213 Cannon 20515-0919; fax 225-5974

COMMITTEES
International Relations
Judiciary

HOMETOWN
Boca Raton

BORN
Jan. 2, 1961, Queens, N.Y.

RELIGION
Jewish

FAMILY
Wife, Laurie Wexler; three children

EDUCATION
Emory U., attended 1978-79; U. of Florida, B.A. 1982 (political science); George Washington U., J.D. 1985

CAREER
Lawyer

POLITICAL HIGHLIGHTS
Fla. Senate, 1990-97

ELECTION RESULTS

2002 GENERAL		
Robert Wexler (D)	156,747	72.2%
Jack Merkl (R)	60,477	27.8%
2002 PRIMARY		
Robert Wexler (D)		unopposed
2000 GENERAL		
Robert Wexler (D)	171,080	71.6%
Morris Kent Thompson (R)	67,789	28.4%

PREVIOUS WINNING PERCENTAGES
1998 (100%); 1996 (66%)

Elected 1996; 4th term

Wexler is one of Capitol Hill's "rhetorical warriors," whose average day may consist of as many television appearances as committee meetings. He came to national prominence in 1998, when as a freshman, he emerged as one of President Clinton's most visible defenders during the Judiciary Committee's impeachment deliberations.

Outspoken and media-savvy, Wexler has been a staple on television interview shows ever since, advancing his views on subjects ranging from prescription drug prices to U.S. policy on Iraq to Palm Beach County's difficulties in administering elections in 2000 and 2002.

But it is on the subject of the Middle East that Wexler has been most vocal. The lawmaker is a staunch defender of Israel, applauding the Bush administration's insistence that the Palestinians oust Yasser Arafat and renounce terrorism. And he urges the administration to take tough actions against nations in the Middle East and South Asia — even erstwhile U.S. allies — when it is in the United States' interest.

"That is the stuff I love talking about," he says, adding that in his district — which includes the heavily Jewish communities of Boca Raton and Palm Beach — Middle East policy is virtually local politics.

Although he backed President Bush only 28 percent of the time in the 107th Congress, slightly below average for a House Democrat, he applauded Bush's tough line on Middle East and South Asia matters. In 2002, he voted to authorize the use of military force against Iraq, "not because I support the irresponsible manner and timing in which President Bush has proceeded with his plans for war . . . but rather, because of the threat posed by Hussein."

There is another aspect to Wexler's congressional persona, which is demonstrated by his membership in the moderate group of lawmakers known as the New Democrat Coalition. In the midst of the Florida presidential election dispute, Wexler declared that once it was resolved, "We ought to be big enough people to join behind the new president."

Wexler nevertheless was highly critical in 2001 and 2002 of the administration of elections by Florida officials, particularly in Palm Beach County. He urged Congress to give local officials help and said that merely providing new equipment was not enough — voters had to be educated and election judges trained.

Wexler blasted the Republicans' plan in 2002 for dealing with the high cost of prescription drugs for senior citizens, saying it was a "disgrace" and "nothing more than a half-hearted attempt to . . . provide themselves with election year cover." He had harsh words for Democrats as well. The Democratic Party, he said, "abdicates its responsibility when we criticize Bush's tax cuts without having the courage to repeal it." Wexler proposed rescinding part of the $1.3 billion tax cut approved by Congress in 2001 to pay for a $300 billion to $350 billion prescription drug program.

Wexler is a staunch foe of the National Rifle Association. He proudly noted that the NRA had targeted him in the 2002 election campaign as one of the "F troop" of lawmakers whose voting records were given failing grades by the gun group. "If the NRA is afraid of me, then I must be doing a good job working to make America's streets safer," he said.

Wexler, who serves on the International Relations Committee, made more than a dozen trips to the Middle East in the 107th Congress, often flying back and forth between Saudi Arabia and Israel to engage in unofficial shuttle diplomacy. He has also visited India, Turkey and Taiwan and is the co-founder and co-chairman of the Taiwan and Turkey caucuses.

In the 107th, Wexler drafted legislation, which became law, directing the Pentagon to review whether the Congressional Medal of Honor had been unjustly denied to Jewish or Hispanic members of the armed forces. A similar review of the service records of Asian-American war veterans resulted in the granting of 22 medals of honor, he said.

Wexler's district is home to American Media Inc., the publisher of supermarket tabloids such as the National Enquirer, and where an employee of one of the tabloids, Bob Stevens, became the first victim of deadly anthrax spread through the mail. Wexler has demanded that the federal government take over the still-quarantined office building and pay to have it cleaned up.

His staff estimates that he was interviewed on television about 100 times during the six months that the impeachment wars raged in Congress. "I got to do in one term what it might have taken 10 terms to do," said Wexler, who rated it an almost entirely positive experience. Not everyone is a fan, however: Political writer Ronald Brownstein of the Los Angeles Times once labeled Wexler "the human advertisement for the mute button."

Born in Queens, Wexler was 10 when his family moved to South Florida. After earning his law degree at George Washington University, he returned to Florida and practiced law in Boca Raton.

In 1990 he unseated a 16-year veteran of the state Senate, Republican Don Childers. In his six years in the Senate, Wexler won generally favorable reviews, but he also attracted criticism for some controversial proposals.

As the chairman of the Senate's Criminal Justice Committee, Wexler proposed castration (via a chemical process, not surgery) for two-time rapists and electrocution for a third rape conviction. He also proposed that women who gave birth to so-called cocaine babies be prevented from having more children. His castration-of-rapists bill was vehemently criticized. The head of the Florida chapter of the American Civil Liberties Union said, "He wants to adopt Islamic-style justice." But Wexler told the Orlando Sentinel, "What I'm proposing is just common sense."

When four-term Democratic Rep. Harry A. Johnston announced he would not seek re-election to his 19th District seat in 1996, Wexler leapt at the opening. In the ensuing four-way primary, he won a plurality of the vote, then handily defeated state Senate Majority Leader Peter Weinstein in the runoff. He rolled up two-thirds of the general-election vote against Republican Beverly Kennedy, a Pompano Beach financial consultant, and has won re-election easily since.

KEY VOTES

2002

- Yes Overhaul campaign finance law; ban "soft money" and restrict advocacy advertising
- Yes Back Bush's defense budget increase
- No Extend 1996 welfare law
- ? Adopt Bush's discretionary spending limit
- No Pass GOP Medicare prescription drug plan
- Yes Create independent Sept. 11 commission
- Yes Extend union protections to Homeland Security Department employees
- No Revive fast-track procedures for trade agreements
- Yes Authorize war against Iraq
- No Advance bankruptcy overhaul opposed by abortion opponents

2001

- No Nullify Clinton Labor Department ergonomics rule
- No Cut taxes by $1.35 trillion through fiscal 2011
- Yes Maintain ban on oil drilling in Arctic National Wildlife Refuge
- No Approve Bush proposal to limit managed-care plan liability for coverage decisions
- Yes Divert money from crop subsidy payments to land conservation
- Yes Expand law enforcement power to investigate suspected terrorists

CQ VOTE STUDIES

	PARTY UNITY		PRESIDENTIAL SUPPORT	
	Support	Oppose	Support	Oppose
2002	89%	11%	29%	71%
2001	94%	6%	27%	73%
2000	91%	9%	79%	21%
1999	93%	7%	84%	16%
1998	92%	8%	90%	10%

INTEREST GROUPS

	AFL-CIO	ADA	CCUS	ACU
2002	100%	100%	32%	9%
2001	100%	100%	30%	4%
2000	100%	85%	52%	17%
1999	89%	100%	20%	8%
1998	100%	100%	18%	0%

FLORIDA 19

Southeast – parts of Coral Springs, Margate and Boca Raton

Two-thirds of the heavily Democratic 19th's residents live in Palm Beach County and one-third live in Broward County, mostly west of Interstate 95, where subdivisions dot the landscape. The 19th stretches from West Palm Beach as far south as Margate and includes parts of Boca Raton and Deerfield Beach. Older, upper-middle-class residents make it one of the most educated and white-collar districts in the state.

Almost exclusively white, the 19th supports Democrats by overwhelming margins at the state and national levels. Sen. Bill Nelson and Democratic presidential candidate Al Gore both won this district with more than 70 percent in the 2000 election. Retirees, including many Jewish condominium residents, provide a consistent base of support throughout much of the district.

The 19th has the highest percentage of residents age 65 or older (30 percent) of any district in the nation, and elderly voters comprise more than 80 percent of the electorate in the 19th's portion of Palm Beach County. Accordingly, the "condo commandos" who run condominium associations serve as local power brokers. Redistricting in 2002 removed some wealthy residents of gated communities in Boca Raton, adding to the 19th's Democratic tilt.

The portion of Boca Raton included in the 19th long has been home to corporate headquarters. Sensormatic Electronics Corp. (acquired by Tyco International in 2001) and Rexall Sundown, a vitamin producer, have major facilities there.

MAJOR INDUSTRY
Health care, electronics, financial services

CITIES
Coral Springs (pt.), 74,195; Margate (pt.), 42,284; Greenacres, 27,569; Tamarac (pt.), 25,756; Coconut Creek (pt.), 24,901

NOTABLE
A photo editor for The Sun, a supermarket tabloid, contracted the first fatal case of anthrax in 2001 while working at the newspaper's Boca Raton office; Boca Raton is known for its pink municipal buildings and the Spanish revival architecture of Addison Mizner.

Rep. Peter Deutsch (D)

CAPITOL OFFICE
225-7931
www.house.gov/deutsch
2303 Rayburn 20515-0920; fax 225-8456

COMMITTEES
Energy & Commerce

HOMETOWN
Fort Lauderdale

BORN
April 1, 1957, Bronx, N.Y.

RELIGION
Jewish

FAMILY
Wife, Lori Ann Deutsch; two children

EDUCATION
Swarthmore College, B.A. 1979 (psychology); Yale U., J.D. 1982

CAREER
Lawyer; nonprofit executive

POLITICAL HIGHLIGHTS
Fla. House, 1983-93

ELECTION RESULTS

2002 GENERAL
Peter Deutsch (D) unopposed

2002 PRIMARY
Peter Deutsch (D) unopposed

2000 GENERAL
Peter Deutsch (D) unopposed

PREVIOUS WINNING PERCENTAGES
1998 (100%); 1996 (65%); 1994 (61%); 1992 (55%)

Elected 1992; 6th term

With an eye toward expanding his influence, and possibly winning statewide office, Deutsch has steadily bolstered the reserves in his campaign treasury even though he has not been seriously challenged since his initial election to the House in 1992. "I'm at a point in my career where I don't want to say I'm just another member of Congress," Deutsch said. "I want to influence the direction of the party."

To that end Deutsch (DOYCH) has formed his own political action committee to support fellow centrist Democrats. In 2000, he used the fund to support Vice President Al Gore's presidential campaign in Florida. He was a vociferous advocate of Gore's position during the state's ballot-counting controversy, going so far as to file a House ethics committee complaint charging that Republican Steve Buyer of Indiana improperly used his House Armed Services Committee seat to obtain information on service members who voted by overseas ballot. Deutsch also joined a cadre of House Democrats who tried to stop the joint session of Congress convened to certify the electoral vote tally that elected George W. Bush the 43rd president.

After Democratic leaders persuaded him to donate a hefty amount to the party's effort to win back the House in 2002, Deutsch lashed out at Minority Leader Richard A. Gephardt for comments that his staff had made alluding to Deutsch's stinginess. Later, as Gephardt prepared to launch his 2004 presidential campaign, Deutsch was an early advocate of Gephardt stepping down from his leadership post, saying that Gephardt could not undertake both high-profile endeavors effectively.

Deutsch makes no apologies for his hard-driving style. "Team player" is not a phrase that comes to mind in describing him. Deutsch is such an ardent pursuer of his causes that even natural allies sometimes keep their distance, fearful that his sharp elbows and strong rhetoric will complicate the building of bipartisan coalitions.

Arguing in federal court against Florida's GOP-drafted congressional redistricting map for this decade, which he saw as unfair to the Democrats, Deutsch was so enthusiastic — and expansive — in his rhetoric that U.S. District Judge Adalberto Jordan admonished the congressman that he could not be "witness, plaintiff, judge and jury all rolled up into one."

On Capitol Hill, Deutsch is most aggressive in advancing Everglades preservation, government programs for senior citizens, a hard-line policy against Cuban leader Fidel Castro and a close U.S. relationship with Israel.

After the Sept. 11, 2001, terrorist attacks, Deutsch hopped a plane with three other lawmakers to personally deliver a resolution expressing support for the Israeli government and condemning Palestinian suicide bombings. To bring the reality of Middle East violence home to his constituents, he returned with a suicide bomber's explosives-lined vest that had been confiscated by Israeli security forces.

In 2000, Deutsch made news when he traveled to Cuba with U.S. permission, but without the consent of Cuban authorities. He made unscheduled house calls on dissidents and, upon returning to the United States, called for continuing the U.S. trade embargo. The Fort Lauderdale Sun-Sentinel quoted Deutsch characterizing as "either naive or crazy" his anti-embargo colleagues in Congress, many of whom are also Democrats.

Deutsch also pursues his objectives legislatively; his seat on the Energy and Commerce Committee, with broad jurisdiction, gives him ample opportunity. In the 107th Congress the House rejected his proposal to permit the creation of human embryos for therapeutic research. After the wave of accounting and corporate governance scandals confronted the 107th, Deutsch promoted legislation to limit the amount of employer stocks in 401(k) retirement accounts to 10 percent.

Deutsch's voting record places him slightly to the left of the average Southern Democrat and slightly to the right of his party's leadership — positions one would expect from a member of the centrist New Democrat Coalition. He has sided with conservatives on proposals to overhaul public housing, to make it easier for property owners to challenge land-use decisions and to crack down on youth violence. During the 106th Congress, he teamed up with Republican Rep. Michael Bilirakis of Florida to try to ease Clinton administration regulations on Medicare HMOs.

But on a range of issues, Deutsch votes a liberal line. He supports abortion rights, backs gun control and generally sides with organized labor. Deutsch takes a dim view of Republican efforts to greatly increase defense spending and limit the authority of the EPA.

In Deutsch's first decade in Congress, his district included large sections of the Everglades, and its restoration is one of his top priorities. He calls the area "America's most threatened ecosystem" and contends it is vital to South Florida's economy. In 2000, Congress authorized the first $1.4 billion of a $7.8 billion federal-state Everglades restoration project that Deutsch helped put together.

As representative for a large elderly population, Deutsch is an outspoken advocate of adding prescription drug coverage to Medicare and champions legislation to allow the reimportation of U.S. drugs from other countries, generally at lower cost.

Deutsch entered Congress at age 35 after a decade in the Florida Legislature. He began gearing up for a congressional candidacy when he became chairman of the state House subcommittee that was supposed to draw the congressional map for the 1990s. A federal court eventually handled the process. When Deutsch learned that the judges' map put his home in the district of Democrat Dante B. Fascell, a 38-year House veteran, he decided to run anyway. Fascell retired, but he and two other departing Florida Democrats, Lawrence J. Smith and William Lehman, endorsed Deutsch's primary opponent, Broward County Commissioner Nicki Englander Grossman.

The campaign turned personal but Deutsch, who enjoyed a big financial advantage, won the nomination handily. He defeated Republican Beverly Kennedy that November by 17 percentage points, his closest House race to date. Republicans have not even fielded a candidate since 1996.

KEY VOTES

2002

- Yes Overhaul campaign finance law; ban "soft money" and restrict advocacy advertising
- Yes Back Bush's defense budget increase
- No Extend 1996 welfare law
- ? Adopt Bush's discretionary spending limit
- No Pass GOP Medicare prescription drug plan
- Yes Create independent Sept. 11 commission
- Yes Extend union protections to Homeland Security Department employees
- No Revive fast-track procedures for trade agreements
- Yes Authorize war against Iraq
- No Advance bankruptcy overhaul opposed by abortion opponents

2001

- No Nullify Clinton Labor Department ergonomics rule
- No Cut taxes by $1.35 trillion through fiscal 2011
- Yes Maintain ban on oil drilling in Arctic National Wildlife Refuge
- No Approve Bush proposal to limit managed-care plan liability for coverage decisions
- Yes Divert money from crop subsidy payments to land conservation
- Yes Expand law enforcement power to investigate suspected terrorists

CQ VOTE STUDIES

	PARTY UNITY		PRESIDENTIAL SUPPORT	
	Support	Oppose	Support	Oppose
2002	86%	14%	41%	59%
2001	91%	9%	37%	63%
2000	87%	13%	71%	29%
1999	88%	12%	80%	20%
1998	88%	12%	82%	18%

INTEREST GROUPS

	AFL-CIO	ADA	CCUS	ACU
2002	89%	85%	45%	12%
2001	100%	90%	43%	8%
2000	100%	65%	57%	28%
1999	78%	95%	40%	8%
1998	90%	95%	35%	4%

FLORIDA 20

Southeast – parts of Hollywood, Sunrise, Davie and Fort Lauderdale

Middle-class suburbs mix with beach communities as the 20th snakes through heavily Democratic territory in Broward and Miami-Dade counties from as far north as Village Park to as far south as Miami Beach. The district takes in a slice of Fort Lauderdale and accounts for about one-third of Broward's population, much of it in suburbs such as Sunrise, Plantation and Davie. Western Broward teems with shopping centers and suburban development as many former Miami residents have moved north in search of suburban life.

Though it takes in those western Broward suburbs, the district wraps around the eastern side of the Miami area. It twists through portions of Hollywood and Hallandale in Broward and moves south into Aventura, with its growing community of young professionals, and North Miami before jumping the Intracoastal Waterway to take in Bal Harbor and a chunk of Miami Beach.

About two-thirds of residents are white and about one-fifth are Hispanic. Some liberal-leaning areas, such as most of Wilton Manors, were added to the 20th in 2002 redistricting. Wilton Manors has a significant gay and lesbian community, and Dania Beach is becoming a more prominent gay resort area. Jewish retirees also contribute to the district's overall Democratic bent.

Davie, with its cattle ranches, has retained some of its rural feel. Plantation has more-expensive homes and light industry. Democrats tend to win elections in Broward County, where they rack up especially large margins in the 20th's parts of Sunrise and Lauderhill. Al Gore took 68 percent of the district's vote in the 2000 presidential election.

MAJOR INDUSTRY

Tourism, business services, retail

CITIES

Hollywood (pt.), 81,921; Sunrise (pt.), 71,670; Davie (pt.), 70,142; Plantation (pt.), 66,264; Weston, 49,286; Pembroke Pines (pt.), 37,466

NOTABLE

Wilton Manors has a gay mayor and a gay-majority city council; The architecture in downtown Davie is designed to resemble the Old West, and the local McDonald's has a hitching post for horses.

Rep. Lincoln Diaz-Balart (R)

CAPITOL OFFICE
225-4211
www.house.gov/diaz-balart
2244 Rayburn 20515-0921; fax 225-8576

COMMITTEES
Rules
Select Homeland Security
(Rules - chairman)

HOMETOWN
Miami

BORN
Aug. 13, 1954, Havana, Cuba

RELIGION
Roman Catholic

FAMILY
Wife, Cristina Diaz-Balart; two children

EDUCATION
U. of South Florida, B.A. 1976 (international relations); Case Western Reserve U., J.D. 1979

CAREER
Lawyer; state prosecutor

POLITICAL HIGHLIGHTS
Democratic nominee for Fla. House, 1982; Fla. House, 1987-89; Fla. Senate, 1989-92

ELECTION RESULTS

2002 GENERAL	
Lincoln Diaz-Balart (R)	unopposed
2002 PRIMARY	
Lincoln Diaz-Balart (R)	unopposed
2000 GENERAL	
Lincoln Diaz-Balart (R)	unopposed

PREVIOUS WINNING PERCENTAGES
1998 (75%); 1996 (100%); 1994 (100%); 1992 (100%)

Elected 1992; 6th term

About 40 percent of the population of Florida's 21st District is of Cuban descent — Diaz-Balart among them — so it is not surprising that U.S.-Cuba relations are his top priority. But for Diaz-Balart, opposition to Fidel Castro is more than a matter of political expediency. Rather, it has been more akin to a holy crusade, with Diaz-Balart (DEE-az ba-LART) spending much of his first decade in the House looking for any occasion to turn up the heat on his nemesis. The Cuban dictator has responded in kind — even sending spies to penetrate Diaz-Balart's district offices.

It is not only Castro that Diaz-Balart and the three other Cuban-American members of the House — his freshman congressman brother, Mario, their Republican colleague from Miami Ileana Ros-Lehtinen, and Democrat Robert Menendez of New Jersey — are fighting. They also face growing pressures from farm-state lawmakers to lift the four-decade-old U.S. embargo on trade with Cuba.

"Those of us who want to keep the embargo as leverage to force a democratic transition are in a race against time," Diaz-Balart said in 2002.

Diaz-Balart can count on steady support from the White House to withstand the assault. President Bush's political aides credited Diaz-Balart's Cuban-American constituents for putting Bush over the top in the vital battle to win Florida's 25 electoral votes in the 2000 presidential election. Bush's brother, Jeb, was eager to retain the same voters during his successful bid for a second term as Florida's governor.

In one sign of administration favor, Attorney General John Ashcroft yielded to pleas from Diaz-Balart and Ros-Lehtinen to try and strip Eriberto Mederos, a Cuban-American in Miami, of his U.S. citizenship for allegedly torturing political prisoners at a psychiatric hospital in Havana in the 1970s. It was the first such case in more than two decades.

Diaz-Balart is a skillful inside player; drawing on his background as a prosecutor, he can be persuasive in face-to-face meetings. Republican leaders quickly noted those skills, naming him in only his second term to the Rules Committee, the agent of the GOP leadership in setting the ground rules for debate on the House floor. In 2001, Speaker J. Dennis Hastert followed up by naming him to the Republican Policy Committee, the GOP's official sounding board for legislative proposals and strategies. He serves as chairman of the group's Subcommittee on the Americas.

In the 108th, Diaz-Balart added a seat on the new Homeland Security panel, which oversees the new Cabinet department of the same name.

Because of his Rules Committee assignment, Diaz-Balart frequently leads House floor debates, a plus for Republicans eager to showcase one of only four Hispanic members of their party in the House in the 108th Congress. In 2000, a nationwide poll published in Hispanic Magazine cited Diaz-Balart as one of the 10 most influential Hispanics in the nation.

Diaz-Balart has used that status — and the effort by leaders of both parties to woo Hispanic voters — to push for immigration policies that he says are the "great unifier" among Latinos, not just Cuban-Americans. This is a plus in a district that includes a substantial number of other Latinos. He played a key role during the 107th Congress in persuading House GOP leaders to drop efforts to make it more difficult for legal immigrants to obtain food stamps. He also has sought to forestall deportation from the United States of thousands of refugees from Central and South America.

In the 106th Congress, he played a high-profile role in the debates on

Capitol Hill over the fate of the Cuban youngster Elián González. He argued that the boy, who had been rescued from the ocean after his mother drowned while attempting to defect to the United States, should have remained in this country. When federal agents seized Elián from the home of his Miami relatives, Diaz-Balart was outraged.

In 2000, he supported the Cuban American National Foundation when it targeted campaign advertisements against lawmakers — including some Republicans — whom it regarded as insufficiently anti-Castro.

To his political adversaries, Diaz-Balart's obsession with toppling Castro means he often ignores other pressing matters. Diaz-Balart bristles at the notion that he is a one-issue member, but the fact remains that matters involving Cuba are of high importance to his constituents.

Florida's Cuban community is heavily Republican, but the working-class nature of the 21st District can lead Diaz-Balart to stray from the GOP line. He was one of the few GOP House candidates in 1994 who declined to sign the "Contract With America" campaign platform and he has bucked his party on a number of social programs, including the 1996 welfare overhaul, which imposed new restrictions on benefits to legal as well as illegal immigrants.

Diaz-Balart's grandfather, father and uncle served in Cuba's House before the family fled to the United States in 1959, the year of the revolution, when the future congressman was 5 years old. His father's sister was married to Castro in the late 1940s and early 1950s, but they divorced and there was a political falling-out between the families long before Castro took control.

After law school, Diaz-Balart worked for a Miami legal services organization that provided free legal help for the poor. He served as a Dade County prosecutor in the early 1980s under Janet Reno, whom he frequently criticized during her time as attorney general under President Clinton.

A Democrat when he first ran, unsuccessfully, in 1982 for the Florida Legislature, Diaz-Balart was a co-chairman of the Democrats for Reagan campaign in Florida in 1984 and switched to the GOP in 1985, easily winning a state House seat in 1986. He served three years in the House and three in the state Senate.

When the courts redrew Florida's congressional maps after the 1990 census, a second Hispanic-majority district was created. Diaz-Balart easily bested a fellow Cuban-American state senator in a two-way Republican primary. He drew no Democratic foe that November, and since then has been re-elected with little or no competition. In 2002, as in 2000, he was the only candidate on the ballot.

KEY VOTES

2002

No Overhaul campaign finance law; ban "soft money" and restrict advocacy advertising
Yes Back Bush's defense budget increase
Yes Extend 1996 welfare law
Yes Adopt Bush's discretionary spending limit
Yes Pass GOP Medicare prescription drug plan
No Create independent Sept. 11 commission
No Extend union protections to Homeland Security Department employees
Yes Revive fast-track procedures for trade agreements
Yes Authorize war against Iraq
? Advance bankruptcy overhaul opposed by abortion opponents

2001

Yes Nullify Clinton Labor Department ergonomics rule
Yes Cut taxes by $1.35 trillion through fiscal 2011
No Maintain ban on oil drilling in Arctic National Wildlife Refuge
Yes Approve Bush proposal to limit managed-care plan liability for coverage decisions
No Divert money from crop subsidy payments to land conservation
Yes Expand law enforcement power to investigate suspected terrorists

CQ VOTE STUDIES

	PARTY UNITY		PRESIDENTIAL SUPPORT	
	Support	Oppose	Support	Oppose
2002	94%	6%	87%	13%
2001	94%	6%	88%	12%
2000	84%	16%	35%	65%
1999	78%	22%	33%	67%
1998	80%	20%	33%	67%

INTEREST GROUPS

	AFL-CIO	ADA	CCUS	ACU
2002	14%	15%	83%	88%
2001	8%	5%	86%	84%
2000	40%	20%	65%	56%
1999	44%	25%	60%	64%
1998	70%	25%	72%	68%

FLORIDA 21

Southeast – most of Hialeah and Kendall

The Hispanic-dominated 21st is a dependable Republican district that includes middle-class suburbs in central-west Miami-Dade County, from part of Miami Lakes in the north through most of Hialeah in its center and much of Kendall to the south. It includes one-fourth of Miami-Dade's population and a slice of southwestern Broward County. Traditionally, the district's politics center around opposition to Fidel Castro. But economic and foreign policy conservatism are balanced somewhat by residents' more moderate views on labor and social policy matters.

Many residents commute from Hialeah, a vibrant, blue-collar residential area filled with Cuban-Americans, to other parts of the 21st. Transportation-related businesses, including Carnival Cruise Lines, have set up facilities close to Miami International Airport, which was moved into the 21st during 2002 redistricting. Officials say the area is well-positioned to capitalize on trade pacts with Latin American countries.

South Florida's healthy economic scene during the 1990s meant more jobs and homes for the 21st and neighboring districts. The 21st also picks up parts of Miramar and Pembroke Pines, which boast many young professionals from Latin America.

The district's large, suburban Cuban-American community accounts for its Republican bent in statewide and federal elections. Few areas in Florida are as heavily Republican as Hialeah, which has a large contingent of elderly Cuban-American voters and which gave Republican Gov. Jeb Bush more than 80 percent of the vote in the 2002 election. Bob Dole only narrowly won the district in 1996, but George W. Bush carried the 21st by 16 percentage points in 2000.

MAJOR INDUSTRY

Trade, technology, small business

CITIES

Hialeah (pt.), 208,552; Kendall (pt.), 59,676; Pembroke Pines (pt.), 54,426; Fountainbleau (pt.), 52,244; Country Club, 36,310; University Park, 26,538

NOTABLE

Hialeah boasts 15,000 multilingual businesses; Amelia Earhart's final flight began in 1937 in Hialeah.

Rep. E. Clay Shaw Jr. (R)

CAPITOL OFFICE
225-3026
www.house.gov/shaw
2408 Rayburn 20515-0922; fax 225-8398

COMMITTEES
Ways & Means
(Social Security - chairman)
Joint Taxation

HOMETOWN
Fort Lauderdale

BORN
April 19, 1939, Miami, Fla.

RELIGION
Roman Catholic

FAMILY
Wife, Emilie Shaw; four children

EDUCATION
Stetson U., B.S. 1961 (business); U. of Alabama, M.B.A. 1963 (accounting); Stetson U., J.D. 1966

CAREER
Nurseryman; lawyer; city prosecutor

POLITICAL HIGHLIGHTS
Fort Lauderdale associate municipal judge, 1969-71; Fort Lauderdale City Commission, 1971-73; vice mayor of Fort Lauderdale, 1973-75; mayor of Fort Lauderdale, 1975-81

ELECTION RESULTS

2002 GENERAL		
E. Clay Shaw Jr. (R)	131,930	60.8%
Carol Roberts (D)	83,265	38.4%
2002 PRIMARY		
E. Clay Shaw Jr. (R)		unopposed
2000 GENERAL		
E. Clay Shaw Jr. (R)	105,855	50.1%
Elaine Bloom (D)	105,256	49.9%

PREVIOUS WINNING PERCENTAGES
1998 (100%); 1996 (62%); 1994 (63%); 1992 (52%); 1990 (98%); 1988 (66%); 1986 (100%); 1984 (66%); 1982 (57%); 1980 (55%)

Elected 1980; 12th term

With one of the largest percentages of elderly constituents of any congressman, Shaw serves as something of a weather vane for other Republicans running on the issue of overhauling the Social Security system. While he clung to his seat in 2000 by only 599 votes, Shaw increased that margin to 48,665 in 2002 while continuing the debate about the program's future on the campaign trail.

"It's time for Congress — the people you elect — to legislate for the next generation and not the next election," he told officials of AARP at their annual legislative meeting in 2002.

Shaw has been a central figure in the debate as chairman of the Ways and Means Subcommittee on Social Security since 1999; under GOP term limits the 108th Congress will be his last with that gavel.

His 61 percent landslide in 2002 was eased by redistricting, which made the 22nd District politically competitive for this decade after it had trended Democratic in the 1990s. But Shaw's victory nonetheless adds to President Bush's confidence that the supposed third rail of politics has lost much of its juice. Like the president, Shaw now seems less vulnerable to the argument Democrats make to senior citizens that Republican proposals to allow workers to invest some of their payroll taxes in individual investment accounts would threaten the long-term fiscal health of Social Security, the federal retirement income benefit.

Still, it does not seem likely the president will push his proposal unless he is re-elected in 2004, mindful of the $1 trillion, 10-year cost estimate for his plan to move into a system of private accounts while still paying current benefits. With a return of federal deficits, it would be even more difficult to pay for Shaw's plan, which would have the government borrowing and investing money in the private accounts.

Shaw, who would become eligible for full Social Security benefits upon his 65th birthday in 2004, holds much of the GOP's institutional memory on another major social policy change: the 1996 rewrite of the welfare system. As chairman of the Ways and Means Human Resources Subcommittee in the 104th Congress, he was one of the lawmakers who molded President Clinton's promise to "end welfare as we know it" into a law that almost all Republicans and many Democrats supported. Although he no longer chairs the panel that oversees welfare, Shaw was an important behind-the-scenes force in urging Congress to preserve most of those changes as its work to update the law intensified in 2003.

At the same time, he endorsed Bush's proposal to impose a longer, 40-hour workweek requirement to qualify for welfare benefits, without counting vocational training. "By increasing standards, we show a greater expectation for those we are trying to help, and as we have seen, people will rise to our expectations of them," he said.

His work on welfare was in keeping with Shaw's reputation for trying to craft legislation that will attract bipartisan backing. During the lengthy and often contentious welfare debate of the 104th, Shaw made sure Democrats' viewpoints got a fair hearing. But he also helped advance the GOP position that localities and states should have more authority over welfare policy, a view anchored in his 13 years' experience in municipal government, including six years as the mayor of Fort Lauderdale.

Shaw takes risks trying to rein in entitlement spending, but he also knows the political value of increasing benefits for senior citizens in an election year. In 2002, the House passed his bill to ease eligibility rules to help 120,000 disabled and elderly widows and divorced retirees whose spouses die and leave them with reduced Social Security benefits. The vote was preceded by a tart exchange with Robert T. Matsui of California, the Social Security Subcommittee's top Democrat, who proposed instead expanding benefits for 5 million widows, at a cost of $73 billion over 10 years, by guaranteeing payments equal to 75 percent of combined benefits paid when both spouses were alive. Shaw said he supported that more-generous approach but concluded that the budget could not support it.

The fight was part of Democrats' strategy to press the issue of the future of seniors' entitlements, which ultimately doomed Shaw's bill for the 107th. GOP leaders blocked Senate action on the measure, fearing it would become an opportunity for the Democrats to renew debate on creating a Medicare prescription drug benefit.

Shaw had more luck in 2000, when he presided over a repeal of Social Security's so-called earnings penalty. The law ended a Depression-era policy that reduced benefits for those people ages 65 through 69 whose wages exceeded an annual limit. He also sponsored legislation requiring Medicare to pay for annual mammograms and pap exams to help older women detect the early signs of breast or cervical cancer.

Shaw himself was operated on for lung cancer in January 2003, but the procedure did not slow him down much: He spent his recovery time lobbying colleagues for a provision in the wrapup 2002 spending law to have the government assume the estimated $20 million cost of cleaning up anthrax contamination at a tabloid newspaper company in Boca Raton that was the target of mail sabotage in 2001.

Also close to home, Shaw has been part of negotiations on the massive project to restore the Everglades, and he has pushed several bills designed to curb the flow of illegal drugs into South Florida.

After stints as a municipal judge, city commissioner, vice mayor and mayor of Fort Lauderdale, Shaw was unopposed for the GOP nomination when he first ran for the House in 1980. He capitalized on Democratic squabbling to secure what was then the 12th District. Democratic primary voters dumped 70-year-old Rep. Edward J. Stack for a younger candidate, former state Rep. Alan Becker. Bragging that during his tenure as mayor he had cut spending, broadened the economic base and helped give Fort Lauderdale a more cosmopolitan image, Shaw won with 55 percent.

He was re-elected relatively easily until 2000, when Democratic state Rep. Elaine Bloom pounced on his plan for revising Social Security.

KEY VOTES

2002

- No Overhaul campaign finance law; ban "soft money" and restrict advocacy advertising
- Yes Back Bush's defense budget increase
- Yes Extend 1996 welfare law
- Yes Adopt Bush's discretionary spending limit
- Yes Pass GOP Medicare prescription drug plan
- No Create independent Sept. 11 commission
- No Extend union protections to Homeland Security Department employees
- Yes Revive fast-track procedures for trade agreements
- Yes Authorize war against Iraq
- No Advance bankruptcy overhaul opposed by abortion opponents

2001

- Yes Nullify Clinton Labor Department ergonomics rule
- Yes Cut taxes by $1.35 trillion through fiscal 2011
- No Maintain ban on oil drilling in Arctic National Wildlife Refuge
- Yes Approve Bush proposal to limit managed-care plan liability for coverage decisions
- Yes Divert money from crop subsidy payments to land conservation
- Yes Expand law enforcement power to investigate suspected terrorists

CQ VOTE STUDIES

	PARTY UNITY		PRESIDENTIAL SUPPORT	
	Support	Oppose	Support	Oppose
2002	93%	7%	92%	8%
2001	92%	8%	95%	5%
2000	87%	13%	31%	69%
1999	86%	14%	37%	63%
1998	88%	12%	34%	66%

INTEREST GROUPS

	AFL-CIO	ADA	CCUS	ACU
2002	11%	10%	95%	88%
2001	8%	10%	100%	76%
2000	0%	10%	80%	68%
1999	11%	20%	88%	60%
1998	10%	10%	100%	72%

FLORIDA 22

Southeast – coastal Broward and Palm Beach counties, parts of Fort Lauderdale and Boca Raton

The 22nd follows picturesque Route A1A down the Southeast coast from northern Palm Beach County to Fort Lauderdale in Broward County. Though its projections reach inland in places to pick up middle-class suburbs and gated communities, the district is mostly identifiable by its upscale beachfront cities and towns, including parts of Boca Raton. The 22nd no longer has the highest percentage of elderly residents in the state after 2002 redistricting, but one-fifth of its population is 65 or older.

The district's residents are mostly well-off and overwhelmingly white. Republicans count Palm Beach, Pompano Beach and Fort Lauderdale as their base. Many of the old 22nd's Democratic strongholds — including all of the district's territory in Miami-Dade County — were excised during redistricting to help bolster GOP candidates here.

Both Palm Beach, where a majority of residents live, and Broward counties lean Democratic, but redistricting lassoed in enough Republican precincts to transform the 22nd from a Democratic-leaning district that favored Al Gore by 21 percentage points in the 2000 presidential election into a politically competitive battleground that backed Gore by just 5 percentage points. Rep. Shaw, who won by fewer than 600 votes under the old lines in 2000, captured 61 percent of the vote in the new district in 2002.

Exclusive hotels and shopping centers lie within the district, while the ports of Palm Beach and Fort Lauderdale attract shipping and cruise line business. The area's elderly population supports several large hospitals. The wealth of many district residents helps insulate them from economic pressures, but the area depends heavily on tourism.

MAJOR INDUSTRY

Health care, tourism, shipping

CITIES

Fort Lauderdale (pt.), 61,509; Boca Raton (pt.), 55,946; Coral Springs (pt.), 43,354; Pompano Beach (pt.), 34,925; Palm Beach Gardens (pt.), 30,649

NOTABLE

The International Swimming Hall of Fame Museum is in Fort Lauderdale.

Rep. Alcee L. Hastings (D)

CAPITOL OFFICE
225-1313
alcee.pubhastings@mail.house.gov
www.house.gov/alceehastings
2235 Rayburn 20515-0923; fax 225-1171

COMMITTEES
Rules
Select Intelligence

HOMETOWN
Miramar

BORN
Sept. 5, 1936, Altamonte Springs, Fla.

RELIGION
African Methodist Episcopal

FAMILY
Divorced; three children

EDUCATION
Fisk U., B.S. 1958 (zoology & botany); Howard U., attended 1958-60 (law); Florida A&M U., J.D. 1963

CAREER
Judge; lawyer

POLITICAL HIGHLIGHTS
Sought Democratic nomination for U.S. Senate, 1970; U.S. District Court judge, 1979-89; Democratic nominee for Fla. secretary of state, 1990

ELECTION RESULTS

2002 GENERAL		
Alcee L. Hastings (D)	96,347	77.5%
Charles Laurie (R)	27,986	22.5%
2002 PRIMARY		
Alcee L. Hastings (D)		unopposed
2000 GENERAL		
Alcee L. Hastings (D)	89,179	76.3%
Bill Lambert (R)	27,630	23.7%

PREVIOUS WINNING PERCENTAGES
1998 (100%); 1996 (73%); 1994 (100%); 1992 (59%)

Elected 1992; 6th term

Any biography of Hastings will include his House impeachment in 1988 and his Senate conviction the next year, which stripped him of a federal trial court judgeship for allegedly extorting a bribe. But his recent career in Congress has revealed more of the ambition and doggedness that helped to revive his career, and which seems likely to push his impeachment toward the back pages of his life story.

A champion of liberal causes, a force in the Congressional Black Caucus and a harsh critic of the 2000 presidential election contest in Florida, in the 107th Congress Hastings made a seat on the highly partisan Rules Committee his principal forum. From there he uses his fiery oratorical style to protest the substance of Republican legislation as well as the procedures that GOP leaders want to use to push their proposals through. When his protests are in vain, as they usually are, Hastings takes his anger out to the House floor and often sets the rhetorical tone for the Democratic side of the debate.

"I hope the American worker is braced for the sucker punch they are about to receive," Hastings said on the last night the House met before its 2002 summer vacation, as the GOP majority prepared to muscle through legislation carrying out President Bush's request for more trade negotiating latitude from Capitol Hill.

Earlier that night, he criticized the GOP ground rules for debating legislation to set up the Department of Homeland Security. He voted against the bill, but he nonetheless favored the concept; he had been behind the first bipartisan measure introduced after the attacks of Sept. 11, 2001, calling for the creation of a "National Office for Combating Terrorism." And the 2002 legislation included his provision to require the department to abide by Equal Employment Opportunity laws and provide whistleblower protections.

Indeed, the 107th Congress was one in which Hastings was at the center of much of the action, legislative as well as political.

It ended with Hastings trying to improve relations between African-American and Jewish House members, which became strained after two Southern black incumbents were defeated in 2002 Democratic primaries because pro-Israel donors heavily supported their opponents. The 107th had begun with a joint session of Congress, presided over by Vice President Al Gore, to formally elect George W. Bush as president. As Florida's 25 disputed and decisive electoral votes were awarded, Hastings led a walk-out by members of the Congressional Black Caucus. "'We did all we could," Hastings called out to Gore. "The chair thanks the gentleman from Florida," the vice president replied with a smile.

Hastings arrived in the House in 1993 determined to impress the lawmakers who had impeached him five years before as courteous, respectful and hard-working. "Succeeding is the best revenge," he once said. "My goal was to get beyond people viewing me as an impeached judge."

To that end he concentrated on issues of particular concern to his constituents — funding for Medicare, job training, Head Start and sugar subsidies — and on developing an expertise in foreign affairs. At the start of the 107th, Hastings was the top Democrat on the International Relations' Europe Subcommittee, and he had earned kudos from members on both sides for attention to committee business.

He left the committee for Rules in the middle of 2001. By that time he had traveled to more than two dozen countries on official business, including a half-dozen trips to Africa. He realized that there was little political gain from his work on matters such as peace between Ethiopia and Eritrea or the African AIDS epidemic — especially when some of his constituents, as he once put it, "are as interested in day-to-day survival as the people in Sudan are."

His standing as the only impeached judge in Congress made him an especially sought-after lawmaker during the impeachment proceedings against President Clinton in 1998. He left no doubt that he thought that Independent Counsel Kenneth W. Starr's probe of the president was out of bounds, offering a resolution asking the House to impeach Starr for "gross prosecutorial misconduct."

Hastings showed he is a team player by temporarily giving up his seat on the Intelligence Committee for much of 2002 in order to give a political boost to Alabama Democrat Robert E. "Bud" Cramer. But his work on intelligence issues continued, particularly after the 2001 terrorist attacks, when he pushed for more cultural and ethnic diversity in recruiting new spies.

The congressman's local activism includes resisting what he sees as efforts by some white Florida Democrats to shift the state party to a right-of-center stance, diminishing the influence of black voters. He has several times urged blacks to consider voting for Republicans as a means of sending the party a signal that it should not take black support for granted.

The only child of under-educated parents who mostly toiled as domestic workers, Hastings earned a degree in zoology and botany at Fisk University and was accepted to medical school, but he chose to pursue a law career instead.

In 1979, President Carter nominated him to fill a U.S. District Court seat in Miami and he became the first black federal judge in Florida. In 1983 a jury acquitted Hastings of charges that he solicited a $150,000 bribe in exchange for granting a lenient sentence, but a federal judicial panel later concluded he had lied and made up evidence to secure that verdict. The vote was 413-3 in the House to impeach him and 69-26 in the Senate to remove him from office. In 1997, by which time Hastings was in his third term in the House, there were reports that the FBI had misled Congress and the courts on forensic tests used as evidence in the case.

Although he lost a bid for Florida secretary of state in 1990, Hastings won a majority in the precincts of the new 23rd District, which was drawn for the 1990s with a slight black majority. State Rep. Lois Frankel, a liberal white Democrat, took 35 percent to his 28 percent in the primary, but Hastings won the nomination in a runoff with 58 percent. He won in November with 59 percent against GOP real estate developer Ed Fielding, and in his five subsequent re-elections he has never polled below 73 percent.

KEY VOTES

2002

- Yes Overhaul campaign finance law; ban "soft money" and restrict advocacy advertising
- Yes Back Bush's defense budget increase
- No Extend 1996 welfare law
- No Adopt Bush's discretionary spending limit
- No Pass GOP Medicare prescription drug plan
- Yes Create independent Sept. 11 commission
- Yes Extend union protections to Homeland Security Department employees
- No Revive fast-track procedures for trade agreements
- No Authorize war against Iraq
- No Advance bankruptcy overhaul opposed by abortion opponents

2001

- No Nullify Clinton Labor Department ergonomics rule
- No Cut taxes by $1.35 trillion through fiscal 2011
- Yes Maintain ban on oil drilling in Arctic National Wildlife Refuge
- No Approve Bush proposal to limit managed-care plan liability for coverage decisions
- No Divert money from crop subsidy payments to land conservation
- No Expand law enforcement power to investigate suspected terrorists

CQ VOTE STUDIES

	PARTY UNITY		PRESIDENTIAL SUPPORT	
	Support	Oppose	Support	Oppose
2002	93%	7%	27%	73%
2001	91%	9%	18%	82%
2000	95%	5%	82%	18%
1999	97%	3%	82%	18%
1998	95%	5%	90%	10%

INTEREST GROUPS

	AFL-CIO	ADA	CCUS	ACU
2002	100%	95%	42%	0%
2001	100%	100%	29%	8%
2000	100%	80%	55%	4%
1999	100%	80%	22%	0%
1998	100%	80%	22%	5%

FLORIDA 23

Southeast – parts of Fort Lauderdale, West Palm Beach and Lauderhill

One of two black-majority districts in the state, the heavily Democratic 23rd stretches westward from working-class Fort Pierce to the eastern shores of Lake Okeechobee and back east toward some of the coastal hubs, such as West Palm Beach and Fort Lauderdale. Most residents live in Broward County, and much of the area west of Interstate 95 is rural and unpopulated. A significant portion of the Everglades was added to the 23rd in 2002 redistricting. The eastern borders of the 23rd tend to be several blocks off the coast, with the neighboring 22nd taking in much of the prime beachfront property.

Most urban areas in the 23rd — such as Lauderhill, Lauderdale Lakes, Riviera Beach and portions of West Palm Beach — contain largely black neighborhoods and attract local government employees, educators and other middle-class professionals. The 23rd is growing more diverse, drawing in people from around the world. Hispanics make up 14 percent of the population. Citrus, sugar cane and rice growers work the large but sparsely populated rural portions of the district. The 23rd lacks a major employment sector, and the vulnerability of citrus crops to bad weather contributes to making it one of the poorest districts in the state.

Democrats outnumber Republicans by a ratio of more than 3-to-1, and voters routinely give Democratic candidates more than 75 percent of the vote in competitive statewide elections. Indeed, many heavily black precincts — including some in western Fort Lauderdale and Lauderdale Lakes — gave Democratic gubernatorial nominee Bill McBride more than 90 percent of the vote in 2002.

MAJOR INDUSTRY

Agriculture, local government, small business

CITIES

Fort Lauderdale (pt.), 57,387; West Palm Beach (pt.), 52,330; Lauderhill (pt.), 47,371; North Lauderdale, 32,264; Lauderdale Lakes (pt.), 30,895

NOTABLE

Lake Okeechobee, part of which is in the 23rd, is the second-largest freshwater lake contained wholly within the United States; Lauderdale Lakes has 22 churches within its four square miles.

Rep. Tom Feeney (R)

Elected 2002; 1st term

Fresh off a two-year stint as speaker of the Florida House of Representatives, Feeney expressed awareness that he would "have to shift gears" and "be more patient" as a freshman in the 108th Congress.

The self-described Reagan Republican says he understands both the responsibility for governance borne by the House GOP majority and the luxury to criticize that comes with the Democrats' minority status. He served in both the minority and majority during his decade in the state House.

It was Feeney's initial two terms as a rhetorical "bomb-thrower" in a state legislature then controlled by Democrats that helped land him a spot as running mate with 1994 Republican gubernatorial candidate Jeb Bush. The bid vaulted Feeney into prominence, even though it ended in a narrow defeat for Bush (who rebounded to win the office in 1998 and 2002).

Feeney, who had left his legislative seat open in 1994, was returned to the state House in the 1996 election. Four years later, with Republicans holding the majority, his colleagues elected him speaker.

That post gave Feeney a big role in the pre-2002 redistricting and leverage to help design the 24th District — one of Florida's two new House seats. The conservative-leaning, Orlando-based district includes the Kennedy Space Center, where Feeney's wife works.

In his first contest for federal office Feeney took 62 percent of the vote to easily defeat Democrat Harry Jacobs, a wealthy trial lawyer.

A friend of Pennsylvania Republican Sen. Rick Santorum from their undergraduate days at Penn State, Feeney's contacts in Washington and friends in the Florida delegation may have given him a leg up over other freshmen in the 108th Congress. He won a post on the Science panel, as well as seats on Judiciary and Financial Services.

He was also selected as an assistant whip and represents the freshman class as a liaison to the House leadership. Recalling his days as speaker, Feeney noted, "You set the agenda. You only have to be in one place at [a] time."

CAPITOL OFFICE
225-2706
tom feeney@mail.house.gov
www.house.gov/feeney
323 Cannon 20515-0924; fax 226-6299

COMMITTEES
Financial Services
Judiciary
Science

HOMETOWN
Oviedo

BORN
May 21, 1958, Abington, Pa.

RELIGION
Presbyterian

FAMILY
Wife, Ellen Stewart Feeney; two children

EDUCATION
Penn State U., B.A. 1980 (political science);
U. of Pittsburgh, J.D. 1983

CAREER
Lawyer

POLITICAL HIGHLIGHTS
Fla. House, 1990-94; Republican nominee for lieutenant governor, 1994; Fla. House, 1996-2002 (Speaker, 2000-2002)

ELECTION RESULTS

2002 GENERAL		
Tom Feeney (R)	135,576	61.8%
Harry Jacobs (D)	83,667	38.2%
2002 PRIMARY		
Tom Feeney (R)		unopposed

FLORIDA 24

East central – Orlando suburbs, part of Space Coast

Created following the 2000 census, the 24th takes in much of the area between the GOP-leaning Orlando suburbs and the so-called Space Coast, drawing nearly equally from Orange, Seminole and Volusia counties, with just a bit less than one-fifth of its population coming from its portion of Brevard County.

Fashioned out of slices of the old Republican-held 7th, 8th and 15th districts, the 24th is a potentially competitive district with a small but distinct Republican lean. The GOP nominee won the 1992, 1996 and 2000 presidential contests among voters in the 24th, with George W. Bush capturing 52 percent of the vote in 2000.

The Space Coast, home of the Kennedy Space Center, is an economic driver in the region, providing a tourist attraction and a base for technology companies.

North of the Space Coast are popular beach communities and the city of Daytona Beach, most of which is in the neighboring 7th District. College students and bikers flock to Daytona's famous coastline during spring and summer.

The 24th takes in one of Daytona Beach's jewels — Daytona International Speedway, which is home to NASCAR's Daytona 500 stock car race.

The district, which has a relatively young population for Florida, sweeps west to pick up suburban communities outside Orlando, including most of Altamonte Springs and all of Oviedo.

MAJOR INDUSTRY
Aerospace, technology, tourism

CITIES
Port Orange, 45,823; Titusville, 40,670; Altamonte Springs (pt.), 30,130; Oviedo, 26,316; Deltona (pt.), 22,510

NOTABLE
Star Systems, an electronic payments network utilizing ATMs and retailers, is based in Maitland (shared with the 7th).

Rep. Mario Diaz-Balart (R)

CAPITOL OFFICE
225-2778
www.house.gov/mariodiaz-balart
313 Cannon 20515-0925; fax 226-0346

COMMITTEES
Budget
Transportation & Infrastructure

HOMETOWN
Miami

BORN
Sept. 25, 1961, Fort Lauderdale, Fla.

RELIGION
Roman Catholic

FAMILY
Single

EDUCATION
U. of South Florida, attended 1979-82

CAREER
Marketing firm executive; mayoral aide

POLITICAL HIGHLIGHTS
Fla. House, 1988-92; Fla. Senate, 1992-2000; Fla. House, 2000-02

ELECTION RESULTS

2002 GENERAL		
Mario Diaz-Balart (R)	81,845	64.7%
Annie Betancourt (D)	44,757	35.4%
2002 PRIMARY		
Mario Diaz-Balart (R)		unopposed

Elected 2002; 1st term

Elected to represent a new House district in 2002, Diaz-Balart will never have to look far to find a close friend in the House. His older brother, fellow Republican Lincoln Diaz-Balart, has represented a South Florida congressional district since 1993.

The younger Diaz-Balart (DEE-az ba-LART) doesn't need much fraternal coaching on the ways of lawmaking, though. He sandwiched three terms in the state House around two terms in the state Senate. Diaz-Balart went back to the state House after Florida's term-limit law barred him from running again for the Senate.

After watching Diaz-Balart get Florida Gov. Jeb Bush on the phone to discuss Florida's fiscal situation, GOP Rep. Ileana Ros-Lehtinen told the Miami Herald, "Mario doesn't put things on a to-do list. He just does them."

Diaz-Balart's family was in public life in Cuba, then emigrated to the United States when Fidel Castro took power there. Anti-Castro sentiment remains strong in his Hispanic-majority district.

Diaz-Balart says his chief priority in his freshman term is supporting President Bush and American forces in the war on terrorism. But he says he has other policy goals. He supports the Republican-drafted prescription-drug benefit legislation that the House passed in 2002 and says he is committed to delivering relief for senior citizens.

Diaz-Balart also said he wants to address other health care concerns, specifically to pass a $3,000 tax credit for families who purchase health insurance. He sought — and won — seats on the Budget and Transportation and Infrastructure committees.

Though Diaz-Balart's return to the state House might have been seen as a step back, it enabled him to chair the redistricting committee involved in drawing the 25th — one of two new districts Florida received in reapportionment. Entering the 2002 race as a solid favorite, Diaz-Balart raised six times more money than the Democratic nominee, state Rep. Annie Betancourt, and he won with 65 percent of the vote.

FLORIDA 25

South – western Miami-Dade County, the Everglades

One of two seats Florida gained following the 2000 census, the 25th takes in a broad swath of land covering the western portion of Miami-Dade County, most of Collier County and almost all of Monroe County. Geographically, it is centered in Everglades National Park and Big Cypress National Preserve.

The district was constructed to elect a Republican of Cuban descent. A majority of residents are Hispanic — many of them Cuban-American — and Republicans have a 43 percent to 35 percent registration edge over Democrats. Though Bill Clinton won the district with a plurality in his 1996 re-election bid, Republicans have won the area in most statewide elections, especially those involving members of the Bush family.

Nearly 90 percent of the district's population lives in Miami-Dade County, much of it on the western edge of the Miami region and in communities south of the city.

National parks give the 25th an ecosystem and an array of wildlife — everything from manatees to panthers — not commonly found in North America. Restoration of the Everglades, oil drilling and the pace of development promise to remain contentious issues here for some time.

Republican support for a hard line against Fidel Castro-led Cuba has helped the GOP forge a longstanding alliance with South Florida's large Cuban-American community.

MAJOR INDUSTRY
Tourism

CITIES
Kendale Lakes, 56,901; Tamiami, 54,788; The Hammocks, 47,379; Kendall West, 38,034

NOTABLE
Everglades National Park covers 1.5 million acres — which is just a small portion of the Everglades.

GEORGIA

Gov. Sonny Perdue (R)

First elected: 2002
Length of term: 4 years
Term expires: 1/07
Salary: $127,303
Phone: (404) 656-1776
Hometown: Bonaire
Born: Dec. 20, 1946; Perry, Ga.
Religion: Baptist
Family: Wife, Mary Perdue; four children
Education: U. of Georgia, D.V.M. 1971
Military Service: Air Force, 1971-74
Career: Fertilizer and grain business owner; veterinarian
Political highlights: Houston County Planning and Zoning Board, 1978-90; Ga. Senate, 1991-2001 (president pro tempore, 1997-99)
Election results:

2002 GENERAL		
Sonny Perdue (R)	1,042,221	51.4%
Roy Barnes (D)	937,335	46.2%
Garrett Hayes (LIBERT)	47,968	2.4%

Lt. Gov. Mark Taylor (D)

First elected: 1998
Length of term: 4 years
Term expires: 1/07
Salary: $83,148
Phone: (404) 656-5030

STATE LEGISLATURE

General Assembly: Meets January-March
House: 180 members, 2-year terms
2003 breakdown: 72R, 107D, 1I; 142 men, 38 women
Salary: $16,200
Phone: (404) 656-5082
Senate: 56 members, 2-year terms
2003 breakdown: 30R, 26D; 43 men, 13 women
Salary: $16,200
Phone: (404) 656-0028

STATE TERM LIMITS

Governor: 2 terms
Senate: No
House: No

URBAN STATISTICS

CITY	POPULATION
Atlanta	416,474
Augusta-Richmond County	199,775
Columbus	186,291
Savannah	131,510
Athens-Clarke County	101,489

REGISTERED VOTERS

Voters do not register by party.

POPULATION

2002 population (est.)	8,560,310
2000 population	8,186,453
1990 population	6,478,216
Percent change (1990-2000)	+26.4%
Rank among states (2002)	10
Median age	33.4
Born in state	57.8%
Foreign born	7.1%
Violent crime rate	505/100,000
Poverty level	13%
Federal workers	93,207
Military	96,952

REDISTRICTING

Georgia gained two House seats in reapportionment. The legislature drew a new, 13-district map, which the governor signed on Oct. 1, 2001.

MISCELLANEOUS

Web: www.state.ga.us
Capital: Atlanta

STATE ELECTION OFFICIAL
(404) 656-2871

DEMOCRATIC HEADQUARTERS
(404) 885-1998

REPUBLICAN HEADQUARTERS
(404) 257-5559

District Statistics

DIST.	2000 VOTE FOR PRESIDENT BUSH	GORE	NADER	WHITE	BLACK	ASIAN	HISP	MEDIAN INCOME	WHITE COLLAR	BLUE COLLAR	SERVICE INDUSTRY	OVER 64	UNDER 18	COLLEGE EDUCATION	RURAL	SQ. MILES
1	65%	35%	n/a	71%	23%	1%	4%	$36,158	53%	32%	15%	11%	28%	18%	42%	11,232
2	50.4	49.6	n/a	50	44	1	3	$29,354	50	33	17	12	28	14	41	9,724
3	52	48	n/a	56	40	1	3	$31,433	49	34	17	12	26	13	51	10,915
4	29	71	n/a	32	53	4	9	$49,307	67	20	13	8	25	36	0	251
5	27	73	n/a	34	56	2	6	$39,725	68	17	15	9	22	37	0	252
6	69	31	n/a	83	7	4	5	$75,611	80	11	9	7	28	51	2	435
7	72	28	n/a	82	7	4	5	$63,455	69	21	10	6	29	32	14	1,195
8	70	30	n/a	83	13	1	2	$52,406	61	28	12	9	27	23	42	3,512
9	68	32	n/a	81	14	1	3	$39,987	53	34	13	12	26	19	66	6,947
10	71	29	n/a	85	3	1	9	$42,037	51	38	11	10	26	16	48	3,741
11	51	49	n/a	62	28	1	7	$37,582	52	34	14	11	26	17	28	3,701
12	45	55	n/a	52	42	1	3	$31,108	54	29	18	11	25	19	26	5,224
13	41	59	n/a	42	41	5	10	$43,429	56	30	14	7	28	19	8	777
STATE	**55**	**43**	**1**	**63**	**28**	**2**	**5**	**$42,433**	**59**	**27**	**13**	**10**	**27**	**24**	**28**	**57,906**
U.S.	**47.9**	**48.4**	**3**	**69**	**12**	**4**	**13**	**$41,994**	**60**	**25**	**15**	**12**	**26**	**24**	**21**	**3,537,438**

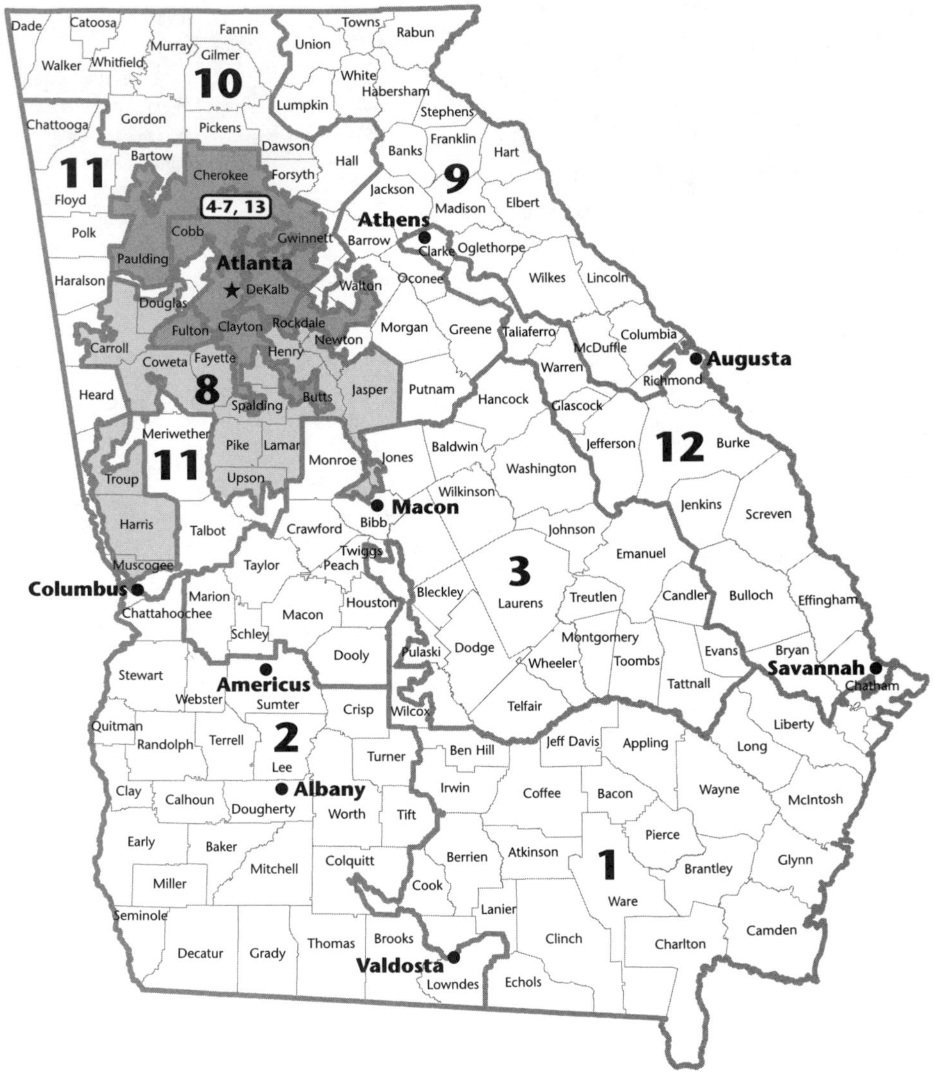
Dade
Catoosa
Walker
Whitfield
Murray
Fannin
Gilmer
Towns
Union
Rabun
10
White
Habersham
Lumpkin
Stephens
Chattooga
Gordon
Pickens
Franklin
Banks
Hart
Dawson
Hall
11
Bartow
Cherokee
Forsyth
9
Floyd
Jackson
Madison
Elbert
4-7, 13
Polk
Cobb
Athens
Gwinnett
Barrow
Clarke
Oglethorpe
Paulding
Atlanta
Wilkes
Lincoln
Haralson
DeKalb
Walton
Oconee
Douglas
Fulton
Clayton
Rockdale
Morgan
Greene
Taliaferro
Columbia
Carroll
Newton
McDuffie
Coweta
Fayette
Henry
Warren
Augusta
Richmond
8
Jasper
Putnam
Heard
Butts
Hancock
Glascock
Spalding
Meriwether
Jefferson
12
Burke
Pike
Lamar
Baldwin
11
Monroe
Jones
Troup
Washington
Upson
Wilkinson
Macon
Jenkins
Screven
Harris
Talbot
Crawford
Bibb
Johnson
Emanuel
Twiggs
Muscogee
Taylor
Peach
3
Columbus
Marion
Bleckley
Laurens
Treutlen
Candler
Bulloch
Effingham
Chattahoochee
Houston
Macon
Schley
Montgomery
Evans
Bryan
Dooly
Pulaski
Dodge
Wheeler
Toombs
Savannah
Stewart
Americus
Tattnall
Chatham
Webster
Sumter
Crisp
Wilcox
Telfair
Quitman
Liberty
Randolph
Terrell
2
Turner
Ben Hill
Jeff Davis
Appling
Long
Lee
Albany
Irwin
Coffee
Bacon
Wayne
Clay
Calhoun
McIntosh
Dougherty
Worth
Tift
Pierce
Early
Baker
Atkinson
1
Mitchell
Colquitt
Berrien
Brantley
Glynn
Miller
Cook
Ware
Seminole
Lanier
Camden
Decatur
Grady
Thomas
Brooks
Clinch
Charlton
Valdosta
Lowndes
Echols

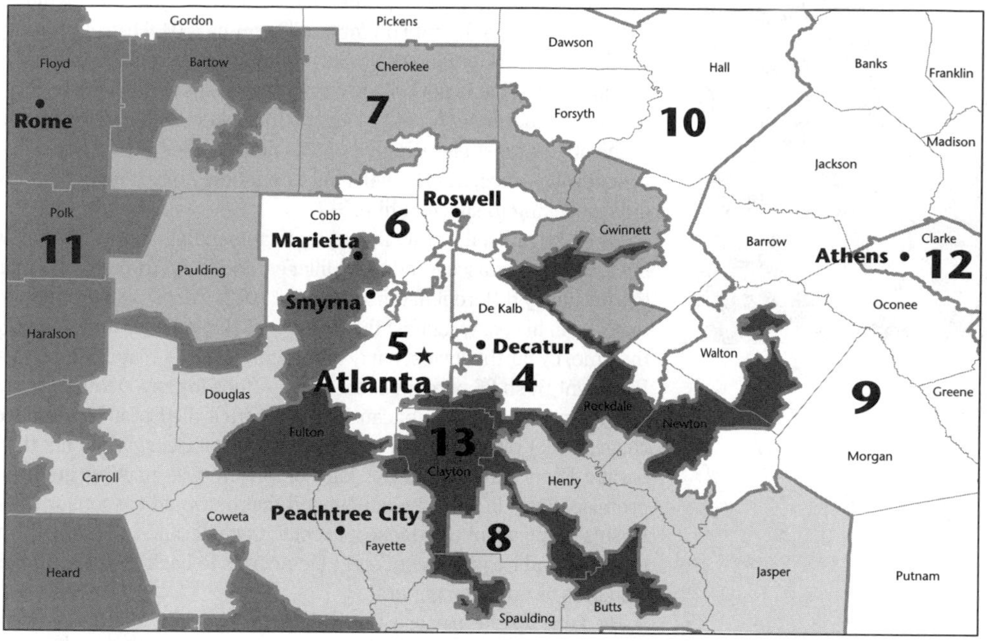
Gordon
Pickens
Dawson
Floyd
Bartow
Cherokee
Hall
Banks
Franklin
Rome
7
Forsyth
10
Madison
Jackson
Polk
Cobb
Roswell
6
Gwinnett
11
Marietta
Barrow
Clarke
Athens
12
Paulding
Smyrna
De Kalb
Oconee
Haralson
5
Decatur
Walton
Atlanta
4
9
Greene
Douglas
Rockdale
Fulton
Newton
13
Clayton
Morgan
Carroll
Henry
Coweta
Peachtree City
Fayette
8
Heard
Jasper
Putnam
Butts
Spaulding

Sen. Zell Miller (D)

CAPITOL OFFICE
224-3643
miller.senate.gov
257 Dirksen 20510-1006; fax 228-2090

COMMITTEES
Agriculture, Nutrition & Forestry
Banking, Housing & Urban Affairs
Veterans' Affairs

HOMETOWN
Young Harris

BORN
Feb. 24, 1932, Young Harris, Ga.

RELIGION
Methodist

FAMILY
Wife, Shirley Ann Miller; two children

EDUCATION
Young Harris College, A.A. 1951; U. of Georgia, A.B. 1957 (political science), M.A. 1958 (history)

MILITARY SERVICE
Marine Corps, 1953-56

CAREER
Professor; state government official

POLITICAL HIGHLIGHTS
Mayor of Young Harris, 1959-60; Ga. Senate, 1961-65; sought Democratic nomination for U.S. House, 1964, 1966; lieutenant governor, 1975-91; sought Democratic nomination for U.S. Senate, 1980; governor, 1991-99

ELECTION RESULTS

2000 SPECIAL		
Zell Miller (D)	1,413,224	58.1%
Mack Mattingly (R)	920,478	37.9%
Paul MacGregor (LIBERT)	25,942	1.1%

Elected 2000; 1st term

Appointed July 2000

Miller's conservatism has made him the least reliable Democratic vote for the party leadership since he arrived in the Senate in 2000, but his colleagues have tolerated his maverick ways in the closely divided chamber.

It thus came as a blow to the Democratic Party in 2003 when Miller announced he would not run for a full term in 2004. His retirement plans complicated the Democrats' already uphill effort to reclaim the majority of the chamber. That is not only because of a recent Republican tide in Georgia but also because the folksy and plain-spoken Miller, who remains one of the state's most enduringly popular figures after almost three decades in statewide office, says he will neither endorse nor campaign for any candidate seeking to succeed him.

When he arrived in July 2000, Democrats initially hoped for a new ally, but they quickly discovered that Miller's trademark cowboy boots marched to a decidedly different drumbeat. In the 107th Congress, he voted with the majority in his party against the majority of Republicans only 41 percent of the time, by far the lowest party unity score of any senator. And he backed President Bush 86 percent of the time — tops for any Democrat.

Appointed after Republican Paul Coverdell died of a cerebral hemorrhage, Miller pledged to represent the people of Georgia and not the Democratic Party. And it was not long before he was making good on that promise. Early in 2001, he announced that he would cosponsor President Bush's proposal for the deepest tax cut in two decades, the only Democrat to do so. And he was one of eight Democrats to back John Ashcroft's confirmation as attorney general.

He kept up the pattern through the end of the 107th Congress. He pushed through an amendment to an energy policy bill that was designed to hold down the required minimum gas mileage for pickup trucks, arguing that increasing fuel efficiency would raise the price. And he worked with Bush and the Republican leadership on the bill creating the Homeland Security Department, all the while chiding the Democratic leadership for holding up enactment over provisions important to organized labor.

"I didn't come up here to be a dissident or contrarian," Miller has said. "I came up here to vote how the people of Georgia would want me to vote. I didn't realize that would cause a problem."

His record repeatedly has fueled speculation that Miller would switch to the GOP — a possibility Miller just as repeatedly has denied. "What part of 'no' don't you understand?" he told a reporter asking the question in the fall of 2002.

Miller says he is used to alienating his fellow Democrats. As a state senator in the 1960s, he broke with many in his party when he supported keeping the University of Georgia open during integration.

But he also has a strong partisan side and a long record of assisting Democratic candidates in Georgia. His support helped Bill Clinton win Georgia's 1992 presidential primary, and he was rewarded with the role of keynote speaker at that year's Democratic convention. He also campaigned feverishly in 2002 for the state's two other most prominent Democrats, Sen. Max Cleland and Gov. Roy Barnes, although both were swept out of office in a statewide GOP landslide.

Miller often finds himself at the center of the most contentious policy debates in the Senate — largely because of the narrow partisan balance, which has made him a potential swing vote on most issues. Many senators seek him out as a cosponsor of their proposals. In the 107th, he was at the forefront in the debate over creating Medicare coverage of prescription drugs, writing the primary Senate Democratic plan with Florida's Bob Graham. Though the proposal did not clear a 60-vote procedural hurdle, it garnered 52 votes. Miller also voted for another, less generous compromise plan by Graham, but he opposed two GOP alternatives.

Before the Senate took up the issue, however, Miller pointedly chastised his fellow Democrats for wanting "an issue, not a result." He has complained frequently that there are "too many presidential candidates" on the Senate floor, and that they are more concerned with image than legislating.

Miller has carefully tended his state's parochial interests. From his seat on the Agriculture Committee, for example, he worked to make sure the 2002 farm bill protected Georgia peanut growers.

As governor, Miller had pushed the establishment of the HOPE college scholarship program, funded by state lottery revenue, for high school graduates with at least a "B" average. In the Senate, Miller introduced legislation to give tax breaks for teachers as a way to boost their pay. Miller also championed a bill to force the Education Department to cut in half the paperwork it requires of teachers.

Chiefly, Miller says he follows his instincts on legislative issues. That was readily apparent when Congress began writing a resolution allowing the president to go after the perpetrators of the Sept. 11, 2001, attacks. Asked by a reporter what Bush should do to the terrorists, Miller bluntly stated, "Bomb the hell out of them." Though a connection between the attacks and famed terrorist Osama bin Laden had not yet been established, Miller passionately advocated military action in Afghanistan, where bin Laden was believed to be hiding. He cited the ample evidence that bin Laden was the mastermind of other terrorist attacks against U.S. interests overseas.

His father, a college dean, died when Miller was 17 days old. After a couple of years of college, Miller joined the Marine Corps. He often cites lessons he learned in the military; his 1997 autobiography is titled, "Corp Values: Everything You Need to Know, I Learned in the Marines."

Miller entered politics in 1959 with a term as mayor of his small North Georgia hometown of Young Harris. In 1960, at age 28, he was elected to the state Senate. But his political rise was not without stumbles: He lost bids for Congress in 1964 and 1966. He was elected in 1974 as lieutenant governor — an office he would hold for 16 years — but lost a 1980 primary challenge to Democratic Sen. Herman Talmadge.

In 1990, Miller won election as governor. His approval rating at the end of his second term was 85 percent, but term limits barred him from seeking another four years. Miller and his wife, Shirley, moved back to the stone house his mother had built 60 years earlier, and he taught history and politics to students at three colleges while serving on seven corporate boards.

He also had more time for his hobbies, which include baseball and music. Miller's fondness for country music is well-known; his parties at the governor's mansion were raucous affairs featuring an array of country music singers.

When Coverdell, at age 51, died in the middle of his eighth year as a senator, Miller initially rebuffed Barnes' offer of an appointment to the Senate, saying he was enjoying his retirement. But Miller finally agreed when Barnes made it clear he did not have any other candidates in mind. A little more than three months after his appointment, Miller was elected to serve the four remaining years of Coverdell's term, winning by 20 percentage points over Republican Mack Mattingly, who had spent one term in the Senate that ended in 1987.

KEY VOTES

2002

Yes Pass farm bill reversing crop subsidy limits
Yes Postpone tougher automobile fuel efficiency standards
Yes Overhaul campaign finance law; ban "soft money" and restrict advocacy advertising
Yes Set federal election standards
Yes Support oil drilling in Arctic National Wildlife Refuge
Yes Revive fast-track procedures for trade agreements
Yes Create federal insurance coverage for catastrophic terrorist losses
Yes Tighten federal accounting and corporate governance regulation
Yes Advance bipartisan Medicare prescription drug plan
Yes Create independent Sept. 11 commission
No Back Democratic Homeland Security Department proposal
Yes Authorize war against Iraq

2001

Yes Confirm John Ashcroft as attorney general
Yes Nullify Clinton Labor Department ergonomics rule
Yes Cut taxes by $1.35 trillion through fiscal 2011
Yes Pass Democratic bill to bolster rights of patients in managed-care plans
Yes Permit a new round of military base closings
Yes Expand law enforcement power to investigate suspected terrorists

CQ VOTE STUDIES

	PARTY UNITY		PRESIDENTIAL SUPPORT	
	Support	Oppose	Support	Oppose
2002	40%	60%	92%	8%
2001	42%	58%	82%	18%
2000	25%	75%	100%	0%

INTEREST GROUPS

	AFL-CIO	ADA	CCUS	ACU
2002	58%	30%	79%	47%
2001	56%	35%	85%	60%
2000	33%	0%	100%	—

Sen. Saxby Chambliss (R)

CAPITOL OFFICE
224-3521
416 Russell 20510-1005; fax 224-0072

COMMITTEES
Agriculture, Nutrition & Forestry
Armed Services
(Personnel - chairman)
Judiciary
(Border Security, Immigration & Citizenship - chairman)
Rules & Administration
Select Intelligence
Joint Printing

HOMETOWN
Moultrie

BORN
Nov. 10, 1943, Warrenton, N.C.

RELIGION
Episcopalian

FAMILY
Wife, Julianne Chambliss; two children

EDUCATION
Louisiana Tech U., attended 1961-62; U. of Georgia, B.B.A. 1966 (business administration); U. of Tennessee, J.D. 1968

CAREER
Lawyer; hotel owner; firefighter

POLITICAL HIGHLIGHTS
Sought Republican nomination for U.S. House, 1992; U.S. House, 1995-2003

ELECTION RESULTS

2002 GENERAL		
Saxby Chambliss (R)	1,071,352	52.7%
Max Cleland (D)	932,422	45.9%
Claude Thomas (LIBERT)	27,830	1.4%
2002 PRIMARY		
Saxby Chambliss (R)	300,371	61.1%
Bob Irvin (R)	132,132	26.9%
Robert "Bob" Brown (R)	59,109	12.0%

PREVIOUS WINNING PERCENTAGES
2000 House Election (59%); 1998 House Election (62%); 1996 House Election (53%); 1994 House Election (63%)

Elected 2002; 1st term

Having won one of the most symbolically important Republican victories of 2002, Chambliss has positioned himself in the Senate to pick up where his work left off in the House: advocating generous spending on the military, prodding the government's spy agencies and defending federal help for Southern farmers.

To make his career continuity easier, Chambliss took assignments to three committees — Armed Services, Select Intelligence and Agriculture — that directly paralleled those he held at the end of his eight-year House career. He also was named to the Rules and Administration Committee, which spends most of its time serving the Senate's logistical needs, and the Judiciary Committee, which has broad latitude over legislation that might thwart terrorists operating inside the United States. But Chambliss said he was particularly interested in immersing himself in the committee's work advancing President Bush's nominees for the federal judiciary, one of the more polarizing items on the closely divided Senate's agenda in the runup to the 2004 election.

Chambliss came to Washington in 1995 after more than two decades of business and civic involvement in southern Georgia, where he was a small town attorney specializing in agriculture law, a motel owner in Moultrie and an activist in local economic development efforts. So, he has a well-practiced interest in putting federal dollars to work for parochial interests. He will be seeking to assure generous funding levels to, among other facilities, the headquarters of the Centers for Disease Control and Prevention in Atlanta and the Federal Law Enforcement Training Center in Brunswick.

First and foremost, Chambliss will be looking out for the needs of the 13 military installations in the state, which have blossomed since World War II, in part because there has been a nearly continuous presence of a Georgian on Senate Armed Services. Democrat Max Cleland, whom Chambliss defeated, spent his one term on the panel — and was insufficiently attentive to Georgia's military spending needs, in the view of candidate Chambliss. Cleland succeeded Sam Nunn, who chaired the panel for eight years ending in 1994. Nunn, in turn, held the seat of Richard B. Russell, the chairman for many years at the height of the Cold War in the 1950s and 1960s.

Chambliss, who was named chairman of the Personnel Subcommittee for the 108th Congress, will be seeking to protect Georgia facilities from the round of base closings scheduled for 2005. Chambliss is well-versed in the politics of base closings; as a civic activist, he helped preserve the mission of Robins Air Force Base during an earlier round, in 1993. As a House member, he tussled with House GOP leaders and President Clinton over an election season proposal to tinker with the 1995 base closings by keeping Texas and California maintenance bases functioning instead of closing them — and moving much of the work to Georgia.

Three days after the attacks of Sept. 11, 2001, Chambliss' nascent Senate campaign was given a public relations boost when he was picked by Speaker J. Dennis Hastert to chair a new Intelligence Subcommittee on Terrorism and Homeland Security. The credibility of the panel — which was assigned to recommend ways the CIA, FBI and National Security Agency could prevent future attacks — was cast into question that fall, when Chambliss quipped that one route to security would be if local sheriffs were to "arrest every Muslim that comes across the state line."

In 2002, the panel issued its recommendations, which Chambliss plans to promote in the Senate: emphasize the work of spies over technology, recruit more non-governmental informants overseas, hire more linguists for eavesdropping and do a better job of sharing intelligence among the agencies. To bolster his point that the current system is unfathomably diffuse, aides to Chambliss put together a Byzantine government flow chart that illustrated, to comic effect, the range of government offices that now have some hand in ensuring domestic safety.

As the new farm bill was being written by the 107th Congress, Chambliss also chaired the House Agriculture Subcommittee on General Farm Commodities and Risk Management. As in the 1996 farm bill rewrite, Chambliss showed he was not afraid to mix it up with leaders of his own party when the interests of Georgia's peanut, cotton and tobacco growers are concerned. (A Brown & Williamson tobacco plant employed more than 2,000 of his House constituents.) But Chambliss was unable to save the peanut subsidy system, despite his role as a negotiator on the bill's final form. Instead, he and likeminded lawmakers were only able to include language to provide farmers with coverage for their losses over the next five years.

An avid hunter of quail, duck and dove, Chambliss co-chaired the Congressional Sportsmen's Caucus in the 106th Congress and sponsored legislation to establish a federal policy to promote hunting. Among the items on his civic résumé is time in his 20s as a volunteer firefighter and as a longtime coach of YMCA basketball and Little League baseball. (He was a second-baseman on the University of Georgia baseball team.) The son of an Episcopal priest, Chambliss says his family's frequent moves when he was a boy helped him learn to make friends quickly, an asset in his political career.

Chambliss has said he would like to eliminate the current federal tax code, but he has remained noncommittal on the two leading alternatives: a flat-rate income tax and a national sales tax.

On the special House Intelligence panel, as on a task force in 2000 on options for reducing Medicare waste and fraud, Chambliss has shown an ability to work with Democrats. But in his votes, he has almost always followed the party line. He backed 98 percent of the legislation to carry out the GOP's "Contract With America" in his freshman year in the House, and he stood with most Republicans against most Democrats 98 percent of the time in his final House term.

But his loyalty was not sufficient to allow him to climb into the House hierarchy; having passed on entreaties that he run for the Senate against Democrat Zell Miller in 2000, he lost a four-way race that fall to become House Budget Committee chairman.

Chambliss lost his first bid for public office, too, when in 1992 he sought the Republican nomination against Democratic Rep. J. Roy Rowland. But when Rowland retired in 1994, Chambliss captured an easy pickup for the GOP in that landslide year by defeating Democrat Craig Mathis, a lawyer and the son of former Rep. Dawson Mathis. He was the first Republican to represent his rural "middle Georgia" district since Reconstruction.

His 2002 win was no less symbolic. Although he had been recruited by the White House, many doubted at first that Chambliss could defeat Cleland, a legislative moderate and one of the most prominent disabled veterans of the Vietnam War. But Chambliss went on the attack, alleging that Cleland had gone soft on national defense by opposing portions of President Bush's plans for creating the Department of Homeland Security. Chambliss endured criticism from those who said he unfairly impugned Cleland as unpatriotic, and his focused campaign — combined with a massive Republican voter turnout effort — propelled him to victory by an unexpectedly wide 7 percentage point margin.

KEY VOTES

House Service:

2002

- No Overhaul campaign finance law; ban "soft money" and restrict advocacy advertising
- Yes Back Bush's defense budget increase
- Yes Extend 1996 welfare law
- Yes Adopt Bush's discretionary spending limit
- Yes Pass GOP Medicare prescription drug plan
- No Create independent Sept. 11 commission
- No Extend union protections to Homeland Security Department employees
- Yes Revive fast-track procedures for trade agreements
- Yes Authorize war against Iraq
- No Advance bankruptcy overhaul opposed by abortion opponents

2001

- Yes Nullify Clinton Labor Department ergonomics rule
- Yes Cut taxes by $1.35 trillion through fiscal 2011
- No Maintain ban on oil drilling in Arctic National Wildlife Refuge
- Yes Approve Bush proposal to limit managed-care plan liability for coverage decisions
- No Divert money from crop subsidy payments to land conservation
- Yes Expand law enforcement power to investigate suspected terrorists

CQ VOTE STUDIES

House Service:

	PARTY UNITY		PRESIDENTIAL SUPPORT	
	Support	Oppose	Support	Oppose
2002	98%	2%	90%	10%
2001	98%	2%	93%	7%
2000	95%	5%	24%	76%
1999	94%	6%	26%	74%
1998	95%	5%	22%	78%
1997	96%	4%	26%	74%
1996	96%	4%	35%	65%
1995	98%	2%	17%	83%

INTEREST GROUPS

House Service:

	AFL-CIO	ADA	CCUS	ACU
2002	0%	0%	90%	100%
2001	17%	0%	95%	100%
2000	0%	0%	90%	91%
1999	33%	10%	80%	80%
1998	0%	0%	94%	96%
1997	0%	5%	88%	88%
1996	0%	0%	100%	100%
1995	0%	0%	100%	96%

Rep. Jack Kingston (R)

CAPITOL OFFICE
225-5831
jack.kingston@mail.house.gov
www.house.gov/kingston
2242 Rayburn 20515-1001; fax 226-2269

COMMITTEES
Appropriations
(Legislative Branch - chairman)
Joint Library

HOMETOWN
Savannah

BORN
April 24, 1955, Bryan, Texas

RELIGION
Episcopalian

FAMILY
Wife, Libby Kingston; four children

EDUCATION
U. of Georgia, B.A. 1978 (economics)

CAREER
Insurance broker

POLITICAL HIGHLIGHTS
Ga. House, 1984-92

ELECTION RESULTS

2002 GENERAL		
Jack Kingston (R)	103,661	72.1%
Don Smart (D)	40,026	27.9%
2002 PRIMARY		
Jack Kingston (R)		unopposed
2000 GENERAL		
Jack Kingston (R)	131,684	69.1%
Joyce Marie Griggs (D)	58,776	30.9%

PREVIOUS WINNING PERCENTAGES
1998 (100%); 1996 (68%); 1994 (77%); 1992 (58%)

Elected 1992; 6th term

Kingston was one of the biggest winners in the House Republican leadership overhaul at the start of the 108th Congress — assuming a pair of posts from which to pursue his dual goals of spreading the party message nationwide and bringing federal dollars home.

He won easy election as vice chairman of the Republican Conference, a party organization that seeks to enhance the GOP's public image. And his seniority on the Appropriations Committee enabled him to become a "cardinal," one of the 13 chairmen of the appropriations subcommittees who draft annual spending bills. Kingston took the gavel of the panel that writes the budget for Congress and its affiliated agencies.

Informal and easygoing, Kingston has a quick sense of humor that he uses to zing liberal Democratic proposals. His job in the Republican Conference is a logical step from his previous post as chairman of the House GOP's "Theme Team," a group of lawmakers responsible for spreading the party's message, mostly in speeches on the floor before and after the day's legislative business. He had been the group's chairman since 1997.

As head of the Theme Team, he told his colleagues to keep their message short and simple. "It's not lofty or esoteric, it's understandable," he said of their rhetorical goal. A challenge, he said, is to overcome the notion that the GOP does not understand or care about the impact of its policies on those with modest or small incomes. "One of my goals is to try to get Republicans to be a little more warm and fuzzy," he told the Atlanta Journal-Constitution.

Kingston's voting record reflects his conservative views across a range of social and economic issues. He is seen frequently on the floor attacking Democratic stands on topics ranging from federal spending to the 2002 federal appeals court ruling that the "one nation, under God" phrase in the pledge of allegiance is unconstitutional. He seldom strays from his party's position. In the 107th Congress, for example, he backed President Bush 89 percent of the time and sided with the GOP on 98 percent of the votes that pitted one party against the other.

Kingston's personality and communications skills have brought him a steady stream of offers to appear on television. He was a guest several times, for instance, on "Politically Incorrect," a late-night talk show that aired on ABC. The show's liberal host, Bill Maher, said he appreciated Kingston's ability to set forth his conservative views as well as his one-liners.

As the only Georgia Republican on Appropriations, where he has served since his second term began in 1995, he works to secure funds for statewide needs, such as Atlanta mass transit projects. Kingston also caters to his district by seeking funding for government programs that support agriculture and defense, two pillars of the South Georgia economy.

On the Agriculture Subcommittee, Kingston has been especially protective of the state's peanut and cotton farmers. This position has sometimes put him at odds with those Republicans who view federal crop subsidy programs as antithetical to free enterprise. "We need to keep in mind that the people who are being subsidized are not necessarily the farmers," Kingston responds. "They are the American consumers."

He has also sought federal funds to deepen the harbors at Savannah and Brunswick and money for a visitors center and repair work on structures on Cumberland Island, site of a historic slave settlement. That effort, along with federal funds he obtained for research on a disease that endangers Vidalia onions, earned him a rebuke in the 107th from Citizens Against Government Waste. He did not take the criticism lightly, as he has made a concerted effort to cultivate an image as a frugal guardian of the federal purse. An Associated Press survey in 2002 found that Kingston's district ranked first in the state and 22nd nationally in federal spending.

In his freshman term, when Democrats complained that Republican proposals would cut spending in necessary programs, Kingston disagreed. "When we say there is going to be a cut, what we mean is there is going to be a decrease in the projected increase, not a real cut the way you and I would think of a cut in our household" budgeting, he said.

Kingston cast a high-profile dissenting vote in 1997 on the spending component of a balanced-budget deal between the Clinton administration and congressional Republicans, arguing that it included too much money for new, liberal-backed programs. He was among just 32 House Republicans to buck the party line. In addition to supporting his party's tax cut plans, he backed a controversial measure that would have scrapped income taxes altogether.

Kingston cuts his own personal cost of living by using his Capitol Hill office as a bedroom when he is in Washington. He enjoys a good laugh. He has been known to participate in such projects as infiltrating a colleague's office late one night to plaster pictures of an endangered species of mouse all over the place.

Born in Texas, where his father was an art professor, Kingston and his family spent a few months in Ethiopia before they settled in Georgia while he was still in diapers. Kingston claims Georgia as his home state, telling a reporter once, "If you're potty-trained in a state, I think that gives you native status."

After earning an undergraduate degree in economics, Kingston moved to Savannah to sell insurance. He won his first election in 1984 to the state House, where he served eight years. When Democrat Lindsay Thomas retired in 1992, Kingston was well-positioned to woo voters into the Republican column in a House race; many of them already had been voting Republican for president. Kingston drew minor primary opposition, then dispatched Democrat Barbara Christmas, a school principal. His 58 percent share of the vote that year remains his lowest election percentage.

Redistricting after the 2000 census put both Kingston and his 8th District GOP colleague Saxby Chambliss in the 1st District, but Chambliss decided to run for the Senate instead. The new map gave the 1st an even more Republican flavor, and Kingston won by 44 percentage points. As the 108th began, Kingston was among several Republicans being mentioned as likely candidates for the Senate in 2004, when Democrat Zell Miller is retiring.

KEY VOTES

2002

- No Overhaul campaign finance law; ban "soft money" and restrict advocacy advertising
- Yes Back Bush's defense budget increase
- Yes Extend 1996 welfare law
- Yes Adopt Bush's discretionary spending limit
- Yes Pass GOP Medicare prescription drug plan
- No Create independent Sept. 11 commission
- No Extend union protections to Homeland Security Department employees
- Yes Revive fast-track procedures for trade agreements
- Yes Authorize war against Iraq
- Yes Advance bankruptcy overhaul opposed by abortion opponents

2001

- Yes Nullify Clinton Labor Department ergonomics rule
- Yes Cut taxes by $1.35 trillion through fiscal 2011
- No Maintain ban on oil drilling in Arctic National Wildlife Refuge
- Yes Approve Bush proposal to limit managed-care plan liability for coverage decisions
- No Divert money from crop subsidy payments to land conservation
- Yes Expand law enforcement power to investigate suspected terrorists

CQ VOTE STUDIES

	PARTY UNITY		PRESIDENTIAL SUPPORT	
	Support	Oppose	Support	Oppose
2002	98%	2%	85%	15%
2001	98%	2%	93%	7%
2000	95%	5%	17%	83%
1999	93%	7%	14%	86%
1998	94%	6%	20%	80%

INTEREST GROUPS

	AFL-CIO	ADA	CCUS	ACU
2002	0%	0%	85%	96%
2001	8%	5%	95%	100%
2000	10%	5%	80%	100%
1999	22%	0%	75%	95%
1998	0%	0%	82%	100%

GEORGIA 1

Southeast – Savannah suburbs, part of Valdosta

The 1st takes in a swath of southeast Georgia and its entire coastline, stretching from South Carolina to Florida. In the redistricting plan enacted in 2001, the 1st was altered to become a Republican-leaning district with a substantial military population. Like much of the rest of Georgia, the district is ancestrally Democratic but trends Republican in federal races. George W. Bush received 65 percent of the vote here in 2000.

The 1st has no population center; redistricting removed the urban, Democratic areas of Savannah that were the nucleus of the old 1st. The district now has large, mostly rural chunks, reaching into the Republican suburbs of Savannah and parts of Valdosta. It also travels up Interstate 75, taking in parts of Warner Robins, the Republican areas outside of Macon and Robins Air Force Base. The district includes five of the state's 12 major military bases.

Despite a drought, storms and hurricanes that severely hurt the area's farmers in 1998, peanuts, onions, cotton, tobacco and other crops help sustain the economy, as do timber, defense, shrimping and tourism. The district's ports and coastline make trade and coastal conservation dominant issues.

Georgia's coast is becoming a popular destination for retirees and is seeing an influx of new residents settling between Hilton Head, S.C., and Florida. This growing part of the population adds to the Republican lean of the district, outnumbering older, agricultural Democrats.

MAJOR INDUSTRY

Agriculture, military, manufacturing

MILITARY BASES

Fort Stewart (Army), 15,020 military, 1,844 civilian (2000) (shared with the 3rd and the 12th); Robins Air Force Base, 5,655 military, 13,460 civilian (2001); Kings Bay Naval Submarine Base, 5,334 military, 2,801 civilian; Hunter Army Airfield, 4,201 military, 78 civilian (1999); Moody Air Force Base, 2,800 military, 600 civilian

CITIES

Hinesville, 30,392; Brunswick, 15,600; Valdosta (pt.), 15,442

NOTABLE

The Okefenokee Swamp, which covers 436,000 acres, is home to an estimated 35,000 alligators and 234 species of birds.

Rep. Sanford D. Bishop Jr. (D)

CAPITOL OFFICE
225-3631
bishop.email@mail.house.gov
www.house.gov/bishop
2429 Rayburn 20515-1002; fax 225-2203

COMMITTEES
Appropriations

HOMETOWN
Albany

BORN
Feb. 4, 1947, Mobile, Ala.

RELIGION
Baptist

FAMILY
Wife, Vivian Creighton Bishop; one stepchild

EDUCATION
Morehouse College, B.A. 1968 (political science); Emory U., J.D. 1971

MILITARY SERVICE
Army, 1971

CAREER
Lawyer

POLITICAL HIGHLIGHTS
Ga. House, 1977-91; Ga. Senate, 1991-93

ELECTION RESULTS

2002 GENERAL		
Sanford D. Bishop Jr. (D)	unopposed	
2002 PRIMARY		
Sanford D. Bishop Jr. (D)	unopposed	
2000 GENERAL		
Sanford D. Bishop Jr. (D)	96,430	53.5%
Dylan Glenn (R)	83,870	46.5%

PREVIOUS WINNING PERCENTAGES
1998 (57%); 1996 (54%); 1994 (66%); 1992 (64%)

Elected 1992; 6th term

Bishop's middle-of-the-road political philosophy is evident across a wide spectrum of issues, and his voting record shows him to be the most conservative black member of Congress. He breaks Democratic ranks more often than any other member of the Congressional Black Caucus, and he has won commendations from groups such as the National Federation of Independent Business and the American Legion for his legislative stands.

He fits in comfortably with the "Blue Dog" coalition of conservative House Democrats, where he and Harold E. Ford Jr. of Tennessee are the only black members. In the 107th Congress, he was one of only 13 Democrats who backed the initial House version of President Bush's tax cut bill and one of just 36 Democrats who voted to lift a prohibition on drilling in the Arctic National Wildlife Refuge.

Bishop has cosponsored a proposed constitutional amendment to guarantee freedom of religious expression in public places, including prayer in schools. He also supports legislation to prohibit desecration of the flag.

With his independent voting record, Bishop has resisted racial pigeonholing throughout his congressional career. Attention to his constituents' agriculture and military interests has enabled him to build a base of support beyond the black community. And on certain core Democratic issues, Bishop votes with his party. He supports abortion rights and has taken labor's side in disputes with the business-oriented Republican majority.

As the 108th Congress convened, Bishop voted for Democrat Nancy Pelosi for Speaker, despite pressure that he and several other Blue Dogs got from some conservative groups to withhold support — and despite his unhappiness that Pelosi had not stepped down from her top Democratic post on the Intelligence Committee when she became whip in 2002. Bishop ranked just below her on that panel's Democratic roster. (Pelosi won the post of minority leader for the 108th.)

Bishop and another Blue Dog, Marion Berry of Arkansas, were named to the Appropriations Committee in 2003 as part of an effort by Pelosi to award choice committee assignments to all factions of the party. To take the seat, Bishop had to leave Intelligence, where he had served since 1997, and Agriculture.

Building on his work on the Intelligence panel, Bishop was named in late 2001 to the House Democrats' Homeland Security Task Force. He chaired a subcommittee that developed recommendations for protecting the country's infrastructure — including refineries, power plants, government buildings and computer networks — from terrorist attacks.

Bishop has always supported a healthy defense budget and looked out for the interests of the 2nd District's Fort Benning, the Army's huge infantry training base, as well as Moody Air Force Base, which was in the 2nd before redistricting put it just across the 1st District line.

In 1999, Bishop was one of only two Democrats to vote for the foreign operations appropriations bill. He said he backed the bill because it contained funding for what was then known as the School of the Americas, located at Fort Benning. The school has often been the target of attacks from other lawmakers, who argue that it has trained South and Central American military officers who have been implicated in allegations of human rights abuses. Bishop says the school does not teach or condone such actions. The school was reorganized and renamed the Defense Institute for Hemispheric Security Cooperation in the 106th Congress.

On Agriculture, Bishop played a crucial role in protecting peanut farmers when their subsidy program was overhauled during debate on the 2002 farm bill. More peanuts are grown in the 2nd District than in any other congressional district — considerably more than a quarter of the nation's output. The farm bill did away with the peanut quota, which was becoming less valuable in the face of imports from Mexico under the North American Free Trade Agreement. In addition to a cash payment as a buy-out of the peanut quota, Bishop was able to include a new market support program and requirements that foreign peanuts be labeled. He also supported more funding to help small and disadvantaged farmers.

Bishop grew up in Mobile, Ala., where his parents were both educators. His father was the president of a community college that is now named for him — Bishop State Community College — and his mother was the college librarian. The younger Bishop made a name for himself as a civil rights lawyer in Columbus, Ga., before winning election to the state legislature in 1976, where he served for 16 years.

Bishop was on the Reapportionment Committee that, with stern urgings from the Justice Department, in 1992 drew new congressional district maps that made the 2nd District the third black-majority district in the state. Columbus business leaders persuaded Bishop to seek the new seat and helped finance his challenge to white Democratic Rep. Charles Hatcher, who had been identified as one of the chief abusers of the House's private bank, with 819 overdrafts. In a primary runoff against Hatcher, Bishop won the nomination with 53 percent of the vote; in November, he coasted past Republican physician Jim Dudley.

In 1995, a federal court ruled the boundaries of the 2nd to be an unconstitutional "racial gerrymander" and handed down a new map, altering the racial composition of his constituency and putting Columbus in the 3rd District. The black share of the population in the redrawn 2nd dropped from 51 percent to 39 percent. Bishop moved about 90 miles southeast to Albany, in the center of the 2nd.

He weathered some tough re-election fights in 1996, 1998 and 2000. In his closest battle, in 2000, Bishop narrowly defeated former Senate aide Dylan Glenn, who is also black.

But redistricting following the 2000 census was good to Bishop, putting part of Muscogee County, his longtime home, back in the 2nd District and increasing the black share of the population to 44 percent. The resulting Democratic district scared off all potential challengers, and Bishop was unopposed in both the 2002 primary and general election.

KEY VOTES

2002

- Yes Overhaul campaign finance law; ban "soft money" and restrict advocacy advertising
- Yes Back Bush's defense budget increase
- No Extend 1996 welfare law
- No Adopt Bush's discretionary spending limit
- No Pass GOP Medicare prescription drug plan
- Yes Create independent Sept. 11 commission
- Yes Extend union protections to Homeland Security Department employees
- No Revive fast-track procedures for trade agreements
- Yes Authorize war against Iraq
- No Advance bankruptcy overhaul opposed by abortion opponents

2001

- No Nullify Clinton Labor Department ergonomics rule
- ? Cut taxes by $1.35 trillion through fiscal 2011
- No Maintain ban on oil drilling in Arctic National Wildlife Refuge
- No Approve Bush proposal to limit managed-care plan liability for coverage decisions
- No Divert money from crop subsidy payments to land conservation
- Yes Expand law enforcement power to investigate suspected terrorists

CQ VOTE STUDIES

	PARTY UNITY		PRESIDENTIAL SUPPORT	
	Support	Oppose	Support	Oppose
2002	80%	20%	52%	48%
2001	71%	29%	50%	50%
2000	65%	35%	55%	45%
1999	73%	27%	64%	36%
1998	71%	29%	58%	42%

INTEREST GROUPS

	AFL-CIO	ADA	CCUS	ACU
2002	78%	75%	55%	40%
2001	100%	70%	65%	39%
2000	60%	50%	78%	43%
1999	89%	65%	56%	28%
1998	70%	70%	61%	44%

GEORGIA 2

Southwest – Albany, part of Columbus and Valdosta

Georgia's 2nd takes in the state's entire southwest corner and extends south from Columbus to the Florida border. It contains parts of Columbus and Valdosta and all of Albany, Bainbridge and Thomasville.

Although it was once a black-majority district, redistricting in 1995 reduced its black population, changing it from a strongly Democratic area to one in which Republicans were competitive. Redistricting changes enacted in 2001 made the 2nd significantly more Democratic again, adding predominantly black areas of Columbus to the district. Forty-four percent of the voting age population is black.

Democrats hold most local offices and are strong in the northwestern counties that have higher black populations. Pockets of GOP strength exist in Lee County, in the central part of the 2nd, as well as in Thomasville and other southern parts of the district. Dougherty County, with Albany as the county seat, is the district's most populous and is reliably Democratic. Nonetheless, George W. Bush narrowly won the district in 2000, with 50.4 percent of the vote.

The 2nd's largely rural and heavily agricultural regions have struggled economically for decades and are heavily dependent on farm loan assistance. Farming and livestock are key to the economy, and the district grows more peanuts than any other place in the United States.

MAJOR INDUSTRY

Agriculture, military, manufacturing, health care

MILITARY BASES

Fort Benning (Army), 33,521 military, 7,582 civilian (shared with the 11th) (2002); Marine Corp Logistics Base, 601 military, 2,442 civilian (2001)

CITIES

Columbus (pt.), 83,973; Albany, 76,939; Valdosta (pt.), 28,282

NOTABLE

Jackie Robinson, who broke baseball's color barrier in 1947, was born in Cairo; Plains is the hometown of former President Jimmy Carter.

Rep. Jim Marshall (D)

CAPITOL OFFICE
225-6531
jim.marshall@mail.house.gov
www.house.gov/marshall
502 Cannon 20515-1003; fax 225-3013

COMMITTEES
Agriculture
Armed Services
Small Business

HOMETOWN
Macon

BORN
March 31, 1948, Ithaca, N.Y.

RELIGION
Roman Catholic

FAMILY
Wife, Camille Marshall; two children

EDUCATION
Princeton U., A.B. 1972 (politics); Boston U., J.D. 1977

MILITARY SERVICE
Army, 1968-70

CAREER
Lawyer; law professor; logging business owner

POLITICAL HIGHLIGHTS
Mayor of Macon, 1995-99; Democratic nominee for U.S. House, 2000

ELECTION RESULTS

2002 GENERAL		
Jim Marshall (D)	75,394	50.5%
Calder Clay (R)	73,866	49.5%
2002 PRIMARY		
Jim Marshall (D)	26,614	53.6%
Chuck Byrd (D)	16,542	33.3%
Joe N. Lester (D)	5,663	11.4%
Sig Dayan (D)	851	1.7%

Elected 2002; 1st term

Marshall, a former Army Ranger and Vietnam veteran, says he will focus his attentions on military and veterans issues as a freshman, and his seat on the Armed Services panel — a post that Democratic leaders promised him before the election — enables him to do that.

Citing his own experience with air power in infantry combat, Marshall contends that ensuring that Warner Robins Air Logistics Center retains its maintenance capability is key to any national defense strategy. Part of the logistics center is in the 3rd District.

Marshall says he will make privacy rights and personal freedom a centerpiece of his tenure, including the protection of the right to bear arms. He adds that his military upbringing and background lead him to support amending the Constitution to prohibit desecration of the U.S. flag. He maintains that such an amendment would not significantly limit the freedom to engage in political speech or protest and that the amendment would be a deserved tribute to those who serve the country in the armed forces.

A former mayor of Macon, Marshall prevailed in his second consecutive try for Congress. When he ran in 2000 for the 8th District seat held by Republican Saxby Chambliss, Marshall was touted early on as a strong Democratic challenger because of his military record, conservative views and urban base in Macon. But Chambliss proved too popular and won by 18 percentage points.

Marshall, though, got two breaks that set the stage for his win in 2002. Chambliss decided on the Senate bid that resulted in his upset of Democratic incumbent Max Cleland, and Macon was included in the redrawn 3rd District, which had a stronger Democratic lean than the district in which Marshall previously ran.

Despite a spirited and well-funded challenge by Republican Calder Clay, a Bibb County commissioner, Marshall won by a 1,528-vote margin, the third-closest House race in 2002.

GEORGIA 3

Middle Georgia – Macon

Created to encompass the rural heart of Georgia, the 3rd takes in mostly agricultural counties in the center of the state. Farm issues are paramount here, increasingly so since drought has put the area's economy in peril.

The district stretches from Marion County in the west to Hancock County in the north, while Telfair and Tattnall counties flank its southern border. Peaches, pecans and cotton are primary crops in the center of the district. Peanuts dominate the southern area, and onions and tobacco are prevalent in the southeast. Forestry also is a major industry. Aerospace jobs and textile manufacturing have helped sustain the economy, though some textile plants have closed in recent years.

The 3rd was drawn in redistricting after the 2000 census to elect a Democrat. But like much of the South, voters will support Republicans, and the 3rd can be politically competitive — George W. Bush received 52 percent of the vote here in the 2000 presidential election. Blacks make up 37 percent of the voting age population.

The 3rd is almost split in two by a gash up its center, in which the 1st District takes in Warner Robins Air Force Base and Republican suburbs south of Macon. The 8th also descends into the area, taking in Republican suburbs north of Macon. The 3rd includes the rest of Macon, including the heavily Democratic city center.

MAJOR INDUSTRY
Agriculture, distribution, aerospace

MILITARY BASES
Fort Stewart (Army), 15,020 military, 1,844 civilian (2000) (shared with the 1st and 12th)

CITIES
Macon (pt.), 89,507; Warner Robins (pt.), 38,969; Milledgeville, 18,757

NOTABLE
Milledgeville served as the state capital from 1803 until 1868, when the capital was moved to Atlanta during Reconstruction; Vidalia is known for its sweet onions; Claxton is known for its fruitcake.

Rep. Denise L. Majette (D)

CAPITOL OFFICE
225-1605
www.house.gov/majette
1517 Longworth 20515-1004; fax 226-0691

COMMITTEES
Budget
Education & Workforce
Small Business

HOMETOWN
Stone Mountain

BORN
May 18, 1955, Brooklyn, N.Y.

RELIGION
African Methodist Episcopal

FAMILY
Husband, Rogers J. Mitchell Jr.; two children

EDUCATION
Yale U., B.A. 1976 (history); Duke U., J.D. 1979

CAREER
Lawyer

POLITICAL HIGHLIGHTS
Ga. state court judge, 1993-2002

ELECTION RESULTS

2002 GENERAL		
Denise L. Majette (D)	118,045	77.0%
Cynthia Van Auken (R)	35,202	23.0%
2002 PRIMARY		
Denise L. Majette (D)	68,612	58.3%
Cynthia A. McKinney (D)	49,058	41.7%

Elected 2002; 1st term

Majette scored a distinctive upset with her 2002 primary win over five-term Democratic Rep. Cynthia A. McKinney in Georgia's 4th District.

Majette (muh-JET) says she actually does not differ much from her predecessor. "I am pro-choice, anti-death penalty, for protecting rights of workers and making sure that everyone has access on a level playing field." Yet Majette does diverge from McKinney in tone and on some issues affecting African-Americans: She doesn't favor reparations for slavery and has been ambiguous on affirmative action.

One sign of their different approaches came early in Majette's tenure when she joined the House centrists known as the New Democrat Coalition.

Appointed to the Education and the Workforce panel, she advocates federal government incentives for people to teach in certain areas of the nation and supports forgiving student loans for college graduates who take teaching jobs.

Majette also will work to protect a vital contributor to homeland security that is located in the 4th District: the federal Centers for Disease Control and Prevention. She says her experience as a judge will help her in Congress. "It's about listening to different points of view and recognizing that sometimes you have to chose your battles wisely," she says.

McKinney's fiercely liberal rhetoric and pro-Palestinian stance made her an incendiary figure. Majette capitalized on that notoriety: She took in almost $400,000 in donations at the end of the primary race, much of it from Jewish donors.

While McKinney scored points during debates with her command of specific issues, Majette's soft-spoken and measured manner won over voters. She parried McKinney's efforts to persuade the 4th District's Democratic constituency that Republican enemies had put the challenger up to run. She also benefited from the GOP crossover vote. Majette swept to an easy primary victory with 58 percent, then defeated little-known GOP nominee Cynthia Van Auken, a homemaker, by more than a 3-to-1 ratio.

GEORGIA 4

Atlanta suburbs — DeKalb County

Already decidedly Democratic, the DeKalb County-based 4th became more so in redistricting after the 2000 census. It is now Georgia's second black-majority district, though the majority is a slight one — African-Americans make up 50.2 percent of the voting age population.

DeKalb County, which sits just east of Atlanta, accounts for almost 97 percent of the district's population and is the most Democratic county in the state. Democratic candidates receive a warm reception in the county's racially diverse central and western portions, while Republicans run well in northern DeKalb's more white, affluent areas.

Like the rest of Atlanta, south DeKalb — which has one of the nation's most affluent concentrations of African-Americans — is seeing rapid growth. This growth has changed the tenor of the 4th, bringing more moderate, business-oriented African-Americans into the district and lessening the influence of more-liberal voices, such as that of five-term Rep. Cynthia A. McKinney, who was defeated in the 2002 primary.

Jobs in the 4th center around health care and higher education. Emory University, home to a university hospital, is a major employer. The Centers for Disease Control and Prevention also employs a sizable number of the area's health care workers. Decatur was a 19th century commercial hub until it lost out as a railroad center to Atlanta, but it still has many government-related jobs.

MAJOR INDUSTRY
Retail, health care, government

CITIES
North Atlanta, 38,579; Redan, 33,841; Dunwoody, 32,808; Candler-McAfee, 28,294

NOTABLE
Stone Mountain Park features a huge granite outcropping into which a sculpture of Robert E. Lee and other Confederate heroes is carved.

Rep. John Lewis (D)

CAPITOL OFFICE
225-3801
www.house.gov/johnlewis
343 Cannon 20515-1005; fax 225-0351

COMMITTEES
Budget
Ways & Means

HOMETOWN
Atlanta

BORN
Feb. 21, 1940, Troy, Ala.

RELIGION
Baptist

FAMILY
Wife, Lillian Lewis; one child

EDUCATION
American Baptist Theological Seminary, B.A. 1961 (theology); Fisk U., B.A. 1963 (religion & philosophy)

CAREER
Civil rights activist

POLITICAL HIGHLIGHTS
Sought Democratic nomination for U.S. House (special election), 1977; Atlanta City Council, 1982-86

ELECTION RESULTS

2002 GENERAL		
John Lewis (D)		unopposed
2002 PRIMARY		
John Lewis (D)		unopposed
2000 GENERAL		
John Lewis (D)	137,333	77.2%
Hank Schwab (R)	40,606	22.8%

PREVIOUS WINNING PERCENTAGES
1998 (79%); 1996 (100%); 1994 (69%); 1992 (72%); 1990 (76%); 1988 (78%); 1986 (75%)

Elected 1986; 9th term

In 2002 Lewis received the NAACP Spingarn Medal — the highest honor the organization can bestow — for his lifetime of contributions to civil rights. Typically, Lewis said that he was accepting it not just for himself, "but for the countless individuals who are not here," who were killed or jailed during the nation's civil rights struggle.

For the dean of the Georgia congressional delegation, who has never been comfortable in the spotlight, it was another case of deflecting the attention that comes his way as one of the icons of the civil rights movement. But for many of his colleagues in the House, the honor was long overdue.

"I've never been the kind of person who naturally attracts the limelight," Lewis wrote in his autobiography, "Walking With the Wind." "I'm not a handsome guy. I'm not flamboyant. I'm not what you would call elegant. . . . I simply have never been the kind of guy who draws attention."

Somehow, the shy youth who attended segregated schools learned to be a leader. He was one of the Freedom Riders who took dangerous, integrated bus rides through the Deep South in 1961. He became chairman of the Student Nonviolent Coordinating Committee in 1963 and spoke at the March on Washington. In fact, his original speech was so fiery that other civil rights leaders made him tone it down. The most famous speaker that day, the Rev. Martin Luther King Jr., told him, "John, that doesn't sound like you."

By March 1965, he had found enough steel to stand at the front of hundreds of marchers on the Edmund Pettus Bridge in Selma, Ala., facing down charging state troopers without moving a muscle. The images from the "Bloody Sunday" march that day, in which Lewis suffered a severe concussion from the crack of a trooper's billy club, helped jolt Congress into passing the Voting Rights Act.

Anyone who hears the thundering timbre of his preacher's voice on the House floor — with a cadence that sounds eerily like King's — knows that Lewis has found the confidence he needed to make it in politics.

Whether Lewis likes it or not, he is a national figure. Activist groups and Democratic Party leaders call on him for everything from comments at ribbon-cutting ceremonies at housing projects to high stakes fundraising. Even Trent Lott, hoping to keep his job as Senate Republican leader, sought forgiveness from Lewis in late 2002 after his off-the-cuff remarks praising Sen. Strom Thurmond's 1948 pro-segregation presidential campaign ignited a firestorm. Lewis indicated he might be willing to give Lott a second chance, but the uproar was too great and Lott had to step down.

Lewis still considers himself a shy person. But he says that as a young man at the heart of the civil rights movement, he was "forced to grow up" as he and others took responsibility for the groups of people who sat in at lunch counters and for the Freedom Riders. These days, Lewis says, the act of campaigning in Atlanta draws him out, and the political battles in Congress embolden him by spurring him to "get in the way" — a civil rights expression for physically placing oneself in the way of injustice and forcing the perpetrators to change. "I think the movement liberated me," Lewis says, "and I think being in Congress liberated me more."

A liberal stalwart in the House, Lewis has risen to the ranks of the Democratic leadership, serving as the senior chief deputy whip. On the Ways and Means panel, Lewis sounds off about health care for poor people and the uninsured, about Republican tax policy and about the consequences of liberalized trade for labor rights in the Third World. He serves on Democratic task forces on health care, education and Social Security, helping to solidify the party's positions on those bread-and-butter social issues.

Lewis is not the kind of legislator who puts out 15-point policy initiatives. Instead, he works as the motivator, rallying other lawmakers to recognize a problem and work up the will to solve it. He generally does not spend a lot of time writing legislation; rather, he seeks to be a voice of conscience, using his office as a bully pulpit to speak for racial reconciliation and healing.

There have been some specific projects on Lewis' plate, however. In the 106th Congress, for example, he cosponsored legislation to reduce racial disparities in health care, and in the 107th, he won enactment of his bill that will lead to the establishment of a National Museum of African American History and Culture on the Mall in Washington.

As Congress approved sweeping new powers for law enforcement in the aftermath of the Sept. 11, 2001, terrorist attacks, Lewis voted "no," worrying that the new domestic surveillance powers could mark a return to the days when the government spied on him and other civil rights leaders.

Since 1997, Lewis and GOP Rep. Amo Houghton have co-chaired the Faith and Politics Institute, an interfaith, nonpartisan organization that sponsors forums on racial issues. They have heard from such speakers as Colin L. Powell, now secretary of state, and Jim Lawson, Lewis' mentor in the non-violent protest tactics that drove the civil rights movement. The institute also sponsors an annual civil rights pilgrimage to Alabama, where Lewis, often joined by House colleagues, recreates his famous walk across the bridge.

One of 10 children of sharecroppers in rural Alabama, Lewis still retains many of the frugal habits of his youth. He told the Atlanta Journal-Constitution that he buys his suits on sale and cuts coupons before he visits the grocery store. "I hate paying full price for anything," he said.

He first ran for Congress in 1977, for the seat Andrew Young left to become U.N. ambassador. He lost to Wyche Fowler, who went on to serve 10 years in the House and six in the Senate. Lewis won election to the Atlanta City Council in 1981, and when Fowler ran for the Senate in 1986, Lewis tried again for the House. He captured the Democratic nomination in a tough battle against state Sen. Julian Bond and then breezed to a 3-to-1 victory in November.

Lewis has won eight times since with better than two-thirds of the vote. His district remained solidly Democratic in the remapping that followed the 2000 census, and the GOP did not field an opponent in 2002.

KEY VOTES

2002

Yes Overhaul campaign finance law; ban "soft money" and restrict advocacy advertising
? Back Bush's defense budget increase
No Extend 1996 welfare law
No Adopt Bush's discretionary spending limit
No Pass GOP Medicare prescription drug plan
Yes Create independent Sept. 11 commission
Yes Extend union protections to Homeland Security Department employees
No Revive fast-track procedures for trade agreements
No Authorize war against Iraq
No Advance bankruptcy overhaul opposed by abortion opponents

2001

No Nullify Clinton Labor Department ergonomics rule
No Cut taxes by $1.35 trillion through fiscal 2011
Yes Maintain ban on oil drilling in Arctic National Wildlife Refuge
No Approve Bush proposal to limit managed-care plan liability for coverage decisions
Yes Divert money from crop subsidy payments to land conservation
No Expand law enforcement power to investigate suspected terrorists

CQ VOTE STUDIES

	PARTY UNITY		PRESIDENTIAL SUPPORT	
	Support	Oppose	Support	Oppose
2002	96%	4%	21%	79%
2001	97%	3%	15%	85%
2000	96%	4%	80%	20%
1999	96%	4%	84%	16%
1998	99%	1%	87%	13%

INTEREST GROUPS

	AFL-CIO	ADA	CCUS	ACU
2002	100%	80%	31%	0%
2001	100%	100%	26%	0%
2000	100%	95%	42%	4%
1999	100%	95%	9%	0%
1998	100%	90%	13%	0%

GEORGIA 5

Atlanta

The heart of the 5th lies in downtown Atlanta, the symbolic capital of the New South and the commercial center of the Southeast. The district takes in almost all of the city of Atlanta and much of surrounding Fulton County. The most populous county in Georgia, Fulton is reliably Democratic. A few pockets of GOP strength exist in the district's wealthier northern suburbs, such as Buckhead.

The 5th is one of two black-majority districts in the state. Its 56 percent black population — concentrated mostly in the southern part of the district — keeps it a Democratic bastion, though whites have flooded into the recently revitalized Midtown area. A large gay population in Midtown also has a significant influence on local politics.

During the 1990s, Atlanta saw a 13 percent increase in white residents, while the black population declined by 3 percent. Overall, the city's population grew by about 6 percent. New apartment buildings and condominiums are going up almost daily as the city attempts to keep up with the increase.

Along with Atlanta's downtown business district, Hartsfield Atlanta International Airport in Clayton County is the 5th's major economic generator. The airport, a small part of which is located in the 13th District, is one of the nation's busiest and employs more than 44,000 people. The 5th's strategic location also has made it the headquarters for transportation-related industries, distribution companies and other major firms. At the same time, air pollution, gridlock and urban sprawl from the expanding economy are a concern.

MAJOR INDUSTRY

Transportation, distribution

MILITARY BASES

Fort McPherson (Army), 1,694 military; 2,283 civilian (2001)

CITIES

Atlanta (pt.), 403,925; Sandy Springs (pt.), 44,738; East Point, 39,595; Smyrna (pt.), 26,781; College Park (pt.), 18,348; North Druid Hills, 16,132

NOTABLE

Martin Luther King Jr. was born in Atlanta and served as a pastor of Ebenezer Baptist Church; Atlanta hosted the 1996 Summer Olympics; Coca-Cola and CNN headquarters are in Atlanta.

Rep. Johnny Isakson (R)

CAPITOL OFFICE
225-4501
ga06@mail.house.gov
www.house.gov/isakson
132 Cannon 20515-1006; fax 225-4656

COMMITTEES
Education & Workforce
Transportation & Infrastructure

HOMETOWN
Marietta

BORN
Dec. 28, 1944, Atlanta, Ga.

RELIGION
Methodist

FAMILY
Wife, Dianne Isakson; three children

EDUCATION
U. of Georgia, B.B.A. 1966

MILITARY SERVICE
Ga. Air National Guard, 1966-72

CAREER
Real estate company president

POLITICAL HIGHLIGHTS
Candidate for Cobb County Commission, 1974; Ga. House, 1977-90 (Republican leader, 1983-90); Republican nominee for governor, 1990; Ga. Senate, 1994-96; sought Republican nomination for U.S. Senate, 1996; Ga. Board of Education chairman, 1996-99

ELECTION RESULTS

2002 GENERAL		
Johnny Isakson (R)	163,525	79.9%
Jeff Weisberger (D)	41,204	20.1%
2002 PRIMARY		
Johnny Isakson (R)		unopposed
2000 GENERAL		
Johnny Isakson (R)	256,595	74.8%
Brett DeHart (D)	86,666	25.3%

PREVIOUS WINNING PERCENTAGES
1999 Special Election (65%)

Elected February 1999; 2nd full term

Although he is a junior lawmaker, Isakson is teaching his colleagues a thing or two about education. A consensus builder trusted by fellow Republicans and even many Democrats, Isakson helped provide the impetus for compromise in the contentious House debate over President Bush's education initiative.

Isakson, chairman of the Georgia Board of Education from 1996 to 1999, played an important role in guiding through the House the education overhaul of 2001. The legislation for the first time ties federal aid to schools to improvements in student performance on annual standardized tests. As a member of the ad hoc House-Senate committee that negotiated a final version of the bill, Isakson persuaded colleagues to give schools more flexibility in using federal money and to allow them to transfer money among a variety of programs. He also was instrumental in getting conferees to adopt a requirement that one-fourth of technology funds be used for teacher classroom training.

Isakson still occasionally gets ribbed by colleagues for his un-Newtness — a reference to his predecessor, House Speaker Newt Gingrich, who represented the affluent suburban Atlanta district for 20 years. Gingrich, although a dynamic leader, was autocratic and abrasive; Isakson is humble, conciliatory and even-tempered. The comparisons are becoming less frequent as Isakson gains influence because of his detailed knowledge of education policy and his ability to legislate.

His ambitions extend beyond the House, however. Isakson announced in early 2003 plans to run for the seat of Democratic Sen. Zell Miller when Miller retires in 2004.

Though he is a conservative, Isakson says he is not captive to ideology. He sides faithfully with GOP leaders on tax-cutting bills, and his background as a millionaire real estate executive puts him on the side of business in most cases. But he sometimes takes a more moderate stance than other conservatives on social issues. For instance, he opposes a constitutional amendment to ban abortion and is wary of a Bush proposal to partially privatize Social Security. "I like to look at each issue and do what I think is right, and when you do that, you run the risk of failing someone's litmus test," he says.

But Isakson is in no danger of being mistaken for a Democrat. He opposes gun control and supports a ban on a procedure its critics call "partial birth" abortion. He voted against a bipartisan bill in 1999 giving patients greater powers to sue their managed-care plans, though the leading sponsor was fellow Georgia Republican Charlie Norwood. On national security issues, Isakson is a strong Bush defender. As the House debated in 2002 whether to authorize the administration to use force against Iraq, Isakson called Bush's approach a "doctrine of liberation."

During 17 years as a state legislator — 14 years in the Georgia House and three in the Senate — Isakson developed a reputation as a skillful arbitrator capable of bridging factions within the Republican Party and forging links with state Democrats. "He figured out early on that if you wanted to leave any kind of fingerprint on public policy, you have to be able to work with people," says Charles Bullock, a University of Georgia political scientist.

Isakson began his focus on education early in his House career. Though he was the lowest-ranking Republican on the Education and the Workforce Committee in the 106th Congress, he was the driving force behind a party proposal to help states pay for such federally mandated school modernization costs as asbestos removal and outfitting buildings for disabled students. Republicans on the committee had resisted Democratic proposals for the federal government to shoulder the cost of school repairs.

Recognizing the potential impact of the school construction issue, Isakson persuaded GOP Chairman Bill Goodling of Pennsylvania that Republicans would lose the debate without their own proposal. Instead of refusing to back any federal role in fixing schools, Isakson proposed more limited federal help. Goodling rewarded Isakson by bypassing more senior Republicans to give him a seat on Congress' Web-Based Education Commission, formed to advise the president and Congress on using the Internet to improve student achievement.

In the 107th Congress, Isakson threw himself into the Bush education initiative. But like any good junior lawmaker, he kept one eye on district concerns. Isakson promoted federal grants for programs like one in Dalton, Ga., in which Mexican teachers are hired to teach immigrant students who cannot speak English. And he used his other committee assignment, on the Transportation and Infrastructure panel, to prod the Transportation Department to restore highway funds for traffic-clogged Atlanta. He also badgered Georgia officials to bring Atlanta into compliance with the Clean Air Act, a requirement for restoring the highway funds.

His rising national profile stands in stark contrast to his first days as a congressman. Not every freshman lawmaker has to step into the shoes of a former Speaker, especially one as controversial and powerful as Gingrich. But Isakson, although little known nationally, was already a fixture in Georgia politics.

When Gingrich resigned under fire from his Republican colleagues after the party's loss of seats in the 1998 midterm elections, Isakson was the state's school board chairman. He immediately became the front-runner to succeed Gingrich. With huge advantages in name identification and campaign funds, Isakson took 65 percent against five opponents in the special election in 1999. He cruised to easy re-election wins in 2000 and 2002.

Winning the seat was the first time in a while that positioning himself as a relative moderate in the predominantly conservative Georgia Republican Party worked for Isakson. He had lost a bid for governor to conservative Democrat Miller in 1990. He ran for the GOP Senate nomination in 1996, but lost in a runoff to conservative businessman Guy Millner. His reputation for bipartisanship eventually paid off in 1996, when Miller, as governor, appointed Isakson chairman of Georgia's Board of Education.

KEY VOTES

2002

No Overhaul campaign finance law; ban "soft money" and restrict advocacy advertising
Yes Back Bush's defense budget increase
Yes Extend 1996 welfare law
Yes Adopt Bush's discretionary spending limit
Yes Pass GOP Medicare prescription drug plan
No Create independent Sept. 11 commission
No Extend union protections to Homeland Security Department employees
Yes Revive fast-track procedures for trade agreements
Yes Authorize war against Iraq
Yes Advance bankruptcy overhaul opposed by abortion opponents

2001

Yes Nullify Clinton Labor Department ergonomics rule
\+ Cut taxes by $1.35 trillion through fiscal 2011
No Maintain ban on oil drilling in Arctic National Wildlife Refuge
Yes Approve Bush proposal to limit managed-care plan liability for coverage decisions
No Divert money from crop subsidy payments to land conservation
Yes Expand law enforcement power to investigate suspected terrorists

CQ VOTE STUDIES

	PARTY UNITY		PRESIDENTIAL SUPPORT	
	Support	Oppose	Support	Oppose
2002	94%	6%	85%	15%
2001	97%	3%	90%	10%
2000	91%	9%	30%	70%
1999	87%	13%	29%	71%

INTEREST GROUPS

	AFL-CIO	ADA	CCUS	ACU
2002	0%	5%	100%	96%
2001	9%	5%	100%	88%
2000	0%	5%	85%	72%
1999	13%	10%	91%	66%

GEORGIA 6

Atlanta suburbs – Roswell, part of Marietta

Anchored in Atlanta's burgeoning northern suburbs, the 6th covers parts of three counties that are home to Republican voters who work in technology and other white-collar occupations. The 2000 census showed the old 6th as the most highly populated district in the state, a reflection of the massive growth taking place here.

The mostly white 6th is one of Georgia's most affluent, educated and Republican districts. Office parks, malls and housing subdivisions dominate the landscape. This area is referred to as the Golden Crescent: It is sandwiched between three of the state's major highways — Interstate 75, Interstate 85 and the Interstate 285 perimeter highway. Cobb County, northwest of Atlanta, accounts for more than 50 percent of the district's vote, and many of its residents work at Lockheed Martin, across the district line in the 11th.

Along with its defense industry, Marietta (shared with the 11th) provides Cobb County with its own thriving commercial center. Numerous corporations have office space in the "Platinum Triangle," shared with the 5th, a huge employment center that has begun to rival Atlanta's business district. But the growth and prospering economy also have brought gridlock and air pollution, causing some businesses to reconsider locating here.

In the central part of the 6th are solidly GOP suburbs in northern Fulton County. Alpharetta was once home to large farms that since have been converted into suburban developments. Roswell, formerly a cotton-milling center, is now a booming bedroom community in Fulton County.

MAJOR INDUSTRY

Communications, aerospace, finance, technology

CITIES

Roswell (pt.), 71,848; Sandy Springs (pt.), 41,043; Alpharetta, 34,854; Kennesaw, 21,675; Marietta (pt.), 18,614; Acworth, 13,422

NOTABLE

Former Republican Rep. Newt Gingrich represented the 6th from 1979-99 and served as House Speaker from 1995-99; Confederate troops defeated Northern Gen. William Sherman's army on June 27, 1864, at what is now Kennesaw Mountain National Battlefield Park.

Rep. John Linder (R)

CAPITOL OFFICE
225-4272
john.linder@mail.house.gov
linder.house.gov
1727 Longworth 20515-1007; fax 225-4696

COMMITTEES
House Administration
Rules
(Technology & the House - chairman)
Select Homeland Security
Joint Printing

HOMETOWN
Duluth

BORN
Sept. 9, 1942, Deer River, Minn.

RELIGION
Presbyterian

FAMILY
Wife, Lynne Linder; two children

EDUCATION
U. of Minnesota, Duluth, B.S. 1963; U. of Minnesota, D.D.S. 1967

MILITARY SERVICE
Air Force, 1967-69

CAREER
Financial executive; dentist

POLITICAL HIGHLIGHTS
Ga. House, 1975-81; Republican nominee for Ga. Senate, 1980; Ga. House, 1983-91; Republican nominee for U.S. House, 1990

ELECTION RESULTS

2002 GENERAL		
John Linder (R)	138,997	78.9%
Michael R. Berlon (D)	37,124	21.1%
2002 PRIMARY		
John Linder (R)	56,892	64.5%
Bob Barr (R)	31,374	35.5%
2000 GENERAL		
John Linder (R)		unopposed

PREVIOUS WINNING PERCENTAGES
1998 (69%); 1996 (64%); 1994 (58%); 1992 (51%)

Elected 1992; 6th term

Once a rising Republican star, Linder spent a good deal of time in the 107th Congress fighting to keep his seat. Redistricting threw him into a redrawn district and a primary contest against Rep. Bob Barr, a fellow conservative with a higher national profile. The soft-spoken Linder prevailed in 2002 by an unexpectedly large margin, perhaps auguring better days ahead for the six-term lawmaker.

Linder had been in the top GOP ranks in the 1990s, but his fortunes declined when his closest political ally, House Speaker Newt Gingrich, was forced to resign after the party's dismal showing in the 1998 congressional elections. Linder's support similarly evaporated, and less than two weeks after Gingrich quit, Linder lost the chairmanship of the National Republican Congressional Committee, the organization that helps recruit and fund GOP candidates for the House.

Since then, Linder has had to be satisfied with the influence he retains as a senior member of the Rules Committee. He could take the helm when Chairman David Dreier of California hits the six-year term limit on chairmen at the end of the 108th Congress. The second-ranking Republican, Porter J. Goss of Florida, has said he is going to retire.

Another recent bright spot for Linder was securing a seat on the new Homeland Security Committee in early 2003. The panel promises to be a hub of the government's efforts to revamp domestic security agencies and policies in the wake of the Sept. 11, 2001, terrorist attacks.

Linder is as conservative a Republican as they come. He is anti-tax and pro-business. His No. 1 issue is abolishing the existing tax code and replacing it with a national sales tax. He earned a perfect, 100 percent score from the U.S. Chamber of Commerce in 2001. The year was typical of Linder's voting record: He supported an overhaul of bankruptcy laws that favored creditors, repeal of a new ergonomics rule aimed at protecting workers from repetitive stress injuries and a trade measure giving the president expedited power to negotiate trade pacts. He again had a 100 percent rating from the business group in 2002.

Linder is equally conservative on social issues. He opposes abortion and is a cosponsor of legislation to ban a procedure its opponents call "partial birth" abortion. He is against most new gun control proposals and in 2002 voted in favor of arming commercial pilots with handguns to discourage terrorists.

In the 107th Congress, Linder focused on what for him is a local issue: increasing funding for the Atlanta-based Centers for Disease Control and Prevention. And he continued to push his national sales tax proposal, which he first introduced in 1999.

Linder's plan calls for the repeal of income and payroll taxes, abolition of the Internal Revenue Service and enactment of a national sales tax administered primarily by the states. His proposal was overshadowed, as most other tax plans were, by President Bush's $1.35 trillion tax cut, which in 2001 slashed income tax rates, eliminated the "marriage penalty" and cut estate taxes — all of which Linder supported.

The political alliance between Linder and Gingrich dates to the mid-1970s, when the two worked to rebuild the Georgia Republican Party. After Gingrich led Republicans to their historic takeover of Congress in 1995, the new Speaker rewarded Linder by putting him in charge of the NRCC, the congressional committee that works to elect more Republicans.

When the GOP instead lost five seats in 1998, the rank and file's long-simmering dissatisfaction with Gingrich's leadership and his ethics problems peaked. Without a strong base among House Republicans to call his own, Linder too was swept out of the leadership, losing a bid to remain in the NRCC top post to Virginia's Thomas M. Davis III.

Linder grew up in a small Minnesota town, the son of a car salesman. Though not politically active, his father was interested in public affairs. Linder recalls listening to the 1952 election returns on the family's huge Philco radio set. He worked his way through college at the University of Minnesota in Duluth, starting in pre-med but switching to dentistry after observing dentists at a speech clinic working with children with cleft palates.

After graduating from dental school, Linder joined the Air Force, where he practiced dentistry in San Antonio. Linder and his wife then moved to suburban Atlanta. He set up a dentistry practice but remained interested in politics. He subscribed to the Congressional Record, saying he was fascinated by the good ideas he found in the Record's Extension of Remarks section.

Linder ran successfully for a seat in the Georgia House in 1974 and wound up serving 14 years in the state legislature. In 1977, he founded a lending institution that specialized in providing financial assistance to small businesses and eventually he left dentistry. While in the state House, he earned a reputation for battling with the Democratic leadership.

Linder first ran for Congress in 1990, losing a tight battle with Democratic Rep. Ben Jones in the 4th District. Two years later, redistricting gave the district a more Republican tilt, and Linder tried again. He narrowly edged state Sen. Cathey Steinberg, 51 percent to 49 percent, while Jones ran for re-election in the 10th District.

After a Supreme Court decision invalidated Georgia's congressional map as racial gerrymandering, Linder in 1995 wound up representing a redrawn 11th District. It included some of the Atlanta suburbs and rural areas.

He enjoyed easy re-elections until forced to face off against Barr in the 2002 primary in the newly drawn 7th District. Barr, a consummate conservative like Linder, was known for his role as a leader in the House GOP effort to impeach President Clinton and as an outspoken voice on national television talk shows. But Republican voters ultimately rejected his acerbic style and polarizing politics in favor of the button-down Linder, who prevailed by 29 percentage points. Linder went on to win in November with 79 percent of the vote.

KEY VOTES

2002

No Overhaul campaign finance law; ban "soft money" and restrict advocacy advertising
Yes Back Bush's defense budget increase
Yes Extend 1996 welfare law
Yes Adopt Bush's discretionary spending limit
Yes Pass GOP Medicare prescription drug plan
No Create independent Sept. 11 commission
No Extend union protections to Homeland Security Department employees
Yes Revive fast-track procedures for trade agreements
Yes Authorize war against Iraq
Yes Advance bankruptcy overhaul opposed by abortion opponents

2001

Yes Nullify Clinton Labor Department ergonomics rule
Yes Cut taxes by $1.35 trillion through fiscal 2011
No Maintain ban on oil drilling in Arctic National Wildlife Refuge
Yes Approve Bush proposal to limit managed-care plan liability for coverage decisions
No Divert money from crop subsidy payments to land conservation
Yes Expand law enforcement power to investigate suspected terrorists

CQ VOTE STUDIES

	PARTY UNITY		PRESIDENTIAL SUPPORT	
	Support	Oppose	Support	Oppose
2002	98%	2%	90%	10%
2001	99%	1%	98%	2%
2000	96%	4%	22%	78%
1999	95%	5%	18%	82%
1998	96%	4%	21%	79%

INTEREST GROUPS

	AFL-CIO	ADA	CCUS	ACU
2002	11%	0%	100%	100%
2001	8%	0%	100%	96%
2000	0%	0%	90%	87%
1999	0%	10%	92%	87%
1998	0%	0%	100%	100%

GEORGIA 7

North of Atlanta — outer Atlanta suburbs

The 7th takes in overflow from many of the Atlanta suburbs contained in the 6th District. Forming a horseshoe shape around the top of Atlanta, the district is characterized by rapid suburban growth, including many newcomers to the state. As the suburbs close to the city become increasingly populated, the areas represented by the 7th are becoming outer suburbs. Many of the towns are transitioning from rural to suburban.

In addition to those who commute to Atlanta, many who live in the district work at Lockheed Martin in the nearby 11th or at one of a host of technology companies in Norcross. The homebuilding industry is burgeoning as the explosion of housing developments and wealthy subdivisions extends farther north from the city.

Voters in the 7th range from social conservatives living in rural areas to fiscal conservatives living in suburban areas. Redistricting following the 2000 census shifted the district's politics further right, as many Democratic and swing voters were removed, leaving a solid GOP base.

In 2000, George W. Bush received 72 percent of the vote in the new 7th, more than in any other district in the state. The bulk of voters live in Gwinnett County, considered the most-moderate and fastest-growing county in the district.

Water use is a major issue. The state has been affected by droughts, and the increasing population is depleting the area's water supply. Lake Lanier (shared with the 10th) and Allatoona Lake are major bodies of water in the district.

MAJOR INDUSTRY

Technology, retail, homebuilding, manufacturing

CITIES

Duluth, 22,122; Lawrenceville (pt.), 18,269; Snellville (pt.), 15,346

NOTABLE

Mall of Georgia, in Buford, covers 2 million square feet and features themed courtyards that represent areas of the state; Duluth elected the first woman mayor in Georgia, Alice H. Strickland, in 1921; She promised to "clean up Duluth and rid it of demon rum."

Rep. Mac Collins (R)

CAPITOL OFFICE
225-5901
www.house.gov/maccollins
1131 Longworth 20515-1008; fax 225-2515

COMMITTEES
Ways & Means
Select Intelligence

HOMETOWN
Jackson

BORN
Oct. 15, 1944, Jackson, Ga.

RELIGION
Methodist

FAMILY
Wife, Julie Collins; four children

EDUCATION
Jackson H.S., graduated 1962

MILITARY SERVICE
Ga. National Guard, 1964-70

CAREER
Trucking company owner

POLITICAL HIGHLIGHTS
Butts County Commission, 1977-81 (chairman); candidate for Ga. Senate, 1984, 1986; Ga. Senate, 1989-93

ELECTION RESULTS

2002 GENERAL		
Mac Collins (R)	142,505	78.3%
Angelos Petrakopoulos (D)	39,422	21.7%
2002 PRIMARY		
Mac Collins (R)		unopposed
2000 GENERAL		
Mac Collins (R)	150,200	63.5%
Gail Notti (D)	86,309	36.5%

PREVIOUS WINNING PERCENTAGES
1998 (100%); 1996 (61%); 1994 (66%); 1992 (55%)

Elected 1992; 6th term

Now in his second decade on Capitol Hill, the plain-talking Collins has worked his way up to the middle tier of the Ways and Means Committee. His conservative, anti-tax views and his frugal notions on federal spending have caused him to oppose even some Republican fiscal initiatives.

He says he would just as soon see the federal government get out of the way of business. To explain his pro-business philosophy, Collins is fond of paraphrasing the bank robber Willy Sutton: "Because that's where the jobs are." The Republican leadership has come to appreciate not only his votes — particularly on taxes and defense spending — but also his rhetoric.

Generally pleasant and approachable, Collins also is known for being blunt. In 2002, he lambasted another member of the Georgia delegation, Democrat Cynthia A. McKinney, for implying that Bush administration officials may have known in advance of the Sept. 11, 2001, terrorist attacks. "Basically, you have a publicity seeker with zero evidence making unfounded claims about something which she knows nothing," Collins said.

He also took off after Senate Democratic leader Tom Daschle, describing him in one news release as a socialist and charging Daschle with "obstructing policy for political gain."

Despite his casual ways and abrupt talk, Collins is no fool when it comes to politics. As a boy in Flovilla, Ga., politics was family table talk, and his mother was the first woman elected to the city council there. Collins himself served eight years in public office before coming to Washington — four as a Butts County commissioner and four as a state senator, starting out as a Democrat.

On Ways and Means, Collins usually introduces a wide range of bills designed to cut taxes. Some focus on relatively minor changes in depreciation formulas, others are sweeping proposals to reduce income tax rates.

In the 107th Congress, his aversion to what he regards as wasteful federal spending led him to vote against a number of measures that enjoyed widespread Republican support, including the GOP version of a prescription drug plan for senior citizens, which Collins called "irresponsible," and a bill to establish Radio Free Afghanistan. On the latter measure, he was one of only two House members to vote "no."

Concerned about lost jobs in Georgia's textile industry, Collins consistently has voted against legislation to lower trade barriers, including the 1993 law implementing the North American Free Trade Agreement, the 1994 law creating the World Trade Organization and the 2000 law to normalize trade relations with China. But in the 107th Congress, Collins voted for the law giving the president fast-track authority to negotiate trade agreements that Congress cannot amend. He said he was assured by the Bush administration that negotiators would look out for textile interests.

Although agriculture is an important part of Georgia's economy, Collins voted against the 2002 farm bill, complaining that it moved away from the free market system. Also in the 107th, Collins was one of just two House Republicans who opposed the initial version of an aviation security bill because he said it proposed a "bloated, time-consuming bureaucracy." He argued that the "government needs to create high security standards and leave the implementation to the local airport authority. Any airport that fails to meet those standards would be subject to closure."

In the 108th, Collins won appointment to the Intelligence Committee. Like many Southern Republicans, Collins strongly supports robust spending on the military. Just south of the district line in Columbus, in the southwest part of the state, is Fort Benning, Georgia's largest base.

Collins raised objections in 2002 when the Army announced that it was moving the headquarters of its forces for the Caribbean and Central and South America from Puerto Rico to Fort Sam Houston in Texas. He had lobbied for Fort Benning's designation, and he complained that the Army had failed to show why the San Antonio fort was picked instead.

A member of the unofficial congressional Boot Caucus (he wears them every day), Collins presents a "regular guy" persona, occasionally lacing his comments with allusions to his background in the trucking business. Once when he took a tightly scheduled fact-finding trip to Bosnia that involved 20 hours of flying in less than two days, he described the experience as "kind of like a West Coast turnaround in an 18-wheeler."

Collins started his business after high school, when he was 18, hauling logs and building it into a thriving enterprise. His two sons now run the company. After four years as a county commissioner and four more in the General Assembly, the post-1990 census redistricting gave Collins his opening to Congress. The 3rd District was dramatically altered, giving it a mixture of independent voters, Reagan Democrats and GOP suburbanites who did not know 10-year incumbent Democrat Richard Ray.

Stumping in jeans and boots and spending less than $250,000, Collins attacked Ray as a politician who had lost touch with the folks back home. He won with 55 percent, by far his lowest percentage. Since then, he has flirted with the notion of making a statewide run for senator or governor. Collins is among several Republicans in the House delegation considering a bid to replace Democrat Zell Miller, who announced he would not run for re-election to the Senate in 2004.

Georgia's political map changed considerably in 2002 as the state added two more House seats. Collins' district, now the 8th, meanders from Columbus in the southwest to the southern Atlanta suburbs, intertwining itself at several points with the perhaps even more oddly shaped 13th District. In fact, Collins' house is now in the 13th, while his neighbors just across the road are in the 8th.

But the new map caused Collins no electoral distress. Even though no part of his home county of Butts, where he has lived for most of his congressional tenure, was in his district until the 108th Congress, he never had to cope with the carpetbagger label. He lived in the 11th District in his early years in Congress and, after court-ordered redistricting in 1995, his home was in the 10th. In 2003, for the first time, he represented his boyhood home of Flovilla.

KEY VOTES

2002

No Overhaul campaign finance law; ban "soft money" and restrict advocacy advertising
Yes Back Bush's defense budget increase
Yes Extend 1996 welfare law
Yes Adopt Bush's discretionary spending limit
No Pass GOP Medicare prescription drug plan
No Create independent Sept. 11 commission
? Extend union protections to Homeland Security Department employees
Yes Revive fast-track procedures for trade agreements
Yes Authorize war against Iraq
Yes Advance bankruptcy overhaul opposed by abortion opponents

2001

Yes Nullify Clinton Labor Department ergonomics rule
Yes Cut taxes by $1.35 trillion through fiscal 2011
No Maintain ban on oil drilling in Arctic National Wildlife Refuge
Yes Approve Bush proposal to limit managed-care plan liability for coverage decisions
? Divert money from crop subsidy payments to land conservation
Yes Expand law enforcement power to investigate suspected terrorists

CQ VOTE STUDIES

	PARTY UNITY		PRESIDENTIAL SUPPORT	
	Support	Oppose	Support	Oppose
2002	96%	4%	82%	18%
2001	98%	2%	86%	14%
2000	96%	4%	19%	81%
1999	95%	5%	14%	86%
1998	95%	5%	12%	88%

INTEREST GROUPS

	AFL-CIO	ADA	CCUS	ACU
2002	22%	0%	85%	100%
2001	17%	5%	91%	96%
2000	10%	5%	76%	96%
1999	33%	15%	80%	92%
1998	0%	0%	83%	100%

GEORGIA 8

West – suburbs of Atlanta, Columbus and Macon

Created in redistricting after the 2000 census, the 8th was drawn to elect a Republican. Mostly within the rough triangle of Macon, Columbus and the south-central suburbs of Atlanta, the 8th jumps all around western Georgia, taking in Republican suburbs of those cities. The 11th and 13th districts wind in and around the 8th, encompassing Democratic areas.

Much of the 8th used to be agricultural but is now suburban, though many rural areas remain. Textile and poultry processing plants dot the landscape, and the timber industry flourishes here. The home building industry also is becoming a larger force in the suburbs, as additional housing developments and malls are constructed.

South of Atlanta, the district includes suburbs that were cut out of the heavily Democratic 13th. Peachtree City, in Fayette County, is a planned community 15 miles south of Atlanta that attracts commuters and home builders. Fayette County is home to many workers at nearby Hartsfield Atlanta International Airport. Henry County, east of Fayette, is the second-fastest-growing county in the state.

Farther east, the district encompasses all of rural Jasper County and snakes into Bibb County, covering the Republican suburbs north of Macon. Some workers from Robins Air Force Base, in the 1st District, live in the 8th, along with commuters to Macon.

The district's western edge includes rural Carroll and Coweta counties and extends south into Harris County, a wealthy bedroom community outside Columbus. The 8th also includes the northern part of Muscogee County and its immediate suburbs of Columbus.

MAJOR INDUSTRY

Textiles, agriculture, timber, poultry processing, home building

CITIES

Columbus (pt.), 53,778; Peachtree City, 31,580; Douglasville (pt.), 13,553; Fayetteville, 11,148; Macon (pt.), 7,748; LaGrange (pt.), 7,618

NOTABLE

Callaway Gardens, a 14,000-acre resort and gardens in Pine Mountain, holds the Sky High Hot Air Balloon Festival every Labor Day.

Rep. Charlie Norwood (R)

CAPITOL OFFICE
225-4101
www.house.gov/norwood
2452 Rayburn 20515-1009; fax 226-5995

COMMITTEES
Education & Workforce
(Workforce Protections - chairman)
Energy & Commerce

HOMETOWN
Evans

BORN
July 27, 1941, Valdosta, Ga.

RELIGION
Methodist

FAMILY
Wife, Gloria Norwood; two children

EDUCATION
Georgia Southern U., B.S. 1964 (biology);
Georgetown U., D.D.S. 1967

MILITARY SERVICE
Army, 1967-69

CAREER
Dentist

POLITICAL HIGHLIGHTS
No previous office

ELECTION RESULTS

2002 GENERAL		
Charlie Norwood (R)	123,313	72.8%
Barry Gordon Irwin (D)	45,974	27.2%
2002 PRIMARY		
Charlie Norwood (R)	42,452	81.7%
Lee Dickerson (R)	9,522	18.3%
2000 GENERAL		
Charlie Norwood (R)	122,590	63.2%
Marion Freeman (D)	71,309	36.8%

PREVIOUS WINNING PERCENTAGES
1998 (60%); 1996 (52%); 1994 (65%)

Elected 1994; 5th term

As Norwood finishes a decade in the House, he is getting used to a new role: life outside the national spotlight.

For most of his congressional career, Norwood has been closely identified with one issue, the patients' bill of rights. He received enormous attention for his maneuvering on legislation to give people more leverage over their medical insurance plans — first working with Democrats and against the House Republican leadership for two years, then reversing field and cutting a deal in secret with President Bush in 2001.

Now that the issue seems likely to go nowhere during the 108th Congress, Norwood is no longer receiving piles of speaking invitations and interview requests. The stubbornness and zeal for dealmaking that he brought to the managed-care debate have receded somewhat behind his country doctor's exterior.

And unlike so many of his Republican colleagues in the Georgia delegation, Norwood has decided against doing something guaranteed to plump up his profile at least through 2004: He is not seeking the Senate seat of retiring Democrat Zell Miller. "I don't want to be doing this until I'm 90 years old," he said in describing that decision. Now in his early 60s, he added, "If I were even 10 years younger, I'd have a different attitude."

A tobacco chewer with a love of fishing and duck hunting, Norwood probably will hew to more traditional Republican issues through the rest of his congressional career than he did as the top GOP champion of an aggressive response to the patients' rights issue. As chairman of the Workforce Protections Subcommittee of Education and the Workforce, he has jurisdiction over occupational safety and wage issues. He plans to revive a longtime Republican quest for legislation that would allow workers to refuse to pay any union dues that would be used for political purposes.

And even though the patients' rights debate has been downgraded as a national issue in light of rising health care costs, Norwood continues to call for at least a scaled-back bill. From his seat on the Energy and Commerce Subcommittee on Health, he continues to be active in health care debates affecting Medicare and Medicaid.

Norwood said his energy has not diminished since a November 2000 car accident that shattered several ribs and bones in his hands. The injuries turned out to be "a great thing," he said, because during his long recovery he scaled back the enthusiastic eating habits that he had developed on Capitol Hill and dropped more than 50 pounds.

Now, he said, his biggest challenge is limiting his priorities and finding new focus. "I have to slap my hand to stay out of some of the things that I'm interested in so that I can focus on things that can actually get done."

Norwood's broad interests may spring from the fact that his political experience came late in life. He had never held public office before his election as part of the "revolutionary" GOP Class of 1994. He ran on the platform that local and state governments are generally better problem solvers than federal bureaucrats. As a dentist, he said, he knew plenty about unnecessary and onerous federal regulation.

Norwood initially became influential on the managed-care issue by working with the leadership, helping to write a consensus GOP package that the House passed in 1998. But when the legislation died in the Senate, Norwood resolved to take a more aggressive stance in the 106th Congress.

He at first tried to work within the system but concluded that top Republicans were inhospitable to compromise. With Commerce's top Democrat, John D. Dingell of Michigan, as his partner, Norwood promoted a bill under which patients could have sued their health plans over coverage decisions — anathema to loyal GOP business and insurance interests. When the House passed the plan with 275 votes, a furious Speaker J. Dennis Hastert refused to appoint Norwood as one of the negotiators with the Senate, and the legislation died again at the end of 2000.

In the 107th Congress, Norwood strayed on the issue anew, this time abandoning the Dingell fold. Torn between his Democratic allies on the issue and Bush, whom he considered a friend, Norwood gambled that picking the president would boost momentum for his cause. Their surprise accord allowed a bill with a GOP stamp to pass the House, but the measure died once more when priorities shifted after the Sept. 11, 2001, attacks.

Norwood has shown a rebellious streak on other issues as well, particularly trade. He opposed Bush's campaign in the 107th for the power to negotiate trade deals on a fast track. And he worked actively against the GOP leadership and President Clinton in the 106th to oppose enactment of the law permanently granting China normal trade status.

Despite his high-profile defections, Norwood is generally a loyal party foot soldier. In each of his first four terms he stood with Republicans on party-line votes at least 95 percent of the time. And he backed Bush 85 percent of the time in the 107th, squarely in the middle of the House GOP.

He opposes abortion, supports school vouchers and school prayer, and is a staunch advocate for the rights of gun owners — a position that he says was cemented by an incident when he was 16 years old. He and a high school friend were playing with a .22-caliber pistol when it discharged while in Norwood's hands, killing the other boy. Norwood said the experience convinced him that no amount of gun control could have prevented such an accident.

After serving as a combat medic in Vietnam, Norwood opened his dental practice. His election two decades later — he trounced one-term incumbent Democrat Don Johnson by 2-to-1 in the 1994 GOP landslide — made him the first Republican to represent the Augusta area in the House since Reconstruction. With the exception of 1996, he has retained his seat by generally comfortable margins.

Reapportionment after the 2000 census resulted in a considerable makeover in the state's congressional map; the seat in the northeastern corner was made more reliably Republican and renumbered (it had been the 10th), and Norwood won his most lopsided victory ever.

KEY VOTES

2002

No Overhaul campaign finance law; ban "soft money" and restrict advocacy advertising
Yes Back Bush's defense budget increase
Yes Extend 1996 welfare law
Yes Adopt Bush's discretionary spending limit
Yes Pass GOP Medicare prescription drug plan
No Create independent Sept. 11 commission
No Extend union protections to Homeland Security Department employees
No Revive fast-track procedures for trade agreements
Yes Authorize war against Iraq
No Advance bankruptcy overhaul opposed by abortion opponents

2001

Yes Nullify Clinton Labor Department ergonomics rule
Yes Cut taxes by $1.35 trillion through fiscal 2011
No Maintain ban on oil drilling in Arctic National Wildlife Refuge
Yes Approve Bush proposal to limit managed-care plan liability for coverage decisions
No Divert money from crop subsidy payments to land conservation
Yes Expand law enforcement power to investigate suspected terrorists

CQ VOTE STUDIES

	PARTY UNITY		PRESIDENTIAL SUPPORT	
	Support	Oppose	Support	Oppose
2002	96%	4%	82%	18%
2001	96%	4%	88%	12%
2000	97%	3%	17%	83%
1999	94%	6%	14%	86%
1998	96%	4%	18%	82%

INTEREST GROUPS

	AFL-CIO	ADA	CCUS	ACU
2002	22%	5%	68%	96%
2001	25%	10%	81%	96%
2000	10%	5%	71%	100%
1999	44%	10%	71%	88%
1998	10%	5%	83%	100%

GEORGIA 9

Northeast – part of Augusta

The 9th starts in northeastern Georgia, encompassing agricultural and mountain areas, and travels down the South Carolina border to take in parts of Augusta. It also extends west to take in some suburbs east of Atlanta.

Created following the 2000 census, the 9th is solidly Republican. An arm from the neighboring 12th cuts north into the center of the district to strip out liberal Athens and the University of Georgia. A growing suburban population contributes to the GOP bent, and George W. Bush received 68 percent of the district's vote in the 2000 presidential election.

Suburban areas around Augusta and Athens are less developed than those bordering Atlanta. The district takes in part of the city of Augusta as well, including much of the Augusta National Golf Club (shared with the 12th). Many of the 9th's suburbs are rural in character, dotted with dairy farms and ranches. The mountainous northern region is the most rural, with dairy, timber and mining industries sustaining the economy. The area also depends on tourism dollars from visitors to a chain of lakes on the South Carolina border: Lake Russell, Lake Thurmond and Lake Hartwell.

The Savannah River valley makes water a major issue. Legislators representing this part of the state often have fought against exporting water to Atlanta, hoping to keep the resources on their own turf.

MAJOR INDUSTRY

Agriculture, tourism, retail

MILITARY BASES

Fort Gordon (Army), 12,168 military, 4,819 civilian (2001) (shared with the 12th)

CITIES

Augusta-Richmond (pt.), 36,679; Martinez, 27,749; Evans, 17,727

NOTABLE

Augusta National Golf Club (shared with the 12th) hosts the annual Masters golf tournament; The movies "Deliverance" and "Smokey and the Bandit" were set in Rabun County; Helen, a hamlet in White County, is a replica of a Swiss village; Elberton is known as the granite capital of the world.

Rep. Nathan Deal (R)

CAPITOL OFFICE
225-5211
www.house.gov/deal
2437 Rayburn 20515-1010; fax 225-8272

COMMITTEES
Energy & Commerce
Government Reform

HOMETOWN
Gainesville

BORN
Aug. 25, 1942, Millen, Ga.

RELIGION
Baptist

FAMILY
Wife, Sandra Dunagan Deal; four children

EDUCATION
Mercer U., B.A. 1964, J.D. 1966

MILITARY SERVICE
Army, 1966-68

CAREER
Lawyer; state prosecutor

POLITICAL HIGHLIGHTS
Hall County Juvenile Court judge, 1971-72; Hall County attorney, 1977-79; Ga. Senate, 1981-93 (served as a Democrat; president pro tempore, 1991-93)

ELECTION RESULTS

2002 GENERAL		
Nathan Deal (R)		unopposed
2002 PRIMARY		
Nathan Deal (R)		unopposed
2000 GENERAL		
Nathan Deal (R)	183,171	75.2%
James Harrington (D)	60,360	24.8%

PREVIOUS WINNING PERCENTAGES
1998 (100%); 1996 (66%); 1994 (58%); 1992 (59%)
*Elected as a Democrat 1992-1994

Elected 1992; 6th term

Now the senior party-switcher in the House, Deal at the start of the 108th Congress had been a member of the Republican Party more than three times as long as he served in the House as a Democrat. But his conservatism has shifted only marginally along the way, suggesting that the change of affiliation was more about marketing himself to his rural North Georgia constituents than about signaling an altered ideology.

Deal changed sides near the beginning of his second term in 1995, three months after the House came under GOP control for the first time in 40 years. Four other conservative Democrats switched later that year, but among them only Louisiana's Billy Tauzin is still in Congress. And all of them essentially followed the rhetorical lead of Deal, who declared that "the Democratic Party's attitude wasn't in tune with me or my constituents' beliefs" and that its leaders were "unwilling to change their liberal philosophy" to pay more heed to the desires of culturally and fiscally conservative Southern Democrats.

The switch has only enhanced Deal's political security at home. He won both his elections to the House as a Democrat with less than 60 percent of the vote, the customary threshold used in defining a "safe" seat. His share of the vote has never dipped below about two-thirds in the four elections since, and Deal was unopposed in 1998 and in 2002. The latter election came in a redrawn and renumbered district — it was the 9th in the 1990s — that ambles southward toward Atlanta but has retained its overwhelmingly conservative, and national Republican, loyalties.

Deal's legislative efforts mostly are behind the scenes on the Energy and Commerce Committee, the panel to which he was assigned by the Republicans as a reward for his new allegiance. As a lawmaker comfortably in sync with the GOP, Deal is seldom seen on the House floor except for votes, and many of the appearances he does make are as the presiding officer. Deal's demeanor is low-key and approachable, a regular-guy persona that dates at least as far back as his street-level, walk-in law practice at home in Gainesville, Ga.

He is as fiscally frugal now as he was in his first term, when he and about 20 other freshman Democrats formed the Fiscal Caucus to pressure the Clinton administration to cut spending. That caucus was one of the forerunners to the "Blue Dog" coalition of conservative Democrats, which Deal helped found just before he jumped parties.

In the 107th Congress, Deal reversed his past course and gave his all-important support to the law re-establishing fast-track trade procedures, under which Congress must consider the trade agreements reached by presidents on an expedited timetable and without amendments. The House endorsed the measure by only a three-vote majority in 2002, and Deal provided one of those votes, after exacting assurances from administration officials that they would look out for his area's poultry industry in the future.

During the Clinton administration, Deal had opposed fast-track authority, contending that trade deals threatened vital textile interests in his district. But many textile manufacturers have left North Georgia in recent years and have been replaced by high-tech industries that rely on global commerce to survive.

At first glance, the landlocked and mostly rural area might seem an unlikely hot spot for concern about immigration. But the poultry and carpet businesses rely on foreign workers — illegal and legal — and Deal has long served on a GOP immigration task force. His particular interest lies in beefing up enforcement against illegal immigrants, including those who enter the United States legally but stay longer than permitted. After the Sept. 11, 2001, attacks, he was even more adamant that the Immigration and Naturalization Service improve its processes for approving visas, not just to weed out potential terrorists but also to make sure immigrants are legally entitled to be in the United States. "To make us feel secure," he said, Congress must "do something about the fiasco that exists in the INS."

While the 10th District takes in part of the rapidly growing Atlanta metropolitan area, its heart remains rural, so issues such as logging and satellite television access are important. In the 106th Congress, Deal was a leader on legislation to help local counties whose revenues from timber harvesting on federal lands have dwindled.

The district's economy also relies on tourist dollars — it takes in both Lake Lanier and Lake Allatoona, prime summertime vacation spots for suburbanites — and Deal has pressed to have those making decisions on federal lake management take into account the likely impact on recreational activities. Because water from the lakes is sometimes diverted for other uses, Deal believes tourism in the area has suffered.

His views on most national issues are in line with the dominant conservative wing of the GOP, including his opposition to gun control and abortion, his support of a healthy defense budget and his backing for a constitutional amendment to ban flag desecration.

Deal is the only child of two public school teachers (his wife is a teacher as well), and although his parents were not active in politics, they impressed on him the importance of being active in public life. "After all, teaching is a type of public service," he says.

He was a successful high school and college debater, and he went on to law school. Fulfilling a commitment he made as a four-year member of the ROTC during college, he joined the Army and served two years in the Judge Advocate General's corps before opening his law practice back in Gainesville. He served as a prosecutor and a juvenile court judge and then, at the urging of friends, ran for an open state Senate seat in 1980.

He had put together a string of effortless re-elections by the time Ed Jenkins, a fellow conservative Democrat, announced in 1992 that he was retiring from the House. Deal's Republican opponent that year was Daniel Becker, who made abortion the focus of a "morality in government" campaign; he aired anti-abortion TV ads featuring graphic photos of allegedly aborted fetuses. Becker's appeal proved to be limited; he managed only 41 percent.

KEY VOTES

2002

No Overhaul campaign finance law; ban "soft money" and restrict advocacy advertising
Yes Back Bush's defense budget increase
Yes Extend 1996 welfare law
Yes Adopt Bush's discretionary spending limit
Yes Pass GOP Medicare prescription drug plan
No Create independent Sept. 11 commission
No Extend union protections to Homeland Security Department employees
Yes Revive fast-track procedures for trade agreements
Yes Authorize war against Iraq
Yes Advance bankruptcy overhaul opposed by abortion opponents

2001

Yes Nullify Clinton Labor Department ergonomics rule
Yes Cut taxes by $1.35 trillion through fiscal 2011
No Maintain ban on oil drilling in Arctic National Wildlife Refuge
Yes Approve Bush proposal to limit managed-care plan liability for coverage decisions
No Divert money from crop subsidy payments to land conservation
Yes Expand law enforcement power to investigate suspected terrorists

CQ VOTE STUDIES

	PARTY UNITY		PRESIDENTIAL SUPPORT	
	Support	Oppose	Support	Oppose
2002	96%	4%	82%	18%
2001	98%	2%	93%	7%
2000	95%	5%	15%	85%
1999	92%	8%	16%	84%
1998	94%	6%	16%	84%

INTEREST GROUPS

	AFL-CIO	ADA	CCUS	ACU
2002	11%	0%	90%	100%
2001	9%	5%	90%	100%
2000	10%	5%	71%	96%
1999	22%	10%	84%	80%
1998	10%	10%	67%	88%

GEORGIA 10

North — Dalton, Gainesville

Anchored by North Georgia's mountains, the 10th runs across the western half of the state's northern border. It includes the Cloudland Canyon, the man-made Lake Lanier and several growing Atlanta suburbs, as well as bedroom communities outside of Chattanooga, Tenn.

Residents are overwhelmingly white and strongly Republican; only 3 percent of the district's voting age population is black. While Democrats have long dominated local politics, the GOP allegiance in some north-central counties is unwavering and dates to the Civil War. George W. Bush received 71 percent of the district's vote in 2000.

Economically, the 10th has benefited from a population boom. A surge of new residents in the south has brought white-collar and service-sector jobs to the district but is straining local water resources. Many of the new residents are Hispanic immigrants who work in the district's poultry processing and carpet-making industries in Hall and Whitfield counties. Tourist dollars also play a role in the economy, as visitors flock to Lake Lanier (shared with the 7th).

The district also dips down into the Atlanta area, where it takes in Republican suburbs north and east of the city, most of them dominated by housing subdivisions and shopping malls.

MAJOR INDUSTRY

Poultry processing, carpet manufacturing, textiles

CITIES

Dalton, 27,912; Gainesville, 25,578; Calhoun, 10,667; Fort Oglethorpe, 6,940

NOTABLE

Dalton is known as the carpet capital of the world; Gainesville, dubbed the poultry capital of the world, displays the Georgia Poultry Federation's monument to the industry in the center of town: an obelisk with a chicken statue on top; Springer Mountain is the southern terminus of the Appalachian National Scenic Trail, which is 2,167 miles long and extends to Maine.

Rep. Phil Gingrey (R)

Elected 2002; 1st term

An obstetrician who has delivered 5,200 babies, Gingrey says he hopes to use his experience as a doctor to tackle the issue of health care affordability. As a fiscal and social conservative, he can be expected to pursue a Republican prescription for the problem.

For example, Gingrey has said he favors an overhaul of federal tort laws. He echoes the argument many have made: the routine costs of medical malpractice suits are forcing too many doctors out of business.

As a state legislator, Gingrey worked to cut taxes, promote gun owners' rights and toughen teen driving laws. He opposes abortion, including in the cases of rape or incest.

Gingrey's résumé includes four years as chairman of the Marietta school board. He advocates parental involvement in schools, favors state and local control over most education matters, and argues for a longer school year.

On fiscal issues, he supports abolishing the IRS and would like to see a national retail sales tax enacted to replace the federal income tax.

He sought and won a seat on the Armed Services panel, where he looks after the interests of Georgia's numerous military installations and Lockheed Martin, a leading defense contractor and one of the 11th District's major employers. He also serves on the Science and the Education and the Workforce committees.

Gingrey's 2002 win over well-funded Democratic businessman Roger Kahn was a bit of an upset, since the Democrats who controlled the state's redistricting had drawn the 11th District to boost their nominee's chances of winning. But the district overall is conservative, and Gingrey succeeded in appealing to right-leaning voters, many of them religious conservatives from rural areas. Gingrey won by 3 percentage points despite spending less than $2 million to Kahn's more than $3.6 million.

Shortly after his election, Gingrey added a new perspective to his views on medicine: He underwent double heart bypass surgery in mid-December. But he was on hand for the Jan. 7 opening day of the 108th Congress.

CAPITOL OFFICE
225-2931
gingrey.ga@mail.house.gov
www.house.gov/gingrey
1118 Longworth 20515-1011; fax 225-2944

COMMITTEES
Armed Services
Education & Workforce
Science

HOMETOWN
Marietta

BORN
July 10, 1942, Augusta, Ga.

RELIGION
Roman Catholic

FAMILY
Wife, Billie Gingrey; four children

EDUCATION
Georgia Institute of Technology, B.S. 1965 (chemistry); Medical College of Georgia, M.D. 1969

CAREER
Physician

POLITICAL HIGHLIGHTS
Marietta Board of Education, 1993-97 (chairman, 1994-97); Ga. Senate, 1999-2003

ELECTION RESULTS

2002 GENERAL		
Phil Gingrey (R)	69,427	51.6%
Roger Kahn (D)	65,007	48.4%
2002 PRIMARY RUNOFF		
Phil Gingrey (R)	9,930	63.6%
Cecil Staton (R)	5,692	36.4%
2002 PRIMARY		
Phil Gingrey (R)	12,377	40.1%
Cecil Staton (R)	9,750	31.6%
Bob Herriott (R)	8,717	28.3%

GEORGIA 11

Northwest – Rome, parts of Columbus and Marietta

Running south along the Alabama border from northwest Georgia to Columbus, the oddly shaped 11th stretches east to take in Atlanta's northwestern suburbs and connect several Democratic areas. While the district includes all or part of 17 counties, the majority of its voters live in three — Cobb (suburbs of Atlanta and part of Marietta), Floyd (Rome) and Muscogee (Columbus).

The 11th was drawn following the 2000 census to lean Democratic. Although 26 percent of the voting age population is African-American, the district's white population tends to be socially conservative and supportive of GOP candidates. George W. Bush captured 51 percent of the district's vote in the 2000 presidential election.

Cobb County is a collection of largely white-collar, middle-income suburbs with a rapidly growing minority population. The 11th takes in southern parts of the county and much of Marietta (shared with the 6th). Small businesses and corporate headquarters, as well as military- and aerospace-related jobs in Marietta, spark the economy. Lockheed Martin employs many. Other major industries include electrical wire in Carroll County and carpet manufacturing in the north.

Areas outside the district's three cities are largely agricultural, and some small towns are reliant on textile trades. The beef and timber industries and a few manufacturers provide jobs for workers along the border.

MAJOR INDUSTRY
Defense, carpet manufacturing, electronics

MILITARY BASES
Naval Air Station Atlanta, 1,160 military, 192 civilian; Fort Benning (Army), 33,521 military, 7,582 civilian (shared with the 2nd) (2002)

CITIES
Columbus (pt.), 48,030; Marietta (pt.), 40,133; Rome, 34,980; Mableton (pt.), 28,140

NOTABLE
Like its Italian namesake, Rome is built on seven hills.

Rep. Max Burns (R)

CAPITOL OFFICE
225-2823
www.house.gov/burns
512 Cannon 20515-1012; fax 225-3377

COMMITTEES
Agriculture
Education & Workforce
Transportation & Infrastructure

HOMETOWN
Sylvania

BORN
Nov. 8, 1948, Millen, Ga.

RELIGION
Baptist

FAMILY
Wife, Lora Burns; two children

EDUCATION
Georgia Institute of Technology, B.I.E. 1973 (industrial engineering); Georgia State U., M.B.I.S. 1977 (business information systems), Ph.D. 1987 (business administration)

MILITARY SERVICE
Army Reserve, 1973-81

CAREER
Professor; information systems manager; airline engineer

POLITICAL HIGHLIGHTS
Screven County Commission, 1994-98 (chairman, 1997-98)

ELECTION RESULTS

2002 GENERAL		
Max Burns (R)	77,479	55.2%
Charles Walker Jr. (D)	62,904	44.8%
2002 PRIMARY		
Max Burns (R)	13,956	50.5%
Barbara Dooley (R)	13,700	49.5%

Elected 2002; 1st term

Burns favors a "massive overhaul" of government fiscal policy that includes eliminating the IRS and creating a national sales tax. Yet the freshman — who still lives on the farm where he grew up — says in his first term he will focus on a less ideological issue: economic development for the 12th District.

He got both of his preferred committee assignments, Agriculture and Transportation. He also has a seat on the Education and the Workforce panel and was elected president of the freshman class.

An educator for 20 years and a professor of information systems at Georgia Southern University when he entered the 2002 race, Burns says he would like to make long-distance learning more available to students.

He says he opposes "the radical gay rights agenda" as well as " 'hate crimes' legislation that discriminates against traditional religious values." On his Web site, he makes his views on gun control clear: "Individual citizens have a constitutional right to keep and bear arms. Period." He was endorsed by anti-abortion groups.

Democrats, who controlled the state's redistricting process, designed Georgia's 12th District to elect their party's nominee. So it initially appeared that Burns' conservative views on social and fiscal issues might put the seat out of reach for Republicans.

But Burns was helped to victory by the difficulties of the Democratic nominee, Charles "Champ" Walker Jr., an entrepreneur and the son of former state Senate Majority Leader Charles Walker. In the last few weeks of the campaign, local newspapers revealed that the younger Walker had been charged with shoplifting and leaving the scene of an accident years earlier.

Burns appealed to the district's white rural voters, who are situated between the 12th's three urban areas that give the district its Democratic lean — Athens, Augusta and Savannah. He pulled out a 10 percentage point upset over Walker. The victory made him the Republican with the highest percentage of black constituents. Democrats are expected to mount a competitive challenge in 2004 for a seat that they consider in their camp.

GEORGIA 12

East — Athens, most of Augusta and Savannah

The 12th resembles the Statue of Liberty, with Athens at the torch, Augusta at the head, and Savannah at the feet. It covers the southern half of Georgia's border with South Carolina, extending down from Augusta into Chatham County to cover most of the city of Savannah. The district's arm travels through agricultural communities to take in Athens and the University of Georgia's main campus.

Drawn during redistricting following the 2000 census to elect a Democrat, the 12th encompasses Savannah's city center, including the inner city and historic areas. While all of Savannah was included in the old 1st District, the new map split the city to separate predominantly Democratic and Republican areas. Thirty-nine percent of the 12th's voting age population is black.

Effingham, a rapidly growing Savannah suburb, is the most Republican part of the district. Farther north, the 12th takes in the urban areas of Augusta. Most of Augusta National Golf Club is in the 9th, but the 13th hole, part of "Amen Corner," is in the 12th.

The agricultural areas south of Athens are heavily African-American, specializing in row farming and timber production. Textile factories had a presence here, but many have shut down in recent years. The Medical College of Georgia is in the district.

MAJOR INDUSTRY
Agriculture, manufacturing, timber

MILITARY BASES
Fort Stewart (Army), 15,020 military, 1,844 civilian (shared with the 1st and 3rd); Fort Gordon (Army), 12,168 military, 4,819 civilian (2001) (shared with the 9th); Navy Supply Corps School, 136 military, 157 civilian (2002)

CITIES
Augusta-Richmond (pt.), 158,503; Savannah (pt.), 126,598; Athens-Clarke, 101,489

NOTABLE
Part of the movie "Forrest Gump" was filmed at Chippewa Square in Savannah.

Rep. David Scott (D)

CAPITOL OFFICE
225-2939
david.scott@mail.house.gov
www.house.gov/davidscott
417 Cannon 20515-1013; fax 225-4628

COMMITTEES
Agriculture
Financial Services

HOMETOWN
Atlanta

BORN
June 27, 1946, Aynor, S.C.

RELIGION
Baptist

FAMILY
Wife, Alfredia Scott; two children

EDUCATION
Florida A&M U., B.A. 1967 (English & speech); U. of Pennsylvania, M.B.A. 1969

CAREER
Advertising agency owner; management consultant

POLITICAL HIGHLIGHTS
Ga. House, 1975-83; Ga. Senate, 1983-2003

ELECTION RESULTS

2002 GENERAL		
David Scott (D)	70,011	59.6%
Clay Cox (R)	47,405	40.4%
2002 PRIMARY		
David Scott (D)	22,624	53.8%
Greg K. Hecht (D)	8,384	19.9%
David Worley (D)	5,568	13.2%
Donzella J. James (D)	4,703	11.2%
Embry Malone (D)	762	1.8%

Elected 2002; 1st term

Scott's persuasive political skills come from an almost evangelical sense of purpose. As a Democratic state lawmaker for more than a quarter-century, he worked hard to promote values and religion in society, and even harder to cross racial boundaries in his appeal.

Scott says one of his proudest accomplishments is Georgia's "moment of silence" law, which requires schools to set aside time for reflection and prayer at the start of each day. He says he will continue his fight for prayer in schools as a member of Congress. "It has done wonders in curbing violence here," he says of his home state.

Scott was raised in relatively humble conditions as the son of a minister. The first college graduate in his family and an alumnus of the University of Pennsylvania's Wharton School of Business, he started his own advertising company, Dayn-Mark, in 1979. But much of his career has been spent serving in public office, including eight years in the Georgia House and 20 years in the state Senate. He was on the redistricting committee that helped draw the 13th as a winding Atlanta-area district favorable to Democrats.

As a state legislator, he sponsored bills to fund breast cancer research, to require a background check before gun purchases, and to restrict landfills in residential areas of Atlanta.

Upon his arrival in Congress, Scott joined the "Blue Dog" coalition of conservative Democrats and was elected a regional whip. He says he agrees with President Bush on the need for a strong military and supported the tax cut Bush pushed through Congress in 2001.

Scott won the Democratic nomination outright in Georgia's Aug. 20 primary, avoiding a September runoff. He easily defeated businessman Clay Cox in the general election. His famous brother-in-law, baseball great Hank Aaron, appeared in campaign ads for him.

His victory in the white-plurality 13th District — one of two new seats gained by fast-growing Georgia as a result of the 2000 census — made him one of four black members, all Democrats, in the state's House delegation.

GEORGIA 13

Southern Atlanta suburbs

One of two new districts created in Georgia following the 2000 census, the 13th covers a spidery area south of Atlanta with tentacles extending outward from the city. The district was created by Democratic state legislators to represent the growing black population on the outskirts of Atlanta.

The district has a slim white plurality: 42 percent of the 13th's population is white, while 41 percent is African-American. Roughly 10 percent of residents are Hispanic, though voter turnout is much lower among that population. Solidly Democratic, 59 percent of residents voted for Al Gore in the 2000 presidential election.

The 13th takes in an array of middle-income urban, suburban and rural areas. Many residents in the urban areas — the two fingers that run along Interstate 85, north of Atlanta in Gwinnett County and south of the city in Fulton County — live in apartment communities and commute to Atlanta. The heart of the district is suburban Clayton County, which formerly was populated by blue-collar white residents and is now a haven for African-American families moving south from Atlanta. The 13th's fingers run through some Republican areas to reach rural, Democratic-leaning towns at the district's fingertips.

The 13th includes a small section of Atlanta and a small part of Hartsfield Atlanta International Airport. The airport, one of the nation's busiest, helps bolster the economy.

MAJOR INDUSTRY
Agriculture, distribution, aerospace

MILITARY BASES
Fort Gillem (Army), 478 military, 1,713 civilian (2001)

CITIES
Forest Park, 21,447; Griffin (pt.), 17,783; Atlanta (pt.), 12,515; Riverdale, 12,478

NOTABLE
Jonesboro was the setting for Tara, the plantation in Margaret Mitchell's novel "Gone With the Wind"; TV show "Dukes of Hazzard" was filmed in Covington.

HAWAII

Gov. Linda Lingle (R)

First elected: 2002
Length of term: 4 years
Term expires: 12/06
Salary: $94,780
Phone: (808) 586-0034
Hometown: Honolulu
Born: June 4, 1953; St. Louis, Mo.
Religion: Jewish
Family: Divorced
Education: California State U., Northridge, B.A. 1975 (journalism)
Career: Newspaper owner; journalist
Political highlights: Maui County Council, 1981-91; mayor of Maui, 1991-98; Republican nominee for governor, 1998; Hawaii Republican Party chairwoman, 1999-2002
Election results:

2002 GENERAL		
Linda Lingle (R)	197,009	51.6%
Mazie Hirono (D)	179,647	47.0%

Lt. Gov. James 'Duke' Aiona (R)

First elected: 2002
Length of term: 4 years
Term expires: 12/06
Salary: $90,041
Phone: (808) 586-0255

STATE LEGISLATURE

Legislature: Meets January-April
House: 51 members, 2-year terms
2003 breakdown: 15R, 36D; 37 men, 14 women
Salary: $32,000
Phone: (808) 586-6400
Senate: 25 members, 4-year terms
2003 breakdown: 5R, 20D; 18 men, 7 women
Salary: $32,000
Phone: (808) 586-6720

STATE TERM LIMITS

Governor: 2 consecutive terms
House: No
Senate: No

URBAN STATISTICS

CITY	POPULATION
Honolulu	371,657
Hilo	40,759
Kailua	36,513
Kaneohe	34,970
Waipahu	33,108

REGISTERED VOTERS

Voters do not register by party.

POPULATION

2002 population (est.)	1,244,898
2000 population	1,211,537
1990 population	1,108,229
Percent change (1990-2000)	+9.3%
Rank among states (2002)	42
Median age	36.2
Born in state	56.9%
Foreign born	17.5%
Violent crime rate	244/100,000
Poverty level	10.7%
Federal workers	29,276
Military	53,632

REDISTRICTING

Hawaii retained its two House seats in reapportionment. The Hawaii Reapportionment Commission adopted a new map on Nov. 30, 2001.

MISCELLANEOUS

Web: www.state.hi.us
Capital: Honolulu

STATE ELECTION OFFICIAL
(808) 453-8683

DEMOCRATIC HEADQUARTERS
(808) 596-2980

REPUBLICAN HEADQUARTERS
(808) 593-8180

District Statistics

DIST.	2000 VOTE FOR PRESIDENT BUSH	GORE	NADER	WHITE	BLACK	ASIAN	HISP	MEDIAN INCOME	WHITE COLLAR	BLUE COLLAR	SERVICE INDUSTRY	OVER 64	UNDER 18	COLLEGE EDUCATION	RURAL	SQ. MILES
1	39%	55%	5%	18%	2%	54%	5%	$50,798	64%	16%	20%	15%	22%	29%	1%	191
2	36	56	7	28	2	28	9	$48,686	57	21	22	11	27	23	16	6,232
STATE	37	56	6	23	2	41	7	$49,820	60	19	21	13	24	26	9	6,423
U.S.	47.9	48.4	3	69	12	4	13	$41,994	60	25	15	12	26	24	21	3,537,438

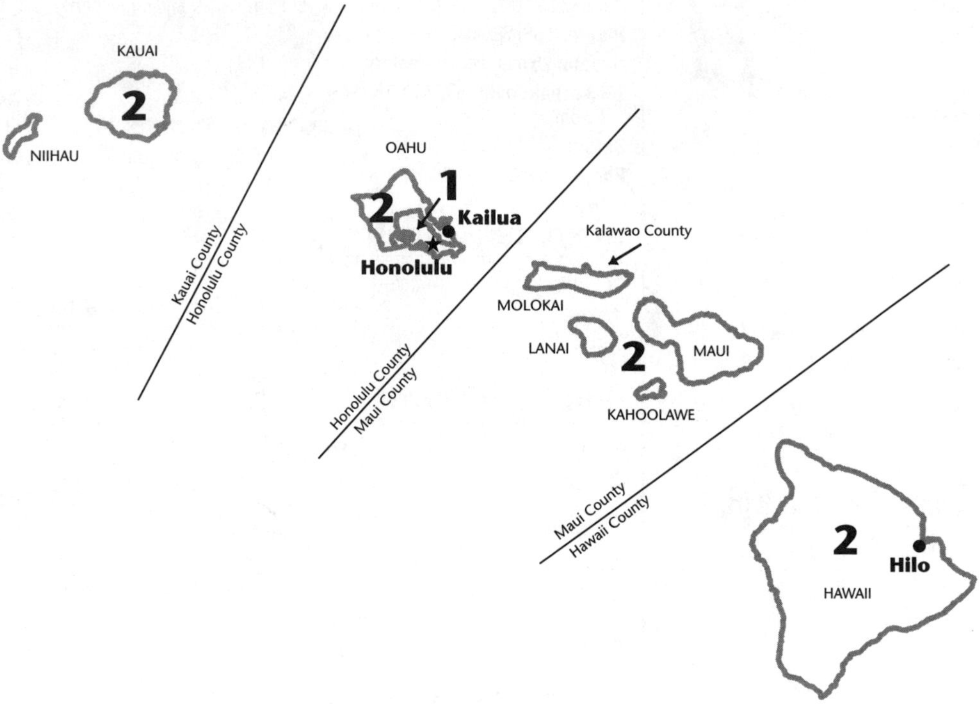
KAUAI
2
NIHAU
Kauai County
Honolulu County
OAHU
2
1
Kailua
Honolulu
Honolulu County
Maui County
Kalawao County
MOLOKAI
LANAI
2
MAUI
KAHOOLAWE
Maui County
Hawaii County
2
Hilo
HAWAII

Sen. Daniel K. Inouye (D)

Elected 1962; 7th term

CAPITOL OFFICE
224-3934
inouye.senate.gov
722 Hart 20510-1102; fax 224-6747

COMMITTEES
Appropriations
Commerce, Science & Transportation
Indian Affairs - ranking member
Rules & Administration
Joint Printing

HOMETOWN
Honolulu

BORN
Sept. 7, 1924, Honolulu, Hawaii

RELIGION
Methodist

FAMILY
Wife, Margaret Shinobu Inouye; one child

EDUCATION
U. of Hawaii, A.B. 1950 (government & economics); George Washington U., J.D. 1952

MILITARY SERVICE
Army, 1943-47

CAREER
Lawyer; city prosecutor

POLITICAL HIGHLIGHTS
Hawaii Territorial House, 1954-58 (majority leader); Hawaii Territorial Senate, 1958-59; U.S. House, 1959-63

ELECTION RESULTS

1998 GENERAL		
Daniel K. Inouye (D)	315,252	79.2%
Crystal Young (R)	70,964	17.8%
Lloyd Jeffery Mallan (LIBERT)	11,908	3.0%
1998 PRIMARY		
Daniel K. Inouye (D)	105,130	92.8%
Richard H. Thompson (D)	8,105	7.2%

PREVIOUS WINNING PERCENTAGES
1992 (57%); 1986 (74%); 1980 (78%); 1974 (83%); 1968 (83%); 1962 (69%); 1960 House Election (74%); 1959 Special Election House Election (68%)

A deeply private man in a highly public job, Inouye is a living link between Hawaii's past as a U.S. territory and its future as the nation's vibrant, multicultural bridge to the Pacific Rim. He has represented Hawaii in Congress since the archipelago joined the union in 1959, and he has done so with a quiet dignity that belies his behind-the-scenes influence with his colleagues. In the Senate since 1963, at the start of the 108th Congress he was the sixth-longest-serving senator in the nation's history.

On the rare occasions when Inouye (ih-NO-way) speaks out publicly, his words convey a sense of gravity and command attention. When the Senate was debating in 2002 whether to grant President Bush the authority to attack Iraq, Inouye made front-page headlines when he took exception to a Bush comment that Democrats were not concerned about national security. Inouye, who lost an arm fighting Nazi Germany in World War II and won the Congressional Medal of Honor in 2000 for his bravery, rose on the Senate floor to protest.

"It grieves me when my president makes statements that would divide this nation," he said. "This is not a time for Democrats and Republicans to say we got more medals than you, we've lost more limbs than you, we've shed more blood than you."

Inouye eventually ended up voting against the resolution that authorized Bush to go after Iraq. And his longstanding commitment to the military and national defense also did not stop him from voting against legislation creating a new Homeland Security Department later that year. Along with his home-state colleague, Democrat Daniel K. Akaka, Inouye voiced concern that the department could use its ability to compile information on citizens to encroach on civil liberties.

The first Japanese-American elected to Congress, Inouye believes strongly in the notion of honor — one of the attributes that identifies him as the product of an earlier political era, when cloakroom collegiality was valued more than partisan combativeness and reverence for the Senate as an institution was the norm. He declined to cast a tie-breaking vote in favor of a Democratic-backed amendment to the 2001 Bush tax bill, for example, in order to keep his promise to "pair" his votes that day with his friend Ted Stevens, a Republican who would have voted the other way but was home in Alaska speaking at a granddaughter's high school graduation.

Though Inouye typically votes the Democratic party line, his colleagues have come to rely on him to handle delicate tasks that require the appearance of impartiality and unquestioned probity. He took center stage during two congressional investigations of executive branch misdeeds. His 1987 appointment to chair the Senate committee investigating the Iran-contra affair stemmed not only from his evenhanded manner but also from the esteem accorded him during the 1973 Watergate hearings, which led to the downfall of President Nixon. Inouye earned a reputation as a tough but judicious interrogator of Nixon's aides and associates.

When Chairman Harry Reid of Nevada recused himself in 2002, Inouye stepped in to head the Ethics Committee's investigation of fellow Democrat Robert G. Torricelli. The panel ended up voting unanimously to "severely admonish" the New Jersey senator for accepting cash and gifts from a businessman — the harshest ethical rebuke of a senator in seven years, and one that ultimately led Torricelli to drop his re-election bid.

The No. 2 Democrat on the Appropriations Committee and long the top

Democrat on its Defense Subcommittee, Inouye has secured billions of dollars in federal spending for his state. His efforts have made him a prime target of the nonprofit watchdog group Citizens Against Government Waste, which has attacked him for annually producing Hawaii line items not sought by the White House. Inouye is unapologetic about helping to boost the economy back home. "The criticism," he said in 2000, "is to me an indication that I am doing the job I was elected to do."

Building on equally successful efforts in previous years, Inouye secured nearly $700 million in defense spending for Hawaii in 2002, with nearly $202 million going to upgrade and repair the Pearl Harbor Naval Shipyard. He also secured $257 million for military construction projects for Hawaii's missile range facility and military bases. Some of Inouye's funding efforts have also benefited his alma mater, the University of Hawaii.

Inouye shares with Stevens, the chairman of Appropriations and its Defense Subcommittee, an interest in shifting military priorities away from a longstanding concentration on Europe and toward the Pacific. Citing his state's relative proximity to Asia, he has been among the handful of Senate Democrats to support a Republican effort to create a national missile defense system.

Inouye and Stevens also see eye-to-eye on most issues affecting indigenous populations. The prospect that native Alaskans might benefit from oil exploration in the Arctic National Wildlife Refuge caused Inouye to support Stevens' unsuccessful efforts in 2002 to open the refuge to oil drilling. Most Democrats opposed the controversial Bush-sponsored provision, saying it could damage Alaska's fragile wildlife and environment.

Inouye has used his position as top Democrat on the Senate Indian Affairs panel to advance legislation important to American Indians and native Hawaiians. In the 107th Congress, Inouye and the panel's top Republican, Coloradan Ben Nighthorse Campbell, battled Connecticut Democrats Christopher J. Dodd and Joseph I. Lieberman when they sought to put a moratorium on the recognition of new American Indian tribes.

Despite his popularity and longevity, Inouye has had trouble ascending the Senate leadership ladder. His 1989 bid for majority leader attracted only 14 of the 55 Democratic votes; Inouye never expanded his base beyond old hands and colleagues on the Appropriations Committee.

Inouye is revered by Hawaii's large Japanese-American community. In 1943, as an 18-year-old pre-med student at the University of Hawaii, he enlisted in the famed "Go for Broke" all-nisei 442nd Regimental Combat Team, and fought across Italy and France. When he advanced alone to take out a machine gun that had pinned down his men, he lost his right arm and spent 20 months in military hospitals. Prevented by his injury from becoming a surgeon, he went first into law and then into politics. He won his first election in 1954, to Hawaii's territorial House, and helped guide Hawaii to statehood. He was elected that year as the state's first U.S. House member, and in 1962 Inouye won election to the Senate.

He scored four more landslide wins over modest GOP opposition. But in 1992, Inouye's pedestal was shaken by state Sen. Rick Reed, his Republican opponent. Reed ran a radio ad featuring claims by Inouye's barber that Inouye had forced sex on her 17 years earlier and had made unwanted advances since. That prompted nine other women to make similar accusations, which Inouye called "unmitigated lies." The Ethics Committee dropped a review of the charges when the accusers declined to participate in its investigation. But the allegation likely contributed to his lowest winning percentage ever in a congressional race: 57 percent.

Inouye's political decline proved short-lived, however. His re-election numbers returned to form in 1998, when he drew 79 percent.

KEY VOTES

2002

Yes Pass farm bill reversing crop subsidy limits
No Postpone tougher automobile fuel efficiency standards
Yes Overhaul campaign finance law; ban "soft money" and restrict advocacy advertising
Yes Set federal election standards
Yes Support oil drilling in Arctic National Wildlife Refuge
? Revive fast-track procedures for trade agreements
Yes Create federal insurance coverage for catastrophic terrorist losses
Yes Tighten federal accounting and corporate governance regulation
Yes Advance bipartisan Medicare prescription drug plan
? Create independent Sept. 11 commission
Yes Back Democratic Homeland Security Department proposal
No Authorize war against Iraq

2001

No Confirm John Ashcroft as attorney general
No Nullify Clinton Labor Department ergonomics rule
No Cut taxes by $1.35 trillion through fiscal 2011
Yes Pass Democratic bill to bolster rights of patients in managed-care plans
No Permit a new round of military base closings
Yes Expand law enforcement power to investigate suspected terrorists

CQ VOTE STUDIES

	PARTY UNITY		PRESIDENTIAL SUPPORT	
	Support	Oppose	Support	Oppose
2002	90%	10%	76%	24%
2001	98%	2%	66%	34%
2000	91%	9%	94%	6%
1999	91%	9%	86%	14%
1998	93%	7%	87%	13%
1997	91%	9%	87%	13%
1996	87%	13%	86%	14%
1995	84%	16%	85%	15%
1994	92%	8%	95%	5%
1993	92%	8%	95%	5%

INTEREST GROUPS

	AFL-CIO	ADA	CCUS	ACU
2002	92%	80%	41%	0%
2001	100%	90%	43%	9%
2000	60%	60%	69%	23%
1999	88%	95%	50%	0%
1998	88%	80%	44%	9%
1997	83%	75%	50%	4%
1996	86%	85%	33%	11%
1995	100%	95%	41%	0%
1994	88%	75%	20%	0%
1993	100%	85%	20%	13%

Sen. Daniel K. Akaka (D)

CAPITOL OFFICE
224-6361
senator@akaka.senate.gov
akaka.senate.gov
141 Hart 20510-1103; fax 224-2126

COMMITTEES
Armed Services
Energy & Natural Resources
Governmental Affairs
Indian Affairs
Veterans' Affairs
Select Ethics

HOMETOWN
Honolulu

BORN
Sept. 11, 1924, Honolulu, Hawaii

RELIGION
Congregationalist

FAMILY
Wife, Mary Mildred Akaka; five children

EDUCATION
U. of Hawaii, B.Ed. 1952, M.Ed. 1966

MILITARY SERVICE
Army Corps of Engineers, 1945-47

CAREER
Gubernatorial aide; state economic grants official; elementary school principal and teacher

POLITICAL HIGHLIGHTS
Sought Democratic nomination for lieutenant governor, 1974; U.S. House, 1977-90

ELECTION RESULTS

2000 GENERAL		
Daniel K. Akaka (D)	251,215	72.7%
John S. Carroll (R)	84,701	24.5%
Lauri A. Clegg (NL)	4,220	1.2%
2000 PRIMARY		
Daniel K. Akaka (D)	150,507	90.2%
Arturo P. Reyes (D)	16,312	9.8%

PREVIOUS WINNING PERCENTAGES
1994 (72%); 1990 Special Election (54%); 1988 House Election (89%); 1986 House Election (76%); 1984 House Election (82%); 1982 House Election (89%); 1980 House Election (90%); 1978 House Election (86%); 1976 House Election (80%)

Elected 1990; 2nd full term

Appointed April 1990

While his low-key style means that Akaka is among the least-known senators in Washington, at home he is seen as an active member of a cohesive state delegation that protects Hawaii's interests. During the 107th Congress, for instance, he and the state's other veteran Democratic senator, Daniel K. Inouye, voted the same way 95 percent of the time.

The only native Hawaiian ever to serve in Congress (his mother is Hawaiian and his father is of Chinese and Hawaiian ancestry), Akaka (uh-KAH-kuh) gets involved in the nitty-gritty of the issues important to his state — some as serious as preserving the islands' role in national security, and others less weighty, such as creating a postage stamp with surfing legend Duke Kahanamoku's likeness.

Akaka often builds legislation from the ground up, meeting with scientists and local officials to gather information, then assembling support on the federal level. He has a quiet, deliberative working style — more in tune with traditional Hawaiian ways than with the modern media operations run by many in the Senate — described by one Pacific islander official as "island-style."

The 12-hour plane rides from Washington to Honolulu make it difficult for Akaka to return home, but he is never far from his roots. Every morning he meets with visiting constituents over coffee and pastries.

Native issues are often Akaka's focus. He helped craft a landmark measure in 2000 to set in motion a process to recognize native Hawaiians as a distinct indigenous group with federally guaranteed rights, and he introduced a similar bill in 2001, only to find it blocked by conservative Republicans on the Senate floor. The legislation would establish an Office of Hawaiian Affairs in the Interior Department and would set up a system by which native Hawaiians could gain rights similar to those of Indian tribes. "This is a question of fundamental fairness," Akaka said, and he introduced the bill again in the 108th.

The senator has long promoted the rights of indigenous peoples, especially native Hawaiians. An Akaka law enacted in the 104th Congress compensates native Hawaiians by transferring federal land to a trust in return for lands seized by the United States during the state's territorial period. The law builds on a measure that Akaka helped steer through the Senate in 1992: an apology to Hawaiians for the 1893 U.S. overthrow of the native government. But when that apology helped fuel an independence movement in Hawaii, Akaka the conciliator was quick to clarify that his intention was quite the opposite. "I look at the apology resolution as the first step toward healing, not creating new barriers," he said in 1998.

Akaka is a loyal Democrat. Over the years, he has joined the liberal wing of the party in opposing welfare overhaul, a balanced-budget constitutional amendment, the line-item veto and a ban on a procedure its opponents call "partial birth" abortion. But his commitment to native peoples can supersede his party ties.

In 2002, Akaka cited the Inupiat Eskimos' desire for economic development as his main reason for eschewing the concerns of environmentalists and supporting President Bush's proposal to allow oil drilling in Alaska's Arctic National Wildlife Refuge. He also said his longstanding friendship with Alaska Republican Frank H. Murkowski, a main proponent of the proposal, had factored into his support. When the issue came before the Senate and Akaka voted with Murkowski, Majority Leader Tom Daschle went through convoluted maneuvers to ensure that Akaka, the second-most-senior Democrat on the Energy panel, was not on the conference committee named to write a compromise House-Senate energy bill.

Over the years, Akaka has also made some waves in foreign policy. As Bush stepped up his efforts after the Sept. 11, 2001, bombings to punish Iraq for harboring terrorists, Akaka called on the administration to revive United Nations inspections of Iraqi weapons sites. "We should continue to push to get U.N. inspectors back on the ground," Akaka said at a hearing. "Keeping Saddam Hussein bottled up and forcing him to confront obstacles in every direction is not a bad thing." Later on, he opposed legislation authorizing the president to use force in Iraq.

In 2000, Akaka met with Cuban leader Fidel Castro for 10 hours after the senator and some of his colleagues traveled to the communist nation. Akaka, a former school teacher and principal, stressed the importance of increasing educational exchanges between the two countries. That same year, he steered a measure through the Senate to impose federal immigration laws on the Northern Mariana Islands, a U.S. territory that had become a haven for clothing industry sweatshops. "I speak as a friend and neighbor when I say that this policy cannot continue," Akaka said on the Senate floor. "The . . . system of indentured immigrant labor is morally wrong and violates basic democratic principles."

A protector of Hawaii's sugar industry, Akaka has successfully fought recurrent efforts to do away with federal sugar programs. In 1996 and again in 2001, he opposed efforts by New Hampshire Republican Judd Gregg to lessen the government's support of sugar producers. In 1990, Akaka won a larger victory for sugar subsidies against Democrat Bill Bradley of New Jersey, a lanky former basketball star. Of that fight, Akaka told a newspaper, "I'm only 5-feet-7, but I slam-dunked him."

The remark recalls an incident earlier in Akaka's career. In 1984, the House Democratic leadership was one vote short on a crucial roll call as it sought to block President Reagan's request for production of the MX missile. With time running out, Illinois Democrat Marty Russo located Akaka, who had been recorded as a pro-MX vote, lifted him out of a phone booth and escorted — some witnesses said carried — him into the chamber. Akaka then changed his vote, giving the anti-MX forces a key victory.

Akaka's career is a study in the quiet but steady perseverance of a quintessential team player. From teacher to assistant principal, principal, state bureaucrat, House member and ultimately senator, he has climbed the ladder one rung at a time.

Akaka rose through the Honolulu education bureaucracy before entering politics in 1971 as appointed head of the state Office of Economic Opportunity. In 1976, he captured the 2nd District seat after a difficult primary contest. He rose to the middle tier of seniority on the Appropriations Committee, where he concentrated almost entirely on fulfilling parochial needs. When Democrat Spark M. Matsunaga died in April 1990, Akaka was a logical choice to fill the Senate vacancy. Not only was he on good terms with Democratic Gov. John Waihee III, who made the appointment, he was also close to the state Democratic Party leadership and had received support throughout his career from Japanese-Americans, a crucial voting bloc.

However, with Akaka facing a special election in November 1990 to fill the remaining four years of Matsunaga's term, there was a degree of trepidation about Akaka's ability to hold the seat in the face of a challenge by Republican Rep. Patricia F. Saiki. Akaka had been a rather sedate figure during his House career and was not readily identifiable to many Hawaiians. But by playing to his strengths — his low-key personality and his ability to deliver federal largess to Hawaii — he won with a surprisingly solid 54 percent. He won his next two Senate elections far more easily.

KEY VOTES

2002

Yes Pass farm bill reversing crop subsidy limits
No Postpone tougher automobile fuel efficiency standards
Yes Overhaul campaign finance law; ban "soft money" and restrict advocacy advertising
Yes Set federal election standards
Yes Support oil drilling in Arctic National Wildlife Refuge
No Revive fast-track procedures for trade agreements
Yes Create federal insurance coverage for catastrophic terrorist losses
Yes Tighten federal accounting and corporate governance regulation
Yes Advance bipartisan Medicare prescription drug plan
Yes Create independent Sept. 11 commission
Yes Back Democratic Homeland Security Department proposal
No Authorize war against Iraq

2001

No Confirm John Ashcroft as attorney general
No Nullify Clinton Labor Department ergonomics rule
X Cut taxes by $1.35 trillion through fiscal 2011
Yes Pass Democratic bill to bolster rights of patients in managed-care plans
Yes Permit a new round of military base closings
Yes Expand law enforcement power to investigate suspected terrorists

CQ VOTE STUDIES

	PARTY UNITY		PRESIDENTIAL SUPPORT	
	Support	Oppose	Support	Oppose
2002	91%	9%	63%	37%
2001	98%	2%	70%	30%
2000	98%	2%	97%	3%
1999	96%	4%	89%	11%
1998	96%	4%	91%	9%
1997	97%	3%	90%	10%
1996	95%	5%	88%	12%
1995	95%	5%	89%	11%
1994	94%	6%	97%	3%
1993	95%	5%	94%	6%

INTEREST GROUPS

	AFL-CIO	ADA	CCUS	ACU
2002	100%	80%	53%	0%
2001	100%	95%	50%	13%
2000	86%	85%	46%	12%
1999	89%	100%	41%	4%
1998	100%	85%	41%	10%
1997	71%	95%	60%	4%
1996	100%	95%	31%	5%
1995	100%	95%	24%	0%
1994	88%	85%	20%	0%
1993	91%	90%	18%	4%

Rep. Neil Abercrombie (D)

CAPITOL OFFICE
225-2726
neil.abercrombie@mail.house.gov
www.house.gov/abercrombie
1502 Longworth 20515-1101; fax 225-4580

COMMITTEES
Armed Services
Resources

HOMETOWN
Honolulu

BORN
June 26, 1938, Buffalo, N.Y.

RELIGION
Unspecified

FAMILY
Wife, Nancie Caraway

EDUCATION
Union College, B.A. 1959; U. of Hawaii, M.A. 1964, Ph.D. 1974 (American studies)

CAREER
Educator

POLITICAL HIGHLIGHTS
Sought Democratic nomination for U.S. Senate, 1970; Hawaii House, 1974-78; Hawaii Senate, 1978-86; U.S. House, 1986-87; defeated in primary for re-election to U.S. House, 1986; Honolulu City Council, 1988-90

ELECTION RESULTS

2002 GENERAL		
Neil Abercrombie (D)	131,673	72.9%
Mark Terry (R)	45,032	24.9%
James H. Bracken (LIBERT)	4,028	2.2%
2002 PRIMARY		
Neil Abercrombie (D)		unopposed
2000 GENERAL		
Neil Abercrombie (D)	108,517	69.0%
Philip L. Meyers (R)	44,989	28.6%
Gerard Murphy (LIBERT)	3,688	2.4%

PREVIOUS WINNING PERCENTAGES
1998 (62%); 1996 (50%); 1994 (54%); 1992 (73%); 1990 (61%)

Elected 1990; 7th full term

Also served Sept. 1986-Jan. 1987

Abercrombie arrived in Congress in the early 1990s as an archetype from three decades earlier: the longhaired war protester pushing the left edge of the American ideological envelope at every turn. And, taken as a whole, his voting record reflects his membership in the Progressive Caucus, the most liberal faction of House Democrats.

But on some high-profile issues, ranging from business tax deductions to the size of the Pentagon budget, Abercrombie departs from liberal orthodoxy to represent a part of the country where the economic pillars are tourism and the military.

The ponytail was shorn in 1997, when Abercrombie concluded, "It was getting in the way of getting the job done." But aside from that concession, his public persona has not changed since he arrived in Congress. He still sports the bushy beard reminiscent of his days as a Vietnam War opponent. He is still a friendly, intense and burly fellow. And he still is incorrigibly irreverent, as he demonstrated by showing up at a White House reception with a shopping bag full of chocolate-covered macadamia nuts and Kona coffee — two of his state's delicacies — to give to the president.

He even talks like the professor he once was (although in 2001 he declined a nomination by the University of Hawaii's faculty union to become the school's president). When a federal appeals court ruled that schoolchildren could not be required to recite the pledge of allegiance because it contains the phrase "under God," Abercrombie joined all but three House members in voting to condemn the decision. But Abercrombie — who has opposed a constitutional ban on flag-burning — explained his vote in terms of the sociological importance of rituals such as the pledge in promoting values such as freedom and patriotism.

Some of his most striking deviations from the liberal line are on tax policies important to the travel and tourism industries that account for a large share of his state's employment. Abercrombie has pushed hard for legislation allowing a tax deduction for the full cost of business meals and entertainment as well as for travel costs of a spouse going along on a business trip. He also backed the long GOP-led campaign to repeal the estate tax, which he said is particularly harmful to Hawaii's many family-owned businesses.

The 2001 tax cut includes an Abercrombie-sponsored provision allowing shareholders in the Campbell Estate — Hawaii's seventh-largest private landowner — up to 14 years to pay the taxes they will owe when the trust is dissolved in 2007.

Still, Abercrombie's instinct is to side with workers over business. He voted against the House version of a bill to establish a Department of Homeland Security, objecting to provisions waiving certain Civil Service protections for employees of the new department and to others he said would grant overly broad protection against product liability suits to manufacturers of pharmaceuticals and emergency equipment.

Hawaii is the hub of U.S. military operations in the Pacific and East Asia, so it was natural that Abercrombie would take a seat on the Armed Services panel. Early in his tenure, he backed unsuccessful bids to restrain Pentagon spending. But more recently, he has sided with the committee's pro-defense majority on the overall budget issue. He was a leading advocate of legislation that provided military retirees with more-generous medical benefits while remaining skeptical of certain big-ticket weapons such as the

B-2 "stealth" bomber and a proposed anti-missile defense system.

In the 108th Congress, Abercrombie is the top-ranking Democrat on the Tactical Air and Land Forces Subcommittee, which has jurisdiction over Army and Air Force programs, as well as Navy and Marine Corps tactical aviation.

He also is a senior member of the Readiness Subcommittee, which has general oversight authority over military construction as well as jurisdiction over Navy shipyards, including Pearl Harbor Naval Shipyard. In 2002, a new tugboat that services Navy vessels at Pearl Harbor was named after him.

Abercrombie and fellow Hawaii Democrat Daniel K. Inouye, the top-ranking Democrat on the Senate Defense Appropriations Subcommittee, routinely add several hundred million dollars annually to the Pentagon budget for construction or research projects in their state.

Another top priority for Abercrombie has been protecting civilian federal employees against what he sees as a "pro-privatization" bias in the process the government uses to decide whether to outsource work. And he has pushed legislation that would recognize native Hawaiians as a distinct indigenous group with the right to self-determination.

Abercrombie has not abandoned his skepticism toward the wisdom of using military force when other options are available. Though he backed the military operations in Afghanistan after the Sept. 11, 2001, attacks, he warned against getting U.S. troops involved in counterinsurgency operations in the Philippines. And he voted against the 2002 law authorizing President Bush to use force against Iraq.

The man who now represents Waikiki got his start in Buffalo, N.Y. After college, he taught school for a time before moving to Hawaii for graduate school. He became a practitioner of protest politics, taking 13 percent of the 1970 Democratic Senate primary vote as an anti-Vietnam War candidate. Four years later he won election to the state House.

After 11-plus years in the legislature, Abercrombie briefly served in the House when he won a special election in 1986 to fill a vacancy. But he narrowly lost the primary election for a full term, which was held the same day. He got a second chance when the seat opened up in 1990, winning the Democratic primary with 46 percent of the vote and cruising to an easy victory in November.

But he faced difficult re-election battles in 1994 and 1996 and struggled to fend off charges that he was an extreme liberal. Since then, however, he has won by comfortable margins.

KEY VOTES

2002

Yes	Overhaul campaign finance law; ban "soft money" and restrict advocacy advertising
Yes	Back Bush's defense budget increase
No	Extend 1996 welfare law
No	Adopt Bush's discretionary spending limit
No	Pass GOP Medicare prescription drug plan
Yes	Create independent Sept. 11 commission
Yes	Extend union protections to Homeland Security Department employees
No	Revive fast-track procedures for trade agreements
No	Authorize war against Iraq
No	Advance bankruptcy overhaul opposed by abortion opponents

2001

No	Nullify Clinton Labor Department ergonomics rule
Yes	Cut taxes by $1.35 trillion through fiscal 2011
Yes	Maintain ban on oil drilling in Arctic National Wildlife Refuge
No	Approve Bush proposal to limit managed-care plan liability for coverage decisions
Yes	Divert money from crop subsidy payments to land conservation
?	Expand law enforcement power to investigate suspected terrorists

CQ VOTE STUDIES

	PARTY UNITY		PRESIDENTIAL SUPPORT	
	Support	Oppose	Support	Oppose
2002	89%	11%	32%	68%
2001	79%	21%	35%	65%
2000	86%	14%	72%	28%
1999	89%	11%	71%	29%
1998	92%	8%	82%	18%

INTEREST GROUPS

	AFL-CIO	ADA	CCUS	ACU
2002	100%	85%	45%	12%
2001	92%	90%	39%	8%
2000	90%	80%	42%	12%
1999	100%	100%	17%	4%
1998	100%	95%	22%	12%

HAWAII 1

Oahu — Honolulu, Waipahu, Pearl City

Located on the southern coast of Oahu Island, the compact 1st takes in the narrow plain south of the Koolau mountain range, encompassing the city of Honolulu — the engine that drives all of Hawaii. Redistricting following the 2000 census added only one town, Waipahu, which lies west of Honolulu. Pearl Harbor is the district's unforgettable landmark.

Honolulu is Hawaii's capital, home to most of its business and about a third of its people. To the east lies Waikiki and the heart of Hawaii's leading industry: tourism. The state experienced a downturn in the mid-1990s as Asia's economic problems meant fewer Japanese visitors and less Japanese investment in the state. The Sept. 11 terrorist attacks also hurt tourism, but it has largely rebounded. The district's other major economic plank — the military — managed to escape major cuts and is holding steady.

The 1st is a Democratic stronghold and has elected only one Republican to Congress in its history. Japanese-Americans — particularly of the older generation — dominate the Democratic Party and are joined by many other non-white constituents who form the majority of the 1st's residents. Locally, Democrats do very well in elections, although some moderate Republican enclaves exist in the suburbs of East Honolulu and Waikiki. But even in traditionally GOP areas, Democratic Rep. Abercrombie garners support.

MAJOR INDUSTRY

Tourism, military, construction

MILITARY BASES

Hickam Air Force Base, 4,395 military, 1,559 civilian; Pearl Harbor Naval Shipyard and Intermediate Maintenance Facility, 610 military, 3,673 civilian; Camp H.M. Smith, 633 military, 62 civilian; Pearl Harbor Naval Submarine Base, 2,830 military, 59 civilian; Tripler Army Medical Center, 1,469 military, 1,477 civilian; Fort Shafter, 603 military, 1,481 civilian; Pearl Harbor Naval Station, 567 military, 440 civilian (2000)

CITIES

Honolulu, 371,657; Waipahu, 33,108; Pearl City, 30,976; Waimalu, 29,371

NOTABLE

Iolani Palace in Honolulu is believed to be the only palace in the United States; Ala Wai Golf Course in Waikiki, now with roughly 165,000 rounds a year, has been rated "busiest course" by the Guiness Book of Records.

Rep. Ed Case (D)

CAPITOL OFFICE
225-4906
ed.case@mail.house.gov
www.house.gov/case
128 Cannon 20515-1102; fax 225-4987

COMMITTEES
Agriculture
Education & Workforce
Small Business

HOMETOWN
Honolulu

BORN
Sept. 27, 1952, Hilo, Hawaii

RELIGION
Protestant

FAMILY
Wife, Audrey Case; four children

EDUCATION
Williams College, B.A. 1975 (psychology); U. of California, Hastings College of Law, J.D. 1981

CAREER
Lawyer; congressional aide

POLITICAL HIGHLIGHTS
Manoa Neighborhood Board, 1985-89; Democratic nominee for Hawaii House, 1986, 1988; Hawaii House, 1995-2002 (majority leader, 1999-2001); sought Democratic nomination for governor, 2002

ELECTION RESULTS

2003 SPECIAL		
Ed Case (D)	33,002	43.7%
Matt Matsunaga (D)	23,050	30.5%
Colleen Hanabusa (D)	6,046	8.0%
Barbara Marumoto (R)	4,497	6.0%
Bob McDermott (R)	4,298	5.7%
Others	823	1.1%
2002 SPECIAL		
Ed Case (D)	23,576	51.4%
John Mink (D)	16,624	36.3%
John S. Carroll (R)	1,933	4.2%
Others	1,233	2.7%
Whitney T. Anderson (R)	942	2.1%

Elected 2002; 1st full term

Case represents a new wave in Hawaii congressional politics. Elected at age 50, he is the youngest person in the state's delegation by 14 years and the first newcomer to the delegation in more than a decade. He also ran on a pledge to shake up the state's long-dominant Democratic establishment.

Case says his views — liberal on social issues, centrist on economic issues — align with those of Congress' coalition of New Democrats. He focused heavily on education in his bid for the House, noting that standardized tests show Hawaii's public school system to be one of the worst performers in the nation; and he won a seat on the Education and the Workforce panel in Congress. Another committee assignment, Agriculture, will allow him to look out for the cattle ranches, coffee farms and sugar and pineapple plantations of the 2nd District, which includes most of Oahu outside Honolulu and all of the other Hawaiian islands.

Case, a lawyer who worked with Hawaii's largest law firm, said his life apart from politics has made him a better legislator. "I bring the expertise of moving easily between the world of business and the world of government," said Case, whose first cousin Steve Case was a founder of AOL. "I've lived with one foot in each of those worlds for decades now."

After seven years in the state House, Case narrowly lost a longshot bid for the Democratic gubernatorial nomination in 2002. But he leveraged that effort to become the front-runner to succeed Patsy T. Mink, the first nonwhite woman elected to Congress, who died in September 2002. Case garnered an outright majority of 51 percent of the vote against 36 other aspirants to win a November special election for the final weeks of Mink's 12th full term. Although the 107th Congress had adjourned and Case was never officially sworn in, his first victory nonetheless allowed him to run as the incumbent in the January 2003 special election to replace Mink in the 108th Congress. (She had won re-election posthumously in November.) In a field of 44 candidates, he bested runner-up Matt Matsunaga, a former state senator, by 13 percentage points.

HAWAII 2

Suburban and Outer Oahu; 'Neighbor Islands'

Some visitors call these Pacific islands paradise. With beaches, volcanoes, rain forests and deserts, the 2nd is amazing in its geographic diversity. It includes part of Oahu and all of the other seven major islands that make up the state.

The 2nd's economy struggled through rough times in the 1990s with both of its major industries, tourism and agriculture, in crisis. The more luxury-oriented tourism offered in the 2nd was not as hard-hit as Honolulu. But the Japanese yen's depreciation and Asia's economic woes resulted in Asian visitors spending less in the latter part of the decade — a worrisome development in a state that welcomes more than one-fourth of its tourists from Japan. A wave of sugar plantation closures also shook the economy, but growers are diversifying by adding more coffee, macadamia nuts and bananas. Tax incentives have helped attract biotech and information technology companies.

The 2nd has large Asian sections and is heavily Democratic. While there are some predominately white, conservative-leaning communities on Oahu and Maui, these areas barely make a dent. Economic problems can give the GOP grounds to make inroads at the local level, but the liberal 2nd has kept Democrats in office.

MAJOR INDUSTRY
Tourism, agriculture, military

MILITARY BASES
Schofield Barracks (Army), 13,090 military, 1,623 civilian (2002); Marine Corps Base Hawaii, 6,970 military, 1,650 civilian; Naval Computer and Telecommunications Area Master Station Pacific, 584 military, 224 civilian (1998); Lualualei Naval Magazine, 232 military, 403 civilian (2000)

CITIES
Hilo, 40,759; Kailua (unincorporated), 36,513; Kaneohe, 34,970; Kahului, 20,146

NOTABLE
Kauai's Waialeale, the wettest spot on earth, averages 300 inches of rain annually.

IDAHO

Gov. Dirk Kempthorne (R)

First elected: 1998
Length of term: 4 years
Term expires: 1/07
Salary: $98,500
Phone: (208) 334-2100
Hometown: Boise
Born: Oct. 29, 1951; San Diego, Calif.
Religion: Methodist
Family: Wife, Patricia Kempthorne; two children
Education: U. of Idaho, B.A. 1975 (political science)
Career: Public affairs manager; securities representative; political consultant; building association executive
Political highlights: Mayor of Boise, 1986-92; U.S. Senate, 1993-99
Election results:

2002 GENERAL		
Dirk Kempthorne (R)	231,566	56.3%
Jerry M. Brady (D)	171,711	41.7%
Daniel L.J. Adams (LIBERT)	8,187	2.0%

Lt. Gov. Jim Risch (R)

First elected: 2002
Length of term: 4 years
Term expires: 1/07
Salary: $26,750
Phone: (208) 334-2200

STATE LEGISLATURE

Legislature: Meets January-March
House: 70 members, 2-year terms
2003 breakdown: 54R, 16D; 47 men, 23 women
Salary: $15,646; $1,700/year in expenses
Phone: (208) 332-1140
Senate: 35 members, 2-year terms
2003 breakdown: 28R, 7D; 31 men, 4 women
Salary: $15,646; $1,700/year in expenses
Phone: (208) 332-1309

STATE TERM LIMITS

Governor: 2 terms; can run eight years later
Senate: 4 terms in a 15-year period
House: 4 terms in a 15-year period

URBAN STATISTICS

CITY	POPULATION
Boise	185,787
Nampa	51,867
Pocatello	51,466
Idaho Falls	50,730
Meridian	34,919

REGISTERED VOTERS

Voters do not register by party.

POPULATION

2002 population (est.)	1,341,131
2000 population	1,293,953
1990 population	1,006,749
Percent change (1990-2000)	+28.5%
Rank among states (2002)	39
Median age	33.2
Born in state	47.2%
Foreign born	5%
Violent crime rate	253/100,000
Poverty level	11.8%
Federal workers	12,939
Military	9,730

REDISTRICTING

Idaho retained its two House seats in reapportionment. The Idaho Commission on Redistricting adopted a new map on Aug. 22, 2001.

MISCELLANEOUS

Web: www.state.id.us
Capital: Boise

STATE ELECTION OFFICIAL
(208) 334-2300

DEMOCRATIC HEADQUARTERS
(208) 336-1815

REPUBLICAN HEADQUARTERS
(208) 343-6405

District Statistics

DIST.	2000 VOTE FOR PRESIDENT BUSH	GORE	NADER	WHITE	BLACK	ASIAN	HISP	MEDIAN INCOME	WHITE COLLAR	BLUE COLLAR	SERVICE INDUSTRY	OVER 64	UNDER 18	COLLEGE EDUCATION	RURAL	SQ. MILES
1	68%	28%	n/a	89%	0%	1%	7%	$38,364	56%	28%	15%	12%	28%	20%	34%	39,525
2	64	26	n/a	87	0	1	9	$36,934	57	27	16	11	29	23	33	43,222
STATE	67	28	2	88	0	1	8	$37,572	57	28	16	11	29	22	34	82,747
U.S.	47.9	48.4	3	69	12	4	13	$41,994	60	25	15	12	26	24	21	3,537,438

Boundary
Bonner
Coeur d'Alene
Kootenai
Benewah
Shoshone
Moscow
Latah
Clearwater
Nez Perce
Lewiston
Lewis
Idaho
1
Adams
Valley
Lemhi
Washington
Custer
2
Clark
Fremont
Payette
Gem
Boise
Jefferson
Madison
Teton
Canyon
Butte
Boise
Idaho Falls
Bonneville
Ada
Elmore
Camas
Blaine
Bingham
Gooding
Lincoln
Caribou
Jerome
Minidoka
Power
Bannock
Owyhee
Twin Falls
Cassia
Twin Falls
Oneida
Franklin
Bear Lake

Sen. Larry E. Craig (R)

CAPITOL OFFICE
224-2752
craig.senate.gov
520 Hart 20510-1203; fax 228-1067

COMMITTEES
Appropriations
Energy & Natural Resources
(Public Lands & Forests - chairman)
Judiciary
Veterans' Affairs
Special Aging - chairman

HOMETOWN
Payette

BORN
July 20, 1945, Council, Idaho

RELIGION
Methodist

FAMILY
Wife, Suzanne Craig; three children

EDUCATION
U. of Idaho, B.A. 1969 (political science); George Washington U., attended 1969-70 (U.S. foreign policy)

MILITARY SERVICE
Idaho National Guard, 1970-72

CAREER
Farmer; rancher

POLITICAL HIGHLIGHTS
Idaho Senate, 1975-81; U.S. House, 1981-91

ELECTION RESULTS

2002 GENERAL		
Larry E. Craig (R)	266,215	65.2%
Alan Blinken (D)	132,975	32.6%
Donovan Bramwell (LIBERT)	9,354	2.3%
2002 PRIMARY		
Larry E. Craig (R)		unopposed

PREVIOUS WINNING PERCENTAGES
1996 (57%); 1990 (61%); 1988 House Election (66%); 1986 House Election (65%); 1984 House Election (69%); 1982 House Election (54%); 1980 House Election (54%)

Elected 1990; 3rd term

Building on a pioneer heritage of rugged individualism, Craig represents a strongly conservative and thoroughly modern West anxious to throw off a century of regulations over its ranches, farms and forests.

His unwavering conservatism, combined with flawless diction and masterful debating skills, lifted Craig to the chairmanship of the Republican Policy Committee, the fourth-ranking GOP leadership position, at the start of his second term in 1997 — a post he was forced to relinquish in the 108th Congress because of party-imposed leadership term limits.

Instead, he took over as the appointed chairman of the GOP Committee on Committees and resumed the chairmanship of the Aging Committee, which he chaired for the first five months of the 107th Congress, until the Democrats took control of the Senate. Craig also added the Judiciary Committee to his portfolio in the 108th.

Craig has been an unambiguous advocate of the "multiple use" of public lands in the West, fighting efforts by Democrats and some moderate Republicans to limit or eliminate grazing, mining, oil and gas drilling and road-building on the millions of acres owned by the United States government. "Like a lot of Westerners, I come from pioneer stock. My grandmother rode west in a covered wagon," Craig wrote in a statement of his Western agenda. Where pioneers tamed the West to mine the gold, timber and other natural riches, Craig sees a new wave of "amenity migrants" arriving in search of an outdoor lifestyle. "In their own way, these people are tied to the land like the pioneers of old," he wrote. What ties the old and new together, he said, is "an appreciation for the resources and the value that multiple uses contribute to our livelihoods and communities."

Throughout his decade in the House and first dozen years in the Senate, Craig has taken aim at environmental laws — most notably the Endangered Species Act — that he says trample on private property rights and inhibit job growth. Thus, it was with particular zeal that he staged a loud but unsuccessful fight with Senate Democrats in the 107th to allow selective logging in national forests to reduce the risk of wildfires.

Craig furiously advocated a Bush administration proposal designed to reduce legal and administrative barriers to thinning underbrush and small trees, as well as commercially valuable old-growth trees. It also would have blocked environmentalists and community activists from seeking court orders to temporarily block proposed logging and other fire-prevention programs in national forests.

Craig joined the Appropriations Committee in 1997 and used the post, with limited success, to fight the Clinton administration's penchant for regulatory changes affecting public lands. In the 106th, he scored a big win for Idaho by helping push to enactment a bill to compensate rural counties that had lost revenue because of decreased timber sales from public lands. But he has never earned sufficient seniority on any subcommittee to win elevation as its chairman.

His conservative views place Craig in the mainstream among Senate Republicans, but his aggressive advocacy and talkative ways can sometimes irk colleagues. At the start of the 107th, Craig nearly lost his Policy Committee chairmanship to Pete V. Domenici of New Mexico on a narrow vote. Later in 2001, Vermont's James M. Jeffords left the Republican Party to protest what he saw as the party's increasingly extreme conservative positions on an array of issues.

Craig is not blindly partisan. He made a highly publicized break with the president in 2002, when the Senate debated Bush's legislation requiring Congress to approve or reject presidential trade agreements, without alteration. Craig wanted to give the Senate power to vote separately on portions of trade pacts that would weaken U.S. laws barring foreign countries from dumping cheap products on U.S. markets. He teamed with Minnesota Democrat Mark Dayton and won adoption of such language by the Senate. Bush threatened to veto the bill unless the provision was removed, and in the end Craig settled for provisions that require trade negotiators to preserve U.S. anti-dumping laws if possible and to report to Congress if they have to weaken or eliminate them to reach a deal.

Craig in 2002 also was one of the first Republicans to question Bush's initial saber-rattling against Iraq. "The president must make the case before the American people and the Congress," Craig said. "And when that case is made, we will all make a judgment based on the evidence provided to us. The business of war is mighty serious business."

Craig is on the board of the National Rifle Association and in the Senate he zealously guards the rights of gun owners. After a student massacre at Colorado's Columbine High School in 1999, Craig led the campaign against proposals to require background checks on prospective purchasers at gun shows. The Senate backed them anyway, but the bill was never enacted. In the 107th Congress, Craig teamed with fellow Republican John McCain of Arizona and two Democrats, Charles E. Schumer of New York and Edward M. Kennedy of Massachusetts, to push legislation strengthening instant background checks to better keep guns from felons and the mentally ill. (They called themselves the "Odd Quad.")

Craig showed an early appetite for politics. Born on his family's ranch, which was homesteaded in 1899 by his grandfather, he served as the Idaho state president and national vice president of the Future Farmers of America and as head of the Idaho Young Republicans before running successfully for the state Senate in 1974. In the legislature, he was known as something of a moderate. But in his initial House campaign in 1980, he tied himself to Steve Symms, the district's conservative incumbent then campaigning for the Senate. After winning a tough primary, Craig was rated a solid favorite. But Democrat Glenn W. Nichols drew attention by walking the length of the district, from Canada to Nevada, and held Craig to 54 percent.

As part of the first wave of the "Reagan revolution," Craig helped move that chamber far enough to the right to pass President Reagan's tax and spending plans in the 97th Congress. But his unspectacular showing in a strong Republican year guaranteed a tough challenge in 1982. Democrats chose Larry LaRocco, who had worked as northern Idaho field representative for Democratic Sen. Frank Church. But Craig again won with 54 percent. After that, he won about two-thirds of the vote in three subsequent House races.

The retirement of Republican James A. McClure after three terms in 1990 gave Craig his opportunity to advance to the Senate. He got into the race early and easily bested state Attorney General Jim Jones, winning 59 percent of the vote in the GOP primary. In the general election, Craig roared past Democrat Ron Twilegar, a former state legislator and Boise City Council member, with 61 percent.

In 1996, Craig's Democratic opponent was Walt Minnick, a former executive at a Boise lumber company with strong GOP credentials; he was a one-time aide in the Nixon White House. Democrats had a brief flurry of hope, but Craig campaigned vigorously and ended up capturing 57 percent. He had even less trouble winning a third term in 2002, collecting 65 percent of the vote against Democrat Alan Blinken, who had been President Clinton's ambassador to Belgium, and Libertarian Donovan Bramwell.

KEY VOTES

2002

- No Pass farm bill reversing crop subsidy limits
- Yes Postpone tougher automobile fuel efficiency standards
- No Overhaul campaign finance law; ban "soft money" and restrict advocacy advertising
- Yes Set federal election standards
- Yes Support oil drilling in Arctic National Wildlife Refuge
- Yes Revive fast-track procedures for trade agreements
- No Create federal insurance coverage for catastrophic terrorist losses
- \+ Tighten federal accounting and corporate governance regulation
- No Advance bipartisan Medicare prescription drug plan
- Yes Create independent Sept. 11 commission
- No Back Democratic Homeland Security Department proposal
- Yes Authorize war against Iraq

2001

- Yes Confirm John Ashcroft as attorney general
- Yes Nullify Clinton Labor Department ergonomics rule
- Yes Cut taxes by $1.35 trillion through fiscal 2011
- No Pass Democratic bill to bolster rights of patients in managed-care plans
- No Permit a new round of military base closings
- Yes Expand law enforcement power to investigate suspected terrorists

CQ VOTE STUDIES

	PARTY UNITY		PRESIDENTIAL SUPPORT	
	Support	Oppose	Support	Oppose
2002	93%	7%	95%	5%
2001	96%	4%	97%	3%
2000	100%	0%	40%	60%
1999	97%	3%	29%	71%
1998	99%	1%	29%	71%
1997	97%	3%	54%	46%
1996	98%	2%	32%	68%
1995	98%	2%	20%	80%
1994	98%	2%	30%	70%
1993	97%	3%	15%	85%

INTEREST GROUPS

	AFL-CIO	ADA	CCUS	ACU
2002	8%	5%	90%	100%
2001	13%	0%	100%	96%
2000	0%	0%	93%	100%
1999	0%	0%	88%	96%
1998	0%	5%	100%	84%
1997	0%	5%	100%	84%
1996	0%	0%	100%	95%
1995	0%	0%	100%	96%
1994	13%	0%	80%	100%
1993	18%	5%	91%	100%

Sen. Michael D. Crapo (R)

CAPITOL OFFICE
224-6142
crapo.senate.gov
111 Russell 20510-1205; fax 228-1375

COMMITTEES
Agriculture, Nutrition & Forestry
(Forestry, Conservation & Rural Revitalization - chairman)
Banking, Housing & Urban Affairs
Budget
Environment & Public Works
(Fisheries, Wildlife & Water - chairman)
Small Business & Entrepreneurship

HOMETOWN
Idaho Falls

BORN
May 20, 1951, Idaho Falls, Idaho

RELIGION
Mormon

FAMILY
Wife, Susan Crapo; five children

EDUCATION
Brigham Young U., B.A. 1973 (political science); Harvard U., J.D. 1977

CAREER
Lawyer

POLITICAL HIGHLIGHTS
Idaho Senate, 1985-93 (president pro tempore, 1989-93); U.S. House, 1993-99

ELECTION RESULTS

1998 GENERAL		
Michael D. Crapo (R)	262,966	69.5%
Bill Mauk (D)	107,375	28.4%
George J. Mansfeld (NL)	7,833	2.1%
1998 PRIMARY		
Michael D. Crapo (R)	110,205	87.3%
Matt Alan Lambert (R)	16,075	12.7%

PREVIOUS WINNING PERCENTAGES
1996 House Election (69%); 1994 House Election (75%); 1992 House Election (61%)

Elected 1998; 1st term

Conservative in his political philosophy and moderate in his demeanor, Crapo focuses his efforts largely on matters of local concern while casting dependable votes for the Senate Republican leadership and President Bush.

He is reluctant to personalize political disagreements, and he usually can count on a receptive audience when he seeks to cross party lines to gain a compromise or cosponsors. As he approaches the end of his first term, he is still described by many of his colleagues as "a nice guy."

His mild manner belies an ambition, largely fueled by his dedication to a deceased older brother, that is reflected in the climb that Crapo (CRAY-poe) has made up the political ladder. A cum laude graduate of Harvard Law School, he was elected to the state Senate at age 33 and chosen its president pro tempore just four years later. He won the 2nd District's House seat in 1992 and was tapped to be the freshman class representative to the GOP leadership. In 1998, he breezed into an open Senate seat. In the 107th Congress, he was named a GOP deputy whip.

Throughout his public life, Crapo has been guided by his desire to fulfill dreams his oldest brother, Terry, could not. An Idaho state legislator and wunderkind who was also Michael Crapo's mentor and law partner, Terry Crapo died just two weeks after he was diagnosed with leukemia in 1982. In a written response to an Idaho newspaper's question about the motivations of political candidates in 1996, Crapo said, "I began to reflect on how Terry might face this battle if the roles were reversed. I knew without a doubt that he would be in there fighting until the very last moment."

Crapo faced his own trial with cancer in 2000, when doctors diagnosed prostate cancer and operated. He recovered quickly and now sponsors health screening booths at fairs across the state.

Crapo always has maintained good relations with the Republican leadership. In the House, he was given a seat on the Energy and Commerce Committee in his first term. He later was assigned to the Resources Committee, which deals with a broad range of Western concerns. In the Senate, Crapo is well-placed to continue his work on resource issues. He has subcommittee chairmanships on both the Environment and Agriculture committees and also has seats on the Budget, Banking and Small Business panels.

In the 107th, Crapo was among those lawmakers who successfully fought for a delay in proposed EPA regulations affecting bodies of water considered to be polluted from agricultural runoff.

As Congress worked to rewrite the farm bill in the 107th, Crapo was a leader in the fight against a conservation proposal to let the government buy water rights from farmers. He also was opposed to proposed changes in the dairy program that he said would put Idaho dairymen at a disadvantage. On both issues, he and Republican Larry E. Craig, Idaho's senior senator, let it be known they would not give in easily and their opposition persuaded sponsors to water down both proposals.

Crapo's opposition also stalled for an entire year a bill to speed the cleanup of polluted industrial sites, known as brownfields. Crapo said he feared that a stand-alone brownfields bill would reduce the momentum for a broader overhaul of the federal superfund law. He relented in 2001 and the legislation became law, after it was changed to limit the EPA's authority over ongoing cleanup work. Crapo says he favors more community involvement in cleanup efforts.

Crapo supported an environmental measure that first was enacted in

1999 as an Idaho pilot project to provide federal grants to small communities that need help complying with water treatment, clean air and other environmental regulations. He broadened the program in the 107th, and included it in the farm legislation enacted in 2002.

Like many Western legislators, Crapo is wary of Canadian policies toward timber and agricultural trade with the United States. He bucked the majority of his party and opposed legislation to implement both the 1993 North American Free Trade Agreement and the 1994 General Agreement on Tariffs and Trade. He attended the protest-plagued 1999 World Trade Organization meeting in Seattle to ensure that farmers were not given short shrift in trade negotiations. Since then he has voted to enact the 2000 law making permanent the normalized U.S.-China trade relationship and the 2002 law giving the president fast track authority to negotiate trade deals.

Crapo also has worked successfully with Democrats to promote certain education initiatives. The main goals of several of his proposals, to improve rural education, technology and teacher training, were made part of the education policy overhaul that became law in 2002. Other education measures he has introduced were endorsed by the National Education Association, a group often at odds with the GOP.

The youngest of six children of an Idaho Falls postmaster and his homemaker wife, Crapo graduated from Brigham Young University with a degree in political science. He was an intern with GOP Rep. Orval Hansen of Idaho during the summer that the Watergate scandal began and later watched the televised hearings with great interest. "It bothered me to see that happening . . . but I was also fascinated with the political process and the fact that our system had a mechanism" to deal with the crisis, he later told the Spokane (Wash.) Spokesman-Review.

Crapo thought about becoming a doctor and after graduating from college spent a year in a pre-med program. But he changed his mind after gaining admission to Harvard Law School. After graduating and working as a law clerk, Crapo returned to his hometown to practice law.

A devout Mormon, Crapo says his experiences with the church, which gives its lay leaders considerable responsibilities in dealing with personal and community issues, helped prepare him for public office. Friendly and casual, he is more at ease wearing boots, jeans and a plaid shirt. He says he is sorry that his days of riding dirt bikes, a favorite pastime in college, are now behind him.

During his tenure in the state legislature, Crapo was a calming presence in an otherwise boisterous body and showed a willingness to seek consensus. More than once, colleagues who remembered his brother would mistakenly call him Terry.

In 1992, he ran for the House seat being vacated by Democrat Richard Stallings, who ran unsuccessfully for the Senate instead. In the GOP-leaning 2nd, Crapo was aided by George Bush's top-of-the-ticket presence as the GOP presidential candidate, and he defeated Democrat J.D. Williams by 26 percentage points.

Crapo never has had a difficult time winning re-election, and when Republican Sen. Dirk Kempthorne decided to run for governor in 1998, Crapo quickly became the ordained front-runner as his successor. Following a relatively effortless primary, Crapo's general popularity and a strong Republican tide enabled him to crush Bill Mauk, a former Democratic state chairman, by more than 40 points.

At the start of the Bush administration, there was discussion that he might be interested in a federal judgeship. Crapo didn't deny that he might someday be interested in that or in running for governor, perhaps, but he said the talk was premature. He called the Senate his "dream job."

KEY VOTES

2002

No Pass farm bill reversing crop subsidy limits
Yes Postpone tougher automobile fuel efficiency standards
No Overhaul campaign finance law; ban "soft money" and restrict advocacy advertising
Yes Set federal election standards
Yes Support oil drilling in Arctic National Wildlife Refuge
Yes Revive fast-track procedures for trade agreements
Yes Create federal insurance coverage for catastrophic terrorist losses
\+ Tighten federal accounting and corporate governance regulation
No Advance bipartisan Medicare prescription drug plan
Yes Create independent Sept. 11 commission
No Back Democratic Homeland Security Department proposal
Yes Authorize war against Iraq

2001

Yes Confirm John Ashcroft as attorney general
Yes Nullify Clinton Labor Department ergonomics rule
Yes Cut taxes by $1.35 trillion through fiscal 2011
No Pass Democratic bill to bolster rights of patients in managed-care plans
No Permit a new round of military base closings
Yes Expand law enforcement power to investigate suspected terrorists

CQ VOTE STUDIES

	PARTY UNITY		PRESIDENTIAL SUPPORT	
	Support	Oppose	Support	Oppose
2002	92%	8%	96%	4%
2001	94%	6%	96%	4%
2000	100%	0%	41%	59%
1999	97%	3%	30%	70%
House Service:				
1998	89%	11%	30%	70%
1997	94%	6%	20%	80%
1996	95%	5%	30%	70%
1995	97%	3%	21%	79%
1994	96%	4%	40%	60%
1993	96%	4%	33%	67%

INTEREST GROUPS

	AFL-CIO	ADA	CCUS	ACU
2002	9%	10%	94%	94%
2001	19%	10%	100%	92%
2000	0%	0%	93%	100%
1999	0%	0%	88%	100%
House Service:				
1998	22%	10%	94%	83%
1997	13%	0%	70%	92%
1996	0%	0%	100%	95%
1995	0%	5%	100%	92%
1994	11%	5%	83%	90%
1993	8%	5%	91%	96%

Rep. C. L. 'Butch' Otter (R)

CAPITOL OFFICE
225-6611
www.house.gov/otter
1711 Longworth 20515-1201; fax 225-3029

COMMITTEES
Energy & Commerce

HOMETOWN
Star

BORN
May 3, 1942, Caldwell, Idaho

RELIGION
Roman Catholic

FAMILY
Divorced; four children

EDUCATION
College of Idaho, B.A. 1967 (political science)

MILITARY SERVICE
Idaho National Guard, 1967-73

CAREER
Agribusiness company executive; oil company partner

POLITICAL HIGHLIGHTS
Idaho House, 1973-77; sought Republican nomination for governor, 1978; lieutenant governor, 1987-2001

ELECTION RESULTS

2002 GENERAL		
C. L. "Butch" Otter (R)	120,743	58.6%
Betty Richardson (D)	80,269	38.9%
Steve Gothard (LIBERT)	5,129	2.5%
2002 PRIMARY		
C. L. "Butch" Otter (R)		unopposed
2000 GENERAL		
C. L. "Butch" Otter (R)	173,743	64.8%
Linda Pall (D)	84,080	31.4%
Ronald G. Wittig (LIBERT)	6,093	2.3%
Kevin Philip Hambsch (REF)	4,200	1.6%

Elected 2000; 2nd term

Otter came to Congress as an advocate for a limited federal role on almost all issues. He tries to keep Washington from restricting private property rights, infringing on civil liberties in the name of anti-terrorism protection and forcing states to raise the legal drinking age.

Otter's libertarian inclination seems to go over well with Idaho voters, who elected him to the Idaho House twice and as lieutenant governor four times before sending him to Washington. His views match those of many of his constituents, as Idaho can claim to be the nation's most Republican-dominated state.

A back-slapping, guitar-strumming cowboy at heart, Otter's personal appeal also explains how he has been able to sustain Idahoans' support despite a drunken driving conviction and a divorce from his wife of 30 years.

Much of Idaho's land is under federal control, and like many Western lawmakers, Otter is an ardent advocate of state management of federal lands. A millionaire businessman and rancher, Otter has had his own run-ins with the federal government. He was fined $50,000 by the Environmental Protection Agency in 2001 for filling in wetlands on his ranch along the Boise River. It was his third EPA citation.

Otter's tangles with EPA over the work he has done on his ranch illustrate his attitude about the government's reach into private property rights. "I think the EPA is way out of control," he told the Spokane (Wash.) Spokesman-Review, adding that he does not believe he has done anything wrong. He argues that "sound science" should guide the implementation of EPA regulations and the Endangered Species Act.

One of his priorities in Congress is to require the federal government to complete studies of potential wilderness areas within 10 years. He contends that some wilderness studies drag on for more than a decade, and the land is effectively off-limits for many uses while the study is on-going. Otter also worked in the 107th Congress to give ranchers greater access, during weather emergencies, to lands set aside for conservation purposes.

Displaying his libertarian bent, Otter was one of just three Republicans who voted in 2001 against anti-terrorism legislation that gave law enforcement agencies sweeping new powers. "Some of the provisions . . . place more power in the hands of law enforcement than our Founding Fathers could ever have dreamt, and several compromise the civil liberties of law-abiding Americans," he said.

In the 108th Congress, Otter won appointment to the powerful Energy and Commerce Committee. To take the post, he had to relinquish seats on the Government Reform, Resources and Transportation panels. On Transportation, he was instrumental in the 107th in obtaining funding to upgrade U.S. 95, which runs north and south from near Boise to the Canadian border.

Otter played a leading role on 2002 legislation that authorized the U.S. Treasury to buy silver in order to continue production of the American eagle silver dollar, a popular, money-making collectible coin made by the U.S. Mint. Idaho is one of the country's leading silver-producing states.

Sixth in a family of nine children, Otter grew up in Caldwell, just west of Boise. According to a profile in the Spokesman-Review, he dropped out of high school to help his mother run the family farm when his father and brother were injured. Mounting medical bills forced the Otters to sell the farm, and he went back to school, studying at a Catholic monastery for two years before giving up the idea of entering the priesthood. He continued his studies at the College of Idaho, becoming the first member of his family to complete college.

While there, he met Gay Simplot and soon went to work for her father. He spent 30 years working his way up the ranks at the Boise-headquartered J.R. Simplot agribusiness company.

Otter's father was a union electrician, and he says his family members were Democrats. But he remembers comparing Democratic and Republican campaign literature as he prepared to vote for the first time in 1964. He told the Spokesman-Review that he recalls thinking, "Boy, my dad's not going to like this very well, but I don't think I'm a Democrat. I feel more like a Barry Goldwater Republican."

In 1972, at the urging of his father-in-law and a well-known libertarian, Ralph Smeed, Otter ran for the state House on a platform of reducing the size of government. Frustrated after two terms, he left the legislature and continued his upward climb at J.R. Simplot.

In 1986, he was back before the voters, running for the first of his four terms as the state's lieutenant governor. In office less than two months, Otter had a chance to demonstrate his libertarian approach as acting governor while his boss, Democratic Gov. Cecil D. Andrus, was briefly out of the state.

At the time, Idaho was under pressure from the federal government to raise the drinking age or lose millions of dollars in highway money. The legislature passed a bill to raise the state's legal drinking age from 19 to 21. Otter vetoed the measure, decrying what he termed the government's blackmail attempt. The legislature passed the bill again, and Andrus signed it; but owing to Otter's personal charm, no one was angry with him.

Otter's divorce from Simplot and a drunken driving conviction put an end to his thoughts of running for governor in 1994. He decided to run again for lieutenant governor and was re-elected two more times.

In 2000, when outspoken conservative Rep. Helen Chenoweth-Hage fulfilled her pledge to limit her House service to three terms, Otter entered the race to succeed her. He overcame seven GOP opponents in the primary, rebuffing his primary foes' criticism that his libertarian views were not sufficiently conservative to make him a legitimate heir to Chenoweth-Hage. He refused, for example, to adopt a strict anti-abortion policy, saying, "I don't want the government involved in a decision with the life of an innocent child."

After handily winning the primary, Otter breezed to an easy general-election victory by a ratio of more than 2-to-1. In 2002, he beat former U.S. Attorney Betty Richardson by 20 percentage points.

KEY VOTES

2002

No Overhaul campaign finance law; ban "soft money" and restrict advocacy advertising
Yes Back Bush's defense budget increase
Yes Extend 1996 welfare law
Yes Adopt Bush's discretionary spending limit
Yes Pass GOP Medicare prescription drug plan
? Create independent Sept. 11 commission
No Extend union protections to Homeland Security Department employees
Yes Revive fast-track procedures for trade agreements
Yes Authorize war against Iraq
No Advance bankruptcy overhaul opposed by abortion opponents

2001

Yes Nullify Clinton Labor Department ergonomics rule
Yes Cut taxes by $1.35 trillion through fiscal 2011
No Maintain ban on oil drilling in Arctic National Wildlife Refuge
Yes Approve Bush proposal to limit managed-care plan liability for coverage decisions
No Divert money from crop subsidy payments to land conservation
No Expand law enforcement power to investigate suspected terrorists

CQ VOTE STUDIES

	PARTY UNITY		PRESIDENTIAL SUPPORT	
	Support	Oppose	Support	Oppose
2002	94%	6%	87%	13%
2001	96%	4%	81%	19%

INTEREST GROUPS

	AFL-CIO	ADA	CCUS	ACU
2002	0%	0%	90%	96%
2001	8%	0%	87%	96%

IDAHO 1

West – Nampa, Panhandle, part of Boise

Stretching the 500-mile height of western Idaho, from British Columbia in the north to Nevada in the south, the 1st is mostly rural, punctuated by urban pockets. White-collar workers in Idaho's capital, Boise (shared with the 2nd), combine with agricultural voters to give it a GOP base. Redistricting after the 2000 census had little effect on the district, with the 1st losing a small part of Boise.

Boise and its surroundings contain about one-fourth of the district's population and house the headquarters of many lumber, paper, food processing, electronics and construction companies. The strongest Democratic voting bloc is found among the timber and metal miners in the panhandle and around Coeur d'Alene, but Democrats are outnumbered in nearly every other part of the district.

The 1st's midsize cities have attracted new high-tech businesses, such as Hewlett-Packard in Boise, and created new white-collar jobs. Some technology companies also reside along the Interstate 90 corridor in the northern part of the district. Nampa, west of Boise, has experienced high growth due to cheaper housing and a solid job market. Some small towns have not fared as well, as the 1st has become increasingly urbanized. Small timber mills have suffered, and the mining industry has struggled with low prices. Many rural communities are attempting to attract tourists to the state's forests, lakes and mountains.

Republicans dominate the district. Since 1967, Democrats have held the congressional seat for only four years (1991-95). Only three counties — Latah, Shoshone and Nez Perce — supported Bill Clinton in his two presidential elections. Al Gore fared even worse in 2000, as George W. Bush swept all of the counties in the 1st.

MAJOR INDUSTRY
Manufacturing, agriculture, timber

CITIES
Boise City (pt.), 59,680; Nampa, 51,867; Meridian, 34,919; Coeur d'Alene, 34,514; Lewiston, 30,904; Caldwell, 25,967; Moscow, 21,291

NOTABLE
The Sunshine Mine Memorial near Kellogg in Shoshone County memorializes the 1972 Sunshine Mine fire, which killed 91 miners; At nearly 20 carats, one of the largest diamonds found in the United States was discovered near McCall.

Rep. Mike Simpson (R)

CAPITOL OFFICE
225-5531
www.house.gov/simpson
1339 Longworth 20515-1202; fax 225-8216

COMMITTEES
Appropriations

HOMETOWN
Blackfoot

BORN
Sept. 8, 1950, Burley, Idaho

RELIGION
Mormon

FAMILY
Wife, Kathy Simpson

EDUCATION
Utah State U., attended 1968-72 (pre-dentistry); Washington U. (Mo.), D.D.S. 1977; Utah State U., B.S. 2002

CAREER
Dentist

POLITICAL HIGHLIGHTS
Blackfoot City Council, 1980-84; Idaho House, 1985-99 (Speaker, 1993-99)

ELECTION RESULTS

2002 GENERAL		
Mike Simpson (R)	135,605	68.2%
Edward W. Kinghorn (D)	57,769	29.1%
John H. Lewis (LIBERT)	5,508	2.8%
2002 PRIMARY		
Mike Simpson (R)		unopposed
2000 GENERAL		
Mike Simpson (R)	158,912	70.7%
Craig Williams (D)	58,265	25.9%
Donovan Bramwell (LIBERT)	7,542	3.4%

PREVIOUS WINNING PERCENTAGES
1998 (53%)

Elected 1998; 3rd term

A conservative small-town dentist who stumbled into local politics nearly two decades before being elected to Congress in 1998, Simpson has taken his brand of up-close-and-personal politicking straight into the offices of his congressional colleagues.

An ambitious goal of meeting every one of his 434 House peers during his first term brought him a wave of press attention. He actually met with about 350 lawmakers, a feat that underscored his commitment to working equally with ideological soul mates and partisan opposites. As chairman of the Veterans' Affairs Subcommittee on Benefits, for instance, he convened a hearing in 2002 in the Texas district of the panel's top-ranking Democrat, Silvestre Reyes.

"A legislative body functions on relationships. You may have the best idea in the world, but if you can't convince 218 people to agree with you, you're out of luck," he told the Boise Idaho Statesman soon after arriving in Congress. He points to his 12-point "Simpson's Rules," which include "hear both sides before judging" and "never, never make an enemy needlessly."

He has followed the same philosophy back home, briefly joining the American Civil Liberties Union and the Idaho Conservation League and regularly attending meetings with environmental groups with whom he often disagrees. In the 108th Congress, he won appointment to the Appropriations Committee, a panel where personal relationships help grease the skids. He has a seat on the subcommittee that funds energy and water development programs.

Simpson says he represents the views of rural Western lawmakers, whose perspectives on water and land-use issues are often misunderstood by Easterners. He says Westerners "must resist the temptation to turn local decision-making power over to the federal government in return for assistance in funding."

To take the Appropriations post, he had to relinquish all of his other assignments, including the Veterans' Affairs Committee. On that panel in the 107th, he pushed legislation to boost employment programs for veterans. And on the Resources Committee, he sponsored a bill to restrict the president's ability to create national monuments by executive order.

In the 106th, Simpson won enactment of a law increasing funding for southern Idaho's Minidoka Water Project and another measure expanding the City of Rocks National Reserve. He opposes breaching the four Snake River dams as a method of restoring the region's salmon population, but he was able to win $40 million for other resource restoration efforts in Idaho.

He also proposed legislation to reintroduce the Eastern timber wolf into New York's Catskill Mountains. Some members viewed the measure as a tit-for-tat response to the release of Canadian wolves in Idaho, but he insists that he is serious about applying the Endangered Species Act nationwide.

A co-chairman of a bipartisan congressional caucus to advance the interests of farmers and ranchers in World Trade Organization negotiations, Simpson attended WTO talks in Seattle in 1999. He watches out for his district's sugar beet growers, who are concerned about subsidized competition from abroad. Simpson also favors expanded trade ties with China, which is a promising market for Northwest wheat sales.

Simpson casts conservative votes on most issues, but he broke ranks with the GOP in supporting legislation in the 106th Congress that would have mandated trigger locks for guns. He also was critical of GOP leaders for not negotiating more seriously with President Clinton on a number of tax proposals.

Upon his arrival in Washington, Simpson had intended to work for free in inner-city dental clinics, but he found that licensing requirements made that too complicated. He also discovered that he did not have time to see patients during his visits back home, so he reluctantly sold his share of the dental practice.

An avid golfer who boasts a six handicap, Simpson also paints in his spare time. "He works hard and plays hard," said one aide.

Simpson grew up in the eastern Idaho town of Blackfoot, where his father and uncle had a dental practice. He met his wife in high school, and they both attended Utah State University. (Simpson did not earn his degree until 2002, however, when he arranged to have some credits from dental school at Washington University in St. Louis transferred to Utah State.)

Returning to Blackfoot to join the family dental practice, Simpson decided to run for a city council seat, a nonpartisan job, only after he noticed no one else was. He says that his interest in politics was first sparked by a high school teacher who was a staunch Democrat, but when he decided to run for the state legislature four years later, Simpson had to choose a party affiliation and concluded he was more comfortable with the GOP.

Simpson started out with a reputation as an occasionally angry maverick, but he mellowed and made a name for himself in Boise, rising through the ranks and serving as Speaker of the House during his last six years there.

He had given some thought to seeking the governorship in 1998 but decided against it when Republican Sen. Dirk Kempthorne chose to run. Republican Rep. Michael D. Crapo made a bid for Kempthorne's Senate seat, which created an opening for Simpson in the 2nd District. He won a four-way GOP primary despite criticism from social conservatives that he was insufficiently ardent on their issues.

During the campaign, Simpson was more worried about voters learning of his memberships in the ACLU and the Idaho Conservation League than of his use of marijuana in college 30 years before. And he made no effort to hide the fact that he is a lapsed Mormon who once smoked and still drinks occasionally. But these revelations seemed to have little effect on the heavily Mormon, but also Republican, electorate. He went on to defeat conservative Democrat Richard Stallings, who had held the seat from 1985 to 1993, by 8 percentage points. He cruised to re-election in 2000 and again in 2002. He has not ruled out a future run for governor.

KEY VOTES

2002

No Overhaul campaign finance law; ban "soft money" and restrict advocacy advertising
Yes Back Bush's defense budget increase
Yes Extend 1996 welfare law
Yes Adopt Bush's discretionary spending limit
Yes Pass GOP Medicare prescription drug plan
No Create independent Sept. 11 commission
No Extend union protections to Homeland Security Department employees
Yes Revive fast-track procedures for trade agreements
Yes Authorize war against Iraq
Yes Advance bankruptcy overhaul opposed by abortion opponents

2001

Yes Nullify Clinton Labor Department ergonomics rule
Yes Cut taxes by $1.35 trillion through fiscal 2011
No Maintain ban on oil drilling in Arctic National Wildlife Refuge
Yes Approve Bush proposal to limit managed-care plan liability for coverage decisions
No Divert money from crop subsidy payments to land conservation
Yes Expand law enforcement power to investigate suspected terrorists

CQ VOTE STUDIES

	PARTY UNITY		PRESIDENTIAL SUPPORT	
	Support	Oppose	Support	Oppose
2002	95%	5%	92%	8%
2001	98%	2%	88%	12%
2000	94%	6%	29%	71%
1999	91%	9%	24%	76%

INTEREST GROUPS

	AFL-CIO	ADA	CCUS	ACU
2002	11%	0%	100%	92%
2001	17%	5%	100%	84%
2000	0%	0%	90%	88%
1999	11%	10%	100%	84%

IDAHO 2

East — Pocatello, Idaho Falls, part of Boise

Covering eastern and central Idaho, the 2nd includes part of Boise, a few midsize towns and a vast swath of agricultural land irrigated by the Snake River. To the west, in Elmore County, is the Mountain Home Air Force Base. But most of the district subsists on agriculture, primarily potatoes, sugar beets and grain. Blackfoot, in Bingham County, is known as the potato-producing capital of the world.

The 2nd's manufacturing economy revolves around food processing, including Ore-Ida's frozen french fries. The district also is home to technology firms, including Micron, which provide thousands of jobs. The 2nd's fortunes have risen and fallen on agriculture, with farms faring poorly but expected to benefit from the 2002 farm law that reinstated federal subsidies for staple crops. Farmers have expanded into dairy, beef and cheese processing, especially in Twin Falls and Jerome counties.

Tourism is the district's third-leading industry. With natural wonders such as Shoshone Falls, and ski resorts such as Sun Valley, the 2nd attracts a steady stream of vacationers.

The district consistently votes Republican at the state and national level. Members of The Church of Jesus Christ of Latter-day Saints make up the largest religious group; like most Mormon areas, the district is strongly conservative. Since 1992, only Blaine County, with its resorts, has voted Democratic in presidential elections. The district gained only a small part of Boise in redistricting, which did little to alter its political makeup.

MAJOR INDUSTRY
Agriculture, food processing, tourism

MILITARY BASES
Mountain Home Air Force Base, 4,464 military, 425 civilian; Boise Air Terminal Air Guard Station, 1,253 military, 149 civilian (1999)

CITIES
Boise City (pt.), 126,107; Pocatello, 51,466; Idaho Falls, 50,730; Twin Falls, 34,469; Rexburg, 17,257

NOTABLE
Nearly 85 percent of all commercial trout sold in the United States is produced in the Hagerman Valley near Twin Falls; Sun Valley was America's first ski resort; In 1955, Arco became the first town powered solely by atomic energy — for one hour.

ILLINOIS

Gov. Rod R. Blagojevich (D)

First elected: 2002
Length of term: 4 years
Term expires: 1/07
Salary: $150,691
Phone: (217) 782-0244
Hometown: Chicago
Born: Dec. 10, 1956; Chicago, Ill.
Religion: Eastern Orthodox
Family: Wife, Patricia Blagojevich; two children
Education: Northwestern U., B.A. 1979 (history); Pepperdine U., J.D. 1983
Career: Lawyer
Political highlights: Assistant Cook County state's attorney, 1986-88; Ill. House, 1993-97; U.S. House, 1997-2003
Election results:

2002 GENERAL		
Rod R. Blagojevich (D)	1,847,040	52.2%
Jim Ryan (R)	1,594,960	45.1%
Cal Skinner (LIBERT)	73,794	2.1%

Lt. Gov. Pat Quinn (D)

First elected: 2002
Length of term: 4 years
Term expires: 1/07
Salary: $115,235
Phone: (217) 782-7884

STATE LEGISLATURE

General Assembly: Meets January-June
House: 118 members, 2-year terms
2003 breakdown: 52R, 66D; 82 men, 36 women
Salary: $57,619
Phone: (217) 782-8223
Senate: 59 members, rotates between 2 and 4-year terms
2003 breakdown: 26R, 32D, 1I; 48 men, 11 women
Salary: $57,619
Phone: (217) 782-5715

STATE TERM LIMITS

Governor: No
Senate: No
House: No

URBAN STATISTICS

CITY	POPULATION
Chicago	2,896,016
Rockford	150,115
Aurora	142,990
Naperville	128,358
Peoria	112,936

REGISTERED VOTERS

Voters do not register by party.

POPULATION

2002 population (est.)	12,600,620
2000 population	12,419,293
1990 population	11,430,602
Percent change (1990-2000)	+8.6%
Rank among states (2002)	5
Median age	34.7
Born in state	67.1%
Foreign born	12.3%
Violent crime rate	657/100,000
Poverty level	10.7%
Federal workers	91,284
Military	57,753

REDISTRICTING

Illinois lost one House seat in reapportionment. The state legislature drew a new, 19-district map, which the governor signed on May 31, 2001.

MISCELLANEOUS

Web: www.state.il.us
Capital: Springfield

STATE ELECTION OFFICIAL
(217) 782-4141

DEMOCRATIC HEADQUARTERS
(217) 546-7404

REPUBLICAN HEADQUARTERS
(217) 525-0011

District Statistics

DIST.	2000 VOTE FOR PRESIDENT BUSH	GORE	NADER	WHITE	BLACK	ASIAN	HISP	MEDIAN INCOME	WHITE COLLAR	BLUE COLLAR	SERVICE INDUSTRY	OVER 64	UNDER 18	COLLEGE EDUCATION	RURAL	SQ. MILES
1	16%	82%	2%	27%	65%	1%	5%	$37,222	61%	22%	17%	13%	28%	19%	0%	98
2	17	81	2	26	62	1	10	$41,330	60	24	16	12	29	18	0	185
3	39	57	3	68	6	3	21	$48,048	58	28	14	14	26	21	0	124
4	19	76	4	18	4	2	74	$35,935	43	39	17	6	32	14	0	39
5	33	63	4	66	2	6	23	$48,531	65	22	14	12	20	34	0	57
6	53	44	2	75	3	8	12	$62,640	70	20	10	10	26	35	0	213
7	16	81	2	27	62	4	6	$40,361	71	16	14	10	27	32	0	56
8	55	42	2	79	3	6	11	$62,762	67	22	11	8	28	32	4	618
9	30	66	3	62	11	12	12	$46,531	70	16	14	16	21	40	0	75
10	47	51	2	75	5	6	12	$71,663	76	15	10	12	27	48	0	250
11	50	48	2	84	8	1	7	$47,800	55	30	15	12	27	19	22	4,241
12	43	53	3	80	16	1	2	$35,198	55	27	18	14	25	17	23	4,425
13	55	42	2	82	5	7	5	$71,686	75	16	9	9	28	42	1	355
14	54	42	3	74	5	2	18	$56,314	60	27	13	9	29	26	14	2,852
15	54	42	3	88	6	2	2	$38,583	58	27	15	14	23	23	36	10,072

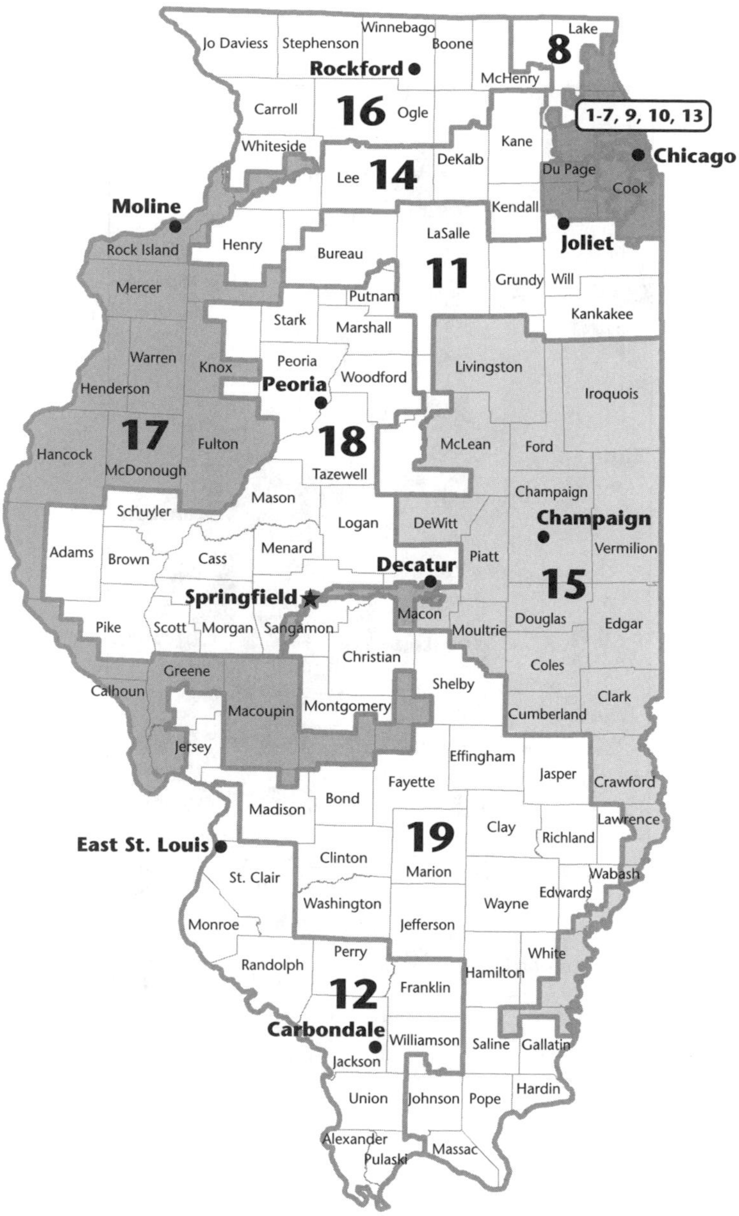

District Statistics

DIST.	2000 VOTE FOR PRESIDENT BUSH	GORE	NADER	WHITE	BLACK	ASIAN	HISP	MEDIAN INCOME	WHITE COLLAR	BLUE COLLAR	SERVICE INDUSTRY	OVER 64	UNDER 18	COLLEGE EDUCATION	RURAL	SQ. MILES
16	54%	43%	2%	86%	5%	1%	6%	$48,960	57%	30%	13%	12%	28%	21%	22%	4,098
17	43	53	3	87	7	1	4	$35,066	52	31	18	16	24	15	29	8,120
18	54	43	2	90	6	1	2	$41,934	59	25	15	15	24	21	32	8,186
19	55	41	3	94	3	0	1	$38,955	55	29	16	15	24	17	48	11,519
STATE	43	55	2	68	15	3	12	$46,590	62	24	14	12	26	26	12	55,584
U.S.	47.9	48.4	3	69	12	4	13	$41,994	60	25	15	12	26	24	21	3,537,438

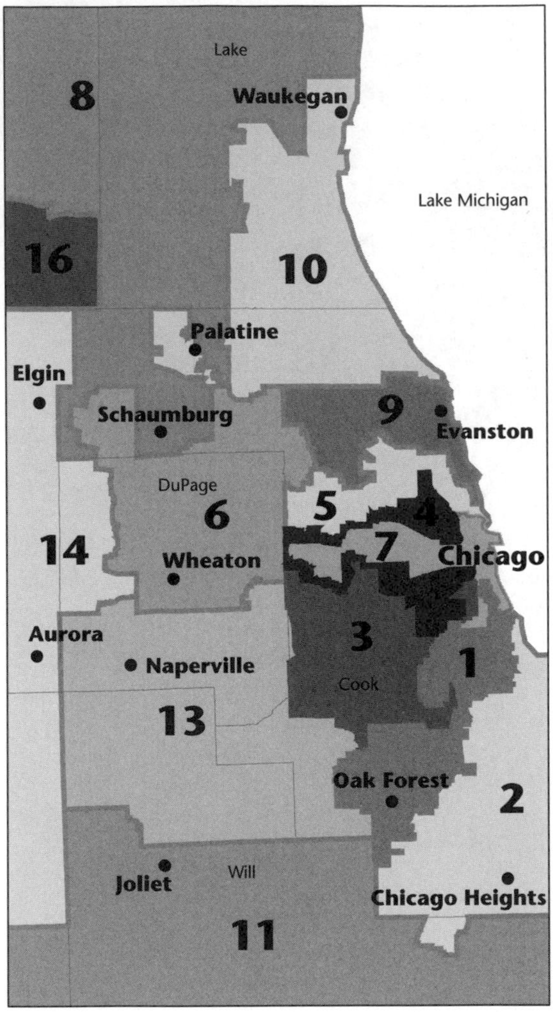
Lake
8
Waukegan
Lake Michigan
16
10
Palatine
Elgin
Schaumburg
9
Evanston
DuPage
6
5
4
14
7
Chicago
Wheaton
3
Aurora
Naperville
1
Cook
13
Oak Forest
2
Joliet
Will
Chicago Heights
11

Sen. Richard J. Durbin (D)

CAPITOL OFFICE
224-2152
dick@durbin.senate.gov
durbin.senate.gov
332 Dirksen 20510-1304; fax 228-0400

COMMITTEES
Appropriations
Governmental Affairs
Judiciary
Rules & Administration
Select Intelligence

HOMETOWN
Springfield

BORN
Nov. 21, 1944, East St. Louis, Ill.

RELIGION
Roman Catholic

FAMILY
Wife, Loretta Schaefer Durbin; three children

EDUCATION
Georgetown U., B.S.F.S. 1966 (international affairs & economics), J.D. 1969

CAREER
Lawyer; congressional and state legislative aide

POLITICAL HIGHLIGHTS
Democratic nominee for Ill. Senate, 1976; Democratic nominee for lieutenant governor, 1978; U.S. House, 1983-97

ELECTION RESULTS

2002 GENERAL		
Richard J. Durbin (D)	2,103,766	60.3%
Jim Durkin (R)	1,325,703	38.0%
Steven Burgauer (LIBERT)	57,382	1.7%
2002 PRIMARY		
Richard J. Durbin (D)		unopposed

PREVIOUS WINNING PERCENTAGES
1996 (56%); 1994 House Election (55%); 1992 House Election (57%); 1990 House Election (66%); 1988 House Election (69%); 1986 House Election (68%); 1984 House Election (61%); 1982 House Election (50%)

Elected 1996; 2nd term

One conversation with Durbin makes it clear why Minority Leader Tom Daschle tapped him to shape the message of the week for Senate Democrats. Durbin has the knack for matching his rhetoric to the occasion: catchy when the subject is broad political themes, detailed when the subject is the nuts and bolts of legislation. He can shift gears between details and the big picture in a way that few members of Congress can. Somehow, he stops short of sounding like a robot — but it is also clear that it is virtually impossible to knock him off message.

Durbin serves as the assistant Democratic floor leader, but that title understates the true role he plays in the party. He runs the "Speakers' Group," where Senate Democrats brainstorm, generally on Tuesday or Wednesday mornings, about what issues they should talk about during the week and how they should present them. Durbin also brings in outside speakers to brief the senators on timely issues.

It is the same role he played during the last of his seven terms in the House. When Richard A. Gephardt became minority leader in 1995, he put Durbin in charge of reshaping the House Democrats' political message for their new and unaccustomed role of the minority. After Durbin was elected to the Senate the next year, Daschle asked him to reprise the role on the north side of the Capitol.

A sharp-tongued debater, Durbin knows how to develop a communications strategy, his colleagues say. But the 13 years he spent as parliamentarian of the Illinois Senate also helped him to master the rules and practices of the United States Senate and the substance of a wide range of legislative issues. As such, Durbin aspires to move up in the leadership someday. (Durbin also gained a measure of national attention in 2000 when that year's Democratic nominee, Al Gore, considered him as a possible running mate.)

For the most part, Durbin is a reliably liberal voice in the Senate. Since 1997, he has never failed to back his party at least 95 percent of the time that the two parties have been in opposition. It was Durbin's amendment to the 2002 farm bill that restored Food Stamp benefits to legal immigrants, making them eligible for a vital public benefit they had lost in the 1996 welfare overhaul. Durbin also tried, unsuccessfully, to amend the 2002 economic recovery package to provide unemployment compensation to part-time workers who normally do not qualify for the benefit.

And he teamed with two Senate colleagues, Edward M. Kennedy of Massachusetts and Mike DeWine of Ohio, to introduce a bill that would give the Food and Drug Administration the authority to regulate tobacco products, an effort to revive an anti-tobacco crusade that lost steam after President Clinton left office. On trade, though, Durbin occasionally has strayed from the wishes of his liberal base. He took heat from unions in 1993 for supporting the North American Free Trade Agreement, and again in 2000 for backing the Clinton administration on granting China permanent normal trade status; in 2002, however, he opposed reviving fast-track procedures for congressional consideration of trade deals.

After the Sept. 11, 2001, terrorist attacks, Durbin was especially valuable to Daschle in defending the Senate's prerogative to disagree with President Bush over issues ranging from airport security to the economy. "Under the Constitution, we always have a role to play in national crises," Durbin said in late 2001. "We only have one commander in chief, and I'm going to stand by him, but Congress is always going to have a say as well."

Durbin brought himself up to speed quickly when the issues before Congress changed after the attacks. Already pushing for stricter food safety regulations, after the anthrax attacks of October 2001 he easily shifted gears to present food safety as a key battleground in efforts to prevent bioterrorism. Airport security was also a major concern — one that hit particularly close to home after private security guards at Chicago's O'Hare International Airport nearly let a passenger board a flight with seven knives, a stun gun and a can labeled "pepper spray." Durbin won the addition of language to the 2001 aviation security law requiring more extensive background checks of airport workers and the use of new technology to detect explosives.

From the start of his seven House terms in 1983, Durbin positioned himself to be a reliable ally of both the outgoing and incoming generations of Democratic leaders. Relying on his knowledge of legislative procedure, Durbin even in his first term often presided over contentious debates, a role rare in its day for a freshman, and in his second term he was rewarded with an Appropriations Committee seat. All the while, he met regularly with two leaders of the then-junior Democrats, Gephardt and Tony Coelho of California. His fealty to the concept of following the leadership helped him win a coveted Appropriations seat as soon as he became a senator.

Though Durbin generally has had a close working relationship with Illinois' other senator, Republican Peter G. Fitzgerald, that relationship was endangered in 2002 when the two clashed over Durbin's legislation to expand O'Hare. Durbin said the expansion was needed to modernize the world's busiest airport, but Fitzgerald said the proposed design would have placed the runways dangerously close together and he blocked the bill. That battle resumed in the 108th Congress.

Durbin was 14 when his chain-smoking father died of lung cancer, and Durbin has dedicated much of his congressional career to crusading against tobacco companies. But he plays down that personal aspect of the debate. "I am not unique," he said of the loss of his father. "I know it's a big issue to millions of Americans and their families who have lost loved ones to tobacco."

As a member of the House, Durbin led the successful effort in the late 1980s to ban smoking on most domestic airline flights. Later, as chairman and then top-ranking member on the House Agriculture Appropriations Subcommittee, he tried to scale back government support for tobacco farmers, falling just two votes short in a floor vote in 1996. As a senator, he has pressed to make Senate office buildings smoke-free, a proposal that drew a cool response from senators from tobacco states.

While working for Sen. Paul Douglas, an Illinois Democratic icon, Durbin earned undergraduate and law degrees from Georgetown University. He then went to work at the state capital as Senate parliamentarian, counsel to the state Senate judiciary committee and aide to Lt. Gov. Paul Simon, a Democrat who went on to a 22-year career in Congress.

In 1982, redistricting allowed Durbin to unseat 11-term GOP Rep. Paul N. Findley by 1,410 votes in a Springfield-based House district. He won re-election six times by comfortable, if not overwhelming, margins.

When his old mentor, Simon, announced he would not seek re-election to the Senate in 1996, Durbin jumped into the race. With endorsements from Simon and Illinois' other Democratic senator, Carol Moseley-Braun, Durbin had little trouble winning the primary. In the general election, he faced off against state Rep. Al Salvi, a little-known conservative with firm anti-abortion and gun owners' rights views. Durbin characterized him as an extreme conservative and won the election by 15 percentage points.

By 2002, Durbin's seat was safe enough that he coasted to a second term. No top-tier Republican considered the race seriously and he ended up defeating centrist GOP state Rep. Jim Durkin by 22 points.

KEY VOTES

2002

Yes Pass farm bill reversing crop subsidy limits
No Postpone tougher automobile fuel efficiency standards
Yes Overhaul campaign finance law; ban "soft money" and restrict advocacy advertising
Yes Set federal election standards
No Support oil drilling in Arctic National Wildlife Refuge
No Revive fast-track procedures for trade agreements
Yes Create federal insurance coverage for catastrophic terrorist losses
Yes Tighten federal accounting and corporate governance regulation
Yes Advance bipartisan Medicare prescription drug plan
Yes Create independent Sept. 11 commission
Yes Back Democratic Homeland Security Department proposal
No Authorize war against Iraq

2001

No Confirm John Ashcroft as attorney general
No Nullify Clinton Labor Department ergonomics rule
No Cut taxes by $1.35 trillion through fiscal 2011
Yes Pass Democratic bill to bolster rights of patients in managed-care plans
No Permit a new round of military base closings
Yes Expand law enforcement power to investigate suspected terrorists

CQ VOTE STUDIES

	PARTY UNITY		PRESIDENTIAL SUPPORT	
	Support	Oppose	Support	Oppose
2002	97%	3%	67%	33%
2001	95%	5%	62%	38%
2000	99%	1%	97%	3%
1999	95%	5%	87%	13%
1998	95%	5%	90%	10%
1997	97%	3%	92%	8%
House Service:				
1996	91%	9%	82%	18%
1995	93%	7%	83%	17%
1994	98%	2%	78%	22%
1993	94%	6%	78%	22%

INTEREST GROUPS

	AFL-CIO	ADA	CCUS	ACU
2002	100%	95%	50%	0%
2001	94%	95%	31%	0%
2000	75%	95%	50%	4%
1999	89%	100%	35%	4%
1998	100%	95%	50%	8%
1997	100%	100%	40%	4%
House Service:				
1996	91%	80%	27%	0%
1995	100%	85%	25%	8%
1994	78%	95%	25%	0%
1993	92%	90%	27%	13%

Sen. Peter G. Fitzgerald (R)

CAPITOL OFFICE
224-2854
senator_fitzgerald@fitzgerald.senate.gov
fitzgerald.senate.gov
555 Dirksen 20510-1305; fax 228-1372

COMMITTEES
Agriculture, Nutrition & Forestry
(Research, Nutrition & General Legislation - chairman)
Commerce, Science & Transportation
(Consumer Affairs & Product Safety - chairman)
Governmental Affairs
(Financial Management, Budget & International Security - chairman)
Small Business & Entrepreneurship
Special Aging

HOMETOWN
Inverness

BORN
Oct. 20, 1960, Elgin, Ill.

RELIGION
Roman Catholic

FAMILY
Wife, Nina Fitzgerald; one child

EDUCATION
Dartmouth College, A.B. 1982 (classics);
Aristotelian U. (Greece), attended 1983;
U. of Michigan, J.D. 1986

CAREER
Lawyer

POLITICAL HIGHLIGHTS
Sought Republican nomination for Ill. House, 1988; Ill. Senate, 1993-99; sought Republican nomination for U.S. House, 1994

ELECTION RESULTS

1998 GENERAL		
Peter G. Fitzgerald (R)	1,709,041	50.3%
Carol Moseley-Braun (D)	1,610,496	47.4%
Don A. Torgersen (REF)	74,704	2.2%
1998 PRIMARY		
Peter G. Fitzgerald (R)	372,916	51.8%
Loleta Didrickson (R)	346,606	48.2%

Elected 1998; 1st term

On the day he was elected in 1998, Fitzgerald gathered his supporters at a victory celebration and played the Tom Petty song, "I Won't Back Down." The title is an apt assessment of how he is often viewed in the Senate.

Fitzgerald's supporters say he fights passionately for what he believes in, but his critics say his approach is ill-suited to a chamber that values give and take. They add that Fitzgerald picks politically popular targets that generate good headlines. Either way, Fitzgerald is not likely to change his tune. "When I'm doing what I think is right, I don't back down," he said.

But in April 2003, saying he was unwilling to embark on the full-time campaign that would be required for him to have a chance of winning re-election, Fitzgerald announced he would not run in 2004.

At some point Fitzgerald has angered just about everyone he serves with — including the two most powerful members of the Illinois delegation: Republican J. Dennis Hastert, the Speaker of the House, and Democrat Richard J. Durbin, the state's senior senator. He has also had words with Chicago Mayor Richard M. Daley, a Democrat, and former Illinois Gov. George Ryan, a Republican. Fitzgerald says each of the disputes simply represents a disagreement over a specific issue. And in truth, there are many instances in which he has agreed with Hastert, Durbin, Daley and Ryan.

It is not so much Fitzgerald's independence that bothers some of his colleagues, but rather the way he has gone about things. Hastert, who had a run-in with Fitzgerald in 2001 over funding for a Lincoln Library in the state capital, angrily accused Fitzgerald of "political grandstanding." And Durbin was peeved over Fitzgerald's tactics on legislation involving the long-running dispute over whether Chicago's O'Hare Airport should be expanded.

Yet the two senators continue to host a weekly breakfast gathering for visiting constituents, and they agree on an arrangement that lets them both have influence over presidential nominations for jobs in the state. But Illinois political observers report that their relationship is strained.

Arizona Republican Sen. John McCain, who himself attracts notice for his maverick behavior, had a well-publicized spat with Fitzgerald in 1999 over limits on flights to O'Hare. McCain told Business Week in 2002 that he views Fitzgerald as "a refreshingly independent-minded young man."

A rumpled, balding and brainy lawyer, Fitzgerald is one of the wealthiest members of the Senate, though he is said to be sensitive about being called rich. He prefers to be known as a doting father who enjoys fishing and playing catch with his son. Fitzgerald is not aloof; he will chat at length about almost anything, from arcane budget rules to the Chicago Cubs.

Fitzgerald, whose multimillion-dollar fortune is in bank stock, declined to place his assets in trust when he came to the Senate. To avoid a conflict of interest, he recuses himself on banking issues and he turned down a seat on the Banking Committee, just as he had done in the Illinois Senate.

In the 107th Congress, Fitzgerald played a leading role in the congressional probes of the collapse of the Enron Corp. and the subsequent accounting scandals at other large companies. He spent hours sifting through the thousands of pages of Enron documents delivered to Capitol Hill. "I've concluded that you're perhaps the most accomplished confidence man since Charles Ponzi," he later told former Enron CEO Kenneth L. Lay at a hearing. "I'd say you were a carnival barker, except that wouldn't be fair to carnival barkers."

Fitzgerald proposed a measure requiring stock analysts to disclose their ties with companies whose stock they rate, and he was a lead sponsor of a bill to require companies to count the cost of stock options against their earnings.

A staunch conservative, both on fiscal and social issues, Fitzgerald is not always a dependable Republican. In the 107th Congress, he voted in agreement with the majority of his party only 78 percent of the time against a majority of Democrats. Only six other GOP senators had lower party unity scores.

Fitzgerald values his image as an independent, proudly pointing out instances in which he has split from the majority of Senate Republicans on issues such as health care and the environment.

He has voted with the Democrats to give patients more clout in their dealings with their managed-care providers and to oppose drilling for oil in the Arctic. He cast the only vote in the Senate against the financial bailout for the airline industry enacted after the Sept. 11, 2001, terrorist attacks. The measure did not ask enough of the airlines in return, Fitzgerald said, and it did nothing to help the thousands of airline workers laid off in the cutbacks that followed the attacks.

Fitzgerald can also point to some legislative successes. As the 108th began, he was the lead sponsor of a law enacted to extend unemployment benefits. In the 107th, he won Senate passage of a bill aimed at boosting use of child safety seats in cars and was an active player in efforts to ban MTBE, a gasoline additive that has contaminated groundwater and is a suspected carcinogen.

His bill to exempt survivors of the Holocaust from federal taxes on compensation payments was made part of the 2001 tax cut. In the 106th, he guided to enactment bills to permit consumers to use electronic food stamps for out-of-state transactions and to allow farmers to file their paperwork with the Agriculture Department electronically.

Fitzgerald is the youngest of five children of a man who built a large suburban Chicago-area bank from scratch, selling out to a larger bank in 1994 for $246 million. His father, Gerald, was active in local politics, including raising money for Republican Rep. Philip R. Crane; and Fitzgerald interned for the congressman while in college.

He spent his early years in the northwest Chicago suburb of Inverness, then went off to a Rhode Island boarding school run by Benedictine monks. He majored in classics at Dartmouth and remains fluent in Greek. As a corporate attorney two years out of law school, Fitzgerald made his first bid for elective office, narrowly losing the GOP primary for a state House seat in 1988. In 1992, he won election to an open state Senate seat.

Barely a year later, Fitzgerald surprised local political observers by challenging Crane's renomination to the House, saying that his old mentor was ineffective and had been in office too long. But Crane won the 1994 Republican primary by 7 percentage points, and Fitzgerald continued to serve in Springfield, where he was one of a group of young, conservative, reform-minded lawmakers known as the Fab 5. He challenged no-bid deals for lucrative riverboat casino licenses and sponsored a bill to ban same-sex marriages.

Fitzgerald won election to the Senate in 1998 by defeating Democrat Carol Moseley-Braun, the nation's first African-American woman senator, who was dogged throughout her one term by a string of ethics accusations. Spending $7 million of his own money on his primary campaign, Fitzgerald edged past the Republican establishment's preferred candidate by less than 4 percentage points and went on to oust Moseley-Braun by 3 points. Overall, Fitzgerald spent $17.7 million to win his seat, much of it his own money.

KEY VOTES

2002

Yes Pass farm bill reversing crop subsidy limits
Yes Postpone tougher automobile fuel efficiency standards
Yes Overhaul campaign finance law; ban "soft money" and restrict advocacy advertising
Yes Set federal election standards
No Support oil drilling in Arctic National Wildlife Refuge
Yes Revive fast-track procedures for trade agreements
Yes Create federal insurance coverage for catastrophic terrorist losses
Yes Tighten federal accounting and corporate governance regulation
No Advance bipartisan Medicare prescription drug plan
Yes Create independent Sept. 11 commission
No Back Democratic Homeland Security Department proposal
Yes Authorize war against Iraq

2001

Yes Confirm John Ashcroft as attorney general
Yes Nullify Clinton Labor Department ergonomics rule
Yes Cut taxes by $1.35 trillion through fiscal 2011
Yes Pass Democratic bill to bolster rights of patients in managed-care plans
No Permit a new round of military base closings
Yes Expand law enforcement power to investigate suspected terrorists

CQ VOTE STUDIES

	PARTY UNITY		PRESIDENTIAL SUPPORT	
	Support	Oppose	Support	Oppose
2002	77%	23%	95%	5%
2001	79%	21%	96%	4%
2000	81%	19%	51%	49%
1999	87%	13%	37%	63%

INTEREST GROUPS

	AFL-CIO	ADA	CCUS	ACU
2002	31%	20%	90%	85%
2001	38%	15%	71%	78%
2000	25%	25%	71%	95%
1999	33%	15%	88%	92%

Rep. Bobby L. Rush (D)

CAPITOL OFFICE
225-4372
www.house.gov/rush
2416 Rayburn 20515-1301; fax 226-0333

COMMITTEES
Energy & Commerce

HOMETOWN
Chicago

BORN
Nov. 23, 1946, Albany, Ga.

RELIGION
Protestant

FAMILY
Wife, Carolyn Rush; five children (one deceased)

EDUCATION
Roosevelt U., B.A. 1973; U. of Illinois, Chicago, attended 1975-77, M.A. 1994 (political science); McCormick Seminary, M.A. 1998 (theological studies)

MILITARY SERVICE
Army, 1963-68

CAREER
Insurance broker; political aide

POLITICAL HIGHLIGHTS
Candidate for Chicago City Council, 1975; sought Democratic nomination for Ill. House, 1978; Chicago City Council, 1983-93; candidate for mayor of Chicago, 1999

ELECTION RESULTS

2002 GENERAL		
Bobby L. Rush (D)	149,068	81.2%
Raymond G. Wardingley (R)	29,776	16.2%
Dorothy G. Tsatsos (LIBERT)	4,812	2.6%
2002 PRIMARY		
Bobby L. Rush (D)		unopposed
2000 GENERAL		
Bobby L. Rush (D)	172,271	87.8%
Raymond G. Wardingley (R)	23,915	12.2%

PREVIOUS WINNING PERCENTAGES
1998 (87%); 1996 (86%); 1994 (76%); 1992 (83%)

Elected 1992; 6th term

Rush's life took numerous twists and turns before landing him in Congress. There, he has a platform for work on behalf of his low-income South Side Chicago constituents, from his seat on the Energy and Commerce Committee and his affiliation with the Progressive Caucus and the Black Caucus, two of the most liberal groups in the House.

Born in southern Georgia, Rush grew up in Chicago, where his mother moved when he was 7 after her marriage broke up. She worked as a Republican activist because whites dominated the Democratic machine. Rush was in an integrated Boy Scout troop and volunteered for the Army, but when he became disillusioned by a commanding officer whom he viewed as racist, he joined the Student Non-Violent Coordinating Committee.

He soon founded the Illinois chapter of the militant Black Panthers organization. Belying the Panthers' violent image, however, Rush coordinated a Panthers-run program that provided free breakfasts for children and a medical clinic that developed a mass screening effort for sickle cell anemia.

When he was in his 20s, Rush was imprisoned for six months for illegal possession of weapons. As a congressman, however, he has been an advocate of strict restrictions on firearms. Rush has sponsored a number of gun control measures, and in the 107th Congress he lent his support to legislation that would require background checks at gun shows.

Rush's commitment to tighter gun restrictions has been strengthened by personal experience. In 1999, his son Huey (named after Black Panther Huey Newton) was shot and killed in a Chicago sidewalk robbery. Shortly before his son's accused murderers were found guilty in 2002, Rush's nephew was charged with murder after what police said was a drug deal gone bad. "These kinds of stories have no winners, only losers, and occur far too often in our communities," Rush said.

Legislation is a small part of the solution to the problem of gun deaths, Rush told the Chicago Tribune a few weeks after his son's death. "Nowadays, we've got a spectator community, not an active community. What we've got to do is create opportunities to take those spectators onto the field and say, 'Look, you do have power. You can do something about solving a problem.' "

Rush has spoken out against the death penalty, particularly in Illinois, where several innocent people have been placed on death row.

After graduating from college, Rush quit the Panthers, sold insurance and then entered local politics, challenging the party machinery and losing two races — first for the Chicago City Council and later for the state House. In 1983, however, he won election to the City Council, riding the coattails of 1st District Democratic Rep. Harold Washington, who was elected in an upset that year as Chicago's first black mayor.

Rush was elected to Congress in 1992, ousting Democrat Charles A. Hayes, who had replaced Washington in the House but who was susceptible to Rush's charge that he had not been providing sufficient leadership in Congress. A gifted political organizer, Rush quickly impressed his party leaders; by his second term, he had a seat on the coveted Commerce Committee (now Energy and Commerce), which has one of the broadest legislative portfolios in Congress.

Rush devotes much of his energy to the oratory of frustration, lashing out at Republican efforts to cut spending for social programs and fuming at those in his own party whom he sees as giving up too much ground to the GOP.

The primary focus of Rush's legislative work is to help his economically struggling urban constituents. Upon his arrival in the 103rd Congress, he pursued urban economic revitalization from a seat he had during his first term on the Banking Committee. He maintains that "massive disinvestment" by lenders has caused economic abandonment in many urban areas, bringing high unemployment that spawns a host of social problems.

In the 107th, he was the driving force behind a provision in the broadband deregulation bill to require the regional Bell companies to offer high-speed Internet service to low-income areas. The House passed a bill in 2002 that included the proposal, but the legislation died in the Senate.

Rush can work with colleagues who stand nowhere near him on the ideological spectrum. In addressing the shortage of health care workers in urban hospitals, for example, Rush allied himself with a prominent conservative, Republican home-state colleague Henry J. Hyde, on a bill to establish a special visa classification for foreign nurses. During the summer of 2001, Rush teamed up with Republican Roy Blunt of Missouri to introduce a bill aimed at stabilizing gasoline prices.

Rush is active in the Congressional Black Caucus; he was its secretary in the 107th and lost to Maryland Democrat Elijah E. Cummings for the chairmanship in the 108th.

Because of his past association with the Black Panthers, the media instantly focused on Rush after the 1992 election, making him a TV celebrity before his first term even began. But Rush seldom mentions his Panther past, except on issues concerning increased police powers. He was a vocal opponent of legislation swept to enactment soon after the Sept. 11, 2001, terrorist attacks that increased law enforcement's ability to investigate and prosecute suspected terrorists. "I feel like I'm in a time warp," Rush told the Chicago Tribune. "So much of what Bush and [Attorney General John] Ashcroft are saying sounds identical to the language the FBI used 32 years ago" to investigate the Black Panthers and other groups.

Rush has won every general election with ease. However, he had a poor showing in his 1999 challenge to the re-election of Democrat Richard M. Daley as mayor, receiving just 28 percent in the primary. In the race Rush accused Daley of neglecting the city's poorer neighborhoods. Following that defeat, Rush had to face an emboldened field of challengers in 2000 but was renominated with 61 percent of the vote, tantamount to re-election in the overwhelmingly Democratic district. In 2002 Rush ran uncontested in the primary and easily won the general election.

KEY VOTES

2002

- Yes Overhaul campaign finance law; ban "soft money" and restrict advocacy advertising
- Yes Back Bush's defense budget increase
- No Extend 1996 welfare law
- No Adopt Bush's discretionary spending limit
- No Pass GOP Medicare prescription drug plan
- Yes Create independent Sept. 11 commission
- Yes Extend union protections to Homeland Security Department employees
- No Revive fast-track procedures for trade agreements
- No Authorize war against Iraq
- No Advance bankruptcy overhaul opposed by abortion opponents

2001

- No Nullify Clinton Labor Department ergonomics rule
- ? Cut taxes by $1.35 trillion through fiscal 2011
- Yes Maintain ban on oil drilling in Arctic National Wildlife Refuge
- No Approve Bush proposal to limit managed-care plan liability for coverage decisions
- No Divert money from crop subsidy payments to land conservation
- No Expand law enforcement power to investigate suspected terrorists

CQ VOTE STUDIES

	PARTY UNITY		PRESIDENTIAL SUPPORT	
	Support	Oppose	Support	Oppose
2002	95%	5%	28%	72%
2001	91%	9%	26%	74%
2000	98%	2%	91%	9%
1999	97%	3%	86%	14%
1998	95%	5%	84%	16%

INTEREST GROUPS

	AFL-CIO	ADA	CCUS	ACU
2002	100%	85%	50%	0%
2001	100%	75%	35%	10%
2000	100%	90%	36%	0%
1999	89%	100%	23%	0%
1998	100%	95%	33%	8%

ILLINOIS 1

Chicago — South Side and southwest

The nation's first black-majority district, the 1st covers much of Chicago's South Side. It begins at 26th Street in the historic black hub and spreads out to the south and west through mainly residential neighborhoods. The district narrows considerably through the southwestern Chicago neighborhoods of Washington Heights, Beverly and Morgan Park, then expands outside the city to scoop up close-in suburbs. About 70 percent of the 1st's residents live in Chicago (down from 90 percent under the district's 1990s configuration).

Long a relatively compact district, the 1st's boundaries have expanded gradually in the past few decades to adjust for declining populations in some of the area's most economically distressed neighborhoods. Redistricting following the 2000 census stretched the 1st as far south as Cook County's border with Will County.

When the steel industry left the South Side in the 1970s, it decimated the district's middle class and many black-owned businesses. Now the 1st is home to some of the city's largest subsidized housing projects, and about 20 percent of the population lives in poverty. The district still has several solidly middle-class black neighborhoods, including Chatham and Avalon Park. The north end takes in part of Bronzeville, which has seen young black professionals move in and rehabilitate old houses instead of leaving for the suburbs. Blue Island, one close-in southwest suburb, is 40 percent Hispanic and 25 percent black.

The 1st, represented by black congressmen since 1929, has the nation's largest percentage of African-Americans (65 percent). White voters are concentrated outside the city or in some southwestern neighborhoods. The 1st is perhaps the state's most Democratic district. It gave 2000 presidential nominee Al Gore his best showing in Illinois (82 percent).

MAJOR INDUSTRY

Hospitals, higher education, manufacturing

CITIES

Chicago (pt.), 451,488; Oak Forest (pt.), 28,041; Orland Park (pt.), 27,342; Tinley Park (pt.), 23,863; Blue Island (pt.), 23,436; Evergreen Park, 20,821

NOTABLE

The 1st is home to the national headquarters of Jesse Jackson's Rainbow/PUSH Coalition; The University of Chicago is in the Hyde Park neighborhood.

Rep. Jesse L. Jackson Jr. (D)

CAPITOL OFFICE
225-0773
webmaster@jessejacksonjr.org
www.jessejacksonjr.org
2419 Rayburn 20515-1302; fax 225-0899

COMMITTEES
Appropriations

HOMETOWN
Chicago

BORN
March 11, 1965, Greenville, S.C.

RELIGION
Baptist

FAMILY
Wife, Sandi Jackson; one child

EDUCATION
North Carolina A&T U., B.S. 1987 (business management); Chicago Theological Seminary, M.A. 1990 (theology); U. of Illinois, J.D. 1993

CAREER
Lawyer

POLITICAL HIGHLIGHTS
No previous office

ELECTION RESULTS

2002 GENERAL		
Jesse L. Jackson Jr. (D)	151,443	82.3%
Doug Nelson (R)	32,567	17.7%
2002 PRIMARY		
Jesse L. Jackson Jr. (D)	100,370	85.3%
Yvonne Christian-Williams (D)	11,757	10.0%
Anthony W. Williams (D)	5,501	4.7%
2000 GENERAL		
Jesse L. Jackson Jr. (D)	175,995	89.8%
Robert Gordon III (R)	19,906	10.2%

PREVIOUS WINNING PERCENTAGES
1998 (89%); 1996 (94%); 1995 Special Election (76%)

Elected December 1995; 4th full term

Initially benefiting from his universally known name, Jackson has been able to separate himself from his dynamic father, the civil rights leader, and develop his own philosophy. Now in his fourth full term in the House, Jackson says he sees America "through the eyes of race," but he adds, "I believe that Americans hear all political dialogue through the hearing aid of the economy."

To that end, Jackson, along with his staff aide Frank Watkins, wrote a book, "A More Perfect Union: Advancing New American Rights," where they advanced the theory that the regional differences between the North and South have played a key role in shaping the kind of country the United States is now — politically, economically and socially. The divide between North and South still shapes the views of many lawmakers on whether states' rights should take precedence over federal authority, Jackson contends. He writes that this regional split is far more relevant to the future of the country than the differing ideologies of the political parties, the role of labor unions or women's movements, or the impact of immigration.

Jackson also argues in the book that states' rights should be superseded by human rights. Turning his thoughts into action, Jackson in the 107th Congress proposed seven amendments to the Constitution to guarantee basic human rights to American citizens. These basic rights are the right to a job, to quality health care, to decent housing, to quality education, to a clean environment, to vote, and reproductive rights. And Jackson added an eighth proposed amendment — the right to be subjected to progressive taxation.

The book also offers admissions of his mistakes and assessments of his colleagues. He reveals that many of his best friends are people with whom he has little in common politically. Jackson says he and former Majority Leader Dick Armey of Texas had a wonderful time on a fishing trip, for example.

It is not Jackson's first book. Earlier, he and his father (whom he refers to as "the Reverend") wrote "It's About the Money," a book that offers practical advice on personal financial matters. It discusses credit card use and various strategies for investing and saving money. He also has written another book with his father, "Legal Lynching: The Death Penalty and America's Future," which forms the basis for his legislation to impose a moratorium on the imposition of the death penalty.

Jackson does not have his father's looming physical presence nor the pulpit cadences of his oratory, but the congressman is becoming a key Capitol Hill player in his own right.

In his second term, he won a seat on the Appropriations Committee, and the reviews of his performance on the spending committee are improving. Some Chicago observers said earlier that they had detected an unwillingness in Jackson to engage in the committee's dealmaking and to carry the water for other Illinois Democrats, who rely on him to represent their interests. Jackson takes some issue with that assessment, pointing out that he was a rookie appropriator from the minority party.

But it is also true that his disagreement with Mayor Richard M. Daley over Chicago airport issues has colored their relationship on other matters. Daley has turned to other Democrats in the delegation, particularly William O. Lipinski, to make the pitches for funding for Chicago projects.

Jackson's interest in economic expansion explains his deep involvement in the bruising battle over whether to expand Chicago's O'Hare Airport or to build another major airport for the region on rural land at Peotone, just south of Jackson's district. The new airport venture has the potential to provide thousands of jobs for Jackson's many unemployed constituents. He has joined with Illinois Republicans Rep. Henry J. Hyde and Sen. Peter G. Fitzgerald to push for the Peotone plan, while fellow Democrat Daley advocates expanding O'Hare. "This is the one reason Mayor Daley and I don't talk," Jackson quips.

Jackson takes voting seriously: He has missed just one roll call vote in his House career. He says he was talking to a reporter in the Rayburn Building and did not hear the bells signifying a vote on March 1, 2001. He rushed to the floor, but was too late. Upset about the missed vote, Jackson vowed not to "miss any more."

Jackson acknowledges that he is both blessed and cursed with the expectations that come with being the son of the Rev. Jesse L. Jackson. Many people have expected him to travel the country, speaking and marching and trying to build his own national reputation. "They thought I'd be a young man in a hurry. . . . But I'm not in a hurry, except to fix some things in my district." He proudly points to funds he has obtained for local projects, such as safe drinking water for Ford Heights.

Jackson holds few news conferences and picks his spots when asked to make speeches or comment on current events that have a race relations aspect. Jackson's rhetoric usually sounds less passionate than his father's — one observer characterizes the congressman as the "accountant for the Rainbow Coalition."

CBS News once filmed Jackson vacuuming the carpet in his Capitol Hill office, and Jackson confessed he does it all the time. "It's relaxing for me. It's a way for me to think and reflect," he said. He also has earned a black belt in tae kwon do.

A lawyer who graduated from Washington's elite St. Alban's School, Jackson presents himself as a vibrant member of a new generation of black leadership. He followed in his father's footsteps, serving as vice president at-large of Operation PUSH (People United to Serve Humanity) and as national field director for the Rainbow Coalition.

Jackson came to Congress in a 1995 special election to replace Democrat Mel Reynolds, who resigned after being convicted of sexual misconduct. Jackson countered criticism that he was too young for the job by arguing that being the son of Jesse Jackson amounted to a lifetime of political experience. After winning a hard-fought primary against state Sen. Emil Jones Jr., Jackson had no difficulty in that fall's general election or in subsequent races.

KEY VOTES

2002

- Yes Overhaul campaign finance law; ban "soft money" and restrict advocacy advertising
- No Back Bush's defense budget increase
- No Extend 1996 welfare law
- No Adopt Bush's discretionary spending limit
- No Pass GOP Medicare prescription drug plan
- Yes Create independent Sept. 11 commission
- Yes Extend union protections to Homeland Security Department employees
- No Revive fast-track procedures for trade agreements
- No Authorize war against Iraq
- No Advance bankruptcy overhaul opposed by abortion opponents

2001

- No Nullify Clinton Labor Department ergonomics rule
- No Cut taxes by $1.35 trillion through fiscal 2011
- Yes Maintain ban on oil drilling in Arctic National Wildlife Refuge
- No Approve Bush proposal to limit managed-care plan liability for coverage decisions
- Yes Divert money from crop subsidy payments to land conservation
- No Expand law enforcement power to investigate suspected terrorists

CQ VOTE STUDIES

	PARTY UNITY		PRESIDENTIAL SUPPORT	
	Support	Oppose	Support	Oppose
2002	96%	4%	25%	75%
2001	95%	5%	16%	84%
2000	96%	4%	83%	17%
1999	95%	5%	82%	18%
1998	96%	4%	83%	17%

INTEREST GROUPS

	AFL-CIO	ADA	CCUS	ACU
2002	100%	90%	25%	0%
2001	100%	95%	23%	0%
2000	100%	100%	23%	4%
1999	100%	100%	8%	8%
1998	100%	100%	22%	8%

ILLINOIS 2

Chicago — far South Side; Chicago Heights

The 2nd begins in Chicago's South Side along Lake Michigan and extends south along the Indiana border and southwest to take in Chicago Heights and Cook County suburbs. Redistricting following the 2000 census extended the southern border into University Park in Will County.

About 40 percent of district residents live in Chicago. The 2nd runs from the Hyde Park area near the University of Chicago, south through such neighborhoods as South Shore, South Chicago, East Side, Roseland and Pullman. East Side is heavily Hispanic.

U.S. Steel was once a dominant employer in the 2nd. When the steel industry collapsed in the late 1970s, it devastated the district's industrial-based economy. Ford Motor Co. is one of the few large manufacturing businesses remaining in the district.

A proposed new airport in nearby Peotone (in the 11th District) could rejuvenate the 2nd's economy. Advocates hope the airport would attract corporate headquarters, hotels, distributors and other new businesses. Unemployment remains high, and many residents have fled the South Side to find jobs. Before redistricting in 2001, the 2nd had the smallest population of any Illinois district.

In Chicago's south suburbs it is not unusual to find heavily black areas like Harvey, Dolton and Ford Heights, or largely white areas like Homewood, Flossmoor and Thornton. Other areas are more racially mixed — in Chicago Heights, whites and blacks are about equal in population, and one-fourth of residents are Hispanic.

Overall, the 2nd's 62 percent black population and working-class base shape a staunchly Democratic district.

MAJOR INDUSTRY

Automotive and wire manufacturing, steel production, health care

CITIES

Chicago (pt.), 265,814; Calumet City, 39,071; Chicago Heights, 32,776

NOTABLE

Pullman, now part of Chicago near Lake Calumet, originally was a factory town built by the Pullman Palace Car Co., maker of railroad sleeping cars.

Rep. William O. Lipinski (D)

Elected 1982; 11th term

CAPITOL OFFICE
225-5701
www.house.gov/lipinski
2188 Rayburn 20515-1303; fax 225-1012

COMMITTEES
Transportation & Infrastructure

HOMETOWN
Chicago

BORN
Dec. 22, 1937, Chicago, Ill.

RELIGION
Roman Catholic

FAMILY
Wife, Rose Marie Lipinski; two children

EDUCATION
Loras College, attended 1956-57

MILITARY SERVICE
Army Reserve, 1961-67

CAREER
Parks supervisor

POLITICAL HIGHLIGHTS
Chicago City Council, 1975-83

ELECTION RESULTS

2002 GENERAL		
William O. Lipinski (D)	unopposed	
2002 PRIMARY		
William O. Lipinski (D)	unopposed	
2000 GENERAL		
William O. Lipinski (D)	145,498	75.6%
Karl Groth (R)	47,005	24.4%

PREVIOUS WINNING PERCENTAGES
1998 (72%); 1996 (65%); 1994 (54%); 1992 (64%); 1990 (66%); 1988 (61%); 1986 (70%); 1984 (64%); 1982 (75%)

As he begins his third decade in Congress, Lipinski remains the picture of an old-style urban pol. Wiry and fast-talking, he seems more comfortable negotiating deals in back rooms than touting the party line to the press. A Roman Catholic of Polish and Irish lineage from working-class roots, he sees his job as sticking up for the "little guy" against monied interests.

"I have nothing against people in this economy becoming millionaires, becoming billionaires," he once said. "But I believe that it is really the duty and the responsibility of the . . . government to try to create an economy that improves the standard of living of all the citizens of this country."

But he also can be a thorn in the side of liberals who populate the party leadership. Like the middle-class white ethnic groups that dominate his suburban Chicago district, Lipinski holds conservative views on social issues and is firmly convinced that U.S. trade liberalization is a calamity for American industrial workers.

A member of the "Blue Dogs," a coalition of conservative Democrats, Lipinski opposes abortion, wants to outlaw desecration of the American flag and supports the Republican call for tuition vouchers and medical savings accounts. Although he consistently sides with labor, he voted with President Bush's position 53 percent of the time and against his party's majority more than 30 percent of the time in the 107th Congress. He was one of nine House Democrats who voted for the first economic stimulus bill the Republicans drafted after the Sept. 11, 2001, terrorist attacks, which was designed to spur consumer and business spending with tax cuts; and he was one of 12 Democrats who voted against the campaign finance law enacted in 2002.

Such independence has encouraged GOP leaders to cooperate in other areas with Lipinski, who is dean of the Illinois Democratic delegation. He is friends with Speaker J. Dennis Hastert, and on a 1999 train ride between Chicago and Seattle they began discussing ways to redraw the state's congressional lines for the current decade. Illinois lost a seat in reapportionment, and the pair ultimately came up with a map designed to protect as many incumbents as possible — especially Lipinski, who was given even more like-minded constituents. Lipinski agreed to lines that sacrificed one House Democrat, David Phelps, who lost re-election to GOP Rep. John Shimkus in solidly Republican southern Illinois territory.

Throughout his House career, Lipinski has focused chiefly on matters of parochial interest to Chicago. He sits on the Transportation and Infrastructure Committee, a good place to look out for a range of Chicago concerns, including the welfare of O'Hare Airport, the fate of aging Midway Airport (in Lipinski's district), and flooding and erosion along the city's 24-mile Lake Michigan shoreline.

In the 108th Congress Lipinski had a choice between two key Transportation subcommittees — Aviation and Highways, each of which face work on major bills. He chose the Highways panel, leaving Aviation, where he had been the top Democrat since midway through the 104th Congress.

In taking his leave, Lipinski urged Transportation Secretary Norman Y. Mineta, a former committee colleague, to consider re-regulating the aviation industry.

As the top-ranking Democrat on the Aviation Subcommittee, Lipinski fought efforts by Chicago lawmakers to get federal funding for a third metropolitan airport. In the 107th and again in the 108th, he sponsored a bill to strip the state of Illinois of its veto power over new runways at

O'Hare. He also works hard to help colleagues secure funding for highway and mass transit projects, dismissing critics who decry such spending as "pork." Early in the 107th, he took a leading role in drafting a wish list of nearly 250 local projects for which Illinois members wanted Bush's support in funding.

After the Sept. 11 attacks, Lipinski joined the effort to enact the law federalizing all airport passenger and baggage screeners. "Airport screeners are overworked, underpaid, undertrained and invariably work for the lowest-bidding private security firm," he said. Lipinski had been pushing since 1987 to make screeners federal employees.

Although Lipinski works closely with Republicans on some issues, he has turned on the GOP when debate has shifted to worker-management matters. He led the opposition to a Republican measure making it more difficult for Federal Express employees to unionize. And he opposed a GOP push in 1996 to allow businesses to offer workers compensatory time off in lieu of pay for overtime work.

Lipinski is also an unyielding foe of lowering international trade barriers. He has opposed efforts to give fast-track trade negotiation authority to the president. He says the North American Free Trade Agreement has "sacrificed 400,000 American jobs at the altar of free trade." He opposed making China a permanent normal trading partner, saying that the United States "should treat China as a totalitarian regime."

A lifelong Chicago resident, Lipinski dropped out of college after he hurt his back. His injury was mild enough that he could work as a weekend athletic instructor in the Parks Department. He spent 17 years there, eventually rising to an administrative position. In 1975, Lipinski was elected to the city council, where he lobbied for the establishment of the Southwest Rapid Transit Line. As chairman of the council's Education Committee, he opposed mandatory busing, a hot-button issue for his heavily ethnic constituency.

During an intraparty split in 1982, Lipinski defeated Rep. John G. Fary in the Democratic primary. He had to survive another intramural battle a decade later, when redistricting compelled him to run against fellow Democratic Rep. Marty Russo. Lipinski called on the muscle of the city's Democratic organization, as he has throughout the years when necessary, and defeated Russo with 58 percent of the vote. (Lipinski still leads the party's 23rd Ward organization.) In his general-election victories, Lipinski has never gotten less than 54 percent of the vote and on several occasions has won with more than 70 percent. In 2002, he was unopposed.

KEY VOTES

2002

- No — Overhaul campaign finance law; ban "soft money" and restrict advocacy advertising
- Yes — Back Bush's defense budget increase
- No — Extend 1996 welfare law
- ? — Adopt Bush's discretionary spending limit
- No — Pass GOP Medicare prescription drug plan
- Yes — Create independent Sept. 11 commission
- Yes — Extend union protections to Homeland Security Department employees
- ? — Revive fast-track procedures for trade agreements
- No — Authorize war against Iraq
- No — Advance bankruptcy overhaul opposed by abortion opponents

2001

- No — Nullify Clinton Labor Department ergonomics rule
- ? — Cut taxes by $1.35 trillion through fiscal 2011
- ? — Maintain ban on oil drilling in Arctic National Wildlife Refuge
- ? — Approve Bush proposal to limit managed-care plan liability for coverage decisions
- No — Divert money from crop subsidy payments to land conservation
- Yes — Expand law enforcement power to investigate suspected terrorists

CQ VOTE STUDIES

	PARTY UNITY		PRESIDENTIAL SUPPORT	
	Support	Oppose	Support	Oppose
2002	75%	25%	47%	53%
2001	62%	38%	61%	39%
2000	73%	27%	52%	48%
1999	66%	34%	58%	42%
1998	58%	42%	50%	50%

INTEREST GROUPS

	AFL-CIO	ADA	CCUS	ACU
2002	67%	55%	53%	32%
2001	80%	40%	50%	55%
2000	90%	45%	40%	37%
1999	78%	55%	28%	45%
1998	50%	45%	50%	48%

ILLINOIS 3

Chicago — southwest side; south and west suburbs

The 3rd covers the southwest corner of Chicago and adjacent suburbs, part of a working-class region known as the "Bungalow Belt" that is stocked with voters of Eastern European, Italian and Irish descent.

This once urban, Chicago-machine district shifted west into suburban territory when a new Hispanic-majority district was created to its north in 1991 redistricting. The change inserted an ample GOP vote from the district's more affluent suburbs, especially in western Cook County. The townships of Lyons, Palos and Riverside voted for Republican George W. Bush in the 2000 presidential election.

Further redistricting following the 2000 census added more of Chicago; city residents now comprise about 40 percent of the district population. The 3rd includes the historically Irish neighborhood of Bridgeport, which is the former home and political base of the powerful Daley family, and southwest Chicago neighborhoods such as Beverly, West Lawn, Clearing and Garfield Ridge (where Midway Airport is located). The West Lawn and West Eldson neighborhoods have experienced rapid Hispanic growth. The 3rd has more Hispanics than all but two districts in Illinois.

Crisscrossed by highways, railroads and the Chicago Sanitary and Ship Canal, the 3rd is a center of manufacturing and distribution. Expansion at Midway has broadened the district's retail and service base and created new jobs for district residents.

In national elections, the 3rd typically votes Democratic, but not by the same wide margins as in other Chicago-based districts. Many working- and middle-class voters lean to the right on social issues.

MAJOR INDUSTRY

Metals and other heavy manufacturing, trucking, warehouses

CITIES

Chicago (pt.), 266,264; Oak Lawn, 55,245; Berwyn (pt.), 51,179; Burbank, 27,902; Brookfield (pt.), 18,980; Palos Hills, 17,665

NOTABLE

The Berwyn Houby Festival, celebrating Czech heritage, is named after the Czech word for mushroom.

Rep. Luis V. Gutierrez (D)

CAPITOL OFFICE
225-8203
luisgutierrez.house.gov
2367 Rayburn 20515-1304; fax 225-7810

COMMITTEES
Financial Services
Veterans' Affairs

HOMETOWN
Chicago

BORN
Dec. 10, 1953, Chicago, Ill.

RELIGION
Roman Catholic

FAMILY
Wife, Soraida Arocho Gutierrez; two children

EDUCATION
Northeastern Illinois U., B.A. 1975 (liberal arts)

CAREER
Teacher; social worker

POLITICAL HIGHLIGHTS
Chicago City Council, 1986-93

ELECTION RESULTS

2002 GENERAL		
Luis V. Gutierrez (D)	67,339	79.7%
Anthony Lopez-Cisneros (R)	12,778	15.1%
Marjorie Kohls (LIBERT)	4,396	5.2%
2002 PRIMARY		
Luis V. Gutierrez (D)	38,338	68.2%
Martin R. Castro (D)	12,008	21.4%
John Joseph Holowinski (D)	5,849	10.4%
2000 GENERAL		
Luis V. Gutierrez (D)	89,487	88.6%
Stephanie Sailor (LIBERT)	11,476	11.4%

PREVIOUS WINNING PERCENTAGES
1998 (82%); 1996 (94%); 1994 (75%); 1992 (78%)

Elected 1992; 6th term

Gutierrez is used to being lonely. He is a liberal in a conservative-run House; he is the first Hispanic member of Congress from Illinois; and he represents one of the poorest, least-educated districts in the nation. If he can't be on the inside cutting deals on legislation, Gutierrez is determined to be on the outside rattling the doorknob, in his self-assigned role as critic of the majority party and defender of liberal values.

Tough-sounding rhetoric has been a favorite weapon of Gutierrez (goo-tee-AIR-ez) since his earliest days in the House. As a freshman, his nationally televised criticism of Congress drew angry responses from even Democratic colleagues, hurting his chances of getting a seat on a top-tier committee. His central issue is easing immigration limits, not a wildly popular idea in a Republican-held Congress. On the environment, education, labor-management relations and abortion, Gutierrez sees the GOP agenda as a threat to his Hispanic-majority district in Chicago, which has among the highest percentages of non-citizens and the lowest per capita income in the nation.

As chairman of the Congressional Hispanic Caucus' Task Force on Immigration and Citizenship, Gutierrez devotes much of his time to fighting GOP efforts to limit the numbers of immigrants and their government benefits. In the 107th Congress, he sponsored a bill granting permanent legal residency to immigrants who had been in the United States since 1996, rather than 1972 as was the case under existing law. The bill also called for a national study of immigrant trafficking and exploitation. Another of his bills requires paid immigration consultants to be licensed by the U.S. Immigration and Naturalization Service.

One of just three House members of Puerto Rican descent, Gutierrez has waged a campaign to force the U.S. Navy to abandon its training facility on the small island of Vieques, just off the coast of Puerto Rico, after a civilian was killed in a bombing accident. In 2000, Gutierrez was among a group of more than 100 protesters, including New York Democratic Rep. Nydia M. Velázquez, who were forcibly removed from the facility. He was arrested in another protest in 2001 and later sentenced to three hours in jail and six months of probation.

Gutierrez had a high profile during the House debate in the 105th Congress on a bill to let Puerto Rico choose either statehood, independence or continued status as a U.S. commonwealth. Gutierrez, who went to high school in Puerto Rico and first registered to vote there, says, "I want Puerto Rico to be a free and independent nation."

As a reminder of the difficulties faced by non-white Americans, Gutierrez likes to cite something that happened to him at the Capitol in 1996. Returning to his office from a reception with his daughter and niece, Gutierrez was confronted by a security officer who questioned whether he indeed was a member of Congress. The officer made matters worse by being rude and insulting, Gutierrez says.

A 2002 Chicago Sun-Times editorial called Gutierrez "arguably . . . the most influential Latino political leader in Chicago history." He can be passionate in his defense of society's underdogs. After President Clinton struck what Gutierrez considered a bad deal on the budget with congressional Republicans in 1997, he said, "A low-income veteran who took a bullet or two at Iwo Jima or Vietnam has to make another sacrifice to help an investor who wants to take a profit on Wall Street."

Gutierrez's legislative goals include a number of proposals aimed at improving mass transit and making it more affordable, outlawing certain handguns, and requiring the insurance and securities affiliates of large financial houses to do business in poor neighborhoods.

In 2002, Gutierrez parted ways with colleagues in the Illinois Democratic delegation by endorsing freshman Rep. Rahm Emanuel for a seat on the Ways and Means Committee; the other Democrats supported Rep. Danny K. Davis. Gutierrez also played a key role in the intraparty battle for the Democratic nomination in the 2002 Illinois gubernatorial race. He was one of the first prominent politicians to endorse House colleague Rod R. Blagojevich, who went on to win the nomination and the governorship.

Gutierrez sits on the same two committees he got when he first came to Congress in 1993: Financial Services (formerly Banking) and Veterans' Affairs. In the 107th, he claimed the top Democratic post on the Financial Services panel's Oversight and Investigations Subcommittee.

His chances of a higher-profile assignment have foundered since 1994, when Gutierrez denounced Congress' shortcomings in an appearance on the CBS program "60 Minutes." He drew raves from congressional critics, and his office logged more than 500 phone calls and faxes praising his integrity and candor. But his House colleagues judged his performance to be self-serving, especially for someone who wasn't exactly a career reform politician. After all, they were quick to note, he came up through the rough-and-tumble world of Chicago city politics.

Born in Chicago, Gutierrez returned there after high school in Puerto Rico to attend college. He worked for more than a decade as a teacher, social worker and community activist.

In 1983, he backed the insurgent mayoral bid of Democrat Harold Washington, who defeated incumbent Mayor Jane Byrne and Illinois States Attorney Richard M. Daley, son of the longtime mayor, in the Democratic primary. Washington became Chicago's first African-American mayor. In 1986, Gutierrez was elected to the city council, where he was nicknamed "El Gallito," Spanish for "the little fighting rooster," for his tenacity.

After Washington died and Daley became mayor, he and Gutierrez reconciled. When the oddly shaped Hispanic-majority 4th District was created for the 1992 election (incumbent Democratic Rep. George E. Sangmeister was moved to the 11th District), Daley backed Gutierrez for the seat. Daley's support practically guaranteed Gutierrez the non-Hispanic white vote, and he won easily in the heavily Democratic district. Since then, he generally has faced a primary challenge and then has breezed to re-election in the fall.

KEY VOTES

2002

- Yes Overhaul campaign finance law; ban "soft money" and restrict advocacy advertising
- Yes Back Bush's defense budget increase
- No Extend 1996 welfare law
- No Adopt Bush's discretionary spending limit
- No Pass GOP Medicare prescription drug plan
- \+ Create independent Sept. 11 commission
- Yes Extend union protections to Homeland Security Department employees
- No Revive fast-track procedures for trade agreements
- No Authorize war against Iraq
- No Advance bankruptcy overhaul opposed by abortion opponents

2001

- No Nullify Clinton Labor Department ergonomics rule
- No Cut taxes by $1.35 trillion through fiscal 2011
- Yes Maintain ban on oil drilling in Arctic National Wildlife Refuge
- No Approve Bush proposal to limit managed-care plan liability for coverage decisions
- Yes Divert money from crop subsidy payments to land conservation
- Yes Expand law enforcement power to investigate suspected terrorists

CQ VOTE STUDIES

	PARTY UNITY		PRESIDENTIAL SUPPORT	
	Support	Oppose	Support	Oppose
2002	95%	5%	31%	69%
2001	95%	5%	28%	72%
2000	96%	4%	84%	16%
1999	93%	7%	76%	24%
1998	93%	7%	83%	17%

INTEREST GROUPS

	AFL-CIO	ADA	CCUS	ACU
2002	100%	95%	42%	0%
2001	100%	95%	35%	16%
2000	100%	90%	38%	9%
1999	100%	95%	16%	0%
1998	100%	90%	28%	16%

ILLINOIS 4

Chicago — parts of North Side, southwest side

Surrounding the black-majority 7th District in the center of Chicago, the horseshoe-shaped 4th was drawn to unite the city's Hispanic neighborhoods into one voting bloc. Slightly less than 90 percent of district residents live in Chicago.

The district, created after the 1990 census revealed that the city's Hispanic population had passed 500,000, is three-fourths Hispanic, and after slight boundary revisions in 2001 includes 45 percent of Cook County's 1.1 million Hispanics. Solidly Democratic, the 4th is plagued by low voter turnout.

A narrow strip of land — about 10 miles in length and running along railroad tracks, highways and cemeteries — attaches the Puerto Rican neighborhood of Logan Square in the northern part of the 4th to Mexican-American communities in Little Village and Pilsen in the southern part. In 1998, the Supreme Court declined to hear a suit alleging that the district had been unconstitutionally drawn with race as the major factor.

More than 90 percent of residents are Hispanic in parts of the Lower West Side and South Lawndale neighborhoods around Cermak Road. Hispanic growth also has been impressive in some close-in suburbs: Cicero, a once heavily Slavic town infamous for being the center of operations for Al Capone's mob and the site of a 1966 race riot, is now three-fourths Hispanic. Stone Park, located in the district's northwestern corner (near the DuPage County line), was once largely Italian but is now four-fifths Hispanic.

The 4th has the state's largest percentage of blue-collar workers, and includes significant immigrant populations in both its Hispanic communities and adjacent Ukrainian and Polish neighborhoods. It also takes in part of Back of the Yards, an area in Chicago that declined when the city's famed stockyards closed in the early 1970s.

MAJOR INDUSTRY
Light manufacturing, county administration, electronics

CITIES
Chicago (pt.), 560,373; Cicero (pt.), 73,209; Melrose Park (pt.), 5,756

NOTABLE
The Mexican Fine Arts Center Museum is located in the Lower West Side neighborhood.

Rep. Rahm Emanuel (D)

CAPITOL OFFICE
225-4061
rahm.emanuel@mail.house.gov
www.house.gov/emanuel
1319 Longworth 20515-1305; fax 225-5603

COMMITTEES
Budget
Financial Services

HOMETOWN
Chicago

BORN
Nov. 29, 1959, Chicago, Ill.

RELIGION
Jewish

FAMILY
Wife, Amy Rule; three children

EDUCATION
Sarah Lawrence College, B.A. 1981 (liberal arts); Northwestern U., M.A. 1985 (speech & communication)

CAREER
Investment bank executive; senior White House official; campaign aide and finance director

POLITICAL HIGHLIGHTS
No previous office

ELECTION RESULTS

2002 GENERAL		
Rahm Emanuel (D)	106,514	66.8%
Mark A. Augusti (R)	46,008	28.9%
Frank Gonzalez (LIBERT)	6,913	4.3%
2002 PRIMARY		
Rahm Emanuel (D)	46,774	50.5%
Nancy Kaszak (D)	35,716	38.6%
Peter Dagher (D)	4,145	4.5%
Stanley Niziolek (D)	1,698	1.8%
Mark A. Fredrickson (D)	1,202	1.3%
Ray Lear (D)	1,094	1.2%
Paul A. Rauner (D)	1,043	1.1%
Joseph Slovinec (D)	953	1.0%

Elected 2002; 1st term

Emanuel's 2002 election to Illinois' open 5th District seat returned him to Washington, where as a senior adviser to President Clinton he had developed a reputation as a sharp-elbowed political tactician. Nicknamed "Rahmbo" after the take-no-prisoners action hero, Emanuel once sent a rotting fish to a pollster.

Yet Emanuel's knowledge of the ways of Washington was quickly noted by House Democratic leaders, who made him part of the party's whip organization. It is a job for which he needed no on-the-job training: Emanuel helped direct successful Clinton administration efforts to pass the 1993 North American Free Trade Agreement and the 1996 overhaul of welfare law.

Emanuel left the White House in early 1999 to become an investment banker in Chicago. But he jumped at the opportunity to run for Congress when three-term Democratic Rep. Rod R. Blagojevich made an ultimately successful bid for governor.

Emanuel effectively clinched the election with a primary victory over former state Rep. Nancy Kaszak, who lost to Blagojevich in the 1996 primary. Chicago Mayor Richard M. Daley backed Emanuel, who had helped Daley raise money for his own past campaigns.

Feeling assured of victory in the solidly Democratic North Side Chicago district, Emanuel gave cash from his bountiful campaign treasury to other Democratic House candidates, including at least five of his Class of 2002 colleagues. Emanuel proudly noted after the general election that he outperformed 2000 Democratic presidential nominee Al Gore in the 5th District.

Emanuel won seats on the Financial Services and Budget committees, solid second-choice assignments. He had angled for a plum spot on the Ways and Means Committee — whose former chairman, Democrat Dan Rostenkowski, represented the 5th for 36 years — but he realized it was a long shot for a freshman.

ILLINOIS 5

Chicago — North Side

The 5th spans the North Side of Chicago, from Lake Michigan to near O'Hare International Airport (located in the 6th District). One of the city's few remaining active industrial sectors runs through the middle of the district, along the north branch of the Chicago River. The district's 2 percent black population is the lowest in the state.

On the east side, the 5th includes most of Lincoln Park, a wealthy community of "lakefront liberals" known for their expensive homes and opposition to Democratic machine politics. Voters here rarely support establishment candidates in the primary but then vote Democratic in general elections.

The west side of the district covers part of the "Bungalow Belt," a strip of 1930s brick homes built by Central and Eastern European families. This section of town is still dominated by middle- and working-class German and Polish neighborhoods, but has seen an increasing number of Hispanic newcomers. Voters here also lean Democratic but sometimes vote for Republicans in the general election.

The west's working-class base routinely supports candidates trumpeting populist-style economic causes. But far-west side neighborhoods also have been known to elect a few Republicans to local offices. On the federal level, the district supported Democratic presidential candidates in 1992, 1996 and 2000.

MAJOR INDUSTRY
Warehousing and storage, electronics, manufacturing, health care

CITIES
Chicago (pt.), 549,762; Elmwood Park (pt.), 23,741; Franklin Park, 19,434

NOTABLE
Wrigley Field is home to baseball's Chicago Cubs; Famous gangster death sites: the S.M.C. Cartage Co. garage, where Al Capone ordered "Bugs" Moran's gangsters shot in the 1929 St. Valentine's Day Massacre; and the Biograph Theatre, where federal agents gunned down outlaw John Dillinger in 1934.

Rep. Henry J. Hyde (R)

CAPITOL OFFICE
225-4561
www.house.gov/hyde
2110 Rayburn 20515-1306; fax 225-1166

COMMITTEES
International Relations - chairman
Judiciary

HOMETOWN
Bensenville

BORN
April 18, 1924, Chicago, Ill.

RELIGION
Roman Catholic

FAMILY
Widowed; four children

EDUCATION
Duke U., attended 1943-44; Georgetown U., B.S. 1947 (history); Loyola U., J.D. 1949

MILITARY SERVICE
Navy, 1944-46; Naval Reserve, 1946-68

CAREER
Lawyer

POLITICAL HIGHLIGHTS
Republican nominee for U.S. House, 1962; Ill. House, 1967-75 (majority leader, 1971-73)

ELECTION RESULTS

2002 GENERAL		
Henry J. Hyde (R)	113,174	65.1%
Tom Berry (D)	60,698	34.9%
2002 PRIMARY		
Henry J. Hyde (R)		unopposed
2000 GENERAL		
Henry J. Hyde (R)	133,327	58.9%
Brent Christensen (D)	92,880	41.1%

PREVIOUS WINNING PERCENTAGES
1998 (67%); 1996 (64%); 1994 (73%); 1992 (66%); 1990 (67%); 1988 (74%); 1986 (75%); 1984 (75%); 1982 (68%); 1980 (67%); 1978 (66%); 1976 (61%); 1974 (53%)

Elected 1974; 15th term

Having won national renown and the undying support of conservatives for playing two career-making roles — anti-abortion crusader and Clinton impeachment prosecutor — Hyde is finishing his third decade in the House trying to do an altogether different job: shepherd Republican foreign policy in a time of international unrest.

Hyde has chaired the International Relations Committee since 2001, taking the gavel of a panel where he had not had much impact since the arms control and Central America policy debates of the 1980s. When the GOP won control of the House in 1994, Hyde was picked to chair the Judiciary Committee and move much of the party's socially conservative agenda. But his most historic task was to steer the impeachment of President Clinton through the House and serve as lead prosecutor in the Senate trial.

Republican-imposed term limits compelled Hyde to give up the Judiciary chairmanship at the start of the 107th Congress, but he was able to leverage his seniority and stature to take over International Relations. Leading that panel has turned out to be a mixed blessing. The committee's GOP membership is considerably more centrist than the House as a whole, and Republican moderates on the panel have been as inclined to cast their ballots with Democrats as with a conservative such as Hyde.

A seminal moment occurred in May 2001 when, during Hyde's first major outing as chairman, moderate Republicans and Democrats teamed up over Hyde's objections to overturn some anti-abortion restrictions that President Bush had imposed on some foreign aid. That vote not only undermined Hyde's authority as chairman, but it also was a personal blow to a lawmaker with a reputation for thwarting abortion rights.

Subsequently, Hyde made sure he had the support of top-ranking Democrat Tom Lantos of California before moving any legislation through his panel. As a team, they pushed to House passage bills to combat AIDS overseas, repay U.S. debt to the United Nations and provide aid to Afghanistan. But many of Hyde's initiatives, such as the AIDS bill and a measure to improve government-sponsored exchange and broadcasting programs, ran aground in the Democratic-controlled Senate. And Bush preferred to tackle the most significant foreign policy issues — such as relations with Israel and the showdown with Iraq — directly with the top House leaders.

At the same time, Hyde has been a generally loyal backer of Bush's plans for waging the war on terrorism, at home and abroad. Soon after hearing of the terrorist attacks of Sept. 11, 2001 (while exercising at Washington's Fort McNair to ease the arthritic pain in his back), Hyde concluded that a lessening of complacency about terrorist threats in the national psyche might be the event's tiniest of silver linings.

Among his colleagues, Hyde is respected as an old-fashioned wit, one of the sharpest legal minds on Capitol Hill, a genuinely nice man and a leading defender of the institution of Congress. Hyde, who attended Georgetown University on a basketball scholarship, is a hulk of a man with a rousing oratorical style. He is often the most impressive spokesman in legislative battles, pouncing on flaws in foes' arguments with all the repartee and sarcasm he once used as a Chicago trial lawyer.

While now viewed as an elder statesman among House Republicans, his highest position among his GOP peers was as chairman of the Republican Policy Committee in the early 1990s. Still, his name comes up whenever there is discussion about possible candidates for Speaker if the rank-and-file some day loses faith in the current GOP leadership.

Hyde performed yeoman's service in the "Republican revolution," swiftly adapting himself to the influx of conservatives elected in the 1990s — and also helping them adapt to the House. Still, he has had some high-profile differences with the party's right wing. He gave a pivotal speech on the House floor in 1990 in favor of what later became the Family and Medical Leave Act. He voted to ban certain assault-style weapons in 1994 and 1996. And he adamantly opposes term limits, although he allowed proposed constitutional amendments on the issue to move through his committee.

On the legislative front, he is best-known for the "Hyde amendment," initially written in 1976 during his first term to bar the federal funding of abortions. It has since been altered to create exceptions when the woman has become pregnant because of incest or rape, or if her life is endangered by maintaining the pregnancy.

To the public, Hyde will always be remembered for leading — with unswerving determination — the prosecution of Clinton for alleged perjury and obstruction of justice stemming from his affair with Monica Lewinsky, a former White House intern. When GOP colleagues counseled against zealous pursuit of the popular president, Hyde insisted that the nation's chief law enforcement officer deserved to be removed from office for undermining "the rule of law." Hyde became a favorite target of Democratic partisans, who revealed that when he was in his 40s Hyde had carried on a five-year affair with a married woman. He dismissed his transgression as a "youthful indiscretion." Though Hyde convinced the House to impeach Clinton on two counts in 1998, GOP leaders sought to bring the 1999 Senate trial to a quick conclusion because it was clear they did not have the two-thirds majority needed for convictions.

While Hyde has no great reputation for championing parochial concerns, he places much importance on seeing to the construction of a third airport to serve the Chicago area. He opposed the 2000 federal aviation law because it allowed more flights at O'Hare, which is in his district.

Hyde grew up in Chicago as an Irish Catholic Democrat. He began having doubts about the Democratic Party in the late 1940s; by 1952, he had switched to the GOP. Elected to the state House in 1966, he was one of its most outspoken and articulate debaters, rising to majority leader but losing a bid for Speaker. In 1974, longtime GOP Rep. Harold Collier retired from his suburban Chicago House seat. Capitalizing on his fundraising prowess and his army of precinct workers, Hyde bucked the post-Watergate tide and won with 53 percent. He has been invincible ever since.

KEY VOTES

2002

No Overhaul campaign finance law; ban "soft money" and restrict advocacy advertising
Yes Back Bush's defense budget increase
Yes Extend 1996 welfare law
Yes Adopt Bush's discretionary spending limit
Yes Pass GOP Medicare prescription drug plan
No Create independent Sept. 11 commission
No Extend union protections to Homeland Security Department employees
Yes Revive fast-track procedures for trade agreements
Yes Authorize war against Iraq
Yes Advance bankruptcy overhaul opposed by abortion opponents

2001

Yes Nullify Clinton Labor Department ergonomics rule
Yes Cut taxes by $1.35 trillion through fiscal 2011
No Maintain ban on oil drilling in Arctic National Wildlife Refuge
Yes Approve Bush proposal to limit managed-care plan liability for coverage decisions
No Divert money from crop subsidy payments to land conservation
Yes Expand law enforcement power to investigate suspected terrorists

CQ VOTE STUDIES

	PARTY UNITY		PRESIDENTIAL SUPPORT	
	Support	Oppose	Support	Oppose
2002	97%	3%	92%	8%
2001	95%	5%	88%	12%
2000	89%	11%	35%	65%
1999	89%	11%	31%	69%
1998	92%	8%	20%	80%

INTEREST GROUPS

	AFL-CIO	ADA	CCUS	ACU
2002	13%	0%	100%	88%
2001	17%	5%	96%	92%
2000	20%	10%	71%	76%
1999	22%	15%	75%	72%
1998	0%	0%	88%	92%

ILLINOIS 6

Northwest and west Chicago suburbs

Just west of Chicago, the 6th includes northern DuPage County and part of northwest Cook County. It is full of older, mostly built-out bedroom communities along commuter rail lines running into the city. Many of these suburbs have been revitalizing their downtown districts.

Most residents of the 6th traditionally have commuted to Chicago, but some now travel to booming northwest satellite cities. The district's eastern boundary is O'Hare International Airport (an extension of the city of Chicago), which is one of the nation's busiest airports and the focus of the 6th's commercial district. Hotels and other travel-related businesses, and companies seeking close airport access, are located in the area.

The district has a reputation as a Republican bastion, historically working in opposition to Chicago's Democrats. It includes slightly more than half of DuPage County, which accounts for three-fourths of the population. DuPage is decidedly Republican (it backed George W. Bush by 13 percentage points in the 2000 presidential election), but not as heavily so as in the 1980s, when it backed Ronald Reagan and George Bush by better than 2-to-1 ratios. Overall, George W. Bush won the 6th with 53 percent of the vote in 2000.

The 6th is one-eighth Hispanic, and DuPage is becoming more racially diverse. Addison and Bensenville have many Hispanic residents, and Asians and Hispanics each tally 20 percent in Glendale Heights. Many Hispanics came to the district when agriculture was a dominant industry and stayed as Chicago's suburbs crept westward in the 1970s and 1980s and took over farmland.

The Cook County portions of the district also have a conservative lean. Under redistricting following the 2000 census, the 6th ceded nearly all of Maine township (Des Plaines, Park Ridge) to the 9th District and gained most of Hanover township (the westernmost township in Cook) from the 8th District.

MAJOR INDUSTRY

Airport, light manufacturing, health care

CITIES

Wheaton, 55,416; Elmhurst, 42,762; Lombard, 42,322; Carol Stream, 40,438

NOTABLE

United Airlines headquarters is in Elk Grove Village.

Rep. Danny K. Davis (D)

CAPITOL OFFICE
225-5006
www.house.gov/davis
1222 Longworth 20515-1307; fax 225-5641

COMMITTEES
Education & Workforce
Government Reform
Small Business

HOMETOWN
Chicago

BORN
Sept. 6, 1941, Parkdale, Ark.

RELIGION
Baptist

FAMILY
Wife, Vera Davis; two children

EDUCATION
Arkansas AM&N College, B.A. 1961 (history & education); Chicago State U., M.A. 1968 (guidance); Union Institute, Ph.D. 1977 (public administration)

CAREER
Health care consultant; teacher

POLITICAL HIGHLIGHTS
Chicago City Council, 1979-90; sought Democratic nomination for U.S. House, 1984, 1986; Cook County Commission, 1990-97; candidate for mayor of Chicago, 1991

ELECTION RESULTS

2002 GENERAL		
Danny K. Davis (D)	137,933	83.2%
Mark Tunney (R)	25,280	15.3%
Martin Pankau (LIBERT)	2,543	1.5%
2002 PRIMARY		
Danny K. Davis (D)		unopposed
2000 GENERAL		
Danny K. Davis (D)	164,155	85.9%
Robert Dallas (R)	26,872	14.1%

PREVIOUS WINNING PERCENTAGES
1998 (93%); 1996 (82%)

Elected 1996; 4th term

Davis has never seen Congress from the vantage point of the majority. But unlike many who have been stuck in the House's minority party year after year, Davis has not trimmed his aims to fit within the limits of his power. He has taken on causes to the left of most of his party and admits that he thinks about the long term — the very long term — when it comes to many of his priorities. He doesn't worry about the hot issues of the day. Those matters, he says, will be addressed regardless of what he does.

"I have a tendency to take on those things that may not be as sexy and appealing," he says.

Still, Davis has had his victories. He was a principal mover in 2000 behind a package of anti-poverty initiatives to revitalize poor neighborhoods. And in 1998 the House voted in favor of his proposal to help low-income workers commute to their jobs.

But during the 107th Congress, Davis took on an issue he knows will require a long battle: the effort to integrate ex-convicts into their communities with jobs, housing and voting rights. "All of the issues associated with poverty are pronounced in my district," Davis says. "Rather than run from it, or hope someone else is going to do it, we took a vote that the ex-offender issue is going to be the top issue."

Davis is not expecting his efforts to turn into laws any time soon. But he notes that to build a house you must first lay a solid foundation, and he hopes to build the support necessary to construct new policies down the line.

His committee assignments have given him little say over criminal justice or social programs, although he won a seat on Education and the Workforce in the 108th. Many of his Illinois Democratic colleagues backed him for appointment to Ways and Means, though 5th District freshman Rahm Emanuel also wanted the post. It went to Stephanie Tubbs Jones of Ohio.

While his liberal views allow him to work comfortably in the Congressional Progressive Caucus, Davis also draws on his church-going upbringing to examine policy questions. He backs the principle, if not the specifics, of President Bush's faith-based initiative to provide new tax breaks for charitable giving and to permit federal funding of religious groups that provide social services. Many social advances for blacks — since and including the abolition of slavery — have their origins in the church, he says.

Davis often sprinkles his arguments with humorous stories and light asides. A gregarious, enthusiastic man with a deep, melodious voice, he laces his talk with tidbits of personal philosophy, drawing heavily on his childhood as one of 11 children born to sharecroppers who picked cotton in southeastern Arkansas, one of the poorest regions of the country. He says he and his brothers and sisters went to a segregated school only four or five months of the year, spending the rest of the time in the fields.

Sometimes stubborn when pressing his priorities, Davis says he learned perseverance from his father and empathy from his mother. "They instilled whatever drive and desire I may have had," he notes.

His district in the heart of Chicago is different in some obvious ways from his rural roots, but Davis says he sees many of the same problems in both places. He pleads for "economic policies that will also create jobs for which people can actually work and earn a decent wage, a livable wage." He has pushed legislation to improve transportation, housing, health care and education for his heterogeneous district, which includes not only huge public housing projects but also some well-to-do suburbs, plush high rises and the business center downtown.

Davis joined in a bill to require local and state governments to reduce taxes and regulatory requirements on companies operating in designated urban and rural renewal areas. In the Congressional Black Caucus, where he is the secretary in the 108th, Davis has pushed for a serious look at police brutality and racial profiling, seeking "equal application of the law" — which he sees as a major focus in the future of the ongoing civil rights struggle.

A member of the Government Reform Committee, Davis worked to increase participation in the 2000 census, particularly in low-income areas. He also pressed the U.S. Postal Service (where he once worked as a clerk) to move more ethnic minorities into management jobs. In 2001, he was among the first who called on Congress to honor postal workers who died after handling anthrax-tainted mail and he said the incident should spur Congress to look at improving the postal service in general.

Davis says he went off to college in Arkansas with the idea of becoming a teacher. After graduation, with $50 given to him by his father, Davis set off for California where a job awaited. But his money ran out, and he got no farther than Chicago. He stayed with an older sister for a time, working in the post office and at other jobs before landing a teaching job. Davis soon realized he wanted to be more involved in the community, and his activism eventually led him to become president of the National Association of Community Health Centers. In 1979, Davis headed a committee of neighborhood leaders looking for a candidate to challenge the Democratic political machine in a city council race, but he failed to turn up anyone. "So I said, 'what the hell,' and decided to run myself," he said.

Davis won — the first black alderman who was not part of the regular party machinery — and served until 1990, when he became a Cook County commissioner. On the city council, Davis was a close associate of Harold Washington, a former House member and the city's first black mayor, who also had challenged the Democratic machine.

In 1984, Davis opposed 7th District Rep. Cardiss Collins in the Democratic primary; he lost by 10 percentage points but held her to less than a majority. Davis opposed Collins again in 1986 but lost decisively. And in 1991, Davis was the decided underdog in a Democratic primary campaign for mayor against the incumbent, Richard M. Daley.

Davis never gave up. When Collins announced plans to retire in 1996, Davis jumped into the race. He faced a crowded primary field and opposition from some elements of the party machine, but he cleared those hurdles and won with ease that November. He has not been seriously challenged since.

KEY VOTES

2002

Yes Overhaul campaign finance law; ban "soft money" and restrict advocacy advertising
Yes Back Bush's defense budget increase
No Extend 1996 welfare law
No Adopt Bush's discretionary spending limit
No Pass GOP Medicare prescription drug plan
Yes Create independent Sept. 11 commission
Yes Extend union protections to Homeland Security Department employees
No Revive fast-track procedures for trade agreements
No Authorize war against Iraq
No Advance bankruptcy overhaul opposed by abortion opponents

2001

No Nullify Clinton Labor Department ergonomics rule
No Cut taxes by $1.35 trillion through fiscal 2011
Yes Maintain ban on oil drilling in Arctic National Wildlife Refuge
No Approve Bush proposal to limit managed-care plan liability for coverage decisions
Yes Divert money from crop subsidy payments to land conservation
No Expand law enforcement power to investigate suspected terrorists

CQ VOTE STUDIES

	PARTY UNITY		PRESIDENTIAL SUPPORT	
	Support	Oppose	Support	Oppose
2002	96%	4%	24%	76%
2001	97%	3%	17%	83%
2000	97%	3%	88%	12%
1999	97%	3%	84%	16%
1998	95%	5%	85%	15%

INTEREST GROUPS

	AFL-CIO	ADA	CCUS	ACU
2002	100%	90%	42%	0%
2001	100%	100%	35%	4%
2000	100%	100%	33%	4%
1999	100%	100%	17%	0%
1998	100%	95%	28%	8%

ILLINOIS 7

Chicago – downtown, West Side; west suburbs

East to west, the 7th stretches from the Loop, Chicago's downtown business district, almost to the DuPage County line, taking in the well-to-do western suburbs of Oak Park and River Forest. North to south, the district runs from the upscale Lincoln Park neighborhood to 57th Street on the South Side.

The eastern end of the 7th houses some of Chicago's gems, including the Sears Tower, the plush high-rises of River North, several museums and about a dozen colleges and universities. Chicago's "Magnificent Mile" on Michigan Avenue includes some prestigious shops and first-rate hotels and museums. Business giants such as Boeing, Sara Lee and Quaker Foods and Beverages have their corporate headquarters in the 7th.

But most of the district lives in the poverty-stricken neighborhoods that stretch from the western Loop to the edge of the county. Except for a few communities of middle-class blacks, the West Side has had problems with gang violence, unemployment and crumbling infrastructure. The situation is beginning to change in the West Loop, once dominated by the Cabrini-Green housing project, where young couples and development companies have rehabilitated old apartment buildings and warehouses, turning them into condos and lofts.

The district fills with white commuters during the day, but more than 60 percent of the district's permanent residents are black. A reliably Democratic district across the ballot, the only genuine political contests in the 7th are the Democratic primaries.

MAJOR INDUSTRY

Insurance, banking, accounting

CITIES

Chicago (pt.), 502,445; Oak Park, 52,524; Maywood (pt.), 24,895

NOTABLE

The United Center, arena for the Chicago Bulls and Blackhawks, Soldier Field, stadium for the Chicago Bears and Fire, and Comiskey Park (U.S. Cellular Field), stadium for the Chicago White Sox, are in the district; The Ernest Hemingway birthplace and museum are in Oak Park; Oprah Winfrey's Harpo Productions is in Chicago; Architect Frank Lloyd Wright's home and studio are in Oak Park.

Rep. Philip M. Crane (R)

CAPITOL OFFICE
225-3711
www.house.gov/crane
233 Cannon 20515-1308; fax 225-7830

COMMITTEES
Ways & Means
(Trade - chairman)
Joint Taxation

HOMETOWN
Wauconda

BORN
Nov. 3, 1930, Chicago, Ill.

RELIGION
Protestant

FAMILY
Wife, Arlene Catherine Crane; eight children (one deceased)

EDUCATION
DePauw U., attended 1948-50; Hillsdale College, B.A. 1952 (history & psychology); U. of Michigan, attended 1952-54; U. of Vienna (Austria), attended 1953, attended 1956; Indiana U., M.A. 1961, Ph.D. 1963 (history)

MILITARY SERVICE
Army, 1954-56

CAREER
Professor; author; advertising executive

POLITICAL HIGHLIGHTS
Sought Republican nomination for president, 1980

ELECTION RESULTS

2002 GENERAL		
Philip M. Crane (R)	95,275	57.4%
Melissa L. Bean (D)	70,626	42.6%
2002 PRIMARY		
Philip M. Crane (R)		unopposed
2000 GENERAL		
Philip M. Crane (R)	141,918	61.0%
Lance Pressl (D)	90,777	39.0%

PREVIOUS WINNING PERCENTAGES
1998 (69%); 1996 (62%); 1994 (65%); 1992 (56%); 1990 (82%); 1988 (75%); 1986 (78%); 1984 (78%); 1982 (66%); 1980 (74%); 1978 (80%); 1976 (73%); 1974 (61%); 1972 (74%); 1970 (58%); 1969 Special Election (58%)

Elected November 1969; 17th full term

As chairman of the Ways and Means Subcommittee on Trade, Crane would be expected to be a central figure in any debate on key trade matters. But in the 107th Congress he sat on the sidelines as GOP leaders muscled President Bush's top trade priority through the House. Instead it was Ways and Means Chairman Bill Thomas who orchestrated the campaign to enact the law granting the president expanded authority to negotiate trade deals. And that is as clear a reflection as any of what life is now like for the longest-serving Republican in the House.

Crane has really never recovered from the huge disappointment he suffered as the 107th Congress began. He lost a battle for what would have been the biggest prize of his congressional career — the chairmanship of Ways and Means — and ever since he has reverted to the low-profile role he has generally played since arriving in Congress in 1969.

His unsuccessful bid for chairman was made all the more bitter by the fact that the Republican who won the post, California's Thomas, had nine years less seniority in the House than Crane. And the vote of the leadership panel that selects chairmen was unanimous for Thomas.

As a small consolation, Crane was granted a waiver from GOP term limits and allowed to remain at the helm of the Trade Subcommittee. But that softened the blow minimally for Crane, who had spent months working against his reputation of the past two decades by lobbying GOP leaders, actively promoting legislation and raising campaign funds for other Republican lawmakers in hopes of enhancing his chairmanship bid.

Crane and Thomas joined to sponsor legislation to carry out Bush's top trade priority — requiring Congress to vote, without amendment, on trade deals struck by a president — but it was not the version that moved through Congress. Crane did successfully flex his muscle against the chairman at least once in the 107th, helping engineer an underground crusade that beat back Thomas' efforts to repeal a popular export tax brake.

Given Thomas' hands-on leadership style, Crane would have found it difficult to assert himself more routinely, had he really wanted to. While respected for his intelligence — he holds a doctorate in history and has written three books on politics — Crane has never established himself as a party insider. For years now, the House GOP agenda has been set by leaders who are a decade or two younger than Crane, the only House Republican whose congressional career began in the 1960s.

In March 2000, Crane checked himself into a clinic where he underwent treatment for alcoholism. He entered the facility after a group of friends confronted him in his office and urged him to seek help. Crane said he was drinking as many as 10 beers a night. While he plays down the drinking problem, calling it a bad "habit" similar to smoking and even boasting that he left the clinic several days ahead of schedule, many of his colleagues said the drinking had caused him to lose any effectiveness as a legislator.

After his treatment, Crane made a quick comeback in the House. On April 12, one day after returning to work, he did something he had never done in his previous 32 years in office: He presided over the House. His office said it was just a coincidence that such a visible honor should occur upon his return to work, but it kicked off a series of high-profile events for Crane.

In May, Congress sent President Clinton a bill, written by Crane, to increase imports from the Caribbean, Central America and sub-Saharan Africa. It was similar to legislation Crane had first introduced in 1995.

(Even months later, Crane proudly kept in his breast pocket a blue pen inscribed with Clinton's signature given to him after the signing ceremony.) In June, with Crane serving as floor manager, the House passed legislation, enacted later in 2000, making China a permanent normal U.S. trade partner. Through that pair of trade laws, Crane can take partial credit for expanding U.S. trade to about 40 percent of the world's population.

A former chairman of the American Conservative Union, Crane has been criticized by some GOP colleagues for pursuing unrealistic legislative goals and failing to assemble a record of legislative accomplishment. "There are four functions of government that we should fund: Defense, State, Justice and the Treasury," Crane told the Chicago Sun-Times in 1995. "Even the Department of Agriculture, which was created in the 1850s, is not essential."

An ardent tax foe, Crane has proposed plans to create a 10 percent flat tax and eliminate all other taxes, such as the income tax. Immediately after losing his bid for Ways and Means chairman, he urged Thomas to pursue deep tax cuts from his post as leader of the committee, and during the 107th he was an unstinting supporter of Bush's tax cut agenda.

Crane's political career has thrived in the conservative environment of the affluent northwest Chicago suburbs. In 1969, he ran in a special election that followed President Nixon's appointment of GOP Rep. Donald H. Rumsfeld — secretary of defense in the current administration — to head the Office of Economic Opportunity. Crane topped a seven-candidate field with 22 percent. His Democratic foe tried to paint him as an ideological extremist, but Crane's soft-spoken and articulate manner helped him win with 58 percent.

In the 1970s, Crane was a wunderkind among conservatives. After Jimmy Carter won the presidency in 1976, Crane aspired to lead the national conservative Republican counterattack. Dashingly handsome, well-spoken and still shy of 50, he launched a bid for the 1980 GOP presidential nomination. But after he spent a year trying to organize support for the New Hampshire primary, William Loeb, then the acerbic Manchester Union Leader publisher and political baron, ran articles accusing Crane of heavy drinking and womanizing. By the time New Hampshire voted, Crane was a minor candidate and received 1.8 percent of the vote. He won five convention delegates but withdrew and endorsed Ronald Reagan.

From 1972 through 1990, he won re-election easily, never dropping below 60 percent. In the early 1990s, however, he began to draw serious intraparty challenges from more-moderate Republicans. Crane survived the primaries by relying on his conservative base. His seat has been safe since, although his 15-point victory margin in 2002 was his smallest since 1992.

KEY VOTES

2002

No Overhaul campaign finance law; ban "soft money" and restrict advocacy advertising
? Back Bush's defense budget increase
Yes Extend 1996 welfare law
Yes Adopt Bush's discretionary spending limit
Yes Pass GOP Medicare prescription drug plan
No Create independent Sept. 11 commission
No Extend union protections to Homeland Security Department employees
Yes Revive fast-track procedures for trade agreements
Yes Authorize war against Iraq
Yes Advance bankruptcy overhaul opposed by abortion opponents

2001

Yes Nullify Clinton Labor Department ergonomics rule
Yes Cut taxes by $1.35 trillion through fiscal 2011
No Maintain ban on oil drilling in Arctic National Wildlife Refuge
Yes Approve Bush proposal to limit managed-care plan liability for coverage decisions
No Divert money from crop subsidy payments to land conservation
Yes Expand law enforcement power to investigate suspected terrorists

CQ VOTE STUDIES

	PARTY UNITY		PRESIDENTIAL SUPPORT	
	Support	Oppose	Support	Oppose
2002	98%	2%	86%	14%
2001	99%	1%	93%	7%
2000	94%	6%	24%	76%
1999	96%	4%	16%	84%
1998	96%	4%	24%	76%

INTEREST GROUPS

	AFL-CIO	ADA	CCUS	ACU
2002	11%	0%	94%	100%
2001	8%	0%	96%	100%
2000	0%	0%	85%	100%
1999	0%	5%	91%	100%
1998	0%	0%	81%	96%

ILLINOIS 8

Northwest Cook County – Schaumburg; part of Lake and McHenry Counties

Most of the 8th's population lies in the affluent, well-established suburbs northwest of Chicago, although population growth has spurred new developments farther north through western Lake County and into the Chain-O-Lakes vacation communities near the Wisconsin border.

The district became a huge employment center in the late 1980s, drawing commuters away from Chicago and causing serious traffic problems. The 8th is still struggling with these negatives that come with rapid development and suburban sprawl.

As in other northwestern Chicago suburban districts, some of the 8th's cities, such as Palatine (which is shared with the 10th) and Schaumburg, have lured corporate headquarters. Motorola is based in Schaumburg. The biggest development boom in Cook County has been abetted by access to Interstates 90 and 290 and proximity to O'Hare International Airport (in the 6th District).

Redistricting in 2001 gave the 8th more of Lake County, where a slight majority of district residents live. The district now takes in all of Lake County's border with Wisconsin. This area is mostly upscale and well-educated; in the southwest Lake townships of Cuba and Ela, the median family income is more than $100,000. Redistricting also added the northeastern part of fast-growing McHenry County, located west of Lake.

The 8th's strong Republican tradition — it gave George W. Bush 55 percent of the vote in 2000 — has been moderated only slightly by newcomers and a small but growing minority population. Hispanics make up one-tenth of district residents.

MAJOR INDUSTRY
Health care, insurance, retail

CITIES
Schaumburg (pt.), 71,577; Palatine (pt.), 47,077; Hoffman Estates (pt.), 39,568; Mundelein (pt.), 28,416; Round Lake Beach, 25,859

NOTABLE
Six Flags Great America amusement park is in Gurnee; The Volo Illinois Auto Museum features classic and celebrity cars.

Rep. Jan Schakowsky (D)

Elected 1998; 3rd term

When Schakowsky began hearing horror stories about long lines and poor service at the Immigration and Naturalization Service's downtown Chicago office, she decided to look into it. She traveled to the office one morning and, without identifying herself as a member of Congress, stood in line for more than 3 1/2 hours before being told to go home. When she didn't leave fast enough, she recalls, a worker told her to get moving or get ready to go to jail. When the worker asked who Schakowsky was, the congresswoman replied: "First of all, I'm a human being."

The incident led to a House subcommittee hearing and subsequent improvements in the federal office. It also cemented Schakowsky's growing reputation among Democrats as a tough-minded and ambitious activist who is willing to roll up her sleeves to get results.

Schakowsky (shuh-KOW-ski) is a firm believer in using the power of government to enhance citizens' lives. She describes Medicare as a spectacular success and wants to expand it to pay the medical bills of all Americans. As befits a former elementary school teacher, she clamors for a stronger federal investment in public education. She supports gun control and a new approach to fighting drug abuse, telling one political columnist that there is a growing acknowledgment that the drug war hasn't worked.

Schakowsky was the most loyal House Democrat in the 107th Congress, backing her party 99.3 percent of the time on votes that pitted the two parties against each other. And she was an early supporter of Nancy Pelosi of California, who was elected Democratic whip in 2002 and then moved up to be the party's leader in the 108th.

It was therefore not surprising when Schakowsky got a coveted assignment to the Energy and Commerce Committee, and was named the top Democrat on the panel's Consumer Protections Subcommittee. She also is one of seven chief deputy whips, a post she first got when Pelosi advanced to the whip job in 2002.

The Consumer Protection post enables her to continue the work she began three decades ago on behalf of consumers. In the 107th, she introduced a comprehensive bill to end automatic-teller surcharges and exorbitant bank fees. She proposed a bill to crack down on lenders who prey on the poor and elderly by charging high rates and fees for mortgage loans.

Amid the recurring talk about the need for both parties to govern from the center, Schakowsky remains an outspoken advocate of pushing the agenda to the left. "It's more important than ever for there to be a very clear, unapologetic progressive voice," she said. "We need to correctly define what the middle of America is; I believe the progressive position is the middle position."

The redrawing of her district for this decade incorporates some traditionally Republican suburbs northwest of Chicago, but that has had little impact on her liberal leanings. "When it comes to paying attention to local issues and local needs, I want people out there to feel confident that my office will be there for them," she said of her new suburban constituents.

Schakowsky has supported the Bush administration's fight against terrorism in Afghanistan, but she said it must be coupled with increased foreign aid to economically distressed nations. "That has to be included in the calculation of the war on terrorism," she said. "There is no security in the world without economic justice."

Schakowsky is not satisfied to simply espouse progressive causes. A vet-

CAPITOL OFFICE
225-2111
jan.schakowsky@mail.house.gov
www.house.gov/schakowsky
515 Cannon 20515-1309; fax 226-6890

COMMITTEES
Energy & Commerce

HOMETOWN
Evanston

BORN
May 26, 1944, Chicago, Ill.

RELIGION
Jewish

FAMILY
Husband, Robert Creamer; three children

EDUCATION
U. of Illinois, B.S. 1965 (elementary education)

CAREER
Senior citizens group director; consumer advocate; teacher

POLITICAL HIGHLIGHTS
Candidate for Cook County Commission, 1986; Ill. House, 1991-99 (floor leader, 1994-99)

ELECTION RESULTS

2002 GENERAL		
Jan Schakowsky (D)	118,642	70.3%
Nicholas M. Duric (R)	45,307	26.8%
Stephanie Sailor (LIBERT)	4,887	2.9%
2002 PRIMARY		
Jan Schakowsky (D)		unopposed
2000 GENERAL		
Jan Schakowsky (D)	147,002	76.4%
Dennis J. Driscoll (R)	45,344	23.6%

PREVIOUS WINNING PERCENTAGES
1998 (75%)

eran activist of more than 25 years, she seeks to teach organizing skills to others. "I believe that progressives need to develop a winning, not whining strategy for the new millennium . . .," she wrote in The Nation in 2000.

Indeed, Schakowsky was doing leadership work even before she won her seat in Congress. With her husband, Robert Creamer, a longtime Chicago political organizer, she set up a training program for political advocates that has become a model for the party and was replicated nationwide. The program used newspaper advertisements and word of mouth to draw volunteers — many of them college students — to Chicago, where a "campaign school" gave them instruction and political tools and then put them in the field to work on several House races.

Schakowsky's activist approach began as a stay-at-home mother in the early 1970s, when she helped launch a successful nationwide campaign to require freshness dates on food products. Following her work for consumer and senior citizen advocacy groups, she was elected to the state House, where she fought for labor unions, family leave benefits and changes in medical insurance law sought by consumer groups. She worked on toughening Illinois' hate crimes law and guaranteeing homeless people the right to vote. Her work earned her the chairmanship of the state House Labor and Commerce Committee and the position of Democratic floor leader.

In seeking to replace Sidney R. Yates, a liberal Democrat who held the 9th District seat for 48 years before retiring, Schakowsky easily won the staunchly Democratic district in 1998 after besting state Sen. Howard W. Carroll and Hyatt hotel heir Jay "J.B." Pritzker, both more centrist politically, in the primary. She won lopsided re-election victories in 2000 and 2002.

Schakowsky has drawn attention within Democratic circles for her fundraising prowess. Her contacts with donors interested in women's issues, including female business executives, paid off when feminist organizations backed her in the 1998 primary.

Without any serious challengers in the past two elections, Schakowsky has been able to devote substantial efforts to her party's attempt to regain control of the House. She was by far the biggest party fundraiser among first-term House members in 2000 and one of the biggest among all Democrats. "She spends every free moment dialing for dollars," one admiring House aide told the Chicago Tribune. She reportedly turned down an offer to head the House Democrats' campaign committee in the 108th.

Schakowsky had been considering a run for the Senate in 2004 until she got the Energy and Commerce post.

KEY VOTES

2002

Yes Overhaul campaign finance law; ban "soft money" and restrict advocacy advertising
No Back Bush's defense budget increase
No Extend 1996 welfare law
No Adopt Bush's discretionary spending limit
No Pass GOP Medicare prescription drug plan
Yes Create independent Sept. 11 commission
Yes Extend union protections to Homeland Security Department employees
No Revive fast-track procedures for trade agreements
No Authorize war against Iraq
No Advance bankruptcy overhaul opposed by abortion opponents

2001

No Nullify Clinton Labor Department ergonomics rule
No Cut taxes by $1.35 trillion through fiscal 2011
Yes Maintain ban on oil drilling in Arctic National Wildlife Refuge
No Approve Bush proposal to limit managed-care plan liability for coverage decisions
Yes Divert money from crop subsidy payments to land conservation
No Expand law enforcement power to investigate suspected terrorists

CQ VOTE STUDIES

	PARTY UNITY		PRESIDENTIAL SUPPORT	
	Support	Oppose	Support	Oppose
2002	99%	1%	25%	75%
2001	99%	1%	17%	83%
2000	97%	3%	85%	15%
1999	95%	5%	82%	18%

INTEREST GROUPS

	AFL-CIO	ADA	CCUS	ACU
2002	100%	100%	30%	0%
2001	100%	100%	27%	0%
2000	100%	85%	40%	4%
1999	100%	100%	20%	4%

ILLINOIS 9

Chicago — North Side lakefront; Evanston

The 9th starts in upscale Wilmette (shared with the 10th), runs south through the liberal suburbs of Evanston and Skokie and Chicago's multiethnic North Side, and then drops into one of the city's most prosperous lakefront neighborhoods. It also extends west to industrial and blue-collar Des Plaines and Rosemont (both shared with the 6th).

Roughly two-thirds of the district's population is white, with the remainder almost evenly divided among Asians, blacks and Hispanics. More than one in five who live in Skokie, Morton Grove and Lincolnwood are Asian.

Slightly less than half of the district's population lives in Chicago. The neighborhoods of Rogers Park, Edgewater and Uptown once housed Eastern European and Irish immigrants; they are now an eclectic mix of Asian, European and African immigrants. Rogers Park, tucked in the city's northeast corner, takes in the campus of Loyola University. Uptown is mainly working-class, with some low-income areas. Southeast Asians, the area's newest arrivals, have opened shops and restaurants, revitalizing the area's economy.

Lakeview, the district's southernmost point, includes a large gay population. The area near Wrigley Field (which lies in the adjacent 5th District) is a mecca for affluent young professionals and is home to a hot real estate market.

Most of the other Chicagoans in the 9th live in the far northwestern part of the city, near O'Hare Airport (which is located in the neighboring 6th).

The mix of immigrants, affluent urbanites and Northwestern University students makes the 9th solidly Democratic. Although the "lakefront liberals" tend not to vote for machine candidates, they are reliably Democratic. The district's suburbs contain a sizable Jewish population.

MAJOR INDUSTRY
Health care, insurance, light manufacturing

CITIES
Chicago (pt.), 299,868; Evanston, 74,239; Skokie, 63,348; Des Plains (pt.), 39,632; Park Ridge, 37,775; Niles, 30,068; Morton Grove, 22,451

NOTABLE
The North Shore Center for the Performing Arts is in Skokie.

Rep. Mark Steven Kirk (R)

CAPITOL OFFICE
225-4835
rep.kirk@mail.house.gov
www.house.gov/kirk
1531 Longworth 20515-1310; fax 225-0837

COMMITTEES
Appropriations

HOMETOWN
Highland Park

BORN
Sept. 15, 1959, Champaign, Ill.

RELIGION
Congregationalist

FAMILY
Wife, Kimberly Vertolli-Kirk

EDUCATION
Cornell U., B.A. 1981 (history); London School of Economics, M.S. 1982; Georgetown U., J.D. 1992

MILITARY SERVICE
Naval Reserve, 1989-present

CAREER
Congressional committee counsel; congressional aide; lawyer; State Department aide; World Bank officer

POLITICAL HIGHLIGHTS
No previous office

ELECTION RESULTS

2002 GENERAL		
Mark Steven Kirk (R)	128,611	68.8%
Henry H. Perritt Jr. (D)	58,300	31.2%
2002 PRIMARY		
Mark Steven Kirk (R)		unopposed
2000 GENERAL		
Mark Steven Kirk (R)	121,582	51.2%
Lauren Beth Gash (D)	115,924	48.8%

Elected 2000; 2nd term

Kirk arrived on Capitol Hill in 2001 determined to pursue an agenda focused on service to his district, to show his constituents that he was capable of delivering for them after winning a narrow election victory to succeed his one-time boss, 10-term GOP Rep. John Edward Porter.

Kirk's priorities included keeping the North Chicago veterans hospital open, alleviating suburban Chicago transportation problems, addressing mercury pollution in Lake Michigan, and cleaning up a former Nike missile site in Vernon Hills and a shuttered nuclear power plant in Zion.

Then came Sept. 11, 2001. In a Congress suddenly faced with decisions on fighting international terrorism, reshaping the nation's military, and developing a new foreign policy mind-set, Kirk's colleagues quickly noticed that his training and background gave him a certain perspective and expertise on the new issues.

Kirk spent more than a dozen years as an intelligence officer in the Naval Reserve, which included several tours of duty in hot spots around the world — such as Panama, Haiti, Bosnia and the northern no-fly zone in Iraq. He earned a degree from the London School of Economics and once worked for a member of Parliament. He has visited more than 40 countries.

He also served as the legislative counsel for the House International Relations Committee and worked at the World Bank and the State Department. His boss on International Relations, former New York GOP Rep. Benjamin A. Gilman, says that Kirk "has a great leadership potential. Give him as many responsibilities as possible." That is just what GOP leaders did: Kirk took advantage of all the attention not usually afforded a freshman, and his performance won him a seat on the Appropriations Committee in the 108th Congress.

Kirk has been among those lawmakers who pointed to shortcomings in military intelligence that allowed the Sept. 11 attacks to occur. He notes that while the U.S. government has directed massive amounts of money into creating surveillance technology that can track ships anywhere in the world, investments in human intelligence — the kind needed to crack terrorist cells — has lagged.

In 2001, as Congress debated a resolution authorizing force to respond to the Sept. 11 attacks, Kirk urged his colleagues to support President Bush. "People who worry about a Gulf of Tonkin resolution don't have a sense of history. That was two shots that missed. This was an attack on our homeland," he said.

In 2002, Kirk was one of nine House members chosen by Bush to work on the resolution authorizing the use of force against Iraq. Kirk said the congressional group "modified his position considerably" by limiting the scope of the resolution and insisting on support from the United Nations.

On an aviation security bill enacted after Sept. 11, Kirk's contributions included provisions requiring airport baggage screeners to be U.S. citizens and establishing a "Sky 911" program to ensure that emergency calls from airplanes are handled by trained personnel.

Kirk still managed to focus on issues important to his constituents in the 107th Congress. On the Transportation Committee, Kirk and his allies were able to get $55 million to expand the Chicago area's Metra commuter rail system, including the purchase of new stations and double tracks. He also worked to preserve local medical care for Chicago-area veterans and helped arrange the merger of the North Chicago veterans hospital with the hospital at the Great Lakes Naval Station. And he convinced the owner of the Chicago Bulls to build a community basketball facility in North Chicago to give young people an after-school and nighttime activity.

Kirk is moderate across a wide range of domestic issues, and he broke with his party on a number of high-profile votes in the 107th Congress. He was one of only nine Republicans who voted against a bill to outlaw a procedure its opponents call "partial birth" abortion. He also backs the use of stem cells in medical research. He voted to maintain the prohibition on drilling for oil in Alaska's Arctic National Wildlife Refuge, and he supported campaign finance overhaul legislation. But despite those defections, Kirk backed the GOP about 85 percent of the time in the 107th.

Kirk's years as a congressional staff member helped reduce his learning curve as a lawmaker, but he told the Chicago Daily Herald he still needs to adjust to being a congressman. "When you're a staffer, you can show up wearing a sweater, you can have your hair mussed up. As long as the work is done, that's fine. When you're a member of Congress, you have to look the part."

Kirk grew up in the northern Chicago suburbs and says that a brush with death at age 16 — he nearly drowned in Lake Michigan — shaped his future. "To be given a second chance means it has to mean something," he told the Chicago Tribune. "For me, that means making a difference through public service."

He built an impressive educational and professional résumé, and in 1989, while working for Porter, he joined the Naval Reserve after a project piqued his interest in the military.

When Porter announced in October 1999 that he would not seek re-election, Kirk jumped into the race, along with 10 other Republican candidates, including several millionaires. Kirk was not the front-runner, but he impressed voters with his grasp of policy and his ties to Porter, who endorsed him. He beat his closest competitor, printing company heiress Shawn Margaret Donnelley, by 16 percentage points.

In the general election, Kirk faced a formidable opponent in state Rep. Lauren Beth Gash, but he was able to prevail by 2 percentage points.

To buttress his chances for re-election in 2002, Kirk undertook an aggressive fundraising effort in his first term. The new district map drawn by the state legislature gave him a slightly more Republican constituency. Kirk, buoyed by endorsements from the Sierra Club, Planned Parenthood and the Illinois Education Association, won handily with 69 percent.

KEY VOTES

2002

Yes Overhaul campaign finance law; ban "soft money" and restrict advocacy advertising
Yes Back Bush's defense budget increase
Yes Extend 1996 welfare law
Yes Adopt Bush's discretionary spending limit
Yes Pass GOP Medicare prescription drug plan
No Create independent Sept. 11 commission
No Extend union protections to Homeland Security Department employees
Yes Revive fast-track procedures for trade agreements
Yes Authorize war against Iraq
Yes Advance bankruptcy overhaul opposed by abortion opponents

2001

Yes Nullify Clinton Labor Department ergonomics rule
Yes Cut taxes by $1.35 trillion through fiscal 2011
Yes Maintain ban on oil drilling in Arctic National Wildlife Refuge
Yes Approve Bush proposal to limit managed-care plan liability for coverage decisions
Yes Divert money from crop subsidy payments to land conservation
Yes Expand law enforcement power to investigate suspected terrorists

CQ VOTE STUDIES

	PARTY UNITY		PRESIDENTIAL SUPPORT	
	Support	Oppose	Support	Oppose
2002	85%	15%	85%	15%
2001	85%	15%	74%	26%

INTEREST GROUPS

	AFL-CIO	ADA	CCUS	ACU
2002	11%	20%	95%	76%
2001	25%	25%	83%	48%

ILLINOIS 10

North and northwest Chicago suburbs – Waukegan

The mostly upscale 10th hugs Lake Michigan, taking in southeast Lake County and northeast Cook County. Along the lakefront, Chicagoland's old-money elite live in exclusive towns like Wilmette (shared with the 9th), Kenilworth and Winnetka, where homes routinely sell for $500,000 or more.

To the north, the district's industrial sector, in Waukegan and North Chicago, found new life in 1994 when nearby Great Lakes Naval Training Center became the nation's only naval recruit training facility. Most of the district's minorities live in Waukegan, which is about 45 percent Hispanic and 20 percent black. Minorities also make up a majority in North Chicago, located just south of Waukegan. There also is a large Jewish constituency in the district.

Suburban and working-class residents combine to make the 10th a moderate "swing" district — fiscally conservative but socially liberal, especially on abortion rights and gun control. With the 10th's proximity to Lake Michigan, environmental protection is a major issue.

Within the 10th, Cook County is slightly more populous than Lake County. In 2001 redistricting, the 10th shed part of Wilmette to the south and some communities on the Wisconsin border (which had been the district's northern boundary). The western border was extended to pick up part of Palatine and Inverness. The revised 10th is slightly more Republican than its 1990s configuration, though residents within the new lines narrowly backed Bill Clinton in 1996 and Al Gore in 2000.

MAJOR INDUSTRY
Pharmaceutical research, insurance, military

MILITARY BASES
Naval Training Center Great Lakes, 4,945 military, 4,226 civilian (2000)

CITIES
Waukegan (pt.), 79,726; Arlington Heights (pt.), 69,414; Buffalo Grove, 42,909; North Chicago, 35,918; Wheeling, 34,496; Northbrook, 33,435

NOTABLE
Berto Center, the Chicago Bulls basketball training facility, is in Deerfield; The Chicago Botanic Garden is in Glencoe.

Rep. Jerry Weller (R)

CAPITOL OFFICE
225-3635
www.house.gov/weller
1210 Longworth 20515-1311; fax 225-3521

COMMITTEES
International Relations
Ways & Means

HOMETOWN
Morris

BORN
July 7, 1957, Streator, Ill.

RELIGION
Christian

FAMILY
Single

EDUCATION
Joliet Junior College, attended 1977; U. of Illinois, B.S. 1979 (agriculture)

CAREER
Congressional aide; state and federal official; hog farmer; sales representative

POLITICAL HIGHLIGHTS
Republican nominee for Ill. House, 1986; Ill. House, 1989-95

ELECTION RESULTS

2002 GENERAL		
Jerry Weller (R)	124,192	64.3%
Keith S. Van Duyne (D)	68,893	35.7%
2002 PRIMARY		
Jerry Weller (R)		unopposed
2000 GENERAL		
Jerry Weller (R)	132,384	56.4%
James P. Stevenson (D)	102,485	43.6%

PREVIOUS WINNING PERCENTAGES
1998 (59%); 1996 (52%); 1994 (61%)

Elected 1994; 5th term

Whether campaigning for the Republican leadership or for a reduction in married couples' taxes, Weller is nothing if not persistent.

He pours great effort into both the policy and political sides of his job, and he rarely wavers once he has staked out a position. While this makes him a reliable ally for the GOP and particularly for Speaker J. Dennis Hastert, a fellow Illinoisan, Weller's penchant for repeating his speeches dozens of times tries the patience of even his allies.

When the Ways and Means Committee in 2001 took up Weller's bill to repeal portions of the tax code that cause some two-earner married couples to owe more than they would had they stayed single, Weller produced his usual props — poster-size photos of a young couple from Joliet, Ill., who faced the so-called marriage penalty. But before Weller could recite his well-rehearsed speech about the plight of Shad and Michelle Hallihan, Chairman Bill Thomas jokingly declared that Weller's time had expired, adding, "I believe I know them."

Weller apparently took the ribbing to heart. The next year, time and again he told the story of a different Joliet couple, José and Magdalene Castillo. Weller said he just wanted to put a fresh face on the tax debate. But his desire to move up in the party is never far below the surface, and his attempt to tailor his appeal to Hispanic voters — as the GOP is seeking to do nationally — could not hurt.

As finance chairman of the National Republican Congressional Committee, Weller helped the party raise a record $163 million for its successful 2002 campaign. But he was thwarted in his efforts to move up. Soon after the midterm election, House Republicans instead voted 119-90 to put New York's Thomas M. Reynolds in charge of the House GOP campaign organization for 2004.

As partial consolation, Weller was given a seat on the International Relations Committee in addition to Ways and Means, a post that normally precludes any other committee assignments. Weller also was named a deputy whip and retained his seat on the Republican Policy Committee.

Weller came to Congress as part of the conservative-dominated Republican takeover Class of 1994 and soon won some plum assignments. With Hastert's backing, in his freshman term he served on the Steering Committee, which makes GOP committee assignments. Two years later, Weller won his coveted Ways and Means seat and was elected president of his sophomore class. But his first bid to move into the ranks of the GOP leadership also failed; he finished last in a field of four when he ran for secretary of the Republican Conference in the 105th Congress.

At that point, Weller turned his energies on his main policy goal, minimizing the marriage penalty. His proposal became a mainstay of the tax bills that the House GOP used to goad the cautious Senate and skeptical Clinton White House in the late 1990s. Once President Bush took office, the measure finally appeared destined for enactment, but its inclusion in his $1.35 trillion package was not a certainty. Questions had been raised about whether one-earner families who already received a "marriage bonus" at tax time should also benefit from a cut designed to help those two-earner couples that most often suffered a tax penalty. Weller joined with Republican Sen. Kay Bailey Hutchison of Texas to press negotiators to retain the cuts for both groups, and in large measure they prevailed.

Because the 2001 tax cuts are set to expire after 2010, Weller's crusade is not over; he and other Republicans are pushing legislation in the 108th to extend the provisions indefinitely.

In addition, Weller is a leading advocate on Ways and Means for allowing businesses to more quickly claim deductions for technology purchases. He also is urging creation of a 20 percent tax credit for homeowners who install up to $10,000 in windows, insulation, air conditioners or heaters that will lead to energy savings.

Trade is the one policy area where Weller has been known to waver. In the 105th, he was one of only two Ways and Means Republicans who opposed giving President Clinton authority to negotiate trade agreements without fear of congressional amendment. He reversed course in the 107th, however, and backed enactment of the law reviving those fast-track procedures for Bush.

Even though redistricting after the 2000 census gave the 11th District many more Republicans for this decade, Weller still represents plenty of blue-collar workers. As a result, he tends to be more moderate than many Republicans on issues important to organized labor. He has voted to increase the minimum wage, and in 2002 he led an unsuccessful effort to break a post-election impasse over extending unemployment benefits.

Weller spends a great deal of time tending the interests of his constituents outside Chicago. His main parochial accomplishment has been persuading the Army to turn over the Joliet Arsenal for local use, including a prairie preserve and a veterans cemetery. Weller has had less success in winning federal help to establish a third Chicago airport in Peotone, in large part because many of his congressional colleagues, including Hastert, prefer to enlarge Chicago O'Hare instead. Hastert's lobbying on the issue has been so strong that Weller ended up voting for a measure to pave the way for a $6.6 billion runway expansion and reconfiguration at O'Hare, saying he wanted to see both it and Peotone improved.

Weller worked as a congressional aide and a Department of Agriculture staffer before making his first bid for the General Assembly in 1986. Declared the winner by four votes, he took office in January, but then the state House's Democratic majority ordered a recount. When the new tally showed Weller losing by four votes, the young legislator was sent home.

He won the seat two years later, however, and he stayed there until his election to the House. When Democrat George E. Sangmeister retired after four terms, Weller picked up the seat for the GOP with a surprisingly easy 3-to-2 victory over state Rep. Frank Giglio. He held off his stiffest challenge two years later, from former state Rep. Clem Balanoff. With his district redrawn, Weller won his biggest majority yet in 2002.

KEY VOTES

2002

No Overhaul campaign finance law; ban "soft money" and restrict advocacy advertising
Yes Back Bush's defense budget increase
Yes Extend 1996 welfare law
Yes Adopt Bush's discretionary spending limit
Yes Pass GOP Medicare prescription drug plan
No Create independent Sept. 11 commission
No Extend union protections to Homeland Security Department employees
Yes Revive fast-track procedures for trade agreements
Yes Authorize war against Iraq
Yes Advance bankruptcy overhaul opposed by abortion opponents

2001

Yes Nullify Clinton Labor Department ergonomics rule
Yes Cut taxes by $1.35 trillion through fiscal 2011
No Maintain ban on oil drilling in Arctic National Wildlife Refuge
Yes Approve Bush proposal to limit managed-care plan liability for coverage decisions
No Divert money from crop subsidy payments to land conservation
Yes Expand law enforcement power to investigate suspected terrorists

CQ VOTE STUDIES

	PARTY UNITY		PRESIDENTIAL SUPPORT	
	Support	Oppose	Support	Oppose
2002	96%	4%	88%	12%
2001	96%	4%	93%	7%
2000	86%	14%	41%	59%
1999	88%	12%	24%	76%
1998	88%	12%	26%	74%

INTEREST GROUPS

	AFL-CIO	ADA	CCUS	ACU
2002	11%	5%	95%	92%
2001	17%	0%	100%	92%
2000	22%	15%	68%	66%
1999	22%	15%	88%	80%
1998	40%	15%	88%	92%

ILLINOIS 11

South Chicago exurbs – Joliet; part of Bloomington-Normal

Beginning south of Chicago in suburban Will County, the 11th heads west through the old industrial city of Joliet and into farming country, with a sliver making a left turn in LaSalle County to run south parallel to Interstate 39 as it heads to Bloomington-Normal.

Will County (shared mostly with the 13th District) is the district's most populous jurisdiction and has seen an influx of young suburban families. Will had a 41 percent growth rate in the 1990s and voted narrowly for GOP presidential nominee George W. Bush in 2000. The county is at the nexus of a plan to build a third Chicago metro-area airport in Peotone. Residents in the 11th's northern reaches say a new airport would boost the suburbs, though rural residents worry it may disrupt their way of life.

South of Will, the 11th includes Kankakee County before assuming a more rural posture west of those two counties as it takes in a small portion of Livingston County, all of Grundy and LaSalle counties and most of Bureau County before its jaunt south to Bloomington.

In the 1990s, the 11th was the most eclectic district in Illinois, running from southeastern Chicago through some racially diverse Cook County suburbs and ending in LaSalle's farming communities. But 2001 redistricting made the district less urban and suburban by moving the Cook County portions to the 2nd and adding the southern leg to McLean County's Bloomington-Normal region, which is home to Illinois State University and is shared with the 15th District.

The 11th remains politically competitive on the numbers, but the removal of Democratic-leaning southern Cook County lessened the district's Democratic influence. The old 11th voted for Al Gore in 2000 by 8 percentage points; the new district backed Bush by 2 points.

MAJOR INDUSTRY

Farm equipment manufacturing, agriculture

CITIES

Joliet (pt.), 105,052; Normal (pt.), 30,662; Bloomington (pt.), 30,298; Kankakee, 27,491; Ottawa, 18,307

NOTABLE

The Midewin National Tallgrass Prairie is in Will County.

Rep. Jerry F. Costello (D)

CAPITOL OFFICE
225-5661
www.house.gov/costello
2454 Rayburn 20515-1312; fax 225-0285

COMMITTEES
Science
Transportation & Infrastructure

HOMETOWN
Belleville

BORN
Sept. 25, 1949, East St. Louis, Ill.

RELIGION
Roman Catholic

FAMILY
Wife, Georgia Cockrum Costello; three children

EDUCATION
Belleville Area College, A.A. 1971; Maryville College of the Sacred Heart, B.A. 1973

CAREER
Law enforcement official

POLITICAL HIGHLIGHTS
St. Clair County Board chairman, 1980-88

ELECTION RESULTS

2002 GENERAL		
Jerry F. Costello (D)	131,580	69.3%
David Sadler (R)	58,440	30.8%
2002 PRIMARY		
Jerry F. Costello (D)		unopposed
2000 GENERAL		
Jerry F. Costello (D)		unopposed

PREVIOUS WINNING PERCENTAGES
1998 (60%); 1996 (72%); 1994 (66%); 1992 (71%); 1990 (66%); 1988 (53%); 1988 Special Election (51%)

Elected August 1988; 8th full term

An elected official who has represented the struggling industrial communities of southwest Illinois for 20 years, first as a county chief executive and then as a member of Congress, Costello long ago decided that the dwindling steel mill, stockyard and coal mining jobs that were the traditional backbone of the district's economy were not likely to return. Instead, he believes that improving the region's transportation infrastructure will retain and attract new jobs. From his posts on the Transportation and Science committees, Costello has set about doing that, with some success.

He has brought millions of federal dollars to his district and the region for industrial parks, visitors centers and transportation projects. He helped steer nearly $600 million in federal funding for the MetroLink light rail, which connects the "Metro East" area of Illinois with St. Louis, and has sought to upgrade and replace bridges across the Mississippi River. He also is trying to develop MidAmerica St. Louis Airport just north of Scott Air Force Base as a "feeder" destination for Lambert-St. Louis International Airport, despite difficulties attracting regularly scheduled commercial passenger service. Costello hopes linking MidAmerica with Lambert via the light rail system will make the smaller airfield more viable.

He continues to look out for the interests of Scott Air Force Base, a candidate in past rounds of military base closings. The base is home to air mobility and transportation commands that could figure in future consolidations. In the aftermath of the Sept. 11, 2001, terrorist attacks, Costello argued that keeping Air Force assets deployed across centrally located installations such as Scott is preferable to concentrating them in fewer locations.

Such advocacy has kept Costello strong politically, even when tainted by an ethics problem. He was named an "unindicted co-conspirator" in the 1997 trial of his childhood friend and former business partner Amiel Cueto, who was convicted of trying to block the federal investigation of a convicted racketeer. Republicans have never tired of reminding voters of the connection, but to no avail. The GOP did not even field a candidate against him in 2000, and in 2002, running in a newly drawn district, he got 69 percent of the vote.

Costello denied wrongdoing in the Cueto matter. At the trial, government witnesses testified that Costello was a silent partner in two casino deals and that he helped pass a bill in Congress to aid an Indian tribe that owned the land where one of the casinos was to be built. Costello was not implicated in any crime and said that being named an unindicted co-conspirator was merely a prosecutorial tool to ensure that certain testimony was admissible.

He got more unfavorable publicity early in 2002, when media reports revealed that Illinois Secretary of State Jesse White hired Costello's 26-year-old son for a $50,000-a-year job over a more experienced candidate after Costello had called on behalf of his son. Costello described the incident as a routine job reference call, adding that he had not directly spoken to White about his son's candidacy. He attributed the flap, in part, to a long-running feud with his hometown newspaper, the Belleville News-Democrat, which obtained state documents on the hiring.

Costello, who rarely speaks on the House floor, is not a completely dependable vote for party leaders. He supports the party line about three-fourths of the time. He is a staunch labor ally, opposing overseas trade agreements that he says will cost U.S. jobs. He opposes Clean Air Act regulations, saying that they have devastated the southern Illinois coal industry.

On social policy issues, Costello reflects his constituency's cultural conservatism. He was one of 10 House members who lobbied to add language expressing tolerance of anti-abortion views to the 1996 Democratic Party platform. He supports gun owners' rights — in 1998, he backed legislation to exempt retired police officers from state laws restricting concealed weapons.

Costello was a member of the Budget Committee until the 106th Congress. From that post in the 104th, he objected to GOP plans that would have reduced the growth of domestic programs of interest to his core constituents, such as Medicare and the Legal Services Corporation.

The lawmaker keeps working to direct as much of the federal pie to the 12th District as he can. In addition to his work on infrastructure needs, Costello won approval of legislation to set aside federal land for a visitors center devoted to the journey of explorers Meriwether Lewis and William Clark, near the site where the expedition departed on its westward journey in 1804. The center opened late in 2002.

Costello grew up in East St. Louis in a politically active family. In 1960, when he was 11, the young Irish Catholic Costello was intrigued by the campaign appearance in his hometown of another Irish Catholic — John F. Kennedy, who was running for president.

While attending a local community college, Costello began a career in law enforcement during which he rose from court bailiff to become administrator of the region's court system. In 1980, he was elected chairman of the St. Clair County Board. He became well-known in his heavily Democratic region, serving at one point as chairman of the metropolitan St. Louis Council of Governments.

His high profile made him heir apparent to Democrat Melvin Price, an elderly House veteran who did not seek re-election in 1988. But in the primary, Madison County Auditor Pete Fields portrayed Costello as an old-style, hardball "boss" in the St. Clair County Democratic machine. Costello survived because of a huge financial advantage, but had only a 46 percent plurality.

When Price died in April, Costello squared off against Republican college official Robert H. Gaffner in a special election. Gaffner suggested voters call Costello and quiz him about his ethics. Costello barely won the special election, then went on to win in November with 53 percent of the vote. He was not seriously challenged again until 1998, when Republican Bill Price, an orthopedic surgeon and the son of Melvin Price, announced his candidacy. Costello again overcame questions about his connections with Cueto and charged that Price represented a threat to Social Security and Medicare. Costello took 60 percent of the vote.

KEY VOTES

2002

- Yes Overhaul campaign finance law; ban "soft money" and restrict advocacy advertising
- Yes Back Bush's defense budget increase
- No Extend 1996 welfare law
- No Adopt Bush's discretionary spending limit
- No Pass GOP Medicare prescription drug plan
- Yes Create independent Sept. 11 commission
- Yes Extend union protections to Homeland Security Department employees
- No Revive fast-track procedures for trade agreements
- No Authorize war against Iraq
- No Advance bankruptcy overhaul opposed by abortion opponents

2001

- No Nullify Clinton Labor Department ergonomics rule
- No Cut taxes by $1.35 trillion through fiscal 2011
- Yes Maintain ban on oil drilling in Arctic National Wildlife Refuge
- No Approve Bush proposal to limit managed-care plan liability for coverage decisions
- No Divert money from crop subsidy payments to land conservation
- Yes Expand law enforcement power to investigate suspected terrorists

CQ VOTE STUDIES

	PARTY UNITY		PRESIDENTIAL SUPPORT	
	Support	Oppose	Support	Oppose
2002	80%	20%	40%	60%
2001	72%	28%	37%	63%
2000	76%	24%	52%	48%
1999	73%	27%	63%	37%
1998	76%	24%	68%	32%

INTEREST GROUPS

	AFL-CIO	ADA	CCUS	ACU
2002	100%	70%	50%	36%
2001	100%	80%	48%	44%
2000	90%	55%	47%	33%
1999	100%	65%	24%	24%
1998	100%	90%	28%	25%

ILLINOIS 12

Southwest – Belleville, East St. Louis, Carbondale

The 12th begins in the St. Louis suburbs along the Mississippi River and extends south along the river to the end of the state, where the Mississippi and Ohio rivers converge near Cairo.

Illinois' worst urban blight isn't in Chicago — it is 300 miles southwest in East St. Louis, where severe white flight and industrial decay nearly bankrupted the city. In the late 1980s, the city cut off most municipal services, including trash collection. Federal and state intervention, coupled with new revenue from casino gambling, restored most city services by the mid-1990s, but residents still face high unemployment and poverty.

Other cities in the 12th also stand on precarious ground. Alton had to bolster its industrial base with riverboat gambling. Residents of Belleville, where nearby Scott Air Force Base is the largest employer, worry about defense cutbacks. Coal mining has almost disappeared from the hilly, southern end of the district with the mechanization of the industry and enactment of the 1990 Clean Air Act. Higher education remains one of the few steadfast employers: Jackson County's economy is bolstered by Southern Illinois University in Carbondale, which has 22,000 students.

The district's economic anxiety and relatively large minority population (blacks make up 16 percent of the population) make it solid Democratic turf. Democrat Rod R. Blagojevich carried nine of the 11 counties wholly or partly within the 12th in his 2002 race for governor. St. Clair County, which includes East St. Louis, is the only Illinois county other than Chicago-based Cook to vote Democratic in the past seven presidential elections. Some corn and hog farmers in western counties lean Republican, but they are too few to sway the district.

MAJOR INDUSTRY
Manufacturing, higher education, riverboat gambling, agriculture

MILITARY BASES
Scott Air Force Base, 7,634 military, 2,199 civilian (1999)

CITIES
Belleville, 41,410; East St. Louis, 31,542; Granite City, 31,301; Alton, 30,496; O'Fallon, 21,910; Carbondale, 20,681

NOTABLE
Cahokia Mounds, a prehistoric civilization, was designated by the United Nations as a World Heritage Site in 1982.

Rep. Judy Biggert (R)

CAPITOL OFFICE
225-3515
www.house.gov/biggert
1213 Longworth 20515-1313; fax 225-9420

COMMITTEES
Education & Workforce
Financial Services
Science
(Energy - chairwoman)
Standards of Official Conduct

HOMETOWN
Hinsdale

BORN
Aug. 15, 1937, Chicago, Ill.

RELIGION
Episcopalian

FAMILY
Husband, Rody Biggert; four children

EDUCATION
Stanford U., A.B. 1959 (international relations); Northwestern U., J.D. 1963

CAREER
Lawyer

POLITICAL HIGHLIGHTS
Hinsdale Board of Education, 1982-85 (president, 1983-85); Village of Hinsdale Plan Commission, 1989-93; Ill. House, 1993-99

ELECTION RESULTS

2002 GENERAL		
Judy Biggert (R)	139,546	70.3%
Thomas Mason (D)	59,069	29.7%
2002 PRIMARY		
Judy Biggert (R)		unopposed
2000 GENERAL		
Judy Biggert (R)	193,250	66.2%
Thomas Mason (D)	98,768	33.8%

PREVIOUS WINNING PERCENTAGES
1998 (61%)

Elected 1998; 3rd term

Biggert came to the House with more than two decades of civic and political activities under her belt and a thorough understanding of the difficulties women can face in the professional and political world.

She describes herself as a moderate, and she supports abortion rights and broadening educational opportunities. But Biggert also opposes additional stringent gun control laws. She views her abortion and gun votes as consistent — because both signal her view that the government should intrude less often into people's lives.

An accomplished skeet shooter who owns several guns, Biggert still engages in trap shooting at a rustic club in Michigan when she can find the time. Molded by this personal experience, her views on gun control are decidedly more conservative than many of her colleagues expect. Biggert believes existing laws against illegal uses of guns should be vigorously enforced, but says there is no need for sweeping new legislation.

She affiliates with other GOP moderates in the Tuesday Group and the Republican Main Street Partnership. But she was not among the majority of partnership members who voted to enact the 2002 campaign finance law.

Biggert is from a generation when the career choices pursued by women were limited. She recalls that her sister originally said she wanted to be a nurse and only considered medical school when their father, a business executive, told her that girls also could be doctors. Biggert said when she applied to a master's in business degree program, she received a letter from the school informing her that women were not accepted, but that she was welcome to take a few night classes.

She enrolled in law school instead and practiced law for more than 20 years, working out of her home as she raised four children. She also involved herself in countless community organizations and boards, dealing with such concerns as education, health care and crime.

Biggert has been dogged in her work on a number of child-related issues, including schooling for homeless children, helping children who have eating disorders and financing school construction.

She was able to get her measure providing schooling for homeless children included in the sweeping education law enacted in 2002. Her portion of the statute authorized $70 million to help ensure that homeless children can be schooled — either in the closest facility or by staying in the school they attended before becoming homeless — without facing delays and red tape in winning admission. Biggert also wrote a second provision, providing more money for training teachers of math and science.

In the 107th Congress, Biggert co-chaired the Congressional Caucus on Women's Issues. When the plight of women and children in Afghanistan received widespread notice, the caucus made them its top priority. Biggert helped to win U.S. education and health care aid to help Afghan women and children cope with the woeful conditions in their war-torn country.

In 1999 Fortune magazine identified Biggert as one of the congressional newcomers most likely to become a star. But she has been unsuccessful trying to prove the prophecy. She first ran for GOP Conference secretary at the start of the 107th, reminding her colleagues that she had advanced to the leadership of the Illinois House in just her second term there and that she had been a prolific fundraiser for the National Republican Congressional Committee in 2000. She lost to Barbara Cubin of Wyoming, 123-76. At the start of the 108th, Biggert made a second and short-lived bid for the secretary's job, dropping out when she concluded Californian John T. Doolittle had the election wrapped up.

She had also run for president of her GOP freshman class in 1999. She attributed that loss, in part, to being the only woman in her class.

Describing herself as a negotiator and consensus builder, in the 107th she and conservative colleague Mark Souder of Indiana were co-chairmen of weekly "unity dinners" designed to bring together disparate factions of House Republicans whenever an issue loomed that threatened intraparty discord. Even if consensus cannot be reached, lawmakers say they leave the dinners feeling better about the opportunity to air their views.

She is also a team player. In the 107th, Speaker J. Dennis Hastert asked her to serve on the ethics committee in addition to her three other committees — Financial Services, Education and the Workforce, and Science.

One arena where her ambition to move up has not been thwarted is on the Science panel, where in the 108th she chairs the Energy Subcommittee, whose jurisdiction includes the Argonne and Fermi national laboratories. Argonne plays a key role in fuel cell research.

After clerking for a federal judge, Biggert opened her own home-based law practice, specializing in real estate and estate planning. Having had three children in three years — a fourth came several years later — she concluded such a practice was the only way she could remain active professionally. Biggert also threw herself into the PTA, Sunday school, the Junior League and the Visiting Nurse Association.

Her community activities eventually led her to serve on the Hinsdale planning commission and the board of education, including a stint as president of the latter group from 1983 to 1985. Elected to the Illinois House in 1992, she focused on women's and children's issues and was elected assistant Republican leader after just one term in Springfield.

Biggert was the handpicked successor of Republican Harris W. Fawell, who retired in 1998 after holding his House seat for 14 years. Biggert's daughter, Adrienne, worked for Fawell as a legislative assistant at the end of his tenure. Biggert defeated five men vying for the GOP nomination and went on to win the seat with 61 percent of the vote.

Memories of her early success in the Illinois House led Biggert to pledge to observe a six-year term limit when she first ran for Congress. But soon after arriving in Washington, she retracted the pledge, saying it was a mistake and she had not been aware of the powerful seniority system in Congress. Biggert's solidly Republican district — its tilt was maintained by redistricting in 2000 — gave her 70 percent in 2002.

KEY VOTES

2002

No Overhaul campaign finance law; ban "soft money" and restrict advocacy advertising
Yes Back Bush's defense budget increase
Yes Extend 1996 welfare law
Yes Adopt Bush's discretionary spending limit
Yes Pass GOP Medicare prescription drug plan
No Create independent Sept. 11 commission
No Extend union protections to Homeland Security Department employees
Yes Revive fast-track procedures for trade agreements
Yes Authorize war against Iraq
Yes Advance bankruptcy overhaul opposed by abortion opponents

2001

Yes Nullify Clinton Labor Department ergonomics rule
Yes Cut taxes by $1.35 trillion through fiscal 2011
No Maintain ban on oil drilling in Arctic National Wildlife Refuge
Yes Approve Bush proposal to limit managed-care plan liability for coverage decisions
Yes Divert money from crop subsidy payments to land conservation
Yes Expand law enforcement power to investigate suspected terrorists

CQ VOTE STUDIES

	PARTY UNITY		PRESIDENTIAL SUPPORT	
	Support	Oppose	Support	Oppose
2002	89%	11%	82%	18%
2001	90%	10%	84%	16%
2000	82%	18%	43%	57%
1999	78%	22%	37%	63%

INTEREST GROUPS

	AFL-CIO	ADA	CCUS	ACU
2002	11%	15%	100%	84%
2001	17%	20%	100%	56%
2000	0%	20%	100%	68%
1999	11%	30%	96%	60%

ILLINOIS 13

Southwest Chicago suburbs – Naperville

More than half of the suburban Chicago-based 13th's population lives in the southern part of booming DuPage County. The district's most populous city is Naperville, which has tripled its population since 1980. Sprawling subdivisions and a newly refurbished downtown characterize this fairly young suburb.

Argonne National Laboratory, in southeast DuPage, and Fermi National Accelerator Laboratory, just over the border in the 14th District, have made the area a scientific research hub and provide a prime source of jobs for district residents.

Naperville and Oak Brook have become leading business centers outside Chicago and are home to a growing number of corporate headquarters. Oak Brook, home to headquarters for McDonald's, is about 10 miles south of O'Hare Airport and sits near the nexus of Interstates 88, 294 and 290, which has abetted its development. These cities increasingly draw in commuters, creating serious traffic problems in suburban communities.

Nearly one-third of the population lives in northern Will County communities such as Bolingbrook and Romeoville. The rest live in the southwestern corner of Cook. Redistricting in 2001 required the 13th, Illinois' fastest-growing district in the 1990s, to shed more than 100,000 people (mostly to the 1st and 11th districts).

Voters in the 13th tend to be white-collar executive types, loyal to free enterprise. It is a reliably Republican district that comfortably backed George W. Bush in the 2000 presidential election. Many residents, however, hold moderate views on family and women's issues (such as equal pay and child care) and environmental protection.

MAJOR INDUSTRY

Scientific research, health care, insurance

CITIES

Naperville, 128,358; Bolingbrook, 56,321; Downers Grove (pt.), 45,139; Aurora (pt.), 40,846; Woodridge, 30,934; Orland Park (pt.), 23,729

NOTABLE

Hamburger University, McDonald's management training center, is located in Oak Brook.

Rep. J. Dennis Hastert (R)

CAPITOL OFFICE
225-2976
dhastert@mail.house.gov
www.house.gov/hastert
235 Cannon 20515-1314; fax 225-0697

COMMITTEES
Speaker of the House – no committee assignments

HOMETOWN
Plano

BORN
Jan. 2, 1942, Aurora, Ill.

RELIGION
Methodist

FAMILY
Wife, Jean Hastert; two children

EDUCATION
Wheaton College, A.B. 1964 (economics); Northern Illinois U., M.A. 1967 (education)

CAREER
Teacher; restaurateur

POLITICAL HIGHLIGHTS
Ill. House, 1981-86

ELECTION RESULTS

2002 GENERAL		
J. Dennis Hastert (R)	135,198	74.1%
Laurence J. Quick (D)	47,165	25.9%
2002 PRIMARY		
J. Dennis Hastert (R)		unopposed
2000 GENERAL		
J. Dennis Hastert (R)	188,597	74.0%
Vern Deljonson (D)	66,309	26.0%

PREVIOUS WINNING PERCENTAGES
1998 (70%); 1996 (64%); 1994 (76%); 1992 (67%); 1990 (67%); 1988 (74%); 1986 (52%)

Elected 1986; 9th term

With little fanfare, Hastert has become a powerful and effective Speaker of the House, putting to rest early assumptions he would be an interim figurehead until a more dynamic, telegenic Republican could be groomed for the job. Hastert is now the primary legislative driver for the Bush administration in Congress, while maintaining a regular-guy image among his loyal rank and file.

As a testament to his staying power, House Republicans in 2003 repealed the eight-year term limit on the Speaker, which would have required Hastert to leave the job in 2006. It was a strong signal of their preference for Hastert's low-profile style, a marked contrast to his polarizing, better-known predecessor, Newt Gingrich of Georgia, who was forced to resign after a series of political missteps. He appears content to leave the flash and fancy rhetoric to others and present himself as an ordinary man shaping legislation out of public view.

By the start of the 108th Congress, Hastert had been Speaker longer than Gingrich was, and in four years at the helm, he had consolidated his hold on power by staying a step ahead of the competing factions in the GOP and efficiently guiding the legislative machinery without calling attention to himself. He is no longer thought of as the weaker of the two top House leaders. Tom DeLay, the influential majority leader from Texas, overshadowed him in the early part of his speakership, but Hastert now leaves no doubt that he is in charge.

He is deeply conservative on issues but prefers to let committee chairmen and other leaders work with minimal intrusion. He presses them to settle their intraparty differences with as little pre-emption from him as possible. Unlike earlier Speakers, Hastert did not come to the job with a policy agenda of his own, with the exception of health care, in which he has long had an interest.

Hastert, who cultivates the trust of fellow Republicans, rarely seeks out the media spotlight or Washington's social swirl. When he does decide to assert himself, he typically does so with effect. His non-threatening style, his allies say, comes with a self-assurance and resolve that House Republicans do not underestimate.

Hastert has a unique, power-sharing relationship with DeLay as a result of the symbiotic path the two followed into leadership. When Republicans became the majority party in 1995, Gingrich became Speaker and DeLay was elected whip, though Gingrich preferred his ally, Robert S. Walker of Pennsylvania, for the post. Hastert ran DeLay's successful upset campaign for whip, and DeLay made Hastert his chief deputy, an appointive post.

Then in 1998, Gingrich was ousted after a series of gaffes and the GOP's drubbing in the midterm election. At the time, the Republicans had many promising young leaders but no ready replacement for the top job. Appropriations Chairman Robert L. Livingston of Louisiana was initially chosen, but he withdrew after revealing he had had extramarital affairs. Other potential candidates, notably DeLay and Dick Armey, the majority leader at the time, were seasoned but damaged by their roles in an earlier, failed attempt to remove Gingrich. So Hastert emerged as the consensus choice. DeLay helped his deputy round up the votes to win, guaranteeing himself a strong position in the Hastert era.

Hastert was elected as the 51st Speaker after just a dozen years in the House, the fastest rise since 1891. He is also the first person since 1919 to become Speaker without holding a prior elected leadership job.

His first two years in the post, 1999 and 2000, were unspectacular legislatively. He got caught in an election-eve budget battle that Republicans feared would hurt them politically. But the party held its majority and captured the White House. In the first two years of the Bush administration, Hastert aggressively pressed the president's agenda, helping him win victories on tax cuts, education, homeland security, trade liberalization and the war on terrorism. Hastert's stature increased when Republicans defied historic trends and gained seats in the midterm 2002 election.

In the 107th, solid margins of support for President Bush's conservative agenda in the House could often pressure Republican Senate moderates to go along. That gave the president an edge in the narrowly divided Senate. And it enabled the Speaker to be bolder than he had been in the past. He sometimes railed against Republican senators and the administration when they chose pragmatic compromise with Democrats instead of standing behind more conservative GOP principles.

Hastert is masterful at inoculating his party against Democratic attacks by pushing legislation addressing the opposition's touchstone issues. In 2001, House Republicans passed a Medicare prescription drug benefit bill that had no chance of winning Senate passage but that took the punch out of the Democrats' top campaign issue.

While Gingrich became the divisive face of the GOP, the paunchy former wrestling coach in department store suits is barely recognized by tourists as he lumbers through the Capitol. During four years as DeLay's deputy, Hastert developed a knack for pushing the party line without making colleagues feel pressured. He is considered a good listener who can handle lawmakers with difficult egos and persuade the reluctant to vote the party line. To many of his colleagues, he is "Denny," an amiable former high school teacher who seemed more at home with the regular-order style of his mentor, former Minority Leader Robert H. Michel of Illinois, than with the self-styled GOP revolutionaries that Gingrich led to power in 1995.

Hastert travels the country diligently to campaign for colleagues and collect cash — and he brought in more money for his party in the run-up to the 2002 election than any previous Speaker of either party.

Hastert was a high school social studies teacher and wrestling coach for 16 years before being appointed in 1981 to the state legislature to fill a vacancy. When GOP Rep. John E. Grotberg retired because of illness in 1986, Hastert was elected as his successor with just 52 percent of the vote. He has drawn at least two-thirds of the vote in all but one election since.

KEY VOTES

2002

No Overhaul campaign finance law; ban "soft money" and restrict advocacy advertising
Yes Back Bush's defense budget increase
Yes Extend 1996 welfare law
Yes Adopt Bush's discretionary spending limit
Yes Pass GOP Medicare prescription drug plan
No Create independent Sept. 11 commission
S Extend union protections to Homeland Security Department employees
Yes Revive fast-track procedures for trade agreements
Yes Authorize war against Iraq
Yes Advance bankruptcy overhaul opposed by abortion opponents

2001

Yes Nullify Clinton Labor Department ergonomics rule
Yes Cut taxes by $1.35 trillion through fiscal 2011
No Maintain ban on oil drilling in Arctic National Wildlife Refuge
Yes Approve Bush proposal to limit managed-care plan liability for coverage decisions
No Divert money from crop subsidy payments to land conservation
S Expand law enforcement power to investigate suspected terrorists

CQ VOTE STUDIES

	PARTY UNITY		PRESIDENTIAL SUPPORT	
	Support	Oppose	Support	Oppose
2002	100%	0%	100%	0%
2001	100%	0%	100%	0%
2000	100%	0%	28%	72%
1999	95%	5%	17%	83%
1998	96%	4%	21%	79%

INTEREST GROUPS

	AFL-CIO	ADA	CCUS	ACU
2002	0%	—	100%	8%
2001	0%	0%	100%	100%
2000	0%	0%	81%	100%
1999	0%	0%	100%	90%
1998	0%	0%	100%	100%

ILLINOIS 14

North Central – Aurora, Elgin, DeKalb

Most people in the 14th live on the district's eastern side, in established towns along the Fox River valley. West of the river, prairies and farms stretch to the district's end in Henry County, nearly to the Mississippi River. Rich in hay, soybeans and corn, the flat landscape is interrupted only by Northern Illinois University in DeKalb.

The district's population center is Kane County, a fast-growing area on the outskirts of metropolitan Chicago. The district's largest cities, Aurora and Elgin, suffered a period of heavy manufacturing decline in the 1980s but have recovered by promoting industrial parks and opening riverboat casinos. One of Aurora's major employers is the heavy-equipment manufacturer Caterpillar. The cities also have benefited from job growth in nearby Naperville and Schaumburg, suburban cities that have emerged as business centers outside Chicago.

Both Elgin and Aurora are about one-third Hispanic, a vestige of the days when DuPage County farms were cultivated by migrant labor. Those farms have now been paved over and built upon, but many of the migrant workers remained in the area. Only three other Illinois districts — the Chicago-area 3rd, 4th and 5th — have a greater Hispanic population than the 14th, which is almost one-fifth Hispanic.

While the minority influence tends to help Democrats, the 14th overall has a strong Republican tilt, due mostly to the GOP leanings of Kane County, Kendall County (which includes Speaker Hastert's hometown of Yorkville), and northwestern DuPage County. GOP-friendly suburban and rural voters far outnumber the cities' blue-collar and minority Democrats. George W. Bush carried the district by 12 percentage points in the 2000 presidential election.

MAJOR INDUSTRY

Farm machinery and other manufacturing, riverboat gambling, agriculture

CITIES

Aurora (pt.), 102,144; Elgin (pt.), 74,013; DeKalb, 39,018; Carpentersville, 30,586; St. Charles, 27,896; Batavia, 23,866

NOTABLE

Former President Ronald Reagan's birthplace in Tampico and boyhood home in Dixon are operated as local museums.

Rep. Timothy V. Johnson (R)

CAPITOL OFFICE
225-2371
www.house.gov/timjohnson
1229 Longworth 20515-1315; fax 226-0791

COMMITTEES
Agriculture
Science
Transportation & Infrastructure

HOMETOWN
Urbana

BORN
July 23, 1946, Champaign, Ill.

RELIGION
Assemblies of God

FAMILY
Divorced; nine children

EDUCATION
U.S. Military Academy, attended 1964; U. of Illinois, B.A. 1969, J.D. 1972

CAREER
Lawyer; realtor

POLITICAL HIGHLIGHTS
Urbana City Council, 1971-75; Ill. House, 1977-2000

ELECTION RESULTS

2002 GENERAL		
Timothy V. Johnson (R)	134,650	65.2%
Joshua T. Hartke (D)	64,131	31.0%
Carl Estabrook (GREEN)	7,836	3.8%
2002 PRIMARY		
Timothy V. Johnson (R)		unopposed
2000 GENERAL		
Timothy V. Johnson (R)	125,943	53.2%
Mike Kelleher (D)	110,679	46.8%

Elected 2000; 2nd term

In Washington, if Johnson is not in a committee meeting or on the floor of the House, it's a good bet that he is in the members-only gym, swimming laps or pounding out the miles on a treadmill or stationary bike while catching up on his reading or making some of the dozens of phone calls he makes to constituents every day.

He says the devotion to exercise keeps him energized for his busy schedule. Agriculture policy is Johnson's leading interest, since crops and food processing are the economic lifeblood for thousands of his constituents.

Johnson landed a seat on the Agriculture Committee in his first term, replacing the retired Thomas W. Ewing, his predecessor. Johnson says his political philosophy is similar to Ewing's. "Both of us have an acute awareness of the importance of agriculture and small business within the district," Johnson told the Bloomington Pantagraph in 2001.

Fulfilling a campaign pledge, the first bill Johnson introduced in the 107th Congress was a measure to eliminate the use of MTBE, a gasoline additive that is blamed for polluting groundwater. Johnson wants to see more use of two MTBE rivals: ethanol, which is made from corn, and biodiesel, which is derived from soybeans. Both plants are grown in abundance in the 15th District. Johnson also worked to increase funding for Agriculture Department export promotion activities; nearly half of the corn, soybeans and other grains grown in the state are exported.

Environmentalists, however, have praised Johnson for his legislation to ban MTBE and for his votes against drilling for oil in the Arctic National Wildlife Refuge and to protect national park and offshore areas from drilling.

Johnson also went against party philosophy by voting for the 2002 campaign finance overhaul and against the Republican-drafted language in a patients' bill of rights that would have limited liability and damage awards. He worries that the anti-terrorism package written after the attacks of Sept. 11, 2001, gives authorities too much latitude to infringe on civil rights.

He is more conservative on social issues. During the campaign finance debate, Johnson voted for an amendment, which failed, to exclude restrictions on advertising when the topic was the Second Amendment. Johnson is staunchly opposed to abortion. He does, however, support stem cell research in certain circumstances. Johnson's father had diabetes and his grandfather suffered from Parkinson's disease.

A member of the Main Street Partnership, a group of moderate and pro-business Republicans, he backed President Bush only 77 percent of the time in the 107th Congress, one of the two dozen lowest percentages among House Republicans. He had promised to limit himself to three terms in Congress but, just before the 2002 election, he revoked that pledge, telling the Champaign News-Gazette, "I have learned that the pledge is limiting my effectiveness."

Johnson's multitasking while on the treadmill is a perfect illustration of his organized daily routine as well as his self-described compulsion to make phone calls, sometimes several hundred a day. Swimming is a mid-day "mental health break," he told an Illinois Magazine reporter. An avid basketball fan, he played the game all the time before a slipped disc that developed during his 2000 campaign sidelined him.

In addition to his ambitious exercise regimen, Johnson has what he admits are "very, very eccentric eating habits." He skips breakfast and lunch and survives on a diet of fruit, rice cakes, granola, vitamin supplements, fresh squeezed juice and a kind of farmer's cheese. "I eat the same thing every single meal of my life," he told Illinois Magazine.

His thin physique evokes an occasional observation that he resembles another central Illinois politician — Abraham Lincoln. The resemblance was perhaps more striking when Johnson had a beard. Even after shaving his beard late in 2001, the Lincoln comparisons still are made. Johnson's staff says it was just an accident that a prominent backdrop at a campaign appearance in Urbana was a statue of a young, clean-shaven Lincoln.

Johnson grew up in a political family. His mother and her parents were active in McLean County Republican politics. His father, though originally a Democrat, switched parties and served on the Urbana City Council. Johnson says he began passing out campaign literature when he was 3 or 4 years old.

He became a GOP precinct committeeman at age 21, while he was still in college. By 24, he was on the Urbana City Council, and at 30, he was elected to the Illinois House, where he stayed for 24 years. Outside the legislature, Johnson worked in real estate and founded a law practice.

During his long tenure in Springfield, Johnson worked to toughen penalties for drunken driving and sex offenses. He briefly considered running for Congress in 1992 against Ewing, then just a freshman. By 2000, Johnson was looking for something new, and he leapt into the 15th District race when Ewing announced his retirement.

Known as an indefatigable campaigner who is now undefeated in 17 elections, Johnson was the first candidate to jump into the race. But the GOP primary field grew to four, and three of the most influential Illinois Republicans backed different candidates. Gov. George Ryan endorsed Johnson, Speaker J. Dennis Hastert backed state Rep. Bill Brady and incumbent Ewing supported his son, Sam Ewing. Johnson, running on high name recognition and ample personal funds, won the contest with 44 percent of the vote.

The 15th leans Republican and Johnson entered the fall race as a strong favorite. But he faced a tougher-than-expected battle with his Democratic foe, university instructor Mike Kelleher, a first-time candidate and former Capitol Hill aide. Johnson prevailed, though with a modest 53 percent.

Given his low margin of victory, Johnson's 2002 re-election prospects seemed uncertain, as redistricting promised to change the shape of the district dramatically. Indeed, the new map put Democratic Rep. David Phelps' home in the 15th District, but Phelps elected to run against Republican John Shimkus in the 19th instead. When Kelleher declined to run again, Johnson cruised to a 2-to-1 triumph over political novice Joshua T. Hartke.

KEY VOTES

2002

Yes Overhaul campaign finance law; ban "soft money" and restrict advocacy advertising
Yes Back Bush's defense budget increase
Yes Extend 1996 welfare law
Yes Adopt Bush's discretionary spending limit
Yes Pass GOP Medicare prescription drug plan
No Create independent Sept. 11 commission
No Extend union protections to Homeland Security Department employees
Yes Revive fast-track procedures for trade agreements
Yes Authorize war against Iraq
No Advance bankruptcy overhaul opposed by abortion opponents

2001

Yes Nullify Clinton Labor Department ergonomics rule
Yes Cut taxes by $1.35 trillion through fiscal 2011
Yes Maintain ban on oil drilling in Arctic National Wildlife Refuge
No Approve Bush proposal to limit managed-care plan liability for coverage decisions
No Divert money from crop subsidy payments to land conservation
Yes Expand law enforcement power to investigate suspected terrorists

CQ VOTE STUDIES

	PARTY UNITY		PRESIDENTIAL SUPPORT	
	Support	Oppose	Support	Oppose
2002	85%	15%	80%	20%
2001	85%	15%	74%	26%

INTEREST GROUPS

	AFL-CIO	ADA	CCUS	ACU
2002	11%	15%	85%	76%
2001	33%	15%	74%	68%

ILLINOIS 15
East central – Champaign, Bloomington, Danville

Agriculture is the dominant industry in the 15th, which takes in all or part of 22 counties. Corn and soybean fields cover much of this area, and the crop yields are the state's highest in the counties south of Champaign, the district's main population center. Farmers produce feed and raw material for food products manufactured just over the border at Decatur-based Archer Daniels Midland Co. in the 17th District.

Scattered amid the farms are several midsize towns, including Danville, that are centered around agribusiness and manufacturing. Higher education is big business in this district, with 38,000 students at the University of Illinois flagship campus in Urbana-Champaign. Bloomington-Normal has Illinois State and Illinois Wesleyan universities, which are just outside the district in the 11th. Bloomington, home to State Farm Insurance, leads downstate Illinois in insurance and finance.

Redistricting in 2001 altered the 15th's boundaries after slow growth in downstate Illinois cost the state one seat in reapportionment. Mapmakers dismantled the southeastern 19th District, and the remnants that were attached to the 15th form a long, narrow appendage that hugs the Indiana border. North to south, the 15th runs for more than 250 miles.

The district has a strong GOP lean. Republicans typically run strongest in counties north of Champaign, including Iroquois, Livingston and Ford counties, which gave presidential candidate George W. Bush in 2000 and GOP gubernatorial nominee Jim Ryan in 2002 at least 60 percent of the vote, though both lost Illinois. Champaign County's academic community helps keep Democrats competitive: Champaign was the only county east of Decatur and south of Chicago that Bush lost in Illinois in 2000, though only narrowly; Ryan carried it in 2002.

MAJOR INDUSTRY
Agriculture, higher education, food processing

CITIES
Champaign, 67,518; Urbana, 36,395; Bloomington (pt.), 34,510; Danville, 33,904; Charleston, 21,039; Mattoon, 18,291

NOTABLE
The Lincoln Log Cabin State Historic Site in Coles County preserves the last home of Abraham Lincoln's father and stepmother.

Rep. Donald Manzullo (R)

CAPITOL OFFICE
225-5676
www.house.gov/manzullo
2228 Rayburn 20515-1316; fax 225-5284

COMMITTEES
Financial Services
Small Business - chairman

HOMETOWN
Egan

BORN
March 24, 1944, Rockford, Ill.

RELIGION
Baptist

FAMILY
Wife, Freda Manzullo; three children

EDUCATION
American U., B.A. 1967 (political science); Marquette U., J.D. 1970

CAREER
Lawyer

POLITICAL HIGHLIGHTS
Sought Republican nomination for U.S. House, 1990

ELECTION RESULTS

2002 GENERAL		
Donald Manzullo (R)	133,339	70.6%
John Kutsch (D)	55,488	29.4%
2002 PRIMARY		
Donald Manzullo (R)		unopposed
2000 GENERAL		
Donald Manzullo (R)	178,174	66.7%
Charles W. Hendrickson (D)	88,781	33.2%

PREVIOUS WINNING PERCENTAGES
1998 (100%); 1996 (60%); 1994 (71%); 1992 (56%)

Elected 1992; 6th term

A family background in small business — his family lived in a one-room apartment above the struggling grocery store that his father owned in Rockford — has shaped Manzullo's tenure as chairman of the Small Business Committee, a post in which he has continued to build upon his solid pro-business and socially conservative record.

In the 107th Congress, Manzullo (man-ZOO-low) worked to lower tax rates for the owners of small businesses and make it easier for them to bid on federal contracts. And he helped pass legislation that gave federal aid to small-business owners affected by the Sept. 11, 2001, terrorist attacks. Private enterprise, Manzullo believes, plays a key role in the social and economic well-being of the community, and so regulations on small-business owners should not be too numerous or burdensome.

During his first term as chairman, however, Manzullo made his biggest splash by facing down the chief Medicare and Medicaid administrator, Thomas Scully, in a rare public standoff between a top congressional Republican and the Bush administration. When Scully refused to testify in 2002 on the same panel with witnesses critical of his agency, Manzullo issued a subpoena. When Scully defied it, the chairman threatened to draft a contempt of Congress citation. In the end, Scully relented and issued his mea culpa before the committee as he sat next to the medical industry witnesses he had tried to avoid.

While Manzullo's pro-business philosophy is often in harmony with Republican party leaders, he has defied them on occasion. He voted against a GOP leadership measure in the 107th to create a Medicare prescription drug benefit, fearing it would hurt independent pharmacists in his area. And he is at odds with the Bush administration over steel tariffs that have hurt local manufacturers who rely on imported steel.

Manzullo says his views were shaped by the example of his father, who was generous in extending grocery store credit to new arrivals from displaced persons camps in Europe and otherwise served as a "one-man social services agency," helping the newcomers to America insulate their homes with cardboard and organizing community activities such as boxing tournaments.

Off the committee, Manzullo sponsored a 2001 law qualifying more sick veterans for disability compensation, and making the eligibility retroactive to cover veterans previously denied care for Persian Gulf War syndrome. Manzullo said the death of a 36-year-old Gulf War veteran in his district inspired him to pursue the legislation. Similarly, the complaints of an Illinois fire chaplain led him to push for enactment in the 107th a law allowing line-of-duty death benefits for firefighters, police and their chaplains to be paid to whomever is listed on the victim's life insurance policy. He was joined in that effort by liberal New York Democrat Jerrold Nadler, who sought the change to benefit gay public safety officers. Manzullo distanced himself from that cause and said he was seeking equity for Roman Catholic priests, who cannot be married and have "surviving spouses."

Manzullo strongly supports federal funding for the Export-Import Bank and the Overseas Private Investment Corporation, government agencies that assist businesses in expanding exports and are sometimes criticized as "corporate welfare." Manzullo argues that they are an essential counterbalance to foreign governments that invest much more heavily than the United States in helping their businesses increase exports.

He has championed an initiative he calls "America's Jobs First," which encourages procurement officers and purchasing agents to buy supplies from American companies — preferably small businesses. And Manzullo has pressed hard to prevent "bundling," a process where federal agencies consolidate contracts for goods and services to improve efficiency. Critics say the practice puts small businesses at a disadvantage because they are too small or too specialized.

Manzullo is a pillar of the Republican right on a range of domestic issues, including taxation, education, the environment and abortion. He belongs to the Republican Study Committee, a faction of the most conservative House GOP members. Manzullo — who earlier in his career helped start crisis pregnancy centers in Rockford and picketed clinics that performed abortions — also has proposed that federally funded family planning clinics be required to get parental notification before they provide contraceptives to minors.

Freda Manzullo, a microbiologist, taught the couple's three children at home until the eighth grade, when they went to a small Christian high school in suburban Virginia. Manzullo says that home-schooling is not for everyone, but that his family decided it was the best way to keep everyone together under the circumstances of a congressional schedule. When Congress is in recess the family heads for their small beef cattle farm in Illinois.

Manzullo recalls deciding, at age 4, to become a lawyer when he grew up. At age 10, he also decided that it would be nice to be a member of Congress. He followed through on the first vow by spending 20 years in law practice, most of them as a small-town lawyer who handled many family cases. When Republican Rep. Lynn Martin decided to run for the Senate in 1990, Manzullo jumped into the House race and, with a door-to-door campaign, made a respectable 46 percent showing in the GOP primary.

The Republican nominee, John W. Hallock Jr., had the dubious distinction of losing the general election to John W. Cox Jr. — the first Democratic congressional victory in that part of Illinois in the 20th century — and Manzullo decided to keep right on campaigning. It was expected that Republicans would challenge Cox in 1992 with state Sen. Jack Schaffer, a contender with party establishment backing and more money than Manzullo. But Manzullo and his corps of volunteers, many from families helped by his father years before, went hard after Schaffer and won the primary with 56 percent of the vote. In November, the district reverted to its traditional GOP form, electing Manzullo by 12 percentage points over Cox. Manzullo has not been seriously challenged since.

KEY VOTES

2002

No Overhaul campaign finance law; ban "soft money" and restrict advocacy advertising
Yes Back Bush's defense budget increase
Yes Extend 1996 welfare law
Yes Adopt Bush's discretionary spending limit
No Pass GOP Medicare prescription drug plan
No Create independent Sept. 11 commission
No Extend union protections to Homeland Security Department employees
Yes Revive fast-track procedures for trade agreements
Yes Authorize war against Iraq
No Advance bankruptcy overhaul opposed by abortion opponents

2001

Yes Nullify Clinton Labor Department ergonomics rule
Yes Cut taxes by $1.35 trillion through fiscal 2011
No Maintain ban on oil drilling in Arctic National Wildlife Refuge
Yes Approve Bush proposal to limit managed-care plan liability for coverage decisions
No Divert money from crop subsidy payments to land conservation
Yes Expand law enforcement power to investigate suspected terrorists

CQ VOTE STUDIES

	PARTY UNITY		PRESIDENTIAL SUPPORT	
	Support	Oppose	Support	Oppose
2002	95%	5%	82%	18%
2001	94%	6%	77%	23%
2000	95%	5%	22%	78%
1999	92%	8%	15%	85%
1998	95%	5%	21%	79%

INTEREST GROUPS

	AFL-CIO	ADA	CCUS	ACU
2002	13%	5%	95%	100%
2001	17%	0%	96%	92%
2000	0%	5%	90%	95%
1999	0%	15%	96%	92%
1998	0%	0%	94%	92%

ILLINOIS 16

North – Rockford, part of McHenry County

The 16th spans most of the Illinois-Wisconsin border, taking in Rockford and covering the rolling northern prairie where family farmers grow corn and raise dairy cows.

At its eastern end, the district includes most of McHenry County, the fastest-growing county in Illinois during the 1990s at 42 percent. Located at the edge of Chicago's flourishing northwest counties, McHenry is quickly filling up with new suburban bedroom communities. Solidly GOP, it voted for George W. Bush by 20 percentage points in the 2000 presidential election. To the west is Boone County, which also is fast-growing and Republican-leaning.

About one-fourth of the district's voters live in Rockford (Winnebago County), an industrial hub and the state's second-largest city. Once the self-styled tool and die capital of the world, in the 1980s it became a poster child of Rust Belt decline, with unemployment often exceeding 20 percent. The city recovered by upgrading to high-tech manufacturing and expanding its exports to China, Mexico and Canada.

Other counties in the 16th are among Illinois' leading dairy producers. Jo Daviess County, in the northwest corner, is a state leader in raising beef cattle and producing hay. Galena, in rolling hills near the Mississippi River, has a tourist-based economy.

Redistricting following the 2000 census made the 16th somewhat more rural by shedding part of McHenry to the 8th District and adding parts of the counties to the southwest.

More than 90 percent of the district's black residents live in Rockford, giving the city a base of loyal Democrats. But the 16th covers mostly conservative, Republican territory. Only once in the 20th century did district voters elect a Democrat to the House.

MAJOR INDUSTRY

Manufacturing, aircraft and machine parts, agriculture, trade

CITIES

Rockford,150,115; Crystal Lake (pt.), 37,740; Freeport, 26,443; Lake in the Hills, 23,152; Belvidere, 20,820; Machesney Park, 20,759

NOTABLE

The Ulysses S. Grant Home is in Galena; Rockford is known as the world's largest producer of fasteners.

Rep. Lane Evans (D)

CAPITOL OFFICE
225-5905
lane.evans@mail.house.gov
www.house.gov/evans
2211 Rayburn 20515-1317; fax 225-5396

COMMITTEES
Armed Services
Veterans' Affairs - ranking member

HOMETOWN
Rock Island

BORN
Aug. 4, 1951, Rock Island, Ill.

RELIGION
Roman Catholic

FAMILY
Single

EDUCATION
Augustana College (Ill.), B.A. 1974 (political science); Georgetown U., J.D. 1978

MILITARY SERVICE
Marine Corps, 1969-71

CAREER
Lawyer

POLITICAL HIGHLIGHTS
No previous office

ELECTION RESULTS

2002 GENERAL		
Lane Evans (D)	127,093	62.4%
Peter Calderone (R)	76,519	37.6%
2002 PRIMARY		
Lane Evans (D)		unopposed
2000 GENERAL		
Lane Evans (D)	132,494	54.9%
Mark Baker (R)	108,853	45.1%

PREVIOUS WINNING PERCENTAGES
1998 (52%); 1996 (52%); 1994 (55%); 1992 (60%); 1990 (67%); 1988 (65%); 1986 (56%); 1984 (57%); 1982 (53%)

Elected 1982; 11th term

An unapologetic Democrat when he represented a swing district with strong Republican roots, Evans has become even more outspoken in expressing his economic populism and socially liberal views now that redistricting has pushed the 17th District solidly into the Democratic column for the current decade.

From 1994 to 2000, Evans was one of the more endangered House incumbents, winning re-election with 55 percent or less of the vote in four straight contests. A combination of hard work, an engaging manner and an active constituent service effort enabled him to hold onto the seat he had captured in a stunning 1982 upset, but it was rarely easy.

That changed, however, after the Illinois General Assembly — required to wipe away one House seat because of reapportionment — remade the district, moving out many of the rural areas and small towns where Evans had struggled and replacing them with Democratic-leaning urban neighborhoods from Decatur and Springfield. (The voters in the old 17th had preferred George W. Bush by 6 percentage points in 2000; the voters Evans now represents had preferred Al Gore by 10 points.) As a result, Republicans mounted only token opposition to Evans, who cruised to his 11th term in 2002. His 62 percent was his best showing since 1990.

But while that gift of a safe seat may have emboldened Evans to sharpen his partisan rhetoric — Republicans "don't really care" about veterans, he said at a Democratic rally for prescription drug benefits in 2002 — it probably will not lead to changes in the main themes of his House career, which has been shaped by his military service, his working-class family background, his years as a poverty lawyer and his own experience with serious illness.

In 1998, Evans revealed that he had suffered from Parkinson's disease for three years, prompting concerns about his ability to keep up with the rigorous House schedule. Although he sometimes has problems with balance and often cannot force his facial muscles into a smile, Evans says his condition has stabilized enough to allow him to continue his work. In fact, the regular jogger argues that his illness "has made me an even better congressman. I understand the difficulties people face every day."

The impact of his struggle with Parkinson's is also evident in his stand on controversial social issues, such as President Bush's decision in 2001 to fund research only on stem cells already extracted from human embryos — an endorsement of limited research that pleased neither the scientific community nor abortion foes. While many opponents of legal abortion supported a ban on such research, Evans noted that it held out hope for curing his and other crippling conditions. "I know many people feel strongly about the right to life. But for me, there's also a right to live," he said.

The centerpiece of Evans' legislative career, however, has been his work on veterans programs. As the top-ranking Democrat on the Veterans' Affairs Committee since 1997, Evans perhaps has become best-known among his colleagues for his tireless work to beef up benefits for others who have served in uniform. In the 107th Congress, for example, he pushed veterans-related measures to aid the homeless, boost federal job placement assistance and expand health outreach services.

While veterans matters traditionally have been seen as less partisan than other issues, Evans has not hesitated to criticize Republicans when he believes they are holding back on needed benefits. During House consideration of a veterans education bill in 2001, for example, he assailed the GOP leadership for blocking consideration of his amendment to increase authorized funding to $24 billion from $9 billion.

Evans is the first Vietnam-era veteran to hold the top slot on Veterans' Affairs. Although he was not assigned to Vietnam during his two years in the Marine Corps, he emerged a few years ago as a leading proponent of federal programs benefiting veterans of that conflict. He has been a crusader in helping veterans suffering from diseases linked to Agent Orange, a defoliant used during the Vietnam War. His four-year effort to gain medical compensation for these veterans paid off when his bill was enacted in the 102nd Congress.

Evans sought to buck the seniority system and take the gavel of the Veterans' panel in 1992 after years of locking horns with Chairman G.V. "Sonny" Montgomery of Mississippi. Younger veterans, who perceived Montgomery as dragging his feet on compensation for Agent Orange-related diseases, saw the World War II and Korean War veteran as intent on protecting his own generation's programs at the expense of those who had served in Vietnam. In a secret ballot of House Democrats, Evans fell four votes short in his bid to oust Montgomery, who had held the gavel for a dozen years. Evans prepared for a 1994 rematch, but when Republicans won control of the House that year he decided against challenging Montgomery for the chairmanship. Montgomery retired two years later.

Evans, who also serves on the Armed Services Committee, and Vermont's Democratic Sen. Patrick J. Leahy have tried since 1992 to mobilize U.S. government support for an international agreement to ban the use of land mines. Humanitarian concerns also were evident in Evans' 2001 campaign to press Japan to apologize for sexually abusing Asian "comfort women" during World War II.

Evans points to his parents — his father was a firefighter, his mother a nurse — as the inspiration for his liberal views, saying, "They saved people's lives. I fight for ordinary people and I identify with ordinary people. I think there is something real in my ability to connect with working families."

In 1982, Evans emerged from his community legal clinic in Rock Island to make his first run for public office. It was an effort that seemed futile until the March Republican primary, when former state Sen. Kenneth G. McMillan, a New Right stalwart, defeated moderate eight-term Rep. Tom Railsback. That set up a clear ideological choice in November, one that benefited Evans in the recession year of 1982. Urging voters in the economically troubled district to "send Reagan a message," Evans won with 53 percent of the vote.

KEY VOTES

2002

Yes Overhaul campaign finance law; ban "soft money" and restrict advocacy advertising
Yes Back Bush's defense budget increase
No Extend 1996 welfare law
No Adopt Bush's discretionary spending limit
No Pass GOP Medicare prescription drug plan
Yes Create independent Sept. 11 commission
Yes Extend union protections to Homeland Security Department employees
No Revive fast-track procedures for trade agreements
No Authorize war against Iraq
No Advance bankruptcy overhaul opposed by abortion opponents

2001

No Nullify Clinton Labor Department ergonomics rule
No Cut taxes by $1.35 trillion through fiscal 2011
Yes Maintain ban on oil drilling in Arctic National Wildlife Refuge
No Approve Bush proposal to limit managed-care plan liability for coverage decisions
No Divert money from crop subsidy payments to land conservation
Yes Expand law enforcement power to investigate suspected terrorists

CQ VOTE STUDIES

	PARTY UNITY		PRESIDENTIAL SUPPORT	
	Support	Oppose	Support	Oppose
2002	97%	3%	24%	76%
2001	93%	7%	26%	74%
2000	94%	6%	76%	24%
1999	94%	6%	80%	20%
1998	92%	8%	83%	17%

INTEREST GROUPS

	AFL-CIO	ADA	CCUS	ACU
2002	100%	100%	40%	0%
2001	100%	100%	27%	0%
2000	100%	95%	38%	8%
1999	100%	100%	16%	0%
1998	100%	90%	22%	16%

ILLINOIS 17

West — Moline, Rock Island; part of Decatur and Springfield

The 17th is a vivid demonstration of the extremes Illinois mapmakers went to in 2001 to draw safe districts for incumbent House members. In the 1990s, the 17th was a relatively compact district that split just two counties. The redrawn 17th is a geographic monstrosity, taking in nine full counties and parts of 14 others, hugging much of Illinois' border with the Mississippi River but reaching with tentacle-like appendages as far inland as Springfield and Decatur.

In 1837, John Deere developed the first self-cleaning steel plow in the present-day 17th, which includes rich farmland along the Mississippi and the cities of Rock Island and Moline, two of the four industrial Quad Cities that straddle the river into Iowa. Defense cutbacks have drained jobs from one of the district's industrial mainstays, the Rock Island Arsenal.

Corn, soybeans and hogs fuel most of the rest of the district's economy. Even the industrial sector depends on agriculture: It is dominated by the nation's two largest farm equipment manufacturers. Sliding farm profits have forced the Quad Cities to recruit new types of manufacturing.

Redistricting gave the 17th, a politically competitive district in the 1990s, a decided Democratic tilt. Six of the nine counties wholly within the 17th voted for Al Gore in the 2000 presidential election. The Democratic vote in Rock Island, coupled with the Democratic lean of the parts of Springfield and Decatur that were drawn into the district, are enough to overcome the Republican tendencies of some rural areas.

MAJOR INDUSTRY
Farm equipment manufacturing, agriculture, defense

MILITARY BASES
Rock Island Arsenal (Army), 133 military, 3,719 civilian (1999)

CITIES
Decatur (pt.), 58,701; Moline, 43,768; Quincy, 40,366; Rock Island, 39,684; Galesburg, 33,706; Springfield (pt.), 28,952; East Moline, 20,333

NOTABLE
The Carl Sandburg Home in Galesburg is where the late poet was born; Wyatt Earp was born in Monmouth; Bishop Hill was established in 1846 by Swedish religious dissidents searching for a "utopia on the prairie."

Rep. Ray LaHood (R)

CAPITOL OFFICE
225-6201
www.house.gov/lahood
1424 Longworth 20515-1318; fax 225-9249

COMMITTEES
Appropriations
Select Intelligence
(Terrorism & Homeland Security - chairman)

HOMETOWN
Peoria

BORN
Dec. 6, 1945, Peoria, Ill.

RELIGION
Roman Catholic

FAMILY
Wife, Kathleen LaHood; four children

EDUCATION
Spoon River Community College, attended 1963-65; Bradley U., B.S. 1971 (education)

CAREER
Congressional aide; youth bureau director; urban planning commission director; teacher

POLITICAL HIGHLIGHTS
Ill. House, 1982-83; defeated for election to Ill. House, 1982

ELECTION RESULTS

2002 GENERAL		
Ray LaHood (R)	unopposed	
2002 PRIMARY		
Ray LaHood (R)	unopposed	
2000 GENERAL		
Ray LaHood (R)	173,706	67.1%
Joyce Harant (D)	85,317	32.9%

PREVIOUS WINNING PERCENTAGES
1998 (100%); 1996 (59%); 1994 (60%)

Elected 1994; 5th term

LaHood is a moderate who has endeared himself to a broad swath of the House GOP by working hard to master House rules, display evenhandedness and usually err on the side of the party leadership. As a result, other moderates have promoted him for election to the leadership, while party leaders have entrusted him with high-profile assignments.

A member of both the Appropriations and Intelligence committees, LaHood frequently is at the center of the action on Capitol Hill, particularly since the terrorist attacks of Sept. 11, 2001. But his efforts to secure more prominence for himself have come up short. When it became clear in 2001 that Tom DeLay would move up from party whip to floor leader in the 108th Congress, LaHood launched a campaign for whip as an antidote to DeLay's hard-charging conservatism. When his bid failed to gain traction after three months, LaHood gave up and effusively endorsed DeLay's anointed successor, Roy Blunt of Missouri.

Still, LaHood remains something of a nationally respected figure, at least to the loyal audience of thousands that tunes in congressional debates on C-SPAN. His aides believe LaHood has presided over the House more frequently than any other member since his arrival in 1995 — never more prominently than in 1998, when he wielded the gavel as the House debated the impeachment of President Clinton.

Using the knowledge of both parliamentary procedure and political dynamics gained during a decade as the chief of staff to his predecessor in the House, Republican Leader Robert H. Michel, LaHood has a bipartisan reputation as both forceful and evenhanded when tapped by the Speaker to take the chair. The GOP leadership is confident that LaHood's rulings, which are confident and quick, help maintain order during complicated or emotionally charged debates.

LaHood drew considerable notice in 2002, when the House and Senate intelligence panels joined forces to investigate intelligence-related failures before the terrorist attacks. LaHood was at times both a friend and a foe of the Bush administration. He criticized the White House for refusing to declassify records that, in his view, would have revealed how much the White House knew prior to the attacks. At the same time, LaHood unsuccessfully fought creation of the independent commission to investigate government lapses before the attacks, terming it "a set-up deal to blame the president."

The grandson of an immigrant from Lebanon and a one-time junior high school teacher, LaHood considers himself a watchdog for minority rights, and he has expressed concern about the level of sophistication among his colleagues in their knowledge of the Middle East. "There is a pretty fair understanding about Israel and the Palestinians," he says, "but there is only a sketchy understanding of other countries in the region including Syria, Egypt and Lebanon."

While many of his colleagues in the GOP takeover Class of 1994 revel in their outsider backgrounds and won election by lambasting Congress as an institution, LaHood has never shied from his role as an insider. In 2002, he pressed for the creation of a workout facility for House aides, and he was among the few members willing to fret publicly about the loss of coveted parking spaces at the foot of the Capitol steps, which were removed to facilitate construction of the new visitors center.

Hoping to bolster the public's respect for Congress, since 1997 LaHood has organized bipartisan retreats at the start of each Congress in hope of promoting civility, or at least understanding, between lawmakers of both parties. "It is hard to demonize a political opponent if you have held his 2-year-old daughter on your knee," he said in a 1999 commencement speech.

LaHood is part of a small, informal group of Republican advisers to Speaker J. Dennis Hastert, another Michel protégé. He usually is a reliable vote for the party on core issues. Yet at times, LaHood has split from his leadership. He was one of only three House Republicans elected in 1994 who did not sign the "Contract With America," the party's winning campaign manifesto that year. LaHood voiced concern then that the House GOP agenda of tax cuts and defense spending would worsen the federal deficit. He expressed similar concern over George W. Bush's presidential campaign platform of 2000, but he ended up supporting Bush's $1.35 trillion tax cut enacted in 2001.

A member of the Appropriations Committee and its Agriculture Subcommittee since the 107th Congress, LaHood is in a good position to look out for his thousands of constituents who grow or sell corn and soybeans. Among other things, he has pressed for broader use of ethanol, the corn-based fuel additive.

He was a delegate from the Appropriations panel to the Budget Committee in the 107th. GOP budget writers typically are among the most tight-fisted members of Congress, while GOP appropriators generally are amenable to additional spending. LaHood is more sympathetic to the latter approach. He boasts of infrastructure dollars he has brought home to Illinois. And when the budget-writing process melted down in 2002, he nonchalantly remarked that the annual budget resolution was of little consequence, because the appropriators generally get their way regardless of what the document says.

Echoing the move by outgoing Republican Gov. George Ryan to commute all death sentences in Illinois in 2003, LaHood has pushed legislation to improve death row prisoners' access to DNA testing that might prove their innocence.

In the 105th and 106th Congresses, LaHood sponsored legislation to abolish the Electoral College and allow the president to be chosen by the popular vote. "The existence of the college needs to be addressed before we are embroiled in a crisis in which a president is elected without winning the popular vote," he said in 1997, three years before Al Gore won the popular vote but Bush was elected by virtue of his narrow Electoral College majority.

LaHood first declared his candidacy for Congress in 1993, one day after Michel announced his retirement after 30 years in the House. He won with 60 percent of the vote and has never faced a serious challenge since.

KEY VOTES

2002

- No Overhaul campaign finance law; ban "soft money" and restrict advocacy advertising
- Yes Back Bush's defense budget increase
- Yes Extend 1996 welfare law
- Yes Adopt Bush's discretionary spending limit
- Yes Pass GOP Medicare prescription drug plan
- No Create independent Sept. 11 commission
- No Extend union protections to Homeland Security Department employees
- Yes Revive fast-track procedures for trade agreements
- Yes Authorize war against Iraq
- No Advance bankruptcy overhaul opposed by abortion opponents

2001

- Yes Nullify Clinton Labor Department ergonomics rule
- Yes Cut taxes by $1.35 trillion through fiscal 2011
- Yes Maintain ban on oil drilling in Arctic National Wildlife Refuge
- Yes Approve Bush proposal to limit managed-care plan liability for coverage decisions
- No Divert money from crop subsidy payments to land conservation
- Yes Expand law enforcement power to investigate suspected terrorists

CQ VOTE STUDIES

	PARTY UNITY		PRESIDENTIAL SUPPORT	
	Support	Oppose	Support	Oppose
2002	92%	8%	82%	18%
2001	90%	10%	74%	26%
2000	87%	13%	32%	68%
1999	83%	17%	26%	74%
1998	83%	17%	28%	72%

INTEREST GROUPS

	AFL-CIO	ADA	CCUS	ACU
2002	11%	0%	89%	92%
2001	33%	15%	86%	72%
2000	10%	15%	95%	72%
1999	22%	15%	84%	66%
1998	40%	20%	83%	60%

ILLINOIS 18

Central – Peoria, part of Springfield and Decatur

When Richard M. Nixon spoke to the silent majority, his message hit home in Peoria, an American Everytown filled with hard-working, conservative, middle-class folks.

Thirty years later, Peoria is a politically competitive region in a sea of mostly rural Republicanism. A large black population on the south side and a substantial union constituency allow Democratic candidates to prevail in Peoria, as Al Gore did in the city and its namesake county in the 2000 presidential election. Republicans run stronger to the north: GOP gubernatorial nominee Jim Ryan's strong showing there helped him carry the city and county in 2002.

The 18th takes in all or part of 20 counties in central and western Illinois, with Peoria County accounting for nearly 30 percent of the population. In the south, the 18th takes in the northern part of Springfield, the state capital, some Republican-leaning suburbs north and west of the city, and rural turf that stretches west of the capital almost to the Mississippi River. In its southeastern reaches, the 18th runs to north Decatur.

In much of this predominantly agricultural district, voters worry about crop prices, ethanol, free trade and estate taxes. But the district's economic health still depends largely on Peoria-based Caterpillar Inc., which manufactures earth-moving equipment and other heavy machinery.

The Republican lean of the rural areas, primarily those north and east of Peoria and north of Springfield, tips the 18th to the GOP. Woodford County, which abuts Peoria to the east, gave Ryan his third-best showing in the state in 2002, and it was George W. Bush's fourth-best Illinois county in the 2000 presidential election.

MAJOR INDUSTRY

Construction machinery, ethanol and grain products, agriculture

CITIES

Peoria, 112,936; Springfield (pt.), 57,209; Pekin, 33,857; East Peoria, 22,638; Jacksonville, 18,940; Decatur (pt.), 15,571

NOTABLE

Pekin (Tazewell County) was the hometown of former Senate Minority Leader Everett McKinley Dirksen; Abraham Lincoln's tomb in Springfield is a state historic site.

Rep. John Shimkus (R)

CAPITOL OFFICE
225-5271
www.house.gov/shimkus
513 Cannon 20515-1319; fax 225-5880

COMMITTEES
Energy & Commerce

HOMETOWN
Collinsville

BORN
Feb. 21, 1958, Collinsville, Ill.

RELIGION
Lutheran

FAMILY
Wife, Karen Shimkus; three children

EDUCATION
U.S. Military Academy, B.S. 1980; Southern Illinois U., M.B.A. 1997

MILITARY SERVICE
Army, 1980-86; Army Reserve, 1986-present

CAREER
High school teacher

POLITICAL HIGHLIGHTS
Candidate for Madison County Board, 1988; Collinsville Township Board of Trustees, 1989-93; Madison County treasurer, 1990-97; Republican nominee for U.S. House, 1992

ELECTION RESULTS

2002 GENERAL		
John Shimkus (R)	133,956	54.8%
David Phelps (D)	110,517	45.2%
2002 PRIMARY		
John Shimkus (R)		unopposed
2000 GENERAL		
John Shimkus (R)	161,393	63.1%
Jeffrey Cooper (D)	94,382	36.9%

PREVIOUS WINNING PERCENTAGES
1998 (61%); 1996 (50%)

Elected 1996; 4th term

Burly and athletic, Shimkus was not only the star GOP pitcher in the 2002 congressional baseball game against the Democrats, he was named the Most Valuable Player.

Shimkus had been a catcher, dating back to his junior varsity days at West Point. But he ably filled the big void left by former Oklahoma Republican Rep. Steve Largent, a National Football League Hall-of-Famer, and excelled in the 9-2 Republican victory. He pitched seven innings, struck out four and was hit by a pitch — proving he is not afraid to take one for the team.

Shimkus is a combination of serious competitor and affable colleague, whether on the field or on the House floor. A deeply committed social conservative, he is regularly out front on controversial issues. He is among the most outspoken House opponents of a procedure referred to by its opponents as "partial birth" abortion. "As a pro-life Christian, I find partial-birth abortion a most cruel and gruesome act against another living human being," Shimkus said.

But Shimkus also is interested in working in a bipartisan fashion on less controversial issues. In the 107th Congress, for instance, he worked with Illinois Democratic Sen. Richard J. Durbin and others on a measure to improve car booster seats for children, and with Massachusetts Democrat Edward J. Markey and others on a bill to create a child-friendly Internet domain, known as ".kids.us."

Shimkus is a pragmatic conservative in the same mold as another Illinois Republican, Speaker J. Dennis Hastert. In the 106th Congress, he played a central role in efforts to craft a bipartisan package that would have paired a Democratic-backed minimum wage hike with Republican-backed tax cuts. When the 107th began, he listed an increase in the minimum wage as one of his top legislative priorities, although no increase was passed.

While he supported the resolution authorizing the use of force in Iraq in the 107th Congress, Shimkus joined other Republicans in the 106th in opposing the military intervention in Kosovo. A fourth-generation Lithuanian, Shimkus is co-chairman of the House Baltic Caucus. A U.S. delegate to the NATO Parliamentary Assembly, he was active in the 107th Congress in supporting NATO expansion to include the Baltic states of Lithuania, Latvia and Estonia.

Republican leaders had Shimkus' narrow 1996 victory in mind when they awarded him a choice committee seat in the 105th Congress on what is now the Energy and Commerce Committee. The panel's broad jurisdiction gives its members contacts with lobbying interests eager to contribute to incumbents' re-election campaigns. Shimkus landed the prize with help from Hastert, who used his status as a member of the GOP leadership and as a senior member of the committee to champion Shimkus' cause.

On one key issue before his committee — deregulation of the electric utility industry — Shimkus aims to protect the interests of his home state, which already has enacted a law deregulating the utility industry. "I am inclined to see that the new Illinois regulations hold in place," he said.

He was instrumental in passing a law in the 106th Congress establishing "911" as the nationwide emergency service number and promoting wireless emergency service.

Shimkus repays his leadership's kind treatment by voting a reliably Republican line even on trade, a tough issue in southern Illinois. The district has a large population of factory workers wary of foreign competition, but he also wants to promote agricultural exports from his district and state. Illinois ranks among the top 10 states in agricultural exports.

In the 107th Congress, Shimkus backed the White House on legislation to give the president fast-track trade negotiating authority. Under fast-track, trade agreements are sent to Congress for an up-or-down vote and cannot be amended. The measure was favored by agriculture interests. But Shimkus also backed stiff tariffs on imported steel, which were sought by domestic steel producers.

From his seat on the Energy and Commerce panel, Shimkus pursues legislation to promote an alternative fuel called biodiesel, which is refined from soybeans, a crop grown in his district. "Biodiesel is good for the environment, good for family farmers and good for the economy," he says. "Meanwhile, soybean farmers are given a new market in which to sell their product."

Related to that is Shimkus' effort to promote ethanol, made from corn, and to ban the fuel additive MTBE, which competes with ethanol as a gasoline additive to reduce emissions. Opponents say MTBE has been found to have contaminated groundwater supplies.

Shimkus graduated from West Point, served in the Army from 1980 to 1986, and then returned to his Illinois hometown of Collinsville. (He still serves in the Army Reserve, with the rank of lieutenant colonel.) After teaching high school history and government, he entered local politics, winning election in 1989 to the Collinsville Township Board of Trustees.

The next year, he won the post of Madison County treasurer, and he was easily re-elected in 1994. In 1992, he challenged Democratic Rep. Richard J. Durbin, who had represented the 20th for the previous 10 years. Shimkus took 44 percent of the vote in a losing effort. When Durbin made a move for the Senate in 1996, Shimkus again mounted a House campaign.

In the general election, he faced state Rep. Jay C. Hoffman, who emphasized his work on anti-crime legislation in the state legislature. Shimkus portrayed Hoffman as an opponent of tax relief and billed himself as a pro-business voice who would roll back taxes and government regulations. Although President Clinton carried the district by 7 percentage points, Shimkus won by 1,238 votes.

In 2002, when reapportionment cost Illinois one of its House seats, the new congressional map threw Shimkus and Democrat David Phelps together in the new 19th District. The district's demographics favored Shimkus, and he won the incumbent vs. incumbent matchup by almost 10 percentage points.

KEY VOTES

2002

No Overhaul campaign finance law; ban "soft money" and restrict advocacy advertising
Yes Back Bush's defense budget increase
Yes Extend 1996 welfare law
Yes Adopt Bush's discretionary spending limit
Yes Pass GOP Medicare prescription drug plan
No Create independent Sept. 11 commission
No Extend union protections to Homeland Security Department employees
Yes Revive fast-track procedures for trade agreements
Yes Authorize war against Iraq
No Advance bankruptcy overhaul opposed by abortion opponents

2001

Yes Nullify Clinton Labor Department ergonomics rule
Yes Cut taxes by $1.35 trillion through fiscal 2011
No Maintain ban on oil drilling in Arctic National Wildlife Refuge
Yes Approve Bush proposal to limit managed-care plan liability for coverage decisions
No Divert money from crop subsidy payments to land conservation
Yes Expand law enforcement power to investigate suspected terrorists

CQ VOTE STUDIES

	PARTY UNITY		PRESIDENTIAL SUPPORT	
	Support	Oppose	Support	Oppose
2002	94%	6%	80%	20%
2001	95%	5%	86%	14%
2000	93%	7%	29%	71%
1999	92%	8%	21%	79%
1998	93%	7%	25%	75%

INTEREST GROUPS

	AFL-CIO	ADA	CCUS	ACU
2002	11%	0%	90%	100%
2001	25%	5%	100%	92%
2000	20%	10%	80%	80%
1999	22%	15%	96%	80%
1998	30%	10%	94%	88%

ILLINOIS 19

South — southern rural counties; part of Springfield

Following a decade of slow population growth, Illinois lost one of its 20 House districts in 2001 reapportionment. In general, the new map merged the 19th and 20th districts, creating a sprawling district in southern Illinois that touches three states (Missouri, Indiana and Kentucky) and takes in all or part of 30 counties.

The northern counties cover typical Midwestern country — acres of corn and soybean fields dotted by small towns. This area leans Republican, as do more-populous areas such as the 19th's share of Madison County and the Sangamon County suburbs of Springfield, the state capital.

The southern half looks more like Appalachia than Midwestern prairie. Its hilly, forested counties depend on timber and coal mining. Unemployment is an endemic problem in much of the region. Mechanization of mining has caused job losses and reduced demand for the region's high-sulfur coal. Pope County, the state's least populous, is almost entirely within the Shawnee National Forest.

The district has an ancestrally conservative Democratic tradition but leaned Republican in the 2000 presidential election, backing George W. Bush with 55 percent of the vote. While the economic populism of the region can help conservative Democrats win, voters will cast a GOP ballot if they perceive Democrats as too liberal on cultural issues. In the 2000 election, Wayne and Effingham counties gave Bush his top vote percentages in the state. Edwards County, which is shared with the 15th District, gave 2002 GOP gubernatorial nominee Jim Ryan a statewide high of 70 percent.

MAJOR INDUSTRY

Agriculture, coal mining, manufacturing, food products

CITIES

Springfield (pt.), 25,293; Collinsville (pt.), 21,803; Edwardsville (pt.), 21,478

NOTABLE

Metropolis (Massac County) was declared the official hometown of Superman by the Illinois House in 1972 — the town is closer to Birmingham, Ala., than to Chicago.

INDIANA

Gov. Frank L. O'Bannon (D)

First elected: 1996
Length of term: 4 years
Term expires: 1/05
Salary: $95,000
Phone: (317) 232-4567
Hometown: Indianapolis
Born: Jan. 30, 1930; Louisville, Ky.
Religion: Methodist
Family: Wife, Judy O'Bannon; three children
Education: Indiana U., B.A. 1952 (government), J.D. 1957
Military Service: Air Force, 1952-54
Career: Lawyer; publisher
Political highlights: Ind. Senate, 1971-89 (Democratic floor leader, 1978-89); lieutenant governor, 1989-97
Election results:

2000 GENERAL

Frank L. O'Bannon (D)	1,232,525	56.6%
David M. McIntosh (R)	908,285	41.7%
Andrew Horning (LIBERT)	38,458	1.8%

Lt. Gov. Joe Kernan (D)

First elected: 1996
Length of term: 4 years
Term expires: 1/05
Salary: $76,000
Phone: (317) 232-4545

STATE LEGISLATURE

Legislature: Meets January-April in odd-numbered years; January-March in even-numbered years
House: 100 members, 2-year terms
2003 breakdown: 49R, 51D; 85 men, 15 women
Salary: $11,600
Phone: (317) 232-9600
Senate: 50 members, 4-year terms
2003 breakdown: 32R, 18D; 37 men, 13 women
Salary: $11,600
Phone: (317) 232-9400

STATE TERM LIMITS

Governor: 2 terms
Senate: No
House: No

URBAN STATISTICS

CITY	POPULATION
Indianapolis	791,926
Fort Wayne	205,727
Evansville	121,582
South Bend	107,789
Gary	102,746

REGISTERED VOTERS

Voters do not register by party.

POPULATION

2002 population (est.)	6,159,068
2000 population	6,080,485
1990 population	5,544,159
Percent change (1990-2000)	+9.7%
Rank among states (2002)	14
Median age	35.2
Born in state	69.3%
Foreign born	3.1%
Violent crime rate	349/100,000
Poverty level	9.5%
Federal workers	37,567
Military	22,639

REDISTRICTING

Indiana lost one House seat in reapportionment. The state legislature failed to agree on a plan and Democratic Gov. Frank L. O'Bannon signed an executive order adopting the new, nine-district map on May 16, 2001.

MISCELLANEOUS

Web: www.state.in.us
Capital: Indianapolis

STATE ELECTION OFFICIAL
(317) 232-3939

DEMOCRATIC HEADQUARTERS
(317) 231-7100

REPUBLICAN HEADQUARTERS
(317) 635-7561

District Statistics

	2000 VOTE FOR PRESIDENT															
DIST.	BUSH	GORE	NADER	WHITE	BLACK	ASIAN	HISP	MEDIAN INCOME	WHITE COLLAR	BLUE COLLAR	SERVICE INDUSTRY	OVER 64	UNDER 18	COLLEGE EDUCATION	RURAL	SQ. MILES
1	42%	57%	n/a	70%	18%	1%	10%	$44,087	53%	31%	15%	13%	27%	17%	13%	2,209
2	54	45	n/a	84	8	1	5	$40,381	51	35	14	13	26	17	27	3,679
3	66	33	n/a	88	6	1	4	$44,013	52	36	12	11	28	18	35	3,240
4	67	32	n/a	94	1	1	3	$45,947	57	30	13	11	26	22	32	4,016
5	69	30	n/a	93	3	1	2	$52,800	63	25	12	11	27	31	26	3,266
6	59	40	n/a	93	4	0	1	$39,002	50	35	15	14	25	15	41	5,550
7	43	55	n/a	63	29	1	4	$36,522	58	26	16	11	26	21	0	262
8	57	42	n/a	94	4	1	1	$36,732	52	32	16	14	24	16	42	7,042
9	56	42	n/a	94	2	1	2	$39,011	51	35	14	12	24	17	48	6,603
STATE	57	41	1	86	8	1	4	$41,567	54	32	14	12	26	19	29	35,867
U.S.	47.9	48.4	3	69	12	4	13	$41,994	60	25	15	12	26	24	21	3,537,438

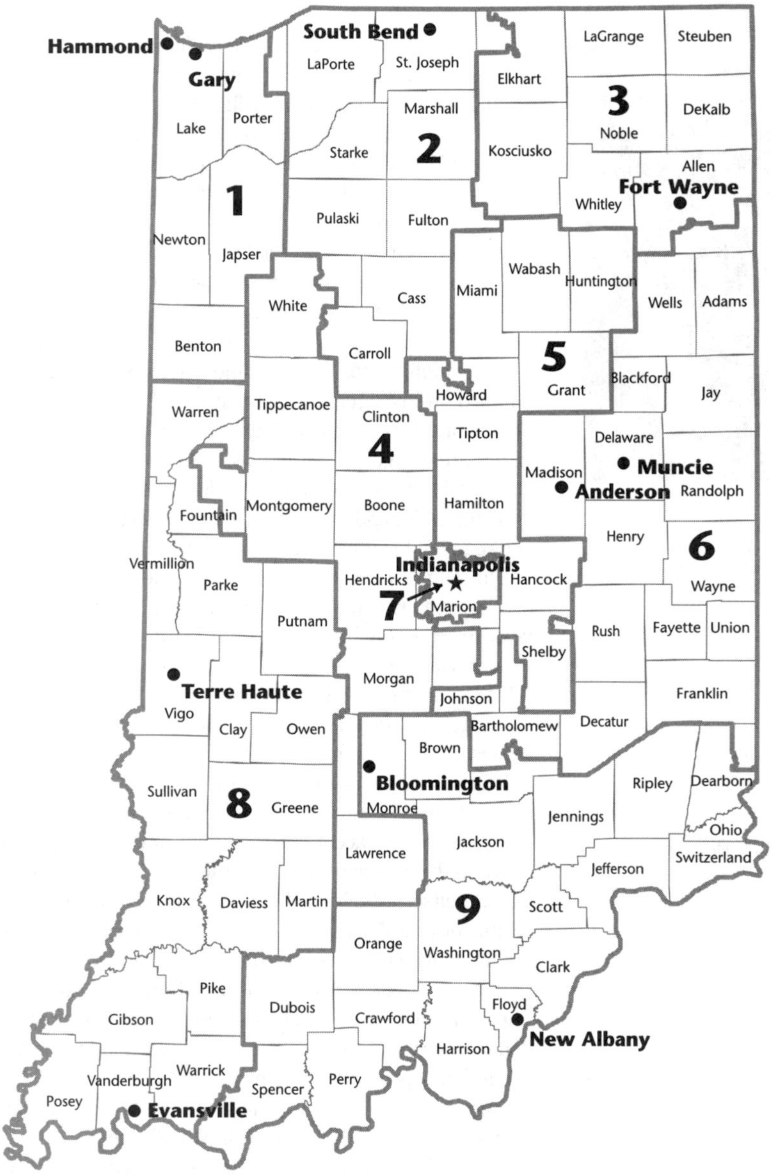
Hammond
Gary
South Bend
LaPorte
St. Joseph
Elkhart
LaGrange
Steuben
Lake
Porter
Marshall
3
DeKalb
Noble
Starke
2
Kosciusko
Allen
Fort Wayne
1
Whitley
Pulaski
Fulton
Newton
Japser
Wabash
Huntington
Miami
Cass
White
Wells
Adams
Benton
Carroll
5
Grant
Blackford
Howard
Jay
Warren
Tippecanoe
Clinton
Tipton
Delaware
4
Muncie
Madison
Anderson
Randolph
Fountain
Montgomery
Boone
Hamilton
Henry
6
Vermillion
Indianapolis
Hancock
Parke
Hendricks
Wayne
7
Marion
Putnam
Rush
Fayette
Union
Shelby
Morgan
Terre Haute
Johnson
Franklin
Vigo
Clay
Owen
Decatur
Bartholomew
Brown
Bloomington
Ripley
Dearborn
Sullivan
8
Greene
Monroe
Jennings
Ohio
Jackson
Lawrence
Switzerland
Jefferson
Knox
Daviess
Martin
9
Scott
Orange
Washington
Clark
Pike
Gibson
Dubois
Crawford
Floyd
New Albany
Harrison
Warrick
Perry
Vanderburgh
Spencer
Posey
Evansville

Sen. Richard G. Lugar (R)

CAPITOL OFFICE
224-4814
senator_lugar@lugar.senate.gov
lugar.senate.gov
306 Hart 20510-1401; fax 228-0360

COMMITTEES
Agriculture, Nutrition & Forestry
Foreign Relations - chairman

HOMETOWN
Indianapolis

BORN
April 4, 1932, Indianapolis, Ind.

RELIGION
Methodist

FAMILY
Wife, Charlene Lugar; four children

EDUCATION
Denison U., B.A. 1954; Oxford U., B.A., M.A. 1956 (Rhodes scholar)

MILITARY SERVICE
Navy, 1957-60

CAREER
Farm manager; manufacturing executive

POLITICAL HIGHLIGHTS
Indianapolis School Board, 1964-67; mayor of Indianapolis, 1968-75; Republican nominee for U.S. Senate, 1974; sought Republican nomination for president, 1996

ELECTION RESULTS

2000 GENERAL		
Richard G. Lugar (R)	1,427,944	66.6%
David L. Johnson (D)	683,273	31.9%
Paul Hager (LIBERT)	33,992	1.6%
2000 PRIMARY		
Richard G. Lugar (R)		unopposed

PREVIOUS WINNING PERCENTAGES
1994 (67%); 1988 (68%); 1982 (54%); 1976 (59%)

Elected 1976; 5th term

In 2003, Lugar got his chance to disprove the old cliche that "there are no second acts in American politics." For 16 years, he had waited to return as chairman of the Senate Foreign Relations Committee — a post he held in the 99th Congress of 1985-86. He was finally able to seize that opportunity after the 2002 election. The retirement of Republican Jesse Helms of North Carolina and the GOP takeover of the Senate allowed Lugar to reclaim a job he truly loves and in which he had won great acclaim — what he jokingly referred to as the "golden days."

In taking charge, Lugar made clear that he wants to spend the 108th Congress restoring the prestige of a panel whose luster has faded since the end of the Cold War. He has sought to have Congress pass a foreign assistance authorization bill for the first time since his previous chairmanship, move forward on his signature issue of nonproliferation, and probe deeply the Bush administration's handling of controversial foreign policy issues. It was an ambitious agenda for any lawmaker — and it was viewed as a particular stretch by some of Lugar's colleagues, who view him as too nice to be a strong leader and too moderate to keep pace with the Bush White House and many of his more conservative Senate colleagues.

But politics is an intellectual calling for Lugar, who cites his access to intelligence briefings and classified foreign policy documents as one of his favorite aspects of being a senator. Lugar has built his career on a serious, sober style that has cost him opportunities to ascend to higher office. But if his gold-plated résumé and a seemingly unending supply of navy blue suits have not propelled Lugar to the White House, or even to the Cabinet, he has earned high regard in the Senate.

With all the energy and self-discipline of a long-distance runner — in his early 70s, he still runs 12 to 15 miles a week — he has racked up a long and impressive list of accomplishments: Phi Beta Kappa at Denison University, where he was co-president of the student body with his wife-to-be, Charlene Smeltzer; Rhodes Scholar at Oxford; naval intelligence officer; popular mayor of Indianapolis; longest-serving senator in Indiana history; and architect of a landmark overhaul in federal agriculture policy.

Regarded as a virtual icon back home, Lugar manages to blend his Capitol Hill image as an elder statesman with a reputation for close attention to issues back home. While he admits that the intricacies of foreign policy do not capture the imagination of Indiana voters, his meticulous work on campaigns and his diligent attention to constituent service give him license to steer his own course in Washington.

"Most of my constituents are not interested in the specifics of foreign policy, or the leadership of the various countries . . . or really how policies flow," Lugar said in 2001. But because he places equal importance on the concerns of constituents, he added, "they have been prepared to give me a great deal of latitude to do the things that I think are important and interest me."

That latitude has allowed Lugar to be a witness to, and often a vital participant in, some of the most gripping foreign policy events of the past three decades. On foreign affairs and other issues, he has a reputation as an independent thinker who studies at length before taking a position and who then speaks his mind plainly, if rather woodenly.

When Lugar first chaired Foreign Relations, he was President Reagan's pick in 1986 to head a U.S. delegation monitoring the tumultuous Philippine election between President Ferdinand E. Marcos and challenger Corazon

C. Aquino. Lugar was an influential force in persuading Reagan that Marcos had stolen the election and should step down. That same year, Lugar also dealt Reagan one of his worst foreign policy defeats on Capitol Hill when he joined with Democrats to pass a measure imposing sanctions against South Africa. When Reagan vetoed the measure, Lugar led the effort for a successful override.

Lugar scored one of the most heralded U.S. foreign policy victories of the decade in 1991, when he and Sen. Sam Nunn, a Georgia Democrat, sponsored an initiative to dismantle thousands of nuclear weapons in the former Soviet Union. During its first 10 years, the program eliminated more than 5,000 Soviet nuclear warheads and earned Lugar and Nunn a nomination for the Nobel Peace Prize.

An unabashed proponent of a strong U.S. global presence, Lugar has advocated bold actions to bring about stable conditions around the world. During the Persian Gulf crisis of 1990-91, he gained national attention for suggesting that Iraqi leader Saddam Hussein "must either leave or be removed." Lugar supported President Bush's efforts to force a confrontation in 2001 with Saddam, but argued publicly and privately that the confrontation should occur through the United Nations.

Lugar's accomplishments and high-profile role in the foreign policy arena have come about in spite of political setbacks that have cost him chances to run for national office — and to take a more prominent Senate role during the late 1980s and early 1990s. When the GOP lost control of the Senate in the 1986 election, Helms asserted his seniority to take the top Republican spot on Foreign Relations, and Lugar lost a fight challenging the seniority system. Briefly considered as a vice presidential prospect in 1980, he was stung somewhat eight years later when the No. 2 spot on the ticket went to his junior Indiana colleague in the Senate, Dan Quayle. Lugar also ran an abbreviated presidential campaign in 1996 but was doomed by his dry manner, complex policy speeches and insistence on highlighting international, rather than domestic, issues.

As chairman of the Agriculture Committee from 1995 to 2001, however, he used his own experience as a farmer — for 46 years he has run a 604-acre corn, soybean and walnut tree farm that belonged to his father — to shape agriculture policy. The high point of his tenure there came in 1996, when he won enactment of a sweeping farm bill that replaced New Deal-era crop subsidies with a seven-year schedule of fixed payments, moving farmers toward a free-market system. But the dramatic changes in that law were largely undone by the new farm bill enacted in 2002.

Lugar is not averse to breaking from the GOP line. His environmental record is more moderate than that of many Senate Republicans, and he has supported some gun control legislation. The senator also has pushed to protect nutrition programs, such as food stamps and school lunches. But he rates as a solid conservative on most issues, favoring tax cuts and military spending and opposing abortion in most cases. In the 107th, he was the only senator to support President Bush 100 percent of the time — a reflection of his belief in a strong presidency vis-à-vis the Congress.

Lugar's long record of electoral success is remarkable, given his modest gifts as a campaigner. He meets crowds rather stiffly, and his style borders on lecturing. But he has always impressed Indiana voters as a man of substance. Even in 1974, running for the Senate in a Watergate-dominated year with a reputation as "Richard Nixon's favorite mayor," Lugar came within a respectable 75,000 votes of Democratic incumbent Birch Bayh (whose son, Evan, is now Indiana's junior senator). In 1976, against a much weaker Democratic incumbent, Vance Hartke, Lugar won handily, and he has been re-elected four times — the most in Indiana history.

KEY VOTES

2002

No Pass farm bill reversing crop subsidy limits
Yes Postpone tougher automobile fuel efficiency standards
Yes Overhaul campaign finance law; ban "soft money" and restrict advocacy advertising
Yes Set federal election standards
Yes Support oil drilling in Arctic National Wildlife Refuge
Yes Revive fast-track procedures for trade agreements
Yes Create federal insurance coverage for catastrophic terrorist losses
Yes Tighten federal accounting and corporate governance regulation
No Advance bipartisan Medicare prescription drug plan
No Create independent Sept. 11 commission
No Back Democratic Homeland Security Department proposal
Yes Authorize war against Iraq

2001

Yes Confirm John Ashcroft as attorney general
Yes Nullify Clinton Labor Department ergonomics rule
Yes Cut taxes by $1.35 trillion through fiscal 2011
No Pass Democratic bill to bolster rights of patients in managed-care plans
Yes Permit a new round of military base closings
Yes Expand law enforcement power to investigate suspected terrorists

CQ VOTE STUDIES

	PARTY UNITY		PRESIDENTIAL SUPPORT	
	Support	Oppose	Support	Oppose
2002	91%	9%	100%	0%
2001	92%	8%	100%	0%
2000	86%	14%	65%	35%
1999	88%	12%	40%	60%
1998	84%	16%	54%	46%
1997	83%	17%	62%	38%
1996	90%	10%	31%	69%
1995	92%	8%	28%	72%
1994	78%	22%	45%	55%
1993	88%	12%	34%	66%

INTEREST GROUPS

	AFL-CIO	ADA	CCUS	ACU
2002	31%	5%	95%	90%
2001	13%	15%	100%	92%
2000	0%	10%	100%	84%
1999	0%	5%	100%	88%
1998	0%	0%	94%	68%
1997	0%	30%	90%	64%
1996	0%	5%	85%	95%
1995	0%	5%	100%	77%
1994	0%	10%	90%	76%
1993	0%	10%	100%	72%

Sen. Evan Bayh (D)

CAPITOL OFFICE
224-5623
senator@bayh.senate.gov
bayh.senate.gov
463 Russell 20510-1404; fax 228-1377

COMMITTEES
Armed Services
Banking, Housing & Urban Affairs
Energy & Natural Resources
Small Business & Entrepreneurship
Select Intelligence
Special Aging

HOMETOWN
Indianapolis

BORN
Dec. 26, 1955, Shirkieville, Ind.

RELIGION
Episcopalian

FAMILY
Wife, Susan Bayh; two children

EDUCATION
Indiana U., B.S. 1978 (business economics); U. of Virginia, J.D. 1981

CAREER
Lawyer

POLITICAL HIGHLIGHTS
Ind. secretary of state, 1986-89; governor, 1989-97

ELECTION RESULTS

1998 GENERAL		
Evan Bayh (D)	1,012,244	63.7%
Paul Helmke (R)	552,732	34.8%
R. Sink-Burris (LIBERT)	23,641	1.5%
1998 PRIMARY		
Evan Bayh (D)		unopposed

Elected 1998; 1st term

Bayh is cut from the mold of the centrists who rose to prominence in Democratic politics in the 1990s. And as chairman of the Democratic Leadership Council — the primary affinity group for those trying to move the party away from its traditional liberalism — he is in a position to shape the policies that moderate Democrats will follow in the 2000s.

During his first Senate term, Bayh (BYE) has made a point of seeking compromises that blur party lines and partisan credit. Though his father, Birch, was one of the Senate's leading liberal voices during an 18-year career that ended in 1980, the younger Bayh is much more in tune with the Hoosier State's conservative bent. He says he always looks for the center, because that is where deals are made. Still, he has occasionally veered further to the right than some of his Democratic colleagues would like.

During the 2002 debate on whether to grant President Bush authority to attack Iraq, for example, Bayh joined forces with other defense hawks to push for adoption of a White House-backed resolution that recommended but did not require that Bush consult with the world community before taking action.

Along with Connecticut Democrat Joseph I. Lieberman, Arizona Republican John McCain and Virginia Republican John W. Warner, Bayh effectively halted efforts by Majority Leader Tom Daschle to win more concessions from the administration before the Senate vote.

Bayh was among the first Democrats to call for pre-emptive action against Iraq in order to prevent Saddam Hussein from developing weapons of mass destruction. "They're waiting for a threat to materialize," he said of those who urged caution. "I'm not sure we'll find a smoking gun here, but if we wait until it's cocked and loaded, it's probably too late."

Bayh, who got a seat on the Armed Services Committee in the 108th Congress to complement his assignment to Intelligence, suggested in 2002 that the United States might want to lift its ban on assassinations in order to go after Iraq's leader. Such views sit well with Indiana's senior senator, Republican Richard G. Lugar, who says Bayh is easy to work with because their politics are not that far apart. In fact, in Indiana, Bayh's moderate politics have earned him the moniker of "Republicrat."

Still, Bayh does not always disagree with the Democratic mainstream. He was one of the first to oppose Bush's choice of John Ashcroft to be attorney general, saying, "He will bring some of his more strident views to bear in that office in ways that will cause great confrontation and controversy." Bayh was also an early critic of the president's $1.6 trillion, 10-year tax cut plan, and he voted against the $1.35 trillion version ultimately enacted in 2001.

In 2002, he voted with the majority of Democrats to remove a series of provisions — inserted at the last minute by House Republicans — in the measure that established the Homeland Security Department. Even though a major beneficiary, Eli Lilly and Co., is one of Indiana's most important corporate forces, Bayh sought to remove provisions that would insulate vaccine-makers from lawsuits.

Bayh generally takes a cautious approach to his politics. He tends to inch ahead rather than rush forward, preferring to examine all sides of an issue carefully before taking a stand. His floor speeches are rare and prosaic affairs, filled with calls for compromise and a reliance on "Hoosier values." While many fellow senators gave impassioned speeches just before voting on President Clinton's fate in the 1999 impeachment trial, Bayh, who voted to acquit, delivered remarks that sounded like a legal brief.

Critics say that caution comes from his attempts to accumulate political capital rather than risk his neck on bold substantive initiatives. "I'll never have the political capital or popularity of Evan Bayh," Indiana state Rep. Mark Kruzan, a Democrat, told The Indianapolis Star in 1996, when Bayh was ending his two terms as governor. "But I've often sensed that polling information and pressure from advisers was helping to steer the ship."

Bayh is a believer in accountability, both institutional and personal. He has been a forceful advocate of boosting federal spending to education but tying the aid to performance, and he pressed legislation designed to promote responsible fatherhood. "Hundreds of thousands of young men," he said in 2001, "bring children into the world and walk away from one of the most profound responsibilities that anyone could ever take on."

After the Sept. 11, 2001, terrorist attacks, Bayh used his seat on the Banking Committee to spearhead enactment of a law allowing the government to track and regulate terrorist financing that used an informal system of brokers known as a "hawala." And he championed provisions in a bioterrorism law that helped states fund their bioterror response plans. But his opposition to using the war on terrorism as an excuse to inflate spending bills led him to vote against most of the spending bills passed at the end of 2001.

On other fronts, Bayh has championed legislation, which became law, aimed at protecting senior citizens from fraud — including deceptive sweepstakes offers, investment schemes and telemarketing come-ons.

Bayh's movie-star good looks and cross-party appeal keep his favorability ratings high back home in Indiana. That in turn drives speculation that his sights will someday turn on the White House. He briefly considered a 2004 campaign but concluded his twin sons were too young for him to be an absent father for the better part of two years.

Many say Bayh's path to the Senate had been charted for years. Born in the small town of Shirkieville, he moved to Washington at age 7, when his father was elected to the Senate. While attending the elite St. Albans School, among his babysitters was Lynda Bird Johnson, the president's older daughter. Bayh met his wife, Susan, while she was a summer intern for the House Ways and Means Committee. Bayh's most important political setback came early; while in law school, he managed his father's losing campaign for a fourth term in 1980, when he was swept out in the Reagan landslide.

After clerking for a federal judge and practicing law, at age 30 Bayh was elected Indiana secretary of state. Two years later, in 1988, he became the youngest governor in the nation and stayed popular for eight years, in part by riding the crest of a robust economy.

He delivered the keynote address at the 1996 Democratic convention and, term-limited as governor at the end of that year, began readying his Senate campaign for two years thence. GOP incumbent Daniel R. Coats decided to retire rather than face Bayh, and in November Bayh trounced Mayor Paul Helmke of Fort Wayne by a nearly 2-to-1 margin.

Bayh briefly considered mounting a bid to return to the governor's mansion in 2004 but then decided to seek to stay in Washington, notwithstanding the severe damages to his family's home in a 2002 fire.

Bayh's Senate security clearance did him no good when he sought to coach his sons' basketball team and was told he would have to be fingerprinted and undergo background checks from two law enforcement agencies. "What's good enough for the CIA, NSA and FBI isn't good enough for the YMCA," he told the Indianapolis Star.

KEY VOTES

2002

Yes Pass farm bill reversing crop subsidy limits
Yes Postpone tougher automobile fuel efficiency standards
Yes Overhaul campaign finance law; ban "soft money" and restrict advocacy advertising
Yes Set federal election standards
No Support oil drilling in Arctic National Wildlife Refuge
Yes Revive fast-track procedures for trade agreements
Yes Create federal insurance coverage for catastrophic terrorist losses
Yes Tighten federal accounting and corporate governance regulation
Yes Advance bipartisan Medicare prescription drug plan
Yes Create independent Sept. 11 commission
Yes Back Democratic Homeland Security Department proposal
Yes Authorize war against Iraq

2001

No Confirm John Ashcroft as attorney general
No Nullify Clinton Labor Department ergonomics rule
No Cut taxes by $1.35 trillion through fiscal 2011
Yes Pass Democratic bill to bolster rights of patients in managed-care plans
Yes Permit a new round of military base closings
Yes Expand law enforcement power to investigate suspected terrorists

CQ VOTE STUDIES

	PARTY UNITY		PRESIDENTIAL SUPPORT	
	Support	Oppose	Support	Oppose
2002	70%	30%	79%	21%
2001	82%	18%	69%	31%
2000	92%	8%	98%	2%
1999	88%	12%	89%	11%

INTEREST GROUPS

	AFL-CIO	ADA	CCUS	ACU
2002	85%	70%	65%	30%
2001	100%	100%	50%	32%
2000	75%	80%	60%	16%
1999	89%	90%	59%	12%

Rep. Peter J. Visclosky (D)

CAPITOL OFFICE
225-2461
www.house.gov/visclosky
2313 Rayburn 20515-1401; fax 225-2493

COMMITTEES
Appropriations

HOMETOWN
Merrillville

BORN
Aug. 13, 1949, Gary, Ind.

RELIGION
Roman Catholic

FAMILY
Divorced; two children

EDUCATION
Indiana U. Northwest, B.S. 1970 (accounting); U. of Notre Dame, J.D. 1973; Georgetown U., LL.M. 1982

CAREER
Lawyer; congressional aide

POLITICAL HIGHLIGHTS
No previous office

ELECTION RESULTS

2002 GENERAL		
Peter J. Visclosky (D)	90,443	66.9%
Mark J. Leyva (R)	41,909	31.0%
Timothy P. Brennan (LIBERT)	2,759	2.0%
2002 PRIMARY		
Peter J. Visclosky (D)	57,099	85.6%
Ralph Spelbring (D)	9,621	14.4%
2000 GENERAL		
Peter J. Visclosky (D)	148,683	71.6%
Jack Reynolds (R)	56,200	27.1%
Christopher Nelson (LIBERT)	2,907	1.4%

PREVIOUS WINNING PERCENTAGES
1998 (73%); 1996 (69%); 1994 (56%); 1992 (69%); 1990 (66%); 1988 (77%); 1986 (73%); 1984 (71%)

Elected 1984; 10th term

During almost two decades as a congressman, nothing has stirred the passions of the otherwise low-key Visclosky nearly so much as issues related to the steel industry. Though steel-making jobs in northwestern Indiana have plummeted from about 70,000 two decades ago to fewer than half as many now, Visclosky's blue-collar district produces more steel than any other area in the nation.

As vice chairman of the Congressional Steel Caucus, Visclosky (vis-KLOSS-key) has pushed legislation under which the government would help pay the health and pension costs of steel company retirees. In the 107th Congress he urged President Bush to place tariffs of 40 percent on foreign steel imports, saying anything less would be "meaningless and unacceptable" — before the president imposed lesser tariffs. Visclosky also has generally opposed trade liberalization: He voted in 1993 against the North American Free Trade Agreement, in 2000 against making China a permanent normal U.S. trade partner, and in 2001 against reviving fast-track procedures for congressional action on trade deals.

After the Sept. 11, 2001, terrorist attacks, Visclosky said a weakened steel industry could undermine the nation's national security. "It is those specialty steels made by the domestic steel industry that are necessary for those nuclear-attack submarines and those armored vehicles," he said on the House floor. "Unfortunately, we have an industry in distress."

Visclosky's other abiding interest in Congress is leveraging his seniority on the Appropriations Committee to deliver money for Indiana transportation and infrastructure projects. His secondary legislative priorities have included crime-fighting efforts, bids to accelerate the servicing of the national debt and local action to permit floating casinos in Gary, his district's population center, in hopes of spurring more lakeshore development.

Visclosky is a Catholic seminary drop-out who later went on to complete two degrees at Catholic institutions, Notre Dame and Georgetown. He has spent most of his adult life in politics. After finishing law school in 1973 at Notre Dame, he linked his fortunes to Adam Benjamin Jr., then a state senator and rising political star in Indiana. Visclosky coordinated Benjamin's successful campaign for Congress in 1976 and served as one of his top aides in Washington for the next six years.

When Benjamin died in September 1982, Democrats were without a candidate for the November election. As the 1st District Democratic chairman, Richard G. Hatcher — Gary's longtime mayor — was in a position to choose the Democratic nominee, and he picked Katie Hall, a state senator and loyal ally. She won easily but when she sought renomination in 1984, Visclosky and another candidate challenged her.

Visclosky put on dozens of $2 "dog and bean" dinners to attract the young, the elderly and the unemployed. His "Slovak kid" background helped, as did the memory that older voters had of the candidate's father, John, Gary's mayor in 1962 and 1963. Visclosky bested Hall in the primary by 2 percentage points, then swamped the Republican in November. He has had little trouble winning his subsequent nine re-elections.

Visclosky's low-key approach and sharp focus on a shortlist of issues keeps him out of the spotlight. The one committee to which he belongs, Appropriations, generally works in a bipartisan fashion. A detail-minded legislator, he is devoted to the idea that politics is about resolving disputes through discussion and compromise. And he is an unassuming man whose infrequent floor speeches are likely to be tributes to people back home or to a civic organization.

Still, Visclosky is the only Hoosier on an Appropriations panel, so the other 10 members of the Indiana delegation look to him to see that their spending priorities are taken care of as well as his own. In the 107th, he sought millions of dollars for improvements to the Gary/Chicago Airport to help make it a more viable alternative to crowded O'Hare and Midway airports in Chicago. He also pushed for money to upgrade the Chicago, South Shore and South Bend Railroad lines. In 2000, Visclosky claimed credit for winning allocations worth tens of millions of dollars for projects in his district.

From his first day in the House, a slot on Appropriations was Visclosky's goal, as he sought to follow in Benjamin's footsteps. Visclosky made it onto the panel in October 1991 — six years, nine months and nine days after he made his first bid for such an appointment, Visclosky later recalled, revealing just how focused he was on the goal.

In his quest to deter crime in the 1st District, historically known as one of the most dangerous areas in the Midwest, Visclosky got northwest Indiana designated as a High Intensity Drug Trafficking Area. He obtained money to fight the flow of drugs and gang violence in Gary, Hammond and East Chicago. He worked to arrange for the Indiana National Guard to help tear down neighborhood crack houses.

In the 104th Congress, Visclosky secured funds to provide 600 bulletproof vests to northwest Indiana law enforcement officers. Then, learning the problem was a national one — an estimated 25 percent of U.S. police officers do not have access to vests — Visclosky in 1998 joined with New Jersey Republican Frank A. LoBiondo to authorize a new Justice Department grant program and has worked to keep funding forthcoming.

In representing his reliably Democratic district, Visclosky generally votes the party line. But he is a fiscal conservative who breaks with his leadership on some budgetary matters. He supported a balanced-budget constitutional amendment and was among the few lawmakers who pressed for strict enforcement mechanisms to ensure that the 1997 balanced-budget agreement was faithfully implemented. Visclosky declares that the government has "a moral responsibility" to balance the budget.

He also has shown a conservative bent on some social issues, such as his support of a ban on a procedure its opponents call "partial birth" abortion, although earlier he had voted against the ban. He opposed the GOP's initial welfare overhaul legislation, but backed the final compromise President Clinton signed in 1996 over some liberal Democrats' objections.

KEY VOTES

2002

Yes Overhaul campaign finance law; ban "soft money" and restrict advocacy advertising
Yes Back Bush's defense budget increase
No Extend 1996 welfare law
No Adopt Bush's discretionary spending limit
No Pass GOP Medicare prescription drug plan
Yes Create independent Sept. 11 commission
Yes Extend union protections to Homeland Security Department employees
No Revive fast-track procedures for trade agreements
No Authorize war against Iraq
No Advance bankruptcy overhaul opposed by abortion opponents

2001

No Nullify Clinton Labor Department ergonomics rule
No Cut taxes by $1.35 trillion through fiscal 2011
Yes Maintain ban on oil drilling in Arctic National Wildlife Refuge
No Approve Bush proposal to limit managed-care plan liability for coverage decisions
? Divert money from crop subsidy payments to land conservation
No Expand law enforcement power to investigate suspected terrorists

CQ VOTE STUDIES

	PARTY UNITY		PRESIDENTIAL SUPPORT	
	Support	Oppose	Support	Oppose
2002	92%	8%	22%	78%
2001	86%	14%	33%	67%
2000	92%	8%	75%	25%
1999	87%	13%	77%	23%
1998	83%	17%	79%	21%

INTEREST GROUPS

	AFL-CIO	ADA	CCUS	ACU
2002	100%	90%	35%	12%
2001	100%	85%	39%	17%
2000	100%	75%	33%	12%
1999	100%	95%	4%	12%
1998	100%	80%	28%	12%

INDIANA 1
Northwest — Gary, Hammond

Bordered to the north by Lake Michigan and to the west by Illinois, the 1st is home to steelworkers and large union and minority populations that offer Democrats solid support. More steel is produced here than in any other district in the nation — more than 30,000 steelworkers reside in Gary, Hammond and East Chicago. Most of the 1st's population lives in the far northwest corner, where more than 80 percent of Gary residents are black and more than half of East Chicago residents are Hispanic. The 1st also is home to many Eastern European ethnic neighborhoods.

Residents around Gary still struggle with the effects of unemployment, suburban flight and urban decay that began when the steel industry took a dive in the early 1980s. As recently as 1970, Gary and Fort Wayne (located in the 3rd) were equal in population. Thirty years later, Gary had only half the population of Fort Wayne.

Another crisis hit in 1998 when cheap, imported steel flooded the U.S. market in record amounts. At least one steel company went out of business and there were thousands of layoffs. The district has attracted some lake boat gambling, but so far it is not a replacement for steel's place in the economy.

Democrats carry congressional and presidential elections by strong margins. Republicans have a meager base in growing Porter County and in Lake County suburbs such as Crown Point and Merrillville, where an influx of white Chicago commuters has raised incomes.

Redistricting following the 2000 census added southern Lake County and three rural counties, and altered the district's portion of Porter County.

MAJOR INDUSTRY
Steel, manufacturing, gaming

CITIES
Gary, 102,746; Hammond, 83,048; Portage, 33,496; East Chicago, 32,414; Merrillville, 30,560; Valparaiso (pt.), 27,362; Hobart, 25,363; Schererville, 24,851; Highland, 23,546

NOTABLE
Indiana Dunes National Lakeshore; Singer Michael Jackson was raised in Gary; John Dillinger's infamous jailbreak occurred in Crown Point.

Rep. Chris Chocola (R)

Elected 2002; 1st term

Few House freshmen are likely to be as supportive of President Bush as Chocola, who benefited from two presidential campaign visits in 2002 en route to defeating a former congresswoman, Democrat Jill Long Thompson, for Indiana's open 2nd District seat.

Chocola (cha-KO-luh), who had never held political office before, said he intends to "bring some real-life experience to Washington." His seats on the Agriculture and Small Business committees allow him to draw on his background as a former CEO and chairman of CTB International Corp., which makes feeding, water and storage systems for the poultry, egg, pork and grain industries.

Chocola follows a fairly conservative line on economic and social policy. He says his top priority is to help make the Bush tax cuts permanent. Although he identifies himself as a free-trade supporter, as a candidate he backed Bush's decision in 2001 to impose tariffs on foreign steel imports. That position played well in a district where steel employment has declined in part because of foreign competition.

Several road construction projects, including an upgrade of the highway between South Bend and Indianapolis, are high on Chocola's priority list, and he sought, and won, a seat on the Transportation Committee to further those goals.

Chocola's near-upset in 2000 of veteran Democratic Rep. Tim Roemer set the stage for his successful campaign in 2002. Shortly after Roemer announced in January 2001 that he would not seek a seventh term, Chocola declared his candidacy.

Chocola managed to win despite a redistricting map that shifted some Republican-voting areas from Roemer's conservative-leaning district and put Chocola's Elkhart County home just outside the district line.

Thompson, who as Jill Long had represented a northeastern Indiana district from 1989 to 1995, attacked Chocola for supporting a system of private accounts under Social Security, calling it an effort to privatize the program. But Bush's popularity helped boost Chocola to a 5 percentage point victory.

CAPITOL OFFICE
225-3915
www.house.gov/chocola
510 Cannon 20515-1402; fax 225-6798

COMMITTEES
Agriculture
Small Business
Transportation & Infrastructure

HOMETOWN
Bristol

BORN
Feb. 24, 1962, Jackson, Mich.

RELIGION
Presbyterian

FAMILY
Wife, Sarah Chocola; two children

EDUCATION
Hillsdale College, B.A. 1984 (business administration & political economy); Thomas M. Cooley Law School, J.D. 1988

CAREER
Agricultural manufacturing company executive; lawyer; cleaning materials company credit manager; foreign exchange trader

POLITICAL HIGHLIGHTS
Republican nominee for U.S. House, 2000

ELECTION RESULTS

2002 GENERAL		
Chris Chocola (R)	95,081	50.5%
Jill Long Thompson (D)	86,253	45.8%
Sharon Metheny (LIBERT)	7,112	3.8%
2002 PRIMARY		
Chris Chocola (R)	30,176	78.2%
Lewis Farmer Hass (R)	8,417	21.8%

INDIANA 2

North central – South Bend, parts of Elkhart and Kokomo

The 2nd touches a southeastern corner of Lake Michigan and stretches across Indiana's northern border, but also drops south to Kokomo. Traditionally a politically competitive area, it has been considered a barometer of national political trends.

The district takes in St. Joseph County (South Bend), which is home to an ideologically diverse and economically disparate population. Here, the wealthy, Catholic Notre Dame community is joined by low-income, minority populations downtown, as well as blue-collar communities east of the city. Farther west, Michigan City's steel-producing areas and blue-collar La Porte provide solid Democratic support.

Farming and business in Elkhart County (shared with the 3rd) — a national center for the manufactured housing industry — create a faithful conservative constituency. Elkhart's large Amish population helps make it the state's leading milk producer.

The 2nd takes in some rural, Republican-leaning counties in north-central Indiana. Redistricting following the 2000 census extended the district (numbered the 3rd in the 1990s) south to Kokomo in Howard County. Kokomo (shared with the 5th) is dependent on the automobile industry, with Delphi and Daimler Chrysler as the area's dominant employers, and has a working-class, Democratic orientation. The 2nd is less GOP-leaning than the old 3rd, but George W. Bush won it by 9 points in the 2000 presidential election.

MAJOR INDUSTRY
Manufacturing, higher education, agriculture

CITIES
South Bend, 107,789; Elkhart (pt.), 48,783; Mishawaka, 46,557; Michigan City, 32,900

NOTABLE
The College Football Hall of Fame and Studebaker National Museum are located in South Bend.

Rep. Mark Souder (R)

CAPITOL OFFICE
225-4436
souder@mail.house.gov
www.house.gov/souder
1227 Longworth 20515-1403; fax 225-3479

COMMITTEES
Government Reform
(Criminal Justice, Drug Policy & Human Resources - chairman)
Resources
Select Homeland Security

HOMETOWN
Fort Wayne

BORN
July 18, 1950, Fort Wayne, Ind.

RELIGION
Evangelical

FAMILY
Wife, Diane Souder; three children

EDUCATION
Indiana U., B.S. 1972 (business administration); Notre Dame, M.B.A. 1974

CAREER
Congressional aide; furniture company executive; general store owner

POLITICAL HIGHLIGHTS
No previous office

ELECTION RESULTS

2002 GENERAL		
Mark Souder (R)	92,566	63.1%
Jay Rigdon (D)	50,509	34.5%
Michael Donlan (LIBERT)	3,531	2.4%
2002 PRIMARY		
Mark Souder (R)	53,186	59.6%
Paul Helmke (R)	33,038	37.0%
William R. Larsen (R)	3,079	3.5%
2000 GENERAL		
Mark Souder (R)	131,051	62.3%
Mike Foster (D)	74,492	35.4%
Michael Donlan (LIBERT)	4,887	2.3%

PREVIOUS WINNING PERCENTAGES
1998 (63%); 1996 (58%); 1994 (55%)

Elected 1994; 5th term

Souder was a compassionate conservative before George W. Bush made it cool to be a compassionate conservative. He is far right in ideology but tackles issues that traditionally have belonged to the left, such as helping the less fortunate and combating drug abuse. "If you scratch behind any of my positions, you find my religious beliefs," Souder says.

As a result, it is hard to typecast Souder (rhymes with NOW-dur). His positions are sometimes unpredictable and are always influenced by his Christian faith. It is not contradictory in Souder's world therefore to bolt GOP orthodoxy and vote with Democrats for tougher environmental laws. "As a Christian, part of what you do is be a steward of all creation," he says.

Similarly, he is an enthusiastic backer of Israel in the Middle East conflict — even though he shares his constituents' skepticism about foreign aid in general — because in the Bible, God promised land to Abraham and his descendants, the Jews.

Souder was not an early or vocal supporter of Bush's presidential bid, and he bucked the White House on elements of the president's faith-based charity legislation and education bill in the 107th Congress. He and other conservatives were especially resistant to Bush's proposed mandate for annual progress tests in public schools. Such tests, they argued, would be the first step toward a nationally mandated curriculum, one possibly hostile to a Biblical interpretation of man's origins. But Souder fell into line and voted for the final versions of both bills.

A wonkish and amiable personality, Souder immerses himself in the details of his issues and so is rarely caught flat-footed on the facts. His passion for policy, however, has not translated into leadership roles. He has no appetite for the year-round fundraising demanded of leaders. "I don't like to raise money, and I never will," Souder says. "I'd much rather read a book, read a bill or sit through a three-hour hearing."

A former congressional aide, he is content to work behind the scenes to keep nudging the leadership his way. "You don't have to be in leadership to determine the health care plan at the margins," Souder says. "There are multiple ways to lead."

Souder, who came to the House with the radicalized Class of 1994, notes that in spite of frequent setbacks, conservatives scored significant victories in recent years in changing the welfare system and slashing federal income taxes. "If you're expecting in government dramatic changes constantly, you'll be frustrated," he says. "If you capitalize on key moments of transition in politics, you'll move government."

Souder's work on the president's faith-based charities initiative in the 107th likewise produced incremental results for the religious right. The bill was intended to remove barriers preventing religiously influenced groups from getting federal money for their programs helping the disadvantaged and the poor. Souder had argued privately to the White House that the original proposal was too ambitious and urged early compromise with liberal Democrats and civil rights groups. When Bush decided to press ahead, Souder fought for the president's plan. The final version, Souder says, "may not have as much impact, but it sets the principles."

He also lost a battle with the White House over federally mandated testing. As a member of the Education and the Workforce Committee, Souder opposed a central element of the president's education bill requiring public school students to take annual math and reading tests.

Long active in anti-drug efforts, Souder chairs the Government Reform Subcommittee on Criminal Justice, Drug Policy and Human Resources. He supports interdiction, but he also believes the federal government should fund prevention programs. He has averaged one trip a year to Colombia for the last eight years.

In the 108th Congress he got a seat on the new Homeland Security panel charged with overseeing the newly created Cabinet department; he had to give up his Education seat.

The Souders were among the earliest settlers of Allen County, Ind., in the 1840s. The family's original harness shop grew into a series of family businesses in Grabill that made the Souder name well-known. The modern-day Souders, mostly religious conservatives, were generally not inclined to step into the temporal realm of politics. That changed the day Sen. Daniel R. Coats, another Indiana conservative, dropped in at the family store to buy some furniture.

Coats, then a member of the House, believed in ideas that appealed to Souder, such as using the tax code to further conservative causes. In 1984, Souder became Coats' staff director on the Select Committee on Children, Youth and Families and later was deputy chief of staff in Coats' Senate office.

In 1994, Souder decided to run for Coats' former House seat. He faced a tough, six-candidate primary. All the major contenders in the GOP field that year were staunchly conservative, and Souder's low-key demeanor made him appear less hard-line.

After winning the primary, Souder went on the attack early, starting with summer radio ads that portrayed the incumbent, Democratic Rep. Jill L. Long, as a Washington insider beholden to special interests. Souder also made every attempt to tie Long to the Clinton administration. The strategy paid off; he beat Long by 11 percentage points.

Souder's declaration in 1998 that he opposed impeaching President Clinton earned him a serious primary opponent in 2000. (He said Clinton should be prosecuted as a private citizen.) Souder eventually bested Allen County chief deputy prosecutor Michael Loomis with 62 percent of the vote; he garnered 62 percent in the general election as well.

He attracted serious primary competition again in 2002, this time as a result of redistricting. The new map threw 200,000 new people into the 4th District. Though it remained heavily Republican, former Fort Wayne Mayor Paul Helmke decided to oppose Souder, presenting him with a challenger with name identification nearly as high as his own. However, Souder won the nomination by a healthy margin and cruised to re-election in November.

KEY VOTES

2002

- No Overhaul campaign finance law; ban "soft money" and restrict advocacy advertising
- Yes Back Bush's defense budget increase
- Yes Extend 1996 welfare law
- Yes Adopt Bush's discretionary spending limit
- Yes Pass GOP Medicare prescription drug plan
- No Create independent Sept. 11 commission
- No Extend union protections to Homeland Security Department employees
- Yes Revive fast-track procedures for trade agreements
- Yes Authorize war against Iraq
- No Advance bankruptcy overhaul opposed by abortion opponents

2001

- Yes Nullify Clinton Labor Department ergonomics rule
- Yes Cut taxes by $1.35 trillion through fiscal 2011
- No Maintain ban on oil drilling in Arctic National Wildlife Refuge
- Yes Approve Bush proposal to limit managed-care plan liability for coverage decisions
- No Divert money from crop subsidy payments to land conservation
- Yes Expand law enforcement power to investigate suspected terrorists

CQ VOTE STUDIES

	PARTY UNITY		PRESIDENTIAL SUPPORT	
	Support	Oppose	Support	Oppose
2002	94%	6%	89%	11%
2001	96%	4%	86%	14%
2000	91%	9%	19%	81%
1999	94%	6%	16%	84%
1998	90%	10%	25%	75%

INTEREST GROUPS

	AFL-CIO	ADA	CCUS	ACU
2002	11%	10%	85%	88%
2001	9%	10%	91%	96%
2000	10%	10%	71%	88%
1999	33%	5%	80%	80%
1998	20%	15%	76%	83%

INDIANA 3
Northeast – Fort Wayne

Agricultural communities with deep-rooted religious beliefs shape the character of the 3rd, a solidly Republican district in Indiana's northeast corner. The district's long tradition of social conservatism begins in the large Amish communities to the northwest, which are not overtly politically active but form and reflect the area's traditional values. Rural voters bolster the state's Republican leanings.

The 3rd's population center is Allen County, which includes Fort Wayne and accounts for nearly half of the district population. Fort Wayne, the state's most populous city after Indianapolis, has white-collar suburban neighborhoods and German-Americans that cement the 3rd's conservative loyalties. Like many midsize Midwestern cities, Fort Wayne has a substantial manufacturing sector. While the surrounding area has lost thousands of manufacturing jobs since the late 1990s, the region has been cushioned somewhat by a strong white-collar service sector. Technology and financial-service jobs have attracted professionals into Allen County, which had a slightly higher growth rate in the 1990s than Indiana at large. Noble County, northwest of Allen, grew by 22 percent in the 1990s.

After Allen, the district's next most populous counties are Elkhart (shared with the 2nd) and Kosciusko, which were added to the 3rd in redistricting following the 2000 census. Both counties are solidly conservative: Kosciusko gave George W. Bush a statewide high of 76 percent of the vote in the 2000 election. East of Elkhart is LaGrange County, where nearly one-third of residents speak a language at home other than English; the county's Amish population speaks a German dialect.

Democrats find support in minority and blue-collar neighborhoods in Fort Wayne, but little backing elsewhere. In 2000, George W. Bush won every county in the 3rd with at least 60 percent of the vote.

MAJOR INDUSTRY

Manufacturing, agriculture, health care

CITIES

Fort Wayne (pt.), 202,769; Goshen, 26,611

NOTABLE

Author and naturalist Gene Stratton-Porter's former home is a state historical site on Sylvan Lake in Noble County.

Rep. Steve Buyer (R)

CAPITOL OFFICE
225-5037
www.house.gov/buyer
2230 Rayburn 20515-1404; fax 225-2267

COMMITTEES
Energy & Commerce
Veterans' Affairs
(Oversight & Investigations - chairman)

HOMETOWN
Monticello

BORN
Nov. 26, 1958, Rensselaer, Ind.

RELIGION
Methodist

FAMILY
Wife, Joni Buyer; two children

EDUCATION
The Citadel, B.S. 1980 (business administration); Valparaiso U., J.D. 1984

MILITARY SERVICE
Army Reserve, 1980-84; Army, 1984-87; Army Reserve, 1987-present

CAREER
Lawyer; Army prosecutor

POLITICAL HIGHLIGHTS
No previous office

ELECTION RESULTS

2002 GENERAL		
Steve Buyer (R)	112,760	71.4%
Bill Abbott (D)	41,314	26.2%
Jerry L. Susong (LIBERT)	3,934	2.5%
2002 PRIMARY		
Steve Buyer (R)	44,608	54.6%
Brian Kerns (R)	24,443	29.9%
Michael R. Young (R)	6,605	8.1%
Thomas J. Herr (R)	2,684	3.3%
Tim Baynard (R)	1,754	2.2%
Bob Smith (R)	1,589	2.0%
2000 GENERAL		
Steve Buyer (R)	132,051	60.9%
Greg Goodnight (D)	81,427	37.5%
Scott Benson (LIBERT)	3,507	1.6%

PREVIOUS WINNING PERCENTAGES
1998 (63%); 1996 (65%); 1994 (70%); 1992 (51%)

Elected 1992; 6th term

After a decade in Washington, Buyer is known as a tough-talking conservative who enjoys sparring with liberals on abortion, gun control or whatever else is the most polarizing issue of the moment. He was picked in 1998 by Speaker Newt Gingrich to rally somewhat reluctant House Republicans for their impeachment crusade against President Clinton, and he remained defiant when the effort fell short the next year.

At the Senate trial, Buyer (BOO-yer) was one of the 13 "managers" who unsuccessfully argued the House's case that Clinton should be removed from office for perjury and obstruction of justice. Three years later, Buyer says, Democrats were still seeking payback, as demonstrated by what he calls the mean-spirited dismantling of his old congressional territory in a redistricting process controlled by Indiana Democrats.

"They even took away where I grew up," Buyer says. (It is Liberty Township, less than 10 miles from where he now lives.) "No one in my family can vote for me."

But Buyer's often pugnacious partisanship puts off many. Late in 2000, with the presidential outcome hanging in the balance, Buyer spent nine days in Florida pressing local officials to count military ballots mailed from overseas, most of which were presumed to be for George W. Bush and many of which had been ruled invalid on technical grounds. Florida Democratic Rep. Peter Deutsch filed a complaint with the House ethics committee, alleging that Buyer had used his contacts with the Pentagon to obtain information on military absentee voters and had then given the records to Florida Republican officials. The complaint against Buyer was dismissed, but the panel concluded that a congressional aide had improperly relayed information.

Buyer has learned, however, to reach across the aisle to achieve his legislative goals. In the 106th Congress, Buyer was chairman of the Armed Services Subcommittee on Military Personnel. He played a pivotal role — with bipartisan support — in the enactment of pay raises, a more generous retirement system and an expanded health care system for military retirees. The package helped to boost military morale.

As the 107th Congress opened, Buyer took the unusual step of giving up his seniority on Armed Services and starting over at the bottom of the ladder on the Energy and Commerce Committee. He did win permission to keep his seat on Veterans' Affairs, where he chairs the Oversight and Investigations Subcommittee.

Buyer said he wanted to switch committees because he had accomplished three major goals on Armed Services — altering the military's retirement system, changing its pay tables and creating the Tricare for Life health care and prescription drug benefit. He said he wanted to apply his experience with military health care issues to the array of health concerns under Energy and Commerce's jurisdiction.

Buyer came to Congress fresh from duty with the Army Reserve in the Persian Gulf War, where he was a lawyer providing legal advice on the treatment of prisoners, detained civilians and refugees. In 2003, Buyer, still in the reserves, got notice that he would be called to active duty in the second conflict against Iraq. But the Pentagon decided that his presence in the region would cause too many security problems and his activation was canceled.

Buyer was near an Iraqi munitions depot that U.S. forces destroyed in 1991, and he suffered ill health for years afterward. He told a Capitol Hill hearing and news conference in 1993 that a month after he returned home from the gulf, he noticed he could not jog short distances "without feeling exhausted." He also had kidney problems and two cases of pneumonia and spent much of the last month of the 1992 campaign in bed. In 2000, Buyer was notified by the Defense Department that he likely had been exposed to chemical agents that drifted in the smoke cloud from the depot.

Buyer's father, brother and sister are dentists, but he majored in business administration at The Citadel, the military college of South Carolina. By coincidence, however, his first posting in the Army was with a medical detachment, where he was assigned to the dental clinic.

Buyer's active duty was deferred while he attended law school in Indiana. He became an Army lawyer, first on active duty and then as a reservist. He was called to serve in the Persian Gulf War in 1990 on three days' notice.

Soon after he returned, Buyer decided to run for Congress against three-term Democrat Jim Jontz. "When I came back home," he once told a church congregation, "I saw things happening with my country that bothered me deeply, and I could either sit back and complain about it or get off my duff and do something about it." Buyer criticized Jontz's vote against giving President George Bush authority to commit troops to the gulf. He also drew attention to Jontz's four overdrafts at the private bank for House members. His 4,500-vote win was among the biggest House race upsets of 1992. Buyer won easily in his first four re-elections.

Reapportionment after the 2000 census took one House seat away from Indiana, however, forcing a substantial redrawing of the political lines to account for only nine districts. Buyer's 5th District was parceled out to six districts. Only 3 percent of his former constituents were put in the 4th, but his hometown was there as well. Buyer decided that that is where he would seek re-election, although some local Republicans suggested he run in the GOP-leaning (and vacant) 2nd District.

To introduce himself to his new constituents, Buyer embarked on a 260-mile run across the new district. He declared the journey a success, reporting that he went through two pairs of shoes and encountered one angry pit bull and 51 dead opossums. (Rebounding from his illnesses, Buyer has run seven marathons, and he regularly competes in congressional golf, football, baseball and basketball events.)

Buyer's energetic approach to the campaign was in marked contrast to his chief GOP opponent, first-term Rep. Brian Kerns, who put up a seemingly lackluster fight. Buyer carried all 12 counties and won the primary by 25 percentage points. He cruised to a 45-point win in November.

KEY VOTES

2002

- No Overhaul campaign finance law; ban "soft money" and restrict advocacy advertising
- Yes Back Bush's defense budget increase
- ? Extend 1996 welfare law
- Yes Adopt Bush's discretionary spending limit
- Yes Pass GOP Medicare prescription drug plan
- No Create independent Sept. 11 commission
- No Extend union protections to Homeland Security Department employees
- Yes Revive fast-track procedures for trade agreements
- Yes Authorize war against Iraq
- Yes Advance bankruptcy overhaul opposed by abortion opponents

2001

- Yes Nullify Clinton Labor Department ergonomics rule
- Yes Cut taxes by $1.35 trillion through fiscal 2011
- No Maintain ban on oil drilling in Arctic National Wildlife Refuge
- Yes Approve Bush proposal to limit managed-care plan liability for coverage decisions
- No Divert money from crop subsidy payments to land conservation
- Yes Expand law enforcement power to investigate suspected terrorists

CQ VOTE STUDIES

	PARTY UNITY		PRESIDENTIAL SUPPORT	
	Support	Oppose	Support	Oppose
2002	97%	3%	83%	17%
2001	97%	3%	93%	7%
2000	94%	6%	22%	78%
1999	92%	8%	24%	76%
1998	91%	9%	24%	76%

INTEREST GROUPS

	AFL-CIO	ADA	CCUS	ACU
2002	13%	0%	94%	91%
2001	18%	0%	96%	96%
2000	10%	5%	85%	84%
1999	22%	10%	88%	91%
1998	22%	15%	94%	88%

INDIANA 4

West central – Indianapolis suburbs, Lafayette

Traversing the 4th by car requires a 175-mile trip through a slender district that takes in a mixture of farmland, small towns and suburbs. It spans from White County, which is roughly halfway between Chicago and Indianapolis, south to Lawrence County, which is about halfway between Indianapolis and Louisville.

The 4th, as redrawn following the 2000 census, includes remnants of the 7th District that existed under the 1990s map. White, the district's northernmost county (and which is shared with the 2nd District), tops the state in corn and soybean production. Farther south, Montgomery and Clinton counties also produce corn and soybeans. In between is Tippecanoe County, the district's most populous, which takes in Lafayette and West Lafayette. The latter is home to the main campus of Purdue University, which has an enrollment of more than 38,000. The school's engineering bent helps give Tippecanoe a conservative hue.

South and east of fast-growing, GOP-friendly Boone and Hendricks counties, the 4th takes in a western sliver of Marion County (Indianapolis) and curves south of Indianapolis to take in most of Johnson County, which is filling up with young, well-educated families.

Moving west and south, the district encompasses all of mostly rural Morgan County before narrowing considerably to take in western Monroe County (but not Bloomington, which is in the 9th District). South of Monroe is Lawrence County.

The 4th includes some of the most overwhelmingly Republican territory in Indiana. In the 2000 election, Boone and Hendricks gave George W. Bush 72 percent of the vote, a performance he surpassed in just two other Indiana counties. Bush did not lose a single county in the 4th.

MAJOR INDUSTRY
Higher education, agriculture, manufacturing

CITIES
Lafayette, 56,397; Indianapolis (pt.), 39,244; Greenwood, 36,037

NOTABLE
Ben-Hur Museum is in Crawfordsville; Tippecanoe Battlefield was where troops led by then-governor (and later president) William Henry Harrison fought off an American Indian attack in 1811.

Rep. Dan Burton (R)

CAPITOL OFFICE
225-2276
www.house.gov/burton
2185 Rayburn 20515-1405; fax 225-0016

COMMITTEES
Government Reform
(Wellness & Human Rights - chairman)
International Relations

HOMETOWN
Indianapolis

BORN
June 21, 1938, Indianapolis, Ind.

RELIGION
Christian

FAMILY
Widowed; three children

EDUCATION
Indiana U., attended 1958-59; Cincinnati Bible College, attended 1959-60

MILITARY SERVICE
Army, 1956-57; Army Reserve, 1957-62

CAREER
Real estate and insurance agent

POLITICAL HIGHLIGHTS
Ind. House, 1967-69; Ind. Senate, 1969-71; Republican nominee for U.S. House, 1970; sought Republican nomination for U.S. House, 1972; Ind. House, 1977-81; Ind. Senate, 1981-83

ELECTION RESULTS

2002 GENERAL		
Dan Burton (R)	129,442	72.0%
Katherine Fox Carr (D)	45,283	25.2%
Christopher Adkins (LIBERT)	5,130	2.9%
2002 PRIMARY		
Dan Burton (R)	65,022	83.8%
George Thomas Holland (R)	12,560	16.2%
2000 GENERAL		
Dan Burton (R)	199,207	70.4%
Darin Patrick Griesey (D)	74,881	26.4%
Joe Hauptmann (LIBERT)	9,087	3.2%

PREVIOUS WINNING PERCENTAGES
1998 (72%); 1996 (75%); 1994 (77%); 1992 (72%); 1990 (63%); 1988 (73%); 1986 (68%); 1984 (73%); 1982 (65%)

Elected 1982; 11th term

After gaining influence as a gadfly and firebrand during the Clinton years, the self-described "pit bull" of the House Republicans finds himself increasingly marginalized and viewed with suspicion by the leadership of his own party.

As he began his third decade in Congress in 2003, Burton was forced by the six-year GOP term limit rules to give up the gavel of the Government Reform Committee, which he had used as an investigative cudgel on the White House, and not only when President Clinton was its occupant. Then the International Relations Committee chairman, Illinois Republican Henry J. Hyde, rearranged his subcommittee structure, at least in part to prevent Burton from chairing the panel with oversight of South Asia. That cost Burton a forum to showcase his close ties to Pakistan — which in the past have angered Pakistan's rival, India.

Instead, Burton was forced to settle for the chairmanship of a new Wellness and Human Rights Subcommittee on Government Reform. He plans to use the panel to pursue his interest in expanding the rights of people who claim they have been harmed by vaccines to seek compensation. (Burton blames vaccines for the autism that a grandson developed as a toddler.)

Some of Burton's diminished stature can be traced to his revelation in 1988 that he fathered a son out of wedlock in the early 1980s. The admission came as Burton was leading a committee investigation of Clinton's personal behavior during the Monica Lewinsky scandal. But Burton's somewhat unpredictable and zealous partisanship also is increasingly viewed as a liability. When President Bush called in 2002 for the creation of the Homeland Security Department, House GOP leaders quickly moved to take the job of writing the authorizing legislation away from Burton's committee, creating a select committee for the task instead.

Although a fellow Republican is now in the White House, Burton still shows a tendency to challenge the executive branch. In the 107th Congress, he led an ultimately unsuccessful congressional challenge to the president's decision to restrict the release, scheduled by law, of archived material from the Reagan administration. "I don't want the American people to think that the government is becoming secretive," he said in siding with the public's right to know over executive privilege.

Burton was a founder of the Conservative Action Team, or CATs, the caucus of the most conservative Republicans who have since renamed themselves the Republican Study Committee. Burton does little to cover his fierce partisanship: He once called Clinton a "scum bag" and described his Democratic critics as "squealing pigs."

But his pursuit of alleged Democratic wrongdoing has opened Burton to similar political attacks. As he probed Democratic fundraising in 1997, there were reports that he improperly raised money for his own campaign. "I know of only one person who was perfect, and he was nailed to a cross," Burton said of the charges. Burton later told the Indianapolis Star that he believed his undaunted pursuit of Democratic wrongdoing had made him a target of surveillance and potential physical harm.

While most Republicans reined in their political attacks on Clinton after his 1999 Senate impeachment trial acquittal, Burton was not deterred. He used his chairmanship of Government Reform to pummel the administration throughout the 106th Congress with subpoenas and investigations into such issues as campaign fundraising; the deadly 1993 shootout in Waco,

Texas, between federal agents and Branch Davidians; and Clinton's 1999 pardon of 16 Puerto Rican militants.

Most famously, he suggested that presidential counsel Vincent W. Foster Jr.'s death in 1994 was a murder. He conducted his own investigation in his backyard with the help of a homicide detective, firing a gun into what he would only refer to as "a head-like object" — reportedly a pumpkin or a watermelon — to see if the sound could be heard at a distance.

Burton's tenacity and combativeness developed early in life. His 6-foot, 8-inch father regularly beat him and his mother and was eventually jailed for abuse. His family lived in hotels and trailer parks, and by the time he was 12, Burton had lived in 38 states, Mexico and Canada.

"I never stopped worrying that Dad would come back after he got out of jail," he told People magazine in 1994. "One day, when I was 13, he did. I was baby-sitting my younger brother and sister when I saw him come up the front walk. I was petrified and yelled, 'Don't come up here.' . . . I grabbed a shotgun we kept beside the front door. When he saw the gun, he turned around. I'm glad he did because I might have shot him."

After enlisting in the Army at 18 and later attending Cincinnati Bible College, Burton worked as an insurance agent; at the time he considered himself an independent but often voted Democratic. He says he entered politics after seeing an interview in 1964 with Norman Thomas, a socialist who had run for president six times. As Burton recalls it, Thomas' message was that the socialist philosophy would ultimately infiltrate American politics under the label of the Democratic Party. The next day Burton went to the local library and used the Congressional Record to see what legislation Democrats supported. Concluding that Thomas was onto something, Burton immediately called the local GOP and volunteered. Two years later, at age 28, he won a seat in the state legislature as a Republican.

Burton first made national headlines in 1987 when he proposed mandatory blood tests for everyone in the United States to track the AIDS virus. Associates describe Burton as being phobic about the virus. One former House colleague, Democrat Andy Jacobs Jr. of Indianapolis, has told reporters that Burton refuses to eat soup in restaurants for fear of being infected with HIV.

Still, his flamboyant conservatism remains a good fit for his wealthy suburban district. He has won his past six re-elections with more than 70 percent of the vote, including 2002 when Indiana's congressional map for this decade — which renumbered his district from the 6th to the 5th — made his constituency slightly less Republican.

KEY VOTES

2002

- No Overhaul campaign finance law; ban "soft money" and restrict advocacy advertising
- \+ Back Bush's defense budget increase
- Yes Extend 1996 welfare law
- \+ Adopt Bush's discretionary spending limit
- Yes Pass GOP Medicare prescription drug plan
- Yes Create independent Sept. 11 commission
- No Extend union protections to Homeland Security Department employees
- Yes Revive fast-track procedures for trade agreements
- Yes Authorize war against Iraq
- No Advance bankruptcy overhaul opposed by abortion opponents

2001

- Yes Nullify Clinton Labor Department ergonomics rule
- Yes Cut taxes by $1.35 trillion through fiscal 2011
- No Maintain ban on oil drilling in Arctic National Wildlife Refuge
- Yes Approve Bush proposal to limit managed-care plan liability for coverage decisions
- – Divert money from crop subsidy payments to land conservation
- ? Expand law enforcement power to investigate suspected terrorists

CQ VOTE STUDIES

	PARTY UNITY		PRESIDENTIAL SUPPORT	
	Support	Oppose	Support	Oppose
2002	97%	3%	84%	16%
2001	97%	3%	87%	13%
2000	98%	2%	17%	83%
1999	94%	6%	13%	87%
1998	93%	7%	21%	79%

INTEREST GROUPS

	AFL-CIO	ADA	CCUS	ACU
2002	13%	0%	80%	100%
2001	9%	5%	87%	100%
2000	13%	5%	89%	91%
1999	33%	5%	83%	95%
1998	0%	5%	93%	96%

INDIANA 5
East central – part of Indianapolis and suburbs

Dominated by Indianapolis suburbanites and rural farmers, the 5th is Indiana's wealthiest district and is staunchly Republican turf. The trend might well continue; the suburbanites, who are rapidly taking the region's countryside, have been a largely GOP constituency.

The district's most affluent residents and its few minorities live in northern Indianapolis (Marion County) and in the Hamilton County suburbs of Carmel, Fishers and Noblesville. Here, growing populations of white-collar workers in electronics and financial services bring median incomes well above state and national averages. Hamilton's median family income, $80,000 in 1999, was the state's highest and was nearly $20,000 above the next-highest county, Hancock (which is east of Indianapolis and also in the 5th District).

Hamilton, Marion and Hancock counties make up more than half of the 5th's population. Southeast of Indianapolis, the district also takes in most of Shelby County and northeastern Johnson County.

The suburban affluence does not extend to the northern part of the district, which is more middle-class. Miami County lost population in the 1990s, in part because of the 1994 realignment of what is now Grissom Air Reserve Base. Wabash and Grant, adjacent to Miami, also lost population in the 1990s. The district also takes in most of Howard County, including parts of working-class Kokomo (shared with the 2nd).

While the rural communities are not as affluent as their suburban counterparts, they too are solidly Republican. George W. Bush won all of the counties at least partly within the 5th in the 2000 presidential election. Four of the counties were among his 10 best statewide.

MAJOR INDUSTRY
Financial services, electronics, agriculture

CITIES
Indianapolis (pt.), 130,195; Fishers, 37,835; Carmel, 37,733; Marion, 31,320

NOTABLE
The Dan Quayle Center and U.S. Vice Presidential Museum is in Quayle's hometown of Huntington; Peru is the birthplace of Cole Porter and the site of the International Circus Hall of Fame; The Elwood Haynes Museum, in Kokomo, honors the inventor who was among the first to build a gasoline-powered automobile.

Rep. Mike Pence (R)

CAPITOL OFFICE
225-3021
mike.pence@mail.house.gov
mikepence.house.gov
1605 Longworth 20515-1406; fax 225-3382

COMMITTEES
Agriculture
International Relations
Judiciary

HOMETOWN
Edinburgh

BORN
June 7, 1959, Columbus, Ind.

RELIGION
Christian

FAMILY
Wife, Karen Pence; three children

EDUCATION
Hanover College, B.A. 1981 (history); Indiana U., J.D. 1986

CAREER
Radio broadcasting consultant; radio broadcaster; think tank president; lawyer

POLITICAL HIGHLIGHTS
Republican nominee for U.S. House, 1988, 1990

ELECTION RESULTS

2002 GENERAL		
Mike Pence (R)	118,436	63.8%
Ann Melina Fox (D)	63,871	34.4%
Doris Robertson (LIBERT)	3,346	1.8%
2002 PRIMARY		
Mike Pence (R)		unopposed
2000 GENERAL		
Mike Pence (R)	106,023	50.9%
Bob Rock (D)	80,885	38.8%
William G. Frazier (I)	19,077	9.2%
Michael Anderson (LIBERT)	2,422	1.2%

Elected 2000; 2nd term

There is nothing middle-of-the-road about Pence. As a former talk radio host who says Rush Limbaugh was the inspiration for his radio career, Pence is one of the most conservative members of Congress.

He can usually be relied on to support the GOP leadership and President Bush, except when he stakes out positions to the right of them. He was among the band of conservative Republicans who handed their leaders a defeat at the end of the 107th Congress by killing a bankruptcy overhaul bill because they wanted it to offer protections to anti-abortion protesters.

Pence was also among the dozen fiscal conservatives who insisted, throughout the 107th, on holding Republican leaders responsible for keeping government spending down. In 2001, Pence voted against a large education bill because, he said, it called for a 22 percent increase in federal spending. In 2002, Pence and his allies forced the leadership to adjust its timetable for considering annual spending bills, a move many of his GOP colleagues criticized. But Pence said, "What we accomplished was to stop the bleeding" by preventing bills with increased funding from coming up for a vote.

A social conservative as well, Pence cited moral values as a key campaign issue in both his 2000 and 2002 races. Despite his zeal in promoting his views, he has a soft-spoken, almost placid manner. He remains in good graces with the GOP leadership despite his periodic opposition to their policies.

When he arrived in the House in 2001, Pence was named to the GOP whip team. In the 108th Congress he was promoted to deputy whip and got a seat on the Republican Policy Committee.

Pence was the only House freshman in the 107th Congress to chair a subcommittee. He took the gavel of the Small Business Committee's Regulatory Reform and Oversight Subcommittee, where he conducted hearings on topics ranging from access to Internet communications, to the effects of government regulations on small businesses, to health insurance issues. He left the Small Business panel in the 108th to take a seat on International Relations.

The 6th District has a large rural constituency, and Pence tends to the interests of the farming community from his seat on the Agriculture Committee. In October 2001, Pence was named to a vacant seat on the Judiciary Committee just as it was gearing up to draft anti-terrorism legislation in response to the Sept. 11 attacks against the United States, and he retained that seat in the 108th.

Pence was tapped to lead an ad hoc group of members of the conservative Republican Study Committee to keep an eye on the drafting of a bill to establish a Department of Homeland Security. He announced that the group of "cantankerous conservatives" would raise objections to any provisions that increased federal spending or the size of the bureaucracy.

When anthrax-laced letters were delivered to Capitol Hill offices in the fall of 2001, Pence's office was one of four in a cluster on the sixth and seventh floors of the Longworth Building that were found to be contaminated. Although most House members were displaced for a short while as the extent of the contamination was assessed, Pence and his staff were homeless for more than two months. Pence worked out of Majority Whip Tom DeLay's personal office in the Rayburn Building, while his staff set up shop in a basement room normally used for banquets.

Although Arizona Republican Sen. John McCain campaigned for Pence in 2000, the two had a falling out over McCain's push for campaign finance legislation. Pence eventually accused McCain of working too closely with the Democrats. The Indianapolis Star reported that Pence told his GOP colleagues, "McCain is so deep in bed with the Democrats that his feet are coming out of the bottom of the sheets." Pence joined as a plaintiff in a lawsuit challenging the constitutionality of the campaign finance law enacted in 2002.

Drawing on his radio experience, Pence has set up a small radio studio in his House office where he records commentaries that are available on his Web site. He is also a frequent guest on radio and television interview shows.

A Democrat in his younger days, Pence made a run for the House in 1988 at age 29 with a challenge to veteran Democratic Rep. Philip R. Sharp. He lost by 6 percentage points. Two years later, he tried again, this time losing by almost 19 points.

In the latter race, Pence ran a harshly negative campaign against Sharp. The following year, Pence wrote an article entitled "Confessions of a Negative Campaigner" in which he said, "Negative campaigning, I now know, is wrong." He added, "It is wrong, quite simply, to squander a candidate's priceless moment in history . . . on partisan bickering."

It was during that period that Limbaugh captured Pence's imagination. "I was inspired by those dulcet tones to seek a career in radio and television," he recalls. Pence's first radio show aired in 1989 in Rushville, Ind. He eventually built up a syndicated talk show that was heard on 18 stations across the state. On many of those stations, he said, he was Limbaugh's "warm-up act."

Pence's years as a radio broadcaster and as host of a public affairs television show in Indianapolis kept his name before the public. When he decided in 2000 to run for the seat of GOP Rep. David M. McIntosh, who ran, unsuccessfully, for governor, Pence easily beat state Rep. Jeff Linder and four other opponents in the GOP primary. He then topped Democratic lawyer Bob Rock by 12 percentage points in November.

Redistricting after the 2000 census helped Pence. State Democrats who controlled the remapping process sought to bolster vulnerable Democratic Rep. Baron P. Hill in the neighboring 9th District. In shaping the new 6th District, the Democrats gave Pence some of Hill's Republican-leaning rural territory in southeastern Indiana. They put forth an active challenger in Melina Fox, a farmer and party activist who was running for office for the first time, but Pence cruised to a 29-point victory in a race that was noted for its civility.

KEY VOTES

2002

- No Overhaul campaign finance law; ban "soft money" and restrict advocacy advertising
- Yes Back Bush's defense budget increase
- Yes Extend 1996 welfare law
- Yes Adopt Bush's discretionary spending limit
- Yes Pass GOP Medicare prescription drug plan
- No Create independent Sept. 11 commission
- No Extend union protections to Homeland Security Department employees
- Yes Revive fast-track procedures for trade agreements
- Yes Authorize war against Iraq
- No Advance bankruptcy overhaul opposed by abortion opponents

2001

- Yes Nullify Clinton Labor Department ergonomics rule
- Yes Cut taxes by $1.35 trillion through fiscal 2011
- No Maintain ban on oil drilling in Arctic National Wildlife Refuge
- Yes Approve Bush proposal to limit managed-care plan liability for coverage decisions
- No Divert money from crop subsidy payments to land conservation
- Yes Expand law enforcement power to investigate suspected terrorists

CQ VOTE STUDIES

	PARTY UNITY		PRESIDENTIAL SUPPORT	
	Support	Oppose	Support	Oppose
2002	99%	1%	84%	16%
2001	97%	3%	91%	9%

INTEREST GROUPS

	AFL-CIO	ADA	CCUS	ACU
2002	11%	5%	84%	100%
2001	0%	0%	96%	100%

INDIANA 6

East – Muncie, Anderson, Richmond

Covering most of Indiana's eastern border with Ohio, the 6th is a mix of farm, midsize city and suburban populations. The district's major population centers are Muncie and Anderson, in the center of the district.

In the 1920s Muncie was the model for "Middletown," a study of small-town American life. Today, it is home to Ball State University, as well as two large automotive plants. The city's economy was unsteady for much of the 1990s, with unemployment rates well above the state average. Delaware and adjacent Blackford were among the 11 Indiana counties that lost population in the 1990s. Anderson, another former auto manufacturing hub, also has seen industrial decline.

South and east of Muncie and Anderson, the 6th takes in Wayne and Henry counties, where the percentage of residents over age 65 is among the highest in Indiana. Richmond, in Wayne County, is the main city on the 6th's eastern edge. Rush County is a top state producer of corn and soybeans.

Redistricting following the 2000 census elongated the district (previously numbered the 2nd). The new 6th extends as far south as Dearborn County, just a few miles from the Ohio River, and stretches as far north as Allen County, just south of Fort Wayne.

The 6th has a Democratic past but now leans conservative, in part because the decline of manufacturing weakened the district's Democratic labor base. Bill Clinton carried Delaware and Madison counties, where Muncie and Anderson are located, respectively, in the 1996 presidential election, but George W. Bush carried all 19 counties that lie wholly or partly in the 6th in 2000.

MAJOR INDUSTRY
Auto manufacturing, agriculture, light industry

CITIES
Muncie, 67,430; Anderson, 59,734; Richmond, 39,124

NOTABLE
The Indiana Basketball Hall of Fame is in New Castle; David Letterman is an alumnus of Ball State University; Elwood was the hometown of 1940 GOP presidential nominee Wendell Willkie.

Rep. Julia Carson (D)

CAPITOL OFFICE
225-4011
rep.carson@mail.house.gov
www.house.gov/carson
1535 Longworth 20515-1407; fax 225-5633

COMMITTEES
Financial Services
Transportation & Infrastructure

HOMETOWN
Indianapolis

BORN
July 8, 1938, Louisville, Ky.

RELIGION
Baptist

FAMILY
Divorced; two children

EDUCATION
Martin U., attended 1994-95 (political science)

CAREER
Clothing store owner; human resources manager; congressional aide

POLITICAL HIGHLIGHTS
Ind. House, 1973-77; Ind. Senate, 1977-91; Center Township trustee, 1991-97

ELECTION RESULTS

2002 GENERAL		
Julia Carson (D)	77,478	53.1%
Brose McVey (R)	64,379	44.1%
Andrew Horning (LIBERT)	3,919	2.7%
2002 PRIMARY		
Julia Carson (D)	24,807	90.8%
Bobby Hidalgo (D)	2,515	9.2%
2000 GENERAL		
Julia Carson (D)	91,689	58.5%
Marvin B. Scott (R)	62,233	39.7%
Na'llah Ali (LIBERT)	2,780	1.8%

PREVIOUS WINNING PERCENTAGES
1998 (58%); 1996 (53%)

Elected 1996; 4th term

When Carson urges people in poverty to find a way to support themselves, she can offer her own life as an example. Born to a teenage single mother, she waited tables, delivered newspapers and did farm labor to generate income as a youth. Later, as a divorced young mother of two, she pinched every penny.

Carson's doctrine of self-reliance might seem to fit right in with the philosophy of the typical congressional Republican, but in fact her experiences have led her to very different conclusions about how to help the poor. In the six years before her election to Congress, she held the job of Center Township trustee, administering municipal social services to low-income people in downtown Indianapolis. "We got people off of welfare and put them into jobs and into training and into educational experiences," Carson recalled. "We did not do that by being cruel." She typically takes a dim view of the GOP's proposals, using adjectives like "cruel" and "regressive" to describe them.

In the 108th Congress Carson traded the seat she had held on the Veterans' Affairs Committee since her freshman year for assignment to the Transportation and Infrastructure Committee, where her priorities include funding for expansion of the Indianapolis airport and a waterfront project in downtown Indianapolis.

Fragile health led her to miss 82 roll calls during her third term, or 8 percent of all the recorded votes in the 107th Congress. But in her speeches and in the votes that she did cast, Carson continued her pattern of generally — although not consistently — aligning with fellow members of the Progressive Caucus, the most liberal faction of the House Democrats. She has been a fairly reliable supporter of organized labor, environmental protections, abortion rights, gun control and health care programs. From her seat on the Financial Services Committee, she has resisted such GOP initiatives as an overhaul of the federal public housing program, which included a requirement that unemployed tenants perform eight hours of community service per month.

In 2002 Carson opposed President Bush's request for broad authority to wage war against Iraq. She argued that an attack not specifically blessed by the U.N. Security Council and a congressional declaration of war would violate both the U.N. Charter and the Constitution.

Her record on trade liberalization has been mixed. In the 107th, she joined most Democrats against Bush's bid to revive fast-track procedures for congressional action on trade agreements. But in the 106th, she bowed to intense lobbying by the Clinton White House, put aside her concerns about human rights violations and voted to make permanent the normal trade relations between the United States and China. "I feel like I have been put in a Maytag washer and put on the spin cycle," she said before the vote.

In the 107th, Carson sponsored a bill aimed at promoting "responsible fatherhood" by financing media campaigns and grants to state and local governments and other entities. She said the bill was needed because "too many kids spend their entire lives without any contact with their fathers." She also introduced legislation that would require safety devices for newly made handguns.

Carson has worked with Republicans on measures to expand the reach of social programs. In the 106th she and Indiana's senior senator, Republican Richard G. Lugar, introduced legislation to encourage schools, child care facilities and federal nutrition programs to share efforts to identify children who could qualify for Medicaid or for the newer Children's Health Insurance Program.

But Carson often sharply criticizes GOP initiatives. She argued that Bush had "perpetrated a fraud upon the people" by maintaining that the budget could accommodate not only his 2001 tax cut but also adequate social spending and a reduction of the national debt. She characterized as "incomprehensible" that Republicans would want to close the Legal Services Corporation in the 1990s and leave legal representation for the indigent in the hands of private attorneys. She has said that creating government vouchers that could pay tuition at private or religious schools would be a "cruel hoax" on the public school system.

In the 106th Congress, Carson won enactment of a measure awarding the Congressional Gold Medal to civil rights figure Rosa Parks. The bill initially won little support beyond members of the Congressional Black Caucus, but Carson stirred up media coverage and eventually enlisted more than 300 cosponsors in her successful campaign for the measure.

In 2002, she introduced legislation that would make all of her state, rather than just a haphazard portion of it, subject to daylight-saving time from April through October. She argued that the measure was needed to improve energy efficiency and reduce pollution.

Carson began her congressional career as a secretary, and then a district aide, for Democratic Rep. Andrew Jacobs Jr. of Indianapolis. In 1972, she won the first of two state House terms, and in 1976 she moved up to the state Senate, where she served until 1991 and sat on the Finance Committee. During her years in the General Assembly, she worked as human resources director at Cummins Engine and later opened a dress shop in Indianapolis that failed and left her saddled with debt. (She had her state Senate wages garnished to partially pay off the debts.)

While she was Center Township trustee, the office's overhead went up. But she improved the agency's financial standing overall, while reducing taxes and halving the roster of people receiving financial assistance.

When Jacobs retired in 1996 after 15 terms, he endorsed Carson to succeed him, helping her win a tough nomination battle and hold off a vigorous Republican attempt to capture the 10th District. She won her next two re-election contests by comfortable margins. Redistricting for this decade made her district — which had been labeled the 10th — somewhat less Democratic. Although she withstood a tough campaign by Republican Brose McVey, a former congressional aide, Carson's 9 percentage point victory was her closest since her initial win in 1996.

KEY VOTES

2002

Yes Overhaul campaign finance law; ban "soft money" and restrict advocacy advertising
Yes Back Bush's defense budget increase
No Extend 1996 welfare law
No Adopt Bush's discretionary spending limit
No Pass GOP Medicare prescription drug plan
Yes Create independent Sept. 11 commission
Yes Extend union protections to Homeland Security Department employees
No Revive fast-track procedures for trade agreements
No Authorize war against Iraq
No Advance bankruptcy overhaul opposed by abortion opponents

2001

No Nullify Clinton Labor Department ergonomics rule
No Cut taxes by $1.35 trillion through fiscal 2011
Yes Maintain ban on oil drilling in Arctic National Wildlife Refuge
No Approve Bush proposal to limit managed-care plan liability for coverage decisions
Yes Divert money from crop subsidy payments to land conservation
Yes Expand law enforcement power to investigate suspected terrorists

CQ VOTE STUDIES

	PARTY UNITY		PRESIDENTIAL SUPPORT	
	Support	Oppose	Support	Oppose
2002	96%	4%	19%	81%
2001	95%	5%	26%	74%
2000	96%	4%	84%	16%
1999	97%	3%	81%	19%
1998	96%	4%	89%	11%

INTEREST GROUPS

	AFL-CIO	ADA	CCUS	ACU
2002	100%	100%	37%	0%
2001	100%	100%	35%	4%
2000	90%	90%	40%	4%
1999	100%	95%	18%	0%
1998	100%	95%	22%	0%

INDIANA 7
Most of Indianapolis

Indiana's largest concentration of minorities lives in the urban 7th, which boasts one of the state's biggest white-collar work forces but also has one of its lowest median incomes. Almost four times bigger than Fort Wayne, the state's next most-populous city, Indianapolis is the state's capital as well as its banking and commercial center. Heavy industry also plays a role in the city's economy, with a few automotive plants hanging on despite industry downturns.

Redistricting in 2001 changed the district's number (from 10 to 7) and slightly reduced the district's black population and Democratic lean. But even with those changes, the 7th gave Al Gore a solid 55 percent of the vote in the 2000 presidential election, and its substantial minority influence makes it hard for a Republican to win.

Large minority populations, particularly African-Americans, in central Indianapolis form the 7th's Democratic core. The joint Indiana University-Purdue University campus is here, and some neighborhoods are up to 65 percent black. In the city's northern tier, white-collar residents are some of the wealthiest in the state and are more receptive to Republican candidates. In the southern part of the district, blue-collar, mostly white populations built around the city's manufacturing industry are more socially conservative and generally supported Republicans on the local level in the 1990s.

Indianapolis has a reputation for being one of the nation's more conservative metropolitan areas: Richard G. Lugar (now senator), William Hudnut and Stephen Goldsmith kept the mayor's office in Republican hands for 32 years, until Democrat Bart Peterson took office in 2000. On the federal level, George W. Bush carried Marion County (which is shared with the 4th and 5th districts) by slightly more than 1 percentage point in 2000, a smaller margin than Bob Dole took in 1996.

MAJOR INDUSTRY
Manufacturing, health care, higher education

CITIES
Indianapolis (pt.), 612,431; Lawrence (pt.), 27,868

NOTABLE
Indianapolis Motor Speedway; President Benjamin Harrison, John Dillinger, poet James Whitcomb Riley, three vice presidents and 10 Indiana governors are buried in the Crown Hill Cemetery.

Rep. John Hostettler (R)

Elected 1994; 5th term

CAPITOL OFFICE
225-4636
john.hostettler@mail.house.gov
www.house.gov/hostettler
1214 Longworth 20515-1408; fax 225-3284

COMMITTEES
Armed Services
Judiciary
(Immigration, Border Security & Claims - chairman)

HOMETOWN
Blairsville

BORN
July 19, 1961, Evansville, Ind.

RELIGION
General Baptist

FAMILY
Wife, Elizabeth Ann Hostettler; four children

EDUCATION
Rose-Hulman Institute of Technology, B.S. 1983 (mechanical engineering)

CAREER
Mechanical engineer

POLITICAL HIGHLIGHTS
No previous office

ELECTION RESULTS

2002 GENERAL		
John Hostettler (R)	98,952	51.3%
Bryan L. Hartke (D)	88,763	46.0%
Pam Williams (LIBERT)	5,150	2.7%
2002 PRIMARY		
John Hostettler (R)		unopposed
2000 GENERAL		
John Hostettler (R)	116,879	52.7%
Paul Perry (D)	100,488	45.3%
Thomas Tindle (LIBERT)	4,342	2.0%

PREVIOUS WINNING PERCENTAGES
1998 (52%); 1996 (50%); 1994 (52%)

Hostettler is one of the most conservative members of the House, where he contends that the Constitution is all too frequently ignored by both Congress and the courts.

Opposing major changes to the Constitution is one of the few viewpoints he shares with the Democrats. He voted with Democratic lawmakers against constitutional amendments requiring a balanced budget and imposing term limits — two elements of the House GOP's 1995 "Contract With America."

Hostettler (HO-stet-lur) came to Washington in 1995 as one of the "true believers" among the Republican lawmakers who vowed to adhere to core conservative principles. In that vein, he opposes abortion, advocates for gun owners' rights and seeks to reduce the role of government in people's lives.

Although Hostettler lines up with the GOP leadership more than 90 percent of the time, there are occasions when he takes a more conservative stance than party leaders want, particularly on budget issues. He voted against a number of spending bills in the 107th Congress because he said their funding levels were too high.

Later in 2002, he was one of only six House Republicans to vote against a measure authorizing President Bush to wage war against Iraq. Hostettler argued that while the president had made the case that Iraq posed a threat, he concluded that "it does not pose an *imminent* [his emphasis] threat that justifies a pre-emptive military strike." In a House floor speech outlining his views, Hostettler quoted the Constitution, Winston Churchill and St. Augustine. He ranked in the top 10 list of House Republicans opposing President Bush in 2002.

Hostettler has also feuded with his hometown newspaper, the Evansville Courier & Press, refusing to talk with its reporters after it wrote (incorrectly, Hostettler says) that he had offended a group of breast cancer survivors who visited his office to lobby for research funding. The newspaper quoted the women as saying that Hostettler was rude and insisted on talking about possible links between abortion and breast cancer.

Although he is considered one of the more frugal House members, when it comes to transportation and defense funding Hostettler backs some spending initiatives, particularly when they benefit Indiana. He is a co-chairman of the Interstate 69 Caucus, a group of lawmakers who work for completion of the mid-continent highway from the Canadian border in eastern Michigan to the Mexican border at Laredo, Texas. The portion of the highway in Indiana runs only from the Michigan border to Indianapolis. When built, the southern section that will run through Indiana will traverse Hostettler's district.

From his seat on the Armed Services Committee, he supports Republican efforts to boost the Pentagon's funding; he also watches out for the Crane Naval Surface Warfare Center in his district. In 2002, Hostettler was a leader in the Capitol Hill effort to force the Pentagon to back down from its requirement that female service members stationed in Saudi Arabia wear traditional Muslim abayas, garments that cover the face and body, when off their base.

He also led an unsuccessful drive in 2002 to require the Transportation Security Agency to train airline pilots so they could carry guns on board.

Before coming to Congress, Hostettler's chief experience in the public arena was as a member of the board of deacons at the Twelfth Avenue General Baptist Church in Evansville, where he taught Bible study and led prayer meetings. His strongly held religious beliefs translate into conservative views on most social policy issues.

During his first House term, Hostettler split openly with Speaker Newt Gingrich, contending early and often that Gingrich's ethics woes and general unpopularity made him a hindrance in spreading the GOP gospel. In 1997, Hostettler was among five Republican lawmakers to vote "present" in the election of Gingrich to be Speaker, and he later participated in an abortive plan to oust Gingrich from his leadership post.

Hostettler grew up with nine siblings in the same southern Indiana county where he now lives. After getting a degree in mechanical engineering from the Rose-Hulman Institute of Technology in Terre Haute, he married his high school sweetheart and went to work for Southern Indiana Gas & Electric Co.

Hostettler's interest in politics dates to the election of Bill Clinton in 1992, and by 1994 he decided he had to challenge the local congressman, six-term Democratic Rep. Frank McCloskey. He had little money, but relying on a grass-roots organization drawn primarily from area churches, Hostettler won the six-candidate GOP primary. He went on to defeat McCloskey by almost 5 percentage points in the watershed Republican electoral breakthrough. The cake at his victory celebration read, "To God Give the Glory."

With Democrats targeting his seat, Hostettler struggled in the next three elections, never capturing more than 53 percent and posting winning margins of 2, 6 and 7 points.

Close races in the 8th District pre-date Hostettler. It has seen a series of contests so narrowly decided that it is often referred to as the "Bloody Eighth." Since 1982, only once (in 1988) has the winner captured more than 55 percent of the vote, and after the 1984 election it took almost six months for the House to decide the victor, following a bitter battle that resulted in hard feelings between the two parties that lingered long after.

Redistricting for the 2002 election changed the district's geography — adding Terre Haute and dropping Bloomington — but did little to alter the 8th's political competitiveness. Although the Democratic candidate, newcomer Bryan Hartke, was not regarded as the party's best choice, the race was nevertheless another close one: Hostettler got 51 percent of the votes and won by just 5 percentage points.

KEY VOTES

2002

- No Overhaul campaign finance law; ban "soft money" and restrict advocacy advertising
- Yes Back Bush's defense budget increase
- No Extend 1996 welfare law
- Yes Adopt Bush's discretionary spending limit
- No Pass GOP Medicare prescription drug plan
- No Create independent Sept. 11 commission
- No Extend union protections to Homeland Security Department employees
- No Revive fast-track procedures for trade agreements
- No Authorize war against Iraq
- No Advance bankruptcy overhaul opposed by abortion opponents

2001

- Yes Nullify Clinton Labor Department ergonomics rule
- Yes Cut taxes by $1.35 trillion through fiscal 2011
- No Maintain ban on oil drilling in Arctic National Wildlife Refuge
- Yes Approve Bush proposal to limit managed-care plan liability for coverage decisions
- No Divert money from crop subsidy payments to land conservation
- Yes Expand law enforcement power to investigate suspected terrorists

CQ VOTE STUDIES

	PARTY UNITY		PRESIDENTIAL SUPPORT	
	Support	Oppose	Support	Oppose
2002	88%	12%	72%	28%
2001	94%	6%	85%	15%
2000	92%	8%	17%	83%
1999	91%	9%	11%	89%
1998	91%	9%	24%	76%

INTEREST GROUPS

	AFL-CIO	ADA	CCUS	ACU
2002	22%	15%	80%	84%
2001	11%	15%	85%	92%
2000	30%	15%	76%	88%
1999	44%	15%	83%	96%
1998	10%	10%	78%	92%

INDIANA 8
West – Evansville, Terre Haute

Indiana's southwest corner, formed by the converging Wabash and Ohio rivers, houses the 8th District, characterized by laborers and social conservatives. It is known in political circles as the "Bloody Eighth" for its aggressive and close elections, including a 1984 barnburner in which four votes separated the candidates.

Evansville, an Ohio River port and the state's third-largest city, is southern Indiana's industrial center. It is located in Vanderburgh County, the district's most populous, and is home to the 8th's only substantial minority and liberal populations.

North of Evansville the district takes on a more rural and culturally conservative flavor. Gibson and Knox counties are among Indiana's top corn producing areas. Nearly one in six people in Daviess County, east of Knox, speak a language other than English at home. The county also has a large Amish population. Martin County, east of Daviess, includes the Naval Surface Warfare Center in Crane.

Owen County, northwest of Bloomington and about 50 miles southwest of Indianapolis, has just 22,000 residents but had a higher population growth rate in the 1990s than all but three other Indiana counties. West of Owen is Vigo County, the district's other major population center and home of Indiana State University in Terre Haute. Redistricting following the 2000 census extended the district's northern boundary to Warren County, which is closer to Chicago than to Evansville.

The 8th's manufacturing base and history as a mining center long gave Democrats an edge. But cultural issues, including gun control, strongly thrust the 8th in George W. Bush's direction in 2000; he carried every county in the district except for sparsely populated Vermillion.

MAJOR INDUSTRY
Manufacturing, agriculture, higher education

MILITARY BASES
Naval Surface Warfare Center, Crane Division, 55 military, 3,248 civilian (2002)

CITIES
Evansville, 121,582; Terre Haute, 59,614; Vincennes, 18,701

NOTABLE
Labor leader Jimmy Hoffa was born in Brazil.

Rep. Baron P. Hill (D)

Elected 1998; 3rd term

CAPITOL OFFICE
225-5315
www.house.gov/baronhill
1024 Longworth 20515-1409; fax 226-6866

COMMITTEES
Agriculture
Armed Services
Joint Economic

HOMETOWN
Seymour

BORN
June 23, 1953, Seymour, Ind.

RELIGION
Christian Church

FAMILY
Wife, Betty Hill; three children

EDUCATION
Furman U., B.A. 1975 (history)

CAREER
Financial adviser; state legislative aide; insurance company manager

POLITICAL HIGHLIGHTS
Ind. House, 1983-91; Democratic nominee for U.S. Senate, 1990; State Student Assistance Commission of Indiana director, 1992

ELECTION RESULTS

2002 GENERAL		
Baron P. Hill (D)	96,654	51.2%
Mike Sodrel (R)	87,169	46.1%
Jeff Melton (GREEN)	2,745	1.5%
Al Cox (LIBERT)	2,389	1.3%
2002 PRIMARY		
Baron P. Hill (D)		unopposed
2000 GENERAL		
Baron P. Hill (D)	126,420	54.2%
Michael Everett Bailey (R)	102,219	43.8%
Sara Chambers (LIBERT)	4,644	2.0%

PREVIOUS WINNING PERCENTAGES
1998 (51%)

Hill's conservative bent on some social policy issues and his high school basketball heroics in hoops-crazy Indiana have helped him win three close elections in a district that can be shaky territory for a Democrat. And, in 2003, he began to move up the ranks of the House Democratic hierarchy.

House Minority Leader Nancy Pelosi named representatives of the various party factions to the top levels of the whip organization in the 108th Congress, and Hill, a leader of a coalition of the most conservative House Democrats known as the "Blue Dogs," won appointment as one of seven chief deputy whips.

Yet politics was not Hill's first love. A basketball star at Seymour High School, he was inducted into the Indiana Basketball Hall of Fame in 2000, along with NBA legend Larry Bird. "When I was growing up in Seymour, all I could think of was basketball and girls. Politics was the furthest thing from my mind," he recalls.

Hill says he picked up the political bug while in college, watching the Watergate hearings on television and becoming fascinated by the process of government. He first ran for office after a friend of his from the Jaycees retired from his state House seat. He says he likes the competitive aspect of politics, which reminds him of sports.

As one of three Blue Dog co-chairmen in the 108th, Hill joins with his conservative colleagues in cautioning against budget deficits — arguing for restraint in both spending and cutting taxes.

He is not shy about breaking ranks with the Democratic leadership. During his first two terms in the House, Hill sided with the Democrats about three-quarters of the time on votes that pitted the two parties against each other. In the 107th Congress, for instance, he went against party wishes on such matters as cloning embryos for medical research, giving the president more authority on personnel matters involving the new Department of Homeland Security, and pushing for overseas trade markets.

Hill supports expanded foreign trade, which he says would benefit his district's farmers as well as major shippers, such as United Parcel Service, whose hub just across the Ohio River in Louisville employs many of his constituents. In the 107th Hill was one of only 25 Democrats who voted for legislation to give the president fast-track authority to negotiate trade agreements that Congress cannot amend.

Hill sits on the Agriculture Committee, where he applauded the farm bill enacted in 2002, saying it was important that farmers get predictable support from the federal government. He said that the measure was a significant improvement over the previous farm bill of 1996, which replaced crop subsidies with fixed payments that declined over time regardless of market conditions.

The 9th District is one of the nation's top tobacco producers, and Hill favors an end to the longstanding quota system for burley tobacco, which is grown in Indiana and nearby states. He proposes a federal buyout of quotas, saying the money should be paid to farmers to help them make the transition to another crop. Under Hill's plan, farmers could continue to grow tobacco but without federal support.

Hill is married to a middle-school math teacher, and he often weighs in on education issues. He maintains that schools would be safer if they were smaller. He says social scientists have found that students perform better and feel more comfortable when they attend a smaller school. Dating back to his first year in Congress, after the massacre at Colorado's Columbine High School, Hill wrote legislation providing federal grants to local districts to help them shrink the size of schools. He persevered, and his Smaller Schools, Stronger Communities legislation became law in 2001 as part of a larger education bill.

On the Armed Services Committee, Hill was involved in successful negotiations to turn the Army's shuttered Jefferson Proving Ground in his district into a national wildlife refuge.

The youngest of seven children whose parents worked in a shoe factory, Hill went to Furman University on a basketball scholarship. He says the scholarship was the only way he could have gone to college.

After getting his degree in history, Hill returned home to the small town of Seymour and ran an insurance and real estate business. He served eight years in the state House, leaving in 1990 to wage an uphill battle for the U.S. Senate. He attracted some notice by walking 400 miles from the Ohio River to Lake Michigan, where he celebrated by jumping into the 60-degree water. He lost to Republican Daniel R. Coats but did surprisingly well, capturing 46 percent of the vote.

Encouraged by the showing, Hill briefly entered the 1992 Senate race and the 1994 gubernatorial race, but he pulled out both times in the interest of Democratic Party unity. After his 1990 defeat, Hill was appointed director of Indiana's State Student Assistance Commission and worked as a state legislative aide before joining Merrill Lynch as a financial analyst.

When Democratic Rep. Lee H. Hamilton let him know he'd be vacating the 9th District seat in 1998, after 17 terms, Hill decided to make the run. Voters remembered his high school basketball exploits nearly three decades earlier, and he defeated former state Sen. Jean Leising, who had run against Hamilton in 1994 and 1996, by about 3 percentage points.

In 2000, the surprise Republican nominee was Michael Everett Bailey, who had gained notoriety in 1992 by running graphic TV ads about abortion during his campaign against Hamilton. Bailey ran the same ads against Hill, to no better effect, and Hill prevailed by 10 points.

Reapportionment after the 2000 census cost Indiana one of its 10 House seats. Yet during redistricting, the 9th was the least affected of the Hoosier State districts. The new map, which added Bloomington (home of Indiana University) and dropped some Republican-leaning areas near Cincinnati, resulted in a slightly more Democratic district. Although the national GOP targeted the seat in 2002 for special attention, Hill won a hard-fought race by 5 points over businessman Mike Sodrel.

KEY VOTES

2002

- Yes Overhaul campaign finance law; ban "soft money" and restrict advocacy advertising
- Yes Back Bush's defense budget increase
- No Extend 1996 welfare law
- No Adopt Bush's discretionary spending limit
- No Pass GOP Medicare prescription drug plan
- Yes Create independent Sept. 11 commission
- No Extend union protections to Homeland Security Department employees
- Yes Revive fast-track procedures for trade agreements
- Yes Authorize war against Iraq
- Yes Advance bankruptcy overhaul opposed by abortion opponents

2001

- No Nullify Clinton Labor Department ergonomics rule
- No Cut taxes by $1.35 trillion through fiscal 2011
- Yes Maintain ban on oil drilling in Arctic National Wildlife Refuge
- No Approve Bush proposal to limit managed-care plan liability for coverage decisions
- No Divert money from crop subsidy payments to land conservation
- ? Expand law enforcement power to investigate suspected terrorists

CQ VOTE STUDIES

	PARTY UNITY		PRESIDENTIAL SUPPORT	
	Support	Oppose	Support	Oppose
2002	76%	24%	45%	55%
2001	72%	28%	34%	66%
2000	81%	19%	76%	24%
1999	74%	26%	65%	35%

INTEREST GROUPS

	AFL-CIO	ADA	CCUS	ACU
2002	44%	70%	65%	28%
2001	82%	75%	50%	32%
2000	70%	70%	60%	16%
1999	78%	75%	56%	16%

INDIANA 9
Southeast — Bloomington, New Albany

Bordering the Ohio River to the south, the 9th shares socially conservative roots and, more recently, competitive politics with other river valley districts. Manufacturing forms the district's economic foundation, although agriculture and retail trade also are prevalent in Indiana's southeastern quadrant.

The 9th's northeastern counties are seeing an influx of Cincinnati migrants, who have started to change the district from rural to slightly suburban. To the south, Clark and Floyd counties are adding residents due to Louisville metropolitan area growth. Clark is the 9th's most populous county.

Much of Monroe, the next most-populous county, was drawn into the 9th following the 2000 census, including Bloomington. Indiana University's presence gives the city a Democratic lean, and in some city precincts the write-in tally for Green Party presidential candidate Ralph Nader was higher than that of George W. Bush in 2000.

While the university makes Monroe one of Indiana's best-educated counties, the 9th as a whole is blue-collar with a low percentage of college graduates. Unemployment in some counties, including Orange and Crawford, can run substantially above Indiana's otherwise low average, and areas of rural poverty exist in the district. Crawford has the state's second-highest poverty rate and the longest commute time: many residents work in Louisville, due east on Interstate 64.

While the 9th has a Democratic heritage, the area's deep conservatism on cultural issues propelled Bush to a double-digit victory in 2000. Although Bush's statewide showing was only 10 percentage points higher than that of Republican Bob Dole four years earlier, in the 9th Bush exceeded Dole's 1996 numbers by more than 16 percentage points in Dubois, Crawford, Jennings, Orange, Switzerland and Ohio counties.

MAJOR INDUSTRY
Manufacturing, agriculture, retail

CITIES
Bloomington (pt.), 66,459; New Albany, 37,603; Jeffersonville, 27,362

NOTABLE
Basketball star Larry Bird is from French Lick; Corydon, hometown of Gov. Frank L. O'Bannon, was Indiana's first state capital (1816-25).

IOWA

Gov. Tom Vilsack (D)

First elected: 1998
Length of term: 4 years
Term expires: 1/07
Salary: $104,794
Phone: (515) 281-5211
Hometown: Mt. Pleasant
Born: Dec. 13, 1950; Pittsburgh, Pa.
Religion: Roman Catholic
Family: Wife, Christie Vilsack; two children
Education: Hamilton College (N.Y.), A.B. 1972; Albany Law School, J.D. 1975
Career: Lawyer
Political highlights: Mayor of Mt. Pleasant, 1987-92; Iowa Senate, 1993-99
Election results:

2002 GENERAL		
Tom Vilsack (D)	540,449	52.7%
Doug Gross (R)	456,612	44.5%
Jay Robinson (GREEN)	14,628	1.4%
Clyde Cleveland (LIBERT)	13,098	1.3%

Lt. Gov. Sally Pederson (D)

First elected: 1998
Length of term: 4 years
Term expires: 1/07
Salary: $73,047
Phone: (515) 281-0225

STATE LEGISLATURE

General Assembly: Meets January-May
House: 100 members, 2-year terms
2003 breakdown: 54R, 46D; 75 men, 25 women
Salary: $21,380
Phone: (515) 281-3221
Senate: 50 members, 4-year terms
2003 breakdown: 29R, 21D; 43 men, 7 women
Salary: $21,380
Phone: (515) 281-3371

STATE TERM LIMITS

Governor: No
Senate: No
House: No

URBAN STATISTICS

CITY	POPULATION
Des Moines	198,682
Cedar Rapids	120,758
Davenport	98,359
Sioux City	85,013
Waterloo	68,747

REGISTERED VOTERS

Nonaffiliated	38%
Republican	33%
Democrat	30%

POPULATION

2002 population (est.)	2,936,760
2000 population	2,926,324
1990 population	2,776,755
Percent change (1990-2000)	+5.4%
Rank among states (2002)	30
Median age	36.6
Born in state	74.8%
Foreign born	3.1%
Violent crime rate	266/100,000
Poverty level	9.1%
Federal workers	18,928
Military	14,329

REDISTRICTING

Iowa retained its five seats in reapportionment. The Legislative Service Bureau drew a new map, which the state legislature approved and the governor signed on June 22, 2001.

MISCELLANEOUS

Web: www.state.ia.us
Capital: Des Moines

STATE ELECTION OFFICIAL
(515) 281-5865

DEMOCRATIC HEADQUARTERS
(515) 244-7292

REPUBLICAN HEADQUARTERS
(515) 282-8105

District Statistics

DIST.	2000 VOTE FOR PRESIDENT BUSH	GORE	NADER	WHITE	BLACK	ASIAN	HISP	MEDIAN INCOME	WHITE COLLAR	BLUE COLLAR	SERVICE INDUSTRY	OVER 64	UNDER 18	COLLEGE EDUCATION	RURAL	SQ. MILES
1	45%	52%	2%	92%	4%	1%	2%	$38,727	56%	29%	15%	14%	25%	20%	34%	7,217
2	43	53	3	92	2	2	3	$40,121	59	27	14	13	24	25	34	7,566
3	48	49	2	90	3	2	3	$43,176	62	24	14	13	26	25	27	6,979
4	49	48	2	95	1	1	3	$38,242	56	29	15	16	24	20	49	15,760
5	57	40	2	94	1	1	4	$36,773	53	31	16	17	26	16	51	18,348
STATE	48	49	2	93	2	1	3	$39,469	57	28	15	15	25	21	39	55,869
U.S.	47.9	48.4	3	69	12	4	13	$41,994	60	25	15	12	26	24	21	3,537,438

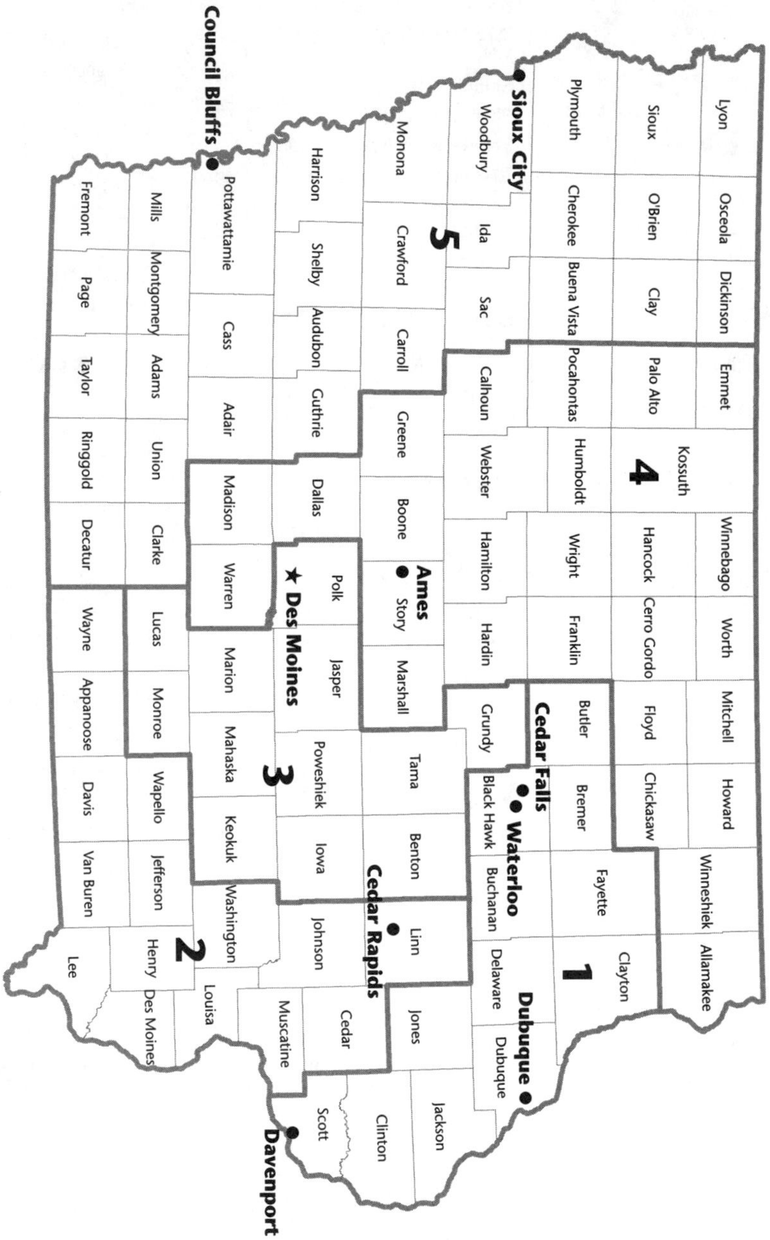
Sioux City
Council Bluffs
Ames
Des Moines
Cedar Falls
Waterloo
Cedar Rapids
Dubuque
Davenport
1
2
3
4
5
Lyon
Osceola
Dickinson
Emmet
Kossuth
Winnebago
Worth
Mitchell
Howard
Winneshiek
Allamakee
Sioux
O'Brien
Clay
Palo Alto
Hancock
Cerro Gordo
Floyd
Chickasaw
Fayette
Clayton
Plymouth
Cherokee
Buena Vista
Pocahontas
Humboldt
Wright
Franklin
Butler
Bremer
Black Hawk
Buchanan
Delaware
Dubuque
Woodbury
Ida
Sac
Calhoun
Webster
Hamilton
Hardin
Grundy
Monona
Crawford
Carroll
Greene
Boone
Story
Marshall
Tama
Benton
Linn
Jones
Jackson
Harrison
Shelby
Audubon
Guthrie
Dallas
Polk
Jasper
Poweshiek
Iowa
Johnson
Cedar
Clinton
Pottawattamie
Cass
Adair
Madison
Warren
Marion
Mahaska
Keokuk
Washington
Louisa
Muscatine
Scott
Mills
Montgomery
Adams
Union
Clarke
Lucas
Monroe
Wapello
Jefferson
Henry
Des Moines
Fremont
Page
Taylor
Ringgold
Decatur
Wayne
Appanoose
Davis
Van Buren
Lee

Sen. Charles E. Grassley (R)

CAPITOL OFFICE
224-3744
chuck_grassley@grassley.senate.gov
grassley.senate.gov
135 Hart 20510-1501; fax 224-6020

COMMITTEES
Agriculture, Nutrition & Forestry
Budget
Finance - chairman
Judiciary
Joint Taxation

HOMETOWN
New Hartford

BORN
Sept. 17, 1933, New Hartford, Iowa

RELIGION
Baptist

FAMILY
Wife, Barbara Grassley; five children

EDUCATION
U. of Northern Iowa, B.A. 1955, M.A. 1956 (political science); U. of Iowa, attended 1957-58 (graduate studies)

CAREER
Farmer

POLITICAL HIGHLIGHTS
Republican nominee for Iowa House, 1956; Iowa House, 1959-75; U.S. House, 1975-81

ELECTION RESULTS

1998 GENERAL		
Charles E. Grassley (R)	648,480	68.4%
David Osterberg (D)	289,049	30.5%
1998 PRIMARY		
Charles E. Grassley (R)		unopposed

PREVIOUS WINNING PERCENTAGES
1992 (70%); 1986 (66%); 1980 (54%); 1978 House Election (75%); 1976 House Election (57%); 1974 House Election (51%)

Elected 1980; 4th term

As he returned to the chairmanship of the Finance Committee for the 108th Congress, Grassley faced frequently conflicting pressures to be a loyal member of the conservative Republican leadership while also standing guard on pocketbook issues vital to his constituents.

As fiscally conservative as any Republican and a champion for small businesses and free trade, Grassley also is a plain-spoken advocate for populist themes that transcend party lines, such as the defense of government whistleblowers and attacks on companies that dodge taxes. He is a social conservative, too, opposing abortion and gun control, and has been a crusader against deficits on the Budget Committee. But Grassley also works to fund Iowa projects and has developed a reputation as a pragmatic dealmaker on efforts to improve social services and aid for farmers.

On Finance, Grassley has been able to draw support for tax measures from moderates in both parties, especially those from rural states. Max Baucus of Montana, the panel's top-ranking Democrat, is a frequent ally. Grassley's success as a broker, both as chairman for the first five months of 2001 and as top Republican when Baucus took the gavel for the rest of the 107th Congress, helped to advance the Bush administration's economic program. "The tradition of the committee has been bipartisan. We have continued that tradition," Grassley said of his relationship with Baucus.

Agreements between the pair helped clear the way for two of President Bush's top legislative achievements of the 107th: the 10-year, $1.35 trillion tax cut of 2001 and the 2002 law renewing the president's fast-track authority to negotiate trade deals that cannot be amended by Congress.

Early in the 108th, Grassley backed Bush's effort to extend his signature tax cut, which will otherwise expire by 2011. He initially questioned whether Bush's proposal to eliminate taxation of corporate dividends was politically viable but later reversed course. "I think I should have kept my mouth shut back in January," Grassley said after meeting with the president. He continued to insist, however, that bipartisan compromise would be needed to enact Bush's second round of ambitious tax cuts.

But overall, during the first two years of the Bush administration Grassley backed the president on the floor 97 percent of the time, 10th among senators returning for the 108th.

Grassley is not a lawyer — "I'm just a farmer from Butler County," he likes to say — but on the Judiciary Committee he holds his own by mastering legislative details and building coalitions on his priorities. Since 1997 these have included a campaign to rewrite bankruptcy law, primarily to make it harder for people to wipe away their debts in bankruptcy court. Still unfulfilled, the quest has been quintessential Grassley; although no one at the Capitol views him as particularly smooth in his delivery or sophisticated in his argument, many identify him as the most persistent senator around.

Through much of his congressional career, Grassley has led high-profile investigations of government waste and misconduct. "Frankly, it takes too much time to pass legislation on some issues," he says. "With oversight, it's direct and immediate, and you see results much more quickly."

In the 107th, he worked on Judiciary with Chairman Patrick J. Leahy, a Vermont Democrat, to probe allegations that rank-and-file FBI employees were being held to tougher standards of conduct than bureau managers. Grassley also pushed successfully in 2002 to extend whistleblower protection requirements to the new Department of Homeland Security.

During the 1980s, Grassley publicized some extraordinary Pentagon expenditures, including $7,600 for a coffeemaker. He has worked on overhauling the IRS and trimming the number of federal judgeships. And he has made the work of Capitol Hill itself a priority, pushing the 1995 law making Congress abide by the labor and safety rules it imposes on businesses, trying to require public disclosure of "holds" placed on legislation by individual senators and investigating the health and safety effects from the cleanup after the 2001 anthrax attack on the Capitol.

Grassley is more open than many top Senate Republicans to finding common ground with moderate and even liberal Democrats. Late in the 107th, he attempted to cut a deal with Massachusetts Democrat Edward M. Kennedy to curb requirements that workers hold employer stock in their retirement accounts. In the 106th, he and Kennedy pushed a proposal to give parents Medicaid assistance for disabled children.

Grassley also has developed close ties to other moderates and liberals in both parties, and was forgiving when James M. Jeffords of Vermont left the GOP to become an independent in 2001. "We took too much of our relationships for granted, we Republicans," he said.

While he has a consistently conservative voting record, Grassley is not always a friend of business. During the 107th, he worked to limit tax breaks and federal contracts for companies that move their headquarters to offshore tax havens. "Imagine the nerve," Grassley said. "They create phony foreign headquarters in a file folder or a mail box to escape taxes and then use other peoples' taxes to turn a profit."

Grassley backs aggressive enforcement of antitrust laws. He has expressed alarm at the rate of mergers in the meat processing industry and has pushed the Agriculture Department to take a tougher stand against anti-competitive practices. With Iowa's other senator, Democrat Tom Harkin, he has moved to spur more airline competition, in part by writing into a 2000 law the guarantee of two slots at Washington's crowded Reagan National Airport for a carrier offering nonstop service to Des Moines.

Grassley has had a seat on more than half the Senate's committees, serving long stints on Agriculture and Aging — with obvious parochial benefits — and shorter tenures on Small Business, Labor, Governmental Affairs and Appropriations. Since the 107th he has held the same four seats: Budget and Joint Taxation in addition to Finance and Judiciary. In the 108th, he got back on Agriculture as well.

The son of Waterloo-area farmers, Grassley is proud of his deep rural roots and his status as the Senate's only working farmer. He still returns to work the family corn and soybean fields on weekends and when the Senate is in recess — though he has been known to plow with a cell phone tucked inside his cap so he can feel the vibrations of an incoming call from Washington. He views himself as one of the few farmer-statesmen left in a country founded by them, and is not one to put on airs or attempt to spin.

He began predicting a career in politics for himself while he was in high school, although he initially dreamed only of a seat in the Iowa House. After graduating from the University of Northern Iowa, he did graduate work at two Iowa universities and paid the bills by working in a factory — where he was a Machinists union member. A few years later, he and his wife, Barbara, took over his family's grain and livestock operation.

At the age of 25, he began a 16-year stint in the General Assembly, where he rose to become chairman of the House Appropriations Committee. He moved to Congress as the successor of H.R. Gross, a revered Republican figure in the state who retired in 1974. Six years later he took 54 percent of the vote to unseat liberal Democratic Sen. John C. Culver. His share of the vote has not fallen below 66 percent in his three subsequent re-elections.

KEY VOTES

2002

- Yes Pass farm bill reversing crop subsidy limits
- Yes Postpone tougher automobile fuel efficiency standards
- No Overhaul campaign finance law; ban "soft money" and restrict advocacy advertising
- Yes Set federal election standards
- Yes Support oil drilling in Arctic National Wildlife Refuge
- Yes Revive fast-track procedures for trade agreements
- No Create federal insurance coverage for catastrophic terrorist losses
- Yes Tighten federal accounting and corporate governance regulation
- No Advance bipartisan Medicare prescription drug plan
- Yes Create independent Sept. 11 commission
- No Back Democratic Homeland Security Department proposal
- Yes Authorize war against Iraq

2001

- Yes Confirm John Ashcroft as attorney general
- Yes Nullify Clinton Labor Department ergonomics rule
- Yes Cut taxes by $1.35 trillion through fiscal 2011
- No Pass Democratic bill to bolster rights of patients in managed-care plans
- Yes Permit a new round of military base closings
- Yes Expand law enforcement power to investigate suspected terrorists

CQ VOTE STUDIES

	PARTY UNITY		PRESIDENTIAL SUPPORT	
	Support	Oppose	Support	Oppose
2002	88%	12%	95%	5%
2001	93%	7%	99%	1%
2000	94%	6%	42%	58%
1999	90%	10%	33%	67%
1998	86%	14%	39%	61%
1997	91%	9%	60%	40%
1996	92%	8%	32%	68%
1995	92%	8%	26%	74%
1994	87%	13%	34%	66%
1993	91%	9%	25%	75%

INTEREST GROUPS

	AFL-CIO	ADA	CCUS	ACU
2002	15%	10%	95%	95%
2001	13%	5%	100%	92%
2000	0%	0%	100%	96%
1999	0%	0%	94%	92%
1998	0%	5%	83%	80%
1997	0%	5%	100%	80%
1996	0%	15%	92%	90%
1995	0%	5%	100%	91%
1994	0%	15%	90%	92%
1993	0%	20%	91%	88%

Sen. Tom Harkin (D)

CAPITOL OFFICE
224-3254
tom_harkin@harkin.senate.gov
harkin.senate.gov
731 Hart 20510-1502; fax 224-9369

COMMITTEES
Agriculture, Nutrition & Forestry - ranking member
Appropriations
Health, Education, Labor & Pensions
Small Business & Entrepreneurship

HOMETOWN
Cumming

BORN
Nov. 19, 1939, Cumming, Iowa

RELIGION
Roman Catholic

FAMILY
Wife, Ruth Harkin; two children

EDUCATION
Iowa State U., B.S. 1962 (government & economics); Catholic U. of America, J.D. 1972

MILITARY SERVICE
Navy, 1962-67; Naval Reserve, 1968-74

CAREER
Lawyer; congressional aide

POLITICAL HIGHLIGHTS
Democratic nominee for U.S. House, 1972; U.S. House, 1975-85; sought Democratic nomination for president, 1992

ELECTION RESULTS

2002 GENERAL		
Tom Harkin (D)	554,278	54.2%
Greg Ganske (R)	447,892	43.8%
Timothy A. Harthan (GREEN)	11,340	1.1%
2002 PRIMARY		
Tom Harkin (D)		unopposed

PREVIOUS WINNING PERCENTAGES
1996 (52%); 1990 (54%); 1984 (56%); 1982 House Election (59%); 1980 House Election (60%); 1978 House Election (59%); 1976 House Election (65%); 1974 House Election (51%)

Elected 1984; 4th term

Harkin, a veteran senator, still lives his convictions as one of a dwindling number of influential liberals in Congress. As his party has increasingly moderated its policies with leaders like President Clinton, Harkin has remained unbowed. "What used to be known as the center has moved to the right, and I think that's unhealthy for the country," Harkin said in 2003.

"The so-called conservative tax and social policies of the right really make us a more divided society. They put more and more emphasis on those few who have a lot. It's an erosion of the American dream."

Though old-school liberals are often sidelined these days, Harkin's influence is felt on an unusually wide range of issues, from health policy to farm subsidies. He frequently joins with moderates to strike deals, the result often being more left-leaning legislation.

A floor battle at the start of the 108th Congress was typical for Harkin. Pushing for more money for public schools, he said Republicans had a choice between honoring their commitment in the 2001 education overhaul — a President Bush initiative — or using the money for tax cuts for investors, another Bush proposal. "Instead of focusing on dividends for millionaires, we should be focusing on making sure our kids can multiply and divide," he said. The Senate voted additional money for schools, but only half of what Harkin had sought.

Harkin was a vocal foe of the president's $1.35 trillion tax cut in 2001, which he said unduly favored the wealthy over the middle and lower classes. A small group of endangered Senate Democrats voted for the tax cut, but Harkin remained steadfast.

A rare spot of political ambiguity for him is trade; a strong friend of labor, he nonetheless finds himself voting for free-trade agreements in deference to Iowa farmers and their demands for loose export rules.

With Republican Sen. Chuck Hagel of Nebraska, Harkin is a leader in the fight for full funding for special education programs, which the federal government mandates but pays for only in part.

Harkin frequently teams with his friend, Sen. Arlen Specter, a Pennsylvania Republican, who shares his intense interest in health care policy. As the two top leaders on the Appropriations Committee's Labor, Health and Human Services, and Education panel, they managed to double funding for medical research at the National Institutes of Health over the five years beginning in 1998. They are also cosponsors of a proposal in the debate over replicating human stem cells; the plan would allow human embryos to be used for medical treatments but not to clone people.

Harkin has long advocated letting the Food and Drug Administration regulate tobacco, and he was a leader in unsuccessful tobacco lawsuit settlement bills in 1998 and 1999. In the 108th Congress, he proposed taking nationwide a pilot federal program that provides free fruit and vegetables to public school children in four states.

Harkin's signal achievement in the health arena was the 1990 Americans with Disabilities Act, which extended broad civil rights protections to an estimated 54 million Americans with mental and physical disabilities. Harkin says he was inspired by his deaf brother, Frank, and he gave part of his floor speech in sign language in Frank's honor. "Many times he told me, 'Gosh, I wish I'd had this when I started out,' " Harkin says.

Given Iowa's importance in the Farm Belt, agriculture is another of Harkin's keen interests. And his leadership in this area helped him fend off a serious Republican challenge to his seat in the last election.

Harkin was facing a tough contest in 2002 against GOP Rep. Greg Ganske. Harkin fortuitously became chairman of the Agriculture Committee in 2001 when GOP Sen. James Jeffords of Vermont suddenly became an independent and threw the Senate into Democratic hands.

Harkin was a major force behind a six-year farm bill that restored some certainty for farmers by ensuring continued government subsidies. Those payments were threatened by the Republicans' 1996 "Freedom to Farm" law, which sought to wean American farmers off big government subsidies over time.

Enactment of the bill just before the election showcased his work for the state's important agriculture sector. He was helped, too, by his populist appeal to a big segment of the state's voters. Harkin, considered one of the most vulnerable incumbents because of Iowa's swing politics, defeated Ganske by 10 percentage points despite a last-minute appeal to voters by Bush. He became the longest-serving Democratic senator in Iowa history.

The son of a coal miner, Harkin grew up in a small, crowded house in the town of Cumming. His mother, a Slovenian immigrant, died when he was 10. He worked his way through college and law school, and spent five years in Vietnam as a Navy pilot.

In 1969, he was hired by Iowa Democratic Rep. Neal Smith as an aide on the House select committee investigating the U.S. military's progress in Vietnam. He made a name for himself with his discovery of South Vietnam's "tiger cages."

By outwitting a South Vietnamese official on a guided tour of a prison camp, Harkin found, behind a hidden door, hundreds of men, women and children crammed into underground cells. The cells had open grates on top through which guards poured skin-searing doses of lime. Harkin photographed the political prisoners and tape-recorded their stories.

Skittish members of the committee sought to suppress his documentation of abuses by America's ally in the war. But Harkin insisted on going public, and his photographs and story in Life magazine energized the antiwar movement in this country and forced South Vietnam to shutter the tiger cages. The move cost the 30-year-old Harkin his job, but a few years later he found his way back to Capitol Hill.

Harkin first ran for Congress in 1972, against entrenched GOP incumbent William Scherle. He attracted publicity with his gimmick of "work days," toiling alongside farmers, teachers and welfare caseworkers — a technique still used in campaigns today. He lost narrowly but tried again and toppled Scherle by a slim margin in 1974, this time building a stronger organization and raising more money. In four House re-elections, he captured about 60 percent of the vote.

His Senate campaigns have been tougher. He won his seat in 1984 by ousting GOP Sen. Roger W. Jepsen with 56 percent of the vote. In 1990, GOP challenger Rep. Tom Tauke threatened Harkin by accusing him of abusing congressional mailing privileges and voting for excessive spending. Harkin eventually won by 9 percentage points. In 1996, he won a third term by defeating GOP Rep. Jim Ross Lightfoot by 5 percentage points.

Harkin ran briefly for the Democratic nomination for president in 1992, winning the Iowa caucuses handily but staggering in subsequent primaries. In 2000, Democratic presidential nominee Al Gore considered making Harkin his running mate but settled on Democratic Sen. Joseph I. Lieberman of Connecticut.

Harkin says he no longer wants to run for president. But he wants to continue to influence the Democratic Party, and perhaps move it back to the left.

KEY VOTES

2002

Yes Pass farm bill reversing crop subsidy limits
No Postpone tougher automobile fuel efficiency standards
Yes Overhaul campaign finance law; ban "soft money" and restrict advocacy advertising
Yes Set federal election standards
No Support oil drilling in Arctic National Wildlife Refuge
Yes Revive fast-track procedures for trade agreements
Yes Create federal insurance coverage for catastrophic terrorist losses
Yes Tighten federal accounting and corporate governance regulation
No Advance bipartisan Medicare prescription drug plan
Yes Create independent Sept. 11 commission
Yes Back Democratic Homeland Security Department proposal
Yes Authorize war against Iraq

2001

No Confirm John Ashcroft as attorney general
No Nullify Clinton Labor Department ergonomics rule
– Cut taxes by $1.35 trillion through fiscal 2011
Yes Pass Democratic bill to bolster rights of patients in managed-care plans
Yes Permit a new round of military base closings
Yes Expand law enforcement power to investigate suspected terrorists

CQ VOTE STUDIES

	PARTY UNITY		PRESIDENTIAL SUPPORT	
	Support	Oppose	Support	Oppose
2002	92%	8%	69%	31%
2001	97%	3%	63%	37%
2000	97%	3%	92%	8%
1999	97%	3%	91%	9%
1998	98%	2%	88%	12%
1997	92%	8%	87%	13%
1996	91%	9%	85%	15%
1995	91%	9%	90%	10%
1994	97%	3%	92%	8%
1993	93%	7%	93%	7%

INTEREST GROUPS

	AFL-CIO	ADA	CCUS	ACU
2002	100%	80%	45%	15%
2001	100%	100%	38%	8%
2000	75%	95%	57%	4%
1999	89%	100%	47%	4%
1998	100%	95%	50%	5%
1997	71%	85%	70%	12%
1996	86%	80%	38%	10%
1995	92%	95%	44%	9%
1994	88%	100%	30%	0%
1993	73%	90%	27%	0%

Rep. Jim Nussle (R)

CAPITOL OFFICE
225-2911
nussleia@mail.house.gov
www.house.gov/nussle
303 Cannon 20515-1501; fax 225-9129

COMMITTEES
Budget - chairman
Ways & Means

HOMETOWN
Manchester

BORN
June 27, 1960, Des Moines, Iowa

RELIGION
Lutheran

FAMILY
Wife, Karen Nussle; two children

EDUCATION
Luther College, B.A. 1983; Drake U., J.D. 1985

CAREER
Lawyer

POLITICAL HIGHLIGHTS
Delaware County attorney, 1986-90

ELECTION RESULTS

2002 GENERAL		
Jim Nussle (R)	112,280	57.2%
Ann Hutchinson (D)	83,779	42.7%
2002 PRIMARY		
Jim Nussle (R)		unopposed
2000 GENERAL		
Jim Nussle (R)	139,906	55.4%
Donna L. Smith (D)	110,327	43.7%

PREVIOUS WINNING PERCENTAGES
1998 (55%); 1996 (53%); 1994 (56%); 1992 (50%); 1990 (50%)

Elected 1990; 7th term

Nussle has settled in as an influential player and a reliable GOP leadership ally on fiscal policy. Since becoming chairman of the Budget Committee in the 107th Congress, he has smoothed some of the rough edges of his demeanor and legislative style that, earlier in his career, drew the ire not just of Democrats but also of House Republican leaders.

Nussle bested three other contenders to take the Budget gavel, including two who had more seniority on the panel. He promptly returned the favor to Republican leaders early in 2001 by writing a budget resolution much to their liking, closely following President Bush's initial budget proposal and setting the stage for the $1.35 trillion tax cut enacted that spring. With a $5.6 trillion surplus forecast by the end of the decade, Nussle argued strongly that it was the government's duty to give some of it back to taxpayers.

A year later, with the economy faltering, tax revenue shrinking and the aftermath of the Sept. 11, 2001, terrorist attacks draining resources, Nussle vociferously defended the tax cut against Democratic attacks that it was fiscally irresponsible. "Do not come down here and blame the tax cuts without having the courage or the guts to give us a plan to raise those taxes back up again," he said. He wrote another budget resolution that pleased Bush and House Republican leaders, which called for big increases in defense spending and tightly restrained domestic spending.

The president rewarded Nussle with a pair of trips to Iowa to support his 2002 re-election campaign. Although he seemed to be one of the more vulnerable GOP incumbents, Nussle ended up scoring a decisive victory over Democrat Ann Hutchinson, the mayor of Bettendorf, who sought to make the race a referendum on the struggling economy.

Nussle is seen by many colleagues as less divisive than his predecessor, John R. Kasich of Ohio, who offered the minority party little substantive input on the budgets written during his six-year tenure. Democrats acknowledge that Nussle is running a more open shop than Kasich did, allowing them more influence and more resources. And he has sought to polish his relationship with news media, frequently stopping for impromptu interviews.

Nussle has tangled often with the Congressional Budget Office over its budget forecasts, contending that they are frequently far off the mark. He also feuded publicly with CBO Director Dan L. Crippen, who disagreed with Nussle and opposed "dynamic scoring," in which the projected costs of some legislation, particularly tax cuts, are reduced on the budget books because they are seen as having such a guaranteed positive effect on the economy. A dispirited Crippen chose not to seek a second term and left in 2003. He was replaced with a Nussle-backed dynamic scoring advocate.

Nussle and Speaker J. Dennis Hastert seem to get along. They occasionally refer to one other as "cousin" — Nussle is the maiden name of Hastert's mother. (The two do not believe they are actually related.)

In the past, Nussle has had a more rocky relationship with members of both parties. He still is remembered for the time in 1991 when, during a floor speech, he placed a brown paper bag over his head to decry the Democratic leadership's decision not to make public the roster of lawmakers who had overdrawn their accounts at the private bank for House members. The moment — telecast by C-SPAN and extensively covered by the national media — came to symbolize the image problem Congress then faced. It also was viewed, in both cloakrooms, as demeaning grandstanding particularly inappropriate from a colleague.

Nussle was then one of the "Gang of Seven," a group of Republican freshmen in the 102nd Congress who agitated for changes in the way the Democratic-run House operated. When the GOP won control in 1994, Nussle became the point man for incoming Speaker Newt Gingrich's plan to remake the House, which included cutting committee staffs and eliminating such institutional traditions as daily ice delivery to members' offices. Time magazine named him one of the top 50 rising political leaders in the nation. But once the 104th Congress got under way, Nussle faded from view, becoming just another foot soldier in the Republican "revolution."

Nussle was vice chairman of the National Republican Congressional Committee in the 104th, and he harbored aspirations of running the campaign organization in the 105th. But the job went to John Linder, a Georgia neighbor of Gingrich, and a few months later Nussle lost another bid for the leadership when another Gingrich-backed candidate, Washington's Jennifer Dunn, was elected vice chairman of the GOP Conference.

Nussle normally is a ready vote for his party on social and environmental issues, but as a proponent of reduced government spending he has broken with the leadership at times to oppose big-ticket military items. He often pushes for spending cuts to offset the expenses of emergencies — even including flood relief for Iowa.

Like many of his colleagues, however, Nussle has learned to fight for items of clear interest back home, and he earns plaudits for his constituent service. As a representative of farm country, he favors increasing agricultural exports — he is a solid vote for trade liberalization — and has worked to expand domestic markets for ethanol, a fuel additive made from corn.

Nussle, whose eldest child has Down syndrome, is a strong supporter of federal special education programs and the Special Olympics.

Nussle was interested in government and politics from an early age; he was a 30-year-old lawyer with just one term as a county attorney under his belt when he ran in 1990 for the House seat that Republican Tom Tauke (for whom Nussle once interned) gave up to run for the Senate. Nussle eked out a 1,642-vote victory. Two years later he had to run against another incumbent, Democrat Dave Nagle, when reapportionment cost Iowa a House seat. Nussle again squeaked by, and Democrats have continued to mount serious challenges every two years. His 57 percent in 2002 was a career high.

Iowa political observers have already begun touting him for a bid for governor in 2006, when his term as Budget chairman is due to end.

KEY VOTES

2002

No Overhaul campaign finance law; ban "soft money" and restrict advocacy advertising
Yes Back Bush's defense budget increase
Yes Extend 1996 welfare law
Yes Adopt Bush's discretionary spending limit
Yes Pass GOP Medicare prescription drug plan
No Create independent Sept. 11 commission
No Extend union protections to Homeland Security Department employees
Yes Revive fast-track procedures for trade agreements
Yes Authorize war against Iraq
Yes Advance bankruptcy overhaul opposed by abortion opponents

2001

Yes Nullify Clinton Labor Department ergonomics rule
Yes Cut taxes by $1.35 trillion through fiscal 2011
No Maintain ban on oil drilling in Arctic National Wildlife Refuge
Yes Approve Bush proposal to limit managed-care plan liability for coverage decisions
No Divert money from crop subsidy payments to land conservation
Yes Expand law enforcement power to investigate suspected terrorists

CQ VOTE STUDIES

	PARTY UNITY		PRESIDENTIAL SUPPORT	
	Support	Oppose	Support	Oppose
2002	93%	7%	88%	12%
2001	95%	5%	88%	12%
2000	93%	7%	25%	75%
1999	87%	13%	22%	78%
1998	89%	11%	27%	73%

INTEREST GROUPS

	AFL-CIO	ADA	CCUS	ACU
2002	11%	0%	100%	92%
2001	17%	0%	100%	88%
2000	10%	15%	95%	84%
1999	11%	20%	100%	80%
1998	10%	10%	100%	84%

IOWA 1

East — Davenport, Waterloo, Dubuque

The 1st takes in half of Iowa's Mississippi River counties and is dominated by three midsize industrial cities: Davenport, Waterloo and Dubuque.

Davenport and Bettendorf in Scott County (Iowa's half of the Quad Cities that straddle the river into Illinois) are old, industrial river cities whose economies suffered badly during the 1980s but are recovering by capitalizing on tourists drawn to riverboat gambling. Waterloo, slightly more than 100 miles northwest of Davenport, grew up around the farm-implement and meatpacking industries. While hogs still are slaughtered here, the economy diversified in the 1990s to include finance and insurance. Neighboring Cedar Falls relies on the influence of the University of Northern Iowa.

Dubuque, built against the bluffs facing the Mississippi River, is Iowa's oldest city. Its economic base shifted in the 1990s from manufacturing and meatpacking to service, including insurance, finance and telecommunications.

Democrats outnumber Republicans in the 1st, but voters have tended to demonstrate their independence at the polls in recent years. Black Hawk County, with Cedar Falls and Waterloo, has a strong Democratic base from its labor and academic communities. Scott County narrowly voted for Al Gore in 2000 but has a centrist Republican tradition. Democrats have the advantage in Clinton County, located north of Scott. Overall, Gore carried the district with 52 percent of the vote.

Dubuque County, which is heavily Catholic, gave Gore a greater percentage of the vote than any other county in the 1st. Dubuque has a culturally conservative lean, though, and Rep. Nussle has consistently outperformed Republican presidential candidates there. The rest of the 1st's residents live in rural areas that by and large are Republican-leaning but politically competitive.

MAJOR INDUSTRY

Farm machinery, meatpacking, health care, agriculture

CITIES

Davenport, 98,359; Waterloo, 68,747; Dubuque, 57,686; Cedar Falls, 36,145

NOTABLE

Dyersville is home to the baseball field in the movie "Field of Dreams."

Rep. Jim Leach (R)

CAPITOL OFFICE
225-6576
talk2jim@mail.house.gov
www.house.gov/leach
2186 Rayburn 20515-1502; fax 226-1278

COMMITTEES
Financial Services
International Relations
(Asia & the Pacific - chairman)

HOMETOWN
Iowa City

BORN
Oct. 15, 1942, Davenport, Iowa

RELIGION
Episcopalian

FAMILY
Wife, Elisabeth Ann "Deba" Leach; two children

EDUCATION
Princeton U., A.B. 1964 (political science); Johns Hopkins U., M.A. 1966 (Soviet politics); London School of Economics, attended 1966-68 (economics & Soviet politics)

CAREER
Propane gas company executive; foreign service officer; congressional aide

POLITICAL HIGHLIGHTS
Republican nominee for U.S. House, 1974

ELECTION RESULTS

2002 GENERAL		
Jim Leach (R)	108,130	52.2%
Julie Thomas (D)	94,767	45.7%
Kevin Litten (LIBERT)	4,178	2.0%
2002 PRIMARY		
Jim Leach (R)		unopposed
2000 GENERAL		
Jim Leach (R)	164,972	61.8%
Bob Simpson (D)	96,283	36.1%
Russ Madden (LIBERT)	5,564	2.1%

PREVIOUS WINNING PERCENTAGES
1998 (57%); 1996 (53%); 1994 (60%); 1992 (68%); 1990 (100%); 1988 (61%); 1986 (66%); 1984 (67%); 1982 (59%); 1980 (64%); 1978 (64%); 1976 (52%)

Elected 1976; 14th term

No matter what the topic, Leach tends to adopt a calm, professorial air that sets him apart from his back-slapping colleagues. His didactic manner, low-key style and colorless speaking tone — along with the sweaters he favors under his suit jackets — suggest an academic's appearance. In fact, Leach was briefly rumored to be in the running for the presidency of the University of Iowa after he won re-election with just 52 percent in 2002, his closest race since his initial election to the House in 1976.

In some ways, since relinquishing the Banking Committee gavel in 2001, Leach has been returning to his roots. As chairman of International Relations' Subcommittee on East Asia and the Pacific, he has focused on foreign affairs, including North Korea's nuclear presence. In the 108th Congress, the subcommittee was given added oversight over policy toward India and Pakistan, whose deep rivalry and nuclear weaponry could combine into a tinderbox even as Pakistan remains a key U.S. ally in the war on terrorism.

Leach's career started in 1965 as an aide to Republican Rep. Donald H. Rumsfeld of Illinois. (The pair became close enough that Rumsfeld's daughter once stayed with the Leach family for a year.) Four decades on, Leach says that he respects tremendously Rumsfeld's work as secretary of defense, although they often disagree on foreign affairs. In 2002, he was one of only six House Republicans to vote against the resolution authorizing President Bush to launch a military campaign against Iraq.

Leach was a foreign service officer in 1971 and 1972. He played a high-level role in negotiating a number of international treaties — including the Biological and Toxic Weapons Convention of 1972 — while working for the Arms Control and Disarmament Agency. Over the years, Leach has held leadership posts on a number of significant international panels, including Parliamentarians for Global Action, an international nonprofit organization of elected leaders from more than 100 nations, and the United States Commission on Improving the Effectiveness of the United Nations.

International concerns were less of a priority for Leach during his six years chairing the Banking Committee, which was renamed Financial Services after his tenure ended because of term limits in 2001. Leach was a principal architect of the landmark law enacted in the 106th Congress that lowered the regulatory barriers that had separated banks, brokerages and insurers since the Depression. The path to a deal on the bill was notoriously complicated until the end — the affected industries squabbled as they vied for competitive advantage, and the Federal Reserve and the Treasury fought over regulatory power — yet Leach managed to succeed where many others had failed in decades of previous attempts.

Leach was No. 2 in GOP seniority and hoped to take the helm of International Relations in the chairmanship shuffle of 2001, but the gavel went instead to Henry J. Hyde of Illinois, who was No. 3 in seniority and had served six years as Judiciary Committee chairman.

The snub is emblematic of Leach's situation after more than a quarter-century in the House. He has rarely shied away from bucking the Republican leadership when he disagrees with its course, and his search for bipartisanship has at times come at the expense of the GOP agenda. In the 107th, he strayed from his party and voted with Democrats more often than all but one other Republican. And he supported President Bush's position just 65 percent of the time, a lower score than all but two other House Republicans.

His renegade record combined with his erudite manner make Leach a bit of an oddity in the House. He shuns the party circuit, makes comparatively few floor statements and does not seek out media publicity. One of the Capitol's gentler souls, he treats friend and foe in the same measured, polite way and approaches issues with more than the usual introspection.

Leach's independent streak was manifest early on. Although his job in the Foreign Service had nothing to do with Watergate, when he was 31 he resigned in protest over President Nixon's "Saturday night massacre" firing of Archibald Cox, the special prosecutor. In the House, Leach joined nine other Republicans at the start of the 105th Congress in casting their votes for Speaker for people other than Newt Gingrich, the GOP incumbent whose conduct was then the subject of a House ethics committee investigation. Leach voted for retired House Minority Leader Robert H. Michel of Illinois. (Two of the other dissidents voted for Leach.)

Though he split his vote on the two articles of impeachment against President Clinton adopted by the House in 1998 — voting for the perjury charge but against the obstruction of justice charge — Leach played a lead role in congressional inquiries into President and Mrs. Clinton's behavior in a series of investments known by the shorthand Whitewater.

Leach lost his first bid for the House, in 1974, against Democratic incumbent Edward Mezvinsky. But he won their 1976 rematch and was easily re-elected until 1996, when he was held to 53 percent by Democrats portraying him as having lost his moderation in the GOP "revolution."

Leach was touted for a top State Department or Treasury post in the Bush administration, but his chances were hurt by the Democratic nature of eastern Iowa. Al Gore carried the 1st District, which Leach was representing at the time, by 10 percentage points in 2000. Redistricting for this decade — which was handled by a nonpartisan state legislative agency — then put Leach and his Republican colleague Jim Nussle in a newly configured 1st.

The district would have favored Nussle in the 2002 GOP primary, so Leach moved from Davenport to Iowa City, a Democratic stronghold dominated by the University of Iowa. One-third of voters in the 2nd District were new to him — and he kept to his practice of refusing contributions from political action committees or people outside Iowa — but Leach squeezed past family physician Julie Thomas, touted by Democrats for her health care expertise and endearing image.

Leach said he was planning for another campaign in 2004. When he does retire, though, Leach does not plan to stay in Washington. "I can spell Nirvana for you," he says. "IOWA CITY."

KEY VOTES

2002

- Yes Overhaul campaign finance law; ban "soft money" and restrict advocacy advertising
- Yes Back Bush's defense budget increase
- Yes Extend 1996 welfare law
- Yes Adopt Bush's discretionary spending limit
- Yes Pass GOP Medicare prescription drug plan
- Yes Create independent Sept. 11 commission
- No Extend union protections to Homeland Security Department employees
- Yes Revive fast-track procedures for trade agreements
- No Authorize war against Iraq
- Yes Advance bankruptcy overhaul opposed by abortion opponents

2001

- Yes Nullify Clinton Labor Department ergonomics rule
- Yes Cut taxes by $1.35 trillion through fiscal 2011
- Yes Maintain ban on oil drilling in Arctic National Wildlife Refuge
- No Approve Bush proposal to limit managed-care plan liability for coverage decisions
- No Divert money from crop subsidy payments to land conservation
- Yes Expand law enforcement power to investigate suspected terrorists

CQ VOTE STUDIES

	PARTY UNITY		PRESIDENTIAL SUPPORT	
	Support	Oppose	Support	Oppose
2002	71%	29%	70%	30%
2001	73%	27%	60%	40%
2000	73%	27%	45%	55%
1999	70%	30%	38%	62%
1998	63%	37%	53%	47%

INTEREST GROUPS

	AFL-CIO	ADA	CCUS	ACU
2002	11%	30%	85%	56%
2001	42%	45%	78%	25%
2000	20%	30%	80%	58%
1999	22%	55%	76%	48%
1998	44%	45%	89%	32%

IOWA 2

Southeast – Cedar Rapids, Iowa City

The 2nd, a Democratic-leaning region of 15 southeastern Iowa counties, takes in part of the state's eastern border with the Mississippi River and about half of the state's southern border with Missouri.

In the district's north is Cedar Rapids (in Linn County), the most populous city in the district and, after the state capital of Des Moines, the most populous in the state. Long a center for grain processing, Cedar Rapids has weathered hard economic times of late with help from telecommunication equipment firms.

Iowa City (Johnson County), located south of Cedar Rapids, is home to the University of Iowa and a growing number of high-tech companies. The academic community gives Iowa City a strong liberal tilt; one of the city's precincts gave more votes to Ralph Nader than George W. Bush in the 2000 presidential election. Johnson County has not backed a Republican presidential nominee since Richard M. Nixon in 1960.

The 2nd's other population center runs along the Mississippi River in the district's southeast, in Des Moines and Lee counties. Unions retain some influence in the area, but an economy once centered on manufacturing is headed toward tourism and riverboat gambling.

The counties that form the district's southwestern arm are predominantly rural; the economy here relies on exporting agricultural products, including corn, tomatoes, soybeans and pork. With the exception of Wapello County (Ottumwa), this area leans Republican.

Linn, Johnson and the river counties together give the 2nd a decidedly Democratic tilt. But Republican Rep. Leach has held onto the district by mixing fiscal conservatism with moderate-to-liberal social views.

MAJOR INDUSTRY

Electronics, telecommunications, health care, grain processing

CITIES

Cedar Rapids, 120,758; Iowa City, 62,220; Burlington, 26,839; Marion, 26,294; Ottumwa, 24,998; Muscatine, 22,697

NOTABLE

University of Iowa Hospitals and Clinics is one of the largest teaching hospitals in the world; Cedar Rapids' government buildings are located on an island in the center of the city.

Rep. Leonard L. Boswell (D)

CAPITOL OFFICE
225-3806
rep.boswell.ia03@mail.house.gov
www.house.gov/boswell
1427 Longworth 20515-1503; fax 225-5608

COMMITTEES
Agriculture
Transportation & Infrastructure
Select Intelligence

HOMETOWN
Des Moines

BORN
Jan. 10, 1934, Harrison County, Mo.

RELIGION
Reorganized Church of Jesus Christ of Latter Day Saints

FAMILY
Wife, Dody Boswell; three children

EDUCATION
Graceland College, B.A. 1969 (business administration)

MILITARY SERVICE
Army, 1956-76

CAREER
Farmer

POLITICAL HIGHLIGHTS
Iowa Senate, 1985-97 (president, 1992-97); sought Democratic nomination for U.S. House, 1986; Iowa Democratic Central Committee, 1992-96; Democratic nominee for lieutenant governor, 1994

ELECTION RESULTS

2002 GENERAL		
Leonard L. Boswell (D)	115,367	53.4%
Sam Thompson (R)	97,285	45.0%
Jeffrey J. Smith (LIBERT)	2,689	1.3%
2002 PRIMARY		
Leonard L. Boswell (D)		unopposed
2000 GENERAL		
Leonard L. Boswell (D)	156,327	62.8%
Jay B. Marcus (R)	83,810	33.7%
Sue Atkinson (INDC)	5,563	2.2%

PREVIOUS WINNING PERCENTAGES
1998 (57%); 1996 (49%)

Elected 1996; 4th term

To prevail in the toughest challenge of his congressional career, in 2002, Boswell had to move — literally and figuratively — from the farm to the city. As a rural conservative, he had gained a steady political foothold in the fields of southern Iowa since his initial election in 1996. But redistricting for this decade compelled him to move to Des Moines, where he had to show the state's most liberal Democrats that he could represent their interests, too.

That he was able to do so is a testament to Boswell's knack for forging political alliances. A member of the "Blue Dogs," a coalition of like-minded House lawmakers, his career voting record puts him in the moderate-to-conservative ranks of House Democrats. He voted for several Republican spending and tax proposals in his first term and broke with most Democrats on an array of social policy questions during his first four years in office, when he backed President Clinton only two-thirds of the time.

In the 107th Congress, Boswell rebuffed overtures from the GOP to switch parties, then took a noticeable turn to the left. He voted more often with a majority of his party than ever before and he backed President Bush less than two-fifths of the time. His AFL-CIO approval rating jumped substantially, while the U.S. Chamber of Commerce gave him his lowest marks ever. He and Sen. Tom Harkin, the only other Democrat in the delegation, were the only Iowans to oppose the $1.35 trillion tax cut of 2001 and the 2002 law granting the president fast-track trade negotiating power.

Boswell's varied background enables him to offer expertise in a number of fields, including military affairs, agriculture and the appropriations process. His legislative career began in 1985 in the state Senate, where he chaired the Appropriations Committee and eventually became president. He was disappointed at the start of the 108th when a promised seat on the Appropriations panel failed to materialize, partly because the person who had promised it, Richard A. Gephardt, had stepped aside as minority leader.

Drafted in 1956, when he was 22, Boswell became a helicopter pilot and did two tours in Vietnam, earning a pair of Distinguished Flying Crosses and a pair of Bronze Stars. Upon his retirement as a lieutenant colonel, Boswell returned home to farm cattle on 475 acres in his native Decatur County. His involvement in community affairs spurred his neighbors to urge him to enter politics, first as a member of the local farmers' co-op and grain elevator board and then in the General Assembly.

That breadth and depth of experience set him apart from his colleagues when he arrived in Washington in 1997, at 63 the oldest House freshman in the 105th Congress. Boswell's age, easygoing and steady demeanor, and career credentials brought him early respect from Democratic leaders, who put him on the party panel that makes committee assignments.

The Des Moines Register describes his conversational style as giving "quick, short responses . . . followed by more detailed explanations." And U.S. News & World Report once described him as "a farmer who looks like Archie Bunker, only more rumpled."

Boswell's legislative agenda is focused on the matters before the committees on which he serves — Agriculture and Transportation. He also is the top Democrat on the Intelligence panel's Human Intelligence, Analysis and Counterintelligence Subcommittee.

On Agriculture, Boswell was the only Iowan to vote against the original six-year farm bill rewrite passed by the House in 2001; he said it did not provide enough for small family farms, and it did not include language to minimize livestock ownership by meatpackers in order to improve market access for smaller operators. But when the final bill was written without ameliorating some of his concerns, he declared it the "best deal" possible for Iowa farmers and voted for its enactment in 2002.

In the 106th Congress, Boswell was a tireless advocate of ethanol, an alternative fuel source made from corn. He championed research efforts in Iowa to develop alternative fuels from other crops as well. Although he voted against the fast-track trade bill in the 107th, in the 106th he voted for the law to normalize the U.S.-China trade relationship, hoping it would expand the export market for his constituents' grain and animals.

On Transportation, Boswell works to improve commercial airline service to Des Moines, which like many medium-size cities must deal with limited options and high fares. He was a negotiator in 2000 on an aviation law that authorized funds for airport construction and earmarked money for more than a dozen airports in the 3rd District. He also has fought to preserve Amtrak service to southern Iowa.

Together with Republican Rep. Tom Osborne of Nebraska, Boswell has sought to alter the Medicare reimbursement system. Iowa ranks last in such reimbursements, and the pair want to ensure that no state gets payments more than 5 percent above or below the national average.

In 1996, Boswell gave in to the urging of supporters and entered the race for the 3rd District seat just two days before the filing deadline. The Republican incumbent, Jim Ross Lightfoot, was giving up the seat after a dozen years to run against Harkin for the Senate.

Capitalizing on his name recognition from years in the state legislature and campaigns for lieutenant governor in 1994 and for Congress in 1986 — when he lost to Lightfoot in a bid for the Democratic nomination — Boswell won the primary easily. Against Mike Mahaffey, a county prosecutor and former state GOP chairman, Boswell eked out a November win with the endorsement of the Iowa Farm Bureau, unusual for a Democrat.

In the 2002 race against Republican lawyer Stan Thompson, who cochaired George W. Bush's Iowa campaign in 2000, Boswell was attacked as a liberal who opposed school prayer. Boswell countered that he was for voluntary school prayer. He used his hefty campaign war chest to beat back campaign appearances by Bush administration heavyweights on behalf of Thompson and won with 54 percent of the vote.

Boswell initially said he would serve only four terms; he has rethought that pledge and early in 2003 was considering another run.

KEY VOTES

2002

Yes Overhaul campaign finance law; ban "soft money" and restrict advocacy advertising
Yes Back Bush's defense budget increase
No Extend 1996 welfare law
No Adopt Bush's discretionary spending limit
Yes Pass GOP Medicare prescription drug plan
Yes Create independent Sept. 11 commission
Yes Extend union protections to Homeland Security Department employees
No Revive fast-track procedures for trade agreements
Yes Authorize war against Iraq
Yes Advance bankruptcy overhaul opposed by abortion opponents

2001

No Nullify Clinton Labor Department ergonomics rule
No Cut taxes by $1.35 trillion through fiscal 2011
Yes Maintain ban on oil drilling in Arctic National Wildlife Refuge
No Approve Bush proposal to limit managed-care plan liability for coverage decisions
No Divert money from crop subsidy payments to land conservation
Yes Expand law enforcement power to investigate suspected terrorists

CQ VOTE STUDIES

	PARTY UNITY		PRESIDENTIAL SUPPORT	
	Support	Oppose	Support	Oppose
2002	81%	19%	40%	60%
2001	78%	22%	37%	63%
2000	69%	31%	60%	40%
1999	69%	31%	67%	33%
1998	65%	35%	65%	35%

INTEREST GROUPS

	AFL-CIO	ADA	CCUS	ACU
2002	78%	80%	55%	32%
2001	92%	85%	48%	24%
2000	70%	55%	65%	41%
1999	88%	70%	50%	32%
1998	70%	65%	83%	36%

IOWA 3

Central and east central — Des Moines

The 12-county 3rd is somewhat microcosmic of the Hawkeye state. It includes relatively well-off urban and suburban areas, as well as rural counties, industrial cities and scattered towns with hopes for economic development. It is roughly one-third urban, suburban and rural.

The district is anchored in Des Moines, the state's largest city and the region's commercial, financial and governmental center. Almost two-thirds of the district's residents live in Des Moines and the surrounding towns in Polk County. The capital has flourished since the 1980s, partly because of its diverse, white-collar employment base and its partial independence from agriculture. There is a sizable African-American and Hispanic population north of downtown, between Interstate 235 and Drake University.

Outside of Polk the 3rd takes on a more rural and conservative flavor. No other county has more than 40,000 residents, and George W. Bush won nine of the district's 11 other counties in the 2000 presidential election. Mahaska and Grundy counties are among the most heavily Republican territories in Iowa.

But the 3rd is competitive in its voting: It gave Al Gore a 49 percent plurality of its votes, as did Iowa as a whole. The influence of Des Moines and surrounding Polk County gives the 3rd its slight Democratic lean. Polk has been more reliably Democratic than many parts of the nation, even supporting Democratic presidential nominees in the GOP presidential landslides of 1984 and 1988. Polk has not given a Republican presidential candidate a majority of its votes since Richard M. Nixon in 1972.

MAJOR INDUSTRY

Insurance, health care, manufacturing

CITIES

Des Moines, 198,682; West Des Moines (pt.), 42,525; Urbandale (pt.), 28,745; Ankeny, 27,117; Newton, 15,579

NOTABLE

F.L. Maytag built the first mechanized washer in Newton; Legendary Western lawman and gunfighter Wyatt Earp grew up in Pella; Pella is home to window and door manufacturer Pella Corp.

Rep. Tom Latham (R)

CAPITOL OFFICE
225-5476
tom.latham@mail.house.gov
www.house.gov/latham
440 Cannon 20515-1504; fax 225-3301

COMMITTEES
Appropriations

HOMETOWN
Alexander

BORN
July 14, 1948, Hampton, Iowa

RELIGION
Lutheran

FAMILY
Wife, Kathy Latham; three children

EDUCATION
Wartburg College, attended 1967; Iowa State U., attended 1967-70 (agriculture & business)

CAREER
Seed company executive; insurance agency marketing representative; insurance agent; bank teller

POLITICAL HIGHLIGHTS
Franklin County Republican chairman, 1984-91

ELECTION RESULTS

2002 GENERAL		
Tom Latham (R)	115,430	54.8%
John Norris (D)	90,784	43.1%
Terry L. Wilson (LIBERT)	2,952	1.4%
2002 PRIMARY		
Tom Latham (R)	38,321	88.5%
Gail E. Boliver (R)	4,956	11.5%
2000 GENERAL		
Tom Latham (R)	159,367	68.8%
Mike Palecek (D)	67,593	29.2%
Ben L. Olson (LIBERT)	2,875	1.2%

PREVIOUS WINNING PERCENTAGES
1998 (99%); 1996 (65%); 1994 (61%)

Elected 1994; 5th term

The land — and what can be grown on it — shapes a large part of Latham's life and his work in Congress. He and his brothers own their family's seed company and three farms. He jokes that he lives in the suburbs — his north-central Iowa home is a mile outside a town that has 165 people.

With the family farmer in mind, one of Latham's top priorities in Congress is to roll back federal regulations and taxes. In the 107th Congress, Latham not only backed House-passed legislation to repeal the estate tax permanently, but he authored a resolution, which passed the House, urging the Senate to act on the measure. Latham said that large estate tax bills have forced some heirs to sell the family farm.

Latham tells how he and his brothers once had to spend $12,000 to measure dust microns on their small soybean farm outside Alexander to comply with the Clean Air Act. "It is exactly why any small-business person today is much more concerned about someone from the government walking in and saying they want to help than [about] any competitor down the street."

Latham is loyal to the House GOP leadership. He supports the party line about 95 percent of the time when the two parties are pitted against each other. In the 108th Congress, as he has been since the 105th, Latham is on the Republican Steering Committee, which makes committee assignments.

Since his arrival in the House, Latham has had committee posts that play to his background and the interests of his district, home to some of the nation's most productive farmland.

As a freshman in the 104th Congress, he was given a seat on the Agriculture Committee, which was then wrestling with fashioning a major overhaul of farm programs to bring them more in line with free-market principles. Latham was a strong backer of the "Freedom to Farm" bill, enacted in 1996, which he said would give farmers greater planting flexibility.

Responding to the plummeting prices hog farmers were getting in the late 1990s, Latham in the 106th Congress won approval of a new system of mandatory reporting of livestock prices nationally, aimed at helping producers match supply and demand. As Congress worked on a new farm bill in the 107th, he tried to ensure small livestock producers equal treatment from meatpacking houses. He also sought to reduce the maximum federal payment a farmer could receive.

Both efforts were aimed at helping the family farmer, but neither proposal was included in the final version of the bill, which Latham argued mostly benefited large, corporate farm operations. He voted against the bill, one of 73 Republicans who did so.

In the 105th, Latham moved to the Appropriations Committee, where his post on the Agriculture Subcommittee enables him to continue to watch out for Iowa farm interests. He has directed millions of dollars to a livestock health research facility in Ames, and he has fought to lift U.S. embargoes on the export of food and medicine to countries, such as Cuba, that are under U.S. economic sanctions. "Embargoes have always destroyed the farmers and never really punished the people they were aimed at," he argues.

On the Commerce, Justice, State Appropriations Subcommittee, Latham's priority has been the war against illegal drugs. He is proud of his efforts to win funding for a methamphetamine center in Sioux City, which provides training in the region for local law enforcement officials who must cope with the epidemic of meth labs in rural areas.

Latham and other Iowa lawmakers were unable in the 107th Congress to obtain more Medicare money for the state and health care providers in other rural areas, despite their arguments about the disparities between urban and rural Medicare payments. That issue promises to remain at the top of Latham's agenda during the 108th Congress.

Responding to stories about an Iowa man's design of a flag to honor an Iowa Congressional Medal of Honor recipient, Latham introduced legislation, which became law in 2002, to establish an official flag that will be presented to all medal of honor recipients.

Latham grew up on a farm doing the usual chores and helping in the family seed business. He stayed close to home in his first 20 years — attending Wartburg College about 50 miles east of his hometown of Alexander and then going to Iowa State University, about 60 miles south in Ames.

His interest in politics was sparked by a trip he took in 1990, as a member of a farm delegation that visited Russia and Poland. Latham says he was appalled at the primitive agricultural methods and machinery, and he blames much of that on the totalitarian governments that he says not only mismanaged the economy but "destroyed individual freedom and dignity." He remembers one Polish farmer who tearfully told him that farmers hadn't owned their land since the Nazis seized it in World War II.

Latham decided that a government that so profoundly intruded in individuals' lives and controlled what they did with their land was something to be feared and resisted. He can date his resolve to run for public office to that realization.

Back in Iowa, he chaired the Franklin County Republican Party for seven years but rebuffed entreaties to run for the legislature: The seasonal nature of his seed business conflicted with state legislative sessions. In 1994, however, when GOP Rep. Fred Grandy gave up the 5th District seat to seek the governorship, Latham decided to run. He was a good fit for the district in a strong GOP year, and he breezed to election.

Latham won re-election easily in 1996, 1998 and 2000, but in 2002 new district lines drafted by a nonpartisan state agency made the district more competitive. The new map put Latham's home in the 4th District; but more than half of his constituents were in the 5th, and it was viewed as more favorable to a Republican than the 4th.

Nonetheless, Latham elected to run in the 4th. He was well-known to many of the new constituents, dating back to his days as a traveling salesman for the family seed business. He wound up winning by almost 12 percentage points against Democrat John Norris, a former state party chairman, in a race that attracted considerable national attention.

KEY VOTES

2002

- No Overhaul campaign finance law; ban "soft money" and restrict advocacy advertising
- Yes Back Bush's defense budget increase
- Yes Extend 1996 welfare law
- Yes Adopt Bush's discretionary spending limit
- Yes Pass GOP Medicare prescription drug plan
- No Create independent Sept. 11 commission
- No Extend union protections to Homeland Security Department employees
- Yes Revive fast-track procedures for trade agreements
- Yes Authorize war against Iraq
- Yes Advance bankruptcy overhaul opposed by abortion opponents

2001

- Yes Nullify Clinton Labor Department ergonomics rule
- Yes Cut taxes by $1.35 trillion through fiscal 2011
- No Maintain ban on oil drilling in Arctic National Wildlife Refuge
- Yes Approve Bush proposal to limit managed-care plan liability for coverage decisions
- No Divert money from crop subsidy payments to land conservation
- Yes Expand law enforcement power to investigate suspected terrorists

CQ VOTE STUDIES

	PARTY UNITY		PRESIDENTIAL SUPPORT	
	Support	Oppose	Support	Oppose
2002	92%	8%	85%	15%
2001	97%	3%	90%	10%
2000	94%	6%	26%	74%
1999	91%	9%	23%	77%
1998	94%	6%	24%	76%

INTEREST GROUPS

	AFL-CIO	ADA	CCUS	ACU
2002	11%	5%	100%	88%
2001	8%	0%	100%	91%
2000	10%	5%	95%	88%
1999	0%	5%	96%	88%
1998	0%	0%	100%	92%

IOWA 4
North and central — Ames, Mason City

The vast 4th takes up most of the state's northern border and dips deeply south, past the state capital of Des Moines (in the 3rd District), dividing Republican-leaning western Iowa and Democratic-leaning eastern Iowa.

Ames is the district's most populous city and is home to Iowa State University, about 30 miles north of Des Moines. Ames leans Democratic, but does not have a strong liberal strain. The city, which accounts for almost two-thirds of Story County residents, backed Al Gore by just 7 percentage points in the 2000 presidential election.

Democrats fare well in Cerro Gordo County, which includes Mason City, the 4th's next most-populous city. Two-thirds of Mason City's employers are involved in manufacturing. A third urban center is Fort Dodge in Webster County, an industrial center that has relied on gypsum factories to support the area's economy. The city also emerged as a leader in veterinary pharmaceuticals. There are many Irish Catholic Democrats in this area.

But the 4th may have a slight GOP lean. George W. Bush won the district with 49 percent in 2000, capturing 13 of the 20 counties that have less than 20,000 residents.

The southern reaches of the district buttonhook counterclockwise around Des Moines to take in the Republican-leaning counties of Dallas, Madison and Warren. Dallas is a big exception to Iowa's sluggish population growth; suburban growth west of Des Moines fueled Dallas' 37 percent growth rate in the 1990s, by far the fastest clip in the state. Warren (13 percent) and Madison (12 percent) also registered impressive growth.

MAJOR INDUSTRY

Meatpacking, health care, veterinary pharmaceuticals

CITIES

Ames, 50,731; Mason City, 29,172; Marshalltown, 26,009; Fort Dodge, 25,136; Indianola, 12,998; Boone, 12,803

NOTABLE

Film star John Wayne was born in Winterset; Madison County's covered bridges were popularized in Robert James Waller's book; Mason City inspired native son Meredith Willson to compose the musical "The Music Man."

Rep. Steve King (R)

CAPITOL OFFICE
225-4426
steve.king@mail.house.gov
www.house.gov/steveking
1432 Longworth 20515-1505; fax 225-3193

COMMITTEES
Agriculture
Judiciary
Small Business

HOMETOWN
Kiron

BORN
May 28, 1949, Storm Lake, Iowa

RELIGION
Roman Catholic

FAMILY
Wife, Marilyn King; three children

EDUCATION
Northwest Missouri State U., attended 1967-70

CAREER
Construction company owner

POLITICAL HIGHLIGHTS
Iowa Senate, 1997-2002

ELECTION RESULTS

2002 GENERAL		
Steve King (R)	113,257	62.2%
Paul Shomshor (D)	68,853	37.8%
2002 PRIMARY		
Steve King (R)	16,503	30.3%
John Redwine (R)	13,428	24.6%
Brent Siegrist (R)	12,978	23.8%
Jeff Ballenger (R)	11,563	21.2%

Elected 2002; 1st term

King is eager to make a conservative imprint on both social and economic policy. His political philosophy is heavily influenced by his background as the owner of a construction company he founded in 1975. He says the government regulates and taxes businesses too heavily.

"I saw that government weight cause me to take more and more of my resources and hire people to fill out paperwork and meet their requirements," said King.

He brings to Congress the same tax-cutting zeal he exemplified in the state Senate. He says the current tax code inflicts a burden that "saps the resources" of businesses and "takes away incentive for entrepreneurs."

King similarly espouses strongly conservative views on social issues, particularly in his opposition to abortion rights. He denounces affirmative action as constituting "preferential treatment policies" that are the "last bastion of institutionalized racism in this country."

A backer of a national right-to-work law limiting union activity, King also wants to repeal the 1931 Davis-Bacon Act, a Depression-era law that requires federal contractors to pay "local prevailing wages" to employees. "I tell people that I don't get to die until that is repealed," he says.

King's priorities include agricultural development, where his seat on the Agriculture Committee is vital, and transportation issues, including upgrading U.S. Route 20 to a four-lane highway from Sioux City to Dubuque.

Running in an overwhelmingly Republican, largely rural district, King coasted to victory in November after a grueling nominating campaign. He got the GOP nod in a post-primary convention after none of the four contenders met the 35 percent vote threshold to win outright in the June primary.

He received considerable financial backing from the anti-tax Club for Growth and endorsements from such prominent conservative activists as Steve Forbes, Gary Bauer and Alan Keyes.

IOWA 5

West – Sioux City, Council Bluffs

The 32-county 5th takes in miles of fertile soil and gently undulating hills in the western part of the state. The bountiful land has allowed the region to remain more like the Iowa of old than any other part of the state.

Sioux City, the district's largest metropolitan center, has developed into a service center for a region that includes part of Nebraska and South Dakota. Some Sioux City businesses have moved across the river to take advantage of more-favorable tax laws in other states, but Woodbury County has sprouted numerous bedroom communities where many workers live. Sioux City long has leaned Republican, and surrounding rural towns are home to many independent farmers who tend to vote Republican.

The district's second-largest city, Council Bluffs, also is located on the state's western border, though farther south. Built against bluffs, the city was a bustling crossroads for three westward trails in the early 1800s, and five railroads later met there. Today, many workers cross the Missouri River to work for Omaha businesses that have been lured to Nebraska by lower tax rates.

Southwest Iowa is less wedded to social conservatism than the northwest region and is more likely to back GOP-establishment candidates. This area gave big percentages to George W. Bush in the 2000 caucuses, and it backed state House Speaker Brent Siegrist in the 2002 5th District primary over more-conservative challengers.

Overall, the solidly Republican district backed Bush by 17 percentage points in the 2000 general election. Bush's six top-performing counties in Iowa, and 11 of his best 13, are in the 5th District (topped by Sioux County with 83 percent of the vote).

MAJOR INDUSTRY
Meatpacking, agriculture

CITIES
Sioux City, 85,013; Council Bluffs, 58,268

NOTABLE
The annual Donna Reed Festival is held in the actress' hometown of Denison; The largest rural Danish settlement in the United States is in Elk Horn.

KANSAS

Gov. Kathleen Sebelius (D)

First elected: 2002
Length of term: 4 years
Term expires: 1/07
Salary: $94,036
Phone: (785) 296-3232
Hometown: Topeka
Born: May 15, 1948; Cincinnati, Ohio
Religion: Roman Catholic
Family: Husband, Gary Sebelius; two children
Education: Trinity College (D.C.), B.A. 1970 (political science); U. of Kansas, M.P.A. 1977
Career: Law association director; state corrections department official
Political highlights: Kansas Governmental Ethics Commission, 1975-77; Kan. House, 1987-95; Kan. insurance commissioner, 1995-2003

Election results:

2002 GENERAL		
Kathleen Sebelius (D)	441,858	52.9%
Tim Shallenburger (R)	376,830	45.1%
Ted Pettibone (REF)	8,907	1.1%
Ira Dennis Hawver (LIBERT)	8,097	1.0%

Lt. Gov. John E. Moore (D)

First elected: 2002
Length of term: 4 years
Term expires: 1/07
Salary: $109,000 (includes salary for also serving as Kansas' secretary of Commerce and Housing)
Phone: (785) 296-2213

STATE LEGISLATURE

Legislature: Meets from January-June
House: 125 members, 2-year terms
2003 breakdown: 80R, 45D; 90 men, 35 women
Salary: $78/day in session; $85/day expenses; $5,400/year allowance
Phone: (785) 296-7633
Senate: 40 members, 4-year terms
2003 breakdown: 30R, 10D; 31 men, 9 women
Salary: $78/day in session; $85/day expenses; $5,400/year allowance
Phone: (785) 296-7344

STATE TERM LIMITS

Governor: 2 terms
Senate: No
House: No

URBAN STATISTICS

CITY	POPULATION
Wichita	344,284
Overland Park	149,080
Kansas City	146,866
Topeka	122,377

REGISTERED VOTERS

Republican	47%
Democrat	27%
Unaffiliated	26%

POPULATION

2002 population (est.)	2,715,884
2000 population	2,688,418
1990 population	2,477,574
Percent change (1990-2000)	+8.5%
Rank among states (2002)	32
Median age	35.2
Born in state	59.5%
Foreign born	5%
Violent crime rate	389/100,000
Poverty level	9.9%
Federal workers	25,639
Military	29,103

REDISTRICTING

Kansas retained its four House seats in reapportionment. The state legislature drew a new map, which the governor signed on May 31, 2002.

MISCELLANEOUS

Web: www.state.ks.us
Capital: Topeka

STATE ELECTION OFFICIAL
(785) 296-4561

DEMOCRATIC HEADQUARTERS
(785) 234-0425

REPUBLICAN HEADQUARTERS
(785) 234-3456

District Statistics

DIST.	2000 VOTE FOR PRESIDENT BUSH	GORE	NADER	WHITE	BLACK	ASIAN	HISP	MEDIAN INCOME	WHITE COLLAR	BLUE COLLAR	SERVICE INDUSTRY	OVER 64	UNDER 18	COLLEGE EDUCATION	RURAL	SQ. MILES
1	67%	28%	3%	85%	2%	1%	11%	$34,869	53%	31%	16%	16%	26%	18%	48%	57,373
2	54	41	4	87	5	1	4	$37,855	58	27	16	14	25	23	40	14,134
3	53	42	4	80	9	3	7	$51,118	70	17	12	10	27	39	5	778
4	59	37	3	81	7	2	7	$40,917	57	29	14	13	28	23	21	9,531
STATE	58	37	3	83	6	2	7	$40,624	60	26	14	13	27	26	29	81,815
U.S.	47.9	48.4	3	69	12	4	13	$41,994	60	25	15	12	26	24	21	3,537,438

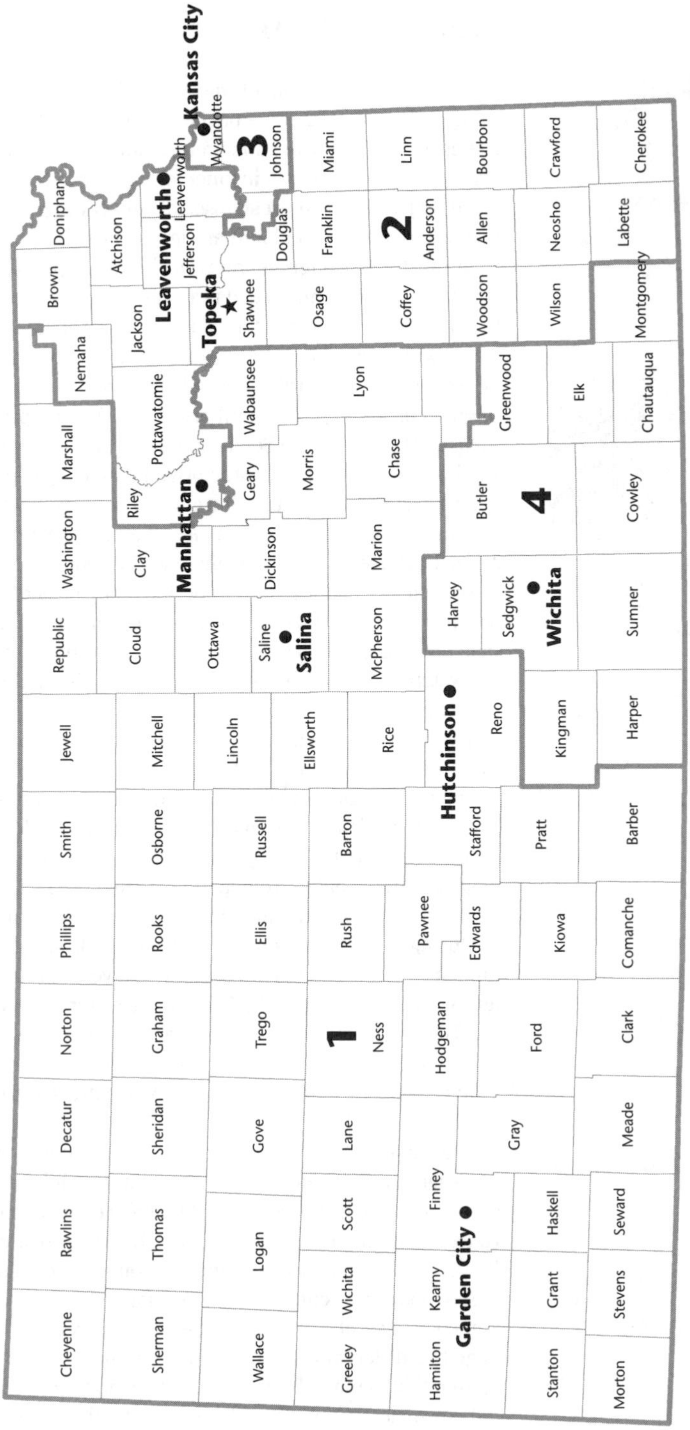
Kansas City
Leavenworth
Topeka
Manhattan
Salina
Hutchinson
Wichita
Garden City
1
2
3
4
Doniphan
Brown
Nemaha
Marshall
Washington
Republic
Jewell
Smith
Phillips
Norton
Decatur
Rawlins
Cheyenne
Atchison
Jackson
Pottawatomie
Riley
Clay
Cloud
Mitchell
Osborne
Rooks
Graham
Sheridan
Thomas
Sherman
Leavenworth
Jefferson
Wyandotte
Johnson
Douglas
Shawnee
Wabaunsee
Geary
Dickinson
Ottawa
Saline
Lincoln
Ellsworth
Russell
Ellis
Trego
Gove
Logan
Wallace
Miami
Franklin
Osage
Lyon
Morris
Marion
McPherson
Rice
Barton
Rush
Ness
Lane
Scott
Wichita
Greeley
Linn
Anderson
Coffey
Chase
Harvey
Reno
Stafford
Pawnee
Hodgeman
Finney
Kearny
Hamilton
Bourbon
Allen
Woodson
Greenwood
Butler
Sedgwick
Kingman
Pratt
Edwards
Ford
Gray
Haskell
Grant
Stanton
Crawford
Neosho
Wilson
Elk
Cowley
Sumner
Harper
Barber
Kiowa
Comanche
Clark
Meade
Seward
Stevens
Morton
Cherokee
Labette
Montgomery
Chautauqua

Sen. Sam Brownback (R)

CAPITOL OFFICE
224-6521
sam_brownback@brownback.senate.gov
brownback.senate.gov
303 Hart 20510-1604; fax 228-1265

COMMITTEES
Appropriations
Commerce, Science & Transportation
(Science, Technology & Space - chairman)
Foreign Relations
(East Asian & Pacific Affairs - chairman)
Joint Economic

HOMETOWN
Topeka

BORN
Sept. 12, 1956, Garnett, Kan.

RELIGION
Roman Catholic

FAMILY
Wife, Mary Brownback; five children

EDUCATION
Kansas State U., B.S. 1979 (agricultural economics); U. of Kansas, J.D. 1982

CAREER
Lawyer; professor; White House fellow; broadcaster

POLITICAL HIGHLIGHTS
Kan. secretary of Agriculture, 1986-93; U.S. House, 1995-96

ELECTION RESULTS

1998 GENERAL

Sam Brownback (R)	474,639	65.3%
Paul Feleciano Jr. (D)	229,718	31.6%
Thomas L. Oyler (LIBERT)	11,545	1.6%
Alvin Bauman (REF)	11,334	1.6%

1998 PRIMARY

Sam Brownback (R)	unopposed

PREVIOUS WINNING PERCENTAGES
1996 Special Election (54%); 1994 House Election (66%)

Elected 1996; 1st full term

In an affable if calculated way, Brownback pursues a broad range of legislative interests that have pushed him into high-profile debates on such issues as Mideast sanctions, immigration and human cloning. The hard-driving lawmaker has an instinct for getting in the center of the action on issues of particular interest to social conservatives, such as violence in the media and international human rights abuses.

In the 108th Congress, he won the only open Republican seat on the Appropriations Committee. It is a panel where pragmatism and willingness to compromise are important, and those are characteristics not often associated with Brownback. In contrast to the person whose seat in the Senate he won in 1996, Majority Leader Bob Dole, Brownback has focused more often on promoting his moral principles than on practicing political pragmatism. His time in the Senate has been marked by passionate rebukes of what the lawmaker has characterized as society's immorality.

"It's part of the overall culture war that we've been in the last 10 years," Brownback says. "Most people feel like they have to defend their families against culture" instead of being enriched by it.

Brownback blames Hollywood for many societal ills. "There are more social workers than serial murderers in America. There are more pastors than prostitutes. But you'd never know it from TV," he said in 1999. "When we watch more and more violence, profanity and sleaze, we eventually grow more violent, profane and coarse."

The senator scored political points when he prompted a Federal Trade Commission investigation of whether the entertainment industry was marketing violent and sexually explicit movies and songs to young teenagers. But Brownback also has voted against limiting violent TV programming to hours when children likely would not be watching. "I think that starts us down a path of content regulation," he told the Los Angeles Times. "What I constantly push is the industry setting its own code of conduct."

During the 107th Congress, Brownback sought to ban all forms of human cloning. The bill never came to a vote, and in the 108th he plans to use his chairmanship of the Commerce Committee's Science, Technology and Space Subcommittee to advance the issue. A staunch abortion foe, Brownback equates research on embryonic stem cells with the taking of a life because the cells would have to be extracted from days-old embryos created in clinics.

Brownback says a 1995 bout with skin cancer focused him on the truly important things in life. He attends midweek Bible readings and prayer sessions and has close personal and political connections to religious conservative activists. In July 2002, he left the Methodist church and became a Roman Catholic. He has declined to comment on his decision.

A supporter of cutting taxes on married couples, Brownback also has argued in favor of streamlining the nation's tax code. "I really think we need to go to a different tax code — just eliminate this one and go to a taxation system that is much broader in its base and reduced in its rate," he says.

Brownback's concern with societal standards sometimes causes him to take unexpected positions. Although he voted to convict President Clinton of misconduct stemming from his affair with a White House intern, he urged his GOP colleagues to show Clinton respect during the 1999 impeachment trial and to attend the president's State of the Union address. "The country will forgive a lot, but not bad manners," he said.

On the Foreign Relations Committee, Brownback has crusaded for lifting restrictions on U.S. aid to the oil-rich former Soviet republic of Azerbaijan. Similarly in 1999, he won enactment of "Silk Road" legislation designed to improve U.S. relations and speed economic development in Central Asia and the Caucasus — another bill strongly backed by energy companies. Despite complaints about China's human rights record, he voted for the 2000 law granting that nation permanent status as a normal U.S. trade partner. The prospects of more grain exports are eagerly embraced by his state's corn and wheat farmers. And pro-Israel groups have lauded him for supporting the Iraqi opposition and attempting to block Iranian cooperation with Russia.

As the top Republican on the Near Eastern and South Asian Affairs Subcommittee, Brownback labored in something of a foreign policy backwater until the Sept. 11, 2001, attacks helped to transform him into a top congressional voice on Afghanistan and the Muslim world. He helped push to enactment a law that year waiving for two years sanctions on Pakistan, a key ally of the Bush administration in its war on terrorism.

And, long before President Bush began to focus on Saddam Hussein, Brownback was pushing for a tougher policy against the Iraqi leader. "I don't want to see Saddam outlast another U.S. president," he said in 1999.

The senator has adopted children from China and Guatemala. But in the 106th, he came under criticism from some adoption advocates for opposing Senate ratification of the Hague Convention on Intercountry Adoption, a treaty designed to impose standards on the often chaotic international adoption process. The treaty, Brownback contended, would create an unwieldy and costly adoption bureaucracy.

One of Brownback's lowest moments in Congress came in 1997 during Senate investigations into Democratic National Committee fundraising practices. Describing a bonus pay scheme that Democrats had arranged with fundraiser John Huang, Brownback mimicked a Chinese accent and said: "No raise money, no get bonus." A moment later, he added that he meant "no slight by my statement," but it was too late. Sharp criticism came from Asian-American groups and California Democratic Sen. Dianne Feinstein, who said: "The United States Senate is no place for racial stereotyping."

Brownback appears to have had politics in his blood since he was president of his eighth-grade class. He was student body president at Kansas State University, a national officer of the Future Farmers of America, a White House fellow in the U.S. Trade Representative's office in the administration of President George Bush, then Kansas secretary of agriculture for six years. Brownback planned to run for governor in 1994, but he decided on a House race instead when Democratic incumbent Jim Slattery gave up his 2nd District seat to run for the governorship. In that year's GOP tidal wave, Brownback easily defeated the state's two-term Democratic governor, John Carlin.

When Dole resigned from the Senate in spring 1996 to run full time for president, Gov. Bill Graves appointed Lt. Gov. Sheila Frahm to fill the seat until a special election could be held. Brownback defeated the more moderate Frahm by 13 percentage points in a special GOP primary by reaching out aggressively to business groups and social conservatives. He won a tough November election against stockbroker Jill Docking, a member of a well-known Kansas political family, with 54 percent of the vote.

In 1998, Brownback easily won a full term and he began the 108th as the prohibitive favorite for re-election in 2004.

Kansas Republicans urged Brownback to run for governor in 2002, but he decided to stay in the Senate.

KEY VOTES

2002

- No Pass farm bill reversing crop subsidy limits
- Yes Postpone tougher automobile fuel efficiency standards
- No Overhaul campaign finance law; ban "soft money" and restrict advocacy advertising
- Yes Set federal election standards
- Yes Support oil drilling in Arctic National Wildlife Refuge
- ? Revive fast-track procedures for trade agreements
- Yes Create federal insurance coverage for catastrophic terrorist losses
- Yes Tighten federal accounting and corporate governance regulation
- No Advance bipartisan Medicare prescription drug plan
- Yes Create independent Sept. 11 commission
- No Back Democratic Homeland Security Department proposal
- Yes Authorize war against Iraq

2001

- Yes Confirm John Ashcroft as attorney general
- Yes Nullify Clinton Labor Department ergonomics rule
- Yes Cut taxes by $1.35 trillion through fiscal 2011
- No Pass Democratic bill to bolster rights of patients in managed-care plans
- No Permit a new round of military base closings
- Yes Expand law enforcement power to investigate suspected terrorists

CQ VOTE STUDIES

	PARTY UNITY		PRESIDENTIAL SUPPORT	
	Support	Oppose	Support	Oppose
2002	94%	6%	98%	2%
2001	94%	6%	99%	1%
2000	98%	2%	40%	60%
1999	95%	5%	31%	69%
1998	96%	4%	37%	63%
1997	96%	4%	56%	44%
House Service:				
1996	92%	8%	32%	68%
1995	96%	4%	22%	78%

INTEREST GROUPS

	AFL-CIO	ADA	CCUS	ACU
2002	15%	5%	100%	100%
2001	19%	0%	93%	96%
2000	0%	0%	100%	100%
1999	0%	5%	94%	95%
1998	0%	0%	94%	92%
1997	0%	0%	100%	100%
House Service:				
1996	0%	5%	93%	100%
1995	8%	0%	100%	92%

Sen. Pat Roberts (R)

CAPITOL OFFICE
224-4774
pat_roberts@roberts.senate.gov
roberts.senate.gov
302 Hart 20510-1605; fax 224-3514

COMMITTEES
Agriculture, Nutrition & Forestry
Armed Services
(Emerging Threats & Capabilities - chairman)
Health, Education, Labor & Pensions
Select Ethics
Select Intelligence - chairman

HOMETOWN
Dodge City

BORN
April 20, 1936, Topeka, Kan.

RELIGION
Methodist

FAMILY
Wife, Franki Roberts; three children

EDUCATION
Kansas State U., B.A. 1958 (journalism)

MILITARY SERVICE
Marine Corps, 1958-62

CAREER
Congressional aide; newspaper reporter, editor

POLITICAL HIGHLIGHTS
U.S. House, 1981-97

ELECTION RESULTS

2002 GENERAL		
Pat Roberts (R)	641,075	82.5%
Steven A. Rosile (LIBERT)	70,725	9.1%
George Cook (REF)	65,050	8.4%
2002 PRIMARY		
Pat Roberts (R)	233,642	83.7%
Thomas L. "Tom" Oyler (R)	45,491	16.3%

PREVIOUS WINNING PERCENTAGES
1996 (62%); 1994 House Election (77%); 1992 House Election (68%); 1990 House Election (63%); 1988 House Election (100%); 1986 House Election (77%); 1984 House Election (76%); 1982 House Election (68%); 1980 House Election (62%)

Elected 1996; 2nd term

Roberts sometimes has been known for stirring up controversy rather than easing it, but for the 108th Congress one of his top goals is to soothe tensions between lawmakers and federal intelligence agencies. That may mean toning down his pithy and sometimes sarcastic tongue, which makes him a favorite among the bookers for the television talk shows.

Twice voted "Funniest Senator" in annual Washingtonian magazine surveys of congressional staff, Roberts is known for unleashing verbal zingers on the floor and off. In 2000, he labeled anti-trade organizations as "the representatives of Ralph Nader, Ross Perot, Pat Buchanan and other various wackos." The next year, he said asking the federal agency that administers Medicare and Medicaid for help would be akin to "asking the Boston Strangler for a necklace."

But, as the new chairman of the Intelligence Committee, Roberts will be pressed to put aside his irascibility and rapier wit in favor of the patient and subtle approaches of a diplomat. Although he has been on Intelligence since becoming a senator in 1997 — and although he chaired the House Agriculture Committee when it rewrote federal farm policy in the 104th Congress — Roberts has never had a role overseeing such an internationally sensitive issue.

"We won't take any pins out of any hand grenades early," promises the former Marine, adding that Intelligence would seek to collaborate with other Senate committees, the White House and House members.

Roberts also aims to work closely with the top Intelligence Committee Democrat, Vice Chairman John D. Rockefeller IV of West Virginia. The two began 2003 in an unusually public spat over the apportionment of staff positions and budget for the panel. But by the next month the rift had been mended, and Roberts and Rockefeller toured five nations together with their counterparts on Senate Armed Services, a committee that has engaged in occasional turf fights with Intelligence.

"I'm not going to be an apologist for the intelligence community, but I do intend to be a champion for their goals," Roberts says. "People are putting their lives on the line. We need to correct any problems" without questioning agents' dedication.

He says too many of the congressional hearings about the intelligence community's work before and after the Sept. 11, 2001, terrorist attacks were designed to create "gotcha" moments that made agents look bad but allowed lawmakers to look tough. Those events made intelligence officials wary of sharing information with Congress, he says, and thus made it more difficult for legislators to come up with the best proposals for change. In a bid to alter that dynamic Roberts plans to move more of his committee's proceedings behind closed doors. What that sacrifices in televised drama, Roberts says, will be made up for in essential witness candor.

In the 108th Roberts also chairs the Armed Services Subcommittee on Emerging Threats and Capabilities, where he has been the top Republican since the 106th. To stay close to the corn and wheat farmers and cattle ranchers of his state, he holds a seat on Senate Agriculture, too.

Roberts was not a particularly influential player on defense questions in the first part of his career. But the interest was there, he insists, and the roots run deep. An uncle who was a military attaché to the U.S. embassy in China survived the 1937 sinking by Japanese planes of the U.S. gunboat *Panay* on the Yangtze River. And Roberts' continued loyalty to his branch of the service exemplifies the old saw that there is no such thing as an "ex-Marine."

Though he does not tout the fact, few members have as good a claim as Roberts to having foreseen the threat of a large-scale terrorist attack before Sept. 11 and having tried to warn his colleagues and the public. On the Emerging Threat subcommittee, he vigorously pressed the Pentagon and Congress to look beyond Cold War-style military conflicts and to prepare for military attacks that would use novel weapons; he also urged preparedness for a gamut of possible terrorist assaults — attacks on civilian populations with nuclear, chemical or biological weapons and cyberattacks on economically critical computer networks.

While he is a reliable GOP vote on such issues as abortion and cutting government rules or taxes, he is less confrontational than some younger Republicans. Instead, Roberts focuses on economic and security issues, often building alliances with Democrats. Like many farm-state Republicans, from the start of his career he displayed an internationalist instinct anchored in an export-oriented world view. He worries that U.S. economic sanctions against other countries are hurting the farm economy. He is an outspoken advocate of free trade and was an ardent proponent of the 2002 law giving President Bush fast-track trade negotiating authority.

Though a relative newcomer to the first string on defense issues, Roberts is an old hand at the legislative power game: By the end of his eight terms in the House, he was known as "The Aggie" for his pivotal role in the farm policy debate. The 1996 "Freedom to Farm" law remains his signature legislative achievement. It replaced traditional farm subsidies with a system of fixed but declining payments to farmers — a concept rural lawmakers championed because they were convinced that strong overseas markets for commodities would offset the smaller government payments.

But prices slumped worldwide instead. Roberts supported bills in the 105th and 106th that pumped billions of dollars into the ailing farm economy. Critics said those bailouts showed that the farm law was flawed, but Roberts blamed the Clinton administration and some in Congress for not doing enough to ease exports, pare regulations, and strengthen crop insurance policies. When the 107th Congress wrote a new farm law that reversed many of the policies of the 104th, Roberts voted against it.

Since 1999 Roberts has been on the Ethics Committee, and as the top-ranking Republican in 2002 he helped mete out the harshest punishment of a senator in seven years. Democrat Robert G. Torricelli dropped his bid for re-election in New Jersey after he was "severely admonished" for accepting gifts from a campaign donor.

A newspaper reporter and editor after his time in the Marines, Roberts earned legislative experience by working as a House aide for 12 years. When his boss, Republican Rep. Keith G. Sebelius, announced his retirement in 1980, Roberts was ready. He cruised to victory in the general election, capitalizing on Sebelius' popularity and referring to "our record" so frequently that he sounded like an incumbent.

As he became one of the most popular politicians in Kansas, Roberts was often likened to former Majority Leader Bob Dole, another Kansan known for a caustic tone and conservative outlook. Roberts initially balked at making a Senate bid in 1996 when Republican Nancy Landon Kassebaum retired, saying he wanted to focus on shepherding a farm bill into law. But he eventually entered the race and handily won the GOP nod. Facing Democratic state Treasurer Sally Thompson in the fall, at one point his temper got the better of him when he labeled his opponent a "bitch." Still, he won with 62 percent of the vote. In 2002, Democrats didn't field a candidate and Roberts took 83 percent against two third-party candidates.

KEY VOTES

2002

- No Pass farm bill reversing crop subsidy limits
- Yes Postpone tougher automobile fuel efficiency standards
- No Overhaul campaign finance law; ban "soft money" and restrict advocacy advertising
- Yes Set federal election standards
- Yes Support oil drilling in Arctic National Wildlife Refuge
- Yes Revive fast-track procedures for trade agreements
- Yes Create federal insurance coverage for catastrophic terrorist losses
- Yes Tighten federal accounting and corporate governance regulation
- No Advance bipartisan Medicare prescription drug plan
- Yes Create independent Sept. 11 commission
- No Back Democratic Homeland Security Department proposal
- Yes Authorize war against Iraq

2001

- Yes Confirm John Ashcroft as attorney general
- Yes Nullify Clinton Labor Department ergonomics rule
- Yes Cut taxes by $1.35 trillion through fiscal 2011
- No Pass Democratic bill to bolster rights of patients in managed-care plans
- No Permit a new round of military base closings
- Yes Expand law enforcement power to investigate suspected terrorists

CQ VOTE STUDIES

	PARTY UNITY		PRESIDENTIAL SUPPORT	
	Support	Oppose	Support	Oppose
2002	96%	4%	96%	4%
2001	95%	5%	99%	1%
2000	97%	3%	38%	62%
1999	94%	6%	29%	71%
1998	95%	5%	35%	65%
1997	90%	10%	59%	41%
House Service:				
1996	92%	8%	37%	63%
1995	96%	4%	19%	81%
1994	96%	4%	40%	60%
1993	94%	6%	34%	66%

INTEREST GROUPS

	AFL-CIO	ADA	CCUS	ACU
2002	15%	0%	100%	100%
2001	13%	0%	93%	100%
2000	0%	0%	100%	92%
1999	0%	0%	94%	88%
1998	0%	0%	100%	84%
1997	0%	15%	90%	68%
House Service:				
1996	0%	5%	94%	95%
1995	0%	0%	96%	80%
1994	0%	0%	92%	100%
1993	0%	0%	100%	100%

Rep. Jerry Moran (R)

CAPITOL OFFICE
225-2715
jerry.moran@mail.house.gov
www.house.gov/moranks01
1519 Longworth 20515-1601; fax 225-5124

COMMITTEES
Agriculture
(General Farm Commodities & Risk Management - chairman)
Transportation & Infrastructure
Veterans' Affairs

HOMETOWN
Hays

BORN
May 29, 1954, Great Bend, Kan.

RELIGION
Protestant

FAMILY
Wife, Robba Moran; two children

EDUCATION
Fort Hays State U., attended 1972-73; U. of Kansas, B.S. 1976 (economics), J.D. 1981

CAREER
Lawyer; banker

POLITICAL HIGHLIGHTS
Kan. Senate, 1989-97 (vice president, 1993-95; majority leader, 1995-97)

ELECTION RESULTS

2002 GENERAL		
Jerry Moran (R)	189,976	91.1%
Jack W. Warner (LIBERT)	18,585	8.9%
2002 PRIMARY		
Jerry Moran (R)		unopposed
2000 GENERAL		
Jerry Moran (R)	214,328	89.3%
Jack W. Warner (LIBERT)	25,581	10.7%

PREVIOUS WINNING PERCENTAGES
1998 (81%); 1996 (73%)

Elected 1996; 4th term

Every year, Moran drives a rental car across the sprawling plains of the 1st District to hold town meetings. The congressman's far-flung "listening tour" is a custom begun three decades ago by Republican Keith G. Sebelius and continued by Republican Pat Roberts, now the state's junior senator. But for this decade the trek has become more difficult to complete than ever before; the Big First, as the district is called, now takes in 69 counties — three more than it did before redistricting for this decade — as the farms and small communities of the Kansas prairie continue to depopulate.

The factors that led to the emptying of the rural Midwest are very much on the minds of Moran's constituents as he stops to hear their views at places such as Daylight Doughnuts in Hugoton, the Beecher Bible and Rifle Church in Wabaunsee and the Blue Bird Cafe in Bird City.

Moran hears often about low crop prices. And, from his seat on the Agriculture Committee, he seeks to help western Kansas' corn and wheat farmers by pushing for more foreign markets for U.S. farm goods and by boosting subsidies to shelter farmers from the effects of drought or plummeting wheat prices. "Ninety-eight percent of the mouths to feed are outside the United States, and many of them are hungry," Moran told the Topeka Capital-Journal newspaper. "So if there is going to be profitability on the farm, in large part it's going to come about as the result of the United States getting aggressive about exports."

In the 2002 farm law, Moran also worked on the addition of provisions to increase production of ethanol, a fuel additive made from corn, and to speed the installation of broadband cables across rural America, which many see as essential to small-town economic survival.

While maintaining an innocuous public profile in Washington, Moran has worked behind the scenes within the Republican caucus and quietly gained influence since he was first elected in 1996. In the 107th Congress, he won coveted spots on the farm bill conference committee and on the Republican Steering Committee, which decides the party's committee assignments.

He is also a co-chair of the 184-lawmaker Rural Health Care Coalition. After the Sept. 11, 2001, terrorist attacks, when the Bush administration stopped a program that gave visas to foreign doctors who promised to work in rural outposts, Moran rallied the opposition. The administration ultimately agreed to process 86 pending applications, including four by doctors who would be sent to Kansas. Moran worked with the administration to resuscitate the program.

In the 108th, Moran got an Agriculture subcommittee chairmanship; he wields the gavel of the General Farm Commodities panel.

To take that post, he had to relinquish, after just one term, his chairmanship of the Veterans' Affairs Subcommittee on Health. There is not a single VA hospital in the 1st District (it has no city large enough to support one), but he has worked to build outpatient clinics in under-served areas. He drafted legislation to rename a VA hospital after Bob Dole, whose career in Washington began as the Big First's congressman.

In 2000, Moran backed a measure to promote the use of communications technology to improve rural medicine by allowing Medicare reimbursement for care and consultation performed via interactive television hookups.

As a member of the Transportation and Infrastructure Committee, in the 108th Congress Moran will push for more rural road-building, especially in Kansas, as the panel updates federal highway and mass transit law for the first time since 1998.

At 53,275 square miles, Moran's is among the nation's largest congressional districts. In the post-census redistricting, the Republican legislature redrew the boundaries of the state's four House seats to make life more electorally difficult for Kansas' lone Democrat, Dennis Moore. A little more territory was added to the 1st, but Moran drew no Democratic opponent in 2002, nor had he drawn major-party opposition two years before.

Moran is a native of the Big First, where his father labored in the oil fields and his mother worked as a secretary with an electric utility. As a high school student body officer, Moran was in charge of inviting the local congressman — Sebelius — to speak at a fundraising dinner. They kept in touch, and several years later Moran went off to Washington as an intern for Sebelius. It was the summer of 1974, the height of the Watergate scandal, and Moran remembers feeling like an eyewitness to history as the House Judiciary Committee held hearings to consider the impeachment of President Nixon.

In 1976, Moran graduated from the University of Kansas with a degree in economics and took a job as a small-town banker. He earned his law degree five years later and opened his own practice in Hays. In 1988, he made a long-shot race for the state Senate against an 18-year incumbent, regarding it as an extension of his other civic involvements. He won by just a few hundred votes. He was unopposed for a second term in 1992.

Moran's time in Topeka included a stint as chairman of the state Senate Judiciary Committee before he became majority leader in 1995. His ascension illustrated Moran's knack for appealing to both the conservative and moderate wings of the Kansas GOP, which spent much of the previous decade in an intense struggle for control of the state party.

Moran ran for Congress in 1996 when Roberts moved up to the Senate to succeed fellow Republican Nancy Landon Kassebaum, who retired. Moran quickly became the front-runner, portraying himself as a pragmatic conservative. In a district with a long Republican tradition, and with Dole topping the GOP ticket as its presidential nominee, Moran rolled to an easy victory with 73 percent of the vote against John Divine, the former mayor of Salina.

The 1st District has been a breeding ground for statewide officeholders — Dole and Roberts are the two most prominent recent examples — and Moran's name is already being mentioned as a potential candidate for governor in 2006.

KEY VOTES

2002

No Overhaul campaign finance law; ban "soft money" and restrict advocacy advertising
Yes Back Bush's defense budget increase
Yes Extend 1996 welfare law
Yes Adopt Bush's discretionary spending limit
Yes Pass GOP Medicare prescription drug plan
No Create independent Sept. 11 commission
No Extend union protections to Homeland Security Department employees
Yes Revive fast-track procedures for trade agreements
Yes Authorize war against Iraq
No Advance bankruptcy overhaul opposed by abortion opponents

2001

Yes Nullify Clinton Labor Department ergonomics rule
Yes Cut taxes by $1.35 trillion through fiscal 2011
No Maintain ban on oil drilling in Arctic National Wildlife Refuge
Yes Approve Bush proposal to limit managed-care plan liability for coverage decisions
No Divert money from crop subsidy payments to land conservation
Yes Expand law enforcement power to investigate suspected terrorists

CQ VOTE STUDIES

	PARTY UNITY		PRESIDENTIAL SUPPORT	
	Support	Oppose	Support	Oppose
2002	89%	11%	72%	28%
2001	90%	10%	77%	23%
2000	93%	7%	25%	75%
1999	86%	14%	18%	82%
1998	90%	10%	29%	71%

INTEREST GROUPS

	AFL-CIO	ADA	CCUS	ACU
2002	0%	5%	90%	96%
2001	25%	5%	96%	88%
2000	0%	0%	90%	92%
1999	33%	20%	88%	84%
1998	10%	10%	100%	92%

KANSAS 1
West – Salina, Hutchinson, Dodge City

The fiscally conservative 1st takes in all of western Kansas and stretches east across farmland to reach Nemaha County in the north and Emporia in the center, covering most of rural Kansas in the process. The district covers 70 percent of the state and in land area is bigger than most U.S. states (including 25 of the 26 states east of the Mississippi River).

The 1st's economy is wedded to agriculture, an industry that suffered from weather disasters in the 1980s and falling commodity prices in the 1990s. More and more rural residents have packed their bags for the city to escape the tough farming life.

The largest population center is in the district's eastern portion. Salina (Saline County) is a traditional farm-market town, but has an industrial element — Raytheon has a factory here. Hutchinson, site of the Kansas State Fair, is dominated by farm- and food-related businesses. Junction City is home to many civilian workers who commute to Fort Riley in the 2nd District. In the west, towns such as Garden City and Dodge City rely on meatpacking and tourism. Thriving beef processing plants continue to draw Mexican and Asian immigrants.

The 1st is comfortably Republican, although it did exhibit an independent streak in the 1992 presidential election, giving Ross Perot 29 percent of the vote. The district overwhelmingly voted for George W. Bush in the 2000 presidential contest, giving him two-thirds of the vote. The GOP also dominates local offices, except in Hays, where Fort Hays State University is located, and in Hutchinson.

MAJOR INDUSTRY
Agriculture, manufacturing, oil and gas

CITIES
Salina, 45,679; Hutchinson, 40,787; Garden City, 28,451; Emporia, 26,760; Dodge City, 25,176; Hays, 20,013; Liberal, 19,666; Junction City, 18,886

NOTABLE
President Dwight D. Eisenhower's burial place and presidential library are in Abilene; Former Senate Majority Leader and 1996 Republican presidential nominee Bob Dole is from Russell.

Rep. Jim Ryun (R)

CAPITOL OFFICE
225-6601
jim.ryun@mail.house.gov
ryun.house.gov
2433 Rayburn 20515-1602; fax 225-7986

COMMITTEES
Armed Services
Budget
Financial Services

HOMETOWN
Jefferson County

BORN
April 29, 1947, Wichita, Kan.

RELIGION
Presbyterian

FAMILY
Wife, Anne Ryun; four children

EDUCATION
U. of Kansas, B.A. 1970 (photojournalism)

CAREER
Motivational speaker; author; product consultant; Olympic athlete

POLITICAL HIGHLIGHTS
No previous office

ELECTION RESULTS

2002 GENERAL		
Jim Ryun (R)	127,477	60.4%
Dan Lykins (D)	79,160	37.5%
Arthur L. Clack (LIBERT)	4,340	2.1%
2002 PRIMARY		
Jim Ryun (R)	unopposed	
2000 GENERAL		
Jim Ryun (R)	164,951	67.4%
Stanley Wiles (D)	71,709	29.3%
Ira Dennis Hawver (LIBERT)	8,099	3.3%

PREVIOUS WINNING PERCENTAGES
1998 (61%); 1996 (52%)

Elected 1996; 4th term

Though his mile run record was shattered long ago, Ryun remains more famous as the athlete he was than as the politician he has become. But that does not seem to bother the congressman, who appears satisfied to advocate his staunch conservatism, and to fight for his constituents' parochial needs, in a decidedly low-key manner.

Ryun had never held elective office before arriving in the House in 1997, but the people of eastern Kansas knew his name as well as any state office-holder's. He first achieved notice as the first high school miler to break the four-minute barrier. He was on the cover of Sports Illustrated as its Sportsman of the Year in 1966, won the Sullivan Award as the nation's top amateur athlete in 1967, was named one of the top 10 young men in the country by the Jaycees in 1968, held the world record for the mile (3:51:1) for seven years, and was on three U.S. Olympic teams — all by the age of 25.

In the quarter-century after his competitive athletic career ended, Ryun worked with sports camps, gave motivational speeches drawing on athletic and religious themes, and worked with a hearing aid manufacturer to help hearing-impaired children. (He has a hearing impairment himself.) Ryun also dabbled in politics, mostly working on behalf of other candidates who shared his conservative views.

He won his House seat when Majority Leader Bob Dole resigned from the Senate to press his bid as the Republican nominee for president in 1996 and the 2nd District's incumbent, Republican Sam Brownback, moved to fill Dole's seat in the Senate. With the backing of the conservative wing of Kansas' divided GOP, Ryun prevailed easily in a three-way primary against two more-moderate candidates. In the fall he won by 7 percentage points over Democratic lawyer John Frieden, who tried to paint Ryun as too extreme for the district. His subsequent three races have been far easier; in 2002, in territory that remained solidly Republican after redistricting, Ryun won by 23 points over Dan Lykins, the state Democratic Party's treasurer.

In his first six years at the Capitol, Ryun has become a nearly pure party loyalist, voting with most Republicans against most Democrats 98 percent of the time in the 107th Congress. On national issues, Ryun's priorities and philosophy generally mirror those of the GOP leadership — in favor of lower taxes, restrained domestic spending, more-robust defense spending, and fewer federal regulations of people and business.

But his party loyalty and conservative politics were not enough to move him into the ranks of the GOP leadership. As House Republicans met to elect their leaders for the 108th Congress, Ryun lost his bid for election as chairman of the House Republican Conference, finishing a poor third behind Deborah Pryce of Ohio and J.D. Hayworth of Arizona.

Ryun has affiliated himself with a group of the most conservative members of his party in the House, now called the Republican Study Group, and on those occasions when he has been at odds with the GOP mainstream he has almost always been on its right. In his first term, for example, he was one of just 32 Republicans who voted against the spending cuts in a budget-balancing deal reached by President Clinton and the GOP leadership, finding fault with some of the spending increases embodied by the deal.

From his seat in the middle tier of GOP seats on the Armed Services Committee, however, Ryun's principal focus is looking out for the troops at Fort Riley and Fort Leavenworth and for local defense contractors. His Web site boasts that in the 107th Congress he secured $41 million for a new barracks complex at Fort Riley and $4 million to buy sectionalized water distributors built by Kline Manufacturing in Fort Scott.

Defense of another Kansas installation, McConnell Air Force Base, led him to buck the Bush administration in 2001. He and another Armed Services Republican, Saxby Chambliss of Georgia, successfully pushed a law blocking Bush's plan to cut the number of B-1 bombers to 60, from 93, and move them from Georgia and Kansas to bases in South Dakota and Texas.

Also in 2001, Ryun saw enactment of his legislation creating a commission to commemorate the 50th anniversary of the most important Supreme Court decision arising from Kansas, the *Brown v. Board of Education* school desegregation decision.

Though not often in the limelight, Ryun stirred some controversy in 1999 with a proposal — prompted by reports that China stole U.S. nuclear secrets — that would bar foreign scientists from nuclear weapons laboratories.

An ardent foe of abortion rights, Ryun opposes federal funding for embryonic stem cell research, noting in a 2001 floor speech that he would prefer instead for embryos created in fertility clinics to be allowed to grow into babies, who could then be adopted. Ryun often refers to the importance of his Christian faith, and in 2002 he and his two sons collaborated on a book, "Heroes Among Us," that was featured in Christian bookstores. Ryun promoted the book on religious broadcasts.

One local issue of interest to Ryun is an effort to amend the "rails-to-trails" act to give the former owners of land under abandoned railroad tracks a chance to get the land back or be paid for it. Currently, many unused railbeds are converted to recreational trails and — while Ryun says he has made good use of such trails as a runner — he argues that the original landowners deserve help against the "Goliath that's denying them all their rights."

In May of 2001, a Reston, Va., prep runner shattered Ryun's high school mile record of 36 years, but the record still dwarfs his reputation as a lawmaker. In the year following, the Washington Post mentioned Ryun 34 times, including once to ask how he felt about losing the record. Only twice did those stories mention that Ryun was a member of Congress.

Still, Ryun never regarded himself as a phenomenon. He had failed to make the basketball and baseball teams, and once described himself as "a nerd" who began running as a teenager to find acceptance.

Ryun continues to run — recreationally, but still faster than most. In an annual Washington fundraising race that attracts many lawmakers, Ryun covers the three-mile course in about 20 minutes.

KEY VOTES

2002

No Overhaul campaign finance law; ban "soft money" and restrict advocacy advertising
Yes Back Bush's defense budget increase
Yes Extend 1996 welfare law
Yes Adopt Bush's discretionary spending limit
Yes Pass GOP Medicare prescription drug plan
No Create independent Sept. 11 commission
No Extend union protections to Homeland Security Department employees
Yes Revive fast-track procedures for trade agreements
Yes Authorize war against Iraq
No Advance bankruptcy overhaul opposed by abortion opponents

2001

Yes Nullify Clinton Labor Department ergonomics rule
Yes Cut taxes by $1.35 trillion through fiscal 2011
No Maintain ban on oil drilling in Arctic National Wildlife Refuge
Yes Approve Bush proposal to limit managed-care plan liability for coverage decisions
No Divert money from crop subsidy payments to land conservation
Yes Expand law enforcement power to investigate suspected terrorists

CQ VOTE STUDIES

	PARTY UNITY		PRESIDENTIAL SUPPORT	
	Support	Oppose	Support	Oppose
2002	98%	2%	88%	12%
2001	99%	1%	91%	9%
2000	98%	2%	25%	75%
1999	97%	3%	17%	83%
1998	96%	4%	21%	79%

INTEREST GROUPS

	AFL-CIO	ADA	CCUS	ACU
2002	11%	0%	95%	100%
2001	8%	0%	96%	100%
2000	0%	0%	90%	100%
1999	0%	0%	84%	96%
1998	0%	0%	100%	100%

KANSAS 2

East — Topeka, Manhattan, Leavenworth

The 2nd runs the length of the state in east Kansas from Nebraska to Oklahoma, passing west of the Kansas City area. This moderately conservative district is a combination of rural farm communities and urbanized areas, including the state capital of Topeka. One-fourth of district residents live in Topeka or surrounding Shawnee County.

Republicans do well in the district's rural regions, while Democrats are more successful in Topeka and the state's blue-collar southeast corner. Although the 2nd is conservative, it is not overwhelmingly Republican; it was the only congressional district in Kansas where native son Bob Dole failed to win 50 percent or more of the vote in the 1996 presidential election. The district also favored Democrat Kathleen Sebelius in the 2002 governor's election. George W. Bush won the district with 54 percent of the vote in the 2000 presidential election.

The 2nd's economy has experienced slow but steady growth, and unemployment is low. Most of the jobs revolve around agriculture, particularly wheat. State government is Topeka's largest employer. Fort Riley and Fort Leavenworth also aid the 2nd's economy, though Fort Riley suffered a round of cutbacks in the mid-1990s.

Redistricting following the 2000 census added part of Lawrence — the Democratic-leaning home of the University of Kansas (the university itself is in the 3rd District) — but the political impact was offset by the 2nd's acquisition of conservative Miami County. The district also includes Manhattan, home to Kansas State University.

MAJOR INDUSTRY
Agriculture, defense, higher education

MILITARY BASES
Fort Riley (Army), 9,951 military, 3,995 civilian; Fort Leavenworth (Army), 3,152 military, 2,171 civilian (2001)

CITIES
Topeka, 122,377; Manhattan, 44,831; Leavenworth, 35,420; Lawrence (pt.), 25,768; Pittsburg, 19,243

NOTABLE
Robert Stroud, the "Birdman of Alcatraz," served 30 years in the federal penitentiary in Leavenworth before being transferred to Alcatraz; The Kansas Museum of History is in Topeka; Mine Creek Battlefield near Pleasanton was the site of Kansas' only major Civil War battle.

Rep. Dennis Moore (D)

CAPITOL OFFICE
225-2865
dennis.moore@mail.house.gov
www.house.gov/moore
431 Cannon 20515-1603; fax 225-2807

COMMITTEES
Budget
Financial Services
Science

HOMETOWN
Lenexa

BORN
Nov. 8, 1945, Anthony, Kan.

RELIGION
Protestant

FAMILY
Wife, Stephene Moore; seven children

EDUCATION
Southern Methodist U., attended 1965; U. of Kansas, B.A. 1967; Washburn U., J.D. 1970

MILITARY SERVICE
Army, 1970; Army Reserve, 1970-73

CAREER
Lawyer

POLITICAL HIGHLIGHTS
Johnson County district attorney, 1977-89; Democratic nominee for Kan. attorney general, 1986

ELECTION RESULTS

2002 GENERAL		
Dennis Moore (D)	110,095	50.2%
Adam Taff (R)	102,882	46.9%
Dawn Bly (REF)	5,046	2.3%
2002 PRIMARY		
Dennis Moore (D)		unopposed
2000 GENERAL		
Dennis Moore (D)	154,505	50.1%
Phill Kline (R)	144,672	46.9%
Chris Mina (LIBERT)	9,533	3.1%

PREVIOUS WINNING PERCENTAGES
1998 (52%)

Elected 1998; 3rd term

Moore has been elected three times by close margins in the suburbs of Kansas City, the first Democrat to win more than one term from the area since 1936. He has survived politically largely because of his credibility on crime, as a former county prosecutor, and because of his willingness to go along with the Republicans — and President Bush, who carried the 3rd District — on some issues, including tax cuts, trade liberalization and authorization for a war in Iraq.

After the GOP-controlled legislature redrew the state's congressional boundaries for this decade, the 3rd became more Republican than before. But Moore prevailed by 3 percentage points in 2002, his same margin of victory as two years before. The campaign became a national ground zero for partisan sniping, with Democrats maintaining that Republicans were trying to politicize the war on terrorism. The charge came after Vice President Dick Cheney, at a fundraiser for former Navy fighter pilot Adam Taff, the GOP nominee, said Taff's military background would make him more helpful to President Bush than Moore.

Still, Moore is a reliable vote for Democratic Party leaders on some core issues, including gun control measures such as trigger locks and background checks. And he has stuck with his party on major health care battles — which are more than political issues to him, since his wife is a nurse.

Moore favors legislation to allow patients to sue their managed-care providers for denial of coverage, but voted against a bill in the 107th Congress that he said would have made it impossible for patients to collect meaningful awards in those lawsuits. He also voted against a Republican bill to provide prescription drug coverage to seniors through private insurance policies and health plans, saying that approach "would force them to deal with the same people that are driving up the cost of health care now."

Moore belongs to both the moderate New Democrat Coalition and the "Blue Dogs," a coalition of the most conservative Democrats. He supported his Blue Dog colleague, Harold E. Ford Jr. of Tennessee, in his unsuccessful race against Nancy Pelosi of California to become the new House Democratic leader in the 108th Congress.

On the Budget Committee, Moore is trying to establish himself as a voice for moderate Democrats on federal fiscal policy. He was one of four Blue Dogs in 2002 to propose an alternative to the Republican budget resolution, a non-binding spending blueprint.

Moore charted a more complicated course on tax cuts, revealing the difficulties of being a moderate Democrat in a GOP district. He voted for Bush's 2001 plan to cut taxes by $1.35 trillion through 2010, noting that it included several individual tax breaks he had favored in the past and arguing that the price of the tax cuts should be acceptable as long as the projected budget surpluses actually appeared. When deficits appeared instead, Moore later voted against making the tax cuts permanent.

In his first term, Moore took on a tough issue: overhaul of the campaign finance system. He was a leading voice urging regulation of political organizations that were not required to disclose their fundraising or spending as long as they did not express support for or opposition to a federal candidate. A disclosure requirement was enacted in 2000, and he was an enthusiastic supporter of the broader campaign finance overhaul enacted in 2002.

For a dozen years, Moore served as the Johnson County district attorney, and he was known for his personal approach. Barbara Daniels, the mother of a teenager murdered by three men, asked Moore to testify whenever one of the killers came up for parole. "If I call, he answers," Daniels told The Kansas City Star. "He's really been a good friend." Moore also took the lead in creating a county victims assistance program.

Moore has played guitar since high school, favoring country rock, the blues and classical music, and he once shared the stage at a Farm Aid concert with Willie Nelson and David Crosby. He made a memorable campaign commercial during his 1998 race in which he humorously interspersed his positions on issues with a few guitar licks.

Like many of his generation, Moore was drawn to politics by the issues of race and the war in Vietnam. In 1965, he was inspired by Sen. J. William Fulbright's convocation speech at Southern Methodist University on the arrogance of the U.S. position in Vietnam. That same year, some friends visiting his dorm told him they were driving to Selma, Ala., to take part in a civil rights march. To his chagrin, Moore took his father's advice and skipped the trip. He says he is glad that later as a congressman he was able to return to the scene with civil rights pioneer John Lewis, now a Democratic House colleague from Georgia, to participate in a re-enactment of the march.

Moore compares his political career with that of his father, a three-term county prosecutor who ran unsuccessfully for Congress in 1958 and 1960. A framed "Walter Moore for Congress" poster hangs in Dennis Moore's Capitol Hill office. But campaigning for his dad "did not give me the bug," he recalls. "In fact, if anything, going door-to-door handing out cards for my dad was not something I enjoyed that much." But he adds, "If you're going to be successful in politics, gradually you have to overcome that."

The 3rd District had long been represented by GOP moderates, but in 1998 Moore was able to unseat the conservative Republican Vince Snowbarger after one term. Moore entered the race when he saw that Snowbarger had not raised much money in his first year in office, a mistake Moore was careful not to repeat. He raised more than $1.5 million for his 2000 race against state Sen. Phill Kline, another conservative.

In 2002, all of the odds seemed to be against Moore. Not only had his district been redrawn to be slightly more Republican, but Taff was also more of a moderate than past nominees against him. But Moore launched a major get-out-the-vote drive in friendly Democratic areas, and he also may have benefited from the National Republican Campaign Committee's decision not to pump money into Taff's race until late in the campaign.

Early in 2003 Moore said that he had "looked hard" at a possible race, but had decided not to challenge GOP Sen. Sam Brownback in 2004.

KEY VOTES

2002

Yes Overhaul campaign finance law; ban "soft money" and restrict advocacy advertising
Yes Back Bush's defense budget increase
No Extend 1996 welfare law
No Adopt Bush's discretionary spending limit
No Pass GOP Medicare prescription drug plan
Yes Create independent Sept. 11 commission
Yes Extend union protections to Homeland Security Department employees
Yes Revive fast-track procedures for trade agreements
Yes Authorize war against Iraq
Yes Advance bankruptcy overhaul opposed by abortion opponents

2001

No Nullify Clinton Labor Department ergonomics rule
Yes Cut taxes by $1.35 trillion through fiscal 2011
Yes Maintain ban on oil drilling in Arctic National Wildlife Refuge
No Approve Bush proposal to limit managed-care plan liability for coverage decisions
No Divert money from crop subsidy payments to land conservation
Yes Expand law enforcement power to investigate suspected terrorists

CQ VOTE STUDIES

	PARTY UNITY		PRESIDENTIAL SUPPORT	
	Support	Oppose	Support	Oppose
2002	82%	18%	40%	60%
2001	77%	23%	40%	60%
2000	76%	24%	68%	32%
1999	82%	18%	77%	23%

INTEREST GROUPS

	AFL-CIO	ADA	CCUS	ACU
2002	78%	85%	60%	20%
2001	75%	85%	57%	20%
2000	50%	65%	66%	24%
1999	78%	100%	52%	12%

KANSAS 3

Kansas City region — Overland Park, eastern Lawrence

Eastern Kansas' 3rd District differs markedly from the state's other districts. Geographically compact, it is almost entirely within the metropolitan sphere of Kansas City, Mo., and most of its population lives either in Kansas City, Kan., or in Johnson County suburbs. It boasts three of the state's five most-populous cities.

The district is hardly uniform in its economic character. Poverty and unemployment are prevalent in Wyandotte County and Kansas City itself. Overshadowed by its namesake across the Missouri River, Kansas City, Kan., is an industrial town that has had its share of Rust Belt blues because of factory closures and the long-term decline of urban stockyards. But Kansas City maintains a large industrial base and has attracted some growth in its biotechnology sector.

Johnson County is one of the state's richest, with company headquarters, suburban developments and a strong service sector.

While Kansas City lost population in the 1990s, many Johnson County areas are booming. Overland Park grew by one-third, passing Topeka and Kansas City to become the state's second-largest city, and Olathe grew by nearly 50 percent during the decade.

Heading west, the 3rd takes in the eastern part of Douglas County and two-thirds of Lawrence (shared with the 2nd). Lawrence is home to the University of Kansas, which falls within the 3rd's boundaries, and is considered the most liberal area in the state.

Large, wealthy Johnson County is a Republican stronghold, and it gives the 3rd a GOP-lean. But Democratic strength in Wyandotte County and parts of Douglas County keep the district competitive.

MAJOR INDUSTRY

Long-distance phone service, auto manufacturing, service

CITIES

Overland Park, 149,080; Kansas City, 146,866; Olathe, 92,962; Lawrence (pt.), 54, 330; Shawnee, 47,996; Lenexa, 40,238; Leawood, 27,656

NOTABLE

James Naismith, inventor of basketball, was the University of Kansas' first coach and the only one with a losing record.

Rep. Todd Tiahrt (R)

CAPITOL OFFICE
225-6216
www.house.gov/tiahrt
2441 Rayburn 20515-1604; fax 225-3489

COMMITTEES
Appropriations

HOMETOWN
Goddard

BORN
June 15, 1951, Vermillion, S.D.

RELIGION
Assemblies of God

FAMILY
Wife, Vicki Tiahrt; three children

EDUCATION
South Dakota School of Mines and Technology, attended 1969-71; Evangel College, B.A. 1975 (management); Southwest Missouri State U., M.B.A. 1989 (marketing)

CAREER
College instructor; airline company manager

POLITICAL HIGHLIGHTS
Republican nominee for Kan. House, 1990; Kan. Senate, 1993-95

ELECTION RESULTS

2002 GENERAL		
Todd Tiahrt (R)	115,691	60.6%
Carlos Nolla (D)	70,656	37.0%
Maike Warren (LIBERT)	4,616	2.4%
2002 PRIMARY		
Todd Tiahrt (R)		unopposed
2000 GENERAL		
Todd Tiahrt (R)	131,871	54.4%
Carlos Nolla (D)	101,980	42.0%
Steven A. Rosile (LIBERT)	8,732	3.6%

PREVIOUS WINNING PERCENTAGES
1998 (58%); 1996 (50%); 1994 (53%)

Elected 1994; 5th term

As his hometown newspaper, the Wichita Eagle, once observed, Tiahrt "has turned out to be just as advertised. A fiscal conservative, a social conservative, a religious conservative." On Capitol Hill, such views usually translate into dependable votes for the GOP leadership and the Bush administration, but Tiahrt (TEE-hart) is not always a loyal minion.

On more than one occasion, Tiahrt's insistence on pursuing his conservative agenda has given the leadership heartburn, and he is not shy about berating the administration when he thinks it has gone off course. He will also go straight to the Oval Office to plead his case.

The GOP leadership dealt with the matter by making Tiahrt one of them. In the 107th Congress, he was appointed one of 18 deputy whips, requiring him to persuade other lawmakers to back the party's agenda and giving him less time to engage in floor fights on conservative social policy amendments. It was widely believed that Tiahrt was in the running for appointment as chief deputy whip in the 108th Congress, and was disappointed when the job went to Eric Cantor of Virginia.

His pursuit of conservative principles is often played out by adding social policy proposals to the annual appropriations bills. His amendments have targeted U.S. funding for foreign family planning organizations, needle-exchange programs for drug abusers, and adoptions by gay couples. These amendments are not always viewed favorably by his party's leaders, particularly when the fight throws the legislative calendar off schedule or threatens a bill's chance of passage.

His new responsibilities in the 107th led Tiahrt to scale back his efforts to amend spending bills, although he did offer a proposal to permit the administration to withhold some international family planning funds and another requiring signs at a Washington airport subway station to reflect the airport's name change honoring President Reagan.

Tiahrt has served on the Appropriations Committee since 1997, and although he sometimes argues for spending restraint, he has used his seat to win an array of federal grants for his district, particularly for defense, transportation and water development projects, and disaster relief for farmers.

Tiahrt joined the Defense Appropriations Subcommittee in the 107th, where he teamed with Washington Democrat Norm Dicks to win approval of a plan allowing the Air Force to lease 100 Boeing 767 aircraft for use as aerial refueling tankers. The modifications on the planes are to be done at Boeing's Wichita facility and should provide an estimated 2,500 jobs. Tiahrt worked as a contract manager with Boeing before coming to Congress.

As an added bonus, some of the refueling tankers are expected to be stationed at McConnell Air Force Base in Wichita — a significant consolation prize for the Air National Guard unit at McConnell, which lost its detachment of B-1 bombers. Tiahrt had appealed directly to President Bush to keep the bombers at McConnell.

From May 2001 until June 2002, Tiahrt fought to free two Kansas missionaries — Martin and Gracia Burnham — kidnapped by Philippine rebels. Tiahrt continually pressured the Bush administration and the Philippine government to remember the plight of the two missionaries. He urged U.S. officials to use any means, including U.S. military involvement or the payment of ransom, to free the Burnhams. The 377-day saga ended in a jungle shootout in which Martin Burnham was killed and Gracia Burnham was rescued. Tiahrt then called on Congress to review U.S. policy on the kidnapping of Americans.

Tiahrt is a member of the Republican Study Committee, a group of the most conservative House Republicans. He is strongly anti-abortion, and spoke in 2003 at the annual March for Life rally in Washington, D.C.

Born in South Dakota, Tiahrt grew up on a family farm in the southeast part of the state. His father served on the local school board. He played football in college, and is one of the stars of the annual congressional charity baseball and basketball games.

He enrolled at the South Dakota School of Mines and Technology but transferred to Evangel College in Springfield, Mo., which describes itself as a Christian liberal arts university. It is run by the Assembly of God church, of which Tiahrt is a member.

After college, Tiahrt embarked on a career in the aerospace industry with Boeing. As a contract manager, he was involved in talks between Boeing and the federal government on a number of projects, including NASA's space station, Air Force One and many military aircraft.

Tiahrt originally registered as a Democrat. His grandfather had impressed him with the story of how the federal government had helped with the purchase of the family farm during the Depression. Tiahrt says he did not give his party affiliation much thought until he set out to run for the Kansas House in 1990. He decided then that the Republican Party was a closer match for his strong religious views and switched parties.

Tiahrt lost that race for the state House, succumbing in a recount after initial tallies showed him with a 24-vote lead. He remained active in local party politics, and two years later he was elected to the state Senate, where he was best-known for pushing legislation allowing people to carry concealed weapons.

In 1994, Tiahrt decided to wage a long-shot challenge to popular nine-term Democratic Rep. Dan Glickman. Glickman's polls throughout the summer showed him with a lead in the 30-point range; but Tiahrt mobilized a grass-roots network that drew heavily from the ranks of the anti-abortion movement, in which his wife was active, and which had engaged in protests and blockades in Wichita.

Tiahrt chipped away at Glickman, linking him to the unpopular Clinton administration. He ended up winning by 6 percentage points.

He had a serious re-election battle in 1996, eventually defeating moderate Democrat Randy Rathbun by just 3 percentage points. Democrats harbor some hope of capturing the district again, but Tiahrt has won his subsequent re-elections by 20, 12 and 24 percentage points, respectively.

KEY VOTES

2002

No Overhaul campaign finance law; ban "soft money" and restrict advocacy advertising
Yes Back Bush's defense budget increase
Yes Extend 1996 welfare law
Yes Adopt Bush's discretionary spending limit
Yes Pass GOP Medicare prescription drug plan
No Create independent Sept. 11 commission
No Extend union protections to Homeland Security Department employees
Yes Revive fast-track procedures for trade agreements
Yes Authorize war against Iraq
No Advance bankruptcy overhaul opposed by abortion opponents

2001

Yes Nullify Clinton Labor Department ergonomics rule
Yes Cut taxes by $1.35 trillion through fiscal 2011
No Maintain ban on oil drilling in Arctic National Wildlife Refuge
Yes Approve Bush proposal to limit managed-care plan liability for coverage decisions
No Divert money from crop subsidy payments to land conservation
Yes Expand law enforcement power to investigate suspected terrorists

CQ VOTE STUDIES

	PARTY UNITY		PRESIDENTIAL SUPPORT	
	Support	Oppose	Support	Oppose
2002	96%	4%	88%	12%
2001	97%	3%	88%	12%
2000	94%	6%	24%	76%
1999	95%	5%	18%	82%
1998	96%	4%	20%	80%

INTEREST GROUPS

	AFL-CIO	ADA	CCUS	ACU
2002	11%	5%	95%	96%
2001	0%	0%	96%	96%
2000	0%	0%	95%	91%
1999	11%	5%	88%	95%
1998	0%	0%	94%	100%

KANSAS 4
South central – Wichita

Seeing an airplane is about as commonplace as seeing a bird to residents of the 4th. The moderately conservative district is centered around the state's largest city, Wichita, with its large aviation industry. Much of the rest of the 4th is farmland.

Boeing, one of the state's largest employers, has a plant here. Cessna, Raytheon Aircraft and Bombardier Aerospace are among the other airplane manufacturers that have operations in the Wichita area. Although the industry has helped keep the economy healthy, aviation business downturns have led the city to look for ways to diversify. Wichita also benefits from a regional medical center and universities.

Sumner County, on the Oklahoma border, is one of Kansas' leading wheat-growing counties. Wheat also is important in Harper and Kingman counties to the west. Cattle graze in sparsely populated Greenwood, Elk and Chautauqua counties to the east.

Redistricting in the 1990s made the politically marginal 4th more favorable to Republicans by taking out Democratic-leaning Reno County and bringing in Republican-oriented Montgomery County (in the district's far southeast corner). This change helped Republicans win the district in 1994 and keep it since then. Redistricting following the 2000 census made minor changes and did not alter the 4th's political outlook. Locally, Republicans usually win here, but Democrats capture some offices. Cowley County, in the south-central part of the district, tilts more Democratic.

MAJOR INDUSTRY
Aviation, defense, agriculture

MILITARY BASES
McConnell Air Force Base, 2,771 military, 726 civilian (2002)

CITIES
Wichita, 344,284; Derby, 17,807; Newton, 17,190

NOTABLE
Almon Strowger, who invented the dial telephone, lived for a time in El Dorado; Omar Knedlik of Coffeyville invented the first frozen carbonated drink machine in 1961; Old Cowtown Museum in Wichita recreates life in Sedgwick County and Wichita from 1865 to 1880.

KENTUCKY

Gov. Paul E. Patton (D)

First elected: 1995
Length of term: 4 years
Term expires: 12/03
Salary: $104,619
Phone: (502) 564-2611
Hometown: Pikeville
Born: May 26, 1937; Fallsburg, Ky.
Religion: Presbyterian
Family: Wife, Judi Patton; four children
Education: U. of Kentucky, B.S. 1959 (mechanical engineering)
Career: Coal company executive
Political highlights: Ky. deputy transportation secretary, 1979; Ky. Democratic Party chairman, 1981-83; Pike County judge-executive, 1982-91; lieutenant governor, 1991-95
Election results:

1999 GENERAL		
Paul E. Patton (D)	349,798	61.5%
Wanda "Peppy" Martin (R)	133,485	23.5%

Lt. Gov. Stephen L. Henry (D)

First elected: 1995
Length of term: 4 years
Term expires: 12/03
Salary: $91,075
Phone: (502) 564-2611

STATE LEGISLATURE

General Assembly: Meets January-April in even-numbered years; January-March in odd-numbered years
House: 100 members, 2-year terms
2003 breakdown: 65R, 35D; 89 men, 11 women
Salary: $166/day in session; $93/day expenses; $1,580/month out of session
Phone: (502) 564-8100
Senate: 38 members, 4-year terms
2003 breakdown: 22R, 16D; 34 men, 4 women
Salary: $166/day in session; $93/day expenses; $1,580/month out of session
Phone: (502) 564-8100

STATE TERM LIMITS

Governor: 2 terms
Senate: No
House: No

URBAN STATISTICS

CITY	POPULATION
Lexington-Fayette	260,512
Louisville	256,231
Owensboro	54,067

REGISTERED VOTERS

Democrat	59%
Republican	35%
Other	6%

POPULATION

2002 population (est.)	4,092,891
2000 population	4,041,769
1990 population	3,685,296
Percent change (1990-2000)	+9.7%
Rank among states (2002)	26
Median age	35.9
Born in state	73.7%
Foreign born	2%
Violent crime rate	295/100,000
Poverty level	15.8%
Federal workers	36,234
Military	50,134

REDISTRICTING

Kentucky retained its six House seats in reapportionment. The state legislature drew a new map, which the governor signed on Jan. 31, 2002.

MISCELLANEOUS

Web: www.state.ky.us
Capital: Frankfort
STATE ELECTION OFFICIAL
(502) 573-7100
DEMOCRATIC HEADQUARTERS
(502) 695-4828
REPUBLICAN HEADQUARTERS
(502) 875-5130

District Statistics

DIST.	2000 VOTE FOR PRESIDENT BUSH	GORE	NADER	WHITE	BLACK	ASIAN	HISP	MEDIAN INCOME	WHITE COLLAR	BLUE COLLAR	SERVICE INDUSTRY	OVER 64	UNDER 18	COLLEGE EDUCATION	RURAL	SQ. MILES
1	58%	40%	1%	90%	7%	0%	1%	$30,360	47%	39%	15%	15%	24%	12%	63%	11,683
2	61	37	1	91	6	1	2	$35,724	50	36	14	12	26	14	53	7,567
3	48	50	2	76	19	1	2	$39,468	62	24	14	14	24	25	2	367
4	61	37	2	95	2	0	1	$40,150	56	30	14	12	26	18	40	5,679
5	57	42	1	97	1	0	1	$21,915	48	36	15	12	25	10	79	10,676
6	56	42	2	87	8	1	2	$37,544	59	27	14	11	23	25	29	3,757
STATE	57	41	2	89	7	1	1	$33,672	54	32	14	13	25	17	44	39,728
U.S.	47.9	48.4	3	69	12	4	13	$41,994	60	25	15	12	26	24	21	3,537,438

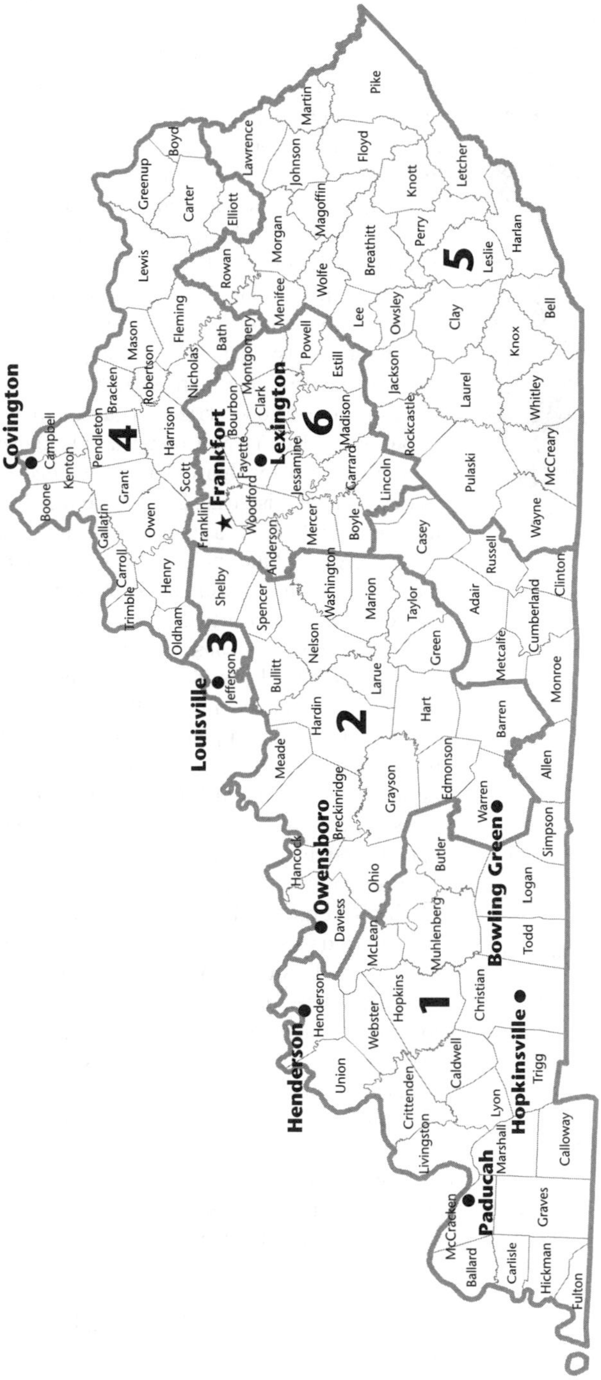
Covington
Louisville
Frankfort
Lexington
Owensboro
Henderson
Bowling Green
Hopkinsville
Paducah
1
2
3
4
5
6
Boone
Campbell
Kenton
Pendleton
Bracken
Mason
Lewis
Greenup
Boyd
Carter
Elliott
Lawrence
Martin
Pike
Johnson
Floyd
Magoffin
Morgan
Rowan
Fleming
Robertson
Harrison
Grant
Gallatin
Owen
Carroll
Trimble
Henry
Oldham
Scott
Nicholas
Bath
Montgomery
Menifee
Wolfe
Breathitt
Knott
Letcher
Perry
Leslie
Harlan
Owsley
Lee
Powell
Estill
Clark
Bourbon
Fayette
Woodford
Franklin
Jessamine
Madison
Garrard
Jackson
Rockcastle
Clay
Laurel
Knox
Bell
Whitley
McCreary
Pulaski
Lincoln
Boyle
Mercer
Anderson
Shelby
Spencer
Jefferson
Bullitt
Nelson
Washington
Marion
Casey
Wayne
Russell
Clinton
Cumberland
Adair
Taylor
Green
Metcalfe
Monroe
Barren
Hart
Larue
Hardin
Meade
Breckinridge
Grayson
Edmonson
Allen
Warren
Simpson
Butler
Logan
Todd
Ohio
Hancock
Daviess
McLean
Muhlenberg
Christian
Hopkins
Webster
Henderson
Union
Crittenden
Caldwell
Trigg
Lyon
Livingston
Marshall
Calloway
McCracken
Graves
Ballard
Carlisle
Hickman
Fulton

Sen. Mitch McConnell (R)

CAPITOL OFFICE
224-2541
senator@mcconnell.senate.gov
mcconnell.senate.gov
361A Russell 20510-1702; fax 224-2499

COMMITTEES
Agriculture, Nutrition & Forestry
Appropriations
(Foreign Operations - chairman)
Rules & Administration

HOMETOWN
Louisville

BORN
Feb. 20, 1942, Sheffield, Ala.

RELIGION
Baptist

FAMILY
Wife, Elaine L. Chao; three children

EDUCATION
U. of Louisville, B.A. 1964; U. of Kentucky, J.D. 1967

CAREER
Lawyer; Justice Department official; congressional aide

POLITICAL HIGHLIGHTS
Jefferson County judge-executive, 1978-85

ELECTION RESULTS

2002 GENERAL		
Mitch McConnell (R)	731,679	64.7%
Lois Combs Weinberg (D)	399,634	35.3%
2002 PRIMARY		
Mitch McConnell (R)		unopposed

PREVIOUS WINNING PERCENTAGES
1996 (55%); 1990 (52%); 1984 (50%)

Elected 1984; 4th term

In the waning days of the 107th Congress, McConnell stood on the Senate floor to pay tribute to retiring conservative icon Jesse Helms and uttered an epitaph that perfectly describes his own career. "There is a tendency . . . particularly of those in public life to want to be liked, to want to be appreciated," he said. "Sen. Helms has resisted that temptation."

McConnell can be a formidable opponent — conservative, tough, competitive and tireless. Frequently opting to stand by his conservative principles over the more politically prudent or popular position, he will swim against even the most inevitable political tides if he disagrees strongly enough with a proposed policy. He has shown that most forcefully in his long fight against changing the campaign finance system; having finally been overpowered in Congress in 2002 after stopping such legislation for 15 years, he has now carried his quest into the federal courts.

But unlike Helms, McConnell also is known as an effective backstage operator, a realist with a well-regulated ego willing to bargain when necessary to attain his goals. Even those who have fought him on campaign finance describe him as approachable and willing to reach out to senators with divergent philosophies. It was McConnell who brokered one of the major bipartisan compromises of 2002; his deal between Democrats, who wanted to make access to the polls easier, and Republicans, who wanted to make cheating at the polls more difficult, led to the law setting the first federal standards for the conduct of elections, with the aim of avoiding disputes such as those that had marred the election of President Bush.

After outflanking a pair of rivals behind the scenes, McConnell was unopposed for election as the Senate majority whip in the 108th Congress; he succeeded Oklahoma's Don Nickles, who was term-limited under GOP rules. In the No. 2 job in the senatorial hierarchy, McConnell is called upon to count votes, broker compromises and bridge coalitions. With the GOP in control, the pressure is on McConnell to work with Majority Leader Bill Frist to sell Bush's agenda and then get it passed. (In early 2003 Frist helped ensure that he would have McConnell by his side by persuading the Kentuckian to undergo heart bypass surgery.)

In the independent-minded and closely divided Senate, the whip's job is to play the tough cop while also tending to the care and feeding of his colleagues' particular wishes — on policy as well as logistics. It means playing the partisan, and fighting to keep his colleagues unified, while at the same time acting as a bridge builder, reaching for the Democratic votes the GOP often needs to form majorities for the president's agenda.

Senate Republican leaders have "almost all carrot, and no stick," McConnell says, so he and Frist "spend a lot of time pleading and cajoling, bringing about the maximum degree of cooperation, knowing that there's not a great deal of punishment that can be doled out."

McConnell was elevated into the leadership even though, during his four years as chairman of the Senate Republican campaign organization, the roster of GOP senators declined from 55 to 50.

In his first three terms, McConnell was best-known as the archenemy of proposals to restrict the influence of money in politics. As soon as Bush reluctantly signed the 2002 law banning "soft money" contributions and restricting issue advocacy advertising, McConnell assembled some of the nation's great legal minds and sued to overturn the statute, which he views as an unconstitutional restriction on the use of money as a form of political speech protected by the First Amendment.

He mounted his first successful filibuster in the 100th Congress and mustered other Republicans to block campaign finance bills of various iterations more than 20 times. Along the way he became an increasingly divisive figure in the Senate, even in the GOP cloakroom. And the enmity that formed there between McConnell and the campaign finance proposals' most visible proponent, Republican John McCain of Arizona, shows no signs of abating.

Although it is less well-known, McConnell has made an equally forceful stand against what he views as greedy trial lawyers. He was among those who won some new restrictions on civil lawsuits in the 2002 law creating a federal terrorism insurance program. Also in the 107th, he offered an amendment to a Medicare prescription drug bill to limit malpractice lawsuit damages and lawyers' fees. And he unsuccessfully tried to restrict unsolicited contact by personal injury lawyers with victims or their families.

Having overcome polio as a child, McConnell never lacked for toughness or tenacity. He has risen through the ranks of the Republican leadership, at least in part because he takes on unpopular jobs. In 1995, for example, he chaired the Senate Ethics Committee when it voted to expel Republican Bob Packwood of Oregon over charges of sexual misconduct. Packwood subsequently resigned.

From 1999 through 2002 McConnell chaired the Rules Committee, which handles internal Senate housekeeping matters as well as campaign finance and election legislation. Since 1993, he has played a key role in determining levels of U.S. foreign aid from his perch as the top Republican on the Appropriations Subcommittee on Foreign Operations. Using that post, he took a forceful role in guiding Middle Eastern policy in the 107th. As one of Israel's strongest supporters, he introduced legislation with California Democrat Dianne Feinstein to sever ties with the Palestinian Authority. He also has been a leading advocate for increased U.S. aid to Ukraine, Georgia and Armenia, seeing them as bulwarks against a potentially resurgent Russia.

McConnell was the student body president in high school and college and president of his law school class. After earning his law degree in 1967, he worked for Republican Sen. Marlow Cook of Kentucky and then served as a deputy assistant attorney general in the Ford administration. He served two terms as the chief executive of Jefferson County, which includes Louisville, before waging his winning 1984 Senate race.

His campaign against two-term Democratic incumbent Walter D. Huddleston struggled until McConnell hit upon a clever, homey gimmick to get across his view that the incumbent had limited influence and was often absent from committee meetings. McConnell aired television advertising showing bloodhounds sniffing frantically around Washington in search of the incumbent. Many concluded that McConnell had a point — they were not exactly sure what Huddleston had been doing in Congress. Aided by President Reagan's long re-election coattails, McConnell won by four-tenths of a percentage point.

In 1990, McConnell was tabbed as one of the most vulnerable Republicans up for re-election. He brought back the TV bloodhounds, this time to bark up the fact that he had made 99 percent of the votes cast during his first term; he won with 52 percent of the vote. McConnell's margin of victory has grown in each of his subsequent races. He took 55 percent in 1996 against former Lt. Gov. Steven L. Beshear, and 65 percent in 2002 against Lois Combs Weinberg, an education activist.

Midway through his second term he married Elaine L. Chao, who went on to be George W. Bush's secretary of labor.

KEY VOTES

2002

- No Pass farm bill reversing crop subsidy limits
- Yes Postpone tougher automobile fuel efficiency standards
- No Overhaul campaign finance law; ban "soft money" and restrict advocacy advertising
- Yes Set federal election standards
- Yes Support oil drilling in Arctic National Wildlife Refuge
- Yes Revive fast-track procedures for trade agreements
- No Create federal insurance coverage for catastrophic terrorist losses
- Yes Tighten federal accounting and corporate governance regulation
- No Advance bipartisan Medicare prescription drug plan
- Yes Create independent Sept. 11 commission
- No Back Democratic Homeland Security Department proposal
- Yes Authorize war against Iraq

2001

- Yes Confirm John Ashcroft as attorney general
- Yes Nullify Clinton Labor Department ergonomics rule
- Yes Cut taxes by $1.35 trillion through fiscal 2011
- No Pass Democratic bill to bolster rights of patients in managed-care plans
- No Permit a new round of military base closings
- Yes Expand law enforcement power to investigate suspected terrorists

CQ VOTE STUDIES

	PARTY UNITY		PRESIDENTIAL SUPPORT	
	Support	Oppose	Support	Oppose
2002	97%	3%	96%	4%
2001	98%	2%	97%	3%
2000	99%	1%	42%	58%
1999	95%	5%	33%	67%
1998	95%	5%	39%	61%
1997	97%	3%	59%	41%
1996	95%	5%	39%	61%
1995	95%	5%	24%	76%
1994	92%	8%	37%	63%
1993	94%	6%	28%	72%

INTEREST GROUPS

	AFL-CIO	ADA	CCUS	ACU
2002	23%	0%	95%	100%
2001	6%	5%	93%	96%
2000	0%	5%	92%	100%
1999	0%	0%	88%	84%
1998	0%	0%	94%	92%
1997	0%	5%	100%	88%
1996	14%	10%	85%	95%
1995	0%	0%	100%	91%
1994	0%	5%	90%	92%
1993	0%	15%	100%	79%

Sen. Jim Bunning (R)

CAPITOL OFFICE
224-4343
bunning.senate.gov
316 Hart 20510-1703; fax 228-1373

COMMITTEES
Banking, Housing & Urban Affairs
(Economic Policy - chairman)
Budget
Energy & Natural Resources
Finance
Veterans' Affairs

HOMETOWN
Southgate

BORN
Oct. 23, 1931, Southgate, Ky.

RELIGION
Roman Catholic

FAMILY
Wife, Mary Bunning; nine children

EDUCATION
Xavier U., B.S. 1953 (economics)

CAREER
Investment broker; sports agent; professional baseball player

POLITICAL HIGHLIGHTS
Fort Thomas City Council, 1977-79; Ky. Senate, 1979-83; Republican nominee for governor, 1983; U.S. House, 1987-99

ELECTION RESULTS

1998 GENERAL		
Jim Bunning (R)	569,817	49.7%
Scotty Baesler (D)	563,051	49.2%
Charles R. Arbegust (REF)	12,546	1.1%
1998 PRIMARY		
Jim Bunning (R)	152,493	74.3%
Barry Metcalf (R)	52,798	25.7%

PREVIOUS WINNING PERCENTAGES
1996 House Election (68%); 1994 House Election (74%); 1992 House Election (62%); 1990 House Election (69%); 1988 House Election (74%); 1986 House Election (55%)

Elected 1998; 1st term

Bunning achieved fame in baseball, where he was an eight-time All-Star, won more than 100 games in each major league, struck out more than 1,000 batters in each league and pitched a no-hitter in each league, including a perfect game for the Philadelphia Phillies against the New York Mets in 1964. Inducted into the Hall of Fame in 1996, the Phillies retired his No. 14 uniform number five years later.

Those who watched Bunning's baseball career generally described him as a tough, stubborn competitor — someone who hated to lose and never liked to yield an inch of the plate to an opponent. And those who have watched his political career see many of the same characteristics. To his allies he is determined and diligent; to anyone who even comes close to getting in his way, he can appear gratuitously argumentative and acerbic.

The persistence that fueled Bunning's athletic ascent is also evident in his congressional persona. It took him five years to work his way to the majors after his minor league career began as an 18-year-old, $150-a-month right-hander in the Class D Ohio-Indiana League. Even then, he had his eye on life beyond the game, taking economics classes at Xavier University. He skipped spring training sessions a few times to finish his degree in 1953.

There is no doubt that baseball gave Bunning some of the greatest thrills of his life, but he still finds satisfaction in the Senate — and so he plans on seeking a second term in 2004. "I'm in the Hall of Fame. My number is retired. The next thing to do is die," he said in the spring of 2001. "We'll hold off on that for a while, especially since there is a tie in the Senate."

The Senate is no longer tied, and the return of a Republican majority in the 108th Congress allowed Bunning to take seats on five committees as he prepared to run for re-election. First among them is Finance, which writes tax, trade, Medicare, welfare and Social Security legislation. He is Kentucky's first senator on Finance since Republican Thruston B. Morton retired in 1968, although in the House Bunning sat on the Ways and Means Committee and chaired its Social Security Subcommittee for four years.

After two years away, Bunning returned in 2003 to Energy, where he vowed to promote an expansion of clean coal technology incentives, an obvious priority in Kentucky, as part of any energy policy overhaul. He also took seats on Veterans' Affairs and Budget while keeping his assignment to Banking. In return, he dropped his seat on Armed Services, where in the 107th Congress he backed increased spending for missile defense programs and sought to protect and enhance the mission of his state's military complexes, including Fort Knox and Fort Campbell. He also sought unsuccessfully to prevent another round of military base closures set for 2005. He says that "the Pentagon has never been able to show concrete savings from the first round of closings."

With characteristic curtness, Bunning took Defense Secretary Donald H. Rumsfeld to task in 2002 over the administration's strategy in the war against terrorism. "You have come to us to ask approval of almost $380 billion worth of expenditures," he told Rumsfeld. "I'd like to have a little more assurance that you're going to finish the job that you started after Sept. 11."

On Banking, Bunning chairs the Economic Policy Subcommittee, which oversees the monetary policies of the Federal Reserve, and in the 107th he described his role as "to keep Alan Greenspan's feet to the fire." He criticized the Fed's decisions to lower interest rates as too timid in the face of an economic weakening as the decade began.

A strong opponent of abortion and gun control, Bunning fits in comfortably with the Senate's ideological conservatives. His voting record typically rates 90 percent-plus scores from the American Conservative Union and 10 percent or less from the liberal Americans for Democratic Action.

He occasionally displays a populist streak, particularly on trade. Although in 2002 he voted to give President Bush fast-track trade negotiating authority, in 2000 he had split with most Republicans in opposing a law permanently granting China the same low tariff rates as most other nations. And in the House, he had opposed the 1993 North American Free Trade Agreement.

Bunning's lifetime rating of slightly more than 10 percent in the AFL-CIO's analysis of his votes in Congress may indicate his generally pro-business bent, but he was also a key figure in the mid-1960s in the creation of the Major League Baseball Players Association, which represents the players in their dealings with the team owners.

Bunning also guards the interests of his state's bread-and-butter industries — tobacco and horse racing. He introduced legislation in the 106th Congress to exempt from federal taxes all payments made to tobacco farmers under a 1997 settlement between states and the tobacco industry. The payments were meant to compensate farmers for reduced sales to cigarette companies forced to cut back on production and distribution under the settlement. In the 107th, he was the Senate leader in efforts to help horse farmers affected by the mysterious "mare reproductive loss syndrome," which resulted in the deaths of large numbers of foals and cost the Kentucky horse industry hundreds of millions of dollars.

The father of nine children, Bunning has a personal interest in foster care and adoption issues, as two of his daughters have adopted children. In 2002, Bunning's son David, who had been a federal prosecutor, won confirmation at age 35 as U.S. District Court judge in Covington.

Bunning was born and reared in the Kentucky suburbs of Cincinnati. He retired from baseball in 1971, ending a 17-year career in which he played primarily for the Detroit Tigers and the Phillies. After managing several seasons in the minor leagues, Bunning returned home and turned full time to his work as an investment broker and agent to professional athletes.

Bunning won a seat on the Fort Thomas City Council in 1977. Just two years later, he unseated a longtime Democratic state senator. In 1983, in the last year of his four-year state Senate term, he challenged the Republican floor leader and won the leadership post by one vote. Later that year, at the behest of party leaders, he ran for governor, but lost to Democratic Lt. Gov. Martha Layne Collins, 54 percent to 44 percent — a respectable showing in a state that usually elects Democratic governors by large margins.

In 1986, GOP officials again enlisted Bunning. This time, he was pressed to run for the House when veteran Republican Gene Snyder announced his retirement from the 4th District, an area connecting the Louisville and Cincinnati suburbs. Bunning won that November with 55 percent of the vote, and then began a streak of five re-election wins in which he averaged 69 percent.

The 1998 Senate election to succeed Democrat Wendell H. Ford, who was retiring after 24 years, pitted Bunning against Democrat Scotty Baesler, a three-term House member from the adjacent 6th District. The race was a magnet for spending from outside groups. The Christian Coalition and the Campaign for Working Families intervened to attack Baesler's support of abortion rights. Bunning ultimately won the general election by 6,766 votes out of more than 1.1 million cast. His victory margin was the second smallest of any 1998 Senate race.

KEY VOTES

2002

No Pass farm bill reversing crop subsidy limits
Yes Postpone tougher automobile fuel efficiency standards
No Overhaul campaign finance law; ban "soft money" and restrict advocacy advertising
Yes Set federal election standards
Yes Support oil drilling in Arctic National Wildlife Refuge
Yes Revive fast-track procedures for trade agreements
Yes Create federal insurance coverage for catastrophic terrorist losses
Yes Tighten federal accounting and corporate governance regulation
No Advance bipartisan Medicare prescription drug plan
Yes Create independent Sept. 11 commission
No Back Democratic Homeland Security Department proposal
Yes Authorize war against Iraq

2001

Yes Confirm John Ashcroft as attorney general
Yes Nullify Clinton Labor Department ergonomics rule
Yes Cut taxes by $1.35 trillion through fiscal 2011
No Pass Democratic bill to bolster rights of patients in managed-care plans
No Permit a new round of military base closings
Yes Expand law enforcement power to investigate suspected terrorists

CQ VOTE STUDIES

	PARTY UNITY		PRESIDENTIAL SUPPORT	
	Support	Oppose	Support	Oppose
2002	97%	3%	96%	4%
2001	97%	3%	96%	4%
2000	98%	2%	33%	67%
1999	95%	5%	24%	76%
House Service:				
1998	92%	8%	20%	80%
1997	95%	5%	27%	73%
1996	96%	4%	33%	67%
1995	98%	2%	19%	81%
1994	96%	4%	31%	69%
1993	96%	4%	27%	73%

INTEREST GROUPS

	AFL-CIO	ADA	CCUS	ACU
2002	31%	0%	95%	100%
2001	13%	0%	93%	100%
2000	13%	5%	78%	100%
1999	11%	0%	82%	100%
House Service:				
1998	0%	0%	94%	92%
1997	0%	0%	90%	92%
1996	9%	5%	81%	100%
1995	0%	0%	96%	92%
1994	11%	5%	83%	95%
1993	8%	10%	91%	100%

Rep. Edward Whitfield (R)

CAPITOL OFFICE
225-3115
www.house.gov/whitfield
301 Cannon 20515-1701; fax 225-3547

COMMITTEES
Energy & Commerce

HOMETOWN
Hopkinsville

BORN
May 25, 1943, Hopkinsville, Ky.

RELIGION
Methodist

FAMILY
Wife, Constance Whitfield; one child

EDUCATION
U. of Kentucky, B.S. 1965 (business); Wesley Theological Seminary, attended 1966; U. of Kentucky, J.D. 1969

MILITARY SERVICE
Army Reserve, 1967-73

CAREER
Lawyer; oil distributor; railroad executive

POLITICAL HIGHLIGHTS
Ky. House, 1974-75 (served as a Democrat)

ELECTION RESULTS

2002 GENERAL		
Edward Whitfield (R)	117,600	65.3%
Klint Alexander (D)	62,617	34.8%
2002 PRIMARY		
Edward Whitfield (R)		unopposed
2000 GENERAL		
Edward Whitfield (R)	132,115	58.0%
Brian Roy (D)	95,806	42.0%

PREVIOUS WINNING PERCENTAGES
1998 (55%); 1996 (54%); 1994 (51%)

Elected 1994; 5th term

The 1994 elections that brought Whitfield to the House marked a transformation for him and for Kentucky politics. A former Democrat, he became the first Republican ever to represent the district. The six-member House delegation that Democrats had controlled by a 4-to-2 margin flipped to become 4-to-2 Republican.

Since eking out that first victory with 51 percent of the vote, Whitfield has clamped a GOP lock on the seat, mainly by paying close attention to local tobacco and energy interests. The GOP now holds all but one of Kentucky's House seats and both Senate seats.

A Democrat when he served in the state legislature in the mid-1970s, Whitfield found an early political mentor in Democrat Edward Breathitt, a longtime family friend who served a term as Kentucky's governor in the 1960s. After being out of elective office for almost 20 years, Whitfield was convinced to run again in 1994, this time as a Republican, by Kentucky GOP Sen. Mitch McConnell.

Now, with a 65 percent win in 2002, Whitfield has emerged as one of five House Republicans from Kentucky who look to McConnell, the Senate's new majority whip, for political guidance and aid. In turn, the House members have proved their loyalty to McConnell, notably with their unanimous opposition to the campaign finance law enacted in 2002 that McConnell opposed in Congress and the courts.

Whitfield denounced the measure on the House floor as an "incumbent protection act," saying it would do nothing but protect sitting lawmakers from challengers by limiting access to big-dollar "soft money" campaign contributions — used for party-building activities and issue ads — that could help counter the incumbent's edge.

During the two decades between his elected offices, Whitfield lived mostly in Florida and Washington, D.C., where he was a top railroad executive, a job he initially landed with some help from Breathitt. For a few years in the early 1990s, he served as a lawyer for the Interstate Commerce Commission.

As a member of the Energy and Commerce panel, Whitfield has been a consistent supporter of coal-powered electricity and has fiercely defended the tobacco industry against regulation by the Food and Drug Administration. In the 107th Congress, he helped shape the House-passed version of the energy bill, which included provisions from bills he had sponsored authorizing funding and tax credits to encourage research, development and investment in "clean-coal" technology aimed at making coal burn with fewer harmful emissions.

Whitfield also has taken an active role in shaping health care legislation, advocating free-market solutions during debates on patients' rights and creation of a Medicare drug benefit. He and California Democrat Lois Capps led the effort in the House for one of the few significant health bills passed in the 107th Congress — the Nurse Reinvestment Act, designed to increase the nation's capacity to train nurses and encourage practicing nurses to remain in the profession.

Whitfield usually votes with the GOP majority but has deviated on occasion, such as when he opposed a Republican plan to provide education vouchers. He also opposed electricity industry deregulation, reflecting the fact that his constituents benefit from low-cost power from the Tennessee Valley Authority (TVA). He supported legislation compensating nuclear plant workers for past exposure to radiation because it would help employees at the uranium enrichment plant at Paducah, in the 1st District.

Although GOP leaders were initially reluctant to act because of the compensation bill's price tag, Whitfield and his allies eventually were able to win a $150,000 lump-sum payment and lifetime medical benefits for ailing workers, with the government forced to bear the burden of proof to show that workers were not eligible. The package also included $78 million for cleanup at the Paducah facility.

Among Whitfield's local legislative accomplishments was money for a new lock at the Kentucky Dam to accommodate barge traffic and funds for the U.S. Forest Service to oversee the popular Land Between the Lakes recreation area. Land Between the Lakes had been managed by TVA, but Whitfield, McConnell and other area lawmakers were able to ease the transition to Forest Service management.

Whitfield also was a key player in a 1997 overhaul of the Food and Drug Administration, concentrating on the regulation of food products. Deregulating margarine was a pet concern. The 1950s regulation of the butter substitute was outdated, he argued, because it was a relic of protectionist laws erected by dairy interests. He represents an area that produces soybeans, a key ingredient in margarine.

Whitfield won a slot on the Commerce Committee (now called Energy and Commerce) in his first term. Chairman Thomas J. Bliley Jr. of Virginia was looking to bring friends of the tobacco industry on board, and tobacco is an important crop in the 1st District. When the Clinton administration filed a lawsuit against tobacco companies, Whitfield objected to what he called the administration's "punitive and vindictive pursuit of a legal business and farmers who grow a legal crop."

Born in Hopkinsville, near the Tennessee border and Ft. Campbell, Whitfield practiced law and ran an oil distribution company in western Kentucky. He declined to seek re-election to the state House after just one term and soon moved east, where he spent 12 years as a railroad official, including several years as a lobbyist for railroad giant CSX Corp. After leaving his post at the Interstate Commerce Commission, he briefly practiced law in Florida but soon decided to move back to Kentucky to run for the House.

Whitfield's challenge to one-term Democratic Rep. Tom Barlow looked like an uphill battle, even to McConnell, given the district's deep Democratic roots. But Whitfield has established himself securely since that first race, adding to his margin of victory with each election.

KEY VOTES

2002

- No Overhaul campaign finance law; ban "soft money" and restrict advocacy advertising
- Yes Back Bush's defense budget increase
- Yes Extend 1996 welfare law
- Yes Adopt Bush's discretionary spending limit
- Yes Pass GOP Medicare prescription drug plan
- No Create independent Sept. 11 commission
- No Extend union protections to Homeland Security Department employees
- Yes Revive fast-track procedures for trade agreements
- Yes Authorize war against Iraq
- No Advance bankruptcy overhaul opposed by abortion opponents

2001

- Yes Nullify Clinton Labor Department ergonomics rule
- Yes Cut taxes by $1.35 trillion through fiscal 2011
- No Maintain ban on oil drilling in Arctic National Wildlife Refuge
- Yes Approve Bush proposal to limit managed-care plan liability for coverage decisions
- No Divert money from crop subsidy payments to land conservation
- Yes Expand law enforcement power to investigate suspected terrorists

CQ VOTE STUDIES

	PARTY UNITY		PRESIDENTIAL SUPPORT	
	Support	Oppose	Support	Oppose
2002	94%	6%	87%	13%
2001	96%	4%	93%	7%
2000	90%	10%	29%	71%
1999	89%	11%	24%	76%
1998	90%	10%	24%	76%

INTEREST GROUPS

	AFL-CIO	ADA	CCUS	ACU
2002	0%	0%	94%	100%
2001	8%	0%	100%	96%
2000	0%	0%	90%	87%
1999	22%	10%	100%	80%
1998	20%	5%	88%	96%

KENTUCKY 1

West — Hopkinsville, Henderson, Paducah

Located in the western part of the Bluegrass state, Kentucky's rural, 34-county 1st is a hub of agricultural activity. Here, slaves once helped cultivate cotton and tobacco crops, and tobacco still dominates the economy (particularly in the counties south of the Ohio River city of Henderson), though its future is uncertain. The 1st also has seen a steady decline in its coal industry to the north.

The Ohio River port of Paducah (McCracken County) traditionally has been the political and population center of western Kentucky, but its population has been surpassed by Hopkinsville (Christian County), an agricultural market center dependent on nearby Fort Campbell, and by Henderson.

While the 1st has seen its coal and mining industries decline precipitously, Hopkins County has weathered the loss by evolving into a regional industrial and medical center. Tourism and recreation also play a role in the economy, especially near the Land Between the Lakes recreation area, where management functions in 1999 were transferred from the Tennessee Valley Authority to the Forest Service.

The 1st's Confederate legacy traditionally translated into Democratic votes, but the 1994 GOP wave sent the district's first Republican to Congress. While conservative Democrats continue to dominate local offices in western Kentucky, the region votes for Republican presidential candidates. George W. Bush carried 30 of the district's 34 counties in the 2000 election. Redistricting following the 2000 census changed the district little, but marginally increased the 1st's conservative lean by giving it some GOP-voting rural counties in south-central Kentucky.

MAJOR INDUSTRY
Agriculture, manufacturing

MILITARY BASES
Fort Campbell, 23,227 military, 4,251 civilian (2001) (shared with Tennessee's 7th District)

CITIES
Hopkinsville, 30,089; Henderson, 27,373; Paducah, 26,307

NOTABLE
The Jefferson Davis Monument, located at his birthplace in Fairview, is a 351-foot obelisk; The nation's only plant that turns uranium into nuclear fuel is operated by USEC Inc. in Paducah.

Rep. Ron Lewis (R)

CAPITOL OFFICE
225-3501
www.house.gov/ronlewis
2418 Rayburn 20515-1702; fax 226-2019

COMMITTEES
Government Reform
Ways & Means

HOMETOWN
Cecilia

BORN
Sept. 14, 1946, Greenup County, Ky.

RELIGION
Baptist

FAMILY
Wife, Kayi Lewis; two children

EDUCATION
Morehead State U., attended; U. of Kentucky, B.A. 1969 (political science & history); Morehead State U., M.A. 1981 (higher education)

MILITARY SERVICE
Navy, 1972

CAREER
Christian bookstore owner; minister; college instructor

POLITICAL HIGHLIGHTS
Sought Republican nomination for Ky. House, 1971

ELECTION RESULTS

2002 GENERAL		
Ron Lewis (R)	122,773	69.6%
David L. Williams (D)	51,431	29.2%
Robert Guy Dyer (LIBERT)	2,084	1.2%
2002 PRIMARY		
Ron Lewis (R)		unopposed
2000 GENERAL		
Ron Lewis (R)	160,800	67.7%
Brian Pedigo (D)	74,537	31.4%

PREVIOUS WINNING PERCENTAGES
1998 (64%); 1996 (58%); 1994 (60%); 1994 Special Election (55%)

Elected May 1994; 5th full term

In his early years in the House, Lewis, a former minister and owner of a Christian bookstore, often used the pulpit of the House floor to sermonize about the decline of moral values in contemporary America. He decried the primacy of personal gratification and the lack of personal responsibility, and blasted "a morally corrupt culture" that fosters teenage pregnancy, abortion and drug use.

Lewis still feels strongly about family values, but, befitting his seat on the Ways and Means Committee, where he has the opportunity to pursue legislation to help shape family values, he has focused his efforts more on legislating — on issues such as welfare legislation and tax policies that affect married couples, foster care and adoption.

In the 107th Congress, he won approval of a bill to encourage adults to become foster parents by excluding payments for foster care expenses from taxable income. Lewis' oldest child is adopted, and he pushed to increase the adoption tax credit.

Lewis has a perfect career score from the Christian Coalition, and he has served in leadership posts in such conservative groups as the Conservative Opportunity Society, the House Family Caucus and the House Pro-Life Caucus. He affiliates with the Republican Study Committee (formerly the Conservative Action Team), a group of lawmakers that anchors the GOP right wing in the House. Lewis' dependably conservative voting record and his campaign work for other GOP candidates helped him win the assignment on the Ways and Means panel beginning in 1999.

Lewis' position is firmly to the right on most social issues. He lays a large share of the blame for what he believes is a decline in moral values on the Democratic Party. "For 40 years we had a tax-and-spend Congress. . . . For 30 years there has been a war on poverty, $5 trillion has been spent. And what have we got?" he asks. "We have more in poverty, we have more welfare, more illegitimacy, lower education, higher crime, more poverty, more drugs."

Although the tobacco country of western central Kentucky had been represented by Democrats for more than a century, Democratic voters did not have to make a big ideological leap to support Lewis, because the culturally conservative views he holds long have been the local norm.

Lewis also tends carefully to home-state concerns. He champions the development of alternative fuels that make use of district crops, helps direct federal funds to district projects and fiercely protects the interests of tobacco farmers. Backed by Kentucky farm organizations, Lewis introduced legislation in the 107th to promote increased use of ethanol and biodiesel, made from corn and soybeans, through tax incentives for fuel retailers and consumers.

Although he is a fiscal conservative on most issues, he is a believer in the Appalachian Regional Commission (ARC), a Great Society program to build roads and spur economic development in 13 Appalachian states. Lewis grew up in Appalachia. "I remember the little one-lane roads, the dusty dirt roads, the lack of utilities, the small one-room schools," he told his House colleagues. The ARC, he said, had brought "tremendous improvement" to Eastern Kentucky and "now there are nice highways, nice schools, utilities reaching into the homes, paved highways." In the 107th, Lewis wrote legislation to add two Kentucky counties to those eligible for assistance from the ARC.

Lewis also worked with GOP Sen. Jim Bunning to win an Army commitment for a $200 million investment in military housing at Fort Knox, the government's gold repository and the Army's tank center, which is in the 2nd.

Tobacco growers have an unflinching advocate in Lewis. He has recognized, however, that political support for federal tobacco programs is dwindling and has urged farmers to take advantage of any federal buyout offer rather than insisting on fighting for continued federal price supports.

In the 107th, he linked his support for tobacco with his strong anti-abortion stance. During the debate on whether to permit human stem cell research, Lewis said he could never support any medical research that involves the destruction of human embryos. But adult stem cell research, Lewis argues, is different. He told his colleagues that researchers in Kentucky had stimulated growth of adult stem cells with proteins taken from tobacco plants. " 'Tobacco helps cure cancer' could be a headline you read some day," Lewis said.

The son of a tobacco farmer, Lewis says that he is "one politician who can truly claim he was born in a log cabin." He worked his way through college, which included doing stints at a steel company, a hospital and the highway department.

After graduation, Lewis was a salesman before beginning a five-year teaching stint at a small Louisville business college. He later attended a seminary and became an ordained Baptist minister. He also operated a Christian bookstore. He had never before held office when he sought the 1994 GOP nomination against Democratic Rep. William H. Natcher. When Natcher died that March, in his 41st year in the House, party officials chose Lewis to run in the resulting special election.

The unassuming Lewis made a favorable impression on many skeptical Democratic voters, who had expected him to be more doctrinaire. He tied his Democratic opponent, former state Sen. Joseph Prather, to the unpopular Clinton White House. With about $200,000 in funding from the national GOP, Lewis won with 55 percent of the vote, an outcome that gave a hint of the Republican electoral tide that would sweep the GOP into control of the House that fall.

Lewis was the winner in the fall general-election contest with 60 percent and has won re-election easily since.

Lewis had pledged to serve no more than four terms, but in 1998 he said the promise had been a mistake. "It's not fair for people to invest six or eight years in a representative who would be a lame duck his last two years and could not be as effective as he should be or could be," he said.

KEY VOTES

2002

- No Overhaul campaign finance law; ban "soft money" and restrict advocacy advertising
- Yes Back Bush's defense budget increase
- Yes Extend 1996 welfare law
- Yes Adopt Bush's discretionary spending limit
- Yes Pass GOP Medicare prescription drug plan
- No Create independent Sept. 11 commission
- No Extend union protections to Homeland Security Department employees
- Yes Revive fast-track procedures for trade agreements
- Yes Authorize war against Iraq
- No Advance bankruptcy overhaul opposed by abortion opponents

2001

- Yes Nullify Clinton Labor Department ergonomics rule
- Yes Cut taxes by $1.35 trillion through fiscal 2011
- No Maintain ban on oil drilling in Arctic National Wildlife Refuge
- Yes Approve Bush proposal to limit managed-care plan liability for coverage decisions
- No Divert money from crop subsidy payments to land conservation
- Yes Expand law enforcement power to investigate suspected terrorists

CQ VOTE STUDIES

	PARTY UNITY		PRESIDENTIAL SUPPORT	
	Support	Oppose	Support	Oppose
2002	98%	2%	85%	15%
2001	98%	2%	93%	7%
2000	94%	6%	25%	75%
1999	95%	5%	17%	83%
1998	94%	6%	20%	80%

INTEREST GROUPS

	AFL-CIO	ADA	CCUS	ACU
2002	11%	0%	90%	96%
2001	8%	0%	96%	100%
2000	0%	0%	90%	96%
1999	11%	5%	100%	92%
1998	0%	0%	100%	100%

KENTUCKY 2

West central – Owensboro, Bowling Green

The mostly rural 2nd, anchored in Kentucky's west-central heartland, takes in some suburban areas near Louisville and runs through rolling tobacco country, ending in the river country to the west.

While tobacco remains the district's dominant crop, the 2nd's economy relies on more than agriculture. Oil and coal help make Owensboro western Kentucky's leading trade center, while the General Motors Corvette plant in Bowling Green also provides jobs. Although substantially smaller than either Louisville or Lexington, the two cities are the state's third and fourth most populous. Away from the main population areas, the economic picture has been somewhat grim. In Taylor County, the closing of a textile plant in the late 1990s helped ratchet its unemployment rate above 20 percent at one point. An Amazon.com facility has helped steady the area.

The eastern portion of the district includes several of the distilleries that comprise Kentucky's "Bourbon Trail." Bardstown, in Nelson County, bills itself as the bourbon capital of the world (there is a whiskey museum in the city). Redistricting following the 2000 census brought the 2nd's northern boundary to Shelby County, which is sandwiched between Louisville and the state capital of Frankfort.

The 2nd includes the birthplace of Abraham Lincoln (in Larue County), the first Republican president, and district voters now side with the GOP in federal elections after a long period of Democratic dominance following the Reconstruction era. In the 2000 election, George W. Bush did not lose any of the 19 counties that lie wholly within the 2nd District, and just five gave him less than 60 percent of the vote.

MAJOR INDUSTRY
Tobacco, tourism, manufacturing

MILITARY BASES
Fort Knox, 6,386 military, 5,486 civilian (2001)

CITIES
Owensboro, 54,067; Bowling Green, 49,296; Elizabethtown, 22,542

NOTABLE
The U.S. bullion depository at Fort Knox, or "Gold Vault," houses the largest portion of the U.S. gold reserve; Mammoth Cave National Park; Bardstown includes Federal Hill Mansion, which inspired Stephen Foster to compose the ballad "My Old Kentucky Home."

Rep. Anne M. Northup (R)

CAPITOL OFFICE
225-5401
northup.house.gov
1004 Longworth 20515-1703; fax 225-5776

COMMITTEES
Appropriations

HOMETOWN
Louisville

BORN
Jan. 22, 1948, Louisville, Ky.

RELIGION
Roman Catholic

FAMILY
Husband, Robert Wood Northup; six children

EDUCATION
Saint Mary's College (Ind.), B.A. 1970 (economics & business)

CAREER
Teacher

POLITICAL HIGHLIGHTS
Ky. House, 1987-96

ELECTION RESULTS

2002 GENERAL		
Anne M. Northup (R)	118,228	51.6%
Jack Conway (D)	110,846	48.4%
2002 PRIMARY		
Anne M. Northup (R)		unopposed
2000 GENERAL		
Anne M. Northup (R)	142,106	52.9%
Eleanor Jordan (D)	118,785	44.2%
Donna Mancini (LIBERT)	7,804	2.9%

PREVIOUS WINNING PERCENTAGES
1998 (52%); 1996 (50%)

Elected 1996; 4th term

Northup holds the unwanted distinction of representing one of the most heavily Democratic House districts held by a Republican. Registered Democrats in the Louisville area outnumber Republicans by about 2-to-1, but that has not stopped Northup — who labels herself a "compassionate conservative" — from winning a quartet of nail-biter elections.

Her thin victory margins (her high-water mark was 53 percent in 2000) have required her utmost attention to the particular needs of the 3rd District, and have thereby prevented her from pursuing a one-time goal of moving up in the Republican leadership ranks. Instead, she uses a seat on the Appropriations Committee for frequently parochial purposes.

In 1998 Northup ran for vice chairman of the caucus of House Republicans, finishing second in a field of four to Florida's Tillie Fowler. She did win appointment, however, as one of six vice chairmen of the National Republican Congressional Committee, the organization that seeks to elect Republicans to the House. When Fowler announced her retirement, Northup planned to run for vice chairman again in 2000. But when Deborah Pryce of Ohio entered the race, Northup switched and campaigned for secretary of the Republican Conference instead. One day before the balloting she dropped out of the leadership sweepstakes altogether, saying she had concluded she needed to focus entirely on holding her House seat.

Northup comes to the task with a background that makes her a GOP campaign strategist's dream: She is a telegenic mother of six, a seasoned legislator and an articulate proponent of pragmatic conservatism — a made-to-order candidate for a party that often has image problems with women voters. So she was identified as a potential GOP star from the moment she arrived on Capitol Hill, given a prized seat on Appropriations as a freshman and frequently tapped by the leadership to give the "working mother" perspective on issues.

"All soccer moms don't think alike," she told The Christian Science Monitor. "I do not believe the Republican philosophy and perspective is in general anti-minority, anti-women . . . but it is certainly portrayed that way."

To bring what she calls a "family ethic" to policy debates, Northup often prefaces her remarks with, "As a mother of six children. . . ." When adding her support to GOP education overhaul proposals, she has talked about how she sold quilts to pay for special tutoring programs for several of her children, who had learning disabilities. She ascribes her willingness to compromise to her upbringing in a large family. She often reads to students during school visits back home in Louisville.

Northup is pro-business, and her voting record has grown increasingly conservative over the years, which she both acknowledges and defends. "I believe I represent the broad-based middle of this community," she said in a 2002 campaign debate.

For a brief time she worked as a teacher, and Northup is the founder of the House Reading Caucus. She authored legislation creating the National Reading Panel, which was charged with determining which of the dozens of federally funded reading programs were most effective. The panel's findings were incorporated into the education policy law enacted in 2002, and President Bush praised her efforts.

Northup, who adopted two of her children as infants, traveled to China in the 107th Congress to help persuade the government to lift its cap on the number of Chinese children foreigners are permitted to adopt. One of

Northup's adopted children is African-American, the other is of mixed race. Northup argues that Democrats do not have all the answers for the African-American community. "Look what they've created — a zillion programs and more hopelessness than ever," she told Insight magazine.

On Appropriations, she tries to balance her professed fiscal conservatism with her desire to make sure Louisville gets its share of federal spending. To that end she has won money for two new bridges across the Ohio River, medical research grants for local hospitals and the University of Louisville, social service programs for black churches and research and recording work by the American Printing House for the Blind in Louisville, which was in dire financial straits.

Five days before the 2002 election, Northup announced that the Ohio River bridges project had been granted "accelerated environmental review" by the Bush administration, meaning the project will be allowed to move on a much faster track.

Northup played a lead role in the 2000 battle over whether the Occupational Safety and Health Administration could issue a new rule requiring businesses to set up programs to prevent repetitive motion injuries. She argued that the ergonomics rule would be too expensive for most businesses and "simply isn't feasible." The regulation was of particular interest to United Parcel Service, which has a large distribution hub in Louisville and has many workers who perform repetitive tasks.

Northup has one brother and nine sisters, including Olympic champion swimmer Mary T. Meagher. Her father was involved in local Republican politics. When her youngest child started school, Northup rekindled her own interest in politics — she had been active in student government in high school and college — by taking a job in the state legislature. She was elected to the state House in 1987. Her record there was conservative but with an independent streak. For example, even though tobacco is key to Kentucky's economy, Northup led an effort to impose stricter laws against the sale of tobacco to children.

With the help of religious conservatives, Northup, who opposes abortion rights, won her House seat by 1,299 votes in 1996 by defeating freshman Democratic Rep. Mike Ward — making her the only GOP challenger in the nation to oust a Democrat in a district President Clinton carried that year. Democrats have put up top-tier candidates against her ever since: former state Attorney General Chris Gorman in 1998; state Rep. Eleanor Jordan, the only black woman in the state legislature, in 2000; and telegenic and well-funded lawyer Jack Conway in 2002.

KEY VOTES

2002

No Overhaul campaign finance law; ban "soft money" and restrict advocacy advertising
Yes Back Bush's defense budget increase
Yes Extend 1996 welfare law
Yes Adopt Bush's discretionary spending limit
Yes Pass GOP Medicare prescription drug plan
No Create independent Sept. 11 commission
No Extend union protections to Homeland Security Department employees
Yes Revive fast-track procedures for trade agreements
Yes Authorize war against Iraq
Yes Advance bankruptcy overhaul opposed by abortion opponents

2001

Yes Nullify Clinton Labor Department ergonomics rule
Yes Cut taxes by $1.35 trillion through fiscal 2011
No Maintain ban on oil drilling in Arctic National Wildlife Refuge
Yes Approve Bush proposal to limit managed-care plan liability for coverage decisions
No Divert money from crop subsidy payments to land conservation
Yes Expand law enforcement power to investigate suspected terrorists

CQ VOTE STUDIES

	PARTY UNITY		PRESIDENTIAL SUPPORT	
	Support	Oppose	Support	Oppose
2002	95%	5%	90%	10%
2001	99%	1%	98%	2%
2000	89%	11%	32%	68%
1999	89%	11%	28%	72%
1998	91%	9%	25%	75%

INTEREST GROUPS

	AFL-CIO	ADA	CCUS	ACU
2002	11%	0%	100%	88%
2001	8%	0%	100%	96%
2000	0%	0%	95%	72%
1999	0%	5%	100%	68%
1998	10%	0%	100%	88%

KENTUCKY 3

Louisville and suburbs

With the Ohio River forming its western border, the 3rd sprawls across ethnically and economically diverse neighborhoods in Jefferson County, taking in Louisville. Compared with the rest of the state, Louisville has a sizable black population (nearly one-third of the state's blacks live in the city), as well as a large Catholic community, a legacy of a massive German immigration in the mid-19th century. The city of Louisville was scheduled to merge with the county government in 2003.

Despite some job losses from industrial decline, labor strength runs deep among the blue-collar, white residents of the South End. Blacks, who live near downtown in the West End, also make up a strong Democratic voting bloc. Republicans live in the affluent East End by the Ohio River. The bulk of the 3rd's recent population growth came in northeastern and southeastern Jefferson County.

Although tobacco is a part of the 3rd's hearty economy, other sectors, such as the service industry, have rivaled it. Louisville claims a booming health care industry, and the United Parcel Service operates an air-freight hub out of Louisville International Airport. A Ford assembly plant provides thousands of jobs. Tourism, already big, was boosted by the 1998 opening of a massive floating casino on the Indiana bank of the Ohio River.

The 3rd is Kentucky's most Democratic district in electoral performance, but it is politically competitive. Democrats run well at the local level, especially in downtown Louisville. But more-upscale areas favor Republicans, and the increasing muscle of white-collar suburbanites appears to be swinging the 3rd closer to the GOP. Redistricting following the 2000 census added more Republicans to the district.

MAJOR INDUSTRY

Service, manufacturing, trade, tobacco

CITIES

Louisville, 256,231; Jeffersontown, 26,633; Pleasure Ridge, 25,776

NOTABLE

The Kentucky Derby, called "the greatest two minutes in sports," is held at Churchill Downs in south Louisville; Louisville is the birthplace of Muhammad Ali (1942) and the cheeseburger (1934), and is home to the Louisville Slugger Museum.

Rep. Ken Lucas (D)

CAPITOL OFFICE
225-3465
www.house.gov/kenlucas
1205 Longworth 20515-1704; fax 225-0003

COMMITTEES
Agriculture
Financial Services
Select Homeland Security

HOMETOWN
Richwood

BORN
Aug. 22, 1933, Covington, Ky.

RELIGION
Christian Church

FAMILY
Wife, Mary Lucas; five children

EDUCATION
U. of Kentucky, B.S. 1955; Xavier U., M.B.A. 1970

MILITARY SERVICE
Air Force, 1955-57; Ky. Air National Guard, 1957-67

CAREER
Banking executive; university regent; financial planner

POLITICAL HIGHLIGHTS
Florence City Council, 1967-74; Boone County Commission, 1974-82; Boone County judge-executive, 1992-98

ELECTION RESULTS

2002 GENERAL		
Ken Lucas (D)	87,776	51.1%
Geoff Davis (R)	81,651	47.6%
John Grote (LIBERT)	2,308	1.3%
2002 PRIMARY		
Ken Lucas (D)		unopposed
2000 GENERAL		
Ken Lucas (D)	125,872	54.3%
Don Bell (R)	100,943	43.5%
Ken Sain (GR)	3,662	1.6%

PREVIOUS WINNING PERCENTAGES
1998 (53%)

Elected 1998; 3rd term

The sole remaining Democrat from Kentucky in Congress, Lucas flirted with a party switch after the 2002 election. But he not only decided to remain a Democrat, he also said he would seek re-election in 2004, renouncing a pledge to serve only three terms. And he made both decisions after barely eking out election to his third House term.

Lucas defended his pledge-breaking by declaring that support for term limits, which soared a decade ago, had dwindled. "The movement has all but ended," he said. "While I still believe that public service is a calling that is temporary, these are not ordinary times in America, and I cannot in good conscience step away from my work."

If Lucas' decision to remain a Democrat cheered his party, it did not signal any rapprochement with its liberal core. The party's tilt "is very discouraging to me," Lucas says. "The center is where it is in this country." He was one of the 29 lawmakers who backed one of his colleagues in the "Blue Dog" coalition of the most conservative Democrats, Harold E. Ford Jr. of Tennessee, for House minority leader at the end of 2002. When the 108th Congress convened eight weeks later, Lucas was one of the four Democrats who refused to vote for Nancy Pelosi, the new minority leader, in the election for House Speaker. He voted "present" instead.

Pelosi did not hold either vote against him, however. She gave him one of 23 Democratic seats on the newly created Homeland Security Committee.

Lucas is the first from his party to represent the northern reaches of the state in 32 years, and he served notice the day he took office in 1999 that he would not be a Democratic team player. He joined only four other Democrats in voting to approve the roster of 13 Judiciary Committee members assigned to prosecute the House's case against President Clinton in the Senate's impeachment trial.

Since then, Lucas has offered little comfort to his party leaders. In the 107th Congress, he voted with a majority of fellow Democrats against a majority of Republicans only 44 percent of the time — the second-lowest party unity score of any House Democrat returned to the 108th Congress.

During the 107th, Lucas — who is anti-abortion, anti-gun control and pro-tobacco — supported President Bush's $1.35 trillion tax cut package, as well as measures to ban a procedure its opponents call "partial birth" abortion and to make it a federal crime to circumvent state parental consent laws and transport a girl across state lines for an abortion. In the 106th, he supported legislation to require a two-thirds majority vote in Congress to increase taxes, as well as a bill to allow states to post the Ten Commandments in state government buildings.

But Lucas shares some bellwether positions with his Democratic colleagues. He backs efforts to allow patients to sue their managed-care plans for denial of coverage, he favors Democratic proposals to protect Social Security, and he opposes federally funded vouchers for low-income families to send their children to private schools.

Lucas supported the education policy overhaul that was a top priority for Bush in 2001. Lucas' wife, Mary, is a former schoolteacher, and two of his five children are teachers. Lucas is pressing his own education proposals, including a bill to award competitive grants of $10 million or more to local schools for computer training for teachers. He says that teachers should get up to a $1,000 tax credit to take technology classes or buy computer equipment to use at home. Drawing on his business experience, Lucas also wants to give companies greater incentives to donate equipment to schools.

Elected at age 65, Lucas was the oldest member of the Class of 1998. He makes no secret of his lack of political ambition; in fact, he frequently attributes his maverick style to his moment in life. "Age allows you to maybe be more independent than you might be," Lucas said during the 107th. "It allows me to vote my conscience and the will of my district, and not worry too much about the consequences."

A self-described "common-sense conservative" who grew up on a dairy and tobacco farm in the 4th District's Grant County, Lucas says his work in Congress is guided by his community's needs. As a freshman on Agriculture, he cosponsored a bill with fellow Kentuckian Ernie Fletcher that would have given tax relief to tobacco farmers hurt by lawsuits against their industry. He also has pushed measures to protect dairy farmers, including one to create a dairy compact for Southeastern states — including Kentucky — to set minimum milk prices above the federally established level.

In the 107th, Lucas traded his seat on the Budget Committee for one on Financial Services, with the aim of enhancing economic development and homeownership opportunities in his district, and bolstering privacy laws.

A prominent figure in northern Kentucky business and local political circles, Lucas says running for Congress was "an offshoot, really, of my civic work." Throughout his career as a financial planner, Lucas was involved in his community, including serving as a city councilman, a county commissioner, county executive and a regent at his alma mater, the University of Kentucky — where there is a building named after him and he has received an honorary doctorate.

His emphasis in Congress on public education and economic development can be traced to his roots in Florence, just south of Cincinnati, where he founded and led several economic development organizations.

It was in college that Lucas met the person who ultimately persuaded him to run for Congress. Paul E. Patton, a fraternity brother, would go on to win two elections as the Democratic governor — with plenty of campaign help from Lucas — and later talk his friend into pursuing a seat in the House. While serving as the executive of Boone County, his time came when Republican Jim Bunning moved up to the Senate in 1998; Lucas defeated Republican state Sen. Gex "Jay" Williams by 7 percentage points.

In 2000, he prevailed over Republican Don Bell, a retired Secret Service agent, by almost 11 percentage points. But in 2002, he was held to only 51 percent by Republican Geoff Davis, the owner of a high-tech manufacturing consulting firm, who has vowed to seek a rematch in 2004.

KEY VOTES

2002

Yes Overhaul campaign finance law; ban "soft money" and restrict advocacy advertising
Yes Back Bush's defense budget increase
Yes Extend 1996 welfare law
No Adopt Bush's discretionary spending limit
Yes Pass GOP Medicare prescription drug plan
Yes Create independent Sept. 11 commission
No Extend union protections to Homeland Security Department employees
Yes Revive fast-track procedures for trade agreements
Yes Authorize war against Iraq
Yes Advance bankruptcy overhaul opposed by abortion opponents

2001

No Nullify Clinton Labor Department ergonomics rule
Yes Cut taxes by $1.35 trillion through fiscal 2011
No Maintain ban on oil drilling in Arctic National Wildlife Refuge
Yes Approve Bush proposal to limit managed-care plan liability for coverage decisions
No Divert money from crop subsidy payments to land conservation
Yes Expand law enforcement power to investigate suspected terrorists

CQ VOTE STUDIES

	PARTY UNITY		PRESIDENTIAL SUPPORT	
	Support	Oppose	Support	Oppose
2002	42%	58%	78%	22%
2001	47%	53%	81%	19%
2000	54%	46%	41%	59%
1999	46%	54%	41%	59%

INTEREST GROUPS

	AFL-CIO	ADA	CCUS	ACU
2002	11%	10%	90%	84%
2001	33%	25%	91%	76%
2000	40%	25%	80%	60%
1999	63%	40%	88%	64%

KENTUCKY 4

North – Covington, Florence, Ashland

About half of the 4th's residents live in Cincinnati's suburbs, which helps explain the district's dual economic personality and its consistently conservative politics. Starting near the industrial city of Ashland along the Ohio River, the 4th picks up tobacco farms and small towns and passes through the Ohio commuters' region in northern Kentucky, eventually reaching the suburbs northeast of Louisville.

Covington (Kenton County) and the northern part of the district have enjoyed steady economic growth, partly because of Cincinnati-Northern Kentucky International Airport located in Boone County. Covington also serves as a regional center for the IRS, a major employer. Boone County increased its population by about 50 percent in the 1990s. Suburban Boone, Campbell and Kenton counties account for just less than half of the 4th's population.

At the district's western end is Oldham County, which abuts Jefferson County (Louisville) and has the highest median income in the state. Oldham joins the Cincinnati-area counties in voting reliably Republican.

The economic picture is gloomier in the eastern counties. Ashland struggled to cope with the relocation of Ashland Inc. to Covington and the downsizing of other businesses, and the city has become a declining industrial hub. Boyd County, which includes Ashland, was the only county in the 4th to lose population in the 1990s.

The district is rivaled only by the west-central 2nd District in its steadfast backing of Republican presidential candidates. George W. Bush topped 60 percent of the vote in the 4th, and Al Gore carried just two counties, both in the far east: Elliott, which has voted Democratic for president since before 1920 and where 97 percent of registered voters are Democrats, and Boyd, which Bush only narrowly lost. The Covington-area district had sent a Republican to Congress since 1967 until a conservative Democrat won in 1998.

MAJOR INDUSTRY
Service, manufacturing, health care

CITIES
Covington, 43,370; Florence, 23,551; Ashland, 21,981; Newport, 17,048; Erlanger, 16,676; Fort Thomas, 16,495; Independence, 14,982

NOTABLE
The Kentucky Speedway racetrack is near Sparta in Gallatin County.

Rep. Harold Rogers (R)

CAPITOL OFFICE
225-4601
Talk2Hal@mail.house.gov
www.house.gov/rogers
2406 Rayburn 20515-1705; fax 225-0940

COMMITTEES
Appropriations
(Homeland Security - chairman)
Select Homeland Security

HOMETOWN
Somerset

BORN
Dec. 31, 1937, Barrier, Ky.

RELIGION
Baptist

FAMILY
Wife, Cynthia Doyle Rogers; three children

EDUCATION
Western Kentucky U., attended 1956-57; U. of Kentucky, B.A. 1962, LL.B. 1964

MILITARY SERVICE
Ky. National Guard, 1956-57; N.C. National Guard, 1957-58; Ky. National Guard, 1958-63

CAREER
Lawyer

POLITICAL HIGHLIGHTS
Pulaski and Rockcastle counties commonwealth attorney, 1969-80; Republican nominee for lieutenant governor, 1979

ELECTION RESULTS

2002 GENERAL		
Harold Rogers (R)	137,986	78.3%
Sidney Bailey-Bamer (D)	38,254	21.7%
2002 PRIMARY		
Harold Rogers (R)	77,615	91.8%
Billy Ray Wilson (R)	6,948	8.2%
2000 GENERAL		
Harold Rogers (R)	145,980	73.6%
Sidney Bailey-Bamer (D)	52,495	26.5%

PREVIOUS WINNING PERCENTAGES
1998 (78%); 1996 (100%); 1994 (79%); 1992 (55%); 1990 (100%); 1988 (100%); 1986 (100%); 1984 (76%); 1982 (65%); 1980 (68%)

Elected 1980; 12th term

After two decades of generally low-profile labor in the deal-cutting fields of the appropriators, Rogers has been awarded stewardship of one of the most influential and high-profile new power centers of the 108th Congress. He is the first chairman of the House Appropriations subcommittee with control over spending at the Department of Homeland Security.

The panel was formed to write an annual bill to fund the first new Cabinet department created since 1988, which was born out of the largest governmental reorganization since the start of the Cold War. A trusted lieutenant of full Committee Chairman C.W. Bill Young, a Florida Republican, Rogers was given the authority to consolidate some of the jurisdiction that had been shared by eight of the 13 Appropriations subcommittees.

He brings to the job a reputation for holding the line on spending, although not in a way sufficiently zealous to satisfy the most fiscally conservative of his fellow Republicans. He also takes the gavel after having developed expertise in the budgets — and management — of several of the biggest agencies that the department is absorbing.

Rogers chaired the Appropriations Transportation Subcommittee in the 107th Congress, when the Transportation Security Administration was created after the terrorist attacks of Sept. 11, 2001. During floor debate on legislation to create the new agency, Rogers supported calls to federalize passenger and baggage screening but opposed hiring new federal workers to handle those tasks, and he voted against a Democratic proposal that would have federalized those functions. House Republicans lost that battle, and Rogers supported the final version of the bill, which allowed the new agency to hire and manage the baggage screeners.

From his perch on Appropriations, he then took aim at the new agency, which was originally part of the Transportation Department, for paying law enforcement officers too much and submitting a series of budget requests that appeared dubious — including a request for 3,400 employees to handle passenger clothing when it was removed for screening and 1,400 workers to tell passengers to remove cellular telephones and pagers when they pass through the metal detectors. "We will not give them money to hire a standing army of almost 70,000 people to take off your shoes, check your briefcase three times, and perform intensive checks of white-haired grandmothers in wheelchairs," Rogers said.

The 2002 law creating the Department of Homeland Security settled a longstanding debate, in which Rogers played a leading role, over how to improve the performance of the Immigration and Naturalization Service. The agency was split in half, with one bureau to guard the nation's borders and another to process immigration paperwork. Both bureaus were placed in the new department.

Rogers had promoted such a plan, with minimal success, during the six years he spent as chairman of the Commerce, Justice and State Appropriations Subcommittee, which then had the INS in its purview. Critics of the former agency, including Rogers, had long contended that it was ineffective in enforcing deportation of illegal immigrants and too slow in approving paperwork for new legal residents.

In addition, the homeland security law included language by Rogers allowing the department to set up interagency task forces, modeled on drug interdiction task forces in Florida and California, to anticipate terrorist threats against the United States and take action to head them off.

"Hal" Rogers tends toward a pragmatic conservatism. He is an easygoing, old-style Republican pol who understands the art of cutting a legislative deal — and he has honed his skills capably since joining Appropriations in his second term. When the newly ascendent GOP majority squared off against President Clinton over domestic spending priorities in the latter half of the 1990s, it was Rogers who mediated many of the settlements.

Rogers has never been enthusiastic about budget-cutting for its own sake, and has not been seen as especially tough on controlling spending on lawmakers' projects. But he has been enough of a watchdog against bureaucratic waste that he was safe at the start of the 108th, when the more fiscally conservative GOP leadership won the power to decide who would remain Appropriations subcommittee chairmen, known as "cardinals" because of the power they wield out of public view.

Off the committee, Rogers has not been afraid to go against the partisan grain when parochial concerns have conflicted with the wishes of the GOP leadership. This has proved especially true on trade. Southeastern Kentucky's declining coal and tobacco industries have made the 5th the poorest district in the state, and one of the poorest in the country represented by a Republican. As a consequence, Rogers has voted against three of the four marquee trade liberalization laws of the past decade.

And in the 107th, he was one of the 23 Republicans who initially voted against the fourth one, too — a measure to grant the president fast-track trade negotiating authority. Rogers reversed course and joined a narrow House majority to enact the final version of the law, however, because it had been amended to provide aid to those who lost their jobs because of trade accords.

After earning undergraduate and law degrees at the University of Kentucky, Rogers made a name for himself in the southeastern part of the state as a civic activist, promoting industrial development. In 1969, he took over as the commonwealth's attorney in that part of the state and continued to play a conspicuous role in politics as prosecutor for Pulaski and Rockcastle counties. Although he lost a 1979 campaign for lieutenant governor, the name recognition he earned paid off when he ran for the House in 1980 to succeed retiring Republican Tim Lee Carter. Rogers won a 10-person GOP primary and then waltzed to victory in November with 68 percent of the vote.

He has posted a lower vote percentage only once: Running in a district that was made much more Democratic by the redistricting after the 1990 census, he was held to 55 percent in 1992. Redistricting for this decade should keep the seat safely in Rogers' hands.

KEY VOTES

2002

No	Overhaul campaign finance law; ban "soft money" and restrict advocacy advertising
Yes	Back Bush's defense budget increase
Yes	Extend 1996 welfare law
Yes	Adopt Bush's discretionary spending limit
Yes	Pass GOP Medicare prescription drug plan
No	Create independent Sept. 11 commission
No	Extend union protections to Homeland Security Department employees
Yes	Revive fast-track procedures for trade agreements
Yes	Authorize war against Iraq
Yes	Advance bankruptcy overhaul opposed by abortion opponents

2001

Yes	Nullify Clinton Labor Department ergonomics rule
Yes	Cut taxes by $1.35 trillion through fiscal 2011
No	Maintain ban on oil drilling in Arctic National Wildlife Refuge
Yes	Approve Bush proposal to limit managed-care plan liability for coverage decisions
No	Divert money from crop subsidy payments to land conservation
Yes	Expand law enforcement power to investigate suspected terrorists

CQ VOTE STUDIES

	PARTY UNITY		PRESIDENTIAL SUPPORT	
	Support	Oppose	Support	Oppose
2002	95%	5%	87%	13%
2001	96%	4%	93%	7%
2000	91%	9%	23%	77%
1999	93%	7%	21%	79%
1998	92%	8%	23%	77%

INTEREST GROUPS

	AFL-CIO	ADA	CCUS	ACU
2002	13%	0%	100%	88%
2001	17%	10%	91%	88%
2000	10%	5%	76%	80%
1999	33%	5%	88%	80%
1998	11%	5%	88%	92%

KENTUCKY 5

East and southeast – Somerset, Middlesboro

No area of Kentucky has lower levels of income and education than the rural 5th, which takes in eastern Kentucky's hardscrabble coal country and whose largest city, Somerset, has a population of 11,000.

Coal mining once was a thriving industry in this sparsely populated, Appalachian region, but its decline has brought even harder times to the region's mountain people. Mining still provides thousands of jobs in the area — particularly in high-producing coal areas such as Pike, Perry, Harlan and Knott counties — but the eastern counties are trying to diversify their economies. Some community leaders are trying to attract tourists by highlighting the area's country music heritage, building new arts centers and showcasing the area's coal history.

Population in the western section is concentrated in Pulaski and Laurel counties. Like the rest of the west, Somerset relies heavily on tourism and recreation. Lake Cumberland is nearby, as is the Big South Fork National River and Recreation Area. The Daniel Boone National Forest extends from Rowan County in the north to the Tennessee border.

The 5th is secure GOP territory — Democrats have not represented the southeast Kentucky district since 1889. Republicans run particularly well in the more populous central and western parts. Jackson and Owsley counties, in the west, gave George W. Bush more than 80 percent of the vote in 2000, and five other counties in the southern part gave Bush more than 70 percent. Bush carried the district overall with 57 percent.

Democrats maintain a strong presence in the far eastern coal counties where the United Mine Workers of America union is strong. Seven of the 15 Kentucky counties Al Gore won in 2000 are in the 5th; Democratic voter registration tops 90 percent in some of the counties. But Bush cracked the Democratic dominance by winning Menifee, Morgan and Wolfe counties in 2000.

MAJOR INDUSTRY

Health care, service, tourism, coal

CITIES

Somerset, 11,352; Middlesboro, 10,384; Corbin, 7,742; Pikeville, 6,295

NOTABLE

The 5th has the nation's highest percentage of white residents (97 percent); Colonel Harland Sanders began making what would later be known as Kentucky Fried Chicken at his service station in Corbin.

Rep. Ernie Fletcher (R)

CAPITOL OFFICE
225-4706
www.house.gov/fletcher
1117 Longworth 20515-1706; fax 225-2122

COMMITTEES
Energy & Commerce

HOMETOWN
Lexington

BORN
Nov. 12, 1952, Mount Sterling, Ky.

RELIGION
Baptist

FAMILY
Wife, Glenna Fletcher; two children

EDUCATION
U. of Kentucky, B.S 1974 (mechanical engineering), M.D. 1984

MILITARY SERVICE
Air Force, 1974-80

CAREER
Physician

POLITICAL HIGHLIGHTS
Ky. House, 1995-96; Republican nominee for U.S. House, 1996

ELECTION RESULTS

2002 GENERAL		
Ernie Fletcher (R)	115,622	72.0%
Gatewood Galbraith (I)	41,753	26.0%
Mark Gailey (LIBERT)	3,313	2.1%
2002 PRIMARY		
Ernie Fletcher (R)		unopposed
2000 GENERAL		
Ernie Fletcher (R)	142,971	52.8%
Scotty Baesler (D)	94,167	34.8%
Gatewood Galbraith (I)	32,436	12.0%

PREVIOUS WINNING PERCENTAGES
1998 (53%)

Elected 1998; 3rd term

The Republican leadership has called on Fletcher to be one of their frontmen on the politically sensitive subject of patients' rights. That was his main niche during his first four years in the House, and now Fletcher hopes it will help propel him to the Kentucky governor's mansion at the end of 2003.

Also working in his favor is the patronage of the state's top elected Republican, Sen. Mitch McConnell, and Fletcher's success at turning a swing district into reliably Republican territory.

Smart, well-spoken and not overly doctrinaire — as well as a family physician — Fletcher was an obvious choice to help the GOP come up with a plan that would give patients more clout in dealing with their managed-care plans and also protect the interests of two key constituencies of the party, health insurers and employers. By the 107th Congress he was the main author of the leadership bill, along the way risking the wrath of the American Medical Association, which had helped get him elected in 1998.

"As I saw it, my job was to ripen the situation," he said of that effort. He considers one of his skills to be a willingness to reason and see other sides of an issue. "Some people want to scream in your face, which I don't think is very effective," he told The Washington Post in 2000. "I'm one who works by sitting down with people to make a consensus and compromise."

Still, his bill never had a chance of passing. After the Senate produced its patients' rights measure in 2001, the House moved only when another House Republican, dentist Charlie Norwood of Georgia, reached an agreement with the White House that propelled a bill to narrow party-line passage. But a compromise never came close to emerging in the 107th.

Unlike other doctors in Congress, Fletcher often trains his sights narrowly on other health care issues, such as stem cell research and anthrax. Now a member of the Energy and Commerce Committee — a post he was given in early 2002 — Fletcher will have plenty of opportunities to weigh in on the host of health issues that are under the panel's purview. His appointment allowed the GOP to keep a doctor on the dais, as surgeon Greg Ganske of Iowa left after the 107th to run for the Senate.

A litmus test that Fletcher applies to congressional health care proposals is this: Will it increase or decrease the number of people with medical insurance? More than 40 million Americans do not have coverage, and Fletcher cites one study that found that an uninsured person was three times more likely to die in the hospital than someone with coverage.

He argued that the Democrats' legislation for a patients' bill of rights would cause many insurers to drop coverage altogether, fearing huge potential liabilities from lawsuits. Fletcher also has sponsored other proposals, including bills to encourage states to develop so-called risk pools, which provide insurance to some people who cannot otherwise find coverage. And he championed legislation to permit small businesses and farmers to join together to offer health insurance to their workers.

Although he is a physician, Fletcher makes no apologies for defending tobacco farmers. He sees them as an important constituency that must be protected, and he opposes requiring the tobacco industry to bear the costs of smoking-related illnesses.

Horse breeding is a multibillion-dollar industry in Kentucky, and Fletcher was quick to respond in 2001 when hundreds of foals died or were still-born as a result of what was called mare reproductive loss syndrome, costing the industry at least $200 million. On the Agriculture Committee, where he served before joining Energy and Commerce, Fletcher helped get federal loans or loan guarantees for affected horse breeders.

Fletcher won praise in 2001 for his efforts to save federal funding for "Between the Lions," a public television show that helps teach children to read. He also has won some federal support to expand into the central part of the state a program known by the acronym PRIDE, for Personal Responsibility In a Desirable Environment. Proposed by fellow GOP Kentucky Rep. Harold Rogers, it helps mobilize people to clean up litter and trash in their communities as well as dumps, and it covers southeastern Kentucky.

Fletcher grew up in Lexington and his father, who did not graduate from college, turned down a promotion in order to stay in the city so his son could afford to attend the University of Kentucky.

While studying mechanical engineering, Fletcher worked on a NASA contract with the school to study the impact of space travel on astronauts' bodily fluids; the job gave rise to his desire to join the space program. He went through college on an ROTC scholarship, then spent six years flying Air Force jets to repay the obligation. Still interested in NASA at that point, he decided a medical degree would look good on his résumé. As his children grew older, the space program lost some of its allure, and Fletcher settled into a career in family practice. (Along the way, he worked as a missionary doctor in India.)

While treating single mothers, Fletcher says he became irritated with government policies that sometimes made their predicament worse. He was occasionally badgered by friends to run for office until finally, in 1994, he permitted a friend to file state House candidacy papers on his behalf. After he was elected, he became hooked on politics and two years later ran for Congress.

After taking a respectable 44 percent in 1996 against Democrat Scotty Baesler, who had held the seat since 1992, Fletcher tried again two years later. When Baesler gave up his seat to run unsuccessfully for the Senate, Fletcher wound up facing Democratic state Sen. Ernesto Scorsone, capturing 17 of 19 counties and winning by 7 percentage points.

The 2000 rematch between Fletcher and Baesler became one of the year's most closely watched contests. Fletcher took advantage of some missteps by Baesler and swamped the Democrat by 18 points. The strong showing discouraged Democrats from fielding a candidate in 2002 and planted the seed of Fletcher's 2003 gubernatorial quest.

KEY VOTES

2002

No Overhaul campaign finance law; ban "soft money" and restrict advocacy advertising
Yes Back Bush's defense budget increase
Yes Extend 1996 welfare law
Yes Adopt Bush's discretionary spending limit
Yes Pass GOP Medicare prescription drug plan
No Create independent Sept. 11 commission
No Extend union protections to Homeland Security Department employees
Yes Revive fast-track procedures for trade agreements
Yes Authorize war against Iraq
Yes Advance bankruptcy overhaul opposed by abortion opponents

2001

Yes Nullify Clinton Labor Department ergonomics rule
Yes Cut taxes by $1.35 trillion through fiscal 2011
No Maintain ban on oil drilling in Arctic National Wildlife Refuge
Yes Approve Bush proposal to limit managed-care plan liability for coverage decisions
No Divert money from crop subsidy payments to land conservation
Yes Expand law enforcement power to investigate suspected terrorists

CQ VOTE STUDIES

	PARTY UNITY		PRESIDENTIAL SUPPORT	
	Support	Oppose	Support	Oppose
2002	96%	4%	87%	13%
2001	97%	3%	93%	7%
2000	92%	8%	22%	78%
1999	93%	7%	19%	81%

INTEREST GROUPS

	AFL-CIO	ADA	CCUS	ACU
2002	11%	0%	95%	92%
2001	8%	0%	100%	96%
2000	0%	5%	80%	84%
1999	0%	0%	96%	84%

KENTUCKY 6

East central – Lexington, Frankfort

The 6th embodies the culture and economic pursuits that most outsiders associate with the state of Kentucky. This is the heart of the Bluegrass region, which spawns Kentucky Derby champions and is host to considerable tobacco and liquor interests.

A patchwork of urban, suburban and rural areas, the 6th experienced steady economic growth in the 1990s. Lexington, the district's largest city, continues to have a strong equine industry and is known as the thoroughbred capital of the world. The city is home to the University of Kentucky, where the basketball team plays at Rupp Arena. A Toyota manufacturing facility in Georgetown, just north of Lexington, is one of the largest employers in the state.

Tobacco, always a highly charged subject in this region, held strong in the 1990s despite mounting concerns about its future. Kentucky's top three producers of burley tobacco in 2000 — Bourbon, Fayette and Madison counties — are in the 6th District.

The 6th swung sharply to George W. Bush in the 2000 election after narrowly backing Bill Clinton in 1996. As in other Kentucky districts, the cultural themes of the 2000 election helped the GOP. District voters tend to be socially conservative, especially on gun control. The House seat switched from Republican to Democrat and back again in the 1990s.

Government workers in Frankfort contribute to Franklin County's Democratic lean; it was the only county in the 6th to back Al Gore for president in 2000. Democratic support dips in Woodford and Scott counties, which border Franklin and have among the highest incomes in Kentucky. Republicans run up big margins in the farmland south of Lexington — Bush took districtwide highs of 69 percent in Garrard County and 67 percent in Jessamine County.

MAJOR INDUSTRY
Manufacturing, service, tobacco, retail

MILITARY BASES
Bluegrass Army Depot, 394 military, 643 civilian (1999)

CITIES
Lexington-Fayette, 260,512; Frankfort, 27,741; Richmond, 27,152

NOTABLE
The whiskey bourbon was named after Bourbon County.

LOUISIANA

Gov. Mike Foster (R)

First elected: 1995
Length of term: 4 years
Term expires: 1/04
Salary: $95,000
Phone: (225) 342-7015
Hometown: Franklin
Born: July 11, 1930; Shreveport, La.
Religion: Episcopalian
Family: Wife, Alice Foster; two children, two stepchildren
Education: Louisiana State U., B.S. 1952 (chemistry)
Military Service: Air Force, 1952-55
Career: Sugar cane farmer; contracting business owner; sugar company executive
Political highlights: La. Senate, 1988-96
Election results:

1999 GENERAL		
Mike Foster (R)	805,203	62.2%
William J. Jeffferson (D)	382,445	29.5%

Lt. Gov. Kathleen Babineaux Blanco (D)

First elected: 1995
Length of term: 4 years
Term expires: 1/04
Salary: $85,000
Phone: (225) 342-7009

STATE LEGISLATURE

Legislature: Meets March-June in odd-numbered years; April-June in even-numbered years
House: 105 members, 4-year terms
2003 breakdown: 34R, 70D, 1I; 85 men, 20 women
Salary: $16,800
Phone: (225) 342-6945
Senate: 39 members, 4-year terms
2003 breakdown: 15R, 24D; 36 men, 3 women
Salary: $16,800
Phone: (225) 342-2040

STATE TERM LIMITS

Governor: 2 terms
Senate: 3 terms
House: 3 terms

URBAN STATISTICS

CITY	POPULATION
New Orleans	484,674
Baton Rouge	227,818
Shreveport	200,145
Lafayette	110,257
Lake Charles	71,757

REGISTERED VOTERS

Democrat	58%
Republican	23%
Other	19%

POPULATION

2002 population (est.)	4,482,646
2000 population	4,468,976
1990 population	4,219,973
Percent change (1990-2000)	+5.9%
Rank among states (2002)	23
Median age	34
Born in state	79.4%
Foreign born	2.6%
Violent crime rate	681/100,000
Poverty level	19.6%
Federal workers	34,590
Military	41,392

REDISTRICTING

Louisiana retained its seven House seats in reapportionment. The state legislature drew a new map, which the governor signed on Oct. 19, 2001.

MISCELLANEOUS

Web: www.state.la.us
Capital: Baton Rouge
STATE ELECTION OFFICIAL
(225) 342-4971
DEMOCRATIC HEADQUARTERS
(225) 336-4155
REPUBLICAN HEADQUARTERS
(225) 928-2998

District Statistics

	2000 VOTE FOR PRESIDENT															
DIST.	BUSH	GORE	NADER	WHITE	BLACK	ASIAN	HISP	MEDIAN INCOME	WHITE COLLAR	BLUE COLLAR	SERVICE INDUSTRY	OVER 64	UNDER 18	COLLEGE EDUCATION	RURAL	SQ. MILES
1	66%	31%	1%	80%	13%	2%	5%	$40,948	65%	21%	14%	13%	25%	27%	20%	2,402
2	22	76	1	28	64	3	4	$27,514	56	22	22	10	28	19	1	266
3	52	45	1	70	25	1	2	$34,463	50	35	15	11	29	11	27	7,010
4	55	43	1	62	33	1	2	$31,085	53	29	18	13	27	17	41	10,765
5	57	40	1	63	34	1	1	$27,453	54	29	18	13	27	16	47	13,775
6	55	43	1	63	33	1	2	$37,931	61	24	15	10	27	24	24	3,076
7	55	42	1	72	25	1	1	$31,453	55	29	17	12	28	17	31	6,268
STATE	53	45	1	63	32	1	2	$32,566	57	27	17	12	27	19	27	43,562
U.S.	47.9	48.4	3	69	12	4	13	$41,994	60	25	15	12	26	24	21	3,537,438

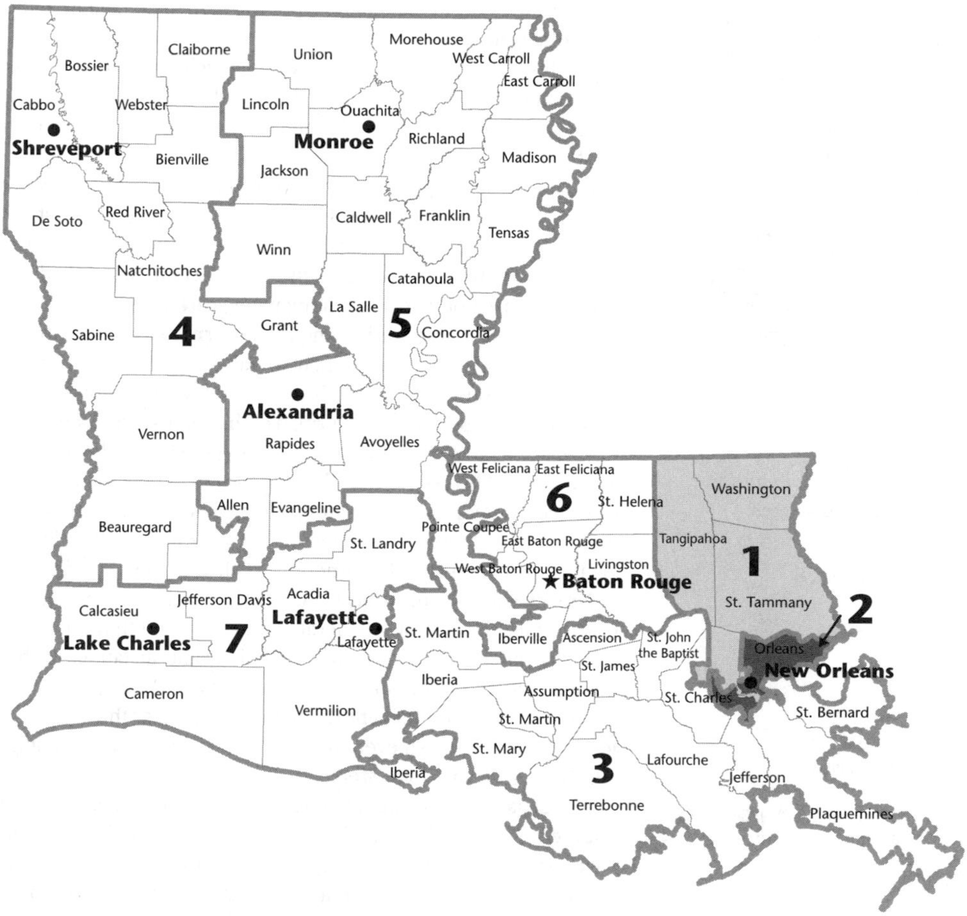

Bossier
Claiborne
Union
Morehouse
West Carroll
East Carroll
Cabbo
Webster
Lincoln
Ouachita
Shreveport
Monroe
Bienville
Richland
Madison
Jackson
De Soto
Red River
Caldwell
Franklin
Tensas
Winn
Natchitoches
Catahoula
La Salle
Sabine
4
Grant
5
Concordia
Alexandria
Vernon
Rapides
Avoyelles
West Feliciana
East Feliciana
Washington
Allen
Evangeline
6
St. Helena
Beauregard
Pointe Coupee
Tangipahoa
St. Landry
East Baton Rouge
1
West Baton Rouge
Livingston
Baton Rouge
Jefferson Davis
Acadia
St. Tammany
Calcasieu
2
Lafayette
Lake Charles
7
Lafayette
St. Martin
Iberville
Ascension
St. John the Baptist
Orleans
New Orleans
St. James
Iberia
Cameron
Assumption
St. Charles
St. Bernard
Vermilion
St. Martin
St. Mary
3
Lafourche
Iberia
Jefferson
Terrebonne
Plaquemines

Sen. John B. Breaux (D)

CAPITOL OFFICE
224-4623
senator@breaux.senate.gov
breaux.senate.gov
503 Hart 20510-1803; fax 228-2577

COMMITTEES
Commerce, Science & Transportation
Finance
Rules & Administration
Special Aging - ranking member

HOMETOWN
Crowley

BORN
March 1, 1944, Crowley, La.

RELIGION
Roman Catholic

FAMILY
Wife, Lois Breaux; four children

EDUCATION
U. of Southwestern Louisiana, B.A. 1964 (political science); Louisiana State U., J.D. 1967

CAREER
Lawyer; congressional aide

POLITICAL HIGHLIGHTS
U.S. House, 1972-87

ELECTION RESULTS

1998 GENERAL

John B. Breaux (D)	620,502	64.0%
Jim Donelon (R)	306,616	31.6%
Raymond Brown (X)	12,203	1.3%
Sam Houston Melton Jr. (D)	9,893	1.0%

PREVIOUS WINNING PERCENTAGES
1992 (72%); 1986 (53%); 1984 House Election (86%); 1982 House Election (79%); 1980 House Election (100%); 1978 House Election (60%); 1976 House Election (83%); 1974 House Election (89%); 1972 House Election (100%); 1972 House Special Election (55%)

Elected 1986; 3rd term

The Senate's top centrist Democrat likes to say "all solutions start from the center." In an era of slender margins of control in the chamber, Breaux has become an important power broker between the two major parties on issues ranging from creation of a prescription drug benefit to the shaping of a homeland security bill.

But his compromise solutions, while headline-grabbing, are frequently undercut by the intransigence of the Republican White House and Democratic leaders in Congress, who find more political value in continuing the fight until the next election.

In the 108th Congress, Breaux (BRO) had a powerful new ally on the health care issues close to his heart. Tennessee Sen. Bill Frist, with whom he has often cosponsored legislation, ascended to majority leader after the GOP took control of the Senate in the 2002 election. Breaux had teamed with Frist in the past on bills holding managed-care companies responsible for poor patient care and overhauling the government's Medicare program.

An early leader of the movement to pull the Democratic Party to the center, Breaux is one of the Senate's most vocal advocates of the disappearing art of compromise. He was chairman of the centrist Democratic Leadership Council — a position Bill Clinton used to help launch his bid for the presidency — and he co-chairs with Republican Olympia Snowe of Maine the Centrist Coalition, a bipartisan group of moderate senators. He is also a member of the Senate New Democrats. "I've never felt inclined to switch parties," Breaux says. "I'd rather try to change the party from within."

Breaux has been his party's chief deputy whip in the Senate since 1993, despite misgivings among liberal Democrats who think he's too quick to split the difference on issues. His high-profile flirtations with the Bush administration only compounded their unease. Breaux was the first Democrat to meet with President Bush one-on-one after the divisive 2000 presidential election. Bush even offered Breaux a job in his administration as a Cabinet secretary, but Breaux declined.

The senator also is often at odds with core Democratic supporters. He angered organized labor in the 107th Congress by helping to defeat a new ergonomics standard protecting workers from repetitive stress injuries. He also clashed with environmentalists by supporting Bush's proposal to open areas of the Arctic wilderness to oil drilling. In 1998, the watchdog group Public Citizen gave Breaux their annual "Golden Leash" award for accepting large contributions from energy firms while opposing bills to clamp down on smog and emissions thought to contribute to global warming.

All told, Breaux in the 107th split from his party colleagues 42 percent of the time — more often than all but two other Senate Democrats. And his 82 percent support of President Bush marked him as the No. 2 Senate Democrat in fealty to the chief executive.

After serving 14 years in the House and 16 in the Senate, Breaux sees himself as a bridge to independent voters. "That is the balance of power in the country politically," he says. "They look to the ideas more than the party."

Breaux is a senior member of the Finance Committee and the top Democrat on the Aging Committee. In 2002, he tried to end the partisan gridlock over prescription drug coverage for senior citizens by cosponsoring a "tripartisan" plan with Iowa Republican Charles E. Grassley and independent James M. Jeffords of Vermont. While Republicans said they could support the plan, most Democrats said it was inadequate, and it was voted down. In the 106th, Breaux and Frist floated a plan to revamp Medicare that included a new drug benefit. But Democrats insisted on adding the benefit without structural change in Medicare, and the Breaux-Frist bill failed.

Breaux's efforts date to 1998 and 1999, when he chaired the National Bipartisan Commission on the Future of Medicare. Then, he tried unsuccessfully to get the commission to unify behind a prescription drug benefit tied to structural changes aimed at saving the program from potential insolvency as the baby boom generation began to retire. But he could muster only 10 of the 11 votes required to send the plan on to Congress.

Breaux also played a major role in the 107th in trying to break the stalemate over personnel rules that was stalling Senate passage of the homeland security bill. Bush wanted authority to hire and fire workers in the new department, but Democrats and federal employee unions opposed the idea. Breaux, with Democrat Ben Nelson of Nebraska and Republican Lincoln Chafee of Rhode Island, proposed a compromise allowing the administration to exclude workers from union contracts under limited circumstances.

But the stalemate dragged on, and when Republicans won control of the Senate in the 2002 elections, Breaux and his colleagues lost their leverage.

He often has had to be satisfied with incremental changes in policy. Breaux may not have stopped Bush's massive tax cut plan in 2002, but he was instrumental in cutting it from $1.6 trillion to $1.35 trillion. In 1996, he won a compromise on the health insurance portability bill allowing people to transfer their insurance from job to job. The same year, he helped forge compromises that led to passage of the historic welfare overhaul bill.

Breaux is the latest in a long line of colorful politicians from Louisiana, the state that produced populist Huey Long and Gov. Edwin Edwards, Breaux's political mentor who was convicted for corruption. The only child of an oil field laborer and a dressmaker, Breaux was born in Crowley, the same hometown as Edwards, in the heart of Cajun country.

The region was settled by French-Catholic Acadians ("Cajuns"), who still dominate the southern half of the state in everything from food to politics. Breaux retains a hint of a Cajun accent, and with his sharp wit and sociable nature, he is a popular figure at Mardi Gras, where he plays a washboard. Posted on his Web site is a recipe for his mother-in-law's rice dressing.

In 1981, a House member at the time, Breaux memorably explained why he had supported President Reagan's social spending cuts in return for concessions on natural gas policy and sugar subsidies. His vote, he said, could not be bought, but "it can be rented."

Breaux started out in politics as a top aide to Edwards in the House. When Edwards ran for governor in 1972, he pushed Breaux as his successor. With the help of his mentor's organization, Breaux defeated five other candidates to win a special election. He had no GOP opposition in November to secure a full term; he was easily re-elected to the House six times.

Breaux had a tougher time in his 1986 bid to replace retiring Democratic Sen. Russell B. Long. Louisiana's oil industry was foundering and Edwards' image had suffered during two corruption trials. Those circumstances gave the GOP one of its best openings in years, and GOP Rep. W. Henson Moore began airing ads charging that Democrats had squandered the state's resources and prostituted the political system to their own advantage.

Ultimately, however, the national political situation helped to bail out Breaux: He warned voters that Moore's first allegiance was to his party and to Reagan, not to Louisiana. Breaux won 42 of 64 parishes, taking 53 percent of the vote. Since then, his seat has been safe.

First elected at age 28, Breaux's 30-plus years in Congress makes him one of the small number of members who have spent more than half their life on Capitol Hill.

KEY VOTES

2002

Yes Pass farm bill reversing crop subsidy limits
Yes Postpone tougher automobile fuel efficiency standards
No Overhaul campaign finance law; ban "soft money" and restrict advocacy advertising
Yes Set federal election standards
Yes Support oil drilling in Arctic National Wildlife Refuge
Yes Revive fast-track procedures for trade agreements
Yes Create federal insurance coverage for catastrophic terrorist losses
Yes Tighten federal accounting and corporate governance regulation
No Advance bipartisan Medicare prescription drug plan
Yes Create independent Sept. 11 commission
Yes Back Democratic Homeland Security Department proposal
Yes Authorize war against Iraq

2001

Yes Confirm John Ashcroft as attorney general
Yes Nullify Clinton Labor Department ergonomics rule
Yes Cut taxes by $1.35 trillion through fiscal 2011
Yes Pass Democratic bill to bolster rights of patients in managed-care plans
No Permit a new round of military base closings
Yes Expand law enforcement power to investigate suspected terrorists

CQ VOTE STUDIES

	PARTY UNITY		PRESIDENTIAL SUPPORT	
	Support	Oppose	Support	Oppose
2002	55%	45%	88%	12%
2001	59%	41%	77%	23%
2000	73%	27%	85%	15%
1999	75%	25%	77%	23%
1998	73%	27%	79%	21%
1997	65%	35%	81%	19%
1996	70%	30%	78%	22%
1995	73%	27%	77%	23%
1994	78%	22%	85%	15%
1993	80%	20%	86%	14%

INTEREST GROUPS

	AFL-CIO	ADA	CCUS	ACU
2002	77%	65%	79%	42%
2001	75%	55%	71%	48%
2000	25%	50%	86%	40%
1999	67%	80%	56%	17%
1998	63%	75%	59%	20%
1997	14%	55%	70%	20%
1996	71%	60%	62%	20%
1995	75%	70%	56%	22%
1994	63%	55%	44%	17%
1993	82%	40%	27%	24%

Sen. Mary L. Landrieu (D)

CAPITOL OFFICE
224-5824
landrieu.senate.gov
724 Hart 20510-1804; fax 224-9735

COMMITTEES
Appropriations
Energy & Natural Resources
Small Business & Entrepreneurship

HOMETOWN
New Orleans

BORN
Nov. 23, 1955, Arlington, Va.

RELIGION
Roman Catholic

FAMILY
Husband, Frank Snellings; two children

EDUCATION
Louisiana State U., B.A. 1977 (sociology)

CAREER
Realtor

POLITICAL HIGHLIGHTS
La. House, 1980-88; La. treasurer, 1988-96; candidate for governor, 1995

ELECTION RESULTS

2002 GENERAL RUNOFF		
Mary L. Landrieu (D)	638,654	51.7%
Suzanne Haik Terrell (R)	596,642	48.3%
2002 GENERAL		
Mary L. Landrieu (D)	573,347	46.0%
Suzanne Haik Terrell (R)	339,506	27.2%
John Cooksey (R)	171,752	13.8%
Tony Perkins (R)	119,776	9.6%
Raymond Brown (D)	23,553	1.9%

PREVIOUS WINNING PERCENTAGES
1996 (50%)

Elected 1996; 2nd term

Landrieu has always had an arm's-length relationship with the majority of the Senate Democratic caucus. She is a moderate who departs from the party line on many crucial votes, a practice that is necessary to get elected in Louisiana but often makes the rest of the party wary of her next move.

She will have more goodwill in the 108th Congress than she has had in years, thanks to her morale-boosting re-election victory in 2002, a pleasant surprise for Democrats who had just lost the Senate majority. But she can be expected to test that goodwill repeatedly as she continues to vote a more conservative line than the rest of her party.

In a year of Democratic losses, Landrieu (LAN-drew) bucked the trend. Despite President Bush's vigorous support for Republican challenger Suzanne Haik Terrell, one month after the Democrats lost control of the Senate Landrieu triumphed in a runoff election that was required under Louisiana's unique congressional election system. Bush's appearances on behalf of other Republicans helped to reclaim the Senate, but some analysts said that his efforts, along with those of the national Republican Party organization, began to look like overkill in the Landrieu race and actually may have helped her win.

Landrieu's victory did not translate into better committee assignments. As the minority party, Democrats had fewer committee seats to give out in the 108th, so Landrieu had to make a choice between keeping her seat on the Appropriations Committee or staying on Armed Services. She chose the former. She also retained seats on Energy and Natural Resources, where she promotes the wishes of her state's substantial oil and gas interests, and Small Business.

Still, her re-election could give her a bigger role in the 108th in a number of ways, such as being tapped to shepherd more prominent Democratic amendments or to act as spokesman for the party's core issues. At the very least, Senate Democrats expect her to be pressed into service campaigning for her colleagues — something she has proven she knows how to do.

In her re-election campaign Landrieu promised that she would not be a "rubber stamp" for Bush. In reality, though, Landrieu increased her support for the president and distanced herself from Democrats as the election drew near. In 2002 she backed Bush 84 percent of the time, up from 74 percent in 2001. And she broke with Democrats on party-line votes 35 percent of the time, up from 19 percent in 2001. She was among the five Senate Democrats who voted against her party most often.

In the 107th, Landrieu voted for the $1.35 trillion Bush tax cut and sided with Republicans in a vote to permanently repeal the estate tax, complicating Democratic leaders' efforts to blame the tax cut for the nation's economic woes. She also sided with Republicans on allowing exploration for oil and gas in Alaska's Arctic National Wildlife Refuge. She cosponsored a measure with Republican Sen. Sam Brownback of Kansas that would have banned all human cloning, opposing Democrats and some Republicans who wanted to allow cloning to create human tissue for biomedical research.

Landrieu affiliates with both the Senate New Democrats and the bipartisan Centrist Coalition. "Too often here in Washington, the loudest voices are the ones on the far left and far right," she said in 2000 as the New Democrats — she dubbed them the "mod squad" — were organized. "That is why this group was formed, to give voice to those in the sensible center."

She has a proven ability to take on complex issues that benefit her state.

In 2001, Landrieu played a role in securing language in the education policy overhaul that targets new federal funds to school districts with the highest concentrations of poor children. Winning support for the provision, which is especially important to a high-poverty state like Louisiana, was an uphill battle against appropriators, who had allowed the funds to continue to flow to districts that were no longer poor. Landrieu pointed out that one in five school districts where 50 percent to 75 percent of students were poor received no such funds, while some wealthier districts were getting a disproportionate share.

In the 106th, Landrieu used both her persistence and her charm in the first major legislative campaign of her Senate career — an effort to guarantee that $3 billion annually for 15 years in offshore drilling revenue would be spent on a host of federal and state conservation programs. In a key move, Landrieu won over Energy Chairman Frank H. Murkowski, an Alaska Republican, after taking him to dinner at New Orleans' famed Commander's Palace. In the end, Landrieu and other supporters had to settle for a smaller measure subject to annual appropriations, but even the partial victory was more than some had expected.

The senator has tried to balance her support of traditionally liberal programs such as child care with careful attention to Louisiana's parochial interests. In 1998, she cosponsored a bill to boost protection of private property rights, to the dismay of environmentalists and the applause of her state's real estate interests. She and the state's other senator, Democrat John B. Breaux, frequently issue joint news releases touting federal dollars they have secured for Louisiana projects.

In 2000, she collaborated on a book, "Nine and Counting," with her eight female Senate colleagues in the 106th Congress. After that she announced that she would not campaign against any of those women, Democrat or Republican. In 1998 she wrote a column, "Mothers Make Good Senators Too," in defense of her Democratic Senate colleague from Arkansas, Blanche Lincoln, the mother of twins. During her first term Landrieu and her husband, Frank Snellings, built a house on Capitol Hill in which to raise their two adopted children.

Landrieu is no stranger to politics. She is the oldest of nine children of Moon Landrieu, who served as mayor of New Orleans and was secretary of the Department of Housing and Urban Development in the Carter administration. But the younger Landrieu's own political road has hardly been a smooth one. After serving in the state legislature and as Louisiana treasurer, she made an unsuccessful run for governor in 1995. Despite that loss, she was back in the arena a year later, this time seeking the Senate seat that Democrat J. Bennett Johnston was relinquishing after four terms.

When Landrieu won by the slimmest margin ever in a Louisiana Senate race — just 5,788 votes out of 1.7 million cast — her election was challenged by the loser, conservative Louis "Woody" Jenkins. He alleged voter fraud and Republicans on the Senate Rules Committee voted for a broad investigation of the election; the bitter and divisive probe dragged on until October 1997 before the panel voted to end it. "Never again should a legally certified senator be held hostage by wild, reckless and unproven allegations from a disgruntled loser," Landrieu said afterward.

In 2002, Landrieu was forced into the Dec. 7 runoff because she fell short of the 50 percent needed under state law to claim victory on Nov. 5. She had finished first, with 46 percent, in the nine-candidate field, which included three well-known Republicans: Terrell, the state elections commissioner; Rep. John Cooksey, who received 14 percent; and state Rep. Tony Perkins, who took 10 percent. In the runoff she increased the size of her 1996 margin of victory seven-fold — to 42,012, or 3 percentage points.

KEY VOTES

2002

Yes Pass farm bill reversing crop subsidy limits
Yes Postpone tougher automobile fuel efficiency standards
Yes Overhaul campaign finance law; ban "soft money" and restrict advocacy advertising
Yes Set federal election standards
Yes Support oil drilling in Arctic National Wildlife Refuge
Yes Revive fast-track procedures for trade agreements
Yes Create federal insurance coverage for catastrophic terrorist losses
Yes Tighten federal accounting and corporate governance regulation
Yes Advance bipartisan Medicare prescription drug plan
Yes Create independent Sept. 11 commission
? Back Democratic Homeland Security Department proposal
Yes Authorize war against Iraq

2001

No Confirm John Ashcroft as attorney general
Yes Nullify Clinton Labor Department ergonomics rule
Yes Cut taxes by $1.35 trillion through fiscal 2011
Yes Pass Democratic bill to bolster rights of patients in managed-care plans
Yes Permit a new round of military base closings
\+ Expand law enforcement power to investigate suspected terrorists

CQ VOTE STUDIES

	PARTY UNITY		PRESIDENTIAL SUPPORT	
	Support	Oppose	Support	Oppose
2002	65%	35%	84%	16%
2001	81%	19%	74%	26%
2000	88%	12%	85%	15%
1999	81%	19%	86%	14%
1998	89%	11%	86%	14%
1997	77%	23%	87%	13%

INTEREST GROUPS

	AFL-CIO	ADA	CCUS	ACU
2002	83%	70%	84%	35%
2001	88%	85%	69%	28%
2000	63%	80%	73%	16%
1999	67%	95%	59%	4%
1998	88%	90%	67%	8%
1997	29%	70%	70%	16%

Rep. David Vitter (R)

CAPITOL OFFICE
225-3015
david.vitter@mail.house.gov
vitter.house.gov
414 Cannon 20515-1801; fax 225-0739

COMMITTEES
Appropriations
Budget

HOMETOWN
Metairie

BORN
May 3, 1961, New Orleans, La.

RELIGION
Roman Catholic

FAMILY
Wife, Wendy Vitter; four children

EDUCATION
Harvard U., A.B. 1983; Oxford U., B.A. 1985 (Rhodes scholar); Tulane U., J.D. 1988

CAREER
Business lawyer; adjunct law professor

POLITICAL HIGHLIGHTS
La. House, 1992-99

ELECTION RESULTS

2002 GENERAL		
David Vitter (R)	147,117	81.5%
Monica L. Monica (R)	20,268	11.2%
Robert "Bob" Namer (R)	7,229	4.0%
Ian P. Hawkhurst (I)	5,956	3.3%
2000 GENERAL		
David Vitter (R)	191,379	80.5%
Michael A. Armato (D)	29,935	12.6%
Cary J. Deaton (D)	10,982	4.6%
Martin A. Rosenthal (NL)	3,129	1.3%

PREVIOUS WINNING PERCENTAGES
1999 Special Election (51%)

Elected May 1999; 2nd full term

Known in Louisiana for his willingness to challenge the status quo and be seen as a reform-minded maverick, in Washington, Vitter has been more of a team player — most of the time.

He has been a dependable vote for the Republican leadership and a supporter of President Bush on most issues; and, despite his reputation back home, Vitter was rewarded with a seat on the Appropriations Committee and an appointment to the Republican Policy Committee in 2001, at the start of his first full term. These are positions party leaders do not give to someone they view as a loose cannon.

The only member of the Louisiana delegation to sit on House Appropriations — Mary L. Landrieu, a Democrat, has a spot on Senate Appropriations — Vitter has worked to gain funding to assist in the state's economic development, including support for area military bases and defense contractors and a variety of transportation projects. Although the Appropriations panel is known for its collegial atmosphere, as members rely on each other to get the spending they want approved, Vitter appears content to cultivate his lone-wolf reputation.

For example, he favors regional governance of the New Orleans airport, arguing that its importance stretches far beyond the city limits. The Louisiana delegation is seriously divided over the issue, but Vitter continues to offer numerous amendments to spending bills to block expansion of the airport in hopes of forcing action on the matter.

Some political observers have called Vitter's actions political grandstanding, and the smart but brash conservative has been dubbed a pariah in some circles. Republican state House Speaker Pro Tempore C.E. "Peppi" Bruneau Jr. once said Vitter was "incapable of working with anybody." Vitter seems not to mind his reputation. "I've rocked the boat and that's caused some resentment," he says, "but that's only in the political establishment."

Vitter also has been involved in a longstanding feud with his state's top Republican, Gov. Mike Foster. Their differences center on legalized gambling, which Vitter opposes. In the 107th Congress, they traded barbs over the issue, including wrangling over a proposal for an Indian casino near Lake Charles that was eventually turned down.

Vitter charges that Foster and his allies, in retaliation, drafted state campaign finance legislation aimed at members of Congress who run for local office. (Though he finally decided against it, Vitter seriously considered running for governor in 2003.) He lobbied against the bill, testifying in Baton Rouge, but his tactics reportedly angered state lawmakers and were counterproductive. "He didn't do the cause a great deal of good," the congressional delegation's dean, Republican Billy Tauzin, told the Baton Rouge Advocate.

Tauzin told the newspaper he had talked with Vitter about his problems back home, but added that he had been pleased with Vitter's team efforts in the House. Shortly before he took office in 1999, Vitter told The New Orleans Times Picayune that if people "are expecting some grand confrontational style, they will be sorely disappointed."

In 2002, Vitter joined the rest of the Louisiana delegation in opposing the Bush administration's imposition of tariffs on imported steel, which he said posed a serious problem for the Port of New Orleans. About 40 percent of the port's revenue is from arriving steel shipments, he said. He warned that the decision to impose tariffs had caused him to rethink his support for giving the president fast-track authority to negotiate trade agreements without

Congressional amendment. But Vitter ultimately voted for the bill.

Vitter had big shoes to fill when he came to Congress. His predecessor was Robert L. Livingston, who chaired Appropriations for four years and then was picked by his GOP colleagues at the end of 1998 to replace Newt Gingrich as Speaker in the 106th Congress. But the next month Livingston decided to resign from the House after admitting extramarital affairs.

Vitter had a brief taste of the House while at Harvard, serving as an intern for Massachusetts Democrat Joe Moakley. After continuing his education as a Rhodes scholar and receiving his law degree, he practiced business law and taught at both Tulane and Loyola universities.

Vitter said he was unhappy with the questionable reputation of Louisiana politics, and he decided to try to do something about it. In 1991 he won the state House seat vacated by former Ku Klux Klan leader David Duke, who ran for governor.

In Baton Rouge, Vitter proved his willingness to ruffle some feathers. He filed an ethics complaint against a close friend of Democratic Gov. Edwin Edwards, and then spearheaded a recall petition effort against the governor. He won passage of a measure limiting the terms of state lawmakers, while also opposing a pay raise for legislators. And he led a successful fight to end a Tulane scholarship program that allowed state legislators to choose recipients, denouncing the program as an abuse of power.

While he has angered many fellow politicians, Vitter's constituents generally give him high marks and supporters praise his integrity and courage. He was unopposed for re-election to the state House in 1995.

When Livingston announced his resignation, Vitter was one of nine candidates in a special election to replace him. Despite his seven years in the legislature, Vitter was still able to portray himself as an outsider in his race against David Treen, a former House member and governor.

Treen had the support of most of the political establishment — including Livingston and Foster — and came in first with 25 percent. Having resigned his state House seat, Vitter brought about a special election for that seat on the same day as the primary. He thus increased turnout in his old district, and came in second in the primary with 22 percent, edging out Duke, who was third with 19 percent. The runoff was largely about political style and the benefits of the immediate seniority the 70-year-old Treen would have from his seven years in Congress, as against the 38-year-old Vitter's prospects of accumulating even more seniority in the future. Vitter emerged with a narrow, 2 percentage point victory.

He captured more than four-fifths of the vote in 2000 and 2002.

KEY VOTES

2002

- No Overhaul campaign finance law; ban "soft money" and restrict advocacy advertising
- Yes Back Bush's defense budget increase
- Yes Extend 1996 welfare law
- Yes Adopt Bush's discretionary spending limit
- Yes Pass GOP Medicare prescription drug plan
- No Create independent Sept. 11 commission
- No Extend union protections to Homeland Security Department employees
- Yes Revive fast-track procedures for trade agreements
- Yes Authorize war against Iraq
- No Advance bankruptcy overhaul opposed by abortion opponents

2001

- Yes Nullify Clinton Labor Department ergonomics rule
- Yes Cut taxes by $1.35 trillion through fiscal 2011
- No Maintain ban on oil drilling in Arctic National Wildlife Refuge
- Yes Approve Bush proposal to limit managed-care plan liability for coverage decisions
- No Divert money from crop subsidy payments to land conservation
- Yes Expand law enforcement power to investigate suspected terrorists

CQ VOTE STUDIES

	PARTY UNITY		PRESIDENTIAL SUPPORT	
	Support	Oppose	Support	Oppose
2002	99%	1%	85%	15%
2001	98%	2%	93%	7%
2000	92%	8%	25%	75%
1999	92%	8%	20%	80%

INTEREST GROUPS

	AFL-CIO	ADA	CCUS	ACU
2002	11%	0%	95%	100%
2001	8%	0%	100%	100%
2000	0%	0%	85%	88%
1999	14%	5%	88%	83%

LOUISIANA 1

East – Metairie, part of Florida Parishes

A short distance from festive downtown New Orleans, the conservative 1st skims the edges of the city and reaches north across Lake Pontchartrain to the Mississippi border. The mostly white-collar population is among the wealthiest and most educated in the state.

The 1st's population center is on the south side of the lake and includes the upscale Metairie suburbs. The area is packed with white-collar conservatives who generally vote Republican.

North of the lake, the 1st includes three of the "Florida Parishes," so named because they were part of Spanish Florida until 1810. Once a community of seasonal homes for residents escaping the heat and humidity of New Orleans, the north shore is now a booming suburban haven, replete with suburbanites who commute across Lake Pontchartrain Causeway to their jobs in New Orleans. St. Tammany Parish was the fastest-growing area in the 1st during the 1990s. Local developments include petrochemical and oil industries, and leaders hope to attract high-tech firms related to the expansion of the Avondale Shipyard in the 2nd. The northern parishes are still heavily agricultural, producing mainly cotton, corn and soybeans.

Democrats held the 1st for a little more than a century before it became a GOP possession in 1977. Now, residents warmly welcome Republicans on the local and federal level. George W. Bush took 66 percent of the district's vote in 2000, making the 1st the only Louisiana district to give him more than 57 percent. Reliably Democratic African-Americans make up 13 percent of the 1st's population — the only district in the state with less than 24 percent. Democrats do manage to win a few local offices in the northern, rural Washington and Tangipahoa parishes.

MAJOR INDUSTRY

Petrochemicals, oil, agriculture, tourism

CITIES

Metairie (pt.), 140,916; Kenner (pt.), 46,007; New Orleans (pt.), 37,451; Slidell, 25,695; Hammond, 17,639; Terrytown (pt.), 15,232

NOTABLE

Lake Pontchartrain Causeway, the world's longest highway bridge over water, spans about 23.9 miles; Former Ku Klux Klansman David Duke held the Metairie state House seat from 1989 to 1993; Pop singer Britney Spears is from Kentwood in Tangipahoa Parish.

Rep. William J. Jefferson (D)

CAPITOL OFFICE
225-6636
jeffersonmc@mail.house.gov
www.house.gov/jefferson
240 Cannon 20515-1802; fax 225-1988

COMMITTEES
Ways & Means

HOMETOWN
New Orleans

BORN
March 14, 1947, Lake Providence, La.

RELIGION
Baptist

FAMILY
Wife, Andrea Green Jefferson; five children

EDUCATION
Southern U. and A&M College, B.A. 1969 (English & political science); Harvard U., J.D. 1972; Georgetown U., LL.M. 1996 (taxation)

MILITARY SERVICE
Army, 1969-75

CAREER
Lawyer; congressional aide

POLITICAL HIGHLIGHTS
La. Senate, 1980-91; candidate for mayor of New Orleans, 1982, 1986; candidate for governor, 1999

ELECTION RESULTS

2002 GENERAL		
William J. Jefferson (D)	90,310	63.5%
Irma Muse Dixon (D)	28,480	20.0%
Silky Sullivan (R)	15,440	10.9%
Clarence "Buddy" Hunt (D)	4,137	2.9%
Wayne E. Clement (I)	3,789	2.7%
2000 GENERAL		
William J. Jefferson (D)		unopposed

PREVIOUS WINNING PERCENTAGES
1998 (86%); 1996 (100%); 1994 (75%); 1992 (73%); 1990 (53%)

Elected 1990; 7th term

A tax attorney educated at Harvard and Georgetown, Jefferson has a calm, understated manner. Raised in rural northeast Louisiana in a family of 10 children, he has gained impressive insider's credentials over the years. He is a member of the powerful Ways and Means Committee.

But at the start of the 108th Congress, he was disappointed when the new Democratic leader in the House, Nancy Pelosi, did not accept his application to chair the party's campaign organization, the Democratic Congressional Campaign Committee. Jefferson had been a stalwart fundraiser for the party in the run-up to the 2002 election, and he sought the post with the backing of many members of the Congressional Black Caucus. Pelosi picked fellow Californian Robert T. Matsui instead.

The top Democrat on Ways and Means, Charles B. Rangel of New York, described Jefferson for the New Orleans Times-Picayune as "no nonsense . . . not a backslapping politician . . . a very serious legislator." Notably industrious, Jefferson went to night school for three years — after being elected to Congress. He graduated from Georgetown with a master's of law in taxation. Rangel often refers to Jefferson as "my tax counsel."

He also is one of the more conservative members of the Black Caucus. His frequent support for business interests sets him apart from many black members of the House. In the 107th Congress, Jefferson backed President Bush 42 percent of the time; only Sanford D. Bishop Jr. of Georgia had a more conservative voting record among black Democrats.

The most loyal proponent of trade liberalization among black lawmakers, Jefferson and Harold E. Ford Jr. of Tennessee were the only African-Americans among the 25 House Democrats who voted to enact the 2002 law giving the president authority to negotiate trade deals that Congress may not amend. He also voted to make permanent the normal U.S.-China trade relationship in 2000, to create the World Trade Organization in 1994 and to embrace the North American Free Trade Agreement in 1993. And he was a major player in writing the 2000 trade law to promote economic development and U.S. investment in sub-Saharan Africa and the Caribbean.

Oil and gas interests are big business in Louisiana, and Jefferson is a firm supporter of the energy industry. He voted to allow oil drilling in Alaska's Arctic National Wildlife Refuge, and he joined with a coalition of energy industry and business leaders to urge the United States to look more toward sub-Saharan Africa for its future oil needs.

Jefferson was a prominent critic of Bush's decision in 2001 to impose tariffs on steel imports at the behest of domestic steelmakers. He said the tariffs threatened the maritime and port industries, particularly in New Orleans where steel shipments are the port's leading revenue source. But only 18 Democrats and 12 Republicans voted in the House for his resolution to overturn Bush's tariff policy.

His alliances with the Republicans are not strictly limited to business issues. Jefferson has joined with Republicans in backing a constitutional amendment to ban flag burning and voted for a GOP plan to repeal estate taxes. After the Sept. 11, 2001, terrorist attacks, he supported legislation to allow guns in commercial airliner cockpits. He voted against the initial House anti-terrorism legislation in 2001, saying that it would put civil liberties in peril, but he voted for the compromise that became law.

As chairman of the Congressional Black Caucus Foundation in the 107th, Jefferson led a foundation initiative aimed at increasing home ownership by minorities. The program also helped would-be homeowners navigate the process of finding an affordable mortgage.

When Jefferson arrived in Washington in 1991 after more than a decade in the Louisiana Senate, he made a good first impression on Democratic leaders. Their desire to diversify the membership of top-tier committees helped him earn a seat on Ways and Means in just his second term. He was briefly displaced from the panel in the 104th Congress when the GOP takeover of the House reduced the number of Democratic slots, but he was returned to the committee in the 105th.

Jefferson was born and brought up in poverty in far northeast Louisiana, where he did his fair share of chopping cotton. His mother was adamant about the need for education, and Jefferson proved to be a high achiever. He was class president in high school and student body president at Southern University in Baton Rouge. He then won a scholarship to Harvard Law School. He also clerked for a federal judge in Louisiana and worked on Capitol Hill for Democratic Sen. J. Bennett Johnston of Louisiana. He moved to New Orleans in 1976 to join a law firm.

Elected to the state Senate in 1979, he represented a racially mixed New Orleans district that included much of the affluent Uptown area, and he developed a reputation as a nuts-and-bolts expert on fiscal matters and a promoter of economic development. He waged unsuccessful campaigns to become mayor of New Orleans in 1982 and again in 1986, but because of the timing of the elections he did not have to give up his Senate seat.

Jefferson was well-positioned to succeed Democrat Lindy Boggs in 1990 when she retired after representing New Orleans in the House for 18 years. Jefferson finished first in the crowded primary; in a bitterly fought runoff, he narrowly defeated lawyer Marc Morial, the son of New Orleans' first black mayor, Ernest N. "Dutch" Morial. Since then, Jefferson has won re-election handily.

In 1999, he ran for governor against the GOP incumbent, Mike Foster. Again, because of the timing of the election, he did not have to relinquish his House seat to run, but he curtailed his schedule in the months leading up to the October election. He got 30 percent, far behind Foster's 62 percent.

Political events did not start out well for Jefferson in 2002. He played a high-profile, hands-on role in the unsuccessful mayoral campaign of Richard Pennington in March, and then saw one of his five daughters, Jalila, lose in a special election for a vacant seat in the state legislature. But those defeats did not carry over to November, when Jefferson left his nearest rival behind by 43 percentage points.

KEY VOTES

2002

Yes Overhaul campaign finance law; ban "soft money" and restrict advocacy advertising
Yes Back Bush's defense budget increase
No Extend 1996 welfare law
No Adopt Bush's discretionary spending limit
? Pass GOP Medicare prescription drug plan
Yes Create independent Sept. 11 commission
Yes Extend union protections to Homeland Security Department employees
Yes Revive fast-track procedures for trade agreements
Yes Authorize war against Iraq
No Advance bankruptcy overhaul opposed by abortion opponents

2001

No Nullify Clinton Labor Department ergonomics rule
No Cut taxes by $1.35 trillion through fiscal 2011
No Maintain ban on oil drilling in Arctic National Wildlife Refuge
No Approve Bush proposal to limit managed-care plan liability for coverage decisions
Yes Divert money from crop subsidy payments to land conservation
Yes Expand law enforcement power to investigate suspected terrorists

CQ VOTE STUDIES

	PARTY UNITY		PRESIDENTIAL SUPPORT	
	Support	Oppose	Support	Oppose
2002	92%	8%	40%	60%
2001	87%	13%	44%	56%
2000	90%	10%	80%	20%
1999	91%	9%	85%	15%
1998	91%	9%	83%	17%

INTEREST GROUPS

	AFL-CIO	ADA	CCUS	ACU
2002	86%	75%	58%	20%
2001	91%	80%	70%	21%
2000	89%	70%	66%	13%
1999	71%	75%	40%	4%
1998	100%	80%	43%	13%

LOUISIANA 2
New Orleans

French street names, strands of Spanish moss and snake-bearing, fortune-telling voodoo queens add to New Orleans' unique cultural mix. But beyond its reputation as the "Big Easy," the comfortably Democratic 2nd, which takes in much of the city and some middle-class suburbs, has dealt with serious issues. While the crime rate has fallen, widespread poverty continues to cause some flight from the city. Since its peak in 1960, New Orleans' population has declined by almost one-fourth.

Famed for its food and jazz traditions, New Orleans is one of the most popular tourist destinations in the country. Mardi Gras and the annual Jazz & Heritage Festival alone attract millions of visitors and billions of dollars each year.

Other staples of the 2nd's economic diet — the New Orleans port, shipbuilding and petroleum industries — have held strong in recent years. The Avondale shipyard, recently purchased by defense contractor Northrop Grumman, built a new high-tech center that has created jobs and drawn businesses to the area. Meanwhile, after a decade of decline, the oil and gas industry experienced a resurgence in the 1990s that has leveled off in recent years.

Three rounds of redistricting in the 1990s left the 2nd as Louisiana's only black-majority district. Revisions following the 2000 census did not alter that status, and left the district 64 percent black. Democratic presidential candidates routinely garner more than 60 percent of the vote here. In 2000, Al Gore received 76 percent.

MAJOR INDUSTRY
Tourism, shipbuilding, oil and gas

MILITARY BASES
Naval Support Activity New Orleans, 3,865 military, 2,700 civilian (1999); several Coast Guard stations, 684 military, 118 civilian (1998)

CITIES
New Orleans (pt.), 447,223; Marrero (pt.), 35,796; Kenner (pt.), 24,510

NOTABLE
The St. Charles Streetcar Line, created in 1835, is the oldest continuously operating line in the world; Lindy Boggs, mother of newscaster Cokie Roberts and widow of Rep. Hale Boggs, was elected to the U.S. House in 1973 and held the 2nd until Rep. Jefferson was elected in 1990.

Rep. Billy Tauzin (R)

CAPITOL OFFICE
225-4031
www.house.gov/tauzin
2183 Rayburn 20515-1803; fax 225-0563

COMMITTEES
Energy & Commerce - chairman
Resources
Select Homeland Security

HOMETOWN
Thibodaux

BORN
June 14, 1943, Chackbay, La.

RELIGION
Roman Catholic

FAMILY
Wife, Cecile Tauzin; five children

EDUCATION
Nicholls State U., B.A. 1964 (English); Louisiana State U., J.D. 1967

CAREER
Lawyer

POLITICAL HIGHLIGHTS
La. House, 1972-80 (served as a Democrat); candidate for governor, 1987

ELECTION RESULTS

2002 GENERAL		
Billy Tauzin (R)	130,323	86.7%
William Beier (I)	12,964	8.6%
David Iwanico (I)	7,055	4.7%
2000 GENERAL		
Billy Tauzin (R)	143,446	78.0%
Edwin J. "Eddie" Albares (I)	16,908	9.2%
Anita Rosenthal (NL)	13,488	7.3%
Dion Bourque (LIBERT)	10,118	5.5%

PREVIOUS WINNING PERCENTAGES
1998 (100%); 1996 (100%); 1994 (76%); 1992 (82%); 1990 (88%); 1988 (89%); 1986 (100%); 1984 (100%); 1982 (100%); 1980 (85%); 1980 Special Election (53%)
*Elected as a Democrat 1980-94

Elected May 1980; 12th full term

Now passing through the midpoint of his time chairing the Energy and Commerce Committee, Tauzin has made his mark as an aggressive investigator of corporate fraud and has enhanced his reputation as a legislative compromiser nonpareil. But he has yet to achieve breakthroughs on the broad telecommunications, energy, health care and environmental measures that would become cornerstones of his legislative legacy.

Tauzin has a keen sense of his function as a catalyst for action by a panel with extraordinary reach over the U.S. economy. He takes pride in his role as steward of the oldest legislative committee in Congress. And since the day he took over in 2001, he has been an activist chairman in the manner of the most recent Democrat to hold the gavel, John D. Dingell of Michigan. Tauzin has a taste for the limelight and makes no bones about his eagerness to apply his shrewdness and his policy acumen to move legislation.

Already, his zeal for the deal has led to speculation that several high-profile groups — giant telecommunications companies and Hollywood studio moguls among them — will seek to woo Tauzin (TOE-zan) to leave Congress and become their top lobbyist when his chairmanship is concluded because of GOP term limits at the end of 2006.

Once known primarily as a champion of his state's oil and gas industry, a mainstay of the "old" economy, Tauzin has positioned himself to play a pivotal part on issues central to the "new" economy and to homeland security. During more than two decades in the House, Tauzin has favored what he calls "marketplace solutions" to government regulation. He has taken a two-pronged approach to oversight: stressing the traditional GOP goal of loosening federal controls over industry, while moving into traditionally Democratic territory as a champion for consumer protection.

Tauzin's career has been marked by a desire to be a playmaker and to build support for his point of view — often shifting his point of view in the process. To the consternation of some conservatives, for example, he responded to corporate fraud scandals during the 107th Congress by seizing the issue and the spotlight. As he did in response to the Firestone tire recalls of 2000, Tauzin advised Republicans that failure to take tough steps would be politically tone-deaf in an election year and that the GOP should sometimes embrace legislation to shape the behavior of American industry.

His aides obtained key testimony alleging accounting fraud from corporate whistleblowers at energy trader Enron Corp. and telecommunications giant WorldCom Inc. Tauzin also probed the alleged use of insider information in the trading of shares of drug maker ImClone Systems Inc. by the company's former top executive and by style maven Martha Stewart.

Critics suggest that Tauzin's quest for publicity may not only ruffle GOP conservatives but also cause him to lose control of whatever legislation he is trying to shepherd. Tauzin says any deals he makes are acceptable to the Republican leadership.

His animated, back-slapping style conceals an intense competitiveness and a diligence when it comes to learning the nuances of policy. He calls himself the Cajun ambassador to Congress, while his constituents call him the "Swamp Fox." He shifts effortlessly from English to French, and his Web site is bilingual. Recipes from his book, "Cook and Tell," are featured at the fundraisers that help him raise money for the GOP. Several of Tauzin's lobbyist friends are members of the hunt club he operates from a mobile home near a wildlife preserve on Maryland's Eastern Shore. His

Capitol Hill office is decorated with hunting trophies, one of them an alligator head with its jaw stuffed with Mardi Gras beads.

A founding member of the conservative "Blue Dog" coalition of House Democrats, Tauzin switched parties in 1995 after winning his House seat nine times as a Democrat. He acted seven months after the Republican takeover of Congress — and after he was promised he could keep the seniority he had accrued on Energy and Commerce. That set the stage for his rivalry that still lingers with Michael G. Oxley of Ohio, a lifelong Republican with comparable seniority. In their initial face-off, at the start of the 105th Congress, a subcommittee both lawmakers wanted to chair was split; at the start of the 107th, GOP leaders awarded Tauzin the Energy and Commerce chairmanship, but the panel's jurisdiction over securities and insurance was moved to a new Financial Services Committee chaired by Oxley.

Since then Tauzin has asserted his panel's jurisdiction over parts of the homeland security agenda, winning increased funding for efforts to combat biological attacks and helping to pass tighter safety requirements for 2.2 million miles of natural gas and oil pipelines.

At the start of the 108th, Tauzin hoped to renew a campaign with Dingell, his committee's top Democrat, to allow the regional Bell operating companies to provide Internet access on long-distance telephone lines. The pair also readied legislation to encourage a quicker transition to widespread use of high-definition television sets and broadcasting systems. Tauzin planned to revive a comprehensive energy bill that died in the 107th after negotiators failed to reach consensus on clean air mandates and language that would open the Arctic National Wildlife Refuge to oil drilling. And he prepared to propose a prescription drug benefit for Medicare participants and legislation to protect the privacy of online consumers.

Tauzin is reliably conservative on fiscal and social matters. He has called for replacement of the federal income tax with a national sales tax.

A native of South Louisiana's Cajun country, Tauzin had a law practice in the bayou towns of Houma and Thibodaux. He won a state legislative seat in 1971, and during eight years in the post emerged as Gov. Edwin W. Edwards' protégé. He served as floor leader in the state House and came to Washington after winning a 1980 special election to replace GOP Rep. David C. Treen, who had been elected governor. In 1987, Tauzin finished fourth in his one bid for higher office — governor of Louisiana. But he has never had a problem holding his House seat — in either party. In 1996, he became the first member of Congress to win re-election without opposition after switching parties. No Democrat has run against him since.

KEY VOTES

2002

- No Overhaul campaign finance law; ban "soft money" and restrict advocacy advertising
- Yes Back Bush's defense budget increase
- Yes Extend 1996 welfare law
- Yes Adopt Bush's discretionary spending limit
- Yes Pass GOP Medicare prescription drug plan
- No Create independent Sept. 11 commission
- No Extend union protections to Homeland Security Department employees
- Yes Revive fast-track procedures for trade agreements
- Yes Authorize war against Iraq
- No Advance bankruptcy overhaul opposed by abortion opponents

2001

- Yes Nullify Clinton Labor Department ergonomics rule
- Yes Cut taxes by $1.35 trillion through fiscal 2011
- No Maintain ban on oil drilling in Arctic National Wildlife Refuge
- Yes Approve Bush proposal to limit managed-care plan liability for coverage decisions
- No Divert money from crop subsidy payments to land conservation
- Yes Expand law enforcement power to investigate suspected terrorists

CQ VOTE STUDIES

	PARTY UNITY		PRESIDENTIAL SUPPORT	
	Support	Oppose	Support	Oppose
2002	97%	3%	88%	12%
2001	99%	1%	95%	5%
2000	92%	8%	26%	74%
1999	93%	7%	21%	79%
1998	92%	8%	23%	77%

INTEREST GROUPS

	AFL-CIO	ADA	CCUS	ACU
2002	11%	0%	95%	96%
2001	17%	0%	100%	96%
2000	0%	0%	85%	84%
1999	0%	5%	100%	84%
1998	0%	5%	100%	88%

LOUISIANA 3

South central – New Iberia, Houma

A maze of interconnected bayous, swamps and marshes, the southern 3rd District runs along the coast of the Gulf of Mexico and takes in the Mississippi River delta and the eastern half of Cajun country. Folks here know the intricate details of catching and cleaning fish, a major industry in the 3rd, and are adept at stockpiling canned goods and plywood during hurricane season. River Road, a highway running the length of the Mississippi River, originates in the 3rd and is lined by symbols of the Old South — antebellum sugar plantations.

After a decade of decline, the 3rd rebounded somewhat in the 1990s, due in large part to the oil and gas industry, which is especially big in parishes along the Gulf. The district helps the state lead the nation in crawfish, catfish, blue crab and shrimp production. Further inland, petrochemical plants along the Mississippi have recovered since the 1980s but still struggle with declining overseas demand. Sugar cane, which dominated the regional economy into the 20th century, continues to be profitable. Employment remains seasonal, and the unemployment rate soars in the off-season.

Democrats dominated the region for nearly a century, with a Progressive Party interlude, but the Catholic 3rd now favors Republicans. The historical tendency of the district, however, remains: Conservative Democrats fare well in local elections.

MAJOR INDUSTRY
Oil and gas, petrochemicals, fishing, shipbuilding, sugar cane

MILITARY BASES
Naval Air Station Joint Reserve Base New Orleans, 2,100 military, 900 civilian (1999)

CITIES
New Iberia, 32,623; Houma, 32,393; Chalmette, 32,069; Laplace, 27,684

NOTABLE
Morgan City hosts the Louisiana Shrimp & Petroleum Festival each Labor Day; New Iberia is home to the Conrad Rice Mill, the oldest working rice mill in the United States; The main Battle of New Orleans, fought on Chalmette battlefield Jan. 8, 1815, was waged after a peace treaty had been signed by the United States and Great Britain.

Rep. Jim McCrery (R)

CAPITOL OFFICE
225-2777
jim.mccrery@mail.house.gov
www.house.gov/mccrery
2104 Rayburn 20515-1804; fax 225-8039

COMMITTEES
Ways & Means
(Select Revenue Measures - chairman)

HOMETOWN
Shreveport

BORN
Sept. 18, 1949, Shreveport, La.

RELIGION
Methodist

FAMILY
Wife, Johnette McCrery; two children

EDUCATION
Louisiana Tech U., B.A. 1971 (English & history);
Louisiana State U., J.D. 1975

CAREER
Lobbyist; lawyer; congressional aide

POLITICAL HIGHLIGHTS
Candidate for Leesville City Council, 1978

ELECTION RESULTS

2002 GENERAL		
Jim McCrery (R)	114,649	71.6%
John Milkovich (D)	42,340	26.5%
Bill Jacobs (I)	3,104	1.9%
2000 GENERAL		
Jim McCrery (R)	122,678	70.5%
Phillip R. Green (D)	43,600	25.1%
Michael "Mike" Taylor (I)	4,059	2.3%
James Ronals Skains (I)	3,630	2.1%

PREVIOUS WINNING PERCENTAGES
1998 (100%); 1996 (71%); 1994 (80%); 1992 (63%); 1990 (55%); 1988 (69%); 1988 Special Election (51%)

Elected April 1988; 8th full term

McCrery is not one for impassioned speeches on the House floor or for other types of political theater. But while most Americans have never heard of him, his expertise and ability to operate on both sides of the aisle have made him a player on an impressive list of legislative issues.

As chairman of the Select Revenue Measures Subcommittee, McCrery works closely with Ways and Means Chairman Bill Thomas — who hand-picked him for that post at the start of the 107th Congress. In that role he helped write the $1.35 trillion tax cut package of 2001, the economic stimulus package that followed the Sept. 11, 2001, terrorist attacks, and the tax incentives that were a major portion of an energy policy overhaul that died at the end of 2002. He was a member of GOP task forces on Social Security, managed health care and prescription drugs. He has cemented his political clout by doling out campaign funds to colleagues.

For all of this, McCrery's name often is mentioned when talk turns to who will chair Ways and Means starting in 2007, when Thomas will be compelled by GOP term limits to yield the gavel.

McCrery seems to waver between the zeal of a convert (he began his political career as a Democrat) and the non-ideological pragmatism of a chief operating officer. While he is a Republican partisan, his even-tempered demeanor allows him to work with Democrats more frequently and with more ease than the more combative Thomas. "It's not a good cop, bad cop routine," McCrery says. "But each of us is aware that the other has strengths and weaknesses, and we do try to complement those as best we can."

Like Thomas, McCrery immerses himself in the complexities of the issues he tackles; he says that helps him handle the unrelenting pressure that a member of Congress faces from colleagues, constituents and lobbyists to take stands on tough questions. "The main way I deal with it is just to make sure that I have accumulated enough information to make an informed decision," he says. "Then at least I have conviction and I know what I'm talking about."

In 2000, at the request of The Atlantic Monthly magazine, McCrery agreed to a lengthy discussion with Washington Democratic Rep. Jim McDermott on whether the two philosophically opposed lawmakers could agree on a plan to provide health insurance coverage for every American. Throughout the discussion, which showcased each man's grasp of the subject, McCrery made it clear he realizes significant compromises are needed. "If we want to save the private health care system, Republicans are going to have to accept some things that normally would be contrary to our basic philosophy," McCrery said. He said he would require everyone to purchase insurance and would equalize premiums, regardless of a person's age, sex or medical history, to spread the risks broadly.

Writing plans to prevent the eventual insolvencies of Social Security, Medicare and Medicaid are McCrery's legislative dreams. He would transform Medicare into a group of subsidized health care plans for senior citizens in much the same way workers choose their medical insurance from among plans offered by employers. The more basic the plan selected, the lower the out-of-pocket expense. McCrery would replace the current Social Security system with personal accounts and invest those funds in the stock and bond markets.

His attention is not focused entirely on national issues. He still looks out for the interests of Fort Polk and Barksdale Air Force Base, and during the rewrite of the highway law in the 108th Congress, he is sure to press to accelerate spending on Interstate 69, a newly designated Michigan-to-Mexico highway that cuts across the 4th District.

McCrery's fascination with politics began at a young age. In 1960, he proudly waved a homemade "Nixon for president" sign in front of his Houston home while passersby made rude gestures. As a slight, fair-haired young man, McCrery won election as high school student body president by defeating a popular quarterback. He set up his first telephone bank and talked to 800 other students.

After graduation from law school, McCrery joined a firm in his hometown of Leesville, then put in two years as an assistant city attorney in Shreveport. As a Democrat in 1981, he signed on with Democratic Rep. Buddy Roemer, working first in the district office in Shreveport and then as Roemer's legislative director in Washington. McCrery returned to Louisiana in 1984 to lobby for Georgia-Pacific Corp. in the state capital.

In 1987 he joined the list of Southern conservative Democrats switching to the GOP. After Roemer was elected governor, McCrery jumped into the 1988 special election to be his successor. Although initially the least-known candidate in the field, McCrery stood out as the only Republican and impressed many with his knowledge of the issues. He finished first in the primary and took 51 percent to defeat Democratic state Sen. Foster L. Campbell Jr. in the general-election runoff. McCrery had little time to prepare to defend the seat in November, but Democratic efforts to unseat him fizzled.

His most significant re-election challenge came in 1992, when redistricting matched him against fellow incumbent Jerry Huckaby, an eight-term Democrat. Huckaby chaired the Agriculture Subcommittee on Cotton, Rice and Sugar — commodities of great importance to Louisiana —but he was disadvantaged by the demographics of the new district and had 88 overdrafts at the private bank for House members. McCrery won with 63 percent and has not been as seriously challenged since.

Since 1997 McCrery has been a vice chairman of the National Republican Congressional Committee, the House Republican campaign organization. With minimal Democratic opposition in recent years, he has poured the proceeds of his fundraising efforts into the Committee for the Preservation of Capitalism, his political action committee. During the 2002 campaign, McCrery's PAC raised more than $900,000 and contributed more than $500,000 to colleagues — who are likely to be reminded of McCrery's generosity if he eventually seeks the Ways and Means chairmanship.

KEY VOTES

2002

No Overhaul campaign finance law; ban "soft money" and restrict advocacy advertising
Yes Back Bush's defense budget increase
Yes Extend 1996 welfare law
Yes Adopt Bush's discretionary spending limit
Yes Pass GOP Medicare prescription drug plan
No Create independent Sept. 11 commission
No Extend union protections to Homeland Security Department employees
Yes Revive fast-track procedures for trade agreements
Yes Authorize war against Iraq
Yes Advance bankruptcy overhaul opposed by abortion opponents

2001

Yes Nullify Clinton Labor Department ergonomics rule
Yes Cut taxes by $1.35 trillion through fiscal 2011
No Maintain ban on oil drilling in Arctic National Wildlife Refuge
Yes Approve Bush proposal to limit managed-care plan liability for coverage decisions
No Divert money from crop subsidy payments to land conservation
Yes Expand law enforcement power to investigate suspected terrorists

CQ VOTE STUDIES

	PARTY UNITY		PRESIDENTIAL SUPPORT	
	Support	Oppose	Support	Oppose
2002	97%	3%	87%	13%
2001	98%	2%	98%	2%
2000	90%	10%	27%	73%
1999	92%	8%	25%	75%
1998	94%	6%	26%	74%

INTEREST GROUPS

	AFL-CIO	ADA	CCUS	ACU
2002	13%	0%	100%	92%
2001	8%	5%	100%	92%
2000	0%	5%	95%	83%
1999	0%	0%	96%	80%
1998	10%	5%	100%	96%

LOUISIANA 4

Northwest and west – Shreveport, Bossier City

Removed from the Cajun influence that much of Louisiana is known for, the mostly white-collar 4th identifies more with Dallas than New Orleans. Covering most of western Louisiana, the conservative district takes in Shreveport at its north end and wanders into timber country in Beauregard and Allen parishes in the south.

The oil industry that fueled the economy in the 4th fizzled in the 1980s. But Shreveport and Bossier City responded to a 1995 gambling proposal that allowed for 15 casinos in the state; five riverboat casinos now are docked on the Red River that separates the two cities. A wave of riverfront renewal, accompanied by a large influx of retail and service industries, has helped drive the economy in recent years. Other industries remain intact: General Motors has invested millions in a new Shreveport facility, and the city has remained a health care hub for northern Louisiana as well as for eastern Texas and southern Arkansas. The Barksdale Air Force Base near Bossier City also is a major employer for both cities. Forestry and poultry production scattered throughout the 4th adds to the economy.

Redistricted three times in the 1990s, the old 4th briefly had a black majority, but African-Americans now make up a third of the population. The area sent conservative Democrats to Congress from 1874 until a 1988 special election. The GOP incumbent has won comfortably since (briefly in the old 5th), even though registered Democrats outnumber Republicans. Locally, the 4th still favors Democrats, although the suburbs around Shreveport and Bossier City have elected some Republicans in recent elections.

MAJOR INDUSTRY

Military, riverboat gambling, health care, timber

MILITARY BASES

Fort Polk (Army), 8,911 military, 1,867 civilian; Barksdale Air Force Base, 7,217 military, 541 civilian (1999)

CITIES

Shreveport, 200,145; Bossier City, 56,461; Natchitoches, 17,865

NOTABLE

Bank robbers Bonnie and Clyde were gunned down south of Gibsland in 1934 — the town re-enacts the shooting every year.

Rep. Rodney Alexander (D)

CAPITOL OFFICE
225-8490
www.house.gov/alexander
316 Cannon 20515-1805; fax 225-5639

COMMITTEES
Agriculture
Armed Services

HOMETOWN
Quitman

BORN
Dec. 5, 1946, Quitman, La.

RELIGION
Baptist

FAMILY
Wife, Nancy Alexander; three children

EDUCATION
Louisiana Tech U., attended 1965

MILITARY SERVICE
Air Force Reserve, 1965-71

CAREER
Insurance agent; road construction contractor

POLITICAL HIGHLIGHTS
Jackson Parish Police Jury, 1972-87 (president, 1980-87); La. House, 1988-2002

ELECTION RESULTS

2002 GENERAL RUNOFF		
Rodney Alexander (D)	86,718	50.3%
Lee Fletcher (R)	85,744	49.7%
2002 GENERAL		
Rodney Alexander (D)	52,952	28.7%
Lee Fletcher (R)	45,278	24.5%
Clyde C. Holloway (R)	42,573	23.1%
Robert J. Barham (R)	34,533	18.7%
Sam Houston Melton Jr. (D)	4,595	2.5%
Jack Wright (R)	3,581	1.9%

Elected December 2002; 1st term

Reserved and conservative, Alexander was one of the few Democrats who arrived for the 108th Congress having taken a House seat from the GOP.

As a result, he was given his first choice of committee assignment: Agriculture, from which Alexander says his priority will be promoting the cotton and sugar cane growers of strongly conservative but economically challenged northern Louisiana. He was not able to win a seat on the Transportation panel, where he wanted to pursue funding for a long list of public works and put his experience in the family road construction business to use.

One of Alexander's first acts in the House was to join the "Blue Dog" coalition of the most conservative Democrats, which had provided his campaign with financial support and sent two of its members, Charles W. Stenholm of Texas and Mike Ross of Arkansas, to aid his campaign.

Alexander campaigned against federal regulation and promised to oppose an expansion of abortion rights or new gun controls. He described his ideology as "pro-business, pro-life and pro-gun," but then modified it somewhat: "Pro-two-gun if someone wants to carry two."

Alexander, who left college after a year, spent 15 years on the Jackson Parish Police Jury, which is akin to county council, before winning election to the state House in 1988. There he co-wrote a law that helped rural hospitals obtain a larger share of Medicare and Medicaid reimbursements than urban hospitals, and he sponsored the creation of a program to help low-income families obtain pediatric medical insurance coverage.

His opening to Congress came when GOP incumbent John Cooksey gave up his seat after three terms to run for the Senate. Alexander was first among seven candidates in the initial round of balloting, on the national Election Day. Under Louisiana's unique congressional election system, the top two finishers advanced to a December runoff. Lee Fletcher, who had been Cooksey's chief of staff, was favored in the GOP-leaning district. But Alexander, who portrayed the contest as between "blue jeans and a blue blood," prevailed by 974 votes — the second-closest House race of the year.

LOUISIANA 5

Northeast and central — Monroe, Alexandria

Taking in most of northeastern and central Louisiana, the conservative 5th District stretches from the delta parishes along the Mississippi River to central Louisiana — a region known as the Crossroads for its mix of American Indians, Cajuns and European settlers.

Although the rich, black soil along the Mississippi produces much of the state's cotton and soybeans, poor education and transportation systems slow economic growth — poverty and unemployment in the delta parishes can affect as many as one-fourth of residents. A move toward larger farms has altered the economy of Monroe, the 5th's largest city. Located between the delta farms in the east and the small lumber and paper mills that dot the western parishes, Monroe now depends increasingly on health care, service and retail industries.

The central part of the state is focused around Alexandria in Rapides Parish. Although military base closings in the 1990s hurt the regional economy, the 1992 conversion of England Air Force Base into an industrial park has helped the area.

This historically Democratic district leans Republican, but voters will support conservatives of either party. Democrats hold some local offices. George W. Bush took 57 percent of the 5th's vote in the 2000 presidential election. Most residents classify themselves as conservative Democrats, but the Baptists and Pentecostals in the north are more likely to vote for Republicans than the Catholics in the south. About one-third of residents are African-American.

MAJOR INDUSTRY
Agriculture, health care

CITIES
Monroe, 53,107; Alexandria, 46,342

NOTABLE
Former Gov. and Sen. Huey Long was born in Winn Parish in 1893; Delta Air Lines started in Monroe and was based there until moving to Atlanta in 1941.

Rep. Richard H. Baker (R)

CAPITOL OFFICE
225-3901
www.house.gov/baker
341 Cannon 20515-1806; fax 225-7313

COMMITTEES
Financial Services
(Capital Markets, Insurance & GSEs - chairman)
Transportation & Infrastructure
Veterans' Affairs

HOMETOWN
Baton Rouge

BORN
May 22, 1948, New Orleans, La.

RELIGION
Methodist

FAMILY
Wife, Kay Baker; two children

EDUCATION
Louisiana State U., B.A. 1971 (political science)

CAREER
Real estate broker

POLITICAL HIGHLIGHTS
La. House, 1972-86 (served as a Democrat, 1972-85)

ELECTION RESULTS

2002 GENERAL		
Richard H. Baker (R)	146,932	84.0%
Rick Moscatello (I)	27,898	16.0%
2000 GENERAL		
Richard H. Baker (R)	165,637	68.0%
Kathy J. Rogillio (D)	72,192	29.7%
Michael S. Wolf (LIBERT)	5,649	2.3%

PREVIOUS WINNING PERCENTAGES
1998 (51%); 1996 (69%); 1994 (81%); 1992 (51%); 1990 (100%); 1988 (100%); 1986 (51%)

Elected 1986; 9th term

Baker says he was drawn to a life in public service by the example of his father, a Methodist preacher in Louisiana: Watching his dad work with people, he says, made him want to do the same. Although he tried his own hand at being a lay preacher, Baker concluded that he was "not cut out for pastoral service" and entered politics instead.

"My mission is to make change," Baker says. "Hopefully, it will be viewed as change for the good."

His chosen path put him at odds with the popular perception of the back-slapping, flamboyant Louisiana politician. "You'd be hard-pressed to catch Richard Baker, were he a football player, dancing in the end zone after scoring a touchdown. It's just not his style," The Financial Services Roundtable magazine once observed. Indeed, not until he had been in Congress a dozen years, and faced a 1998 election scare, did he become convinced he needed a press secretary to publicize his legislative accomplishments.

And he is as conservative as he is solemn. The liberal Americans for Democratic Action has given Baker a 0 rating for 12 consecutive years, while the U.S. Chamber of Commerce has given him a 95 percent grade.

Since the Republicans took over in the 104th Congress, Baker has chaired the Financial Services subcommittee with jurisdiction over capital markets, deposit insurance and the secondary mortgage market. (Because the jurisdictions of both the full committee, which had been called Banking, and the subcommittee have changed over the years, Baker has not run afoul of the party-imposed six-year term limit on chairmanships.)

From his subcommittee perch, Baker — who began his career as a pro-labor Democrat, but now views himself as a free-market conservative — played an important role in the laws enacted in 2002 to bolster corporate accountability and make the federal government the insurer of last resort against terrorism.

In 2001, he held hearings on conflicts of interest among Wall Street stock analysts, an issue that came to the fore with the subsequent high-profile bankruptcies of Enron Corp. and WorldCom Inc. "Maybe there hasn't been complete erosion in the Chinese walls that traditionally shielded analysts from investment banking interests," Baker said at one hearing. "Or maybe somebody's just been handing out a whole lot of Chinese ladders for people to climb back and forth as they please."

The modest anti-corporate-fraud bill that Baker and Financial Services Chairman Michael G. Oxley, an Ohio Republican, shepherded through the House early in 2002 had the tacit backing of the White House. But the wave of corporate accounting misbehavior continued and made their proposals politically inoperative. The measure that became law that summer was mostly written by the majority Senate Democrats, although it included a Baker provision that directed monetary penalties paid by corporate executives into a fund for defrauded shareholders and employees.

Along with Oxley, Baker subsequently launched a probe of investment banking practices, particularly regarding initial public stock offerings. Baker is a staunch believer that the federal government, and not the states, should regulate the securities industry. After New York Attorney General Eliot Spitzer reached a $100 million settlement with Merrill Lynch over alleged conflicts of interest by analysts, Baker wrote to the attorneys general of the other 49 states urging them not to take similar action and threatening legislation to curb their jurisdiction.

He has also used his gavel to take on powerful forces in the home loan industry, seeking increased regulation of Fannie Mae and Freddie Mac, the government-chartered mortgage giants, in a battle that also pitted him and his allies at large banks against consumer groups, the real estate industry, small banks — and Oxley, who has held Baker at bay on the issue.

Baker says his philosophy of business regulation is "to make sure whatever A can do to B under the rules, B can do to A." He says his top priority is to prevent another bailout of an economic sector akin to the savings and loan debacle of the late 1980s and early 1990s. He carried that philosophy into the debate on the law establishing a federal backstop for commercial property and casualty insurers against terrorist attacks, insisting on a provision requiring at least a partial payback of any government aid.

Baker concedes that "99.9 percent of what I do is of no interest to people in the district," but he argues that it is important to them. "My concern is that taxpayers not be called upon to pay off a bill they didn't create."

He does look out for the 6th District. He saw to it that the Baton Rouge Metropolitan Airport received $7 million in federal funding to reduce the noise of airport operations in 2002. That same year he also secured $2.2 million to fund a new anti-terrorism training center in Louisiana. And he was the driving force behind the creation of a training camp for at-risk youngsters and a health facility for veterans — on the grounds of an old federal leprosarium that he had transferred to state control.

After his graduation from Louisiana State University, Baker started his own real estate business and won election to the legislature at age 23 — as a Democrat. He made a name for himself in Baton Rouge by writing a law that created objective criteria for allocating state highway funds; the money had been doled out based on political favoritism.

The GOP leaders who persuaded Baker to switch parties in 1985 perceived him as their best chance to retain the House seat being vacated the next year by Republican W. Henson Moore, who ran for the Senate. And they were right: Baker put together an unusual coalition of country club Republicans and blue-collar Democrats to defeat a better-financed Democrat, state Sen. Thomas Hudson, by 6 percentage points.

In 1992, reapportionment cost Louisiana a House seat, and Baker was reelected by only 2,700 votes when he was forced to run in the same district as another House Republican from the Class of 1986, Clyde C. Holloway. Baker's only other close call was in 1998, when he prevailed by 2,800 votes in a race against Democrat Marjorie McKeithen, the daughter and granddaughter of big players in Louisiana politics.

KEY VOTES

2002

- No Overhaul campaign finance law; ban "soft money" and restrict advocacy advertising
- Yes Back Bush's defense budget increase
- Yes Extend 1996 welfare law
- Yes Adopt Bush's discretionary spending limit
- Yes Pass GOP Medicare prescription drug plan
- No Create independent Sept. 11 commission
- No Extend union protections to Homeland Security Department employees
- Yes Revive fast-track procedures for trade agreements
- Yes Authorize war against Iraq
- Yes Advance bankruptcy overhaul opposed by abortion opponents

2001

- Yes Nullify Clinton Labor Department ergonomics rule
- Yes Cut taxes by $1.35 trillion through fiscal 2011
- No Maintain ban on oil drilling in Arctic National Wildlife Refuge
- Yes Approve Bush proposal to limit managed-care plan liability for coverage decisions
- No Divert money from crop subsidy payments to land conservation
- Yes Expand law enforcement power to investigate suspected terrorists

CQ VOTE STUDIES

	PARTY UNITY		PRESIDENTIAL SUPPORT	
	Support	Oppose	Support	Oppose
2002	96%	4%	82%	18%
2001	99%	1%	100%	0%
2000	90%	10%	26%	74%
1999	94%	6%	17%	83%
1998	94%	6%	20%	80%

INTEREST GROUPS

	AFL-CIO	ADA	CCUS	ACU
2002	11%	0%	95%	100%
2001	9%	0%	100%	96%
2000	0%	0%	85%	75%
1999	0%	0%	96%	80%
1998	0%	0%	100%	100%

LOUISIANA 6
East central — Baton Rouge

Centered around the state capital of Baton Rouge, the socially conservative 6th takes in a slew of petrochemical plants along the Mississippi River as well as rural parishes along the Mississippi border. Baton Rouge's economic and population growth has spilled over into neighboring parishes, which attract commuters with superior schools and lower crime rates.

The decline of the domestic oil industry in the 1980s made Baton Rouge's government and university employees even more vital to the district's economy — Southern and Louisiana State universities are both located in the city. While oil and petrochemicals rebounded in the 1990s, local officials were concerned with the exodus of white-collar workers. A 1996 "Plan Baton Rouge" to redevelop downtown brought more tourism to the area — aided by the addition of two docked riverboat casinos. Although the port is no longer the centerpiece of the 6th's economy, it remains important.

Agriculture fuels the rural parishes on the outskirts of the district — sugar cane is produced in the west, while the northeastern part is lined with paper mills and potato farms.

As in most of the South, socially conservative suburban and rural voters have shifted toward the GOP. But the minority and blue-collar residents of Baton Rouge still vote Democratic. Rounds of redistricting in the 1990s gave the 6th more and more of Baton Rouge, transforming it into a politically competitive district. Democrats fare well locally in the northern and western parts of the 6th, while East Baton Rouge, Livingston and Ascension parishes consistently vote Republican. George W. Bush received 55 percent of the district's vote in 2000.

MAJOR INDUSTRY

Government, higher education, petrochemicals

CITIES

Baton Rouge, 227,818; Shenandoah, 17,070; Baker, 13,793

NOTABLE

The state capitol, completed in 1932, is the tallest in the United States; Gov. Huey Long, who led the fight for the new capitol, was assassinated there in 1935 and is buried on the capitol grounds; The five-campus Southern University System is the only historically black university system in the country.

Rep. Chris John (D)

CAPITOL OFFICE
225-2031
christopher.john@mail.house.gov
www.house.gov/john
403 Cannon 20515-1807; fax 225-5724

COMMITTEES
Energy & Commerce

HOMETOWN
Crowley

BORN
Jan. 5, 1960, Crowley, La.

RELIGION
Roman Catholic

FAMILY
Wife, Payton John; two children

EDUCATION
Louisiana State U., B.A. 1982 (business administration)

CAREER
Trucking company owner

POLITICAL HIGHLIGHTS
Crowley City Council, 1984-88; La. House, 1988-96; candidate for lieutenant governor, 1995

ELECTION RESULTS

2002 GENERAL		
Chris John (D)	138,659	86.8%
Roberto Valletta (I)	21,051	13.2%
2000 GENERAL		
Chris John (D)	152,796	83.3%
Michael P. Harris (LIBERT)	30,687	16.7%

PREVIOUS WINNING PERCENTAGES
1998 (100%); 1996 (53%)

Elected 1996; 4th term

One of the half-dozen most conservative Democrats in the House, John organized support for Harold E. Ford Jr. of Tennessee in his longshot bid against Nancy Pelosi to become House Democratic leader in the 108th Congress. John said that the Democrats needed to change their national reputation as supporters of abortion rights and gun control — which Pelosi backs, but which are still anathema across much of the South.

John and Ford are colleagues in the "Blue Dog" coalition of the most conservative Democrats. "When did it stop being cool to be a Democrat?" John asked the Baton Rouge Advocate. Many of his fellow Blue Dogs are young Democrats, he observed, "and there aren't many of us left anymore."

Ford, whose campaign was based on the argument that Pelosi is too liberal to lead the Democrats back into the majority, received only 29 votes in the secret balloting; presumably, most came from the Blue Dogs. John said he knew his colleague from San Francisco would win overwhelmingly, but said he backed Ford's candidacy to emphasize that the party has a broad membership base and that all factions need a voice in leadership.

John's voting record in the 107th Congress proves how disparate his views are from the majority of his party. He sided with President Bush 64 percent of the time — on trade, the federal budget, tax cuts and energy development, among other issues. Only four other Democrats voted with the president more often. And only six other Democrats broke from the fold more often on mostly party-line votes in 2001 and 2002; John did so 42 percent of the time.

His last three re-elections have been endorsed by the U.S. Chamber of Commerce and — perhaps more telling — his ratings from the Americans for Democratic Action and the American Conservative Union are similar: about 40 percent from the liberals and 50 percent from the conservatives. He sides more often with business interests than with organized labor.

John has benefited from his party's awareness that it must reach out to its conservative wing. Minority Leader Richard A. Gephardt made good on a promise and awarded John a coveted seat on the Energy and Commerce Committee in the 107th Congress — soon after John turned down Republican entreaties to switch parties. "They had some nice offers," John said of the GOP in an interview with the New Orleans Times-Picayune, "but the fact is, philosophically I'm a Democrat and will always be one."

When he arrived in the House in 1997 with a background in business and politics, John joined up with the Blue Dogs and was soon given a prominent role in announcing the group's plan for achieving a balanced budget. In the next four years, he was one of three co-chairmen of the group and helped to present Blue Dog proposals on prescription drugs, campaign finance and the budget. He rotated off the leadership in the 108th, but he remains active in the group.

His focus on bridge building across party lines, he told the Baton Rouge paper, is "what people want — moderates who can be effective, and not someone hellbent on a dogmatic line from which they cannot vary. They don't want to see a lot of fights between donkeys and elephants."

John introduced six bills in the 107th Congress, bringing his six-year, career total to one dozen. "I prefer to sit and compromise and to lobby my colleagues," John said when he was first elected. He had a similar track record in the state legislature, where he developed a reputation as someone who was a willing listener, a hard worker and a legislator well-versed on a few key issues, particularly oil and gas matters.

In 2002 and again in 2003, John offered legislation to provide matching grants to local governments to help them deal with a deadly outbreak of West Nile virus. On Commerce, he teamed with the panel's senior Democrat, John D. Dingell of Michigan, to push legislation to shield gun manufacturers and dealers from lawsuits stemming from use of their weapons.

To take the seat on Energy and Commerce, John had to give up seats on the Agriculture and Resources committees, which were good fits for his district, where farming, oil and gas development, and coastal preservation are important issues. In the 107th he worked to help Louisiana's rice farmers, who are facing financial difficulties. (John and his brothers own two rice and crawfish farms they inherited from their grandparents.)

Locally, John clashed with Republican Gov. Mike Foster over his preliminary approval of an Indian casino in the 7th District, near the Texas border. John, who had supported casino and riverboat gambling during his years in the state House, said that Foster had made key decisions on the casino without giving local authorities a chance to comment.

Before coming to Washington, John helped run his family's trucking company, and he has sought highway improvements that would benefit the 7th District. He was able to win a high-priority designation for a project to upgrade U.S. 90 from Lafayette to New Orleans, making it an extension of Interstate 49. In 2002, John managed to direct $6 million in federal funds for an interstate interchange in Lafayette.

After earning a degree in business administration from Louisiana State University, John returned to his native Crowley and the family's businesses — not only trucking but also politics. He had also worked as a legislative aide for his father, who was serving in the state House.

John spent four years on the Crowley City Council, and in 1987 won the state House seat his father had held. He served eight years in Baton Rouge. In 1995, he gave up the seat to run, unsuccessfully, for lieutenant governor; but a year later he was back on the ballot. With Republican Jimmy Hayes leaving the House after a decade to run for the Senate, the race for the 7th District drew a field of eight. As the only legislator on the ballot, and with his run for lieutenant governor fresh in voters' minds, John was the best-known candidate.

He emerged from the all-party primary in first place but fell far short of the requisite majority. He beat the second-place finisher, another Democrat, lawyer Hunter Lundy, to win the election by 6 percentage points. He had no opposition in 1998 and only third-party foes in 2000 and 2002.

KEY VOTES

2002

- Yes Overhaul campaign finance law; ban "soft money" and restrict advocacy advertising
- ? Back Bush's defense budget increase
- No Extend 1996 welfare law
- No Adopt Bush's discretionary spending limit
- No Pass GOP Medicare prescription drug plan
- Yes Create independent Sept. 11 commission
- Yes Extend union protections to Homeland Security Department employees
- Yes Revive fast-track procedures for trade agreements
- Yes Authorize war against Iraq
- No Advance bankruptcy overhaul opposed by abortion opponents

2001

- Yes Nullify Clinton Labor Department ergonomics rule
- Yes Cut taxes by $1.35 trillion through fiscal 2011
- No Maintain ban on oil drilling in Arctic National Wildlife Refuge
- No Approve Bush proposal to limit managed-care plan liability for coverage decisions
- No Divert money from crop subsidy payments to land conservation
- Yes Expand law enforcement power to investigate suspected terrorists

CQ VOTE STUDIES

	PARTY UNITY		PRESIDENTIAL SUPPORT	
	Support	Oppose	Support	Oppose
2002	64%	36%	58%	42%
2001	52%	48%	69%	31%
2000	65%	35%	49%	51%
1999	53%	47%	58%	42%
1998	56%	44%	50%	50%

INTEREST GROUPS

	AFL-CIO	ADA	CCUS	ACU
2002	67%	45%	74%	46%
2001	45%	40%	83%	63%
2000	50%	30%	90%	41%
1999	63%	45%	83%	50%
1998	60%	50%	76%	45%

LOUISIANA 7

Southwest — Lafayette, Lake Charles

Anchored by blue-collar Lake Charles in the west, white-collar Lafayette in the east and the Gulf of Mexico in the south, the 7th takes in both coastal and city life. A sizable Catholic citizenry bolsters the district's socially conservative leanings.

The 7th's economy is firmly centered around agriculture, as well as oil and gas production. After the statewide petroleum depression in the 1980s, local officials worked to diversify the economy. But with recovery in the 1990s, attention has refocused on the offshore and inland oil wells. The rural parishes between Lafayette and Lake Charles produce rice and soybeans. Rice farmers also have had success raising crawfish in fallow rice fields.

Dotted with waterfowl and wildlife refuges, the 7th's Gulf edge serves sports and commercial fishermen. Lake Charles, a refining and chemical-producing hub in Calcasieu Parish, offers a sharp industrial contrast to the district's coastal and rural areas.

Despite the 7th's conservative tenor, the area tends to vote for moderate Democrats and has sent a Democrat to Congress in every election since 1884. Lafayette Parish, in the eastern part of the district, is the most Republican-leaning area.

Three stabs at redistricting in the 1990s did little to change the 7th, and the redraw following the 2000 census also left the district largely intact. The only changes in 2001 were the removal of the old 7th's portions of Allen and St. Martin parishes. George W. Bush captured 55 percent of the 7th's vote in 2000. In 1996, the district regained some black neighborhoods in Lafayette Parish that it had lost in 1992. African-Americans now make up one-fourth of the population.

MAJOR INDUSTRY

Oil and gas, petrochemicals, agriculture, fishing

CITIES

Lafayette, 110,257; Lake Charles, 71,757; Opelousas, 22,860

NOTABLE

Former Gov. Edwin W. Edwards and Sen. John B. Breaux represented the 7th; Dr. Michael E. DeBakey, born in Lake Charles, was the first person to successfully use an artificial heart in a patient; Rayne, the self-proclaimed frog capital of the world, hosts an annual frog festival.

MAINE

Gov. John Baldacci (D)

First elected: 2002
Length of term: 4 years
Term expires: 1/07
Salary: $70,000
Phone: (207) 287-3531
Hometown: Bangor
Born: Jan. 30, 1955; Bangor, Maine
Religion: Roman Catholic
Family: Wife, Karen Baldacci; one child
Education: U. of Maine, B.A. 1986 (history)
Career: Restaurant operator
Political Highlights: Bangor City Council, 1978-81; Maine Senate, 1982-94; U.S. House, 1995-2003

Election Results:

2002 GENERAL		
John Baldacci (D)	238,179	47.1%
Peter E. Cianchette (R)	209,496	41.5%
Jonathan K. Carter (GI)	46,903	9.3%
John M. Michael (I)	10,612	2.1%

Senate President Beverly C. Daggett (D)

(no lieutenant governor)
Phone: (207) 287-1500

STATE LEGISLATURE

Legislature: Meets January-June in odd-numbered years; January-April in even-numbered years
House: 151 members, 2-year terms
2003 breakdown: 67R, 80D, 3I, 1GREEN; 114 men, 37 women
Salary: $19,686/2-year term
Phone: (207) 287-1400
Senate: 35 members, 2-year terms
2003 breakdown: 17R, 18D; 22 men, 13 women
Salary: $19,686/2-year term
Phone: (207) 287-1540

STATE TERM LIMITS

Governor: 2 consecutive terms
House: 4 terms
Senate: 4 terms

URBAN STATISTICS

CITY	POPULATION
Portland	64,249
Lewiston	35,690
Bangor	31,473
South Portland	23,325
Auburn	23,203

REGISTERED VOTERS

Unenrolled	37%
Democrat	32%
Republican	30%

POPULATION

2002 population (est.)	1,294,464
2000 population	1,274,923
1990 population	1,227,928
Percent change (1990-2000)	+3.8%
Rank among states (2002)	40
Median age	38.6
Born in state	67.3%
Foreign born	2.9%
Violent crime rate	110/100,000
Poverty level	10.9%
Federal workers	13,542
Military	10,200

REDISTRICTING

Maine retained its two House seats in reapportionment. The state will draw a new map in 2003.

MISCELLANEOUS

Web: www.state.me.us
Capital: Augusta

STATE ELECTION OFFICIAL
(207) 287-4186

DEMOCRATIC HEADQUARTERS
(207) 622-6233

REPUBLICAN HEADQUARTERS
(207) 622-6247

District Statistics

DIST.	2000 VOTE FOR PRESIDENT BUSH	GORE	NADER	WHITE	BLACK	ASIAN	HISP	MEDIAN INCOME	WHITE COLLAR	BLUE COLLAR	SERVICE INDUSTRY	OVER 64	UNDER 18	COLLEGE EDUCATION	RURAL	SQ. MILES
1	43%	51%	6%	96%	1%	1%	1%	$41,585	61%	24%	15%	14%	24%	28%	50%	3,617
2	46	48	5	97	0	0	1	$32,678	53	31	16	15	23	18	71	27,244
STATE	44	49	6	96	1	1	1	$37,240	57	27	15	14	24	23	60	30,862
U.S.	47.9	48.4	3	69	12	4	13	$41,994	60	25	15	12	26	24	21	3,537,438

Aroostook
Piscataquis
2
Somerset
Penobscot
Washington
Franklin
Bangor
Hancock
Oxford
Kennebec
Waldo
Augusta
Androscoggin
Lewiston
Lincoln
Knox
Sagadahoc
Cumberland
1
1
Portland
York

Sen. Olympia J. Snowe (R)

CAPITOL OFFICE
224-5344
olympia@snowe.senate.gov
snowe.senate.gov
154 Russell 20510-1903; fax 224-1946

COMMITTEES
Commerce, Science & Transportation
(Oceans, Fisheries & Coast Guard - chairwoman)
Finance
Small Business & Entrepreneurship - chairwoman
Select Intelligence

HOMETOWN
Falmouth

BORN
Feb. 21, 1947, Augusta, Maine

RELIGION
Greek Orthodox

FAMILY
Husband, John R. McKernan Jr.

EDUCATION
U. of Maine, B.A. 1969 (political science)

CAREER
Congressional aide; city employee

POLITICAL HIGHLIGHTS
Maine House, 1973-77; Maine Senate, 1977-79; U.S. House, 1979-95

ELECTION RESULTS

2000 GENERAL

Olympia J. Snowe (R)	437,689	68.9%
Mark Lawrence (D)	197,183	31.1%

2000 PRIMARY

Olympia J. Snowe (R)	unopposed

PREVIOUS WINNING PERCENTAGES
1994 (60%); 1992 House Election (49%); 1990 House Election (51%); 1988 House Election (66%); 1986 House Election (77%); 1984 House Election (76%); 1982 House Election (67%); 1980 House Election (79%); 1978 House Election (51%)

Elected 1994; 2nd term

Snowe is one of the Senate's most powerful and influential centrists, a role she relishes and plays wisely. She has been a player on nearly every piece of major legislation that has come before the chamber, from tax cut and Medicare prescription drug legislation to defense spending and homeland security. Regardless of the issue, she has made finding the middle ground a hallmark of her more than two decades in Congress.

With a casual, approachable style, Snowe is known as a modest senator in a chamber filled with big egos. She is popular with her colleagues, and both parties court her heavily, knowing she is well-regarded. She enjoys preparing for committee hearings, often spending hours at the task, and aides describe her as tough but fair.

While Snowe does not always get everything she wants, she is often successful at slipping strategically targeted provisions into final legislation. Though she sometimes has to threaten to withhold her vote to prevail, she succeeds on many occasions by building coalitions with centrist Democrats and relying on her personal charm. For example, when the Bush administration pushed its sweeping tax cut plan early in the 107th Congress, Snowe's consistent persuasion helped broaden a provision on child tax credits. After striking compromises, Snowe generally supports GOP legislation in its final form.

Snowe's knowledge and power have brought her national stature. She was the first Republican woman ever to sit on the Senate's powerful tax-writing Finance Committee. In the 2002 Miss America pageant, a contestant cited Snowe as a role model, along with Bush administration national security adviser Condoleezza Rice. Washingtonian Magazine in 2001 named her as one of the city's 100 most powerful women.

As chairwoman of the Small Business Committee, Snowe plans to use her post to encourage women entrepreneurs and pursue a wide-ranging legislative agenda. Roughly 97 percent of Maine's 37,000 employers are small businesses with fewer than 20 employees. She also chairs the Commerce panel's subcommittee on Oceans, Atmosphere and Fisheries, where a top legislative priority will be reauthorization of the Magnuson-Stevens fisheries conservation law. The law is important to Maine, which has 3,500 miles of coastline and where fishing is an important industry. Snowe also continues to look out for the interests of Bath Iron Works, the giant builder of Navy ships that is the state's largest employer.

Snowe co-chairs the Centrist Coalition, a group of about 30 Republican and Democratic senators who strive to find common ground on issues such as tax policy and campaign finance reform. She has pushed Republican leaders to focus more on the party's moderates, and has made clear to sometimes reluctant GOP leaders that they need to do a better job of reaching across the aisle. In the 107th, she sided with Democrats more often than all but two other Senate Republicans.

She demonstrated her independence during tense negotiations in the 107th on legislation to create a homeland security department. Snowe, fellow Maine Republican Susan Collins and Republican Lincoln Chafee of Rhode Island took issue with special-interest provisions in the bill that, among other things, would help shield vaccine manufacturers from lawsuits. The three withheld their vote for the bill until winning assurances from House and Senate GOP leaders that the provisions would be stripped from the bill early in the 108th.

Earlier in the 107th, Snowe, with Vermont independent James M. Jeffords, wrote an amendment to campaign finance legislation to prohibit direct use of union or corporate money for election ads in the weeks leading to elections. The language became part of the final bill.

Also in the 107th, Snowe co-authored a "tripartisan" Medicare prescription drug bill with Republicans, Democrats and the independent Jeffords that would have looked to the private market to provide drug coverage for seniors. She insisted that any bill provide a uniform benefit for the elderly — preferably one that pays for drug coverage for every beneficiary, regardless of income.

She has taken a cautious approach on tax relief, urging Bush and Republicans to make their 2001 tax cuts contingent on reductions in government debt, also known as a "trigger" mechanism. When that idea failed to gain traction, she insisted instead that the package's child tax credit be made refundable, so that even those paying little or no tax could benefit from it. That provision was made part of the bill that became law.

Though she strongly supports abortion rights, Snowe has tried to broker compromises with conservatives, joining with Democrats in seeking an alternative to the GOP's desired ban on a procedure its opponents call "partial birth" abortion. She also has joined with Democrats on a proposal requiring federal workers' health insurance plans to pay for contraceptives.

Snowe often joins with Democrats on environmental matters; she opposes drilling in the Arctic National Wildlife Refuge and works to require sport utility vehicles to get better gas mileage.

Snowe arrived in the Senate in the 1994 electoral sweep that gave control of Congress to the GOP, and she was notable as the only newly elected Senate GOP moderate. But she also stood out for having a personal story as compelling as many of the military heroes who have come to the chamber.

The daughter of first- and second-generation Greek immigrants, Snowe was orphaned at age 9 and raised by an aunt and uncle in blue-collar surroundings. She was married to state Rep. Peter Snowe and working as an aide to U.S. Rep. William S. Cohen in 1973 when Peter Snowe was killed in an automobile accident. A month later, she was elected to succeed him in the state House. She won election to the state Senate in 1976, and just two years later, won a close House race to succeed Cohen, who had moved on to the Senate.

While Snowe was representing the northern 2nd District, another personable moderate Republican, John R. McKernan Jr., won the 1st District seat in 1982. Four years later, he was elected to the first of two terms as governor. He won Snowe's heart along the way, and the two were married in 1989.

In the book "Nine and Counting," a collaboration of the nine women serving in the Senate in 2000, Snowe said her life experiences shaped her political outlook. "With the devastation of Peter's death came a sensitivity to the tremendous difficulties that other women in similar situations face — such as raising children alone," she wrote. "Later that was brought to bear on issues such as pension reform, child care and displaced homemakers."

After winning election to the House in 1978, Snowe enjoyed a series of easy victories until 1990, when a deepening recession led to restlessness among voters. She eventually defeated Democratic state Rep. Patrick K. McGowan, 51 percent to 49 percent. A 1992 rematch was even closer; she won with a 49 percent plurality.

Despite the close outcomes, Snowe was the presumed GOP nominee when Senate Majority Leader George J. Mitchell, a Democrat, announced his surprise retirement early in 1994. Snowe prevailed with 60 percent of the vote. In 2000, she overwhelmed state Senate President Mark Lawrence with nearly 69 percent of the vote.

KEY VOTES

2002

Yes Pass farm bill reversing crop subsidy limits
No Postpone tougher automobile fuel efficiency standards
Yes Overhaul campaign finance law; ban "soft money" and restrict advocacy advertising
Yes Set federal election standards
No Support oil drilling in Arctic National Wildlife Refuge
Yes Revive fast-track procedures for trade agreements
Yes Create federal insurance coverage for catastrophic terrorist losses
Yes Tighten federal accounting and corporate governance regulation
No Advance bipartisan Medicare prescription drug plan
Yes Create independent Sept. 11 commission
No Back Democratic Homeland Security Department proposal
Yes Authorize war against Iraq

2001

Yes Confirm John Ashcroft as attorney general
Yes Nullify Clinton Labor Department ergonomics rule
Yes Cut taxes by $1.35 trillion through fiscal 2011
Yes Pass Democratic bill to bolster rights of patients in managed-care plans
No Permit a new round of military base closings
Yes Expand law enforcement power to investigate suspected terrorists

CQ VOTE STUDIES

	PARTY UNITY		PRESIDENTIAL SUPPORT	
	Support	Oppose	Support	Oppose
2002	57%	43%	90%	10%
2001	64%	36%	84%	16%
2000	71%	29%	62%	38%
1999	69%	31%	49%	51%
1998	65%	35%	55%	45%
1997	59%	41%	78%	22%
1996	72%	28%	53%	47%
1995	70%	30%	42%	58%
House Service:				
1994	67%	33%	60%	40%
1993	68%	32%	41%	59%

INTEREST GROUPS

	AFL-CIO	ADA	CCUS	ACU
2002	31%	30%	85%	65%
2001	50%	40%	79%	60%
2000	0%	30%	73%	80%
1999	33%	45%	59%	60%
1998	38%	35%	78%	40%
1997	43%	55%	70%	44%
1996	29%	35%	77%	70%
1995	25%	40%	84%	39%
House Service:				
1994	56%	30%	67%	57%
1993	42%	40%	64%	67%

Sen. Susan Collins (R)

CAPITOL OFFICE
224-2523
senator@collins.senate.gov
collins.senate.gov
172 Russell 20510-1904; fax 224-2693

COMMITTEES
Armed Services
Governmental Affairs - chairwoman
Special Aging
Joint Economic

HOMETOWN
Bangor

BORN
Dec. 7, 1952, Caribou, Maine

RELIGION
Roman Catholic

FAMILY
Single

EDUCATION
St. Lawrence U., B.A. 1975 (government)

CAREER
Business center director; congressional aide

POLITICAL HIGHLIGHTS
Maine commissioner of financial regulation, 1987-91; Small Business Administration official, 1992-93; Maine deputy treasurer, 1993; Republican nominee for governor, 1994

ELECTION RESULTS

2002 GENERAL		
Susan Collins (R)	295,041	58.4%
Chellie Pingree (D)	209,858	41.6%
2002 PRIMARY		
Susan Collins (R)		unopposed

PREVIOUS WINNING PERCENTAGES
1996 (49%)

Elected 1996; 2nd term

In a Senate fraught with partisan tensions, Collins tries to avoid the fray. Her well-earned reputation as a Republican centrist has brought her security at home in Maine, where political moderation is cherished and where Democrats are highly competitive: Collins in 2002 easily won a second Senate term over a well-regarded Democratic challenger, former state Sen. Chellie Pingree, by focusing on issues such as health care, education and consumer protection that have traditionally benefited Democrats.

As one of a handful of top Republican woman lawmakers, Collins increasingly finds herself showcased by her party's national leaders as they try to expand the appeal of the party to moderate voters. Collins' growing stature is symbolized by her chairmanship of the Governmental Affairs Committee in the 108th Congress. A prime responsibility is oversight of the new Department of Homeland Security; in fact, her first session as chairwoman was the confirmation hearing for Homeland Security Secretary Tom Ridge.

Collins plans to maintain Governmental Affairs' oversight function by investigating consumer and Medicare fraud and government waste. Two days after winning re-election, Collins called the Defense Department comptroller to discuss ways to overhaul the Pentagon's financial systems and reduce misuse of government credit cards by department personnel.

Collins chaired the Governmental Affairs Permanent Subcommittee on Investigations in the 106th Congress and part of the 107th and made a name as a consumer advocate. In the 106th, she won passage of a bill cracking down on deceptive practices of small sweepstakes companies. In 2000, she obtained fake identification cards to draw notice to Web sites that offer bogus credentials. She also pressed for tougher rules against unauthorized charges imposed on callers by long-distance phone companies.

Strict attention to the nuts and bolts of governing could be expected of Collins, a former Senate aide and state regulator. Collins also has displayed shrewd political skills, winning concessions from conservatives when her support was critical to move a bill through the narrowly divided Congress.

Collins gave a good example of her approach during the latter stages of the 107th Congress, when the Democrats who then controlled the Senate were fighting the Bush administration over its proposal to create a Homeland Security Department with rules to limit civil service protections.

Collins kept her vote closely guarded until she gained concessions from President Bush on two major issues: labor rights and coastal resources. She obtained a promise from Ridge — then the director of the predecessor White House Office of Homeland Security — to set up a grievance process for workers denied union protections on national security grounds. She also won assurances that the Coast Guard's responsibilities for preventing terrorism would not diminish resources for fisheries enforcement, boating safety and other functions vital to her coastal state.

By conducting her negotiations discreetly and not publicly confronting the administration, Collins demonstrated an independent streak while never raising serious questions about her party loyalty.

That approach also can be seen on some health care issues. In the 107th, she supported the Republican version of a patients' bill of rights and favored a largely private sector approach, as Republican leaders did, to adding a prescription drug benefit to Medicare. But she joined many members of both parties in supporting a Senate bill that would give generic drug makers faster access to brand-name pharmaceuticals. The issue is important to Maine's population, which is older than the national average.

Collins also has taken on more-modest health care initiatives. In 1999, she won unanimous backing for a measure urging the National Institutes of Health to put greater emphasis on diabetes research. She also introduced a measure to toughen government inspection of imported food.

Collins sides with party conservatives on some high-profile issues. She resists gun control initiatives, and voted in 1999 against a proposal that would have required background checks on buyers at gun shows.

On fiscal policy, too, she generally sides with the political right, supporting a balanced-budget constitutional amendment and requiring a two-thirds majority vote of Congress to raise taxes. She backs a constitutional amendment to limit congressional terms and has said she plans to serve just 12 years in the Senate. She has been skeptical of tax cut plans that threaten to impose long-range budget deficit pressures.

Collins often sides with Democrats on environmental issues, including opposition to oil drilling in the Arctic National Wildlife Refuge.

But on some social policies, Collins is likely to join fellow Maine Republican Sen. Olympia J. Snowe among centrists who urge a go-slow approach. That resonates in a state where independents are the biggest voting bloc, and where Democratic registrants outnumber Republicans.

Criticizing a proposal to ban a procedure its opponents call "partial birth" abortion, she once told The Boston Globe: "Everybody knows these laws are unconstitutional on their face." As an alternative, Collins, Snowe and other moderates have proposed restricting late-term abortions except to prevent "grievous injury" to the woman's health.

Collins plied her own course over the impeachment of President Clinton. She first proposed that the Senate in early 1999 adopt "findings of fact" that would detail Clinton's misconduct in his affair with intern Monica Lewinsky, thereby allowing those who did not want to remove Clinton from office to nonetheless show disapproval. Her idea won support from a number of Republicans but not enough Democrats. Later, Collins was one of five Republican senators to vote "not guilty" on both impeachment articles.

Politics is in Collins' blood: Both her parents served terms as mayor of the small northern Maine town of Caribou. Her father, grandfather, great-grandfather and great-great-grandfather served as Maine legislators.

Collins visited the U.S. Capitol as a high school senior and spent two hours talking with a Republican woman trailblazer, Maine Sen. Margaret Chase Smith. "I remember leaving her office and thinking that if she can be in the Senate, women can do anything. It really was in some ways a transformational experience," Collins has said.

After college, Collins returned to Washington in the mid-1970s and worked for a dozen years as an adviser on business issues to Maine Republican Sen. William S. Cohen. She then served as commissioner of Maine's Department of Professional and Financial Regulation.

Collins' first venture as a political candidate was disappointing. She won the 1994 Republican nomination for governor but ran far behind victorious independent Angus King and Democratic nominee Joseph E. Brennan, a former governor and House member.

After Cohen announced that he would retire in 1996, Collins climbed back in the ring. A clearly improved campaigner, she won the GOP primary handily. In the general-election contest, she faced Brennan, who never regained his political footing after losses in the 1990 and 1994 gubernatorial elections. Collins defeated Brennan by 5 percentage points in a year in which Democrats won both of Maine's House districts and the presidential contest. She beat 2002 opponent Pingree by 17 points.

KEY VOTES

2002

- Yes Pass farm bill reversing crop subsidy limits
- No Postpone tougher automobile fuel efficiency standards
- Yes Overhaul campaign finance law; ban "soft money" and restrict advocacy advertising
- Yes Set federal election standards
- No Support oil drilling in Arctic National Wildlife Refuge
- Yes Revive fast-track procedures for trade agreements
- Yes Create federal insurance coverage for catastrophic terrorist losses
- Yes Tighten federal accounting and corporate governance regulation
- Yes Advance bipartisan Medicare prescription drug plan
- Yes Create independent Sept. 11 commission
- No Back Democratic Homeland Security Department proposal
- Yes Authorize war against Iraq

2001

- Yes Confirm John Ashcroft as attorney general
- Yes Nullify Clinton Labor Department ergonomics rule
- Yes Cut taxes by $1.35 trillion through fiscal 2011
- Yes Pass Democratic bill to bolster rights of patients in managed-care plans
- No Permit a new round of military base closings
- Yes Expand law enforcement power to investigate suspected terrorists

CQ VOTE STUDIES

	PARTY UNITY		PRESIDENTIAL SUPPORT	
	Support	Oppose	Support	Oppose
2002	57%	43%	88%	12%
2001	67%	33%	88%	12%
2000	74%	26%	57%	42%
1999	74%	26%	49%	51%
1998	67%	33%	63%	37%
1997	61%	39%	76%	24%

INTEREST GROUPS

	AFL-CIO	ADA	CCUS	ACU
2002	31%	35%	85%	55%
2001	50%	35%	79%	64%
2000	0%	25%	80%	76%
1999	11%	25%	76%	64%
1998	38%	35%	78%	36%
1997	14%	50%	80%	48%

Rep. Tom Allen (D)

CAPITOL OFFICE
225-6116
rep.tomallen@mail.house.gov
www.house.gov/allen
1717 Longworth 20515-1901; fax 225-5590

COMMITTEES
Energy & Commerce

HOMETOWN
Portland

BORN
April 16, 1945, Portland, Maine

RELIGION
Protestant

FAMILY
Wife, Diana Allen; two children

EDUCATION
Bowdoin College, B.A. 1967 (English); Oxford U., B.Phil. 1970 (Rhodes scholar); Harvard U., J.D. 1974

CAREER
Policy consultant; lawyer; congressional aide

POLITICAL HIGHLIGHTS
Portland City Council, 1989-95 (mayor, 1991-92); sought Democratic nomination for governor, 1994

ELECTION RESULTS

2002 GENERAL		
Tom Allen (D)	172,646	63.8%
Steven Joyce (R)	97,931	36.2%
2002 PRIMARY		
Tom Allen (D)		unopposed
2000 GENERAL		
Tom Allen (D)	202,823	59.8%
Jane Amero (R)	123,915	36.5%
J. Frederic Staples (I)	12,356	3.6%

PREVIOUS WINNING PERCENTAGES
1998 (60%); 1996 (55%)

Elected 1996; 4th term

Allen has established himself as an attractive, well-informed liberal spokesman on a variety of high-profile issues, including President Bush's missile defense program, prescription drugs for the elderly and several environmental policy questions. In the 108th Congress he has a new platform from which to address several of those issues: the Energy and Commerce Committee. It has one of the broadest legislative portfolios of any House panel, ranging from clean air to health care.

Allen cut his teeth on one of the hottest issues before Congress in the past decade: the campaign finance system. As co-chairman of the freshman task force on the issue in the 105th Congress, Allen pushed to ban "soft money," the unlimited and minimally regulated contributions that were becoming a dominant force in federal elections. He also sought to require more timely reporting of donations and spending, and to raise limits on contributions. When pressure from rank-and-file members forced the House leadership to bring campaign finance legislation to the floor in 1998, however, the freshman plan was defeated in favor of a less sweeping alternative.

Allen stayed active in the cause, generally behind the scenes, until changes to campaign finance law were enacted in 2002. But long before then he was in the middle of what he calls his "signature issue": what to do about the high price of prescription medications. Allen says the importance of the issue became clear to him at a town meeting late in 1997, when a retired firefighter — somebody he knew from an early campaign — talked about his $300 per month bill for prescription drugs. Allen enlisted the Democratic staff of the Government Reform Committee, where he then served, to investigate the matter. Its studies were among the earliest to show that senior citizens without prescription coverage to supplement Medicare often spend large portions of their income on medicine.

In the 106th Congress, Allen joined the Democratic whip organization and was named to the party's prescription drug task force, where he drafted one of a number of competing bills to address the issue. Initially, his solution was to require drug companies to make prescription drugs available to Medicare beneficiaries at the same discounted price offered to federal agencies, which get better deals because of bulk purchasing.

In the 107th, he fine-tuned his ideas to capitalize on the fact that pharmaceutical companies typically charge lower prices abroad. As revised, Allen's bill would have required the government to negotiate on behalf of Medicare beneficiaries for drug prices that are equal to the average prices charged in the other major industrialized countries.

Allen also has proposed grants to help states figure out how to subsidize health care insurance premiums for low-income employees of small businesses. The problem is especially acute in Maine, where much of the state is rural territory in which doctors and other health care providers are few and far between. "They don't really compete with each other," he said, "and the insurance companies don't want to be here, anyway."

His general liberalism did not prevent Allen from embracing more-hawkish positions on the Armed Services Committee, where he spent his first three terms. His district includes the Bath Iron Works — one of the six commercial shipyards building vessels for the Navy as well as Maine's largest private employer — and like more-conservative members from other shipbuilding districts, Allen belabored the Bush administration in the 107th Congress for buying too few ships to meet the goal of keeping a fleet of more than 300 vessels.

Like most members of Armed Services, Allen unsuccessfully opposed Bush's demand for another round of base closures, now scheduled to climax in 2005. A Navy air base in Brunswick and the Portsmouth Navy Shipyard in New Hampshire, just across the Piscataqua River from Kittery, had narrowly dodged the ax in previous base closures and are widely viewed as vulnerable in the coming process.

But Allen also joined more-senior committee Democrats on more ideologically charged partisan issues, as in the unsuccessful effort to slow the Bush administration's push to deploy a nationwide anti-missile defense. He and other Democrats were equally unsuccessful in their efforts to weaken some of the Republican majority's initiatives — ones Allen said might increase U.S. dependence on nuclear weapons to destroy attacking missiles or root out deeply buried enemy installations.

Allen also has been a strong proponent of tough environmental regulations, a position he shares with many members of both parties who represent the Northeast. In 2002, he joined a bipartisan House group from the region protesting the Bush administration's decision to relax clean air standards for older power plants; and air quality is a main focus of his work on Energy and Commerce in the 108th.

He was a co-founder in the 106th of the Oceans Caucus, which he hopes will advance legislation to protect Maine's fisheries and coastline.

Allen comes from a political family: His father and grandfather were both on the Portland City Council, and his mother was active in politics as well. After studying in England, Allen worked a short time in 1970 for Democratic Sen. Edmund S. Muskie, both on a campaign in Maine and on Muskie's Senate staff.

After practicing law for almost 20 years in Portland, Allen's first elective office was as a member of the Portland City Council, where he served for six years, including one year as the council-elected mayor. Allen chaired Bill Clinton's campaign in Maine in 1992 and was an adviser on agriculture issues during the presidential transition.

Following an unsuccessful 1994 bid for the Democratic gubernatorial nomination, in 1996 Allen challenged freshman GOP Rep. James B. Longley Jr. With a million-dollar assist from the AFL-CIO, the Sierra Club and other groups that ran campaign ads on his behalf, Allen mobilized key elements of his party's base while successfully tying Longley to the "extreme" Republican "Contract With America" agenda. He won by 10 percentage points. He has won by a wider margin three times since — in 2002 he cruised to a 28 percentage point victory.

KEY VOTES

2002

- Yes Overhaul campaign finance law; ban "soft money" and restrict advocacy advertising
- Yes Back Bush's defense budget increase
- No Extend 1996 welfare law
- No Adopt Bush's discretionary spending limit
- No Pass GOP Medicare prescription drug plan
- Yes Create independent Sept. 11 commission
- Yes Extend union protections to Homeland Security Department employees
- No Revive fast-track procedures for trade agreements
- No Authorize war against Iraq
- No Advance bankruptcy overhaul opposed by abortion opponents

2001

- No Nullify Clinton Labor Department ergonomics rule
- No Cut taxes by $1.35 trillion through fiscal 2011
- Yes Maintain ban on oil drilling in Arctic National Wildlife Refuge
- No Approve Bush proposal to limit managed-care plan liability for coverage decisions
- Yes Divert money from crop subsidy payments to land conservation
- Yes Expand law enforcement power to investigate suspected terrorists

CQ VOTE STUDIES

	PARTY UNITY		PRESIDENTIAL SUPPORT	
	Support	Oppose	Support	Oppose
2002	95%	5%	36%	64%
2001	96%	4%	28%	72%
2000	94%	6%	84%	16%
1999	96%	4%	86%	14%
1998	93%	7%	84%	16%

INTEREST GROUPS

	AFL-CIO	ADA	CCUS	ACU
2002	100%	95%	53%	0%
2001	100%	95%	30%	0%
2000	90%	85%	52%	4%
1999	78%	95%	28%	0%
1998	100%	100%	39%	0%

MAINE 1
South — Portland, Augusta

Rural oceanfront property draws residents to the 1st, a district incorporating the southern reaches of Maine that are also bustling with new technology jobs. Residents of Maine's largest city, Portland, are moving into outlying areas, replacing farmland and uninterrupted forests with single-family homes.

Although textile- and shoe-manufacturing plants have been downsized or closed, a high-tech boom has kept unemployment low. Companies seeking a strong infrastructure and a high quality of life have moved to southern Maine, where Interstate 95 offers a straight shot to Boston. Well-to-do and largely seasonal residents live on the coast, where former President George Bush travels for retreats at his Kennebunkport estate.

Tourism is important in the lower part of the state, as residents from across New England and Canada head to popular beaches and shopping areas along the York County coast. The military's influence also is strong in the 1st.

In a state with one of the weakest party systems in the nation, personalities play the largest role in elections; little difference exists between Democrats and Republicans in many local elections. A plurality of the state's voters register as "unenrolled" or independent. Grounded in Maine's strong communities, the state's voting participation is second only to Minnesota – 67 percent in 2000.

MAJOR INDUSTRY
Military shipbuilding, fishing, high-tech

MILITARY BASES
Portsmouth Naval Shipyard, 114 military, 4,100 civilian (2002); Brunswick Naval Air Station, 3,909 military, 689 civilian (2002)

CITIES
Portland, 64,249; South Portland, 23,324; Biddeford, 20,942; Augusta, 18,560; Saco, 16,822; Westbrook, 16,142; Waterville, 15,605

NOTABLE
The 1st helped lead the Prohibition crusade when a mid-19th century Portland businessman, Neal Dow, discontinued the traditional "rum break" for his tannery workers because it interfered with productivity; Dow was the Prohibition Party's presidential candidate in 1880.

Rep. Michael H. Michaud (D)

CAPITOL OFFICE
225-6306
www.house.gov/michaud
437 Cannon 20515-1902; fax 225-2943

COMMITTEES
Small Business
Transportation & Infrastructure
Veterans' Affairs

HOMETOWN
East Millinocket

BORN
Jan. 18, 1955, Millinocket, Maine

RELIGION
Roman Catholic

FAMILY
Single

EDUCATION
Schenck H.S., graduated 1973

CAREER
Paper mill worker

POLITICAL HIGHLIGHTS
Maine House, 1981-94; Maine Senate, 1995-2002 (president, 2001)

ELECTION RESULTS

2002 GENERAL		
Michael H. Michaud (D)	116,868	52.0%
Kevin L. Raye (R)	107,849	48.0%
2002 PRIMARY		
Michael H. Michaud (D)	12,230	31.4%
Susan W. Longley (D)	10,800	27.7%
Sean F. Faircloth (D)	7,829	20.1%
John M. Nutting (D)	4,751	12.2%
David Costello (D)	1,773	4.6%
Lori M. Handrahan (D)	1,623	4.2%

Elected 2002; 1st term

The impact of foreign trade on Maine's big industries contributed to long-time millworker Michaud's decision to run for Congress in 2002, and the issue will probably remain one of his top priorities in the House.

Michaud (ME-shoo) blames what he views as unfair practices under recent trade liberalization agreements for damaging his state's economy and bankrupting businesses, including his former employer, the Great Northern Paper Co. Michaud started in the factory right after high school and worked there for 29 years — even as he built a 22-year career in the Maine Legislature that culminated in a stint as state Senate president.

The successor to Democrat John Baldacci, who was elected governor in 2002, Michaud touted his blue-collar background and legislative experience in capturing the politically competitive 2nd District. His Franco-American roots also connect him with much of the culture and community spirit of his constituents.

His close ties to organized labor have helped him throughout his political career and abetted his narrow win over Republican Kevin Raye — whose former boss, Republican Olympia J. Snowe, represented the 2nd District from 1979 until she became a senator in 1995. The AFL-CIO made Michaud's victory one of its top political priorities in 2002.

Michaud favors a prescription drug benefit modeled on a state law he championed, which was subsequently challenged in court. Like many Democratic politicians from the northern tier of states, he has crossed the Canadian border with seniors to buy cheaper medication. His opposition to abortion rights sets him apart from many of his Democratic colleagues, however, and he is one of the few Northerners to join the "Blue Dog" coalition of conservative House Democrats.

Michaud sought and won a seat on the Transportation and Infrastructure Committee, a base from which he can pursue Maine's efforts to improve east-west transportation routes. He also took seats on the Veterans' Affairs and Small Business panels.

MAINE 2

North — Lewiston, Bangor

Millions of acres of trees surround the small towns of northern Maine's 2nd, one of the most politically independent districts in the nation. The largest district in a state east of the Mississippi, the 2nd attracts millions of visitors to Acadia National Park, Baxter State Park and Maine's many lakes and ski resorts.

A billion-dollar lobster industry dominates the East Coast, and the timber industry reigns in the rest of the 2nd. Sparsely populated in parts, the region is less wealthy than the 1st, which has benefited from an influx of high-tech jobs. Aroostook County, on the Canadian border, lost more than 10,000 people after Loring Air Force Base closed in the 1990s, though recent revitalization efforts have brought 1,000 new jobs to the 8,700-acre base. As the national economy has become more service-based, the 2nd has felt the pinch. Manufacturing jobs, especially in shoes and textiles, have gone overseas, and residents are heading south for jobs. Farming is in decline as well, though the district remains one of the largest producers of potatoes and blueberries in the nation. When redistricting takes place before the 2004 elections, the 2nd will expand southward to pick up more people.

Democrats and Yankee Republicans often vote across party lines in a state with weak party loyalties. In 1992, Ross Perot finished second in the presidential election, behind Bill Clinton but ahead of George Bush. Active participation in town activities helps encourage one of the highest voter turnouts in the nation.

MAJOR INDUSTRY
Logging, fishing, textile manufacturing, tourism, higher education

CITIES
Lewiston, 35,690; Bangor, 31,473; Auburn, 23,203; Presque Isle, 9,511

NOTABLE
Author Stephen King lives in Bangor; Abraham Lincoln's first vice president, Hannibal Hamlin, was born in Paris Hill; E.B. White, author of "Charlotte's Web," lived on a farm in North Brooklin.

MARYLAND

Gov. Robert L. Ehrlich Jr. (R)

First elected: 2002
Length of term: 4 years
Term expires: 1/07
Salary: $135,000
Phone: (410) 974-3901
Hometown: Timonium
Born: Nov. 25, 1957; Baltimore, Md.
Religion: Methodist
Family: Wife, Kendel Sibiski Ehrlich; one child
Education: Princeton U., A.B. 1979; Wake Forest U., J.D. 1982
Career: Lawyer
Political highlights: Md. House, 1987-95; U.S. House, 1995-2003
Election results:

2002 GENERAL		
Robert L. Ehrlich Jr. (R)	879,592	51.6%
Kathleen Kennedy Townsend (D)	813,422	47.7%

Lt. Gov. Michael S. Steele (R)

First elected: 2002
Length of term: 4 years
Term expires: 1/07
Salary: $112,000
Phone: (410) 974-2804

STATE LEGISLATURE

General Assembly: Meets January-April
House: 141 members, 4-year terms
2003 breakdown: 43R, 98D; 94 men, 47 women
Salary: $34,500
Phone: (410) 841-3700
Senate: 47 members, 4-year terms
2003 breakdown: 14R, 33D; 32 men, 15 women
Salary: $34,500
Phone: (410) 841-3800

STATE TERM LIMITS

Governor: 2 terms
Senate: No
House: No

URBAN STATISTICS

CITY	POPULATION
Baltimore	651,154
Frederick	52,767
Gaithersburg	52,613
Bowie	50,269
Rockville	47,388

REGISTERED VOTERS

Democrat	56%
Republican	30%
Other	14%

POPULATION

2002 population (est.)	5,458,137
2000 population	5,296,486
1990 population	4,781,468
Percent change (1990-2000)	+10.8%
Rank among states (2002)	18
Median age	36
Born in state	49.3%
Foreign born	9.8%
Violent crime rate	787/100,000
Poverty level	8.5%
Federal workers	151,044
Military	50,137

REDISTRICTING

Maryland retained its eight House seats in reapportionment. The state legislature drew a new map, which the governor signed on May 6, 2002.

MISCELLANEOUS

Web: www.state.md.us
Capital: Annapolis

STATE ELECTION OFFICIAL
(410) 269-2840

DEMOCRATIC HEADQUARTERS
(410) 280-8818

REPUBLICAN HEADQUARTERS
(410) 269-0113

District Statistics

DIST.	2000 VOTE FOR PRESIDENT BUSH	GORE	NADER	WHITE	BLACK	ASIAN	HISP	MEDIAN INCOME	WHITE COLLAR	BLUE COLLAR	SERVICE INDUSTRY	OVER 64	UNDER 18	COLLEGE EDUCATION	RURAL	SQ. MILES
1	57%	40%	3%	85%	11%	1%	2%	$51,918	63%	23%	14%	13%	25%	27%	36%	3,653
2	41	57	2	66	27	2	2	$44,309	61	23	15	12	26	20	2	355
3	41	56	3	76	16	3	3	$52,906	72	16	12	13	23	37	1	293
4	21	77	2	28	57	6	8	$57,727	71	15	14	7	28	33	2	315
5	41	57	2	60	30	4	3	$62,661	68	19	13	9	26	29	25	1,504
6	61	36	3	92	5	1	1	$50,957	61	24	14	12	26	24	39	3,062
7	24	73	3	34	59	4	2	$38,885	67	16	17	12	26	28	5	294
8	31	66	3	56	16	11	14	$68,306	77	11	12	12	24	54	1	297
STATE	40	56	3	62	28	4	4	$52,868	68	18	14	11	26	31	14	9,774
U.S.	47.9	48.4	3	69	12	4	13	$41,994	60	25	15	12	26	24	21	3,537,438

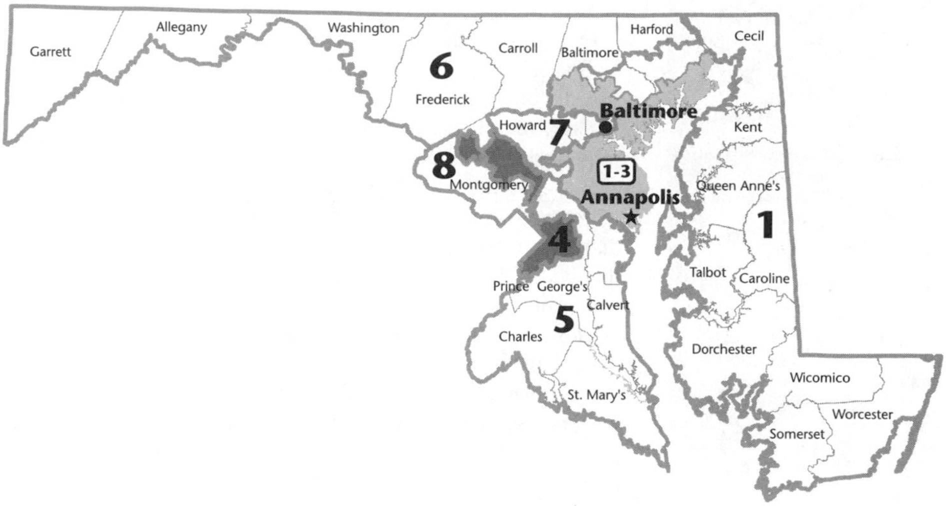
Garrett
Allegany
Washington
Carroll
Harford
Cecil
Baltimore
6
Frederick
Baltimore
Howard
7
Kent
8
Montgomery
1-3
Annapolis
Queen Anne's
1
4
Talbot
Caroline
Prince George's
Calvert
5
Charles
Dorchester
Wicomico
St. Mary's
Worcester
Somerset

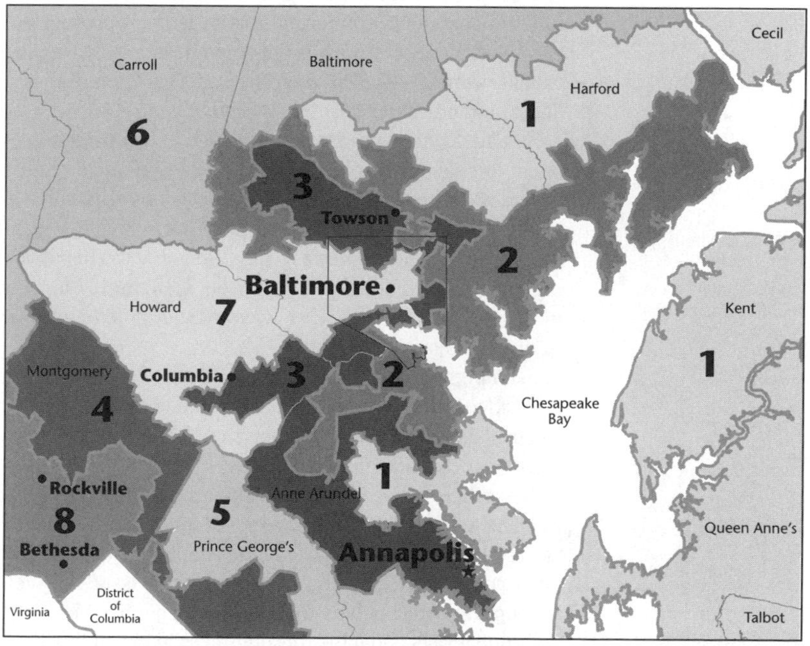
Cecil
Carroll
Baltimore
Harford
1
6
3
Towson
2
Baltimore
Kent
Howard
7
1
Montgomery
Columbia
3
2
4
Chesapeake
Bay
1
Rockville
Anne Arundel
5
8
Queen Anne's
Bethesda
Prince George's
Annapolis
District
of
Columbia
Virginia
Talbot

Sen. Paul S. Sarbanes (D)

CAPITOL OFFICE
224-4524
senator@sarbanes.senate.gov
sarbanes.senate.gov
309 Hart 20510-2002; fax 224-1651

COMMITTEES
Banking, Housing & Urban Affairs - ranking member
Budget
Foreign Relations
Joint Economic

HOMETOWN
Baltimore

BORN
Feb. 3, 1933, Salisbury, Md.

RELIGION
Greek Orthodox

FAMILY
Wife, Christine Sarbanes; three children

EDUCATION
Princeton U., A.B. 1954 (public & international affairs); Oxford U., B.A. 1957 (Rhodes scholar); Harvard U., LL.B. 1960

CAREER
Lawyer; White House aide

POLITICAL HIGHLIGHTS
Md. House, 1967-71; U.S. House, 1971-77

ELECTION RESULTS

2000 GENERAL		
Paul S. Sarbanes (D)	1,230,013	63.2%
Paul Rappaport (R)	715,178	36.7%
2000 PRIMARY		
Paul S. Sarbanes (D)	384,748	83.2%
George English (D)	45,984	10.0%
Sidney Altman (D)	31,502	6.8%

PREVIOUS WINNING PERCENTAGES
1994 (59%); 1988 (62%); 1982 (64%); 1976 (57%); 1974 House Election (84%); 1972 House Election (70%); 1970 House Election (70%)

Elected 1976; 5th term

On the eve of the Senate Banking Committee debate on corporate fraud legislation in 2002, it seemed certain that Sarbanes, the panel chairman, would at best win only narrow party-line approval for his proposals. Momentum for a tough regulatory bill was fading, and top Republicans on the panel were working with business lobbyists to scuttle the measure altogether.

But legislation was approved that day, 17-4, after Sarbanes did something increasingly rare in the modern Congress. Not only did he strike a late-night deal by reaching across the aisle, but he also did so with such stealth that both K Street and GOP leaders were taken by surprise. The maneuver epitomizes Sarbanes, whom the Baltimore Sun has described as the "silver fox," a cautious man who has learned how to get things done in Congress "quietly but with shrewd skillfulness."

As it turned out, Sarbanes' timing was accidentally impeccable. A week later, telecommunications giant WorldCom Inc. announced that it had misstated $3.9 billion in costs as expenses, a revelation that transformed his bill into one of the marquee, must-pass bills of the 107th Congress. After decades of obscure toil on Capitol Hill, Sarbanes suddenly found himself the darling of the television talk show circuit. He essentially dictated terms to Republicans during abbreviated conference negotiations, and the statute that was enacted stands as the most sweeping overhaul of securities law since the Great Depression.

One of the Senate's most penetrating intellects, Sarbanes has the skills to leave opponents sputtering, but he is not a provocateur. He generally shows little appetite for legislative gamesmanship, relying instead on an expansive mind — he has degrees from Princeton, Harvard and Oxford — and a methodical approach to policymaking.

Sarbanes often appears disinterested in campaigning, comes off as diffident in dealing with his colleagues, can be prickly in his relations with advocacy groups and usually has little use for the attention of reporters. But he is nonetheless a straightforward Democratic vote, a signature advantage in a state with nearly twice as many Democrats as Republicans, and he gets high marks from liberal interest groups. In the 107th, he was the second-most loyal Senate Democrat on votes that pitted a majority of one party against a majority of the other.

Seemingly comfortable with his detached manner, Maryland voters respond to his efforts on their behalf — to keep federal jobs in the state, protect the Chesapeake Bay, transform public housing programs and keep personal financial information private.

Nevertheless, Sarbanes' painstaking approach to analyzing issues and his reticent style have frustrated some of his admirers, who feel that the Senate's seventh-most-senior Democrat should be more of a leader. Instead, he often vexes colleagues by targeting minor issues for zealous attention, leading some to conclude that his judgment on the importance of subjects does not always equal his thoroughness in examining them.

While other congressional committee chairmen were hauling business executives under the TV lights in early 2002 to testify about accounting scandals, Sarbanes embarked on a painstaking series of 10 hearings on arcane issues surrounding corporate governance and accounting. Before the WorldCom scandal broke, backers of stringent new corporate regulations fretted that he was squandering political momentum.

Other than the corporate fraud bill, Sarbanes scored few legislative accomplishments in his 18 months as Banking chairman. After the Sept. 11, 2001, terrorist attacks, he quickly moved an anti-money-laundering bill through the committee and into law. Sarbanes also oversaw the reauthorization of the Export-Import Bank. But he stayed in the background on legislation to create a federal terrorism insurance program, allowing other Senate Democrats to take the lead on the bill.

As Banking chairman, Sarbanes took little substantive action on his own longstanding priorities, such as financial privacy and legislation to curb so-called predatory mortgage lending to low-income homebuyers. And it is unclear how he will seek to advance his personal agenda now that he is the top-ranking minority member of the panel in the 108th Congress.

From that position in the 106th Congress, Sarbanes helped the Clinton administration win concessions from the GOP on the path to enacting an overhaul of the laws governing the nation's financial services industry. In particular, he helped fight a Republican-led attempt to exempt small rural banks from the Community Reinvestment Act, a law aimed at forcing banks to make loans in poor neighborhoods.

Politically, Democratic leaders turn to Sarbanes when they need a spokesman who can hold up against partisan attack: In 1987, he was selected for the panel investigating the Iran-contra arms-for-hostages scandal. In 1995, he was the top Democrat on the Senate Whitewater Committee, where he challenged Republican Alfonse M. D'Amato of New York at every opportunity. He argued that the committee hearings into the death of Deputy White House Counsel Vincent W. Foster Jr. and the conduct of the White House staff produced no evidence of wrongdoing.

He also played a critical role in the 1974 proceedings on the impeachment of President Nixon. As a junior member of the House Judiciary Committee, Sarbanes drafted its most important article of impeachment, charging the president with obstruction of justice.

In 1986, Sarbanes launched the first filibuster of his career over legislation that would have transferred control over two of the major airports serving Washington, D.C., from the federal government to a regional authority. Marylanders saw the bill as an economic threat to their state's major airport, Baltimore-Washington International. Sarbanes talked for five days, with an uncharacteristic enthusiasm that won concessions aimed at providing some protection for Maryland's interests.

The son of Greek immigrant parents, Sarbanes grew up on Maryland's Eastern Shore, attended Princeton and won a Rhodes scholarship to Oxford. After graduating from Harvard Law School in 1960 — where he befriended Michael S. Dukakis, the 1988 Democratic presidential nominee — Sarbanes practiced law briefly before jumping into public life as an administrative assistant in President Kennedy's Council of Economic Advisers. He practiced law again and won a state House seat in 1966.

Running as an anti-war, anti-machine insurgent, Sarbanes headed for Congress in 1970 by winning a primary challenge to Democratic Rep. George H. Fallon, the aging chairman of the Public Works Committee, who had represented Baltimore in the House for 13 terms. With Democrats enjoying a nearly 4-to-1 registration advantage in the multiethnic 4th District, Sarbanes won the seat with ease in the fall.

He moved to the Senate by unseating one-term Republican J. Glenn Beall Jr. in 1976. Republicans put Sarbanes on their 1982 target list, but he raised money aggressively and state GOP leaders failed to enlist a big-name challenger. In 1988, he trounced Alan L. Keyes, a former State Department official and more recently a presidential candidate. In 1994, Sarbanes defeated national GOP chairman Bill Brock; and in 2000, he triumphed easily over Republican attorney Paul Rappaport.

KEY VOTES

2002

- Yes Pass farm bill reversing crop subsidy limits
- No Postpone tougher automobile fuel efficiency standards
- Yes Overhaul campaign finance law; ban "soft money" and restrict advocacy advertising
- Yes Set federal election standards
- No Support oil drilling in Arctic National Wildlife Refuge
- No Revive fast-track procedures for trade agreements
- Yes Create federal insurance coverage for catastrophic terrorist losses
- Yes Tighten federal accounting and corporate governance regulation
- Yes Advance bipartisan Medicare prescription drug plan
- Yes Create independent Sept. 11 commission
- Yes Back Democratic Homeland Security Department proposal
- No Authorize war against Iraq

2001

- No Confirm John Ashcroft as attorney general
- No Nullify Clinton Labor Department ergonomics rule
- No Cut taxes by $1.35 trillion through fiscal 2011
- Yes Pass Democratic bill to bolster rights of patients in managed-care plans
- No Permit a new round of military base closings
- Yes Expand law enforcement power to investigate suspected terrorists

CQ VOTE STUDIES

	PARTY UNITY		PRESIDENTIAL SUPPORT	
	Support	Oppose	Support	Oppose
2002	98%	2%	65%	35%
2001	99%	1%	63%	37%
2000	99%	1%	95%	5%
1999	97%	3%	86%	14%
1998	99%	1%	92%	8%
1997	98%	2%	87%	13%
1996	94%	6%	90%	10%
1995	96%	4%	90%	10%
1994	98%	2%	95%	5%
1993	98%	2%	96%	4%

INTEREST GROUPS

	AFL-CIO	ADA	CCUS	ACU
2002	100%	100%	40%	0%
2001	100%	95%	36%	8%
2000	88%	95%	40%	12%
1999	100%	100%	35%	4%
1998	100%	95%	44%	4%
1997	100%	100%	30%	0%
1996	100%	95%	23%	0%
1995	100%	100%	21%	0%
1994	88%	95%	20%	0%
1993	91%	95%	18%	0%

Sen. Barbara A. Mikulski (D)

CAPITOL OFFICE
224-4654
mikulski.senate.gov
709 Hart 20510-2003; fax 224-8858

COMMITTEES
Appropriations
Health, Education, Labor & Pensions
Select Intelligence

HOMETOWN
Baltimore

BORN
July 20, 1936, Baltimore, Md.

RELIGION
Roman Catholic

FAMILY
Single

EDUCATION
Mount Saint Agnes College, B.A. 1958 (sociology); U. of Maryland, M.S.W. 1965

CAREER
Social worker

POLITICAL HIGHLIGHTS
Baltimore City Council, 1971-77; Democratic nominee for U.S. Senate, 1974; U.S. House, 1977-87

ELECTION RESULTS

1998 GENERAL		
Barbara A. Mikulski (D)	1,062,810	70.5%
Ross Z. Pierpont (R)	444,637	29.5%
1998 PRIMARY		
Barbara A. Mikulski (D)	349,382	84.4%
Ann L. Mallory (D)	43,120	10.4%
Kauko H. Kokkonen (D)	21,658	5.2%

PREVIOUS WINNING PERCENTAGES
1992 (71%); 1986 (61%); 1984 House Election (68%); 1982 House Election (74%); 1980 House Election (76%); 1978 House Election (100%); 1976 House Election (75%)

Elected 1986; 3rd term

As the Senate's senior woman, Mikulski takes seriously her role in mentoring the women who have come after her. In that den mother role, she reveals a side of her personality that seems a closer match to her early days as a social worker in Baltimore than her dominant image as a feisty, blue-collar, partisan, liberal lawmaker.

But there is a hard-edged purpose to the women's bonding — to get beyond the good intentions that spurred them to get involved in public life and to develop strategies to get things accomplished now that they are in the Senate.

And that's what Mikulski has done. She first got involved in public life in a neighborhood battle to stop a highway project. At one point, she recalls, she jumped on a table and gave a fiery speech and everyone cheered.

But, she says, talk is not enough — there also has to be a plan, to "operationalize good intentions." "If you only talk and don't produce . . . you contribute to the cynicism," she wrote in "Nine and Counting," a collaborative book written by the nine women serving in the Senate in 2000.

That foray into public life was instructive: "When I was a social worker, I wanted to help people, but it was difficult to do because I didn't have all of the resources I wanted. Now I am a social worker with power."

Mikulski is an unabashed "blue collar" liberal who rarely shies away from the straightforward approach. She does not suffer fools easily, and while she is sometimes criticized for being brusque — she is known for being a particularly demanding boss, even within a universe of demanding bosses at the Capitol — even critics admit that she does well at getting results. In a Washingtonian magazine poll, she was listed among the "meanest" lawmakers, but the same magazine also called her, in its September 2001 issue, one of the 100 most powerful women in Washington. She is now the fourth-longest-serving woman in congressional history.

Mikulski is the secretary of the Senate Democratic Conference, and for more than a decade now she has been the top Democrat on the Appropriations subcommittee that drafts the annual spending bill that funds federal housing, veterans, space, environment and science programs. She chaired the panel from 1989 through 1994 and for the final 18 months of the 107th Congress, when the Democrats had control of the chamber.

She is able to sprinkle visible pockets of money for Maryland throughout the annual VA-HUD spending bill, including economic development grants, money for Baltimore's sewer system and various Chesapeake Bay cleanup projects. The subcommittee bill also funds NASA, and Mikulski has been an ardent defender of the space program.

Mikulski works with federal housing officials to protect Baltimore residents from property "flipping," in which speculators buy homes, often in distressed neighborhoods, make cosmetic repairs, and quickly sell the houses to unsuspecting buyers at inflated prices. She received some criticism in 2002 when she voted against an increase in automobile fuel economy standards in an effort to help keep open a marginal General Motors plant in Baltimore.

Mikulski also does what she can for the steel industry, pushing for protections against subsidized imports of foreign steel. She also wants additional medical insurance coverage for domestic steelworkers who have recently retired from financially strapped companies.

The senator's record has rarely disappointed women's groups. She is a strong supporter of abortion rights and has tried to ensure that federal health care plans provide abortion coverage. She helped push to enactment the 1990 law that created the women's health research office at the National Institutes of Health. And in 1995, she was the first member of the Ethics Committee to call for public hearings on sexual harassment allegations against Republican Bob Packwood of Oregon, a turning point in a three-year case that ultimately led to Packwood's resignation from the Senate.

Increased federal funding for research on women's health issues and diseases, such as Alzheimer's, also is important to Mikulski. In the 107th, she played a key role in legislation to address a national shortage of nurses. She also continued her efforts to include birth control coverage in government health insurance plans.

From the time she arrived in 1987 until 1992, Mikulski and Republican Nancy Landon Kassebaum of Kansas were the only two women in the Senate. As the ranks jumped to five in 1993, to nine in 1999 and to 14 in 2003, Mikulski has offered the new women her own introductory seminars and dispensed advice on everything from organizing their offices to setting long-term goals. In "Nine and Counting," Mikulski recalls: "I didn't come to politics by the traditional male route, being in a nice law firm or belonging to the right clubs. Like most of the women I've known in politics, I got involved because I saw a community need."

Mikulski grew up in the working-class east Baltimore neighborhood of Highlandtown. Her parents ran a grocery store — Willy's Market — across the street from their row house. Nearby, her Polish immigrant grandmother operated a bakery legendary for its jelly doughnuts and raisin bread.

Inspired by a movie about Marie Curie, Mikulski decided to become a chemist. But reality set in when she got to college: "I got a C in chemistry and an A in social sciences. I decided that I would go with my strengths." She became a social worker, earning a master's degree in 1965. Parts of her neighborhood were torched in anger after the 1968 assassination of the Rev. Martin Luther King Jr. As a social worker, Mikulski delivered food to the needy during the riots, sometimes by riding atop a tank.

She then was involved in what became a multiethnic, multiracial fight against a freeway that would have leveled several city neighborhoods. Building on the successful battle against the highway, Mikulski won a city council seat in 1971 and became prominent in the feminist movement.

In the post-Watergate election of 1974, she took 43 percent in a Senate challenge to the heavily favored incumbent Republican, Charles McC. Mathias Jr. That race positioned her well for 1976, when Democrat Paul S. Sarbanes gave up his seat as Baltimore's congressman to run his successful initial campaign for the Senate. She won the seat and served five terms in the House, where, from her seat on the Energy and Commerce Committee, she was known as a champion of consumer causes.

She also attracted notice on the national political scene, including some support for her selection as Walter F. Mondale's running mate in 1984; the nod went to another congresswoman, New York's Geraldine Ferraro.

Mikulski won her Senate seat in 1986, when Mathias retired. She easily defeated Rep. Michael D. Barnes and outgoing Gov. Harry R. Hughes in the primary. Republicans nominated conservative Linda Chavez, a staff director of the U.S. Commission on Civil Rights under President Reagan. Mikulski won by 22 percentage points, then followed up with 40-plus point victories in both 1992 (over black conservative activist Alan L. Keyes) and 1998.

Mikulski has teamed with writer Marylouise Oates to pen two mystery novels, both featuring Eleanor Gorzack, a Pennsylvania senator. When Gorzack is appointed to the Senate after her husband's death, she seeks the counsel of Hilda Mendelssohn, a more-senior Senate colleague. The advice she receives sounds like an introductory seminar offered by Mikulski.

KEY VOTES

2002

Yes	Pass farm bill reversing crop subsidy limits
Yes	Postpone tougher automobile fuel efficiency standards
Yes	Overhaul campaign finance law; ban "soft money" and restrict advocacy advertising
Yes	Set federal election standards
No	Support oil drilling in Arctic National Wildlife Refuge
No	Revive fast-track procedures for trade agreements
Yes	Create federal insurance coverage for catastrophic terrorist losses
Yes	Tighten federal accounting and corporate governance regulation
Yes	Advance bipartisan Medicare prescription drug plan
Yes	Create independent Sept. 11 commission
Yes	Back Democratic Homeland Security Department proposal
No	Authorize war against Iraq

2001

No	Confirm John Ashcroft as attorney general
No	Nullify Clinton Labor Department ergonomics rule
No	Cut taxes by $1.35 trillion through fiscal 2011
Yes	Pass Democratic bill to bolster rights of patients in managed-care plans
No	Permit a new round of military base closings
Yes	Expand law enforcement power to investigate suspected terrorists

CQ VOTE STUDIES

	PARTY UNITY		PRESIDENTIAL SUPPORT	
	Support	Oppose	Support	Oppose
2002	96%	4%	68%	32%
2001	98%	2%	66%	34%
2000	97%	3%	92%	8%
1999	96%	4%	86%	14%
1998	97%	3%	91%	9%
1997	92%	8%	91%	9%
1996	92%	8%	90%	10%
1995	87%	13%	89%	11%
1994	90%	10%	93%	7%
1993	92%	8%	95%	5%

INTEREST GROUPS

	AFL-CIO	ADA	CCUS	ACU
2002	100%	100%	47%	0%
2001	100%	95%	43%	12%
2000	88%	95%	46%	8%
1999	89%	100%	59%	4%
1998	100%	90%	53%	4%
1997	86%	95%	44%	4%
1996	86%	95%	23%	0%
1995	100%	90%	39%	4%
1994	75%	85%	33%	0%
1993	100%	85%	27%	4%

Rep. Wayne T. Gilchrest (R)

CAPITOL OFFICE
225-5311
www.house.gov/gilchrest
2245 Rayburn 20515-2001; fax 225-0254

COMMITTEES
Resources
(Fisheries Conservation, Wildlife & Oceans - chairman)
Science
Transportation & Infrastructure

HOMETOWN
Kennedyville

BORN
April 15, 1946, Rahway, N.J.

RELIGION
Methodist

FAMILY
Wife, Barbara Gilchrest; three children

EDUCATION
Wesley College, A.A. 1971; Delaware State U., B.A. 1973 (history); Loyola College (Md.), attended 1990

MILITARY SERVICE
Marine Corps, 1964-68

CAREER
High school teacher

POLITICAL HIGHLIGHTS
Republican nominee for U.S. House, 1988

ELECTION RESULTS

2002 GENERAL		
Wayne T. Gilchrest (R)	192,004	76.7%
Ann D. Tamlyn (D)	57,986	23.2%
2002 PRIMARY		
Wayne T. Gilchrest (R)	35,599	60.0%
Dave Fischer (R)	21,524	36.3%
Bradlyn McClanahan (R)	2,185	3.7%
2000 GENERAL		
Wayne T. Gilchrest (R)	165,293	64.4%
Bennett Bozman (D)	91,022	35.5%

PREVIOUS WINNING PERCENTAGES
1998 (69%); 1996 (62%); 1994 (68%); 1992 (51%); 1990 (57%)

Elected 1990; 7th term

Look for the guy on Capitol Hill who seems the most like your high school principal, and you most likely will have found Gilchrest, a quiet and quirky Republican who has established a reputation as one of his party's leading environmentalists in Congress.

An avid outdoorsman who makes no secret of the fact that he prefers wandering the wilderness to strolling the halls of the Capitol, Gilchrest seems almost entirely without affectation. In his first dozen years in Congress, the former public school teacher and house painter demonstrated he was willing to defy his party on some issues — he has favored gun control and abortion rights, and champions environmental regulation — while hewing to conservative principles on fiscal policy and education.

His wide-eyed demeanor, wrinkled shirts and sometimes bent or broken eyeglasses all convey the image of a man who stumbled into public life and is a little bewildered to find that he is still there. He refers to himself as an "accidental" congressman. Still, Gilchrest has amassed enough policy expertise and seniority to make up for his apparent lack of interest in political maneuvering. He was sufficiently aware of the dynamics within his own caucus that he did not enter the race to chair the Resources Committee in the 108th Congress; his environmental views left him no prospect of winning.

Instead, he retained for a second term the chairmanship of the Fisheries Conservation, Wildlife and Oceans Subcommittee — a forum for addressing his top priority, the preservation of the Chesapeake Bay wetlands and waterways that give the 1st District its extraordinary shape.

When the 107th Congress debated the farm bill, Gilchrest banded together with environmentalists from both parties to try to divert billions of dollars from commodity subsidy payments into conservation programs, such as those that pay farmers to idle environmentally sensitive land and to protect wildlife and wetlands. The effort was unsuccessful, but it was a watershed moment nonetheless: It marked the first time in years that suburban and Northeastern lawmakers had worked so actively and come so close to shaping agriculture policy against the wishes of Farm Belt lawmakers.

Gilchrest did come away from the 2002 farm bill with an important parochial victory: a federal pilot program that will send agricultural conservation funding to the most environmentally and economically sensitive land on the Chesapeake's eastern Delmarva Peninsula.

In the 106th, he won approval of legislation to restore 1 million acres of habitat in estuaries such as the Chesapeake. Gilchrest also has consistently fought attempts by GOP conservatives to scale back substantially the 1973 Endangered Species Act. But instead of always favoring environmental controls, Gilchrest says he likes to seek practical solutions that take economic interests into account. He told the Baltimore Sun, "Somebody has to stand up for the critters," at a time when GOP environmental policy is mostly the handiwork of deregulatory lawmakers from the West.

Gilchrest is not afraid to challenge GOP leaders. He was one of only about two dozen House Republicans who initially signed on to a bipartisan health care initiative in 1999 allowing patients to sue their health plans for coverage decisions. Breaking with the bulk of national Republican figures, he backed John McCain for the GOP presidential nomination in 2000 and chaired the Arizona senator's campaign in Maryland. Both are Vietnam veterans, and Gilchrest lauded McCain for "serving his country and standing on principle." In the 107th, Gilchrest voted against President Bush 27 percent of the time, more often than all but eight other House Republicans.

Born in New Jersey, Gilchrest joined the Marine Corps right out of high school. He plays down the 1967 battle that won him the Bronze Star and the chest and shoulder wound that earned him a Purple Heart, portraying his conduct as more foolhardy than brave. He attended several colleges, mixing in a job as a chicken plucker in Maine and studying rural poverty in Kentucky. After graduating from Delaware State University, he held a series of teaching jobs, ending up at Kent County High School on Maryland's Eastern Shore in 1979.

Gilchrest did two stints with the Forest Service in Idaho and supplemented his teacher's income by moonlighting as a house painter. When he first ran for the House in 1988, he rushed to Annapolis in paint-covered clothes to file for election after he read in a newspaper that the GOP was having trouble finding a candidate.

In addition to his moderate environmental views, Gilchrest has voted for gun control measures on a number of occasions, and he supports abortion rights. He backed the campaign finance law of 2002 that was ardently opposed by the Republican leadership.

But Gilchrest votes with the conservative majority on labor issues, and despite his background as a public school teacher he supports conservatives' push to give parents taxpayer-financed vouchers to pay for private school education. He says competition will force public schools to improve.

He lost his first bid for Congress against Rep. Roy Dyson, a conservative Democrat. But he won their 1990 rematch with ease. Dyson had been weakened by reports of ties to a Pentagon procurement scandal and revelations that, despite his hawkish stance on military matters, he had been a conscientious objector during the Vietnam War.

Gilchrest's only general-election scare was two years later, when redistricting put him in a contest against three-term Democratic Rep. Tom McMillan, a basketball star with the University of Maryland, the U.S. Olympic team and the Washington Bullets. Portraying McMillen as a rich Washington insider and himself as an average guy, Gilchrest won with 51 percent.

In 2002, attorney David Fischer captured 36 percent of the Republican primary vote against Gilchrest with the backing of the conservative Club for Growth — one of the first forays of the group in attempting to unseat a moderate incumbent Republican. Gilchrest's campaign was complicated by his policy of not accepting money from political action committees or from donors outside Maryland.

KEY VOTES

2002

- Yes Overhaul campaign finance law; ban "soft money" and restrict advocacy advertising
- Yes Back Bush's defense budget increase
- Yes Extend 1996 welfare law
- Yes Adopt Bush's discretionary spending limit
- Yes Pass GOP Medicare prescription drug plan
- Yes Create independent Sept. 11 commission
- No Extend union protections to Homeland Security Department employees
- Yes Revive fast-track procedures for trade agreements
- Yes Authorize war against Iraq
- Yes Advance bankruptcy overhaul opposed by abortion opponents

2001

- Yes Nullify Clinton Labor Department ergonomics rule
- Yes Cut taxes by $1.35 trillion through fiscal 2011
- Yes Maintain ban on oil drilling in Arctic National Wildlife Refuge
- Yes Approve Bush proposal to limit managed-care plan liability for coverage decisions
- Yes Divert money from crop subsidy payments to land conservation
- Yes Expand law enforcement power to investigate suspected terrorists

CQ VOTE STUDIES

	PARTY UNITY		PRESIDENTIAL SUPPORT	
	Support	Oppose	Support	Oppose
2002	86%	14%	80%	20%
2001	86%	14%	67%	33%
2000	79%	21%	50%	50%
1999	72%	28%	41%	59%
1998	71%	29%	38%	62%

INTEREST GROUPS

	AFL-CIO	ADA	CCUS	ACU
2002	13%	10%	94%	78%
2001	17%	25%	87%	48%
2000	20%	15%	80%	58%
1999	22%	50%	72%	52%
1998	20%	35%	89%	44%

MARYLAND 1

East — Eastern Shore, part of Anne Arundel County

The 1st includes the rural counties of the Eastern Shore and, across the Chesapeake Bay, some of the fast-growing suburbs of Anne Arundel County. It also moves across the Susquehanna River in the northeastern part of the state and claims large chunks of Harford County, including Bel Air, and Baltimore County.

Although the district's regions are different in many ways, they share a conservative lean that benefits Republicans. The 1st supported the Republican presidential candidate in 1992, 1996 and 2000. During redistricting following the 2000 census, some GOP-leaning voters were pushed into the 1st from the 2nd and 3rd districts.

The Eastern Shore, which holds about three-fifths of the district's population, has a steady economic grounding in agriculture. The central, more rural, part of the Eastern Shore is GOP heartland. The northern counties, closer to Baltimore and Philadelphia, and southern counties, with larger black and working-class populations, are more Democratic. Ocean City is a popular beach town that swells with visitors during the summer months.

Across the bay, some conservative parts of Anne Arundel County remain in the district. Annapolis, the Democratic-leaning state capital, was removed during redistricting. Part of Baltimore's fast-growing, GOP-leaning northern suburbs also are included in the district.

MAJOR INDUSTRY

Agriculture, manufacturing, tourism

MILITARY BASES

U.S. Naval Academy/Annapolis Naval Station, 1,010 military, 1,599 civilian (1999) (shared with 3rd District)

CITIES

Bel Air South (unincorporated) (pt.), 35,353; Severna Park (unincorporated) (pt.), 26,646; Bel Air North (unincorporated) (pt.), 25,372; Salisbury, 23,743; Arnold (unincorporated), 23,422

NOTABLE

Wild ponies can be seen roaming Assateague Island, a barrier island on the Atlantic Ocean; Residents of Smith Island, which calls itself Maryland's only inhabited offshore island in the Chesapeake Bay, speak an Elizabethan English-based dialect.

Rep. C.A. Dutch Ruppersberger (D)

Elected 2002; 1st term

Ruppersberger must use a different set of political skills to thrive as a lawmaker after eight years as the powerful executive of Maryland's populous Baltimore County. But he has made major adjustments before.

A former U.S. lacrosse team member, Ruppersberger dates the dawning of his political consciousness to a late-night journey to the Capitol to pay his respects as assassinated President Kennedy lay in state. Twelve years later, a near-fatal car accident in 1975 prompted Ruppersberger, then a prosecutor, to run for office. He has said he devoted himself to public service at the bidding of a University of Maryland doctor who saved his life, and he has become a leading advocate for the university's Shock Trauma unit in Baltimore.

Ruppersberger lost a state Senate bid in 1978, but he went on to serve on the Baltimore County Council and was twice elected county executive. His major areas of focus included economic development and education.

Facing a term limit as county executive in 2002, Ruppersberger considered a run for governor but decided instead to seek the 2nd District seat being vacated by Republican Rep. Robert L. Ehrlich Jr., who was making his own gubernatorial bid.

In the redistricting process, the Democratic-controlled legislature reshaped the 2nd into a district favoring a Democrat — so much so that some observers dubbed it the "Dutch" district. Republicans countered by putting up popular former Rep. Helen Delich Bentley, who represented the 2nd from 1985 to 1995. But the remapping changes and Ruppersberger's well-known name helped the Democrat win by a margin of almost 9 percentage points.

Ruppersberger won appointment to the Intelligence Committee, a coup for the freshman whose district is home to the National Security Agency. He also has a seat on the Government Reform panel, and he was selected to represent GOP freshmen on the Democratic Steering Committee, which doles out committee assignments.

CAPITOL OFFICE
225-3061
www.house.gov/ruppersberger
1630 Longworth 20515-2002; fax 225-3094

COMMITTEES
Government Reform
Select Intelligence

HOMETOWN
Cockeysville

BORN
Jan. 31, 1946, Baltimore, Md.

RELIGION
Methodist

FAMILY
Wife, Kay Ruppersberger; two children

EDUCATION
U. of Maryland, attended 1963-67; U. of Baltimore, J.D. 1970

CAREER
Lawyer; county prosecutor

POLITICAL HIGHLIGHTS
Democratic nominee for Md. Senate, 1978; Baltimore County Council, 1985-94; Baltimore County executive, 1994-2002

ELECTION RESULTS

2002 GENERAL		
C.A. Dutch Ruppersberger (D)	105,718	54.2%
Helen Delich Bentley (R)	88,954	45.6%
2002 PRIMARY		
C.A. Dutch Ruppersberger (D)	32,967	50.3%
Oz Bengur (D)	23,729	36.2%
Kenneth T. Bosley (D)	5,104	7.8%
Brian Hollister Davis (D)	2,285	3.5%
James Edward DeLoach Jr. (D)	1,508	2.3%

MARYLAND 2

Part of Baltimore and suburbs – Dundalk, Essex

The 2nd includes northern and eastern parts of Baltimore, suburbs in most directions around the city and most of the territory east of Interstate 95 between Baltimore and the Susquehanna River.

Redrawn during redistricting following the 2000 census to increase Democratic strength, the 2nd ranges northeast from Baltimore along the Chesapeake Bay and south into Anne Arundel County, where it picks up Baltimore-Washington International Airport and Fort George G. Meade (including the National Security Agency). The district's northwest branch moves through the GOP-heavy northern suburbs and then hooks into largely African-American suburbs west of Baltimore, such as Randallstown. Blacks make up 27 percent of the 2nd's population.

In eastern Baltimore County, the blue-collar industrial sector — including Dundalk — has struggled with unemployment. But Bethlehem Steel, one of the county's major employers, opened a new mill in 2000 at its Sparrows Point complex, which is seen as a valuable asset for the area's economy. A General Motors plant in White Marsh employs several hundred people.

The 2nd gave Al Gore 57 percent of its vote in the 2000 presidential election. But many Democrats in the Baltimore suburbs have favored GOP candidates in past House races.

MAJOR INDUSTRY
Manufacturing, defense, product distribution

MILITARY BASES
Fort George G. Meade (Army), 10,377 military, 17,177 civilian; Aberdeen Proving Ground (Army), 2,680 military, 5,096 civilian (2001)

CITIES
Baltimore (pt.), 111,715; Dundalk (unincorporated), 62,306

NOTABLE
The stadium complex in Aberdeen is home to Cal Ripken Baseball, a youth division of the amateur Babe Ruth League.

Rep. Benjamin L. Cardin (D)

CAPITOL OFFICE
225-4016
rep.cardin@mail.house.gov
www.house.gov/cardin
2207 Rayburn 20515-2003; fax 225-9219

COMMITTEES
Ways & Means
Select Homeland Security

HOMETOWN
Baltimore

BORN
Oct. 5, 1943, Baltimore, Md.

RELIGION
Jewish

FAMILY
Wife, Myrna Edelman Cardin; two children

EDUCATION
U. of Pittsburgh, B.A. 1964 (economics); U. of Maryland, LL.B. 1967

CAREER
Lawyer

POLITICAL HIGHLIGHTS
Md. House, 1967-87 (Speaker, 1979-87)

ELECTION RESULTS

2002 GENERAL		
Benjamin L. Cardin (D)	145,589	65.7%
Scott Alan Conwell (R)	75,721	34.2%
2002 PRIMARY		
Benjamin L. Cardin (D)	62,938	90.0%
John Rea (D)	6,986	10.0%
2000 GENERAL		
Benjamin L. Cardin (D)	169,347	75.7%
Colin Harby (R)	53,827	24.1%

PREVIOUS WINNING PERCENTAGES
1998 (78%); 1996 (67%); 1994 (71%); 1992 (74%); 1990 (70%); 1988 (73%); 1986 (79%)

Elected 1986; 9th term

Both his father and uncle held office in Maryland in the 1950s, and on the strength of his family name Cardin began his uninterrupted string of election victories one month after he turned 23. "I looked like I was about 12," he recalls.

But Cardin says he has "worked hard to warrant his seat ever since," and in Annapolis as well as Washington he has often done so on the most complex questions of the day. An acknowledged expert on such complicated issues as pension regulation and the Social Security system, he wears the label "policy wonk" as a badge of honor. And his appetite for policy discourse seems limitless: He listens to National Public Radio as he drives himself the 75 minutes from his home in Baltimore to the Capitol each morning.

His political philosophy is difficult to pigeonhole; Cardin characterizes himself as a fiscally conservative progressive. "I don't believe the private sector left to its own devices will clean our air and water. I believe in an active government, but I don't believe that we can violate basic discipline," he says. "I am for balancing the budget."

Still, he votes a relatively loyal Democratic line. He stands with his party on nine out of 10 party-line votes, and in the 107th Congress he opposed President Bush's wishes 65 percent of the time, more often than most other Democrats. The liberal Americans for Democratic Action gives him a lifetime rating of 88; the American Conservative Union rates him at 6.

At the same time, he works closely with Republicans on contentious issues, from tax and budget matters to the social policies of health care and welfare. Cardin has endured some partisan sniping along the way, particularly for the smooth statute-writing machine he has constructed with Republican Rob Portman of Ohio, the main conduit between the Bush White House and the offices of the House GOP leadership; their latest retirement savings proposal promises to be a top-tier bill in the 108th Congress.

Their first joint effort was on minor changes in the regulation of hospice care in 1993. Five years later, they teamed up to draft the language that formed the basis of the 1998 law overhauling the IRS, and since then they have been concentrating on the pension system; their package of incentives for retirement savings was the only major component of the 2001 tax law that was not proposed by Bush.

In the 106th Congress, Cardin teamed with another Republican, E. Clay Shaw Jr. of Florida, on a plan to allow some private investment of Social Security savings. That partnership irked Democrats, too, because it may have helped Shaw prevail in one of the tightest House races of 2000.

Still, there are many issues on which Cardin strongly disagrees with the Republican line. On the Ways and Means Committee, for example, he has argued against efforts to terminate the tax code, and he opposes establishing tax-sheltered education savings accounts that parents could use for private school expenses. He also has been a regular critic of the bulk of Bush's tax proposals.

Generally, Cardin takes a nuanced non-ideological approach to society's problems. On Social Security, for example, he wants to help younger Americans save for themselves to put less pressure on the dwindling trust fund. He thinks medical coverage could be extended to all by building on the current system of private health insurance.

In the 108th, he got a seat on the new Homeland Security Committee, where security at America's ports will be a top Cardin concern.

Organized labor has long been a force in Baltimore politics, but international commerce also plays a key role in the port city's economy. So Cardin walks a careful line on trade issues, trying to promote trade while guarding against the loss of U.S. jobs to lower-cost operations overseas. He voted to implement the North American Free Trade Agreement in 1993 and to create the World Trade Organization in 1994. He initially opposed the 2000 law permanently granting China normal trade status but eventually came on board, saying his concerns about that country's human rights record had been addressed. But he opposed the 2002 law granting the president fast-track authority to negotiate trade pacts that Congress cannot amend.

As an ethics committee member in the 104th, Cardin was the lead Democrat on a four-member panel that investigated alleged ethics violations by Speaker Newt Gingrich. He subsequently co-chaired a 12-member task force that recommended changes to the ethics process. Cardin voted against the final package, in part because it banned ethics complaints from outsiders unless they could obtain the sponsorship of a member of Congress.

Cardin keeps a close eye on home-state interests. He has had a hand in preserving the Coast Guard base at Curtis Bay and securing funds to restore Fort McHenry in Baltimore. He helped secure funding for Amtrak and development assistance for a light rail system in Baltimore.

Since he arrived in Annapolis in 1967, several months before he graduated first in his class at the University of Maryland Law School, Cardin has been known as someone who intellectualizes policy problems. While representing the white-collar, heavily Jewish precincts of northwest Baltimore, he earned a reputation as a master conciliator and a budgetary expert. By age 32, he was chairman of the state House Ways and Means Committee, and four years later he became the youngest speaker in the history of the House of Delegates. During his eight years in that job, he promoted extra spending on education and mass transit, and promoted bipartisan compromise on banking regulations and pension law.

Cardin initially hoped to run for governor in 1986, but when Baltimore Mayor William Donald Schaefer decided to seek the job (he won and served eight years) Cardin shifted his sights to the House seat that Barbara A. Mikulski was vacating to run for the Senate. He won in a rout, has done so ever since and remains a potent figure on the Maryland political stage. His flirtation with a 1998 gubernatorial candidacy had both the incumbent Democrat and his leading GOP challenger on edge. It was not the first time Cardin pondered a statewide campaign and, considering he was only 59 as the 108th Congress began, it may not be the last.

KEY VOTES

2002

Yes Overhaul campaign finance law; ban "soft money" and restrict advocacy advertising
Yes Back Bush's defense budget increase
No Extend 1996 welfare law
No Adopt Bush's discretionary spending limit
No Pass GOP Medicare prescription drug plan
Yes Create independent Sept. 11 commission
Yes Extend union protections to Homeland Security Department employees
No Revive fast-track procedures for trade agreements
No Authorize war against Iraq
No Advance bankruptcy overhaul opposed by abortion opponents

2001

No Nullify Clinton Labor Department ergonomics rule
No Cut taxes by $1.35 trillion through fiscal 2011
Yes Maintain ban on oil drilling in Arctic National Wildlife Refuge
No Approve Bush proposal to limit managed-care plan liability for coverage decisions
Yes Divert money from crop subsidy payments to land conservation
Yes Expand law enforcement power to investigate suspected terrorists

CQ VOTE STUDIES

	PARTY UNITY		PRESIDENTIAL SUPPORT	
	Support	Oppose	Support	Oppose
2002	90%	10%	35%	65%
2001	89%	11%	35%	65%
2000	92%	8%	94%	6%
1999	92%	8%	83%	17%
1998	91%	9%	78%	22%

INTEREST GROUPS

	AFL-CIO	ADA	CCUS	ACU
2002	100%	95%	55%	0%
2001	100%	100%	35%	4%
2000	90%	90%	42%	8%
1999	89%	100%	28%	0%
1998	100%	95%	25%	8%

MARYLAND 3

Part of Baltimore; eastern Columbia; Annapolis

Like a Z-shaped lightning bolt, the 3rd District flashes through three of Maryland's largest urban centers — Baltimore, Columbia and Annapolis.

Starting in the traditionally Jewish suburbs northwest of Baltimore, the district snakes east, then south, to pick up parts of northeastern Baltimore's suburbs and parts of downtown Baltimore, including Fells Point and the stadiums that house Baltimore's major-league sports teams: baseball's Orioles and football's Ravens. Many of eastern Baltimore's ethnic neighborhoods are included in the district, but it lost much of downtown to the neighboring 7th in redistricting following the 2000 census. The 3rd then twists south and west through suburban Arbutus and Elkridge on its way to the eastern part of Columbia. Finally, the district moves southeast toward Annapolis.

State and local governments provide employment in Annapolis, which is both the state capital and the Anne Arundel County seat, while technology, financial services and health care businesses push the economy of the Columbia area. Fort George G. Meade — including the National Security Agency — and Baltimore-Washington International Airport, which are both located in the neighboring 2nd District, attract defense-related companies to the region.

The district includes some GOP-leaning areas in Anne Arundel and Baltimore counties, including recently added Towson, but was designed to favor Democratic candidates for federal office.

MAJOR INDUSTRY
Government, technology, defense-related business

MILITARY BASES
U.S. Naval Academy/Annapolis Naval Station, 1,010 military, 1,599 civilian (1999) (shared with 1st District)

CITIES
Baltimore (pt.), 168,687; Columbia (unincorporated) (pt.), 40,311; Annapolis, 35,838; Pikesville (unincorporated), 29,123

NOTABLE
The Preakness Stakes, the second event in horse racing's Triple Crown, is held at Pimlico in northwestern Baltimore; Both of Maryland's senators, Democrats Paul S. Sarbanes and Barbara A. Mikulski, represented the 3rd before their election to the Senate.

Rep. Albert R. Wynn (D)

CAPITOL OFFICE
225-8699
www.house.gov/wynn
434 Cannon 20515-2004; fax 225-8714

COMMITTEES
Energy & Commerce

HOMETOWN
Mitchellville

BORN
Sept. 10, 1951, Philadelphia, Pa.

RELIGION
Baptist

FAMILY
Wife, Gaines Clore Wynn; one child, one stepchild

EDUCATION
U. of Pittsburgh, B.S. 1973 (political science); Howard U., attended 1973-74 (public administration); Georgetown U., J.D. 1977

CAREER
Lawyer

POLITICAL HIGHLIGHTS
Md. House, 1983-87; Md. Senate, 1987-93

ELECTION RESULTS

2002 GENERAL		
Albert R. Wynn (D)	131,644	78.6%
John B. Kimble (R)	34,890	20.8%
2002 PRIMARY		
Albert R. Wynn (D)	66,225	83.3%
Don Williams (D)	13,299	16.7%
2000 GENERAL		
Albert R. Wynn (D)	172,624	87.2%
John B. Kimble (R)	24,973	12.6%

PREVIOUS WINNING PERCENTAGES
1998 (86%); 1996 (85%); 1994 (75%); 1992 (75%)

Elected 1992; 6th term

When Wynn first came to Congress a decade ago, he represented a district drawn by state General Assembly Democrats to maximize the clout of minority voters. But the same redistricting process that propelled a record number of African-Americans into office nationwide in 1992 also helped Republicans win control of the House in the next election. Wynn found himself locked out of power, as did the Congressional Black Caucus, which the new GOP leadership stripped of staff and funding along with other legislative service organizations.

"Losing the majority has been my biggest frustration," Wynn said.

So when district lines were redrawn for this decade, he put his party loyalty, and his desire to get some power back, ahead of his personal political security. He encouraged mapmakers to take some of the suburban Democrats from the 4th District and move them to the 8th District, hoping to help force neighboring Republican Constance A. Morella from office. Two of Wynn's three assumptions came true: He still won another landslide reelection and Morella was defeated, but Republicans scored a net gain of seats in the House nonetheless.

Although generally a party loyalist, Wynn has emerged as a wild card on some crucial issues.

In the 107th Congress he signed on as cosponsor of an ultimately unsuccessful Republican alternative to the campaign finance overhaul package that was enacted in 2002. As chairman of the Black Caucus campaign finance task force, he argued that minority candidates needed to maintain access to unrestricted "soft money" donations in order to pay for get-out-the-vote efforts. Wynn ultimately voted for the campaign finance bill, but his gambit drew a commitment from House Democratic leaders to make up some of the money that Wynn believes black candidates will watch disappear.

Wynn also voted for the 1996 welfare overhaul opposed by many liberal Democrats after President Clinton endorsed the final version. "The fact that we did have a Democratic president and he was very good in reaching out to the Black Caucus enabled him to chart a more moderate path through Congress," Wynn said.

And his 2002 vote for the resolution authorizing Bush to launch a military campaign against Iraq was one of only four cast by members of the Black Caucus. Wynn told constituents he was concerned about the safety of more than 70,000 federal workers who are his constituents and could become terrorist targets at work. "I went to the memorial service of the two postal workers who were killed by anthrax and attended the funerals of many constituents who perished on Sept. 11," he said. "We must do all we can to safeguard our citizens and ensure that history never repeats itself."

Wynn earned a reputation as a political kingmaker in 1998, when he used his voter mobilization skills to help Democrat Parris N. Glendening win reelection as governor by a healthy margin. Wynn filled a void left when the state's two top black politicians withdrew their support of Glendening and helped business leaders recruit a primary candidate against the incumbent. In 2002, Wynn played a dominant role in Prince George's County politics, offering key endorsements of the new county executive, Jack Johnson, and most of the new county council.

Wynn's strong political base has helped him move up in the ranks of the Black Caucus; he ran its political action committee for the 2002 campaign. But he was rebuffed in 1998, when he was soundly defeated in his one bid to move into the leadership of the Democratic caucus.

Four years later, Wynn endorsed the long-shot candidacy of Harold E. Ford Jr. of Tennessee to be party leader in the 108th. Ford lost in a landslide to Nancy Pelosi but Wynn appeared to emerge unscathed, becoming a regional whip in the organization of fellow Marylander Steny H. Hoyer. Wynn also sits on the powerful Energy and Commerce Committee.

Bordering the nation's capital on the north, east and south, the 4th was the first black-majority district dominated by middle-class suburbanites. As a result, its residents' priorities differ from those of many other districts where most people are African-American. Many of Wynn's constituents are small-business owners who contract with the federal government, and he tends to be more pro-business than many of his Black Caucus colleagues.

As Congress debated the 2002 measure creating the Department of Homeland Security, however, Wynn objected to the authority granted the administration to impose new rules on federal workers shifted into the department. "This is supposed to be a bill about fighting terrorism," he said. "This bill puts the administration at war with federal employees."

Mindful of the 4th's high concentration of minorities and government workers, Wynn stresses the importance of enforcing anti-discrimination laws in the federal workplace. He has called discrimination in federal agencies "a long-festering sore," and says, "Corporate America cannot be expected to integrate until the federal government does."

Born in Philadelphia, Wynn spent his early years in North Carolina, where his father farmed and his mother taught school. When he was 7 his father was hired by the Department of Agriculture and the family moved back north, first to Washington and later to the Maryland suburbs. Wynn attended segregated schools until he was in the ninth grade. He was elected president of his high school senior class. "I have always been pretty good at mobilizing," Wynn recalls.

Wynn excelled at the trombone and was a debater at the University of Pittsburgh. After earning a law degree from Georgetown University in 1977, Wynn ran the Prince George's County Consumer Protection Commission. He immersed himself in local politics, working on other candidates' campaigns. In 1982, his door-to-door campaigning skills and party contacts helped him unseat an incumbent state representative.

After 10 years in Annapolis, Wynn was one of 13 Democrats who lined up for the newly drawn 4th District. He won the primary, which was tantamount to election, with 1,300 more votes than Alexander Williams Jr., the Prince George's County prosecutor. That remains his only tough race.

KEY VOTES

2002

Yes	Overhaul campaign finance law; ban "soft money" and restrict advocacy advertising
Yes	Back Bush's defense budget increase
No	Extend 1996 welfare law
No	Adopt Bush's discretionary spending limit
No	Pass GOP Medicare prescription drug plan
Yes	Create independent Sept. 11 commission
Yes	Extend union protections to Homeland Security Department employees
No	Revive fast-track procedures for trade agreements
Yes	Authorize war against Iraq
Yes	Advance bankruptcy overhaul opposed by abortion opponents

2001

No	Nullify Clinton Labor Department ergonomics rule
?	Cut taxes by $1.35 trillion through fiscal 2011
Yes	Maintain ban on oil drilling in Arctic National Wildlife Refuge
No	Approve Bush proposal to limit managed-care plan liability for coverage decisions
Yes	Divert money from crop subsidy payments to land conservation
Yes	Expand law enforcement power to investigate suspected terrorists

CQ VOTE STUDIES

	PARTY UNITY		PRESIDENTIAL SUPPORT	
	Support	Oppose	Support	Oppose
2002	87%	13%	32%	68%
2001	88%	12%	31%	69%
2000	95%	5%	84%	16%
1999	91%	9%	82%	18%
1998	93%	7%	83%	17%

INTEREST GROUPS

	AFL-CIO	ADA	CCUS	ACU
2002	100%	85%	50%	8%
2001	100%	90%	35%	4%
2000	100%	85%	57%	12%
1999	89%	100%	22%	4%
1998	100%	100%	33%	4%

MARYLAND 4

Inner Prince George's County; part of Montgomery County

The only suburban district in the nation with a black majority, the 4th includes Washington, D.C.'s eastern suburbs in Prince George's County and a sizable swath of northern Montgomery County. Democrats have a strong hold on the district's largely middle-class, black population.

The 4th's thriving economy is built on small business and the spillover of high-tech firms from Montgomery County and Northern Virginia. The district includes major parts of the Prince George's County High Technology Triangle, home to companies such as Raytheon and anchored by the University of Maryland and NASA (both nearby in the 5th). Prince George's is a national leader for black business formation, home ownership and education. Many of its residents are federal employees who have made the exodus from Washington. The 4th has the nation's highest percentage of government employees (29 percent).

But some of Prince George's County's low-income areas inside the Capital Beltway, which surrounds Washington, share the capital's problems of drug trafficking and violent crime.

Mapmakers altered the 4th in redistricting following the 2000 census in order to make the neighboring 8th District more Democratic. They exchanged some of the 4th's heavily minority neighborhoods in western Prince George's County and eastern Montgomery County for farther-out Montgomery County suburbs and exurbs, like Burtonsville, Olney and Sandy Spring. Nearly 40 percent of the new 4th's population resides in Montgomery County, and 57 percent of residents are black.

MAJOR INDUSTRY
Retail grocery, computers, recreation, technology

MILITARY BASES
Andrews Air Force Base, 4,400 military, 1,300 civilian; Adelphi Army Research Laboratory, 20 military, 880 civilian (2001)

CITIES
Silver Spring (unincorporated) (pt.), 46,910; Oxon Hill-Glassmanor (unincorporated), 35,355; Suitland-Silver Hill (unincorporated), 33,515

NOTABLE
Air Force One is kept at Andrews Air Force Base; FedEx Field is the home of the NFL's Washington Redskins.

Rep. Steny H. Hoyer (D)

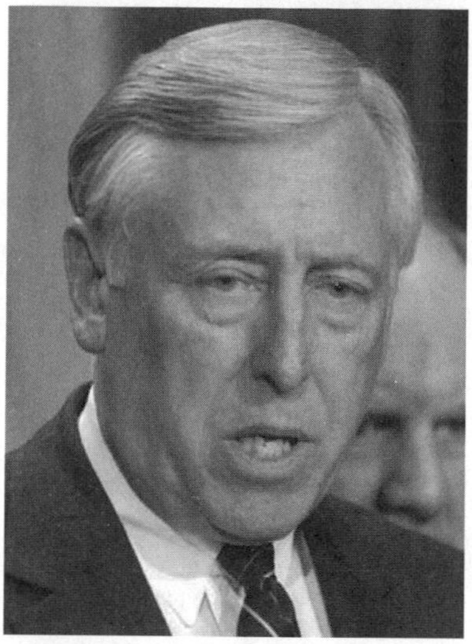

CAPITOL OFFICE
225-4131
www.house.gov/hoyer
1705 Longworth 20515-2005; fax 225-4300

COMMITTEES
Appropriations

HOMETOWN
Mechanicsville

BORN
June 14, 1939, Manhattan, N.Y.

RELIGION
Baptist

FAMILY
Widowed; three children

EDUCATION
U. of Maryland, B.S. 1963 (political science); Georgetown U., J.D. 1966

CAREER
Lawyer

POLITICAL HIGHLIGHTS
Md. Senate, 1967-79 (president, 1975-79); sought Democratic nomination for lieutenant governor, 1978; Md. Board of Higher Education, 1978-81

ELECTION RESULTS

2002 GENERAL		
Steny H. Hoyer (D)	137,903	69.3%
Joseph T. Crawford (R)	60,758	30.5%
2002 PRIMARY		
Steny H. Hoyer (D)		unopposed
2000 GENERAL		
Steny H. Hoyer (D)	166,231	65.1%
Thomas E. "Tim" Hutchins (R)	89,019	34.9%

PREVIOUS WINNING PERCENTAGES
1998 (65%); 1996 (57%); 1994 (59%); 1992 (53%); 1990 (81%); 1988 (79%); 1986 (82%); 1984 (72%); 1982 (80%); 1981 Special Election (55%)

Elected May 1981; 11th full term

More than two decades after arriving in the House, Hoyer fulfilled a long-time dream when he secured the No. 2 job in the Democratic leadership in the 108th Congress. He was elected minority whip, a reversal of fortune for Hoyer after a series of unsuccessful attempts to move up the ladder.

It was a welcome rebound for a lawmaker who, halfway through the 107th Congress, risked being branded a has-been. In the fall of 2001, he was soundly defeated in an election for the Democratic whip's post. A dozen Democrats who he believed were committed to him voted for his rival, Nancy Pelosi of California. She won, 118-95. It was Hoyer's second failed bid for the job. He had lost to David E. Bonior of Michigan 10 years earlier, 160-109.

A third opportunity for him to run for whip arose in late 2002 when Pelosi became the favorite to step up to minority leader, succeeding Richard A. Gephardt, who was leaving the party leader's post to run for president. Hoyer had anticipated such a scenario; he had never truly stopped campaigning for the job. By the time the party election rolled around, he had the votes lined up. This time, Hoyer had no opposition, and Democrats resoundingly chose him as whip.

Considered a hard worker willing to reach out to new members and veteran lawmakers alike, Hoyer needs those skills more than ever. House Democrats have been out of the majority for nearly a decade, and liberal and conservative members of the party disagree sharply on how to start winning elections again. House Democrats "need a message that will resonate with the base and the swing voters," Hoyer says, adding that if they fail to appeal to both groups, they will lose.

Hoyer wants to expand the whip's role beyond the customary duties of vote-counting and persuasion. He sees his job as cultivating support for the party's positions earlier in the process, long before legislation hits the floor. Success would not only guarantee a more unified party, but help Democrats stop President Bush's conservative agenda from getting through the House.

Charming and impeccably dressed, Hoyer has well-honed skills as an inside operator and a smoothness in front of the cameras that makes him a favorite party spokesman. Though Pelosi has shot ahead of him on the leadership track, there are few more-seasoned veterans than Hoyer. In 1986, he helped Tony Coelho of California win the first-ever election for Democratic whip; the position previously had been appointive. Hoyer became a deputy whip for Coelho. Three years later, Hoyer was elected chairman of the Democratic Caucus, a job he held for four years.

Hoyer is a member of the Democratic Steering Committee, which makes the party's committee assignments. His political action committee, AmeriPAC, is one of the most active leadership PACs among House Democrats. A native New Yorker who moved to suburban Washington as a child, Hoyer, now in his 60s, still has the energetic and confident manner of somebody who is on his way somewhere.

At Pelosi's insistence, he gave up his slot as top Democrat on the House Administration Committee, which handles internal housekeeping and Capitol security issues. His service on that panel led to Hoyer's greatest legislative achievement in the 107th Congress: enactment of a law that set the first national standards for the conduct of elections. Hoyer and Chairman Bob Ney, an Ohio Republican, negotiated tirelessly with Senate leaders in both parties to overcome partisan suspicions and strike a deal in 2002.

A self-described "John Kennedy Democrat," Hoyer throughout the 1980s had no trouble holding his seat in the mostly liberal, heavily Democratic district in suburban Prince George's County outside of Washington. With a seat on the Appropriations Committee, Hoyer fights relentlessly for the federal workers who make up a large voting bloc in his district. He has won them pay raises and lower retirement contribution rates in recent years.

He rebuffed entreaties to give up the committee when he became whip because of the value of the post to his constituents. "I have a primary responsibility: to work for the people who hired me," Hoyer said. "And where I serve them is on the committee." He is the senior Democrat on the newly constituted Transportation and Treasury Subcommittee.

Hoyer began moderating his views after redistricting in the 1990s added a conservative swath of southern Maryland to his district. Held to 53 percent in 1992, he has since pushed his victory margins consistently higher. To do so, he shifted his personal ideology toward the center on some issues, a bit of pragmatic politics he doesn't bother to conceal.

Hoyer generally votes a pro-labor, pro-environment line. A strong proponent of abortion rights, he has argued vigorously against the conservative-backed policy that prohibits federal employees' health care plans from providing coverage for most abortions.

He is more routinely pro-defense than most House Democrats. Like Gephardt, he split with the majority of his peers in 2002 to vote to authorize the use of military force against Iraq. And although he opposed the 2002 law giving the president expedited powers in negotiating trade agreements, he voted for the other three bellwether trade laws of the past decade: approving permanent normal trade status for China in 2000, creating the World Trade Organization in 1994 and implementing the North American Free Trade Agreement in 1993.

Hoyer showed leadership potential long before his service in Congress. He was president of the Maryland Young Democrats, and in 1963, was named the University of Maryland's "Outstanding Male Graduate."

Three years later, he graduated from Georgetown Law School and immediately won election, at age 27, to the Maryland Senate. A few years later, when he turned 35, he became that body's youngest president ever.

He was 41 when he won his House seat in a special election to replace Democrat Gladys Noon Spellman, who was in an irreversible coma. As a reward for his loyalty to the leadership as a freshman, he was awarded a coveted seat on the Appropriations Committee in his second term.

KEY VOTES

2002

Yes Overhaul campaign finance law; ban "soft money" and restrict advocacy advertising
Yes Back Bush's defense budget increase
No Extend 1996 welfare law
No Adopt Bush's discretionary spending limit
No Pass GOP Medicare prescription drug plan
Yes Create independent Sept. 11 commission
Yes Extend union protections to Homeland Security Department employees
No Revive fast-track procedures for trade agreements
Yes Authorize war against Iraq
No Advance bankruptcy overhaul opposed by abortion opponents

2001

No Nullify Clinton Labor Department ergonomics rule
No Cut taxes by $1.35 trillion through fiscal 2011
Yes Maintain ban on oil drilling in Arctic National Wildlife Refuge
No Approve Bush proposal to limit managed-care plan liability for coverage decisions
Yes Divert money from crop subsidy payments to land conservation
Yes Expand law enforcement power to investigate suspected terrorists

CQ VOTE STUDIES

	PARTY UNITY		PRESIDENTIAL SUPPORT	
	Support	Oppose	Support	Oppose
2002	89%	11%	32%	68%
2001	91%	9%	30%	70%
2000	93%	7%	90%	10%
1999	89%	11%	82%	18%
1998	89%	11%	81%	19%

INTEREST GROUPS

	AFL-CIO	ADA	CCUS	ACU
2002	100%	95%	42%	4%
2001	100%	95%	43%	9%
2000	90%	80%	47%	12%
1999	89%	90%	20%	8%
1998	100%	95%	28%	4%

MARYLAND 5
Outer Prince George's County; southern Maryland

The 5th includes part of Prince George's County, southern Anne Arundel County and all of the three rapidly growing southern counties of Charles, Calvert and St. Mary's. The mix of liberals in Prince George's County and conservative Democrats and Republicans throughout much of the rest of the district gives the 5th a broad array of political interests.

Prince George's County, which accounts for half the district's population — and nearly 60 percent of its registered Democrats — includes many liberal black communities and College Park, home of the University of Maryland's main campus. "P.G." County, as locals call it, was the only county in the 5th to back Bill Clinton in 1996, allowing Democrats to carry the district. In 2000, a growing black population helped Al Gore take largely exurban Charles County while winning the 5th handily. The GOP holds a slight registration edge among the Anne Arundel residents in the district, but Democrats have the advantage in every other county.

The district is enjoying a moderate amount of economic success due to the technology boom, both in Prince George's County and in Southern Maryland. Many residents and companies have left the Washington, D.C., metropolitan area for the southern counties, attracted by the abundance of land and the military presence. Its proximity to Washington gives the 5th the nation's second-highest percentage of government workers, behind the neighboring 4th District. The Tri-County area retains its Southern rural character, however, with tobacco as its major crop and a conservative, but strongly Democratic tradition.

MAJOR INDUSTRY
Defense, agriculture, technology

MILITARY BASES
Naval Air Station Patuxent River, 2,670 military, 6,640 civilian (2000); Naval Surface Warfare Center, Indian Head Division, 1,141 military, 2,291 civilian (2002)

CITIES
Bowie (pt.), 47,714; St. Charles (unincorporated), 33,379; Clinton (unincorporated), 26,064; College Park, 24,657

NOTABLE
NASA Goddard Space Flight Center; Cliffs along the Chesapeake Bay in Calvert County contain more than 600 species of fossils; St. Mary's was the first capital of Maryland.

Rep. Roscoe G. Bartlett (R)

CAPITOL OFFICE
225-2721
www.house.gov/bartlett
2412 Rayburn 20515-2006; fax 225-2193

COMMITTEES
Armed Services
(Projection Forces - chairman)
Science
Small Business

HOMETOWN
Frederick

BORN
June 3, 1926, Moreland, Ky.

RELIGION
Seventh-Day Adventist

FAMILY
Wife, Ellen Louise Bartlett; 10 children

EDUCATION
Columbia Union College, B.S. 1947 (theology & biology); U. of Maryland, M.S. 1948 (physiology), Ph.D. 1952 (physiology)

CAREER
Real estate developer; scientific research company owner; farmer; biomedical engineer; professor

POLITICAL HIGHLIGHTS
Sought Republican nomination for U.S. Senate, 1980; Republican nominee for U.S. House, 1982

ELECTION RESULTS

2002 GENERAL		
Roscoe G. Bartlett (R)	147,825	66.1%
Donald M. DeArmon (D)	75,575	33.8%
2002 PRIMARY		
Roscoe G. Bartlett (R)		unopposed
2000 GENERAL		
Roscoe G. Bartlett (R)	168,624	60.7%
Donald DeArmon (D)	109,136	39.3%

PREVIOUS WINNING PERCENTAGES
1998 (63%); 1996 (57%); 1994 (66%); 1992 (54%)

Elected 1992; 6th term

Growing up as a tenant farmer's son during the Depression, Bartlett developed callouses on his hand and a conservative political philosophy that extols self-reliance. Six decades later, the self-styled citizen-legislator, who commutes about 50 miles every day to Capitol Hill from his farm near Frederick, Md., retains both characteristics.

His aversion to government intrusiveness runs deep, as one might expect of a man whose mother used feed sacks to make clothes and bed sheets for the family while his father refused government assistance. Although considerably older than many of the conservative young Republican firebrands who joined the House in the 1990s, the septuagenarian Bartlett is every bit their equal in ideological fervor. When Republicans took control of the House in the 104th Congress, Bartlett voted for every item in the House GOP's "Contract With America" legislative lineup. Over six terms, he has been a reliable proponent of the House Republicans' conservative agenda, voting to scale back government and reduce taxes.

But Bartlett's Main Street conservatism, rooted in his hardscrabble childhood, strongly held religious beliefs and his experience as a small-businessman, coexists with other facets of his makeup that occasionally separate him from fellow Republicans.

A strict constitutional constructionist, he was one of 27 House Republicans in 2002 who voted, unsuccessfully, against giving the president fast-track authority to negotiate international trade agreements that Congress can either accept or reject but not amend. "I don't think you can give to the president power [to regulate foreign trade] constitutionally given to Congress," he told a reporter, pulling a copy of the Constitution out of his coat pocket.

A stalwart defense hawk, Bartlett is an equally staunch libertarian who regretted his 2001 vote for the so-called USA-PATRIOT Act, enacted after the Sept. 11 terrorist attacks to give the government sweeping new powers to track, arrest and prosecute suspected terrorists. "Probably the least patriotic thing I've done since I got here," he lamented in an interview several months later. "If the price of catching another terrorist or two is an erosion of our civil liberties, they will have won," he said.

Bartlett's independence is particularly striking on technical issues that engage his flair for science. On the Science panel, he is well-versed in the subject of global energy resources. Unlike most in his party, he opposes drilling for oil in Alaska's Arctic National Wildlife Refuge, arguing that the amount of oil that could be recovered is too small to help end the country's dependence on foreign oil. He backs increased funding for basic research, saying in 2003 that President Bush's budget proposal was "far from adequate."

Other themes that highlight Bartlett's congressional record are more conventional. A member of the National Federation of Independent Businesses, the small-business lobby, he has used his seat on the Small Business Committee to reduce regulatory requirements for businesses and to prevent the government from "bundling" contracts in such large packages that small firms cannot compete for them.

His support for gun owners' rights leads him to introduce a measure every Congress stipulating that Americans have the right to use firearms to defend their families and homes. In 2001, he also introduced a resolution urging the president to reject any agreement reached by a United Nations conference on small arms that would infringe on the Second Amendment right to bear arms.

On the Armed Services Committee, where he is a subcommittee chairman in the 108th, Bartlett is known for being "politically incorrect . . . and proud of it," to quote a large button he sometimes carries in his coat pocket. He has vigorously opposed a 1994 Pentagon decision to allow the services to put male and female recruits through basic training together, blaming several high-profile military sex scandals on a policy of allowing the sexes to live and train together.

He also authored a proposal in 1996 that he said would end the practice of "Uncle Sam subsidizing smut at defense facilities." The measure to bar the sale of "lascivious" magazines or videotapes on military bases was included in that year's defense authorization bill and withstood a lengthy legal challenge by Penthouse magazine publisher Bob Guccione. But Bartlett's straight-laced, paternalistic concern for the well-being of the troops goes beyond matters of sex. In 2000, he got Congress to require a Pentagon study of whether the thousands of slot machines installed in U.S. bases overseas were harming the troops' morale and finances.

Born on his grandfather's farm in Kentucky, Bartlett saw his father work as a tenant farmer in western Pennsylvania during the Depression era. He originally intended to become a minister but instead pursued a graduate education in physiology at the University of Maryland, eventually earning a master's degree and a doctorate in human physiology.

He taught in both California and Washington, D.C., and conducted research for the National Institutes of Health and the Navy's School of Aviation Medicine, where his mechanical skill led him into engineering. He holds 20 patents for his invention of respiratory support and safety devices used by pilots, astronauts and rescue workers. In 1999, Bartlett was honored for his lifetime service by the American Institute of Aeronautics and Astronautics.

In 1961, Bartlett moved to a dairy farm in Frederick County and continued to work at the Johns Hopkins Applied Physics Laboratory and teach in Frederick. He later entered the home building business.

He ran unsuccessfully for the House in 1982 but was back a decade later, after closing his home building firm and leaving his teaching career. He narrowly won a three-way GOP primary in 1992 and was expecting to face an uphill general-election battle against conservative Democrat Beverly B. Byron, a seven-term incumbent, who had held Bartlett to just 26 percent in 1982. But Byron was upset in the primary by challenger Thomas H. Hattery, and in November Bartlett capitalized on confusion in Democratic ranks to beat Hattery by 8 percentage points. He has won re-election easily since then.

KEY VOTES

2002

No Overhaul campaign finance law; ban "soft money" and restrict advocacy advertising
Yes Back Bush's defense budget increase
Yes Extend 1996 welfare law
Yes Adopt Bush's discretionary spending limit
Yes Pass GOP Medicare prescription drug plan
Yes Create independent Sept. 11 commission
No Extend union protections to Homeland Security Department employees
No Revive fast-track procedures for trade agreements
Yes Authorize war against Iraq
No Advance bankruptcy overhaul opposed by abortion opponents

2001

Yes Nullify Clinton Labor Department ergonomics rule
Yes Cut taxes by $1.35 trillion through fiscal 2011
Yes Maintain ban on oil drilling in Arctic National Wildlife Refuge
Yes Approve Bush proposal to limit managed-care plan liability for coverage decisions
No Divert money from crop subsidy payments to land conservation
Yes Expand law enforcement power to investigate suspected terrorists

CQ VOTE STUDIES

	PARTY UNITY		PRESIDENTIAL SUPPORT	
	Support	Oppose	Support	Oppose
2002	94%	6%	79%	21%
2001	91%	9%	74%	26%
2000	97%	3%	17%	83%
1999	94%	6%	9%	91%
1998	95%	5%	19%	81%

INTEREST GROUPS

	AFL-CIO	ADA	CCUS	ACU
2002	22%	10%	80%	96%
2001	17%	15%	78%	88%
2000	10%	5%	71%	100%
1999	33%	10%	84%	96%
1998	10%	5%	78%	100%

MARYLAND 6

North and west – Frederick, Hagerstown

The 6th reaches across the northern tier of the state from Western Maryland to the Susquehanna River. It takes in all of Garrett, Allegany, Washington, Frederick and Carroll counties, as well as significant portions of Baltimore and Harford counties and a small, exurban slice of Montgomery County. The 6th has a rural tradition and a conservative bent that often benefit the GOP. Though Frederick and Carroll counties are thriving economically, the demise of old-line industry has left the Appalachian Mountain area struggling. Some local leaders have tried to promote the region as a destination for vacationers.

Frederick and Carroll are experiencing rapid growth from new residents escaping the city and inner suburbs and commuting to Baltimore and Washington, D.C. Carroll County, however, still has an agricultural economy and remains a Republican stronghold.

During redistricting following the 2000 census, northern portions of Baltimore and Harford counties, where Republicans and old-line conservative Democrats reign, were taken out of the 2nd and folded into the district, bolstering the GOP's hold on the 6th.

The three western counties are less populous and remain solidly conservative. Washington County, with its strong manufacturing base, is the only one experiencing economic prosperity. With companies such as Kelly-Springfield closing their operations, Allegany and Garrett counties both are struggling and have become dependent on tourism.

MAJOR INDUSTRY

Manufacturing, technology, agriculture, tourism

MILITARY BASES

Fort Detrick (Army), 1,280 military, 4,981 civilian (2000)

CITIES

Frederick, 52,767; Hagerstown, 36,687; Eldersburg (unincorporated), 27,741; Cumberland, 21,518; Westminster, 16,731

NOTABLE

Camp David, the president's retreat; Whittaker Chambers' pumpkin patch in Westminster produced evidence for Richard M. Nixon during the Alger Hiss trial; Fort Detrick specializes in biomedical research and development.

Rep. Elijah E. Cummings (D)

CAPITOL OFFICE
225-4741
www.house.gov/cummings
1632 Longworth 20515-2007; fax 225-3178

COMMITTEES
Government Reform
Transportation & Infrastructure

HOMETOWN
Baltimore

BORN
Jan. 18, 1951, Baltimore, Md.

RELIGION
Baptist

FAMILY
Separated; three children

EDUCATION
Howard U., B.A. 1973 (political science);
U. of Maryland, J.D. 1976

CAREER
Lawyer

POLITICAL HIGHLIGHTS
Md. House, 1983-96 (Speaker pro tempore, 1995)

ELECTION RESULTS

2002 GENERAL		
Elijah E. Cummings (D)	137,047	73.5%
Joseph E. Ward (R)	49,172	26.4%
2002 PRIMARY		
Elijah E. Cummings (D)	67,850	89.4%
A. Robert Kaufman (D)	4,891	6.4%
Charles U. Smith (D)	1,745	2.3%
Charles C. McPeek (D)	1,449	1.9%
2000 GENERAL		
Elijah E. Cummings (D)	134,066	87.1%
Kenneth Kondner (R)	19,773	12.8%

PREVIOUS WINNING PERCENTAGES
1998 (86%); 1996 (83%); 1996 Special Election (81%)

Elected April 1996; 4th full term

Cummings enjoys a new prominence in the 108th Congress as the chairman of the Congressional Black Caucus. He was in line for the post after serving a term as caucus secretary and another as vice chairman, but he won it only after fending off a spirited challenge from Bobby L. Rush, a fellow Democrat from Illinois.

Elected chairman in December 2002, Cummings was thrust immediately into the national spotlight as a prominent African-American critic of Trent Lott of Mississippi. Just a week before, Lott had suggested that the country would have been better off had Strom Thurmond been elected president in 1948, when he ran on a segregationist platform. The furor ultimately cost Lott his job as the Senate Republican leader.

Cummings then led the Black Caucus in protesting President Bush's decision to renominate Lott's protégé, federal District Judge Charles W. Pickering Sr., for the 5th Circuit Court of Appeals. The Democratic-controlled Senate Judiciary Committee had rejected Pickering's nomination in March 2002, criticizing his civil rights record. Black Caucus members said Bush's decision to renominate Pickering in 2003 "fails to live up to" the spirit of Bush's condemnation of Lott's remarks about Thurmond. "The continuing de facto segregation and inequality in America cannot be whitewashed by the president's words," Cummings said.

As leader of the Black Caucus, Cummings said he would seek ways to energize young voters "so they can see the relevancy of Democratic Party politics." Too often, he said, "we have young people who decide they don't want to be involved in politics."

In the 107th, Cummings and a number of other Black Caucus members withheld support for the campaign finance overhaul package until they were assured that Democratic leaders would provide adequately for get-out-the-vote efforts if the bill became law and would press for enactment of a separate bill setting national voting system standards. "If we're going to talk about reform and talk about elections, we need to first start off with the fundamental rights given to us by the Constitution," Cummings said. "That is, that everybody be allowed to vote." Both measures were enacted in 2002.

He was a vocal opponent of the resolution authorizing the use of force against Iraq. "It is not a declaration of war, it is a blank check to use force without the moral or political authority of a declaration of war. Congress must not abandon its authority under the Constitution," Cummings said on the House floor.

He was equally concerned about the fight against terrorism at home, which he feared could lead to violations of civil rights and civil liberties. Cummings was one of 66 House members, and the only one from Maryland, to vote against the 2001 law that greatly enhanced the power of law enforcement agents to investigate suspected terrorists.

Cummings got a direct taste of the impact that bioterrorism could have when he and three colleagues were forced to evacuate their Longworth Building offices after the October 2001 anthrax mailings contaminated the Senate's Hart Building and a smattering of House facilities. They could not move back until January 2002, after all traces of anthrax were eliminated and the furnishings and equipment replaced.

A public official for two decades, Cummings' political successes have been marred by economic hardships. Owing thousands of dollars in back taxes and other debts when he arrived at the Capitol, he warded off fore-closure proceedings on his house and spent two winters without heat because he could not afford to fix his furnace.

He blamed his shaky finances on conditions that dated back many years — starting his own law firm, trying to support three children, lacking car insurance when he got into an accident — but he told The Baltimore Sun in 1999 that he had finally paid off most of his debts. "I have a moral conscience that is real central," he told The Sun. "I didn't ask the federal government or anyone else to do me any favors."

Cummings, whose mostly urban district has a black majority, says the communities he represents need ample federal assistance to combat illegal drugs and violent crime, improve education and health care, and stimulate economic development. In the 107th, Cummings won expanded federal support for a nursing program at Coppin State College in Baltimore. He also has won federal grants for a University Technical Assistance Center at Morgan State University, and money to rehabilitate several Baltimore-area school playgrounds.

A member of the Congressional Steel Caucus, Cummings introduced legislation in the 107th to provide health insurance aid for retired steel workers. About 13,000 Bethlehem Steel Corp. retirees live in Baltimore.

Cummings looks for ways to improve the lot of his constituents without relying on congressional action. He holds job fairs and seminars to help constituents learn about college aid programs.

A Baltimore native, Cummings was one of seven children in a working-class family. His parents had migrated from South Carolina, where they were sharecroppers, and he recalls that, "As a young boy in south Baltimore . . . we did not have many opportunities. We did not play on grass. We played on asphalt." But he says he was set on a productive course by "two very strong parents," who scrimped and saved to buy their own home in a city neighborhood that was integrating.

He graduated Phi Beta Kappa from Howard University and earned a law degree from the University of Maryland in 1976. Six years later, he was elected to the state House. During 13 years there, he rose to the chamber's second-ranking position, at the time the highest Maryland office ever held by an African-American. In 1996, he outpaced 26 other Democrats and five Republicans to replace Democrat Kweisi Mfume, who resigned from the House to become president of the NAACP. Since then, his November election tally has never dropped below 70 percent — a consistency of support that has led to Cummings' name being mentioned as a possible candidate for mayor of Baltimore in 2004.

KEY VOTES

2002

Yes Overhaul campaign finance law; ban "soft money" and restrict advocacy advertising
Yes Back Bush's defense budget increase
No Extend 1996 welfare law
No Adopt Bush's discretionary spending limit
No Pass GOP Medicare prescription drug plan
Yes Create independent Sept. 11 commission
Yes Extend union protections to Homeland Security Department employees
No Revive fast-track procedures for trade agreements
No Authorize war against Iraq
No Advance bankruptcy overhaul opposed by abortion opponents

2001

No Nullify Clinton Labor Department ergonomics rule
No Cut taxes by $1.35 trillion through fiscal 2011
Yes Maintain ban on oil drilling in Arctic National Wildlife Refuge
No Approve Bush proposal to limit managed-care plan liability for coverage decisions
Yes Divert money from crop subsidy payments to land conservation
No Expand law enforcement power to investigate suspected terrorists

CQ VOTE STUDIES

	PARTY UNITY		PRESIDENTIAL SUPPORT	
	Support	Oppose	Support	Oppose
2002	95%	5%	25%	75%
2001	95%	5%	19%	81%
2000	97%	3%	88%	12%
1999	98%	2%	85%	15%
1998	95%	5%	83%	17%

INTEREST GROUPS

	AFL-CIO	ADA	CCUS	ACU
2002	100%	95%	45%	0%
2001	100%	95%	27%	4%
2000	100%	85%	47%	4%
1999	89%	100%	21%	0%
1998	100%	100%	28%	4%

MARYLAND 7

Downtown Baltimore; part of Columbia

The 7th takes in both the low-income neighborhoods of West Baltimore and much of downtown, including the bustling retail center of the Inner Harbor. The 7th follows the black migration west to include Baltimore County's middle-class southwestern suburbs, and it also includes the bulk of Howard County, including the western portion of Columbia, a liberal-leaning planned community between Baltimore and Washington.

The 7th's black majority (almost 60 percent) gives Democrats a distinct advantage in national and local contests through much of the district. But Republicans regularly win on the local level in the more rural parts of Howard County.

Efforts to improve Baltimore's poor neighborhoods have been slow, and urban problems, such as crime, drug abuse, teen pregnancy and unemployment, have prompted many of the city's middle-class residents to head to the suburbs.

But the picture within the city is not all bleak. Many of Baltimore's most identifiable landmarks and businesses are in the 7th. The gentrified Mount Vernon area, home of the Walters Art Museum and the Peabody Institute, are within its boundaries. Farther north are Johns Hopkins University and the Baltimore Museum of Art.

In addition to the revitalized Inner Harbor waterfront, the old retail section west of the downtown hub still survives; Lexington Market and the Baltimore Arena are here. There are middle-class black communities along Liberty Heights Road in West Baltimore.

The University of Maryland, Baltimore County, in Catonsville and its adjacent research area are attracting technology firms.

MAJOR INDUSTRY

Health care, manufacturing, technology

CITIES

Baltimore (pt.), 370,752; Ellicott City (unincorporated) (pt.), 56,231; Columbia (unincorporated) (pt.), 47,943; Catonsville (unincorporated), 39,820; Woodlawn (unincorporated), 36,079

NOTABLE

The 7th's portion of Baltimore is home to NAACP national headquarters, author Edgar Allan Poe's gravesite and the National Aquarium.

ep. Chris Van ollen (D)

CAPITOL OFFICE
225-5341
chris.vanhollen@mail.house.gov
www.house.gov/vanhollen
1419 Longworth 20515-2008; fax 225-0375

COMMITTEES
Education & Workforce
Government Reform

HOMETOWN
Kensington

BORN
Jan. 10, 1959, Karachi, Pakistan

RELIGION
Episcopalian

FAMILY
Wife, Katherine Wilkens Van Hollen; three children

EDUCATION
Swarthmore College, B.A. 1983 (philosophy); Harvard U., M.P.P. 1985; Georgetown U., J.D. 1990

CAREER
Lawyer; gubernatorial aide; congressional aide

POLITICAL HIGHLIGHTS
Md. House, 1991-95; Md. Senate, 1995-2003

ELECTION RESULTS

2002 GENERAL		
Chris Van Hollen (D)	112,788	51.7%
Constance A. Morella (R)	103,587	47.5%

2002 PRIMARY		
Chris Van Hollen (D)	37,494	43.5%
Mark K. Shriver (D)	35,022	40.6%
Ira S. Shapiro (D)	10,956	12.7%
Deborah A. Vollmer (D)	2,149	2.5%

Elected 2002; 1st term

Whether on the campaign trail or in legislative chambers, Van Hollen finds a way to win — as he showed in 2002 when he ousted popular Republican incumbent Constance A. Morella, who had long frustrated Democrats' designs on Maryland's strongly Democratic 8th District.

In the state Senate, Van Hollen engineered a strategy to funnel education dollars to Montgomery County, his home base, and brokered a deal on legislation to require trigger locks on handguns sold in the state. His efforts won him the loyal backing of a strong corps of activists and numerous advocacy groups.

Aside from his successes as a lawmaker, Van Hollen was able to campaign on his policy experience as a political aide. As a Senate Foreign Relations Committee staff member, he chronicled Iraqi President Saddam Hussein's use of chemical weapons against Iraq's Kurdish population. Van Hollen later worked for Democrat William Donald Schaefer, then Maryland's governor.

Van Hollen says his priorities in the 108th Congress include helping the Democratic Party develop a strong economic platform and working to fully fund the sweeping education law enacted during the 107th Congress.

His committee assignments — Education and Government Reform — match his legislative experience on education issues and the keen interest of his constituents, many of whom are federal workers, in federal personnel matters.

The son of a foreign service officer, Van Hollen was born in Pakistan and spent much of his youth abroad, living in India, Sri Lanka and Turkey.

Van Hollen's 43.5 percent in the four-way Democratic primary enabled him to edge past his main opponent, state Rep. Mark K. Shriver — a member of the Kennedy clan — by less than 2,500 votes. Van Hollen then one-upped himself by toppling the well-regarded Morella, a 16-year veteran who was widely viewed as the most liberal House Republican. Benefiting from a redistricting plan drawn by fellow Democrats who controlled the state legislature, Van Hollen prevailed by 4 percentage points.

MARYLAND 8

Part of Montgomery County — Bethesda, Gaithersburg

The 8th contains wealthy Montgomery County suburbs northwest of Washington, D.C., such as Bethesda, Chevy Chase and Potomac, as well as less-affluent suburbs in eastern Montgomery and western Prince George's County. It also includes rural areas northwest of Potomac and the Interstate 270 technology corridor, a hotbed for high-tech and biotechnology companies that runs through Rockville and Gaithersburg.

The district was redrawn to elect a Democrat in redistricting following the 2000 census. Mapmakers removed some GOP-leaning areas in northern Montgomery County and added liberal Takoma Park, as well as heavily black and Hispanic neighborhoods in western Prince George's County.

Government is the dominant employer in the 8th, where federal agencies abound and Rockville is the Montgomery County seat. The large contingent of educated professionals supports a thriving economy that is bolstered by a wide array of big-name business interests, including Lockheed Martin, Marriott and IBM.

Potomac, in the western part of the district, is known for its horse farms and expensive estates. In the far west, officials struggle to preserve an agricultural heritage.

MAJOR INDUSTRY
Government, technology, services, retail

MILITARY BASES
National Naval Medical Center, 2,273 military, 1,396 civilian (2002); National Imagery and Mapping Agency, 7,000; Naval Surface Warfare Center, Carderock Division, 7 military, 1,600 civilian (2003)

CITIES
Wheaton-Glenmont (unincorporated), 57,694; Bethesda (unincorporated), 55,277; Gaithersburg, 52,613; Rockville, 47,388

NOTABLE
Author F. Scott Fitzgerald is buried in Rockville.

MASSACHUSETTS

Gov. Mitt Romney (R)

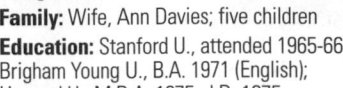

First elected: 2002
Length of term: 4 years
Term expires: 1/07
Salary: $135,000
Phone: (617) 727-3600
Hometown: Belmont
Born: March 12, 1947; Detroit, Mich.
Religion: Mormon
Family: Wife, Ann Davies; five children
Education: Stanford U., attended 1965-66; Brigham Young U., B.A. 1971 (English); Harvard U., M.B.A. 1975; J.D. 1975
Career: Salt Lake Olympic organizing committee president; venture capitalist
Political highlights: Republican nominee for U.S. Senate, 1994

Election results:

2002 GENERAL

Mitt Romney (R)	1,091,988	49.8%
Shannon P. O'Brien (D)	985,981	44.9%
Jill Stein (GREEN)	76,530	3.5%
Carla Howell (LIBERT)	23,044	1.1%

Lt. Gov. Kerry Healey (R)

First elected: 2002
Length of term: 4 years
Term expires: 1/07
Salary: $120,000
Phone: (617) 727-3600

STATE LEGISLATURE

General Court: Meeting time varies; usually year-round
House: 160 members, 2-year terms
2003 breakdown: 23R, 136D, 1I; 120 men, 40 women
Salary: $53,380
Phone: (617) 722-2356
Senate: 40 members, 2-year terms
2003 breakdown: 6R, 34D; 28 male, 12 female
Salary: $60,880
Phone: (617) 722-1276

STATE TERM LIMITS

Governor: 2 terms
Senate: No
House: No

URBAN STATISTICS

CITY	POPULATION
Boston	589,141
Worcester	172,648
Springfield	152,082
Lowell	105,167
Cambridge	101,355

REGISTERED VOTERS

Unenrolled	50%
Democrat	36%
Republican	13%

POPULATION

2002 population (est.)	6,427,801
2000 population	6,349,097
1990 population	6,016,425
Percent change (1990-2000)	+5.5%
Rank among states (2002)	13
Median age	36.5
Born in state	66.1%
Foreign born	12.2%
Violent crime rate	476/100,000
Poverty level	9.3%
Federal workers	53,161
Military	23,516

REDISTRICTING

Massachusetts retained its 10 House seats in reapportionment. The state legislature drew a new map, which the governor allowed to become law without her signature on Feb. 11, 2002.

MISCELLANEOUS

Web: www.state.ma.us
Capital: Boston

STATE ELECTION OFFICIAL
(617) 727-2828

DEMOCRATIC HEADQUARTERS
(617) 472-0637

REPUBLICAN HEADQUARTERS
(781) 224-7461

District Statistics

DIST.	2000 VOTE FOR PRESIDENT BUSH	GORE	NADER	WHITE	BLACK	ASIAN	HISP	MEDIAN INCOME	WHITE COLLAR	BLUE COLLAR	SERVICE INDUSTRY	OVER 64	UNDER 18	COLLEGE EDUCATION	RURAL	SQ. MILES
1	33%	56%	9%	89%	2%	2%	6%	$42,570	60%	24%	16%	14%	24%	25%	31%	3,101
2	35	58	7	82	5	1	9	$44,386	61	24	15	14	26	23	15	922
3	35	59	6	86	3	3	6	$50,223	66	21	14	13	25	31	7	581
4	29	65	5	88	2	3	3	$53,169	68	20	13	14	24	37	12	732
5	37	56	6	80	2	5	12	$56,217	67	21	12	11	27	34	7	566
6	36	57	6	90	2	2	4	$57,826	70	18	13	14	24	35	5	480
7	29	64	6	84	3	6	5	$56,110	73	14	13	16	21	40	0	170
8	15	74	10	49	22	8	16	$39,300	71	13	17	9	18	40	0	41
9	34	59	5	79	8	4	5	$55,407	69	17	14	14	24	34	2	313
10	39	54	6	92	2	3	1	$51,928	67	18	15	17	23	34	8	934
STATE	33	60	6	82	5	4	7	$50,502	67	19	14	14	24	33	9	7,840
U.S.	47.9	48.4	3	69	12	4	13	$41,994	60	25	15	12	26	24	21	3,537,438

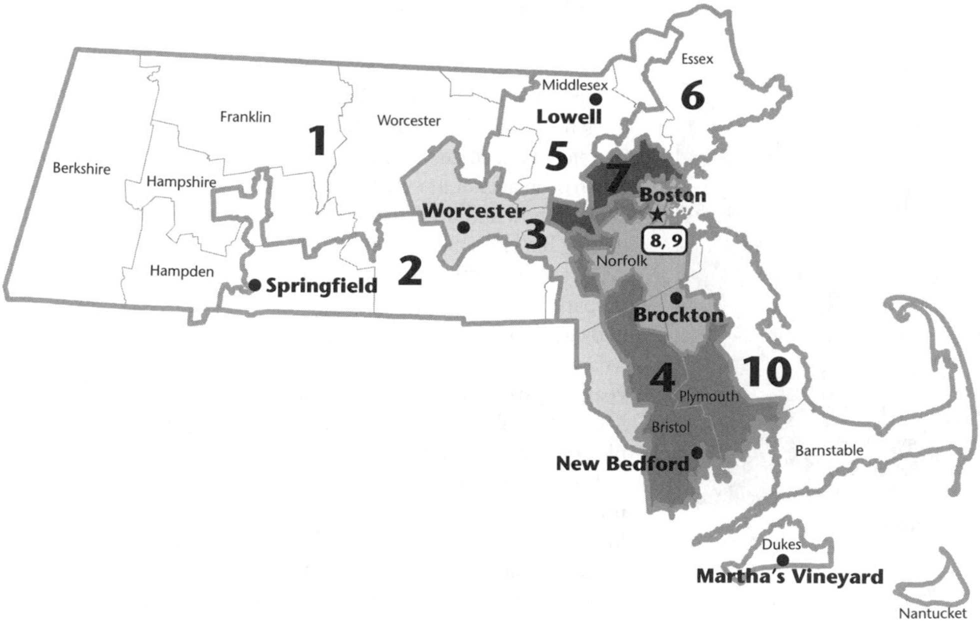
Essex
6
Middlesex
Lowell
Franklin
1
Worcester
5
Berkshire
Hampshire
7
Boston
Worcester
3
8, 9
Norfolk
Hampden
Springfield
2
Brockton
4
10
Plymouth
Bristol
New Bedford
Barnstable
Dukes
Martha's Vineyard
Nantucket

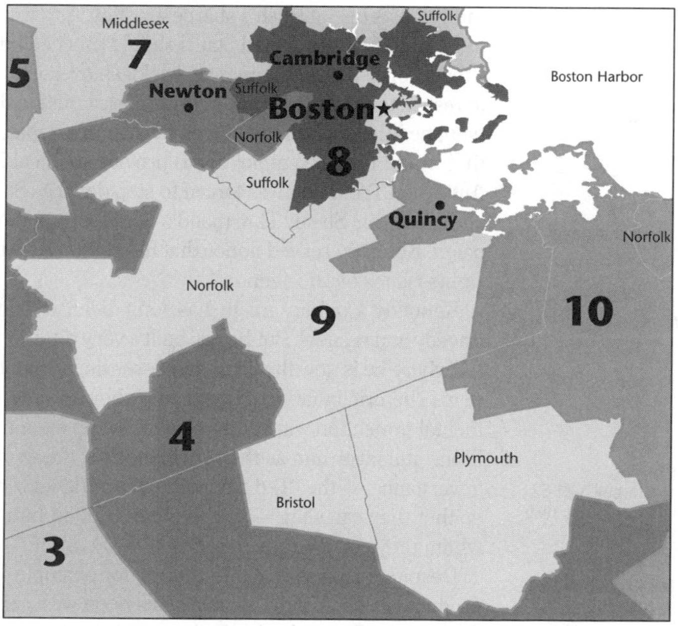
Middlesex
Suffolk
7
Cambridge
Boston Harbor
5
Newton
Suffolk
Boston
Norfolk
8
Suffolk
Quincy
Norfolk
Norfolk
9
10
4
Plymouth
Bristol
3

Sen. Edward M. Kennedy (D)

CAPITOL OFFICE
224-4543
senator@kennedy.senate.gov
kennedy.senate.gov
317 Russell 20510-2101; fax 224-2417

COMMITTEES
Armed Services
Health, Education, Labor & Pensions - ranking member
Judiciary
Joint Economic

HOMETOWN
Hyannis Port

BORN
Feb. 22, 1932, Boston, Mass.

RELIGION
Roman Catholic

FAMILY
Wife, Victoria Reggie Kennedy; three children, two stepchildren

EDUCATION
Harvard U., A.B. 1956 (government); International Law School, The Hague (The Netherlands), attended 1958; U. of Virginia, LL.B. 1959

MILITARY SERVICE
Army, 1951-53

CAREER
Lawyer

POLITICAL HIGHLIGHTS
Suffolk County assistant district attorney, 1961-62; sought Democratic nomination for president, 1980

ELECTION RESULTS

2000 GENERAL		
Edward M. Kennedy (D)	1,889,494	72.7%
Jack E. Robinson III (R)	334,341	12.9%
Carla Howell (LIBERT)	308,860	11.9%
Philip Lawler (CNSTP)	42,113	1.6%
2000 PRIMARY		
Edward M. Kennedy (D)		unopposed

PREVIOUS WINNING PERCENTAGES
1994 (58%); 1988 (65%); 1982 (61%); 1976 (69%); 1970 (62%); 1964 (74%); 1962 Special Election (55%)

Elected 1962; 7th full term

At a time when his family's political dynasty seems diminished by a string of recent election defeats, Kennedy still towers as one of Washington's most influential legislators and one of the Democratic Party's most forceful spokesmen. As he begins his fifth decade in the Senate, he is as much of an anchor as ever for his party's liberal base, and he retains a keen sense of how and when to compromise to turn bills into laws without abandoning his principles.

A case in point came during the 107th Congress, as President Bush prepared his education overhaul proposal. The new president invited Kennedy to the White House in early 2001 for popcorn and a movie to show his willingness to reach across the aisle — even to Kennedy. By the end of the year, they had won enactment of a law tying federal school aid more directly to test results. "I've come to admire him," Bush said. "He's a smart, capable senator. You want him on your side, I can tell you that."

But the following year, when Bush and Republicans backed off from promises to fully fund the programs, Kennedy called the education law "hollow talk," and set the stage for a fierce budget battle in the 108th Congress. "That legislation was signed into law with great fanfare," Kennedy said. "But when the klieg lights go out and the bunting comes down and the cameras leave, the money isn't there. Needed resources for education are denied, even as new tax breaks for the wealthy are sought."

On a broad range of issues, Kennedy positioned himself at the start of the 108th as one of Bush's sharpest critics. As a war with Iraq approached, he warned that the United States should proceed only with United Nations support or risk an anti-American backlash overseas. As Republicans sought to restructure Medicare and provide a prescription drug benefit for seniors, he upped the ante on the overall health care debate, calling for legislation that would require employers to provide medical insurance for workers. And when Trent Lott was forced to step down as Senate Republican leader after praising Strom Thurmond's 1948 segregationist presidential campaign, Kennedy served notice that he would pressure Bush to elevate civil rights issues on the agenda.

Kennedy's public image has long been defined by family triumph, tragedy and scandal. But he has built a very different reputation at the Capitol, where he is now the fifth-longest-serving senator ever. The earnestness of his rhetoric in favor of organized labor, health care for all and environmental protection win grudging admiration even from opponents. Republicans still favor him as their metaphor for the wrong approach to federal governance — the "Ted Kennedy liberal" label remains the most cutting epithet they can sling — but they have found him to be a Democrat with whom they can deal.

Despite philosophical differences, for example, one of Kennedy's most productive and friendly alliances has been with conservative Utah Republican Orrin G. Hatch, the chairman of the Judiciary Committee. Among other achievements, the two collaborated on the Religious Freedom Restoration Act and the Americans with Disabilities Act.

In 1999, it was an agreement between Kennedy and Texas Republican Phil Gramm, a staunch conservative, that broke a partisan standoff over the ground rules for President Clinton's impeachment trial. "Stranger things have happened in politics, but the Kennedy-Gramm alliance is one of the strangest," GOP Sen. John McCain of Arizona said at the time.

Kennedy long ago understood what might be called the Iron Law of the Senate: Little can be accomplished without the 60 votes needed to overcome filibusters. And that requires compromises that cross party lines.

"Kennedy has built a career on that understanding," New York Times reporter Adam Clymer wrote in a 1999 biography, "winning victories over three decades on civil rights, election law, health care, crime and other subjects, in a series of alliances with key Republicans from Howard Baker to Bob Dole to Hugh Scott to Strom Thurmond."

For all his willingness to cut a deal when half a loaf appears within his grasp, Kennedy still fights losing battles with zeal — seeking patients' rights protections, minimum wage increases, a ban on employment discrimination against gays and more. From his desk at the rear of the Senate, he can raise the somnolent with his thunderous roar, his face reddening and his voice needing no electronic amplification as he attacks.

It is impossible to talk about his career without also recalling Kennedy's penchant for reckless behavior: the 1969 auto accident at Chappaquiddick in which the passenger in his car, Mary Jo Kopechne, drowned; a long period of carousing at Capitol Hill restaurants in the 1980s; his 1991 revelry with his son Patrick and nephew William Kennedy Smith at a Florida nightclub where Smith met a woman who subsequently accused him of rape. (Smith was acquitted after a highly publicized trial.)

Kennedy's image was so tainted that he felt compelled to sit mute at the 1991 confirmation hearings for Supreme Court Justice Clarence Thomas, who was accused of sexual harassment. His silence disappointed women and others who, in different days, would have counted on him. But his family life appears to have stabilized since 1992, when Kennedy was married for the second time, to Washington attorney Victoria Reggie.

Doubts about Kennedy's judgment fueled Republican hopes of defeating him in 1994. Republican venture capitalist Mitt Romney (who was elected Massachusetts governor in 2002) tapped his personal fortune to fill the airwaves with television ads portraying the senator as tired and haggard. Kennedy fought back, touring the state delivering federal checks and painting Romney as unprepared for Congress. He bucked the year's GOP tide and won with 58 percent. In 2000, he won his seventh full term with 73 percent against another wealthy businessman, Jack E. Robinson III.

While a niece and a nephew lost gubernatorial and congressional races in Maryland in 2002, Kennedy's younger son, Patrick, won re-election to a fifth term in the House from Rhode Island.

The youngest of nine children of Rose Fitzgerald, a congressman's daughter, and Joseph P. Kennedy, an ambassador to Britain and the first chairman of the Securities and Exchange Commission, Kennedy was first elected in 1962, at age 30, to fill the remaining two years of President John F. Kennedy's Senate term. (The president had arranged for family friend Benjamin A. Smith to be appointed until his youngest brother was old enough under the Constitution to serve.)

After the president was assassinated in 1963 and Sen. Robert F. Kennedy of New York was assassinated while seeking the Democratic presidential nomination in 1968, Kennedy felt intense pressure to take up his brothers' fallen banner. But when he challenged President Carter in 1980, memories of Chappaquiddick were still too fresh, and the candidate failed to articulate a clear idea of why he wanted to be president.

For all the years of anticipation that preceded it, the most memorable moment of Kennedy's only presidential bid came at its finale, in a speech to the Democratic National Convention. After conceding defeat, he vowed that "for all those whose cares have been our concern, the work goes on, the cause endures, the hope still lives, and the dream shall never die."

KEY VOTES

2002

Yes Pass farm bill reversing crop subsidy limits
No Postpone tougher automobile fuel efficiency standards
Yes Overhaul campaign finance law; ban "soft money" and restrict advocacy advertising
Yes Set federal election standards
No Support oil drilling in Arctic National Wildlife Refuge
No Revive fast-track procedures for trade agreements
Yes Create federal insurance coverage for catastrophic terrorist losses
Yes Tighten federal accounting and corporate governance regulation
Yes Advance bipartisan Medicare prescription drug plan
Yes Create independent Sept. 11 commission
Yes Back Democratic Homeland Security Department proposal
No Authorize war against Iraq

2001

No Confirm John Ashcroft as attorney general
No Nullify Clinton Labor Department ergonomics rule
No Cut taxes by $1.35 trillion through fiscal 2011
Yes Pass Democratic bill to bolster rights of patients in managed-care plans
Yes Permit a new round of military base closings
Yes Expand law enforcement power to investigate suspected terrorists

CQ VOTE STUDIES

	PARTY UNITY		PRESIDENTIAL SUPPORT	
	Support	Oppose	Support	Oppose
2002	97%	3%	64%	36%
2001	97%	3%	66%	34%
2000	98%	2%	94%	6%
1999	97%	3%	93%	7%
1998	100%	0%	96%	4%
1997	97%	3%	88%	12%
1996	94%	6%	88%	12%
1995	96%	4%	92%	8%
1994	94%	6%	95%	5%
1993	96%	4%	97%	3%

INTEREST GROUPS

	AFL-CIO	ADA	CCUS	ACU
2002	100%	100%	29%	0%
2001	100%	100%	38%	4%
2000	86%	90%	40%	12%
1999	88%	95%	47%	4%
1998	100%	95%	47%	0%
1997	100%	100%	40%	4%
1996	100%	90%	38%	0%
1995	100%	100%	33%	4%
1994	88%	90%	20%	0%
1993	82%	90%	36%	4%

Sen. John Kerry (D)

CAPITOL OFFICE
224-2742
john_kerry@kerry.senate.gov
kerry.senate.gov
304 Russell 20510-2102; fax 224-8525

COMMITTEES
Commerce, Science & Transportation
Finance
Foreign Relations
Small Business & Entrepreneurship - ranking member

HOMETOWN
Boston

BORN
Dec. 11, 1943, Denver, Colo.

RELIGION
Roman Catholic

FAMILY
Wife, Teresa Heinz Kerry; two children, three stepchildren

EDUCATION
Yale U., B.A. 1966 (political science); Boston College, J.D. 1976

MILITARY SERVICE
Navy, 1966-70

CAREER
Lawyer; county prosecutor

POLITICAL HIGHLIGHTS
Democratic nominee for U.S. House, 1972; lieutenant governor, 1983-85

ELECTION RESULTS

2002 GENERAL		
John Kerry (D)	1,605,976	80.0%
Michael E. Cloud (LIBERT)	369,807	18.4%
Randall Forsberg (write-in)	24,898	1.2%
2002 PRIMARY		
John Kerry (D)		unopposed

PREVIOUS WINNING PERCENTAGES
1996 (52%); 1990 (57%); 1984 (55%)

Elected 1984; 4th term

Kerry has been on the shortlist of possible Democratic presidential or vice presidential candidates for more than a decade, so it was little surprise when he became one of the first in the party to enter the 2004 presidential race. In doing so, the Vietnam veteran who turned into a protester against the war ensured that much of what he says and does in the 108th Congress will be judged by how it affects his chances in a crowded field of challengers to President Bush.

At some level, though, Kerry has already been in this position for years. A tall man with carefully styled hair and a long, chiseled jaw, Kerry has been expected to run someday since long before he arrived in the Senate — partly because of his sharp intellect and his appeal as a war veteran, and partly because he has never been known for keeping a low profile. (In Boston, his nickname is "Live Shot," a reference to his fondness for television cameras.) He opted against running for the White House in 1992 and again in 2000, although he made Al Gore's shortlist of potential running mates that year.

Kerry's war background took on new relevance for the Democrats as they sought to mount a credible challenge to a wartime Republican president, and the evolution of his thinking since Vietnam has been the subject of an 11,000-word profile in The New Yorker. But he is also trying hard to shake an image as a stiff blue-blood who has cultivated too much of a likeness to John F. Kennedy.

Still, his Vietnam experience, and the knowledge of international affairs he has picked up through his service on the Foreign Relations Committee, made him one of the most forceful Democratic spokesmen against Bush's argument that the United States should be prepared to attack Iraq alone to eliminate its weapons of mass destruction.

"I think you have to build legitimacy when you go to war," Kerry said in September 2002. Noting that Bush only sought the involvement of the United Nations at the urging of several GOP foreign policy elder statesmen, Kerry said, "I'd rather have a president who would do that initially, and didn't just do that as a matter of compromise. Through its own clumsiness throughout the summer . . . they created a debate about the administration rather than about Saddam Hussein."

In the end, Kerry voted for the resolution authorizing Bush to launch military action after the administration agreed to language that expressed a preference for involving other nations. He has defended his 1991 vote against the resolution authorizing the Persian Gulf War, calling it "the right vote at that moment in time." Noting that the war was ultimately successful, Kerry said, "I was not against using force. I was against moving so precipitously that we didn't have the consent . . . of the American people."

A leader of Vietnam Veterans Against the War, Kerry joined with other demonstrators in 1971 as they threw their medals over the White House fence. (He takes pains to explain that he opposed the returning of medals as a tactic and saved his own — three Purple Hearts, a Silver Star and a Bronze Star. Instead, he tossed over the ribbons of another veteran who could not travel to Washington.)

Kerry, who had risen to the rank of lieutenant in the Navy, got front-page coverage when he asked the Senate Foreign Relations Committee, "How do you ask a man to be the last man to die for a mistake?" He tried to exploit the publicity by moving to Lowell and running for an open House seat in

1972. He won his 10-way primary but lost in the fall to Republican Paul Cronin. During this time, Kerry received his first inquiry about a presidential run from CBS television reporter Morley Safer.

After his defeat, he went to law school and then worked as an assistant district attorney in Middlesex County. In 1982, he was elected lieutenant governor in a challenge of the Democratic establishment. Two years later, he beat Democratic Rep. James M. Shannon for the nomination to replace retiring Sen. Paul E. Tsongas. He won the general election over conservative businessman Raymond Shamie with 55 percent.

Twenty-five years after his service in Vietnam, the conflict still colored Kerry's actions and his life in Congress. In the mid-1990s, he teamed up with another Vietnam veteran and ex-POW, GOP Sen. John McCain of Arizona, to push for normalized U.S. relations with Vietnam. In 1994, Kerry and McCain worked to clear the way for President Clinton to lift the longstanding trade embargo with Vietnam. The action came a year after Kerry's Select Committee on POW-MIA Affairs concluded that there was "no compelling evidence" that any American remained alive in captivity in Southeast Asia.

More recently, Kerry has turned to domestic concerns. A participant in the original Earth Day in 1970, Kerry helped organize the 30th Earth Day celebration in 2000 and promoted environmentally friendly energy policies in Congress. He has undertaken difficult long-term assignments, such as building support in a skeptical Senate for the pollution restrictions of the 1997 Kyoto protocol on global warming, and he has been harshly critical of Bush for abandoning that treaty.

In 1998, he drafted a plan to overhaul public education that was heavy on ideas troublesome to traditional Democratic supporters. His plan would have transformed every public school into a charter school. It endorsed "public school choice," giving parents the option of sending children to public schools other than those in their geographic district.

Kerry also has embraced concepts at odds with powerful teachers unions, including raising teaching standards and making it easier for potential teachers with liberal arts degrees to get certified without many of the courses in education theory now required. He also has sought to change the tenure system, making it easier to fire bad teachers.

On crime, Kerry has drawn from his experience as a prosecutor to back get-tough tactics. He has proposed a "two strikes and you're out" bill and a mandatory life sentence for crimes against children.

In his role as the top Democrat on the Small Business Committee, Kerry has paid special attention to cutting federal red tape even while expanding some federal initiatives. He has touted the Small Business Administration's micro-loan program, which provides small loans to businesses that are having a hard time getting bank financing. In the 107th, he won Senate passage of a bill to offer emergency loans to small businesses hurt by rising utility costs, but the House never acted on it.

Early in his Senate career, Kerry's reputation suffered somewhat from his apparent preoccupation with image. He got known for caring about how things looked, and when he had corrective jaw surgery, it was regarded by some as an effort to improve his appearance.

In 1996, he faced his toughest challenge yet from William F. Weld, then the state's popular GOP governor. On the campaign trail, Weld's affable, down-to-earth style contrasted well with Kerry's stiff, aloof persona. And Kerry had to battle allegations of impropriety over his rent-free use of a lobbyist's apartment in Washington. But his late spending and solid performance in a series of debates carried him to victory by 7 percentage points. In 2002, the Republicans did not even bother to run a candidate against him.

KEY VOTES

2002

Yes Pass farm bill reversing crop subsidy limits
No Postpone tougher automobile fuel efficiency standards
Yes Overhaul campaign finance law; ban "soft money" and restrict advocacy advertising
Yes Set federal election standards
No Support oil drilling in Arctic National Wildlife Refuge
Yes Revive fast-track procedures for trade agreements
\+ Create federal insurance coverage for catastrophic terrorist losses
Yes Tighten federal accounting and corporate governance regulation
Yes Advance bipartisan Medicare prescription drug plan
Yes Create independent Sept. 11 commission
Yes Back Democratic Homeland Security Department proposal
Yes Authorize war against Iraq

2001

No Confirm John Ashcroft as attorney general
No Nullify Clinton Labor Department ergonomics rule
– Cut taxes by $1.35 trillion through fiscal 2011
Yes Pass Democratic bill to bolster rights of patients in managed-care plans
Yes Permit a new round of military base closings
Yes Expand law enforcement power to investigate suspected terrorists

CQ VOTE STUDIES

	PARTY UNITY		PRESIDENTIAL SUPPORT	
	Support	Oppose	Support	Oppose
2002	92%	8%	72%	28%
2001	98%	2%	65%	35%
2000	96%	4%	97%	3%
1999	95%	5%	93%	7%
1998	95%	5%	94%	6%
1997	97%	3%	87%	13%
1996	92%	8%	92%	8%
1995	92%	8%	87%	13%
1994	94%	6%	90%	10%
1993	94%	6%	93%	7%

INTEREST GROUPS

	AFL-CIO	ADA	CCUS	ACU
2002	92%	85%	55%	20%
2001	100%	95%	38%	4%
2000	75%	90%	53%	12%
1999	78%	95%	53%	0%
1998	100%	95%	50%	4%
1997	71%	95%	50%	0%
1996	86%	95%	31%	5%
1995	100%	95%	32%	4%
1994	88%	95%	30%	0%
1993	82%	90%	45%	12%

Rep. John W. Olver (D)

CAPITOL OFFICE
225-5335
www.house.gov/olver
1027 Longworth 20515-2101; fax 226-1224

COMMITTEES
Appropriations

HOMETOWN
Amherst

BORN
Sept. 3, 1936, Honesdale, Pa.

RELIGION
Unspecified

FAMILY
Wife, Rose Olver; one child

EDUCATION
Rensselaer Polytechnic Institute, B.S. 1955; Tufts U., M.S. 1956; Massachusetts Institute of Technology, Ph.D. 1961 (chemistry)

CAREER
Professor

POLITICAL HIGHLIGHTS
Mass. House, 1969-73; Mass. Senate, 1973-91

ELECTION RESULTS

2002 GENERAL		
John W. Olver (D)	137,841	67.6%
Matthew W. Kinnaman (R)	66,061	32.4%
2002 PRIMARY		
John W. Olver (D)		unopposed
2000 GENERAL		
John W. Olver (D)	169,375	68.2%
Pete Abair (R)	73,580	29.7%
Robert Potvin (I)	5,157	2.1%

PREVIOUS WINNING PERCENTAGES
1998 (72%); 1996 (53%); 1994 (99%); 1992 (52%); 1991 Special Election (50%)

Elected June 1991; 6th full term

Olver, a former chemistry professor, likes to take on challenges — he rock climbs despite his fear of heights, saying it gives him a feeling of control. And despite his quiet and decidedly low-key personality, he has embraced a career requiring that he mix and mingle with constituents on the campaign trail and his fellow lawmakers in the House.

Hardworking with a knack for detail, Olver has never lost an election in more than 30 years. Yet his solitary style has caused friction within the state's delegation at times, as he is the only Massachusetts lawmaker on the Appropriations Committee, where dealmaking and good relationships with other legislators are considered essential. The top-ranking Democrat on the subcommittee that funds the Treasury Department and transportation programs, he is expected not only to work for spending to benefit his western Massachusetts district, but also to carry water for his home-state colleagues.

In 1999, Joe Moakley, the dean of the state's House delegation, let it be known that he felt Olver should be doing more. Moakley suggested that Olver's personality was not suited to the give-and-take atmosphere of the Appropriations panel. "Some people are born salesmen, others are born librarians," Moakley told the Boston Herald. "He means well. He's a nice guy, bright enough, but he's not collegial," Moakley said.

Olver takes such criticisms to heart, and he has tried to be more of a team player. It is clear, however, that he likes the policy aspect of the job more than the political one, and many of his Bay State colleagues still prefer to go to other appropriators for help with a pet project. Olver has made some efforts to join forces with other Massachusetts lawmakers on common interests — with Rep. Edward J. Markey and Sen. John Kerry on environmental issues and with Rep. Martin T. Meehan on campaign finance, for instance.

Olver says he believes in the government's responsibility to solve society's problems and to play a part in economic development. He has been called the Massachusetts delegation's "most liberal liberal," even in a contingent that includes such pillars of the Democratic left as Rep. Barney Frank and Sen. Edward M. Kennedy. He affiliates with the Progressive Caucus, the most liberal faction of House Democrats, and he sided with his party on votes that pitted Democrats against Republicans 98.5 percent of the time in the 107th Congress. His votes on fiscal matters made him one of eight House members who received a zero score in 2001 from the anti-spending group Citizens Against Government Waste.

Environmental protection is one of Olver's priorities. He spends much of his free time outdoors hiking, rock climbing, wind surfing or cross-country skiing. He continually presses the Bush administration to do more to reduce greenhouse gas emissions and to increase automobile fuel economy. Olver and Maryland Republican Wayne T. Gilchrest formed and co-chair the House's Climate Change Caucus, in which members work to develop bipartisan agreements on climate issues.

In the 107th Congress, Olver, Gilchrest and other caucus members introduced a bill to require the Environmental Protection Agency to collect and publish information about greenhouse gas emissions. Though the White House made it clear that it would not implement agreements reached in the 1997 Kyoto Protocol on global warming, Olver keeps pushing for incremental steps.

He also works for continued funding of the Silvio O. Conte National Wildlife Refuge along the Connecticut River, named after his predecessor in the House. In the 107th, Olver offered legislation proposing a study to determine whether a number of hiking trails in Connecticut and Massachusetts should be added to the National Trails System. During a hearing on the bill, Olver showed up with his own enlarged photos of scenic spots along the trails and gave a mini-seminar on the geologic and botanic highlights of the area.

As the top Democrat on Appropriations' Military Construction Subcommittee in the 106th and 107th Congresses, Olver's attention to detail was well-known. Once, while trying to determine how the Pentagon sets priorities for spending on new National Guard and reserve facilities, he brought his own extensive worksheet to a committee meeting, passed out copies and provoked a lengthy discussion with the military officials who had come to testify.

Olver has pushed for funding to build and run a number of community health centers and, as a member of the Rural Health Care Coalition, he worked in the 106th Congress to increase Medicare funds for home health care, hospitals and medical providers that were particularly affected by cuts in Medicare reimbursements in 1997.

Born on a farm in Pennsylvania, Olver headed north for graduate school, earning a doctorate from the Massachusetts Institute of Technology at age 24. He taught chemistry at the University of Massachusetts' Amherst campus for eight years before making his first foray into elective politics and winning — a state House race in 1968.

Four years later, he bucked the national GOP trend, unseating an incumbent Republican state senator. He stayed in the state Senate until 1991 when Conte, a liberal Republican, died in the middle of his 17th term.

Olver won a 10-way Democratic primary with surprising ease, then he collected endorsements from his defeated rivals as well as from union members, teachers, environmentalists, women's groups and abortion rights supporters. He won the special election by fewer than 2,000 votes, marking the first time since 1892 that the area had sent a Democrat to the House. After that he alternated close races in 1992 and 1996 (when he defeated Jane Swift, who would later serve as governor) with re-election romps in 1994 and 1998.

The 2000 election broke that pattern, when Olver won by 39 percentage points. His territory left largely intact by redistricting, he won by 35 points in 2002.

KEY VOTES

2002

- Yes Overhaul campaign finance law; ban "soft money" and restrict advocacy advertising
- No Back Bush's defense budget increase
- No Extend 1996 welfare law
- No Adopt Bush's discretionary spending limit
- No Pass GOP Medicare prescription drug plan
- Yes Create independent Sept. 11 commission
- Yes Extend union protections to Homeland Security Department employees
- No Revive fast-track procedures for trade agreements
- No Authorize war against Iraq
- No Advance bankruptcy overhaul opposed by abortion opponents

2001

- No Nullify Clinton Labor Department ergonomics rule
- No Cut taxes by $1.35 trillion through fiscal 2011
- Yes Maintain ban on oil drilling in Arctic National Wildlife Refuge
- No Approve Bush proposal to limit managed-care plan liability for coverage decisions
- Yes Divert money from crop subsidy payments to land conservation
- No Expand law enforcement power to investigate suspected terrorists

CQ VOTE STUDIES

	PARTY UNITY		PRESIDENTIAL SUPPORT	
	Support	Oppose	Support	Oppose
2002	99%	1%	27%	73%
2001	98%	2%	12%	88%
2000	97%	3%	83%	17%
1999	96%	4%	88%	12%
1998	99%	1%	88%	12%

INTEREST GROUPS

	AFL-CIO	ADA	CCUS	ACU
2002	100%	95%	37%	0%
2001	100%	100%	23%	0%
2000	100%	90%	38%	4%
1999	89%	95%	13%	0%
1998	100%	95%	24%	0%

MASSACHUSETTS 1

West – Pittsfield, Leominster, Westfield

The oranges of autumn, the whites of winter and the greens of spring and summer attract vacationers to the 1st. The Berkshire Mountains of western Massachusetts once protected American Indians from encroaching whites. But three hundred years later, the area serves as home to a shrinking blue-collar and stable rural population.

Tourist areas include the kind of serene New England towns depicted in films, books and Norman Rockwell paintings. Tanglewood, the summer home of the Boston Symphony Orchestra, also attracts jazz and chamber music fans to its outdoor theater in Lenox. The Yankee Candle Company, one of the largest manufacturers of scented candles, is based in South Deerfield.

After decades as a dominant textile mill area and the world's top plastics producer, factory closures and downsizing decimated the region during the recession of the late 1980s and early 1990s. Pittsfield and Fitchburg suffered the most. While the economy of Pittsfield is diversifying, General Electric reduced its defense-related work force there from 11,000 in the 1980s to 2,000 a decade later. A strong retail and plastics industry has spurred growth in Leominster, a western outgrowth of the Boston suburbs that sits on the crossing of two major highways at the eastern edge of the district.

Once a Republican stronghold, the 1st was held by liberal GOP Rep. Silvio Conte for more than three decades until his death in 1991. Some rural areas east of Interstate 91 support Republicans, but the sparse population is overwhelmed by Democratic union voters in the northeast and university liberals around Amherst, where the state's flagship university is located. Seven of the 13 cities and towns in which 2002 Democratic gubernatorial nominee Shannon O'Brien received at least two-thirds of the vote are in the 1st.

MAJOR INDUSTRY

Plastics, paper, tourism, higher education

CITIES

Pittsfield, 45,793; Leominster, 41,303; Westfield, 40,072; Holyoke, 39,838; Fitchburg, 39,102; Amherst (unincorporated), 34,874

NOTABLE

John Chapman, known as Johnny Appleseed, was born in Leominster; NAACP founder W.E.B. DuBois (1868-1963) was born in Great Barrington.

Rep. Richard E. Neal (D)

CAPITOL OFFICE
225-5601
www.house.gov/neal
2133 Rayburn 20515-2102; fax 225-8112

COMMITTEES
Budget
Ways & Means

HOMETOWN
Springfield

BORN
Feb. 14, 1949, Worcester, Mass.

RELIGION
Roman Catholic

FAMILY
Wife, Maureen Neal; four children

EDUCATION
American International College, B.A. 1972 (political scinece); U. of Hartford, M.P.A. 1976

CAREER
College lecturer; teacher; mayoral aide

POLITICAL HIGHLIGHTS
Springfield City Council, 1978-84 (president, 1979); mayor of Springfield, 1984-89

ELECTION RESULTS

2002 GENERAL		
Richard E. Neal (D)		unopposed
2002 PRIMARY		
Richard E. Neal (D)		unopposed
2000 GENERAL		
Richard E. Neal (D)	196,670	98.9%
write-ins	2,176	1.1%

PREVIOUS WINNING PERCENTAGES
1998 (98%); 1996 (72%); 1994 (59%); 1992 (53%); 1990 (100%); 1988 (80%)

Elected 1988; 8th term

It is a somewhat misleading characterization, but Neal may well be the most conservative person in the all-Democratic congressional delegation for Massachusetts. Yet he is a strong supporter of the environment and labor and, from his seat on the Ways and Means Committee, he works hard to close corporate tax loopholes.

On certain social issues, however, Neal takes a less-traveled road than most of his home-state colleagues. He opposes federal funding of abortions and has voted to ban a procedure its opponents call "partial birth" abortion. He also supported a constitutional amendment allowing Congress to outlaw desecration of the U.S. flag. But these positions would be expected from many people in the 2nd District, particularly in Springfield's blue-collar and Irish Catholic precincts, where most of the district's voters live.

Neal has opposed Republican efforts, however, to advance constitutional amendments requiring a balanced budget and congressional term limits. He routinely stays with the Democrats on more than 90 percent of party-line votes each year and won a seat on the Budget panel in the 108th Congress.

His top priority in the 107th was legislation to close loopholes in the law that offer huge tax benefits to companies that move their headquarters out of the United States. Such moves are a "slap in the face to individual taxpayers," Neal said as his quest became a hot campaign-season cause of the Democrats in 2002. He resumed the battle in the 108th.

An opponent of the $1.35 trillion, 10-year tax cut President Bush pushed to enactment in 2001, Neal argued from the outset of the debate — presciently — that the new, lower tax rates would force millions more people to pay the alternative minimum tax, which was originally designed to ensure that the very richest people would have to pay some taxes despite all the credits and deductions they might claim. Neal has advocated repealing the parallel tax system. In Ways and Means and on the House floor, he also sought to expand the tax package's new benefits for contributing to retirement accounts, which he said would do too little for those of modest income.

Neal also has worked to simplify the tax code, sponsoring a measure to eliminate more than 200 lines from individual tax forms or worksheets.

As a member of Ways and Means' Trade Subcommittee, Neal has cast a swing vote on trade. Siding with labor and environmental groups, he opposed the 2002 fast-track law giving the president authority to negotiate trade agreements that Congress can approve or reject but not amend. And he voted against the 1993 North American Free Trade Agreement. But in 2000, he voted to grant China permanent normal trade status, one of only two in the Massachusetts House delegation to do so. Amid concerns about China's human rights record, Neal described his vote to The Wall Street Journal as "a leap of faith," but he added: "Having said that, the Massachusetts economy is perfectly positioned to take advantage of this" move to open up trade with China.

In the 107th, his aversion to circumventing the regular legislative procedures of the House drew some attention when he appeared to be thwarting the effort of his Massachusetts colleague — and Capitol Hill roommate — Martin T. Meehan to bring campaign finance legislation to the floor. When GOP leaders refused to bring up the bill, Meehan and his Republican cosponsor, Christopher Shays of Connecticut, sought to assemble the signatures of a majority of House members on a discharge petition to force the bill before the House. Though a supporter of the measure, Neal initially declined to sign, arguing that legislative chaos would result if such grassroots campaigns were to succeed on a regular basis. Still, he promised Meehan and their party's leaders that if they could get 217 signatures, he would provide the pivotal 218th — which is what happened.

Neal has been a leader of congressional efforts to keep the United States involved in the search for peace in Northern Ireland. His paternal grandparents are from Ireland, while his maternal grandparents are from Northern Ireland, and Neal is co-chairman of the Ad Hoc Congressional Committee on Irish Affairs. In 1999, he urged a major restructuring of the predominantly Protestant Northern Ireland police force, the Royal Ulster Constabulary. In 1998, his name was floated as a potential candidate for ambassador to Ireland, and in 2002 he was given the American Ireland Fund's International Leadership Award.

What the golf course is for many businessmen and civic leaders, the basketball court is for Neal — a place to develop personal relationships that go beyond political interests and to cut a deal now and then while he is working up a healthy sweat. Neal spends plenty of time in the members-only House gymnasium and at the Springfield YMCA competing in what his staff describes as "spirited" full court games. As a former high school player and the father of two sons who are good enough to play at the college level, Neal's passion for the game goes well beyond any sense of obligation he may feel as the representative of the city where basketball was invented.

Reared by an aunt after both of his parents died before he reached his early teens, Neal says he has always been fascinated by politics. He majored in political science in college, and later he was the co-chairman of George McGovern's 1972 presidential campaign in western Massachusetts. After serving as an aide to Springfield Mayor William C. Sullivan, he won three elections to the city council. He also taught history and government at a high school and at area colleges. In 1983, he won the first of three elections as mayor, drawing favorable notices for stimulating downtown rehabilitation and neighborhood revitalization.

In 1988, when Democrat Edward P. Boland announced his retirement after 36 years in the House, Neal was quick off the mark. He won the nomination unopposed and crushed a weak GOP foe. In his first re-election bid, he survived a primary challenge from former Springfield Mayor Theodore E. Dimauro. Two years later, he was held to 53 percent in November — a consequence of redistricting, anti-incumbent fever and Neal's 87 overdrafts at the private bank for House members. But Neal has had little trouble holding the seat since; Republicans have not fielded a challenger since 1996.

KEY VOTES

2002

- Yes Overhaul campaign finance law; ban "soft money" and restrict advocacy advertising
- Yes Back Bush's defense budget increase
- No Extend 1996 welfare law
- No Adopt Bush's discretionary spending limit
- No Pass GOP Medicare prescription drug plan
- Yes Create independent Sept. 11 commission
- Yes Extend union protections to Homeland Security Department employees
- No Revive fast-track procedures for trade agreements
- No Authorize war against Iraq
- No Advance bankruptcy overhaul opposed by abortion opponents

2001

- No Nullify Clinton Labor Department ergonomics rule
- No Cut taxes by $1.35 trillion through fiscal 2011
- Yes Maintain ban on oil drilling in Arctic National Wildlife Refuge
- No Approve Bush proposal to limit managed-care plan liability for coverage decisions
- Yes Divert money from crop subsidy payments to land conservation
- Yes Expand law enforcement power to investigate suspected terrorists

CQ VOTE STUDIES

	PARTY UNITY		PRESIDENTIAL SUPPORT	
	Support	Oppose	Support	Oppose
2002	96%	4%	28%	72%
2001	92%	8%	26%	74%
2000	92%	8%	83%	17%
1999	91%	9%	78%	22%
1998	95%	5%	80%	20%

INTEREST GROUPS

	AFL-CIO	ADA	CCUS	ACU
2002	88%	90%	37%	4%
2001	92%	85%	27%	13%
2000	90%	80%	38%	8%
1999	78%	95%	32%	4%
1998	100%	95%	35%	12%

MASSACHUSETTS 2

South central – Springfield, Chicopee, Northampton

The rolling hills and thick forests of the 2nd extend along the state's southern border from Springfield and Northampton in the west to Bellingham in the east. Springfield dwarfs all other communities in the 2nd; small, rural towns and intermittent farms fill out the rest of south-central Massachusetts.

Much of Springfield's economic success in the 1990s was tied to its history as a hub for inventions, although the region's future rests with the insurance and health care industries — most notably Mass Mutual and Baystate Health System — which have replaced some of the city's shrinking manufacturing base. Service and government jobs, some of which are generated by Chicopee's Westover Air Reserve Base, are important to the region's economy. The construction of a new home for the Basketball Hall of Fame and restoration of the civic center should bring more visitors to Springfield.

Hispanics — many of whom moved to the 2nd in the 1950s to work in the tobacco fields — once gravitated to Springfield's North End but are now more dispersed through the city. Most African-Americans live near the city's center.

Residents in and around Springfield, many of whom are blue-collar and Irish Catholic, vote Democratic and dominate the district's elections. Smith College produces a strongly liberal vote in Northampton, which gave 2000 Green Party presidential nominee Ralph Nader a greater share of the vote than Republican George W. Bush. Despite the district's strong Democratic lean, some Republicans can be competitive, particularly among small-town and rural voters. Mitt Romney, the 2002 GOP gubernatorial nominee, narrowly won the 2nd.

MAJOR INDUSTRY

Insurance, health care, higher education, tourism

CITIES

Springfield, 152,082; Chicopee, 54,653; Northampton, 28,978

NOTABLE

Important local inventions or "firsts" include the U.S. Armory (1794), Pullman rail car (1850), monkey wrench (1854), basketball (1892), and the gasoline-powered car (1893).

Rep. Jim McGovern (D)

CAPITOL OFFICE
225-6101
www.house.gov/mcgovern
430 Cannon 20515-2103; fax 225-5759

COMMITTEES
Rules

HOMETOWN
Worcester

BORN
Nov. 20, 1959, Worcester, Mass.

RELIGION
Roman Catholic

FAMILY
Wife, Lisa McGovern; two children

EDUCATION
American U., B.A. 1981 (history), M.P.A. 1984

CAREER
Congressional aide

POLITICAL HIGHLIGHTS
Sought Democratic nomination for U.S. House, 1994

ELECTION RESULTS

2002 GENERAL		
Jim McGovern (D)	155,697	98.8%
write-ins	1,848	1.2%
2002 PRIMARY		
Jim McGovern (D)		unopposed
2000 GENERAL		
Jim McGovern (D)	213,065	98.8%
write-ins	2,496	1.2%

PREVIOUS WINNING PERCENTAGES
1998 (57%); 1996 (53%)

Elected 1996; 4th term

McGovern became a member of Congress in 1997 already exceptionally well-versed in the ways of the Capitol, and with a network of highly placed Democratic lawmakers to guide him as he moved onto the political stage after almost two decades behind the scenes.

As an aide to the former South Dakota senator and presidential candidate George McGovern (no relation), and to Rep. Joe Moakley, who chaired the Rules Committee for 5 1/2 years and was dean of the Massachusetts House delegation at his death in 2001, McGovern developed an appreciation for the importance of both grand visions and pragmatism in politics. "McGovern taught me it was OK to be an idealist," he told the Boston Globe. "Moakley taught me how to get things done."

When Moakley died, McGovern moved quickly to gain his mentor's seat on the Rules Committee, a powerful arm of the leadership because of its power to set the parameters for debates on the House floor. He received the assignment from Democratic leaders, then agreed to allow Alcee L. Hastings of Florida to take the seat in mid-2001. McGovern nonetheless got on Rules a year later, when Tony P. Hall of Ohio stepped aside before resigning from Congress to take an ambassadorship. Since then McGovern has not shied away from combat in the often tartly partisan debates of the committee. "I don't see any reason why you and you alone . . . should rewrite our trade adjustment laws and do it so badly," McGovern told Republican Ways and Means Committee Chairman Bill Thomas of California during a particularly contentious 2002 hearing on legislation renewing presidential fast-track trade negotiating authority.

McGovern affiliates with the Progressive Caucus, the most left-leaning faction of the House Democrats. But he works with lawmakers in both parties on nuts-and-bolts issues of economic development, education and health care. He has fought to improve Medicare payments for home health care, increase Pell Grants for college students and provide U.S. support for a United Nations program to provide school lunches.

As a freshman in the 105th Congress, McGovern was chosen for a spot in the party whip organization and won a seat on the Transportation Committee as it rewrote surface transportation policy. He leapfrogged over 22 more-senior Democrats on the panel when he was appointed one of the House negotiators on the final version of the bill, known as TEA-21. He was able to win funding for a variety of Worcester-area highway, transit and bikeway projects then — and, even though he no longer serves on Transportation, he surely will be advocating another round of earmarks for his district when the law is rewritten in the 108th.

McGovern takes a keen interest in foreign affairs, particularly in Latin America. He has traveled to Cuba twice and, in 2002, was among the 17 Democrats and 17 Republicans to form the House's Cuba Working Group, which pressed for elimination of the ban on travel to Cuba, removal of financing restrictions on sales of food to the island and generally closer ties. He also has opposed increased military aid to Colombia in that nation's fight against left-wing rebels, even in the context of an international anti-terrorism effort.

At the request of a group of high school student constituents, McGovern became involved in conditions in East Timor, which struggled to break away from Indonesian rule. In 1999, he traveled there to observe a plebiscite on independence. East Timor was a Portuguese colony for hundreds of years, and the 3rd District includes a substantial Portuguese community.

While he was a top aide to Moakley, McGovern was a key staff member on a 1990 House task force that looked into the murders the year before of six Jesuit priests and two women in El Salvador. Several of the Salvadoran military officers who were implicated in the case had graduated from the U.S. Army School of the Americas at Fort Benning, which trains Latin American military officers. Since then, McGovern has persistently tried to eliminate funding for the school, which he says "continues to train military officers who harm and kill the innocent people of Latin America." The school was reorganized and renamed the Western Hemispheric Institute for Security Cooperation in the 106th but remains in business.

McGovern knows it is wise to keep in touch back home, in ways both grand and small. During the Clinton administration, he convened an economic summit in Worcester, the largest city he represents, to bring together local, state and federal government officials, academics and leaders of the private sector to discuss strategies to revitalize the local economy. In 2002, he was on Worcester Common to welcome home the local team that was runner-up to the U.S. champion in the Little League World Series.

During his childhood in Worcester — his father ran a liquor store and his mother was a dance teacher — the McGoverns followed politics closely, especially where the Kennedys were involved. When Sen. Robert F. Kennedy was assassinated in 1968, he recalls, "my father gathered us around the kitchen table and we wrote sympathy cards to Ethel."

McGovern had his first brush with politics as a junior high schooler in 1972, when he found himself defending presidential candidate George McGovern because they shared the same last name. He then became involved in the campaign. Later, as an American University student, he worked in McGovern's Senate office. In 1984, when the South Dakotan launched another presidential bid, Jim McGovern was his campaign manager in Massachusetts and made the nominating speech at the Democratic National Convention in San Francisco. The elder McGovern returned the favor in 1996 and campaigned for Jim McGovern in Massachusetts.

McGovern went to work for Moakley in 1981 and served on his personal staff and in the Rules Committee office until 1996.

He unsuccessfully sought the Democratic nomination for the 3rd District seat in 1994. In 1996, in an election considered something of an upset, he defeated two-term Republican Peter I. Blute by 8 percentage points. In 1998, Republicans viewed McGovern as vulnerable, but he beat moderate state Sen. Matthew J. Amorello by 15 points. The incumbent has faced no GOP opposition in his two re-elections since.

KEY VOTES

2002

Yes Overhaul campaign finance law; ban "soft money" and restrict advocacy advertising
No Back Bush's defense budget increase
No Extend 1996 welfare law
No Adopt Bush's discretionary spending limit
No Pass GOP Medicare prescription drug plan
Yes Create independent Sept. 11 commission
Yes Extend union protections to Homeland Security Department employees
No Revive fast-track procedures for trade agreements
No Authorize war against Iraq
No Advance bankruptcy overhaul opposed by abortion opponents

2001

No Nullify Clinton Labor Department ergonomics rule
No Cut taxes by $1.35 trillion through fiscal 2011
Yes Maintain ban on oil drilling in Arctic National Wildlife Refuge
No Approve Bush proposal to limit managed-care plan liability for coverage decisions
Yes Divert money from crop subsidy payments to land conservation
No Expand law enforcement power to investigate suspected terrorists

CQ VOTE STUDIES

	PARTY UNITY		PRESIDENTIAL SUPPORT	
	Support	Oppose	Support	Oppose
2002	99%	1%	22%	78%
2001	97%	3%	16%	84%
2000	98%	2%	86%	14%
1999	96%	4%	82%	18%
1998	97%	3%	80%	20%

INTEREST GROUPS

	AFL-CIO	ADA	CCUS	ACU
2002	100%	100%	30%	0%
2001	100%	90%	35%	4%
2000	100%	100%	33%	0%
1999	89%	100%	20%	0%
1998	100%	100%	39%	4%

MASSACHUSETTS 3

Central and south — Worcester, Attleboro, part of Fall River

The 3rd District cuts a diagonal sliver from the mountains of Princeton to the fishing community of Fall River, winding its way from areas north and west of Boston almost to the Atlantic Ocean south of the city.

Worcester, a working-class city with a strong biotechnology presence, is the 3rd's population hub and has been revitalizing its downtown. A late-1990s project centralizing its respected hospitals, research institutes and some drug manufacturing plants into a medical center has sparked economic development. Still, Worcester registered slow population growth in the 1990s. Hispanics and blacks are displacing whites. Communities to the north and south are filling up with suburbanites who commute to jobs in Boston or Providence, R.I.

At the district's southern end, Fall River (shared with the 4th District) has long been a bastion of blue-collar white ethnic Democrats. The city has long had one of the highest unemployment rates in the state.

The Democratic dominance in Worcester and Fall River allows Democrats to overcome the ring of Republican support that binds the towns surrounding Worcester, including Paxton, Holden, the Boylstons and Shrewsbury. George W. Bush came close to winning those areas, as well as Princeton and the well-off towns of Southborough and Hopkinton in the north-central part of the district, but he failed to carry a single city or town in the 3rd in the 2000 presidential election.

Despite the dominance of Democratic presidential candidates, the 3rd can support moderate-to-liberal Republicans, as shown by its backing of Mitt Romney in the 2002 gubernatorial election. Romney won every city and town in the 3rd except Fall River, Worcester and two others.

MAJOR INDUSTRY

Biotechnology, health care, heavy manufacturing, retail

CITIES

Worcester, 172,648; Fall River (pt.), 53,704; Attleboro, 42,068

NOTABLE

Worcester boasts two important "firsts," more than two centuries apart: the publication of the first American novel, William Hill Brown's "The Power of Sympathy," in 1789, and the successful cloning of human embryos by a Worcester-based biotech company in 2001.

Rep. Barney Frank (D)

CAPITOL OFFICE
225-5931
www.house.gov/frank
2252 Rayburn 20515-2104; fax 225-0182

COMMITTEES
Financial Services - ranking member
Select Homeland Security

HOMETOWN
Newton

BORN
March 31, 1940, Bayonne, N.J.

RELIGION
Jewish

FAMILY
Single

EDUCATION
Harvard U., A.B. 1962 (government), J.D. 1977

CAREER
Lawyer; mayoral and congressional aide

POLITICAL HIGHLIGHTS
Mass. House, 1973-81

ELECTION RESULTS

2002 GENERAL		
Barney Frank (D)		unopposed
2002 PRIMARY		
Barney Frank (D)		unopposed
2000 GENERAL		
Barney Frank (D)	200,638	74.9%
Martin D. Travis (R)	56,553	21.1%
David J. Euchner (LIBERT)	10,553	3.9%

PREVIOUS WINNING PERCENTAGES
1998 (98%); 1996 (72%); 1994 (100%); 1992 (68%); 1990 (66%); 1988 (70%); 1986 (89%); 1984 (74%); 1982 (60%); 1980 (52%)

Elected 1980; 12th term

For eight years, Frank took ample pleasure in being the caustic foil to the House Republican leadership, overmatching their wit in debate even when he could not overpower them in the legislative clutches. But in the 108th Congress, Frank is taking on an additional role — top Democrat on the Financial Services Committee — that should allow him to put his quick mind to work on legislative offense as much as on rhetorical defense.

From his new perch, Frank will seek to steer the panel's attention to housing issues, including predatory mortgage lending to the poor, and global commerce, especially stepped-up oversight of the International Monetary Fund and the World Bank.

At the behest of Minority Leader Nancy Pelosi, who was seeking to open up seats for junior members on desirable committees, in the 108th Frank took a leave from the Judiciary Committee, where he had long been one of the most assertive and effective members of either party and had risen to No. 2 in Democratic seniority. Pelosi softened the loss of that seat by naming Frank to the new Homeland Security Committee.

Frank has never allowed his committee assignments — or lack thereof — to circumscribe his intellectual engagement or his activism. And the Democrats' loss of the House majority did nothing to muffle his voice. "I'm used to being in the minority," he told The New York Times Magazine after the GOP took charge. "I'm a left-handed, gay Jew. I've never felt, automatically, a member of any majority."

The comment is quintessential Barney Frank: candid, self-deprecating, combative and clever, too. After 11 terms in the House, he has amassed an encyclopedic knowledge of public policy and parliamentary rules, which he employs with precision in his battles. And whatever their political stripes, people all over Washington enjoy his shtick. Frank was named funniest and smartest member of Congress in the 2000 Washingtonian magazine poll of Capitol Hill aides.

It is easy to see why. In an era when floor "debate" is often just a recitation of boilerplate rhetoric, Frank is spontaneous combustion, passionately making his liberal case with off-the-cuff, rapid-fire — and tightly reasoned — arguments. In the waning hours of the 107th Congress, the GOP leadership sought to resuscitate a bankruptcy overhaul bill by eliminating a provision that had caused the House to condemn it to oblivion only hours before. Frank tartly observed "the separation anxiety on the Republican side of not being continuously in the bosom, if not the pocket, of large financial interests."

Frank's sarcasm is legendary. During a hearing on the accounting scandals of 2002, he congratulated one witness "on your ability to evade so calmly." He frequently chides the GOP majority for dictating policy to the states in areas such as prison construction and gambling regulation, even as they claim the mantle of champions of states' rights. He savors opportunities to expose rifts within the Republican Party, gleefully observing that, "The right hand doesn't know what the far right hand is doing."

From his Judiciary seat, Frank was center stage during the 1998 impeachment proceedings against President Clinton. Echoing the famous Watergate question of a quarter-century before — Sen. Howard H. Baker Jr.'s "What did the president know, and when did he know it?" — Frank's most memorable line was, "What did he touch, and when did he touch it?" That rhetorical question served as the Democrats' most ironic condemnation of the fervent GOP pursuit of details about the president's relationship with the former White House intern Monica Lewinsky.

Frank, who was the first member of Congress ever to announce his homosexuality, pushed for a censure of the president, similar to the reprimand the House had handed him in 1990 after revelations that a male prostitute Frank had hired as a household employee was running a prostitution business from Frank's apartment. The House voted 408-18 to reprimand Frank for bringing discredit on the House.

His willingness to use himself as an example illustrates the matter-of-fact way Frank has handled controversy about his personal life. "I answer every other question I'm asked," he said in disclosing his sexual orientation in 1987. In the 104th Congress, Frank led the unsuccessful opposition to a law discouraging gay marriages. In the 103rd, he angered some gay rights groups by offering a policy on homosexuals in the military only slightly more tolerant than Clinton's.

In the 107th, he opposed President Bush 89 percent of the time, more often than any other member. But for all the attention he attracts by provoking the GOP, he also is willing to work with Republicans to reach compromise. "If you're not able to work closely with people you despise, you can't really work here," he told The Boston Globe while working with conservatives in a bid to prevent enactment of the 2000 law normalizing the U.S.-China trade relationship.

In 2002, Frank worked with Republican Judiciary Chairman F. James Sensenbrenner of Wisconsin on a bill to allow some permanent resident aliens who had lived in the United States for seven years and who had committed minor crimes to seek to remain in the country rather than be deported. In 2003, he fostered a collegial relationship with Financial Services Chairman Michael G. Oxley, an Ohio Republican; the two began the year sponsoring a bill together to renew a lapsed federal flood insurance program.

After growing up in Bayonne, N.J., Frank went to Harvard and stuck around to teach government and do graduate work. Between 1968 and 1972, he worked for Boston Mayor Kevin White and was administrative assistant to Democratic Rep. Michael Harrington of Massachusetts, gaining contacts that helped him win a seat in the state House. He had been there eight years when Democratic Rep. Robert F. Drinan, a liberal Catholic priest, bowed to a papal prohibition on clergymen holding public office. Frank won the seat with 52 percent against a Republican who portrayed him as too liberal.

His toughest re-election battle was his first, when Massachusetts lost a seat in reapportionment for the 1980s, and Frank was forced to run in 1982 against Republican Rep. Margaret M. Heckler. He won with 60 percent.

KEY VOTES

2002

- Yes Overhaul campaign finance law; ban "soft money" and restrict advocacy advertising
- No Back Bush's defense budget increase
- No Extend 1996 welfare law
- No Adopt Bush's discretionary spending limit
- No Pass GOP Medicare prescription drug plan
- Yes Create independent Sept. 11 commission
- Yes Extend union protections to Homeland Security Department employees
- No Revive fast-track procedures for trade agreements
- No Authorize war against Iraq
- No Advance bankruptcy overhaul opposed by abortion opponents

2001

- No Nullify Clinton Labor Department ergonomics rule
- No Cut taxes by $1.35 trillion through fiscal 2011
- Yes Maintain ban on oil drilling in Arctic National Wildlife Refuge
- No Approve Bush proposal to limit managed-care plan liability for coverage decisions
- Yes Divert money from crop subsidy payments to land conservation
- No Expand law enforcement power to investigate suspected terrorists

CQ VOTE STUDIES

	PARTY UNITY		PRESIDENTIAL SUPPORT	
	Support	Oppose	Support	Oppose
2002	97%	3%	14%	86%
2001	97%	3%	9%	91%
2000	94%	6%	84%	16%
1999	92%	8%	80%	20%
1998	94%	6%	81%	19%

INTEREST GROUPS

	AFL-CIO	ADA	CCUS	ACU
2002	100%	100%	26%	8%
2001	100%	100%	22%	0%
2000	100%	95%	33%	12%
1999	100%	100%	21%	0%
1998	100%	100%	33%	4%

MASSACHUSETTS 4

New Bedford; Boston suburbs – Newton; Taunton

Downtowns replete with 18th- and 19th-century town hall buildings dot the Yankee communities in the 4th, several of which have celebrated their 300th or 350th anniversaries. The district encompasses thickly settled Boston suburbs, rural cranberry bogs and urban New Bedford and Fall River (shared with the 3rd District).

The economic health of the 4th reflects a split between the northern and southern tiers of the district. The northern well-to-do towns and Boston suburbs benefited from a strong economy in the 1990s, due in large part to the Route 128 high-tech corridor, though moderate unemployment started to affect the area at the end of the 1990s. The southern fishing and former textile mill communities, including Fall River and New Bedford, struggled to stave off double-digit unemployment as the textile industry declined to almost nothing and commercial fishermen faced sparse catches. In the 4th's center, the cranberry bogs in Middleboro and biotechnology firms farther north provide a strong economic base.

The blue-collar, immigrant-laden southern section of the district gives the 4th a strong Democratic lean. New Bedford, which has the lowest median household income in the state, and Fall River are heavily Portuguese and vote solidly Democratic. So does the district's wealthiest community, Westport, located south of Fall River and west of New Bedford. The wealthy northwestern towns of Wellesley, Dover and Sherborn tend to lean Republican, but the well-to-do and densely populated Newton and Brookline opt for liberal Democrats.

MAJOR INDUSTRY

Fishing, cranberries, health care, textile manufacturing

CITIES

New Bedford, 93,768; Newton, 83,829; Brookline (unincorporated), 57,107; Taunton, 55,976; Fall River (pt.), 38,234; Dartmouth (unincorporated), 30,666; Wellesley (unincorporated), 26,613

NOTABLE

Fig Newtons originated in Newton; Former Gov. Michael S. Dukakis commuted downtown by trolley from his home in Brookline; Ocean Spray is headquartered in Lakeville-Middleboro.

Rep. Martin T. Meehan (D)

CAPITOL OFFICE
225-3411
martin.meehan@mail.house.gov
www.house.gov/meehan
2229 Rayburn 20515-2105; fax 226-0771

COMMITTEES
Armed Services
Judiciary

HOMETOWN
Lowell

BORN
Dec. 30, 1956, Lowell, Mass.

RELIGION
Roman Catholic

FAMILY
Wife, Ellen T. Murphy; two children

EDUCATION
U. of Massachusetts, Lowell, B.S. 1978 (political science & education); Suffolk U., M.P.A. 1981, J.D. 1986

CAREER
County prosecutor; state securities investigator; state legislative aide; congressional aide

POLITICAL HIGHLIGHTS
No previous office

ELECTION RESULTS

2002 GENERAL		
Martin T. Meehan (D)	122,562	60.2%
Charles McCarthy (R)	69,337	34.0%
Ilana Freedman (LIBERT)	11,729	5.8%
2002 PRIMARY		
Martin T. Meehan (D)		unopposed
2000 GENERAL		
Martin T. Meehan (D)	199,601	98.0%
write-ins	4,040	2.0%

PREVIOUS WINNING PERCENTAGES
1998 (71%); 1996 (99%); 1994 (70%); 1992 (52%)

Elected 1992; 6th term

A self-described "street kid from Lowell," Meehan faced the twin political fights of his life during the 107th Congress and came out standing both times. At the same time he was cajoling the House to accept his seven-year crusade to overhaul the campaign finance system, Meehan was forced to lobby his state's legislature to save his congressional district.

With Connecticut Republican Christopher Shays, Meehan in 2002 pushed through the House legislation to ban unlimited corporate and labor donations to the political parties and to restrict issue advertisements — even as Speaker J. Dennis Hastert proclaimed that their bill would "end democracy as we know it." Because Shays and Meehan had worked closely with their Senate counterparts, John McCain of Arizona and Russell D. Feingold of Wisconsin, the Senate soon followed suit and President Bush grudgingly signed the measure.

And Meehan successfully persuaded the Massachusetts assembly to reject the efforts of State House Speaker Tom Finneran to make Meehan and fellow Democratic Rep. John Tierney fight for the same House seat as part of redistricting for this decade. Meehan had irked Finneran by supporting a Massachusetts initiative that allows candidates for statewide office to receive public funds if they agree to limit their spending and do not accept contributions above $100. Meehan, who had to sell his car and take out two mortgages on his home to finance his first race for Congress, also supports government-financed campaigns.

Although the map eventually was shaped so that Meehan and Tierney could run in separate districts, Meehan's efforts cost him a chance to be governor in 2002. Finneran had said he wanted to change the boundaries because Meehan, who was ahead in gubernatorial polls, was not likely to seek re-election to the House. When his congressional district was challenged, Meehan pledged that he would forgo the statewide race and run again for Congress.

His desire to stay in Washington has been a sore spot. When he won a Democratic primary against four-term incumbent Chester G. Atkins on the way to his first election in 1992, Meehan promised he, too, would serve only four terms. He reneged on the pledge in 2000 but easily won re-election.

Nonetheless, the issue did not endear Meehan to some in the state. Others in the top tier of the state's Democratic political class sometimes have been aggravated by his courting of the press. And Meehan angered many constituents after Sept. 11, 2001, when he was quoted in the Boston Herald questioning whether Air Force One was targeted that day and speculating on the president's motives for being away from Washington that day. Meehan's office in Lowell received so many threatening phone calls that a police guard was posted outside. Meehan said the paper misrepresented his views.

Despite his victory on campaign finance, which won him a great deal of positive national attention, he was held to 60 percent in 2002, his smallest share of the vote since he won the seat with 52 percent over former GOP Rep. Paul W. Cronin at a time when the seat had a slight Republican edge.

The fast-talking Meehan is the son of working-class Irish Americans. When President Kennedy came on television in the 1960s, he recalls, the Meehan household fell silent. Meehan named his first son Robert Francis after the president's younger brother who was attorney general.

Like many Massachusetts politicians, Meehan earned his stripes by attending the Suffolk University Law School. Afterward, he worked as an assistant to the mayor of Lowell, as an aide to Democratic Rep. James M. Shannon and as a state Senate aide. He was a prosecutor in the early 1990s and then won acclaim for stepping up oversight of securities laws when he served as the deputy secretary of state in Massachusetts for securities and corporations.

Perhaps more than most members of Congress, Meehan is candid about how much personal experience influences his legislative priorities. When he is not winning money for Lowell and Lawrence, old textile towns attempting to switch to high-tech enterprises, Meehan focuses on an issue near and dear to his heart: discouraging the use of tobacco. He describes how his father, a typesetter at the Lowell newspaper, was so addicted that he "smoked a cigarette on the way home from being told he was going to die if he didn't stop."

The elder Meehan eventually quit, but his son has spent much of his congressional career attempting to expose the motives of tobacco companies and finding ways to keep teenagers away from cigarettes. In 1994, after tobacco executives testified that nicotine was not addictive, Meehan drafted a 111-page memo asking Attorney General Janet Reno to convene a grand jury to consider perjury and fraud charges. Later, he and Utah Republican James V. Hansen introduced several anti-smoking bills, including one to remove nicotine gradually from all tobacco products sold in the United States and another to ban sales of tobacco over the Internet.

Meehan also sponsored legislation to expand federal workers' health care insurance to cover fertility treatments. Meehan and his wife had sought help from a fertility clinic.

Although Meehan is within the mainstream of his party, his voting record defies easy labeling. Like an earlier 5th District congressman, Democrat Paul E. Tsongas, Meehan is a social policy liberal and a budget cutter. He often rates among the most fiscally responsible members of Congress in the Concord Coalition's annual survey of votes. Concord, the site of the famous early Revolutionary War battle, is in the 5th District, and it is where in 1992 Tsongas and New Hampshire Republican Sen. Warren B. Rudman launched the coalition to press for a balanced federal budget.

Meehan is also active on national security issues. In the 108th Congress he is the top Democrat on the new Terrorism, Unconventional Threats and Capabilities Subcommittee. He was one of a handful of members who traveled to Afghanistan to examine military conditions there during the campaign against al Qaeda.

KEY VOTES

2002

- Yes Overhaul campaign finance law; ban "soft money" and restrict advocacy advertising
- Yes Back Bush's defense budget increase
- No Extend 1996 welfare law
- No Adopt Bush's discretionary spending limit
- No Pass GOP Medicare prescription drug plan
- Yes Create independent Sept. 11 commission
- ? Extend union protections to Homeland Security Department employees
- ? Revive fast-track procedures for trade agreements
- Yes Authorize war against Iraq
- No Advance bankruptcy overhaul opposed by abortion opponents

2001

- No Nullify Clinton Labor Department ergonomics rule
- No Cut taxes by $1.35 trillion through fiscal 2011
- Yes Maintain ban on oil drilling in Arctic National Wildlife Refuge
- No Approve Bush proposal to limit managed-care plan liability for coverage decisions
- Yes Divert money from crop subsidy payments to land conservation
- Yes Expand law enforcement power to investigate suspected terrorists

CQ VOTE STUDIES

	PARTY UNITY		PRESIDENTIAL SUPPORT	
	Support	Oppose	Support	Oppose
2002	98%	2%	26%	74%
2001	97%	3%	29%	71%
2000	92%	8%	81%	19%
1999	96%	4%	84%	16%
1998	97%	3%	88%	12%

INTEREST GROUPS

	AFL-CIO	ADA	CCUS	ACU
2002	100%	75%	44%	9%
2001	100%	90%	29%	0%
2000	90%	90%	45%	12%
1999	78%	100%	20%	0%
1998	100%	100%	31%	4%

MASSACHUSETTS 5

North central — Lowell, Lawrence, Haverhill

More than a generation ago, billowing smokestacks put Lawrence and Lowell among the nation's leading industrial centers. Today, the cities continue to be the population hubs for the 5th, but the wealthy suburbs and rural communities — home to technology workers and some of the nation's most prestigious prep schools — give the district a more upscale flavor.

Textiles are still vital to struggling Lawrence, where immigration has put its sizable Hispanic population — comprised mostly of Dominicans and Puerto Ricans — in the majority. Lowell and surrounding suburbs, meanwhile, continue to reinvent themselves. The early 1990s recession hobbled Digital Equipment Corporation and toppled computer giant Wang, both major employers in the area, but the subsequent Internet boom attracted software firms and other high-tech companies. The upswing spurred growth in small towns, as aging buildings that once housed textile mills, and then defense contractors, became home to start-ups and financial services firms.

While political rivalries between European immigrants are giving way to contests featuring Puerto Ricans, Dominicans and Cambodians, the blue-collar and low-income minority residents of Lowell and Lawrence vote strongly Democratic, as do many well-educated suburban liberals.

The southern part of the 5th is generally wealthy, with Carlisle, Sudbury, Harvard and Bolton all registering six-figure median household incomes. These areas demonstrated their political independence in backing Al Gore in the 2000 presidential election and Republican Mitt Romney in the 2002 gubernatorial election.

MAJOR INDUSTRY

Computer software, defense, textiles

CITIES

Lowell, 105,167; Lawrence, 72,043; Haverhill, 58,969; Methuen, 43,789; Billerica (unincorporated), 38,981; Chelmsford (unincorporated), 33,858

NOTABLE

Concord was the site of the first day of fighting in the Revolutionary War on April 19, 1775 (now celebrated each year as Patriot's Day); Paul Revere's ride and the first Revolutionary battles in towns in the 5th and 7th districts are re-enacted every year; Walden Pond served as temporary home to Henry David Thoreau.

Rep. John F. Tierney (D)

CAPITOL OFFICE
225-8020
www.house.gov/tierney
120 Cannon 20515-2106; fax 225-5915

COMMITTEES
Education & Workforce
Government Reform

HOMETOWN
Salem

BORN
Sept. 18, 1951, Salem, Mass.

RELIGION
Unspecified

FAMILY
Wife, Patrice Tierney

EDUCATION
Salem State College, B.A. 1973 (political science); Suffolk U., J.D. 1976

CAREER
Lawyer; chamber of commerce official

POLITICAL HIGHLIGHTS
Democratic nominee for U.S. House, 1994

ELECTION RESULTS

2002 GENERAL		
John F. Tierney (D)	162,900	68.3%
Mark C. Smith (R)	75,462	31.6%
2002 PRIMARY		
John F. Tierney (D)	unopposed	
2000 GENERAL		
John F. Tierney (D)	205,324	71.0%
Paul McCarthy (R)	83,501	28.9%

PREVIOUS WINNING PERCENTAGES
1998 (55%); 1996 (48%)

Elected 1996; 4th term

Tierney wants to improve access to health care, protect retirees' benefits, clean up political campaigns, strengthen public schools and find out whether genetically engineered foods are safe.

He is persistent in his efforts — coming back every Congress to author the same bills to achieve those top legislative goals. Unfortunately for Tierney, he has met with little success, at least on his major initiatives.

The problem, of course, is that Tierney is a liberal Democrat in a House that has been run by conservative Republicans throughout his career, now in its fourth term.

And the rhetoric he aims at the majority party probably doesn't help. During House debate in 2002 on a spending package for military and homeland security programs, Tierney castigated Republicans for insinuating that Democrats who opposed portions of the bill were not patriotic. Tierney railed against "the shameful spectacle of the Speaker of this House, and others" questioning Democratic motives. "That was disgraceful, even for a majority that has made the disparagement of the democratic process an art form," Tierney said.

Tierney has introduced a "Clean Money, Clean Elections" bill every Congress since he arrived in 1997. The bill, which would provide public financing and free broadcast time for candidates who agree not to use personal funds or accept contributions and which would limit expenditures by political parties, has never even been considered at the subcommittee level. Tierney usually signs up three or four dozen cosponsors, but has not been able to entice a single Republican to join his effort.

The same holds true with his bills to prevent companies from canceling or reducing their retirees' health benefits and to provide incentives to states to develop universal health care programs: No Republican support, no committee action.

Usually, Tierney's roster of cosponsors does not go much beyond the membership of the Progressive Caucus, a group of about five dozen of the most liberal members of the House that includes Tierney.

Tierney's liberal initiatives and rhetorical jibes are bold moves for a man whose first election victory came by a slim 371 votes against a Republican incumbent.

Tierney is the only Massachusetts lawmaker on the Education and the Workforce Committee, where he champions measures to make college more affordable by increasing federal funding for Pell Grants and maintaining low-interest student loans. He also wants to use federal money to help local school districts hire more teachers so that class sizes in elementary and secondary schools can be reduced. In 2002, he used his committee seat to obtain a $3 million grant for job training and placement for about 800 workers who lost jobs at a closed Lucent Technologies plant in his district.

Tierney also serves on the Government Reform Committee. He joined with the committee's top-ranking Democrat, Henry A. Waxman of California, to inquire into the Bush administration's list of federal regulations deemed to be especially burdensome to business. He also tried to obtain a study that purported to outline severe deficiencies in the Pentagon's multibillion-dollar missile defense system, which Tierney ardently opposes. In 2002, he was the author of a proposal to prohibit development of space-based missile programs. It was soundly rejected by the House.

In the 107th Congress, Tierney became the top Democrat on Government Reform's Energy Policy, Natural Resources and Regulatory Affairs Subcommittee. He focused much of his efforts there on policies involving the environment and energy supplies. Tierney has been a vigorous proponent of steps to increase the availability and hold down the price of home heating oil, a vital commodity in New England.

Tierney has also developed an interest in a specific health concern: the safety of genetically engineered food. In both the 106th and 107th Congresses, he sought to require the Department of Agriculture to study the health risks associated with genetically altered crops.

Although Tierney served a year as president of the Salem Chamber of Commerce, he does not usually see eye-to-eye with the U.S. Chamber of Commerce, backing the business group's position less than a quarter of the time. The National Federation of Independent Business says it approves of fewer than 10 percent of Tierney's votes.

Tierney first became interested in politics as a boy growing up in Salem. His uncle served as a ward councilor in Peabody, and Tierney used to campaign with him door-to-door in the community. He worked to put himself through college, where he majored in political science. After law school, he worked for a private law practice and became active in Salem civic affairs.

Although the 6th District contains much of the territory of the oddly shaped district that spawned the term "gerrymander" two centuries ago, it is now one of the most regularly shaped and compact of the state's 10 House districts. In redistricting after the 2000 census, state House Speaker Thomas Finneran, who was feuding with Democratic Rep. Martin T. Meehan, initially proposed a plan that would have thrown Tierney and Meehan together in a substantially redrawn 6th. That plan did not fly, however, and the district's new boundaries are little different from what they have been since the early 1990s.

After pondering an electoral bid for years, Tierney launched his first political campaign in 1994 and came within 4 percentage points of defeating freshman Republican Rep. Peter G. Torkildsen, whose ability to hold on to the seat was aided by that year's Republican tide. Tierney tried again in 1996, and with President Clinton running up a 28 percentage point victory margin in the district, he eked out a 371-vote win.

Torkildsen was back for a rematch in 1998, stressing his moderate stands on such issues as abortion and gay rights and some gun controls. GOP party strategists identified the race as a priority, but Tierney won by 12 points. He has breezed to a pair of lopsided re-election wins since, in 2002 besting security consultant Mark Smith with 68 percent.

KEY VOTES

2002

- Yes Overhaul campaign finance law; ban "soft money" and restrict advocacy advertising
- No Back Bush's defense budget increase
- No Extend 1996 welfare law
- No Adopt Bush's discretionary spending limit
- No Pass GOP Medicare prescription drug plan
- Yes Create independent Sept. 11 commission
- Yes Extend union protections to Homeland Security Department employees
- No Revive fast-track procedures for trade agreements
- No Authorize war against Iraq
- No Advance bankruptcy overhaul opposed by abortion opponents

2001

- No Nullify Clinton Labor Department ergonomics rule
- No Cut taxes by $1.35 trillion through fiscal 2011
- Yes Maintain ban on oil drilling in Arctic National Wildlife Refuge
- No Approve Bush proposal to limit managed-care plan liability for coverage decisions
- Yes Divert money from crop subsidy payments to land conservation
- No Expand law enforcement power to investigate suspected terrorists

CQ VOTE STUDIES

	PARTY UNITY		PRESIDENTIAL SUPPORT	
	Support	Oppose	Support	Oppose
2002	99%	1%	23%	77%
2001	98%	2%	19%	81%
2000	97%	3%	81%	19%
1999	95%	5%	79%	21%
1998	98%	2%	83%	17%

INTEREST GROUPS

	AFL-CIO	ADA	CCUS	ACU
2002	100%	100%	32%	0%
2001	100%	100%	26%	0%
2000	100%	95%	28%	4%
1999	89%	100%	12%	4%
1998	100%	100%	22%	4%

MASSACHUSETTS 6

North Shore – Lynn, Peabody

Pristine beaches line the cool ocean of Boston's North Shore, home to some of the state's largest homes. Country clubs, fox hunting and polo matches are popular diversions for residents of the northern inland, where the population is sparse but wealthy.

The population is denser along the Route 128 high-tech corridor, which cuts through the southern part of the district. Like much of Massachusetts in the 1990s, communities along Route 128 turned from manufacturing to an information-based economy. Fueled in part by Boston's universities, technology firms have flourished from Burlington (where Sun Microsystems has offices) to Gloucester, which also supports a major fishing industry. Burlington has a major new industrial park, reflecting the continued growth of the district's economy.

Lynn, the 6th's largest community, is home to aerospace and defense contractors and includes a General Electric jet engine plant. Urban dwellers are concentrated mostly in Lynn and Peabody and provide blue-collar and minority votes for Democrats. Other population centers in the district include the adjacent coastal cities of Beverly, which residents describe as the birthplace of the Navy because its first commissioned ship sailed from the city's harbor, and Salem, which has a rich history as the hometown of Nathaniel Hawthorne and the locale of the 1692 witch trials. Salem is middle-class and has a Democratic slant, while Beverly is more politically independent.

Republicans can do well in upscale towns such as Boxford, Lynnfield, Topsfield and Wenham, which gave 2002 GOP gubernatorial nominee Mitt Romney more than two-thirds of the vote. While the district has a Democratic tilt, it is not overwhelming, and the GOP can win by attracting independent-minded "unenrolled" voters.

MAJOR INDUSTRY
Computer software, defense, fishing

MILITARY BASES
Hanscom Air Force Base, 1,561 military, 1,420 civilian (2000)

CITIES
Lynn, 89,050; Peabody, 48,129; Salem, 40,407; Beverly, 39,862

NOTABLE
The 6th includes territory that spawned the original "gerrymander," a state legislative district named for Gov. Elbridge Gerry in 1812.

Rep. Edward J. Markey (D)

CAPITOL OFFICE
225-2836
www.house.gov/markey
2108 Rayburn 20515-2107; fax 226-0092

COMMITTEES
Energy & Commerce
Resources
Select Homeland Security

HOMETOWN
Malden

BORN
July 11, 1946, Malden, Mass.

RELIGION
Roman Catholic

FAMILY
Wife, Susan Blumenthal

EDUCATION
Boston College, B.A. 1968, J.D. 1972

MILITARY SERVICE
Army Reserve, 1968-73

CAREER
Lawyer

POLITICAL HIGHLIGHTS
Mass. House, 1973-77

ELECTION RESULTS

2002 GENERAL		
Edward J. Markey (D)	170,968	98.2%
write-ins	2,206	1.3%
2002 PRIMARY		
Edward J. Markey (D)	73,014	84.9%
James O. Hall (D)	12,964	15.1%
2000 GENERAL		
Edward J. Markey (D)	211,543	98.9%
write-ins	2,268	1.1%

PREVIOUS WINNING PERCENTAGES
1998 (71%); 1996 (70%); 1994 (64%); 1992 (62%); 1990 (100%); 1988 (100%); 1986 (100%); 1984 (71%); 1982 (78%); 1980 (100%); 1978 (85%); 1976 Combined General and Special Election (77%)

Elected 1976; 14th full term

A casual visitor to the Energy and Commerce and Resources Committee hearing rooms might conclude that Markey has made his mark in the House as one of its quickest quipsters. And he has. But he also has a reputation of long standing as one of its foremost experts on technology issues and one of its staunchest advocates for consumer protection.

A milk truck driver's son who has been a member of Congress since he was 30, Markey is now the dean of the Massachusetts House delegation and is tenth overall in Democratic seniority in the chamber. His seniority has afforded him influence on a pair of committees that between them touch almost every aspect of domestic policy. He is the No. 3 Democrat on Energy and Commerce. And he has served more time on Resources than anyone else in the 108th Congress. He also got a prized spot in the 108th on the new Homeland Security panel.

Since 1987, Markey has been the top Democrat on the Energy and Commerce subcommittee that deals with telecommunications issues, a perch from which he can indulge his longstanding fascination with electronic gizmos and communications devices; promote the interests of companies and workers in the high-tech Route 128 corridor in his district; and champion the personal privacy concerns of the information age.

Because of their broad legislative portfolio, members of Energy and Commerce are magnets for campaign dollars, and Markey is no exception. What had been unusual about him is that for years he took money only from individuals, not political action committees.

Markey's proven ability to raise cash from people — at a time when corporate and union giving may be curtailed by the 2002 campaign finance law — prompted Minority Leader Nancy Pelosi to offer Markey the chairmanship of the House Democratic campaign organization in the runup to the 2004 election. After word of the offer was leaked to The Boston Globe, to Pelosi's annoyance, he turned her down. He also said he would take PAC money in his 2004 re-election campaign.

Markey deploys a wry wit and well-honed sarcasm to skewer opponents and to make his points. Pointing to Chairman Billy Tauzin, a Louisiana Republican with whom he maintains a strong working relationship, Markey once accused cable television companies at an Energy and Commerce hearing of "tipping my father and Billy's mother upside down and shaking money out." Addressing Federal Communications Commission Chairman Michael K. Powell, the son of Secretary of State Colin L. Powell, Markey said, "People are always asking me to compare you to your father. What I always tell them is you're just as smart as your father, but you have a lot more power to affect the world."

Markey has gained some of his most noted victories and learned new coalition-building skills since the Republican takeover took away most of his legislative clout. With Rep. Dan Burton, a conservative Indiana Republican, he pushed the requirement for "v-chip" circuitry in new televisions to allow parents to block violent or sexually explicit programs.

He also has championed a requirement that online businesses obtain consent before sharing customers' personal information with others. Markey helped found the bipartisan Congressional Privacy Caucus in the 106th and worked with liberals and libertarians to promote privacy protection. He has worked with conservatives to protect children from Hollywood violence. In the 106th, he worked with Tauzin on a law requiring the auto industry to provide the government with more information about product defects.

Markey remains a champion for the 1996 telecommunications overhaul that he helped write. A steep drop in the stock market in the 107th swept away many upstart companies that the law was supposed to nurture. But Markey argues that the law has failed because of lax FCC enforcement. In the 107th, he fought a proposal by Tauzin and Democrat John D. Dingell of Michigan to loosen the law's requirements that regional Bell telephone companies open their local networks to rivals before they can engage in the lucrative delivery of high-speed Internet service.

Markey belongs to a loose coalition of liberal, urban Democrats who align against conservative Republicans and rural lawmakers to advocate strong pollution controls and restrictions on the exploitation of public lands. In the 107th, Markey opposed broad energy legislation backed by the Bush administration and supported an unsuccessful effort to raise fuel efficiency standards for automobiles and light trucks. He led House opposition to opening the Arctic National Wildlife Refuge to oil drilling.

In his early days in Congress, Markey acquired a minor national following as a crusader against domestic nuclear power and nuclear weaponry. After the Sept. 11, 2001, attacks, he pushed for language in an anti-terrorism law calling for federal distribution of potassium iodide, an antidote for radiation sickness, in case nuclear plants were damaged by terrorists.

Markey became expert in securities issues when he chaired the combined Telecommunications and Financial Services Subcommittee in the 1990s. He opposed the financial services overhaul law of 1999, saying it wrongly allowed customers' personal information to be passed among the bank, brokerage and insurance affiliates in the expected new wave of financial service conglomerates.

On a range of issues, Markey uses his clout to defend New England interests. On Resources, for example, he worked to protect the New England coastal ecology and the depleted Georges Bank fishing area.

Elected to the state House at 26, he served two terms, battling his party's leadership on occasion. Once, they retaliated by kicking him off the Judiciary Committee, and one opponent went so far as to throw the furniture from Markey's office into the hallway. Markey came to Congress in 1976 by winning a special election to succeed Democrat Torbert H. MacDonald, who died. Markey's only tough campaign since then was in 1984, when his opponent questioned his commitment to the job after Markey briefly ran for the Senate seat opened by the retirement of Democrat Paul E. Tsongas.

KEY VOTES

2002

- Yes Overhaul campaign finance law; ban "soft money" and restrict advocacy advertising
- No Back Bush's defense budget increase
- No Extend 1996 welfare law
- No Adopt Bush's discretionary spending limit
- No Pass GOP Medicare prescription drug plan
- Yes Create independent Sept. 11 commission
- Yes Extend union protections to Homeland Security Department employees
- No Revive fast-track procedures for trade agreements
- Yes Authorize war against Iraq
- No Advance bankruptcy overhaul opposed by abortion opponents

2001

- No Nullify Clinton Labor Department ergonomics rule
- No Cut taxes by $1.35 trillion through fiscal 2011
- Yes Maintain ban on oil drilling in Arctic National Wildlife Refuge
- No Approve Bush proposal to limit managed-care plan liability for coverage decisions
- Yes Divert money from crop subsidy payments to land conservation
- Yes Expand law enforcement power to investigate suspected terrorists

CQ VOTE STUDIES

	PARTY UNITY		PRESIDENTIAL SUPPORT	
	Support	Oppose	Support	Oppose
2002	99%	1%	25%	75%
2001	96%	4%	26%	74%
2000	98%	2%	88%	12%
1999	96%	4%	79%	21%
1998	95%	5%	82%	18%

INTEREST GROUPS

	AFL-CIO	ADA	CCUS	ACU
2002	100%	100%	30%	4%
2001	100%	100%	36%	4%
2000	100%	85%	29%	4%
1999	100%	100%	16%	0%
1998	100%	90%	31%	4%

MASSACHUSETTS 7

Northwest Boston suburbs — Framingham

The affluent strip along Route 128-Interstate 95, a Silicon Valley of the East, shapes the 7th's character. Stretching east from an urban retail center on Route 9 in Framingham, north along Route 128 as it rings Boston and then north of the city to reach the middle-class coastal town of Revere, the district includes some of the state's most well-to-do communities. The area takes pride in its history; each year, Lexington re-enacts Paul Revere's ride and the first Revolutionary War battles (which took place in towns in the 7th and 5th districts) on Patriots Day.

The economy is driven by a strong software and Internet industry. Many Medford and Malden residents commute to blue-collar jobs in Boston. Malden has a rapidly growing Asian community. For decades, Revere has attracted middle-class vacationers to its beaches.

The 7th's political roots are a mix of Protestant Yankee Republican and Irish Democrat. But like all Massachusetts districts, the 7th votes Democratic in federal races. Redistricting following the 2000 census only increased the 7th's already strong Democratic leanings. Al Gore won the 2000 presidential vote here; George W. Bush's best showing was in Weston, the only locale in the 7th that gave him even 40 percent of the vote.

The wealthy sections of the 7th vary from the more conservative Weston to liberal Lincoln. Democrats also draw votes from a blue-collar, middle-class base in Framingham and in the district's east, including Revere, Everett and Malden.

MAJOR INDUSTRY
Computer software, telecommunications, defense

MILITARY BASES
Army Soldier Systems Center (Natick), 200 military, 1,700 civilian (2003)

CITIES
Framingham (unincorporated), 66,910; Waltham, 59,226; Malden, 56,340; Medford, 55,765; Revere, 47,283; Arlington (unincorporated), 42,389

NOTABLE
James Pierpont is said to have written "Jingle Bells" in 1850 while visiting Medford Square; Richard B. Fitzgibbon Jr. and Richard B. Fitzgibbon III of Stoneham were the only known American father and son to die in the Vietnam War.

Rep. Michael E. Capuano (D)

CAPITOL OFFICE
225-5111
www.house.gov/capuano
1232 Longworth 20515-2108; fax 225-9322

COMMITTEES
Financial Services
Transportation & Infrastructure

HOMETOWN
Somerville

BORN
Jan. 9, 1952, Somerville, Mass.

RELIGION
Roman Catholic

FAMILY
Wife, Barbara Teebagy Capuano; two children

EDUCATION
Dartmouth College, B.A. 1973 (psychology); Boston College, J.D. 1977

CAREER
Lawyer; state legislative aide

POLITICAL HIGHLIGHTS
Somerville Board of Aldermen, 1977-79; candidate for mayor of Somerville, 1979, 1981; Somerville Board of Aldermen, 1985-89; mayor of Somerville, 1990-99; sought Democratic nomination for Mass. secretary of state, 1994

ELECTION RESULTS

2002 GENERAL	
Michael E. Capuano (D)	unopposed
2002 PRIMARY	
Michael E. Capuano (D)	unopposed
2000 GENERAL	
Michael E. Capuano (D)	unopposed

PREVIOUS WINNING PERCENTAGES
1998 (82%)

Elected 1998; 3rd term

After serving as a Massachusetts alderman and a suburban mayor, Capuano arrived on Capitol Hill with little patience for the role expected of freshmen under the House's seniority system. "I made more decisions in a day as mayor than all last year," he told the Boston Herald in 2000, one year into his tenure representing part of Boston and its suburbs. He vowed to quickly "short-circuit" the system.

In his second term, Capuano (CAP-you-AH-no) landed a seat on the Transportation and Infrastructure Committee — a timely move as work proceeds on the Big Dig construction project, which will put Boston's central highway system underground. He also joined the Democratic leadership team as a regional whip and a member of the Democratic Steering Committee, which makes committee assignments.

And Capuano created a national profile with his comments on the accounting scandals that helped to shape the legislative agenda of the 107th Congress. When officials of Global Crossing Ltd., a bankrupt communications company, appeared before the Financial Services Committee, newspapers across the country reported Capuano's unambiguous indictment. "The whole thing you're talking about is nothing more than a much more fancy and larger Ponzi scheme," he said.

Although known for a sharp tongue, Capuano lacks the celebrity of his predecessors. Capuano won the seat after Joseph P. Kennedy II, the son of Robert F. Kennedy and nephew of John F. Kennedy, gave it up after six terms. The House seat was the first political post President Kennedy ever won. Further back, the Kennedy brothers' grandfather, John F. Fitzgerald, represented the district at the turn of the century.

And while Capuano is half Irish, his Italian-American surname is a change from the Irish identification of the Kennedys and others who have held the seat since World War II: James Michael Curley and former Speaker Thomas P. "Tip" O'Neill Jr. Capuano inherited O'Neill's mammoth desk when another Boston Democrat, Rep. Joe Moakley, died in 2001. "Joe and I had similar backgrounds. Similar personalities on some levels, and similar constituencies," Capuano says.

Although Capuano upholds his district's Democratic tradition, he takes less consistently liberal positions and brings to the office a blue-collar pragmatism honed during two decades in local politics.

Capuano has street smarts that belie his Ivy League education. And while he occasionally uses rough language that accentuates his brash personality, he also carefully alphabetizes his files. Trained as a tax attorney, he dives into the minutiae of budget and tax issues. His legislative approach is a pragmatic one: "I want to figure out what I think I can win and push the envelope a little." He says he tends to focus on "stuff that flies under the radar screen."

That strategy has allowed Capuano to score some legislative successes. A bill passed by the House during his first term included Capuano's provision to allow teachers and uniformed municipal workers to buy homes through subsidized housing programs — even if their incomes were above the poverty level. In 2002, he won adoption of an amendment requiring that the public be represented on the five-member oversight board created under the new accounting regulation law. And he pushed to include the families of the victims of the 2001 anthrax attacks among those compensated after the Sept. 11 terrorist attacks.

Capuano once joked that he wanted to be "the Democratic Tom DeLay," recognizing that his hard-driving, partisan style of campaigning might be similar to that of the new House majority leader. Were Capuano to have his way, he would dispense with political posturing and simply state his views. "I'm regularly frustrated by the amount of rhetoric that we have. I understand it, I accept it as part of the reality, but I don't want to participate in it any more than I have to," he says.

Capuano voted against the 2002 education law, a measure largely negotiated between President Bush and Democratic Sen. Edward M. Kennedy, the elder statesman from the family so closely tied to his district. Although he joined the president and the senator at the bill signing, Capuano declared, "I thought we could do a lot better."

Capuano's most unwelcome publicity probably resulted from an article in Vanity Fair magazine in 2001 that described the aggressive pursuit of social interaction with congressmen by Washington interns. The story put Capuano in a Capitol Hill restaurant drinking and singing with a group of colleagues and young women two days after the Sept. 11 attacks. Capuano described the portrayal as "full of false innuendoes" and "incredibly far off the truth," though he does have a standing Thursday evening of socializing with a group of fellow Democratic congressmen.

Capuano must navigate in a district where political tensions continually work their way to the surface. As mayor of Somerville, he drew criticism from detractors who described his style as "tyrannical" and said he managed the city like a ward boss, hiring friends and relatives and running enemies out of public agencies. Capuano called the attacks on his leadership style "a sign of a good executive." Soon after being sworn into the House, Capuano criticized black leaders in his district for not giving his 1998 campaign much support. Then, citing a need to save money and centralize operations, he closed a district office in Roxbury, a neighborhood with a significant black population. After protests, he reopened an office there.

Capuano triumphed in a 10-person Democratic donnybrook created by Kennedy's unexpected 1998 retirement in the solidly Democratic district. The presumed front-runner was Raymond L. Flynn, a former Boston mayor and ambassador to the Vatican who had abandoned a flagging run for governor. But Capuano needled Flynn on his education and housing policies as mayor; others attacked Flynn's anti-abortion position. Although greatly outspent by two other candidates, Capuano was lifted to victory by a strong turnout in Somerville. He breezed by a Republican opponent that November, and the GOP has not fielded a candidate since.

KEY VOTES

2002

- Yes Overhaul campaign finance law; ban "soft money" and restrict advocacy advertising
- No Back Bush's defense budget increase
- No Extend 1996 welfare law
- No Adopt Bush's discretionary spending limit
- No Pass GOP Medicare prescription drug plan
- Yes Create independent Sept. 11 commission
- Yes Extend union protections to Homeland Security Department employees
- No Revive fast-track procedures for trade agreements
- No Authorize war against Iraq
- No Advance bankruptcy overhaul opposed by abortion opponents

2001

- No Nullify Clinton Labor Department ergonomics rule
- No Cut taxes by $1.35 trillion through fiscal 2011
- Yes Maintain ban on oil drilling in Arctic National Wildlife Refuge
- No Approve Bush proposal to limit managed-care plan liability for coverage decisions
- Yes Divert money from crop subsidy payments to land conservation
- No Expand law enforcement power to investigate suspected terrorists

CQ VOTE STUDIES

	PARTY UNITY		PRESIDENTIAL SUPPORT	
	Support	Oppose	Support	Oppose
2002	98%	2%	21%	79%
2001	96%	4%	17%	83%
2000	98%	2%	87%	13%
1999	95%	5%	81%	19%

INTEREST GROUPS

	AFL-CIO	ADA	CCUS	ACU
2002	89%	95%	28%	4%
2001	100%	95%	32%	4%
2000	100%	100%	33%	0%
1999	100%	100%	16%	0%

MASSACHUSETTS 8

Parts of Boston and suburbs – Cambridge, Somerville

The 8th combines Boston's historic Revolutionary War sites with neighborhoods that reflect its evolving future. From the North End and South End — the neighboring 9th takes in places in between like Beacon Hill and the financial district — the 8th grabs much of the city west of Interstate 93. In doing so, it picks up the Back Bay area, Chinatown and many largely black and Hispanic neighborhoods in areas like Roxbury, Dorchester and Jamaica Plain, making it the state's only district where a majority of residents are minorities.

Among the many Beantown sights found in the 8th are the Old North Church, Bunker Hill, the U.S.S. Constitution and Logan International Airport (shared with the 7th). Most of the land involved in the "Big Dig," a long-running transportation project that will route the city's central highway underground, is in the 8th.

Two of the world's most respected universities — Harvard and the Massachusetts Institute of Technology — lie across the Charles River in Cambridge. Typifying the district's monolithically liberal politics, Cambridge gave George W. Bush just 13 percent of the vote in the 2000 presidential election — a showing topped by Green Party nominee Ralph Nader.

The district also takes in dozens of other colleges and universities, which drive much of the economy, whether through blue-collar service employees who work at the schools and teaching hospitals or through biotechnology software firms that employ local talent. Somerville, just north of Cambridge, has a thriving arts community, while Chelsea, with more-affordable housing and blue-collar jobs, has seen its Hispanic population expand to comprise one-half of the city's residents.

MAJOR INDUSTRY

Biotechnology, higher education, health care, tourism

CITIES

Boston (pt.), 420,922; Cambridge, 101,355; Somerville, 77,478

NOTABLE

The 8th is the descendant of the district once represented by John F. Kennedy (1947-53) and Thomas P. "Tip" O'Neill Jr. (1953-87).

Rep. Stephen F. Lynch (D)

CAPITOL OFFICE
225-8273
stephen.lynch@mail.house.gov
www.house.gov/lynch
319 Cannon 20515-2109; fax 225-3984

COMMITTEES
Financial Services
Government Reform

HOMETOWN
Boston

BORN
March 31, 1955, Boston, Mass.

RELIGION
Roman Catholic

FAMILY
Wife, Margaret Lynch; one child

EDUCATION
Wentworth Institute of Technology, B.S. 1988 (construction management); Boston College, J.D. 1991; Harvard U., M.A. 1998 (public administration)

CAREER
Lawyer; ironworker

POLITICAL HIGHLIGHTS
Mass. House, 1995-96; Mass. Senate, 1996-2001

ELECTION RESULTS

2002 GENERAL		
Stephen F. Lynch (D)		unopposed
2002 PRIMARY		
Stephen F. Lynch (D)	69,244	80.6%
William Ferguson Jr. (D)	16,643	19.4%
2001 SPECIAL		
Stephen F. Lynch (D)	44,943	65.0%
Jo Ann Sprague (R)	22,645	32.7%
Susan Gallagher-Long (C)	827	1.2%

Elected October 2001; 1st full term

Most House members, especially from the minority party, spend their first few years keeping a relatively low profile, since their lack of seniority makes it hard for them to do anything else. Lynch had a tougher start than most.

He came to the House in the fall of 2001 to replace an especially beloved congressman: Joe Moakley, a Democrat who held the seat from 1973 until his death of leukemia. Anyone would have had a hard time filling the shoes of such a veteran, but Lynch also faced extraordinary timing: He won the Democratic nomination for the seat on Sept. 11, 2001.

Lynch is no longer at the bottom of the seniority list, and he is building an identity of his own as one of the few lawmakers who can speak from personal experience about how Congress' policies affect the working class. Having grown up in one of South Boston's poorest housing projects, he worked as an ironworker for 18 years while putting himself through school, and he served as president of his local union. That experience immersed him deeply in South Boston's tangled politics of class and race, which sometimes has cast an uncomfortable shadow on his political career. But it also allows him to escape the derisive stereotype of members of Congress as wealthy, white lawyers.

Neither does Lynch fit the stereotype of the Massachusetts liberal. He describes himself as a moderate, and in his first full term he backed President Bush's wishes one-third of the time; about half of House Democrats did so more often and half less often. He parted ways with most in the caucus to support the authorization of a war against Iraq. And his opposition to abortion rights was an issue in his initial campaign, as his Democratic opponents tried to paint him as too conservative for the district.

"After Sept. 11, there was a sobering impact on the nation, and certainly on my own district," Lynch says. "People want someone who's going to be strong on defense, strong on security, someone who's no-nonsense, who's not going to go off on some liberal escapade. They just want someone who's going to make them safe."

Lynch fits comfortably in the party mainstream on most issues. In June 2002, he joined three other Massachusetts Democrats — Barney Frank, John F. Tierney and Michael E. Capuano — on the now-standard politicians' trip to Canada to help senior citizens buy prescription drugs at lower prices. He has traveled to Cuba and is a strong advocate of lifting the sanctions against that country. He has expressed support for civil unions for gay couples and extensions of medical benefits to domestic partners.

As a former labor leader, it was no surprise that Lynch opposed the law enacted in 2002 granting the president fast-track authority to negotiate trade deals Congress cannot amend. In his first floor speech in 2001, Lynch talked about how he had worked at the Quincy shipyard near Boston and a General Motors plant in Framingham, both of which closed because of foreign competition. Under fast-track, lawmakers "give up those rights and those responsibilities to the very people who sent us here," Lynch said. "It flies in the face of our responsibility, both under the Constitution and as a moral obligation to the people who we represent."

On the Veterans' Affairs Committee until the end of the 107th, he minded the interests of the three VA medical facilities in his district and its shelter for homeless veterans. He sponsored legislation to establish a mentoring program for registered nurses to address the nursing shortage at VA hospitals in New England, and another bill to launch a pilot program allowing the VA to fill prescriptions written by private physicians — at a probable cost savings for those receiving the medicine.

In the 108th Congress, Lynch traded in his Veterans' Affairs seat for a spot on Financial Services. He retained his seat on Government Reform.

For Lynch not all politics is local. In 2002 he went to Cuba with five other lawmakers and dined with Fidel Castro. He left Havana convinced that U.S. sanctions had helped Castro blame the outside world for all of Cuba's problems, including the extreme poverty that has gripped the nation for decades. He said he went to Cuba in an effort to carry on the work in Latin American affairs begun by Moakley, who headed a commission that exposed the involvement of high-ranking military officials in the 1989 deaths of six Jesuit priests in El Salvador.

Lynch's father was an ironworker for 40 years. At age 30, Lynch was elected as the youngest president Ironworkers Local 7 had ever had. At the same time he attended law school, which was his ticket out of the unstable and often dangerous work of his trade. He joined a law firm, continuing his practice, begun in law school, of representing housing project residents for free. His pro bono interests eventually prompted friends to encourage him to run for the Massachusetts legislature.

Lynch unseated incumbent state Rep. Paul Gannon in 1994, and in April 1996 he won a special election to fill the state Senate seat of Senate President William M. Bulger, who became president of the University of Massachusetts system. That position gave Lynch a solid launching pad to run for Congress when Moakley died soon after his 15th term began.

It was not a clear shot, however. He was up against six Democratic opponents, several of whom criticized him for his opposition to abortion. And two of his opponents, state Sen. Cheryl A. Jacques and state Sen. Brian A. Joyce, raised questions about an incident from Lynch's days as an attorney, when he defended 14 white teenagers accused of physically and verbally abusing a white girl and her Hispanic boyfriend. Lynch responded that someone needed to defend the teens and protect their rights, but the incident was a reminder of the racial tensions that have long been an unwelcome undercurrent to life in South Boston.

Still, Lynch benefited from his personal story of working his way out of poverty, as well as the publicity from a painful act of generosity: He donated 60 percent of his liver to his brother-in-law, who had liver cancer. Lynch won the primary with 39 percent of the vote to Jacques' 29 percent, and went on to defeat Republican state Sen. Jo Ann Sprague with 65 percent. In 2002, no Republican challenged him for re-election.

KEY VOTES

2002

Yes Overhaul campaign finance law; ban "soft money" and restrict advocacy advertising
Yes Back Bush's defense budget increase
No Extend 1996 welfare law
No Adopt Bush's discretionary spending limit
No Pass GOP Medicare prescription drug plan
Yes Create independent Sept. 11 commission
Yes Extend union protections to Homeland Security Department employees
No Revive fast-track procedures for trade agreements
Yes Authorize war against Iraq
No Advance bankruptcy overhaul opposed by abortion opponents

2001

Yes Expand law enforcement power to investigate suspected terrorists

CQ VOTE STUDIES

	PARTY UNITY		PRESIDENTIAL SUPPORT	
	Support	Oppose	Support	Oppose
2002	94%	6%	33%	67%
2001	97%	3%	37%	63%

INTEREST GROUPS

	AFL-CIO	ADA	CCUS	ACU
2002	100%	90%	40%	13%
2001	100%	—	44%	0%

MASSACHUSETTS 9

Part of Boston; southern suburbs – Brockton, Braintree

The 9th begins with a central swath of downtown Boston, covering Beacon Hill, the West End and the financial district. The statehouse and brokerage houses — the 9th is home to one of the world's largest centers for mutual fund investing — are dominant in this part of Boston. They share the area with sprawling Boston Common park and several of New England's major tourist attractions. Faneuil Hall Marketplace anchors the retail industry. Some of the wealthiest neighborhoods in the state are along the Charles River.

From central Boston the district hops the Fort Point Channel into South Boston — long referred to as "Southie" — and closely hugs Interstate 93 on its way into Milton. It connects through Dedham to West Roxbury, a mostly white suburban enclave in the southwestern part of Boston.

The "Brahmin" homes of Beacon Hill are counterbalanced by the poor and working-class neighborhoods of traditionally Irish Southie and middle-class suburban communities south and west of the city. Though solidly Democratic, Southie's political tradition is one of supporting pro-labor Democrats who are more conservative on social issues.

The 9th's areas outside of Boston are relatively conservative for Massachusetts. While the district's suburbs have helped elect Republicans to the governor's mansion in recent years, the district's mostly blue-collar base in Boston and Brockton keeps it solidly Democratic in federal elections.

MAJOR INDUSTRY

Financial services, government, tourism

CITIES

Boston (pt.), 168,219; Brockton, 94,304; Braintree (unincorporated), 33,698; Randolph (unincorporated), 30,963; Norwood (unincorporated), 28,587

NOTABLE

Patriots tossed boxes of tea into Boston Harbor during the Boston Tea Party in 1773, a catalyst for the Revolutionary War; The John F. Kennedy Library and Museum is in Boston; A new federal courthouse in South Boston was named for the late Rep. Joe Moakley, who represented the district from 1973 until his death in 2001.

Rep. Bill Delahunt (D)

CAPITOL OFFICE
225-3111
william.delahunt@mail.house.gov
www.house.gov/delahunt
1317 Longworth 20515-2110; fax 225-5658

COMMITTEES
International Relations
Judiciary

HOMETOWN
Quincy

BORN
July 18, 1941, Quincy, Mass.

RELIGION
Roman Catholic

FAMILY
Divorced; two children

EDUCATION
Middlebury College, B.A. 1963; Boston College, J.D. 1967

MILITARY SERVICE
Coast Guard, 1963; Coast Guard Reserve, 1963-71

CAREER
Lawyer

POLITICAL HIGHLIGHTS
Quincy City Council, 1971-73; Mass. House, 1973-75; Norfolk County district attorney, 1975-97

ELECTION RESULTS

2002 GENERAL		
Bill Delahunt (D)	179,238	69.2%
Luiz Gonzaga (R)	79,624	30.7%
2002 PRIMARY		
Bill Delahunt (D)		unopposed
2000 GENERAL		
Bill Delahunt (D)	234,675	74.1%
Eric V. Bleicken (R)	81,192	25.7%

PREVIOUS WINNING PERCENTAGES
1998 (70%); 1996 (54%)

Elected 1996; 4th term

Outgoing and affable, Delahunt is a reliable liberal vote and an important Democratic voice on the International Relations and Judiciary committees. Although an aggressive partisan debater at times, he has a knack for cultivating relationships with colleagues who have far different ideological outlooks, such as conservative Southern Republicans Cass Ballenger of North Carolina and Spencer Bacchus of Alabama. International Relations Committee Chairman Henry J. Hyde of Illinois says Delahunt brings "a maturity, leavened with a good sense of humor" to Congress.

Delahunt (DELL-a-hunt) says he is part of the generation inspired to enter politics by John F. Kennedy. At Middlebury College, Delahunt was co-chairman of a Vermont students-for-Kennedy group. The other chairman (and also a fraternity brother of Delahunt's) was the late Ronald H. Brown, secretary of Commerce under President Clinton.

After his service in the state House, Delahunt spent more than 20 years as a district attorney just south of Boston, and his experience as a prosecutor has made him an influential voice for his party on Judiciary. "Billy has locked up more people than everyone else on the committee put together," Barney Frank of Massachusetts, for years the panel's No. 2 Democrat, told The Boston Globe. "He is a liberal with his head on his shoulders."

In the 107th Congress, that reputation helped Delahunt, along with cosponsor Ray LaHood of Illinois, put together a solid bipartisan majority for legislation that sought to ensure that those facing the death penalty in federal cases had adequate legal representation and access to new, sophisticated DNA tests if they could prove their innocence. State death row inmates' rights to DNA tests also would be guaranteed.

Delahunt, a Coast Guard veteran, also has emerged as one of the agency's leading advocates in Congress, and in the 107th he was pivotal to its positioning as a key element in the nation's homeland security forces.

Among his other legislative priorities, Delahunt has pushed to lift a moratorium on Internet taxes, saying the prohibition drains funds from local governments that could be used to finance schools and essential services, such as police and fire departments. He has attacked Japanese whaling practices and has sponsored measures, favored by environmentalists, to preserve the North Atlantic Right Whale. And he has worked to toughen the Clean Air Act and continue enforcement of environmental standards at military facilities. One issue that earned him considerable notice in 2002 was his opposition to a proposed electricity-generating windmill farm in Nantucket Sound.

On International Relations, Delahunt has helped organize a 40-member Cuba Working Group to press for an end to the four-decade embargo against the island ruled by Fidel Castro. He has pushed the White House to include human rights conditions on military aid to Colombia. And he has opposed President Bush's decision to withdraw from the establishment of an International Criminal Court that would try alleged perpetrators of genocide and war crimes.

In a rhetorical face-off with Republicans, Delahunt often can be unsparing. Despite his heated words, however, he frequently collaborates with Republicans. He often travels with Ballenger to Latin America. He established the Cuba Working Group with conservative Jeff Flake of Arizona and worked with South Carolina's Lindsey Graham on an election process overhaul package during the 107th.

Although "politics may make odd bedfellows," Delahunt's bedfellows are actually reliable liberals — as was made clear by "The Little House on the Hill," a short-lived television show put together by the comedian Al Franken and aired in 2002. It portrayed the domestic hijinks of Delahunt and his three Democratic housemates: Sens. Charles E. Schumer of New York and Richard J. Durbin of Illinois and Rep. George Miller of California.

Delahunt, who adopted an abandoned Vietnamese baby girl in 1975, has been a force behind legislation to ease overseas adoptions. In the 106th, he won a major victory with passage of his bill to grant automatic citizenship to children adopted from abroad, as well as to foreign-born children of U.S. parents. He also won enactment of legislation allowing parents to get vaccinations for their adopted children in this country, instead of having to wait for shots overseas.

Delahunt's fondness for baseball, particularly the Boston Red Sox, has crept into his political work. At a 1999 reception for Venezuelan President Hugo Chavez, Delahunt sought to court the controversial Venezuelan leftist with an unusual gift: a framed baseball card of Luis Aparacio, a Venezuelan and Hall of Fame shortstop who played for the Red Sox. Delahunt also has used his Judiciary Committee post to argue against baseball's antitrust exemption after Florida financier John Henry won control of the Red Sox in a controversial sale.

A Quincy native, Delahunt became a city councilman at 30. Elected to the state House in 1972, he shared an office with a couple of other Beacon Hill rookies, Barney Frank and Edward J. Markey, now senior members of the state's congressional delegation. Two years later, however, Gov. Michael S. Dukakis named him the district attorney for suburban Norfolk County, of which Quincy is the major municipality.

In 1996, when Democrat Gerry E. Studds announced his retirement from the House after a dozen terms, Delahunt was regarded as the Democratic front-runner from the start. But in a hard-fought September primary contest, he trailed state Rep. Phil Johnston by about 300 votes. Delahunt went to court, charging that ballots that should have been counted for him were mistakenly counted as blank. A state judge concurred, and Delahunt was certified the primary winner just 28 days before Election Day. He went on to win the general election by 13 percentage points.

Delahunt has had no trouble retaining his seat since. Redistricting following the 2000 census preserved his core constituencies, and he won a fourth term in 2002, taking 69 percent against Cape Cod businessman Luiz Gonzaga.

KEY VOTES

2002

Yes Overhaul campaign finance law; ban "soft money" and restrict advocacy advertising
No Back Bush's defense budget increase
No Extend 1996 welfare law
No Adopt Bush's discretionary spending limit
No Pass GOP Medicare prescription drug plan
Yes Create independent Sept. 11 commission
Yes Extend union protections to Homeland Security Department employees
No Revive fast-track procedures for trade agreements
No Authorize war against Iraq
No Advance bankruptcy overhaul opposed by abortion opponents

2001

No Nullify Clinton Labor Department ergonomics rule
No Cut taxes by $1.35 trillion through fiscal 2011
Yes Maintain ban on oil drilling in Arctic National Wildlife Refuge
No Approve Bush proposal to limit managed-care plan liability for coverage decisions
Yes Divert money from crop subsidy payments to land conservation
Yes Expand law enforcement power to investigate suspected terrorists

CQ VOTE STUDIES

	PARTY UNITY		PRESIDENTIAL SUPPORT	
	Support	Oppose	Support	Oppose
2002	97%	3%	24%	76%
2001	94%	6%	21%	79%
2000	95%	5%	80%	20%
1999	95%	5%	81%	19%
1998	97%	3%	83%	17%

INTEREST GROUPS

	AFL-CIO	ADA	CCUS	ACU
2002	100%	90%	39%	0%
2001	100%	95%	26%	4%
2000	89%	85%	47%	8%
1999	100%	100%	24%	0%
1998	100%	100%	28%	8%

MASSACHUSETTS 10
South Shore – Quincy, Cape Cod, islands

Cool coastal breezes in the summer and warm ocean air in the winter attract retirees and tourists to the 10th, where most towns border the ocean. The area that spawned the nation's puritanical streak and the Thanksgiving holiday still retains a Yankee flavor, but the northern part of the 10th has attracted residents from Boston's ethnic neighborhoods. A rail line from Boston to several South Shore communities is contributing to the area's population boom. The old 10th was the fastest-growing Massachusetts district in the 1990s.

Other than tourism, maritime technology and research are burgeoning industries along the Cape, especially in Woods Hole. To the north, a booming software industry helped the area recover from a recession in the early 1990s.

The mainland coastal towns of the 10th are commonly referred to as the South Shore. With the exception of a handful of thriving cranberry bogs, most of the South Shore towns consist of bedroom developments for Boston's professionals or Quincy's blue-collar workers. The state's most liberal population lives on the far end of Cape Cod, where Provincetown, a predominantly gay artists' colony, thrives. Provincetown gave 75 percent of the vote to Democrat Shannon O'Brien in the 2002 gubernatorial race, her statewide high, and 80 percent to Al Gore in 2000, his second-highest state total.

But those totals belie the 10th's overall political character, which is more politically independent than Democratic. The state's least heavily Democratic district in the 2000 presidential race, the 10th opted for Republican Mitt Romney by 17 points in the 2002 gubernatorial race, thanks to GOP strength in coastal communities southeast of Quincy and northwest of Plymouth.

MAJOR INDUSTRY
Marine technology, biotechnology, health care, tourism

CITIES
Quincy, 88,025; Weymouth, 53,988; Plymouth (unincorporated), 51,701; Barnstable, 47,821; Falmouth (unincorporated), 32,660

NOTABLE
Presidents John Adams (1797-1801) and John Quincy Adams (1825-1829) were from Quincy; Plymouth Rock; The John Alden House in Duxbury is named for the Pilgrim who sailed on the Mayflower.

MICHIGAN

Gov. Jennifer M. Granholm (D)

First elected: 2002
Length of term: 4 years
Term expires: 1/07
Salary: $172,000
Phone: (517) 373-3400
Hometown: Northville
Born: Feb. 5, 1959; Richmond, Canada
Religion: Roman Catholic
Family: Husband, Daniel G. Mulhern; three children
Education: U. of California, Berkeley, B.A. 1984 (political science & French); Harvard U., J.D. 1987
Career: Federal prosecutor; campaign aide; lawyer
Political highlights: Wayne County Corporation Counsel, 1994-98; Mich. attorney general, 1999-2003
Election results:

2002 GENERAL		
Jennifer M. Granholm (D)	1,633,796	51.4%
Dick Posthumus (R)	1,506,104	47.4%

Lt. Gov. John Cherry (D)

First elected: 2002
Length of term: 4 years
Term expires: 1/07
Salary: $125,900
Phone: (517) 373-3400

STATE LEGISLATURE

Legislature: Meets January-June and September-December
House: 110 members, 2-year terms
2003 breakdown: 62R, 47D, 1 vacancy; 85 men, 24 women
Salary: $79,650; $12,000/year expenses
Phone: (517) 373-0135
Senate: 38 members, 4-year terms
2003 breakdown: 22R, 16D; 27 men, 11 women
Salary: $79,650; $12,000/year expenses
Phone: (517) 373-2400

STATE TERM LIMITS

Governor: 2 terms
Senate: 2 terms
House: 3 terms

URBAN STATISTICS

CITY	POPULATION
Detroit	951,270
Grand Rapids	197,800
Warren	138,247
Flint	124,943
Sterling Heights	124,471

REGISTERED VOTERS

Voters do not register by party.

POPULATION

2002 population (est.)	10,050,446
2000 population	9,938,444
1990 population	9,295,297
Percent change (1990-2000)	+6.9%
Rank among states (2002)	8
Median age	35.5
Born in state	75.4%
Foreign born	5.3%
Violent crime rate	555/100,000
Poverty level	10.5%
Federal workers	54,604
Military	21,833

REDISTRICTING

Michigan lost one House seat in reapportionment. The state legislature drew a new, 15-district map, which the governor signed on Sept. 11, 2001.

MISCELLANEOUS

Web: www.state.mi.us
Capital: Lansing

STATE ELECTION OFFICIAL
(517) 373-2540

DEMOCRATIC HEADQUARTERS
(517) 371-5410

REPUBLICAN HEADQUARTERS
(517) 487-5413

District Statistics

DIST.	2000 VOTE FOR PRESIDENT BUSH	GORE	NADER	WHITE	BLACK	ASIAN	HISP	MEDIAN INCOME	WHITE COLLAR	BLUE COLLAR	SERVICE INDUSTRY	OVER 64	UNDER 18	COLLEGE EDUCATION	RURAL	SQ. MILES
1	53%	47%	n/a	94%	1%	0%	1%	$34,076	51%	30%	19%	17%	23%	16%	67%	24,887
2	61	39	n/a	87	4	1	5	$42,589	51	34	15	12	28	18	44	5,365
3	61	39	n/a	82	8	2	6	$45,936	57	30	13	11	28	24	23	1,854
4	55	45	n/a	93	2	1	2	$39,020	54	29	17	14	25	19	59	7,451
5	38	62	n/a	75	18	1	4	$39,675	51	32	17	12	27	15	21	1,754
6	54	46	n/a	84	9	1	4	$40,943	53	32	15	12	26	21	42	3,331
7	53	47	n/a	88	6	1	3	$45,181	54	32	15	12	26	19	46	4,295
8	52	48	n/a	88	5	2	3	$52,510	63	23	14	9	26	29	30	2,254
9	52	48	n/a	81	8	6	3	$65,358	75	15	10	12	24	44	1	311
10	55	45	n/a	94	1	1	2	$52,690	55	32	13	11	27	17	34	3,549
11	52	48	n/a	90	4	3	2	$59,177	65	24	12	12	25	29	3	399
12	38	62	n/a	82	12	2	1	$46,784	60	27	14	16	23	20	0	160

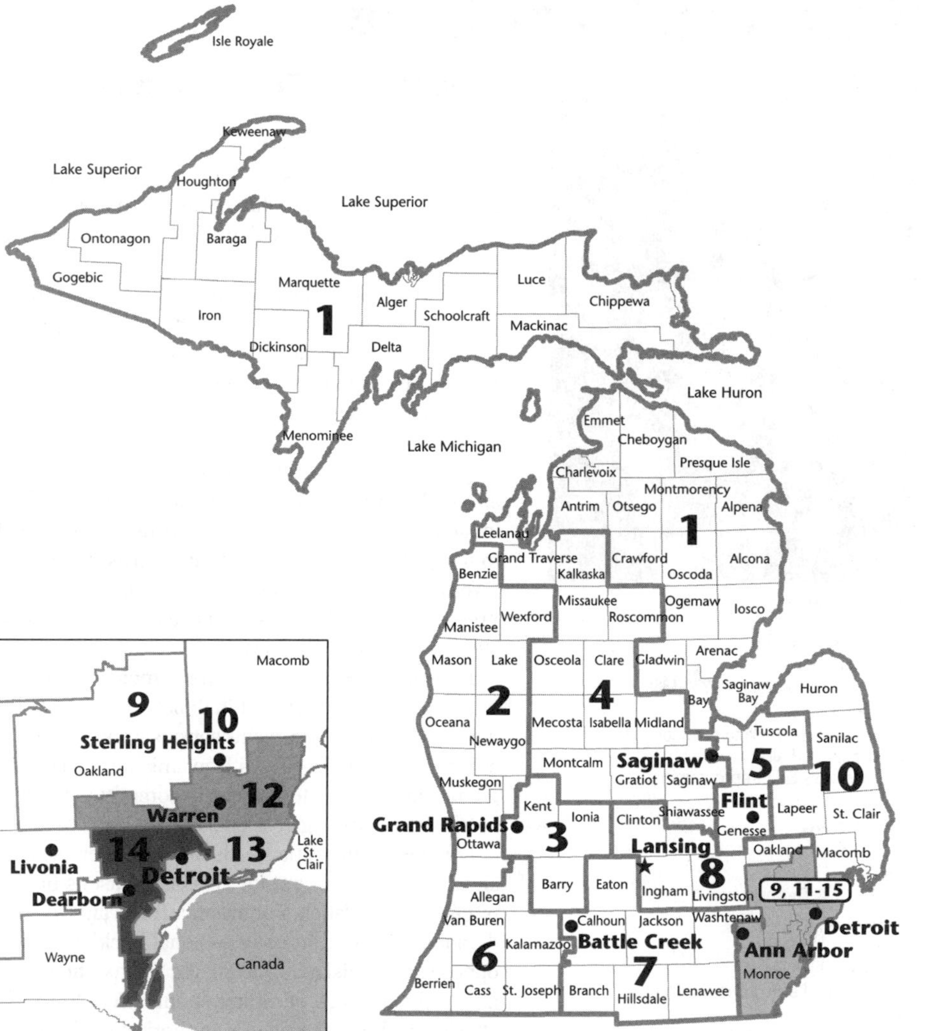

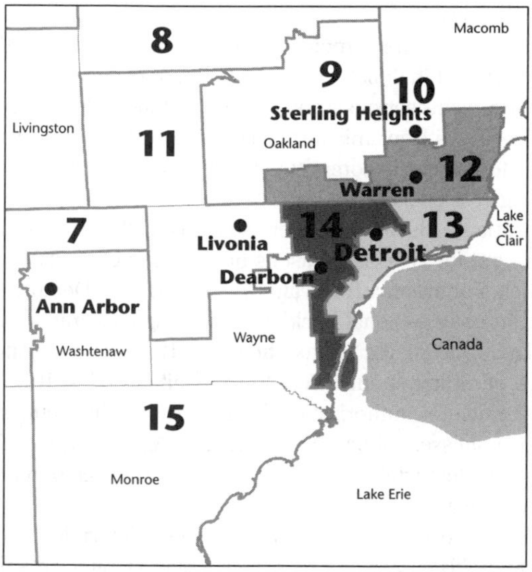

District Statistics

DIST.	2000 VOTE FOR PRESIDENT BUSH	GORE	NADER	WHITE	BLACK	ASIAN	HISP	MEDIAN INCOME	WHITE COLLAR	BLUE COLLAR	SERVICE INDUSTRY	OVER 64	UNDER 18	COLLEGE EDUCATION	RURAL	SQ. MILES
13	19%	81%	n/a	29%	60%	1%	7%	$31,165	51%	29%	20%	11%	30%	14%	0%	108
14	18	82	n/a	32	61	1	2	$36,099	53	29	18	12	29	14	0	123
15	39	61	n/a	79	12	4	3	$48,963	59	26	14	10	25	28	12	961
STATE	**46**	**51**	**2**	**79**	**14**	**2**	**3**	**$44,667**	**57**	**28**	**15**	**12**	**26**	**22**	**25**	**56,804**
U.S.	47.9	48.4	3	69	12	4	13	$41,994	60	25	15	12	26	24	21	3,537,438

Sen. Carl Levin (D)

CAPITOL OFFICE
224-6221
senator2@levin.senate.gov
levin.senate.gov
269 Russell 20510-2202; fax 224-1388

COMMITTEES
Armed Services - ranking member
Governmental Affairs
Small Business & Entrepreneurship
Select Intelligence

HOMETOWN
Detroit

BORN
June 28, 1934, Detroit, Mich.

RELIGION
Jewish

FAMILY
Wife, Barbara Levin; three children

EDUCATION
Swarthmore College, B.A. 1956 (political science); Harvard U., LL.B. 1959

CAREER
Lawyer

POLITICAL HIGHLIGHTS
Michigan Civil Rights Commission general counsel, 1964-67; Detroit chief appellate defender, 1968-69; Detroit City Council, 1970-77 (president, 1974-77)

ELECTION RESULTS

2002 GENERAL		
Carl Levin (D)	1,896,614	60.6%
Andrew Raczkowski (R)	1,185,545	37.9%
2002 PRIMARY		
Carl Levin (D)		unopposed

PREVIOUS WINNING PERCENTAGES
1996 (58%); 1990 (57%); 1984 (52%); 1978 (52%)

Elected 1978; 5th term

Levin's trademarks — the reading glasses perched at the end of his nose, the famously rumpled style, his talent for mastering complex issues — were on view as never before during the 107th Congress when Democratic control of the Senate coincided with major crises that fell squarely within Levin's jurisdiction.

As Armed Services Committee chairman, Levin was a spokesman for the party's effort to pressure President Bush to seek U.N. and congressional authority for an attack on Iraq. And as head of the Governmental Affairs Investigations Subcommittee, Levin ran one of the major congressional probes into the collapse of Houston-based energy conglomerate Enron Corp.

Levin is keeping those committee assignments in the 108th Congress, although as ranking Democrat once again he will not have quite as much influence in initiating policy. Instead, he has signaled he will not be adverse to using the filibuster to wage an aggressive defense for the Democrats. "We can stop, we can prevent, we can clarify issues," Levin told the Detroit Free Press. "The Senate is an unusual place because 41 senators can at least stop bad stuff from happening."

Levin's comprehension of the complicated issues he deals with is the foundation of his clout. But in debate, he leverages that expertise by taking his opponents' arguments seriously and digging methodically for inconsistencies. And he does it with an amiable tenacity, making him dogged but genial, both as an interrogator in committee hearings and as a negotiator in legislative drafting sessions.

On international affairs, his bedrock premise is that collaboration with allies is essential — not for idealistic reasons but because of hard-nosed, pragmatic calculation. For instance, even after Bush yielded to Democrats' demands and sought congressional backing for war against Iraq, Levin opposed the legislation, calling it a "blank check" for Bush to act unilaterally in the absence of an imminent threat to the United States. If Bush attacked without specific U.N. authorization, Levin warned, other countries might refuse the use of essential bases and airspace. Moreover, he said, potential allies might be less willing to help shoulder the burden of reconstructing Iraq after the war.

By similar reasoning, Levin staunchly opposed Bush's determination to discard the 1972 Anti-Ballistic Missile Treaty and deploy a limited anti-missile defense. Levin was skeptical of the system's technical feasibility. And he warned — long before Sept. 11, 2001 — that a defense against a rogue state's ballistic missiles would be useless against far more likely terrorist attacks. But his fundamental argument was that if the United States deployed a missile defense without regard to the views of other countries, they might respond with new weapons of their own, paradoxically making the United States less secure with a missile defense than without one.

In the summer of 2001, Levin and his fellow Armed Services Committee Democrats sought to use the annual defense authorization bill to prevent Bush from unilaterally scrapping the ABM pact. After Sept. 11, Levin dropped the provision in the interest of national unity. But he conceded that the president probably would have beaten it back, even if the terrorist strikes had not occurred.

On the other hand, Bush's demand that Congress authorize another round of military base closings put him in line with a position Levin had pushed unsuccessfully for years. President Clinton had undercut his own chances of winning additional closures by maneuvering in 1995, before his re-election campaign, to save jobs at bases to be closed in Texas and California. Enraged Republicans vowed never to let the president preside over base closures. Levin and Republican John McCain of Arizona pushed to resume base closures after Clinton's term expired, but they were unsuccessful. Backed by Defense Secretary Donald H. Rumsfeld, in 2001 Levin secured another round of base closings, although it took a Bush veto threat to overcome GOP opposition in the House.

Untangling the causes of Enron's collapse was a job tailor-made for Levin's methodical approach. And the Investigations Subcommittee gave him the ideal instrument. In a series of hearings, he traced the web of financial transactions the company used to conceal mounting losses. Levin was particularly critical of Enron's use of stock options — which do not have to be declared as expenses — as compensation for senior management. He had decried the practice for years, but the Senate ultimately rejected his proposal for tighter accounting standards when it enacted the corporate oversight law of 2002.

On social issues, Levin clearly stands left of center. He voted against banning a procedure its opponents call "partial birth" abortion, and he opposes the ban on abortions at overseas military hospitals. While he supported barring job discrimination on the basis of sexual orientation, he did vote to prohibit federal recognition of same-sex marriage. He was among the most ardent advocates of the gun control package Congress considered after the 1999 teenage shooting spree at Columbine High School in Colorado, which ultimately was scuttled by disagreement.

In the 107th Congress his most conspicuous departure from liberal orthodoxy was when he joined the successful opposition, along with 18 other Democrats, to a Senate proposal to increase dramatically the average mileage U.S. auto manufacturers would be required to achieve. The measure, which would have disrupted Detroit's marketing of the current generation of minivans and SUVs, was vehemently opposed by the industry, which remains the economic anchor of Levin's home state.

In the 1970s, Levin made a name for himself on the Detroit City Council, where he teamed with Mayor Coleman A. Young to demolish thousands of abandoned buildings.

Levin won his Senate seat in 1978 by defeating Republican incumbent Robert P. Griffin, who had initially planned to retire after losing a bid to become party leader the previous year. By the time he reversed course and decided to run, Griffin had missed one-third of the Senate votes over an entire year. Levin said Griffin was obviously tired of the job, and the voters agreed that Griffin deserved a rest. Levin won by 4 percentage points.

Levin, whose older brother Sander represents Michigan in the House, has an avuncular manner, but he can and will play political hardball. In 1984, he aired an ad showing his GOP opponent, former astronaut Jack Lousma, warming up a Japanese audience a year earlier by telling them about the Toyota he owned — an obvious faux pas in a state where the phrase "Japanese car" translates as joblessness. President Reagan carried Michigan with 59 percent, but Levin held on to win with 52 percent.

In his three succeeding re-election efforts, Levin's margin of victory has steadily improved. By 2002, he was well enough entrenched that several GOP heavyweights declined to make what was assumed to be a futile run. At one point, Republicans seriously weighed nominating a one-time contestant in the TV reality game show "Survivor." Ultimately, state Rep. Andrew Raczkowski took up the GOP banner, but he garnered just 38 percent of the vote.

KEY VOTES

2002

Yes Pass farm bill reversing crop subsidy limits
Yes Postpone tougher automobile fuel efficiency standards
Yes Overhaul campaign finance law; ban "soft money" and restrict advocacy advertising
Yes Set federal election standards
No Support oil drilling in Arctic National Wildlife Refuge
No Revive fast-track procedures for trade agreements
Yes Create federal insurance coverage for catastrophic terrorist losses
Yes Tighten federal accounting and corporate governance regulation
Yes Advance bipartisan Medicare prescription drug plan
Yes Create independent Sept. 11 commission
Yes Back Democratic Homeland Security Department proposal
No Authorize war against Iraq

2001

No Confirm John Ashcroft as attorney general
No Nullify Clinton Labor Department ergonomics rule
No Cut taxes by $1.35 trillion through fiscal 2011
Yes Pass Democratic bill to bolster rights of patients in managed-care plans
Yes Permit a new round of military base closings
Yes Expand law enforcement power to investigate suspected terrorists

CQ VOTE STUDIES

	PARTY UNITY		PRESIDENTIAL SUPPORT	
	Support	Oppose	Support	Oppose
2002	95%	5%	66%	34%
2001	98%	2%	65%	35%
2000	97%	3%	92%	8%
1999	97%	3%	89%	11%
1998	98%	2%	93%	7%
1997	95%	5%	90%	10%
1996	94%	6%	86%	14%
1995	97%	3%	89%	11%
1994	92%	8%	90%	10%
1993	97%	3%	93%	7%

INTEREST GROUPS

	AFL-CIO	ADA	CCUS	ACU
2002	100%	95%	40%	0%
2001	100%	100%	36%	8%
2000	75%	90%	66%	12%
1999	89%	95%	53%	4%
1998	100%	90%	44%	0%
1997	86%	95%	50%	0%
1996	86%	85%	23%	5%
1995	100%	100%	26%	0%
1994	88%	95%	20%	0%
1993	91%	95%	18%	8%

Sen. Debbie Stabenow (D)

CAPITOL OFFICE
224-4822
senator@stabenow.senate.gov
stabenow.senate.gov
702 Hart 20510-2204; fax 228-0325

COMMITTEES
Agriculture, Nutrition & Forestry
Banking, Housing & Urban Affairs
Budget
Special Aging

HOMETOWN
Lansing

BORN
April 29, 1950, Clare, Mich.

RELIGION
United Methodist

FAMILY
Husband, Tom Athans; two children

EDUCATION
Michigan State U., B.A. 1972, M.S.W. 1975

CAREER
Leadership training consultant

POLITICAL HIGHLIGHTS
Ingham County Commission, 1975-78 (chairwoman, 1977-1978); Mich. House, 1979-91; Mich. Senate, 1991-94; sought Democratic nomination for governor, 1994; Democratic nominee for lieutenant governor, 1994; U.S. House, 1997-2001

ELECTION RESULTS

2000 GENERAL

Debbie Stabenow (D)	2,061,952	49.5%
Spencer Abraham (R)	1,994,693	47.9%

2000 PRIMARY

Debbie Stabenow (D)	unopposed

PREVIOUS WINNING PERCENTAGES
1998 House Election (57%); 1996 House Election (54%)

Elected 2000; 1st term

Stabenow has moved quickly to the fore in the Senate, leading Democrats through one of Capitol Hill's most volatile political debates — how to add prescription drug coverage to Medicare. As chairwoman of her party's prescription drug task force, Stabenow played a prominent role in the attempt in the 107th Congress to include drug coverage in the federal entitlement program that serves nearly 40 million elderly and disabled Americans. She heads the Senate Democrats' Health Care Task Force in the 108th.

Stabenow (STAB-uh-now) jumped deeper into the political fray in the 108th by taking on responsibility for returning Democrats to the majority in the Senate. Party leaders chose her at the end of 2002 to be vice chairwoman of the Democratic Senatorial Campaign Committee, the chief fundraising and recruiting organization for Senate candidates. Democrats must defend 19 Senate seats in 2004 while Republicans are trying to keep 15.

The senator knows a thing or two about difficult odds. She narrowly unseated Republican Spencer Abraham in 2000, becoming the first woman senator elected from Michigan. She is part of the coalition of centrist New Democrats in the Senate, as she was during her two terms in the House. In the 107th Congress, she chaired the party's Women's Senate Network, which provides money to encourage women to run for office.

She has consistently challenged prescription drugmakers, a powerful and wealthy industry that heavily supports Republicans. She literally rode the Medicare prescription drug issue to victory in 2000, ushering busloads of Michigan seniors to Canada where they could buy their medication for far less than in the United States.

In the 107th, Stabenow helped pass legislation to allow the "reimportation" of U.S.-made drugs from Canada and to make it easier for generic drugs, which usually sell for less than their brand-name counterparts, to get to the marketplace.

She also proposed limiting what drug companies could deduct on their tax returns for direct-to-consumer advertising, capping such deductions at the amount companies spend on research and development of new drugs.

"We pay the pharmaceutical corporations at the prescription counter and through billions of dollars in taxpayer subsidies," she said. "And they, in turn, spent more than twice as much on advertising and marketing techniques as they do on research and development. This is simply not acceptable."

In the 108th Congress, Stabenow went up against the drug industry again, working to delete provisions in the 2002 homeland security law that would have helped shield vaccine makers from lawsuits.

Foreign steel imports were also a big concern for Stabenow in the 107th. Thousands of her constituents work in the steel industry in Michigan's Upper Peninsula, and to protect those jobs, Stabenow pushed President Bush to slap a four-year, 50 percent tariff on imported steel. While she praised Bush's decision to levy a 30 percent tariff, she was disappointed that it was not higher. Anything less than 40 percent, she said, is like "splitting the baby, which is not good enough."

Stabenow has shown her willingness to join with Republicans on a number of issues. In the Senate, she partnered with Republican Olympia J. Snowe of Maine in a failed attempt to pass legislation that would have delayed future tax cuts if expected budget surpluses did not materialize. Stabenow also was one of three Budget Committee Democrats to support an effort by Republican Pete V. Domenici of New Mexico to extend existing budget caps for another year.

In the House, Stabenow voted for GOP-sponsored measures to restructure the nation's public housing system and to encourage states to prosecute violent juvenile offenders as adults. She also supported a GOP-backed constitutional amendment to outlaw desecration of the U.S. flag.

Yet Stabenow has been true to traditional Democratic positions on such matters as abortion rights, education, gun control and public funding for the arts. She has shown strong support for labor, a key Democratic constituency. In 2002, she voted against giving Bush fast-track authority to negotiate trade agreements that Congress cannot amend, something labor strongly opposed.

Stabenow, along with home-state Democratic colleague Carl Levin, also clashed with Bush over the president's judicial nominees. In the 107th Congress, she and Levin prevented most of Bush's nominees for the 6th U.S. Circuit Court of Appeals, which includes Michigan, from getting even a hearing in the Judiciary Committee. Their goal was to stonewall the Bush nominees until former President Clinton's picks for the court, blocked by Republicans during the 106th Congress, received hearings.

Stabenow opposed Bush's move to store nuclear waste at Nevada's Yucca Mountain, arguing that the material would still have to be stored in "cooling pools" in the Great Lakes for at least five years. She said the administration's proposal to transport the waste was unclear and could pose security risks in the states the waste would pass through, including Michigan.

One of Stabenow's first actions as a freshman senator was to help the man she had defeated, Abraham, win Senate confirmation as Bush's secretary of energy. She introduced Abraham to the Senate Energy Committee, which votes on the appointment.

Stabenow's narrow victory to unseat Abraham in 2000 was the latest progression in a successful political career that has spanned more than half her life. She established herself as a fixture in Michigan Democratic politics with three years on the Ingham County Commission, a seat she first won in 1975 at age 25. She went on to serve 12 years in the Michigan House and four years in the state Senate.

She has had one down year in politics. In 1994, she lost the Democratic gubernatorial primary to veteran Democratic Rep. Howard Wolpe. She then accepted Wolpe's invitation to join his ticket as a candidate for lieutenant governor, but incumbent GOP Gov. John Engler swept to re-election in what turned out to be a very good year for Republicans.

Stabenow made a comeback in 1996, ending Republican Rep. Dick Chrysler's one-term hold on the politically competitive 8th District. She was easily re-elected to her seat in the House in 1998.

That win set up Stabenow's Senate challenge to Abraham. Neither candidate had primary opposition. Stabenow was a vice chairwoman of the Democratic presidential convention in Los Angeles — an indication of the importance that her party placed on her takeover bid. Abraham launched a summertime campaign blitz that gave him a big lead in polls, and some Democratic strategists fretted that they might have to write off the race. But Stabenow and allied groups staged a late counteroffensive that enabled her campaign to peak at the right time.

Stabenow had a campaign chest of $8 million. She was the top recipient of money from EMILY's list, the Democratic women's political action committee that supports abortion rights. She also benefited from a strong turnout by blacks and union members and a Michigan victory by Democratic presidential nominee Al Gore. Stabenow won by slightly more than 67,000 votes out of more than 4.1 million cast.

KEY VOTES

2002

- Yes Pass farm bill reversing crop subsidy limits
- Yes Postpone tougher automobile fuel efficiency standards
- Yes Overhaul campaign finance law; ban "soft money" and restrict advocacy advertising
- Yes Set federal election standards
- No Support oil drilling in Arctic National Wildlife Refuge
- No Revive fast-track procedures for trade agreements
- Yes Create federal insurance coverage for catastrophic terrorist losses
- Yes Tighten federal accounting and corporate governance regulation
- Yes Advance bipartisan Medicare prescription drug plan
- Yes Create independent Sept. 11 commission
- Yes Back Democratic Homeland Security Department proposal
- No Authorize war against Iraq

2001

- No Confirm John Ashcroft as attorney general
- No Nullify Clinton Labor Department ergonomics rule
- No Cut taxes by $1.35 trillion through fiscal 2011
- Yes Pass Democratic bill to bolster rights of patients in managed-care plans
- Yes Permit a new round of military base closings
- Yes Expand law enforcement power to investigate suspected terrorists

CQ VOTE STUDIES

	PARTY UNITY		PRESIDENTIAL SUPPORT	
	Support	Oppose	Support	Oppose
2002	95%	5%	66%	34%
2001	96%	4%	64%	36%
House Service:				
2000	82%	18%	74%	26%
1999	87%	13%	78%	22%
1998	87%	13%	78%	22%
1997	88%	12%	81%	19%

INTEREST GROUPS

	AFL-CIO	ADA	CCUS	ACU
2002	100%	95%	45%	0%
2001	100%	100%	43%	8%
House Service:				
2000	90%	90%	47%	16%
1999	78%	95%	44%	4%
1998	90%	100%	61%	9%
1997	100%	95%	50%	12%

Rep. Bart Stupak (D)

CAPITOL OFFICE
225-4735
stupak@mail.house.gov
www.house.gov/stupak
2352 Rayburn 20515-2201; fax 225-4744

COMMITTEES
Energy & Commerce

HOMETOWN
Menominee

BORN
Feb. 29, 1952, Milwaukee, Wis.

RELIGION
Roman Catholic

FAMILY
Wife, Laurie Stupak; two children (one deceased)

EDUCATION
Northwestern Michigan Community College, A.A. 1972; Saginaw Valley State College, B.S. 1977 (criminal justice); Thomas M. Cooley Law School, J.D. 1981

CAREER
Lawyer; state trooper; patrolman

POLITICAL HIGHLIGHTS
Mich. House, 1989-91; sought Democratic nomination for Mich. Senate, 1990

ELECTION RESULTS

2002 GENERAL		
Bart Stupak (D)	150,701	67.7%
Don Hooper (R)	69,254	31.1%
John W. Loosemore (LIBERT)	2,732	1.2%
2002 PRIMARY		
Bart Stupak (D)	unopposed	
2000 GENERAL		
Bart Stupak (D)	169,649	58.4%
Chuck Yob (R)	117,300	40.4%

PREVIOUS WINNING PERCENTAGES
1998 (59%); 1996 (71%); 1994 (57%); 1992 (54%)

Elected 1992; 6th term

Now starting his second decade in the House, Stupak seems to have found his political niche in the frequently frigid climes of Michigan's Upper Peninsula. He casts a reliable vote for the Democratic leadership except on the biggest of bellwether votes, when he strays frequently enough to preserve his standing as a centrist back home.

A former police officer and state trooper, a supporter of gun owners, an opponent of abortion rights and a steadfast ally of organized labor, Stupak (STU-pack) appeals to many social conservatives while also pleasing the working-class, union-label Democrats with his populist views on trade and economic policy. And his rough-and-ready style seems a good fit in the rural reaches of the 1st District, where voters are far from the big cities and regard themselves as rugged individualists.

His social conservatism was on prominent display as the 108th Congress began, when one of the first bills the House passed in 2003 was legislation Stupak wrote with Dave Weldon, a Florida Republican, to make it illegal to clone a human embryo or to import clone embryos or any product derived from them. The House passed a similar bill by Stupak and Weldon in 2001, but the Senate never debated the measure.

Stupak has bolstered his local political standing with his work on the Energy and Commerce Committee. From his seat on the Health Subcommittee, he has pressed for the Food and Drug Administration to impose tighter regulation on the acne medication Accutane, and in the 108th Congress he was vowing to push legislation if the agency did not act. Stupak believes that Accutane was the likeliest reason that his son B.J. — a popular high school athlete and student leader who aspired to replace his father in the House someday — committed suicide at age 17 in 2000. Stupak was able to obtain a two-year committee investigation about the drug's effects that has lent credence to his belief.

Stupak is the founder of the Congressional Law Enforcement Caucus, a natural pursuit for someone who was a law enforcement officer for 12 years. (An injury in the line of duty forced him to retire in 1984; despite a bad knee ever since, Stupak is a star of the Democrats' baseball team.) He often focuses on neighborhood crime prevention, including community and school policing. In the 107th Congress, he won enactment of his legislation to limit public access to body armor, which emboldens some criminals to engage in shootouts with police. In 1999, he was named to a bipartisan task force to study school violence.

Though Stupak has been a member of the National Rifle Association, in the wake of the shootings at Colorado's Columbine High School in 1999 he voted for the strictest of several proposals to require background checks at gun shows. The move drew opposition from many in northern Michigan, where gun ownership is common and hunting is a popular pastime. The NRA, which had endorsed Stupak in the past, backed his Republican challenger in 2000 and endorsed neither candidate in 2002.

As redrawn and enlarged for this decade, the 1st District is 24,887 square miles — almost 45 percent of the state's land area and the third-largest district east of the Mississippi River. Touching three of the Great Lakes, the district has 1,556 miles of freshwater shoreline — more than any other district in the continental United States. And Stupak walks a fine line on environmental issues. Economically struggling communities in the district would like to attract more industry, but encouraging development threatens the natural environment, which attracts much-needed tourist dollars.

In the late 1990s, he voted with Republicans to continue road building subsidies for the logging industry. In 2002, he opposed efforts to ban road building in one-third of U.S. national forests. And he criticized the National Park Service for proposing a ban on snowmobiles in its parks — environmentalists fault the recreational vehicles for the noise and pollution they create. He argued that each park should set its own policy.

But Stupak sided with environmentalists in the 107th when he won enactment of a federal ban on oil drilling beneath the Great Lakes., which was matched soon after with a ban enacted by the Michigan Legislature.

In the 108th, Stupak was seeking to promote a plan, drawn with state officials, to restrict the ability of bottled-water companies to draw from the lakes and to prevent commercial ships from dumping ballast water in the lakes. Such water often contains animal life not native to the region and thereby disruptive to the ecosystem.

Another parochial priority of Stupak's has been redevelopment of K.I. Sawyer Air Force Base, which was ordered closed in 1993. Stupak got federal funds to help convert the base to civilian use, and Sawyer has been cited as a model for other military base conversion efforts.

As a lifelong resident of the Upper Peninsula (known by locals as the UP), Stupak prides himself on his "Yooper" background. While serving as an Escanaba police officer, he earned an undergraduate degree in criminal justice. Still a trooper, he obtained a law degree, which served him well after his forced retirement from the state police. He entered private law practice and got involved in local civic and political affairs. He won a state House seat in 1988 but gave it up after two years for a state Senate bid, in which he narrowly lost the Democratic primary.

Stupak's opportunity to try for Congress came in 1992, when Republican Rep. Robert W. Davis retired after seven terms. Davis' departure was hastened when the House Ethics Committee labeled him one of the 22 abusers of the private bank then maintained for House members: Davis had 878 overdrafts. Stupak defeated a former Republican House member, Philip E. Ruppe, with 54 percent of the vote.

Only twice since has Stupak won more than 60 percent of the vote. The most recent time was in 2002, when he polled 68 percent in a reconfigured district made slightly more Democratic. On the same day, however, Democrat Laurie Stupak was defeated for election to the state House seat that her husband had held — the first time the GOP had won the seat in more than a decade. Her eight years as mayor of Menominee end in December 2003.

KEY VOTES

2002

Yes Overhaul campaign finance law; ban "soft money" and restrict advocacy advertising
Yes Back Bush's defense budget increase
No Extend 1996 welfare law
No Adopt Bush's discretionary spending limit
No Pass GOP Medicare prescription drug plan
Yes Create independent Sept. 11 commission
Yes Extend union protections to Homeland Security Department employees
No Revive fast-track procedures for trade agreements
No Authorize war against Iraq
No Advance bankruptcy overhaul opposed by abortion opponents

2001

? Nullify Clinton Labor Department ergonomics rule
No Cut taxes by $1.35 trillion through fiscal 2011
Yes Maintain ban on oil drilling in Arctic National Wildlife Refuge
No Approve Bush proposal to limit managed-care plan liability for coverage decisions
Yes Divert money from crop subsidy payments to land conservation
Yes Expand law enforcement power to investigate suspected terrorists

CQ VOTE STUDIES

	PARTY UNITY		PRESIDENTIAL SUPPORT	
	Support	Oppose	Support	Oppose
2002	89%	11%	33%	67%
2001	81%	19%	31%	69%
2000	83%	17%	67%	33%
1999	83%	17%	70%	30%
1998	83%	17%	75%	25%

INTEREST GROUPS

	AFL-CIO	ADA	CCUS	ACU
2002	100%	80%	45%	16%
2001	100%	75%	38%	38%
2000	100%	65%	30%	22%
1999	100%	85%	16%	16%
1998	100%	90%	17%	20%

MICHIGAN 1
Upper Peninsula; northern Lower Michigan

Rolling, forested hills and some Upper Peninsula (UP) mountains that get hundreds of inches of snow make the 1st one of the few places suited to skiing in the Midwest. Beaches and resorts around Petoskey also lure summer vacationers from Detroit, Chicago and Cleveland, feeding the area's tourist industry. But most of the district saw its economic foundations erode in the 1990s.

The UP, surrounded by three of the Great Lakes and connected to the rest of the state by the Mackinac Bridge, is still recovering from the closure of K. I. Sawyer Air Force Base in the 1990s. Mining, which once drew immigrants to remote parts of the state, has not been a growth industry since the early 20th century. NAFTA has effectively killed most remaining copper, paper and iron production.

Tourism and timber products companies are the only growth industries. Snowmobiling makes up at least 40 percent of winter revenues for restaurants and hotels. Slow population growth in northern Michigan and the UP gradually has led to the expansion of the district's territory to encompass more than 40 percent of the state's land mass. After the 2000 census, the 1st needed to add about 23,000 people to meet the population equality requirement; a new map drawn in 2001 did this by shedding some northwestern Michigan counties (including Grand Traverse) and adding some northeastern counties along the Saginaw Bay. The 1st reaches nearly as far south as Bay City (which is in the 5th).

As a whole, the 1st backs Democrats, but there is a strong strain of social conservatism, particularly on gun rights. A long tradition of union organization among miners and mill workers has left the western and central UP strongly Democratic, a preference shared by the eastern counties in the northern part of the state. But George W. Bush made major inroads in the area in the 2000 presidential election, decisively winning counties that Bob Dole had lost in 1996. The northern counties at the top of the "mitten" also tend to support Republicans.

MAJOR INDUSTRY
Mining, logging, tourism, auto parts

CITIES
Marquette, 19,661; Sault Ste. Marie, 16,542; Escanaba, 13,140

NOTABLE
Isle Royale National Park; The National Ski Hall of Fame is in Ishpeming.

Rep. Peter Hoekstra (R)

CAPITOL OFFICE
225-4401
tellhoek@mail.house.gov
www.house.gov/hoekstra
2234 Rayburn 20515-2202; fax 226-0779

COMMITTEES
Education & Workforce
(Select Education - chairman)
Transportation & Infrastructure
Select Intelligence
(Technical & Tactical Intelligence - chairman)

HOMETOWN
Holland

BORN
Oct. 30, 1953, Groningen, Netherlands

RELIGION
Christian Reformed Church

FAMILY
Wife, Diane Hoekstra; three children

EDUCATION
Hope College, B.A. 1975 (political science);
U. of Michigan, M.B.A. 1977

CAREER
Furniture company executive

POLITICAL HIGHLIGHTS
No previous office

ELECTION RESULTS

2002 GENERAL		
Peter Hoekstra (R)	156,937	70.4%
Jeffrey A. Wrisley (D)	61,749	27.7%
Laurie L. Aleck (LIBERT)	2,680	1.2%
2002 PRIMARY		
Peter Hoekstra (R)		unopposed
2000 GENERAL		
Peter Hoekstra (R)	186,762	64.4%
Bob Shrauger (D)	96,370	33.2%

PREVIOUS WINNING PERCENTAGES
1998 (69%); 1996 (65%); 1994 (75%); 1992 (63%)

Elected 1992; 6th term

Hoekstra has little use for government and its regulatory ways. So when news about illegal and unethical corporate conduct hit Capitol Hill with full force during the 107th Congress, the former furniture company executive was angry. "If business does not do self-correcting, then there will be more oversight," he said. "You cannot legislate trust and integrity, but we may try."

He also sent leading business executives around the country a draft of his proposed "Shareholders' Bill of Rights" — an ethics and accountability code to be practiced by corporate chiefs. To his chagrin, some executives demurred.

As the business scandals showed, Hoekstra (HOOK-struh) is irked by irresponsible behavior. But he does not think much of government either. As chairman for six years of the Education and the Workforce Oversight Subcommittee, he came up with what he believed were damning tales of federal agencies unable to document how they were spending taxpayer money. Hoekstra hoped that public outrage would bolster his efforts to reform government spending practices. But with dozens of congressional investigations vying for public notice — many of them much sexier than his businesslike probes of the departments of Labor and Education — Hoekstra found that his work was largely overlooked.

In the 107th Congress, Hoekstra's assignments to the Budget, Education and the Workforce, and Intelligence committees put him in a prime position to shape debates on fiscal policy, education and the new war on terrorism. He served as vice chairman of the Intelligence Terrorism and Homeland Security Subcommittee, which issued a classified report that criticized the performance of the CIA, FBI and the National Security Agency before Sept. 11, 2001. In the 108th, he traded his seat on Budget for one on the Transportation and Infrastructure Committee.

While he is a promoter of his party's core conservative message, Hoekstra has gone his own way on some high-profile issues. He voted against President Bush's request for fast-track trade negotiating authority in the 107th, worried that new trade deals could disadvantage western Michigan's fruit and vegetable farmers. He also voted against the 2002 farm bill, which Bush supported but which Hoekstra viewed as overly expensive.

Most publicly, in 2001 he fought to kill a central tenet of Bush's education overhaul proposal: mandatory annual testing in reading and math in grades 3 through 8. Hoekstra viewed those as an inappropriate federal mandate, and he and Massachusetts Democrat Barney Frank sought to delete the testing requirements from the House bill. They lost after some of the most intensive White House lobbying of the year. Upset by his defeat and irked by the lack of any voucher provision to support private schooling, Hoekstra voted against enacting the law.

Also in the 107th, Hoekstra opposed the law letting pilots carry guns in cockpits, noting that taxpayers would have to pay for training and equipment, and that the program was a federal mandate on private businesses.

But he does compromise, usually while keeping to his conservative principles. For example, he carefully audited President Clinton's AmeriCorps community service program when he chaired the Education and the Workforce's Oversight Subcommittee. In 2002, as the new chairman of the Education Subcommittee, he and top-ranking Democrat Tim Roemer of Indiana crafted the "Citizen Service Act" sought by Bush that would reauthorize and expand AmeriCorps and other national volunteer service programs. The legislation called for greater accountability in awarding AmeriCorps grants, to reduce fraud and abuse, and it prohibited members from engaging in political activities, campaigns or unions. The bill died because it was opposed by other GOP leaders.

Hoekstra's congressional career has included a sometimes seamless blending of local concerns with national interests. When he was in charge of the Oversight panel, he headed a probe of election corruption within the Teamsters union for which he was criticized by members of both parties — Democrats argued that he was seeking partisan political advantage and Republicans contended that he was not being political enough.

But in 2000, the Michigan Teamsters endorsed Hoekstra and he helped nurture a political relationship between the union and the White House. That led to the union's backing of Bush's proposal to drill for oil in Alaska's Arctic National Wildlife Refuge, which the union said would create jobs. In 2002, the Teamsters again endorsed Hoekstra.

Hoekstra has been a leading critic of Federal Prison Industries Inc., a corporation that uses inmates to make products for the federal government. He says that its low-cost labor enables it to compete unfairly with private business. In 2002 he charged that it was a major factor in the closing of C.F. Hathaway Co.'s last U.S. shirt-making plant. His interest stems from his previous job with Herman Miller Inc., a maker of office furniture headquartered in his district that also competed with Prison Industries.

Hoekstra was born in the Netherlands and immigrated to the United States with his family when he was 3, settling in the town of Holland in a heavily Dutch part of Michigan. After receiving an MBA from the University of Michigan, Hoekstra embarked on an executive career.

In 1992, Hoekstra decided he could do a better job than 13-term Republican Rep. Guy Vander Jagt — for whom Hoekstra once interned. Hoekstra accused Vander Jagt of neglecting his constituents' needs in favor of enjoying the Washington high life and raising money for the National Republican Congressional Committee, which he chaired. Hoekstra ousted Vander Jagt in the GOP primary by 6 percentage points. In November he won the seat handily and has not been challenged seriously since.

Hoekstra had said he would serve no more than six terms, but in December 2002 he announced he would run for re-election in 2004. He said his term-limit pledge had been a mistake, but denied becoming a captive of Capitol Hill. He pointed out that he does not own or rent property in Washington, but instead sleeps in his office while the House is in session. He spends the remainder of his time in Michigan.

KEY VOTES

2002

No Overhaul campaign finance law; ban "soft money" and restrict advocacy advertising
Yes Back Bush's defense budget increase
Yes Extend 1996 welfare law
Yes Adopt Bush's discretionary spending limit
Yes Pass GOP Medicare prescription drug plan
No Create independent Sept. 11 commission
No Extend union protections to Homeland Security Department employees
No Revive fast-track procedures for trade agreements
Yes Authorize war against Iraq
No Advance bankruptcy overhaul opposed by abortion opponents

2001

Yes Nullify Clinton Labor Department ergonomics rule
Yes Cut taxes by $1.35 trillion through fiscal 2011
No Maintain ban on oil drilling in Arctic National Wildlife Refuge
Yes Approve Bush proposal to limit managed-care plan liability for coverage decisions
Yes Divert money from crop subsidy payments to land conservation
Yes Expand law enforcement power to investigate suspected terrorists

CQ VOTE STUDIES

	PARTY UNITY		PRESIDENTIAL SUPPORT	
	Support	Oppose	Support	Oppose
2002	91%	9%	88%	12%
2001	91%	9%	74%	26%
2000	93%	7%	23%	77%
1999	93%	7%	15%	85%
1998	93%	7%	24%	76%

INTEREST GROUPS

	AFL-CIO	ADA	CCUS	ACU
2002	11%	5%	85%	92%
2001	17%	10%	91%	88%
2000	10%	10%	90%	88%
1999	0%	5%	88%	88%
1998	10%	5%	82%	100%

MICHIGAN 2
West – Muskegon, Holland

The 2nd stretches 140 miles along Lake Michigan, covering counties full of cherry trees and asparagus farms. Pioneers, most of them Dutch, were drawn to the region by rich logging opportunities. Now, heavy industrial manufacturing dominates the most populated counties, including Ottawa, Muskegon and Allegan, but the early settlers' pioneering spirit persists. Dutch independence has made the 2nd one of the most staunchly Republican districts in Michigan.

That Republicanism is led by Ottawa County, which gave George W. Bush a statewide high of 71 percent of the vote in the 2000 presidential election. Ottawa added more than 50,000 residents in the 1990s, more than all but three other Michigan counties, and grew by 27 percent. More than 35 percent of district residents live in Ottawa County.

Support for Democratic candidates can be found among minority voters in the district's largest city, Muskegon, which has struggled to keep manufacturing jobs. But local tax incentives have drawn in new automotive parts suppliers, helping the economy rebound. Western Michigan also hosts several of the nation's top office furniture makers, including Herman Miller in Zeeland and Haworth in Holland.

Holland, south of Muskegon, is a conservative, Dutch-settled port town that draws tourists from all over the Midwest. It is the westernmost point of the "Dutch Triangle," formed by Holland, Grand Rapids and Kalamazoo. The Dutch lifestyle of the early 20th century is recreated in Dutch Village theme park, complete with wooden shoes and klompen dancers. Holland's annual tulip festival draws hundreds of thousands of visitors every May.

Redistricting following the 2000 census did not significantly alter the 2nd's borders. The new map added Benzie County, a fast-growing area in northwest Michigan, and reconfigured the boundaries in the south.

MAJOR INDUSTRY
Metal, furniture, tourism, agriculture

CITIES
Muskegon, 40,105; Holland, 35,048; Norton Shores, 22,527

NOTABLE
The world's largest weather vane is in Montague; Oceana County hosts the National Asparagus Festival.

Rep. Vernon J. Ehlers (R)

CAPITOL OFFICE
225-3831
www.house.gov/ehlers
1714 Longworth 20515-2203; fax 225-5144

COMMITTEES
Education & Workforce
House Administration
Science
(Environment, Technology & Standards - chairman)
Transportation & Infrastructure
Joint Library

HOMETOWN
Grand Rapids

BORN
Feb. 6, 1934, Pipestone, Minn.

RELIGION
Christian Reformed Church

FAMILY
Wife, Johanna Ehlers; four children

EDUCATION
Calvin College, attended 1952-55; U. of California, Berkeley, A.B. 1956 (physics), Ph.D. 1960 (physics)

CAREER
Professor; physicist

POLITICAL HIGHLIGHTS
Kent County Commission, 1975-83 (chairman, 1979-82); Mich. House, 1983-85; Mich. Senate, 1985-93 (president pro tempore)

ELECTION RESULTS

2002 GENERAL		
Vernon J. Ehlers (R)	153,131	70.0%
Kathryn D. Lynnes (D)	61,987	28.3%
Tom Quinn (LIBERT)	2,613	1.2%
2002 PRIMARY		
Vernon J. Ehlers (R)		unopposed
2000 GENERAL		
Vernon J. Ehlers (R)	179,539	65.0%
Tim Steele (D)	91,309	33.1%

PREVIOUS WINNING PERCENTAGES
1998 (73%); 1996 (69%); 1994 (74%); 1993 Special Election (67%)

Elected December 1993; 5th full term

In the world of politics, few problems are solved by scientific means. But Ehlers, the first research physicist elected to Congress, always seems to be seeking ways to apply science or logic to political and legislative puzzles.

His search is often frustrated by Congress' slow pace. Asked what he considers his major achievements, Ehlers (AY-lurz) reaches back to before his decade in Congress and cites two laws he helped write as a state legislator: one to implement a Michigan-wide 911 emergency system, the other to create an infant testing program for metabolic diseases.

In Washington, Ehlers' analytical reasoning generally lands him on middle ground. He is conservative on fiscal matters, although he is a leading advocate for increased funding for scientific research, and more liberal on social questions. But his scientific background and loyalty to the GOP leadership sometimes conflict, creating awkward moments.

In the 107th Congress, Ehlers voted against President Bush's proposal to drill for oil in the Arctic National Wildlife Refuge. That stance, combined with his support for increasing fuel efficiency standards for light trucks and sport utility vehicles — an unpopular position in auto-reliant Michigan — highlighted the independence that earned him his first Sierra Club endorsement for re-election in 2002. In the end, however, he backed the final House version of an energy policy bill that called for drilling in the refuge.

His clarity on matters of science also can become blurred when Ehlers' religion suggests a different approach. The son of a minister and a devout Christian himself, he has helped write several books that meld theology and science as guides to managing the environment. He also refers to his religious beliefs when he ponders the ethical issues surrounding cloning.

Ehlers did not take a position in 2001 when Bush decided to allow federal funding for limited embryonic stem cell research, but he credited the president's stance with minimizing political fallout among both church groups and the scientific community.

His background has shaped the role he has played on the five House committees on which he sits — but none more so than the Science Committee, where he has chaired the Environment, Technology and Standards Subcommittee since the 107th. Its jurisdiction includes the Environmental Protection Agency and the National Institute of Standards and Technology. Ehlers helped thwart the administration's proposed transfer of NIST's computer security division to the new Homeland Security Department, arguing it would dilute the agency's role in civilian affairs.

Since 1999, another research physicist has been in the House with Ehlers: Democrat Rush D. Holt of New Jersey. They have joined to promote science education and expand research. "We're not trying to produce nerds," Ehlers once said of their campaign, "even though I still wear my plastic pocket protector."

Regarded by his colleagues as one of the smartest lawmakers in Washington, Ehlers is often called on by Republican leaders to apply his scientific expertise in the policy arena. During his time as a college physics professor, he was a science adviser to Gerald R. Ford when Ford represented Grand Rapids in the House. When Ehlers came to Congress, the GOP leadership asked him to help House members make better use of the then-fledgling Internet. He offered training, helped equip offices with network software and new hardware, and advised lawmakers about how to set up Web sites to communicate with constituents.

In the 107th Congress, Ehlers sought more funding for the National Science Foundation, which he argued has grown stagnant over the previous decade. He makes the same arguments about the Department of Energy, which he says is a Cold War relic that needs an overhaul to emphasize research. In 2002, the House passed bills written in Ehlers' subcommittee to create a better inland flooding warning system, set standards for electronically linking manufacturers and suppliers, reauthorize the National Sea Grant College Program, and create a new EPA deputy administrator for science and technology.

On the Transportation and Infrastructure Committee in the 107th, Ehlers opposed giving Bush the power to decide whether baggage screeners should be federal workers or private contract employees, because he thought it was an inappropriate yielding of congressional prerogative. Ehlers also opposed the 2002 law allowing firearms in airliner cockpits.

Despite his non-confrontational mien, Ehlers has been drawn into partisan dust-ups. He headed a task force of two Republicans and one Democrat that investigated the contested 1996 election victory in southern California by Democrat Loretta Sanchez over Republican incumbent Robert K. Dornan. The panel concluded hundreds of votes had been cast by non-citizens — but not enough to change the outcome of the election.

Due to severe asthma and allergies, both mitigated now by medication, Ehlers was schooled at home until college. After receiving a doctorate in physics from the University of California at Berkeley when he was 26, Ehlers stayed as a lecturer and research physicist for six years. In 1966, he traded that liberal atmosphere for the conservative, religious-oriented campus of Calvin College in Grand Rapids, where he had spent three years as an undergraduate.

In 1982, Ehlers won election to the state House, succeeding Republican Paul B. Henry, a former colleague at Calvin, who had moved to the state Senate. Over the next dozen years, Ehlers followed Henry up the political ladder, succeeding him in the state Senate and finally in Congress.

In 1993, Ehlers was president pro tempore of the Michigan Senate. Nearly 60 years old, he was looking for new challenges and weighing a 1994 campaign for the Senate seat then held by Democrat Donald W. Riegle Jr. But when Henry died of brain cancer that July, Ehlers launched a House bid and quickly moved to the front of an eight-person Republican pack. He won with 67 percent in the special election and has never faced a significant challenge to his re-election.

KEY VOTES

2002

- No Overhaul campaign finance law; ban "soft money" and restrict advocacy advertising
- Yes Back Bush's defense budget increase
- Yes Extend 1996 welfare law
- Yes Adopt Bush's discretionary spending limit
- Yes Pass GOP Medicare prescription drug plan
- No Create independent Sept. 11 commission
- No Extend union protections to Homeland Security Department employees
- Yes Revive fast-track procedures for trade agreements
- Yes Authorize war against Iraq
- No Advance bankruptcy overhaul opposed by abortion opponents

2001

- Yes Nullify Clinton Labor Department ergonomics rule
- Yes Cut taxes by $1.35 trillion through fiscal 2011
- Yes Maintain ban on oil drilling in Arctic National Wildlife Refuge
- Yes Approve Bush proposal to limit managed-care plan liability for coverage decisions
- Yes Divert money from crop subsidy payments to land conservation
- Yes Expand law enforcement power to investigate suspected terrorists

CQ VOTE STUDIES

	PARTY UNITY		PRESIDENTIAL SUPPORT	
	Support	Oppose	Support	Oppose
2002	85%	15%	87%	13%
2001	88%	12%	81%	19%
2000	78%	22%	38%	62%
1999	83%	17%	29%	71%
1998	78%	22%	33%	67%

INTEREST GROUPS

	AFL-CIO	ADA	CCUS	ACU
2002	11%	15%	95%	80%
2001	8%	10%	91%	68%
2000	20%	20%	80%	64%
1999	0%	20%	96%	60%
1998	30%	25%	89%	56%

MICHIGAN 3

West central — Grand Rapids

Grand Rapids, Michigan's second-most-populous city, teems with auto plants and metals manufacturing, but it's a world away from Detroit. Conservative Dutch Republicans — not auto union Democrats — control the district, making the 3rd one of Michigan's heaviest GOP regions. Its staunch conservatism is rivaled only by the neighboring 2nd; both districts gave 61 percent of the two-party vote to George W. Bush in the 2000 presidential election.

Also unlike Detroit, Grand Rapids has escaped complete dependence on the auto industry. The city is a leading producer of metal office furniture, in addition to making avionics systems, tools and home appliances. The city's economy prospered in the 1970s when modular furniture became popular, but it suffered in the early 1990s when companies began to downsize their managerial staffs and cut back on office space. In a major effort to revitalize downtown Grand Rapids, the city built a new arena and recruited three minor league sports teams.

Gerald R. Ford made his way to the House and then the presidency from Grand Rapids (the area airport is named for the 38th president), and his brand of small-government Republicanism and fiscal restraint still holds sway in the 3rd. One of the district's largest employers, Amway, based in Ada, consistently contributes to Republicans around the nation. This direct sales company, which markets personal- and home-care products, promotes its philosophy of private philanthropy by donating generously to area universities, hospitals and churches.

More than 80 percent of residents live in Kent County, which grew by 15 percent in the 1990s largely because of rapid growth outside of Grand Rapids (which grew by just 5 percent). The rest live in Ionia and Barry counties, located east and southeast of Kent, respectively. Redistricting following the 2000 census made minimal changes to the 3rd.

MAJOR INDUSTRY

Office furniture, auto parts, metals manufacturing

CITIES

Grand Rapids, 197,800; Wyoming, 69,368; Kentwood, 45,255; Walker, 21,842; Forest Hills (unincorporated), 20,942

NOTABLE

The Norton Mound Group, one of the best-preserved burial centers of the Hopewell culture, is in Grand Rapids.

Rep. Dave Camp (R)

CAPITOL OFFICE
225-3561
www.house.gov/camp
137 Cannon 20515-2204; fax 225-9679

COMMITTEES
Ways & Means
Select Homeland Security
(Infrastructure & Border Security - chairman)

HOMETOWN
Midland

BORN
July 9, 1953, Midland, Mich.

RELIGION
Roman Catholic

FAMILY
Wife, Nancy Camp; three children

EDUCATION
Albion College, B.A. 1975 (economics); U. of San Diego, J.D. 1978

CAREER
Lawyer; congressional aide

POLITICAL HIGHLIGHTS
Mich. House, 1989-91

ELECTION RESULTS

2002 GENERAL		
Dave Camp (R)	149,090	68.2%
Lawrence D. Hollenbeck (D)	65,950	30.2%
Sterling Johnson (GREEN)	2,261	1.0%
2002 PRIMARY		
Dave Camp (R)		unopposed
2000 GENERAL		
Dave Camp (R)	182,128	68.0%
Lawrence D. Hollenbeck (D)	78,019	29.1%
Alan Gamble (GREEN)	3,790	1.4%

PREVIOUS WINNING PERCENTAGES
1998 (91%); 1996 (65%); 1994 (73%); 1992 (63%); 1990 (65%)

Elected 1990; 7th term

Conservative in his politics, understated in his political style and loyal to his party leadership, Camp worked his way onto the top row of the Ways and Means Committee dais well before his 50th birthday — a reflection of a long political career that belies his youthful appearance. Indeed, in his demeanor on Capitol Hill, Camp more closely resembles the veteran members with whom he shares seniority than the junior members who are generally closer to his age.

When he arrived in the House in 1991, Camp was on the leading edge of the wave of youthful Republican conservatives who since have flooded the chamber. But while so many of those lawmakers have continued to cultivate their images as political outsiders, Camp has made his mark in Congress a more old-fashioned way — landing a choice committee assignment, digging into some complex legislative issues and taking on a variety of chores for party elders.

He ran J. Dennis Hastert's whirlwind campaign to become Speaker at the end of 1998 and remains a part of the Speaker's inner circle. Hastert named him to a party task force to address the high cost of prescription drugs and he put Camp on the House ethics committee for one term — a burdensome honor, perhaps, but one that was evidence that Camp had the leadership's trust and a willingness to handle thankless tasks on behalf of the party.

Camp has several other, more formal leadership posts. He is an assistant deputy whip and serves on the GOP Steering Committee, which makes House committee assignments for the party. In the run-up to the 2000 election, he chaired the executive committee of the National Republican Congressional Committee, which seeks to elect Republicans to the House. And he has headed a panel appointed by the leadership that recommends "corrections" bills for floor action — measures to repeal federal regulations or laws that GOP leaders deem unnecessary. In the 108th Congress, he added a seat on the newly formed Homeland Security panel, which oversees the new Cabinet department of the same name.

But it is on Ways and Means, where Camp has served since his second term, that he has been most influential. He had a key role in the 1996 enactment of the law overhauling the welfare system; he has had a hand in writing law to expand adoptions; he has helped sell the Republicans' prescription drug benefit proposals; and he has been a leader in the GOP's quest to make permanent the package of tax cuts enacted in 2001, which otherwise will expire in 10 years after costing the Treasury $1.35 trillion.

When the Republicans took over the House in the 104th Congress, the GOP leadership's strategy was to link welfare overhaul with big changes in the Medicaid system. But Camp mounted a campaign against that idea, working to convince his colleagues that moving the welfare package by itself would improve its chances for enactment. That was the course ultimately taken, and after further compromise with the White House, Republicans finally agreed on the plan that President Clinton signed in 1996.

In the 107th Congress, as the House developed its version of the welfare bill extension, Camp joined Republican colleagues in rejecting the restoration of most welfare benefits to legal immigrants. Camp said doing so would "erode the principles" of the 1996 law, which the GOP counts as one of its signature achievements.

Camp relied on his experience as a domestic law attorney in Michigan to play a leading role during the 105th Congress in the writing of a law promoting the adoption of children in foster care. And in the 106th Congress, he was a driving force behind a bill to ease adoptions of children from other countries.

During debate on energy legislation in the 107th, Camp pressed for tax breaks to promote the collection, and use as energy, of landfill gas, and to encourage purchases of advanced technology and alternative fuel vehicles.

While not as vocal as some Republicans, Camp's point of departure on most issues is firmly conservative. If the matter involves spending federal funds, it's a good bet that he will come down on the side that costs the least.

Camp has long promoted legislation to apply any lawmaker's unused office and staff funds to paying down the deficit or the national debt, and during his tenure he has returned to the Treasury about $1 million in unused office account money, though lawmakers are not required to do so. He also donates his congressional cost-of-living pay increases to scholarships for college students every other year.

Camp's office in Washington features a rack of several dozen men's neckties — a curiosity for visiting constituents, who paw through the collection looking for a tie that represents a favorite school or organization. He began building the collection when The Detroit News reported that Camp had arrived in Congress with just three ties and invited readers to supplement the congressman's collection.

His interest in politics began at an early age, and Camp got his initial hands-on experience volunteering on the local judicial campaign of a lawyer for whom he was interning.

After practicing law for five years, Camp became chief of staff for Republican Bill Schuette, a childhood friend, during his first term in the House. Camp returned to Michigan in 1986 to manage Schuette's re-election campaign and resume his law career. But in 1988, he ran for and won an open state House seat based in Midland. He had barely found his chair in the legislature, however, when GOP strategists persuaded Schuette to run for the Senate against Democrat Carl Levin in 1990 and suggested that Camp would make a fine successor to Schuette in the House.

Aided by Schuette's endorsement, Camp eked out a close primary victory against four opponents. The Democrats nominated Joan L. Dennison, who espoused support for some of the ideas of political extremist Lyndon H. LaRouche Jr. Camp coasted to victory with 65 percent of the vote. His re-election contests since have been easy. In 2002, he trounced retired teacher Lawrence D. Hollenbeck for a second straight time in a newly drawn district that retained a Republican tilt.

KEY VOTES

2002

- No Overhaul campaign finance law; ban "soft money" and restrict advocacy advertising
- Yes Back Bush's defense budget increase
- Yes Extend 1996 welfare law
- Yes Adopt Bush's discretionary spending limit
- Yes Pass GOP Medicare prescription drug plan
- No Create independent Sept. 11 commission
- No Extend union protections to Homeland Security Department employees
- Yes Revive fast-track procedures for trade agreements
- Yes Authorize war against Iraq
- Yes Advance bankruptcy overhaul opposed by abortion opponents

2001

- Yes Nullify Clinton Labor Department ergonomics rule
- Yes Cut taxes by $1.35 trillion through fiscal 2011
- No Maintain ban on oil drilling in Arctic National Wildlife Refuge
- Yes Approve Bush proposal to limit managed-care plan liability for coverage decisions
- No Divert money from crop subsidy payments to land conservation
- Yes Expand law enforcement power to investigate suspected terrorists

CQ VOTE STUDIES

	PARTY UNITY		PRESIDENTIAL SUPPORT	
	Support	Oppose	Support	Oppose
2002	95%	5%	85%	15%
2001	96%	4%	91%	9%
2000	91%	9%	24%	76%
1999	90%	10%	23%	77%
1998	92%	8%	27%	73%

INTEREST GROUPS

	AFL-CIO	ADA	CCUS	ACU
2002	11%	0%	100%	96%
2001	17%	0%	100%	96%
2000	0%	5%	90%	84%
1999	0%	15%	96%	79%
1998	0%	10%	100%	96%

MICHIGAN 4

North central — Midland, Traverse City

Forests and farms cover much of the 14 central Michigan counties that lie wholly or partly in the 4th, which is the state's second-largest district in land area. The white pine forests north of Midland, the district's largest city, were once some of the most bountiful logging lands in the state. Now, retirees and vacationers build second homes in the sparsely populated woods, and tourists come to ski, camp and hunt in these remote counties.

Midland, on the district's eastern border, is home to Dow Chemical and Dow Corning, makers of chemicals, plastics and silicone products. Dow Chemical headquarters sits on a 2,150-acre campus in Midland, giving the city more engineers, chemists and metallurgists per capita than any other city in the nation. The area is vulnerable to Dow's corporate restructuring, but also has benefited from Dow's generous philanthropy, with churches, schools and libraries built by the Dow fortune.

West and south of Midland, the district turns agricultural. Farmers — who till fields of sugar beets, dry beans, corn, wheat and oats — worry about free trade, price supports and crop insurance. The number of farms and small towns throughout the 4th gives it a Republican lean.

Redistricting following the 2000 census gave the 4th some solidly Republican, sparsely populated but fast-growing counties in northwest Michigan. The proximity to Lake Michigan and distance from noisy population centers makes the area especially attractive to retirees. Leelanau County, in the northwest corner, grew by 28 percent in the 1990s, and Grand Traverse County (Traverse City), grew by 21 percent. Almost every county in the 4th that is west and north of Midland saw its population grow by at least 15 percent.

MAJOR INDUSTRY

Agriculture, chemical and plastics manufacturing, tourism

CITIES

Midland (pt.), 41,463; Mount Pleasant, 25,946; Owosso, 15,713; Traverse City, 14,532

NOTABLE

Interlochen Center for the Arts, south of Traverse City, includes a camp and an academy for students of the arts; Prominent alumni include CBS News correspondent Mike Wallace, actors Tom Hulce and Linda Hunt, and soprano Jessye Norman.

Rep. Dale E. Kildee (D)

CAPITOL OFFICE
225-3611
www.house.gov/kildee
2107 Rayburn 20515-2205; fax 225-6393

COMMITTEES
Education & Workforce
Resources

HOMETOWN
Flint

BORN
Sept. 16, 1929, Flint, Mich.

RELIGION
Roman Catholic

FAMILY
Wife, Gayle Kildee; three children

EDUCATION
Sacred Heart Seminary, B.A. 1952; U. of Detroit, attended 1954 (teaching certificate); U. of Peshawar (Pakistan), attended 1958-59 (Rotary fellowship); U. of Michigan, M.A. 1961 (history)

CAREER
Teacher

POLITICAL HIGHLIGHTS
Mich. House, 1965-75; Mich. Senate, 1975-77

ELECTION RESULTS

2002 GENERAL		
Dale E. Kildee (D)	158,709	91.6%
Clint Foster (LIBERT)	9,344	5.4%
Harley Mikkelson (GREEN)	5,188	3.0%
2002 PRIMARY		
Dale E. Kildee (D)		unopposed
2000 GENERAL		
Dale E. Kildee (D)	158,184	61.1%
Grant Garrett (R)	92,926	35.9%
Laurie M. Martin (LIBERT)	5,337	2.1%

PREVIOUS WINNING PERCENTAGES
1998 (56%); 1996 (59%); 1994 (51%); 1992 (54%); 1990 (68%); 1988 (76%); 1986 (80%); 1984 (93%); 1982 (75%); 1980 (93%); 1978 (77%); 1976 (70%)

Elected 1976; 14th term

To understand Kildee's political philosophy, it helps to know three things about him. He is the son of an autoworker who hails from the home of General Motors Corp., making him a fierce protector of the auto industry and labor unions. He is a seminary graduate who taught Latin after abandoning plans to become a Roman Catholic priest, a basis for his conservative views on abortion-related matters and his strong advocacy for education. And he founded the House's Native American Caucus, a reflection of a concern for American Indians that goes back to his childhood.

His blue-collar credentials are rock-solid, and his political views reflect his roots. As the No. 2 Democrat on both the Education and the Workforce and the Resources committees, Kildee is well-placed to push for an activist federal role in helping people in need — including American Indians — and to defend the rights of organized labor.

Representing a district that has suffered severe job losses, Kildee does more than just sympathize. Like fellow Michigan Democrat John D. Dingell, he requires his congressional employees who drive to work to have a car manufactured by United Auto Worker members. "If I walked into an office of a member from Florida, I would not expect to see oranges from Brazil in a big bowl there," Kildee once said on Fox News. "We tend to be sensitive to the needs of our people in our districts."

Kildee entered politics with election to the state House in 1964 — the heyday of Lyndon B. Johnson's Great Society war on poverty, civil rights crusades and other social reforms — and he remains a staunch liberal on most issues unrelated to abortion. But he is prepared to compromise when necessary. In the 107th Congress, he was a negotiator on the final terms of President Bush's elementary and secondary education overhaul. Conservative Republicans opposed it, partly because it called for a huge increase in federal spending. Kildee helped block an effort to combine drug-abuse prevention and after-school programs into one block grant.

In the 105th Congress, he played an active role in a bipartisan compromise on a law cutting student loan rates, authorizing more federal aid to college students and starting a federal grant program for teacher training and recruitment. In 1996, he voted for the law that imposed the first-ever work requirements on welfare recipients — anathema to most liberals. Kildee said Democrats had won enough concessions to make the measure acceptable.

In the 106th Congress, he backed a Republican fetal protection bill that opponents said would undermine the Supreme Court's 1973 *Roe v. Wade* decision. In 2002, Kildee supported a House-passed bill that would let hospitals and insurance companies refuse to perform or pay for abortions without forfeiting Medicare and other federal funding, thus shielding Catholic hospitals and other providers that oppose abortion.

Still, Kildee has championed many women's issues and in 2002, he sought to join the all-female Congressional Caucus for Women's Issues. He was rebuffed, gently. "Mr. Kildee had expressed an interest early on," said an aide to California Democrat Juanita Millender-McDonald, the caucus co-chairman. "But regrettably, he's of the wrong gender."

His father's hometown is near the Grand Traverse reservation, and as a child, Kildee was impressed with his father's concern for the condition of its residents. A previous generation of Kildees had traded with the Indians. As a state legislator, Kildee wrote a law allowing Michigan's American Indians to attend its state colleges for free. In his suit pocket are copies not only of the Constitution but also of the landmark 1832 Supreme Court decision that gave the federal government exclusive jurisdiction over Indian affairs, and thus responsibility for Indians' welfare.

In the House, that jurisdiction is generally exercised by the Resources Committee. When Congress in 1997 started talking about levying a tax on Indian-run gambling operations, Kildee founded the Native American Caucus. In honor of all his efforts, the Grand Traverse Band of Ottawa and Chippewa Indians in 1998 named April 15 "Dale Kildee Day."

Kildee can champion individuals as well as groups. He worked for five years to secure a presidential pardon — granted on President Clinton's final day in office — for one of his former ninth grade civics students, a local businessman convicted of international money laundering in 1981. The case captured Kildee's interest after the federal judge who sentenced the businessman petitioned the Justice Department for the pardon.

Starting in late 1985, Kildee voted "yes" or "no" on more than 6,000 consecutive roll call votes on the House floor over the next 13 years, the longest streak of any active member. By Congressional Quarterly's strict accounting, the streak ended in June 1998, when he joined more than 60 lawmakers in voting "present" on a campaign finance proposal. The Detroit News contends the streak did not end until October 2000, at 8,141, when Kildee was in an Education Committee meeting and missed a routine vote to approve the congressional journal. Kildee did not miss a single roll call in the 107th.

After a decade in the state House, Kildee won a state Senate seat in 1974. He was elected to Congress with 70 percent of the vote just two years later to succeed fellow Democrat Donald W. Riegle Jr., who left the House for a successful bid for the Senate. A string of similarly easy victories ran through his 1990 re-election. But he had close calls in 1992 and 1994, when Republican Megan O'Neill, who had worked in the White House under President George Bush, ran strong campaigns. In the 1992 race, Kildee had to answer for 100 overdrafts at the private bank for House members; more generally, redistricting for the 1990s had left him a redrawn 9th District in which almost half the people were new to him.

Redistricting for this decade again made Kildee potentially vulnerable. The Republican-controlled legislature drew a map that made Kildee a resident of a redesigned 5th District; a five-term incumbent, Democrat James A. Barcia, also lived in the new 5th. But Kildee's hefty campaign war chest and seniority prompted Barcia to run for the Michigan state Senate rather than face Kildee in a 2002 primary. In November, Barcia was elected to the legislature, and Kildee faced no GOP opposition for a 14th term.

KEY VOTES

2002

Yes Overhaul campaign finance law; ban "soft money" and restrict advocacy advertising
Yes Back Bush's defense budget increase
No Extend 1996 welfare law
No Adopt Bush's discretionary spending limit
No Pass GOP Medicare prescription drug plan
Yes Create independent Sept. 11 commission
Yes Extend union protections to Homeland Security Department employees
No Revive fast-track procedures for trade agreements
No Authorize war against Iraq
No Advance bankruptcy overhaul opposed by abortion opponents

2001

No Nullify Clinton Labor Department ergonomics rule
No Cut taxes by $1.35 trillion through fiscal 2011
Yes Maintain ban on oil drilling in Arctic National Wildlife Refuge
No Approve Bush proposal to limit managed-care plan liability for coverage decisions
Yes Divert money from crop subsidy payments to land conservation
Yes Expand law enforcement power to investigate suspected terrorists

CQ VOTE STUDIES

	PARTY UNITY		PRESIDENTIAL SUPPORT	
	Support	Oppose	Support	Oppose
2002	89%	11%	38%	62%
2001	88%	12%	37%	63%
2000	87%	13%	72%	28%
1999	87%	13%	71%	29%
1998	84%	16%	74%	26%

INTEREST GROUPS

	AFL-CIO	ADA	CCUS	ACU
2002	100%	80%	40%	8%
2001	100%	85%	35%	32%
2000	100%	75%	42%	20%
1999	100%	90%	20%	12%
1998	100%	95%	33%	16%

MICHIGAN 5
East – Flint, Saginaw, Bay City

Flint, the birthplace of General Motors in 1908, gave rise to the modern labor movement 30 years later when sit-down strikes at two Flint plants forced the auto giant to recognize the power of the United Auto Workers (UAW) union. Farther north, the 5th takes in Saginaw and Bay City.

From the turn of the century until the late 1960s, Flint, the largest city in the 5th, grew along with the U.S. auto industry. Then the 1970s oil shock and an increase in inexpensive imports undercut demand for GM cars and drove the economy into a downward spiral. The industry recovered from that slump, but automation and overseas production have reduced the number of jobs. Although GM jobs are not as plentiful, a number of small, spin-off companies employ a significant number of people.

The district's blue-collar voters are populist on economics and more conservative on cultural issues, but they identify strongly with the Democratic Party. Genesee County, which accounts for two-thirds of the district's population, is strongly influenced by the UAW and gave 63 percent of its vote to Al Gore in the 2000 presidential election, his second-best showing in Michigan. Gore received 84 percent in Flint, which is majority-black. The Green Party's Ralph Nader, despite his anti-corporate stance, took just 2 percent of the vote in Genesee.

Auto workers and Democratic voters also are plentiful in Saginaw, which backed Gore by a better than 3-to-1 ratio. The district also includes parts of Bay County and all of Tuscola County, part of Michigan's "Thumb."

Redistricting following the 2000 census cut counties from the old 5th's north and east. Mapmakers expanded the district's southern border to include the remainder of Genesee County, including Flint. The county had been split between the 5th, 8th and 9th districts in the 1990s.

MAJOR INDUSTRY
Auto parts manufacturing, agriculture, sugar processing

CITIES
Flint, 124,943; Saginaw, 61,799; Bay City, 36,817; Burton, 30,308

NOTABLE
Famous natives include Stevie Wonder (Saginaw) and Madonna (Bay City); Bay City was once known as the "Lumber Capital of the World"; Flint native Michael Moore's documentary film, "Roger & Me," chronicled the effect of GM's layoffs in the 1980s.

Rep. Fred Upton (R)

CAPITOL OFFICE
225-3761
talk2.fsu@mail.house.gov
www.house.gov/upton
2161 Rayburn 20515-2206; fax 225-4986

COMMITTEES
Education & Workforce
Energy & Commerce
(Telecommunications and the Internet - chairman)

HOMETOWN
St. Joseph

BORN
April 23, 1953, St. Joseph, Mich.

RELIGION
Protestant

FAMILY
Wife, Amey Upton; two children

EDUCATION
U. of Michigan, B.A. 1975 (journalism)

CAREER
Congressional aide; budget analyst

POLITICAL HIGHLIGHTS
No previous office

ELECTION RESULTS

2002 GENERAL		
Fred Upton (R)	126,936	69.2%
Gary C. Giguere Jr. (D)	53,793	29.3%
Richard M. Overton (REF)	2,788	1.5%
2002 PRIMARY		
Fred Upton (R)	44,487	66.0%
Dale L. Shugars (R)	21,580	32.0%
Gloria Krueger Ham (R)	1,321	2.0%
2000 GENERAL		
Fred Upton (R)	159,373	67.9%
James Bupp (D)	68,532	29.2%
William Bradley (LIBERT)	3,573	1.5%

PREVIOUS WINNING PERCENTAGES
1998 (70%); 1996 (68%); 1994 (73%); 1992 (62%); 1990 (58%); 1988 (71%); 1986 (62%)

Elected 1986; 9th term

By blending fiscal conservatism with more-centrist views on some social issues, Upton has been able to stake a claim in several camps — even when those allegiances conflict.

Upton generally aligns himself with the loose coalition of maverick moderate Republicans, but he is also the chairman of an influential subcommittee and as such must stay in the good graces of the House GOP leadership. He views himself as a natural-born compromiser — someone who takes his time making decisions on almost everything and has the capacity for dealing with Democrats — but he also wants to be perceived as a party loyalist in the clutch.

He turned 50 in 2003 and wrinkles are beginning to form around his eyes, yet he still looks far too boyish to be in his ninth term. And his insistence to everyone he meets to "just call me Fred" perpetuates the image. President Bush at first dubbed him "Freddy Boy" and later shortened the nickname to "Freddy."

While he usually sides with Bush, he is not afraid to disagree. In 2001, for example, when the administration's energy plan left open the possibility of drilling for gas and oil in the Great Lakes, Upton helped pass a ban on such exploration. He told the White House from the House floor, "Gentlemen, you should look elsewhere."

In 2002, Upton was among 20 Republican moderates who protested to Speaker J. Dennis Hastert when, at the insistence of conservatives, Hastert put a halt to action on the year's biggest domestic spending bill until its price tag was reduced to an amount acceptable to Bush. The moderates said they might vote against the bill unless its education, health and labor funding was increased to levels above the president's wishes. The result was a standoff that pushed the 107th Congress' budget debate two months into the 108th, but in the end some domestic programs — especially for education — were increased.

Upton bucked his party leaders to vote for the campaign finance overhaul of 2002. To the dismay of some conservatives, he has sided with a minority of Republicans in voting for tighter curbs on firearms purchases at gun shows. He is a vocal advocate of allowing research on fetal tissue, arguing that it may help find a cure for serious diseases, but he backed Bush's decision to limit embryonic stem cell research to existing stocks of cell lines.

Upton has been chairman of the Energy Subcommittee on Telecommunications and the Internet since the 107th Congress, when he shepherded to enactment a law creating a ".kids" domain on the Internet that would be free from pornography and other harmful materials. He also renewed his call to recording industry executives to improve labeling of violent or sexually explicit material, and he won inclusion of abstinence education provisions in the welfare policy bill the House passed in 2002.

When public outrage swelled in 2000 over the deaths of more than 100 people using vehicles equipped with Firestone tires, Upton — a member of the Energy and Commerce Committee since his third term — won passage of a landmark bill to impose prison terms on auto industry officials if they withhold information about defects.

As part of the wrapup spending law enacted in early 2003, Upton won inclusion of a provision — sought by college and professional sports organizations after the Sept. 11, 2001, terrorist attacks — restricting airplanes with banners from flying over stadiums during events. (Upton in 1982 had hired just such a plane to fly over a Baltimore Orioles game with a banner making his marriage proposal to his wife, Amey.)

Though he watches federal spending, Upton once blocked the Coast Guard's plans to save money by dismantling the Great Lakes foghorn network. He said he owed the horns a debt of gratitude: Once, out sailing with friends when a fog rolled in, Upton and his shipmates were led home by the foghorns' blasts.

Upton comes from one of Michigan's wealthier Republican families; his grandfather helped found Whirlpool Corp., which is based in Upton's district. A sense of social responsibility was instilled in the young Upton early on. His parents took care of as many as two dozen foster children at various times, and one of Upton's first jobs was in a day care center.

He arrived in Congress in 1987 by ousting an incumbent Republican in a primary — Mark D. Siljander, a Christian conservative activist. But Upton's credentials as a fiscal conservative were solid: He had spent a decade working for David A. Stockman, when Stockman was southwestern Michigan's congressman and later at the Office of Management and Budget, where Stockman was President Reagan's top budgeteer and Upton was the budget office's liaison to Capitol Hill.

In Congress, Upton became a deputy to Newt Gingrich when Gingrich was elected GOP whip in 1989, and the next year he joined Gingrich in castigating President George Bush for agreeing to raise taxes as part of a deal to reduce the deficit. Upton resigned as a deputy whip in 1993 because he disliked Gingrich's confrontational style. Since the GOP takeover of 1995, Upton generally has cast his lot with a loose coalition of mostly moderate Republicans.

Upton's political positioning has helped give him a virtual lock on his House seat; he has won his past five November elections with better than two-thirds of the vote. But in 2002, his stance attracted a Republican primary challenge from state Sen. Dale L. Shugars, who charged that Upton was not conservative enough, especially on abortion-related issues. Upton spent more than $1 million in his first contested primary since 1990. He criticized Shugars for waging a negative campaign and urged his constituents to reject such tactics. They did, renominating Upton with 66 percent of the vote. He won in November with 69 percent.

As the 108th Congress began, Upton had not missed a roll call on the floor since mid-1997 and had cast 3,058 consecutive votes — the longest active voting participation streak in the House.

KEY VOTES

2002

- Yes Overhaul campaign finance law; ban "soft money" and restrict advocacy advertising
- Yes Back Bush's defense budget increase
- Yes Extend 1996 welfare law
- Yes Adopt Bush's discretionary spending limit
- Yes Pass GOP Medicare prescription drug plan
- No Create independent Sept. 11 commission
- No Extend union protections to Homeland Security Department employees
- Yes Revive fast-track procedures for trade agreements
- Yes Authorize war against Iraq
- Yes Advance bankruptcy overhaul opposed by abortion opponents

2001

- Yes Nullify Clinton Labor Department ergonomics rule
- Yes Cut taxes by $1.35 trillion through fiscal 2011
- No Maintain ban on oil drilling in Arctic National Wildlife Refuge
- Yes Approve Bush proposal to limit managed-care plan liability for coverage decisions
- Yes Divert money from crop subsidy payments to land conservation
- Yes Expand law enforcement power to investigate suspected terrorists

CQ VOTE STUDIES

	PARTY UNITY		PRESIDENTIAL SUPPORT	
	Support	Oppose	Support	Oppose
2002	92%	8%	82%	18%
2001	88%	12%	77%	23%
2000	79%	21%	39%	61%
1999	80%	20%	32%	68%
1998	79%	21%	33%	67%

INTEREST GROUPS

	AFL-CIO	ADA	CCUS	ACU
2002	11%	5%	95%	92%
2001	25%	10%	100%	76%
2000	10%	25%	85%	60%
1999	0%	25%	92%	68%
1998	20%	15%	89%	56%

MICHIGAN 6

Southwest – Kalamazoo, Portage, Benton Harbor

Lush forests in Michigan's southwest corner make the 6th a prime spot for tourists and orchards. Cherries and peaches grow in the fruit belt that extends north from St. Joseph and Benton Harbor — once a stop on the Underground Railroad — through Van Buren County. Many affluent Chicagoans keep second homes in the wooded area along the Lake Michigan shoreline, which has become known as "Harbor County."

Kalamazoo, the 6th's most-populous city, has a strong and diverse manufacturing economy. Cities throughout the district have escaped dependence on Detroit's automaker economy.

Home appliance manufacturer Whirlpool is based in Benton Harbor, and pharmaceutical maker Pharmacia has facilities in Kalamazoo. Education is another economic pillar, led by Western Michigan University's 29,000 students.

Kalamazoo's blue-collar work force makes it one of the few Democratic parts of the 6th; Al Gore carried the city by a 25 percentage point margin in the 2000 presidential election, helping him narrowly win Kalamazoo County.

But the city's voters are no match for the Republican influences in the district — namely, its conservative Dutch heritage, white-collar corporate managers and rural conservatives. Berrien County, the district's second-most-populous county, went decisively for George W. Bush (though heavily black Benton Harbor went for Gore by 2,461 to 81).

The 6th also includes all of Republican-leaning Van Buren, St. Joseph and Cass counties (the latter abuts the Indiana state line near South Bend and Elkhart). Redistricting gave the district more of Allegan County, a solidly Republican lake county between Kalamazoo and Grand Rapids.

MAJOR INDUSTRY

Manufacturing, higher education, agriculture

CITIES

Kalamazoo, 77,145; Portage, 44,897; Niles, 12,204; Sturgis, 11,285; Benton Harbor, 11,182

NOTABLE

The first outdoor pedestrian shopping mall in the United States was built in Kalamazoo in 1959.

Rep. Nick Smith (R)

CAPITOL OFFICE
225-6276
www.house.gov/nicksmith
2305 Rayburn 20515-2207; fax 225-6281

COMMITTEES
Agriculture
International Relations
Science
(Research - chairman)

HOMETOWN
Addison

BORN
Nov. 5, 1934, Addison, Mich.

RELIGION
Congregationalist

FAMILY
Wife, Bonnalyn Smith; four children

EDUCATION
Michigan State U., B.A. 1957; U. of Delaware, M.S. 1959 (agricultural economics)

MILITARY SERVICE
Air Force, 1959-61

CAREER
Dairy farmer

POLITICAL HIGHLIGHTS
Somerset Township Board of Trustees, 1962-66; Hillsdale County Board of Supervisors, 1966-68; Mich. House, 1979-83; Mich. Senate, 1983-93

ELECTION RESULTS

2002 GENERAL		
Nick Smith (R)	121,142	59.7%
Mike Simpson (D)	78,412	38.6%
Kenneth L. Proctor (LIBERT)	3,515	1.7%
2002 PRIMARY		
Nick Smith (R)		unopposed
2000 GENERAL		
Nick Smith (R)	147,369	61.2%
Jennie Crittendon (D)	86,080	35.7%

PREVIOUS WINNING PERCENTAGES
1998 (57%); 1996 (55%); 1994 (65%); 1992 (88%)

Elected 1992; 6th term

Smith operates a 2,000-acre dairy and grain farm and his down-to-earth style has helped him win re-election easily in the small towns and farm communities that are a mainstay of his constituency. When he completes this term, Smith will call it quits in the House, abiding by a commitment he made in 1995, when the congressional term-limits movement was in full swing. He promised then to serve no more than a dozen years in the House. But he has not ruled out a run for the Senate in 2006.

Smith is chairman of the Science Committee's Research Subcommittee, and he has become one of Capitol Hill's leading proponents of plant research and genetically engineered foods. He also weighs in knowledgeably on agriculture issues from his senior post on the Agriculture Committee and on the House GOP Policy Committee. But he has a wide range of eclectic interests that includes the long-term solvency of the Social Security system, mandatory military service for young men, firefighting and fire prevention, and tae kwon do, the Korean self-defense art (he is a second-degree black belt).

Despite his ardent fiscal conservatism, Smith favors big increases in the National Science Foundation's budget. "I generally maintain a philosophy of limited government, and I intend to continue to push for increased private investment in research," he told the Battle Creek Enquirer in 2002, "but I think tax-funded basic research has been a very worthwhile investment." His interests in farming and scientific research merged in the 107th Congress when he sponsored a bill to authorize National Science Foundation grants for regional plant genome research centers, which would develop new varieties of food crops and plant varieties that could be used as alternative fuel sources.

Although many environmentalists worry that changing the gene structure of plants can have unforeseen and potentially dangerous consequences, Smith plants genetically altered corn and soybeans on his farm and thinks the government should encourage others to do the same; he says the technology reduces dependence on insecticides. "Agricultural biotechnology has come of age," he wrote to a colleague in 2000. "The potential benefits to mankind are limited only by the resourcefulness of our scientists."

Smith casts a dependably conservative vote on social issues. But he sometimes goes against the grain, straying from the party line on matters such as campaign finance and, in 2000, the GOP's prescription drug plan.

In the 107th Congress, he was deemed enough of a problematic team player that he was left off the roster of House negotiators assigned to write the final version of the new farm bill with a group of senators. Smith's seniority on Agriculture would normally have guaranteed him a seat at the bargaining table, but his support for a limit on how much a farmer could receive annually from the federal government, along with his opposition to a dairy compact sought by Upper Midwest dairy farmers, reportedly kept him off the negotiating committee. That may also have been a factor in GOP leaders' bypassing him in the 108th to choose Virginian Robert W. Goodlatte as Agriculture Committee chairman.

During work on the farm bill, Smith led the battle to renew a law that allows bankrupt family farmers to restructure their debt without losing their land. He sponsored several short-term extensions of the statute until a longer-term renewal could be enacted with the farm bill in 2002.

Smith served on the Budget Committee from 1995 to 2001 and sought the panel's chairmanship in the 107th Congress, promising to hold down spending to provide money for tax cuts. He lost out, in a four-way race, to Jim Nussle of Iowa, then left the committee and picked up a seat on International Relations.

Just as he did during 14 years as a state legislator, Smith advocates tax cuts and spending restraint, backing GOP plans to eliminate the current tax code and to require a two-thirds majority vote in both chambers to raise taxes. His frugality begins in his own congressional office. He regularly returns to the Treasury a large portion of the funds appropriated to him for staff salaries and expenses.

An Air Force veteran, Smith introduced legislation in 2002 to require all young men to spend at least six months in basic military training. He said doing so would yield reinforcements for the potentially lengthy war against terrorism and provide a shared experience that would benefit the nation.

When the hard edges of his insistent conservatism are not in evidence, Smith has a laconic demeanor that hints at his farm upbringing; and his plain-spoken ways often stand in sharp contrast to the formality and procedural precision that are hallmarks of Congress.

Born on the same farm in southern Michigan as his father and grandfather, Smith spent his early years moving around the country, as his father moved from one assignment to another with the U.S. Geological Survey.

He worked his way through Michigan State, studying economics, psychology and political science. He also participated in wrestling, gymnastics and cheerleading.

Following his stint in the Air Force, Smith planned to work for U.S. Steel, but while waiting for a management program to start, he came across a farm for sale just five miles from where he grew up. He bought the 600-acre spread, has tripled its size and continues to be active in its operation.

Smith served four years in the Michigan House and a decade in the state Senate. When a federal court redrew Michigan's map for the 1990s, the 7th District appeared so solidly Republican that no Democrat bothered to run in 1992. Nor did any incumbent House Republican make a bid, creating an open seat that would effectively be won on primary day. Smith, well-known from his service in Lansing, took 43 percent of the vote in a four-person field. He has since won re-election with relative ease, all the while eschewing contributions from political action committees. With his territory's GOP tilt protected in redistricting, Smith in 2002 defeated restaurateur Mike Simpson by 21 percentage points.

KEY VOTES

2002

Yes Overhaul campaign finance law; ban "soft money" and restrict advocacy advertising
Yes Back Bush's defense budget increase
Yes Extend 1996 welfare law
Yes Adopt Bush's discretionary spending limit
No Pass GOP Medicare prescription drug plan
No Create independent Sept. 11 commission
No Extend union protections to Homeland Security Department employees
Yes Revive fast-track procedures for trade agreements
Yes Authorize war against Iraq
Yes Advance bankruptcy overhaul opposed by abortion opponents

2001

Yes Nullify Clinton Labor Department ergonomics rule
Yes Cut taxes by $1.35 trillion through fiscal 2011
No Maintain ban on oil drilling in Arctic National Wildlife Refuge
Yes Approve Bush proposal to limit managed-care plan liability for coverage decisions
No Divert money from crop subsidy payments to land conservation
Yes Expand law enforcement power to investigate suspected terrorists

CQ VOTE STUDIES

	PARTY UNITY		PRESIDENTIAL SUPPORT	
	Support	Oppose	Support	Oppose
2002	89%	11%	90%	10%
2001	93%	7%	81%	19%
2000	93%	7%	24%	76%
1999	90%	10%	22%	78%
1998	88%	12%	26%	74%

INTEREST GROUPS

	AFL-CIO	ADA	CCUS	ACU
2002	22%	5%	85%	92%
2001	8%	5%	87%	92%
2000	10%	10%	84%	91%
1999	0%	10%	79%	84%
1998	30%	20%	83%	76%

MICHIGAN 7

South central – Battle Creek, Jackson

The southern Michigan counties that make up the 7th take in small towns, farming communities and a few mid-size cities. Kellogg's Tony the Tiger makes his home in Battle Creek, the district's largest city. The cereal giant is not only one of the city's largest employers, but it also maintains one of the nation's top philanthropic organizations, donating some gifts to the Battle Creek area.

Outside Battle Creek, auto parts manufacturing drives small-town economies, especially in Jackson. Agriculture dominates most of the rest of the 7th, with soybeans and corn as the staple crops. The farming counties of Branch, Eaton, Hillsdale, Jackson and Lenawee have been fertile ground for the GOP: George W. Bush and former Sen. Spencer Abraham carried all five in 2000 even as they were losing statewide.

Rural and small-town voters tend to overwhelm the influence of the cities' blue-collar population, but even Democrats tend to be socially conservative. Unlike Detroit's auto workers, many of those living here have roots in the surrounding Republican countryside. Hillsdale County is home to Hillsdale College, which does not accept federal funding and has a free-market orientation.

The district's political and social culture has been shaped by Quaker settlements that made the area a station on the Underground Railroad and left many residents sensitive to issues such as racial segregation and the Vietnam War.

Redistricting following the 2000 census did not make major changes to the 7th, though the district needed to gain population due to the state's one-seat loss in reapportionment. The 7th took on a larger slice of Washtenaw County (though county seat Ann Arbor is in the 15th District) and abuts the Detroit-area Wayne County.

MAJOR INDUSTRY
Agriculture, food processing, auto parts manufacturing, health care

CITIES
Battle Creek, 53,364; Jackson, 36,316; Adrian, 21,574

NOTABLE
Sojourner Truth lived in Battle Creek; Battle Creek's annual Cereal Festival culminates in the world's longest breakfast table; Grand Ledge, a late-1800s resort town, featured a merry-go-round on one of its islands.

Rep. Mike Rogers (R)

CAPITOL OFFICE
225-4872
www.house.gov/mikerogers
133 Cannon 20515-2208; fax 225-5820

COMMITTEES
Energy & Commerce

HOMETOWN
Brighton

BORN
June 2, 1963, Livonia, Mich.

RELIGION
Methodist

FAMILY
Wife, Diane Rogers; two children

EDUCATION
Adrian College, B.A. 1985 (sociology & criminal justice)

MILITARY SERVICE
Army, 1985-88

CAREER
Home construction company owner; FBI agent

POLITICAL HIGHLIGHTS
Mich. Senate, 1995-2001 (majority floor leader, 1999-2001)

ELECTION RESULTS

2002 GENERAL		
Mike Rogers (R)	156,525	67.9%
Frank McAlpine (D)	70,920	30.8%
Thomas Yeutter (LIBERT)	3,152	1.4%
2002 PRIMARY		
Mike Rogers (R)		unopposed
2000 GENERAL		
Mike Rogers (R)	145,190	48.8%
Dianne Byrum (D)	145,079	48.8%
Bonnie Bucqueroux (GREEN)	3,467	1.2%

Elected 2000; 2nd term

Rogers won his seat by 111 votes, the closest House election in the nation in 2000. So he spent much of his first term in Congress bolstering his political prospects with persistent fundraising, loyalty to the leadership and a focus on district issues. And as the House considered legislation to counter terrorism, Rogers was able to put to good use his unique congressional background as both an Army veteran and an FBI special agent.

He solidified his standing back home to such a degree that he won his second term with 68 percent of the vote. With a conservative bent on most issues, he proved himself a dependable vote for the GOP in the 107th Congress while working as one of 18 deputy majority whips. He was such a loyal lieutenant in the whip organization that his name was mentioned as a possible chief deputy to Roy Blunt in the 108th. His prize instead was appointment to the Energy and Commerce panel, one of the most coveted posts.

Because of his first-hand experience in wiretapping, Rogers was asked for his input as the Justice Department developed its anti-terrorism package — including proposals to broaden wiretap authority — just after the Sept. 11, 2001, attacks. As the plan moved toward enactment that fall, his colleagues sought out Rogers for guidance on wiretapping and other law enforcement issues.

When President Bush first raised the issue of war with Iraq, Rogers urged a go-slow approach until several key questions were answered. The administration subsequently satisfied Rogers' concerns, and he joined in voting to back the war resolution sought by Bush. Rogers' own Army service, and the fact that one of his brothers is a colonel with the 101st Airborne, gave him credibility with the Bush administration.

To take his Energy and Commerce seat — where his priorities include legislation to regulate garbage shipments from Canada — Rogers had to relinquish his spots on the Transportation and Financial Services panels.

On Financial Services, in the 107th he wrote legislation to coordinate the collection and sharing of information by regulators in the banking, insurance and securities industries. Working with Chairman Michael G. Oxley of Ohio (a fellow FBI veteran), Rogers developed a bill to permit more than 250 state, federal and private regulatory organizations to coordinate their databases, including the FBI's fingerprint files, to combat fraud. Of particular interest was the collection of data on money laundering, which law enforcement officials have linked to illegal drug operations and terrorism.

Rogers also drafted legislation to help first-time homebuyers by offering grants to help them come up with a down payment. His efforts to make housing more affordable have roots in his family's business. He and his father and brothers own a company that assembles modular homes. In fact, he lives in one of the company's dwellings.

Rogers, whose district includes Michigan State University, has proposed federal tax incentives to encourage families to save money for higher education, along the lines of a measure he shepherded through the Michigan Legislature. Similar provisions were included in the 2001 tax cut law, which lasts through 2011; Rogers would like to see those extended indefinitely.

After the Sept. 11 attacks, but before the anthrax attacks of that October, Rogers called for police, firefighters and medical technicians to be given vaccinations against anthrax. Rogers had a specific interest in making the prescient proposal: BioPort Corp., located in the 8th District, was embroiled in a lengthy dispute with the Food and Drug Administration as the company sought approval to make an anthrax vaccine.

Rogers grew up in Livingston County, just west of Detroit. His father was a high school vice principal, football coach and a town supervisor. His mother ran a local chamber of commerce and served on the county commission. The youngest of five boys, Rogers says he wanted to be an FBI agent from the time he was in his teens.

He majored in sociology and criminal justice at Adrian College. At the same time, he enrolled in Army ROTC at the University of Michigan. After graduation, he spent three years in the Army and then entered the FBI Academy. He finished at the top of his class, earning a coveted assignment to the field office in Chicago, where he was responsible for unraveling a complex case involving public officials in the Chicago suburb of Cicero.

In 1994, after deciding to move back to Michigan to raise his family, Rogers almost immediately jumped into a race for the state Senate. The longtime GOP incumbent had decided to retire, and in the strongly Republican district, Rogers cruised to victory. He was re-elected in 1998. He served as majority floor leader in the 1999-2000 session. In Lansing, he sponsored a bill to shield children from the dangers of the Internet, targeting pornography and pedophiles who try to meet children on-line.

When Democrat Debbie Stabenow decided to give up the 8th District seat to run for the Senate in 2000, Rogers and a state Senate colleague, Democrat Dianne Byrum, were their parties' nominees to succeed her. Their expensive but civil campaign in one of the nation's premier "swing" districts went down to the wire — and beyond. Rogers' win was not official until December, when Byrum conceded after a partial recount failed to erase her opponent's slim lead.

Because of the recount, Rogers missed the lottery that assigned Capitol Hill office space, and he wound up in the attic of the Cannon Building, as far away from the House floor as any office. Rogers dealt with his "penthouse" digs with humor, telling the Grand Rapids Press of a deal with the custodian: "If I wring his mops for him, I get half of his desk space."

Rogers immediately set out to solidify his hold on the district. He raised almost $750,000 in his first six months in office — more than any other freshman in the history of the House, his staff was told. But the effort may not have been necessary. The redrawing of Michigan's congressional map for this decade, managed by Republicans, added thousands of GOP voters to the 8th District. Byrum declined to run again, and Rogers had an almost free ride against Democratic attorney Frank McAlpine, who entered the race on the last possible day and raised little money.

KEY VOTES

2002

- No Overhaul campaign finance law; ban "soft money" and restrict advocacy advertising
- Yes Back Bush's defense budget increase
- Yes Extend 1996 welfare law
- Yes Adopt Bush's discretionary spending limit
- Yes Pass GOP Medicare prescription drug plan
- No Create independent Sept. 11 commission
- No Extend union protections to Homeland Security Department employees
- Yes Revive fast-track procedures for trade agreements
- Yes Authorize war against Iraq
- No Advance bankruptcy overhaul opposed by abortion opponents

2001

- Yes Nullify Clinton Labor Department ergonomics rule
- Yes Cut taxes by $1.35 trillion through fiscal 2011
- No Maintain ban on oil drilling in Arctic National Wildlife Refuge
- Yes Approve Bush proposal to limit managed-care plan liability for coverage decisions
- No Divert money from crop subsidy payments to land conservation
- Yes Expand law enforcement power to investigate suspected terrorists

CQ VOTE STUDIES

	PARTY UNITY		PRESIDENTIAL SUPPORT	
	Support	Oppose	Support	Oppose
2002	96%	4%	85%	15%
2001	95%	5%	88%	12%

INTEREST GROUPS

	AFL-CIO	ADA	CCUS	ACU
2002	0%	0%	90%	92%
2001	17%	5%	96%	84%

MICHIGAN 8

Central — Lansing

Michigan's capital district, where Ransom Eli Olds founded Olds Motor Vehicle Co. in 1897, covers Lansing, East Lansing and some agricultural communities to the east. The local dominance of General Motors, which makes Chevrolets, Cadillacs and Pontiacs, is matched only by state government. Together, they employ thousands of people in the 8th.

Michigan State, the nation's first land-grant university, gave birth to the district's second-largest city, East Lansing. State government workers, university students, faculty and autoworkers make Ingham County strongly Democratic. In 2000 elections, Al Gore took 57 percent in Ingham (his fourth-best showing in Michigan) and then-Rep. Debbie Stabenow took 58 percent in her Senate race.

Ingham's liberal leanings are nearly counterbalanced by the strong GOP tendencies of Livingston County, a fast-growing area just to the east. Livingston increased its population by 36 percent in the 1990s and has been absorbing whites leaving Detroit, Flint, Lansing and Pontiac. In contrast to Livingston, Ingham lost population in the 1990s. Combined, the two counties account for two-thirds of residents in the 8th District.

Most of the rest of the 8th's voters live in northern Oakland County, an upscale region that is closer to Flint and Detroit than to Lansing. The 8th also includes Clinton County, just north of Lansing, and parts of Shiawassee County, located between Lansing and Flint.

In redistricting following the 2000 census, Republican mapmakers drew more of Oakland into the 8th to give a GOP lean to a district that was highly competitive in the 1990s. The old 8th's share of Genesee County, including many Democratic voters, was shifted to the 5th District.

MAJOR INDUSTRY

State government, auto manufacturing, higher education

CITIES

Lansing (pt.), 114,321; East Lansing, 46,525; Okemos (unincorporated), 22,805

NOTABLE

Basketball star Earvin "Magic" Johnson hails from Lansing and played college ball at Michigan State University; Howell celebrates the honeydew harvest with its annual Melon Festival.

Rep. Joe Knollenberg (R)

CAPITOL OFFICE
225-5802
rep.knollenberg@mail.house.gov
www.house.gov/knollenberg
2349 Rayburn 20515-2209; fax 226-2356

COMMITTEES
Appropriations
(Military Construction - chairman)

HOMETOWN
Bloomfield Township

BORN
Nov. 28, 1933, Mattoon, Ill.

RELIGION
Roman Catholic

FAMILY
Wife, Sandie Knollenberg; two children

EDUCATION
Eastern Illinois U., B.S. 1955 (social science)

MILITARY SERVICE
Army, 1955-57

CAREER
Insurance broker

POLITICAL HIGHLIGHTS
Oakland County Republican Party chairman, 1978-86

ELECTION RESULTS

2002 GENERAL		
Joe Knollenberg (R)	141,102	58.1%
David Fink (D)	96,856	39.9%
Robert Schubring (LIBERT)	4,922	2.0%
2002 PRIMARY		
Joe Knollenberg (R)	45,696	86.6%
Bart Baron (R)	7,044	13.4%
2000 GENERAL		
Joe Knollenberg (R)	170,790	55.8%
Matthew Frumin (D)	124,053	40.5%
Marilyn MacDermaid (GREEN)	4,191	1.4%
Dick Gach (LIBERT)	3,371	1.1%

PREVIOUS WINNING PERCENTAGES
1998 (64%); 1996 (61%); 1994 (68%); 1992 (58%)

Elected 1992; 6th term

In his single term as chairman of the District of Columbia Appropriations Subcommittee, Knollenberg won kudos for his efforts to produce a less controversial spending bill. The measure that funds the capital city is often the scene of partisan bickering and a favored proving ground for congressional policy proposals. But Knollenberg, as loyal a Republican as the next, presided over the legislation in a calm and even-handed way.

In the 108th Congress, Knollenberg has moved on to chair the Military Construction Subcommittee, where his approach should work with ease. The panel has long been known as particularly bipartisan and collegial because the only real tension over its annual handiwork is between fulfilling all the wishes of the Pentagon and addressing the desire of lawmakers to add additional appropriations for barracks, runway upgrades and maintenance sheds back home.

The D.C. spending bill not only provides about $400 million in federal funds, it also gives congressional approval for the District to spend its own tax revenue. It has historically been the vehicle for the conservative GOP majority in Congress to mandate or prohibit actions by the far more liberal District government on issues such as abortion, drugs, health insurance, gay rights and legal representation for the poor. The number of these riders dropped from 67 in 2000 to 34 in 2001, Knollenberg's first year as chairman, although many controversial ones remained.

Acknowledging the political reality of the GOP-run House, the city's delegate, Democrat Eleanor Holmes Norton, issued a statement in 2002 declaring that the subcommittee's work on the bill was "the smoothest of my 12 years in Congress."

The responsibilities of chairing an Appropriations panel have caused Knollenberg to reorder his legislative priorities, which had centered previously on his unflagging opposition to many government regulations. He is best-known for his crusade against federal standards that have limited post-1992 toilets to 1.6 gallons per flush, less than half the volume of the previous standard, and have also restricted the output of new showerheads.

In the 106th Congress, Knollenberg was able to get a House subcommittee vote on his bill. He lost, 12-13, but said he remained "committed to fighting frivolous federal laws and regulations." He introduced the toilet mandate bill again in the 107th, along with similar measures dealing with air conditioners, washing machines and heat pumps, but he did not campaign hard for action on them.

Although he usually rails against wasteful spending, Knollenberg has used his Appropriations post to direct money to projects he likes. He has sought federal funds for artificial-kidney research at the University of Michigan, and obtained $60 million for cleanup of the Rouge River. And he seeks annually to earmark funds for local roads projects.

Concerned about security-induced bottlenecks at the Canadian border that have stalled commerce, Knollenberg led a charge in the 107th Congress to hire more customs, immigration and border patrol agents. Michigan received a substantial percentage of the new agents.

Knollenberg's conservative views on regulatory, business and environmental issues reflect his experiences as a small-business owner. His positions are also in line with the interests of the auto manufacturers and high-technology companies that fuel his district's economy. Knollenberg opposed the steel tariffs imposed in 2002 by President Bush, pointing to the harm that higher prices were causing the automobile industry. In the 108th, he wants the administration to review the tariffs "and how they are hurting steel users."

He is equally opposed to raising the fuel economy standards for Detroit's cars. He has used his Appropriations seat to provide research grants to help develop more fuel-efficient technologies, but he argues that the government should not mandate new technologies that are not ready for commercial use.

In 1999, Knollenberg served on a leadership-appointed task force that concluded that North Korea had not lived up to its agreement to discontinue its nuclear weapons program. The panel said no further aid should be provided to North Korea until it complied, and Knollenberg has continued his opposition to any U.S. aid to Pyongyang.

His opposition to abortion and his backing of other conservative social policy initiatives earn Knollenberg high ratings from groups such as the Christian Coalition and the American Conservative Union. Knollenberg, whose son, Steve, is gay, earns low marks for his voting record from the Human Rights Campaign, an issue advocacy group for homosexuals. Knollenberg says his son's "sexual orientation is a personal matter" and that he "unequivocally" supports him "with all the love and respect that a family possibly can."

The fifth of 13 children reared on a farm in central Illinois, Knollenberg attended college near home. But after graduating and spending two years in the Army, he moved to the Detroit area in 1959 to work for Allstate Insurance. He eventually opened his own branch office. His community activities in the north Detroit suburbs included chairing a local PTA, chairing the Oakland County GOP organization and heading the campaign of Republican Rep. William S. Broomfield.

When Broomfield retired in 1992 after 18 terms, Knollenberg won the GOP nomination in a three-way race. He then defeated Democrat Walter O. Briggs IV, nephew of former Democratic Sen. Philip A. Hart, by 18 percentage points in the upscale Republican 11th District. His next four re-election wins came easily — his smallest victory margin was 15 points in 2000.

After redistricting for this decade, Knollenberg sought re-election in the 9th District, with a constituency that was 60 percent new. He was matched dollar-for-dollar by wealthy Democratic lawyer David Fink in one of the most expensive House races in Michigan history, but he won by 18 points.

When he first ran in 1992, he said he would serve only 12 years. He has since said he does not believe in term limits, but he did not signal early on whether he would run again in 2004.

KEY VOTES

2002

No Overhaul campaign finance law; ban "soft money" and restrict advocacy advertising
Yes Back Bush's defense budget increase
Yes Extend 1996 welfare law
Yes Adopt Bush's discretionary spending limit
Yes Pass GOP Medicare prescription drug plan
– Create independent Sept. 11 commission
No Extend union protections to Homeland Security Department employees
Yes Revive fast-track procedures for trade agreements
Yes Authorize war against Iraq
Yes Advance bankruptcy overhaul opposed by abortion opponents

2001

Yes Nullify Clinton Labor Department ergonomics rule
Yes Cut taxes by $1.35 trillion through fiscal 2011
No Maintain ban on oil drilling in Arctic National Wildlife Refuge
Yes Approve Bush proposal to limit managed-care plan liability for coverage decisions
No Divert money from crop subsidy payments to land conservation
Yes Expand law enforcement power to investigate suspected terrorists

CQ VOTE STUDIES

	PARTY UNITY		PRESIDENTIAL SUPPORT	
	Support	Oppose	Support	Oppose
2002	96%	4%	92%	8%
2001	99%	1%	98%	2%
2000	92%	8%	32%	68%
1999	90%	10%	30%	70%
1998	94%	6%	24%	76%

INTEREST GROUPS

	AFL-CIO	ADA	CCUS	ACU
2002	0%	0%	100%	88%
2001	8%	0%	100%	92%
2000	0%	0%	90%	80%
1999	0%	5%	92%	80%
1998	10%	0%	100%	96%

MICHIGAN 9

Suburban Detroit — eastern Oakland County

Michigan's 9th — the wealthiest and most-educated district in the state — is wholly contained within Oakland County, one of the most affluent counties in the nation and home to the American headquarters for DaimlerChrysler (in Auburn Hills) and Kmart (in Troy). The district includes more than half the 1.2 million people who lived in Oakland County at the time of the 2000 census.

Communities such as Farmington Hills, north of the northern Detroit boundary cut by 8 Mile Road, form a corridor between Grand River Avenue and the Northwestern Highway that has served as one of the major routes for white exodus from Detroit. Troy, in the southeast corner of the district, has benefited from growth in high-tech automotive research and design, and is also a major office center. The area has a large Asian population.

Troy, Bloomfield and Rochester Hills give the district its Republican lean, but Democrats fare well in Pontiac, where blacks are a plurality. Al Gore narrowly carried Farmington Hills, the most-populous city in the district, and easily won West Bloomfield in the 2000 presidential election.

Republican candidates have slipped somewhat in Oakland County. In the 1980s, Ronald Reagan and George Bush ran 6 to 8 percentage points ahead of their statewide vote share. In 2000, George W. Bush received 48 percent of the Oakland County vote, which was only marginally higher than his 46 percent showing statewide. Redistricting following the 2000 census shuffled the county's congressional districts, as Michigan lost one seat in reapportionment. The redrawn 9th contains part of the old 9th, 11th and 12th districts.

MAJOR INDUSTRY

Auto manufacturing, engineering, health care, insurance

CITIES

Farmington Hills, 82,111; Troy, 80,959; Rochester Hills, 68,825; Pontiac, 66,337; Waterford (pt.) (unincorporated), 66,316; West Bloomfield (unincorporated), 64,862; Royal Oak (pt.), 54,536

NOTABLE

The first Holocaust museum built in the United States is in West Bloomfield; The Rev. Charles Coughlin broadcast his controversial weekly radio programs from the Shrine of the Little Flower church in Royal Oak in the 1930s.

Rep. Candice S. Miller (R)

Elected 2002; 1st term

Serving someday in Congress was not on Miller's mind when she dropped out of college to sell boats at a family-owned marina business on Michigan's Clinton River. But when the local township board proposed a tax increase on marinas, she became a self-described "noisy activist" and found "that whole experience very stimulating."

At 24, Miller was elected to fill a vacancy on the Harrison Township Board of Trustees — defying advice that a Republican could not win in the area, and beginning a political career that would lead to her 2002 election in Michigan's open 10th District.

Within a year after her trustee election, Miller entered a crowded field for township supervisor and unseated the incumbent. In her next race, she defeated the 24-year incumbent treasurer to become the first Republican in a half-century to win countywide office in suburban Detroit's Macomb County. She then defeated another 24-year incumbent to become Michigan's secretary of state, taking charge of a technologically backward agency that did not have a single copy or fax machine in any of its branch offices.

Her seat on the Government Reform Committee may allow her to address bureaucratic problems on the federal level. Miller expressed a strong interest during the campaign in national security issues and was rewarded with a seat on the Armed Services Committee as well.

As one who regularly leads the cheers at statewide Republican rallies, Miller can be expected to be a team player for the Bush administration. She describes herself as a social and fiscal conservative.

Miller had long eyed a seat in Congress but was blocked by the popularity of Democratic Rep. David E. Bonior. She lost badly in a 1986 bid to unseat Bonior, then backed out of an expected challenge in 2000.

But she was ready in 2002 when the Republican-controlled state legislature redrew the 10th District, and as Bonior bid for governor, Miller's well-known name and strong fundraising enabled her to easily defeat the Democratic nominee, Macomb County prosecutor Carl Marlinga.

CAPITOL OFFICE
225-2106
www.house.gov/candicemiller
508 Cannon 20515-2210; fax 226-1169

COMMITTEES
Armed Services
Government Reform

HOMETOWN
Harrison Township

BORN
May 7, 1954, Detroit, Mich.

RELIGION
Presbyterian

FAMILY
Husband, Donald Miller; one child

EDUCATION
Macomb Community College, attended 1973-74; Northwood Institute, attended 1974

CAREER
Boat saleswoman

POLITICAL HIGHLIGHTS
Harrison Township Board of Trustees, 1979-80; Harrison Township supervisor, 1980-92; Republican nominee for U.S. House, 1986; Macomb County treasurer, 1993-95; Mich. secretary of state, 1995-2002

ELECTION RESULTS

2002 GENERAL		
Candice S. Miller (R)	137,339	63.3%
Carl J. Marlinga (D)	77,053	35.5%
Renae Coon (LIBERT)	2,536	1.2%
2002 PRIMARY		
Candice S. Miller (R)		unopposed

MICHIGAN 10

Southeast – northern Macomb County, Port Huron, most of the 'Thumb'

Stretching from Sterling Heights in the Macomb County suburbs north of Detroit to the Michigan "Thumb," the 10th combines suburban, lakefront and rural communities. Statewide candidates who carry Macomb, an electoral bellwether where half of the 10th's residents live, usually win the state.

Macomb, while still home to some auto plants, largely has shed its blue-collar past and "Reagan Democrat" reputation and is becoming more white-collar and upscale. Democrats have made major inroads in northern-state suburban counties such as Macomb. But Republican lawmakers who controlled Michigan's redistricting process following the 2000 census were careful to draw Macomb's most solidly Republican territories, including Shelby, Macomb and Washington townships, into the 10th.

Mapmakers put Democratic-leaning southern Macomb in the 12th District.

North of Macomb is St. Clair County, a politically competitive region where one-fourth of residents live. Port Huron, a source of blue-collar Democratic votes, has grown with the expansion of Detroit's metropolitan area. Water quality issues are important to residents along Lake Huron and Lake St. Clair. The 10th also has thriving small businesses based on the boating industry.

The rest of the district has a rural feel, with communities that are dependent on fruit, soybeans, corn and dairy products. The 10th has some of the most productive navy bean and sugar beet fields in the state. Sanilac County leads Michigan in dairy production.

MAJOR INDUSTRY
Auto manufacturing, agriculture, recreation

CITIES
Sterling Heights (pt.), 86,536; Shelby (unincorporated), 65,159; Port Huron, 32,338

NOTABLE
The 10th has the highest number of registered recreational boats per capita in the nation.

Rep. Thaddeus McCotter (R)

CAPITOL OFFICE
225-8171
www.house.gov/mccotter
415 Cannon 20515-2211; fax 225-2667

COMMITTEES
Budget
International Relations

HOMETOWN
Livonia

BORN
Aug. 22, 1965, Detroit, Mich.

RELIGION
Roman Catholic

FAMILY
Wife, Rita McCotter; three children

EDUCATION
U. of Detroit, B.A. 1987 (political science), J.D. 1990

CAREER
Lawyer

POLITICAL HIGHLIGHTS
Schoolcraft College Board of Trustees, 1989-92; Wayne County Commission, 1993-98; Mich. Senate, 1999-2002

ELECTION RESULTS

2002 GENERAL		
Thaddeus McCotter (R)	126,050	57.2%
Kevin Kelley (D)	87,402	39.7%
William Boyd (GREEN)	4,243	1.9%
Daniel E. Malone (USTAX)	2,710	1.2%
2002 PRIMARY		
Thaddeus McCotter (R)	25,940	69.1%
David C. Hagerty (R)	11,619	30.9%

Elected 2002; 1st term

A lifelong resident of the current 11th District, located north and west of Detroit, McCotter never set out to become a politician. He spent many years as a semi-professional musician playing guitar in several bands, including one called Sir Funk-a-Lot and the Knights of the Terrestrial Jam.

But, persuaded by a friend to get involved in the 1988 presidential campaign, he went to the Republican National Convention as a delegate pledged to George Bush. This led McCotter to a successful bid for a seat on the Wayne County Commission in 1992 and election to the state Senate in 1998.

McCotter said he is eager to support President Bush's agenda. He favors making permanent the tax cuts Bush pushed to enactment in 2001. He also wants to respond to the clamor he heard on the campaign trail for a prescription drug benefit.

Appointed to seats on the Budget and International Relations committees, McCotter said he is interested in how American foreign policy affects the economy.

But he is likely to put much of his focus on home-state issues. He says Michigan needs to continue to diversify its economy and forestall a "brain drain" of college graduates leaving the state in search of employment. As a state lawmaker, McCotter, a self-described conservationist, cosponsored a Great Lakes protection bill. He also took up a constituent's suggestion to boost interest in the sciences by designating the mastodon the "official fossil of Michigan."

McCotter was a beneficiary of a Republican-controlled redistricting process that crafted the 11th as a GOP-leaning district with no incumbent. He established himself as the favorite and easily fended off Democratic nominee Kevin Kelley, a township supervisor who had a long political résumé but began his campaign late.

Though McCotter chaired two committees in the Michigan Senate, he has no illusions about calling the shots as a freshman member of Congress. "I know I can't come in and ask for anything and expect to get it," he said.

MICHIGAN 11

Southeast – Livonia, Westland, Novi

The 11th, which takes in suburbs west and north of Detroit, stands out as a Republican-leaning area in a region renowned for its support of pro-labor Democrats.

Although Detroit's presence makes Wayne County, where 70 percent of the district's residents live, a Democratic stronghold, the 11th's portion of Wayne is politically competitive. Residents here split their presidential votes almost evenly in 2000 between George W. Bush and Al Gore.

Republicans run well in upper-middle-class communities such as Livonia, the most populous city in the district, and Canton, a rapidly developing residential area in western Wayne County, east of Ann Arbor (located in the 15th). While Wayne County lost population in the 1990s, Canton's population increased by more than one-third.

Also rapidly growing are Northville and Plymouth townships, which are upscale areas just west of Livonia. Bush took about 60 percent of the vote in these areas.

Democrats run better in more middle-class areas such as Redford Township, just west of Detroit, and Westland, an area south of Livonia that gave 58 percent to Gore.

The 11th also covers southwestern Oakland County. The area is more Republican-leaning: Bush captured almost all of this territory in 2000. Novi, the most populous Oakland County jurisdiction in the 11th, grew by 47 percent in the 1990s.

Auto manufacturing is important here, with several Ford facilities among the area plants.

MAJOR INDUSTRY
Auto manufacturing, engineering, health care, insurance

CITIES
Livonia, 100,545; Westland, 86,602; Canton (unincorporated), 76,366

NOTABLE
Novi, first settled around 1825, is said to have been named for being the sixth stop — VI in Roman numerals — on a stagecoach route.

Rep. Sander M. Levin (D)

CAPITOL OFFICE
225-4961
www.house.gov/levin
2300 Rayburn 20515-2212; fax 226-1033

COMMITTEES
Ways & Means

HOMETOWN
Royal Oak

BORN
Sept. 6, 1931, Detroit, Mich.

RELIGION
Jewish

FAMILY
Wife, Victoria Levin; four children

EDUCATION
U. of Chicago, B.A. 1952; Columbia U., M.A. 1954 (international relations); Harvard U., LL.B. 1957

CAREER
Lawyer; U.S. Agency for International Development official

POLITICAL HIGHLIGHTS
Oakland Board of Supervisors, 1961-64; Mich. Senate, 1965-71 (minority leader, 1969-70); Democratic nominee for governor, 1970, 1974

ELECTION RESULTS

2002 GENERAL		
Sander M. Levin (D)	140,970	68.3%
Harvey R. Dean (R)	61,502	29.8%
Dick Gach (LIBERT)	2,694	1.3%
2002 PRIMARY		
Sander M. Levin (D)	71,881	78.8%
William J. Callahan (D)	16,926	18.6%
Mario Nesr Fundarski (D)	2,444	2.7%
2000 GENERAL		
Sander M. Levin (D)	157,720	64.3%
Bart Baron (R)	78,795	32.1%
Thomas Ness (GREEN)	4,137	1.7%
Andrew Le Cureaux (LIBERT)	3,630	1.5%

PREVIOUS WINNING PERCENTAGES
1998 (56%); 1996 (57%); 1994 (52%); 1992 (53%); 1990 (70%); 1988 (70%); 1986 (76%); 1984 (100%); 1982 (67%)

Elected 1982; 11th term

Long before he started his third decade in the House in 2003, Levin had established himself as perhaps the most pivotal Democratic vote in the House on trade.

And that is not only because he has been his party's top-ranking member on the Ways and Means Trade Subcommittee since 1999. Mild-mannered yet tenacious, Levin also is known for throwing his intellectual might into understanding the details of legislation — and their practical implication. And he represents one of the most renowned political proving grounds in the nation: Macomb County outside Detroit, where the term "Reagan Democrat" was coined and where the exporting aspirations of automakers and a growing service economy often conflict with the fears that union members have about watching jobs being shipped overseas.

So in the 107th Congress it was an important warning signal to President Bush when Levin came out against one of the administration's top first-term priorities: reviving procedures that compel Congress to approve or reject, without amendment, the trade deals struck by the president. Levin wanted the legislation to guarantee that enforceable labor rights and environmental quality standards would be required of each nation participating in any trade deal moved along such a fast-track.

When his concerns were not sufficiently addressed, he voted against the package enacted in 2002 — and so did seven out of eight House Democrats, the most lopsided opposition from that caucus to any of the four major trade liberalization laws of the past decade. "Trade policy built on partisanship is built on sand and will sink," Levin warned at the time.

It was a far different story in the 106th Congress, when Levin was a central player in securing enactment of the law making China a permanent normal U.S. trading partner. Passage by the House was deeply in doubt until Levin and Nebraska Republican Doug Bereuter struck a deal to include language establishing a congressional-executive branch commission to monitor China's behavior on human rights and compliance with trade rules. (He later was appointed to the commission he helped to create.)

Levin split his vote on the two big trade laws enacted in the 1990s. He opposed the 1993 measure implementing the North American Free Trade Agreement, saying the new benefits to Mexico would "tilt the playing field against American workers." But he voted the next year for the law endorsing a global trade agreement and creating the World Trade Organization, saying it would be a net benefit to the domestic economy.

Levin votes a liberal line on most social policy issues, earning high marks from civil rights groups and environmentalists. He supports gun control and abortion rights, and has voted against outlawing the procedure called "partial birth" abortion by its opponents.

From his position on Ways and Means, in the 104th Congress he scored some success in modifying the GOP welfare overhaul plan. Rather than try to defeat the package, as many Democrats wanted, Levin accepted the idea of ending the federal guarantee of providing welfare checks to eligible low-income mothers and children. He became an expert on the details and worked to secure revisions. When President Clinton signed the law in 1996, Levin was among a handful of Democratic lawmakers at the Rose Garden bill-signing ceremony.

In the 105th, Levin played an important role in revising the aspect of the welfare law that Democrats most disliked: its removal of benefits for sick and elderly legal immigrants. "This is not about welfare reform, it is about community responsibility," Levin argued. "It is not about moving a young parent from welfare to work, but about elderly people who cannot work."

As debate on updating the welfare law began in the 107th, Levin proposed improving health care access for those leaving the welfare system, and also making it easier for states to receive credit from the federal government for moving people off welfare and into jobs.

Levin has been actively involved in legislation combating illegal drugs, including a bipartisan matching grant initiative, the Drug-Free Communities Act. With a Republican colleague on Ways and Means, Sam Johnson of Texas, Levin has proposed establishing a tax credit for companies that conduct clinical testing research at U.S. medical schools and teaching hospitals. And he asked the General Accounting Office to investigate Michigan's poor-performing child care inspection services after the state announced cutbacks in its child care licensing inspector work force.

After four years as an appointed supervisor in Oakland County, Levin won his first elected office in 1964, a suburban Detroit state Senate seat. He was minority leader in Lansing, served as state Democratic Party chairman in the late 1960s and was viewed as a rising star when he was the party's gubernatorial nominee in 1970 and 1974. But his low-key manner did not shine in the statewide races, and he lost both.

After a stint as assistant administrator in the Agency for International Development, Levin announced for the House seat of retiring Democratic Rep. William M. Brodhead in 1982. With his well-known surname — his younger brother, Carl, had been in the Senate almost four years by then — and support from the party establishment, Levin overcame five primary opponents and won his first general election with two-thirds of the vote.

Levin has survived challenges at the polls because he is a prolific fundraiser who can tout his influence on legislation on important topics and because of long and close involvement in community affairs in the northern Detroit suburbs. Although he coasted in the 1980s, after redistricting for the 1990s he had four consecutive competitive re-election races. The Republican-led state legislature redrew Levin's district for this decade to make it more conservative, but in 2002 Levin prevailed with 68 percent of the vote, his best showing since 1990.

His chief rival was his Democratic primary opponent, state Rep. William Callahan. But Callahan suffered mightily after contending that Levin, who is Jewish, should not be re-elected because the district had become more conservative and Roman Catholic.

KEY VOTES

2002

Yes Overhaul campaign finance law; ban "soft money" and restrict advocacy advertising
Yes Back Bush's defense budget increase
No Extend 1996 welfare law
No Adopt Bush's discretionary spending limit
No Pass GOP Medicare prescription drug plan
Yes Create independent Sept. 11 commission
Yes Extend union protections to Homeland Security Department employees
No Revive fast-track procedures for trade agreements
No Authorize war against Iraq
No Advance bankruptcy overhaul opposed by abortion opponents

2001

No Nullify Clinton Labor Department ergonomics rule
No Cut taxes by $1.35 trillion through fiscal 2011
Yes Maintain ban on oil drilling in Arctic National Wildlife Refuge
No Approve Bush proposal to limit managed-care plan liability for coverage decisions
No Divert money from crop subsidy payments to land conservation
Yes Expand law enforcement power to investigate suspected terrorists

CQ VOTE STUDIES

	PARTY UNITY		PRESIDENTIAL SUPPORT	
	Support	Oppose	Support	Oppose
2002	95%	5%	28%	72%
2001	93%	7%	30%	70%
2000	93%	7%	90%	10%
1999	93%	7%	87%	13%
1998	93%	7%	83%	17%

INTEREST GROUPS

	AFL-CIO	ADA	CCUS	ACU
2002	100%	95%	40%	0%
2001	100%	95%	43%	4%
2000	90%	90%	52%	8%
1999	67%	95%	24%	4%
1998	100%	100%	33%	8%

MICHIGAN 12

Suburban Detroit – Warren, Clinton, Southfield

Well-settled suburbs north of 8 Mile Road, Detroit's northern boundary, form Michigan's 12th. The district is fertile ground for Democratic candidates and depends heavily on automobile manufacturing, making the United Auto Workers union a potent political force.

Roughly 70 percent of district residents live in Macomb County, once a largely blue-collar area that typified the "Reagan Democrats," those socially conservative, ancestrally Democratic blue-collar voters who had strong union loyalties but overwhelmingly backed Republican presidential candidates in the 1980s. But Macomb is becoming more white-collar, and Democrats have made progress here: Bill Clinton won Macomb in 1996, and Al Gore and now-Sen. Debbie Stabenow narrowly carried the county in 2000.

The district is lined with auto manufacturing facilities. Warren, the district's most populous city and a traditional Democratic stronghold (it voted for Gore by 56 percent to 41 percent in 2000), is home to the General Motors Technical Center, a 330-acre design and engineering campus. The Army's Tank Automotive Command also is in Warren.

The western part of the district takes in several areas in southern Oakland County, near the Detroit boundary, that are heavily Democratic and African-American: Southfield, which has become a haven for black urban professionals escaping Detroit's crime, Lathrup Village, Oak Park and Royal Oak. Other Oakland County communities in the 12th include Ferndale, Hazel Park and Madison Heights, which also are solidly Democratic but mostly white.

Redistricting following the 2000 census pushed the largely Democratic district firmly into the Democrats' column. Republican mapmakers removed some GOP-leaning areas from the 12th to improve their party's chances in adjacent districts.

MAJOR INDUSTRY

Auto and tank manufacturing, auto research and design

CITIES

Warren, 138,247; Clinton (unincorporated), 95,648; Southfield, 78,296; St. Clair Shores, 63,096; Roseville, 48,129; Sterling Heights (pt.), 37,935

NOTABLE

The Detroit Zoo is in Royal Oak.

Rep. Carolyn Cheeks Kilpatrick (D)

CAPITOL OFFICE
225-2261
www.house.gov/kilpatrick
1610 Longworth 20515-2213; fax 225-5730

COMMITTEES
Appropriations

HOMETOWN
Detroit

BORN
June 25, 1945, Detroit, Mich.

RELIGION
African Methodist Episcopal

FAMILY
Divorced; two children

EDUCATION
Ferris State U., A.A. 1965; Western Michigan U., B.S. 1968 (education); U. of Michigan, M.A. 1972 (education)

CAREER
Teacher

POLITICAL HIGHLIGHTS
Mich. House, 1979-97; candidate for Detroit City Council, 1991; sought Democratic nomination for Mich. Senate, 1994

ELECTION RESULTS

2002 GENERAL		
Carolyn Cheeks Kilpatrick (D)	120,869	91.6%
Raymond H. Warner (LIBERT)	11,072	8.4%
2002 PRIMARY		
Carolyn Cheeks Kilpatrick (D)		unopposed
2000 GENERAL		
Carolyn Cheeks Kilpatrick (D)	140,609	88.6%
Chrysanthea D. Boyd-Fields (R)	14,336	9.0%
Raymond H. Warner (LIBERT)	1,690	1.1%

PREVIOUS WINNING PERCENTAGES
1998 (87%); 1996 (88%)

Elected 1996; 4th term

Kilpatrick is upfront about the challenges facing the center-city Detroit portion of her district, which "has the best and worst of America in it," as she told the Detroit News soon after her election. She is in a good position to do something about the problems facing her constituents.

Now in her fourth term in the House, Kilpatrick is already serving her third on the Appropriations Committee. She and Republican Joe Knollenberg are the only Michiganders on the panel, but she is the one on the Transportation Subcommittee. From that seat, Kilpatrick will be in a good position to press for funding for Detroit's transportation once local officials have developed a framework for creating a regionwide transportation master plan.

Transportation tops Kilpatrick's long list of needs that call out for government attention in her district, by far the poorest in the state. She has helped in the development of a coordinated Detroit area transportation strategy that includes a sizable contribution from mass transit, something that has been sorely lacking in the "Motor City." Kilpatrick says Detroit's transit system is inadequate, particularly in meeting the needs of many "reverse" commuters who live in the city and work in the suburbs. Meanwhile, she has been able to obtain some federal funds for more buses, renovation projects and better access roads for the Detroit airport, along with money to study the possibility of creating a light rail system.

Although her territory has a new number — it was the 15th District in the 1990s — remapping after the 2000 census did little to change her constituency's essential characteristics. Expansion of the boundaries north and south along Lake St. Clair and the Detroit River, and exclusion of some of Detroit, reduced the district's African-American population to about 60 percent, from about 70 percent in 1990. But the 13th still includes wide swaths of impoverished center-city neighborhoods and is overwhelmingly Democratic.

Unlike many lawmakers, who seek to portray their constituency only in positive terms, Kilpatrick is frank about the problems facing her district, including high infant mortality, high unemployment, high school drop-out rates and blighted neighborhoods and substandard housing. The federal government should play a key role in addressing all those problems, she says.

Mindful of her constituents' needs and their dependence on federal programs, Kilpatrick is one of Congress' more steadfast liberal voices, though slightly less so than her Democratic colleague from Detroit, John Conyers Jr. In 2001, she cast one of the 66 votes in the House against the final version of the anti-terrorism package written in response to the Sept. 11, 2001, terrorist attacks, arguing that its enactment severely curtailed civil liberties. She also voted against the package of aid to the airline industry, which was crippled after the attacks, because, she said, "It contains nothing for 100,000 employees who were laid off."

She does break from the liberal ranks when it comes to automobile fuel economy standards, which are anathema to the Detroit-area automobile industry. She voted against a proposal to increase those standards in the 107th Congress, and in the 106th she teamed with Knollenberg in opposing moves to use appropriations legislation to increase the standards. "I understand the concerns of my colleagues," she said in 2000. "But the industry has made some giant steps since 1996."

On Appropriations' Foreign Operations Subcommittee, she has raised questions about the effectiveness of the United States' anti-drug strategy in South America and about U.S. policy in the Israeli-Palestinian conflict.

Kilpatrick has undertaken a crusade to get corporate America and the federal government to spend more of their advertising dollars with women- and minority-owned media outlets and advertising agencies. In 2000, using a General Accounting Office study as ammunition, she and New Jersey Democratic Rep. Robert Menendez helped persuade President Clinton to sign an executive order aimed at giving minority firms a bigger piece of the federal ad budget. In the 107th and again in the 108th Congresses, Kilpatrick worked on legislation to codify the Clinton order.

Kilpatrick also is responsible for a family political legacy. Her son, Kwame, who was her campaign manager at an early age, succeeded her in the state legislature when she came to Congress and then, in 2001, was elected mayor of Detroit at the age of 31. The new mayor credited his mother and father (a leading Wayne County government official) for instilling in him the obligations of public service.

A Detroit native, Kilpatrick holds a master's degree in education, and as a teacher in the Detroit public schools for eight years, she taught business and vocational classes. Often in floor debate, she makes her points by discussing the needs of children. She won the first of nine terms in the state House, a full-time job, in 1978. In Lansing, she was the first black woman to serve on the Appropriations Committee, and she once led a coalition of Democratic and Republican lawmakers seeking to block a proposal by popular Republican Gov. John Engler to halt state funding for local transportation programs. But she generally was not regarded as a key player on most issues.

She has hit a few bumps in her political career, losing a 1991 bid for the Detroit City Council when questions arose about whether she was sufficiently independent from Mayor Coleman Young, and failing, after changing her mind several times, to win a spot on the 1994 state Senate ballot.

Her predecessor in Congress, Democrat Barbara-Rose Collins, did not cut much of a legislative figure in Washington. But Kilpatrick was somewhat reluctant to challenge Collins, a one-time political ally. However, when Collins in 1996 became the subject of separate investigations by the House ethics committee and the Justice Department into allegations of ethical and financial misconduct, Kilpatrick stepped forward. Kilpatrick took a majority of the primary vote and beat Collins by 20 percentage points. The November outcome was preordained in the heavily Democratic district, and Kilpatrick has since won re-election with ease.

KEY VOTES

2002

Yes Overhaul campaign finance law; ban "soft money" and restrict advocacy advertising
No Back Bush's defense budget increase
No Extend 1996 welfare law
No Adopt Bush's discretionary spending limit
No Pass GOP Medicare prescription drug plan
Yes Create independent Sept. 11 commission
Yes Extend union protections to Homeland Security Department employees
No Revive fast-track procedures for trade agreements
No Authorize war against Iraq
No Advance bankruptcy overhaul opposed by abortion opponents

2001

No Nullify Clinton Labor Department ergonomics rule
No Cut taxes by $1.35 trillion through fiscal 2011
Yes Maintain ban on oil drilling in Arctic National Wildlife Refuge
No Approve Bush proposal to limit managed-care plan liability for coverage decisions
Yes Divert money from crop subsidy payments to land conservation
? Expand law enforcement power to investigate suspected terrorists

CQ VOTE STUDIES

	PARTY UNITY		PRESIDENTIAL SUPPORT	
	Support	Oppose	Support	Oppose
2002	98%	2%	27%	73%
2001	93%	7%	15%	85%
2000	96%	4%	83%	17%
1999	98%	2%	88%	12%
1998	96%	4%	88%	12%

INTEREST GROUPS

	AFL-CIO	ADA	CCUS	ACU
2002	100%	95%	42%	0%
2001	100%	100%	39%	4%
2000	100%	85%	42%	8%
1999	89%	100%	16%	0%
1998	100%	90%	28%	0%

MICHIGAN 13

Part of Detroit; Lincoln Park; Wyandotte

General Motors helped build Detroit through a thriving American auto industry over the first half of the 20th century. Then riots in 1967 and the oil crisis of the 1970s decimated the city's economy and turned it into a virtual war zone. The 13th suffered the worst of the 1967 riots in terms of property damage and deaths. For a time, Detroit was even known as the "Beirut of America." The city still has a reputation for crime and relatively high taxes, and many of the affluent suburbs that surround Detroit have become regional office centers and have lured companies away from the city.

Detroit is divided between the 13th and 14th districts, with a slightly larger share of the city's population living in the 13th. The 13th is a black-majority district, and about three-fourths of its residents live in Detroit. The city steadily declined in population in the 1990s, and fell below 1 million in the 2000 census.

Detroit remains overwhelmingly Democratic (Al Gore won the city with 94 percent in 2000) and black (80 percent of Detroit's population). Pockets of poverty exist, and the 13th has the state's highest percentage of households with incomes under $10,000. Wealthy communities to the northeast, such as Grosse Pointe, also are losing population.

Downtown Detroit and the waterfront, covered by the 13th, have been a target for intensive redevelopment. There are two new sporting venues downtown that are part of a massive entertainment complex — Comerica Park opened in 2000 for baseball's Detroit Tigers, and Ford Field opened in 2002 for the National Football League's Detroit Lions. There also are several new casinos.

Redistricting following the 2000 census renumbered the district from the 15th to the 13th and added the cities of Wyandotte and Lincoln Park, but the changes did not shift the district's overwhelmingly Democratic tilt.

MAJOR INDUSTRY
Auto and auto parts manufacturing, government

CITIES
Detroit (pt.), 511,449; Lincoln Park, 40,008; Wyandotte, 28,006

NOTABLE
The Belle Isle Zoo and the Charles H. Wright Museum of African-American History are in the 13th.

Rep. John Conyers Jr. (D)

CAPITOL OFFICE
225-5126
john.conyers@mail.house.gov
www.house.gov/conyers
2426 Rayburn 20515-2214; fax 225-0072

COMMITTEES
Judiciary - ranking member

HOMETOWN
Detroit

BORN
May 16, 1929, Detroit, Mich.

RELIGION
Baptist

FAMILY
Wife, Monica Conyers; two children

EDUCATION
Wayne State U., B.A. 1957, LL.B. 1958

MILITARY SERVICE
Mich. National Guard, 1948-50; Army, 1950-54; Army Reserve, 1954-57

CAREER
Lawyer; congressional aide

POLITICAL HIGHLIGHTS
Candidate for mayor of Detroit, 1989, 1993

ELECTION RESULTS

2002 GENERAL		
John Conyers Jr. (D)	145,285	83.2%
Dave Stone (R)	26,544	15.2%
2002 PRIMARY		
John Conyers Jr. (D)		unopposed
2000 GENERAL		
John Conyers Jr. (D)	168,982	89.1%
William A. Ashe (R)	17,582	9.3%
Constance J. Catalfio (LIBERT)	2,113	1.1%

PREVIOUS WINNING PERCENTAGES
1998 (87%); 1996 (86%); 1994 (81%); 1992 (82%); 1990 (89%); 1988 (91%); 1986 (89%); 1984 (89%); 1982 (97%); 1980 (95%); 1978 (93%); 1976 (92%); 1974 (91%); 1972 (88%); 1970 (88%); 1968 (100%); 1966 (84%); 1964 (84%)

Elected 1964; 20th term

As he approaches his 40th year in Congress, Conyers is the second-longest-serving member of the House after another Detroit-area Democrat, John D. Dingell. And, like his fellow veteran of the Great Society and Watergate eras at the Capitol, Conyers has found it frequently difficult to adapt to life under Republican control of the House.

But since 2001, he has at least found it more pleasant to operate from his position of power as the top-ranking Democrat on the Judiciary Committee. Conyers has worked closely behind the scenes with the panel's Republican Chairman, F. James Sensenbrenner Jr. of Wisconsin, despite their frequent public disagreements. That is a sharp departure from the much stormier relationship that Conyers had during his six years with the previous GOP chairman, Henry J. Hyde of Illinois.

His liberal convictions undaunted, Conyers continues to position himself as a champion of the downtrodden, the same way he did when he was swept into office alongside Lyndon B. Johnson in 1964. He spends much of his time trying to thwart what he views as GOP efforts to weaken individual rights at the behest of business or law enforcement.

Having fought almost every social policy battle at least once before, Conyers' delivery has become less fiery of late but his voice remains strongly partisan. So does his voting record. In the 107th Congress, he opposed President Bush 86 percent of the time, more often than all but two other House members. And he sided with the Democrats 97 percent of the time on votes in which the two parties were in opposition.

Still, Conyers worked with Sensenbrenner in 2001 on a plan to give law enforcement greater legal leeway to fight terrorism in the aftermath of the attacks of Sept. 11. But the House Republican leadership abruptly scrapped the bipartisan bill in favor of its own version, which was quickly rammed through the House. Conyers opposed it as well as the subsequent compromise with the Senate that became law.

The next year, Conyers also opposed the legislation establishing the Department of Homeland Security, saying that it did too little to maintain civil service and union protections for federal workers.

A co-founder of the Congressional Black Caucus, Conyers has championed the causes of civil rights, minorities and the poor. He introduced legislation to make the birthday of the Rev. Dr. Martin Luther King Jr. a national holiday four days after the civil rights leader's assassination in 1968, and he pushed the bill until it was enacted in 1983. In 2001, he introduced a bill to ban racial profiling by law enforcement.

In each Congress during the past decade, Conyers has introduced legislation to set up a commission to study whether the federal government owes reparations to African-American descendants of slaves. His bill has yet to receive a hearing.

Conyers won the gratitude of other Democrats for his vociferous defense of President Clinton during the 1998 impeachment proceedings. He accused Republicans of a politically inspired attempt to remove a twice-elected president. By that time, Conyers was the only remaining member of Judiciary from 1974, when the panel had voted for the impeachment of President Nixon. Conyers had been on the Nixon administration's infamous "enemies list."

In defending Clinton, Conyers said there was no comparison between the president's covering up his affair with former White House intern Monica

Lewinsky and Nixon's covering up his complicity in the Watergate affair. Clinton "can't be impeached without devaluing the rule of law and degrading [the meaning of] impeachable offenses," Conyers said.

Conyers' foreign policy agenda focuses on fostering democracy in Haiti. He has led several congressional delegations to the island nation to study the challenges facing its government and to monitor elections.

Conyers voted against the 2002 resolution authorizing the use of military force against Iraq, arguing that "we should avoid the horrors of war unless war is really necessary." He joined with New York Democrat Charles B. Rangel in suggesting that the military draft should be revived, which he said might appropriately dampen enthusiasm for war.

After serving with the Army in Korea, Conyers went home to Detroit and got involved in politics while in law school there. The creation in 1964 of a second black-majority congressional district in the city provided an opening for Conyers, who won a primary race against accountant Richard H. Austin by 108 votes. He won the Democratic district in a rout that November and has won his 19 subsequent terms the same way.

In the House, Conyers has often seemed less interested in legislative brokerage than in being a liberal voice of protest. Twice in the early 1970s, he waged symbolic campaigns for Speaker against Carl Albert of Oklahoma, whom he accused of "stagnation and reaction." Conyers also was seen as being sarcastic and abrasive, which did not make it easy for him to assemble the coalitions required to move legislation.

And his two quixotic bids to become mayor of Detroit did not enhance his reputation. In 1989, he challenged Mayor Coleman A. Young and finished third in a primary. A 1993 run also failed.

With the Republican takeover of the House in 1995, Conyers turned his attention to blocking the portions of the GOP agenda that came through the Judiciary panel. He said in 1996 that, "The Republican Party is now completely led by extremists." He opposed the GOP campaign to rewrite welfare law, the party's market-oriented 1996 farm law, all of its efforts to restrict abortion rights and its efforts in the 106th and 107th Congresses to overhaul bankruptcy law — in his view to reward banks at the expense of consumers.

Conyers has a strong interest in jazz and frequently takes time out to listen to music in his office, where posters of jazz artists are displayed. In 1987, he successfully sponsored a House resolution declaring jazz a "rare and valuable national American treasure." A Washington, D.C., jazz club, HR-57, is named for the resolution.

KEY VOTES

2002

Yes Overhaul campaign finance law; ban "soft money" and restrict advocacy advertising
No Back Bush's defense budget increase
No Extend 1996 welfare law
No Adopt Bush's discretionary spending limit
No Pass GOP Medicare prescription drug plan
Yes Create independent Sept. 11 commission
Yes Extend union protections to Homeland Security Department employees
No Revive fast-track procedures for trade agreements
No Authorize war against Iraq
No Advance bankruptcy overhaul opposed by abortion opponents

2001

No Nullify Clinton Labor Department ergonomics rule
No Cut taxes by $1.35 trillion through fiscal 2011
Yes Maintain ban on oil drilling in Arctic National Wildlife Refuge
No Approve Bush proposal to limit managed-care plan liability for coverage decisions
Yes Divert money from crop subsidy payments to land conservation
No Expand law enforcement power to investigate suspected terrorists

CQ VOTE STUDIES

	PARTY UNITY		PRESIDENTIAL SUPPORT	
	Support	Oppose	Support	Oppose
2002	99%	1%	21%	79%
2001	96%	4%	7%	93%
2000	98%	2%	85%	15%
1999	97%	3%	84%	16%
1998	95%	5%	90%	10%

INTEREST GROUPS

	AFL-CIO	ADA	CCUS	ACU
2002	100%	100%	21%	0%
2001	100%	90%	23%	4%
2000	100%	95%	30%	0%
1999	89%	100%	17%	8%
1998	100%	80%	20%	0%

MICHIGAN 14
Parts of Detroit and Dearborn

The auto industry kept Detroit humming for most of this century. The early factories drew people from rural Michigan, Appalachia, the South and Eastern Europe. Then race riots during the summer of 1967 and the oil crisis of the early 1970s sparked an evacuation of the Motor City. Many residents fled to the suburbs, and automakers moved to Mexico and non-union U.S. towns, leaving Detroit with some of the poorest and most crime-ridden neighborhoods in the nation. In 1960, 1.7 million people lived in Detroit; in 2000, its population was 951,000.

The 14th covers the residential neighborhoods that sprang up north of Detroit's auto plants. It includes slightly less than half of Detroit, which accounts for two-thirds of the district's total population. Long an economically distressed area, the district has seen a few signs of renewal. Property values are beginning to pick up, and crime rates are starting to fall — additional signs that Detroit's worst days may be past.

As redrawn following the 2000 census, the 14th includes two-thirds of Dearborn, which is home to Ford Motor Co. and its River Rouge factory — once the largest in the world. Dearborn has a large Arab-American population, with 30 percent of city residents claiming Arab ancestry. The district also includes two areas enveloped by Detroit: Hamtramck, an ethnically diverse enclave where more than 10 percent of residents consider themselves biracial, and Highland Park, an overwhelmingly African-American area that in 2000 had the highest poverty rate (38 percent) in metropolitan Detroit.

The 14th has the nation's seventh-largest percentage of black residents (61 percent), and is safely Democratic. Detroit's unyielding Democratic bent keeps Republicans from carrying the seat or Wayne County.

MAJOR INDUSTRY
Auto and auto parts manufacturing, health care

CITIES
Detroit (pt.), 439,821; Dearborn (pt), 64,759; Southgate, 30,136; Allen Park, 29,376; Hamtramck, 22,976

NOTABLE
Woodward Avenue, between 6 Mile and 7 Mile roads, was the nation's first paved road (1909); The Henry Ford Museum houses the rocking chair that President Abraham Lincoln sat in when he was assassinated at Ford's Theatre in Washington, D.C., on April 14, 1865.

Rep. John D. Dingell (D)

CAPITOL OFFICE
225-4071
www.house.gov/dingell
2328 Rayburn 20515-2215; fax 226-0371

COMMITTEES
Energy & Commerce - ranking member

HOMETOWN
Dearborn

BORN
July 8, 1926, Colorado Springs, Colo.

RELIGION
Roman Catholic

FAMILY
Wife, Debbie Dingell; four children

EDUCATION
Georgetown U., B.S. 1949 (chemistry), J.D. 1952

MILITARY SERVICE
Army, 1944-46

CAREER
County prosecutor

POLITICAL HIGHLIGHTS
No previous office

ELECTION RESULTS

2002 GENERAL		
John D. Dingell (D)	136,518	72.2%
Martin Kaltenbach (R)	48,626	25.7%
Gregory Stempfle (LIBERT)	3,919	2.1%
2002 PRIMARY		
John D. Dingell (D)	58,120	58.7%
Lynn Rivers (D)	40,832	41.3%
2000 GENERAL		
John D. Dingell (D)	167,142	71.0%
William Morse (R)	62,469	26.5%
Edward Hlavac (LIBERT)	2,814	1.2%

PREVIOUS WINNING PERCENTAGES
1998 (67%); 1996 (62%); 1994 (59%); 1992 (65%); 1990 (67%); 1988 (97%); 1986 (78%); 1984 (64%); 1982 (74%); 1980 (70%); 1978 (77%); 1976 (76%); 1974 (78%); 1972 (68%); 1970 (79%); 1968 (74%); 1966 (63%); 1964 (73%); 1962 (83%); 1960 (79%); 1958 (79%); 1956 (74%); 1955 Special Election (76%)

Elected December 1955; 24th full term

For all the influence Dingell wields as dean of the House and top-ranking Democrat on the powerful Energy and Commerce Committee, it was an effort by Democratic liberals to deny him a 24th full term that drew his heaviest media attention in the 107th Congress.

When post-census reapportionment took a House seat away from Michigan and the Republican-controlled state legislature redrew the congressional map for this decade, Dingell was compelled to seek the 2002 Democratic nomination against another incumbent House Democrat, eight-year veteran Lynn Rivers. Feminists, environmentalists and gun control advocates teamed up with Rivers and gave Dingell the fight of his long political life.

But he fought back — and won the primary with 59 percent — with a hefty campaign war chest and a muscular coalition of National Rifle Association members, the auto industry and its union members, business lobbyists and longtime grass-roots activists. "I don't ever worry about elections," he said afterward. "I work like hell."

The race split House Democrats: Nancy Pelosi, the soon-to-be minority leader, backed Rivers — a choice Dingell will not soon forget. But the size of Dingell's win only fortified his standing as a power to be reckoned with.

Republican control has kept him from the gavel at Energy and Commerce, which he helped transform into Capitol Hill's most influential regulatory committee as chairman from 1981 through 1994. But, as he approaches the latter half of his eighth decade in life and his fifth decade in the House, Dingell's complex personality and keen political sense still inspire fear among those whom he has in his sights.

If his imposing frame is not enough to intimidate any guileless visitors or political foes who wander into his office, a stuffed menagerie of animals who once crossed Dingell's path might do the trick. Although the avid hunter resigned from the NRA board in 1994 during debate on a crime bill, his aggressive and successful pursuit of big game is key to understanding his cunning, sometime mercilessness and reputation for ruthless accretion of power. He says he has adopted as his own the aphorism the Corleone family made famous in "The Godfather, Part II": "Keep your friends close, but your enemies closer."

It is a style he learned from his father, John D. Sr., a New Deal champion of national health insurance as a Detroit congressman for 22 years until his death in 1955, when the son took over. But his word is his bond; when Dingell seals a deal, he can be counted on to keep it.

As Energy and Commerce chairman, Dingell built a remarkable fiefdom, running the committee with an iron fist and becoming a potent symbol of the Old Bull Democratic chairmen who made life miserable for the minority. He amassed the broadest committee jurisdiction of any chairman in the postwar era, covering energy, health, communications, transportation, waste disposal and numerous regulatory agencies. Many Republicans hated his imperious style, but they saw him as a leadership model to emulate when they took control in the 104th Congress.

Dingell often cites as one of the major accomplishments of his chairmanship the 1990 rewrite of the federal clean air law. He had blocked it during most of the 1980s, and did not give in until he thought he had gotten a good deal for the automakers that are the lifeblood of his district and state.

Although in the minority since 1995, Dingell has frequently outwitted, outsmarted, outmaneuvered and outlasted Republicans and Democrats alike on major issues. Against his fervent desire, he watched Republicans tear down the Depression-era regulatory barriers that had separated banks, brokerages and insurance companies. But he proved to GOP leaders he would not be ignored, crafting legislation on issues ranging from telecommunications to drinking water quality — and blocking ideas he opposed, such as electric utility deregulation.

His major effort in the 107th Congress was with the GOP chairman of Energy and Commerce, Billy Tauzin of Louisiana, to deregulate the market for high-speed Internet services over local telephone lines. Their bill was passed by the House but died in the Senate after one of the most intensive and well-publicized lobbying campaigns in recent years.

Dingell keeps tabs on the executive branch — whether in Republican or Democratic hands — through a seemingly constant stream of letters known as "Dingell-grams." Several months into the Bush administration, Dingell took the House floor to poke fun at the new staff in the White House for lacking political savvy and responding to his missives with form letters. "I even got better responses from Richard Nixon," he said. The White House soon began answering Dingell's letters, and President Bush reportedly told Dingell he was the "biggest pain in the ass" on Capitol Hill.

But a part of this crusade unwittingly jeopardized the ability of Congress to oversee the workings of the executive branch. With Henry A. Waxman of California, his close investigatory colleague on Energy and Commerce, Dingell asked the General Accounting Office in 2001 to probe the involvement of energy companies in the formulation of administration energy policy. The GAO ended up filing an unprecedented lawsuit to compel Vice President Dick Cheney to release records. But the quest ended in 2003, when the GAO declined to appeal a federal judge's ruling that the congressional agency lacked the legal standing to bring such a suit — a potential setback for Congress' investigatory reach.

Aside from his abortion and gun views, on most issues Dingell stands with liberal Democrats, supporting civil rights, Great Society programs and expansion of the federal government's role. (He presided over the House in 1965 when the bill that created Medicare was passed.)

In two dozen general elections, Dingell has slipped below 60 percent only once, when the GOP took control of Congress in 1994. He shows no signs of retiring, but if he does there are two people who could logically maintain the family hold on the seat: the incumbent's wife, Debbie, president of the General Motors Foundation, and his son Chris, who was elected a state judge in 2002 after 16 years as a state senator.

KEY VOTES

2002

Yes Overhaul campaign finance law; ban "soft money" and restrict advocacy advertising
Yes Back Bush's defense budget increase
No Extend 1996 welfare law
No Adopt Bush's discretionary spending limit
No Pass GOP Medicare prescription drug plan
Yes Create independent Sept. 11 commission
Yes Extend union protections to Homeland Security Department employees
No Revive fast-track procedures for trade agreements
No Authorize war against Iraq
No Advance bankruptcy overhaul opposed by abortion opponents

2001

No Nullify Clinton Labor Department ergonomics rule
No Cut taxes by $1.35 trillion through fiscal 2011
Yes Maintain ban on oil drilling in Arctic National Wildlife Refuge
No Approve Bush proposal to limit managed-care plan liability for coverage decisions
Yes Divert money from crop subsidy payments to land conservation
No Expand law enforcement power to investigate suspected terrorists

CQ VOTE STUDIES

	PARTY UNITY		PRESIDENTIAL SUPPORT	
	Support	Oppose	Support	Oppose
2002	96%	4%	26%	74%
2001	88%	12%	29%	71%
2000	89%	11%	81%	19%
1999	85%	15%	77%	23%
1998	89%	11%	82%	18%

INTEREST GROUPS

	AFL-CIO	ADA	CCUS	ACU
2002	100%	90%	42%	4%
2001	100%	95%	41%	24%
2000	100%	80%	33%	16%
1999	89%	80%	24%	12%
1998	100%	85%	28%	8%

MICHIGAN 15

Southeast – Ann Arbor, Taylor, parts of Dearborn and Dearborn Heights

Situated on the flat land west and south of Detroit, the 15th contains a mix of auto workers, engineers and academics. As redrawn following the 2000 census, the 15th is a Democratic bastion that takes in parts of the old 13th, based in Ann Arbor, and the old 16th, based in Wayne County outside Detroit.

Interstate 94, which joins the eastern and western ends of the 15th in the north, has emerged as an engineering and research corridor where robotics companies, developing ways to automate auto manufacturing, have helped turn Detroit assembly line jobs into highly skilled, computerized work.

At the district's northwestern corner is Ann Arbor, the district's most populous city and home to the University of Michigan's academic community. Ann Arbor votes reliably Democratic: Al Gore took 69 percent of the vote here in the 2000 presidential election. Ypsilanti, a working-class town southeast of Ann Arbor, is home to Eastern Michigan University and also reliably backs Democratic candidates.

A little more than 40 percent of the district's residents live in the blue-collar, reliably Democratic suburbs of Wayne County. The 15th's most populous city here is Taylor, which is just east of Detroit Metropolitan Wayne County Airport in Romulus. Dearborn, the western third of which is in the 15th, Dearborn Heights (shared with the 11th) and Inkster form the district's northeast corner.

Monroe County, south of Wayne and Washtenaw counties, borders Lake Erie to the east and the Toledo, Ohio, area to the south.

MAJOR INDUSTRY

Auto and auto parts manufacturing, higher education, medical research, steel

CITIES

Ann Arbor, 114,024; Taylor, 65,868; Dearborn Heights (pt.), 44,694; Dearborn (pt.), 33,016; Inkster, 30,115; Romulus, 22,979; Ypsilanti, 22,362

NOTABLE

NOAA's Great Lakes Environmental Research Laboratory is in Ann Arbor.

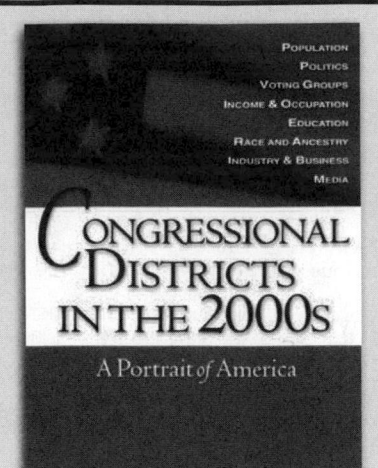

MINNESOTA

Gov. Tim Pawlenty (R)

First elected: 2002
Length of term: 4 years
Term expires: 1/07
Salary: $120,303
Phone: (651) 296-0121
Hometown: Eagan
Born: Nov. 27, 1960; South St. Paul, Minn.
Religion: Protestant
Family: Wife, Mary Pawlenty; two children
Education: U. of Minnesota, B.A. 1983 (political science), J.D. 1986
Career: Internet consulting firm executive; lawyer
Political Highlights: Eagan Planning Commission, 1988-89; Eagan City Council, 1990-92; Minn. House, 1993-2003
Election results:

2002 GENERAL		
Tim Pawlenty (R)	999,473	44.4%
Roger Moe (D)	821,268	36.5%
Timothy J. Penny (INDC)	364,534	16.2%
Ken Pentel (GREEN)	50,589	2.3%

Lt. Gov. Carol Molnau (R)

First elected: 2002
Length of term: 4 years
Term expires: 1/07
Salary: $78,196
Phone: (651) 297-8353

STATE LEGISLATURE

Legislature: Meets January-May in odd-numbered years; February-April in even-numbered years
House: 134 members, 2-year terms
2003 breakdown: 82R, 52D; 102 men, 32 women
Salary: $31,140
Phone: (651) 296-2146
Senate: 67 members, 4-year terms
2003 breakdown: 31R, 35D, 1I; 44 men, 23 women
Salary: $31,140
Phone: (651) 296-0504

STATE TERM LIMITS

Governor: No
Senate: No
House: No

URBAN STATISTICS

CITY	POPULATION
Minneapolis	382,618
St. Paul	287,151
Duluth	86,918
Rochester	85,806
Bloomington	85,172

REGISTERED VOTERS

Voters do not register by party.

POPULATION

2002 population (est.)	5,019,720
2000 population	4,919,479
1990 population	4,375,099
Percent change (1990-2000)	+12.4%
Rank among states (2002)	21
Median age	35.4
Born in state	70.2%
Foreign born	5.3%
Violent crime rate	281/100,000
Poverty level	7.9%
Federal workers	32,833
Military	19,625

REDISTRICTING

Minnesota retained its eight House seats in reapportionment. The state legislature failed to agree on a plan and a state Supreme Court special redistricting panel adopted a new map on March 19, 2002.

MISCELLANEOUS

Web: www.state.mn.us
Capital: St. Paul
STATE ELECTION OFFICIAL
(651) 215-1440
DEMOCRATIC HEADQUARTERS
(651) 293-1200
REPUBLICAN HEADQUARTERS
(651) 222-0022

District Statistics

	2000 VOTE FOR PRESIDENT															
DIST.	BUSH	GORE	NADER	WHITE	BLACK	ASIAN	HISP	MEDIAN INCOME	WHITE COLLAR	BLUE COLLAR	SERVICE INDUSTRY	OVER 64	UNDER 18	COLLEGE EDUCATION	RURAL	SQ. MILES
1	50%	46%	4%	93%	1%	2%	3%	$40,941	57%	28%	15%	15%	25%	22%	44%	13,322
2	51	45	4	92	2	2	3	$61,344	65	23	12	8	30	31	20	3,035
3	50	46	4	89	4	4	2	$63,816	73	17	10	10	27	40	4	468
4	37	57	6	78	6	8	5	$46,811	67	19	14	12	26	33	0	202
5	29	63	8	71	13	5	6	$41,569	67	18	15	12	22	35	0	124
6	53	42	5	95	1	1	1	$56,862	60	27	12	8	29	25	36	3,081
7	55	41	4	93	0	1	3	$36,453	53	31	16	17	26	16	66	31,796
8	45	50	5	95	1	0	1	$37,911	53	30	17	16	25	18	63	27,583
STATE	46	48	5	88	3	3	3	$47,111	62	24	14	12	26	27	29	79,610
U.S.	47.9	48.4	3	69	12	4	13	$41,994	60	25	15	12	26	24	21	3,537,438

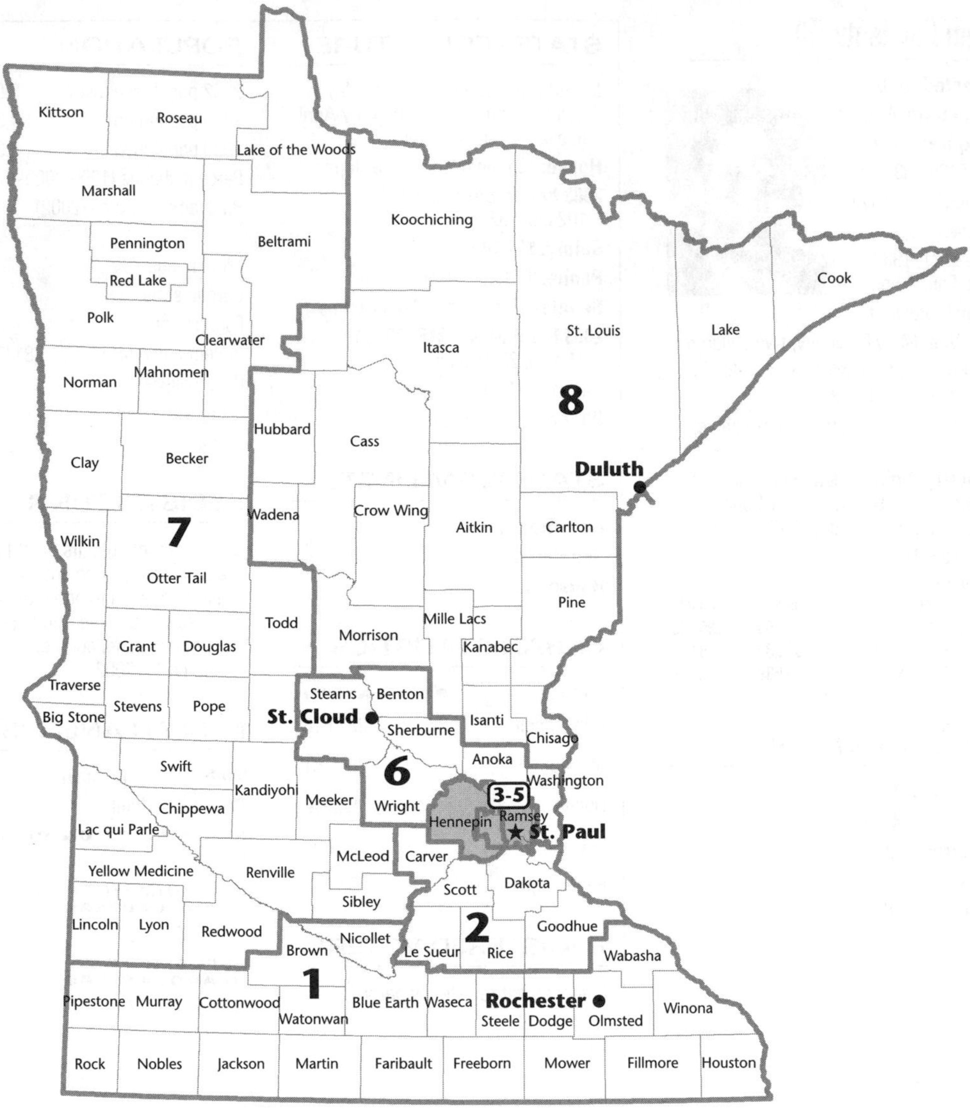
Kittson
Roseau
Lake of the Woods
Marshall
Koochiching
Pennington
Beltrami
Red Lake
Polk
Cook
Clearwater
St. Louis
Lake
Itasca
Norman
Mahnomen
8
Hubbard
Cass
Clay
Becker
Duluth
7
Wadena
Crow Wing
Aitkin
Carlton
Wilkin
Otter Tail
Pine
Todd
Mille Lacs
Grant
Douglas
Morrison
Kanabec
Traverse
Stearns
Benton
Big Stone
Stevens
Pope
St. Cloud
Isanti
Sherburne
Chisago
Swift
Anoka
6
Washington
Kandiyohi
Meeker
3-5
Chippewa
Wright
Hennepin
Ramsey
St. Paul
Lac qui Parle
McLeod
Carver
Yellow Medicine
Renville
Dakota
Scott
Sibley
Lincoln
Lyon
Redwood
2
Goodhue
Nicollet
Brown
Le Sueur
Rice
Wabasha
1
Pipestone
Murray
Cottonwood
Blue Earth
Waseca
Rochester
Winona
Watonwan
Steele
Dodge
Olmsted
Rock
Nobles
Jackson
Martin
Faribault
Freeborn
Mower
Fillmore
Houston

Wright
6
Anoka
Washington
Hennepin
Coon Rapids
Brooklyn Park
Ramsey
3
4
Plymouth
Minneapolis
St. Paul
Minnetonka
5
Eden Prairie
Bloomington
Eagan
Carver
Scott
2
Dakota

Sen. Mark Dayton (D)

CAPITOL OFFICE
224-3244
dayton.senate.gov
346 Russell 20510-2305; fax 228-2186

COMMITTEES
Agriculture, Nutrition & Forestry
Armed Services
Governmental Affairs
Rules & Administration
Joint Printing - ranking member

HOMETOWN
Minneapolis

BORN
Jan. 26, 1947, Minneapolis, Minn.

RELIGION
Presbyterian

FAMILY
Divorced; two children

EDUCATION
Yale U., B.A. 1969 (psychology)

CAREER
Investment company president; runaway youth home director; congressional and gubernatorial aide; social worker; science teacher

POLITICAL HIGHLIGHTS
Minn. commissioner of economic development, 1978; Democratic nominee for U.S. Senate, 1982; Minn. commissioner of energy and economic development, 1983-86; Minn. auditor, 1991-95; sought Democratic nomination for governor, 1998

ELECTION RESULTS

2000 GENERAL		
Mark Dayton (D)	1,181,553	48.8%
Rod Grams (R)	1,047,474	43.3%
James Gibson (INDC)	140,583	5.8%
2000 PRIMARY		
Mark Dayton (D)	178,972	41.3%
Michael Ciresi (D)	96,874	22.4%
Jerry R. Janezich (D)	90,074	20.8%
Rebecca Yanisch (D)	63,289	14.6%

Elected 2000; 1st term

Born into privilege and heir to the Target Corp. retailing fortune, Dayton has devoted his life to public service and liberal causes in the tradition of Minnesota's Democratic icons Hubert H. Humphrey and Walter F. Mondale. He espouses universal health care, federally subsidized computers in every school and a broad expansion of government aid for the poor.

During his first two years in office, his ideology and his voting record tracked closest with those of his home-state colleague Paul Wellstone, generally regarded as the most liberal member of the Senate until his death in October 2002. The two senators voted the same way 97 percent of the time. In the 107th Congress Dayton opposed President Bush 37 percent of the time; Wellstone was the only senator who broke with Bush more often.

Dayton has been in the spotlight considerably less often than Wellstone was. He is awkward in crowds, displays little affinity for the camaraderie of the Capitol corridors and remains something of an enigma back home. In a February 2002 poll, 41 percent told the Star Tribune newspaper that they did not know anything Dayton had done in his first year in office.

Dayton appeared to be making a conscious effort to raise his visibility as the 108th Congress began. He introduced 10 progressive social policy bills in as many days, nearly matching the amount of legislation he had proposed during the 107th. But he says: "I knew Paul Wellstone and I liked Paul Wellstone. And I know I'm no Paul Wellstone. You've got to be yourself."

Actually, Dayton has been active as a legislator. From his seat on the Agriculture Committee, he helped rewrite the 1996 farm law, which was designed to make farmer income more in tune with market forces and less reliant on federal subsidies. Dayton termed it a failure. He described the update enacted in 2002, which promised a generous boost in government aid, as "an economic recovery bill for our rural communities."

Dayton caught the White House's attention in a big way in 2002 when he teamed with Republican Larry E. Craig of Idaho to win adoption of a Senate amendment that had the potential to torpedo one of Bush's top objectives, reviving fast-track procedures for trade agreements. Their language would have allowed a majority of senators to delete from trade agreements any provision that blocked enforcement of U.S. anti-dumping laws. The amendment, dropped from the final legislation in the face of a veto threat, would have substantially weakened the central tenet of fast-track policy: Congress must accept or reject, but cannot alter, the trade deals a president negotiates.

"It's the most prominent role I've had," Dayton told the Star Tribune. Still, as a first-term senator who was relegated to the minority after an 18-month taste of the majority, he has felt more frustration than power. "Trying to get something moving here is like trying to push the Sta-Puf marshmallow man up Mount Everest," he says.

Dayton's liberal leanings go back to his college days at Yale. While his parents supported Republican Richard M. Nixon for president in 1960 and 1968, Dayton's political hero was Robert F. Kennedy. He protested the Vietnam War and applied the family fortune to left-wing causes. His rebelliousness led the young Dayton to be investigated by the FBI, targeted by the IRS and named to President Nixon's enemies list.

Senior citizens, farmers and labor union members form Dayton's political base. He is a strong advocate of the Democrats' plan to require Medicare to cover the cost of prescription drugs; it was his defining campaign issue. To pay for such coverage, Dayton proposed scrapping Bush's tax cut for people in the top tax bracket. He also floated the idea of taxing drug companies to offset the cost.

After Sept. 11, 2001, Dayton wrote to FBI Director Robert S. Mueller to find out why Mueller refused to disclose allegations of Colleen Rowley, the Minnesota FBI agent who went public with information about how her superiors had thwarted the investigation of Zacarias Moussaoui, later charged with conspiracy in the terrorist hijackings. Dayton has subsequently promoted whistleblower protection legislation from his seat on the Governmental Affairs Committee.

Dayton has been an eager pupil of Robert C. Byrd of West Virginia's in learning the Senate's rules and customs, and in the 107th he was one of the chamber's most attentive and diligent presiding officers — a job generally seen as a thankless task to which freshmen must be assigned.

And he has not been shy about following Byrd's lead and using a single senator's powers to put a hold on some of Bush's nominations — either to express his opposition to their confirmations or to obtain other concessions. In the spring of 2002, for example, he lifted his objections to confirmation of a new head of the Air National Guard only after the organization agreed to give the 148th Fighter Wing in Duluth newer F-16C fighter jets to replace its aging fleet. In the summer, he held up confirmation of more than 60 nominees until he was granted a meeting with administration officials to allay his concerns that the Immigration and Naturalization Service was treating unfairly couples seeking to adopt Cambodian children.

Making it easier for students to pay for college is a long-term goal for Dayton. While more federal spending to solve this problem is a classically liberal solution, he also says he wants to end "overregulation" that bogs down educators in paperwork. Pointing to his copy of libertarian Philip Howard's book, "The Death of Common Sense," Dayton has said, "I agree with it."

His great-grandfather George Dayton started a dry goods store in Minneapolis in 1902 that grew into the nation's fifth-largest retailer, encompassing the Marshall Field's, Mervyn's and Target chains. Dayton Hudson Corp. became Target in 2000. Dayton briefly dabbled in the family business, but he quickly gravitated to public service, working as a science teacher in New York City's Lower East Side and as a counselor of runaway children in Boston. He served as an aide to Mondale and did a stint as state economic development commissioner. He was the state auditor for four years ending in 1995.

Dayton first ran for the Senate in 1982, spending $7 million and garnering 47 percent against GOP incumbent David Durenberger. Frugal Minnesotans derided him as a rich boy who tried to buy a Senate seat. Dayton also failed in a 1998 bid to win the Democratic gubernatorial nomination.

In 2000 Dayton spent $12 million from his own accounts to win election to the Senate by 6 percentage points against one-term conservative Republican Rod Grams. Once again criticized for his heavy campaign spending, Dayton countered that because he had plenty of his own money, he would not be beholden to special-interest groups. "Persistence pays," he says. "I think eventually people saw that I've been committed to public service."

To underscore that commitment, he accepts only $1 of his annual salary and donates the rest to a senior citizen advocacy group in Minnesota. In 2003 he began making himself available for community service work, inviting constituents to sign him up for jobs at their schools, hospitals or small businesses.

KEY VOTES

2002

Yes Pass farm bill reversing crop subsidy limits
No Postpone tougher automobile fuel efficiency standards
Yes Overhaul campaign finance law; ban "soft money" and restrict advocacy advertising
Yes Set federal election standards
No Support oil drilling in Arctic National Wildlife Refuge
Yes Revive fast-track procedures for trade agreements
Yes Create federal insurance coverage for catastrophic terrorist losses
Yes Tighten federal accounting and corporate governance regulation
Yes Advance bipartisan Medicare prescription drug plan
Yes Create independent Sept. 11 commission
Yes Back Democratic Homeland Security Department proposal
No Authorize war against Iraq

2001

No Confirm John Ashcroft as attorney general
No Nullify Clinton Labor Department ergonomics rule
No Cut taxes by $1.35 trillion through fiscal 2011
Yes Pass Democratic bill to bolster rights of patients in managed-care plans
Yes Permit a new round of military base closings
Yes Expand law enforcement power to investigate suspected terrorists

CQ VOTE STUDIES

	PARTY UNITY		PRESIDENTIAL SUPPORT	
	Support	Oppose	Support	Oppose
2002	95%	5%	68%	32%
2001	99%	1%	60%	40%

INTEREST GROUPS

	AFL-CIO	ADA	CCUS	ACU
2002	100%	95%	45%	11%
2001	100%	100%	36%	4%

Sen. Norm Coleman (R)

CAPITOL OFFICE
224-5641
320 Hart 20510-2303; fax 224-8438

COMMITTEES
Agriculture, Nutrition & Forestry
Foreign Relations
(Western Hemisphere, Peace Corps & Narcotics Affairs - chairman)
Governmental Affairs
(Permanent Investigations - chairman)
Small Business & Entrepreneurship

HOMETOWN
St. Paul

BORN
Aug. 17, 1949, Brooklyn, N.Y.

RELIGION
Jewish

FAMILY
Wife, Laurie Coleman; four children (two deceased)

EDUCATION
Hofstra U., B.A. 1971 (political science); Brooklyn Law School, attended 1972-74; U. of Iowa, J.D. 1976

CAREER
Lawyer; state prosecutor and solicitor general; city welfare aide

POLITICAL HIGHLIGHTS
Sought Democratic nomination for mayor of St. Paul, 1989; mayor of St. Paul, 1994-2002 (served as a Democrat 1994-96); Republican nominee for governor, 1998

ELECTION RESULTS

2002 GENERAL		
Norm Coleman (R)	1,116,697	49.5%
Walter F. Mondale (D)	1,067,246	47.3%
Jim Moore (INDC)	45,139	2.0%
2002 PRIMARY		
Norm Coleman (R)	195,630	94.4%
Jack Shepard (R)	11,678	5.6%

Elected 2002; 1st term

Coleman is a Brooklyn native whose accent betrays his roots: He was a high school classmate of New York Democratic Sen. Charles E. Schumer. But the distance he traveled en route to a Senate seat in Minnesota is just a small part of Coleman's unusual political trajectory.

Coleman was a bona fide 1960s liberal who attended Woodstock, led barefoot student protests against the Vietnam War and served as a roadie for the long-forgotten rock group Ten Years After. He eventually earned a law degree and became a state prosecutor and solicitor general in Minnesota before being elected mayor of St. Paul — as a Democrat.

Yet Coleman switched to the Republican Party in December 1996, was re-elected mayor in 1997 and was the party's unsuccessful nominee in the 1998 election for governor won by independent Jesse Ventura.

By 2002, he had become President Bush's handpicked challenger to Democrat Paul Wellstone, a staunch liberal with whom Coleman once was allied. And steadfast White House support helped Coleman to victory despite the sympathy engendered by Wellstone's death when his campaign plane crashed just 11 days before he was to stand for a third term in the Senate. The Democrats replaced Wellstone on the ballot with an icon of Minnesota politics, Walter F. Mondale, who was a Minnesota senator for more than a decade, vice president under Jimmy Carter and the 1984 Democratic presidential nominee.

Coleman's victory by 2 percentage points — less than 50,000 votes — which helped the GOP clinch control of the Senate for the 108th Congress, completed his transformation into a Baby Boomer fiscal and social conservative. Still, he is seeking to position himself as a moderate voice in the Republican Party — something he may have to achieve to obtain electoral security in politically volatile Minnesota.

His ideological shift came about gradually. Coleman points to the deaths of two of his children as infants as inspiring him to oppose abortion and support "pro-family" issues. As mayor of St. Paul during the economic boom of the 1990s, he developed increasingly pro-business sentiments while working to revitalize a city where Democratic voters predominate. His party switch spurred catcalls from Democrats who accused him of political opportunism, but it earned him the warm GOP embrace that lingered long enough to help send him to the Senate.

Coleman lines up with Bush on most defense, trade and tax issues, including support for fast-track trade negotiating authority and reduced regulations on businesses. In 2002 and after, Coleman supported the White House proposals for creating a federal prescription drug benefit, establishing the Homeland Security Department, waging a war against Iraq and permitting workers to invest some of their Social Security set-asides in personal accounts. He also supports making permanent the 2001 Bush tax cut. Yet Coleman said the second wave of tax cuts the president proposed in 2003 were too costly and would not stimulate the economy quickly enough. He joined 10 moderate senators to draft an alternative plan.

In two other breaks with the president, Coleman opposes oil drilling in the Arctic National Wildlife Refuge and would lift the trade embargo of Cuba, in part to bolster export of Minnesota farm goods.

From his first days in the Senate, Coleman indicated that his would be a pragmatic approach. After voting for a narrowly focused drought aid plan, Coleman said he supported it because it had a better chance of enactment than more comprehensive — and expensive — legislation. "When I was running for the United States Senate I promised to get something done for disaster relief for Minnesota farmers," Coleman said in his first Senate speech. "I didn't promise to vote for something everyone knows is going nowhere and then shrug my shoulders and say, 'Gee whiz, I tried.' "

Coleman changed tacks on farm aid in the campaign, at first supporting Bush's position of restraint, then backing a push for new relief. The switch underscores the efforts Coleman has had to make to attract rural voters: With his New York accent, blow-dried hair and gleaming smile, his big-city image was difficult to shake on the campaign trail.

His appointment to the Agriculture Committee may help. Coleman wants to expand farm loans and create a grant program for rural small businesses. And he has spoken in support of alternative energy sources, particularly ethanol and biodiesel made from Minnesota corn and soybeans.

Coleman scored an early coup as a freshman when he was named chairman of the Governmental Affairs Committee's Permanent Subcommittee on Investigations, one of the more powerful forums in Congress for inquiries into government, business and political malfeasance.

His Senate victory did not climax an unbroken record of electoral success. Coleman lost his first race for mayor in 1989; nine years later, he came in 3 points behind Ventura, with a rather unimpressive 34 percent of the vote. Yet the statewide name identification he developed in that race — and his potential to cut into the Democratic vote in St. Paul and other cities — convinced GOP strategists that he was their pick to take on Wellstone. It took some lobbying: Coleman had his sights set on another run for governor, while Republican state legislative leader Tim Pawlenty planned to run for the Senate. But Vice President Dick Cheney called Pawlenty and persuaded him to instead enter the governor's race (which he won) pushing Coleman toward the Senate contest instead.

An eight-year record as mayor was at the heart of Coleman's campaign. The city experienced job growth, new downtown investment and the return of pro hockey to Minnesota for the first time since the North Stars left for Dallas in 1993 — all without raising property taxes. Coleman contended that he had a bipartisan approach that would make him more effective than Wellstone, who was always better known for standing by his principles than for racking up legislative accomplishment.

In reply, Wellstone was able to point to the hearty endorsement his own 1996 re-election has received from Coleman at a state Democratic convention just months before the mayor's party switch. Paradoxically, Coleman's speech at that convention was used in a television advertisement to suggest that his word could not be trusted.

The contest was seemingly deadlocked when Wellstone, his wife, daughter, three aides and two pilots died in the crash of their small chartered plane in northern Minnesota.

Shocked and grieving Democrats turned to Mondale, who would have been the seventh former vice president to later become a senator; the most recent was Hubert H. Humphrey, who after serving under President Johnson was a senator for seven years until his death in 1978.

Many Democrats expected that the Minnesota situation would be something of a replay of what had happened in Missouri's Senate race in 2000, when Democrat Mel Carnahan also died in a campaign plane crash but was elected posthumously. But the tide turned when a televised memorial for Wellstone turned overtly partisan and began a backlash against Mondale. Angered by the service's tone, after the general election Ventura appointed fellow independent Dean Barkley to fill out the rest of Wellstone's term in the 107th Congress.

Rep. Gil Gutknecht (R)

CAPITOL OFFICE
225-2472
gil@mail.house.gov
www.house.gov/gutknecht
425 Cannon 20515-2301; fax 225-3246

COMMITTEES
Agriculture
(Department Operations, Oversight, Nutrition & Forestry - chairman)
Budget
Science

HOMETOWN
Rochester

BORN
March 20, 1951, Cedar Falls, Iowa

RELIGION
Roman Catholic

FAMILY
Wife, Mary Gutknecht; three children

EDUCATION
U. of Northern Iowa, B.A. 1973 (business)

CAREER
Real estate broker; school supplies salesman; auctioneer; computer software salesman

POLITICAL HIGHLIGHTS
Minn. House, 1983-95

ELECTION RESULTS

2002 GENERAL		
Gil Gutknecht (R)	163,570	61.5%
Steve Andreasen (D)	92,165	34.7%
Greg Mikkelson (GREEN)	9,964	3.8%
2002 PRIMARY		
Gil Gutknecht (R)		unopposed
2000 GENERAL		
Gil Gutknecht (R)	159,835	56.4%
Mary Rieder (D)	117,946	41.6%
Rich Osness (LIBERT)	5,440	1.9%

PREVIOUS WINNING PERCENTAGES
1998 (55%); 1996 (53%); 1994 (55%)

Elected 1994; 5th term

Gutknecht likes to read military histories, and he can cite details from biographies of Abraham Lincoln and Winston Churchill. But he also is known to have a weakness for Spam, the oft-derided processed meat loaf produced by his constituents at Hormel Foods Corp. in Austin, Minn. He passes out tins to his colleagues and in 2000 persuaded the Library of Congress to hold an exhibit on the product's place in American life.

The outgoing Gutknecht (GOOT-neck) portrays himself as a commonsense fellow who doesn't put on airs. He has moderated his views since arriving in Washington with the Republican takeover Class of 1994, and he now focuses on Medicare funding and reducing drug costs as well as on such GOP benchmark causes as tax reduction.

He chairs the subcommittee on the Agriculture panel with jurisdiction over dairy, biofuels research and the food stamp program.

A member of the Agriculture Committee since 1999, Gutknecht and other Midwestern lawmakers scored a victory in the new 2002 farm law, which included a three-and-a-half year, $1.3 billion dairy price support program. He defends genetically modified food products that have come under fire from some consumer and environmental groups. He also votes for disaster assistance for farmers and has supported trade liberalization legislation.

On the Budget panel, he sounds a note of caution about tax cuts and increased spending that threaten to balloon the federal deficit only a few years after that beast had seemingly been tamed.

He was one of 31 House Republicans who voted early in 2003 against a huge spending bill that encompassed most of the government's budget, except defense spending, saying that it had "too much spending and too many gimmicks." And, against the backdrop of rising budget deficits, he argued that President Bush should scale back his proposed 2003 tax cuts. "I'm not sure that my average taxpayer out there says, 'What I really need is another $300 in tax relief.'"

Gutknecht believes that controlling spending will be the key to eventually bringing about the return of surpluses. "The demand for spending is enormous," he said. "And it comes from all quarters. Those of us who believe we have to continue to apply fiscal discipline are many times outnumbered."

Gutknecht, who likes to remind his constituents that his name means "good hired hand" in German, goes to great lengths to lobby for the agricultural interests in his district, which is home not only to Spam but also to the Jolly Green Giant of processed-vegetable fame. In 1999, he was so outraged by a year-end spending bill that granted higher subsidies to Northeastern dairy producers, at the expense of those in the upper Midwest, that he quit his position as GOP regional whip.

Prescription drugs manufactured in the United States often are sold at much lower prices in other countries than in the United States, and Gutknecht wants pharmacies and drug wholesalers to be able to re-import them. In 2002, he founded the Republican Caucus for Affordable Pharmaceuticals. In 2002, he angered GOP House leaders when he was one of only eight Republicans who voted against a GOP version of a Medicare prescription drug program because it did not include re-importation language.

When he came to Washington, Gutknecht happily joined his fellow "Republican revolutionaries" in pushing the congressional debate on fiscal policy and social issues to the right. He has tempered that voting record since. In 1998, he was one of only 11 Republicans to vote against a GOP plan to cut taxes by $80 billion over five years, citing concern that doing so would cut into funds needed to shore up Social Security. In 1999, he voted to require background checks for purchases at some gun shows.

And Gutknecht has been more skeptical than many in his party about large increases in military spending. He says he believes in a strong defense, "But just look at the Defense Department and the amount of waste and duplication and mismanagement that we see." Still, he backed the military buildup in the wake of the Sept. 11, 2001, terrorist attacks.

Gutknecht has invested much energy in an effort that is politically appealing even if it irritates some of his colleagues: cutting back on House members' pensions. He wants to bar members from accruing additional pension benefits after they have served six terms — providing incentive for members to leave after a dozen years in office.

A native of Cedar Rapids, Iowa, and a graduate of the University of Northern Iowa there, Gutknecht was active in Republican campaigns from an early age. He is a skilled pitchman — for years he sold school supplies, then worked as an auctioneer. After college, his sales job took him to southeastern Minnesota. He won a seat in the Minnesota House at 31 and spent a dozen years there as a loyal team player in the Independent-Republican caucus, attracting attention for his considerable oratorical ability and rising to the post of party floor leader.

After exploring a bid for an open Senate seat in 1994, he shifted his focus to winning a House seat when Democrat Timothy J. Penny decided to leave Congress after six terms. With his base in the district's leading population center, Rochester, and his ties to the GOP hierarchy, Gutknecht easily got the party's nod and overwhelmed former Republican Rep. Arlen I. Erdahl's comeback bid in the primary. In the general election, Gutknecht won with 55 percent against state Sen. John C. Hottinger, who sought to perpetuate the fiscally conservative Democratic tradition of Penny.

As the 1st District was configured in the 1990s, it was a classic swing district, and Gutknecht never captured more than 56 percent of the vote in his first four elections. The map drawn following the 2000 census gave the 1st a slightly more Republican lean, allowing Gutknecht to relax a bit in his 2002 re-election race; he took 62 percent against Steve Andreasen, a senior National Security Council aide during the Clinton administration.

With the state's population increasingly clustered in and around the Twin Cities, the district, which now stretches across the southern part of the state from South Dakota to Wisconsin, remains primarily rural in character.

KEY VOTES

2002

- No Overhaul campaign finance law; ban "soft money" and restrict advocacy advertising
- Yes Back Bush's defense budget increase
- Yes Extend 1996 welfare law
- Yes Adopt Bush's discretionary spending limit
- No Pass GOP Medicare prescription drug plan
- Yes Create independent Sept. 11 commission
- No Extend union protections to Homeland Security Department employees
- Yes Revive fast-track procedures for trade agreements
- Yes Authorize war against Iraq
- No Advance bankruptcy overhaul opposed by abortion opponents

2001

- Yes Nullify Clinton Labor Department ergonomics rule
- Yes Cut taxes by $1.35 trillion through fiscal 2011
- No Maintain ban on oil drilling in Arctic National Wildlife Refuge
- Yes Approve Bush proposal to limit managed-care plan liability for coverage decisions
- No Divert money from crop subsidy payments to land conservation
- Yes Expand law enforcement power to investigate suspected terrorists

CQ VOTE STUDIES

	PARTY UNITY		PRESIDENTIAL SUPPORT	
	Support	Oppose	Support	Oppose
2002	94%	6%	78%	22%
2001	94%	6%	84%	16%
2000	92%	8%	24%	76%
1999	94%	6%	18%	82%
1998	92%	8%	24%	76%

INTEREST GROUPS

	AFL-CIO	ADA	CCUS	ACU
2002	22%	0%	85%	100%
2001	17%	0%	83%	96%
2000	0%	5%	80%	92%
1999	11%	15%	96%	92%
1998	10%	5%	94%	92%

MINNESOTA 1
South – Rochester, Mankato

One of Minnesota's three rural districts, the 1st runs across the state's entire southern border from South Dakota to the Mississippi River, cut horizontally by Interstate 90 and vertically by Interstate 35. While the rural areas continue to lose population, cities such as Rochester, home to the Mayo Clinic and an IBM facility, and Mankato thrive. But the district's economy is dominated by agriculture and food processing.

Corn, soybeans, sugar beets, hogs and dairy are staples of the agricultural economy. Food processing — from fresh turkey to canned soups — is more prevalent in the western half of the district, where there is no town with more than 20,000 people. Though still more than 90 percent white, Spanish, Hmong, Lao and Somali immigrants have come to take agricultural jobs in towns such as Worthington, which has the state's second-highest enrollment of non-English speakers in its schools, following St. Paul.

While many towns and small farmers support the Democratic-Farmer-Labor Party, Republicans have made gains by preaching fiscal conservatism and stressing rural and farm issues. George W. Bush took just over half of the district's vote in the 2000 presidential election.

Larger farms — particularly dairy — in the east support Republicans. Redistricting following the 2000 census added western farmlands that support Democrats and may make the 1st more competitive in the future. Rochester, once solidly Republican, also has begun to support some Democrats. Blue-collar workers from the Austin-based Hormel meatpacking company, as well as the city of Albert Lea, form a Democratic stronghold. College communities in Mankato (Minnesota State University) and Winona (Winona State University) also support Democrats.

MAJOR INDUSTRY
Agriculture, food processing, health care

CITIES
Rochester, 85,806; Mankato, 32,427; Winona, 27,069; Austin, 23,314; Owatonna, 22,434

NOTABLE
Austin, the birthplace of Spam, is home to the Spam Museum.

Rep. John Kline (R)

CAPITOL OFFICE
225-2271
john.kline@mail.house.gov
www.house.gov/kline
1429 Longworth 20515-2302; fax 225-2595

COMMITTEES
Armed Services
Education & Workforce

HOMETOWN
Lakeville

BORN
Sept. 6, 1947, Allentown, Pa.

RELIGION
Methodist

FAMILY
Wife, Vicky Kline; two children

EDUCATION
Rice U., B.A. 1969 (biology); Shippensburg U., M.S. 1988 (public administration)

MILITARY SERVICE
Marine Corps, 1969-94

CAREER
Think tank executive; farmer; management consultant; Marine officer

POLITICAL HIGHLIGHTS
Republican nominee for U.S. House, 1998, 2000

ELECTION RESULTS

2002 GENERAL		
John Kline (R)	152,970	53.3%
Bill Luther (D)	121,121	42.2%
Samuel D. Garst (NNT)	12,430	4.3%
2002 PRIMARY		
John Kline (R)		unopposed

Elected 2002; 1st term

His election in a newly drawn suburban district outside the Twin Cities returned Kline to the Washington area, where he spent nearly 10 of his 25 years in the Marine Corps — with assignments that included carrying the "football," a briefcase containing the codes that would be used to launch a nuclear attack, for Presidents Carter and Reagan.

Kline's concerns about the future of the Marines inspired his interest in political office, and he points to his time in the military as his most important job-training experience. Appointed to the Armed Services Committee, Kline says the House could benefit from the knowledge of more veterans. "We need to restructure the armed forces," he has said, "so that we're spending money in the right places for the right things."

Still, he expressed diverse interests during his three tough campaigns against Democratic incumbent Bill Luther. Kline won by 32,000 votes in 2002 after losing by 5,000 votes in 2000 and 12,000 votes in 1998.

Also appointed to the Education and the Workforce panel, Kline is a strong fiscal and social conservative who spent the two years before coming to Congress heading a think tank that supports free markets and lower taxes. He backs making permanent the tax cut enacted in 2001 and says workers should be allowed to invest some of their Social Security tax payments as they choose. He also portrays himself as an environmentalist devoted to setting land aside for conservation and recreation.

Kline's two previous bids against Luther made him one of the nation's most seasoned challengers in 2002; he also benefited greatly from Minnesota's congressional map for this decade. The first two Kline-Luther matchups were in the 6th District, which was a differently shaped and somewhat Democratic suburban district in the 1990s. But the redistricting done by a judicial panel recast the 2nd District as Republican-leaning territory. It appeared at first that Luther would face off with Republican Rep. Mark Kennedy in the redrawn 6th, but instead Luther decided to move his residence so that he could face Kline again.

MINNESOTA 2
Southern Twin Cities suburbs

Located south of the Twin Cities, the 2nd includes all or part of seven rapidly growing counties. Transformed from largely rural to suburb-dominated during redistricting following the 2000 census, the district now reflects the 1990s population influx to the Minneapolis-St. Paul metro area.

Residents can hop on Interstate 35 and shoot into the Twin Cities from Dakota and Scott counties (Scott is the fastest-growing county in the state). New, expensive housing developments underscore the area's higher incomes, and population increases in Carver, Scott and particularly Dakota (shared with the 4th District) have made these counties younger and wealthier.

Goodhue, Le Sueur and Rice counties retain an agricultural feel, though people are beginning to move here as well. The cost of living has not yet skyrocketed, however.

Scott and Carver counties propel conservative Republicans to office, while Dakota County has some working-class areas that are faithful Democratic-Farmer-Labor Party supporters. But their political voice is competing with growing numbers of young families, who tend to vote socially progressive but fiscally conservative.

The Rice County towns of Northfield — home to St. Olaf and Carleton colleges — and Faribault also provide Democratic votes, while Goodhue County remains a conservative farming area.

Despite a downturn in the airline industry, Northwest Airlines remains an economic linchpin for the area. Casinos are big business for the Shakopee Mdewakanton Sioux tribe in Prior Lake.

MAJOR INDUSTRY
Manufacturing, casinos, aviation

CITIES
Eagan, 63,557; Burnsville, 60,220; Apple Valley, 45,527; Lakeville, 43,128

NOTABLE
The late Sen. Paul Wellstone was a professor at Carleton College; Green Giant was founded in Le Sueur.

Rep. Jim Ramstad (R)

CAPITOL OFFICE
225-2871
mn03@mail.house.gov
www.house.gov/ramstad
103 Cannon 20515-2303; fax 225-6351

COMMITTEES
Ways & Means

HOMETOWN
Minnetonka

BORN
May 6, 1946, Jamestown, N.D.

RELIGION
Protestant

FAMILY
Single

EDUCATION
U. of Minnesota, B.A. 1968; George Washington U., J.D. 1973

MILITARY SERVICE
Army Reserve, 1968-74

CAREER
Lawyer; professor; congressional and state legislative aide

POLITICAL HIGHLIGHTS
Minn. Senate, 1981-91

ELECTION RESULTS

2002 GENERAL		
Jim Ramstad (R)	213,334	72.0%
Darryl Tyree Stanton (D)	82,575	27.9%
2002 PRIMARY		
Jim Ramstad (R)		unopposed
2000 GENERAL		
Jim Ramstad (R)	222,571	67.6%
Sue Shuff (D)	98,219	29.9%
Bob Odden (LIBERT)	5,302	1.6%

PREVIOUS WINNING PERCENTAGES
1998 (72%); 1996 (70%); 1994 (73%); 1992 (64%); 1990 (67%)

Elected 1990; 7th term

From his senior seat on the Ways and Means Committee, Ramstad has been an unwavering supporter of President Bush's campaigns for lower taxes and liberalized trade. But he steers a far more moderate course than most of the rest of the Republican Conference on a broad range of domestic issues — including abortion, environmental protection, health care, education and gun control.

As a result, he voted against Bush more than a quarter of the time in the 107th Congress, an opposition score higher than all but 10 other House Republicans.

He acknowledges that it isn't easy being a centrist in the often ideologically polarized House. "When controversial votes come up, I often get heat," he has said. But a genial personality and a non-confrontational approach have helped Ramstad plot a quiet course toward acceptance by the Republican leadership.

A recovering alcoholic, Ramstad is keenly interested in boosting treatment for drug and alcohol addicts, and has repeatedly pressed legislation that would require insurance companies to cover the costs of such care. He also pushes for expanded insurance coverage for a range of mental disorders.

Ramstad speaks freely about his struggles. He says he started drinking as a college senior, and he recognized that he needed to do something about his addiction in 1981 when he woke up in jail in Sioux Falls, S.D., after a night of drinking, fighting and a blackout. "Every day, I have to recover," he has said. "Every day I do healthy, positive things so I won't take another drink."

Ramstad's district is home to several medical companies, and he uses his Ways and Means seat to pursue a strong interest in health issues. Concerned that Medicare, the federal medical insurance program for the elderly and disabled, sometimes takes years to approve reimbursement for new medical devices, he introduced legislation in the 107th and 106th Congresses to speed up the process. He also sought to improve access to Medicare+Choice plans for special-needs beneficiaries by allowing plans to target enrollment to such people.

While loyally backing the GOP line, Ramstad took a low-profile role on the two issues that dominated the Ways and Means panel's work in the 107th: Bush's 1.35 trillion, 10-year tax cut package of 2001 and enactment in 2002 of the law reviving fast-track trade negotiating procedures.

But Ramstad had one tax policy victory of his own in the 107th. Just a month after it was introduced, and without a hint of dissent, Congress cleared his legislation to preserve the tax-free treatment of housing allowances for clergy members. The law had the effect of stopping a federal appeals court from deciding whether such a special tax benefit for preachers violated the First Amendment.

In the 106th Congress, Ramstad had won enactment of another narrow change in the tax code. That law guaranteed that parents still could claim the standard child deduction for a son or daughter who had been kidnapped, reversing an IRS policy in the case of a Minnesota couple.

Ramstad seeks to steer a moderate course on abortion rights, backing legalized abortion but also supporting "reasonable limits" on access to the procedure. He would ban the procedure described by its opponents as "partial birth" abortion, labeling it "repulsive and extreme." He supports federal funding for embryonic stem cell research, he says, in part to prevent the private sector from deciding the related legal and moral issues.

After the Sept. 11, 2001, terrorist attacks, Ramstad was among only seven Republicans who defied the GOP leadership and voted to federalize passenger and baggage screeners at the country's bigger airports. (Bush opposed the idea as well, but relented when it was clear Congress would insist on it.)

The upscale, suburban and solidly Republican nature of Ramstad's constituency was not altered by redistricting following the 2000 census, and 3rd District voters still signal a strong desire for gun control and environmental protections. Ramstad reflects those interests. He voted for the package of weapons restrictions that ultimately died in the 106th Congress. In the 105th, he opposed GOP efforts to ease water pollution regulations and restrict the Environmental Protection Agency's regulatory authority. He also has worked with a group of moderates to produce a compromise rewrite of the Endangered Species Act, and he has battled against proposals to allow increased motorboat traffic through northern Minnesota's Boundary Waters Canoe Area Wilderness.

Ramstad's effort to strike a balance between right and left was evident when the House impeached President Clinton. The lawmaker voted for the two articles that were approved by the House and against the two that were rejected.

Government has been an interest of Ramstad's since boyhood. His Web page carries the famous photo of a young Clinton shaking hands with President Kennedy at the White House in 1963. Also in that photo is Ramstad, who was with Clinton in the American Legion Boys Nation contingent that day. Even all these years later, Ramstad has been known to brag that back in 1963, he beat Clinton in a basketball game.

(Adding to his store of presidential relationship trivia, Ramstad in 2002 confided to The Hill, a Capitol Hill newspaper, that President Bush had given him advice on where to buy a suit.)

Ramstad came to Washington three decades ago to study law at George Washington University and work as an aide to a Republican congressman from North Dakota, Thomas S. Kleppe. In 1980, he won a seat in the Minnesota Senate, serving there until he ran for the 3rd District seat vacated in 1990 by veteran Republican Bill Frenzel.

Although his abortion rights stance placed him at odds with many at the party convention, he ultimately defeated four candidates after seven ballots. Ramstad won in November with 67 percent against Democratic investment executive Lewis DeMars and has easily held his seat since; in 2002, he trounced Democrat Darryl Stanton, who listed his occupation as "inventor."

KEY VOTES

2002

Yes Overhaul campaign finance law; ban "soft money" and restrict advocacy advertising
Yes Back Bush's defense budget increase
Yes Extend 1996 welfare law
Yes Adopt Bush's discretionary spending limit
Yes Pass GOP Medicare prescription drug plan
No Create independent Sept. 11 commission
No Extend union protections to Homeland Security Department employees
Yes Revive fast-track procedures for trade agreements
Yes Authorize war against Iraq
Yes Advance bankruptcy overhaul opposed by abortion opponents

2001

Yes Nullify Clinton Labor Department ergonomics rule
Yes Cut taxes by $1.35 trillion through fiscal 2011
Yes Maintain ban on oil drilling in Arctic National Wildlife Refuge
Yes Approve Bush proposal to limit managed-care plan liability for coverage decisions
Yes Divert money from crop subsidy payments to land conservation
Yes Expand law enforcement power to investigate suspected terrorists

CQ VOTE STUDIES

	PARTY UNITY		PRESIDENTIAL SUPPORT	
	Support	Oppose	Support	Oppose
2002	84%	16%	82%	18%
2001	77%	23%	65%	35%
2000	78%	22%	41%	59%
1999	77%	23%	34%	66%
1998	68%	32%	43%	57%

INTEREST GROUPS

	AFL-CIO	ADA	CCUS	ACU
2002	11%	15%	95%	92%
2001	17%	20%	87%	52%
2000	10%	30%	90%	68%
1999	11%	40%	80%	72%
1998	0%	20%	94%	60%

MINNESOTA 3

Hennepin County suburbs — Bloomington, Brooklyn Park, Plymouth

Minnesota's most affluent district, the 3rd encompasses Minneapolis' western suburbs, where large white-collar populations are grounded in fiscal conservatism but adhere to moderate views on social issues, particularly abortion.

With an abundant technology industry, white-collar workers, golf courses and middle-class homes, the 3rd is a classic picture of suburban living. Several Fortune 500 corporations, such as State Farm Insurance, have their headquarters in the district, and many residents commute to large companies just outside the 3rd, such as Northwest Airlines and General Mills. Traffic snarls for commuters driving east from the Lake Minnetonka area have worsened considerably from sustained regional growth.

Brooklyn Park was governed in the early 1990s by Mayor Jesse Ventura, who later became governor with the 3rd's electoral blessing, though the white-collar areas did not favor him. Unlike the faster-growing, more conservative outlying suburbs in the 2nd and 6th districts, the 3rd has sent moderate Republicans to Congress since 1970. The district also elects Republicans to the state legislature, but supported Bill Clinton for president in 1992 and 1996. George W. Bush defeated Al Gore, 50 percent to 46 percent, here in the 2000 presidential election.

Brooklyn Park, Coon Rapids (shared with the 6th) and Brooklyn Center's blue-collar residents are older, conservative Democratic-Farmer-Labor Party voters, but the affluent, Republican south and west portions of the 3rd cast most of the votes, giving the 3rd a tilt to the right.

MAJOR INDUSTRY

Electronics, manufacturing, food processing

CITIES

Bloomington, 85,172; Brooklyn Park, 67,388; Plymouth, 65,894; Coon Rapids (pt.), 58,396; Eden Prairie, 54,901; Minnetonka, 51,301

NOTABLE

Southdale, in Edina, was the nation's first fully enclosed shopping mall (1956); The Mall of America in Bloomington, the nation's largest shopping mall at 4.2 million square feet, attracts more than 40 million visitors a year and employs more than 11,000.

Rep. Betty McCollum (D)

CAPITOL OFFICE
225-6631
www.house.gov/mccollum
1029 Longworth 20515-2304; fax 225-1968

COMMITTEES
Education & Workforce
International Relations
Resources

HOMETOWN
St. Paul

BORN
July 12, 1954, Minneapolis, Minn.

RELIGION
Roman Catholic

FAMILY
Divorced; two children

EDUCATION
Inver Hills Community College, A.A. 1980; College of St. Catherine, B.A. 1987 (education)

CAREER
Substitute teacher; retail saleswoman

POLITICAL HIGHLIGHTS
Candidate for North St. Paul City Council, 1984; North St. Paul City Council, 1987-92; Minn. House, 1993-2001

ELECTION RESULTS

2002 GENERAL		
Betty McCollum (D)	164,597	62.2%
Clyde Billington (R)	89,705	33.9%
Scott J. Raskiewicz (GREEN)	9,919	3.8%
2002 PRIMARY		
Betty McCollum (D)		unopposed
2000 GENERAL		
Betty McCollum (D)	130,403	48.0%
Linda Runbeck (R)	83,852	30.9%
Tom Foley (INDC)	55,899	20.6%

Elected 2000; 2nd term

McCollum is the first woman to represent Minnesota in the House in more than 40 years. The last congresswoman from the state, Coya Knutson, lost in 1958 when she was famously urged by her husband to end her political career and "come home." But McCollum seems determined to stay in Congress awhile.

After winning a second term in 2002, McCollum began searching for "a one-room efficiency" to buy in Washington. She has also sought to continue the work of her predecessor, liberal environmentalist Bruce F. Vento. Her liberal, progressive views seem to sit well with the mostly liberal, progressive residents of St. Paul.

They sit well with Democratic leaders as well: When Nancy Pelosi ran for party whip in 2001, she asked McCollum to give the nominating speech. "It was very exciting because I haven't been a big talker in the caucus. It reinforced that I'm building good relationships," she told The Star-Tribune newspaper. When Pelosi ascended to party leader in the 108th Congress, she named McCollum to the Steering Committee, which makes committee assignments. And McCollum's upper Midwest colleagues selected her to be their regional whip.

In the 107th, she was the freshman class representative on the House Democratic campaign committee and was named by House Democratic leaders to the National Council on the Arts.

When she arrived on Capitol Hill in 2001, McCollum asked for and won a seat on the Resources Committee, where Vento had waged his heartfelt battles to protect public lands and clean up the air and water.

McCollum had served on the Environment and Natural Resources Committee during her eight years in the state House, and on Capitol Hill she introduced legislation to study whether the entire stretch of the Mississippi River — from its headwaters in Minnesota to the Gulf of Mexico — should be included in the National Trails System. She also visited the north slope of Alaska to view proposed oil drilling sites. She says she is opposed to drilling in the Arctic National Wildlife Refuge.

A former substitute teacher, McCollum sits on the Education and the Workforce Committee. In the 107th she led a determined but unsuccessful effort by Minnesota lawmakers to change key provisions of the measure that rewrote most federal education law. Officials in Minnesota said the state would lose millions of dollars under the plan, particularly because of the cost of administering annual testing for students and the fact that federal funding formulas were revised. McCollum, the only Minnesotan on the Education panel, was one of only six House Democrats to vote against the final bill. (Only one Minnesotan in the House voted for it.)

McCollum spent much of her first term keeping the public spotlight on the plight of two Nigerian women sentenced to death by stoning. One was found guilty of adultery, the other for having sex out of wedlock. McCollum offered a House resolution condemning the sentences, which were handed out under a strict reading of Islamic code, and urging Nigerian authorities not to carry out the executions.

In her first House term, McCollum compiled a solidly Democratic voting record, backing her party on 97 percent of the votes on which the two parties were opposed. She has a 100 percent rating from the liberal Americans for Democratic Action.

McCollum says her public policy views were shaped by her upbringing in a penny-pinching middle-class household, and by her background as a teacher and sales clerk. She says her retail background — she worked at such stores as J.C. Penney, Sears and Dayton's — taught her a lesson that has proven equally valuable in politics. "Retail teaches you to listen to people. It's not about what I want to give you. It's about what you need to make your life better," she told the Star-Tribune.

McCollum was born and raised in the Twin Cities area. She studied at a community college and received her bachelor's degree when she was 32, at about the time she was venturing into politics.

She has continued her education since arriving on Capitol Hill, taking Spanish classes offered by the Agriculture Department. Although her district is only 5 percent Hispanic, McCollum told Roll Call, a Capitol Hill newspaper, that learning a new language helped her understand the problems faced by those for whom English is not their native language. Her district also includes a large contingent of Hmong refugees from Laos.

McCollum says she decided to become politically active when, as the mother of young children, she approached the city manager of North St. Paul to demand repairs to playground equipment. "He showed me this gazillion-year park repair project and I said, 'No. We need to make this more of a priority,' " she told the Star-Tribune.

She ran for city council, lost that first bid, but won in a second attempt. She moved to the legislature six years later, beating two incumbents thrown into the same district by decennial redistricting. McCollum rose through party ranks to become one of four assistant majority leaders.

Despite her 14 years in elective office, McCollum says she had not thought of running for Congress until Vento announced in 2000 that he would not run for a 13th term and revealed that he had a rare form of lung cancer. Although six other Democrats sought to succeed Vento, McCollum gained an essential edge for the September primary when she won the state Democratic Party's endorsement at its convention in June.

McCollum drew a seasoned Republican foe in state Sen. Linda Runbeck, but her biggest worry seemed to be the possible siphoning of Democratic votes by independent candidate Tom Foley, a former Democrat and longtime Ramsey County attorney. But Foley, who ran as a fiscal conservative, appeared to draw votes from both candidates.

Though McCollum missed a majority with 48 percent of the vote — the second-lowest percentage for any 2000 House winner — she easily outran Runbeck, who took 31 percent. Foley finished with 21 percent. In 2002 McCollum was re-elected with 62 percent of the vote.

KEY VOTES

2002

- Yes Overhaul campaign finance law; ban "soft money" and restrict advocacy advertising
- Yes Back Bush's defense budget increase
- No Extend 1996 welfare law
- No Adopt Bush's discretionary spending limit
- No Pass GOP Medicare prescription drug plan
- Yes Create independent Sept. 11 commission
- Yes Extend union protections to Homeland Security Department employees
- No Revive fast-track procedures for trade agreements
- No Authorize war against Iraq
- No Advance bankruptcy overhaul opposed by abortion opponents

2001

- No Nullify Clinton Labor Department ergonomics rule
- No Cut taxes by $1.35 trillion through fiscal 2011
- Yes Maintain ban on oil drilling in Arctic National Wildlife Refuge
- No Approve Bush proposal to limit managed-care plan liability for coverage decisions
- Yes Divert money from crop subsidy payments to land conservation
- Yes Expand law enforcement power to investigate suspected terrorists

CQ VOTE STUDIES

	PARTY UNITY		PRESIDENTIAL SUPPORT	
	Support	Oppose	Support	Oppose
2002	98%	2%	25%	75%
2001	96%	4%	28%	72%

INTEREST GROUPS

	AFL-CIO	ADA	CCUS	ACU
2002	89%	100%	40%	4%
2001	100%	100%	39%	4%

MINNESOTA 4

Ramsey County – St. Paul and suburbs

St. Paul's liberal university communities, bedroom neighborhoods, state government and labor populations provide a consistent stronghold for the Democratic-Farmer-Labor Party. Represented in Congress by a Democrat since 1949, voters in the 4th — slightly less than half of whom live in St. Paul — have elected DFL candidates at all levels of government. But as with much of central Minnesota, the district has an independent streak, as demonstrated by support for Ross Perot in the 1992 presidential election and Jesse Ventura in the 1998 gubernatorial race.

St. Paul gained population in the 1990s, though it grew much slower than surrounding areas. The district includes independent and moderate voters in parts of fast-growing Washington County and affluent northern suburbs such as North Oaks and White Bear Lake.

St. Paul is a traditionally Democratic city with a large German and Irish-Catholic population. The city developed as a major port and railroading center and still has a strong labor tradition. Today, blue-collar, black and Hispanic communities contribute to the city's Democratic flavor. It also is a center of Hmong culture in the United States. Forty percent of students in St. Paul's schools are non-English speakers.

Home to the state capital and the headquarters of 3M, the 4th has a large percentage of white-collar workers who live in middle- and high-income neighborhoods. Several colleges, including the University of Minnesota's agriculture school, are located in affluent communities around St. Paul. The limited Republican base is in the growing suburbs to the north of the city that have drawn city residents and newcomers.

MAJOR INDUSTRY

State government, higher education, manufacturing

CITIES

St. Paul, 287,151; Maplewood, 34,947; Roseville, 33,690; Oakdale, 26,653; Shoreview, 25,924; White Bear Lake, 24,325; New Brighton, 22,206

NOTABLE

Supreme Court Justices Warren E. Burger and Harry A. Blackmun grew up in St. Paul; St. Paul was originally called Pig's Eye Landing, after bootlegger Pierre "Pig's Eye" Parrant; In 2002, the area elected Mee Moua to the state Senate, making her the first Hmong state legislator in the United States.

Rep. Martin Olav Sabo (D)

CAPITOL OFFICE
225-4755
martin.sabo@mail.house.gov
www.house.gov/sabo
2336 Rayburn 20515-2305; fax 225-4886

COMMITTEES
Appropriations

HOMETOWN
Minneapolis

BORN
Feb. 28, 1938, Crosby, N.D.

RELIGION
Lutheran

FAMILY
Wife, Sylvia Ann Sabo; two children

EDUCATION
Augsburg College, B.A. 1959 (history); U. of Minnesota, attended 1960

CAREER
Public official

POLITICAL HIGHLIGHTS
Minn. House, 1961-79 (minority leader, 1969-73, Speaker, 1973-79)

ELECTION RESULTS

2002 GENERAL		
Martin Olav Sabo (D)	171,572	67.0%
Daniel Nielsen Mathias (R)	66,271	25.9%
Tim Davis (GR)	17,825	7.0%
2002 PRIMARY		
Martin Olav Sabo (D)		unopposed
2000 GENERAL		
Martin Olav Sabo (D)	176,629	69.2%
Frank Taylor (R)	58,191	22.8%
Rob Tomich (INDC)	11,323	4.4%
Renee Lavoi (CNSTP)	4,522	1.8%
Chuck P. Charnstrom (LIBERT)	4,480	1.8%

PREVIOUS WINNING PERCENTAGES
1998 (67%); 1996 (64%); 1994 (62%); 1992 (63%); 1990 (73%); 1988 (72%); 1986 (73%); 1984 (70%); 1982 (66%); 1980 (70%); 1978 (62%)

Elected 1978; 13th term

One of the most senior Democrats in the House, Sabo is also one of the most influential, in spite of his natural reserve and aversion to self-promotion. With the esteem he enjoys back home in Minneapolis, he has no need to toot his own horn.

Endorsing his 2002 re-election bid, the Minneapolis Star-Tribune said that his 24 years in Congress made Sabo "a Minnesota state treasure." He certainly has done more than the obligatory work of a local congressman. He has brought to the state millions of dollars for transit and environmental projects, while also developing a reputation on the national level as an authority on the federal budget.

The new Democratic leadership under Nancy Pelosi of California rewarded him at the start of the 108th Congress with the job of top-ranking Democrat of the new Homeland Security Appropriations Subcommittee, a position likely to enhance his influence. He had served as ranking member of the Transportation Subcommittee in the 107th.

In his politics, Sabo is as liberal as they come, which may endear him to his left-leaning party leadership but limits his effectiveness in a House run by conservative Republicans. It's hard to imagine some of his proposals becoming law anytime soon. Sabo would change the tax laws to discourage "excessive executive pay." He wants to limit the tax deductibility of an executive's pay to 25 times the amount paid a company's lowest-paid worker, which he says would send the message "that those who work on the factory floor are as important to a company's success as those who work in the executive suite."

Sabo also would guarantee health insurance to all Americans through a single-payer, tax-financed system. He backs public financing of political campaigns as a solution to persistent concerns about influence-buying by big private donors.

Though low-key in manner, preferring one-on-one contacts with colleagues over talking before a camera lens, Sabo nonetheless knows how to work a spending bill when he wants to send a message. He made his point loud and clear when President Bush in 2001 sought to implement a North American Free Trade Agreement ruling requiring that all U.S. roads be open to Mexican trucks. The administration initially ignored Sabo's proposal requiring that the trucks be certified according to U.S. safety standards. But the White House was forced to strike a deal after Sabo won adoption of a killer amendment to the fiscal 2002 Transportation spending bill that would have banned Mexican truckers entirely by cutting off funds to process their applications.

Sabo plans to closely scrutinize the Homeland Security Department from his new subcommittee post. He has voiced concern about moving already troubled agencies — the Transportation Security Administration, in particular — into a new department with other agencies that have not been performing well.

Sabo's natural reserve sets him apart from more-combative liberals in the House, though he is a true believer in government's ability to improve the lot of working Americans. The Star Tribune once wrote, "Sabo's conduct as a legislator suggests a variation of an old Norwegian joke: He's a politician who cares so passionately about an issue that he'll almost speak out about it."

For a time, Sabo aspired to a larger role in the House leadership. He was a deputy whip and chairman of the Democratic Study Group, a collection of liberal members. But when he sought the Democratic whip post for the 100th Congress, he ran a laconic campaign and ultimately gave up when he figured he did not have the votes to win.

Sabo's political values are rooted in his upbringing. He was born of Norwegian immigrant parents on a North Dakota farm. (His last name means "farm by the sea.") His family donated land for the community's school, where his mother volunteered as a cook; Sabo was valedictorian of a graduating class of three. He recalls how grateful his family was to finally get electricity from the Roosevelt-era Rural Electrification Administration.

Sabo is a staunch proponent of pay equity for workers. He has fought to increase the minimum wage, and in 2000 cosponsored a bill that would have required federal contractors to pay a "living wage" necessary for a family of four to live at the federal poverty level, at the time $8.20 per hour. Sabo has used his seat on the Appropriations Committee to fight proposed budget cuts in low-income heating assistance, housing, education and environmental protection programs. He is a strong supporter of federal funding for mass transit and alternative transportation such as bicycling.

Despite his advocacy of government spending, Sabo was an important contributor to the elimination of the budget deficit in the late 1990s. As chairman of the Budget Committee in the 103rd Congress, he helped build the case for President Clinton's tax-raising, deficit-cutting budget plan. Its passage in 1993, without a single Republican vote, was a factor in the declining deficits and economic growth that followed.

Well-liked by Budget Committee staff members, Sabo's quickness with numbers borders on legendary. He left aides gaping once when he was handed a long table of numbers. He glanced down the columns, handed it back and said, "It doesn't add up."

His favorite numbers are baseball statistics. A huge Minnesota Twins fan, he listens to broadcasts of games over the Internet on his office computer. He also coaches the Democrats' team in the annual congressional baseball game.

Sabo was first elected to the state House at age 22, serving for 18 years, including six as speaker. When Democrat Donald Fraser left the House for an unsuccessful Senate bid in 1978, Sabo easily won his party's nomination and was elected comfortably in the dependably Democratic 5th District. His re-election races have been routine, except for an intraparty challenge in 1992 when a faction of liberals complained that Sabo had opposed across-the-board defense cuts. Sabo won the primary with 67 percent.

KEY VOTES

2002

- Yes Overhaul campaign finance law; ban "soft money" and restrict advocacy advertising
- Yes Back Bush's defense budget increase
- No Extend 1996 welfare law
- No Adopt Bush's discretionary spending limit
- No Pass GOP Medicare prescription drug plan
- Yes Create independent Sept. 11 commission
- Yes Extend union protections to Homeland Security Department employees
- No Revive fast-track procedures for trade agreements
- No Authorize war against Iraq
- No Advance bankruptcy overhaul opposed by abortion opponents

2001

- No Nullify Clinton Labor Department ergonomics rule
- No Cut taxes by $1.35 trillion through fiscal 2011
- Yes Maintain ban on oil drilling in Arctic National Wildlife Refuge
- No Approve Bush proposal to limit managed-care plan liability for coverage decisions
- No Divert money from crop subsidy payments to land conservation
- No Expand law enforcement power to investigate suspected terrorists

CQ VOTE STUDIES

	PARTY UNITY		PRESIDENTIAL SUPPORT	
	Support	Oppose	Support	Oppose
2002	96%	4%	25%	75%
2001	91%	9%	14%	86%
2000	96%	4%	90%	10%
1999	92%	8%	86%	14%
1998	90%	10%	89%	11%

INTEREST GROUPS

	AFL-CIO	ADA	CCUS	ACU
2002	89%	100%	35%	0%
2001	92%	100%	26%	0%
2000	90%	100%	38%	0%
1999	75%	95%	13%	0%
1998	100%	90%	24%	0%

MINNESOTA 5

Minneapolis and suburbs

Established at the northernmost navigable point on the Mississippi River, Minneapolis accounts for most of the 5th's vote and has supported liberal Rep. Sabo since 1978. The 2000 round of redistricting may have made the district even more Democratic, moving the affluent suburb of Edina into the 3rd District and adding first-ring northern suburbs. For the first time in a half-century, Minneapolis gained population in the 1990s, though it grew much slower than surrounding areas.

Minneapolis is home to many large corporations, such as General Mills, Target Corp. and U.S. Bancorp. The 5th attracted well-educated white-collar workers in the economic boom of the 1990s, but the shift has not changed the area's liberal-mindedness. Minneapolis has the highest number of theater seats per capita in the United States outside of New York City. This strong arts community's liberal lean is bolstered by the University of Minnesota in eastern Minneapolis. Residents who flock to the area's many lakes also support environmental protections. Green Party presidential candidate Ralph Nader received 8 percent of the 5th's vote in 2000 — one of his best showings in the nation.

Traffic and the lack of affordable housing have become large problems here. Though Minneapolis was dubbed "murderapolis" by the New York Times in 1996, the city has managed to cut crime and redevelop downtown riverfront areas.

Although Minneapolis is known for its Scandinavian heritage, the 5th is the state's most racially diverse district. Asian and black communities — including a sizable Somali population — contribute to the district's Democratic-Farmer-Labor voter rolls. The district's poorer communities lie north of downtown.

MAJOR INDUSTRY

Corporate administration, banking, higher education

CITIES

Minneapolis, 382,618; St. Louis Park, 44,126; Richfield, 34,439

NOTABLE

The Minneapolis Sculpture Garden at Walker Art Center features an enormous metal spoon holding a cherry; Democrat Hubert H. Humphrey was elected mayor of Minneapolis in 1945; Minneapolis was the locale of the "Mary Tyler Moore Show."

Rep. Mark Kennedy (R)

CAPITOL OFFICE
225-2331
mark.kennedy@mail.house.gov
markkennedy.house.gov
1415 Longworth 20515-2306; fax 225-6475

COMMITTEES
Financial Services
Transportation & Infrastructure

HOMETOWN
Watertown

BORN
April 11, 1957, Benson, Minn.

RELIGION
Roman Catholic

FAMILY
Wife, Debbie Kennedy; four children

EDUCATION
Saint John's U. (Minn.), B.A. 1978 (accounting); U. of Michigan, M.B.A. 1983

CAREER
Giftware company financial executive; food company financial director; accountant

POLITICAL HIGHLIGHTS
No previous office

ELECTION RESULTS

2002 GENERAL		
Mark Kennedy (R)	164,747	57.3%
Janet Robert (D)	100,738	35.1%
Dan Becker (INDC)	21,484	7.5%
2002 PRIMARY		
Mark Kennedy (R)		unopposed
2000 GENERAL		
Mark Kennedy (R)	138,957	48.1%
David Minge (D)	138,802	48.0%
Gerald W. Brekke (INDC)	7,875	2.7%

Elected 2000; 2nd term

Kennedy has now served a term in the House and won a decisive re-election victory, putting to rest doubts about whether his first election was a fluke; in 2000 he unseated a Democratic incumbent by only 155 votes.

In his initial campaign, Kennedy jokingly urged voters to send him to Congress to prove there are Kennedys who are Republicans. The Minnesota Kennedy had a grandmother named Rose, and he comes from a large Roman Catholic family with plenty of involvement in politics: His grandfather was mayor of Murdoch, in rural Swift county, and his father was on the county school board. But that is where any similarity ends between him and the Massachusetts political family of the same name. All of Mark Kennedy's relatives in public life have been Republicans, and his own ideology reflects the mostly conservative and rural constituency of southwestern Minnesota that initially sent him to Congress.

In 2002, a new congressional map drawn by a state court for this decade dramatically relocated the 2nd District, which Kennedy then represented, and put his house just across the border in the newly configured 6th District. Kennedy told the St. Paul Pioneer Press that a group of friends had offered to "hoist up my home and drag it" the necessary half-mile, but he decided instead to run in the 6th — which arcs around three sides of the Minneapolis-St. Paul metropolitan area and extends as far west as St. Cloud. Though that district is home to only about 15 percent of his old constituents, its voting patterns made it appear somewhat more friendly to him than the new 2nd.

Although the 6th District's incumbent, Democrat Bill Luther, decided to run in the 2nd, Kennedy wound up facing a well-funded Democrat anyway: attorney Janet Robert, who was spending mainly her own money. The campaign was bruising, but Kennedy cruised to a 22 percentage point victory in a race that most observers had believed would be much closer.

Kennedy, who says, "I am for better or worse a businessman," was named to the Financial Services Committee in the 108th Congress. He says his priorities include enhancing the stock of affordable housing and further bolstering corporate accountability. During the debate in the 107th, after the collapses of Enron Corp. and WorldCom Inc., he was among those pressing for tough punishment for guilty executives and stricter corporate accounting standards.

Financial Services is a good fit with his background. He earned an undergraduate degree in accounting and worked as a CPA for Arthur Andersen for several years. He then got a master's in business administration and took a job with Pillsbury's international treasury department. He was an executive at Federated Department Stores in Cincinnati and then at ShopKo in Green Bay, Wis., before returning to Minnesota in 1995 as chief financial officer with Department 56, the specialty giftware company.

To take the Financial Services spot, Kennedy left the Agriculture Committee, where he was heavily involved in the debate on the 2002 farm bill. He did his best to look out for the interests of the corn, soybean and dairy farmers in his rural district. Kennedy told the Minneapolis Star Tribune, however, that he is "not a farmer, but a rural person." His house is on 60 acres just outside Watertown, about 40 miles west of Minneapolis. He rents some of the land out for farming and rhapsodizes about the wildlife that wanders through his property. He told the newspaper he gets choked up when he watches "Hoosiers," a movie set in a small town in Indiana.

He has persevered in efforts to gain federal funding for his district's transportation needs. A member of the Transportation and Infrastructure Committee, in his first term he hosted both Republican Tom Petri of Wisconsin, the chairman of the committee's Highway Subcommittee, and Transportation Secretary Norman Y. Mineta to show them his district's transportation needs. Mineta was so struck by the freshman lawmaker's pitch that he gave him the nickname "Roads" Kennedy. Kennedy was able to obtain funds for several projects in and around St. Cloud in the 107th.

While casting a generally dependable vote for his party and President Bush, Kennedy in the 107th voted against allowing drilling in the Arctic National Wildlife Refuge and against the Bush administration's education bill. Most members of the Minnesota delegation opposed the education measure, objecting to its intrusion on local controls.

Kennedy won a partial victory in 2002 when elements of the first bill he introduced — to improve rural emergency medical service training and equipment — were included in another bill that became law. He also won House passage of a bill he wrote that would protect the privacy of the records of home-schooled students.

Kennedy has three brothers and three sisters, and he spent much of his childhood in Pequot Lakes, a small town in the north-central part of the state where his father was the local banker and sat on the school board for 27 years. Kennedy was a sports star in high school and active in the 4-H Club. In college he worked on Republican Rudy Boschwitz's successful 1978 Senate campaign, and he says he always knew that one day he would run for office because of his family's history of involvement in politics.

That day came in 2000. Kennedy decided to make his electoral debut in a race for the House against four-term Democratic incumbent David Minge. "The things I really care about are largely impacted by the federal government," he told the Star Tribune, mentioning defense and foreign policy as well as programs that affect rural areas. He won the GOP nomination with ease and was able to focus on Minge, who was something of a moderate. Minge's incumbency almost rescued him, but the election night tally showed Kennedy the winner by 155 votes. Minge asked for a recount, but withdrew the request more than a month later when it became clear he would not reverse the outcome.

That made Kennedy one of two Republicans to unseat a House Democratic incumbent in 2000. Having won the second-closest House race in 2000, Kennedy moved aggressively to supplement his campaign war chest as soon as he took office.

KEY VOTES

2002

- No Overhaul campaign finance law; ban "soft money" and restrict advocacy advertising
- \+ Back Bush's defense budget increase
- Yes Extend 1996 welfare law
- Yes Adopt Bush's discretionary spending limit
- Yes Pass GOP Medicare prescription drug plan
- No Create independent Sept. 11 commission
- No Extend union protections to Homeland Security Department employees
- Yes Revive fast-track procedures for trade agreements
- Yes Authorize war against Iraq
- No Advance bankruptcy overhaul opposed by abortion opponents

2001

- Yes Nullify Clinton Labor Department ergonomics rule
- Yes Cut taxes by $1.35 trillion through fiscal 2011
- Yes Maintain ban on oil drilling in Arctic National Wildlife Refuge
- Yes Approve Bush proposal to limit managed-care plan liability for coverage decisions
- No Divert money from crop subsidy payments to land conservation
- Yes Expand law enforcement power to investigate suspected terrorists

CQ VOTE STUDIES

	PARTY UNITY		PRESIDENTIAL SUPPORT	
	Support	Oppose	Support	Oppose
2002	97%	3%	90%	10%
2001	93%	7%	86%	14%

INTEREST GROUPS

	AFL-CIO	ADA	CCUS	ACU
2002	11%	0%	95%	96%
2001	17%	10%	91%	88%

MINNESOTA 6
North and east Twin Cities suburbs; St. Cloud

One of Minnesota's three suburban-oriented districts, the 6th stretches from east and north of the Twin Cities through conservative, developing areas northwest to St. Cloud. The district is tied together by Interstate 94, which runs from St. Cloud through the Twin Cities to Wisconsin, and the burgeoning Northstar Corridor that runs along the Mississippi River. Officials hope a planned 82-mile commuter train line to link Rice in Benton County with the Twin Cities will help alleviate traffic congestion along the corridor and create jobs.

Development has not yet made St. Cloud a Twin Cities suburb, though the former granite quarrying city is one of the fastest-growing in the state. Home to a mix of blue-collar Democrats and white-collar Republicans, it lies within heavily Catholic Stearns County.

Anoka and Wright counties, to the north and west of Minneapolis and its first-ring suburbs, include new, wealthy suburban developments and also exurban hobby farms. Washington County, to the east and north of St. Paul, includes Woodbury (a small part of which is in the 2nd), which doubled in population in the 1990s, and the cosmopolitan small town of Stillwater on the St. Croix River, which marks the Wisconsin border. Sherburne County grew by more than 50 percent in the 1990s.

The 6th is a competitive district with a slight GOP lean. Young, high-income families that fuel the region's growth tend to favor fiscal conservatism except on social issues such as public safety and education. Transplants from the north are more liberal on government spending but are likely to be socially conservative. Blue-collar communities in the suburbs of Anoka and Washington counties are faithful Democratic-Farmer-Labor Party supporters. Anoka as a whole is a swing county that also includes conservative Democrats and young Republicans. Independent Jesse Ventura won every county in the 6th during his 1998 gubernatorial bid.

MAJOR INDUSTRY
Corporate administration, manufacturing

CITIES
St. Cloud, 59,107; Blaine, 44,942; Woodbury (pt.), 44,767; Andover, 26,588; Ramsey, 18,510

NOTABLE
Writer and radio show host Garrison Keillor was born in Anoka.

Rep. Collin C. Peterson (D)

CAPITOL OFFICE
225-2165
www.house.gov/collinpeterson
2159 Rayburn 20515-2307; fax 225-1593

COMMITTEES
Agriculture
Select Intelligence

HOMETOWN
Detroit Lakes

BORN
June 29, 1944, Fargo, N.D.

RELIGION
Lutheran

FAMILY
Divorced; three children

EDUCATION
Moorhead State U., B.A. 1966 (accounting)

MILITARY SERVICE
Minn. National Guard, 1963-69

CAREER
Accountant

POLITICAL HIGHLIGHTS
Minn. Senate, 1977-87; sought Democratic nomination for U.S. House, 1982; Democratic nominee for U.S. House, 1984, 1986; sought Democratic nomination for U.S. House, 1988

ELECTION RESULTS

2002 GENERAL		
Collin C. Peterson (D)	170,234	65.3%
Dan Stevens (R)	90,342	34.6%
2002 PRIMARY		
Collin C. Peterson (D)		unopposed
2000 GENERAL		
Collin C. Peterson (D)	185,771	68.7%
Glen Menze (R)	79,175	29.3%
Owen Sivertson (CNSTP)	5,550	2.1%

PREVIOUS WINNING PERCENTAGES
1998 (72%); 1996 (68%); 1994 (51%); 1992 (50%); 1990 (54%)

Elected 1990; 7th term

Peterson is a fiscal conservative. He is also pro-business, anti-abortion and anti-gun control. He likes the idea of a constitutional amendment on school prayer. As a result, his fellow Democrats routinely mention him as a potential party-switcher. But, while he ranks among the top 10 Democrats for crossing party lines on House votes, Peterson said after the 2002 election that he isn't interested in joining the GOP.

He would rather work through the "Blue Dogs," the group of conservative Democrats that Peterson helped found and that is often at odds with liberal party leaders. "We are the only people willing to work with the Republicans and actually legislate," he says. "The Democrats just trash everything they are trying to do."

Peterson and the Blue Dogs can sometimes be more conservative than the majority of Republicans. Given a choice between a balanced budget and tax cuts, they'd take a balanced budget.

In 2001, Peterson was one of just 10 Democrats who voted for a $958 billion package of tax cuts proposed by President Bush. But he declined to go along with a larger proposal calling for $1.6 trillion in tax cuts over 10 years. Peterson also backed an unsuccessful amendment that would have delayed or canceled parts of the tax cuts if Congress failed to pass spending cuts to keep the budget in balance. He said, "We need to remember how far we've come from the days of huge yearly federal deficits." When Republicans came back in 2002 with proposals to make the tax cuts permanent, Peterson voted no.

On the issues of taxes, Peterson is to the right of even most Republicans. He teamed up with Georgia Republican John Linder in the 106th Congress to propose abolishing the Internal Revenue Service and replacing federal income and payroll taxes with a 23 percent national sales tax. A former accountant, Peterson says the tax code is overly complex and that simplification would cure a host of economic ills.

"It could solve our balance of trade problems because our exports will not have taxes built into their prices. And, it will be good for the family farmers who want their children to inherit the farm because there will be no inheritance tax."

On other issues, too, Peterson is a dissident among dissidents, breaking with his fellow Blue Dogs. In 1999, he was one of only two Democrats to vote against bipartisan legislation empowering patients of HMOs, including enabling them to sue their medical plans over the denial or delay of care. When the debate resurfaced in 2001, Peterson cosponsored a Republican leadership alternative that did not expand patients' rights to sue their health plans. The following year, he was one of just eight Democrats who voted for a GOP bill creating a drug benefit for Medicare beneficiaries by relying on private insurers.

Peterson departs from fiscal conservatism in a couple of ways. He supports public financing of election campaigns, and he is a fierce defender of big government spending on the farm subsidies that are popular in his agriculture-dependent district.

A member of the Agriculture Committee, he was part of the House-Senate conference committee that wrote the final 2002 farm bill boosting spending by $73.5 billion over 10 years. The measure reversed a 1996 law designed to wean farmers from federal price supports, a longtime goal of fiscal conservatives. Peterson declared the bill a triumph, even as the federal budget slipped back into deficit. "We've renewed our commitment to rural America," he said.

Peterson likes to share in the credit for defeating the perennial amendment to the agriculture spending bill to kill the sugar price-support program. The 7th District is home to many sugar beet farmers. But he has been less successful in protecting upper Midwestern dairy farmers from national pricing structures that favor producers in other regions.

Peterson tends to follow big labor's preferences on international trade, voting in 2002 against granting the president fast-track authority to negotiate trade agreements. In 2000, he opposed permanently granting China normal trade status.

Peterson draws high marks from both the National Right to Life Committee and the National Rifle Association. An avid sportsman, he is the co-chairman of the Congressional Sportsmen's Caucus and once boasted he has "more dead animals on my wall than anybody in this Congress, except for [Alaska Republican] Don Young." Outdoor Life magazine featured him in 2000 as a friend of the sportsman in its voter guide. During an interview with the magazine, he reinforced the point by pulling out two guns he keeps in a closet in his Capitol Hill office.

Environmentalists attacked Peterson in the 106th Congress for pushing a bill allowing states to establish hunting seasons for cormorants, which Peterson blamed for devastating game fish populations. But he also worked with the Humane Society on a measure to ban the interstate transport of birds for cockfighting.

A pilot and a musician, Peterson was a trombonist in the Army National Guard band for six years. He enjoys performing at small venues, such as fundraisers, as a country-rock guitarist and singer. He once appeared with country singer Willie Nelson at a Farm Aid concert.

Before his election to the House, Peterson served for 10 years in the Minnesota Senate. In the 1980s, he made four unsuccessful bids for a House seat; in two of those attempts, he failed to get even the Democratic nomination.

Peterson decided to run again in 1990 when Republican Rep. Arlan Stangeland faced criticism over using his House credit card to charge several calls to or from the phone of a female Virginia lobbyist. Peterson was careful to present himself as a "new Collin Peterson," and he took 54 percent of the vote.

After scratching out close re-election victories in 1992 and 1994, Peterson has since won easily.

KEY VOTES

2002

- No Overhaul campaign finance law; ban "soft money" and restrict advocacy advertising
- Yes Back Bush's defense budget increase
- Yes Extend 1996 welfare law
- No Adopt Bush's discretionary spending limit
- Yes Pass GOP Medicare prescription drug plan
- Yes Create independent Sept. 11 commission
- Yes Extend union protections to Homeland Security Department employees
- No Revive fast-track procedures for trade agreements
- Yes Authorize war against Iraq
- No Advance bankruptcy overhaul opposed by abortion opponents

2001

- No Nullify Clinton Labor Department ergonomics rule
- Yes Cut taxes by $1.35 trillion through fiscal 2011
- No Maintain ban on oil drilling in Arctic National Wildlife Refuge
- Yes Approve Bush proposal to limit managed-care plan liability for coverage decisions
- No Divert money from crop subsidy payments to land conservation
- No Expand law enforcement power to investigate suspected terrorists

CQ VOTE STUDIES

	PARTY UNITY		PRESIDENTIAL SUPPORT	
	Support	Oppose	Support	Oppose
2002	64%	36%	54%	46%
2001	63%	37%	42%	58%
2000	60%	40%	49%	51%
1999	51%	49%	39%	61%
1998	54%	46%	55%	45%

INTEREST GROUPS

	AFL-CIO	ADA	CCUS	ACU
2002	56%	45%	70%	48%
2001	75%	50%	55%	43%
2000	60%	60%	52%	32%
1999	67%	40%	72%	52%
1998	80%	60%	56%	56%

MINNESOTA 7

West – Moorhead, Willmar

Stretching 330 miles from north to south, the vast 7th spans almost all of the state's western third. It shifts from flat prairie in the west to hills, lakes and heavy forests in the middle of the state. Besides Willmar in the southern part of the district, the 7th's population centers, Moorhead and East Grand Forks, are on the Red River, which forms the border between Minnesota and North Dakota, and have much larger companion cities across the border.

While the river irrigates some of the nation's blackest soil, floods in 1997 and 2001 capped a decade of agricultural struggle in the area. Though it lost some population, East Grand Forks largely has been rebuilt since 1997. Sugar beets and sunflowers are the dominant crops in the fertile west, while soybeans, wheat, corn and other staples are more prevalent in the east and south. The district also is a top producer of turkeys. Concern over the sugar market, the floods, drought and crop disease has left farmers looking to diversify and has sent younger residents fleeing. The Prairie Correctional Facility, a private prison taking inmates from as far away as Hawaii, is located in Appleton.

The district's manufacturing firms lend some stability to the area. The 7th produces hockey sticks, windows, skis and snowmobiles. Lakes in the north and east drive many resorts catering to retirees.

The 7th was George W. Bush's strongest Minnesota district in 2000, but residents will support either party, and the 7th is the state's most competitive district in statewide races. Traditional small-farm and labor support for Democrats still exists, particularly in the south, but these voters tend to oppose gun control and abortion. The district's most conservative voters live along the state's western border.

MAJOR INDUSTRY

Agriculture, light manufacturing, recreation

CITIES

Moorhead, 32,177; Willmar, 18,351; Fergus Falls, 13,471

NOTABLE

Writer Sinclair Lewis, the first American to win the Nobel Prize in Literature, grew up in Sauk Center; Walnut Grove was the childhood home of "Little House on the Prairie" author Laura Ingalls Wilder.

Rep. James L. Oberstar (D)

CAPITOL OFFICE
225-6211
www.house.gov/oberstar
2365 Rayburn 20515-2308; fax 225-0699

COMMITTEES
Transportation & Infrastructure - ranking member

HOMETOWN
Chisholm

BORN
Sept. 10, 1934, Chisholm, Minn.

RELIGION
Roman Catholic

FAMILY
Wife, Jean Oberstar; six children

EDUCATION
College of St. Thomas, B.A. 1956 (French & political science); College of Europe (Belgium), M.A. 1957 (comparative government)

CAREER
Language teacher; congressional aide

POLITICAL HIGHLIGHTS
Sought Democratic nomination for U.S. Senate, 1984

ELECTION RESULTS

2002 GENERAL		
James L. Oberstar (D)	194,909	68.7%
Robert Lemen (R)	88,673	31.2%
2002 PRIMARY		
James L. Oberstar (D)		unopposed
2000 GENERAL		
James L. Oberstar (D)	210,094	67.9%
Robert Lemen (R)	79,890	25.8%
Mike Darling (I)	19,667	6.4%

PREVIOUS WINNING PERCENTAGES
1998 (66%); 1996 (67%); 1994 (66%); 1992 (59%); 1990 (73%); 1988 (75%); 1986 (73%); 1984 (67%); 1982 (77%); 1980 (70%); 1978 (87%); 1976 (100%); 1974 (62%)

Elected 1974; 15th term

The son of a blue-collar mining family in Minnesota's Iron Range, Oberstar is a policy wonk who has been known to wax on about the elegance of his favorite legislative language. A New Deal liberal, he has one of the longest service records in the House, having spent 11 years as a top congressional aide before he was elected in his own right in 1974. He now ranks seventh among House Democrats in seniority and is one of only three Democratic "Watergate babies" remaining in the House.

All that experience has made him a savvy, hands-on legislator. His background, passions and style are well-suited to the Transportation and Infrastructure Committee, where he has been the top-ranking Democrat since 1995. That role will keep him busy in the 108th Congress, when the committee plans to rewrite both the 1998 surface transportation law and the 2000 aviation law that accelerated spending for airport improvements.

Oberstar's mentor and predecessor in the House was Democrat John A. Blatnik, who rose to chair what was then called the Public Works and Transportation Committee. As Blatnik's chief aide, Oberstar learned how to bring federal largess back home. And Blatnik was never shy about earmarking funds to benefit his colleagues' districts.

Oberstar still defends that practice, although as debate on the highway bill got under way in 2003 he and the committee's chairman, Republican Don Young of Alaska, thought to constrain the system somewhat. They required each member of the panel to justify, in a 21-point questionnaire, each request for an earmark.

His knowledge of transportation programs served Oberstar well after the Sept. 11, 2001, terrorist attacks. He was front and center as Congress moved to strengthen aviation security and bail out the ailing airline industry that fall. A fierce ally of unions, Oberstar repeatedly fought to help airline workers laid off in the aftermath of the terrorist attacks.

The needs of workers never seem to be too far from his mind. On a panel that has been renowned for its bipartisan collegiality in the pursuit of more public works, Oberstar's essentially unwavering labor loyalties can be a rare source of friction.

Even in the midst of the homeland security debate following the terrorist attacks and the saber rattling with Iraq during the 107th Congress, Oberstar urged passage of a labor funding bill. President Bush "has made an awful lot of noise about Iraq and homeland security, but this is the real security," he told the Minneapolis Star Tribune. "There are funds in there for job training, vocational training, all of which are needed in a time when we have 9.5 million people unemployed."

Oberstar's father was an iron ore miner and union official who worked in both underground mine shafts and open pits, where Oberstar labored as a teenager. His mother worked in a shirt factory. Proving he has not forgotten his roots or the needs of his constituents, Oberstar has supported the creation of a health insurance safety net for retired steel workers.

Oberstar had a strong working relationship with Transportation's previous Republican chairman, Bud Shuster of Pennsylvania, who resigned from the House in 2001 to become a transportation lobbyist. Young is more openly partisan, and there have been occasional squabbles between the minority and the majority in recent years. But in the 107th, Oberstar joined forces with Young to argue that their panel's jurisdiction should not be whittled away by Bush's plan to consolidate 22 agencies into the new

Department of Homeland Security. The Transportation Committee voted to oppose efforts to move the Federal Emergency Management Agency and the Coast Guard into the new department, but it lost that battle.

While he is a loyal Democrat, Oberstar has scuffled with the liberal wing of the party on the issues of abortion and gun owners' rights. A devout Roman Catholic, he has proposed a constitutional amendment to ban abortions except in cases where the woman's life is in danger.

Oberstar is an advocate of adoption and co-chairs the Congressional Coalition on Adoption; his oldest child was adopted. He has pushed for more federal funding for breast cancer research and education. His first wife died in 1991 after an eight-year battle with the disease, and he has since married a woman who had lost her first husband to cancer. On that front in the 107th, he wrote legislation to provide financial relief, including a tax credit, to caregivers of sick family members.

He generally sides with Democrats in fighting Republican efforts to scale back environmental protections. In 2002, for instance, he introduced legislation aimed at overturning a Supreme Court decision that in his view had diminished the protection of wetlands. He said the decision went against nearly 30 years of interpretation and opened "an opportunity for waters across the nation to be destroyed and degraded."

But Oberstar will oppose environmental groups if their positions clash with the interests of his constituents. In 1998, for example, he worked to maintain funding for construction of logging roads on federal lands, which environmentalists say damages forest ecosystems. "This is not an issue between corporate giants and little guys. This is silk-stocking environmentalists against us hicks from the sticks, and I am fed up with it," he said.

A dedicated bicyclist, Oberstar included in the 1998 highway law numerous provisions to encourage biking and enhance bicycle safety and education. In the 1991 highway law, he won an authorization of federal funds to convert abandoned railways into recreational bike paths.

Oberstar takes delight in demonstrating his facility with foreign languages, including French and Creole, which he taught to U.S. Navy personnel in Haiti in the early 1960s before coming to Washington. The congressman, who has a graduate degree from the College of Europe in Brussels, also speaks some Spanish, Italian, Slovenian and Serbo-Croatian.

When Blatnik retired and sought to anoint Oberstar as his successor in 1974, a rival Democratic faction led by Minnesota's Perpich political dynasty sought to derail the plan. But Oberstar won the primary and has never looked back since.

KEY VOTES

2002

- Yes Overhaul campaign finance law; ban "soft money" and restrict advocacy advertising
- No Back Bush's defense budget increase
- No Extend 1996 welfare law
- No Adopt Bush's discretionary spending limit
- No Pass GOP Medicare prescription drug plan
- Yes Create independent Sept. 11 commission
- Yes Extend union protections to Homeland Security Department employees
- No Revive fast-track procedures for trade agreements
- No Authorize war against Iraq
- No Advance bankruptcy overhaul opposed by abortion opponents

2001

- No Nullify Clinton Labor Department ergonomics rule
- ? Cut taxes by $1.35 trillion through fiscal 2011
- No Maintain ban on oil drilling in Arctic National Wildlife Refuge
- No Approve Bush proposal to limit managed-care plan liability for coverage decisions
- Yes Divert money from crop subsidy payments to land conservation
- No Expand law enforcement power to investigate suspected terrorists

CQ VOTE STUDIES

	PARTY UNITY		PRESIDENTIAL SUPPORT	
	Support	Oppose	Support	Oppose
2002	94%	6%	28%	72%
2001	87%	13%	34%	66%
2000	92%	8%	80%	20%
1999	88%	12%	73%	27%
1998	90%	10%	85%	15%

INTEREST GROUPS

	AFL-CIO	ADA	CCUS	ACU
2002	100%	80%	26%	4%
2001	100%	75%	35%	24%
2000	100%	75%	25%	8%
1999	88%	75%	23%	12%
1998	100%	95%	24%	13%

MINNESOTA 8
Northeast – Duluth, Iron Range

The expansive 8th covers Minnesota's northeast quadrant, including Duluth and the Iron Range — taconite mining communities that stretch across the middle of the state through Cass, Crow Wing and St. Louis counties. It is the only one of Minnesota's three rural districts to include any of the Minneapolis-St. Paul metro area, though that area makes up only 12 percent of its population.

Logging and mining still provide a solid base for the region, though the work force is less than half what it was in the 1980s. These blue-collar workers with strong ties to labor cement the 8th's long affiliation with the Democratic-Farmer-Labor Party. The 8th has not sent a Republican to Congress since the 1944 election.

Duluth, the largest city, is the shipping point for much of the grain from the Plains states, and the westernmost deep sea port to the Atlantic. It remains a Democratic stronghold. The rural areas also are Democratic, but voters favor a hands-off approach to federal land management and tend to oppose gun control and abortion.

The southern end of the district grew in the 1990s by attracting Twin Cities commuters. The GOP is making inroads in this rapidly expanding area, where voters are willing to stray from the 8th's solid Democratic stance.

The district has the most varied terrain in the state, from farms in the south and west through the Iron Range and a watery northern border to rugged terrain in the northeastern arrowhead region. Huge tracts of land are designated as state and national forests, and the Boundary Waters Canoe Area along the Canadian border is noted for its motor-free beauty.

MAJOR INDUSTRY

Mining, timber, recreation

CITIES

Duluth, 86,918; Hibbing, 17,071; Brainerd, 13,178

NOTABLE

Actress Judy Garland hailed from Grand Rapids; The nation's only gas station designed by Frank Lloyd Wright is in Cloquet; Eveleth is home to the U.S. Hockey Hall of Fame; Little Falls was the boyhood home of aviator Charles Lindbergh; International Falls calls itself "the icebox of the nation" and claims to be the coldest spot in the lower 48 states.

MISSISSIPPI

Gov. Ronnie Musgrove (D)

First elected: 2000
Length of term: 4 years
Term expires: 1/04
Salary: $101,800
Phone: (601) 359-3150
Hometown: Batesville
Born: July 29, 1956; Tocowa, Miss.
Religion: Baptist
Family: Wife, Melanie Musgrove; two children
Education: Northwest Mississippi Community College, A.A. 1976; U. of Mississippi, B.S. 1978, J.D. 1981
Career: Lawyer
Political highlights: Miss. Senate, 1988-96; lieutenant governor, 1996-2000
Election results:

1999 GENERAL*		
Ronnie Musgrove (D)	379,034	49.6%
Mike Parker (R)	370,691	48.5%

* Under the state constitution, since neither candidate received both a majority of popular votes and a majority of the 122 state House districts, the Mississippi House voted to elect Musgrove on Jan. 4, 2000.

Lt. Gov. Amy Tuck (R)

First elected: 1999*
Length of term: 4 years
Term expires: 1/04
Salary: $60,000
Phone: (601) 359-3200
*Elected as a Democrat

STATE LEGISLATURE

Legislature: Meets January-April
House: 122 members, 4-year terms
2003 breakdown: 36R, 83D, 3I; 106 men, 16 women
Salary: $10,000; $1,500/month out of session; $85/day in session
Phone: (601) 359-3360
Senate: 52 members, 4-year terms
2003 breakdown: 21R, 31D; 46 men, 6 women
Salary: $10,000; $1,500/month out of session; $85/day in session
Phone: (601) 359-3202

STATE TERM LIMITS

Governor: 2 terms
Senate: No
House: No

URBAN STATISTICS

CITY	POPULATION
Jackson	184,256
Gulfport	71,127
Biloxi	50,644
Hattiesburg	44,779
Greenville	41,633

REGISTERED VOTERS

Voters do not register by party.

POPULATION

2002 population (est.)	2,871,782
2000 population	2,844,658
1990 population	2,573,216
Percent change (1990-2000)	+10.5%
Rank among states (2002)	31
Median age	33.8
Born in state	74.3%
Foreign born	1.4%
Violent crime rate	361/100,000
Poverty level	19.9%
Federal workers	25,318
Military	35,850

REDISTRICTING

Mississippi lost one House seat in reapportionment. The state legislature failed to agree on a plan and a three-judge federal panel implemented a new, four-district map on Feb. 4, 2002.

MISCELLANEOUS

Web: www.state.ms.us
Capital: Jackson

STATE ELECTION OFFICIAL
(601) 359-6357

DEMOCRATIC HEADQUARTERS
(601) 969-2913

REPUBLICAN HEADQUARTERS
(601) 948-5191

District Statistics

DIST.	2000 VOTE FOR PRESIDENT BUSH	GORE	NADER	WHITE	BLACK	ASIAN	HISP	MEDIAN INCOME	WHITE COLLAR	BLUE COLLAR	SERVICE INDUSTRY	OVER 64	UNDER 18	COLLEGE EDUCATION	RURAL	SQ. MILES
1	59%	40%	1%	71%	26%	0%	1%	$32,535	49%	39%	12%	12%	27%	14%	62%	11,413
2	41	57	2	35	63	0	1	$26,894	52	31	17	11	29	17	37	13,625
3	64	35	0	64	33	1	1	$31,907	57	30	13	13	26	20	60	13,168
4	64	34	0	73	22	1	2	$33,023	52	31	17	12	27	17	46	8,701
STATE	58	41	1	61	36	1	1	$31,330	52	33	15	12	27	17	51	46,907
U.S.	47.9	48.4	3	69	12	4	13	$41,994	60	25	15	12	26	24	21	3,537,438

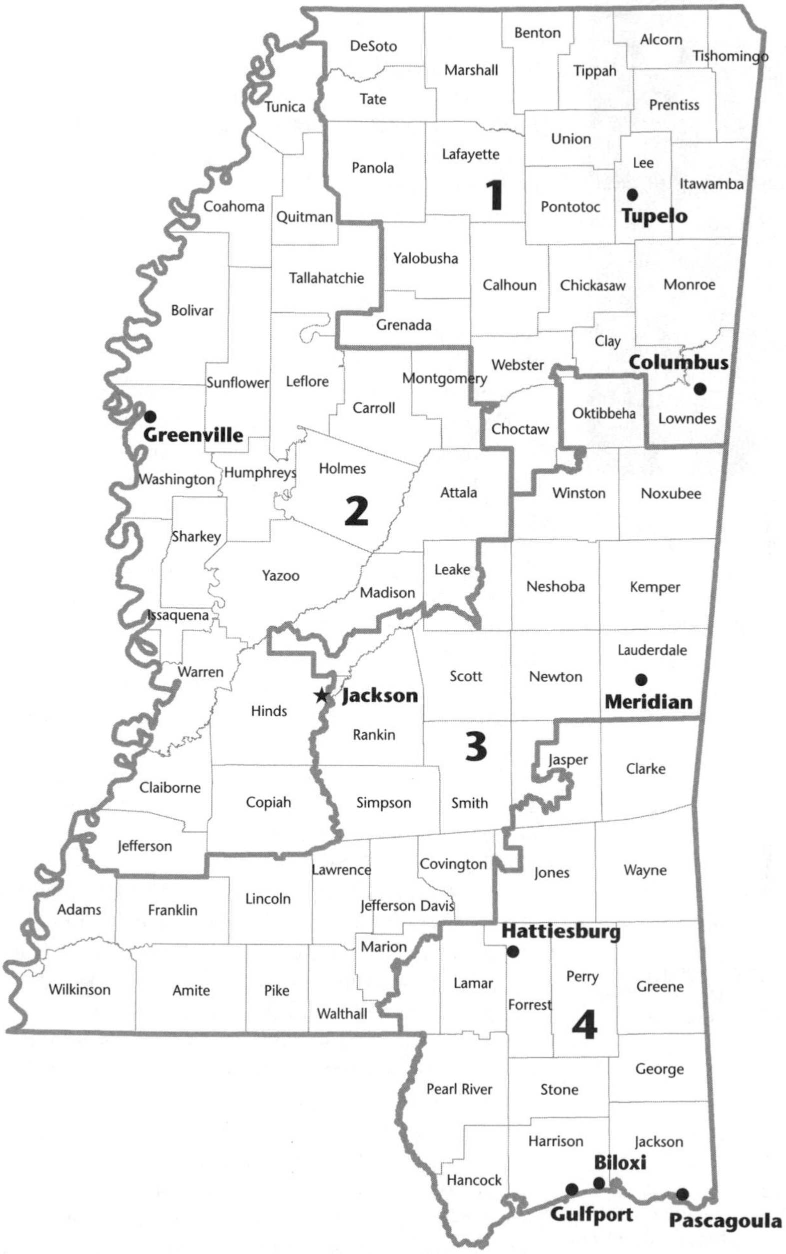
DeSoto
Benton
Marshall
Tippah
Alcorn
Tishomingo
Tunica
Tate
Prentiss
Union
Lafayette
Panola
Lee
Itawamba
1
Pontotoc
Tupelo
Coahoma
Quitman
Yalobusha
Tallahatchie
Calhoun
Chickasaw
Monroe
Bolivar
Grenada
Clay
Webster
Columbus
Montgomery
Sunflower
Leflore
Carroll
Oktibbeha
Lowndes
Choctaw
Greenville
Holmes
Humphreys
Washington
Attala
Winston
Noxubee
2
Sharkey
Yazoo
Leake
Neshoba
Kemper
Madison
Issaquena
Lauderdale
Warren
Scott
Newton
Jackson
Meridian
Hinds
Rankin
3
Jasper
Clarke
Claiborne
Copiah
Simpson
Smith
Jefferson
Covington
Lawrence
Jones
Wayne
Adams
Franklin
Lincoln
Jefferson Davis
Hattiesburg
Marion
Wilkinson
Amite
Pike
Lamar
Perry
Greene
Forrest
Walthall
4
George
Pearl River
Stone
Harrison
Jackson
Biloxi
Hancock
Gulfport
Pascagoula

Sen. Thad Cochran (R)

CAPITOL OFFICE
224-5054
senator@cochran.senate.gov
cochran.senate.gov
113 Dirksen 20510-2402; fax 224-9450

COMMITTEES
Agriculture, Nutrition & Forestry - chairman
Appropriations
(Homeland Security - chairman)
Rules & Administration
Joint Library
Joint Printing

HOMETOWN
Jackson

BORN
Dec. 7, 1937, Pontotoc, Miss.

RELIGION
Baptist

FAMILY
Wife, Rose Cochran; two children

EDUCATION
U. of Mississippi, B.A. 1959 (psychology); Trinity College (U. of Dublin, Ireland), attended 1963-64 (international law); U. of Mississippi, J.D. 1965

MILITARY SERVICE
Navy, 1959-61

CAREER
Lawyer

POLITICAL HIGHLIGHTS
U.S. House, 1973-78

ELECTION RESULTS

2002 GENERAL

Thad Cochran (R)	533,269	84.6%
Shawn O'Hara (REF)	97,226	15.4%

2002 PRIMARY

Thad Cochran (R)	unopposed

PREVIOUS WINNING PERCENTAGES
1996 (71%); 1990 (100%); 1984 (61%); 1978 (45%); 1976 House Election (76%); 1974 House Election (70%); 1972 House Election (48%)

Elected 1978; 5th term

Cochran is his state's senior senator, but only now is he clearly eclipsing his fellow Mississippian and rival of three decades, Trent Lott.

While Lott was forced out as Republican leader for the 108th Congress, Cochran assumed a pair of influential chairmanships. He took over the Agriculture Committee, eliminating the distinction he had held for four years as the most senior GOP senator who had never been a committee chairman. And he laid claim to the gavel at an emerging center of power in Washington: the new Appropriations subcommittee assigned to write the annual budget for the Department of Homeland Security.

Those two chairmanships could be but a quick springboard, however, to the prize of Cochran's career. If Republicans retain their Senate majority for the 109th Congress, GOP-imposed term limits will require Alaska's Ted Stevens to turn over the gavel of the Appropriations Committee to Cochran in 2005.

The homeland panel offers Cochran ample opportunity to prepare for the big step up. One of the full committee chairman's most important jobs is to carve up the total available funding among 13 annual spending bills — and to mediate disputes among lawmakers over priorities. In the 108th Cochran will take on a scaled-down version of that task, as his subcommittee divides some $30 billion among 22 agencies that used to belong to other parts of the government — and that were accustomed to having their budgets written by eight different Appropriations subcommittees.

Urbane, thoughtful and accessible, Cochran appears up to the job. His courtly Southern manner stands out in the modern Senate, where sharp, partisan rhetoric more often holds sway. That is part of the reason the soft-spoken Cochran remained in the background while Lott and other younger Republican conservatives brought their more confrontational style to the chamber. But his influence in the Senate and as a facilitator within the GOP should not be underestimated.

For 22 years he was either chairman or top-ranking Republican on the Agriculture Appropriations Subcommittee. In the 107th Congress, he was at the center of the rewrite of the law that authorizes federal agriculture subsidy, conservation and nutrition programs. He was one of the lead sponsors of a plan backed by the Bush administration as an alternative to the Democratic bill, although he abandoned his proposals rather than be labeled an obstructionist when the Democrats vowed to block the proposal.

Before leaving the Governmental Affairs Committee in 2003, Cochran parlayed a subcommittee chairmanship into leadership of the drive to deploy a nationwide anti-missile defense system, one of the signature GOP defense issues. Eschewing confrontation, which had not worked, Cochran won a major victory for the Bush administration in 2002 by carefully laying out the case for missile defense and then courting Democratic support.

And it was Cochran's change of heart that proved a turning point in the long drive to alter campaign finance law. His announcement in January 2001 that he had switched sides and would support the bill that GOP leaders were fighting hard started a steady erosion in the ranks of Republican opposition; the law was enacted 14 months later. "It became obvious to me that the influence of 'soft money' and independent groups was overwhelming the efforts of candidates," Cochran said.

Elected to the House in President Nixon's re-election landslide of 1972, Cochran quickly established himself as one of the bright lights among the new breed of GOP conservatives who were dissolving the Democrats' "Solid South." But while Nixon's vaunted "Southern Strategy" included a none-too-subtle pitch to whites perturbed by the empowerment of blacks, Cochran avoided alienating black constituents. Though his electoral base was the Jackson area's younger, upwardly mobile white population, he made an effort to maintain contact with the black communities that made up almost half of his constituency.

Yet Cochran is no liberal. In 1990, he was able to oust John H. Chafee of Rhode Island as secretary of the Republican Conference — the third-ranking slot in the Senate GOP hierarchy — because the caucus's increasingly numerous conservatives were unhappy with Chafee's defection on a range of lightning rod issues for the party.

Still, his approach has been largely conciliatory as he focuses on the more pragmatic business of legislating. He has plied his skills in the parceling out of federal money to Mississippi, particularly for agriculture programs. His easygoing manner has made him a natural for the collegial, bipartisan culture of the Appropriations Committee. As the 108th began, Cochran won kudos for assembling a $3.1 billion drought relief package that satisfied both the big grain farmers of the Midwest and the cotton, peanut, rice and sugar farmers of the South.

A rivalry between Cochran and Lott probably was inevitable, given that both are smart, attractive politicians in the same party in a relatively small state and that they are nearly contemporaries. Cochran was four years ahead of Lott at the University of Mississippi, where both were presidents of fraternities as well as cheerleaders — an elected position that was the starting point in many a Mississippi political career.

The son of two educators, Cochran was known even at Ole Miss as diplomatic and quiet, a leader who was rarely demanding. He was also an honor student, and he made partner in his Jackson law firm when he was less than three years out of school.

Cochran had been active in local party politics during his law career and was a key state figure in Nixon's 1968 campaign. Four years later, when Democratic Rep. Charles R. Griffin retired, Cochran won a narrow victory. Lott was elected to the House the same year, and the two young congressmen soon became the leaders of warring factions within the state party. The pragmatists, led by Cochran, and the ideologues, led by Lott, feuded with increasing intensity for the better part of two decades.

Although Lott wanted to run in 1978, when Democrat James O. Eastland retired after almost 36 years in the Senate, Cochran muscled him out of the way and became Mississippi's first GOP senator in a century. He won with 45 percent of the vote, as an independent black candidate drew much of the black vote away from Democrat Maurice Dantin, a former Columbia mayor.

All of Cochran's Senate re-elections have been easy affairs; Democrats did not even field a challenger in 1990 or 2002. The only election he has lost along the way was in 1996. When Bob Dole left the Senate to concentrate on his presidential campaign, the only two candidates for majority leader were Mississippi's senators. Lott, who was then the GOP whip, was first out of the gate in rounding up commitments of support and won, 44-8.

When Lott was forced out as party leader at the end of 2002, after a furor over a racially divisive remark, Cochran stayed in the background. Other Southern Republicans publicly clamored for new leadership, but Cochran confined himself to urging the GOP to reach out to minorities while staying true to conservative principles. "What's important to all Americans, African-Americans and others, is the economy, more jobs, better-paying jobs," he said. "And we need to stick to basic conservative approaches to dealing with issues like the economy."

KEY VOTES

2002

- No Pass farm bill reversing crop subsidy limits
- Yes Postpone tougher automobile fuel efficiency standards
- Yes Overhaul campaign finance law; ban "soft money" and restrict advocacy advertising
- Yes Set federal election standards
- Yes Support oil drilling in Arctic National Wildlife Refuge
- Yes Revive fast-track procedures for trade agreements
- Yes Create federal insurance coverage for catastrophic terrorist losses
- Yes Tighten federal accounting and corporate governance regulation
- No Advance bipartisan Medicare prescription drug plan
- No Create independent Sept. 11 commission
- No Back Democratic Homeland Security Department proposal
- Yes Authorize war against Iraq

2001

- Yes Confirm John Ashcroft as attorney general
- Yes Nullify Clinton Labor Department ergonomics rule
- Yes Cut taxes by $1.35 trillion through fiscal 2011
- No Pass Democratic bill to bolster rights of patients in managed-care plans
- No Permit a new round of military base closings
- Yes Expand law enforcement power to investigate suspected terrorists

CQ VOTE STUDIES

	PARTY UNITY		PRESIDENTIAL SUPPORT	
	Support	Oppose	Support	Oppose
2002	86%	14%	96%	4%
2001	84%	16%	96%	4%
2000	98%	2%	45%	55%
1999	94%	6%	38%	62%
1998	86%	14%	53%	47%
1997	82%	18%	68%	32%
1996	93%	7%	40%	60%
1995	93%	7%	34%	66%
1994	82%	18%	45%	55%
1993	91%	9%	26%	74%

INTEREST GROUPS

	AFL-CIO	ADA	CCUS	ACU
2002	23%	25%	100%	90%
2001	25%	15%	86%	88%
2000	0%	0%	100%	92%
1999	0%	0%	88%	84%
1998	0%	0%	100%	76%
1997	0%	15%	90%	56%
1996	0%	5%	91%	94%
1995	8%	0%	95%	83%
1994	13%	10%	90%	92%
1993	9%	0%	91%	84%

Sen. Trent Lott (R)

CAPITOL OFFICE
224-6253
senatorlott@lott.senate.gov
lott.senate.gov
487 Russell 20510-2403; fax 224-2262

COMMITTEES
Commerce, Science & Transportation (Aviation - chairman)
Finance
Rules & Administration - chairman
Select Intelligence
Joint Library

HOMETOWN
Pascagoula

BORN
Oct. 9, 1941, Grenada County, Miss.

RELIGION
Baptist

FAMILY
Wife, Patricia Elizabeth Lott; two children

EDUCATION
U. of Mississippi, B.P.A. 1963 (public administration), J.D. 1967

CAREER
Lawyer; congressional aide

POLITICAL HIGHLIGHTS
U.S. House, 1973-89

ELECTION RESULTS

2000 GENERAL		
Trent Lott (R)	654,941	65.9%
Troy Brown (D)	314,090	31.6%
2000 PRIMARY		
Trent Lott (R)		unopposed

PREVIOUS WINNING PERCENTAGES
1994 (69%); 1988 (54%); 1986 House Election (82%); 1984 House Election (85%); 1982 House Election (79%); 1980 House Election (74%); 1978 House Election (100%); 1976 House Election (68%); 1974 House Election (73%); 1972 House Election (55%)

Elected 1988; 3rd term

Forty-five words delivered off the cuff at the birthday party of a beloved colleague brought Lott's two dozen years in the Republican congressional leadership to a cataclysmic end. He was left with little more than crumbs of influence in the 108th Congress, and his party was subjected to revived public skepticism about its commitment to civil rights.

On Dec. 5, 2002, Lott gave a brief extemporaneous speech at the 100th birthday celebration of South Carolina Republican Strom Thurmond that praised the retiring senator's pro-segregation presidential campaign in 1948. "I want to say this about my state: When Strom Thurmond ran for president, we voted for him. We're proud of it," Lott said. "And if the rest of the country had followed our lead, we wouldn't have had all these problems over all these years, either."

Lott's remarks ignited a political firestorm. He issued several public apologies and even appeared on Black Entertainment Television to declare his support for affirmative action policies. It was for naught. Fellow Republicans, angry at seeing the party cast as insensitive to minorities, distanced themselves. President Bush, not a close ally of Lott's to begin with, personally sealed his fate by publicly rebuking him, calling his remarks "offensive."

Lott nevertheless worked assiduously to stop a behind-the-scenes White House effort to replace him with Bill Frist of Tennessee, a Bush ally and a polished politician who better symbolized the New South, especially for younger Republicans. After Frist announced he would challenge Lott at a special GOP caucus to reconsider the party's leadership, Lott, his political options exhausted, stepped down. That ended a 6 1/2-year run as Republican leader just as he was about to be elevated to majority leader again.

Lott now has the unwanted distinction of being the first senator to be forced out of such a high-ranking post since the leadership took its current form in the early part of the 20th century.

Unlike the three top House leaders toppled in the past two decades — Democratic Speaker Jim Wright in 1989, GOP Speaker Newt Gingrich and his designated successor, Robert L. Livingston, in 1998 — Lott did not resign his seat in Congress. Instead, he signaled a willingness to try to rehabilitate himself in his new role as rank-and-file legislator. He set to work in 2003 securing money to jump-start a controversial flood control project in Mississippi. Lott also did his party an overdue favor. By staying, he kept the seat Republican. If he had immediately resigned, the Democratic governor of Mississippi would have appointed a successor.

To cushion his fall, Republican leaders arranged for Lott to chair the Rules and Administration Committee. The panel mainly handles Senate housekeeping, such as the assignment of office space. So as chairman, Lott remains a party insider. And if the GOP keeps its Senate majority in the 109th Congress, Lott's chairmanship of Rules automatically makes him the master of ceremonies at the 2005 presidential inaugural.

Lott also used his seniority to bump Kay Bailey Hutchison of Texas out of the chairmanship of the Commerce Subcommittee on Aviation, giving him a central role in important debates over aviation security and the future of the financially troubled commercial airline industry.

Lott remains a study in contrasts. The son of a shipyard worker, he favors pinstriped suits and tightly knotted silk ties. His precision haircuts are a target of late-night comics. A courtly Southerner, he talks faster than many of his Northern colleagues. A committed conservative, he often sought to cut deals with Democratic leader Tom Daschle to keep the Senate moving.

His fall from grace was sudden, but Lott had a history of ill-considered remarks. Most caused only passing embarrassment, yet needlessly angered colleagues. When Republicans lost five Senate seats in 2000, leaving them in a historic 50-50 tie with Democrats, many in the GOP grumbled that Lott had been more interested during the 106th Congress in shielding vulnerable incumbents from having to cast difficult votes than in passing legislation that could have burnished the Republican legislative record.

The grousing turned to near revolt after Lott struck a power-sharing deal with Daschle in 2001 that gave the parties an equal number of seats on committees and an equal amount of staff and office space. Lott said he wanted to avoid a messy floor fight over inside-the-Senate issues just as Bush assumed office.

Lott did succeed in pushing through Bush's top legislative priority. Although GOP moderates were able to pare the president's tax cut proposal by $270 billion to $1.35 trillion over 10 years, the bill picked up a dozen Senate Democratic votes and became law.

A single-minded focus on forcing bills to passage, and a sometimes dictatorial approach, created internal strife in his own caucus. But it was his threat of retribution against those who strayed on the tax cut that backfired badly for the party. Moderate James M. Jeffords of Vermont quit the GOP in a huff, became an independent and caucused with the Democrats, handing that party control of the Senate in June 2001.

Lott's colleagues were prepared to forgive and forget once they recaptured the majority in the 2002 election. They swiftly re-elected the entire leadership team. "I'm getting a second chance to do this job," Lott said a month before his ouster.

When Lott arrived on the Capitol's north side in 1989, he was part of a wave of aggressive conservatives moving over from the House eager to push a more overtly conservative agenda in the clubby Senate. Lott won election as Republican Conference secretary in 1993, and two years later he ousted the more moderate Alan K. Simpson of Wyoming to become GOP whip. Eighteen months after that, when Majority Leader Bob Dole resigned to focus on his 1996 presidential campaign, Lott sought the top job, vowing more aggressive leadership. His opponent was longtime political rival Thad Cochran, a fellow Mississippian. The mild-tempered Cochran offered the GOP a chance to vote against the changes in political style. The party voted for change and for Lott, 44-8.

Despite his conservative views and sometimes sharply partisan rhetoric, Lott often worked comfortably with Democrats to help enact major legislation, including bills to overhaul welfare and to make health insurance portable job to job. He was credited with walking a fine line with Democrats to make President Clinton's 1999 Senate trial far less acrimonious than the House's impeachment proceedings.

Lott has been a political animal at least since his days at the University of Mississippi, where he was a cheerleader and president of the Interfraternity Council. He came to Washington in 1968 as top aide to House Rules Committee Chairman William M. Colmer, a Mississippi Democrat. When Colmer retired in 1972, Lott switched parties and ran as a Republican to succeed him. He won with 55 percent of the vote against Democratic state Sen. Ben Stone and was easily re-elected seven times. In 1981, he became the first House Republican whip from the Deep South.

When Democrat John C. Stennis retired in 1988 after 41 years in the Senate, Lott was elected with 54 percent over Democratic Rep. Wayne Dowdy. Democrats have put up a minimal fight in Lott's two subsequent contests.

KEY VOTES

2002

No Pass farm bill reversing crop subsidy limits
Yes Postpone tougher automobile fuel efficiency standards
No Overhaul campaign finance law; ban "soft money" and restrict advocacy advertising
Yes Set federal election standards
Yes Support oil drilling in Arctic National Wildlife Refuge
Yes Revive fast-track procedures for trade agreements
Yes Create federal insurance coverage for catastrophic terrorist losses
Yes Tighten federal accounting and corporate governance regulation
No Advance bipartisan Medicare prescription drug plan
No Create independent Sept. 11 commission
No Back Democratic Homeland Security Department proposal
Yes Authorize war against Iraq

2001

Yes Confirm John Ashcroft as attorney general
Yes Nullify Clinton Labor Department ergonomics rule
Yes Cut taxes by $1.35 trillion through fiscal 2011
? Pass Democratic bill to bolster rights of patients in managed-care plans
No Permit a new round of military base closings
Yes Expand law enforcement power to investigate suspected terrorists

CQ VOTE STUDIES

	PARTY UNITY		PRESIDENTIAL SUPPORT	
	Support	Oppose	Support	Oppose
2002	98%	2%	100%	0%
2001	98%	2%	96%	4%
2000	98%	2%	45%	55%
1999	97%	3%	32%	68%
1998	96%	4%	39%	61%
1997	94%	6%	56%	44%
1996	97%	3%	34%	66%
1995	98%	2%	23%	77%
1994	97%	3%	40%	60%
1993	96%	4%	20%	80%

INTEREST GROUPS

	AFL-CIO	ADA	CCUS	ACU
2002	15%	0%	100%	100%
2001	0%	0%	85%	96%
2000	0%	5%	93%	100%
1999	0%	0%	82%	96%
1998	0%	0%	94%	92%
1997	0%	5%	90%	72%
1996	0%	5%	85%	100%
1995	0%	0%	100%	96%
1994	0%	5%	90%	100%
1993	9%	5%	100%	92%

Rep. Roger Wicker (R)

CAPITOL OFFICE
225-4306
roger.wicker@mail.house.gov
www.house.gov/wicker
2455 Rayburn 20515-2401; fax 225-3549

COMMITTEES
Appropriations
Budget

HOMETOWN
Tupelo

BORN
July 5, 1951, Pontotoc, Miss.

RELIGION
Southern Baptist

FAMILY
Wife, Gayle Wicker; three children

EDUCATION
U. of Mississippi, B.A. 1973 (political science & journalism), J.D. 1975

MILITARY SERVICE
Air Force, 1976-80; Air Force Reserve, 1980-present

CAREER
County public defender; lawyer; congressional aide

POLITICAL HIGHLIGHTS
Miss. Senate, 1988-94

ELECTION RESULTS

2002 GENERAL		
Roger Wicker (R)	95,404	71.4%
Rex N. Weathers (D)	32,318	24.2%
Brenda Blackburn (REF)	3,477	2.6%
Harold M. Taylor (LIBERT)	2,368	1.8%
2002 PRIMARY		
Roger Wicker (R)		unopposed
2000 GENERAL		
Roger Wicker (R)	145,967	69.8%
Joey Grist (D)	59,763	28.6%
C. Lawrence (LIBERT)	3,310	1.6%

PREVIOUS WINNING PERCENTAGES
1998 (67%); 1996 (68%); 1994 (63%)

Elected 1994; 5th term

As a member of the Appropriations Committee facing the prospect of a series of wartime deficits, Wicker took to posing a tough question to the administration, the voters and — not least of all — to himself as the 108th Congress began. "Can the nation afford both guns and butter?" he asked in various forums.

Whatever the answer, simply posing the question reflected his struggle to balance competing domestic concerns with an expensive never-ending hunt for terrorists, a looming war against Iraq and efforts to shore up domestic security. "The war on terrorism has forced Congress and President Bush to redirect many of our budget priorities," he said as the House adopted its first budget after the Sept. 11, 2001, attacks.

In finding a fiscal balance he can live with, Wicker has taken cues from his fellow Mississippian and former boss, Sen. Trent Lott. Both are defense hawks who take great pride in bringing home the federal bacon to their impoverished state, which always ranks high in the "12 Porkiest States" list published by Citizens Against Government Waste.

That fits with Wicker's view of himself as a pragmatic legislator. Although he served as president of the GOP freshman class elected in the 1994 "Republican revolution," when the party took control of the House for the first time in 40 years, Wicker is no firebrand. "I didn't come to Washington to burn all the buildings down. We were all unfairly painted with the same brush," he said in 1998. "Most of us in our own ways are much more pragmatic and results-oriented." That is not to say he is not a loyal and conservative Republican; in the entire 107th Congress he broke with a majority of his party on the House floor only six times — a 98.5 percent loyalty score. He also boasts a lifetime rating of 0 percent from the Americans for Democratic Action and a 3 percent lifetime mark from the AFL-CIO.

After landing an Appropriations seat as a freshman, he flexed his muscles there to help advance controversial conservative legislation. He wrote language setting National Institutes of Health (NIH) guidelines that blocked federal funding of embryonic stem cell research until Bush announced a new policy in 2001 clearing the way for studies using only a limited number of embryos that already had been harvested.

Wicker certainly does not fit the profile of a fire-breathing ideologue. He's an easygoing, approachable man who sings in his church choir, acts in community theater groups and once chaired the Mississippi Senate's Public Health and Welfare Committee even though the Democrats controlled the chamber.

His seniority on Appropriations puts him next in line to join the "college of cardinals," the 13 subcommittee chairmen who develop the initial drafts of each of the annual spending bills. As a member of the Appropriations panel that funds the Health and Human Services, Education and Labor departments, Wicker takes a special interest in beefing up funding for disease research. He helped lead efforts to double the NIH budget over five years and has championed spending more to fight polio and Muscular Dystrophy research and to help improve the lives of cancer survivors.

Closer to home, Wicker makes certain that constituents know about every road improvement he has helped win money for and every contract he has helped steer to his alma mater, the University of Mississippi. And in the 107th, Wicker, Lott and Sen. Thad Cochran of Mississippi, who is No. 2 in GOP seniority on Senate Appropriations, persuaded a reluctant NIH to create a new National Institute of Biomedical Imaging and Bioengineering with an initial appropriation of $112 million — and with the ultimate goal of landing an institute campus at Ole Miss.

Ever protective of his state's interests, Wicker convinced his fellow freshmen in the 104th Congress that the Appalachian Regional Commission — an inviting target for some GOP budget-cutters — was vital to the development of areas such as the stretch of northern Mississippi he represents, and the agency was spared. In the 106th, he backed a bipartisan plan to create a regional authority to foster economic development in the Mississippi Delta. Still, Wicker staunchly asserts his fiscal conservatism. In 1999, he backed a proposal to impose an across-the-board spending cut, declaring, "There are no winners and losers, and I don't know of any accounts that couldn't take a small hit."

Raised in a political family — his father was a county attorney, a state senator and then a circuit judge for 20 years — Wicker organized the local Teenage Republican club in high school. Although his father was a Democrat, as was virtually every office-holder in the South in those days, Wicker says, "There's not a dime's worth of difference in his philosophy of government and mine."

Wicker was the first Republican ever to be elected student body president at Ole Miss. While still in college, he was a delegate to the 1972 Republican National Convention and came to know a young Trent Lott as the latter was making his first run for Congress.

Wicker was in the Air Force ROTC and after law school served four years on active duty as a prosecutor before going to work for Lott in Washington in 1980. He came home to practice law and, in 1987, won his own state Senate seat. In Jackson he helped write Mississippi's strict abortion law and push through an education overhaul that included a controversial school-choice provision. He served with another young lawyer, who went on to become a successful author — John Grisham. He remembers Grisham selling his first novel out of the trunk of his car and so far has resisted his wife's entreaties that he also try his hand at writing.

When Democrat Jamie L. Whitten retired in 1994 after 53 years in the House — the longest service in the chamber's history — the conservative-minded 1st District was ripe for GOP picking. Wicker emphasized his legislative experience and edged out Grant Fox, a former Cochran aide, for the Republican nomination. In November he won with 63 percent of the vote and has not been seriously challenged since. As might be expected of Whitten's successor, Wicker does not support congressional term limits.

KEY VOTES

2002

No Overhaul campaign finance law; ban "soft money" and restrict advocacy advertising
Yes Back Bush's defense budget increase
Yes Extend 1996 welfare law
No Adopt Bush's discretionary spending limit
Yes Pass GOP Medicare prescription drug plan
No Create independent Sept. 11 commission
No Extend union protections to Homeland Security Department employees
Yes Revive fast-track procedures for trade agreements
Yes Authorize war against Iraq
No Advance bankruptcy overhaul opposed by abortion opponents

2001

Yes Nullify Clinton Labor Department ergonomics rule
Yes Cut taxes by $1.35 trillion through fiscal 2011
No Maintain ban on oil drilling in Arctic National Wildlife Refuge
Yes Approve Bush proposal to limit managed-care plan liability for coverage decisions
No Divert money from crop subsidy payments to land conservation
Yes Expand law enforcement power to investigate suspected terrorists

CQ VOTE STUDIES

	PARTY UNITY		PRESIDENTIAL SUPPORT	
	Support	Oppose	Support	Oppose
2002	99%	1%	85%	15%
2001	99%	1%	95%	5%
2000	93%	7%	22%	78%
1999	95%	5%	22%	78%
1998	94%	6%	24%	76%

INTEREST GROUPS

	AFL-CIO	ADA	CCUS	ACU
2002	11%	0%	90%	100%
2001	8%	0%	96%	96%
2000	0%	0%	85%	84%
1999	0%	0%	96%	92%
1998	0%	0%	100%	96%

MISSISSIPPI 1

North — Tupelo, Southaven, Columbus

The northeastern Hill Country and rich farmland on the edge of the Delta region in northwestern Mississippi support an agricultural economy in the 1st, while manufacturing dominates in Lee County (Tupelo) and surrounding areas.

Tupelo, the region's largest city, is a major producer of upholstered furniture; it hosts a biannual national furniture market that draws enough visitors to temporarily double the local population. Fortune 500 companies abound, drawing job-seekers from poorer parts of the state. The Tennessee-Tombigbee Waterway, which cuts through the 1st's eastern edge, has spawned a boom of forestry-related business.

In the district's northwest corner, De Soto County is becoming a haven for residents who commute to Memphis over the Tennessee border. De Soto is the district's most populous county and its fastest growing: Its population expanded by nearly 50 percent in the 1990s. Just to the east, Marshall and Benton counties are home to many of the district's African-Americans, a group that makes up more than one-fourth of the population.

Redistricting following the 2000 census did little to change the district's boundaries, politics or economy, but the 1st did pick up Lowndes County, which includes Columbus and Columbus Air Force Base.

Democrats held the congressional seat for more than a century until a Republican captured it in 1994. Voters have gradually turned away from Democrats in federal elections, favoring GOP presidential candidates in 1992, 1996 and 2000. Democrats, however, dominate state and local elections, stemming from the party's provincial political monopoly since Reconstruction.

MAJOR INDUSTRY
Furniture, agriculture, manufacturing

MILITARY BASES
Columbus Air Force Base, 1,506 military, 432 civilian (2002)

CITIES
Tupelo, 34,211; Southaven, 28,977; Columbus, 25,944; Olive Branch, 21,054

NOTABLE
Jamie L. Whitten, who represented the district from 1941 to 1995, was the House's longest-serving member — 53 years and two months.

Rep. Bennie Thompson (D)

CAPITOL OFFICE
225-5876
thompsonms2nd@mail.house.gov
www.house.gov/thompson
2432 Rayburn 20515-2402; fax 225-5898

COMMITTEES
Agriculture
Select Homeland Security

HOMETOWN
Bolton

BORN
Jan. 28, 1948, Bolton, Miss.

RELIGION
Methodist

FAMILY
Wife, London Thompson; one child

EDUCATION
Tougaloo College, B.A. 1968 (political science); Jackson State College, M.S. 1972 (educational administration)

CAREER
Teacher

POLITICAL HIGHLIGHTS
Bolton Board of Aldermen, 1969-73; mayor of Bolton, 1973-79; Hinds County Board of Supervisors, 1980-93

ELECTION RESULTS

2002 GENERAL		
Bennie Thompson (D)	89,913	55.1%
Clinton B. LeSueur (R)	69,711	42.8%
Lee F. Dilworth (REF)	3,426	2.1%
2002 PRIMARY		
Bennie Thompson (D)	47,893	73.5%
George E. Irvin Sr. (D)	17,277	26.5%
2000 GENERAL		
Bennie Thompson (D)	112,777	65.1%
Hardy Caraway (R)	54,090	31.2%
William G. Chipman (LIBERT)	4,305	2.5%
Lee F. Dilworth (REF)	2,135	1.2%

PREVIOUS WINNING PERCENTAGES
1998 (71%); 1996 (60%); 1994 (54%); 1993 Special Runoff Election (55%)

Elected April 1993; 5th full term

Thompson has made it his mission to try to push civil rights issues and other minority concerns onto the congressional agenda. His drive stems from his early experience as a black politician in Mississippi and the makeup of his constituency — largely black, rural and poor.

When Thompson entered politics three decades ago, the electoral system in Mississippi was bitterly divided over race, and black officeholders were few. In 1968, at age 20, he ran successfully for alderman in his native Bolton, but white officials prevented him from taking the seat until a court order forced the town to relent.

The state's political landscape has changed much since then, with many blacks holding office. But in Thompson's view, too much has stayed the same. He still feels that minorities wage an uphill battle against the wealthy and the powerful, and he has called for aggressive federal action to combat discrimination. Even Thompson's own Democratic Party does not escape criticism; he says African-Americans "have been taken for granted."

Indeed, Thompson has not been afraid to take on his party's leadership. Speaking for the Congressional Black Caucus, he argued at a meeting with House Minority Leader Richard A. Gephardt in the 107th Congress that the caucus' loyalty should be rewarded with better committee assignments. (He himself did not get a hoped-for seat on the Appropriations Committee in the 108th, but he did get a post on the new Homeland Security panel.)

But he saves most of his barbs for Republicans. When home-state senator Trent Lott lauded Strom Thurmond's segregationist 1948 presidential campaign, Thompson, the state's only black congressman, condemned the remarks, and noted that Lott had never sought him ought in the decade they had both served in Congress.

And Thompson was a leading voice against the confirmation — both in the 107th and 108th Congresses — of Mississippi federal judge Charles W. Pickering (the father of Thompson's House colleague) to a post on the federal court of appeals. Thompson said Judge Pickering's "record speaks for itself. If you are female or a member of a racial minority, your issues are likely to be frowned upon."

When Thompson hears the conservative House GOP majority malign affirmative action, he bristles. He once told his colleagues, "For most of us who are over 45, we never had new textbooks in our community, we never had the opportunity to play in a public playground or swim in a public swimming pool, and so some of us take very seriously the notion of affirmative action because this was the only opportunity that many of us ever received."

He has joined other Black Caucus members from largely rural districts in protesting that the Agriculture Department has long been guilty of discriminating against blacks in the administration of federal farm and loan programs. "There just might be a conspiracy which our government is participating in to do away with African-American farmers in this country," he said in 1998. In 2001, he introduced legislation to compensate black farmers for such discrimination.

He has harsh words for GOP budget priorities: "It makes no sense to force the poorest Americans to go without food stamps, school lunches and baby formula in order to balance the budget and then turn around and give wealthy campaign contributors . . . a huge tax cut," he said in 1997.

The rural, black-majority 2nd District is one of the poorest in the nation. Thompson has been able to secure some federal funding to improve the region's infrastructure, rural housing and health care. He made use of visits by President Clinton and other members of his administration to secure federal funds. Even with a Republican in the White House, Thompson has continued to lobby for federal money. In 2002, $6.2 million in federal grants was awarded to Central Mississippi Inc., which runs a Head Start program in Winona.

Farming has long been the dominant sector of the 2nd District's economy, and Thompson uses his seat on the Agriculture Committee to watch out for those interests. In recent years, riverboat casinos have sprung up in Tunica County and now are a leading source of jobs.

The move that brought Thompson the most publicity in the 107th was his refusal to join most of the Black Caucus in supporting campaign finance overhaul legislation. One of only two caucus members to vote against the bill, he cited his support for publicly financed campaigns as the reason for his vote.

In his home state, Thompson has been active in the 27-year-old legal battle over desegregation of Mississippi's universities. He was one of the original plaintiffs in a 1975 lawsuit. In 2002, a settlement was finally approved that would bring $503 million to three of the state's historically black colleges. Thompson said the settlement rewrote "another unfortunate chapter in Mississippi's past."

Born in 1948, Thompson was educated in segregated elementary and secondary schools in Mississippi. At Tougaloo College, he met civil rights activist Fannie Lou Hamer, who inspired him to pursue a political career. Thompson graduated from Tougaloo in 1968 and that same year won a seat on the Bolton Board of Aldermen. Four years later, he was elected mayor of Bolton, and at age 32, he took a seat on the Board of Supervisors for Hinds County, which includes the state capital, Jackson.

The House seat Thompson won in a 1993 special election had been held since 1987 by Mike Espy, Mississippi's first black in Congress since Reconstruction. Espy resigned in January 1993 to become Clinton's secretary of agriculture. In the special election to replace Espy, the first-place finisher in the initial balloting was Republican Hayes Dent, an adviser to GOP Gov. Kirk Fordice. Dent took 34 percent, while Thompson ran second with 28 percent. Thompson prevailed in the runoff, 55 percent to 45 percent.

In his 1994 bid for a full term, Thompson faced Bill Jordan, a black attorney and ordained minister. Thompson was able to outspend Jordan and won by 15 percentage points. His next three re-election victories were by comfortable margins, but in 2002 he was held to a surprisingly low 55 percent by underfunded and little-known Clinton B. LeSueur, who is also black.

KEY VOTES

2002

- No Overhaul campaign finance law; ban "soft money" and restrict advocacy advertising
- Yes Back Bush's defense budget increase
- No Extend 1996 welfare law
- No Adopt Bush's discretionary spending limit
- No Pass GOP Medicare prescription drug plan
- Yes Create independent Sept. 11 commission
- Yes Extend union protections to Homeland Security Department employees
- No Revive fast-track procedures for trade agreements
- No Authorize war against Iraq
- No Advance bankruptcy overhaul opposed by abortion opponents

2001

- No Nullify Clinton Labor Department ergonomics rule
- No Cut taxes by $1.35 trillion through fiscal 2011
- No Maintain ban on oil drilling in Arctic National Wildlife Refuge
- No Approve Bush proposal to limit managed-care plan liability for coverage decisions
- No Divert money from crop subsidy payments to land conservation
- No Expand law enforcement power to investigate suspected terrorists

CQ VOTE STUDIES

	PARTY UNITY		PRESIDENTIAL SUPPORT	
	Support	Oppose	Support	Oppose
2002	94%	6%	22%	78%
2001	87%	13%	29%	71%
2000	92%	8%	77%	23%
1999	94%	6%	82%	18%
1998	95%	5%	82%	18%

INTEREST GROUPS

	AFL-CIO	ADA	CCUS	ACU
2002	100%	90%	55%	8%
2001	100%	85%	48%	12%
2000	100%	90%	50%	8%
1999	100%	100%	17%	0%
1998	100%	95%	18%	13%

MISSISSIPPI 2

West central — Jackson, Mississippi Delta

The 2nd combines most of Jackson, the state's capital and largest city, with the nutrient-rich flatlands of the Mississippi Delta. The agricultural economy stemming from the Delta has promoted landowner/tenant relationships that have made the 2nd one of the poorest districts in the nation. Parts of the Delta still lack centralized running water.

Most of the district lies west of Interstate 55 and north of Interstate 20. Traveling west from Jackson, the 2nd moves into Vicksburg on the Louisiana border. Just north of Vicksburg, the road drops 15 feet in Issaquena County, marking the beginning of the flat Delta, where some of the nation's most fertile soil supports cotton and soybeans. Although some low-income white residents call the 2nd home, it is the only black-majority district in a state with the highest percentage of black residents in the nation.

While casinos in Tunica County — a popular gaming destination — have helped erase its standing as the nation's poorest county, many casino workers don't live in the district and instead commute from the Memphis region. Since the end of the 1990s, the 2nd has lost many manufacturing jobs to Mexico, which has contributed to high unemployment in some areas. But government, service and small-scale manufacturing jobs have kept unemployment in check in Jackson. Vicksburg is another economic bright spot, where a mixture of tourism, casinos and a Mississippi River port have fostered local prosperity. WorldCom is headquartered in Clinton.

Democratic since 1987, the 2nd's politics are dominated by the African-American vote, though Republicans hold small areas around Jackson and the district's northeast.

MAJOR INDUSTRY

Agriculture, government, casinos

CITIES

Jackson (pt.), 152,424; Greenville, 41,633; Vicksburg, 26,407; Clinton, 23,347; Clarksdale, 20,645; Greenwood, 18,425

NOTABLE

The Delta was the real birthplace of blues music: Blues pioneer Muddy Waters was born in Rolling Fork in 1915, and blues legend B.B. King was born in Indianola in 1925.

Rep. Charles W. 'Chip' Pickering Jr. (R)

Elected 1996; 4th term

CAPITOL OFFICE
225-5031
www.house.gov/pickering
229 Cannon 20515-2403; fax 225-5797

COMMITTEES
Agriculture
Energy & Commerce

HOMETOWN
Laurel

BORN
Aug. 10, 1963, Laurel, Miss.

RELIGION
Baptist

FAMILY
Wife, Leisha Jane Pickering; five children

EDUCATION
Mississippi College, attended 1981-82; U. of Mississippi, B.A. 1986 (business administration); Baylor U., M.B.A. 1989

CAREER
Congressional aide; U.S. Agriculture Department official

POLITICAL HIGHLIGHTS
No previous office

ELECTION RESULTS

2002 GENERAL		
Charles Pickering Jr. (R)	139,329	63.6%
Ronnie Shows (D)	76,184	34.8%
2002 PRIMARY		
Charles Pickering Jr. (R)		unopposed
2000 GENERAL		
Charles Pickering Jr. (R)	153,899	73.2%
William Clay Thrash (D)	54,151	25.7%
Jonathan R. Golden (LIBERT)	2,313	1.1%

PREVIOUS WINNING PERCENTAGES
1998 (85%); 1996 (61%)

Though the earnest and youthful-looking Pickering is often still taken for the congressional aide that he once was, he took office for his fourth term having established a reputation as a savvy legislator, particularly on high-tech issues, as well as a political survivor.

His previous jobs — four years as a legislative aide to Sen. Trent Lott preceded by two years as an Agriculture Department political appointee — gave Pickering an early advantage when it came to understanding the legislative process and choosing issues on which to make his name. So, too, did his political support from the rest of the "Mississippi mafia" of Thad Cochran, the state's senior senator, and Haley Barbour, the former Republican National Committee chairman.

When Pickering first came to Congress, he wanted a seat on what is now called the Energy and Commerce committee. But his Senate connections weren't much help, and he had to wait two years – a shorter wait than most. His seat on that committee, which helps to regulate much of the nation's business, helped give him a leg up in his 2002 re-election race.

Because Mississippi lost a seat in post-2000 census reapportionment, a federal court redistricting plan forced Pickering into a race against Democrat Ronnie Shows, a four-year House veteran. Though some analysts said the folksy Shows could be competitive by appealing to rural voters, the district lines favored the GOP and Pickering won by 29 percentage points — the most lopsided of the four general-election matchups between incumbents in 2002.

One way in which Pickering's congressional life has been complicated by his depth of political connectedness is his standing as the son of one of President Bush's most controversial judicial nominees. The elder Pickering's record on civil rights helped sink his nomination to the 5th Circuit Court of Appeals in the 107th Congress. And that record, combined with his close personal relationship with Lott, made Pickering's confirmation upon his renomination in the 108th problematic after Lott lost the majority leader's job because of remarks widely perceived as backing segregation.

The younger Pickering spent hours on the Senate side of the Capitol lobbying on his father's behalf. Just before the vote against him in 2002, he even imported two other Mississippians to plead his father's case: Democrat Frank Hunger, former Vice President Al Gore's brother-in-law, and former Democratic Mississippi Gov. William Winter.

Pickering won a spot on the Republican Policy Committee as a freshman, when House leaders recognized him as a well-connected junior member who could be trusted to vote a dependably conservative line. After a federal court ruled that it was unconstitutional to require schoolchildren to recite the Pledge of Allegiance because of its phrase "under God," Pickering introduced a constitutional amendment that would explicitly allow the pledge to be recited anywhere, including in schools.

His Washington connections may help explain Pickering's stand against two causes that draw strong support from Republicans hostile toward career politicians: He opposes term limits for members of Congress and has supported, on several occasions, cost of living pay raises for members.

On Energy and Commerce, Pickering was able to call on the expertise he developed as the telecommunications aide for Lott, who serves on the Senate Commerce Committee. Pickering was one of the pivotal staff players during the debate over the 1996 rewrite of telecommunications law.

In 2002, the big telecommunications fight was over whether to allow the four regional Bell companies to offer the broadband Internet services over telephone lines without first opening their local markets to competitors, an important requirement of 1996 law. MCI WorldCom, a long-distance company headquartered near Pickering's district just outside of Jackson, opposed the bill, and Pickering sided with them. He argued it would kill competition in the telecommunications market, a position at odds with his committee chairman, Republican Billy Tauzin of Louisiana, a main sponsor of the bill. Though the House easily passed it, the Senate did not act.

Early in his tenure on Capitol Hill, Pickering served on the Science Committee, where he looked out for the varied aeronautical and scientific activities of the John C. Stennis Space Center in southern Mississippi and for federally supported research work at Mississippi colleges.

Pickering, who says he is a seventh-generation Mississippian, comes from a prominent family in Jones County, of which his father remains the patriarch. But the congressman said he "kind of rebelled against" politics as a youth. He went to the small, Baptist-run Mississippi College for two years, where he played free safety on the football team.

He worked for a year on the family dairy and catfish farm, which was run by his uncle and grandfather, and then went off to the University of Mississippi to study business. After college, Pickering was a trailblazer in establishing a Baptist missionary presence beyond the Iron Curtain, in Hungary. Then it was back to another Baptist institution, Baylor University, for a master's degree with an emphasis on international business.

In the first Bush administration's Agriculture Department, he specialized in export promotion. He envisioned putting his missionary work, college training and USDA experience to good use in a career in international business. But other events intervened: Pickering started a family — his five sons are prominently featured in his campaigns, when he tells constituents that if they can't give him their vote, they should at least offer their sympathy — and Lott offered him a staff job.

There is a tradition in Mississippi of congressional aides moving into elective office; Lott did so, as did 1st District Republican Rep. Roger Wicker. So when Democrat G.V. "Sonny" Montgomery announced that he would not seek a 16th term in 1996, Pickering jumped at the chance to join that group. His political contacts and well-known name propelled him to first place in the nine-candidate GOP primary, and he won the runoff against former state Rep. Bill Crawford. In November, Pickering posted 61 percent against Democrat John Arthur Eaves Jr., a lawyer who also had grown up in a political family. He won two other lopsided re-elections before facing Shows in 2002.

KEY VOTES

2002

No Overhaul campaign finance law; ban "soft money" and restrict advocacy advertising
Yes Back Bush's defense budget increase
Yes Extend 1996 welfare law
Yes Adopt Bush's discretionary spending limit
Yes Pass GOP Medicare prescription drug plan
No Create independent Sept. 11 commission
No Extend union protections to Homeland Security Department employees
Yes Revive fast-track procedures for trade agreements
Yes Authorize war against Iraq
No Advance bankruptcy overhaul opposed by abortion opponents

2001

Yes Nullify Clinton Labor Department ergonomics rule
Yes Cut taxes by $1.35 trillion through fiscal 2011
No Maintain ban on oil drilling in Arctic National Wildlife Refuge
Yes Approve Bush proposal to limit managed-care plan liability for coverage decisions
No Divert money from crop subsidy payments to land conservation
Yes Expand law enforcement power to investigate suspected terrorists

CQ VOTE STUDIES

	PARTY UNITY		PRESIDENTIAL SUPPORT	
	Support	Oppose	Support	Oppose
2002	97%	3%	85%	15%
2001	95%	5%	84%	16%
2000	97%	3%	25%	75%
1999	95%	5%	21%	79%
1998	95%	5%	20%	80%

INTEREST GROUPS

	AFL-CIO	ADA	CCUS	ACU
2002	11%	0%	90%	100%
2001	17%	5%	91%	96%
2000	0%	0%	90%	100%
1999	22%	0%	88%	92%
1998	0%	0%	94%	100%

MISSISSIPPI 3
East central to southwest – Jackson suburbs

The 3rd sprawls across 28 counties, moving from Oktibbeha and Noxubee counties in the east central part of the state to the Mississippi River in the southwest corner. The GOP stronghold picks up Jackson's northeast corner and some of its mostly white northern and eastern suburbs.

Timber is dominant in the 3rd, but health care and defense also are important industries, especially in Meridian. A new Nissan plant — just outside the district in the neighboring 2nd — is expected to boost Jackson's economy. Small rural communities, filled with poultry and dairy farms, are prevalent. Rankin County is one of the fastest-growing regions of the state, spurred by nearby Jackson residents moving to the suburbs. Kemper and Noxubee counties on the eastern border include areas as poor as the Delta.

The recession of the late 1980s and early 1990s decimated Natchez's oil and gas industry, but tourism helped the southwestern outpost's economy stay afloat; the small river city, with its antebellum homes and dockside casinos, attracts nearly 150,000 visitors per year.

Republicans now dominate the federal politics of the 3rd, as Democrats did for most of the 20th century. George W. Bush took 64 percent of the vote in 2000. The new 3rd, created in redistricting following the 2000 census, combines the old 3rd and 4th districts to create a GOP district.

MAJOR INDUSTRY
Timber, poultry, agriculture

MILITARY BASES
Naval Air Station Meridian, 556 military, 313 civilian (2001)

CITIES
Meridian, 39,968; Jackson (pt.), 31,832; Pearl, 21,961; Starkville, 21,869

NOTABLE
Some call Natchez, the oldest settled city on the Mississippi River (1716), the "City of Five Flags" — it has been controlled by the French, British, Spanish, the Confederacy and the United States; Neshoba County is known as the site of an annual fair in Philadelphia, and as the place where three civil rights workers were murdered by members of the Ku Klux Klan in 1964, an event partly fictionalized for the movie "Mississippi Burning."

Rep. Gene Taylor (D)

CAPITOL OFFICE
225-5772
www.house.gov/genetaylor
2311 Rayburn 20515-2404; fax 225-7074

COMMITTEES
Armed Services
Transportation & Infrastructure

HOMETOWN
Bay St. Louis

BORN
Sept. 17, 1953, New Orleans, La.

RELIGION
Roman Catholic

FAMILY
Wife, Margaret Taylor; three children

EDUCATION
Tulane U., B.A. 1976 (history & political science); U. of Southern Mississippi, Gulf Park, attended 1978-80 (business & economics)

MILITARY SERVICE
Coast Guard Reserve, 1971-84

CAREER
Sales representative

POLITICAL HIGHLIGHTS
Bay St. Louis City Council, 1981-83; Miss. Senate, 1983-89; Democratic nominee for U.S. House, 1988

ELECTION RESULTS

2002 GENERAL		
Gene Taylor (D)	121,742	75.2%
Karl Mertz (R)	34,373	21.2%
Wayne Parker (LIBERT)	3,311	2.1%
Thomas R. Huffmaster (REF)	2,442	1.5%
2002 PRIMARY		
Gene Taylor (D)		unopposed
2000 GENERAL		
Gene Taylor (D)	153,264	78.8%
Randy McDonnell (R)	35,309	18.2%
Wayne Parker (LIBERT)	3,002	1.5%
Katie Perrone (REF)	2,820	1.5%

PREVIOUS WINNING PERCENTAGES
1998 (78%); 1996 (58%); 1994 (60%); 1992 (63%); 1990 (81%); 1989 Special Runoff Election (65%)

Elected October 1989; 7th full term

His jaw often set with indignation, Taylor has never shied away from staking out a lonely and often self-righteous place for himself in the House. He is one of the most conservative Democrats in a liberal-leaning caucus, but he does not have much use for President Bush or the Republicans who run Congress, either.

His anti-establishment credentials are rock solid. On two out of every five floor votes in the 107th that pitted most Democrats against most Republicans, Taylor broke ranks and sided with the GOP — and that was the least often he had strayed since arriving in 1989. But he backed the president's position only 45 percent of the time.

As the 108th convened, Taylor was one of four conservative Democrats who refused to cast their symbolic vote for Minority Leader Nancy Pelosi in the election for Speaker. But unlike the others, who voted "present," Taylor cast his protest ballot for John P. Murtha of Pennsylvania — who did not seek a leadership post of any sort. It was a repeat of his performance two years earlier, when Taylor voted for Murtha and all the other Democrats stood with Minority Leader Richard A. Gephardt.

In 1998, he was the only Democrat who voted in favor of both articles of impeachment the House brought against President Clinton and also the two that the House rejected. He has waged campaigns, annoying to members on both sides of the aisle, to limit the amount of speechmaking on the House floor and the range of perquisites for congressional leaders. In 1995, when the Republicans took over the House, Taylor declined to vote for either Gephardt or Newt Gingrich for Speaker. "I'm sick and tired of being heard and not listened to," he said.

But he spurned offers to join the five colleagues who switched to the GOP at the time. Instead, he helped pull together the coalition of the most conservative House Democrats known as the "Blue Dogs."

Although he is turning 50 in the 108th, Taylor's appearance is still that of the angry young man, and he is rarely more angry than when it comes to federal deficits, which he abhors. Still, he voted against both the 1990 deficit-reduction deal between President George Bush and a Democratic Congress and Clinton's 1993 deficit-reduction plan. He did, however, back the budget-balancing deal between Clinton and the GOP in 1997.

While a big and long-lasting surplus was forecast in 2001, Taylor opposed the 10-year, $1.35 trillion Bush tax cut. "Quit sticking my kids with your bills," Taylor said a year later, when deficits were back and congressional Republicans were pushing to make the 2001 cuts permanent. "I liked you guys so much better when you were for a balanced budget."

He has been caustic on the campaign trail as well. In 2002, he suggested that his GOP opponent, Karl Mertz, belonged in a mental hospital.

Observing him only in public, one would readily assume that Taylor is a humorless man. "If he was like he appears on TV, none of us would work for the S.O.B.," an aide once said. But Taylor's personality is exactly the opposite. He is an easygoing, fun-loving guy, according to those who know him, particularly those who have attended his annual Mardi Gras party on Capitol Hill, complete with miniature floats, outlandish costumes, liquid refreshment and Taylor's homemade jambalaya.

Taylor is an energetic champion of his district's military interests, its blue-collar factory workers and its socially conservative values. He is right in step with the Republican majority on many high-profile issues — banning flag desecration, cutting off federal arts subsidies, protecting gun owners' rights and curbing environmental regulation.

Taylor pursues a protectionist course on trade, arguing that working people are harmed by trade liberalization while the monied establishment benefits. He has opposed all four of the most controversial trade laws enacted while he has been in Congress.

As the top Democrat on Armed Services' Projection Forces Subcommittee, Taylor looks after Keesler Air Force Base, the naval station in Pascagoula, the naval construction center in Gulfport and Ingalls Shipbuilding, the state's largest private employer. In 2002, he played a key role in a Biloxi City Council decision to reject a proposed high-rise condominium near the flight path of Keesler, which could have deepened the base's vulnerability in the round of military base closings set to climax in 2005.

On the Transportation and Infrastructure Committee, Taylor is an enthusiastic supporter of federal spending on highway construction, harbor dredging and other public works projects — especially those in Mississippi, where the growth of the casino industry along the Gulf Coast has exacerbated transportation problems.

During 13 years in the Coast Guard Reserves, Taylor twice won commendations for his work skippering a 41-foot patrol boat on the Mississippi River, and he continues to have an interest in things nautical. Earlier in his congressional career he lived on a boat while in Washington. Taylor protects the interests of his district's shrimpers and fishermen, urges increased Coast Guard funding, and promotes measures to help the U.S. shipbuilding and cruise ship industries compete against foreign companies.

Taylor went to Catholic schools, and he recalls the nuns wheeling in a television set so the students could watch the inauguration of the first Catholic president, John F. Kennedy. Taylor was only 7 years old, but he recalls that moment as the beginning of his interest in politics.

He majored in political science and history at Tulane and then was a salesman for a box company. In 1981, he won a seat on the Bay St. Louis City Council and two years later he started a six-year turn in the state Senate.

The Democratic Party had little interest in Taylor's first campaign for Congress, for the seat Republican Trent Lott left open in 1988 to run for the Senate. But he surprised them with a strong, 45 percent showing against Republican Larkin Smith. Less than a year later, Smith died in a plane crash. In the special-election campaign, national Democratic support was again slim, but Taylor prevailed over Lott's longtime aide Tom Anderson Jr. and Democratic Attorney General Mike Moore. He has won with ease since.

KEY VOTES

2002

Yes Overhaul campaign finance law; ban "soft money" and restrict advocacy advertising
Yes Back Bush's defense budget increase
Yes Extend 1996 welfare law
No Adopt Bush's discretionary spending limit
No Pass GOP Medicare prescription drug plan
Yes Create independent Sept. 11 commission
No Extend union protections to Homeland Security Department employees
No Revive fast-track procedures for trade agreements
Yes Authorize war against Iraq
No Advance bankruptcy overhaul opposed by abortion opponents

2001

Yes Nullify Clinton Labor Department ergonomics rule
No Cut taxes by $1.35 trillion through fiscal 2011
No Maintain ban on oil drilling in Arctic National Wildlife Refuge
No Approve Bush proposal to limit managed-care plan liability for coverage decisions
No Divert money from crop subsidy payments to land conservation
Yes Expand law enforcement power to investigate suspected terrorists

CQ VOTE STUDIES

	PARTY UNITY		PRESIDENTIAL SUPPORT	
	Support	Oppose	Support	Oppose
2002	63%	37%	45%	55%
2001	56%	44%	45%	55%
2000	57%	43%	40%	60%
1999	44%	56%	39%	61%
1998	41%	59%	33%	67%

INTEREST GROUPS

	AFL-CIO	ADA	CCUS	ACU
2002	67%	50%	45%	48%
2001	64%	55%	39%	64%
2000	60%	45%	38%	56%
1999	67%	50%	68%	72%
1998	33%	30%	41%	79%

MISSISSIPPI 4

Southeast — Gulf Coast, Hattiesburg

The pristine white Gulf Coast beaches of the 4th are surrounded by casino resorts that have popped up since Hancock and Harrison counties changed their gaming laws in 1992. Despite slow statewide population growth during the 1990s, many parts of the 4th, including Hancock, experienced population booms. Small forested rural communities dominate where strip malls and suburban sprawl do not. The district's healthy economy and general lack of poverty differentiate it from the rest of the state.

The military, defense-related businesses — most notably Northrop Grumman's Ingalls shipbuilding yard in Pascagoula — and casinos are the dominant industries. Large medical facilities at Keesler Air Force Base and the University of Southern Mississippi, as well as new golf courses, have attracted retirees to the region.

The 4th, which includes the core of the old 5th District, picked up Clarke County, the rest of Wayne County and parts of Marion, Jones and Jasper counties in redistricting following the 2000 census, but the additions are unlikely to change the political outlook of the district.

A conservative Democrat holds the 4th's congressional seat, but the district tends to swing between the parties locally. Republican presidential candidates won the district in 1992, 1996 and 2000.

MAJOR INDUSTRY

Military, shipbuilding, casinos

MILITARY BASES

Keesler Air Force Base, 12,110 military, 3,576 civilian (2000); Naval Construction Battalion Center Gulfport, 4,521 military, 426 civilian (2001); Naval Station Pascagoula, 2,101 military, 208 civilian (2002); Naval Oceanographic Office, 36 military, 863 civilian (2000)

CITIES

Gulfport, 71,127; Biloxi, 50,644; Hattiesburg, 44,779; Pascagoula, 26,200

NOTABLE

Sen. Trent Lott was the only Republican since 1877 to hold the area's congressional seat for more than one year — he held it from 1973 until 1989; Harrison County claims to have the largest manmade beach in the nation at 26 miles; Barq's Root Beer was created in 1898 by Edward Barq Sr. of Biloxi.

MISSOURI

Gov. Bob Holden (D)

First elected: 2000
Length of term: 4 years
Term expires: 1/05
Salary: $120,086
Phone: (573) 751-3222
Hometown: Jefferson City
Born: August 24, 1949; Kansas City, Mo.
Religion: Disciples of Christ
Family: Wife, Lori Hauser Holden; two children
Education: Southwest Missouri State U., B.A. 1973 (political science)
Military Service: Mo. National Guard, 1971-75
Career: Congressional aide; assistant to the state treasurer
Political highlights: Mo. House, 1983-89; Mo. treasurer, 1993-2001
Election results:

2000 GENERAL		
Bob Holden (D)	1,152,752	49.1%
Jim Talent (R)	1,131,307	48.2%

Lt. Gov. Joe Maxwell (D)

First elected: 2000
Length of term: 4 years
Term expires: 1/05
Salary: $77,184
Phone: (573) 751-4727

STATE LEGISLATURE

General Assembly: Meets January-May
House: 163 members, 2-year terms
2003 breakdown: 90R, 73D; 128 men, 35 women
Salary: $31,351
Phone: (573) 751-3659
Senate: 34 members, 4-year terms
2003 breakdown: 20R, 14D; 27 men, 7 women
Salary: $31,351
Phone: (573) 751-3766

STATE TERM LIMITS

Governor: 2 terms
Senate: 2 terms
House: 4 terms

URBAN STATISTICS

CITY	POPULATION
Kansas City	441,545
St. Louis	348,189
Springfield	151,580
Independence	113,288
Columbia	84,531

REGISTERED VOTERS

Voters do not register by party.

POPULATION

2002 population (est.)	5,672,579
2000 population	5,595,211
1990 population	5,117,073
Percent change (1990-2000)	+9.3%
Rank among states (2002)	17
Median age	36.1
Born in state	67.8%
Foreign born	2.7%
Violent crime rate	490/100,000
Poverty level	11.7%
Federal workers	57,783
Military	38,091

REDISTRICTING

Missouri retained its nine House seats in reapportionment. The state legislature drew a new map, which the governor signed on June 1, 2001.

MISCELLANEOUS

Web: www.state.mo.us
Capital: Jefferson City
STATE ELECTION OFFICIAL
(573) 751-2301
DEMOCRATIC HEADQUARTERS
(573) 636-5241
REPUBLICAN HEADQUARTERS
(573) 636-3146

District Statistics

DIST.	2000 VOTE FOR PRESIDENT BUSH	GORE	NADER	WHITE	BLACK	ASIAN	HISP	MEDIAN INCOME	WHITE COLLAR	BLUE COLLAR	SERVICE INDUSTRY	OVER 64	UNDER 18	COLLEGE EDUCATION	RURAL	SQ. MILES
1	26%	71%	2%	46%	50%	2%	1%	$36,314	62%	21%	17%	14%	26%	22%	1%	217
2	58	39	2	93	2	2	1	$61,416	71	18	11	11	27	38	8	1,248
3	43	54	2	86	9	2	2	$41,091	60	24	15	13	25	23	13	1,247
4	58	39	2	92	3	1	2	$34,541	51	33	16	14	25	16	60	14,544
5	37	60	2	66	24	1	6	$38,311	62	23	15	13	26	23	4	512
6	52	43	3	92	3	1	2	$41,225	59	27	15	13	25	21	34	13,032
7	62	36	2	93	1	1	3	$32,929	55	29	16	14	24	19	41	5,480
8	58	37	4	92	4	0	1	$27,865	48	36	16	16	25	12	60	18,681
9	54	42	3	93	4	1	1	$36,693	54	31	15	13	25	20	54	13,925
STATE	50	47	2	84	11	1	2	$37,934	58	27	15	14	26	22	31	68,886
U.S.	47.9	48.4	3	69	12	4	13	$41,994	60	25	15	12	26	24	21	3,537,438

Atchison
Nodaway
Worth
Harrison
Mercer
Putnam
Schuyler
Scotland
Clark
Holt
Gentry
Grundy
Sullivan
Adair
Knox
Lewis
Andrew
DeKalb
Daviess
6
Linn
Macon
Shelby
Marion
St. Joseph
Buchanan
Clinton
Caldwell
Livingston
Chariton
Monroe
Ralls
Randolph
9
Platte
Clay
Ray
Carroll
Pike
Saline
Audrain
Lincoln
Kansas City
Independence
Howard
Boone
2
1
Lafayette
Columbia
Jackson
Cooper
Callaway
Montgomery
St. Charles
5
Johnson
Pettis
Warren
Cass
Moniteau
St. Louis
St. Louis
Jefferson City
Gasconade
Cole
Henry
Benton
Morgan
Osage
Franklin
Jefferson
Bates
4
Miller
3
Maries
St. Clair
Camden
Crawford
Vernon
Hickory
Washington
Ste. Genevieve
Pulaski
Phelps
Cedar
St. Francois
Perry
Dallas
Laclede
Iron
Polk
Dent
Barton
Dade
Reynolds
Madison
Cape Girardeau
Greene
Bollinger
Texas
Jasper
Springfield
Webster
Wright
8
Cape Girardeau
Shannon
Wayne
Scott
Lawrence
Christian
Newton
Douglas
Carter
Stoddard
Mississippi
7
Howell
Stone
Butler
McDonald
Barry
Taney
Ozark
Oregon
Ripley
New Madrid
Pemiscot
Dunklin

Sen. Christopher S. Bond (R)

CAPITOL OFFICE
224-5721
kit_bond@bond.senate.gov
bond.senate.gov
274 Russell 20510-2503; fax 224-8149

COMMITTEES
Appropriations
(VA, HUD & Independent Agencies - chairman)
Environment & Public Works
(Transportation & Infrastructure - chairman)
Health, Education, Labor & Pensions
(Aging - chairman)
Small Business & Entrepreneurship
Select Intelligence

HOMETOWN
Mexico

BORN
March 6, 1939, St. Louis, Mo.

RELIGION
Presbyterian

FAMILY
Wife, Linda Bond; one child

EDUCATION
Princeton U., A.B. 1960; U. of Virginia, LL.B. 1963

CAREER
Lawyer

POLITICAL HIGHLIGHTS
Republican nominee for U.S. House, 1968; Mo. auditor, 1971-73; governor, 1973-77; defeated for re-election as governor, 1976; governor, 1981-85

ELECTION RESULTS

1998 GENERAL		
Christopher S. Bond (R)	830,625	52.7%
Jay Nixon (D)	690,208	43.8%
Tamara A. Millay (LIBERT)	31,876	2.0%
1998 PRIMARY		
Christopher S. Bond (R)	213,569	86.9%
Joyce P. Lea (R)	9,685	3.9%
Joseph "Joe" France (R)	6,178	2.5%
John R. Alsup (R)	5,824	2.4%
Douglas E. Jones (R)	5,596	2.3%
Joseph A. Schwan (R)	4,991	2.0%

PREVIOUS WINNING PERCENTAGES
1992 (52%); 1986 (53%)

Elected 1986; 3rd term

Perhaps it is fitting that clay has played such a substantial role in Bond's life, for he views legislation as a malleable product to be shaped according to the practical and political necessities of the moment rather than a work that must be cast in a rigid ideological frame.

The clay soil of Bond's hometown of Mexico, 90 miles northwest of St. Louis, provided the source of local industry, and the man credited with exploiting this natural resource was Bond's grandfather, brick-making magnate Allen Percy Green. Until it closed in 2002, the A.P. Green Fire Brick Co. was a mainstay of the community.

The senator's hometown — population 11,320 in 2000 — still figures prominently in his life. When not in Washington, he indulges his love of the outdoors by fishing and planting trees there. He has had several low-grade skin cancers removed through the years, which he has attributed to the time he spends outdoors. Bond even provided the meal for the rehearsal dinner preceding his second marriage, to GOP political consultant Linda Pell in 2002. Attendees dined on a 55-pound salmon Bond had caught on an Alaskan fishing trip.

Still known by his childhood nickname, "Kit," Bond is also known for his love of cigars and for the Senate gym; he has been known to arrive at the Senate in sweaty athletic garb when votes interrupt his workouts.

Behind his outdoorsy and sometimes gruff exterior, Bond is a soft-edged conservative, happy to spend money on government programs that benefit his state and willing to cooperate with Democrats if necessary to do so. He has a reputation as a low-key workhorse, yet his fellow Republicans have been reluctant to elect him to a leadership post; he has lost three attempts to become chairman of the Senate Republican caucus.

Bond appears to delight in the work of the Appropriations Committee. Since 1997 he has been the top Republican on the subcommittee that writes the second-largest of the annual domestic spending bills — covering veterans, housing, space, environmental and science programs. As chairman again in the 108th Congress, he planned to reassess NASA's priorities in light of the destruction of the space shuttle Columbia in 2003.

Despite their strikingly different ideologies, Bond regularly finds consensus with the panel's top Democrat, Barbara A. Mikulski of Maryland, who like Bond is eager to deliver federal money back home.

Few federal dollars make as big a splash as highway funds, and Bond is well-positioned in the 108th to look out for Missouri's interests as Congress rewrites surface transportation law. He ensured himself an influential seat at the table by declining the chairmanship of the Small Business Committee to head the Environment and Public Works panel's Transportation, Infrastructure and Nuclear Safety Subcommittee. "Highways are all-consuming," he said. "We will draft a national highway bill that assures equal treatment," Bond told highway officials during a December 2002 meeting in Kansas City, "but we want to get a little more equal treatment for Missouri."

Bond is unashamed about bringing home the bacon. When the watchdog group Citizens Against Government Waste gave him a "License to Pork" in 1999 for having brought home more than $50 million in federal dollars the year before, Bond was more proud than offended. "If they think it's pork, it's an awfully healthy diet for the people of Missouri, and I'm proud to participate in it," Bond told the Associated Press. "Just tell 'em, 'In the next batch, I'll bring along my own barbecue sauce.' "

In standing up for Missouri, Bond has sometimes found himself in the midst of major controversy. While much of the nation was focused on the Florida ballot snafus that threw the 2000 presidential election into disarray, St. Louis was reeling from findings that thousands of its voters were registered in more than one place.

Missouri Republicans were convinced that fraud had cost them a Senate seat and the governor's mansion. When the 107th Congress produced an election law overhaul in 2002, it contained a Bond provision requiring voters to show proof of residence either when they register or when they vote. Although he publicly fumed at several points along the way, Bond negotiated with the Democrats for six months on language each side could live with.

Bond was involved in a major environmental dispute in 2000, when he tried to stop the Army Corps of Engineers from altering the flow of water on the Missouri River in order to help endangered species and tourism in the Dakotas. The move threatened barge traffic on the river as it flows through Missouri, and Bond won language in a spending bill to prevent it. But President Clinton vetoed the measure.

Bond — who gave up a seat on the Budget Committee for a seat on Select Intelligence in the 108th — stood for election to his current term having suggested a repeal of the 1976 ban on political assassination. "One bullet at Hitler at the right time might have saved millions of people," he said at a 1998 debate, sponsored by the Jewish Community Relations Council of St. Louis. "I believe when you have a head of state, perhaps such as Saddam Hussein, who is bent on carrying out evil and continues to do so, you may cause far less human suffering if you go after that leader."

Despite his occasional forays into bipartisanship, Bond is usually a conservative Republican who receives low marks from labor and high ones from the Chamber of Commerce. And in the 107th, his votes backed President Bush's desires 98 percent of the time; only four other GOP senators supported Bush more often.

Bond has never been an overwhelming favorite of Missouri voters, and there is talk he might retire from public life when his current term ends in 2005. He has won by more than 10 percentage points only once — his first victory in 1970.

Bond broke into politics in 1968, unsuccessfully seeking a seat in the House from northeastern Missouri. But two years later, he won the office of state auditor. In 1972, he was elected the state's first GOP governor since World War II — and, at 33, he was immediately labeled a rising Republican star. In 1976, he lost a re-election bid to Democrat Joseph P. Teasdale, but he avenged that loss in 1980.

In 1986, Bond battled Democratic Lt. Gov. Harriett Woods in a bitter contest for the Senate seat being vacated after three terms by Democrat Thomas F. Eagleton. Bond offered himself as a budget-conscious conservative and painted Woods as a liberal with values out of sync with most Missourians. She called Bond a passive governor, an aloof aristocrat and a likely rubber stamp for President Reagan. Bond won with 53 percent.

In 1992, Bond's opponent, St. Louis County Council member Geri Rothman-Serot, sought to capitalize on the "Year of the Woman" tide. But Bond's campaign treasury was four times larger than Rothman-Serot's, and he prevailed with 52 percent — Missouri's only victorious statewide GOP candidate that year. Six years later, the Democrats touted Missouri Attorney General Jay Nixon, but his campaign stumbled when he angered black voters by moving to end a court-ordered school desegregation plan. Bond prevailed with 53 percent.

KEY VOTES

2002

- No Pass farm bill reversing crop subsidy limits
- Yes Postpone tougher automobile fuel efficiency standards
- No Overhaul campaign finance law; ban "soft money" and restrict advocacy advertising
- Yes Set federal election standards
- Yes Support oil drilling in Arctic National Wildlife Refuge
- Yes Revive fast-track procedures for trade agreements
- Yes Create federal insurance coverage for catastrophic terrorist losses
- Yes Tighten federal accounting and corporate governance regulation
- No Advance bipartisan Medicare prescription drug plan
- No Create independent Sept. 11 commission
- No Back Democratic Homeland Security Department proposal
- Yes Authorize war against Iraq

2001

- Yes Confirm John Ashcroft as attorney general
- Yes Nullify Clinton Labor Department ergonomics rule
- Yes Cut taxes by $1.35 trillion through fiscal 2011
- No Pass Democratic bill to bolster rights of patients in managed-care plans
- No Permit a new round of military base closings
- Yes Expand law enforcement power to investigate suspected terrorists

CQ VOTE STUDIES

	PARTY UNITY		PRESIDENTIAL SUPPORT	
	Support	Oppose	Support	Oppose
2002	89%	11%	98%	2%
2001	94%	6%	99%	1%
2000	96%	4%	46%	54%
1999	93%	7%	34%	66%
1998	88%	12%	38%	62%
1997	89%	11%	62%	38%
1996	95%	5%	37%	63%
1995	93%	7%	36%	64%
1994	78%	22%	49%	51%
1993	85%	15%	33%	67%

INTEREST GROUPS

	AFL-CIO	ADA	CCUS	ACU
2002	15%	10%	100%	84%
2001	19%	10%	93%	88%
2000	0%	0%	100%	92%
1999	0%	0%	94%	84%
1998	13%	15%	89%	72%
1997	0%	15%	100%	76%
1996	29%	10%	100%	90%
1995	8%	5%	100%	70%
1994	13%	20%	100%	83%
1993	10%	25%	100%	80%

Sen. Jim Talent (R)

CAPITOL OFFICE
224-6154
senator_talent@talent.senate.gov
493 Russell 20510-2505; fax 228-1518

COMMITTEES
Agriculture, Nutrition & Forestry
(Marketing, Inspection & Product Promotion - chairman)
Armed Services
(Seapower - chairman)
Energy & Natural Resources
Special Aging

HOMETOWN
Chesterfield

BORN
Oct. 18, 1956, Des Peres, Mo.

RELIGION
Presbyterian

FAMILY
Wife, Brenda Lyons Talent; three children

EDUCATION
Washington U., B.A. 1978 (political science); U. of Chicago, J.D. 1981

CAREER
Lobbyist; lawyer

POLITICAL HIGHLIGHTS
Mo. House, 1985-93 (minority leader, 1989-93); U.S. House, 1993-2001; Republican nominee for governor, 2000

ELECTION RESULTS

2002 SPECIAL		
Jim Talent (R)	935,032	49.8%
Jean Carnahan (D)	913,778	48.7%
2002 PRIMARY SPECIAL		
Jim Talent (R)	395,994	89.6%
Joseph A. May (R)	18,525	4.2%
Doris Bass Landfather (R)	14,074	3.2%
Scott Craig Babbitt (R)	7,705	1.7%
Martin Lindstedt (R)	5,773	1.3%

PREVIOUS WINNING PERCENTAGES
1998 House Election (70%); 1996 House Election (61%); 1994 House Election (67%); 1992 House Election (50%)

Elected 2002; 1st term

Talent narrowly prevailed in one of the bellwether Senate races of 2002 by hewing to the same conservative stands — on taxes, regulation, defense and social policy — that defined his eight years in the House and his close but unsuccessful 2000 campaign to be governor of Missouri.

His return to the Capitol marks one of the more notable political comebacks of recent years, and yet Talent had only recently celebrated his 46th birthday when he was sworn in as a senator for a term ending in 2006. He took office in November 2002, because his victory that month over incumbent Democrat Jean Carnahan was in a special election. She had been sent to Washington in place of her husband, Gov. Mel Carnahan, who died in a plane crash three weeks before his election to the Senate in 2000. The governor's appointment of Carnahan was only until the next general election.

Missouri is one of the nation's principal swing states, and as a Senate candidate Talent promised to seek bipartisan compromises. Yet he associated himself mainly with the conservative activist wing of the Republican Party during his years as a House member, when he was a close adviser to the conservative GOP leadership. Senate Republican leaders also expect Talent to be a loyal lieutenant; they named him an assistant majority whip shortly after his arrival.

Talent was named to a quartet of committees and subsequently was handed the gavel of two subcommittees. On Agriculture he will chair the Marketing panel, an obvious fit for a senator whose constituents are at the buckle of the farm belt. On Armed Services he will chair the Seapower panel, with little obvious parochial benefit to a landlocked state — especially now that the Navy's long-term plans do not include the F-18s that had been constructed by Boeing Corp. in suburban St. Louis.

Talent had fought to save that program when he sat on Armed Services in the House. But he made his main mark on the Small Business Committee. He was 40 when he became chairman in 1997, the youngest person to chair a House standing committee in more than four decades.

During his four years with the gavel, Talent's philosophy as an economic conservative was clearly etched as a major part of his political persona. He promoted Republican goals as he sought to draw more attention to the low-profile committee. He advocated private-sector solutions to economic and social problems. He denigrated federal regulations he portrayed as strangling small businesses. And he created a new Empowerment Subcommittee with the goal of calling attention to the view that individual enterprise and initiative should be paramount in American life and that government should play a much smaller role.

Talent favors more tax cuts, including making permanent the repeal of estate taxes and the reduction in the "marriage penalty" enacted as part of the sweeping 2001 tax law. He wants to fight workplace ergonomics rules and other regulations that he believes are too onerous and costly, particularly for small businesses. In the House he opposed the 1993 law guaranteeing job security for workers who take leaves for family or medical reasons.

Talent contends that he "designed the most comprehensive anti-poverty initiatives ever considered by Congress," including the starting point for the welfare overhaul that Republicans worked out with President Clinton in the 104th Congress. Foreshadowing the Bush administration's drive in the 108th Congress, Talent supported tougher work requirements for welfare recipients than were included in the 1996 law. In the House he also sponsored legislation to cut off federal assistance for unmarried mothers younger than 21 and eventually for those under 25 — a plan even more stringent than that proposed in the "Contract With America," the conservative agenda adopted by House candidates in their triumphant 1994 campaign.

From his seat on the Senate Energy and Natural Resources Committee, Talent has promised to support construction of a national nuclear waste repository at Yucca Mountain in Nevada and oil exploration in Alaska's Arctic National Wildlife Refuge.

Talent is particularly conservative on social issues. He has opposed a law that makes it a federal offense to use force or threats to prevent women from entering abortion clinics, and he opposes additional gun control.

To help shrink the ranks of those without medical insurance, Talent would allow businesses to unite in nationwide alliances that would give them greater clout in negotiating cheaper insurance rates. It is a solution, he says, that "doesn't cost the taxpayer a dime."

He advocates giving patients greater rights to sue their health insurance companies, but in a more limited way than many Democrats favor. An unrestricted right to sue would drive up premiums and force businesses to drop coverage, he says. He also would oppose any bill that does not protect businesses from being sued for decisions made by HMOs.

A member of the Aging Committee, Talent favors a plan to add prescription drug coverage to Medicare that he says would combine the best of Democratic and Republican proposals. It would look mainly to the private sector to design a benefit, but include a mix of government oversight and subsidies.

Talent was born just outside St. Louis and went to college there. He then went to Chicago, earned his law degree and stayed to clerk for Judge Richard A. Posner, a prominent conservative on the 7th Circuit Court of Appeals. He was 28 when he won a state House seat. He spent eight years there, four of them as minority leader, at one point bucking Republican Gov. John Ashcroft's proposal for a tax increase to support better education.

After winning a Republican primary against George Herbert Walker III, a cousin of President George Bush, Talent was elected to the House in 1992 by defeating one-term Democrat Joan Kelly Horn in the 2nd District, covering the mostly affluent St. Louis suburbs. In the House he stayed with the GOP on 94 percent of mostly party-line votes and opposed Clinton's wishes about three-quarters of the time.

He gave up his House seat in 2000 to run for governor when Mel Carnahan decided to try to move from Jefferson City to Washington. But Talent lost by 21,445 votes to the Democratic state treasurer, Bob Holden, in a race many Missouri Republicans maintain was tilted by voter fraud.

Soon thereafter Talent went to work for Arent Fox, a Washington law and lobbying firm — a job Democrats said amounted to an improper subsidy for his Senate campaign. Talent represented small businesses and grain processors, among other clients, but he said he complied with a one-year prohibition on former members directly lobbying Congress. He also said he had not decided to run for the Senate when he took the job.

But Republicans were already looking to Talent as their best candidate against Carnahan. Well-known as an adviser to her husband throughout his career, she was sustained by his lingering popularity and sympathy over her personal loss. But she had only two years to establish her own legislative and policy record, and often found herself caught between the push of the Senate Democratic leadership and the pull of the centrist political imperative of her state. This time Talent won — and by almost the same margin that he had lost by two years before: 21,254 votes.

CQ VOTE STUDIES

House Service:

	PARTY UNITY		PRESIDENTIAL SUPPORT	
	Support	Oppose	Support	Oppose
2000	94%	6%	23%	77%
1999	91%	9%	22%	78%
1998	93%	7%	20%	80%
1997	95%	5%	27%	73%
1996	93%	7%	32%	68%
1995	98%	2%	15%	85%
1994	95%	5%	51%	49%
1993	93%	7%	34%	66%

INTEREST GROUPS

House Service:

	AFL-CIO	ADA	CCUS	ACU
2000	0%	10%	78%	91%
1999	11%	15%	92%	84%
1998	0%	5%	100%	96%
1997	0%	5%	80%	100%
1996	9%	10%	100%	100%
1995	0%	0%	100%	96%
1994	0%	5%	100%	95%
1993	8%	10%	82%	96%

Rep. William Lacy Clay (D)

CAPITOL OFFICE
225-2406
www.house.gov/clay
131 Cannon 20515-2501; fax 225-1725

COMMITTEES
Financial Services
Government Reform

HOMETOWN
St. Louis

BORN
July 27, 1956, St. Louis, Mo.

RELIGION
Roman Catholic

FAMILY
Wife, Ivie Lewellen Clay; two children

EDUCATION
U. of Maryland, B.S. 1983 (government & politics)

CAREER
Paralegal; congressional aide

POLITICAL HIGHLIGHTS
Mo. House, 1983-91; Mo. Senate, 1991-2000

ELECTION RESULTS

2002 GENERAL		
William Lacy Clay (D)	133,946	70.1%
Richard Schwadron (R)	51,755	27.1%
James Higgins (LIBERT)	5,354	2.8%
2002 PRIMARY		
William Lacy Clay (D)	41,405	74.3%
Carl E. Harris (D)	14,322	25.7%
2000 GENERAL		
William Lacy Clay (D)	149,173	75.2%
Zellner Dwight Billingsly (R)	42,730	21.5%
Brenda Reddick (GREEN)	3,099	1.6%
Tamara A. Millay (LIBERT)	2,253	1.1%

Elected 2000; 2nd term

With 17 years as an elected official under his belt by the time his namesake father announced his retirement after 32 years in the House, the younger Clay was able to both embrace his father and declare his independence when he entered the race to succeed him. "Although I am not my father, I am my father's son, in that we share the same values . . . and commitment to principles, such as fairness and justice," said Clay, who is known by his middle name.

Clay shares his father's liberal agenda — he is a member of the Progressive Caucus, a group of about five dozen of the most liberal lawmakers — but he is widely regarded as more mellow than his contentious and rough-edged father. Although Clay is an avid cook and a golf fanatic, his mother told the St. Louis Post-Dispatch that politics "has been his life. That's the only thing he knows."

In order to pay for his education at the University of Maryland, Clay was a House of Representatives doorman for seven years. The hours he spent watching the action from the cloakrooms and the Speaker's lobby gave him ample insight into the ways of Congress. Clay's experience so impressed his colleagues in the Democratic Class of 2000 that they elected him president of their group for the 107th Congress.

During his first term, Clay was preoccupied with a range of campaign and election issues. He had joined in a lawsuit on Election Day that resulted in polls in St. Louis being kept open an extra 45 minutes to take on the long lines of waiting voters. He and other Democrats complained that day of a "concerted attempt to suppress votes" in poor, predominately Democratic neighborhoods; the Republicans charged there was voter fraud. The same arguments surfaced in March 2001 in the St. Louis mayoral primary, and investigations and legislative hearings on what do about the conduct of elections in Missouri dragged on for months.

Clay's involvement in the Missouri cases dovetailed with his assignment to the Congressional Black Caucus' working group on voting rights and the electoral process. Legislation to revamp the nation's voting procedures did become law and, although the Democrats-only group was generally not directly involved in the negotiations, it did play an important role in keeping up pressure for eventual congressional action on a much watered-down measure.

He cast a reluctant vote for another law enacted in 2002 to overhaul the nation's campaign finance system. Clay had originally signed a discharge petition to bring the bill to the House floor, but he later withdrew his signature, declaring that it was only a halfway measure "that would do more harm than good." Clay and a number of other African-American lawmakers said they were concerned that a ban on "soft money," unregulated donations that do not go directly to candidates, would hurt get-out-the-vote drives in minority communities.

Back in Missouri, as the legislature tackled the decennial chore of drawing new congressional district boundaries to account for population shifts, Clay declared himself ashamed of the way the Democratic Party was "leading the charge to dilute minority strength." At the core of that allegation was a dispute over how to draw the lines in the St. Louis area setting the boundaries between the constituents of Clay and Democratic Leader Richard A. Gephardt. The two ultimately reached an agreement under which the black population of the 1st District was reduced to half the district total, down from the three-fifths it had reached by the late 1990s.

Concerns over campaigns and elections did not occupy all of Clay's time in the 107th. On the Government Reform Committee, he sought a congressional probe of nursing home conditions in his district after four people died of heat stress in 2001. The inquiry, by the committee's Democratic staff, found that all 30 of the homes that care for Medicaid or Medicare recipients had violated federal safety and health standards, and that half of them had serious violations.

One of Clay's priorities is to spur economic development in urban St. Louis County — where crime and a troubled public school system have contributed to a steady decline in population. In 2001, Clay was able to earmark $5 million in the defense spending bill for cleanup work at the abandoned St. Louis Army Ammunitions Plant. The 21-acre site is in a prime location for commercial development and will be a valuable piece of real estate once the toxic wastes have been removed. He and other area lawmakers are also keeping tabs on the big Ford Motor Co. Hazelwood plant in the 1st District, which Ford has said it plans to close.

Economic development is a family effort. Clay's wife, Ivie, works for the St. Louis Development Corporation, the city's economic development agency.

Clay was 12 when his father was elected to Congress, and he spent his teenage years in suburban Maryland, attending high school in Silver Spring and college in College Park. A government and politics major, Clay also earned a paralegal certificate. He was just starting law school at Howard University when an opening in the Missouri House drew him back to St. Louis to run in a special election.

He spent the next 17 years in the General Assembly, serving eight years in the state House before winning a 1991 special election for a state Senate vacancy. He supplemented his part-time legislator's salary by working in real estate and as a paralegal.

In Jefferson City, Clay helped push through measures benefiting welfare recipients, imposing new penalties for hate crimes and creating tax breaks for those saving for education and home ownership. When the Ku Klux Klan announced that its members would "adopt" a stretch of Interstate 55 to keep it clean, Clay orchestrated legislative action to name that segment of the road after civil rights icon Rosa Parks.

Clay was the presumed heir to the 1st District seat from the moment his father announced his retirement. He won his first term with 75 percent of the vote and captured 70 percent in 2002 against Republican Richard Schwadron, a Boeing project manager.

KEY VOTES

2002

Yes	Overhaul campaign finance law; ban "soft money" and restrict advocacy advertising
?	Back Bush's defense budget increase
No	Extend 1996 welfare law
No	Adopt Bush's discretionary spending limit
?	Pass GOP Medicare prescription drug plan
?	Create independent Sept. 11 commission
Yes	Extend union protections to Homeland Security Department employees
No	Revive fast-track procedures for trade agreements
No	Authorize war against Iraq
No	Advance bankruptcy overhaul opposed by abortion opponents

2001

No	Nullify Clinton Labor Department ergonomics rule
No	Cut taxes by $1.35 trillion through fiscal 2011
Yes	Maintain ban on oil drilling in Arctic National Wildlife Refuge
No	Approve Bush proposal to limit managed-care plan liability for coverage decisions
Yes	Divert money from crop subsidy payments to land conservation
?	Expand law enforcement power to investigate suspected terrorists

CQ VOTE STUDIES

	PARTY UNITY		PRESIDENTIAL SUPPORT	
	Support	Oppose	Support	Oppose
2002	94%	6%	32%	68%
2001	95%	5%	21%	79%

INTEREST GROUPS

	AFL-CIO	ADA	CCUS	ACU
2002	100%	80%	44%	4%
2001	100%	100%	35%	8%

MISSOURI 1

North St. Louis; northeast St. Louis County

Flanked by the Mississippi and Missouri rivers, the St. Louis-based 1st is a mixture of poor center-city communities and middle-class suburbs. Redistricting following the 2000 census extended the district further west in St. Louis County to offset a population decline fueled by crime and deteriorating housing conditions.

The 1st takes in the northern half of St. Louis, including most of the city's popular attractions, such as the Gateway Arch and Forest Park, which attracts more than 12 million visitors a year. Many of the area's largest employers are scattered throughout the 1st, including BJC HealthCare, one of the largest nonprofit health care organizations in the United States.

Suburbs in St. Louis County include the region's main airport (one of the nation's 10 busiest) and a Boeing jet plant added in redistricting. Residents here are concerned by Ford's plan to close its Hazelwood assembly plant by mid-decade.

By far the state's most heavily Democratic district, the 1st handed Al Gore a 45-point victory in 2000. Local and state contests almost always favor Democrats. The black population, which stood at just under 60 percent after the 1990 census, has decreased considerably, though African-Americans still make up almost 50 percent of district voters.

Deep state budget cuts have led to cutbacks in city spending, making education, health care and housing key issues for voters at the polls. Allegations of voting fraud in the 2000 Senate and gubernatorial elections thrust St. Louis into the national debate over an election standards bill, and made officials eager to replace the district's aging voting equipment.

MAJOR INDUSTRY

Manufacturing, aircraft, higher education

CITIES

St. Louis (pt.), 163,020; Florissant, 50,497; Hazelwood, 26,206; University City (pt.), 24,075; Ferguson, 22,406

NOTABLE

The Missouri History Museum, St. Louis Art Museum, St. Louis Zoo and St. Louis Science Center are located in 1400-acre Forest Park, which calls itself the nation's seventh-largest urban park.

Rep. Todd Akin (R)

CAPITOL OFFICE
225-2561
rep.akin@mail.house.gov
www.house.gov/akin
117 Cannon 20515-2502; fax 225-2563

COMMITTEES
Armed Services
Science
Small Business
(Workforce, Empowerment & Government Programs - chairman)

HOMETOWN
Town & Country

BORN
July 5, 1947, Manhattan, N.Y.

RELIGION
Christian

FAMILY
Wife, Lulli Akin; six children

EDUCATION
Worcester Polytechnic Institute, B.S. 1971 (engineering); Covenant Theological Seminary, M.Div. 1985

MILITARY SERVICE
Army, 1972-80

CAREER
University lecturer; steel company manager; computer company marketing executive

POLITICAL HIGHLIGHTS
Mo. House, 1989-2000

ELECTION RESULTS

2002 GENERAL		
Todd Akin (R)	167,057	67.1%
John Hogan (D)	77,223	31.0%
Darla R. Maloney (LIBERT)	4,548	1.8%
2002 PRIMARY		
Todd Akin (R)		unopposed
2000 GENERAL		
Todd Akin (R)	164,926	55.3%
Ted House (D)	126,441	42.4%

Elected 2000; 2nd term

A conservative's conservative, Akin does not mince words. "We need Republican congressmen who have the backbone to challenge the failed liberal dogma of our recent past," proclaimed the Web site for his initial campaign for the House in 2000.

At the time, he was in his 12th year as a state legislator, where he was known for his aggressive pursuit of conservative principles, both social and fiscal. Akin is steadfastly opposed to abortion, same-sex marriage and gun control. He served on the board of Missouri Right to Life. His six children are educated at home, and he advocates more local control of schools. He also wants to give parents more choice over the schools their children attend.

When he failed to prevail in the Missouri General Assembly, Akin went to the courthouse. He unsuccessfully sued the State of Missouri after the legislature approved a schools bill that included $310 million in tax increases. Later, wary of the social impact of expanded gambling, he brought suit against the state's approval of "riverboat" casino licenses for several vessels permanently anchored in man-made ponds near the Missouri River. The court battle eventually led to a referendum on the issue that, while permitting such arrangements, served to tighten state regulation of the industry.

Akin says he bases his political philosophy on his considerable study of the early history of the United States. He has concluded that the nation's early covenants, including the Mayflower Compact and the Constitution, between the people and those who govern set the United States apart.

The role of government, he says, is to make distinctions between good ideas and bad ones and to be the servant of the people. He wants to curb the size and scope of the federal government by seeking a constitutional amendment to restrict the growth of revenue flowing to the Treasury. Much of federal spending, with the exception of money for the military, is suspect in Akin's eyes.

In the 108th Congress, Akin's prospects for legislative success are improved with his new chairmanship of the Small Business panel's Subcommittee on Workforce, Empowerment, and Government Programs.

In his first term, he concentrated on the work of the Armed Services Committee, a good match for a former Army lieutenant. He worked to look out for the interests of Boeing Co., which has large plants in St. Charles County, in the 2nd District, as well as in St. Louis, in the 1st. As the Pentagon in 2001 weighed competing bids by Boeing and Lockheed Martin Corp. for a contract to build the Joint Strike Fighter, Akin and Republican Sen. Christopher S. Bond of Missouri called for both companies to share the work. Akin argued that the loser might drop out of the jet-fighter business, hurting national security in the long run. Lockheed won the contract, but firms in the St. Louis area wound up getting some peripheral work from the job. Boeing also won a contract with South Korea for another fighter.

On the Science Committee, Akin and Illinois Democrat Jerry F. Costello teamed to push for accelerated research in developing technologies to burn coal with less pollution.

In the 107th Congress, Akin was the author of a successful amendment to an education bill that required any federally mandated tests to measure "objective knowledge rather than opinions or beliefs." He explained the rationale for his proposal by saying: "I do not believe . . . it is reasonable for us to be testing a kid and measuring them up or down based on what their religious persuasion is or their political persuasion." Akin also believes the federal government should pay a higher share of the costs of educating disabled children — a costly mandate that it has imposed on local schools.

He was in the minority of Republicans who voted against the new farm law enacted in 2002, saying it cost too much. He argued that the measure represented a step backward as it allowed for more government involvement in agriculture, which GOP conservatives had hoped to end in the 1996 "Freedom to Farm" law.

Akin's great-grandfather founded the Laclede Steel Co. of St. Louis, and his father worked there as well. Akin grew up in the St. Louis area but went to college in Massachusetts, where he studied engineering and joined the Army ROTC. After serving as an Army combat engineer, Akin sold large computers for IBM in Massachusetts, where he met his wife, Lulli. After four years, Akin returned home to Missouri. He worked for a while at Laclede Steel and then decided to enter divinity school.

Akin says the combination of his engineering and seminary training gives him the scientific problem-solving skills and the theological reference points that enable him to study the "mechanics of how our system was put together." His academic training also helps him determine how officials should judge which public policy ideas are good and which are not, he says.

Akin's reputation in Springfield as a doctrinaire state legislator spurred opponents to label him as ideologically isolated when he launched his campaign for the House seat being vacated by Republican Jim Talent, who left Congress in 2000 to run for governor. But ardent grass-roots support enabled Akin to narrowly prevail in a five-way primary, defeating former St. Louis County Executive Gene McNary by 56 votes. Many observers credited Akin's victory to bad weather on Election Day that hurt turnout for McNary. But Akin told the St. Louis Post-Dispatch, "My base will show up in earthquakes."

The Democratic nominee, state Sen. Ted House, who holds conservative views on social issues such as abortion, characterized Akin's views on health care and education as "far extreme," but an energetic campaign style and the district's GOP leanings carried Akin to a 13-point victory.

Akin was the lone member of the nine-member Missouri House delegation to oppose the congressional redistricting map for the state drawn after the 2000 census. The plan was a result of a compromise among the other members of the delegation. Although his district became more Republican, Akin objected to changes that split some suburban St. Louis communities. In 2002, he easily dispatched perennial candidate John Hogan, who runs for some office every two years, by better than 2-to-1.

KEY VOTES

2002

No Overhaul campaign finance law; ban "soft money" and restrict advocacy advertising
Yes Back Bush's defense budget increase
Yes Extend 1996 welfare law
Yes Adopt Bush's discretionary spending limit
Yes Pass GOP Medicare prescription drug plan
No Create independent Sept. 11 commission
No Extend union protections to Homeland Security Department employees
Yes Revive fast-track procedures for trade agreements
Yes Authorize war against Iraq
No Advance bankruptcy overhaul opposed by abortion opponents

2001

Yes Nullify Clinton Labor Department ergonomics rule
Yes Cut taxes by $1.35 trillion through fiscal 2011
No Maintain ban on oil drilling in Arctic National Wildlife Refuge
Yes Approve Bush proposal to limit managed-care plan liability for coverage decisions
No Divert money from crop subsidy payments to land conservation
Yes Expand law enforcement power to investigate suspected terrorists

CQ VOTE STUDIES

	PARTY UNITY		PRESIDENTIAL SUPPORT	
	Support	Oppose	Support	Oppose
2002	98%	2%	90%	10%
2001	97%	3%	86%	14%

INTEREST GROUPS

	AFL-CIO	ADA	CCUS	ACU
2002	11%	0%	85%	100%
2001	0%	5%	91%	100%

MISSOURI 2

Western St. Louis County; north and eastern St. Charles County — St. Charles

Composed mostly of upper-middle-class white suburbanites, the 2nd is one of the state's richest and fastest-growing districts. Western St. Louis and St. Charles counties continue to prosper from a westward migration started by mass population departures from St. Louis in the 1980s.

Commuter traffic into the St. Louis business district remains heavy, but local residents are increasingly finding lucrative jobs away from the city. Boeing employs many 2nd District residents, though redistricting following the 2000 census moved the company's main manufacturing facility into the neighboring1st District. DaimlerChrysler and a General Motors plant in Wentzville are major employers, along with biotechnology and financial services companies. A dwindling but diverse agriculture industry supports the northern fringes around the Mississippi-Missouri river junction.

Although Democrats held the 2nd during most of the latter part of the 20th century, Republicans have dominated in recent years. GOP presidential candidates won the district in 1992, 1996 and 2000, and Republicans have an edge in state and local races.

Wealthy communities such as Ladue and Frontenac are unshakably Republican, and the removal of union-laden Florissant, St. Ann and Bridgeton during redistricting moved the district further into the GOP column. Lincoln County, added in redistricting, threw a Democratic-leaning constituency into the mix, but the 2nd supported George W. Bush by a 58 percent to 39 percent tally in the 2000 presidential race, a 7 percentage point gain over Bush's victory margin under the old boundaries.

MAJOR INDUSTRY

Auto manufacturing, biotechnology, agriculture

CITIES

St. Charles, 60,321; St. Peters (pt.), 50,001; Chesterfield, 46,802; O'Fallon (pt.), 44,949; Wildwood, 32,884; Ballwin, 31,283

NOTABLE

Route 66 State Park near Eureka is located on what was Times Beach, the site of an environmental disaster where soil became tainted with dioxin.

Rep. Richard A. Gephardt (D)

CAPITOL OFFICE
225-2671
www.house.gov/gephardt
1236 Longworth 20515-2503; fax 225-7452

COMMITTEES
No committee assignments

HOMETOWN
St. Louis

BORN
Jan. 31, 1941, St. Louis, Mo.

RELIGION
Baptist

FAMILY
Wife, Jane Byrnes Gephardt; three children

EDUCATION
Northwestern U., B.S. 1962; U. of Michigan, J.D. 1965

MILITARY SERVICE
Mo. Air National Guard, 1965-71

CAREER
Lawyer

POLITICAL HIGHLIGHTS
St. Louis Board of Aldermen, 1971-76; sought Democratic nomination for president, 1988

ELECTION RESULTS

2002 GENERAL		
Richard A. Gephardt (D)	122,181	59.1%
Catherine S. Enz (R)	80,551	38.9%
Dan Byington (LIBERT)	4,146	2.0%
2002 PRIMARY		
Richard A. Gephardt (D)	44,535	73.6%
Michael Bram (D)	16,014	26.5%
2000 GENERAL		
Richard A. Gephardt (D)	147,222	57.8%
William J. Federer (R)	100,967	39.7%
Mary Maroney (GREEN)	3,266	1.3%

PREVIOUS WINNING PERCENTAGES
1998 (56%); 1996 (59%); 1994 (58%); 1992 (64%); 1990 (57%); 1988 (63%); 1986 (69%); 1984 (100%); 1982 (78%); 1980 (78%); 1978 (82%); 1976 (64%)

Elected 1976; 14th term

For what looms as his final term in Congress, Gephardt has stepped down as Democratic leader after 13 1/2 years, the longest run since John W. McCormack of Massachusetts held the job for most of two decades ending in 1962. Gephardt is pursuing the goal he set for himself long before he joined the House hierarchy — winning the White House.

His second presidential quest effectively compelled him to give up his leadership post after the 107th Congress. Gephardt was the House majority leader from June 1989 until the GOP takeover of 1995 and minority leader for eight years after that. His colleagues, frustrated by setbacks in the 2002 election, made clear they would not allow Gephardt to remain as leader if he pursued the party's 2004 presidential nomination. They wanted someone who would focus on regaining control of the House, a goal that has eluded them in spite of Gephardt's best efforts in four elections.

Gephardt is only the second Democratic leader since the 1920s who has failed to become Speaker. The other was Hale Boggs of Louisiana, who died in office in 1972. But as he yielded the leader's job to Nancy Pelosi of California, he expressed relief that he would no longer have to speak for the often-fractious House Democrats. "I'm looking forward to the freedom to speak for myself and talk about my vision for America's future," he said.

Gephardt came to Congress in 1977 as a moderate-to-conservative Democrat, opposed to abortion rights and school busing and in favor of President Reagan's 1981 tax cut. He shifted to the left in preparation for his first presidential bid in 1988. He hewed to a liberal line as he considered running again in 2000, opposing President Clinton on trade, welfare and the budget.

But during the 107th, he moved back toward the center. He sided with President Bush 31 percent of the time, putting him squarely in the middle of all House Democrats' presidential support scores.

Most notably, he teamed with Bush in 2002 to write the resolution authorizing the use of force against Iraq. Gephardt long had spoken out on the need for regime change in Baghdad, but his deal with the White House angered many Democrats, in part because it undercut Senate Majority Leader Tom Daschle's effort to force Bush to work through the United Nations. Gephardt insisted his presidential aspirations played no part in the decision. He said he regretted his 1991 vote against the war that drove Iraq from Kuwait, and he implored all Democrats to vote their conscience without "questioning others' motives." A majority of his peers voted against him.

More often than not, however, Gephardt was in step with House Democrats. He earned praise from colleagues for his tireless fundraising and campaigning in their behalf, and for his ability to unify Democrats on key votes despite deep differences between liberals and moderates. Some critics say his drive to find a House Democratic consensus often left his party with a muddled message, or none at all. The House, for example, advanced parts of Bush's tax cut in 2001 with unexpectedly large numbers of Democratic votes, a result of what some saw as Gephardt's failure to set a cohesive party strategy for dealing with the new president.

GOP leaders in recent years often excoriated him, portraying Gephardt as unduly partisan. His allies say his biggest flaw politically is appearing stiff and emotionally distant. He is not one to show his feelings publicly. While hailed as a good listener, it is rare to catch him in an unguarded moment, joking with colleagues or revealing disappointment or anger.

Gephardt and Speaker J. Dennis Hastert maintained a particularly icy relationship well into the 107th Congress. It thawed somewhat in the surge of bipartisanship after the Sept. 11, 2001, terrorist attacks. The two were evacuated by helicopter to spend much of that day together in a military bunker in the Virginia wilderness. They also bonded after they were branded "wimps" by the New York Post for their handling of the anonymous anthrax-tainted letter attacks against targeted lawmakers in 2001.

Gephardt eschewed a presidential run in the 2000 election and spurned overtures to be Al Gore's running mate in order to concentrate on recapturing the House. The issues seemed to be breaking the Democrats' way. For a final pre-election meeting of House Democrats, he donned the breastplate and facial war paint of the Scottish freedom fighter depicted in the film "Braveheart." He raised $37 million for Democratic House candidates and pressured senior incumbents to postpone retirements.

Gephardt was seen by colleagues as working diligently for their cause again two years later, but the shifting of his interest to his own national race was palpable. In the 2002 election, the party lost five seats — the first reversal of the steady gains it had been making since losing control in 1994.

In his first race for the nomination in 1988, Gephardt won the Democratic presidential caucus in Iowa but dropped out soon after finishing second in the New Hampshire primary to Massachusetts Gov. Michael S. Dukakis, the eventual nominee. He may be hard to peg in his second national campaign. An ally of labor unions and environmentalists, he also helped found the moderate, pro-business Democratic Leadership Council.

As his 2004 bid began, Gephardt was relying heavily on a series of personal anecdotes to promote his agenda and soften his image with human touches. He never fails to mention that his father, Lou, was a milk truck driver and a member of the Teamsters union.

When he talks about medical care for the uninsured, he notes how hard it would have been to pay for the childhood cancer treatment of his son, Matt, without a good insurance plan. He has proposed subsidizing college tuition for would-be teachers, he says, because of the low salary his daughter Kate earns as a teacher. And he wants to make pension plans portable between jobs because of his mother, Loreen. He says she received only $42 each month in pension because she changed jobs so frequently.

Gephardt first was elected to Congress in 1976, to the seat of retiring Democrat Leonor K. Sullivan. He won on the strength of his reputation as a young activist on the machine-dominated St. Louis Board of Aldermen, where he served six years. He has struggled some in recent years, winning with less than 60 percent of the vote in six of his last seven elections.

KEY VOTES

2002

Yes Overhaul campaign finance law; ban "soft money" and restrict advocacy advertising
Yes Back Bush's defense budget increase
No Extend 1996 welfare law
No Adopt Bush's discretionary spending limit
No Pass GOP Medicare prescription drug plan
Yes Create independent Sept. 11 commission
Yes Extend union protections to Homeland Security Department employees
No Revive fast-track procedures for trade agreements
Yes Authorize war against Iraq
No Advance bankruptcy overhaul opposed by abortion opponents

2001

No Nullify Clinton Labor Department ergonomics rule
No Cut taxes by $1.35 trillion through fiscal 2011
Yes Maintain ban on oil drilling in Arctic National Wildlife Refuge
No Approve Bush proposal to limit managed-care plan liability for coverage decisions
Yes Divert money from crop subsidy payments to land conservation
Yes Expand law enforcement power to investigate suspected terrorists

CQ VOTE STUDIES

	PARTY UNITY		PRESIDENTIAL SUPPORT	
	Support	Oppose	Support	Oppose
2002	93%	7%	33%	67%
2001	94%	6%	29%	71%
2000	93%	7%	83%	17%
1999	94%	6%	88%	12%
1998	93%	7%	82%	18%

INTEREST GROUPS

	AFL-CIO	ADA	CCUS	ACU
2002	100%	90%	35%	8%
2001	100%	95%	30%	13%
2000	100%	90%	28%	13%
1999	89%	100%	24%	0%
1998	100%	90%	24%	12%

MISSOURI 3

South St. Louis; southeast St. Louis County; Jefferson and Ste. Genevieve counties

Bordered on the east by the Mississippi River, the 3rd includes the southern half of St. Louis, as well as older, established suburbs and newer, sprawling ones. Most of the suburban middle-class residents commute to St. Louis County's business district, although there are traces of small-scale farming, manufacturing and river trading.

Whereas St. Louis as a whole (shared with the 1st District) has declined in population in the past few decades, south St. Louis' residential areas have remained stable. Large Italian and German neighborhoods continue to present a strong voice. To the south, Jefferson County has been one of the state's fastest-growing areas since 1980. Bedroom communities such as Arnold and Imperial continue to prosper.

Many suburban residents work outside the district. Anheuser-Busch, headquartered in the 3rd's portion of St. Louis, is a major provider of jobs to the region. The National Imagery and Mapping Agency also has facilities in the district. Farther south, on the fringes of Ste. Genevieve County, small farming complements a sizable trading industry along the docks of the Mississippi River, where chemical facilities also are located.

The district's blue-collar base favors Democrats, although the GOP finds significant support in middle-class communities such as Arnold and a large Catholic contingent gives the district an anti-abortion tilt. The 3rd's communities often fight over education and economic development funding. Redistricting following the 2000 census removed some traditionally conservative areas, such as Sunset Hills. The revised 3rd gave Al Gore 54 percent of the vote in the 2000 presidential election.

MAJOR INDUSTRY

Beer manufacturing, defense, health care

CITIES

St. Louis (pt.), 185,169; Oakville (unincorporated), 35,309; Mehlville (unincorporated) (pt.), 27,055; Webster Groves, 23,230

NOTABLE

The Missouri Botanical Garden is in St. Louis.

Rep. Ike Skelton (D)

CAPITOL OFFICE
225-2876
ike.skelton@mail.house.gov
www.house.gov/skelton
2206 Rayburn 20515-2504; fax 225-2695

COMMITTEES
Armed Services - ranking member

HOMETOWN
Lexington

BORN
Dec. 20, 1931, Lexington, Mo.

RELIGION
Christian Church

FAMILY
Wife, Susan Skelton; three children

EDUCATION
Wentworth Military Academy, A.A. 1951; U. of Edinburgh (United Kingdom), attended 1953; U. of Missouri, A.B. 1953 (history), LL.B. 1956

CAREER
Lawyer; state prosecutor

POLITICAL HIGHLIGHTS
Lafayette County prosecuting attorney, 1957-60; Mo. Senate, 1971-77

ELECTION RESULTS

2002 GENERAL		
Ike Skelton (D)	142,204	67.6%
James A. Noland Jr. (R)	64,451	30.7%
Daniel Roy Nelson (LIBERT)	3,583	1.7%
2002 PRIMARY		
Ike Skelton (D)		unopposed
2000 GENERAL		
Ike Skelton (D)	180,634	66.9%
James A. Noland Jr. (R)	84,406	31.3%
Thomas L. Knapp (LIBERT)	2,878	1.1%

PREVIOUS WINNING PERCENTAGES
1998 (71%); 1996 (64%); 1994 (68%); 1992 (70%); 1990 (62%); 1988 (72%); 1986 (100%); 1984 (67%); 1982 (55%); 1980 (68%); 1978 (73%); 1976 (56%)

Elected 1976; 14th term

With a Republican in the White House, Skelton came into his own in the 107th Congress as a leading Democratic voice on defense. On the two most significant national security issues that President Bush presented to Congress — his request for authority to go to war with Iraq and his decision to deploy a nationwide anti-missile defense — House Democratic leaders turned to Skelton to help determine the party's position.

Skelton's hawkish views gave them political cover against their party's post-Vietnam reputation for being soft on defense. In more than two decades on the Armed Services panel, where he has been senior Democrat since 1998, Skelton has been a reliable supporter of high defense budgets with a particular concern for the welfare of the troops and their combat-readiness.

Familiar with the broad sweep of military affairs, Skelton helped shape hard-nosed, practical critiques of Bush's proposals behind which Democrats of widely varying ideological stripes could rally. Weeks before the House voted to authorize war with Iraq, Skelton was badgering Bush to lay out a strategy for encouraging the emergence of a politically stable post-war regime in Iraq. "I have no doubt that our military would decisively defeat Iraq's forces and remove Saddam," he wrote the president, "but like the proverbial dog chasing the car, we must consider what we would do after we caught it."

Ultimately, nearly two-thirds of House Democrats voted against the Iraq resolution, which Skelton supported. But unlike Bush's initial proposal, Skelton contended, the resolution that was adopted reflected Democrats' preference for acting multilaterally, if possible, and for staying the course after a military victory to rebuild a peaceable Iraq.

On missile defense, Skelton and other Democratic centrists supported the eventual deployment of a system that could fend off small numbers of missiles launched by North Korea or other rogue states. But they insisted the system undergo adequate testing before deployment and that it not be funded at the expense of more-pressing defense requirements, particularly pay and other factors bearing on the troops' quality of life.

"I see the need to increase budgets for re-enlistment bonuses, special pays, recruiting and family housing," he said, commenting on Bush's decision to deploy the first phase of a missile defense by 2004. This call for "increased funding to deploy an untested missile defense system gives me concern about their priorities."

Indeed, Skelton has been critical of Bush — as he had been of President Clinton — for spreading U.S. troops too thin. He has sponsored various legislative initiatives that would at least give the administration the option of increasing the number of active-duty personnel. But the Bush team has been no more receptive to the idea than their Democratic predecessors.

Although a childhood bout with polio kept Skelton from military service, he has had a lifelong interest in military history. And much of his desire to maintain military readiness stems from his study of the years between the World Wars — years that saw the allies disarm too much too soon. Convinced the military was not producing the kind of strategic thinkers who won World War II, in the 1980s Skelton helped push through legislation that changed the emphasis in war colleges from management skills to strategic thinking.

In 1985, Skelton and other defense-minded majority Democrats on Armed Services replaced the panel's aged and ailing chairman, Melvin Price of Illinois, with Les Aspin of Wisconsin, who made the committee an active force in shaping defense policy. He later joined Aspin to write the law that shifted power from the separate armed services to senior commanders responsible for military operations around the world; the measure sought to improve coordination among the services and to give the president more coherent military advice. That law was widely credited with the smooth integration of forces during the 1991 Persian Gulf War.

Skelton viewed Clinton's defense budgets as anemic and goaded the administration to request more money and more troops. But he also parried some GOP attacks on Clinton. Like many Republicans, Skelton warned that Clinton was wearing out U.S. forces by frequently sending them overseas while cutting manpower. But he opposed congressional efforts to force a pullout once troops were in the field.

In 2000, Skelton endorsed a new challenge to conventional Pentagon thinking, calling on the Navy to supplement its fleet of large warships with smaller, less expensive vessels that could be built in greater numbers.

On most social issues, Skelton is in tune with his constituents and, thus, at odds with his more liberal Democratic colleagues. He has opposed abortion in most cases, voted to repeal the ban on certain semiautomatic assault-style weapons, and backed the overhaul of the welfare system. On votes pitting most Democrats against most Republicans, he stuck with his party only 67 percent of the time in the 107th Congress. In 1993, as chairman of the Armed Services subcommittee dealing with personnel, Skelton — who had qualms about Clinton's proposal to revoke the military's ban on homosexuals — was one of the key Democrats who pushed the "don't ask, don't tell" compromise that Clinton accepted.

Skelton's father, a friend of Harry S. Truman, brought his son to Washington for the 1949 inauguration. Truman has continued to occupy a central role in Skelton's political life: He was endorsed by Truman's widow, chaired a joint session of Congress on the day it observed Truman's 100th birthday, and fought a Smithsonian exhibit on the dropping of the first atomic bomb because he viewed it as unfairly questioning Truman's motives toward the Japanese.

After six years in the state Senate, Skelton ran for the House in 1976, seeking to succeed retiring Democrat William Randall. As a rural state legislator with a narrow political base, Skelton did not look particularly well-positioned when the campaign began, but he won with 56 percent. That was his closest race, except for a 1982 post-redistricting contest when he was forced to run against GOP freshman Rep. Wendell Bailey. Skelton benefited from greater familiarity with the new district's voters, and he won with 55 percent.

KEY VOTES

2002

- Yes Overhaul campaign finance law; ban "soft money" and restrict advocacy advertising
- Yes Back Bush's defense budget increase
- No Extend 1996 welfare law
- No Adopt Bush's discretionary spending limit
- No Pass GOP Medicare prescription drug plan
- Yes Create independent Sept. 11 commission
- Yes Extend union protections to Homeland Security Department employees
- Yes Revive fast-track procedures for trade agreements
- Yes Authorize war against Iraq
- Yes Advance bankruptcy overhaul opposed by abortion opponents

2001

- Yes Nullify Clinton Labor Department ergonomics rule
- No Cut taxes by $1.35 trillion through fiscal 2011
- No Maintain ban on oil drilling in Arctic National Wildlife Refuge
- No Approve Bush proposal to limit managed-care plan liability for coverage decisions
- No Divert money from crop subsidy payments to land conservation
- Yes Expand law enforcement power to investigate suspected terrorists

CQ VOTE STUDIES

	PARTY UNITY		PRESIDENTIAL SUPPORT	
	Support	Oppose	Support	Oppose
2002	73%	27%	58%	42%
2001	61%	39%	56%	44%
2000	70%	30%	61%	39%
1999	61%	39%	64%	36%
1998	64%	36%	58%	42%

INTEREST GROUPS

	AFL-CIO	ADA	CCUS	ACU
2002	67%	60%	70%	32%
2001	67%	50%	64%	64%
2000	80%	40%	66%	40%
1999	78%	55%	52%	41%
1998	90%	65%	65%	36%

MISSOURI 4

West central – Kansas City suburbs, Jefferson City

Laden with lakes, rivers and farmland, the 4th follows the Missouri River on much of its northern border. Besides portions of southeast Kansas City suburbs, state capital Jefferson City and medium-size Sedalia, the district typifies rural and small-town Missouri.

Most residents work at small-scale farming — row crops, soybeans and livestock — or moderate-size manufacturing of household goods. The farming communities generally have recovered from "hundred-year" Missouri River floods in 1993 and 1995. Tourism helps the rural areas. In Camden County, the Lake of the Ozarks region (shared with the 9th), with modern hotels and retail outlets, attracts 300,000 boaters a weekend during peak times. The lake areas also draw many retirees.

The 4th's piece of the Kansas City suburbs has not grown as fast as the area north of the city (in the 6th), and the suburbs are not as affluent, but they provide some blue-collar manufacturing jobs. Across the district, in Jefferson City, state government employs more than 15,000 people.

Congressional elections heavily favor Democrats in the western counties while Republican votes can be tilled farther east, especially in Webster and Camden counties, and in counties in the southwest, such as Cedar and Barton, which were added from the old 7th during 2001 redistricting. The district may be trending Republican — GOP state legislators outnumber their Democratic counterparts 2-to-1 in the state districts covering the 4th, and George W. Bush took 58 percent of the vote in the 2000 presidential election.

MAJOR INDUSTRY

Government, defense, agriculture, manufacturing

MILITARY BASES

Fort Leonard Wood, 5,716 military, 2,302 civilian; Whiteman Air Force Base, 5,084 military, 1,164 civilian (2002)

CITIES

Jefferson City (pt.), 39,611; Sedalia, 20,339; Warrensburg, 16,340

NOTABLE

President Harry S Truman was born in Lamar; Sedalia hosts the Scott Joplin Ragtime Festival each June; The restored home of George Caleb Bingham in Arrow Rock honors the late American artist.

Rep. Karen McCarthy (D)

CAPITOL OFFICE
225-4535
www.house.gov/karenmccarthy
1436 Longworth 20515-2505; fax 225-4403

COMMITTEES
Energy & Commerce
Select Homeland Security

HOMETOWN
Kansas City

BORN
March 18, 1947, Haverhill, Mass.

RELIGION
Roman Catholic

FAMILY
Divorced

EDUCATION
U. of Kansas, B.S. 1969; U. of Birmingham, England, attended 1974; U. of Missouri, Kansas City, M.A. 1976; U. of Kansas, M.B.A. 1986

CAREER
Investment banking analyst; teacher

POLITICAL HIGHLIGHTS
Mo. House, 1977-95

ELECTION RESULTS

2002 GENERAL		
Karen McCarthy (D)	122,645	65.9%
Steve Gordon (R)	60,245	32.4%
Jeanne F. Bojarski (LIBERT)	3,277	1.8%
2002 PRIMARY		
Karen McCarthy (D)	40,532	86.3%
Charles Lindsey (D)	6,460	13.8%
2000 GENERAL		
Karen McCarthy (D)	159,826	68.9%
Steve Gordon (R)	66,439	28.6%
Charles Reitz (GREEN)	2,548	1.1%
Alan Newberry (LIBERT)	2,350	1.0%

PREVIOUS WINNING PERCENTAGES
1998 (66%); 1996 (67%); 1994 (57%)

Elected 1994; 5th term

Her district is famous for its sultry blues, tangy barbecue and Jesse James outlaw lore, but McCarthy registers as being as unassuming and manifestly moderate as they come in Congress. It is a recipe that so far appears to have served her well.

A career politician, she came to Washington in 1995 after toiling in the Missouri State House for 18 years. As a Democrat who won her seat in Congress in the teeth of the Republican revolution, McCarthy prides herself on being a non-ideological consensus builder. And as she moves toward the end of her first decade in the House, her political philosophy and voting record offer something to each of the three main factions in the Democratic Caucus — traditional liberals, conservative "Blue Dogs," and centrists who call themselves the New Democrat Coalition.

McCarthy belongs to the New Democrat group, which says it seeks "mainstream, bipartisan solutions." She joined most lawmakers in this group in backing measures that liberal Democrats generally rejected, such as the 1996 welfare overhaul. In her freshman year, she backed the GOP "Contract with America" 59 percent of the time, joining Republicans in votes to limit unfunded federal mandates and to require a balanced budget.

On some issues, however, McCarthy leans to the left. She is a strong supporter of environmental regulations, gun control and women's rights such as equal pay. A divorced Catholic, McCarthy supports abortion rights and stem cell research. She also has staunchly opposed the budget priorities of the Republican majority and President Bush.

Yet she joined with the GOP majority and the Democratic Blue Dogs in two of their constitutional amendment crusades — to mandate a balanced federal budget and to permit Congress to ban desecration of the U.S. flag. The fiscally conservative Concord Coalition gives her high marks.

Her experience in state government gives her a measure of sympathy for the GOP view that state and local officials should have more authority. Still, she maintains that "government does have a responsibility to see that each individual has opportunity." As she once told the Kansas City Star: "Sometimes people need boots in order to pull themselves up by those bootstraps. I see government's role as getting out of the way once that's accomplished."

McCarthy applies the notion of limited government to her own office, where she employs fewer staff aides than most other members and keeps her use of her free mail privileges to a minimum. Such practices have permitted her to spend nearly $180,000 less than the average member of Congress annually and earned her the National Taxpayers Union's ranking as one of the House's most thrifty members.

Since the 105th Congress, McCarthy has served on the Energy and Commerce Committee, where she has dealt with many of the wide range of issues under the panel's purview, including telecommunications, the environment, energy, Medicare and welfare. In the 107th Congress, she joined forces with the Republican members of Congress from her state on an initiative designed to increase the use of fuel made with soybeans, a huge cash crop in Missouri. The polluted abandoned industrial or military sites known as brownfields have been one of her particular interests, and McCarthy played a key role in 1997 in providing tax incentives for businesses to clean up these sites.

In the 108th, she added a seat on the new Homeland Security Committee, where she will focus on the needs of first responders in dealing with emergencies or acts of terrorism.

McCarthy says she generally favors free trade. But she has voted "no" on recent trade liberalization measures: to grant China permanent status as a normal U.S. trading partner in the 106th Congress, and in the 107th against reviving fast-track procedures for congressional consideration of trade pacts.

On Capitol Hill, she has continued the work she began in Jefferson City in championing a compact between Missouri and Kansas that permits taxation in the Kansas City area to fund cultural facilities and restore historic structures, such as historic Union Station, which has been transformed into a science museum and children's learning center. In 2000, she wrote legislation to renew the state compact and worked to obtain federal grants to assist local projects.

At heart, McCarthy is a local politician. She is known for being attentive to constituent service and local road projects, such as a $41 million four-lane bridge across the Missouri River. And when market forces threatened to drive the Kansas City Royals out of business, McCarthy, an avid baseball fan, proposed legislation to share revenues between small- and big-market teams.

Born in Massachusetts, McCarthy lived on a farm there until she was 14, when her family moved to a Kansas City suburb. She can pinpoint the day she became interested in public service: her 21st birthday, in 1968, when Robert F. Kennedy spoke at the University of Kansas, where McCarthy was majoring in English. His speech "stays with me even now," she told the Kansas City Star. "So I knew from that day forward I would work for him, and thus would be a Democrat."

After graduation in 1969, she got a job teaching high school English but remained interested in politics. She was elected to the state House at age 29, and in the next 18 years she advanced steadily, becoming chairman of the Ways and Means Committee — all the while working as an analyst for an investment banking firm and later as a government affairs consultant.

She was the front-runner for her House seat from the start in 1994, when incumbent Democrat Alan Wheat chose to run for the Senate instead. After taking 41 percent of the primary vote against 10 rivals, she won the general election by 14 percentage points over conservative black Republican Ron Freeman, a former professional football player who worked for years as an urban youth coordinator.

Each of her four re-election victories since has been with 66 percent of the vote or better. Redistricting following the 2000 census added more Cass County suburbs to her territory, but these did not substantially alter the overall urban, left-leaning character of her constituency.

KEY VOTES

2002

- Yes Overhaul campaign finance law; ban "soft money" and restrict advocacy advertising
- Yes Back Bush's defense budget increase
- No Extend 1996 welfare law
- No Adopt Bush's discretionary spending limit
- No Pass GOP Medicare prescription drug plan
- \+ Create independent Sept. 11 commission
- Yes Extend union protections to Homeland Security Department employees
- No Revive fast-track procedures for trade agreements
- No Authorize war against Iraq
- No Advance bankruptcy overhaul opposed by abortion opponents

2001

- No Nullify Clinton Labor Department ergonomics rule
- – Cut taxes by $1.35 trillion through fiscal 2011
- Yes Maintain ban on oil drilling in Arctic National Wildlife Refuge
- No Approve Bush proposal to limit managed-care plan liability for coverage decisions
- Yes Divert money from crop subsidy payments to land conservation
- Yes Expand law enforcement power to investigate suspected terrorists

CQ VOTE STUDIES

	PARTY UNITY		PRESIDENTIAL SUPPORT	
	Support	Oppose	Support	Oppose
2002	95%	5%	29%	71%
2001	92%	8%	29%	71%
2000	94%	6%	87%	13%
1999	94%	6%	80%	20%
1998	92%	8%	81%	19%

INTEREST GROUPS

	AFL-CIO	ADA	CCUS	ACU
2002	100%	95%	40%	0%
2001	91%	95%	48%	4%
2000	100%	95%	52%	4%
1999	75%	95%	44%	0%
1998	89%	100%	56%	0%

MISSOURI 5

Kansas City and suburbs

Mostly middle-class Democratic residents live in Kansas City and the Jackson and Cass County suburbs that make up the 5th. Although the city's suburban growth is greatest in its Kansas portion, Missouri communities have prospered.

A diverse economic base has enabled Kansas City to grow from a cow town to a transportation and telecommunications hub. Steel and automobile production facilities highlight a solid industrial base. Many district residents travel to Kansas or neighboring districts to work at companies such as Sprint Communications and General Motors. The federal government also is a large employer. The city remains a viable market for feeder cattle and winter wheat, although on a smaller scale than in years past.

Hallmark Cards, one of Kansas City's largest employers, built a popular entertainment complex in the downtown area. Resurgence in high-end loft communities has lured younger, well-to-do residents to the city. Still, the contrasting neighborhoods on opposite sides of Troost Avenue remind residents of the economic disparity in the city, which largely runs along racial lines. Taking in nearly all of Kansas City's black neighborhoods, the district has a 24 percent black population. About half its voters are in Kansas City, half in the suburbs. Offshoot cities such as Lee's Summit and the 5th's portion of Cass County experienced rapid population growth during the first half of the 1990s. The city of Independence (a small part of which is in the 6th) still accounts for about one-fifth of the district's vote.

The 5th is reliably Democratic and socially moderate. Democrats have held the Kansas City seat since 1931, and Al Gore captured 60 percent of the district's vote in the 2000 presidential election.

MAJOR INDUSTRY

Auto manufacturing, agriculture

MILITARY BASES

Marine Corps Support Activity, 371 military, 242 civilian (2001)

CITIES

Kansas City (pt.), 322,910; Independence (pt.), 110,822; Lee's Summit (pt.), 65,498; Raytown, 30,388; Grandview, 24,881; Belton, 21,730

NOTABLE

President Harry S Truman hailed from Independence.

Rep. Sam Graves (R)

CAPITOL OFFICE
225-7041
sam.graves@mail.house.gov
www.house.gov/graves
1513 Longworth 20515-2506; fax 225-8221

COMMITTEES
Agriculture
Small Business
(Rural Enterprises, Agriculture & Technology - chairman)
Transportation & Infrastructure

HOMETOWN
Tarkio

BORN
Nov. 7, 1963, Fairfax, Mo.

RELIGION
Baptist

FAMILY
Wife, Lesley Graves; three children

EDUCATION
U. of Missouri, B.S. 1986 (agronomy)

CAREER
Farmer

POLITICAL HIGHLIGHTS
Mo. House, 1993-95; Mo. Senate, 1995-2001

ELECTION RESULTS

2002 GENERAL		
Sam Graves (R)	131,151	63.0%
Cathy Rinehart (D)	73,202	35.2%
Erik Buck (LIBERT)	3,735	1.8%
2002 PRIMARY		
Sam Graves (R)		unopposed
2000 GENERAL		
Sam Graves (R)	138,925	50.9%
Steve Danner (D)	127,792	46.8%
James Dykes (LIBERT)	3,696	1.4%
Marie Richey (NL)	2,788	1.0%

Elected 2000; 2nd term

During his two years in the Missouri House and six in the state Senate, Graves was known as a quiet conservative on both fiscal and social matters. But he made headlines occasionally — staging a filibuster that threatened a school desegregation bill that he thought did not contain enough for rural districts, successfully easing state automobile inspection requirements and proposing that prisoners be required to work on chain gangs.

Graves is best-known, however, for his commitment to farming. When he graduated with a degree in agronomy from the University of Missouri in 1986, Graves returned to the family farm in the far northwest corner of the state, becoming the sixth generation of Graveses to till the soil there.

Graves' dedication to farming despite the continuing exodus of farmers from the land was noteworthy enough that NBC's "Today" show featured him in 1987 to tell their viewers why he had chosen a career in farming. He said he wanted to continue his family's heritage, and he intended to make money from farming.

With Graves now in Congress, his younger brother, Danny, and his father, Sam Sr., are in charge of the day-to-day operations on the family's combined 2,400 acres of farmland, where they raise corn, soybeans and cattle. Although he now spends most of his days in the marble halls of Congress, Graves is still a farmer at heart — he can wax rhapsodic about the many uses of baling wire and about climbing up on the old 1968 John Deere 4020 tractor that his grandfather had bought new.

Graves became involved in politics through the Missouri Farm Bureau. In his hometown of Tarkio, he was active in the Bureau, winning recognition as the organization's national outstanding young farmer, and in the Atchison County young farmer and rancher committee.

Graves argues that farmers are at the mercy of many factors beyond their control — including the national policy of providing low-cost food to consumers — so federal government involvement is essential. Graves sits on the Agriculture Committee, and when the panel considered a major overhaul of farm programs in the 107th Congress, he won inclusion of a provision to boost farmers' earnings by easing their entry into other stages of food production, such as food processing and the transportation of crops.

Graves was a leader in the fight to block the Corps of Engineers from changing its management of the Missouri River to create a "spring rise" that mimics the natural flow of the river. Critics of the proposal say it poses threats to agriculture and river barge traffic.

Although agricultural issues top Graves' agenda, he proudly points to two of his proposals that were included in the large education bill that became law in 2002. One was a requirement that 95 percent of federal education dollars be spent in the classroom and the other provided protection for teachers from frivolous lawsuits arising from disciplining students. The 95 percent requirement was one of Graves' campaign pledges. His wife, Lesley, is a kindergarten teacher.

One of his proposals that raised some eyebrows was his request for a $273,000 grant to combat "Goth culture" in the Kansas City suburb of Blue Springs. Graves said the reported "self-mutilation and other sorts of violent acts" in the subculture, noted for dark clothing and makeup, "is a behavioral problem that is in need of treatment." Critics of government spending seized on the request as a prime example of federal pork-barreling.

Graves also sits on the Transportation and Small Business committees, which are useful assignments for someone who represents a rural constituency.

The Graves family has been active in northwest Missouri public affairs for many years. Graves' great-grandfather (also named Sam) was a stalwart Democrat and served on the county commission. Most family members were Democrats (conservative Democrats, Graves hastens to point out) until they, like many other area residents, gravitated to the GOP.

Graves' younger brother, Todd, was appointed by President Bush to be the U.S. attorney for western Missouri, shortly after Sam Graves entered the House. Todd Graves had worked for a Republican attorney general, managed a statewide GOP campaign for attorney general, won election as Platte County prosecutor, and was the 2000 GOP nominee for state treasurer.

Just six months before the 2000 election, Sam Graves appeared to be headed again to the state Senate in Jefferson City. He had no intention of running for Congress, because Pat Danner — a popular conservative Democrat who had represented the 6th District for four terms — had filed for re-election.

But Danner unexpectedly announced in May that she would retire. The filing period for candidates for the seat was reopened, and GOP officials coaxed eight-year state legislator Graves into entering the race. He quickly overshadowed several lesser-known Republican hopefuls.

The Democrats nominated the congresswoman's son, Steve Danner. But Graves' assertive campaign and conservative politics gave him momentum in a district that, outside of its portion of Kansas City, consists mainly of small towns and farms. The 6th is regarded as a swing district.

Graves' down-home image was enhanced by his extended family's habit of having dinner together every night. (They often take vacations together, as well.) Aided by visits from top House Republicans, including Speaker J. Dennis Hastert, he was able to counter Democrats' campaign charges that he was too much of a conservative ideologue and he prevailed over Danner by 4 percentage points, a victory that came on Graves' 37th birthday.

In 2002, aided by a favorable redrawing of the district's boundaries in the decennial redistricting, Graves easily defeated Clay County Assessor Cathy Rinehart, taking 63 percent of the vote.

The Tarkio airfield is surrounded by the Graves' farmland, and the congressman satisfies his longstanding fascination with flying by piloting a "classic" 1946 Piper Cub, both for pleasure and on business trips around the district.

KEY VOTES

2002

- No Overhaul campaign finance law; ban "soft money" and restrict advocacy advertising
- Yes Back Bush's defense budget increase
- Yes Extend 1996 welfare law
- Yes Adopt Bush's discretionary spending limit
- Yes Pass GOP Medicare prescription drug plan
- No Create independent Sept. 11 commission
- No Extend union protections to Homeland Security Department employees
- Yes Revive fast-track procedures for trade agreements
- Yes Authorize war against Iraq
- Yes Advance bankruptcy overhaul opposed by abortion opponents

2001

- Yes Nullify Clinton Labor Department ergonomics rule
- Yes Cut taxes by $1.35 trillion through fiscal 2011
- No Maintain ban on oil drilling in Arctic National Wildlife Refuge
- Yes Approve Bush proposal to limit managed-care plan liability for coverage decisions
- No Divert money from crop subsidy payments to land conservation
- Yes Expand law enforcement power to investigate suspected terrorists

CQ VOTE STUDIES

	PARTY UNITY		PRESIDENTIAL SUPPORT	
	Support	Oppose	Support	Oppose
2002	95%	5%	79%	21%
2001	96%	4%	90%	10%

INTEREST GROUPS

	AFL-CIO	ADA	CCUS	ACU
2002	11%	0%	95%	100%
2001	17%	5%	100%	88%

MISSOURI 6

Northwest – St. Joseph, part of Kansas City

A mixture of suburbanites and farmers, the 6th is bordered by Iowa to the north, Nebraska and Kansas to the west, and the Missouri River to the west and most of the south.

Kansas City's suburban boom in the 1980s provided steady growth for the middle-class residents of Platte, Clay and eastern Jackson counties, who work mainly for the city's steel, transportation and communications companies. Kansas City International Airport in Platte County and American Airlines also are large employers, and the Kansas City area is home to Farmland, a large farm cooperative, and the Dairy Farmers of America, a large cooperative milk supplier. The suburbs have attracted some insurance, financial services and agribusiness companies.

Outside of the metropolitan area, the river town of St. Joseph serves as the economic hub. In the 1990s, the economy began to speed up, but agrarian life still prevails in most of the district's counties, where corn and livestock are pervasive. New processing plants have created a growing market for soybeans as well.

Although historically Democratic, the district was competitive during the last quarter of the 20th century. The 6th now seems in strong GOP hands. Democrat Bill Clinton won the 1992 and 1996 presidential elections, but GOP Senate candidates did well during the same period, and George W. Bush carried the district with 52 percent of the vote in 2000. Republicans seeking state office also have fared better recently, especially in the northern, rural areas.

MAJOR INDUSTRY

Agriculture, international shipping, manufacturing

CITIES

Kansas City (pt.), 118,635; St. Joseph, 73,990; Blue Springs (pt.), 39,698; Gladstone, 26,365; Liberty, 26,232

NOTABLE

Jesse James was raised near Kearney and is buried there; The Jesse James Home in St. Joseph was where the outlaw was shot and killed in 1882; The Pony Express carried mail between St. Joseph and California from April 1860 through October 1861.

Rep. Roy Blunt (R)

CAPITOL OFFICE
225-6536
www.house.gov/blunt
217 Cannon 20515-2507; fax 225-5604

COMMITTEES
Energy & Commerce

HOMETOWN
Strafford

BORN
Jan. 10, 1950, Niangua, Mo.

RELIGION
Baptist

FAMILY
Separated; three children

EDUCATION
Southwest Baptist U., B.A. 1970 (history); Southwest Missouri State U., M.A. 1972 (history & government)

CAREER
University president; teacher

POLITICAL HIGHLIGHTS
Greene County clerk, 1973-84; Republican nominee for lieutenant governor, 1980; Mo. secretary of state, 1985-93; sought Republican nomination for governor, 1992

ELECTION RESULTS

2002 GENERAL		
Roy Blunt (R)	149,519	74.8%
Ron Lapham (D)	45,964	23.0%
Doug Burlison (LIBERT)	4,378	2.2%
2002 PRIMARY		
Roy Blunt (R)		unopposed
2000 GENERAL		
Roy Blunt (R)	202,305	73.9%
Charles Christrup (D)	65,510	23.9%
Doug Burlison (LIBERT)	2,965	1.1%

PREVIOUS WINNING PERCENTAGES
1998 (73%); 1996 (65%)

Elected 1996; 4th term

He is quite literally the man who blunts the sharp edge of House Republican Majority Leader Tom DeLay. Blunt is the affable third-ranking House leader who enjoys the genteel game of croquet and is credited with easing the sometimes tense relationships among House Republicans.

After just three terms in the House, Blunt skyrocketed to whip, the job Delay held from 1995 to 2002. And though Blunt comes across as the softer man, the one who mediates between angry factions in an easy-listening voice, he is just as indomitable a political strategist as his mentor. Perhaps more so. When Blunt took over as whip, former whip DeLay, nicknamed "The Hammer," presented him with a hammer wrapped in velvet, noting Blunt's "softer touch." Blunt responded, "A velvet-covered hammer hurts just as much. It just makes less noise."

Unlike DeLay, Blunt has cultivated close ties with the Bush White House. Over breakfast every few weeks, he plots legislative strategy with Karl Rove, the president's top political adviser.

Blunt developed his non-combative style as a matter of political survival in Missouri, a presidential battleground state that leans Democratic. So to this day, people on Capitol Hill do not realize just how conservative Blunt is. A former president of Southwest Baptist University in Missouri, he earns support score percentages in the 90s from the American Conservative Union.

He spearheaded the drive to turn back President Clinton's ergonomics rules; he has advocated severing relations with Palestinian leader Yasser Arafat. Yet Blunt is viewed as a pragmatist and dealmaker. After the Sept. 11, 2001, terrorist attacks, Speaker J. Dennis Hastert dispatched Blunt as his emissary to negotiate a $15 billion airline bailout with Senate Democratic leaders.

Blunt also led the Battleground 2002 campaign finance strategy, a Republican effort that channeled $24 million from lawmakers to needy candidates and helped widen the party's slim majority of 223 to a comfortable 229.

Blunt rose fast through the ranks by allying himself with DeLay, then building his own loyalty base by allocating campaign funds to vulnerable lawmakers — a strategy used by DeLay in his own rise to power. Blunt's political action committee, Rely on Your Beliefs (RoyB for short), delivered $207,000 to GOP candidates in the 2000 election cycle. Blunt further cemented bonds with the rank-and-file by snaring a seat on the influential Republican Steering Committee, which doles out committee assignments.

He then proved his mettle by developing a legislative strategy that worked on this principle: Ignore Democrats, keep House Republicans united, and pass the most conservative legislation possible. The approach helped House Republicans deal with a narrowly divided Senate. "The House has to go further than the president would be willing to go, so that you have a chance in conference to get where the president would like to be," Blunt says.

The key to keeping Republicans united in the House is what Blunt calls "listening sessions." He brings in a dozen lawmakers and creates a microcosm of the discordant GOP in his office. That lets both moderates and conservatives see how difficult the road to reconciliation is.

Blunt quietly handles matters behind the scenes. He persuaded the White House to back off and not voice its opposition to arming airline pilots in 2002. The year before, Blunt helped win over reluctant Republicans from depressed textile-making districts to support a bill giving Bush fast-track authority to negotiate trade agreements with foreign countries.

Blunt has nurtured his own career with the same insider's savvy. He locked up the race to become House Republican whip in 2003 in February of 2002, after the only competitor, Ray LaHood of Illinois, bowed out.

He was one of the earliest backers of Bush's presidential campaign and served as chief liaison between the candidate and the House GOP. In his office Blunt displays a wooden gavel, a gift from Bush.

Blunt's detractors, mostly moderates, grumble that their top leadership is too closely affiliated with DeLay. Before becoming Speaker, Hastert was DeLay's chief deputy whip, the same as Blunt's previous position. Still, even his critics say Blunt is a steady, patient leader.

The son of a dairy farmer and a state legislator, Blunt was raised on a farm near Springfield. He still lives on a farm near there, raising Angus cattle and a few horses. Each summer he conducts an agricultural tour of the district, visiting farms and ranches and bringing in foreign trade representatives from Asia.

Like a good junior legislator, Blunt spent his first two terms catering to his rural constituents. In 1999, he helped dairy farmers by blocking a proposed new Department of Agriculture pricing system that would have reduced dairy prices. He also was able to stop the Environmental Protection Agency in 1999 from including propane, a major source of heating fuel in southwest Missouri, on its list of toxic substances.

Blunt's first job after college was as a high school government and history teacher. He was active in politics at an early age, working in 1972 on an unsuccessful congressional bid by John Ashcroft, who went on to become governor, senator and then attorney general. A year later, Blunt was appointed Greene County clerk by GOP Gov. Christopher S. Bond, now the state's senior senator. Blunt was re-elected to that post twice.

After an unsuccessful run for lieutenant governor in 1980, he won the first of two terms as secretary of state in 1984. (Blunt's oldest son, Matt, is involved in politics, also serving as Missouri's secretary of state. He is considered a likely gubernatorial candidate in 2004.)

After losing the Republican gubernatorial primary in 1992, Blunt accepted the presidency of his alma mater, Southwest Baptist University. But he jumped back into politics in 1996, when GOP Rep. Mel Hancock announced his retirement. Blunt won a narrow primary victory over Gary Nodler, a former congressional aide. In the general election, Blunt cruised to victory with 65 percent of the vote in the reliably Republican district. His re-election races have been cakewalks.

KEY VOTES

2002

- No Overhaul campaign finance law; ban "soft money" and restrict advocacy advertising
- Yes Back Bush's defense budget increase
- Yes Extend 1996 welfare law
- Yes Adopt Bush's discretionary spending limit
- Yes Pass GOP Medicare prescription drug plan
- ? Create independent Sept. 11 commission
- ? Extend union protections to Homeland Security Department employees
- ? Revive fast-track procedures for trade agreements
- Yes Authorize war against Iraq
- Yes Advance bankruptcy overhaul opposed by abortion opponents

2001

- Yes Nullify Clinton Labor Department ergonomics rule
- Yes Cut taxes by $1.35 trillion through fiscal 2011
- No Maintain ban on oil drilling in Arctic National Wildlife Refuge
- Yes Approve Bush proposal to limit managed-care plan liability for coverage decisions
- No Divert money from crop subsidy payments to land conservation
- Yes Expand law enforcement power to investigate suspected terrorists

CQ VOTE STUDIES

	PARTY UNITY		PRESIDENTIAL SUPPORT	
	Support	Oppose	Support	Oppose
2002	98%	2%	91%	9%
2001	98%	2%	95%	5%
2000	98%	2%	25%	75%
1999	95%	5%	19%	81%
1998	95%	5%	17%	83%

INTEREST GROUPS

	AFL-CIO	ADA	CCUS	ACU
2002	14%	0%	100%	100%
2001	17%	5%	95%	96%
2000	0%	0%	90%	96%
1999	13%	10%	96%	87%
1998	0%	0%	82%	100%

MISSOURI 7

Southwest – Springfield, Joplin

Two decades of rapid growth helped lift southwest Missouri from a rural hideaway to a burgeoning resort and industrial region. Since the 1970s, this part of Missouri has outpaced the rest of the state in population growth, increasing by 24 percent in the 1990s.

Springfield, in Greene County, is the 7th's industrial and commercial center and has become a manufacturing hub. More than 40 percent of district residents live in Greene or neighboring Christian County on the 7th's eastern edge. Large hospital facilities in Springfield draw patients from as far as Arkansas. The district's other population center, Joplin, is across the district in Jasper County. Once a lead and zinc mining town, it is now a manufacturing and trucking center.

Branson, in the southeast corner, leads the 7th's thriving tourism industry as a magnet for country music fans. A town of 6,000, it draws more than six million visitors a year and boasts more than 40 theaters, including the Andy Williams and Mel Tillis theaters. The area also relies on the resort industry surrounding Table Rock and Taneycomo lakes.

The southwest corner of the district supports beef and dairy cattle, along with poultry. Many of the small, rural communities in the Ozarks have not quite yielded to development. Expansion along U.S. Highway 71, which runs from Kansas City into Arkansas, is expected to improve the area's accessibility and economic prospects.

The 7th has been long considered a Republican bastion. The Assemblies of God, headquartered in Springfield, is among the active religious organizations that reflect the area's devout, conservative population. Springfield has become slightly more Democratic since the 1980s, partly because of the influx of new residents, but the city still leans Republican.

MAJOR INDUSTRY

Manufacturing, agriculture, tourism

CITIES

Springfield, 151,580; Joplin, 45,504; Carthage, 12,668; Nixa, 12,124

NOTABLE

Springfield is home to Fantastic Caverns, which calls itself the nation's only ride-through cave; George Washington Carver's boyhood home is now a national monument in Diamond; Wilson's Creek National Battlefield Park is in Republic.

Rep. Jo Ann Emerson (R)

CAPITOL OFFICE
225-4404
www.house.gov/emerson
2440 Rayburn 20515-2508; fax 226-0326

COMMITTEES
Appropriations

HOMETOWN
Cape Girardeau

BORN
Sept. 16, 1950, Washington, D.C.

RELIGION
Presbyterian

FAMILY
Husband, Ron Gladney; two children, six stepchildren

EDUCATION
Ohio Wesleyan U., B.A. 1972 (political science)

CAREER
Public affairs executive; lobbyist

POLITICAL HIGHLIGHTS
No previous office

ELECTION RESULTS

2002 GENERAL		
Jo Ann Emerson (R)	135,144	71.8%
Gene Curtis (D)	50,686	26.9%
Eric Van Oostrom (LIBERT)	2,491	1.3%
2002 PRIMARY		
Jo Ann Emerson (R)	50,605	87.1%
Richard A. Kline (R)	7,499	12.9%
2000 GENERAL		
Jo Ann Emerson (R)	162,239	69.3%
Bob Camp (D)	67,760	29.0%

PREVIOUS WINNING PERCENTAGES
1998 (63%); 1996 (50%); 1996 Special Election (63%)

Elected 1996; 4th full term

Emerson has demonstrated a deft ability to buck her Republican leadership on a number of hot-button issues and still remain true to the political leanings of an increasingly conservative district.

The blunt-spoken Appropriations Committee member, who succeeded her husband, Bill Emerson, in the 8th District after he died of lung cancer in 1996, makes no apologies for reaching across party lines in an effort to solve problems that plague her constituents. "I'm all about finding the best mechanism to do something," she says.

That means that Emerson sometimes reaches beyond her core concerns as a leader of rural lawmakers and wades into battles that others treat as tests of party loyalty.

She has teamed up with Democrats, for example, in an effort to allow importation of prescription drugs approved by U.S. regulators that are sold more cheaply abroad and to rewrite patent laws to speed low-cost generic drugs to market. With prescription drug costs soaring, Emerson said lawmakers needed to "stop listening to the scare tactics of drug companies" and pay more attention to the needs of average citizens.

She also supported, in the aftermath of the Sept. 11, 2001, terrorist attacks, an ultimately successful Senate proposal to federalize aviation security workers, despite initial opposition from the White House and House Republican leaders.

While she has voted with her party about 90 percent of the time in recent years, she supported President Bush just 82 percent of the time during the 107th Congress — the lowest score of any Missouri Republican.

Despite Emerson's willingness to break Republican ranks on occasion, she frequently is mentioned as a potential Senate candidate. And she continues to score high both with conservative groups and with her GOP colleagues. She stumped with former Missouri GOP Rep. James M. Talent during his successful 2002 Senate campaign against incumbent Democrat Jean Carnahan; and the 7th District's GOP Rep. Roy Blunt returned the favor by introducing her to constituents he had lost to Emerson through redistricting.

Emerson is adept at balancing priorities that often produce fiscal contradictions, such as taking a leading role in passing a massive increase in farm support spending even as she argues that Congress should be more careful about spending money.

As a suburban Washington native who spent 20 years as a lobbyist in the capital, Emerson was not a natural fit for her rural constituents in southeast Missouri. But she has worked hard to connect, and she makes a point of experiencing how they work and live. In 2001 she passed up a meeting with Bush when he visited her district because she was in the midst of a tour taking turns filling in at various jobs, from bagging groceries to delivering the weather news.

Emerson teamed up in 2000 with North Carolina Democrat Eva Clayton to revive the disbanded Congressional Rural Caucus to ensure that rural areas are considered in all relevant federal policy and appropriations measures. She and Clayton co-chaired the caucus in the 107th.

Emerson has taken on both the Clinton and Bush administrations in pushing to open up the Cuban market to help farmers in her district and across the nation. "The one thing I've learned over all these years is the importance of listening," she says. "When my farmers say that Congress and the administration have made it impossible to sell rice to Cuba, I'm going to learn all I can about that and try to fix it." She carefully built a bipartisan coalition to press the issue.

Emerson supports property owners' rights over efforts to increase environmental protections, and she argues that states should have primacy in land management decisions. She denounced President Clinton's plan to designate certain waterways as American Heritage Rivers and has opposed a number of wetlands protection measures.

Emerson — who spent two decades as a lobbyist for the American Insurance Association, the National Restaurant Association and others — learned bedrock Republican principles early on. She grew up in Bethesda, Md., and had a perfect GOP political tutor in her father, Ab Hermann, who for many years served as the executive director of the Republican National Committee.

But it was also her father who taught Emerson how to get along with Democrats, including neighbor and family friend Hale Boggs, the powerful longtime representative from Louisiana who rose to majority leader before he disappeared on a plane flight in Alaska in 1972. Emerson remained friends with Boggs' widow, Lindy, and drew inspiration from the Democrat's successful race to succeed her husband after his death and from the long, successful House career that Lindy Boggs built for herself.

After graduating from Ohio Wesleyan, Emerson returned to the Washington area, where she worked for the National Republican Congressional Committee and then began a career as a lobbyist. In Washington, she met Bill Emerson, a former congressional staffer who also was a lobbyist.

Bill Emerson, first elected in 1980, was a candidate for a ninth House term when he died. His widow reluctantly entered the race to succeed him and had to run as an independent because the filing deadline for the primary had closed. But her entry was eased by endorsements of the House Republican leadership and the Missouri Republican Party.

She won with 50 percent of the vote, finishing 13 percentage points ahead of Democrat Emily Firebaugh and 39 points ahead of the official GOP candidate, Richard A. Kline. (She won a special election that same day to fill the last two months of her husband's term.)

Since then, Emerson routinely has been re-elected by strong margins, helped by her careful attention to constituent service. From her husband, Emerson learned the importance of delivering federal dollars to her district, as symbolized by his legacy project, a new $100 million Mississippi bridge linking Missouri and Illinois named after him. In 2000, Emerson married St. Louis Democratic labor lawyer Ron Gladney.

KEY VOTES

2002

No Overhaul campaign finance law; ban "soft money" and restrict advocacy advertising
Yes Back Bush's defense budget increase
Yes Extend 1996 welfare law
+ Adopt Bush's discretionary spending limit
No Pass GOP Medicare prescription drug plan
No Create independent Sept. 11 commission
No Extend union protections to Homeland Security Department employees
Yes Revive fast-track procedures for trade agreements
Yes Authorize war against Iraq
Yes Advance bankruptcy overhaul opposed by abortion opponents

2001

Yes Nullify Clinton Labor Department ergonomics rule
Yes Cut taxes by $1.35 trillion through fiscal 2011
No Maintain ban on oil drilling in Arctic National Wildlife Refuge
Yes Approve Bush proposal to limit managed-care plan liability for coverage decisions
No Divert money from crop subsidy payments to land conservation
Yes Expand law enforcement power to investigate suspected terrorists

CQ VOTE STUDIES

	PARTY UNITY		PRESIDENTIAL SUPPORT	
	Support	Oppose	Support	Oppose
2002	93%	7%	81%	19%
2001	91%	9%	83%	17%
2000	91%	9%	24%	76%
1999	88%	12%	21%	79%
1998	92%	8%	22%	78%

INTEREST GROUPS

	AFL-CIO	ADA	CCUS	ACU
2002	22%	0%	95%	96%
2001	17%	5%	91%	83%
2000	10%	0%	80%	80%
1999	33%	10%	80%	80%
1998	10%	5%	83%	92%

MISSOURI 8

Southeast – Cape Girardeau, Ozark Plateau

Some of the state's most bountiful farmland can be found in the 8th, which takes in the mountains, forests and Mississippi Valley towns of Missouri's southeastern corner.

The district spans the political spectrum from solidly Republican counties in the west and northeast along the Mississippi River to "Yellow Dog" Democratic territory in the southeast area, dubbed the boot heel because of its shape. Voters tend to be socially conservative on issues such as abortion and gun control and leery of environmental regulations, and the GOP has made inroads in the boot heel in elections for offices higher than the county level.

The 8th is slowly recovering from a decline in the textile industry since the 1980s. Agriculture and lead mining fuel the central counties, while the boot heel is a former wheat-growing region that now produces soybean, corn, cotton and rice.

Major growth centers in the district include the northern counties of Phelps and St. Francois, which have been boosted by light manufacturing and defense subcontracts. Lumber also features heavily in the 8th's industry, and four-fifths of Mark Twain National Forest's 1.5 million acres lies in the 8th.

Frequent flooding and earthquakes from the New Madrid fault line that runs through southeast Missouri make the 8th a disaster-prone region, though reinforced levees and highways have reduced the risk. The last major flooding of the Mississippi River was in 1995, but preparation for smaller floods is still an annual spring ritual in the border towns.

MAJOR INDUSTRY

Agriculture, lead mining, lumber

CITIES

Cape Girardeau, 35,349; Sikeston, 16,992; Poplar Bluff, 16,651; Rolla, 16,367

NOTABLE

The Census Bureau estimates that the population center of the United States is near Edgar Springs; Laura Ingalls Wilder wrote her "Little House" series of books in Mansfield; Astronaut Linda M. Godwin, who has logged more than 38 days in space, was born in Cape Girardeau; The New Madrid region has more earthquakes than any other part of the United States east of the Rocky Mountains.

Rep. Kenny Hulshof (R)

CAPITOL OFFICE
225-2956
www.house.gov/hulshof
412 Cannon 20515-2509; fax 225-5712

COMMITTEES
Budget
Standards of Official Conduct
Ways & Means

HOMETOWN
Columbia

BORN
May 22, 1958, Sikeston, Mo.

RELIGION
Roman Catholic

FAMILY
Wife, Renee Hulshof; two children

EDUCATION
U. of Missouri, B.S. 1980 (agriculture economics); U. of Mississippi, J.D. 1983

CAREER
State and city prosecutor; public defender

POLITICAL HIGHLIGHTS
Sought Republican nomination for Boone County prosecutor, 1992; Republican nominee for U.S. House, 1994

ELECTION RESULTS

2002 GENERAL		
Kenny Hulshof (R)	146,032	68.2%
Donald M. Deichman (D)	61,126	28.6%
Keith Brekhus (GREEN)	4,262	2.0%
John Mruzik (LIBERT)	2,705	1.3%
2002 PRIMARY		
Kenny Hulshof (R)		unopposed
2000 GENERAL		
Kenny Hulshof (R)	172,787	59.3%
Steven R. Carroll (D)	111,662	38.3%
Robert Hoffman (LIBERT)	3,608	1.2%

PREVIOUS WINNING PERCENTAGES
1998 (62%); 1996 (49%)

Elected 1996; 4th term

Hulshof's bright-eyed aspect and frequently flashed grin bespeak his status as a rising Republican star, with considerable influence in the House and statewide ambitions in Missouri. But underneath the polished veneer is a skilled former state prosecutor with a record of fighting both local skirmishes for his constituents and the broader national battles on tax cuts, education and farm policy that are crucial to his party's success.

Although he represents an area that has morphed in recent years from a rural Democratic mainstay to an increasingly suburban swing district, Hulshof (HULLZ-hoff) nevertheless hews to conservative principles. From his coveted perch on the Ways and Means Committee, he has been a leading proponent of making President Bush's 2001 tax cut permanent, and of creating tax-advantaged savings accounts for education and for farmers. He introduced Bush's limited proposal for altering campaign finance law and was tapped in 2001 to head the Republican Policy Committee's panel on retirement security capital markets and tax policy.

In the 108th, Hulshof added a seat on the Budget panel to his portfolio.

But the parochial needs of his constituents have prompted Hulshof to stray sometimes from strict Republican tenets. "Generally, my goals do not conflict with those of the party," Hulshof said upon his arrival. But, he added, "There have been times when, in the interest of my constituents, I have bucked the Republican leadership."

He has been a major player in farm states' campaign to use tax credits to create markets for renewable fuels such as ethanol and biodiesel, both of which are derived from agricultural products. As a freshman, Hulshof even took on the powerful chairman of his committee at the time, Bill Archer of Texas, when Archer tried to phase out the ethanol tax break. When Archer abandoned the plan the next year, Hulshof — as a negotiator on that year's big rewrite of highway and mass transit law — and other farm-state lawmakers were able to win a seven-year extension of the ethanol credit.

He comes by his agricultural ties honestly; Hulshof grew up on a farm near the boot heel of southeastern Missouri and still recalls getting an uncomfortably personal lesson in how politics influences agriculture when his parents almost lost their farm in the early 1980s because of the U.S. grain embargo of the Soviet Union.

Hulshof joined a bipartisan group of lawmakers from steel-producing states in 2001 to push legislation to revitalize the U.S. steel industry by lowering imports and establishing a federal loan guarantee program to help strapped firms.

Hulshof has been gaining influence steadily in Washington since the day he defeated Democrat Harold L. Volkmer, a two-decade veteran in a district that had last sent a Republican to Washington in 1920. Not only did he receive an appointment to Ways and Means by GOP elders, a rare plum for a freshman, but his first-term GOP colleagues elected him class president. Hulshof made a concerted effort in that role to define himself and his peers as not only conservative but also pragmatic and cooperative — and not given to the kind of ideological brinkmanship that characterized the class first elected in 1994, when the GOP won control of Congress. Soon after the 105th Congress convened, Hulshof was a leading force behind the first in a series of biannual and bipartisan "civility" retreats, where the objective is for Republicans and Democrats to get acquainted with each other in a non-confrontational setting.

In the 106th Congress, Hulshof was a key player in the enactment of a law permitting the disabled to work and earn money without losing their medical benefits.

As his third term began in 2001, Hulshof spent considerable time in the Senate, where he was right in the middle of the highly politicized fight over the attorney general nomination of John Ashcroft, who had just been defeated for re-election as a senator from Missouri. Hulshof appeared at the Ashcroft confirmation hearings in an effort to discredit an influential Ashcroft critic, Ronnie White, the first African-American to serve on the Missouri Supreme Court.

White testified that Ashcroft had unfairly blocked his nomination to a federal trial court judgeship by mischaracterizing his record on the death penalty. Hulshof, who had been the prosecutor in a 1992 murder case in which White was the lone dissenter on appeal, rebutted the judge's account, saying his ruling in the 1992 case was grounds enough for Ashcroft to oppose White's confirmation.

Hulshof also has flirted with seeking more of the national spotlight for himself. The state's senior GOP officeholder, Sen. Christopher S. Bond, and other prominent Republicans tried in 2001 to persuade Hulshof to challenge Democrat Jean Carnahan's bid for a full term in the Senate: He demurred, citing family reasons. After his easy win in 2002, Hulshof briefly considering a run for governor in 2004. But the birth of a daughter, the death of his father, and his mother's desire to keep the family farm operating convinced Hulshof, an only child, to focus on personal matters and not make the statewide run.

A former high school athlete, Hulshof stars as the first baseman for the Republicans in the annual charity baseball game against the Democrats, and as a guard and a forward on the congressional basketball team that plays a team of lobbyists for charity. He also sings and plays the drums in his church choir.

An agricultural economics graduate of the University of Missouri, Hulshof went on to the University of Mississippi for law school. Upon graduation, he worked as a public defender, and then as a prosecutor in Cape Girardeau County before moving to Columbia to work for the state attorney general.

Hulshof was a fill-in candidate in 1994 against Volkmer, tapped by party leaders to run when the GOP front-runner bowed out after the filing deadline. Despite being a political neophyte with no name recognition, Hulshof lost by just 5 percentage points. When he tried again in 1996, he first overcame a stiff primary challenge from wealthy ophthalmologist Harry Eggleston, then edged Volkmer by slightly less than 6,000 votes in November.

KEY VOTES

2002

- No Overhaul campaign finance law; ban "soft money" and restrict advocacy advertising
- Yes Back Bush's defense budget increase
- Yes Extend 1996 welfare law
- Yes Adopt Bush's discretionary spending limit
- Yes Pass GOP Medicare prescription drug plan
- No Create independent Sept. 11 commission
- No Extend union protections to Homeland Security Department employees
- Yes Revive fast-track procedures for trade agreements
- Yes Authorize war against Iraq
- Yes Advance bankruptcy overhaul opposed by abortion opponents

2001

- Yes Nullify Clinton Labor Department ergonomics rule
- Yes Cut taxes by $1.35 trillion through fiscal 2011
- No Maintain ban on oil drilling in Arctic National Wildlife Refuge
- Yes Approve Bush proposal to limit managed-care plan liability for coverage decisions
- No Divert money from crop subsidy payments to land conservation
- Yes Expand law enforcement power to investigate suspected terrorists

CQ VOTE STUDIES

	PARTY UNITY		PRESIDENTIAL SUPPORT	
	Support	Oppose	Support	Oppose
2002	95%	5%	88%	12%
2001	94%	6%	95%	5%
2000	96%	4%	19%	81%
1999	88%	12%	22%	78%
1998	89%	11%	25%	75%

INTEREST GROUPS

	AFL-CIO	ADA	CCUS	ACU
2002	11%	10%	100%	96%
2001	17%	5%	100%	92%
2000	0%	5%	85%	96%
1999	13%	25%	88%	84%
1998	0%	15%	100%	88%

MISSOURI 9

Northeast – Columbia, St. Louis exurbs

Besides Columbia and some western St. Louis suburbs, the 9th consists of small towns spread among farmlands. Residents include many middle-class, socially conservative Democrats, but the arrival of new wealth has led to rapid suburban growth and a rise in Republican-leaning areas.

The 9th splits St. Charles County with the neighboring 2nd District and encompasses all of nearby Warren and Franklin counties. A General Motors plant and a Boeing hub in nearby districts provide jobs, but much of the area's growth has come from small businesses. A wine industry that dates back to the 19th century provides income for Gasconade and surrounding counties.

Columbia, a steadily growing and mostly middle-class city across the district from St. Charles County, is home to the University of Missouri's flagship campus and a handful of medical facilities, including the Harry S Truman Memorial Veterans Hospital. Despite a significant exodus of young people from farming families, the district's economy still thrives on cattle, soybean, corn and winter wheat.

Traditionally Democratic, the 9th is becoming increasingly Republican with the growth of suburban St. Louis and the decline of "Yellow Dog" Democrats in rural communities. Before 1996, voters elected a Republican member of Congress only once in the 20th century, in 1920. Still predominantly Democratic at the local level, the district expanded southwest in 2001 redistricting to gain new counties that have contributed to a GOP base for state offices. George W. Bush carried the redrawn district by 12 percentage points in the 2000 presidential election.

MAJOR INDUSTRY

Higher education, electronics, agriculture

CITIES

Columbia, 84,531; Hannibal, 17,757; Kirksville, 16,988; Washington, 13,243

NOTABLE

Samuel Clemens (Mark Twain) was born in Florida in Monroe County and grew up in Hannibal, which attracts visitors to Twain's boyhood home; Westminster College in Fulton was the site of Winston Churchill's "Iron Curtain" speech after World War II; The August A. Busch wildlife area in St. Charles County was purchased by the state in 1947 after Busch's widow made a donation toward the purchase.

MONTANA

Gov. Judy Martz (R)

First elected: 2000
Length of term: 4 years
Term expires: 1/05
Salary: $88,190
Phone: (406) 444-3111
Hometown: Helena
Born: July 28, 1943; Big Timber, Mont.
Religion: Christian Church
Family: Husband, Harry Martz; two children
Education: Eastern Montana College, attended 1964-65
Career: Commercial solid waste disposal company owner; congressional aide; sporting goods retailer; Olympic athlete
Political highlights: Lieutenant governor, 1997-2001
Election results:

2000 GENERAL		
Judy Martz (R)	209,135	51.0%
Mark O'Keefe (D)	193,131	47.1%
Stan Jones (LIBERT)	7,926	1.9%

Lt. Gov. Karl Ohs (R)

First elected: 2000
Length of term: 4 years
Term expires: 1/05
Salary: $62,471
Phone: (406) 444-3111

STATE LEGISLATURE

Legislature: Meets January-April in odd-numbered years
House: 100 members, 2-year terms
2003 breakdown: 53R, 47D; 71 men, 29 women
Salary: $76/day in session; $97/day in session allowance
Phone: (406) 444-4819
Senate: 50 members, 4-year terms
2003 breakdown: 29R, 21D; 42 men, 8 women
Salary: $76/6 days per week in session; $90/day in session allowance
Phone: (406) 444-4880

STATE TERM LIMITS

Governor: 2 terms in a 16-year period
Senate: 2 terms in a 16-year period
House: 4 terms in a 16-year period

URBAN STATISTICS

CITY	POPULATION
Billings	89,847
Missoula	57,053
Great Falls	56,690
Butte-Silver Bow	34,606
Bozeman	27,509

REGISTERED VOTERS

Voters do not register by party.

POPULATION

2002 population (est.)	909,453
2000 population	902,195
1990 population	799,065
Percent change (1990-2000)	+12.9%
Rank among states (2002)	44
Median age	37.5
Born in state	56.1%
Foreign born	1.8%
Violent crime rate	241/100,000
Poverty level	14.6%
Federal workers	13,044
Military	8,349

REDISTRICTING

Montana retained its one House seat in reapportionment.

MISCELLANEOUS

Web: www.state.mt.us
Capital: Helena

STATE ELECTION OFFICIAL
(406) 444-4732

DEMOCRATIC HEADQUARTERS
(406) 442-9520

REPUBLICAN HEADQUARTERS
(406) 442-6469

District Statistics

DIST.	2000 VOTE FOR PRESIDENT BUSH	GORE	NADER	WHITE	BLACK	ASIAN	HISP	MEDIAN INCOME	WHITE COLLAR	BLUE COLLAR	SERVICE INDUSTRY	OVER 64	UNDER 18	COLLEGE EDUCATION	RURAL	SQ. MILES
AL	58%	33%	6%	90%	0%	1%	2%	$33,024	59%	24%	17%	13%	26%	24%	46%	145,552
STATE	58	33	6	90	0	1	2	$33,024	59	24	17	13	26	24	46	145,552
U.S.	47.9	48.4	3	69	12	4	13	$41,994	60	25	15	12	26	24	21	3,537,438

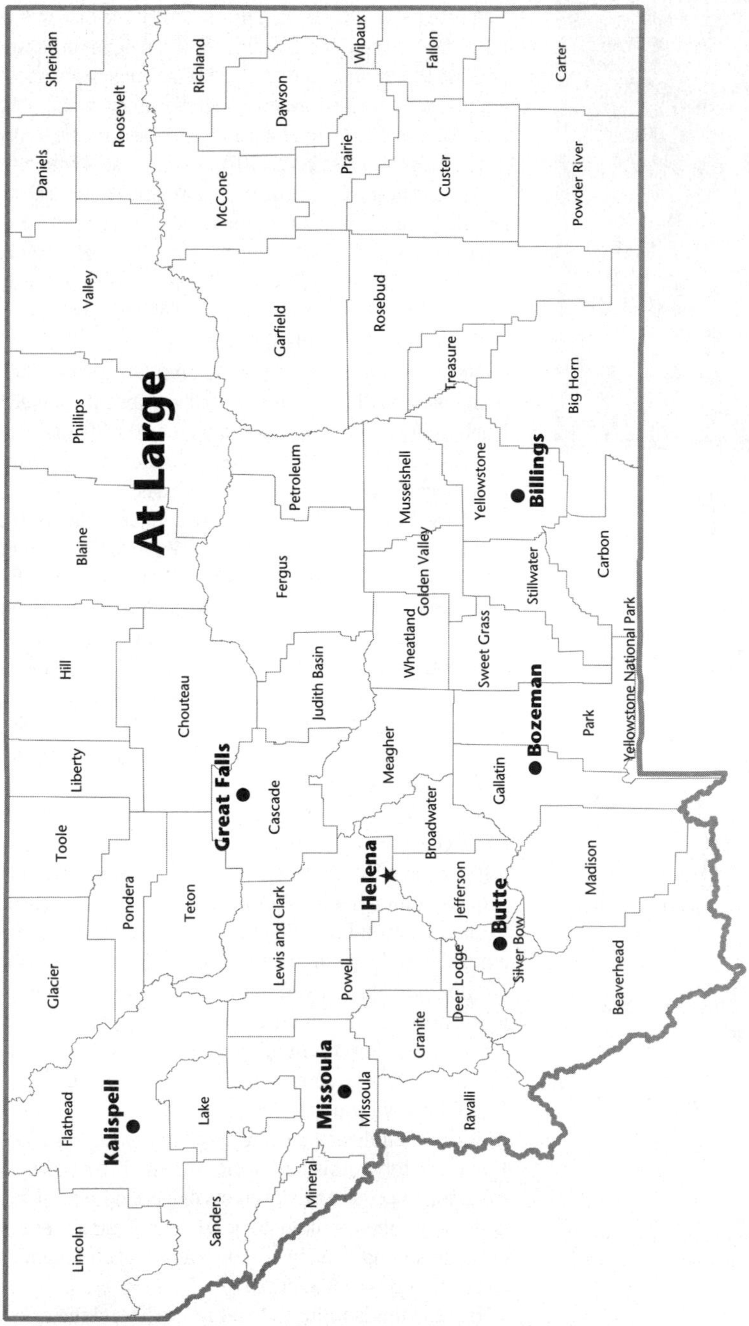
At Large
Sheridan
Daniels
Roosevelt
Richland
Dawson
Wibaux
Fallon
Carter
McCone
Prairie
Custer
Powder River
Valley
Garfield
Rosebud
Treasure
Big Horn
Phillips
Petroleum
Musselshell
Yellowstone
Billings
Blaine
Fergus
Golden Valley
Stillwater
Carbon
Hill
Chouteau
Judith Basin
Wheatland
Sweet Grass
Yellowstone National Park
Liberty
Great Falls
Cascade
Meagher
Gallatin
Bozeman
Park
Toole
Broadwater
Helena
Pondera
Teton
Lewis and Clark
Jefferson
Butte
Madison
Glacier
Powell
Deer Lodge
Silver Bow
Beaverhead
Flathead
Kalispell
Lake
Missoula
Granite
Ravalli
Mineral
Lincoln
Sanders

Sen. Max Baucus (D)

CAPITOL OFFICE
224-2651
max@baucus.senate.gov
baucus.senate.gov
511 Hart 20510-2602; fax 228-3687

COMMITTEES
Agriculture, Nutrition & Forestry
Environment & Public Works
Finance - ranking member
Joint Taxation - ranking member

HOMETOWN
Helena

BORN
Dec. 11, 1941, Helena, Mont.

RELIGION
United Church of Christ

FAMILY
Wife, Wanda Baucus; one child

EDUCATION
Stanford U., A.B. 1964 (economics), LL.B. 1967

CAREER
Lawyer

POLITICAL HIGHLIGHTS
Mont. House, 1973-75; U.S. House, 1975-78

ELECTION RESULTS

2002 GENERAL		
Max Baucus (D)	204,853	62.7%
Mike Taylor (R)	103,611	31.7%
Stan Jones (LIBERT)	10,420	3.2%
Bob Kelleher (GR)	7,653	2.3%
2002 PRIMARY		
Max Baucus (D)		unopposed

PREVIOUS WINNING PERCENTAGES
1996 (50%); 1990 (68%); 1984 (57%); 1978 (56%); 1976 House Election (66%); 1974 House Election (55%)

Elected 1978; 5th term

A placard on the desk in his Senate office declares that "Montana Comes First" for Baucus, and that has proved true in more ways than one. Not only does he assiduously pursue tax breaks, policy changes and spending to benefit his state, he also walks an extraordinarily fine political line to keep winning elections as Montana trends increasingly Republican and conservative.

His balancing act in the 107th Congress — which frequently flummoxed and frustrated the rest of the Democratic hierarchy — culminated in his landslide election to a fifth term in 2002, an astonishing achievement for a Democrat in today's Rocky Mountain West. But Baucus was the chairman of the Finance Committee at the time, so his centrist straddling greatly hampered the Senate Democratic majority's efforts to counter President Bush's policies and to promote its own.

Nothing better illustrates the double edges of Baucus' recent behavior than his co-writing of the $1.35 trillion tax cut enacted in the spring of 2001, Bush's biggest domestic policy victory during his first year in office. As the top-ranking Democrat on Finance at the time, Baucus worked closely with Republican Chairman Charles E. Grassley of Iowa and the White House to move the bill seamlessly through a Senate split 50-50 between Republicans and Democrats. Montana voters embraced the tax relief. But their senator's collaboration irked Democrats nationwide, because the party's ability to criticize Bush's tax cut in the 2002 campaign was hobbled by the fact that Baucus' deal had won the votes of 12 Democratic senators.

Skepticism about Baucus' party loyalty continued to dog him when he became Finance chairman in June 2001. There were whispers that Majority Leader Tom Daschle, who was particularly infuriated over Baucus' role in the Bush tax cut, wanted to take the gavel away from him.

From the outset, the new chairman struggled to assert his leadership. His approach was characteristically ambivalent, and he let it show. He came close to losing control of several previously choreographed bill drafting sessions. His comments in public were often halting — as if he was still reflecting on what he should say even as the words left his mouth.

Baucus tried but failed to work out an agreement with Republicans on a new tax relief package for small businesses and rural development. And Democratic leaders did not risk allowing Finance to consider their Medicare prescription drug plan — fearing that Baucus would allow it to wind up looking too much like the House Republicans' version. Daschle instead took a Democratic plan straight to the floor. It failed, as did the Republican versions.

With Republicans back in control for the 108th, Baucus is back to being Finance's top-ranking minority member. Grassley and he share a determination to protect the interests of rural communities, especially on health care, so Baucus is likely to score some gains there. But his fellow Democrats, including Daschle — who also sits on Finance — are watching him warily on tax and Medicare overhaul issues.

Baucus tends to hew closer to the liberal majority of his party between elections. In the 107th, he sided with his party on just 67 percent of the votes pitting majorities of the two parties against one another; only three other Democrats strayed from the fold more often. But in the 106th, when his next campaign was three and four years away, his party unity score was 20 percentage points higher. It was the same when he ran for a fourth term in the 104th Congress; his party unity score was 70 percent, compared with

82 percent in the 103rd.

Baucus' ideological inconsistencies reflect the historic political divide in his sparsely populated state. Democrats traditionally have dominated in the stunningly picturesque mountainous western half, while Republicans rule in the open ranchland of the eastern half. His constituents share the sometimes conflicting goals of protecting the beauty around them while relying on natural resources for their livelihood. Baucus scored 56 percent on the 2002 League of Conservation Voters scorecard, down from 75 percent in 2001.

Baucus also must juggle the interests of the conservative ranching and business communities with those of the unionized miners and educators who make up his base. In 2001, he was one of six Democrats to vote for a measure overturning Clinton administration ergonomics regulations — rules promoted by organized labor but opposed by business. That same year, however, he voted with the rest of his caucus to approve patients' bill of rights legislation that business and insurance groups fought.

Baucus faced heat at home for reversing his career-long opposition to gun control by voting in 1993 for the Brady law, which mandated a waiting period and background check before the purchase of a handgun, and the 1994 crime law, which included a ban on certain semiautomatic assault-style weapons. But in 1999, Baucus was the only Senate Democrat who voted "no" on the key amendment to that year's gun control bill that would have required background checks for firearms purchases at gun shows.

As a senior member of the Environment and Public Works Committee, Baucus is in a prime position to steer highway dollars to Montana during the rewrite of the surface transportation law scheduled for the 108th. During the last rewrite, in 1998, he helped push through a new funding formula that aided Western states.

Baucus' brother and sister-in-law now run the sprawling family ranch north of Helena. Even though the Sieben Ranch Co. bears the senator's middle name, it was clear early on that Baucus was going to take a different career path. He entered public life after finishing Stanford Law School in 1967, serving as an attorney for the Securities and Exchange Commission in Washington for three years. He returned home to Montana in 1971 to coordinate the state's constitutional convention, and the next year he won a seat in the state legislature.

Two years later, he dislodged a two-term Republican incumbent to win a House seat in the post-Watergate sweep of 1974. He arrived in the Senate at the end of 1978, four days after his 37th birthday, after winning a primary against Paul Hatfield, a Democrat who had been appointed to the seat.

Holding his seat in the Senate has not always been easy, and in 1996 Baucus won by fewer than 20,000 votes over Republican Denny Rehberg, then the lieutenant governor and now Montana's sole House member.

Bush carried Montana by 25 percentage points in 2000, and Republicans tried hard to recruit popular former Gov. Marc Racicot to run against Baucus in 2002. Racicot demurred — he was later named Republican National Committee chairman — and Baucus cruised to victory with 63 percent of the vote against GOP state Sen. Mike Taylor. He was confident enough of victory that he was spotted jogging along the Potomac River on some weekend afternoons close to the election.

Baucus was criticized in 2002 by Republicans and editorial pages after a federal building in Helena was named for him. Federal and state officials said it was an appropriate honor because Baucus was instrumental in ensuring the building was built downtown. But critics said it was unseemly to name a building for a sitting elected official — especially one in the middle of running for re-election.

KEY VOTES

2002

Yes Pass farm bill reversing crop subsidy limits
Yes Postpone tougher automobile fuel efficiency standards
Yes Overhaul campaign finance law; ban "soft money" and restrict advocacy advertising
Yes Set federal election standards
No Support oil drilling in Arctic National Wildlife Refuge
Yes Revive fast-track procedures for trade agreements
Yes Create federal insurance coverage for catastrophic terrorist losses
Yes Tighten federal accounting and corporate governance regulation
Yes Advance bipartisan Medicare prescription drug plan
? Create independent Sept. 11 commission
Yes Back Democratic Homeland Security Department proposal
Yes Authorize war against Iraq

2001

No Confirm John Ashcroft as attorney general
Yes Nullify Clinton Labor Department ergonomics rule
Yes Cut taxes by $1.35 trillion through fiscal 2011
Yes Pass Democratic bill to bolster rights of patients in managed-care plans
No Permit a new round of military base closings
Yes Expand law enforcement power to investigate suspected terrorists

CQ VOTE STUDIES

	PARTY UNITY		PRESIDENTIAL SUPPORT	
	Support	Oppose	Support	Oppose
2002	67%	33%	88%	12%
2001	67%	33%	71%	29%
2000	88%	12%	97%	3%
1999	87%	13%	81%	19%
1998	84%	16%	81%	19%
1997	73%	27%	87%	13%
1996	73%	27%	90%	10%
1995	68%	32%	79%	21%
1994	86%	14%	89%	11%
1993	85%	15%	90%	10%

INTEREST GROUPS

	AFL-CIO	ADA	CCUS	ACU
2002	69%	75%	70%	37%
2001	81%	80%	71%	28%
2000	75%	85%	46%	16%
1999	78%	95%	59%	4%
1998	75%	80%	56%	5%
1997	29%	65%	70%	4%
1996	71%	85%	46%	20%
1995	83%	75%	47%	13%
1994	100%	85%	20%	0%
1993	73%	85%	20%	16%

Sen. Conrad Burns (R)

CAPITOL OFFICE
224-2644
burns.senate.gov
187 Dirksen 20510-2603; fax 224-8594

COMMITTEES
Appropriations
(Interior - chairman)
Budget
Commerce, Science & Transportation
(Communications - chairman)
Energy & Natural Resources
Small Business & Entrepreneurship

HOMETOWN
Billings

BORN
Jan. 25, 1935, Gallatin, Mo.

RELIGION
Lutheran

FAMILY
Wife, Phyllis Burns; two children

EDUCATION
U. of Missouri, attended 1952-54 (agriculture)

MILITARY SERVICE
Marine Corps, 1955-57

CAREER
Radio and television broadcaster; auctioneer

POLITICAL HIGHLIGHTS
Yellowstone County Commission, 1987-89

ELECTION RESULTS

2000 GENERAL		
Conrad Burns (R)	208,082	50.6%
Brian Schweitzer (D)	194,430	47.2%
Gary Lee (REF)	9,089	2.2%
2000 PRIMARY		
Conrad Burns (R)		unopposed

PREVIOUS WINNING PERCENTAGES
1994 (62%); 1988 (52%)

Elected 1988; 3rd term

Burns is a dichotomy. One half of his personality is stalled in the old West with his cowboy boots, folksy manner and blunt talk. The walls of his office are covered with large color photos of cattle drives and cowboys. Yet the other half of his life is squarely focused on the future, as he continually earns praise from the computer community — the so-called digerati — for his championship of the telecommunications industry.

Burns has been at the forefront in congressional debates so far in the Information Age, promoting modern technology issues such as high-speed Internet access and fighting 21st century annoyances such as electronic junk mail. Since 1997 he has been either the chairman or senior Republican minority member of the Commerce panel's Communications Subcommittee.

His background as a radio broadcaster helped him see, long before most of his colleagues, the importance of embracing and fostering new communications technologies. In 1996, Burns chaired the first interactive hearing on Capitol Hill and several times he has been cited as one of the Senate's most "'Net-friendly" members. In the 107th Congress, he was a co-chairman of the Congressional Internet Caucus.

Modern communication is of particular importance in sparsely populated states such as Montana. In fact, many of the most technology-savvy senators — including Burns and Vermont's Patrick J. Leahy, Wyoming's Michael B. Enzi and Alaska's Ted Stevens — represent mostly rural states located far from the nation's traditional communications and technology centers. Burns argues that such technology is vital to the economic well-being of Montana, by providing its residents the same access to information and electronic commerce opportunities as the residents of larger states. Long-distance learning and telemedicine are also important in rural areas, where professors and doctors are especially scarce.

In the 107th, Burns offered a "Tech 7" communications agenda that included such issues as protecting Internet privacy, offering incentives to build the high-speed Internet network, allocating the broadcast spectrum to accommodate the growth of wireless communications, increasing the public's access to the workings of the government, and curbing unwanted e-mail, known as spam. His "can the spam" legislation to permit recipients to take their names off e-mail lists and to penalize e-mail marketers that do not comply has been a particular interest.

Burns' effort to increase Internet access, including wireless broadband, involved not only the Commerce Committee but also the 2002 rewrite of the farm bill. Burns was a leader in the effort to include funds in the measure for grants or loans from the Department of Agriculture's Rural Utilities Service to spur deployment of broadband service in rural areas.

A former auctioneer — he had to auction off the farms of friends during a previous farm crisis — Burns also pays attention to other rural issues such as aid for farmers and ranchers, lower rail rates for Montana shippers, federal assistance to small airports, and energy development. Burns sides with the farmers and cattlemen of his state, who complain that large meatpackers do not offer them fair prices, and that railroads hold them captive to unfairly high rates. In the 107th he pushed for generous emergency drought aid in the face of budget constraints, saying, "I am unable to overlook an industry that is as important to America as the military."

His main forum for addressing his constituents' parochial needs is the Appropriations Committee, where he chairs the Interior Subcommittee in the 108th Congress. Burns' Web site enumerates 103 earmarks totaling $151.5 million for Montana in the mammoth domestic spending law enacted in early 2003, ranging from $6 million for a fish hatchery in Fort Peck to $100,000 for railroad track work in Billings.

Burns served for three years in the Marine Corps in Japan and Korea, often sleeping in a sweltering Quonset hut, which left a lasting impression. He says the all-volunteer military, which competes with private industry for personnel, should upgrade family housing, especially given the increase in married recruits since his days as an $82-a-month corporal.

After the terrorist attacks of Sept. 11, 2001, Burns' military background helped shape his view that airline pilots should be given weapons to defend the cockpit from would-be hijackers. He played a leading role in the law enacted in 2002 to that end. He also argued that the United States should stop importing "rogue oil" from Middle East nations that use the revenue to support terrorists. And he convinced the Treasury Department to issue "Patriot Bonds" after the terrorist attacks to fund the war on terrorism and to help rebuild New York City and the Pentagon.

As tales of corporate bookkeeping scandals saturated the news in 2001 and 2002, Burns suggested that the federal law that permits the government to seize the assets of "drug kingpins" should be extended to "corporate kingpins" convicted of financial crimes.

Burns has had trouble with his "folksy" image, mostly from the residents of Montana, who fear that Burns' chaw of tobacco and plain-spoken manner will give the state a bad name. Soon after he joined the Senate, Burns walked up to a police horse and examined its mouth to see how old the animal was. "Thanks, Conrad, thanks for telling the world what hicks we are," editorialized The Billings Gazette. Burns drew unwanted attention again in 1994 by telling the Bozeman Chronicle an anecdote about a rancher who used a racial epithet when referring to African-Americans. When Mississippi Sen. Trent Lott's laudatory comments in late 2002 about Strom Thurmond's segregationist 1948 presidential race stirred up controversy, Burns felt compelled to issue a blanket apology: "I deeply regret the things I've said in the past. My remarks were wrong and repugnant and I apologize for them once again."

Burns grew up on a small Missouri farm, where his mother was a Democratic Party worker. He first went to Montana as a teenager for a summer job as a firefighter. He studied agriculture at the University of Missouri for two years and then enlisted in the Marines. In 1962 he got a job with an agricultural magazine and moved to Billings. He later worked for the Billings Livestock Commission and did radio and television farm and ranch reports before co-founding the Northern Agricultural Network, which began with four radio stations.

After winning election as a Yellowstone County Commissioner in 1986, he sold his interest in the network, which by then had grown to more than three dozen radio and television stations in Montana and Wyoming.

Soon, Burns' name was mentioned as a potential challenger in 1988 to two-term Democratic Sen. John Melcher. Despite being tagged as an underdog with no expertise on national or international issues, his broadcasting life gave him wide name recognition. With strong backing from the Senate GOP campaign organization and President Reagan's timely veto of a wilderness bill Melcher wrote — giving credence to Burns' view that the incumbent lacked clout in Washington — Burns won with 52 percent of the vote. It was the biggest Senate upset of the year.

He breezed to a second term with 62 percent against Jack Mudd, a former University of Montana law school dean. But in 2000 he won by only 3 percentage points against farmer Brian Schweitzer, a political neophyte who focused his campaign on the high cost of prescription drugs.

KEY VOTES

2002

No Pass farm bill reversing crop subsidy limits
Yes Postpone tougher automobile fuel efficiency standards
No Overhaul campaign finance law; ban "soft money" and restrict advocacy advertising
No Set federal election standards
Yes Support oil drilling in Arctic National Wildlife Refuge
Yes Revive fast-track procedures for trade agreements
No Create federal insurance coverage for catastrophic terrorist losses
Yes Tighten federal accounting and corporate governance regulation
No Advance bipartisan Medicare prescription drug plan
Yes Create independent Sept. 11 commission
No Back Democratic Homeland Security Department proposal
Yes Authorize war against Iraq

2001

Yes Confirm John Ashcroft as attorney general
Yes Nullify Clinton Labor Department ergonomics rule
Yes Cut taxes by $1.35 trillion through fiscal 2011
No Pass Democratic bill to bolster rights of patients in managed-care plans
No Permit a new round of military base closings
Yes Expand law enforcement power to investigate suspected terrorists

CQ VOTE STUDIES

	PARTY UNITY		PRESIDENTIAL SUPPORT	
	Support	Oppose	Support	Oppose
2002	88%	12%	93%	7%
2001	96%	4%	97%	3%
2000	90%	10%	51%	49%
1999	94%	6%	24%	76%
1998	94%	6%	38%	62%
1997	94%	6%	57%	43%
1996	97%	3%	29%	71%
1995	95%	5%	26%	74%
1994	84%	16%	43%	57%
1993	92%	8%	24%	76%

INTEREST GROUPS

	AFL-CIO	ADA	CCUS	ACU
2002	31%	10%	90%	100%
2001	19%	10%	100%	96%
2000	0%	5%	93%	87%
1999	11%	0%	88%	96%
1998	0%	0%	100%	84%
1997	14%	15%	78%	88%
1996	0%	5%	85%	100%
1995	0%	0%	100%	83%
1994	13%	0%	70%	92%
1993	18%	20%	91%	96%

Rep. Denny Rehberg (R)

CAPITOL OFFICE
225-3211
denny.rehberg@mail.house.gov
www.house.gov/rehberg
516 Cannon 20515-2601; fax 225-5687

COMMITTEES
Agriculture
Resources
Transportation & Infrastructure

HOMETOWN
Billings

BORN
Oct. 5, 1955, Billings, Mont.

RELIGION
Episcopalian

FAMILY
Wife, Janice Lenhardt Rehberg; three children

EDUCATION
Montana State U., attended 1973-74; Washington State U., B.A. 1977 (political science)

CAREER
Rancher; congressional aide; realtor

POLITICAL HIGHLIGHTS
Mont. House, 1985-91; lieutenant governor, 1991-97; Republican nominee for U.S. Senate, 1996

ELECTION RESULTS

2002 GENERAL		
Denny Rehberg (R)	214,100	64.6%
Steve Kelly (D)	108,233	32.7%
Mike Fellows (LIBERT)	8,988	2.7%
2002 PRIMARY		
Denny Rehberg (R)		unopposed
2000 GENERAL		
Denny Rehberg (R)	211,418	51.5%
Nancy Keenan (D)	189,971	46.3%
James J. Tikalsky (LIBERT)	9,132	2.2%

Elected 2000; 2nd term

As his state's only representative, Rehberg has more constituents than anyone else in the House: 902,000 at the time of the 2000 census. Even though Montana's population grew by 13 percent in the previous decade, it fell short of winning back a second House seat, which had been taken away in the 1992 reapportionment.

Responding to the needs of so many people — the typical member represents about two-thirds as many — makes Rehberg's job unlike that of most other lawmakers in the House. For Rehberg (REE-berg), the answer is to keep his base of knowledge broad, something he says he learned to do during his six years as Montana's lieutenant governor in the 1990s.

His voting record shows him to be someone the GOP leadership and President Bush can usually depend on; he is solidly pro-business and pro-development. But some of Rehberg's legislative interests stray from the Republican line. He not only wants better prescription drug coverage for senior citizens and more special education funding for Montana's public schools but also billions of dollars to fund land conservation. "I take seriously my job to represent the entire state," he told the Great Falls Tribune. "It doesn't serve any purpose for me . . . to represent one narrow position."

Rehberg gained a seat on the Agriculture Committee in his first term, a logical choice for the fifth-generation rancher. He set out to help farmers and ranchers cope with the West's devastating drought and to open agricultural markets to foreign trade. During committee debate on the rewrite of the farm bill, Rehberg won inclusion of a plan aimed at helping farmers participate in business ventures beyond producing raw commodities. He also pushed for more funding in a 2001 agriculture assistance bill than Bush wanted, saying, "I fear that many producers in my state may not make it to the next farm bill."

Rural states such as Montana face unique challenges in providing economic development, education and health care opportunities. As lieutenant governor, Rehberg chaired the state's Rural Development Council. In Congress, he helps small communities take advantage of federal grants.

Montana stretches more than 500 miles from east to west and 250 miles from north to south, a vast expense that can make travel difficult between the state's many small and widely scattered population enters. On the Transportation Committee, Rehberg in his first term was able to win funding for Montana highway projects and federal grants to help small airports upgrade their facilities. And he led a successful effort to convince the Postal Service to continue airmail service in Montana.

The federal Essential Air Service program is important to the state — commercial airline service to seven Montana towns exists because of EAS subsidies. In addition, air service to Montana's larger cities is limited. As part of the airline bailout package enacted after the Sept. 11, 2001, terrorist attacks, Rehberg won language directing the Department of Transportation to ensure that smaller communities received adequate airline service. He also championed legislation to permit pilots to carry firearms.

Rehberg also has to cope with his own travel logistics. Once he gets to Montana, he still often drives hundreds of miles to reach his destination. In his first year in Congress, he estimates he drove 60,000 miles in the state in order to fulfill a pledge to visit all 56 of its counties.

Rehberg is intent on using his seat to strengthen the public school system. Most towns in Montana offer no option other than a public school. Rehberg says one of his priorities is to force the federal government to pay its agreed-upon share for special education programs for disabled students. He also wants to provide rural areas with convenient and affordable access to modern health care and to address the nationwide problem of the uninsured.

Rehberg says he has a keen personal interest in seeing Congress enact a permanent repeal of the estate tax because his family had to sell part of its ranch holdings to pay taxes due after his great-grandmother died in 1976.

Rehberg grew up on the family beef cattle and cashmere goat ranch, competing in gymnastics and cultivating a passion for playing the drums. His percussion skills still intact, he was among the 10 or so lawmakers in the "Congressional All-Stars" band that played a benefit concert to raise money for Sept. 11 terrorist attack relief efforts.

His mother taught elementary school and his father, in addition to running the ranch, took on a number of other jobs to help support the family. His father, Jack, was a GOP nominee for a Montana House seat in 1970 but took just 36 percent against Democrat John Melcher.

After earning a degree in political science, with emphasis on public administration, from Washington State University, Rehberg worked as an intern in the Montana Senate, sold real estate for two years and then moved to Washington in 1979 to work for GOP Rep. Ron Marlenee of Montana. Returning to the family ranch three years later, he ended up serving six years in the state House and managing political campaigns for Marlenee in 1986 and the successful Senate bid of Republican Conrad Burns in 1988.

Rehberg was appointed lieutenant governor in 1991 when Lt. Gov. Allen Kolstad quit to join the Bush administration, and he was elected to a four-year term in 1992. In 1996, Rehberg came within 5 percentage points of defeating Democratic Sen. Max Baucus, whose $3.7 million in spending on the race was almost triple what Rehberg spent.

In 2000, he was unopposed for the GOP nomination when Republican Rick Hill retired after just two House terms, citing poor health. Rehberg looked to be the underdog against Democratic state school superintendent Nancy Keenan, but after a somewhat vitriolic campaign he won by 5 points.

National GOP strategists sounded Rehberg out about another race against Baucus in 2002, but he nixed that idea and was essentially given a pass by the Democrats for election to a second House term. He won by 32 points over Steve Kelly, an art gallery owner in Bozeman.

During his first House race, Rehberg removed himself from the management of the family ranch after arranging to have its herd of 600 goats moved to the Baucus family ranch. The two families now share the profits.

KEY VOTES

2002

No Overhaul campaign finance law; ban "soft money" and restrict advocacy advertising
Yes Back Bush's defense budget increase
Yes Extend 1996 welfare law
Yes Adopt Bush's discretionary spending limit
Yes Pass GOP Medicare prescription drug plan
No Create independent Sept. 11 commission
No Extend union protections to Homeland Security Department employees
Yes Revive fast-track procedures for trade agreements
Yes Authorize war against Iraq
No Advance bankruptcy overhaul opposed by abortion opponents

2001

Yes Nullify Clinton Labor Department ergonomics rule
Yes Cut taxes by $1.35 trillion through fiscal 2011
No Maintain ban on oil drilling in Arctic National Wildlife Refuge
Yes Approve Bush proposal to limit managed-care plan liability for coverage decisions
No Divert money from crop subsidy payments to land conservation
Yes Expand law enforcement power to investigate suspected terrorists

CQ VOTE STUDIES

	PARTY UNITY		PRESIDENTIAL SUPPORT	
	Support	Oppose	Support	Oppose
2002	95%	5%	85%	15%
2001	96%	4%	88%	12%

INTEREST GROUPS

	AFL-CIO	ADA	CCUS	ACU
2002	11%	0%	95%	100%
2001	17%	5%	100%	84%

MONTANA

At large

Montana's Big Sky country has long been a place where pioneers traveled to strike it rich. Once explored by Lewis and Clark and later by fur trappers and gold seekers, Montana is now a prime destination for celebrities and telecommuters who want to buy their own small piece of the frontier.

After the 1990 census, Montana lost one of its two congressional seats. The resulting statewide district combines the state's politically independent halves into one unpredictable voting bloc. The western, mountainous half of the state leans Democratic, with an environmental base and a union tradition in mining and lumber mills. It also is home to the state's university community in Missoula. The area has been shifting to support more natural resources-based development in recent years. The eastern half, a flat plain where wheat and cattle are raised, follows a tradition of rural Republicanism.

Despite these differences, both halves can be conservative and independent. The state elected Jeannette Rankin, the first woman in Congress, in 1916. Ross Perot had some of his best showings in the nation here in both the 1992 and 1996 presidential elections.

With an economy based on natural resources, Montana finds itself exploiting its terrain while also striving to protect it. In ballot initiatives, voters have rejected some environmental regulations. Yet Butte, the site of years of mining, is the center of a massive superfund clean-up effort. George W. Bush captured 58 percent of the state's vote in the 2000 presidential election.

MAJOR INDUSTRY

Agriculture, tourism, forestry

MILITARY BASES

Malmstrom Air Force Base, 3,363 military, 370 civilian (2002)

CITIES

Billings, 89,847; Missoula, 57,053; Great Falls, 56,690; Butte-Silver Bow, 34,606; Bozeman, 27,509; Helena, 25,780

NOTABLE

Glacier National Park is located in the northwest part of the state; Jordan was the site of a 1996 standoff between federal authorities and an anti-tax group called The Freemen.

NEBRASKA

Gov. Mike Johanns (R)

First elected: 1998
Length of term: 4 years
Term expires: 1/07
Salary: $85,000
Phone: (402) 471-2244
Hometown: Lincoln
Born: June 18, 1950; Osage, Iowa
Religion: Roman Catholic
Family: Wife, Stephanie Johanns; two children
Education: St. Mary's College (Minn.), B.A. 1971 (communication and arts); Creighton U., J.D. 1974
Career: Lawyer
Political highlights: Lancaster County Commission, 1982-86; Lincoln City Council, 1989-91; mayor of Lincoln, 1991-99
Election results:

2002 GENERAL		
Mike Johanns (R)	330,349	68.7%
Stormy Dean (D)	132,348	27.5%
Paul A. Rosberg (NEB)	18,294	3.8%

Lt. Gov. Dave Heineman (R)

First elected: 2002
Length of term: 4 years
Term expires: 1/07
Salary: $60,000
Phone: (402) 471-2256

STATE LEGISLATURE

Unicameral Legislature: Meets 90 days in odd-numbered years; 60 days in even-numbered years
Legislature: 49 non-partisan members, 4-year terms
2003 breakdown: 40 men, 9 women
Salary: $12,000
Phone: (402) 471-2271

STATE TERM LIMITS

Governor: 2 consecutive terms
Legislature: 2 consecutive terms

URBAN STATISTICS

CITY	POPULATION
Omaha	390,007
Lincoln	225,581
Bellevue	44,382
Grand Island	42,940
Kearney	27,431

REGISTERED VOTERS

Republican	50%
Democrat	35%
Nonpartisan	14%

POPULATION

2002 population (est.)	1,729,180
2000 population	1,711,263
1990 population	1,578,385
Percent change (1990-2000)	+8.4%
Rank among states (2002)	38
Median age	35.3
Born in state	67.1%
Foreign born	4.4%
Violent crime rate	328/100,000
Poverty level	9.7%
Federal workers	15,620
Military	15,040

REDISTRICTING

Nebraska retained its three House seats in reapportionment. The state legislature drew a new map, which the governor signed on May 30, 2001.

MISCELLANEOUS

Web: www.state.ne.us
Capital: Lincoln
STATE ELECTION OFFICIAL
(402) 471-3229
DEMOCRATIC HEADQUARTERS
(402) 434-2180
REPUBLICAN HEADQUARTERS
(402) 475-2122

District Statistics

	2000 VOTE FOR PRESIDENT															
DIST.	BUSH	GORE	NADER	WHITE	BLACK	ASIAN	HISP	MEDIAN INCOME	WHITE COLLAR	BLUE COLLAR	SERVICE INDUSTRY	OVER 64	UNDER 18	COLLEGE EDUCATION	RURAL	SQ. MILES
1	59%	36%	4%	91%	1%	2%	4%	$40,021	58%	27%	15%	13%	25%	24%	35%	11,951
2	57	39	4	80	10	2	6	$45,235	67	20	13	10	27	31	2	411
3	71	25	3	92	0	0	6	$33,866	54	31	15	17	26	17	54	64,511
STATE	62	33	4	87	4	1	6	$39,250	59	26	15	14	26	24	30	76,872
U.S.	47.9	48.4	3	69	12	4	13	$41,994	60	25	15	12	26	24	21	3,537,438

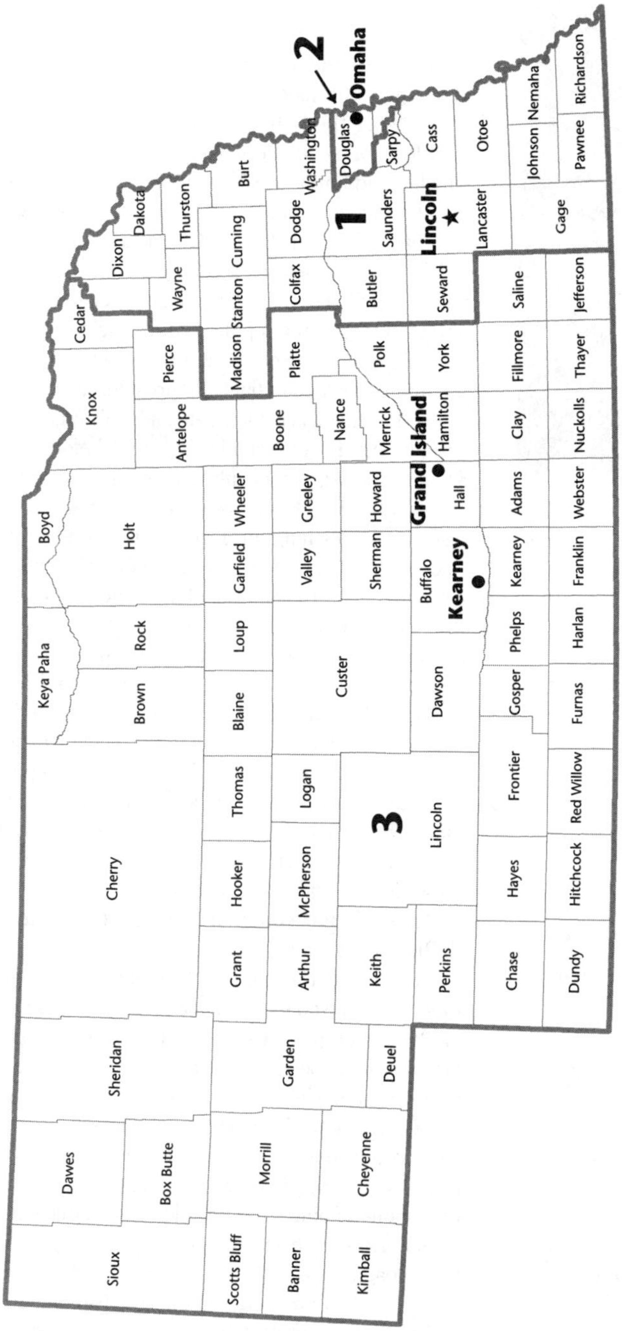
1
2
3
Omaha
Lincoln
Grand Island
Kearney
Dixon
Dakota
Thurston
Burt
Washington
Douglas
Sarpy
Cass
Otoe
Nemaha
Johnson
Richardson
Pawnee
Cedar
Wayne
Cuming
Dodge
Saunders
Lancaster
Gage
Knox
Pierce
Madison
Stanton
Colfax
Butler
Seward
Saline
Jefferson
Antelope
Platte
Polk
York
Fillmore
Thayer
Boone
Nance
Merrick
Hamilton
Clay
Nuckolls
Boyd
Holt
Wheeler
Greeley
Howard
Hall
Adams
Webster
Garfield
Valley
Sherman
Buffalo
Kearney
Franklin
Keya Paha
Rock
Loup
Custer
Phelps
Harlan
Brown
Blaine
Dawson
Gosper
Furnas
Thomas
Logan
Lincoln
Frontier
Red Willow
Cherry
Hooker
McPherson
Hayes
Hitchcock
Grant
Arthur
Keith
Perkins
Chase
Dundy
Sheridan
Garden
Deuel
Dawes
Box Butte
Morrill
Cheyenne
Sioux
Scotts Bluff
Banner
Kimball

Sen. Chuck Hagel (R)

CAPITOL OFFICE
224-4224
chuck_hagel@hagel.senate.gov
hagel.senate.gov
248 Russell 20510-2705; fax 224-5213

COMMITTEES
Banking, Housing & Urban Affairs
(International Trade & Finance - chairman)
Foreign Relations
(International Economic Policy, Export & Trade Promotion - chairman)
Select Intelligence

HOMETOWN
Omaha

BORN
Oct. 4, 1946, North Platte, Neb.

RELIGION
Episcopalian

FAMILY
Wife, Lilibet Hagel; two children

EDUCATION
U. of Nebraska, Omaha, B.A. 1971 (history)

MILITARY SERVICE
Army, 1967-68

CAREER
Investment bank executive; cellular phone company founder; lobbyist; congressional aide; radio talk show host

POLITICAL HIGHLIGHTS
Veterans Administration deputy administrator, 1981-82

ELECTION RESULTS

2002 GENERAL		
Chuck Hagel (R)	397,438	82.8%
Charlie A. Matulka (D)	70,290	14.6%
John J. Graziano (LIBERT)	7,423	1.6%
Phil Chase (I)	5,066	1.1%
2002 PRIMARY		
Chuck Hagel (R)		unopposed

PREVIOUS WINNING PERCENTAGES
1996 (56%)

Elected 1996; 2nd term

Despite his relatively short tenure in the Senate, Hagel appears so frequently on national television talk shows that he comments knowingly about how the food provided by NBC's "Meet the Press" stacks up to CBS's "Face the Nation" or ABC's "This Week."

Television schedulers like Hagel for his telegenic looks, engaging personality and blunt yet substantive remarks on national issues. He is also a popular guest because of his willingness to challenge top members of his own party, from the Senate GOP leadership to President Bush.

But Hagel is not just a talking head. With considerable luck as well as political skill and determination, the second-term lawmaker has emerged as a leader on foreign policy issues, rising to become the second-ranking Republican on the Foreign Relations Committee in 2003. He even has been mentioned as a potential GOP presidential candidate in 2008.

An affable and articulate self-made millionaire and decorated Vietnam veteran, he had never held elective office before his long-shot 1996 victory in a Senate race against popular Democratic Gov. Ben Nelson. (Nelson won the state's other Senate seat when it came open in 2000.) But Hagel got off to a fast start in Washington, earning high praise from his new colleagues.

One of his key decisions came soon after he was elected: He agreed to a request from Indiana Republican Richard G. Lugar, a senior member of the Foreign Relations Committee, to join the panel at a time when few lawmakers showed interest in foreign affairs. A series of retirements and election losses allowed Hagel to rise quickly to the top of the committee hierarchy, putting him in a key position just when the Sept. 11, 2001, terrorist attacks placed a premium on foreign policy expertise.

Hagel expanded his knowledge by traveling extensively overseas, meeting with top foreign leaders and slogging through hour after hour of committee hearings. That commitment — and his close ideological affinity with Lugar's "realist" brand of foreign policy — have helped the panel's two senior Republicans forge a close working relationship. He also has had few problems finding common ground with the panel's top Democrat, Joseph R. Biden Jr. of Delaware.

In fact, Hagel is more likely to square off against Bush, though in 2000 Bush interviewed him as a potential vice presidential running mate. During the 107th Congress, Hagel questioned Bush's plans to attack Iraq, invoking his Vietnam experience to warn of the potentially dangerous consequences of an invasion. He blasted Bush's characterization of Iran as part of an "axis of evil," saying the United States should be seeking warmer ties with Tehran. He introduced legislation to beef up U.S. military and economic assistance to post-war Afghanistan, contending that the Bush administration's aversion to "nation-building" threatened to return that country to chaos.

Hagel's visibility and independence have grated on some of his more senior colleagues. In 1998, he challenged Mitch McConnell of Kentucky in his bid for re-election as chairman of the National Republican Senatorial Committee, the organization responsible for recruiting GOP candidates and raising the money to get them elected. With Majority Leader Trent Lott's tacit backing, McConnell trounced Hagel, 39-13.

In his willingness to buck the White House and Senate leadership, Hagel resembles Arizona Sen. John McCain, and he was an enthusiastic supporter of McCain's 2000 bid for the Republican presidential nomination. Commentators noted that the two senators had much in common: heroic war service, plain-spoken candor and impatience with the status quo in government. What Hagel lacked, it was widely observed, was McCain's visible temper. Hagel has been called "McCain without the attitude."

But the two have another, more fundamental difference. Hagel supports a business-oriented brand of conservatism, sometimes at odds with McCain's increasingly populist impulses. Hagel embraces the longstanding Republican tenets of tax cuts and reductions in federal government spending. He has little patience for the foreign policy views of some on the GOP right who support unyielding economic sanctions on foreign nations guilty of human rights abuses.

With a perspective rooted in business, Hagel stresses the importance of the global village and the virtues of internationalism, espousing the benefits of "dynamic, global, interconnected" markets. He has furthered these views as the chairman of the Foreign Relations Committee's International Economic Policy Subcommittee and the Banking panel's International Trade Subcommittee.

While Hagel's primary focus has been overseas, he also has been an important player on some domestic issues, notably health care. He was among the first Senate Republicans to recognize the political popularity of creating a prescription drug benefit for Medicare recipients, introducing a bill in 2000 to address the issue. In the 107th Congress, he tried to bridge differences in the Senate with legislation that would have provided a large share of benefits to the poor and those with high drug costs.

Hagel's compelling personal story has contributed to his rapid political rise. He grew up in a small town in Nebraska, where he started working as a carhop at a drive-in restaurant when he was 9 years old. After his father died when he was 16, Hagel, as the oldest child, played a key role in the upbringing of his younger siblings. In high school, he successfully ran for student council president, attracting attention through stunts such as tying a chicken to the hood of his car and driving around blaring out his positions as the chicken cackled.

Later, Hagel enlisted in the Army and spent a year as an infantryman in Vietnam, serving side-by-side with his brother, Tom. Hagel was seriously wounded twice and received two Purple Hearts, suffering burns that required a decade to heal completely.

After graduating from college in 1971, he landed a job with Republican Rep. John Y. McCollister of Nebraska, and rose to become his top aide. Hagel then became a lobbyist for the Firestone Tire & Rubber Company and campaigned heavily in 1980 for Ronald Reagan, who rewarded him with a top job at the Veterans Administration. He left government in 1982 to start a business on a shoestring, selling his seven-year-old Buick and two insurance bonds and investing his net worth of $5,000 in a cellular phone company that he began with two partners. That company, Vanguard Cellular Systems Inc., became the country's second-largest independent cell phone company and made Hagel a multimillionaire. Hagel received the 2001 Horatio Alger Award, which recognizes self-made business leaders who have overcome adversity.

He entered the 1996 Senate primary as the underdog against Attorney General Don Stenberg but spent lavishly from his personal funds and swept the nomination with more than 60 percent of the vote. In the fall, Hagel made the centerpiece of his bid the argument that federal tax cuts would stimulate economic growth, something he contended would do more to address problems in society than any government program. Helped by GOP criticism that Nelson was breaking an earlier pledge to serve out his term as governor, Hagel won by 14 percentage points.

In 2002, Hagel's 68-point margin of victory over Democrat Charlie Matulka was the largest in Nebraska Senate election history.

KEY VOTES

2002

No Pass farm bill reversing crop subsidy limits
Yes Postpone tougher automobile fuel efficiency standards
No Overhaul campaign finance law; ban "soft money" and restrict advocacy advertising
Yes Set federal election standards
Yes Support oil drilling in Arctic National Wildlife Refuge
Yes Revive fast-track procedures for trade agreements
Yes Create federal insurance coverage for catastrophic terrorist losses
Yes Tighten federal accounting and corporate governance regulation
No Advance bipartisan Medicare prescription drug plan
Yes Create independent Sept. 11 commission
No Back Democratic Homeland Security Department proposal
Yes Authorize war against Iraq

2001

Yes Confirm John Ashcroft as attorney general
Yes Nullify Clinton Labor Department ergonomics rule
Yes Cut taxes by $1.35 trillion through fiscal 2011
No Pass Democratic bill to bolster rights of patients in managed-care plans
Yes Permit a new round of military base closings
Yes Expand law enforcement power to investigate suspected terrorists

CQ VOTE STUDIES

	PARTY UNITY		PRESIDENTIAL SUPPORT	
	Support	Oppose	Support	Oppose
2002	94%	6%	98%	2%
2001	92%	8%	96%	4%
2000	94%	6%	49%	51%
1999	92%	8%	36%	64%
1998	89%	11%	42%	58%
1997	92%	8%	59%	41%

INTEREST GROUPS

	AFL-CIO	ADA	CCUS	ACU
2002	23%	10%	95%	95%
2001	25%	25%	100%	84%
2000	0%	0%	100%	88%
1999	0%	5%	100%	88%
1998	0%	0%	94%	72%
1997	0%	5%	100%	80%

Sen. Ben Nelson (D)

CAPITOL OFFICE
224-6551
bennelson.senate.gov
720 Hart 20510-2706; fax 228-0012

COMMITTEES
Agriculture, Nutrition & Forestry
Armed Services
Veterans' Affairs

HOMETOWN
Omaha

BORN
May 17, 1941, McCook, Neb.

RELIGION
Methodist

FAMILY
Wife, Diane Nelson; four children

EDUCATION
U. of Nebraska, B.A. 1963 (philosophy), M.A. 1965 (philosophy), J.D. 1970

CAREER
Lawyer; insurance company executive

POLITICAL HIGHLIGHTS
Neb. director of insurance, 1975-76; governor, 1991-99; Democratic nominee for U.S. Senate, 1996

ELECTION RESULTS

2000 GENERAL		
Ben Nelson (D)	353,093	51.0%
Don Stenberg (R)	337,977	48.8%
2000 PRIMARY		
Ben Nelson (D)	105,661	92.1%
Al Hamburg (D)	8,482	7.4%

Elected 2000; 1st term

He may not be as flashy as Bob Kerrey, his war hero predecessor, but Nelson is no less a maverick. He toes the party line even less frequently than Kerrey or Chuck Hagel, the state's independent-minded Republican senator. During his first two years in the Senate, Nelson voted against Democratic leaders almost 46 percent of the time and sided with Republican President Bush 81 percent — the third-most of any Senate Democrat. But he has not burned his bridges: In the 108th Congress he is one of four Democrats of varying political persuasions on a new executive committee to hone the party's agenda and unify members.

In a Senate so closely divided, Nelson's willingness to cross party lines gives him an unusual amount of power for a freshman. He estimates that he has met personally with President Bush at least a half-dozen times, including flying with him twice on Air Force One. Bush, who is known for bestowing nicknames, calls Nelson "Nelly," though the senator says he would prefer a more "macho" moniker.

While Nelson sometimes complains of being worked over by the president or party leaders, he generally plays down the role such lobbying has in his decisions. He invoked his standard line — "The only pressure I feel is internal pressure to do what's right" — when pondering in the 107th Congress whether to support banning "soft money" campaign contributions to political parties. He eventually sided with Republicans on that issue, one of only two Senate Democrats to vote against the law enacted in 2002.

As an alternative, Nelson promoted a proposal to limit soft-money contributions to $60,000 per donor — the work of Hagel, who had bested him in a tight race for the Senate in 1996.

Nelson's speed in burying the hatchet with Hagel and in charting a course as a player on an array of issues shows an astute political strategist at work. Unlike some politicians whose glad-handing style propels them into public office, Nelson's rise to the Senate is mostly the product of perseverance. Since age 17, when he was elected governor of a model Nebraska high school legislature, Nelson has yearned for statewide office. The election of his high school superintendent and debate coach, Ralph Brooks, to be Nebraska's governor persuaded Nelson that "you didn't have to be from a big city to have an opportunity in politics."

Nelson was reared in McCook, a remote small town where his mother, Birdella, started a local taxpayers' watchdog group. Her attention to how tax revenue was spent was not lost on her son. "Watching the purse strings is the most important basic thing you can do in government," he says.

Such a mindset is in line with that of the majority of Nebraskans, who tend to have a strong conservative, as well as independent, streak. Nelson's understanding of the state's political dynamic was on display just one month into his Senate career, when he joined Republicans and only seven other Democrats in voting to confirm former Missouri GOP Sen. John Ashcroft as attorney general.

In addition, the Nebraskan sided with most Republicans in voting against the Democrats' plans to extend health insurance to retired steelworkers. He voted for President Bush's signature tax cuts and the Republicans' 2002 budget plan, which made the tax cuts possible. He also supported Republican measures to ban cloning.

On the Agriculture Committee, Nelson's agenda starts with the drought that has plagued the Nebraska farmer. In an effort to draw more attention to its devastating effects, he gave the drought a name — David — just as hurricanes have been named. "An emergency is an emergency," he said.

A two-term governor, Nelson is a frequent advocate of states' rights. When the Senate considered Bush's education overhaul, Nelson teamed up with Missouri Democrat Jean Carnahan to propose an amendment that would have canceled annual testing of schoolchildren unless the federal government picked up the tab. The provision was rejected.

While some might accuse Nelson of siding with the opposing party too much, his Democratic stripes come through when the Senate is considering Social Security, Medicare or farm programs. Nelson has cited his support of the entitlement programs for the elderly as the crux of his party affiliation. And he was an avid proponent of the Democrats' $410 billion plan to boost farm incomes, though he lamented that too many wealthy farmers would benefit from its payments.

On many issues, Nelson works actively with a group of moderates generally led by Louisiana Democrat John B. Breaux and Maine Republican Olympia J. Snowe. When the Bush tax plan took center stage, Nelson quickly sided with the group, which chipped away at the president's $1.6 trillion proposal until it reached a level — $1.35 trillion — that a bloc of like-minded moderates could support in a time of surplus. But he did not prevail in his bid to create a "circuit breaker," under which Congress would have reconsidered the cut in the event of a return to deficits.

Nelson's support for many conservative proposals has led some in the Republican Party to view him as a possible convert. Efforts to persuade Nelson to switch became particularly frequent after Vermont's James M. Jeffords left the GOP in 2001 to become a Senate independent. Nelson gives no sign that he is any more interested in changing his stripes than he was when approached by the Nebraska GOP. "I've had people talking to me about that for a decade or more," Nelson says matter-of-factly.

Nelson prides himself on being a practical joker. As governor, he participated in a segment of the TV show "Candid Camera" in which he told visitors to his office that he was planning to change the state's name to "something much more modern . . . something like Zenmar or Quentron." He also held a party for others named Ben Nelson. Twelve from Nebraska, 10 from other states and one dog attended. The senator goes by his middle name — his first name is Earl — but he still gets phone calls for other Ben Nelsons.

Nelson returns to Nebraska often but was forced to make some unwanted trips in 2002 to testify on the state's behalf in a lawsuit filed by a company denied a license for a low-level radioactive waste facility. The company alleged that Nelson improperly used his political power to ensure the license would not be granted. The judge ordered Nebraska to pay $151 million in damages; the state has appealed.

While Nelson has held politics in high esteem since an early age, he considered joining the ministry while at the University of Nebraska. He opted instead for law school and, upon graduation, began a long career in insurance law. He ran an insurance company, headed a national association of insurance regulators and directed his state's insurance department. In 1990, he launched his first statewide run for office, surviving the Democratic primary for governor by just 42 votes. He went on to defeat the incumbent, Republican Kay Orr, by 4,000 votes.

After eight years as governor he returned in 1999 to his law firm, Kaufman-Nelson-Pattee, where he helped states develop Washington lobbying strategies. But when Kerrey announced he would retire the next year, Nelson was the shoo-in Democratic nominee as his successor. He ended up defeating Attorney General Don Stenberg by 2 percentage points — the closest Senate election in Nebraska history.

KEY VOTES

2002

Yes Pass farm bill reversing crop subsidy limits
Yes Postpone tougher automobile fuel efficiency standards
No Overhaul campaign finance law; ban "soft money" and restrict advocacy advertising
Yes Set federal election standards
No Support oil drilling in Arctic National Wildlife Refuge
Yes Revive fast-track procedures for trade agreements
Yes Create federal insurance coverage for catastrophic terrorist losses
Yes Tighten federal accounting and corporate governance regulation
No Advance bipartisan Medicare prescription drug plan
Yes Create independent Sept. 11 commission
Yes Back Democratic Homeland Security Department proposal
Yes Authorize war against Iraq

2001

Yes Confirm John Ashcroft as attorney general
No Nullify Clinton Labor Department ergonomics rule
Yes Cut taxes by $1.35 trillion through fiscal 2011
Yes Pass Democratic bill to bolster rights of patients in managed-care plans
No Permit a new round of military base closings
Yes Expand law enforcement power to investigate suspected terrorists

CQ VOTE STUDIES

	PARTY UNITY		PRESIDENTIAL SUPPORT	
	Support	Oppose	Support	Oppose
2002	51%	49%	91%	9%
2001	58%	42%	74%	26%

INTEREST GROUPS

	AFL-CIO	ADA	CCUS	ACU
2002	62%	50%	63%	55%
2001	81%	70%	71%	56%

Rep. Doug Bereuter (R)

CAPITOL OFFICE
225-4806
www.house.gov/bereuter
2184 Rayburn 20515-2701; fax 225-5686

COMMITTEES
Financial Services
International Relations
(Europe - chairman)
Transportation & Infrastructure
Select Intelligence
(Intelligence Policy & National Security - chairman)

HOMETOWN
Cedar Bluffs

BORN
Oct. 6, 1939, York, Neb.

RELIGION
Lutheran

FAMILY
Wife, Louise Bereuter; two children

EDUCATION
U. of Nebraska, B.A. 1961; Harvard U., M.C.P. 1966 (city planning), M.P.A. 1973

MILITARY SERVICE
Army, 1963-65

CAREER
City planner; professor; state official

POLITICAL HIGHLIGHTS
Neb. Legislature, 1975-79

ELECTION RESULTS

2002 GENERAL		
Doug Bereuter (R)	133,013	85.4%
Robert Eckerson (LIBERT)	22,831	14.7%
2002 PRIMARY		
Doug Bereuter (R)		unopposed
2000 GENERAL		
Doug Bereuter (R)	155,485	66.3%
Alan Jacobsen (D)	72,859	31.0%
David Oenbring (LIBERT)	6,147	2.6%

PREVIOUS WINNING PERCENTAGES
1998 (73%); 1996 (70%); 1994 (63%); 1992 (60%); 1990 (65%); 1988 (67%); 1986 (64%); 1984 (74%); 1982 (75%); 1980 (79%); 1978 (58%)

Elected 1978; 13th term

One of the House's most influential Republicans in the international policy arena, Bereuter is an advocate of trade liberalization, vigorous U.S. participation in international organizations and a strong but limited role for the U.S. military abroad. He also played a leading role in examining and revamping the U.S. intelligence agencies that were unable to warn in advance of al Qaeda's plan to attack the United States on Sept. 11, 2001.

His Wall Street internationalism has made Bereuter a well-respected voice in foreign policy circles at home and overseas, where he often leads delegations of lawmakers to meetings with their counterparts, particularly in Europe. Late in 2002, he was elected president of the NATO Parliamentary Assembly, a body of legislators from NATO member nations that advises the military alliance. In 2003, he became chairman of the International Relations Subcommittee on Europe.

But his non-ideological, pro-business foreign policy has not endeared him to the House Republican leadership. His views have distanced him especially from Majority Leader Tom DeLay, the most influential of the religious conservatives at the Capitol who are exercising growing control over congressional foreign policy. And so GOP leaders rebuffed Bereuter when he sought to ascend to one committee chairmanship in the 107th Congress and a different committee chairmanship in the 108th.

In 2001, the top spot on the International Relations panel came open because of a six-year term limit on Chairman Benjamin A. Gilman of New York. Bereuter, who had served as the panel's vice chairman, had been biding his time for the moment to step up — even twice turning down home state GOP entreaties that he run for higher office. But GOP leaders gave the gavel instead to Henry J. Hyde of Illinois, who was compelled by the same Republican term-limit rule to step down as Judiciary chairman that year.

Party leaders tried to appease Bereuter by naming him chairman of the Financial Services Committee's International Monetary Policy and Trade Subcommittee — a post he relinquished in 2003 — and vice chairman of the Intelligence Committee, an appointment that put him in line to take the chairmanship of that panel in the 108th.

But a year later, Republican leaders again dashed Bereuter's aspirations, persuading Porter J. Goss of Florida to reverse his announced plans to retire by saying they needed him to continue chairing the Intelligence Committee in 2003 and 2004 despite the term-limit rule.

Despite his differences with Republican leaders, Bereuter is hardly a rebel. The GOP leadership and the U.S. business community continue to look to him as an important adviser on foreign policy, particularly with regard to intelligence and Sino-American relations. And Bereuter has steered a moderate course on intelligence matters. For example, he viewed creation of the Department of Homeland Security as a useful response to the failure of existing intelligence agencies. But he has been wary of an expansion of domestic agency spying powers as a potential intrusion on civil liberties. And he advocates more responsibilities for the intelligence committees in monitoring the often-covert government operations that are required as part of the war on terrorism.

In the 106th Congress, Bereuter, as chairman of International Relations' Asia and the Pacific Subcommittee, used his knowledge on trade and his friendships with Democrats to broker a deal that was pivotal to enactment of the law making permanent the normal U.S.-China trade relationship.

When it became apparent that a House majority for the proposal was failing to solidify, Bereuter and Michigan Democrat Sander M. Levin developed a legislative package that successfully assuaged lawmakers' concerns about rewarding a nation with a history of human rights violations, labor abuses and military posturing.

Bereuter votes a centrist line on social policy, and his manner is thoughtful and non-confrontational. In debate, his focus is on substance, rather than rhetorical fireworks.

On the Financial Services panel, Bereuter clashed with President Bush's first Treasury secretary, Paul H. O'Neill, when he sought during the 107th to restrict Treasury's control over Export-Import Bank loans and to press the department for greater accountability of U.S. funding to a half-dozen multilateral lending organizations. In the end, Bereuter backed down in the face of a Bush administration threat to veto the underlying bill to reauthorize the Ex-Im Bank.

Beyond the international focus of his subcommittee, Bereuter has emphasized housing, community development and the health of small banks. His background is unusual for a Nebraska politician — he was the state's top urban planner in the late 1960s — and he was eager to put his expertise in urban affairs to use when he arrived in Washington. In his second term, he won a seat on what was then called the Banking Committee, which oversees many urban issues, and two years later he became top Republican on the subcommittee with jurisdiction over international financial institutions — a close fit with his International Relations work.

Bereuter was elected to the state legislature in 1974, and he won a reputation as one of its more liberal members by sponsoring a land-use planning bill opposed by farmers and ranchers. But he ran as a conservative to win election to the House four years later, besting a conservative state senator in the primary and then uniting Republican support and a large independent vote to win 58 percent against Hess Dyas, a former state Democratic Party chairman.

Since then, he has won re-election with ease. Democrats did not even field an opponent in 2002.

In 2000, Bereuter had the inside track for a Senate seat when Democrat Bob Kerrey announced his retirement. But as in 1998, when Nebraska Republicans sought a gubernatorial candidate, Bereuter stayed put, hoping re-election to a 12th term would bring the International Relations chairmanship. Now, he is indicating that he intends to retire from Congress by 2008, if not sooner.

KEY VOTES

2002

Yes Overhaul campaign finance law; ban "soft money" and restrict advocacy advertising
Yes Back Bush's defense budget increase
Yes Extend 1996 welfare law
Yes Adopt Bush's discretionary spending limit
Yes Pass GOP Medicare prescription drug plan
No Create independent Sept. 11 commission
No Extend union protections to Homeland Security Department employees
Yes Revive fast-track procedures for trade agreements
Yes Authorize war against Iraq
Yes Advance bankruptcy overhaul opposed by abortion opponents

2001

Yes Nullify Clinton Labor Department ergonomics rule
Yes Cut taxes by $1.35 trillion through fiscal 2011
No Maintain ban on oil drilling in Arctic National Wildlife Refuge
Yes Approve Bush proposal to limit managed-care plan liability for coverage decisions
No Divert money from crop subsidy payments to land conservation
Yes Expand law enforcement power to investigate suspected terrorists

CQ VOTE STUDIES

	PARTY UNITY		PRESIDENTIAL SUPPORT	
	Support	Oppose	Support	Oppose
2002	86%	14%	85%	15%
2001	90%	10%	83%	17%
2000	82%	18%	32%	68%
1999	79%	21%	35%	65%
1998	84%	16%	28%	72%

INTEREST GROUPS

	AFL-CIO	ADA	CCUS	ACU
2002	11%	10%	90%	72%
2001	17%	10%	91%	72%
2000	10%	10%	90%	64%
1999	11%	35%	92%	62%
1998	0%	5%	100%	64%

NEBRASKA 1

East – Lincoln, Fremont, Norfolk

The 1st takes in eastern Nebraska, excluding Omaha and its suburbs. The region includes the state's capital, Lincoln, and the University of Nebraska's Memorial Stadium, which could qualify as the district's second-largest city and the state's third-largest when filled to its 74,000-seat capacity during a home football game. Despite the area's small-town reputation, growing industry in Omaha exurbs, including Lincoln, Norfolk and South Sioux City, is helping to make the eastern portion of the state more urban.

Lincoln, in particular, is thriving and has seen a major population increase led by the expanding state and city governments and the university. Hospitals and a banking and insurance industry also help sustain the city's economy.

Although the district was home to populist William Jennings Bryan and many supporters of his politics at the turn of the 20th century, the 1st now votes consistently Republican at all levels. The University of Nebraska's main campus in Lincoln makes the city more liberal, but voter registration favors the GOP in both the city and surrounding Lancaster County. The strongest Democratic areas are in the northeast, in Dakota County, with a sizable blue-collar contingent, and in Thurston County, made up of the Winnebago and Omaha Indian reservations. Democratic-leaning Saline County was moved from the 1st District to the western 3rd in redistricting following the 2000 census.

The region depends on agriculture but with a modern twist. Traditional crop and hog farming are supplemented by other agribusiness, such as meat processing, food packaging and fertilizer production. Telemarketing and polling companies, such as the Gallup Organization, also add to white-collar job opportunities. Flood control is a problem in the area.

MAJOR INDUSTRY
Agriculture, meat processing, health care, government

CITIES
Lincoln, 225,581; Fremont, 25,174; Norfolk, 23,516; Beatrice, 12,496

NOTABLE
Johnny Carson, former host of "The Tonight Show," grew up in Norfolk; Arbor Day was first celebrated in Nebraska City in 1872; A phone booth in Wahoo has been the fictional home office for "The Late Show with David Letterman" since 1996.

Rep. Lee Terry (R)

CAPITOL OFFICE
225-4155
Talk2Lee@mail.house.gov
leeterry.house.gov
1524 Longworth 20515-2702; fax 226-5452

COMMITTEES
Energy & Commerce

HOMETOWN
Valley

BORN
Jan. 29, 1962, Omaha, Neb.

RELIGION
Methodist

FAMILY
Wife, Robyn Terry; three children

EDUCATION
U. of Nebraska, B.S. 1984 (political science); Creighton U., J.D. 1987

CAREER
Lawyer

POLITICAL HIGHLIGHTS
Omaha City Council, 1991-99 (president, 1994-95)

ELECTION RESULTS

2002 GENERAL		
Lee Terry (R)	89,917	63.3%
Jim Simon (D)	46,843	33.0%
Doug Paterson (GREEN)	3,236	2.3%
Dave Stock (LIBERT)	2,018	1.4%
2002 PRIMARY		
Lee Terry (R)		unopposed
2000 GENERAL		
Lee Terry (R)	148,911	65.8%
Shelley Kiel (D)	70,268	31.1%
John J. Graziano (LIBERT)	6,856	3.0%

PREVIOUS WINNING PERCENTAGES
1998 (66%)

Elected 1998; 3rd term

In a sense Terry is a natural-born representative for Omaha and its suburbs. He is a hometown boy who learned politics from his parents. At age 10, he analyzed President Nixon's landslide victory for his folks on election night 1972. His father was an elections commissioner of Douglas County, which surrounds Omaha, and in 1976 was the Republican nominee for the House seat that his son now holds. Terry's mother ran unsuccessfully for the county board six years later.

By that time Terry was at the state university in Lincoln, having mapped out a life plan for himself centered on a career in politics. Unlike so many Nebraskans, who devote their suppertime discussions to the joys and sorrows of Husker football, talk around the Terry table was often about the wayward ways of a liberal Congress. Four years after earning his law degree at Omaha's Creighton University, Terry was on the city council, and during eight years there he rose to be the group's president and played a role in lowering property taxes. He waltzed into his House seat in 1998 and has faced no serious challenge since.

Terry is a stalwart conservative who votes relatively consistently with the Republican leadership and backed President Bush on seven out of every eight votes in the 107th Congress. In recognition, GOP leaders gave Terry a bottom-rung post on the leadership ladder, an assignment as one of several dozen assistant whips.

Terry has held a seat since the 107th on the Energy and Commerce Committee, which has jurisdiction to regulate a broad swath of the American economy, from the railroads to the Internet. He has used his assignment to push initiatives aimed at helping Nebraskans, such as legislation to create a rural affairs advisory board at the Federal Communications Commission. He says development of a national energy policy — a Bush administration initiative that died in the 107th Congress — is one of his top goals on the panel in the 108th.

No 2nd District representative can ignore Offutt Air Force Base, located just south of Omaha. With more than 9,000 military and civilian personnel, it is as much a part of the community as Creighton or the Mutual of Omaha insurance company. Offutt is the home of the U.S. Strategic Command, where any nuclear war would be planned, and Bush went there for part of Sept. 11, 2001. Terry has looked out for the base's interests, including helping to secure $11 million in 2002 for a new fire and crash rescue station.

Moreover, in a move inspired by many of the roughly 8,400 military retirees in the community near Offutt, Terry sponsored a resolution in the 107th calling for Veterans Day to remain on Nov. 11, the anniversary of the World War I armistice. Terry was reacting to suggestions by a federal commission and others in Congress that Veterans Day be moved a week earlier to coincide with Election Day in a bid to boost voter turnout.

Omaha is also home to the headquarters of Union Pacific Railroad, making rail issues of obvious concern to Terry. He was a sponsor of the law enacted in 2001, at the behest of both labor and management, to restructure the federal railroad pension system to allow some of the funds to be invested in stocks and bonds.

Unlike the more combative conservatives who came to the House earlier in the 1990s, the smiling and fresh-faced Terry has positioned himself as a pragmatist. "I want to fight the good fight on abortion, but that doesn't mean I drag down an appropriations bill," he told The Omaha World-

Herald after his election. Still, Terry sought to embarrass Democrats in 1999 by forcing a vote on $19 billion in tax increases that he lifted from President Clinton's budget. Put into the awkward position of opposing their own president, Democrats joined with Republicans in voting down the measure overwhelmingly. Minority Leader Richard A. Gephardt denounced Terry's effort at the time as "another gimmick."

Though the 2nd District is the state's most urban and suburban, Terry keeps an eye on agricultural issues. When the 107th took up a rewrite of farm law, he expressed an interest in maintaining the free-market philosophy of the statute enacted in 1996. But in the end, he voted to enact a replacement in 2002 that reverted to providing substantial farm subsidies.

Terry casts a conservative vote on social issues. He has denounced a procedure that its opponents describe as "partial birth" abortion, and he supports school vouchers, a priority of the Bush administration.

But Terry struggles with the question of gun owners' rights. Although he voted in 1999 against mandatory trigger locks, he said early in 2000 he could support such a step, as well as waiting periods for purchases at gun shows, because he was dismayed by the nation's repeated school shootings. "You can't go through this last year without being touched in some way and at least say, 'Are there other reasonable steps we should be taking,' " he told the World-Herald.

In 1998 Terry's position on the Omaha City Council made him the clear front-runner for the House seat that Republican Jon Christensen was vacating after two terms to wage an ultimately unsuccessful run for governor. Terry won the four-way primary by 10 percentage points and then triumphed by 31 points in November over underfunded Democrat Mike Scott, a newscaster.

The slightly closer of Terry's subsequent re-elections was in 2002, when Democrats held out some hope in Jim Simon, a wealthy former AOL executive. Terry complicated his own future when, one month before the election, he appeared in a Pfizer Inc. television advertisement promoting a discount prescription drug program for senior citizens. The campaign finance watchdog group Common Cause said Terry's appearance violated a law barring a campaign from benefiting directly from a corporation. Terry said he thought the ad was a public service announcement, although he asked the company to stop running it. He won with 63 percent of the vote.

When he first ran for office, Terry pledged to serve no more than three terms, but he backed away from that promise soon after arriving in Washington. He said he quickly realized the benefits that come with seniority.

KEY VOTES

2002

- No Overhaul campaign finance law; ban "soft money" and restrict advocacy advertising
- Yes Back Bush's defense budget increase
- Yes Extend 1996 welfare law
- Yes Adopt Bush's discretionary spending limit
- Yes Pass GOP Medicare prescription drug plan
- No Create independent Sept. 11 commission
- No Extend union protections to Homeland Security Department employees
- Yes Revive fast-track procedures for trade agreements
- Yes Authorize war against Iraq
- No Advance bankruptcy overhaul opposed by abortion opponents

2001

- Yes Nullify Clinton Labor Department ergonomics rule
- Yes Cut taxes by $1.35 trillion through fiscal 2011
- No Maintain ban on oil drilling in Arctic National Wildlife Refuge
- Yes Approve Bush proposal to limit managed-care plan liability for coverage decisions
- No Divert money from crop subsidy payments to land conservation
- Yes Expand law enforcement power to investigate suspected terrorists

CQ VOTE STUDIES

	PARTY UNITY		PRESIDENTIAL SUPPORT	
	Support	Oppose	Support	Oppose
2002	92%	8%	84%	16%
2001	95%	5%	91%	9%
2000	96%	4%	25%	75%
1999	92%	8%	21%	79%

INTEREST GROUPS

	AFL-CIO	ADA	CCUS	ACU
2002	11%	5%	85%	88%
2001	8%	0%	91%	96%
2000	0%	5%	95%	96%
1999	0%	5%	88%	83%

NEBRASKA 2

East – Omaha and suburbs

Formerly the eastern terminus of the Union Pacific Railroad, Omaha is the heart of the 2nd. Omaha grew up as a blue-collar city: a railroad center, a Missouri River port and a place where cattle became steaks. To outsiders, this broad-shouldered, gritty image remains. But the city has become mainly a place of downtown office buildings and white-collar jobs in agriculture and insurance businesses. It also is known as the nation's 1-800 capital, thanks to a glut of telecommunications and credit processing companies.

As its core has filled with people through the years, the 2nd has become more compact. The district lost its slice of Cass County and much of Sarpy County in redistricting following the 2000 census, and now contains just Douglas County and eastern Sarpy County.

Although the district votes consistently Republican, Omaha's dwindling blue-collar base still supports some Democrats, and victory in the city's south side is essential for Democrats to win statewide. The 2nd has always been anti-abortion, but social conservatives are gaining ground once held by more-moderate European immigrants.

Douglas County is reliably Republican, having voted for the GOP presidential candidate every time but once since Harry S Truman. Omaha is home to three-fourths of Nebraska's growing black population, but the state's first black candidate for Congress lost the district by more than 30 percent in 1998. George W. Bush took 57 percent of the 2nd's vote in the 2000 presidential election, his lowest tally in the state.

MAJOR INDUSTRY
Toll-free service centers, food processing

MILITARY BASES
Offutt Air Force Base, 7,574 military, 3,260 civilian (2002)

CITIES
Omaha, 390,007; Bellevue, 44,382; Papillion, 16,363

NOTABLE
President Gerald R. Ford and political activist Malcolm X were born in Omaha; Father Flanagan's Boys Town, incorporated in 1936, was the only village in the nation run by children; Billionaire investor Warren Buffett lives in Omaha — his father, Republican Howard Buffett, represented Omaha in the House in 1943-49 and 1951-53.

Rep. Tom Osborne (R)

CAPITOL OFFICE
225-6435
www.house.gov/osborne
507 Cannon 20515-2703; fax 226-1385

COMMITTEES
Agriculture
Education & Workforce
Resources

HOMETOWN
Lemoyne

BORN
Feb. 23, 1937, Hastings, Neb.

RELIGION
Methodist

FAMILY
Wife, Nancy Osborne; three children

EDUCATION
Hastings College, B.A. 1959 (history); U. of Nebraska, M.A. 1963, Ph.D. 1965 (educational psychology)

MILITARY SERVICE
Neb. National Guard, 1960-66

CAREER
College football coach; professional football player

POLITICAL HIGHLIGHTS
No previous office

ELECTION RESULTS

2002 GENERAL		
Tom Osborne (R)	163,939	93.2%
Jerry Hickman (LIBERT)	12,017	6.8%
2002 PRIMARY		
Tom Osborne (R)		unopposed
2000 GENERAL		
Tom Osborne (R)	182,117	82.0%
Rollie Reynolds (D)	34,944	15.7%
Jerry Hickman (LIBERT)	4,909	2.2%

Elected 2000; 2nd term

Osborne has little trouble with name recognition in Nebraska. He is a legend for having coached the University of Nebraska football team to 255 wins and three national championships. In 2000, when he switched careers and ran for Congress, his Democratic opponent more than once referred to Osborne as "my hero."

But Osborne is also someone who wore a name tag at his own election night victory party that year, as if there were anyone in the entire state, where Big Red football is a religion, who did not know who he was.

At a time in life when most people are looking toward retirement, Osborne is now in his second term in his second career. He told The Associated Press shortly after he arrived that not many in Washington are impressed by a former football coach, "nor should they be."

Osborne also got the last pick of House offices for the 107th Congress, finishing dead last in the freshmen drawing for office space and ending up in the southeast corner of the Cannon Building's garret-like fifth floor. He brought along few mementos of his storied coaching career, just one photograph of him giving an interview and a few football-themed prints.

But Osborne says he applies many of his coaching techniques to his new life on Capitol Hill. Communicating ideas, formulating a plan and fostering teamwork toward a common goal are applicable in coaching and Congress, he believes. Although both endeavors are highly competitive, he says, coaching offered more immediate feedback. "As a coach, you call a play and it's done in five seconds," he told USA Today. In the House, however, "you have to be much more patient."

Also, in football the location of the goal line is beyond dispute, he says, while in legislating that line keeps moving. For instance, Osborne thought one of his top agenda items — the Mentoring for Success program — was included in the federal education policy overhaul enacted at the end of his first year in office. The program was allocated $17.5 million for its first year, and Osborne saw its future as secure. But a few months later, President Bush's budget made no mention of the mentoring program. He persevered, however, and Bush highlighted the program in his 2003 State of the Union speech and asked for $450 million over three years.

The mentoring proposal is an outgrowth of a program, called TeamMates, that Osborne began in Nebraska in the early 1990s. That program, which initially matched his football players with middle school students who were having difficulty in school, convinced Osborne that effective mentoring can combat "absenteeism from school, teenage pregnancy, and drug and alcohol dependence." His seat on the Education and the Workforce Committee gives him a forum in which to continue to pursue that idea and another priority, the Rural Education Achievement Program.

Osborne is also convinced that something must be done to arrest the flight from rural areas. Forty-seven of the 69 counties he represents — more than 64,000 square miles — lost population in the 1990s; many who left were young adults looking for better economic opportunities.

Bolstering the farm economy and bringing new businesses to rural areas form a large chunk of Osborne's agenda on the Agriculture Committee. He says electronic commerce could thrive in rural locations if the access to computer broadband were improved. Like many rural legislators, he also votes to promote liberalized trade as a way to expand crop exports. "There never have been more people hanging on by their fingernails,"

Osborne said when the committee took up the farm bill rewrite in the 107th.

He knows full well the precarious nature of farming; his grandparents lost their farm near St. Paul, north of Grand Island, during the Depression.

Osborne casts a generally conservative vote and seldom strays from the positions taken by the GOP leadership and Bush. But when it came to overhauling the campaign finance system, he was one of the nine GOP freshmen — 41 House Republicans altogether — to vote for the measure enacted in 2002 over strenuous leadership objections.

Osborne has no patience for unscrupulous sports agents or gambling on sports. He told a Senate hearing that his mailbox had been blown up, and he had received death threats and obscene phone calls in the middle of the night "from people who held me personally responsible for their gambling losses." He continued, "Coaches and their players are expected to win twice. First, they must win the game, and then they must beat the point spread."

Osborne's weekly trips home are a marathon. Whether his flight from Washington lands in Omaha or Denver, it is still a drive of three hours or more to his cabin in tiny Lemoyne, on the shore of Lake McConaughy. Yet because he can dictate his own schedule on the weekends, he says, a congressman's life is actually more family-friendly than that of a Big Twelve coach.

A high school sports star in Hastings, Neb., Osborne played football for Hastings College and then three seasons with the Washington Redskins and San Francisco 49ers. He returned to the University of Nebraska and became a graduate assistant football coach while pursuing a master's in educational psychology. He stayed on at the Lincoln campus, working his way through the assistant coaching ranks while earning a doctorate in educational psychology.

He became head coach in 1973, and over the next 25 seasons he led the Cornhuskers to 13 conference championships to go with the three national crowns. Osborne retired from coaching after the 1997 season, was inducted into the College Football Hall of Fame in 1998 — and soon realized that fishing and other retirement activities were not enough for him. Two years later, when Republican Bill Barrett called it quits after five House terms, Osborne decided to run, because he "still has some energy left."

His Democratic foe, real estate agent Rollie Reynolds, acknowledged he had little chance for victory in heavily Republican western Nebraska, especially against "a worldwide hero" whose "face recognition is about like Muhammad Ali." Osborne won with 82 percent of the vote. Two years later, the Democrats declined to field a challenger in the district, which was only minimally altered by redistricting.

KEY VOTES

2002

- Yes Overhaul campaign finance law; ban "soft money" and restrict advocacy advertising
- Yes Back Bush's defense budget increase
- Yes Extend 1996 welfare law
- Yes Adopt Bush's discretionary spending limit
- Yes Pass GOP Medicare prescription drug plan
- No Create independent Sept. 11 commission
- No Extend union protections to Homeland Security Department employees
- Yes Revive fast-track procedures for trade agreements
- Yes Authorize war against Iraq
- No Advance bankruptcy overhaul opposed by abortion opponents

2001

- Yes Nullify Clinton Labor Department ergonomics rule
- Yes Cut taxes by $1.35 trillion through fiscal 2011
- No Maintain ban on oil drilling in Arctic National Wildlife Refuge
- Yes Approve Bush proposal to limit managed-care plan liability for coverage decisions
- No Divert money from crop subsidy payments to land conservation
- Yes Expand law enforcement power to investigate suspected terrorists

CQ VOTE STUDIES

	PARTY UNITY		PRESIDENTIAL SUPPORT	
	Support	Oppose	Support	Oppose
2002	89%	11%	88%	12%
2001	94%	6%	88%	12%

INTEREST GROUPS

	AFL-CIO	ADA	CCUS	ACU
2002	11%	10%	90%	80%
2001	17%	5%	100%	84%

NEBRASKA 3

West – Grand Island, North Platte, Scottsbluff

Scouting what would later become the Oregon Trail, early 19th century explorers described this section of the country as the "Great American Desert." Most of the 3rd's land is arid, and most of the district's population lives along the meager Platte River.

Grand Island, North Platte and Scottsbluff each serve as regional centers, providing for the retail and health care needs of the surrounding counties. Industry and manufacturing also locate around these areas, as well as in Columbus, Hastings and Kearney. The rest of the land in the district's 69 counties is left to cattle ranchers and sugar beet and wheat farmers. The economy is susceptible to changes in the region's climate. Droughts in the early part of the 1990s battered western Nebraska. The district has a number of the nation's poorest counties.

The 3rd is fiercely independent politically — it gave more votes to Ross Perot than Bill Clinton in 1992 — but the majority is conservative and strongly Republican. In the 2000 presidential contest, George W. Bush carried the district with 71 percent of the vote. Reflecting the area's isolation, most voters are against government intervention. The 1st and 2nd districts dominate state politics, leaving the 3rd resentful that despite its massive land size, its interests, such as farm subsidies and property taxes, are not top priorities.

Saline County, a Democratic-leaning pocket, was added to the 3rd in redistricting following the 2000 census, but the change is not expected to alter the district's outlook.

MAJOR INDUSTRY

Agriculture, food processing, tourism

CITIES

Grand Island, 42,940; Kearney, 27,431; Hastings, 24,064; North Platte, 23,878; Columbus, 20,971; Scottsbluff, 14,732

NOTABLE

Pulitzer Prize-winning author Willa Cather grew up in Red Cloud and based several of her novels in the central-southern region of the state; Carhenge, a full-size replica of Britain's Stonehenge made of cars, stands in Alliance; Fort Robinson near Crawford, now a state park, served as a German prisoner-of-war camp during World War II; The Great Platte River Road Archway Monument, across Interstate 80 near Kearney, was built to memorialize westward expansion.

NEVADA

Gov. Kenny Guinn (R)

First elected: 1998
Length of term: 4 years
Term expires: 1/07
Salary: $117,000
Phone: (775) 684-5670
Hometown: Las Vegas
Born: Aug. 24, 1936; Garland, Ark.
Religion: Protestant
Family: Wife, Dema Guinn; two children
Education: California State U., Fresno, B.A. 1957, M.A. 1958 (physical education); Utah State U., Ph.D. 1970 (education)
Career: Bank chairman; interim university president; utility company chairman; school superintendent
Political highlights: No previous office
Election results:

2002 GENERAL		
Kenny Guinn (R)	344,001	68.2%
Joe Neal (D)	110,935	22.0%
"None of these candidates"	23,674	4.7%
Dick Geyer (LIBERT)	8,104	1.6%
David G. Holmgren (IA)	7,047	1.4%
Jerry L. Norton (I)	5,543	1.1%
A. Charles Laws (GREEN)	4,775	1.0%

Lt. Gov. Lorraine Hunt (R)

First elected: 1998
Length of term: 4 years
Term expires: 1/07
Salary: $50,000
Phone: (775) 684-5637

STATE LEGISLATURE

Legislature: Meets February-June in odd-numbered years
House: 42 members, 2-year terms
2003 breakdown: 19R, 23D; 31 men, 11 women
Salary: $130/day in session; $85/day allowance
Phone: (775) 684-8555
Senate: 21 members, 4-year terms
2003 breakdown: 13R, 8D; 13 men, 8 women
Salary: $130/day in session; $85/day allowance
Phone: (775) 684-1437

STATE TERM LIMITS

Governor: 2 terms
Senate: 3 terms
House: 6 terms

URBAN STATISTICS

CITY	POPULATION
Las Vegas	478,434
Reno	180,480
Henderson	175,381
North Las Vegas	115,488

REGISTERED VOTERS

Republican	42%
Democrat	41%
Nonpartisan	15%

POPULATION

2002 population (est.)	2,173,491
2000 population	1,998,257
1990 population	1,201,833
Percent change (1990-2000)	+66.3%
Rank among states (2002)	35
Median age	35
Born in state	21.3%
Foreign born	15.8%
Violent crime rate	524/100,000
Poverty level	10.5%
Federal workers	14,701
Military	11,932

REDISTRICTING

Nevada gained one House seat in reapportionment. The state legislature drew a new, three-district map, which the governor signed on June 15, 2001.

MISCELLANEOUS

Web: www.state.nv.us
Capital: Carson City

STATE ELECTION OFFICIAL
(775) 684-5705

DEMOCRATIC HEADQUARTERS
(702) 737-8683

REPUBLICAN HEADQUARTERS
(702) 258-9182

District Statistics

	2000 VOTE FOR PRESIDENT															
DIST.	BUSH	GORE	NADER	WHITE	BLACK	ASIAN	HISP	MEDIAN INCOME	WHITE COLLAR	BLUE COLLAR	SERVICE INDUSTRY	OVER 64	UNDER 18	COLLEGE EDUCATION	RURAL	SQ. MILES
1	40%	56%	n/a	52%	12%	5%	28%	$39,480	48%	23%	29%	10%	27%	15%	0%	177
2	57	37	n/a	75	2	3	15	$43,879	55	25	20	11	26	19	21	105,079
3	47.8	48.4	n/a	69	5	6	16	$50,749	57	18	25	12	24	20	4	4,570
STATE	50	46	2	65	7	4	20	$44,581	53	22	25	11	26	18	8	109,826
U.S.	47.9	48.4	3	69	12	4	13	$41,994	60	25	15	12	26	24	21	3,537,438

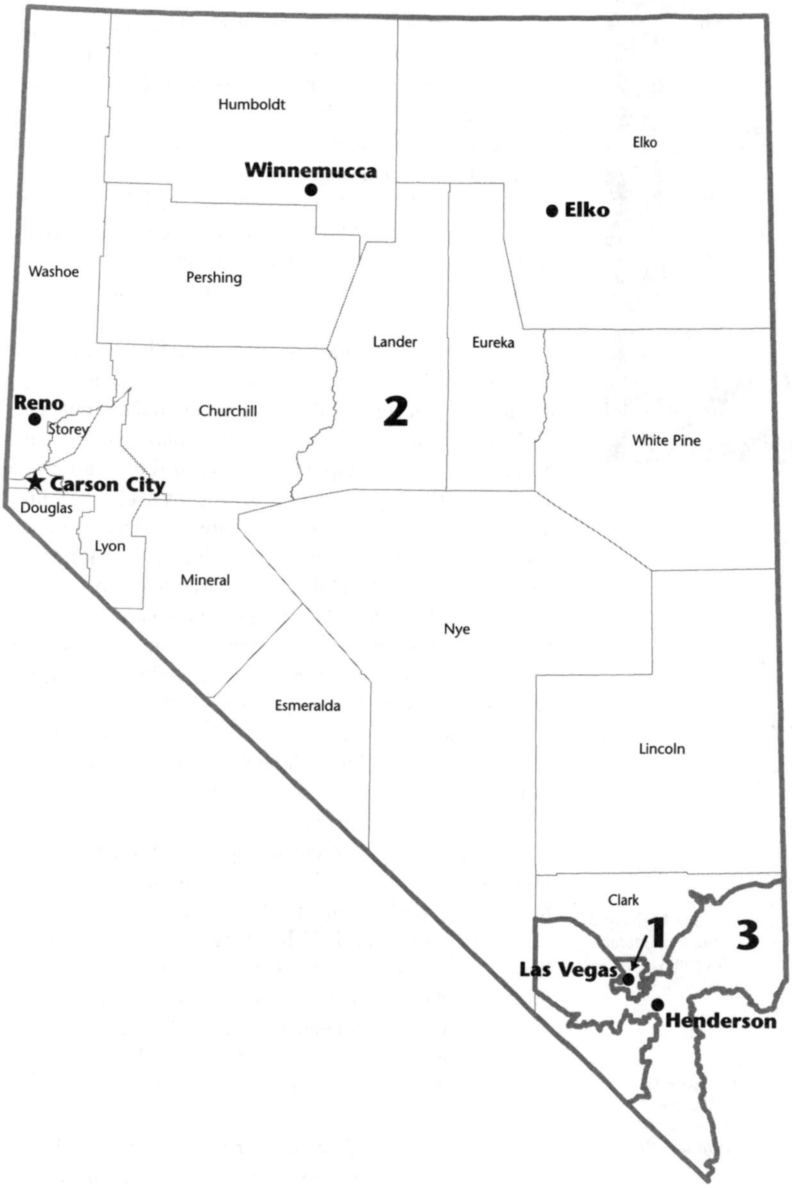

Humboldt
Winnemucca
Elko
Elko
Washoe
Pershing
Lander
Eureka
Reno
Storey
Churchill
2
White Pine
Carson City
Douglas
Lyon
Mineral
Nye
Esmeralda
Lincoln
Clark
1
3
Las Vegas
Henderson

Sen. Harry Reid (D)

CAPITOL OFFICE
224-3542
reid.senate.gov
528 Hart 20510-2803; fax 224-7327

COMMITTEES
Appropriations
Environment & Public Works
Indian Affairs
Select Ethics - vice chairman
Special Aging

HOMETOWN
Searchlight

BORN
Dec. 2, 1939, Searchlight, Nev.

RELIGION
Mormon

FAMILY
Wife, Landra Reid; five children

EDUCATION
Southern Utah State College, A.S. 1959; Utah State U., B.A. 1961 (history & political science); George Washington U., J.D. 1964; U. of Nevada, Las Vegas, attended 1969-70

CAREER
Lawyer

POLITICAL HIGHLIGHTS
Nev. Assembly, 1969-71; lieutenant governor, 1971-75; Democratic nominee for U.S. Senate, 1974; candidate for mayor of Las Vegas, 1975; Nevada Gaming Commission chairman, 1977-81; U.S. House, 1983-87

ELECTION RESULTS

1998 GENERAL		
Harry Reid (D)	208,650	47.9%
John Ensign (R)	208,222	47.8%
"None of the Above"	8,125	1.9%
Michael Cloud (LIBERT)	8,044	1.8%
1998 PRIMARY		
Harry Reid (D)		unopposed

PREVIOUS WINNING PERCENTAGES
1992 (51%); 1986 (50%); 1984 House Election (56%); 1982 House Election (58%)

Elected 1986; 3rd term

As minority whip, Reid is the second-highest-ranking Democrat in the Senate. Although he is overshadowed by popular Minority Leader Tom Daschle, he has carved out a powerful role for himself. He never strays far from the Senate floor, where he guards the Democrats' prerogatives. And he frequently acts as message-bearer to the Republican majority when partisan tensions run high.

Reid has ambitions to take over the top job someday. He had hoped to move up as early as 2004, when Daschle was expected to run for president. In early 2003, Reid quietly lined up 40 votes, enough to win, but put his plans on hold when Daschle opted not to seek the Democratic nomination.

Reid's future is clouded by the fact that he is unusually vulnerable for a third-term senator and former House member. He barely eked out re-election in 1998 and could draw a serious Republican challenger again in 2004.

Currently, he remains an important player in the Senate, more so than his predecessor as whip, Wendell H. Ford of Kentucky. Since getting the job in 1999, Reid has enhanced the role by spending more time on the floor than any other senator. "I felt that if there was a continuous presence on the floor, so someone knew what was going on at all times, things would work better," Reid says. "And that has proven to be so."

He has cultivated working relationships with Republicans, which are helpful during the closely divided Senate's frequent partisan meltdowns. Helping pressure Democrats to resist offering politically charged amendments or employing constant delaying tactics are among the tasks that fall to him.

Reid is not reluctant to play hardball when party imperatives demand it, however. After GOP presidential candidate George W. Bush appeared at Bob Jones University, Reid cosponsored a resolution condemning the school for alleged racist policies.

More than just a vote-counter, Reid is a loyal, trusted lieutenant to Daschle, who routinely delegates to him many of the day-to-day duties of floor leader. He lines up speakers and coordinates with the GOP on the schedule. He also fills in if the Democratic floor manager of a bill wants to leave the chamber. His efforts to accommodate other senators' schedules have earned him his colleagues' gratitude. He can be solicitous with fellow senators, but also has been known to bring the hammer down on an uncooperative colleague. Republican Orrin G. Hatch of Utah describes him as "pleasant, unassuming, but tough. . . . I have a lot of respect for him. Harry's a straight shooter."

Reid is not the ideal politician. He is an average debater. He prefers reading books to attending fundraising dinners. And he shuns the nonstop self-promotion that drives many lawmakers. "I don't like parades. I don't like banquets. I don't like public gatherings," says Reid, who spends his free time with his wife, five children and grandchildren.

In addition to his work as whip, Reid remains the top-ranking Democrat on the Ethics Committee, and is the top Democrat on Appropriations' Energy and Water Development Subcommittee, where he has successfully pressed for additional funds for renewable energy research. A technology buff, he is chairman of the Senate's High-Tech Working Group, which brings legislators together with industry leaders.

As a leader, Reid rarely bucks his party, but he does go his own way on a couple of issues. A practicing Mormon, he typically votes with Republicans in favor of restrictions on abortion. In 1999, he was one of two Democrats to oppose an amendment expressing support for the Supreme Court's 1973 *Roe v. Wade* decision legalizing abortion. Reid has supported the GOP in efforts to ban what opponents describe as "partial birth" abortion, a medical procedure that aborts a fetus late in the term.

Organized labor is an important constituency in Nevada, and Reid has sided with the unions on big trade votes in recent years. In 2000, he opposed granting China permanent normal trade status.

Environmentalists generally like Reid, and several national groups helped him in his tight 1998 race. In 2001, he cosponsored the successful "brownfields" bill boosting the federal commitment to cleaning up contaminated industrial sites. But ranchers and miners hold sway in Nevada, and Reid often defends their interests on land use issues.

By far his biggest effort on behalf of his constituents is trying to stop the opening of a national nuclear waste depository at Yucca Mountain, 100 miles northwest of Las Vegas. Reid suffered a serious defeat in 2002 when Congress endorsed President Bush's decision to store 77,000 tons of spent reactor fuel under the mountain's volcanic rock. Reid lobbied fellow senators hard, telling them their votes mattered to him personally. But the key Senate vote was a filibuster-proof 60-39. In 2003, he was able to cut the level of funding for the program from nearly $600 million to $460 million in the omnibus spending bill.

Reid grew up in a cabin without indoor plumbing in the tiny Nevada mining town of Searchlight. His mother was a high school dropout. His father was a hard-drinking miner who later killed himself. Searchlight did not have a high school, so Reid boarded with other families in nearby Henderson to attend school there. He worked his way through college, moonlighting as a Capitol police officer while attending law school at George Washington University in Washington, D.C.

Reid returned to Henderson as city attorney. In 1968, at age 28, he won election to the Nevada State Assembly. His political mentor was Democrat Mike O'Callaghan, who first got to know Reid in Henderson, where he was Reid's high school civics teacher and boxing coach. Two years later Reid was elected lieutenant governor, the youngest in the state's history, on the same ticket as O'Callaghan, who was elected governor. In 1974, Reid lost a close race for the Senate to Republican Paul Laxalt.

O'Callaghan named Reid chairman of the Nevada Gaming Commission to oversee the state's top industry at a time when it was heavily influenced by organized crime. It was an eye-opening experience. "They put bombs on my car, there were threatening phone calls at night, people tried to bribe me and went to jail," Reid told the Las Vegas Review-Journal.

Reid served two House terms before running again for the Senate in 1986, winning the first of three close elections. He carried only two of the state's 16 counties against Rep. Jim Santini, a Democrat turned Republican. But one of those was Clark County, Reid's political base and home to the majority of Nevada voters in or near Las Vegas. Reid won with 50 percent of the vote.

In 1992, Charles Woods, a wealthy broadcast executive, held Reid to 53 percent in the primary. In the general election, Reid outspent GOP rancher Demar Dahl 5-to-1 and pulled off the win with just 51 percent.

In his last re-election contest in 1998, Reid won by just 428 votes over Republican John Ensign, a House member from Las Vegas. Their contest was bitter. Reid called Ensign "an embarrassment to the state," and Ensign's advertising described Reid as an "old card shark." After Ensign was elected in 2000 to the state's other Senate seat, the two reconciled and these days frequently cosponsor legislation of interest to the state.

KEY VOTES

2002

Yes Pass farm bill reversing crop subsidy limits
No Postpone tougher automobile fuel efficiency standards
Yes Overhaul campaign finance law; ban "soft money" and restrict advocacy advertising
Yes Set federal election standards
No Support oil drilling in Arctic National Wildlife Refuge
No Revive fast-track procedures for trade agreements
Yes Create federal insurance coverage for catastrophic terrorist losses
Yes Tighten federal accounting and corporate governance regulation
Yes Advance bipartisan Medicare prescription drug plan
Yes Create independent Sept. 11 commission
Yes Back Democratic Homeland Security Department proposal
Yes Authorize war against Iraq

2001

No Confirm John Ashcroft as attorney general
No Nullify Clinton Labor Department ergonomics rule
No Cut taxes by $1.35 trillion through fiscal 2011
Yes Pass Democratic bill to bolster rights of patients in managed-care plans
Yes Permit a new round of military base closings
Yes Expand law enforcement power to investigate suspected terrorists

CQ VOTE STUDIES

	PARTY UNITY		PRESIDENTIAL SUPPORT	
	Support	Oppose	Support	Oppose
2002	94%	6%	71%	29%
2001	96%	4%	65%	35%
2000	94%	6%	92%	8%
1999	92%	8%	82%	18%
1998	81%	19%	79%	21%
1997	83%	17%	84%	16%
1996	79%	21%	78%	22%
1995	74%	26%	75%	25%
1994	88%	12%	90%	10%
1993	86%	14%	88%	12%

INTEREST GROUPS

	AFL-CIO	ADA	CCUS	ACU
2002	100%	85%	45%	10%
2001	100%	100%	43%	20%
2000	88%	90%	40%	12%
1999	100%	90%	35%	12%
1998	75%	90%	56%	20%
1997	86%	85%	50%	8%
1996	71%	85%	31%	15%
1995	100%	80%	37%	9%
1994	100%	85%	20%	4%
1993	82%	60%	18%	24%

Sen. John Ensign (R)

CAPITOL OFFICE
224-6244
ensign.senate.gov
379A Russell 20510-2805; fax 228-2193

COMMITTEES
Armed Services
(Readiness & Management Support - chairman)
Budget
Commerce, Science & Transportation
Health, Education, Labor & Pensions
Small Business & Entrepreneurship
Veterans' Affairs

HOMETOWN
Las Vegas

BORN
March 25, 1958, Roseville, Calif.

RELIGION
Christian

FAMILY
Wife, Darlene Ensign; three children

EDUCATION
U. of Nevada, Las Vegas, attended 1976-79; Oregon State U., B.S. 1981; Colorado State U., D.V.M. 1985

CAREER
Veterinarian; casino manager

POLITICAL HIGHLIGHTS
U.S. House, 1995-99; sought Republican nomination for U.S. Senate, 1998

ELECTION RESULTS

2000 GENERAL		
John Ensign (R)	330,687	55.1%
Ed Bernstein (D)	238,260	39.7%
write-ins	11,503	1.9%
Kathryn Rusco (GREEN)	10,286	1.7%
2000 PRIMARY		
John Ensign (R)	95,904	88.0%
Richard Hamzik (R)	6,202	5.7%
write-ins	5,290	4.9%
Fernando Platin (R)	1,543	1.4%

PREVIOUS WINNING PERCENTAGES
1996 House Election (50%); 1994 House Election (48%)

Elected 2000; 1st term

Ensign entered the Senate in 2001 promising to provide crucial influence with a new Republican White House and the Senate Republicans on issues of overriding importance to Nevada: keeping nuclear waste out of the state, and preserving the gaming industry in it. Although he has had mixed success so far, Ensign has not held it against his GOP colleagues, and he remains a reliable conservative vote for his party.

While Ensign and Harry Reid, the Democratic whip, work closely together on Nevada-specific legislation, in the 107th Congress they tied with two North Carolinians — Democratic presidential hopeful John Edwards and retiring Republican firebrand Jesse Helms — as the Senate delegation least likely to stick together. Nevada's senators nonetheless insist that, while they voted the same way only 56 percent of the time, and ran against each other in a bitter 1998 campaign that Reid ultimately won, they maintain an amiable personal relationship.

But no matter how solidly they stood in opposition to a federal plan to bury radioactive nuclear waste in Nevada, it was not enough.

Nevadans have long viewed the government plan to store spent fuel rods from nuclear power plants under Yucca Mountain as an attempt to "Screw Nevada." Republicans, in general, have been the driving force behind the effort to store the waste in that repository, less than a two-hour drive from Las Vegas. But Ensign found himself in the cross hairs of the standoff in 2002, after the House overwhelmingly ratified an Energy Department recommendation that nuclear waste from 38 states be shipped to Yucca Mountain.

Majority Leader Tom Daschle put the onus of killing the plan squarely on Ensign's shoulders, declaring that it was up to the GOP freshman to find sufficient votes in the Senate to stop it. By his own account, Ensign sat down with all 48 of his Republican colleagues, but he learned that most had already made up their minds. The Senate endorsed the plan with 10 votes to spare, and President Bush signed the order for shipments to begin as soon as legal and regulatory hurdles were cleared.

Ensign has so far fared better on the gambling front. From his seat on the Commerce Committee, he has been able to fight a rearguard action against legislation by the panel's top Republican, John McCain of Arizona, to outlaw gambling on college sports — wagering that is legal in Nevada. And Ensign has made it a top priority to limit the growth of Internet gambling, a practice that has cut into casino revenues.

Ensign's links to the influential Nevada industry go beyond political necessity. He is a former casino manager and his stepfather is chairman of Mandalay Resort Group, the Las Vegas company that owns the Monte Carlo and Circus Circus casino hotels.

In the 107th, Ensign worked on a number of other issues before the Commerce Committee, including his cosponsorship of a law that aims to create a "safe zone" for children on the Internet by creating a so-called dot-kids domain free from material unsuitable for youngsters. He also worked to give airports, including Las Vegas' McCarran International, additional time to install new baggage screening equipment to detect explosives.

In the 108th Congress, Ensign was named chairman of a 10-member Senate GOP High Tech Task Force. But aside from Commerce, Ensign undertook a wholesale reshuffling of his committee assignments, trading posts on the Banking and Aging panels for assignments to Armed Services, Budget and Health, Education, Labor and Pensions.

Outside of his fights on Nevada-specific issues, Ensign has energetically sought to increase his influence within the Senate on a broader array of issues. He weighed in on the wave of corporate scandals that upended the political landscape in 2002. At a hearing on the failure of energy giant Enron Corp., Ensign told former Enron chief executive officer Kenneth Lay, "I think deplorable, one, that either you didn't know or two, that if you did know what was going on, how did you think that you could get away with it? . . . At some point, you have to pay the piper, as they say."

With Democrat Joseph I. Lieberman of Connecticut, Ensign co-wrote a law to authorize new funding and incentives for nursing students, an attempt to address a national shortage of nurses. And he teamed up with Nebraska Republican Chuck Hagel on a plan that would have provided a limited prescription drug benefit under Medicare for low-income patients. Although the proposal drew 51 votes, it fell short of the 60 votes needed to overcome procedural hurdles in the Senate.

Ensign favors flexibility in immigration laws to reward some longtime illegal immigrants with permanent residency. "You do have to recognize reality — that we need them," says Ensign. "The economy in the Southwest would fall apart without illegal aliens."

Ensign strongly opposes abortion rights — a somewhat risky position in Nevada, where voters in 1990 wrote into state law the Supreme Court's 1973 *Roe v. Wade* decision that made abortion legal in the United States.

As a supporter of the partial privatization of Social Security, Ensign argues that private accounts would put younger workers in a better position to build wealth for their retirement. And he supports provisions to scrap the current tax code and replace it with one that would minimize the role of the INS.

Ensign — whose mane of thick silver hair looks like a senatorial coif from central casting — is also one of the Senate's better athletes. In the annual congressional charity baseball game of 2002, he turned several fine plays at shortstop and drove in two runs. He was the only senator who played. The same year, he posted the third-fastest time of congressional entrants in an annual 3-mile charity running race, with a time of 21:12.

After getting a degree in veterinary medicine, Ensign opened the first 24-hour animal hospital in Las Vegas and was the general manager at two Las Vegas casinos. GOP leaders urged him to run for the House in 1994 and, although he was a political novice, he assembled an impressive organization of volunteers and embarked on an energetic precinct-walking effort. In the Republicans' takeover sweep that year, he overcame a large Democratic registration advantage to squeeze past four-term Democrat James Bilbray in the Las Vegas-based 1st District by just 1,436 votes.

As a freshman, he landed a spot on the Ways and Means Committee, where he took an active part in work on the overhaul of the nation's welfare system that was one of the singular achievements of the "Republican revolution." To bolster his argument for the law, he would sketch his own autobiography: When he was a preschooler, his biological father abandoned his family. Although she qualified for public assistance, his mother instead took a $12-a-day job making change in a Reno casino. "That taught me a work ethic that we are robbing from welfare families today," he said.

Ensign gave up his House seat to challenge Reid in 1998, losing by just 428 votes. But early in 1999, Democrat Richard H. Bryan announced he would not run for a third Senate term. Ensign kept his campaign apparatus running and, although Democrat Ed Bernstein, an attorney, was an aggressive opponent, Ensign was able to spend twice as much money on the campaign and won with 55 percent in 2000 — the best showing of his four congressional races.

KEY VOTES

2002

No Pass farm bill reversing crop subsidy limits
Yes Postpone tougher automobile fuel efficiency standards
No Overhaul campaign finance law; ban "soft money" and restrict advocacy advertising
Yes Set federal election standards
Yes Support oil drilling in Arctic National Wildlife Refuge
No Revive fast-track procedures for trade agreements
Yes Create federal insurance coverage for catastrophic terrorist losses
Yes Tighten federal accounting and corporate governance regulation
No Advance bipartisan Medicare prescription drug plan
Yes Create independent Sept. 11 commission
No Back Democratic Homeland Security Department proposal
Yes Authorize war against Iraq

2001

Yes Confirm John Ashcroft as attorney general
Yes Nullify Clinton Labor Department ergonomics rule
Yes Cut taxes by $1.35 trillion through fiscal 2011
No Pass Democratic bill to bolster rights of patients in managed-care plans
Yes Permit a new round of military base closings
Yes Expand law enforcement power to investigate suspected terrorists

CQ VOTE STUDIES

	PARTY UNITY		PRESIDENTIAL SUPPORT	
	Support	Oppose	Support	Oppose
2002	90%	10%	96%	4%
2001	88%	12%	97%	3%
House Service:				
1998	82%	18%	27%	73%
1997	87%	13%	30%	70%
1996	80%	20%	40%	60%
1995	89%	11%	18%	82%

INTEREST GROUPS

	AFL-CIO	ADA	CCUS	ACU
2002	15%	15%	95%	85%
2001	19%	20%	93%	84%
House Service:				
1998	20%	25%	83%	88%
1997	0%	5%	80%	100%
1996	18%	5%	88%	85%
1995	0%	0%	100%	96%

Rep. Shelley Berkley (D)

CAPITOL OFFICE
225-5965
shelley.berkley@mail.house.gov
www.house.gov/berkley
439 Cannon 20515-2801; fax 225-3119

COMMITTEES
International Relations
Transportation & Infrastructure
Veterans' Affairs

HOMETOWN
Las Vegas

BORN
Jan. 20, 1951, Manhattan, N.Y.

RELIGION
Jewish

FAMILY
Husband, Larry Lehrner; two children

EDUCATION
U. of Nevada, Las Vegas, B.A. 1972 (political science); U. of San Diego, J.D. 1976

CAREER
Lawyer

POLITICAL HIGHLIGHTS
Nev. Assembly, 1983-85; University and Community College System of Nevada Board of Regents, 1990-98

ELECTION RESULTS

2002 GENERAL		
Shelley Berkley (D)	64,312	53.7%
Lynette Boggs-McDonald (R)	51,148	42.7%
Steven Dempsey (I)	2,861	2.4%
W. Lane Startin (GR)	1,393	1.2%
2002 PRIMARY		
Shelley Berkley (D)		unopposed
2000 GENERAL		
Shelley Berkley (D)	118,469	51.7%
Jon Porter (R)	101,276	44.2%
Charles Schneider (LIBERT)	4,011	1.8%
Christopher Hansen (IA)	3,933	1.7%

PREVIOUS WINNING PERCENTAGES
1998 (49%)

Elected 1998; 3rd term

In her first four years in the House, Berkley had an approach that seemed to mirror Las Vegas. Like her hometown, she made no bones about being fast-paced and eager to stand out in a crowd.

"I tend to have a very effusive personality," she said soon after her election in 1998, when Nevada's governor predicted that everyone on Capitol Hill would know about Berkley within a month of her arrival. Despite her desire to continue to make a name for herself, Berkley discovered in her early months that she drew less attention to her policy positions than to her personal life. She gained publicity for showing up at a news conference wearing white tennis shoes with high heels, for example, and for her 1999 wedding to a local physician at Bally's casino — in which Berkley was attended by no fewer than 19 bridesmaids.

As she has settled into her life in Congress, Berkley has worked hard to prove she is a serious legislator. She doggedly tends to parochial concerns, most notably by protecting jobs at the state's nuclear test site and joining in the Nevada congressional delegation's longstanding and so far unsuccessful fight to keep nuclear waste out of the state.

"They know I'm not afraid of anybody or anything," she says of her constituents. "I'm a lioness who takes care of her cubbies."

Berkley has drawn confidence from the House Democratic leadership, although not so much as she would like. When he was Minority Leader, Richard A. Gephardt signaled his interest in putting Berkley on the Ways and Means Committee, where she could look out for the state's gaming industry. But when Gephardt stepped aside after the party's 2002 election losses and Nancy Pelosi became party leader, she picked two other Democrats.

That is not to say Berkley is on Pelosi's bad side. In fact, the Californian has helped to steer millions of dollars in appropriations to projects in southern Nevada. And, when she was Democratic whip, Pelosi made Berkley one of her 24 regional assistants, a post Berkley continues to hold in the 108th.

In 2001 Democratic leaders gave Berkley permission to sit on a third committee, adding International Relations to Veterans' Affairs and Transportation and Infrastructure. In the 108th, she remains on all three panels. On International Relations, Berkley sits on the Middle East and Central Asia Subcommittee, allowing her to pursue her interest in Israel. She also got a seat in the 108th on the panel's Terrorism Subcommittee.

Berkley's longstanding interest in politics is fueled, she says, by her desire to give something back after her parents emigrated to the United States from Eastern Europe. She moved to Las Vegas at age 6, later attending the University of Nevada at Las Vegas, where she served as student body president before graduating with a political science degree.

After earning a law degree in San Diego, Berkley returned to Las Vegas to start a career. She spent two years in the state Assembly but became better known as a state university regent, a position that helped her become familiar with education issues. She also served on civic and legal boards before running for Congress.

Although Berkley became known in Nevada as a Democratic Party activist, she bills herself as a moderate who can work with members on both sides of the aisle and is a member of the centrist New Democrat Coalition. She joined with Pennsylvania Republican Patrick J. Toomey in 2001 in sponsoring a bill that would restrict the power of Medicare administrators to cut off payments to health care providers and would give those accused of improper billing enhanced rights to appeal such rulings. At the same time, Berkeley has contended that Republican attempts to rewrite medical malpractice law would be too restrictive, and she has urged Congress to instead approve bipartisan legislation similar to Nevada's law.

Berkley describes herself as an opponent of gun control, a position echoed by many Western politicians. But some gun rights activists criticized her for voting in the 106th Congress for a variety of proposals championed by gun control advocates. She responded that her support of such safety measures did not conflict with her belief that the federal government should not prevent citizens from owning guns.

Diagnosed with an advanced case of osteoporosis at about the time she was first elected to the House, Berkley has championed legislation to require insurance coverage for bone mass measurements.

All Nevadans in Congress suffered a major setback in 2002 when, after years of blocking such a bill, they could not prevent a law from being enacted to allow spent fuel from commercial nuclear power plants to be stored at Yucca Mountain, about 90 miles northwest of Las Vegas. But Berkley has vowed to fight the measure through the courts. "I will line up in front of the railroad ties to keep nuclear waste from going to Yucca Mountain," she said. She has also promised to try to defeat legislation to ban betting on college sports, a proposal she said would have a devastating impact on the state's gambling industry.

Berkley won her initial race when Republican John Ensign gave up the 1st District House seat in 1998 to run — unsuccessfully, that year — for the Senate. Though regarded as the front-runner, she squeaked by Republican Don Chairez, a former county judge, by just 3 percentage points after battling ethics questions involving memos she had written several years before advising a legal client to make campaign contributions to judges as a way of currying favor. In 2000, fending off the same ethics questions, she defeated GOP state Sen. Jon Porter by 8 points.

Berkley avoided a tough rematch in 2002 when Nevada gained a House seat in reapportionment and the 1st District — which included the nation's fastest-growing metropolitan area — was split in two. The largely urban and Democratic constituents that have formed the core of her support stayed in the 1st, while the rural and suburban Republican areas around Las Vegas were turned into the new 3rd District. Porter ran there and won handily. Challenged instead by Las Vegas City Councilwoman Lynette Maria Boggs-McDonald, whom the Republicans touted as their most competitive African-American nominee in the nation, Berkley prevailed by 11 points.

KEY VOTES

2002

Yes Overhaul campaign finance law; ban "soft money" and restrict advocacy advertising
Yes Back Bush's defense budget increase
No Extend 1996 welfare law
No Adopt Bush's discretionary spending limit
No Pass GOP Medicare prescription drug plan
Yes Create independent Sept. 11 commission
Yes Extend union protections to Homeland Security Department employees
No Revive fast-track procedures for trade agreements
Yes Authorize war against Iraq
No Advance bankruptcy overhaul opposed by abortion opponents

2001

No Nullify Clinton Labor Department ergonomics rule
Yes Cut taxes by $1.35 trillion through fiscal 2011
Yes Maintain ban on oil drilling in Arctic National Wildlife Refuge
No Approve Bush proposal to limit managed-care plan liability for coverage decisions
No Divert money from crop subsidy payments to land conservation
Yes Expand law enforcement power to investigate suspected terrorists

CQ VOTE STUDIES

	PARTY UNITY		PRESIDENTIAL SUPPORT	
	Support	Oppose	Support	Oppose
2002	87%	13%	42%	58%
2001	88%	12%	37%	63%
2000	81%	19%	63%	37%
1999	89%	11%	79%	21%

INTEREST GROUPS

	AFL-CIO	ADA	CCUS	ACU
2002	89%	85%	50%	16%
2001	92%	90%	43%	12%
2000	80%	65%	57%	28%
1999	78%	100%	36%	4%

NEVADA 1
Las Vegas

Neon lights and the chance of easy money continue to reel pleasure seekers into the 1st, which includes Las Vegas and its immediate areas. The city, the state's largest, experienced phenomenal growth in the 1990s; the metropolitan area has been the fastest growing in the nation. One of the downsides is that traffic congestion is now a major concern.

Gambling and tourism drive the 1st's economy. With a healthy economy in the late 1990s, large and small gaming companies continued to thrive. Several new luxury resorts were built on Las Vegas Boulevard, the newest part of the famed "Strip." About 36 million people visited Las Vegas in 2000, with an economic impact of $31 billion.

The Sept. 11 attacks sharply affected tourism in 2001, forcing many workers out of jobs. One year later most service workers were cautiously optimistic that business was starting to pick back up. Discussions in California about opening more casinos adds to the industry's worries, but local leaders are excited over the Las Vegas Monorail project, a four-mile line slated to open in early 2004 that will run along the east side of the Strip.

Besides the gambling industry, the 1st also attracts tourists to its surrounding national parks and desert topography. The area's record growth has made home building a major industry as well, and the city relies on distribution and trade because of its central Western location.

The 1st was a competitive swing district that attracted quite a bit of national attention and money in recent elections, but it became significantly more Democratic in redistricting after the 2000 census when many of the rapidly growing suburbs of the city were placed in the new 3rd District. Though some pockets of Republicans live in the district, the 1st has a strong Democratic base in unionized service workers.

MAJOR INDUSTRY

Tourism, casinos, conventions

CITIES

Las Vegas (pt.), 362,908; North Las Vegas, 115,488; Paradise (unincorporated) (pt.), 77,893

NOTABLE

The Little White Wedding Chapel on Las Vegas Boulevard has a drive-through window for weddings.

Rep. Jim Gibbons (R)

CAPITOL OFFICE
225-6155
mail.gibbons@mail.house.gov
www.house.gov/gibbons
100 Cannon 20515-2802; fax 225-5679

COMMITTEES
Armed Services
Resources
Select Homeland Security
(Intelligence & Counterterrorism - chairman)
Select Intelligence
(Human Intelligence, Analysis & Counterintelligence - chairman)

HOMETOWN
Reno

BORN
Dec. 16, 1944, Sparks, Nev.

RELIGION
Mormon

FAMILY
Wife, Dawn Gibbons; three children

EDUCATION
U. of Nevada, Reno, B.S. 1967 (geology), M.S. 1973 (mining geology); Southwestern U., J.D. 1979

MILITARY SERVICE
Air Force, 1967-71; Nev. Air National Guard, 1975-95

CAREER
Airline pilot; lawyer; geologist

POLITICAL HIGHLIGHTS
Nev. Assembly, 1989-94 (minority whip, 1993); Republican nominee for governor, 1994

ELECTION RESULTS

2002 GENERAL		
Jim Gibbons (R)	149,574	74.3%
Travis O. Souza (D)	40,189	20.0%
Janine Hansen (IA)	7,240	3.6%
Brendan Trainor (LIBERT)	3,413	1.7%
2002 PRIMARY		
Jim Gibbons (R)		unopposed
2000 GENERAL		
Jim Gibbons (R)	229,608	64.5%
Tierney Cahill (D)	106,379	29.9%

PREVIOUS WINNING PERCENTAGES
1998 (81%); 1996 (59%)

Elected 1996; 4th term

A decorated fighter pilot popular at home and with the Bush White House, Gibbons appears to have a political future as bright as any House member's. He is mentioned often as a possible candidate for higher office.

Despite his ties to the White House, Gibbons does not always march in step with fellow Republicans. He has devoted his Capitol Hill career to fighting many members of his party on the marquee issue in Nevada politics — the push to establish a national, high-level radioactive waste site at Yucca Mountain, 90 miles northwest of Las Vegas.

When the House voted in 2002 in favor of President Bush's decision to put the waste dump at Yucca, Gibbons, a geologist, tried to convince lawmakers that the project was unsafe. He also argued that Nevadans should not be forced to accept waste they did not generate and do not want. After the vote, he vowed to work with the rest of the Nevada delegation to seek to block further progress in court.

Even among 434 fellow legislators, Gibbons is not hard to find. Most days he is on the floor as the House begins its daily session, wearing his trademark cowboy boots. He is among the most active of the five dozen or so members of the GOP "theme team," who articulate the Republican view of the world in one-minute speeches before the day's legislative business.

His committee assignments mesh well with his background, which includes degrees in mining and law, and experience as a combat pilot. Gibbons sits on four committees: Resources, Armed Services, Intelligence and Homeland Security.

On the Intelligence panel, Gibbons now chairs the Human Intelligence, Analysis and Counterintelligence Subcommittee. In the 107th Congress, he was vice chairman of a Terrorism and Homeland Security Subcommittee formed after the Sept. 11, 2001, terrorist attacks and was among the first to support creation of a Homeland Security Department. He has been a vocal supporter of CIA Director George Tenet, a Clinton-era holdover.

In the 108th, Gibbons was appointed to the new Homeland Security Committee and was named vice chairman of Resources. The latter was a consolation prize after he was blocked from chairing the Energy and Mineral Resources Subcommittee. GOP leaders gave Barbara Cubin of Wyoming a waiver from the six-year limit, allowing her to keep that gavel for another two years.

Gibbons is co-chairman of the Congressional Mining Caucus, which lobbies in support of the mining industry. The 2nd District encompasses about 96 percent of the state's land area, and almost 90 percent of the land is owned by the federal government. Federal water and grazing regulations and federal mining policies play key roles in the economic development of the state. The Yucca Mountain battle is about the only common ground Gibbons has with environmentalists. He usually sympathizes with property rights advocates and business interests in their disputes with environmental groups over endangered species and other land-related issues.

Gibbons is an avid defender of Nevada's gambling industry. Often pitted against fellow Republicans, he has fought proposals to outlaw gambling on college sports, to ban automated teller machines from casinos, to withhold a portion of bingo and keno winnings for federal income taxes, and to tax casino workers for the value of employer-provided meals.

The congressman sometimes stands apart from the free-trade enthusiasts who are a majority in the House GOP. He voted against permanently granting China normal trade status, and he opposed giving President Clinton fast-track authority to negotiate trade agreements that Congress cannot amend. With George W. Bush in the White House, however, he voted for the fast-track negotiating authority.

Gibbons was born in Sparks, just outside of Reno. His father, who had an eighth-grade education, was a laborer for the Southern Pacific Railroad, and the family had little money. Their house was located along the flight path of the local airport, and Gibbons dreamed of being a pilot.

His father died the day he graduated from high school, and Gibbons says his mother pushed him to go to college, where he studied earth science and geology. Faced with a draft notice after graduation, Gibbons joined the Air Force. A combat pilot, he flew A-37 close-air support planes during a tour in Vietnam. (Recalled to active duty during the Gulf War, Gibbons won a Distinguished Flying Cross.)

After the service, Gibbons wanted to become a commercial pilot, but the airlines weren't hiring at the time. So he pursued geology and earned a master's degree before deciding he "didn't want to be packing rocks up a hill like my dad did." He entered law school and earned his degree about the same time he was hired as a pilot. He spent most of the next two decades flying for Western Airlines and then for Delta. In the last three Congresses, he has offered legislation to raise the mandatory retirement age for commercial pilots from 60 to 65.

In 1987, Gibbons helped his wife, Dawn, lobby the state legislature on a matter related to her business. That rekindled his interest in public affairs, piqued years earlier when his mother ran for mayor of Sparks. In 1988, Gibbons won the first of three elections to the state Assembly.

After losing a 1994 race for governor to incumbent Democrat Bob Miller, Gibbons was the best-known of the Republicans who made a play for the 2nd District in 1996, when veteran GOP Rep. Barbara F. Vucanovich retired. He won a six-way primary with 42 percent of the vote and went on to carry the Republican-leaning district by 23 percentage points. It did no harm that he shared the ballot with his own proposed amendment to the state constitution requiring a two-thirds majority vote of the legislature for any tax increase. The amendment, put on the ballot as a result of a petition drive led by Gibbons, also won. Since then, he has had little trouble holding onto the seat.

Gibbons is a potential challenger in 2004 to Harry Reid, the Senate's No. 2 Democrat. Nevada political insiders say he has a chance of unseating Reid, who has a history of razor-thin re-election margins despite his leadership status. Gibbons also is talked about as a strong contender for governor in 2006.

KEY VOTES

2002

No Overhaul campaign finance law; ban "soft money" and restrict advocacy advertising
Yes Back Bush's defense budget increase
Yes Extend 1996 welfare law
Yes Adopt Bush's discretionary spending limit
Yes Pass GOP Medicare prescription drug plan
No Create independent Sept. 11 commission
No Extend union protections to Homeland Security Department employees
Yes Revive fast-track procedures for trade agreements
Yes Authorize war against Iraq
Yes Advance bankruptcy overhaul opposed by abortion opponents

2001

Yes Nullify Clinton Labor Department ergonomics rule
Yes Cut taxes by $1.35 trillion through fiscal 2011
No Maintain ban on oil drilling in Arctic National Wildlife Refuge
Yes Approve Bush proposal to limit managed-care plan liability for coverage decisions
? Divert money from crop subsidy payments to land conservation
Yes Expand law enforcement power to investigate suspected terrorists

CQ VOTE STUDIES

	PARTY UNITY		PRESIDENTIAL SUPPORT	
	Support	Oppose	Support	Oppose
2002	96%	4%	88%	12%
2001	97%	3%	93%	7%
2000	92%	8%	29%	71%
1999	91%	9%	20%	80%
1998	93%	7%	22%	78%

INTEREST GROUPS

	AFL-CIO	ADA	CCUS	ACU
2002	11%	5%	90%	92%
2001	17%	5%	96%	96%
2000	20%	30%	61%	88%
1999	44%	15%	68%	84%
1998	20%	20%	89%	92%

NEVADA 2

Reno, Carson City and the 'Cow Counties'

The conservative-leaning 2nd takes in everything outside of Las Vegas and its suburbs — almost all of the state's vast rural areas. Reno and the capital, Carson City, anchor the 2nd in the west, and in the district's "Cow Counties," agriculture, mining and ranching dominate. Nearly 90 percent of the district's land is federally owned.

In the 1800s, the gold rush attracted fortune seekers to Reno. Fortune seekers now are more inclined to try their luck in the city's casinos or head to Lake Tahoe. Gambling has not fared as well in Reno in recent years, and the industry is concerned that customers will flock to new Indian reservation casinos in California. Yucca Mountain, the proposed national nuclear waste storage site located northwest of Las Vegas in Nye County, also has been a contentious issue in the 2nd.

The 2nd has sent Republicans to Congress since its creation in 1982. It votes mostly Republican in local elections and is becoming increasingly conservative. Redistricting in 2001 further increased the district's Republican voting base by removing some urban territory in Clark County to create the new 3rd District.

Though the 3rd was drawn to take in most of the Las Vegas suburbs, the 2nd dips into two areas of Clark County in the southern part of the state. It takes in Nellis Air Force Base and much of the northern part of Clark, as well as a few suburban communities in the southwestern area of the county.

MAJOR INDUSTRY

Gambling, mining, manufacturing, warehousing

MILITARY BASES

Nellis Air Force Base, 6,859 military, 904 civilian (2001); Naval Air Station Fallon, 1,038 military, 542 civilian (2001)

CITIES

Reno, 180,480; Sparks, 66,346; Carson City, 52,457; Pahrump (unincorporated), 24,631

NOTABLE

White King, a 10-foot, 4-inch tall polar bear on display in Elko, is said to be the world's largest polar bear; Battle Mountain was selected by the Washington Post Magazine in 2001 as "the armpit of America."

Rep. Jon Porter (R)

CAPITOL OFFICE
225-3252
www.house.gov/porter
218 Cannon 20515-2803; fax 225-2185

COMMITTEES
Education & Workforce
Transportation & Infrastructure

HOMETOWN
Henderson

BORN
May 16, 1955, Fort Dodge, Iowa

RELIGION
Roman Catholic

FAMILY
Wife, Laurie Porter; two children

EDUCATION
Briar Cliff College, attended 1973-77 (theology)

CAREER
Farm insurance company branch manager; farm insurance agent; electronics repairman and distributor

POLITICAL HIGHLIGHTS
City Council of Boulder City, 1983-93 (mayor, 1987-1991); Nev. Senate, 1995-2002; Republican nominee for U.S. House, 2000

ELECTION RESULTS

2002 GENERAL		
Jon Porter (R)	100,378	56.1%
Dario Herrera (D)	66,659	37.2%
Pete O'Neil (I)	6,842	3.8%
Neil Scott (LIBERT)	3,421	1.9%
2002 PRIMARY		
Jon Porter (R)	25,446	68.6%
Barry D. Bilbray (R)	6,179	16.7%
Susan Kiger (R)	3,407	9.2%
Bob Daily (R)	2,052	5.5%

Elected 2002; 1st term

Porter's is an unusual résumé among House freshman: A suburban mayor for four years and a state senator for eight more, he also has marketed and repaired electronics and sold farm insurance.

But he has been a regular Republican along the way, and his loyalty has earned him a seat on the House GOP Policy Committee, a leadership forum for setting legislative positions and mediating intraparty disputes.

At the same time, after taking office Porter joined the centrist-oriented Republican Main Street Partnership — a reflection of the political nature of the 3rd District, which Nevada gained in the reapportionment after the 2000 census. The state legislature made the new seat's voters as evenly divided between Republican and Democrat as possible.

Porter said he would work in Congress to provide resources for his district, which is dealing with the impact of rapid growth. Having won a seat on the Transportation and Infrastructure Committee, one of his priorities will be directing money back home in the new highway and mass transit law that Congress expects to write in the 108th Congress. His assignment to the Education and the Workforce Committee will allow Porter to pursue issues on which he made a mark during his time in the state Senate, where he worked to secure money for new school construction.

Porter has a stated interest in environmental issues, boasting that as mayor of Boulder City he helped slow sprawl by creating a wildlife preservation area. But he also takes many pro-business positions and has said he will join the GOP fight to limit damage awards in civil lawsuits.

Porter's 44 percent share of the vote as the GOP nominee against Democratic Rep. Shelley Berkley in 2000 made him the party's preferred candidate in the 3rd District in 2002. Democrats hoped the low-key Porter would be eclipsed by their energetic candidate, Clark County Commissioner Dario Herrera. But Porter's steady approach turned out to be a major strength after a series of news reports that questioned Herrera's ethics, and he won by an unexpectedly wide margin of 19 percentage points.

NEVADA 3

Las Vegas suburbs

Roughly pinwheel-shaped, the new 3rd District is located in Clark County, which has absorbed much of the 66 percent population gain that made Nevada the nation's fastest-growing state in the 1990s. The district includes a chunk of Las Vegas, but it is mainly composed of suburbs such as Henderson and Boulder City.

Though most of the city's casinos are located in the urban 1st District, the 3rd is home to many who work in the gambling industry and are part of the area's strong union structure. The district has a 16 percent Hispanic population. It also contains the busy Las Vegas airport.

The 3rd was drawn to be a partisan swing district. When it was created in 2001, its voting makeup was 42 percent Democratic and 42 percent Republican, with the rest of the voters unaffiliated. Al Gore narrowly beat George W. Bush in the 2000 presidential contest here by 48.4 percent to 47.8 percent.

Republicans may have an advantage in the future, however, as the GOP suburban areas are expanding rapidly. The district takes in most of the suburbs, including Summerlin to the west, a massive planned community along the western rim of Las Vegas Valley. These areas are populated with many white-collar new arrivals to the state, as well as one of the fastest-growing elderly populations in the country. To the east, along the Arizona border near Utah, the population is largely Mormon — an influence that has spread into suburbs such as Henderson. In the south, the district contains lightly populated mining communities around Laughlin on the Arizona border.

CITIES
Henderson, 175,381; Spring Valley (unincorporated), 117,390; Las Vegas (pt.), 115,526

MAJOR INDUSTRY
Mining, gambling, ranching

NOTABLE
Hoover Dam, about 30 miles southeast of Las Vegas, often is called one of the greatest engineering works in history.

NEW HAMPSHIRE

Gov. Craig Benson (R)

First elected: 2002
Length of term: 2 years
Term expires: 1/05
Salary: $100,000
Phone: (603) 271-2121
Hometown: Rye
Born: Oct. 8, 1954; New York, N.Y.
Religion: Roman Catholic
Family: Wife, Denise Benson; two children
Education: Babson College, B.S. 1977 (finance); Syracuse U., M.B.A. 1979
Career: Technology manufacturing company founder
Political highlights: No previous office
Election results:

2002 GENERAL		
Craig Benson (R)	259,663	58.6%
Mark Fernald (D)	169,277	38.2%
John Babiarz (LIBERT)	13,028	2.9%

Senate President Thomas Eaton (R)

(no lieutenant governor)
Phone: (603) 271-2111

STATE LEGISLATURE

General Court: Meets January-June
House: 400 members, 2-year terms
2003 breakdown: 282R, 118D; 286 men, 114 women
Salary: $100
Phone: (603) 271-3661
Senate: 24 members, 2-year terms
2003 breakdown: 18R, 6D; 20 men, 4 women
Salary: $100
Phone: (603) 271-2111

STATE TERM LIMITS

Governor: No
Senate: No
House: No

URBAN STATISTICS

CITY	POPULATION
Manchester	107,006
Nashua	86,605
Concord	40,687
Derry	34,021
Rochester	28,461

REGISTERED VOTERS

Republican	36.9%
Unenrolled	36.8%
Democrat	26%

POPULATION

2002 population (est.)	1,275,056
2000 population	1,235,786
1990 population	1,109,252
Percent change (1990-2000)	+11.4%
Rank among states (2002)	41
Median age	37.1
Born in state	43.3%
Foreign born	4.4%
Violent crime rate	175/100,000
Poverty level	6.5%
Federal workers	7,933
Military	4,435

REDISTRICTING

New Hampshire retained its two House seats in reapportionment. The state legislature drew a new map, which the governor signed on April 8, 2002.

MISCELLANEOUS

Web: www.state.nh.us
Capital: Concord

STATE ELECTION OFFICIAL
(603) 271-3242

DEMOCRATIC HEADQUARTERS
(603) 225-6899

REPUBLICAN HEADQUARTERS
(603) 225-9341

District Statistics

DIST.	2000 VOTE FOR PRESIDENT BUSH	GORE	NADER	WHITE	BLACK	ASIAN	HISP	MEDIAN INCOME	WHITE COLLAR	BLUE COLLAR	SERVICE INDUSTRY	OVER 64	UNDER 18	COLLEGE EDUCATION	RURAL	SQ. MILES
1	49%	46%	4%	95%	1%	1%	2%	$50,135	63%	24%	13%	12%	25%	29%	33%	2,449
2	47	48	4	95	1	1	2	$48,762	62	25	13	12	25	29	48	6,519
STATE	48	47	4	95	1	1	2	$49,467	62	25	13	12	25	29	41	8,968
U.S.	47.9	48.4	3	69	12	4	13	$41,994	60	25	15	12	26	24	21	3,537,438

Coos
Grafton
Carroll
2
1
Belknap
Strafford
Sullivan
Merrimack
Rochester
Concord
Dover
Portsmouth
Manchester
Rockingham
Cheshire
Hillsborough
Nashua

Sen. Judd Gregg (R)

Elected 1992; 2nd term

CAPITOL OFFICE
224-3324
mailbox@gregg.senate.gov
gregg.senate.gov
393 Russell 20510-2904; fax 224-4952

COMMITTEES
Appropriations
(Commerce, Justice, State & Judiciary - chairman)
Budget
Health, Education, Labor & Pensions - chairman

HOMETOWN
Rye

BORN
Feb. 14, 1947, Nashua, N.H.

RELIGION
Congregationalist

FAMILY
Wife, Kathleen Gregg; three children

EDUCATION
Columbia U., A.B. 1969; Boston U., J.D. 1972, LL.M. 1975

CAREER
Lawyer

POLITICAL HIGHLIGHTS
N.H. Governor's Executive Council, 1979-81; U.S. House, 1981-89; governor, 1989-93

ELECTION RESULTS

1998 GENERAL		
Judd Gregg (R)	213,477	67.8%
George Condodemetraky (D)	88,883	28.2%
Brian Christeson (LIBERT)	7,603	2.4%
Roy Kendel (IA)	4,733	1.5%
1998 PRIMARY		
Judd Gregg (R)	64,121	85.6%
Phil Weber (R)	10,818	14.4%

PREVIOUS WINNING PERCENTAGES
1992 (48%); 1986 House Election (74%); 1984 House Election (76%); 1982 House Election (71%); 1980 House Election (64%)

As the new chairman of the Health, Education, Labor and Pensions Committee, Gregg has taken the gavel from a fellow New Englander with diametrically opposite views on most of the major social policy issues of the day. But even though he and Edward M. Kennedy could not be more different in philosophy and temperament, Gregg has managed to forge a solid working relationship with the Massachusetts Democrat.

Gregg is a man of some reserve, not often given to backroom bonhomie. When presidential candidate George W. Bush picked Gregg to play the part of his opponent, Al Gore, for debating practice in the fall of 2000, campaign aides told The Washington Post that Gregg was the right person for the job because he was smart, stiff and dour — the very characteristics that GOP operatives delighted in ascribing to Gore.

But Gregg has experience and relationships resulting from previous service in the House and as New Hampshire's governor that have proved useful to the Senate GOP leadership. During his eight years in the House, he was an early participant in the Conservative Opportunity Society, a group founded by Republican Newt Gingrich of Georgia with the aim of toppling the House Democratic majority — a goal achieved in 1994, by which point Gregg already was a senator.

In the 107th Congress Gregg worked closely with Kennedy and other Democrats on bills to speed government reviews of new medical devices, to encourage banks to cut down on identity theft by using something other than Social Security numbers to identify their customers, and to force food manufacturers to note allergens on labels. In each of these cases, Gregg tilted the legislation more toward the liking of business interests.

In 2001 Gregg and Kennedy, working with their counterparts from the House Education and the Workforce Committee, overcame partisan differences to write the final version of President Bush's education overhaul initiative. As part of the mammoth domestic spending law of early 2003 — completing budget work held over from the 107th — Gregg was instrumental in obtaining $2 billion more than Bush had initially sought for education programs.

Still, only three GOP senators voted the way Bush wanted more often than Gregg in the 107th; he did so 99 percent of the time.

Gregg is a longtime advocate of increased federal funding for special education, a cause he is expected to pursue as his committee rewrites the Individuals with Disabilities Education Act in the 108th Congress.

He starts the 108th in a much stronger position to shape legislation acceptable to anti-regulatory business interests and to social conservatives. Not only will Gregg guide the drafting of health, education and labor bills in the HELP Committee, he also will have substantial control over some crucial federal funding as chairman of the Appropriations Subcommittee that finances the Commerce, Justice and State departments and the federal judiciary.

Gregg is a staunch fiscal conservative. He has even bucked some in the GOP by proposing strict spending caps and budget-balancing enforcement mechanisms. He has tried, unsuccessfully, to eliminate the federal crop insurance program for tobacco farmers. An opponent of tax breaks and subsidies for businesses, he led an unsuccessful fight in the 105th to rescind a tax break for hard-rock mining companies. He also opposes price supports for peanuts and sugar and the annual subsidy that helps U.S. companies market agricultural products overseas.

On social issues, he has battled legislation designed to ban job discrimination against homosexuals, arguing that a federal law should not overturn state rulings on the matter. He has also been a longtime ally of anti-abortion forces. As governor from 1989 to 1993, he vetoed bills that would have bolstered abortion rights provisions in New Hampshire law. In the Senate, he has voted to ban the procedure its opponents call "partial birth" abortion.

In the 106th Congress, Gregg emerged as a leading player in the debate over Social Security, teaming with Democrat John B. Breaux of Louisiana to propose using a portion of the payroll tax for individual savings accounts. Such a step, the pair said, would enable the government to maintain the program's solvency without raising taxes or cutting benefits. But the proposal saw no action. Gregg warned that without a White House-congressional summit, agreement on a Social Security fix was "a long way off."

Gregg occasionally follows his New Hampshire libertarian leanings. Pairing with Democrat Patrick J. Leahy of neighboring Vermont, in the 105th he successfully opposed a plan to limit the tobacco industry's overall liability in future lawsuits to $8 billion in exchange for advertising restrictions and other concessions. Gregg assailed the plan as an "artificial, inappropriate legislative protection" that would be "totally outside the traditional manner in which we have managed our marketplace."

He also has strayed from the party line on matters of regional concern. New England is downwind from coal-fired power plants in the Midwest, which have been blamed for acid rain and other pollution in the Northeast. In 2003, Gregg and several other Northeastern Republicans joined Democrats in an unsuccessful effort to delay new administration rules weakening air pollution requirements.

The son of a former GOP governor of New Hampshire — Hugh Gregg, who served from 1953 to 1955 — Gregg has spent most of his life in public service. He practiced law only a short time before launching his political career in 1978, when he unseated a Republican incumbent to join the five-member state Executive Council. Two years later, he won the House seat of retiring Republican James C. Cleveland. His training as a tax attorney helped win him a seat on the Ways and Means Committee, but he manifested a straight-laced Yankee distaste for deal-cutting and had little role in the tax code overhaul of 1986.

Two years later, he left Congress for the first of a pair of two-year terms as governor. In each race, he took at least 60 percent of the vote.

When Gregg sought to return to Washington in 1992, however, he ran into stiff opposition. New Hampshire's economic woes fired up an angry electorate, helping Bill Clinton carry the state for president and putting pro-business Democrat John Rauh in a position to give Gregg his toughest electoral fight as they vied to succeed Republican Warren B. Rudman, who was stepping down after two terms.

While acknowledging the state's economic hardships, Gregg frequently noted that he had kept a tight lid on spending and remained staunchly opposed to state income and sales taxes. Gregg lost most of the counties in his old congressional district on the rural western side of New Hampshire, but he carried the populous southeast corner and the GOP "North Country" and prevailed by 3 percentage points.

Gregg won an easy re-election in 1998, even after his opponent, George Condodemetraky, accused him of draft-dodging. Gregg vehemently denied the accusations — he received a valid medical deferment, he said — and refused to debate his opponent on television. Gregg walked away with 68 percent of the vote.

KEY VOTES

2002

No Pass farm bill reversing crop subsidy limits
No Postpone tougher automobile fuel efficiency standards
No Overhaul campaign finance law; ban "soft money" and restrict advocacy advertising
Yes Set federal election standards
Yes Support oil drilling in Arctic National Wildlife Refuge
No Revive fast-track procedures for trade agreements
Yes Create federal insurance coverage for catastrophic terrorist losses
Yes Tighten federal accounting and corporate governance regulation
No Advance bipartisan Medicare prescription drug plan
No Create independent Sept. 11 commission
No Back Democratic Homeland Security Department proposal
Yes Authorize war against Iraq

2001

Yes Confirm John Ashcroft as attorney general
Yes Nullify Clinton Labor Department ergonomics rule
Yes Cut taxes by $1.35 trillion through fiscal 2011
No Pass Democratic bill to bolster rights of patients in managed-care plans
No Permit a new round of military base closings
Yes Expand law enforcement power to investigate suspected terrorists

CQ VOTE STUDIES

	PARTY UNITY		PRESIDENTIAL SUPPORT	
	Support	Oppose	Support	Oppose
2002	81%	19%	96%	4%
2001	96%	4%	100%	0%
2000	98%	2%	38%	62%
1999	94%	6%	33%	67%
1998	91%	9%	43%	57%
1997	87%	13%	63%	37%
1996	91%	9%	34%	66%
1995	94%	6%	22%	78%
1994	84%	16%	42%	58%
1993	90%	10%	24%	76%

INTEREST GROUPS

	AFL-CIO	ADA	CCUS	ACU
2002	15%	10%	100%	85%
2001	13%	0%	100%	88%
2000	0%	0%	86%	100%
1999	0%	0%	76%	91%
1998	0%	5%	89%	76%
1997	0%	10%	100%	76%
1996	0%	5%	92%	75%
1995	0%	0%	95%	87%
1994	0%	15%	90%	79%
1993	0%	10%	91%	92%

Sen. John E. Sununu (R)

CAPITOL OFFICE
224-2841
mailbox@sununu.senate.gov
111 Russell 20510-2903; fax 224-1353

COMMITTEES
Banking, Housing & Urban Affairs
Commerce, Science & Transportation
Foreign Relations
(International Operations & Terrorism - chairman)
Governmental Affairs
Joint Economic

HOMETOWN
Bedford

BORN
Sept. 10, 1964, Boston, Mass.

RELIGION
Roman Catholic

FAMILY
Wife, Kitty Sununu; three children

EDUCATION
Massachusetts Institute of Technology, B.S., M.S. 1987 (mechanical engineering); Harvard U., M.B.A. 1991

CAREER
Corporate financial officer; management consultant; mechanical engineer

POLITICAL HIGHLIGHTS
U.S. House, 1997-2003

ELECTION RESULTS

2002 GENERAL		
John E. Sununu (R)	227,229	50.8%
Jeanne Shaheen (D)	207,478	46.4%
Clarence G. Blevens (LIBERT)	9,835	2.2%
2002 PRIMARY		
John E. Sununu (R)	81,920	53.5%
Robert C. Smith (R)	68,608	44.8%
Kenneth Scot Stremsky (R)	2,694	1.8%

PREVIOUS WINNING PERCENTAGES
2000 House Election (52%); 1998 House Election (67%); 1996 House Election (50%)

Elected 2002; 1st term

With his election to the Senate at 38 — a victory that required him to defeat incumbent Republican Sen. Robert C. Smith in the primary and incumbent Democratic Gov. Jeanne Shaheen in the general election — Sununu provided an extension of his family's budding political dynasty.

His father, John H. Sununu, was governor from 1983 to 1989 and then was chief of staff to the first President Bush for three years; his mother, Nancy, is a longtime state Republican activist. And Sununu's involvement in his parents' political activities seems to have left him not only with an eagerness to be involved, but also with useful knowledge about the nuts and bolts of campaigning — the importance of grass-roots support and personal interaction with voters, for instance.

Yet while the younger Sununu may come to politics naturally, he is not quite a natural politician. He credits his background in mechanical engineering with giving him an analytical approach to problem-solving that separates him from the lawyerly crowd in Washington.

Soft-spoken and reserved in public settings, Sununu nonchalantly strolled the halls of the House during his six years there, usually with his hands in his pockets. He did not make incendiary floor speeches and he rarely attended news conferences. Passersby took him for a 30-something congressional aide. But his measured approach made him a valued bridge builder between the often conflicting worlds of his two committees: Budget, where Republicans try to hold down spending, and Appropriations, where members of both parties are willing to let spending rise.

Unlike some of his harder-line conservative House colleagues, though, Sununu did not regard compromise as capitulation. "There's nothing contradictory about being fiscally conservative and pragmatic," he said.

As the youngest senator in the 108th Congress, Sununu will now seek to influence money matters on the Commerce, Science and Transportation Committee, the Banking, Housing and Urban Affairs Committee and the Joint Economic Committee. He also won assignments to Governmental Affairs and Foreign Relations, where he chairs the International Operations and Terrorism Subcommittee.

Sununu says he does not seek legislative advice from his father, and that he speaks to him "no more or no less than anyone else who has a good relationship with their father." But he is not shy about stating that he has personal ties to the upper echelons of the current Bush administration, including the president himself, that may help him achieve his goals. "I have a great personal relationship," he says, with White House Chief of Staff Andrew H. Card Jr.

But in his first publicized foray as a senator, Sununu worked against the White House, joining other Northeastern Republicans and most Democrats early in 2003 in an unsuccessful bid to delay a Bush administration rule that weakens air pollution regulations.

Sununu's ability to succeed in the Senate may depend on his ability to adapt from the House — where his approach as a party loyalist and quiet inside-dealmaker served him well — to the more freewheeling and individualistic side of the Capitol. Sununu said he looked forward to the challenge. "In the Senate, given the openness of the rules, it's easier for an individual to shape legislation that doesn't necessarily move through committee," he said.

Asked what he plans to focus on the most, however, Sununu returns to the issues on which he concentrated in the House: "tax cuts, getting the budget back to balance, and modernizing Social Security."

To Sununu, "modernizing Social Security" means allowing people to manage some of their Social Security tax dollars in private accounts. He did not conceal this position in his Senate campaign, even though proposing changes to Social Security is often politically risky. He said shortly after his election that voters who see a candidate taking a firm stand on Social Security "can count on you not to shy away from tough issues."

Restraint in taxation and government spending is a bedrock belief of New Hampshire Republicans. Sununu, typically, is frugal on fiscal issues and wants to reduce the scope and reach of federal government.

Even serving on House Appropriations, a place that has weakened the fiscal resolve of many in the past, did not change Sununu's outlook. He said his goal continued to be "focusing on controlling the size of the federal bureaucracy" so that taxes could be cut.

Sununu favors a flat tax, arguing that the federal government uses the current tax code to "engineer the way we live."

While in junior high school, Sununu observed firsthand his mother's work as a school board member; her experiences in that capacity taught him the importance and difficulties of public service. He turned his aptitudes for science and math into engineering degrees at MIT and a business degree at Harvard. After that he was chief financial officer for Teletrol Systems Inc., an innovative heating and cooling equipment maker in New Hampshire owned by Dean Kamen, inventor of the Segway motorized two-wheel scooter.

Sununu's opportunity to enter the family business came in 1996, when after three terms Republican Bill Zeliff gave up the 1st District House seat to run unsuccessfully for the GOP gubernatorial nomination. Sununu benefited from his widely known name and won a seven-person GOP primary by 476 votes. In the general election, Sununu edged Joseph F. Keefe, the state Democratic chairman, by 3 percentage points.

Sununu cruised to a second term in 1998 with 67 percent. But in 2000, he did not campaign aggressively and won by only 8 points against Democratic state Rep. Martha Fuller Clark.

While his modest victory in that race raised some eyebrows, Republican operatives did not hesitate to turn to Sununu soon after — when they sensed that the incumbent's vulnerability could hamper the party's ability to win back control of the Senate in 2002. Smith, an aggressive and unpredictable conservative, had flummoxed party strategists by embarking in 1999 on a quixotic presidential bid, which he began as a Republican and ended as an independent during an abrupt though brief separation from the GOP.

Sununu jumped into the Senate race in the fall of 2001. Smith attacked him for waging a battle that would leave Republicans divided after the primary and work to the Democrats' benefit. Sununu countered that Republicans needed to put forward their strongest candidate to take on Shaheen, who had been a popular governor, and touted endorsements he had received from some of Smith's Republican colleagues in the Senate.

Sununu won the GOP nomination in September by 9 points — the first person to unseat an elected senator in a primary since 1992, when Carol Moseley-Braun won the Democratic Senate nomination in Illinois over two-term incumbent Alan J. Dixon.

Sununu's high-profile victory eight weeks before the general election gave him a bounce in public opinion polls. Shaheen closed the gap in October, but a strong turnout of Republican voters helped propel Sununu to a 4-point victory.

KEY VOTES

House Service:

2002

No Overhaul campaign finance law; ban "soft money" and restrict advocacy advertising
Yes Back Bush's defense budget increase
Yes Extend 1996 welfare law
Yes Adopt Bush's discretionary spending limit
Yes Pass GOP Medicare prescription drug plan
No Create independent Sept. 11 commission
No Extend union protections to Homeland Security Department employees
Yes Revive fast-track procedures for trade agreements
Yes Authorize war against Iraq
No Advance bankruptcy overhaul opposed by abortion opponents

2001

Yes Nullify Clinton Labor Department ergonomics rule
Yes Cut taxes by $1.35 trillion through fiscal 2011
No Maintain ban on oil drilling in Arctic National Wildlife Refuge
Yes Approve Bush proposal to limit managed-care plan liability for coverage decisions
Yes Divert money from crop subsidy payments to land conservation
Yes Expand law enforcement power to investigate suspected terrorists

CQ VOTE STUDIES

House Service:

	PARTY UNITY		PRESIDENTIAL SUPPORT	
	Support	Oppose	Support	Oppose
2002	93%	7%	92%	8%
2001	93%	7%	95%	5%
2000	95%	5%	28%	72%
1999	95%	5%	18%	82%
1998	91%	9%	25%	75%
1997	95%	5%	29%	71%

INTEREST GROUPS

House Service:

	AFL-CIO	ADA	CCUS	ACU
2002	13%	0%	90%	92%
2001	0%	0%	100%	92%
2000	10%	10%	85%	96%
1999	0%	0%	88%	100%
1998	0%	0%	94%	92%
1997	0%	5%	100%	92%

Rep. Jeb Bradley (R)

CAPITOL OFFICE
225-5456
www.house.gov/bradley
1218 Longworth 20515-2901; fax 225-5822

COMMITTEES
Armed Services
Small Business
Veterans' Affairs

HOMETOWN
Wolfeboro

BORN
Oct. 20, 1952, Rumford, Maine

RELIGION
Episcopalian

FAMILY
Wife, Barbara Bradley; four children

EDUCATION
Tufts U., B.A. 1974 (sociology)

CAREER
Real estate developer; natural food store owner; magician; painting company owner

POLITICAL HIGHLIGHTS
Wolfeboro Planning Board, 1986-90; Wolfeboro Budget Committee, 1990-93; N.H. House, 1991-2002

ELECTION RESULTS

2002 GENERAL		
Jeb Bradley (R)	128,993	58.1%
Martha Fuller Clark (D)	85,426	38.5%
Dan Belforti (LIBERT)	7,387	3.3%
2002 PRIMARY		
Jeb Bradley (R)	23,012	31.4%
John A. Stephen (R)	16,956	23.1%
Sean Mahoney (R)	13,861	18.9%
Vivian Clark (R)	6,889	9.4%
Wayne Barrows (R)	6,008	8.2%
Francine Wendelboe (R)	4,947	6.8%
Gary Scott Hoffman (R)	1,101	1.5%

Elected 2002; 1st term

An avid outdoorsman with a tough constitution, Bradley has climbed many of New Hampshire's tallest peaks and whenever possible takes a daily dip in the family lake. "When the water is below 40 degrees, it feels like your skin is burning. If you focus on that mentally, you feel warm," Bradley said. "I've been doing it for years. If you can do that, you can do anything."

Bradley hopes that same New England self-discipline and determination will sustain him in Congress. He also arrived with a reputation as one of the more moderate GOP House freshmen, which he underscored by joining the centrist Republican Main Street Partnership.

His GOP blend of fiscal conservatism and social policy moderation is dwindling nationwide, but it remains a viable strain in the Northeast. He supports abortion rights, opposes school vouchers and wants the Arctic National Wildlife Refuge left alone. He favors a tax and regulatory climate in which the economy will prosper, and says that a fiscal philosophy of "lower taxes and lower spending wherever possible" can help spur growth.

Bradley's wide-ranging interests include modernizing the military, which he can pursue from his seats on the Armed Services and Veterans' Affairs committees. He also was assigned to the Small Business panel.

While developing real estate, owning a painting company and a natural food store and working as a magician, Bradley worked his way up in politics from the city planning board in a town of 5,000 beside Lake Winnipesaukee to a dozen years in the state House.

He captured the 1st District seat by breaking open what had appeared to be a close race, trouncing Democratic state Rep. Martha Fuller Clark by almost 20 percentage points. His easy win belied the nervousness some Republicans felt about holding the seat Republican John E. Sununu gave up to pursue his Senate seat. Clark was well-funded and had come within 8 points of Sununu in 2000. But Bradley's legislative record helped propel him to victory in an eight-candidate primary, and in the fall his Republican Party backers effectively portrayed Clark as too liberal for the district.

NEW HAMPSHIRE 1

East — Manchester, Rochester

Nestled in the southeast corner of the state, the 1st covers about one-fourth of New Hampshire's land yet contains 12 of the 17 most populous communities, including the largest, Manchester.

Most people live in and around Manchester or in Rockingham County along the coast. Some residents of southeastern towns, such as Dover, Portsmouth, Hampton and Exeter, commute to Boston.

Manchester, which boasts many technology and manufacturing companies, grew slowly in the 1990s. But the city is surrounded by rapidly growing areas such as upper-income Bedford to the southwest and Hooksett to the north.

In the eastern part of the district, the Portsmouth Naval Shipyard, across the state line in Kittery, Maine, has served as an economic anchor. Portsmouth experienced a big population drop in the 1990s, in part due to the closing of Pease Air Force Base.

Democratic-leaning Strafford County, where Durham (home to the University of New Hampshire) and Dover are located, gives Democrats healthy margins at the polls. Carroll County, in the north end of the district, is a rural, GOP-friendly area that thrives primarily on tourism and farming.

The 1st exhibits a Republican lean, albeit a small one. Republicans do well in medium-size and small towns, but no longer roll up big margins in population centers such as Manchester, which elected a Democratic mayor in 1999 and backed Al Gore in the 2000 presidential election.

MAJOR INDUSTRY
Health care, insurance, computer manufacturing

CITIES
Manchester, 107,006; Rochester, 28,461; Dover, 26,884; Derry, 22,661

NOTABLE
Franklin Pierce, the 14th president, was born in Hillsborough; Robert Frost operated a farm in Derry that is now a state historic site.

Rep. Charles Bass (R)

CAPITOL OFFICE
225-5206
cbass@mail.house.gov
www.house.gov/bass
2421 Rayburn 20515-2902; fax 225-2946

COMMITTEES
Energy & Commerce

HOMETOWN
Peterborough

BORN
Jan. 8, 1952, Boston, Mass.

RELIGION
Episcopalian

FAMILY
Wife, Lisa L. Bass; two children

EDUCATION
Dartmouth College, A.B. 1974

CAREER
Congressional aide; architectural products executive

POLITICAL HIGHLIGHTS
Sought Republican nomination for U.S. House, 1980; N.H. House, 1983-89; N.H. Senate, 1989-93; defeated in primary for re-election to N.H. Senate, 1992

ELECTION RESULTS

2002 GENERAL		
Charles Bass (R)	125,804	56.8%
Katrina Swett (D)	90,479	40.9%
John Babiarz (LIBERT)	5,051	2.3%
2002 PRIMARY		
Charles Bass (R)	61,473	86.6%
Eugene Douglass (R)	9,486	13.4%
2000 GENERAL		
Charles Bass (R)	152,581	56.2%
Barney Brannen (D)	110,367	40.6%
Brian Christeson (LIBERT)	6,188	2.3%

PREVIOUS WINNING PERCENTAGES
1998 (53%); 1996 (50%); 1994 (51%)

Elected 1994; 5th term

A former building products company executive, Bass brought a reputation for independence and a strong family political tradition to Washington. He takes a deep interest in consumer protection and technology-related issues as a member of the Energy and Commerce Committee, where he first took a seat in the 107th Congress.

A reserved but amiable man, Bass is a member of the moderate Republican Main Street Partnership. He sides with GOP leaders on most economic issues, such as free trade and lower taxes. But he has shown independence on several environmental and social policy questions. And he angered his leadership by becoming one of the decisive final four lawmakers to sign the petition that compelled the House to act in 2002 on the campaign finance package that most Republicans opposed.

Bass was born into a political family. From 1955 to 1963 his father, Perkins Bass, held the congressional seat he now occupies. His grandfather, Robert P. Bass, was the state's governor from 1911 to 1913.

Bass still keeps a banner that he says inspired him to run for the House in 1994. Made by his two children, it bears their handprints and a slogan: "The future of the world is in hands so small." He has made increased federal funding for special education a signature issue, saying that should be the federal government's top education priority.

On Energy and Commerce, Bass tends to the diverse needs of his district's consumers and business interests, which include defense, electronics, computer and health care companies. On the Telecommunications Subcommittee, he supports the effort to permit the regional Bell Telephone companies to transmit high-speed Internet traffic over telephone lines outside their service regions without first having to open their local phone systems to competition.

In an effort to protect consumers from solicitations by fraudulent charities seeking to capitalize on the Sept. 11, 2001, terrorist attacks, Bass won House passage of his proposal to double civil penalties against scam artists during times of national emergencies. But the bill died in the Senate.

Like most Republicans, Bass argues that the federal government often discourages economic development by saddling business with too many regulations. Harboring a fascination with gadgets that dates to his childhood, he has become a champion for one of his state's most prominent businessmen, inventor Dean Kamen, who has dubbed Bass the "gearhead congressman." Bass backs legislation to allow Kamen's motorized two-wheel scooter, the Segway Human Transporter, to roll on federally funded paths and sidewalks in states that have approved its use. He also hopes to clear away any regulatory hurdles for another Kamen invention: a powerful electric generator for homes and businesses that could provide a cheap alternative source of electricity. "We don't want technology to be blocked by the stroke of a bureaucrat's pen," Bass says.

Like many other Northeastern Republicans, Bass sometimes backs environmental protection measures. As the 108th began, he was sounding off against President Bush's proposals to relax air quality standards and to drill for oil in the Arctic National Wildlife Refuge. In the 107th, he supported gradual increases in fuel efficiency standards for cars and light trucks. In the 105th, he voted against a Republican bill to make it easier for landowners to challenge federal environmental regulations that adversely affect the use of their land.

In the 107th, Bass backed efforts to erase the tax advantages for companies — including his New Hampshire corporate constituent, Tyco International Inc. — that move their official corporate headquarters to offshore tax havens. Tyco has offices in Concord, but technically it moved its headquarters to Bermuda in 1997.

Bass has been a staunch fiscal conservative, winning plaudits from the Concord Coalition, a budget watchdog group. A former member of the Budget Committee, he has backed a two-year budget cycle, in which money would be appropriated only in alternate years. He urged Bush to veto the 2002 farm bill on grounds that it would help big corporate farms and "drive family farmers out."

One pet peeve has been what he terms "cowboy welfare" — an Agriculture Department program that seeks to protect Western livestock by killing coyotes and other predators. "We have coyotes on my farm in New Hampshire, but nobody has given me a dime to get rid of them," he says.

At his farm, Bass keeps chickens and a collection of antique cars, including his prize Ford Model A. His chickens can regularly be heard in the background when he is doing radio interviews from his home.

After graduating from Dartmouth, Bass served first as a field worker for Republican Rep. William S. Cohen of Maine and then was chief of staff for GOP Rep. David F. Emery of Maine. His first attempt to win a seat in Congress was in 1980, when Republican Rep. James C. Cleveland retired. But Bass was outmaneuvered by another of the state's political "blue bloods," Judd Gregg, whose father had been governor in the 1950s.

While chairman of a company that fabricates decorative facades for buildings, Bass won election two years later to the state House, where he served six years. In 1988, he won a seat in the state Senate, where he wrote the New Hampshire law on voluntary campaign spending limits.

In 1992, Bass lost his state Senate seat when a conservative beat him in the GOP primary. Two years later he tried for Congress again, winning his party's nomination with just 29 percent of the vote; two conservatives divided nearly half of the total. In November, the Republican takeover tide helped Bass oust Democratic Rep. Dick Swett by 5 percentage points.

In both 1996 and 1998, Bass drew primary challenges from conservatives and went on to post narrow victories in the fall. In 2000, he avoided a primary challenge and took 56 percent against a well-funded Democratic newcomer, Barney Brannen. In 2002, Bass was outspent by his opponent, Democrat Katrina Swett, the wife of the man he unseated in 1994 and a daughter of Rep. Tom Lantos of California, but he won with 57 percent.

KEY VOTES

2002

- Yes Overhaul campaign finance law; ban "soft money" and restrict advocacy advertising
- Yes Back Bush's defense budget increase
- Yes Extend 1996 welfare law
- Yes Adopt Bush's discretionary spending limit
- Yes Pass GOP Medicare prescription drug plan
- No Create independent Sept. 11 commission
- No Extend union protections to Homeland Security Department employees
- Yes Revive fast-track procedures for trade agreements
- Yes Authorize war against Iraq
- Yes Advance bankruptcy overhaul opposed by abortion opponents

2001

- Yes Nullify Clinton Labor Department ergonomics rule
- Yes Cut taxes by $1.35 trillion through fiscal 2011
- Yes Maintain ban on oil drilling in Arctic National Wildlife Refuge
- Yes Approve Bush proposal to limit managed-care plan liability for coverage decisions
- Yes Divert money from crop subsidy payments to land conservation
- Yes Expand law enforcement power to investigate suspected terrorists

CQ VOTE STUDIES

	PARTY UNITY		PRESIDENTIAL SUPPORT	
	Support	Oppose	Support	Oppose
2002	85%	15%	82%	18%
2001	85%	15%	79%	21%
2000	85%	15%	34%	66%
1999	83%	17%	27%	73%
1998	78%	22%	33%	67%

INTEREST GROUPS

	AFL-CIO	ADA	CCUS	ACU
2002	0%	15%	90%	80%
2001	17%	25%	91%	60%
2000	0%	20%	90%	75%
1999	0%	20%	88%	68%
1998	10%	10%	94%	63%

NEW HAMPSHIRE 2

West – Nashua, Concord

The 2nd encompasses the entire western half of New Hampshire and most of the state's southern border with Massachusetts, spanning from white-collar territory in the southern tier to the mountains and forests of the sparsely populated "North Country."

The district has an economy as varied as its population. Many of the upwardly mobile refugees who fled Massachusetts' higher tax rates reside along the populous southern tier of the district in towns such as Salem, Windham and Atkinson, but still work across the state line. Nashua, the 2nd's most populous city, has experienced ups and downs with industries deeply involved in computers and electronics.

The economy of the heavily forested "North Country" is closely tied to paper manufacturing and wood products. In the far northern reaches of the state, about 20 miles from the border with Quebec, is tiny Dixville Notch, where residents cast the nation's first votes at the stroke of midnight Election Day. In between lie smaller blue-collar towns, many of which depend on tourist dollars from lake visitors and skiers.

Once rock-ribbed Republican, the 2nd has become more competitive in recent years. Al Gore carried the district in 2000, thanks to the Democratic lean of Nashua and the liberalism of Concord, the state capital, and the college towns of Hanover and Keene. Other population centers are politically competitive: George W. Bush carried Salem by 2 votes and lost Hudson by 46 votes in 2000. The northern counties tend to lean Republican.

Redistricting in 2002 made minimal changes to the 2nd, which retained all of its territory from the 1990s map but added the Merrimack County towns of Epsom and Pittsfield, just east of Concord.

MAJOR INDUSTRY

Electronics, computer technology, health care

CITIES

Nashua, 86,605; Concord, 40,687; Keene, 22,563; Claremont, 13,151

NOTABLE

"Old Man of the Mountain" stone profile – the source for the state emblem – is in Franconia Notch in the White Mountains; The State House in Concord is the oldest legislative building in America in which both houses continue to sit in their original chambers; Daniel Webster's birthplace is in Franklin.

NEW JERSEY

Gov. James E. McGreevey (D)

First elected: 2001
Length of term: 4 years
Term expires: 1/06
Salary: $175,000
Phone: (609) 777-2500
Hometown: Woodbridge
Born: Aug. 6, 1957; Jersey City, N.J.
Religion: Roman Catholic
Family: Wife, Dina McGreevey; two children
Education: Columbia U., B.A. 1978 (political science); Georgetown U., J.D. 1981; Harvard U., M.A. 1982 (education)
Career: Pharmaceutical company executive; state parole board executive director; county prosecutor
Political highlights: N.J. Assembly, 1990-92; mayor of Woodbridge, 1992-2002; N.J. Senate, 1994-97; Democratic nominee for governor, 1997

Election results:

2001 GENERAL		
James E. McGreevey (D)	1,256,853	56.4%
Bret Schundler (R)	928,174	41.7%
Bill Schluter (I)	24,084	1.1%

Senate Presidents John O. Bennett (R) and Richard J. Codey (D)

(no lieutenant governor)
Phone: (609) 292-5199
Because control of the Senate is evenly split, the two parties rotate the position.

STATE LEGISLATURE

Legislature: Meets year-round
House: 80 members, 2-year terms
2003 breakdown: 36R, 43D, 1GREEN; 66 men, 14 women
Salary: $49,000
Phone: (609) 292-5339
Senate: 40 members, 4-year terms
2003 breakdown: 20R, 20D; 35 men, 5 women
Salary: $49,000
Phone: (609) 292-5199

STATE TERM LIMITS

Governor: 2 consecutive terms
Senate: No
House: No

URBAN STATISTICS

CITY	POPULATION
Newark	273,546
Jersey City	240,055
Paterson	149,222
Elizabeth	120,568
Edison	97,687

REGISTERED VOTERS

Unaffiliated	55%
Democrat	25%
Republican	19%

POPULATION

2002 population (est.)	8,590,300
2000 population	8,414,350
1990 population	7,730,188
Percent change (1990-2000)	+8.9%
Rank among states (2002)	9
Median age	36.7
Born in state	53.4%
Foreign born	17.5%
Violent crime rate	384/100,000
Poverty level	8.5%
Federal workers	64,174
Military	27,982

REDISTRICTING

New Jersey retained its 13 House seats in reapportionment. The New Jersey Redistricting Commission adopted a new map on Oct. 26, 2001

MISCELLANEOUS

Web: www.state.nj.us
Capital: Trenton

STATE ELECTION OFFICIAL
(609) 292-3760

DEMOCRATIC HEADQUARTERS
(609) 392-3367

REPUBLICAN HEADQUARTERS
(609) 989-7300

District Statistics

DIST.	2000 VOTE FOR PRESIDENT BUSH	GORE	NADER	WHITE	BLACK	ASIAN	HISP	MEDIAN INCOME	WHITE COLLAR	BLUE COLLAR	SERVICE INDUSTRY	OVER 64	UNDER 18	COLLEGE EDUCATION	RURAL	SQ. MILES
1	34%	66%	n/a	71%	16%	3%	8%	$47,473	62%	23%	15%	12%	27%	21%	1%	335
2	44	56	n/a	72	14	2	10	$44,173	54	24	23	14	25	18	21	1,982
3	45	55	n/a	83	9	3	4	$55,282	68	19	14	17	24	27	4	926
4	48	52	n/a	81	8	2	8	$54,073	65	20	14	16	25	25	7	719
5	54	46	n/a	86	1	7	4	$72,781	73	16	11	13	26	39	17	1,099
6	36	64	n/a	62	16	8	12	$55,681	66	20	14	12	24	30	0	196
7	51	49	n/a	79	4	8	7	$74,823	74	16	10	13	25	42	10	595
8	38	63	n/a	54	13	5	26	$51,954	64	23	13	13	25	28	0	107
9	35	65	n/a	61	7	11	19	$52,437	67	20	13	15	21	30	0	93
10	16	84	n/a	21	57	4	15	$38,177	58	24	18	11	27	18	0	66
11	56	45	n/a	83	3	6	7	$79,009	76	14	10	12	25	45	7	610
12	42	58	n/a	72	11	9	5	$69,668	76	14	10	13	25	42	7	633
13	26	74	n/a	32	11	6	48	$37,129	56	28	16	11	23	21	0	57
STATE	40	56	3	66	13	6	13	$55,146	66	20	14	13	25	30	6	7,417
U.S.	47.9	48.4	3	69	12	4	13	$41,994	60	25	15	12	26	24	21	3,537,438

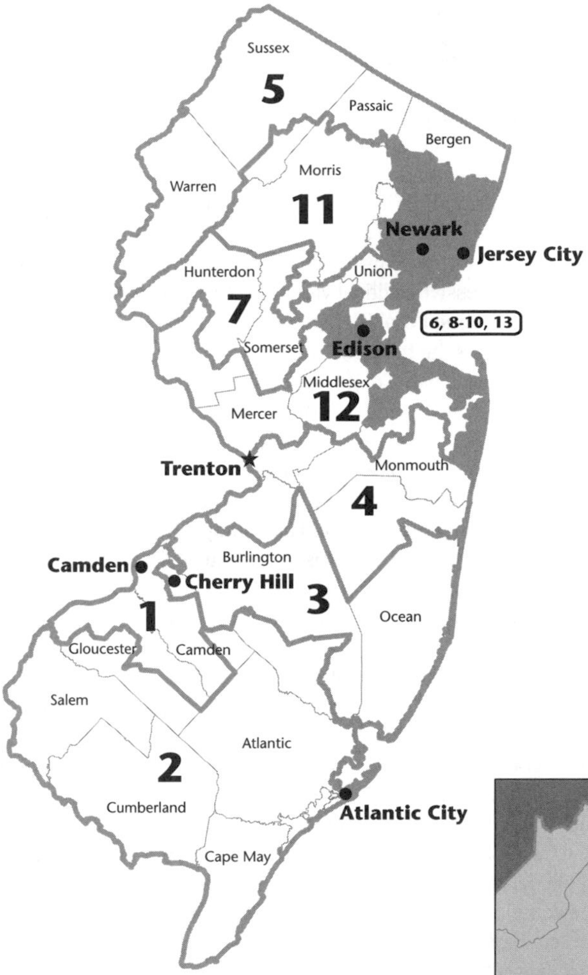
Sussex
5
Passaic
Bergen
Warren
Morris
11
Newark
Jersey City
Hunterdon
Union
7
6, 8-10, 13
Somerset
Edison
Middlesex
12
Mercer
Trenton
Monmouth
4
Camden
Burlington
Cherry Hill
3
1
Ocean
Gloucester
Camden
Salem
Atlantic
2
Cumberland
Atlantic City
Cape May

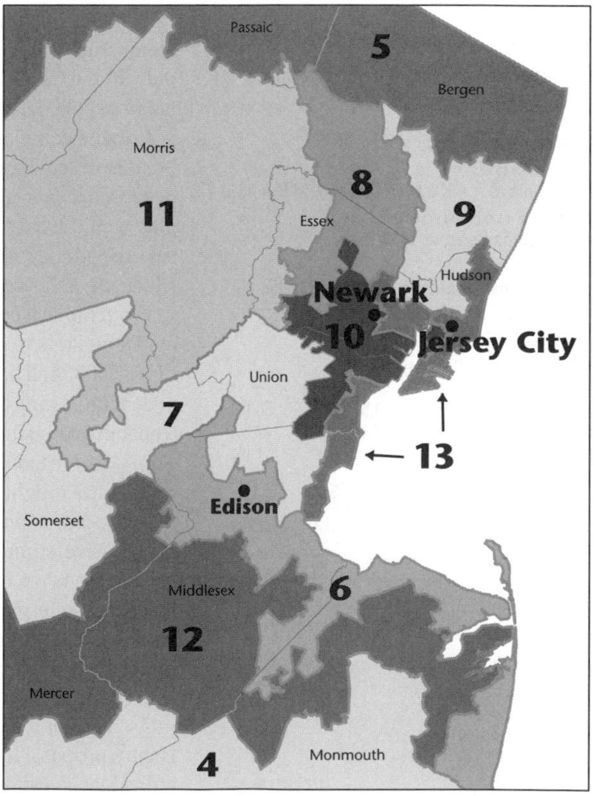
Passaic
5
Bergen
Morris
8
11
Essex
9
Hudson
Newark
10
Jersey City
Union
7
13
Edison
Somerset
Middlesex
6
12
Mercer
Monmouth
4

Sen. Jon Corzine (D)

CAPITOL OFFICE
224-4744
corzine.senate.gov
502 Hart 20510-3004; fax 228-2197

COMMITTEES
Banking, Housing & Urban Affairs
Budget
Foreign Relations

HOMETOWN
Hoboken

BORN
Jan. 1, 1947, Taylorville, Ill.

RELIGION
Christian non-denominational

FAMILY
Separated; three children

EDUCATION
U. of Illinois, B.A. 1969; U. of Chicago, M.B.A. 1973

MILITARY SERVICE
Marine Corps Reserve, 1969-75

CAREER
Investment bank CEO, manager; bond trader

POLITICAL HIGHLIGHTS
No previous office

ELECTION RESULTS

2000 GENERAL		
Jon Corzine (D)	1,511,237	50.1%
Bob Franks (R)	1,420,267	47.1%
Bruce Afran (I)	32,841	1.1%
2000 PRIMARY		
Jon Corzine (D)	251,216	58.0%
James J. Florio (D)	182,212	42.0%

Elected 2000; 1st term

Corzine had an unusually rapid rise toward prominence during the first two years of his freshman term in the Senate.

When he first arrived at the Capitol, the former investment banking executive was known primarily for spending more than $60 million of his own money to win his Senate seat, a self-financing record. But Corzine (COR-zyne) holds not only an enormous Wall Street fortune but also unwaveringly progressive political views. Like the Roosevelts, Kennedys and his Senate colleague Frank R. Lautenberg, Corzine has convinced the party faithful that, despite his wealth, he has the interests of the working class at heart. In the 107th Congress, he did this by taking on virtually all the issues important to the business community — and taking the opposite side.

While becoming a top spokesman for the Democratic leadership on a panoply of economic and regulatory measures, Corzine is increasingly speaking out on other issues as well. His voting record during the 107th placed him among his party's partisan stalwarts. Only three senators voted against President Bush more often. And Corzine's siding with the Democrats on 96 percent of party-line votes was matched or exceeded by only a dozen colleagues.

He has used his wealth to help other Democrats, donating hundreds of thousands of dollars to candidates and organizations. But in the run-up to the 2004 election, Corzine will play a much larger political role: chairman of the Democratic Senatorial Campaign Committee, the party's Senate candidate recruitment and fundraising organization. It is a tall order — Democrats will have 19 seats to defend as Bush seeks re-election versus only 15 for the GOP — but if he exceeds expectations his standing as a national political player will be cemented.

Corzine came out swinging as an economic populist from the moment he took office. Early in 2001 he spoke out against Bush's proposals for the deepest tax cuts in two decades. Although he calculated that the president's plan would have reduced his taxes by about $1 million annually, Corzine said the money would do more good if it were spent on Social Security, Medicare and education.

From his seat on the Banking Committee, Corzine joined with other Senate Democrats to introduce an early version of a corporate accountability bill in 2002, well before the telecommunications giant WorldCom Inc. conceded it had improperly accounted for billions of dollars in expenses. That transformed such a bill into must-pass legislation, and Majority Leader Tom Daschle tapped Corzine as a spokesman for Senate Democrats in promoting the toughest measure that was politically possible.

In the face of anemic economic growth in late 2002, Corzine proposed a progressive stimulus package that included a payroll tax holiday, a 13-week extension of unemployment benefits and increased aid to cash-strapped state governments. To help pay for those proposals, Corzine would freeze the reductions in the top two income tax rates scheduled under the Bush tax cut package of 2001. Corzine was gearing up to fight Bush's second big tax cut proposal in the 108th.

As head of a Democratic Social Security task force, Corzine opposes Bush's proposal to use a portion of the Social Security payroll tax to set up individual investment accounts. And he teamed up with Democrat Edward M. Kennedy of Massachusetts on a Senate bill that would require all businesses with 100 or more workers to provide health insurance.

When he won his seat in 2000, Corzine's platform included universal health care for children and a $3,000 tax credit for senior citizens and for families caring for an aging parent. He advocated rewarding high school students who earn at least a B average by using federal money to pay for their college tuition. And he favored abortion rights and the legalization of gay marriage.

Like Lautenberg — who held his Senate seat before him, and who returned to sit beside him in the 108th — Corzine is a staunch supporter of gun control. He backs proposals to license and register all firearms, ban sales of firearms at gun shows, impose safety standards on gun manufacturers, and limit individuals' handgun purchases to one each month.

Corzine did part company with most Democrats on a couple of high-profile votes in the 107th. He was one of two Democrats to oppose the 2002 farm bill, which he considered too costly, and he was among only 21 Democrats opposing the law authorizing war against Iraq.

The GOP takeover of the Senate in the 108th cost Corzine his seat on the Environment and Public Works Committee. But he hung onto his Budget and Banking committee assignments, although he is now low man on the Democratic roster on both panels. (Hillary Rodham Clinton of New York, who ranked just above him, gave up her Budget seat to keep Corzine on the committee.) Corzine also was appointed to the Foreign Relations Committee for the 108th.

Corzine is not the product of inherited wealth. He grew up on a small farm in the central Illinois community of Willey's Station. His father farmed and sold insurance; his mother was a teacher. Corzine says he took his first job at age 13 to help the family make ends meet.

After graduating Phi Beta Kappa from the University of Illinois, Corzine enlisted in the Marine Corps Reserve, where he rose to the rank of sergeant. After his active duty, he began working as a portfolio analyst at the Continental Illinois National Bank in Chicago. He earned a graduate business degree from the University of Chicago and went to work at Bank Ohio, a regional bank in Columbus.

In 1975, Corzine moved to New Jersey after he was hired as a bond trader at Goldman Sachs. He became a partner in 1980 and was chosen chairman and chief executive officer in 1994, when Goldman was one of the world's most competitive and profitable investment banks. He left in 1999 after converting the firm from a private partnership to a public company. In a manner befitting his wealth, he remains a trustee of an array of arts and educational institutions.

When Lautenberg announced that he was retiring after three terms in 2000, Corzine's willingness to spend freely from his personal fortune was the principal reason he was able to win his first campaign for public office.

Corzine was not known to New Jersey voters when he entered the race, and he did not make an easy transition from business to politics. He came across as both plain-spoken and ill at ease. Yet his appeal as a fresh face — along with his big spending — enabled him to trounce his Democratic primary opponent, James J. Florio, by 16 percentage points. After 15 years in the House, Florio had been defeated after one term as governor because of an unpopular tax increase, and he never was able to resurrect his image.

The Republican nominee was Rep. Bob Franks. He trailed badly in polls throughout much of the race, but was able to make it a close contest with a drumbeat of themes: that Corzine was trying to "buy" a Senate seat, was reluctant to release his tax returns, and lacked experience in public life. But Corzine was able to use his outsize campaign treasury to dominate the television airwaves, and he prevailed by 3 percentage points.

KEY VOTES

2002

- No Pass farm bill reversing crop subsidy limits
- No Postpone tougher automobile fuel efficiency standards
- Yes Overhaul campaign finance law; ban "soft money" and restrict advocacy advertising
- Yes Set federal election standards
- No Support oil drilling in Arctic National Wildlife Refuge
- No Revive fast-track procedures for trade agreements
- Yes Create federal insurance coverage for catastrophic terrorist losses
- Yes Tighten federal accounting and corporate governance regulation
- Yes Advance bipartisan Medicare prescription drug plan
- Yes Create independent Sept. 11 commission
- Yes Back Democratic Homeland Security Department proposal
- No Authorize war against Iraq

2001

- No Confirm John Ashcroft as attorney general
- No Nullify Clinton Labor Department ergonomics rule
- No Cut taxes by $1.35 trillion through fiscal 2011
- Yes Pass Democratic bill to bolster rights of patients in managed-care plans
- Yes Permit a new round of military base closings
- Yes Expand law enforcement power to investigate suspected terrorists

CQ VOTE STUDIES

	PARTY UNITY		PRESIDENTIAL SUPPORT	
	Support	Oppose	Support	Oppose
2002	96%	4%	64%	36%
2001	96%	4%	63%	37%

INTEREST GROUPS

	AFL-CIO	ADA	CCUS	ACU
2002	100%	100%	50%	5%
2001	100%	100%	36%	0%

Sen. Frank R. Lautenberg (D)

CAPITOL OFFICE
224-3224
frank_lautenberg@lautenberg.senate.gov
lautenberg.senate.gov
324 Hart 20510-3003; fax 224-8567

COMMITTEES
Commerce, Science & Transportation
Governmental Affairs

HOMETOWN
Cliffside Park

BORN
Jan. 23, 1924, Paterson, N.J.

RELIGION
Jewish

FAMILY
Divorced; four children

EDUCATION
Columbia U., B.S. 1949 (economics)

MILITARY SERVICE
Army, 1942-46

CAREER
Paycheck processing firm founder

POLITICAL HIGHLIGHTS
U.S. Senate, 1983-2001

ELECTION RESULTS

2002 GENERAL

Frank R. Lautenberg (D)	1,138,193	53.9%
Doug Forrester (R)	928,439	44.0%
Ted Glick (GREEN)	24,308	1.2%

1994 GENERAL

Frank R. Lautenberg (D)	1,033,487	50.3%
Garabed Haytaian (R)	966,244	47.0%

PREVIOUS WINNING PERCENTAGES
1988 (54%); 1982 (51%)

Elected 1982; 4th term

Did not serve 2001-2003

Lautenberg's declaration that he was retiring from public life in 2000 rang down the curtain on an 18-year career in the Senate — or so he intended at the time. But, at the age of 78, he was summoned back just two years later by a Democratic Party desperate to find a stand-in for the state's scandal-fallen senator, Robert G. Torricelli.

Now, Lautenberg is by far the most experienced federal legislator among the freshmen of the 108th Congress. He is the fourth-oldest senator. While 31 other popularly elected senators have left the Capitol only to return again, Lautenberg is the first to do so after saying he was out of politics for good. And he is settling the score in one of the nastiest and most public congressional feuds in modern times.

Yet Lautenberg's return to the arena is a mixed blessing for him.

On the one hand, he had to campaign for only a month and essentially was liberated from fundraising obligation, the aspect of congressional life most distasteful to him. Having won, he has been hailed by other Democrats as a savior. Almost no one expects him to run for re-election when he is 84, so he has something of a political free rein for the next six years. And while he and Torricelli were fabled enemies, there is every reason to believe Lautenberg can get along with the state's other senator, Jon Corzine. Both are self-made millionaires in the financial services industry, and both are Democrats with reliably liberal voting records.

On the other hand, Lautenberg has none of the perquisites or guaranteed legislative sway that would have been his had he remained in the Senate without interruption. His accrued seniority won him almost no consideration, and he ended up as the lowest-ranking minority party member on the Commerce Committee, where he last sat in 1984, and on the Governmental Affairs Committee, where he had never served.

Had he won a fourth consecutive term in 2000, he would have had a much better choice. He could have been the top Democrat on either the Budget Committee, as it considers President Bush's economic program, or on the Environment and Public Works Committee, as it writes new federal highway, mass transit and aviation policies. He also would have been fifth in Democratic seniority on Appropriations, where he was the top Democrat on the Transportation Subcommittee for 14 years.

His return also meant that, at least for now, Congress has set aside its plan to name a Federal Aviation Administration building in Atlantic City after him. Such tributes to former lawmakers are not infrequent, however, and during his time away, a New Jersey Transit commuter rail station was named in his honor.

Tenaciousness as an advocate for his home state was a hallmark of Lautenberg's first stint in the Senate; he won in 1982 with the slogan "New Jersey first." He battled frequently and successfully to protect Amtrak, whose major Northeast route goes through his state. In 1998 he pressed the Clinton administration to back away from plans to lower the passenger railroad's federal subsidies. During initial 1997 debate on the current highway law, which expires in the 108th, he threatened to filibuster the massive package unless it was altered to provide more for New Jersey.

Long before the Sept. 11, 2001, terrorist attacks, Lautenberg was a proponent of increased funding for aviation security, winning more money for such efforts than the Clinton administration sought.

Lautenberg has gained renown for taking on two of Washington's most influential forces, the tobacco and gun lobbies. A former two-pack-a-day smoker, he was the driving force in the Senate behind the 1989 law that banned smoking on domestic airline flights. And he subsequently led the crusade to restrict smoking in most federal buildings. In 1997 he pushed through language barring anyone convicted of domestic violence, including spousal or child abuse, from possessing a firearm. And he won a Senate vote in 1999 to require background checks on all people who buy firearms at gun shows — the high-water mark in a drive for gun control legislation that foundered by the end of the 106th Congress.

Lautenberg's liberalism in his initial Senate service was most notable on social issues. He often took more-conservative stances on fiscal matters: From his senior seat on the Budget Committee, in 1997 he gave crucial Democratic congressional backing to the budget-balancing deal that had been struck mainly between President Clinton and the GOP.

A son of an immigrant silk mill worker, Lautenberg transformed his company, Automatic Data Processing, from a three-man business into a world leader in processing paychecks. Although involved for years as a Democratic activist and fundraiser — his $90,000 contribution to George McGovern's 1972 campaign earned him a place on President Nixon's enemies list — he had never sought office before his 1982 bid for an open Senate seat. (Veteran Democrat Harrison A. Williams Jr. had been convicted in the Abscam corruption probe.)

Spending $4 million of his own money, an unusually large sum in that era, he took 51 percent to defeat Republican Rep. Millicent Fenwick. In 1988, he won with 54 percent against an aggressive challenge from Republican Pete Dawkins, once the Army's youngest brigadier general. Lautenberg survived the 1994 GOP tide with a 3 percentage point victory over conservative state Assembly Speaker Garabed "Chuck" Haytaian.

For much of the 105th and 106th Congresses, when Lautenberg and Torricelli were their state's senators, they barely spoke — in large part because Lautenberg viewed his first-term colleague as insufficiently deferential and overly brash. Lobbyists complained that straightforward matters of parochial concern were going unacknowledged because the two would not sign off on them together. The feud was joined for good at a 1999 meeting of Senate Democrats, when Torricelli threatened in vulgar terms to castrate Lautenberg in retaliation for what he viewed as an insulting and inaccurate charge.

So five weeks before Election Day 2002, Lautenberg eagerly promoted himself as the replacement Democratic nominee when Torricelli abandoned his campaign. Inquiries by federal prosecutors into Torricelli's fundraising practices, which culminated in the exposure of his improper dealings with a campaign donor, had led to a Senate Ethics Committee rebuke in July that effectively ended his chance of winning a second term.

When two House members, Robert Menendez and Frank Pallone Jr., declined to become the replacement candidate, the personally wealthy and universally known Lautenberg became the party's choice.

Republicans unsuccessfully argued in the New Jersey Supreme Court that the nominee switch was being made too late under state law; the court held that the voter interest in having viable candidates from both major parties superceded a literal reading of that law, and the U.S. Supreme Court declined to reconsider that decision.

Republicans had nominated wealthy businessman Doug Forrester, whose main campaign theme had been that he did not have Torricelli's ethical baggage. He retooled his message to make it about the legitimacy of Lautenberg's candidacy, but the once-and-future senator cruised to victory by a margin of 10 percentage points.

CQ VOTE STUDIES

	PARTY UNITY		PRESIDENTIAL SUPPORT	
	Support	Oppose	Support	Oppose
2000	98%	2%	98%	2%
1999	96%	4%	93%	7%
1998	97%	3%	90%	10%
1997	94%	6%	87%	13%
1996	93%	7%	90%	10%
1995	94%	6%	87%	13%
1994	84%	16%	82%	18%
1993	86%	14%	85%	15%
1992	92%	8%	22%	78%
1991	89%	11%	31%	69%

INTEREST GROUPS

	AFL-CIO	ADA	CCUS	ACU
2000	75%	90%	46%	4%
1999	78%	100%	44%	0%
1998	88%	95%	50%	4%
1997	71%	95%	60%	0%
1996	100%	95%	15%	0%
1995	100%	100%	16%	0%
1994	88%	95%	30%	4%
1993	82%	95%	45%	24%
1992	92%	100%	30%	4%
1991	67%	95%	10%	5%

Rep. Robert E. Andrews (D)

CAPITOL OFFICE
225-6501
rob.andrews@mail.house.gov
www.house.gov/andrews
2439 Rayburn 20515-3001; fax 225-6583

COMMITTEES
Education & Workforce
Select Homeland Security

HOMETOWN
Haddon Heights

BORN
Aug. 4, 1957, Camden, N.J.

RELIGION
Episcopalian

FAMILY
Wife, Camille Spinello Andrews; two children

EDUCATION
Bucknell U., B.A. 1979 (political science); Cornell U., J.D. 1982

CAREER
Lawyer; professor

POLITICAL HIGHLIGHTS
Camden County Board of Freeholders, 1987-90 (director, 1988-90); sought Democratic nomination for governor, 1997

ELECTION RESULTS

2002 GENERAL		
Robert E. Andrews (D)	121,846	92.7%
Timothy Haas (LIBERT)	9,543	7.3%
2002 PRIMARY		
Robert E. Andrews (D)		unopposed
2000 GENERAL		
Robert E. Andrews (D)	167,327	76.2%
Charlene Cathcart (R)	46,455	21.2%
Catherine L. Parrish (I)	3,090	1.4%

PREVIOUS WINNING PERCENTAGES
1998 (73%); 1996 (76%); 1994 (72%); 1992 (67%); 1990 (54%); 1990 Special Election (55%)

Elected 1990; 7th full term

Andrews has earned a reputation as a smart, fresh-thinking lawmaker who can frame classic Democratic arguments in new ways and help his colleagues achieve consensus. So it is perhaps surprising that he has not risen higher in the party's ranks. The problem Andrews faces, should he have such aspirations, is that he was viewed for years as something of a lone wolf, with his own agenda and little interest in anything else. After a decade in the House, however, in the 107th Congress he started taking overt steps to build stronger bridges with his colleagues, and his standing in the caucus seems to be on the ascent.

A turning point may have come in 1997, when Andrews narrowly lost a bid for governor; in an upset, the Democratic nomination was won by James E. McGreevey, then a state senator. Andrews took the loss hard. He withdrew for a time from party politics and had harsh words not only for some party leaders but for the political system, saying that "people who control vast sums of money have undue leverage." But since then, he has worked more actively with other Democrats on the party's core issues and has become more vocal in caucus meetings, where he is credited with coming up with insightful arguments that have helped fine-tune party positions.

In the 107th, Andrews played a prominent role on some of the hottest issues at the Capitol. During the 2001 debate over airport security, he was in the midst of the action on a proposal to federalize baggage screeners. "When we all came into this building today and walked through screeners to get here, it was licensed law enforcement officers who protected us in the Capitol, not rent-a-cops," he told the Chicago Tribune. "If it's good enough for the members of Congress and visitors to the Capitol, it's good enough for every person who wants to fly."

He was an early advocate of the creation of a House committee to oversee the work of the newly formed Department of Homeland Security, and in the 108th, when such a panel was formed, Andrews was put on it.

Andrews took the lead on another important issue, opposing a Republican bill to allow businesses to offer their workers access to professional investment advice for their retirement savings. As the top Democrat on the Education and the Workforce Subcommittee on Employer-Employee Relations, Andrews sponsored an alternative that would have required firms with a conflict of interest to refer workers to another firm for advice. His plan was defeated, and the Republican bill passed, but the Senate never acted.

Andrews also was a member of the conference committee that wrote the final version of the sweeping education overhaul bill in 2001. And, as he has in previous years, Andrews played an active role in pushing for the so-called patients' bill of rights, though that bill's proposed overhaul of managed care ultimately died just as it did in the 106th and 105th Congresses.

Long known as one of the House's most prolific legislators, Andrews introduced 107 bills and resolutions in the 107th Congress, on issues ranging from child support to federal budget policy. One bill would have raised to five years, from one, the time former members of Congress must wait before lobbying their ex-colleagues.

When a regional postal facility in the 1st District was found to be contaminated with anthrax during the fall 2001 attacks, Andrews got the inspector general of the Postal Service to investigate why the facility was reopened twice before it had been completely inspected and cleaned. Andrews also has displayed a professional interest in, to his ear, the declining quality of radio music. He asked the Justice Department for an antitrust investigation of Clear Channel Communications Inc., which owns 1,200 stations.

Personally, Andrews does not schmooze with his colleagues very much, but he is pleasant and approachable and displays a dry sense of humor. "I guess they want to build a mud castle," he once said of a Delaware River dredging project that would have deposited most of the sludge in his district. At night, he usually takes the train home to Haddon Heights to be with his wife and two young daughters; he says they have been instrumental in making him less of a workaholic.

The son of a former shipyard worker, Andrews generally takes the side of organized labor, opposing free-trade agreements that he believes could cost U.S. workers their jobs. He is a fairly conventional Northeastern Democrat, taking stands in support of environmental protection, abortion rights and gun control.

When Andrews was a 14-year-old in the Jersey suburbs of Philadelphia, his father lost his shipyard job. His mother went to work as a secretary, and his father eventually got a janitor's job. In a 1997 interview with Gannett News Service, Andrews recalled telling his newly unemployed father: "Maybe there's someone in the government who could help you." When his father dismissed the suggestion as unlikely, Andrews remembers thinking: "What were they doing, if not helping people like him?"

The first in his family to go to college, Andrews was a teaching assistant in his senior year at Bucknell and wrote this question as the entire final exam for an introductory political science class: "Politics is everything. Explain."

After a half-dozen years practicing law, at age 29 Andrews won a seat on the Camden County governing board. He became known as a young reformer and two years later was chosen to head the board.

He was a protégé of liberal Democratic Rep. James J. Florio. After Florio was elected governor in 1989, Andrews moved to take his place in the House, winning a 1990 special election (and a full term the same day) despite voter anger at Florio over a big state tax increase that year. Andrews refrained from directly repudiating the governor but took a "no new taxes" pledge for his first term.

Andrews won three easy re-elections, making him the initial favorite in the 1997 gubernatorial race. His narrow, bitter loss has had no carry-over effect in his three subsequent House bids, but the ill will between Andrews and McGreevey has lingered. When Sen. Robert G. Torricelli dropped his 2002 re-election bid five weeks before Election Day, the governor vetoed the idea of making Andrews the replacement Democratic nominee.

KEY VOTES

2002

Yes Overhaul campaign finance law; ban "soft money" and restrict advocacy advertising
Yes Back Bush's defense budget increase
No Extend 1996 welfare law
No Adopt Bush's discretionary spending limit
No Pass GOP Medicare prescription drug plan
Yes Create independent Sept. 11 commission
Yes Extend union protections to Homeland Security Department employees
No Revive fast-track procedures for trade agreements
Yes Authorize war against Iraq
No Advance bankruptcy overhaul opposed by abortion opponents

2001

No Nullify Clinton Labor Department ergonomics rule
No Cut taxes by $1.35 trillion through fiscal 2011
Yes Maintain ban on oil drilling in Arctic National Wildlife Refuge
No Approve Bush proposal to limit managed-care plan liability for coverage decisions
Yes Divert money from crop subsidy payments to land conservation
Yes Expand law enforcement power to investigate suspected terrorists

CQ VOTE STUDIES

	PARTY UNITY		PRESIDENTIAL SUPPORT	
	Support	Oppose	Support	Oppose
2002	88%	12%	41%	59%
2001	88%	12%	35%	65%
2000	88%	12%	75%	25%
1999	86%	14%	76%	24%
1998	86%	14%	77%	23%

INTEREST GROUPS

	AFL-CIO	ADA	CCUS	ACU
2002	89%	90%	32%	8%
2001	100%	90%	41%	20%
2000	90%	75%	38%	20%
1999	89%	95%	25%	20%
1998	90%	95%	44%	12%

NEW JERSEY 1

Southwest – Camden, Pennsauken

Across the Delaware River from Philadelphia, in southwestern New Jersey, the 1st is a Democratic stronghold. The largest concentration of its population lives in the troubled city of Camden, one of the poorest in the nation. Almost two-thirds of the district's residents live in Camden County, with most of the rest in Gloucester County and a handful in the southwestern edge of Burlington County.

For decades, Camden has been plagued by the departure of residents and businesses, a shrinking tax base, surging unemployment and crime, particularly drug trafficking. The state government assumed control of the city's finances and in 2002 approved a $175 million plan to redevelop and revitalize the area.

There are some good signs for the city. An aquarium and a 25,000-seat outdoor amphitheater have attracted more tourists to Camden's waterfront. In 2000, the waterfront was the site of a welcoming ceremony for the Republican National Convention. The city also joined its port facilities with Philadelphia's to create one of the largest on the Eastern Seaboard, and the EPA launched a redevelopment initiative to clean up industrial waste. Camden also is home to the Campbell Soup Company.

As distressed as the city is, the southern suburbs that fill out the 1st — like Gloucester and Collingswood — are developing. Voorhees Township also grew at a steady clip in the 1990s.

Blacks and Hispanics form a majority of the population in Camden, while many whites live in the surrounding suburbs. Overall, blacks make up 16 percent of district residents and Hispanics total 8 percent. The 1st has a large working-class contingent, and Al Gore took nearly two-thirds of the vote here in the 2000 presidential election.

MAJOR INDUSTRY
Shipping, manufacturing, education, health care

CITIES
Camden, 79,904; Pennsauken (unincorporated), 35,737; Glassboro, 19,068; Lindenwold, 17,414

NOTABLE
Poet Walt Whitman lived in Camden at the time of his death; Former Gov. James J. Florio represented the 1st for 15 years.

Rep. Frank A. LoBiondo (R)

CAPITOL OFFICE
225-6572
lobiondo@mail.house.gov
www.house.gov/lobiondo
225 Cannon 20515-3002; fax 225-3318

COMMITTEES
Armed Services
Transportation & Infrastructure
(Coast Guard & Maritime Transportation - chairman)

HOMETOWN
Vineland

BORN
May 12, 1946, Bridgeton, N.J.

RELIGION
Roman Catholic

FAMILY
Wife, Jan LoBiondo; two children

EDUCATION
St. Joseph's U., B.S. 1968 (business administration)

CAREER
Trucking company operations manager

POLITICAL HIGHLIGHTS
Cumberland County Board of Freeholders, 1985-87; N.J. Assembly, 1988-94; Republican nominee for U.S. House, 1992

ELECTION RESULTS

2002 GENERAL		
Frank A. LoBiondo (R)	116,834	69.2%
Steven A. Farkas (D)	47,735	28.3%
Roger Merle (LIBERT)	1,739	1.0%
Michael Matthews (GREEN)	1,720	1.0%
2002 PRIMARY		
Frank A. LoBiondo (R)		unopposed
2000 GENERAL		
Frank A. LoBiondo (R)	155,187	66.4%
Edward G. Janosik (D)	74,632	31.9%
Robert Gabrielsky (I)	3,252	1.4%

PREVIOUS WINNING PERCENTAGES
1998 (66%); 1996 (60%); 1994 (65%)

Elected 1994; 5th term

LoBiondo's grandfather and father, both immigrants, established a trucking company in South Jersey to transport farm produce to market, and today LoBiondo represents the district that accounts for more than 40 percent of the Garden State's agricultural production.

An economically diverse area, the 2nd District includes small farms and the beach communities of Cape May and Atlantic City, with its large hotels and casinos and its crime-ridden poorer sections. LoBiondo's legislative efforts are wide-ranging, in keeping with his district's diversity, and include coastal protections, tourism, gambling and agriculture. He is the only New Jersey member of the Congressional Rural Caucus.

In some respects, LoBiondo (lo-bee-ON-dough) fits in well with his colleagues in the conservative House GOP Class of 1994. On fiscal policy, abortion and gun control, he hews to the right. The National Rifle Association was a key backer of his first winning House bid. He supports the GOP position about 80 percent of the time.

But he is more moderate than party leaders and has deserted them on key votes — supporting, for example, the Shays-Meehan campaign finance bill though Speaker Dennis Hastert strongly opposed it. Not one to seek a reputation as a party maverick, LoBiondo says his departures from the conservative line are simply in response to his district's interests. He is a low-key politician who prefers to work quietly behind the scenes. Reporters who cover him regularly say he can come across as aloof.

His stands on the environment, labor and on some social policy issues also put him in the small subset of Northeastern moderates in the House GOP. In his last three re-election campaigns, he has received substantial support from labor unions, who like his record on increasing the minimum wage; opposing foreign trade agreements; and backing the Davis-Bacon wage law, which requires federal construction contractors to pay workers the prevailing local wage.

LoBiondo is a champion of the Meals on Wheels program, whose success he observed firsthand during his days as a county official. He says the program will save the federal government money by lowering future Medicare and veterans health care costs. And he favors continued funding for the National Endowment for the Arts, saying it is important to his district's efforts to extend tourism beyond the summer months.

In the 107th Congress, he took the gavel of the Transportation Committee's Coast Guard and Maritime Transportation Subcommittee, giving him an oversight role in the Coast Guard's base at Cape May. The chairmanship also gave LoBiondo a chance to get involved in the homeland security debate after the Sept. 11, 2001, terrorist attacks. He cosponsored a port security bill requiring the Coast Guard to conduct vulnerability assessments of U.S. ports while evaluating the effectiveness of security at some foreign ones. Congress cleared the legislation in 2002, but was unable to agree on how to pay for it.

LoBiondo got a chance to expand his work on national security issues after being appointed to the Armed Services Committee in the 108th Congress. The plum assignment was a reward from Republican leaders who were pleased with his decision in 2001 to forego a challenge to Democratic Sen. Robert Torricelli, who was becoming increasingly vulnerable as a result of an ethics probe. GOP leaders were happy not to have to defend LoBiondo's House seat in the 2002 election, when the two major parties were vying for control of the narrowly divided House.

As a co-founder of the Congressional Gaming Caucus, LoBiondo watches out for the interests of Atlantic City's gambling establishments in the face of increasing competition from the Internet. "The gaming entertainment industry is an economic engine that is helping drive the economy of states with legalized gaming, and it is doing this job in a very responsible way," he said in 2001.

LoBiondo is strongly committed to spending restraint, and has voted against a number of government programs that many Republicans support, including NASA's International Space Station. He opposes price supports for peanuts, sugar and tobacco; he also has criticized as "corporate welfare" the Market Promotion Program, which provides subsidies to companies to advertise their products overseas.

LoBiondo grew up in the small South Jersey town of Rosenhayn in what would be a dream environment for many young boys — working around the trucks at LoBiondo Brothers Motor Express Inc., while also spending time on local farms owned by other members of his extended family.

His father was involved in local politics and served as mayor of Deerfield Township. He instilled in his son the idea that public involvement, in civic organizations as well as in politics, is an important aspect of life. But the LoBiondo children also were expected to join the family business, and for 26 years after college, LoBiondo worked in the family's trucking company.

In the early 1980s, LoBiondo ran for the Cumberland County Board of Freeholders. He served one term and was ready to run for another when party leaders convinced him to run instead for an unexpected opening in the General Assembly. He served in the statehouse for seven years.

Then in 1992, he challenged longtime Democratic Rep. William J. Hughes, whose moderate image and personal popularity offset the GOP's advantage in voter registration. LoBiondo lost, capturing just 41 percent of the vote. Two years later, Hughes retired and LoBiondo tried again. He easily overcame the better-funded William L. Gormley, longtime Atlantic County GOP boss and a member of the state Senate, by tagging him as a "closet Democrat." He went on to defeat a little-known Democrat, Louis N. Magazzu, in the general election.

LoBiondo has won re-election with ease since then, including a 41-point victory in 2002. He says he will serve no more than 12 years in the House. That would take him to 2006, when Democratic Sen. Jon Corzine would be up for re-election.

KEY VOTES

2002

- Yes Overhaul campaign finance law; ban "soft money" and restrict advocacy advertising
- Yes Back Bush's defense budget increase
- Yes Extend 1996 welfare law
- Yes Adopt Bush's discretionary spending limit
- Yes Pass GOP Medicare prescription drug plan
- Yes Create independent Sept. 11 commission
- No Extend union protections to Homeland Security Department employees
- No Revive fast-track procedures for trade agreements
- Yes Authorize war against Iraq
- No Advance bankruptcy overhaul opposed by abortion opponents

2001

- No Nullify Clinton Labor Department ergonomics rule
- Yes Cut taxes by $1.35 trillion through fiscal 2011
- Yes Maintain ban on oil drilling in Arctic National Wildlife Refuge
- Yes Approve Bush proposal to limit managed-care plan liability for coverage decisions
- Yes Divert money from crop subsidy payments to land conservation
- Yes Expand law enforcement power to investigate suspected terrorists

CQ VOTE STUDIES

	PARTY UNITY		PRESIDENTIAL SUPPORT	
	Support	Oppose	Support	Oppose
2002	84%	16%	80%	20%
2001	82%	18%	79%	21%
2000	77%	23%	35%	65%
1999	80%	20%	18%	82%
1998	75%	25%	35%	65%

INTEREST GROUPS

	AFL-CIO	ADA	CCUS	ACU
2002	22%	15%	75%	80%
2001	42%	30%	70%	60%
2000	30%	20%	57%	64%
1999	67%	40%	68%	80%
1998	40%	30%	78%	68%

NEW JERSEY 2

South — Atlantic City, Vineland

One of the state's most politically and economically diverse districts, the 2nd stretches from the Philadelphia suburbs in Gloucester County to the beach communities of Ocean City and Cape May, taking in much of the southern tier of the state. This is a Republican-leaning district, and locals generally support smaller government and oppose gun control. However, Democrats fare well in statewide elections and have a stronghold in south Cumberland County and in some of the district's more industrial towns.

The western corner of the 2nd is largely rural Salem County, home to a nuclear energy plant run by PSEG. The district's center includes Cumberland and Atlantic counties, where farmers' markets and small agrarian communities grow peaches, blueberries, cranberries, tomatoes and soybeans. South Cumberland County is the 2nd's most industrial area, although the economy is shifting from glass and plastics manufacturing to service. The area has been plagued with an unemployment rate higher than the state average.

Tourism is the cash crop in shore communities, where environmental and economic issues are one and the same; the local economy was hit hard when medical waste washed ashore in the late 1980s.

The 2nd includes one of the nation's most well-known gambling resort destinations, Atlantic City, where hotels and casinos create huge numbers of jobs, but where the poorer parts of the city are ravaged by crime and urban blight.

The Delaware River's busy port and one of the nation's largest petroleum centers also contribute to the economy.

MAJOR INDUSTRY

Gambling, tourism, agriculture, petroleum, manufacturing

CITIES

Vineland, 56,271; Atlantic City, 40,517; Millville, 26,847; Bridgeton, 22,771

NOTABLE

The main federal air marshal training facility is in Pomona at Atlantic City International Airport; Delaware Memorial Bridge, the world's longest twin suspension bridge, crosses the Delaware River from Salem County; Cape May Lighthouse, at the southern tip of New Jersey, was built in 1859 and is still in operation.

Rep. H. James Saxton (R)

CAPITOL OFFICE
225-4765
www.house.gov/saxton
339 Cannon 20515-3003; fax 225-0778

COMMITTEES
Armed Services
(Terrorism, Unconventional Threats & Capabilities - chairman)
Resources
Joint Economic - vice chairman

HOMETOWN
Mount Holly

BORN
Jan. 22, 1943, Nicholson, Pa.

RELIGION
Methodist

FAMILY
Divorced; two children

EDUCATION
East Stroudsburg State College, B.A. 1965 (education); Temple U., attended 1967-68 (education)

CAREER
Real estate broker; elementary school teacher

POLITICAL HIGHLIGHTS
N.J. Assembly, 1976-82; N.J. Senate, 1982-84

ELECTION RESULTS

2002 GENERAL		
H. James Saxton (R)	123,375	65.0%
Richard Strada (D)	64,364	33.9%
2002 PRIMARY		
H. James Saxton (R)		unopposed
2000 GENERAL		
H. James Saxton (R)	157,053	57.3%
Susan Bass Levin (D)	112,848	41.2%

PREVIOUS WINNING PERCENTAGES
1998 (62%); 1996 (64%); 1994 (66%); 1992 (59%); 1990 (58%); 1988 (69%); 1986 (65%); 1984 (61%); 1984 Special Election (65%)

Elected 1984; 10th full term

Saxton in the 108th Congress took the gavel of a newly created Armed Services subcommittee on terrorism and other unconventional threats to national security — a potentially high-profile consolation for not being awarded the chairmanship of the Resources Committee.

He is the longest-serving member of Resources without another full committee chairmanship. But in picking new chairmen, the GOP leadership made plain that loyalty and ideology could trump such seniority, and there was never much doubt but that Saxton would be passed over.

He had two strikes against him: where he is from and how he votes. An Easterner on a panel that historically has been chaired by a Westerner, he was viewed by many of his GOP colleagues as much too environmentally friendly. His approval rating from the pro-environment League of Conservation Voters for the 107th Congress was 59 percent; the Californian who was elected chairman instead, Richard W. Pombo, got a score of 9 from the same group. Saxton announced that he would take the Armed Services post and technically dropped out of the race before the GOP Steering Committee met to pick a new chairman.

Spectacled and soft-spoken, Saxton has long had an interest in the role of the military in homeland security. He served as chairman of a special oversight panel on terrorism in the 107th and has become an influential voice on homeland defense.

As chairman of Armed Services' Military Installations Subcommittee in the 107th, Saxton championed more defense spending and advocated expanded roles for the 3rd District's Fort Dix and McGuire Air Force Base to strengthen homeland security. In 2002, he fought against plans for a new commission to recommend base closures — arguing that bases should be retained as assets to fight terrorism. In a compromise, a law was enacted to delay the next round of closures until 2005.

Saxton retains his membership on the Resources panel, where, as one of the GOP's most prominent "greens," he has been willing to fight Western Republicans who favor development over environmental protection and are critical of the Environmental Protection Agency. He is not shy about criticizing the Bush administration for not doing more to reduce air pollution and arsenic levels in drinking water, and the Sierra Club calls him "a steadfast leader" for his defense of wilderness areas, including the Arctic National Wildlife Refuge.

On the committee, Saxton is a proponent for causes important to a constituency that lives in a belt that stretches from the Philadelphia suburbs across Barnegat Bay to the Jersey Shore. In the 107th, he pushed for new time and area restrictions on commercial long-line fishermen to protect migratory white marlin. He won passage of legislation in the 106th directing EPA to develop new standards for pollutants in coastal waters. And he has been a leading advocate for imposing tighter regulations on the noise and water pollution generated by personal watercraft.

He also has opposed property rights activists who sought to scale back the Endangered Species Act. They argued that the law protects wildlife at great cost to landowners and the economy. But Saxton warned that proposals to compensate owners for any sharp drop in land values caused by protecting endangered species would bust the budget.

Saxton keeps to the middle on social policy issues. He generally opposes abortion and has backed legislation to ban a procedure its opponents call "partial birth" abortion. He also opposes allowing federal employees' health plans to cover abortions. But he has backed some gun control measures, including a ban on certain types of assault-style weapons.

A conventional conservative on fiscal policy, Saxton sponsored a bill in the 107th to exclude from an individual's taxable income up to $3,000 in mutual fund capital gains distributions. He pushed for elimination of a requirement that retirees withdraw funds from tax-deferred individual retirement accounts at age 70-and-a-half. As a senior member of the Joint Economic Committee — which he chaired in 2001 and 2002 — he advocates lower taxes on savings and promotes the use of inflation targets by the Federal Reserve when setting monetary rules. He argues that explicit price stability goals will make it easier for the central bank to duplicate practices of Federal Reserve Chairman Alan Greenspan, after he retires. But Greenspan has opposed setting such formal targets.

A staunch advocate for Israel, Saxton in the 107th pushed for passage of a House resolution that supported the Israeli government. On a trip to Israel in 2002, Saxton criticized Palestinian Authority Chairman Yasser Arafat. "He is a motivator of terrorism," Saxton said.

Saxton backed a bill, passed by the House in 1996, aimed at limiting the president's ability to place U.S. troops under U.N. command. "When U.S. lives are at stake, the American public expects and demands that Americans are at the helm," Saxton said. In 1997, he supported setting a deadline for withdrawing U.S. troops from Bosnia.

A former real estate broker and elementary school teacher, Saxton served in the state legislature for eight years before making a bid for the House. In his first race, he struggled to win the nomination for the seat left open in 1984 with the death of another environmentally friendly Republican in the House, Edwin B. Forsythe.

Saxton came into the campaign with support from the strong GOP organization in Burlington County, but he faced Republicans from Ocean and Camden counties as well. Saxton ran ads on Philadelphia TV stations to attract voters in Camden County. After surviving the primary, by drawing support from his large state Senate constituency, he had little trouble winning the general election in what was then a heavily Republican district.

Saxton had his toughest re-election races in 2000, when longtime Cherry Hill Mayor Susan Bass Levin held him to 57 percent, and 1990, when he took just 58 percent against former Cherry Hill City Council member John H. Adler. He won his 10th full term by 31 points in 2002 in a district slightly reconfigured in 2001 but drawn with incumbent protection in mind.

KEY VOTES

2002

No Overhaul campaign finance law; ban "soft money" and restrict advocacy advertising
Yes Back Bush's defense budget increase
Yes Extend 1996 welfare law
Yes Adopt Bush's discretionary spending limit
Yes Pass GOP Medicare prescription drug plan
No Create independent Sept. 11 commission
No Extend union protections to Homeland Security Department employees
Yes Revive fast-track procedures for trade agreements
Yes Authorize war against Iraq
No Advance bankruptcy overhaul opposed by abortion opponents

2001

No Nullify Clinton Labor Department ergonomics rule
Yes Cut taxes by $1.35 trillion through fiscal 2011
Yes Maintain ban on oil drilling in Arctic National Wildlife Refuge
Yes Approve Bush proposal to limit managed-care plan liability for coverage decisions
Yes Divert money from crop subsidy payments to land conservation
Yes Expand law enforcement power to investigate suspected terrorists

CQ VOTE STUDIES

	PARTY UNITY		PRESIDENTIAL SUPPORT	
	Support	Oppose	Support	Oppose
2002	91%	9%	87%	13%
2001	89%	11%	82%	18%
2000	78%	22%	40%	60%
1999	80%	20%	32%	68%
1998	80%	20%	32%	68%

INTEREST GROUPS

	AFL-CIO	ADA	CCUS	ACU
2002	13%	0%	90%	92%
2001	33%	15%	82%	64%
2000	30%	20%	61%	56%
1999	22%	25%	68%	68%
1998	38%	25%	81%	63%

NEW JERSEY 3

South central – Cherry Hill, Toms River

Covering one of New Jersey's oldest and wealthiest areas, the 3rd crosses the south-central section of the state from the southern shores of Ocean County to the Philadelphia suburbs along the Delaware River. It includes most of Burlington County and Cherry Hill in Camden County.

Industrial growth dominates the short strip of land that abuts the Delaware River and encompasses the affluent, Republican-leaning suburbs of Cinnaminson, Delran and Moorestown. Across the district near the Atlantic Ocean, communities around Toms River are concerned that offshore waste disposal and other environmental issues may affect their beach tourist industry. Local officials, most of whom are Republicans, emphasize their "green" credentials.

McGuire Air Force Base and Fort Dix (shared with the 4th District) make defense another salient issue in the 3rd. During the 1990s, the federal government funneled more than $500 million into modernization projects at McGuire, once slated to be closed, including $20 million for a new air terminal.

This politically competitive district has lots of wealthy elderly voters, many of whom live in retirement communities along Route 70, and the lowest percentage of Hispanic residents of any district in the state. Municipal and school budgets, as well as tax rates, are among the lowest in the state — in part because of the high turnout by elderly voters.

MAJOR INDUSTRY

Retail sales, health care, agriculture

MILITARY BASES

McGuire Air Force Base, 5,548 military, 1,419 civilian (2003); Fort Dix (Army), 3,124 military, 1,322 civilian (2001) (shared with the 4th)

CITIES

Toms River (unincorporated), 86,327; Springdale (unincorporated), 14,409; Holiday City-Berkeley (unincorporated), 13,884

NOTABLE

Burlington County, three-fourths of which is in the 3rd District, is the second-largest cranberry-producing county in the nation; Toms River was one of two American teams to win the Little League World Series in the 1990s.

Rep. Christopher H. Smith (R)

CAPITOL OFFICE
225-3765
www.house.gov/chrissmith
2373 Rayburn 20515-3004; fax 225-7768

COMMITTEES
International Relations
Veterans' Affairs - chairman

HOMETOWN
Robbinsville

BORN
March 4, 1953, Rahway, N.J.

RELIGION
Roman Catholic

FAMILY
Wife, Marie Smith; four children

EDUCATION
Trenton State College, B.A. 1975 (business)

CAREER
Sporting goods executive; state anti-abortion group director

POLITICAL HIGHLIGHTS
Republican nominee for U.S. House, 1978

ELECTION RESULTS

2002 GENERAL		
Christopher H. Smith (R)	115,293	66.2%
Mary Brennan (D)	55,967	32.1%
2002 PRIMARY		
Christopher H. Smith (R)		unopposed
2000 GENERAL		
Christopher H. Smith (R)	158,515	63.2%
Reed Gusciora (D)	87,956	35.1%
Stuart Chaifetz (I)	3,627	1.5%

PREVIOUS WINNING PERCENTAGES
1998 (62%); 1996 (64%); 1994 (68%); 1992 (62%); 1990 (63%); 1988 (66%); 1986 (61%); 1984 (61%); 1982 (53%); 1980 (57%)

Elected 1980; 12th term

Smith's ticket to prominence in the House remains his energetic and steadfast opposition to abortion, an issue that provokes battles almost every year. And every time, Smith can be found manning the barricades, whether trying to prevent federal funds from paying for the abortions of poor women, or to keep foreign aid from going to agencies that may counsel women about abortions, or to protect the legal rights of abortion protesters, or to outlaw the procedure that doctors call "dilation and extraction" — but that Smith and his allies describe as "partial birth" abortion.

While President Bush's election marked a victory for Smith's views, it also has meant he is now playing second fiddle to the president as an anti-abortion crusader. Bush's mantra of "compassionate conservatism," however, seems to mesh nicely with Smith's unusual combination of opposition to abortion, support for the causes of labor unions and concern for human rights around the world — a mix that grows from both New Jersey's political realities and Smith's deeply felt Roman Catholic beliefs.

Not surprisingly, Smith has given the president more support than he gave either Bush's father or Ronald Reagan. Still, he has not been afraid to break with the Republican mainstream and the White House — and he did so more often in the 107th Congress than all but a score of other Republicans. He backed Bush only three-quarters of the time and sided with the GOP on party-line votes 87 percent of the time.

Once again in the 107th, it was Smith's unwavering stand against an expansion of abortion rights that led to his most prominent maverick behavior. Virtually single-handedly, he undid a compromise on abortion restrictions on foreign aid reached by appropriators and supported by Secretary of State Colin L. Powell. This forced the president to back Smith's hard-line stance, rather than face the wrath of his anti-abortion base.

And at the end of 2002, Smith triumphed — over the vaunted House GOP whip organization, the White House and even Republican Rep. Henry J. Hyde of Illinois, himself a patron saint of abortion foes — to scuttle a comprehensive overhaul of the nation's bankruptcy laws that had been moving by fits and starts toward enactment since 1997. Abortion opponents, led by Smith, objected to a provision in the compromise bill that would have prevented abortion protesters from filing for federal bankruptcy protection in order to avoid paying court-ordered judgments.

Since the 107th, Smith has chaired the Veterans' Affairs Committee, where he has exhibited the same energy and tenacity that has helped him rise in the House. The panel was previously regarded as a legislative backwater, but under Smith's gavel the committee has helped win new support for veterans issues and Department of Veterans Affairs facilities. He has won congressional backing to boost spending on veterans programs, garnered the largest increase ever for veterans educational funding under the GI bill, and provided new job training opportunities for homeless vets.

Shaken by the Sept. 11, 2001, terrorist attacks and by anthrax-laced letters to Congress believed to have originated in Trenton, in his district, Smith also saw Bush sign a law giving the VA a role in the war on terrorism; the measure calls for establishing four centers at veterans hospitals to research and develop responses to biological, chemical or radiological attacks.

And Smith is eyeing further changes. His ultimate goal is to make a greater percentage of the spending on veterans an entitlement — akin to Social Security or Medicare — meaning it would not be subject to annual review as part of the discretionary appropriations process.

Smith's energetic devotion to veterans issues yields benefits both on and off Capitol Hill. Within the GOP ranks, his leadership on the Veterans' panel has strengthened his bona fides for the job he would ultimately like to hold — chairman of the International Relations Committee, where he is now vice chairman. His advocacy also has yielded benefits at home, where aging veterans are a major constituency.

Veterans' support is another ingredient in a potent political mix that has allowed Smith to win election to the House a dozen times, despite repeated attempts by his political opponents to paint him as so obsessed with abortion that he does not adequately represent other interests. Smith has secured his position with diligent constituent work and careful attention to the needs of blue-collar workers and their unions. On labor matters, the environment and gun control, in fact, Smith often breaks from his party's conservative majority.

Smith was executive director of the New Jersey Right to Life Committee before coming to Congress, at age 27, after defeating 13-term Democrat Frank Thompson Jr., who had been caught up in the Abscam bribery scandal. Ever since, Smith has been working to move federal legislation that would chip away at the constitutional right to abortion guaranteed by the Supreme Court in *Roe v. Wade*. A major victory in that cause — a federal law to outlaw the partial birth abortion procedure — seemed within reach as the 108th Congress began.

As chairman of the International Relations Subcommittee on International Operations and Human Rights from 1995 through 2000, Smith became well-known for his efforts to combat religious persecution abroad. In 1998, he won enactment of a law establishing a federal program to help victims of torture both in the United States and abroad. Smith has continued his human rights work as co-chairman of the Congressional Commission on Security and Cooperation in Europe, an organization set up to monitor the progress of human rights in Europe after the signing of the 1975 Helsinki Final Act between the United States and the Soviet Union.

Smith has a special interest in the rights of children and has sponsored legislation to monitor child labor conditions abroad and crack down on abuses. He often refers in conversation to his own four children, whose photographs are prominently displayed in his congressional office. In the 106th Congress, he won enactment of a law to combat trafficking in women and children, who are often forced into prostitution; the statute also doubled the authorized funding for the Violence Against Women Act.

KEY VOTES

2002

- No Overhaul campaign finance law; ban "soft money" and restrict advocacy advertising
- Yes Back Bush's defense budget increase
- Yes Extend 1996 welfare law
- Yes Adopt Bush's discretionary spending limit
- Yes Pass GOP Medicare prescription drug plan
- Yes Create independent Sept. 11 commission
- No Extend union protections to Homeland Security Department employees
- No Revive fast-track procedures for trade agreements
- Yes Authorize war against Iraq
- No Advance bankruptcy overhaul opposed by abortion opponents

2001

- No Nullify Clinton Labor Department ergonomics rule
- Yes Cut taxes by $1.35 trillion through fiscal 2011
- Yes Maintain ban on oil drilling in Arctic National Wildlife Refuge
- No Approve Bush proposal to limit managed-care plan liability for coverage decisions
- Yes Divert money from crop subsidy payments to land conservation
- Yes Expand law enforcement power to investigate suspected terrorists

CQ VOTE STUDIES

	PARTY UNITY		PRESIDENTIAL SUPPORT	
	Support	Oppose	Support	Oppose
2002	89%	11%	80%	20%
2001	84%	16%	70%	30%
2000	73%	27%	42%	58%
1999	76%	24%	27%	73%
1998	79%	21%	27%	73%

INTEREST GROUPS

	AFL-CIO	ADA	CCUS	ACU
2002	22%	10%	80%	80%
2001	50%	30%	61%	56%
2000	50%	30%	47%	64%
1999	56%	40%	64%	79%
1998	30%	25%	61%	72%

NEW JERSEY 4

Central – part of Trenton, Lakewood

The 4th spreads across the center of the state, where the Garden State begins its transition from South to North Jersey, extending from Trenton and the Delaware River to the Jersey Shore and coastal communities such as Point Pleasant and Spring Lake.

The district includes much of the southern and eastern portions of the state capital, Trenton. Democratic-leaning parts of the city, including largely black neighborhoods, were shifted into the 12th District in redistricting following the 2000 census, making the 4th more Republican and the 12th more Democratic.

Most of Trenton's white residents live in the reconfigured 4th, which includes the historically Italian neighborhood of Chambersburg. But the area is not without diversity. More than 25 percent of the 4th's Trenton population is black, while 30 percent is Hispanic.

The Republican lean of the 4th is strengthened by more-conservative areas in the eastern half of the district. But voters here can exhibit an independent streak in local elections, although they tend to prefer Republicans for federal office.

Military bases are important to the economy, but the district does not rely solely on defense. Trenton and its suburbs have a diverse range of businesses, and the towns along the Jersey Shore in Ocean and Monmouth counties depend heavily on tourism.

MAJOR INDUSTRY
State government, tourism, manufacturing

MILITARY BASES
Fort Dix (Army), 3,124 military, 1,322 civilian (shared with the 3rd); Naval Air Systems Command Lakehurst, 1,105 military, 1,688 civilian (2001)

CITIES
Trenton (pt.), 37,745; Lakewood (unincorporated), 36,065; Mercerville-Hamilton Square (unincorporated), 26,419; Point Pleasant, 19,306

NOTABLE
Trenton, a Revolutionary War battleground, was temporarily the U.S. capital; John A. Roebling and his sons, of Trenton, made the cable for the Brooklyn, Manhattan, George Washington and Golden Gate bridges, among others; An illuminated sign on a bridge over the Delaware River proclaims, "Trenton Makes, The World Takes."

Rep. Scott Garrett (R)

CAPITOL OFFICE
225-4465
www.house.gov/garrett
1641 Longworth 20515-3005; fax 225-9048

COMMITTEES
Budget
Financial Services

HOMETOWN
Wantage

BORN
July 9, 1959, Englewood, N.J.

RELIGION
Protestant

FAMILY
Wife, Mary Ellen Garrett; two children

EDUCATION
Montclair State College, B.A. 1981 (political science); Rutgers U., J.D. 1984

CAREER
Lawyer

POLITICAL HIGHLIGHTS
N.J. Assembly, 1990-2003; sought Republican nomination for U.S. House, 1998, 2000

ELECTION RESULTS

2002 GENERAL		
Scott Garrett (R)	118,881	59.5%
Anne Sumers (D)	76,504	38.3%
Michael J. Cino (LTI)	4,466	2.2%
2002 PRIMARY		
Scott Garrett (R)	16,234	45.0%
David C. Russo (R)	9,299	25.8%
Gerald Cardinale (R)	9,109	25.3%
Akram Yosri Abdelrahman (R)	773	2.1%
Brian Fox (R)	665	1.8%

Elected 2002; 1st term

Garrett is not often ambiguous in advocating deregulation and a winnowing of the federal bureaucracy.

On the first significant legislative vote of his congressional career, Garrett was one of only four House members to oppose enacting a 2003 law extending federal unemployment insurance benefits, saying that he was concerned about the cost. Though he expressed support for the Bush administration's expansive education policies late in his 2002 campaign, he had called for cutting the Education Department in the past.

A social conservative, Garrett opposes abortion and advocates gun owners' rights. And his anti-tax message makes him a favorite of the Club for Growth, a conservative activist group.

His emphasis on fiscal issues helped him win seats on the Budget and Financial Services committees, where he can represent the interests of his many constituents who commute to New York for brokerage and banking jobs. And he was among the first freshmen in the 108th to see a bill he wrote passed by the House; the measure would give the Securities and Exchange Commission emergency powers to suspend or impose regulations to keep the markets functioning in a national emergency.

The decision by moderate Republican Marge Roukema to retire in 2002 after 11 House terms opened the way for the much more conservative Garrett to win election to Congress on his third try. He had lost the GOP nomination to Roukema by 2,000 votes in the 2000 primary and by only 1,700 votes in the 1998 primary.

As a state assemblyman since 1990, Garrett had been a dogged advocate of lower taxes and became a darling of the most conservative faction of the New Jersey GOP. He immediately became the front-runner to succeed Roukema and was easily able to brush aside criticism that he was too far to the right for the suburban to somewhat rural 5th District. He won a five-way primary with 45 percent of the vote, and in November defeated Democrat Anne Sumers, an ophthalmologist, by 19 percentage points.

NEW JERSEY 5

North and west — Bergenfield, Paramus

Taking in the northernmost portion of New Jersey, the 5th is largely suburban and includes some of the most scenic and affluent areas of the state. It stretches from northern Bergen County through parts of Passaic and the hill-enclosed regions of Sussex County, crossing the Appalachian Mountains and running southwest into Warren County. It has the smallest minority population of New Jersey's 13 districts.

Property values and income levels are among the highest in the state, and no municipality here has more than 30,000 residents. About three-fifths of the district's population is in wealthy Bergen County, which includes Saddle River and its multimillion-dollar homes. The scenic back country of Sussex and Warren counties traditionally has been rural but grew about 10 percent in the 1990s as young professionals from New York City moved to the area. Warren County continues to experience significant housing development.

Many businesses make northern New Jersey their home, including Sony Electronics America and the Hertz rental car company in Park Ridge, Toys "R" Us in Paramus and M&M/Mars in Hackettstown.

The 5th tends to vote Republican, though most voters register as independent. GOP strength lies more in the growing western areas than in older Bergen County areas. At the local level, pockets of Democratic strength include Phillipsburg in south Warren County and sections of Bergen County, where races are often close. George W. Bush captured 54 percent of the district's vote in the 2000 presidential election, his second-highest percentage in the state.

MAJOR INDUSTRY
Pharmaceuticals, electronics, shipping

CITIES
West Milford (unincorporated), 26,410; Bergenfield, 26,247; Paramus, 25,737

NOTABLE
President Nixon retired to Park Ridge.

Rep. Frank Pallone Jr. (D)

CAPITOL OFFICE
225-4671
frank.pallone@mail.house.gov
www.house.gov/pallone
420 Cannon 20515-3006; fax 225-9665

COMMITTEES
Energy & Commerce
Resources

HOMETOWN
Long Branch

BORN
Oct. 30, 1951, Long Branch, N.J.

RELIGION
Roman Catholic

FAMILY
Wife, Sarah Pallone; three children

EDUCATION
Middlebury College, B.A. 1973 (history & French);
Tufts U., M.A. 1974 (international relations);
Rutgers U., J.D. 1978

CAREER
Lawyer

POLITICAL HIGHLIGHTS
Long Branch City Council, 1982-88; N.J. Senate, 1984-88

ELECTION RESULTS

2002 GENERAL		
Frank Pallone Jr. (D)	91,379	66.5%
Ric Medrow (R)	42,479	30.9%
Richard D. Strong (GREEN)	1,819	1.3%
2002 PRIMARY		
Frank Pallone Jr. (D)		unopposed
2000 GENERAL		
Frank Pallone Jr. (D)	141,698	67.5%
Brian T. Kennedy (R)	62,454	29.8%
Earl Gray (I)	4,252	2.0%

PREVIOUS WINNING PERCENTAGES
1998 (57%); 1996 (61%); 1994 (60%); 1992 (52%); 1990 (49%); 1988 (52%); 1988 Special Election (52%)

Elected 1988; 8th full term

Pallone is a dogged promoter of his party's positions on the expansion of federal medical insurance and stricter environmental protection. Ambitious and often aggressively partisan, he is an energetic critic of almost all Republican domestic policies and one who is most frequently found on the House floor at the end of the day, speaking out on a wide range of topics after almost all other lawmakers have left the chamber.

Pallone (puh-LOAN) is one of the most ardent Democratic opponents of Republican proposals for adding prescription drug coverage to the benefits under Medicare, the federal health insurance program for the elderly and disabled. He derided as a "sham" the bill the GOP forced through the House in 2002, which would have provided subsidies to private insurers to encourage them to offer coverage to seniors.

As part of the Democratic Party's campaign to rein in the cost of drugs, Pallone pushed legislation to place limits on tax deductions that pharmaceutical companies can take for advertising expenses. And in the 106th Congress, he was one of eight House Democratic negotiators on the patients' rights bill that died at the end of 2000 — a measure supporters say would give patients more leverage in dealing with their insurance companies.

Pallone has served on several party leadership committees, including the Steering and Policy panels, which make committee assignments and advise the leadership on legislation. He has won for himself assignments to a pair of committees that handle a broad swatch of domestic policy — Energy and Commerce and Resources — and he rails at what he sees as injustices done to consumers by powerful business interests, such as insurance companies and industrial polluters. When Democrats want to paint the picture of big business cozying up to Republicans for favors, Pallone is more than willing to help.

In the 107th, when Energy and Commerce took up Medicare drug coverage legislation, Pallone seized the offensive when the Republicans adjourned the drafting session in order to attend a fundraiser cosponsored by a drug maker. If a "Republican is not sure what . . . one of the pharmaceutical companies thinks of a certain amendment," he sneered, "they can simply ask for an opinion tonight over wine and cheese."

Pallone also has been among the Democrats most assertive in portraying the GOP as determined, in his view, "to gut environmental laws" such as the Clean Water Act, the Clean Air Act, the superfund hazardous waste law and the Safe Drinking Water Act. A native of the Jersey Shore town of Long Branch, and as the representative of a significant swath of the coastline, Pallone's top legislative priorities usually include coastal environmental issues, a cause he brought with him to Washington from his days as a member of the state Senate, where he sponsored bills to limit ocean dumping of garbage and sewage sludge.

He has promoted the continuation of the federal program to bulk up the beaches with additional sand. He has opposed plans to mine sand and gravel in the Atlantic — he argued that would hurt marine life — and he and others in the New Jersey delegation have opposed a Bush administration proposal to study the economic and environmental impact of allowing oil drilling off the Jersey coast.

Pallone has called for an end to the use of a gasoline additive, MTBE, that has contaminated drinking water supplies. And he has fought President Bush's attempts to scale back the number of superfund sites in New Jersey.

In the 107th, he was named to the Democrats' environmental policy "rapid response" team. In part because of his concerns about the potential environmental damage from expanded global trade, Pallone has opposed all major trade liberalization laws enacted since his arrival.

He also tends to the interests of the sizable Indian-American community in the 6th District. He is one of the founders of the House India Caucus, along with several other New Jersey lawmakers.

Pallone inherited his political interest from his father, who was a police officer in Long Branch and a longtime activist in local Democratic politics, including the campaigns of Democratic Rep. James J. Howard. Howard urged the younger Pallone, a maritime lawyer, to run for the Long Branch City Council in 1982. Just one year later, Pallone won a state Senate seat.

In March 1988, Howard, who was chairman of the Public Works Committee, died of a heart attack. Many Democratic insiders, including Howard's widow, lined up behind Pallone. In November, he won two elections on the same day — a special election to fill the vacancy and a full term in his own right — each by 5 percentage points.

He has faced several other electoral challenges since. In 1990, Democrats across New Jersey hunkered down, fearing the wrath of voters angry about Democratic Gov. James J. Florio's $2.8 billion tax increase. Pallone's little-known Republican challenger, lawyer Paul A. Kapalko, milked the anti-tax fury for all it was worth, and Pallone survived by only 4,258 votes.

New Jersey lost a House seat in reapportionment for the 1990s, and Pallone's shore-based district was merged with another district anchored inland, in Middlesex County, where Pallone was not as well-known. He got a break when the Democratic incumbent there, Bernard J. Dwyer, retired; but Pallone still had to win a primary against a state legislator that Dwyer had endorsed before going on to notch a 7-point victory in November.

Since then, his re-election margins have been more comfortable. He seriously considered running for the Senate in 2000 but decided against it, partly at the behest of national Democratic leaders, who urged him to seek re-election as part of their push to regain control of the House.

In September 2002, after scandal-plagued Democratic Sen. Robert G. Torricelli pulled out of his re-election race just five weeks before Election Day, Democratic Gov. James E. McGreevey asked Pallone to fill in. Pallone briefly agreed, but demurred within an hour.

Redistricting after the 2000 census, with the lines drawn by a bipartisan commission, protected all the state's incumbents and in 2002 Pallone scored a 36-point victory over Ric Medrow, a historian and journalist.

KEY VOTES

2002

- Yes Overhaul campaign finance law; ban "soft money" and restrict advocacy advertising
- Yes Back Bush's defense budget increase
- No Extend 1996 welfare law
- No Adopt Bush's discretionary spending limit
- No Pass GOP Medicare prescription drug plan
- Yes Create independent Sept. 11 commission
- Yes Extend union protections to Homeland Security Department employees
- No Revive fast-track procedures for trade agreements
- No Authorize war against Iraq
- No Advance bankruptcy overhaul opposed by abortion opponents

2001

- No Nullify Clinton Labor Department ergonomics rule
- No Cut taxes by $1.35 trillion through fiscal 2011
- Yes Maintain ban on oil drilling in Arctic National Wildlife Refuge
- No Approve Bush proposal to limit managed-care plan liability for coverage decisions
- Yes Divert money from crop subsidy payments to land conservation
- Yes Expand law enforcement power to investigate suspected terrorists

CQ VOTE STUDIES

	PARTY UNITY		PRESIDENTIAL SUPPORT	
	Support	Oppose	Support	Oppose
2002	95%	5%	30%	70%
2001	93%	7%	28%	72%
2000	91%	9%	77%	23%
1999	94%	6%	79%	21%
1998	92%	8%	78%	22%

INTEREST GROUPS

	AFL-CIO	ADA	CCUS	ACU
2002	89%	100%	35%	4%
2001	100%	95%	30%	16%
2000	100%	85%	30%	12%
1999	100%	95%	24%	8%
1998	100%	100%	28%	12%

NEW JERSEY 6

East central – New Brunswick, Plainfield, part of Edison

Wedged in the heart of the suburbs south of New York and Newark, the 6th combines industrial communities in Middlesex County with a long, thin stretch that incorporates beach towns in Monmouth County.

Like much of the state, the district was previously politically competitive but has leaned toward Democrats in recent years. Redistricting following the 2000 census added Democratic areas. The 6th now hops the Union County line to take in Plainfield and crosses the Somerset County line to grab most of Somerset. Al Gore captured 64 percent of the revised district's vote in the 2000 presidential election.

In the southwest corner, New Brunswick consolidates two Democratic voting blocs: students from Rutgers University and African-Americans. Nearby Piscataway and the wealthier suburb of Highland Park also favor Democrats. Major area employers include Johnson & Johnson, headquartered in New Brunswick, and Telcordia Technologies, a communications technology firm that has multiple facilities around Piscataway.

Middle-class and independent-voting residents cluster around Edison (shared with the 7th), the district's largest city and home to corporate offices and some manufacturing. Two-thirds of Edison's population lives in the 6th. Exceptionally fast growth in this area after World War II established Middlesex County as the state's leader in industrial growth.

In Monmouth County, the problems of Asbury Park are an exception to the area's generally sunny outlook. Once a vacation site made famous by rocker Bruce Springsteen, the town saw crime grow as the local economy declined.

MAJOR INDUSTRY

Higher education, technology, pharmaceuticals, manufacturing

CITIES

Edison (unincorporated) (pt.), 65,782; New Brunswick, 48,573; Plainfield, 47,829; Sayreville, 40,377; Long Branch, 31,340

NOTABLE

Edison was named after inventor Thomas Edison; The Sandy Hook Light, opened in 1764, is the nation's oldest standing lighthouse.

Rep. Mike Ferguson (R)

CAPITOL OFFICE
225-5361
www.house.gov/ferguson
214 Cannon 20515-3007; fax 225-9460

COMMITTEES
Energy & Commerce

HOMETOWN
Warren

BORN
July 22, 1970, Ridgewood, N.J.

RELIGION
Roman Catholic

FAMILY
Wife, Maureen Ferguson; three children

EDUCATION
U. of Notre Dame, B.A. 1992 (government); Georgetown U., M.P.P. 1995 (education policy)

CAREER
College instructor; education consulting firm owner

POLITICAL HIGHLIGHTS
Republican nominee for U.S. House, 1998

ELECTION RESULTS

2002 GENERAL		
Mike Ferguson (R)	106,055	58.0%
Tim Carden (D)	74,879	40.9%
Darren Young (LIBERT)	2,068	1.1%
2002 PRIMARY		
Mike Ferguson (R)		unopposed
2000 GENERAL		
Mike Ferguson (R)	128,434	51.6%
Maryanne S. Connelly (D)	113,479	45.6%
Jerry L. Coleman (I)	5,444	2.2%

Elected 2000; 2nd term

Ferguson favors boosting federal aid for education and enhancing federal protection of the environment, issues more regularly associated with the other side of the aisle. Yet he is often pigeonholed as a conservative, he says, because of his strong opposition to abortion, even in the case of rape or incest.

"It's unfortunate that if you happen to be conservative on one issue you're labeled a conservative," he once told the Newark Star-Ledger. "I think it's important to look at someone's entire spectrum of positions on issues. In general, I'm a pretty good mix for New Jersey."

At one point Ferguson taught political science at a community college, but he says his brief stint as a history teacher and basketball coach in the Bronx is when he decided he wanted to serve in Congress. He staked out a position as a GOP moderate in his first term and joined the Main Street Partnership, a group that includes about 50 House members whose goal is "to serve as a voice for centrist Republicans." Breaking with President Bush on several key labor and environmental questions, he voted on the House floor the way the president wanted 88 percent of the time — squarely in the middle of the House GOP spectrum for the 107th Congress.

He was among only 34 House Republicans who voted to continue the prohibition on drilling for oil in the Arctic National Wildlife Refuge. He favors better fuel economy for sport utility vehicles, and he pushed for tougher air quality standards for power plants.

Ferguson supports an increase in the minimum wage and approves of the Davis-Bacon prevailing wage standards that apply to workers on federally funded construction projects. He was one of 13 House Republicans who voted against the repeal in 2001 of workplace ergonomics standards issued at the end of the Clinton administration.

The Teamsters union endorsed him in 2002, as did the League of Conservation Voters, which graded his votes in the 107th Congress as a 59; the average score for a House Republican was 17.

But the House GOP leadership and the Bush White House — aware that Ferguson is seeking to succeed in a swath of northern New Jersey where the electorate is split almost down the middle — have not let his occasional transgressions dissuade them from doing what they could to enhance his standing back home. He was given a seat on the powerful Energy and Commerce Committee in the 108th Congress.

Ferguson's wife, Maureen, delivered their third child in February 2003 just a few days after doctors participated in a work slowdown to protest rising malpractice insurance premiums. At about the same time, he signed on as a cosponsor of legislation offered by GOP Rep. James C. Greenwood of Pennsylvania to cap malpractice awards.

Education was at the top of his agenda in his first term. He promoted additional federal aid, including providing more money for Pell Grants for college students and for teacher training and reading programs. He also proposed tax benefits for families to save for their children's education. With Rhode Island Democrat Patrick J. Kennedy, he pushed legislation to more than triple the federal funding for special education programs for students with disabilities.

Ferguson also was able to tout his success in getting federal funds for a number of local projects, including flood control work in Green Brook, revitalization of the historic part of Fanwood, and environmental cleanup in Manville.

Eighty-one people from the 7th District died in the Sept. 11, 2001, terrorist attacks, and Ferguson and his wife visited the families of everyone who died. Ferguson said he told the families he would do everything he could to make sure something like Sept. 11 never happened again.

Ferguson earned a master's degree in education policy. In addition to teaching he has directed a national school reform advocacy group and founded an educational consulting firm. He first ran for the House in 1998 in the neighboring 6th District, where he was helped by the fundraising prowess of his father, politically well-connected public relations executive Thomas Ferguson. Although he spent more than $1 million, he lost to incumbent Democrat Frank Pallone Jr. by almost 17 percentage points.

Far from being discouraged, Ferguson moved to the 7th District after he found out that the incumbent, Republican Bob Franks, was abandoning the seat to run for the Senate in 2000. Ferguson confronted the carpetbagger label directly. "It's because I want to go to Congress, because I want to serve," he said when asked why he was buying a new home. "It's not fun to pack up your family over Christmas and move them in a haphazard way. That's not something anyone would do for fun."

In the campaign Ferguson worked to deflect attention from his views on abortion, presenting a broader picture that emphasized his middle-of-the-road views on other issues. He defeated three rivals — including Tom Kean Jr., son of the former New Jersey governor — for the GOP nomination. In November his Democratic opponent was the former mayor of Fanwood, Maryanne S. Connelly, who had mounted a competitive challenge to Franks in 1998. Ferguson's argument that his views were mainstream helped him to a 6-point win.

At age 30, he was the second-youngest freshman in the 107th Congress; in the 108th, he ranks as the fourth-youngest.

Redistricting in New Jersey after the 2000 census was favorable to all House incumbents, but Ferguson may have benefited the most. The new map gave the 7th some heavily Republican areas. Where the old district had favored Al Gore by 12 percentage points in the 2000 presidential election, voters who live within the boundaries of the new 7th went for George W. Bush by a narrow margin.

Still, Ferguson was identified as one of the most vulnerable GOP lawmakers in 2002, and he received special attention from the White House, including visits with the president. He defeated Democratic businessman Tim Carden by 17 points.

KEY VOTES

2002

- Yes Overhaul campaign finance law; ban "soft money" and restrict advocacy advertising
- Yes Back Bush's defense budget increase
- Yes Extend 1996 welfare law
- Yes Adopt Bush's discretionary spending limit
- Yes Pass GOP Medicare prescription drug plan
- Yes Create independent Sept. 11 commission
- No Extend union protections to Homeland Security Department employees
- Yes Revive fast-track procedures for trade agreements
- Yes Authorize war against Iraq
- No Advance bankruptcy overhaul opposed by abortion opponents

2001

- No Nullify Clinton Labor Department ergonomics rule
- Yes Cut taxes by $1.35 trillion through fiscal 2011
- Yes Maintain ban on oil drilling in Arctic National Wildlife Refuge
- Yes Approve Bush proposal to limit managed-care plan liability for coverage decisions
- Yes Divert money from crop subsidy payments to land conservation
- Yes Expand law enforcement power to investigate suspected terrorists

CQ VOTE STUDIES

	PARTY UNITY		PRESIDENTIAL SUPPORT	
	Support	Oppose	Support	Oppose
2002	87%	13%	88%	12%
2001	87%	13%	88%	12%

INTEREST GROUPS

	AFL-CIO	ADA	CCUS	ACU
2002	11%	5%	85%	84%
2001	33%	20%	87%	58%

NEW JERSEY 7

North central – Woodbridge Township

Beginning in Woodbridge Township near the border with New York City, the 7th meanders west through north central New Jersey, taking in parts of Union, Somerset and Hunterdon counties before reaching the Delaware River on the Pennsylvania border. Many of its residents live in bedroom communities and commute to Newark or New York.

Redistricting following the 2000 census removed Democratic areas such as Plainfield and added wealthy, heavily Republican areas in Somerset and Hunterdon counties. The district now leans Republican, and George W. Bush captured a slight majority of the vote here in the 2000 presidential election. Redistricting decreased the minority population from nearly one-third to about one-fifth.

Although the new, western areas of the district are less densely populated, the entire 7th has experienced some corporate and industrial growth. Parts of Somerset and Hunterdon counties, once dotted by horse farms, have been developed into office parks and shopping malls. Drug manufacturers fuel the economy, led by Merck & Co. in Whitehouse Station. Telecommunications giant Lucent Technologies is based in Murray Hill (Union County).

All four of the district's counties boast long histories, with charters dating back centuries. During the Revolutionary War, New Providence residents dumped the town's supply of salt into a brook to prevent the British from taking it.

The district has several of New Jersey's superfund toxic waste sites, and residents tend to be environmentally conscious. Other important local issues include aircraft noise from nearby Newark Liberty International Airport (in the 10th and 13th districts) and money for infrastructure.

MAJOR INDUSTRY

Pharmaceuticals, manufacturing, telecommunications

CITIES

Edison (unincorporated) (pt.), 31,905; Westfield, 29,644; Union (unincorporated) (pt.), 27,066; Scotch Plains (unincorporated), 22,732

NOTABLE

Gov. James E. McGreevey, elected in 2001, was the longtime mayor of Woodbridge Township.

Rep. Bill Pascrell Jr. (D)

CAPITOL OFFICE
225-5751
bill.pascrell@mail.house.gov
www.house.gov/pascrell
1722 Longworth 20515-3008; fax 225-5782

COMMITTEES
Transportation & Infrastructure
Select Homeland Security

HOMETOWN
Paterson

BORN
Jan. 25, 1937, Paterson, N.J.

RELIGION
Roman Catholic

FAMILY
Wife, Elsie Marie Pascrell; three children

EDUCATION
Fordham U., B.A. 1959 (journalism), M.A. 1961 (philosophy)

MILITARY SERVICE
Army, 1961; Army Reserve, 1962-67

CAREER
City official; teacher

POLITICAL HIGHLIGHTS
Paterson Board of Education, 1977-81 (president, 1981); N.J. Assembly, 1988-97; mayor of Paterson, 1990-97

ELECTION RESULTS

2002 GENERAL		
Bill Pascrell Jr. (D)	88,101	66.8%
Jared Silverman (R)	40,318	30.6%
Joseph A. Fortunato (GREEN)	3,400	2.6%
2002 PRIMARY		
Bill Pascrell Jr. (D)		unopposed
2000 GENERAL		
Bill Pascrell Jr. (D)	134,074	67.0%
Anthony Fusco Jr. (R)	60,606	30.3%
Joseph A. Fortunato (I)	4,469	2.2%

PREVIOUS WINNING PERCENTAGES
1998 (62%); 1996 (51%)

Elected 1996; 4th term

Pascrell grew up in the working-class town of Paterson, now the heart of the territory he represents. It is where his Italian immigrant grandparents had settled. It is where he served as head of the school board, mayor and a state legislator. And it is where he still has his home, a modest house in a middle-class neighborhood. So his claim to being close to the constituency he represents is difficult to refute.

As mayor and in the General Assembly, Pascrell (pass-KRELL) devoted his attention to jobs, public safety and education. In Congress, his legislative priorities have included trade, prescription drug coverage for the elderly, and shoring up Social Security and Medicare. He generally backs Democratic Party positions on matters such as gun control and education funding. But he has voted for tougher penalties for juvenile offenders, a Republican-written overhaul of the nation's public housing system and a ban on the medical procedure described by its opponents as "partial birth" abortion.

Pascrell, who has witnessed an exodus of manufacturing jobs from Paterson over the years, has doggedly opposed ceding congressional authority over trade issues to the executive branch. Citing studies showing that the 1993 North American Free Trade Agreement has caused trade deficits and the loss of more than 3 million American jobs, he voted in the 107th Congress against giving President Bush the power to negotiate trade deals that Congress could approve or reject, but not amend.

And in the 106th Congress, he voted against making permanent China's normalized trade relationship with the United States. "Congress must not hand over its responsibility to 'regulate commerce with foreign nations,' " as dictated by the Constitution, Pascrell wrote in an op-ed piece.

A main focus of Pascrell's congressional career has been steering federal funds to local fire departments. In 2000, he shepherded through Congress a new federal program to direct hundreds of millions of dollars to hire, train and equip local firefighters. He continued his advocacy for firefighters by sponsoring a measure in the 107th to provide federal mortgage assistance to volunteer firefighters. He also introduced a bill that would require colleges receiving federal funds to publish fire safety reports.

A veteran of the Army Reserve, Pascrell sponsored legislation that would require the Veterans Affairs Department to more fully inform veterans of available federal benefits, and a bill that would exempt small businesses owned by recently discharged veterans from paying certain loan fees. He also called for a moment of silence or a public service announcement on radio and television stations at 11 a.m. every Veterans Day, Nov. 11.

After the Sept. 11, 2001, terrorist attacks on the World Trade Center and the Pentagon, Pascrell proposed a bill that would allow taxpayers to designate $3 of their tax liability to fund the federal government's homeland security efforts. He also chaired a House Democratic bioterrorism task force established after the attacks.

In the 108th Congress, building on his task force work, Pascrell won appointment to the new Homeland Security Committee. He had hoped for a seat on Ways and Means, and was energetic in his fund-raising efforts on behalf of other Democrats in 2002, but the continued GOP control of the House limited the openings.

A champion of environmental issues such as the greater use of non-gasoline-powered motor vehicles, Pascrell opposed a natural gas pipeline planned by the Transcontinental Pipeline Co. that would have run through his district, arguing that it was unnecessary and environmentally dangerous.

In 2001, Pascrell helped found the Congressional Brain Injury Task Force, a bipartisan effort to steer federal funding to brain injury research and heighten awareness of the more than a million traumatic brain injuries that occur in the United States every year.

Pascrell, whose father worked for the railroad, was the first member of his family to go to high school, and his neighborhood pals razzed him when he went off to college. He worked his way through Fordham, earning a bachelor's degree in journalism and a master's in philosophy.

Then he embarked on a 12-year career as a high school teacher in neighboring Paramus, interrupted by a stint in the Army. In 1974, he began working for the city of Paterson, first as director of the public works department and then heading up the planning and development office.

At the same time, he got involved in local politics, as a campaign volunteer for Democratic Rep. Robert A. Roe and others. He was appointed to the Paterson Board of Education and was eventually elected its president.

He won a seat in the state General Assembly in 1987 and, as is permitted by New Jersey law, he simultaneously served as mayor of Paterson beginning in 1990. As mayor, Pascrell promoted tough law enforcement measures, particularly in drug trafficking. To make it more difficult for dealers to communicate with their customers, he personally ripped out the lines and receivers of pay telephones that had not been issued a city permit.

In 1996, his New Jersey mayoral colleagues elected him "mayor of the year," a bipartisan honor that he touted as proof of his record in helping Paterson rebound from the loss of manufacturing jobs. He also said his colleagues' support was evidence of his ability to go beyond party politics and work with lawmakers on both sides of the aisle to solve problems.

Pascrell was his party's choice to take on Rep. Bill Martini in 1996, two years after the freshman Republican's narrow victory ended 34 years of Democratic hegemony in the 8th District.

The national party gave Pascrell a boost, inviting him to speak at the 1996 Democratic National Convention, where he offered his views on the role of Congress: "Congress should be about giving people reason to have faith in their government again. It's not about taking from one group and giving to another." The AFL-CIO targeted the race as a key labor battlefield. Pascrell needed every bit of help he could get: He toppled Martini by just 6,200 votes. In acknowledgment of his tenuous hold on the seat, Pascrell immediately began amassing a war chest for 1998 and that dissuaded Martini from running. Pascrell's last three re-election contests have been routine.

KEY VOTES

2002

Yes Overhaul campaign finance law; ban "soft money" and restrict advocacy advertising
Yes Back Bush's defense budget increase
No Extend 1996 welfare law
No Adopt Bush's discretionary spending limit
No Pass GOP Medicare prescription drug plan
Yes Create independent Sept. 11 commission
Yes Extend union protections to Homeland Security Department employees
No Revive fast-track procedures for trade agreements
Yes Authorize war against Iraq
No Advance bankruptcy overhaul opposed by abortion opponents

2001

No Nullify Clinton Labor Department ergonomics rule
No Cut taxes by $1.35 trillion through fiscal 2011
Yes Maintain ban on oil drilling in Arctic National Wildlife Refuge
No Approve Bush proposal to limit managed-care plan liability for coverage decisions
Yes Divert money from crop subsidy payments to land conservation
Yes Expand law enforcement power to investigate suspected terrorists

CQ VOTE STUDIES

	PARTY UNITY		PRESIDENTIAL SUPPORT	
	Support	Oppose	Support	Oppose
2002	89%	11%	48%	52%
2001	87%	13%	37%	63%
2000	84%	16%	66%	34%
1999	86%	14%	80%	20%
1998	86%	14%	70%	30%

INTEREST GROUPS

	AFL-CIO	ADA	CCUS	ACU
2002	100%	90%	50%	12%
2001	100%	95%	39%	20%
2000	100%	75%	35%	20%
1999	100%	95%	25%	18%
1998	100%	95%	33%	16%

NEW JERSEY 8

Northeast — Paterson, Clifton, Passaic

The 8th begins in Pompton Lakes and moves south through the southern part of Passaic County into northern Essex County, extending into parts of Livingston, West Orange and South Orange, just to the west of Newark. The district is a diverse combination of urban centers and suburban towns, and includes Paterson, the state's third-largest city, as well as Clifton and Passaic.

Paterson was once known for silk mills that made it a leading textile producer in the late 19th century. But after labor strife and the introduction of rayon and other materials, the city experienced a serious economic downfall from which it never fully recovered. Today, Paterson suffers from chronic unemployment and poverty.

The district's Essex County portion, by contrast, is mostly suburban, from wealthy Montclair to the blue-collar and middle-class towns of Nutley and Belleville. Italian Catholics make up a large segment of this area, and there also are pockets of Jewish voters in Essex and Passaic counties. Many residents commute into Newark or New York.

The district is politically competitive, but recently its voters have favored Democrats in federal elections. Al Gore won 63 percent of the vote in the 2000 presidential election.

Overall the district is more than one-fourth Hispanic and 13 percent black, but Paterson, home to dozens of ethnic groups, is half Hispanic and nearly one-third black. The city has a deep-seated labor tradition, making it voter-rich territory for Democratic candidates.

MAJOR INDUSTRY

Pharmaceuticals, manufacturing, communications

CITIES

Paterson, 149,222; Clifton, 78,672; Passaic, 67,861; Wayne (unincorporated), 54,069; Bloomfield (unincorporated), 47,683; West Orange (unincorporated) (pt.), 43,835; Belleville (unincorporated), 35,928

NOTABLE

George Washington made his headquarters at Dey Mansion in Wayne during the Revolutionary War for much of the summer and fall of 1780; Samuel Colt patented his first Colt revolver in Paterson and opened his first factory there in 1836; The tough methods principal Joe Clark employed at Eastside High School in Paterson were portrayed by Morgan Freeman in the movie "Lean on Me."

Rep. Steven R. Rothman (D)

CAPITOL OFFICE
225-5061
www.house.gov/rothman
1607 Longworth 20515-3009; fax 225-5851

COMMITTEES
Appropriations

HOMETOWN
Fair Lawn

BORN
Oct. 14, 1952, Englewood, N.J.

RELIGION
Jewish

FAMILY
Divorced; two children

EDUCATION
Syracuse U., B.A. 1974 (political philosophy); Washington U., J.D. 1977

CAREER
Lawyer

POLITICAL HIGHLIGHTS
Mayor of Englewood, 1983-89; Democratic nominee for Bergen County Board of Freeholders, 1989; Bergen County surrogate court judge, 1993-96

ELECTION RESULTS

2002 GENERAL		
Steven R. Rothman (D)	97,108	69.8%
Joseph Glass (R)	42,088	30.2%
2002 PRIMARY		
Steven R. Rothman (D)		unopposed
2000 GENERAL		
Steven R. Rothman (D)	140,462	67.9%
Joseph Tedeschi (R)	61,984	30.0%
Lewis Pell (I)	2,273	1.1%

PREVIOUS WINNING PERCENTAGES
1998 (65%); 1996 (56%)

Elected 1996; 4th term

Rothman's densely populated district lies across the Hudson River from Manhattan and, like the rest of suburban New York, it suffers from pollution and congestion. A quiet and diligent lawmaker, Rothman wants to use his seat on the Appropriations Committee to help reduce the noise and traffic that cross the river into northern New Jersey.

In the 107th Congress, Rothman worked to obtain hundreds of millions of dollars for the New York-New Jersey area to restore and expand commuter rail and ferry service in the aftermath of the Sept. 11, 2001, terrorist attacks, which crippled the tangled web of mass transit systems that had converged around the World Trade Center. He also helped obtain money for light rail projects in Bergen County, particularly the Hudson-Bergen mass transit project, and for a variety of highway improvements.

Rothman has been a leader in a longstanding local battle against aircraft noise at the bustling Teterboro Airport. Convenient to Manhattan, the airport handles about 500 flights a day, many of them corporate jets. He has offered a range of solutions, including mandating an evening curfew on arrivals and departures, soundproofing area schools and requiring corporate jets to switch to new, quieter engines. In 2002, he announced he finally had succeeded in banning the noisiest and largest of the private jets that use the airfield. Rothman also used his Appropriations seat to gain approval of $12.5 million for the Federal Aviation Administration to redesign metropolitan New York aviation routes.

He also has weighed in against train noise, offering a bill to give local authorities more clout in stopping locomotives from idling. Arguing early in his House career for more federal highway and mass transit money for New Jersey, Rothman took a swipe at conservatives who begrudge those dollars but support other spending to benefit their own districts. "We don't have many military bases, we don't have hurricanes and other natural disasters, but we have traffic nightmares . . . and a decaying infrastructure. Our roads and transit systems are our disasters, and the country has an obligation to support us in rebuilding them," he said.

Another of Rothman's goals is the preservation of the remaining 8,400 acres of undeveloped land in the Meadowlands, by the stadium where the Giants and Jets play their National Football League home games. He would like to see the land become a park, with bird-watching platforms and nature trails throughout the wetlands. He obtained some federal money to begin buying the land, and he also has arranged for several federal agencies to study the feasibility of protecting the rest, which otherwise would be a prime target for development.

Inspired in the 106th Congress by a request from a middle school in his district, Rothman wrote the law that established a federal-local matching program to pay for metal detectors, security cameras or other safety precautions to keep guns out of schools. "The fact that we have to discuss metal detectors in schools at all sends a signal that our society has become too violent and that children have too easy access to guns," he said. His "secure our schools" proposal has received $5 million in each of its first two years.

Rothman votes with the majority of his party on issues such as abortion rights, environmental protection, gun control and expanded medical care for the uninsured. He has, however, made an occasional foray into Republican territory. He was in the minority of Democrats who voted in favor of a constitutional amendment to ban desecration of the U.S. flag. "People can find plenty of ways to denigrate this country and still maintain their freedom of speech, but they can do it without desecrating the flag," Rothman told a veterans gathering.

Rothman served for three years as a Bergen County surrogate court judge and has voted with the GOP on occasion to require tougher treatment in the courts of violent juvenile offenders. He supports the death penalty.

During the 107th Congress, he joined with Republican Thomas M. Davis III of Virginia in offering legislation to overhaul the administration of elections. Some of the provisions were incorporated in the election overhaul that became law in 2002.

Rothman is described by his colleagues as soft-spoken and thoughtful, a noticeable demeanor on the often partisan and argumentative Judiciary Committee, where Rothman served during his first two terms. During the panel's impeachment proceedings against President Clinton in 1998, Rothman won recognition by both sides as a voice of calm and reason. He did not excuse the president's behavior in the sex and coverup scandal that led to his impeachment, but he was critical of the extensive investigation of the president by special counsel Kenneth W. Starr.

An assessment of Rothman offered midway through his first term by California Democratic Rep. Cal Dooley still applies. Dooley, a leader of the New Democrat Coalition of moderate Democrats — to which Rothman belongs — told The Bergen Record newspaper that Rothman is the type of lawmaker who will "get underneath the hood and get their hands dirty and really get things done."

Rothman was born in Englewood. After leaving New Jersey for college and law school, he returned in 1978 to practice law. He immediately got involved in local Democratic Party politics. In 1983, he won the Englewood mayoralty and served in that post, working to balance the city's budget and reduce crime. He gave up the job in 1989, when he ran instead in an unsuccessful bid for Bergen County freeholder, or councilman.

His won his next campaign, for the Surrogate Court judgeship, in 1993. But he gave up that job to run for Congress in 1996, when he won the Democratic organization's backing to succeed Robert G. Torricelli — who was giving up his House seat that year for his quest to succeed the retiring Democrat Bill Bradley in the Senate.

Rothman has won more-lopsided victories three times since then. In 2002, in a solidly Democratic territory left largely alone during the redistricting process, he took 70 percent against Republican telecommunications firm marketing executive Joe Glass.

KEY VOTES

2002

Yes Overhaul campaign finance law; ban "soft money" and restrict advocacy advertising
Yes Back Bush's defense budget increase
No Extend 1996 welfare law
No Adopt Bush's discretionary spending limit
No Pass GOP Medicare prescription drug plan
Yes Create independent Sept. 11 commission
Yes Extend union protections to Homeland Security Department employees
No Revive fast-track procedures for trade agreements
Yes Authorize war against Iraq
Yes Advance bankruptcy overhaul opposed by abortion opponents

2001

No Nullify Clinton Labor Department ergonomics rule
No Cut taxes by $1.35 trillion through fiscal 2011
Yes Maintain ban on oil drilling in Arctic National Wildlife Refuge
No Approve Bush proposal to limit managed-care plan liability for coverage decisions
Yes Divert money from crop subsidy payments to land conservation
Yes Expand law enforcement power to investigate suspected terrorists

CQ VOTE STUDIES

	PARTY UNITY		PRESIDENTIAL SUPPORT	
	Support	Oppose	Support	Oppose
2002	87%	13%	32%	68%
2001	91%	9%	27%	73%
2000	89%	11%	80%	20%
1999	89%	11%	82%	18%
1998	87%	13%	83%	17%

INTEREST GROUPS

	AFL-CIO	ADA	CCUS	ACU
2002	89%	95%	42%	12%
2001	100%	85%	26%	13%
2000	100%	90%	38%	12%
1999	89%	100%	28%	4%
1998	100%	100%	29%	8%

NEW JERSEY 9

Northeast – Hackensack, part of Jersey City

Across the Hudson River from northern Manhattan, the 9th is a predominantly wealthy district, but it falls in the middle of New Jersey's generally affluent suburbs. The most prestigious neighborhoods lie to the north, including Englewood and Fort Lee. High rises have sprung up along the river for New York City commuters. The district becomes more middle-class and blue-collar as it runs south into Lyndhurst and Jersey City.

Redevelopment has strengthened this district's already solid economy. Anchored by the Meadowlands Sports Complex in East Rutherford, the southern part of the district has seen increased commercial and residential development. But concerns about wetlands preservation have kept growth at a moderate pace. Lipton is based in Englewood Cliffs in the district's northeast corner.

With a strong Hispanic population around Jersey City (shared with the 10th and 13th) and a sizable proportion of black and Asian voters, Democrats far outnumber Republicans. In the district's southern areas, the working-class towns of North Arlington, Lyndhurst and Kearny (shared with the 13th) provide a strong Democratic vote. The large population of Jewish voters in the northern towns of Teaneck and Fair Lawn also supports Democrats. Bergen County as a whole tends to lean Republican, though several of the older, affluent towns in the county have a history of Democratic voting. Al Gore took nearly two-thirds of the 9th's vote in the 2000 presidential election.

MAJOR INDUSTRY

Manufacturing, health care, shipping, stadium events

CITIES

Jersey City (pt.), 58,129; Hackensack, 42,677; Teaneck (unincorporated), 39,260; Kearny (pt.), 38,250; Fort Lee, 35,461; Fair Lawn, 31,637

NOTABLE

The Meadowlands Sports Complex includes Continental Airlines Arena, Giants Stadium and Meadowlands Racetrack, which play host to football, basketball, hockey, soccer, horse racing and concerts; Teterboro Airport is home to the Aviation Hall of Fame and Museum of New Jersey; The George Washington Bridge crosses the Hudson River into Manhattan from Fort Lee; The New Jersey Naval Museum is in Hackensack.

Rep. Donald M. Payne (D)

Elected 1988; 8th term

CAPITOL OFFICE
225-3436
donald.payne@mail.house.gov
www.house.gov/payne
2209 Rayburn 20515-3010; fax 225-4160

COMMITTEES
Education & Workforce
International Relations

HOMETOWN
Newark

BORN
July 16, 1934, Newark, N.J.

RELIGION
Baptist

FAMILY
Widowed; three children

EDUCATION
Seton Hall U., B.A. 1957 (social studies)

CAREER
Computer forms company executive; company community affairs director; high school teacher

POLITICAL HIGHLIGHTS
Essex County Board of Freeholders, 1972-78; sought Democratic nomination for Essex County executive, 1978; sought Democratic nomination for U.S. House, 1980; Newark Municipal Council, 1982-88; sought Democratic nomination for U.S. House, 1986

ELECTION RESULTS

2002 GENERAL		
Donald M. Payne (D)	86,433	84.5%
Andrew Wirtz (R)	15,913	15.6%
2002 PRIMARY		
Donald M. Payne (D)	33,851	84.1%
Edward A. Allen (D)	3,583	8.9%
Edmund Proctor (D)	2,818	7.0%
2000 GENERAL		
Donald M. Payne (D)	133,073	87.5%
Dirk B. Weber (R)	18,436	12.1%

PREVIOUS WINNING PERCENTAGES
1998 (84%); 1996 (84%); 1994 (76%); 1992 (78%); 1990 (81%); 1988 (77%)

Payne is generally a low-key operator, working out of the spotlight on issues of importance to his constituents and trying to chip away at Republican legislation that would limit government programs for the poor.

"I would not call myself electrifying," he said a decade ago about his subdued style. "But I think there is a lot of dignity in being able to achieve things without having to create rapture."

Still, Payne does not always avoid publicity. In 2001, he chained himself to the gates of the Sudanese embassy to protest that country's brutal civil war, which has killed an estimated 2 million people and displaced 4 million others. That is part of a very public crusade Payne has helped lead to impose new sanctions on the predominantly Muslim government in Khartoum, which has been accused of tolerating slavery, bombing innocent civilians and cutting off food aid shipments in a decades-old conflict against Christians and animists in Sudan's south.

Payne's high-profile efforts on Sudan reflect his ability to vary his tactics to advance his legislative agenda. But it also shows the passionate commitment he has long held for Africa. He serves as the top Democrat on International Relations' Africa Subcommittee, travels regularly to the continent and has pushed administration after administration to pay more attention to relations with the continent and provide more aid to the region.

As part of his efforts to keep the United States engaged in Africa, he has worked hard to defend his panel's turf. During the spate of committee downsizing begun by the Democrats in the 103rd Congress and continued by the Republicans in the 104th, Payne was a key figure in the successful effort to maintain the Africa Subcommittee as a distinct entity. During the 107th, he objected when Republicans chose to have Egypt — the largest recipient of aid on the continent — fall under the jurisdiction of the Middle East and South Asia Subcommittee instead of his panel.

Payne's behind-the-scenes influence reached a high point during Bill Clinton's presidency. He persuaded Clinton to travel to Africa and accompanied him on a 1998 visit to the continent, and in 2000 he helped in the negotiations that led to enactment of a law expanding trade with the nations of sub-Saharan Africa.

Under President Bush, Payne does not enjoy the same access to the White House, but he still works patiently on traditional Democratic social programs such as education, labor and human rights, and on police treatment of minorities. He has brought his concern for human rights to domestic issues as well, deploring police brutality, racial profiling and the burning of black churches.

He remains one of the most liberal members of the House; in the 107th he opposed Bush 86 percent of the time, the second most of any House Democrat. From his seat on the Education and the Workforce Committee, Payne has fought to continue the practice of targeting federal funds to low-income districts, in the face of Republican plans to give states more flexibility in deciding how to spend the money. He argues that the nation's great economic prosperity "has not spread to our inner cities," and that the government should not be abandoning its responsibilities to help all its citizens in the rush to balance the budget.

Payne's strategy of quiet persuasiveness faced one its biggest tests in 1995, when he became chairman of the Congressional Black Caucus just as the newly in control GOP cut off congressional funding for such caucuses. Payne helped raise money privately to maintain caucus operations.

Payne credits much of his own success in life to an organization known as The Leaguers, and to its founders, Reynold and Mary Burch, both leading members of the Newark black community. Burch used her contacts with Seton Hall University to help Payne win a four-year scholarship to the school. Payne was the first president of The Leaguers, which celebrated its 50th anniversary in 1999. The group's goals are to provide Newark inner-city teenagers with encouragement, education and work opportunities, and social outlets.

A high school history teacher and football coach after college, Payne moved into business in 1963 as community affairs director for the Newark-based Prudential Insurance Co. Later, he was vice president of a computer forms company founded by his brother.

The head of a "storefront YMCA" in Newark in the late 1950s, Payne became the first black president of the National Council of YMCAs in 1970 and later served two four-year terms as chairman of the YMCA's International Committee on Refugees. While participating in these activities, the widowed Payne was raising his three children and building his political career. He served six years as an Essex County freeholder, essentially a county councilman, and another six on the Newark Municipal Council.

Perseverance enabled Payne to pull himself up from poverty, and it also took perseverance — three campaigns — to win election in the black-majority 10th District. His path was blocked by the legendary Democrat Peter W. Rodino Jr., who had held the seat since 1949. As chairman of the Judiciary Committee, Rodino had achieved fame during the 1974 impeachment proceedings against President Nixon, but it was Rodino's steadfast advocacy of civil rights legislation that earned him the votes of the district's blacks.

Nevertheless, Payne tried in 1980 and 1986 to unseat Rodino, arguing that a black person could better represent the district and that Rodino was a roadblock to black political advancement. Jesse L. Jackson campaigned for Payne in 1986, arguing that Payne "has a kinship with this community [Rodino] does not have." But Rodino won the primary with 59 percent.

When Rodino decided to retire in 1988, party officials got behind Payne. His only opposition came in the Democratic primary from city council colleague Ralph T. Grant Jr. But Payne's advantages — party support, a sizable campaign treasury and name recognition — easily brought him the nomination. Payne's November victory was a formality in this overwhelmingly Democratic district, making him the first black representative from New Jersey. He has won easily ever since.

KEY VOTES

2002

Yes	Overhaul campaign finance law; ban "soft money" and restrict advocacy advertising
No	Back Bush's defense budget increase
No	Extend 1996 welfare law
No	Adopt Bush's discretionary spending limit
No	Pass GOP Medicare prescription drug plan
Yes	Create independent Sept. 11 commission
Yes	Extend union protections to Homeland Security Department employees
No	Revive fast-track procedures for trade agreements
No	Authorize war against Iraq
No	Advance bankruptcy overhaul opposed by abortion opponents

2001

No	Nullify Clinton Labor Department ergonomics rule
No	Cut taxes by $1.35 trillion through fiscal 2011
Yes	Maintain ban on oil drilling in Arctic National Wildlife Refuge
No	Approve Bush proposal to limit managed-care plan liability for coverage decisions
Yes	Divert money from crop subsidy payments to land conservation
No	Expand law enforcement power to investigate suspected terrorists

CQ VOTE STUDIES

	PARTY UNITY		PRESIDENTIAL SUPPORT	
	Support	Oppose	Support	Oppose
2002	98%	2%	16%	84%
2001	98%	2%	12%	88%
2000	97%	3%	86%	14%
1999	97%	3%	88%	12%
1998	97%	3%	89%	11%

INTEREST GROUPS

	AFL-CIO	ADA	CCUS	ACU
2002	100%	90%	30%	0%
2001	100%	100%	22%	0%
2000	100%	95%	33%	0%
1999	89%	100%	21%	0%
1998	100%	90%	20%	9%

NEW JERSEY 10

Northeast – parts of Newark and Jersey City

Covering a multiracial, urban region centered in Newark, the black-majority 10th provides a solid base for Democrats. Outside Newark (which is shared with the 13th), the district extends into Essex County's working-class suburbs of Irvington, East Orange and Orange. Largely blue-collar and packed with minorities, the district's cities contribute to its Democratic leanings. It takes in portions of Jersey City (shared with the 9th and 13th districts) and Elizabeth (shared with the 13th).

The 10th's portion of Newark is made up of the largely black central, south and west wards of the city. The central ward was decimated in the 1967 riots and never fully recovered. The decade after the riots saw a steep decline in the number of jobs and an increase in the number of departing whites. As the Irish and Italians headed to the suburbs, blacks became a majority and grabbed the reins of power at City Hall; African-Americans have held the mayoralty since 1970.

Although deep poverty continues to be a problem in some spots, efforts to revitalize the area have had some success. An infusion of new housing is helping some of Newark's worst neighborhoods. The population exodus largely has ceased, and the city has several major employers, including Prudential Financial. A large performing arts center that opened in 1997 is helping, as are new retail outlets in Essex County. Newark Liberty International Airport (a small part of which is in the 13th) is a transportation hub for travelers to New York City and is home to large Continental Airlines facilities that employ thousands of residents. Port Newark-Elizabeth (in the 13th) also provides jobs for the region.

The district votes consistently Democratic at all levels, though Rahway and Roselle include some Republicans. Bill Clinton won by comfortable margins in the 1992 and 1996 presidential contests, and Al Gore topped 80 percent, his statewide high, here in 2000.

MAJOR INDUSTRY
Aviation, shipping, insurance, higher education, pharmaceuticals

CITIES
Newark (pt.), 155,413; Elizabeth (pt.), 74,984; East Orange, 69,824; Jersey City (pt.), 63,725; Irvington (unincorporated), 60,695

NOTABLE
Thomas Edison's first shop opened in Newark in 1871.

Rep. Rodney Frelinghuysen (R)

CAPITOL OFFICE
225-5034
rodney.frelinghuysen@mail.house.gov
www.house.gov/frelinghuysen
2442 Rayburn 20515-3011; fax 225-3186

COMMITTEES
Appropriations
(District of Columbia - chairman)

HOMETOWN
Harding

BORN
April 29, 1946, Manhattan, N.Y.

RELIGION
Episcopalian

FAMILY
Wife, Virginia T. Frelinghuysen; two children

EDUCATION
Hobart College, B.A. 1969; Trinity College (Conn.), attended 1971 (American history)

MILITARY SERVICE
Army, 1969-71

CAREER
County board aide

POLITICAL HIGHLIGHTS
Morris County Board of Freeholders, 1974-83 (director, 1980); sought Republican nomination for U.S. House, 1982; N.J. Assembly, 1983-94; sought Republican nomination for U.S. House, 1990

ELECTION RESULTS

2002 GENERAL		
Rodney Frelinghuysen (R)	132,938	72.4%
Vij Pawar (D)	48,477	26.4%
Richard S. Roth (LIBERT)	2,263	1.2%
2002 PRIMARY		
Rodney Frelinghuysen (R)		unopposed
2000 GENERAL		
Rodney Frelinghuysen (R)	186,140	68.0%
John P. Scollo (D)	80,958	29.6%
John Pickarski (I)	5,199	1.9%

PREVIOUS WINNING PERCENTAGES
1998 (68%); 1996 (66%); 1994 (71%)

Elected 1994; 5th term

Frelinghuysen's voting record in the 107th Congress shows he took a step to the right — moving from the more liberal end of the Republican spectrum to a position closer to the party mainstream.

In the 106th Congress, he broke ranks with his party more often than all but six of his colleagues. In the 107th, his party unity score on votes that pitted the two parties against each other placed him squarely in the middle ranks of the GOP. Many special interest groups, ranging from the National Taxpayers Union to the American Federation of Teachers to the NAACP, also ranked Frelinghuysen (FREE-ling-high-zen) as more conservative in the 107th Congress than in the 106th.

Frelinghuysen insists, however, that his views have not changed despite the shift in his voting record. He is still moderate on many social issues such as the environment, gun control and abortion, and more conservative on taxes, labor issues, trade and welfare. Frelinghuysen's staff suggests that with a Republican in the White House, the votes were more often presented in terms that emphasized the congressman's core GOP beliefs.

In the 108th Congress, he became one of the Appropriations Committee's 13 "cardinals" — the subcommittee chairmen in charge of drafting the annual spending bills. Frelinghuysen chairs the District of Columbia spending bill, which generally goes to the newest cardinal.

Frelinghuysen has always been more moderate on environmental regulations than most of his GOP colleagues — an issue that resonates with his upscale, suburbanite constituents. In the 107th, he continued to place pollution and hazardous waste cleanup and beach and wetlands protection at the top of his legislative agenda.

He has been particularly interested in preserving the Highlands, areas of mountainous and scenic watershed lands throughout northern New Jersey, New York and Connecticut. The federal purchase of lands in the Sterling Forest in 1996 was due to his efforts, and in the 107th, Frelinghuysen won additional federal money to set aside more of the Highlands. Also in the 107th, from his seat on the Appropriations Committee, Frelinghuysen secured funds for an updated Forest Service study on Highlands conservation. He was among only a half-dozen Republicans who won early 2002 re-election endorsements from the League of Conservation Voters.

As the only Republican from New Jersey on the Appropriations Committee, he is responsible for carrying water for his Garden State colleagues. Frelinghuysen, who at one time chaired the New Jersey Assembly's Appropriations Committee, has pursued federal dollars for local mass transit projects, New York Harbor dredging and changes in Veterans Affairs Department funding formulas to direct more health care spending to New Jersey. He sits on the panel's Defense Subcommittee where he keeps a watchful eye on the Army's Picatinny Arsenal in his district. He also has seats on the subcommittees that fund the Pentagon and energy and water project spending.

Even before the Sept. 11, 2001, terrorist attacks and the spread of anthrax through the mail, Frelinghuysen emphasized the possible threat of terrorism as the impetus for more spending at New Jersey's military establishments, including "smart" weapons research at the Picatinny Arsenal and communications research at Fort Monmouth. In the 106th and 107th, he was able to get federal funds for bioterrorism defense efforts in New Jersey with the money directed at research and the training of emergency personnel.

Frelinghuysen has made consumer privacy one of his top issues, whether it is protecting personal information consumers provide in Internet transactions or requiring cell phone users' consent for the location of their calls to be tracked. He also wants to stop telemarketers from blocking consumers' caller identification devices.

In 2002, Frelinghuysen led the fight to preserve one of the oldest trees on the Capitol grounds, an English elm that was endangered by work on a new visitors center.

He could argue that some of his ancestors may well have enjoyed the shade of that ancient English elm: The Frelinghuysen family has a long record of public service stretching back to the Revolutionary War era. Six Frelinghuysens have served in Congress. The first was in the Continental Congress; another also was secretary of state; one ran for vice president on a ticket with Henry Clay; and one was Frelinghuysen's father, Peter, who served in the House for 22 years, until 1975.

Noting that he was 6 years old when his father first ran for Congress, Frelinghuysen observed in a newspaper interview that, "A lot of what you do in life is the direct result of those who bring you up. It either drives you toward this life or drives you away." More interested in governing than in ideological purity, he decries the practice of "damning the institution of Congress."

Frelinghuysen started his political career after college and a stint in the Army during the Vietnam War by going to work for Dean Gallo, then a Morris County freeholder and later a member of the House. Frelinghuysen became a freeholder himself in 1974. In 1982, he lost a GOP primary for the 12th District seat, but in 1983, he won a state Assembly seat. In 1990, he failed again in a contest for the 12th District, running third in the Republican primary won by Dick Zimmer, who went on to serve three terms in the House.

When Frelinghuysen finally won election to the House in 1994, victory was bittersweet, because it followed the death of his friend and mentor Gallo. Ill health had forced Gallo in August 1994 to abandon his campaign for a sixth term. Gallo anointed Frelinghuysen, who had been managing the re-election bid, as his successor.

After New Jersey GOP insiders overwhelmingly ratified Gallo's choice at a special nominating convention, Frelinghuysen sailed to victory in the Republican-dominated 11th. Gallo died two days before the November election, which Frelinghuysen won with 71 percent over Democrat Frank Herbert, a former state senator. He has easily won re-election since then, although there has been some talk of a challenge from the conservative wing of the GOP.

KEY VOTES

2002

Yes Overhaul campaign finance law; ban "soft money" and restrict advocacy advertising
Yes Back Bush's defense budget increase
Yes Extend 1996 welfare law
Yes Adopt Bush's discretionary spending limit
Yes Pass GOP Medicare prescription drug plan
Yes Create independent Sept. 11 commission
No Extend union protections to Homeland Security Department employees
Yes Revive fast-track procedures for trade agreements
Yes Authorize war against Iraq
Yes Advance bankruptcy overhaul opposed by abortion opponents

2001

Yes Nullify Clinton Labor Department ergonomics rule
Yes Cut taxes by $1.35 trillion through fiscal 2011
Yes Maintain ban on oil drilling in Arctic National Wildlife Refuge
Yes Approve Bush proposal to limit managed-care plan liability for coverage decisions
Yes Divert money from crop subsidy payments to land conservation
Yes Expand law enforcement power to investigate suspected terrorists

CQ VOTE STUDIES

	PARTY UNITY		PRESIDENTIAL SUPPORT	
	Support	Oppose	Support	Oppose
2002	84%	16%	85%	15%
2001	89%	11%	88%	12%
2000	73%	27%	48%	52%
1999	69%	31%	45%	55%
1998	77%	23%	37%	63%

INTEREST GROUPS

	AFL-CIO	ADA	CCUS	ACU
2002	11%	15%	95%	80%
2001	0%	20%	91%	60%
2000	10%	25%	71%	56%
1999	11%	40%	68%	48%
1998	10%	10%	83%	52%

NEW JERSEY 11

North central – Morris County

Exclusive, pastoral estates and Fortune 500 firms make the 11th one of the most privileged districts in the nation. Located in northern New Jersey and centered in Morris County, the district has the nation's second-highest median income. Its voters tend to be socially moderate, family-centered and ardently fiscally conservative, and the 11th is one of the most solidly Republican districts in the northeast. George W. Bush captured 56 percent of the vote here in the 2000 presidential election, his highest total in the state.

Downsizing in the telecommunications industry increased the amount of empty office space in Morris County. But overall the district's office market is still strong. Corporate giants AT&T (in Basking Ridge), Nabisco (in East Hanover), Honeywell (in Morristown) and BASF (in Mount Olive) have facilities here. Pharmaceutical companies have found the 11th particularly attractive, with Pfizer (Morris Plains) and Novartis (East Hanover) basing major operations in the district and Wyeth headquartered in Madison.

In addition to all of Morris County, the district takes in chunks of Essex County in the east, Somerset County in the south, Sussex County in the northwest and a sliver of Passaic County in the northeast.

Some district residents commute to Manhattan, but the region's attractiveness to large employers and high-paying white-collar jobs means fewer residents are leaving the area for work. Dover's Picatinny Arsenal experienced some cutbacks in the 1990s, but appears to be safe from further cuts.

MAJOR INDUSTRY
Pharmaceuticals, finance, telecommunications, manufacturing

MILITARY BASES
Picatinny Arsenal (Army), 89 military, 3,385 civilian (2003)

CITIES
Morristown, 18,544; Dover, 18,188; Madison, 16,530; Livingston (unincorporated), 16,224

NOTABLE
Morristown National Historical Park, the first national historic park established by the federal government, includes George Washington's 1779-80 Revolutionary War headquarters.

Rep. Rush D. Holt (D)

CAPITOL OFFICE
225-5801
holt.house.gov
1019 Longworth 20515-3012; fax 225-6025

COMMITTEES
Education & Workforce
Select Intelligence

HOMETOWN
Hopewell

BORN
Oct. 15, 1948, Weston, W.Va.

RELIGION
Quaker

FAMILY
Wife, Margaret Lancefield; three children

EDUCATION
Carleton College, B.A. 1970; New York U., M.S. 1980, Ph.D. 1981 (physics)

CAREER
University research assistant director; physics professor

POLITICAL HIGHLIGHTS
Sought Democratic nomination for U.S. House, 1996

ELECTION RESULTS

2002 GENERAL		
Rush D. Holt (D)	104,806	61.0%
DeForest Soaries (R)	62,938	36.7%
Carl J. Mayer (GREEN)	1,871	1.1%
2002 PRIMARY		
Rush D. Holt (D)		unopposed
2000 GENERAL		
Rush D. Holt (D)	146,162	48.7%
Dick Zimmer (R)	145,511	48.5%
Carl J. Mayer (I)	5,811	1.9%

PREVIOUS WINNING PERCENTAGES
1998 (50%)

Elected 1998; 3rd term

"My congressman *is* a rocket scientist," proclaim the bumper stickers that Holt supporters hand out. Actually, the congressman says, he is more of an energy scientist. As the former assistant director of the Princeton Plasma Physics Laboratory, he researched alternative energy sources.

Either way, Holt is one of the few elected scientists in Washington, and he believes Congress could use more of them. "With all due respect to lawyers, we need more diversity among legislators," he once told The New York Times. "It's not that scientists have a corner on the truth, but a science background is important for understanding the limitations of some policies . . . to define what is possible."

Holt's doctoral dissertation was on the outer layer of the sun. He holds a patent for improving the efficiency of solar ponds, a source of thermal energy. He says he picked up his interest in science at an early age from his mother, who earned a master's degree in zoology and taught science at a junior college. She also was a West Virginia legislator and served two years as the state's secretary of state.

His father, Rush Dew Holt Sr., was active in West Virginia politics for all of his adult life and served a total of 13 years as a state legislator. But he reached the pinnacle of his career early on: Elected to the Senate in 1934 at age 29, he had to wait six months to be sworn in because, under the Constitution, senators must be 30 years old. (He was defeated for renomination to a second term.)

The younger Holt was a Congressional Science Fellow in the office of Pennsylvania Democratic Rep. Bob Edgar in the early 1980s and consulted with the State Department on arms control, space activities and international science. He says that his impetus for running for office was a distaste for the "shortsightedness and mean-spiritedness of the Gingrich Congress." He told the Newark Star-Ledger that one of his goals in Congress would be "to restore trust in government, to take a less cynical view of politics."

Not surprisingly, Holt's legislative agenda includes placing a stronger national emphasis on math and science education as well as providing lawmakers with better scientific advice when they must consider cutting-edge science and technology issues. His background also gives him the expertise to weigh in on two top-tier current issues — homeland and energy security. The Democratic leadership gave him a seat on the Intelligence Committee in the 108th Congress.

Holt says the government should pay more attention to biotechnology and all of its potential uses, which can range from improving the food supply to spreading mass death in a terrorist attack. He urged the government to study the genetic composition of all potential pathogens, including anthrax and smallpox, in order to be prepared in case of an attack.

He came uncomfortably close to such an attack as his office on the sixth floor of the Longworth House Office Building was contaminated with anthrax in 2001 and was closed for three months. (A giant postal processing center that serves his constituents handled all three of the known letters containing anthrax mailed that fall.)

One of his priorities has been to reinstate the Office of Technology Assessment, which advised Congress on scientific and technology issues for a quarter-century before the GOP-run Congress closed it in 1995. For this effort, Holt was named by Scientific American magazine in 2002 as one of its 50 "visionaries from the worlds of research, industry and politics whose accomplishments point toward a brighter technological future."

Other items on his agenda include banning snowmobiles from national parks and pushing the National Park Service to add a number of New Jersey Revolutionary War battle sites to its list of national heritage areas.

Holt can usually be counted on to vote in accord with the Democratic leadership, but he has strayed on a few occasions. Although he opposed the overall Bush tax cut of 2001, he supported two of its components: eliminating the estate tax and lessening the "marriage penalty," a quirk in the tax code that results in some two-earner couples paying higher income taxes. He affiliates with the centrist New Democrat Coalition.

Holt is a five-time champion of the TV quiz show "Jeopardy" and is bemused by the attention that brings. After his 1998 election, he told the Charleston, W. Va., Daily Mail that he didn't think his game show success was particularly relevant to the campaign but from the interest it received from journalists, "it must be the most significant thing I've done."

Holt first ran for the House in 1996, losing in the Democratic primary to David N. Del Vecchio, who in turn lost a close race to Republican Michael Pappas. Two year later, Holt portrayed socially conservative Pappas as too far to the right for the district. Pappas also inadvertently hurt his own cause by taking to the House floor to sing a song, set to the tune of "Twinkle Twinkle Little Star," in praise of President Clinton's legal adversary, Independent Counsel Kenneth W. Starr. Holt won by about 5,000 votes, one of only six challengers to unseat an incumbent in 1998.

The narrowness of that victory made Holt one of the GOP's most-targeted incumbents in 2000. Republican ads portrayed him as little more than a tax-and-spend liberal with Ivy League bona fides. To blunt contentions that he was fiscally irresponsible, Holt pointed to his support of a plan that would keep surplus Social Security funds from being spent on other government programs. His campaign against moderate Republican Dick Zimmer — who had held the House seat for three terms ending in 1996 — turned bitter, and the outcome was in doubt for three weeks after Election Day. Holt was eventually declared the victor by 651 votes.

Once again, the GOP kept the 12th District on its target list for 2002. But the state commission that redrew the congressional lines for this decade gave incumbents of both parties more-favorable constituencies. The GOP offered up an attractive candidate, DeForest "Buster" Soaries, an African-American Baptist minister who had served as New Jersey's secretary of state. But Holt won with 61 percent.

KEY VOTES

2002

Yes Overhaul campaign finance law; ban "soft money" and restrict advocacy advertising
No Back Bush's defense budget increase
No Extend 1996 welfare law
No Adopt Bush's discretionary spending limit
No Pass GOP Medicare prescription drug plan
Yes Create independent Sept. 11 commission
Yes Extend union protections to Homeland Security Department employees
No Revive fast-track procedures for trade agreements
No Authorize war against Iraq
No Advance bankruptcy overhaul opposed by abortion opponents

2001

No Nullify Clinton Labor Department ergonomics rule
No Cut taxes by $1.35 trillion through fiscal 2011
Yes Maintain ban on oil drilling in Arctic National Wildlife Refuge
No Approve Bush proposal to limit managed-care plan liability for coverage decisions
Yes Divert money from crop subsidy payments to land conservation
Yes Expand law enforcement power to investigate suspected terrorists

CQ VOTE STUDIES

	PARTY UNITY		PRESIDENTIAL SUPPORT	
	Support	Oppose	Support	Oppose
2002	94%	6%	30%	70%
2001	92%	8%	35%	65%
2000	88%	12%	67%	33%
1999	91%	9%	79%	21%

INTEREST GROUPS

	AFL-CIO	ADA	CCUS	ACU
2002	100%	90%	40%	8%
2001	92%	90%	43%	0%
2000	80%	80%	47%	16%
1999	78%	95%	24%	4%

NEW JERSEY 12

Central – part of Trenton, East Brunswick, Princeton

Set in the middle of the state, the 12th begins in Hunterdon County, hitting ethnically diverse Trenton (shared with the 4th) and East Brunswick as it winds east to Monmouth County. It ends in shore communities such as Rumson just short of the Atlantic Ocean.

Despite its jagged shape, many of the district's towns are similar. Office parks dominate the landscape in these affluent and white communities. But there are pockets of blue-collar diversity. Redistricting following the 2000 census made the 12th more Democratic by exchanging part of predominantly white Hunterdon County for a sizable portion of the state capital, Trenton, where more than 70 percent of the residents are black. Plainsboro in Middlesex County has a large Asian population.

The 12th has benefited from economic growth, though midsize towns such as Ewing must contend with the side effects of suburban sprawl. Delaware River towns, such as Frenchtown and Lambertville, offer quaint antique shops and bed and breakfasts. In addition to the Capitol, the district also boasts the governor's official residence, the stately and imposing Drumthwacket in Princeton.

Old money and suburban affluence made the area historically Republican, except for a small Democratic constituency anchored by Princeton's academic community. But due to an influx of independents, the 12th became politically competitive even before mapmakers pushed it to the left in redistricting. Al Gore took 58 percent of the new district's vote in the 2000 presidential election, 7 percentage points higher than under the old lines.

MAJOR INDUSTRY
Higher education, military, pharmaceuticals

MILITARY BASES
Fort Monmouth (Army), 312 military, 5,243 civilian (2001)

CITIES
Trenton (pt.), 47,658; East Brunswick (unincorporated), 46,756; North Brunswick (unincorporated), 36,287; Ewing (unincorporated), 35,707

NOTABLE
The Lenox Inc. china company, founded in Trenton, is based in Lawrenceville.

Rep. Robert Menendez (D)

CAPITOL OFFICE
225-7919
menendez@mail.house.gov
menendez.house.gov
2238 Rayburn 20515-3013; fax 226-0792

COMMITTEES
International Relations
Transportation & Infrastructure

HOMETOWN
Union City

BORN
Jan. 1, 1954, Manhattan, N.Y.

RELIGION
Roman Catholic

FAMILY
Separated; two children

EDUCATION
St. Peter's College, B.A. 1976 (political science); Rutgers U., J.D. 1979

CAREER
Lawyer

POLITICAL HIGHLIGHTS
Union City Board of Education, 1974-82; mayor of Union City, 1986-92; N.J. Assembly, 1987-91; N.J. Senate, 1991-93

ELECTION RESULTS

2002 GENERAL		
Robert Menendez (D)	72,605	78.3%
James Geron (R)	16,852	18.2%
Pat Henry Faulkner (GREEN)	1,195	1.3%
2002 PRIMARY		
Robert Menendez (D)		unopposed
2000 GENERAL		
Robert Menendez (D)	117,856	78.7%
Theresa de Leon (R)	27,849	18.6%
Claudette C. Meliere (I)	2,741	1.8%

PREVIOUS WINNING PERCENTAGES
1998 (80%); 1996 (79%); 1994 (71%); 1992 (64%)

Elected 1992; 6th term

Menendez has dreamed of becoming a U.S. senator since childhood. But when the ideal opportunity seemed to crop up in 2002, he took a pass and chose not to run for the seat of fellow Democrat Robert G. Torricelli, who abandoned his campaign in the face of deepening ethical troubles. Menendez calculated he had better odds of moving into the top-tier Democratic leadership in the House than of winning a Senate seat. It turns out he made a good bet.

Brash and ambitious, Menendez campaigned successfully for chairman of the House Democratic Caucus. He beat a seasoned rival, Rosa DeLauro of Connecticut, by a single vote to become the highest-ranking Hispanic in the history of Congress.

That 104-103 victory gave Menendez the No. 3 position in the Democratic hierarchy in the 108th Congress. He also is the first Hispanic elected to Congress from New Jersey, the only Cuban-American Democrat in Congress and one of the party's most articulate spokesmen. As the vice chairman of the party caucus in both the 106th and 107th Congresses, Menendez built an impressive power base by giving the competing groups in the caucus a voice in policymaking, which often helped unite ideological, geographic and ethnic factions.

In beating DeLauro, a favorite of those who wanted more gender diversity in the leadership, Menendez argued that Democrats needed to have a Hispanic in the top echelon if they were going to effectively court the fastest-growing ethnic voting bloc and counter the appeal of the Spanish-speaking president among Latino voters. Several Hispanic groups outside Congress promoted Menendez's candidacy, warning that his defeat would send the wrong message to Hispanic voters. At the same time, Menendez's leadership political action committee donated $689,000 to Democratic candidates for Congress in 2002, three times as much as DeLauro's PAC.

In the end, a confluence of two odd circumstances helped him in the final stretch. Menendez and DeLauro agreed to permit Colorado Democrat Mike Feeley to vote, even though his membership in the House was in doubt. (After a lengthy recount, he lost to Republican Bob Beauprez.) Feeley backed Menendez, while one of DeLauro's supporters, Darlene Hooley of Oregon, missed the vote because of knee surgery.

In the 107th Congress, Menendez was his party's leading spokesman on homeland security. He was fatefully positioned for the role; his district includes Newark International Airport, the origin of United Airlines Flight 93, which was hijacked by terrorists on Sept. 11, 2001, and then retaken by rebel passengers before crashing in rural Pennsylvania, killing all aboard. Menendez also sits on Transportation's Aviation Subcommittee, which drafted a bailout for the major airlines, which were hard hit by the drop-off in air travel after the attacks.

As head of the Democrats' Homeland Security Task Force, Menendez assembled legislation to bolster bioterrorism defenses and establish a Department of Homeland Security, putting Democrats out in front of the GOP leadership's legislative response to the attacks. Menendez later became a member of the committee that rewrote President Bush's homeland security proposal in the House. He used his positions to call for stringent deadlines to bolster airline security.

Menendez often joins with the House's three other Cuban-Americans, who are Republicans, in criticizing the Castro regime. He was a valued adviser to President Clinton and to 2000 Democratic presidential nominee Al Gore on the complex politics of the Cuban-American community.

Menendez is a powerful voice on the gamut of Latino issues and remains active in organizations tapped into New Jersey's steadily increasing Hispanic population. He has often castigated Republicans for pursuing policies that he says show a bias against Hispanics and other immigrant groups. Yet he does not want to be pigeonholed as a Hispanic leader, and he cultivates a larger role for himself as a Democratic statesman. He once warned a New Jersey public television station that he would refuse interview requests if they continued to question him only on ethnic issues such as immigration.

Menendez is a liberal and a believer in activist government. He sides with organized labor, backs abortion rights, supports gun control and faults Republicans as proponents of tax breaks for the wealthy. Tapped to deliver the Democrats' weekly radio address early in 2001, Menendez blasted Bush's tax cut proposal, arguing that "families who depend on a paycheck — not an inheritance" would see little of the benefits.

Menendez was among the most vocal critics of the way the House GOP investigated Democrat Loretta Sanchez's narrow 1996 victory over Republican incumbent Robert K. Dornan in what was then California's 46th District. He called the probe a "witch hunt" and a waste of taxpayers' money.

A native New Yorker and the son of Cuban immigrants, Menendez won election to the Union City School Board in 1974 while he was still in college. He was elected as Union City mayor in 1986 and to the state Assembly in 1987, serving in both offices simultaneously. He was named to fill a state Senate vacancy in early 1991 and that November won the seat.

Redistricting for the 1990s nearly doubled the Hispanic population in the 13th District. When Democrat Frank J. Guarini decided to retire after 14 years in the House, Menendez quickly emerged as the front-runner for the seat. He won the primary with 68 percent of the vote and the general election with 64 percent. He has done exceedingly well in his subsequent re-elections, and redistricting after the 2000 census kept the 13th almost half Hispanic and overwhelmingly Democratic.

While making his mark in the House, Menendez had kept an eye on the Senate and raised millions of dollars for a possible campaign. He planned to run for an open seat in 2000, but dropped out when Torricelli instead backed Jon Corzine, who went on to win. After Torricelli was rebuked by the Senate Ethics Committee and dropped his bid for a second term in September 2002, state party leaders approached Menendez about becoming the replacement nominee, but he turned them down.

KEY VOTES

2002

Yes Overhaul campaign finance law; ban "soft money" and restrict advocacy advertising
Yes Back Bush's defense budget increase
No Extend 1996 welfare law
No Adopt Bush's discretionary spending limit
No Pass GOP Medicare prescription drug plan
Yes Create independent Sept. 11 commission
Yes Extend union protections to Homeland Security Department employees
No Revive fast-track procedures for trade agreements
No Authorize war against Iraq
No Advance bankruptcy overhaul opposed by abortion opponents

2001

No Nullify Clinton Labor Department ergonomics rule
No Cut taxes by $1.35 trillion through fiscal 2011
Yes Maintain ban on oil drilling in Arctic National Wildlife Refuge
No Approve Bush proposal to limit managed-care plan liability for coverage decisions
Yes Divert money from crop subsidy payments to land conservation
Yes Expand law enforcement power to investigate suspected terrorists

CQ VOTE STUDIES

	PARTY UNITY		PRESIDENTIAL SUPPORT	
	Support	Oppose	Support	Oppose
2002	87%	13%	28%	72%
2001	89%	11%	30%	70%
2000	91%	9%	78%	22%
1999	91%	9%	81%	19%
1998	90%	10%	78%	22%

INTEREST GROUPS

	AFL-CIO	ADA	CCUS	ACU
2002	89%	95%	42%	8%
2001	100%	95%	35%	16%
2000	100%	95%	38%	8%
1999	100%	100%	24%	4%
1998	100%	95%	33%	12%

NEW JERSEY 13

Northeast — parts of Jersey City and Newark

Covering a long, thin swath from North Bergen to Perth Amboy along the Hudson River, Newark Bay and Arthur Kill, the diverse 13th takes in parts of Jersey City and Newark. Hispanics, many of whom came in a wave of immigration from Central and South America that followed a loosening of restrictions in 1965, constitute a plurality, though just short of a majority. The 13th was drawn in 1992 to combine scattered Hispanic neighborhoods, and the district elected the state's first Hispanic congressman, Rep. Menendez, that year.

Within sight of some of the nation's best-known landmarks, including the Statue of Liberty and Manhattan's gleaming skyscrapers, the 13th now has a major landmark on its own turf — Ellis Island. After a protracted legal battle, the U.S. Supreme Court decided in 1998 that New Jersey can lay claim to 80 percent of the immigration gateway, whose lure has helped form the 13th's colorful character.

Russian, Indian, Korean and Filipino communities add to the district's diversity and its overwhelming Democratic vote. A few Republican presidential ballots are cast by members of Cuban communities in West New York, Union City, North Bergen and Guttenberg, though much of the Cuban population has moved to Bergen County.

The district is a transportation hub, with Port Newark-Elizabeth and a small part of Newark Liberty International Airport (shared with the 10th). Several lines, including Hudson-Bergen Light Rail, carry commuters across the district, and PATH trains, ferries and tunnels bring passengers to and from New York. Hoboken has seen gentrification, as young professionals and financial services companies have moved across the river from Manhattan. Officials are hoping to turn long-suffering Jersey City into "Wall Street West."

MAJOR INDUSTRY

Transportation, health care, retail, financial securities

CITIES

Jersey City (pt.), 118,201; Newark (pt.), 118,133; Union City, 67,088; Bayonne (pt.), 56,465; Perth Amboy, 47,303; West New York, 45,768

NOTABLE

Bayonne Bridge, the world's longest steel arch bridge from 1931 until 1977, connects Bayonne and Staten Island over the Kill Van Kull; Frank Sinatra was born and raised in Hoboken.

NEW MEXICO

Gov. Bill Richardson (D)

First elected: 2002
Length of term: 4 years
Term expires: 1/07
Salary: $110,000
Phone: (505) 827-3000
Hometown: Santa Fe
Born: Nov. 15, 1947; Pasadena, Calif.
Religion: Roman Catholic
Family: Wife, Barbara Richardson
Education: Tufts U., B.A. 1970 (political science & French), M.A. 1971 (international relations)
Career: International trade consultant; state party official; congressional aide
Political highlights: Democratic nominee for U.S. House, 1980; U.S. House, 1983-97; United Nations ambassador, 1997-98; Energy secretary, 1998-2001
Election results:

2002 GENERAL		
Bill Richardson (D)	268,674	55.5%
John A. Sanchez (R)	189,090	39.1%
David E. Bacon (GREEN)	26,465	5.5%

Lt. Gov. Diane Denish (D)

First elected: 2002
Length of term: 4 years
Term expires: 1/07
Salary: $85,000
Phone: (505) 827-3050

STATE LEGISLATURE

Legislature: Meets January-March in odd-numbered years; January-February in even-numbered years
House: 70 members, 2-year terms
2003 breakdown: 27R, 43D; 49 men, 21 women
Salary: $145/day
Phone: (505) 986-4751
Senate: 42 members, 4-year terms
2003 breakdown: 18R, 24D; 30 men, 12 women
Salary: $145/day
Phone: (505) 986-4714

STATE TERM LIMITS

Governor: 2 consecutive terms
Senate: No
House: No

URBAN STATISTICS

CITY	POPULATION
Albuquerque	448,607
Las Cruces	74,267
Santa Fe	62,203
Rio Rancho	51,765
Roswell	45,293

REGISTERED VOTERS

Democrat	52%
Republican	33%
No party	12%

POPULATION

2002 population (est.)	1,855,059
2000 population	1,819,046
1990 population	1,515,069
Percent change (1990-2000)	+20.1%
Rank among states (2002)	36
Median age	34.6
Born in state	51.5%
Foreign born	8.2%
Violent crime rate	758/100,000
Poverty level	18.4%
Federal workers	28,772
Military	17,163

REDISTRICTING

New Mexico retained its three House seats in reapportionment. GOP Gov. Gary E. Johnson vetoed the state legislature's plan and a state judge adopted a new map on Jan. 2, 2002.

MISCELLANEOUS

Web: www.state.nm.us
Capital: Santa Fe

STATE ELECTION OFFICIAL
(505) 827-3621

DEMOCRATIC HEADQUARTERS
(505) 830-3650

REPUBLICAN HEADQUARTERS
(505) 998-5254

District Statistics

DIST.	2000 VOTE FOR PRESIDENT BUSH	GORE	NADER	WHITE	BLACK	ASIAN	HISP	MEDIAN INCOME	WHITE COLLAR	BLUE COLLAR	SERVICE INDUSTRY	OVER 64	UNDER 18	COLLEGE EDUCATION	RURAL	SQ. MILES
1	47%	48%	4%	49%	2%	2%	43%	$38,413	65%	19%	16%	11%	26%	30%	9%	4,717
2	54	43	2	44	2	1	47	$29,269	53	29	18	13	29	17	29	69,493
3	43	52	4	41	1	1	36	$35,058	60	23	17	11	29	24	37	47,146
STATE	47.8	47.9	4	45	2	1	42	$34,133	60	23	17	12	28	24	25	121,356
U.S.	47.9	48.4	3	69	12	4	13	$41,994	60	25	15	12	26	24	21	3,537,438

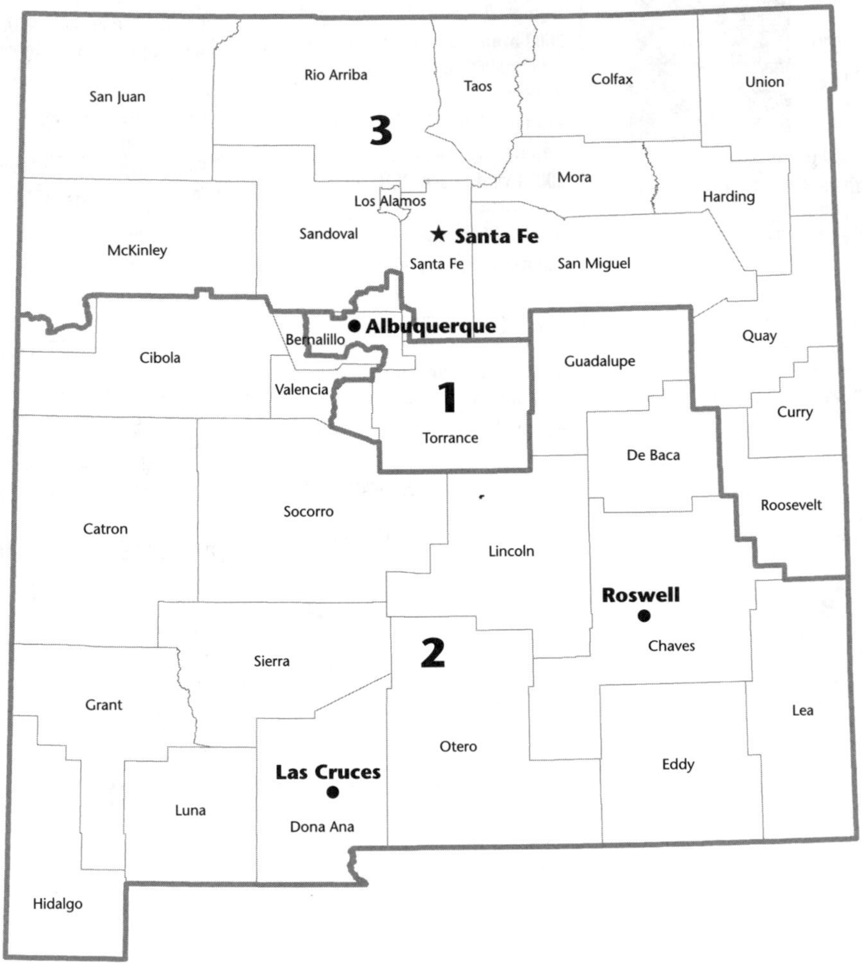
San Juan
Rio Arriba
Taos
Colfax
Union
3
Mora
Harding
Los Alamos
Sandoval
★ Santa Fe
Santa Fe
San Miguel
McKinley
● Albuquerque
Bernalillo
Cibola
Quay
Guadalupe
Valencia
1
Torrance
Curry
De Baca
Roosevelt
Catron
Socorro
Lincoln
Roswell
Chaves
Sierra
2
Grant
Lea
Otero
Eddy
Las Cruces
Luna
Dona Ana
Hidalgo

Sen. Pete V. Domenici (R)

CAPITOL OFFICE
224-6621
senator_domenici@domenici.senate.gov
domenici.senate.gov
328 Hart 20510-3101; fax 228-0900

COMMITTEES
Appropriations
(Energy & Water Development - chairman)
Budget
Energy & Natural Resources - chairman
Indian Affairs

HOMETOWN
Albuquerque

BORN
May 7, 1932, Albuquerque, N.M.

RELIGION
Roman Catholic

FAMILY
Wife, Nancy Domenici; eight children

EDUCATION
U. of Albuquerque, attended 1950-52; U. of New Mexico, B.S. 1954; U. of Denver, LL.B. 1958

CAREER
Lawyer

POLITICAL HIGHLIGHTS
Albuquerque City Commission, 1966-70 (chairman and ex-officio mayor, 1967-70); Republican nominee for governor, 1970

ELECTION RESULTS

2002 GENERAL		
Pete V. Domenici (R)	314,193	65.0%
Gloria Tristani (D)	168,863	35.0%
2002 PRIMARY		
Pete V. Domenici (R)		unopposed

PREVIOUS WINNING PERCENTAGES
1996 (65%); 1990 (73%); 1984 (72%); 1978 (53%); 1972 (54%)

Elected 1972; 6th term

After 30 years in the Senate, the intense and influential Domenici is one of Congress' most respected elder statesmen, particularly on budgetary and energy matters. But he has never been able to translate his clout and credibility into becoming part of the GOP leadership.

A hardworking fiscal conservative with a moderate streak on social issues, Domenici (doe-MEN-ih-chee) has continually been left behind as Senate Republicans have moved to the right to pick their leaders. He watched his close ally Bob Dole overtake him in a 1990 bid for majority leader and later lost two races for the chairmanship of the Republican Policy Committee, in 1990 and 2000.

Domenici nevertheless is highly regarded enough to have been considered twice for vice president. In 1988, George H.W. Bush included Domenici on his shortlist of prospects; 12 years later, Majority Leader Trent Lott publicly floated his name to George W. Bush for consideration.

In the 108th Congress, Domenici assumed the chairmanship of the Energy and Natural Resources Committee, relinquishing the gavel of the Budget Committee. He had been the top Republican on that panel for 22 years, making a name for himself with his dedication to fiscal discipline and balanced budgets. Replacing him was Don Nickles of Oklahoma, a product of the Reagan revolution of 1980 who had defeated Domenici for the policy committee chairmanship in 1990, and who was viewed as more in line with the Bush administration on tax and spending priorities.

Domenici settled for taking the helm of the Energy and Natural Resources Committee in the 108th Congress. The job enables him to continue his longtime efforts as Congress' chief apostle for nuclear power, an energy source he says has been unjustly overlooked. "Nuclear power is safe, if not safer than some of the other energy sources, and it is environmentally sound," he said in 2001.

He is further able to push his energy agenda as chairman of the Energy and Water Appropriations Subcommittee. Two of the Energy Department's nuclear weapons laboratories, Sandia and Los Alamos, are in his state, and he has been such an ardent protector of the agency that some of its employees refer to him as "St. Pete."

Despite his influential status, Domenici has maintained a regular-guy image in Washington. A driven yet sensitive man, he appears genuinely distressed when a colleague is angry at him. He does not suffer criticism lightly and can bristle at those who question his actions. But he is deeply loyal to his staff, treating them like extended family members, and likewise displays considerable respect toward colleagues. "He understands that you don't do irreparable harm to relationships with anyone," former Republican Sen. Warren B. Rudman of New Hampshire, a close friend, once told The Washington Post. "If Pete has a fault, it's that he worries too much."

Domenici's fiscally conservative yet socially moderate approach has enabled him to work with a broad spectrum of lawmakers. He teamed with conservative Sen. Phil Gramm, a Texas Republican, on Social Security legislation and worked with the liberal Paul Wellstone, Minnesota's Democratic senator, on mental health issues. Domenici has a daughter who suffers from schizophrenia, and her struggles caused him to lead the push to make health insurance providers treat mental illness as any other ailment.

Domenici says he has been persistent in letting his GOP colleagues know when he thinks a bill is overly partisan: "I tell them not once but twice, and if I can tell them three times, I do." And it was Domenici who convinced Republicans to elect Bill Frist as majority leader by acclamation over the telephone in late 2002 instead of waiting to hold a regular election. The move followed Lott's praise for Strom Thurmond's 1948 segregationist presidential campaign.

Domenici's political acumen has not prevented him from tangling with some of his more conservative colleagues. He has opposed a push for "dynamic scoring," in which the cost of tax cuts to the Treasury are mitigated by economic growth that the cuts would be designed to induce. As an appropriator, he also has been less willing than Nickles and other conservatives to consider chopping programs.

The senator's advocacy of fiscal restraint was passed down by his father, an Italian immigrant grocer. When Domenici was accepted into law school, his father agreed to finance his education but demanded to be repaid if his son brought home an "F."

Domenici first was thrust into the limelight on budget issues in the 1980s, when the GOP controlled the Senate and he served his first stint as Budget Committee chairman, leading the panel in its three-way battles with the Reagan administration and the Democratic-controlled House. He was more interested in balancing the budget than in providing the fiscal stimulus sought by "supply side" conservatives — Reagan budget director David A. Stockman called him a "Hooverite."

During the 12 years that Republicans Ronald Reagan and George Bush held the White House, Domenici was expected at times to muffle his call to cut the budget. After spending four years criticizing President Clinton's administration, Domenici helped lead a team of GOP negotiators in May 1997 in producing an agreement to balance the budget by fiscal 2002. The sprawling pact bore Domenici's stamp of pragmatism by containing something for both sides — tax cuts along with limited new money for selected Democratic priorities such as health care for children.

Enduringly popular with voters across the spectrum of his state's diverse population, he has not faced an even remotely difficult re-election race in more than 20 years. He goes to great lengths not to be perceived as an out-of-touch Beltway insider, a label that a number of opponents have tried unsuccessfully to pin on him.

The most recent opponent who sought to make that argument was Gloria Tristani, a member of the Federal Communications Commission under Clinton and granddaughter of former New Mexico Sen. Dennis Chavez. Nevertheless, Domenici had little trouble winning re-election in 2002, garnering 65 percent of the vote.

One of five children of Italian immigrants, Domenici worked in his father's wholesale grocery business as a youth. He was a good enough pitcher in college to receive a contract from a Brooklyn Dodgers farm team in 1954. He gave up baseball after a season, taught math for a year and then went to law school.

Domenici's early background is in municipal government. As an Albuquerque city official in the late 1960s, he prided himself on holding neighborhood meetings to hear residents' complaints. After four years in city government, he ran for governor in 1970, losing to Democrat Bruce King by 5 percentage points.

Undeterred, Domenici came back in 1972, this time running for the Senate seat being vacated by Democrat Clinton P. Anderson. He linked his Democratic foe, banker and former state Rep. Jack Daniels, to the unpopular presidential candidacy of George McGovern and won, with 54 percent. He struggled to win re-election in 1978, but since then, he has not faced a strong challenge for his seat.

KEY VOTES

2002

- ? Pass farm bill reversing crop subsidy limits
- Yes Postpone tougher automobile fuel efficiency standards
- Yes Overhaul campaign finance law; ban "soft money" and restrict advocacy advertising
- Yes Set federal election standards
- Yes Support oil drilling in Arctic National Wildlife Refuge
- Yes Revive fast-track procedures for trade agreements
- Yes Create federal insurance coverage for catastrophic terrorist losses
- Yes Tighten federal accounting and corporate governance regulation
- No Advance bipartisan Medicare prescription drug plan
- Yes Create independent Sept. 11 commission
- No Back Democratic Homeland Security Department proposal
- Yes Authorize war against Iraq

2001

- Yes Confirm John Ashcroft as attorney general
- Yes Nullify Clinton Labor Department ergonomics rule
- # Cut taxes by $1.35 trillion through fiscal 2011
- ? Pass Democratic bill to bolster rights of patients in managed-care plans
- No Permit a new round of military base closings
- Yes Expand law enforcement power to investigate suspected terrorists

CQ VOTE STUDIES

	PARTY UNITY		PRESIDENTIAL SUPPORT	
	Support	Oppose	Support	Oppose
2002	89%	11%	96%	4%
2001	89%	11%	96%	4%
2000	94%	6%	51%	49%
1999	93%	7%	33%	67%
1998	83%	17%	57%	43%
1997	85%	15%	67%	33%
1996	90%	10%	42%	58%
1995	93%	7%	26%	74%
1994	78%	22%	53%	47%
1993	86%	14%	34%	66%

INTEREST GROUPS

	AFL-CIO	ADA	CCUS	ACU
2002	25%	15%	100%	88%
2001	21%	10%	100%	90%
2000	0%	0%	100%	95%
1999	11%	5%	94%	88%
1998	13%	5%	100%	70%
1997	0%	25%	100%	60%
1996	14%	20%	83%	85%
1995	8%	5%	100%	78%
1994	13%	25%	90%	84%
1993	9%	20%	100%	80%

Sen. Jeff Bingaman (D)

CAPITOL OFFICE
224-5521
senator_bingaman@bingaman.senate.gov
bingaman.senate.gov
703 Hart 20510-3102; fax 224-2852

COMMITTEES
Energy & Natural Resources - ranking member
Finance
Health, Education, Labor & Pensions
Joint Economic

HOMETOWN
Silver City

BORN
Oct. 3, 1943, El Paso, Texas

RELIGION
Methodist

FAMILY
Wife, Anne Kovacovich Bingaman; one child

EDUCATION
Harvard U., A.B. 1965 (government); Stanford U., J.D. 1968

MILITARY SERVICE
Army Reserve, 1968-74

CAREER
Lawyer

POLITICAL HIGHLIGHTS
N.M. attorney general, 1979-83

ELECTION RESULTS

2000 GENERAL

Jeff Bingaman (D)	363,744	61.7%
Bill Redmond (R)	225,517	38.3%

2000 PRIMARY

Jeff Bingaman (D)	unopposed

PREVIOUS WINNING PERCENTAGES
1994 (54%); 1988 (63%); 1982 (54%)

Elected 1982; 4th term

Bingaman is among those Democrats more at ease with the intricacies of policy than the glamour of politics. He avoids the television talk-show circuit, rarely takes part in news conferences and often lets other New Mexico lawmakers take the lead in putting out press releases on statewide matters. Although he is cordial in his relations with the news media, one of his former aides joked that she sometimes "bribed" Bingaman with candy to encourage him to return reporters' calls.

As chairman of the Senate Energy and Natural Resources Committee in the 107th Congress, Bingaman successfully avoided the spotlight even in the thick of debate over a high-profile national energy policy. He allowed colleagues with presidential ambitions such as Connecticut's Joseph I. Lieberman and Massachusetts' John Kerry to grab headlines over the marquee issues of drilling for oil in Alaska's Arctic National Wildlife Refuge and raising automobile fuel efficiency standards.

Majority Leader Tom Daschle eventually took the bill away from Bingaman's committee and brought it directly to the floor in an effort to prevent the panel from approving a provision barring oil exploration in the Alaskan refuge. When the measure finally landed in a House-Senate conference, Bingaman tried but failed to reach a compromise for a stripped-down bill with the House Energy Committee chairman, Republican Billy Tauzin of Louisiana.

Bingaman is the Energy Committee's top-ranking Democrat in the 108th Congress. He has forged a respectful relationship with his home-state Republican colleague Pete V. Domenici, who took over as chairman. The two work closely on issues that mirror their common interests, which include promoting the use of nuclear power and furthering energy research.

Bingaman and Domenici have disagreed over the years on a variety of energy-related matters, such as how to restructure the Energy Department to protect its nuclear weapons secrets. But both men have gone out of their way to avoid being confrontational or overly critical of each other.

In addition to mastering such complex topics as energy technology and nuclear weapons, Bingaman has delved into issues at the core of the Democratic agenda, including education and pensions. For that reason, he has become a trusted adviser to Daschle and belongs to a small "message group" that meets weekly to shape the party's stands and priorities.

Insiders credit Bingaman with persuading other Democratic senators and the Bush administration to rally around "accountability" language in the education authorization bill enacted in 2002 that forces schools receiving federal funding to raise their standards.

Bingaman also has teamed with Majority Leader Bill Frist to introduce legislation aimed at reducing obesity among children and adolescents.

Republicans and Democrats alike have taken note of Bingaman's sensible, non-partisan and thoughtful manner. "When he speaks up to the [Democratic] caucus or policy committee or message group, he's very influential because he's always thought it through," said Joel Johnson, a White House official under President Clinton who had previously worked for Daschle.

Bingaman augmented his portfolio in the 107th Congress with a seat on the Finance Committee, which writes tax, trade and health care legislation. He worked to extend unemployment benefits and provide training to workers who lose their jobs because of U.S. trade policy.

With Democrats forced to reduce their membership on committees in the 108th Congress after the GOP takeover, Bingaman had to relinquish his seat on the Armed Services Committee, where his workmanlike devotion to detail earned him comparisons to the panel's venerated retired chairman, Democrat Sam Nunn of Georgia. Bingaman kept a watchful eye on New Mexico's military bases and was a strong proponent of putting defense technologies to use in the private sector.

That position is popular in New Mexico — home to two of the Energy Department's national laboratories, Sandia and Los Alamos, which have sought new missions with the end of the Cold War.

In the Senate, Bingaman has taken on a variety of unglamorous but important assignments. Daschle has appointed him to task forces studying high-wage job creation, Social Security, and the settlement between tobacco companies and the states. Almost without exception, though, Bingaman has let other panel members grab the headlines on those issues.

"He never seeks to advance himself; he never says, 'Look at me,' " said North Dakota Democrat Kent Conrad, who chaired the tobacco group and notes that Bingaman is among those he turns to for advice on difficult issues. "I find him to be one of the colleagues I respect the most," Conrad said.

A pragmatic, results-oriented lawmaker, Bingaman has compiled a moderate-to-liberal voting record as a senator. He was among the Senate Democrats who most strongly supported Clinton's agenda, but under the Bush administration he has become more inclined to vote against the majority of his party.

In October 2002, Bingaman voted against the resolution authorizing Bush to use military force if necessary to disarm Iraq. He urged the Bush administration to let U.N. inspectors look for more evidence of weapons of mass destruction before invading Iraq. "We should not short-circuit that process by a premature military action," he said in January 2003.

Like many of his colleagues, Bingaman has lamented the growing partisanship in the Senate. But he has remained persistent in pushing his ideas despite having less success with Democrats in the minority. "Bitterness is not a word for him," his wife, Anne, once said. "It's not in his nature. His family is from Kansas, from Midwestern stock, and they're just very stoic."

Bingaman's family helped point him toward a political career. He grew up in the New Mexico mining town of Silver City, the son of a professor and nephew of John Bingaman, a confidant of the state's 24-year Democratic senator, Clinton Anderson. At Stanford Law School, Bingaman worked for Sen. Robert F. Kennedy's 1968 presidential campaign. Returning to New Mexico, he served as counsel to the 1969 state constitutional convention, joined a politically connected law firm and ran successfully for attorney general in 1978.

When he launched his 1982 Senate campaign, he was little-known outside the political and legal communities but politically unscarred. He won 54 percent to topple incumbent GOP Sen. Harrison H. Schmitt, a former Apollo astronaut, who appeared more interested in pet subjects such as 21st century technology than in the state's struggling economy.

In three re-election races since, only one has featured a serious challenger — Colin McMillan, a former Pentagon official, who used much of his own money in 1994 to attack aggressively Bingaman's stance on fees for grazing on public lands and his support for Clinton's budget policy. In the end, McMillan could not make sufficient inroads in Democratic counties, and Bingaman won with 54 percent.

KEY VOTES

2002

Yes Pass farm bill reversing crop subsidy limits
No Postpone tougher automobile fuel efficiency standards
Yes Overhaul campaign finance law; ban "soft money" and restrict advocacy advertising
Yes Set federal election standards
No Support oil drilling in Arctic National Wildlife Refuge
Yes Revive fast-track procedures for trade agreements
Yes Create federal insurance coverage for catastrophic terrorist losses
Yes Tighten federal accounting and corporate governance regulation
Yes Advance bipartisan Medicare prescription drug plan
Yes Create independent Sept. 11 commission
Yes Back Democratic Homeland Security Department proposal
No Authorize war against Iraq

2001

No Confirm John Ashcroft as attorney general
No Nullify Clinton Labor Department ergonomics rule
X Cut taxes by $1.35 trillion through fiscal 2011
Yes Pass Democratic bill to bolster rights of patients in managed-care plans
No Permit a new round of military base closings
Yes Expand law enforcement power to investigate suspected terrorists

CQ VOTE STUDIES

	PARTY UNITY		PRESIDENTIAL SUPPORT	
	Support	Oppose	Support	Oppose
2002	78%	22%	79%	21%
2001	91%	9%	68%	32%
2000	87%	13%	95%	5%
1999	88%	12%	84%	16%
1998	87%	13%	87%	13%
1997	88%	12%	92%	8%
1996	88%	12%	84%	16%
1995	84%	16%	91%	9%
1994	84%	16%	89%	11%
1993	80%	20%	86%	14%

INTEREST GROUPS

	AFL-CIO	ADA	CCUS	ACU
2002	92%	90%	60%	17%
2001	100%	90%	50%	29%
2000	75%	85%	64%	16%
1999	78%	100%	59%	4%
1998	75%	85%	56%	0%
1997	57%	90%	60%	0%
1996	100%	95%	15%	0%
1995	100%	90%	42%	0%
1994	75%	60%	50%	16%
1993	73%	70%	36%	20%

Rep. Heather A. Wilson (R)

CAPITOL OFFICE
225-6316
ask.heather@mail.house.gov
www.house.gov/wilson
318 Cannon 20515-3101; fax 225-4975

COMMITTEES
Armed Services
Energy & Commerce

HOMETOWN
Albuquerque

BORN
Dec. 30, 1960, Keene, N.H.

RELIGION
Methodist

FAMILY
Husband, Jay Hone; three children

EDUCATION
Air Force Academy, B.S. 1982 (international politics); Oxford U., M.Phil. 1984 (Rhodes scholar), D.Phil. 1985 (international relations)

MILITARY SERVICE
Air Force, 1978-89

CAREER
Management consultant; National Security Council staff member

POLITICAL HIGHLIGHTS
N.M. Children, Youth and Families secretary, 1995-98

ELECTION RESULTS

2002 GENERAL		
Heather A. Wilson (R)	95,711	55.3%
Richard Romero (D)	77,234	44.7%
2002 PRIMARY		
Heather A. Wilson (R)		unopposed
2000 GENERAL		
Heather A. Wilson (R)	107,296	50.3%
John Kelly (D)	92,187	43.3%
Daniel Kerlinsky (GREEN)	13,656	6.4%

PREVIOUS WINNING PERCENTAGES
1998 (48%); 1998 Special Election (45%)

Elected June 1998; 3rd full term

A former Air Force officer, a Rhodes scholar and a national security official who walks the corridors of the Capitol with military bearing, the no-nonsense Wilson has carved out a niche for herself among Republicans as a fresh voice and party spokeswoman on defense issues.

Wilson — who delivers serious speeches in her signature low, even tone — established a conservative voting record, but a slightly more moderate public face, during her first four and a half years in Congress; she has made improving health care and education top priorities. Much of the rest of her time on Capitol Hill is spent toiling to protect and promote the energy industry, an all-important force in her state.

Wilson is a protégé of one of Congress' most powerful figures: Pete V. Domenici, a senator from New Mexico for three decades and now chairman of the Energy and Natural Resources panel. Domenici had a strong hand in plucking Wilson from her spot as secretary of New Mexico's Children, Youth and Families Department and propelling her toward Congress in 1998, calling her "the most brilliantly qualified candidate" running for the House at the time.

Perhaps more importantly, Republicans view Wilson as a representative right out of central casting for Albuquerque. That is largely because Wilson — the first woman veteran to serve in Congress — is steeped in the military issues that most concern her defense-dominated district. Her hometown paper once described her as someone who "with short-cropped hair and her back ramrod straight . . . looks like she still would be at home in the Air Force blues she wore until 1989."

Since 2001, she has chaired the Republican Policy Committee's National Security and Foreign Affairs panel, where she helped hone the party's message on defense issues after the terrorist attacks of Sept. 11, 2001, and in the preparation for an invasion of Iraq. Her panel spent nearly a year on a report, released in February 2003, that challenged the government to do a better job of sustaining its nuclear weapons complex, investing more in research and development, and refining anti-proliferation programs.

Wilson also sits on the two committees that matter most for her district: Armed Services, where she can look out for the interests of Kirtland Air Force Base, and Energy and Commerce, where she fights for Sandia National Laboratories. The two are major employers in the Albuquerque area. In 2001, Wilson voted against the annual defense authorization measure because it established a timetable for a new round of military base closures culminating in 2005.

Nuclear power is big business in New Mexico and — in lock step with Domenici — Wilson used her seat on Energy and Commerce to try to boost the role for nuclear power in the energy policy overhaul lawmakers debated, without finishing, in the 107th Congress. She won House passage of a provision, crucial to the industry's survival, to extend the federal nuclear liability system, which exists to provide insurance compensation to the public in the event of a nuclear accident, and to cap the industry's payments. And, in the 2002 law creating the Homeland Security Department, she won inclusion of language mandating a reassessment of nuclear reactor safety nationwide.

Health care and education issues played a major role in setting her course in public service. During the 107th and again in the 108th, she has worked to advance measures that would increase Medicare reimbursement rates for doctors in rural areas.

She criticized President Bush in 2002 when he threatened to veto legislation that would have allowed disabled veterans to receive military retirement pay and disability compensation at the same time. In the end, only the most seriously injured of veterans and those wounded under enemy fire were allowed to collect both payments.

Wilson tends to stick with her party when it comes to holding down government spending. But she has sought to bolster resources for education, joining a bipartisan group in the 107th that called for increasing Head Start spending by more than $330 million and advocating a tax credit for teachers who agree to work in low-income areas. As the debate on rewriting welfare law started in 2002, Wilson pressed with other Republican women for a $2 billion increase in child care block grants.

Wilson was a high school junior in New Hampshire when the Air Force Academy opened its doors to women, and she decided she wanted to be a pilot, like her father and grandfather. She graduated from the academy in 1982, the third class that included women. She never got around to getting a pilot's license, however, as she went to Oxford as a Rhodes scholar. There she earned master's and doctoral degrees in international relations.

After serving in the Air Force in Europe, Wilson took a job in 1989 with the National Security Council in the first Bush White House. In 1991, she married and moved to New Mexico. She started a consulting firm and joined GOP Gov. Gary E. Johnson's Cabinet in 1995.

She resigned that post early in 1998 to run for the House when Republican Steven H. Schiff, fighting a battle against skin cancer, said his fifth term would be his last. She entered the race with the endorsements of Schiff and Domenici.

When Schiff died in March, Wilson became the GOP nominee for the special election to finish Schiff's term. She prevailed by 5 percentage points against multimillionaire businessman and Democratic state Sen. Phillip J. Maloof, while liberal Green Party nominee Robert L. Anderson took 15 percent of the vote. The trio went at it again in the regular fall election, which Wilson won by 7 points. She won by 7 points again in 2000.

In 2002 — in territory that retained its Democratic lean after redistricting — Wilson won by 11 points over state Sen. Richard Romero. He hoped for a boost from the district's sizeable Hispanic population, but Wilson got significant help from the White House, including visits from President Bush and several Cabinet-level officials. Election night returns showed Romero ahead, but a flood of absentee ballots accounted for her final healthy margin.

KEY VOTES

2002

- No Overhaul campaign finance law; ban "soft money" and restrict advocacy advertising
- Yes Back Bush's defense budget increase
- Yes Extend 1996 welfare law
- Yes Adopt Bush's discretionary spending limit
- Yes Pass GOP Medicare prescription drug plan
- No Create independent Sept. 11 commission
- No Extend union protections to Homeland Security Department employees
- Yes Revive fast-track procedures for trade agreements
- Yes Authorize war against Iraq
- Yes Advance bankruptcy overhaul opposed by abortion opponents

2001

- Yes Nullify Clinton Labor Department ergonomics rule
- Yes Cut taxes by $1.35 trillion through fiscal 2011
- No Maintain ban on oil drilling in Arctic National Wildlife Refuge
- Yes Approve Bush proposal to limit managed-care plan liability for coverage decisions
- No Divert money from crop subsidy payments to land conservation
- Yes Expand law enforcement power to investigate suspected terrorists

CQ VOTE STUDIES

	PARTY UNITY		PRESIDENTIAL SUPPORT	
	Support	Oppose	Support	Oppose
2002	90%	10%	90%	10%
2001	94%	6%	88%	12%
2000	87%	13%	33%	67%
1999	84%	16%	32%	68%
1998	87%	13%	22%	78%

INTEREST GROUPS

	AFL-CIO	ADA	CCUS	ACU
2002	11%	5%	100%	84%
2001	17%	5%	91%	84%
2000	10%	10%	80%	80%
1999	11%	15%	88%	68%
1998	25%	0%	100%	83%

NEW MEXICO 1
Central — Albuquerque

Built around Albuquerque, New Mexico's largest city, the 1st is the only urban district in a sparsely populated, desert state. Since the Manhattan Project set the region on a technology-driven course in the 1940s, Albuquerque has grown from 35,000 people before WWII to more than 440,000 in 2000.

Sandia National Laboratories — born out of the Manhattan Project — is the basis for a steady defense industry. Sandia, which employs 7,000 workers, coordinates with the two other major employers in the district — the University of New Mexico and Kirtland Air Force Base — to conduct nuclear and national security research. Sandia's success has contributed to a surge in computer, laser and other high-tech companies in the area, including Muse Technologies, Emcore, Phillips Laboratory at Kirtland and nearby Intel (located in the 3rd). The city's concentration of technology firms draws a disproportionate number of PhDs to the area.

Although the 1st became slightly more conservative as a result of redistricting following the 2000 census, the large government work force and predominantly Hispanic South Valley provide registered Democrats with a slight edge. Democrats hold most local offices and the district's Hispanics, who make up 43 percent of the population, overwhelmingly favor Democrats. The Green Party also makes a strong showing, reaching double-digit percentages in some congressional races. But the GOP has held the congressional seat since its creation in 1968; the area traditionally sends fiscally conservative, defense-oriented moderate Republicans to Congress. Much of the GOP vote comes from the mainly white, upper-middle-class Northeast Heights section of Albuquerque.

MAJOR INDUSTRY
Higher education, scientific research, government

MILITARY BASES
Kirtland Air Force Base, 4,829 military, 1,833 civilian (2001)

CITIES
Albuquerque (pt.), 442,365; South Valley (unincorporated) (pt.), 39,060; North Valley (unincorporated), 11,923

NOTABLE
Albuquerque's annual International Balloon Fiesta is the world's largest hot air balloon event; The National Atomic Museum in Albuquerque is owned by the Department of Energy and operated by Sandia Labs.

Rep. Steve Pearce (R)

CAPITOL OFFICE
225-2365
www.house.gov/pearce
1408 Longworth 20515-3102; fax 225-9559

COMMITTEES
Resources
Transportation & Infrastructure

HOMETOWN
Hobbs

BORN
Aug. 23, 1947, Lamesa, Texas

RELIGION
Baptist

FAMILY
Wife, Cynthia Pearce; one child

EDUCATION
New Mexico State U., B.B.A. 1970 (economics); Eastern New Mexico U., M.B.A. 1991

MILITARY SERVICE
Air Force, 1971-76

CAREER
Oil well services company owner; corporate pilot

POLITICAL HIGHLIGHTS
N.M. House, 1997-2001; sought Republican nomination for U.S. Senate, 2000

ELECTION RESULTS

2002 GENERAL		
Steve Pearce (R)	79,631	56.2%
John Arthur Smith (D)	61,916	43.7%
2002 PRIMARY		
Steve Pearce (R)	12,346	35.1%
Edward R. Tinsley (R)	9,587	27.3%
Phelps Anderson (R)	8,432	24.0%
C. Earl Greer (R)	2,428	6.9%
Leo Martinez (R)	2,389	6.8%

Elected 2002; 1st term

Behind an outwardly dry personality are tactical political skills that Pearce put to work both before and after his election to the House. He outmaneuvered and out-organized his opponents in 2002. Shortly thereafter, he was named an assistant whip by the House Republican leadership.

His selection for that job indicated that Pearce plans to keep fairly close to the party line. He backs President Bush's economic program and his plans for pre-emptive action against Iraq. He is in the GOP mainstream in opposing more gun control and expanded abortion rights. But he also has sent signals that he might stray from time to time. His support for the war on terrorism is tempered, for example, by concern that the new Homeland Security Department might have too much power to thwart individual liberty in the name of security.

A four-year veteran of the state House and an Air Force veteran who served in Vietnam, Pearce owns a Mooney airplane that he flies for fun these days, although he also has been a corporate pilot. He was named one the top 100 members of the past century in the farm-oriented youth education group, 4-H. He rises at 4:30 a.m. daily to read the Bible.

Many of Pearce's concerns are local. In his campaign he lamented the water shortages that endanger farms and small businesses in southern New Mexico. He also says public lands should be "multiple use," and he supports oil exploration in the district. Pearce will pursue these issues from his seats on the Resources and Transportation and Infrastructure committees. Ultimately he would like to be on Appropriations like his predecessor, Republican Joe Skeen.

Skeen's failing health led to his retirement after 22 years in 2002. While conservative-leaning, the 2nd has a large Hispanic population that helps yield a Democratic voter registration edge. And the socially conservative views of their nominee, state Sen. John Arthur Smith, gave the party hope that he might have crossover appeal. But Pearce had a money advantage and Bush administration help, and he won by 12 percentage points.

NEW MEXICO 2

South – Las Cruces, Roswell

Before hosting the first atomic bomb explosion in 1945, the mostly rural 2nd, covering the southern half of the state, looked like the old American West. Since then, the area has attracted nuclear research and waste facilities to the Chihuahua Desert's deep salt beds and remote location. The first permanent underground low-level nuclear waste repository opened in abandoned salt mines near Carlsbad in 1999.

Towns in the 2nd have built a stable economy on traditional Western industries: copper and lead mining in the Mexican Highlands along the Arizona border, and oil and gas, as well as cattle and sheep ranching, in the southeastern corner of the state, dubbed Little Texas after the Texans who settled the region in the early 20th century. The northern New Mexico technology industry has spilled over into the 2nd, supported by New Mexico State and other universities. Severe water shortages have prevented large-scale industrial development and larger corporate farming, although the northern part of the district is a major producer of pistachios.

Beginning in the 1970s, ranchers and conservative Democrats steered away from a long liberal tradition. Democrats hold the vast majority of local offices, but the district is now competitive at the national level.

MAJOR INDUSTRY
Agriculture, mining, oil and gas production

MILITARY BASES
Holloman Air Force Base, 3,879 military, 1,159 civilian; White Sands Missile Range, 513 military, 2,422 civilian (2002)

CITIES
Las Cruces, 74,267; Roswell, 45,293; Alamogordo, 35,582; Hobbs, 28,657

NOTABLE
White Sands National Monument is the world's largest gypsum dune field; Roswell hosts an annual UFO festival near the site where a UFO allegedly crashed in 1947; Ted Turner, one of the nation's largest private landowners, owns more than 1.1 million acres in New Mexico, much of it in the 2nd.

Rep. Tom Udall (D)

CAPITOL OFFICE
225-6190
tom.udall@mail.house.gov
www.house.gov/tomudall
1414 Longworth 20515-3103; fax 226-1331

COMMITTEES
Resources
Small Business
Veterans' Affairs

HOMETOWN
Santa Fe

BORN
May 18, 1948, Tuscon, Ariz.

RELIGION
Mormon

FAMILY
Wife, Jill Z. Cooper; one stepchild

EDUCATION
Prescott College, B.A. 1970 (government & political science); Cambridge U., B.L.L. 1975; U. of New Mexico, J.D. 1977

CAREER
Lawyer

POLITICAL HIGHLIGHTS
Assistant U.S. attorney, 1978-81; sought Democratic nomination for U.S. House, 1982; Democratic nominee for U.S. House, 1988; N.M. attorney general, 1991-99

ELECTION RESULTS

2002 GENERAL		
Tom Udall (D)	unopposed	
2002 PRIMARY		
Tom Udall (D)	unopposed	
2000 GENERAL		
Tom Udall (D)	135,040	67.2%
Lisa L. Lutz (R)	65,979	32.8%

PREVIOUS WINNING PERCENTAGES
1998 (53%)

Elected 1998; 3rd term

As the cousin of a current congressman, the nephew of a former congressman, and the son of a former congressman and Interior secretary, Udall can claim a family legacy of public service beyond practically anyone whose last name is not Kennedy. Now in his third term, however, he has yet to send signals that he will transcend backbencher status and become a prominent legislative force in the mold of his father and uncle.

Udall and his Colorado cousin, Democrat Mark Udall, were elected to the House on the same day in 1998, bringing to Congress a second generation of their family. Tom's father, Stewart, represented Arizona in the House in the late 1950s before serving as secretary of Interior under Presidents Kennedy and Johnson. Morris K. Udall, Tom's uncle and Mark's father, succeeded his brother, Stewart, in the House in 1961 and was a prominent force there for the next 30 years. "From the time I was six, I heard my father and uncle talk about public service," Tom recalls.

The telegenic Udall, who carries himself with his father's straight-backed assurance and even talks like him, says that while his last name has helped him in Congress it has not allowed him to coast. "It opens doors, but then I think I have to do the work to persuade whoever it is that I'm fighting for a righteous cause," he says. "I'm not going to trade on what I haven't earned, but I am going to try to build on what I've been given."

Although he and his cousin have similar personalities and interests — both are avid mountaineers and both sit on the Resources Committee — he says his eight-year experience as New Mexico's attorney general "gives me a different perspective, a statewide perspective, on how the federal government interacts with the state." He acknowledges, though, that it has not always been easy making the transition from an attorney general's office with 150 employees to a congressional office with an ever-changing staff of about 20.

Udall also has found it hard to accept the partisan rancor in the closely divided House. "I'm a little disillusioned," he said early in 2002. "We can be less partisan, concentrating more on the substance of legislation in committee markups and in working groups rather than trying to just set down a marker for the election."

The Udall cousins have paired up on legislation, including an effort to create a national environmental stewardship program encouraging volunteers to help preserve parks, forests and other sensitive tracts. Continuing a practice he started as attorney general, the New Mexican has relied on his wife, Jill Z. Cooper, also an attorney, as a political confidante. Cooper, who was a consultant for the Presidential Commission on Holocaust Assets in 2000, stands in for her husband at events and serves as a sounding board.

Udall has spent much of his time concentrating on matters of local interest, a practical approach for a relatively junior House member in the minority. He worked with other members of the New Mexico delegation to get the federal government to purchase the picturesque 95,000-acre Baca Ranch in his district. Udall, who speaks Spanish, reintroduced a measure his predecessor, Republican Bill Redmond, had sponsored creating a commission to review the claims of heirs to Hispanic land grants.

Udall also has introduced bills to give poor people monthly stipends to cover their gasoline costs and to improve the Jicarilla Apache Reservation water system. The 2002 farm bill contains country-of-origin meat labeling requirements championed by Udall.

A reliable Democratic vote, Udall has aligned himself with his party's leaders in the House. He became a cog in the Democratic whip organization, working to round up votes for the leadership on key measures. He serves on Democratic Caucus task forces on education, energy, health, economics and homeland security. In the 108th Congress, he was elected by regional colleagues to the Steering Committee, which makes Democratic committee assignments.

As chairman of a Democratic campaign finance task force in the 106th Congress, Udall helped his party press GOP leaders to call up campaign finance legislation. In the 107th, he helped to write some of the provisions in the package that became law in 2002.

Udall has worked on his party's other priorities, including health care, releasing a study showing discrepancies in prescription drug prices in his district. He also worked with California's George Miller, the Education and the Workforce Committee's top Democrat, on the education reauthorization law enacted in 2002. Udall considers Miller, a liberal firebrand who nonetheless is skilled in the art of deal-making, one of the colleagues he most admires. Another role model is Michigan Democrat Sander M. Levin, a fellow liberal from a political family with close ties to organized labor.

Udall takes pains to stay in touch with his constituents, who range from nuclear scientists at Los Alamos National Laboratory to wealthy liberals in Santa Fe to rural Hispanics and Indians living in areas where unemployment remains fixed above 40 percent. He holds frequent town meetings across the district, which encompasses northern New Mexico and is roughly the size of Pennsylvania. "I believe very much in access," he says. "The main thing for me is striving to reach new people and get new ideas."

Udall has carved out a safe niche for himself in the district, which is easily New Mexico's most liberal. His 1998 House campaign was his third try: He lost a 1982 Democratic primary for the seat to Bill Richardson, who went on to win and serve there for more than 14 years. In 1988, Udall was the Democratic nominee in the adjacent 1st District but lost to Republican Steven H. Schiff. In 1998, Udall returned to the 3rd, as local Democrats were eager to oust Redmond, a conservative Republican minister who had won a three-way special election in May 1997 to replace Richardson when he left to become President Clinton's U.N. ambassador.

Udall won an eight-candidate Democratic primary; in the general election, he attacked Redmond as too conservative and won by a comfortable, 10 percentage point margin in the state's most Democratic district.

In 2000, Udall cruised to victory, by a ratio of more than 2-to-1. District lines were altered only slightly by redistricting, and Udall was unopposed in 2002.

KEY VOTES

2002

Yes Overhaul campaign finance law; ban "soft money" and restrict advocacy advertising
Yes Back Bush's defense budget increase
No Extend 1996 welfare law
No Adopt Bush's discretionary spending limit
No Pass GOP Medicare prescription drug plan
Yes Create independent Sept. 11 commission
Yes Extend union protections to Homeland Security Department employees
No Revive fast-track procedures for trade agreements
No Authorize war against Iraq
No Advance bankruptcy overhaul opposed by abortion opponents

2001

No Nullify Clinton Labor Department ergonomics rule
No Cut taxes by $1.35 trillion through fiscal 2011
Yes Maintain ban on oil drilling in Arctic National Wildlife Refuge
No Approve Bush proposal to limit managed-care plan liability for coverage decisions
Yes Divert money from crop subsidy payments to land conservation
No Expand law enforcement power to investigate suspected terrorists

CQ VOTE STUDIES

	PARTY UNITY		PRESIDENTIAL SUPPORT	
	Support	Oppose	Support	Oppose
2002	98%	2%	20%	80%
2001	96%	4%	23%	77%
2000	91%	9%	77%	23%
1999	92%	8%	78%	22%

INTEREST GROUPS

	AFL-CIO	ADA	CCUS	ACU
2002	89%	100%	35%	0%
2001	100%	100%	30%	4%
2000	90%	80%	35%	9%
1999	100%	95%	24%	0%

NEW MEXICO 3

North — Santa Fe, Rio Rancho, Farmington

Since artist Georgia O'Keeffe began painting northern New Mexico in 1929, the 3rd District's breathtaking scenery and unique Spanish and American Indian heritage have attracted thousands of artists and beauty seekers. Today, galleries and ski resorts still attract tourists, while an influx of retirees made the district the most rapidly growing part of the state in the 1990s.

But the 3rd is a district of extremes. Alongside the bountiful art trade is extraordinary poverty. Gallup, in McKinley County, boasts the most millionaires per capita in the world, while the county itself remains one of the poorest in the nation. Large American Indian populations in the northwest struggle with modest farming and ranching ventures in the same area that provides lofty incomes for oil and gas producers. Many western reservations are plagued with alcoholism, while Rio Arriba County in the north has the highest drug mortality rate in the nation.

Hispanics and American Indians — alongside a wealthy, liberal base in the state capital of Santa Fe — give Democrats a 2-to-1 edge in voter registration. Conservative pockets exist in areas such as Rio Rancho, where Intel employs more than 5,500 workers; Los Alamos, where the A-bomb was developed during WWII; and among energy producers in San Juan County in the district's northwest.

MAJOR INDUSTRY

State government, ranching, farming, tourism

MILITARY BASES

Cannon Air Force Base, 3,400 military, 597 civilian (2003)

CITIES

Santa Fe, 62,203; Rio Rancho (pt.), 46,701; Farmington, 37,844; Clovis, 32,667; Gallup, 20,209

NOTABLE

Santa Fe, the nation's second-oldest city, was founded in 1607, 13 years before the Pilgrims landed at Plymouth Rock; Roughly 100 tribes show their work at the Santa Fe Indian Market each August; The Aztec Ruins National Monument in Aztec features structures and artifacts from the 1100s and 1200s; Camel Rock, near Tesuque, is a natural sandstone formation that the elements have eroded into the shape of a camel; Officials said in 2003 they plan to renumber Route 666, now known as the "devil's highway," which runs north from Gallup into Colorado and Utah.

NEW YORK

Gov. George E. Pataki (R)

First elected: 1994
Length of term: 4 years
Term expires: 1/07
Salary: $179,000
Phone: (518) 474-8390
Hometown: Garrison
Born: June 24, 1945; Peekskill, N.Y.
Religion: Roman Catholic
Family: Wife, Elizabeth "Libby" Pataki; four children
Education: Yale U., B.A. 1967; Columbia U., J.D. 1970
Career: Lawyer; farm owner
Political highlights: Mayor of Peekskill, 1982-84; N.Y. Assembly, 1985-92; N.Y. Senate, 1993-95
Election results:

2002 GENERAL		
George E. Pataki (R, C)	2,262,255	49.4%
H. Carl McCall (D, WFM)	1,534,064	33.5%
Blase Tom Golisano (INDC)	654,016	14.3%
Gerard J. Cronin (RTL)	44,195	1.0%

Lt. Gov. Mary Donohue (R)

First elected: 1998
Length of term: 4 years
Term expires: 1/07
Salary: $151,000
Phone: (518) 474-4623

STATE LEGISLATURE

Legislature: Officially meets year-round; main session January-June
Assembly: 150 members, 2-year terms
2003 breakdown: 47R, 103D; 115 men, 35 women
Salary: $79,500
Phone: (518) 455-4218
Senate: 62 members, 2-year terms
2003 breakdown: 38R, 24D; 51 men, 11 women
Salary: $79,500
Phone: (518) 455-3216

STATE TERM LIMITS

Governor: No
Senate: No
House: No

URBAN STATISTICS

CITY	POPULATION
New York City	8,008,278
Buffalo	292,648
Rochester	219,773
Yonkers	196,086
Syracuse	147,306

REGISTERED VOTERS

Democrat	47%
Republican	28%
Other parties/Unaffiliated	20%

POPULATION

2002 population (est.)	19,157,532
2000 population	18,976,457
1990 population	17,990,455
Percent change (1990-2000)	+5.5%
Rank among states (2002)	3
Median age	35.9
Born in state	65.3%
Foreign born	20.4%
Violent crime rate	554/100,000
Poverty level	14.6%
Federal workers	133,980
Military	57,987

REDISTRICTING

New York lost two House seats in reapportionment. The state legislature drew a new, 29-district map, which the governor signed on June 5, 2002.

MISCELLANEOUS

Web: www.state.ny.us
Capital: Albany

STATE ELECTION OFFICIAL
(518) 474-6220

DEMOCRATIC HEADQUARTERS
(212) 725-8825

REPUBLICAN HEADQUARTERS
(518) 462-2601

District Statistics

DIST.	2000 VOTE FOR PRESIDENT														
	BUSH	GORE	NADER	WHITE	BLACK	ASIAN	HISP	MEDIAN INCOME	WHITE COLLAR	BLUE COLLAR	SERVICE INDUSTRY	OVER 64	UNDER 18	COLLEGE EDUCATION	RURAL	SQ. MILES
1	43%	53%	4%	84%	4%	2%	8%	$61,884	64%	21%	15%	12%	26%	27%	6%	646
2	39	58	3	72	10	3	14	$71,147	66	20	14	12	27	31	0	239
3	44	53	3	87	2	3	7	$70,561	69	17	14	15	24	31	0	183
4	37	60	3	62	18	4	14	$66,799	68	17	15	14	25	31	0	90
5	29	68	3	44	5	24	23	$51,156	65	18	17	15	22	34	0	66
6	11	88	1	13	52	9	17	$43,546	57	21	22	11	27	18	0	40
7	21	76	3	28	17	13	40	$36,990	57	21	22	13	24	20	0	26
8	18	76	6	69	5	11	12	$47,061	79	10	11	14	18	48	0	15
9	30	68	3	64	4	15	14	$45,426	68	18	14	17	21	31	0	37
10	8	88	3	16	60	3	17	$30,212	60	18	22	10	30	18	0	18
11	9	87	4	21	59	4	12	$34,082	61	16	23	9	27	25	0	12
12	15	79	6	23	9	16	49	$29,195	51	28	21	9	26	17	0	19
13	44	53	3	71	6	9	11	$50,092	65	18	17	13	24	24	0	65
14	23	72	5	66	5	11	14	$57,152	82	8	10	13	13	57	0	13
15	7	89	4	16	31	3	48	$27,934	64	15	21	11	24	25	0	10

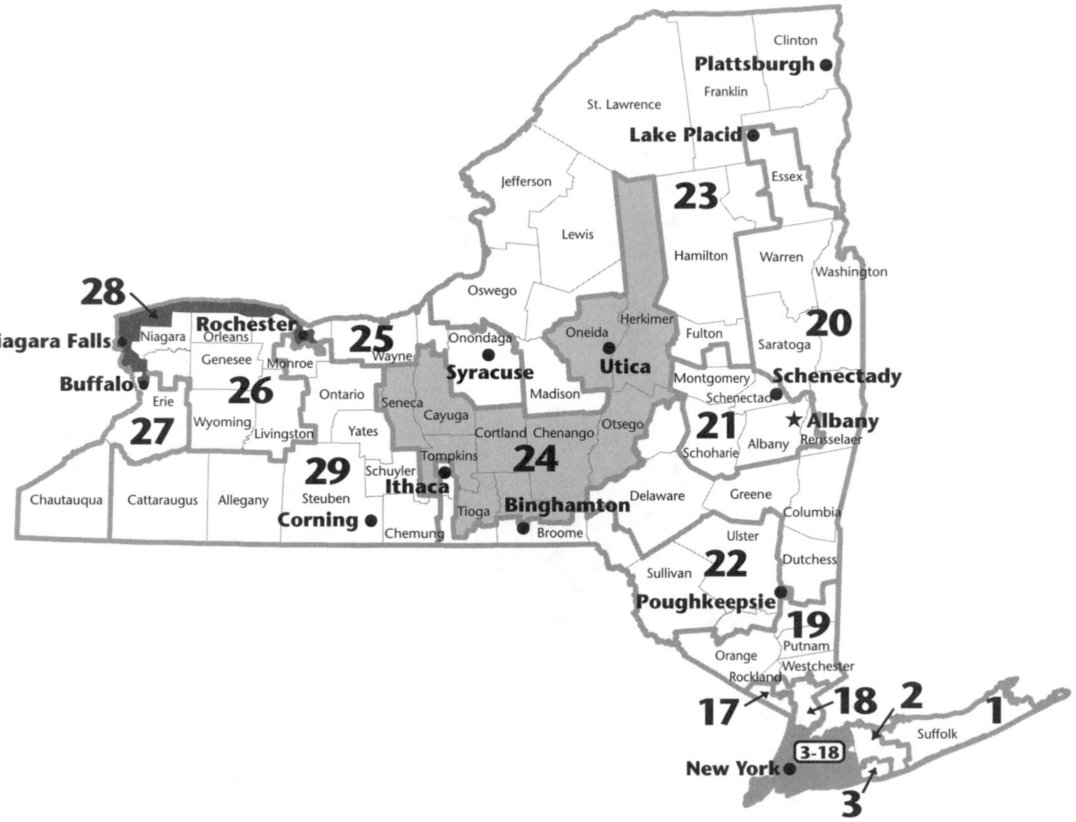

District Statistics

DIST.	2000 VOTE FOR PRESIDENT BUSH	GORE	NADER	WHITE	BLACK	ASIAN	HISP	MEDIAN INCOME	WHITE COLLAR	BLUE COLLAR	SERVICE INDUSTRY	OVER 64	UNDER 18	COLLEGE EDUCATION	RURAL	SQ. MILES
16	6%	93%	2%	3%	30%	2%	63%	$19,311	46%	24%	30%	7%	35%	8%	0%	12
17	26	71	3	41	30	5	20	$44,868	65	16	19	13	27	29	0	127
18	38	59	3	67	9	5	16	$68,887	73	13	14	14	25	44	1	222
19	49	47	4	84	5	2	8	$64,337	67	19	14	11	27	32	21	1,401
20	51	45	5	93	2	1	2	$44,239	61	24	15	14	24	25	55	7,018
21	39	56	5	85	7	2	3	$40,254	66	19	15	15	23	27	16	1,935
22	42	52	6	80	8	3	8	$38,586	61	22	17	14	24	24	32	3,246
23	49	47	4	93	3	1	2	$35,434	52	29	19	12	25	16	65	13,235
24	48	47.6	4	92	3	1	2	$36,082	57	25	17	15	24	19	49	6,164
25	45	51	4	87	7	2	2	$43,188	65	21	14	14	26	28	21	1,620
26	52	45	4	92	3	2	2	$46,653	62	24	14	14	25	26	29	2,731
27	41	55	4	89	4	1	5	$36,884	58	26	16	16	24	20	18	1,830
28	33	63	4	62	29	1	6	$31,751	58	23	18	14	26	21	7	534
29	54	43	3	93	3	2	1	$41,875	61	24	15	14	25	26	42	5,660
STATE	35	60	4	62	15	5	15	$43,393	64	20	17	13	25	27	13	47,214
U.S.	47.9	48.4	3	69	12	4	13	$41,994	60	25	15	12	26	24	21	3,537,438

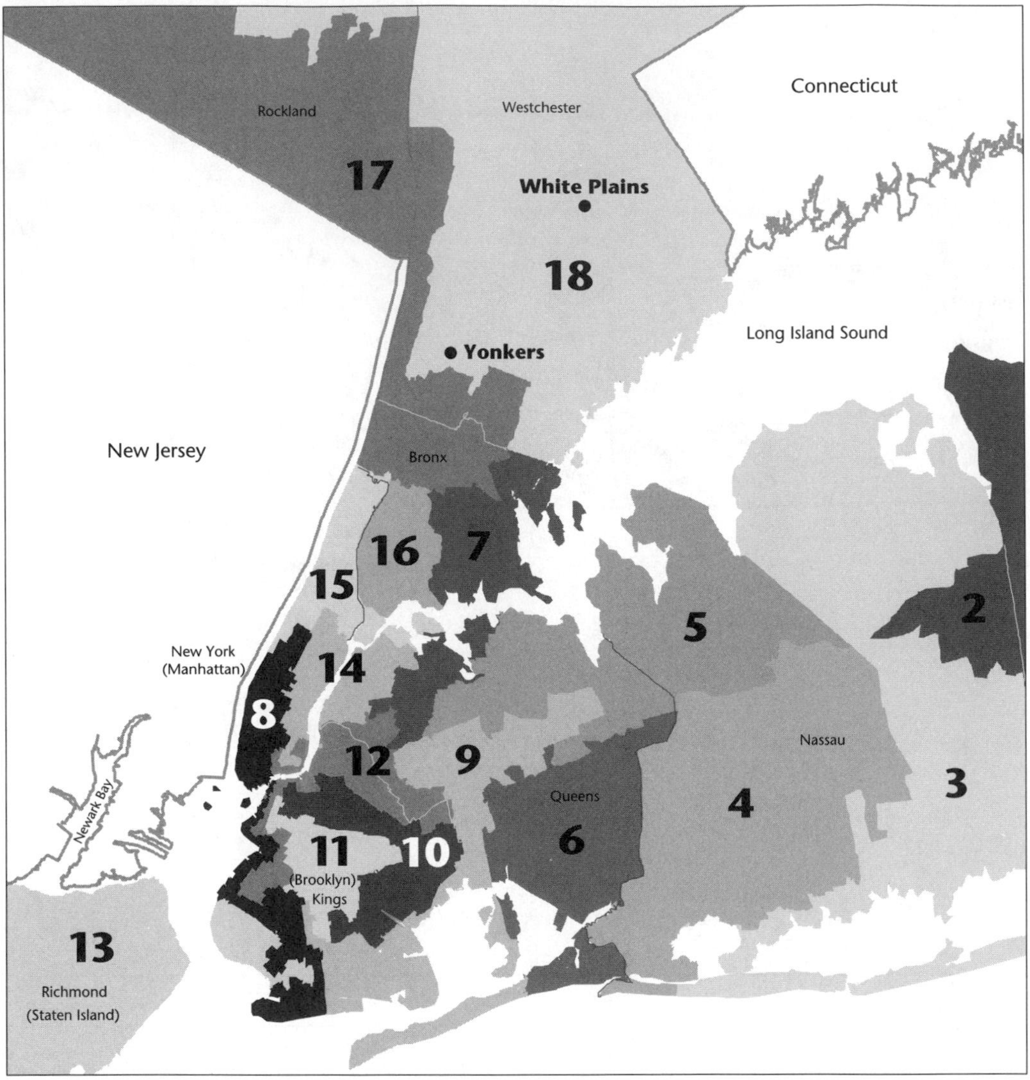
Rockland
Westchester
Connecticut
17
White Plains
18
Long Island Sound
Yonkers
New Jersey
Bronx
16
7
15
5
2
New York
(Manhattan)
14
8
Nassau
12
9
3
Newark Bay
Queens
4
11
10
6
(Brooklyn)
Kings
13
Richmond
(Staten Island)

Sen. Charles E. Schumer (D)

CAPITOL OFFICE
224-6542
schumer.senate.gov
313 Hart 20510-3203; fax 228-3027

COMMITTEES
Banking, Housing & Urban Affairs
Energy & Natural Resources
Judiciary
Rules & Administration
Joint Library

HOMETOWN
Brooklyn

BORN
Nov. 23, 1950, Brooklyn, N.Y.

RELIGION
Jewish

FAMILY
Wife, Iris Weinshall; two children

EDUCATION
Harvard U., A.B. 1971, J.D. 1974

CAREER
Lawyer

POLITICAL HIGHLIGHTS
N.Y. Assembly, 1975-81; U.S. House, 1981-99

ELECTION RESULTS

1998 GENERAL		
Charles E. Schumer (D, INDC, L)	2,551,065	54.6%
Alfonse M. D'Amato (R, C, RTL)	2,058,988	44.1%
1998 PRIMARY		
Charles E. Schumer (D)	388,701	50.8%
Geraldine A. Ferraro (D)	201,625	26.4%
Mark Green (D)	145,819	19.1%
Eric Ruano Melendez (D)	28,493	3.7%

PREVIOUS WINNING PERCENTAGES
1996 House Election (75%); 1994 House Election (73%); 1992 House Election (89%); 1990 House Election (80%); 1988 House Election (78%); 1986 House Election (93%); 1984 House Election (72%); 1982 House Election (79%); 1980 House Election (77%)

Elected 1998; 1st term

Former Senate Republican leader Bob Dole once joked that the most dangerous place to stand was between Schumer and a TV camera. Schumer's incessant stream of news releases and clever quotes makes his one of the fastest-spinning congressional publicity mills. But it is a measure of his intellect and hard work that Schumer can talk with authority about a wide range of public policies, and his negotiating skills far from the camera's glare have produced a long string of legislative successes.

In the 108th Congress, discouraged by the party's losses in the 2002 elections, Minority Leader Tom Daschle named Schumer to a new four-member executive committee to hone the party's agenda and its public message.

A member of the Judiciary Committee in the Senate, as he was during his 18-year House career, Schumer has led opposition to several of President Bush's judicial nominees, describing them as "out of the mainstream." Schumer argues that a potential federal judge's ideology should be taken into consideration by senators — a view contrary to the customary belief that presidents should be given wide latitude to shape the federal courts.

Schumer staked out his role in the confirmation wars from the opening days of the Bush administration, when he battled the nomination of John Ashcroft — a former colleague on Senate Judiciary — to be attorney general. He declared that the fight against Ashcroft was "a shot across the bow," aimed at discouraging the president from making similarly divisive judicial nominations in the future.

As the 107th Congress began, Schumer was grudgingly prepared to operate in a relative shadow, while a glare of international celebrity surrounded his new home-state colleague in the Senate, fellow Democrat Hillary Rodham Clinton. The pair remain competitive and turf-conscious — over both legislative territory in Washington and Democratic primacy back home — but after the Sept. 11, 2001, terrorist attacks they were able to work together on behalf of the victims, most of whom they counted as constituents.

Schumer also joined with Republican Sen. Don Nickles of Oklahoma to expand a compensation fund for victims of the 2001 attacks to benefit families of those killed or injured in the 1995 Oklahoma City federal building bombing and a 1993 World Trade Center bombing. And he partnered with Arizona Republican Jon Kyl on a bill to ease the authorization for warrants under the Foreign Intelligence Surveillance Act. The proposal, which got no further than hearings in the 107th, drew criticism from civil libertarians.

Schumer's work on the surveillance bill was characteristic of his longstanding support for giving law enforcement more power to pursue criminals. In the House, where he chaired the Judiciary Crime Subcommittee for four years, he was a main sponsor of the 1994 anti-crime law. It created President Clinton's program to put 100,000 new officers on the beat, banned 19 assault weapons, expanded the federal death penalty and created a "three-strikes" mandatory life sentence for repeat violent offenders. Building on a bill Schumer sponsored, the law also called for enhanced sentences for "hate crimes" motivated by bias.

An ardent gun control advocate, Schumer was the chief sponsor of the 1993 Brady law that required a background check for the purchase of any handgun. When the National Rifle Association once called him "the criminal's best friend," Schumer shot back: "I wear this like a badge of honor."

Much of Schumer's anti-crime work is aimed at helping victims. In 2002,

Schumer lambasted the Justice Department for requiring rape victims to help pay for the collection of forensic evidence against their attackers, which he likened to "asking the family of a homicide victim to pay for the autopsy." He won Senate passage of a bill aimed at making the recovery process easier for victims, but it did not advance in the House.

His interests are by no means limited to crime. Early in 2003, he urged that any economic stimulus package include a one-time, $40 billion boost in direct aid to state and local governments. He proposed a $10 billion plan to outfit all commercial airliners with anti-missile equipment. And he resurrected a bill with Republican John McCain of Arizona, which the Senate had passed in 2002, to speed generic drugs to market by making it more difficult for brand-name drugmakers to extend their patents.

On the Banking Committee, Schumer tries to serve both business interests and average New Yorkers. He worked to reverse a federal plan that would have required investment banks to set up alternate headquarters outside New York as a contingency in case of another terrorist attack. He has pressed to reduce securities transaction fees and also argued for more protection for consumers with bad credit, prompting the American Banker newsletter to describe Schumer as "one of the few members of the often-polarized Senate Banking and Judiciary committees that can make both industry and community groups happy."

Schumer has been central to the debate, ongoing since 1997, over revamping the nation's bankruptcy code. In the 107th, he added a provision designed to block abortion protesters from filing for bankruptcy to avoid paying court-ordered fines and judgments. Ultimately, the bankruptcy bill sank because of resistance among anti-abortion lawmakers to compromise language Schumer wrote with Illinois Republican Rep. Henry J. Hyde.

Schumer was a familiar face on television as a defender of President Clinton at the time of his impeachment. He was the only person to cast votes on the matter in three venues — as a member of the House Judiciary Committee, then on the House floor at the end of 1998 and then during the trial at the start of his service in the Senate in 1999.

Brooklyn born and bred, Schumer was elected to represent the borough in the state Assembly just before he turned 24, the fall after his graduation from Harvard Law School. Six years later, he was easily elected to Congress with the endorsement of Elizabeth Holtzman, who gave up her Brooklyn House seat to be the 1980 Democratic nominee for the Senate.

She lost that year to Republican Alfonse M. D'Amato, and after husbanding his statewide ambitions for 18 years Schumer decided to take on D'Amato. He won the Democratic nomination with 51 percent against former Rep. Geraldine A. Ferraro, the 1984 vice presidential nominee, and New York City Public Advocate Mark Green.

In the fall D'Amato branded Schumer as a liberal and attacked him for missing more than 100 floor votes while campaigning. Schumer deflected D'Amato's charges, pointing to his anti-crime and gun control efforts, and also recounted D'Amato's history of ethics problems. Though D'Amato spent more than $24 million, Schumer was competitive, spending almost $17 million. He won by almost 500,000 votes.

Facing re-election in 2004, Schumer had stockpiled almost $13.6 million in cash by the end of 2002. And he was maintaining the peripatetic operating style that had sustained his congressional career. He meets with the New York press corps almost every Sunday, the New York Times wrote in a profile, "often to talk about small-bore issues that might get him headlines on what is traditionally a slow news day: restoring telephone service to a block in Harlem; urging the National Football League to bring the Super Bowl to New York, exhorting New Yorkers to donate blood."

KEY VOTES

2002

Yes Pass farm bill reversing crop subsidy limits
No Postpone tougher automobile fuel efficiency standards
Yes Overhaul campaign finance law; ban "soft money" and restrict advocacy advertising
Yes Set federal election standards
No Support oil drilling in Arctic National Wildlife Refuge
No Revive fast-track procedures for trade agreements
Yes Create federal insurance coverage for catastrophic terrorist losses
Yes Tighten federal accounting and corporate governance regulation
Yes Advance bipartisan Medicare prescription drug plan
Yes Create independent Sept. 11 commission
Yes Back Democratic Homeland Security Department proposal
Yes Authorize war against Iraq

2001

No Confirm John Ashcroft as attorney general
No Nullify Clinton Labor Department ergonomics rule
No Cut taxes by $1.35 trillion through fiscal 2011
Yes Pass Democratic bill to bolster rights of patients in managed-care plans
No Permit a new round of military base closings
Yes Expand law enforcement power to investigate suspected terrorists

CQ VOTE STUDIES

	PARTY UNITY		PRESIDENTIAL SUPPORT	
	Support	Oppose	Support	Oppose
2002	95%	5%	68%	32%
2001	92%	8%	65%	35%
2000	97%	3%	98%	2%
1999	94%	6%	91%	9%
House Service:				
1998	94%	6%	85%	15%
1997	90%	10%	83%	17%
1996	91%	9%	83%	17%
1995	89%	11%	87%	13%
1994	94%	6%	83%	17%
1993	97%	3%	83%	17%

INTEREST GROUPS

	AFL-CIO	ADA	CCUS	ACU
2002	92%	85%	50%	10%
2001	100%	95%	43%	16%
2000	75%	95%	53%	12%
1999	89%	100%	53%	4%
House Service:				
1998	100%	100%	36%	9%
1997	100%	85%	40%	19%
1996	90%	90%	31%	5%
1995	100%	80%	32%	4%
1994	75%	90%	58%	5%
1993	100%	95%	9%	9%

Sen. Hillary Rodham Clinton (D)

CAPITOL OFFICE
224-4451
senator@clinton.senate.gov
clinton.senate.gov
476 Russell 20510-3204; fax 228-0282

COMMITTEES
Armed Services
Environment & Public Works
Health, Education, Labor & Pensions

HOMETOWN
Chappaqua

BORN
Oct. 26, 1947, Chicago, Ill.

RELIGION
Methodist

FAMILY
Husband, Bill Clinton; one child

EDUCATION
Wellesley College, B.A. 1969; Yale U., J.D. 1973

CAREER
First lady; lawyer; law school professor

POLITICAL HIGHLIGHTS
No previous office

ELECTION RESULTS

2000 GENERAL		
Hillary R. Clinton (D, L, WFM)	3,747,310	55.3%
Rick A. Lazio (R, C)	2,915,730	43.0%
2000 PRIMARY		
Hillary R. Clinton (D)	565,353	82.0%
Mark McMahon (D)	124,315	18.0%

Elected 2000; 1st term

Since arriving in the Senate, Clinton has consciously transformed herself from a national lightning rod to a pragmatic legislator willing to reach across party lines. She has won respect in the Senate by keeping a relatively low profile and demonstrating a willingness to take a backseat to some of her less-prominent colleagues.

But by the start of the 108th Congress, there were signs that Clinton was ready to move to the foreground. She led Democrats in a push to extend unemployment benefits at the end of 2002, and she expressed interest in taking on a leadership role in her party. Democratic leader Tom Daschle named her to chair the Steering and Coordination Committee, which serves as a liaison between Senate Democrats and other Democratic officials and organizations around the country.

It was hard to imagine a senator elected with as much fanfare as former first lady Clinton — hailed by her loyalists as a policy innovator and survivor of brutal conservative attacks against her and President Clinton, derided by critics as an overly ambitious, scandal-prone carpetbagger who had no business running for the Senate in New York.

Clinton secured her place in history in 2000, when she became the only first lady elected to a federal office. But that lofty distinction was balanced by a distinct disadvantage: She had to operate, negotiate and legislate among many colleagues who long ago had formed their opinions about her personality and politics.

During her campaign, GOP Sen. Don Nickles of Oklahoma, who was then majority whip, attended a fundraiser at the Capitol Hill restaurant La Colline that garnered $100,000 for her opponent, Rep. Rick A. Lazio. Two years later, in November 2002, Nickles joined with Clinton to cobble together a compromise on extending unemployment benefits for three months. President Bush endorsed the plan, and it eventually became law early in 2003.

Her collaboration with Nickles on the issue was just one example of her ability to work with the GOP. On the Environment and Public Works Committee, Clinton has frequently teamed up with Republican senators such as George V. Voinovich of Ohio and James M. Inhofe of Oklahoma. Other former critics, such as Republican Sens. Mike DeWine of Ohio and Pat Roberts of Kansas, also have penned legislation with her.

When she was first lady, Clinton's policy passion was health care, but she has placed less emphasis on that topic as a senator. Instead, she has tended closely to the needs of New York, a state where she never resided until deciding to run for office.

Behind the scenes, Clinton runs a sophisticated operation, more like that of a senior senator. Her chief of staff is a seasoned Capitol Hill veteran. Her top health care legislative aide hails from the Clinton White House. She employs the power of her office in back channels, writing letters to executive branch agencies, asking questions.

Aides on both sides of the aisle describe Clinton as a model freshman student of the Senate, who has worked hard to learn its rules and customs. She arrives at her subcommittee hearings and committee legislative sessions well-prepared. Her attention to detail extends to thank-you notes for helpful staffers.

In the 108th, Clinton won appointment to the Armed Services panel, the first New Yorker to serve on the committee in its 56-year history.

She also sits on the Health, Education, Labor and Pensions panel. During consideration of an education bill in the 107th Congress, Clinton offered five amendments on teacher training. All five won approval — an impressive feat for a freshman legislator. She acknowledged she is eyeing assignment to one of the more coveted committees — either Finance or Appropriations — when it is her turn.

Clinton still has a zest for partisan combat from time to time on high-profile issues. During confirmation hearings on Tommy G. Thompson's nomination to be secretary of health and human services, Clinton plunged into one of the most controversial issues facing the nominee by questioning him about the drug mifepristone, also known as RU486. The drug blocks the action of progesterone, which is necessary to sustain a pregnancy. Noting that the drug "was approved by the FDA [Food and Drug Administration] as a safe and effective method of early medical abortion," Clinton asked Thompson: "Will you take any action to undo the FDA approval of RU486, which was based on strong scientific evidence?" Thompson was noncommittal.

Clinton likes to point to federal projects that she has helped to win for her adopted state. The list starts with $20 billion in emergency funding for New York after the Sept. 11, 2001, terrorist attacks. The senator says she worked not only to help secure the funds, but to push for their rapid disbursement.

However, Clinton has suffered some prominent legislative setbacks. She and other New York lawmakers tried and failed to extract billions more from the White House in response to the attacks. On health care, Clinton's biggest initiative in the 107th Congress — a bill to require drugmakers to conduct pediatric safety tests when their products are prescribed for children — did not advance beyond committee.

Singed by the failure of her health care task force in the first two years of her husband's presidency, Clinton has restrained her ambitions in that area as a senator.

"Right now I'm focused on the incremental changes that could damage our existing health care system, like the cutbacks in Medicare funding for our teaching hospitals and our rural hospitals, payments to doctors, the nursing shortage," she said in 2002.

But Clinton still dreams of returning to a broader health care fight someday. "Nobody has really tackled the big question about how we're going to do a better job of funding health care and trying to provide a system that is more cost effective and offers the chance for everyone to be insured. I will certainly weigh in on that," she said in 2002.

Indeed, Clinton remains a prominent national figure, a fact that was reinforced after Bush's State of the Union address in 2002. Every year lawmakers seek national attention by responding to the president's speech, and they flock to reporters stationed in the Capitol to be interviewed. While the Speaker of the House, J. Dennis Hastert, was waiting patiently in a television queue for his turn, producers whisked Clinton to the front of one of the lines.

Despite her efforts to work with Republicans, her tenure as first lady of Arkansas and then of the United States leaves no doubt about her liberal views. She advocates an activist government on issues such as education, health care and gun control. In her 1996 book "It Takes a Village," Clinton wrote: "In a democracy, government is not 'them' but 'us,' an endeavor that joins with volunteerism and the efforts of the private sector in sustaining our mutual obligations to our children, families and communities."

She was praised by supporters as bold and brilliant, but reviled by opponents as a social engineer who would inject government into all realms of Americans' private lives. Clinton surprised those critics, who thought her liberal views made her a soft target, by handily defeating Lazio by 12 percentage points.

KEY VOTES

2002

Yes Pass farm bill reversing crop subsidy limits
No Postpone tougher automobile fuel efficiency standards
Yes Overhaul campaign finance law; ban "soft money" and restrict advocacy advertising
Yes Set federal election standards
No Support oil drilling in Arctic National Wildlife Refuge
No Revive fast-track procedures for trade agreements
Yes Create federal insurance coverage for catastrophic terrorist losses
Yes Tighten federal accounting and corporate governance regulation
Yes Advance bipartisan Medicare prescription drug plan
Yes Create independent Sept. 11 commission
Yes Back Democratic Homeland Security Department proposal
Yes Authorize war against Iraq

2001

No Confirm John Ashcroft as attorney general
No Nullify Clinton Labor Department ergonomics rule
No Cut taxes by $1.35 trillion through fiscal 2011
Yes Pass Democratic bill to bolster rights of patients in managed-care plans
No Permit a new round of military base closings
Yes Expand law enforcement power to investigate suspected terrorists

CQ VOTE STUDIES

	PARTY UNITY		PRESIDENTIAL SUPPORT	
	Support	Oppose	Support	Oppose
2002	93%	7%	67%	33%
2001	97%	3%	61%	39%

INTEREST GROUPS

	AFL-CIO	ADA	CCUS	ACU
2002	92%	95%	45%	10%
2001	100%	95%	43%	12%

Rep. Timothy H. Bishop (D)

Elected 2002; 1st term

Bishop is one of just four freshmen who unseated an incumbent in November, upsetting one-term GOP Rep. Felix J. Grucci Jr.

But that is really nothing new for New York's 1st District, which takes up the eastern end of Long Island. Since 1999, the 1st has had three different representatives and switched party hands three times.

A longtime provost at Southampton College, Bishop won assignment to the Education and the Workforce Committee, where he can bring his professional background in education to bear. Bishop also got a coveted spot on the Transportation Committee.

As a board member of the Eastern Long Island Coastal Conservation Alliance, Bishop says he will work to fund the acquisition of land threatened by development, adding that Washington is not up-to-date on what localities are doing about sprawl. Other priorities include ensuring support for the Brookhaven National Laboratory and an animal disease research facility on Plum Island, in the 1st.

Bishop, whose district has a large senior citizen population, takes liberal stands on health care issues. He says he will work for universal health care programs.

Bishop says he also will insist on a balanced budget. Rather than back a total abolition of the estate tax — as called for in tax cut legislation that President Bush pushed to enactment in 2001 — he wants to exempt family farms passed from generation to generation.

During the campaign, Bishop pointed out Grucci's poor marks from the League of Conservation Voters and accused the Grucci family's fireworks company of polluting groundwater. Bishop's emphasis on environmental protection won him a constituency in the coastal district.

But his boost into contention was the result of a gaffe by Grucci, whose campaign ad accusing Bishop of turning his back on rape victims during his tenure as a college official was refuted and widely vilified. Bishop won by less than 2 percentage points; Grucci did not concede the victory until nine days after the election.

CAPITOL OFFICE
225-3826
tim.bishop@mail.house.gov
www.house.gov/timbishop
1133 Longworth 20515-3201; fax 225-3143

COMMITTEES
Education & Workforce
Transportation & Infrastructure

HOMETOWN
Southampton

BORN
June 1, 1950, Southampton, N.Y.

RELIGION
Roman Catholic

FAMILY
Wife, Kathryn Bishop; two children

EDUCATION
College of the Holy Cross, B.A. 1972; Long Island U., M.P.A. 1981

CAREER
College provost; college administrator

POLITICAL HIGHLIGHTS
No previous office

ELECTION RESULTS

2002 GENERAL

Timothy H. Bishop (D, WFM)	84,276	50.2%
Felix J. Grucci Jr. (R, C, INDC, RTL)	81,524	48.6%
Lorna Salzman (GREEN)	1,991	1.2%

2002 PRIMARY

Timothy H. Bishop (D)	unopposed

NEW YORK 1

Eastern Suffolk County — Hamptons, Smithtown

Covering the eastern two-thirds of Long Island's Suffolk County, the 1st reaches out into the Atlantic Ocean. At its far eastern end, the district takes in the elite estates of some of New York's wealthiest in the Hamptons and Shelter Island. The rural end of the island has retained its pastoral character, with fishing villages, farms and wineries scattered throughout. Many duck farms have disappeared, but Long Island's wine industry has expanded rapidly.

Moving west, the 1st takes in some blue-collar towns, populated by conservative Irish-Catholics and Italian-Americans. Farther west, Smithtown and Brookhaven have boomed with suburban growth. Defense once dominated the economy, but many of those jobs have been replaced by scientific research, attracted by the State University of New York at Stony Brook and Brookhaven National Laboratory.

The 1st's lingering rural temperament and small-town feel make it one of the most conservative districts near New York City. Registration favors Republicans, but many residents have more liberal views on abortion and gun laws. Environmental issues rank high, as many towns depend on the ocean for fish and tourism.

Although Republicans dominate at the local level, Democrats make the 1st competitive in federal elections. Voters have sent a Democrat to the House in 14 of the previous 22 elections. Al Gore outpolled George W. Bush by a 53 percent to 43 percent tally in the 2000 presidential election, and Bill Clinton carried the district in 1996.

MAJOR INDUSTRY
Higher education, medicine, research

CITIES
Coram (unincorporated), 34,923; Centereach (unincorporated), 27,285

NOTABLE
The Montauk Point Lighthouse, built in 1796, was the first lighthouse in New York State.

Rep. Steve Israel (D)

CAPITOL OFFICE
225-3335
www.house.gov/israel
429 Cannon 20515-3202; fax 225-4669

COMMITTEES
Armed Services
Financial Services

HOMETOWN
Huntington

BORN
May 30, 1958, Brooklyn, N.Y.

RELIGION
Jewish

FAMILY
Engaged to Marlene Budd; two children

EDUCATION
Nassau Community College, A.A. 1978 (liberal arts); Syracuse U., attended 1978-79; George Washington U., B.A. 1982 (political science)

CAREER
Public relations and marketing firm manager; assistant county executive; university fundraising director; Jewish advocacy group county director; congressional aide

POLITICAL HIGHLIGHTS
Democratic nominee for Suffolk County Legislature, 1987; Huntington Town Board, 1993-2001 (majority leader, 1997-2001)

ELECTION RESULTS

2002 GENERAL		
Steve Israel (D, INDC, WFM)	85,451	58.5%
Joseph P. Finley (R, C, RTL)	59,117	40.5%
John Keenan (GREEN)	1,558	1.1%
2002 PRIMARY		
Steve Israel (D)		unopposed
2000 GENERAL		
Steve Israel (D)	90,438	47.9%
Joan B. Johnson (R)	65,880	34.9%
Robert T. Walsh Sr. (RTL)	11,224	6.0%
Richard Thompson (C)	10,824	5.7%
David Bishop (INDC, GREEN, WFM)	10,266	5.4%

Elected 2000; 2nd term

Israel made it to Congress in 2001 in the politically competitive 2nd District through a series of events shaped by other New York politicians.

When New York Mayor Rudolph Giuliani announced that he had prostate cancer and was dropping his much-anticipated Senate bid, the 2nd District's four-term GOP Rep. Rick Lazio stepped into the race, leaving the House seat open. Israel immediately joined the campaign for the open seat. The 2nd District includes many independent voters, and they like their lawmakers to remain in the center, regardless of party affiliation. Israel fits that description as a fiscal conservative who is moderate on social issues.

With an eye to keeping his seat, Israel makes a point of working across party lines — in the 107th he often teamed up with his Long Island neighbor, 1st District Republican Felix J. Grucci Jr. — and backing President Bush almost half the time, a mark that put him among the top three dozen Democratic supporters of the president in the 107th Congress.

Israel's tenure on the Huntington Town Board was also marked by his bipartisanship and fiscal conservatism, as he worked to cut the town's long-term debt in half. When he reached the House, Israel signed on with the centrist New Democrat Coalition and the more conservative "Blue Dog" coalition. Israel is the only New Yorker and one of only three Northeast lawmakers in the Blue Dogs, and he is one of the most liberal, according to the assessments of the liberal Americans for Democratic Action and the American Conservative Union.

Mindful of Israel's politically competitive district, the Democratic leadership helped him establish himself early. They gave Israel a seat on the Financial Services Committee and chose him as the only freshman representative on the Democratic Steering Committee, which doles out committee assignments. Later in the 107th Congress, party leaders put Israel on their Homeland Security Task Force. In the 108th, he is the only New York Democrat on the Armed Services Committee.

Israel has said that health care is one of his top legislative concerns, and his first bill was aimed at giving health maintenance organizations incentives to serve senior citizens and penalizing HMOs if they discontinued coverage. Israel contends that many Long Island senior citizens have been rejected by their HMOs, because reimbursement rates for Suffolk County were set too low under Medicare spending rates approved by Congress in 1997.

Assertive and energetic, Israel buttonholed the president late in 2001 about the Medicare issue when Bush visited Capitol Hill to pass along Christmas wishes. "I just planted myself at the exit of the room. He was going to have to knock me down to get past," Israel told The New York Times. The confrontation earned him meetings with administration officials who vowed to try to resolve the HMO problem. He also has worked on the issue with Connecticut Republican Nancy L. Johnson, who chairs the Ways and Means Subcommittee on Health, irking some Democratic leaders.

Israel was rebuked by fellow New Yorker Charles B. Rangel, the top-ranking Democrat on Ways and Means, for his support of GOP legislation to eliminate the so-called marriage penalty tax. Later, Israel was one of only nine Democrats to vote for a GOP economic stimulus bill.

On the Financial Services panel, Israel has worked to ensure the availability of affordable housing, a longtime interest and an issue of concern to suburban Long Islanders. As the committee worked on a money-laundering bill, it approved an Israel amendment calling for more attention to the links between international terrorism and ostensible charities.

Israel became involved in politics in high school, riding his bicycle after school to the campaign headquarters of Democrat Franklin Ornstein, who waged an unsuccessful challenge in 1974 to GOP Rep. Norman F. Lent. As a political science student at George Washington University, Israel worked briefly for California Democratic Rep. Robert T. Matsui and then spent three years with Rep. Richard L. Ottinger, a New York Democrat.

Israel returned to Long Island in 1983, where he worked as a fundraiser for Touro College, a Jewish-sponsored institution. In 1987, he lost a bid for the Suffolk County legislature, but then he went to work as an aide to the county executive.

He later formed his own fundraising and public relations firm. Israel was the director of the Institute on the Holocaust and the Law, which is affiliated with Touro and the American Jewish Congress. He stayed active in local politics, winning a seat on the Huntington Town Board in a 1993 special election. During his seven years on the town board, Israel worked with Republicans to put the town on a sound fiscal footing — cutting the long-term debt by almost half and improving the bond rating while opposing a property tax increase. He was the first local official to offer information about his activities on the Internet, establishing his own Web page.

During his years in Long Island politics, Israel said, he always had in mind a return to Washington. "I learned as a congressional aide how effective you can be, and I always hoped to have the opportunity," he told Newsday.

His chance came in 2000 when Lazio entered the Senate race to challenge Democrat Hillary Rodham Clinton. Israel narrowly defeated Suffolk County legislator David Bishop for the Democratic nomination. In a five-way race in November, Israel received the smallest percentage of the vote of any House winner that year — 47.9 percent — but won by 13 points over Islip Town Clerk Joan B. Johnson, the GOP nominee.

Israel's hold on the seat seemed tenuous in 2002. There was talk that redistricting might put him and Grucci in the same district. There was also the specter of a challenge from the popular Lazio, who was being urged by GOP strategists to make a comeback. Neither of these events came to pass. Lazio announced in March that he would not run.

The new district lines discouraged another potentially tough GOP challenger, county legislator Allan Binder. That left the field to firefighter Joe Finley and Israel easily prevailed, by 18 percentage points.

KEY VOTES

2002

- Yes Overhaul campaign finance law; ban "soft money" and restrict advocacy advertising
- Yes Back Bush's defense budget increase
- No Extend 1996 welfare law
- No Adopt Bush's discretionary spending limit
- Yes Pass GOP Medicare prescription drug plan
- Yes Create independent Sept. 11 commission
- Yes Extend union protections to Homeland Security Department employees
- No Revive fast-track procedures for trade agreements
- Yes Authorize war against Iraq
- Yes Advance bankruptcy overhaul opposed by abortion opponents

2001

- No Nullify Clinton Labor Department ergonomics rule
- Yes Cut taxes by $1.35 trillion through fiscal 2011
- Yes Maintain ban on oil drilling in Arctic National Wildlife Refuge
- No Approve Bush proposal to limit managed-care plan liability for coverage decisions
- Yes Divert money from crop subsidy payments to land conservation
- Yes Expand law enforcement power to investigate suspected terrorists

CQ VOTE STUDIES

	PARTY UNITY		PRESIDENTIAL SUPPORT	
	Support	Oppose	Support	Oppose
2002	83%	17%	41%	59%
2001	82%	18%	48%	52%

INTEREST GROUPS

	AFL-CIO	ADA	CCUS	ACU
2002	67%	75%	58%	32%
2001	75%	90%	43%	8%

NEW YORK 2

Long Island – Brentwood, Commack

Taking in the central part of Long Island and covering almost all of western Suffolk County, the 2nd is full of suburban communities that popped up all over the county's potato fields during the post-World War II suburban boom. Now the 2nd, which also takes in a small piece of east-central Nassau County, has a burgeoning computer sector and the state's highest median income.

Much of the district's white-collar work force commutes to New York City, and the indigenous industry has long been blue-collar. Defense plants hummed during the height of the Cold War, but cutbacks brought job losses. Computer and electronics firms have helped fill the void. The 2nd houses a relatively diverse population, mixing well-to-do communities like Dix Hills with solidly middle- and working-class neighborhoods. During the summer many New Yorkers flock to Fire Island, a beach community which lies partly in the 2nd.

Redistricting in 2002 gave the 2nd all of Huntington — which it previously shared with the 5th — and stripped it of more-conservative coastal communities in Islip and Babylon to the south. The 2nd also acquired most of Plainview and part of Jericho in Nassau County, both of which have large Jewish populations.

With a nearly 30 percent minority population, a significant Jewish community and a blue-collar base, the 2nd has a substantial, but not overwhelming, Democratic vote. A Republican held the seat for most of the 1990s before it reverted to Democratic control in 2000. The district remains competitive, but redistricting did push it leftward. Al Gore captured 58 percent of the vote here in the 2000 presidential election.

MAJOR INDUSTRY

Computers, electronics, service

CITIES

Brentwood (unincorporated), 53,917; Commack (unincorporated), 36,363; Central Islip (unincorporated), 31,950; Huntington Station (unincorporated), 29,910

NOTABLE

Fire Island National Seashore separates the Atlantic Ocean from the Great South Bay; Islip Long Island MacArthur Airport is near Ronkonkoma; The Walt Whitman Birthplace State Historic Site and Interpretive Center is in West Hills (South Huntington).

Rep. Peter T. King (R)

CAPITOL OFFICE
225-7896
pete.king@mail.house.gov
www.house.gov/king
436 Cannon 20515-3203; fax 226-2279

COMMITTEES
Financial Services
(Domestic & International Monetary Policy, Trade & Technology - chairman)
International Relations
Select Homeland Security

HOMETOWN
Seaford

BORN
April 5, 1944, Manhattan, N.Y.

RELIGION
Roman Catholic

FAMILY
Wife, Rosemary King; two children

EDUCATION
St. Francis College, B.A. 1965 (history); U. of Notre Dame, J.D. 1968

MILITARY SERVICE
N.Y. National Guard, 1968-73

CAREER
Lawyer

POLITICAL HIGHLIGHTS
Hempstead Town Council, 1978-81; Nassau County comptroller, 1981-93; Republican nominee for N.Y. attorney general, 1986

ELECTION RESULTS

2002 GENERAL		
Peter T. King (R, C, INDC, RTL)	121,537	71.9%
Stuart L. Finz (D)	46,022	27.2%
2002 PRIMARY		
Peter T. King (R)	11,932	78.0%
Robert Previdi (R)	3,357	22.0%
2000 GENERAL		
Peter T. King (R, INDC, C, RTL)	143,126	59.5%
Dal LaMagna (D, GREEN, WFM)	95,787	39.8%

PREVIOUS WINNING PERCENTAGES
1998 (64%); 1996 (55%); 1994 (59%); 1992 (50%)

Elected 1992; 6th term

King has rightly earned a reputation for straight talk and a willingness to buck the Republican establishment, even though politically he is somewhat more conservative than many of his Northeast GOP colleagues.

He bemoans the declining ranks of Northeast Republicans in the House, saying that "to be a real national party, you can't isolate yourself from any region." In the last decade or so, King says, the GOP has had "a voice and face that scared off many [voters] in the Northeast. There was a judgmental tone, a harshness."

Although his maverick stances do not always endear him to the GOP leadership, his Long Island constituents seem to approve. He has won his last three elections by margins of at least 20 percentage points.

King also has played a significant role in the effort to bring peace to Northern Ireland, an experience he has drawn upon in writing two novels. An outspoken advocate of ending British rule in Northern Ireland, he has had a long and close relationship with Gerry Adams, the leader of Sinn Fein, the political wing of the Irish Republican Army.

Despite his occasional criticism of the GOP establishment, King votes with his party on most fiscal and social issues, supporting expanded trade opportunities and school vouchers, while opposing abortion. In the 107th Congress, he sided with the GOP on 92 percent of party-line votes, his highest score in five terms in the House. He backed President Bush 89 percent of the time, and the president has favored him with a nickname: Pedro.

On other issues, King is difficult to categorize politically. He supports drilling in Alaska's Arctic National Wildlife Refuge, saying, "You can't always cave in to the environmental wackos." But he joined with the Democrats to back increased automotive fuel economy standards, and he favors some gun control measures. He also supported labor unions' efforts to raise the minimum wage, to require employers to meet ergonomic standards for their workers, and to impose steel import quotas. After voting initially for a Democratic plan to give patients more clout in their dealings with health maintenance organizations, King voted in 2001 for the GOP plan.

King chairs the Financial Services panel's Domestic and International Monetary Policy Subcommittee. In the 107th Congress, he shepherded legislation to renew the Defense Production Act, which grants executive agencies the power to buy needed goods quickly in emergencies, such as natural disasters and terrorist attacks. King, like many metropolitan New York lawmakers, has put in considerable time and effort on the compensation fund for relatives of victims of the Sept. 11, 2001, terrorist attacks. In the 108th, he sits on the new Homeland Security Committee.

King supports immigration (his parents are from Ireland), but he favors making English the official language of the United States. He also urges tough measures to combat the smuggling of illegal aliens into the country.

A veteran of the rough-and-tumble politics in Nassau County, King says confrontation and partisanship are natural elements of legislative and political business. "I really believe that democracy is a contact sport," he once told Newsday.

The litany of King's shoot-from-the-hip comments is extensive. During the 2000 presidential race, he denounced GOP candidate George W. Bush for speaking at Bob Jones University, a bastion of religious conservatism, and switched his support from Bush to Arizona GOP Sen. John McCain.

In 2002, he harshly criticized Saudi Arabia and Muslim clerics in the United States, saying that "anti-Semitism and anti-Americanism are, in effect, government policy in Saudi Arabia."

In 2003 King suggested that French leaders go to Baghdad "to instruct the Iraqis in how to surrender," noting that France "set a world record in World War II for the quickest surrender by a world power."

He also argued strenuously in the media in 1998 that pursuing President Clinton's impeachment was not the proper course and told The Washington Post that GOP Whip Tom DeLay had intimidated party moderates to get them to fall in with the party line. King was one of only four Republicans who voted against all four articles of impeachment.

King's involvement in Northern Ireland politics dates back to his time in local government, a fact that drew criticism from some who said it had nothing to do with being the Nassau County comptroller. King made many trips to Northern Ireland to protest British policies and struck up a relationship with Adams. Years later, that relationship led to his role as an intermediary in meetings between Adams and British Prime Minister Tony Blair. King also worked closely with President Clinton on Northern Ireland, helping to bring about the 1998 Good Friday peace accords.

King, who is co-chairman of the Ad Hoc Committee for Irish Affairs, has written two novels about the Northern Ireland peace efforts, with heavy doses of real names and events. Clinton wrote a flattering blurb for the second book.

King grew up in a blue-collar Queens neighborhood, where his father was a police officer. He borrowed money to go to law school at Notre Dame. Afterward, he interned (along with Rudolph Giuliani) at Richard Nixon's New York law firm. He entered public life in 1972 as a deputy Nassau County attorney and eventually became the county comptroller, serving three terms. During his tenure, the ambitious King lost a 1986 run for New York attorney general.

When veteran GOP Rep. Norman F. Lent announced in 1992 that he would not seek re-election, King moved with characteristic dispatch to establish himself as Lent's successor, contending that his government experience would help him get things done in Washington.

After coasting through the primary, King narrowly survived a contest against the much-better-funded Democrat, Steve A. Orlins. In the GOP-leaning district, King's long history of involvement in local civic and political affairs helped him win by 3 percentage points. He has since won re-election by more comfortable margins. After winning in 2002 by 45 points, he was seriously considering running in 2004 against Democratic Sen. Charles E. Schumer.

KEY VOTES

2002

- No — Overhaul campaign finance law; ban "soft money" and restrict advocacy advertising
- Yes — Back Bush's defense budget increase
- ? — Extend 1996 welfare law
- Yes — Adopt Bush's discretionary spending limit
- Yes — Pass GOP Medicare prescription drug plan
- No — Create independent Sept. 11 commission
- No — Extend union protections to Homeland Security Department employees
- Yes — Revive fast-track procedures for trade agreements
- Yes — Authorize war against Iraq
- Yes — Advance bankruptcy overhaul opposed by abortion opponents

2001

- No — Nullify Clinton Labor Department ergonomics rule
- ? — Cut taxes by $1.35 trillion through fiscal 2011
- No — Maintain ban on oil drilling in Arctic National Wildlife Refuge
- Yes — Approve Bush proposal to limit managed-care plan liability for coverage decisions
- Yes — Divert money from crop subsidy payments to land conservation
- Yes — Expand law enforcement power to investigate suspected terrorists

CQ VOTE STUDIES

	PARTY UNITY		PRESIDENTIAL SUPPORT	
	Support	Oppose	Support	Oppose
2002	92%	8%	84%	16%
2001	92%	8%	93%	7%
2000	77%	23%	45%	55%
1999	79%	21%	32%	68%
1998	82%	18%	31%	69%

INTEREST GROUPS

	AFL-CIO	ADA	CCUS	ACU
2002	0%	10%	85%	83%
2001	27%	10%	83%	84%
2000	40%	15%	55%	64%
1999	44%	30%	54%	75%
1998	30%	10%	82%	76%

NEW YORK 3

Long Island – Levittown, Hicksville, Long Beach

Most of Long Island's eastern Nassau County and the south shore of western Suffolk County make up the 3rd, where extravagant estates mingle with some of the nation's oldest middle-class suburbs. The district boasts New York State's second-highest median income.

The Republican Party has long been a potent force in the 3rd, and redistricting in 2002 strengthened the party's hand even further by adding southwestern Suffolk. The addition was headlined by the acquisition of coastal portions of Islip and Babylon. Even with the district's significant labor presence from construction and professional unions, most of the 3rd's elected officials are Republicans, though Democrats have made some gains in Nassau County overall. Pockets of Democratic support in Plainview and Jericho, where many of the residents are Jewish, were moved into the neighboring 2nd District in redistricting.

While Democratic presidential candidates have held a modest edge districtwide in recent years (Al Gore captured 53 percent of the vote here in 2000), they have not done as well as in other Long Island districts. The 3rd easily favors Republicans in state and congressional races.

The economy faltered in the 1980s when aircraft and electronics manufacturing giant Northrup Grumman downsized following post-Cold War defense cutbacks. But the 3rd has rebounded, expanding its information technology base and enjoying a low unemployment rate.

The district is overwhelmingly white, with the lowest percentage of black residents (2 percent) in the state and the lowest percentage of Hispanics (7 percent) in the New York City area.

MAJOR INDUSTRY

Information technology, higher education

CITIES

Levittown (unincorporated), 53,067; Hicksville (unincorporated) (pt.), 39,670; Long Beach, 35,462; West Islip (unincorporated) (pt.), 27,171; Lindenhurst (pt.), 27,162; Glen Cove, 26,622

NOTABLE

Bethpage State Park hosted the 2002 U.S. Open golf tournament; President Theodore Roosevelt's Sagamore Hill estate is in Oyster Bay; Roosevelt's grave is at nearby Youngs Memorial Cemetery.

Rep. Carolyn McCarthy (D)

CAPITOL OFFICE
225-5516
www.house.gov/carolynmccarthy
106 Cannon 20515-3204; fax 225-5758

COMMITTEES
Education & Workforce
Financial Services

HOMETOWN
Mineola

BORN
Jan. 5, 1944, Brooklyn, N.Y.

RELIGION
Roman Catholic

FAMILY
Widowed; one child

EDUCATION
Glen Cove Nursing School, L.P.N. 1964

CAREER
Nurse

POLITICAL HIGHLIGHTS
No previous office

ELECTION RESULTS

2002 GENERAL		
Carolyn McCarthy (D, INDC, WFM)	94,806	56.3%
Marilyn F. O'Grady (R, C, RTL)	72,882	43.2%
2002 PRIMARY		
Carolyn McCarthy (D)	unopposed	
2000 GENERAL		
Carolyn McCarthy (D, INDC, WFM)	136,703	60.6%
Greg R. Becker (R, C, RTL)	87,830	38.9%

PREVIOUS WINNING PERCENTAGES
1998 (53%); 1996 (57%)

Elected 1996; 4th term

Now in her fourth term, McCarthy is branching out and moving up within the Democratic Caucus. Reaching beyond her signature gun control issues to education, health care and financial services, she also is starting to climb the hierarchy within her party.

In the 108th Congress, Minority Leader Nancy Pelosi put McCarthy on the Steering Committee, the leadership-dominated panel that makes committee assignments for the House Democrats, and named her an assistant whip. McCarthy joked to Newsday that being an assistant whip was somewhat similar to being a nurse, which was her career for more than 30 years before she entered politics. "We're just sent out to take the temperature of our fellow Democrats, and report back to the 'doctor,' " she said.

In the 108th, McCarthy gave up a seat on the Budget Committee after one term in order to take a place on the Financial Services Committee, a panel with jurisdiction over many of the businesses that employ her commuter constituency. She also remains on the Education and the Workforce Committee, where she played an active role in the 107th as the panel drafted President Bush's overhaul of federal education programs. McCarthy joined forces with Dale Kildee, a Michigan Democrat, and Mark Souder, an Indiana Republican, to defeat an attempt to consolidate drug-abuse prevention and after-school programs into a single block grant.

Having struggled with dyslexia as a child, McCarthy also has pressed for more federal aid for school districts to cope with the costs of educating learning-disabled children. She has backed multibillion-dollar Democratic plans to pay for new teachers and renovate aging schools, while opposing GOP proposals for school vouchers.

Although her Democratic roots are shallow — she was a lifelong Republican until the year she was elected to Congress — McCarthy appears to fit comfortably in the mainstream of her House caucus. She is a backer of abortion rights and environmental protections, and she is a steady friend of labor. But she sometimes tilts toward conservatism: She has backed constitutional amendments outlawing desecration of the U.S. flag and requiring a two-thirds congressional majority to raise federal taxes, for example. In the 107th, she voted to repeal the estate tax, although she opposed the overall Bush tax. And she voted to authorize a war against Iraq.

Still, McCarthy likely always will be identified first and foremost with the tragedy that propelled her into public life and inspired her continuing crusade for tougher gun controls. "I've come to peace with the fact that that will be in my obituary," she told The Associated Press.

It all started in December 1993, when a deranged gunman opened fire on a Long Island Rail Road commuter train. Among the victims were McCarthy's husband, Dennis, who was killed, and her adult son, Kevin, who was seriously wounded.

When her congressman, freshman Republican Daniel Frisa, voted in 1996 to eliminate a 1994 ban on semiautomatic weapons, McCarthy was incensed. Local GOP officials squelched her inquiries about mounting a primary challenge to Frisa, so she quit the Republican Party and launched a Democratic campaign to unseat him.

She raised more than $1 million and outspent Frisa, whom she described as out of the mainstream and in the mold of Speaker Newt Gingrich. She campaigned on gun control and health policy, and Frisa seemed at a loss for an effective response. McCarthy won by 17 percentage points. In 2000, she bumped her margin to 22 points. Facing a tougher challenge in 2002, she still won by 13 points over GOP ophthalmologist Marilyn F. O'Grady.

McCarthy's personal tragedy gives her speeches on gun control unusual emotional force. When she rose to speak on the House floor at 1 a.m. June 18, 1999, a hush fell over the chamber. With tears flowing down her cheeks, McCarthy implored her colleagues to support her amendment to toughen background check requirements for would-be purchasers at gun shows. "I am Irish and I am not supposed to cry in front of anyone. But I made a promise a long time ago" to her late husband and her son, she said. "If there was anything that I could do to prevent one family from going through what I have gone through, then I have done my job."

McCarthy thought she had connected emotionally, particularly in the aftermath of a mass shooting at Columbine High School in Colorado. But her amendment lost, as most of her gun control efforts have.

In her first term, McCarthy and others sought to press a floor amendment to a juvenile crime bill requiring childproof trigger locks on all guns. The GOP leadership blocked the move. But the debate provoked enough public response for the Clinton administration to win concessions from eight major gun manufacturers, which agreed voluntarily to a White House call for trigger locks on all guns made in the United States.

In 2001, she tried again as an Education and the Workforce subcommittee considered a bill to authorize juvenile justice programs. Her amendment to establish a $75 million, five-year program to equip guns with child-safety trigger locks was rejected.

In March 2002, a fatal shooting in a church in McCarthy's district gave her further reason to continue her fight. A priest and a parishioner were shot and killed at a Mass by a former church employee who had bought his gun four days earlier, even though he had a history of mental illness and was under a restraining order. Under federal law, he should have been ineligible to buy a rifle. But when a gun store owner performed a background check, nothing turned up. McCarthy developed legislation with Democratic Sen. Charles E. Schumer of New York authorizing grants to states to help them automate mental health databases so the information could be shared with the criminal background check system. She titled it the "Our Lady of Peace Act" after the church in which the shooting occurred. The bill passed the House by voice vote but died in the Senate.

McCarthy is determined to keep trying, especially after the birth of her first grandson, named for her slain husband. "I've come to the realization this is going to take a while," she told Newsday in 2000.

KEY VOTES

2002

- Yes Overhaul campaign finance law; ban "soft money" and restrict advocacy advertising
- Yes Back Bush's defense budget increase
- No Extend 1996 welfare law
- No Adopt Bush's discretionary spending limit
- No Pass GOP Medicare prescription drug plan
- Yes Create independent Sept. 11 commission
- Yes Extend union protections to Homeland Security Department employees
- No Revive fast-track procedures for trade agreements
- Yes Authorize war against Iraq
- Yes Advance bankruptcy overhaul opposed by abortion opponents

2001

- No Nullify Clinton Labor Department ergonomics rule
- Yes Cut taxes by $1.35 trillion through fiscal 2011
- Yes Maintain ban on oil drilling in Arctic National Wildlife Refuge
- No Approve Bush proposal to limit managed-care plan liability for coverage decisions
- Yes Divert money from crop subsidy payments to land conservation
- Yes Expand law enforcement power to investigate suspected terrorists

CQ VOTE STUDIES

	PARTY UNITY		PRESIDENTIAL SUPPORT	
	Support	Oppose	Support	Oppose
2002	84%	16%	45%	55%
2001	83%	17%	44%	56%
2000	84%	16%	68%	32%
1999	89%	11%	77%	23%
1998	82%	18%	68%	32%

INTEREST GROUPS

	AFL-CIO	ADA	CCUS	ACU
2002	67%	80%	60%	32%
2001	83%	85%	48%	17%
2000	70%	65%	65%	24%
1999	75%	90%	44%	8%
1998	80%	90%	61%	24%

NEW YORK 4

Southwest Nassau County — Hempstead

The 4th's diverse array of residents includes wealthy New York City suburbanites and Wall Street commuters, as well as low- and middle-income residents. The district consumes the southwest corner of Long Island's Nassau County and borders eastern Queens.

With the largest minority population of Long Island's four congressional districts, the 4th has a Democratic base, particularly in Hempstead and Uniondale, which include large black and Hispanic communities. The affluent and largely Jewish "Five Towns" (Inwood, Lawrence, Cedarhurst, Woodmere and Hewlett), in the 4th's southwestern corner, also lean Democratic. But overall voter registration favors the GOP.

District politics were competitive in the 1990s, with independent and socially moderate voters electing four different representatives during the decade. The 4th elected Republicans until 1996, when voters chose pro-gun control Democratic Rep. McCarthy; they have re-elected her to three more terms. The district voted for Bill Clinton in both of his presidential bids, overwhelmingly so in 1996. And in the 2000 presidential contest, Al Gore secured the district with 60 percent of the vote.

Some of the political upheaval may be tied to economic turmoil that began in the 1980s with the decline of the defense industry, on which Long Island was heavily dependent. The 4th continues to rebuild and diversify, focusing on technology and small businesses. A number of working-class residents are employed by John F. Kennedy International Airport (across the district line in Queens' 6th District), Belmont Park race track, and large shopping centers such as Roosevelt Field Mall in Garden City.

Pocketbook issues and unique regional concerns — such as airplane noise — dominate political discussion in the 4th and help keep it competitive.

MAJOR INDUSTRY
Health care, technology, higher education

CITIES
Hempstead, 56,554; East Meadow (unincorporated), 37,461; Valley Stream, 36,368; Freeport (pt.), 34,958; Elmont (unincorporated), 32,657

NOTABLE
Nassau Coliseum is home to the New York Islanders hockey team.

Rep. Gary L. Ackerman (D)

CAPITOL OFFICE
225-2601
gary_ackerman@mail.house.gov
www.house.gov/ackerman
2243 Rayburn 20515-3205; fax 225-1589

COMMITTEES
Financial Services
International Relations

HOMETOWN
Queens

BORN
Nov. 19, 1942, Brooklyn, N.Y.

RELIGION
Jewish

FAMILY
Wife, Rita Ackerman; three children

EDUCATION
Queens College, B.A. 1965

CAREER
Teacher; publisher and editor; advertising executive

POLITICAL HIGHLIGHTS
Sought Democratic nomination for N.Y. City Council at large, 1977; N.Y. Senate, 1979-83

ELECTION RESULTS

2002 GENERAL		
Gary Ackerman (D, INDC, L, WFM)	68,773	92.3%
Perry S. Reich (C)	5,718	7.7%
2002 PRIMARY		
Gary Ackerman (D)		unopposed
2000 GENERAL		
Gary Ackerman (D, INDC, L, WFM)	137,684	68.0%
Edward Elkowitz (R, C)	61,084	30.2%
Anne T. Robinson (RTL)	3,846	1.9%

PREVIOUS WINNING PERCENTAGES
1998 (65%); 1996 (64%); 1994 (55%); 1992 (52%); 1990 (100%); 1988 (100%); 1986 (77%); 1984 (69%); 1983 Special Election (50%)

Elected March 1983; 10th full term

Ackerman, the boutonniere-sporting dean of New York's Long Island contingent, is known for using his sharp wit and agility with parliamentary procedures to promote his liberal views and to gig the Republican majority.

His caustic broadsides sometimes are aimed at corporate chieftains and others he suspects of abuses of power. Typical was his rebuke of Bernard J. Ebbers, former chief executive officer of WorldCom Inc., during a 2002 hearing on alleged accounting manipulation by the telecommunications giant. "Do you sleep well at night?" Ackerman demanded as Ebbers sat tight-lipped at the witness table.

When the House took up a constitutional amendment in 1999 to ban desecration of the U.S. flag, Ackerman came to the floor wearing a tie depicting the flag and said his neckwear would be banned under the amendment. In an interview on the Howard Stern radio show, he described himself as "naked and draped in the flag." The real threat, he said, was not the occasional burning of a flag, "but the permanent banning of the burners."

His staunchly liberal views on education, health care and the environment seldom prevail, but persistence helps him be heard above the fray. During the tense moments before lawmakers voted in 1998 on whether to launch an impeachment inquiry against President Clinton, Ackerman said, "I move that when the House adjourn, we do so to Salem, a quaint village in the Commonwealth of Massachusetts, whose history beckons us thence." His reference to the site of the infamous 17th century witch trials drew hisses from Republicans but elicited a wry smile from GOP Speaker Newt Gingrich.

Ackerman scoffs at pretension and convention. His residence in Washington is a houseboat on the Potomac called the Unsinkable II. He says that the original Unsinkable sank.

A senior member of the International Relations Committee, Ackerman is a respected voice on foreign policy, arguing that the United States should play an active role in promoting democracy abroad. He travels overseas often, and invokes his firsthand experiences when urging measured responses to developments in India, North Korea and China.

During the 107th Congress, Ackerman forged an unlikely alliance with conservative Republicans to try to build support for Israel's hard-line policies toward the Palestinians. Ackerman, who is Jewish, joined with Tom DeLay of Texas and Roy Blunt of Missouri, both Christian conservatives, on a resolution that would have severed ties between the United States and Yasser Arafat's Palestinian Authority. The measure was toned down at the Bush administration's request.

Ackerman contends that to promote global security, the United States must remain actively engaged in dialogue even with nations such as China and North Korea that are allegedly involved in weapons proliferation. Breaking with his allies in labor, he voted in 2000 to grant China permanent normal trade status. Similarly, he voted against a 1998 proposal to ban the export of U.S. satellites to China. The measure was pushed by Republicans, and embraced by many Democrats, in response to evidence that technology transfers had helped China develop nuclear weapons capability.

Ackerman also successfully battled repeated efforts by conservative GOP Rep. Dan Burton of Indiana to cut aid to India. He blocked a Republican proposal to ban most aid to nations that fail to support U.S. positions on at least one out of every four roll call votes at the U.N. General Assembly. He called it a thinly disguised attempt to slash aid to India, one of four nations that did not meet that standard. The other three, Cuba, Syria and North Korea, were already barred from U.S. aid in other ways.

In addition to pursuing his international interests, Ackerman tends to the parochial concerns of his sprawling and diverse 5th District. He saved the U.S. Coast Guard station at Eatons Neck from threatened closure; he pushed for resolution of the 1994 Long Island Rail Road strike; and he lobbies relentlessly for funds to clean up Long Island Sound. In 2002, he proudly noted in a press release that the 5th was No. 1 in New York in the amount of federal spending — $9.5 billion, according to the Associated Press.

Despite his liberalism, Ackerman has the capacity to work with ideological opposites, as he demonstrated in the 104th Congress when he joined conservative Tom Coburn of Oklahoma in passing a measure to provide AIDS testing for newborns. "You have to be willing to compromise," Ackerman told Newsday in the 105th. "Part of the problem is there is a group of Republicans down here who believe they are locked in a battle, not between good and bad, but between good and evil. Those who believe that way, they can't compromise with evil."

Ackerman, a former social studies teacher, first ventured into public policy in 1969, when, as a new father, he successfully sued the New York City Board of Education for the right of a father to receive unpaid leave. At the time, time off to care for newborns was offered only to women. He subsequently had run-ins with the Queens Democratic machine as a publisher of a weekly newspaper (of which he now owns a share). He challenged a city council incumbent in 1977 and lost.

But the next year, he captured a state Senate seat. After Democratic Rep. Benjamin S. Rosenthal died in 1983, Ackerman convinced Democratic leaders to support him in the special-election race against a wealthy independent, pollster Douglas Schoen, and a less competitive GOP candidate. Ackerman won with 50 percent of the vote and cruised through four re-elections in the then-7th District, a mainly urban constituency that included many loyally Democratic Jewish and Hispanic voters.

In the 1992 election, however, redistricting had removed much of his base in Queens and thrown him into the more conservative suburban Long Island 5th District. Ackerman faced a more difficult re-election battle. He was also hurt by revelations that he had 111 overdrafts at the House Bank, during the scandal over special checking privileges for lawmakers. But he prevailed by 7 percentage points over GOP Suffolk County Legislator Allan E. Binder by rolling up a big margin in what remained of his Queens district. He has since won by comfortable margins.

KEY VOTES

2002

Yes Overhaul campaign finance law; ban "soft money" and restrict advocacy advertising
Yes Back Bush's defense budget increase
No Extend 1996 welfare law
No Adopt Bush's discretionary spending limit
No Pass GOP Medicare prescription drug plan
Yes Create independent Sept. 11 commission
Yes Extend union protections to Homeland Security Department employees
No Revive fast-track procedures for trade agreements
Yes Authorize war against Iraq
No Advance bankruptcy overhaul opposed by abortion opponents

2001

No Nullify Clinton Labor Department ergonomics rule
? Cut taxes by $1.35 trillion through fiscal 2011
Yes Maintain ban on oil drilling in Arctic National Wildlife Refuge
No Approve Bush proposal to limit managed-care plan liability for coverage decisions
Yes Divert money from crop subsidy payments to land conservation
Yes Expand law enforcement power to investigate suspected terrorists

CQ VOTE STUDIES

	PARTY UNITY		PRESIDENTIAL SUPPORT	
	Support	Oppose	Support	Oppose
2002	93%	7%	32%	68%
2001	94%	6%	29%	71%
2000	96%	4%	94%	6%
1999	97%	3%	87%	13%
1998	97%	3%	86%	14%

INTEREST GROUPS

	AFL-CIO	ADA	CCUS	ACU
2002	100%	95%	37%	4%
2001	100%	80%	35%	4%
2000	90%	80%	41%	13%
1999	78%	100%	29%	0%
1998	100%	100%	35%	0%

NEW YORK 5

Northeast Queens; northwest Nassau County

The 5th stretches east from south of LaGuardia Airport in Queens into northwestern Nassau County, reaching Roslyn and East Hills. Redistricting in 2002 made significant alterations to the district, which previously had skirted Long Island Sound's North Shore into Suffolk County to take in part of Huntington. By removing Suffolk and adding more of Queens, the new district is more Democratic. Almost 80 percent of the 5th's residents live in Queens and 20 percent live in Nassau.

The minority population grew substantially with redistricting, particularly in Hispanic and Asian communities. Half of New York City's Asians live in Queens, and Elmhurst, downtown Flushing, Murray Hill and Queensboro Hill have a heavy Asian presence. The neighborhoods of North Corona and South Corona have a strong Hispanic influence.

Although pockets of low-income neighborhoods exist in the 5th, northeastern Queens has affluent areas such as the Douglaston and Little Neck neighborhoods near the Nassau County line. Before fanning eastward into Nassau, the district buttonhooks to the south and west along the Grand Central Parkway to take in some communities around St. John's University (which itself is in the 6th District).

Many of the district's residents commute to white-collar jobs outside the 5th, but the local economy is boosted by the U.S. Merchant Marine Academy at Kings Point, Shea Stadium (home to the Mets baseball team) and the USTA National Tennis Center in Flushing Meadows-Corona Park, where the U.S. Open tennis tournament is held each year.

Nassau tends to be politically competitive, but the strong Democratic tilt of Queens contributes to the district's more than 2-to-1 Democratic registration advantage.

MAJOR INDUSTRY

Higher education, health care, small business

CITIES

New York (pt.), 517,889; Port Washington (unincorporated), 15,215; Great Neck, 9,538

NOTABLE

In 1662, religious freedom advocate John Bowne was arrested for allowing Quakers to worship in his Flushing home, which is now one of the oldest remaining structures in New York State.

Rep. Gregory W. Meeks (D)

Elected February 1998; 3rd full term

Reared in the public housing of East Harlem, Meeks says education, affordable child care and economic development are essential ingredients in helping his constituents improve their lot. He owes his interest in public affairs to his mother, who resumed her education when her four children were in their teens and inspired him to become involved alongside her in community improvement projects.

A staunch liberal, Meeks is a fierce defender of affordable housing and a biting critic of police violence against ethnic minorities. But he has sometimes found himself forging alliances with the business community in his constant focus on jobs creation. Adept at winning funds for his constituents, he keeps a keen eye on the concerns of John F. Kennedy International Airport, which is in the 6th District in southernmost Queens.

His desire to balance liberal philosophy in Washington against economic development back home could be seen in the weeks after the Sept. 11, 2001, attacks by terrorist hijackers. Though he and other Democrats were unable to obtain aid for the thousands of airline workers who faced layoffs after the attacks hobbled the travel industry, Meeks backed the law providing up to $15 billion in aid for the airlines.

He and other New York lawmakers also spearheaded US Airways' successful effort to receive a $900 million federal loan guarantee under the law. He suggested that some of the steps ordered under a separate aviation security law enacted that fall might be "window dressing" and should be reviewed to determine their detrimental effects on airline operations and passenger comfort.

His seat on the Financial Services Committee is Meeks' main forum for promoting affordable housing. As a result he has opposed proposals to tighten regulation of Fannie Mae and Freddie Mac, the government-chartered mortgage giants, calling them "a model of transparency and efficiency."

On the International Relations Committee, and its subcommittee on Africa, Meeks is well-positioned to participate in many of the debates about the war on terrorism and is at the forefront of efforts to provide humanitarian aid to Africa. He also backs private sector financing of exports to Cuba, which are prohibited by a longstanding trade embargo.

Meeks aspired to raise his profile substantially in the 108th Congress, seeking election to the vice chairmanship of the House Democratic Caucus. But on the day of the balloting, he and another candidate, Zoe Lofgren of California, conceded defeat to James E. Clyburn of South Carolina before the votes were tabulated. Soon after, Meeks was forced — under the 2002 campaign finance overhaul law, which he supported — to step down as chairman of New York's Council of Black Elected Democrats, made up of federal, state and city officials. The law prohibits federal lawmakers from leading groups that accept the sort of "soft money" campaign donations banned from federal campaigns under the law.

Meeks has been a swing vote on trade. During the 2000 debate on whether to make permanent the normal U.S.-China trade relationship, he took a trip arranged by the Clinton administration to observe the Chinese economy. He returned and agreed to vote "yes," in part because he had concluded the society there was not as oppressive as he had believed — and in part because of the prospect of increased trade going through JFK. He opposed the 2002 law expanding the administration's trade negotiating

CAPITOL OFFICE
225-3461
congmeeks@mail.house.gov
www.house.gov/meeks
1710 Longworth 20515-3206; fax 226-4169

COMMITTEES
Financial Services
International Relations

HOMETOWN
Far Rockaway

BORN
Sept. 25, 1953, Harlem, N.Y.

RELIGION
Baptist

FAMILY
Wife, Simone-Marie Meeks; three children

EDUCATION
Adelphi U., B.A. 1975; Howard U., J.D. 1978

CAREER
Workers' compensation board judge; city prosecutor

POLITICAL HIGHLIGHTS
N.Y. Assembly, 1993-98

ELECTION RESULTS

2002 GENERAL		
Gregory W. Meeks (D, L, WFM)	72,799	96.5%
Rey Clarke (INDC)	2,632	3.5%
2002 PRIMARY		
Gregory W. Meeks (D)	22,209	78.7%
Rey Clarke (D)	6,024	21.3%
2000 GENERAL		
Gregory W. Meeks (D, WFM)		unopposed

PREVIOUS WINNING PERCENTAGES
1998 (100%); 1998 Special Election (56%)

authority, citing the same concerns as most other Democrats about inadequate environmental and labor protections.

Legal rights of individuals are also a top concern for Meeks. In 2000, after the National Collegiate Athletic Association investigated St. John's University in Queens, he introduced legislation that would give student athletes some legal rights and guarantee that they have independent legal counsel. "These young people are subjected to having their lives dissected before the public on mere allegations and without any independent legal representation during the investigation," Meeks warned.

Meeks is deeply involved with his party's black activist constituency. He was one of more than a dozen African-American leaders arrested outside the Supreme Court in 1998 as they protested the court's paucity of law clerks from minority groups. After four New York City police officers shot and killed a Guinean immigrant in 1999, he joined other black leaders in protesting police violence against minorities. In 2002, he spoke on the House floor in support of preserving a collection of Malcolm X documents that had become embroiled in a family dispute.

After graduating from Howard University Law School, Meeks began his career as a Queens County assistant district attorney and as a narcotics crime prosecutor. After a brief stint on the State Investigation Commission, which probes wrongdoing by state officials and organized crime figures, Meeks was appointed as a state workers' compensation judge and later moved up to the position of supervising law judge.

During those years, Meeks became involved in a variety of community matters — neighborhood cleanups, street repairs, traffic problems, street safety — in the working-class neighborhood of Far Rockaway where his parents were eventually able to move.

Meeks says he always thought his involvement in politics would be behind the scenes, but community activist colleagues persuaded him to run for office. In 1992, he won the first of three terms to the state Assembly, where he held seats on a range of committees that oversaw state codes, the judiciary, insurance, small business and government operations.

When Democrat Floyd H. Flake resigned his 6th District seat during his sixth term in 1997 to devote himself to leading an influential African Methodist Episcopal church in Queens, he endorsed Meeks to be his successor. Propelled by additional key endorsements, Meeks got the Democratic nomination. He then captured 56 percent of the vote in a four-way general election that was marked by low voter turnout. He has not drawn Republican opposition in any of his three subsequent elections.

KEY VOTES

2002

- Yes Overhaul campaign finance law; ban "soft money" and restrict advocacy advertising
- No Back Bush's defense budget increase
- No Extend 1996 welfare law
- No Adopt Bush's discretionary spending limit
- No Pass GOP Medicare prescription drug plan
- Yes Create independent Sept. 11 commission
- Yes Extend union protections to Homeland Security Department employees
- No Revive fast-track procedures for trade agreements
- No Authorize war against Iraq
- Yes Advance bankruptcy overhaul opposed by abortion opponents

2001

- No Nullify Clinton Labor Department ergonomics rule
- No Cut taxes by $1.35 trillion through fiscal 2011
- Yes Maintain ban on oil drilling in Arctic National Wildlife Refuge
- No Approve Bush proposal to limit managed-care plan liability for coverage decisions
- Yes Divert money from crop subsidy payments to land conservation
- Yes Expand law enforcement power to investigate suspected terrorists

CQ VOTE STUDIES

	PARTY UNITY		PRESIDENTIAL SUPPORT	
	Support	Oppose	Support	Oppose
2002	94%	6%	26%	74%
2001	94%	6%	20%	80%
2000	95%	5%	92%	8%
1999	96%	4%	86%	14%
1998	97%	3%	90%	10%

INTEREST GROUPS

	AFL-CIO	ADA	CCUS	ACU
2002	89%	85%	45%	4%
2001	100%	85%	36%	5%
2000	90%	95%	50%	8%
1999	89%	95%	29%	0%
1998	100%	85%	33%	5%

NEW YORK 6

Southeast Queens – Jamaica, St. Albans

A black-majority, mostly middle-class area, the 6th is economically focused around John F. Kennedy International Airport on Jamaica Bay in southeastern Queens. It is the only district wholly within the 2.2 million-resident borough of Queens.

Redistricting in 2002 only marginally changed the lines of the 6th, which is bound roughly by Cross Bay Boulevard to the west, Grand Central Parkway to the north and the Nassau County line to the east. South of the airport, across Jamaica Bay, the 6th takes in part of Rockaway, including Edgemere and Far Rockaway. Included in the 6th's boundaries are St. John's University, located at the far north, and Aqueduct Racetrack, at the far west.

More than a generation ago, communities such as Springfield Gardens and St. Albans were settled by a burgeoning Irish and Italian Roman Catholic middle class. Today, while the economic profile of these areas is not much different, the demographics are completely changed — most of the residents are black.

The 6th is one of the nation's most economically sound black-majority districts, though some areas like South Jamaica have been troubled by unemployment and other urban ills. JFK Airport, its largest employer, provides a steady job base and, combined with health care, municipal government and construction jobs, helps create a strong union constituency.

With a sizable Hispanic constituency to go along with its black majority, the district has an overwhelmingly Democratic lean: Al Gore won 88 percent of the vote here in the 2000 presidential election, and Democrats outnumber Republicans 14-to-1 in voter registration.

MAJOR INDUSTRY
Airport, health care, education

CITIES
New York (pt.), 654,361

NOTABLE
Roy Wilkins Park in Jamaica is named for the civil rights leader; Floyd H. Flake, who represented the 6th from 1987 until he resigned in 1997, is the senior pastor at the 15,000-member Greater Allen Cathedral of New York in Jamaica; Residents of the 6th have the nation's longest average travel time to work: more than 47 minutes, according to the 2000 census.

Rep. Joseph Crowley (D)

CAPITOL OFFICE
225-3965
write2joecrowley@mail.house.gov
www.house.gov/crowley
312 Cannon 20515-3207; fax 225-1909

COMMITTEES
Financial Services
International Relations

HOMETOWN
Elmhurst

BORN
March 16, 1962, Elmhurst, N.Y.

RELIGION
Roman Catholic

FAMILY
Wife, Kasey Crowley; two children

EDUCATION
Queens College, B.A. 1985 (communications & political science)

CAREER
State legislator

POLITICAL HIGHLIGHTS
N.Y. Assembly, 1987-99

ELECTION RESULTS

2002 GENERAL		
Joseph Crowley (D, WFM)	50,967	73.3%
Kevin Brawley (R, C)	18,572	26.7%
2002 PRIMARY		
Joseph Crowley (D)	15,166	64.0%
Dennis Coleman (D)	8,516	36.0%
2000 GENERAL		
Joseph Crowley (D)	78,207	71.7%
Rose Robles Birtley (R)	24,592	22.5%
Robert E. Hurley (C)	3,131	2.9%
Paul Gilman (GREEN)	1,999	1.8%
Garafalia Christea (RTL)	1,172	1.1%

PREVIOUS WINNING PERCENTAGES
1998 (69%)

Elected 1998; 3rd term

Crowley had an easy road to Congress because of his family's political connections, but his hard work on behalf of his constituents has helped convince early skeptics that he now belongs there.

In the 108th Congress, Crowley moved up in the leadership ranks when he was named one of seven chief deputy whips. He was also appointed to the Steering Committee, which makes Democratic committee assignments.

Like most New York City-area lawmakers, Crowley spent much of the 107th dealing with the aftermath of the Sept. 11, 2001, terrorist attacks. He estimates that 105 families in his district lost a family member in the collapse of the World Trade Center towers. Crowley has family ties to the New York City police and fire departments. His father was at one time a police detective; his cousin, firefighter John Moran, died in the attacks. Crowley, whose district includes Queens and part of the Bronx, worked to ensure compensation for victims' families, health care monitoring of those exposed to toxic dust, and recognition for the efforts of rescue workers.

Based on congressional field hearings, a dozen town hall meetings and information from local officials, Crowley wrote a 100-page blueprint on New York City's security needs to guard against future attacks. "The federal government must make New York City a top priority when it allocates funds for homeland security," Crowley said, adding that it could cost as much as $10 billion to fund all of his recommendations. In the 107th, he was named to the Democrats' Homeland Security Task Force.

Upon his arrival on Capitol Hill in 1999, Crowley lobbied his peers to win election to one of four six-month terms as president of the Democratic freshman class, a leadership role that gave him access to top party officials. He credits such political networking as a factor in his selection for a seat on the Financial Services panel in the 107th, a post he sought avidly.

"Joe influences people not with his formidable size [he's a burly 6-foot-4], but with his personality and sense of humor," his Class of 1998 New York colleague Anthony Weiner told Newsday.

Gregarious and easygoing, Crowley displays a talent for cultivating influential politicians. He scored a notable success late in 1999 when first lady Hillary Rodham Clinton — then on the verge of declaring her candidacy for the Senate — hosted a fundraiser for him.

Crowley is a bit more conservative than other New York Democrats, but he stands with his party on about 90 percent of party-line votes.

As a member of the International Relations Committee, he has plunged deeply into international politics, a longstanding personal interest and a concern of his constituents. Crowley, whose mother is from Northern Ireland, has played a particularly large role in trying to keep the peace process in Northern Ireland moving forward. He is one of four co-chairmen of the congressional Ad Hoc Committee for Irish Affairs.

He is also co-chairman of the India caucus; Crowley's district has a large South Asian population, and he has traveled to India and Bangladesh, as well as Israel, Colombia and Kosovo.

Crowley is personally opposed to abortion but has supported some abortion rights measures, such as allowing female military personnel stationed abroad to have abortions at military hospitals.

Closer to home, he has been in the forefront, dating back to 1999, in getting the federal government involved in combating West Nile virus, which made its first U.S. appearance in New York City. At his urging, President

Clinton appointed a West Nile "czar" to coordinate the effort.

Another important local topic has been congestion, noise and air pollution at LaGuardia Airport. In the 107th Congress, he was able to win approval of a study of noise and air pollution in the vicinity of the airport, and he has won $40 million to help soundproof local schools.

A guitar player, Crowley once belonged to a band called "The Budget Blues" with three friends from his days in the New York Assembly. He has been known to perform a perfect imitation of Van Morrison singing "Wild Nights." He occasionally sings in public, including the national anthem once before a New York Knicks basketball game.

Reared in a political family, Crowley says that one of his earliest memories is handing out pamphlets with his family for Democrat Mario M. Cuomo after church. His uncle, Walter Crowley, was a well-known Queens politician who served on the New York City Council.

Crowley was first elected to the state Assembly just a year after his graduation from college. He was in Albany for 12 years, serving on the Banking and Ways and Means panels. He made news in 1996 when he offered legislation to require New York schools to teach about starvation in Ireland during the 1840s potato famine.

His predecessor in the 7th District, Democrat Thomas J. Manton, was a longtime friend of Crowley's father and uncle. Manton surprised his fellow Democrats in 1998 when he announced his retirement several days after the election filing deadline. That allowed party officials, including Manton, the Queens Democratic chairman, to handpick Crowley as the nominee. Crowley then swamped the Republican candidate, corporate security manager James J. Dillon, in the general election.

But Manton's tactics angered other Democrats who had wanted a shot at the seat. Several vowed to unseat Crowley in the 2000 Democratic primary, and, after months of behind-the-scenes wrangling, they united behind Queens Councilman Walter McCaffrey. But McCaffrey was fighting an uphill battle. During his first term in office, Crowley seized every opportunity to increase his stature and diminish the threat from potential opponents. He was so effective, it hardly seemed to matter when McCaffrey surprisingly pulled out of the race right before the September primary, citing campaign funding difficulties. Crowley coasted to victory in the general election, winning more than 70 percent of the vote.

In 2002, Crowley had a serious primary challenge from community activist and former state Sen. Dennis Coleman, but he prevailed with 64 percent, and breezed to re-election in November.

KEY VOTES

2002

Yes Overhaul campaign finance law; ban "soft money" and restrict advocacy advertising
Yes Back Bush's defense budget increase
No Extend 1996 welfare law
No Adopt Bush's discretionary spending limit
No Pass GOP Medicare prescription drug plan
Yes Create independent Sept. 11 commission
Yes Extend union protections to Homeland Security Department employees
No Revive fast-track procedures for trade agreements
Yes Authorize war against Iraq
Yes Advance bankruptcy overhaul opposed by abortion opponents

2001

No Nullify Clinton Labor Department ergonomics rule
No Cut taxes by $1.35 trillion through fiscal 2011
Yes Maintain ban on oil drilling in Arctic National Wildlife Refuge
No Approve Bush proposal to limit managed-care plan liability for coverage decisions
Yes Divert money from crop subsidy payments to land conservation
Yes Expand law enforcement power to investigate suspected terrorists

CQ VOTE STUDIES

	PARTY UNITY		PRESIDENTIAL SUPPORT	
	Support	Oppose	Support	Oppose
2002	93%	7%	39%	61%
2001	89%	11%	30%	70%
2000	91%	9%	82%	18%
1999	91%	9%	81%	19%

INTEREST GROUPS

	AFL-CIO	ADA	CCUS	ACU
2002	78%	95%	50%	8%
2001	91%	80%	43%	20%
2000	100%	85%	38%	20%
1999	89%	95%	32%	8%

NEW YORK 7

Part of Queens and the Bronx

Few districts in the nation are as ethnically and racially diverse as the 7th, which takes in part of northern Queens and the eastern part of the Bronx. Blacks, Hispanics and Asians each compose more than 10 percent of the population, with Hispanics a clear plurality of residents at 40 percent.

The rapid-growth 7th was one of the few New York districts to see substantial change in 2002 redistricting: Under the district's 1990s configuration, nearly three-fourths of the registered votes came out of Queens. Now, two-thirds of registered voters come from the Bronx.

The district climbs north from near the intersection of the Brooklyn-Queens and Long Island expressways (in the neighboring 12th) to take in Woodside, Jackson Heights, East Elmhurst and LaGuardia Airport. This fast-growing area is heavily Hispanic and spurred much of Queens' 14 percent population growth rate in the 1990s.

The district continues northeast to the College Point neighborhood, then jumps across the Whitestone Bridge to envelop parts of the Bronx, reaching as far west as the Bronx Zoo and the New York Botanical Garden and as far north as Co-op City and the Westchester County line. The Bronx portion of the district includes Morris Park and Pelham Bay, which have an Italian influence. While the Bronx overall has economic struggles, the areas around Eastchester Bay have some of the borough's highest incomes.

Like most New York City districts, the 7th has a strong Democratic lean, though a bit less monolithically so. It is mostly middle class and residential, though steady growth tied to the city has spurred new businesses. LaGuardia makes the Queens area a transportation hub, and the health care industry is a major employer in the Bronx.

MAJOR INDUSTRY
Airport, health care, service

CITIES
New York (pt.), 654,360

NOTABLE
The Maritime Industry Museum and SUNY-Maritime College are at Fort Schuyler in Throgs Neck, where the East River meets Long Island Sound.

Rep. Jerrold Nadler (D)

CAPITOL OFFICE
225-5635
jerrold.nadler@mail.house.gov
www.house.gov/nadler
2334 Rayburn 20515-3208; fax 225-6923

COMMITTEES
Judiciary
Transportation & Infrastructure

HOMETOWN
Manhattan

BORN
June 13, 1947, Brooklyn, N.Y.

RELIGION
Jewish

FAMILY
Wife, Joyce L. Miller; one child

EDUCATION
Columbia U., A.B. 1969 (government); Fordham U., J.D. 1978

CAREER
Lawyer; state legislative aide

POLITICAL HIGHLIGHTS
N.Y. Assembly, 1976-92; candidate for Manhattan borough president, 1985; candidate for New York City comptroller, 1989

ELECTION RESULTS

2002 GENERAL		
Jerrold Nadler (D, L, WFM)	81,002	76.1%
Jim Farrin (R, INDC)	19,674	18.5%
Alan Jay Gerber (C)	3,361	3.2%
Dan Wentzel (GREEN)	1,918	1.8%
2002 PRIMARY		
Jerrold Nadler (D)		unopposed
2000 GENERAL		
Jerrold Nadler (D, L, WFM)	150,273	81.2%
Marian S. Henry (R)	27,057	14.6%
Dan Wentzel (GREEN)	4,765	2.6%

PREVIOUS WINNING PERCENTAGES
1998 (86%); 1996 (82%); 1994 (82%); 1992 (81%); 1992 Special Election (100%)

Elected 1992; 6th full term

Nowhere was the terrorist onslaught of Sept. 11, 2001, felt more than in the congressional district that Nadler has represented for a decade, which takes in the World Trade Center. The destruction changed the landscape and thousands of lives in the 8th District forever, and rebuilding the area and aiding the victims has become Nadler's overriding objective.

But the attacks did not push Nadler to the right politically, as they did many of his colleagues. He has spent his career as an outspoken voice for liberalism and has continued in that role without swerving. Just weeks after the attacks, Nadler voted against giving the government enhanced authority to spy on suspected terrorists, one of just 66 members of the House to oppose the bill. In 2002, he voted "present" on a resolution that called on the courts to keep the words "under God" in the pledge of allegiance.

Whether it is an attempt to ban a procedure its opponents call "partial birth" abortion, to bar human cloning or to restrict flag burning, Nadler is a leader among Democrats in fighting for civil liberties and individual rights. Nadler's philosophy fits well in his district, which stretches from Manhattan's Upper West Side through Greenwich Village and into Brooklyn. The 8th has one of the largest concentrations of liberal Jewish voters and gay and lesbian political activists in America, and few of them are happy that Republicans control Congress. Neither is Nadler.

A member of the Progressive Caucus, the most liberal faction of House Democrats, he has close to a 100 percent career vote rating from the liberal Americans for Democratic Action — of which he is an honorary vice president — and a lifetime rating of 3 percent from the American Conservative Union.

Nadler is quick to join in partisan debate and eager to expound on his views, often in nugget-size sound bites. In the Judiciary Committee in particular, he is always at the ready with an amendment or an argument, or both, as the panel considers GOP proposals to alter social policy, the Constitution, the criminal justice system, consumer regulations or civil rights. He is the top-ranking Democrat on Judiciary's Constitution Subcommittee.

Nadler strongly opposed legislation, which died at the end of the 107th Congress, to overhaul the nation's bankruptcy laws; he described it as "a bill of, by and for the credit card companies, which have waged a long and expensive campaign for it." The measure would have required more bankruptcy filers to try to pay back at least some of their debt. Nadler and other consumer advocates contend that there would be fewer bankruptcies if credit card companies and banks would stop extending credit to poor risks.

Nadler takes a strong stand on issues of interest to the homosexual community. After the Sept. 11 attacks, he and conservative Republican Donald Manzullo of Illinois led a successful effort to change federal law to allow benefits paid out for firefighters, police and chaplains to be directed to whoever is listed on a victim's life insurance policy, thus allowing homosexuals to collect on policies. Nadler also has pressed for added funding for housing programs for people with AIDS. And he criticized President Clinton for not insisting on an unambiguous end to the ban on gays in the military, saying the " 'don't ask, don't tell, don't get caught' policy represents a reaffirmation of the policy of official bigotry by the United States."

But Nadler fervently defended Clinton against Judiciary Republicans, who led the House in impeaching the president in 1998 for lying about his affair with White House intern Monica Lewinsky. Nadler accused the GOP of "running a lynch mob."

On the Transportation Committee, Nadler's long-range goal is to increase freight rail service to New York City by building a new tunnel under New York Harbor. In the 107th Congress, he marked progress in that effort, which he says would foster economic development, ease pollution and lower consumer costs in the city.

Nadler made an immediate impression when he arrived in the House in 1993. He persuaded his Democratic colleagues to approve an organizational reform that spreads out party power: The "Nadler rule" prohibits the top Democrat on a full committee from also holding the party's No. 1 seat on a subcommittee.

Born in Brooklyn, Nadler spent his early years on a New Jersey poultry farm. His family moved back to New York City after the farm failed. He earned a degree in government from Columbia and a law degree from Fordham, which he attended at night while working at an off-track betting office during the day.

Politics has been a lifelong passion for Nadler. In high school, he became friends with Dick Morris — later to gain fame and then notoriety as a political consultant to Clinton — and roomed with Morris at Columbia. Nadler organized students against the Vietnam War to campaign for Eugene J. McCarthy in the 1968 New Hampshire Democratic presidential primary. He was an aide to a New York state senator and he campaigned for liberal Democrat Ted Weiss' election to Congress. In 1976, Nadler won a seat in the state Assembly. He served there for 16 years.

When Weiss died on the eve of the 1992 Democratic primary, voters renominated him nonetheless, giving party officials the right to pick a successor. That set off a scramble among the district's ample cadre of Democratic activists, with six candidates jumping into the frenetic nine-day race for the nomination. While others, such as former Rep. Bella S. Abzug, were better known to the public, Nadler had longstanding ties to the insiders who would cast the votes. He got the nomination and went on to win the special election and the general-election contest for a full term on the same day.

In the overwhelmingly Democratic 8th District, the partisan nature of which was not altered by post-2000 census redistricting, Nadler has been re-elected with ease.

In August 2002, he underwent stomach reduction surgery, a radical step to reduce his obesity and attendant health problems that he worried would limit his congressional career. Nadler, who says his goal is to drop from a high of 338 pounds to about 160, had lost 70 pounds by early 2003.

KEY VOTES

2002

Yes Overhaul campaign finance law; ban "soft money" and restrict advocacy advertising
No Back Bush's defense budget increase
No Extend 1996 welfare law
No Adopt Bush's discretionary spending limit
No Pass GOP Medicare prescription drug plan
Yes Create independent Sept. 11 commission
Yes Extend union protections to Homeland Security Department employees
No Revive fast-track procedures for trade agreements
No Authorize war against Iraq
No Advance bankruptcy overhaul opposed by abortion opponents

2001

No Nullify Clinton Labor Department ergonomics rule
No Cut taxes by $1.35 trillion through fiscal 2011
Yes Maintain ban on oil drilling in Arctic National Wildlife Refuge
No Approve Bush proposal to limit managed-care plan liability for coverage decisions
Yes Divert money from crop subsidy payments to land conservation
No Expand law enforcement power to investigate suspected terrorists

CQ VOTE STUDIES

	PARTY UNITY		PRESIDENTIAL SUPPORT	
	Support	Oppose	Support	Oppose
2002	97%	3%	18%	82%
2001	98%	2%	21%	79%
2000	95%	5%	84%	16%
1999	98%	2%	84%	16%
1998	96%	4%	79%	21%

INTEREST GROUPS

	AFL-CIO	ADA	CCUS	ACU
2002	100%	95%	26%	0%
2001	100%	95%	26%	0%
2000	100%	95%	28%	4%
1999	100%	100%	12%	0%
1998	100%	100%	24%	8%

NEW YORK 8

West Side Manhattan; Borough Park; Coney Island

Starting just west of Central Park, the 8th moves south through Manhattan's West Side, taking in part of the Theater District and Times Square, then Chelsea, Greenwich Village, SoHo and Wall Street. It continues across the East River to skim Brooklyn's western waterfront, followed by some working-class areas, much of Brighton Beach and some of Brooklyn's south coastline in Coney Island.

It was in the 8th that terrorists crashed commercial airliners into the twin towers of the World Trade Center on Sept. 11, 2001, killing thousands of people and leveling the buildings. Despite the generally varied interests of the winding district, the logistics of rebuilding Lower Manhattan promise to dominate political and economic discussion in the 8th for some time to come.

The manufacturing industry that once sustained Brooklyn has been neglected in a surge of white-collar financial growth, though most of Brooklyn's well-to-do neighborhoods are in other districts.

Manhattan's heavily Democratic West Side has sent liberal representatives to Congress for decades. The Brooklyn portion, added in 1992 redistricting, increased the district's diversity, and Green Party presidential candidate Ralph Nader received 6 percent of the 8th's vote in 2000, his highest percentage in the state.

The 8th's politically active communities — gay, Jewish, minority, artistic and student — have supported Democratic presidential candidates overwhelmingly in recent years. Some GOP voters live in Brooklyn's middle-class neighborhoods, like Borough Park and Bensonhurst, backing candidates with more-conservative views.

MAJOR INDUSTRY

Finance, tourism, manufacturing, small business

CITIES

New York (pt.), 654,360

NOTABLE

The Statue of Liberty, Empire State Building, Governors Island, South Street Seaport, American Museum of Natural History, Lincoln Center, Penn Station, Madison Square Garden, City Hall, New York University and Coney Island's KeySpan Park, home to minor-league baseball's Brooklyn Cyclones, are in the 8th.

Rep. Anthony Weiner (D)

CAPITOL OFFICE
225-6616
weiner@mail.house.gov
www.house.gov/weiner
1122 Longworth 20515-3209; fax 226-7253

COMMITTEES
Judiciary
Science
Transportation & Infrastructure

HOMETOWN
Brooklyn

BORN
Sept. 4, 1964, Brooklyn, N.Y.

RELIGION
Jewish

FAMILY
Single

EDUCATION
State U. of New York, Plattsburgh, B.A. 1985

CAREER
Congressional aide

POLITICAL HIGHLIGHTS
New York City Council, 1992-99

ELECTION RESULTS

2002 GENERAL		
Anthony Weiner (D, L, WFM)	60,737	65.7%
Alfred F. Donohue (R, C)	31,698	34.3%
2002 PRIMARY		
Anthony Weiner (D)		unopposed
2000 GENERAL		
Anthony Weiner (D, L)	98,983	68.4%
Noach Dear (R, C)	45,649	31.6%

PREVIOUS WINNING PERCENTAGES
1998 (66%)

Elected 1998; 3rd term

Weiner is much like his mentor, Sen. Charles E. Schumer, the fellow Democrat he succeeded in the House. Not only do they have distinctive Brooklyn accents and even look something alike, but both possess liberal convictions, are comfortable in the political hurly-burly and can quickly sum up the day's events with a sound bite for the nightly news.

The New York City media, predictably, delight in being able to describe Weiner (WEE-ner) as a "political hot dog." They speculate that he harbors ambitions to become mayor — an idea that Weiner claims to have discussed only with his cat Matisse.

When the USA Network announced in late 2002 that its film based on the life of New York Mayor Rudolph Giuliani would be shot in Montreal so the network could benefit from Canadian tax incentives, Weiner's protest drew headlines. Shooting scenes of the Big Apple in Montreal "is tantamount to shooting a movie about the battle of the Alamo in Vancouver," he wrote to Barry Diller, the network's chief, in a letter that the tabloids lapped up. "What's next — a USA remake of 'Pride of the Yankees' to be filmed at the Skydome?"

Young, energetic and ambitious, Weiner found his footing quickly in the House. As a 34-year-old freshman, he won approval in 1999 of $30 million over three years to encourage aircraft builders to design quieter engines — a key concern for his constituents, who live beneath the takeoff and final approach paths of both LaGuardia and John F. Kennedy airports. Weiner was also among the New York members who fought a move in the 106th to allow more takeoffs and landings at those airports; their success locked in the existing numbers until 2007.

And after a 2001 jet crash that devastated a residential Long Island neighborhood (the plane lost its tailfin assembly shortly after takeoff from JFK), Weiner worked with the Federal Aviation Administration to redesign departure procedures to avoid populated areas whenever possible.

Weiner's influence over transportation policy is likely to grow in the 108th. He won a seat on the Transportation and Infrastructure Committee as it prepared to reauthorize the federal government's multibillion-dollar surface transportation and aviation programs.

The Sept. 11, 2001, terrorist attacks also deepened his activism on issues close to home and in the Middle East. The 2002 State Department authorization law included a Weiner provision requiring department recognition of Jerusalem as the capital of Israel. Palestinian leader Yasser Arafat denounced the provision and President Bush has declined to enforce it.

Weiner also cosponsored a House bill by fellow New Yorker Sherwood Boehlert, a Republican, to create special teams within the National Institute of Standards and Technology to investigate building failures and protect potentially valuable evidence. Weiner argued that bureaucratic infighting and mishandled evidence had impeded the probe into why the World Trade Center's twin towers collapsed so readily.

As a member of the Judiciary Committee, Weiner added language to the 2002 law creating the Department of Homeland Security that permits federal authorities to share security intelligence with local law enforcement. He also successfully included language in the 2001 anti-terrorism law to speed up implementation of a federal program to track foreign students and to increase the death benefits for federal public safety officers.

Weiner came to politics with a run for student government at the State

University of New York at Plattsburgh. His first campaign gave him a chance to hone a skill that has stood him in good stead: a self-deprecating sense of humor. Among his slogans were "Vote for Weiner. He'll be frank," "Weiner's on a roll" and "You'll relish Weiner." Still, he lost his bid.

He served for six years as a congressional aide in Schumer's Brooklyn and Washington offices. Then in 1991, at age 27, he became the youngest person at the time ever elected to the New York City Council. He worked with at-risk teenagers to create an anti-graffiti cleanup group known as "Weiner's Cleaners." Seven years later, he was among the youngest members of the 106th Congress and was elected by his freshman class to the Democratic whip organization.

Though he was seen as the protégé of Schumer, Weiner did not have an easy path to his party's nomination when the incumbent made his 1998 Senate run. Weiner won the Democratic nomination in a tight four-way primary by 489 votes. But he coasted in the overwhelmingly Democratic district in November and has easily won re-election since.

Although an activist liberal in the tradition of Democrats on Judiciary, on occasion Weiner has reached across the aisle to work with Republicans, a rarity for Democrats on that sharply partisan panel. He helped write a deal with Republicans in 2000 on a law making it more difficult for the government to seize private property from suspected criminals, for example.

Weiner also has championed consumer interests — parochial and national. He and fellow New York Democrat Joseph Crowley have pushed a bill to require telephone companies and the Federal Communications Commission to speed up 911 technology to pinpoint distress calls from cell phones. As a representative for a substantial elderly population, he has proposed a bill to give bigger annual cost of living increases for Social Security beneficiaries in the most expensive cities. In the fall of 2002, he made it his business to try to find a new operator for a supermarket in the Sheepshead Bay neighborhood of Brooklyn after its major grocer pulled out.

Always ready to take on Bush's policies, Weiner is a favorite of schedulers on the cable news shows. (His official biography notes that as a freshman, he made more television appearances than any other first-termer in the 106th.) As some Democrats shied away from challenging Bush on national security in 2002, Weiner in a Fox News interview questioned the success of the war on terrorism: "Show me a victory," he declared.

Weiner is an aggressive fundraiser and was one of a dozen House Democrats who transferred at least $100,000 from his personal campaign account to the Democratic Congressional Campaign Committee in 2002.

KEY VOTES

2002

Yes Overhaul campaign finance law; ban "soft money" and restrict advocacy advertising
No Back Bush's defense budget increase
No Extend 1996 welfare law
No Adopt Bush's discretionary spending limit
No Pass GOP Medicare prescription drug plan
Yes Create independent Sept. 11 commission
Yes Extend union protections to Homeland Security Department employees
No Revive fast-track procedures for trade agreements
Yes Authorize war against Iraq
No Advance bankruptcy overhaul opposed by abortion opponents

2001

No Nullify Clinton Labor Department ergonomics rule
No Cut taxes by $1.35 trillion through fiscal 2011
Yes Maintain ban on oil drilling in Arctic National Wildlife Refuge
No Approve Bush proposal to limit managed-care plan liability for coverage decisions
Yes Divert money from crop subsidy payments to land conservation
Yes Expand law enforcement power to investigate suspected terrorists

CQ VOTE STUDIES

	PARTY UNITY		PRESIDENTIAL SUPPORT	
	Support	Oppose	Support	Oppose
2002	95%	5%	24%	76%
2001	95%	5%	26%	74%
2000	94%	6%	90%	10%
1999	95%	5%	88%	12%

INTEREST GROUPS

	AFL-CIO	ADA	CCUS	ACU
2002	100%	100%	32%	8%
2001	100%	95%	35%	0%
2000	90%	85%	40%	8%
1999	78%	100%	24%	0%

NEW YORK 9

Part of Brooklyn and Queens – Forest Hills, Rockaway, Sheepshead Bay

The Democratic-leaning 9th takes in north-central and western Queens and segues into southeastern Brooklyn. The district was divided almost equally between Brooklyn and Queens in the late 1990s, but 2002 redistricting left the 9th with 70 percent of its registered voters living in Queens.

The new map extended the 9th farther east in Queens, past the Grand Central Parkway and through the Hillcrest and Fresh Meadows neighborhoods to the edge of Oakland Gardens, which is only a few exits from Nassau County on the Long Island Expressway. Many of Queens' wealthiest communities are in the northern part of the 9th. Median household incomes in this area top $100,000.

The 9th narrows and runs south from Forest Park, taking in part of the Woodhaven, Ozone Park and Lindenwood neighborhoods. A decade ago, these areas were mostly white. Hispanics now outnumber whites, and the Asian population is rapidly expanding.

The 9th also takes in much of the Rockaway area in far southwestern Queens along the Atlantic Ocean. In Brooklyn, the district includes Floyd Bennett Field and most of Gateway National Recreation Area on Jamaica Bay. Farther west, the Sheepshead Bay area has seen an influx of Russian immigrants.

A sizable Jewish population contributes to the district's Democratic heft. Registered Democrats outnumber Republicans by a 3-to-1 ratio, and Al Gore topped two-thirds of the vote here in 2000.

MAJOR INDUSTRY
Service, finance, insurance, manufacturing

CITIES
New York (pt.), 654,360

NOTABLE
Kings Plaza Shopping Center and Marina, billed as the first indoor mall in New York City, opened in 1970 near Mill Basin; American Airlines Flight 587, from John F. Kennedy International Airport to the Dominican Republic, crashed into Belle Harbor on Nov. 12, 2001.

Rep. Edolphus Towns (D)

CAPITOL OFFICE
225-5936
congressmantowns@mail.house.gov
www.house.gov/towns
2232 Rayburn 20515-3210; fax 225-1018

COMMITTEES
Energy & Commerce
Government Reform

HOMETOWN
Brooklyn

BORN
July 21, 1934, Chadbourn, N.C.

RELIGION
Baptist

FAMILY
Wife, Gwendolyn Towns; two children

EDUCATION
North Carolina A&T State U., B.S. 1956; Adelphi U., M.S.W. 1973

MILITARY SERVICE
Army, 1956-58

CAREER
Professor; hospital administrator

POLITICAL HIGHLIGHTS
Brooklyn borough deputy president, 1976-82

ELECTION RESULTS

2002 GENERAL		
Edolphus Towns (D, L)	73,859	97.8%
Herbert F. Ryan (C)	1,639	2.2%
2002 PRIMARY		
Edolphus Towns (D)		unopposed
2000 GENERAL		
Edolphus Towns (D, L)	120,700	90.2%
Ernestine M. Brown (R)	6,852	5.1%
Barry Ford (WFM)	5,530	4.1%

PREVIOUS WINNING PERCENTAGES
1998 (92%); 1996 (91%); 1994 (89%); 1992 (96%); 1990 (93%); 1988 (89%); 1986 (89%); 1984 (85%); 1982 (84%)

Elected 1982; 11th term

Towns has served more than 20 years in the House, where he has quietly built up a record of legislative successes and has brought home considerable largess to his Brooklyn district. In the 107th Congress, for example, he procured $153 million for a federal courthouse and acquired a $150 million reconstruction bond for the borough's Interfaith Hospital.

Affable and low-key, Towns is the sixth-ranking Democrat on the Energy and Commerce Committee, and he has been the chairman or ranking minority member of a subcommittee, either on that panel or on the Government Reform Committee, since the 103rd Congress. He was chairman of the Congressional Black Caucus in the 102nd Congress. Despite these positions, he often eludes the spotlight.

He gained some notice in 1997 when he endorsed Republican Rudolph Giuliani for re-election as mayor of New York City. Critics argue he has not achieved as much of a presence on Capitol Hill as might be expected from a lawmaker with his longevity. But Towns easily ignores his critics and goes about pursuing his own interests and helping his Brooklyn district.

One such interest is telecommunications. In the 1996 Telecommunications Act, he sponsored language creating a venture capital fund for minorities. In 2002, he cosponsored a key amendment that facilitated House passage of legislation aimed at allowing the regional Bell phone companies to more quickly deploy high-speed Internet connections. He also has backed a bill to narrow the "digital divide" — giving urban and rural communities access to new information technologies.

Another of Towns' concerns is the rights of student athletes. In the 107th Congress, he cosponsored legislation that would bring sports agents under the auspices of the Federal Trade Commission, allowing unscrupulous agents to be sued in state courts for misleading student athletes or offering them bribes or gifts.

Towns also has been active on health care issues such as creating a prescription drug benefit under the Medicare program. He introduced legislation in the 107th Congress that would increase Medicare reimbursements for midwife services. His priorities in the 106th Congress included not only a range of preventive health and nutrition measures but also legislation to encourage teachers to live in the same communities where they work.

Towns also authored a bill to ban the sale of toys that resemble real guns. Later, after two teenagers were shot and killed when they pointed a realistic-looking toy gun at two police officers, he persuaded a drug store chain to stop selling the toys.

The New York Daily News in a 1998 survey rating the New York City congressional delegation ranked Towns near the bottom. His lowest scores came in the categories of "national presence" and "clout." His highest scores were for constituent service and work ethic. In 2000, The New York Times endorsed his challenger in the Democratic primary, commenting that "after 18 years, [Towns'] record in Congress has been minimal and his support for tobacco and other special interests is troubling."

Towns' support for the tobacco industry may be rooted in his upbringing. The son of a sharecropper in North Carolina, where tobacco is a major crop, Towns argues that anti-tobacco legislation affects small farmers as well as the large manufacturers. He only stopped taking campaign donations from the tobacco industry in 2000 after considerable pressure.

In an overwhelmingly Democratic district such as the 10th, the Democratic primary is the real election, and the 10th has a long history of party infighting. The 2000 primary, in which Towns turned back Harvard-trained lawyer Barry Ford by a 57 percent to 43 percent tally, was fought amid grumblings from some of Towns' critics that the congressman was going too far in trying to position his son, Darryl, a state assemblyman, as the heir to the district seat.

Towns also endured a spate of negative publicity when the House bank controversy unfolded in the 102nd Congress. He had 408 overdrafts at the private bank for House members; Towns explained, however, that his receptionist had embezzled $28,000 from his account to support a drug habit. But publicity from the incident — combined with 1991 news reports that the Black Caucus (which Towns chaired from 1991 to 1993) had used funds from the office account of a retiring member to pay delinquent taxes — gave a perception that Towns and the caucus should have paid closer attention to their financial affairs.

Towns was born in Chadbourn in southeastern North Carolina and graduated from historically black North Carolina A & T in Greensboro. After a two-year Army stint, he came north and began the career that eventually led him into elective politics in Brooklyn. He worked as a teacher and hospital administrator and earned a master's degree in social work from Adelphi University. In 1976, he was appointed Brooklyn Borough deputy president, and while working at Borough Hall, he established links to numerous community organizations.

Towns' chance to run for the House came in 1982 after redistricting gave the 11th District an almost even split of blacks and Hispanics. The new district included some Brooklyn territory that had been represented by white Democratic Rep. Frederick W. Richmond. But Richmond, who had been indicted on charges of income tax evasion and possession of marijuana, resigned. (Richmond was later convicted.)

In the turbulent world of Brooklyn politics, Towns benefited from a lack of enemies. He drew support from party regulars as well as from a rival faction calling for a change. Towns fended off two Hispanic primary contenders to win nomination with 50 percent. He won easily in November, starting an unbroken string of general-election landslides in the Democratic stronghold. Redistricting in 1992 put him in a newly drawn but just as Democratic 10th District, where he has faced tough primary battles three times, including the 2000 contest.

In 2002, however, he was unopposed in the Democratic primary and took 98 percent of the vote in November against a third-party candidate.

KEY VOTES

2002

- Yes Overhaul campaign finance law; ban "soft money" and restrict advocacy advertising
- No Back Bush's defense budget increase
- No Extend 1996 welfare law
- No Adopt Bush's discretionary spending limit
- ? Pass GOP Medicare prescription drug plan
- Yes Create independent Sept. 11 commission
- Yes Extend union protections to Homeland Security Department employees
- No Revive fast-track procedures for trade agreements
- No Authorize war against Iraq
- No Advance bankruptcy overhaul opposed by abortion opponents

2001

- No Nullify Clinton Labor Department ergonomics rule
- ? Cut taxes by $1.35 trillion through fiscal 2011
- No Maintain ban on oil drilling in Arctic National Wildlife Refuge
- No Approve Bush proposal to limit managed-care plan liability for coverage decisions
- Yes Divert money from crop subsidy payments to land conservation
- Yes Expand law enforcement power to investigate suspected terrorists

CQ VOTE STUDIES

	Party Unity		Presidential Support	
	Support	Oppose	Support	Oppose
2002	94%	6%	32%	68%
2001	91%	9%	34%	66%
2000	97%	3%	89%	11%
1999	94%	6%	79%	21%
1998	93%	7%	85%	15%

INTEREST GROUPS

	AFL-CIO	ADA	CCUS	ACU
2002	100%	80%	40%	4%
2001	100%	65%	50%	14%
2000	100%	95%	50%	4%
1999	78%	95%	28%	4%
1998	100%	95%	31%	9%

NEW YORK 10

Part of Brooklyn – Bedford-Stuyvesant, Canarsie, Downtown Brooklyn, East New York

The 10th begins just inland of Brooklyn's industrial waterfront and heads east before bounding back southwest after reaching the Queens border. The district encompasses one of New York's most economically and ethnically diverse constituencies, but is homogeneously Democratic, with a 13-to-1 Democratic registration advantage. Al Gore took 88 percent of the area's vote in the 2000 presidential contest.

Redistricting in 2002 brought the black-majority 10th west of Flatbush Avenue to include part of Midwood in south-central Brooklyn. East of this area, the district takes in growing Georgetown and Canarsie. Canarsie's racial composition has changed dramatically, as many blacks of Caribbean descent are moving to an area that was once predominantly white. Many of these families have solid middle-class incomes, which is the exception rather than the rule for most of the district. At its northwest corner, the 10th cups the Brooklyn Navy Yard (located in the 12th) to take in Fort Greene and part of Williamsburg — diverse areas with large black and Hispanic populations.

Joblessness has aggravated poverty, violent crime and racial tensions in some working-class and low-income communities like East New York and Bedford-Stuyvesant. Erosion in the 10th's manufacturing base has caused unemployment, though government jobs in Downtown Brooklyn, which includes Borough Hall and several court facilities, and education jobs at the district's colleges, which include Brooklyn College and Long Island University-Brooklyn, aid the economy.

Aging infrastructure is a problem, as water and sewer lines are prone to collapse and heavy truck traffic is eroding the Brooklyn-Queens Expressway and residential streets leading to the Brooklyn and Manhattan bridges (both in the 12th District).

MAJOR INDUSTRY

Government, higher education, small business, pharmaceuticals

CITIES

New York (pt.), 654,361

NOTABLE

Spike Lee's film, "Do The Right Thing," is set in Bedford-Stuyvesant.

Rep. Major R. Owens (D)

CAPITOL OFFICE
225-6231
major.owens@mail.house.gov
www.house.gov/owens
2309 Rayburn 20515-3211; fax 226-0112

COMMITTEES
Education & Workforce
Government Reform

HOMETOWN
Brooklyn

BORN
June 28, 1936, Memphis, Tenn.

RELIGION
Baptist

FAMILY
Wife, Maria Cuprill-Owens; five children

EDUCATION
Morehouse College, B.A. 1956 (math); Atlanta U., M.L.S. 1957

CAREER
City community development commissioner; librarian

POLITICAL HIGHLIGHTS
N.Y. Senate, 1975-83

ELECTION RESULTS

2002 GENERAL		
Major R. Owens (D, WFM)	76,917	86.6%
Susan Cleary (R, INDC)	11,149	12.6%
2002 PRIMARY		
Major R. Owens (D)		unopposed
2000 GENERAL		
Major R. Owens (D, WFM)	112,050	87.0%
Susan Cleary (R)	8,406	6.5%
Una Clarke (L)	7,366	5.7%

PREVIOUS WINNING PERCENTAGES
1998 (90%); 1996 (92%); 1994 (89%); 1992 (94%); 1990 (95%); 1988 (93%); 1986 (91%); 1984 (91%); 1982 (91%)

Elected 1982; 11th term

Owens is passionate, uncompromising and sometimes even belligerent about issues affecting people he believes are oppressed or discriminated against. "I am one of those who is not ashamed to be called a liberal," he says. "In fact, I am proud of it. I am a liberal, I am progressive, all of those kinds of things that people seem to shrink away from. Our group has not disappeared."

Owens is also known as "the rapping congressman." He pens poetry and rap lyrics to mock the conservative initiatives of the Republican majority, saying this gives him "an outlet for political frustrations." Owens says he brings the rhythm of the streets to the Capitol with his rap poems, which are printed in the Congressional Record and displayed on his congressional Web site.

Among his offerings in the 107th Congress was "Message to the Republican Mob," about the unfolding corporate accounting scandals. Owens argued that "our constituents are ahead of the lawmakers in demanding justice." The poem began, "Before you merely mauled welfare mothers/ But now you're messing with / The Great American Middle Class / We'll kick your rear."

One of his favorite poems was titled, "Let's Roll America," which Owens said is not only a military call to action but also a challenge to the United States to spread democracy and feed the hungry. Another poem was a tribute to those killed in the Sept. 11, 2001, terrorist attacks on the World Trade Center towers, which included these lines: "Thousands of honored dead/ Perished in pain/ But not in vain."

As the top Democrat on the Education and the Workforce panel's Workforce Protections Subcommittee, Owens has tried to beat back Republican attacks on organized labor and efforts to relax health and safety regulations on business. He has supported minimum wage increases, blocked attempts to eliminate cash payments for overtime, opposed the repeal of the Davis-Bacon prevailing wage law, and protested the effort to dismantle the Occupational Safety and Health Administration.

In the past two Congresses, while many Democrats sought action on a measure to subsidize the interest on school construction bonds, Owens advocated a bill that would have authorized more than $20 billion in direct federal payments over five years. He argued that poor communities would never be able to sell the construction bonds in the first place. In the 107th Congress, his proposal, in the form of an amendment to a large education authorization bill, was defeated by the Education and the Workforce Committee by a 22-25 vote.

Owens was more successful in winning additional funding for libraries in the education bill. As a former librarian, he said the funds would be of particular benefit to "underserved communities and more importantly Central Brooklyn."

In addition to his leadership role on the Education and the Workforce Committee, Owens also is chairman of the Congressional Black Caucus's Education Braintrust and was named by party leaders in the 107th to be on the House Democratic Caucus education message team.

Owens is also a leader of the Progressive Caucus, the most liberal faction of House Democrats. A staunch proponent of gun control, he has proposed rewriting or even repealing the Second Amendment, which guarantees the right of Americans to bear arms. In the 107th, he voted with the majority of Democrats 98 percent of the time, while he opposed President Bush's position 81 percent of the time.

The 11th District is home to a large Caribbean immigrant population, and Owens advocates policies to aid immigrating Haitians. In the last two Congresses, for instance, he has introduced a bill to prevent the Immigration and Naturalization Service from deporting people with American-born children under 18 and to allow children under 12 without parents to become U.S. citizens.

Responding to the effort in the 107th Congress to require airport screeners to be U.S. citizens, Owens suggested that anyone who is eligible to serve in the armed forces — including non-citizens — should be eligible for an airport security job.

Born in Memphis and educated in the South as a librarian, Owens was a community organizer in Brooklyn's economically depressed Brownsville section in the 1960s when he was tapped by Mayor John V. Lindsay to head New York City's anti-poverty program. He made his first bid for elected office in 1974, winning a state Senate seat that he held for eight years.

When Owens set his sights on the House in 1982 — upon the retirement of Democrat Shirley Chisholm after seven terms — he faced a tough opponent: Vander Beatty, who as deputy Democratic leader in the state Senate had built a patronage empire in the Brooklyn black community. But Owens capitalized on Beatty's unsavory connections and his own reputation for honesty. He won the primary narrowly and easily won the general election in November.

Republicans have never posed a threat to Owens, whose solidly Democratic district is composed largely of African-Americans and other minorities. He usually has earned at least 90 percent of the vote in the general election; in both 2000 and 2002 he received 87 percent.

But in 2000, with his district tilting increasingly toward West Indian immigrants, he had to fight hard in a primary battle against City Councilwoman Una Clarke, who was born in Jamaica. Clarke contended that Owens had failed to win a federal empowerment zone for the district and did not respond to constituents who needed help with immigration procedures or other matters. With the help of prominent Democrats, including first lady and New York Senate candidate Hillary Rodham Clinton, Owens won the primary by almost 9 percentage points.

Some believed that showing might have signaled that Owens' hold on the district was weakening, but he was unopposed for renomination in 2002.

KEY VOTES

2002

- Yes Overhaul campaign finance law; ban "soft money" and restrict advocacy advertising
- No Back Bush's defense budget increase
- No Extend 1996 welfare law
- No Adopt Bush's discretionary spending limit
- No Pass GOP Medicare prescription drug plan
- Yes Create independent Sept. 11 commission
- Yes Extend union protections to Homeland Security Department employees
- No Revive fast-track procedures for trade agreements
- No Authorize war against Iraq
- No Advance bankruptcy overhaul opposed by abortion opponents

2001

- No Nullify Clinton Labor Department ergonomics rule
- No Cut taxes by $1.35 trillion through fiscal 2011
- Yes Maintain ban on oil drilling in Arctic National Wildlife Refuge
- No Approve Bush proposal to limit managed-care plan liability for coverage decisions
- Yes Divert money from crop subsidy payments to land conservation
- No Expand law enforcement power to investigate suspected terrorists

CQ VOTE STUDIES

	PARTY UNITY		PRESIDENTIAL SUPPORT	
	Support	Oppose	Support	Oppose
2002	98%	2%	21%	79%
2001	98%	2%	17%	83%
2000	98%	2%	88%	12%
1999	97%	3%	85%	15%
1998	97%	3%	88%	12%

INTEREST GROUPS

	AFL-CIO	ADA	CCUS	ACU
2002	100%	90%	25%	4%
2001	100%	95%	19%	4%
2000	100%	90%	42%	0%
1999	89%	100%	21%	0%
1998	100%	100%	22%	0%

NEW YORK 11

Part of Brooklyn — Flatbush, Crown Heights, Brownsville, Park Slope

A black-majority residential district in central Brooklyn, the 11th is predominantly working-class but also contains some of the borough's wealthiest neighborhoods.

Redistricting in 2002 did not significantly alter the district's boundaries, other than to extend it westward through Carroll Gardens into parts of Cobble Hill and Brooklyn Heights to compensate for slow population growth in the 1990s. The changes did not affect the district's reliably Democratic vote: Democrats outnumber Republicans by a 12-to-1 ratio. George W. Bush finished with only 9 percent of the vote here in the 2000 presidential election.

At the heart of the district is Flatbush, a working-class black and Hispanic neighborhood that has become home to numerous Caribbean immigrants from Jamaica, Haiti, the Dominican Republic and Trinidad and Tobago. The 11th's West Indian Carnival Parade attracts hundreds of thousands of visitors each year, a feature that economic development officials hope to exploit to draw tourists into Brooklyn.

In the district's north is Crown Heights, made infamous in 1991 when a car driven by an orthodox rabbi's assistant struck and killed a black child, setting off four days of riots between African-Americans and Hasidic Jews.

While New York City gained population in the 1990s, the Crown Heights region lost population during that period. Brownsville, east of Crown Heights, also is heavily black. Pockets of affluence in the 11th include Park Slope, just northwest of Prospect Park, and part of Brooklyn Heights near the Brooklyn Bridge.

MAJOR INDUSTRY

Health care, retail

CITIES

New York (pt.), 654,361

NOTABLE

Ebbets Field, where the Brooklyn Dodgers played from 1913 to 1957, was demolished in 1960 and is now a housing complex; The Brooklyn Museum of Art and Brooklyn Botanic Garden are in the 11th.

Rep. Nydia M. Velázquez (D)

CAPITOL OFFICE
225-2361
www.house.gov/velazquez
2241 Rayburn 20515-3212; fax 226-0327

COMMITTEES
Financial Services
Small Business - ranking member

HOMETOWN
Brooklyn

BORN
March 28, 1953, Yabucoa, P.R.

RELIGION
Roman Catholic

FAMILY
Husband, Paul Bader

EDUCATION
U. of Puerto Rico, B.A. 1974 (political science); New York U., M.A. 1976 (political science)

CAREER
Puerto Rican Community Affairs Department director; congressional aide; professor

POLITICAL HIGHLIGHTS
New York City Council, 1984-85; defeated for re-election to New York City Council, 1984

ELECTION RESULTS

2002 GENERAL		
Nydia M. Velázquez (D, WFM)	48,408	95.8%
Cesar Estevez (C)	2,119	4.2%
2002 PRIMARY		
Nydia M. Velázquez (D)		unopposed
2000 GENERAL		
Nydia M. Velázquez (D, WFM)	81,699	86.5%
Rosemary Markgraf (R)	10,052	10.6%
Paul Pederson (SW)	1,025	1.1%

PREVIOUS WINNING PERCENTAGES
1998 (84%); 1996 (85%); 1994 (92%); 1992 (77%)

Elected 1992; 6th term

The first Hispanic woman to serve as the ranking member of a House committee, Velázquez has used her post on the Small Business Committee as a bully pulpit to badger the federal government to do more business with small firms, especially those owned by minorities and women. She is the first woman of Puerto Rican descent to be elected to Congress.

Velázquez's district has the second-highest percentage of blue-collar workers in New York, so she pays particular attention to government and private programs aimed at helping people improve their lives through better access to education, health care, housing and jobs. She continues to press for a variety of economic development programs for her district and other low-income communities. And with more than 100,000 Puerto Rican constituents in the 12th District, Velázquez (veh-LASS-kez) also pays particular attention to matters affecting the island commonwealth.

A number of other House committees outrank Small Business in terms of prestige and clout, but Velázquez has worked hard to make the panel relevant. Using her top-ranking position, she has pushed to increase the share of government business that goes to small firms, to help small-business owners provide health insurance and pensions for their employees, and to direct them to loans and other sources of capital.

After the Sept. 11, 2001, terrorist attacks, Velázquez proposed legislation to ensure the involvement of small business in the cleanup and rebuilding of lower Manhattan. And she offered a bill to involve local businesses and other groups in developing plans for use of polluted former industrial sites, known as brownfields, after they are cleaned up.

In 2000, she directed a Small Business Democratic staff study of the procurement practices at 21 government agencies that do substantial business with private industry. The study resulted in a "report card" that gave the agencies generally low marks on using small firms. She has made the report card an annual event, noting in 2002 that the government's overall grade had actually fallen (from C-minus to D) despite contracting goals set by the Clinton and Bush administrations.

She and Small Business Chairman Donald Manzullo, R-Ill., generally work well together, agreeing on the federal contracting issue. Velázquez laments, "For many small businesses, an iron curtain hangs around federal procurement offices that reads, 'small businesses need not apply.' "

In the 107th Congress, Velázquez took up the case of a woman who was fired from a Brooklyn garment factory after she complained about working conditions and abuse of workers. Velázquez made the point that not all sweatshop operations are overseas. The Department of Labor eventually moved against the company, but Velázquez said, "I know there are hundreds of other cases like this one that go unresolved in my district alone."

Velázquez also has a seat on the Financial Services Committee, where she is the only New York City Democrat on the Housing Subcommittee. She won the panel's approval in the 107th of a pilot program in New York to provide loan counseling to prospective homebuyers in areas where mortgage foreclosures have been a problem. Many of the foreclosures are a result of unscrupulous lenders charging high interest rates and fees and imposing unrealistic terms, she said. She also got the committee to clarify the federal law that requires that a portion of public housing maintenance and construction funds be used to hire residents to do the work.

Velázquez has a keen interest in immigration issues. From 1986 until her election to the House, she worked as a liaison between the Puerto Rican government and Latino communities in the United States. And, in Congress, most casework in her district office relates to immigration matters.

Velázquez also joined other Puerto Rican lawmakers in demanding that the Navy stop using the island of Vieques, just off Puerto Rico, for bombing practice. She was once arrested during a protest of the shelling.

Velázquez was born and raised in a sugar cane region in southeastern Puerto Rico with her twin sister and seven other siblings. Her father cut sugar cane and her mother helped the family make ends meet by selling food to the other cane workers. Her father also ran a small business that made cinder blocks, and so he had to deal with the regulations, labor standards and taxes that confront all small businesses.

Although he had only a third-grade education, Velázquez says her father sparked her interest in public life and politics. She says she remembers him discussing workers' rights issues at the dinner table. She told The New York Times that he delivered passionate speeches from the back of a flatbed truck and founded a political party in their hometown of Yabucoa. "I always wanted to be like my father," she told The Times.

After graduating from the University of Puerto Rico — the first in her family to receive a college diploma — Velázquez came to New York City for graduate school. She then taught Puerto Rican studies at Hunter College, worked as a special assistant to Democratic Rep. Edolphus Towns and served briefly on the New York City Council before taking the Puerto Rico liaison job in 1986.

Her local name recognition increased dramatically shortly before her 1992 House race, when she ran a Hispanic voter registration effort financed by the Puerto Rican government. She said the effort registered 200,000 voters nationwide, but critics said she targeted the Brooklyn sections that later became part of her newly drawn Hispanic-majority congressional district.

Her biggest obstacle in the Democratic primary was nine-term Democratic Rep. Stephen J. Solarz, whose district had been dismantled in redistricting. Solarz hired Hispanic advisers and learned a few Spanish phrases, but as an unknown to many of his would-be constituents, he was branded a wealthy carpetbagger. Velázquez defeated him by 5 percentage points in the primary, then captured 77 percent of the vote in the general election.

Since then, Velázquez has won handily, even after court-ordered redistricting in 1997 reduced the Hispanic population in the 12th District from 58 percent to 49 percent. Redistricting in 2002 made few changes in the 12th, which is still 49 percent Hispanic.

KEY VOTES

2002

- Yes Overhaul campaign finance law; ban "soft money" and restrict advocacy advertising
- No Back Bush's defense budget increase
- No Extend 1996 welfare law
- No Adopt Bush's discretionary spending limit
- No Pass GOP Medicare prescription drug plan
- Yes Create independent Sept. 11 commission
- Yes Extend union protections to Homeland Security Department employees
- No Revive fast-track procedures for trade agreements
- No Authorize war against Iraq
- No Advance bankruptcy overhaul opposed by abortion opponents

2001

- No Nullify Clinton Labor Department ergonomics rule
- No Cut taxes by $1.35 trillion through fiscal 2011
- Yes Maintain ban on oil drilling in Arctic National Wildlife Refuge
- No Approve Bush proposal to limit managed-care plan liability for coverage decisions
- Yes Divert money from crop subsidy payments to land conservation
- No Expand law enforcement power to investigate suspected terrorists

CQ VOTE STUDIES

	PARTY UNITY		PRESIDENTIAL SUPPORT	
	Support	Oppose	Support	Oppose
2002	99%	1%	24%	76%
2001	96%	4%	26%	74%
2000	97%	3%	85%	15%
1999	95%	5%	76%	24%
1998	96%	4%	81%	19%

INTEREST GROUPS

	AFL-CIO	ADA	CCUS	ACU
2002	89%	95%	35%	0%
2001	92%	90%	35%	0%
2000	100%	90%	40%	4%
1999	100%	100%	24%	4%
1998	100%	95%	33%	8%

NEW YORK 12

Lower East Side of Manhattan; parts of Brooklyn and Queens

The 12th, which touches parts of Manhattan, Brooklyn and Queens, was created in 1992 to form a Hispanic-majority district under the Voting Rights Act. Once known as the Bullwinkle District because of its resemblance to the cartoon moose, the 12th was redrawn by court decree in 1998 to have a more compact shape and a decreased Hispanic population. Marginal changes in 2002 retained the district's basic contours and pegged its Hispanic population at 49 percent.

Even with a significant immigrant population that is not eligible to vote and low turnout among Hispanic voters, the 12th elected and continues to send a Puerto Rican representative to Congress. The district's numerous working-class and minority residents make it a Democratic bastion.

Two-thirds of the 12th's registered voters live in Brooklyn. In its southwest corner, the district begins in Sunset Park, which has a large Hispanic population, then segues north along the East River and jumps across the Brooklyn and Manhattan bridges into Manhattan to take in Chinatown, part of Little Italy and the Lower East Side. Nearly one in five registered voters lives in Manhattan.

Back in northern Brooklyn (the 12th also includes the Williamsburg Bridge), it takes in Greenpoint, which has a large Polish population, and moves east along the Brooklyn-Queens border to the heavily Hispanic neighborhoods of East Williamsburg, Bushwick and Cypress Hills. In Queens, the 12th takes in parts of the Sunnyside and Woodside neighborhoods, which are experiencing rapid Hispanic growth.

MAJOR INDUSTRY
Health care, manufacturing, service

CITIES
New York (pt.), 654,360

NOTABLE
Brooklyn's Green-Wood Cemetery, where the more than 560,000 interred include Leonard Bernstein, Horace Greeley and notorious 19th century New York politician William M. "Boss" Tweed; Brooklyn Navy Yard; The Brooklyn Heights Promenade, built over the Brooklyn-Queens Expressway, looks out at the lower Manhattan skyline.

Rep. Vito J. Fossella (R)

CAPITOL OFFICE
225-3371
vito.fossella@mail.house.gov
www.house.gov/fossella
1239 Longworth 20515-3213; fax 226-1272

COMMITTEES
Energy & Commerce
Financial Services

HOMETOWN
Great Kills

BORN
March 9, 1965, South Beach, N.Y.

RELIGION
Roman Catholic

FAMILY
Wife, Mary Pat Fossella; two children

EDUCATION
U. of Pennsylvania, B.S. 1987; Fordham U., J.D. 1993

CAREER
Management consultant; lawyer

POLITICAL HIGHLIGHTS
New York City Council, 1994-97

ELECTION RESULTS

2002 GENERAL		
Vito J. Fossella (R, C, RTL)	72,204	69.6%
Arne M. Mattsson (D, L, WFM)	29,366	28.3%
Anita Lerman (INDC)	1,427	1.4%
2002 PRIMARY		
Vito J. Fossella (R)		unopposed
2000 GENERAL		
Vito J. Fossella (R, C, RTL)	109,806	64.6%
Katina M. Johnstone (D, WFM)	57,603	33.9%
Anita Lerman (INDC, GREEN)	2,653	1.6%

PREVIOUS WINNING PERCENTAGES
1998 (65%); 1997 Special Election (61%)

Elected November 1997; 3rd full term

Glib, telegenic and easygoing, Fossella cannot help but invite comparisons with his predecessor, Susan Molinari, who was prominent in the GOP leadership during the mid-1990s. So, Fossella gets more than his share of attention for a relatively junior member without a major piece of legislation under his belt. He is the beneficiary of a waiver from Speaker J. Dennis Hastert allowing him to sit on Financial Services as well as Energy and Commerce, which is normally an "exclusive" committee posting.

He is the only Republican in Congress representing New York City and, from his perch on Financial Services, Fossella (Fuh-SELL-ah) is trying to build a portfolio on issues that affect Wall Street, a big employer of his constituents. He enjoyed a first taste of success when the House passed his bill in 2001 slashing the federal fees on stock trades, a move he said would help spur more market activity for both large and small investors. The bill also increased salaries for employees of the Securities and Exchange Commission, the agency in the middle of a political storm over corporate ethics.

Fossella is more conservative than most Northeastern Republicans, who tend to be labor friendly, pro-abortion rights moderates. He favors most free-trade agreements and opposes new ergonomics regulations for the computer-dominated workplace. He opposes an expansion of abortion rights and supports oil drilling in the Arctic wilderness.

But he is not as driven by ideology as others in the predominately conservative House GOP. He tends to be a pragmatist who keeps a sharp eye on the dollars-and-cents concerns of his district. During the battle over education in the 107th Congress, for instance, Fossella was less involved in the touchstone school choice issue than he was in a behind-the-scenes wrestling match with Democratic Sen. Hillary Clinton of New York over funding for poor schools. When a Clinton proposal threatened to take $10 million from schools in Staten Island, Queens and Brooklyn, Fossella successfully called on some senior Republicans to squelch it.

"I am a simple guy," says Fossella, whom the New York Daily News has described as having a "self-deprecating, smart-aleck" style. "My job every day is defined by how I can best serve the people of Brooklyn and Staten Island."

Fossella's attention to local concerns has helped him tighten his grip on the seat in his third full term, but it also took on heightened importance after the Sept. 11, 2001, terrorist attacks. He lost several friends and high school classmates in the World Trade Center that day, as well as 30 fellow parishioners from St. Clare's Roman Catholic Church on Staten Island. It would be hard to find a family in Fossella's district that was not likewise personally touched. He spent a lot of time attending funerals that fall, and working on the New York City bailout plan hammered out in three-way meetings of the White House, the mayor's office and the House GOP leadership.

One of Fossella's pet projects since Sept. 11 has been the establishment of a national memorial at the Fresh Kills landfill on Staten Island, a closed facility that was temporarily reopened as the place for sorting debris from the trade center, including the incinerated remains of victims.

Fossella was an early backer of President Bush in the primaries and has reaped the benefits. Though unknown nationally, he was given a prime-time speech at the Republican National Convention in 2000, which put him on many GOP radar screens as a comer.

When he arrived on Capitol Hill in late 1997 after a special-election victory, Fossella won assignment to the Transportation and Infrastructure Committee. He was able to secure $32 million for new ferries to run between Staten Island and Manhattan, the first new vessels in many years. Transportation is a big issue on Staten Island, linked to the rest of the city by only one bridge and the storied ferry service.

Fossella also worked to reduce noise from aircraft flying low over Staten Island after takeoff from Newark. The noise issue has been hotly contested for years and pits New York against New Jersey.

In his first year in the House, Fossella played a lead role in the House's decision to denounce President Clinton's decision to grant clemency to Puerto Rican militant nationalists imprisoned for a string of bombings and robberies in the 1970s and 1980s. One of the victims was a police officer constituent, and Fossella said he was outraged that convicted terrorists were able to negotiate the terms of their release. In 1999, he protested a Brooklyn Museum of Art exhibit of the Virgin Mary in which elephant dung was used. "Nowhere does it say that the American taxpayer has to subsidize so-called art that desecrates one religion," he said.

Fossella hails from a well-known Italian-American political family on Staten Island, and he is close to another one, the Molinaris. Fossella's father, Vito Sr., served in Mayor Ed Koch's administration; an uncle, Frank Fossella, was a New York City Council member. From 1935 until his death in 1944, Fossella's great-grandfather James O'Leary was a Democratic House member from New York. Though he comes from a long line of Democrats, Fossella's conservatism prompted him to switch parties in 1990.

When Susan Molinari announced in 1997 that she was resigning from the House for a career in television, her father, Guy, a former House member himself and the Staten Island GOP borough president, immediately tapped Fossella as the heir apparent, referring to him as "my son."

Fossella already had a respectable political résumé. A Fordham University-trained lawyer and graduate of the University of Pennsylvania, he was on the City Council — in the same seat once held by his uncle. As part of an overmatched GOP minority, Fossella had managed to win notice in the conservative and insular borough of Staten Island by securing the island's first new public schools.

During the 1997 special-election campaign for the House seat, which coincided with the New York mayoral race, Fossella marched alongside GOP Mayor Rudolph W. Giuliani's re-election bandwagon. Giuliani's landslide margins within the district helped propel Fossella to an easy victory. His re-election contests since have been uneventful.

KEY VOTES

2002

No Overhaul campaign finance law; ban "soft money" and restrict advocacy advertising
Yes Back Bush's defense budget increase
Yes Extend 1996 welfare law
Yes Adopt Bush's discretionary spending limit
Yes Pass GOP Medicare prescription drug plan
No Create independent Sept. 11 commission
No Extend union protections to Homeland Security Department employees
Yes Revive fast-track procedures for trade agreements
Yes Authorize war against Iraq
Yes Advance bankruptcy overhaul opposed by abortion opponents

2001

Yes Nullify Clinton Labor Department ergonomics rule
Yes Cut taxes by $1.35 trillion through fiscal 2011
No Maintain ban on oil drilling in Arctic National Wildlife Refuge
Yes Approve Bush proposal to limit managed-care plan liability for coverage decisions
Yes Divert money from crop subsidy payments to land conservation
Yes Expand law enforcement power to investigate suspected terrorists

CQ VOTE STUDIES

	PARTY UNITY		PRESIDENTIAL SUPPORT	
	Support	Oppose	Support	Oppose
2002	94%	6%	87%	13%
2001	92%	8%	93%	7%
2000	91%	9%	26%	74%
1999	89%	11%	26%	74%
1998	91%	9%	23%	77%

INTEREST GROUPS

	AFL-CIO	ADA	CCUS	ACU
2002	11%	0%	95%	92%
2001	9%	0%	100%	88%
2000	0%	0%	80%	80%
1999	0%	15%	91%	83%
1998	0%	0%	100%	96%

NEW YORK 13

Staten Island; part of southwest Brooklyn

Staten Island's large retired population and white, upper-middle-class suburban residents make the 13th more amenable to Republicans than any of New York City's other districts. The 13th's predominantly Italian-American and Catholic conservatives that live on both sides of the Verrazano Narrows Bridge, which connects Staten Island and Brooklyn, have elected a Republican representative since 1982. While Democrat Al Gore carried Staten Island with 52 percent in the 2000 presidential election, Republican Michael R. Bloomberg took 77 percent en route to his mayoral victory in 2001. Gore won the 13th overall with 53 percent.

Staten Island was so disenchanted with New York City's Democratic leadership that in 1993 residents overwhelmingly approved a referendum to secede from the city, though the state legislature blocked its enactment. Chief among Staten Island's complaints had been the presence of the Fresh Kills landfill, which the city sanitation department closed in March 2001 but which some have argued should be reopened at least temporarily.

The least diverse of the five boroughs, Staten Island is the only one in which non-Hispanic whites make up a majority of the residents (71 percent). The Hispanic and black populations are concentrated mostly in the borough's northeastern neighborhoods. There is an Asian presence in some of the borough's north-central neighborhoods.

Almost three-fourths of registered voters live in Staten Island. The Brooklyn portions of the district include Bay Ridge, Dyker Heights and part of Bensonhurst near the Verrazano Narrows Bridge. South of Bensonhurst, the 13th buttonhooks south of Cropsey Avenue and moves east to Ocean Parkway, taking in the Gravesend neighborhood.

MAJOR INDUSTRY

Health care, retail, communications

MILITARY BASES

Fort Hamilton (Army), 603 military, 285 civilian (2001)

CITIES

New York (pt.), 654,631

NOTABLE

Bay Ridge was the setting for the 1977 disco movie "Saturday Night Fever"; Todt Hill is touted as the highest point on the Eastern Seaboard south of Maine.

Rep. Carolyn B. Maloney (D)

CAPITOL OFFICE
225-7944
rep.carolyn.maloney@mail.house.gov
www.house.gov/maloney
2331 Rayburn 20515-3214; fax 225-4709

COMMITTEES
Financial Services
Government Reform
Joint Economic

HOMETOWN
Manhattan

BORN
Feb. 19, 1948, Greensboro, N.C.

RELIGION
Presbyterian

FAMILY
Husband, Clifton H.W. Maloney; two children

EDUCATION
Greensboro College, A.B. 1968

CAREER
State legislative aide; teacher

POLITICAL HIGHLIGHTS
New York City Council, 1982-93

ELECTION RESULTS

2002 GENERAL		
Carolyn Maloney (D, INDC, L, WFM)	95,931	75.3%
Anton Srdanovic (R, C)	31,548	24.8%
2002 PRIMARY		
Carolyn Maloney (D)	unopposed	
2000 GENERAL		
Carolyn Maloney (D, L)	148,080	73.9%
Carla Rhodes (R)	45,453	22.7%
Sandra Stevens (GREEN)	4,869	2.4%

PREVIOUS WINNING PERCENTAGES
1998 (77%); 1996 (72%); 1994 (64%); 1992 (50%)

Elected 1992; 6th term

Maloney is a tireless, persistent advocate for her New York City constituents and for the rights of women, here and abroad. She likes to speak her mind, which has a decidedly liberal bent, and she has become so effective in the role of a gadfly that the Democratic Party has used her talents to criticize the positions of the Bush administration.

Maloney was particularly unhappy with the Bush administration after the Sept. 11, 2001, terrorist attacks on the World Trade Center. Maloney, who represents Queens and a good portion of the east side of Manhattan, was the first to complain that President Bush was reneging on his promise of $20 billion in federal funds to help rebuild New York City. To quantify the city's economic losses, she commissioned studies from the Federal Reserve, the General Accounting Office and the Congressional Research Service.

She also teamed up with New York Democratic Sen. Hillary Rodham Clinton to complain about the Federal Emergency Management Agency's poor response to victims of the attacks. Mitchell E. Daniels Jr., director of the Office of Management and Budget, derided the two women lawmakers as money grubbers, but Maloney's fears proved true and her efforts were praised by the New York press.

Maloney has long been an advocate for abortion rights, the equal rights amendment and the right of women to breast-feed in public. She is devoted to the causes of women worldwide. She demonstrated the plight of Afghan women under the Taliban by coming to the House floor in a head-to-toe blue burqa. Her point partly backfired when Islamic groups condemned her for being insensitive to the women who voluntarily wear those garments for religious reasons.

Maloney has condemned President Bush over his decision to cut U.S. contributions to the United Nations Population Fund, which helps to deliver birth control information and services to women in Third World nations. She said that the funding cut "sends a message that when push comes to shove, the administration's right-wing base comes first."

Since the 105th Congress, Maloney has introduced an equal rights constitutional amendment. In the 107th Congress, and again in the 108th, she even persuaded Democratic Rep. John Dingell of Michigan, who had opposed the ERA in the past, to sign on. Her high mark for cosponsors has been 211, in the 107th, well short of the two-thirds needed.

She has introduced a number of bills to ensure the right of women to breast-feed while at work. "Breast-feeding is not a crime," she said. "But mothers . . . have been made to feel as if they are engaging in some sort of lewd behavior." Her legislation to permit breast-feeding on federal property, which she introduced after some nursing women were asked to leave the Capitol, federal museums and parks, was signed into law in 1999.

Some congressional observers say Maloney appears unfocused, both in conversation and in her legislative work. She introduced 52 bills and resolutions in the 107th Congress, many representing priority issues for the women's caucus, which she used to co-chair. Some of her measures became law, however, including a bill to reduce fees charged by the Securities and Exchange Commission. Other bills passed the House, such as one that would allow authorities to use wiretaps to combat child pornography and sexual exploitation.

Maloney sits on the Government Reform Committee, where she puts her

New York City Council expertise on procurement and government contracting policies to use. She had been the city government's top watchdog against government waste, chairing the Committee on Contracts.

In the 105th, Democratic leaders gave Maloney primary responsibility for making the case that the GOP was playing politics with the 2000 census. As the top Democrat on the Census Subcommittee, she waged battle with Republicans on whether the Census Bureau should be permitted to use statistical sampling to augment the traditional head count. Statistical sampling is a technique that scientifically estimates population in areas where traditional head counting methods do not yield an accurate tally.

Calling it "the civil rights issue of the 1990s," Maloney accused the GOP of blocking sampling because it might boost the count of minorities and give Democrats an edge in redistricting. "The Republican leadership should not be afraid of counting blacks, Hispanics and Asians," she said.

Maloney lost her battle on statistical sampling in court and in Congress, but she won more federal dollars for the Census Bureau to hire extra census takers to go door-to-door to make the count as complete as possible.

Maloney also has a seat on the Financial Services Committee, where she focuses on holding down credit card interest rates, protecting the elderly from financial fraud and giving senior citizens in public housing the right to own household pets. In the 108th, she is the top Democrat on the Domestic and International Monetary Policy, Trade and Technology Subcommittee.

Maloney hails from Greensboro, N.C. She came to New York City for a visit in her early 20s and stayed, eventually teaching adult education in East Harlem and joining the city's vast educational bureaucracy. Maloney says she realized that government had a larger impact than any teacher on the education of the city's youth. She then moved to Albany to work for the state legislature. Five years later, she was elected to the New York City Council, where she served 10 years.

When Maloney ran against seven-term GOP Rep. Bill Green in 1992, media hype about the "Year of the Woman" lent momentum to her underdog challenge. She also benefited from redistricting, which forced Green to campaign on some unfamiliar turf. She beat him narrowly, 50 percent to 48 percent.

Her re-election races since then have been runaway victories. In 2002, her opponent in the Democratic primary was a publisher of sex-themed guide books, who boasted of not having voted since 1997. He was disqualified from the race 10 days before the election. Maloney won in November by a 3-to-1 ratio.

KEY VOTES

2002

Yes Overhaul campaign finance law; ban "soft money" and restrict advocacy advertising
Yes Back Bush's defense budget increase
No Extend 1996 welfare law
No Adopt Bush's discretionary spending limit
No Pass GOP Medicare prescription drug plan
Yes Create independent Sept. 11 commission
Yes Extend union protections to Homeland Security Department employees
No Revive fast-track procedures for trade agreements
Yes Authorize war against Iraq
Yes Advance bankruptcy overhaul opposed by abortion opponents

2001

No Nullify Clinton Labor Department ergonomics rule
No Cut taxes by $1.35 trillion through fiscal 2011
Yes Maintain ban on oil drilling in Arctic National Wildlife Refuge
No Approve Bush proposal to limit managed-care plan liability for coverage decisions
Yes Divert money from crop subsidy payments to land conservation
Yes Expand law enforcement power to investigate suspected terrorists

CQ VOTE STUDIES

	PARTY UNITY		PRESIDENTIAL SUPPORT	
	Support	Oppose	Support	Oppose
2002	93%	7%	34%	66%
2001	90%	10%	33%	67%
2000	92%	8%	82%	18%
1999	93%	7%	82%	18%
1998	93%	7%	82%	18%

INTEREST GROUPS

	AFL-CIO	ADA	CCUS	ACU
2002	89%	100%	53%	4%
2001	92%	95%	35%	0%
2000	90%	90%	45%	12%
1999	78%	100%	36%	4%
1998	100%	100%	33%	8%

NEW YORK 14

East Side Manhattan; western Queens

Wealthy Republicans engineered politics on Manhattan's East Side when this "Silk Stocking District" was created. But starting in the 1960s, the old-money elite was gradually supplanted by "limousine liberals," highly educated young professionals devoted to the arts. The 14th has the nation's highest percentage of residents with at least a bachelor's degree (57 percent) and the highest percentage who walk to work.

Republicans can still compete locally, and the 14th supported GOP Mayor Rudolph Giuliani in 1997. But the district sent a Democrat to Congress in 1992, and its residents have given overwhelming support to Democratic presidential candidates in recent years.

Taking in all of Central Park in the district's northwest corner, the 14th's western edge then roughly follows Broadway south toward Union Square before narrowing to reach the Lower East Side. Landmarks include Carnegie Hall, Rockefeller Center, Grand Central Terminal, the United Nations, the Chrysler Building, Trump Tower and Fifth Avenue's Museum Mile, which includes the Metropolitan Museum of Art.

But the tony neighborhoods of Manhattan's East Side do not tell the whole story of a district that crosses Roosevelt Island to pick up ethnic working-class sections of Queens, such as Astoria, and some poorer sections. Long Island City, once an industrial powerhouse, experienced decline but is seeing some resurgence as a haven for artists. It is also home to Queens West — a massive new commercial and residential development along the riverfront.

Though redistricting in 2002 changed some of the eastern contours of the 14th, it still includes most of the northwestern edge of Queens, which has a mix of ethnic communities. In the 1980s and 1990s, the region attracted immigrants from abroad, particularly Greeks, Asians and Hispanics. Now it draws Manhattanites in search of more-affordable housing.

MAJOR INDUSTRY
Finance, publishing, communications, advertising, health care, tourism

CITIES
New York (pt.), 654,361

NOTABLE
The American Museum of the Moving Image is in Astoria; Republican John V. Lindsay and Democrat Edward I. Koch held the East Side congressional seat at the time each was elected mayor of New York.

Rep. Charles B. Rangel (D)

CAPITOL OFFICE
225-4365
www.house.gov/rangel
2354 Rayburn 20515-3215; fax 225-0816

COMMITTEES
Ways & Means - ranking member
Joint Taxation

HOMETOWN
Harlem

BORN
June 11, 1930, Harlem, N.Y.

RELIGION
Roman Catholic

FAMILY
Wife, Alma Rangel; two children

EDUCATION
New York U., B.S. 1957; St. John's U., LL.B. 1960

MILITARY SERVICE
Army, 1948-52

CAREER
Lawyer

POLITICAL HIGHLIGHTS
Assistant U.S. attorney, 1961-62; N.Y. Assembly, 1967-71; sought Democratic nomination for N.Y. City Council president, 1969

ELECTION RESULTS

2002 GENERAL		
Charles B. Rangel (D, WFM)	84,367	88.5%
Jessie Fields (R, INDC)	11,008	11.5%
2002 PRIMARY		
Charles B. Rangel (D)		unopposed
2000 GENERAL		
Charles B. Rangel (D, L, WFM)	130,161	91.9%
Jose A. Suero (R)	7,346	5.2%
Dean Loren (GREEN)	2,134	1.5%

PREVIOUS WINNING PERCENTAGES
1998 (93%); 1996 (91%); 1994 (97%); 1992 (95%); 1990 (97%); 1988 (97%); 1986 (96%); 1984 (97%); 1982 (97%); 1980 (96%); 1978 (96%); 1976 (97%); 1974 (97%); 1972 (96%); 1970 (87%)

Elected 1970; 17th term

With Democrats having failed to take back the House in four tries, it appears Rangel may never reach the pinnacle of power he long has sought: chairman of the Ways and Means Committee, arguably the most powerful panel in Congress, in charge of writing tax, trade, welfare, health care, Social Security and Medicare legislation.

The extent of Rangel's disappointment after the 2002 election was clear, and he expressed doubt about his own willingness to keep working on party-building efforts in the hope of taking the gavel. "I've got to find out what the road map is before I decide how long I'll be on the ride," he said.

Now the fourth-most-senior Democrat in the House, Rangel has worked doggedly since 1995 for his party's effort to win back the majority. He has spent much of his time on the road, helping Democrats in districts with large black populations, organizing get-out-the-vote campaigns and raising money. But his fundraising slowed in the run-up to the midterm election. He brought in $5 million — an enormous sum, but only half what he collected for the 2000 campaign.

An aggressive partisan before the public, the raspy-voiced Rangel takes glee in lacerating most GOP initiatives. But he is described as good-natured in private by many of the same people he has skewered publicly. And at times — especially when a Democrat has been in the White House — corporate lobbyists have come to know Rangel more frequently as a deal-cutting pragmatist than as a liberal ideologue. An outsize personality and lawyerly powers of persuasion have helped. So has his sense of humor. His sly delivery and bombastic punch lines prompted one former aide to describe him as "a black Jackie Gleason."

Rangel's relationship with Ways and Means Chairman Bill Thomas, a California Republican, has been like a troubled marriage, with each accusing the other of intransigence. Rangel lambasted Bush's 2001 tax cut as a gift to the rich that would squander the surplus, though he backed a smaller tax cut targeted to working families. As the 108th began, he chided the president's second round of tax cuts as "a recipe for passing along our problems to other Congresses, other presidents, and other generations."

But Rangel has been willing to work behind the scenes toward compromise, and he has a friendly relationship of longstanding with Republican Charles E. Grassley of Iowa, the Senate Finance Committee chairman. Rangel helped engineer the 2002 economic stimulus package, which paired narrow tax breaks for business with extended unemployment benefits for laid-off workers. And his willingness to buck labor unions and endorse a permanent normalization of trade relations with China was key to the business lobby securing one of its top priorities for 2000.

Rangel has voted against the other three hard-fought trade liberalization laws of the past decade: the North American Free Trade Agreement of 1993; the creation of the World Trade Organization in 1994; and the revival of fast-track congressional procedures for trade deals in 2002. But he was a driving force behind the 2000 law liberalizing trade with nations of the Caribbean, Central America and sub-Saharan Africa, and he has been a staunch foe of the trade embargo against Cuba.

Efforts to spur economic development in downtrodden neighborhoods have resulted in much of Rangel's legislative success. He was a principal author of the 1993 "empowerment zones" law providing tax credits to businesses that move into blighted areas, the 1986 tax credit for developers who build low-income housing, and the 1978 tax credit for businesses that hire hard-to-place workers such as ex-convicts and inner-city youth.

After the Sept. 11, 2001, terrorist attacks, Rangel helped steer into law tax breaks to help rebuild lower Manhattan. He was also the driving force behind the decision to hold a special meeting of Congress in New York to mark the first anniversary of the attacks.

His commitment to parochial matters led him to press Bill Clinton to open his post-presidential office in Harlem. And he was among the earliest to encourage first lady Hillary Rodham Clinton to run for the Senate in 2000.

A founder of the Congressional Black Caucus, Rangel has a reliably liberal record on social policy. He champions gun control, affirmative action and abortion rights, and he was a passionate critic of the 1996 law ending welfare's status as an entitlement. He has backed a commission to promote reparations for descendants of former slaves.

At the start of the 108th, he introduced legislation to reinstate the military draft, arguing that, "A disproportionate number of the poor and members of minority groups make up the enlisted ranks of the military, while the most privileged Americans are underrepresented or absent."

Raised by his seamstress mother and her family in Harlem, Rangel dropped out of high school at 16, later joined the Army and won a Purple Heart and Bronze Star after surviving firefights in the Korean War that claimed much of his unit. After the war, he finished high school, and then went to college and law school under the G.I. Bill. His political career got its start when he appealed to the last of the Tammany Hall bosses to allow his grandfather to keep his job operating elevators at city hall. He succeeded, which led Rangel to put his persuasive talents to work helping his friends and neighbors.

After four years in the state Assembly, Rangel was elected to the House in 1970 after ousting Rep. Adam Clayton Powell Jr. in the Democratic primary, ending one of the most flamboyant congressional careers of modern times. Rangel has had only one significant challenger since: Powell's son and namesake, in the 1994 primary. In 2002, Rangel was re-elected with 88 percent of the vote, the lowest showing since his initial election in 1970.

Rangel's time in Congress has not been without travail. He was soundly defeated in a bid to become the House Democratic whip in 1986, and he was among the last members cleared of wrongdoing in the House bank scandal of the early 1990s. In 1999 he was entangled in a financial scandal at Harlem's historic Apollo Theater; the state of New York dropped a lawsuit against Rangel and others on the theater board, saying they acted in good faith.

KEY VOTES

2002

- Yes Overhaul campaign finance law; ban "soft money" and restrict advocacy advertising
- No Back Bush's defense budget increase
- No Extend 1996 welfare law
- No Adopt Bush's discretionary spending limit
- No Pass GOP Medicare prescription drug plan
- Yes Create independent Sept. 11 commission
- Yes Extend union protections to Homeland Security Department employees
- No Revive fast-track procedures for trade agreements
- No Authorize war against Iraq
- No Advance bankruptcy overhaul opposed by abortion opponents

2001

- No Nullify Clinton Labor Department ergonomics rule
- No Cut taxes by $1.35 trillion through fiscal 2011
- Yes Maintain ban on oil drilling in Arctic National Wildlife Refuge
- No Approve Bush proposal to limit managed-care plan liability for coverage decisions
- Yes Divert money from crop subsidy payments to land conservation
- Yes Expand law enforcement power to investigate suspected terrorists

CQ VOTE STUDIES

	PARTY UNITY		PRESIDENTIAL SUPPORT	
	Support	Oppose	Support	Oppose
2002	98%	2%	24%	76%
2001	91%	9%	23%	77%
2000	93%	7%	97%	3%
1999	96%	4%	81%	19%
1998	95%	5%	88%	12%

INTEREST GROUPS

	AFL-CIO	ADA	CCUS	ACU
2002	100%	95%	32%	0%
2001	100%	90%	25%	4%
2000	90%	90%	41%	4%
1999	78%	90%	29%	0%
1998	100%	90%	29%	9%

NEW YORK 15

Northern Manhattan – Harlem, Washington Heights

Harlem was a nexus of black political and cultural power during its heyday in the 1920s and 1930s. But by the time the district was created in 1944, the Great Depression, an influx of poor migrants and race riots had contributed to severe decline. Two highly popular black Democrats — Adam Clayton Powell Jr. and Rep. Rangel — have controlled the 15th since its creation; Powell served 12 terms and part of a 13th; Rangel has been elected 17 times. A solidly Democratic district, Bill Clinton won overwhelming majorities here in 1992 and 1996, and Al Gore got nearly 90 percent of the vote in 2000.

The past 20 years have brought substantial change to the 15th, with Puerto Rican and Dominican immigration supplanting the district's African-American majority. Hispanics now far outnumber non-Hispanic blacks, but low voter participation among Hispanics means the smaller black population (31 percent of residents) continues to dominate the district's politics.

Harlem's 1996 designation as a federal empowerment zone has brought the beginning of an economic resurgence. Refurbished brownstones, new restaurants, national retail chains and prominent corporations are moving into the area. In early 2001, Harlem also received a public relations boon when Clinton decided to lease office space in a building on 125th Street, the area's main thoroughfare.

The district's hospitals and colleges, along with many small businesses, provide much of the employment. But for less-educated residents, many of the jobs are out of reach. The district's doctors, lawyers and other professionals reside in Harlem's affluent black neighborhoods like Strivers Row, the white, affluent Upper West Side or around Columbia University in Morningside Heights.

MAJOR INDUSTRY
Health care, higher education, retail

CITIES
New York (pt.), 654,361

NOTABLE
Legendary venues such as the Cotton Club and the Apollo Theater drew jazz greats and comedians; The district includes Randalls, Wards and Rikers islands.

Rep. José E. Serrano (D)

CAPITOL OFFICE
225-4361
jserrano@mail.house.gov
www.house.gov/serrano
2227 Rayburn 20515-3216; fax 225-6001

COMMITTEES
Appropriations

HOMETOWN
Bronx

BORN
Oct. 24, 1943, Mayaguez, P.R.

RELIGION
Roman Catholic

FAMILY
Wife, Mary Staucet; five children

EDUCATION
Dodge Vocational H.S., graduated 1961; Lehman College, attended 1961

MILITARY SERVICE
Army Medical Corps, 1964-66

CAREER
School district administrator; banker

POLITICAL HIGHLIGHTS
N.Y. Assembly, 1975-90; sought Democratic nomination for Bronx borough president, 1985

ELECTION RESULTS

2002 GENERAL

José E. Serrano (D, WFM)	50,716	92.1%
Frank Dellavalle (R, C)	4,366	7.9%

2002 PRIMARY

José E. Serrano (D)	unopposed

2000 GENERAL

José E. Serrano (D, L)	103,041	95.8%
Aaron Justice (R)	3,934	3.7%

PREVIOUS WINNING PERCENTAGES
1998 (95%); 1996 (96%); 1994 (96%); 1992 (91%); 1990 (93%); 1990 Special Election (92%)

Elected March 1990; 7th full term

With more than a dozen years on Capitol Hill under his belt, Serrano combines his insider status as a top Democratic appropriator with an unrepentant liberalism and outspoken involvement in issues important to the Hispanic community.

When the National Journal in 2001 issued its rankings of the most liberal members of the House, Serrano's news release bragged that he had tied for first. "My entire career I've been known as a liberal. I embrace that label," he said, because it "reflects my concern for people like those in my community who don't always share in the economic prosperity of the country."

As one measure of his placement on the political spectrum, the American Conservative Union gives Serrano's career voting record in the House an approval score of 2 percent. As one gauge of his standing with the party leadership, in the 108th Congress he was made one of the three vice chairmen of the Democratic Steering Committee, which makes the party's committee assignments.

Serrano grew up in the Millbrook Houses, a public housing project in the Bronx. As the representative of one of the poorest and most Democratic districts in the nation, Serrano says his principal legislative priority "is ensuring that the South Bronx gets its fair share for education, jobs, housing and economic development."

His main venue for seeking that funding is the Appropriations Committee. Since 1999 he has been the top Democrat on the subcommittee that directs spending at the Commerce, Justice and State departments and the federal courts, one of the most routinely controversial of the 13 annual spending measures. In the 108th, he also took a seat on the new Homeland Security Appropriations Subcommittee.

The Puerto Rican-born Serrano (sa-RAH-no, with a rolled 'R') also weighs in on an array of issues of importance to the island commonwealth, whose delegate to Congress — known as the resident commissioner — has no vote on the House floor. About 183,000 of Serrano's 16th District constituents are of Puerto Rican descent. Backing the view of many Puerto Ricans, Serrano has waged a high-profile battle to lift or at least lessen the Cuban trade embargo and travel restrictions. He has worked against efforts to make English the official national language. On the question of whether Puerto Rico should be granted statehood or independence, he says the citizens of the island should decide.

Using his Appropriations seat, Serrano was able to obtain funding for a scholarship program aimed at training students in the Bronx for foreign service careers. He has also obtained federal money to clean up the Bronx River, plant trees in the borough and reduce air pollution from trucks, believed to be a contributing factor in the high incidence of asthma among his constituents. Serrano has helped San Juan obtain federal funding for its light rail system, while failing to get funds for New York City to jump-start construction of its long-dormant Second Avenue subway route. Newsday quoted an anonymous lawmaker and two aides as complaining, "Is he the congressman for the Bronx or for Puerto Rico?"

In 2002, when the House voted on a feel-good resolution marking the 50th anniversary of the constitution of the Puerto Rican commonwealth, Serrano demurred. While the relationship between Puerto Rico and the United States "has had some wonderful moments, it has never stopped, in my opinion, being a colonial relationship," he said. Serrano was pleased when 31 of his colleagues also voted against the measure, as he thought he would cast the lone dissenting vote.

In 2000, Serrano was arrested outside the White House for protesting the Navy's continued use of the island of Vieques, just off the coast of Puerto Rico, for training exercises using live bombs. On the Vieques issue and some others Serrano has aligned himself with the activist Al Sharpton, a candidate for the 2004 Democratic presidential nomination, saying that Sharpton "does not fear the political downside of speaking the truth."

Serrano also is a strong advocate of liberalized immigration laws, backing extension of a program that allows some immigrants to apply for residency even if they are in the country illegally. In the 107th Congress, he was able to win approval of a measure granting posthumous citizenship to those who were in the process of becoming citizens when they died in the Sept. 11, 2001, terrorist attacks.

Beginning in the 104th Congress, Serrano has offered "English-plus" legislation, which encourages all residents of the United States not only to become proficient in English but also to preserve or gain skills in other languages as well. The measure began as a response to proposals to make English the official language, reflecting what Serrano views as an English-only attitude. "Multilingualism is an asset, not a liability," he says.

His parents emigrated from Puerto Rico when he was 7, and Serrano says he learned English by listening to Frank Sinatra records that his father brought back from the Army. Serrano became a big fan, amassing a large collection of Sinatra records and sponsoring the 1997 measure that awarded Sinatra a congressional gold medal.

After graduating from a vocational high school and serving in the Army, Serrano took a job in a New York City bank and began making political contacts in his work for a Bronx school district. Those contacts helped him win a state Assembly seat in 1974. His tenure in Albany — including service as chairman of the Assembly Education Committee — made him a fixture in New York Hispanic politics. (His son, José Marco Serrano, was elected to the New York City Council in 2001.)

When Democratic Rep. Robert Garcia resigned his seat in 1990 after he was convicted of defense contract extortion, Serrano moved quickly to stake his claim. He breezed to victory with 92 percent of the vote in the special election against black Republican businessman Simeon Golar and won a full term with 93 percent that November. He has won all his subsequent re-elections with at least 91 percent.

KEY VOTES

2002

- Yes Overhaul campaign finance law; ban "soft money" and restrict advocacy advertising
- No Back Bush's defense budget increase
- No Extend 1996 welfare law
- No Adopt Bush's discretionary spending limit
- No Pass GOP Medicare prescription drug plan
- Yes Create independent Sept. 11 commission
- Yes Extend union protections to Homeland Security Department employees
- No Revive fast-track procedures for trade agreements
- No Authorize war against Iraq
- No Advance bankruptcy overhaul opposed by abortion opponents

2001

- No Nullify Clinton Labor Department ergonomics rule
- No Cut taxes by $1.35 trillion through fiscal 2011
- Yes Maintain ban on oil drilling in Arctic National Wildlife Refuge
- No Approve Bush proposal to limit managed-care plan liability for coverage decisions
- Yes Divert money from crop subsidy payments to land conservation
- No Expand law enforcement power to investigate suspected terrorists

CQ VOTE STUDIES

	PARTY UNITY		PRESIDENTIAL SUPPORT	
	Support	Oppose	Support	Oppose
2002	96%	4%	26%	74%
2001	92%	8%	29%	71%
2000	93%	7%	90%	10%
1999	93%	7%	70%	30%
1998	95%	5%	85%	15%

INTEREST GROUPS

	AFL-CIO	ADA	CCUS	ACU
2002	100%	90%	37%	0%
2001	92%	85%	35%	0%
2000	90%	90%	42%	0%
1999	89%	95%	12%	4%
1998	100%	90%	25%	0%

NEW YORK 16
South Bronx

The 16th, which covers the distressed neighborhoods of the South Bronx, is the nation's poorest district in terms of median income. One-third of families live on a household income of less than $10,000, and the area is plagued by urban ills and low rates of home ownership. But some South Bronx neighborhoods have started to turn around, thanks to grass-roots community work and federal empowerment zone money.

The South Bronx, overtaken by a post-World War II influx of Hispanics to New York City, has since 1970 elected men of Puerto Rican origin to the House. The Puerto Rican influence has long been strong in the 16th, though the district also is home to many African and South and Central American immigrants. The district's 3 percent non-Hispanic white population is the lowest in the nation.

Democratic presidential candidates regularly top 90 percent of the vote in the 16th, which might be the most strongly Democratic district in the nation. But like many districts with large minority and immigrant populations, voter turnout is low. Redistricting in 2002 made the 16th a bit longer and narrower in shape; the district now reaches almost as far north as the convergence of the Harlem and Hudson rivers.

Like frontier settlements, several downtown developments of single-family homes and low-rise housing have been built on vacated lots by subsidized economic development organizations, and they are occupied by people who grew up in the district, worked their way out and are now returning to help rebuild the neighborhoods.

Light manufacturing firms also have set up shop, replacing some of the heavy industry that moved out decades ago. Local baseball fans hope New York Yankees owner George Steinbrenner does not make good on threats to move the team out of the Bronx. Fordham University is in the 16th as well.

MAJOR INDUSTRY
Health care, light manufacturing

CITIES
New York (pt.), 654,360

NOTABLE
The Edgar Allan Poe Cottage in the Bronx (the writer's last home) is owned by New York City.

Rep. Eliot L. Engel (D)

CAPITOL OFFICE
225-2464
www.house.gov/engel
2264 Rayburn 20515-3217; fax 225-5513

COMMITTEES
Energy & Commerce
International Relations

HOMETOWN
Bronx

BORN
Feb. 18, 1947, Bronx, N.Y.

RELIGION
Jewish

FAMILY
Wife, Patricia Ennis Engel; three children

EDUCATION
Hunter-Lehman College, B.A. 1969 (history); City U. of New York, Lehman College, M.A. 1973 (guidance & counseling); New York Law School, J.D. 1987

CAREER
Teacher; guidance counselor

POLITICAL HIGHLIGHTS
Bronx Democratic district leader, 1974-77;
N.Y. Assembly, 1977-88

ELECTION RESULTS

2002 GENERAL		
Eliot L. Engel (D, L, WFM)	77,535	62.6%
C. Scott Vanderhoef (R, C, INDC)	42,634	34.4%
Arthur L. Gallagher (RTL)	1,931	1.6%
Elizabeth Shanklin (GREEN)	1,743	1.4%
2002 PRIMARY		
Eliot L. Engel (D)		unopposed
2000 GENERAL		
Eliot L. Engel (D, L)	115,093	89.7%
Patrick McManus (C, R)	13,201	10.3%

PREVIOUS WINNING PERCENTAGES
1998 (88%); 1996 (85%); 1994 (78%); 1992 (80%); 1990 (61%); 1988 (56%)

Elected 1988; 8th term

Engel says he has always been a political junkie and adds that as a boy, he memorized the names of all the current 100 senators. One basic political lesson he clearly learned is to pay attention to local needs. Yet with a district composed of dozens of ethnic groups, Engel also sees the world as a place to provide constituent service.

He frequently issues press releases objecting to rising local cable television rates and cuts in weekend express bus service, but he will follow those with a statement accusing the Saudi government of aiding terrorist attacks against Americans. Foreign affairs is one of Engel's principal interests in Washington, as his district is home to Irish, Italians and Eastern Europeans and rising numbers of Hispanics and African-Americans.

He is a vocal member of the International Relations Committee, where he takes the position of a liberal interventionist. He believes the United States should take steps to stop humanitarian tragedies. He was an early advocate of U.S. intervention in the civil war in Yugoslavia. In 1993, he joined a bipartisan group of lawmakers who urged the Clinton administration to take sides in Bosnia against the Serbs, who were being accused of perpetrating widespread atrocities in the name of "ethnic cleansing" — the forced removal of Muslims to create all-Serbian communities.

In 2000, he opposed granting China normal trade status because of the country's human rights abuses. "Are we only for the almighty dollar or are we for morality and doing what's right?" he asked.

In 2002, he advocated continued U.S. sanctions against Iran. "Right now the Taliban is our real enemy and the Iranian government and the Taliban have not gotten along. . . . Iran, or some elements in Iran, may see this as a hook to try to improve relations with the United States. . . . I think that's something we should not slam the door on," he told the Associated Press.

Engel says a high priority in the 108th Congress will be a measure he sponsored in the 107th with Majority Leader Dick Armey to impose economic and diplomatic sanctions on Syria, unless it can be certified that Damascus has halted support for terrorism, destroyed any stocks of weapons of mass destruction and ended its occupation of Lebanon.

Like Engel, many of the 17th District's residents are Jewish, and he is a strong supporter of Israel. He was the prime sponsor of a congressional resolution recognizing Jerusalem as the "undivided capital of Israel."

In keeping with his constituents' political inclinations, Engel follows a traditionally Democratic course. He sides with labor unions, fights for civil rights and defends the United Nations, the Corporation for Public Broadcasting and the National Endowment for the Humanities against GOP attacks. He supports the Democratic Party position more than 90 percent of the time.

Engel also sits on the Energy and Commerce Committee, where he is active on policies related to mental health, illegal drugs, housing, and energy availability and price. He sometimes quotes his mother, who he says is "my best adviser in terms of health care, particularly the importance of prescription drug coverage and Medicare."

Engel is usually content to stand in the background and attend to constituent service and the nuts-and-bolts of legislation. But on one day every year, he has a brief moment on the national stage: He arrives early in the House chamber for the annual State of the Union address to be sure to grab an aisle seat so he can greet the president and renew acquaintances with a number of ambassadors. He began the tradition as a freshman when he greeted President George Bush and continued with it when George W. Bush gained the White House. After he greeted Bush in 2003, he said, "The constituents love it. And as long as they love it, I love it."

Constituent service is second nature to Engel, who grew up in the Bronx and earned his political spurs in local Democratic clubs. An Engel aide proudly points to a 1996 Wall Street Journal profile where the writer noted that Engel is known in his working-class district as "The Mayor," a tribute to Engel's attention to urban concerns, such as congested subway routes or broken traffic lights.

Engel's father was a welder, but father and son were both interested in politics and world affairs, and they walked picket lines together. He attended New York City public schools, where he later worked as a teacher and guidance counselor. He was elected to the state Assembly in 1977, when he defeated the candidate endorsed by the Democratic Party.

In the Assembly, he worked on housing and substance abuse issues and established his credentials in the "reform" wing of the Bronx Democratic organization. Thus, it was not completely unexpected when he announced in 1988 that he was giving up his Assembly seat to challenge Democratic Rep. Mario Biaggi, who was then on trial for bribery, conspiracy and extortion. Nevertheless, it was the gamble of his career. Biaggi remained highly popular, and most Democrats stood aside when Biaggi defiantly announced he would seek re-election in 1988.

But in August, Biaggi was convicted and resigned his seat. His name remained on the ballot, however, for both the primary and the general election (the latter because he regularly received the endorsement of district Republicans). Engel won both contests, taking 56 percent in the general election to Biaggi's 27 percent.

He easily rebuffed a Biaggi comeback attempt in 1992, but since then has felt growing pressure from Hispanic and black challengers. Engel is one of the few non-minority lawmakers who represent a district in which a majority of the populace belongs to a racial or ethnic minority. In 2000, Engel survived a nasty and racially tinged primary challenge from state Sen. Larry Seabrook, who is black and who received backing from Bronx Democratic Party leader Roberto Ramirez. Engel managed to win, 50 percent to 41 percent.

His district was remapped in 2002 to include part of Rockland County as well as parts of the Bronx and Westchester counties, and Engel had no primary opposition. He won re-election in November easily, with 63 percent.

KEY VOTES

2002

Yes Overhaul campaign finance law; ban "soft money" and restrict advocacy advertising
Yes Back Bush's defense budget increase
No Extend 1996 welfare law
No Adopt Bush's discretionary spending limit
No Pass GOP Medicare prescription drug plan
Yes Create independent Sept. 11 commission
Yes Extend union protections to Homeland Security Department employees
No Revive fast-track procedures for trade agreements
Yes Authorize war against Iraq
No Advance bankruptcy overhaul opposed by abortion opponents

2001

No Nullify Clinton Labor Department ergonomics rule
No Cut taxes by $1.35 trillion through fiscal 2011
Yes Maintain ban on oil drilling in Arctic National Wildlife Refuge
No Approve Bush proposal to limit managed-care plan liability for coverage decisions
Yes Divert money from crop subsidy payments to land conservation
Yes Expand law enforcement power to investigate suspected terrorists

CQ VOTE STUDIES

	PARTY UNITY		PRESIDENTIAL SUPPORT	
	Support	Oppose	Support	Oppose
2002	89%	11%	44%	56%
2001	94%	6%	35%	65%
2000	94%	6%	87%	13%
1999	94%	6%	84%	16%
1998	97%	3%	82%	18%

INTEREST GROUPS

	AFL-CIO	ADA	CCUS	ACU
2002	100%	90%	50%	12%
2001	100%	85%	32%	4%
2000	100%	85%	38%	22%
1999	89%	95%	24%	0%
1998	100%	95%	24%	4%

NEW YORK 17

North Bronx; part of Westchester and Rockland counties — Mount Vernon, part of Yonkers

The 17th is an economically, racially and ethnically diverse territory that takes in the northwestern part of the Bronx and parts of Westchester and Rockland counties northwest of New York City. Blacks and Hispanics together constitute a majority of residents in the district.

Riverdale, a heavily Jewish neighborhood, sits at the western edge of the Bronx and is one of New York's most affluent areas. East of Riverdale, on the other side of Van Cortlandt Park and Woodlawn Cemetery, there is a large black population. The 17th reaches almost as far east as the mammoth Co-op City apartment complex (in the 7th District). About 45 percent of district residents live in the Bronx.

In Westchester County, home to one-fourth of the 17th's residents, the district takes in all of Mount Vernon, which is heavily black, some black and Hispanic communities in western Yonkers, and predominantly white communities, many of Italian and Irish descent, in southeastern Yonkers.

The 17th narrows significantly in northern Yonkers, meandering north along Route 9 and the Hudson River to cross the Tappan Zee Bridge into Rockland County, parts of which were appended to the 17th in 2002 redistricting. Rockland leans Democratic, but not overwhelmingly so.

The new district lines excised some of the Bronx's Democratic faithful, but Al Gore nonetheless took 71 percent of the vote here in the 2000 presidential election, and Democrats hold a substantial registration edge over the GOP.

MAJOR INDUSTRY

Health care, higher education, city government

CITIES

New York (pt.), 292,423; Yonkers (pt.), 87,617; Mount Vernon, 68,381; Spring Valley, 25,464

NOTABLE

Duke Ellington, Elizabeth Cady Stanton, F.W. Woolworth, Nellie Bly and "Bat" Masterson are among those buried in Woodlawn Cemetery in the Bronx.

Rep. Nita M. Lowey (D)

CAPITOL OFFICE
225-6506
nita.lowey@mail.house.gov
www.house.gov/lowey
2329 Rayburn 20515-3218; fax 225-0546

COMMITTEES
Appropriations
Select Homeland Security

HOMETOWN
Harrison

BORN
July 5, 1937, Bronx, N.Y.

RELIGION
Jewish

FAMILY
Husband, Stephen Lowey; three children

EDUCATION
Mount Holyoke College, B.A. 1959 (marketing)

CAREER
State government aide; homemaker

POLITICAL HIGHLIGHTS
N.Y. assistant secretary of state, 1985-87

ELECTION RESULTS

2002 GENERAL		
Nita M. Lowey (D, WFM)	98,957	92.0%
Michael J. Reynolds (RTL)	8,558	8.0%
2002 PRIMARY		
Nita M. Lowey (D)		unopposed
2000 GENERAL		
Nita M. Lowey (D)	126,878	67.3%
John G. Vonglis (R, C)	58,022	30.8%
Florence T. O'Grady (RTL)	3,747	2.0%

PREVIOUS WINNING PERCENTAGES
1998 (83%); 1996 (64%); 1994 (57%); 1992 (56%); 1990 (63%); 1988 (50%)

Elected 1988; 8th term

Lowey's personal warmth and unassuming manner belie the influence she has wielded as head of the Democratic Congressional Campaign Committee, the House Democrats' campaign arm, and as the top-ranking Democrat on the Appropriations subcommittee that doles out foreign aid.

Her path to more power, however, has been blocked to some degree by an even more powerful woman — one of her newer constituents, Hillary Rodham Clinton. After 12 years in the House, Lowey saw her plans to move up the political ladder in 2000 quashed when Clinton jumped into the race to replace retiring New York Democratic Sen. Daniel Patrick Moynihan. Lowey had been patiently awaiting the opportunity for years, amassing campaign cash for a Senate run.

But after Clinton threw her hat into the ring, Lowey (LOW-ee) loyally and gracefully stepped aside. She seconded Clinton's nomination at the New York Democratic convention, and her chief of staff went on to become the press secretary for Clinton's Senate campaign. The classy way in which Lowey handled the awkward situation earned her praise from fellow Democrats and even a few Republicans.

Furthermore, for the 2000 elections, Lowey helped raise more than $6 million for the House Democrats' effort to recruit and elect women candidates. And she contributed more than $160,000 from her own campaign treasury to aid other Democrats. Her fundraising prowess gained notice from Democratic leaders, who rewarded her in the 107th Congress with the chairmanship of the campaign committee.

Lowey set fundraising records during her tenure, the last year before new campaign finance regulations took effect. But citing the demanding nature of the job, she opted to step down after the 107th Congress. She and other Democratic leaders were criticized for failure to craft a coherent message, but she argued, "This election was a referendum on a popular wartime president and the wind was in our face."

Replacing the campaign committee in Lowey's portfolio in the 108th Congress is an appointment to the new Homeland Security Committee.

During her lengthy House career, the high-energy Lowey has established herself as a leading advocate for women's rights and other liberal causes. She has pushed family planning issues, fiercely opposing Republican efforts to eliminate appropriations for international family planning programs and to outlaw a procedure its opponents call "partial birth" abortion.

She gained a new pulpit for these views in the 107th Congress, when she became the top Democrat on the Foreign Operations Appropriations Subcommittee. In that post, she unsuccessfully battled Bush's decisions to restrict funds for U.S. family planning groups and the U.N. family planning program. She was more successful in winning funds for post-war Afghanistan, for basic education, and for preventing and treating AIDS overseas.

Although Lowey has frequently found herself on the losing end of abortion battles in the Republican-controlled House, she did enjoy an unexpected triumph in 1998 when she won contraceptive coverage for federal workers whose insurance plans cover pharmaceuticals. She called contraceptive coverage a "basic women's health benefit."

She was less successful in winning House approval of bipartisan legislation she introduced in the 107th Congress to expand the State Children's Health Insurance Program (S-CHIP) to cover pregnant women. Her bill would have covered pre- and post-natal care for low-income women not eligible for Medicaid, but a Bush administration regulation issued in 2001 allowed states to expand S-CHIP to "unborn children" and does not fully cover pregnant women before, during or after delivery.

While Lowey proudly wears her liberal credentials, she also has become recognized as an inside player who maneuvers skillfully through the appropriations process. As a member of the Appropriations Committee, she knows how to deal, whether the issue is family planning funding, aid to Israel, or money for projects in New York, including funds to help the city pay the costs of the Sept. 11, 2001, terrorist attacks. She initially won her seat on Appropriations in 1993 by aggressively lobbying the Democratic leadership.

Lowey got her start in politics a quarter-century ago. She was a homemaker in Queens when she volunteered in a neighbor's 1974 campaign for lieutenant governor. That neighbor was Mario M. Cuomo. Though Cuomo lost the primary, new Democratic Gov. Hugh L. Carey appointed him as New York's secretary of state. Cuomo, in turn, hired Lowey to work in his department's anti-poverty division.

By the mid-1980s, Cuomo was governor and Lowey was the top aide to new Secretary of State Gail Shaffer. Lowey made an impressive debut in electoral politics in 1988 when she unseated two-term GOP Rep. Joseph J. DioGuardi in the then-20th District.

Lowey survived a primary against Hamilton Fish III, publisher of The Nation magazine and son of a GOP House member, and against businessman Dennis Mehiel. She raised $1.3 million, a huge sum for a challenger.

DioGuardi outspent her in the general election, but a newspaper reported in October that a New Rochelle auto dealer had funneled $57,000 in corporate contributions to DioGuardi's campaign through his employees. DioGuardi denied knowledge of the pass-through scheme, but the disclosures damaged him and Lowey won narrowly.

DioGuardi returned for a rematch in 1990, but by then Lowey's legislative work, constituent service and fundraising skills had established her as a strong favorite, and she won decisively. Since then, she has outdistanced all competition, capped by a 92 percent share in 2002 over a third-party foe.

In her campaigns, Lowey has benefited from her personal wealth, largely derived from her husband's stake in the law firm of Lowey Dannenberg Bemporad & Selinger. As a result of reapportionment after the 2000 census, New York lost two districts. The new map drawn by the state legislature gave Lowey a larger share of New York City's northern suburbs. The GOP declined to field a candidate in 2002.

KEY VOTES

2002

- Yes Overhaul campaign finance law; ban "soft money" and restrict advocacy advertising
- Yes Back Bush's defense budget increase
- No Extend 1996 welfare law
- No Adopt Bush's discretionary spending limit
- No Pass GOP Medicare prescription drug plan
- Yes Create independent Sept. 11 commission
- Yes Extend union protections to Homeland Security Department employees
- No Revive fast-track procedures for trade agreements
- Yes Authorize war against Iraq
- No Advance bankruptcy overhaul opposed by abortion opponents

2001

- No Nullify Clinton Labor Department ergonomics rule
- No Cut taxes by $1.35 trillion through fiscal 2011
- Yes Maintain ban on oil drilling in Arctic National Wildlife Refuge
- No Approve Bush proposal to limit managed-care plan liability for coverage decisions
- Yes Divert money from crop subsidy payments to land conservation
- Yes Expand law enforcement power to investigate suspected terrorists

CQ VOTE STUDIES

	PARTY UNITY		PRESIDENTIAL SUPPORT	
	Support	Oppose	Support	Oppose
2002	94%	6%	26%	74%
2001	96%	4%	28%	72%
2000	94%	6%	91%	9%
1999	94%	6%	86%	14%
1998	94%	6%	83%	17%

INTEREST GROUPS

	AFL-CIO	ADA	CCUS	ACU
2002	100%	90%	40%	4%
2001	100%	95%	38%	0%
2000	90%	75%	52%	9%
1999	78%	100%	16%	4%
1998	100%	100%	35%	8%

NEW YORK 18

Most of Westchester County – New Rochelle, most of Yonkers

The 18th encompasses most of southern and central Westchester County, excluding parts of Yonkers bordering the Hudson River and the Bronx, and all of Mount Vernon. The district hops the Hudson to pick up most of New City and Congers and all of Haverstraw in Rockland County. Redistricting in 2002 pushed the district completely out of New York City, where it had taken in a swath of the Bronx and Queens.

The 18th is a well-to-do residential district that leans Democratic, but not overwhelmingly. Westchester County has a Republican base but enough affluent Democrats to make it competitive. Wealthy New York suburbs such as Scarsdale and Mamaroneck are the district's hallmark. Many of the district's residents enjoy an easy commute to white-collar jobs in Manhattan.

But the district also takes in working-class communities, including Port Chester and urban sections of White Plains and New Rochelle. Al Gore carried the reconfigured district with nearly 60 percent of the vote in the 2000 presidential election. The 18th has the largest portion of Yonkers, Westchester's most populous city. It also includes Ossining, site of Sing Sing prison — its location north of the city on the Hudson River led New Yorkers to refer to prison-bound criminals being "sent up the river."

Hospitals and colleges provide employment opportunities in the district, and officials are trying to attract more technology firms to the region, particularly Yonkers. Purchase is home to PepsiCo., IBM's corporate headquarters are in Armonk and Reader's Digest is based in Pleasantville.

MAJOR INDUSTRY

Health care, higher education

CITIES

Yonkers (pt.), 108,469; New Rochelle, 72,182; White Plains, 53,077

NOTABLE

North Tarrytown was renamed Sleepy Hollow in honor of the Washington Irving story set there; Thomas Paine Cottage and Museum is in New Rochelle; Former President Bill Clinton and Sen. Hillary Rodham Clinton have a home in Chappaqua.

Rep. Sue W. Kelly (R)

CAPITOL OFFICE
225-5441
dearsue@mail.house.gov
www.house.gov/suekelly
1127 Longworth 20515-3219; fax 225-3289

COMMITTEES
Financial Services
(Oversight & Investigations - chairwoman)
Small Business
Transportation & Infrastructure

HOMETOWN
Katonah

BORN
Sept. 26, 1936, Lima, Ohio

RELIGION
Presbyterian

FAMILY
Husband, Edward W. Kelly; four children

EDUCATION
Denison U., B.A. 1958 (botany & bacteriology); Pace Law School, attended 1976-77; Sarah Lawrence College, M.A. 1985 (health advocacy)

CAREER
Professor; teacher; hospital administrative aide; medical researcher; retailer

POLITICAL HIGHLIGHTS
No previous office

ELECTION RESULTS

2002 GENERAL		
Sue W. Kelly (R, C, INDC)	121,129	70.0%
Janine M.H. Selendy (D)	44,967	26.0%
Christine M. Tighe (RTL)	4,374	2.5%
Jonathan M. Wright (GREEN)	2,642	1.5%
2002 PRIMARY		
Sue W. Kelly (R)		unopposed
2000 GENERAL		
Sue W. Kelly (R, C)	145,532	60.9%
Larry Otis Graham (D, L, WFM)	85,871	35.9%
Frank X. Lloyd (RTL)	4,086	1.7%
Mark R. Jacobs (GREEN)	3,662	1.5%

PREVIOUS WINNING PERCENTAGES
1998 (62%); 1996 (46%); 1994 (52%)

Elected 1994; 5th term

With political views shaped by a wide array of real-world experience before she entered politics, it is not surprising that Kelly practices a pragmatic brand of politics, one in which her congressional record offers most interest groups something to praise and something to criticize.

"I've been called a liberal, a strong centrist and a member of the vast right-wing conspiracy," she once told Gannett News Service.

In 2002, for example, Kelly was endorsed by the League of Conservation Voters but not by the Sierra Club, while the American Wilderness Coalition's report card judged her voting record worthy of only a "C." At the same time, her bid for a fifth term was endorsed by the Republican Pro-Choice Coalition, even as the Westchester Coalition for Legal Abortion lamented that Kelly "has joined the anti-choice majority . . . and in so doing both baffled and alienated the pro-choice women who elected her."

Her evolving voting pattern reflects a shift. She sided with the Republicans on 85 percent of mostly party-line votes in the 107th Congress — at the lower end of the GOP party unity scores in the House, but still a significantly higher percentage than in her previous two terms.

Indeed, she has moved into the Republican mainstream on several bellwether votes in recent years. In her first term, for example, she voted against banning the procedure its opponents call "partial birth" abortion, but since then she has voted for such legislation. In 1998 and 1999, she voted in favor of campaign finance overhaul legislation offered by Republican Christopher Shays of Connecticut and Democrat Martin T. Meehan of Massachusetts. In 2002, she stood with the GOP leadership and voted against the Shays-Meehan measure that became law.

She took the side of labor unions and backed an increase in the minimum wage in 1996, but voted against a similar plan in 2000. Similarly, she sided with unions and environmentalists in the 105th by voting against reviving fast-track presidential trade negotiating authority. When President Bush pushed a similar proposal in the 107th, however, she voted yes.

The daughter of a doctor, Kelly majored in botany and bacteriology in college and then worked as a medical researcher. She got married and raised four children. She co-founded a local chapter of the League of Women Voters, served as a PTA president, and volunteered as a rape crisis counselor and patients' advocate at a New York City hospital. She taught junior high school science and math, had a florist shop and ran a business that rehabilitated real estate. She took two years of law school classes, earned a master's degree in health advocacy and was a part-time professor at Sarah Lawrence College.

Her legislative agenda is influenced by her eclectic background, particularly her hospital work and her small-business experience.

In the 107th, she worked to increase Medicare payments to hospitals in the 19th District, and she joined with Democratic Sen. Hillary Rodham Clinton on legislation to rectify a national nursing shortage. Reminded that in the 2000 Senate campaign she had called Clinton a "carpetbagger" with a "radical liberal agenda," Kelly told the New York Post in 2001, "I work for the people of my district — even Mrs. Clinton." (Under redistricting for this decade, the Clintons' Chappaqua home was moved out of the 19th.)

Kelly, who has long been a key player in congressional efforts to combat breast cancer, sponsored legislation to broaden insurance coverage of treatments, including reconstructive breast surgery. Her bill to renew the special breast cancer stamp — which costs more than a regular first-class stamp, with the extra money going to breast cancer research — became law in 2001 as part of a larger measure.

As a former small-business owner, Kelly holds anti-regulatory views that are shared by many in the business community. At the start of the 107th, however, she lost her bid to chair the Small Business Committee. The leadership picked the more senior Donald Manzullo of Illinois.

She then assumed the chairmanship of Financial Services' Oversight and Investigations Subcommittee. From there, she offered a bill to lift the prohibition on interest payments on business checking accounts. She also offered a number of bills aimed at helping small businesses recover from the aftermath of the Sept. 11, 2001, terrorist attacks. And she introduced a bill to broaden the definition of stalking to include "cyberstalking," which includes harassment by e-mail, telephone or the Internet. Her panel held a number of hearings that focused on such topics as federal housing programs, identity theft, corporate fraud, and the financing of international terrorism.

Although Kelly had more than three decades of political and civic experience — including work in the campaigns of Republicans at the local, state and national level — she had never run for office until 1994, when moderate Republican Hamilton Fish retired after 26 years in the House. Positioning herself as the moderate in the race, she won the seven-person GOP primary with 23 percent of the vote, while two more-conservative candidates trailed narrowly.

But she prevailed with only 52 percent in the fall. Her Democratic opponent was Hamilton Fish Jr., the incumbent's son, whom the GOP incumbent endorsed and who was seeking to perpetuate a line of Hamilton Fishes in Congress dating to 1843. The Conservative and Right to Life parties' nominee was Joseph J. DioGuardi, one of the losers of the GOP primary, who had represented a nearby House district from 1985 to 1989.

DioGuardi ran again in 1996 and helped hold Kelly to a 46 percent plurality win. She prevailed somewhat more easily in the subsequent two elections, and then won her easiest victory to date in 2002. She did so even after post-census reapportionment cost New York two House seats, and the state legislature placed Kelly and 30-year veteran Republican Rep. Benjamin A. Gilman in the same district. Gilman, the oldest member of the House in the 107th, decided to retire, although he briefly weighed a switch to the Democratic Party to oppose Kelly.

KEY VOTES

2002

No Overhaul campaign finance law; ban "soft money" and restrict advocacy advertising
Yes Back Bush's defense budget increase
Yes Extend 1996 welfare law
Yes Adopt Bush's discretionary spending limit
Yes Pass GOP Medicare prescription drug plan
No Create independent Sept. 11 commission
No Extend union protections to Homeland Security Department employees
Yes Revive fast-track procedures for trade agreements
Yes Authorize war against Iraq
Yes Advance bankruptcy overhaul opposed by abortion opponents

2001

Yes Nullify Clinton Labor Department ergonomics rule
Yes Cut taxes by $1.35 trillion through fiscal 2011
Yes Maintain ban on oil drilling in Arctic National Wildlife Refuge
Yes Approve Bush proposal to limit managed-care plan liability for coverage decisions
Yes Divert money from crop subsidy payments to land conservation
Yes Expand law enforcement power to investigate suspected terrorists

CQ VOTE STUDIES

	PARTY UNITY		PRESIDENTIAL SUPPORT	
	Support	Oppose	Support	Oppose
2002	90%	10%	80%	20%
2001	80%	20%	77%	23%
2000	75%	25%	46%	54%
1999	69%	31%	41%	59%
1998	66%	34%	41%	59%

INTEREST GROUPS

	AFL-CIO	ADA	CCUS	ACU
2002	11%	20%	85%	88%
2001	25%	25%	91%	40%
2000	20%	35%	76%	56%
1999	33%	50%	80%	56%
1998	50%	45%	83%	48%

NEW YORK 19

Hudson Valley – Peekskill, West Point

Wedged between Connecticut and New Jersey, the 19th follows a sizable portion of the Hudson River. On the east side of the river, the 19th spans the southern tier of Dutchess County, all of Putnam County and the northern section of Westchester County. It also takes in some land west of the Hudson in Orange County and the northern edge of Rockland County.

The southeastern, Westchester County, portion of the district is known for its elegant exurban homes and horse country that attract wealthy professionals and celebrities from Manhattan, where some residents work. The median family income approaches $200,000 in some places. Nearly 85 percent of the district's residents are white. Racially, ethnically and economically diverse Peekskill, with a working- and middle-class base, sits on the eastern shore of the Hudson River in northwestern Westchester.

The wealth in the southern part of the district and the rural character of its northern and western reaches — which extend to the foothills of the Catskill Mountains — help give the 19th a solidly Republican tilt. Although Republican George W. Bush did not receive a majority of the district's vote in the 2000 presidential election, his plurality here made the 19th one of only six New York districts he carried.

Drawn by the groundwork built by IBM — a longtime presence in Yorktown — technical and research firms have moved into the lower Hudson Valley. Dutchess County, Putnam County and Orange County, where farmers grow onions, lettuce and celery, are more rural. The U.S. Military Academy at West Point, which celebrated its bicentennial in 2002, also aids the district's economy.

MAJOR INDUSTRY

Computers, telecommunications, agriculture

MILITARY BASES

U.S. Military Academy, 1,376 military, 2,930 civilian (2003)

CITIES

Peekskill, 22,441; Jefferson Valley-Yorktown, 14,891; Beacon, 13,808

NOTABLE

The home of John Jay, Continental Congress president and first chief justice of the United States, is in Katonah.

Rep. John E. Sweeney (R)

CAPITOL OFFICE
225-5614
john.sweeney@mail.house.gov
www.house.gov/sweeney
416 Cannon 20515-3220; fax 225-6234

COMMITTEES
Appropriations
Select Homeland Security

HOMETOWN
Clifton Park

BORN
Aug. 9, 1955, Troy, N.Y.

RELIGION
Roman Catholic

FAMILY
Divorced; three children

EDUCATION
Hudson Valley Community College, A.A. 1978 (liberal arts); Russell Sage College, B.A. 1981 (political science & criminal justice); Western New England College, J.D. 1990

CAREER
Gubernatorial adviser; lawyer; county public safety program director

POLITICAL HIGHLIGHTS
N.Y. Republican Party executive director, 1992-95; N.Y. labor commissioner, 1995-97

ELECTION RESULTS

2002 GENERAL		
John E. Sweeney (R, C)	140,238	73.3%
Frank Stoppenbach (D)	45,878	24.0%
Margaret Lewis (GREEN)	5,162	2.7%
2002 PRIMARY		
John E. Sweeney (R)		unopposed
2000 GENERAL		
John E. Sweeney (R, C)	167,368	67.9%
Ken McCallion (D, GREEN, WFM)	79,111	32.1%

PREVIOUS WINNING PERCENTAGES
1998 (55%)

Elected 1998; 3rd term

Sweeney has been on the fast track since his arrival on Capitol Hill in 1999, winning spots on the Republican Steering Committee and the party whip team in his first term and an appointment to the Appropriations Committee in his second.

He is usually a dependable member of the GOP, but on occasion he will buck the direction of the leadership and President Bush.

In the 107th Congress, for example, Sweeney and several other New York Republicans joined with state Democrats to insist that New York immediately receive the full $20 billion they believed was promised to cope with the Sept. 11, 2001, terrorist attacks. At the same time, Sweeney also pressed for more state highway funding than the Bush administration sought, arguing that proposed cuts would be part of a "triple whammy" for New York, coupled with disaster relief needs and health insurance costs.

After the New York aid fight, Sweeney said, "I don't think I'll be invited to any of the leaders' Christmas parties this year." Asked about the controversies, Sweeney told the Albany Times Union, "Hey, it's better than being insignificant." His high-profile battles also brought stories about his political ambitions, and he does not reject the notion that he might be interested in higher office.

Despite those parochial disagreements, Sweeney supports the GOP leadership about 90 percent of the time.

Gregarious and approachable, Sweeney makes a point of cultivating relationships with fellow lawmakers. He has made friends across the aisle, earning praise from Democrat Jose E. Serrano, an Appropriations Committee colleague. He often joins forces with fellow Class of 1998 New York Republican Thomas M. Reynolds, whom he has known for years. A New York political columnist, writing under the pseudonym Enos Throop, said of Sweeney: "Smart, brash and tough, Sweeney is one of the few hard-edged partisans savvy enough to get things done for his district."

One dispute that did not go his way involved the Environmental Protection Agency. Sweeney waged a long, ultimately losing battle against EPA's plan to dredge the Hudson River to remove cancer-causing polychlorinated biphenyls, or PCBs, dumped there legally for three decades by General Electric plants along the river. Sweeney argued, unsuccessfully, that the dredging might well stir up more PCBs that were safely trapped on the bottom. He was able, however, to insist on certain safeguards during the work.

In the 108th Congress, Sweeney continued his crusade, along with his upstate New York GOP colleagues John M. McHugh and Sherwood Boehlert, to reduce emissions from power plants. The efforts of the "acid rain team" are aimed at dealing with the harmful effects of air pollution on the Adirondack region.

Sweeney introduced 43 bills during his first term. In the 107th, he continued his prolific pace, introducing 39 bills and resolutions (the 15th-most among House members) on a wide range of subjects. A number of the measures were related to terrorism, including a proposal for the Treasury Department to issue "Freedom Bonds" to enable investors to aid in the battle against terrorism. His bill provided the impetus for the Treasury to offer "Patriot Bonds" for just that purpose.

Sweeney has focused much of his energy on cutting taxes and boosting the economy of his upstate New York district. He pushed for tax breaks for small businesses as a way to stimulate economic development. Although he was raised in a union household and served for two years as the New York state labor commissioner, he generally holds pro-business views.

In his first term, Sweeney had a seat on the Transportation Committee, which helped him deliver much-needed funding for the airport in Albany, a main link to the rest of the world for many of his constituents. In the 107th, his new seat on Appropriations and the panel's Transportation Subcommittee enabled him to continue his efforts.

Sweeney's early years were spent in a public housing project in Troy. His father worked in a shirt factory and was a local union official, and his mother worked at a hospital. He says his father and mother instilled a strong work ethic and the notion that children should feel obligated to do better than their parents. He told The Hill, a Capitol Hill newspaper, that becoming a Republican was his form of youthful rebellion.

He attended the local community college off and on, getting his two-year degree at the age of 22 and then earning a bachelor's degree through night classes at Russell Sage College. Sweeney's first job out of college was as head of a local drunken-driving prevention program and later as an aide to the Rensselaer County executive. He then decided to become a lawyer. He commuted several hours a day to law school in Springfield, Mass., about 85 miles each way, and earned his law degree in 1990. He was 34.

He had become friends with William Powers, a local GOP official, who Sweeney says was his political mentor. Powers became state party chairman, and Sweeney became the party's lawyer and then the party's executive director.

When Republican George E. Pataki became governor in 1995, he named Sweeney to head the state's Labor Department. Sweeney quickly cleaned house, aiming to show that the department should not be viewed as pro-labor and anti-business. Later, Sweeney became one of Pataki's personal aides.

When 10-term GOP Rep. Gerald B.H. Solomon announced his retirement from the 22nd District in 1998, he handpicked Sweeney as his successor. Sweeney sailed through the four-candidate GOP primary. He took full advantage of the district's GOP leanings, winning comfortably over Democratic publisher and Red Hook Councilwoman Jean Parvin Bordewich.

His two re-election campaigns since then have been breezes. In 2000, he defeated Democratic attorney Kenneth McCallion by better than 2-to-1. In 2002, redistricting did little to change the GOP slant of Sweeney's district, now numbered the 20th, and he cruised to victory with 73 percent.

KEY VOTES

2002

No Overhaul campaign finance law; ban "soft money" and restrict advocacy advertising
Yes Back Bush's defense budget increase
Yes Extend 1996 welfare law
Yes Adopt Bush's discretionary spending limit
Yes Pass GOP Medicare prescription drug plan
No Create independent Sept. 11 commission
No Extend union protections to Homeland Security Department employees
Yes Revive fast-track procedures for trade agreements
Yes Authorize war against Iraq
Yes Advance bankruptcy overhaul opposed by abortion opponents

2001

Yes Nullify Clinton Labor Department ergonomics rule
Yes Cut taxes by $1.35 trillion through fiscal 2011
Yes Maintain ban on oil drilling in Arctic National Wildlife Refuge
Yes Approve Bush proposal to limit managed-care plan liability for coverage decisions
Yes Divert money from crop subsidy payments to land conservation
Yes Expand law enforcement power to investigate suspected terrorists

CQ VOTE STUDIES

	PARTY UNITY		PRESIDENTIAL SUPPORT	
	Support	Oppose	Support	Oppose
2002	91%	9%	85%	15%
2001	92%	8%	83%	17%
2000	89%	11%	32%	68%
1999	86%	14%	25%	75%

INTEREST GROUPS

	AFL-CIO	ADA	CCUS	ACU
2002	11%	5%	95%	88%
2001	18%	15%	96%	68%
2000	20%	10%	76%	72%
1999	56%	25%	76%	72%

NEW YORK 20

North Hudson Valley – Saratoga Springs

New York's 20th runs along the state's eastern border, starting just outside Poughkeepsie and stretching into the Adirondack Mountains. It covers much of the primarily residential Hudson River Valley, including the site of the Battle of Saratoga, America's first significant victory against the British in the Revolutionary War. A western branch of the 20th picks up rural territory as far west as Delaware and Otsego Counties.

The 20th's population hub is in its center, in the Albany-Schenectady-Troy metropolitan area. The district includes none of those cities (they are all in the 21st), but does claim much of their GOP suburbia. The three cities helped fuel a suburban boom in southern Saratoga County in the 1980s. Saratoga Springs, synonymous with world-class horse racing, attracts tourists during the summer months.

The district follows Interstate 87 north into mountainous, scenic Adirondack Park and the resort areas of Lake George and Essex County. Lake Placid, site of the 1932 and 1980 Winter Olympics, is in Essex County at the northern tip of the district.

The southern end is made up of mainly rural and mountainous territory in Otsego, Delaware, Greene, Columbia and northern Dutchess counties. It includes mansions built along the Hudson River by the nation's elite, including the Vanderbilts, Martin Van Buren and Franklin Delano Roosevelt.

A heavy presence of unionized state workers outside Albany makes labor an important constituency, but dairy farmers and small-town voters give the GOP a solid edge. The 20th (previously the 22nd) has the lowest minority percentage in the state, and was one of only three districts to give George W. Bush a majority in the 2000 presidential election.

MAJOR INDUSTRY
Agriculture, tourism, paper manufacturing

CITIES
Saratoga Springs, 26,186; Glens Falls, 14,354

NOTABLE
Franklin Roosevelt lost Dutchess County, site of his Hyde Park home, in seven of nine general elections in which he competed.

Rep. Michael R. McNulty (D)

CAPITOL OFFICE
225-5076
mike.mcnulty@mail.house.gov
www.house.gov/mcnulty
2210 Rayburn 20515-3221; fax 225-5077

COMMITTEES
Ways & Means

HOMETOWN
Green Island

BORN
Sept. 16, 1947, Troy, N.Y.

RELIGION
Roman Catholic

FAMILY
Wife, Nancy Ann McNulty; four children

EDUCATION
College of the Holy Cross, B.A. 1969 (political science)

CAREER
Public official

POLITICAL HIGHLIGHTS
Green Island supervisor, 1970-77; Democratic nominee for N.Y. Assembly, 1976; mayor of Green Island, 1977-83; N.Y. Assembly, 1983-89

ELECTION RESULTS

2002 GENERAL		
M. McNulty (D, C, INDC, WFM)	161,329	75.1%
Chuck Rosenstein (R)	53,525	24.9%
2002 PRIMARY		
M. McNulty (D)		unopposed
2000 GENERAL		
M. McNulty (D, INDC, C)	175,339	74.4%
Thomas G. Pillsworth (R)	60,333	25.6%

PREVIOUS WINNING PERCENTAGES
1998 (74%); 1996 (66%); 1994 (67%); 1992 (63%); 1990 (64%); 1988 (62%)

Elected 1988; 8th term

A product of machine politics since birth — he is the scion of the Democratic dynasty in the gritty blue-collar town of Green Island — McNulty always has been an organization man. At 22 he was elected town supervisor, a post his grandfather and father had held. After six years as mayor and six more in the state Assembly, he was handpicked by the Albany area's Democratic bosses in 1988 to take the state capital's seat in Congress.

McNulty has been a back-bencher in the House ever since. He spent his first two terms toiling quietly as a vote-counter in the Democratic whip organization, and was rewarded for it with a seat on the Ways and Means panel. After a decade on that high-profile panel — which writes tax, trade, health care, Social Security and welfare legislation — McNulty, the top Democrat on the Select Revenue Measures Subcommittee, has cemented his standing as its lowest-profile Democrat. He rarely speaks out, either from the committee dais or on the House floor, preferring to tend to business in the Capitol's backrooms and to husband his career through attentive constituent service.

McNulty has his differences with party doctrine on some social issues. But when it comes to matters important to organized labor, he rarely strays from the Democratic line. He is regularly among the first to press for increases in the minimum wage. He has opposed allowing employers to offer workers compensatory time off instead of overtime pay.

And he has sided with unions, which fear loss of jobs to workers overseas, in voting against three of the principal trade liberalization laws of the past decade: the 1993 codification of the North American Free Trade Agreement, the 2000 statute permanently granting China normal trade status, and the 2002 fast-track measure giving the president authority to negotiate trade agreements that Congress must approve or reject but cannot amend.

Bucking most lawmakers in both parties, however, McNulty was a vocal opponent of the 2001 law allowing the president to extend normal trade relations status to Vietnam. McNulty, whose brother Bill was killed in the Vietnam War, argues that the country should not be rewarded with that economic benefit because it has insufficiently accounted for U.S. military personnel still missing since the conflict.

McNulty has shown his independence on other occasions. He was one of only two Ways and Means members in 1996 to oppose legislation aimed at punishing foreign firms that aid the oil industries of Iran and Libya, saying he favored a stronger version approved by the International Relations Committee. In the 106th Congress, he initially voted with the GOP (one of 65 Democrats to do so) to repeal the estate tax. He returned to the Democratic fold when the House sustained President Clinton's veto of the measure, however, and in 2001 he opposed all the aspects of President Bush's tax cut, including its phaseout of the estate tax.

The closest McNulty has come to pushing his own legislation into law came in 1998. That year, he joined with a fellow New Yorker on Ways and Means, Republican Amo Houghton, on a bill to exempt from federal taxes the $1 million reward paid to David Kaczynski for turning in his brother, Theodore, better known as the Unabomber. David Kaczynski, a constituent of McNulty's, promised to donate the reward to the families of the Unabomber's victims but had to pay $300,000 in taxes. The measure was stripped out of the session-ending catchall spending bill at the last minute.

The conservative strain in McNulty's voting record surfaces most often on social policy. He would outlaw a procedure described as "partial birth" abortion by its opponents; would prohibit federal workers' health plans from paying for abortions; and would prevent public funding of the procedure except in cases of rape, incest or danger to the life of the woman. McNulty also voted for the 1996 law barring federal recognition of gay marriages. He backed three-fifths of the legislation to carry out the "Contract With America," the fiscally and socially conservative campaign manifesto on which the Republicans reclaimed the House in 1994 — the highest level of support among New York state Democrats.

More routinely, however, McNulty is in the Democratic mainstream. He voted against the 1996 welfare overhaul and has supported some gun control measures, and in the 107th he aligned himself with the party leadership against Republican efforts to stimulate the economy — which he viewed as too generous to business — and to add a prescription drug benefit to Medicare, which he viewed as inadequate.

The McNulty name has been a force in local upstate New York politics since 1914, when the congressman's grandfather, John J. McNulty, was elected Green Island tax collector. He went on to serve as town supervisor, county board chairman and county sheriff. The congressman's father, Jack McNulty Jr., served as town supervisor starting in 1949 and was mayor until the end of 2002. He was succeeded as mayor of Green Island by his daughter, the congressman's sister, Ellen McNulty-Ryan.

In his long political career, Congressman McNulty has waged only one unsuccessful campaign: a 1976 challenge to a GOP assemblyman. But he bounced back to win the first of his three terms in the legislature in 1982. While an assemblyman, McNulty once introduced legislation to make Uncle Sam the official state patriot. The icon is believed to have been modeled after Sam Wilson, a meatpacker from Troy, which is in McNulty's district.

McNulty's opening to move to Washington came with the sudden retirement in 1988 of 30-year Democratic incumbent Samuel S. Stratton, whose health was failing. Within hours of the announcement, the district's Democratic leaders met and chose McNulty to replace him on the ballot. McNulty defeated local Republican official Peter Bakal with 62 percent — his lowest share ever in a congressional general election.

Following the 2000 census, the 21st District was enlarged slightly because of reapportionment, in which New York gave up two House seats. But its solid Democratic cast was not altered, and in 2002, McNulty won his eighth term by 50 points over Republican attorney Chuck Rosenstein.

KEY VOTES

2002

- Yes Overhaul campaign finance law; ban "soft money" and restrict advocacy advertising
- Yes Back Bush's defense budget increase
- No Extend 1996 welfare law
- No Adopt Bush's discretionary spending limit
- No Pass GOP Medicare prescription drug plan
- Yes Create independent Sept. 11 commission
- Yes Extend union protections to Homeland Security Department employees
- No Revive fast-track procedures for trade agreements
- Yes Authorize war against Iraq
- No Advance bankruptcy overhaul opposed by abortion opponents

2001

- No Nullify Clinton Labor Department ergonomics rule
- No Cut taxes by $1.35 trillion through fiscal 2011
- Yes Maintain ban on oil drilling in Arctic National Wildlife Refuge
- No Approve Bush proposal to limit managed-care plan liability for coverage decisions
- Yes Divert money from crop subsidy payments to land conservation
- Yes Expand law enforcement power to investigate suspected terrorists

CQ VOTE STUDIES

	PARTY UNITY		PRESIDENTIAL SUPPORT	
	Support	Oppose	Support	Oppose
2002	90%	10%	28%	72%
2001	87%	13%	36%	64%
2000	88%	12%	75%	25%
1999	89%	11%	77%	23%
1998	89%	11%	76%	24%

INTEREST GROUPS

	AFL-CIO	ADA	CCUS	ACU
2002	100%	85%	30%	12%
2001	100%	80%	32%	24%
2000	100%	55%	57%	17%
1999	88%	90%	21%	8%
1998	100%	75%	23%	21%

NEW YORK 21
Capital District — Albany, Schenectady, Troy

As the terminus of the Erie Canal, which connects the Great Lakes to the Hudson River, New York's Capital District was one of the state's earliest industrial centers. Blue-collar workers and state employees give the Albany-Schenectady-Troy area a substantial union population and a solidly Democratic vote — unusual for an upstate district.

Albany is home to one of the nation's last big-city political machines, formed in 1921. During the heyday of Daniel O'Connell and Mayor Erastus Corning II, the Albany machine used to ensure Democratic victories throughout the area, but it now holds less sway over the area's ever-expanding suburbs. Few of the district's Democrats can be described as liberal. Most are quite conservative when it comes to social issues. Indeed, Rep. McNulty runs on the Conservative and Independence party lines, in addition to the Democratic Party line.

The 21st was expanded during 2002 redistricting and now includes all of Albany, Schenectady, Schoharie and Montgomery counties, as well as parts of Fulton, Saratoga and Rensselaer counties.

Despite large-scale industrial losses in the 1980s and 1990s, manufacturing remains a force. Job losses have been mitigated by an intensive effort to recruit small manufacturing and technology firms. Retail and wholesale jobs saw a real boom during the 1990s, and service jobs now account for about one-third of non-farm employment.

MAJOR INDUSTRY
State government, services, manufacturing, retail

MILITARY BASES
Watervliet Arsenal (Army), 6 military, 723 civilian (2001)

CITIES
Albany, 95,658; Schenectady, 61,821; Troy, 49,170; Rotterdam, 20,536

NOTABLE
The Mohawk and Hudson Rail Road, chartered in 1826 and opened in 1831, ran between Albany and Schenectady and was the state's first railroad; Samuel Wilson, a meatpacker who provided the Army with much of its rations during the War of 1812, is believed to be the inspiration for "Uncle Sam" and is buried in Troy; The original Shaker settlement was established in Watervliet in 1776.

Rep. Maurice D. Hinchey (D)

CAPITOL OFFICE
225-6335
mhinchey@mail.house.gov
www.house.gov/hinchey
2431 Rayburn 20515-3222; fax 226-0774

COMMITTEES
Appropriations

HOMETOWN
Saugerties

BORN
Oct. 27, 1938, Manhattan, N.Y.

RELIGION
Roman Catholic

FAMILY
Separated; three children

EDUCATION
State U. of New York, New Paltz, B.S. 1968 (political science & English), M.A. 1970 (English)

MILITARY SERVICE
Navy, 1956-59

CAREER
State employee

POLITICAL HIGHLIGHTS
Democratic nominee for N.Y. Assembly, 1972; N.Y. Assembly, 1975-93

ELECTION RESULTS

2002 GENERAL		
M. Hinchey (D, INDC, L, WFM)	113,280	64.2%
Eric Hall (R, C)	58,008	32.9%
Steven Greenfield (GREEN)	2,723	1.5%
Paul J. Laux (RTL)	2,473	1.4%
2002 PRIMARY		
Maurice D. Hinchey (D)		unopposed
2000 GENERAL		
M. Hinchey (D, INDC, WFM, L)	140,395	62.0%
Bob Moppert (R, C)	83,856	37.0%
Paul J. Laux (RTL)	2,328	1.0%

PREVIOUS WINNING PERCENTAGES
1998 (62%); 1996 (55%); 1994 (49%); 1992 (50%)

Elected 1992; 6th term

Now in his sixth term in the House, Hinchey's politics remain true to his working-class roots. He has earned a 99 percent career rating from the AFL-CIO, and he has never received less than a 95 percent rating from the liberal Americans for Democratic Action. He has a 95 percent lifetime rating from the League of Conservation Voters. He is also a member of the Progressive Caucus, which is the most liberal of the policy groups in the House.

Hinchey is generally a dependable vote for Democratic Party positions. In the 108th Congress, he was rewarded for his loyalty by being elected one of 12 regional whips. In the 106th Congress, he was given a seat on the Appropriations Committee, where he sits on the Interior and Agriculture subcommittees.

Hinchey is not usually inclined to seek out partisan confrontation, a good approach to take on Appropriations where bipartisan behavior is often rewarded. He will join with his upstate New York Republican colleagues on issues of common interest. That cooperation was most in evidence after the Sept. 11, 2001, terrorist attacks, when upstate lawmakers joined with the rest of the state delegation to try to gain federal money to help rebuild lower Manhattan. Hinchey and Republican John E. Sweeney, who is also on Appropriations, took the lead in trying to secure more aid for New York in the fiscal 2002 defense spending measure than the Bush administration and GOP leaders wanted. Their efforts were eventually defeated, however.

On the Agriculture subcommittee, Hinchey works to open Cuba to agricultural exports from the United States, which would be an important new market for his district's farmers. In the 107th Congress, Hinchey was able to secure aid for New York apple growers and obtain a host of grants for specific development projects. He also works to gain federal funding to build the new east-west Interstate 86, which he says is important to the region's economic development.

Hinchey's pragmatism and cooperative manner are indicative of political reality: Democrats are easily outnumbered by Republicans in the upstate districts. But he is still willing to go to bat for his constituents' interests. Hinchey publicly sparred with Republican Sue W. Kelly during debate over the fiscal 2002 supplemental spending bill. Kelly had won inclusion of a provision that would have boosted Medicare reimbursements for hospitals in Duchess and Orange counties, located in her district. Hinchey led the charge against the provision arguing that it did not cover Ulster and Sullivan counties, located in his district. He said any reimbursement provision should cover all the region's hospitals. Kelly's provision was eventually stripped out during the bill's House-Senate conference.

Environmental policies remain Hinchey's principal interest outside of Appropriations. An environmental fight in the 1970s over the development of a huge power plant on the Hudson River was the primary reason for Hinchey's entry into electoral politics. In the state Assembly, Hinchey chaired the Environmental Conservation Committee investigating the "Love Canal" contamination scandal and drafting bills to combat acid rain and to create the Hudson River Valley Greenway.

Once in Congress, Hinchey followed up his efforts on the Greenway by winning passage of his bill to designate much of the region as a National Heritage Area. He also has been involved in a long-running effort to require General Electric to clean up toxic polychlorinated biphenyls, or

PCBs, discharged into the Hudson River from its plant north of Albany.

Hinchey deviates from the majority of his party on the issue of gun owners' rights. He was the only New York Democrat to vote in 1996 to repeal the ban on certain semiautomatic assault-style weapons. Yet he did support the 1993 Brady bill, which calls for a five-day waiting period for handgun purchases. A member of the Congressional Sportsmen's Caucus, Hinchey received some unwelcome attention during his first House term when he was charged with carrying a loaded handgun in his baggage at Washington's National Airport. He eventually pleaded no contest and was given a suspended sentence.

Hinchey grew up in a working-class home, joined the Navy out of high school, worked in a local cement plant for five years and then paid his way through college by working nights collecting tolls on the New York State Thruway. In the House, he is noticed for his silver hair, pin-striped suits and elegant silk ties.

Hinchey's parents had been active in local party politics, and after his graduation from college, he was encouraged to get involved in behind-the-scenes political activities while starting a career in education. He lost his first bid for the state Assembly, in 1972, but came back two years later to begin an 18-year tenure in Albany.

In 1992, when nine-term Democratic Rep. Matthew F. McHugh retired, Hinchey sought to move up to Congress. He started as the underdog in the Democratic primary, facing Binghamton Mayor Juanita M. Crabb. But Hinchey prevailed by pushing a plan to revitalize the economy of the recession-hit region.

In November that year, Hinchey faced Republican Bob Moppert, a six-year county legislator. As Bill Clinton was carrying the 26th by 10 percentage points, Hinchey edged Moppert by 8,819 votes. The close race and competitive nature of the district made Hinchey a top GOP target for 1994, with Moppert back for a rematch. Hinchey survived again, winning by slightly more than 1,200 votes. In subsequent re-election bids, however, Hinchey has enjoyed more comfortable margins. In 2000, he beat Moppert again, this time by 25 points.

In 2002, he won re-election by a ratio of almost 2-to-1 in the new 22nd District, which was not so different from his old 26th District, retaining, for example, the college town of Ithaca, a haven for liberal activists. The New York districts were reconfigured after the 2000 census when a loss of population cost New York two House seats. Hinchey's victory came over first-time GOP candidate Eric Hall.

KEY VOTES

2002

Yes Overhaul campaign finance law; ban "soft money" and restrict advocacy advertising
No Back Bush's defense budget increase
No Extend 1996 welfare law
No Adopt Bush's discretionary spending limit
No Pass GOP Medicare prescription drug plan
Yes Create independent Sept. 11 commission
Yes Extend union protections to Homeland Security Department employees
No Revive fast-track procedures for trade agreements
No Authorize war against Iraq
No Advance bankruptcy overhaul opposed by abortion opponents

2001

No Nullify Clinton Labor Department ergonomics rule
No Cut taxes by $1.35 trillion through fiscal 2011
Yes Maintain ban on oil drilling in Arctic National Wildlife Refuge
No Approve Bush proposal to limit managed-care plan liability for coverage decisions
Yes Divert money from crop subsidy payments to land conservation
Yes Expand law enforcement power to investigate suspected terrorists

CQ VOTE STUDIES

	PARTY UNITY		PRESIDENTIAL SUPPORT	
	Support	Oppose	Support	Oppose
2002	99%	1%	20%	80%
2001	96%	4%	21%	79%
2000	98%	2%	94%	6%
1999	94%	6%	87%	13%
1998	96%	4%	83%	17%

INTEREST GROUPS

	AFL-CIO	ADA	CCUS	ACU
2002	100%	100%	30%	4%
2001	100%	100%	26%	0%
2000	100%	95%	23%	0%
1999	88%	95%	16%	4%
1998	100%	100%	22%	4%

NEW YORK 22

South central – Binghamton, Poughkeepsie, Ithaca

The elongated 22nd reaches from the hills above Cayuga Lake to the east bank of the Hudson River. Most residents are found at those extremes: the Ithaca and Binghamton areas in the west and the Hudson Valley region, including Poughkeepsie, Newburgh and Kingston, on the eastern edge.

In general, the district is rural, with a large portion of the Catskill Mountains in the center and apple and dairy farms throughout. Taking in all of Sullivan and Ulster counties and parts of six others, the mixture of cities and farmland creates a politically competitive environment, though Democrats enjoy a slight advantage.

Ithaca, in the 22nd's far northwest, is home to Cornell University, Ithaca College and a corps of liberal activists. Residents elected a socialist mayor three times in the 1990s, and Republican George W. Bush took just 28 percent of the vote here in the 2000 presidential election.

The district extends along the Pennsylvania border from Tioga County to Sullivan County, taking in Broome County's Triple Cities — Binghamton, Johnson City and Endicott. Once an industrial hub, Binghamton saw a decline in manufacturing jobs during the 1980s and 1990s, and the economy has been hit hard by recessions. Defense companies are still a major force, though IBM, which at one time was headquartered in Endicott, has significantly reduced operations in the area. Officials now hope to use the state university in Binghamton as an anchor for economic development.

The Catskills' Borscht Belt, a prominent Jewish resort area, declined as tourists began vacationing in more exotic locales. Officials hope to lure tourists back with casinos that have been approved by the state.

MAJOR INDUSTRY
Higher education, agriculture, electronics

CITIES
Binghamton, 47,380; Poughkeepsie, 29,871; Ithaca, 29,287

NOTABLE
Gen. George Washington had his headquarters and residence in Newburgh from 1782 to 1783; Bethel was the site of the marathon Woodstock rock concert in 1969; Mohonk Mountain House, near New Paltz, has hosted four presidents since its opening in 1869.

Rep. John M. McHugh (R)

CAPITOL OFFICE
225-4611
www.house.gov/mchugh
2333 Rayburn 20515-3223; fax 226-0621

COMMITTEES
Armed Services
(Total Force - chairman)
Government Reform
International Relations

HOMETOWN
Pierrepont Manor

BORN
Sept. 29, 1948, Watertown, N.Y.

RELIGION
Roman Catholic

FAMILY
Divorced

EDUCATION
Utica College of Syracuse U., B.A. 1970 (political science); State U. of New York, Albany, M.P.A. 1977

CAREER
State legislative aide; city official; insurance broker

POLITICAL HIGHLIGHTS
N.Y. Senate, 1985-93

ELECTION RESULTS

2002 GENERAL		
John M. McHugh (R, C)	unopposed	
2002 PRIMARY		
John M. McHugh (R)	unopposed	
2000 GENERAL		
John M. McHugh (R, C)	138,322	74.3%
Neil P. Tallon (D)	42,698	22.9%
Willard E. Smith (INDC, GREEN)	5,167	2.8%

PREVIOUS WINNING PERCENTAGES
1998 (79%); 1996 (71%); 1994 (79%); 1992 (61%)

Elected 1992; 6th term

McHugh is at home with the behind-the-scenes, nuts-and-bolts work of governing and writing legislation, and he has little need for face time on television. His colleagues describe him as a "worker bee," and he is often spotted sitting just off the House floor, puffing on a cigar and doing his legislative homework.

He had more homework in the 107th Congress as he was named chairman of the Armed Services Military Personnel Subcommittee — a place he had never served. But true to his industrious nature, he went to work learning the issues and quickly became an influential voice on them. In the 108th, he retains the gavel of the personnel panel, restructured slightly and renamed the Total Force Subcommittee.

A career politician, McHugh began working in government soon after graduating from college with a degree in political science. As might be expected from someone who has made public service his career, McHugh seeks not to dismantle or shrink the federal government but to make it work better. His tireless effort to reorganize the U.S. Postal Service is a good example. As chairman of Government Reform's Postal Service Subcommittee from 1995 to 2001, McHugh labored in vain to advance legislation that would help the Postal Service remain competitive in an era when technology has transformed the way people communicate. After the Government Reform Committee defeated it in 2002 following heavy lobbying against the bill by the United Parcel Service, McHugh lamented, "I feel a little bit like Robert E. Lee. Everybody said he was . . . a good general, then built a cemetery in his front yard."

He continues to pursue the issue. At the start of the 108th Congress, new Government Reform Chairman Thomas M. Davis III of Virginia named McHugh chairman of a Special Panel on Postal Reform and Oversight. He was to work with a nine-member commission appointed by President Bush and report directly to Davis, making postal reform a full committee issue. McHugh says that new technologies, including e-mail, fax and the Internet, have supplanted the Postal Service in transmitting documents that were once the mainstay of the mail business. Electronic billing and competition from private mail and package delivery companies also threaten the future of the Postal Service unless it can adapt, McHugh argues. "Simply put, the current structure of the Postal Service is not suited for the dynamic communications marketplace of today," he said.

McHugh still seeks cooperation with Democrats and does not have a notably ideological voting record. He supports labor on a number of issues and has won AFL-CIO endorsement several times. But on fiscal policy and most social issues, he casts a dependably Republican vote.

McHugh's vast upstate district is one of New York's poorest. It is heavily dependent on defense spending at Fort Drum and on agriculture, particularly dairy farming and apple growing, all areas in which the federal government plays a key role. In the 107th, McHugh offered a package of economic development bills dealing with agriculture, tourism and technology, such as increasing rural access to the Internet.

The 10th Mountain Division, based at Fort Drum, was one of the first Army units deployed in Afghanistan in 2001 to help topple the Taliban and search for al Qaeda terrorists. McHugh has been able to direct funding to maintain Fort Drum's standing as one of the Army's most modern bases. He argues that the 1995 military base closures were not always based on sound criteria, and pushed hard to prevent another round. Having failed in that quest, in the 107th he played an influential role on Armed Services in developing more specific guidelines for the base-closing commission to follow before proposing that installations be shut in 2005.

McHugh and his New York GOP colleagues John E. Sweeney and Sherwood Boehlert are concerned about the effect of acid rain on the Adirondack region, joining forces each Congress to offer legislation aimed at reducing emissions from power plants.

Throughout his House career, McHugh has voted against giving the president fast-track trade negotiating authority, saying he does not think the dairy industry would be adequately protected in the resulting trade liberalization treaties. "Dairy is going to lose. It always loses," he said in announcing his opposition to the 2002 trade law.

McHugh and his dairy industry allies were satisfied with the farm bill written by the 107th. While it did not include an interstate compact for Northeast dairy farmers to help them compete with Midwest milk producers, it did add a national program and included a payment scheme for Northeast dairymen.

McHugh has long argued for a bolstered Customs Service presence on the Canadian border — a historically low priority that has been given new attention by the Homeland Security Department created after the Sept. 11, 2001, terrorist attacks.

McHugh grew up in a middle-class family in Watertown, majored in political science in college, and after a brief stint as an insurance broker, got a job as an assistant to the city manager in Watertown. He moved to the staff of state Sen. H. Douglas Barclay, where his duties included serving as a liaison to local governments in the district — a job that helped McHugh prepare for a successful run for the state Senate when Barclay retired in 1984.

When Republican David O'B. Martin decided to retire in 1992 after a dozen years in the House, McHugh jumped into the race. He won the primary over a more conservative opponent, Morrison J. Hosley Jr., a local business owner and Hamilton town supervisor. That was tantamount to winning election in the historically Republican North Country; he won his first term with 61 percent and has done better than that ever since.

Redistricting for this decade was surprisingly favorable to McHugh. New York lost two seats in reapportionment, and several plans for a revised map would have put McHugh in the same district with other incumbents or drastically altered his constituency. But in the end, the state legislature gave McHugh everything he wanted — and no one ran against him in 2002.

KEY VOTES

2002

- Yes Overhaul campaign finance law; ban "soft money" and restrict advocacy advertising
- Yes Back Bush's defense budget increase
- Yes Extend 1996 welfare law
- Yes Adopt Bush's discretionary spending limit
- Yes Pass GOP Medicare prescription drug plan
- No Create independent Sept. 11 commission
- No Extend union protections to Homeland Security Department employees
- No Revive fast-track procedures for trade agreements
- Yes Authorize war against Iraq
- Yes Advance bankruptcy overhaul opposed by abortion opponents

2001

- No Nullify Clinton Labor Department ergonomics rule
- Yes Cut taxes by $1.35 trillion through fiscal 2011
- No Maintain ban on oil drilling in Arctic National Wildlife Refuge
- Yes Approve Bush proposal to limit managed-care plan liability for coverage decisions
- Yes Divert money from crop subsidy payments to land conservation
- Yes Expand law enforcement power to investigate suspected terrorists

CQ VOTE STUDIES

	PARTY UNITY		PRESIDENTIAL SUPPORT	
	Support	Oppose	Support	Oppose
2002	90%	10%	85%	15%
2001	89%	11%	88%	12%
2000	87%	13%	34%	66%
1999	81%	19%	29%	71%
1998	80%	20%	35%	65%

INTEREST GROUPS

	AFL-CIO	ADA	CCUS	ACU
2002	22%	15%	85%	79%
2001	42%	15%	91%	68%
2000	20%	5%	80%	73%
1999	56%	35%	76%	72%
1998	40%	25%	89%	68%

NEW YORK 23
North — Watertown, Plattsburgh, Oswego

The vast 23rd covers roughly one-fourth of the state, bordering Lake Champlain, the St. Lawrence Seaway and Lake Ontario. The waterways provide an inexpensive source of electricity, which has lured some heavy industry to the district and given it a number of blue-collar voters. But most of the district is rural, full of small towns, dairy farms, maple syrup producers and colleges. It reaches south to Oneida Lake and Madison County.

Fort Drum (near Watertown, the district's largest city) is one of the largest and most modern Army facilities on the East Coast. It thus far has been safe from post-Cold War base closures, but district residents did experience some economic hardship when Plattsburgh Air Force Base shut down in 1995. A business park has sprung from its ashes, attracting roughly 60 tenants.

Still, unemployment remains a problem throughout the district; harsh winters and high transportation costs make attracting jobs difficult. Bright spots include seasonal tourism — the 23rd covers much of the Adirondack Mountains. The proximity to waterways and forests made paper production a major industry for a long while, but many mills have been forced to close their doors, though Georgia Pacific retains its presence in Plattsburgh. Officials see the expansion of broadband Internet access as a means of stoking economic development.

The northeast corner of the state has sent Republicans to the House since the 1872 election. But George W. Bush barely won here in the 2000 presidential election, and Democrats have had increasing success at the local level in recent years.

MAJOR INDUSTRY
Agriculture, manufacturing, tourism, defense

MILITARY BASES
Fort Drum, 11,217 military, 1,411 civilian (2001)

CITIES
Watertown, 26,705; Plattsburgh, 18,816; Oswego, 17,954

NOTABLE
In 1775, Ethan Allen led the Green Mountain Boys — and Benedict Arnold — in seizing Fort Ticonderoga from the British; Whiteface Mountain is a top East Coast skiing destination.

Rep. Sherwood Boehlert (R)

CAPITOL OFFICE
225-3665
rep.boehlert@mail.house.gov
www.house.gov/boehlert
2246 Rayburn 20515-3224; fax 225-1891

COMMITTEES
Science - chairman
Transportation & Infrastructure
Select Homeland Security
Select Intelligence

HOMETOWN
New Hartford

BORN
Sept. 28, 1936, Utica, N.Y.

RELIGION
Roman Catholic

FAMILY
Wife, Marianne Willey Boehlert; four children

EDUCATION
Utica College, A.B. 1961 (public relations)

MILITARY SERVICE
Army, 1956-58

CAREER
Congressional aide; public relations executive

POLITICAL HIGHLIGHTS
Sought Republican nomination for U.S. House, 1972; Oneida County executive, 1979-82

ELECTION RESULTS

2002 GENERAL		
Sherwood Boehlert (R)	108,017	70.7%
David L. Walrath (C)	32,991	21.6%
Mark Dunau (GREEN)	6,660	4.4%
Kathleen M. Peters (RTL)	5,109	3.3%
2002 PRIMARY		
Sherwood Boehlert (R)	21,504	53.4%
David L. Walrath (R)	18,773	46.6%
2000 GENERAL		
Sherwood Boehlert (R, INDC)	124,132	60.5%
David Vickers (C, RTL)	42,854	20.9%
Richard W. Englebrecht (D)	38,049	18.6%

PREVIOUS WINNING PERCENTAGES
1998 (81%); 1996 (64%); 1994 (71%); 1992 (64%); 1990 (84%); 1988 (100%); 1986 (69%); 1984 (73%); 1982 (56%)

Elected 1982; 11th term

The only unvarnished moderate House Republican to hold a full committee chairmanship — and several moderates have been passed over — Boehlert is regarded as an important envoy between the House GOP leadership and the chamber's increasingly independent Republican swing voters. Known best for his strong pro-environment positions, he is someone the Bush White House has to keep a sharp eye on. Respected among his peers, Boehlert has the ability to influence the votes of about 30 GOP moderates on "green" issues.

Though relatively new as a committee chairman — he took over the Science Committee in the 107th Congress — Boehlert has steered the second-tier panel into new territory, such as anti-terrorism and cyberspace policy. He boosted the professionalism of the staff by hiring scientists for key subcommittees and has tried to ensure that the panel's recommendations are based on science, not ideology. Boehlert envisions extending the panel's mission to efforts to upgrade science, math and technology education.

The panel is under increased scrutiny in the 108th Congress as the nation's space program undergoes a thorough re-examination in the wake of the February 2003 space shuttle disaster.

Under Boehlert's guidance in the 107th, the committee pushed through the House bills to boost funding for the National Science Foundation by 15 percent and to set aside $1 billion for research on Internet security.

Approachable and low-key, Boehlert is a former congressional staffer and forceful debater with a ready command of the facts. Though often at war with the conservative-dominated leadership, he knows when to strike a deal and so is never at risk of being considered irrelevant. He tells district audiences good-naturedly: "When I vote against the Republican leadership, you can assume they're wrong."

Boehlert regularly departs from the GOP to seek alliances with Democrats on a range of issues. Annual vote surveys show him to be among the most independent-minded House Republicans, although in 2002 — faced with a strong primary challenge from a conservative — he voted with the GOP more than ever before, in addition to posting his highest-ever rating from the American Conservative Union and his lowest-ever score from the liberal Americans for Democratic Action.

His vote in the 107th Congress was pivotal to the passage of a sweeping campaign finance overhaul bill that both the White House and the GOP leadership fought. Earlier, Boehlert was one of four moderate Republicans who proposed a Senate censure of President Clinton rather than removal from office.

Boehlert is mostly at odds with President Bush and his party on environmental issues. In direct conflict with Bush, Boehlert supports restrictions on carbon dioxide emissions, opposes drilling for oil in the Arctic National Wildlife Refuge and has pushed for tougher fuel emissions standards for popular sport utility vehicles. He has tried without result to overhaul the federal superfund hazardous waste program to ensure that more money is spent on cleanup of the nation's worst toxic waste sites.

He honed his role as protector of the environment during the heyday of Republican anti-regulatory fervor under Speaker Newt Gingrich. In 1995, Boehlert rallied a coalition of Democrats and GOP moderates against conservatives' efforts to scale back clean air and clean water laws. He helped eliminate 17 controversial provisions that made federal appropriations to the Environmental Protection Agency contingent on new curbs on the agency's regulatory powers. The episode angered anti-regulatory GOP Westerners, who see him as insensitive to the economic realities of their region.

Boehlert continues to fight for more stringent controls on emissions that cause acid rain, smog and haze that plague his upstate New York district, pushing for reductions in pollutants released by power plants in the Midwest. "If I weren't an environmentalist, my constituents would find someone else to represent them," Boehlert is quoted as saying.

On fiscal policy, Boehlert generally concurs with his party's conservative majority. He supported Bush's centerpiece economic bill, the $1.35 trillion tax cut package passed by Congress in 2001.

In other areas, Boehlert often votes with Democrats. He has favored increasing the minimum wage, sided with unions on labor matters and opposed banning a procedure its opponents call "partial birth" abortion. He also favors some new controls on guns and voted against easing restrictions on the purchase of weapons at gun shows.

Boehlert, known to practically everyone as "Sherry," was a Capitol Hill aide for 15 years. His own political ambitions were deferred for a decade after an initial defeat in 1972. That year, he had hoped to succeed his boss, retiring GOP Rep. Alexander Pirnie, but he lost to Donald J. Mitchell, an assemblyman, in a Republican primary. Boehlert swallowed his disappointment and went to work for Mitchell.

In 1979, he relaunched his political career by winning the Oneida County executive post. By 1982, Mitchell was ready to retire. Boehlert was driving along a highway in Oneida County when he heard the news. He pulled into a rest stop, called a radio station and announced his candidacy.

As county executive, he had earned high marks from labor unions, and he was one of only two New York Republicans to get the state AFL-CIO's endorsement in the 1982 election. After winning the Republican primary comfortably, Boehlert capitalized on a huge organizational and financial advantage to defeat Democrat Anita Maxwell, with 56 percent. Every November since then he has captured at least 60 percent of the vote.

But Boehlert's left-of-center Republican philosophy leaves him vulnerable to a conservative backlash in the primaries. In 2002, he survived a surprising close call at the hands of conservative challenger David L. Walrath, a Cayuga County legislator. Boehlert hung on to win, 53 percent to 47 percent.

A rabid baseball fan, Boehlert aptly represents a district that houses the Baseball Hall of Fame in Cooperstown. At one time, he owned a small share of the Utica Blue Sox, a minor league team then in his hometown.

KEY VOTES

2002

Yes Overhaul campaign finance law; ban "soft money" and restrict advocacy advertising
Yes Back Bush's defense budget increase
Yes Extend 1996 welfare law
Yes Adopt Bush's discretionary spending limit
Yes Pass GOP Medicare prescription drug plan
No Create independent Sept. 11 commission
No Extend union protections to Homeland Security Department employees
Yes Revive fast-track procedures for trade agreements
Yes Authorize war against Iraq
Yes Advance bankruptcy overhaul opposed by abortion opponents

2001

No Nullify Clinton Labor Department ergonomics rule
Yes Cut taxes by $1.35 trillion through fiscal 2011
Yes Maintain ban on oil drilling in Arctic National Wildlife Refuge
Yes Approve Bush proposal to limit managed-care plan liability for coverage decisions
Yes Divert money from crop subsidy payments to land conservation
Yes Expand law enforcement power to investigate suspected terrorists

CQ VOTE STUDIES

	PARTY UNITY		PRESIDENTIAL SUPPORT	
	Support	Oppose	Support	Oppose
2002	79%	21%	78%	22%
2001	79%	21%	74%	26%
2000	68%	32%	61%	39%
1999	60%	40%	52%	48%
1998	59%	41%	60%	40%

INTEREST GROUPS

	AFL-CIO	ADA	CCUS	ACU
2002	11%	25%	90%	64%
2001	33%	35%	83%	32%
2000	30%	40%	80%	40%
1999	44%	65%	60%	40%
1998	90%	60%	61%	24%

NEW YORK 24

Central – Utica, Rome, Auburn

The J-shaped 24th starts at the western edge of the Adirondack Mountains, sweeps through the central part of the state — south of Syracuse and north of Binghamton — and extends into the Finger Lakes region. Pristine countryside is dotted by the small towns and rural hamlets of central New York. James Fenimore Cooper's tales of the frontier days gave central New York its nickname, the "Leatherstocking Region." Along with dairy farms, the 24th contains halls of fame and other historical gems, including the Women's Rights Convention and the National Women's Hall of Fame in Seneca Falls and the National Baseball Hall of Fame in Cooperstown.

Utica and Rome, aging industrial cities on the Mohawk River, suffered as manufacturing jobs left the state, but blue-collar jobs remain critical to these cities and give the 24th many of its Democratic voters.

The region took a major hit when Griffiss Air Force Base closed in 1995. An effort to turn the Mohawk River Valley into a high-tech information center — aided by the Air Force's Rome research laboratory, which works with many of the state's universities — has replaced some of those jobs.

The 24th also is home to the Oneida Indian Nation, which runs a profitable casino in Verona and has a long-running lawsuit against the state to reclaim its native lands. In the western part of the district, the Cayuga Indian Nation won $250 million in damages from New York in a similar claim, but the state is appealing the award.

The district's natural beauty gives voters a proclivity for earth-friendly policies, but they are traditional Yankee Republicans. The 24th gives solid support to Republican congressional candidates, and voters favored George W. Bush by a slim margin in the 2000 presidential election.

MAJOR INDUSTRY

Higher education, agriculture, tourism, manufacturing

CITIES

Utica, 60,651; Rome, 34,950; Auburn, 28,574; Cortland, 18,740

NOTABLE

The National Soccer Hall of Fame is in Oneonta, and the National Distance Running Hall of Fame is in Utica.

Rep. James T. Walsh (R)

CAPITOL OFFICE
225-3701
rep.james.walsh@mail.house.gov
www.house.gov/walsh
2369 Rayburn 20515-3225; fax 225-4042

COMMITTEES
Appropriations
(VA, HUD & Independent Agencies - chairman)

HOMETOWN
Syracuse

BORN
June 19, 1947, Syracuse, N.Y.

RELIGION
Roman Catholic

FAMILY
Wife, DeDe Ryan Walsh; three children

EDUCATION
St. Bonaventure U., B.A. 1970 (history)

CAREER
Marketing executive; social worker; Peace Corps volunteer

POLITICAL HIGHLIGHTS
Syracuse Common Council, 1978-88 (president, 1986-88); sought nomination for Onondaga County executive, 1987

ELECTION RESULTS

2002 GENERAL		
James T. Walsh (R, C, INDC)	144,610	72.3%
Stephanie Aldersley (D)	53,290	26.6%
Francis J. Gavin (WFM)	2,131	1.1%
2002 PRIMARY		
James T. Walsh (R)		unopposed
2000 GENERAL		
James T. Walsh (R, INDC, C)	151,880	69.0%
Francis J. Gavin (D)	64,533	29.3%
Howie Hawkins (GREEN)	3,830	1.7%

PREVIOUS WINNING PERCENTAGES
1998 (69%); 1996 (55%); 1994 (58%); 1992 (56%); 1990 (63%); 1988 (57%)

Elected 1988; 8th term

A second-generation congressman, Walsh is one of the most influential members of the Empire State's congressional delegation by virtue of chairing the Appropriations subcommittee that drafts the third-largest of the annual spending bills. Not even the state's famous junior senator, Democrat Hillary Rodham Clinton, has as prominent role in allocating federal dollars.

Walsh's subcommittee, known as VA-HUD, provides the funding for the Department of Housing and Urban Development (HUD), whose programs are particularly important to New York City; the Department of Veterans Affairs (VA), which serves more than 1.3 million veterans in the state; the Environmental Protection Agency, which oversees the cleanup of the Hudson River and Onondaga Lake, a heavily polluted body of water in Walsh's hometown of Syracuse; as well as NASA and many other independent agencies. Walsh has been able to steer hundreds of millions of dollars to New York, including tens of millions for projects in Syracuse.

In the 108th, a thorough review of NASA spending needs will highlight his work, in the aftermath of the Columbia space shuttle disaster. Walsh had aided students in his district in placing a scientific experiment on the flight. "We'll find out what happened, we'll fix it and we'll go on," he told the Syracuse Post-Standard.

Aided in part by senior Republicans who knew his father, former Rep. William F. Walsh, the younger Walsh has made friends on both sides of the aisle. He is known for a sense of fairness. The irascible Appropriations Committee senior Democrat, David R. Obey of Wisconsin, calls Walsh a "first-class legislator" who is willing to work with the minority.

While Walsh sides with the GOP leadership at key moments, he is frequently more moderate than the party hierarchy. In 2001 Walsh quietly deleted from the VA-HUD bill a Republican provision that barred spending to implement provisions of the 1997 U.N. Kyoto Protocol on Global Warming. The Bush administration opposed the treaty, as did many GOP lawmakers who didn't like its binding standards for greenhouse gas emissions imposed on industrialized countries.

In 2002 Walsh broke with his party to vote for an overhaul of campaign finance laws and to vote against fast-track trade legislation that gives the president broad negotiating authority. In 2000, he voted for a two-year increase in the minimum wage, which GOP leaders opposed. During final negotiations on a spending bill in 2000, Walsh changed the eligibility requirements for food stamps, allowing 500,000 more Americans to qualify at a cost of about $1.6 billion over five years.

Walsh assumed a high profile defending New York's interests after the the Sept. 11, 2001, terrorist attacks. Over White House objections, he and others in the delegation led a campaign for $9.7 billion in emergency spending, as part of Congress' pledge to provide $20 billion for recovery and rebuilding efforts. After being rebuffed in the Appropriations Committee, the New Yorkers threatened to stall the defense appropriations bill unless they received a House vote on their proposal. That brought the White House to the negotiating table, and the two sides eventually came to an agreement on aid for New York.

Walsh is not shy about using his subcommittee chairmanship to help Syracuse and other parts of central New York suffering economic decline. He notes that the practice of earmarking funds for local needs is a long congressional tradition. "Does it have warts? Yes. Are there abuses? Yes, there are," he told the Syracuse Herald American. "But it's as good a process as you can find because it gives members an opportunity to directly impact on problems and concerns they have in their districts."

Walsh also sits on the Agriculture Appropriations Subcommittee, which has jurisdiction over milk price supports, important to upstate dairy farmers. In the 106th Congress, Walsh included a provision in an appropriations bill that blocked new federal milk-pricing rules, a move that protected New York dairy farmers but infuriated lawmakers from the Upper Midwest. He also secured disaster aid for New York apple growers.

Before his seniority allowed him to claim the VA-HUD gavel, Walsh in the 104th chaired the District of Columbia spending subcommittee. In that role, he helped write the 1995 law that created a financial control board to steer the capital city out of longstanding fiscal problems. He also imposed a limit on the local government's budget deficit. But he stopped efforts by GOP budget-cutters who sought to reduce federal financial support for the city. Walsh said, "We should not shirk our responsibilities to our nation's capital."

Walsh has endorsed funding increases for the Peace Corps, where he spent two years teaching rice-growing techniques in Nepal. He also quietly opposed GOP efforts to eliminate AmeriCorps, the national service program modeled in some ways after the Peace Corps. The program's funding is covered by the VA-HUD bill, and whenever the House has voted to cut it, Walsh has worked behind the scenes to restore it.

A gun owner and hunter, Walsh is a member of the Congressional Sportsmen's Caucus. In 1999, he backed a measure to allow quick background checks for purchases at some gun shows, a proposal that was defeated in part because gun control advocates labeled it too weak. He also opposed a 1994 ban on certain semiautomatic assault-style weapons and voted to repeal the ban in 1996. But in 1993, Walsh voted for the Brady law imposing a five-day waiting period on handgun purchases.

Walsh is chairman of the Friends of Ireland congressional caucus and travels often to Ireland in peace efforts. He sponsored the law allowing poor residents of Northern Ireland to get job training in the United States, which has come to be known as the "Walsh visa."

His father was mayor of Syracuse and later served in the House, so it's not surprising that Walsh got interested in politics. He served more than a decade on the Syracuse City Council, including three years as council president. He entered Congress on his first try in 1988, when four-term GOP incumbent George C. Wortley was nudged into retirement by local party leaders. His percentage has hovered around 70 percent in his last three races.

KEY VOTES

2002

Yes	Overhaul campaign finance law; ban "soft money" and restrict advocacy advertising
Yes	Back Bush's defense budget increase
Yes	Extend 1996 welfare law
Yes	Adopt Bush's discretionary spending limit
Yes	Pass GOP Medicare prescription drug plan
No	Create independent Sept. 11 commission
No	Extend union protections to Homeland Security Department employees
No	Revive fast-track procedures for trade agreements
Yes	Authorize war against Iraq
Yes	Advance bankruptcy overhaul opposed by abortion opponents

2001

Yes	Nullify Clinton Labor Department ergonomics rule
?	Cut taxes by $1.35 trillion through fiscal 2011
Yes	Maintain ban on oil drilling in Arctic National Wildlife Refuge
Yes	Approve Bush proposal to limit managed-care plan liability for coverage decisions
Yes	Divert money from crop subsidy payments to land conservation
Yes	Expand law enforcement power to investigate suspected terrorists

CQ VOTE STUDIES

	PARTY UNITY		PRESIDENTIAL SUPPORT	
	Support	Oppose	Support	Oppose
2002	88%	12%	87%	13%
2001	92%	8%	88%	12%
2000	79%	21%	43%	57%
1999	78%	22%	32%	68%
1998	73%	27%	36%	64%

INTEREST GROUPS

	AFL-CIO	ADA	CCUS	ACU
2002	22%	15%	84%	75%
2001	10%	10%	91%	76%
2000	10%	20%	85%	56%
1999	33%	35%	72%	64%
1998	40%	30%	89%	44%

NEW YORK 25

North central – Syracuse, most of Irondequoit

Located in the center of the state, Syracuse is the only major city and economic hub of the 25th, which stretches from Onondaga County west along Lake Ontario to Irondequoit, a suburb of Rochester. Small towns and farms fill out the rest of the area in this moderately conservative district.

Syracuse is still suffering from a steep decline in manufacturing jobs that began in the 1980s and continued through the 1990s, though the city has held on to some blue-collar jobs by encouraging light manufacturing. Other growth comes from service-related work in hospitals and universities. State officials are working to turn upstate New York cities into university-based technology centers, and they hope Syracuse (home to Syracuse University) will become such a hub for environmental systems. Outside of Syracuse, small towns rely on dairy farming.

In this previously strong Republican territory, the area's GOP organization once held the loyalties of Irish, Italian, Polish and Jewish constituencies in and around Syracuse. The electorate's Republican leanings were reinforced by the typical upstate antipathy toward Democratic New York City. But the Republican machine has faded; economic stagnation in the 1990s and the decline of the city's industrial sector have helped the Democratic Party gain ground. Minorities and blue-collar workers contribute to the Democratic vote in Syracuse, as does an upscale Jewish population in DeWitt.

Redistricting in 2002 added parts of Monroe County and all of Wayne County, padding the sizable Republican base in Syracuse's suburbs and outlying areas. The revised 25th gave a slight majority to Al Gore in the 2000 presidential election, but by a smaller margin than under the old lines.

MAJOR INDUSTRY

Agriculture, service, manufacturing, higher education

CITIES

Syracuse, 147,306; Irondequoit (pt.), 32,661; Fairmount, 10,795

NOTABLE

The Brannock Device — used to measure feet for shoe size — was invented by Syracuse native Charles F. Brannock, and the company is based in Liverpool, a Syracuse suburb; Joseph Smith, founder of the Mormon Church, grew up and had his first visions in Palmyra.

Rep. Thomas M. Reynolds (R)

CAPITOL OFFICE
225-5265
www.house.gov/reynolds
332 Cannon 20515-3226; fax 225-5910

COMMITTEES
House Administration
Rules

HOMETOWN
Springville

BORN
Sept. 3, 1950, Belfonte, Pa.

RELIGION
Presbyterian

FAMILY
Wife, Donna Reynolds; four children

EDUCATION
Griffith Institute H.S., graduated 1968; Kent State U., attended 1968-69

MILITARY SERVICE
N.Y. Air National Guard, 1970-76

CAREER
Real estate and insurance broker; state legislative aide

POLITICAL HIGHLIGHTS
Concord Town Council, 1974-82; Erie County Legislature, 1982-88 (Republican leader, 1987-88); N.Y. Assembly, 1989-99 (minority leader, 1995-98)

ELECTION RESULTS

2002 GENERAL		
Thomas Reynolds (R, C, INDC)	135,089	73.6%
Ayesha F. Nariman (D)	41,140	22.4%
Shawn Harris (RTL)	4,084	2.2%
Paul E. Fallon (GREEN)	3,146	1.7%
2002 PRIMARY		
Thomas Reynolds (R)		unopposed
2000 GENERAL		
Thomas Reynolds (R, C)	157,694	69.3%
Thomas W. Pecoraro (D)	69,870	30.7%

PREVIOUS WINNING PERCENTAGES
1998 (57%)

Elected 1998; 3rd term

In just his third term, Reynolds has rapidly climbed the House Republican leadership ladder, with his election to chair the National Republican Campaign Committee in the 108th Congress the latest step. He is particularly successful at the inside game in the House, and unlike many of his GOP colleagues who proudly declare themselves not to be politicians, Reynolds embraces the job.

"My vocation, avocation and hobby is government and politics," he told The Washington Post. Reynolds has been involved in government and politics since he was an aide to a state assemblyman at the age of 22.

Reynolds conducted a yearlong, low-key campaign to head the NRCC, the House GOP's candidate recruitment and fundraising organization. He succeeded Thomas M. Davis III of Virginia, who held the post for two terms. Reynolds defeated Illinois' Jerry Weller by a 119-90 tally.

"People regard him as one of the rising stars," New York Democratic Sen. Charles E. Schumer told The New York Times. Schumer said he wouldn't be surprised if Reynolds became Speaker one day.

In his first term, Reynolds became the second Republican freshman appointed to the Rules Committee in 75 years. He also was the only freshman named as one of 18 GOP deputy whips. Reynolds said his work in Tom DeLay's whip organization helped him understand the behind-the-scenes intricacies of legislating. In the 108th, he remains in the whip organization.

Reynolds' loyalty to the party leadership was evident in 2001 when he angered many New Yorkers by helping the GOP pass an anti-terrorism supplemental spending bill. The measure contained less money than New Yorkers said they had been promised for terrorism recovery aid. As a member of the Rules Committee, Reynolds led the debate on the House floor, saying that the full amount of the money pledged would eventually be provided but not all of it would be made available right then.

Reynolds' stance put him at odds with many of his New York colleagues, such as Republican John E. Sweeney, a close friend for almost two decades. But his party loyalty earned him credit with the GOP leadership and the White House. Reynolds pressed for help for New York in other ways, including supporting a package of tax breaks to encourage redevelopment in lower Manhattan and to entice people to spend money in New York City restaurants and theaters.

Reynolds also has attended to the needs of his upstate constituents, which he cites as his top priority. He has helped struggling apple growers and dairy farmers and looked after the health care needs of veterans. He has worked to balance the demands of truckers who want prompt crossings at the U.S.-Canadian border with the need to beef up border security to protect the nation against terrorism. He also sought to improve the quality of the Great Lakes, by combating the spread of toxins and invasive species, including the big head carp.

Reynolds had shown fundraising and organizational acumen as a party leader in western New York and in the state Assembly. It was no surprise, therefore, when Speaker J. Dennis Hastert chose Reynolds as co-chairman for Battleground 2000, an unprecedented effort by the NRCC to raise money to help embattled incumbents, challengers and open-seat candidates. Reynolds pressed lawmakers who had large cash reserves and safe seats to write checks; he talked others into conducting special fundraisers.

The drive brought in nearly $22 million, considerably more than the target. In 2002, Reynolds chaired the NRCC's spring dinner, which raised $7.5 million. Those successes presaged his election as NRCC chairman.

As evidence of the high regard with which he is held by party leaders and of his political savvy, Reynolds won appointment to the Ways and Means Committee in the 107th Congress. He immediately took a leave of absence from the panel because House rules prohibit someone on Rules from serving on any other major committee.

Reynolds grew up in southern Erie County. He entered Kent State University as a business major, but left when his mother became ill. He returned home to help his traveling salesman father raise his younger siblings. He never graduated from college, but he told The Hill, a Capitol Hill newspaper, "It hasn't impaired me." He worked in the real estate and insurance businesses and, at age 22, became an aide to a state assemblyman.

A year later, he was elected to the Concord Town Council, in southern Erie County. After eight years, he moved up to the Erie County Legislature, following Bill Paxon, whom he had met through their service in the Young Republicans. Paxon had just won election to the state Assembly. In 1988, Reynolds won election to fill Paxon's seat in the state legislature. During his decade in Albany, Reynolds earned a reputation as a hard-working conservative. He chaired the GOP's affordable housing task force and paid close attention to constituent service.

In 1994, as the Republican Party leader in Erie County, long a Democratic stronghold, Reynolds was instrumental in moving the county to the GOP column as George E. Pataki was elected governor. He was on Pataki's transition team. In 1995, Reynolds was chosen leader of the Assembly's Republican minority, a position he held until he ran for Congress in 1998 when Paxon stepped down.

Throughout Paxon's House career, Reynolds had served as his campaign manager, and Paxon returned the favor by managing Reynolds' House campaign. A shoo-in for the heavily Republican district, Reynolds was so flush with campaign cash that he was able to donate $50,000 to the House GOP campaign committee two weeks before his election. He easily won a 15 percentage point victory over history professor Bill Cook, even though he didn't live in the district.

New York legislators drew a new district map (renumbered the 26th) that gave Reynolds a larger Republican margin than initial proposals had contained. As one GOP strategist told The New York Times, Reynolds "wanted a district that would allow him to vote like a Southern conservative" and back the party leadership. In 2002, he won re-election by better than 3-to-1.

KEY VOTES

2002

- No Overhaul campaign finance law; ban "soft money" and restrict advocacy advertising
- Yes Back Bush's defense budget increase
- Yes Extend 1996 welfare law
- Yes Adopt Bush's discretionary spending limit
- Yes Pass GOP Medicare prescription drug plan
- No Create independent Sept. 11 commission
- No Extend union protections to Homeland Security Department employees
- Yes Revive fast-track procedures for trade agreements
- Yes Authorize war against Iraq
- Yes Advance bankruptcy overhaul opposed by abortion opponents

2001

- Yes Nullify Clinton Labor Department ergonomics rule
- Yes Cut taxes by $1.35 trillion through fiscal 2011
- No Maintain ban on oil drilling in Arctic National Wildlife Refuge
- Yes Approve Bush proposal to limit managed-care plan liability for coverage decisions
- Yes Divert money from crop subsidy payments to land conservation
- Yes Expand law enforcement power to investigate suspected terrorists

CQ VOTE STUDIES

	PARTY UNITY		PRESIDENTIAL SUPPORT	
	Support	Oppose	Support	Oppose
2002	96%	4%	92%	8%
2001	94%	6%	93%	7%
2000	93%	7%	25%	75%
1999	88%	12%	25%	75%

INTEREST GROUPS

	AFL-CIO	ADA	CCUS	ACU
2002	11%	0%	100%	92%
2001	17%	5%	96%	88%
2000	0%	0%	85%	84%
1999	11%	15%	92%	79%

NEW YORK 26

Suburban Buffalo and Rochester; rural west

The Republican-leaning 26th spreads from the Buffalo to the Rochester suburbs, scooping up mainly rural areas in between and to the south. It takes in all or part of seven counties, but slightly less than half of residents live in Niagara and Erie counties in the westernmost part of the district.

The population is anchored in Amherst, a white-collar suburb northeast of Buffalo. The State University of New York at Buffalo and corporate office parks are mainstays. Amherst and Lancaster, a town to the southeast, voted narrowly for Al Gore in the 2000 presidential election. Less-populous areas in northeastern Erie, including Clarence and Newstead, lean Republican.

The 26th's share of Niagara County, including Lockport and North Tonawanda, was added during 2002 redistricting, which renumbered the district from the 27th. As in Erie, the Niagara portion is politically competitive, with registered Republicans only slightly outnumbering Democrats.

The New York State Thruway links Erie County to the Rochester suburbs of western Monroe County, which include Greece and have a Republican lean.

Between Buffalo and Rochester are the dairy, vegetable and grain farms of rural western New York. Wyoming County is solidly Republican and heavily agricultural, with an abundance of dairy farms. Wyoming also has a facility that is distinctly unbucolic: the state penitentiary at Attica, which in 1971 had one of the worst prison riots in U.S. history. Livingston County, east of Wyoming, includes Conesus Lake, which is at the western edge of New York's Finger Lakes region, and part of the Genesee River, which flows north into Rochester.

MAJOR INDUSTRY

Manufacturing, agriculture, service

CITIES

North Tonawanda, 33,262; Lockport, 22,279; Batavia, 16,256

NOTABLE

The Herschell Carrousel Factory Museum in North Tonawanda hosts about 20,000 visitors a year; The Jell-O museum in LeRoy celebrates the beginnings of the famous gelatin dessert.

Rep. Jack Quinn (R)

CAPITOL OFFICE
225-3306
www.house.gov/quinn
2448 Rayburn 20515-3227; fax 226-0347

COMMITTEES
Transportation & Infrastructure
(Railroads - chairman)
Veterans' Affairs

HOMETOWN
Hamburg

BORN
April 13, 1951, Buffalo, N.Y.

RELIGION
Roman Catholic

FAMILY
Wife, Mary Beth Quinn; two children

EDUCATION
Siena College, B.A. 1973 (English education); State U. of New York, Buffalo, M.Ed. 1983

CAREER
Teacher

POLITICAL HIGHLIGHTS
Town of Hamburg Council, 1982-84; Hamburg town supervisor, 1985-93

ELECTION RESULTS

2002 GENERAL		
Jack Quinn (R, C)	120,117	69.1%
Peter Crotty (D, WFM)	47,811	27.5%
Thomas Casey (RTL)	3,586	2.1%
Albert N. LaBruna (GREEN)	2,405	1.4%
2002 PRIMARY		
Jack Quinn (R)		unopposed
2000 GENERAL		
Jack Quinn (R, C, INDC)	138,452	67.1%
John Fee (D, L, WFM)	67,819	32.9%

PREVIOUS WINNING PERCENTAGES
1998 (68%); 1996 (55%); 1994 (67%); 1992 (52%)

Elected 1992; 6th term

Quinn's tight relationship with organized labor and his charismatic personality make him one of the most well-known of the dwindling number of House Republican moderates.

He spent much of his first decade in Congress battling the GOP leadership — and earning accolades from Democrats — not only on minimum wage, trade and other labor issues, but also on campaign finance, gun control and the budget. During the 107th Congress, he served as the chairman of the House Republican Working Group on Labor; the position helped endear him to his constituents in Buffalo, one of the most unionized cities in the country.

While such advocacy may win him votes at home, it has made many Republicans in Washington uncomfortable. Still, GOP leaders know that Quinn's positions on labor are essential to his political survival, an important consideration in a closely divided House. And his joviality in the clubby confines of the House have made Quinn one of the more personally popular members on either side of the aisle.

He has racked up an impressive string of electoral victories in the mostly Democratic, union-heavy precincts of downtown Buffalo. On four occasions, he has won re-election with two-thirds of the vote or better — including in 2000, when George W. Bush lost the 30th District, which Quinn then represented, by 24 percentage points. In 2002, he won with a career-high 69 percent in the 27th District, which was reconfigured in the redistricting for this decade to be slightly more friendly to the GOP.

In the 107th, Quinn displayed his pro-labor bent by continuing his long-running efforts to drive up the minimum wage, introducing legislation that calls for a $1-an-hour increase over two years. Quinn was instrumental in forcing the Republican leaders of the 104th Congress to enact the most recent increase, to $5.15. At his urging, the House passed another wage increase in the 106th Congress, but it died in a series of disputes with the Senate. Quinn hopes to coordinate efforts with Senate supporters of a minimum wage increase in the 108th.

He also polished his labor credentials during the 107th by opposing the GOP leadership as it engineered the repeal of the workplace ergonomics regulations issued in the final days of the Clinton administration. And he has taken the union view in voting against all four of the most controversial trade liberalization laws enacted during his time in Congress.

Quinn comes from a union background — his father was a longtime engineer on the trains that served Buffalo's steel mills. "There are five sons in my family, and my mother jokes that all of our birthdays coincide with each time my father was on strike," he once said. Quinn says he became a Republican almost by chance: His uncle, a local GOP elections official, happened to be the one who sent him his voter registration papers while he was in college — with the box for Republican Party affiliation already checked off.

Quinn was a dependable Republican vote early in his career, including 1995, when he backed the GOP "Contract With America." And even in the 107th he backed Bush's positions and stood with the GOP on party-line votes about 85 percent of the time, high enough numbers to keep him out of the ranks of the most maverick Republicans.

To illustrate his camaraderie with the president, whose nickname for Quinn is "Big Man from Buffalo," the 6-foot, 5-inch congressman likes to recall how he telephoned the White House after a record winter storm in upstate New York in 2001 to report that "the snow is over the Big Man's head." Quinn was not nearly as pleased with the White House a year later, however, when he complained about cuts in aid to low-income people to help them pay their heating bills.

In 2001, Quinn stood with a united House GOP caucus in backing Bush's signature campaign promise, a $1.35 trillion tax cut. But two years before, Quinn was one of only four House Republicans to vote against the GOP's $792 billion tax cut, which died with President Clinton's veto. He argued that the cut was too deep and would increase the national debt.

Buffalo constituents also are concerned about economic development. Since the 107th, when Quinn took the chairmanship of the Transportation and Infrastructure Subcommittee on Railroads, he has pushed his GOP colleagues to accept increased funding for Amtrak, which connects Buffalo to Chicago and New York. Quinn's support for Amtrak stems from both fond personal memories of his father's work on the South Buffalo Railroad and his own vested interest in a current project that will boost Buffalo's economy. Plans to reinvigorate the city's harbor include a new transportation center, which is likely to include a new Amtrak station.

Probably none of Quinn's votes have been as important to the GOP leadership as his 1998 votes in favor of Clinton's impeachment. Quinn, who had developed a close friendship with the president — one year they watched the Super Bowl and ate pizza together at the White House — changed his mind on the charges a few days before the House vote. "The more I learn about the serious details of perjury and obstruction of justice, the more I am concerned about the president's failure to tell the truth under oath," he said.

That decision was widely regarded as a major factor in the pro-impeachment votes of several other moderate Republicans who had been undecided. After the vote, an unidentified White House aide told the New York Daily News how Clinton had become only the second president ever to be impeached: "Two words: Jack Quinn."

Before entering politics, Quinn taught high school English, coached basketball and track, and got a master's degree in education. In 1992, he was the Hamburg chief executive when he took on Erie County Executive Dennis Gorski for the House seat being vacated by Democrat Henry J. Nowak. Sensing that year's anti-incumbent mood, Quinn focused his campaign on proposals to limit congressional perquisites. He also described his opponent as a typical politician who represented "more of the same." Quinn won with 52 percent of the vote.

KEY VOTES

2002

- Yes Overhaul campaign finance law; ban "soft money" and restrict advocacy advertising
- Yes Back Bush's defense budget increase
- Yes Extend 1996 welfare law
- Yes Adopt Bush's discretionary spending limit
- Yes Pass GOP Medicare prescription drug plan
- No Create independent Sept. 11 commission
- No Extend union protections to Homeland Security Department employees
- No Revive fast-track procedures for trade agreements
- Yes Authorize war against Iraq
- Yes Advance bankruptcy overhaul opposed by abortion opponents

2001

- No Nullify Clinton Labor Department ergonomics rule
- ? Cut taxes by $1.35 trillion through fiscal 2011
- No Maintain ban on oil drilling in Arctic National Wildlife Refuge
- Yes Approve Bush proposal to limit managed-care plan liability for coverage decisions
- Yes Divert money from crop subsidy payments to land conservation
- Yes Expand law enforcement power to investigate suspected terrorists

CQ VOTE STUDIES

	PARTY UNITY		PRESIDENTIAL SUPPORT	
	Support	Oppose	Support	Oppose
2002	84%	16%	84%	16%
2001	87%	13%	85%	15%
2000	76%	24%	43%	57%
1999	74%	26%	38%	62%
1998	76%	24%	32%	68%

INTEREST GROUPS

	AFL-CIO	ADA	CCUS	ACU
2002	13%	15%	84%	64%
2001	50%	20%	82%	70%
2000	40%	15%	70%	70%
1999	67%	50%	72%	60%
1998	40%	30%	76%	48%

NEW YORK 27

West – most of Buffalo, south and east suburbs

Tucked along the shores of Lake Erie in western New York, the 27th contains all of Erie County south of Buffalo and all but the northeastern portion of the city itself. Most of Buffalo's minority residents are in the neighboring 28th.

The region has battled to shed its high unemployment rate and Rust Belt image. Auto manufacturing remains important in the area, and the city has a large concentration of blue-collar workers. Buffalo has seen an increase in finance, insurance and real estate industry jobs — driven mostly by two thriving banks, HSBC and M&T. As part of a larger plan to help the beleaguered economy of upstate New York, officials hope university-based research will turn the Buffalo region into a bioinformatics center, promoting the use of computer technology to study genomes, proteins and biomolecules.

Adelphia, a major cable telecommunications company, planned to move its headquarters — and high-paying executive jobs — to the waterfront from Pennsylvania, but the plan was scrapped when the company filed for bankruptcy in 2002. Still, local leaders see the waterfront as the locus for Buffalo's renaissance. Sports teams, particularly the NFL's Buffalo Bills, who play in Orchard Park, are the pride of the city. The rest of Erie County and Chautauqua County, a grape-growing region, are mostly rural.

The 27th has a Democratic tradition but was made more Republican in 2002 redistricting: An incumbent-protection plan added the GOP stronghold of Chautauqua County to the old 30th, which was renumbered the 27th. Residents already had shown a willingness to vote for a moderate Republican with union sympathies — as they have done in sending Rep. Quinn to Congress for six terms.

MAJOR INDUSTRY

Auto manufacturing, government, agriculture, tourism

CITIES

Buffalo (pt.), 163,179; Cheektowaga, 79,988; West Seneca, 45,943; Jamestown, 31,730

NOTABLE

All major cities in the northeastern part of North America are within a 500-mile radius of Buffalo; President Franklin D. Roosevelt gave his 1936 "I Hate War" speech at the Chautauqua Institution.

Rep. Louise M. Slaughter (D)

CAPITOL OFFICE
225-3615
louiseny@mail.house.gov
www.house.gov/slaughter
2469 Rayburn 20515-3228; fax 225-7822

COMMITTEES
Rules
Select Homeland Security

HOMETOWN
Fairport

BORN
Aug. 14, 1929, Harlan County, Ky.

RELIGION
Episcopalian

FAMILY
Husband, Robert Slaughter; three children

EDUCATION
U. of Kentucky, B.S. 1951 (microbiology), M.P.H. 1953

CAREER
State government aide; market researcher; microbiologist

POLITICAL HIGHLIGHTS
Monroe County Legislature, 1975-79; N.Y. Assembly, 1983-87

ELECTION RESULTS

2002 GENERAL		
Louise M. Slaughter (D, WFM)	99,057	62.5%
Henry F. Wojtaszek (R, C, INDC)	59,547	37.5%
2002 PRIMARY		
Louise M. Slaughter (D)		unopposed
2000 GENERAL		
Louise M. Slaughter (D)	151,688	65.7%
Mark C. Johns (R, C)	75,348	32.6%

PREVIOUS WINNING PERCENTAGES
1998 (65%); 1996 (57%); 1994 (57%); 1992 (55%); 1990 (59%); 1988 (57%); 1986 (51%)

Elected 1986; 9th term

As lawmakers find themselves drawn deeply into health care's ethical and budgetary complexities, Slaughter has emerged as a key Democratic voice on prescription drugs, genetic discrimination, antibiotic resistance and abortion. A bacteriologist with a master's degree in public health, she often is tapped by Democratic leaders to make their case during health care debates with a forceful and learned argument.

Slaughter actually has a voice on nearly all major legislation to come before the House. She is the second-most-senior Democrat on the Rules Committee, which serves as the traffic cop for bills headed to the House floor. And she has now served in the House longer than any other Democratic woman except Marcy Kaptur of Ohio, elected four years before her.

In the 108th, Minority Leader Nancy Pelosi named Slaughter to one of the 23 Democratic seats on the new Committee on Homeland Security, a plum assignment that will enhance her visibility.

Slaughter is a Southerner who represents a district in upstate New York. She lives in a suburb of Rochester where she spent most of her adult life, but she was brought up in the mountains of Kentucky's Harlan County, a genuine coal miner's daughter.

When Slaughter came to Congress in 1987, House Democratic leaders quickly took a liking to her warmth, grit and liberal views. They gave her a seat on the Rules Committee in 1989 and on the Budget Committee in 1991. Slaughter's rise through the party then slowed. She narrowly lost a race for the vice chairmanship of the Democratic Caucus in the 104th Congress. She failed in a bid to become top-ranking Democrat on the Budget Committee in the 105th Congress and left the panel when her term expired.

While Pelosi was party whip, she named Slaughter as her point person on "issues that concern women" in 2002, from abortion rights to health care and education; in the 108th she is the Democratic co-chairman of the Congressional Caucus for Women's Issues. Slaughter is front and center in a fight against GOP efforts to restrict abortion and family planning funds. She once called a Republican plan to curtail family planning aid to developing countries "inhumane," and she has attacked as "shameful" the effort to ban a procedure its opponents call "partial birth" abortion.

Her legislative successes include the establishment of a national task force to ensure that children get proper care in the event of a terrorist attack, and a bill to increase education about the health risks of the anti-miscarriage drug DES, which has caused cancer and abnormalities in the children of some women who took the drug.

One of Slaughter's top concerns is that advanced understanding of the human genome system, which offers promise of dramatic medical breakthroughs, could lead to discrimination against people with genetic disorders. She repeatedly has introduced legislation to protect people from being fired from their jobs or dropped by their insurers as the result of a genetic test. "Every human being has between five and 50 faulty genes," Slaughter said. "Genetic discrimination is not something that might happen to a hypothetical group of people. . . . We are talking about ourselves."

While working on national issues, Slaughter also carefully tends to the companies in her district, which include Eastman Kodak and Xerox. That list once included telecommunications company Global Crossing Ltd., which went bankrupt amid accusations of questionable accounting techniques. The company laid off 1,600 workers and left most employees with empty 401(k) retirement accounts. Slaughter helped prompt a House investigation. "Many former employees have been economically devastated as a result of corporate greed," she said.

Slaughter also remains involved in the district's fight to win more frequent and less expensive airline service. "This aeronautics structure was built with the tax dollars of the United States," she said in 2001. "Then deregulation came along, and we went from about 13 airlines in Rochester to about six. We can get service, but we pay the highest fares also in the country." Slaughter helped lure low-cost carrier JetBlue to Rochester in 2000 and Air Tran Airways in 2002. The new service helped bring down costs, but Rochester's fares remain among the highest in the nation.

She also is working to establish ferry service across Lake Ontario from Toronto to Rochester.

Slaughter moved to New York in the 1950s, when her husband went to work as an executive with a local corporation. Her first brush with public policy came in 1971 when she joined with some neighbors to try to save a stand of trees from development. It was a losing battle. "I thought in my best Kentucky fashion that if I would put on my best dress and go and be very nice and polite and ask them to save this forest that they would say, 'Well, why not?' " she later told the Associated Press. "And they just handed me my hat."

The episode sparked an interest in politics. She served as a Monroe County legislator and as an assistant to Mario M. Cuomo, then New York's secretary of state. In 1982, she ousted a Republican incumbent to move to the state Assembly, where she served four years before winning her seat in the House with 51 percent of the vote against conservative first-term Republican Fred J. Eckert. Actor Richard Gere, with whom she shared an interest in Central American issues, campaigned door-to-door with her. (They are friends still; he headlined a 2002 fundraiser for her.)

It was not until 1998, in her seventh House election, that Slaughter began drawing better than 60 percent of the vote, the customary threshold for being viewed as a lopsided winner. She did so in 2000 and again in 2002, after the 28th District was redrawn considerably for this decade.

Reapportionment after the 2000 census cost New York a pair of House seats, and the state legislature placed Slaughter in the same district as 14-term Democratic incumbent John J. LaFalce. When efforts to alter the remap failed, LaFalce chose to retire rather than face Slaughter in a primary. She won by 25 points in November and wasted no time in opening offices in Buffalo and in Niagara Falls, both new to her district, and in touting federal funding and grants for projects in both communities.

KEY VOTES

2002

- Yes Overhaul campaign finance law; ban "soft money" and restrict advocacy advertising
- Yes Back Bush's defense budget increase
- No Extend 1996 welfare law
- No Adopt Bush's discretionary spending limit
- No Pass GOP Medicare prescription drug plan
- ? Create independent Sept. 11 commission
- Yes Extend union protections to Homeland Security Department employees
- No Revive fast-track procedures for trade agreements
- No Authorize war against Iraq
- No Advance bankruptcy overhaul opposed by abortion opponents

2001

- No Nullify Clinton Labor Department ergonomics rule
- No Cut taxes by $1.35 trillion through fiscal 2011
- Yes Maintain ban on oil drilling in Arctic National Wildlife Refuge
- No Approve Bush proposal to limit managed-care plan liability for coverage decisions
- Yes Divert money from crop subsidy payments to land conservation
- Yes Expand law enforcement power to investigate suspected terrorists

CQ VOTE STUDIES

	PARTY UNITY		PRESIDENTIAL SUPPORT	
	Support	Oppose	Support	Oppose
2002	98%	2%	16%	84%
2001	96%	4%	29%	71%
2000	96%	4%	87%	13%
1999	96%	4%	81%	19%
1998	96%	4%	82%	18%

INTEREST GROUPS

	AFL-CIO	ADA	CCUS	ACU
2002	100%	100%	22%	0%
2001	100%	95%	35%	0%
2000	100%	90%	38%	4%
1999	100%	100%	21%	4%
1998	100%	100%	39%	8%

NEW YORK 28

Northwest – Rochester, part of Buffalo

A small strip of land along the shore of Lake Ontario serves as a connector for the ends — Buffalo and Rochester — of the telephone receiver-shaped 28th. The old Rochester-based 28th and Buffalo-based 29th were merged during 2002 redistricting to create one district that encompasses the northeastern portion of Buffalo, all of Niagara Falls and almost all of Rochester, giving the new 28th most of the Democratic-rich voting areas in western New York.

Blacks make up more than one-fourth of the population, and minorities combined total more than one-third, giving the district a far higher proportion of minority residents than any of the surrounding districts.

While manufacturing powered by the Niagara River long has been the base of Buffalo's economy, Rochester has been a technology center. Both cities are trying to recover from economic decline in the 1990s.

Optic and imaging manufacturing firms drive Rochester's economy, joined by high-tech start-up companies that benefit from proximity to the area's major corporations, Eastman Kodak and Xerox Corp., and academic institutions.

Rochester suffered from high unemployment during the 1990s, but the situation has been improving. While much of the slack in the manufacturing sector has been picked up by the service industries, the lower salaries have exacerbated the problems of Rochester's low-income residents.

Unlike many northeastern cities with blue-collar bases, the Rochester area long held to a moderate Republican tradition typical of upstate New York. But it has begun to lean the other way. Both the old 28th and old 29th supported Democratic presidential candidates in 1992, 1996 and 2000. Al Gore won the new district by 30 percentage points in 2000.

MAJOR INDUSTRY

Service, manufacturing, tourism

CITIES

Rochester (pt.), 219,729; Buffalo (pt.), 129,469; Niagara Falls, 55,593

NOTABLE

About 50,000 honeymooners visit Niagara Falls each year; The Rochester home of women's rights activist Susan B. Anthony is now a museum.

Rep. Amo Houghton (R)

CAPITOL OFFICE
225-3161
www.house.gov/houghton
1111 Longworth 20515-3229; fax 225-5574

COMMITTEES
International Relations
Ways & Means
(Oversight - chairman)

HOMETOWN
Corning

BORN
Aug. 7, 1926, Corning, N.Y.

RELIGION
Episcopalian

FAMILY
Wife, Priscilla Houghton; four children, three stepchildren

EDUCATION
Harvard U., A.B. 1950, M.B.A. 1952

MILITARY SERVICE
Marine Corps, 1945-46

CAREER
Glassworks company executive

POLITICAL HIGHLIGHTS
No previous office

ELECTION RESULTS

2002 GENERAL		
Amo Houghton (R, C)	127,657	73.1%
Kisun J. Peters (D)	37,128	21.3%
Wendy M. Johnson (RTL)	5,836	3.3%
Rachel Treichler (GREEN)	4,010	2.3%
2002 PRIMARY		
Amo Houghton (R)		unopposed
2000 GENERAL		
Amo Houghton (R, C)	154,238	77.3%
Kisun J. Peters (D)	45,193	22.7%

PREVIOUS WINNING PERCENTAGES
1998 (68%); 1996 (72%); 1994 (85%); 1992 (71%); 1990 (70%); 1988 (96%); 1986 (60%)

Elected 1986; 9th term

Seventeen years ago, Houghton planned to step down as chief executive officer of Corning Glass and embark on a new career as a missionary to Zimbabwe. He instead wound up running for Congress. In a way, Houghton's work in the House is similar to what he had in mind in Africa: promoting civility, faith and understanding between the races.

He is a driving force behind the semiannual civility retreats for members and their families. He and Democrat John Lewis of Georgia co-chair the Faith & Politics Institute, an interfaith, nonpartisan organization that tries to improve communication between the races and encourages lawmakers to apply spiritual values to political life. Houghton (HO-tun) joins Lewis each March in leading a congressional contingent to Selma, Ala., to commemorate the famous civil rights march across the Edmund Pettus Bridge.

But Houghton's previous life among the corporate elite still sometimes shows through. He maintains a membership in the exclusive Augusta National Golf Club in Georgia, which does not admit women, despite pressure from women's groups to do so.

His voting record shows Houghton to be an independent, moderate voice in the House GOP. He was a founder and now serves as a member of the executive committee of the Republican Main Street Partnership, which seeks to promote centrist policymaking.

Despite his business background, Houghton often deviates from the GOP script. A supporter of abortion rights, he takes a dim view of social and religious conservatives who he thinks wield too much influence on Republican leaders. "The people who are posing as firefighters for the Republican Party, in a way, are really the pyromaniacs," he once said.

In 2001, Houghton was one of three Republicans to vote with Democrats on the International Relations Committee to restore funding for overseas family planning organizations that counsel clients on abortion. The money had been eliminated by an executive order from President Bush.

The following year, Houghton was one of only six House Republicans to vote against a resolution that Bush sought authorizing the use of U.S. military force against Iraq. Houghton said he favored a multilateral approach to dealing with Iraq and feared that a solo offensive by the United States would spur terrorist attacks.

And Houghton has clashed with social and religious conservatives on free-trade issues. He is against efforts to impose economic sanctions on countries in order to change their behavior. He opposed, for instance, legislation that would punish countries that persecute religious minorities.

In 1998, Houghton was one of only four Republicans to vote against all four articles of impeachment against President Clinton.

With a seat on the influential tax-writing Ways and Means panel, Houghton advocates research and development tax credits to help business. His reference point is his experience at Corning, where he strongly supported research that led to the firm's breakthroughs in fiber optics.

Houghton helped steer through the House billions of dollars in federal tax incentives to help New York City after the Sept. 11, 2001, terrorist attacks.

In the 106th Congress, Houghton became the chairman of the Ways and Means Oversight Subcommittee. He wrote what was designed to be the GOP response to Democratic efforts to require disclosure of political fundraising and spending by certain nonprofit organizations known as "527s," a reference to a section of the tax code. The debate was highly partisan, and although the Houghton measure eventually became law, it was narrowed in scope by GOP leaders.

From his perch on the International Relations Committee, Houghton pursues his longstanding interest in Africa. Though he never got to be a missionary, he provides financial assistance to a rural mission school in Zimbabwe, which he often visits. In 1999, the extent of the AIDS plague on the African continent hit home when he discovered that a friend, the superintendent of the school, had lost his son to the disease.

Ranked by Forbes magazine as one of the richest American politicians, Houghton is unassuming and colleagues find him personable. Several staffers have stuck with him for more than a decade, an eternity on Capitol Hill.

Houghton is carrying on the traditions of a patrician family that for years has run Corning Inc. in Steuben County. He served 19 years as chief executive officer of the company founded by the Houghton family in 1851. He also has been on the boards of Procter & Gamble, IBM Corp. and Citibank. Houghton's father and grandfather were in public service, his father as ambassador to France, his grandfather as a member of the House and then as ambassador to Germany and Great Britain.

Political opportunity knocked for Houghton after he had turned 60, just as he was planning to leave the United States for educational and religious work in Zimbabwe. In 1986, New York Gov. Mario M. Cuomo tapped Democratic Rep. Stan Lundine to run for lieutenant governor, leaving what was then the 34th District seat open.

Houghton was popular in his hometown of Corning, where Corning Glass is the major employer. Among other civic contributions, the company helped finance the restoration of the city after a devastating flood in 1972. While he had never been particularly active in local Republican affairs, Houghton had little trouble securing the GOP nomination. He pointed to his experience creating jobs and easily deflected attempts by his Democratic opponent, Cattaraugus County District Attorney Larry Himelein, to portray him as an elitist. He has returned to the House every two years since with at least two-thirds of the vote.

He had planned to leave Congress in 2000, but decided to be in position to wage what turned out to be a successful campaign to retain the small-town focus of the district (then the 31st) during redistricting. He launched a save-the-district petition drive and raised money for GOP state lawmakers drawing the new lines. After he won re-election in 2002 by a 52-point margin, Houghton again was pondering his electoral future.

KEY VOTES

2002

Yes Overhaul campaign finance law; ban "soft money" and restrict advocacy advertising
Yes Back Bush's defense budget increase
Yes Extend 1996 welfare law
Yes Adopt Bush's discretionary spending limit
Yes Pass GOP Medicare prescription drug plan
No Create independent Sept. 11 commission
No Extend union protections to Homeland Security Department employees
Yes Revive fast-track procedures for trade agreements
No Authorize war against Iraq
? Advance bankruptcy overhaul opposed by abortion opponents

2001

Yes Nullify Clinton Labor Department ergonomics rule
? Cut taxes by $1.35 trillion through fiscal 2011
Yes Maintain ban on oil drilling in Arctic National Wildlife Refuge
Yes Approve Bush proposal to limit managed-care plan liability for coverage decisions
? Divert money from crop subsidy payments to land conservation
Yes Expand law enforcement power to investigate suspected terrorists

CQ VOTE STUDIES

	PARTY UNITY		PRESIDENTIAL SUPPORT	
	Support	Oppose	Support	Oppose
2002	78%	22%	77%	23%
2001	84%	16%	73%	27%
2000	76%	24%	55%	45%
1999	70%	30%	49%	51%
1998	66%	34%	49%	51%

INTEREST GROUPS

	AFL-CIO	ADA	CCUS	ACU
2002	14%	20%	82%	62%
2001	18%	30%	82%	30%
2000	20%	20%	85%	52%
1999	11%	45%	87%	40%
1998	56%	30%	100%	29%

NEW YORK 29

Southern Tier – Elmira, Corning; Rochester suburbs

The 29th blankets much of the southwestern portion of New York known as the Southern Tier, encompassing a mix of forests, lakes and farms. Small towns and villages dot the countryside. It also reaches north to take in Rochester suburbs.

The district has a large presence of blue-collar workers and is home to diverse manufacturing interests including glassware, furniture and diesel engines. Agriculture also helps drive the economy, mostly through dairy farms and wineries. The Finger Lakes and surrounding parks draw thousands of visitors annually. Like much of the upstate region, the district's population was stagnant in the 1990s, with four counties losing population and the other four registering single-digit growth.

The 29th curls north and west to take in southern parts of Monroe County outside Rochester, where a plurality of the district's residents live. It wraps around the west, south and east sides of the city, taking in mostly GOP-leaning towns such as Chili, Pittsford and Perinton.

With Chautauqua County (Jamestown) moved to the Buffalo-area 27th in 2002 redistricting, the 29th's westernmost point is Cattaraugus County, a rural area that includes Allegany State Park and St. Bonaventure University. To the east, the GOP holds a better than 2-to-1 registration advantage over Democrats in Allegany, Steuben and Yates counties. Steuben County contains Corning, one of America's better-known company towns because of its glass products and costly crystal pieces.

Republicans hold an edge over Democrats in voter registration, and George W. Bush received 54 percent of the area's vote in the 2000 presidential election — his best showing in the state. The 29th also has the lowest percentage of Hispanic residents in any New York district.

MAJOR INDUSTRY
Agriculture, manufacturing, tourism

CITIES
Elmira, 30,940; Brighton (pt.), 25,869; Olean, 15,347

NOTABLE
The Corning Museum of Glass is a major tourist attraction.

NORTH CAROLINA

Gov. Michael F. Easley (D)

First elected: 2000
Length of term: 4 years
Term expires: 1/05
Salary: $118,430
Phone: (919) 733-4240
Hometown: Rocky Mount
Born: March 23, 1950; Nash County, N.C.
Religion: Roman Catholic
Family: Wife, Mary Easley; one child
Education: U. of North Carolina, B.A. 1972 (political science); North Carolina Central U., J.D. 1976
Career: Lawyer
Political highlights: Brunswick, Bladen and Columbus County district attorney, 1982-92; sought Democratic nomination for U.S. Senate, 1990; N.C. attorney general, 1993-2001
Election results:

2000 GENERAL		
Michael F. Easley (D)	1,530,324	52.0%
Richard Vinroot (R)	1,360,960	46.3%
Barbara J. Howe (LIBERT)	42,674	1.5%

Lt. Gov. Beverly Perdue (D)

First elected: 2000
Length of term: 4 years
Term expires: 1/05
Salary: $104,523
Phone: (919) 871-6482

STATE LEGISLATURE

General Assembly: Meets January-June
House: 120 members, 2-year terms
2003 breakdown: 60R, 60D; 92 men, 28 women
Salary: $13,951
Phone: (919) 733-3451
Senate: 50 members, 2-year terms
2003 breakdown: 22R, 28D; 43 men, 7 women
Salary: $13,951
Phone: (919) 733-6854

STATE TERM LIMITS

Governor: 2 consecutive terms
Senate: No
House: No

URBAN STATISTICS

CITY	POPULATION
Charlotte	540,828
Raleigh	276,093
Greensboro	223,891
Durham	187,035
Winston-Salem	185,776

REGISTERED VOTERS

Democrat	48%
Republican	34%
Unaffiliated	17%

POPULATION

2002 population (est.)	8,320,146
2000 population	8,049,313
1990 population	6,628,637
Percent change (1990-2000)	+21.4%
Rank among states (2002)	11
Median age	35.3
Born in state	63%
Foreign born	5.3%
Violent crime rate	498/100,000
Poverty level	12.3%
Federal workers	60,331
Military	118,281

REDISTRICTING

North Carolina gained one House seat in reapportionment. The state legislature drew a new 13-district map. The governor had no role in the process and the map was enacted on Dec. 5, 2001.

MISCELLANEOUS

Web: www.state.nc.us
Capital: Raleigh
STATE ELECTION OFFICIAL
(919) 733-7173
DEMOCRATIC HEADQUARTERS
(919) 821-2777
REPUBLICAN HEADQUARTERS
(919) 828-6423

District Statistics

DIST.	2000 VOTE FOR PRESIDENT BUSH	GORE	NADER	WHITE	BLACK	ASIAN	HISP	MEDIAN INCOME	WHITE COLLAR	BLUE COLLAR	SERVICE INDUSTRY	OVER 64	UNDER 18	COLLEGE EDUCATION	RURAL	SQ. MILES
1	41%	58%	0%	44%	50%	0%	3%	$28,410	46%	37%	18%	14%	26%	12%	52%	7,199
2	53	47	0	59	30	1	8	$36,510	52	34	14	10	26	16	50	3,956
3	65	35	0	76	17	1	4	$37,510	56	29	15	12	24	20	47	6,192
4	47	52	0	69	21	4	5	$53,847	75	14	11	8	25	48	17	1,253
5	67	32	0	88	7	1	4	$39,710	54	34	12	13	23	20	57	4,402
6	68	32	0	85	9	1	4	$43,503	56	33	11	14	24	23	48	2,944
7	51	48	0	63	23	0	4	$33,998	50	34	16	13	25	18	55	6,087
8	53	46	0	62	27	2	7	$38,390	53	33	14	11	26	18	31	3,283
9	64	35	0	83	10	2	4	$55,059	69	20	10	10	25	36	16	991
10	65	34	0	85	9	1	3	$37,649	45	42	12	13	24	14	50	3,302
11	58	41	0	90	5	0	3	$34,720	52	32	16	18	21	21	56	6,025
12	39	60	0	45	45	2	7	$35,775	52	32	16	11	26	19	11	821
13	49	50	0	63	27	2	6	$41,060	60	26	13	11	23	27	26	2,256
STATE	56	43	0	70	21	1	5	$39,184	56	31	14	12	24	23	40	48,711
U.S.	47.9	48.4	3	69	12	4	13	$41,994	60	25	15	12	26	24	21	3,537,438

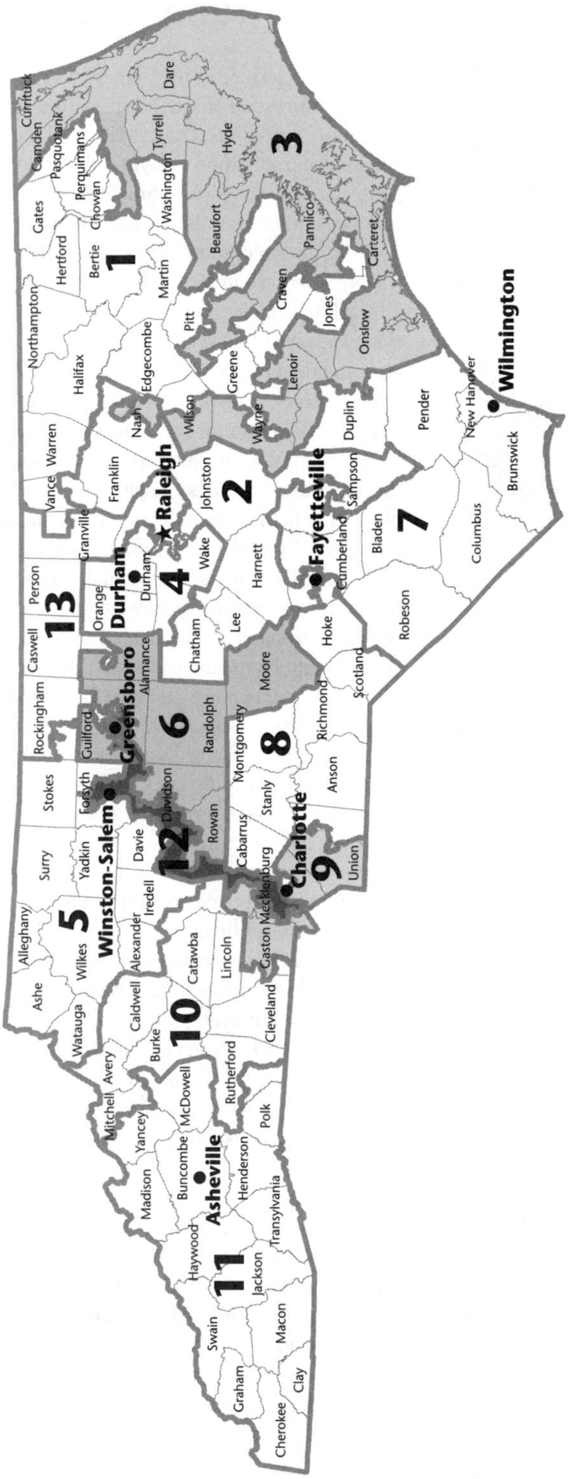

1
2
3
4
5
6
7
8
9
10
11
12
13
Wilmington
Raleigh
Durham
Greensboro
Winston-Salem
Fayetteville
Charlotte
Asheville
Currituck
Camden
Pasquotank
Perquimans
Chowan
Gates
Hertford
Bertie
Dare
Tyrrell
Washington
Hyde
Beaufort
Pamlico
Carteret
Craven
Jones
Onslow
Martin
Pitt
Northampton
Halifax
Edgecombe
Greene
Lenoir
Wilson
Nash
Wayne
Duplin
Pender
New Hanover
Brunswick
Warren
Vance
Franklin
Johnston
Sampson
Granville
Wake
Harnett
Cumberland
Bladen
Columbus
Person
Durham
Orange
Caswell
Alamance
Chatham
Lee
Hoke
Robeson
Moore
Scotland
Richmond
Rockingham
Guilford
Randolph
Montgomery
Anson
Stokes
Forsyth
Davidson
Stanly
Rowan
Cabarrus
Union
Mecklenburg
Surry
Yadkin
Davie
Iredell
Alleghany
Wilkes
Alexander
Catawba
Lincoln
Gaston
Ashe
Watauga
Caldwell
Burke
Cleveland
Avery
Rutherford
Mitchell
McDowell
Yancey
Polk
Madison
Buncombe
Henderson
Haywood
Transylvania
Swain
Jackson
Macon
Graham
Cherokee
Clay

Sen. John Edwards (D)

CAPITOL OFFICE
224-3154
edwards.senate.gov
225 Dirksen 20510-3306; fax 228-1374

COMMITTEES
Health, Education, Labor & Pensions
Judiciary
Small Business & Entrepreneurship
Select Intelligence

HOMETOWN
Raleigh

BORN
June 10, 1953, Seneca, S.C.

RELIGION
Methodist

FAMILY
Wife, Elizabeth Anania Edwards; four children (one deceased)

EDUCATION
North Carolina State U., B.S. 1974 (textiles); U. of North Carolina, J.D. 1977

CAREER
Lawyer

POLITICAL HIGHLIGHTS
No previous office

ELECTION RESULTS

1998 GENERAL		
John Edwards (D)	1,029,237	51.2%
Lauch Faircloth (R)	945,943	47.0%
Barbara J. Howe (LIBERT)	36,963	1.8%
1998 PRIMARY		
John Edwards (D)	277,468	51.4%
David Grier "D.G." Martin (D)	149,049	27.6%
Ella Scarborough (D)	55,486	10.3%
Robert Junior Ayers (D)	22,477	4.2%
Mike Robinson (D)	20,178	3.7%
James Everette Carmack (D)	8,200	1.5%
Gene Gay (D)	7,173	1.3%

Elected 1998; 1st term

When he arrived in the Senate in 1999, the self-assured Edwards immediately impressed his colleagues and the Democratic leadership as an articulate, ambitious, charismatic and moderate voice from the South — a felicitous combination of style, substance and drive. So it came as little surprise when Edwards, with ample encouragement, started exploring his current presidential candidacy early in his freshman term.

From his successful life as a plaintiffs' lawyer, Edwards came seemingly from nowhere in 1998 to win his seat in the Senate. It was his first foray into politics and he continues to cultivate an image as the plainspoken outsider. He says he sees the political middle as more representative of the public than conservative or liberal ideologies and talks frequently of the need to find a consensus on legislation. His oft-repeated phrase is that he wants to be a "champion for the regular people."

He affiliates with two moderate groups, the Senate New Democrats and the bipartisan Centrist Coalition, and he works closely with other like-minded senators, including Republican Olympia J. Snowe of Maine and Democrat Evan Bayh of Indiana, who also is his frequent jogging partner.

Edwards' status as a newcomer to the center stage of national politics, which makes him so attractive to many, is also potentially his greatest weakness. To sustain a presidential candidacy he will have to convince voters — starting with Democratic Party insiders and financial backers — that he has the domestic and international policy heft, and the stomach for political combat at its most ferocious, to lead the nation in a way that inspires confidence.

"He has all the ingredients you're looking for" save one, John B. Breaux of Louisiana, a leading centrist Democrat in the Senate, told the New York Times. "What is missing is a great deal of seasoning or experience in the business of government."

In his first term, Edwards, like many lawmakers, has stressed the need to protect Social Security and Medicare, to improve public education and to provide better health care delivery. He emerged early as a lead sponsor of legislation to give patients new rights in dealing with their managed-care plans, working closely with Democrat Edward M. Kennedy of Massachusetts and Republican John McCain of Arizona. His willingness to work with Republicans while remaining a loyal Democrat on most issues has won him friends and influenced colleagues. So has his deft touch during debates, particularly on the issue of patients' rights — a skill that reflects his background as one of the nation's most successful trial lawyers.

In the months leading to his decision to run for president, Edwards gave a series of policy addresses designed to raise his profile and boost his credibility on other issues, including national security and foreign affairs. In a speech at the Brookings Institution, he called for a new domestic intelligence agency, more money for border control information technology and more staffing for immigration, border patrol and consular offices. "Washington is not doing enough to make America safe," Edwards said.

From his seat on the Intelligence Committee, Edwards also has worked to sharpen his foreign policy credentials with fact-finding trips abroad, including stops in London and Brussels.

Despite his lack of political experience, Edwards was quickly viewed as a star in his freshman class. After he arrived in 1999, his first order of business was the impeachment trial of President Clinton. The proceedings were a defining event — a chance to show off his skills as an orator and litigator —

and Edwards was picked by Minority Leader Tom Daschle for the three-person team that deposed key players in the House's case against the president, including former White House intern Monica Lewinsky. The experience, coming on a weekend in which the nation was captivated by the nationally televised trial, gave Edwards unusual early exposure to the public. But many senators say it was actually his speech — during the closed-door deliberations — that first impressed them. In his remarks, Edwards laid out the case for not removing the president from office.

"I think we saw firsthand why he made so much money talking to jurors," said Republican Gordon H. Smith of Oregon, a frozen foods company executive, "and why I had to make my money selling frozen peas."

Edwards' impeachment role was just the first exercise of his powers of persuasion. He was credited with upstaging Republican opponents from the first when the chamber debated patients' rights legislation. In the 107th, he and McCain announced a bipartisan patients' rights proposal, which GOP leaders, including President Bush, denounced.

With Republican Susan Collins of Maine, Edwards also brokered a deal on legislation to make it more difficult to repeatedly extend patent protections on pharmaceuticals. With fellow moderate Democrat Joseph I. Lieberman of Connecticut, one of his 2004 rivals, he helped lead the fight against Bush's plans to revise the Clean Air Act.

Edwards has proposed an education plan that, among other things, would boost federal aid for teacher training and guarantee free college tuition to students who commit to teach at least five years in communities that are short of teachers. He has called for trimming the non-national security federal work force by 10 percent over the next decade and for tax cuts for small businesses that he says would jump start the economy.

When Edwards was growing up in Robbins, N.C., a small Piedmont town, his father was a textile worker and his mother ran a small furniture refinishing shop. He was the first in his family to attend college, working his way through North Carolina State University, earning his law degree from the University of North Carolina and graduating with honors from both schools. He then went on to earn millions of dollars from his share of lawsuit settlements, often representing families suing insurance companies and other large corporations.

In 1996 Edwards' 16-year-old son, Wade, was killed in a car crash — just weeks after being named a national finalist in a "What it means to be an American" essay contest. After a visit at the White House with first lady Hillary Rodham Clinton, Wade went on to Capitol Hill, where he ended up spending more than an hour in conversation with North Carolina's Republican Sen. Jesse Helms. Helms, who had never met John Edwards, later eulogized the boy on the Senate floor as "one of the most impressive young men I have ever met."

Two years later Edwards relied largely on his personal fortune to fund his Senate campaign. One-term GOP incumbent Lauch Faircloth tried to attack Edwards' trial lawyer background, but the Democrat proudly pointed out that he had spent his adult life "being an advocate for people, mostly children and mostly families." Edwards painted himself as a political outsider and ran a well-scripted campaign. He defeated Faircloth by 4 percentage points, becoming one of only three challengers to unseat an incumbent that year.

The victory continued a pattern going back five Senate elections. Not since Democrat Sam J. Ervin Jr. held the seat from 1954 through 1974 has anyone occupying it been able to last more than one term. That streak will continue in 2004 if Edwards makes a presidential bid and does not seek a second Senate term. Under North Carolina law, he can run for both offices simultaneously, but some advisers say that may be politically risky.

KEY VOTES

2002

Yes Pass farm bill reversing crop subsidy limits
No Postpone tougher automobile fuel efficiency standards
Yes Overhaul campaign finance law; ban "soft money" and restrict advocacy advertising
Yes Set federal election standards
No Support oil drilling in Arctic National Wildlife Refuge
Yes Revive fast-track procedures for trade agreements
Yes Create federal insurance coverage for catastrophic terrorist losses
Yes Tighten federal accounting and corporate governance regulation
Yes Advance bipartisan Medicare prescription drug plan
Yes Create independent Sept. 11 commission
Yes Back Democratic Homeland Security Department proposal
Yes Authorize war against Iraq

2001

No Confirm John Ashcroft as attorney general
No Nullify Clinton Labor Department ergonomics rule
No Cut taxes by $1.35 trillion through fiscal 2011
Yes Pass Democratic bill to bolster rights of patients in managed-care plans
No Permit a new round of military base closings
Yes Expand law enforcement power to investigate suspected terrorists

CQ VOTE STUDIES

	PARTY UNITY		PRESIDENTIAL SUPPORT	
	Support	Oppose	Support	Oppose
2002	84%	16%	76%	24%
2001	91%	9%	67%	33%
2000	94%	6%	92%	8%
1999	92%	8%	87%	13%

INTEREST GROUPS

	AFL-CIO	ADA	CCUS	ACU
2002	100%	70%	55%	30%
2001	100%	95%	50%	16%
2000	75%	85%	40%	12%
1999	100%	90%	41%	8%

Sen. Elizabeth Dole (R)

CAPITOL OFFICE
224-6342
120 Russell 20510-3301; fax 228-1339

COMMITTEES
Agriculture, Nutrition & Forestry
(Production & Price Competitiveness - chairwoman)
Armed Services
Banking, Housing & Urban Affairs
Special Aging

HOMETOWN
Salisbury

BORN
July 29, 1936, Salisbury, N.C.

RELIGION
Presbyterian

FAMILY
Husband, Bob Dole

EDUCATION
Duke U., B.A. 1958 (political science); Harvard U., M.A. 1960 (education & government), J.D. 1965

CAREER
Red Cross president; lawyer; White House aide

POLITICAL HIGHLIGHTS
Federal Trade Commission, 1973-79; U.S. Transportation secretary, 1983-87; U.S. Labor secretary, 1989-90; sought Republican nomination for president, 2000

ELECTION RESULTS

2002 GENERAL		
Elizabeth Dole (R)	1,248,664	53.6%
Erskine B. Bowles (D)	1,047,983	45.0%
Sean Haugh (LIBERT)	33,807	1.5%
2002 PRIMARY		
Elizabeth Dole (R)	342,631	80.4%
Jim Snyder (R)	60,477	14.2%
Jim Parker (R)	8,752	2.1%
Ada M. Fisher (R)	6,045	1.4%

Elected 2002; 1st term

Dole brings a decidedly more temperate tone to the Senate than did her five-term predecessor, conservative Republican firebrand Jesse Helms. Yet there will likely be a less dramatic contrast in their voting records: Dole is a Republican loyalist who expresses mainly conservative views on issues, albeit with much less fervor than Helms.

Although she does not consider herself to be a product of the feminist movement, Dole is a pioneer among women and boasts one of the strongest résumés in politics. She has worked in the administrations of the six presidents who preceded Bill Clinton. Yet Dole will have to persuade some skeptics of her gravitas as a freshman senator.

Returning to her native North Carolina after nearly 40 years on the Washington political scene, Dole was propelled to front-runner status by her past tenures as secretary of two Cabinet agencies; her eight years as president of the American Red Cross; her marriage to Bob Dole, longtime Kansas senator and 1996 presidential candidate; and her own bid for the 2000 Republican presidential nomination.

Boosted by her effusive Southern charm and her persistent celebrity, she overcame a well-grounded Democratic opponent in former White House Chief of Staff Erskine Bowles to win election in 2002.

She was greeted in the Senate as an old friend; she has socialized with and testified before many of her colleagues in her previous incarnations as Cabinet secretary and senatorial wife.

On most issues, Dole toes the Republican line. She favors making permanent the 10-year, $1.35 trillion tax cut that President Bush pushed to enactment in 2001, touts the Republicans' prescription drug benefits proposal and supported giving Bush authority for military intervention in Iraq.

She also backs the president's proposal to add "personal retirement accounts" to Social Security, a position that state Democrats spent millions of dollars during the campaign trying to discredit by branding the idea as "privatization" of the federal pension system for senior citizens.

Dole advocates local control of education, proposing to attract more teachers by giving them tax breaks, protecting them from lawsuits and forgiving some student loans. She said in the campaign that her first priority in Congress would be adding a line-item veto to the Constitution so the president could trim wasteful spending. She says she has always been "pro-life" and would oppose efforts to further restrict gun ownership.

After graduating from Harvard Law School, Dole began her Washington career as a consumer affairs aide to President Johnson and then to President Nixon. Originally a Democrat, she switched her party affiliation when she married Bob Dole in 1975. She then served as a member of the Federal Trade Commission under Presidents Ford and Carter and as assistant for public liaison in the administration of President Reagan.

In February 1983, she became the first woman to serve as secretary of transportation. In January 1989, she was sworn in as secretary of labor under the first President George Bush. She did not enter the private sector until 1991, when she became president of the American Red Cross.

Though she was regarded in the run-up to 2000 as the first woman to make a serious bid for the presidency, critics derided her campaign appearances as overly controlled and dubbed her a political lightweight. She abandoned her campaign in October 1999, before a single primary or caucus vote was cast, citing the overwhelming fundraising advantage that party front-runner George W. Bush had established.

Dole had not lived in North Carolina since she graduated from Duke University in 1958, and in the 2002 Senate campaign some opponents tried to portray her as a Washington insider and a carpetbagger. But this criticism was blunted by the fact that Democratic nominee Bowles' main political credential also meant that he had spent his recent years elsewhere — as chief of staff to Clinton.

Seeking to parry questions about her depth of knowledge on issues, the Republican nominee drafted a "Dole Plan." It contained specific proposals to create jobs in the state, which was experiencing higher-than-average unemployment because of the decline of the once-thriving textile industry. With the economy slumping, Dole also said she would seek to cut taxes and reduce regulation on businesses to promote job growth.

Her plan backed the Bush administration's pro-trade agenda. Bowles hit Dole hard for her support of authorizing fast-track trade negotiating authority for the president, saying the measure would further decimate the textile industry in the state. But Dole defended her stand, saying negotiations with other nations would give the state's workers a level playing field on which to compete. "I would never vote for a plan that would hurt our North Carolina industries," she said. "But also, I want vigorous enforcement of existing agreements. This was not done in the Clinton administration."

Another part of her plan was a tobacco quota buyout proposal, which would give tobacco growers higher payments per pound by using the existing 15-cents per pack excise tax on cigarettes. She said the plan, which she borrowed from Helms, would infuse the state's rural economy with billions of dollars. In the 108th, Dole chairs the Agriculture Committee's Production and Price Competitiveness Subcommittee, whose jurisdiction includes tobacco and other agricultural commodities such as dairy products, peanuts, sugar, rice and soybeans.

Dole was able to make good on her promise to get a seat on the Armed Services Committee, a pivotal position for a state with several military bases. And she got a third major committee — Banking — which is a good match with Charlotte's interests as a regional financial center.

Despite her reliably Republican rhetoric, Dole often had to walk a fine line between emphasizing her GOP credentials and trying not to alienate middle-of-the-road voters and conservative Democrats.

One case in point was her position on the Family and Medical Leave Act, which guarantees workers time off to attend to major personal matters. Though she opposed the measure when Clinton signed it into law in 1993 and when she ran for president in 1999, she said in 2002 that it had proven itself over 10 years and that she would like to see it expanded.

As in her presidential bid, Dole again was criticized from some quarters as too scripted, but she relaxed substantially, spending much of her time holding barbeques and showing her interest in local issues by visiting the state's 100 counties. She adopted a folksy tone that ingratiated her to the state's working-class voters.

Dole benefited from the fact that she had only minor opposition in the September 2002 Republican primary, while Bowles had serious opposition for the Democratic nomination. That allowed Dole to spend the summer touring the state and accruing almost universally positive publicity, especially from many small newspapers that published adoring accounts of her visits to their towns.

Rural voters had much to do with her impressive 9 percentage point win over Bowles, as did the strong early endorsement she received from former political rival Bush. Her 53.6 percent tally was the highest percentage any North Carolina Senate candidate had received since 1978.

Rep. Frank W. Ballance Jr. (D)

Elected 2002; 1st term

Arriving with 19 years of experience in the North Carolina Legislature, Ballance was elected by his colleagues as president of the Democratic freshman Class of 2002. But he served notice that his style would be different from that of his predecessor in the House, fellow Democrat Eva Clayton.

"I don't think I can be as kind and nice as she is," he said. "She can give and take with anyone. But my style is different. I don't want to say I'm abrasive, but I don't mind mixing it up a bit."

Both are African-American political trailblazers. Ballance was elected in 1982 as the first black state representative for his area since Reconstruction. A decade later, Clayton and Democrat Melvin Watt became the first blacks sent to Congress by North Carolina in the modern era. Ballance ran with the endorsement of Clayton, a close friend since they attended law school together in the early 1960s. Both were political activists in the 1960s and 1970s in northeastern North Carolina. It was a time, Ballance recalls, when the area "was majority black, but blacks had no political power."

Ballance says his congressional votes largely will fall in line with Clayton's mainly liberal pattern. He shares her priority of directing money — especially federal education aid — to the 1st District, which has a large share of poor residents and some of the nation's biggest annual peanut, tobacco and cotton harvests. Ballance, who grew up on a farm, sought and won a seat on the Agriculture Committee, where Clayton also had served.

As a state senator, Ballance was behind a measure aimed at decreasing racial profiling by requiring officers to maintain a record of people they stop, the reason for searching and whether anything was found. He also sponsored a bill, which eventually became law, that made it illegal to execute the mentally retarded in North Carolina.

Ballance won a four-person Democratic House primary with 47 percent of the vote; the only white candidate, Pasquotank County Commissioner Sam Davis, finished second with 26 percent. In the fall, Ballance trounced Republican Greg Dority, a security consultant, by 29 percentage points.

CAPITOL OFFICE
225-3101
frank.ballance@mail.house.gov
www.house.gov/ballance
413 Cannon 20515-3301; fax 225-3354

COMMITTEES
Agriculture
Small Business

HOMETOWN
Warrenton

BORN
Feb. 15, 1942, Windsor, N.C.

RELIGION
Baptist

FAMILY
Wife, Bernadine S. Ballance; three children

EDUCATION
North Carolina Central U., B.A. 1963 (political science), J.D. 1965

MILITARY SERVICE
N.C. National Guard, 1968-71

CAREER
Lawyer; law professor

POLITICAL HIGHLIGHTS
N.C. House, 1983-87; sought Democratic nomination for N.C. Senate, 1986; N.C. Senate, 1989-2002

ELECTION RESULTS

2002 GENERAL		
Frank W. Ballance Jr. (D)	93,157	63.7%
Greg Dority (R)	50,907	34.8%
Mike Ruff (LIBERT)	2,093	1.4%
2002 PRIMARY		
Frank W. Ballance Jr. (D)	37,833	47.0%
Sam Davis (D)	20,758	25.8%
Janice McKenzie Cole (D)	14,410	17.9%
Christine L. Fitch (D)	7,526	9.4%

NORTH CAROLINA 1

Northeast – part of Goldsboro, Rocky Mount and Greenville

Situated among the tobacco fields and Baptist churches of eastern North Carolina, the 1st is a poor, rural Democratic stronghold. It has the lowest education and income levels of any North Carolina congressional district.

The main body of the district rests along the Virginia border, with appendages winding south to take in parts of several of the region's commercial centers — Goldsboro, Greenville and Kinston. Redistricting following the 2000 census kept the 1st's basic shape intact, and it remains the most heavily black district in North Carolina (50 percent).

The area's economy is based overwhelmingly on manufacturing and agriculture. Cotton and peanut fields prevail in the northern counties, while tobacco, hogs and poultry dominate farther south. Manufacturing, primarily of textiles and lumber products, is scattered throughout.

Registered Democrats outnumber Republicans by more than 4-to-1 in the 1st, which backed Democrat Michael F. Easley with 70 percent in the 2000 governor's race. Many white voters claim the Democratic roots of their forefathers but often support GOP candidates at the state and national level. Republicans also find support in the increasingly affluent coastal areas of Beaufort and Craven counties.

MAJOR INDUSTRY
Agriculture, manufacturing, health care

MILITARY BASES
Seymour Johnson Air Force Base, 4,298 military, 542 civilian (2002)

CITIES
Goldsboro (pt.), 36,187; Rocky Mount (pt.), 32,062; Wilson (pt.), 25,068; Greenville (pt.), 22,028

NOTABLE
Caleb Bradham started selling "Brad's Drink" in 1898 at his New Bern drug store — the beverage is now known as Pepsi Cola.

Rep. Bob Etheridge (D)

CAPITOL OFFICE
225-4531
www.house.gov/etheridge
1533 Longworth 20515-3302; fax 225-5662

COMMITTEES
Agriculture
Select Homeland Security

HOMETOWN
Lillington

BORN
Aug. 7, 1941, Sampson County, N.C.

RELIGION
Presbyterian

FAMILY
Wife, Faye Cameron Etheridge; three children

EDUCATION
Campbell U., B.S. 1965 (business administration)

MILITARY SERVICE
Army, 1965-67

CAREER
Hardware store owner; tobacco farmer

POLITICAL HIGHLIGHTS
Harnett County Commission, 1973-77 (chairman, 1975-77); N.C. House, 1979-87; N.C. superintendent of Public Instruction, 1989-96

ELECTION RESULTS

2002 GENERAL		
Bob Etheridge (D)	100,121	65.4%
Joseph L. Ellen (R)	50,965	33.3%
Gary Minter (LIBERT)	2,098	1.4%
2002 PRIMARY		
Bob Etheridge (D)		unopposed
2000 GENERAL		
Bob Etheridge (D)	146,733	58.3%
Doug Haynes (R)	103,011	40.9%

PREVIOUS WINNING PERCENTAGES
1998 (57%); 1996 (53%)

Elected 1996; 4th term

Etheridge is a centrist Southern Democrat who departs from many in his party on trade issues. His district is a dichotomy: It is home to the state capital of Raleigh and its high-tech Research Triangle Park as well as more-rural counties where family tobacco and hog farms dot the landscape.

Etheridge was the only Democrat in the North Carolina delegation voting in 2002 to give President Bush fast-track trade negotiating authority, which limits Congress' role in trade agreements. North Carolina's powerful textile lobby, which fears that fast-track authority will cause the state to lose jobs to foreign competitors, promised retribution at the voting booth for Etheridge.

But the 2nd District is not so concerned with textiles. Etheridge has a strong base among tobacco farmers and others in agribusiness, and the Raleigh area is more interested in attracting new technology firms to the state. Etheridge has wisely backed both of these interests.

He pressed for a trade agreement to allow tobacco farmers to export their product to China. In 2000, Etheridge voted for legislation permanently granting China normal trade relations with the United States, contending that it would provide the North Carolina economy with expanded markets. "Gaining access to China, the largest market in the world, will only help our state and our nation expand our economic leadership and extend our ideals of liberty, democracy and freedom to those who have been shut off from such basic rights and values for far too long," he said.

Etheridge opposes those in his own party who seek to clamp down on the tobacco industry. A part-time tobacco farmer himself, Etheridge has long fought against efforts to end the federal support program for tobacco, arguing that growers could not switch profitably to another crop and that land values in tobacco communities would plummet. People will continue to smoke, he says, but without the existing support system, small farmers will give way to large corporate farms owned and operated by cigarette manufacturers. He sits on the Agriculture Committee, where he can look after the interests of his district's farmers.

Etheridge was disappointed when compensation for tobacco farmers was left out of the 2002 farm bill. But he made another attempt to aid them, sponsoring legislation with Republican Ernie Fletcher of Kentucky to provide payments to tobacco growers and quota holders.

Etheridge has also fought the perennial effort in the House to curtail spending on the federal price-support program for peanuts, another key crop in North Carolina. Critics of the federal peanut program say it inflates the price of peanuts at the expense of consumers. Etheridge played a key role in the 2002 farm bill overhaul of the peanut program, which replaced quotas with marketing loans, direct payments and counter-cyclical payments to provide funds when market prices fall.

Etheridge splits his votes evenly between his party and the White House. He supported President Bush's position 47 percent of the time in the 107th. It is never far from his mind that the 2nd District has conservative leanings; the district voted for Bob Dole in 1996 and George W. Bush in 2000. When he attacks Republicans, it is generally over issues that resonate in his district, such as GOP attempts to restrict spending for disaster relief or schools.

Before coming to Congress, Etheridge was the top man in North Carolina's public school system for almost eight years. He has spoken frequently and at length on the House floor of his desire to "build on what is working well in our public schools, rather than scapegoating public school principals, teachers, parents and children."

Etheridge favors proposals to develop voluntary national tests for elementary school students, but he opposes private school tuition voucher plans that "will only divert attention away from improving public schools." He believes the federal government should devote more dollars to the repair and construction of schools. "I have seen multimillion-dollar prisons next door to crummy, crumbling, decaying public schools," Etheridge once said, "and then we have the gall to tell our children that education is important. They can see the difference in where we put our money."

On the Science Committee in the 107th, Etheridge won approval of his bill to improve hurricane forecasting, especially for inland areas where flooding can be a serious problem. Etheridge argued that fewer lives would have been lost in the wake of Hurricane Floyd in 1999 if inland residents had had a better sense of what was in store. Etheridge took a leave from the Science Committee in the 108th Congress when he was appointed to the Homeland Security Committee.

Born, raised and educated in east-central North Carolina, Etheridge was a hardware store owner and tobacco farmer when he first entered politics in 1972. He won election to the Harnett County Commission, serving for four years, the last two as chairman. In 1978, he won the first of four terms in the North Carolina General Assembly, where he rose to chair the Appropriations Committee. Then he moved to statewide office, holding the school superintendency for eight years.

That background made Etheridge the choice of 2nd District Democrats to contest the 1996 re-election of freshman Republican David Funderburk, who had been a zealous supporter of the House GOP's conservative agenda in the 104th Congress. Following the national Democratic script, Etheridge called Funderburk a threat to entitlement programs such as Social Security, Medicare and Medicaid. Etheridge's deep local roots helped him win with 53 percent of the vote.

In 1998, conservative state Sen. Dan Page and the national GOP went after Etheridge aggressively. Page was the first GOP candidate to air attack ads tying the Democratic candidate to President Clinton and his White House sex scandal. But Etheridge had given Republicans little opportunity to tag him as a liberal, and he won by 16 percentage points.

He increased his victory margin to 17 points in 2000, defeating GOP candidate Doug Haynes, a local businessman. In 2002, with the district made substantially more Democratic by redistricting, Etheridge posted his best showing, gaining a 32-point victory over first-time candidate Joseph Ellen.

KEY VOTES

2002

- Yes Overhaul campaign finance law; ban "soft money" and restrict advocacy advertising
- Yes Back Bush's defense budget increase
- No Extend 1996 welfare law
- No Adopt Bush's discretionary spending limit
- No Pass GOP Medicare prescription drug plan
- Yes Create independent Sept. 11 commission
- Yes Extend union protections to Homeland Security Department employees
- Yes Revive fast-track procedures for trade agreements
- Yes Authorize war against Iraq
- Yes Advance bankruptcy overhaul opposed by abortion opponents

2001

- No Nullify Clinton Labor Department ergonomics rule
- No Cut taxes by $1.35 trillion through fiscal 2011
- Yes Maintain ban on oil drilling in Arctic National Wildlife Refuge
- No Approve Bush proposal to limit managed-care plan liability for coverage decisions
- No Divert money from crop subsidy payments to land conservation
- Yes Expand law enforcement power to investigate suspected terrorists

CQ VOTE STUDIES

	PARTY UNITY		PRESIDENTIAL SUPPORT	
	Support	Oppose	Support	Oppose
2002	87%	13%	50%	50%
2001	83%	17%	44%	56%
2000	84%	16%	65%	35%
1999	79%	21%	67%	33%
1998	81%	19%	73%	27%

INTEREST GROUPS

	AFL-CIO	ADA	CCUS	ACU
2002	78%	80%	60%	24%
2001	92%	85%	57%	36%
2000	70%	60%	66%	28%
1999	89%	85%	48%	24%
1998	89%	80%	65%	28%

NORTH CAROLINA 2

Central — parts of Raleigh and Fayetteville

From the thriving state capital of Raleigh, the 2nd pinwheels east, north and south to take in several surrounding rural counties and part of Fayetteville. While the high-tech Research Triangle Park, the area's economic hub, lies in the neighboring 4th, its influence radiates through the low hills of this eastern Piedmont district.

Research Triangle techies, university academics and government employees live in Raleigh and form the basis of the district's Democratic tilt. Much of the region consists of booming and increasingly urban bedroom communities such as Garner. Sprawl has begun to infiltrate surrounding counties as well, but they still rely primarily on tobacco farming (especially in Johnston and Harnett counties) and blue-collar manufacturing jobs. Redistricting after the 2000 census added a strong military presence, as the 2nd now contains Pope Air Force Base and part of Fort Bragg, located at the southwestern edge of the district.

Redistricting also lessened the 2nd's conservative lean by excising parts of Wake and Nash counties and adding a black-majority section of Fayetteville. The 2nd contains the mostly black and strongly Democratic southeastern section of Raleigh, and it has a higher percentage of Hispanics residents (8 percent) than any other district in the state. While the Democrats' 30-point registration advantage exaggerates the party's edge — Republicans run well in areas such as Johnston County even though Democrats have more registrants — the GOP has a tough time here.

MAJOR INDUSTRY

State government, higher education, agriculture

MILITARY BASES

Fort Bragg (Army), 46,463 military, 4,245 civilian (shared with the 8th District); Pope Air Force Base, 5,300 military, 677 civilian (2002)

CITIES

Fayetteville (pt.), 49,899; Raleigh (pt.), 45,368; Fort Bragg (unincorporated), 29,183; Sanford, 23,220

NOTABLE

A highway sign outside Sanford claims that it is the brick capital of the United States; The Harnett County town of Erwin grew up around a denim plant, formerly called itself the "denim capital of the world," and still holds a fall festival called "Denim Days."

Rep. Walter B. Jones (R)

CAPITOL OFFICE
225-3415
congjones@mail.house.gov
www.house.gov/jones
422 Cannon 20515-3303; fax 225-3286

COMMITTEES
Armed Services
Financial Services
Resources

HOMETOWN
Farmville

BORN
Feb. 10, 1943, Farmville, N.C.

RELIGION
Roman Catholic

FAMILY
Wife, Joe Anne Jones; one child

EDUCATION
North Carolina State U., attended 1962-65; Atlantic Christian College, B.A. 1967 (history)

MILITARY SERVICE
N.C. National Guard, 1967-71

CAREER
Lighting company executive; insurance benefits company executive

POLITICAL HIGHLIGHTS
N.C. House, 1983-93 (served as a Democrat); sought Democratic nomination for U.S. House, 1992

ELECTION RESULTS

2002 GENERAL		
Walter B. Jones (R)	131,448	90.7%
Gary Goodson (LIBERT)	13,486	9.3%
2002 PRIMARY		
Walter B. Jones (R)		unopposed
2000 GENERAL		
Walter B. Jones (R)	121,940	61.4%
Leigh Harvey McNairy (D)	74,058	37.3%
David F. Russell (LIBERT)	2,457	1.2%

PREVIOUS WINNING PERCENTAGES
1998 (62%); 1996 (63%); 1994 (53%)

Elected 1994; 5th term

Jones grew up in a political household and early on started following in his father's footsteps, first into the family business and later into politics. But the younger Jones, now approaching the end of a decade in the House, is blazing his own political career in eastern North Carolina — one far off the path of Walter B. Jones Sr.

The most obvious departure is that the father, who died in 1992 as he was preparing to retire after 26 years in Congress, was a Democrat. The incumbent congressman switched parties and joined the Republicans in 1993, a year before winning election to the House on his second try. A member of the Republican Study Group, the House GOP's most conservative members, he is far more conservative than his father, routinely garnering ratings of 95 percent or more from the American Conservative Union. (His father's annual scores were closer to 20 percent at the end of his career.)

And unlike the senior Jones — whose service with an earlier generation of lawmakers and whose post as a committee chairman served to promote pragmatic, result-oriented dealings — the younger Jones is one of the few unreconstructed "true believers" of the GOP takeover Class of 1994. That class was marked by its members' uncompromising insistence, at least initially, that the party stand firm for the core conservative principles they espoused in their campaigns. Jones, in a gentlemanly, understated style, still holds to this course, even after many of his colleagues have decided that a dose of pragmatism and compromise is necessary.

His conservatism is evident in his efforts to ensure that religious leaders can preach or speak about political candidates or topics. Jones says a little-known 1954 law means that religious leaders risk losing their tax-exempt status if they campaign for specific candidates. He wants to repeal that provision. The bill was defeated in the House in 2002, but Jones introduced it again in the 108th Congress.

After graduating from college in 1967, Jones became an executive with the family's office supply company, later moving on to other business ventures. It was not until he was almost 40 that Jones first sought elective office.

He started out small, winning a seat in the state House, where he served for a decade. And when he did try to follow his father in the national political arena — seeking to be his successor in 1992 — he was rebuffed, losing a runoff in the Democratic primary to Eva Clayton in a district that had been redrawn as black-majority after the 1990 census.

Jones comes down on the conservative side of most issues, including allowing prayer in public schools, providing school vouchers to help parents pay for private school tuition and increasing military spending. He frequently takes to the House floor to demand tax cuts and advocates a phase-out of the tax code. Jones was an eager backer of the House GOP "Contract With America" legislative agenda in his first term, and he votes a dependable Republican line, siding with his party nearly 90 percent of the time. A notable exception has been his consistent opposition to measures to liberalize foreign trade.

On the Armed Services Committee, Jones looks out for the military installations of the 3rd District and has written a number of bills aimed at improving pay, benefits and housing for military personnel, including one in the 106th Congress to give a $500 tax credit to military families who are eligible for food stamps. He undertook a crusade in the 106th Congress to block a Pentagon requirement that armed forces personnel be given an anthrax vaccination. Citing reports casting doubt on the safety of the vaccine, Jones proposed legislation to make the vaccination voluntary.

For all his conservative credentials, Jones, who represents a long swath of the Carolina coast, touts his concern for environmental protection when it comes to coastal matters. His district includes the tourist-rich Outer Banks barrier islands. During the 1998 campaign, he ran television advertising in which he was featured walking on the beach saying, "It's everybody's responsibility to make sure that our rivers and waterways are clean now and for future generations."

Jones succeeded in the 105th in enacting a law designed to preserve the wild horses of Shackleford Banks, a part of the Cape Lookout National Seashore. The National Park Service had been studying the horses' impact on area fauna, but Jones was not convinced the park service was doing enough to protect the animals. His measure requires the agency to work with a local foundation to ensure that the equine population does not go below 100.

Jones is a member of the Resources Committee and, in a show of bipartisanship, has joined with Democratic members who represent coastal districts to fight to retain the ban on offshore oil and gas drilling. He also was involved in the decade-long battle to preserve the 1870 lighthouse at Cape Hatteras. He pushed to build a stronger seawall to protect the landmark against beach erosion, but it was eventually decided that the lighthouse should be moved.

Jones is a fiscal conservative, often more so than his party's leaders. He voted against the massive transportation authorization bill in 1998 and the more massive end-of-year catchall spending bill, measures that were criticized by fiscal conservatives for breaking spending caps agreed to in 1997.

He has not been reticent, however, in speaking up for federal programs that are important to his district, such as the federal price-support program for peanut growers. He also has been vocal in protecting another important crop in his district — tobacco. During the Clinton administration, he said the Food and Drug Administration was conducting a "witch hunt" against the tobacco farmer. "This is Big Brother at its worst. What's next — prohibition of alcohol, caffeine, chocolate?" he railed on the House floor. "The government has no business in those decisions, and the FDA and commissioner have no authority to classify nicotine as a drug."

After switching to the GOP and setting his sights on the 3rd District, instead of his father's old 1st District seat, Jones in 1994 won 53 percent of the general-election vote to oust four-term Democrat H. Martin Lancaster. He has won re-election easily since then.

KEY VOTES

2002

No Overhaul campaign finance law; ban "soft money" and restrict advocacy advertising
Yes Back Bush's defense budget increase
Yes Extend 1996 welfare law
Yes Adopt Bush's discretionary spending limit
Yes Pass GOP Medicare prescription drug plan
Yes Create independent Sept. 11 commission
No Extend union protections to Homeland Security Department employees
No Revive fast-track procedures for trade agreements
Yes Authorize war against Iraq
No Advance bankruptcy overhaul opposed by abortion opponents

2001

Yes Nullify Clinton Labor Department ergonomics rule
? Cut taxes by $1.35 trillion through fiscal 2011
No Maintain ban on oil drilling in Arctic National Wildlife Refuge
Yes Approve Bush proposal to limit managed-care plan liability for coverage decisions
No Divert money from crop subsidy payments to land conservation
Yes Expand law enforcement power to investigate suspected terrorists

CQ VOTE STUDIES

	PARTY UNITY		PRESIDENTIAL SUPPORT	
	Support	Oppose	Support	Oppose
2002	89%	11%	72%	28%
2001	88%	12%	78%	22%
2000	92%	8%	19%	81%
1999	91%	9%	19%	81%
1998	92%	8%	21%	79%

INTEREST GROUPS

	AFL-CIO	ADA	CCUS	ACU
2002	22%	10%	63%	96%
2001	18%	10%	80%	92%
2000	10%	5%	61%	96%
1999	50%	15%	72%	100%
1998	10%	5%	72%	100%

NORTH CAROLINA 3

East – Jacksonville, part of Greenville, Outer Banks

The 3rd runs along the eastern shore from the Virginia border to north of Wilmington, sweeping from the fragile barrier islands of the Outer Banks to the tobacco and peanut fields of the coastal plain. It is a large swath of rural land inlaid with waterways, affluent vacation towns and military facilities; the closest thing to skyscrapers here are historic lighthouses that dot the shoreline.

Many residents earn their living through fishing, farming and tourism. The district's military bases have a large impact on the economy, notably Camp Lejeune, which deployed a high percentage of its Marines abroad in 2002-03. At the southern end, two fingers of land stretch west, taking in turkey, hog and wheat farms.

Redistricting following the 2000 census did not significantly overhaul the district's jagged shape. One leg of the 3rd stretches from Onslow County in the south, where Jacksonville and Camp Lejeune are located, all the way north to Nash County, including part of Rocky Mount.

The remap enhanced the 3rd's conservative lean by ceding to the 1st some northeastern counties with large black populations. In the 2002 Senate race, Republican Elizabeth Dole topped 60 percent of the vote in Onslow, Wayne and Cartaret counties, three of the four most-populous jurisdictions in the 3rd.

MAJOR INDUSTRY

Military, agriculture, tourism

MILITARY BASES

Camp Lejeune Marine Corps Base, 41,500 military, 4,861 civilian (2000); Cherry Point Marine Corps Air Station and Naval Air Depot, 8,223 military, 4,816 civilian (2003); New River Marine Corps Air Station, 5,866 military, 135 civilian (2000)

CITIES

Jacksonville, 66,715; Greenville (pt.), 38,448; Wilson (pt.), 19,337

NOTABLE

Kitty Hawk is where Wilbur and Orville Wright made their first flight; Dare County is named for Virginia Dare, the first child born of English parents in America (1587).

Rep. David E. Price (D)

CAPITOL OFFICE
225-1784
www.house.gov/price
2162 Rayburn 20515-3304; fax 225-2014

COMMITTEES
Appropriations

HOMETOWN
Chapel Hill

BORN
Aug. 17, 1940, Erwin, Tenn.

RELIGION
Baptist

FAMILY
Wife, Lisa Price; two children

EDUCATION
Mars Hill College, attended 1957-59; U. of North Carolina, B.A. 1961 (American history & math); Yale U., B.D. 1964 (theology), Ph.D. 1969 (political science)

CAREER
Professor

POLITICAL HIGHLIGHTS
N.C. Democratic Party chairman, 1983-84; U.S. House, 1987-95; defeated for re-election to U.S. House, 1994

ELECTION RESULTS

2002 GENERAL		
David E. Price (D)	132,185	61.2%
Tuan A. Nguyen (R)	78,095	36.2%
Ken Nelson (LIBERT)	5,766	2.7%
2002 PRIMARY		
David E. Price (D)		unopposed
2000 GENERAL		
David E. Price (D)	200,885	61.7%
Jess Ward (R)	119,412	36.6%
C. Brian Towey (LIBERT)	5,573	1.7%

PREVIOUS WINNING PERCENTAGES
1998 (57%); 1996 (54%); 1992 (65%); 1990 (58%); 1988 (58%); 1986 (56%)

Elected 1986; 8th term
Did not serve 1995-97

Price represents one of the South's more politically progressive districts and, on a wide range of issues, this political science professor-turned-politician has compiled a more liberal voting record than the typical Southern Democrat. The 4th District is home to the Raleigh-Durham-Chapel Hill Research Triangle Park, where many academics and Northern transplants have come to work.

Now well into his second stint in the House, Price assiduously tends to his district's needs from a seat on the Appropriations Committee, a priority that has taken on increasing importance as the Bush administration has sought to restrain the growth of many domestic research enterprises to shift additional funds toward defense. Price is particularly watchful of funding levels at the National Science Foundation, which in recent years has channeled hundreds of grants to Research Triangle facilities. In the 108th Congress, Price is on both sides of the guns vs. butter tussle: He added an assignment on the new Homeland Security Appropriations Subcommittee.

He also cites education as a top concern, particularly teacher recruitment. "We need 2.3 million teachers in the next 10 years in this country, and I don't think we have any idea where they're coming from," Price says.

Although Price pursues a centrist course on politically charged home-state issues such as tobacco regulation, he generally votes with the majority of his party. He consistently backs abortion rights and environmental protection measures, and he was a vocal opponent of President Bush's 2001 tax cut.

One way Price keeps his constituents happy is by using his seat on Appropriations to funnel federal dollars to his district. In the 107th Congress, for example, he earmarked funds in the Labor-Health and Human Services-Education spending bill for a new $500,000 magnetic resonance imaging facility at Durham County Regional Hospital, $250,000 to enhance technology at rural and low-income North Carolina schools, and another $250,000 for technology grants to the North Carolina Community College System. In the 106th, he battled for disaster relief funds in the wake of Hurricane Floyd, and he also landed $49 million for an Environmental Protection Agency facility in Research Triangle.

Price frequently sides with organized labor, although he has split with the unions on trade policy at times. He voted for legislation in 2000 granting China permanent normal trade status. He contended that the measure would bolster American jobs through increased exports. "Our markets are already largely open, so all the opening is on their side."

However, Price joined the overwhelming majority of House Democrats in opposing legislation in the 107th Congress to grant the president fast-track trade negotiating authority. And he supported Bush's decision in 2002 to impose temporary tariffs on imports of most foreign steel to fight what the domestic industry said was unfair foreign competition.

Price has tried to find a middle ground on tobacco, a touchy issue in a state where the leaf has been hallowed for three centuries. He backs tough restrictions on teenagers' access to cigarettes and chewing tobacco, but he calls for a "stabilization mechanism" so that tobacco growers don't go belly-up.

In 1997, he voted against a Democratic amendment to eliminate the federal crop insurance subsidy for tobacco farmers. Price began his floor remarks by saying, "I am not a reflexive defender of the tobacco industry." Then he gave an academic analysis of his state's longtime cash cow and continued, "Denying crop insurance or disaster relief to these individuals will not change their geography or climate or the economic facts of life. It will not miraculously enable them to turn to some other crop or line of work. It will simply ruin many of them economically, especially those on the margin of profitability — those on the small farms."

Improving education is a personal interest for Price, who was a university professor. It is also good politics in the 4th District, with its concentration of universities, research facilities and high-technology firms. In 1997, Price scored a major legislative win when Congress cleared education affordability legislation that he had been advocating for several years. The law made interest on student loans tax deductible and permitted penalty-free withdrawals from IRAs for education expenses.

Price has opposed GOP efforts to provide taxpayer-financed tuition vouchers that parents could use to send their children to private school. "The Republican voucher plan . . . would divert us from the challenge of making public education all that it can and must be," he said on the House floor.

Democratic leaders called on Price's political science background early in the 107th Congress when he won appointment to an ad hoc committee to recommend improvements in election procedures, and he claims credit for helping to shape the truth-in-advertising provisions of the campaign finance law enacted in 2002.

Born in East Tennessee to a high school principal father and English teacher mother, Price got his undergraduate degree at the University of North Carolina and then went to Yale for graduate study, earning political science and divinity degrees. While teaching political science at Duke University in the 1970s, he became heavily involved in state Democratic politics. He served as chairman of the state party in 1983 and 1984, and in 1985 became a founding member of the national Democratic Leadership Council, which sought to expand the influence of party moderates.

The contacts Price made in his party work helped him raise money and attract supporters for a successful House race in 1986. After beating out three opponents for the Democratic nomination, he ousted freshman GOP Rep. Bill Cobey by 12 percentage points. He won re-election three times by comfortable margins but lost to former Raleigh Police Chief Fred Heineman by 1,215 votes in the GOP takeover landslide of 1994.

Price avenged that defeat in the next election, waging an aggressive campaign that emphasized door-to-door canvassing and plenty of personal contact with voters. He won by almost 11 percentage points in 1996 and has prevailed easily in subsequent elections. In a district made more comfortably Democratic after reapportionment, Price won in 2002 with 61 percent.

KEY VOTES

2002

- Yes Overhaul campaign finance law; ban "soft money" and restrict advocacy advertising
- Yes Back Bush's defense budget increase
- No Extend 1996 welfare law
- No Adopt Bush's discretionary spending limit
- No Pass GOP Medicare prescription drug plan
- Yes Create independent Sept. 11 commission
- Yes Extend union protections to Homeland Security Department employees
- No Revive fast-track procedures for trade agreements
- No Authorize war against Iraq
- Yes Advance bankruptcy overhaul opposed by abortion opponents

2001

- No Nullify Clinton Labor Department ergonomics rule
- No Cut taxes by $1.35 trillion through fiscal 2011
- Yes Maintain ban on oil drilling in Arctic National Wildlife Refuge
- No Approve Bush proposal to limit managed-care plan liability for coverage decisions
- Yes Divert money from crop subsidy payments to land conservation
- Yes Expand law enforcement power to investigate suspected terrorists

CQ VOTE STUDIES

	PARTY UNITY		PRESIDENTIAL SUPPORT	
	Support	Oppose	Support	Oppose
2002	92%	8%	38%	62%
2001	88%	12%	35%	65%
2000	90%	10%	80%	20%
1999	87%	13%	74%	26%
1998	87%	13%	77%	23%

INTEREST GROUPS

	AFL-CIO	ADA	CCUS	ACU
2002	78%	95%	55%	0%
2001	100%	95%	43%	4%
2000	80%	85%	61%	4%
1999	89%	95%	40%	4%
1998	80%	95%	61%	8%

NORTH CAROLINA 4

Central – Durham, Chapel Hill, part of Raleigh

With more than three-fourths of the district's population living in Durham and Wake counties, to understand Research Triangle Park is to understand the 4th. The medical and technological research park was created in the 1950s by a group of academics, politicians and businessmen who saw the need to diversify the state's economy beyond the traditional tobacco and textile industries. To tap the brainpower of the three surrounding universities — Duke University in Durham, the University of North Carolina in Chapel Hill, and North Carolina State University in Raleigh — the park was located in the center of the triangle the schools create.

As the park grew, especially in the 1980s, the Durham of James B. Duke's Lucky Strike cigarettes largely disappeared. And as developers began converting tobacco warehouses into apartment buildings, concerns arose over quality-of-life issues. While the district leans to the left, its highly educated voters — one in five holds a post-graduate or professional degree — can be independent-minded. Democrats are boosted by the large black population in the city of Durham. Redistricting following the 2000 census made the 4th slightly more Democratic by cutting out some GOP areas in Wake County. Residents of the 4th voted narrowly for Al Gore in the 2000 presidential election.

The new map also slimmed the shape of the 4th, which sits halfway between the ocean and the Blue Ridge Mountains. While based primarily in the Triangle, the district still passes through rolling hills of evergreen forests. But some rural territory was excised in redistricting, and the 4th has a smaller rural element than all but two North Carolina districts (the 9th and the 12th).

MAJOR INDUSTRY

Technology research, higher education

CITIES

Durham, 187,035; Cary (pt.), 83,478; Chapel Hill, 48,715; Raleigh (pt.), 38,149

NOTABLE

Home to the Durham Bulls baseball team; The 1988 movie, "Bull Durham," starring Kevin Costner, was filmed here; The nation's first state university, The University of North Carolina at Chapel Hill, was chartered in 1789 and opened to students in 1795.

Rep. Richard M. Burr (R)

CAPITOL OFFICE
225-2071
richard.burrnc05@mail.house.gov
www.house.gov/burr
1526 Longworth 20515-3305; fax 225-2995

COMMITTEES
Energy & Commerce
Select Intelligence

HOMETOWN
Winston-Salem

BORN
Nov. 30, 1955, Charlottesville, Va.

RELIGION
Methodist

FAMILY
Wife, Brooke Burr; two children

EDUCATION
Wake Forest U., B.A. 1978 (communications)

CAREER
Marketing manager; kitchen appliance salesman

POLITICAL HIGHLIGHTS
Republican nominee for U.S. House, 1992

ELECTION RESULTS

2002 GENERAL		
Richard M. Burr (R)	137,879	70.2%
David Crawford (D)	58,558	29.8%
2002 PRIMARY		
Richard M. Burr (R)		unopposed
2000 GENERAL		
Richard M. Burr (R)	172,489	92.8%
Steven LeBoeuf (LIBERT)	13,366	7.2%

PREVIOUS WINNING PERCENTAGES
1998 (68%); 1996 (62%); 1994 (57%)

Elected 1994; 5th term

The health care and technology sectors have supplanted tobacco as the dominant economic force in the 5th District, and Burr's legislative agenda reflects that. Since the terrorist attacks of Sept. 11, 2001, he has also focused on terrorism, as a member of the Intelligence Committee.

The 108th Congress will be Burr's last in the House. He said he would not seek re-election, and early in 2003 he began seriously pursuing a bid for the Senate in 2004.

Burr has brought his knowledge of health care issues to the biological warfare debate. In the 107th Congress he chaired an Intelligence subcommittee on bioterrorism, and was vice chairman of the Energy and Commerce Committee — in essence the handpicked jack-of-all trades lieutenant of Chairman Billy Tauzin, a Louisiana Republican who named him vice chairman again in the 108th. Burr was also a conferee on legislation, enacted in 2002, to strengthen the nation's defenses against a biological or chemical attack.

Personable and telegenic, Burr has over the years concentrated his efforts on prescription drug prices, rural health care, food safety warnings and biomedical research, as well as on trying to stem the defection of teachers and nurses from their professions into higher-paying high-tech jobs.

Burr focused in the previous two Congresses on working with other Republicans to develop a proposal to deal with the rising cost of prescription drugs for Medicare beneficiaries, declaring that younger generations have some obligation to help seniors finance their pharmaceutical needs.

Burr is well-situated to deal with his health care priorities from his seat on Energy and Commerce's Health Subcommittee, a position he got as a freshman in 1995, when he arrived as part of the "Contract With America" class that made the GOP the House majority. From that post, he is able to look out for his district's medical technology, medical education and pharmaceutical industries.

A native of Winston-Salem, home to the R.J. Reynolds Tobacco Co., Burr must continue to defend the interests not only of cigarette manufacturers but of the many farmers in the district who depend on tobacco for their livelihood. After the 105th Congress spent much time debating legislation to increase federal regulation of tobacco and failed to reach a consensus, the issue moved off the front burner. That outcome was just the way Burr wanted it. In the 107th and 108th Congresses, Burr's interests have been increasing government assistance for tobacco exports and a tobacco quota buyout program aimed at helping farmers who want to quit growing tobacco to transition out of the business while permitting remaining growers to be competitive. (Burr quit smoking cigarettes in 1998 after making a televised vow to do so.)

Though he watches out for the textile industry, which is vital to his state's economy, in the 107th Burr supported legislation to revive fast-track procedures for congressional consideration of trade agreements, without amendment.

Burr attracted favorable attention early in his congressional career when he was given a key role in the development of legislation to streamline the Food and Drug Administration's policies for approving drugs and medical devices, such as pacemakers. He began that work in the 104th Congress and was rewarded in the 105th, when President Clinton signed into law FDA overhaul legislation that included Burr's language to establish a speedier approval process for drugs that treat life-threatening illnesses.

Although Burr is every bit as conservative as the typical member of the GOP Class of 1994, his patience and pragmatism in molding the FDA bill into something that could win congressional and presidential backing showed that he was more interested in the business of legislating than some of his classmates, who styled themselves "revolutionaries" and insisted on adhering to their core conservative principles rather than compromising.

That interest in legislating, he says, was a major factor in his decision early in 1999 to pass on a run for governor in 2000, which a number of Republicans back home had urged. The North Carolina governor's job is too administrative for his tastes, says Burr, who reports that he still gets goose bumps on viewing the illuminated Capitol when flying into Washington at night. He considered a Senate run in 2002, but deferred to Elizabeth Dole.

Burr's preliminary preparations for a 2004 Senate campaign, so far in advance of the election, is something new for Burr, who as a salesman for a wholesale distributor of kitchen appliances came home one day and announced to his wife that he wanted to run for Congress. That was in 1991, and Burr recalls, "I'd never been active politically, and I certainly didn't even know how much a congressman made."

He lost that race, against Democrat Stephen L. Neal in 1992, but garnered 46 percent of the vote. After a stint as co-chairman of North Carolina Taxpayers United — and angered by the 1993 congressional vote to raise taxes — he was back in 1994. Neal decided to retire, and Burr won with 57 percent, his closest election.

His goal back then was to balance the federal budget. Nevertheless, in 1997, when he got a chance to vote on the massive balanced-budget spending-cut bill, he was among the minority of Republicans to vote against it; he said the package cut too much from federal health care spending.

Born in Virginia, Burr moved to Winston-Salem when he was 6. His father was a Presbyterian minister. In retrospect, Burr has concluded that his understanding of the important role personal contact and constituent service play in a congressman's success began in his childhood.

He played football at Wake Forest and then went into sales — pushing Amana by day and teaching housewives how to cook with their new-fangled microwave ovens at night. Burr's outgoing personality and the skills he learned in the sales job are put to good use in his current occupation. He says he loves to campaign for re-election. One technique he favors is a periodic "take this job and try it" program, in which he asks constituents to invite him to work alongside them in their jobs. He's flipped hamburgers, delivered parcels and observed open-heart surgery.

KEY VOTES

2002

No Overhaul campaign finance law; ban "soft money" and restrict advocacy advertising
Yes Back Bush's defense budget increase
Yes Extend 1996 welfare law
Yes Adopt Bush's discretionary spending limit
Yes Pass GOP Medicare prescription drug plan
No Create independent Sept. 11 commission
No Extend union protections to Homeland Security Department employees
Yes Revive fast-track procedures for trade agreements
Yes Authorize war against Iraq
Yes Advance bankruptcy overhaul opposed by abortion opponents

2001

Yes Nullify Clinton Labor Department ergonomics rule
Yes Cut taxes by $1.35 trillion through fiscal 2011
No Maintain ban on oil drilling in Arctic National Wildlife Refuge
Yes Approve Bush proposal to limit managed-care plan liability for coverage decisions
No Divert money from crop subsidy payments to land conservation
Yes Expand law enforcement power to investigate suspected terrorists

CQ VOTE STUDIES

	PARTY UNITY		PRESIDENTIAL SUPPORT	
	Support	Oppose	Support	Oppose
2002	95%	5%	92%	8%
2001	95%	5%	93%	7%
2000	92%	8%	22%	78%
1999	93%	7%	17%	83%
1998	92%	8%	24%	76%

INTEREST GROUPS

	AFL-CIO	ADA	CCUS	ACU
2002	11%	0%	100%	96%
2001	17%	10%	96%	88%
2000	10%	5%	80%	88%
1999	33%	5%	84%	87%
1998	10%	5%	82%	92%

NORTH CAROLINA 5
Northwest – part of Winston-Salem

In this northern Piedmont district, Mayberry meets R.J. Reynolds. The district's northern counties, which run along the Virginia border, are filled with small rural towns such as Mount Airy, the childhood home of Andy Griffith and the inspiration for the fictional setting of his 1960s television series. The district's major population center is Winston-Salem and surrounding Forsyth County, home to R.J. Reynolds Tobacco Co. The company's corporate headquarters is in the 12th District (which has most of Winston-Salem), but its largest plant is in the 5th, in the appropriately named town of Tobaccoville.

The economy of Forsyth County has changed over the past few years, veering away from its one-time mainstays, textiles and tobacco. While tobacco production still employs several thousand, it now ranks second to health care, partly because of Wake Forest University's medical center. Banking also is on the rise. Textile and blue-collar manufacturing still prevail throughout the other counties, and grazing cattle wander over Surry County's low, rolling hills.

Redistricting following the 2000 census moved the 5th's lines to the west and south to make room for the state's new 13th District, which includes some territory that had been in the northeastern part of the old 5th. But the new map kept the 5th's strong Republican leanings intact. The district backed Republican Richard Vinroot by a 12-point margin in the 2000 governor's race, and the GOP has a voter-registration advantage. Republicans dominate in Davie and Yadkin counties, located west of Winston-Salem, which were two of the three counties to give Republican Elizabeth Dole more than 70 percent of the vote in the 2002 Senate race. Even the 5th's share of Forsyth leans Republican, as most of Winston-Salem's sizable black population was drawn into the 12th.

MAJOR INDUSTRY

Health care, tobacco, textiles, agriculture

CITIES

Winston-Salem (pt.), 69,790; Statesville (pt.), 23,280; Kernersville, 17,126; Clemmons, 13,827

NOTABLE

Ashe County's "New River," in existence for roughly 300 million years, is regarded as one of the oldest rivers in the United States.

Rep. Howard Coble (R)

Elected 1984; 10th term

A cigar-smoking former prosecutor, Coble uses blunt talk and negotiating savvy to cut bipartisan deals as a senior member of both the Judiciary and Transportation and Infrastructure committees.

But his tendency to be outspoken can get him in trouble. It did so at the start of the 108th Congress, soon after Coble took the gavel of Judiciary's newly constituted Crime, Terrorism and Homeland Security Subcommittee. Democrats called for him to resign that chairmanship after Coble told a radio interviewer that he agreed with the U.S. government's internment of Japanese-Americans during World War II. Coble said he was "taken aback" by the controversy that attended his comment and refused to give up the chairmanship, but he offered that internment was "the wrong decision and an action that should never be repeated."

His tough talk also won him headlines during Judiciary's 1998 impeachment proceedings. When Democratic Rep. Robert F. Drinan of Massachusetts, a Catholic priest who was on the Judiciary panel during Watergate, suggested at a hearing that conservatives were looking for "vengeance" against President Clinton, Coble retorted that, "If anybody thinks vengeance is involved, I'll meet them in the parking lot."

Under the straw hat he often wears to protect his sun-sensitive skin, Coble is a solid conservative on social and fiscal issues. With an old-fashioned backslapping approach, he strongly advocates for the tobacco industry and fights to protect the economic viability of his state's textile mills from his position as a leader in the House Textile Caucus. He emphasizes his experience in business as a former insurance claims adjuster and state tax collector. He cultivates friends in both parties on the Navy Yard tennis courts, where he competes with other lawmakers in weekly doubles matches.

He describes himself as an "AM guy in an FM world," seldom using a computer and preferring to write his speeches in longhand.

Coble took over the Crime Subcommittee in the 108th after the maximum allowable six-year turn as chairman of the Courts, the Internet and Intellectual Property Subcommittee. But he had begun focusing on homeland security issues in the 107th, emphasizing his background as a prosecutor and a Coast Guard veteran. He was one of only nine lawmakers to oppose the post-Sept. 11 aviation security law, which made aviation security workers federal employees; Coble argued that the measure would cost too much and had been "driven by hysteria." He pushed hard for putting more federal money into port security. "I have a deep feeling the messengers of evil will come next time through a port or harbor," Coble said.

On Judiciary, disputes with consumer groups and some businesses stymied two Coble initiatives in 2002: a proposal to penalize unauthorized use of private databases, and another to allow Hollywood to employ techniques used by hackers to block consumers from using Internet sites that provide access to pirated copies of movies and music.

In the 105th, Coble helped develop a landmark law to augment copyright protection for digital works such as computer software and compact discs. In the 106th, he helped write laws to allow delivery of local television channels via satellite and to move toward international standardization of patent applications.

Coble, who is a fan of bluegrass music, won praise from musicians such as Bruce Springsteen and Bonnie Raitt for reversing himself on an impor-

CAPITOL OFFICE
225-3065
howard.coble@mail.house.gov
www.house.gov/coble
2468 Rayburn 20515-3306; fax 225-8611

COMMITTEES
Judiciary
(Crime, Terrorism & Homeland Security - chairman)
Transportation & Infrastructure

HOMETOWN
Greensboro

BORN
March 18, 1931, Greensboro, N.C.

RELIGION
Presbyterian

FAMILY
Single

EDUCATION
Appalachian State U., attended 1949-50 (history); Guilford College, A.B. 1958 (history); U. of North Carolina, J.D. 1962

MILITARY SERVICE
Coast Guard, 1952-56; Coast Guard Reserve, 1960-82; Coast Guard, 1977-78

CAREER
Lawyer; insurance claims supervisor

POLITICAL HIGHLIGHTS
N.C. House, 1969; assistant U.S. attorney, 1969-73; N.C. Department of Revenue secretary, 1973-77; Republican nominee for N.C. treasurer, 1976; N.C. House, 1979-83

ELECTION RESULTS

2002 GENERAL		
Howard Coble (R)	151,430	90.4%
Tara Grubb (LIBERT)	16,067	9.6%
2002 PRIMARY		
Howard Coble (R)		unopposed
2000 GENERAL		
Howard Coble (R)	195,727	91.0%
Jeffrey D. Bentley (LIBERT)	18,726	8.7%

PREVIOUS WINNING PERCENTAGES
1998 (89%); 1996 (73%); 1994 (100%); 1992 (71%); 1990 (67%); 1988 (62%); 1986 (50%); 1984 (51%)

tant recording industry issue in 2000. He won passage of a law that nullified language he had sponsored in 1999 classifying sound recordings as "works for hire." The singers said the 1999 law prevented them from taking ownership of popular songs from recording companies after copyrights expire. "Never in my wildest dreams did I think this would have become such a big deal," Coble said in explaining his change of heart.

But Coble can be uncompromising on issues that hit close to home, including his defense of the tobacco industry, a powerful presence in his state. "It is lawfully grown, lawfully sold and lawfully consumed. It's a lawful product," he said when the Food and Drug Administration suggested regulating nicotine as a drug in 1995. "Therefore, as a smoker, I assume the risks of consuming that lawful product."

As the son of a department store manager and a textile worker, Coble votes in ways that support the textile industry. He opposed both the 2002 law granting the president fast-track trade negotiating authority and the 2000 law permanently normalizing the U.S.-China trade relationship.

An enduring quest for Coble has been to attack wasteful spending. He has called for extending the service requirement for graduates of military academies to eight years from five years, saying the current payback for such a government-financed education is inadequate. Closer to home, he is one of the few lawmakers who declines to participate in the congressional pension program, calling it "a taxpayer ripoff."

Coble was a federal prosecutor and then the state's chief tax collector in the mid-1970s. After four years as a state representative, he contemplated a run for governor in 1984, but switched course and decided to seek the GOP nomination against freshman Democratic Rep. Robin Britt. He won the primary by a scant 164 votes against former state Sen. Walter C. Cockerham, a millionaire construction company owner who had been stumping in the district and courting GOP votes for months before Coble entered the race.

In the fall, Coble stressed his fiscal conservatism while painting Britt as an extravagant liberal who had voted against President Reagan on two of every three votes in 1983. Tapping into the flow of conservative Democrats who were crossing party lines in Reagan's re-election landslide that year, Coble won by 2,662 votes.

Britt quickly plotted a comeback, and on Election Day 1986 only 79 votes separated the winner and the loser. Britt challenged the election results, but he was unsuccessful. Coble has had little to worry about since; 1996 was the last time the Democrats fielded a challenger.

KEY VOTES

2002

No Overhaul campaign finance law; ban "soft money" and restrict advocacy advertising
Yes Back Bush's defense budget increase
Yes Extend 1996 welfare law
Yes Adopt Bush's discretionary spending limit
Yes Pass GOP Medicare prescription drug plan
No Create independent Sept. 11 commission
No Extend union protections to Homeland Security Department employees
No Revive fast-track procedures for trade agreements
Yes Authorize war against Iraq
Yes Advance bankruptcy overhaul opposed by abortion opponents

2001

Yes Nullify Clinton Labor Department ergonomics rule
Yes Cut taxes by $1.35 trillion through fiscal 2011
No Maintain ban on oil drilling in Arctic National Wildlife Refuge
Yes Approve Bush proposal to limit managed-care plan liability for coverage decisions
No Divert money from crop subsidy payments to land conservation
Yes Expand law enforcement power to investigate suspected terrorists

CQ VOTE STUDIES

	PARTY UNITY		PRESIDENTIAL SUPPORT	
	Support	Oppose	Support	Oppose
2002	95%	5%	82%	18%
2001	95%	5%	86%	14%
2000	96%	4%	21%	79%
1999	92%	8%	12%	88%
1998	93%	7%	16%	84%

INTEREST GROUPS

	AFL-CIO	ADA	CCUS	ACU
2002	11%	10%	75%	92%
2001	17%	10%	87%	92%
2000	10%	15%	76%	86%
1999	38%	15%	78%	100%
1998	11%	10%	89%	96%

NORTH CAROLINA 6
Central – parts of Greensboro and High Point

Located in the heart of the state, the 6th takes in part of the city of Greensboro and surrounding Guilford County and then spreads south to include the famed golf course towns of Southern Pines and Pinehurst, near Fort Bragg. Already solid GOP turf, the 6th became even more Republican after redistricting following the 2000 census.

The new map shed about 100,000 people in Guilford, mainly to facilitate the creation of the state's new 13th District, and added territory in Alamance County to the east. As redrawn, the 6th takes in two large chunks of Guilford that are connected at a single point, on the Reedy Fork Creek in the northeastern part of the county.

Greensboro, the third-most-populous city in the state, is home to a blend of manufacturing and service companies. Textiles, furniture and tobacco processing long have been the economic backbone of both the city and the district, including Lorillard Tobacco Company, the manufacturer of Kent and Newport cigarettes. However, the influence of tobacco on the economy has somewhat decreased. Insurance companies, an American Express regional credit card service center and six colleges and universities have helped to diversify Greensboro's economy. Nearby High Point is a furniture manufacturing hub.

As in much of North Carolina, trade issues loom large in the 6th District, particularly in textiles and furniture manufacturing. An increase in furniture imports nationwide at the expense of Greensboro's industry has become a major concern.

The 6th includes all of Randolph County, a heavily Republican area located south of Greensboro, and most of Alamance, which votes Republican in part because of the union-resistant textile industry. Moore County includes the upscale golf and retirement centers in Pinehurst and Southern Pines. The rest of the district is mostly rural, tobacco country.

MAJOR INDUSTRY
Tobacco, textiles, furniture manufacturing

CITIES
Greensboro (pt.), 59,010; High Point (pt.), 33,404; Asheboro, 21,672

NOTABLE
The Richard Petty Museum in Level Cross honors the NASCAR legend, who was the Republican nominee for secretary of state in 1996.

Rep. Mike McIntyre (D)

CAPITOL OFFICE
225-2731
congmcintyre@mail.house.gov
www.house.gov/mcintyre
228 Cannon 20515-3307; fax 225-5773

COMMITTEES
Agriculture
Armed Services

HOMETOWN
Lumberton

BORN
Aug. 6, 1956, Lumberton, N.C.

RELIGION
Presbyterian

FAMILY
Wife, Dee McIntyre; two children

EDUCATION
U. of North Carolina, B.A. 1978 (political science), J.D. 1981

CAREER
Lawyer

POLITICAL HIGHLIGHTS
No previous office

ELECTION RESULTS

2002 GENERAL		
Mike McIntyre (D)	118,543	71.1%
James Adams (R)	45,537	27.3%
David Brooks (LIBERT)	2,574	1.6%
2002 PRIMARY		
Mike McIntyre (D)		unopposed
2000 GENERAL		
Mike McIntyre (D)	160,185	69.8%
James Adams (R)	66,463	28.9%
Bob Burns (LIBERT)	3,018	1.3%

PREVIOUS WINNING PERCENTAGES
1998 (91%); 1996 (53%)

Elected 1996; 4th term

McIntyre often tells people they should follow their dreams. He points to Bill McArthur, another native of southeast North Carolina, who became an astronaut despite being rejected by NASA six times. And McIntyre himself is not a bad example of someone who fulfilled a childhood ambition.

His father was a Lumberton city councilman and involved in Democratic politics when they happened to attend a November 1972 victory party for newly elected Democratic Rep. Charlie Rose. McIntyre recalls telling his father that he wanted to be the congressman from the 7th District when he grew up. When Rose retired 24 years later, McIntyre replaced him.

Organized, earnest and with conservatives stances on most issues, McIntyre now appears to have a lock on the seat. He is in fact one of the most conservative Democrats in the House — even by the standards of the "Blue Dogs," the group of Democrats who occupy their party's right flank. Even before his election to the House, McIntyre had agreed to join the group.

But McIntyre's politics fit nicely with his constituency, which wants a congressman who will look out for the interests of tobacco farmers, boost the military, reduce taxes, fight against abortion rights and gun control and advocate for school prayer and protection of the flag.

Republicans sounded him out about switching parties when he first arrived on Capitol Hill. But McIntyre said he was not interested, pointing to his deep Democratic roots. Instead of looking to leave the party, McIntyre has worked, particularly through his membership in the Blue Dogs and the slightly less conservative New Democrat Coalition, to move the party toward the center.

On trade policy, McIntyre joins with labor unions and many Democrats to oppose legislation to liberalize international commerce. "Free trade has been anything but free," McIntyre says. "It's been very costly" to North Carolina's textile and apparel industries. His district has been hit hard by the loss of textile jobs overseas and — with six hurricanes hitting the 7th in McIntyre's first four years in office — a drop in tourism in the coastal areas.

That is why rural economic development is at the top of his legislative priorities. In the 107th Congress, he wrote legislation to expand the federal Trade Adjustment Assistance programs designed to retrain and relocate workers who lost jobs as a result of trade actions. And he developed legislation, introduced again in the 108th, to create a seven-state Southeast Crescent Authority, modeled after the Appalachian Regional Council, to assist economically distressed counties in the Southeast United States.

He also wants to boost tourism in his area, and he is adamant that there be substantial federal funding to help restore storm-damaged beaches along the North Carolina coast. In the 108th, he offered a bill to give federal recognition to the Lumbee Indians, which could lead to a casino in his part of the state.

McIntyre has seats on the Agriculture and Armed Services panels. Both assignments are useful to his district, where farming — especially tobacco — is big business and the military is a major influence; Fort Bragg is just west of the district, while Camp Lejeune is just over the 3rd District line to the east.

He has been a stout defender of the federal tobacco program, which he says is essential to preserving small family farms that grow the leaf. In the 107th, however, declaring "it is time for a new approach," he developed a controversial plan to buy out tobacco growers and to give the Food and

Drug Administration authority over the manufacture, sale and distribution of tobacco products. McIntyre's bill would give holders of federal tobacco quotas the equivalent of about four years' worth of government payments, during which time they could move to the production of another crop. He will try again in the 108th, aided by his post as the top Democrat on the Agriculture subcommittee with jurisdiction over tobacco programs.

McIntyre is a staunch defender of NASA. He remembers being fascinated by space when he was young, and that interest was rekindled by one of his sons, who aspires to be an astronaut and has attended the Space Camp in Huntsville, Ala.

McIntyre has spent his life as a model Southern Democrat. He was chairman of the Teen Democrats in high school, vice president of the College Democrats in college and law school, and an organizer of the Robeson County Young Democrats after that. He was a student government officer in both high school and college.

He spent the summer after his junior year in Washington, D.C., at a congressional seminar program, and it was then that his ambition to be in Congress was cemented. He was standing at the back of the room the day White House lawyer John Dean testified before the Senate Watergate Committee, chaired by Sam J. Ervin Jr. of North Carolina. McIntyre followed Watergate closely and, instead of being turned off of politics by the scandal, he decided more people should involve themselves in the political process. The next summer, he returned to Capitol Hill as an intern in Rose's office.

He majored in political science at the University of North Carolina. After law school, McIntyre continued to involve himself in dozens of community, church, civic and professional activities as he built a law practice in his hometown of Lumberton.

When Rose announced his retirement in 1996, McIntyre was one of seven Democratic primary entrants. He took 23 percent of the vote, 7 percentage points behind Rose Marie Lowry-Townsend, a well-known American Indian and teachers union president. Shortly before the runoff, McIntyre won the backing of several influential leaders in the district's black community, and their support helped him win the nomination with 52 percent.

McIntyre's Republican opponent was Bill Caster, a New Hanover County commissioner and retired Coast Guard officer. McIntyre's conservative stance on most issues helped blunt the GOP attacks, and he won with 53 percent. That was his last race of any note. His district's political makeup minimally altered by the post-census redistricting, he took 71 percent in a rematch against GOP lawyer and engineer James Adams.

KEY VOTES

2002

- Yes Overhaul campaign finance law; ban "soft money" and restrict advocacy advertising
- Yes Back Bush's defense budget increase
- No Extend 1996 welfare law
- No Adopt Bush's discretionary spending limit
- No Pass GOP Medicare prescription drug plan
- Yes Create independent Sept. 11 commission
- Yes Extend union protections to Homeland Security Department employees
- No Revive fast-track procedures for trade agreements
- Yes Authorize war against Iraq
- No Advance bankruptcy overhaul opposed by abortion opponents

2001

- Yes Nullify Clinton Labor Department ergonomics rule
- ? Cut taxes by $1.35 trillion through fiscal 2011
- Yes Maintain ban on oil drilling in Arctic National Wildlife Refuge
- No Approve Bush proposal to limit managed-care plan liability for coverage decisions
- No Divert money from crop subsidy payments to land conservation
- Yes Expand law enforcement power to investigate suspected terrorists

CQ VOTE STUDIES

	PARTY UNITY		PRESIDENTIAL SUPPORT	
	Support	Oppose	Support	Oppose
2002	72%	28%	54%	46%
2001	70%	30%	52%	48%
2000	61%	39%	40%	60%
1999	54%	46%	46%	54%
1998	61%	39%	52%	48%

INTEREST GROUPS

	AFL-CIO	ADA	CCUS	ACU
2002	67%	55%	53%	48%
2001	82%	60%	57%	64%
2000	60%	35%	66%	48%
1999	89%	55%	52%	52%
1998	70%	60%	72%	52%

NORTH CAROLINA 7

Southeast – Wilmington, part of Fayetteville

The 7th stretches from the well-off historic port city of Wilmington in the southeast to the military-based commercial hub of Fayetteville in the north. In between lie tobacco fields, hog farms and manufacturing plants.

Fort Bragg is just outside the 7th (it is shared by the 2nd and 8th districts), but the huge military base is integral to the Fayetteville area. Tobacco, agriculture, and textiles also drive the district's economy, though textile declines have given some counties high unemployment. Free-trade agreements are viewed with suspicion here.

Like Fayetteville (shared with the 2nd and 8th), Wilmington grew significantly in the 1990s, reflected in its expanding medical center and emerging biotechnology industry.

Wealthy condo-dwellers in Wilmington and surrounding New Hanover County exert a rightward influence. But the region's poor farmers, Lumbee Indians (mainly in Robeson County), and cohesive black community in Fayetteville and rural Bladen and Columbus counties give the district a small Democratic lean. The 7th voted narrowly for George W. Bush in the 2000 presidential election but went decisively for Democrat Michael F. Easley in the 2000 governor's race.

Redistricting following the 2000 census made minimal changes to the 7th, but did give the district all of Robeson County. As a result, the new 7th has the fifth-largest percentage of American Indians of any district in the nation, and the largest percentage of any district east of the Mississippi River. The Hispanic population is rising. Duplin County (shared with the 3rd), in the northeast, was profiled in a 2002 New York Times story about how rural school districts have few qualified people to teach English to immigrants.

MAJOR INDUSTRY

Agriculture, military, manufacturing, tourism

CITIES

Wilmington, 75,838; Lumberton, 20,795; Fayetteville (pt.), 19,418

NOTABLE

Wilmington has a strong film and television production industry, with such movies as "Sleeping with the Enemy," "Blue Velvet" and "Domestic Disturbance" and the TV series "Dawson's Creek" filmed there; Basketball star Michael Jordan grew up in Wilmington.

Rep. Robin Hayes (R)

CAPITOL OFFICE
225-3715
www.house.gov/hayes
130 Cannon 20515-3308; fax 225-4036

COMMITTEES
Agriculture
(Livestock & Horticulture - chairman)
Armed Services
Transportation & Infrastructure

HOMETOWN
Concord

BORN
Aug. 14, 1945, Concord, N.C.

RELIGION
Presbyterian

FAMILY
Wife, Barbara Hayes; two children

EDUCATION
Duke U., B.A. 1967 (history)

CAREER
Hosiery mill owner

POLITICAL HIGHLIGHTS
Concord Board of Aldermen, 1975-78 (served as a Democrat); N.C. House, 1993-97; Republican nominee for governor, 1996

ELECTION RESULTS

2002 GENERAL		
Robin Hayes (R)	80,298	53.6%
Chris Kouri (D)	66,819	44.6%
Mark Johnson (LIBERT)	2,619	1.8%
2002 PRIMARY		
Robin Hayes (R)		unopposed
2000 GENERAL		
Robin Hayes (R)	111,950	55.0%
Mike Taylor (D)	89,505	44.0%

PREVIOUS WINNING PERCENTAGES
1998 (51%)

Elected 1998; 3rd term

Hayes' grandfather Charles Cannon was one of the founding giants of North Carolina's textile industry. Now Hayes, an heir to the Cannon Mills fortune and himself the owner of a small hosiery mill, represents a part of the country reeling from the loss of thousands of jobs as companies move stitching operations overseas. Protecting the livelihoods of the workers who remain is central to his agenda — as well as a political imperative, as Hayes learned in the 107th Congress.

Under immense pressure from GOP leaders, he cast one of the deciding votes in the House in 2001 in favor of granting one of President Bush's top wishes: authority to negotiate trade agreements that Congress must approve or reject without alteration. Hayes, who was in tears as he voted to pass the fast-track measure, said he had used his vote to secure valuable protections for textile dyeing and finishing operations.

But the decision haunted him through his 2002 campaign. A backlash from unions and textile workers had him on the defensive, forcing him to spend time reassuring voters that he could be trusted to defend the interests of textile workers — even after he switched sides and voted against the revised version of the fast-track measure enacted in 2002. Hayes said he objected to the addition of a trade agreement with Andean nations that in his view would hurt U.S. textile and apparel makers. But it also was true that GOP leaders were able to clear the bill without his vote and let him off the hook in advance.

Hayes also has earned a reputation at home and on Capitol Hill as one of Congress' staunchest defenders of tobacco, another industry that has been important to his state's economy for generations. He has lobbied the Bush administration to include tobacco companies and farmers in trade deals, despite pressure to keep the industry away from the table.

His committee assignments in the 108th Congress should ensure that he can tend to the needs of his politically competitive district, which had elected a Democrat, W. G. "Bill" Hefner, for a dozen terms until his retirement in 1998. Hayes continues on the Armed Services Committee, a post important to the 8th District's Fort Bragg and Pope Air Force Base (nearby in the 2nd), and the Agriculture Committee, where tobacco tends to get a sympathetic hearing. He assumed the chairmanship of the panel's Livestock and Horticulture Subcommittee in the 108th.

He also has a seat on the Transportation Committee, enabling him to look out for his district's infrastructure needs, particularly as Congress considers a reauthorization of highway and mass transit programs. He is pursuing highway projects and light rail for an urban slice of Charlotte added to the 8th as part of redistricting for this decade.

On Armed Services he pursues better equipment along with better pay and housing for military personnel. He also says he would like to see the Pentagon streamline its bidding process and adopt cost-saving innovations developed in the business world. With an eye toward parochial industries, he won a provision in the 2002 defense authorization law requiring that the Department of Defense look first to U.S. producers and suppliers when buying textiles, specialty metals or agriculture products.

He also has championed a proposal that would provide tax incentives to companies that expand in rural areas.

Hayes is an unpretentious, affable and reliably conservative Republican. He supports school vouchers and charter schools. He opposes abortion.

His passion for hunting and fishing also is well-known to his friends and colleagues. In 2003, he took over as co-chairman of the Congressional Sportsmen's Caucus, composed of about 300 fellow outdoors enthusiasts on Capitol Hill. Not surprisingly, he is a strong supporter of the rights of gun owners. A devout NASCAR fan, he once was part-owner of a racing team, and in 2001 he helped arrange an Air Force flyover honoring the late NASCAR driver Dale Earnhardt before a race at North Carolina Speedway. He has rewarded campaign donors by taking them to a racing school for training to drive a Winston Cup car.

He is also a licensed pilot, and for a time he ran a business in Alaska flying freight and passengers in and out of the bush. He now owns a small air charter business in his hometown.

Growing up in Concord, Hayes says he was "a typical Southern conservative Democrat, raised in a family with a strong work ethic and family beliefs." After college he began a business career that included jobs in the textile, trucking and highway contracting businesses. He inherited a share of his family's textile fortune and eventually bought his own mill. The Capitol Hill newspaper Roll Call estimated his wealth in 2002 at $62 million, the eighth-highest among members of Congress at the time.

His first taste of politics was three years as a town alderman in the 1970s. By the time he ran for a seat in the state House in 1992, he had been a Republican for two years. In 1994, just as the GOP was winning control of Congress, Hayes played a key role in North Carolina's version of the "Republican revolution." He helped organize a GOP takeover of the state House, and his colleagues rewarded him by electing him whip.

Hayes made a statewide name for himself with a 1996 bid for governor. He trounced the establishment's choice for the GOP nomination, former Charlotte Mayor Richard Vinroot, but he took only 43 percent in the general election against Democratic incumbent James B. Hunt.

In his initial bid for Congress two years later, Hayes outspent Democratic lawyer Mike Taylor by a 3-to-1 margin and won with 51 percent of the vote. He took 55 percent in a rematch with Taylor in 2000. But remapping for this decade added Democrats to the 8th District, and the new demographics, combined with his trade vote, made Hayes look more vulnerable than ever in 2002. With fundraising help from Bush and other leading Republicans, however, he won with 54 percent against a Democratic unknown, Charlotte lawyer Chris Kouri.

As the 108th began, Hayes was contemplating a possible statewide run in 2004, either for governor again or for the Senate.

KEY VOTES

2002

- No Overhaul campaign finance law; ban "soft money" and restrict advocacy advertising
- Yes Back Bush's defense budget increase
- Yes Extend 1996 welfare law
- Yes Adopt Bush's discretionary spending limit
- Yes Pass GOP Medicare prescription drug plan
- No Create independent Sept. 11 commission
- No Extend union protections to Homeland Security Department employees
- No Revive fast-track procedures for trade agreements
- Yes Authorize war against Iraq
- No Advance bankruptcy overhaul opposed by abortion opponents

2001

- Yes Nullify Clinton Labor Department ergonomics rule
- Yes Cut taxes by $1.35 trillion through fiscal 2011
- No Maintain ban on oil drilling in Arctic National Wildlife Refuge
- Yes Approve Bush proposal to limit managed-care plan liability for coverage decisions
- No Divert money from crop subsidy payments to land conservation
- Yes Expand law enforcement power to investigate suspected terrorists

CQ VOTE STUDIES

	PARTY UNITY		PRESIDENTIAL SUPPORT	
	Support	Oppose	Support	Oppose
2002	97%	3%	82%	18%
2001	98%	2%	91%	9%
2000	89%	11%	19%	81%
1999	94%	6%	17%	83%

INTEREST GROUPS

	AFL-CIO	ADA	CCUS	ACU
2002	22%	5%	75%	96%
2001	8%	5%	87%	96%
2000	10%	5%	76%	76%
1999	33%	5%	88%	96%

NORTH CAROLINA 8

South central – parts of Charlotte, Fayetteville, Concord and Kannapolis

The 8th connects the worlds of eastern and western North Carolina, spanning from Charlotte in the west to military-dominated Fayetteville in the east. This is a district split along geographic, economic and political lines. Redistricting following the 2000 census extended the 8th west to take in a large portion of Charlotte, giving the previously suburban and rural district an urban component.

Cabarrus, a fast-growing county north of Charlotte, and Cumberland, which includes the 8th's share of Fayetteville, are the district's most-populous counties. Cabarrus is largely white and heavily Republican. Cumberland is more politically competitive.

In Mecklenburg County, which includes Charlotte and is the 8th's third major population center, the district reaches as far west as Memorial Stadium and Independence Park, nearly reaching downtown Charlotte. The 8th's share of Charlotte is almost 40 percent black, giving the district's portion of Mecklenburg a decidedly Democratic lean.

Textile-based economies in the cities along Interstate 85, notably Concord and Kannapolis, have suffered major losses over the last few years as manufacturing jobs have headed overseas. In the east, the district becomes poorer and more rural as it reaches into the Sandhills region. This part of the 8th also has a strong military flavor — Fort Bragg (shared with the 2nd) takes up land in Hoke and Cumberland counties.

The 8th is politically competitive. In 2000, George W. Bush took 53 percent of the vote in the presidential election, while Democrat Michael F. Easley captured 53 percent in the gubernatorial contest.

MAJOR INDUSTRY
Military, manufacturing, agriculture, livestock

MILITARY BASES
Fort Bragg (Army), 46,463 military, 4,245 civilian (2002) (shared with the 2nd)

CITIES
Charlotte (pt.), 100,756; Concord (pt.), 55,938; Fayetteville (pt.), 51,698

NOTABLE
North Carolina Speedway and Rockingham Dragway, known collectively as "The Rock," can draw 250,000 NASCAR fans to races.

Rep. Sue Myrick (R)

CAPITOL OFFICE
225-1976
myrick@mail.house.gov
myrick.house.gov
230 Cannon 20515-3309; fax 225-3389

COMMITTEES
Rules

HOMETOWN
Charlotte

BORN
Aug. 1, 1941, Tiffin, Ohio

RELIGION
Evangelical Methodist

FAMILY
Husband, Ed Myrick; two children, three stepchildren

EDUCATION
Heidelberg College, attended 1959-60 (elementary education)

CAREER
Advertising executive

POLITICAL HIGHLIGHTS
Candidate for Charlotte City Council, 1981; Charlotte City Council, 1983-85; sought Republican nomination for mayor of Charlotte, 1985; mayor of Charlotte, 1987-91; sought Republican nomination for U.S. Senate, 1992

ELECTION RESULTS

2002 GENERAL		
Sue Myrick (R)	140,095	72.4%
Ed McGuire (D)	49,974	25.8%
Christopher S. Cole (LIBERT)	3,374	1.7%
2002 PRIMARY		
Sue Myrick (R)		unopposed
2000 GENERAL		
Sue Myrick (R)	181,161	68.6%
Ed McGuire (D)	79,382	30.0%

PREVIOUS WINNING PERCENTAGES
1998 (69%); 1996 (63%); 1994 (65%)

Elected 1994; 5th term

Myrick represents the re-energized conservatives who are flexing their stronger political muscle in a Congress controlled by Republicans.

As the new head of the Republican Study Committee — about 70 of the most fiscally and socially conservative House Republicans — Myrick criticized President Bush's proposal to increase domestic spending in 2004 by 3.8 percent, calling it "overly generous." She also sponsored a change in rules for the 108th Congress that curbed the power of House Appropriations subcommittee chairmen, a group of lawmakers viewed by conservatives as arrogant and too eager to spend money.

Myrick is one of the members of the celebrated GOP Class of 1994 that helped Republicans take control of the House after 40 years of Democratic rule. She tries to maintain that revolutionary spirit. She is a consistent conservative, and even as many of her Class of 1994 colleagues have tended toward pragmatism, she often has preferred confrontation to compromise.

Some of her biggest legislative victories have not come from conservative causes, however, but from a personal battle that turned her into a leading advocate of legislation to expand cancer research and health care coverage of cancer treatment. Myrick, a breast cancer survivor, shepherded a measure, which became law in 2000, that provides treatment for low-income women diagnosed with breast or cervical cancer under the Centers for Disease Control and Prevention's early detection program.

Myrick underwent surgery for her cancer in December 1999 and received treatments for about six months, cutting back on her workload and occasionally showing up for floor votes wearing a pink surgical mask to reduce the risk of infection. She said her experience with cancer had helped her keep things in perspective and persuaded her to work "very hard not to get back in the same rat race."

Her focus on cancer legislation continued, and at the start of the 107th Congress, she took over a leadership role in the House Cancer Caucus, pledging as co-chairwoman to work to double the funding for the National Cancer Institute.

Myrick scored another victory in 2000 on a measure prompted by the 1997 disappearance of a North Carolina college student who vanished a few weeks after her 18th birthday. President Clinton signed her legislation authorizing grants to help create a national information database on missing adults, like the clearinghouse for missing and exploited children.

Her ardent conservatism and her distinct status as the only Southern Republican woman in the Class of 1994, caught the attention of party leaders when she first arrived in Congress. She got a seat on the Budget Committee in her first term and a post on the Rules Committee in her second.

But in 1997, she met with a small group of disgruntled conservatives who, impatient with the pace of the "Republican revolution" and their leaders' willingness to compromise, plotted to depose Newt Gingrich as Speaker. The coup was foiled — coincidentally, about the same time House Republicans met to elect two new leaders. Myrick was a candidate for secretary of the Republican Conference, but she finished second to Deborah Pryce of Ohio.

Myrick tried for a leadership job again before the start of the 106th Congress, when the Republican Conference vice chairmanship opened up, but she finished fourth. During her leadership bids, Myrick argued that her experience as an advertising executive would help her shape a successful Republican Party message, but her true-believer fervor may have worked against her.

Eventually, she joined the party's message-making team. In the 106th, she began serving with the Republican Conference's Communications Working Group, a role she continued in the 107th. Myrick co-chaired the Republican national platform committee, helping to write the GOP's message during the 2000 national elections. In the 107th, she also was vice chairman of the Republican Study Committee, which disrupted the annual appropriations process in 2002 when it demanded holding the line on federal spending.

Myrick has made economic development a high priority as unemployment plagues her textile-producing state. She was one of several Republicans who cast the deciding votes on legislation in the 107th granting President Bush fast-track trade negotiating authority and limiting Congress' role on trade pacts to an up or down vote. Myrick backed the bill after Bush pledged to help the beleaguered domestic textile industry.

Myrick drew criticism in early 2003 for a comment she made during a speech on domestic security threats. As the United States prepared for war in the Middle East, the congresswoman stepped on American-Arab relations when she noted, "Look at who runs all the convenience stores across the country."

Born in Tiffin, Ohio, Myrick attended Heidelberg College in her hometown for just a year before her parents decided their limited financial resources should be used for the schooling of her three brothers. They figured "I'd just get married," Myrick said. She took a series of jobs in Ohio, beginning with secretarial positions.

Myrick had no political aspirations until the early 1980s, when she and her husband sparred with the Charlotte City Council over the purchase of a property for use as a combination home and business. She ran for the city council in 1981 and lost, but was victorious two years later. In 1985, she lost a bid to become mayor of Charlotte; but in 1987, she won the office, ousting Harvey B. Gantt.

After five-term GOP Rep. Alex McMillan announced his retirement from the 9th District in 1994, Myrick's political experience gave her wide name recognition in a five-way Republican primary. Still, she struggled to win the nomination, prevailing only when news broke that her principal opponent, state House Minority Leader David Balmer, had falsified his résumé. That November, she met only modest Democratic resistance. She has easily won re-election since then.

KEY VOTES

2002

No Overhaul campaign finance law; ban "soft money" and restrict advocacy advertising
Yes Back Bush's defense budget increase
Yes Extend 1996 welfare law
Yes Adopt Bush's discretionary spending limit
Yes Pass GOP Medicare prescription drug plan
No Create independent Sept. 11 commission
No Extend union protections to Homeland Security Department employees
Yes Revive fast-track procedures for trade agreements
Yes Authorize war against Iraq
Yes Advance bankruptcy overhaul opposed by abortion opponents

2001

Yes Nullify Clinton Labor Department ergonomics rule
Yes Cut taxes by $1.35 trillion through fiscal 2011
No Maintain ban on oil drilling in Arctic National Wildlife Refuge
Yes Approve Bush proposal to limit managed-care plan liability for coverage decisions
No Divert money from crop subsidy payments to land conservation
Yes Expand law enforcement power to investigate suspected terrorists

CQ VOTE STUDIES

	PARTY UNITY		PRESIDENTIAL SUPPORT	
	Support	Oppose	Support	Oppose
2002	97%	3%	88%	12%
2001	96%	4%	95%	5%
2000	96%	4%	26%	74%
1999	92%	8%	14%	86%
1998	94%	6%	19%	81%

INTEREST GROUPS

	AFL-CIO	ADA	CCUS	ACU
2002	11%	0%	100%	96%
2001	0%	0%	95%	96%
2000	0%	0%	90%	95%
1999	13%	5%	84%	91%
1998	10%	5%	83%	88%

NORTH CAROLINA 9

South central — parts of Charlotte and Gastonia

Redistricting following the 2000 census strengthened the 9th's ties to Charlotte, the largest metropolitan area in the state. Nearly 40 percent of district residents live within its city limits and nearly 60 percent live in Mecklenburg County, which includes Charlotte.

The primarily white suburbs on the southern side of Charlotte feed the city many of its bankers, brokers, accountants, health care professionals and other white-collar workers. Most of Charlotte's black residents are in the 8th and 12th districts. The 9th has the highest median household income in North Carolina, thanks to upper-middle-class areas such as Huntersville, in northern Mecklenburg.

The region's tremendous growth, much of it sparked by 1990s consolidation in the banking industry, has brought the traffic congestion, shopping malls and higher home values that usually accompany suburban sprawl. Charlotte is now known as the nation's biggest banking center after New York.

To the west, Gastonia and its surrounding towns have been hurt by the continuing decline of the textile industry. But the 9th has decreased its dependence on manufacturing and textiles, and Gastonia's population still grew by 20 percent in the 1990s.

Redistricting kept the 9th's Republican lean intact. The district's GOP registration advantage increased with the addition of most of Union County, a suburban bedroom community located southeast of Charlotte, and the excision of Democratic-leaning Cleveland County in the west. Republican Richard Vinroot, a former Charlotte mayor, received his best vote percentages in the state from the 9th in the 2000 gubernatorial election.

MAJOR INDUSTRY

Finance, service, retail, manufacturing

CITIES

Charlotte (pt.), 243,947; Gastonia (pt.), 60,498; Huntersville, 24,960

NOTABLE

After six years of planning, a Gaston County veterans group in December 1998 succeeded in hoisting the largest flying American flag in the nation — 114 by 65 feet.

Rep. Cass Ballenger (R)

CAPITOL OFFICE
225-2576
cass.ballenger@mail.house.gov
www.house.gov/ballenger
2182 Rayburn 20515-3310; fax 225-0316

COMMITTEES
Education & Workforce
International Relations
(Western Hemisphere - chairman)

HOMETOWN
Hickory

BORN
Dec. 6, 1926, Hickory, N.C.

RELIGION
Episcopalian

FAMILY
Wife, Donna Ballenger; three children

EDUCATION
U. of North Carolina, attended 1944-45; Amherst College, B.A. 1948

MILITARY SERVICE
Naval Air Corps, 1944-45

CAREER
Plastics company executive

POLITICAL HIGHLIGHTS
Catawba County Commission, 1966-74 (chairman, 1970-74); N.C. House, 1975-77; N.C. Senate, 1977-86

ELECTION RESULTS

2002 GENERAL		
Cass Ballenger (R)	102,768	59.3%
Ron Daugherty (D)	65,587	37.9%
Christopher S. Cole (LIBERT)	4,937	2.9%
2002 PRIMARY		
Cass Ballenger (R)		unopposed
2000 GENERAL		
Cass Ballenger (R)	164,182	68.2%
Delmas Parker (D)	70,877	29.5%
Deborah Eddins (LIBERT)	5,599	2.3%

PREVIOUS WINNING PERCENTAGES
1998 (86%); 1996 (70%); 1994 (72%); 1992 (63%); 1990 (62%); 1988 (61%); 1986 (58%); 1986 Special Election (58%)

Elected 1986; 9th full term

A millionaire businessman and one of the richer members of Congress, Ballenger's politics often reflect the almost four decades he spent heading his own plastic packaging company before arriving in the House at age 60. He has drawn on that background to push for changes in federal labor laws, some of which are almost as old as he is. The laws should be modernized, he says, to reflect dramatic changes in the work force since the Depression.

As chairman of the Education and the Workforce Subcommittee on Workforce Protections for six years, Ballenger was often the standard-bearer for the Republicans on labor issues, pushing legislation to provide compensatory time off for workers instead of overtime pay and opposing Democratic efforts to increase the minimum wage.

But Ballenger's agenda goes well beyond pro-business concerns. He and his wife, Donna, have a longstanding interest in Latin America, which Republican leaders recognized in the 107th Congress by handing him the chairmanship of International Relations' Western Hemisphere Subcommittee.

Ballenger first traveled to Latin America more than 30 years ago, when he joined his father-in-law on a trip for an organization that sent U.S. businessmen to help their South American counterparts. Since then, he and his wife have traveled extensively through South and Central America for charitable and humanitarian causes. The Ballengers have helped build homes in Nicaragua and Honduras, provided six shipping containers of school furniture to Venezuela and Ecuador, and established a family foundation that has helped build hospitals throughout Central America.

The congressman says he knows almost every leader in the region. He even established a friendship with Venezuelan President Hugo Chavez, a controversial strongman whose ties to Cuban President Fidel Castro have angered the Bush administration. Chavez visited one of Ballenger's factories, and Ballenger likes to tell the story about how Chavez, who speaks little English, once walked up to Ballenger's wife and said, "I love you very much."

He also has devoted a great deal of attention to Colombia, where the government is struggling to control the illegal drug trade, fight left-wing guerrillas and rein in right-wing paramilitaries. Top State Department officials point to him as the head of an informal "Andean Caucus" that they meet with regularly to address relations with Bogota.

Ballenger won points from the White House in the 107th for casting one of the decisive votes to give President Bush authority to negotiate trade agreements that Congress can accept or reject but not amend. The vote was a tough one for Ballenger, whose district includes several textile plants that could be threatened by liberalized trade. He agreed to support the fast-track bill only after Bush assured him and other textile-state lawmakers that U.S. negotiators would protect their interests in future trade talks. Ballenger portrayed his vote as one of partisan loyalty, not parochial concerns. "He's my president," he said, "I didn't get any roads. I didn't get any bridges. I didn't get my shoes shined."

He did get a stiff re-election challenge, however, from textile plant owner, Ronnie Daugherty, who cited Ballenger's trade vote as his reason for trying to oust him in 2002. Ballenger's 59 percent of the vote, while giving him a 21 percentage point victory, was his worst showing since 1986.

Ballenger is conservative across the board but rarely speaks out on social policy matters. One time that he did, he quickly wished he hadn't: As the airwaves were full of discussion about Mississippi Sen. Trent Lott's laudatory comments about the 1948 pro-segregation presidential campaign of Strom Thurmond, Ballenger acknowledged having "segregationist feelings" himself after run-ins with black Georgia Democratic Rep. Cynthia McKinney. Ballenger quickly apologized, but some groups called for him to resign.

Ballenger is a longtime member of the board that advises the National Endowment for the Arts. He once voted to shut down the agency, but after several months on the arts council, he reported "that significant and positive changes have been made by this agency and Congress to ensure that taxpayers' funds are spent wisely and not on obscene and offensive art."

As chairman of the Workforce Protections panel, Ballenger had ambitions to enact pro-business legislation, but his plans met with stiff resistance from pro-labor Democrats. In response, he showed a willingness to shift to a more pragmatic approach, offering proposals for incremental change. Of special interest to Ballenger was the Occupational Safety and Health Administration, which he says places "excessive emphasis on penalties and citations" and should refashion itself as a consultant to help businesses make workplaces more safe.

On home-state matters, Ballenger is proud of his sponsorship of a bill to designate a segment of Wilson Creek in North Carolina as a component of the National Wild and Scenic Rivers System.

Ballenger served in the Navy during World War II, then went on to college. He returned home to Hickory, where he ran a company that made boxes and later founded Plastic Packaging Inc., which has become a substantial area employer and is still in the family.

He spent eight years in county government and nearly 12 years in the state legislature. Ballenger sought to advance to Congress in 1986 when Republican Rep. James T. Broyhill announced his retirement. Promising to emulate Broyhill, Ballenger won the GOP primary by 11 percentage points over state Rep. George S. Robinson, who argued that because he was 20 years younger than Ballenger he would be better able to build seniority.

Then, Broyhill was appointed to the Senate to replace GOP Sen. John East, who died, setting up a special election for Broyhill's seat. In November, Ballenger comfortably won the special and general elections against Democrat Lester D. Roark, a former mayor of Shelby.

A pleasant, low-profile man, Ballenger in years past could often be found in the Speaker's Lobby just off the House floor, cadging a cigarette from a doorman. With his wife badgering him to give up smoking, Ballenger never bought cigarettes, except when it came time to repay the doorman. He says he has finally been able to give up the habit.

KEY VOTES

2002

- No Overhaul campaign finance law; ban "soft money" and restrict advocacy advertising
- Yes Back Bush's defense budget increase
- Yes Extend 1996 welfare law
- Yes Adopt Bush's discretionary spending limit
- Yes Pass GOP Medicare prescription drug plan
- No Create independent Sept. 11 commission
- No Extend union protections to Homeland Security Department employees
- Yes Revive fast-track procedures for trade agreements
- Yes Authorize war against Iraq
- No Advance bankruptcy overhaul opposed by abortion opponents

2001

- Yes Nullify Clinton Labor Department ergonomics rule
- Yes Cut taxes by $1.35 trillion through fiscal 2011
- No Maintain ban on oil drilling in Arctic National Wildlife Refuge
- Yes Approve Bush proposal to limit managed-care plan liability for coverage decisions
- No Divert money from crop subsidy payments to land conservation
- Yes Expand law enforcement power to investigate suspected terrorists

CQ VOTE STUDIES

	PARTY UNITY		PRESIDENTIAL SUPPORT	
	Support	Oppose	Support	Oppose
2002	96%	4%	90%	10%
2001	97%	3%	93%	7%
2000	96%	4%	23%	77%
1999	94%	6%	25%	75%
1998	94%	6%	22%	78%

INTEREST GROUPS

	AFL-CIO	ADA	CCUS	ACU
2002	13%	0%	90%	96%
2001	0%	0%	95%	88%
2000	0%	0%	94%	91%
1999	22%	5%	84%	80%
1998	0%	5%	82%	91%

NORTH CAROLINA 10
West – Hickory

Set among the small towns of the western part of the state, the 10th has a rustic, small-business and conservative flavor.

While the 10th includes some suburban communities near Charlotte, it is mostly rural — only one town, Hickory, has a population of more than 20,000. The economy of the southern counties is based largely on textile and furniture manufacturing. Redistricting following the 2000 census added some cotton-growing areas. High-tech manufacturing is on the upswing, especially involving fiber-optic cable. Tourists visit the mountains near the Tennessee state line and ski in areas like Banner Elk (Avery County).

Some suburban sprawl has reached into the eastern and southern edges of the 10th, especially in Hickory, where the furniture industry employs a large part of the work force. Iredell County is mostly rural and agricultural, with some manufacturing.

Redistricting removed a swath of rock-ribbed Republican counties to the north and east and added cotton-producing, politically competitive Cleveland County. The changes reduced the GOP registration advantage, but many Democratic voters are conservatives who will support Republicans in federal races.

The 10th's GOP lean is set by Catawba County (Hickory), the district's most populous, which backed Republican Elizabeth Dole by a 30-point margin in the 2002 Senate race. Democrats run better in Cleveland and Burke counties, but Caldwell and Lincoln counties lean heavily Republican. Mitchell and Avery counties, on the Tennessee border, are strongly Republican as well. Avery was Dole's best county in the state (73 percent) in 2002.

MAJOR INDUSTRY
Manufacturing, agriculture, livestock

CITIES
Hickory, 37,222; Shelby, 19,477; Mooresville (pt.), 18,782; Morganton, 17,310; Lenoir, 16,793

NOTABLE
In 1917, the Elliott-Carnegie Public Library in Hickory was the last public library in the country to receive a grant from the Carnegie Foundation.

Rep. Charles H. Taylor (R)

CAPITOL OFFICE
225-6401
www.house.gov/charlestaylor
231 Cannon 20515-3311; fax 226-6422

COMMITTEES
Appropriations
(Interior - chairman)

HOMETOWN
Brevard

BORN
Jan. 23, 1941, Brevard, N.C.

RELIGION
Baptist

FAMILY
Wife, Elizabeth Taylor; three children

EDUCATION
Wake Forest U., B.A. 1963, J.D. 1966

CAREER
Tree farmer; banker

POLITICAL HIGHLIGHTS
N.C. House, 1967-73 (minority leader, 1969-71); N.C. Senate, 1973-75 (minority leader, 1973-75); Republican nominee for U.S. House, 1988

ELECTION RESULTS

2002 GENERAL		
Charles H. Taylor (R)	112,335	55.5%
Sam Neill (D)	86,664	42.9%
Eric Henry (LIBERT)	3,261	1.6%
2002 PRIMARY		
Charles H. Taylor (R)		unopposed
2000 GENERAL		
Charles H. Taylor (R)	146,677	55.1%
Sam Neill (D)	112,234	42.1%
C. Barry Williams (LIBERT)	7,466	2.8%

PREVIOUS WINNING PERCENTAGES
1998 (57%); 1996 (58%); 1994 (60%); 1992 (55%); 1990 (51%)

Elected 1990; 7th term

As House Republican leaders sought to put pro-business lawmakers in charge of environment-related committees in the 108th Congress, Taylor was seen as a good fit. The only registered forester in Congress, he was named chairman of the Interior Appropriations Subcommittee.

His conservative environmental record, including his 1995 bill that temporarily removed restrictions on some timber harvests, helped him move from the Legislative Branch Subcommittee to Interior, in the face of a challenge for the post from Republican George Nethercutt of Washington. Nethercutt unsuccessfully argued to party leaders that the shuffle of leadership posts threatened to leave Westerners without chairmanships on panels that oversee land use and natural resources.

Taylor has not been known for intellectual rigor or legislative acumen. But he has shown a knack for political survival, overcoming some off-kilter judgments on Capitol Hill and questions about his personal business dealings back home. A bank executive as well as tree farmer — and one of the House's wealthier members — Taylor is strongly pro-business, anti-Washington and socially conservative. But he also has won federal dollars to promote economic growth in his district, including millions of dollars for Internet-related education programs and biotech research, as well as money for an Alzheimer's care unit at the veterans hospital near Asheville.

Initially elected on a "reform Congress" platform, in his first term Taylor joined with six other GOP freshmen to form the "Gang of Seven," which gained national attention for their rabble-rousing campaign against congressional perquisites and for full disclosure during the House bank overdraft scandal of the 102nd Congress.

Taylor's dim view of federal government — he once declared on the House floor that "the government will mess up a one-car funeral" — sometimes causes the GOP leadership heartburn. For example, as the chairman of the Legislative Branch Subcommittee, which writes the bill that pays for congressional overhead, Taylor stirred things up in 2000 by proposing deep cuts in the budgets of several agencies, including the Capitol Police. (He toyed with the idea of requiring Capitol air conditioners to be turned off after July 1 to encourage adjournment each year by Independence Day.) House leaders later added money to the bill after lawmakers objected to Taylor's version.

Taylor wound up with the Legislative Branch gavel in the 106th after being turned down for the Military Construction Subcommittee, partly because of his unhappy stewardship of the District of Columbia Subcommittee, which writes the smallest of the 13 regular spending bills. During his first turn at chairing an Appropriations subcommittee, Taylor in 1997 and 1998 loaded the D.C. bill with so many policy add-ons reflecting his own conservative views that the legislation met with intense opposition. House GOP leaders ultimately took over negotiations on the measure and stripped most of the Taylor's "riders."

The congressman has been known to spar with members of his state's delegation. During consideration of a 2000 spending bill, he questioned the need for a $1.5 million study for hurricane flooding protection requested by North Carolina Democrat Eva Clayton. When the Congressional Black Caucus protested on behalf of one of its members, the GOP leadership gave her what she wanted.

Taylor has bucked his party leaders on other occasions, too, taking a protectionist stand on trade legislation to try to help an area that has seen many of its textile and furniture-making jobs sent overseas. He has opposed every free-trade bill during his tenure in Congress, from the 1993 North American Free Trade Agreement to the 2002 law granting President Bush fast-track trade negotiating authority.

Environmentalists criticized Taylor's elevation to the Interior Subcommittee chairmanship. Taylor, whose district includes the Great Smoky Mountains National Park and Blue Ridge Parkway, owns thousands of acres of timberland. He has consistently backed efforts to permit increased logging on public lands, and he pushed through the 1995 measure that waived environmental laws for 18 months to allow the removal of dead and dying trees from national forests. Environmentalists maintained green trees in the Northwest also were harvested.

"I am conservative, and that makes me an enemy of some of the ultra-liberal, radical, so-called environmental organizations, and I don't expect that to change," Taylor told The Asheville Citizen-Times.

Taylor won his first election to a state House seat in 1966, fresh out of law school. He later served in the state Senate, becoming minority leader in each chamber. After losing to Democratic Rep. James McClure Clarke in 1988, Taylor won a 1990 rematch for the House seat with 51 percent. Before 2000, he had won four re-elections with ease.

But that year and in 2002, he had to work hard to maintain the trust of voters. Both times, he was opposed by Democrat Sam Neill, a local lawyer, and both times he won with 55 percent of the vote.

His alleged failure to pay almost $48,000 in overdue property taxes on timberland he owns did not come up during his 2002 campaign as it did two years earlier. In 2000, he paid some of the taxes under protest after one county tax collector threatened to garnish his House salary. The dust-up led Majority Leader Dick Armey to issue a call at the state GOP convention: "Charlie Taylor, wherever you are — pay your taxes."

Taylor also faced criticism after revelations that he had extensive business ventures in Russia — including stakes in a potato warehouse, an apartment building and a chain of convenience stores — while he was cosponsoring a bill to create a program of U.S. aid for Russian home mortgages. At the same time, a federal grand jury was probing loans by Blue Ridge Savings Bank, where he is the chairman of the board. The loans, made to a longtime political ally of the congressman, exceeded thrift loan limits. The issue is still under investigation, but it did not hurt his re-election to the House.

KEY VOTES

2002

No Overhaul campaign finance law; ban "soft money" and restrict advocacy advertising
Yes Back Bush's defense budget increase
Yes Extend 1996 welfare law
Yes Adopt Bush's discretionary spending limit
Yes Pass GOP Medicare prescription drug plan
No Create independent Sept. 11 commission
No Extend union protections to Homeland Security Department employees
No Revive fast-track procedures for trade agreements
Yes Authorize war against Iraq
Yes Advance bankruptcy overhaul opposed by abortion opponents

2001

Yes Nullify Clinton Labor Department ergonomics rule
Yes Cut taxes by $1.35 trillion through fiscal 2011
No Maintain ban on oil drilling in Arctic National Wildlife Refuge
Yes Approve Bush proposal to limit managed-care plan liability for coverage decisions
No Divert money from crop subsidy payments to land conservation
Yes Expand law enforcement power to investigate suspected terrorists

CQ VOTE STUDIES

	PARTY UNITY		PRESIDENTIAL SUPPORT	
	Support	Oppose	Support	Oppose
2002	97%	3%	85%	15%
2001	97%	3%	86%	14%
2000	94%	6%	21%	79%
1999	96%	4%	16%	84%
1998	95%	5%	18%	82%

INTEREST GROUPS

	AFL-CIO	ADA	CCUS	ACU
2002	14%	5%	90%	96%
2001	8%	10%	82%	92%
2000	11%	5%	72%	92%
1999	22%	5%	78%	100%
1998	20%	5%	88%	96%

NORTH CAROLINA 11
West – Asheville

Based in the Great Smoky Mountain region, the 11th is a largely rural district dotted with tree farms, wood mills and campgrounds. While agriculture and forestry long have played a key role in the region's economy, retail trade, health care and education are becoming major employers. Tourism also has a large role, with people flocking to the area's ski slopes, as well as to the hiking trails in national parks and on Mount Mitchell (the highest peak east of the Mississippi River). Tourists also enjoy the palatial Biltmore House, once home of Cornelius Vanderbilt's grandson.

Asheville — which along with surrounding Buncombe County takes in one-third of the district's residents — is the 11th's economic focal point. Residents recently spruced up the city's downtown, and efforts are underway to attract high-tech businesses. The decline of the textile industry has led to a loss of jobs in the district.

Attractive to retirees, the 11th has the highest median age (41) of any North Carolina district. It also has the smallest black population, as the only sizable African-American constituency is in Asheville. The Cherokee Indian Reservation in Swain and Jackson counties gives the district a larger than average American Indian population.

The 11th leans Republican. Buncombe voted for George W. Bush in the 2000 presidential election, as did every other county in the district. But Buncombe was a classic swing county in the 2002 Senate race, in the end backing Republican Elizabeth Dole by exactly one vote out of more than 63,000 cast. Henderson County, the district's second-most-populous, votes solidly Republican.

MAJOR INDUSTRY

Retail trade, forest products, tourism, health care

CITIES

Asheville, 68,889; Hendersonville, 10,420; Waynesville, 9,232

NOTABLE

Many of the state's Cherokee Indians are descendants of the estimated 1,000 Cherokees who hid in the mountains of western North Carolina to avoid the forced migration to Oklahoma along the path now known as the Trail of Tears; The Billy Graham Evangelistic Association operates a 1,500-acre training center called "The Cove" in Asheville; Movies filmed at Asheville's Biltmore House include "Forrest Gump" and "Hannibal."

Rep. Melvin Watt (D)

CAPITOL OFFICE
225-1510
nc12.public@mail.house.gov
www.house.gov/watt
2236 Rayburn 20515-3312; fax 225-1512

COMMITTEES
Financial Services
Judiciary
Joint Economic

HOMETOWN
Charlotte

BORN
Aug. 26, 1945, Steele Creek, N.C.

RELIGION
Presbyterian

FAMILY
Wife, Eulada Watt; two children

EDUCATION
U. of North Carolina, B.S. 1967 (business administration); Yale U., J.D. 1970

CAREER
Nursing home owner; campaign manager; lawyer

POLITICAL HIGHLIGHTS
N.C. Senate, 1985-86

ELECTION RESULTS

2002 GENERAL		
Melvin Watt (D)	98,821	65.3%
Jeff Kish (R)	49,588	32.8%
Carey Head (LIBERT)	2,830	1.9%
2002 PRIMARY		
Melvin Watt (D)	33,853	84.7%
Kimberly Holley (D)	6,107	15.3%
2000 GENERAL		
Melvin Watt (D)	135,570	64.8%
Joshua "Chad" Mitchell (R)	69,596	33.3%
Anna Lyon (LIBERT)	3,978	1.9%

PREVIOUS WINNING PERCENTAGES
1998 (56%); 1996 (71%); 1994 (66%); 1992 (70%)

Elected 1992; 6th term

Watt has two very different congressional personae. The first — a partisan liberal and staunch defender of the Constitution — is reserved for his dealings on the Judiciary Committee, which considers legislation on many highly contentious social policies. But on Financial Services, Watt's style is more bipartisan, and he frequently pairs with his Republican colleagues in attempts to broker compromise.

"Judiciary is just by its nature a very confrontational and quite often a partisan committee," he says. "It's hard not to have people walk away from those debates with some kind of stereotype of you as uncompromising. So when people see me on the other committee, they think it's Dr. Jekyll and Mr. Hyde."

Watt is capable of playing both roles well. But, as he starts his second decade in the House, his bipartisanship on financial legislation is often eclipsed by his frequently unpopular — and lonely — stands against legislation that he views as unconstitutional or as infringing on civil rights.

Six weeks after the terrorist attacks of Sept. 11, 2001, for example, Watt was among the 66 House members who voted against enacting the law granting law enforcement agents broad new powers. Watt said the measure would erode civil liberties and hand police too much power to monitor the activities of the innocent. "Some of us who have a different history in America with delegation of authority to the government and the abuse of that authority proceed a lot differently than others," Watt said. "We cannot just come in, in the middle of a terrorism episode, and forget all the history that has occurred in our country."

The stand was not unusual for Watt, a civil rights lawyer for 22 years before coming to Congress. And his views sometimes put him in unexpected alliances. In his civil liberties-based opposition to the 2001 anti-terrorism measure, Watt teamed up with Republican Bob Barr of Georgia, whose conservatism was anathema to most Democrats but who was also perhaps the most prominent Republican civil libertarian in the House at the time.

On Judiciary, where he is the top Democrat on the Commercial and Administrative Law Subcommittee, he is known for meticulous attention to legislative detail. He schools himself in the most arcane corners of the law at issue, then makes his case with a combination of lawyerly precision and passionate oratory.

During debate in the 107th and the 106th Congresses over rewriting bankruptcy law, Watt steered clear of the partisan brawling. While other liberal Democrats blasted the GOP plan as anti-consumer and a sellout to the credit card industry, Watt quietly focused on the minutiae of the bill, line-by-line, phrase-by-phrase, to build a case against the Republican package. Upon its reintroduction in the 108th Congress, Watt condemned it as "terrible public policy" that would create two bankruptcy systems, one for the rich and one for the poor.

On Financial Services, Watt eagerly looks for Republicans in search of a deal, often scribbling proposed amendments in the margins of the legislative language under discussion. In 2002, he joined with Vito J. Fossella, a New York Republican, to win inclusion in the terrorism insurance law of a provision allowing terrorists' frozen assets to be used to pay compensatory damages.

Although Watt sees his role on Financial Services as an advocate for the little guy, he is on cordial terms with the business community and takes its views into account. Charlotte's big financial services companies, including Wachovia and Bank of America, would no doubt prefer to have a more conservative congressman, but Watt at least gives their opinions a fair hearing. He occasionally agrees with them — opposing, for example, proposals to raise the $100,000 ceiling on federally insured deposits. "Trying to walk the balance between the banker interests and the consumer interests is very difficult," he says.

Watt is actively involved in the panel's work on housing and urban affairs. In the 107th, he successfully amended housing legislation, though it was never enacted, to develop a new federal database that would serve to inform tenants of affordable housing opportunities.

The underpinning of Watt's dogged determination can be gleaned from a quick reading of his life story. Raised in a fatherless household, he grew up in a tin-roofed shack in rural Mecklenburg County that lacked running water or electricity. After attending a segregated high school he went on to graduate Phi Beta Kappa from the University of North Carolina at Chapel Hill, then earned a law degree from Yale. He interrupted his law practice for a brief stint to serve as an appointed state senator and to manage the 1990 Senate campaign of Democrat Harvey Gantt, who nearly upset GOP incumbent Jesse Helms that year.

In 1992, when a circuitously shaped black-majority district was created, Watt won it with relative ease and became one of the first African-American North Carolinians in Congress since 1901. But the boundaries of Watt's constituency were subject to legal challenge throughout the 1990s, and the 12th District's lines were redrawn twice during the decade in response to lawsuits alleging unconstitutional racial gerrymandering.

In 2001, the state's congressional map was redrawn yet again, this time because North Carolina received an additional House seat as a result of population gains. The Democrats in charge of the process made sure to give Watt an electorally safe territory in which to run. But the changing shape of his district has proved more of a distraction than a political threat: Only once in six elections has he been held to less than three-fifths of the vote.

Watt is a good athlete, and Democrats have relied heavily on him in the annual charity baseball game that pits his party against GOP lawmakers. As a star pitcher, Watt has had trouble controlling his curveball, but he was the Democrats' most valuable player in the 1995 and 1996 games, and he was the winning pitcher and co-MVP in 2000.

KEY VOTES

2002

- Yes Overhaul campaign finance law; ban "soft money" and restrict advocacy advertising
- No Back Bush's defense budget increase
- No Extend 1996 welfare law
- No Adopt Bush's discretionary spending limit
- No Pass GOP Medicare prescription drug plan
- Yes Create independent Sept. 11 commission
- Yes Extend union protections to Homeland Security Department employees
- No Revive fast-track procedures for trade agreements
- No Authorize war against Iraq
- No Advance bankruptcy overhaul opposed by abortion opponents

2001

- No Nullify Clinton Labor Department ergonomics rule
- No Cut taxes by $1.35 trillion through fiscal 2011
- Yes Maintain ban on oil drilling in Arctic National Wildlife Refuge
- No Approve Bush proposal to limit managed-care plan liability for coverage decisions
- No Divert money from crop subsidy payments to land conservation
- No Expand law enforcement power to investigate suspected terrorists

CQ VOTE STUDIES

	PARTY UNITY		PRESIDENTIAL SUPPORT	
	Support	Oppose	Support	Oppose
2002	97%	3%	25%	75%
2001	96%	4%	12%	88%
2000	94%	6%	82%	18%
1999	94%	6%	83%	17%
1998	96%	4%	91%	9%

INTEREST GROUPS

	AFL-CIO	ADA	CCUS	ACU
2002	88%	90%	40%	4%
2001	100%	95%	30%	0%
2000	100%	85%	45%	8%
1999	100%	100%	12%	0%
1998	100%	100%	28%	4%

NORTH CAROLINA 12

Central – parts of Charlotte, Winston-Salem and Greensboro

The 12th became known as the mother of all racial gerrymanders when it was originally drawn for the 1992 elections. Struck down by the courts and widely ridiculed for a serpentine shape that aimed to maximize the black population, the 12th was redrawn twice in the 1990s. Redistricting following the 2000 census made only minimal changes to the district that finally survived challenge. The new 12th includes parts of six counties, is 45 percent black and, among North Carolina districts, is rivaled only by the black-majority 1st in its overwhelming Democratic lean.

While not as wildly contorted as its 1990s predecessors, the current 12th forms a zigzag shape that begins in Charlotte, parallels Interstate 85 north and east to take in part of Salisbury, then branches out to scoop up large black populations in Winston-Salem, High Point and Greensboro. The 12th includes about one-third of Charlotte's population but two-thirds of its black population, and 60 percent of Winston-Salem's population but nearly 90 percent of its black residents. Most black constituents in the 12th are lower- to middle-class.

Charlotte, where nearly one-third of district residents live, has a booming economy. After a decade of consolidation among banks, the city surprised many by becoming the nation's biggest banking center outside of New York — the massive Bank of America is headquartered here. But the city's downtown — known as "uptown" — also has its share of poverty and crime. The Biddleville neighborhood, west of the business district, is a hub of the black community and home to the predominantly black Johnson C. Smith University. Outside of the city, transplants accustomed to New York City real estate prices have built upscale suburban neighborhoods with matching decorative street signs.

MAJOR INDUSTRY

Finance, transportation, health care

CITIES

Charlotte (pt.), 196,125; Winston-Salem (pt.), 115,986; Greensboro (pt.), 62,075; High Point (pt.), 52,429; Salisbury (pt.), 26,399

NOTABLE

A Woolworth's lunch counter in Greensboro was the site of the first major civil rights sit-in in 1960.

Rep. Brad Miller (D)

Elected 2002; 1st term

Eight years in the North Carolina General Assembly — and an ability to win a House seat in a region where Democratic fortunes have been waning — brought Miller to his party colleagues' attention. They chose him as a regional whip in his freshman year.

Miller credits a trip to Washington as a youngster for planting the seeds of his interest in politics. He worked on a local campaign in high school, and he started seeking elective office less than a decade out of law school.

Along the way he earned a master's degree from the London School of Economics, which may help him as he works on behalf of the state's burgeoning banking industry. To that end, he got a seat on the Financial Services Committee. He also won assignment to the Science panel, which oversees programs that steer federal money to the state's Research Triangle.

Miller began his political career ambitiously, with a 1988 run for North Carolina secretary of state. He lost the primary, but he was elected to the state House in 1992. Miller was defeated in the big 1994 Republican surge, but two years later he unseated an incumbent GOP state senator.

Miller did not know until five months before Election Day whether the congressional seat that he was seeking would actually exist: North Carolina's growth earned it an additional seat in the reapportionment after the 2000 census, but Utah alleged in federal court that it should receive the seat because the census methodology was improper. The Supreme Court ruled, 5-4, in North Carolina's favor in June 2002. By that time, Miller, as chairman of the state Senate Redistricting Committee, had helped enact a state law drawing the new 13th District with a Democratic edge and including much of his political base.

In a six-way Democratic primary, Miller won by 16 percentage points over Robin Britt, who had served one term in the House in the early 1980s. In November, Miller defeated Republican businesswoman Carolyn W. Grant by 12 points in an unfriendly contest; she later sued Miller, charging that he libeled her in campaign advertising.

CAPITOL OFFICE
225-3032
www.house.gov/bradmiller
1505 Longworth 20515-3313; fax 225-0181

COMMITTEES
Financial Services
Science
Small Business

HOMETOWN
Raleigh

BORN
May 19, 1953, Fayetteville, N.C.

RELIGION
Episcopalian

FAMILY
Wife, Esther Hall

EDUCATION
U. of North Carolina, B.A. 1975 (political science); London School of Economics, M.S.C. 1978 (comparative government); Columbia U., J.D. 1979

CAREER
Lawyer

POLITICAL HIGHLIGHTS
Sought Democratic nomination for N.C. secretary of state, 1988; N.C. House, 1993-95; defeated for re-election to N.C. House, 1994; N.C. Senate, 1997-2002

ELECTION RESULTS

2002 GENERAL		
Brad Miller (D)	100,287	54.7%
Carolyn W. Grant (R)	77,688	42.4%
Alex MacDonald (LIBERT)	5,295	2.9%
2002 PRIMARY		
Brad Miller (D)	22,130	41.8%
Charles Robin Britt (D)	13,490	25.5%
Bill Martin (D)	8,021	15.1%
Lawrence Davis (D)	6,911	13.0%
Gene Gay (D)	2,459	4.6%

NORTH CAROLINA 13

North central — parts of Raleigh and Greensboro

The newly drawn 13th, awarded to growing North Carolina in the 2000 reapportionment, is defined by its urban anchors of Greensboro and Raleigh, which sandwich several rural counties along the Virginia border. Almost half the population lives in Wake County (Raleigh), including a large number of government employees and recent out-of-state transplants.

The district encompasses northern and central Raleigh, an area that falls into the Research Triangle and is built around an economy of high technology, biotechnology and financial services. The 13th takes in about 70 percent of Raleigh, which it shares with the 2nd and 4th districts. The 13th's slice of the city includes most of downtown and the state Capitol.

While Raleigh and Greensboro have grown rapidly and feature diverse economies, the northern, rural areas of Caswell and Alamance counties still rely heavily on manufacturing and farming, particularly textiles and tobacco.

The 13th has an overall Democratic lean, in part because of a sizable black population and a number of white moderates and liberals in the urban areas. Registered Democrats outnumber Republicans by nearly 2-to-1, but the actual Democratic advantage at the polls is smaller. The potential for swing voting exists in both the cities and suburbs. District voters only narrowly supported Al Gore in the 2000 presidential election, but voted more decisively for Democrat Michael F. Easley in the 2000 gubernatorial race.

MAJOR INDUSTRY
Biotechnology, financial services, textiles, agriculture

CITIES
Raleigh (pt.), 192,576; Greensboro (pt.), 102,806; Burlington (pt.), 23,836

NOTABLE
Caswell County features one of the largest Amish communities in the South.

NORTH DAKOTA

Gov. John Hoeven (R)

First elected: 2000
Length of term: 4 years
Term expires: 12/04
Salary: $85,586
Phone: (701) 328-2200
Hometown: Bismarck
Born: March 13, 1957; Bismarck, N.D.
Religion: Roman Catholic
Family: Wife, Mical Hoeven; two children
Education: Dartmouth College, B.A. 1979 (history & economics); Northwestern U., M.B.A. 1981 (finance & accounting)
Career: Bank CEO
Political highlights: No previous office
Election results:

2000 GENERAL		
John Hoeven (R)	159,255	55.0%
Heidi Heitkamp (D)	130,147	45.0%

Lt. Gov. Jack Dalrymple (R)

First elected: 2000
Length of term: 4 years
Term expires: 12/04
Salary: $66,384
Phone: (701) 328-2200

STATE LEGISLATURE

Legislature: Meets January-April in odd-numbered years
House: 94 members, 4-year terms
2003 breakdown: 66R, 28D; 77 men, 17 women
Salary: $3,000; $125/day in session
Phone: (701) 328-2916
Senate: 47 members, 4-year terms
2003 breakdown: 31R, 16D; 42 men, 5 women
Salary: $3,000; $125/day in session
Phone: (701) 328-2916

STATE TERM LIMITS

Governor: No
Senate: No
House: No

URBAN STATISTICS

CITY	POPULATION
Fargo	90,599
Bismarck	55,532
Grand Forks	49,321
Minot	36,567
Mandan	16,718

REGISTERED VOTERS

Voters do not register by party.

POPULATION

2002 population (est.)	634,110
2000 population	642,200
1990 population	638,800
Percent change (1990-2000)	+0.5%
Rank among states (2002)	48
Median age	36.2
Born in state	72.5%
Foreign born	1.9%
Violent crime rate	81/100,000
Poverty level	11.9%
Federal workers	9,656
Military	12,479

REDISTRICTING

North Dakota retained its one House seat in reapportionment.

MISCELLANEOUS

Web: www.state.nd.us
Capital: Bismarck

STATE ELECTION OFFICIAL
(701) 328-4146

DEMOCRATIC HEADQUARTERS
(701) 255-0460

REPUBLICAN HEADQUARTERS
(701) 255-0030

District Statistics

DIST.	2000 VOTE FOR PRESIDENT BUSH	GORE	NADER	WHITE	BLACK	ASIAN	HISP	MEDIAN INCOME	WHITE COLLAR	BLUE COLLAR	SERVICE INDUSTRY	OVER 64	UNDER 18	COLLEGE EDUCATION	RURAL	SQ. MILES
AL	61%	33%	3%	92%	1%	1%	1%	$34,604	59%	24%	17%	15%	25%	22%	44%	68,976
STATE	61	33	3	92	1	1	1	$34,604	59	24	17	15	25	22	44	68,976
U.S.	47.9	48.4	3	69	12	4	13	$41,994	60	25	15	12	26	24	21	3,537,438

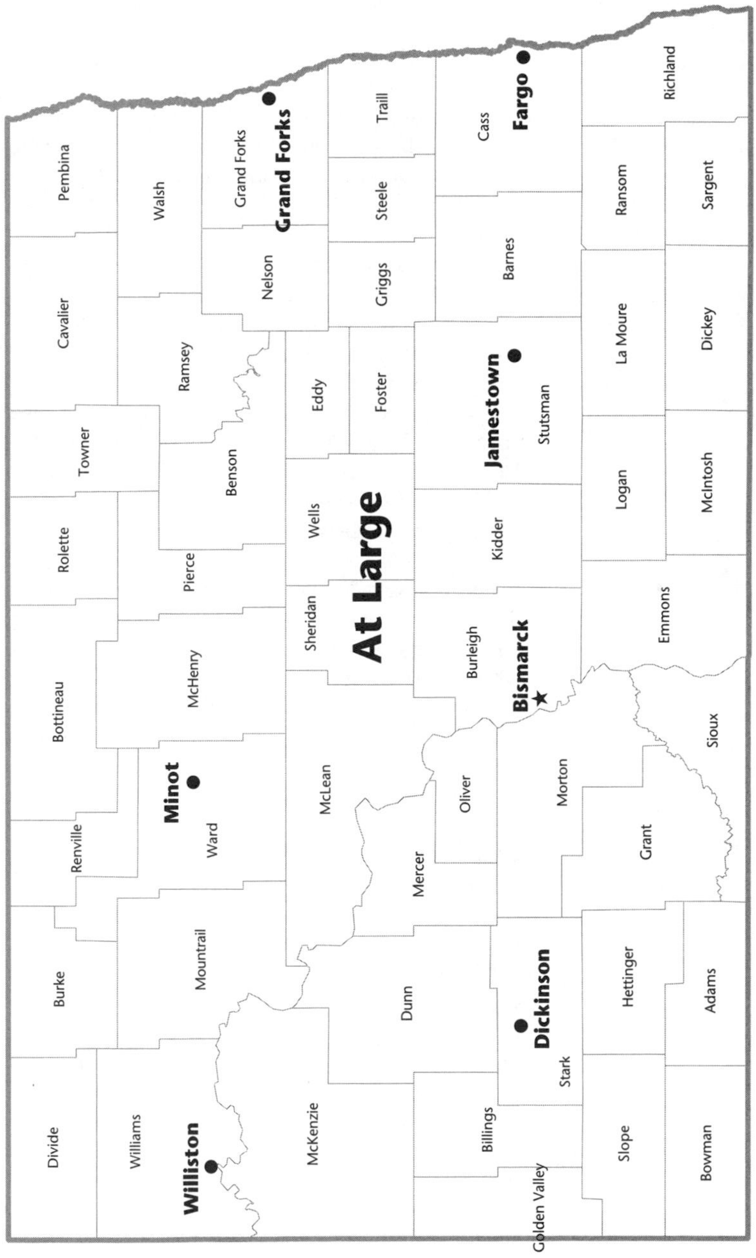
At Large
Pembina
Walsh
Grand Forks
Grand Forks
Traill
Cass
Fargo
Richland
Cavalier
Nelson
Steele
Ransom
Sargent
Griggs
Barnes
Ramsey
Towner
Benson
Eddy
Foster
Jamestown
Stutsman
La Moure
Dickey
Rolette
Pierce
Wells
Kidder
Logan
McIntosh
Bottineau
McHenry
Sheridan
Burleigh
Bismarck
Emmons
Renville
Minot
Ward
McLean
Oliver
Morton
Sioux
Mercer
Grant
Burke
Mountrail
Dunn
Dickinson
Stark
Hettinger
Adams
Divide
Williams
Williston
McKenzie
Billings
Golden Valley
Slope
Bowman

Sen. Kent Conrad (D)

CAPITOL OFFICE
224-2043
senator@conrad.senate.gov
conrad.senate.gov
530 Hart 20510-3403; fax 224-7776

COMMITTEES
Agriculture, Nutrition & Forestry
Budget - ranking member
Finance
Indian Affairs

HOMETOWN
Bismarck

BORN
March 12, 1948, Bismarck, N.D.

RELIGION
Unitarian

FAMILY
Wife, Lucy Calautti; one child

EDUCATION
U. of Missouri, attended 1967; Stanford U., A.B. 1971 (government & political science); George Washington U., M.B.A. 1975

CAREER
Management and personnel director

POLITICAL HIGHLIGHTS
Candidate for N.D. auditor, 1976; N.D. tax commissioner, 1981-87

ELECTION RESULTS

2000 GENERAL

Kent Conrad (D)	176,470	61.5%
Duane Sand (R)	110,420	38.5%

2000 PRIMARY

Kent Conrad (D)	unopposed

PREVIOUS WINNING PERCENTAGES
1994 (58%); 1992 Special Election (63%); 1986 (50%)

Elected 1986; 3rd full term

On the wall of Conrad's office in Bismarck hangs a framed resolution, a gift from the Standing Rock Sioux Tribe. The citation uses Conrad's honorary Sioux name, "Namni Sni," which means, "Never Turns Back."

Friends and foes alike say that title well suits Conrad. He may present himself with the bookish air of someone who was once his state's top tax collector. But Conrad comes across in the Senate as extraordinarily dogged, whether he is hammering away at Republican economic policies from his perch as the Budget Committee's top Democrat or battling on behalf of his state's wheat growers or rural hospitals. He is not averse to reciting the same catchy phrase every day — sometimes, the same one for months on end — to hammer home his views on a topic.

Conrad's persistence was put to the test in the middle of 2001, when the switch of partisan control of the Senate made him the Budget Committee chairman. He had been preparing for the post his entire Senate career. A self-styled budget purist obsessed with fiscal discipline, Conrad was charged with the unenviable task of writing a budget resolution that would please Democrats of all fiscal stripes, from Southern conservatives such as Zell Miller of Georgia to traditional Northeastern liberals such as Edward M. Kennedy of Massachusetts.

In his first big challenge, Conrad managed to get a budget out of his committee on a party-line vote in 2002, but he never came close to rounding up 51 Senate votes for it. As a result, Senate Democratic leaders opted to never bring the measure to the floor. This marked the first time since the advent of the modern budget process in 1974 that the Senate did not adopt a budget resolution, a fact Republicans noted with glee.

But in many respects, Conrad's fate was sealed by forces beyond his control. The Sept. 11, 2001, terrorist attacks ensured bipartisan support for large increases in defense spending. And, with the economy in poor shape, not even fiscal conservatives such as Conrad wanted to push for repealing President Bush's $1.35 billion tax cut. So Conrad was left with no politically palatable way to write a budget plan.

When the Republicans regained control of the Senate in 2003, Conrad returned to his role as the loyal — and vocal — opposition leader on Budget. With his trademark sheath of pie charts and bar graphs at the ready, Conrad stepped up his attacks on Bush's fiscal strategy, calling the 2001 tax cut "a massive raid on the Medicare trust fund and the Social Security trust fund" and blaming it for sending the government "back in the deficit ditch."

Although he is a member of the moderate, pro-business wing of the party known as the New Democrats, Conrad's role as a close ally of Democratic leader Tom Daschle frequently requires him to take on the role of partisan attack dog. Some observers say Conrad seems intent on having the last word in any debate — a trait that sometimes drives his GOP colleagues to distraction. Supporters insist Conrad simply wants to ensure his positions are clear.

Conrad does not fit the stereotype of a "son of the soil"; he looks more like a "Jeopardy" contestant. But he is a relentless advocate for farmers, and he strives to make sure the people of North Dakota and other sparsely populated states are not ignored in Washington. A constant critic of the 1996 farm law, which sought to phase out traditional crop subsidies and replace them with fixed but declining annual payments, Conrad played a central role in writing the 2002 reversal of that policy that provided for a substantial expansion of subsidies.

Conrad concedes that his fiscal sensibilities sometimes conflict with his desire to help out his agrarian constituents. And he participated in several failed attempts by Western lawmakers to provide emergency aid to farmers and ranchers hit by drought in 2001 and 2002.

Conrad also has not been bashful about pressing for millions of dollars in improvements to the Air Force bases in Grand Forks and Minot. He proudly points to the state National Guard's 119th Fighter Wing — nicknamed the Happy Hooligans — whose F-16 fighter pilots were the first scrambled to guard the airspace over Washington on Sept. 11.

His record on international trade tracks Conrad's concerns about the farm economy. He voted against the North American Free Trade Agreement in 1993 because he feared that U.S. wheat prices would drop after an influx of Canadian wheat. He supported the 2000 law making permanent the normal U.S.-China trade relationship, predicting it would lead to an exporting boom for the grain growers of the Great Plains. And he opposed the 2002 law that renewed presidential fast-track trade negotiating powers, arguing that it would put U.S. farmers at a competitive disadvantage. He voted "no" even though the law provides for federal aid to farmers hurt by an influx of imports — a provision he had pursued for years.

Conrad has disappointed conservatives at times by signaling he might support them, then opposing them at the last minute. In the 106th Congress, he and North Dakota's other senator, Democrat Byron L. Dorgan, decided after much deliberation to oppose a constitutional amendment barring flag desecration. In the 104th, Conrad made a late decision to oppose a constitutional amendment mandating a balanced federal budget, which he said he feared could threaten Social Security.

On most social issues, Conrad takes stands that reflect the more conservative side of the prairie populist tradition from which he hails. He voted to override President Clinton's veto of a ban on a procedure its opponents call "partial birth" abortion. He also opposes allowing federal employees' health care plans to cover abortion.

Conrad's early years were marked by the death of his parents, who were killed by a drunken driver when he was 5. He and his brothers were raised by his grandparents. He went to high school at a U.S. military base in Libya, where he lived with family friends. Upon his return to North Dakota, he headed a successful statewide campaign — while still a teenager — to grant voting rights to 19-year-olds.

He was elected state tax commissioner in 1980, and he gained widespread popularity by vigorously auditing out-of-state corporations. In 1986, he unseated Republican Sen. Mark Andrews by 2,000 votes after linking the incumbent to the Reagan administration's unpopular farm policy.

One of Conrad's pledges during that campaign was that he would not seek re-election unless the trade and budget deficits were dramatically reduced during his term in office. In April 1992, Conrad kept his promise by announcing his Senate retirement, even though he joked that he had written the pledge while suffering from a 104-degree fever.

But on Sept. 8, 1992, North Dakota's senior senator, Democrat Quentin N. Burdick, died at age 84 — leaving two years in his Senate term. Democrats urged Conrad to run in a special election the following December, and he was unchallenged for the party's nomination. He won with 63 percent of the vote against Republican state Rep. Jack Dalrymple, and his re-elections in both 1994 and 2000 were by comfortable margins.

Both Conrad and his wife, Lucy Calautti, are avid baseball fans. She became Major League Baseball's lobbyist in Washington in 2000, and Conrad has expressed a desire to be baseball commissioner someday.

KEY VOTES

2002

Yes Pass farm bill reversing crop subsidy limits
Yes Postpone tougher automobile fuel efficiency standards
Yes Overhaul campaign finance law; ban "soft money" and restrict advocacy advertising
Yes Set federal election standards
No Support oil drilling in Arctic National Wildlife Refuge
No Revive fast-track procedures for trade agreements
Yes Create federal insurance coverage for catastrophic terrorist losses
Yes Tighten federal accounting and corporate governance regulation
Yes Advance bipartisan Medicare prescription drug plan
Yes Create independent Sept. 11 commission
Yes Back Democratic Homeland Security Department proposal
No Authorize war against Iraq

2001

Yes Confirm John Ashcroft as attorney general
No Nullify Clinton Labor Department ergonomics rule
No Cut taxes by $1.35 trillion through fiscal 2011
Yes Pass Democratic bill to bolster rights of patients in managed-care plans
No Permit a new round of military base closings
Yes Expand law enforcement power to investigate suspected terrorists

CQ VOTE STUDIES

	PARTY UNITY		PRESIDENTIAL SUPPORT	
	Support	Oppose	Support	Oppose
2002	86%	14%	66%	34%
2001	90%	10%	66%	34%
2000	87%	13%	90%	10%
1999	87%	13%	73%	27%
1998	87%	13%	75%	25%
1997	82%	18%	81%	19%
1996	87%	13%	83%	17%
1995	87%	13%	84%	16%
1994	85%	15%	89%	11%
1993	82%	18%	82%	18%

INTEREST GROUPS

	AFL-CIO	ADA	CCUS	ACU
2002	100%	95%	45%	10%
2001	94%	85%	50%	36%
2000	71%	85%	42%	29%
1999	89%	90%	53%	16%
1998	88%	90%	61%	16%
1997	57%	65%	50%	16%
1996	71%	85%	23%	15%
1995	100%	90%	42%	9%
1994	75%	85%	40%	12%
1993	82%	80%	9%	24%

Sen. Byron L. Dorgan (D)

CAPITOL OFFICE
224-2551
senator@dorgan.senate.gov
dorgan.senate.gov
713 Hart 20510-3405; fax 224-1193

COMMITTEES
Appropriations
Commerce, Science & Transportation
Energy & Natural Resources
Indian Affairs

HOMETOWN
Bismarck

BORN
May 14, 1942, Regent, N.D.

RELIGION
Lutheran

FAMILY
Wife, Kimberly Dorgan; four children (one deceased)

EDUCATION
U. of North Dakota, B.S. 1965; U. of Denver, M.B.A. 1966

CAREER
Aerospace company management trainer

POLITICAL HIGHLIGHTS
N.D. tax commissioner, 1969-80; Democratic nominee for U.S. House, 1974; U.S. House, 1981-92

ELECTION RESULTS

1998 GENERAL		
Byron L. Dorgan (D)	134,747	63.2%
Donna Nalewaja (R)	75,013	35.2%
Harley McLain (REF)	3,598	1.7%
1998 PRIMARY		
Byron L. Dorgan (D)		unopposed

PREVIOUS WINNING PERCENTAGES
1992 (59%); 1990 House Election (65%); 1988 House Election (71%); 1986 House Election (76%); 1984 House Election (79%); 1982 House Election (72%); 1980 House Election (57%)

Elected 1992; 2nd term

Dorgan is a contemporary voice for the prairie populism that swept North Dakota in the 1910s. The Senate's tolerance for lengthy speech-making gives him ample opportunity to rail at the large and distant forces — corporations, foreign governments, international financial institutions — that, he says, don't care a whit for the common folk.

The North Dakotan is a strong public speaker who even one-on-one is passionate about his beliefs, especially when it comes to helping struggling farmers. A true small-town boy, his hometown is the wheat-growing and ranching community of Regent, where, he likes to say, he graduated in the top five in his high school class — of nine.

Despite his clear attachment to his home state, Dorgan is also tied into the Washington elite. He and his family live in the tony suburb of McLean, Va., where the senator often can be seen playing tennis and golfing, sometimes with well-known politicos. His wife, Kimberly, is a senior vice president for the American Council of Life Insurers and was Linda Hall's maid of honor when she married Tom Daschle in 1984. A year later, Mrs. Daschle was maid of honor when Kimberly Olson became Dorgan's second wife.

Dorgan is similarly tight with his North Dakota partner in the Senate. When he first ran for Congress in 1974, his campaign manager was Kent Conrad, and when he won a House seat six years later, Dorgan's successor as state tax commissioner was Conrad. Lucy Calautti, Conrad's wife, was Dorgan's chief of staff for 10 years.

As chairman of the Democratic Policy Committee, Dorgan is a lieutenant of Daschle's in charting the party's legislative and political course in the Senate. It is a post that suits the soundbite-proficient Dorgan well, as he willingly takes to the floor at a moment's notice to explain the party position or to fend off Republican challenges. Dorgan is especially visible during times of agricultural hardship or corporate wrongdoing.

In the 107th Congress the senator was an early and ardent supporter of a generous new farm bill, one that abandoned the GOP precepts of price-support policy enacted in 1996 and reinstituted the types of commodity price supports that had been a main economic safety net under farmers since the New Deal. Dorgan's chief accomplishment was attaching to the Senate version language limiting subsidies to the largest farms, often agents of the corporate entities that Dorgan views as the family farmer's primary enemy. (The language was dropped in negotiations on the final bill.) While other lawmakers derided the law enacted in 2002 as an unnecessary budget-buster, Dorgan called for even more farm spending — his state was besieged by both floods and drought at the time — in the form of an emergency aid package juts a few months later.

While weather is the main bane of North Dakota's agrarian economy, big business often has played the villain's role in the eyes of the state's politicians. The collapse of the energy giant Enron and numerous accounting misdeeds by other multinational corporations gave Dorgan carte blanche to delve into corporate wrongdoing in the 107th. As the chairman of the Commerce Subcommittee on Consumer Affairs, Dorgan called one of the first hearings on the issue and later held a well-publicized session featuring former Enron CEO Jeffrey Skilling. "This is disgusting to me — corporate behavior without a moral base," Dorgan said.

Legislatively, Dorgan spent much of his time in the 107th pushing a bill, known as the Homestead Economic Opportunity Act, to waive taxes and forgive student loans for young people who move back to counties with declining populations. He also had sought to ensure that rural areas are not left out of the technological revolution.

He long has been a leader in the effort to end the embargo on trade with with Cuba, which otherwise would be a market for peas and other North Dakota crops. And he backed the 2000 law making permanent the normal trade relationship between the United States and China, another enormous market for American commodities. But Dorgan opposed the 2002 law granting President Bush expedited trade negotiating authority, predicting the consequence would be agreements that harmed U.S. farmers.

Republicans have branded Dorgan as too liberal for his state, though his voting record puts him toward the conservative end of the Senate Democratic spectrum. He joined Republicans, for example, in supporting the 1996 welfare overhaul. He was one of eight Democrats who voted to confirm John Ashcroft as attorney general in 2001 and was in the minority of Democrats who voted in 2002 to authorize the use of force in Iraq.

But conservatives who hoped Dorgan would side with them on a constitutional amendment to ban flag desecration were infuriated in 2000 when he announced his opposition to the measure. "Almost never have we passed constitutional amendments to take power away from people," Dorgan said. "Most amendments have expanded the concept of freedom."

His reaction to the flag amendment recalled Dorgan's pivotal role in the demise of another proposed constitutional amendment, to require a balanced federal budget. Although Dorgan had voted for such an amendment in 1994, the next year he and Conrad conditioned their continued support on the addition of language to protect Social Security. Republicans would not agree to that, both North Dakotans voted "no," and the amendment fell barely short of the two-thirds majority required.

In general, Dorgan tries to straddle hot-button issues. In the 107th, for example, he attempted to find the middle ground on plans to ban cloning and to repeal the estate tax. In the end, cloning legislation never came up and Dorgan voted against the 2001 tax cut, which phases out the estate tax.

On some issues, however, Dorgan is a nearly solitary voice. He has been one of the most vocal critics of the Federal Reserve's tendency to raise interest rates to fight inflation at the expense of economic growth. In 2000, he was one of just four senators to oppose Fed Chairman Alan Greenspan's confirmation for a fourth term.

Other than a brief stint with a Denver-based aerospace firm, Dorgan has spent virtually all of his career in government. He was working in the state tax department in 1969 when the governor appointed him commissioner, making him the youngest constitutional officer in North Dakota history. By speaking out on an array of issues and suing out-of-state corporations to force them to pay taxes, he made a name for himself with voters.

Dorgan made it clear he had higher political ambitions by taking on GOP Rep. Mark Andrews in 1974. He held Andrews to 56 percent. When Andrews ran for the Senate in 1980, Dorgan won his House seat in a campaign in which he tempered his liberal reputation by supporting an anti-abortion constitutional amendment and decrying government waste. He won five re-elections with ease and became a leading opponent on the Ways and Means Committee of the tax cuts proposed by Presidents Reagan and George Bush.

He won election to the Senate in 1992, after Conrad announced he was retiring to fulfill a campaign pledge to leave the Senate that year unless the deficit was reduced. (Conrad won a Senate seat that year anyway after Sen. Quentin N. Burdick died.) Dorgan cruised to re-election in 1998 against his underfunded GOP foe by touting his success in winning aid for farmers and steering federal funds to North Dakota.

KEY VOTES

2002

Yes Pass farm bill reversing crop subsidy limits
Yes Postpone tougher automobile fuel efficiency standards
Yes Overhaul campaign finance law; ban "soft money" and restrict advocacy advertising
Yes Set federal election standards
No Support oil drilling in Arctic National Wildlife Refuge
No Revive fast-track procedures for trade agreements
Yes Create federal insurance coverage for catastrophic terrorist losses
Yes Tighten federal accounting and corporate governance regulation
Yes Advance bipartisan Medicare prescription drug plan
Yes Create independent Sept. 11 commission
Yes Back Democratic Homeland Security Department proposal
Yes Authorize war against Iraq

2001

Yes Confirm John Ashcroft as attorney general
No Nullify Clinton Labor Department ergonomics rule
No Cut taxes by $1.35 trillion through fiscal 2011
Yes Pass Democratic bill to bolster rights of patients in managed-care plans
No Permit a new round of military base closings
Yes Expand law enforcement power to investigate suspected terrorists

CQ VOTE STUDIES

	PARTY UNITY		PRESIDENTIAL SUPPORT	
	Support	Oppose	Support	Oppose
2002	88%	12%	70%	30%
2001	91%	9%	68%	32%
2000	90%	10%	90%	10%
1999	88%	12%	73%	27%
1998	87%	13%	76%	24%
1997	87%	13%	81%	19%
1996	84%	16%	80%	20%
1995	89%	11%	86%	14%
1994	86%	14%	81%	19%
1993	83%	17%	81%	19%

INTEREST GROUPS

	AFL-CIO	ADA	CCUS	ACU
2002	100%	90%	50%	20%
2001	94%	85%	50%	36%
2000	75%	90%	46%	16%
1999	100%	95%	35%	12%
1998	88%	90%	61%	12%
1997	86%	80%	50%	16%
1996	71%	85%	38%	20%
1995	100%	90%	47%	13%
1994	75%	85%	20%	8%
1993	78%	65%	10%	23%

Rep. Earl Pomeroy (D)

CAPITOL OFFICE
225-2611
rep.earl.pomeroy@mail.house.gov
www.house.gov/pomeroy
1110 Longworth 20515-3401; fax 226-0893

COMMITTEES
Agriculture
Ways & Means

HOMETOWN
Bismarck

BORN
Sept. 2, 1952, Valley City, N.D.

RELIGION
Presbyterian

FAMILY
Divorced; two children

EDUCATION
Valley City State U., attended 1970-71; U. of North Dakota, B.A. 1974 (political science); U. of Durham (United Kingdom), attended 1975 (legal history); U. of North Dakota, J.D. 1979

CAREER
Lawyer

POLITICAL HIGHLIGHTS
N.D. House, 1981-85; N.D. insurance commissioner, 1985-93

ELECTION RESULTS

2002 GENERAL		
Earl Pomeroy (D)	121,073	52.4%
Rick Clayburgh (R)	109,957	47.6%
2002 PRIMARY		
Earl Pomeroy (D)		unopposed
2000 GENERAL		
Earl Pomeroy (D)	151,173	52.9%
John Dorso (R)	127,251	44.6%
Jan Shelver (I)	4,731	1.7%

PREVIOUS WINNING PERCENTAGES
1998 (56%); 1996 (55%); 1994 (52%); 1992 (57%)

Elected 1992; 6th term

With his schoolboy grin and natural friendliness, Pomeroy comes across as a throwback to an earlier era. In spite of repeated GOP attempts to end his 10-year run as the Democratic, lone representative of a GOP-leaning state, Pomeroy keeps proving that nice guys don't always finish last.

His likability helped him eke out a 4.8 percentage point victory over Republican Rick Clayburgh in 2002 and contributed to similarly close wins in previous elections. "He's the kind of guy you sit down with and talk about anything. . . . He's just the kind of person that people in this state like," says Terry Devine, a political columnist for the Fargo Forum, the state's largest newspaper. While in North Dakota to stump for Clayburgh, even Speaker J. Dennis Hastert had to concede that Pomeroy "is a nice guy."

In Washington, Pomeroy has developed an expertise in technical financial issues, particularly in insurance and pension law, helping him move up the congressional ladder. In 2001, he bested about 20 Democrats to win appointment to the party's one open seat on the Ways and Means Committee, which oversees tax, trade, health care and entitlement policy.

In the 108th Congress, he was given added duties: a seat on the Agriculture Committee, where he had served eight years before moving to Ways and Means, and appointment to the Democratic Steering Committee, which makes committee assignments.

Like the state's two Democratic senators, Kent Conrad and Byron Dorgan, Pomeroy has a scholarly mien. The three men have had a close relationship since the 1970s, when Pomeroy, just a year out of college, drove Dorgan around the state as Dorgan ran for the state's House seat. Conrad was Dorgan's campaign manager.

It's no surprise to North Dakotans that Pomeroy has sided with President Bush on several high-profile issues, including creating the Department of Homeland Security and preparing to use military action against Iraq. He also voted to give tax breaks to parents who send their children to private schools and to outlaw a procedure its critics call "partial birth" abortion. He supports gun ownership rights and has been a main proponent, with Texas Republican Lamar Smith, of legislation to ban child pornography and obscenity on the Internet.

Pomeroy teamed up with Republican Tom Osborne of Nebraska to press a portion of Bush's education bill that allows more flexibility for rural school districts. He joined Republican Jim Ramstad of Minnesota to push a measure through Congress ensuring that clergy members' housing allowances remain tax-exempt.

On most economic issues, however, Pomeroy sides with Democrats. He was an unabashed proponent of the $410 billion farm bill that attempted to restore a "safety net" for agricultural producers. And he opposed most of Bush's $1.35 billion in tax cuts as fiscally imprudent for a government trying to ensure funding for Social Security and other costly programs.

Pomeroy's legislative passion is shoring up the retirement system, both the Social Security program and private pension plans. His interest was sparked at a young age. His family relied on Social Security survivor benefits to put him through college after his father died. In the 107th Congress, Pomeroy was appointed to the Democrats' "quick response" team on the politically charged Social Security issue.

Members of both parties working on 401(k) or other private pension laws often seek out Pomeroy's views. He worked with Republican Rob Portman of Ohio and Democrat Benjamin L. Cardin of Maryland on a bipartisan pension overhaul bill that included Pomeroy's proposal to make it easier for workers to transfer their retirement savings to a new job.

Pomeroy honed his knowledge of pension laws during eight years as North Dakota's insurance commissioner. He also served as president of the National Association of Insurance Commissioners. At election time, he receives more political money from the free-spending insurance industry than most other House candidates.

His younger brother, Glenn, succeeded him in both insurance posts and has since moved into an insurance-related job for General Electric. The Pomeroy brothers' ties to the industry raised conflict of interest questions in the 107th, when Pomeroy strongly supported Republican-led plans to make permanent a tax break that allowed U.S. financial services companies and manufacturers to defer taxes on the income they earn overseas. Insurance companies, including General Electric, stood to reap a windfall from the bill. Glenn Pomeroy had lobbied for its passage.

Pomeroy grew up in a small town where his father ran a feed-and-fertilizer store and where he and his brother raised chickens on the family's small farm to make a few extra dollars. He opposes the use of embargoes on food exports as part of economic sanctions leveled against unfriendly countries. "Food should not be used as a weapon and farmers should not be used as fodder in international disputes," he says.

Having lived abroad as a student and worked in the South with the Methodist church, Pomeroy decided in the early 1990s to set politics aside and return to social outreach. As he neared the end of his second term as insurance commissioner, Pomeroy and his wife announced plans to move to Russia to work in the Peace Corps.

Instead, he answered entreaties from the state Democratic Party to run for the House seat after a series of unexpected events leading up to the 1992 election. Conrad announced he would retire from the Senate rather than break his 1986 campaign promise not to seek re-election unless the deficit was reduced. Dorgan, the state's six-term House member, jumped into the Senate contest, leaving the House seat open. Hours before the nominations were to begin, Pomeroy was convinced to run for Dorgan's seat. (Conrad later ran for the other Senate seat after Democrat Quentin N. Burdick died.)

Pomeroy manages a few good international deeds from his House seat. He and his wife adopted two Korean children. In 1999, he helped reunite a family that had been torn apart by the war in Kosovo. In thanks, the family named a newborn baby Dakota.

KEY VOTES

2002

- Yes Overhaul campaign finance law; ban "soft money" and restrict advocacy advertising
- Yes Back Bush's defense budget increase
- Yes Extend 1996 welfare law
- No Adopt Bush's discretionary spending limit
- No Pass GOP Medicare prescription drug plan
- No Create independent Sept. 11 commission
- Yes Extend union protections to Homeland Security Department employees
- No Revive fast-track procedures for trade agreements
- Yes Authorize war against Iraq
- No Advance bankruptcy overhaul opposed by abortion opponents

2001

- No Nullify Clinton Labor Department ergonomics rule
- No Cut taxes by $1.35 trillion through fiscal 2011
- Yes Maintain ban on oil drilling in Arctic National Wildlife Refuge
- No Approve Bush proposal to limit managed-care plan liability for coverage decisions
- No Divert money from crop subsidy payments to land conservation
- Yes Expand law enforcement power to investigate suspected terrorists

CQ VOTE STUDIES

	PARTY UNITY		PRESIDENTIAL SUPPORT	
	Support	Oppose	Support	Oppose
2002	78%	22%	58%	42%
2001	78%	22%	35%	65%
2000	88%	12%	85%	15%
1999	80%	20%	73%	27%
1998	80%	20%	75%	25%

INTEREST GROUPS

	AFL-CIO	ADA	CCUS	ACU
2002	78%	70%	60%	32%
2001	92%	85%	39%	28%
2000	90%	85%	57%	8%
1999	78%	85%	44%	12%
1998	100%	90%	50%	21%

NORTH DAKOTA
At large

North Dakota includes fertile eastern Red River farmlands, wheat-covered plains, arid grasslands farther west and Teddy Roosevelt's beloved ranches near the western border.

The state's agriculture-based economy was shaken in the 1990s by floods, blizzards, foreign competition and the reduction of federal support systems. Agricultural income dropped drastically in the wake of devastating Red River floods and steep declines in the price of wheat. Economic trends intensified a migration of the state's young people away from rural farming communities and into the cities of Fargo and Grand Forks, where a diversified economy and several universities provide greater job choice.

Democrats have represented North Dakota in the House since 1981, and the state's congressional delegation has been entirely Democratic since 1987. Before then, the state had elected only three Democratic representatives (for a total of only six years) since statehood and had supported only five Democratic presidential nominees in the 20th century. Republicans are more numerous and unwavering in the western part of the state, while eastern communities and American Indian reservations are more supportive of Democrats. But Republican roots are strong throughout the state – the state legislature and governorship are GOP-controlled and George W. Bush handily carried the state in 2000.

MAJOR INDUSTRY

Agriculture, health care, higher education

MILITARY

Minot Air Force Base, 4,800 military, 1,200 civilian; Grand Forks Air Force Base, 3,041 military, 500 civilian (2002)

CITIES

Fargo, 90,599; Bismarck, 55,532; Grand Forks, 49,321; Minot, 36,567

NOTABLE

Lewis and Clark met Sacagawea, the Shoshone Indian woman who guided them to the Pacific Ocean, near the Mandan Indian village; Sitting Bull surrendered at Fort Buford in 1881; Gen. George Custer was stationed at Fort Lincoln, near Bismarck, in 1876 when his unit headed west to ultimate defeat at Little Big Horn; The National Buffalo Museum is in Jamestown.

OHIO

Gov. Bob Taft (R)

First elected: 1998
Length of term: 4 years
Term expires: 1/07
Salary: $130,292
Phone: (614) 466-3555
Hometown: Hilliard
Born: Jan. 8, 1942; Boston, Mass.
Religion: Methodist
Family: Wife, Hope Taft; one child
Education: Yale U., B.A. 1963; Princeton U., M.A. 1967 (government); U. of Cincinnati, J.D. 1976
Career: State budget officer; U.S. State Department employee
Political highlights: Ohio House, 1976-80; Hamilton County Commission, 1981-90; Ohio secretary of state, 1991-99
Election results:

2002 GENERAL		
Bob Taft (R)	1,865,007	57.8%
Tim Hagan (D)	1,236,924	38.3%
John A. Eastman (I)	126,686	3.9%

Lt. Gov. Jennette Bradley (R)

First elected: 2002
Length of term: 4 years
Term expires: 1/07
Salary: Does not receive salary as lieutenant governor; earns $120,016 as the director of the Department of Commerce
Phone: (614) 466-3396

STATE LEGISLATURE

General Assembly: Meets January-June in odd-numbered years; January-July in even-numbered years
House: 99 members, 2-year terms
2003 breakdown: 62R, 37D; 76 men, 23 women
Salary: $53,707
Phone: (614) 466-3357
Senate: 33 members, 4-year terms
2003 breakdown: 22R, 11D; 32 men, 1 woman
Salary: $53,707
Phone: (614) 466-4900

STATE TERM LIMITS

Governor: 2 terms
Senate: 2 terms
House: 4 terms

URBAN STATISTICS

CITY	POPULATION
Columbus	711,470
Cleveland	478,403
Cincinnati	331,285
Toledo	313,619
Akron	217,074

REGISTERED VOTERS

Voters do not register by party.

POPULATION

2002 population (est.)	11,421,267
2000 population	11,353,140
1990 population	10,847,115
Percent change (1990-2000)	+4.7%
Rank among states (2002)	7
Median age	36.2
Born in state	74.7%
Foreign born	3%
Violent crime rate	334/100,000
Poverty level	10.6%
Federal workers	80,445
Military	36,713

REDISTRICTING

Ohio lost one House seat in reapportionment. The state legislature drew a new, 18-district map, which the governor signed on Jan. 24, 2002.

MISCELLANEOUS

Web: www.state.oh.us
Capital: Columbus

STATE ELECTION OFFICIAL
(614) 466-2585

DEMOCRATIC HEADQUARTERS
(614) 221-6563

REPUBLICAN HEADQUARTERS
(614) 228-2481

District Statistics

	2000 VOTE FOR PRESIDENT															
DIST.	BUSH	GORE	NADER	WHITE	BLACK	ASIAN	HISP	MEDIAN INCOME	WHITE COLLAR	BLUE COLLAR	SERVICE INDUSTRY	OVER 64	UNDER 18	COLLEGE EDUCATION	RURAL	SQ. MILES
1	53%	47%	n/a	69%	27%	1%	1%	$37,414	60%	23%	16%	13%	26%	22%	5%	416
2	65	35	n/a	92	5	1	1	$46,813	64	23	13	12	26	29	27	2,612
3	54	46	n/a	79	17	1	1	$41,591	60	26	14	14	25	23	15	1,595
4	64	36	n/a	92	5	1	1	$40,100	47	38	15	14	26	13	41	4,620
5	61	39	n/a	94	1	0	4	$41,701	46	40	14	13	26	15	51	6,128
6	51	49	n/a	95	2	0	1	$32,888	52	32	16	15	23	14	50	5,198
7	57	43	n/a	89	7	1	1	$43,248	57	28	14	12	25	19	29	2,848
8	63	37	n/a	92	4	1	1	$43,753	56	30	14	12	26	19	22	2,014
9	43	57	n/a	80	14	1	4	$40,265	55	29	16	14	26	20	14	1,102
10	44	56	n/a	87	4	2	5	$41,841	63	23	14	16	23	23	1	195
11	18	82	n/a	39	56	2	2	$31,998	61	21	17	15	26	23	0	135
12	53	47	n/a	72	22	2	2	$47,289	68	18	13	10	27	32	12	1,016
13	45	55	n/a	82	12	1	4	$44,524	59	27	14	14	26	22	7	531
14	54	46	n/a	94	2	1	1	$51,304	62	25	12	13	26	27	26	1,797
15	54	46	n/a	85	7	3	2	$43,885	66	20	14	10	23	32	9	1,178

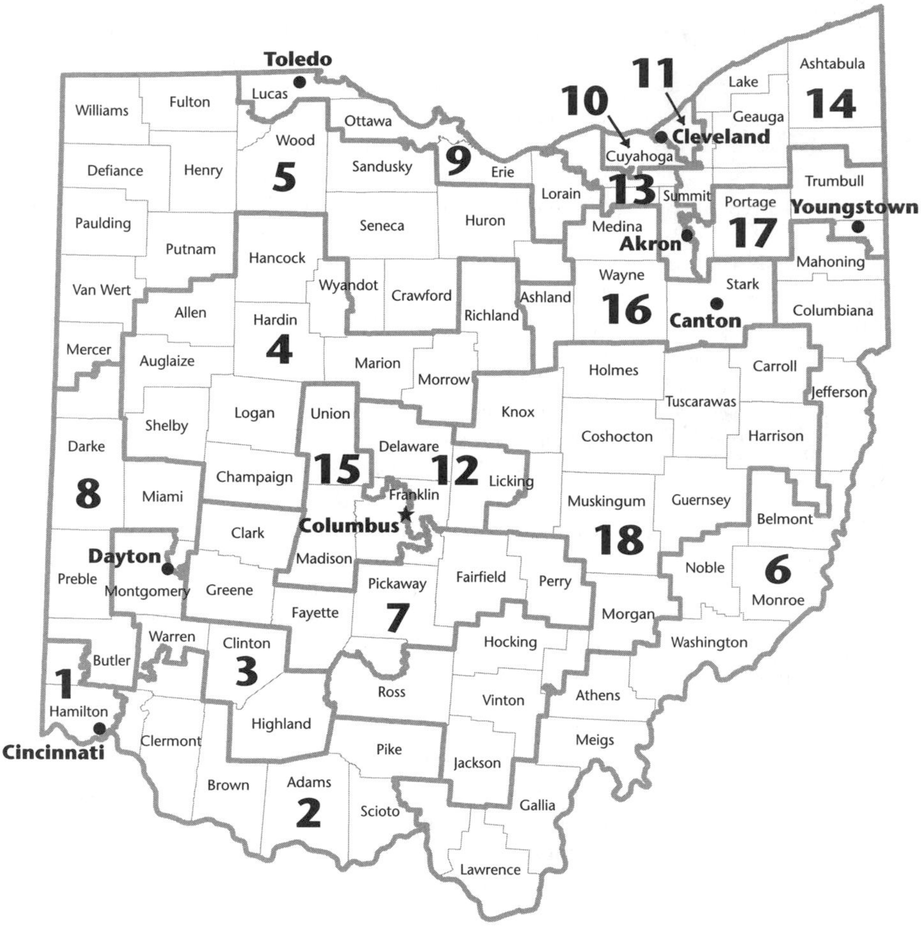

District Statistics

DIST.	2000 VOTE FOR PRESIDENT BUSH	GORE	NADER	WHITE	BLACK	ASIAN	HISP	MEDIAN INCOME	WHITE COLLAR	BLUE COLLAR	SERVICE INDUSTRY	OVER 64	UNDER 18	COLLEGE EDUCATION	RURAL	SQ. MILES
16	56%	44%	n/a	92%	5%	1%	1%	$41,801	55%	31%	14%	14%	26%	19%	26%	1,732
17	37	63	n/a	85	12	1	2	$36,705	52	32	16	15	24	16	16	1,006
18	58	42	n/a	96	2	0	1	$34,462	46	38	16	14	26	11	57	6,826
STATE	50	46	3	84	11	1	2	$40,956	57	28	15	13	25	21	23	40,948
U.S.	47.9	48.4	3	69	12	4	13	$41,994	60	25	15	12	26	24	21	3,537,438

Sen. Mike DeWine (R)

CAPITOL OFFICE
224-2315
senator_dewine@dewine.senate.gov
dewine.senate.gov
140 Russell 20510-3503; fax 224-6519

COMMITTEES
Appropriations
(District of Columbia - chairman)
Health, Education, Labor & Pensions
(Substance Abuse & Mental Health Services - chairman)
Judiciary
(Antitrust, Competition Policy & Consumer Rights - chairman)
Select Intelligence

HOMETOWN
Cedarville

BORN
Jan. 5, 1947, Springfield, Ohio

RELIGION
Roman Catholic

FAMILY
Wife, Fran DeWine; eight children (one deceased)

EDUCATION
Miami U. (Ohio), B.S. 1969; Ohio Northern U., J.D. 1972

CAREER
Lawyer

POLITICAL HIGHLIGHTS
Greene County prosecuting attorney, 1977-81; Ohio Senate, 1981-83; U.S. House, 1983-91; lieutenant governor, 1991-95; Republican nominee for U.S. Senate, 1992

ELECTION RESULTS

2000 GENERAL		
Mike DeWine (R)	2,665,512	59.9%
Ted Celeste (D)	1,595,066	35.9%
John R. McAlister (LIBERT)	116,724	2.6%
2000 PRIMARY		
Mike DeWine (R)	1,029,860	79.5%
Ronald R. Dickson (R)	161,185	12.4%
Frank A. Cremeans (R)	104,219	8.1%

PREVIOUS WINNING PERCENTAGES
1994 (53%); 1988 House Election (74%); 1986 House Election (100%); 1984 House Election (77%); 1982 House Election (56%)

Elected 1994; 2nd term

Republican DeWine is a methodical, deliberate senator who actually reads detailed General Accounting Office reports, and keeps a calculator handy so he can test the mathematical assertions of a report or a piece of legislation. He is remembered for diligently attending every class in law school.

Yet DeWine is no less passionate than some of his flashier colleagues on the left when it comes to his top issue — government's role helping children and families. DeWine frequently joins Democrats in bipartisan efforts to force delinquent parents to pay child support, to help poorly paid child-care workers retire their college loans, and to curb drunken driving. DeWine joined with West Virginia Democrat John D. Rockefeller IV in sponsoring legislation that changed the government's emphasis in custody cases from preserving family structure to protecting the best interests of the children involved.

He also sometimes breaks with the GOP on key environmental votes. In 2002, he was one of eight Republican senators to reject President Bush's proposal to allow oil exploration in Alaska's Arctic National Wildlife Refuge. Environmental advocacy groups praised DeWine's vote against the plan as "courageous." DeWine told The Toledo Blade he was convinced the risks of drilling in fragile wilderness outweigh the benefits.

DeWine has voted consistently against Republican leaders on hate crime legislation to broaden the definition to include victims targeted because of gender or sexual orientation.

The deviations from party doctrine don't make him a full-blooded moderate, but they leave him voting less often with his leaders than other rank-and-file Republicans, about 85 percent of the time. DeWine also cannot be considered one of President Bush's favorites. During the contested GOP primary in 1999 and 2000, DeWine campaigned across Ohio for Bush's opponent, Sen. John McCain of Arizona. He was also one of only four senators to endorse McCain.

But DeWine has turned out to be a loyal ally for Bush on the Judiciary Committee, championing the president's controversial nominees. During the 107th Congress, he gave an exhaustive defense of Charles W. Pickering Sr., countering nearly every claim against the judge from his liberal critics in a lengthy. point-by-point presentation. When the committee in the 108th Congress considered two appeals court nominees from Ohio, DeWine was able to persuade Illinois Democrat Richard J. Durbin to vote for one. Durbin said he trusted DeWine's judgment because of his moderation on other issues.

DeWine most frequently crosses the aisle on legislation involving the welfare of children, often drawing on his own experience as the father of eight children to inform his policy judgments. His own child's use of an asthma inhaler convinced him that drug manufacturers do not know enough about drugs' effects on children. In 2002, he joined with two liberal senators, Democrats Hillary Rodham Clinton of New York and and Edward M. Kennedy of Massachusetts, to push legislation that would compel drugmakers to conduct pediatric safety tests when their products are prescribed for children.

DeWine's third child, Becky, was killed in 1993 in a car accident when she was 22 years old. The event devastated DeWine and his wife, Fran, and he says he still probably doesn't know all the ways that Becky's death has affected him. He counts among his biggest personal achievements a postage stamp encouraging organ and tissue donation. Becky's eyes were donated to two people after her death.

DeWine pushed hard to lower the blood alcohol limit for drivers to .08 percent in 2000. After hearing accounts of the impact of drunken driving on families, DeWine said during debate on the bill, "There is nothing that impacts a legislator more than someone who comes to you with a personal, real-life experience."

He says he also was deeply affected by child-related cases he handled as a Greene County prosecutor in the late 1970s. As the chairman of the District of Columbia Appropriations subcommittee, he has tried to overhaul the Washington, D.C., child welfare system, which has a chronic backlog of abuse cases. DeWine also has successfully pushed legislation making it easier for states to get information about child-support payments and making it a felony to cross state lines to avoid paying child support.

In the 108th, DeWine sought to amend the higher education reauthorization bill with a special provision forgiving the college loans of early childhood educators and child care workers.

DeWine worked with Wisconsin Democrat Russell D. Feingold on an Internet anti-pornography bill and with New York Democrat Daniel Patrick Moynihan on successful legislation to open Nazi war criminal records. His partnership with Democrats Kennedy and the late Paul Wellstone of Minnesota led to a law consolidating more than 50 federal job training programs into three block grants to states while providing individuals with vouchers to pay for training. When the Senate took up a comprehensive anti-smoking bill in the 105th Congress, DeWine successfully teamed with Durbin to stiffen penalties on cigarette manufacturers who fail to reach goals for reducing youth smoking.

On other issues, DeWine generally pursues a conservative agenda. He is a staunch opponent of abortion and voted to ban a procedure its opponents call "partial birth" abortion, in which a fetus is aborted late in the term. In the 107th, he introduced a bill that would make it a federal crime to harm or kill a fetus during the commission of another federal crime.

Latin America has been a special interest of his, and he travels there often. The United States "ignore[s] our own hemisphere at our peril," he says, pointing out that Latin America plays important roles in the matters of drugs, illegal immigration and international trade.

He favors tough anti-drug laws, and has visited Colombia to better understand a major source of the U.S. drug trade. He supports making penalties for powdered cocaine as tough as those for crack cocaine.

DeWine has cemented his hold on his Senate seat by winning funding for facilities in Ohio, including the NASA-Glenn Research Center. In the 107th Congress, he landed a seat on the Appropriations Committee.

His wire-rim glasses and lopsided grin help him look every bit the policy wonk he is. Although low-key in temperament, DeWine has never lacked drive or ambition. After law school, he worked as an assistant county prosecutor before running against his boss and beating him in 1976. In 1980, he won a seat in the Ohio Senate. Just two years later, he won election to the U.S. House, where he served eight years. He left to become lieutenant governor under George V. Voinovich.

In 1992, DeWine challenged Democratic Sen. John Glenn, but lost. Two years later, he ran again, this time for the seat of retiring Democrat Howard M. Metzenbaum. DeWine faced Metzenbaum's son-in-law Joel Hyatt, a political novice who founded the Hyatt Legal Services chain. Stressing his government experience, DeWine won with 53 percent. In 2000, DeWine cruised to an easy, 24-point win over real estate broker Ted Celeste, younger brother of former governor Richard Celeste.

KEY VOTES

2002

No Pass farm bill reversing crop subsidy limits
Yes Postpone tougher automobile fuel efficiency standards
No Overhaul campaign finance law; ban "soft money" and restrict advocacy advertising
Yes Set federal election standards
No Support oil drilling in Arctic National Wildlife Refuge
Yes Revive fast-track procedures for trade agreements
Yes Create federal insurance coverage for catastrophic terrorist losses
Yes Tighten federal accounting and corporate governance regulation
No Advance bipartisan Medicare prescription drug plan
Yes Create independent Sept. 11 commission
No Back Democratic Homeland Security Department proposal
Yes Authorize war against Iraq

2001

Yes Confirm John Ashcroft as attorney general
Yes Nullify Clinton Labor Department ergonomics rule
Yes Cut taxes by $1.35 trillion through fiscal 2011
Yes Pass Democratic bill to bolster rights of patients in managed-care plans
Yes Permit a new round of military base closings
Yes Expand law enforcement power to investigate suspected terrorists

CQ VOTE STUDIES

	PARTY UNITY		PRESIDENTIAL SUPPORT	
	Support	Oppose	Support	Oppose
2002	89%	11%	98%	2%
2001	83%	17%	95%	5%
2000	86%	14%	52%	48%
1999	84%	16%	38%	62%
1998	82%	18%	51%	49%
1997	81%	19%	62%	38%
1996	88%	12%	41%	59%
1995	87%	13%	30%	70%
House Service:				
1990	85%	15%	66%	34%
1989	89%	11%	71%	29%

INTEREST GROUPS

	AFL-CIO	ADA	CCUS	ACU
2002	23%	15%	95%	95%
2001	25%	25%	79%	72%
2000	0%	10%	93%	80%
1999	22%	10%	82%	84%
1998	0%	10%	89%	64%
1997	0%	15%	80%	68%
1996	29%	15%	85%	85%
1995	8%	0%	89%	70%
House Service:				
1990	17%	17%	54%	83%
1989	17%	10%	90%	96%

Sen. George V. Voinovich (R)

CAPITOL OFFICE
224-3353
senator_voinovich@voinovich.senate.gov
voinovich.senate.gov
317 Hart 20510-3504; fax 228-1382

COMMITTEES
Environment & Public Works
(Clean Air, Climate Change & Nuclear Safety - chairman)
Foreign Relations
Governmental Affairs
(Government Management, Federal Workforce & the District of Columbia - chairman)
Select Ethics - chairman

HOMETOWN
Cleveland

BORN
July 15, 1936, Cleveland, Ohio

RELIGION
Roman Catholic

FAMILY
Wife, Janet Voinovich; four children (one deceased)

EDUCATION
Ohio U., B.A. 1958 (government); Ohio State U., J.D. 1961

CAREER
Lawyer; state prosecutor

POLITICAL HIGHLIGHTS
Ohio House, 1967-71; Cuyahoga County auditor, 1971-76; Cuyahoga County Commission, 1977-78; lieutenant governor, 1979; mayor of Cleveland, 1979-89; Republican nominee for U.S. Senate, 1988; governor, 1991-99

ELECTION RESULTS

1998 GENERAL		
George V. Voinovich (R)	1,922,087	56.5%
Mary O. Boyle (D)	1,482,054	43.5%
1998 PRIMARY		
George V. Voinovich (R)	543,833	72.3%
David McCollough (R)	208,011	27.7%

Elected 1998; 1st term

Voinovich is unassuming and amiable, toiling away with little notice on often esoteric but important nuts-and-bolts policy matters. In this time of the television soundbite, Voinovich comes across as Mr. Personnel instead of Mr. Personality like most of his colleagues.

A self-described management wonk, Voinovich (VOY-no-vitch) is known for his detail-oriented approach to work. His interests include protecting the federal civil service system, watching out for the concerns of state and local governments and reducing the national debt.

Voinovich's election to the Senate was merely the latest step in a long career in politics, including 10 years as Cleveland's mayor and eight as Ohio's governor. He has held top leadership posts in both the National League of Cities and the National Governors Association.

"In a roomful of governors, he's easy to miss," observed Governing magazine, which named him one of its Public Officials of the Year in 1995. "Voinovich offers up more of the demeanor of an off-to-the-side gubernatorial assistant." Voinovich himself acknowledges that topics such as the aging federal work force are "boring" to most people, but he makes no apologies for his interest in such mundane government matters.

His main forum for pursuing many of his interests in the 108th Congress is the Governmental Affairs Subcommittee on Oversight of Government Management. And his reputation for evenhanded diligence may serve him well as chairman of the Ethics Committee.

Although Voinovich is seen as a mainstream Republican, he also displays a maverick streak. He has criticized GOP tax policy, cast lonely votes against GOP spending bills and insisted that the views of employee unions be considered in creating the Department of Homeland Security. Although he usually remains low-key, Voinovich can get worked up on occasion, such as when he rails against Congress spending money "like drunken sailors."

A member of the Senate's Centrist Coalition, Voinovich was among the half-dozen least loyal Republican senators in the 106th Congress. In the 107th he continued to show willingness to deviate from the party line on occasion, but his voting record proved to be more dependable; he voted with the majority of Republicans 91 percent of the time.

Voinovich was elected in 1998 on a platform that included criticism of the Republicans' plans to cut taxes by tapping into projected budget surpluses, which he said should be used first to pay down the national debt and shore up Social Security. During his first two and a half years in the Senate, Voinovich crusaded to hold the line on government spending. He was one of just two GOP senators to vote against a $792 billion tax cut in 1999. But he said his view on spending shifted dramatically after the terrorist attacks of Sept. 11, 2001. "In an instant, my priorities . . . shifted from saving for our future to fighting for our future."

He still declares himself to be a "debt hawk," but he says budget deficits are warranted during a war on terrorism. He pressures his colleagues to keep a tight rein on spending, however. He has voted against a number of spending bills since Sept. 11, complaining about "wrapping every pork project in the flag and calling it a national security priority."

Voinovich's long opposition to tax cuts had softened earlier. As 2001 began, he was the first Republican senator to threaten to break publicly with President Bush on his proposal for the deepest tax cut in 20 years. But in March of that year, Voinovich decided a cut was needed to ward off a possible recession.

During the Senate's work on legislation to create the Department of Homeland Security, Voinovich's colleagues often called on his knowledge of government personnel issues. As mayor of Cleveland, he had enlisted the help of the public employee unions in the effort to rescue the city from insolvency. But though he was actively engaged in the debate, which centered on personnel policies, Voinovich was never really included in the inner circle of GOP negotiators. His historically good working relations with government employee unions gave other Republicans pause.

Another personnel issue is on Voinovich's radar as a large segment of the aging federal work force soon will be eligible for retirement. Voinovich wants to make government work more attractive by improving training and giving federal agencies more flexibility in the hiring process.

As a former mayor and governor, Voinovich argues for more local control in deciding how to spend federal funds for programs such as education and environmental protection. He applauded the 1999 "Ed-Flex" law that gave states the flexibility to spend federal education money with fewer strings attached. But in 2001, he cast one of only three Republican "no" votes in the Senate against the major rewrite of education policy because of its "all-out assault on local control."

Of Serbian and Slovenian ancestry, Voinovich in his first year as a senator took a politically risky stance as a vocal opponent of the NATO military action in Kosovo, which involved U.S. forces. He advocated continued diplomatic negotiations with Serb leader Slobodan Milosevic, but he also refused to go to Serbia as long as Milosevic was in control.

To his dismay, the most public attention he got on any issue in 2002 was when he announced he was boycotting a Capitol Hill hearing on coal mining regulations at which a member of the Backstreet Boys was to testify. Voinovich — who had worked hard to bring the Rock and Roll Hall of Fame to Cleveland — said he objected to the use of celebrities to get media attention on an issue. "This isn't about music; it's about substance. Even if this guy was a polka musician, I would still object to him," he said.

A white Republican from a working-class neighborhood in Cleveland's largely black and ethnic East Side, where he still lives, Voinovich's long climb up the government ladder began with a brief stint in the early 1960s as a state assistant attorney general. After serving in the state House and as auditor for Cuyahoga County, he was elected lieutenant governor in 1978. The next year, he unseated Cleveland Mayor Dennis J. Kucinich (now an Ohio congressman) after the city's financial default. With the help of a financial control board, Voinovich reversed some of the city's problems.

Voinovich's initial Senate bid failed miserably; he lost a highly promoted 1988 race to unseat Democratic incumbent Howard M. Metzenbaum, by 14 percentage points. But Voinovich rebounded two years later and won the governorship. During his two terms, he won acclaim for putting the state on a solid financial footing. In 1998, with state law prohibiting a third term as governor, the timing was right for a second Senate run when Democrat John Glenn retired after four terms. Voinovich immediately became the presumptive successor. He was not seriously challenged for the GOP nomination, and in November he won by 13 points over Mary O. Boyle, a former Cuyahoga County commissioner.

After almost two decades as a government executive, Voinovich admits it was tough to adjust to his role as just one senator among 100. His job switch, he says, was akin to "going from being the orchestra leader to a member of the orchestra. And coming to the Senate, you're in the fourth chair, and sometimes you wonder whether or not your instrument is being heard." He says he now works for incremental victories.

KEY VOTES

2002

No Pass farm bill reversing crop subsidy limits
Yes Postpone tougher automobile fuel efficiency standards
No Overhaul campaign finance law; ban "soft money" and restrict advocacy advertising
Yes Set federal election standards
Yes Support oil drilling in Arctic National Wildlife Refuge
Yes Revive fast-track procedures for trade agreements
Yes Create federal insurance coverage for catastrophic terrorist losses
Yes Tighten federal accounting and corporate governance regulation
No Advance bipartisan Medicare prescription drug plan
No Create independent Sept. 11 commission
No Back Democratic Homeland Security Department proposal
Yes Authorize war against Iraq

2001

Yes Confirm John Ashcroft as attorney general
Yes Nullify Clinton Labor Department ergonomics rule
Yes Cut taxes by $1.35 trillion through fiscal 2011
No Pass Democratic bill to bolster rights of patients in managed-care plans
Yes Permit a new round of military base closings
Yes Expand law enforcement power to investigate suspected terrorists

CQ VOTE STUDIES

	PARTY UNITY		PRESIDENTIAL SUPPORT	
	Support	Oppose	Support	Oppose
2002	88%	12%	96%	4%
2001	92%	8%	95%	5%
2000	78%	22%	59%	41%
1999	87%	13%	45%	55%

INTEREST GROUPS

	AFL-CIO	ADA	CCUS	ACU
2002	33%	5%	95%	90%
2001	13%	15%	93%	83%
2000	13%	10%	80%	64%
1999	33%	20%	82%	88%

Rep. Steve Chabot (R)

CAPITOL OFFICE
225-2216
www.house.gov/chabot
129 Cannon 20515-3501; fax 225-3012

COMMITTEES
International Relations
Judiciary
(Constitution - chairman)
Small Business

HOMETOWN
Cincinnati

BORN
Jan. 22, 1953, Cincinnati, Ohio

RELIGION
Roman Catholic

FAMILY
Wife, Donna Chabot; two children

EDUCATION
College of William & Mary, B.A. 1975 (history); Northern Kentucky U., J.D. 1978

CAREER
Lawyer; teacher

POLITICAL HIGHLIGHTS
Independent candidate for Cincinnati City Council, 1979; Republican candidate for Cincinnati City Council, 1983; Cincinnati City Council, 1985-90; Republican nominee for U.S. House, 1988; Hamilton County commissioner, 1990-95

ELECTION RESULTS

2002 GENERAL		
Steve Chabot (R)	110,760	64.8%
Greg Harris (D)	60,168	35.2%
2002 PRIMARY		
Steve Chabot (R)		unopposed
2000 GENERAL		
Steve Chabot (R)	116,768	53.0%
John Cranley (D)	98,328	44.6%
David A. Groshoff (LIBERT)	3,399	1.5%

PREVIOUS WINNING PERCENTAGES
1998 (53%); 1996 (54%); 1994 (56%)

Elected 1994; 5th term

Chabot remains a true believer in the crusade to reduce the scope of the federal government. A member of the Class of 1994, whose election victories swept the Republicans to control of the House, he is among the influential bloc of fiscal conservatives who have stuck by their initial campaign pledge to restrain federal spending — even in some instances when the money would have benefited his district.

In 2001, for example, the last time the House passed distinct versions of all 13 regular appropriations bills, he voted against six of them, arguing that the spending they called for was excessive. "Chabot is as aggressive an anti-tax, anti-regulation, anti-subsidy, anti-abortion conservative as exists in Congress," The Associated Press said in a 2000 profile.

As chairman of Judiciary's Constitution Subcommittee, Chabot was the sponsor of legislation, enacted in 2002, designed to guarantee legal protection to babies "born alive" at any state of development. (Supporters say the bill is needed to protect infants who survive late-term abortions.) Chabot (SHAB-utt) also has been a promoter of legislation, thrice passed by the House, to make it a federal crime for anyone other than a parent to help a girl cross state lines to get an abortion in order to avoid her home state's consent or notification laws. He has been a featured speaker at the annual anti-abortion rally in Washington marking the anniversary of the Supreme Court's *Roe v. Wade* decision that legalized abortion.

From his seat on Judiciary, Chabot seeks to ensure that his colleagues' plans to toughen enforcement of crime and immigration laws do not grant too much new power to the federal government. After the Sept. 11, 2001, attacks, he backed enactment of the law beefing up law enforcement authority to combat terrorism. "People want the full power of the United States to be used against the cowards who carried out these attacks," he said, while cautioning, "We must not cave in to their demands by suspending or weakening our constitutional rights."

Chabot will join hands across the aisle when he sees that Democrats share his commitment to less government intrusion. In the 106th Congress, he teamed up with Democratic Patrick J. Kennedy of Rhode Island on legislation to limit the government's ability to collect DNA samples for a national database, warning that the practice could infringe on Americans' privacy. In the 107th, he continued to champion a constitutional amendment to provide rights for victims of crimes throughout the legal process.

Not shy about voicing his conservative beliefs, Chabot often does so with a soft-spoken demeanor that stands out on Judiciary, where passionate and combative oratory is generally the order of the day. He cast off his normally low-key persona when the spotlight fell on him in 1999 as one of the 13 "managers" who presented the House's case for removing President Clinton from office in the Senate impeachment trial.

The year before, when Judiciary took up the question of whether Clinton should be impeached, no one had to ask Chabot twice to climb on board. During his presentation to the Senate summarizing perjury law, Chabot said of Clinton: "He raised his right hand and swore to tell the truth, the whole truth and nothing but the truth. Then he lied."

Chabot, who has been recognized by conservative groups for his consistent anti-tax voting record, at times shows more zeal than House GOP leaders for reducing the federal budget. In 1999, he denounced a budget agreement negotiated by Clinton and the GOP leadership, saying it spent too much money. His frequent "nay" votes on Republican-written spending bills usually puts him in the company of perhaps only two or three dozen others in his caucus.

Chabot was one of about a dozen members who publicly called in advance for Newt Gingrich's resignation as Speaker after the GOP lost five seats in the 1998 election. That rare setback for the party opposite the president's in a midterm election, GOP conservatives argue, was because Gingrich had lost his ideological moorings and compromised too much with Clinton on spending just before the election.

His father worked as an optician, and Chabot — who lived in a trailer for the first few years of his life — remembers working part-time jobs to help pay the tuition at his parochial high school. He majored in history and earned a teaching certificate at William and Mary College.

Chabot remembers feeling deep disappointment in the Watergate scandal and the subsequent pardoning of President Nixon, whom he had voted for in 1972. The Watergate revelations spurred his move toward a political career, he said, because he felt the public deserved to have leaders they could trust. During the Clinton impeachment trial, Chabot surprised colleagues by acknowledging that he had voted for Democrat Jimmy Carter in the 1976 presidential election instead of President Ford, who had pardoned Nixon.

While teaching middle school students in Cincinnati, Chabot began taking night school law classes across the river at Northern Kentucky University. A few years after getting his law degree, he opened his own neighborhood law practice, with his father serving as his assistant.

Chabot's political career began on the Cincinnati City Council. After two failed bids for a seat on the council, the first at 26 as an independent, Chabot ran as a Republican and won in 1985. He fell short in a congressional bid against Democrat Thomas A. Luken in 1988, then won an election in 1990 to the Hamilton County Board of Commissioners.

Chabot launched his second congressional campaign in 1994 against first-term Democrat David Mann. Emphasizing his blue-collar beginnings and Catholic roots, Chabot campaigned on a platform of lower taxes, less government and change in Washington. With national trends strongly favoring the GOP, he won with 56 percent.

In the next three elections, he had to fend off charges of being too far to the right for his constituents, who voted for Bill Clinton twice and for Al Gore in 2000. He never earned more than 54 percent. But redistricting after the 2000 census made the 1st more Republican, and in 2002 Chabot cruised to a fifth term with 65 percent against volunteerism advocate Greg Harris.

KEY VOTES

2002

No Overhaul campaign finance law; ban "soft money" and restrict advocacy advertising
Yes Back Bush's defense budget increase
Yes Extend 1996 welfare law
Yes Adopt Bush's discretionary spending limit
Yes Pass GOP Medicare prescription drug plan
No Create independent Sept. 11 commission
No Extend union protections to Homeland Security Department employees
Yes Revive fast-track procedures for trade agreements
Yes Authorize war against Iraq
Yes Advance bankruptcy overhaul opposed by abortion opponents

2001

Yes Nullify Clinton Labor Department ergonomics rule
Yes Cut taxes by $1.35 trillion through fiscal 2011
No Maintain ban on oil drilling in Arctic National Wildlife Refuge
Yes Approve Bush proposal to limit managed-care plan liability for coverage decisions
No Divert money from crop subsidy payments to land conservation
Yes Expand law enforcement power to investigate suspected terrorists

CQ VOTE STUDIES

	PARTY UNITY		PRESIDENTIAL SUPPORT	
	Support	Oppose	Support	Oppose
2002	96%	4%	85%	15%
2001	94%	6%	81%	19%
2000	94%	6%	21%	79%
1999	89%	11%	22%	78%
1998	91%	9%	27%	73%

INTEREST GROUPS

	AFL-CIO	ADA	CCUS	ACU
2002	11%	0%	90%	96%
2001	8%	5%	87%	96%
2000	0%	5%	76%	100%
1999	0%	10%	84%	96%
1998	10%	0%	83%	96%

OHIO 1

Western Cincinnati and suburbs

Nestled in Ohio's southwest corner, the 1st contains about three-fourths of Cincinnati's residents. The city's 43 percent black population is critical to Democrats, as Cincinnati's traditional German Catholic conservatives, a growing suburban base and GOP-friendly 2002 redistricting have made the Hamilton County-based 1st politically competitive.

The 1st's southern border is the Ohio River, which serves as a major thoroughfare for barges laden with cargo, helping Cincinnati earn its reputation as a regional center of commerce.

The city's diverse economy prevented it from suffering the degree of hardship that hit other industrial cities in the 1980s, although the region has not been immune to defense cutbacks. Aircraft engine manufacturing and machine toolmaking account for a large portion of blue-collar jobs. The city also houses the headquarters of major U.S. companies (including Procter & Gamble) and is a magnet for research and development firms.

The district takes in Cincinnati's heavily black neighborhoods, including the West End (site of the Laurel Homes housing project, which is being redeveloped.) The 1st also takes in the Over-the-Rhine neighborhood near downtown, where in April 2001 a white police officer shot an unarmed black man, leading to several days of riots.

Redistricting in 2002 drew the 1st to closely resemble its 1980s configuration, when the district also included most of Cincinnati and points north and west. Added to the 1st were GOP-friendly suburbs such as Reading and high-income Evendale and Springdale (which had been in the 2nd District). The redrawn 1st also includes a southwestern piece of Butler County, located north of Hamilton.

MAJOR INDUSTRY

Consumer products development and manufacturing, service

CITIES

Cincinnati (pt.), 257,122; Norwood (pt.), 21,675; Forest Park, 19,463

NOTABLE

Talk show host Jerry Springer is a former council member and mayor of Cincinnati; The Red Stockings — now the Cincinnati Reds — were the nation's first professional baseball team; The National Underground Railroad Freedom Center was set to open in Cincinnati in 2004.

Rep. Rob Portman (R)

CAPITOL OFFICE
225-3164
portmail@mail.house.gov
www.house.gov/portman
238 Cannon 20515-3502; fax 225-1992

COMMITTEES
Budget
Ways & Means

HOMETOWN
Cincinnati

BORN
Dec. 19, 1955, Cincinnati, Ohio

RELIGION
Methodist

FAMILY
Wife, Jane Portman; three children

EDUCATION
Dartmouth College, B.A. 1979; U. of Michigan, J.D. 1984

CAREER
Lawyer

POLITICAL HIGHLIGHTS
White House associate counsel, 1989; White House Legislative Affairs director, 1989-91

ELECTION RESULTS

2002 GENERAL		
Rob Portman (R)	139,218	74.1%
Charles W. Sanders (D)	48,785	26.0%
2002 PRIMARY		
Rob Portman (R)		unopposed
2000 GENERAL		
Rob Portman (R)	204,184	73.6%
Charles W. Sanders (D)	64,091	23.1%
Robert E. Bidwell (LIBERT)	9,266	3.3%

PREVIOUS WINNING PERCENTAGES
1998 (76%); 1996 (72%); 1994 (77%); 1993 Special Election (70%)

Elected May 1993; 5th full term

As the House Republican leadership's designated conduit to President Bush, Portman is one of the few people in the current GOP hierarchy who can be labeled a quintessential Washington insider. When he arrived in Congress a decade ago, at age 37, he had already been exposed to the institutional politics of Washington from vantage points both inside the White House and on K Street.

But Portman is more than a mere messenger shuttling directives between the White House and the Capitol. Although he describes himself as the president's "eyes and ears" in the House, Portman was also handpicked for that job by Speaker J. Dennis Hastert. And it is Hastert who has given Portman the additional responsibility of serving as the chairman of GOP leadership meetings, a literal seat at the table from which he can help shape the message for his party and work to ensure that the White House and congressional Republicans are on the same page.

The duel role allows Portman to take advantage of his first career as a deal-making lawyer for Patton, Boggs and Blow, the politically powerful Washington law firm, and to use some of the techniques he developed as the head of the White House Office of Legislative Affairs under President George Bush. (Some of Portman's political allies from that era are now senior White House aides.)

His friendly style, command of substance and reputation as a fair dealer have brought him praise from both sides of the political aisle. And his knowledge of political parrying was sufficient that, during the 2000 presidential campaign, Portman was called on to play the part of the Democratic vice-presidential nominee, Sen. Joseph I. Lieberman of Connecticut, in Dick Cheney's debate preparations.

Nonetheless, Portman is at a slight disadvantage among the GOP inner circle, because his leadership role is an informal one, and he therefore has no dedicated budget or staff for the work.

A classic example of Portman's steady, persistent approach to building bipartisan consensus was his successful push to include tax incentives for retirement savings in the $1.35 trillion tax cut package enacted in 2001 — the only main component that was not proposed by Bush. Portman attributed the victory to "five years of blood, sweat and tears" with his Democratic ally, Benjamin L. Cardin of Maryland.

Portman says he views alliances with moderate Democrats as essential to getting things done. "It's a way both to come up with good ideas and in a practical manner to move legislation," he says. Portman's ability to bridge partisan differences and his mastery of tax and trade issues has made him an important player on Ways and Means, even though he ranks a lowly 14th in Republican seniority. He is also on the Budget Committee.

In the 108th Congress, he has put a priority on efforts to simplify the tax code by streamlining the capital gains tax and eliminating the alternative minimum tax. Portman says changes are needed because tax law compliance has become too costly and complex.

As Portman's stature in the GOP ranks has grown, he has taken on a number of high-profile assignments aimed at helping to unify his party on contentious issues. After the terrorist attacks of 2001, he was among five Republicans appointed to a committee that developed the House's version of legislation to create the Homeland Security Department. He helped promote Bush's proposal, including controversial provisions to exclude workers in the new department from unions and to waive their civil service protections on national security grounds.

In the 107th, Portman also served on a team that developed the GOP Medicare prescription drug benefit proposal. But he and other Republicans decided to put off efforts to create personal investment accounts in the Social Security program after steep declines in stock prices dampened enthusiasm for the president's proposal.

Portman's clients at Patton, Boggs included Cincinnati-based banana producer Chiquita Brands International Inc. As a stalwart free-trader in Congress, he helped persuade fellow Republicans to support the law enacted in 2002 reviving fast-track procedures for congressional action on trade deals. In 2000 he was a main advocate of making permanent the normalized U.S.-China trade relationship.

Portman has been a champion of a drug-free communities program that supports public education to fight drug abuse. He has called for measures to curb violence in movies and to make it harder for teens to obtain firearms illegally. On environmental issues, he advocates incentives to encourage conservation such as government debt write-offs to prod foreign countries to protect tropical forests.

The son of a lift truck dealer, Portman's family has deep roots in Ohio. His mother's parents bought and refurbished the Golden Lamb, a landmark inn in Lebanon that once hosted Mark Twain and Daniel Webster.

After volunteering on the 1988 Bush campaign and rising through the ranks in the White House lobbying shop, Portman returned to Cincinnati to work as a business lawyer. He came to Congress in 1993 to replace Republican Bill Gradison, who resigned to become president of the Health Insurance Association of America. Portman, who had been an intern in Gradison's office in 1976, won a tight three-way primary against former Rep. Bob McEwen and home builder Jay Buchert. He then won the special election in the solidly conservative suburban district with 70 percent of the vote, his lowest take in a general election to date.

After the GOP took over the House in 1995, Portman quickly made his presence felt by pushing to enact a proposal limiting unfunded policy mandates on state and local governments. The issue was a plank of the "Contract With America," the 1994 House GOP campaign manifesto.

In his spare time, Portman has a passion for whitewater kayaking. He practices paddling in the House pool and in the Little Miami River near his home in Cincinnati. While in college, he navigated the entire 1,800-plus miles of the Rio Grande.

KEY VOTES

2002

No Overhaul campaign finance law; ban "soft money" and restrict advocacy advertising
Yes Back Bush's defense budget increase
Yes Extend 1996 welfare law
Yes Adopt Bush's discretionary spending limit
Yes Pass GOP Medicare prescription drug plan
No Create independent Sept. 11 commission
No Extend union protections to Homeland Security Department employees
Yes Revive fast-track procedures for trade agreements
Yes Authorize war against Iraq
No Advance bankruptcy overhaul opposed by abortion opponents

2001

Yes Nullify Clinton Labor Department ergonomics rule
Yes Cut taxes by $1.35 trillion through fiscal 2011
No Maintain ban on oil drilling in Arctic National Wildlife Refuge
Yes Approve Bush proposal to limit managed-care plan liability for coverage decisions
No Divert money from crop subsidy payments to land conservation
Yes Expand law enforcement power to investigate suspected terrorists

CQ VOTE STUDIES

	PARTY UNITY		PRESIDENTIAL SUPPORT	
	Support	Oppose	Support	Oppose
2002	95%	5%	92%	8%
2001	98%	2%	93%	7%
2000	91%	9%	31%	69%
1999	89%	11%	30%	70%
1998	91%	9%	29%	71%

INTEREST GROUPS

	AFL-CIO	ADA	CCUS	ACU
2002	11%	0%	95%	92%
2001	8%	0%	100%	88%
2000	0%	0%	85%	87%
1999	0%	5%	92%	76%
1998	0%	5%	78%	88%

OHIO 2

Eastern Cincinnati and suburbs; Portsmouth

The 2nd stretches from some of Ohio's wealthiest communities in eastern Cincinnati and Hamilton County in southwest Ohio, to some economically struggling areas in rural southern Ohio. It is perhaps the most solidly Republican district in the state and one with a distinct split between its suburban and rural elements. While Cincinnati's wealthy Republican establishment — including the Taft family — has had significant political influence over the years, the district's rural counties have considerably less political pull.

The area economy revolves around light manufacturing and the retail and service industries, and the district's economic health has been boosted by construction around Cincinnati's downtown.

The 2nd includes less than one-fourth of Cincinnati's residents, including those in the well-heeled neighborhoods of Hyde Park and Mount Lookout. Almost 40 percent of the population lives in Cincinnati or in Hamilton County, including the well-to-do communities of Indian Hills, Madeira, Mariemont and Blue Ash.

To the east, fast-growing Clermont County has become more Republican as it has edged closer to Cincinnati's metropolitan orbit. Once undeveloped farmland is bursting with development. To the north, Warren County is filling up with Dayton-area commuters.

Economically, rural Adams County has suffered, with one of the state's highest unemployment rates. Pike County and most of Scioto County (including its most populous city, Portsmouth), which were added in 2002 redistricting, also are struggling. Pike County includes a uranium enrichment facility that long provided good incomes but ceased operations in 2001.

MAJOR INDUSTRY

Manufacturing, service, retail

CITIES

Cincinnati (pt.), 74,163; Portsmouth, 20,909; Lebanon, 16,962

NOTABLE

An Underground Railroad landmark in Ripley (Brown County): the Rev. John Rankin House, where Harriet Beecher Stowe is believed to have obtained ideas for "Uncle Tom's Cabin"; President Ulysses S. Grant was born in Point Pleasant (Clermont County).

Rep. Michael R. Turner (R)

CAPITOL OFFICE
225-6465
oh03.wyr@mail.house.gov
www.house.gov/miketurner
1740 Longworth 20515-3503; fax 225-6754

COMMITTEES
Armed Services
Government Reform

HOMETOWN
Dayton

BORN
Jan. 11, 1960, Dayton, Ohio

RELIGION
Protestant

FAMILY
Wife, Lori Turner; two children

EDUCATION
Ohio Northern U., B.A. 1982 (political science); Case Western Reserve U., J.D. 1985; U. of Dayton, M.B.A. 1992

CAREER
Real estate developer; lawyer

POLITICAL HIGHLIGHTS
Mayor of Dayton, 1994-2002; defeated for re-election as mayor of Dayton, 2001

ELECTION RESULTS

2002 GENERAL		
Michael R. Turner (R)	111,630	58.8%
Rick Carne (D)	78,307	41.2%
2002 PRIMARY		
Michael R. Turner (R)	46,952	79.6%
Roy E. Brown (R)	8,346	14.2%
Gregory E. Hunter (R)	3,702	6.3%

Elected 2002; 1st term

Turner built a reputation as a Republican who could attract crossover votes when he won two terms as mayor of Dayton, where he focused on downtown redevelopment. "From being a Republican mayor for a 10 percent Republican city, I have a great deal of experience working in a nonpartisan way, working together to pull together a broad coalition," he says.

Turner says he intends to use his facility for working with Democrats to forge partnerships on two priorities: sustaining the high-tech mission of Wright-Patterson Air Force Base just outside of Dayton, and making it easier for companies to redevelop polluted "brownfield" sites in downtown areas by providing federal money to help clean them up and by easing environmental liability concerns.

The House Republican leadership fulfilled a campaign promise by Speaker J. Dennis Hastert and named Turner to the Armed Services Committee. Military spending is critical to the district's economy because so much of what is done at Wright-Patterson involves business and product development by local contractors. Turner hopes to address the potential loss of the civilian workers at the base who are nearing retirement age.

Although he lost his bid for a third mayoral term in 2001 to a popular Democratic state senator, Turner's bipartisan appeal was not lost on GOP congressional candidate recruiters at the time. That is because the Republican-dominated Ohio General Assembly, which needed to get rid of one House district after the 2000 reapportionment, redrew the 3rd District to make it more amenable to a GOP candidate.

Turner quickly emerged as the front-runner when President Bush tapped the 12-term Democratic incumbent, Tony P. Hall, early in 2002 to serve as ambassador to a trio of world hunger-relief organizations. Turner first dismissed a big-spending primary challenge from newspaper publisher Roy Brown, whose father and grandfather had served in the House. In November, Turner took 59 percent of the vote to defeat Democrat Rick Carne, Hall's former chief of staff.

OHIO 3

Southwest – most of Dayton, Kettering

Once one of the state's most successful manufacturing centers, Dayton has suffered economic setbacks. A torrent of departures has displaced its manufacturing base, and efforts to diversify have not yielded results. Montgomery County, which surrounds Dayton, lost population in the 1990s. Still, the area's defense industry, revolving around Wright-Patterson Air Force Base, has had some success in attracting aerospace and technology research companies.

The 3rd leans Republican. Redistricting in 2002 excised parts of northeastern Montgomery County and added GOP territory in Warren County, a fast-growing area outside of Cincinnati, and mostly rural Clinton and Highland counties to the southeast. These three counties give the 3rd its slight Republican tilt.

The district takes in most of Dayton and Montgomery County (both are shared with the 8th), and Dayton's southern suburbs include GOP-inclined, white-collar areas such as Kettering and Centerville. The urban vote — driven by Dayton's black population and large blue-collar work force — makes Montgomery slightly Democratic overall. But the areas added in the remap more than balance this Democratic edge.

MAJOR INDUSTRY
Auto manufacturing, defense, service

MILITARY BASES
Wright-Patterson Air Force Base, 7,600 military, 12,600 civilian (2001) (shared with the 7th District)

CITIES
Dayton (pt.), 137,180; Kettering, 57,502; Trotwood, 27,420; Centerville, 23,024

NOTABLE
The Dayton Peace Agreement to end fighting in the former Yugoslavia was signed in 1995 at Wright-Patterson; Dayton was home to the Wright brothers, who tested several airplanes nearby; Montgomery County claims to be birthplace of the refrigerator, the ice cream cone and the stepladder.

Rep. Michael G. Oxley (R)

CAPITOL OFFICE
225-2676
mike.oxley@mail.house.gov
www.house.gov/oxley
2308 Rayburn 20515-3504; fax 226-0112

COMMITTEES
Financial Services - chairman

HOMETOWN
Findlay

BORN
Feb. 11, 1944, Findlay, Ohio

RELIGION
Lutheran

FAMILY
Wife, Patricia Oxley; one child

EDUCATION
Miami U. (Ohio), B.A. 1966 (government); Ohio State U., J.D. 1969

CAREER
FBI agent; lawyer

POLITICAL HIGHLIGHTS
Ohio House, 1973-81

ELECTION RESULTS

2002 GENERAL		
Michael G. Oxley (R)	120,001	67.5%
Jim Clark (D)	57,726	32.5%
2002 PRIMARY		
Michael G. Oxley (R)	36,889	73.2%
James R. Stahl (R)	13,479	26.8%
2000 GENERAL		
Michael G. Oxley (R)	156,510	67.4%
Daniel L. Dickman (D)	67,330	29.0%
Ralph Mullinger (LIBERT)	8,278	3.6%

PREVIOUS WINNING PERCENTAGES
1998 (64%); 1996 (65%); 1994 (100%); 1992 (61%); 1990 (62%); 1988 (100%); 1986 (75%); 1984 (78%); 1982 (65%); 1981 Special Election (50%)

Elected June 1981; 11th full term

The terrorist attacks and a wave of corporate accounting scandals thrust Oxley into the legislative foreground in the 107th Congress and tested his free-market conservatism in his first term as chairman of the newly constituted Financial Services Committee.

In the sweeping counterterrorism law enacted six weeks after the al Qaeda attacks of Sept. 11, 2001, Oxley won inclusion of a package of measures to combat money laundering as a means of reducing terrorists' access to cash. Just before the 107th adjourned, he steered to enactment a law making the federal government the insurers of last resort for losses due to major terrorist attacks. In between, he played a central role — although he did not get his way — in the writing of the 2002 law setting federal standards for accounting practices and corporate governance.

The motto, "To the victor goes the spoils" is one with which Oxley has long been familiar. He is an unabashed defender of many of the perquisites of membership in Congress. As the chairman of a committee with enormous sway over American business, Oxley has no trouble attracting campaign contributions, many of which he redistributes to other Republicans through his political action committee. He roams as widely as any member to vacation destinations — raising money on the ski slopes of Colorado, attending conferences beside the golf courses of Florida — and he makes no apologies for his travels.

At the Capitol, his wisecracking, backslapping style belies an extraordinary competitiveness and a drive to do things his own way. His approach regularly leaves Democrats on Financial Services annoyed that they have not had a greater say in the panel's work. At the same time, Oxley is deferential to his party's leadership; he accepted the insertion of stringent legal provisions into the terrorism insurance bill, for example, and then acquiesced in a deal on that language that President Bush cut with Senate Democrats but without him.

In Oxley's first year as chairman, his main achievement was a law cutting the fees that the Securities and Exchange Commission charges on securities sales, a top priority of Wall Street. Early the next year, he offered a bill designed to rein in the accounting industry after the highly publicized bankruptcy of Enron Corp. The measure reflected his belief that government should regulate business with the lightest possible touch. Panned by critics as too vague to be effective, Oxley's bill was quickly subsumed to a much more assertive Senate measure after subsequent corporate scandals shifted the political momentum. Oxley fought unsuccessfully to limit the scope of the final version; nevertheless, the law that was eventually enacted — the most sweeping new regulation of publicly traded companies since the Depression — bears his name.

Oxley launched a broad probe of Wall Street investment banks, particularly regarding their handling of initial public offerings of stock. But in keeping with his free-market philosophy, he declared in advance that, if new rules were needed, they should come from the private sector, not Congress.

Personally, Oxley's most important victory of the 107th came at the very start, when he took the gavel of a committee on which he had never served and the panel's jurisdiction was expanded to accommodate his areas of expertise: securities and insurance. That arrangement was the GOP leadership's way of settling a two-year fight between Oxley and Louisiana's Billy Tauzin for the chairmanship of the Energy and Commerce Committee.

Their rivalry did not abate in the 107th, however. Although Tauzin held a series of high-profile hearings on Enron and related issues, Oxley jealously guarded his committee's jurisdiction, seeing to it that Energy and Commerce had no substantive role in writing the corporate fraud bill.

During his final term on Energy and Commerce, Oxley played a significant role in writing the 1999 law repealing Depression-era regulatory barriers separating banks, insurance companies and securities firms. He also helped shepherd to passage a 1995 measure — one of just two enacted over a veto by President Clinton — insulating companies from securities fraud lawsuits when they distributed erroneous but good-faith profit projections. Under his stewardship, the Financial Services Committee largely has avoided examining the ramifications of those two laws in the aftermath of subsequent corporate scandals.

Though tough in political combat, Oxley has a reputation as one of the more jovial members of Congress, known for his quick laugh and megawatt smile. He was a jock in high school, and many of his colleagues know him through golf — he is good enough to have once merited a feature in a golf magazine — as well as basketball, tennis and baseball. For years, he started at shortstop, in the outfield or at first base for the GOP in the annual charity baseball game. But his playing days ended a few years after he broke his wrist in the 1994 game (in a collision at first base with Democrat Sherrod Brown of Ohio) and had to have steel pins inserted in his arm. Oxley has managed the GOP team since 1999.

Oxley traces his conservatism to his upbringing in rural Findlay, Ohio, where his father was a county prosecutor. He sported a flat-top haircut in high school. He recalls jousting with liberal professors in college, where Barry Goldwater's "The Conscience of a Conservative" and free-market economist Milton Friedman were important influences. While many of his generation were protesting the Vietnam War or participating in the social revolution, Oxley went to law school and signed on with the FBI. He later received a commendation for his role in a tense, high-profile arrest of two suspected bank robbers who were members of the Black Panthers.

In 1972, at age 28, he won a seat in the Ohio House. He got an opening to run for Congress in April 1981, when Republican Rep. Tennyson Guyer died. Oxley was an early favorite in the special election, but he had stiff primary competition and won narrowly. Oxley struggled to a 341-vote victory in the general election. He handily won a rematch in 1982 and has not been challenged seriously since.

KEY VOTES

2002

No Overhaul campaign finance law; ban "soft money" and restrict advocacy advertising
Yes Back Bush's defense budget increase
Yes Extend 1996 welfare law
Yes Adopt Bush's discretionary spending limit
Yes Pass GOP Medicare prescription drug plan
No Create independent Sept. 11 commission
No Extend union protections to Homeland Security Department employees
Yes Revive fast-track procedures for trade agreements
Yes Authorize war against Iraq
Yes Advance bankruptcy overhaul opposed by abortion opponents

2001

+ Nullify Clinton Labor Department ergonomics rule
Yes Cut taxes by $1.35 trillion through fiscal 2011
No Maintain ban on oil drilling in Arctic National Wildlife Refuge
Yes Approve Bush proposal to limit managed-care plan liability for coverage decisions
No Divert money from crop subsidy payments to land conservation
Yes Expand law enforcement power to investigate suspected terrorists

CQ VOTE STUDIES

	PARTY UNITY		PRESIDENTIAL SUPPORT	
	Support	Oppose	Support	Oppose
2002	96%	4%	95%	5%
2001	99%	1%	98%	2%
2000	96%	4%	30%	70%
1999	89%	11%	28%	72%
1998	91%	9%	25%	75%

INTEREST GROUPS

	AFL-CIO	ADA	CCUS	ACU
2002	13%	0%	100%	96%
2001	10%	0%	100%	92%
2000	0%	0%	95%	81%
1999	0%	5%	96%	76%
1998	11%	5%	100%	96%

OHIO 4
West central – Mansfield, Lima, Findlay

The 4th is a solid block of Ohio Corn Belt counties. The land supports soybeans, corn, livestock and Republicans. Not one of the 11 counties in the 4th has supported a Democratic presidential candidate since 1964, and seven of them gave Republican George W. Bush at least 60 percent of the vote in 2000. Two of the three most populous, Allen and Hancock counties, last voted Democratic in the Roosevelt-Landon contest of 1936.

Democrats have oases of support, but they are few and far between. Democrats can normally count on votes in Mansfield, the district's largest city, which has a 20 percent black population. While those votes occasionally help a Democrat get elected to local office, they are rarely enough to swing the district in national elections.

Along with corn and soybeans, manufacturing is important to the 4th. While declines in the automobile industry in the 1980s and defense cutbacks in the 1990s caused economic hardships throughout parts of the district, the 4th's small industrial companies and large auto manufacturing plants — including a Ford engine plant in Lima, a General Motors plant in Mansfield and Honda facilities in East Liberty (Logan County) and Anna (Shelby County) — continue to spur the economy. Ada is home to a Wilson Sporting Goods manufacturing facility. Findlay, headquarters of Cooper Tire & Rubber Co. and the joint venture Marathon Ashland Petroleum, is the 4th's most prosperous city.

Redistricting in 2002 did not make significant changes to the 4th. The district picked up some territory in the southwest, adding the rest of Auglaize and Logan counties and all of Champaign and Shelby counties.

MAJOR INDUSTRY

Agriculture, auto manufacturing, oil

CITIES

Mansfield, 49,346; Lima, 40,081; Findlay, 38,967; Marion, 35,318

NOTABLE

Lima was one of the original refinery centers for John D. Rockefeller's Standard Oil; Richland Carrousel Park in downtown Mansfield boasts one of the world's largest carousels; Astronaut Neil Armstrong's hometown of Wapakoneta has a museum in his honor; Marion includes the home and tomb of President Warren G. Harding.

Rep. Paul E. Gillmor (R)

CAPITOL OFFICE
225-6405
www.house.gov/gillmor
1203 Longworth 20515-3505; fax 225-1985

COMMITTEES
Energy & Commerce
(Environment & Hazardous Materials - chairman)
Financial Services

HOMETOWN
Old Fort

BORN
Feb. 1, 1939, Tiffin, Ohio

RELIGION
Methodist

FAMILY
Wife, Karen L. Gillmor; five children

EDUCATION
Ohio Wesleyan U., B.A. 1961; U. of Michigan, J.D. 1964

MILITARY SERVICE
Air Force, 1965-66

CAREER
Lawyer

POLITICAL HIGHLIGHTS
Ohio Senate, 1967-89 (minority leader, 1978-80, 1983-84, president, 1981-82, 1985-88); sought Republican nomination for governor, 1986

ELECTION RESULTS

2002 GENERAL		
Paul E. Gillmor (R)	126,286	67.1%
Roger Anderson (D)	51,872	27.6%
John F. Green (LIBERT)	10,096	5.4%
2002 PRIMARY		
Paul E. Gillmor (R)	41,711	69.3%
Rex A. Damschroder (R)	18,498	30.7%
2000 GENERAL		
Paul E. Gillmor (R)	169,857	69.8%
Dannie Edmon (D)	62,138	25.5%
David J. Schaffer (NL)	5,881	2.4%
John F. Green (LIBERT)	5,464	2.3%

PREVIOUS WINNING PERCENTAGES
1998 (67%); 1996 (61%); 1994 (73%); 1992 (100%); 1990 (68%); 1988 (61%)

Elected 1988; 8th term

He is now in his second term as chairman of a subcommittee with jurisdiction over some high-profile domestic legislation, yet Gillmor's career in Congress has been marked more than anything else by its decidedly low profile.

During his first seven terms, he rarely drew notice in the national media and did not even get much coverage in Ohio. "Gillmor has learned that being steady and cautious can be an asset in a Capitol stuffed with attitude and ego," the Gannett News Service concluded in a 2000 profile.

But having come to Washington after 22 years in the state Senate — the last 10 of them as either minority leader or Senate president — Gillmor knows a legislative body cannot have effective leaders unless it also has loyal followers. He has made a point of being one of the latter, and reliably toes the line laid down by the party's leadership.

He is a solid conservative, both fiscally and socially, but not so ideological that he balks when party leaders say it is time to negotiate and compromise. "I'll leave it to others to say whether I am moderate or conservative or some shade in between," he offered in the Gannett profile.

In the 107th Congress, Gillmor moved into the leadership, taking over the gavel of the Energy and Commerce Subcommittee on the Environment and Hazardous Materials. By the end of his first year as chairman he had shepherded to enactment a law to help clean up and develop contaminated industrial sites known as "brownfields," mainly giving states more control over the process and shielding some small businesses from liability to clean up superfund toxic waste sites. For his efforts, he was named the 2002 legislator of the year by the National Association of Counties.

Gillmor demonstrated his legislative pragmatism when the measure was threatened because some Democrats insisted on clarifying that cleanup programs fell under the requirements of the Davis-Bacon prevailing wage law. Republicans did not care for that provision, but Gillmor went along, in the interest of advancing the bill. Earlier, Gillmor and House leaders had given up on their effort to give states even more authority. "There could be improvements made," Gillmor explained, "but nonetheless it is a good bill and I've decided not to let the perfect be the enemy of the good."

It took some legislative acumen by Gillmor to get the legislation through his own subcommittee. He decided not to press for a broader overhaul of the superfund law because lawmakers had been unable to reach consensus on that for several years. "The time has come to break superfund down into smaller parts and pass those things that we all agree should be done," he said.

As subcommittee chairman, Gillmor also has interest in legislation that would let states regulate shipments of trash coming from other states.

In the 107th, he was one of four members of Energy and Commerce — usually an exclusive committee assignment for Republicans — who also got seats on the newly constituted Financial Services panel at the behest of its new chairman, Ohio's Michael G. Oxley. The committee was given some of the jurisdiction that had resided with the former Commerce Committee.

He has continued to push for a measure that would require mutual funds to show the impact of taxes on performance results, contending that this would help investors identify the funds best for them. He also remains committed to an effort he started earlier to require corporations to disclose charitable donations. Business leaders worry that the measure could discourage donations, but Gillmor contends that shareholders should be informed of such donations since it is their money.

In the 106th Congress, Gillmor played a role on a sweeping rewrite of financial services laws. He worked with Democratic Rep. Edward J. Markey of Massachusetts on legislation that placed restrictions on businesses selling a customer's financial and medical information. (Gillmor's family has an interest in a small banking chain in north central Ohio.)

A swing vote in 2000 on granting China regular status as a U.S. trade partner, Gillmor ultimately backed that bill, contending that "open engagement" would lead to improvements in human rights conditions in China. In 2002, he joined the vast majority of his GOP colleagues in supporting the law reviving fast-track procedures for congressional action on trade bills.

Gillmor made a rare break with GOP leaders in the 106th, cosponsoring legislation to ban "soft money," the unlimited and unregulated contributions used for party-building activities and advocacy advertising. But in the 107th, he was back in the fold and voted against the version of the measure that became law in 2002.

After graduating from law school, Gillmor served a tour of duty in the Air Force as a judge advocate before returning to civilian life. He won his seat in the state Senate the next year, when he was 27. Thirteen years later, after the GOP took over the chamber with a one-vote majority, Gillmor won the Senate presidency over a fiery conservative by stressing the need for negotiation within the GOP as well as with the Democrats, who still controlled the House and governorship.

After losing a 1986 bid for the gubernatorial nomination, Gillmor decided two years later to seek the seat of fellow Republican Delbert L. Latta, who was retiring after 30 years in the House. Gillmor's principal primary opponent turned out to be Latta's son, Robert, a 32-year-old lawyer. In a bitter contest, Gillmor towered over the newcomer in personal recognition, stressing his fiscal conservatism and successes in Columbus. But Latta campaigned aggressively, aided by his father's ready-made organization.

Gillmor won the primary by just 27 votes — the smallest margin in any 1988 House contest. He went on to top 60 percent in the general election, just as he has in every re-election bid since.

In the 2002 Republican primary, Gillmor's challenger was state Rep. Rex Damschroeder, who had finished a distant third in the Gillmor-Latta battle. Damschroeder described Gillmor as an "absentee" congressman whose principal residence is in the Columbus area, where his wife, Karen, serves as a gubernatorial appointee on the state Employment Relations Board. The tactic garnered the challenger just 31 percent of the primary vote.

KEY VOTES

2002

- No Overhaul campaign finance law; ban "soft money" and restrict advocacy advertising
- Yes Back Bush's defense budget increase
- Yes Extend 1996 welfare law
- Yes Adopt Bush's discretionary spending limit
- Yes Pass GOP Medicare prescription drug plan
- No Create independent Sept. 11 commission
- No Extend union protections to Homeland Security Department employees
- Yes Revive fast-track procedures for trade agreements
- Yes Authorize war against Iraq
- Yes Advance bankruptcy overhaul opposed by abortion opponents

2001

- Yes Nullify Clinton Labor Department ergonomics rule
- ? Cut taxes by $1.35 trillion through fiscal 2011
- No Maintain ban on oil drilling in Arctic National Wildlife Refuge
- Yes Approve Bush proposal to limit managed-care plan liability for coverage decisions
- No Divert money from crop subsidy payments to land conservation
- Yes Expand law enforcement power to investigate suspected terrorists

CQ VOTE STUDIES

	PARTY UNITY		PRESIDENTIAL SUPPORT	
	Support	Oppose	Support	Oppose
2002	93%	7%	92%	8%
2001	95%	5%	90%	10%
2000	91%	9%	32%	68%
1999	88%	12%	24%	76%
1998	87%	13%	29%	71%

INTEREST GROUPS

	AFL-CIO	ADA	CCUS	ACU
2002	13%	5%	100%	88%
2001	18%	15%	96%	79%
2000	0%	10%	80%	76%
1999	11%	15%	88%	80%
1998	0%	5%	100%	68%

OHIO 5

Northwest – Bowling Green, Tiffin, Fremont

A mixture of flat farmland, limestone plains and small towns, the 5th runs from Ohio's northwest corner to the north-central portion of the state.

At the district's center is the university town of Bowling Green, located in Wood County, the largest and most populous jurisdiction in the 5th. The Maumee River divides Wood from Toledo-dominated Lucas County (most of which is in the 9th), and more people are finding northern Wood an attractive place to live. Perrysburg increased its population 35 percent in the 1990s. Still, most of Wood's land area is devoted to farming. The county is a top producer of wheat, tomatoes, soybeans and corn.

The remaining constituents are almost evenly divided between counties west and east of Wood. Many of the counties are devoted almost exclusively to agriculture and food packaging. This area is the heart of Ohio's wheat-growing country: the state's five top producers are in northwestern Ohio (Wood, Fulton, Seneca, Henry and Paulding). Migrant workers who live in farm camps during the harvesting months help boost the district's Hispanic population to 4 percent, double the state's average of about 2 percent. Manufacturing is important here as well, with Heinz Ketchup and Arm & Hammer Baking Soda among the products made in the 5th's facilities.

Redistricting in 2002 made some adjustments to the lines in the district's east. The 5th no longer borders Lake Erie; the district boundaries were moved south to give the 5th all of Crawford County and parts of Wyandot and Ashland counties. Sandusky is now in the 9th.

The 5th is strong GOP territory. Fifteen of the 16 counties that lie wholly or partly within the 5th voted for Republican George W. Bush in the 2000 presidential election — the lone exception was Lucas County, a small southwestern chunk of which is in the 5th. Putnam County, located southwest of Wood, gave Bush his best showing in Ohio, 74 percent.

MAJOR INDUSTRY

Agriculture, manufacturing

CITIES

Bowling Green, 29,636; Tiffin, 18,135; Fremont, 17,345; Perrysburg, 16,945

NOTABLE

President Rutherford B. Hayes lived in Fremont (Sandusky County), and the Hayes Presidential Center is located there.

Rep. Ted Strickland (D)

CAPITOL OFFICE
225-5705
www.house.gov/strickland
336 Cannon 20515-3506; fax 225-5907

COMMITTEES
Energy & Commerce
Veterans' Affairs

HOMETOWN
Lucasville

BORN
Aug. 4, 1941, Lucasville, Ohio

RELIGION
Methodist

FAMILY
Wife, Frances Smith Strickland

EDUCATION
Asbury College, B.A. 1963 (history); U. of Kentucky, M.A. 1966 (guidance counseling); Asbury Theological Seminary, M.A. 1967 (divinity); U. of Kentucky, Ph.D. 1980 (counseling psychology)

CAREER
Professor; psychologist; minister

POLITICAL HIGHLIGHTS
Democratic nominee for U.S. House, 1976, 1978, 1980; U.S. House, 1993-95; defeated for re-election to U.S. House, 1994

ELECTION RESULTS

2002 GENERAL		
Ted Strickland (D)	113,972	59.5%
Mike Halleck (R)	77,643	40.5%
2002 PRIMARY		
Ted Strickland (D)	41,351	67.5%
Lou D'Apolito (D)	13,391	21.9%
Charles Brown (D)	6,552	10.7%
2000 GENERAL		
Ted Strickland (D)	138,849	57.7%
Michael Azinger (R)	96,966	40.3%
K. MacCutcheon (LIBERT)	4,759	2.0%

PREVIOUS WINNING PERCENTAGES
1998 (57%); 1996 (51%); 1992 (51%)

Elected 1992; 5th term

Did not serve 1995-97

House members typically keep close tabs on their constituents' views, but Strickland has had particular cause to weigh their concerns heavily: Only after his 2002 re-election could he boast of a winning record in races for Congress. He has now won five and lost four.

But it appears that his future in the House has at last become predictable. He won his current term with 59 percent of the vote — a personal best — against Republican Mike Halleck, a former Columbiana County commissioner, benefiting from a redrawing of the Ohio political map in redistricting that made his constituency's voting patterns reliably Democratic for the first time.

Even before the 6th District was remade for this decade, however, Strickland had succeeded in bolstering his job security by luring federal dollars to the impoverished areas of his rural district and curbing his liberal inclinations on environmental and some social policy issues. His seat on the Energy and Commerce Committee, with its broad legislative jurisdiction, has helped him take a high profile on many of the bread-and-butter economic issues for his constituents.

"Someone once described me as their congressional commissioner," Strickland says. "I take that as a compliment. I represent a part of Appalachia that has lots of poverty, an older population, people with health care problems. People struggle day by day. They need a strong advocate."

The son of a steelworker and one of nine siblings, Strickland has an eclectic professional background. He holds a divinity degree and a doctorate in counseling psychology, and he has worked as a minister, prison psychologist, college professor and director of a Methodist children's home.

Strickland was an unsuccessful nominee for Congress in 1976, 1978 and 1980 before winning in a narrow upset in 1992. He benefited that year from the previous redistricting of Ohio, which resulted in two veteran GOP incumbents vying for the same seat. Strickland narrowly defeated the eventual GOP nominee, Bob McEwen, who had gone through a tough primary against colleague Clarence E. Miller and was damaged by publicity about his 166 overdrafts at the private bank for House members.

Two years later, Strickland was swept out of office in that year's GOP landslide, losing narrowly to conservative Republican businessman Frank A. Cremeans. But he won the seat back in 1996, besting Cremeans in a rematch that was viewed as something of a referendum on Republican stewardship of the 104th Congress.

Strickland had hurt himself with voters by following a moderately liberal line during his first term. He supported abortion rights, voted for President Clinton's tax-raising deficit reduction package and suggested that taxes might have to be raised again to create a universal health care benefit, an idea he supported.

While representing a swing district until the 108th Congress, Strickland has remained a reliable Democratic vote on a number of issues, including education and taxes, and he backs efforts to give managed-care patients the right to sue their health care providers. A staunch ally of labor, he voted in the 107th Congress against reviving fast-track procedures for congressional action on trade treaties, and he voted in 2000 against making permanent the normalized U.S.-China trade relationship.

Along the way, though, Strickland has broken with many in his party in deference to the views of his economically struggling and culturally conservative constituents. He opposed the tougher clean air standards proposed by the Clinton administration, and in the 2002 energy debate he opposed Democratic proposals to curb emissions of carbon dioxide, a "greenhouse gas" that most scientists say contributes to global warming. It is formed by burning fossil fuels such as coal in power plants.

"If I didn't have responsibilities to the people who hire me, I might have a very different attitude," Strickland said. "I feel incredibly torn at times. . . . I want clean air, too, but I've got power plants and coal mines in my district. That has tempered my point of view, because I have to fight for my people and their livelihoods."

In the 107th, Strickland began focusing more intently on steel issues, which figure prominently in his new district. Hoping to protect workers in his region, he strongly endorsed Bush's move to impose tariffs as high as 30 percent on steel imports. He also spent much of his time in the last Congress pushing for expanded coverage of Medicare and Medicaid and more generous veterans' benefits. In the 108th, he can pursue the latter from his new post on the Veterans' Affairs Committee.

In the 106th, Strickland sought a compensation package to help government workers who were exposed to dangerous levels of radiation while building the nation's nuclear arsenal. The issue resonated in southern Ohio, home of the Portsmouth Gaseous Diffusion Plant in Piketon, where hundreds of workers may be eligible for the benefits. Although the plant is no longer in Strickland's district, he said he will continue to monitor the problem. Such workers "played a crucial and sometimes overlooked role in winning the Cold War," Strickland said.

Seeking a middle ground on what he calls "socially divisive issues," he has supported funds for family planning but voted to ban a procedure its critics call "partial birth" abortion. Strickland opposes conservatives' efforts to end federal funding of the National Endowment for the Arts, but he usually sides with them in opposing gun control initiatives.

Drawing on his experience as a psychologist in a maximum security prison, Strickland has regularly introduced legislation to prohibit the privatization of prisons. He warns that such institutions would focus on profits rather than safety.

Strickland opposes a constitutional amendment mandating term limits, citing the recent history of the 6th District as proof that voters have sufficient power to effect turnover. "My district has shown that it is capable of making a decision to elect someone and turn them out and turn them back in," he says. "Why interfere with that?"

KEY VOTES

2002

Yes Overhaul campaign finance law; ban "soft money" and restrict advocacy advertising
Yes Back Bush's defense budget increase
No Extend 1996 welfare law
No Adopt Bush's discretionary spending limit
No Pass GOP Medicare prescription drug plan
Yes Create independent Sept. 11 commission
Yes Extend union protections to Homeland Security Department employees
No Revive fast-track procedures for trade agreements
No Authorize war against Iraq
Yes Advance bankruptcy overhaul opposed by abortion opponents

2001

No Nullify Clinton Labor Department ergonomics rule
No Cut taxes by $1.35 trillion through fiscal 2011
Yes Maintain ban on oil drilling in Arctic National Wildlife Refuge
No Approve Bush proposal to limit managed-care plan liability for coverage decisions
Yes Divert money from crop subsidy payments to land conservation
Yes Expand law enforcement power to investigate suspected terrorists

CQ VOTE STUDIES

	PARTY UNITY		PRESIDENTIAL SUPPORT	
	Support	Oppose	Support	Oppose
2002	90%	10%	32%	68%
2001	89%	11%	26%	74%
2000	85%	15%	67%	33%
1999	84%	16%	63%	37%
1998	85%	15%	66%	34%

INTEREST GROUPS

	AFL-CIO	ADA	CCUS	ACU
2002	89%	90%	40%	12%
2001	100%	90%	35%	16%
2000	100%	90%	31%	12%
1999	100%	85%	20%	12%
1998	100%	85%	33%	32%

OHIO 6

South and east – Boardman, Athens, Steubenville

The 6th parallels the Ohio River for more than 300 miles, bordering three states and enveloping the hardscrabble areas from southern Ohio's Appalachia to the Mahoning Valley near Youngstown.

Many of the district's counties, especially those along the Ohio River in old coal mining territory, suffer high unemployment and have difficulty retaining younger people. Meigs County had Ohio's lowest median household income in 1999; Athens, north of Meigs, and Scioto (shared with the 2nd) and Lawrence, which form the southwest border of the 6th, were not far behind.

Athens County (shared with the 18th) is home to Ohio University and leans Democratic. The Green Party's Ralph Nader received a greater vote share in Athens than any other Ohio county in the 2000 presidential election. East of Athens lies Washington County, which takes in Marietta and is one of the few solidly Republican areas in the district.

North of Washington, the district tilts Democratic. Monroe and Belmont counties have supported Democrats for president since 1976. Jefferson County, which includes Steubenville, also votes dependably Democratic. Jefferson has lost population in the past four censuses and has the highest proportion of elderly residents of any Ohio county.

About one-third of residents live in the northern extreme of the district, in Mahoning and Columbiana counties. The Mahoning portions take in Boardman and Poland, just south of Youngstown.

The 6th has a strong Democratic orientation, though it leans conservative on social issues, particularly on gun control. George W. Bush won seven of the 12 counties that lie wholly or partly within the 6th District in 2000. Redistricting following the 2000 census moved the district's boundaries east and north, strengthening the Democratic edge.

MAJOR INDUSTRY
Service, manufacturing

CITIES
Boardman (unincorporated), 37,215; Athens, 21,342; Steubenville, 19,015

NOTABLE
Marietta was the first European settlement in the Northwest Territories; Entertainer Dean Martin was born in Steubenville.

Rep. David L. Hobson (R)

CAPITOL OFFICE
225-4324
www.house.gov/hobson
2346 Rayburn 20515-3507; fax 225-5688

COMMITTEES
Appropriations
(Energy & Water Development - chairman)

HOMETOWN
Springfield

BORN
Oct. 17, 1936, Cincinnati, Ohio

RELIGION
Methodist

FAMILY
Wife, Carolyn Hobson; three children

EDUCATION
Ohio Wesleyan U., B.A. 1958; Ohio State U., J.D. 1963

MILITARY SERVICE
Ohio Air National Guard, 1958-63

CAREER
Financial executive

POLITICAL HIGHLIGHTS
Candidate for Ohio House, 1982; Ohio Senate, 1982-90 (majority whip, 1986-88, president pro tempore, 1988-90)

ELECTION RESULTS

2002 GENERAL		
David L. Hobson (R)	113,252	67.6%
Kara Anastasio (D)	45,568	27.2%
Frank A. Doden (I)	8,812	5.3%
2002 PRIMARY		
David L. Hobson (R)	30,367	72.7%
Steven Schaefer (R)	6,110	14.6%
John R. Mitchel (R)	3,344	8.0%
Ralph A. Applegate (R)	1,941	4.7%
2000 GENERAL		
David L. Hobson (R)	163,646	67.6%
Donald E. Minor Jr. (D)	60,755	25.1%
John R. Mitchel (I)	13,983	5.8%
Jack Null (LIBERT)	3,802	1.6%

PREVIOUS WINNING PERCENTAGES
1998 (67%); 1996 (68%); 1994 (100%); 1992 (71%); 1990 (62%)

Elected 1990; 7th term

An avuncular, easygoing legislator who prefers to work behind the scenes, Hobson enjoys the trust and respect not only of the Republican leadership but also of members from both sides of the aisle. Elected to his current term at age 66, he has long been known around Capitol Hill as "Uncle Dave" for his calm and effective style as a mediator.

His congressional résumé shows how much the GOP leadership has turned to him since his arrival in 1991. He was appointed to the Rules Committee as a freshman, a rare appointment. He was named to the Appropriations Committee as a sophomore, and he was Speaker Newt Gingrich's personal appointee to the Budget Committee in the 104th and 105th Congresses. (In that role, he served as a conduit between the Speaker and John R. Kasich, his fellow Ohio Republican who chaired Budget at the height of the fiscal policy showdowns with the Clinton administration.)

Hobson arrived with years of experience in politics and business. Not only had he risen to a leadership position in the Ohio General Assembly, but he had also served as chairman of a financial services company and on the boards of a bank, an oil company and a restaurant concern. And he was older than many of the other GOP lawmakers then starting their careers, giving him a different perspective than his younger, more ambitious and less patient colleagues.

Hobson is regarded as a moderate, not so much for his votes — which are largely indistinguishable from the average House Republican's — but for his willingness to compromise as part of the lawmaking process. That has come in particularly handy for him in the horse-trading world of Appropriations, where in the 108th Congress Hobson took over the chairmanship of the Energy and Water Development Subcommittee.

In the previous four years he had chaired the Military Construction Subcommittee, where he supervised a spending bill totaling $10.5 billion in his final year with the gavel. The Energy and Water panel's annual bill is nearly triple in size. Hobson has said that one of his interests is encouraging the Department of Energy to enter into more joint research projects with colleges and universities in search of what he called "innovative energy solutions."

The Military Construction post was useful for Hobson, helping him safeguard key local interests, including Wright-Patterson Air Force Base — the fourth largest employer in the state — as well as the Springfield Air National Guard Base, which he has worked to save from elimination. In the 106th, however, he made a parochially difficult decision to back a move by the House to suspend production of the new F-22 fighter. (The project is managed at Wright-Patterson.) In the end, not only did the fighter survive but the complicated deal to save it produced an additional $94 million for technology programs at the base.

While Hobson's switch in chairmanships may mean less construction money for Wright-Patterson, he will still be able to look out for base concerns from his seat on the Defense Appropriations panel.

He also sits on the subcommittee that allocates funding for veterans, housing, space and environmental programs. He has used that assignment to deliver money to the NASA research center in Cleveland named for former astronaut and Ohio Democratic senator John H. Glenn. And he is likely to take an active role in assessing the space agency's budget in the wake of the shuttle *Columbia's* destruction in 2003.

A former member of the Ohio Air National Guard, Hobson has pressed for improvements in U.S. military bases abroad. After a 2001 trip to the Korean peninsula to examine conditions at U.S. bases there, Hobson began inserting extra funds to modernize the facilities. "At Camp Stanley, many of the troops refer to the old living quarters on post as 'crack houses,' " he recalled about one such base during a July 2001 hearing on the subject.

In addition to his appropriations duties, Hobson maintains an interest in health care issues that he developed as a state senator in the 1980s. In the 108th Congress, he is expected to be a vocal advocate for a Medicare prescription drug benefit that lawmakers failed to enact in the 107th. He has also pushed to obtain higher reimbursement rates for mammograms under Medicare. And he worked with Rep. Tom Sawyer of Ohio, a Democrat defeated in 2002, to enact a law in the 107th streamlining the processing of medical information and financial transactions under the 1996 Health Insurance Portability and Accountability Act. Hobson plans to continue work on that issue in the 108th, seeking to establish an electronic system to make it easier to transfer medical records.

He was one of the last Republicans to make known how he would vote on President Bill Clinton's impeachment in 1998, and his votes then mirrored the action of the House. He voted for the two articles that were adopted and against the two articles that were rejected.

He broke with GOP hard-liners in 1996 when he expressed a willingness to negotiate with Clinton on a balanced-budget plan, rather than risk a government shutdown. The next year, when Congress and the White House struck a balanced-budget deal, he fought to keep lawmakers on that course. He voted against a massive highway bill that authorized more spending than the agreement called for and counseled against tax cuts that might endanger the plan.

In 1982, a month after losing respectably in a state House race, Hobson was appointed to the state Senate seat that Republican Mike DeWine gave up in a successful bid for the U.S. House. After four years in Columbus, Hobson was chosen by his GOP colleagues as majority whip, and his focus was on health care legislation.

Hobson was elected to Congress with 62 percent of the vote in 1990, when DeWine (now Ohio's senior senator) gave up his House seat to run for lieutenant governor. He has won with two-thirds of the vote in each of his last four elections — including in 2002, when the district was reconfigured for this decade and 125,000 voters were people he had not represented before.

KEY VOTES

2002

No Overhaul campaign finance law; ban "soft money" and restrict advocacy advertising
Yes Back Bush's defense budget increase
Yes Extend 1996 welfare law
Yes Adopt Bush's discretionary spending limit
Yes Pass GOP Medicare prescription drug plan
No Create independent Sept. 11 commission
No Extend union protections to Homeland Security Department employees
Yes Revive fast-track procedures for trade agreements
Yes Authorize war against Iraq
Yes Advance bankruptcy overhaul opposed by abortion opponents

2001

Yes Nullify Clinton Labor Department ergonomics rule
Yes Cut taxes by $1.35 trillion through fiscal 2011
No Maintain ban on oil drilling in Arctic National Wildlife Refuge
Yes Approve Bush proposal to limit managed-care plan liability for coverage decisions
No Divert money from crop subsidy payments to land conservation
Yes Expand law enforcement power to investigate suspected terrorists

CQ VOTE STUDIES

	PARTY UNITY		PRESIDENTIAL SUPPORT	
	Support	Oppose	Support	Oppose
2002	94%	6%	90%	10%
2001	95%	5%	88%	12%
2000	90%	10%	33%	67%
1999	85%	15%	29%	71%
1998	91%	9%	28%	72%

INTEREST GROUPS

	AFL-CIO	ADA	CCUS	ACU
2002	11%	0%	100%	88%
2001	17%	15%	96%	80%
2000	0%	0%	90%	72%
1999	38%	20%	83%	80%
1998	20%	5%	82%	88%

OHIO 7

Central — Springfield, Lancaster, part of Columbus

The 7th District begins in Clark County, located west of Columbus and just east of Dayton, then curls south and east past Columbus all the way to rural Perry County, near Zanesville. It exhibits a strong GOP lean, though the excision of several conservative rural counties in redistricting following the 2000 census marginally lessened the 7th's right-of-center voting tendencies.

The district's two most populous counties — Greene and Clark — form the western portion of the district. Wright-Patterson Air Force Base, most of which is in Greene, is the largest single-site employer in Ohio. Greene also has several colleges and universities.

Clark and its county seat, Springfield, suffered economically in the early 1980s but have seen a dramatic turnaround. New companies, including trucking and auto manufacturing plants and distribution firms, now call the area home. Clark voted Democratic for president in 2000, one of just three Ohio counties west of Franklin County (Columbus) to do so.

Residential growth around Columbus has especially affected Clark and Fairfield counties, which serve as bedroom communities and are filling up with white-collar commuters. Fairfield is solidly Republican, as are Fayette and Pickaway counties to its west. Fayette, the least populous county wholly within the 7th, is a major horse-breeding area. Perry, the easternmost county in the 7th, has above-average unemployment.

The 7th was redrawn in 2002 to include about 86,000 people in southeast Franklin County, including a small portion of Columbus.

MAJOR INDUSTRY

Auto manufacturing, military, technology research, agriculture

MILITARY BASES

Wright-Patterson Air Force Base, 7,600 military, 12,600 civilian (2001) (shared with the 3rd District)

CITIES

Springfield, 65,358; Columbus (pt.), 51,097; Beavercreek, 37,984; Lancaster, 35,335; Fairborn, 32,052; Xenia, 24,164

NOTABLE

Gen. William Tecumseh Sherman was born in Lancaster; The modern combine, invented in Springfield, helped revolutionize harvesting and the agriculture industry.

Rep. John A. Boehner (R)

CAPITOL OFFICE
225-6205
john.boehner@mail.house.gov
www.house.gov/boehner
1011 Longworth 20515-3508; fax 225-0704

COMMITTEES
Agriculture
Education & Workforce - chairman

HOMETOWN
West Chester

BORN
Nov. 17, 1949, Cincinnati, Ohio

RELIGION
Roman Catholic

FAMILY
Wife, Debbie Boehner; two children

EDUCATION
Xavier U., B.S. 1977

MILITARY SERVICE
Navy, 1968

CAREER
Plastics and packaging executive

POLITICAL HIGHLIGHTS
Ohio House, 1985-91

ELECTION RESULTS

2002 GENERAL		
John A. Boehner (R)	119,947	70.8%
Jeff Hardenbrook (D)	49,444	29.2%
2002 PRIMARY		
John A. Boehner (R)	27,770	85.2%
Roger A. Thomas (R)	4,839	14.8%
2000 GENERAL		
John A. Boehner (R)	179,756	71.0%
John G. Parks (D)	66,293	26.2%
David R. Shock (LIBERT)	7,254	2.9%

PREVIOUS WINNING PERCENTAGES
1998 (71%); 1996 (70%); 1994 (100%); 1992 (74%); 1990 (61%)

Elected 1990; 7th term

Boehner's expulsion from the House Republican leadership at the end of 1998 might have led another politician to avoid the limelight for a long while, or perhaps seek new career opportunities elsewhere. Not Boehner; he has turned the setback into a steppingstone.

Transforming himself from partisan operator into legislative tactician, he won election two years later as chairman of the Education and the Workforce Committee. One year after that, he stood next to President Bush as he signed one of the landmark laws of the 107th Congress, an overhaul of federal education policy that for the first time ties education aid from Washington to improvement in student test scores.

Along the way, Boehner (BAY-ner) forged alliances with the types of liberal, big-government Democrats whose philosophies he so frequently lambasted during his four years as chairman of the House Republican Conference. In that role he was one of the main message-makers of Newt Gingrich's "Republican revolution"; when the party suffered setbacks in the 1998 election, Boehner was labeled by his colleagues as an ineffectual messenger and was defeated for re-election to his leadership job.

Some measure of his past partisanship left him in the years thereafter, with important results. Preparing for a meeting about education with President-elect Bush late in 2000, Boehner insisted that transition team officials also invite George Miller of California, who was about to become the top Democrat on the panel that Boehner was in line to chair. The unlikely partnership that was born is credited with speeding one of Bush's top domestic priorities into law sooner than many had expected.

While Boehner gives the impression that he is simply happy to go along to get along, answering even the most pointed questions with a shrug or a nod as he puffs on an ever-present cigarette, he is an ambitious politician and a formidable competitor. When he entered Congress in 1991 he was one of the rabble-rousing Gang of Seven, minority party freshmen eager to rein in — or at least rail against — what they saw as the excesses of the House that culminated in its internal bank scandal. His zeal for partisan combat against the entrenched Democratic leadership made him a favorite of the new breed of confrontational Republicans led by Gingrich.

Boehner passed on entreaties that he try and return to the elected GOP leadership in the 108th Congress, in part because acolytes of Tom DeLay — which he pointedly is not — quickly sewed up the top positions. But Boehner's ambitions for more political prominence have not cooled.

In the interim, he has played a leading role in some of the most politically important issues of the day, including retirement savings stabilization, farm subsidies, financial services regulation and patients' rights guarantees.

After the education law, Boehner's most significant legislative accomplishment was enactment of the 1996 farm policy overhaul, which sought to wean farmers off government aid and allow agriculture's fortunes to be tied more closely to the free market. Six years later, he tried unsuccessfully to leverage his senior position on the Agriculture Committee to thwart the replacement statute, which shifted policy back toward a reliance on federal crop subsidies. Boehner did so even though much of the 8th District is corn, soybean, poultry, and livestock farms. And, although the head of the world's largest dairy cooperative is a constituent, Boehner has sought to abolish the federal milk-pricing system.

His willingness to break with the wishes of his electorate reflects his almost religious allegiance to free enterprise. He and a partner built a small plastics and packaging firm, Nucite Sales Inc., into a multimillion-dollar business soon after his graduation from college. The oldest of 11 children and the son of tavern owners, Boehner put himself through school over an eight-year period while working a variety of jobs.

He took on a major legislative task in the 105th Congress when his business contacts prompted Republican leaders to appoint him liaison to the financial services industry. He helped shepherd through the House a bill to rewrite the complex web of laws that govern banks, stock brokerages and insurance firms, but the bill died in the Senate. (A revised measure was enacted in the 106th.) In the 107th, Boehner helped lead the House passage of pension overhaul legislation after the collapse of the Houston energy giant Enron Corp. It stalled in the Senate, but Boehner put it at the top of his agenda again in the 108th.

Post-census redistricting for this decade put the 8th's boundaries much closer to Wright-Patterson Air Force Base, and Boehner undertook a crash program to educate himself about issues related to the base.

Boehner also has kept up his record as a prolific fundraiser for the party and has maintained contacts with the business community. A prime venue for communication with Boehner has been the golf course. A low handicapper (three or four), he is as passionate about the game as he is skilled. He spends much of his free time in Florida, maintaining not only his stroke but also the deep tan he sports all year.

It was one Florida trip that led to a testy legal dispute between Boehner and Democratic Rep. Jim McDermott of Washington. Boehner joined a 1996 conference call in which GOP leaders discussed strategy for dealing with Speaker Gingrich's ethical troubles. A Florida couple intercepted the conversation and taped it. They gave a copy of the tape to McDermott, who was then the ranking Democrat on the House ethics committee. When newspapers ran excerpts, Boehner sued, alleging his privacy had been violated. McDermott says he was within his First Amendment rights. Their dispute has been in litigation ever since.

After six years in the state House, Boehner joined the 1990 GOP primary field against incumbent Donald E. "Buz" Lukens, who had been convicted of a misdemeanor charge stemming from a sexual liaison with a 16-year-old girl. Boehner heavily outspent the front-runner, former Rep. Thomas N. Kindness, and won the primary with 49 percent. In the general election, he won a 3-to-2 victory over former Democratic Mayor Gregory V. Jolivette of Hamilton, and he has done better than that in every subsequent re-election.

KEY VOTES

2002

No Overhaul campaign finance law; ban "soft money" and restrict advocacy advertising
Yes Back Bush's defense budget increase
Yes Extend 1996 welfare law
Yes Adopt Bush's discretionary spending limit
Yes Pass GOP Medicare prescription drug plan
? Create independent Sept. 11 commission
No Extend union protections to Homeland Security Department employees
Yes Revive fast-track procedures for trade agreements
Yes Authorize war against Iraq
Yes Advance bankruptcy overhaul opposed by abortion opponents

2001

Yes Nullify Clinton Labor Department ergonomics rule
Yes Cut taxes by $1.35 trillion through fiscal 2011
No Maintain ban on oil drilling in Arctic National Wildlife Refuge
Yes Approve Bush proposal to limit managed-care plan liability for coverage decisions
No Divert money from crop subsidy payments to land conservation
Yes Expand law enforcement power to investigate suspected terrorists

CQ VOTE STUDIES

	PARTY UNITY		PRESIDENTIAL SUPPORT	
	Support	Oppose	Support	Oppose
2002	97%	3%	92%	8%
2001	99%	1%	98%	2%
2000	95%	5%	30%	70%
1999	93%	7%	27%	73%
1998	96%	4%	25%	75%

INTEREST GROUPS

	AFL-CIO	ADA	CCUS	ACU
2002	11%	0%	100%	88%
2001	8%	0%	100%	96%
2000	0%	5%	85%	87%
1999	0%	10%	92%	91%
1998	0%	0%	89%	96%

OHIO 8
Southwest – Hamilton, most of Middletown

Running along the state's western border, the 8th is fertile GOP ground that is anchored by Butler County, home to the district's two largest cities, Hamilton and Middletown.

Butler has long voted solidly Republican, but the expansion of its suburbs has escalated the rightward trend. The county is known for electing some of Ohio's more conservative state and congressional legislators. George W. Bush took 63 percent of Butler's vote in the 2000 presidential election. One exception to the GOP dominance is Oxford, which includes Miami University and voted narrowly for Al Gore in 2000.

Butler and Miami counties have propelled the district's rapid growth. Union Township, in Butler County, is one of the state's fastest growing suburbs, and many residents there commute to Cincinnati or Dayton. While bad weather and low pork prices hurt the 8th's dominant agriculture industry in the late 1990s, the district's strong manufacturing base, along with new construction and commercial development, helped prevent economic hardship.

About half the 8th's residents live outside Butler County in a string of fertile Corn Belt counties. Corn and soybeans are the major cash crops here, and poultry and livestock also are moneymakers. Mercer (shared with the 5th) and Darke are Ohio's two top-producing soybean and corn counties, and they also yield plenty of Republican votes, backing Bush with 68 percent and 64 percent respectively. Miami County, the district's second most populous, also is reliable GOP turf.

Redistricting in 2002 gave the 8th a bigger chunk of Montgomery County, including parts of northeast Dayton near Wright-Patterson Air Force Base. The new map ceded a small part of southwestern Butler County to the 1st District and moved the 8th's northeast border farther south.

MAJOR INDUSTRY
Agriculture, manufacturing, higher education

CITIES
Hamilton, 60,675; Middletown (pt.), 49,574; Fairfield, 42,097; Huber Heights, 38,212; Dayton (pt.), 28,999

NOTABLE
Hamilton once was known as the "Safe Capital of the World" for the burglar-resistant safes made there; Darke County hosts an Annie Oakley festival each year in honor of their homegrown sharpshooter.

Rep. Marcy Kaptur (D)

CAPITOL OFFICE
225-4146
rep.kaptur@mail.house.gov
www.house.gov/kaptur
2366 Rayburn 20515-3509; fax 225-7711

COMMITTEES
Appropriations

HOMETOWN
Toledo

BORN
June 17, 1946, Toledo, Ohio

RELIGION
Roman Catholic

FAMILY
Single

EDUCATION
U. of Wisconsin, B.A. 1968 (history); U. of Michigan, M.U.P. 1974 (urban planning); Massachusetts Institute of Technology, attended 1981 (urban planning)

CAREER
White House aide; urban planner

POLITICAL HIGHLIGHTS
No previous office

ELECTION RESULTS

2002 GENERAL		
Marcy Kaptur (D)	132,236	74.0%
Edward Emery (R)	46,481	26.0%
2002 PRIMARY		
Marcy Kaptur (D)		unopposed
2000 GENERAL		
Marcy Kaptur (D)	168,547	74.8%
Dwight E. Bryan (R)	49,446	21.9%
Galen Fries (LIBERT)	4,239	1.9%
Dennis Slotnick (NL)	3,096	1.4%

PREVIOUS WINNING PERCENTAGES
1998 (81%); 1996 (77%); 1994 (75%); 1992 (74%); 1990 (78%); 1988 (81%); 1986 (78%); 1984 (55%); 1982 (58%)

Elected 1982; 11th term

Now beginning her third decade in the House, Kaptur is the chamber's senior Democratic woman and the senior woman of either party on the Appropriations Committee, where she has been the ranking Democrat on the Agriculture Subcommittee since 1997.

But her long tenure has not regularly brought with it either influence or legislative success. Indeed, on two of the bellwether issues of the time Kaptur often finds herself openly at odds with her fellow Democrats. Unlike most of her Democratic colleagues in the House — especially the women — Kaptur is not an abortion rights advocate and opposes using federal funds to pay for abortions. And her congressional career has been marked by a steady but often unsuccessful effort to prevent the lowering of international trade barriers. In both areas, her views reflect the concerns of Kaptur's white ethnic constituency, many of whom put stock in the Roman Catholic Church's stance on abortion or fear losing their well-paying blue-collar jobs to low-wage competitors abroad.

Late in 2002, as House Democrats prepared to choose a new leader, Kaptur entered the race just the day before the vote. She said she was under no illusion that she had a chance to win against Californian Nancy Pelosi, but wanted a forum to express her view that the party's emphasis on fundraising had caused it to lose its historical focus on the needs of the working class. Kaptur gave her speech and then withdrew her name.

Kaptur remains emblematic of her Main Street roots. She lives with her brother, Stephen, in the same small house where they were reared, and she attends Mass at the same church where she was baptized. Her parents ran grocery stores in Toledo and nearby Rossford and worked in local auto plants, and Kaptur also was an autoworker to help pay for college. Although she is one of the oldest children born during the Baby Boom, some of her domestic practices are from a bygone era. She maintains the family garden and cans some of the produce that sprouts up; she bakes Polish coffeecakes and makes Polish sausages at the holidays; she paints watercolors; she sews her own curtains.

From her seat on Appropriations, Kaptur engages in the familiar pastime of trying to funnel federal dollars home. Agriculture is Ohio's biggest industry and, as a reminder of that, she sometimes gives her colleagues samples of items — Hirzel spaghetti sauce, Heritage seeds — produced in the state. She also looks out for the interests of the sugar beet growers who are her principal farming constituency. Kaptur has been a leading player in campaigns to save federal sugar subsidies, arguing that without the government's help domestic farmers could lose out to imports from Mexico. It is only fair, in her view, to help U.S. industries survive when they have to comply (appropriately, in her view) with labor, environmental and health standards that are higher than in other nations.

Using similar arguments, Kaptur has been a leader in the campaigns against all the major trade expansion initiatives of President Clinton and President Bush: the 1993 law to carry out the North American Free Trade Agreement, the 1994 law that created the World Trade Organization, the permanent normalization of China's standing as a preferred U.S. trade partner in 2000, and the revival in 2002 of fast-track authority to negotiate trade agreements that Congress cannot amend. "Americans are running like gerbils in a cage because of the pressure of the multinational corporate ethic on the way production is organized and distributed in the world," Kaptur said in

2000. Her high profile in opposing a president of her own party on trade issues led independent presidential candidate Ross Perot to ask her to be his running mate in 1996. Kaptur declined and backed Clinton's re-election.

Her stands on social policies, however, could tarnish her bona fides with some hardcore Democrats who take her side against trade liberalization. In 2002, Kaptur voted "present" on a bill that would allow hospitals to refuse to perform abortions without forfeiting federal money. Kaptur said she did not think health-care facilities that act out of religious faith should have their funding jeopardized, but added she also did not want to bar women from their "full range of choices."

After the 1997 death of her mother, Anastasia, Kaptur and her brother founded the nonprofit Anastasia Fund to promote liberty, community development and free religious expression in the face of political and economic pressures. The fund has helped support groups in Ukraine, China and Mexico. Kaptur also has established the Kaptur Community Fund, which makes charitable donations in Toledo; she regularly contributes her congressional pay raise to the fund.

A staunch defender of the War Powers Act, Kaptur was a plaintiff in a federal lawsuit, which ultimately failed, alleging that Clinton did not obey the law when he ordered bombing in Yugoslavia in 1999.

She had better success in her quest for a national memorial to the veterans of World War II. She first introduced a bill on the issue in 1987, inspired by a constituent, Roger Durbin, who was a veteran of the war. The measure was enacted in 1993, and work began on the memorial — halfway between the Lincoln Memorial and Washington Monument — in 2002.

Kaptur was the first member of her family to attend college. She then worked as a city planner, helping to create community development corporations to revitalize low-income areas of Toledo. That led to a job in the Carter administration as an adviser on urban policy.

Kaptur was working on her doctorate in urban planning at the Massachusetts Institute of Technology when she was recruited to challenge first-term GOP Rep. Ed Weber in 1982. With northwest Ohio in a deep recession, Weber's support for President Reagan's economic agenda proved politically fatal; Kaptur won by 19 percentage points.

She was held to 55 percent in 1984 but has won more than 70 percent of the vote in every race since. Redistricting by the GOP-controlled legislature in 2002 added to the 9th District some Republican-leaning territory to the east — in Ottawa, Erie and Lorain counties — but Kaptur nonetheless took three-quarters of the vote against frequent GOP candidate Ed Emery.

KEY VOTES

2002

- Yes Overhaul campaign finance law; ban "soft money" and restrict advocacy advertising
- Yes Back Bush's defense budget increase
- No Extend 1996 welfare law
- No Adopt Bush's discretionary spending limit
- No Pass GOP Medicare prescription drug plan
- Yes Create independent Sept. 11 commission
- Yes Extend union protections to Homeland Security Department employees
- No Revive fast-track procedures for trade agreements
- No Authorize war against Iraq
- No Advance bankruptcy overhaul opposed by abortion opponents

2001

- No Nullify Clinton Labor Department ergonomics rule
- ? Cut taxes by $1.35 trillion through fiscal 2011
- Yes Maintain ban on oil drilling in Arctic National Wildlife Refuge
- No Approve Bush proposal to limit managed-care plan liability for coverage decisions
- Yes Divert money from crop subsidy payments to land conservation
- Yes Expand law enforcement power to investigate suspected terrorists

CQ VOTE STUDIES

	PARTY UNITY		PRESIDENTIAL SUPPORT	
	Support	Oppose	Support	Oppose
2002	96%	4%	24%	76%
2001	89%	11%	23%	77%
2000	91%	9%	73%	27%
1999	87%	13%	68%	32%
1998	85%	15%	71%	29%

INTEREST GROUPS

	AFL-CIO	ADA	CCUS	ACU
2002	100%	95%	30%	18%
2001	100%	85%	30%	30%
2000	100%	75%	30%	18%
1999	100%	85%	26%	4%
1998	100%	80%	17%	28%

OHIO 9

North – Toledo, Sandusky

The 9th surrounds Toledo, stretching from Lucas County on the Michigan border to southwestern Lorain County. About half of the district's residents live in Toledo, which sits at the mouth of the Maumee River, the largest river flowing into the Great Lakes. Toledo's large concentrations of ethnic blue-collar workers — Germans, Irish, Poles and Hungarians — make it a lonely Democratic outpost in rural, Republican northwestern Ohio.

Republicans are concentrated in the more affluent suburbs on Toledo's west side, such as upscale Ottawa Hills. But Toledo's Democratic voters overwhelm Republicans elsewhere in the district.

Toledo's economy has long depended on the auto industry, which closed several area factories in the 1980s. But the industry is back, albeit in smaller form, with a Jeep assembly plant and a General Motors parts facility. Growth in the city's petroleum and manufacturing industries, including glass and machinery, also has spurred some economic recovery.

To the east of Lucas is Ottawa County, which includes Port Clinton and some islands near Canada's Pelee Island, and Erie County, which includes Sandusky and has a blue-collar feel and a slight Democratic lean. The district's easternmost county is Lorain, parts of which were drawn into the 9th along with Erie County and Sandusky in redistricting following the 2000 census. There is a liberal area around Oberlin College, where residents took a strong anti-slavery stance in the 19th century and continue to crusade for social reforms.

MAJOR INDUSTRY

Auto manufacturing, agriculture, health care

CITIES

Toledo, 313,619; Sandusky, 27,844; Oregon, 19,355; Sylvania, 18,670

NOTABLE

Toledo's historic "Old West End" is known for its Victorian homes and claims to have been the nation's largest residential neighborhood at the turn of the century; Oberlin College, founded in 1833, was the first coeducational institution of higher learning in the United States; Toledo is known to television viewers as the home of Cpl. Max Klinger, a character in the series "M*A*S*H."

Rep. Dennis J. Kucinich (D)

CAPITOL OFFICE
225-5871
www.house.gov/kucinich
1730 Longworth 20515-3510; fax 225-5745

COMMITTEES
Education & Workforce
Government Reform

HOMETOWN
Cleveland

BORN
Oct. 8, 1946, Cleveland, Ohio

RELIGION
Roman Catholic

FAMILY
Divorced; one child

EDUCATION
Case Western Reserve U., B.A., M.A. 1973 (speech communications)

CAREER
Video producer; public power consultant; sportswriter

POLITICAL HIGHLIGHTS
Cleveland City Council, 1969-75; Democratic nominee for U.S. House, 1972; independent candidate for U.S. House, 1974; mayor of Cleveland, 1977-79; defeated for re-election as mayor of Cleveland, 1979; Cleveland City Council, 1983-85; sought Democratic nomination for U.S. House, 1988, 1992; Ohio Senate, 1995-97

ELECTION RESULTS

2002 GENERAL		
Dennis J. Kucinich (D)	129,997	74.1%
Jon A. Heben (R)	41,778	23.8%
Judy Locy (I)	3,761	2.1%
2002 PRIMARY		
Dennis J. Kucinich (D)		unopposed
2000 GENERAL		
Dennis J. Kucinich (D)	167,063	75.0%
Bill Smith (R)	48,930	22.0%
Ron Petrie (LIBERT)	6,762	3.0%

PREVIOUS WINNING PERCENTAGES
1998 (67%); 1996 (49%)

Elected 1996; 4th term

Kucinich first came on the national scene almost a quarter-century ago as the "boy mayor" of Cleveland when it went bankrupt in 1978. But six years before that, he ran hard against the Vietnam war and came within 4,200 votes of upsetting a veteran Republican congressman. And that is the part of his past that Kucinich wants to emulate in the 108th Congress, when he is seeking to become the principal anti-war candidate for the 2004 Democratic presidential nomination.

Of the members of Congress running, Kucinich (ku-SIN-itch) is the only one who characterizes himself as a pacifist — and the only one who worked to prevent Congress from enacting the 2002 law authorizing President Bush to launch a pre-emptive military strike on Iraq. When his attempt to build congressional support for a longer course of diplomacy came up short, Kucinich nonetheless forced the issue on the House floor; his proposal for a delay received 101 votes.

He and five other Democrats then sued to bar Bush from attacking without a specific congressional declaration of war. A federal appeals court tossed out the suit in March 2003. Similarly, in 1999 he joined two dozen other lawmakers in an unsuccessful suit maintaining that President Clinton had illegally committed U.S. troops to a NATO bombing campaign for too long without congressional approval.

Since the 107th Congress, Kucinich has been a chairman of the Congressional Progressive Caucus, the group of the most liberal House Democrats. He is a proponent of a bill to establish a Cabinet-level Department of Peace.

But for all his activism in Washington, Kucinich found that another presidential aspirant, former Vermont Gov. Howard Dean, had staked out the anti-war turf in Iowa and New Hampshire before Kucinich entered the fray in 2003. And Kucinich quickly ran into trouble on another topic important to many Democrats. As a presidential contender, Kucinich described himself as "pro-choice." But as a House member, he had compiled a consistent anti-abortion record until 2002, when he voted "present" on both a bill to outlaw a procedure that opponents call "partial-birth abortion" and on a measure to allow doctors, hospitals and insurance companies to refuse to provide or pay for abortions. Kucinich says his views on abortion had "evolved."

Moreover, his voting record reveals he is not even close to the most liberal House member. While his AFL-CIO lifetime voting approval score is a 98, his overall approval rating from the liberal Americans for Democratic Action is only an 86. And in the 107th Congress, 58 House Democrats opposed Bush more often than Kucinich did.

Where Kucinich distinguishes himself is in his hard-charging approach, perseverance, rhetorical flourishes and self-deprecating wit. When he arrived in Congress, he handed out trading cards featuring himself as a 4-foot 9-inch, 97-pound backup high school quarterback in 1960. Speaking at a journalists' awards dinner a few months later, he brought down the house by promising to civilize Washington through the introduction of three Cleveland staples: kielbasa, polka and bowling.

That glibness was part of an image makeover necessitated by the memories that official Washington retained of Kucinich from his flamboyant and controversial single term as a mayor. The city fell into financial default, and Kucinich's popularity sank so low he wore a bulletproof vest when he threw out the first pitch of the Cleveland Indians' 1978 season. Later that year, he barely survived a recall vote, and the next year he was defeated by Republican George V. Voinovich, now Ohio's junior senator.

But then both Cleveland and its former mayor rebounded. Bucking the GOP tide, Kucinich seized a state Senate seat from a Republican incumbent in 1994. Two years later — in his fifth bid for Congress — he took aim at two-term Republican Martin R. Hoke. Kucinich prevailed by linking the incumbent to House Speaker Newt Gingrich, a polarizing figure by 1996. Kucinich won by 6,000 votes but has breezed through three re-elections.

The son of a truck driver, he earned a master's degree in communications and has worked as a copy editor, sportswriter and political commentator — a background that has helped make him a master at reducing complicated public policy disagreements to easily understood terms.

Kucinich opposed the counterterrorism law enacted soon after the 2001 terrorist attacks, deriding it as an unconscionable erosion of constitutionally guaranteed civil liberties. In a February 2002 speech that generated thousands of mostly supportive e-mail responses, Kucinich railed against Bush's conduct of the campaign against terrorism as a "war without end" that went far beyond what Congress had authorized right after Sept. 11.

"The trappings of a state of siege trap us in a state of fear, ill-equipped to deal with the patriot games, the mind games, the war games of an unelected president and his undetected vice president," Kucinich said, continuing to lament the outcome of the bitterly contested 2000 presidential election and to mock the frequent seclusion of Vice President Dick Cheney.

True to his roots in the labor movement, Kucinich called on Bush in 2002 to impose 40 percent tariffs on imports of foreign steel. After the president imposed tariffs as high as 30 percent, Kucinich hailed the "three-quarters of a victory." He rode into battle the previous year to try to save Ohio's bankrupt LTV Steel, which employed thousands of his constituents.

One of Kucinich's passions is warning Americans about genetically modified food, which would carry government labels under legislation he has proposed since the 106th Congress. "If we are what we eat, shouldn't we know what is in our food, so we know what we will become?" he asked.

Practicing what he preaches, Kucinich made a radical change in his own diet in 1995, becoming a vegetarian after almost five decades in which his diet featured kielbasa and other rich Eastern European fare. Now his meals feature rice, tofu and green tea. "Once I was able to make the transition, I've had enormous amounts of energy, I sleep better, and I don't get tired as much," he said in 2000.

KEY VOTES

2002

Yes Overhaul campaign finance law; ban "soft money" and restrict advocacy advertising
No Back Bush's defense budget increase
No Extend 1996 welfare law
No Adopt Bush's discretionary spending limit
No Pass GOP Medicare prescription drug plan
Yes Create independent Sept. 11 commission
Yes Extend union protections to Homeland Security Department employees
No Revive fast-track procedures for trade agreements
No Authorize war against Iraq
No Advance bankruptcy overhaul opposed by abortion opponents

2001

No Nullify Clinton Labor Department ergonomics rule
No Cut taxes by $1.35 trillion through fiscal 2011
Yes Maintain ban on oil drilling in Arctic National Wildlife Refuge
No Approve Bush proposal to limit managed-care plan liability for coverage decisions
Yes Divert money from crop subsidy payments to land conservation
No Expand law enforcement power to investigate suspected terrorists

CQ VOTE STUDIES

	PARTY UNITY		PRESIDENTIAL SUPPORT	
	Support	Oppose	Support	Oppose
2002	96%	4%	26%	74%
2001	89%	11%	23%	77%
2000	89%	11%	76%	24%
1999	83%	17%	63%	37%
1998	84%	16%	78%	22%

INTEREST GROUPS

	AFL-CIO	ADA	CCUS	ACU
2002	100%	80%	20%	0%
2001	100%	85%	17%	20%
2000	90%	80%	28%	16%
1999	100%	90%	12%	20%
1998	100%	90%	22%	20%

OHIO 10

Cleveland – West Side and suburbs

The 10th includes the western portion of Cleveland and follows the migration of its ethnic residents into the western and southern suburbs. The district, composed mainly of Reagan Democrats, has successfully navigated the transition from an industrial to a service economy.

The line between the 10th and 11th districts generally divides Cleveland's white and black neighborhoods. The 10th contains the state's largest concentration of ethnic voters, mostly Poles, Czechs, Italians, Irish and Germans. Although industry still provides the backbone of the city's economy, the 10th has attracted smaller, high-tech companies and undergone a downtown restoration, helping the district maintain its steady employment base.

The immediate suburbs have a strong union presence and a Democratic lean. The communities of Brooklyn and Lakewood, which abut western Cleveland, are middle-income and lean Democratic. Farther west the incomes rise, as does the level of Republicanism: Bay Village and Westlake residents have above-average incomes and voted solidly for George W. Bush in the 2000 presidential election.

Redistricting following the 2000 census altered the 10th to take in some of central Cuyahoga County — including Brook Park, Middleburg Heights and Parma Heights — that had been in the old 19th District. Brook Park is a blue-collar autoworkers' community that is decidedly Democratic.

The strong Democratic tendencies of Cleveland, coupled with the Republican leanings of some of the city's western and southern suburbs, combine to give the 10th a slight but not overwhelming Democratic lean.

MAJOR INDUSTRY

Manufacturing, banking, technology, auto parts

CITIES

Cleveland (pt.), 190,224; Parma, 85,655; Lakewood, 56,646; North Olmsted, 34,113; Westlake, 31,719

NOTABLE

A publisher dropped an "a" from city founder Moses Cleaveland's name so that it would fit neatly on his page, giving the city's name its current spelling; The city is home to NASA's John H. Glenn Research Center.

Rep. Stephanie Tubbs Jones (D)

CAPITOL OFFICE
225-7032
stephanie.tubbs.jones@mail.house.gov
www.house.gov/tubbsjones
1009 Longworth 20515-3511; fax 225-1339

COMMITTEES
Standards of Official Conduct
Ways & Means

HOMETOWN
Cleveland

BORN
Sept. 10, 1949, Cleveland, Ohio

RELIGION
Baptist

FAMILY
Husband, Mervyn Jones; one child

EDUCATION
Case Western Reserve U., B.A. 1971 (sociology), J.D. 1974

CAREER
Lawyer; municipal judge

POLITICAL HIGHLIGHTS
Cuyahoga County judge, 1983-91; Cuyahoga County prosecutor, 1991-99

ELECTION RESULTS

2002 GENERAL		
Stephanie Tubbs Jones (D)	116,590	76.3%
Patrick A. Pappano (R)	36,146	23.7%
2002 PRIMARY		
Stephanie Tubbs Jones (D)		unopposed
2000 GENERAL		
Stephanie Tubbs Jones (D)	164,134	84.8%
James Sykora (R)	21,630	11.2%
Joel C. Turner (LIBERT)	4,230	2.2%
Sonja K. Glavina (NL)	3,525	1.8%

PREVIOUS WINNING PERCENTAGES
1998 (80%)

Elected 1998; 3rd term

In Cleveland, constituents are not surprised to see their congresswoman pushing a cart in the local supermarket. "I'm not new to people," says Jones, who takes great pride in her cooking and who had a two-decade legal and political career in her hometown before arriving at the Capitol in 1999.

In Washington, Jones, the first black congresswoman to represent Ohio, became in 2003 the first black woman ever appointed to the Ways and Means Committee.

That post, which she got only after a tussle between Democrats and Republicans over the size of the panel, continued her rise through the ranks.

For the second half of the 107th Congress, Jones was the elected president of the sophomore class of the House Democratic Caucus. She served as a liaison between the party's leadership and the other two dozen lawmakers first elected in 1998. Her self-described priorities were promoting the disparate legislative interests of members of the group with the Democratic hierarchy, helping to push the party's legislative agenda and helping colleagues in tough races win re-election, in part by raising money for them. "One of the best attributes of a leader is also being a team player," she says.

When she sought to take a bigger step up at the start of the 108th Congress to the post on Ways and Means, which writes tax, trade, health care and social welfare legislation, she argued that the powerful panel had no African-American women in its ranks and lacked important representation from her Midwest region.

She got the assignment, but only after the GOP avoided embarrassment by reversing plans to reduce the size of the committee, which would have cost Jones the seat.

Although her political leanings are decidedly liberal, Jones has shown a willingness to work across party lines and through established channels of power in the pursuit of her legislative goals, which include helping more Americans become financially secure. "It is time to help our constituencies build wealth — by saving, home-buying, establishing small businesses," she says. "It plays across all of our congressional districts."

She has used her seats on the Financial Services and Small Business committees to help boost economic development in her district, attack predatory lending practices and, most recently, champion laid-off workers who lose severance or pensions when their employers go bankrupt. "Even people with great intelligence got burned on Enron, and they got burned on Global Crossing," Jones says, referring to two high-profile bankruptcies of the early 2000s. She added that insulating people from such losses is "the civil rights issue of the day."

As chairman of the Congressional Black Caucus' Housing Task Force, Jones held hearings on alleged abuses by some lenders who make subprime, or high-risk, loans with high interest rates and fees.

With a district that includes both parts of inner-city Cleveland and some of its more affluent suburbs, Jones says she does not want to be considered a one-track legislator: "My vision is larger than just issues that affect minorities." To that end, she has been seeking to raise congressional awareness of health issues such as fibroids, a condition that affects millions of women but has garnered relatively little research.

Meanwhile, Jones enjoys increasing popularity at home. In a piece of Cleveland and its east side suburbs minimally changed politically by redistricting, she won in 2002 with 76 percent against token GOP opposition.

And she remains a player in local politics. She considered a run for the 2002 Democratic nomination for governor and she briefly entertained entreaties that she make a 2001 bid for Cleveland's mayoralty. She has not ruled out a run for that job in the future.

She first inserted herself into national affairs as a college student, when she was among a group of anti-Vietnam War demonstrators who forced Case Western Reserve University to shut down in the spring of 1970. Such a confrontational approach is still in her political quiver. "Let me be remembered by my constituents that I created a stir trying to get answers to questions that were important to them," she told the Cleveland Plain Dealer in 2001, after she was widely criticized for cutting off Federal Reserve Chairman Alan Greenspan in mid-sentence at a hearing and aggressively questioning Cuban-born Housing Secretary Mel Martinez about where he had lived in the last 10 years.

But she can take a pragmatic legislative approach. In the 107th she tapped her legal background — she was a prosecutor and judge before coming to Congress — to weigh in on post-Sept. 11, 2001, administration policies on bringing suspected terrorists before military tribunals.

Jones believes bolstering the financial soundness of Social Security should be a higher priority than tax cuts, and she opposes raising the program's retirement age. She also wants to make day care more available and less expensive for working families and to invest more money in early-childhood education programs.

After planning for a career in social work, Jones changed her mind and went to law school. Her first job as an attorney was litigating for the Equal Employment Opportunity Commission. Seven years later, in 1981, she was elected to a Cleveland municipal judgeship. Two years after that, she was a gubernatorial appointee to a judgeship that handled felony cases. Jones was elected in 1991 as the Cuyahoga County prosecutor, overseeing a staff of about 300.

In 1998, she won a convincing primary victory and four-fifths of the general-election vote to succeed Louis Stokes, a Democrat who spent 30 years as Ohio's first black member of Congress. Jones called Stokes a "mentor and close friend." He called her his chosen successor, which was a large part of her ticket to initial election.

She also had received nationwide attention that same year for refusing to reopen the case of the late Dr. Sam Sheppard, the basis for "The Fugitive" television series and movie. He was convicted in 1954 of murdering his wife and served 10 years in prison before being acquitted in a retrial.

KEY VOTES

2002

Yes Overhaul campaign finance law; ban "soft money" and restrict advocacy advertising
No Back Bush's defense budget increase
No Extend 1996 welfare law
No Adopt Bush's discretionary spending limit
No Pass GOP Medicare prescription drug plan
Yes Create independent Sept. 11 commission
Yes Extend union protections to Homeland Security Department employees
No Revive fast-track procedures for trade agreements
No Authorize war against Iraq
No Advance bankruptcy overhaul opposed by abortion opponents

2001

No Nullify Clinton Labor Department ergonomics rule
No Cut taxes by $1.35 trillion through fiscal 2011
Yes Maintain ban on oil drilling in Arctic National Wildlife Refuge
No Approve Bush proposal to limit managed-care plan liability for coverage decisions
Yes Divert money from crop subsidy payments to land conservation
No Expand law enforcement power to investigate suspected terrorists

CQ VOTE STUDIES

	PARTY UNITY		PRESIDENTIAL SUPPORT	
	Support	Oppose	Support	Oppose
2002	98%	2%	24%	76%
2001	97%	3%	20%	80%
2000	98%	2%	89%	11%
1999	96%	4%	87%	13%

INTEREST GROUPS

	AFL-CIO	ADA	CCUS	ACU
2002	100%	85%	39%	0%
2001	100%	100%	35%	4%
2000	100%	100%	47%	0%
1999	89%	90%	25%	0%

OHIO 11

Cleveland – East Side and suburbs

The 11th consists of the poor, inner-city areas of Cleveland's East Side and fans out to the east to include upper-middle-class suburbs. The district's black majority and liberal suburbanites combine to make it overwhelmingly Democratic.

The 11th includes 60 percent of Cleveland's residents. Although suburban growth has lured many businesses and residents outside the city, there has been a smattering of commercial and residential development in the downtown area. Redistricting following the 2000 census moved the district line west to take in the Rock and Roll Hall of Fame and the sports stadiums for baseball's Indians, football's Browns and basketball's Cavaliers.

Much of the district's black majority lives in inner-city neighborhoods, mostly below the poverty line. There are some middle-class neighborhoods toward Lake Erie, inhabited mostly by Italians and Eastern Europeans.

The upper-middle-class suburbs of Cleveland Heights, Shaker Heights and University Heights to the east are home to large communities of Jews and young professionals, forming some of Ohio's most liberal and racially integrated areas. Redistricting pushed the 11th farther east to take in communities such as Mayfield Heights, Richmond Heights, Lyndhurst and Pepper Pike, which has one of the highest incomes in the state. Case Western Reserve University is located in University Circle, Cleveland's cultural center.

From the circle area, commuters drive along historic Euclid Avenue to their jobs downtown. While the avenue now bears the marks of poverty, it was known as "Millionaire's Row" at the beginning of the 20th century. Few of the old mansions remain. The one belonging to John D. Rockefeller, founder of Standard Oil, was razed after his death in 1937.

MAJOR INDUSTRY
Health care, manufacturing, utilities

CITIES
Cleveland (pt.), 288,179; Euclid, 52,717; Cleveland Heights, 49,958; Shaker Heights, 29,405; East Cleveland, 27,217; Maple Heights, 26,156

NOTABLE
Shaker Historical Museum; Nation's first indoor shopping mall (1890).

Rep. Pat Tiberi (R)

CAPITOL OFFICE
225-5355
www.house.gov/tiberi
113 Cannon 20515-3512; fax 226-4523

COMMITTEES
Education & Workforce
Financial Services

HOMETOWN
Columbus

BORN
Oct. 21, 1962, Columbus, Ohio

RELIGION
Roman Catholic

FAMILY
Wife, Denice Tiberi

EDUCATION
Ohio State U., B.A. 1985 (journalism)

CAREER
Realtor; congressional aide

POLITICAL HIGHLIGHTS
Ohio House, 1993-2001 (majority leader, 1999-2001)

ELECTION RESULTS

2002 GENERAL		
Pat Tiberi (R)	116,982	64.4%
Edward S. Brown (D)	64,707	35.6%
2002 PRIMARY		
Pat Tiberi (R)		unopposed
2000 GENERAL		
Pat Tiberi (R)	139,242	52.9%
Maryellen O'Shaughnessy (D)	115,432	43.8%
Lawrence N. Hogan (LIBERT)	4,546	1.7%

Elected 2000; 2nd term

After eight years of handling constituent casework for Republican Rep. John R. Kasich and eight more years as a member of the state House, Tiberi was wondering what would come next for him when Kasich decided to step out of public life in 2000. Tiberi (TEA-berry) jumped at the chance to run for the seat, and Kasich quickly endorsed his former staff member.

Some of Kasich's other aides, who had been Tiberi's supervisors and co-workers in the 1980s, now work for the congressman — an unusual display of both staff longevity and loyalty. Tiberi has fostered a collegial atmosphere in the office, as did Kasich, an attitude that is helped by his earnest and approachable manner. One Ohio newspaper columnist called it Tiberi's "gee-whiz enthusiasm."

Tiberi's time as a congressional aide was spent at Kasich's district office in Columbus, not on Capitol Hill, and during the initial years of his new career Tiberi has made diligent constituent service a high priority.

He is still most comfortable, he says, in the Columbus neighborhood where he grew up and has lived most of his life. He resides within walking distance of his 12th District field office, and his polling place is inside the same elementary school that he attended in the 1960s. As one local newspaper columnist said, "Every groundbreaking, every parade, every ribbon-cutting with a pair of scissors to spare . . . is likely to find Pat Tiberi." And, the columnist continued, "that's bad news for the Democrats, who now stand about 4,000 chicken lunches behind Tiberi."

In his first term, Tiberi was a dependable supporter of President Bush and the GOP leadership. He proudly notes the high marks for his voting record from the U.S. Chamber of Commerce and Americans for Tax Reform. Conversely, the liberal Americans for Democratic Action and the AFL-CIO gave him scores of 0 and 5, respectively, in their analyses of his votes.

Tiberi sits on the Education and the Workforce and Financial Services committees. In 2001, he and Delaware Republican Michael N. Castle were able to include in the federal education policy overhaul law a pilot program to give as many as 150 local school districts the authority to combine funding from four separate federal programs to address their own unique needs. To do so, the congressmen had to walk a tight line between the Republican goal of increasing local flexibility and Democrats' insistence on tight federal controls on how the money is spent.

One of Tiberi's chief interests is finding ways to reduce the size and scope of the federal government. When the final compromises behind Bush's $1.35 trillion tax cut included a provision that all the cuts be repealed after 10 years, Tiberi quickly offered legislation to make the rate cuts permanent. But he says his legislation would not go far enough — he favors scrapping the entire federal tax code and starting over.

Tiberi is the eldest of three children of Italian immigrants who arrived in the United States three years before he was born. His father worked as a machinist, while his mother was a seamstress. In describing the formation of his first political allegiances, Tiberi told the Columbus Dispatch that, given their working-class background, he and some high school classmates simply "looked at each other and said, 'I guess we're Democrats.' "

Although he served as his high school's senior class president, Tiberi says he had no interest in politics as a career until a political science class at Ohio State University led to an internship in Kasich's office — and a change of ideological heart. Working for his predecessor, he says, made him reassess his political philosophy. He also realized that "you don't have to be rich or necessarily connected to get into politics," as he told the Dispatch.

Tiberi was working in Kasich's district office and involved in a variety of civic activities when the 1992 remapping of state legislative districts created an open seat that took in his neighborhood. Tiberi's wife, Denice, told the Columbus newspaper that she didn't think her husband had ever really considered running for office before the seat opened up. He met his wife at a Northlands High School marching band alumni gathering — he played trumpet; she played flute.

During his four terms in the General Assembly, Tiberi, who rose to become House majority leader in the 1999-2000 session, developed a reputation as a conservative Republican who was willing and able to work with Democrats. He established a DNA database to track violent criminals and was a prime mover behind a state law that for a time limited large jury awards. The measure later was ruled unconstitutional. Tiberi also wrote legislation requiring performance audits for schools.

Barred by an Ohio term-limit law from seeking re-election to the state House in 2000, Tiberi was considering a career change when Kasich announced he was dropping not only his short-lived campaign for the GOP presidential nomination but also his fall-back plan to seek a 10th term in the House. "I was preparing to go into real estate because I didn't think John Kasich was ever going to leave Congress," Tiberi told the Associated Press. "Then, it was like 'boom,' the opportunity of a lifetime. The right place, right time. I had to run."

Tiberi entered the race for the Republican nomination, as did state Sen. Eugene J. Watts, who once was Tiberi's history professor at Ohio State, and two other candidates. Kasich's support helped Tiberi cruise to an easy primary victory. Democrats have been gaining ground in the Columbus area in recent years, and they offered a formidable opponent, Columbus City Councilwoman Maryellen O'Shaughnessy. Tiberi lost Franklin County (Columbus) but countered that by racking up big margins in the suburban GOP strongholds of Delaware and Licking counties. He won by 9 percentage points.

Although redistricting after the 2000 census made the 12th marginally more Republican, political observers had expected another strong Democratic challenge in 2002. But O'Shaughnessy elected to run for the Franklin County Commission, and Tiberi cruised to a second term by 29 points over Ed Brown, a retired computer engineer and frequent Democratic candidate.

KEY VOTES

2002

- No Overhaul campaign finance law; ban "soft money" and restrict advocacy advertising
- Yes Back Bush's defense budget increase
- Yes Extend 1996 welfare law
- Yes Adopt Bush's discretionary spending limit
- Yes Pass GOP Medicare prescription drug plan
- No Create independent Sept. 11 commission
- No Extend union protections to Homeland Security Department employees
- Yes Revive fast-track procedures for trade agreements
- Yes Authorize war against Iraq
- Yes Advance bankruptcy overhaul opposed by abortion opponents

2001

- Yes Nullify Clinton Labor Department ergonomics rule
- Yes Cut taxes by $1.35 trillion through fiscal 2011
- No Maintain ban on oil drilling in Arctic National Wildlife Refuge
- Yes Approve Bush proposal to limit managed-care plan liability for coverage decisions
- No Divert money from crop subsidy payments to land conservation
- Yes Expand law enforcement power to investigate suspected terrorists

CQ VOTE STUDIES

	PARTY UNITY		PRESIDENTIAL SUPPORT	
	Support	Oppose	Support	Oppose
2002	95%	5%	88%	12%
2001	97%	3%	95%	5%

INTEREST GROUPS

	AFL-CIO	ADA	CCUS	ACU
2002	11%	0%	100%	96%
2001	0%	0%	100%	92%

OHIO 12

Central – Eastern Columbus and suburbs

The 12th includes the eastern half of Columbus and the suburban counties to the north and east of the city. Columbus has become primarily white-collar, and its thriving service economy has led to significant growth in both the city and its adjacent areas. The district has a slight Republican lean, with the strong GOP influence in the Columbus suburbs overcoming the Democratic tilt of the city.

For Democrats to be successful in the 12th, they must command the urban portion of the district, which is heavily black and poorer than the surrounding areas. The 12th includes the bulk of Columbus' black population, which is concentrated east of High Street, near Bexley. These precincts gave large majorities to African-American Democrat Michael B. Coleman in his successful 1999 Columbus mayoral race. Farther east along Broad Street and into the suburbs, black Democratic support diminishes and Republican support goes up. Blacks make up 22 percent of the overall district's residents.

Within Franklin County but outside Columbus, the 12th includes the comfortable suburbs of Dublin, an upscale, solidly Republican area in northwest Franklin that is known to many as the headquarters of Wendy's, whose founder, Dave Thomas, died in 2002. In eastern Franklin, the 15th also takes in Westerville, Gahanna and Reynoldsburg, which also vote dependably Republican.

Delaware County, north of Franklin, has experienced enormous growth and startlingly low unemployment in recent years. Delaware County tops state levels of household income and educational attainment (41 percent have a bachelor's degree). It also experienced the fastest growth by far of any Ohio county in the 1990s, increasing its population by 64 percent. Republicans dominate local offices here. Western Licking County, where the remainder of constituents live, also is experiencing growth.

MAJOR INDUSTRY
Financial services, manufacturing, service

CITIES
Columbus (pt.), 275,882; Westerville, 35,318; Gahanna, 32,636; Reynoldsburg, 32,069; Dublin (pt.), 31,370; Delaware, 25,243

NOTABLE
The Ohio State Fair is held every August at the Ohio Expo Center.

Rep. Sherrod Brown (D)

CAPITOL OFFICE
225-3401
sherrod@mail.house.gov
www.house.gov/sherrodbrown
2332 Rayburn 20515-3513; fax 225-2266

COMMITTEES
Energy & Commerce
International Relations

HOMETOWN
Lorain

BORN
Nov. 9, 1952, Mansfield, Ohio

RELIGION
Lutheran

FAMILY
Divorced; two children

EDUCATION
Yale U., B.A. 1974 (Russian & East European studies); Ohio State U., M.A. 1979 (education), M.A. 1981 (public administration)

CAREER
Teacher

POLITICAL HIGHLIGHTS
Ohio House, 1975-83; Ohio secretary of state, 1983-91; defeated for re-election as Ohio secretary of state, 1990

ELECTION RESULTS

2002 GENERAL		
Sherrod Brown (D)	123,025	69.0%
Ed Oliveros (R)	55,357	31.0%
2002 PRIMARY		
Sherrod Brown (D)		unopposed
2000 GENERAL		
Sherrod Brown (D)	170,058	64.6%
Rick H. Jeric (R)	84,295	32.0%
Michael A. Chmura (LIBERT)	5,837	2.2%
David Kluter (NL)	3,108	1.2%

PREVIOUS WINNING PERCENTAGES
1998 (62%); 1996 (60%); 1994 (49%); 1992 (53%)

Elected 1992; 6th term

Brown has spent his adult life in politics, first elected to the Ohio House in 1974 when he was turning 22. Since winning the 13th District seat in 1992, he has been re-elected with ease in his labor-dominated industrial district. But with the GOP in control of the redistricting process after the 2000 census, Brown's safe perch appeared to be in some jeopardy.

But he "bluff[ed] his way to job security," said the Cleveland Plain Dealer, by threatening to run for governor against Republican Bob Taft if the new district lines were unfavorable. At Taft's direction, the lines were drawn to the congressman's liking.

In the House, Brown has carved out a solid niche for himself by taking on health care issues with down-to-earth, no-nonsense populist fervor. He has an astute political ear for the issues of the moment — issues such as prescription drug benefits under Medicare, tighter regulation of health maintenance organizations, and health coverage for the uninsured. By putting himself at the center of those debates, Brown has become a player in House Democratic circles.

He was reportedly under consideration for appointment in the 108th Congress as chairman of the Democratic Congressional Campaign Committee, the House Democrats' campaign arm, but he said he wasn't interested.

Although his father and grandfather were both physicians, Brown told the Plain Dealer he still had a lot to learn about health care, as someone who "barely knew the difference between Medicare and Medicaid."

He had big shoes to fill when he became the top Democrat on the Commerce Committee's Health Subcommittee in the 105th Congress. He succeeded Henry A. Waxman of California, who had mastered the intricate details of health care programs and was known for his hard-nosed questioning of witnesses he thought were not giving him straight answers.

The Ohioan may be more low-key and affable than Waxman in his personal style, but he ultimately ends up in the same place, promoting the party line by advocating step-by-step expansions of health care coverage while needling Republicans over issues such as prescription drugs for seniors.

In the 107th, Brown focused his attention on detection and treatment of breast and prostate cancer. He and Waxman proposed a bill to phase out the use of popular human antibiotics in animal feed, arguing that it made humans more susceptible to bioterrorism because people build up a resistance to certain antibiotics from overexposure. And he joined with Republican Jo Ann Emerson of Missouri to push for quicker availability of low-cost generic drugs.

Brown normally finds himself in agreement with his party peers in Congress, siding with Democrats on more than 90 percent of the votes that pit one party against the other. On occasion, though, he will break from the majority of House Democrats, as when he backed constitutional amendments to balance the budget and limit congressional terms.

Brown was educated at Yale and holds two graduate degrees, but few can match his populist tone when he thinks jobs are at risk in his district. He long has played a key role in congressional debates over expanded foreign trade. As a freshman in the 103rd, Brown worked tirelessly to defeat the North American Free Trade Agreement (NAFTA) — lobbying fellow freshmen, repeatedly taking the House floor to detail the pact's flaws, and publishing a newsletter that kept track of anti-NAFTA activities.

In the 107th Congress, he continued to argue about NAFTA's defects, complaining about unsafe Mexican trucks operating in the United States. And he said President Bush did not go far enough in 2002 when he imposed tariffs of up to 30 percent on imported steel. He also has been a steadfast opponent of giving the president fast-track authority to negotiate trade agreements that Congress cannot amend.

As co-chairman of the Congressional Taiwan Caucus in the 107th, Brown wrote legislation endorsing Taiwan's participation in the World Health Organization.

Brown has written a book about his congressional experiences entitled, "Congress from the Inside." In a 1999 television interview in which he discussed the book, he listed four important steps for freshmen. Leading the list was getting on the right committee.

And indeed, Brown won a coveted seat on the Energy and Commerce Committee in his first term, after campaigning hard for the post. He recalls in his book that he even parted with a favored baseball card — that of 1950s Boston Red Sox outfielder Jimmy Piersall, who suffered from mental illness. Brown gave the card to influential California Democrat Vic Fazio, with the note, "Don't be crazy. Vote for Sherrod Brown for Energy and Commerce."

Brown's first taste of elective office came as student council president in high school, where he also made time to become an Eagle Scout. He spent summers working on the family dairy farm. His interest in politics was sparked by the Vietnam War, the civil rights movement and the 1968 presidential candidacy of Robert F. Kennedy. He earned a degree in Russian studies from Yale. (He says he once was able to practice his rusty Russian on Raisa Gorbachev, the wife of the Soviet leader, when the couple visited Congress.)

Brown won election to the Ohio House in 1974, and after serving four terms he was elected secretary of state in 1982. He was re-elected to the post in 1986 but lost a re-election bid in 1990 to Bob Taft, the latest in a long line of politically successful Ohio Tafts. Taft was elected governor in 1998.

In 1992, Brown made a bid for the House, joining seven other Democrats in the race for the open 13th District. He was his party's front-runner, though he had moved into the 13th to run, and he easily won the Democratic nomination. In the November election, he handily defeated Republican Margaret R. Mueller, a millionaire social worker who had lost three times to Democrat Dennis E. Eckart in the old 11th. Brown prevailed with just a plurality of the vote in 1994 — a bad year for Ohio Democrats — but has won with ease since. In 2002, with a district favorable to Democrats, Brown cruised to victory with 69 percent.

KEY VOTES

2002

Yes Overhaul campaign finance law; ban "soft money" and restrict advocacy advertising
No Back Bush's defense budget increase
No Extend 1996 welfare law
No Adopt Bush's discretionary spending limit
No Pass GOP Medicare prescription drug plan
Yes Create independent Sept. 11 commission
Yes Extend union protections to Homeland Security Department employees
No Revive fast-track procedures for trade agreements
No Authorize war against Iraq
No Advance bankruptcy overhaul opposed by abortion opponents

2001

No Nullify Clinton Labor Department ergonomics rule
No Cut taxes by $1.35 trillion through fiscal 2011
Yes Maintain ban on oil drilling in Arctic National Wildlife Refuge
No Approve Bush proposal to limit managed-care plan liability for coverage decisions
Yes Divert money from crop subsidy payments to land conservation
No Expand law enforcement power to investigate suspected terrorists

CQ VOTE STUDIES

	PARTY UNITY		PRESIDENTIAL SUPPORT	
	Support	Oppose	Support	Oppose
2002	98%	2%	22%	78%
2001	98%	2%	12%	88%
2000	97%	3%	81%	19%
1999	95%	5%	80%	20%
1998	97%	3%	83%	17%

INTEREST GROUPS

	AFL-CIO	ADA	CCUS	ACU
2002	100%	95%	25%	4%
2001	100%	95%	22%	4%
2000	100%	90%	25%	4%
1999	100%	100%	0%	0%
1998	100%	100%	17%	4%

OHIO 13

Northeast – parts of Akron and suburbs, Cleveland suburbs

The lightning bolt-shaped 13th runs from the shores of Lake Erie west of Cleveland, southeast through the city's mostly middle-class suburbs to Akron. Redistricting following the 2000 census increased the district's Democratic heft by adding western Summit County, including part of Akron. Summit is the most populous county in the 13th, making up 44 percent of the population. The district includes more than 70 percent of Akron's residents, including much of its black population.

Akron had a long history as a blue-collar factory town and was known as the world's rubber capital. Although the tire companies have moved many of their factories, many of their corporate headquarters and research facilities remain, keeping the city alive through tough years.

The city also has been renovating its downtown and recreational areas along the Ohio & Erie Canal. Blue-collar descendants combine with blacks, ethnic whites and the University of Akron's academic community to help the city retain its Democratic character from its blue-collar past.

Bordering Lake Erie at the district's other end is Lorain County, which includes one-third of the 13th's residents and has an industrial, blue-collar heritage. The 13th's portions of Lorain include staunchly Democratic Lorain and Sheffield Lake and Democratic-leaning Elyria. Farther northeast, the Avon and Avon Lake communities are upper middle-class and dependably Republican. Lorain and Avon Lake are home to some of the district's automotive plants.

In the district's middle are some Republican-leaning communities in southern Cuyahoga County and northern Medina County. But Summit and Lorain's dominance gives the 13th a Democratic tilt.

MAJOR INDUSTRY

Auto and auto parts manufacturing, steel, polymer research

CITIES

Akron (pt.), 129,298; Lorain, 68,652; Elyria, 55,953; Cuyahoga Falls (pt.), 39,051; Brunswick, 33,388; Strongsville (pt.), 29,715; North Royalton, 28,648

NOTABLE

The National Inventors Hall of Fame is in Akron; The All-American Soap Box Derby race has been held in Akron since 1935.

Rep. Steven C. LaTourette (R)

CAPITOL OFFICE
225-5731
www.house.gov/latourette
2453 Rayburn 20515-3514; fax 225-3307

COMMITTEES
Financial Services
Government Reform
Standards of Official Conduct
Transportation & Infrastructure
(Economic Development, Public Buildings & Emergency Mgmt. - chairman)

HOMETOWN
Madison

BORN
July 22, 1954, Cleveland, Ohio

RELIGION
Methodist

FAMILY
Wife, Susan LaTourette; four children

EDUCATION
U. of Michigan, B.A. 1976 (history); Cleveland State U., J.D. 1979

CAREER
Lawyer

POLITICAL HIGHLIGHTS
Candidate for Lake County prosecutor, 1984; Lake County prosecutor, 1989-94

ELECTION RESULTS

2002 GENERAL		
Steven C. LaTourette (R)	134,413	72.1%
Dale Virgil Blanchard (D)	51,846	27.8%
2002 PRIMARY		
Steven C. LaTourette (R)		unopposed
2000 GENERAL		
Steven C. LaTourette (R)	206,639	64.8%
Dale Virgil Blanchard (D)	101,842	31.9%
Sid Stone (LIBERT)	10,367	3.3%

PREVIOUS WINNING PERCENTAGES
1998 (66%); 1996 (55%); 1994 (48%)

Elected 1994; 5th term

It was not the kind of debut on the national stage that any politician would have wanted. In July 2002, LaTourette appeared before the House to urge a reprieve for James A. Traficant Jr., his Ohio colleague who was to be expelled from the House after his convictions for taking bribes and kickbacks. LaTourette did not defend his friend's behavior, but he did try to postpone the vote to give Traficant a chance to appeal and ask for a new trial.

The request was rebuffed, and LaTourette (la-tuh-RETT) ultimately voted to expel Traficant that night. But he won grudging respect for his loyalty and his passionate argument. And that act of standing up for a colleague at such an uncomfortable time has come to define LaTourette in the public eye — overwhelming his record as an easygoing and reasonably loyal Republican, though one with a willingness to work with Democrats on a wide range of issues and even vote with them sometimes.

In the 107th Congress, LaTourette opposed giving President Bush fast-track trade negotiating authority, underscoring his standing as one of the most pro-union House Republicans. He called on Republicans to restore food stamp benefits to legal immigrants, and he was seen as a possible swing vote on patients' rights legislation. (He ultimately voted for the version Bush supported.) But he sided with GOP leaders on some other key labor votes, including opposing plans to make baggage screeners at airports members of the government work force.

That should help guarantee him solid standing with his party in the 108th and beyond if LaTourette changes his mind — yet again — about term limits. After promising to serve no more than four terms, LaTourette extended his self-limit to five terms (meaning he would not run in 2004) and later said he promised fellow Ohio Republicans to at least think about a sixth term so the state could reap the benefits of his seniority. His recent re-election bids have yielded handsome 2-to-1 margins.

Another reason to watch LaTourette is his chairmanship of one of the subcommittees that likely will be heavily involved in homeland security. As chairman of the Transportation and Infrastructure Subcommittee on Economic Development, Public Buildings and Emergency Management, he was one of the early voices warning about the disjointed nature of the nation's terrorism defenses; he held hearings on the subject several months before the attacks of Sept. 11, 2001.

The lawmaker stands apart from most of his colleagues in the "revolutionary" takeover GOP Class of 1994. Perhaps it was growing up in the progressive suburb of Cleveland Heights — which declared itself a "nuclear free" zone — that taught him to be inclusive. Or perhaps it is the political character of his constituency. The portion of the northeastern corner of Ohio he represented until redistricting for this decade, known as the 19th District, voted Democratic for president in 1992, 1996 and 2000. (His new territory, renamed the 14th, has a slightly more Republican tilt.)

LaTourette recalls Traficant as one of the only members willing to show him the ropes after his arrival in 1995, and so Traficant's demise posed an awkward situation for LaTourette, a member of the House ethics panel. He decided not to recuse himself from the case, but he described the proceedings as "one of the most unpleasant experiences I could ever recall having."

LaTourette typically concurs with the conservatives on social policy issues. He consistently votes with anti-abortion forces, supported repeal of the ban on certain semiautomatic assault-style weapons and backed the

1996 welfare overhaul. Republican leaders turn to him to preside over contentious floor debates, a role reserved for unflappable members who have a knack for House rules and an understanding of leadership objectives.

LaTourette has fought an unsuccessful battle to strengthen the nation's ailing steel industry. In 2001, he teamed with Ohio Democrat Dennis J. Kucinich on a bill that would have made it easier for steel companies to qualify for federal loan guarantees. They tried to add that language to other legislation in time to save Cleveland-based LTV Steel, which was facing imminent bankruptcy, but they failed and the company went under.

When LaTourette first arrived in the House, he was hoping for a seat on the Judiciary Committee, where he could make use of his background as a private attorney, public defender and prosecutor. (He still says his long-range aspiration is to be a judge.) But Ralph Regula, the dean of the Ohio GOP delegation, told him he would be of more use to the state on the Transportation Committee. On a panel where bipartisan inclinations such as LaTourette's are valued, he has been able to ensure that his district gets its share of highway money.

He also sits on the Financial Services Committee, where to the displeasure of the big Cleveland banks he was a prime mover, along with Democrat Paul E. Kanjorski of Pennsylvania, on legislation loosening restrictions on credit union membership.

LaTourette was raised in a politically active home. Both his mother and grandmother were active volunteers for the Cleveland area's longtime Republican congresswoman, Frances Payne Bolton. He recalls, as a 6-year-old, loading Bolton campaign literature on his little red wagon, which bore a Nixon-Lodge bumper sticker. His grandmother has been the inspiration for several legislative efforts, including a bill to require sweepstakes mailers to disclose the slim odds of winning. He cites the example of his grandmother, in her mid-80s, who subscribed to Field and Stream magazine because she thought it would boost her chances of winning a mail-order sweepstakes.

Even as a youth, LaTourette was not afraid to rock the boat a bit. In high school, he led a petition drive to permit students to wear jeans and grow facial hair. He has sported a beard since he was 18 "because I've always thought my face looked better that way."

LaTourette says working as a public defender taught him how it felt to have "nobody like you." He was in his second term as Lake County prosecutor when he decided to run for Congress. Dubbing Democratic freshman Eric Fingerhut an out-of-touch liberal, LaTourette won by 5 percentage points and has bested that margin in all his re-election races.

KEY VOTES

2002

Yes Overhaul campaign finance law; ban "soft money" and restrict advocacy advertising
Yes Back Bush's defense budget increase
Yes Extend 1996 welfare law
Yes Adopt Bush's discretionary spending limit
Yes Pass GOP Medicare prescription drug plan
Yes Create independent Sept. 11 commission
No Extend union protections to Homeland Security Department employees
No Revive fast-track procedures for trade agreements
Yes Authorize war against Iraq
Yes Advance bankruptcy overhaul opposed by abortion opponents

2001

Yes Nullify Clinton Labor Department ergonomics rule
Yes Cut taxes by $1.35 trillion through fiscal 2011
No Maintain ban on oil drilling in Arctic National Wildlife Refuge
Yes Approve Bush proposal to limit managed-care plan liability for coverage decisions
Yes Divert money from crop subsidy payments to land conservation
Yes Expand law enforcement power to investigate suspected terrorists

CQ VOTE STUDIES

	PARTY UNITY		PRESIDENTIAL SUPPORT	
	Support	Oppose	Support	Oppose
2002	89%	11%	82%	18%
2001	88%	12%	86%	14%
2000	84%	16%	35%	65%
1999	77%	23%	31%	69%
1998	78%	22%	38%	62%

INTEREST GROUPS

	AFL-CIO	ADA	CCUS	ACU
2002	22%	15%	85%	76%
2001	36%	20%	77%	72%
2000	30%	25%	80%	68%
1999	33%	35%	79%	64%
1998	60%	40%	78%	52%

OHIO 14
Northeast – Cleveland and Akron suburbs

The Republican 14th begins south and east of Cleveland and then snakes along the Lake Erie shoreline to include all of Lake and Ashtabula counties in Ohio's northeast corner. The depressed far northeastern communities remain reliant on the ailing steel, chemical and automobile manufacturing industries but have seen some new life from migrants from Cleveland. Plants along Lake Erie have been hurt by foreign competition in steel and chemicals.

Lake County is the district's most populous area (more than one-third of residents live here), despite being Ohio's smallest county in land area. Mentor, the district's largest city and a traditionally industrial swing area, has seen an influx of Republicans with its recent growth. The GOP generally performs better in areas south of Mentor, such as the upper-income Kirtland. Democrats do well in Painesville, where more than half of Lake's blacks and Hispanics live, and in western Lake, including Wickliffe and Willowick.

Ashtabula County, a mostly agricultural region that borders Pennsylvania, is the state's largest county in land area and is known for its covered bridges.

South of Lake are Geauga County, a Republican-leaning, affluent, well-educated area, and northern Portage County. The 14th also includes northeastern Summit County, taking in Stow and Twinsburg.

The 14th is descended from the 1990s-era 19th District that included many of Cuyahoga County's eastern Cleveland suburbs. But redistricting following the 2000 census left the 14th with only a small portion of eastern Cuyahoga, including the upscale communities of Bentleyville and Moreland Hills.

MAJOR INDUSTRY

Auto manufacturing, health care, chemicals

CITIES

Mentor, 50,278; Stow, 32,139; Willoughby, 22,621; Hudson, 22,439; Solon, 21,802; Ashtabula, 20,962; Eastlake, 20,255

NOTABLE

Holden Arboretum, the nation's largest, is in Kirtland; Twinsburg hosts a gathering of twins each August that it calls the largest in the world; There is a President James A. Garfield Historic Site in Mentor.

Rep. Deborah Pryce (R)

CAPITOL OFFICE
225-2015
pryce.oh15@mail.house.gov
www.house.gov/pryce
221 Cannon 20515-3515; fax 225-3529

COMMITTEES
Rules
(Legislative & Budget Process - chairwoman)

HOMETOWN
Upper Arlington

BORN
July 29, 1951, Warren, Ohio

RELIGION
Presbyterian

FAMILY
Divorced; two children (one deceased)

EDUCATION
Ohio State U., B.A. 1973; Capital U., J.D. 1976

CAREER
City prosecutor

POLITICAL HIGHLIGHTS
Franklin County Municipal Court judge, 1985-92

ELECTION RESULTS

2002 GENERAL		
Deborah Pryce (R)	108,193	66.6%
Mark P. Brown (D)	54,286	33.4%
2002 PRIMARY		
Deborah Pryce (R)	22,048	78.0%
Charlie Morrison (R)	6,216	22.0%
2000 GENERAL		
Deborah Pryce (R)	156,792	67.5%
Bill Buckel (D)	64,805	27.9%
Scott T. Smith (LIBERT)	10,700	4.6%

PREVIOUS WINNING PERCENTAGES
1998 (66%); 1996 (71%); 1994 (71%); 1992 (44%)

Elected 1992; 6th term

As chairwoman of the Republican Conference, Pryce is the highest-ranking Republican woman in the House in the 108th Congress — the highest-ranking ever, in fact.

The only other Republican woman who has ever attained even an equivalent post was Margaret Chase Smith of Maine, who headed the Senate Republican Conference for the six years before her retirement in 1972.

Elected to succeed J.C. Watts Jr. of Oklahoma, who retired, Pryce's new role as the House majority party's top communications strategist belies her quiet, workman-like approach to legislation; but her ability to bridge ideological differences while remaining loyal to the party line has served her well.

Even before her victory, over J.D. Hayworth of Arizona and Jim Ryun of Kansas, Pryce's steady climb up the ranks of the House Republicans marked her as a rising star of the GOP. As vice chairwoman of the Republican Conference in the 107th, Pryce mainly served a backup role to Watts at news conferences and GOP leadership meetings. But her new position will thrust her into the national spotlight, in part because some of the other top leaders do not make themselves available to meet regularly with Capitol Hill reporters or appear on television programs. Her main challenge, she has said, is to keep House Republican messages from becoming lost amid a narrowly divided Senate and the cacophony of the 2004 presidential race.

Although she is more moderate than many of her Republican colleagues, and certainly more so than anyone else in the leadership, Pryce's penchant for keeping disagreements private and her background as a consensus-seeking judge have eased her path and kept her firmly within the party fold. Her position on the Rules Committee, which sets the guidelines that govern floor action on individual bills, is one example of her leadership ties. Pryce has long been part of Speaker J. Dennis Hastert's inner circle, where he counts on her to offer unvarnished assessments of what the rank-and-file is thinking.

As she has risen in the ranks, Pryce has increasingly hewed closer to the GOP line on votes that split the parties. Her votes on fiscal policy are reliably Republican and she is among the few social policy moderates who is not viewed with suspicion by GOP conservatives.

As one of only three GOP women elected to the House in the Class of 1992, Pryce was a star from the start. Her first-term colleagues named her their "interim leader" for the early weeks of the 103rd, and when Republicans became the House majority in 1995, she was assigned to the Rules Committee. In 1997, Pryce continued her climb by winning election as Republican Conference secretary, an entry-level rung on the leadership ladder.

In 2000, she was unopposed for the conference vice chairmanship. In the 107th, she headed the Rules panel's Legislative and Budget Process Subcommittee, which oversees the congressional budget process.

Pryce has worked to help Republicans recruit more women candidates for the House and founded the Value In Electing Women Political Action Committee (Viewpac), which helped provide early financial resources to Shelley Moore Capito of West Virginia, Melissa A. Hart of Pennsylvania and Ginny Brown-Waite of Florida. The PAC contributed more than $100,000 to candidates for office in 2002.

Pryce's political success has been clouded by personal tragedy. Her 9-year-old daughter, Caroline, died in 1999 after a battle with cancer. Two years later, she and her husband Randy Walker began divorce proceedings, ending a 21-year marriage. Even as their marriage foundered, however, Pryce and Walker formed Hope Street Kids, a program to support cancer research, and Pryce has taken a more active role on family and health care issues, including efforts to increase federal funding for cancer research. In 2002, Pryce adopted an infant daughter, Mia.

Pryce sponsored the 2000 law to boost funding to prevent child abuse and to investigate such crimes. She also has worked to make adoption easier for qualified applicants. She cosponsored the 1996 law that streamlined adoption procedures for children in foster care.

Pryce has indicated that she may try to build on the Family and Medical Leave Act, which requires businesses to give employees time off to care for relatives. She voted against the original legislation in 1993, fearing it would put a costly burden on employers. She took a leave from the House during her daughter's illness, and says she supports family leave proposals that would help families but "are compatible with good, conservative principles."

While she generally votes the party line, there have been notable exceptions. In 1999, Pryce opposed two impeachment articles brought against President Clinton, and was the only elected GOP leader who did not vote "yes" on all four charges. She has voted in some instances with gun control proponents and abortion rights advocates.

The Speaker in the 105th Congress, Newt Gingrich, selected Pryce to lead a GOP task force on tobacco policy. Rather than calling for new taxes on cigarettes, it proposed redefining the Food and Drug Administration's role in regulating nicotine, establishing an anti-tobacco public service campaign and encouraging states to impose penalties on minors who smoke. The proposal drew fire from all sides, including from within the GOP, with some conservatives saying the regulations went too far and several moderates saying the measure did not go far enough to reduce smoking. The task force's proposal was never formally introduced.

Having studied, worked and lived in the Columbus area for three decades, Pryce is well-versed in the nuances of her congressional district. After attending Ohio State University for her undergraduate degree and Capital University for her law degree, she was a city prosecutor before being elected as a judge on the Franklin County Municipal Court in 1985.

Shortly after she began her second six-year term on the bench, she resigned in 1992 to enter the crowded GOP field vying for the House seat of veteran Republican Chalmers P. Wylie, who was retiring. She won the party's endorsement and prevailed in a tight, three-way general-election race by just 6 percentage points. Since then, she has been re-elected by large margins.

KEY VOTES

2002

- No Overhaul campaign finance law; ban "soft money" and restrict advocacy advertising
- Yes Back Bush's defense budget increase
- Yes Extend 1996 welfare law
- Yes Adopt Bush's discretionary spending limit
- Yes Pass GOP Medicare prescription drug plan
- No Create independent Sept. 11 commission
- No Extend union protections to Homeland Security Department employees
- Yes Revive fast-track procedures for trade agreements
- Yes Authorize war against Iraq
- Yes Advance bankruptcy overhaul opposed by abortion opponents

2001

- Yes Nullify Clinton Labor Department ergonomics rule
- Yes Cut taxes by $1.35 trillion through fiscal 2011
- No Maintain ban on oil drilling in Arctic National Wildlife Refuge
- Yes Approve Bush proposal to limit managed-care plan liability for coverage decisions
- Yes Divert money from crop subsidy payments to land conservation
- Yes Expand law enforcement power to investigate suspected terrorists

CQ VOTE STUDIES

	PARTY UNITY		PRESIDENTIAL SUPPORT	
	Support	Oppose	Support	Oppose
2002	95%	5%	92%	8%
2001	93%	7%	86%	14%
2000	90%	10%	35%	65%
1999	84%	16%	38%	62%
1998	88%	12%	30%	70%

INTEREST GROUPS

	AFL-CIO	ADA	CCUS	ACU
2002	13%	5%	100%	88%
2001	17%	15%	100%	68%
2000	0%	15%	90%	80%
1999	0%	20%	100%	56%
1998	25%	5%	100%	83%

OHIO 15

Western Columbus and suburbs

The 15th is centered on Columbus, the state's centrally located capital. The district includes most of the city, taking in all of Columbus that lies west of High Street, a major north-south thoroughfare. The 15th takes in some city attractions, including the State Capitol building (at High and Broad streets), City Hall, Ohio State University and the Columbus Museum of Art. It also includes the stadium of professional soccer's Crew and the arena of hockey's Blue Jackets.

Columbus is not known to draw large numbers of tourists except on Saturdays in autumn, when Ohio State plays football at home. But the region is generally regarded as a good place to raise a family. Covering much of Franklin County's expanding service sector, which includes several large high-tech research centers, the district has a steady employment base. American Electric Power also is based in the 15th.

Columbus has continued to grow since surpassing Cleveland in the early 1980s to become Ohio's most populous city. The 15th traditionally has been the more Republican of the two districts that divide the capital — the neighboring 12th includes most of the heavily black East Side. Ohio State's academic community and neighborhoods in the nearby West Side of Columbus support Democrats, but they are more than offset by rock-ribbed Republican suburbs west of the Olentangy and Scioto rivers. GOP candidates are strong in comfortable suburbs such as Upper Arlington and Worthington.

Almost 90 percent of district residents live in Franklin County. The rest reside in Madison County, a major corn-producing area to the west, and in Union County, located northwest of Columbus, which last voted Democratic for president in 1932. Marysville, in Union County, is home to a major Honda auto plant and a Honda motorcycle plant.

MAJOR INDUSTRY

Retail trade, health care, research, higher education

CITIES

Columbus (pt.), 384,491; Upper Arlington, 33,686; Grove City, 27,075; Hilliard (pt.), 23,853; Marysville, 15,942

NOTABLE

A full-scale replica of Christopher Columbus' ship, the Santa Maria, is in Columbus; The historic German Village reflects the architecture and character of a 19th-century German neighborhood.

Rep. Ralph Regula (R)

CAPITOL OFFICE
225-3876
www.house.gov/regula
2306 Rayburn 20515-3516; fax 225-3059

COMMITTEES
Appropriations
(Labor, Health & Human Services & Education - chairman)

HOMETOWN
Navarre

BORN
Dec. 3, 1924, Beach City, Ohio

RELIGION
Episcopalian

FAMILY
Wife, Mary Regula; three children

EDUCATION
Mount Union College, B.A. 1948 (business administration); William McKinley School of Law, LL.B. 1952

MILITARY SERVICE
Navy, 1944-46

CAREER
Lawyer; high school teacher; principal

POLITICAL HIGHLIGHTS
Ohio Board of Education, 1960-64; Ohio House, 1965-67; Ohio Senate, 1967-73

ELECTION RESULTS

2002 GENERAL		
Ralph Regula (R)	129,734	68.9%
Jim Rice (D)	58,644	31.1%
2002 PRIMARY		
Ralph Regula (R)		unopposed
2000 GENERAL		
Ralph Regula (R)	162,294	69.2%
William Smith (D)	62,709	26.8%
Richard L. Shetler (LIBERT)	6,166	2.6%
Brad Graef (NL)	3,231	1.4%

PREVIOUS WINNING PERCENTAGES
1998 (64%); 1996 (69%); 1994 (75%); 1992 (64%); 1990 (59%); 1988 (79%); 1986 (76%); 1984 (72%); 1982 (66%); 1980 (79%); 1978 (78%); 1976 (67%); 1974 (66%); 1972 (57%)

Elected 1972; 16th term

There are three political parties on Capitol Hill, the saying goes: the Republican Party, the Democratic Party and the appropriating party. Regula has made his mark in the House as a "cardinal" — a chairman of one of the 13 Appropriations subcommittees — who is particularly adept at steering his bills through partisan and ideological minefields.

As a powerful pragmatist with a low-key approach, Regula (REG-you-luh) has had no trouble making friends among lawmakers during his three full decades in Congress, which now make him the third-most-senior Republican in the House. His moderation on spending issues has sometimes disappointed the most conservative Republicans, but his calm shrewdness in seeking the middle ground on controversial matters allows him to maneuver deftly among GOP factions and across party lines.

"He's the congressman's congressman," says fellow Ohio Republican Michael G. Oxley. "He really understands how to work within the system." The top Democrat on Appropriations, David R. Obey of Wisconsin, describes Regula as "one of the most laid-back members" of the House.

After six years as chairman of the Interior Appropriations Subcommittee, Regula was forced by Republican term-limit rules to give up that gavel as the 107th Congress began. As the second-ranking Republican on Appropriations, he had his pick among six other subcommittees and chose the panel that handles the most expensive — and contentious — of the annual domestic spending measures, covering the departments of Labor, Health and Human Services and Education. Regula calls it the "people's bill," in reference to the medical research and teacher aid programs it funds, but the Labor-HHS bill is also a focal point of the running battle between appropriators from both parties and a Republican White House intent on restraining the growth of domestic spending.

As the budget process ground to a halt in 2002, Regula carried the flag for Appropriations Chairman C.W. Bill Young, a Florida Republican, and sparred publicly with White House Budget Director Mitchell E. Daniels Jr. over Bush administration efforts to impose its spending preferences. "We also want to reflect the members' priorities. I think that's part of our responsibility," Regula said. But after the gentlemanly skirmish, Regula returned to form and invited Daniels to his office for a chat. The two men found that they got along very well, Regula reported.

That political facility has at times provoked suspicion among some Republicans and conservative groups who have pegged Regula, who lives on a farm in Ohio and calls himself a "tree hugger," as too liberal. Regula has handled the charges — hurled most violently by Western private property rights advocates after he took over the Interior chairmanship in 1995 — with disarming candor. He met with his detractors to listen to their criticism, traveled to the West to witness the roots of their concerns and attended meetings of the Western Caucus.

Some conservative lawmakers have raised concerns not only about Regula's willingness to compromise on environmental issues but also about a few other moderate streaks in his record: He has supported a minimum wage increase and family planning programs and resisted proposals for taxpayer-financed private school vouchers. But overall, he was in the House GOP mainstream in the 107th in the frequency with which he backed President Bush and stood with the GOP on party-line votes. (And the League of Conservation Voters gave him only an 18 percent score for his 2001-02 votes.)

In the modern Congress, with its preoccupation with fundraising, Regula is something of an anomaly. He does not accept money from political action committees of businesses, trade associations or ideological groups, although in the run-up to the 2002 election he took $2,000 from the AFL-CIO's PAC and $24,000 from other Republican House lawmakers' PACs or campaign funds. The money was enough to cover most of his obligation, assessed because he is chairman of an influential panel, to donate to the House and Senate GOP campaign organizations.

Regula is dean of the Ohio Republican delegation, and his popularity among House colleagues has proved useful in bipartisan efforts by Ohio lawmakers to stand united on parochial issues. He defends federal support of clean coal technology research, a program of particular interest in his area, where most electricity is produced by coal-fired plants. He also has been a champion of aggressive moves to support the domestic steel industry, which remains a potent economic force in northeastern Ohio. He was a champion of Bush's imposition of tariffs on steel imports in 2001.

His hometown causes also include preserving the memory of President McKinley, Canton's most famous son. Regula — who graduated from a now-defunct law school named after the 25th president — helped engineer the purchase of a house where McKinley lived when he was a congressman, and since 1998 the building has been home to the National First Ladies' Library, which was founded by Regula's wife, Mary. Regula has directed more than $1 million in spending earmarks to the library.

He also preserves McKinley's memory in other ways. For years, he gave red carnations to his House colleagues each Jan. 29, McKinley's birthday. And at the beginning of each Congress, Regula introduces a bill that has the effect of preventing Alaskans from changing the name of Mount McKinley — the nation's tallest peak — to Denali, its Indian name.

Regula is the son of an Ohio farmer, and he returns every weekend to his family's cattle farm in Navarre. Regula also was a schoolteacher and principal and served on the Ohio Board of Education for four years before his election to the General Assembly, where he represented a large swath of Stark County — the heart of the 16th District.

When Republican Frank Bow retired in 1972 after 22 years in the House, Regula was viewed as the logical successor. He won with 57 percent of the vote and has had a solid hold on the seat since. He has been held to less than three-fifths of the vote only once — in 1990, when college professor Warner D. Mendenhall won a surprising 41 percent of the vote. Redistricting for this decade did not alter the GOP nature of the 16th District.

KEY VOTES

2002

- No Overhaul campaign finance law; ban "soft money" and restrict advocacy advertising
- Yes Back Bush's defense budget increase
- Yes Extend 1996 welfare law
- Yes Adopt Bush's discretionary spending limit
- Yes Pass GOP Medicare prescription drug plan
- No Create independent Sept. 11 commission
- No Extend union protections to Homeland Security Department employees
- No Revive fast-track procedures for trade agreements
- Yes Authorize war against Iraq
- Yes Advance bankruptcy overhaul opposed by abortion opponents

2001

- Yes Nullify Clinton Labor Department ergonomics rule
- Yes Cut taxes by $1.35 trillion through fiscal 2011
- No Maintain ban on oil drilling in Arctic National Wildlife Refuge
- Yes Approve Bush proposal to limit managed-care plan liability for coverage decisions
- No Divert money from crop subsidy payments to land conservation
- Yes Expand law enforcement power to investigate suspected terrorists

CQ VOTE STUDIES

	PARTY UNITY		PRESIDENTIAL SUPPORT	
	Support	Oppose	Support	Oppose
2002	94%	6%	90%	10%
2001	95%	5%	88%	12%
2000	88%	12%	36%	64%
1999	83%	17%	32%	68%
1998	87%	13%	28%	72%

INTEREST GROUPS

	AFL-CIO	ADA	CCUS	ACU
2002	22%	5%	95%	88%
2001	25%	20%	91%	76%
2000	10%	10%	80%	76%
1999	22%	25%	84%	64%
1998	40%	20%	89%	64%

OHIO 16
Northeast – Canton

A region of traditional Midwestern values and work ethic, the 16th takes in Canton's Stark County and territory to the west.

Although the boundaries have changed over the years, the Canton-based 16th was represented by William McKinley from 1877 to 1884 and 1885 to 1891. McKinley launched his governorship from the area and ran much of his 1896 presidential campaign from a front porch in Canton.

Canton has a rich manufacturing and steel-producing history, and high-skill manufacturing remains at the core of the region's steadily prosperous economy. But it is a working-class city, with a median income more than $10,000 below the state average. That, coupled with a more than 20 percent black population, makes Canton solidly Democratic. The city backed Al Gore with 61 percent of the vote in 2000.

But Canton has been less important to the 16th's political outlook as its population has declined since the 1950s. The city now accounts for just one-fifth of Stark's population. Massillon and Alliance, the county's next-most-populous cities, grew only marginally in population in the 1990s and lean Democratic. Northern Stark County is upper-middle-class and GOP-leaning. Stark overall voted narrowly for George W. Bush.

West of Stark, the district becomes more rural and solidly Republican. Wayne County, just west of Stark, produced more oats than any other Ohio county in 2000. The 16th also takes in most of Ashland County, which is even more solidly conservative than Wayne.

Redistricting following the 2000 census added two-thirds of Medina County, a dependably Republican area that is northwest of Canton and west of Akron. The area solidified the 16th's GOP orientation.

MAJOR INDUSTRY
Steel, bearings manufacturing, health care

CITIES
Canton, 80,806; Massillon, 31,325; Medina, 25,139; Wooster, 24,811

NOTABLE
The Professional Football Hall of Fame is in Canton; President William McKinley's burial site is in a Canton park; Massillon was the hometown of Jacob Coxey, whose "army" of unemployed men marched to Washington, D.C., after the Panic of 1893.

Rep. Tim Ryan (D)

CAPITOL OFFICE
225-5261
tim.ryan@mail.house.gov
www.house.gov/timryan
222 Cannon 20515-3517; fax 225-3719

COMMITTEES
Armed Services
Education & Workforce
Veterans' Affairs

HOMETOWN
Niles

BORN
July 16, 1973, Niles, Ohio

RELIGION
Roman Catholic

FAMILY
Single

EDUCATION
Bowling Green State U., B.A. 1995 (political science); Franklin Pierce Law Center, J.D. 2000

CAREER
Congressional aide

POLITICAL HIGHLIGHTS
Ohio Senate, 2001-02

ELECTION RESULTS

2002 GENERAL		
Tim Ryan (D)	94,441	51.1%
Ann Womer Benjamin (R)	62,188	33.7%
James A. Traficant Jr. (I)	28,045	15.2%
2002 PRIMARY		
Tim Ryan (D)	28,922	41.3%
Tom Sawyer (D)	19,247	27.5%
Anthony A. Latell (D)	13,858	19.8%
Maridee Costanzo (D)	5,148	7.4%
Joe Louis Teague (D)	2,044	2.9%
Bryan Taafe (D)	787	1.1%

Elected 2002; 1st term

Ryan says his mission in Congress is nothing less than to "redefine a community that has been devastated economically and politically."

The 17th District includes the industrially downtrodden and corruption-plagued Youngstown, and Ryan's aim is to restore the Mahoning Valley's luster by being at the vanguard of a new, younger generation of leadership. He was a 29-year-old freshman state senator when he was elected to the House and is the third-youngest member of the 108th Congress.

Unlike many small cities of the Rust Belt, Youngstown's three colleges and a medical school mean it has retained some concentration of young people, whom Ryan sees as key to an economic reversal. Ryan will be able to look out for the interests of those higher education institutions from a seat on the Education and the Workforce Committee. And he can advocate the interests of the Air Force Reserve Station in Youngstown from a seat on Armed Services. He also has a seat on Veterans' Affairs. His freshman congressional priorities include winning federal money to renovate downtown Youngstown and improving local highways.

Ryan will break with party orthodoxy on some social issues: He opposes abortion and gun control measures. But he lines up with most Democratic colleagues on economic policy and in his affinity with organized labor.

One of the area's best-known native sons — and a recent symbol of its corrupt ways — is James A. Traficant Jr., who became only the second House member expelled since the Civil War after his conviction in 2002 on 10 federal charges, including bribery and racketeering.

To get to Congress, Ryan defeated not one but two House incumbents. He won the Democratic primary by 14 percentage points against eight-term Democrat Tom Sawyer, whose political base had been cannibalized in redistricting and who had alienated organized-labor interests by supporting free-trade bills. In November, Ryan defeated Republican state Sen. Ann Women Benjamin by 17 points. But Traficant, who ran from federal prison as an independent, still took 15 percent of the vote.

OHIO 17

Northeast — Youngstown, Warren, part of Akron

Bordering Pennsylvania in the northeast part of the state, the 17th is a Democratic bastion that takes in part of the Mahoning Valley, including Youngstown. Once a leading steel-producing area, the valley now symbolizes industrial decline; the remaining steel mills are predominantly silent and abandoned.

Despite some economic diversification, young people searching for opportunities often look elsewhere, and the population of most cities has declined. Youngstown's population hovered around 170,000 from the 1930s to the 1960s; the 2000 census found just 82,000 people.

Officials hope the manufacturing industry is starting to turn around. Several auto plants are in the area, and the regional airport, which houses a large Air Force Reserve base, is undergoing expansion that is expected to turn it into an air cargo hub.

Trumbull County (shared with the 14th) is home to a plurality of residents. This area is staunchly Democratic: Warren, Trumbull's most populous city, backed Al Gore with 69 percent of the vote in 2000, and Niles and Girard backed Gore by more than 2-to-1.

Redistricting in 2002 added parts of Summit and Portage counties, which are west of Youngstown and are less solidly Democratic. The Portage portion includes Kent and Ravenna. The Summit portion includes the eastern half of Akron, a city that once produced 90 percent of the nation's tires.

MAJOR INDUSTRY
Automobile assembly, manufacturing

CITIES
Akron (pt.), 87,776; Youngstown, 82,026; Warren, 46,832

NOTABLE
Mill Creek Park in Youngstown covers 2,530 acres; Kent State University was the site of four deaths during a 1970 anti-war protest.

Rep. Bob Ney (R)

CAPITOL OFFICE
225-6265
bobney@mail.house.gov
www.house.gov/ney
2438 Rayburn 20515-3518; fax 225-3394

COMMITTEES
Financial Services
(Housing & Community Opportunity - chairman)
House Administration - chairman
Transportation & Infrastructure
Joint Library
Joint Printing - chairman

HOMETOWN
St. Clairsville

BORN
July 5, 1954, Wheeling, W.Va.

RELIGION
Roman Catholic

FAMILY
Wife, Elizabeth Ney; two children

EDUCATION
Ohio U., attended 1972-74; Ohio State U., B.S. 1976 (history)

CAREER
State health and education program manager; local safety director; educator

POLITICAL HIGHLIGHTS
Ohio House, 1981-83; defeated for re-election to Ohio House, 1982; Ohio Senate, 1984-95

ELECTION RESULTS

2002 GENERAL		
Bob Ney (R)		unopposed
2002 PRIMARY		
Bob Ney (R)		unopposed
2000 GENERAL		
Bob Ney (R)	152,325	64.4%
Marc D. Guthrie (D)	79,232	33.5%
John R. Bargar Sr. (LIBERT)	4,948	2.1%

PREVIOUS WINNING PERCENTAGES
1998 (60%); 1996 (50%); 1994 (54%)

Elected 1994; 5th term

When he became chairman of the House Administration Committee at the start of the 107th Congress, Ney expected to spend most of his time on the logistical business that is the committee's traditional stock-in-trade: approving committee budgets, assessing computer systems, assigning parking spaces and otherwise keeping the internal machinery of the House well-greased.

That chairman's role — sometimes called the mayor of the House — was transformed in the fall of 2001, however, by the terrorist attacks on the United States and the anthrax mailings to Capitol Hill. Ney (pronounced NAY) and his nine-member, leadership-appointed committee abruptly found themselves responsible for ensuring the safety of members of Congress, their staffs and the throngs of tourists who visit the Capitol every year.

Building on the lessons learned in those back-to-back crises, Ney helped win adoption of a new Capitol evacuation plan. He successfully pushed for all House members and their top aides to be given handheld e-mail devices for use in the event that land-line and cellular telephone communications were disrupted again. He arranged the purchase of 435 laptop computers, so members could keep working away from the Capitol. He initiated a pilot program to scan congressional mail, delivering the images electronically until the letters themselves could be irradiated for safety. Then, he made his own office one of the initial 12 participants.

"There's no doubt that security is going to continue to dominate," Ney said of his job going forward. "It's no longer just fires and bomb threats. Now, it's flying bombs and biochemical agents and anthrax. Our eyes have opened up to the need to take care of these things, and that creates a lot more advance planning."

Capitol security was not the only issue Ney tackled in the 107th. As chairman of the committee with legislative jurisdiction, and also acting as an agent of the GOP leadership, he helped wage a vigorous and ultimately losing battle against the campaign finance overhaul enacted in 2002. Then, without missing a beat, he worked in harmony with the top Democrat on his committee, Steny H. Hoyer of Maryland, and the bipartisan leadership of the Senate Rules Committee to win enactment of Congress' response to the disputed 2000 election: a landmark law setting the first federal standards for the conduct of federal elections and authorizing federal funding to help the states upgrade their voting systems. Ney insisted that the measure not include federal mandates but rather give local officials broad authority over the administration of elections.

Ney's district may be the only one in the nation that considers the House Administration Committee a power center. One of its own, Democrat Wayne L. Hays, chaired the panel for five years and was able to leverage its authority over funding for other committees to win projects for eastern Ohio. "Down home, this committee is known as the most important in the House," Ney recalled in 2001, so he made it his top priority as a freshman to win a seat on the panel.

Although he chairs the ultimate insider's committee, however, Ney says he has spent just one full weekend in Washington since his first election to Congress, nearly always driving the seven hours to his eastern Ohio district. He has connections to the world outside the 18th District, however. Fluent in Farsi, Ney taught English in Iran in 1978; he left before that country's revolution, but he continues to meet with prominent exiles when they come to Washington.

Reliably conservative on most issues, Ney is nonetheless vocal in his support for labor unions, which have a sizable constituency in his district, home to most of Ohio's remaining coal and steel producers. He assiduously looks out for those industries and their workers, whether by blocking tougher air emission regulations, opposing trade deals or opposing more visas for high-technology workers — all of which he believes can threaten jobs. His attention to such issues is one reason he has won election five times in a district that previously had not elected a Republican in 48 years.

In 2000, Ney was the only Republican among 71 congressional incumbents who received a promise of financial aid from the AFL-CIO. He sided with unions in the 106th Congress by leading GOP opposition to legislation that President Clinton sought granting China permanent status as a normal U.S. trading partner.

In agreement with most labor unions, Ney supported the Bush administration's decision to impose tariffs on foreign steel imports. But in the 107th, he split with labor and voted at the behest of the GOP leadership to grant the president fast-track trade negotiating authority. The bill passed the House by a single vote in 2001, and the version that became law squeaked through the following summer by three votes.

Ney is a strong foe of federal regulations, especially those that require businesses to undertake costly efforts to reduce pollution. In 2000, he won a House vote for cutting the EPA administrative budget by $5 million and transferring the funds to veterans health care programs. Over-regulation of the coal industry, Ney has said, has "taken food off of the tables of people in southern Ohio." He contends that Ohioans and other Midwesterners have "suffered tremendously" under the Clean Air Act, particularly from provisions targeting emissions that cause acid rain.

Raised in a middle-class family — his father was a camera operator for a television station and his mother worked in a liquor store — Ney worked his way through college and got his start in elective politics at age 26, winning a seat in the state House in 1980 by defeating Hays, who was attempting a political comeback. In 1984, Ney won election to the state Senate, where he eventually rose to be chairman of its Finance Committee.

After nine-term Democrat Douglas Applegate retired in 1994, the well-funded Ney easily dispatched five rivals in the GOP primary and then defeated conservative Democratic state Rep. Greg L. DiDonato. After a close call two years later, Ney has won handily. He drew no opponent at all in 2002 after his district had been redrawn for the decade to enhance his electability.

KEY VOTES

2002

- No Overhaul campaign finance law; ban "soft money" and restrict advocacy advertising
- Yes Back Bush's defense budget increase
- Yes Extend 1996 welfare law
- Yes Adopt Bush's discretionary spending limit
- Yes Pass GOP Medicare prescription drug plan
- No Create independent Sept. 11 commission
- No Extend union protections to Homeland Security Department employees
- Yes Revive fast-track procedures for trade agreements
- Yes Authorize war against Iraq
- Yes Advance bankruptcy overhaul opposed by abortion opponents

2001

- Yes Nullify Clinton Labor Department ergonomics rule
- Yes Cut taxes by $1.35 trillion through fiscal 2011
- No Maintain ban on oil drilling in Arctic National Wildlife Refuge
- Yes Approve Bush proposal to limit managed-care plan liability for coverage decisions
- Yes Divert money from crop subsidy payments to land conservation
- No Expand law enforcement power to investigate suspected terrorists

CQ VOTE STUDIES

	PARTY UNITY		PRESIDENTIAL SUPPORT	
	Support	Oppose	Support	Oppose
2002	95%	5%	90%	10%
2001	91%	9%	79%	21%
2000	88%	12%	29%	71%
1999	89%	11%	16%	84%
1998	85%	15%	27%	73%

INTEREST GROUPS

	AFL-CIO	ADA	CCUS	ACU
2002	11%	0%	100%	92%
2001	25%	10%	96%	88%
2000	40%	20%	61%	83%
1999	44%	10%	92%	84%
1998	30%	15%	83%	80%

OHIO 18

East – Zanesville, Chillicothe

Ohio's most geographically vast district, the 18th envelops 12 whole counties and parts of four others in southern and eastern Ohio. It starts in the rolling hills just south of Canton and runs southwest to the rugged areas in Appalachia. The district, which roughly parallels but does not touch the Ohio River, depends on the steel and coal industries and includes a large Catholic population of Eastern European and Greek immigrants. It has a conservative lean, and contains the highest percentage of white residents (96 percent) and the smallest percentage of college graduates (11 percent) in the state.

The northern part of the 18th includes Tuscarawas County, the district's most populous. West of Tuscarawas (derived from an Indian word meaning "open mouth"), are several solidly Republican counties. Newark (shared with the 12th), in Licking County, survived the closure of an Air Force Base in the 1990s and has become a growing manufacturing and research center.

Carroll, Harrison and Guernsey counties on the district's eastern border are ancestrally Democratic areas that tend to be populist on economics but strongly conservative on cultural issues. Harrison in 2000 voted Republican for president for the first time since 1984. The district scoops up a northern sliver of Belmont County southeast of Harrison. In redistricting following the 2000 census, GOP mapmakers intentionally drew the 18th's boundaries to include Rep. Ney's hometown of St. Clairsville and to place the bulk of Democratic-leaning Belmont in the 6th.

The 18th narrows south of Muskingum County (Zanesville) to reach Morgan County and northwestern Athens County (though not the portion that includes Ohio University). Moving westward, the 18th remains rural as it crosses forests to take in most of Ross County, including Chillicothe.

MAJOR INDUSTRY

Steel, manufacturing, agriculture, coal

CITIES

Zanesville, 25,586; Chillicothe, 21,796; Newark (pt.), 21,118

NOTABLE

Astronaut and former Sen. John Glenn was born in New Concord; A memorial to baseball pitcher Cy Young is in Newcomerstown; There was an Underground Railroad stop in Leesville; A basket-shaped building serves as headquarters for the Longaberger basket company in Newark.

OKLAHOMA

Gov. Brad Henry (D)

First elected: 2002
Length of term: 4 years
Term expires: 1/07
Salary: $101,140
Phone: (405) 521-2342
Hometown: Shawnee
Born: July 10, 1963; Shawnee, Okla.
Religion: Baptist
Family: Wife, Kim Henry; three children
Education: U. of Oklahoma, B.A. 1985 (economics), J.D. 1988
Career: Lawyer
Political highlights: Okla. Senate, 1993-2002
Election results:

2002 GENERAL		
Brad Henry (D)	448,143	43.3%
Steve Largent (R)	441,277	42.6%
Gary L. Richardson (I)	146,200	14.1%

Lt. Gov. Mary Fallin (R)

First elected: 1994
Length of term: 4 years
Term expires: 1/07
Salary: $85,000
Phone: (405) 521-2161

STATE LEGISLATURE

Legislature: Meets February-May
House: 101 members, 2-year terms
2003 breakdown: 48R, 53D; 92 men, 9 women
Salary: $38,400
Phone: (405) 521-2711
Senate: 48 members, 4-year terms
2003 breakdown: 20R, 27D, 1 vacancy; 41 men, 6 women
Salary: $38,400
Phone: (405) 524-0126

STATE TERM LIMITS

Governor: 2 terms
Senate: No more than 12 years combined
House: No more than 12 years combined

URBAN STATISTICS

CITY	POPULATION
Oklahoma City	506,132
Tulsa	393,049
Norman	95,694
Lawton	92,757
Broken Arrow	74,859

REGISTERED VOTERS

Democrat	53%
Republican	37%
Independent	10%

POPULATION

2002 population (est.)	3,493,714
2000 population	3,450,654
1990 population	3,145,585
Percent change (1990-2000)	+9.7%
Rank among states (2002)	28
Median age	35.5
Born in state	62.6%
Foreign born	3.8%
Violent crime rate	498/100,000
Poverty level	14.7%
Federal workers	44,984
Military	41,575

REDISTRICTING

Oklahoma lost one House seat in reapportionment. The state legislature failed to agree on a plan and a county judge implemented a new, five-district map on May 31, 2002.

MISCELLANEOUS

Web: www.state.ok.us
Capital: Oklahoma City
STATE ELECTION OFFICIAL
(405) 521-2391
DEMOCRATIC HEADQUARTERS
(405) 427-3366
REPUBLICAN HEADQUARTERS
(405) 528-3501

District Statistics

	2000 VOTE FOR PRESIDENT															
DIST.	BUSH	GORE	NADER	WHITE	BLACK	ASIAN	HISP	MEDIAN INCOME	WHITE COLLAR	BLUE COLLAR	SERVICE INDUSTRY	OVER 64	UNDER 18	COLLEGE EDUCATION	RURAL	SQ. MILES
1	62%	38%	n/a	74%	9%	1%	5%	$38,610	63%	23%	14%	12%	26%	26%	10%	1,737
2	53	47	n/a	70	4	0	2	$27,885	48	35	17	15	26	13	64	20,563
3	66	34	n/a	81	4	1	5	$32,098	54	30	16	14	26	18	49	34,089
4	61	39	n/a	78	7	2	5	$35,510	57	27	16	12	26	20	37	10,212
5	62	38	n/a	68	14	3	8	$33,893	61	24	15	13	26	25	12	2,067
STATE	60	38	0	74	7	1	5	$33,400	57	28	16	13	26	20	35	68,667
U.S.	47.9	48.4	3	69	12	4	13	$41,994	60	25	15	12	26	24	21	3,537,438

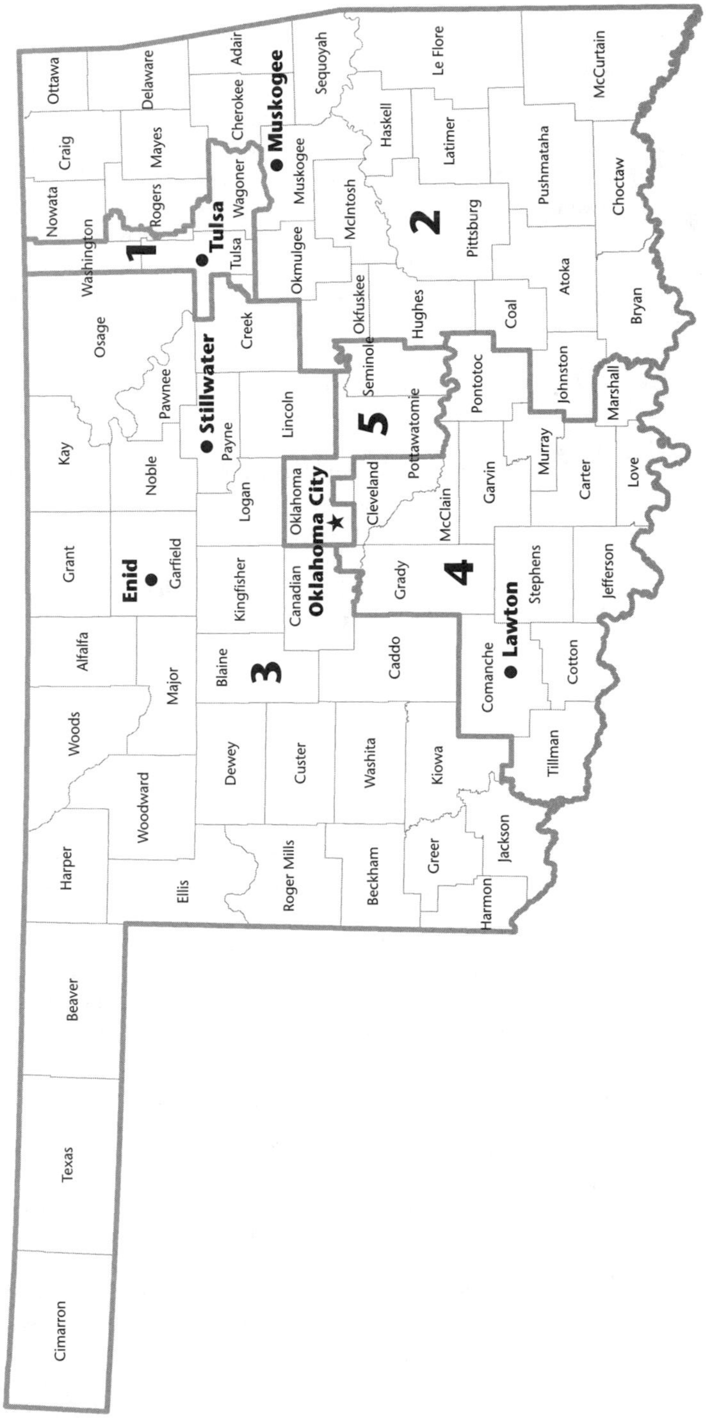

Ottawa
Delaware
Adair
Craig
Mayes
Cherokee
Sequoyah
Le Flore
McCurtain
Nowata
Rogers
Wagoner
Muskogee
Muskogee
Haskell
Latimer
Pushmataha
Choctaw
Washington
Tulsa
Tulsa
Okmulgee
McIntosh
Pittsburg
Atoka
Bryan
Osage
Creek
Okfuskee
Hughes
Coal
Pawnee
Stillwater
Payne
Lincoln
Seminole
Pontotoc
Johnston
Marshall
Kay
Noble
Pottawatomie
Murray
Carter
Love
Logan
Oklahoma
Oklahoma City
Cleveland
McClain
Garvin
Grant
Enid
Garfield
Kingfisher
Canadian
Grady
Stephens
Jefferson
Alfalfa
Lawton
Comanche
Cotton
Blaine
Caddo
Woods
Major
Dewey
Custer
Washita
Kiowa
Tillman
Woodward
Jackson
Harper
Ellis
Roger Mills
Beckham
Greer
Harmon
Beaver
Texas
Cimarron
1
2
3
4
5

Sen. Don Nickles (R)

CAPITOL OFFICE
224-5754
senator@nickles.senate.gov
nickles.senate.gov
133 Hart 20510-3602; fax 224-6008

COMMITTEES
Budget - chairman
Energy & Natural Resources
Finance
(Taxation & IRS Oversight - chairman)
Rules & Administration
Joint Taxation

HOMETOWN
Ponca City

BORN
Dec. 6, 1948, Ponca City, Okla.

RELIGION
Roman Catholic

FAMILY
Wife, Linda Nickles; four children

EDUCATION
Oklahoma State U., B.B.A. 1971

MILITARY SERVICE
Okla. National Guard, 1970-76

CAREER
Machine company executive

POLITICAL HIGHLIGHTS
Okla. Senate, 1979-81

ELECTION RESULTS

1998 GENERAL		
Don Nickles (R)	570,682	66.4%
Don E. Carroll (D)	268,898	31.3%
Mike Morris (I)	15,516	1.8%
1998 PRIMARY		
Don Nickles (R)		unopposed

PREVIOUS WINNING PERCENTAGES
1992 (59%); 1986 (55%); 1980 (54%)

Elected 1980; 4th term

After years of flirting with a bid for the top Senate Republican leadership post, Nickles passed up the opportunity to make a run for the job in the 108th Congress — not once but twice within a period of two months.

Nickles had considered running against Trent Lott of Mississippi as long ago as 1996, when Bob Dole stepped down as majority leader to run full time for president. Instead, Nickles settled for the No. 2 position of assistant majority leader, the formal title that the Republicans give to their whip, after negotiating with Lott for more staff members and a plum office just off the Senate floor.

Nickles floated the idea of a challenge to Lott at almost every opportunity since then — if only to remind the party leader to better attend to the concerns of conservatives such as himself. Most influentially, it was Nickles who late in 2002 first publicly suggested that Lott should step aside as the incoming majority leader, after Lott made racially polarizing remarks at a 100th birthday party for retiring Republican Sen. Strom Thurmond of South Carolina. But then, as before, Nickles decided not to seek the post after canvassing his colleagues and coming away convinced that he did not have the votes to win.

Instead, forced from the whip's job as a consequence of six-year GOP term limits, Nickles chose to chair the Budget Committee. It is his first full committee chairmanship, even though he ranks ninth in Republican seniority. Lobbyists and aides suggested that, if he dislikes the job, he will seriously contemplate retirement in 2004 after 24 years as a senator.

But those who write the annual congressional budget resolution have substantial influence over which big-ticket proposals, such as tax cuts and changes to entitlements such as Medicare and Social Security, are afforded a special shield from filibuster. That protection means such legislation can advance with as few as 51 votes — a huge leg up in the closely divided Senate. So Nickles' Budget gavel will be one of the most influential tools at the Capitol for shaping policy and setting the strategy to steer President Bush's agenda toward enactment.

Nickles got to work straight away, cutting a deal with Democrat Hillary Rodham Clinton of New York to produce the first law of the 108th. The measure, to extend unemployment benefits, diffused a potential political problem for Bush as 2003 began.

Although he is better-known for throwing some of the sharpest partisan elbows in Congress, dealing with Democrats in the cause of political pragmatism is a strategy Nickles has embraced in the past. With Republicans about to lose control of the Senate in the spring of 2001, he helped engineer a quick final compromise on the shape of the $1.35 trillion, 10-year tax cut that carried out the centerpiece of Bush's presidential campaign. In so doing, Nickles pushed GOP conservatives to swallow their pride and agree to a package designed to benefit those of modest means far more than Bush and the vast majority of Republicans advocated. As the No. 3 Republican on the Finance Committee in the 108th, one of Nickles' top desires is to indefinitely extend the provisions in the 2001 law.

On the Budget panel, Nickles succeeds Pete V. Domenici of New Mexico, who had been the only Republican chairman since the committee was established under the 1974 law that set the modern federal budget process. But before he became chairman, Nickles had sat on the committee for 15 years, cultivating his reputation as an undiminished enthusiast for the supply-side and limited-government views that helped sweep him to Washington in the Ronald Reagan landslide. While pushing hard for a Bush tax agenda, he was expected to push the president just as hard to restrain the growth of domestic discretionary spending — even if that meant aggravating the appropriators of his own party.

A self-described policy wonk, Nickles has come to master a broad array of subjects, earning respect from those in both parties for his knowledge of legislative nuance. But that did not make him particularly suited to his vote-counting responsibilities as whip, and he spent little time managing legislation on the floor or prodding colleagues to support a party line. His ill fit with the position was compounded by his uneasy relationship with Lott, whom Nickles regarded as far too willing to compromise conservative principles in order to add to the roster of Senate-completed bills.

When Nickles did focus on policy during his six years as No. 2 in the leadership, he was known more for killing bills than for passing them. He helped scuttle efforts in the 105th Congress to regulate tobacco. As architect of a Senate patients' rights bill substantially different from the House's in the 106th Congress, he succeeded mainly in sinking the whole effort. Two years later, in 2001, the House and Senate again passed competing bills — and again, the legislation died in a partisan standoff in which Nickles played a central role. All the while, he has taken great satisfaction in sidetracking Democratic proposals for increasing the minimum wage, which he has railed against since arriving in Washington.

In the 107th Congress, Nickles briefly went on the offensive, most notably maneuvering behind the scenes to engineer a congressional repeal of regulations on repetitive motion injuries that had been issued during the final days of the Clinton administration — the type of federal rules for businesses that Nickles has abhorred since his first career as a machine company executive.

Once Democrats took control for the final 18 months of the 107th Congress, Nickles used budgetary arguments and procedural devices to try to block a series of proposals. During the battle after Sept. 11, 2001, over an economic stimulus package, he helped scuttle popular proposals to give all laid-off workers a 50 percent federal subsidy to help them buy continued medical insurance coverage under their former employers' plans. Still, the concept became law in 2002, although only to benefit those who lose their jobs to liberalized trade. And Nickles was unable to stop a restructuring of the federal railroad pension system in 2001 that he decried as a budgetary boondoggle.

Nickles has been active in Republican politics since graduating from college. Just two years after his first run for public office, election to the state Senate in 1978, he entered the Republican primary to replace Republican Henry Bellmon, who was retiring from the U.S. Senate after two terms. He attracted the support of the Moral Majority and other conservative Christian groups, and they came to his aid with volunteers and voter registration drives. Nickles won a close, five-way Republican primary. Drawing on the electoral strength of the GOP presidential candidate, Nickles captured a 10 percentage point victory in November. He has been re-elected three times by steadily increasing margins.

When he arrived in the Senate as a 32-year-old, Nickles' baby face helped define him as a poster boy for the younger generation of Reagan conservatives. A few lines now crease that visage, but two decades later he remains in fine cardiovascular shape. In 2002, he finished seventh among members of Congress in a 3-mile charity race. And his time was four minutes faster than Bill Frist, who would bypass him to become majority leader at the end of the year.

KEY VOTES

2002

No Pass farm bill reversing crop subsidy limits
Yes Postpone tougher automobile fuel efficiency standards
No Overhaul campaign finance law; ban "soft money" and restrict advocacy advertising
Yes Set federal election standards
Yes Support oil drilling in Arctic National Wildlife Refuge
Yes Revive fast-track procedures for trade agreements
No Create federal insurance coverage for catastrophic terrorist losses
Yes Tighten federal accounting and corporate governance regulation
No Advance bipartisan Medicare prescription drug plan
Yes Create independent Sept. 11 commission
No Back Democratic Homeland Security Department proposal
Yes Authorize war against Iraq

2001

Yes Confirm John Ashcroft as attorney general
Yes Nullify Clinton Labor Department ergonomics rule
Yes Cut taxes by $1.35 trillion through fiscal 2011
No Pass Democratic bill to bolster rights of patients in managed-care plans
Yes Permit a new round of military base closings
Yes Expand law enforcement power to investigate suspected terrorists

CQ VOTE STUDIES

	PARTY UNITY		PRESIDENTIAL SUPPORT	
	Support	Oppose	Support	Oppose
2002	99%	1%	98%	2%
2001	96%	4%	96%	4%
2000	97%	3%	40%	60%
1999	98%	2%	27%	73%
1998	98%	2%	23%	77%
1997	97%	3%	59%	41%
1996	99%	1%	34%	66%
1995	98%	2%	22%	78%
1994	94%	6%	25%	75%
1993	95%	5%	18%	82%

INTEREST GROUPS

	AFL-CIO	ADA	CCUS	ACU
2002	15%	0%	95%	100%
2001	13%	10%	100%	92%
2000	0%	0%	86%	100%
1999	0%	0%	88%	96%
1998	0%	0%	83%	96%
1997	0%	0%	100%	96%
1996	0%	0%	100%	100%
1995	0%	0%	100%	100%
1994	0%	5%	90%	100%
1993	0%	5%	91%	96%

Sen. James M. Inhofe (R)

CAPITOL OFFICE
224-4721
inhofe.senate.gov
453 Russell 20510-3603; fax 228-0380

COMMITTEES
Armed Services
Environment & Public Works - chairman
Indian Affairs

HOMETOWN
Tulsa

BORN
Nov. 17, 1934, Des Moines, Iowa

RELIGION
Presbyterian

FAMILY
Wife, Kay Inhofe; four children

EDUCATION
U. of Tulsa, B.A. 1973

MILITARY SERVICE
Army, 1956-58

CAREER
Real estate developer; insurance executive

POLITICAL HIGHLIGHTS
Okla. House, 1967-69; Okla. Senate, 1969-77; Republican nominee for governor, 1974; Republican nominee for U.S. House, 1976; mayor of Tulsa, 1978-84; defeated for re-election as mayor of Tulsa, 1984; U.S. House, 1987-94

ELECTION RESULTS

2002 GENERAL		
James M. Inhofe (R)	583,579	57.3%
David L. Walters (D)	369,789	36.3%
James Germalic (I)	65,056	6.4%
2002 PRIMARY		
James M. Inhofe (R)		unopposed

PREVIOUS WINNING PERCENTAGES
1996 (57%); 1994 Special Election (55%); 1992 House Election (53%); 1990 House Election (56%); 1988 House Election (53%); 1986 House Election (55%)

Elected 1994; 2nd full term

It would be hard to find a more conservative senator than Inhofe, the new chairman of the Environment and Public Works Committee.

He has received numerous "Taxpayer's Friend" awards from the National Taxpayers' Union for his tax-slashing votes. He has a lifetime "A+" grade from the National Rifle Association, and a zero score for the past three Congresses from the League of Conservation Voters. He consistently has sided with oil and gas producers against "burdensome" Environmental Protection Agency mandates and once referred to that agency and the Occupational Safety and Health Administration as "Gestapo bureaucracies."

In clashing with the late Democratic Sen. Paul Wellstone, Inhofe (INN-hoff) once remarked: "There probably are not two members of the U.S. Senate who are further apart philosophically than the senior senator from Minnesota and myself. I would probably believe him to be an extreme left-wing radical liberal, and he believes me to be an extreme right-wing radical conservative. And I think maybe we are both right."

Inhofe can come across as stiff and even awkward in person, especially in contrast to his Oklahoma colleague, Don Nickles. Inhofe has feuded for years with the editorial page of his hometown newspaper, the Tulsa World, and he remains suspicious of what he sees as the liberal bias of the national news media. "Don't look for any fair treatment — we're not going to get it," he told the Oklahoma delegation to the 2000 Republican National Convention.

Inhofe drew some national media attention of his own in late 2002 when he criticized Trent Lott's efforts to apologize for the remarks about segregation that ultimately drove him out as Republican leader. "I can't imagine if someone had written out a script how he could have handled it worse," Inhofe told CBS. When Bill Frist announced he would challenge Lott, Inhofe was among the first to offer his endorsement.

While Inhofe distanced himself from Lott, the two were largely in accord on civil rights votes. A National Association for the Advancement of Colored People analysis found that Inhofe was one of four senators who had sided with the NAACP even less often than Lott in the preceding decade.

When he took the gavel at Environment and Public Works as the 108th Congress began, Inhofe vowed to make sure that "sound science" underpins any changes in environmental regulation. "The political agenda of extremists must not dictate our efforts to provide common sense protections that are based on science," he said.

But Inhofe said he knows that as chairman he will have to cut deals with Democrats to get things done. He also acknowledged he might lose some battles in committee, where maverick Republican Lincoln Chafee of Rhode Island was expected to side with Democrats on many environmental issues. Early in the 108th, for example, Inhofe conceded that his committee, in reworking the 1990 Clean Air Act, probably would go beyond President Bush's "Clear Skies" proposal to reduce industrial pollution from sulfur dioxide, nitrogen oxides and, for the first time, mercury emissions. Because of Chafee, Inhofe said, the Senate bill probably also would restrict carbon dioxide emissions, a move Bush and he opposed.

Inhofe backed the president 95 percent of the time in the 107th, but as the 108th began he was pushing for significantly higher spending on highways than the administration envisioned in the rewrite of federal surface transportation law. "Conservatives really believe government has certain functions it must perform," Inhofe said. "Certainly infrastructure is way up there at the top."

Inhofe wants to ensure that all states receive at least 95 cents for every dollar they put into the Highway Trust Fund, financed by federal gasoline tax revenues; currently, Oklahoma gets about 91 cents back.

A staunchly pro-defense lawmaker whose state has several military installations, Inhofe also sits on Armed Services, where he has strongly supported a national missile defense system and increased spending to improve the military's readiness for combat. He fought a losing battle in the 107th against the Pentagon's cancellation of the Crusader howitzer system, which was to be manufactured in Oklahoma.

An Army veteran and experienced pilot, Inhofe has had his brushes with danger. While traveling to Oklahoma City in 1999, his private plane lost its propeller, forcing him to glide about seven miles to make an emergency high-speed landing. He said it was his third forced landing in 41 years of flying. A National Transportation Safety Board investigation found no evidence of anything suspicious that could have caused the mishap.

Inhofe's frequently fiery rhetoric from the right has made him a hero to Tulsa's hard-core conservatives, including religious fundamentalists. He predicted in a 1999 speech that President Clinton's affair with one-time White House intern Monica Lewinsky would trigger a moral revolution and end an "age of perversion."

But sometimes his intemperate words have landed him in hot water. In 2001 he told the Senate that Israel had a right to take harsh measures with the Palestinians because God had promised that land to the Jews. He also likened Palestinian terrorist attacks to "satanic evil," prompting an outcry from American Muslim groups. In 1972, he said Democratic presidential nominee George McGovern should "be hanged with Jane Fonda" for implying that American soldiers were guilty of atrocities in Vietnam.

His conservative base of support helped him through 10 years in the state legislature, a mayoral career and four close House election victories, but it did not look sufficient to sustain a statewide campaign until 1994.

While he was a state senator, Inhofe lost a 1974 campaign for governor to Democrat David L. Boren and a 1976 campaign for Congress. Elected mayor of Tulsa in 1978, he was defeated in 1984, but he bounced back two years later and picked up a House seat for the GOP, winning with 55 percent to succeed Democrat James R. Jones, who ran for the Senate. He never did better than 56 percent in four elections in the state's most Republican district. In 1988, his campaign was complicated when he sued his brother over a stock sale involving the family insurance business.

In the 1994 Senate contest, Democratic Rep. Dave McCurdy was the favorite when Boren, who had gone on to serve as senator, announced he would retire in midterm to become president of the University of Oklahoma. McCurdy fit the general mold of conservative Democratic politics, in equal parts a populist and a friend to business.

But McCurdy had made one error that proved fatal in Oklahoma: He became associated with Clinton, whom he introduced at the 1992 Democratic National Convention. The GOP transformed the race into a referendum on Clinton. No matter what McCurdy said about having differences with the president, Inhofe could top it; he had opposed virtually every move Clinton had made. Inhofe won by 15 percentage points.

When he stood for election to a full term, Democrats were deterred by Inhofe's lopsided victory of two years earlier and did not mount a significant challenge. Inhofe defeated Jim Boren, a cousin of the former senator, by 17 points. In 2002, he won by 21 points against former Democratic Gov. David L. Walters, who was hobbled by past campaign finance improprieties.

KEY VOTES

2002

- No Pass farm bill reversing crop subsidy limits
- Yes Postpone tougher automobile fuel efficiency standards
- No Overhaul campaign finance law; ban "soft money" and restrict advocacy advertising
- Yes Set federal election standards
- Yes Support oil drilling in Arctic National Wildlife Refuge
- Yes Revive fast-track procedures for trade agreements
- Yes Create federal insurance coverage for catastrophic terrorist losses
- Yes Tighten federal accounting and corporate governance regulation
- No Advance bipartisan Medicare prescription drug plan
- Yes Create independent Sept. 11 commission
- No Back Democratic Homeland Security Department proposal
- Yes Authorize war against Iraq

2001

- Yes Confirm John Ashcroft as attorney general
- Yes Nullify Clinton Labor Department ergonomics rule
- Yes Cut taxes by $1.35 trillion through fiscal 2011
- No Pass Democratic bill to bolster rights of patients in managed-care plans
- No Permit a new round of military base closings
- Yes Expand law enforcement power to investigate suspected terrorists

CQ VOTE STUDIES

	PARTY UNITY		PRESIDENTIAL SUPPORT	
	Support	Oppose	Support	Oppose
2002	96%	4%	96%	4%
2001	96%	4%	95%	5%
2000	100%	0%	30%	70%
1999	95%	5%	23%	77%
1998	97%	3%	14%	86%
1997	99%	1%	49%	51%
1996	100%	0%	28%	72%
1995	98%	2%	24%	76%
House Service:				
1994	99%	1%	45%	55%
1993	97%	3%	31%	69%

INTEREST GROUPS

	AFL-CIO	ADA	CCUS	ACU
2002	17%	10%	100%	100%
2001	25%	10%	93%	96%
2000	13%	5%	85%	100%
1999	11%	0%	94%	100%
1998	0%	5%	76%	100%
1997	14%	5%	50%	100%
1996	0%	0%	100%	100%
1995	0%	0%	100%	100%
House Service:				
1994	0%	0%	0%	100%
1993	8%	10%	91%	100%

Rep. John Sullivan (R)

CAPITOL OFFICE
225-2211
ok01.sullivan@mail.house.gov
sullivan.house.gov
114 Cannon 20515-3601; fax 225-9187

COMMITTEES
Government Reform
Science
Transportation & Infrastructure

HOMETOWN
Tulsa

BORN
Jan. 1, 1965, Tulsa, Okla.

RELIGION
Roman Catholic

FAMILY
Wife, Judy Sullivan; five children (one deceased)

EDUCATION
Northeastern State U., B.B.A 1992 (marketing)

CAREER
Real estate broker; petroleum marketing executive

POLITICAL HIGHLIGHTS
Okla. House, 1995-2002

ELECTION RESULTS

2002 GENERAL		
John Sullivan (R)	119,566	55.6%
Doug Dodd (D)	90,649	42.2%
Joseph V. Cristiano (LIBERT)	4,740	2.2%
2002 PRIMARY		
John Sullivan (R)	39,992	84.6%
Evelyn L. Rogers (R)	7,280	15.4%
2002 SPECIAL		
John Sullivan (R)	61,694	53.8%
Doug Dodd (D)	50,850	44.3%
Neil Mavis (LIBERT)	1,758	1.5%

Elected January 2002; 1st full term

Sullivan doesn't have his predecessor Republican Steve Largent's football fame, but he carries the same politically conservative beliefs. Sullivan won a January 2002 special election to replace Largent, who resigned after seven years in the House to wage an unsuccessful run for governor.

When asked to compare himself to Largent, a Hall of Famer who played with the Seattle Seahawks, Sullivan said, "Well, he's better-looking than me. And he's a football player and I'm just an average guy. But we're both pretty conservative." Sullivan affiliates with the Republican Study Committee, a group made up of the GOP's conservative wing.

Largent had asked the state legislature to expedite the special-election process and agreed to stay around until his successor was chosen. Sullivan was warmly welcomed into the Republican fold. While the 2002 State of the Union address came after Sullivan's election but before he was sworn in, President Bush invited Sullivan to come to the House chamber to hear the speech. And Speaker J. Dennis Hastert asked Sullivan's wife, Judy, to attend in the visitors gallery, where she was seated with Jean Hastert and New York GOP Gov. George E. Pataki.

A few months after Sullivan took the oath of office, Bush invited the new congressman over to the White House for a chat. Sullivan said that he had "sweaty hands" as he entered the Oval Office, but that he and Bush seemed to hit it off. After the meeting, Sullivan said the president, who has a penchant for giving nicknames, "called me 'Sully.' " During the 30-minute session, the two men discussed issues ranging from water quality in northeast Oklahoma to homeland security to the Middle East, Sullivan told the Tulsa World.

Sullivan's voting record indicates that he stands solidly with Bush and Hastert: On key roll call votes in 2002, he backed the president 88 percent of the time and voted with the House GOP 99 percent of the time.

Sullivan serves on the Transportation Committee. In the 107th Congress, he was able to secure funding for several projects in his district, including widening Interstate 44 in Tulsa. Sullivan also persuaded the Immigration and Naturalization Service (INS) to increase its staffing in Oklahoma. He said that when a van containing 18 illegal aliens was stopped in Oklahoma, the passengers were let go because there was only one INS agent on duty in the whole state.

Water quality issues, including settling an ongoing dispute between Arkansas and Oklahoma, are also high on Sullivan's legislative agenda.

Sullivan had his first taste of politics as a young boy when he accompanied his father around the neighborhood doing campaign work. He says his father was a Republican and his mother a Democrat.

In college, Sullivan initially was a political science major, but after his father died he switched to business administration. He worked his way through college, attending class whenever he could fit it in with work at a trucking firm. He graduated when he was 27.

The congressman occasionally talks to school and to youth groups about the perils of drinking. He was arrested several times for drinking-related offenses, including public intoxication, loitering, and assault and battery. "I used to drink quite a lot when I was in college," he said. He says his parents required him to do additional volunteer work at Catholic charities to atone for his arrests. He no longer drinks at all, he says.

Sullivan also worked as a real estate broker and a petroleum marketing executive and ran a political memorabilia business. He says those experiences have fueled his zeal to cut business taxes, starting with a reduction in taxes on capital gains. "I know what it's like living under government regulation," he says.

He served a term as president of the Tulsa County Young Republicans and worked behind the scenes on several Republican campaigns. In 1994, when the local state legislator ran for Congress, Sullivan at age 29 ran for and won that seat in the Oklahoma House.

During his seven years in the state legislature, he waged a long battle to remove or reduce the sales tax on groceries, backed reductions in the estate tax and championed a sales tax "holiday" — one day every year when school-related purchases would not be taxed. He proposed reducing the size of the state legislature by almost 40 percent, aiming to make it more streamlined.

When Largent decided to resign his seat to focus his attention on running for governor, he initially said he would leave Congress on Nov. 29, 2001. But after the Sept. 11 terrorist attacks, Largent decided to stay on until mid-February 2002, by which time his successor would be chosen.

Largent asked the legislature to change state election law to permit the special-election process to begin before the seat was actually vacant. The legislature quickly approved the change. The timetable called for a primary in December; a party runoff election, if needed, in January; and the general election on Feb. 12.

Cathy Keating, wife of GOP Gov. Frank Keating, was viewed as the front-runner in the five-way Republican primary. But Sullivan, in an upset, bested Keating by 15 percentage points in the Dec. 11 GOP balloting. Although he was the top vote-getter, his 46 percent was not enough to avoid a Jan. 8 runoff with Keating, who came in second. But Keating soon dropped out, saying a runoff battle could harm the party.

Her decision moved the general election up to Jan. 8, where Sullivan faced Democrat Doug Dodd, who had resigned from the Tulsa School Board to run. Both candidates advocated tax cuts, additional defense spending, and local control over education and energy policies.

Sullivan's 9.5 point margin of victory was more narrow than had been expected in the solidly Republican district, which had gone for Bush by 25 points in 2000.

Redistricting for the 2002 election left the 1st District with a healthy GOP lean. Sullivan faced a rematch with Dodd but easily prevailed, this time by 13 points, to win a full term in office.

KEY VOTES

2002

Yes Back Bush's defense budget increase
Yes Extend 1996 welfare law
Yes Adopt Bush's discretionary spending limit
Yes Pass GOP Medicare prescription drug plan
No Create independent Sept. 11 commission
No Extend union protections to Homeland Security Department employees
Yes Revive fast-track procedures for trade agreements
Yes Authorize war against Iraq
No Advance bankruptcy overhaul opposed by abortion opponents

CQ VOTE STUDIES

	PARTY UNITY		PRESIDENTIAL SUPPORT	
	Support	Oppose	Support	Oppose
2002	99%	1%	88%	12%

INTEREST GROUPS

	AFL-CIO	ADA	CCUS	ACU
2002	13%	0%	89%	—

OKLAHOMA 1

Tulsa; Wagoner and Washington counties

Wooden homes on small plots of land in the city's outskirts contrast with the skyscrapers of downtown Tulsa, the heart of the 1st and one of the most solidly Republican enclaves in Oklahoma. More insular and tied to old money than Oklahoma City and the rest of the state, Tulsans like to distinguish themselves from the "dust-on-their-boots" stereotype of the rest of Oklahoma.

Once the "oil capital of the world," Tulsa thrived on drilling for "black gold" until the market dried up in the 1980s. It is now a city seeking an economic identity to fit with its historic self-image. In the late 1980s, an effort to attract a diverse range of businesses through tax breaks and other incentives started to pay off. Tulsa has become a manufacturing hub of flight simulators. While aviation and aerospace manufacturing have remained productive, the telecommunications and financial services industries have helped prolong growth.

With the economy on the mend, real estate prices are beginning to rise as Tulsa expands to the east and south. Young professionals are moving into the more established sections of the city's center. South Tulsa is sprinkled with executive homes, and new subdivisions are springing up in the bedroom communities of Broken Arrow, Owasso and Jenks. Redistricting after the 2000 census added Bartlesville in Washington County to the north and fast-growing suburbs in Wagoner County to the east.

Democrats split the votes in the 1st's local elections, but Republicans dominate at the federal level. The region has voted for a Democratic presidential candidate only twice since 1920. Socially conservative issues play well here, the home of Oral Roberts University.

MAJOR INDUSTRY

Aerospace, defense manufacturing, oil, agriculture

CITIES

Tulsa (pt.), 387,419; Broken Arrow, 74,859; Bartlesville, 34,746; Owasso, 18,502; Sand Springs (pt.), 17,172; Bixby, 13,336

NOTABLE

One of the deadliest race riots in American history took place in the Tulsa neighborhood of Greenwood in June 1921 — nearly 300 people died; Oral Roberts University is known for its 200-foot prayer tower and "Praying Hands" sculpture.

Rep. Brad Carson (D)

CAPITOL OFFICE
225-2701
brad.carson@mail.house.gov
www.house.gov/bradcarson
317 Cannon 20515-3602; fax 225-3038

COMMITTEES
Resources
Transportation & Infrastructure

HOMETOWN
Claremore

BORN
March 11, 1967, Winslow, Ariz.

RELIGION
Baptist

FAMILY
Wife, Julie Carson

EDUCATION
Baylor U., B.A. 1989 (history); Oxford U., M.A. 1991 (Rhodes scholar); U. of Oklahoma, J.D. 1994

CAREER
Lawyer; Defense Department aide

POLITICAL HIGHLIGHTS
No previous office

ELECTION RESULTS

2002 GENERAL		
Brad Carson (D)	146,748	74.1%
Kent Pharaoh (R)	51,234	25.9%
2002 PRIMARY		
Brad Carson (D)	72,612	64.2%
Mike Mass (D)	34,450	30.5%
Dorothy Vandiver (D)	6,040	5.3%
2000 GENERAL		
Brad Carson (D)	107,273	54.9%
Andy Ewing (R)	81,672	41.8%
Neil Mavis (LIBERT)	6,467	3.3%

Elected 2000; 2nd term

The boyish-looking Carson's biography offers a number of interesting characteristics that have helped him win notice in his brief tenure on Capitol Hill. Only 35 years old as he began his second term, Carson is the 10th-youngest member of the House, one of only two Native Americans in the chamber, the lone Democrat in the Oklahoma delegation and one of the small band of rural Democrats. And he is one of the handful of Rhodes Scholars currently serving in Congress. In 2002, the Junior Chamber of Commerce named him one of its 10 outstanding young Americans.

Carson's moderate views fit well with his conservative, but historically Democratic, constituency. On Capitol Hill, he affiliates with both the conservative Blue Dog coalition and the moderate, pro-business New Democrat Coalition. He has twice been endorsed by the National Rifle Association. His support of trade, energy development, and tax cuts have put him in league with Republicans on a number of occasions.

Carson is fiscally frugal. He voted in both 2001 and 2002 against a spending bill because it did not contain language blocking an automatic pay raise for lawmakers. But he has also vowed to make sure the 2nd District gets its "fair share" of federal dollars. "I want to get my teeth into the bone and not give up until they send the bone back to the 2nd District," he says. Economic development for his district — the poorest in the state — is a top priority.

Carson sits on the Transportation Committee, and in 2002 he and Oklahoma GOP Sen. James M. Inhofe joined forces to get $15 million to rebuild a bridge across Interstate 40 that had been damaged in a deadly barge accident and to pay for the related costs of lengthy detours.

Carson also wants to rectify the longstanding situation in which Oklahoma sends more money to Washington in fuel taxes than it gets in return in highway spending. "We are . . . not wealthy enough that we can afford to be a donor state," Carson argues, promising to "plead, cajole, argue, stand down — whatever it takes" to gain the extra highway funding.

A member of the Cherokee Nation, Carson won enactment of legislation aimed at ending a 95-year dispute between the federal government and three Indian tribes — the Cherokee, Choctaw and Chickasaw — over land on the riverbed of the Arkansas River wrongfully taken from the tribes when Oklahoma became a state in 1907. The Supreme Court had ruled in 1970 that the land belonged to the tribes. Carson's bill authorized a $40 million payment to compensate for natural resources taken from the tribes.

Carson also gained approval of his bill to authorize $33 million to help build a Native American educational and cultural center in Oklahoma City. The museum, once built, may become part of the Smithsonian Institution.

Even before his election to the House, Carson was crusading against management problems in Oklahoma nursing homes, and in Congress he has continued to press for greater federal oversight of the industry. Rural health care needs are a priority for him, and in the 107th Congress, Carson served on a Democratic health care task force and the bipartisan Rural Health Care Coalition.

Carson was born in Winslow, Ariz., where his father was working with the Bureau of Indian Affairs on the Navajo reservation. The family returned to his mother's home in eastern Oklahoma when Carson was a child, and he grew up there as the sixth generation of his family to do so. His mother's family, members of the Cherokee Nation, had come to Oklahoma on the infamous Trail of Tears, when the U.S. government in the 1800s uprooted the

Cherokees from their original homeland in the Southeast.

Carson was both smart and ambitious. His mother told the Daily Oklahoman that Carson at age 7 knew he wanted to be a Rhodes Scholar, although she said he spelled it "Roads" in a school paper detailing what he wanted to do when he grew up. He achieved that distinction after graduating with honors from Baylor University. During his college days, Carson served as an intern in the office of 2nd District Democratic Rep. Mike Synar. He told The Associated Press that he "really got the political bug" during his brief time with Synar.

After studying at Oxford, Carson earned a law degree from the University of Oklahoma, where he was named the outstanding law school graduate. Carson was selected as a White House fellow, and he spent more than a year as a special assistant to Defense Secretary William S. Cohen, working on military readiness and gender-integrated training projects. His work at the Pentagon shaped his views, he says, in favor of the missile defense system and increased defense spending.

Soon after he returned to Oklahoma and resumed his legal practice, Carson filed for the 2nd District House seat being vacated in 2000 by three-term GOP Rep. Tom Coburn, who was observing a term-limits pledge. Coburn had been the first Republican to win in the 2nd since 1920.

Carson showed an ease on the campaign trail in 2000 that belied his youth and status as a first-time candidate. Oklahoma has showed a willingness to elect young candidates: When first elected, Synar was 28 and GOP Sen. Don Nickles was 31.

Carson was nominated in a September runoff over a political veteran, state Rep. Bill Settle. Even though the GOP candidate, car dealer Andy Ewing, had the endorsement of popular incumbent Coburn, Carson coasted to a surprising 13-point win in the state's most expensive House race.

Reapportionment after the 2000 census cost Oklahoma one of its six House seats. Democrats were hoping to preserve two Democratic-leaning districts in the eastern part of the state, but the new map carved up the southeastern 3rd, giving much of it to the 2nd and creating one Democratic — albeit strongly conservative — district. The new southeastern portion of the 2nd, known as Little Dixie, is more conservative than the northern segments of the district. The principal challenge to Carson's re-election in 2002 came in the Democratic primary, from state Rep. Mike Mass, who tried to portray Carson as too liberal for his new constituency. Carson prevailed by a ratio of better than 2-to-1. In the November general election, he crushed Republican Kent Pharoah, with 74 percent.

KEY VOTES

2002

Yes Overhaul campaign finance law; ban "soft money" and restrict advocacy advertising
Yes Back Bush's defense budget increase
No Extend 1996 welfare law
No Adopt Bush's discretionary spending limit
No Pass GOP Medicare prescription drug plan
Yes Create independent Sept. 11 commission
Yes Extend union protections to Homeland Security Department employees
Yes Revive fast-track procedures for trade agreements
Yes Authorize war against Iraq
Yes Advance bankruptcy overhaul opposed by abortion opponents

2001

Yes Nullify Clinton Labor Department ergonomics rule
Yes Cut taxes by $1.35 trillion through fiscal 2011
No Maintain ban on oil drilling in Arctic National Wildlife Refuge
No Approve Bush proposal to limit managed-care plan liability for coverage decisions
No Divert money from crop subsidy payments to land conservation
Yes Expand law enforcement power to investigate suspected terrorists

CQ VOTE STUDIES

	PARTY UNITY		PRESIDENTIAL SUPPORT	
	Support	Oppose	Support	Oppose
2002	74%	26%	52%	48%
2001	68%	32%	51%	49%

INTEREST GROUPS

	AFL-CIO	ADA	CCUS	ACU
2002	67%	65%	75%	40%
2001	67%	65%	70%	48%

OKLAHOMA 2

East – Muskogee, 'Little Dixie'

The 2nd has a definite Democratic lean — all nine Oklahoma counties that George W. Bush lost in the 2000 presidential election are here — but partisanship does not disguise a cultural split between the district's north and south regions. Running from Kansas to Texas and hugging Oklahoma's eastern border, the 2nd takes in outlying areas of Tulsa to the north and the "Little Dixie" region in the south. Southeastern Oklahoma relies on farming and is "Yellow Dog" Democratic territory, while Democrats in the northeastern part of the state are more liberal, at least by Oklahoma's conservative standards.

In "Little Dixie," a 1998 drought was as severe as any in the Dust Bowl era of the 1930s, but conservation techniques prevented similar sandstorms. The economy did suffer, however, as farmers were forced to use feed for grazing animals by midsummer, several months earlier than normal. In addition to beef and poultry, farmers cultivate peanuts and wheat, and in rocky southeastern McCurtain County, the timber industry thrives. Marginal oil and natural gas wells compose the energy businesses that survived the 1980s industry depression.

Up north, in the foothills of the Ozark Mountains, the thickly forested section of the 2nd provides northeast Oklahoma with its nickname, the Green Country. It is a poor rural area with Democratic sympathies. The lakes and waterways, the state's most extensive, attract tourists and the elderly, helping to boost the economy. Delaware County, which contains most of Grand Lake O' the Cherokees, was the state's fastest-growing county in the 1990s (32 percent). The 2nd also has one of the largest American Indian population percentages in the nation (17 percent), and includes Tahlequah, the capital of the Cherokee Nation.

MAJOR INDUSTRY

Timber, ranching, oil and gas

MILITARY BASES

McAlester Army Ammunition Plant, 4 military, 909 civilian (2001)

CITIES

Muskogee, 38,310; McAlester, 17,783; Claremore, 15,873; Tahlequah, 14,458; Miami, 13,704

NOTABLE

The American Indian "Trail of Tears" of 1838-39 ended in Tahlequah — nearly 20 percent of the Cherokee Nation died en route.

Rep. Frank D. Lucas (R)

CAPITOL OFFICE
225-5565
www.house.gov/lucas
2342 Rayburn 20515-3603; fax 225-8698

COMMITTEES
Agriculture
(Conservation, Credit, Rural Development & Research - chairman)
Financial Services
Science

HOMETOWN
Cheyenne

BORN
Jan. 6, 1960, Cheyenne, Okla.

RELIGION
Baptist

FAMILY
Wife, Lynda Lucas; three children

EDUCATION
Oklahoma State U., B.S. 1982 (agriculture economics)

CAREER
Farmer; rancher

POLITICAL HIGHLIGHTS
Republican nominee for Okla. House, 1984, 1986; Okla. House, 1989-94

ELECTION RESULTS

2002 GENERAL		
Frank D. Lucas (R)	148,206	75.6%
Robert T. Murphy (LIBERT)	47,884	24.4%
2002 PRIMARY		
Frank D. Lucas (R)	43,887	89.2%
Richard Hovis (R)	5,330	10.8%
2000 GENERAL		
Frank D. Lucas (R)	95,635	59.3%
Randy Beutler (D)	63,106	39.2%
Joseph V. Cristiano (LIBERT)	2,435	1.5%

PREVIOUS WINNING PERCENTAGES
1998 (65%); 1996 (64%); 1994 (70%); 1994 Special Election (54%)

Elected May 1994; 5th full term

A fifth-generation farmer and rancher from sparsely populated western Oklahoma, Lucas has held on to the family spread while many of his neighbors have packed up and moved to the city.

The population of Roger Mills County, where Lucas lives, declined 17 percent from 1990 to 2000 and has dropped 28 percent since 1980. Twelve of the 15 western-most counties in Oklahoma lost population during the '90s — a key reason that reapportionment after the 2000 census took away one of the Sooner State's six House seats.

Lucas' new district encompasses almost half of the state, stretching nearly 400 miles from the New Mexico border in the panhandle to the outskirts of Oklahoma City and Tulsa. It needs to be this large to draw in enough people to form a congressional district. But while many of his constituents are suburbanites, Lucas' main focus is helping to better rural life.

The emptying of rural Oklahoma is an underlying factor in much of his legislative agenda and constituent service, as he works to develop concrete reasons — jobs, health care, education — for people to stay in places such as his hometown of Cheyenne, the county seat, population 778.

Although he has been an elected official for more than a decade, Lucas likes to say he "still tries to earn an honest living" in western Oklahoma, where his great-great-grandfather was a homesteader in 1900. When Lucas is in Washington tending to congressional business, his wife runs their beef cattle and wheat operation on land that has been in the family since 1912.

As chairman of the Agriculture Committee's Conservation Subcommittee, Lucas played a major role in developing the farm bill that Congress enacted in 2002. Although he supported the "Freedom to Farm" measure in 1996, which was supposed to wean farmers from government support, Lucas told the Tulsa World in 2002, "that was never real to start with. . . . It is obvious that we must support legislation which helps provide a reliable safety net for Oklahoma producers."

As Congress moved in 2002 to revisit the programs from the 1996 farm bill, Lucas was a member of the negotiating team that resolved differences between the House and Senate versions of the bill. The resulting measure included conservation provisions authored by his subcommittee as well as substantial federal support for farmers growing wheat and peanuts, both of which are important crops in Lucas' district. As he urged broad support for the farm bill, Lucas said, "The only people who should be concerned about agriculture policy are people who eat."

Lucas is a party loyalist, and he supports the Republicans more than 95 percent of the time. President Bush, who has coined nicknames for many people, refers to the 6-foot-4 Lucas as "Big Frank." But that familiarity has not deterred Lucas from pressing his leaders and the president to move quickly to provide aid to farmers facing financial disaster because of drought and low prices.

Late in 2001, when the White House was expressing reticence about moving on the farm bill because it involved "large new financial commitments," Lucas pressed for speedy action on Capitol Hill, saying, "I just don't think the folks at the administration have a clear idea of where they're going on agriculture policy."

After the Sept. 11, 2001, terrorist attacks and the spread of deadly anthrax through the mail, Lucas wrote a bill to increase protections against a possible bioterrorism attack on the nation's food supply. His bill called for closer monitoring of imported food, more research on animal and plant diseases, and better inspection of domestic meat and poultry. Much of Lucas' proposal was included in a bioterrorism bill that became law in 2002.

Methamphetamines are a serious problem in rural areas, and Lucas has secured some federal money to help local law enforcement authorities track down and clean up meth labs, which pose risks because of the explosive gases and hazardous wastes created. The cost of cleaning up the labs has put a strain on Oklahoma law enforcement budgets, Lucas says. In 2001 he tried, unsuccessfully, to shift $11.7 million that was tagged for international broadcasting to meth lab investigation and cleanup.

Lucas spent a lot of time working on legislation stemming from the April 1995 bombing in downtown Oklahoma City that destroyed the Alfred P. Murrah Federal Building and killed 168 people. The federal building used to be in Lucas' old district, the 6th. In the years since the bombing, Lucas helped secure more than $100 million in federal funds for the relief, recovery and rebuilding of the area affected by the blast. He also won passage of a measure to establish a national memorial on the bombing site.

With his low-key and soft-spoken manner, Lucas was regarded as a hayseed when he first came to Oklahoma City as a legislator in 1989. He projected the same image when he arrived on Capitol Hill after winning a special election in 1994. But supporters say his image is misleading; it is simply that he would rather listen than talk.

Lucas became interested in politics while at Oklahoma State University. He was president of the College Republicans while working on a degree in agricultural economics. After graduating, he returned home to Cheyenne and soon entered politics. He made two unsuccessful bids for a state House seat in what was then a mostly Democratic area, before capturing a seat in a sprawling district in 1988.

When 10-term Democratic Rep. Glenn English resigned the 6th District seat in early 1994 to head a rural electric lobbying association, Lucas made his run for the House. He outpolled four other Republicans to win the nomination; then, stressing his work in agriculture and his lifelong residency in the district, he won 54 percent of the vote in the general election against Democrat Dan Webber Jr., who had spent years in Washington as an aide to Oklahoma Democratic Sen. David L. Boren.

That was his closest election. In 2002, after introducing himself to his new constituents in the Tulsa, Stillwater and Enid areas, Lucas racked up a big victory in the new 3rd District that GOP Gov. Frank Keating had drawn to be favorable to the GOP.

KEY VOTES

2002

- No Overhaul campaign finance law; ban "soft money" and restrict advocacy advertising
- Yes Back Bush's defense budget increase
- Yes Extend 1996 welfare law
- Yes Adopt Bush's discretionary spending limit
- Yes Pass GOP Medicare prescription drug plan
- No Create independent Sept. 11 commission
- No Extend union protections to Homeland Security Department employees
- Yes Revive fast-track procedures for trade agreements
- Yes Authorize war against Iraq
- Yes Advance bankruptcy overhaul opposed by abortion opponents

2001

- Yes Nullify Clinton Labor Department ergonomics rule
- Yes Cut taxes by $1.35 trillion through fiscal 2011
- No Maintain ban on oil drilling in Arctic National Wildlife Refuge
- Yes Approve Bush proposal to limit managed-care plan liability for coverage decisions
- No Divert money from crop subsidy payments to land conservation
- Yes Expand law enforcement power to investigate suspected terrorists

CQ VOTE STUDIES

	PARTY UNITY		PRESIDENTIAL SUPPORT	
	Support	Oppose	Support	Oppose
2002	98%	2%	88%	12%
2001	98%	2%	88%	12%
2000	97%	3%	22%	78%
1999	93%	7%	17%	83%
1998	95%	5%	22%	78%

INTEREST GROUPS

	AFL-CIO	ADA	CCUS	ACU
2002	0%	0%	100%	96%
2001	25%	5%	96%	96%
2000	0%	0%	85%	91%
1999	11%	0%	96%	96%
1998	0%	0%	100%	100%

OKLAHOMA 3

Panhandle, west and north-central Oklahoma

With nothing to stop it on the flat plains, the wind blows with constant force in the 3rd, an area devastated by the Dust Bowl of the 1930s. Few areas felt the boom or the bust of the 1980s oil market more than the 3rd, as those who had made fortunes on oil had their rigs and property auctioned and their Mercedes and Lincolns repossessed. Western Oklahoma had never fully recovered from the Dust Bowl, and the oil bust was another reason to leave the area.

The 3rd contains most of the old 6th District that existed before 2002 redistricting, covering huge swaths of Oklahoma's land in the western and north-central parts of the state, including much of its border with Kansas. In the western areas, more than half of the district's counties lost population in the first half of the 1990s because of the oil market downturn. Locals are striving to diversify beyond agriculture and oil.

Midwestern plains become more evident in the eastern portions of the 3rd, north of Oklahoma City — an area characterized by Bible Belt conservatism.

The three panhandle counties — Cimarron, Texas and Beaver — are perhaps the most heavily Republican-voting in the state: George W. Bush topped 80 percent in each of these counties in the 2000 presidential election, and 2002 GOP gubernatorial nominee Steve Largent surpassed 65 percent in each county. The southern part of the district is home to conservative Democrats whose families relocated from Texas.

MAJOR INDUSTRY

Agriculture, oil

MILITARY BASES

Altus Air Force Base, 2,192 military, 2,492 civilian; Vance Air Force Base, 1,195 military, 193 civilian (2002)

CITIES

Enid, 47,045; Stillwater, 39,065; Ponca City, 25,919; Altus, 21,447; Yukon, 21,043; Sapulpa (pt.), 19,044

NOTABLE

On Nov. 27, 1868, Gen. George A. Custer led an Army contingent in the Battle of Washita, also referred to as the Black Kettle Massacre, in which 103 Indian men, women and children died.

Rep. Tom Cole (R)

Elected 2002; 1st term

Cole is a consummate Republican insider. Before his win in Oklahoma's 4th District, he served as a state senator, Oklahoma's secretary of state, state Republican Party chairman and chief of staff of the Republican National Committee. He also was a successful political consultant who ran numerous high-profile campaigns, including those of Republican J.C. Watts Jr., the man he succeeded in the 4th District.

Cole, whose mother, Helen, served in both the Oklahoma House and Senate, says the local and national connections he built over 20 years give him an edge over some of his less plugged-in freshman colleagues. "I know the Republican leadership very well, and these kinds of things really are invaluable.

His contacts helped him get his top committee pick, Armed Services, which allows him to look out for the interests of Tinker Air Force Base in the 4th District. He also won seats on the Resources and Education committees and appointment to the GOP whip team.

The Oklahoma lawmaker says he is conservative on the "classic issues," including abortion, gun control, the budget and taxes, and he leaves little doubt that he will be a reliable ally for President Bush. "I'd like to make sure the president has the support of this seat," Cole said. "I would be surprised if I were ever really going to be at odds with him."

That does not mean there will not be shades of disagreement: Cole opposed the Bush administration's cancellation of the Army's Crusader cannon, a setback for 4th District defense contractors.

Cole, who traveled the world on two fellowships, has a master's degree from Yale University and a doctorate from the University of Oklahoma, both in British history. He has taught courses at the George Washington University School of Political Management in Washington, D.C.

Cole withstood a tough contest waged by Democratic former state Sen. Darryl Roberts to win his House seat with 54 percent of the vote.

He is the only congressman who is a member of the Chickasaw Nation.

CAPITOL OFFICE
225-6165
tom.cole@mail.house.gov
www.house.gov/cole
501 Cannon 20515-3604; fax 225-3512

COMMITTEES
Armed Services
Education & Workforce
Resources

HOMETOWN
Moore

BORN
April 28, 1949, Shreveport, La.

RELIGION
Methodist

FAMILY
Wife, Ellen Cole; one child

EDUCATION
Grinnell College, B.A. 1971 (history); Yale U., M.A. 1974 (British history); U. of Oklahoma, Ph.D. 1984 (19th Century British history)

CAREER
Political consultant; party official; congressional aide; professor

POLITICAL HIGHLIGHTS
Okla. Republican Party chairman, 1985-89; Okla. Senate, 1989-91; Okla. secretary of state, 1995-99

ELECTION RESULTS

2002 GENERAL		
Tom Cole (R)	106,452	53.8%
Darryl Roberts (D)	91,322	46.2%
2002 PRIMARY		
Tom Cole (R)	21,789	59.7%
Mark Nuttle (R)	11,944	32.7%
Terry Johnson (R)	1,119	3.1%
Tennie Rogers (R)	648	1.8%
Jerry J. Black (R)	600	1.6%
Garlin Newton (R)	426	1.2%

OKLAHOMA 4

South central — Norman, Lawton, part of Oklahoma City

Home to the state's largest university and two military bases, the 4th contains part of Oklahoma City, its southern suburbs and the western edges of "Little Dixie," a part of the state named for its southern influence.

The 4th's once-booming oil economy suffered from the low prices of the 1990s, and a concurrent drought helped decimate the southwest. Still, agriculture remains an essential economic cog. Soybeans, cotton, wheat and peanuts fill many of the district's family farms. Overall, the district's population increased by the close of the 1990s, as the military maintained its ubiquitous presence. The cancellation of the Crusader artillery system was a blow to Fort Sill and the town of Lawton, however, and many worry that Lawton's economy will collapse completely if Fort Sill does not survive the next round of base closures.

The district has epitomized the Oklahoman trend toward voting Republican in national elections. Although once confined in the 4th to presidential elections, this GOP swing now extends to congressional candidates and trickles down to some state legislators. But Democrats remain competitive, especially in the rural, southern parts of the district and around the University of Oklahoma in Norman. Republicans have strength in other parts of Norman. George W. Bush received 61 percent of the 4th District vote in the 2000 presidential election.

MAJOR INDUSTRY
Military, higher education, oil, agriculture

MILITARY BASES
Tinker Air Force Base, 7,265 military, 15,758 civilian; Fort Sill (Army), 8,785 military, 5,011 civilian (2002)

CITIES
Norman, 95,694; Lawton, 92,757; Oklahoma City (pt.), 70,896; Midwest City (pt.), 45,044; Moore, 41,138

NOTABLE
Apache warrior Geronimo was imprisoned at the Fort Sill Military Reservation.

Rep. Ernest Istook (R)

CAPITOL OFFICE
225-2132
istook@mail.house.gov
www.house.gov/istook
2404 Rayburn 20515-3605; fax 226-1463

COMMITTEES
Appropriations
(Transportation & Treasury - chairman)
Select Homeland Security

HOMETOWN
Warr Acres

BORN
Feb. 11, 1950, Fort Worth, Texas

RELIGION
Mormon

FAMILY
Wife, Judy Lee Istook; five children

EDUCATION
Baylor U., B.A. 1971 (journalism); Oklahoma City U., J.D. 1976

CAREER
Lawyer; gubernatorial aide; journalist

POLITICAL HIGHLIGHTS
Warr Acres City Council, 1983-87; Okla. House, 1987-93

ELECTION RESULTS

2002 GENERAL		
Ernest Istook (R)	121,374	62.2%
Lou Barlow (D)	63,208	32.4%
Donna Davis (I)	10,469	5.4%
2002 PRIMARY		
Ernest Istook (R)		unopposed
2000 GENERAL		
Ernest Istook (R)	134,159	68.4%
Garland McWatters (D)	53,275	27.2%
Bill Maguire (I)	5,930	3.0%
Robert T. Murphy (LIBERT)	2,658	1.4%

PREVIOUS WINNING PERCENTAGES
1998 (68%); 1996 (70%); 1994 (78%); 1992 (53%)

Elected 1992; 6th term

Istook is not like most members of Congress. Instead of guarding his words, the former radio reporter freely shares his views on everything from the most contentious social policy debates of the day to the minutiae of the legislation he is managing. And he has been known to oppose parochial federal spending initiatives, even though he is a proud member of the pet-project-friendly Appropriations Committee.

Such a penchant for going against the grain would make Istook a recurrent problem for the Republican leadership were he not such a stalwart conservative. He is an ally of the Christian right and helped found the Conservative Action Team, now called the Republican Study Committee. In March 2003, he attended the Supreme Court's oral arguments on the constitutionality of a law he sponsored in 2000 requiring schools and libraries that receive federal funds to use filters on their computers to block access to Internet pornography. Failure to uphold his law, Istook said, would mean "our libraries will become nothing more than glorified government-funded adult bookstores."

While civil liberties groups opposed that law, it was not as disturbing to them as several other Istook proposals — including a constitutional amendment to permit school prayer and efforts to bar groups that receive federal funding from lobbying Congress, even if they do so with private funds.

One of the 13 Appropriations "cardinals," or subcommittee chairmen, Istook has considerable power to shape federal spending. In the 108th Congress he chairs a new Transportation and Treasury Subcommittee, with jurisdiction over all the non-homeland security programs previously assigned to a Transportation panel and a committee called Treasury-Postal Service, which Istook chaired in the 107th Congress.

The creation of a new Homeland Security Appropriations Subcommittee took away much of Istook's previous spending authority; as a consolation, he was assigned to the new House committee that will oversee the infancy of the federal Homeland Security Department. And his Appropriations panel will retain control over the budget for the operations of the White House, affording Istook some leverage in disagreements with the Bush administration — after Tom Ridge refused to testify before Congress in 2002 about homeland security spending, Istook dropped his support for the White House's bid to have its internal budgetary decisions largely exempted from congressional scrutiny.

With the president's backing, Istook pushed to enactment in the 107th Congress a ban on federal employee medical insurance coverage of almost all abortions, but his efforts to restrict the coverage of contraception came up short. Istook also sought to win more federal funding for abstinence education programs; his proposal was rejected by the House.

As chairman of the District of Columbia Subcommittee in the 106th Congress, Istook used his power to block city ordinances he did not like, including publicly funded abortions and needle-exchange programs. Istook irked some colleagues along the way, but he later made amends by leaving the city's budget — which appropriators must bless — largely intact and softening some of his social positions. "Here is an example of a right-wing ideologue maturing to the point where he should rightfully be considered a serious legislator," James P. Moran, the top Democrat on Istook's subcommittee, told The Washington Post.

Istook sponsored a bill to authorize states to band together to establish a uniform, streamlined tax system for Internet sales. While many Republicans in Washington found the idea anathema to their low-tax ideals, Istook said the federal government should not dictate how states tax commerce.

Although Istook is a reliable fiscal, as well as social, conservative, he does try to look out for Oklahoma's interests. In the 107th, he fought in vain against Bush's decision to stop Army purchases of the Crusader mobile cannon, which had been assembled in Oklahoma. And he stood up for his state when, in the 2002 election law overhaul, new grants were created for buying modernized voting equipment. Istook argued that states such as Oklahoma, which recently had upgraded their machinery, should not be penalized. As a result, the wrapup spending law of early 2003 included $8 million to cover expenses Oklahoma had incurred more than a decade before.

For the most part, however, Istook has been less likely than most members to pursue spending to be sent back home. While he did secure funds to help rebuild the area of Oklahoma City surrounding the federal building destroyed in the 1995 bombing, he wanted the money spent in that part of town, not more widely, so he added language to that effect. He also has opposed federal funding for a trolley system in Oklahoma City, much to the consternation of some city leaders.

Istook's stands have limited his popularity in the state's largest city, and for a time it looked as though he might be in danger of losing his reliable Republican base of support when the Oklahoma Legislature redrew congressional lines for this decade and did away with one House seat, as post-census reapportionment required. But while the 5th District did gain some Democratic areas, Istook won in 2002 with 62 percent of the vote.

Istook's political instincts were stoked when, after graduating from Baylor University, he began to cover the Oklahoma capitol as a radio reporter. At the same time, he attended law school classes at night. After receiving his law degree, he worked as an aide to Democratic Gov. David L. Boren and then went into private practice. He won a city council seat in the Oklahoma City suburb of Warr Acres in 1982, and four years later he won a seat in the state House, where he rose to assistant minority leader.

To get to Congress in 1992, Istook had to get by two better-known Republicans: eight-term Rep. Mickey Edwards and former U.S. Attorney Bill Price. Edwards was tarred in the scandal surrounding a private bank then maintained for House members and did not make the primary runoff, which Istook won by 12 percentage points. He took 53 percent in the general election and has not faced a serious challenge since.

KEY VOTES

2002

- No Overhaul campaign finance law; ban "soft money" and restrict advocacy advertising
- Yes Back Bush's defense budget increase
- Yes Extend 1996 welfare law
- Yes Adopt Bush's discretionary spending limit
- No Pass GOP Medicare prescription drug plan
- No Create independent Sept. 11 commission
- No Extend union protections to Homeland Security Department employees
- Yes Revive fast-track procedures for trade agreements
- Yes Authorize war against Iraq
- No Advance bankruptcy overhaul opposed by abortion opponents

2001

- Yes Nullify Clinton Labor Department ergonomics rule
- Yes Cut taxes by $1.35 trillion through fiscal 2011
- No Maintain ban on oil drilling in Arctic National Wildlife Refuge
- Yes Approve Bush proposal to limit managed-care plan liability for coverage decisions
- No Divert money from crop subsidy payments to land conservation
- Yes Expand law enforcement power to investigate suspected terrorists

CQ VOTE STUDIES

	PARTY UNITY		PRESIDENTIAL SUPPORT	
	Support	Oppose	Support	Oppose
2002	94%	6%	85%	15%
2001	95%	5%	95%	5%
2000	93%	7%	25%	75%
1999	96%	4%	19%	81%
1998	96%	4%	17%	83%

INTEREST GROUPS

	AFL-CIO	ADA	CCUS	ACU
2002	11%	5%	90%	92%
2001	8%	0%	91%	100%
2000	10%	5%	73%	90%
1999	0%	0%	83%	92%
1998	0%	0%	94%	95%

OKLAHOMA 5

Most of Oklahoma City; Pottawatomie and Seminole counties

The 5th contains all of downtown Oklahoma City, which underwent many changes in the 1980s and 1990s. The early-1980s boom swelled the population, but the economic torpor that gripped the area at decade's end forced corporations to scale back, and the population declined in some areas.

By the early 1990s, Oklahoma City's economy diversified by necessity. While oil and gas still compose a large chunk of the economy along with some agriculture, energy corporations have had to expand their businesses to plastics and other industries. Telecommunications companies took hold in the district, though the recent economic downturn has caused some corporate layoffs. Lucent Technologies was once Oklahoma City's largest employer, but the ailing company sold its plant to an electronics company in 2001.

Oklahoma City is indelibly linked to the 1995 bombing at the Alfred P. Murrah Federal Building that killed 168 people. A memorial and the Institute for the Prevention of Terrorism commemorate the site.

The 5th contains the towns of Shawnee and Seminole, both home to large American Indian populations. Though Tinker Air Force Base is in the 4th, many who work there live in the 5th. The district is also home to several colleges and universities in Oklahoma City.

Republicans have dominated federal elections in the 5th. The addition of Shawnee, Seminole County and the largely black northeastern portion of Oklahoma City in redistricting following the 2000 census made the district more Democratic, but not enough to threaten the GOP hold. George W. Bush took 62 percent of the vote here in the 2000 presidential election.

MAJOR INDUSTRY

Oil, computer hardware, state government, education

CITIES

Oklahoma City (pt.), 420,387; Edmond, 68,315; Shawnee, 28,692

NOTABLE

Seminole County is the historic Seminole Nation territory, accepted by the tribes in exchange for their departure from the Florida Territory; The shopping cart and parking meter were invented in Oklahoma City.

OREGON

Gov. Theodore R. Kulongoski (D)

First elected: 2002
Length of term: 4 years
Term expires: 1/07
Salary: $93,600
Phone: (503) 378-3111
Hometown: Portland
Born: Nov. 5, 1940; Missouri
Religion: Roman Catholic
Family: Wife, Mary Oberst; three children
Education: U. of Missouri, B.A. 1967 (political science & public administration), J.D. 1970
Military Service: Marine Corps, 1960-63
Career: Lawyer
Political highlights: Ore. House, 1975-79; Ore. Senate, 1979-81; Democratic nominee for U.S. Senate, 1980; Democratic nominee for governor, 1982; Ore. insurance commissioner, 1987-91; Ore. attorney general, 1993-97; Ore. Supreme Court, 1997-2001
Election results:

2002 GENERAL		
Theodore R. Kulongoski (D)	618,004	49.0%
Kevin L. Mannix (R)	581,785	46.2%
Tom Cox (LIBERT)	57,760	4.6%

Secretary of State Bill Bradbury (D)

(no lieutenant governor)
First elected: Appointed 1999; elected 2000
Length of term: 4 years
Term expires: 1/05
Salary: $72,000
Phone: (503) 986-1523

STATE LEGISLATURE

General Assembly: Meets January-June in odd-numbered years
House: 60 members, 2-year terms
2003 breakdown: 35R, 25D; 40 men, 20 women
Salary: $1,283/month; $85/day in session
Phone: (503) 986-1187
Senate: 30 members, 4-year terms
2003 breakdown: 15R, 15D; 22 men, 8 women
Salary: $1,283/month; $85/day in session
Phone: (503) 986-1187

STATE TERM LIMITS

Governor: 2 terms
Senate: No
House: No

URBAN STATISTICS

CITY	POPULATION
Portland	529,121
Eugene	137,893
Salem	136,924
Gresham	90,205

REGISTERED VOTERS

Democrat	39%
Republican	36%
Non-affiliated	21%

POPULATION

2002 population (est.)	3,521,515
2000 population	3,421,399
1990 population	2,842,321
Percent change (1990-2000)	+20.4
Rank among states (2002)	27
Median age	36.3
Born in state	45.3%
Foreign born	8.5%
Violent crime rate	351/100,000
Poverty level	11.6%
Federal workers	29,090
Military	12,984

REDISTRICTING

Oregon retained its five House seats in reapportionment. Democratic Gov. John Kitzhaber vetoed the state legislature's plan and a county judge implemented a new map on Oct. 19, 2001.

MISCELLANEOUS

Web: www.state.or.us
Capital: Salem

STATE ELECTION OFFICIAL
(503) 986-1518

DEMOCRATIC HEADQUARTERS
(503) 224-8200

REPUBLICAN HEADQUARTERS
(503) 587-9233

District Statistics

DIST.	2000 VOTE FOR PRESIDENT BUSH	GORE	NADER	WHITE	BLACK	ASIAN	HISP	MEDIAN INCOME	WHITE COLLAR	BLUE COLLAR	SERVICE INDUSTRY	OVER 64	UNDER 18	COLLEGE EDUCATION	RURAL	SQ. MILES
1	45%	51%	5%	81%	1%	5%	9%	$48,464	65%	22%	13%	10%	25%	33%	13%	2,941
2	61	35	4	86	0	1	9	$35,600	54	29	17	15	26	19	36	69,491
3	33	62	5	77	5	5	8	$42,063	59	25	16	11	24	25	7	1,021
4	49	45	6	90	1	2	4	$35,796	55	28	17	15	23	21	31	17,181
5	49	47	5	84	1	2	10	$44,409	61	25	15	13	26	27	20	5,362
STATE	46.5	47	5	84	2	3	8	$40,916	59	26	15	13	25	25	21	95,997
U.S.	47.9	48.4	3	69	12	4	13	$41,994	60	25	15	12	26	24	21	3,537,438

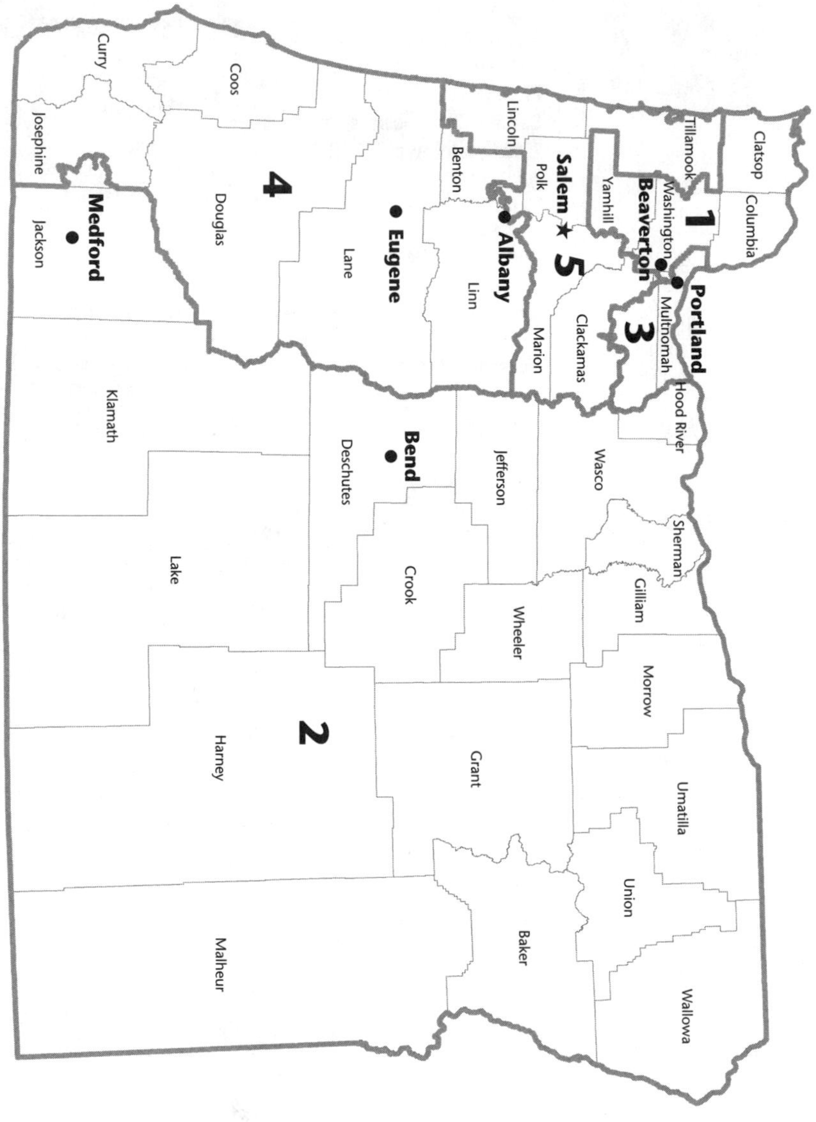
Curry
Coos
Josephine
Jackson
Medford
Douglas
4
Lane
Eugene
Lincoln
Benton
Albany
Linn
Polk
Salem
5
Marion
Yamhill
Clackamas
Tillamook
Washington
Beaverton
1
Clatsop
Columbia
Portland
Multnomah
3
Hood River
Klamath
Deschutes
Bend
Jefferson
Wasco
Sherman
Lake
Crook
Gilliam
Wheeler
Morrow
2
Harney
Grant
Umatilla
Union
Baker
Malheur
Wallowa

Sen. Ron Wyden (D)

CAPITOL OFFICE
224-5244
wyden.senate.gov
516 Hart 20510-3703; fax 228-2717

COMMITTEES
Budget
Commerce, Science & Transportation
Energy & Natural Resources
Environment & Public Works
Select Intelligence
Special Aging

HOMETOWN
Portland

BORN
May 3, 1949, Wichita, Kan.

RELIGION
Jewish

FAMILY
Divorced; two children

EDUCATION
U. of California, Santa Barbara, attended 1967-69; Stanford U., A.B. 1971 (political science); U. of Oregon, J.D. 1974

CAREER
Senior citizen advocacy group state director; lawyer; professor

POLITICAL HIGHLIGHTS
U.S. House, 1981-96

ELECTION RESULTS

1998 GENERAL		
Ron Wyden (D)	682,425	61.1%
John Lim (R)	377,739	33.8%
Karyn Moskowitz (PACIFIC)	22,024	2.0%
Jim Brewster (LIBERT)	18,221	1.6%
1998 PRIMARY		
Ron Wyden (D)	283,654	91.8%
John Sweeney (D)	25,456	8.2%

PREVIOUS WINNING PERCENTAGES
1996 Special Election (48%); 1994 House Election (73%); 1992 House Election (77%); 1990 House Election (81%); 1988 House Election (99%); 1986 House Election (86%); 1984 House Election (72%); 1982 House Election (78%); 1980 House Election (72%)

Elected January 1996; 1st full term

Gangly and rumpled, Wyden hardly cuts the typical figure of a senator. But as he moves toward the end of his first full term, he has established a reputation as a shrewd dealmaker, negotiating skillfully across the aisle to advance education and health programs, and becoming one of the Senate's leading voices on technology issues.

While maintaining the interest in health care, energy and consumer issues that characterized his 15 years in the House, Wyden has been particularly prominent in the Senate in pursuing two major initiatives: updating laws written in the Industrial Age for an economy increasingly dominated by information technology, and trying to protect his state's unique approach to social and political issues.

Wyden acknowledges that his own computer skills are mostly limited to surfing the Internet and playing video games with his children. Nevertheless, he is widely viewed as one of the most tech-savvy members of Congress, in large part because of his work on the Commerce Committee, where he chaired the Science, Technology and Space Subcommittee in the 107th.

Accustomed to pursuing alliances with Republicans on politically charged issues such as health care and taxes, Wyden is particularly open to working with GOP colleagues on technology. "If ever there were issues that are truly bipartisan," he says, "technology really illustrates the point." For example, he has worked closely over the years with Republican Rep. Christopher Cox of California to preserve a moratorium on taxation of Internet transactions.

Despite the concerns of state and local officials, who see their vital sales tax revenues endangered by effectively tax-free online purchases, Wyden argues that requiring Internet businesses to submit to a crazy-quilt of separate tax systems would be fatal to the growth of e-commerce. How would you handle the taxes, he asks, when a consumer in Oregon uses Virginia-based America Online to order perfume from France and ship it to a friend in Canada? On the issue, Wyden lined up with high-tech companies, still a major economic engine of the Pacific Northwest.

In other technology debates, he has sought a middle ground, looking out for the interests of regional giants such as Microsoft Corp. while also recognizing the concerns of consumers.

That centrist approach sometimes wins Wyden more enemies than friends. In 2002, he and Montana Republican Conrad Burns backed an "anti-spam" bill in the Senate designed to curb the flood of unsolicited commercial messages filling consumers' e-mail boxes. But their proposal also included the opt-out approach, angering privacy groups, which favored allowing marketers to send electronic messages only to those who had requested them. In one stroke, the measure's sponsors alienated powerful forces on both sides of the issue.

Wyden also was a central figure in the Senate's overwhelming rejection, early in 2003, of a plan, sought by the Pentagon, that would permit domestic collection — through monitoring of computer activity — of a wide array of personal data on individuals, with the aim of finding terrorists.

In the eyes of many of his constituents, though, one of Wyden's most notable achievements has been his vigorous defense of Oregon's physician-assisted suicide law. He faced an uphill fight in the 106th Congress after House conservatives easily passed a bill prohibiting doctors from prescribing drugs designed to cause a patient's death, and many senators, including

Republican Majority Whip Don Nickles, signaled their support for the measure. But Wyden waged a furious battle to run out the legislative clock in 2000, threatening to filibuster the bill, enlisting the support of influential groups such as the American Cancer Society and combing through other pieces of legislation to ensure that Nickles did not slip the House plan into them.

In the 107th Congress, Wyden fought aggressively to protect Oregon's mail-ballot system from changes under the law overhauling voting procedures that was enacted at the end of 2002. But he is willing to challenge his state when he sees it straying too far from the mainstream, as with a court ruling that effectively banned federal undercover operations in the state. The policy, later dropped, was "an engraved invitation to terrorists and criminals to set up shop in Oregon," Wyden said.

On health care and other issues, Wyden more easily fits the conventional mold of a liberal Democrat. He was a vocal advocate of expanding Medicare to cover prescription drug costs for seniors before that issue became a focus of maneuvering in the 107th, and he has been a longtime critic of managed care.

He also is an outspoken foe of the tobacco industry, a position that garnered television time in 1994 when Wyden, then a senior member of the House Energy and Commerce Committee, asked a panel of tobacco executive witnesses whether they considered tobacco addictive — an assertion they all denied under oath. He repeated the question in 1998 during Senate Commerce hearings, and four of the five CEOs recanted. Wyden was quick to point out the irony.

The Oregon lawmaker's crusades also have included persistent criticism of Senate traditions he finds stifling or unfair. Early in 1999, he was successful in his long campaign to end the secrecy of an informal Senate procedure in which any senator could hold up action on a measure anonymously, without stating the reason. That rule proved ineffective in practice, however, and within two years, he and his ally in the cause, Republican Charles E. Grassley of Iowa, were proposing a new rule requiring those imposing such "holds" to enter their objections in the Congressional Record.

Wyden has forged an unusually close working relationship with Oregon's junior senator, Republican Gordon H. Smith. Smith was his opponent in what was an especially bitter 1996 Senate contest. "We just decided that out of this crucible we had learned a lot about each other," Wyden said. "If anything, we respected each other more for what we had been through." But that friendship put Wyden in a difficult position in the 2002 election, when Democrats mounted a strong challenge to Smith. Wyden made clear he was happy to campaign for the Democratic candidate, Bill Bradbury, but would not say anything negative about Smith.

Wyden was Oregon executive director for the Gray Panthers, an organization promoting senior citizens' interests, when he first ran for the House in 1980. He ousted Democratic Rep. Robert Duncan in the primary and won with 72 percent in November in a Democratic Portland-based district. His victory margin never fell lower in seven subsequent re-elections.

When GOP Sen. Bob Packwood resigned in 1995 rather than face expulsion for personal misconduct, Wyden jumped into the special-election race. Despite some stumbles — most notably on a televised quiz show in which he failed to quote the price of common grocery items — he edged fellow Democratic Rep. Peter A. DeFazio in the primary.

In the general election, Wyden refused to trade in his wrinkled sweaters for natty suits on the campaign trail, despite the urging of his staff. But he narrowly defeated Smith by portraying himself as a reasonable-minded alternative to the conservative state Senate president on such issues as education, the environment, revamping Medicare, and balancing the budget.

KEY VOTES

2002

- Yes Pass farm bill reversing crop subsidy limits
- No Postpone tougher automobile fuel efficiency standards
- Yes Overhaul campaign finance law; ban "soft money" and restrict advocacy advertising
- Yes Set federal election standards
- No Support oil drilling in Arctic National Wildlife Refuge
- Yes Revive fast-track procedures for trade agreements
- Yes Create federal insurance coverage for catastrophic terrorist losses
- Yes Tighten federal accounting and corporate governance regulation
- Yes Advance bipartisan Medicare prescription drug plan
- Yes Create independent Sept. 11 commission
- Yes Back Democratic Homeland Security Department proposal
- No Authorize war against Iraq

2001

- No Confirm John Ashcroft as attorney general
- No Nullify Clinton Labor Department ergonomics rule
- No Cut taxes by $1.35 trillion through fiscal 2011
- Yes Pass Democratic bill to bolster rights of patients in managed-care plans
- Yes Permit a new round of military base closings
- Yes Expand law enforcement power to investigate suspected terrorists

CQ VOTE STUDIES

	PARTY UNITY		PRESIDENTIAL SUPPORT	
	Support	Oppose	Support	Oppose
2002	87%	13%	74%	26%
2001	90%	10%	64%	36%
2000	97%	3%	95%	5%
1999	91%	9%	91%	9%
1998	88%	12%	85%	15%
1997	83%	17%	86%	14%
1996	92%	8%	95%	5%
House Service:				
1995	90%	10%	83%	17%
1994	96%	4%	81%	19%
1993	96%	4%	78%	22%

INTEREST GROUPS

	AFL-CIO	ADA	CCUS	ACU
2002	85%	85%	60%	15%
2001	100%	95%	43%	8%
2000	63%	90%	60%	8%
1999	78%	100%	59%	4%
1998	75%	100%	56%	4%
1997	71%	80%	70%	8%
1996	86%	95%	38%	15%
House Service:				
1995	100%	90%	29%	12%
1994	78%	80%	58%	0%
1993	92%	95%	18%	4%

Sen. Gordon H. Smith (R)

CAPITOL OFFICE
224-3753
gsmith.senate.gov
404 Russell 20510-3704; fax 228-3997

COMMITTEES
Commerce, Science & Transportation
(Competition, Foreign Commerce & Infrastructure - chairman)
Energy & Natural Resources
Finance
(Long-Term Growth & Debt Reduction - chairman)
Indian Affairs
Rules & Administration
Special Aging
Joint Printing

HOMETOWN
Pendleton

BORN
May 25, 1952, Pendleton, Ore.

RELIGION
Mormon

FAMILY
Wife, Sharon Smith; three children

EDUCATION
Brigham Young U., B.A. 1976 (history); Southwestern U., J.D. 1979

CAREER
Frozen food company owner; lawyer

POLITICAL HIGHLIGHTS
Ore. Senate, 1993-97 (president, 1995-97); Republican nominee for U.S. Senate, 1996 (special election)

ELECTION RESULTS

2002 GENERAL		
Gordon H. Smith (R)	712,287	56.2%
Bill Bradbury (D)	501,898	39.6%
Dan Fitzgerald (LIBERT)	29,979	2.4%
Lon Mabon (CNSTP)	21,703	1.7%
2002 PRIMARY		
Gordon H. Smith (R)	306,504	98.9%
write-ins	3,439	1.1%

PREVIOUS WINNING PERCENTAGES
1996 (50%)

Elected 1996; 2nd term

A personally conservative man who represents a state with liberal leanings, Smith works hard to find compromises in the middle, and is sometimes willing to break from the Republican fold along the way.

A former Mormon bishop, he acknowledges that he has strong moral opinions about such socially charged matters as abortion and homosexuality. But he takes care not to inject his personal beliefs into the political arena. "If you want to talk to me about sin, go with me to church," he told the Portland Oregonian. "If you want to talk about public policy, then go with me to the U.S. Senate."

In fact, Smith sometimes seems to go out of his way to promote positions that social conservatives find objectionable. Campaigning for his second term in 2002, he launched a television advertisement touting his support for gay issues, particularly legislation he co-wrote with Democrat Edward M. Kennedy of Massachusetts that would make attacks on homosexuals motivated by their sexual preference a federal crime. That won him the endorsement of the Human Rights Campaign, the national gay rights group, which rarely supports Republicans and is a potent political force in Oregon.

Smith also was a leading backer of stem cell research, which is opposed by anti-abortion groups. He cited personal reasons for his position, saying such research might be helpful in ending his family's history of Parkinson's disease."Everyone will pass away — I know that," Smith said. "But there are some ways that are just beyond hideousness, and this is one."

Smith also has taken a moderate course on health care issues. He pushed to devote budget resources to extend health insurance to the uninsured and co-wrote a bipartisan Senate prescription drug plan with Democrat Bob Graham of Florida; the proposal garnered 49 supporters on the Senate floor during a test vote in which 60 were required.

His stances have made Smith difficult to categorize politically. He earns top marks from business groups and casts frugal votes on fiscal matters. But he reaches across the aisle to forge alliances with Democrats on such divisive issues as gun control and oil drilling in Alaska, and he has worked to bolster funding for education. He made national headlines in 1999 when he led a successful uprising against GOP leaders who attempted to block gun control legislation. Three years later, he was among the first GOP senators to call for Trent Lott to step down as majority leader at the end of 2002 after making seemingly racist remarks.

In many respects, he seeks to emulate the political independence of the Republican he replaced: Mark O. Hatfield, a senator for 30 years. Smith had been interested in following Hatfield onto the Appropriations Committee, which Hatfield had chaired; but he grabbed the opportunity at the beginning of the 108th Congress to take a seat instead on the Finance Committee, where he will be able to pursue his interest in health care matters and taxes — subjects he has focused on since his days in the state Senate. To take the Finance assignment, Smith had to give up a seat on Foreign Relations. He also traded a spot on the Budget panel for new assignments on the Rules and Aging committees.

Personable, telegenic and noted for his eye-catching double-breasted suits that stand out from the traditional Senate garb, Smith is a self-made millionaire who transformed his family's unprofitable frozen vegetable processing company into one of the largest frozen vegetable packers in the country. He calls himself "the biggest pea-picker in American politics" and is a proud member of the Frozen Food Industry Hall of Fame.

He may be one of the most politically resilient members of the Senate. Even though he lost a grueling race for one Oregon Senate seat to Democrat Ron Wyden in January 1996, Smith bounced back immediately to run for a second, tightly contested open seat, winning the race that November. His office proclaims proudly that Smith is the first person ever to run for two Senate seats in the same year.

Now that the bitterness of their 1996 contest has passed, Smith has an especially good working relationship with Wyden. The two crisscrossed Oregon together after the 1999 impeachment trial of President Clinton — Wyden voted to acquit, Smith to convict — to give their constituents a real-life demonstration of bipartisanship. "Our natures are to find solutions, not just confrontations," Smith said. "He simply starts from the left. I start from the right."

But Smith found himself at odds with Wyden and others in the Oregon delegation when the state's physician-assisted suicide law came under fire in the 106th Congress. Torn between representing the will of his constituents, who had voted for the law, and his own belief that human life should not be cut short, Smith announced in 2000 that he would back a bill forbidding doctors to deliberately cause a patient's death. "I admit to having wrestled for a different conclusion on this issue in order that I might once again take comfort in the crowd," an emotional Smith told the Judiciary Committee. "But on a matter of this magnitude — a matter of life and death — I have failed to find comfort with a troubled conscience."

Despite his willingness to seek bipartisan solutions, Smith has proved a loyal Republican when GOP leaders need his support, such as when he switched his vote in 1998 to back an amendment capping fees that attorneys may collect from tobacco litigation; the switch provided the Republicans' margin of victory. Smith also sides with conservatives on some environmental issues. He opposes a plan to breach four dams on the Snake River in order to restore populations of endangered salmon.

Smith is a strong supporter of Israel and co-wrote a Senate-adopted resolution with Joseph I. Lieberman of Connecticut demanding that the Palestinian Authority "dismantle the terrorist infrastructure in the Palestinian areas." As chairman of the Foreign Relations panel's European Affairs Subcommittee in the 106th Congress, Smith supported the U.S. military intervention in early 1999 in Kosovo. He won approval of legislation in the 105th Congress that required congressional action before Clinton could lift economic sanctions against Serbia. He has also been a strong supporter of a large expansion of the NATO alliance.

Smith entered politics in 1992, winning a seat in the state Senate and ascending to the position of Senate president in just two years. His loss to Wyden was in the special election to replace Republican Bob Packwood, whose personal and financial transgressions forced his resignation. Wyden, a veteran House Democrat, attacked Smith for receiving support from groups opposed to abortion and gay rights, for environmental violations at his food processing plant and for his lavish personal spending.

When Hatfield announced his retirement, Smith initially said he would not run again. But national Republicans urged him into the fray. Easily winning the GOP nomination, he eked out a slim 4-point victory over Democratic businessman Tom Bruggere.

Two potentially strong Democratic contenders — Gov. John A. Kitzhaber and Rep. Peter A. DeFazio — opted out of the 2002 race and Smith defeated Oregon Secretary of State Bill Bradbury with 56 percent.

KEY VOTES

2002

No Pass farm bill reversing crop subsidy limits
No Postpone tougher automobile fuel efficiency standards
No Overhaul campaign finance law; ban "soft money" and restrict advocacy advertising
Yes Set federal election standards
No Support oil drilling in Arctic National Wildlife Refuge
Yes Revive fast-track procedures for trade agreements
Yes Create federal insurance coverage for catastrophic terrorist losses
Yes Tighten federal accounting and corporate governance regulation
Yes Advance bipartisan Medicare prescription drug plan
Yes Create independent Sept. 11 commission
No Back Democratic Homeland Security Department proposal
Yes Authorize war against Iraq

2001

Yes Confirm John Ashcroft as attorney general
Yes Nullify Clinton Labor Department ergonomics rule
Yes Cut taxes by $1.35 trillion through fiscal 2011
Yes Pass Democratic bill to bolster rights of patients in managed-care plans
Yes Permit a new round of military base closings
Yes Expand law enforcement power to investigate suspected terrorists

CQ VOTE STUDIES

	PARTY UNITY		PRESIDENTIAL SUPPORT	
	Support	Oppose	Support	Oppose
2002	66%	34%	91%	9%
2001	82%	18%	93%	7%
2000	89%	11%	62%	38%
1999	86%	14%	43%	57%
1998	85%	15%	55%	45%
1997	83%	17%	65%	35%

INTEREST GROUPS

	AFL-CIO	ADA	CCUS	ACU
2002	38%	35%	85%	75%
2001	44%	25%	79%	80%
2000	0%	10%	100%	84%
1999	11%	15%	94%	76%
1998	0%	5%	94%	72%
1997	0%	25%	100%	72%

Rep. David Wu (D)

CAPITOL OFFICE
225-0855
www.house.gov/wu
1023 Longworth 20515-3701; fax 225-9497

COMMITTEES
Education & Workforce
Science

HOMETOWN
Portland

BORN
April 8, 1955, Taiwan

RELIGION
Presbyterian

FAMILY
Wife, Michelle Wu; two children

EDUCATION
Stanford U., B.S. 1977; Harvard Medical School, attended 1978; Yale U., J.D. 1982

CAREER
Lawyer

POLITICAL HIGHLIGHTS
No previous office

ELECTION RESULTS

2002 GENERAL		
David Wu (D)	149,215	62.7%
Jim Greenfield (R)	80,917	34.0%
Beth King (LIBERT)	7,639	3.2%
2002 PRIMARY		
David Wu (D)		unopposed
2000 GENERAL		
David Wu (D)	176,902	58.3%
Charles Starr (R)	115,303	38.0%
Beth King (LIBERT)	10,858	3.6%

PREVIOUS WINNING PERCENTAGES
1998 (50%)

Elected 1998; 3rd term

Now in his third term, Wu has settled into a comfortable stride. He is not an attention-getter, but he comes forward with solid legislative ideas and will occasionally carry the torch on a high-profile Democratic initiative, such as President Clinton's program to put 100,000 new teachers in the classrooms. Every once in a while, he will vote against his fellow Democrats — supporting a repeal of the tax code's "marriage penalty" in 2000 and a Republican welfare bill in 2002, for example — but he generally votes the Democratic line in the increasingly partisan House.

His defining moment in Congress, which still lingers in the memory of many of his constituents, came during his second year in office. As a freshman, Wu faced what may have been the most difficult policy decision of his career and, despite angering many powerful forces in his district, he emerged politically stronger.

Born in Taiwan and the first person of full Chinese ancestry to serve in the House, Wu had said during his 1998 campaign that, unless human rights abuses abated in China, he would vote against permanently granting that nation the same low tariff rates as most other nations. When Clinton submitted a permanent normal trade relations bill to the House in 2000, many doubted Wu would stick to that position. After all, he had been elected by just 7,000 votes to represent part of Oregon's "Silicon Forest," which is heavily dependent on the success of Pacific Rim trade, and he had been the partner of a law firm that represented high-technology businesses on issues including trade. In addition, many of the ethnic Chinese who hailed his victory as a great advance for Asian-Americans wanted to see their homeland move back into the world trading system.

Though Wu was pushed hard, he stuck by his campaign promise. Not only did he vote against the legislation, but he also helped the measure's opponents round up votes in an ultimately unsuccessful bid to defeat it.

Wu's decision so angered the computer-chip behemoth Intel Corp. and the athletic shoe giant Nike Inc. that both gave money to his 2000 opponent, Republican state Sen. Charles Starr. So did some Chinese-American activists. Anticipating such difficulties, however, Wu had maintained a sizable campaign war chest and added to it with increased contributions from labor unions and others who saw a kindred spirit.

Wu outspent Starr, launched a drive to register new Asian-American voters and won re-election by 20 percentage points. In 2002, his constituency minimally altered by redistricting, Wu cruised to a third term over conservative radio talk show host Jim Greenfield.

In the 107th Congress, Wu voted against another trade measure — one that gives the president fast-track authority to negotiate trade agreements that Congress must accept or reject, but cannot amend.

Much of Wu's focus in the House has been on education policy. A member of the Education and the Workforce Committee and the husband of a former Head Start teacher, he took the lead in 2001 in an unsuccessful effort to continue the Clinton program to place 100,000 teachers in the schools. The program, which had been running for three years, was supposed to take seven years to complete. But Republicans always had opposed it, arguing it was an inappropriate role for the federal government. Wu's effort to authorize a fourth year of funding was voted down when the Education panel took up the bill that ultimately became the 2002 education law.

Although Wu has hewed to the party line on most issues, he is a member of the group of pro-business centrists known as the New Democrat Coalition. He practiced this philosophy when he was among just 14 Democrats voting in 2002 for a Republican bill to extend the 1996 welfare law. His main concern was to make sure Oregon could continue its federal waiver to run a different welfare program.

Although Wu served as the chairman of the Congressional Asian Pacific Caucus in the 107th Congress, he strives to be known as more than the only Chinese member of the House. In 2001, however, he drew sympathy over his treatment by a security guard at the Department of Energy. Wu was detained for 15 minutes along with an Asian-American colleague, even after he displayed his congressional identification.

His handling of the China issue and his strong academic credentials — he attended Harvard Medical School and graduated from Yale Law School — suggest Wu may have what it takes to move up the ladder in Congress. But his initial efforts have not borne fruit. He has been unsuccessful in getting an assignment to either the Appropriations or Energy and Commerce panel.

Wu arrived in the United States with his mother and sisters in 1961, when he was 7 years old. The family joined Wu's father, who had come to this country to study when Wu was four months old.

Addressing the 2000 Democratic National Convention, Wu said he had become involved in public life because of the difference that government decisions had made in his own future. He said his family had been able to move to the United States because President Kennedy had expanded quotas that had been used to limit Chinese immigrants. "Public decisions make a difference," he said. "Elections change the course of nations."

In another homage to his adopted homeland, Wu has made a habit of naming those in his household after famous Americans. His son, born on the Fourth of July 1997, is Matthew Jefferson Adams Wu. Family pets have included dogs Sam Rayburn and Teddy Roosevelt and a cat, Lyndon Johnson.

Wu has a musical streak: At a benefit concert at the Hard Rock Cafe a mile from the Capitol, he played violin in a rock and country band with nine other House members to raise relief funds for the victims of the Sept. 11, 2001, attacks on the Pentagon and World Trade Center.

Wu had never held public office when Democrat Elizabeth Furse's retirement opened up a House seat in 1998. He was well-known in the Portland legal and business community and was able to edge past Washington County Commission Chairman Linda Peters in the Democratic primary. In the general election, the district's Democratic leanings lifted Wu to a 3 percentage point victory over public relations consultant Molly Bordonaro.

KEY VOTES

2002

Yes Overhaul campaign finance law; ban "soft money" and restrict advocacy advertising
No Back Bush's defense budget increase
Yes Extend 1996 welfare law
No Adopt Bush's discretionary spending limit
No Pass GOP Medicare prescription drug plan
Yes Create independent Sept. 11 commission
Yes Extend union protections to Homeland Security Department employees
No Revive fast-track procedures for trade agreements
No Authorize war against Iraq
Yes Advance bankruptcy overhaul opposed by abortion opponents

2001

No Nullify Clinton Labor Department ergonomics rule
No Cut taxes by $1.35 trillion through fiscal 2011
Yes Maintain ban on oil drilling in Arctic National Wildlife Refuge
No Approve Bush proposal to limit managed-care plan liability for coverage decisions
Yes Divert money from crop subsidy payments to land conservation
No Expand law enforcement power to investigate suspected terrorists

CQ VOTE STUDIES

	PARTY UNITY		PRESIDENTIAL SUPPORT	
	Support	Oppose	Support	Oppose
2002	88%	12%	42%	58%
2001	81%	19%	30%	70%
2000	83%	17%	67%	33%
1999	87%	13%	78%	22%

INTEREST GROUPS

	AFL-CIO	ADA	CCUS	ACU
2002	89%	95%	45%	16%
2001	92%	100%	30%	8%
2000	90%	90%	52%	20%
1999	89%	100%	24%	4%

OREGON 1

Western Portland and suburbs; Beaverton

Nestled onto the west bank of the Willamette River, Portland's Silicon Forest hums with new companies assembling computer chips. Californians and other migrants have come to Portland in droves, looking for an urban economy with a leisurely lifestyle.

Many of the most affluent urbanites have settled in the city; others are filling up fast-growing suburbs in Washington and Yamhill counties. Aided by a western light rail that stretches to Hillsboro, towns that were once bedroom communities have turned into satellite cities with their own streams of commuters. The populations of Hillsboro, Beaverton and suburbs farther west exploded in the 1990s.

Outside the Portland metro area, the 1st is struggling to keep its traditional industries intact. A highly public battle between loggers and environmentalists over the fate of the spotted owl has dampened forestry. Salmon stocks are dwindling because of excessive harvests and hydroelectric dams. State officials are working to transition workers in both fields to emerging industries in the area.

Electronics, vineyards and nurseries now lead the 1st's economy. Tourism and the remnants of the timber industry round out the job market. With a number of big businesses in the district, international trade is a hot issue.

Redistricting following the 2000 census removed the 1st's share of Clackamas County and reduced its share of Multnomah County (Portland). Washington County, which accounts for 65 percent of the population, epitomizes the 1st's competitiveness: Al Gore won the county by less than 3 percentage points in the 2000 presidential election. Democrats do well in Multnomah and in the far northwestern counties of Clatsop and Columbia, while the GOP has the edge in Yamhill.

MAJOR INDUSTRY

Electronics, computer manufacturing, wine production, nurseries

CITIES

Beaverton, 76,129; Portland (pt.), 74,097; Hillsboro, 70,186; Aloha (unincorporated), 41,741; Tigard, 41,223

NOTABLE

Nike is headquartered in Beaverton; The Lewis and Clark expedition set up a winter camp in 1805-06 in what is now the Fort Clatsop National Memorial, near Astoria.

Rep. Greg Walden (R)

CAPITOL OFFICE
225-6730
greg.walden@mail.house.gov
www.walden.house.gov
1404 Longworth 20515-3702; fax 225-5774

COMMITTEES
Energy & Commerce
Resources

HOMETOWN
Hood River

BORN
Jan. 10, 1957, The Dalles, Ore.

RELIGION
Episcopalian

FAMILY
Wife, Mylene Walden; two children (one deceased)

EDUCATION
U. of Alaska, Fairbanks, attended 1974-75;
U. of Oregon, B.S. 1981 (journalism)

CAREER
Radio station owner; congressional aide

POLITICAL HIGHLIGHTS
Ore. House, 1989-95 (majority leader, 1991-93); Ore. Senate, 1995-97 (assistant majority leader, 1995-97)

ELECTION RESULTS

2002 GENERAL		
Greg Walden (R)	181,295	71.9%
Peter Buckley (D)	64,991	25.8%
Mike Wood (LIBERT)	5,681	2.3%
2002 PRIMARY		
Greg Walden (R)		unopposed
2000 GENERAL		
Greg Walden (R)	220,086	73.6%
Walter A. Ponsford (D)	78,101	26.1%

PREVIOUS WINNING PERCENTAGES
1998 (61%)

Elected 1998; 3rd term

The only Republican in his state's House delegation, Walden has proved himself both an adept negotiator, who has been able to build bipartisan consensus in both the Resources and Energy and Commerce committees, and a steadfast defender of the farming and logging interests vital to the economic well-being of eastern Oregon.

At the start of the 108th Congress, Walden increased his stature in the House GOP by gaining an appointment as a deputy whip and getting a seat on the Energy and Commerce panel's Telecommunications subcommittee. That post allows him to make use of his background in radio and television as Congress tries to keep up with rapidly changing communications issues.

The federal government owns more than half of the land in the 2nd District, including at least part of 10 national forests, and Walden, a critic of federal land-use regulations, has called the area he represents "a district under siege by federal policies." He argues that a range of recreational activities should be allowed on protected land. In his first term, he headed off an effort to make a national monument out of Steens Mountain, a landmark in the southeastern part of the state used by ranchers for grazing. He instead cut a deal to create a cooperative management area. He speaks of the need for better social and environmental policies that nurture growth in small towns.

Hoping to further limit the government's reach into land-use decisions, Walden has pushed legislation that would require the Interior Department to take an additional step — obtaining a consensus of support from the scientific community — before adding new species to those protected by the Endangered Species Act.

On Resources' Water and Power Subcommittee, Walden has sought to maintain adequate water supplies for the farmers and hydropower plants in the 2nd District during the debate over protecting endangered fish. He has worked to prevent another cutoff of irrigation to farms along the Klamath River on the California-Oregon border, a step taken in 2001 to protect endangered suckerfish and other fish.

In the 107th, he joined with other Oregonians in securing aid for Klamath Basin farmers as part of a big farm bill, and he authored a measure to help local irrigation districts who paid operation and maintenance fees even though they received little water. He also has pushed legislation to promote studies of ways to improve fish passage through a dam on the Klamath, and he opposes the removal of dams on the Snake River as a way to bolster the salmon population.

On Energy and Commerce, Walden has been a strong defender of the Bonneville Power Administration, the agency that manages hydroelectric power in the Northwest. He has pushed to ensure regional control over electricity as part of any bill that would create a national power transmission grid. In the 107th, he pushed to enactment a law enabling the Confederated Tribes of Warm Springs to earn revenue by buying a part interest in a new hydroelectric project.

Although agriculture dominates the economy of the district, the area also is becoming a magnet for wind-surfing and snow-boarding tourists. Walden himself enjoys downhill skiing at Mount Hood and sailing on the Columbia River. He co-chairs the House's bipartisan 150-member Renewable Energy Caucus, which advocates use of wind, solar and geothermal power.

Reared on a cherry orchard, Walden has backed legislation that promotes family-owned farms and is a strong supporter of liberalized trade; to boost local exports he won enactment of a law in the 106th allowing the shipment overseas of pears with slight flaws that do not affect taste or shelf life.

On domestic policy, Walden is a steadfast opponent of new gun controls but has adopted a middle-ground position on abortion. He opposes federal funding for abortions and has backed legislation to outlaw a procedure its opponents call "partial birth" abortion. But he does not back a repeal of the Supreme Court's *Roe v. Wade* decision establishing the right to abortion, saying the decision to have an abortion should be left to parents. He says his views on that question were shaped after 1993, when he and his wife, Mylene, considered but rejected aborting a fetus diagnosed with a congenital heart defect. The baby boy was born prematurely and died.

As a youth, Walden earned the rank of Eagle Scout and worked at his father's radio station in Hood River. Having developed his own broadcast voice as a one-time disc jockey and talk-show host, he later bought the family business with his wife. Their company, Columbia Gorge Broadcasters Inc., now operates five popular music and news radio stations. He also worked in television while going to school in Alaska.

Walden got his introduction to politics during a lengthy stint as an aide to former Republican Rep. Denny Smith of Oregon, who was noted for being a political maverick. But Walden has a low-key consensus-building style, honed during eight years in the state legislature, during which he was House majority leader for three years and assistant Senate majority leader for two years. In that way his temperament is more reminiscent of another former House Republican from Oregon named Smith: Walden's predecessor, Bob Smith, who retired as chairman of the Agriculture Committee.

Walden threatened to run for the House as an independent in 1996 to challenge Republican Wes Cooley, who had been accused of lying about his military record in a voter pamphlet after winning the Republican primary two years before. But Smith was lured out of retirement to run for the GOP nomination, with the promise of the Agriculture chairmanship. When Smith agreed to run, both Walden and Cooley bowed out. (In 1997, Cooley was found guilty and ordered to pay fines and perform community service.)

Smith decided to retire once again in 1998, and Walden became the front-runner. He breezed to victory in the GOP primary and easily defeated Democrat Kevin M. Campbell, a former county judge, in the heavily Republican district. He has romped to re-election twice since, and redistricting has maintained the 2nd's solid GOP tilt.

KEY VOTES

2002

- No Overhaul campaign finance law; ban "soft money" and restrict advocacy advertising
- Yes Back Bush's defense budget increase
- Yes Extend 1996 welfare law
- Yes Adopt Bush's discretionary spending limit
- Yes Pass GOP Medicare prescription drug plan
- No Create independent Sept. 11 commission
- No Extend union protections to Homeland Security Department employees
- Yes Revive fast-track procedures for trade agreements
- Yes Authorize war against Iraq
- Yes Advance bankruptcy overhaul opposed by abortion opponents

2001

- Yes Nullify Clinton Labor Department ergonomics rule
- Yes Cut taxes by $1.35 trillion through fiscal 2011
- No Maintain ban on oil drilling in Arctic National Wildlife Refuge
- Yes Approve Bush proposal to limit managed-care plan liability for coverage decisions
- No Divert money from crop subsidy payments to land conservation
- Yes Expand law enforcement power to investigate suspected terrorists

CQ VOTE STUDIES

	PARTY UNITY		PRESIDENTIAL SUPPORT	
	Support	Oppose	Support	Oppose
2002	95%	5%	90%	10%
2001	97%	3%	91%	9%
2000	96%	4%	25%	75%
1999	90%	10%	22%	78%

INTEREST GROUPS

	AFL-CIO	ADA	CCUS	ACU
2002	11%	5%	100%	96%
2001	17%	10%	100%	84%
2000	20%	5%	90%	88%
1999	22%	10%	96%	80%

OREGON 2

East and Southwest – Medford, Bend

The 2nd covers the eastern two-thirds of Oregon, bordering Washington, Idaho, Nevada and California. Most of the land is owned by the federal government, causing considerable strife with the district's residents, who depend on fishing, farming and logging to make a living.

The 2nd lost timber jobs when the spotted owl was deemed an endangered species and its Oregon forest habitat was protected from clear-cutting. Those jobs have been difficult to replace in a district with few urban areas. Farmers produce fruit, wheat and hay in the plateaus and river valleys, but cattle farmers have seen their access to public grazing lands limited. At the same time, the Columbia River's fishing industry has faced restrictions on salmon under the Endangered Species Act. Fishers, farmers and environmentalists have staged high-profile battles over how federal regulators should allocate the Klamath River's water. Shortages led to the loss of crops and thousands of salmon.

During the 1980s, economic difficulties drove enough people from the district that it declined in population, but numbers rebounded in the 1990s as retired couples moved to the area.

With more than 60,000 people, Medford (Jackson County) is the largest city in the 2nd. It is surrounded by pear, cherry and apple orchards in the Rogue River Valley. Less than 20 miles southeast of Medford is Ashland, which has played host to the Oregon Shakespeare Festival since 1935.

Hostility toward the federal government makes the 2nd Oregon's most reliably Republican district. Both George W. Bush in 2000 and gubernatorial nominee Kevin Mannix in 2002 won 19 of the 20 counties wholly or partly within the 2nd (Hood River County was the exception). Democrats are scattered through parts of Ashland and Bend, but they are too few to swing the district.

MAJOR INDUSTRY
Agriculture, forestry, tourism

CITIES
Medford, 63,154; Bend, 52,029; Grants Pass, 23,003; Altamont (unincorporated), 19,603; Ashland, 19,522; Klamath Falls, 19,462

NOTABLE
Crater Lake National Park, designated in 1902, is in Klamath County; The Warm Springs Indian Reservation is in the northwest part of the district.

Rep. Earl Blumenauer (D)

Elected May 1996; 4th full term

As a liberal Democrat in a Republican House, Blumenauer has had his share of frustration since arriving in 1996. But he has found a measure of happiness as a leader of the budding "smart growth" movement, in which he tries to reshape government policies to promote community development in ways that emphasize livability.

An avid bicyclist and runner, Blumenauer (BLUE-men-hour) pursues this goal in a number of ways: by cajoling the Postal Service to keep open older facilities that have become downtown gathering spots; by proposing expanded transit benefits for federal employees and new transit benefits for bicycle commuters; and by lobbying from his Transportation Committee seat to spend billions on mass transit, bicycle trails, historic preservation and other community enhancement projects.

After being advised by former Republican Sen. Mark O. Hatfield of Oregon about the need for freshmen to stand out, he decided to make bow ties his sartorial signature. He has won admiring profiles in USA Today and other widely read publications for his refusal to own a car in Washington. He bikes to his Capitol Hill office from his nearby apartment and cycles to meetings at the White House. And he maintains a library of smart growth books in his office for the use of aides and visitors.

While his livability agenda has not been well-received by Republicans wary of proposals that may resemble 1960s-style "social engineering," Blumenauer says those proposals can place more power in the hands of state and local governments — an argument that dovetails with the GOP desire to shift more decision-making away from Washington. Blumenauer talks of "the power of the collaborative process, sitting down at the table and allowing local voices to be heard." He also works to cast his concerns in a nonpartisan light. "Local officials dealing with police and parks and people's back yards," he says, "can't afford to be gratuitously partisan."

In the last three Congresses, Blumenauer has teamed with GOP Rep. Doug Bereuter of Nebraska on "Two Floods and You're Out" legislation, which aims to discourage homeowners from rebuilding in flood-ravaged areas — a potentially costly proposition for the government flood insurance program. "This is one issue where the fiscal conservatives can join with the environmental protection folks," he says.

Many of Blumenauer's constituents were affected by the bankruptcy of Enron Corp., the energy marketer, because they worked for subsidiary Portland General Electric and had significant amounts of their retirement savings tied up in company stock. In 2002, Blumenauer joined other members of Oregon's congressional delegation in asking their state's Legislative Assembly to prevent state companies from taking out life insurance policies on low-level workers to fund compensation plans for executives and managers. The request came after opponents learned that Portland General Electric had bought "corporate-owned life insurance policies" for nearly 20 years, generating about $80 million for its executives.

In the 105th Congress, when the Transportation Committee last wrote legislation to reauthorize the nation's surface transportation programs — a task it will face again in the 108th Congress — Blumenauer stressed the importance of giving communities a strong voice in deciding how money should be spent. "Our citizens, our constituents, know what they need," he said. "If we engage them in the process of planning for our future, they will respond with innovation and non-traditional solutions." In 2001, he secured

CAPITOL OFFICE
225-4811
write.earl@mail.house.gov
www.house.gov/blumenauer
2446 Rayburn 20515-3703; fax 225-8941

COMMITTEES
International Relations
Transportation & Infrastructure

HOMETOWN
Portland

BORN
Aug. 16, 1948, Portland, Ore.

RELIGION
Unspecified

FAMILY
Divorced; two children

EDUCATION
Lewis and Clark College, B.A. 1970 (political science), J.D. 1976

CAREER
Public official

POLITICAL HIGHLIGHTS
Ore. House, 1973-77; Multnomah County Commission, 1978-86; candidate for Portland City Council, 1980; Portland City Council, 1986-96; candidate for mayor of Portland, 1992

ELECTION RESULTS

2002 GENERAL		
Earl Blumenauer (D)	156,851	66.8%
Sarah Seale (R)	62,821	26.7%
Walter F. "Walt" Brown (S)	6,588	2.8%
Kevin Jones (LIBERT)	4,704	2.0%
David Brownlow (CNSTP)	3,495	1.5%
2002 PRIMARY		
Earl Blumenauer (D)	68,893	87.0%
John Sweeney (D)	9,992	12.6%
2000 GENERAL		
Earl Blumenauer (D)	181,049	66.8%
Jeffrey L. Pollock (R)	64,128	23.7%
Tre Arrow (GREEN)	15,763	5.8%
Bruce Knight (LIBERT)	4,942	1.8%
Walter F. "Walt" Brown (S)	4,703	1.7%

PREVIOUS WINNING PERCENTAGES
1998 (84%); 1996 (67%); 1996 Special Election (70%)

$64 million in federal funding for Portland's 5.8-mile Interstate Max light-rail line extension, which will run between downtown Portland and the Columbia River when completed in 2004.

In keeping with the sentiment of his constituents, Blumenauer consistently votes to protect the environment, boost federal funding of the arts and support abortion rights. In the 107th Congress, he was one of 11 members who voted "present" when the House denounced a court ruling that had declared the pledge of allegiance's "one nation, under God" phrase unconstitutional. He also is active on animal rights issues. He won notice for a provision in the 2002 farm law barring the shipment of fighting birds or dogs across state lines; the language effectively banned cockfighting, which is still legal in Oklahoma, Louisiana and parts of New Mexico.

Blumenauer broke with many in his party, as well as organized labor, to support enactment of the 2000 law making permanent the normal U.S.-China trade relationship — a reflection, he said at the time, that one in five jobs in his district was tied to trade with the Pacific Rim. But on the next marquee trade vote, in the 107th, he opposed the revival of fast-track procedures for congressional consideration of trade deals.

An activist since his teens, Blumenauer was just one year out of college in 1971 when he testified before Congress in support of a constitutional amendment to lower the voting age to 18. Elected to the state House at 24, in four years he rose to chair the Revenue Committee. He then spent eight years on the Multnomah County Commission, followed by a decade on the Portland City Council. In those jobs, he was instrumental in establishing the ambitious and much-praised land-use planning procedures Portland uses to control metropolitan sprawl.

Despite some political stumbles — he failed in a 1980 city council bid and ran unsuccessfully for mayor of Portland in 1992 — his widespread name recognition and appeal put him in a good position to win election to the House in a 1996 special election. The 3rd District seat was vacant after Democrat Ron Wyden won a special Senate election that January to replace Republican Bob Packwood, who had resigned the previous fall rather than face expulsion for sexual harassment and personal misconduct. Blumenauer swamped two opponents in the Democratic primary and — bolstered by the endorsement of Republican Sen. Mark O. Hatfield — cruised past the GOP nominee as well.

He has won re-election with ease ever since. Redistricting did nothing to alter the 3rd's solid Democratic makeup and he won by 40 points in 2002.

KEY VOTES

2002

Yes Overhaul campaign finance law; ban "soft money" and restrict advocacy advertising
No Back Bush's defense budget increase
No Extend 1996 welfare law
No Adopt Bush's discretionary spending limit
No Pass GOP Medicare prescription drug plan
Yes Create independent Sept. 11 commission
Yes Extend union protections to Homeland Security Department employees
No Revive fast-track procedures for trade agreements
No Authorize war against Iraq
No Advance bankruptcy overhaul opposed by abortion opponents

2001

No Nullify Clinton Labor Department ergonomics rule
? Cut taxes by $1.35 trillion through fiscal 2011
Yes Maintain ban on oil drilling in Arctic National Wildlife Refuge
No Approve Bush proposal to limit managed-care plan liability for coverage decisions
Yes Divert money from crop subsidy payments to land conservation
No Expand law enforcement power to investigate suspected terrorists

CQ VOTE STUDIES

	PARTY UNITY		PRESIDENTIAL SUPPORT	
	Support	Oppose	Support	Oppose
2002	96%	4%	25%	75%
2001	89%	11%	19%	81%
2000	93%	7%	88%	12%
1999	90%	10%	80%	20%
1998	92%	8%	85%	15%

INTEREST GROUPS

	AFL-CIO	ADA	CCUS	ACU
2002	100%	100%	35%	4%
2001	91%	90%	30%	0%
2000	90%	90%	42%	0%
1999	78%	95%	40%	4%
1998	100%	95%	41%	4%

OREGON 3

North and east Portland; eastern suburbs

Split by the Willamette River, the city of Portland has two personalities. The eastern portion, covered by the 3rd, still depends on the blue-collar economy that made the city a thriving international port for lumber and fruit. The Port of Portland and Portland International Airport make the city a leading center of trade and distribution. Computer chips and cappuccino drive the city's western side (in the 1st and 5th districts).

Compared to the rest of Portland, the 3rd is a multicultural haven. There is a large African-American population in precincts just east of the Willamette River, near Interstate 5 and Martin Luther King Jr. Blvd., where Democrats regularly win more than 80 percent of the vote in competitive statewide elections. A sizable Hispanic population resides in northeastern Portland and in Gresham and Wood Village east of the city. Asians are numerous in east-central Portland, near 82nd Avenue and Interstate 205.

The 3rd's second-largest city, Gresham, was once a thriving farm community. It is now the easternmost stop on Portland's light rail system and is growing rapidly. Beyond the Portland metropolitan area, the district quickly turns rural. Mount Hood National Forest covers the far eastern part of the district.

Portland's liberal leanings make the 3rd Oregon's most staunchly Democratic district. Democrat Theodore R. Kulongoski won 65 percent of the 3rd's share of Multnomah County in the 2002 gubernatorial election, which he won narrowly. Democrat Bill Bradbury took 56 percent even as he lost decisively statewide to Republican Sen. Gordon H. Smith in 2002. Redistricting following the 2000 census gave the 3rd a larger share of Clackamas County, which is more rural and politically competitive. But any Republican strength there is not large enough to weaken Portland's strong Democratic slant.

MAJOR INDUSTRY
Wholesale trade and distribution, health care, education

CITIES
Portland (pt.), 432,388; Gresham, 90,205; Milwaukie, 20,490

NOTABLE
Forest Park is one of the largest urban parks in the nation; Mount Hood, Oregon's highest peak, reaches 11,239 feet.

Rep. Peter A. DeFazio (D)

CAPITOL OFFICE
225-6416
www.house.gov/defazio
2134 Rayburn 20515-3704; fax 225-0032

COMMITTEES
Transportation & Infrastructure
Select Homeland Security

HOMETOWN
Springfield

BORN
May 27, 1947, Needham, Mass.

RELIGION
Roman Catholic

FAMILY
Wife, Myrnie L. Daut

EDUCATION
Tufts U., B.A. 1969 (economics & political science); U. of Oregon, attended 1969-71 (international studies), M.S. 1977 (public administration & gerontology)

MILITARY SERVICE
Air Force, 1967-71

CAREER
Congressional aide

POLITICAL HIGHLIGHTS
Lane County Commission, 1982-86; sought Democratic nomination for U.S. Senate (special election), 1996

ELECTION RESULTS

2002 GENERAL		
Peter A. DeFazio (D)	168,150	63.8%
Liz VanLeeuwen (R)	90,523	34.4%
Chris Bigelow (LIBERT)	4,602	1.8%
2002 PRIMARY		
Peter A. DeFazio (D)		unopposed
2000 GENERAL		
Peter A. DeFazio (D)	197,998	68.0%
John Lindsey (R)	88,950	30.6%
David G. Duemler (S)	3,696	1.3%

PREVIOUS WINNING PERCENTAGES
1998 (70%); 1996 (66%); 1994 (67%); 1992 (71%); 1990 (86%); 1988 (72%); 1986 (54%)

Elected 1986; 9th term

Each time Republicans celebrate a legislative victory, DeFazio can be counted on to come to the House floor to denounce the moment with a sharp-tongued and often sarcastic speech. In the 107th Congress, he helped lead Democrats in criticizing virtually every major GOP-passed measure as a blow to consumers and taxpayers of modest or minimal means.

But DeFazio (da-FAH-zee-o) has pushed a liberal, populist agenda since the day he arrived in Congress in the House in 1987. He is loud, he is persistent and he is viewed by his critics as a smart aleck — characteristics that earned him a reputation as "long on straight talk and short on political rhetoric," according to an editorial in The World newspaper of Coos Bay.

DeFazio, a leader in the Populist Caucus, a group of about 40 of the most liberal members of Congress, is guided by his belief that his constituents appreciate his rhetoric more than they might a few extra federal dollars. He has encouraged his independent image by driving a 1963 Dodge Dart around Oregon and appearing before his constituents there in jeans or khakis. These gestures appear to have paid off politically, not only with the liberals in the urban part of his district but also with the more conservative voters in the 4th's rural reaches. DeFazio won with 68 percent in 2000 in a district George W. Bush carried with 49 percent. With his constituency minimally altered by redistricting, his percentage in 2002 was 64.

In 2001, DeFazio considered running for governor to succeed fellow Democrat John Kitzhaber, forced by term limits to step down, but he decided against a bid after concluding the post lacked the authority to take on a GOP-controlled legislature. He disappointed national Democrats soon after by also deciding not to challenge the re-election of GOP Sen. Gordon H. Smith.

As a senior Democrat on the Transportation and Infrastructure Committee, which will be rewriting the massive laws that fund aviation, highway and transit programs in the 108th Congress, DeFazio saw greater opportunity in staying where he is. The certainty of a subcommittee chairmanship had the Democrats regained the majority convinced him that the House was "where I thought I could do the most good." He is the top-ranking Democrat on the Aviation Subcommittee in the 108th.

On Transportation, DeFazio is active in aviation and surface transportation matters and on a wide range of consumer issues. During the 107th, he was the top Democrat on the panel's Water Resources and Environment Subcommittee. After the Sept. 11, 2001, terrorist attacks, he led the House Democrats' campaign against the GOP effort to retain private contract workers in airport screening positions as part of the legislation overhauling airline security. The law ultimately enacted not only federalized the baggage screeners but also made a number of other security changes that DeFazio had been urging for years.

His post on the new Homeland Security Committee gives him an additional platform from which to oversee aviation security.

A frequent commuter between the two coasts, DeFazio had pressed in the 106th Congress to require airlines to improve customer service. When the airlines offered to take voluntary steps instead, DeFazio dismissed them: "The flying public has seen these promises made and then broken time and time again and won't be fooled by the latest blast of hot air."

In the 105th, while preparing for a fight over proposals to deregulate the electricity industry, DeFazio pointed out that reduced safety standards, poor service and increased costs had arisen in industries that Congress already had largely freed from federal regulation — aviation, railroads, telecommunications and cable television. In each instance, consumers were getting a raw deal, DeFazio said.

A longtime member of the Resources Committee and its Water and Power Subcommittee, DeFazio, following the Western energy meltdown of 2001 and the Enron accounting fiasco and corporate collapse of 2002, went on the offensive by introducing legislation to re-regulate the energy industry. "Most people don't understand it, and they're still enthralled with the pre-Enron, pre-California idea that markets can do things better than regulators any day of the week," he said.

On Resources, DeFazio often found himself facing a tough juggling act when it came to forest and resource management questions. His constituency includes two groups with strongly conflicting interests on those issues: loggers, who oppose curbs on timber cutting, and environmentalists who want restrictions. He notes wryly that he has been blasted, on a case-by-case basis, by both sides at various times. In the 107th, he worked on getting both camps to agree on a plan for replacing the Clinton-era Northwest forestry plan with one that would allow thinning of previously harvested areas while preserving so-called old growth forests.

DeFazio grew up in Massachusetts, a state where politicians know all about logrolling but not much about timber. DeFazio's first taste of politics came as a youth at the knee of his great-uncle, a classic Boston pol who followed the word Republican with the Boston-accented epithet "bastuhd" so often that it sounded like one word to the young DeFazio.

DeFazio first moved to Oregon to attend the University of Oregon, where he earned a graduate degree in gerontology. After a stint with a community service program for seniors, he went to work for Democratic Rep. Jim Weaver, a hot-tempered populist. He then struck out on his own, winning election to the Lane County Commission in 1982 and earning a reputation for aggressiveness by suing to nullify contracts between Oregon utilities and the Washington Public Power Supply System, whose failed nuclear projects had resulted in utility rate increases.

When Weaver announced he would not seek re-election in 1986, DeFazio stepped in. Portraying himself as heir to Weaver's populist mantle, he narrowly won the Democratic primary. Deflecting criticism that he was too close to the incumbent, he won in the fall with 54 percent and has subsequently held his district with ease. He fell short in a special-election in a hard-fought December 1995 primary. Wyden went on to win the seat.

KEY VOTES

2002

- Yes Overhaul campaign finance law; ban "soft money" and restrict advocacy advertising
- No Back Bush's defense budget increase
- No Extend 1996 welfare law
- No Adopt Bush's discretionary spending limit
- No Pass GOP Medicare prescription drug plan
- Yes Create independent Sept. 11 commission
- Yes Extend union protections to Homeland Security Department employees
- No Revive fast-track procedures for trade agreements
- No Authorize war against Iraq
- No Advance bankruptcy overhaul opposed by abortion opponents

2001

- No Nullify Clinton Labor Department ergonomics rule
- No Cut taxes by $1.35 trillion through fiscal 2011
- Yes Maintain ban on oil drilling in Arctic National Wildlife Refuge
- No Approve Bush proposal to limit managed-care plan liability for coverage decisions
- Yes Divert money from crop subsidy payments to land conservation
- No Expand law enforcement power to investigate suspected terrorists

CQ VOTE STUDIES

	PARTY UNITY		PRESIDENTIAL SUPPORT	
	Support	Oppose	Support	Oppose
2002	94%	6%	24%	76%
2001	96%	4%	19%	81%
2000	86%	14%	67%	33%
1999	92%	8%	73%	27%
1998	93%	7%	80%	20%

INTEREST GROUPS

	AFL-CIO	ADA	CCUS	ACU
2002	100%	95%	30%	12%
2001	100%	100%	25%	16%
2000	100%	90%	25%	8%
1999	100%	100%	12%	8%
1998	100%	95%	12%	16%

OREGON 4
Southwest – Eugene, part of Corvallis

Loggers, fishermen and environmentalists combine to give the 4th a potentially combustible political mix. In the early 1990s, the district was a prime battleground in the fight between lumber mills and environmentalists over the fate of the spotted owl. But after the courts and the Clinton administration turned against the lumber industry, the furor quieted down and most of the unionized mills closed shop.

Fishing, another of the district's economic mainstays, also has dwindled. Most commercial fishermen — in towns such as Charleston, Bandon and Port Orford — are looking for a way out, having been harmed by frequent run closings, short seasons and low prices. While this rural region's unemployment has been decreasing steadily, it is still higher than average, which may explain why the 4th experienced the slowest population growth of any Oregon district in the 1990s. The district increasingly has looked to tourists and expanding retirement communities to aid its economy.

Eugene and Springfield, the district's most populous cities, have fared better. Research at the University of Oregon in Eugene, still a hotbed of environmentalism, has lured high-tech companies. Computer manufacturers, software developers, retailers and the service industry now drive the area's economy.

The electoral success of liberal Rep. DeFazio belies the 4th's political competitiveness. Eugene and Springfield make Lane County reliably Democratic. Linn and Douglas counties vote solidly Republican, and Coos and Curry counties, which once had a strong union tradition, now lean Republican as a result of upper-middle-class retirees flocking from outside the state. (Twenty-six percent of Curry's residents are 65 or older, the highest percentage in the state.) Redistricting following the 2000 census made minimal changes to the 4th, adding more of Benton County in the north and more of Josephine County in the south.

MAJOR INDUSTRY
Forestry, agriculture, fishing, technology, tourism

CITIES
Eugene, 137,893; Springfield, 52,864; Albany (pt.), 36,950; Corvallis (pt.), 32,076; Roseburg, 20,017; Coos Bay, 15,374

NOTABLE
Much of the movie "Stand by Me" was filmed in Lane County.

Rep. Darlene Hooley (D)

CAPITOL OFFICE
225-5711
darlene@mail.house.gov
www.house.gov/hooley
2430 Rayburn 20515-3705; fax 225-5699

COMMITTEES
Budget
Financial Services
Veterans' Affairs

HOMETOWN
West Linn

BORN
April 4, 1939, Williston, N.D.

RELIGION
Lutheran

FAMILY
Divorced; two children

EDUCATION
Pasadena Nazarene College, attended 1957-59 (psychology); Oregon State U., B.S. 1961 (education)

CAREER
Teacher

POLITICAL HIGHLIGHTS
West Linn City Council, 1977-81; Ore. House, 1981-87; Clackamas County Commission, 1987-97

ELECTION RESULTS

2002 GENERAL		
Darlene Hooley (D)	137,713	54.8%
Brian Boquist (R)	113,441	45.1%
2002 PRIMARY		
Darlene Hooley (D)		unopposed
2000 GENERAL		
Darlene Hooley (D)	156,315	56.8%
Brian Boquist (R)	118,631	43.1%

PREVIOUS WINNING PERCENTAGES
1998 (55%); 1996 (51%)

Elected 1996; 4th term

Hooley rushes through her day at the Capitol in a business suit and gym shoes, looking every bit the girls' athletics coach she used to be. She got into politics as a mom fed up with dangerous playground equipment, and as a Democrat in Congress, she pursues a family-oriented agenda. Education, tax policy and the price of prescriptions for the elderly are important issues to Hooley.

She hopes that in the 108th she'll be able to move a little faster than in the 107th, after undergoing double knee replacement surgery in November 2002 to deal with old skiing injuries. Earlier in the year, she had a heart pacemaker implanted. The knee surgery forced her to miss the 2002 end-of-year lame duck session and the opening of the 108th Congress, but she returned before legislative work got under way.

Her trademark sneakers evoke considerable notice and some envy: Democratic Whip Steny H. Hoyer told her that her colleagues say, "We wish we had the gumption to wear them."

Liberal to moderate on issues, she is known as a serious and conciliatory lawmaker, more interested in getting bills passed than in ideological purity. She attributes her narrow 1996 election to the House to her bipartisan style. "I think that's what people are looking for," she said.

Hooley represents a swing district, and is a member of the centrist New Democrat Coalition. She favors limited tax cuts and many free-trade initiatives. But she is more liberal when it comes to social issues such as abortion.

Her interests in Congress include many of the issues she worked on during two decades in local and state government, most notably education. She supports federal spending on early education through Head Start and backs tuition tax credits and government loans for college students. With many other Democrats, she opposes vouchers for private school tuition, contending that the government instead should focus on improving public schools.

Hooley is also involved in the push to make prescription drugs more affordable for senior citizens. One of her ideas is to require drug companies to make prescription medications available to all consumers at the prices they offer their largest buyers. The politically savvy drug industry, strongly opposed to price controls, responded in 1999 with an ad accusing her of playing politics with the issue.

On the environment, Hooley opposes GOP-led efforts to weaken clean air and clean water regulations. But she also has to be politically atuned to her district's economic reliance on logging, agriculture and fishing. Hooley contends that the federal government should set standards but not dictate the ways in which local governments and industry comply.

During debate on the farm bill in 2002, Hooley helped win a significant victory for Oregon fruit and produce farmers. She supported a provision that would require fruit, vegetables, fish and meat to include a label noting the country of origin. The provision had long been opposed by grocery stores, which said it would increase their costs. But U.S. producers believe they would benefit because consumers would be more likely to select U.S.-grown produce.

Hooley must be included on any list of tax cut-loving Democrats. She was more than happy to support Republican President Bush's call for eliminating family-unfriendly elements of the tax code. She joined with just 27 other Democrats in 2001 in voting for his $1.35 trillion package of tax cuts. The bill phased out the estate tax, which is imposed on property and other wealth handed from one generation to the next, and eliminated the marriage penalty, a quirk in the code that forced some married couples to pay more than they would if they filed as singles.

In fact, Hooley's very first bill as a House member was a joint effort with Republican freshman John Cooksey of Louisiana that reduced estate taxes on family-owned small businesses and farms.

Hooley breaks ranks with Democrats on a few other issues, though she generally votes with her party. In 1997, she was among the minority of Democrats to vote for an overhaul of the nation's public housing system. That came after Democrats failed in committee to pass several amendments that would have softened the impact on poor public housing residents.

From her seat on the Financial Services Committee, Hooley campaigns for greater consumer protections and greater corporate accountability. In the 106th Congress, she introduced legislation to require credit card companies to provide customers with the date by which a payment must be postmarked to avoid a late fee. Concerned about "identify theft," she also pursued a plan that would require banks and credit agencies to confirm address changes with customers so the customers would know if their accounts were being used illegally. In the 108th, she chairs a Democratic task force on the issue.

A former reading, music and physical education teacher, Hooley decided to run for a seat on the West Linn City Council in 1977 because she was unhappy with the response she got when she complained that her son had been injured in a fall on a public playground. Told by council members that safety improvements to the playground would be too expensive, she decided to run for the council herself. She won.

After four years on the council, Hooley served in the Oregon House and on the Clackamas County Commission, focusing on issues ranging from recycling to welfare.

In her 1996 House race, she easily outpaced two lesser-known Democrats to claim the party's nomination and the right to take on conservative GOP freshman Rep. Jim Bunn, who had won narrowly in 1994. Hooley quickly gained the support of national Democrats, who helped with a barrage of negative ads portraying Bunn as too conservative for the district and too close to Speaker Newt Gingrich. Bunn, who depended on support from religious conservatives, was also hurt by his divorce and subsequent remarriage to his 31-year-old chief of staff. Hooley won with 51 percent of the vote. Her three re-elections have been by only slightly wider margins — her best showing was 57 percent in 2000.

KEY VOTES

2002

Yes Overhaul campaign finance law; ban "soft money" and restrict advocacy advertising
Yes Back Bush's defense budget increase
No Extend 1996 welfare law
No Adopt Bush's discretionary spending limit
No Pass GOP Medicare prescription drug plan
Yes Create independent Sept. 11 commission
Yes Extend union protections to Homeland Security Department employees
No Revive fast-track procedures for trade agreements
No Authorize war against Iraq
? Advance bankruptcy overhaul opposed by abortion opponents

2001

No Nullify Clinton Labor Department ergonomics rule
Yes Cut taxes by $1.35 trillion through fiscal 2011
Yes Maintain ban on oil drilling in Arctic National Wildlife Refuge
No Approve Bush proposal to limit managed-care plan liability for coverage decisions
Yes Divert money from crop subsidy payments to land conservation
Yes Expand law enforcement power to investigate suspected terrorists

CQ VOTE STUDIES

	PARTY UNITY		PRESIDENTIAL SUPPORT	
	Support	Oppose	Support	Oppose
2002	87%	13%	37%	63%
2001	89%	11%	36%	64%
2000	85%	15%	67%	33%
1999	87%	13%	79%	21%
1998	88%	12%	78%	22%

INTEREST GROUPS

	AFL-CIO	ADA	CCUS	ACU
2002	88%	90%	50%	12%
2001	83%	90%	43%	4%
2000	80%	70%	61%	16%
1999	78%	100%	40%	4%
1998	80%	95%	59%	12%

OREGON 5
Willamette Valley – Salem, part of Portland

Oregon City, the western terminus of the 2,000-mile Oregon Trail, in 1844 became the first incorporated city west of the Mississippi River. For settlers who made the five-month journey from Independence, Mo., the area marked the end of an arduous trek to Oregon's fertile Willamette Valley. The 5th takes in the northern part of that valley and the state capital of Salem, then spills over the Coast Range to cover two Pacific counties, Tillamook and Lincoln. It also includes a small part of Portland (shared with the 1st and 3rd districts).

Clackamas, Marion and Polk counties are at the heart of the Willamette Valley, Oregon's most fertile farmland. The valley is the center of the state's profitable trade in greenhouse crops, seeds and berries. Hops from Marion and Clackamas counties go into some of the nation's finest beers. Polk County grows cherries and wine grapes; wineries dot Polk and Marion counties.

Once exclusively dependent on agriculture and timber, the district's economy has diversified and now supports environmental research, high-tech manufacturing and tourism. Portland's residential suburbs have begun expanding south into Clackamas County.

The 5th is highly competitive. Nearly 75 percent of district residents live in either Marion (Salem) or Clackamas counties, which have many independent voters. Marion, the district's most populous jurisdiction, tends to vote narrowly Republican in competitive statewide races: Gubernatorial candidate Kevin Mannix in 2002 and George W. Bush in 2000 took 52 percent and 51 percent of the county vote in their respective races. Mannix also narrowly carried the 5th's share of Clackamas. Strong Democratic areas include Corvallis (split with the 4th District), which is home to Oregon State University, and southwestern Multnomah County, an area added in redistricting following the 2000 census that hosts some affluent Portland-area liberals around Lewis & Clark College.

MAJOR INDUSTRY
Agriculture, lumber, paper, food processing, state government

CITIES
Salem, 136,924; Lake Oswego (pt.), 35,263; Keizer, 32,203

NOTABLE
The Oregon Coast Aquarium is in Newport; Salem's Willamette University, established in 1842, was the first university in the west.

PENNSYLVANIA

Gov. Edward G. Rendell (D)

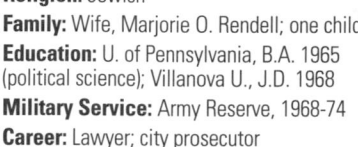

First elected: 2002
Length of term: 4 years
Term expires: 1/07
Salary: $138,270
Phone: (717) 787-2500
Hometown: Philadelphia
Born: Jan. 5, 1944; New York, N.Y.
Religion: Jewish
Family: Wife, Marjorie O. Rendell; one child
Education: U. of Pennsylvania, B.A. 1965 (political science); Villanova U., J.D. 1968
Military Service: Army Reserve, 1968-74
Career: Lawyer; city prosecutor
Political highlights: Philadelphia district attorney, 1978-86; sought Democratic nomination for governor, 1986; sought Democratic nomination for mayor of Philadelphia, 1987; mayor of Philadelphia, 1992-2000; Democratic National Committee chairman, 1999-2001
Election results:

2002 GENERAL		
Edward G. Rendell (D)	1,899,518	53.6%
Mike Fisher (R)	1,566,567	44.2%
Ken V. Krawchuk (LIBERT)	40,923	1.2%
Michael Morrill (GREEN)	38,423	1.1%

Lt. Gov. Catherine B. Knoll (D)

First elected: 2002
Length of term: 4 years
Term expires: 1/07
Salary: $116,147
Phone: (717) 787-3300

STATE LEGISLATURE

General Assembly: Meets year-round
House: 203 members, 2-year terms
2003 breakdown: 108R, 94D, 1 vacancy; 175 men, 27 women
Salary: $64,638
Phone: (717) 787-2372
Senate: 50 members, 4-year terms
2003 breakdown: 29R, 21D; 43 men, 7 women
Salary: $64,638
Phone: (717) 787-5920

STATE TERM LIMITS

Governor: 2 consecutive terms
Senate: No
House: No

URBAN STATISTICS

CITY	POPULATION
Philadelphia	1,517,550
Pittsburgh	334,563
Allentown	106,632
Erie	103,717
Upper Darby	81,821

REGISTERED VOTERS

Democrat	48%
Republican	41%
Other	10%

POPULATION

2002 population (est.)	12,335,091
2000 population	12,281,054
1990 population	11,881,643
Percent change (1990-2000)	+3.4%
Rank among states (2002)	6
Median age	38
Born in state	77.7%
Foreign born	4.1%
Violent crime rate	420/100,000
Poverty level	11%
Federal workers	105,903
Military	43,271

REDISTRICTING

Pennsylvania lost two House seats in reapportionment. The legislature drew a 19-district map, which the governor signed on Jan. 7, 2002. A three-judge panel struck down the map but permitted the 2002 elections to be held under it. The legislature drew a new map, effective for 2004, which the governor signed on April 18, 2002.

MISCELLANEOUS

Web: www.state.pa.us
Capital: Harrisburg

STATE ELECTION OFFICIAL
(717) 787-5280

DEMOCRATIC HEADQUARTERS
(717) 238-9381

REPUBLICAN HEADQUARTERS
(717) 234-4901

District Statistics

DIST.	2000 VOTE FOR PRESIDENT															
	BUSH	GORE	NADER	WHITE	BLACK	ASIAN	HISP	MEDIAN INCOME	WHITE COLLAR	BLUE COLLAR	SERVICE INDUSTRY	OVER 64	UNDER 18	COLLEGE EDUCATION	RURAL	SQ. MILES
1	15%	83%	2%	33%	45%	5%	15%	$28,295	57%	22%	22%	12%	28%	14%	0%	59
2	12	87	2	30	61	4	3	$30,626	66	15	19	14	24	24	0	59
3	50	46	3	94	3	0	1	$35,876	52	31	16	15	24	18	41	3,954
4	52	46	3	94	3	1	1	$43,628	64	23	14	17	24	27	22	1,324
5	59	38	3	96	1	1	1	$33,320	51	33	15	15	22	17	54	10,992
6	48	49	3	87	7	2	3	$55,615	68	21	12	14	25	34	15	839
7	47	50	3	88	5	4	1	$56,154	73	16	11	15	24	36	1	290
8	46	51	3	91	3	2	2	$59,184	68	21	11	13	25	31	9	619
9	64	34	2	96	2	0	1	$34,850	49	36	16	16	24	13	60	7,245
10	56	40	4	95	2	0	1	$35,984	53	32	15	17	23	17	55	6,584
11	43	53	4	93	2	1	3	$34,979	54	30	16	18	22	16	27	2,218
12	43	54	3	95	3	0	1	$30,614	51	31	18	19	21	14	37	2,754
13	42	56	3	86	6	4	3	$49,311	68	19	12	17	24	29	1	248
14	28	69	3	73	23	2	1	$30,140	62	19	20	18	21	21	0	160
15	48	49	4	86	3	2	8	$45,419	60	27	14	16	24	22	13	811

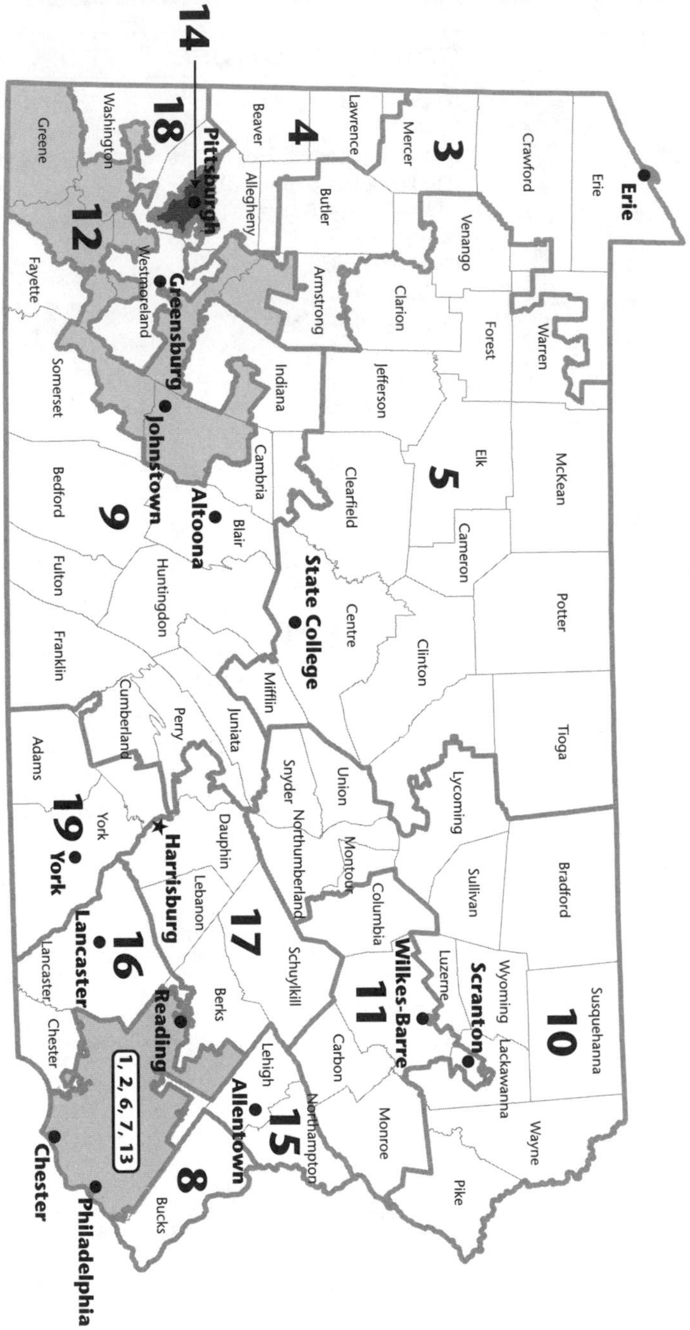

District Statistics

DIST.	2000 VOTE FOR PRESIDENT BUSH	GORE	NADER	WHITE	BLACK	ASIAN	HISP	MEDIAN INCOME	WHITE COLLAR	BLUE COLLAR	SERVICE INDUSTRY	OVER 64	UNDER 18	COLLEGE EDUCATION	RURAL	SQ. MILES
16	62%	35%	3%	84%	4%	1%	9%	$45,941	55%	31%	14%	13%	27%	23%	24%	1,294
17	55	42	3	87	7	1	3	$40,334	55	31	14	16	23	17	30	2,291
18	51	46	3	95	2	1	1	$44,864	66	20	14	18	22	29	16	1,427
19	61	36	3	92	3	1	3	$45,363	57	30	13	14	24	21	29	1,648
STATE	46	51	2	84	10	2	3	$40,106	60	26	15	16	24	22	23	44,817
U.S.	47.9	48.4	3	69	12	4	13	$41,994	60	25	15	12	26	24	21	3,537,438

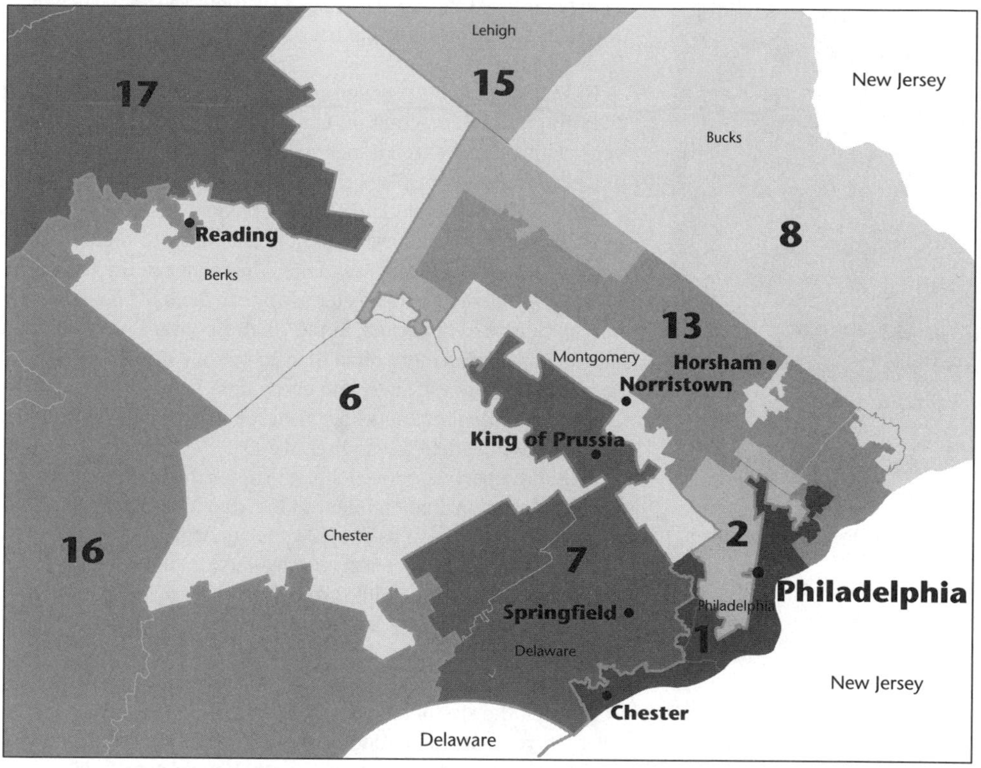
Lehigh
17
15
New Jersey
Bucks
Reading
Berks
8
13
Montgomery
Horsham
Norristown
6
King of Prussia
Chester
16
2
7
Philadelphia
Philadelphia
Springfield
1
Delaware
New Jersey
Chester
Delaware

Sen. Arlen Specter (R)

CAPITOL OFFICE
224-4254
specter.senate.gov
711 Hart 20510-3802; fax 228-1229

COMMITTEES
Appropriations
(Labor, Health & Human Services & Education - chairman)
Governmental Affairs
Judiciary
Veterans' Affairs - chairman

HOMETOWN
Philadelphia

BORN
Feb. 12, 1930, Wichita, Kan.

RELIGION
Jewish

FAMILY
Wife, Joan Specter; two children

EDUCATION
U. of Pennsylvania, B.A. 1951 (international relations); Yale U., LL.B. 1956

MILITARY SERVICE
Air Force, 1951-53

CAREER
Lawyer; professor

POLITICAL HIGHLIGHTS
Philadelphia district attorney, 1966-74; Republican nominee for mayor of Philadelphia, 1967; defeated for re-election as Philadelphia district attorney, 1973; sought Republican nomination for U.S. Senate, 1976; sought Republican nomination for governor, 1978

ELECTION RESULTS

1998 GENERAL		
Arlen Specter (R)	1,814,180	61.3%
Bill Lloyd (D)	1,028,839	34.8%
Dean Snyder (CONSTL)	68,377	2.3%
Jack Iannantuono (LIBERT)	46,103	1.6%
1998 PRIMARY		
Arlen Specter (R)	376,322	67.2%
Larry Murphy (R)	101,120	18.1%
Tom Lingenfelter (R)	82,168	14.7%

PREVIOUS WINNING PERCENTAGES
1992 (49%); 1986 (56%); 1980 (50%)

Elected 1980; 4th term

Sometimes it is hard to remember that this is the same man who grilled Anita Hill so aggressively during the 1991 confirmation hearing of Supreme Court nominee Clarence Thomas. Back then, Specter struck many women voters as insensitive, and he had to fight to keep his Senate seat the following year.

Now, Specter fights to soften anti-abortion language in the GOP platform, tries to outdo Democrats on education spending, and not infrequently votes with Democrats on issues such as extending unemployment benefits and allowing patients to sue their managed-care health plans.

This is the moderate face that the reconstructed Specter believes the Republican Party will have to project if it wants to regain strength in the largely Democratic Northeast. Like other states in the region, Pennsylvania tilts Democratic, and Specter has one of the most liberal voting records among Senate Republicans. In the 107th Congress he bucked his leaders on party-line votes more often than all but one other GOP senator. "I represent a very diverse state, and every time I cast a vote, I run the risk of having 50 percent of the people disagree with me. I'm used to that," Specter told the Philadelphia Inquirer in 2003.

When the party approved a platform for the 2000 elections that called for a constitutional amendment to ban abortion, Specter tried to get the platform committee to back off its stance. As the GOP moderates' liaison to the predominately conservative leadership in the 107th, Specter urged his colleagues to seek middle ground on a host of key issues, from creation of a Homeland Security Department to the use of human stem cells for medical research.

He was one of only three Senate Republicans to insist President Bush scale back the size of his tax cut in 2001 from $1.6 trillion to $1.35 trillion over ten years to make room in the budget for more education spending. Since 1999, he has been one of the few Republicans to join liberal Democrat Edward M. Kennedy of Massachusetts to endorse "hate crime" protections for homosexuals.

Specter possesses one of the quickest minds on Capitol Hill and is not shy about promoting his ideas. He is often the first out with a bill responding to the crisis of the moment. After the terrorist attacks of Sept. 11, 2001, he immediately teamed with another influential centrist, Democrat Joseph I. Lieberman of Connecticut, on legislation calling for a massive reorganization of agencies into a Homeland Security Department. Their bill instituted a Cabinet-level secretary, a move Bush resisted but later conceded was necessary to give the department real teeth. In the 108th Congress, Specter sought and won assignment to the Government Reform panel to become more involved in homeland security issues.

A former prosecutor, Specter often wades into constitutional disputes. He has been a leader in the ongoing effort in Congress to balance civil liberties protections with the need for tighter security, as Attorney General John Ashcroft has sought ever-increasing levels of law enforcement authority.

As chairman of the Appropriations subcommittee that funds the departments of Labor, Health and Human Services, and Education, Specter is well placed to affect the GOP position on domestic policy and makes full use of that power. He has sided with liberal Democrats in demanding that the administration spend enough money to meet the goals of Bush's 2001 "No

Child Left Behind" education bill, which ties federal aid to improvements on test scores. He put together a bill in 2000 that gave the Department of Education more money than President Clinton had requested.

Specter even made peace with Anita Hill — sort of. Passing through the Oklahoma City airport in late 1997, the two ran into each other waiting for the same flight. Hill listened with a mixture of anger and amazement as Specter, who once accused her of "flat-out perjury" in her sexual harassment claims against Thomas, asked Hill if he could stay in touch with her about women's issues. "For me, the hearings were a learning experience," Specter has said. "Out of those hearings came a lot of progress in respecting women."

But in large measure, Specter's tart tongue and blunt manner are simply part of his personality. The senator has a reputation for being abrasive and difficult, especially with employees whom he suspects of not doing their homework. He is just as likely to lecture visitors on constitutional issues — showing off his knowledge and testing theirs — as he is to throw obscure facts about international law into his speeches.

Specter can get away with a lot, however, because even senators who do not like dealing with him personally do not want to get on the wrong side of the Labor-HHS Subcommittee chairman. There is too much money at stake for critical education, health care and job training programs.

Furthermore, he sometimes sets his moderate beliefs aside if party leaders are determined to assert a more conservative position. In 2002, he voted for repeal of the federal ergonomics rule though he had long sided with organized labor on the issue of protecting office workers from repetitive stress injuries. The Bush White House had pressed hard for repeal of the Clinton-era rule.

In 1993, Specter had surgery to remove a brain tumor. The problem was not diagnosed until a procedure known as magnetic resonance imaging was used — prompting Specter to become an outspoken proponent of health tests no matter what the expense. He is a sponsor of legislation to allow cloning of human cells for medical research, putting him at odds with conservatives who support a total ban.

Specter, who has a law degree from Yale University, first made a name for himself in the 1960s as a top aide to the Warren Commission; he helped devise the "single-bullet" theory that a lone gunman was responsible for the 1963 John F. Kennedy assassination. He can still recall from memory the presumed velocity of the bullet at points in its trajectory.

Specter was elected district attorney in Philadelphia twice, in 1965 and 1969, but then suffered several political setbacks, including losing a race for mayor. He decided to make one more attempt when GOP Sen. Richard S. Schweiker announced he would retire in 1980. Luckily for Specter, his Democratic opponent, Pittsburgh Mayor Pete Flaherty, was a two-time statewide loser. Carrying Philadelphia and its suburbs helped Specter overcome Flaherty's strength in the western part of the state.

Specter's next tough race came in 1992, the year after the Clarence Thomas hearings. Democratic challenger Lynn Yeakel, president of a Philadelphia-based women's fundraising organization, looked formidable in light of the anger among women's groups. Specter returned to his moderate roots and campaigned energetically, winning by 3 percentage points.

By 1998, Specter had come back; he won 61 percent of the vote over state Rep. Bill Lloyd. Early in 2003, conservative GOP Rep. Patrick J. Toomey announced that he would challenge Specter in 2004, saying that Specter's views were out of step with the majority of Keystone State Republicans. The White House, which had tried to discourage Toomey from an intraparty battle, quickly endorsed Specter.

KEY VOTES

2002

- Yes Pass farm bill reversing crop subsidy limits
- Yes Postpone tougher automobile fuel efficiency standards
- Yes Overhaul campaign finance law; ban "soft money" and restrict advocacy advertising
- Yes Set federal election standards
- Yes Support oil drilling in Arctic National Wildlife Refuge
- Yes Revive fast-track procedures for trade agreements
- Yes Create federal insurance coverage for catastrophic terrorist losses
- Yes Tighten federal accounting and corporate governance regulation
- Yes Advance bipartisan Medicare prescription drug plan
- Yes Create independent Sept. 11 commission
- No Back Democratic Homeland Security Department proposal
- Yes Authorize war against Iraq

2001

- Yes Confirm John Ashcroft as attorney general
- Yes Nullify Clinton Labor Department ergonomics rule
- Yes Cut taxes by $1.35 trillion through fiscal 2011
- Yes Pass Democratic bill to bolster rights of patients in managed-care plans
- No Permit a new round of military base closings
- Yes Expand law enforcement power to investigate suspected terrorists

CQ VOTE STUDIES

	PARTY UNITY		PRESIDENTIAL SUPPORT	
	Support	Oppose	Support	Oppose
2002	60%	40%	89%	11%
2001	60%	40%	87%	13%
2000	67%	33%	59%	41%
1999	64%	36%	53%	47%
1998	49%	51%	60%	40%
1997	50%	50%	71%	29%
1996	64%	36%	59%	41%
1995	65%	35%	49%	51%
1994	56%	44%	56%	44%
1993	64%	36%	47%	53%

INTEREST GROUPS

	AFL-CIO	ADA	CCUS	ACU
2002	46%	35%	85%	50%
2001	63%	40%	79%	56%
2000	50%	40%	53%	62%
1999	44%	40%	47%	48%
1998	83%	45%	60%	33%
1997	57%	70%	50%	32%
1996	57%	50%	77%	50%
1995	33%	55%	79%	36%
1994	38%	55%	60%	46%
1993	45%	45%	100%	57%

Sen. Rick Santorum (R)

CAPITOL OFFICE
224-6324
santorum.senate.gov
120 Russell 20510-3804; fax 228-0604

COMMITTEES
Banking, Housing & Urban Affairs
Finance
(Social Security & Family Policy - chairman)
Rules & Administration
Special Aging

HOMETOWN
Pittsburgh

BORN
May 10, 1958, Winchester, Va.

RELIGION
Roman Catholic

FAMILY
Wife, Karen Garver Santorum; seven children (one deceased)

EDUCATION
Pennsylvania State U., B.A. 1980 (political science); U. of Pittsburgh, M.B.A. 1981; Dickinson School of Law, J.D. 1986

CAREER
Lawyer; state legislative aide

POLITICAL HIGHLIGHTS
U.S. House, 1991-95

ELECTION RESULTS

2000 GENERAL

Rick Santorum (R)	2,481,962	52.4%
Ron Klink (D)	2,154,908	45.5%

2000 PRIMARY

Rick Santorum (R)		unopposed

PREVIOUS WINNING PERCENTAGES
1994 (49%); 1992 House Election (61%); 1990 House Election (51%)

Elected 1994; 2nd term

An ambitious politician with a well-known taste for hardball partisan politics, Santorum may have found his niche. As chairman of the Senate Republican Conference, the third-ranking position in the leadership, Santorum's job is to help shape the Senate majority's political message — which in the past often meant throwing bombs at the Democrats who controlled the Senate for most of the 107th Congress. He has filled the communications role easily in his first two years on the job, and his influence in the leadership will continue to grow in the 108th Congress as term limits have forced other key leaders to rotate out of the lineup.

When Mississippi's Trent Lott was forced to step down as Senate GOP leader late in 2002, swept away by criticism over his laudatory remarks about the 1948 segregationist presidential campaign of Strom Thurmond, Santorum briefly assayed a run for the top post. But he quickly realized that Tennessee's Bill Frist had the job locked up. To ease Lott's fall, Santorum relinquished his chairmanship of the Rules Committee for the 108th, handing the gavel to Lott. In 2003, Santorum himself came under criticism for remarks that equated homosexual acts with incest and adultery.

In some ways, Santorum seems made for the conference job. As a House member in the early 1990s, he was part of the group of Republicans who preferred the confrontational politics of Newt Gingrich to the pragmatic deal-making politics of the minority leader at that time, Robert H. Michel of Illinois. He was among the "Gang of Seven," a group of junior Republicans who defied their leadership on several occasions. After he moved to the other side of the Capitol in 1995, Santorum continued in that vein, which sometimes placed him out-of-step with the more collegial Senate.

But Santorum's job as conference chairman, in addition to being an advocate for the Bush administration and Republican policies, is to help lead the charge against the Democrats. That is a job Santorum clearly enjoys. He was among the first Republican leaders to try to use one person to illustrate the GOP view that Democrats were "obstructing" Bush's agenda. "The president has stuck out his hand, and Tom Daschle is biting it and chewing it like a rabid dog," Santorum said.

Santorum gained the leadership post at a relatively young age; he was 42 and just starting his second Senate term when he defeated Missouri's Christopher S. Bond for the job. He took on the post with such energy and enthusiasm that some GOP colleagues lamented that Santorum was overdoing it, presenting senators with long lists of assignments to help spread the Republican message. Since then, they say he has learned to turn the volume down, and they credit him with doing a better job of coordinating the Senate GOP message with House Republicans and the White House.

He also has dipped into legislative strategy on occasion. At his suggestion, the leadership conducted "after-action reviews" to see which of the Republican legislative strategies got the best results; the approach was modeled on the reviews that military generals conduct after battles.

As a legislator, however, Santorum is still learning the ropes. He spent much of the 107th Congress working with Connecticut Democrat Joseph I. Lieberman to pass President Bush's faith-based initiative, gradually whittling it down in an attempt to overcome the growing Democratic opposition. But he never did make enough tradeoffs to satisfy their most basic concerns — that federal aid to faith-based groups, without safeguards, could result in subsidizing discrimination and proselytizing — and the bill never made it onto the Senate floor. He and Lieberman are trying again in the 108th and Santorum's new seat on the Finance panel enabled him to push for early committee action on the measure in 2003.

The partnership with Lieberman has a history to it; the two had worked together in 2000 to pass that year's community renewal legislation, an anti-poverty measure that included a narrower provision to provide federal aid to faith-based social services. Still, Santorum has often struggled as the Republican frontman for Bush's broader faith-based package. He seemed annoyed at the compromises he had to make with Democrats.

The son of an Italian immigrant — a Veterans Administration psychologist — the boyish-faced Santorum stresses individual responsibility and self-reliance, not government assistance programs. He can draw on his own experience of holding down a full-time job while attending law school. Santorum also takes care to tend to his constituents' needs, putting his ideology aside when necessary. He has backed programs to help farmers, supported some labor causes such as an increase in the minimum wage, and modified his free-trade views to endorse Bush's 2001 decision to impose tariffs on imported steel. He works hard to stay in touch with his constituents, visiting each of Pennsylvania's 67 counties every year.

He has a working, if not particularly friendly, relationship with his senior Keystone State colleague, the more liberal Republican Arlen Specter. When Rep. Patrick J. Toomey, a conservative in the same mold as Santorum, announced a 2004 primary challenge to Specter in 2004, Santorum quickly announced he would back Specter.

An unalloyed social conservative, Santorum saves his toughest fights for the issue of abortion. He is a leader in the fight to outlaw a procedure that opponents call "partial birth" abortion, which he has called "barbaric" and "the calculated killing of the nearly born." His views are so strong that they prompted one of his few public disagreements with Bush, over the president's decision in 2001 to fund research on stem cells already extracted from human embryos. Santorum keeps a photograph on his desk of an underdeveloped baby — his own late son, Gabriel Michael. The baby was born after only five months of gestation when complications forced an early delivery, and he died two hours later. The Santorums rejected any thought of an abortion, firm in the belief that it would constitute murdering their son.

Santorum has resumed the fight in the 108th. He also is likely to push his so-called born alive bill, which would require that babies born alive at any stage of development be given the same legal rights that all Americans have.

Santorum was smitten by politics as a student at Penn State University, working in congressional campaigns and winning election as state chairman of the College Republicans. After working as an aide in the state legislature for several years, he mounted a long-shot effort in 1990 to unseat Democratic Rep. Doug Walgren, organizing a textbook grass-roots campaign and upsetting the incumbent by 2 percentage points.

In 1994, he took on Democratic Sen. Harris Wofford, who had won a special election in 1991. Santorum ran a fiery campaign that fed on widespread voter discontent with Washington, painting his opponent as an out-of-date liberal and assailing him for supporting gun control measures. He won with 49 percent to Wofford's 47 percent. Democrats targeted Santorum as one of the Senate's most vulnerable incumbents in 2000. They contended he was too conservative for moderate Pennsylvania voters. But a divisive Democratic primary weakened their cause, and the eventual nominee, Rep. Ron Klink, struggled to raise money from deep-pocket Democratic donors. By moderating his image and emphasizing his work on a range of issues, including welfare and Social Security, Santorum won re-election by 7 percentage points.

KEY VOTES

2002

- No Pass farm bill reversing crop subsidy limits
- Yes Postpone tougher automobile fuel efficiency standards
- No Overhaul campaign finance law; ban "soft money" and restrict advocacy advertising
- Yes Set federal election standards
- Yes Support oil drilling in Arctic National Wildlife Refuge
- Yes Revive fast-track procedures for trade agreements
- No Create federal insurance coverage for catastrophic terrorist losses
- Yes Tighten federal accounting and corporate governance regulation
- No Advance bipartisan Medicare prescription drug plan
- Yes Create independent Sept. 11 commission
- No Back Democratic Homeland Security Department proposal
- Yes Authorize war against Iraq

2001

- Yes Confirm John Ashcroft as attorney general
- Yes Nullify Clinton Labor Department ergonomics rule
- Yes Cut taxes by $1.35 trillion through fiscal 2011
- No Pass Democratic bill to bolster rights of patients in managed-care plans
- Yes Permit a new round of military base closings
- Yes Expand law enforcement power to investigate suspected terrorists

CQ VOTE STUDIES

	PARTY UNITY		PRESIDENTIAL SUPPORT	
	Support	Oppose	Support	Oppose
2002	96%	4%	96%	4%
2001	95%	5%	97%	3%
2000	96%	4%	49%	51%
1999	91%	9%	30%	70%
1998	91%	9%	40%	60%
1997	91%	9%	61%	39%
1996	93%	7%	40%	60%
1995	96%	4%	24%	76%
House Service:				
1994	83%	17%	56%	44%
1993	83%	17%	46%	54%

INTEREST GROUPS

	AFL-CIO	ADA	CCUS	ACU
2002	15%	5%	95%	95%
2001	13%	10%	86%	100%
2000	0%	0%	93%	100%
1999	25%	5%	81%	88%
1998	0%	0%	89%	84%
1997	14%	15%	90%	84%
1996	43%	15%	77%	95%
1995	8%	5%	100%	83%
House Service:				
1994	22%	15%	100%	81%
1993	50%	20%	73%	70%

Rep. Robert A. Brady (D)

Elected May 1998; 3rd full term

CAPITOL OFFICE
225-4731
www.house.gov/robertbrady
206 Cannon 20515-3801; fax 225-0088

COMMITTEES
Armed Services
House Administration
Joint Printing

HOMETOWN
Philadelphia

BORN
April 7, 1945, Philadelphia, Pa.

RELIGION
Roman Catholic

FAMILY
Wife, Debra Brady; two children

EDUCATION
St. Thomas More H.S., graduated 1963

CAREER
Union lobbyist; carpenter

POLITICAL HIGHLIGHTS
34th Ward Democratic Executive Committee, 1967-present (leader, 1980-present); candidate for Philadelphia City Council, 1983; Philadelphia Democratic Party chairman, 1986-present

ELECTION RESULTS

2002 GENERAL		
Robert A. Brady (D)	121,076	86.4%
Marie G. Delany (R)	17,444	12.5%
Michael J. Ewall (GREEN)	1,570	1.1%
2002 PRIMARY		
Robert A. Brady (D)		unopposed
2000 GENERAL		
Robert A. Brady (D)	149,621	88.3%
Steven N. Kush (R)	19,920	11.8%

PREVIOUS WINNING PERCENTAGES
1998 (81%); 1998 Special Election (74%)

In addition to his duties as a congressman, Brady also serves as chairman of Philadelphia's Democratic organization, one of the last political machines in the country worthy of the name. On the side, he tends to the needs of his working-class constituents. Brady is effective enough that he has no serious rival in the 1st District, which has the largest percentage of black people of any district in the nation represented by a white person.

But it is Brady's role as local party boss that gives him his clout, as Al Gore confirmed early in his 2000 presidential campaign. As the Philadelphia Inquirer recounted the story, Gore came into the House and walked over to John P. Murtha, the Pennsylvania Democrat who is an acknowledged master of appropriations politics — and Brady's mentor. Not unreasonably, Murtha assumed Gore wanted to talk to him until the vice president asked, "Where's Brady?"

Gore's attentiveness was vindicated on Election Day, when a Brady turn-out-the-vote drive gave the vice president a 350,000-vote margin in Philadelphia — more than offsetting Republican George W. Bush's strength in other parts of the state.

In the House, Brady is as loyal a spear-carrier as the Democratic leadership is likely to find. Indeed, one of the first things he did after he arrived in 1998 was hand Richard A. Gephardt a signed, undated letter of resignation, the most concrete pledge imaginable that he would be there when the minority leader needed him.

His loyalty to organized labor is equally striking, reflecting his working-class roots. Brady was an athlete in his younger days, teaming up once with Wilt Chamberlain in a neighborhood pickup game. But he had to forgo scholarship offers and go to work as a carpenter to help support his family. After 12 years in the trade, he moved into a full-time post with the carpenter's union. Brady still carries a union card and has a lifetime score of 100 percent in the AFL-CIO's rating of members' voting records.

In 2001, he infuriated some longtime environmentalist allies by backing President Bush's proposal to allow oil drilling in Alaska's Arctic National Wildlife Refuge — an idea backed by the Teamsters Union and the AFL-CIO's building trades division.

During the 107th Congress, Brady showed that he could do journeyman legislating by getting a bill passed that would establish a pilot program to help vocational schools teach students how to start a small business. In 2000, he shepherded a measure to study the incidence of hepatitis C among firefighters, paramedics and emergency medical technicians.

Brady also does the routine work of bringing the bacon home to his district. In 2001, for example, he used his seat on the Armed Services Committee to pump an additional $15 million into the scaled-down Navy facility at the former Philadelphia Naval Shipyard. He may have to spend more of his time on that particular type of work in the 108th Congress, because Robert Borski, who had represented Philadelphia's northeast side and was a senior Democrat on the Transportation Committee, retired after redistricting. Accordingly, the city may find itself relying more on Brady to get its share of the federal pie, working through his close friend and patron, appropriations kingpin Murtha. "I'm Murtha's guy. I say to him, 'What do you need me to do,' " Brady declared in 2003.

But Brady spends much of his time operating outside congressional — or even federal — channels to meet his constituents' needs. His tools are his keen negotiating skills, the dense web of contacts he has built up over four decades in union work and politics, and the large pile of markers he holds from people who owe him.

According to Brady's congressional Web site, he was "widely praised as key to the settlement of a labor impasse that threatened to shut down public schools" in his city in 2001. Building on his years of union negotiating experience, Brady hosted a fence-mending session after the bitter 1999 Philadelphia Democratic mayoral primary and brokered the end to a transit strike in 1998.

Brady's approach to the job embodies a lesson he learned years ago. He decided to become involved politically when his mother concluded that the local party boss was being insufficiently attentive to her request for a new bulb in a street lamp. (In 2002, it was Brady who put $600,000 for "security lighting" for a Philadelphia bridge in the annual defense budget bill.)

Twenty-two when he was elected to the 34th Ward Democratic Executive Committee, Brady has been in the local party organization ever since. He held a variety of posts at City Hall, the city's redevelopment agency and the Pennsylvania Turnpike Authority. Many of the positions enabled him to find jobs for people; the Inquirer reported that Brady once dubbed himself "the largest employment agency in Pennsylvania."

Before he ran for the House, Brady had sought elective office just once, losing his bid for a seat on the City Council in 1983. But his grasp of city politics — as well as nominating rules that favored the candidate with the backing of the party machinery — made him a formidable candidate in the 1998 special election when Democratic Rep. Thomas M. Foglietta resigned to become ambassador to Italy. He easily received the Democratic nomination, which practically ensured his victory in the overwhelmingly Democratic district. He won the special election with 74 percent of the vote and has been re-elected with even healthier tallies.

Brady could not vote for himself the first three times he ran for the seat because he lived in the adjacent 2nd District. Brady said he spent his first 37 years as a resident of the 1st District until its lines were redrawn in 1982. "I didn't move, the district moved," he said.

Since the 2000 census cost the state two House seats, there was speculation that Brady's district might be at risk when the lines subsequently were redrawn under a GOP-controlled process. Instead, the new map put two other Philadelphia-area Democrats — Borski and Joseph M. Hoeffel — into the same district. The 1st District was redrawn to once again include Brady's residence, and he won by another landslide.

KEY VOTES

2002

- Yes Overhaul campaign finance law; ban "soft money" and restrict advocacy advertising
- Yes Back Bush's defense budget increase
- No Extend 1996 welfare law
- No Adopt Bush's discretionary spending limit
- No Pass GOP Medicare prescription drug plan
- Yes Create independent Sept. 11 commission
- Yes Extend union protections to Homeland Security Department employees
- No Revive fast-track procedures for trade agreements
- No Authorize war against Iraq
- No Advance bankruptcy overhaul opposed by abortion opponents

2001

- No Nullify Clinton Labor Department ergonomics rule
- No Cut taxes by $1.35 trillion through fiscal 2011
- No Maintain ban on oil drilling in Arctic National Wildlife Refuge
- No Approve Bush proposal to limit managed-care plan liability for coverage decisions
- Yes Divert money from crop subsidy payments to land conservation
- Yes Expand law enforcement power to investigate suspected terrorists

CQ VOTE STUDIES

	PARTY UNITY		PRESIDENTIAL SUPPORT	
	Support	Oppose	Support	Oppose
2002	94%	6%	31%	69%
2001	92%	8%	33%	67%
2000	95%	5%	86%	14%
1999	94%	6%	82%	18%
1998	97%	3%	88%	12%

INTEREST GROUPS

	AFL-CIO	ADA	CCUS	ACU
2002	100%	95%	45%	4%
2001	100%	95%	43%	16%
2000	100%	90%	42%	12%
1999	100%	95%	20%	8%
1998	100%	50%	25%	0%

PENNSYLVANIA 1

South and central Philadelphia; Chester

Home of the Philly cheesesteak, the 1st is known for its patriotic attractions, including the Liberty Bell and Independence Hall, the birthplace of the Constitution. Its Italian population supports a famous market where vendors sell produce, meat and cheese. Many Catholic churches still hold Mass in Italian.

The W-shaped 1st, where almost 90 percent of residents live in Philadelphia, is the state's most racially and ethnically diverse district. Already home to Philadelphia's Chinatown, an influx of Vietnamese and Chinese residents and businesses has boosted the Asian presence. Nearly three-fourths of Philadelphia's Hispanic population resides in the 1st, with the highest concentration in the northern part of the district. But African-Amercians represent the largest population block, at 45 percent.

Veterans Stadium and First Union Center, home to the city's major sports teams, are in the 1st. Lincoln Financial Field, built to replace crumbling Veterans Stadium, was scheduled to house football's Eagles beginning with the 2003 season, and baseball's Phillies also are getting a new park.

Once home to factory workers and a large ethnic blue-collar work force, factory closings have left swaths of the 1st with a bleak economic landscape. While Philadelphia overall won notice for substantial economic recovery in the 1990s and is seeing a surge of construction jobs, major sections have yet to recover from a long period of industrial decay. The 1st has the lowest median income in the state.

The nearby closed Philadelphia Naval Shipyard is home to the booming Kvaerner Philadelphia and Metro Machine shipyards. The region is working to become an important shipbuilding, refurbishing and decommissioning center. Its strong union presence and substantial minority population make the 1st a slam-dunk for Democratic candidates.

MAJOR INDUSTRY

Government, service, health care

CITIES

Philadelphia (pt.), 571,130; Chester, 36,854

NOTABLE

Eastern State Penitentiary, the most expensive upon its opening in 1829, held gangster Al Capone; The Liberty Bell has "Pennsylvania" spelled as "Pensylvania"; Sylvester Stallone's "Rocky" movies were filmed in south Philadelphia.

Rep. Chaka Fattah (D)

CAPITOL OFFICE
225-4001
www.house.gov/fattah
2301 Rayburn 20515-3802; fax 225-5392

COMMITTEES
Appropriations

HOMETOWN
Philadelphia

BORN
Nov. 21, 1956, Philadelphia, Pa.

RELIGION
Baptist

FAMILY
Wife, Renee Chenault-Fattah; three children

EDUCATION
Community College of Philadelphia, attended 1976 (political science); U. of Pennsylvania, M.A. 1986 (government administration)

CAREER
Public official

POLITICAL HIGHLIGHTS
Democratic candidate for Philadelphia City Commission, 1978; Pa. House, 1983-89; Pa. Senate, 1989-95; Consumer Party nominee for U.S. House (special election), 1991

ELECTION RESULTS

2002 GENERAL		
Chaka Fattah (D)	150,623	87.8%
Thomas G. Dougherty (R)	20,988	12.2%
2002 PRIMARY		
Chaka Fattah (D)		unopposed
2000 GENERAL		
Chaka Fattah (D)	180,021	98.0%
Ken V. Krawchuk (LIBERT)	3,673	2.0%

PREVIOUS WINNING PERCENTAGES
1998 (87%); 1996 (88%); 1994 (86%)

Elected 1994; 5th term

Whether he is championing students' interests on Capitol Hill or fighting against school privatization back home in Philadelphia, education never appears to be far from Fattah's mind.

Fattah's commitment to educational equality — his calling card political issue dating back to his time in the Pennsylvania General Assembly — is part of an ambitious liberal agenda that he combines with a longstanding willingness to challenge the powers-that-be. Add the political savvy gained during more than two decades in elective office, and you have the ingredients that make Fattah a self-described "practical idealist."

Fattah (SHOCK-ah fa-TAH) has roots in public life that stretch back to his youthful days as a community activist inspired by his mother. He is full of ideas about things government can do to make the American dream come true for his inner-city constituents. He maintains that many of them have little chance for success as long as Democrats are in the minority, but he says that "you have to put your ideas out there, so that people know where you're coming from and so, when you're in the majority, folks will have an idea of where you want to go."

Fattah is able to form bipartisan alliances and is willing to compromise when legislative success is in sight. The best example of that may be his successful effort to expand nationwide a motivational tool used by private citizens in a number of cities to encourage low-income youths to set their sights on college. The program, dubbed Gear Up, became law in 1998 after Fattah joined with conservative Republican Mark Souder of Indiana and won key support from the Clinton administration. It provides tutoring, mentoring and counseling as early as sixth or seventh grade, and gives schools incentives to offer courses that prepare the students for college.

In the 107th Congress, Fattah got a seat on the Appropriations Committee and immediately became the top-ranking Democrat on the District of Columbia Subcommittee. On that panel he has sought to keep the annual D.C. spending bill clean of social policy add-ons and restrictions on municipal spending often pushed by the GOP. And he works to keep funding flowing for the Gear Up program.

But even as he has learned the ropes of the Capitol's spending process, Fattah says education remains his top priority — "my real passion."

Although he had to leave the Education and the Workforce panel to take the Appropriations assignment, Fattah continued his effort to attract support for legislation that would require states to fund all their public schools equally or to prove that students throughout the state have equal achievement levels. Fattah also has proposed a law that would establish a "student bill of rights" to ensure that students in urban areas have the same access to quality education as do their suburban counterparts.

Fattah is not averse to using non-legislative approaches to important issues, especially when it comes to educational matters in Philadelphia. He founded an annual three-day seminar at which students are encouraged to consider attending graduate school.

But he recalls advice given to him by former Democratic Rep. Louis Stokes of Ohio: Many people can give speeches and do good civic deeds, but only a member of Congress can introduce bills and pass laws. And so, Fattah's emphasis is on legislation. His portfolio includes bills to encourage states to afford all residents access to at least a minimum standard of health care and to prohibit stores from insisting that customers have a credit card as a condition of doing business.

Fattah arrived in Congress in 1995, just as Republicans assumed control. He took the post of whip for the Congressional Black Caucus and wasted no time denouncing the new majority's ideas. During a debate early in the 104th on a GOP proposal to overhaul the welfare system, he said: "We have some tough cowboys here on the floor of the House. This is a new, interesting kind of wagon train in which the cowboys have decided to throw the women and infants and the children and the senior citizens out of the wagon train so they can get where they are going faster. It is cruel."

Named Arthur Davenport at birth, one of six boys in an inner-city household headed by his widowed mother, Fattah's name was changed when his mother married community activist David Fattah. According to a Philadelphia Inquirer profile displayed on his office wall, Fattah's mother named him "Chaka" in honor of a Zulu warrior. Fattah's parents produced a magazine for the black community and established the House of Umoja, which became a neighborhood gathering place and haven for youths trying to work their way out of gang life.

Fattah remembers political discussions and his family's efforts to improve housing in the area. He met Democratic Rep. William H. Gray III and worked on one of his campaigns, and then, at age 22, finished fourth in his bid for a municipal office. Four years later, he successfully challenged a Democratic Party-backed incumbent for a state House seat and, at 25, became the youngest person ever elected to the state legislature.

It was not the last time he bucked the party. After six years in the state House and two in the state Senate, Fattah entered the 1991 special-election race to succeed Gray, who had resigned to become president of the United Negro College Fund. The Democratic Party backed longtime City Councilman Lucien E. Blackwell, and Fattah temporarily quit the party to run on the Consumer Party ticket. Blackwell won with 39 percent to Fattah's 28 percent.

Redistricting for the 1990s — in which Fattah had a hand as a member of the state Senate — reduced the percentage of African-Americans in the 2nd District to 62 percent from 80 percent. That put Blackwell at risk because his appeal was strongest among West Philly's poor and working-class blacks, and in 1994 Fattah challenged Blackwell's renomination. The incumbent had the backing of Mayor Ed Rendell and City Council President John Street. But Fattah outworked Blackwell and claimed the primary victory with an impressive 58 percent. In the overwhelmingly Democratic 2nd — changed only marginally in the most recent redistricting — Fattah has not been seriously challenged in his re-elections.

KEY VOTES

2002

- Yes Overhaul campaign finance law; ban "soft money" and restrict advocacy advertising
- No Back Bush's defense budget increase
- No Extend 1996 welfare law
- No Adopt Bush's discretionary spending limit
- No Pass GOP Medicare prescription drug plan
- Yes Create independent Sept. 11 commission
- Yes Extend union protections to Homeland Security Department employees
- No Revive fast-track procedures for trade agreements
- No Authorize war against Iraq
- No Advance bankruptcy overhaul opposed by abortion opponents

2001

- No Nullify Clinton Labor Department ergonomics rule
- No Cut taxes by $1.35 trillion through fiscal 2011
- Yes Maintain ban on oil drilling in Arctic National Wildlife Refuge
- No Approve Bush proposal to limit managed-care plan liability for coverage decisions
- Yes Divert money from crop subsidy payments to land conservation
- Yes Expand law enforcement power to investigate suspected terrorists

CQ VOTE STUDIES

	PARTY UNITY		PRESIDENTIAL SUPPORT	
	Support	Oppose	Support	Oppose
2002	97%	3%	28%	72%
2001	95%	5%	22%	78%
2000	97%	3%	94%	6%
1999	97%	3%	86%	14%
1998	96%	4%	88%	12%

INTEREST GROUPS

	AFL-CIO	ADA	CCUS	ACU
2002	100%	95%	37%	0%
2001	100%	100%	27%	0%
2000	100%	95%	40%	0%
1999	78%	95%	24%	0%
1998	100%	95%	25%	0%

PENNSYLVANIA 2

West Philadelphia; Chestnut Hill; Cheltenham

From the vantage point of the William Penn statue atop City Hall, one can see the 2nd stretching west and north over some of Philadelphia's long-established neighborhoods. The district encompasses Center City skyscrapers, then moves west across the Schuylkill River past the University of Pennsylvania. West Philadelphia, once Irish, Greek and Jewish, is now nearly all black and features pockets of middle-class and poor communities. Overall, African-Americans represent more than three-fifths of the 2nd's residents.

Except for the Montgomery County township of Cheltenham, the 2nd is wholly within Philadelphia. The district takes in the affluent city neighborhoods of Rittenhouse Square, one of five squares Penn included in his original design of the city, and Chestnut Hill, in the city's northwest corner. It also includes Fairmount Park, which houses the city's art museum, zoo and "Boathouse Row." The park, which flanks the Schuylkill River, runs north along diverse, middle-class neighborhoods, some of which have seen some recent gentrification, and ends in Chestnut Hill. Some of the homes in Center City Philadelphia are among the oldest in the United States.

Economic struggles continue to grip many areas of the district; some of the city's lowest family incomes are found in neighborhoods just north of downtown. The University of Pennsylvania has invested in West Philadelphia, creating incentives for school staff members to live in the neighborhood. This includes financial help for home buyers and the creation of a University of Pennsylvania-assisted public school.

The 2nd's blue-collar work force and large minority population give it an overwhelming Democratic majority. In the 2002 gubernatorial election, Democrat Ed Rendell took more than 85 percent of the vote in 26 of the 27 city wards that are wholly within the district.

MAJOR INDUSTRY
Education, health care, tourism

CITIES
Philadelphia (pt.), 609,486; Glenside (unincorporated) (pt.), 3,093

NOTABLE
The Philadelphia Zoo is home to the nation's only giant river otters; The 30th Street Station is in West Philadelphia.

Rep. Phil English (R)

Elected 1994; 5th term

CAPITOL OFFICE
225-5406
phil.english@mail.house.gov
www.house.gov/english
1410 Longworth 20515-3803; fax 225-3103

COMMITTEES
Ways & Means
Joint Economic

HOMETOWN
Erie

BORN
June 20, 1956, Erie, Pa.

RELIGION
Roman Catholic

FAMILY
Wife, Christiane English

EDUCATION
U. of Pennsylvania, B.A. 1979 (political science)

CAREER
State legislative aide

POLITICAL HIGHLIGHTS
Erie City controller, 1986-89; Republican nominee for Pa. treasurer, 1988

ELECTION RESULTS

2002 GENERAL		
Phil English (R)	116,763	77.7%
AnnDrea M. Benson (GREEN)	33,554	22.3%
2002 PRIMARY		
Phil English (R)		unopposed
2000 GENERAL		
Phil English (R)	135,164	60.8%
Marc Flitter (D)	87,018	39.2%

PREVIOUS WINNING PERCENTAGES
1998 (63%); 1996 (51%); 1994 (49%)

When President Bush was struggling with his decision in 2002 to depart from an aggressive free-trade agenda and protect the nation's ailing steel industry with high tariffs, English persistently warned the administration of the economic and political consequences of not backing steel companies.

English, who has a mostly free-trade voting record, was demonstrating his own brand of political pragmatism — working to reconcile the competing interests of steelmakers in his district, who want protection, and the businesses that use steel, which want low-priced imports.

He was similarly out front in late 2002 and early 2003 in pressing for an extension of unemployment benefits, of particular importance to states such as Pennsylvania.

Although he is now coming to the end of a decade of service in Congress, English must continue to find such a balance on a host of issues if he is to survive politically in the long run.

Although somewhat more Republican since redistricting, the renumbered 3rd District (in the 1990s it was the 21st) still lies within a partisan battleground. Bill Clinton won northwestern Pennsylvania comfortably; George W. Bush carried it narrowly. Organized labor has substantial clout in the region, and English won his first two races with little to spare. His evolving ideology helped him crack 60 percent in his third and fourth elections, however, and in 2002 the Democrats looked at the more GOP-friendly district lines and decided not to field a candidate.

English's moderate political philosophy and track record on bipartisan cooperation placed him outside the norm of the Republicans in the takeover Class of 1994, which was dominated by conservatives who proudly trumpeted their "outsider" status. English, nevertheless, had the credentials on tax issues that helped persuade GOP leaders to put him on the Ways and Means panel, the first Republican freshman in decades to get such a post.

He arrived brimming with ideas, from wide-ranging plans to simplify the tax code to more-focused proposals such as his bill to permit clergymen to join in the Social Security and Medicare systems late in their careers. As would be expected from a former legislative aide, English is conversant with the details of his bills and is a voracious reader who often tests the mettle of his own staff in keeping up with the myriad details of congressional action.

To bolster his credentials with unions, English attended the World Trade Organization meetings in Seattle in 1999 to warn against any softening of anti-dumping regulations that are important to the steel business. He backs trade adjustment assistance programs, which help workers who lose their jobs to foreign competition. In the 104th Congress, he was in the minority of Republicans who backed measures to protect collective bargaining rights of mass transit workers.

But he does not always side with labor. In 1996 he voted to let businesses offer their workers compensatory time off instead of overtime pay. And in the 107th, he voted to revive fast-track procedures for congressional consideration of trade deals and to give the administration more flexibility in dealing with workers at the new Homeland Security Department.

English is a reliable GOP vote on other issues, and his Ways and Means seat allows him to influence policy rather than rely on rhetorical warfare like some of his House generation. "I'm certainly less inclined to throw bombs than someone who is strictly on the sidelines of the process," he says.

In addition to the Trade Subcommittee, English has used other assignments on the Health and Human Resources subcommittees to advance his philosophies. Legislation in 2001 aimed at preventing child abuse and neglect included an English amendment that would allow funds to be used to publicize "safe haven" programs that encourage mothers who do not want to keep their newborns to leave them at a hospital or fire station. English also was part of the GOP team that has formulated the party's proposals for adding a prescription drug benefit under Medicare.

In the wake of the Sept. 11, 2001, terrorist attacks, English advocated a capital gains tax cut to stimulate the economy. He also cosponsored a bill to accelerate business depreciation schedules. A modest version of that bill was in an economic stimulus package enacted in 2002. The return of the budget deficit, however, further dimmed chances for his long-running effort to halve the excise tax on beer.

In 1998, he tried to take on the entire tax code. In front of constituents in Erie, he attempted to cut through the 5,000-page U.S. tax code with a chainsaw. But the chainsaw knocked the book off the table twice. Even after putting the code on the sidewalk, he was just able to nick it with the chainsaw. English finally joked about how tough it was to enact tax reform.

English's interest in politics began at an early age. The son of an Erie lawyer who was active in community affairs, English was a political science major in college and an alternate delegate, at age 20, to the 1976 Republican National Convention. (His sister, Otilie English, has long been involved with overseas issues and was most recently a Washington lobbyist for the Afghan rebels known as the Northern Alliance.)

After college, English spent eight years as a legislative aide for a closely divided Pennsylvania state legislature specializing in tax and social welfare issues. English's career in elective office began in 1985 when he was elected Erie City controller, on a pledge to be a watchdog over the Democratic-dominated government. In 1988, at the midpoint of his four-year term, he ran for state treasurer. While he impressed GOP officials with his knowledge of state fiscal issues, he lost by nearly 500,000 votes.

When his term as controller was over, he moved from candidate to strategist. He helped a little-known underdog, Rick Santorum, organize his 1990 upset of Democratic Rep. Doug Walgren. English then returned to Harrisburg as a legislative staffer, including a stint as chief of staff to a state senator, Melissa A. Hart, who is now a colleague in the House.

He appeared content with his behind-the-scenes career as a top legislative staff member but jumped at the chance to run for an open congressional seat in 1994, when GOP Rep. Tom Ridge ran, successfully, for governor.

KEY VOTES

2002

No Overhaul campaign finance law; ban "soft money" and restrict advocacy advertising
Yes Back Bush's defense budget increase
Yes Extend 1996 welfare law
Yes Adopt Bush's discretionary spending limit
Yes Pass GOP Medicare prescription drug plan
No Create independent Sept. 11 commission
No Extend union protections to Homeland Security Department employees
Yes Revive fast-track procedures for trade agreements
Yes Authorize war against Iraq
Yes Advance bankruptcy overhaul opposed by abortion opponents

2001

Yes Nullify Clinton Labor Department ergonomics rule
Yes Cut taxes by $1.35 trillion through fiscal 2011
No Maintain ban on oil drilling in Arctic National Wildlife Refuge
Yes Approve Bush proposal to limit managed-care plan liability for coverage decisions
No Divert money from crop subsidy payments to land conservation
Yes Expand law enforcement power to investigate suspected terrorists

CQ VOTE STUDIES

	PARTY UNITY		PRESIDENTIAL SUPPORT	
	Support	Oppose	Support	Oppose
2002	93%	7%	87%	13%
2001	89%	11%	81%	19%
2000	83%	17%	38%	62%
1999	84%	16%	24%	76%
1998	81%	19%	36%	64%

INTEREST GROUPS

	AFL-CIO	ADA	CCUS	ACU
2002	11%	0%	95%	92%
2001	25%	10%	95%	68%
2000	30%	25%	76%	56%
1999	38%	25%	76%	72%
1998	50%	35%	89%	68%

PENNSYLVANIA 3

Northwest – Erie

Located in the northwest corner of the state, the 3rd takes in all of Erie County and portions of six others. This historically blue-collar center includes Erie, the state's fourth-most-populous city. A port on Lake Erie, the city has been an industrial center for more than a century.

Although hard hit by economic restructuring in the 1980s, the 3rd remained an industrial area. The number of jobs in the services sector in Erie has nearly doubled since 1980. Fewer steel mills line Mercer County (a small portion of which is in the 4th District); those remaining now operate with a smaller employment base.

Despite those changes, Mercer boasts the largest concentration of pipe and tube production firms in the nation. In Crawford County, scores of tooling and machine shops dominate the landscape. Industrial expansion in Erie also is on the rise with a million-square-foot facility housing a distribution center and manufacturing plant.

Erie County's median household income is slightly below the state median, with the city of Erie well below and townships west and east of the city above the state median. The county, like the district overall, is largely white. Pockets of black residents in northern and central Erie help give the county a Democratic lean. Mercer County, home to one in six district residents, also has a Democratic lean, though George W. Bush nearly won the county in the 2000 presidential election after Bob Dole was trounced there in 1996.

Democratic tendencies in Erie and Mercer are offset by the Republican leanings in Butler and Crawford counties. Overall, the district (numbered the 21st prior to redistricting following the 2000 census) voted narrowly for George W. Bush in 2000.

MAJOR INDUSTRY
Manufacturing, law enforcement, service

CITIES
Erie, 103,717; Sharon, 16,328; Butler, 15,121; Meadville, 13,685

NOTABLE
Former Gov. Tom Ridge is from Erie; The reconstructed U.S. Brig Niagara, a fighting ship from the War of 1812, is docked in Erie; Erie's Presque Isle State Park includes a Coast Guard station and Perry Monument, which is dedicated to those killed in the Battle of Lake Erie (1813).

Rep. Melissa A. Hart (R)

CAPITOL OFFICE
225-2565
rep.hart@mail.house.gov
www.house.gov/hart
1508 Longworth 20515-3804; fax 226-2274

COMMITTEES
Financial Services
Judiciary
Science

HOMETOWN
Bradford Woods

BORN
April 4, 1962, Pittsburgh, Pa.

RELIGION
Roman Catholic

FAMILY
Single

EDUCATION
Washington & Jefferson College, B.A. 1984 (business & German); U. of Pittsburgh, J.D. 1987

CAREER
Lawyer

POLITICAL HIGHLIGHTS
Pa. Senate, 1991-2001

ELECTION RESULTS

2002 GENERAL		
Melissa A. Hart (R)	130,534	64.6%
Stevan Drobac Jr. (D)	71,674	35.5%
2002 PRIMARY		
Melissa A. Hart (R)		unopposed
2000 GENERAL		
Melissa A. Hart (R)	145,390	59.0%
Terry Van Horne (D)	100,995	41.0%

Elected 2000; 2nd term

Ambitious and assertive, the conservative Hart has endeared herself to party leaders by winning elections in historically Democratic-leaning districts. In the House, she has occasionally been a spokeswoman for a Republican leadership eager to showcase women.

In the 108th Congress, Hart ran for the vice chairman slot in the Republican Conference, but lost, 159-56, to Jack Kingston of Georgia, who is in his sixth term. Some members of the party questioned whether Hart, who sought the leadership position after just one congressional term, might not be getting ahead of herself. They wondered why she had not run instead for conference secretary, a lower rung on the leadership ladder.

Hart is both fiscally and socially conservative and her opposition to abortion and support of gun owners' rights are in sync with the socially conservative district she represents. Hart wants to outlaw a procedure its opponents call "partial birth" abortion.

She has offered legislation to withhold federal funds to schools that give students access to a "morning after" birth control pill. At one point in the 107th, she obtained a promise from the GOP leadership for a vote on her proposal, but a communications breakdown led to a brief brouhaha when she tried to offer it as an amendment to a spending bill that appropriators were trying to ease through without controversy. She agreed to withhold the amendment and reintroduced the bill early in the 108th.

The 4th District may be socially conservative, but it has a long history of union support that in the past has kept it in the Democratic column. Hart has joined with other lawmakers from steel-producing areas in urging the administration to impose quotas on imported steel. When she and several other Pennsylvania lawmakers traveled with President Bush on Air Force One en route to Beaver County in her district, Hart made a pitch for an investigation into foreign steel dumping.

That stance pleased area labor unions, but her record otherwise has given them little to cheer. She voted to give the president fast-track authority to negotiate trade agreements that Congress cannot amend, and she backed a bailout of the airline industry that did not include assistance for laid-off workers, including employees of U.S. Airways, which has a hub in Pittsburgh. She did sponsor, along with Democrat Alcee L. Hastings of Florida, separate legislation to help airline workers, but the bill went nowhere. On balance, the AFL-CIO rated her votes in the 107th at 14 percent, while the more conservative Teamsters union endorsed her in 2002.

Hart's chief legislative priority is to foster economic development for her district. Her specific proposals have included providing business tax breaks for hiring new workers, funding Army Corps of Engineers water and sewer projects in the Pittsburgh area and expanding the officially designated boundary of the metropolitan area to include three counties on the fringes of the exurbs, which would increase federal funding to the areas.

She has also proposed a bill to help women who are fleeing domestic violence or other displaced homemakers by providing job training and education. She won passage, as part of larger legislation, of her plan to designate certain safe havens where women could leave unwanted newborns without being prosecuted. She also has backed a measure to make it a federal crime to insert racist, sexist or pornographic material into consumer product packages and language to require the labeling of sexually oriented unsolicited e-mail, known as spam.

Hart grew up in the Pittsburgh suburbs, where her father was a research chemist for PPG Industries. She told the Pittsburgh Post-Gazette that she recalls writing an eighth grade paper entitled, "Why Ronald Reagan is a patriot." After her father died suddenly, Hart and her two siblings had to work their way through school to help out with the family finances.

She majored in business and German in college and joined the Young Republicans. After law school and a few years with a Pittsburgh law firm, Hart, then 28, decided to run for the state Senate. She later told the Press-Gazette that high taxes, particularly a steep property tax increase, had stirred voter discontent. "I had never thought of running for office until . . . I realized the money being taken from us wasn't being spent in an effective way," Hart told the newspaper.

She wasn't expected to win in the traditionally Democratic district, but her aggressive door-to-door campaign surprised even GOP strategists, allowing the GOP to retain its slim control of the state Senate.

Hart made a name for herself during her 10 years in the chamber. She chaired the Finance Committee, where she sponsored a measure to eliminate Pennsylvania's tax on computer company services, such as software design, and offered legislation to facilitate electronic commerce in the state. She mentored Phil English, who was her chief of staff and also worked for the Finance Committee before he was elected to the House from the 21st District in 1994.

Hart, who twice won re-election to her Senate seat, had long been regarded by Republican officials as a rising star, but as lawmakers prepared for the 1999 session of the legislature, she lost a bid to join the GOP leadership to a Senate newcomer, making a run for Congress look more attractive. "I can tell you honestly that I probably wouldn't be running for Congress now if that hadn't happened," she told the Post-Gazette after she entered the 2000 race.

When four-term Democratic Rep. Ron Klink left the seat open to run for the Senate, party leaders cleared the way for Hart's candidacy. As in 1990, Hart faced a tough battle in a Democratic-leaning district, with the GOP's hopes for control of the House at stake. With help from the national Republican Party and the conservative, business-oriented Club for Growth, Hart won impressively with 59 percent over state Rep. Terry Van Horne. She was the first Republican elected in the district since 1976.

Remapping in 2002 gave her a slightly more Republican constituency. The Post-Gazette, which had endorsed her in only one of her previous four races, grudgingly backed her over the untested Democratic candidate, Stevan Drobac Jr. Hart cruised to a 29 percentage point victory.

KEY VOTES

2002

- No Overhaul campaign finance law; ban "soft money" and restrict advocacy advertising
- Yes Back Bush's defense budget increase
- Yes Extend 1996 welfare law
- Yes Adopt Bush's discretionary spending limit
- Yes Pass GOP Medicare prescription drug plan
- No Create independent Sept. 11 commission
- No Extend union protections to Homeland Security Department employees
- Yes Revive fast-track procedures for trade agreements
- Yes Authorize war against Iraq
- Yes Advance bankruptcy overhaul opposed by abortion opponents

2001

- Yes Nullify Clinton Labor Department ergonomics rule
- Yes Cut taxes by $1.35 trillion through fiscal 2011
- No Maintain ban on oil drilling in Arctic National Wildlife Refuge
- Yes Approve Bush proposal to limit managed-care plan liability for coverage decisions
- Yes Divert money from crop subsidy payments to land conservation
- Yes Expand law enforcement power to investigate suspected terrorists

CQ VOTE STUDIES

	PARTY UNITY		PRESIDENTIAL SUPPORT	
	Support	Oppose	Support	Oppose
2002	97%	3%	92%	8%
2001	93%	7%	88%	12%

INTEREST GROUPS

	AFL-CIO	ADA	CCUS	ACU
2002	11%	0%	95%	96%
2001	17%	5%	96%	88%

PENNSYLVANIA 4

West – Pittsburgh suburbs, exurbs

The 4th starts at the western Pennsylvania border in Beaver and Lawrence counties and wraps around the northern and eastern sides of Pittsburgh. Once a top producer of iron and steel, this traditionally blue-collar district is struggling to bounce back from hard economic times.

The area's major highways and proximity to Pittsburgh make the 4th attractive to commuters and expanding companies. Although abandoned steel mills still line the rivers, other sectors are beginning to prosper, bringing some much-needed diversity to the economy. Along with the health care industry, which is a major employer, the 4th has a growing number of computer firms. The district also is dabbling in the biotech industry as surrounding universities expand research grants in the field.

Larger companies, such as U.S. Gypsum and National Gypsum, are bringing more jobs to the area. The district has yet to regain the population of its booming steel days, but some areas, including parts of Butler County, are experiencing rapid residential growth.

Although union tradition has generally kept the district Democratic from the township level to the presidency, socially conservative Republicans can break the Democratic grip. That happened in 2000, when George W. Bush captured the 4th and Rep. Hart easily won the Democratic-held open seat. Much of the district's GOP base can be found in small farming communities, wealthy Pittsburgh suburbs such as Franklin Park, Fox Chapel and Marshall Township, and the southern tier of Butler County. Redistricting following the 2000 census made the 4th slightly more Republican by moving the boundary farther into Allegheny County, where the GOP's strength has increased in recent years.

MAJOR INDUSTRY
Health care, steel, manufacturing

CITIES
Ross Township (unincorporated), 32,551; Shaler Township (unincorporated), 29,757; McCandless Township (unincorporated), 29,022

NOTABLE
Oliver B. Shallenberger invented the electric meter, which indicated the amount of electrical energy dispensed or applied, in Rochester; There were several stops on the Underground Railroad in Lawrence County.

Rep. John E. Peterson (R)

CAPITOL OFFICE
225-5121
john.peterson@mail.house.gov
www.house.gov/johnpeterson
123 Cannon 20515-3805; fax 225-5796

COMMITTEES
Appropriations
Resources

HOMETOWN
Pleasantville

BORN
Dec. 25, 1938, Titusville, Pa.

RELIGION
Methodist

FAMILY
Wife, Saundra Peterson; one child

EDUCATION
Titusville H.S., graduated 1956

MILITARY SERVICE
Army Reserve, 1957-63

CAREER
Supermarket owner

POLITICAL HIGHLIGHTS
Pleasantville Borough Council, 1969-77; Pa. House, 1977-85; Pa. Senate, 1985-97

ELECTION RESULTS

2002 GENERAL		
John E. Peterson (R)	124,942	87.4%
Thomas A. Martin (LIBERT)	18,078	12.6%
2002 PRIMARY		
John E. Peterson (R)		unopposed
2000 GENERAL		
John E. Peterson (R)	147,570	82.7%
Thomas A. Martin (LIBERT)	17,020	9.5%
William M. Belitskus (GREEN)	13,857	7.8%

PREVIOUS WINNING PERCENTAGES
1998 (85%); 1996 (60%)

Elected 1996; 4th term

"I come from rural Pennsylvania," is Peterson's political calling card, his starting point whenever he rises to speak on behalf of his constituents. The 5th District covers almost one quarter of the state's land, sprawling across more than 10,000 square miles of mountains, valleys, hamlets and a sizable national forest. It is the birthplace of America's oil industry and the home of Punxsutawney Phil, the famous groundhog. The largest urban area is a college town — State College, home of Pennsylvania State University.

Peterson's legislative agenda, tailored to his district's needs, includes rural health care, economic development, multiple use of the Allegheny National Forest and development of the 5th's remaining fossil energy reserves. From his seat on the Appropriations Committee, he looks after the needs of Pennsylvania medical schools and regional projects, such as the National Aviary in Pittsburgh. In the 108th Congress, Peterson is co-chairman, along with Florida Democrat Allen Boyd of the 100-plus member Rural Caucus.

Peterson's priorities also reflect his upbringing: Born and raised in the small town of Titusville near where Edwin Drake drilled the country's first oil well, Peterson grew up in a household headed by a steelworker father who never went to high school and who was a recovering alcoholic. The four children went to work to help with family expenses, and college was never an option for Peterson. (In his 30s, he attended a rural leadership training program at Penn State.)

What emerged from that childhood was a strong work ethic, an aversion to alcohol that led to his work combating substance abuse among rural youths, and an interest in improving the educational prospects of the district's children through expanded vocational education and college financial aid. Peterson is among the most vocal advocates of legislation mandating random drug testing for all high school students, saying it could reduce overall drug use and school violence.

Peterson often pleads for help from Washington to boost the economy of his district, which has pockets of rural Appalachian poverty. His Appropriations post puts him in a good position to direct federal dollars to the district. Of particular interest to him has been funding for the Economic Development Administration, which he has described as "the doctor who can give us a transfusion to help us maintain economic life" in rural America.

Peterson also takes an active role advising Pennsylvania universities on federal funding priorities for medical research. As a member of the Appropriations subcommittee with jurisdiction over the National Institutes of Health budget, Peterson has helped Penn State and Pennsylvania's five other medical schools win more than their share of federal research money.

The rural character of the 5th has allied Peterson with Westerners in annual congressional battles over the use of public lands and environmental issues. Peterson in the 107th Congress had the unusual distinction of being named communications director of the 50-member House Western Caucus, the only congressman from the region to be given a leadership position. The group opposes government efforts to restrict development of federal lands, saying key decisions should rest with local officials.

Peterson has warned in the past that environmental extremism tramples the rights of private property owners. "Regulations and laws and declarations have a huge impact on rural life," threatening rural people's "very ability to earn a living and to exist and live where they want to live," he says.

He has badgered the Forest Service to make sure the Allegheny National Forest is kept open for logging and other uses and that local communities are helped in providing fire and emergency services. He also has said he would support expanding the forest's wilderness area to include old-growth forest that has never been logged and some fragile animal habitats.

Peterson's involvement with the Rural Caucus extends to another pet cause — rural health care. He has pushed for legislation to give health care providers financial incentives to serve rural regions, including tax breaks for primary care physicians and higher Medicare payments to rural hospitals and health maintenance organizations.

When it comes to his role in the Republican Conference, Peterson can operate in the fashion of his party's pragmatic legislative dealmakers, but he also has a foot in the camp of its most committed conservative stalwarts. On a broad range of issues, Peterson is as conservative as they come in the House GOP. He opposes abortion, supports gun owners' rights, and wants to give parents taxpayer-financed vouchers to pay tuition at private schools.

A year after completing high school, Peterson joined the Army Reserves and then opened a small grocery store in nearby Pleasantville with his brother and a family friend, who put up the money. Peterson eventually bought out his partners and expanded the store, which he sold in 1984.

Peterson's empathy with retail business was evident in the weeks following the Sept. 11, 2001, terrorist attacks, when he participated in a congressional shopping trip at the behest of the International Mass Retail Association to urge Americans to continue shopping to help the economy. He ran up a $241 bill at a Target store in Northern Virginia.

Peterson entered politics in 1969, at the urging of other local businessmen in Pleasantville, winning a seat on the borough council. After eight years, he was elected to the state House; eight years after that he moved to the state Senate, where he chaired the Public Health and Welfare Committee and the Republican Policy Committee.

When Republican William F. Clinger did not seek re-election in 1996, Peterson was well-situated to succeed him in Congress: His state Senate district covered roughly the western half of the big 5th. Peterson's winning tally in November was 60 percent, but his victory did not come easily. In the spring, he had to fight off three opponents in the Republican primary including Bob Shuster, a son of Bud Shuster, then the veteran congressman from a neighboring district.

His GOP base secure, Peterson has had no re-election difficulty. The Democrats have not fielded a candidate since that first race in 1996.

KEY VOTES

2002

No Overhaul campaign finance law; ban "soft money" and restrict advocacy advertising
Yes Back Bush's defense budget increase
Yes Extend 1996 welfare law
Yes Adopt Bush's discretionary spending limit
Yes Pass GOP Medicare prescription drug plan
No Create independent Sept. 11 commission
No Extend union protections to Homeland Security Department employees
Yes Revive fast-track procedures for trade agreements
Yes Authorize war against Iraq
Yes Advance bankruptcy overhaul opposed by abortion opponents

2001

Yes Nullify Clinton Labor Department ergonomics rule
Yes Cut taxes by $1.35 trillion through fiscal 2011
No Maintain ban on oil drilling in Arctic National Wildlife Refuge
Yes Approve Bush proposal to limit managed-care plan liability for coverage decisions
No Divert money from crop subsidy payments to land conservation
Yes Expand law enforcement power to investigate suspected terrorists

CQ VOTE STUDIES

	PARTY UNITY		PRESIDENTIAL SUPPORT	
	Support	Oppose	Support	Oppose
2002	94%	6%	84%	16%
2001	96%	4%	93%	7%
2000	94%	6%	27%	73%
1999	91%	9%	19%	81%
1998	95%	5%	24%	76%

INTEREST GROUPS

	AFL-CIO	ADA	CCUS	ACU
2002	13%	0%	100%	100%
2001	8%	0%	100%	88%
2000	0%	0%	90%	96%
1999	25%	5%	100%	80%
1998	0%	0%	100%	96%

PENNSYLVANIA 5

North central – State College

The giant, sprawling 5th encompasses part or all of 16 counties and the state's largest university, Pennsylvania State. The district's upper counties border New York State, and its westernmost point is only about 30 miles from the Ohio border. In land framed by the Appalachian Mountains sit struggling towns and pockets of poverty.

State College (Centre County), the district's largest city and home of Penn State, has hopped on the high-tech bandwagon, bringing in manufacturing firms that specialize in electronics and computer products. Its technology-driven development mimics the tide that brought the Silicon Valley to prominence, though on a much smaller scale. The district also boasts a contingent of more than 200 meteorologists.

While State College's work force is technologically advanced, the 5th's other counties remain tied to timber production, manufacturing and oil refining. The district's population is overwhelmingly white. At 96 percent, it has the second-highest percentage in the state.

Much of the 5th — particularly the northern counties — votes Republican, and George W. Bush won all of its counties in 2000. Some exceptions exist: Penn State keeps Centre County competitive for Democrats. Neighboring Clinton County and, farther west, Elk County lean toward Democrats in local elections (but toward Republicans in statewide and federal elections). Jefferson, Tioga, McKean, Clarion and Potter counties are staunchly Republican. Mike Fisher, the Republican gubernatorial nominee in 2002, took 71 percent in Potter and 69 percent in Tioga, his second and fifth-best counties in the state.

MAJOR INDUSTRY
Manufacturing, higher education, timber

CITIES
State College, 38,420; St. Marys, 14,502; Oil City, 11,504

NOTABLE
The town of Punxsutawney (Jefferson County) holds a yearly celebration for groundhog "Punxsutawney Phil," who becomes a national media star on Groundhog Day; Situated amidst about 160,000 acres of the Tioga State Forest lies the Grand Canyon of Pennsylvania; Drake's Well, the first successful oil well in the nation, is on an artificial island in Oil Creek near Titusville.

Rep. Jim Gerlach (R)

CAPITOL OFFICE
225-4315
www.house.gov/gerlach
1541 Longworth 20515-3806; fax 225-8440

COMMITTEES
Small Business
Transportation & Infrastructure

HOMETOWN
Upper Uwchlan Township

BORN
Feb. 25, 1955, Ellwood City, Pa.

RELIGION
Protestant

FAMILY
Divorced; three children

EDUCATION
Dickinson College, B.A. 1977 (political science); Dickinson School of Law, J.D. 1980

CAREER
Lawyer

POLITICAL HIGHLIGHTS
Republican nominee for Pa. House, 1986; Pa. House, 1991-95; Pa. Senate, 1995-2003

ELECTION RESULTS

2002 GENERAL		
Jim Gerlach (R)	103,648	51.4%
Dan Wofford (D)	98,128	48.6%
2002 PRIMARY		
Jim Gerlach (R)		unopposed

Elected 2002; 1st term

During a dozen years as a state legislator, Gerlach became well-regarded in Republican circles for his ability to understand complex issues. But his image as a policy wonk is a bit leavened: He is known for his rendition of "Get Me to the Church on Time" from the musical "My Fair Lady," which he says provided him with his only acting credit in local theater.

Generally a supporter of GOP initiatives, Gerlach (GUR-lock) was the prime sponsor of Pennsylvania's high-profile 1996 welfare law overhaul. But he broke somewhat with Republican Gov. Tom Ridge — now secretary of Homeland Security — by pushing for a pilot program for school choice rather than immediate implementation of a full program.

In Harrisburg, Gerlach also championed legislation to combat suburban sprawl, and he used his state Senate seat to mediate some development disputes between local authorities. That work helped him gain assignment to the Transportation and Infrastructure Committee, where he can advocate in behalf of his constituents in the outer edges of the Philadelphia metropolitan area during the rewrite of highway and mass transit law in the 108th Congress. A main goal of his is to win more federal spending for the preservation of open spaces and farmland.

Having won one of the 10 closest House races of 2002, Gerlach is expected to put a parochial focus on his freshman term to bolster his electoral prospects. His other committee assignment, Small Business, may help.

Though Pennsylvania lost two seats in reapportionment after the 2000 census, Gerlach's colleagues in the Republican-dominated General Assembly redrew the congressional map for this decade with him in mind. No House incumbent chose to run in the redrawn 6th District — which had a close partisan split, but overlapped with much of Gerlach's state Senate constituency — and he was unopposed for the GOP nomination. In November, he won by 5,520 votes over Democratic lawyer Dan Wofford, the son of former Sen. Harris Wofford, whose Washington connections and behind-the-scenes political experience helped him raise money for an effective campaign.

PENNSYLVANIA 6

Southeast – Philadelphia suburbs, part of Reading

The 6th takes in urban, suburban and rural communities stretching from a slice of Montgomery County in the Philadelphia area through northern Chester County and southern and eastern portions of Berks County, including part of Reading and all of Kutztown. Most of the district's land is spread through sparsely populated towns.

Once known for its rails and industrial prowess, the economy of Berks County has branched out in recent years to include service and retail jobs. With its share of historical sites and untouched land, the 6th enjoys a modest tourism industry. Reading is home to a minor league baseball team, and, in the neighboring 16th District, a performing arts center and minor league hockey team.

Growth and water-use issues dominate much of the political discussion in the region, which is mostly situated in the area triangulated by Philadelphia, Reading and Lancaster.

Remnants of an earlier time are evident, as the 6th is home to numerous covered bridges, old mill towns and Pennsylvania Dutch communities, as well as the Hopewell Furnace National Historic Site, a preserved iron plantation in Elverson that dates back to the 18th century.

The GOP-controlled legislature vastly altered the district during redistricting following the 2000 census, redrawing it to give a Republican candidate a small but significant edge. But the new 6th, now much closer to Philadelphia, certainly makes the nation's dwindling list of "swing" districts. Al Gore and George W. Bush ran neck-and-neck here in the 2000 presidential election, with Gore edging Bush by half a percentage point among the district's voters.

MAJOR INDUSTRY
Manufacturing, tourism, retail

CITIES
Reading (pt.), 36,706; Norristown, 31,282

NOTABLE
Daniel Boone was born in Exeter Township.

Rep. Curt Weldon (R)

CAPITOL OFFICE
225-2011
curtpa07@mail.house.gov
www.house.gov/curtweldon
2466 Rayburn 20515-3807; fax 225-8137

COMMITTEES
Armed Services
(Tactical Air & Land Forces - chairman)
Science
Select Homeland Security

HOMETOWN
Aston

BORN
July 22, 1947, Marcus Hook, Pa.

RELIGION
Protestant

FAMILY
Wife, Mary Gallagher Weldon; five children

EDUCATION
West Chester State College, B.A. 1969 (humanities)

CAREER
Teacher; consultant

POLITICAL HIGHLIGHTS
Mayor of Marcus Hook, 1977-82; Delaware County Council, 1981-86 (chairman, 1982-86); Republican nominee for U.S. House, 1984

ELECTION RESULTS

2002 GENERAL		
Curt Weldon (R)	146,296	66.1%
Peter A. Lennon (D)	75,055	33.9%
2002 PRIMARY		
Curt Weldon (R)		unopposed
2000 GENERAL		
Curt Weldon (R)	172,569	64.8%
Peter A. Lennon (D)	93,687	35.2%

PREVIOUS WINNING PERCENTAGES
1998 (72%); 1996 (67%); 1994 (70%); 1992 (66%); 1990 (65%); 1988 (68%); 1986 (61%)

Elected 1986; 9th term

The son of a machinist, Weldon was educated at a small state college and inducted into politics by the patronage-driven Republican Party of Delaware County in suburban Philadelphia. Those are unusual credentials for one of Congress' most respected experts on the military and post-Cold War foreign policy. What he lacks in Ivy League breeding, Weldon makes up for with smarts, boundless confidence and what he calls a "pit bull" personality.

Weldon is one of the most pro-military members of the House, using his seat on Armed Services through four administrations to argue for ever larger defense budgets. He is an unapologetic backer of the controversial anti-missile defense system, which critics maintain is technically infeasible. That makes him a key ally for the Bush administration as it works to secure yearly funding.

The one prize that has eluded Weldon is the chairmanship of a major committee. In the wake of the Sept. 11, 2001, terrorist attacks, Weldon was one of the first lawmakers to push hard for creation of a new homeland security committee. He had a personal career interest at stake; he hoped to head the panel. Republican leaders eventually agreed such a committee was needed, but they gave the gavel to Christopher Cox of California, an ally of Speaker J. Dennis Hastert.

Weldon was similarly disappointed in the 107th Congress. He had campaigned to be the Armed Services chairman, raising campaign funds for fellow Republicans and even spending $17,000 on a glossy booklet touting his vision. But the leadership instead elevated Arizona Republican Bob Stump, who was not nearly as engaged in defense issues as Weldon but who ranked first in seniority on the panel. Weldon complained publicly that Tom DeLay, the GOP whip at the time, had lied by promising him the job. "I can hurt him far more than he can hurt me," Weldon said.

When Stump gave up the gavel in 2002 for health reasons, Weldon again had to step aside for the more senior GOP Rep. Duncan Hunter of California, a much more activist chairman than Stump who shares Weldon's belief in fattening defense budgets. In the 108th Congress, Weldon became the chairman of the panel's Tactical Air and Land Forces Subcommittee, which oversees Army and Air Force programs.

Weldon's interests fit snugly with those of his district, which is heavily blue collar, mostly Republican and in part dependent on the defense industry. Boeing employs more than 4,000 people at a helicopter plant in Ridley Park, Pa. Weldon has been one of the main reasons that Boeing's V-22 Osprey helicopter project remains alive, despite repeated setbacks including two crashes that killed 23 Marines in 2000.

National security issues are Weldon's passion. He has taught a course on international security at three Pennsylvania universities, Widener, Drexel and Eastern.

Early in the 108th, Weldon pushed the Bush administration to open a dialogue with North Korea after revelations that the communist country had restarted its nuclear weapons program. During the Clinton years, he was one of the first in Congress to raise concerns about the missile capacity of North Korea, Iran and Iraq. And in 1999, Congress approved his bill declaring it a national policy to deploy the anti-missile system "as soon as technologically possible." The legislation crowned years of work for Weldon, who had to convince not only President Clinton, but many skeptical Republicans.

Weldon, who speaks Russian, is a friend of top Russian politicians, including several members of the Duma, Russia's parliament. He has visited the country and its former republics 30 times. He advocates strengthening ties through non-strategic means, such as cultivating Russia as an energy supplier.

Weldon has orchestrated numerous meetings between U.S. and Russian public officials, sometimes getting important results. During a meeting he set up in 1999 in Vienna between members of Congress and the Duma, the parties laid out the principles of a peace settlement in Kosovo, which became the blueprint for negotiations between NATO and Yugoslavian strongman Slobodan Milosevic. In 2002, Weldon became the first American to be inducted into the Russian Academy of Social Sciences.

The congressman's blue-collar roots often put him on the side of organized labor in key trade votes. He opposed the 1993 North American Free Trade Agreement and fast-track authority for the president to negotiate trade agreements that Congress cannot amend. He supported bills to ban the permanent replacement of striking workers and to raise the minimum wage. "It's not my style to hurt working people, and business is not always right," Weldon says.

One area where he sometimes is at odds with labor — and closer to traditional Republican thinking — is in his support for changes to the Davis-Bacon Act, which requires the government to pay the prevailing local wage on construction projects.

The youngest of nine children, Weldon grew up in the small, working-class town of Marcus Hook, south of Philadelphia. He graduated from West Chester State College, went into teaching and joined the volunteer fire department. He got the attention of the powerful Delaware County Republican organization after he became mayor of Marcus Hook and helped rescue it from a spiral of factory shutdowns, economic decline and gang warfare. In 1981 he won a seat on the Delaware County Council.

Local Republicans saw Weldon as a good fit for the district's conservative mix of blue- and white-collar workers, and in 1984 nominated him for a run against Democratic Rep. Bob Edgar. His near-win (he lost by only 412 votes) made him the favorite two years later when Edgar ran for the Senate, leaving the House seat open. Weldon prevailed with 61 percent of the vote and has won re-election easily since then.

He never forgot his beginnings in Marcus Hook though. As a House member, Weldon founded the Congressional Fire Services Caucus, which now has several hundred members.

KEY VOTES

2002

Yes Overhaul campaign finance law; ban "soft money" and restrict advocacy advertising
Yes Back Bush's defense budget increase
Yes Extend 1996 welfare law
Yes Adopt Bush's discretionary spending limit
Yes Pass GOP Medicare prescription drug plan
Yes Create independent Sept. 11 commission
No Extend union protections to Homeland Security Department employees
No Revive fast-track procedures for trade agreements
Yes Authorize war against Iraq
No Advance bankruptcy overhaul opposed by abortion opponents

2001

No Nullify Clinton Labor Department ergonomics rule
Yes Cut taxes by $1.35 trillion through fiscal 2011
No Maintain ban on oil drilling in Arctic National Wildlife Refuge
Yes Approve Bush proposal to limit managed-care plan liability for coverage decisions
Yes Divert money from crop subsidy payments to land conservation
Yes Expand law enforcement power to investigate suspected terrorists

CQ VOTE STUDIES

	PARTY UNITY		PRESIDENTIAL SUPPORT	
	Support	Oppose	Support	Oppose
2002	86%	14%	71%	29%
2001	88%	12%	80%	20%
2000	85%	15%	33%	67%
1999	84%	16%	29%	71%
1998	81%	19%	28%	72%

INTEREST GROUPS

	AFL-CIO	ADA	CCUS	ACU
2002	25%	15%	79%	79%
2001	42%	15%	82%	70%
2000	20%	5%	80%	76%
1999	44%	20%	68%	73%
1998	40%	25%	78%	60%

PENNSYLVANIA 7

Suburban Philadelphia – most of Delaware County

Anchored in the suburbs south and west of Philadelphia, the politically competitive 7th takes in vast tracts of middle-class suburbia, including most of Delaware County, the district's population center, as well as southwestern Montgomery and eastern Chester counties.

The 7th attracted significant economic growth in the 1990s. Its defense industry, driven by Lockheed Martin and Boeing, is a large employer, as are the pharmaceutical and technology sectors. New developments, many of which are springing up in the less-populated areas of Chester County, are attracting Philadelphia residents.

Upper Merion Township in Montgomery County has been expanding rapidly since the 1990s opening of the Blue Route (Interstate 476), which links Interstate 95 along the Delaware River with the Schuylkill Expressway near King of Prussia. Farther south, older suburbs such as Norwood, Ridley Park, Media and Upper Darby are mostly white and working class. So is Marcus Hook, an old refinery town along the Delaware River. The 7th has the state's highest percentage of residents with Irish (31 percent) or Italian (20 percent) ancestry.

As recently as 1988, Delaware County voted Republican for president by 21 percentage points. But Delaware now supports Democrats. The county's hefty GOP registration advantage is shrinking, and Al Gore won Delaware in 2000 with 54 percent, the highest total for a Democratic presidential candidate since 1964. The county's strongest Democratic areas, including the mostly black city of Chester, are in the 1st District.

The GOP still does well in the expanding, upper-income areas of Delaware County, including Radnor Township in the north and fast-growing Concord and Bethel townships in the southwest.

MAJOR INDUSTRY

Pharmaceuticals, defense

CITIES

Radnor Township (unincorporated), 30,878; Drexel Hill (unincorporated), 29,364; Springfield (unincorporated), 23,677

NOTABLE

The Thomas Massey House, one of the state's oldest English Quaker homes, is in Marple Township; The King of Prussia Mall is the largest East Coast shopping center.

Rep. James C. Greenwood (R)

CAPITOL OFFICE
225-4276
www.house.gov/greenwood
2436 Rayburn 20515-3808; fax 225-9511

COMMITTEES
Education & Workforce
Energy & Commerce
(Oversight & Investigations - chairman)

HOMETOWN
Erwinna

BORN
May 4, 1951, Philadelphia, Pa.

RELIGION
Presbyterian

FAMILY
Wife, Christina Greenwood; three children

EDUCATION
Dickinson College, B.A. 1973 (social work)

CAREER
Social services agency caseworker; state legislative aide

POLITICAL HIGHLIGHTS
Pa. House, 1981-87; Pa. Senate, 1987-93

ELECTION RESULTS

2002 GENERAL		
James C. Greenwood (R)	127,475	62.6%
Timothy T. Reece (D)	76,178	37.4%
2002 PRIMARY		
James C. Greenwood (R)	31,327	69.1%
Tom Lingenfelter (R)	13,981	30.9%
2000 GENERAL		
James C. Greenwood (R)	154,090	59.2%
Ron Strouse (D)	100,617	38.7%
Philip C. Holmen (REF)	5,394	2.1%

PREVIOUS WINNING PERCENTAGES
1998 (63%); 1996 (59%); 1994 (66%); 1992 (52%)

Elected 1992; 6th term

Until recently, Greenwood was known in Congress primarily for his centrist positions on social issues and his quiet ability to broker bipartisan deals on sensitive topics. All that changed in the 107th Congress, when a coincidence of power politics and financial scandal landed him at the helm of a major congressional investigation that transformed him from behind-the-scenes dealmaker to camera-ready chairman.

The turnabout began in the 107th Congress, when Greenwood was named chairman of the Energy and Commerce Committee's Oversight and Investigations Subcommittee.

Things got more interesting for Greenwood, when from his subcommittee perch, he directed the House probe into the high-profile collapse of the energy trading giant Enron Corp., and for a while became a prime-time regular on national television news programs. Greenwood, who routinely spat out pithy and quotable remarks about the misdeeds of Enron's corporate chieftains, held his fire for no major player in the scandal, addressing an oft-repeated line to fired Arthur Andersen auditor David Duncan that captured the attention of the media and much of the public: "Enron robbed the bank. Arthur Andersen provided the getaway car. They say you were at the wheel."

His panel's team of investigators interviewed scores of executives and securities regulators, and traveled to Enron's headquarters in Houston to unearth evidence about what was then the largest bankruptcy in U.S. history. "It really has completely re-energized me and made my service more interesting by an order of magnitude," Greenwood said of the inquiry.

Later in the 107th, Greenwood's subcommittee also looked into the insider trading scandal involving Martha Stewart and ImClone Systems Inc.

So it is perhaps not surprising that this low-key moderate, who ran for Congress in 1992 as a crusader against entrenched incumbency and pledged to serve only six terms, is now seriously considering breaking his promise and running again in 2004. "At the end of 12 years, I will have amassed such a depth of knowledge on such a breadth of issues that it does become apparent to me that my own constituency would in many ways lose out, both in terms of climbing up the seniority tree and the knowledge tree, if I were to leave," he said in early 2002.

In a Republican Party that controls the House by a slim margin, Greenwood has been called upon often to serve as a liaison between the moderate wing of the GOP, to which he belongs, and the party's leaders or the larger conservative faction of the House GOP. He has worked to bring Democrats and Republicans together on a number of subjects, including a host of environmental and youth violence issues, as well as changing the welfare and Medicare systems.

Greenwood is outspoken on policy issues he cares about, and he sometimes feels ostracized in the ranks of the Republican Conference, where moderate views can be met with resistance. But he sees the struggle as central to the GOP's survival: "If the Republicans are going to stay in the majority for the foreseeable future, it will be the moderates who save the conservative Republicans from themselves," Greenwood said.

His voting record shows Greenwood to be one of the most liberal members of the GOP, particularly on social issues such as abortion rights, family planning, gun control, environmental protections and funding for the National Endowment for the Arts.

He was the sponsor in 2001 and again in 2003 of a key amendment in the House debate about human cloning. His language would have outlawed cloning for the purpose of starting a pregnancy, while allowing cloning to create tissue for medical research. "I think it's a shame that this issue has been co-opted as if it were an abortion issue," Greenwood said in 2003. "We must distinguish between repugnant reproductive cloning and potentially life-saving therapeutic cloning."

In 2000, after the GOP-run Rules Committee refused to permit moderate Republicans to offer alternate language to a bill to outlaw a procedure that opponents call "partial birth" abortion, Greenwood objected. "I got stiffed and I don't like it. It makes me reluctant to bend over backwards the next time somebody needs me," he told Roll Call, a Capitol Hill newspaper.

Although he is a moderate on social issues, Greenwood hews to a conservative line on fiscal policy. He supports a balanced-budget constitutional amendment, for example.

Most of his legislative interests are tied to his committee assignments — Energy and Commerce and Education and the Workforce. He has weighed in on such issues as limiting medical malpractice awards, cleaning up superfund toxic waste sites, providing insurance coverage for prescription contraceptives, funding autism research, and giving oversight to the Food and Drug Administration. Greenwood played a key role in 1997 legislation to revamp the process for FDA review of new prescription drugs. In 2002, he won enactment of a bill to speed up FDA approvals of medical devices.

It was romance that first got Greenwood into politics: His girlfriend's father was a state legislator, and Greenwood worked for him as a legislative assistant and campaign manager. After spending four years as a Bucks County social worker — where he met his wife, also a social worker — he won a seat in the state House in 1980 and moved to the state Senate in 1986.

Greenwood was an activist state legislator. He helped pass a collective bargaining law that addressed a state problem with teacher strikes. He played a large role in passing a solid waste act that mandated recycling and set up a state superfund for compensation for hazardous waste cleanups. And he pursued legislation on housing and children's issues.

Despite his own 12 years in elective office, Greenwood won his House seat on a platform of change against 14-year incumbent Democrat Peter H. Kostmayer, who was not helped by his 50 overdrafts at the private bank for House members. Since then, many of his toughest challenges have come from within the GOP, from candidates who argued he was too liberal.

KEY VOTES

2002

Yes Overhaul campaign finance law; ban "soft money" and restrict advocacy advertising
Yes Back Bush's defense budget increase
Yes Extend 1996 welfare law
Yes Adopt Bush's discretionary spending limit
Yes Pass GOP Medicare prescription drug plan
No Create independent Sept. 11 commission
No Extend union protections to Homeland Security Department employees
Yes Revive fast-track procedures for trade agreements
Yes Authorize war against Iraq
Yes Advance bankruptcy overhaul opposed by abortion opponents

2001

Yes Nullify Clinton Labor Department ergonomics rule
Yes Cut taxes by $1.35 trillion through fiscal 2011
Yes Maintain ban on oil drilling in Arctic National Wildlife Refuge
Yes Approve Bush proposal to limit managed-care plan liability for coverage decisions
Yes Divert money from crop subsidy payments to land conservation
Yes Expand law enforcement power to investigate suspected terrorists

CQ VOTE STUDIES

	PARTY UNITY		PRESIDENTIAL SUPPORT	
	Support	Oppose	Support	Oppose
2002	81%	19%	82%	18%
2001	86%	14%	79%	21%
2000	73%	27%	54%	46%
1999	71%	29%	44%	56%
1998	68%	32%	38%	62%

INTEREST GROUPS

	AFL-CIO	ADA	CCUS	ACU
2002	13%	20%	95%	78%
2001	8%	25%	91%	48%
2000	11%	25%	77%	60%
1999	33%	70%	76%	41%
1998	20%	25%	94%	48%

PENNSYLVANIA 8
Northern Philadelphia suburbs — Bucks County

Nestled mostly north of Philadelphia on the eastern edge of the state, the 8th includes all of Bucks County, a small portion of Montgomery County and a sliver of northeastern Philadelphia. Established in 1682 by William Penn as one of the three original counties in Pennsylvania, Bucks features stately mansions such as Pennsbury Manor, Penn's home. The scenery and charm continue to attract wealthy new residents.

Bucks County grew about 10 percent in the 1990s, on par with its suburban neighbor, Montgomery County. The area's healthy, white-collar economy claims to support more than 20,000 small businesses. But the decade was not without economic problems. Blue-collar workers faced cutbacks in the steel industry, once a significant employer in Bucks County. A new deep-water port has helped, making the 8th something of a distribution and warehouse center. The district also is home to several hospitals. Voters in the 8th tend to be fiscally conservative but support environmentalism and hold moderate stances on some social issues.

Upper Bucks leans Republican — Bedminster Township in north-central Bucks was a rare Philadelphia suburb that did not vote for the former Philadelphia mayor, Democrat Edward G. Rendell, in the 2002 gubernatorial election. The GOP also does well in wealthy Upper and Lower Makefield townships. Democrats fare well in southeastern Bucks, near the Philadelphia line, and in the area just across the Delaware River from Trenton, N.J.

Though Republicans dominate elections for the state legislature in the 8th, Democrats can compete in statewide and federal elections here. Rendell won 63 percent of the Bucks County vote in 2002, and the district gave Al Gore a 5 percentage point cushion in the 2000 presidential election.

MAJOR INDUSTRY
Health care, wholesale and retail trade, tourism

CITIES
Levittown (unincorporated), 53,966; Philadelphia (pt.), 31,549; Morrisville, 10,023

NOTABLE
George Washington's Delaware River crossing is re-enacted in Washington Crossing each Christmas Day; Nobel Prize winning author Pearl S. Buck lived in Bucks County.

Rep. Bill Shuster (R)

CAPITOL OFFICE
225-2431
www.house.gov/shuster
1108 Longworth 20515-3809; fax 225-2486

COMMITTEES
Small Business
Transportation & Infrastructure

HOMETOWN
Hollidaysburg

BORN
Jan. 10, 1961, McKeesport, Pa.

RELIGION
Lutheran

FAMILY
Wife, Rebecca Shuster; two children

EDUCATION
Dickinson College, B.A. 1983 (political science & history); American U., M.B.A. 1987

CAREER
Car dealer; tire company manager

POLITICAL HIGHLIGHTS
No previous office

ELECTION RESULTS

2002 GENERAL		
Bill Shuster (R)	124,184	71.1%
John R. Henry (D)	50,558	28.9%
2002 PRIMARY		
Bill Shuster (R)	33,538	74.0%
David S. Keller (R)	6,319	13.9%
David E. Bahr (R)	5,457	12.0%
2001 SPECIAL		
Bill Shuster (R)	55,549	51.9%
Scott Conklin (D)	47,049	44.0%
Alanna K. Hartzok (GREEN)	4,420	4.1%

Elected May 2001; 1st full term

Since winning a May 2001 special election to succeed his father, veteran Republican Rep. Bud Shuster, the younger Shuster has followed the example of the legendary "king of asphalt" by diligently, if less flamboyantly, seeking money for roads and other public works improvements in his rural Pennsylvania district.

The elder Shuster was the powerful chairman of the Transportation and Infrastructure Committee, and the House's reigning wheeler-dealer of roads and bridges until he left office following an ethics scandal. The younger Shuster is an automobile dealer with no prior experience in elective office. Though he plays down the political value of the family name, it was a potent force in the election, and Shuster has yet to fully emerge from his father's shadow.

"This is about Bill Shuster, and Bill Shuster standing on his own two feet," Shuster told the Chambersburg (Pa.) Public Opinion. "I've been running my own business for the last 11 years. I run my own show." But he acknowledged his father would be a tough act to follow. "He set very high standards that I have to live up to," he said.

Since coming to Washington, the younger Shuster has kept a low media profile. He talks to reporters from newspapers and broadcast stations in his district, but declines interviews with national journalists unless they want to discuss issues related to Pennsylvania.

House Republican leaders gave Shuster an immediate running start by keeping a seat open for him on the Transportation and Infrastructure Committee. By the 2002 election, his campaign Web site boasted of his success in winning funding for 18 projects, including $700,000 for water service improvements in one town and $40,000 for two new girls' softball fields. Shuster has coached Little League baseball and youth soccer and is no slouch as an athlete himself. In the 2002 Roll Call charity baseball game between Democrats and Republicans, he smacked a two-run double.

In the 108th Congress, the committee prepared to update the 1998 surface transportation law, which was his father's greatest legislative legacy. Shuster pledged to work on a bipartisan basis with other members of Pennsylvania's delegation to secure more highway money for his district and the state. Even though the state lost two House seats in redistricting, Shuster noted that Pennsylvanians continue to hold five of the 75 seats on the committee. "We're going to work hard and try to build a coalition to make sure Pennsylvania is not hurt," he said.

Shuster has not limited his legislative efforts to the pursuit of road money. In September 2002, the House overwhelmingly passed a bill he introduced to reauthorize and amend the National Dam Safety Program and provide technical assistance to improve security at dams against potential terrorist attacks. President Bush signed the measure into law.

At the start of the 108th, Republican leaders picked Shuster as one of several dozen assistant whips in new Majority Whip Roy Blunt's operation. But they denied Shuster a requested seat on the Armed Services Committee. The posting would have helped his efforts to protect Letterkenny Army Depot, a target of earlier base-closing rounds. He says keeping the facility from being closed or downsized in the next round of base re-evaluations in 2005 will be "a tough battle."

Shuster has shown an interest in defense and foreign affairs. In 2002, he joined a congressional delegation in traveling to Moscow, Afghanistan and

Uzbekistan to meet with foreign leaders and U.S. troops stationed there. Two months later, he was part of another delegation that visited the Navy's base in Guantanamo Bay, Cuba, where imprisoned al Qaeda and Taliban prisoners were kept, to assess the need for improvements.

For the most part, though, Shuster has stuck to the domestic arena. Like his father and many of his constituents, Shuster is conservative on social issues. During his 2001 bid to succeed his father, he emphasized his opposition to abortion and support for gun owners' rights. Shuster also campaigned on his support for Bush's tax cut plan, and he cited his experience on the board of directors of the Pennsylvania Automotive Association and Chamber of Commerce as evidence of his leadership skills.

The Shuster name is well-known in the south-central Pennsylvania district. Anyone who doubts it need only check the road signs there. Interstate 99, which runs through the district, is named the Bud Shuster Highway after the man who ran the Transportation panel for six years beginning with the GOP takeover of Congress in 1995.

Citing health concerns, Bud Shuster resigned in January 2001 a few months after the House ethics committee rebuked him for "serious official misconduct"; the committee's reprimand was related to his business relationship with his former chief of staff, who became a transportation lobbyist with several clients in need of favors from Shuster.

Bill Shuster was not the first of Bud Shuster's sons to seek a House seat. His brother, Bob, ran in 1996 to succeed retired nine-term Republican Rep. William F. Clinger in the 5th District, which neighbors the 9th. He lost the Republican primary to John E. Peterson, who went on to win and hold the seat. Bob Shuster was mentioned as a possible 9th District candidate after his father's resignation, but Bill emerged as the Shuster of choice.

Despite his family ties, Shuster's initial election victory was closer than expected. He defeated Democrat H. Scott Conklin, a Centre County commissioner, with 52 percent to Conklin's 44 percent. Although greatly outspent by Shuster, conservative Democrat Conklin ran a tireless campaign, driving throughout the expansive district in his own car. Shuster appeared to be hindered by hard feelings from some fellow Republicans who might have run themselves if they had had the same kind of name recognition.

Shuster's re-election in 2002 was considerably less difficult. He easily defeated Democrat John R. Henry, a Breezewood restaurant owner, with 71 percent of the vote. Henry stressed his support for his party's health care agenda, but raised less than $9,000; Shuster spent more than $1 million while touting his work securing federal projects and his constituent service.

KEY VOTES

2002

- No Overhaul campaign finance law; ban "soft money" and restrict advocacy advertising
- Yes Back Bush's defense budget increase
- Yes Extend 1996 welfare law
- Yes Adopt Bush's discretionary spending limit
- Yes Pass GOP Medicare prescription drug plan
- No Create independent Sept. 11 commission
- No Extend union protections to Homeland Security Department employees
- Yes Revive fast-track procedures for trade agreements
- Yes Authorize war against Iraq
- No Advance bankruptcy overhaul opposed by abortion opponents

2001

- Yes Cut taxes by $1.35 trillion through fiscal 2011
- No Maintain ban on oil drilling in Arctic National Wildlife Refuge
- Yes Approve Bush proposal to limit managed-care plan liability for coverage decisions
- Yes Divert money from crop subsidy payments to land conservation
- Yes Expand law enforcement power to investigate suspected terrorists

CQ VOTE STUDIES

	PARTY UNITY		PRESIDENTIAL SUPPORT	
	Support	Oppose	Support	Oppose
2002	98%	2%	88%	12%
2001	95%	5%	89%	11%

INTEREST GROUPS

	AFL-CIO	ADA	CCUS	ACU
2002	11%	0%	95%	96%
2001	30%	5%	94%	94%

PENNSYLVANIA 9
South central — Altoona

Situated in the south-central part of Pennsylvania, the 9th contains no booming metropolis – Altoona, the largest city, is tucked into the Allegheny Mountains and maintains a small-town feel. Most of the 9th's towns have populations under 5,000, making this one of the most rural districts in the nation. The district borders western Maryland and West Virginia to the south and expanded slightly in every other direction as a result of redistricting in 2002.

After decades of decline brought about by the waning of the railroad and mining industries, the area has begun to rebound, and once again residents can thank transportation-related industry for the growth. Bedford County saw its job creation rate shoot up as improvements began on the aging Pennsylvania Turnpike, which opened as the nation's first superhighway in 1940. And the city of Breezewood continues to draw in travelers with its garish display of signs adorning hotels and fast-food restaurants at the turnpike interchange.

Still, the bulk of the district's land is rural and dependent on agriculture.

The 9th has a religious population, one of the most conservative in the state. Voters oppose most gun control and "big government" policies. Its small-business owners and farmers tend also to be fiscally conservative.

Voters went solidly for Republican presidential candidates in 1992, 1996 and 2000. The 9th includes George W. Bush's top two counties in the state in the 2000 election, Fulton (71 percent) and Bedford (70 percent), as well as part of Perry County (70 percent), which was Bush's fourth-best. The GOP controls most local offices.

MAJOR INDUSTRY
Agriculture, manufacturing, services

MILITARY BASES
Letterkenny Army Depot, 2 military, 1,737 civilian (2001)

CITIES
Altoona, 49,363; Chambersburg, 17,760; Waynesboro, 9,614

NOTABLE
A memorial to Flight 93 is in Shanksville, where the hijacked airplane crashed in a field Sept. 11, 2001; President James Buchanan, a native of Mercersburg, vacationed at the Bedford Springs Hotel; Architect Frank Lloyd Wright's Fallingwater house is in Fayette County.

Rep. Don Sherwood (R)

CAPITOL OFFICE
225-3731
www.house.gov/sherwood
1223 Longworth 20515-3810; fax 225-9594

COMMITTEES
Appropriations

HOMETOWN
Tunkhannock

BORN
March 5, 1941, Nicholson, Pa.

RELIGION
Methodist

FAMILY
Wife, Carol Sherwood; three children

EDUCATION
Dartmouth College, B.A. 1963 (economics)

MILITARY SERVICE
Army, 1964-66

CAREER
Car dealer; bank executive; horse farm owner; forestry equipment company owner

POLITICAL HIGHLIGHTS
Tunkhannock Area School Board, 1975-99 (president, 1992-98)

ELECTION RESULTS

2002 GENERAL		
Don Sherwood (R)	152,017	92.9%
Kurt J. Shotko (GREEN)	11,613	7.1%
2002 PRIMARY		
Don Sherwood (R)		unopposed
2000 GENERAL		
Don Sherwood (R)	124,830	52.6%
Patrick Casey (D)	112,580	47.4%

PREVIOUS WINNING PERCENTAGES
1998 (49%)

Elected 1998; 3rd term

Having won his first two terms with considerable difficulty, Sherwood's political standing suddenly has taken a sure turn for the better. To make his electoral life easier, the House Republican leadership gave him a seat on the Appropriations Committee in 2001. And the Republicans who ran Pennsylvania's redistricting process for this decade made Sherwood's territory sufficiently GOP-leaning that the Democrats did not even field a candidate against him in 2002.

His re-election worries safely behind him, Sherwood now seems free to focus on promoting economic development in northeastern Pennsylvania and maintaining the government safety net for the district's elderly.

A sixth-generation resident of the area, Sherwood was 57 when he won his House seat, older than most members newly elected to Congress in recent years. He arrived in Washington with a varied background in business, local school board service and volunteer activities.

As a Republican, Sherwood often faces politically difficult decisions because his district includes a large number of elderly people, and labor unions historically have had a strong influence in the coal and steel factories and railroads that have been the region's economic mainstay. From the start of his House service, Sherwood focused on getting federal help for his economically troubled district. After oil prices spiked in 2000, for example, he worked with other Northeastern lawmakers to get money to put up to 2 million barrels in a Northeastern home heating oil reserve to be used in emergencies, such as severe price increases or interruptions in supply.

To help their elderly constituents, Sherwood and the Democratic lawmaker from the neighboring district, Paul E. Kanjorski, won House passage in 2002 of an increase in Medicare funding for a select list of rural hospitals. That bid ultimately failed, but he came back early in 2003 and was successful. Sherwood was one of 68 House Republicans to go against party leaders by voting for a bipartisan patients' bill of rights measure in 1999, but he returned to the fold in 2001 to vote for a GOP-drafted measure.

Until Sherwood's district was redrawn, it included the blue-collar city of Scranton, where unions long have held sway. Sherwood cast a number of pro-labor votes in his first two terms, including bucking his party leadership to back a minimum wage proposal in the 106th Congress. But he opposed organized labor to vote in 2000 for making China a permanent normal U.S. trade partner, and in 2002 for reviving fast-track procedures for trade agreements that Congress cannot amend.

Before Sherwood got the Appropriations post he sat on the Armed Services panel, where he kept close tabs on issues that affect military bases, as the largest employer in his district was the sprawling Tobyhanna Army Depot, where the army repairs and maintains communications and electronic equipment.

Tobyhanna is now in the neighboring 11th District, but in the 107th he continued to look out for the depot from his Appropriations seat. He also was able to increase Pentagon funding for artillery rounds made at an Army munitions plant in Scranton. And he worked to direct defense funding to a Lockheed Martin plant just outside Scranton.

Noting that his constituents who are dairy farmers were struggling, Sherwood led an unsuccessful effort to authorize the expansion and extension of the Northeast Dairy Compact and the creation of three other regional dairy compacts across the nation during debate on the 2002 farm bill.

Sherwood grew up in the hamlet of Nicholson, where his father operated a car dealership and the neighbor kid three doors down was H. James Saxton Jr., now a New Jersey House colleague. They went to the same school, were in the same Boy Scout troop and recall building a log cabin together on Saxton's property.

After getting his degree in economics from Dartmouth and putting in a stint in the Army, Sherwood settled in Tunkhannock, a dozen miles southwest of Nicholson. At age 26, he opened a car dealership, becoming the youngest Chevrolet dealer on the East Coast. He also became active in local civic affairs. Appointed to the local school board in 1975, he was re-elected six times, serving more than 20 years, including six years as its president. He said that watching many young people move out of the area in search of economic opportunity sparked his interest in national politics.

In 1998, when veteran Republican Joseph M. McDade decided to retire after 36 years in the House, Sherwood jumped into the fray, along with seven other Republicans. He easily outdistanced the GOP field, winning almost half the votes cast.

With McDade's departure, Democrats saw an opportunity that November. They tapped attorney Patrick Casey, a son of former Democratic Gov. Robert P. Casey, hoping the younger Casey's mix of social conservatism and economic populism would dovetail with the district. Sherwood stressed his varied business experience, spent more than $770,000 of his own money on his campaign — and won by 515 votes out of 173,000 cast.

Casey was back for a rematch in 2000, criticizing Sherwood's stances on health care and Social Security and referring to him in advertisements as "millionaire Don Sherwood." The Sierra Club also put Sherwood on its list of incumbents to unseat. But Sherwood emphasized his experience and legislative accomplishments during his first term. In the close race, Sherwood prevailed by 12,000 votes.

Sherwood's hobby for more than a quarter century has been raising Belgian horses. In partnership with another man, Sherwood has won dozens of first-place ribbons in local horse shows. He told the Wilkes-Barre Times Leader that raising and grooming horses "is a release for me, because you can't be showing horses and politicking at the same time."

Sherwood's political fortunes have not been hurt by his sartorial selections, which earned him inclusion in a Pennsylvania political newsletter's roster of best-dressed elected officials. The verdict on Sherwood from PoliticsPA.com: "Dresses for power. His clothing completes the 'Congressional' look."

KEY VOTES

2002

No Overhaul campaign finance law; ban "soft money" and restrict advocacy advertising
Yes Back Bush's defense budget increase
Yes Extend 1996 welfare law
Yes Adopt Bush's discretionary spending limit
Yes Pass GOP Medicare prescription drug plan
No Create independent Sept. 11 commission
No Extend union protections to Homeland Security Department employees
Yes Revive fast-track procedures for trade agreements
Yes Authorize war against Iraq
Yes Advance bankruptcy overhaul opposed by abortion opponents

2001

Yes Nullify Clinton Labor Department ergonomics rule
Yes Cut taxes by $1.35 trillion through fiscal 2011
No Maintain ban on oil drilling in Arctic National Wildlife Refuge
Yes Approve Bush proposal to limit managed-care plan liability for coverage decisions
Yes Divert money from crop subsidy payments to land conservation
Yes Expand law enforcement power to investigate suspected terrorists

CQ VOTE STUDIES

	PARTY UNITY		PRESIDENTIAL SUPPORT	
	Support	Oppose	Support	Oppose
2002	96%	4%	89%	11%
2001	94%	6%	93%	7%
2000	86%	14%	38%	62%
1999	88%	12%	20%	80%

INTEREST GROUPS

	AFL-CIO	ADA	CCUS	ACU
2002	11%	5%	100%	96%
2001	17%	0%	100%	88%
2000	20%	10%	85%	75%
1999	33%	10%	88%	80%

PENNSYLVANIA 10
Northeast – Central Susquehanna Valley

Situated in the upper northeast corner of Pennsylvania, the 10th is home to a portion of the Pocono Mountains region, a popular honeymoon retreat known for its skiing, fishing and golfing.

Redistricting in 2002 significantly expanded the 10th, which ceded Scranton to the neighboring 11th but stretched farther into east-central Pennsylvania to pick up four Central Susquehanna Valley counties — Montour, Northumberland, Union and Snyder. While Scranton was once the 10th's major hub, the four new counties account for about 30 percent of the population. The district retained Williamsport, now its largest city, and Sunberry.

This region includes some of the state's best areas for lumber and agriculture. The latter is particularly prominent in Bradford County, which is among the state and national leaders in dairy production, and in Northumberland and Snyder counties, known for their poultry. Tourism remains strong, especially during the summer months, when visitors come for the scenery and sporting in the eastern part of the district and for the Little League World Series held annually in Williamsport, in the western reaches. Pike County, which increased its population 66 percent in the 1990s, is rapidly filling up with early-rising commuters to New Jersey and New York City who prefer Pike's small-town setting, affordable land and access to interstate highways.

The 10th has large swaths of rural, socially conservative heartland. With Scranton and its strong union ties no longer in the district, the district is more rural and Republican. Democrats still have a presence in areas like Carbondale and Archibald in Lackawanna County and in parts of Northumberland County. But most voters are heavily inclined to support the GOP for federal and state offices. George W. Bush won the 10th by 16 percentage points in 2000.

MAJOR INDUSTRY
Agriculture, manufacturing, tourism

CITIES
Williamsport, 30,706; Back Mountain (unincorporated) (pt.), 22,237

NOTABLE
Little League baseball was founded in Williamsport in 1939; Rep. Sherwood and Rep. H. James Saxton of New Jersey were childhood friends in Nicholson.

Rep. Paul E. Kanjorski (D)

CAPITOL OFFICE
225-6511
paul.kanjorski@mail.house.gov
www.house.gov/kanjorski
2353 Rayburn 20515-3811; fax 225-0764

COMMITTEES
Financial Services
Government Reform

HOMETOWN
Nanticoke

BORN
April 2, 1937, Nanticoke, Pa.

RELIGION
Roman Catholic

FAMILY
Wife, Nancy Kanjorski; one child

EDUCATION
Temple U., attended 1957-62; Dickinson School of Law, attended 1962-65

MILITARY SERVICE
Army, 1960-61

CAREER
Lawyer

POLITICAL HIGHLIGHTS
Sought Democratic nomination for U.S. House (special election), 1980; sought Democratic nomination for U.S. House, 1980

ELECTION RESULTS

2002 GENERAL		
Paul E. Kanjorski (D)	93,758	55.6%
Louis J. Barletta (R)	71,543	42.4%
Thomas J. McLaughlin (REF)	3,304	2.0%
2002 PRIMARY		
Paul E. Kanjorski (D)		unopposed
2000 GENERAL		
Paul E. Kanjorski (D)	131,948	66.4%
Stephen A. Urban (R)	66,699	33.6%

PREVIOUS WINNING PERCENTAGES
1998 (67%); 1996 (68%); 1994 (67%); 1992 (67%); 1990 (100%); 1988 (100%); 1986 (71%); 1984 (59%)

Elected 1984; 10th term

Kanjorski sees his principal duty as a member of Congress as working for economic development in the 11th District as it struggles to move beyond its historical dependence on the coal industry.

By his accounting, he's done pretty well: His 2002 campaign Web site bragged that Kanjorski "has brought more than one billion dollars into Northeastern and Central Pennsylvania."

In 2002, Kanjorski was the lone Democrat to vote to bring up a Republican-drafted spending bill because, he said, the bill contained $39 million for Medicare payments to northeastern Pennsylvania hospitals. He also touts the work he has done to resurrect the $175 million Wyoming Valley Levee Raising Project, a flood control project on the Susquehanna River that had languished for years after its authorization. In the 107th Congress, he worked to ensure that the funding continued, and was able to direct $28 million to the project, bringing the total federal investment to more than $113 million.

Years before, after Kanjorski had convinced President Bill Clinton to revive the long languishing flood control project, the president had called Kanjorski "utterly relentless." He is also leading the drive to fight the closing or downsizing of the veterans hospital in Wilkes-Barre. He has been able to get $48 million in federal funds to renovate the hospital.

A Polish Catholic, Kanjorski reflects the views and concerns of the white, ethnic, working-class people who still dominate politics in his part of Pennsylvania. He holds a conservative view on most social issues. He opposes abortion and gun control and supports school prayer, but he is a loyal Democrat on fiscal matters and a staunch supporter of organized labor.

He continually battles GOP efforts to lower international trade barriers, worrying about how it will affect local blue-collar employment. In the 107th, he voted against a bill to give the president "fast track" authority to negotiate trade agreements that Congress cannot amend.

Kanjorski prefers, however, to seek bipartisan cooperation for his own legislation, such as a measure in the Financial Services Committee that provides incentives for investment in economically distressed areas. He played a lead role in the 107th Congress when the committee drafted a measure on terrorism insurance. Kanjorski worked to protect towns and rural areas from excessive surcharges. He also called attention to the manner in which large investment banks have been allocated opportunities to buy stock in initial public offerings, known as IPOs. Kanjorski is the second-ranking Democrat on the panel in the 108th Congress.

Three perennial priorities on his legislative agenda include finding ways to reduce pollution from burning coal, cleaning up abandoned industrial sites (including coal fields), known as brownfields, and giving states the authority to limit the imports of garbage from other states. Pennsylvania receives more out-of-state trash than any other state in the union.

Kanjorski is not shy about mixing it up in the partisan trenches; he was one of the leading critics of Government Reform Committee Chairman and Indiana Republican Dan Burton in the 105th Congress when Burton led a probe of Democratic fundraising activities. He also was one of only five Democrats in 1998 who voted against any kind of impeachment inquiry of President Clinton.

But he has also warned his own leaders about taking partisan warfare too far. In 2000, he publicly criticized top Democrats for deciding to file a racketeering lawsuit against Republican Tom DeLay of Texas. "This is almost the criminalization of politics," Kanjorski told Roll Call, a Capitol Hill newspaper.

Two years later, Kanjorski was involved in a similar situation. Newspapers reported that the FBI was looking into allegations that Kanjorski had steered federal grants to businesses connected to his family, and some House Republicans considered filing an ethics complaint against him. The FBI never confirmed or denied the reports. The Republican effort was squelched after Democratic leaders reportedly threatened to file a retaliatory complaint against a GOP lawmaker.

Kanjorski was born and grew up in Nanticoke, just southwest of Wilkes-Barre. As a House page in 1954, he was narrowly missed when Puerto Rican terrorists sprayed gunfire on the House chamber from the visitor's gallery.

He attended Temple University and the Dickinson College School of Law, but did not graduate from either. He became a lawyer and worked as an attorney in northeast Pennsylvania for almost 20 years. He was an administrative law judge for workers' compensation cases and served as the unpaid assistant city solicitor for Nanticoke for more than a decade.

After waging a pair of unsuccessful House campaigns in 1980 (one in a special election), he owed his 1984 House victory to an intestinal parasite and a sunny beach. The outcome of his primary challenge to Democratic Rep. Frank Harrison might have been different if not for the discovery that water supplies in parts of the 11th District were contaminated with the giardia parasite. As people boiled their water to make it drinkable, Kanjorski noted that Harrison had flown off on a congressional excursion to Costa Rica, and ran an ad that included a shot of the beach.

Kanjorski pounced on Harrison with a largely self-financed blitz of clever ads portraying the incumbent as an aloof globe-trotter. Harrison tried to ignore Kanjorski and stressed his experience in Washington, but Kanjorski leaped from long shot to victor. In November, Kanjorski handily defeated Republican Robert P. Hudock with 59 percent.

That was his closest election — he has been unopposed twice — until 2002. That year, dogged by newspaper stories about his family business dealings and reports of an FBI investigation, Kanjorski was hard pressed. The national GOP, taking note of the unfavorable publicity, invested heavily in the race. Their candidate, Hazleton Mayor Louis Barletta, pursed the ethics attack aggressively, saying in one televised debate that while Kanjorski may have brought home the bacon, "he put it in his own refrigerator."

But Kanjorski prevailed by 13 percentage points, thanks to a big margin in the Lackawanna County portion of the district, which had been added to the 11th in decennial redistricting earlier in the year.

KEY VOTES

2002

- Yes Overhaul campaign finance law; ban "soft money" and restrict advocacy advertising
- Yes Back Bush's defense budget increase
- No Extend 1996 welfare law
- Yes Adopt Bush's discretionary spending limit
- No Pass GOP Medicare prescription drug plan
- Yes Create independent Sept. 11 commission
- Yes Extend union protections to Homeland Security Department employees
- No Revive fast-track procedures for trade agreements
- Yes Authorize war against Iraq
- No Advance bankruptcy overhaul opposed by abortion opponents

2001

- No Nullify Clinton Labor Department ergonomics rule
- No Cut taxes by $1.35 trillion through fiscal 2011
- No Maintain ban on oil drilling in Arctic National Wildlife Refuge
- No Approve Bush proposal to limit managed-care plan liability for coverage decisions
- Yes Divert money from crop subsidy payments to land conservation
- Yes Expand law enforcement power to investigate suspected terrorists

CQ VOTE STUDIES

	PARTY UNITY		PRESIDENTIAL SUPPORT	
	Support	Oppose	Support	Oppose
2002	79%	21%	42%	58%
2001	75%	25%	47%	53%
2000	82%	18%	80%	20%
1999	83%	17%	72%	28%
1998	86%	14%	82%	18%

INTEREST GROUPS

	AFL-CIO	ADA	CCUS	ACU
2002	100%	75%	50%	24%
2001	100%	65%	43%	36%
2000	100%	65%	42%	16%
1999	89%	75%	24%	16%
1998	100%	85%	22%	12%

PENNSYLVANIA 11
Northeast – Scranton, Wilkes-Barre

Since the turn of the century, the health of the 11th District has been inextricably linked to the production, manufacturing and sale of coal. Demand for the district's anthracite coal peaked in the 1910s and 1920s. Since then, a few cities in this district have disappeared with the long decline of the coal industry and the rise of oil and natural gas. Centralia, site of a burning underground mine, turned into a ghost town after a federally ordered evacuation.

Other towns, such as Jim Thorpe and Wilkes-Barre, have been more prosperous. Jim Thorpe, given that name in 1954 for the decathlon Olympic gold medalist who is buried in town, was a haven for millionaires and has maintained its historic charm as a preservation project of the Department of the Interior. Economic development needs along with an elderly population help drive the push for federal dollars.

The 11th has a decided but not monolithic Democratic lean, the result of a large Irish population and a strong union tradition. Had the reconfigured 11th existed in the 2000 election, Al Gore would have won it by 10 percentage points. Redistricting in 2002 moved Scranton (Lackawanna County) from the neighboring 10th into the 11th, making it even more Democratic. Democrats also do well in Luzerne County, with strong showings in Wilkes-Barre and in smaller cities to the north and east, but not at a level commensurate with their wide registration advantage in the county.

The decline of coal and an investment in technology-driven businesses have helped the GOP, which does well in Columbia County and has a slight edge in voter registration and electoral performance in Monroe County, a fast-growing area in the Poconos where many newcomers commute via Interstate 80 to their jobs in New Jersey and New York.

MAJOR INDUSTRY
Manufacturing, retail trade, tourism

MILITARY BASES
Tobyhanna Army Depot, 123 military, 3,079 civilian (2001)

CITIES
Scranton, 76,415; Wilkes-Barre, 43,123; Hazleton, 23,329

NOTABLE
Berwick prides itself on its high school football team, a perennial power in Pennsylvania that has produced several NFL players.

Rep. John P. Murtha (D)

CAPITOL OFFICE
225-2065
murtha@mail.house.gov
www.house.gov/murtha
2423 Rayburn 20515-3812; fax 225-5709

COMMITTEES
Appropriations

HOMETOWN
Johnstown

BORN
June 17, 1932, New Martinsville, W.Va.

RELIGION
Roman Catholic

FAMILY
Wife, Joyce Murtha; three children

EDUCATION
U. of Pittsburgh, B.A. 1962 (economics)

MILITARY SERVICE
Marine Corps, 1952-55, 1966-67; Marine Corps Reserve, 1967-90

CAREER
Car wash owner and operator

POLITICAL HIGHLIGHTS
Democratic nominee for U.S. House, 1968; Pa. House, 1969-74

ELECTION RESULTS

2002 GENERAL		
John P. Murtha (D)	124,201	73.5%
Bill Choby (R)	44,818	26.5%
2002 PRIMARY		
John P. Murtha (D)	60,687	64.2%
Frank R. Mascara (D)	33,837	35.8%
2000 GENERAL		
John P. Murtha (D)	145,538	70.8%
Bill Choby (R)	56,575	27.5%
James N. O'Neil (REF)	3,324	1.6%

PREVIOUS WINNING PERCENTAGES
1998 (68%); 1996 (70%); 1994 (69%); 1992 (100%); 1990 (62%); 1988 (100%); 1986 (67%); 1984 (69%); 1982 (61%); 1980 (59%); 1978 (69%); 1976 (68%); 1974 (58%); 1974 Special Election (50%)

Elected February 1974; 15th full term

Few lawmakers match, and none surpasses, Murtha's prowess for drafting spending bills and putting behind them a broad, bipartisan coalition of House members, many of whom have a concrete stake in the outcome.

Murtha, in his 15th term, has been either chairman or the ranking minority member of the Defense Appropriations Subcommittee since 1989. He sees himself as indispensible in keeping the wheels of government turning through compromise and judicious applications of legislative lubricant, such as added funds for specific projects of great importance to individual members.

To the GOP "revolutionaries" who took control of the Capitol in 1995, Murtha and his ilk represented a political fifth column, using public largess to lure even some Republicans into preserving and expanding the federal colossus. Statesmen or saboteurs, the appropriators largely prevailed. In the 107th Congress, President Bush's threats to veto higher-than-budgeted spending bills barred Congress from launching any big-ticket programs. But it had little effect on the retail politics of passing a defense bill, because the sum total of members' requests could be accommodated within Bush's overall budget request.

Murtha's effectiveness hinges on finding out what his colleagues want, touching base with interested parties to determine what he realistically can get, and delivering on his commitments. This requires personal attention, which Murtha gives generously. During roll call votes, members who need a sympathetic hearing for some hometown priority usually can find him sitting in a corner of the House chamber, holding court with Democrats from other Rust Belt districts. "You'd think they were handing out candy or something, the way members gravitate over there," Republican James C. Greenwood, a fellow Pennsylvanian, told the Associated Press.

Murtha does not merely grease the legislative wheels. He tries to use his mastery of the process to shape defense policy. His views on the subject have credibility because he works the military establishment the way he works the House — face to face, so he can look his interlocutor in the eye. Impatient with the Power Point presentations beloved by Pentagon briefers, Murtha travels without fanfare to deployments in far-off regions to assess the situation.

He also speaks on military affairs with the moral authority of a decorated veteran of Vietnam ground combat, one of the few in the House. While some congressional veterans use their military experience to rhetorically bludgeon their opponents, Murtha rarely mentions his in public, but his colleagues are well aware of it.

That background explains his strong focus on the troops' quality of life. He was a leader in the successful drive by military brass in the late 1990s to increase pay, liberalize military pensions and expand retirees' health benefits. He also opposed some of the peacekeeping deployments ordered by President Clinton because he felt U.S. forces were being overworked.

Murtha decried Bush's defense budget requests as inadequate, particularly after the terrorist attacks of Sept. 11, 2001. But like other defense hawks of both parties, he ran into a wall of White House opposition when he proposed significant increases in the requests.

In 2002, Murtha's strong defense credentials made him a key figure in shaping the Democrats' response to Bush's push for congressional authorization for military action against Iraq. He applauded Bush's decision to seek a U.N. resolution laying the groundwork for such an attack, warning against a go-it-alone approach. "If we do this unilaterally, it will have a horrendous cost," he said.

Also in 2002, Congress passed his bill establishing a national memorial at the site in Pennsylvania's Somerset County where United Flight 93 crashed after passengers took control of the craft from terrorist hijackers.

Murtha is something of a political throwback, a latter-day version of the lunch-pail liberals who made up a large bloc of House Democrats from the New Deal until the late 1960s, when the party splintered over Vietnam. The coal and steel industries that once were the 12th District's economic lifeblood were decimated by the recessions of the 1980s, but the area's economy is rebounding as high-tech industries move in — many in response to the economic development programs Murtha has squirreled into appropriations laws over the years. In 2002 alone, he claimed credit for steering 1,500 jobs to the district.

The 12th remains a working-class Democratic stronghold, and Murtha is a reliable ally of organized labor, regularly pressing to raise the minimum wage and protect workers against adverse impacts of trade agreements. Once a car-wash operator, he also supports small-business priorities, such as a larger health insurance tax deduction for the self-employed. Reflecting his district's conservatism, Murtha supports gun owners' rights and, as a Catholic, opposes abortion. As a result, his voting record is not as liberal as one might expect. In the 107th Congress, he backed Bush 50 percent of the time, ranking him among the top 20 Democrats in support of the Republican president.

When longtime GOP Rep. John P. Saylor died in 1973, Murtha, then a state legislator, won narrowly over Harry M. Fox, a former Saylor aide, in a special election that focused on the Republicans' Watergate problems. His toughest re-election challenge since was in 1990, when he was almost blindsided in the Democratic primary by lawyer Kenneth B. Burkley, who made the contest a referendum on Murtha's use of congressional power to benefit himself. Murtha won by 8 percentage points.

After Pennsylvania lost two House seats as a result of the 2000 census, the GOP-dominated legislature drew a map that threw Murtha into a primary duel with fellow Democratic Rep. Frank R. Mascara. Four-term veteran Mascara's old district accounted for about half the registered Democrats. But he was swamped by Murtha's fundraising, in which defense contractors, labor unions and Washington politicos played a large role. Murtha won the primary by nearly 2-to-1 and coasted to re-election by nearly 3-to-1.

KEY VOTES

2002

No	Overhaul campaign finance law; ban "soft money" and restrict advocacy advertising
Yes	Back Bush's defense budget increase
?	Extend 1996 welfare law
No	Adopt Bush's discretionary spending limit
No	Pass GOP Medicare prescription drug plan
?	Create independent Sept. 11 commission
Yes	Extend union protections to Homeland Security Department employees
No	Revive fast-track procedures for trade agreements
Yes	Authorize war against Iraq
No	Advance bankruptcy overhaul opposed by abortion opponents

2001

No	Nullify Clinton Labor Department ergonomics rule
No	Cut taxes by $1.35 trillion through fiscal 2011
No	Maintain ban on oil drilling in Arctic National Wildlife Refuge
No	Approve Bush proposal to limit managed-care plan liability for coverage decisions
Yes	Divert money from crop subsidy payments to land conservation
Yes	Expand law enforcement power to investigate suspected terrorists

CQ VOTE STUDIES

	PARTY UNITY		PRESIDENTIAL SUPPORT	
	Support	Oppose	Support	Oppose
2002	75%	25%	55%	45%
2001	66%	34%	47%	53%
2000	70%	30%	74%	26%
1999	67%	33%	58%	42%
1998	73%	27%	73%	27%

INTEREST GROUPS

	AFL-CIO	ADA	CCUS	ACU
2002	100%	55%	61%	32%
2001	100%	65%	52%	48%
2000	100%	55%	45%	24%
1999	89%	60%	43%	24%
1998	100%	75%	47%	21%

PENNSYLVANIA 12
Southwest – Johnstown

Described by an aide to Rep. Murtha as "an upside-down Chinese dragon," the strangely contorted 12th hopscotches in southwestern Pennsylvania across nine counties, eight of which are shared with other districts. A once-booming center of coal, steel and iron production, this area is diversifying to escape economic distress and industrial loss.

The 12th has been the unfortunate victim of floods that devastated Johnstown (Cambria County), the district's largest city, three times in history. The Great Flood of 1889, the most severe, destroyed the town and killed 2,200 people. Again in 1936 and 1977, floods took lives and caused significant damage. The area just celebrated its 25th anniversary of being flood-free, featuring an advertising campaign saying, "The flood's over, come on back!" The 1980s recession also had a devastating effect on the economy. The coal and steel industries declined and the unemployment rate skyrocketed to more than 27 percent.

More recently, the district has bounced back, in part by attracting some high-tech industry, including a Sony plant in Westmoreland and a number of defense and research firms. Capitalizing on past hardships, the Johnstown Flood Museum also draws tourists to the area, and the city's large health care base has remained stable. The unemployment rate in Johnstown has been in the single digits since early 1994, though it generally exceeds the national rate.

This district has been a Democratic stronghold since the New Deal, and Republican mapmakers in 2002 redistricting packed Democrats into the 12th to give the GOP an edge in adjacent districts. Like other towns in the state with an industrial past and an aging population, Johnstown wants federal help, but many voters are more socially conservative than the national Democratic Party. While George W. Bush lost both Cambria and Washington counties in 2000, he received the highest vote share of any GOP presidential candidate there since Richard M. Nixon in 1972.

MAJOR INDUSTRY
Manufacturing, service, health care

CITIES
Johnstown, 23,906; Washington, 15,268; New Kensington, 14,701

NOTABLE
The National Drug Intelligence Center in Johnstown tracks illegal drugs.

Rep. Joseph M. Hoeffel (D)

CAPITOL OFFICE
225-6111
www.house.gov/hoeffel
426 Cannon 20515-3813; fax 226-0611

COMMITTEES
International Relations
Transportation & Infrastructure

HOMETOWN
Abington

BORN
Sept. 3, 1950, Philadelphia, Pa.

RELIGION
Protestant

FAMILY
Wife, Francesca Hoeffel; two children

EDUCATION
Boston U., B.S. 1972 (English); Temple U., J.D. 1986

MILITARY SERVICE
Army Reserve, 1970-76

CAREER
Lawyer

POLITICAL HIGHLIGHTS
Democratic nominee for Pa. House, 1974; Pa. House, 1977-85; Democratic nominee for U.S. House, 1984, 1986; Montgomery County Commission, 1992-98; Democratic nominee for U.S. House, 1996

ELECTION RESULTS

2002 GENERAL		
Joseph M. Hoeffel (D)	107,945	51.0%
Melissa Brown (R)	100,295	47.3%
John P. McDermott (CNSTP)	3,627	1.7%
2002 PRIMARY		
Joseph M. Hoeffel (D)		unopposed
2000 GENERAL		
Joseph M. Hoeffel (D)	146,026	52.8%
Stewart Greenleaf (R)	126,501	45.7%
Ken Cavanaugh (LIBERT)	4,224	1.5%

PREVIOUS WINNING PERCENTAGES
1998 (52%)

Elected 1998; 3rd term

Hoeffel is a savvy pragmatist — a man who despite an understated manner and relative lack of seniority has secured important federal public works projects for his district, succeeded in the hard-hitting field of congressional international affairs, and weathered a Republican effort to redistrict him out of a seat.

Hoeffel (HUFF-ull) struggled to win his first two terms by positioning himself as a moderate Democrat in a moderately Republican district. After redistricting for the decade gave Hoeffel new Democratic turf in the northeastern precincts of Philadelphia to go with his suburban Montgomery County constituency, he still struggled, edging past ophthalmologist Melissa Brown by just 4 points in a surprisingly close, hard-fought contest.

Pennsylvania's GOP-controlled General Assembly, which had to come up with a congressional map that shed two House seats because of post-census reapportionment, drew a new 13th District that combined some territory Hoeffel had represented since 1999 with neighborhoods represented for two decades by another Democrat, Robert A. Borski. The Republicans' intent was to create a primary that would eliminate one incumbent and weaken the other for the fall. That plan backfired when Borski decided to retire from Congress, leaving Hoeffel plenty of time and money to prepare for November.

Hoeffel, who affiliates with the New Democrat Coalition, is moderate on social issues and somewhat more conservative fiscally. He has made it a point to be diligent about constituent concerns and to go after government funds for projects such as the Schuylkill River Heritage Area and highway funding for beleaguered Norristown.

In the 108th Congress, Hoeffel won appointment to the Transportation Committee, where he will watch out for Philadelphia area transit needs as Congress drafts a new transportation authorization bill.

To get on Transportation, he gave up his seat on the Budget Committee, where he opposed GOP tax cut proposals, especially the $1.35 trillion tax cut enacted in 2001. "There is such a thing as too many tax cuts. It's just as fiscally irresponsible as too much spending," he said. But like most Democrats, Hoeffel voted for the final $98 billion economic stimulus and unemployment benefits extension package enacted early in 2002. Hoeffel says he will continue to fight tax breaks and subsidies for big business that he calls "corporate welfare."

A member of the International Relations Committee, Hoeffel has been a strong supporter of Israel, where he traveled during his first term. He also went to Russia early in 2001. He says that while relations had been strained by U.S. plans for a missile defense system, Russia is a "strategic partner and potentially strong ally." Hoeffel also says he would like to see a small-scale Marshall Plan for the Middle East and Central Asia.

On domestic policy, Hoeffel was a proponent of the type of education policy changes enacted in 2002. He is a supporter of abortion rights and an advocate of gun control measures. The husband of a registered nurse, he also advocates regulating health maintenance organizations to allow doctors more leeway and patients more choices. Environmental and labor groups have rewarded him with fundraising dollars and campaign support.

If Hoeffel seems reserved in Washington, he is quite the opposite in his district. In 2000, Hoeffel visited 40 of the district's communities on a walking tour that coincided with the Republican National Convention in Philadelphia. He holds numerous news conferences at home to explain his votes in the House. His outreach techniques also include "Saturdays with Joe," a series of town meetings and supermarket visits he conducts twice a month, and "Cuppa Joe with Joe," when he visits local diners on Saturday mornings to chat with constituents. In 2001, he launched "Joe's Job Days," in which he works at a different job in his district one day a month; that idea was borrowed from Democratic Sen. Bob Graham of Florida.

"This is stuff other guys do, too," Hoeffel says in explaining his high level of activity. "I just really do a lot of it." Early in the 108th, he focused on getting to know his new turf in northeast Philadelphia, where constituents gave him an earful about problems in federally subsidized housing projects.

Hoeffel also has intervened in local disputes, trying unsuccessfully to halt a proposed commuter rail line rate increase for suburban commuters, but securing from President Bush a $2 million budget request for the purchase of a 62-acre tract of land within Valley Forge National Historical Park, on which developers had wanted to build luxury homes.

Hoeffel says his interest in running for public office began with a college course on diplomatic history and the fact that he attended college during the Vietnam War. He made his first run for public office soon after, losing a bid for the state House in 1974. He won two years later and served the next eight years in Harrisburg, leaving in 1984 to run for Congress against GOP Rep. Lawrence Coughlin. He lost to Coughlin in 1986, too, the same year he earned a law degree.

After a five-year hiatus from politics, Hoeffel won a race for Montgomery County commissioner in 1991, serving there until his election to the House. In between, he mounted his third bid for Congress, coming up 84 votes short in 1996 against Jon D. Fox, a member of the GOP takeover Class of 1994.

Two years later, Hoeffel came armed with an ample campaign treasury and won his rematch with Fox by 5 percentage points, persuading voters that his was the type of moderate and independent voice they wanted in Congress. Hoeffel's victory also was impressive because two Republican statewide candidates that year — Gov. Tom Ridge and Sen. Arlen Specter — both carried the 13th District overwhelmingly.

Hoeffel's ability to stick to a moderate course was frustrating to Stewart Greenleaf, veteran state senator and a moderate recruited by the GOP in 2000 as its best shot at returning the district to its roots. (The party had controlled the district for 76 years, until Democrat Marjorie Margolies Mezvinksy was elected in 1992, only to lose to Fox two years later.) Greenleaf characterized Hoeffel as a "liberal," but the attacks did not stick, and Hoeffel won with a percentage of the vote that mirrored that of presidential candidate Al Gore.

KEY VOTES

2002

Yes Overhaul campaign finance law; ban "soft money" and restrict advocacy advertising
Yes Back Bush's defense budget increase
No Extend 1996 welfare law
No Adopt Bush's discretionary spending limit
No Pass GOP Medicare prescription drug plan
Yes Create independent Sept. 11 commission
Yes Extend union protections to Homeland Security Department employees
No Revive fast-track procedures for trade agreements
Yes Authorize war against Iraq
No Advance bankruptcy overhaul opposed by abortion opponents

2001

No Nullify Clinton Labor Department ergonomics rule
– Cut taxes by $1.35 trillion through fiscal 2011
Yes Maintain ban on oil drilling in Arctic National Wildlife Refuge
No Approve Bush proposal to limit managed-care plan liability for coverage decisions
Yes Divert money from crop subsidy payments to land conservation
Yes Expand law enforcement power to investigate suspected terrorists

CQ VOTE STUDIES

	PARTY UNITY		PRESIDENTIAL SUPPORT	
	Support	Oppose	Support	Oppose
2002	93%	7%	38%	62%
2001	91%	9%	36%	64%
2000	91%	9%	87%	13%
1999	91%	9%	85%	15%

INTEREST GROUPS

	AFL-CIO	ADA	CCUS	ACU
2002	100%	95%	50%	4%
2001	100%	100%	35%	0%
2000	100%	90%	42%	8%
1999	78%	100%	20%	4%

PENNSYLVANIA 13

East — northeast Philadelphia, part of Montgomery County suburbs

Nearly evenly divided between Montgomery County and northeast Philadelphia, the 13th combines white-collar suburbia with a portion of the city known for blue-collar grit. While registration is nearly evenly split between the parties, it belies the advantage Democrats have enjoyed in recent statewide and federal races.

Prescription drugs and health care have become prevalent issues in the district thanks to a large senior citizen population in northeast Philadelphia. Education is drawing more attention, as Philadelphia public schools are in worse shape than Montgomery County schools. In the first test of the redrawn district's leanings, public housing has been a subject of debate — many residents are concerned about how federal housing assistance is being administered.

Numerous shopping centers, strip malls and small businesses are housed in northeast Philadelphia, where a riverfront redevelopment project has sparked hopes of stimulating the 13th's dragging economy. This area votes Democratic, but not monolithically so.

Though the GOP still runs well at the local level in Montgomery County, Democrats have made major inroads here in state and federal races. In a dozen years, Montgomery went from voting Republican for president by 22 percentage points to backing Al Gore by 10 points in 2000. Close-in Abington and Upper Dublin (shared with the 8th) now vote Democratic for president, while Republicans run well in northwestern Montgomery, in areas like Upper and Lower Salford, Upper and Lower Frederick and New Hanover.

MAJOR INDUSTRY
Health and business services, chemicals

MILITARY BASES
Willow Grove Naval Air Station, 2,240 military, 109 civilian (2001)

CITIES
Philadelphia (pt.), 305,391; Lansdale, 16,071; Horsham, 14,779

NOTABLE
Pennypack Park is known as the green heart of Northeast Philadelphia.

Rep. Mike Doyle (D)

CAPITOL OFFICE
225-2135
rep.doyle@mail.house.gov
www.house.gov/doyle
401 Cannon 20515-3814; fax 225-3084

COMMITTEES
Energy & Commerce
Standards of Official Conduct

HOMETOWN
Swissvale

BORN
Aug. 5, 1953, Pittsburgh, Pa.

RELIGION
Roman Catholic

FAMILY
Wife, Susan Doyle; four children

EDUCATION
Pennsylvania State U., B.S. 1975 (community development)

CAREER
Insurance company executive; state legislative aide

POLITICAL HIGHLIGHTS
Swissvale Borough Council, 1977-81 (served as a Republican)

ELECTION RESULTS

2002 GENERAL		
Mike Doyle (D)		unopposed
2002 PRIMARY		
Mike Doyle (D)		unopposed
2000 GENERAL		
Mike Doyle (D)	156,131	69.4%
Craig C. Stephens (R)	68,798	30.6%

PREVIOUS WINNING PERCENTAGES
1998 (68%); 1996 (56%); 1994 (55%)

Elected 1994; 5th term

Doyle, whose father and grandfather worked in steel mills, has made aiding the economic resurgence of Pittsburgh his top priority in Congress. He wants to move the city away from a past tied closely to the steel industry to a present-day economy that is more broadly based and includes high-technology manufacturing processes.

From his seat on the Energy and Commerce Committee, Doyle has focused on funneling federal money into local enterprises that develop alternative energy sources and more efficient uses of energy. He also has pressed for the cleanup of polluted industrial sites, known as "brownfields," to permit their use again.

But Doyle also continues to look out for the interests of the steel industry. He urges the federal government to take steps to protect domestic firms from what he regards as unfair foreign competition, and he watches out for retired steel workers whose benefits are in jeopardy. "I'm the first Mike Doyle in the family to not work in the mills, but that's the benefit of their hard work," he told the Greensburg Tribune-Review.

His voting record is similar to those of his Democratic colleagues who affiliate with the "Blue Dogs," a coalition of conservative Democrats, but he says he has never considered joining. His votes on the floor put him in league with the Republicans about a quarter of the time — a relatively high percentage for a Northern Democrat. In the 107th Congress, for example, he sided with Republicans on issues such as cutting taxes for married couples, rejecting an increase in car fuel efficiency standards and making it a federal offense to injure or kill a fetus.

If Doyle is more comfortable with the GOP majority than most Democrats, it may be because he once was one of them. For 16 years, he was chief of staff to a Republican in the Pennsylvania Senate. He was a Republican for many of those years, switching parties in 1992.

But Doyle shows his Democratic stripes by voting with organized labor more than 90 percent of the time and generally backing the party line on issues such as better access to health care and background checks of gun purchasers. He has displayed sufficient party loyalty that he was able to win a seat on Energy and Commerce in the 107th Congress. In the 108th, he has another chance to show his loyalty through his service on the ethics committee, generally regarded as a thankless task.

Joining other lawmakers whose constituents are employed by the auto, steel and coal industries, Doyle has been a frequent and vocal critic of stricter clean air standards proposed by the Environmental Protection Agency, saying the multibillion-dollar cost to business to comply with new pollution limits "is quite a burden to place on our economy."

Although he gave up a seat on the Veterans' Affairs Committee when he won the Energy and Commerce spot, Doyle remains active on veterans issues. In the 107th, he sponsored legislation, which became law, requiring the Department of Veterans Affairs to fully inform the more than half a million surviving spouses and dependents of their eligibility for veterans' benefits and health care services.

Early in the 107th, Doyle and New Jersey GOP Rep. Christopher H. Smith founded a Congressional autism caucus to draw attention to the disorder that affects more than half a million Americans and to push for more federal research funding. Doyle's interest in the matter grew out of his work with Pittsburgh's Center for Autism Research.

In a bid to help revitalize western Pennsylvania's troubled steel towns, Doyle has pressed for legislation creating a national historic park outside Pittsburgh that would highlight the historic role of the steel industry.

Doyle actually did work in the steel mills, during the summers while in college — just enough, he says, to know he wanted to do something else.

After Doyle earned a community development degree from Pennsylvania State, he returned in the mid-1970s to his hometown of Swissvale, just east of Pittsburgh. He entered the insurance business, became involved in community affairs as executive director of the Turtle Creek Valley Citizens Union and was elected to the Swissvale Borough Council, serving as finance and recreation chairman.

For many years, he worked for a Republican state senator, Frank A. Pecora, and out of deference to his boss he switched his party registration to the GOP. In 1992, Pecora switched his affiliation to the Democrats and fought through a crowded House primary to win the right to challenge Republican Rick Santorum, then seeking election to a second House term. Pecora lost decisively. Doyle jumped back to the Democratic Party that same year.

In 1994, when Santorum first ran for the Senate, Doyle took up where his old boss had left off and ran in the open 18th District, surviving a seven-person primary and winning the Democratic nomination with 20 percent of the vote. In the general election, Doyle was not well-known across the district, but neither was GOP nominee John McCarty. Using some of the "time for a change" rhetoric popularized by GOP conservatives, Doyle capitalized on the district's Democratic leanings to win by 10 percentage points. He was one of just four Democrats who swam against the national GOP tide that year to capture a House seat that had been in Republican hands.

Doyle won re-election by 16 points in 1996, even though the Pittsburgh Post-Gazette endorsed the GOP candidate, lawyer David B. Fawcett. Doyle won by 35 points in 1998 and by 39 points in 2000.

Heading into post-census redistricting, Doyle was regarded as one of the more vulnerable incumbents in the nation, given Pennsylvania's loss of two House seats and the GOP's control of the redistricting process. But Doyle caught a series of breaks. Redistricting at first seemed to have dealt him a tough hand, shoving him into the 14th District of fellow Democrat William J. Coyne. But Coyne decided to retire after 11 terms, and none of a number of potentially tough Democratic challengers decided to make a run in 2002. State Republicans, which had made the new 14th heavily Democratic in order to put more Republicans in surrounding districts, declined to field a candidate against Doyle in November.

KEY VOTES

2002

- Yes Overhaul campaign finance law; ban "soft money" and restrict advocacy advertising
- Yes Back Bush's defense budget increase
- No Extend 1996 welfare law
- No Adopt Bush's discretionary spending limit
- No Pass GOP Medicare prescription drug plan
- Yes Create independent Sept. 11 commission
- Yes Extend union protections to Homeland Security Department employees
- No Revive fast-track procedures for trade agreements
- No Authorize war against Iraq
- No Advance bankruptcy overhaul opposed by abortion opponents

2001

- No Nullify Clinton Labor Department ergonomics rule
- No Cut taxes by $1.35 trillion through fiscal 2011
- Yes Maintain ban on oil drilling in Arctic National Wildlife Refuge
- No Approve Bush proposal to limit managed-care plan liability for coverage decisions
- Yes Divert money from crop subsidy payments to land conservation
- Yes Expand law enforcement power to investigate suspected terrorists

CQ VOTE STUDIES

	PARTY UNITY		PRESIDENTIAL SUPPORT	
	Support	Oppose	Support	Oppose
2002	90%	10%	38%	62%
2001	78%	22%	40%	60%
2000	79%	21%	70%	30%
1999	77%	23%	67%	33%
1998	79%	21%	68%	32%

INTEREST GROUPS

	AFL-CIO	ADA	CCUS	ACU
2002	100%	80%	45%	8%
2001	100%	85%	43%	32%
2000	100%	65%	47%	20%
1999	100%	85%	32%	16%
1998	100%	80%	50%	25%

PENNSYLVANIA 14
Pittsburgh and some close-in suburbs

The 14th, which includes all of Pittsburgh and some of its close-in suburbs, has undergone an economic transformation while maintaining its Democratic tradition and ethnic character.

Medical centers and universities, parks, skyscrapers and high-tech industry have replaced the smoke stacks from the steel industry once nestled between the Allegheny, Monongahela and Ohio rivers. A thriving, corporate downtown has grown up in the "Golden Triangle," where the Allegheny and Monongahela rivers meet. Major League Baseball's Pittsburgh Pirates played their first game in their new stadium, PNC Park, in April 2001, and the National Football League's Pittsburgh Steelers also play in a new stadium that opened in 2001, Heinz Field.

Towns such as Monroeville and Penn Hills, only parts of which are in the district, have seen commercial development and some technology jobs move in, while others have languished. Many of Pittsburgh's neighborhoods, such as Bloomfield and Lawrenceville, retain their ethnic roots — mainly German, Italian, Irish and Polish. Squirrel Hill long has been the center of the city's Jewish population.

Even with the diversification of the 14th's economy, the district retains strong Democratic roots. Union strength translates into lopsided Democratic margins, and Democrats far outnumber Republicans, whose outposts in the region are found mostly in the neighboring 4th and 18th districts. Pittsburgh is staunchly Democratic, and the party's candidates also rack up big margins in Wilkinsburg, a heavily black area that abuts Pittsburgh to the east, and McKeesport, West Mifflin and Duquesne, south of the city. Al Gore took 73 percent of the Pittsburgh vote and 69 percent of the district vote in 2000. Democrat Edward G. Rendell took 67 percent in Pittsburgh in the 2002 gubernatorial election.

MAJOR INDUSTRY

Banking, government, health care

CITIES

Pittsburgh, 334,563; Penn Hills (unincorporated) (pt.), 35,864; McKeesport, 24,040; West Mifflin, 22,464; Wilkinsburg, 19,196

NOTABLE

Artist Andy Warhol was born in Pittsburgh; In the 1980s, a bad economy forced Clairton, setting for the movie "The Deer Hunter," to furlough its police and turn off streetlights.

Rep. Patrick J. Toomey (R)

CAPITOL OFFICE
225-6411
rep.toomey.pa15@mail.house.gov
www.house.gov/toomey
224 Cannon 20515-3815; fax 226-0778

COMMITTEES
Budget
Financial Services
Small Business
(Tax, Finance & Exports - chairman)

HOMETOWN
Allentown

BORN
Nov. 17, 1961, Providence, R.I.

RELIGION
Roman Catholic

FAMILY
Wife, Kris Toomey; two children

EDUCATION
Harvard U., A.B. 1984 (political philosophy)

CAREER
Restaurateur; investment banker

POLITICAL HIGHLIGHTS
Allentown Government Study Commission, 1994-96

ELECTION RESULTS

2002 GENERAL		
Patrick J. Toomey (R)	98,493	57.4%
Edward J. O'Brien (D)	73,212	42.6%
2002 PRIMARY		
Patrick J. Toomey (R)		unopposed
2000 GENERAL		
Patrick J. Toomey (R)	118,307	53.3%
Edward J. O'Brien (D)	103,864	46.8%

PREVIOUS WINNING PERCENTAGES
1998 (55%)

Elected 1998; 3rd term

Toomey is an unabashed fiscal conservative who believes his party should do more to reduce the size of the government and maintain fiscal discipline. Having been frustrated in his efforts in the House to make a real dent in spending, Toomey hopes to take his fiscal philosophy to the Senate. He announced in February 2003 that he will challenge Sen. Arlen Specter in the 2004 Republican primary.

The race will prove to be an interesting one, pitting the more moderate Specter against the fiscally hard-line Toomey. Toomey says that Specter is a "consistent liberal," who is "out of step with the Republican Party of Pennsylvania and Pennsylvania as a whole."

The two lawmakers differ on most issues: Specter supports abortion rights, Toomey opposes abortion — a reversal of his stand since his first House run in 1998. Specter voted for the Democratic version of a patient's bill of rights measure in the 107th Congress, while Toomey opposed it. The Club for Growth, a conservative, anti-tax organization, announced its support for Toomey early. But conservative Republican Rick Santorum, Pennsylvania's junior senator, quickly came out in support of Specter.

In the 107th Congress, Toomey and other fiscal conservatives helped reinvigorate the Conservative Action Team (CATs) and then re-named it the Republican Study Group. The 70 members of the coalition began issuing official position papers and demanding a say in GOP leadership decisions about budget and tax policy.

The group brought the budget process to a halt in the middle of 2002, after blasting appropriators for pursuing a path that could balloon discretionary spending. When the first non-defense spending bill came to the floor, a $19.8 billion Interior measure, they balked at $700 million in emergency wildfire spending. "This bill puts us on a pace to bust the budget," Toomey said. He then demanded that the House pass the giant Labor, Health and Human Services, and Education spending bill at the president's requested level — not a higher total favored by GOP moderates — before they would allow any other domestic spending bill to move.

"At some point you [have] to be willing to tighten your belt," Toomey said. The dispute forced the government to operate on stopgap spending measures four months into the fiscal year. Ultimately, Congress approved billions less than appropriators initially favored.

Toomey launched his crusade for fiscal restraint from his seat on the Budget Committee. In 2000, he included language in the annual congressional budget resolution to block passage of a supplemental appropriations bill that year unless its spending was matched with offsetting cuts. The move angered senior members of the Appropriations Committee and for a time threatened funding for peacekeeping operations in Kosovo, drug-fighting efforts in Colombia and disaster aid for hurricane victims. Toomey eventually backed down and agreed to drop his proposal after GOP leaders promised to support future efforts to set aside specific portions of the newfound budget surplus to pay down the national debt.

Despite his sometimes provocative stands, Toomey has earned colleagues' respect on certain financial issues. He sponsored a popular bill, enacted in 2002, to require all government agencies to prepare audited financial statements. He also draws on his background in investment banking in debates before the Financial Services Committee.

Toomey also sits on the Small Business panel, where he is the chairman of the Tax, Finance and Exports Subcommittee. He says his careers in the restaurant business and in investment banking taught him how government agencies and regulations can pose a "real headache" for small businesses.

Toomey's brand of fiscal conservatism plays well in his politically competitive Lehigh Valley district. However, his stands on trade and entitlement programs such as Social Security have put him at odds with some constituencies. His vote in 2000 to grant China permanent normal trade status drew fierce criticism from unions in an area where some blame imports for the closure of a large Bethlehem Steel Corp. plant. He angered them again in the 107th Congress by voting to give the president fast-track authority to negotiate trade pacts that Congress cannot amend.

Toomey spent seven years in the high-pressure world of international finance, trading futures contracts, swaps and other often volatile financial instruments while living in New York, London and Hong Kong. In 1990, he switched his business focus, investing in a chain of sports-themed restaurants in Allentown and Lancaster called Rookies.

Toomey had little political experience prior to his congressional bid other than a summer internship in the office of Republican Sen. John H. Chafee of Rhode Island. But he said the 1994 elections convinced him there was an "opportunity to change the direction of government" and make it more responsive to the citizenry. In 1994, he was elected to a two-year stint on the Allentown Government Study Commission, where he won enactment of a plan making it harder for the city council to raise taxes.

In 1998, Toomey jumped into the open-seat race created by the retirement of three-term moderate Democrat Paul McHale. In a tight six-candidate GOP primary, Toomey edged past the 1996 nominee, Bob Kilbanks, by less than 3 percentage points. He then faced veteran Democratic state Sen. Roy C. Afflerbach, who accused Toomey of having tenuous ties to the district. But the well-funded Toomey portrayed Afflerbach as a tax-raising career politician and won comfortably.

In 2000, Toomey faced a well-financed challenge from former United Steelworkers local president Ed O'Brien, who attacked Toomey's support of the China trade deal and generally depicted him as too conservative for the district. Toomey, benefiting from strong support from business groups, ran ads calling O'Brien an "old-fashioned liberal" and charging that his opponent was in the pocket of labor bosses and trial attorneys. In the end, Toomey captured 53 percent of the vote. In a rematch with O'Brien in 2002, Toomey had fundraising help from GOP heavyweights and won with more than 57 percent of the vote.

KEY VOTES

2002

- No Overhaul campaign finance law; ban "soft money" and restrict advocacy advertising
- Yes Back Bush's defense budget increase
- Yes Extend 1996 welfare law
- Yes Adopt Bush's discretionary spending limit
- Yes Pass GOP Medicare prescription drug plan
- No Create independent Sept. 11 commission
- No Extend union protections to Homeland Security Department employees
- Yes Revive fast-track procedures for trade agreements
- Yes Authorize war against Iraq
- ? Advance bankruptcy overhaul opposed by abortion opponents

2001

- Yes Nullify Clinton Labor Department ergonomics rule
- Yes Cut taxes by $1.35 trillion through fiscal 2011
- No Maintain ban on oil drilling in Arctic National Wildlife Refuge
- Yes Approve Bush proposal to limit managed-care plan liability for coverage decisions
- Yes Divert money from crop subsidy payments to land conservation
- Yes Expand law enforcement power to investigate suspected terrorists

CQ VOTE STUDIES

	PARTY UNITY		PRESIDENTIAL SUPPORT	
	Support	Oppose	Support	Oppose
2002	96%	4%	88%	12%
2001	93%	7%	93%	7%
2000	92%	8%	29%	71%
1999	91%	9%	28%	72%

INTEREST GROUPS

	AFL-CIO	ADA	CCUS	ACU
2002	13%	0%	100%	100%
2001	8%	0%	95%	100%
2000	0%	10%	80%	95%
1999	11%	5%	88%	92%

PENNSYLVANIA 15
East – Allentown, Bethlehem

Centered in the Lehigh Valley about 60 miles north of Philadelphia and abutting the Delaware River, the 15th takes in the cities of Allentown, Bethlehem and Easton — longtime strongholds of heavy industry.

The region once suffered from "Rust Belt" blues that singer Billy Joel enshrined in his 1982 song "Allentown." But the area began to reinvent its economy in the 1990s after unsuccessful attempts to revive the economic might of Bethlehem Steel and Mack Trucks. Bethlehem Steel filed for bankruptcy in 2001 and its company board in 2003 approved a takeover offer by International Steel Group.

Technology office parks and highway freight centers now cover a landscape where factories and small farms once were mainstays. Major employers include Agere Systems, Air Products and Chemicals, and the Lehigh Valley Hospital complex.

Many of the district's towns date to colonial times, some with well-established Pennsylvania Dutch heritages. But the 250-year-old German influence has been diluted by a century of immigration and recent migration from New Jersey and New York. Allentown — the only city among the state's top four not to lose residents in the 1990s — passed Erie during the decade to become Pennsylvania's third-largest city.

Blue-collar, ethnic workers provide a dwindling yet still powerful base for Democrats. But the increasing white-collar constituency and a socially conservative streak among blue-collar Democrats have helped Republicans win 15th District House contests. George W. Bush and Al Gore made multiple trips to the 15th during the 2000 presidential campaign. Gore ultimately captured the district by 1 percentage point.

MAJOR INDUSTRY
Manufacturing, technology, health care

CITIES
Allentown, 106,632; Bethlehem, 71,329; Easton, 26,263

NOTABLE
The Liberty Bell was hidden from the British in an Allentown church; Easton is home to the Crayola crayon factory; Just Born, based in Bethlehem, makes more than 600 million Peeps (brightly colored marshmallow candies) around Easter.

Rep. Joe Pitts (R)

CAPITOL OFFICE
225-2411
www.house.gov/pitts
204 Cannon 20515-3816; fax 225-2013

COMMITTEES
Energy & Commerce
International Relations

HOMETOWN
Kennett Square

BORN
Oct. 10, 1939, Lexington, Ky.

RELIGION
Protestant

FAMILY
Wife, Virginia M. "Ginny" Pitts; three children

EDUCATION
Asbury College, A.B. 1961 (philosophy & religion); West Chester State College, M.Ed. 1972 (comprehensive sciences)

MILITARY SERVICE
Air Force, 1963-69

CAREER
Nursery and landscaping business owner; teacher

POLITICAL HIGHLIGHTS
Pa. House, 1973-97

ELECTION RESULTS

2002 GENERAL		
Joe Pitts (R)	119,046	88.5%
Will Todd (GREEN)	8,720	6.5%
Kenneth Brenneman (CNSTP)	6,766	5.0%
2002 PRIMARY		
Joe Pitts (R)		unopposed
2000 GENERAL		
Joe Pitts (R)	162,403	67.0%
Robert S. Yorczyk (D)	80,177	33.1%

PREVIOUS WINNING PERCENTAGES
1998 (71%); 1996 (59%)

Elected 1996; 4th term

The son of missionaries, Pitts was deeply involved in Central Asian affairs long before the events of Sept. 11, 2001. He has continued to take an interest in that area of the world from his spot on the International Relations Committee and through charitable works that he directs from his Pennsylvania district.

The nexus between his interest in foreign affairs and the domestic issues he strongly supports is his Christian faith, which he says has driven him to reach out to distant peoples. Pitts has organized equipment drives for hospitals in Pakistan, cultural and governmental exchange programs and visits to his Pennsylvania district for officials from the region.

"I think humanitarian aid is effective, when it's people to people," he said. "It says more about who the American people are and what we stand for than many other things."

In the aftermath of the Sept. 11 attacks, he and a handful of other lawmakers formed the Silk Road Caucus, which promotes greater contact between the United States and the newly formed nations in Central Asia. One of Pitts' main roles in the group is to set up meetings between U.S. officials and visiting dignitaries from the area.

In Congress, Pitts follows the same road that he traveled during 24 years in the Pennsylvania legislature — one with few left turns. He is a strong proponent of cutting taxes and limiting the scope of the federal government, and he is a fervent opponent of abortion. As he launched his 2000 re-election bid, Pitts was lauded by the Lancaster New Era, a newspaper in his district, as "a tax cutter, budget balancer and moral crusader."

Pitts' position on abortion earned him serious opposition in his 1996 congressional bid. He also wants to boost prosecutions for violations of obscenity and child exploitation laws. His stance on abortion put him in a leading role in negotiations over legislation to revamp federal bankruptcy law in the 107th Congress. Although supportive of the bill's goal, Pitts and other conservatives objected to a part of the bill aimed at preventing demonstrators — particularly protesters at abortion clinics — from filing for bankruptcy to avoid paying court-ordered fines. Their opposition scuttled the bill at the end of 2002.

Pitts' agenda on Capitol Hill extends well beyond the purview of his committee assignments, reflecting his varied background and his understanding that, as a relatively junior member, the chances of advancing his goals solely through the legislative process are slim. In fact, for the 107th Congress, he completely changed his committees, swapping his former posts on Armed Services, Budget and Small Business for new ones on Energy and Commerce and International Relations.

To further his agenda, Pitts forges alliances with groups that advocate a larger role in civic life for families, businesses and religious and nonprofit groups. These organizations include the Republican Study Committee, the Renewal Alliance, the Fatherhood Promotion Task Force, the Pro-Life Caucus, the Religious Prisoners Congressional Task Force and the Values Action Team, which he leads. He serves as a liaison between two of the groups, delivering weekly reports to the RSC on what the Values Action Team is doing.

He is active in a number of human rights organizations, including the Helsinki Commission. But unlike many lawmakers with strong human rights agendas, he favored the 2000 law normalizing trade with China, arguing that increased engagement would spur China to improve its human rights record.

Pitts' affiliation with a number of non-legislative organizations on the Hill also included his membership in a singing group called the Capitol Four, but it disbanded after the 105th Congress when one of the quartet, Republican Michael Pappas of New Jersey, was defeated.

Many of Pitts' goals derive from his experiences as a child of missionaries and as a young father. Pitts spent most of his youth in the back country of the Philippines, where his parents were engaged in missionary work. He witnessed poverty and devastation close up, as well as the personal satisfaction that a life in public service can bring.

After returning to his native Kentucky, marrying and earning a college degree in philosophy and religion, Pitts embarked on a teaching career along with his wife. When she became pregnant, he discovered that the family could not live on just one teaching salary. So, he joined the Air Force, where he spent five and a half years, including three tours of duty in Southeast Asia in which he flew 116 combat missions as the navigator and electronic warfare officer of a B-52. He considered an Air Force career, but discarded the idea when his 3-year-old son did not recognize him when he returned home from an active duty tour.

After the Air Force, the family moved to Pennsylvania and Pitts returned to teaching — high school math and science. (He has sponsored legislation to require that 95 percent of federal education dollars reach the classroom and not be spent on bureaucracy.) Pitts eventually joined his wife's family's landscape and nursery business and then started his own landscaping firm. While active on local campaigns, Pitts did not think of running for office himself until colleagues convinced him to run for an open state House seat in 1972. He upset the party-endorsed candidate and served in the House for 24 years, including eight years as chairman of the Appropriations Committee.

When Robert S. Walker, a leading figure in the GOP takeover of the House, decided to retire after 10 terms in 1996, Pitts won a hard-fought five-way primary race and, given the GOP's more than 2-to-1 edge in registered voters, prevailed in the general election by 22 percentage points. He has not been challenged seriously in his re-election bids. His territory was made even more Republican in redistricting for this decade, and in 2002 the Democrats did not bother to field a candidate.

Pitts pledged when he first ran for the House in 1996 to serve no more than 10 years, but he announced before the 2002 election that he had changed his mind. Term limits diminish a "lame duck" lawmaker's effectiveness, he says.

KEY VOTES

2002

No Overhaul campaign finance law; ban "soft money" and restrict advocacy advertising
Yes Back Bush's defense budget increase
Yes Extend 1996 welfare law
Yes Adopt Bush's discretionary spending limit
Yes Pass GOP Medicare prescription drug plan
No Create independent Sept. 11 commission
No Extend union protections to Homeland Security Department employees
Yes Revive fast-track procedures for trade agreements
Yes Authorize war against Iraq
No Advance bankruptcy overhaul opposed by abortion opponents

2001

Yes Nullify Clinton Labor Department ergonomics rule
Yes Cut taxes by $1.35 trillion through fiscal 2011
No Maintain ban on oil drilling in Arctic National Wildlife Refuge
Yes Approve Bush proposal to limit managed-care plan liability for coverage decisions
No Divert money from crop subsidy payments to land conservation
Yes Expand law enforcement power to investigate suspected terrorists

CQ VOTE STUDIES

	PARTY UNITY		PRESIDENTIAL SUPPORT	
	Support	Oppose	Support	Oppose
2002	97%	3%	88%	12%
2001	96%	4%	91%	9%
2000	98%	2%	19%	81%
1999	97%	3%	17%	83%
1998	96%	4%	21%	79%

INTEREST GROUPS

	AFL-CIO	ADA	CCUS	ACU
2002	0%	0%	94%	100%
2001	0%	0%	91%	100%
2000	0%	0%	85%	100%
1999	0%	0%	92%	92%
1998	0%	0%	100%	96%

PENNSYLVANIA 16
Southeast – Lancaster, part of Reading

Located in southeast Pennsylvania and bordering Delaware and Maryland to the south, the 16th includes all of Lancaster County, the southern half of Chester County and a slice of Berks County, including part of Reading. Containing much of the so-called "Pennsylvania Dutch Country," the 16th is a Republican bastion.

The strong work ethic of the local labor force and the district's proximity to major roadways attract companies to the area, which is central to the mid-Atlantic's major markets. Economic expansion has attracted new residents, and some of the area's farmland has been built over with tract housing. Rolling and pastoral Chester County was the seventh-fastest-growing county in the state in the 1990s.

Although the 16th welcomes the development, farm preservation remains a major concern, especially in Lancaster, an area ranked among the top nationally in agricultural product sales. Tourism also enhances the 16th's robust economy. Some 4.5 million visitors annually flock to Dutch Country to gaze at Amish horse-drawn carriages, browse at quilt shops and dine in family-style restaurants.

Since the dawn of the Civil War, the areas in the 16th have favored the GOP at all levels. Lancaster County, which accounts for more than 70 percent of the district population, sets the district's conservative political tone with its Amish heritage: George W. Bush won 66 percent of the county vote in the 2000 presidential election. Chester County is more socially moderate, but Bush won nearly every jurisdiction in the 16th's share of the county and topped 60 percent in several townships in western Chester. The only real Democratic strength is in Reading, which is shared with the 6th District and is heavily Democratic as a result of its large Hispanic and black population.

MAJOR INDUSTRY

Agriculture, tourism, manufacturing

CITIES

Lancaster, 56,348; Reading (pt.), 44,501; West Chester, 17,861

NOTABLE

Frank Woolworth's original five-and-ten-cent store opened in Lancaster in 1879; One of the architects of the U.S. Capitol designed the Chester County Courthouse.

Rep. Tim Holden (D)

CAPITOL OFFICE
225-5546
www.house.gov/holden
2417 Rayburn 20515-3817; fax 226-0996

COMMITTEES
Agriculture
Transportation & Infrastructure

HOMETOWN
St. Clair

BORN
March 5, 1957, St. Clair, Pa.

RELIGION
Roman Catholic

FAMILY
Wife, Gwen Holden

EDUCATION
U. of Richmond, attended 1976-77; Bloomsburg U., B.A. 1980 (sociology)

CAREER
Probation officer; insurance broker; realtor

POLITICAL HIGHLIGHTS
Schuylkill County sheriff, 1985-93

ELECTION RESULTS

2002 GENERAL		
Tim Holden (D)	103,483	51.4%
George W. Gekas (R)	97,802	48.6%
2002 PRIMARY		
Tim Holden (D)		unopposed
2000 GENERAL		
Tim Holden (D)	140,084	66.3%
Thomas G. Kopel (R)	71,227	33.7%

PREVIOUS WINNING PERCENTAGES
1998 (61%); 1996 (59%); 1994 (57%); 1992 (52%)

Elected 1992; 6th term

A low-key lawmaker who built his political popularity as a local sheriff, Holden begins his second decade in Congress having distinguished himself as one of the rare bright spots for the Democrats in the 2002 election. He was the party's only winner in the four general-election matchups between House incumbents, defeating 20-year veteran Republican George W. Gekas by 5,681 votes. True to his standing as one of the most conservative congressional Democrats from the Northeast, Holden declared victory at a fish and game club in the town where he has always lived.

His views on social and fiscal issues, plus his attention to those who work Pennsylvania's dwindling farm land, have made Holden popular with a working-class constituency concerned with holding on to their jobs and their guns, and keeping the IRS out of their wallets. His background in law enforcement helps with nominally Republican voters, as does his willingness to stray from the line taken by his party's more polarizing figures. Time magazine once wrote that Holden "would wear a garlic necklace" if it would keep President Clinton away.

Holden sides with most GOP conservatives in opposing abortion rights while supporting the rights of those who own firearms and real estate. But he moves closer to the majority of his party on health care issues, such as expanding Medicare to include a prescription drug benefit, and he votes a pro-union line by opposing trade liberalization.

His middle-of-the-road stance is reflected in his voting record: During his first two years in office, President Bush won Holden's support 49 percent of the time. And Holden stood with fellow Democrats on only 69 percent of votes that split the parties in the 107th Congress, a lower percentage than all but 14 other Democrats.

Holden sits on the Transportation and Agriculture committees, and he is also active in the Congressional Mining Caucus. From those posts, he works quietly to secure funding for local highway and transit projects, to protect the interests of the local dairy industry, and to make the 17th District's large reserves of coal more marketable by spurring researchers to develop technology to burn it more cleanly.

Although he offers remarks on the House floor only a handful of times each year, he will speak out when he feels Pennsylvania's interests are threatened. In 2002, he argued for an extension of bankruptcy protections for family farmers when a broader bankruptcy overhaul that included special language for farmers bogged down. He urged passage of the new farm bill enacted that year, describing it as "a true safety net" for Northeastern and Mid-Atlantic dairy farmers. And he publicly battled federal efforts in 2000 to regulate ash from coal-burning power plants as a hazardous substance, pointing out that it is often used to reclaim Pennsylvania mines.

Holden is a member of the "Blue Dogs," a coalition of conservative House Democrats. On welfare, the budget and other issues, the group has staked out positions to the right of most Democrats but well to the left of the majority of Republicans. Holden opposed the $1.35 trillion, 10-year tax cut enacted in 2001, he said, in the belief that the surplus at the time should be devoted to paying down the national debt while leaving room for an increase in defense spending.

Holden's Democratic stripes are most visible on issues important to organized labor. He typically sides with unions in their disputes with the pro-business GOP leadership — supporting a higher minimum wage and opposing Republican efforts to curb union organizing methods.

Trade issues for Holden are complicated by the fact that his district includes not only union workers, who worry about the loss of jobs to foreign companies, but also export-minded businesses in such industries as communications and steel, as well as a number of firms that must import chemicals for use in their manufacturing processes. Still, he voted against all the landmark trade laws enacted in his first five terms.

During a debate with Gekas in 2002, Holden maintained that the first of these, the 1993 law implementing the North American Free Trade Agreement, had resulted in 36,000 lost manufacturing jobs in the 17th. When Gekas replied that the number of statewide jobs had increased, Holden pounced. "Maybe because of McDonald's and maybe because of Arby's, there were more jobs created. . . . But the good manufacturing jobs that were the heart and soul of Berks County are gone."

Holden's family has a tradition of public service. His father, Joseph "Sox" Holden, was a Schuylkill County commissioner for almost two decades. His great-grandfather, John Siney, founded the Miner's Benevolent Association, the forerunner of the United Mine Workers. When Holden shows up at a firehouse barbecue or a high school football game in the district, he moves with the easy affability of someone who has spent most of his life at such events. Many constituents refer to him as "Timmy."

He was born and still lives in St. Clair, just north of Pottsville in Schuylkill County. A star linebacker, he started college in Virginia on a football scholarship but returned home after a year to recuperate from a bout of tuberculosis and stayed close by to finish school. (He has recently revived his athletic career, in a way; a key hit and aggressive play behind the plate earned him the Democrats' most-valuable-player award in their 2002 charity baseball game against congressional Republicans.)

After working in the insurance and real estate businesses, Holden was a probation officer and sergeant-at-arms in the Pennsylvania House. At 28, he won the first of two terms as Schuylkill County sheriff.

When 12-term Democrat Gus Yatron retired in 1992, Holden won by 4 percentage points in what was then the 6th District, waging a "man of the people" campaign against John E. Jones, a Republican lawyer and judge. Though the district generally votes reliably Republican, Holden won four more times by increasing margins. Still, when reapportionment after the 2000 census took a House seat from Pennsylvania, the Republicans who ran the state's remapping figured Gekas could defeat Holden in the newly drawn 17th — whose voters had preferred Bush by 13 points in 2000.

KEY VOTES

2002

- Yes Overhaul campaign finance law; ban "soft money" and restrict advocacy advertising
- Yes Back Bush's defense budget increase
- Yes Extend 1996 welfare law
- No Adopt Bush's discretionary spending limit
- No Pass GOP Medicare prescription drug plan
- Yes Create independent Sept. 11 commission
- Yes Extend union protections to Homeland Security Department employees
- No Revive fast-track procedures for trade agreements
- Yes Authorize war against Iraq
- No Advance bankruptcy overhaul opposed by abortion opponents

2001

- No Nullify Clinton Labor Department ergonomics rule
- No Cut taxes by $1.35 trillion through fiscal 2011
- Yes Maintain ban on oil drilling in Arctic National Wildlife Refuge
- No Approve Bush proposal to limit managed-care plan liability for coverage decisions
- Yes Divert money from crop subsidy payments to land conservation
- Yes Expand law enforcement power to investigate suspected terrorists

CQ VOTE STUDIES

	PARTY UNITY		PRESIDENTIAL SUPPORT	
	Support	Oppose	Support	Oppose
2002	67%	33%	60%	40%
2001	71%	29%	40%	60%
2000	75%	25%	68%	32%
1999	68%	32%	54%	46%
1998	73%	27%	61%	39%

INTEREST GROUPS

	AFL-CIO	ADA	CCUS	ACU
2002	89%	65%	60%	40%
2001	100%	80%	41%	48%
2000	90%	55%	50%	32%
1999	88%	65%	58%	28%
1998	90%	70%	56%	24%

PENNSYLVANIA 17
East central — Harrisburg, Lebanon, Pottsville

Anchored in the eastern part of south-central Pennsylvania, the 17th is home to Harrisburg, the state capital, which sits 100 miles west of Philadelphia and 200 miles east of Pittsburgh. Here, in GOP-minded central Pennsylvania, state government and manufacturing remain key sources of employment. The district contains all of Dauphin, Lebanon and Schuylkill counties along with parts of Berks and Perry counties.

Harrisburg's skyline is dominated by the Capitol, with a dome inspired by St. Peter's Basilica in Rome. With many state government employees and an African-American majority, the city typically votes Democratic, though the rest of Dauphin County favors Republicans. Those wanting a real taste of Dauphin County skip Harrisburg and go to Hershey, also known as "Chocolatetown, U.S.A." The chocolate factory stands at Hershey's center, emitting the most pleasant of industrial odors.

Computer and electrical components manufacturing drive the economy in Dauphin and Lebanon counties. EDS, Giant Food, Blue Cross/Blue Shield, Bayer Corp. and area hospitals are major employers in the region. The proliferation of service jobs has helped mitigate the impact of other losses. Officials look to balance the needs of agricultural producers with those of industrial workers, making trade a potent issue in the 17th.

The district has a distinct Republican lean, but Rep. Holden demonstrated in 2002 that moderate Democrats can play here. The GOP runs strongly in Lebanon County and in the areas of Dauphin outside Harrisburg. Democrats do well in Schuylkill County, long a coal mining powerhouse, with comfortable margins in Pottsville, Mahanoy and Shenandoah. Holden also easily won the 17th's share of Berks.

MAJOR INDUSTRY
Government, services, manufacturing, agriculture

MILITARY BASES
Fort Indiantown Gap, 577 military, 800 civilian (2000)

CITIES
Harrisburg, 48,950; Lebanon, 24,461; Pottsville, 15,549; Colonial Park (unincorporated), 13,259; Hershey (unincorporated), 12,771

NOTABLE
Streetlights in the town of Hershey are shaped like Hershey Kisses; Pottsville is home to Yuengling, America's oldest active brewery.

Rep. Tim Murphy (R)

CAPITOL OFFICE
225-2301
murphy@mail.house.gov
www.house.gov/murphy
226 Cannon 20515-3818; fax 225-1844

COMMITTEES
Financial Services
Government Reform
Veterans' Affairs

HOMETOWN
Upper St. Clair

BORN
Sept. 11, 1952, Cleveland, Ohio

RELIGION
Roman Catholic

FAMILY
Wife, Nan Missig; one child

EDUCATION
Wheeling College, B.S. 1974; Cleveland State U., M.A. 1976 (psychology); U. of Pittsburgh, Ph.D. 1979 (psychology)

CAREER
Psychologist; professor

POLITICAL HIGHLIGHTS
Pa. Senate, 1997-2003

ELECTION RESULTS

2002 GENERAL		
Tim Murphy (R)	119,885	60.1%
Jack M. Machek (D)	79,451	39.9%
2002 PRIMARY		
Tim Murphy (R)		unopposed

Elected 2002; 1st term

Murphy wants to use his seat in the House to bring highway and mass transit improvements to the greater Pittsburgh area. But the practicing child psychologist suggests that tending to his constituents' well-being will be as important to him as improving their local infrastructure.

When Murphy entered public life by winning a state Senate seat in 1996, he did not set his professional interests aside. Motivated to run by a desire to address problems in managed care, Murphy wrote Pennsylvania's Patients' Bill of Rights. In 2001, he co-wrote a book titled "The Angry Child: Regaining Control When Your Child is Out of Control."

Murphy says he will use his background to tackle the wide range of health care policy debates in the 108th Congress, including how to provide prescription drug coverage for the elderly. Education also is a top priority. As one of 11 children, he cleaned out horse stalls and dug graves to pay his way through school. He wants to help low-income children, whom he believes are not served well by the public education system. He supports vouchers and other programs that could allow low-income families to send their children to private or parochial schools.

His three committee assignments — Financial Services, Government Reform and Veterans' Affairs — will have Murphy pursuing a broader range of interests.

Pennsylvania lost a pair of House seats in reapportionment after the 2000 census. The Republican-controlled General Assembly was nonetheless able to draw a congressional map for this decade with an 18th District south of Pittsburgh configured to favor a Republican — Murphy in particular. He was unopposed for the GOP nomination. He had become the heir presumptive to the seat because the incumbent House member living in the new 18th, four-term Democrat Frank R. Mascara, decided instead to mount an unsuccessful primary challenge to Rep. John P. Murtha.

In November, Murphy took 60 percent of the vote against Democrat Jack Machek, a school tax administrator.

PENNSYLVANIA 18

West – Pittsburgh suburbs, part of Westmoreland County

The 18th is a socially conservative, ancestrally Democratic area that takes in parts of Allegheny, Washington and Westmoreland counties in the orbit of Pittsburgh. The area's access to major waterways made the first half of the 20th century prosperous for parts of the 18th, which was once a prodigious producer of steel. Now, many areas are struggling to make an economic comeback.

The presence of universities and hospitals in the district has led some new technology companies to relocate to the area. However, an economic downturn early in the 21st century and the troubles of several high-tech companies have left the region grasping for a way to deal with unemployment. High property taxes are a volatile issue here.

About 55 percent of the 18th's residents live in Allegheny County, which is dominated by Pittsburgh. The Democratic-leaning city is in the 14th District, and most of Allegheny's wealthy Republican suburbs are in the 4th. The 18th's share includes well-off areas in southwestern Allegheny like Upper St. Clair and Bethel Park, which went solidly for Republican Mike Fisher in the 2002 governor's race, as well as middle- and working-class Democratic enclaves like Carnegie and Dormont, which are just southwest of Pittsburgh.

The 18th also includes most of Westmoreland County, a former Democratic bastion that has moved to the right. George W. Bush won the county by 6 percentage points in the 2000 presidential election.

MAJOR INDUSTRY
Health care, technology, manufacturing, air cargo, steel

CITIES
Bethel Park, 33,556; Mount Lebanon (unincorporated), 33,017; Monroeville (pt.), 24,294

NOTABLE
Singer Perry Como was born in Canonsburg (shared with the 12th).

Rep. Todd R. Platts (R)

CAPITOL OFFICE
225-5836
www.house.gov/platts
1032 Longworth 20515-3819; fax 226-1000

COMMITTEES
Education & Workforce
Government Reform
(Government Efficiency & Financial Management - chairman)
Transportation & Infrastructure

HOMETOWN
York

BORN
March 5, 1962, York, Pa.

RELIGION
Episcopalian

FAMILY
Wife, Leslie Platts; two children

EDUCATION
Shippensburg U., B.S. 1984 (public administration); Pepperdine U., J.D. 1991

CAREER
Lawyer; gubernatorial and state legislative aide

POLITICAL HIGHLIGHTS
Pa. Republican Party finance director, 1988; Pa. House, 1993-2000; sought Republican nomination for York County Commission, 1995

ELECTION RESULTS

2002 GENERAL		
Todd R. Platts (R)	143,097	91.1%
Ben G. Price (GREEN)	7,900	5.0%
Michael L. Paoletta (LIBERT)	6,008	3.8%
2002 PRIMARY		
Todd R. Platts (R)	34,026	76.6%
Tom Glennon (R)	7,150	16.1%
Lester B. Searer (R)	1,921	4.3%
Mike Johnson (R)	1,332	3.0%
2000 GENERAL		
Todd R. Platts (R)	168,722	72.6%
Jeff Sanders (D)	61,538	26.5%

Elected 2000; 2nd term

As a state lawmaker, Platts often annoyed his colleagues with his unwillingness to compromise and his demands that they do away with certain perquisites. "I agree with much of what he does, I just don't like the way he goes about it," one Pennsylvania colleague told the York Daily Record in 1995.

When Platts arrived on Capitol Hill in 2001, he was determined to make a difference. He made campaign finance overhaul a priority, even though it put him at odds with GOP leaders. It may not have been the best way for a freshman to start off his first term in the House, but Platts says he always has been treated fairly by the leadership.

The York newspaper once dubbed him the "King of Clean," referring to Platts' upright image. And he once told the Gettysburg Times that his pet peeve is able-bodied people who park in spots reserved for the disabled.

Platts says he is not unwilling to compromise, but there comes a time when a politician has to take a stand. He may have picked up his stubborn tendencies from his father, who bucked the local Little League establishment with his belief that every child who showed up at practice should play. His father, Dutch, "taught me . . . to work hard, stand up for what you believe in and be honest," Platts says.

He says being a member of Congress has been his ambition since he was a teenager. He worked in local political races while he was in high school, majored in public administration in college, went to law school, and then paid his dues in behind-the-scenes work in local and state politics and civic organizations. He won election to the state legislature at the age of 30.

Platts has long refused to accept political action committee donations. He thus came to Congress intent on changing the campaign finance system. He was one of the 20 Republicans who signed the discharge petition forcing the GOP leadership to bring campaign finance legislation before the House for debate, and then he was one of the 41 Republicans to vote for the measure that became law in 2002.

Even as the term-limits movement continues to wane, Platts in his first term introduced a congressional term-limits constitutional amendment, which would restrict House members to six consecutive terms and senators to two. But Platts himself has not taken a term-limits pledge. He says such a unilateral decision would hurt his constituents by keeping their representative from building valuable seniority. He says working his way through college as a Teamster proved to him the advantages of longevity in a job.

With a seat on the Education and the Workforce panel, Platts follows in the footsteps of his predecessor, Republican Bill Goodling, who was chairman during the last three of his 13 terms in the House.

Platts brings his own education expertise to the panel, as he was chairman of the state House Education Committee's Subcommittee on Basic Education. He argues that the federal government should keep its long-standing promise to pay its full share of the costs of educating disabled students under the Individuals with Disabilities Education Act. The federal contribution would free up more local dollars to provide needed school improvements, such as more teachers to reduce classroom sizes, he says.

In the108th Congress, Platts is on the House GOP Policy Committee and he chairs the Government Reform Committee's Government Efficiency and Financial Management Subcommittee.

Platts' other legislative priorities include funding for his district's transportation projects — on the Transportation Committee he will have a chance to push for the funding when the 108th takes up a rewrite of highway and mass transit law — and support for the armed forces.

Platts says an eighth-grade teacher sparked his fascination with politics. He has an interest in American political history, and he once told the Gettysburg Times that he wished he could have witnessed the signing of the Declaration of Independence. He is in line early for a present-day political event: In both 2002 and 2003, he got to the House chamber three or four hours ahead of time to claim a center aisle seat so he could greet President Bush as he arrived to deliver his State of the Union address.

After working for Republican Gov. Dick Thornburgh and then serving as a legislative committee staff member and assistant finance director for the Republican State Committee, Platts in 1992 made his first bid for elective office, a seat in the state House. He campaigned on a "reform" platform, assembled a large band of volunteers and won comfortably.

Platts' zealous pursuit of institutional changes in Harrisburg and his opposition to a coal-burning power plant in York County struck some colleagues and observers as politically unwise. When he ran for the York County Commission in 1995, some said that Platts was acknowledging his diminished effectiveness in the General Assembly and positioning himself for Goodling's seat in Congress.

Platts rejected that assertion, and when he lost the county commission bid, he twice more sought and won re-election to the state legislature. But in early 1999, when Goodling announced he would not seek re-election in 2000, Platts was the first candidate to jump into the race.

Though greatly outspent in the GOP primary, and still eschewing PAC contributions, Platts won with 33 percent of the vote, 4 percentage points ahead of fellow state Rep. Albert Masland. The district's Republican leanings ensured his victory. He defeated Democrat Jeff Sanders, a college professor, by a nearly 3-to-1 ratio.

Although the state lost two seats in the post-2000 census reapportionment, the remapping was run by a Republican governor and Republican state legislators, and the 19th District's solid GOP tilt was preserved. Platts easily dispatched three foes in the Republican primary in 2002 and had no Democratic opponent in November.

Platts has two young children, and he commutes almost 200 miles daily from his home in York to Capitol Hill and back. He says a hands-free cell phone and books on tape help make the commute possible and that he sleeps in Washington only about a dozen nights a year. He likes to be home so he can be an assistant coach of his son's T-ball team.

KEY VOTES

2002

Yes Overhaul campaign finance law; ban "soft money" and restrict advocacy advertising
Yes Back Bush's defense budget increase
Yes Extend 1996 welfare law
Yes Adopt Bush's discretionary spending limit
Yes Pass GOP Medicare prescription drug plan
No Create independent Sept. 11 commission
No Extend union protections to Homeland Security Department employees
Yes Revive fast-track procedures for trade agreements
Yes Authorize war against Iraq
Yes Advance bankruptcy overhaul opposed by abortion opponents

2001

Yes Nullify Clinton Labor Department ergonomics rule
Yes Cut taxes by $1.35 trillion through fiscal 2011
No Maintain ban on oil drilling in Arctic National Wildlife Refuge
Yes Approve Bush proposal to limit managed-care plan liability for coverage decisions
No Divert money from crop subsidy payments to land conservation
Yes Expand law enforcement power to investigate suspected terrorists

CQ VOTE STUDIES

	PARTY UNITY		PRESIDENTIAL SUPPORT	
	Support	Oppose	Support	Oppose
2002	85%	15%	82%	18%
2001	91%	9%	86%	14%

INTEREST GROUPS

	AFL-CIO	ADA	CCUS	ACU
2002	11%	5%	85%	88%
2001	18%	5%	83%	80%

PENNSYLVANIA 19

South central – York, Gettysburg

Situated west of the Susquehanna River, mostly east of the South Mountains and mostly south of Harrisburg, the 19th's historic landscape has a reliably Republican constituency and flourishing agricultural and manufacturing industries.

Located along several major highways, the district is a prime location for manufacturing and distribution centers, including depots and logistical support facilities for the Department of Defense. York County, where 60 percent of residents live, serves as the 19th's industrial hub. Residential growth, a more recent trend, also can be attributed to the district's location — Marylanders have moved here for the lower taxes and affordable real estate. But many residents, or their forefathers, traveled much farther than from a neighboring state — the 19th has the highest percentage of residents with German ancestry (38 percent) in the state.

Tourism also plays a major role. Nearly 2 million visitors a year come to see the site of the 1863 Battle of Gettysburg in Adams County, a largely agricultural area. Many come for the annual re-enactment of one of the Civil War's most significant battles.

George W. Bush won 61 percent of the 19th's vote in the 2000 presidential election. Cumberland County, which is shared with the 9th, is strongly Republican, with Bush winning all but two precincts in the county. York and Adams also have strong GOP leans, with Democrats only finding strength in the city of York, where blacks and Hispanics together are more than 40 percent of the population, and Gettysburg, which has a large college-age population.

MAJOR INDUSTRY

Agriculture, manufacturing, distribution

MILITARY BASES

Defense Distribution Depot Susquehanna, 128 military, 947 civilian (2001); Carlisle Barracks, 460 military, 537 civilian (1999)

CITIES

York, 40,862; Carlisle, 17,970; Hanover, 14,535

NOTABLE

Birthplace of the Articles of Confederation; York served as the U.S. Capitol from 1777-78 while the British occupied Philadelphia; Harley Davidson's largest manufacturing facility is in York; President Abraham Lincoln gave his famed Gettysburg Address in Adams County.

RHODE ISLAND

Gov. Donald L. Carcieri (R)

First elected: 2002
Length of term: 4 years
Term expires: 1/07
Salary: $100,097
Phone: (401) 222-2080
Hometown: East Greenwich
Born: Dec. 16, 1942; East Greenwich, R.I.
Religion: Roman Catholic
Family: Wife, Sue Carcieri; four children
Education: Brown U., B.A. 1965 (international relations)
Career: Manufacturing company executive; aid relief worker; bank executive; teacher
Political highlights: No previous office
Election results:

2002 GENERAL		
Donald L. Carcieri (R)	181,687	54.8%
Myrth York (D)	150,147	45.3%

Lt. Gov. Charles J. Fogarty (D)

First elected: 1998
Length of term: 4 years
Term expires: 1/07
Salary: $80,000
Phone: (401) 222-2371

STATE LEGISLATURE

General Assembly: Meets January-June
House: 75 members, 2-year terms
2003 breakdown: 9R, 65D, 1I; 64 men, 11 women
Salary: $11,780
Phone: (401) 222-2466
Senate: 38 members, 2-year terms
2003 breakdown: 6R, 32D; 31 men, 7 women
Salary: $11,780
Phone: (401) 222-6655

STATE TERM LIMITS

Governor: 2 terms
Senate: No
House: No

URBAN STATISTICS

CITY	POPULATION
Providence	173,618
Warwick	85,808
Cranston	79,269
Pawtucket	72,958
East Providence	48,688

REGISTERED VOTERS

Voters do not register by party.

POPULATION

2002 population (est.)	1,069,725
2000 population	1,048,319
1990 population	1,003,464
Percent change (1990-2000)	+4.5%
Rank among states (2002)	43
Median age	36.7
Born in state	61.4%
Foreign born	11.4%
Violent crime rate	298/100,000
Poverty level	11.9%
Federal workers	10,207
Military	9,161

REDISTRICTING

Rhode Island retained its two House seats in reapportionment. The state legislature drew a new map, which the governor allowed to become law without his signature on Feb. 20, 2002.

MISCELLANEOUS

Web: www.state.ri.us
Capital: Providence

STATE ELECTION OFFICIAL
(401) 222-2345

DEMOCRATIC HEADQUARTERS
(401) 721-9900

REPUBLICAN HEADQUARTERS
(401) 822-0500

District Statistics

DIST.	2000 VOTE FOR PRESIDENT BUSH	GORE	NADER	WHITE	BLACK	ASIAN	HISP	MEDIAN INCOME	WHITE COLLAR	BLUE COLLAR	SERVICE INDUSTRY	OVER 64	UNDER 18	COLLEGE EDUCATION	RURAL	SQ. MILES
1	31%	63%	6%	83%	4%	2%	7%	$40,616	61%	23%	15%	15%	23%	26%	4%	325
2	34	60	6	81	4	3	10	$44,129	61	23	16	14	25	25	14	720
STATE	32	61	6	82	4	2	9	$42,090	61	23	16	15	24	26	9	1,045
U.S.	47.9	48.4	3	69	12	4	13	$41,994	60	25	15	12	26	24	21	3,537,438

Woonsocket
1
Pawtucket
Providence
Providence
Cranston
Bristol
Warwick
Bristol
2
Kent
Newport
Newport
1
Newport
Washington
2

Sen. Jack Reed (D)

CAPITOL OFFICE
224-4642
jack@reed.senate.gov
reed.senate.gov
320 Hart 20510-3903; fax 224-4680

COMMITTEES
Armed Services
Banking, Housing & Urban Affairs
Health, Education, Labor & Pensions
Joint Economic

HOMETOWN
Cranston

BORN
Nov. 12, 1949, Providence, R.I.

RELIGION
Roman Catholic

FAMILY
Single

EDUCATION
U.S. Military Academy, B.S. 1971 (engineering); Harvard U., M.P.P. 1973, J.D. 1982

MILITARY SERVICE
Army, 1971-79; Army Reserve, 1979-91

CAREER
Lawyer

POLITICAL HIGHLIGHTS
R.I. Senate, 1985-91; U.S. House, 1991-97

ELECTION RESULTS

2002 GENERAL		
Jack Reed (D)	253,774	78.4%
Robert G. Tingle (R)	69,808	21.6%
2002 PRIMARY		
Jack Reed (D)		unopposed

PREVIOUS WINNING PERCENTAGES
1996 (63%); 1994 House Election (68%); 1992 House Election (71%); 1990 House Election (59%)

Elected 1996; 2nd term

The Republican takeover of the Senate in 2003 hurt Reed as much as any single senator. The Democrats were compelled to sacrifice one of their own on the Appropriations Committee, and Reed's scant 18 months of service on the panel made him the odd man out.

It was tough blow for the unassuming senior member of Rhode Island's delegation, who had just cruised to re-election and seemed finally to be gaining notice after a dozen years of demure, steady congressional toil. A blue-collar man in the midst of a delegation historically composed of blue-bloods, Reed had been largely overlooked, as attention focused mostly on members of the Kennedy, Chafee and Pell families — all longtime upper-crust fixtures in the political life of New England.

After years of quiet lobbying, Reed got on Appropriations six months into the 107th Congress, when the departure of Vermont's James M. Jeffords from the GOP put the Democrats at the helm of the Senate and allowed them to add to their committee rosters. For his dependably liberal voting record and his reputation for hard work, Reed had the blessing of both Democratic leader Tom Daschle and Appropriations Chairman Robert C. Byrd. The appointment, the Providence Journal noted, was the "best assignment for a member of the state's delegation in more than 20 years."

Although the seat was taken away, Reed retained his post as the top Senate Democrat on the Joint Economic Committee, and he was named to the Democratic whip organization.

The loss of the Appropriations post increases Reed's focus on the Armed Services panel, where he has been building a reputation as a serious player. His committee seat allows him to push for continued support for the Rhode Island-based Naval Undersea Warfare Center and the Naval Education Training Center. But it is on the issue of missile defense that Reed has been most visible.

Reed graduated from West Point in 1971 and served eight years of active duty in the Army, giving him a background that lends authority to his views on defense matters. He has been a leader of the Democratic opposition to development and deployment of the Bush administration's proposal for a national missile defense system. Reed insists on more congressional oversight of the project and argues that "every billion dollars spent on missile defense is a billion not spent on counterterrorism efforts . . . and a host of other crucial programs."

In the 107th Congress, Reed was chairman of the committee's Strategic Subcommittee, and in the 108th, he is the top-ranking Democrat on the Emerging Threats and Capabilities Subcommittee, which deals with non-traditional threats such as terrorism.

As a columnist for the Providence Journal put it, the lawmaker's critique of the Bush missile defense plan "was vintage Reed: exhaustive, respectful, heavy on the factual findings, light on the polemics." As a Rhode Island political observer told the Boston Globe in 1997: "He is not threatening to the showboats in the Senate."

When President Clinton in 1998 ordered an attack on suspected terrorist sites in Afghanistan and Sudan linked to Osama bin Laden following the bombings of two American embassies in Africa, Reed was supportive. "Taking military action," he said, "is essential to maintaining both our national security and our responsibility as the world superpower."

Reed also takes an active interest in social issues. In the 107th and 106th

Congresses, he took the lead among Senate Democrats in efforts to more closely regulate gun shows, by promoting legislation requiring background checks for people who buy guns from private dealers. Reed noted in 2001 that stronger restrictions on firearms purchases are necessary to homeland security, to prevent "jihad trainees" from readily obtaining weapons in the United States.

Reed is the top Democrat on the Banking panel's Housing Subcommittee, where he has been persistent in educating consumers about lead poisoning. He has also drawn the committee's attention to the national problem of a lack of affordable housing. In the preface to a 2001 report by the National Low Income Housing Coalition, Reed wrote, "Nowhere in the country does the minimum wage work of one person come close to paying the rent."

He recalls that early in his House tenure, before he was on the Banking Committee, he lobbied committee members persistently for help on a specific problem involving Rhode Island credit union depositors. He said he visited with panel members so often that some of them assumed he was a colleague on the committee.

Each year, Reed comes to the aid of the estimated several thousand Liberian refugees who have settled in Rhode Island, part of the more than 10,000 refugees from that country who fled to the United States to escape a long-running civil war. The refugees have not been granted permanent residency, and until they are, Reed annually asks the White House to permit them to stay another year.

Reed grew up in a working-class family in Cranston, where his father was a school custodian and his mother a factory worker. He announced his candidacy for the Senate at the Cranston school administration building, in a room named after his father. His parents placed great importance on education, a value that carries over into Reed's legislative agenda.

He was a serious, studious child. He told the Boston Globe that when he was about 10 he asked his parents for an expensive book — an illustrated history of World War II — which he pored over for hours, studying the accounts of all the battles.

He finished second in his class at his Catholic prep school, where he was an overachieving, 124-pound defensive back who won admission to West Point. He barely met the minimum height requirement. After graduation, the Army put him through a master's program at the John F. Kennedy School of Government at Harvard University. Reed then commanded a company of the Army's 82nd Airborne Division and taught at West Point.

After attaining the rank of captain, he left the Army at age 29 to attend Harvard Law School. He returned home to a job in Rhode Island's biggest corporate law firm. In 1984, he won a seat in the state Senate.

Six years later, Reed took 59 percent of the vote to win the 2nd District House seat, which Republican Claudine Schneider gave up to wage an unsuccessful challenge to Democratic Sen. Claiborne Pell. Before long, Reed was widely regarded as heir-apparent to Pell, whose health was failing.

When Pell announced that he would retire in 1996 after 36 years in office, Reed was well-prepared to run. He overcame a vigorous negative advertising campaign paid for by the National Republican Senatorial Committee, which sought to convince voters that he was a tax-and-spend liberal. He won with 63 percent of the vote against Republican state Treasurer Nancy J. Mayer. In 2002, he won with 78 percent against Republican Robert G. Tingle, a casino pit boss.

Reed enjoys sea kayaking on Narragansett Bay and also keeps in shape by running. In a 3-mile race in 2002 that featured a number of lawmakers, the 52-year-old Reed ran at a pace of better than eight minutes per mile.

KEY VOTES

2002

Yes Pass farm bill reversing crop subsidy limits
No Postpone tougher automobile fuel efficiency standards
Yes Overhaul campaign finance law; ban "soft money" and restrict advocacy advertising
Yes Set federal election standards
No Support oil drilling in Arctic National Wildlife Refuge
No Revive fast-track procedures for trade agreements
Yes Create federal insurance coverage for catastrophic terrorist losses
Yes Tighten federal accounting and corporate governance regulation
Yes Advance bipartisan Medicare prescription drug plan
Yes Create independent Sept. 11 commission
Yes Back Democratic Homeland Security Department proposal
No Authorize war against Iraq

2001

No Confirm John Ashcroft as attorney general
No Nullify Clinton Labor Department ergonomics rule
No Cut taxes by $1.35 trillion through fiscal 2011
Yes Pass Democratic bill to bolster rights of patients in managed-care plans
Yes Permit a new round of military base closings
Yes Expand law enforcement power to investigate suspected terrorists

CQ VOTE STUDIES

	PARTY UNITY		PRESIDENTIAL SUPPORT	
	Support	Oppose	Support	Oppose
2002	98%	2%	66%	34%
2001	99%	1%	64%	36%
2000	97%	3%	95%	5%
1999	96%	4%	89%	11%
1998	98%	2%	90%	10%
1997	99%	1%	86%	14%
House Service:				
1996	88%	12%	81%	19%
1995	92%	8%	82%	18%
1994	97%	3%	91%	9%
1993	96%	4%	83%	17%

INTEREST GROUPS

	AFL-CIO	ADA	CCUS	ACU
2002	100%	100%	40%	0%
2001	100%	100%	36%	4%
2000	75%	95%	46%	12%
1999	100%	100%	47%	4%
1998	88%	95%	56%	0%
1997	100%	100%	44%	0%
House Service:				
1996	82%	80%	31%	5%
1995	100%	90%	25%	12%
1994	78%	85%	50%	5%
1993	100%	90%	18%	9%

Sen. Lincoln Chafee (R)

CAPITOL OFFICE
224-2921
chafee.senate.gov
141-A Russell 20510-3904; fax 228-2853

COMMITTEES
Banking, Housing & Urban Affairs
Environment & Public Works
(Superfund & Waste Management - chairman)
Foreign Relations
(Near Eastern & South Asian Affairs - chairman)

HOMETOWN
Warwick

BORN
March 26, 1953, Warwick, R.I.

RELIGION
Episcopalian

FAMILY
Wife, Stephanie Chafee; three children

EDUCATION
Brown U., B.A. 1975 (classics)

CAREER
Defense company machine shop planner; blacksmith

POLITICAL HIGHLIGHTS
Warwick City Council, 1986-91; Republican nominee for mayor of Warwick, 1990; mayor of Warwick, 1992-99

ELECTION RESULTS

2000 GENERAL		
Lincoln Chafee (R)	222,588	56.9%
Bob Weygand (D)	161,023	41.2%
Christopher Young (REF)	4,107	1.1%
2000 PRIMARY		
Lincoln Chafee (R)		unopposed

Elected 2000; 1st full term

Appointed November 1999

Chafee's shy, timorous demeanor belies his maverick voting record and his willingness to upbraid publicly the far-more-conservative Republicans who dominate the Senate's leadership. His apostasy, forgiven when he was merely filling out the term of his late father, John H. Chafee, has become more problematic for Republican leaders. But given the narrow partisan divide of the Senate and the precedent set by another Republican New Englander, they seem unlikely to punish him.

Convinced that the narrow 2000 election was a national call for moderates to assert themselves, Chafee has bristled at the Bush administration's conservative tilt and what he sees as the unquestioning allegiance to the White House of his GOP colleagues. "My sense is that they take their cue from the administration almost blindly," he said.

The same is certainly not true of Chafee. He has stuck to his moderate and sometimes liberal views despite intense party pressure. And the trend shows no signs of abating in the 108th Congress, when Chafee will be at the midpoint of his first full term. Among the behaviors that have earned him his "Missing Linc" nickname among GOP aides, are his seeming disinterest in deal-cutting and his frequent departures from the party line. He sided with most Republicans against most Democrats only 51 percent of the time in the 107th Congress, by far the lowest party unity score in the Senate GOP. And he backed President Bush only 88 percent of the time, less often than just two other Republicans. Most notably, he was the only GOP senator to vote against authorizing Bush to use military force against Iraq.

Republican Leader Trent Lott took his anger to the press after Chafee decided in 2001 to oppose both Bush's budget and the president's $1.6 trillion tax cut proposal. "You do need to find a way to work with your people, your team, [and] support what we're trying to do to help the country," Lott told reporters. "I'm disappointed in his conduct and his votes."

When Lott's career as party leader came undone 18 months later — after making remarks viewed as an endorsement of segregation — Chafee was the first Republican senator to call publicly for Lott to step down.

As the 108th Congress began, Chafee again was a leading GOP voice urging caution in considering the additional tax cuts Bush proposed, arguing that his fears about the 2001 tax cut had been borne out: "Our government is in deficit, and we have large, expensive challenges ahead."

In the months after moderate Sen. James M. Jeffords of Vermont bolted the GOP and become an independent voting with Democrats — a decision that switched control of the Senate to the Democrats in June 2001 — Chafee said there was a noticeable change for the better in the way GOP conservatives treated him. Colleagues no longer leaned on him as hard as they had before Jeffords switched. "I don't see it as uncomfortable pressure," said Chafee. "There are no threats that are out of bounds."

It is easy to see why his fellow Republicans colleagues find Chafee frustrating. From the budget to a Democratic-led drive to create a patients' bill of rights, Chafee has repeatedly cut against the GOP grain. In 2000, he sided with President Clinton on 88 percent of the votes on which Clinton had taken a position — more than many Democrats.

A look at Rhode Island's Democratic tendencies makes it clear why Chafee votes the way he does. His vote to confirm John Ashcroft, the conservative former senator from Missouri, as Bush's attorney general in 2001 created waves in the Ocean State. "I'm getting hammered back home," Chafee said at the time.

Although Chafee has consistently denied any interest in becoming a Democrat or even caucusing with Democrats — after the 2002 elections he said leaving the GOP was "inconceivable" — he continues to buck the GOP leadership. At the start of the 107th Congress, he voted to shake up his caucus by backing Pete V. Domenici of New Mexico in his bid to replace Idaho's Larry E. Craig as Policy Committee chairman. Domenici lost in a close vote. Chafee, disappointed, said the message was, "We're sticking with the really hard-core conservatives for our leadership."

Chafee follows closely in the footsteps of his father, who held the Senate seat from 1977 until he died in October 1999. The younger Chafee was appointed to the seat, which he won in his own right in 2000.

On the Environment and Public Works Committee, which his father had chaired, Chafee chairs the Superfund Subcommittee and spearheaded enactment in the 107th Congress of a law to promote the redevelopment of brownfields — abandoned, contaminated industrial sites.

On Foreign Relations, he generally follows the internationalist lead of the new GOP chairman in the 108th, Richard G. Lugar of Indiana. After his trip to visit Fidel Castro in Cuba in 2001, Chafee's relations with the previous top Republican, Jesse Helms, cooled markedly.

Labor groups have praised Chafee's support for increasing the minimum wage but were unhappy when he voted for the 2000 law to grant China permanent normal trade status. Chafee also voted for the 2002 law to restore presidential fast-track trade negotiating authority.

Chafee, whose ancestors were among Rhode Island's earliest settlers, has an eclectic background. While studying the classics at Brown University, he spent summers sweeping up after carpenters and bricklayers at construction sites. After graduating, he set off for horseshoeing school at Montana State University. He apprenticed in Kentucky and Florida before heading to the harness tracks of Edmonton and Calgary. He is quite likely the most prominent politician ever mentioned in Hoofcare & Lameness: The Journal of Equine Foot Science. Its August 1999 issue wished the farrier-politician good luck on the hustings. "I wanted to see something of life," Chafee said. "And I enjoyed working at a trade."

After seven years in Canada, Chafee returned to Rhode Island and worked as a machine shop planner for General Dynamics Corp. He followed his father into elective office in 1986 by winning a seat on the Warwick City Council. He lost his first bid for Warwick mayor in 1990 but won the job two years later, becoming the first GOP mayor in 32 years in Rhode Island's second-most populous city, where Democrats outnumber Republicans by a margin of more than 10-to-1.

Chafee began campaigning in March 1999 to succeed his father, who had announced he would not seek a fifth term. When the senator died that fall, Chafee's appointment gave him a leg up in the race, allowing him to establish a moderate voting record in the Senate.

Chafee also benefited in 2000 from a bruising Democratic primary between Rep. Bob Weygand and former Lt. Gov. Richard A. Licht, the party's 1988 nominee against Chafee's father. Weygand won the primary, but his opposition to abortion cost him support among abortion rights Democrats in the general election. Exit polls showed Chafee got support from about half of Rhode Island's Democrats.

In an unusual move, the National Republican Senatorial Committee produced and funded a television spot touting Chafee's votes in support of a patients' rights measure and Medicare coverage of prescription drugs, even though GOP leaders opposed both proposals. The announcer said, "Tell Senator Lincoln Chafee to keep up his independent fight for Rhode Island."

KEY VOTES

2002

- No Pass farm bill reversing crop subsidy limits
- No Postpone tougher automobile fuel efficiency standards
- Yes Overhaul campaign finance law; ban "soft money" and restrict advocacy advertising
- Yes Set federal election standards
- No Support oil drilling in Arctic National Wildlife Refuge
- Yes Revive fast-track procedures for trade agreements
- Yes Create federal insurance coverage for catastrophic terrorist losses
- Yes Tighten federal accounting and corporate governance regulation
- No Advance bipartisan Medicare prescription drug plan
- Yes Create independent Sept. 11 commission
- Yes Back Democratic Homeland Security Department proposal
- No Authorize war against Iraq

2001

- Yes Confirm John Ashcroft as attorney general
- Yes Nullify Clinton Labor Department ergonomics rule
- No Cut taxes by $1.35 trillion through fiscal 2011
- Yes Pass Democratic bill to bolster rights of patients in managed-care plans
- Yes Permit a new round of military base closings
- Yes Expand law enforcement power to investigate suspected terrorists

CQ VOTE STUDIES

	PARTY UNITY		PRESIDENTIAL SUPPORT	
	Support	Oppose	Support	Oppose
2002	54%	46%	93%	7%
2001	50%	50%	84%	16%
2000	37%	63%	88%	12%
1999	56%	44%	100%	0%

INTEREST GROUPS

	AFL-CIO	ADA	CCUS	ACU
2002	46%	45%	63%	53%
2001	63%	65%	64%	44%
2000	50%	70%	66%	44%

Rep. Patrick J. Kennedy (D)

CAPITOL OFFICE
225-4911
patrick.kennedy@mail.house.gov
www.house.gov/patrickkennedy
407 Cannon 20515-3901; fax 225-3290

COMMITTEES
Appropriations

HOMETOWN
Providence

BORN
July 14, 1967, Brighton, Mass.

RELIGION
Roman Catholic

FAMILY
Single

EDUCATION
Providence College, B.A. 1991 (social science)

CAREER
Public official

POLITICAL HIGHLIGHTS
R.I. House, 1989-95

ELECTION RESULTS

2002 GENERAL		
Patrick J. Kennedy (D)	95,233	60.0%
David W. Rogers (R)	59,316	37.3%
Frank A. Carter (I)	4,314	2.7%
2002 PRIMARY		
Patrick J. Kennedy (D)		unopposed
2000 GENERAL		
Patrick J. Kennedy (D)	123,442	66.7%
Steve Cabral (R)	61,522	33.3%

PREVIOUS WINNING PERCENTAGES
1998 (67%); 1996 (69%); 1994 (54%)

Elected 1994; 5th term

In 2002, a year when his family's political mystique was challenged as never before, Kennedy faced his toughest campaign since winning his House seat eight years earlier.

Having built a political record as a masterful Democratic fundraiser — but also a personal record of aberrant behavior — he had to show that his past transgressions had given way to a maturity in office and that his main attention was on his own constituency and not on the political futures of his relatives or the Democratic Party. "His image at home really suffered," said Brown University Professor Darrell West, the author of a book about this particular Kennedy's meteoric ascent. "Rhode Island is a small state where people expect to see their congressman a lot."

Kennedy responded by touting his work bringing home the bacon as a member of the Appropriations Committee. And while two of his first cousins failed in Maryland — Mark Shriver lost a congressional primary and Kathleen Kennedy Townsend lost a race for governor — Kennedy handily won a fifth term in his tony Rhode Island district.

No one else in Congress can boast of such a legendary political lineage, which still counts for something in New England. Kennedy's father is Sen. Edward M. Kennedy of Massachusetts. His late uncles include President John F. Kennedy and Sen. Robert F. Kennedy of New York. A grandfather, Joseph P. Kennedy, was the first Securities and Exchange Commission chairman. A great-grandfather, John Francis Fitzgerald, represented Boston in the House at the end of the 19th century. A cousin, Joseph P. Kennedy II, represented Boston in the House a century later.

The start of Patrick Kennedy's electoral ascent was earlier than any of them. As a 21-year-old student at Providence College, he won election to the state House in 1988. Six years later he was sent to Washington, one of just 13 Democrats elected to the House during the 1994 GOP sweep. He was the youngest person in the 104th Congress.

At the start of his third term, Kennedy was appointed chairman of the Democratic Congressional Campaign Committee — and won his seat on Appropriations for his troubles. (He took a leave from Appropriations during his DCCC tenure.) He used his family's fame to raise almost $100 million on the 2000 campaign, a record that was more than double what had been raised for the party's 1998 effort to win back the House.

"When we're going around the country, it helps get your calls returned," Kennedy said of his surname. And he could reward donors with visits to the family's fabled compound in Hyannis Port, Mass., and entertain others at the grand oceanfront mansions of his Newport constituents. "He's crowding me," Sen. Kennedy grumbled in jest. "I was always measured by my brothers. Now, I'm being measured by my son."

But Kennedy's fundraising prowess was shadowed by embarrassing episodes that kept his name in the tabloids. In 2000, he shoved a Los Angeles International Airport security guard who told him his carry-on bag was too big. She filed a battery suit, but the Los Angeles district attorney's office declined to bring charges. Later that year, the Coast Guard was called to take his distraught date off a chartered yacht following an argument.

By 2002, Republicans were ready to take Kennedy on — in part by calculating that he had spent only 40 nights in Rhode Island during his two years running the House Democratic campaign organization. But their preferred candidates lost the primary to political neophyte David W.

Rogers, whose conservatism was ill-matched to the 1st District. Rogers spent almost $2 million to criticize Kennedy's behavior, but Kennedy spent almost $3 million to defend it and won with 60 percent of the vote.

After stepping down as campaign chairman, Kennedy took his seat on Appropriations in the 107th Congress and began working to funnel millions of federal dollars to Rhode Island. Defense spending helps fuel the economy of his district, which is home to naval facilities that employ about 7,000 people. But his assignments were to a pair of subcommittees that concentrate on domestic spending: Commerce, Justice, State and Judiciary, and Labor, Health and Human Services and Education.

Apart from appropriating, Kennedy has pressed for legislation to enhance childhood development. As someone who openly discusses past battles with depression, Kennedy was a lead sponsor in the 107th of legislation designed to bring insurance coverage for mental illnesses more in line with coverage for physical illnesses. And he has advocated making student loans more widely available and their repayment tax-deductible.

Kennedy has proven slightly more conservative than his father on some issues. He split with the senator and with the other three Rhode Islanders in Congress in backing the 2002 law authorizing a war against Iraq; and in general, the politics of his district require that he cast a more pro-defense vote. He also has voted to outlaw a procedure its opponents call "partial birth" abortion, though he otherwise supports abortion rights.

At the same time, Kennedy has been known to use his father's influence to his advantage. An asthmatic, he persuaded the senator to write into a 1997 law a prohibition on the Food and Drug Administration carrying out its plan to phase out the environmentally unfriendly inhalers that deliver many asthma medications.

In 2000, Kennedy was one of only a dozen House members who voted against a bill to repeal the federal charter of the Boy Scouts of America, a response to the Scouts' ban on homosexuals as troop leaders.

But the most memorable moment of Kennedy's legislative career may have come in 1996, when he took the House floor to urge — in the end, successfully — that Congress stand by its ban on certain semiautomatic assault-style weapons. "Families like mine know all too well what the damage of weapons can do," said a choked-up Kennedy, the nephew of two assassinated public figures. "All I have to say to you is: You play with the devil, you die with the devil. You will never know what it's like because you don't have someone in your family killed. It's not the person who's killed. It's the whole family that's affected."

KEY VOTES

2002

- Yes Overhaul campaign finance law; ban "soft money" and restrict advocacy advertising
- Yes Back Bush's defense budget increase
- No Extend 1996 welfare law
- No Adopt Bush's discretionary spending limit
- No Pass GOP Medicare prescription drug plan
- Yes Create independent Sept. 11 commission
- Yes Extend union protections to Homeland Security Department employees
- No Revive fast-track procedures for trade agreements
- Yes Authorize war against Iraq
- No Advance bankruptcy overhaul opposed by abortion opponents

2001

- No Nullify Clinton Labor Department ergonomics rule
- No Cut taxes by $1.35 trillion through fiscal 2011
- Yes Maintain ban on oil drilling in Arctic National Wildlife Refuge
- No Approve Bush proposal to limit managed-care plan liability for coverage decisions
- Yes Divert money from crop subsidy payments to land conservation
- Yes Expand law enforcement power to investigate suspected terrorists

CQ VOTE STUDIES

	PARTY UNITY		PRESIDENTIAL SUPPORT	
	Support	Oppose	Support	Oppose
2002	89%	11%	40%	60%
2001	93%	7%	29%	71%
2000	97%	3%	81%	19%
1999	96%	4%	78%	22%
1998	91%	9%	79%	21%

INTEREST GROUPS

	AFL-CIO	ADA	CCUS	ACU
2002	100%	90%	40%	8%
2001	100%	95%	32%	4%
2000	100%	90%	15%	16%
1999	100%	90%	25%	4%
1998	100%	95%	33%	12%

RHODE ISLAND 1

East – Pawtucket, part of Providence, Newport

The Democratic 1st occupies the top of Rhode Island, along the Massachusetts border, then moves south to take in Pawtucket and the northeastern part of Providence, the capital, before running along Narragansett Bay to pick up Newport and the island communities in the southeast.

The 1st's industry is mostly centered in northern Rhode Island's Blackstone Valley. Woonsocket, a manufacturing city, is home to the headquarters of CVS, the largest drugstore in the nation.

The district's portion of Providence takes in several colleges, such as Brown University and Providence College, and includes the state capitol. Students and government workers push the 1st's political lean to the left.

The coastal economy south of Providence relies largely on maritime defense. Companies such as Raytheon, which makes components for Navy submarines in Portsmouth, as well as a large naval base and training center in Newport fuel the industry. Large numbers of visitors to Newport, as well as Providence, make tourism an important economic component.

Democrats dominate the district, getting support from ethnic minorities as well as the area's large Catholic majority. Some small, wealthy coastal towns support the GOP, but larger towns lean Democratic. In statewide elections, however, the district has supported Republicans for governor, such as Donald L. Carcieri in 2002, and for U.S. senator, such as Lincoln Chafee in 2000.

MAJOR INDUSTRY
Defense, higher education, manufacturing, tourism, government

MILITARY BASES
Naval Station Newport, 3,000 military, 4,500 civilian (2002)

CITIES
Pawtucket, 72,958; Providence (pt.), 72,102; East Providence, 48,688; Woonsocket, 43,224; North Providence, 32,411; Newport, 26,475

NOTABLE
One of the nation's oldest taverns, the White Horse Tavern, opened in Newport before 1673; The International Tennis Hall of Fame is in Newport; Touro Synagogue in Newport, designed by colonial architect Peter Harrison and dedicated in 1762, is the oldest U.S. synagogue.

Rep. Jim Langevin (D)

CAPITOL OFFICE
225-2735
james.langevin@mail.house.gov
www.house.gov/langevin
109 Cannon 20515-3902; fax 225-5976

COMMITTEES
Armed Services
Select Homeland Security

HOMETOWN
Warwick

BORN
April 22, 1964, Warwick, R.I.

RELIGION
Roman Catholic

FAMILY
Single

EDUCATION
Rhode Island College, B.A. 1990 (political science & public administration); Harvard U., M.P.A. 1994

CAREER
Public official

POLITICAL HIGHLIGHTS
Delegate to R.I. Constitutional Convention, 1986; R.I. House, 1989-95; R.I. secretary of state, 1995-2001

ELECTION RESULTS

2002 GENERAL		
Jim Langevin (D)	129,312	76.4%
John O. Matson (R)	37,740	22.3%
Dorman J. Hayes Jr. (I)	2,323	1.4%
2002 PRIMARY		
Jim Langevin (D)		unopposed
2000 GENERAL		
Jim Langevin (D)	123,805	62.3%
Rodney D. Driver (CFC)	42,625	21.4%
Robert G. Tingle (R)	27,932	14.0%
Dorman J. Hayes Jr. (GREEN)	4,536	2.3%

Elected 2000; 2nd term

Langevin is the first quadriplegic to serve in the House. He says he doesn't mind being a role model for disabled people, and he lets his views be known on gun safety, access to public places and stem cell research — topics that arise from his personal experience. But he insists that he does not intend to be just a congressman for handicapped issues, as witness his memberships on the Armed Services and Homeland Security committees.

Langevin (LAN-juh-vin) told a CNN interviewer that "certainly disability issues are something I have a unique understanding of," but other matters concern him as well. He wants more federal attention paid to training teachers and providing affordable prescription drugs. He also looks after the Electric Boat plant at Quonset Point in his district, which fabricates and assembles large sections of nuclear submarines.

Langevin had a boyhood dream to be a police officer or an FBI agent. He enrolled in a police department cadet program in his hometown of Warwick, riding along with police officers and getting to know the daily police routine. On Aug. 22, 1980, when he was 16 years old, his life and ambitions changed forever. He was in the police locker room with two members of the SWAT team, when one of them inadvertently pulled the trigger of a loaded gun. The bullet ricocheted off a locker and hit Langevin in the neck, severing his spinal cord and leaving him paralyzed. He has no use of his legs and only minimal use of his hands and arms.

Langevin has an aide to help him with domestic chores, and uses a motorized wheelchair to get around. Congressional leaders provided him with a ground-floor office and renovated access to the House chamber to make it easier for him to vote and speak during debates. He uses voice recognition software to dictate letters and write speeches. During the 2001 session, Langevin did not miss a vote, and he missed only two votes in 2002.

Langevin supports stem cell research, believing it holds great promise for millions of people who have diseases such as Parkinson's, Alzheimer's and diabetes, as well as those who have spinal cord injuries such as his own. He says he is convinced he will walk again one day.

Langevin is opposed to abortion except in cases of rape, incest or to save a woman's life. His support of embryonic stem cell research angers anti-abortion activists, who say that destroying an embryo for any reason is wrong. Langevin acknowledges that he has struggled with the issue, but has concluded that it is more "life-affirming" to use aborted embryos to help people.

He has introduced a number of bills on gun safety, including requirements for trigger locks and other safety features on weapons. He reminds his colleagues that if the SWAT team members who were involved in his own shooting can have an accident, then anybody can.

When the U.S. Capitol was hurriedly evacuated on Sept. 11, 2001, after the terrorist attacks on the World Trade Center and the Pentagon, Capitol Hill officials realized they had no plan for evacuating disabled people. Langevin and several wheelchair-bound senators helped develop a plan to evacuate all disabled workers on the Hill.

Langevin also introduced legislation calling for studies on whether Congress could continue to meet in the event of such an evacuation by having lawmakers communicate electronically. The House Administration Committee held a hearing in 2002 on Langevin's "e-Congress" proposal, which might make use of an Internet- and satellite-based communications system.

Early in 2003, he expressed disappointment when President Bush denied Rhode Island's request for a federal disaster declaration after a nightclub fire in West Warwick killed 99 people.

On the Armed Services Committee in the 107th Congress, he led the effort to prevent U.S. military commanders from requiring female service personnel to wear the traditional Muslim garment, the abaya, while stationed in Saudi Arabia. He also worked for the development of a new land mine that can be more easily deactivated.

After Langevin's injury, he and his family were amazed at the hundreds of strangers who pitched in to help. He resolved to somehow repay them, and soon realized that public service and politics was the way he could do that. He volunteered in Frank Flaherty's 1984 campaign for mayor of Warwick, and Flaherty recalls being amazed at how tenacious Langevin was: making phone calls and stuffing envelopes even with limited use of his hands. Later, when Flaherty was still mayor and Langevin was in the legislature, "he'd come in looking for something for his area of the city and he'd drive me crazy, chase me around. I used to threaten to unplug the battery on his wheelchair so I wouldn't have to listen," Flaherty told the Providence Journal.

At age 21, while still a college student, Langevin was elected as a delegate to the Rhode Island Constitutional Convention.

In 1988 he was elected to the first of three terms in the Rhode Island House, where he played a key role in drafting a ballot issue that resulted in a reduction in the size of the state legislature. During his tenure in the legislature, he found time to finish his bachelor's degree in political science and public administration and then commuted to Boston to earn a master's degree in public administration.

In 1994 he successfully ran for secretary of state, vowing to make the state government more accessible to its citizens by upgrading voting machines and modernizing the office to improve access to government information by businesses and citizens. His scathing report on the legislature's compliance with state open meetings laws, titled "Access Denied: Chaos, Confusion and Closed Doors," angered many lawmakers but led to reforms. (As Congress worked in 2002 on legislation to overhaul the election system, Langevin was able to include a requirement that every polling place have a voting machine accessible to a disabled voter.)

In 2000, when 2nd District Democratic Rep. Bob Weygand decided to run for the Senate, Langevin was ready to make a bid for the House. In the solidly Democratic district, Langevin's 62 percent easily outpaced the Republican and a third-party candidate, who actually placed second. In 2002, Langevin cruised again, capturing 76 percent.

KEY VOTES

2002

- Yes Overhaul campaign finance law; ban "soft money" and restrict advocacy advertising
- Yes Back Bush's defense budget increase
- No Extend 1996 welfare law
- No Adopt Bush's discretionary spending limit
- No Pass GOP Medicare prescription drug plan
- Yes Create independent Sept. 11 commission
- Yes Extend union protections to Homeland Security Department employees
- No Revive fast-track procedures for trade agreements
- No Authorize war against Iraq
- No Advance bankruptcy overhaul opposed by abortion opponents

2001

- No Nullify Clinton Labor Department ergonomics rule
- No Cut taxes by $1.35 trillion through fiscal 2011
- Yes Maintain ban on oil drilling in Arctic National Wildlife Refuge
- No Approve Bush proposal to limit managed-care plan liability for coverage decisions
- Yes Divert money from crop subsidy payments to land conservation
- Yes Expand law enforcement power to investigate suspected terrorists

CQ VOTE STUDIES

	PARTY UNITY		PRESIDENTIAL SUPPORT	
	Support	Oppose	Support	Oppose
2002	91%	9%	35%	65%
2001	90%	10%	35%	65%

INTEREST GROUPS

	AFL-CIO	ADA	CCUS	ACU
2002	100%	85%	45%	8%
2001	100%	85%	35%	28%

RHODE ISLAND 2

West – part of Providence, Warwick, Cranston

Bordering Connecticut on one side and the Narragansett Bay on the other, the 2nd occupies the western two-thirds of Rhode Island, covering the upstate rolling hills and most of the metropolitan area around Providence. Washington County, the southernmost part of the district, has beaches and lakes that attract tourists and residents alike. Twelve miles off the southern coast lies Block Island, a scenic vacation spot with more than 365 ponds.

The 2nd's economy is shifting from manufacturing to service. The change has caused a population shift, with people leaving Providence (shared with the 1st District) for Washington County, attracted by the growing businesses centered in the county's idyllic landscape. As white residents have departed the Providence area, more blacks and Hispanics have moved in, increasing the city's already Democratic tendency. The 2nd's portion of Providence includes a few schools, including Johnson & Wales University and Rhode Island College.

General Dynamics' Electric Boat has a submarine facility near Quonset Point in Washington County, and some county residents commute to the company's Groton, Conn., plant as well. Most of the district experienced modest growth during the 1990s, though the median age of the population is getting younger.

The 2nd is home to many working- and middle-class towns, with a substantial union presence that votes Democratic. No Republican presidential candidate has carried the district since Ronald Reagan in 1984. Despite the Democratic dominance, the district's large Catholic population has made abortion a key issue. Redistricting following the 2000 census shifted a few Providence neighborhoods into the 1st District, but the change did not affect the 2nd's political makeup.

MAJOR INDUSTRY

Defense, banking, higher education, government, tourism

CITIES

Providence (pt.), 101,516; Warwick, 85,808; Cranston, 79,269; West Warwick, 29,581; Westerly (unincorporated), 17,682

NOTABLE

The first armed conflict of the American Revolution took place near Warwick in 1772, when patriots in eight longboats captured and burned two British revenue ships.

SOUTH CAROLINA

Gov. Mark Sanford (R)

First elected: 2002
Length of term: 4 years
Term expires: 1/07
Salary: $106,078
Phone: (803) 734-9400
Hometown: Sullivan's Island
Born: May 28, 1960; Fort Lauderdale, Fla.
Religion: Episcopalian
Family: Wife, Jenny Sanford; three children
Education: Furman U., B.A. 1983 (business administration); U. of Virginia, M.B.A. 1988
Military Service: Air Force Reserve, 2002-present
Career: Real estate investor; investment banker
Political highlights: U.S. House, 1995-2001
Election results:

2002 GENERAL		
Mark Sanford (R)	580,459	52.8%
Jim Hodges (D)	518,288	47.1%

Lt. Gov. André Bauer (R)

First elected: 2002
Length of term: 4 years
Term expires: 1/07
Salary: $46,545
Phone: (803) 734-2080

STATE LEGISLATURE

General Assembly: Meets January-June
House: 124 members, 2-year terms
2003 breakdown: 72R, 51D, 1 vacancy; 109 men, 14 women
Salary: $10,400; $95/day in session; $1,000/month expenses
Phone: (803) 734-2010
Senate: 46 members, 4-year terms
2003 breakdown: 24R, 21D, 1 vacancy; 43 men, 2 women
Salary: $10,400; $95/day in session; $1,000/month expenses
Phone: (803) 212-6200

STATE TERM LIMITS

Governor: 2 consecutive terms
Senate: No
House: No

URBAN STATISTICS

CITY	POPULATION
Columbia	116,278
Charleston	96,650
North Charleston	79,641
Greenville	56,002
Rock Hill	49,765

REGISTERED VOTERS

Voters do not register by party.

POPULATION

2002 population (est.)	4,107,183
2000 population	4,012,012
1990 population	3,486,703
Percent change (1990-2000)	+15.1%
Rank among states (2002)	25
Median age	35.4
Born in state	64%
Foreign born	2.9%
Violent crime rate	805/100,000
Poverty level	14.1%
Federal workers	27,923
Military	57,585

REDISTRICTING

South Carolina retained its six House seats in reapportionment. Democratic Gov. Jim Hodges vetoed the state legislature's plan and a three-judge federal panel implemented a new map on March 20, 2002.

MISCELLANEOUS

Web: www.state.sc.us
Capital: Columbia

STATE ELECTION OFFICIAL
(803) 734-9060

DEMOCRATIC HEADQUARTERS
(803) 799-7798

REPUBLICAN HEADQUARTERS
(803) 988-8440

District Statistics

DIST.	2000 VOTE FOR PRESIDENT BUSH	GORE	NADER	WHITE	BLACK	ASIAN	HISP	MEDIAN INCOME	WHITE COLLAR	BLUE COLLAR	SERVICE INDUSTRY	OVER 64	UNDER 18	COLLEGE EDUCATION	RURAL	SQ. MILES
1	59%	38%	2%	74%	21%	1%	3%	$40,713	60%	23%	17%	12%	24%	25%	22%	2,645
2	59	38	2	68	26	1	3	$42,915	63	23	14	11	25	29	34	4,767
3	63	34	1	76	21	1	2	$36,092	49	37	14	13	24	17	50	5,392
4	64	33	2	75	20	1	3	$39,417	56	31	13	12	25	22	26	2,151
5	55	43	1	64	32	1	2	$35,416	48	38	13	12	26	15	53	7,035
6	40	59	1	40	57	1	1	$28,967	48	34	18	12	26	14	52	8,120
STATE	57	41	1	66	29	1	2	$37,082	54	31	15	12	25	20	40	30,109
U.S.	47.9	48.4	3	69	12	4	13	$41,994	60	25	15	12	26	24	21	3,537,438

Greenville
Pickens
Spartanburg
Spartanburg
Greenville
Cherokee
York
Rock Hill
Oconee
Anderson
Anderson
4
Union
Chester
Lancaster
Chesterfield
Marlboro
Laurens
Fairfield
5
Dillon
Darlington
Abbeville
3
Newberry
Kershaw
Lee
Marion
Florence
Greenwood
Saluda
Columbia
Richland
Sumter
Sumter
Florence
Horry
McCormick
1
Lexington
Edgefield
Clarendon
Calhoun
Williamsburg
Aiken
2
6
Georgetown
Orangeburg
Barnwell
Bamberg
Dorchester
Berkeley
1
Allendale
Colleton
Hampton
Charleston
Charleston
Jasper
Beaufort

Sen. Ernest F. Hollings (D)

Elected 1966; 6th full term

CAPITOL OFFICE
224-6121
hollings.senate.gov
125 Russell 20510-4002; fax 224-4293

COMMITTEES
Appropriations
Budget
Commerce, Science & Transportation - ranking member

HOMETOWN
Charleston

BORN
Jan. 1, 1922, Charleston, S.C.

RELIGION
Lutheran

FAMILY
Wife, Rita "Peatsy" Hollings; four children (one deceased)

EDUCATION
The Citadel, B.A. 1942; U. of South Carolina, LL.B. 1947

MILITARY SERVICE
Army, 1942-45

CAREER
Lawyer

POLITICAL HIGHLIGHTS
S.C. House, 1949-55; lieutenant governor, 1955-59; governor, 1959-63; sought Democratic nomination for U.S. Senate, 1962; sought Democratic nomination for president, 1984

ELECTION RESULTS

1998 GENERAL		
Ernest F. Hollings (D)	562,791	52.7%
Bob Inglis (R)	488,132	45.7%
Richard T. Quillian (LIBERT)	16,987	1.6%
1998 PRIMARY		
Ernest F. Hollings (D)		unopposed

PREVIOUS WINNING PERCENTAGES
1992 (50%); 1986 (63%); 1980 (70%); 1974 (70%); 1968 (62%); 1966 Special Election (51%)

With his aristocratic bearing and rumbling baritone, Hollings seems a throwback to an era when Southern Democrats ruled Congress. Appearances aside, the white-haired senator known universally as "Fritz" has stayed current. He is as familiar with Internet privacy today as he was with civil rights legislation in the 1960s, when he came to the Senate during the Johnson administration.

He is the fourth-most-senior member of the Senate, but it wasn't until 2003, with the retirement of Republican Sen. Strom Thurmond, that he became the senior senator from his own state. As the 108th Congress began, there was much speculation about how much longer Hollings would be around; he will be 82 on Election Day 2004, when he is up for reelection. Hollings has not said what his plans are, but the contenders for the job are already preparing, whether or not Hollings runs again.

Hollings holds the top Democratic seat on the Commerce, Science and Transportation Committee, which deals with some of the most technologically challenging issues. He's often at odds with Republican Chairman John McCain of Arizona, with McCain generally favoring deregulation of industry and Hollings expressing reservations about fallout for consumers. "It hasn't worked," Hollings says of the conservative-led trend toward greater deregulation. "We don't need to reverse all the deregulation laws we have passed. It's not that categorical. But we need to go back, review what we've done, and selectively put in place effective regulation."

McCain and Hollings clash on a range of difficult business-related issues confronting Congress. McCain supports a moratorium on taxes on Internet services, but Hollings favors a compromise that would give states more authority to collect sales taxes on online transactions. Hollings also wants tough safeguards to protect consumers on the Internet, including a requirement that online vendors get a consumer's consent before sharing financial data with other companies.

Hollings is a quick-witted debater, using historical anecdotes and humor to drive home his points. In an age when politicians consult opinion polls before uttering a word, Hollings says what's on his mind.

In 2000, Hollings cast the only vote against a proposal to raise the visa quota for skilled foreign workers. A better solution to the shortage of high-tech workers, he argued, was to train people at home. "What we are really facing is a foot race for the high-tech political money. I'm not joining in this charade," he said.

During the 107th Congress, he threatened to force Silicon Valley businesses to get involved helping the government fight intellectual property piracy. The industry voluntarily developed devices to prevent computers, VCRs and DVDs from making illegal copies of movies and music. Hollings also is at odds with traditional Democratic allies in Hollywood over the idea of banning graphic violence in television programs at times when children make up a "substantial portion" of the audience.

The terrorist attacks of Sept. 11, 2001, prompted Hollings to take a lead in promoting transportation security. He supported transferring airline passenger screenings from private contractors to the new Transportation Security Administration. And he won tighter accident prevention requirements for oil and gas pipeline operators.

Even before the attacks, Hollings had introduced legislation to upgrade security at the nation's ports. His bill became law late in 2002, but without the user fees Hollings had urged to pay for the task.

On another level, the terrorist strikes deepened Hollings' longstanding faith in an activist federal government. "The attacks turned the tide," he says. "People are realizing that government is not the enemy."

As a result of the hard-pressed and shrinking textile industry in South Carolina, Hollings has been one of the biggest critics of free-trade pacts. He opposed fast-track trade authority for President Bush in 2002, permanent normal trade status for China in 2000 and the North American Free Trade Agreement in 1993. With the advent of unrestricted trade, he says, the United States is trading full-time manufacturing jobs for part-time jobs.

On many social issues, he is a liberal. He supports abortion rights and is a strong backer of nutrition programs and public health centers. He has supported some restrictions on guns, including mandatory handgun safety locks. A trial lawyer before entering politics, Hollings is also out front in opposing the Bush administration's attempts to limit liability lawsuits.

But on fiscal matters, Hollings is fundamentally conservative and among the most persistent over time in pushing for balanced budgets. He favors paying down the national debt and opposes using the Social Security trust fund for other programs. He has been on the Budget Committee since its creation in 1974. He helped write the groundbreaking Gramm-Rudman-Hollings law in 1985, which established automatic spending cuts if deficit targets were not met. Though Congress and presidents found creative ways to dodge the law, it established the political momentum for the balanced budgets achieved in fiscal years 1998-2001.

Despite his beliefs, Hollings proudly plays the insider's game of scoring projects and money for his state. He happily owned up to securing $45 million to help bring a BMW plant to South Carolina, saying once the overall budget was set every year, "ol' Fritz" was going to get his share.

On foreign policy, Hollings often questions the U.S. role in global peacekeeping operations. In 1991, he opposed the use of military force against Iraq after it invaded Kuwait. But in 2002, he voted for Bush's request to use force against Iraq. He favors a limited national missile defense system and more spending to modernize the military, including the National Guard.

Hollings has been a prominent player in most other important policy debates of his era as well: civil rights, arms control, the defense buildup of the 1980s and the defense retrenchment of the 1990s. Modern times brought new issues to the fore, but Hollings has continued to appeal to a cross-section of voters in what has become a mostly Republican state.

Hollings is the son of a dry goods store owner who lost everything during the Depression. He served as a captain in the Army in World War II and was awarded a Bronze Star. In 1948, at age 26, Hollings won election to the South Carolina House. A decade later, he was elected governor. As a candidate in the late 1950s, Hollings espoused states' rights and condemned school integration. But as governor, he quietly integrated the schools.

In 1962, he challenged Democratic Sen. Olin D. Johnston and lost. Johnston died in 1965, however, and Democratic Gov. Donald Russell appointed himself to the seat. In 1966, Hollings ousted Russell in the special primary to finish Johnston's term. He won a full term two years later and rolled over weak opponents in 1974, 1980 and 1986. In 1992, former GOP Rep. Thomas F. Hartnett portrayed him as an arrogant, entrenched incumbent, but Hollings won with 50 percent, 3 points ahead of Hartnett.

His 1998 re-election campaign encouraged his penchant for speaking out as bluntly as he pleases. Brushing aside a request by his opponent, GOP Rep. Bob Inglis, to pledge to run a courteous campaign, Hollings called Inglis a "goddamned skunk" and said he could "kiss my fanny." Hollings prevailed by 7 percentage points over Inglis.

KEY VOTES

2002

Yes Pass farm bill reversing crop subsidy limits
No Postpone tougher automobile fuel efficiency standards
Yes Overhaul campaign finance law; ban "soft money" and restrict advocacy advertising
Yes Set federal election standards
No Support oil drilling in Arctic National Wildlife Refuge
No Revive fast-track procedures for trade agreements
Yes Create federal insurance coverage for catastrophic terrorist losses
Yes Tighten federal accounting and corporate governance regulation
No Advance bipartisan Medicare prescription drug plan
Yes Create independent Sept. 11 commission
Yes Back Democratic Homeland Security Department proposal
Yes Authorize war against Iraq

2001

No Confirm John Ashcroft as attorney general
Yes Nullify Clinton Labor Department ergonomics rule
No Cut taxes by $1.35 trillion through fiscal 2011
Yes Pass Democratic bill to bolster rights of patients in managed-care plans
Yes Permit a new round of military base closings
Yes Expand law enforcement power to investigate suspected terrorists

CQ VOTE STUDIES

	PARTY UNITY		PRESIDENTIAL SUPPORT	
	Support	Oppose	Support	Oppose
2002	85%	15%	71%	29%
2001	95%	5%	62%	38%
2000	90%	10%	82%	18%
1999	89%	11%	80%	20%
1998	81%	19%	74%	26%
1997	74%	26%	75%	25%
1996	82%	18%	82%	18%
1995	76%	24%	76%	24%
1994	80%	20%	86%	14%
1993	79%	21%	73%	27%

INTEREST GROUPS

	AFL-CIO	ADA	CCUS	ACU
2002	92%	85%	55%	15%
2001	88%	90%	50%	29%
2000	88%	85%	33%	20%
1999	100%	85%	27%	12%
1998	29%	55%	71%	33%
1997	83%	75%	20%	8%
1996	57%	70%	46%	20%
1995	75%	75%	37%	35%
1994	71%	50%	40%	22%
1993	91%	55%	27%	42%

Sen. Lindsey Graham (R)

CAPITOL OFFICE
224-5972
290 Russell 20510-4001; fax 224-1300

COMMITTEES
Armed Services
Health, Education, Labor & Pensions
Judiciary
(Crime, Corrections & Victims' Rights - chairman)
Veterans' Affairs

HOMETOWN
Seneca

BORN
July 9, 1955, Seneca, S.C.

RELIGION
Southern Baptist

FAMILY
Single

EDUCATION
U. of South Carolina, B.A. 1977 (psychology), attended 1977-78 (public administration), J.D. 1981

MILITARY SERVICE
Air Force, 1982-88, 1990; S.C. Air National Guard, 1989-94; Air Force Reserve, 1995-present

CAREER
Lawyer

POLITICAL HIGHLIGHTS
S.C. House, 1993-95; U.S. House, 1995-2003

ELECTION RESULTS

2002 GENERAL

Lindsey Graham (R)	595,218	54.4%
Alex Sanders (D)	484,422	44.2%

2002 PRIMARY

Lindsey Graham (R)	unopposed

PREVIOUS WINNING PERCENTAGES
2000 House Election (68%); 1998 House Election (100%); 1996 House Election (60%); 1994 House Election (60%)

Elected 2002; 1st term

It is never easy replacing a political legend, as Graham is doing as the successor to Strom Thurmond, the Senate's sole centenarian.

But his relative youth and energy should allow Graham to easily eclipse at least the latter-day Thurmond, whose final term was marked by a deepening infirmity. And, as a product of the "New South," Graham appears closer to the model sought by the 21st century Republican Party than his predecessor, who made his national reputation as a champion of the old Southern ways of segregation and states' rights.

Graham's legislative agenda at the outset of his Senate career will not differ greatly from what he pursued during his four terms in the House. And his committee assignments parallel those he had at the end of his House service and those Thurmond had at the end of his career. For the 108th Congress, Graham was assigned to Health, Education, Labor and Pensions; Armed Services; Veterans' Affairs; and Judiciary, where he was handed the gavel of the Crime Subcommittee. In the 107th, Thurmond had seats on the latter three of those panels, while Graham was on the House's Armed Services, Education and the Workforce, and Judiciary panels.

But Graham's voting record may emerge as measurably more moderate than Thurmond's was toward the end of his nearly 48 years in the Senate. Graham portrays himself as a conservative Republican from one of the nation's most conservative and Republican-leaning states, and yet he mixes a large dollop of independence in with his party loyalties. As he ran for the Senate in the 107th Congress, he voted the way President Bush wanted him to on only seven out of eight votes — three-quarters of his GOP colleagues in the House supported the president more often.

And during the turning point days in the campaign for the Republican presidential nomination in 2000, Graham was an ardent and often-quoted supporter of Sen. John McCain of Arizona, even though Bush had the backing of the South Carolina Republican establishment.

Bush's victory in the state's primary effectively doomed the McCain campaign. Two years later, Graham was among only 41 Republicans who voted for the campaign finance overhaul that was at the core of McCain's candidacy. And Bush, ironically, signed the bill into law without fanfare just before traveling to South Carolina to raise money for Graham's Senate bid.

Graham was, at least initially, an apostate on one of the articles of Republican faith at the end of the 1990s: that President Clinton should be removed from office because he had conducted an affair with one-time White House intern Monica Lewinsky and then gone to great lengths to cover it up. "Is this Watergate or Peyton Place?" Graham asked, at first questioning the propriety of probing a public official's private life. But he eventually became convinced that Clinton's obstruction of justice merited his impeachment, and he was chosen over more-senior colleagues for the team of 13 Judiciary Committee Republicans that unsuccessfully prosecuted the House's case in the 1999 Senate trial.

He knows that Clinton's travails will forever be part of his own story. "I don't want to be remembered as the impeachment boy. That shortchanges who I am," he told The New York Times in 2000.

Graham also was one of the leaders of the abortive 1997 effort by a group of disaffected Republicans to depose Newt Gingrich as House Speaker. Graham became de facto leader of the coup plotters, gathering dissidents to air their grievances that Gingrich — who came to power as a confrontationalist — was compromising too often with Clinton. Gingrich learned of the nascent insurrection and moved successfully to stem it.

Yet his role in the coup did not make Graham a pariah within the party. He conceded that his involvement had taught him a thing or two about the difficulties of leadership. "This is a hard crowd to manage on a good day," he said of the House GOP the next year.

Graham came to Washington as part of the "revolutionary" Republican Class of 1994, led by Gingrich, that broke the Democrats' 40-year lock on House control. The first Republican to represent westernmost South Carolina in the House since 1877, he was part of the bloc in that class that campaigned more as reformers than as conservative stalwarts.

He mainly exhibits a strict conservatism, though. In the House, Graham was a staunch opponent of gun control, joined an effort to shut down the National Endowment for the Arts and favored amending the Constitution to outlaw flag desecration. He was the sponsor of the bill the House passed in the 107th to make it a federal crime to harm a fetus while committing any of 68 federal offenses or a crime under military law. He vowed to resurrect that legislation as a senator.

On education issues, Graham backs proposals to give schools more flexibility in spending federal funding. He plans to continue pressing for legislation that would boost the amount of student loans that may be forgiven for teachers in mathematics, science and special education.

Graham typically seeks to limit the scope of the federal government, although he is a proponent of robust defense spending, which play well in a state with six major military bases. And when Graham strays from the party line it is sometimes for reasons that make parochial political sense. Given the presence of the struggling textile industry in his state, it was no surprise he was one of the 27 GOP votes in the House in 2002 against enacting the law putting future trade agreements on a fast-track in Congress.

Born in July 1955, six months after Thurmond was first sworn in to the Senate, Graham maintains a youthful appearance and an aw-shucks manner. After earning his law degree, he joined the Air Force and was a military defense attorney; in his most celebrated case, he defended a demoted officer by exposing flaws in the Air Force's drug tests; the Pentagon tacitly acknowledged these by overhauling the program. Soon thereafter, he was transferred to Germany and was the chief prosecutor for the Air Force in Europe from 1984 to 1998. As a major in the Air National Guard, he was called to active duty and served as a military lawyer in South Carolina during the 1991 Persian Gulf War.

Graham won a state House seat in 1992, but his stay was brief: He saw an opportunity for advancement early in 1994, when 10-term Democratic Rep. Butler Derrick decided to retire. With the 3rd District, like South Carolina as a whole, trending Republican, Graham won easily that fall, beating Democratic state Sen. James Bryan with 60 percent of the vote. He won three more terms with relative ease and began doing fundraising and grass-roots party-building work for a Senate run. (During his campaign in 1996, Thurmond made clear that his seventh full term would be his last and that his aim was to retire a month after turning 100.)

That created the first truly open Senate contest in South Carolina since 1954, when Thurmond himself was first elected as a write-in candidate. By 2002, Graham had become the senior Republican in the state's congressional delegation, and he was unopposed for his party's nomination. The Democrats put up Alex Sanders, a quick-witted former president of the College of Charleston who stressed his conservative credentials. But Graham repeatedly portrayed him as a party loyalist who would vote with "Washington liberals" and won by 10 percentage points.

KEY VOTES

House Service:

2002

Yes Overhaul campaign finance law; ban "soft money" and restrict advocacy advertising
Yes Back Bush's defense budget increase
Yes Extend 1996 welfare law
Yes Adopt Bush's discretionary spending limit
Yes Pass GOP Medicare prescription drug plan
No Create independent Sept. 11 commission
No Extend union protections to Homeland Security Department employees
No Revive fast-track procedures for trade agreements
Yes Authorize war against Iraq
No Advance bankruptcy overhaul opposed by abortion opponents

2001

Yes Nullify Clinton Labor Department ergonomics rule
Yes Cut taxes by $1.35 trillion through fiscal 2011
No Maintain ban on oil drilling in Arctic National Wildlife Refuge
Yes Approve Bush proposal to limit managed-care plan liability for coverage decisions
No Divert money from crop subsidy payments to land conservation
Yes Expand law enforcement power to investigate suspected terrorists

CQ VOTE STUDIES

House Service:

	PARTY UNITY		PRESIDENTIAL SUPPORT	
	Support	Oppose	Support	Oppose
2002	89%	11%	82%	18%
2001	93%	7%	84%	16%
2000	98%	2%	17%	83%
1999	89%	11%	18%	82%
1998	92%	8%	22%	78%
1997	95%	5%	25%	75%
1996	96%	4%	35%	65%
1995	95%	5%	20%	80%

INTEREST GROUPS

House Service:

	AFL-CIO	ADA	CCUS	ACU
2002	22%	15%	70%	83%
2001	17%	15%	78%	88%
2000	10%	5%	70%	100%
1999	56%	20%	50%	88%
1998	10%	15%	76%	88%
1997	0%	5%	90%	92%
1996	0%	0%	100%	100%
1995	0%	5%	96%	96%

Rep. Henry E. Brown Jr. (R)

CAPITOL OFFICE
225-3176
www.house.gov/henrybrown
1124 Longworth 20515-4001; fax 225-3407

COMMITTEES
Budget
Transportation & Infrastructure
Veterans' Affairs
(Benefits - chairman)

HOMETOWN
Hanahan

BORN
Dec. 20, 1935, Bishopville, S.C.

RELIGION
Baptist

FAMILY
Wife, Billye Brown; three children

EDUCATION
Berkeley H.S., graduated 1953

MILITARY SERVICE
S.C. National Guard, 1953-62

CAREER
Grocery chain executive; grocery store data processor; shipyard worker; convenience store employee

POLITICAL HIGHLIGHTS
Hanahan City Council, 1981-85; S.C. House, 1985-2000

ELECTION RESULTS

2002 GENERAL		
Henry E. Brown Jr. (R)	122,518	89.5%
James E. Dunn (UC)	9,560	7.0%
Joseph F. Innella (NL)	4,775	3.5%
2002 PRIMARY		
Henry E. Brown Jr. (R)	47,084	78.8%
Bob Batchelder (R)	12,680	21.2%
2000 GENERAL		
Henry E. Brown Jr. (R)	139,597	60.3%
Andy Brack (D)	82,622	35.7%
Bill Woolsey (LIBERT)	6,010	2.6%

Elected 2000; 2nd term

During his 16 years in the South Carolina House, Brown developed a reputation as a pragmatic and dependable legislator, and in 1995 he became the first Republican in more than 100 years to chair the state's Ways and Means Committee.

The oldest person elected to the House in 2000 — he was 65 at the time — Brown now is positioning himself as an interesting contrast to his predecessor, Republican Mark Sanford, who was elected governor in 2002. Both Brown and Sanford are fiscal conservatives, but Brown does not shy away from trying to bring a "fair share" of federal tax dollars back to eastern South Carolina. He wants the government to help pay for deepening Charleston harbor, replacing the spindly and aging bridge across the Cooper River and pumping additional sand onto South Carolina's tourist-attracting beaches. "The federal government should not lessen its responsibility to protect those natural resources," he argues.

Sanford, in contrast, had fought against earmarking $10 million for the Cooper River bridge as one of a number of "demonstration projects" in a 1998 transportation funding bill. When Brown was given a seat on the Transportation and Infrastructure Committee, he made funding for the new bridge a priority. In addition to championing federal funding for the Cooper River bridge and assistance for the ongoing dredging of the Charleston harbor, Brown joined in the Transportation Committee's effort in the 107th Congress to increase spending from the Highway Trust Fund. The proposal called for an additional $64 million in spending in South Carolina, and Brown called it a "significant investment in our future."

His next major opportunity to boost the quality of roads and bridges back home will come in the 108th Congress, which will update the surface transportation law. A priority is funding for Interstate 73, to Myrtle Beach.

Sanford often gave his party's leadership heartburn with his budget-cutting fervor, but Brown makes it a point to develop relationships with the leaders and chairmen of his committees. "If you want to get things done, you have to get close to the people who make the decisions," he told The Associated Press.

Brown took a 10-day excursion to Alaska with Transportation Chairman Don Young, and he has driven to New Jersey on behalf of Veterans' Affairs Chairman Christopher H. Smith. In addition to those two committees, Brown also has a seat on Budget, where he backs the Bush administration's taxing and spending policies. Brown had hoped being chairman of his state's Ways and Means panel might earn him a spot on the U.S. House committee of the same name, and he undertook a campaign with GOP leaders to win appointment in the 108th Congress. But the only GOP opening went to fellow sophomore Eric Cantor.

On the Veterans' committee, where he assumed the chairmanship of the Benefits Subcommittee in the 108th, Brown has focused on legislation to permit retired members of the military who have a service-connected disability to concurrently receive both military retired pay and disability compensation from the Department of Veterans Affairs. He also sponsored a bill to extend the same treatment to surviving spouses of veterans. Brown also has backed efforts to require military hospitals and VA facilities that are close to each other to share facilities, staff and patients.

Textiles are not as important in the 1st District as elsewhere in the Carolinas, but Brown signed a letter to President Bush from 30 House members urging him to look out for the textile industry in dealing with trade issues. He later voted to back fast-track trade negotiating authority for the president, though a number of Republicans who had signed the letter voted "no." (The port of Charleston expects to be a huge beneficiary of expanded trade.)

Brown won attention in the 107th when his resolution supporting public schools that display the words "God Bless America" won unanimous House approval. Brown had been angered when the American Civil Liberties Union had objected to a "God Bless America" display mounted at a California public school in response to the Sept. 11, 2001, terrorist attacks.

Brown grew up on a farm about 25 miles north of Charleston. In high school, he worked part time in a small general store. He told the South Carolina Business Journal it was that job that taught him the importance of being smart with his money.

After high school, he entered the National Guard and took a job in North Charleston with the local electric company, where he was among the early workers in the budding computer field. Later, Brown took a job at the Charleston Naval Shipyard, where his father had worked. He then began a long career with Piggly Wiggly Carolina Co., the South Carolina franchisee of the Southern grocery chain. Brown took a few classes at The Citadel and continued to move up in the grocery business, eventually becoming a vice president of the firm's computer operations.

Brown was active in civic affairs in the town of Hanahan, north of Charleston; he served first on the planning board and then, in 1981, won a city council seat in a special election, as an independent. Four years later, he won another special election to the state legislature. Brown had invested wisely, and after he began his legislative service, he quit his Piggly Wiggly job.

Sanford had announced at the start of his tenure in Congress that he would serve only six years. So in 1998, just a few days after Brown won reelection to the state House and Sanford won the last of his three terms, Brown filed documents stating his intent to run for Congress in two years. Late in 1999, Brown stepped down from his Ways and Means chairmanship to devote more time to the campaign.

Running against five other Republicans, Brown drew attention to his first name by mailing 20,000 Oh Henry! candy bars to voters. He finished first in the primary and took 55 percent of the vote in a runoff election to defeat former state transportation official Buck Limehouse. Although Democrats nominated a credible candidate in Internet entrepreneur Andy Brack — a longtime aide to Democratic Sen. Ernest F. Hollings — Brown coasted to a 60 percent victory. In 2002, the Democrats did not field a candidate.

KEY VOTES

2002

- No Overhaul campaign finance law; ban "soft money" and restrict advocacy advertising
- Yes Back Bush's defense budget increase
- Yes Extend 1996 welfare law
- Yes Adopt Bush's discretionary spending limit
- Yes Pass GOP Medicare prescription drug plan
- No Create independent Sept. 11 commission
- No Extend union protections to Homeland Security Department employees
- Yes Revive fast-track procedures for trade agreements
- Yes Authorize war against Iraq
- Yes Advance bankruptcy overhaul opposed by abortion opponents

2001

- Yes Nullify Clinton Labor Department ergonomics rule
- Yes Cut taxes by $1.35 trillion through fiscal 2011
- No Maintain ban on oil drilling in Arctic National Wildlife Refuge
- Yes Approve Bush proposal to limit managed-care plan liability for coverage decisions
- No Divert money from crop subsidy payments to land conservation
- Yes Expand law enforcement power to investigate suspected terrorists

CQ VOTE STUDIES

	PARTY UNITY		PRESIDENTIAL SUPPORT	
	Support	Oppose	Support	Oppose
2002	95%	5%	82%	18%
2001	97%	3%	88%	12%

INTEREST GROUPS

	AFL-CIO	ADA	CCUS	ACU
2002	11%	0%	95%	96%
2001	8%	0%	96%	92%

SOUTH CAROLINA 1

East – part of Charleston, Myrtle Beach

Taking in the northeast half of the state's coastline, the 1st is marked by two of South Carolina's landmark tourism cities, Charleston and Myrtle Beach. Horry County, which envelops Myrtle Beach, still has plenty of farmland but is one of the state's fastest-growing areas. The 1st is the least rural of South Carolina's six congressional districts.

Hurricane Hugo wrought devastation all along the state's coastline in 1989, and defense downsizing further hurt Charleston in the early 1990s. But these events also heralded a wave of redevelopment, as the city shifted its economy to manufacturing, shipping, health care and technology. Charleston (80 percent of whose residents live in the 1st) is an icon of the New South but retains its traditional culture. Surrounded by reminders of antebellum history, it is nicknamed the "Holy City" because of the church steeples marking its skyline.

Moving north, tourism and agriculture dominate the 1st. Myrtle Beach's tourist-resort economy welcomes 13 million visitors a year. Horry voted much like South Carolina in the 2002 elections, backing Republicans for governor and the U.S. Senate by solid but not overwhelming margins.

The district's demographics — mostly white, suburban and comfortably middle-class — make it reliable Republican territory. One exception is the strong environmental and anti-development sentiment shared by many coastal residents in response to rapid population growth, rising pollution and beach erosion.

MAJOR INDUSTRY
Tourism, shipping, health care

MILITARY BASES
Charleston Air Force Base, 6,241 military, 1,300 civilian; Charleston Naval Weapons Station, 181 military, 284 civilian (2002)

CITIES
Charleston (pt.), 77,434; Mount Pleasant, 47,609; North Charleston (pt.), 45,530; Goose Creek, 29,208; Summerville, 27,752; Myrtle Beach, 22,759

NOTABLE
Charleston Harbor is home to Fort Sumter, where the Civil War began in April 1861; Fort Moultrie on Sullivan's Island nearby marks the first decisive victory in the War for Independence; 18-year-old Edgar Allan Poe arrived in Charleston in 1827 to enlist at Fort Moultrie.

Rep. Joe Wilson (R)

CAPITOL OFFICE
225-2452
joe.wilson@mail.house.gov
www.house.gov/joewilson
212 Cannon 20515-4002; fax 225-2455

COMMITTEES
Armed Services
Education & Workforce

HOMETOWN
Springdale

BORN
July 31, 1947, Charleston, S.C.

RELIGION
Presbyterian

FAMILY
Wife, Roxanne Wilson; four children

EDUCATION
Washington and Lee U., B.A. 1969 (political science); U. of South Carolina, J.D. 1972

MILITARY SERVICE
Army Reserve, 1972-75; S.C. National Guard, 1975-present

CAREER
Lawyer; campaign manager; U.S. Energy Department official

POLITICAL HIGHLIGHTS
Pine Ridge town judge, 1974-76; Republican nominee for S.C. Senate, 1976; Springdale town judge, 1977-80; S.C. Senate, 1985-2001

ELECTION RESULTS

2002 GENERAL		
Joe Wilson (R)	144,149	84.1%
Mark Whittington (UC)	17,189	10.0%
James R. Legg (LIBERT)	9,650	5.6%
2002 PRIMARY		
Joe Wilson (R)		unopposed
2001 SPECIAL		
Joe Wilson (R)	40,355	73.1%
Brent Weaver (D)	14,034	25.4%

Elected December 2001; 1st full term

Both Wilson's backers and opponents often compare him to longtime GOP Rep. Floyd D. Spence, the man he succeeded in a 2001 special election after the 16-term lawmaker died. And Wilson himself says that his agenda in Congress, and his philosophy about public service, can be traced to Spence, with whom he had worked for more than 30 years.

Calling Spence "my friend and mentor," Wilson says, "I don't see that I would be any different from him; we had so much in common." Wilson had managed five of Spence's re-election campaigns and was involved in many of the statewide GOP campaigns in the Palmetto State throughout the 1980s and 1990s, while working as a real estate lawyer in the Columbia area.

Wilson's first bill in the House was a measure to improve coordination in organ donation. It was a tribute to Spence, who had had both a double lung transplant and a kidney transplant.

Some of Wilson's foes also compare him to Spence, but unfavorably. Wilson once blasted South Carolina Democratic Sen. Ernest F. Hollings for remarks the senator made about Israel's Prime Minister Ariel Sharon and then blew up at California Democratic Rep. Bob Filner of California during a C-SPAN interview, accusing Filner several times of harboring "hatred of America." Several Capitol Hill observers noted that the good-natured Spence would never have been so derisive.

A member of the House GOP "theme team," which helps the party make its points in forums such as C-SPAN interviews and House one-minute speeches, Wilson says he wants to promote conservative Southern values even if it sometimes means public disagreements with colleagues.

Wilson's voting record is almost always in line with the House GOP leadership and President Bush, although his district's textile interests caused him to vote against a bill to give the president fast-track authority to negotiate trade agreements that Congress cannot amend.

After winning the special election, Wilson quickly received a seat on the Armed Services Committee, where Spence had been chairman for six years. His support for the Pentagon comes out of his own experience. In the 108th Congress, Wilson is the only House member in the national guard who actively participates in monthly drills with his unit. One of the first bills he introduced in the 108th was a measure to permit retired members of the national guard and reserves to receive benefits immediately, rather than waiting until age 60. "Of course, I would exempt myself," Wilson said.

Although he does not serve on the International Relations Committee, Wilson has been outspoken in promoting close ties with India, supporting Israel and backing NATO membership for Bulgaria and Romania. His interest in foreign affairs was broadened when Republican National Committee Chairman Lee Atwater appointed him in 1990 to a delegation to observe the first democratic elections for the Bulgarian National Assembly.

Wilson's father was stationed in India with the Flying Tigers during World War II and his stories sparked the congressman's interest in India. He served three years in the Army Reserve and is a colonel in the South Carolina Army National Guard. His background fits well with his district's interests; it is home to Fort Jackson, the Army's largest training base, as well as the Marines' Parris Island training center and a Marine airfield in Beaufort.

Wilson is also interested in promoting renewal of the landmark 1996 welfare law, joining the House GOP's "welfare reform action team" and speaking out on what he views as the law's great successes. His interest in welfare reform is a continuation of work he did in the state Senate, where he chaired a key committee that drafted state welfare legislation.

Wilson's first recollection of politics was when he was a "pop runner" — fetching soft drinks for poll workers. His mother was a Democrat, but Wilson, recalling his great admiration for President Eisenhower, always thought he might be a Republican. He made the transition from working on Democratic races to Republican ones in 1960.

As a 15-year-old high school student, Wilson worked on the losing 1962 Senate campaign of Republican W.D. Workman. A year later, he says, he rode a bus to Washington, D.C., to attend a Draft Goldwater rally.

While in college, Wilson interned in the office of South Carolina's GOP Sen. Strom Thurmond. (His wife and three of their sons also interned for Thurmond at one time.) Later, while in law school, he worked for Spence, beginning a relationship that would last until Spence's death.

Wilson fell short in a close contest for the state Senate in 1976, losing after a recount. In 1984, upon his return to South Carolina after a two-year stint in Washington, D.C., with the Department of Energy, Wilson challenged a Republican incumbent. He won, gaining his first of five victories to the state Senate. In addition to his work on welfare, Wilson's tenure in the legislature was marked by proposals to eliminate property taxes and to cap state spending. He also sought to increase penalties for gun-related felonies, make it easier to impose the death penalty, and require school children to recite portions of the Declaration of Independence.

After Spence died, Wilson said he had his deathbed endorsement. Although Wilson's claim rankled some of his rivals, it was backed up by Spence's widow. Wilson had the backing of most of the party establishment, and he easily raised more than $500,000 for the four-month special-election campaign. Wilson won the five-way GOP primary Oct. 30 with 76 percent of the vote. In the heavily Republican district, he cruised to a healthy 48 percentage point victory in December over Democrat Brent Weaver.

Remapping for 2002 caused him no electoral difficulties. Democrats did not even come up with a challenger, freeing Wilson to devote his time to GOP Rep. Lindsey Graham's successful run for the Senate. He and Graham have worked together for years. Wilson was the staff judge advocate for the Army National Guard while Graham held the same post for the Air Force National Guard.

Wilson's eagerness to take on Hollings fueled speculation that he might be positioning himself to run for the Senate in 2004, when Hollings would be up for re-election. But shortly after he won re-election in 2002, Wilson announced he would not be a Senate candidate.

KEY VOTES

2002

- No Overhaul campaign finance law; ban "soft money" and restrict advocacy advertising
- Yes Back Bush's defense budget increase
- Yes Extend 1996 welfare law
- Yes Adopt Bush's discretionary spending limit
- Yes Pass GOP Medicare prescription drug plan
- No Create independent Sept. 11 commission
- No Extend union protections to Homeland Security Department employees
- No Revive fast-track procedures for trade agreements
- Yes Authorize war against Iraq
- No Advance bankruptcy overhaul opposed by abortion opponents

CQ VOTE STUDIES

	PARTY UNITY		PRESIDENTIAL SUPPORT	
	Support	Oppose	Support	Oppose
2002	97%	3%	82%	18%
2001	100%	0%	100%	0%

INTEREST GROUPS

	AFL-CIO	ADA	CCUS	ACU
2002	22%	10%	80%	92%
2001	—	—	100%	—

SOUTH CAROLINA 2

Central and south — part of Columbia and suburbs, Hilton Head Island

The oddly shaped 2nd winds from the state capital of Columbia down through the middle of the state to a sandy stretch along the coast. The two ends of the district encapsulate some of the state's wealthiest communities: the suburbs of Columbia, in Richland and Lexington counties, and Beaufort and Hilton Head Island on the southern tip.

Columbia's suburbs have grown steadily. While state and local government are still the city's largest employers, its private sector is becoming more of a force. At the southern end of the 2nd, retirees and tourists are drawn to Hilton Head Island. Surrounding Beaufort was the fastest-growing county in population in South Carolina in the 1990s.

Military issues are important here. Just up the shore from the swank resorts, recruits sweat at the Parris Island Marine Corps camp. Fort Jackson in Richland County at the district's northern end and another Marine installation also contribute to the military presence.

The areas between Columbia and Hilton Head are dotted with smaller towns and rural areas that are considerably poorer. Many families in the black-majority counties of Allendale, Hampton and Jasper live below the poverty line, relying on tenant farming and sharecropping.

Heavy Democratic support in the poor areas is offset by wealthy white-collar professionals in the north and south, who push the district firmly into the GOP column. Lexington County, the 2nd's most-populous, voted 2-to-1 for Republican gubernatorial and senatorial candidates in 2002.

MAJOR INDUSTRY

Tourism, government, military, agriculture

MILITARY BASES

Fort Jackson (Army), 5,646 military, 3,842 civilian (2001); Marine Corps Recruitment Depot (Parris Island), 2,046 military, 467 civilian; Beaufort Marine Corps Air Station, 4,400 military, 504 civilian (2002)

CITIES

Columbia (pt.), 59,771; Hilton Head Island, 33,862

NOTABLE

The first federally authorized black unit to fight for the Union, the First South Carolina Volunteers, camped in Beaufort; Hilton Head Island is the site of the largest naval engagement of the Civil War.

Rep. J. Gresham Barrett (R)

CAPITOL OFFICE
225-5301
www.house.gov/barrett
1523 Longworth 20515-4003; fax 225-3216

COMMITTEES
Budget
Financial Services

HOMETOWN
Westminster

BORN
Feb. 14, 1961, Westminster, S.C.

RELIGION
Baptist

FAMILY
Wife, Natalie Barrett; three children

EDUCATION
The Citadel, B.S. 1983 (business administration)

MILITARY SERVICE
Army, 1983-87

CAREER
Furniture store owner

POLITICAL HIGHLIGHTS
S.C. House, 1997-2002

ELECTION RESULTS

2002 GENERAL		
J. Gresham Barrett (R)	119,644	67.1%
George Brightharp (D)	55,743	31.3%
Mike Boerste (LIBERT)	2,785	1.6%
2002 PRIMARY RUNOFF		
J. Gresham Barrett (R)	38,366	65.2%
Jim Klauber (R)	20,505	34.8%
2002 PRIMARY		
J. Gresham Barrett (R)	27,499	43.5%
Jim Klauber (R)	13,865	21.9%
George Ducworth (R)	13,836	21.9%
Bob Waldrep (R)	3,983	6.3%
Stan Jackson (R)	2,702	4.3%
Michael Thompson (R)	1,360	2.2%

Elected 2002; 1st term

Barrett told voters upon his election in 2002 to South Carolina's 3rd District seat that his House record should not be surprising. "I will be a strong conservative member," he said.

A six-year veteran of the state House, Barrett plans to pursue a Republican agenda in his assignments to the Financial Services and Budget committees. He says he will do anything he can to promote business interests.

His conservatism extends to social issues. He touts his efforts to pass state legislation to ban the procedure its opponents call "partial birth" abortion, saying it was "a crowning moment in South Carolina."

Barrett is also proud of the state "Truth-in-Sentencing" bill he backed requiring all convicted felons to serve 85 percent of their sentences. He was a sponsor of a 1998 education measure that established statewide standards for all subjects and grades.

Barrett, who went to the Citadel and graduated from the Army's Airborne school, shares the pro-military views of many South Carolinians. He eventually resigned his commission to join the family furniture business, which he now owns.

His strong Republican loyalties helped earn him a place on the House GOP whip team.

The freshman parts with President Bush on one locally sensitive issue. Representing a district with many textile plants, Barrett says he would not have backed the 2002 bill granting the president fast-track authority to negotiate trade agreements that Congress cannot amend. The measure also was opposed by his House predecessor, Republican Lindsey Graham, who left the 3rd District seat open for a successful Senate bid.

Barrett's involvement in George W. Bush's 2000 South Carolina presidential primary campaign helped him build a strong organization for his own House bid. He easily claimed the Republican nomination over five rivals, then coasted to victory in the general election by a ratio of more than 2-to-1.

SOUTH CAROLINA 3

West — Anderson, Aiken

Encompassing the northwest corner of the state, the 3rd is one of South Carolina's most rural districts. Many voters here are converts to the Republican Party, having shifted over from "Yellow Dog" Democrat status. Former Rep. (and now senator) Lindsey Graham was the first Republican to win this seat since Reconstruction in 1994.

The brimming economy has further boosted opportunities for the GOP. The base of engineers surrounding the Savannah River nuclear complex near Aiken, the district's largest employer, has helped attract Fortune 500 firms to the area, as well as several U.S. divisions of international companies. An example is Fujifilm in Greenwood, which employs 1,500 South Carolinians and has invested more than $1.3 billion in the state. Fujifilm's new medical products plant is the first built outside of Japan.

To the northwest, Anderson has built a more industrial economy, moving away from its rural roots. Many area textile mills have successfully shifted to high-tech fiber manufacturing. Clemson University provides the economic and social nexus for Pickens County at the 3rd's northern tip.

The district votes solidly Republican in federal and statewide races. The 3rd's most populous voting jurisdictions – Anderson, Aiken and Pickens counties – are heavily Republican. Pickens County gave 71 percent of its vote to George W. Bush in 2000. The counties in the 3rd's midsection are more rural, less prosperous and less Republican-leaning. This area includes McCormick County, where the majority of the population is black.

MAJOR INDUSTRY
Manufacturing, textiles, cotton

CITIES
Anderson, 25,514; Aiken (pt.), 22,810; Greenwood, 22,071; Easley, 17,754

NOTABLE
The 70,000-acre Lake Thurmond, previously known as Clarks Hill Lake, was renamed after GOP Sen. Strom Thurmond; Aiken is known as the polo center of the South.

Rep. Jim DeMint (R)

Elected 1998; 3rd term

CAPITOL OFFICE
225-6030
www.demint.house.gov
432 Cannon 20515-4004; fax 226-1177

COMMITTEES
Education & Workforce
Small Business
Transportation & Infrastructure

HOMETOWN
Greenville

BORN
Sept. 2, 1951, Greenville, S.C.

RELIGION
Presbyterian

FAMILY
Wife, Debbie DeMint; four children

EDUCATION
U. of Tennessee, B.S. 1973 (communications); Clemson U., M.B.A. 1981

CAREER
Market research company owner

POLITICAL HIGHLIGHTS
No previous office

ELECTION RESULTS

2002 GENERAL		
Jim DeMint (R)	122,422	69.0%
Peter J. Ashy (D, UC)	52,635	29.7%
C. Faye Walters (NL)	2,176	1.2%
2002 PRIMARY		
Jim DeMint (R)	39,142	61.6%
Phil Bradley (R)	24,423	38.4%
2000 GENERAL		
Jim DeMint (R)	150,436	79.6%
Ted Adams (CNSTP)	16,532	8.7%
April Bishop (LIBERT)	12,757	6.8%
Peter J. Ashy (REF, UC)	6,210	3.3%
C. Faye Walters (NL)	2,640	1.4%

PREVIOUS WINNING PERCENTAGES
1998 (58%)

DeMint exemplifies a new brand of conservatism among House Republicans. While he tends to vote with social conservatives on such issues as abortion (which he opposes) and school vouchers (which he supports), he prefers to emphasize his work on bipartisan legislation that could create more jobs for his constituents or addresses pocketbook issues such as the taxation of working families.

But the 108th Congress will be DeMint's last in the House. Though the term-limits movement was already on the wane in 1998, when he waged his first congressional campaign, he promised then that he would stay in the House for no more than six years. He is a co-founder of the Citizen Legislators Caucus, made up of lawmakers who have agreed to limit their terms voluntarily, a somewhat quiet group that declines to publicly castigate colleagues who renege on such pledges.

But DeMint (da-MENT) wants to stay in Washington; early in 2003 he was gearing up for a run for the Senate in 2004, when Democrat Ernest F. Hollings' term expires.

The GOP needs spokesmen, DeMint says, who "can take the Republican message and communicate it persuasively to swing voters — someone who can say Republicans have a heart and soul, as well as good logic."

DeMint became an expert in positioning a product in a crowded marketplace — be it Homelite chainsaws or St. Pauli Girl beer — while running a market research business in Greenville. In Washington, that background in advertising has served him well as he touts his ideas on economic issues. His marketing savvy helped him gather more than 280 cosponsorships in 2001 on legislation to double the adoption tax credit, to $10,000. "When I present something to the chairman of Ways and Means, I need to show there is overwhelming support, because I am not a member of the committee," DeMint explains. The bipartisan support he showed for the idea helped lead to its inclusion in the $1.35 trillion, 10-year tax cut enacted that year. In the 108th, DeMint is working to make the adoption credit permanent.

Teaming up with Dick Armey, the House majority leader in the 107th Congress, DeMint pushed a proposal to address long-term financing problems for the Social Security system. Their bill would have offered investors a chance to increase their benefits by investing some of their payroll taxes in stocks and bonds, but it also would have guaranteed that benefits did not fall below current levels. "I think a lot of Republicans will want to be on a bill like this that guarantees benefits," he said. "Nobody wants to be associated with benefit cuts." But after the series of corporate scandals — and the stock market swoon that occurred simultaneously — there was little support for the private accounts.

DeMint used his gavel as chairman of the Small Business Subcommittee on Workforce, Empowerment and Government Programs to focus attention on the need for tax breaks and low-interest loans for small business and to promote tax-exempt personal medical insurance accounts for employees. He teamed in the 107th with Democrat John Kerry of Massachusetts, the chairman of the Senate Small Business Committee, on a proposal to help small businesses by allowing them to retain as much as $250,000 in federal income taxes over two years, as long as they paid what they had deferred, with interest, in the subsequent four years.

On the Transportation Committee, DeMint is eager to champion the public works wishes of South Carolina — and the benefits of providing more funding for mass transit in smaller states — as Congress rewrites the highway and public transportation law in the 108th Congress. On the Education and Workforce Committee, DeMint promotes efforts to give states more flexibility in the use of federal education grants.

His loyalty to the GOP pro-business agenda got DeMint into trouble back home in the 107th Congress, when he joined the razor-thin House majority that helped enact the law reviving fast-track congressional procedures for considering trade treaties.

This infuriated the state's powerful textile interests, which see themselves as losers if trade is liberalized. These businesses were not mollified when — in return for their "yes" votes — DeMint and North Carolina Republican Robin Hayes secured the inclusion in a separate law of language to enhance somewhat the domestic textile industry's position in its competition with African and Caribbean clothing makers.

The trade vote became the key issue in DeMint's 2002 primary against former state Rep. Phil Bradley, but the incumbent won with a solid 62 percent. Despite redistricting, the 4th District remained as solidly Republican as it had been in the 1990s, and in 2002 DeMint crushed his Democratic foe by almost 40 percentage points.

DeMint's political positioning has meshed well with the changes in northern South Carolina. Social conservatism runs deep in the 4th, which is squarely in the Bible Belt and home to Bob Jones University, a bastion of evangelicalism. Yet the centerpiece of the district's economy, a sprawling BMW plant outside Spartanburg, manufactures some of the most prized symbols of upward mobility, particularly the trendy Z3 roadster and the X5 sport utility vehicle. Interstate 85, linking Greenville and Spartanburg, is sometimes referred to as the "autobahn." The presence of a major Michelin tire plant drives home the point, and the pro-trade views of the state's automotive businesses have made DeMint's pro-trade stance more politically justifiable.

DeMint entered politics as an unpaid adviser to his predecessor, Republican Bob Inglis, during the 1992 campaign. Six years later, when Inglis gave up the seat for an unsuccessful Senate bid, DeMint won the GOP nomination by 2,000 votes against state Sen. Mike Fair, who had the backing of the standard-bearers of the right such as the Christian Coalition and the Family Research Council. DeMint won by 17 percentage points in the fall.

In Congress, DeMint meets weekly in an interdenominational Bible study group of about 10 men, a practice he's followed for more than 20 years. He says the meeting keeps him focused on spiritual matters.

KEY VOTES

2002

No Overhaul campaign finance law; ban "soft money" and restrict advocacy advertising
Yes Back Bush's defense budget increase
Yes Extend 1996 welfare law
Yes Adopt Bush's discretionary spending limit
Yes Pass GOP Medicare prescription drug plan
No Create independent Sept. 11 commission
No Extend union protections to Homeland Security Department employees
Yes Revive fast-track procedures for trade agreements
Yes Authorize war against Iraq
No Advance bankruptcy overhaul opposed by abortion opponents

2001

Yes Nullify Clinton Labor Department ergonomics rule
Yes Cut taxes by $1.35 trillion through fiscal 2011
No Maintain ban on oil drilling in Arctic National Wildlife Refuge
Yes Approve Bush proposal to limit managed-care plan liability for coverage decisions
No Divert money from crop subsidy payments to land conservation
Yes Expand law enforcement power to investigate suspected terrorists

CQ VOTE STUDIES

	PARTY UNITY		PRESIDENTIAL SUPPORT	
	Support	Oppose	Support	Oppose
2002	97%	3%	85%	15%
2001	98%	2%	95%	5%
2000	98%	2%	22%	78%
1999	97%	3%	11%	89%

INTEREST GROUPS

	AFL-CIO	ADA	CCUS	ACU
2002	11%	0%	90%	100%
2001	0%	0%	96%	100%
2000	0%	0%	90%	100%
1999	11%	0%	92%	91%

SOUTH CAROLINA 4
Northwest – Greenville, Spartanburg

The 4th is South Carolina's most compact district and is centered on Greenville County, the state's most-populous. Greenville and Spartanburg counties together account for 95 percent of the district population. The 4th also takes in Union County, a heavily forested but lightly populated area, and a tiny part of Laurens County.

Successful manufacturing and warehousing ventures have transformed the area from its textile past. The cities of Greenville and Spartanburg are national leaders in per capita investment by foreign corporations. Michelin's North American headquarters are in Greenville, and BMW is a major presence in Spartanburg.

Although no longer the textile capital of the world, the 4th retains a strong textile presence. Industry giant Milliken & Co. is headquartered in Spartanburg. Trade issues are important in the district, though textile companies have less political influence since the industry has declined. Agriculture also plays a role in the Spartanburg area; its sprawling orchards yield one of the biggest peach crops in the South.

Spreading wealth has helped keep this district solidly Republican. But the local GOP has two distinct camps: mainstream, business-oriented conservatives and social conservatives focused around Greenville-based Bob Jones University. In recent years, an influx of professionals has diluted the influence of hard-line social conservatives.

With its rank-and-file textile workers and farm laborers, Spartanburg is less heavily Republican than Greenville. Nonetheless, both counties voted for GOP candidates in key 2002 races by landslide margins. Mark Sanford took 62 percent in Greenville and 59 percent in Spartanburg in the gubernatorial election, and Lindsey Graham took 64 percent and 60 percent in those counties in the Senate election.

MAJOR INDUSTRY
Engineering, manufacturing, textiles, agriculture

CITIES
Greenville, 56,002; Spartanburg, 39,673; Wade Hampton (unincorporated), 20,458; Taylors (unincorporated), 20,125; Greer, 16,843

NOTABLE
Vietnam War Gen. William C. Westmoreland was born in Spartanburg County; Baseball player Shoeless Joe Jackson grew up in Greenville.

Rep. John M. Spratt Jr. (D)

CAPITOL OFFICE
225-5501
www.house.gov/spratt
1401 Longworth 20515-4005; fax 225-0464

COMMITTEES
Armed Services
Budget - ranking member

HOMETOWN
York

BORN
Nov. 1, 1942, Charlotte, N.C.

RELIGION
Presbyterian

FAMILY
Wife, Jane Spratt; three children

EDUCATION
Davidson College, A.B. 1964 (history); Oxford U., M.A. 1966 (philosophy, politics & economics); Yale U., LL.B. 1969

MILITARY SERVICE
Army, 1969-71

CAREER
Lawyer; insurance agency owner

POLITICAL HIGHLIGHTS
No previous office

ELECTION RESULTS

2002 GENERAL		
John M. Spratt Jr. (D)	121,912	85.9%
Doug Kendall (LIBERT)	11,013	7.8%
Steve Lefemine (CNSTP)	8,930	6.3%
2002 PRIMARY		
John M. Spratt Jr. (D)		unopposed
2000 GENERAL		
John M. Spratt Jr. (D)	126,877	58.8%
Carl Gullick (R)	85,247	39.5%
Tom Campbell (LIBERT)	3,665	1.7%

PREVIOUS WINNING PERCENTAGES
1998 (58%); 1996 (54%); 1994 (52%); 1992 (61%); 1990 (100%); 1988 (70%); 1986 (100%); 1984 (92%); 1982 (68%)

Elected 1982; 11th term

In the 108th Congress Spratt serves as Nancy Pelosi's handpicked demographic counterweight in the Democratic leadership — a politically moderate and courtly Southern man to complement the new House minority leader's West Coast liberalism, feminism and high-wattage style.

Pelosi also chose Spratt for the job of assistant to the minority leader because of his top-tier credentials on the budget and national defense, two issues on which the Democrats want to reposition themselves as they seek a new path back to the House majority. A deficit hawk, he is the top Democrat on the Budget Committee at a time when the party is debating the importance of balancing the federal books while also promoting economic recovery efforts and an expansion of Medicare. A defense hawk, he is the No. 2 Democrat on the Armed Services Committee at a time when the party is being pressed to spend whatever it takes to stanch the spread of terrorism and weapons of mass destruction.

Starting his third decade in the House, Spratt has a clear memory for many of its perennial debates, a rarity in a chamber where most members have served less than a decade. His centrist leanings have made him an ideal envoy to negotiate with Republicans, a role that will be more difficult to play now that he is officially part of the Democratic leadership.

Spratt has been a member of Armed Services since 1983, when he first arrived on Capitol Hill. He tends to side with Republicans in support of missile defense but allies himself with liberal Democrats in championing nuclear arms reduction. But after the Sept. 11, 2001, terrorist attacks, Spratt led Democrats to abandon plans to press for cuts in missile defense spending, a tacit acknowledgement that they would lose a fight with President Bush over a system the Pentagon could tout as aiding a nation under siege.

When Bush asked for the authority to invade Iraq, Spratt backed him — but commissioned the Congressional Budget Office to study the costs. He also reminded colleagues that a series of hearings had helped bolster President George Bush's case for attacking Iraq in 1991.

Spratt became the top Democrat on the Budget panel in 1997, and ever since he has acted as the leading Democratic advocate for reversing budget deficits. To that end he has been insistent that Congress not give the Bush administration a blank check for its increased defense and homeland security spending. And, early in 2003, he pressed his party colleagues to unite behind a budget that would eventually generate a small surplus — mainly because it would provide for a less ambitious improvement to Medicare than most Democrats advocate.

A spirited jouster with Republicans in the fiscal policy wars, Spratt has a knack for boiling down complex issues into pithy phrases. He once likened to "a big can opener" a clause in a budget resolution that would have allowed Republicans to increase spending in the middle of the year under certain circumstances.

Spratt has repeatedly called on Bush to convene a budget summit, recalling his role as a lead negotiator for the 1997 balanced-budget deal between President Clinton and the GOP-run 105th Congress that helped wipe out almost three decades of deficits. Spratt describes that budget deal as "the biggest achievement that I can lay any claim to."

Spratt has been to the right of many in his party on fiscal policy. He supported a constitutional amendment to require balanced federal budgets and backed the 1996 law that gave the president line-item veto power. (The

Supreme Court struck it down as unconstitutional in 1998.)

His conservative tilt also has been evident on some issues outside of defense and fiscal matters, such as Spratt's efforts to shield children from unsuitable programming on television. When his more ambitious idea — to yank the federal licenses of TV stations that aired violent programs during prime viewing hours for children — went nowhere, Spratt cosponsored the 1996 law requiring that most new TV sets come with a "v-chip" to allow parents to block violent or otherwise objectionable programming.

Overall in the 107th, he backed Bush on three out of every eight votes — in the top third among all House Democrats for presidential support.

Spratt has been a leading advocate for the textile industry, which helps fuel the 5th District's economy. He voted for the North American Free Trade Agreement in 1993 after the Clinton administration got the Philippines and some other developing countries to accept a longer phaseout of U.S. quotas limiting textile imports. But he opposed the 2000 law making permanent the normal U.S.-China trade relationship and the 2002 law giving the president fast-track trade negotiating power.

In 1998, Spratt broke his right arm in two places after slipping on a spill of some of the Senate's famous bean soup inside the Capitol. The event garnered international chuckles. "We have a story about a congressman by the name of Jack Spratt, believe it or not," intoned the BBC. "It seems he could stay away from the fat, but not the bean soup."

Spratt has generally had to work hard to convince his conservative-leaning constituents that he understands and defends their interests. With his lofty academic credentials (from Davidson, Oxford and Yale) and his background as a lawyer and community bank president, Spratt is not the obvious choice to represent a part of the country where many of the Democratic voters come from poor textile towns and dusty farms.

Winning his first House race in 1982 — on the retirement of Democrat Ken Holland — Spratt persuasively argued that his work with small-town law clients and bank depositors had given him an understanding of their circumstances. He trounced a longtime friend and legal client, Republican John Wilkerson, by 36 percentage points, and he won re-election with ease throughout the 1980s.

But in the 1990s he was often targeted by the national GOP; he survived the Republican sweep of 1994 by just 4 percentage points and did not get above 60 percent in the next three elections. Although the politics of the 5th were kept essentially the same in redistricting after the 2000 census, the GOP did not field a candidate against Spratt in 2002.

KEY VOTES

2002

Yes	Overhaul campaign finance law; ban "soft money" and restrict advocacy advertising
Yes	Back Bush's defense budget increase
No	Extend 1996 welfare law
No	Adopt Bush's discretionary spending limit
No	Pass GOP Medicare prescription drug plan
Yes	Create independent Sept. 11 commission
Yes	Extend union protections to Homeland Security Department employees
No	Revive fast-track procedures for trade agreements
Yes	Authorize war against Iraq
Yes	Advance bankruptcy overhaul opposed by abortion opponents

2001

Yes	Nullify Clinton Labor Department ergonomics rule
No	Cut taxes by $1.35 trillion through fiscal 2011
+	Maintain ban on oil drilling in Arctic National Wildlife Refuge
No	Approve Bush proposal to limit managed-care plan liability for coverage decisions
No	Divert money from crop subsidy payments to land conservation
Yes	Expand law enforcement power to investigate suspected terrorists

CQ VOTE STUDIES

	PARTY UNITY		PRESIDENTIAL SUPPORT	
	Support	Oppose	Support	Oppose
2002	88%	12%	42%	58%
2001	82%	18%	33%	67%
2000	82%	18%	59%	41%
1999	82%	18%	74%	26%
1998	81%	19%	73%	27%

INTEREST GROUPS

	AFL-CIO	ADA	CCUS	ACU
2002	100%	80%	55%	16%
2001	92%	85%	45%	36%
2000	78%	70%	52%	20%
1999	100%	80%	26%	12%
1998	90%	85%	50%	17%

SOUTH CAROLINA 5

North central – Rock Hill

The 5th spans all or part of 14 mostly rural counties in the north-central part of the state, stretching from near Charlotte, N.C., to the Columbia suburbs, with considerable territory spreading east and west. Redistricting following the 2000 census added even more rural sections to the area. The combination of tobacco farmers, white-collar Charlotte commuters and textile workers makes this a conservative district, though it still clings to its traditional Southern Democrat roots.

In the midsection and west, rural counties such as Newberry, Chester, Lancaster and Kershaw produce cotton for the textile mills that historically have dominated the region's economy. The two largest cities, Rock Hill and Sumter (shared with the 6th), add immigrants from the North. Rock Hill, once dependent on the textile industry, now serves as a home for white-collar commuters and Winthrop University.

Many residents of Fairfield County — an area that already had a double-digit unemployment rate — have lost their jobs because of businesses downsizing or moving overseas.

The city of Sumter, once the center of a large agricultural area, is shifting toward industry. Seven miles west of Sumter, Shaw Air Force Base makes up one-third of the area's economy. In the east, Darlington, Dillon and Marlboro counties depend heavily on tobacco farming.

Politically, the 5th tends to vote narrowly Republican in federal races, but conservative Democrats who appeal to the district's numerous poor and rural residents can win here. Democrats also are helped by the district's 32 percent black population, the largest of any South Carolina district except the black-majority 6th.

MAJOR INDUSTRY
Cotton, textiles, tobacco

MILITARY BASES
Shaw Air Force Base, 5,460 military, 465 civilian (2001)

CITIES
Rock Hill, 49,765; Sumter (pt.), 20,518; Gaffney, 12,968

NOTABLE
The Lee County Cotton Festival, held every October, celebrates the agricultural history of "King Cotton"; Home to the Darlington 500 NASCAR race track, where two major races are held; Televangelist Jim Bakker's PTL ministries were located in Fort Mill.

Rep. James E. Clyburn (D)

CAPITOL OFFICE
225-3315
jclyburn@mail.house.gov
www.house.gov/clyburn
2135 Rayburn 20515-4006; fax 225-2313

COMMITTEES
Appropriations

HOMETOWN
Columbia

BORN
July 21, 1940, Sumter, S.C.

RELIGION
African Methodist Episcopal

FAMILY
Wife, Emily Clyburn; three children

EDUCATION
South Carolina State College, B.S. 1962 (social studies)

CAREER
State official; teacher

POLITICAL HIGHLIGHTS
S.C. human affairs commissioner, 1974-92; sought Democratic nomination for S.C. secretary of state, 1978, 1986

ELECTION RESULTS

2002 GENERAL		
James E. Clyburn (D)	115,855	67.0%
Gary McLeod (R)	55,490	32.1%
2002 PRIMARY		
James E. Clyburn (D)	34,106	88.8%
Ben Frasier Jr. (D)	4,304	11.2%
2000 GENERAL		
James E. Clyburn (D)	138,053	71.8%
Vince Ellison (R)	50,005	26.0%
Dianne Nevins (NL)	2,339	1.2%
Lynwood Earl Hines (LIBERT)	1,934	1.0%

PREVIOUS WINNING PERCENTAGES
1998 (73%); 1996 (69%); 1994 (64%); 1992 (65%)

Elected 1992; 6th term

Quietly and pragmatically, Clyburn has become one of the country's most respected African-American politicians. Now in his sixth term, he was elected vice chairman of the Democratic Conference in the 108th Congress, the fourth-highest position in the House Democratic leadership.

Clyburn has risen in the party because of his steady loyalty and fundraising effectiveness. The leading black politician in South Carolina, his support will be needed by those Democrats seeking the presidential nomination to win the 2004 South Carolina Democratic primary — considered a pivotal battleground for the nomination.

Most of the Democratic presidential candidates have either cosponsored a bill with Clyburn or appeared with him at a fundraiser in the past year. Joseph I. Lieberman of Connecticut worked with Clyburn on legislation to boost funding for historically black colleges in the South, and John Kerry of Massachusetts and John Edwards of North Carolina helped Clyburn with a Columbia, S.C., fish fry fundraiser.

Clyburn also was an oft-quoted voice in the debacle surrounding Senate Majority Leader Trent Lott's remarks at the 100th birthday party of Sen. Strom Thurmond of South Carolina. Lott's remarks implied that he supported segregation and led to his removal as Senate majority leader. In one of Lott's several attempted apologies, he tried to take credit for aiding Clyburn's effort to boost funding for historically black colleges. "He's talking the talk but not walking the walk," Clyburn told the Wall Street Journal. In fact, Lott had never cosponsored Lieberman's bill, which was the Senate companion to Clyburn's legislation; Clyburn said Senate Republicans had blocked the measure.

The 6th District is home to a number of historically black colleges, including Clyburn's alma mater, South Carolina State, and Clyburn has been at the forefront of efforts to obtain federal funding to help maintain the schools. He has a strong commitment to higher education. He told The State newspaper that his father loved school so much that he attended the 7th grade three times because blacks in Kershaw County at the time were not allowed to go to high school.

In February 2003, Clyburn was asked to give the Democratic response to President Bush's weekly radio address, where he focused on the president's economic agenda. "African-Americans and Latinos stand to suffer disproportionately from this administration's economic policies that, by all accounts, favor the wealthy," Clyburn said. But he can be equally hard on his own party. After the Republicans increased their majority in the 2002 elections, Clyburn argued that the Democrats did not have enough of a grass-roots presence and relied too heavily on television ads.

Even with his increasing role in Democratic Party politics, Clyburn's priority in the House is advocating for his district — the poorest in South Carolina and among the poorest in the nation. From his seat on the Appropriations Committee, and particularly the Transportation Subcommittee, he seeks federal funds to help the 6th District pay for new bridges, roads, water systems, housing, and economic development.

Even before his appointment to the Appropriations Committee, Clyburn was able to bring federal aid back home as his state's only member of the Transportation and Infrastructure Committee when Congress passed a sweeping surface transportation bill in the 105th. He was proud to report the measure authorized a huge spending increase for the Palmetto State.

As part of that process, Clyburn was able to establish a Transportation Center at South Carolina State University and greatly increase his state's return from the Highway Trust Fund. He also was instrumental in continuing a program that seeks to give 10 percent of construction contracts to disadvantaged businesses.

The first black representative elected from South Carolina since 1896 (when his great-uncle, George Washington Murray, served), Clyburn received some help from the start from House Democratic leaders. In the 106th Congress, he served as chairman of the Congressional Black Caucus, and he played a role in negotiating a purchase of Martin Luther King Jr.'s personal papers by the Library of Congress.

An avid golfer (his current handicap is hovering near 11), Clyburn says you can tell a lot about a person by the way he or she plays golf. He told The Hill newspaper, "You watch a guy who takes risks, or a guy who will lay up rather than going for it. . . . You can tell whether or not he's timid or aggressive."

When Democratic Gov. John West named him a special assistant for human resources in 1971, Clyburn, who had taught school and headed the state's Commission for Farm Workers, was the first black to serve as a gubernatorial appointee in the state in more than 70 years. Three years later, he became the state's Human Affairs commissioner, where he earned a reputation as an able conciliator and established close ties with those in the political power structure.

The son of a minister and a member of one of the most prominent black families in South Carolina politics, Clyburn always had his eye on moving up. In 1978 and 1986, he unsuccessfully sought the Democratic nomination for secretary of state. During his political career in South Carolina, Clyburn saw "the system" become more open to blacks, an evolution confirmed when 1992 redistricting created the black-majority 6th District.

White Democratic incumbent Robin Tallon at first said he would seek reelection. But he backed out, saying he did not want to provoke a racially divisive campaign. Clyburn and four other black Democrats ran in the primary. While all had some political experience, none could match Clyburn's name recognition in the black community or his high-level contacts in the white Democratic Party establishment. Clyburn took 56 percent of the primary vote and rolled up 65 percent in the general election. In the 2002 elections, Clyburn won with 67 percent of the vote, defeating GOP candidate Gary McLeod, who has called the United States a "socialist" country and advocated abolition of direct taxation.

KEY VOTES

2002

Yes Overhaul campaign finance law; ban "soft money" and restrict advocacy advertising
Yes Back Bush's defense budget increase
No Extend 1996 welfare law
No Adopt Bush's discretionary spending limit
No Pass GOP Medicare prescription drug plan
Yes Create independent Sept. 11 commission
Yes Extend union protections to Homeland Security Department employees
No Revive fast-track procedures for trade agreements
No Authorize war against Iraq
No Advance bankruptcy overhaul opposed by abortion opponents

2001

Yes Nullify Clinton Labor Department ergonomics rule
No Cut taxes by $1.35 trillion through fiscal 2011
No Maintain ban on oil drilling in Arctic National Wildlife Refuge
No Approve Bush proposal to limit managed-care plan liability for coverage decisions
No Divert money from crop subsidy payments to land conservation
Yes Expand law enforcement power to investigate suspected terrorists

CQ VOTE STUDIES

	PARTY UNITY		PRESIDENTIAL SUPPORT	
	Support	Oppose	Support	Oppose
2002	97%	3%	31%	69%
2001	84%	16%	33%	67%
2000	91%	9%	75%	25%
1999	95%	5%	85%	15%
1998	95%	5%	83%	17%

INTEREST GROUPS

	AFL-CIO	ADA	CCUS	ACU
2002	100%	95%	50%	0%
2001	92%	70%	61%	20%
2000	100%	85%	57%	8%
1999	100%	85%	13%	0%
1998	100%	95%	28%	4%

SOUTH CAROLINA 6

Central and east – parts of Columbia, Florence and Charleston

A black-majority district designed to take in African-American areas in Columbia, Charleston and elsewhere in the state, the 6th comprises all or part of 15 counties in the eastern half of the state, starting near the North Carolina border and reaching the southeastern coast. With five of South Carolina's six poorest counties, the 6th has the state's lowest median household income.

In the rural portions of the district, many families depend on tobacco and tobacco-related agribusiness for their incomes. In the 1980s, Bamberg, Marion and Williamsburg counties lost population as residents left farms and jobs in the textile industry disappeared. For those who remain, agriculture continues to be the economic mainstay. Many others who live in the district find work in Charleston (shared with the 1st) and Columbia (shared with the 2nd).

Other sectors of the district's economy have fared better. Plastics, pharmaceuticals, textiles and paperboard manufacturing sustain many in the city of Florence (shared with the 5th), which is more middle-class than most of the rest of the 6th. In the coastal parts of the district, maritime industries and tourism provide the economic base. Government services, higher education and manufacturing create jobs in the 6th's midsection.

The 6th gives solid and consistent support to Democrats at all levels. The district's black-majority areas — including the 6th's shares of Columbia and North Charleston, which are more than two-thirds African-American — make this seat a Democratic lock.

MAJOR INDUSTRY

Agriculture, government, textiles, tourism

CITIES

Columbia (pt.), 56,507; North Charleston (pt.), 34,111; Florence (pt.), 26,623; Charleston (pt.), 19,216; Sumter (pt.), 19,125

NOTABLE

All of the state's four historically black colleges and universities are in the district; Clarendon County (pop. 32,502) can claim five South Carolina governors — and all were related.

SOUTH DAKOTA

Gov. Michael Rounds (R)

First elected: 2002
Length of term: 4 years
Term expires: 1/07
Salary: $98,250
Phone: (605) 773-3212
Hometown: Pierre
Born: Oct. 24, 1954; Pierre, S.D.
Religion: Roman Catholic
Family: Wife, Jean Rounds; four children
Education: South Dakota State U., B.S. 1977 (political science)
Career: Insurance and real estate executive; insurance agent; campaign aide
Political highlights: S.D. Senate, 1991-2000 (majority leader, 1995-2000)
Election results:

2002 GENERAL		
Michael Rounds (R)	189,920	56.8%
Jim Abbott (D)	140,263	41.9%

Lt. Gov. Dennis Daugaard (R)

First elected: 2002
Length of term: 4 years
Term expires: 1/07
Salary: $13,404
Phone: (605) 773-3212

STATE LEGISLATURE

Legislature: Meets 40 days in odd-numbered years, beginning in January; 35 days in even-numbered years, beginning in January
House: 70 members, 2-year terms
2003 breakdown: 49R, 21D; 59 men, 11 women
Salary: $12,000/2-year-term; $110/day in session
Phone: (605) 773-3661
Senate: 35 members, 2-year terms
2003 breakdown: 26R, 9D; 31 men, 4 women
Salary: $12,000/2-year-term; $110/day in session
Phone: (605) 773-3251

STATE TERM LIMITS

Governor: 2 consecutive terms
House: 4 consecutive terms
Senate: 2 consecutive terms

URBAN STATISTICS

CITY	POPULATION
Sioux Falls	123,975
Rapid City	59,607
Aberdeen	24,658

REGISTERED VOTERS

Republican	48%
Democrat	39%
Other	13%

POPULATION

2002 population (est.)	761,063
2000 population	754,844
1990 population	696,004
Percent change (1990-2000)	+8.5%
Rank among states (2002)	46
Median age	35.6
Born in state	68.1%
Foreign born	1.8%
Violent crime rate	167/100,000
Poverty level	13.2%
Federal workers	10,803
Military	8,489

REDISTRICTING

South Dakota retained its one House seat in reapportionment.

MISCELLANEOUS

Web: www.state.sd.us
Capital: Pierre

STATE ELECTION OFFICIAL
(605) 773-3537

DEMOCRATIC HEADQUARTERS
(605) 224-1750

REPUBLICAN HEADQUARTERS
(605) 224-7347

District Statistics

DIST.	2000 VOTE FOR PRESIDENT BUSH	GORE	NADER	WHITE	BLACK	ASIAN	HISP	MEDIAN INCOME	WHITE COLLAR	BLUE COLLAR	SERVICE INDUSTRY	OVER 64	UNDER 18	COLLEGE EDUCATION	RURAL	SQ. MILES
AL	60%	38%	0%	88%	1%	1%	1%	$35,282	59%	25%	16%	14%	27%	22%	48%	75,885
STATE	60	38	0	88	1	1	1	$35,282	59	25	16	14	27	22	48	75,885
U.S.	47.9	48.4	3	69	12	4	13	$41,994	60	25	15	12	26	24	21	3,537,438

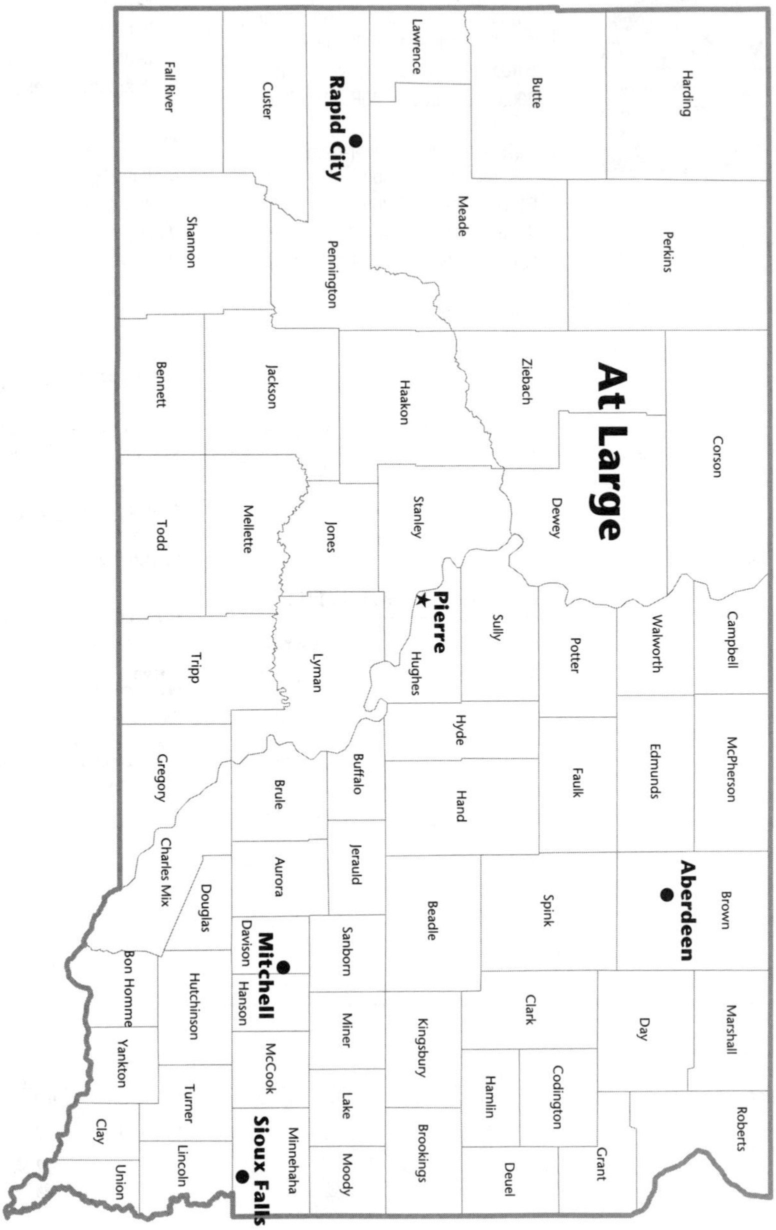

At Large
Rapid City
Pierre
Aberdeen
Mitchell
Sioux Falls
Fall River
Custer
Lawrence
Butte
Harding
Shannon
Pennington
Meade
Perkins
Bennett
Jackson
Haakon
Ziebach
Corson
Todd
Mellette
Jones
Stanley
Dewey
Tripp
Lyman
Hughes
Sully
Potter
Walworth
Campbell
Gregory
Brule
Buffalo
Hyde
Hand
Faulk
Edmunds
McPherson
Charles Mix
Douglas
Aurora
Jerauld
Beadle
Spink
Brown
Davison
Sanborn
Hanson
Bon Homme
Hutchinson
Miner
Kingsbury
Clark
Day
Marshall
Yankton
McCook
Lake
Hamlin
Codington
Roberts
Turner
Clay
Minnehaha
Lincoln
Union
Moody
Brookings
Deuel
Grant

Sen. Tom Daschle (D)

CAPITOL OFFICE
224-2321
tom_daschle@daschle.senate.gov
daschle.senate.gov
509 Hart 20510-4103; fax 224-2047

COMMITTEES
Agriculture, Nutrition & Forestry
Finance
Rules & Administration

HOMETOWN
Aberdeen

BORN
Dec. 9, 1947, Aberdeen, S.D.

RELIGION
Roman Catholic

FAMILY
Wife, Linda Hall Daschle; three children

EDUCATION
South Dakota State U., B.A. 1969 (political science)

MILITARY SERVICE
Air Force, 1969-72

CAREER
Congressional aide

POLITICAL HIGHLIGHTS
U.S. House, 1979-87

ELECTION RESULTS

1998 GENERAL		
Tom Daschle (D)	162,884	62.1%
Ron Schmidt (R)	95,431	36.4%
Byron Dale (LIBERT)	3,796	1.4%
1998 PRIMARY		
Tom Daschle (D)		unopposed

PREVIOUS WINNING PERCENTAGES
1992 (65%); 1986 (52%); 1984 House Election (57%); 1982 House Election (52%); 1980 House Election (66%); 1978 House Election (50%)

Elected 1986; 3rd term

After a topsy-turvy two years in which he went from minority leader to majority leader and back again — and became the Capitol's best-known terrorist target along the way — Daschle is once again leading a caucus of Democratic senators who can do little more than obstruct, delay or modify the agenda of Republican-run Washington.

His decision to remain at the helm of the Senate minority took many of the political elite by surprise; they assumed he would be focusing instead on winning the 2004 Democratic presidential nomination. Daschle was preparing to announce his candidacy in January 2003, but changed his mind the night before the 108th Congress convened. "Right now this is where my heart is, where my passions lie," he told the Senate.

Daschle was viewed across the Capitol as a skilled tactician and a creative leader during his first long run playing defense, when he battled a Republican majority as the Senate minority leader from 1995 until June 2001. But he proved less effective on offense as majority leader during the remaining 18 months of the 107th Congress.

When Vermont's James M. Jeffords left the GOP to become an independent who affiliated with the Democrats, the power balance in the Senate tipped. But the move placed only 51 votes at Daschle's nominal disposal, the smallest Senate majority since 1959 and too narrow a margin to advance legislation over Republican resistance. Nor, in the run-up to a midterm election when so many of his colleagues were vulnerable, could Daschle regularly marshal a united Democratic front to thwart or at least refashion legislation that President Bush demanded.

The consequence was a series of setbacks that outstripped Daschle's roster of victories in the 107th. He could not assemble enough Democrats to prevent the creation of a Homeland Security Department where workers are denied some rights under the civil service system. He could not find a fiscal policy that unified his party, so in 2002 the Senate failed to approve a budget for the first time since the current budget process was adopted in 1974. Nor could he persuade his colleagues on the Finance Committee to agree on a single Medicare prescription drug proposal or a single welfare policy.

And when Daschle tried to lead his caucus to spurn Bush's request for unfettered authority to wage war on Iraq, the president cut a deal with House Minority Leader Richard A. Gephardt. Outflanked, Daschle and most other Senate Democrats ended up voting for the resolution.

All the while, Republicans delighted in labeling Daschle an "obstructionist," even as they used their minority party filibuster power to derail many of the Democrats' legislative initiatives.

The high points for Daschle in the 107th Congress came after the terrorist attacks on Sept. 11, 2001. Determined to contribute to a united governmental front in the aftermath, he and Minority Leader Trent Lott kept their disputes behind closed doors and pushed a number of bills into law in record time. These included an airline bailout, broad new law enforcement powers to fight terrorism and the federalization of most airport security. Bush even gave Daschle a televised embrace after addressing Congress. But all the collegiality had a downside. It hampered Daschle's efforts to distinguish his party's message from the president's.

In October 2001, Congress itself fell victim to a terrorist attack when an aide opened a letter addressed to Daschle and released a cloud of virulent anthrax spores. While helping to orchestrate the evacuation of Capitol Hill and assuage the fears of lawmakers and their staffs, Daschle's own office in the Hart Building was closed for six months for decontamination.

Daschle has never been as well-known outside Washington as other Senate powerhouses, and the anthrax incident was a rare moment in the spotlight for him. In a place full of famous faces and outsize egos, the former altar boy strolls through the Capitol generally unrecognized by the tourists gawking at the Kennedys, Clintons and McCains around him.

Despite policy setbacks, Daschle has shown remarkable success in protecting his party's institutional prerogatives. At the start of the 107th and again in the 108th, he bested first Lott and then new Majority Leader Bill Frist in negotiations to win bigger budgets and more office space for his colleagues than the minority traditionally has been granted.

He also pushed to expand the minority party's powers early in the 108th, leading Democrats into the first prolonged filibuster in modern times against a nominee for a federal appeals court, Miguel Estrada, a Bush pick for the D.C. Circuit Court of Appeals.

Daschle's method is to build consensus among his troops, let debates and negotiations play themselves out, then stand pat until his top priorities are addressed. It served him well in the acid test of his career, the 1999 impeachment trial of President Clinton, the first such proceeding in 131 years. Daschle worked intensively with Lott to avoid a replay of the partisan impeachment brawl in the House. He emerged with his stature enhanced and his clout among Senate Democrats greater than ever; not a single Democrat voted to convict on either of two articles of impeachment.

Daschle's initial election as Democratic leader was underwhelming. He eked out a 24-23 victory over Connecticut's Christopher J. Dodd at the end of 1994, when Majority Leader George J. Mitchell of Maine retired.

Some of the party's old bulls, led by former Majority Leader Robert C. Byrd, were skeptical of his qualifications. But two years later, it was Byrd who nominated Daschle for re-election. To this day, Daschle goes out of his way to accommodate Byrd; he even keeps his copy of the West Virginian's four-volume Senate history on a table in his office beside a photograph of his first grandchild.

Daschle is relentless in promoting his state's interests, and his legislative specialties have hewed closely to South Dakota's economic and political needs: agriculture, veterans' issues, American Indian affairs and rural health care. In the 107th, he paid extraordinary attention to even incremental maneuvering on the farm bill, making sure that corn, wheat and soybean farmers got good deals. Also benefiting politically was home-state colleague Tim Johnson, a Democrat running for a second Senate term.

Daschle is the only military veteran in the top tier of the congressional leadership. During the Vietnam War, he was an Air Force intelligence officer at the Strategic Air Command.

He began his Capitol career as an aide to South Dakota Democratic Sen. James G. Abourezk in the mid-1970s. He moved back home in 1976 to become field director for Abourezk, then ran for a House seat two years later. At age 30, Daschle won the open at-large seat through sheer energy. He and his first wife rang more than 40,000 doorbells in a year; Daschle prevailed by just 139 votes, and only after a final canvass reversed the apparent result on Election Day.

After building a reputation in the House as a diligent defender of his state's agriculture interests, he won his Senate seat with 52 percent of the vote in 1986 by ousting Republican incumbent James Abdnor. His re-elections in 1992 and 1998 against modest competition were nonetheless impressive in a state that has become increasingly Republican. The GOP is eager to find a top-flight challenger to Daschle in 2004.

KEY VOTES

2002

Yes Pass farm bill reversing crop subsidy limits
No Postpone tougher automobile fuel efficiency standards
Yes Overhaul campaign finance law; ban "soft money" and restrict advocacy advertising
Yes Set federal election standards
No Support oil drilling in Arctic National Wildlife Refuge
Yes Revive fast-track procedures for trade agreements
Yes Create federal insurance coverage for catastrophic terrorist losses
Yes Tighten federal accounting and corporate governance regulation
Yes Advance bipartisan Medicare prescription drug plan
Yes Create independent Sept. 11 commission
Yes Back Democratic Homeland Security Department proposal
Yes Authorize war against Iraq

2001

No Confirm John Ashcroft as attorney general
No Nullify Clinton Labor Department ergonomics rule
No Cut taxes by $1.35 trillion through fiscal 2011
Yes Pass Democratic bill to bolster rights of patients in managed-care plans
Yes Permit a new round of military base closings
Yes Expand law enforcement power to investigate suspected terrorists

CQ VOTE STUDIES

	PARTY UNITY		PRESIDENTIAL SUPPORT	
	Support	Oppose	Support	Oppose
2002	80%	20%	75%	25%
2001	98%	2%	69%	31%
2000	93%	7%	95%	5%
1999	93%	7%	84%	16%
1998	90%	10%	90%	10%
1997	92%	8%	92%	8%
1996	94%	6%	93%	7%
1995	93%	7%	92%	8%
1994	91%	9%	94%	6%
1993	90%	10%	93%	7%

INTEREST GROUPS

	AFL-CIO	ADA	CCUS	ACU
2002	92%	85%	58%	22%
2001	100%	100%	43%	8%
2000	71%	85%	71%	8%
1999	89%	90%	56%	8%
1998	88%	90%	61%	4%
1997	71%	80%	60%	4%
1996	86%	90%	38%	0%
1995	100%	95%	37%	4%
1994	63%	80%	40%	4%
1993	91%	75%	20%	12%

Sen. Tim Johnson (D)

CAPITOL OFFICE
224-5842
tim@johnson.senate.gov
johnson.senate.gov
324 Hart 20510-4104; fax 228-5765

COMMITTEES
Appropriations
Banking, Housing & Urban Affairs
Budget
Energy & Natural Resources
Indian Affairs

HOMETOWN
Vermillion

BORN
Dec. 28, 1946, Canton, S.D.

RELIGION
Lutheran

FAMILY
Wife, Barbara Johnson; three children

EDUCATION
U. of South Dakota, B.A. 1969 (political science), M.A. 1970 (political science); Michigan State U., attended 1970-71; U. of South Dakota, J.D. 1975

CAREER
Lawyer; county prosecutor; state legislative aide

POLITICAL HIGHLIGHTS
S.D. House, 1979-83; S.D. Senate, 1983-87; U.S. House, 1987-97

ELECTION RESULTS

2002 GENERAL		
Tim Johnson (D)	167,481	49.6%
John Thune (R)	166,957	49.5%
2002 PRIMARY		
Tim Johnson (D)	65,438	94.8%
Herman Eilers (D)	3,558	5.2%

PREVIOUS WINNING PERCENTAGES
1996 (51%); 1994 House Election (60%); 1992 House Election (69%); 1990 House Election (68%); 1988 House Election (72%); 1986 House Election (59%)

Elected 1996; 2nd term

A quiet and bookish lawyer, the "other" senator from South Dakota is often overshadowed by Democratic leader Tom Daschle. That was never clearer than in 2002, when Johnson's own bid for re-election was viewed across the nation as a referendum on Daschle.

Republicans from President Bush on down went to enormous lengths to help Republican Rep. John Thune defeat Johnson's campaign for a second term. Daschle battled just as hard to save his friend and colleague. The state's 750,000 residents were bombarded with millions of dollars in advertising: Total spending in the election came to about $24 million — $70 per vote. In the end, Johnson survived by 524 votes. Thune declined to seek a recount, but the closeness of the outcome led to immediate pressure on him to run again, against Daschle in 2004.

Throughout the campaign, Johnson's quiet style was compared to that of the more gregarious (and handsome) Thune. The Hill newspaper labeled the contest, "The Hunk Versus the Wonk." Reflecting on that dynamic, Johnson's son Brendan told the Argus Leader newspaper in Sioux Falls that the race was "a little humbling. . . . No one's ever asked my father to pose shirtless for a calendar." In the end, Johnson's camp believed their candidate's down-home style had been a key to his victory.

While most senators covet media attention, Johnson shuns it whenever possible. Instead of staging news conferences or delivering floor speeches, he retires to his office and spends hours poring over dense background materials on subjects such as revamping ground rules for the Federal Deposit Insurance Corporation. "Good policy is good politics" is his mantra.

His private life is no flashier. He and his wife, Barbara, maintain a modest home in the Virginia suburbs. Although Johnson has served as an usher at the local Lutheran church for years, many in the congregation do not know he is a senator. "I've seen him introduce himself as someone who works with the government," the Rev. Thomas Prinz told the Argus Leader.

Instead of focusing on making a name for himself, Johnson has concentrated on providing for his constituents and maintaining a normal family life. One of Johnson's priorities was making it home in time for supper each night as his kids grew up. He introduced legislation in 2003 to bar telemarketers from calling anyone between 5:30 p.m. and 7:30 p.m. Aides said that would help keep family dinner hours "sacred."

When Johnson was elected to the House in 1986, his wife gave up her tenured position as a University of South Dakota social work professor to move the family to Washington. She later became a social worker in the Northern Virginia public schools. All three Johnson children went to school in Virginia but returned to South Dakota for college. The older son, Brooks, joined the Army and serves with the 101st Airborne Division, known as the "Screaming Eagles." Deployed to Bosnia, Kosovo and Afghanistan, Staff Sgt. Johnson shipped out for Kuwait in March 2003 — just as his father had anticipated months earlier when the Senate debated the resolution authorizing an attack on Iraq.

His voice breaking in a rare display of emotion, Johnson said then that he strongly supported Bush's position. "I am willing to cast this vote — one of the most important in my career both as a senator and certainly as a father — because I recognize the threat that Saddam Hussein represents to world peace." Johnson added that he had discussed the issue with his son. "Our understanding as a father and son is, 'You do what is best for the country, and I'll do my job.' "

Family issues almost stopped Johnson from running for the Senate in the first place. With five terms as a House member under his belt, he had a good shot at unseating 18-year Republican incumbent Larry Pressler in 1996. In the middle of the campaign, however, Johnson's wife learned she had breast cancer. He offered to drop out, but she encouraged him to stay in the race. He won by 8,600 votes, the only person to defeat a sitting senator that year.

As a freshman, Johnson immediately landed seats on three Senate committees important to his state: Agriculture, Banking and Energy and Natural Resources. In the 107th he gave up Agriculture for an assignment to one of the most powerful panels, Appropriations. From there, he has attempted to direct federal funds to South Dakota projects, particularly those aimed at helping American Indians and veterans.

Though generally content to tend to state concerns, on occasion Johnson has taken a leading role on broader if little-known national issues. With FDIC reserves steadily declining and a number of banks failing, in the 107th he pushed legislation to increase insurance coverage for depositors. A companion bill passed the House, but the Senate took no action. Johnson vowed to renew his efforts in the 108th.

Johnson has spent his time in Congress tenaciously advocating for his state's farmers and seeking federal funds for local water projects, bridges and roads. He was a strong proponent of the 2002 farm bill that gave producers, particularly those in the Midwest, a sturdier safety net. He also pushed for emergency drought aid for farmers and new funding for a project to bring water to rural areas of Western South Dakota. Efforts to claim credit were complicated, however. The broader spending bill that contained the drought aid drew opposition from Republicans, and only a more-limited version became law early in 2003. And the water project, though it became law in 2002, was sponsored in the House by Thune.

Improving programs for veterans has been another major goal. Johnson has sponsored legislation to make most Department of Veterans Affairs funding mandatory and to extend more health care benefits to veterans. He also has focused on issues affecting senior citizens, an important constituency in a state with a rapidly aging population. He sponsored legislation in the House that would have penalized companies found to charge excessive prices for prescription drugs. He has pressed for creating a Medicare drug benefit for seniors and has supported efforts to allow reimportation of drugs from Canada, where prices are lower.

Johnson can be counted on to vote with Daschle in the clutch most of the time — but far from reliably. In the 107th he was in the bottom third among Senate Democrats when it came to standing with the party on party-line votes, and he was right in the middle when it came to voting the wishes of President Bush. He did so 70 percent of the time, and was one of the dozen Democratic senators (six of them up for re-election) who voted for Bush's $1.35 trillion, 10-year tax cut package.

A fourth-generation South Dakotan, Johnson became familiar with the legislative process by working as a budget analyst in the Michigan state Senate. After returning to his home state and starting a law practice, he ran for the legislature in 1978, serving two terms in the state House and two in the state Senate. He ran for Congress in 1986 when Daschle gave up the state's single House seat to run for the Senate. After a narrow primary victory over a folksy state senator with longstanding farm credentials, Johnson easily won the general election and did not face significant opposition until taking on Pressler.

KEY VOTES

2002

- Yes Pass farm bill reversing crop subsidy limits
- Yes Postpone tougher automobile fuel efficiency standards
- Yes Overhaul campaign finance law; ban "soft money" and restrict advocacy advertising
- Yes Set federal election standards
- No Support oil drilling in Arctic National Wildlife Refuge
- No Revive fast-track procedures for trade agreements
- Yes Create federal insurance coverage for catastrophic terrorist losses
- Yes Tighten federal accounting and corporate governance regulation
- Yes Advance bipartisan Medicare prescription drug plan
- Yes Create independent Sept. 11 commission
- Yes Back Democratic Homeland Security Department proposal
- Yes Authorize war against Iraq

2001

- No Confirm John Ashcroft as attorney general
- No Nullify Clinton Labor Department ergonomics rule
- Yes Cut taxes by $1.35 trillion through fiscal 2011
- Yes Pass Democratic bill to bolster rights of patients in managed-care plans
- Yes Permit a new round of military base closings
- Yes Expand law enforcement power to investigate suspected terrorists

CQ VOTE STUDIES

	PARTY UNITY		PRESIDENTIAL SUPPORT	
	Support	Oppose	Support	Oppose
2002	85%	15%	68%	32%
2001	87%	13%	71%	29%
2000	91%	9%	98%	2%
1999	93%	7%	78%	22%
1998	93%	7%	89%	11%
1997	86%	14%	87%	13%
House Service:				
1996	80%	20%	69%	31%
1995	82%	18%	77%	23%
1994	90%	10%	82%	18%
1993	87%	13%	73%	27%

INTEREST GROUPS

	AFL-CIO	ADA	CCUS	ACU
2002	100%	90%	53%	15%
2001	94%	85%	64%	32%
2000	75%	80%	60%	16%
1999	89%	95%	47%	8%
1998	88%	90%	56%	4%
1997	71%	80%	70%	12%
House Service:				
1996	73%	55%	33%	37%
1995	75%	85%	50%	28%
1994	67%	55%	75%	24%
1993	92%	65%	36%	21%

Rep. Bill Janklow (R)

CAPITOL OFFICE
225-2801
billjanklow@mail.house.gov
www.house.gov/janklow
1504 Longworth 20515-4101; fax 225-5823

COMMITTEES
Agriculture
Government Reform
International Relations

HOMETOWN
Brandon

BORN
Sept. 13, 1939, Chicago, Ill.

RELIGION
Lutheran

FAMILY
Wife, Mary Dean Janklow; three children

EDUCATION
U. of South Dakota, B.S.B.A. 1964 (accounting), J.D. 1966

MILITARY SERVICE
Marine Corps, 1956-59

CAREER
Lawyer; state prosecutor

POLITICAL HIGHLIGHTS
S.D. attorney general, 1975-79; governor, 1979-87; sought Republican nomination for U.S. Senate, 1986; governor, 1995-2003

ELECTION RESULTS

2002 GENERAL		
Bill Janklow (R)	180,023	53.5%
Stephanie Herseth (D)	153,656	45.6%
2002 PRIMARY		
Bill Janklow (R)	60,575	54.9%
Larry Pressler (R)	29,992	27.2%
Tim Amdahl (R)	10,593	9.6%
Roger Hunt (R)	7,799	7.1%
Bert Tollefson Jr. (R)	1,311	1.2%

Elected 2002; 1st term

Janklow says he has no plans to temper his headstrong style even though he is a House freshman instead of a governor, the position he held for 16 of the 24 years before winning his state's sole House seat.

While governor — he twice met South Dakota's two-term limit on consecutive service — Janklow was credited with luring Citibank to set up its credit-card processing facility in Sioux Falls, wiring the state's schools for Internet access and creating a program that employed prison inmates to build low-cost homes. But his critics perceived him as a tyrant, and he was particularly viewed as a foe by many in the state's American Indian community. "He has willed an underpopulated state to achieve beyond its means but left a trail of bitter victims in his wake," said Peter Harriman, a writer for the Sioux Falls Argus Leader.

"I know as much as anybody the controversies I create," Janklow says. "It has always been my responsibility to make sure I try to address problems people can't deal with themselves."

Janklow says his top priority will be legislation to require the federal government to pay local property taxes on land such as national forests and parks, Army Corps of Engineers property and Indian trust land. He was named to the Agriculture Committee — essential to congressional success in a state that is a top producer of corn, wheat and soybeans — and to the International Relations and Government Reform panels.

The 63-year-old Janklow is the only House member in the 108th Congress who served as a governor at the same time as George W. Bush. The president recruited Janklow to run when John Thune gave up the House seat to seek the Senate, and the two embraced as Bush arrived to deliver his 2003 State of the Union address.

As he was finishing his tenure in Pierre, Janklow dispatched his closest primary rival, former Sen. Larry Pressler, by 28 percentage points. He won by 8 points in November against Democratic lawyer Stephanie Herseth, the granddaughter of a former governor.

SOUTH DAKOTA

At large

Low crop prices wounded eastern South Dakota's agriculture-based economy in the 1990s, adding to a steady migration into cities, where finance, computers and health care gradually have overtaken meatpacking as the primary industries. Citibank, Gateway and others moved into the state during the 1990s to take advantage of low taxes and wages. In the west, away from the more populated areas, the arid, hilly portion of the state relies on ranching, mining and tourism — Mount Rushmore, the Black Hills and the Badlands are located here.

South Dakota has one of the nation's highest percentages of American Indians, at just more than 8 percent of the population. The traditionally poor Indian communities found a bright spot in casinos in the 1990s; all nine of the state's Indian reservations grew in population over the decade. But poverty is still a major problem. Shannon County, home of the Pine Ridge Indian Reservation, is one of the poorest counties in the nation.

South Dakotans often vote Republican on the local level, while Democrats are more popular in federal races. But with only three exceptions — 1932, 1936 and 1964 — GOP presidential candidates won the state during the 20th century. The state also has an independent streak, giving Ross Perot 22 percent in 1992 and 10 percent in 1996.

The Missouri River, which splits the state, sometimes is considered a political divide as well — western, ranching Republicans outnumber eastern urban and agricultural Democrats by about 46,000 registered voters. American Indians, found predominantly in the west, traditionally support Democrats.

MAJOR INDUSTRY
Agriculture, finance, tourism

MILITARY
Ellsworth Air Force Base, 3,261 military, 405 civilian (2002)

CITIES
Sioux Falls, 123,975; Rapid City, 59,607; Aberdeen, 24,658; Watertown, 20,237

NOTABLE
More than 200 Sioux were massacred in one day at Wounded Knee in 1890.

TENNESSEE

Gov. Phil Bredesen (D)

First elected: 2002
Length of term: 4 years
Term expires: 1/07
Salary: $85,000
Phone: (615) 741-2001
Hometown: Nashville
Born: Nov. 21, 1943; Oceanport, N.J.
Religion: Presbyterian
Family: Wife, Andrea Conte; one child
Education: Harvard U., S.B. 1967 (physics)
Career: Health insurance company founder; health care executive; computer programmer
Political highlights: Candidate for Mass. Senate, 1970; candidate for mayor of Nashville, 1987; sought Democratic nomination for U.S. House, 1987; mayor of Nashville, 1991-99
Election results:

2002 GENERAL		
Phil Bredesen (D)	837,284	50.6%
Van Hilleary (R)	786,803	47.6%

Lt. Gov. John S. Wilder (D)

(elected by the state Senate)
First elected: 1971
Length of term: 2 years
Term expires: 1/05
Salary: $49,500
Phone: (615) 741-2368

STATE LEGISLATURE

General Assembly: Meets 90 days over 2 years, beginning in January
House: 99 members, 2-year terms
2003 breakdown: 45R, 54D; 80 men, 19 women
Salary: $16,500; $128/day in session; $525/month expenses
Phone: (615) 741-2901
Senate: 33 members, 4-year terms
2003 breakdown: 15R, 18D; 28 men, 5 women
Salary: $16,500; $128/day in session; $525/month expenses
Phone: (615) 741-2730

STATE TERM LIMITS

Governor: 2 terms
Senate: No
House: No

URBAN STATISTICS

CITY	POPULATION
Memphis	650,100
Nashville-Davidson	569,891
Knoxville	173,890
Chattanooga	155,554
Clarksville	103,455

REGISTERED VOTERS

Voters do not register by party.

POPULATION

2002 population (est.)	5,797,289
2000 population	5,689,283
1990 population	4,877,185
Percent change (1990-2000)	+16.7%
Rank among states (2002)	16
Median age	35.9
Born in state	64.7%
Foreign born	2.8%
Violent crime rate	707/100,000
Poverty level	13.5%
Federal workers	50,140
Military	25,585

REDISTRICTING

Tennessee retained its nine House seats in reapportionment. The state legislature drew a new map, which the governor signed on Jan. 17, 2002.

MISCELLANEOUS

Web: www.state.tn.us
Capital: Nashville

STATE ELECTION OFFICIAL
(615) 741-7956

DEMOCRATIC HEADQUARTERS
(615) 327-9779

REPUBLICAN HEADQUARTERS
(615) 329-9595

District Statistics

	2000 VOTE FOR PRESIDENT															
DIST.	BUSH	GORE	NADER	WHITE	BLACK	ASIAN	HISP	MEDIAN INCOME	WHITE COLLAR	BLUE COLLAR	SERVICE INDUSTRY	OVER 64	UNDER 18	COLLEGE EDUCATION	RURAL	SQ. MILES
1	61%	38%	1%	95%	2%	0%	1%	$31,228	50%	35%	15%	15%	22%	15%	45%	4,093
2	59	39	1	90	6	1	1	$36,796	60	26	14	13	23	23	29	2,427
3	57	41	1	85	11	1	2	$35,434	54	32	14	14	23	19	36	3,411
4	49.3	49	1	93	4	0	2	$31,645	45	42	13	14	24	11	68	10,038
5	41	57	1	68	23	2	4	$40,419	64	22	14	11	23	28	11	894
6	49.19	49.15	1	89	6	1	3	$39,721	53	35	12	11	25	16	47	5,480
7	61	38	1	83	11	1	2	$50,090	64	24	12	10	27	29	39	6,292
8	48	51	1	74	22	0	2	$33,001	48	38	15	13	26	13	53	8,262
9	27	72	1	35	59	2	3	$33,806	60	24	15	11	27	22	0	321
STATE	51	47	1	79	16	1	2	$36,360	56	31	14	12	25	20	36	41,217
U.S.	47.9	48.4	3	69	12	4	13	$41,994	60	25	15	12	26	24	21	3,537,438

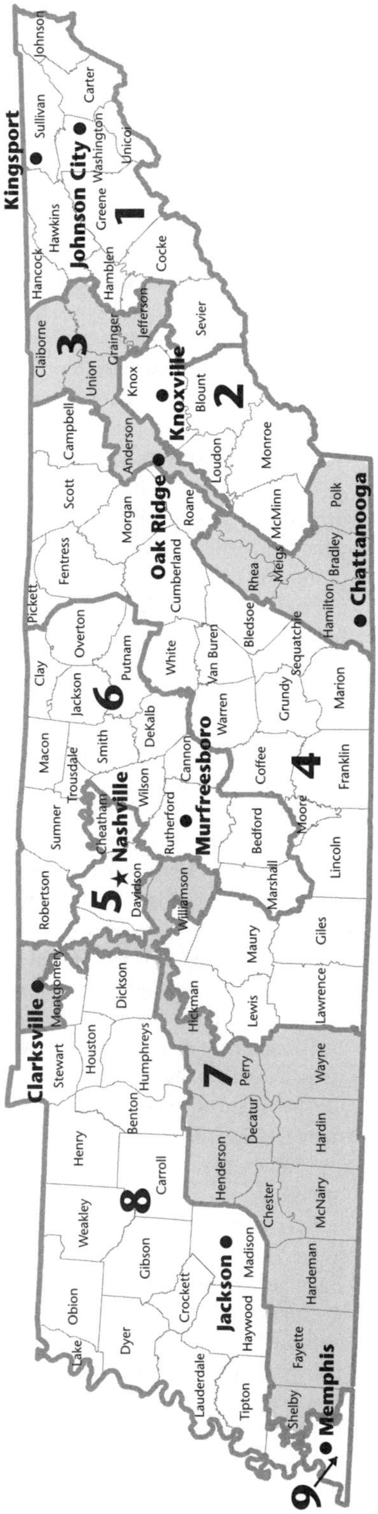
Kingsport
Johnson City
Knoxville
Oak Ridge
Chattanooga
Nashville
Murfreesboro
Clarksville
Jackson
Memphis
1
2
3
4
5
6
7
8
9
Johnson
Carter
Sullivan
Washington
Unicoi
Greene
Hawkins
Hancock
Hamblen
Cocke
Jefferson
Grainger
Claiborne
Union
Sevier
Knox
Blount
Campbell
Anderson
Loudon
Monroe
Scott
Morgan
Roane
Polk
McMinn
Bradley
Meigs
Rhea
Hamilton
Fentress
Cumberland
Pickett
Overton
Clay
Jackson
Putnam
White
Van Buren
Bledsoe
Sequatchie
Marion
Grundy
Warren
DeKalb
Smith
Macon
Trousdale
Wilson
Cannon
Coffee
Franklin
Sumner
Cheatham
Rutherford
Bedford
Moore
Lincoln
Robertson
Davidson
Williamson
Marshall
Maury
Giles
Montgomery
Dickson
Hickman
Lewis
Lawrence
Stewart
Houston
Humphreys
Perry
Wayne
Benton
Decatur
Hardin
Henry
Carroll
Henderson
Chester
McNairy
Weakley
Gibson
Madison
Hardeman
Obion
Crockett
Haywood
Fayette
Lake
Dyer
Lauderdale
Tipton
Shelby

Sen. Bill Frist (R)

CAPITOL OFFICE
224-3344
frist.senate.gov
416 Russell 20510-4205; fax 228-1264

COMMITTEES
Finance
Health, Education, Labor & Pensions
Rules & Administration

HOMETOWN
Nashville

BORN
Feb. 22, 1952, Nashville, Tenn.

RELIGION
Presbyterian

FAMILY
Wife, Karyn Frist; three children

EDUCATION
Princeton U., A.B. 1974; Harvard U., M.D. 1978

CAREER
Surgeon

POLITICAL HIGHLIGHTS
No previous office

ELECTION RESULTS

2000 GENERAL		
Bill Frist (R)	1,255,444	65.1%
Jeff Clark (D)	621,152	32.2%
Tom Burrell (GREEN)	25,815	1.3%
2000 PRIMARY		
Bill Frist (R)		unopposed

PREVIOUS WINNING PERCENTAGES
1994 (56%)

Elected 1994; 2nd term

It is safe to call Frist an overachiever. Already the best weapon Senate Republicans had in health care debates, the transplant-surgeon-turned-politician also spent two years as their chief campaign strategist, a term that ended with his party winning back the Senate in 2002. Brainy, polished and telegenic, Frist quickly became his colleagues' consensus choice to replace Trent Lott as majority leader in December 2002 in the wake of a controversy over off-the-cuff remarks Lott made about segregation.

Frist, who is also an author, a marathon runner and a pilot, has arguably the most difficult and most powerful job on Capitol Hill. That is an unusually large share of influence for a relatively junior lawmaker, but the events leading to his elevation were also unusual.

Before the 108th Congress convened, while lawmakers were still at home, Lott unexpectedly kicked off a firestorm by praising the retiring Sen. Strom Thurmond for his pro-segregation 1948 presidential campaign. During a frenetic several days of telephone calls, GOP senators discussed what to do while the White House waged a behind-the-scenes campaign to dump Lott and replace him with Frist.

Frist was seen as the kind of leader unlikely to make such a mistake. His health care expertise also was a bonus for a party trying to appear more compassionate, and he was an ally of President Bush, whom Frist had known since serving as the Senate liaison to Bush's 2000 presidential campaign.

Despite Lott's efforts to hang on, Frist announced he would challenge him at a special GOP caucus when Congress returned. Republicans hoping to minimize the political fallout from the episode let it be known they backed Frist. His political options gone, Lott stepped down.

In a narrowly divided Senate, Frist's goodwill among Republicans gets him only so far. His physician's self-confidence and equanimity are pluses, though the Senate is a far different management challenge than an operating room. Where one is orderly and subject to a doctor's autocratic rule, the other is inherently undisciplined and tameable only by consensus.

Frist's job is to steer the Bush administration's agenda through a Senate where Republicans hold just 51 seats. He has minimal expertise in the dense and complicated rules of the chamber, which his opponent, Minority Leader Tom Daschle, knows well. Frist is nothing if not a quick study, and he will need to be. In an early test in the 108th Congress, Daschle outmaneuvered him in a showdown over Bush's nomination of Miguel Estrada to the federal appeals bench. Estrada was rejected in a series of Senate votes.

Even as majority leader, Republicans still play up Frist's credential as "the Senate's only doctor," and he doesn't shy from the role. He joined the Finance Committee at the beginning of the 108th, a position that gives him a strong hand in developing the GOP tax cut and a Medicare overhaul. He also loaded the Senate agenda with health care priorities, including an initiative to fight AIDS in Africa and the Caribbean and limits on medical malpractice awards. Early in the 108th, he led the Senate to passage of a ban on a procedure its opponents call "partial birth" abortion.

Over the long term, being majority leader could give Frist more visibility for a race he has not ruled out: a run for the presidency in 2008. He has said he plans to remain in the Senate only through 2006.

For all of his expertise, Frist rarely deviates from the GOP line on health care issues. Instead, he delivers more-detailed and sophisticated versions of the same arguments. He has been an outspoken opponent of letting patients sue their managed-care plans for unrestricted damages, a party-line position. Early in the 107th, he was viewed as potentially able to broker a deal, but his alternative bill got only 36 votes.

Frist got better reviews for his reassuring briefings during the anthrax scare of 2001, when anonymous letters laced with the deadly spores were sent to lawmakers. During the crisis, Frist held daily news briefings with Department of Health and Human Services officials and the Capitol physician. He regularly posted updates of the latest developments on his Senate Web site, advice from medical authorities, and the best precautions for people who suspected they had been exposed. Some Senate critics said Frist tended to overplay his medical expertise, which is in cardiology, by advising workers not to take an anthrax vaccine the government had made available because of the potential side effects.

Afterward, Frist was a key player in enacting a law designed to improve defenses against bioterrorism. In 2002, he published a book on the subject, "When Every Moment Counts: What You Need to Know About Bioterrorism from the Senate's Only Doctor." He donated the profits to the Tennessee Public Health Association to train bioterrorism responders.

Frist has put his medical skills to practical use on numerous occasions. After a gun battle in 1998 left two Capitol Police officers dead, Frist rushed to the scene and helped save the life of the assailant, Russell Eugene Weston Jr. He tended to Thurmond when the South Carolina senator, then 98, collapsed on the Senate floor in 2001. And in 1995, he gave constituent service new meaning by administering cardio-pulmonary resuscitation to a heart attack victim from Tennessee.

Frist served two years as chairman of the National Republican Senatorial Committee — Senate Republicans' campaign arm — and is credited with helping engineer the net two-seat gain that put the chamber back in GOP hands. He ran the committee in a more open manner than his predecessor, Kentucky's Mitch McConnell, now Frist's second-in-command as the majority whip, by allowing other Republican leaders to participate in decisions. When he was elected leader, Frist jumped over higher-ranking peers, including Don Nickles of Oklahoma, who was assistant leader under Lott, and Rick Santorum of Pennsylvania, who was chairman of the Senate Republican Conference.

Some Democrats have suggested Frist stay out of health care policy deliberations because his father founded the hospital chain formerly known as Columbia HCA Corp., now called HCA. Frist has put his stock holdings in a blind trust and argues that such a recusal would be a waste of his knowledge and experience.

Before entering politics, Frist founded and ran Vanderbilt University's transplant center and performed the first successful heart-lung transplant in the South. An interest in public policy, which he studied in college, and public service, which he practiced as a physician, enticed him to seek public office though he had never even registered to vote until he was 36 years old. While a Princeton undergraduate, Frist in 1972 interned for Rep. Joe Evins. When Frist told the Tennessee Democrat that he might want to be in Congress someday, Evins urged Frist to go do something else for about 20 years before going to Washington. Frist took his advice and went into medicine.

Then in 1994, he spent $9.5 million, most of it from his own pocket, to defeat three-term Democrat Jim Sasser. Frist won by 14 percentage points by portraying himself as a political outsider. Sasser could not overcome an image as the sort of Democratic career politician that voters turned against that year. In 2000, Frist was handily re-elected.

KEY VOTES

2002

No Pass farm bill reversing crop subsidy limits
Yes Postpone tougher automobile fuel efficiency standards
No Overhaul campaign finance law; ban "soft money" and restrict advocacy advertising
Yes Set federal election standards
Yes Support oil drilling in Arctic National Wildlife Refuge
Yes Revive fast-track procedures for trade agreements
Yes Create federal insurance coverage for catastrophic terrorist losses
Yes Tighten federal accounting and corporate governance regulation
No Advance bipartisan Medicare prescription drug plan
Yes Create independent Sept. 11 commission
No Back Democratic Homeland Security Department proposal
Yes Authorize war against Iraq

2001

Yes Confirm John Ashcroft as attorney general
Yes Nullify Clinton Labor Department ergonomics rule
Yes Cut taxes by $1.35 trillion through fiscal 2011
No Pass Democratic bill to bolster rights of patients in managed-care plans
Yes Permit a new round of military base closings
Yes Expand law enforcement power to investigate suspected terrorists

CQ VOTE STUDIES

	PARTY UNITY		PRESIDENTIAL SUPPORT	
	Support	Oppose	Support	Oppose
2002	97%	3%	100%	0%
2001	97%	3%	99%	1%
2000	95%	5%	50%	50%
1999	96%	4%	33%	67%
1998	94%	6%	45%	55%
1997	89%	11%	59%	41%
1996	96%	4%	40%	60%
1995	96%	4%	25%	75%

INTEREST GROUPS

	AFL-CIO	ADA	CCUS	ACU
2002	15%	0%	100%	100%
2001	13%	10%	100%	100%
2000	0%	0%	86%	92%
1999	0%	0%	100%	92%
1998	0%	5%	94%	80%
1997	0%	10%	100%	72%
1996	0%	0%	100%	95%
1995	0%	0%	100%	83%

Sen. Lamar Alexander (R)

Elected 2002; 1st term

CAPITOL OFFICE
224-4944
alexander.senate.gov
302 Hart 20510-4204; fax 228-3398

COMMITTEES
Energy & Natural Resources
(Energy - chairman)
Foreign Relations
(African Affairs - chairman)
Health, Education, Labor & Pensions
(Children & Families - chairman)
Joint Economic

HOMETOWN
Nashville

BORN
July 3, 1940, Maryville, Tenn.

RELIGION
Presbyterian

FAMILY
Wife, Honey Alexander; four children

EDUCATION
Vanderbilt U., B.A. 1962 (Latin American history); New York U., J.D. 1965

CAREER
Education consulting firm chairman; lobbyist; university president; White House aide; lawyer

POLITICAL HIGHLIGHTS
Republican nominee for Tenn. governor, 1974; governor, 1979-87; U.S. Education secretary, 1991-93; sought Republican nomination for president, 1996, 2000

ELECTION RESULTS

2002 GENERAL		
Lamar Alexander (R)	891,420	54.3%
Bob Clement (D)	728,295	44.3%
2002 PRIMARY		
Lamar Alexander (R)	295,052	53.8%
Ed Bryant (R)	233,678	42.6%
Mary Taylor Shelby (R)	5,589	1.0%

Even among the Senate's savvy freshman Class of 2002, Alexander stands out for his unusual depth of experience and knowledge of Washington — particularly when it comes to education policy, which has dominated his public career.

Before winning the seat that was vacated by fellow Republican Fred Thompson, Alexander had made improving education a top objective during two terms as governor that spanned most of the 1980s. He went on to serve as president of the University of Tennessee, and then he was secretary of education in the final two years of President George Bush's administration. After leaving Washington he sought the Republican presidential nomination in 1996 and again in 2000.

Upon his arrival in the Senate, however, Alexander sought to play down any expectations that he might push for an early spot in the limelight. He declared himself "perfectly willing to help others take the lead, or to be part of a team, or to simply cast my vote." And, he added, "When you have a lot of experience . . . you don't need to be on center stage just to be there."

But given his background and experience, Alexander is positioned to wield considerable influence over education and other domestic issues. He also is a neighbor and personal friend of Majority Leader Bill Frist. The two live five blocks apart in Nashville and belong to the same church.

When committee assignments were handed out, shortly after Frist's sudden ascension to power in January 2003, Alexander did well. It is unusual for two senators from the same state and the same party to serve on the same committee, but Alexander received special permission to join Frist on the Health, Education, Labor and Pensions Committee, his first choice. He was then named chairman of the Subcommittee on Children and Families.

He also took a seat on the Energy and Natural Resources Committee and chairmanship of its Energy Subcommittee, which will allow him to play a role in energy regulation and other matters important to the Tennessee Valley Authority, a power wholesaler, and Tennessee's Oak Ridge National Laboratory. Alexander says one of his priorities is encouraging clean energy technology. He will work to see that Oak Ridge gets the resources to play a central part in such research.

The Energy Committee also has jurisdiction over national parks, including the Great Smoky Mountains National Park, much of which is in eastern Tennessee. Alexander supports oil drilling in the Arctic National Wildlife Refuge, which he says is necessary to reduce the nation's dependence on Middle Eastern crude. Alexander would like to bolster conservation by dedicating some revenue from drilling to the state grant program of the land and water conservation fund.

With smog a major concern in the Smoky Mountains and the Tennessee River valley, Alexander supports the concept of President Bush's "clear skies" clean air proposal and has said the TVA should take the lead in working with other businesses to cut down on pollution in the region.

Having nurtured an interest in international affairs since his time as governor, when he traveled often to Japan, Alexander asked for and received a Foreign Relations Committee seat. But he says his primary focus will be domestic issues, including health care as well as education.

Alexander always has been viewed with suspicion by some conservatives. But his current education proposals would fit comfortably within the GOP mainstream. He is trying to revive a proposal from his days in the

Cabinet called the "GI Bill for Kids," a school voucher proposal that would give $250 "scholarships" to middle-income and low-income children to help them pay for attendance at any accredited school, including private schools. "This is not like the usual state voucher which takes money from public to private schools," he says. "These are new federal dollars for the schools that help children that need help the most."

In addition, Alexander says he will work to promote charter schools, which are freed from most state and local regulations in exchange for producing better academic performance than other schools.

During his campaign, Alexander pledged to back President Bush "99 percent of the time." To that end he supports an indefinite extension of the tax cuts enacted in 2001, which are all set to expire after 2010. He also says he will continue Thompson's effort to get Congress to adopt a two-year budget, which in his view would allow "less time for wasteful pork barrel spending" and more time for contemplative congressional policymaking.

Like some other Republicans, however, Alexander has shied away from Bush's proposal to allow individuals to invest some of their Social Security money in private savings accounts. He says he could support a pilot program if current benefits are not reduced.

A seventh-generation Tennesseean, Alexander was born and reared in the state's mountainous east. He worked his way through Vanderbilt University where, as a student newspaper editor, he led a campaign to desegregate the school. After graduating with a degree in Latin American history, he earned a law degree at New York University.

At age 34, his first run for office was an unsuccessful 1974 bid for governor against Democrat Roy Blanton. Four years later, with the help and advice of his mentor and friend, Senate Republican Leader Howard H. Baker Jr. of Tennessee, Alexander ran again. This time, he gained national attention by traversing the state on foot — he is a lifelong hiker — in what would become his trademark red-and-black plaid shirt. The voters loved it, electing him with 56 percent over financier Jake Butcher, whom the Democrats nominated when the scandal-scarred Blanton stepped aside.

During his eight years in the governor's mansion, Alexander built a reputation as a pragmatist who lured businesses to Tennessee and pushed a major education package — including a 1-cent sales tax increase — through a Democratic-controlled General Assembly. After a brief break, he spent more than three years as the chief executive of Tennessee's state university system. He joined the Cabinet in 1991 after Bush's first Education secretary, Lauro F. Cavazos, was dismissed as ineffectual.

Alexander started running for president soon after his Cabinet service ended. But his campaign foundered when — fundraising zeal and plaid shirt aside — he had a hard time coming up with memorable campaign themes. He won only slightly more than 3 percent of the total GOP primary vote in 1996, though he dropped out soon after finishing third behind Bob Dole and Patrick J. Buchanan in the New Hampshire primary. He set his sights on the 2000 nomination but stopped campaigning in the summer of 1999, by which point George W. Bush had already become the clear front-runner.

Two years later, when Thompson announced he was retiring after eight years in the Senate, Republicans immediately looked to Alexander to take his place, viewing him as their best chance for maintaining their current political pre-eminence in the state. The Democrats nominated Bob Clement, who had been Nashville's congressman since 1988. With both national parties pumping money into the race, it turned ugly; the candidates dredged up decades-old allegations about each other's business dealings and political history. But Alexander won by 10 percentage points.

Rep. Bill Jenkins (R)

CAPITOL OFFICE
225-6356
www.house.gov/jenkins
1207 Longworth 20515-4201; fax 225-5714

COMMITTEES
Agriculture
(Specialty Crops & Foreign Agriculture - chairman)
Judiciary

HOMETOWN
Rogersville

BORN
Nov. 29, 1936, Detroit, Mich.

RELIGION
Baptist

FAMILY
Wife, Kathryn Jenkins; four children

EDUCATION
Tennessee Technological U., B.B.A. 1958;
U. of Tennessee, J.D. 1961

MILITARY SERVICE
Army, 1959-60; Army Reserve, 1960-69

CAREER
Lawyer; farmer; state conservation department commissioner

POLITICAL HIGHLIGHTS
Tenn. House, 1963-71 (Speaker, 1969-71); sought Republican nomination for governor, 1970; Tennessee Valley Authority Board of Directors, 1971-1978; circuit court judge, 1990-96

ELECTION RESULTS

2002 GENERAL		
Bill Jenkins (R)	127,300	98.8%
write-ins	1,586	1.2%
2002 PRIMARY		
Bill Jenkins (R)	65,421	88.2%
Larry P. Edgell (R)	8,740	11.8%
2000 GENERAL		
Bill Jenkins (R)		unopposed

PREVIOUS WINNING PERCENTAGES
1998 (69%); 1996 (65%)

Elected 1996; 4th term

Jenkins comes off as reticent as a Smoky Mountain bear. He rarely speaks on the House floor, issues few news releases and refrains from sending his constituents taxpayer-funded newsletters. While many lawmakers believe they must deliver clever sound bites for the evening news or the C-SPAN audience, Jenkins does none of that. A veteran of four decades in politics, he presents himself as an old-style Southern politician — polite and unassuming, and concerned much more about the opinion of voters back home than the national intelligentsia.

The low-key manner seems to sit just fine with his constituents. The key moment in Jenkins' path to Congress was when he won the 1996 Republican nomination — with just 18 percent of the vote in an 11-candidate primary field. But in 2000 and 2002, Democrats did not even field a challenger. In the 1st District's solidly Republican counties, which have not sent a Democrat to Congress in more than a century, Jenkins has little need for self-promotion as long as he pays attention to the folks back home. So he is careful to attend to the high-quality constituent service operation inherited from his predecessor, Republican James H. Quillen, who held the seat for 34 years.

While Jenkins has not yet netted the volume of federal aid for the district that Quillen did — a veterans hospital, a courthouse and a highway in the district are named for Quillen — Jenkins says that he is doing his best to meet the needs of his constituents.

A farmer, Jenkins is a reliable vote for liberalized trade, arguing that it would lead to additional farm exports, and he uses his posts on the Agriculture and Judiciary committees to stand vigilant against legislation that would harm the small tobacco farms in his district. In the 108th Congress, he has added clout on Agriculture, having assumed the chairmanship of the Specialty Crops Subcommittee, with jurisdiction over tobacco programs.

He is watchful that any move to deregulate the electricity industry does not harm customers of the Tennessee Valley Authority's power grid. And he casts a fiscally frugal vote, with the exception of backing increased defense spending.

At Agriculture and Judiciary panel meetings, Jenkins typically sits and listens, even though on the campaign trail he promises to bring a "fresh dose of Appalachian straight talk" to the Capitol. When asked about his legislative accomplishments, he refers reporters to his chief of staff. He claims authorship of two laws — naming the courthouse after Quillen and authorizing the Interior Department to issue rights-of-way for natural gas pipelines in Great Smoky Mountains National Park — and issued only about 10 news releases in the 107th. A top priority was to ensure that government loan programs for small businesses and farmers were fully funded.

His main goal on arriving in Washington was to see Congress balance the federal budget, and he explained his vote for the 2001 tax cut by saying the Treasury was generating too much revenue that would have tempted too much spending. He annually returns to the Treasury several thousand dollars of his office overhead allowance. Like other members of the state delegation, he receives season tickets to University of Tennessee football games, but he insists on paying for his.

However, as he told the Knoxville News-Sentinel in 1996, "There are things that every congressional district is entitled to. . . . Water projects, sewer projects, highway projects that will be needed. I certainly think it is legitimate to try to obtain those."

Protecting the 1st District's farmers requires Jenkins to walk a fine line philosophically when it comes to the role of government. He contends that farmers face "difficult and expensive" federal regulatory burdens. But when it stands to benefit his constituents, Jenkins argues in favor of continued federal involvement. One example is his opposition to anti-tobacco forces who sought to end the federal crop insurance subsidy to tobacco growers — a program that benefits many small-scale farming operations in the 1st. Jenkins says that many farmers have no economically feasible alternative to growing tobacco.

Four decades ago, Jenkins was a boy wonder in Tennessee politics. Out of law school just one year, he won election to the state House in 1962. Before the decade was out, with the House split 49-49 and at odds over whom to elect as speaker, Jenkins persuaded an African-American Democrat to switch sides and vote for him in the leadership race and, at 32, Jenkins was elected to the top spot — the only Republican to be elected to that post in the 20th century.

His tenure in the job was brief. In 1970, he tried for the Republican gubernatorial nomination but ran third in the primary. The man who defeated him in that race and went on to become governor, Winfield Dunn, named Jenkins to head the state Department of Conservation, and President Nixon appointed him in 1971 to the three-member Tennessee Valley Authority board, where he served until 1978.

For the next dozen years, Jenkins focused on the law and his beef cattle and burley tobacco farm in Rogersville. But he stayed involved in GOP circles and in 1990 got back into public life, entering the judicial arena with an appointment as a circuit court judge.

In 1996, Quillen's retirement after 17 terms unleashed a lot of pent-up political ambition in northeastern Tennessee. Jenkins touted his status as the only farmer among the leading candidates in the huge Republican field, and he claimed to be the only "dyed-in-the-wool, card-carrying bona fide hillbilly" in the race. Thanks to his many years of political involvement, Jenkins proved to have friends spread across the district. He bested conservative state Sen. Jim Holcomb by a narrow 331 votes for the nomination.

In November, Jenkins won the general-election contest with 65 percent and has been politically safe since. In the overwhelmingly Republican 1st, Jenkins did not encounter a challenger in 2000 or 2002.

KEY VOTES

2002

No Overhaul campaign finance law; ban "soft money" and restrict advocacy advertising
Yes Back Bush's defense budget increase
Yes Extend 1996 welfare law
Yes Adopt Bush's discretionary spending limit
Yes Pass GOP Medicare prescription drug plan
No Create independent Sept. 11 commission
No Extend union protections to Homeland Security Department employees
Yes Revive fast-track procedures for trade agreements
Yes Authorize war against Iraq
Yes Advance bankruptcy overhaul opposed by abortion opponents

2001

Yes Nullify Clinton Labor Department ergonomics rule
Yes Cut taxes by $1.35 trillion through fiscal 2011
No Maintain ban on oil drilling in Arctic National Wildlife Refuge
Yes Approve Bush proposal to limit managed-care plan liability for coverage decisions
No Divert money from crop subsidy payments to land conservation
Yes Expand law enforcement power to investigate suspected terrorists

CQ VOTE STUDIES

	PARTY UNITY		PRESIDENTIAL SUPPORT	
	Support	Oppose	Support	Oppose
2002	97%	3%	86%	14%
2001	96%	4%	91%	9%
2000	94%	6%	22%	78%
1999	91%	9%	16%	84%
1998	95%	5%	20%	80%

INTEREST GROUPS

	AFL-CIO	ADA	CCUS	ACU
2002	0%	0%	95%	100%
2001	8%	5%	87%	96%
2000	0%	0%	80%	91%
1999	33%	15%	84%	87%
1998	10%	5%	89%	100%

TENNESSEE 1

Northeast – Tri-Cities, Morristown

Rolling hills and mountains cover the 1st, which borders Virginia and North Carolina. Thanks to Tennessee Valley Authority power, what were once isolated highland towns and tobacco patches are now scattered small cities with moderate economic growth.

Kingsport, Johnson City and Bristol, known collectively as the Tri-Cities, center their industry on plastics, chemicals and drug manufacturing. East Tennessee State University, a major employer in Johnson City, is a regional medical hub for much of the lower Appalachian region. The Tri-Cities have grown to become the area's economic anchor, while rural areas have lost clout.

Campers, hikers and other visitors seeking the serenity of Great Smoky Mountains National Park must pass through an area jam-packed with large hotels, outlet shopping malls and neon amusement parks. Pigeon Forge and Gatlinburg bring in millions of dollars each year through a booming tourist industry.

In the district's northwest, Hancock and Hawkins counties are severely impoverished. Farmers here raise tobacco, poultry and livestock. There also is zinc and limestone mining, though the coal mining industry's long-ago shutdown has left the area poor.

Like the rest of East Tennessee, the 1st has an overwhelming GOP lean, having sent a Republican to the House for more than a century (since the 1880 election). The rural areas almost always elect Republican state representatives, and the urban areas only sporadically send a Democrat to Nashville. However, mayoral and other local elections are usually nonpartisan.

MAJOR INDUSTRY
Manufacturing, tourism

CITIES
Johnson City, 55,469; Kingsport, 44,905; Morristown, 24,965; Bristol, 24,821

NOTABLE
Dollywood, in Pigeon Forge, is country music star Dolly Parton's theme park; Jonesborough is the state's oldest settlement and is home to the National Storytelling Festival; The Star Cars Museum in Gatlinburg has famous cars from movies; Bristol Motor Speedway, which seats 160,000, has become a major attraction, paralleling the rise of NASCAR.

Rep. John J. 'Jimmy' Duncan Jr. (R)

CAPITOL OFFICE
225-5435
www.house.gov/duncan
2267 Rayburn 20515-4202; fax 225-6440

COMMITTEES
Government Reform
Resources
Transportation & Infrastructure
(Water Resources & Environment - chairman)

HOMETOWN
Knoxville

BORN
July 21, 1947, Lebanon, Tenn.

RELIGION
Presbyterian

FAMILY
Wife, Lynn Duncan; four children

EDUCATION
U. of Tennessee, B.S. 1969 (journalism); George Washington U., J.D. 1973

MILITARY SERVICE
Tenn. National Guard and Army Reserve, 1970-87

CAREER
Judge; lawyer

POLITICAL HIGHLIGHTS
Knox County Criminal Court judge, 1981-88

ELECTION RESULTS

2002 GENERAL		
John J. Duncan Jr. (R)	146,887	79.0%
John Greene (D)	37,035	19.9%
2002 PRIMARY		
John J. Duncan Jr. (R)	67,582	91.7%
Jim Pendergrass (R)	6,095	8.3%
2000 GENERAL		
John J. Duncan Jr. (R)	187,154	89.3%
Kevin J. Rowland (LIBERT)	22,304	10.7%

PREVIOUS WINNING PERCENTAGES
1998 (89%); 1996 (71%); 1994 (90%); 1992 (72%); 1990 (81%); 1988 (56%); 1988 Special Election (56%)

Elected 1988; 8th full term

Although his tenure as chairman of the Transportation and Infrastructure panel's Subcommittee on Aviation ended at the start of the 107th Congress, Duncan was influential in the writing of the aviation security law enacted two months after the Sept. 11, 2001, terrorist attacks.

House GOP rules that limit chairmanships to six years forced Duncan in 2001 to give up the gavel of the subcommittee, where he had become a major player on aviation issues. But far from starting over, Duncan has been able to retain much of his clout on aviation matters while at the same time carving out another area of influence as the chairman of the Transportation panel's Water Resources and Environment Subcommittee, which has jurisdiction over development of dams, ports, water quality and the Tennessee Valley Authority.

Many of the aviation security measure's provisions — including those calling for tighter screening requirements for airports, better equipment to detect explosives, and stronger cockpit doors — had been studied by the subcommittee under Duncan's chairmanship. During debate on the security bill, Duncan sought higher pay for airport screening personnel — at least twice the minimum wage — and a requirement that all screeners be U.S. citizens with no criminal record.

After Congress produced another post-Sept. 11 aviation law, to shore up the financial stability of the airlines, Duncan pleaded with Transportation Secretary Norman Y. Mineta to support resumption of some flights to small- and medium-size cities, such as his hometown of Knoxville. Providing ample air service to all communities long has been a priority for Duncan.

The Transportation Committee as a whole operates in a bipartisan manner, and Duncan has been known to preside over his subcommittees with the fair-handed demeanor of a judge, which he once was.

He is conservative on both fiscal policy and social issues, and he usually votes with the majority of his party. He retains a high regard for the House as an institution, a reflection of the fact that his father, John J. Duncan, held the seat before him. He says he seeks to emulate his father, who made himself a popular congressman for more than 23 years by tending to local concerns and eschewing the national spotlight.

Duncan is serious about cutting federal spending. He says the first thing he asks his staff when they discuss a proposal is, "How much does it cost?" He voted against six of the 13 regular spending bills in 2001, for example, saying that lawmakers were unable to restrain themselves. In the 105th Congress, he voted to abolish crop insurance subsidies for tobacco, even though it is the largest cash crop grown by his constituents.

In the 108th Congress, Duncan hoped to ascend to the chairmanship of the Resources Committee, made vacant by the retirement of James V. Hansen of Utah. But GOP leaders bypassed Duncan and several other more-senior lawmakers to choose Californian Richard Pombo, a conservative who has been more loyal to the leadership and President Bush.

In the 107th, Duncan opposed Bush more than 30 percent of the time, sixth-most among House Republicans, including a "no" vote on authorizing the president to use force against Iraq. Duncan said it was his hardest vote in his 14 years in the House, but he was not convinced of the threat from Iraq.

And although Duncan voted for the North American Free Trade Agreement in 1993, he says he has become increasingly concerned about domestic job losses to overseas manufacturers. He was one of only 27 Republicans who voted against enacting the 2002 law giving the president fast-track authority to negotiate trade agreements that Congress cannot amend. Citing the loss of 900 jobs at a Levi's facility in his district, Duncan told the Knoxville News-Sentinel, "I am sick and tired of seeing all these American jobs go to other countries."

From his seat on the Resources panel, Duncan contends that out-of-control preservationists "will absolutely destroy our standard of living. Unfortunately, we cannot turn our entire nation into a giant tourist attraction."

But he pays close attention to the wilderness in his own backyard — Great Smoky Mountains National Park, the most-visited of the national parks. In the 106th, he offered legislation to allow taxpayers to donate one or more dollars from their annual taxes to benefit the parks.

Having followed his father into politics, Duncan occasionally wonders what his life would have been like if the senior Duncan had chosen another career. His father was part of a group that brought minor league baseball to Knoxville in 1956; young Duncan spent five-and-a-half seasons as the Smokies batboy and was the public address announcer during his first year in college. "I wanted to play baseball, but when I realized I wasn't good enough to make it as a player, I wanted to go into baseball full time," he told the Knoxville newspaper. He said he believes he would have followed his father into sports management, but John Duncan turned down a chance to be president of the South Atlantic League. Instead, his father ran for mayor, leading to a long career in politics.

John Duncan was mayor of Knoxville from 1959 to 1964, when he was elected to the first of his dozen terms in Congress. The younger Duncan, whose uncle was a judge, took the courtroom route into politics. He served seven years as a criminal court judge in Knox County. The years on the bench helped him build enough of a reputation to be a strong candidate in his own right when his father, in failing health, announced that the 100th Congress would be his last. (He died in 1998, shortly after that announcement.)

In his first House campaign, Duncan campaigned primarily as his father's son. Although he is generally known as "Jimmy," he appeared on the ballot as John J. Duncan. He won 56 percent of the vote in both the special and general elections that year and has not been seriously challenged since. A 2001 appearance on the stage at Nashville's Grand Ole Opry apparently did nothing to make him rethink his choice of careers. Duncan, wearing borrowed Western clothes, joined four other House members as backup singers at a nationally broadcast performance. "I don't sing well, but I sing enthusiastically," he said afterward.

KEY VOTES

2002

No Overhaul campaign finance law; ban "soft money" and restrict advocacy advertising
Yes Back Bush's defense budget increase
Yes Extend 1996 welfare law
Yes Adopt Bush's discretionary spending limit
Yes Pass GOP Medicare prescription drug plan
Yes Create independent Sept. 11 commission
No Extend union protections to Homeland Security Department employees
No Revive fast-track procedures for trade agreements
No Authorize war against Iraq
Yes Advance bankruptcy overhaul opposed by abortion opponents

2001

Yes Nullify Clinton Labor Department ergonomics rule
Yes Cut taxes by $1.35 trillion through fiscal 2011
No Maintain ban on oil drilling in Arctic National Wildlife Refuge
Yes Approve Bush proposal to limit managed-care plan liability for coverage decisions
No Divert money from crop subsidy payments to land conservation
Yes Expand law enforcement power to investigate suspected terrorists

CQ VOTE STUDIES

	PARTY UNITY		PRESIDENTIAL SUPPORT	
	Support	Oppose	Support	Oppose
2002	91%	9%	62%	38%
2001	91%	9%	76%	24%
2000	89%	11%	12%	88%
1999	85%	15%	16%	84%
1998	88%	12%	22%	78%

INTEREST GROUPS

	AFL-CIO	ADA	CCUS	ACU
2002	11%	5%	75%	92%
2001	25%	10%	70%	92%
2000	10%	15%	71%	84%
1999	44%	25%	56%	92%
1998	10%	15%	78%	84%

TENNESSEE 2
East – Knoxville

Nestled in the valley of the Great Smoky Mountains at the mouth of the Tennessee River, the 2nd envelopes Knoxville and stretches south and west to include several conservative, rural counties.

State and federal jobs in the district are abundant for residents despite their criticisms of big government year after year. The Tennessee Valley Authority is headquartered in Knoxville, and the Pellissippi Parkway enables commuters to quickly travel west of Knoxville to the Oak Ridge National Laboratory, in the 3rd District.

Knoxvillians will tell you their pride and joy is University of Tennessee athletics. Restaurants, hotels and other businesses thrive on the fans who flock to the university's gargantuan football stadium and basketball arenas each year.

Nonetheless, Knoxville has struggled to revitalize its downtown since playing host to the World's Fair in 1982, after which businesses and hotels began to depart. The Women's Basketball Hall of Fame that opened in 1999 has helped, as have medical facilities that take up the slack from shuttered hospitals outside the city. The rural areas have attracted tourists, while Knoxville itself opened a new convention center in 2002.

Like all of East Tennessee, the mountainous 2nd has a long history of voting Republican. The GOP is entrenched in the district, which has not sent a Democrat to Congress since before the Civil War. In fact, rarely does the Republican incumbent sweat an election. Republicans who are somewhat more moderate mingle freely with a new strain of conservative activist here.

MAJOR INDUSTRY
Higher education, medical services, tourism

CITIES
Knoxville, 173,890; Maryville, 23,120; Farragut, 17,720; Athens, 13,220

NOTABLE
On home football game days, the University of Tennessee's Neyland Stadium becomes the state's fifth-largest city, with more than 104,000 in attendance; A statue in Haley Heritage Square honors "Roots" author Alex Haley, who made his home in Knoxville.

Rep. Zach Wamp (R)

CAPITOL OFFICE
225-3271
www.house.gov/wamp
2447 Rayburn 20515-4203; fax 225-3494

COMMITTEES
Appropriations

HOMETOWN
Chattanooga

BORN
Oct. 28, 1957, Fort Benning, Ga.

RELIGION
Baptist

FAMILY
Wife, Kim Wamp; two children

EDUCATION
U. of North Carolina, attended 1977-78; U. of Tennessee, attended 1978-79; U. of North Carolina, attended 1979-80 (political science)

CAREER
Real estate broker

POLITICAL HIGHLIGHTS
Republican nominee for U.S. House, 1992

ELECTION RESULTS

2002 GENERAL		
Zach Wamp (R)	112,254	64.6%
John Wolfe Jr. (D)	58,824	33.9%
2002 PRIMARY		
Zach Wamp (R)		unopposed
2000 GENERAL		
Zach Wamp (R)	139,840	63.9%
Will Callaway (D)	75,785	34.6%
Trudy A. Austin (LIBERT)	3,235	1.5%

PREVIOUS WINNING PERCENTAGES
1998 (66%); 1996 (56%); 1994 (52%)

Elected 1994; 5th term

More than anything else, Wamp views himself as a "spiritual" man. He uses the word frequently to describe both his personal life and his career on Capitol Hill. His deep religious convictions have made him committed to reaching out to and working with all House members regardless of party affiliation, despite his strongly conservative ideology. "I try to balance time between the physical and spiritual life," he says.

Much of Wamp's energy is devoted to the House Prayer Breakfast, an institution in which several dozen members from both parties meet once a week to sing hymns, discuss their family problems and pray. He co-chaired the group during the 106th Congress and is also a former chairman of the annual National Prayer Breakfast. "It's not about religion. It's about relationships," Wamp says of the House group. "It's the sweet spirit. There's a lot of power in the spiritual realm."

On the other end of the scale — the physical life — Wamp, a self-described "gym rat," is the co-founder, along with Colorado's Mark Udall, of the Congressional Fitness Caucus, which aims to encourage their time-strapped colleagues to make time for fitness activities.

Wamp started down his spiritual path in 1984, when he decided to "clean up" his life and seek help for drug and alcohol abuse. After that he immersed himself in community and church activities, drawing inspiration from a comment by the golfer Chi Chi Rodriguez, "Takers eat well, but givers sleep well."

His religious faith also has carried Wamp through rough waters in Congress. Although he tends to be a loyal GOP vote in the House, Wamp angered his leaders and many of his colleagues in 2002 when he joined with Democrats in backing legislation to overhaul campaign finance laws.

"I felt like I was in the midst of a real hot fire," he says in describing the atmosphere when the House ultimately passed the bill. Still, Wamp cites his efforts on campaign finance as one of his proudest accomplishments. "It was a character-building experience," he says. "I was the first conservative out there committed to campaign finance reform. I've got the scars to prove it."

He also cites his work with the bipartisan Energy Efficiency and Renewable Energy Caucus, which he co-chaired in the 107th, as a highlight of his congressional career. Asked if his efforts on campaign finance and renewable energy were signs he was wavering in his conservative leanings, Wamp countered that both are "smart things, good investments" and that "neither party has the exclusive on good ideas."

But Wamp's interests and voting record generally put him in the heart of the conservative mainstream of House Republicans. He voted in 2001 to overturn the workplace safety regulations instituted by the Clinton administration. He is a member of the House Pro-Life Caucus, which works to thwart abortion rights legislation, and he is a reliable vote in favor of tax cuts. He also has repeatedly pushed, unsuccessfully, for legislation requiring the labeling of entertainment products, such as video games, that contain violent scenes. He was named vice chairman of a Bipartisan Working Group on Youth Violence in the 106th Congress. He also worked with North Carolina Democrat Bob Etheridge on a "Character Counts" bill authorizing federal grants to schools for character education programs aimed at helping children "view the world through a moral lens."

Wamp was first elected to Congress in 1994, when Republicans gained control of the House for the first time in 40 years. A signer of the "Contract With America," he campaigned on a pledge to cut spending in order to balance the budget. But in his first term, he fought GOP efforts to cut spending that included abolishing agencies that are an economic lifeblood of his state — the Tennessee Valley Authority and the Appalachian Regional Commission. At the start of his second term, he became the first Republican from Tennessee since 1910 to sit on the Appropriations Committee.

Wamp describes himself as one of the more fiscally conservative members of Appropriations. But he also says he recognizes that his service on the panel requires compromise to advance the annual spending bills. He and others who once styled themselves GOP "revolutionaries" are "not so dogmatic anymore. Most of us are more pragmatic," Wamp said in 1999. "You can't be a strident idealogue on Appropriations."

As evidence of that, Wamp has been willing to accept some cuts in programs such as the TVA and Appalachian Regional Commission, as long as they are accompanied by cuts to other non-rural development programs.

Wamp was brought up in a Democratic family with deep roots in Southern politics. His great-great-great grandfather spent 40 years in the Alabama Legislature, and his great uncle was a leader in the Alabama General Assembly. Both were Democrats. Wamp himself admits voting for Jimmy Carter in 1976. But he came to the Republican fold four years later, concluding that Ronald Reagan offered a "breath of hope and optimism for America" in the depths of the Iran hostage crisis.

He was so taken with Reagan's campaign that he drove with several University of North Carolina fraternity brothers from Chapel Hill to Washington, D.C., on election night to celebrate the Republican's victory.

Wamp won his first election in high school, as student body president. At 26, he became the youth coordinator for a victorious Chattanooga mayoral candidate. Four years later, he chaired his local Republican organization. Community leaders urged him to run for public office, but he demurred, saying he had "been through too many mud puddles in my life." But when his wife joined in, Wamp decided to run.

He came within 3,000 votes of unseating Democratic Rep. Marilyn Lloyd in 1992. He tried again in 1994, when Lloyd retired after 10 terms. Wamp's primary challenger, state Rep. Kenneth J. Meyer, made use of Wamp's admitted past cocaine addiction. Still, Wamp won the primary with 67 percent of the vote and the general election by 6 percentage points over Democratic property assessor Randy Button. His first re-election was with 56 percent, and he has won more than 60 percent in the last three races.

KEY VOTES

2002

Yes Overhaul campaign finance law; ban "soft money" and restrict advocacy advertising
Yes Back Bush's defense budget increase
Yes Extend 1996 welfare law
P Adopt Bush's discretionary spending limit
Yes Pass GOP Medicare prescription drug plan
No Create independent Sept. 11 commission
No Extend union protections to Homeland Security Department employees
Yes Revive fast-track procedures for trade agreements
Yes Authorize war against Iraq
No Advance bankruptcy overhaul opposed by abortion opponents

2001

Yes Nullify Clinton Labor Department ergonomics rule
Yes Cut taxes by $1.35 trillion through fiscal 2011
No Maintain ban on oil drilling in Arctic National Wildlife Refuge
Yes Approve Bush proposal to limit managed-care plan liability for coverage decisions
No Divert money from crop subsidy payments to land conservation
Yes Expand law enforcement power to investigate suspected terrorists

CQ VOTE STUDIES

	PARTY UNITY		PRESIDENTIAL SUPPORT	
	Support	Oppose	Support	Oppose
2002	90%	10%	82%	18%
2001	95%	5%	88%	12%
2000	93%	7%	19%	81%
1999	90%	10%	14%	86%
1998	89%	11%	18%	82%

INTEREST GROUPS

	AFL-CIO	ADA	CCUS	ACU
2002	0%	5%	80%	96%
2001	9%	15%	87%	88%
2000	10%	10%	71%	87%
1999	44%	20%	60%	96%
1998	10%	15%	76%	84%

TENNESSEE 3

East – Chattanooga, Oak Ridge

The skinny 3rd stretches from Georgia to Kentucky and Virginia but is dominated by Hamilton County, home to the district's largest city, Chattanooga. It was altered in redistricting to give it a more East Tennessee — and hence Republican — flavor.

Once mostly industrial, Chattanooga is attempting to attract high-tech jobs with a "Technology Corridor" similar to Research Triangle Park in North Carolina. The plan encourages collaboration among high-tech companies in Knoxville, Chattanooga and Oak Ridge, and an extensive highway system makes such commuting practical. A recently completed highway linking the Knoxville airport to Oak Ridge — home of nuclear laboratories where World War II weapons were created — has boosted growth.

Oak Ridge, once full of scientists and heavily dependent on federal dollars, has diversified as wealth has moved west of Knoxville. Chattanooga has injected life into its downtown through projects such as the Tennessee Aquarium, the world's largest freshwater aquarium, and new downtown apartments, nightlife and museums. Since the aquarium opened in 1992, the city has attracted hundreds of millions of dollars in downtown investments.

The 3rd historically gives its representatives long tenures in Washington. Republican dominance in the 1960s and early 1970s gave way to Watergate-era disillusionment that led to a 10-term run for Democrats. But Republicans won the House seat in 1994 and continue to win re-election by large margins. Middle Tennessee counties were cut out of the district in remapping following the 2000 census to ensure a Republican hold. George W. Bush captured 57 percent of the district's vote in the 2000 presidential election.

MAJOR INDUSTRY
Nuclear research, high-tech research

CITIES
Chattanooga, 155,554; Cleveland, 37,192; Oak Ridge, 27,387

NOTABLE
Popularized by the Glenn Miller song, the Chattanooga Choo-Choo has been restored as a historic landmark; The Scopes "Monkey" Trial in Dayton in 1925 upheld a ruling making it illegal to teach evolution.

Rep. Lincoln Davis (D)

CAPITOL OFFICE
225-6831
www.house.gov/lincolndavis
504 Cannon 20515-4204; fax 226-5172

COMMITTEES
Agriculture
Science
Transportation & Infrastructure

HOMETOWN
Pall Mall

BORN
Sept. 13, 1943, Pall Mall, Tenn.

RELIGION
Baptist

FAMILY
Wife, Lynda Davis; three children

EDUCATION
Tennessee Technological U., B.S. 1966 (agronomy)

CAREER
Farmer; construction company owner; U.S. Agriculture Department official

POLITICAL HIGHLIGHTS
Mayor of Byrdstown, 1979-83; Tenn. House, 1981-85; sought Democratic nomination for U.S. House, 1984, 1994; Tenn. Senate, 1997-2003

ELECTION RESULTS

2002 GENERAL		
Lincoln Davis (D)	95,989	52.1%
Janice H. Bowling (R)	85,680	46.5%
2002 PRIMARY		
Lincoln Davis (D)	48,843	57.0%
Fran F. Marcum (D)	36,779	42.9%

Elected 2002; 1st term

One of the most socially conservative Democrats elected to Congress in 2002, Davis became familiar on the campaign trail for proclaiming that no candidate would "outgun me, outpray me or outdaddy me."

Davis is a Bible-quoting Baptist, and a highlight of his six years in the state Senate was his sponsorship of the Tennessee law that bans a procedure opponents call "partial birth" abortion. He was endorsed by the National Rifle Association, which mainly backs Republicans — yet another reason he was able to capture a seat for the Democrats that had been in the Republican column for eight years.

Representing a mostly poor and rural slice of central Tennessee, Davis says the nation would be worse off without federal economic development programs such as the Tennessee Valley Authority, and he has promised to keep at least one previously unemployed person on his staff. Davis says he would have opposed recent trade liberalization laws, which he says have sent jobs overseas, and the 2001 tax cut, which he views as helping the rich while hobbling the budget. He has affiliated with the "Blue Dog" coalition of the most conservative House Democrats.

A farmer whose first government jobs were as a soil tester and land assessor for the Agriculture Department, Davis was assigned to the Agriculture Committee. He also got the seat he wanted on Transportation and Infrastructure. And he was named to the Science Committee, where he will look out for the Arnold Engineering Development Center, a federal aircraft testing facility in Tullahoma.

Davis was elected on his third try; he lost Democratic primaries for open House seats in 1984 and 1994. With Republican Van Hilleary leaving the House after four terms to run for governor, Davis worked with the General Assembly in redistricting to increase Democratic strength in the 4th District. He won the primary with 57 percent of the vote against a well-funded opponent running to his left, Fran Marcum. In the fall he won by 6 percentage points against Republican Janice H. Bowling, a former top aide to Hilleary.

TENNESSEE 4

Middle Tennessee — northeast and south

Predominantly rural and poor, the 4th touches Alabama, Georgia and Kentucky and grabs suburbs southwest of Nashville as well as those west of Oak Ridge and Chattanooga. The conservative-leaning district is a melting pot of Tennessee's three regions, as plains turn east into rolling hills that merge with the Cumberland Plateau and eventually the Appalachian Mountains.

The sparsely populated district includes tobacco farms, many of them small, a Saturn plant that employs 7,800 in Spring Hill, and light manufacturing in the south.

The north is equally bereft of economic development. Campbell County in the district's northeast corner has high unemployment and sometimes halts school bus service for lack of funds. Campbell favored Al Gore in the 2000 presidential election, despite sending Republicans to the state legislature. Economic struggles in isolated rural areas such as Morgan and Grundy counties leave water and electricity service unreliable.

Opposition to gun control and abortion, along with a strong religious sentiment, typifies the socially conservative constituency. With the exception of Republican Williamson County (shared with the 7th), the district's conservatives often are Democrats. Gore carried the district narrowly in 2000.

MAJOR INDUSTRY
Agriculture, auto parts, manufacturing

MILITARY BASES
Arnold Air Force Base, 102 military, 254 civilian, 2,470 contractors (2001)

CITIES
Columbia, 33,055; Tullahoma, 17,994

NOTABLE
Jack Daniel's sour mash whiskey distillery in Lynchburg is located in a dry county (Moore); President James K. Polk's home is in Columbia; Mule Day in Columbia attracts 250,000 every April.

Rep. Jim Cooper (D)

CAPITOL OFFICE
225-4311
jim.cooper@mail.house.gov
www.house.gov/cooper
1536 Longworth 20515-4205; fax 226-1035

COMMITTEES
Armed Services
Budget
Government Reform

HOMETOWN
Nashville

BORN
June 19, 1954, Nashville, Tenn.

RELIGION
Episcopalian

FAMILY
Wife, Martha Hayes Cooper; three children

EDUCATION
U. of North Carolina, B.A. 1975 (history & economics); Oxford U., B.A., M.A. 1977 (Rhodes scholar); Harvard U., J.D. 1980

CAREER
Investment firm owner; investment bank managing director; lawyer

POLITICAL HIGHLIGHTS
U.S. House, 1983-95; Democratic nominee for U.S. Senate, 1994

ELECTION RESULTS

2002 GENERAL		
Jim Cooper (D)	108,903	63.7%
Robert Duvall (R)	56,825	33.3%
John Jay Hooker (I)	3,063	1.8%
2002 PRIMARY		
Jim Cooper (D)	32,651	46.7%
John Arriola (D)	16,878	24.2%
Gayle Ray (D)	16,087	23.0%
David Mills (D)	1,657	2.4%
Carlton Cornett (D)	1,096	1.6%
Ronnie Steine (D)	901	1.3%

PREVIOUS WINNING PERCENTAGES
1992 (66.3%); 1990 (69%); 1988 (100%); 1986 (100%); 1984 (75%); 1982 (66%)

Elected 2002; 7th term
Also served 1983-95

Cooper developed a reputation as an accomplished dealmaker and a political moderate during his first tour in the House, a dozen years that ended with an unsuccessful Senate campaign in 1994. And he says he hopes to resurrect that image again in the 108th Congress and beyond.

"I'm not a very ideological person. Practicality is the hallmark," says Cooper. "The level of partisanship and bickering and single-issue stalemate seems so great with very little being accomplished. We've got to learn to get along together and accomplish things."

Although he describes himself as "older, wiser and balder" than when he left Congress, Cooper was still only 48 when he returned. In the intervening years, he managed an investment bank, taught health care policy at Vanderbilt University and founded a company that raises money for Tennessee businesses. He says those experiences helped him better understand what people want and need from government.

Cooper was reassigned to the Budget Committee, where he had served previously, and to the Armed Services and Government Reform panels. He also was elected by his colleagues as a regional whip. While a fine résumé for a freshman, it is a comedown nonetheless from the powerful Energy and Commerce Committee, where in the early 1990s Cooper was a key player on a range of issues, from telecommunications to clean air. He was a major figure in the Clinton-era debate on universal health care coverage.

A governor's son educated at Groton, Harvard and Oxford, Cooper previously had no trouble holding a conservative-leaning, mainly rural district that sprawled across Tennessee. He appears to be just as secure in his new district, which is centered in Nashville and is more reliably Democratic. Democrat Bob Clement gave up the seat to run for the Senate in 2002.

Despite surgery in June to remove a tumor from his colon — doctors said the cancer had not spread — Cooper won the August primary with 47 percent of the vote; the runner-up, state Rep. John Arriola, had 24 percent. In the fall, he won with 64 percent against businessman Robert Duvall.

TENNESSEE 5
Nashville

Home to state capital Nashville, the 5th is Tennessee's second-smallest district geographically, but it looms large in economic, political and cultural value.

"Music City U.S.A." is known for the Grand Ole Opry and homes of country music stars. And while country music is unquestionably Nashville's most famous industry, state government is its top employer. Vanderbilt University and 16 other schools make the district a hub for higher education in the state. And, as a national health care center, the district hosts several insurance companies and research facilities, including the Vanderbilt University Medical Center.

A population boom in Middle Tennessee has kept businesses in downtown Nashville while settlers flock to the Davidson County suburbs. Two large sports stadiums — home to football's Titans and hockey's Predators — opened downtown in the late-1990s. The 5th takes in 96 percent of the county's residents.

Bargain retail stores and other attractions have drawn tourists and locals to suburban Nashville. The Belle Meade suburb long has been one of the state's wealthiest areas, and the hilly district includes parts of more-rural Wilson and Cheatham counties.

The area's economic boom attracted young, Republican-leaning upper-class couples to neighborhoods such as Bellevue and the Hermitage. But the city core, home to many government employees, academics and labor unions, is so strongly Democratic that control of the seat is not in doubt. No Republican won Nashville's congressional seat in the 20th century.

MAJOR INDUSTRY
Government, music, higher education, religious publishing, auto manufacturing

CITIES
Nashville-Davidson (pt.), 542,831; Lebanon (pt.), 12,718; Mount Juliet, 12,366

NOTABLE
"The Hermitage" was the home of President Andrew Jackson; Nashville is home to a life-size reproduction of the Parthenon and to the Country Music Hall of Fame.

Rep. Bart Gordon (D)

CAPITOL OFFICE
225-4231
www.house.gov/gordon
2304 Rayburn 20515-4206; fax 225-6887

COMMITTEES
Energy & Commerce
Science

HOMETOWN
Murfreesboro

BORN
Jan. 24, 1949, Murfreesboro, Tenn.

RELIGION
Methodist

FAMILY
Wife, Leslie Gordon; one child

EDUCATION
Middle Tennessee State U., B.S. 1971; U. of Tennessee, J.D. 1973

MILITARY SERVICE
Army Reserve, 1971-72

CAREER
Lawyer; state party official

POLITICAL HIGHLIGHTS
Tenn. Democratic Party chairman, 1981-83

ELECTION RESULTS

2002 GENERAL		
Bart Gordon (D)	117,119	65.9%
Robert L. Garrison (R)	57,397	32.3%
J. Patrick Lyons (I)	3,065	1.7%
2002 PRIMARY		
Bart Gordon (D)	69,121	91.6%
Harvey Howard (D)	6,255	8.3%
2000 GENERAL		
Bart Gordon (D)	168,861	62.1%
David Charles (R)	97,169	35.7%
Jim Coffer (I)	4,685	1.7%

PREVIOUS WINNING PERCENTAGES
1998 (55%); 1996 (54%); 1994 (51%); 1992 (57%); 1990 (67%); 1988 (76%); 1986 (77%); 1984 (63%)

Elected 1984; 10th term

Gordon is well-known in the House for being the fastest man in Congress. He annually finishes first among lawmakers in the annual three-mile Capital Challenge road race (his 2002 victory was his 13th straight win), beating out such fellow athletes as GOP Rep. Jim Ryun of Kansas, a one-time Olympic silver medalist. "Every year I get one year older, and the competition seems one year younger, so I have to train that much harder," he says.

He runs three to four times a week to keep ahead of his racing foes, and he has moderated his politics to stave off electoral challenges in a district that was becoming increasingly independent in the 1990s. Like many conservatives, he supports tax cuts and gun owners' rights, takes a hard line on immigration and is a fierce critic of efforts to regulate tobacco.

Gordon has strayed from the party line more often since Republicans took control of the House in 1995. He has supported the GOP on a number of issues, including overhauling the welfare system and toughening immigration laws. In 2001, he was one of only 28 Democrats to vote for President Bush's signature tax cut. In 1999, he opposed a Democratic initiative imposing a 72-hour background check on gun show purchases.

But Gordon sides with organized labor in pressing for an increase in the minimum wage and opposing the two most recent trade liberalization measures, the law enacted in 2000 to permanently normalize the U.S.-China trade relationship and the proposal in the 107th Congress to revive fast-track procedures for congressional action on trade agreements.

Mostly, he pays attention to concerns close to home. During the 106th, he urged his colleagues not to prejudge hearings into a massive tire recall by Firestone, which has a plant in his district. After initially siding with environmentalists on increasing funding for farm conservation initiatives, Gordon and other Tennessee Democrats in 2001 voted against shifting $19 billion from crop subsidies to conservation programs, saying it would hurt Tennessee farmers.

Since 1996, Gordon has sponsored legislation modeled on a Tennessee law that would make sports agents subject to fines or imprisonment if they use financial inducements or otherwise knowingly influence an athlete to end his or her college eligibility. Gordon's collaborator and cosponsor is Republican Tom Osborne, the former Nebraska football coach. "When you have a child being promised the moon, it's not too hard to understand why we have the problems we do in college sports," Gordon says.

Gordon cooperates with Republicans on issues that involve space technology and computer security, sponsoring legislation to establish a national policy on digital signatures, which are used to verify the source of an electronic communication and determine whether it has been altered in transit. After a series of NASA mission failures, he urged colleagues in 1999 to study the agency's goals carefully before committing more money to space ventures. And he has questioned whether NASA is doing enough to maintain the viability of its aging space shuttle fleet. Following the Columbia shuttle disaster in 2003, Gordon pressed for a broadly based probe, with investigators drawn from outside of NASA.

In his first decade on Capitol Hill, Gordon earned a place in the Democratic leadership's heart and the party's whip organization with occasional liberal votes on social issues and loyal work on the Rules Committee. He was an architect of compromises in 1990 and 1991 that ultimately led to the Family and Medical Leave Act, requiring businesses to give workers unpaid time off to be with newborn children or ill family members.

But after a 1994 scare at the polls, Gordon became more mindful of his constituents' conservative impulses on certain issues. He fought Clinton's regulations aimed at limiting tobacco's appeal to minors, and he introduced a bill that would have stripped the Food and Drug Administration of its authority to restrict tobacco ads at auto races. "I also oppose trying to treat tobacco as a drug because that's just a backdoor approach to going back to the old Prohibition days. We know that doesn't work," Gordon said.

Gordon won nationwide notice in 1991, when at the request of NBC News, he posed as a prospective vocational education student. He was encouraged at a school in Memphis to sign up for a truck-driving course, using student loans to pay his way. "They were more interested in getting me to sign up for the school than they were in seeing that I would be placed in a good job later or got good training," Gordon said on the NBC show "Exposé." He has since sought to cut off access to the loan program for schools that have high loan default rates.

Gordon picked up a lasting taste for congressional politics as a college student, when he went to work in the 1968 congressional campaign of Democratic state Rep. John Bragg, who lost the race. Fresh out of law school, Gordon won a seat on the state Democratic Executive Committee, and in 1979, he parlayed his contacts into a position as the party's executive director. Two years later, he won the party chairmanship, attracting notice with his computerized mailing lists and fundraising efforts.

When Al Gore gave up his House seat in 1984 to run for the Senate, Gordon was ready. He won a six-way primary with 28 percent. Despite facing the potentially explosive issue of a paternity suit that had been brought against him and later was dismissed, he won all but two counties on Election Day. Gordon generally won re-election by comfortable margins until 1994, the year the Republicans took over Congress; he was held to 51 percent by lawyer Steve Gill, who sought to tie the congressman to Clinton.

His next three re-election victories were also comparatively close. But the Democratic state legislature helped Gordon out substantially in redistricting, adding two Democratic-leaning counties and taking away some heavily GOP territory in the Nashville suburbs. The result was that in 2002 he trounced Robert L. Garrison, a libertarian GOP gadfly, by 34 percentage points.

Although periodically mentioned as a potential Senate candidate, Gordon cited family reasons — a toddler daughter and a wife at a turning point in her own career — in opting out of the race to succeed Republican Fred Thompson, who retired in 2002.

KEY VOTES

2002

- Yes Overhaul campaign finance law; ban "soft money" and restrict advocacy advertising
- Yes Back Bush's defense budget increase
- No Extend 1996 welfare law
- No Adopt Bush's discretionary spending limit
- No Pass GOP Medicare prescription drug plan
- ? Create independent Sept. 11 commission
- Yes Extend union protections to Homeland Security Department employees
- No Revive fast-track procedures for trade agreements
- Yes Authorize war against Iraq
- Yes Advance bankruptcy overhaul opposed by abortion opponents

2001

- No Nullify Clinton Labor Department ergonomics rule
- Yes Cut taxes by $1.35 trillion through fiscal 2011
- Yes Maintain ban on oil drilling in Arctic National Wildlife Refuge
- No Approve Bush proposal to limit managed-care plan liability for coverage decisions
- No Divert money from crop subsidy payments to land conservation
- Yes Expand law enforcement power to investigate suspected terrorists

CQ VOTE STUDIES

	PARTY UNITY		PRESIDENTIAL SUPPORT	
	Support	Oppose	Support	Oppose
2002	74%	26%	54%	46%
2001	66%	34%	54%	46%
2000	71%	29%	50%	50%
1999	68%	32%	62%	38%
1998	74%	26%	62%	38%

INTEREST GROUPS

	AFL-CIO	ADA	CCUS	ACU
2002	75%	70%	68%	40%
2001	83%	65%	65%	42%
2000	80%	60%	71%	44%
1999	88%	70%	71%	36%
1998	80%	90%	72%	36%

TENNESSEE 6

Middle Tennessee — Murfreesboro

Nearby Nashville's population boom has spilled over into much of the 6th District, which wraps around Nashville to the north and east before swinging south.

The hilly countryside includes two university communities: Murfreesboro, which is home to Middle Tennessee State University and has grown rapidly, and Cookeville, where Tennessee Tech University is located. Rutherford County, which includes Murfreesboro, grew by more than 50 percent in the 1990s, and Wilson County east of Nashville grew by almost one-third during the decade. The district has remained fairly loyal to the Democratic Party since the days of Andrew Jackson, who built his political career in the area. Redistricting following the 2000 census allowed the 6th to shed growing conservative areas in Williamson County and increased the chance the seat will stay in Democratic hands. A rural, tobacco-farming base added in northern Robertson County remains staunchly Democratic, as does Bedford County, which was added to the district's southern end.

In the Nashville area's orbit, the economy was strong in the 1990s. A well-developed highway system makes commuting from Nashville, in the 5th District, to Murfreesboro easy. Some residents have government jobs, but employment relies more on automobile parts manufacturers spurred by a Nissan plant in Smyrna and a Saturn plant in the 4th District. Tobacco farming and book distribution also are big businesses.

The 6th supports a Democratic but socially conservative constituency that favors prayer in schools. Though Al Gore represented this area in Congress, he carried it by less than 1 percent of the vote in the 2000 presidential contest.

MAJOR INDUSTRY

Auto and textile manufacturing, book and video distribution

CITIES

Murfreesboro, 68,816; Hendersonville, 40,620; Smyrna, 25,569; Cookeville, 23,923; Gallatin, 23,230

NOTABLE

Cordell Hull practiced law in Celina before beginning his political career, during which he became Franklin Delano Roosevelt's secretary of State from 1933 until 1944; Shelbyville is the heart of Tennessee Walking Horse country; Carthage is the hometown of former Vice President Al Gore.

Rep. Marsha Blackburn (R)

Elected 2002; 1st term

CAPITOL OFFICE
225-2811
www.house.gov/blackburn
509 Cannon 20515-4207; fax 225-2989

COMMITTEES
Education & Workforce
Government Reform
Judiciary

HOMETOWN
Brentwood

BORN
June 6, 1952, Laurel, Miss.

RELIGION
Presbyterian

FAMILY
Husband, Chuck Blackburn; two children

EDUCATION
Mississippi State U., B.S. 1973 (home economics)

CAREER
Retail marketing company owner; state economic development official; sales manager

POLITICAL HIGHLIGHTS
Williamson County Republican Party chairwoman, 1989-91; Republican nominee for U.S. House, 1992; Tenn. Senate, 1999-2002

ELECTION RESULTS

2002 GENERAL		
Marsha Blackburn (R)	138,314	70.7%
Tim Barron (D)	51,790	26.5%
Rick Patterson (I)	5,423	2.8%
2002 PRIMARY		
Marsha Blackburn (R)	36,633	40.3%
David Kustoff (R)	18,392	20.2%
Brent Taylor (R)	14,139	15.6%
Mark Norris (R)	13,104	14.4%
Forrest Shoaf (R)	7,319	8.1%

Blackburn says she will never bend to the political winds. "Nor," says the conservative Blackburn, "do I stay in the middle of the road."

She won Tennessee's 7th District seat in 2002 in part because of her activism against a state income tax as a state senator. Her campaign against the tax included appearing frequently on conservative talk-radio programs and organizing sometimes raucous rallies at the state Capitol during tax debates. She displays a gold-painted ax, with the words "Ax the Tax," in her Capitol Hill office as a reminder of her crusade.

Blackburn was so outspoken on the tax issue that a Memphis newspaper headline asked, "Can Rabble-Rouser Become Team Player?" as Blackburn arrived on Capitol Hill. An early indication that she intends to try came when she was appointed to the House Republican whip team.

While Blackburn acknowledges that the national income tax is a fact of life, she says she will continue to speak out for fiscal conservatism. "The underlying philosophy is the same, regardless of whether it's a state or federal issue: reducing the size of government," she says. She is pushing legislation to allow a sales tax exemption for residents of the nine states, including Tennessee, that do not have an income tax.

She had hoped for a seat on Energy and Commerce or a panel involved in the debate over welfare, but had to settle for Education, Government Reform and Judiciary.

A free-trade advocate, Blackburn opposes tariffs in most situations. She wants to make it harder for illegal immigrants to get a driver's license, which she says they can use to get social services. In one campaign ad, Blackburn cited not just her support for gun owners' rights, but her perfect score on a marksmanship test with her Smith & Wesson .38.

Blackburn leveraged the tax issue and her base in the Nashville suburbs to prevail in a crowded primary field after four-term Republican Rep. Ed Bryant left his 7th District seat open for a Senate bid that would fail. The nomination assured her of victory in the Republican stronghold.

TENNESSEE 7

Eastern Memphis suburbs; most of Clarksville and Franklin

Bordering Kentucky to the north and Mississippi and Alabama to the south, the 7th is anchored by two wealthy, conservative suburban communities: Memphis' Shelby County in the southwest and the Nashville area's Williamson County in the east. It also includes most of the moderately sized city of Clarksville.

White flight from Memphis (in the 9th) has driven growth in suburban Shelby County, where many children attend parochial schools. The migration has transformed traditionally Democratic West Tennessee into a Republican-leaning area dominated by small churches. The new strain of GOP activism is strongly anti-tax and socially conservative.

Heading east and north, agriculture makes for rural counties, where corn, tobacco, hogs and cattle dominate. The rural areas between Memphis and Nashville also are a solid base for Republicans.

"Yellow Dog" Democrats still outweigh Republican voters in Clarksville and surrounding rural sectors. A few miles from the Kentucky border, Clarksville has benefited from diverse manufacturing and the expansion of Fort Campbell, one-third of which is in Kentucky.

The GOP has held the congressional seat since 1973, with support from socially conservative suburban, rural and military contingents.

MAJOR INDUSTRY
Tobacco, cattle, military

MILITARY BASES
Fort Campbell, 23,227 military, 4,251 civilian (2001) (shared with Kentucky's 1st District)

CITIES
Clarksville (pt.), 83,680; Bartlett (pt.), 40,409; Germantown (pt.), 34,200; Franklin (pt.), 33,627

NOTABLE
Shiloh National Military Park memorializes those who died in one of the bloodiest battles of the Civil War.

Rep. John Tanner (D)

CAPITOL OFFICE
225-4714
www.house.gov/tanner
1226 Longworth 20515-4208; fax 225-1765

COMMITTEES
Ways & Means

HOMETOWN
Union City

BORN
Sept. 22, 1944, Halls, Tenn.

RELIGION
Disciples of Christ

FAMILY
Wife, Betty Ann Tanner; two children

EDUCATION
U. of Tennessee, B.S. 1966 (business), J.D. 1968

MILITARY SERVICE
Navy, 1968-72; Tenn. National Guard, 1974-2000

CAREER
Lawyer; insurance company owner

POLITICAL HIGHLIGHTS
Tenn. House, 1977-89

ELECTION RESULTS

2002 GENERAL		
John Tanner (D)	117,811	70.1%
Mat McClain (R)	45,853	27.3%
James L. Hart (I)	4,288	2.6%
2002 PRIMARY		
John Tanner (D)	66,015	86.8%
Richard Ward (D)	10,069	13.2%
2000 GENERAL		
John Tanner (D)	143,127	72.3%
Billy Yancy (R)	54,929	27.7%

PREVIOUS WINNING PERCENTAGES
1998 (100%); 1996 (67%); 1994 (64%); 1992 (84%); 1990 (100%); 1988 (62%)

Elected 1988; 8th term

Tanner has found himself deeply disturbed by the return of federal deficits — but also invigorated by what he sees as the imperative to help get the government back into the black as soon as possible.

As a founding member of the "Blue Dogs," a coalition of the House's most fiscally conservative Democrats, Tanner says he believes he has a responsibility to constantly remind his colleagues that their priorities go beyond fighting terrorism, and to persuade Congress of its moral responsibility to reduce the national debt. "The longer I'm here, the more I am committed to a sane fiscal policy for the United States," Tanner says. "Debt is a real enemy."

Tanner is among the most conservative Democrats in the House. During the first two years that President Bush was in the White House, for example, Tanner voted with the president 52 percent of the time, and against a majority of his own party 33 percent of the time.

He has used his seat on the Ways and Means Committee to try to quietly pull the Democratic Party to the political center — the ground preferred by his rural and small-town constituents. His willingness to work across the aisle has made him a player on a host of bills.

He supported the fast-track trade law in 2002, which gave the president expanded powers to negotiate international trade pacts. Tanner was a key player in inserting a provision limiting the fees the Customs Service charges to inspect packages arriving in the United States from overseas. The provision was sought by Memphis-based FedEx Corp. and other express delivery companies.

Tanner also supported the 2000 law granting China permanent normal trade status. That vote, and an earlier one giving employers the option of offering their workers time off instead of overtime pay, cost Tanner support from some labor groups. But Tanner defended the votes, saying he was looking at the long-term potential for job creation.

In the 104th, he worked with moderate Delaware Republican Michael N. Castle to introduce a bipartisan bill overhauling the welfare system. President Clinton endorsed the Tanner-Castle measure, and elements of their bill eventually became part of the landmark law enacted in 1996.

Tanner supports eliminating all taxation of estates, which he considers a threat to family farms. Still, he voted against the 2001 tax cut package that rolls back and briefly repeals the estate tax, saying its $1.35 trillion cost over 10 years was too steep. He was among the first Democrats to openly talk about whether Congress should reconsider that law in light of the Sept. 11, 2001, terrorist attacks, which contributed to massive defense spending increases and a revenue-sapping recession.

Though a frequent ally of the GOP, Tanner says he gets angry with Republicans who still promote the virtues of the tax cut now that surpluses have turned to deficits. "There's plenty of pressure in the system not to raise taxes," he says. "There's not enough pressure against increasing the debt."

Tanner's voting record in the 106th was conservative enough to attract an endorsement from the U.S. Chamber of Commerce. Yet he was thought to be enough of a loyal Democrat to win appointment to a party task force brainstorming on how the party could win back the House majority. "The perception in the land is that the Democrats are too liberal, the Republicans are too rigid and too conservative, and the Blue Dogs or some group like them are where to go in terms of governing," Tanner once said.

Tanner's votes place him squarely in the middle of the Blue Dogs. The group was formed in 1994, when many conservative Democrats were chafing at what they viewed as indifference to their views by the liberal majority in the Democratic Caucus. Tanner says Democratic leaders now realize they must include a broader range of ideologies in their policymaking if they hope to regain control of the House.

As Democrats organized themselves for the 108th Congress, Tanner backed fellow Blue Dog and fellow Tennessean Harold E. Ford Jr. for Democratic leader against Californian Nancy Pelosi. But after her expected victory, Pelosi, in an outreach effort to create a broadly based leadership team, made Tanner one of three vice chairmen of the Democratic Steering Committee, the panel that makes Democratic committee assignments.

Tanner has been a leader in drafting the Blue Dogs' alternative budget proposals, which have served as a basis for compromise between more-liberal Democrats and the GOP. He called the 1997 balanced-budget deal a "constructive middle ground" that included "significant parts of the Blue Dog budget."

Tanner's father was a farmer and also worked in the family's insurance business. His mother taught school. Tanner attended the University of Tennessee, playing guard on the freshman basketball team and earning bachelor's and law degrees. After four years prosecuting courts-martial in the Navy, Tanner joined a private practice in his hometown of Union City. In 1976, he ran for the state House at the urging of colleagues in the American Legion, where he was a state officer. He also was encouraged by state House Speaker Ned Ray McWherter, a distant relative by marriage.

Tanner served in the General Assembly for 12 years. In 1988, when Democrat Ed Jones, a longtime family friend, retired after nearly two decades in the House, Tanner came out of the blocks fast. He assembled an enviable organization and financial base, boosted by his connections to Jones and McWherter. His relaxed, "good ol' boy" style helped him win over rural and small-town voters. He took 62 percent of the vote against Republican Ed Bryant, a Jackson lawyer, and has rolled to re-election ever since. (Bryant was elected to the House from the neighboring 7th District in 1994.)

After Al Gore was elected vice president in 1992, the Tennessee governor — who happened to be McWherter — needed to appoint an interim replacement to fill Gore's seat in the Senate. The job was said to be Tanner's for the asking, but he told McWherter he preferred to stay on in the House. A decade later, Tanner also quickly killed expectations that he might run for the Senate when Republican Fred Thompson decided to retire.

KEY VOTES

2002

Yes Overhaul campaign finance law; ban "soft money" and restrict advocacy advertising
Yes Back Bush's defense budget increase
? Extend 1996 welfare law
No Adopt Bush's discretionary spending limit
No Pass GOP Medicare prescription drug plan
No Create independent Sept. 11 commission
Yes Extend union protections to Homeland Security Department employees
Yes Revive fast-track procedures for trade agreements
Yes Authorize war against Iraq
Yes Advance bankruptcy overhaul opposed by abortion opponents

2001

Yes Nullify Clinton Labor Department ergonomics rule
No Cut taxes by $1.35 trillion through fiscal 2011
No Maintain ban on oil drilling in Arctic National Wildlife Refuge
No Approve Bush proposal to limit managed-care plan liability for coverage decisions
No Divert money from crop subsidy payments to land conservation
Yes Expand law enforcement power to investigate suspected terrorists

CQ VOTE STUDIES

	PARTY UNITY		PRESIDENTIAL SUPPORT	
	Support	Oppose	Support	Oppose
2002	70%	30%	56%	44%
2001	64%	36%	48%	52%
2000	71%	29%	56%	44%
1999	67%	33%	62%	38%
1998	69%	31%	58%	42%

INTEREST GROUPS

	AFL-CIO	ADA	CCUS	ACU
2002	67%	70%	80%	39%
2001	64%	60%	70%	50%
2000	60%	45%	85%	36%
1999	78%	70%	76%	29%
1998	60%	60%	88%	41%

TENNESSEE 8
West – Jackson, parts of Memphis and Clarksville

The mighty Mississippi to the west and the Tennessee and Cumberland rivers to the east frame the rolling hills and flat farmland that make up the 8th. Except for Memphis' northern suburbs and Jackson, the district is predominantly rural, Democratic and working-class. Democrats, often conservative ones, have held this district seat since Reconstruction. Redistricting following the 2000 census sliced away some growing Republican parts of Shelby County north of Memphis, adding to the Democratic lean. Al Gore carried the 8th in the 2000 presidential contest with 51 percent of the vote.

The district is poor, but a few manufacturing plants prevent the economy from slipping further. A Pringles potato chip plant employs more than 1,300 people in Jackson, and tire, auto and textile manufacturers are scattered throughout less-populated sectors. Mechanization has decreased factory employment but increased production on small farms. Chicken-processing plants give the area some value-added agriculture, while the boll weevil is a longtime scourge to cotton farmers.

State and federal government also provide much-needed jobs via two large state prisons and a downsized, but still significant, naval air station in Millington. Redistricting moved the 8th's eastern border into Clarksville and closer to Nashville.

The northern section of the Tennessee River feeds into Kentucky Lake in the northeast. Tennessee Valley Authority dams and power plants are here, and these waterways also draw many avid hunters and fishermen to the district. Thousands of birdwatchers flock to Reelfoot Lake in the northwest each winter to view the migration of hundreds of bald eagles.

MAJOR INDUSTRY

Manufacturing, agriculture, government

MILITARY BASES

Naval Support Activity Mid-South, 1,412 military, 210 civilian (2001)

CITIES

Jackson, 59,643; Memphis (pt.), 53,080; Clarksville (pt.), 19,775; Dyersburg, 17,452

NOTABLE

Civil War battles were fought at Fort Donelson, Fort Henry and Fort Pillow; A 60-foot tall replica of the Eiffel Tower is in Paris, which also is home to the World's Biggest Fish Fry.

Rep. Harold E. Ford Jr. (D)

CAPITOL OFFICE
225-3265
rep.harold.ford.jr@mail.house.gov
www.house.gov/ford
325 Cannon 20515-4209; fax 225-5663

COMMITTEES
Budget
Financial Services

HOMETOWN
Memphis

BORN
May 11, 1970, Memphis, Tenn.

RELIGION
Baptist

FAMILY
Single

EDUCATION
U. of Pennsylvania, B.A. 1992 (American history); U. of Michigan, J.D. 1996

CAREER
Law clerk; U.S. Commerce Department aide

POLITICAL HIGHLIGHTS
No previous office

ELECTION RESULTS

2002 GENERAL		
Harold E. Ford Jr. (D)	120,904	83.8%
Tony Rush (I)	23,208	16.1%
2002 PRIMARY		
Harold E. Ford Jr. (D)		unopposed
2000 GENERAL		
Harold E. Ford Jr. (D)		unopposed

PREVIOUS WINNING PERCENTAGES
1998 (79%); 1996 (61%)

Elected 1996; 4th term

In one week, Ford transformed himself from a rising star in the Democratic Party into a cautionary tale about the dangers of overreaching. By leaping into a hopeless race against Nancy Pelosi of California to become the new House Democratic leader in the 108th Congress, Ford may have had nothing more in mind than making some points about the future of his party and perhaps building up his name for a future run for the Senate. But he fell far short — winning just 29 votes to Pelosi's 177 — transforming himself, at least temporarily, into damaged goods rather than building himself up for future races.

It would be a mistake, however, to count him out. The energetic, fast-talking Ford can be an eloquent spokesman for the discontent of moderates and young Democrats. Perhaps to dissuade him from becoming a kind of opposition leader within the party, Pelosi named him to the Budget Committee, a platform for him to be a centrist spokesman against Bush administration fiscal policy.

Even after his landslide defeat, Ford does not deny his ambitions to run for statewide office in Tennessee, where his moderation could work to his advantage. "I have long aspired to serve my state in broader ways," Ford said in an online chat with washingtonpost.com after his loss to Pelosi. "God willing and voters permitting, it could be sooner rather than later. But for now, my focus is on helping my party develop a message that will reconnect us with voters nationally."

At the ripe old age of 32, Ford had completed three terms in the House, delivered the keynote address at the 2000 Democratic National Convention, been profiled in Newsweek and flirted twice with running for the Senate, most recently in 2002 when Republican Fred Thompson retired. He had made his mark as a smart, independent-thinking lawmaker. All of that seemed to make him a prime candidate to move into the leadership someday, as leadership aides themselves said before the 2002 election.

The morning after Election Day, in which the Democrats lost six House seats, Ford took to the radio to call for Richard A. Gephardt to step down as minority leader — a move that, well before the election, Gephardt had been expected to make. Two days later, on the same day that Martin Frost of Texas bowed out of the race to succeed Gephardt, Ford jumped in.

By the time he was trounced by Pelosi the next week, the praise he had received for his smarts and independent thinking had turned to jeers for his perceived arrogance and impatience. He sent his colleagues videos reminding them of the party's electoral losses and urging them to give him a chance. He tagged Pelosi as the candidate of the failed old guard. But the rest of his campaign was waged on the airwaves rather than by approaching House Democrats one-on-one.

But as much as Ford called for "new ideas," he offered few specifics. Other than calling for a "payroll tax holiday" to revive the economy by putting quick cash into people's hands, his main difference with Pelosi was that he had voted for the law authorizing President Bush to wage war against Iraq. That position alienated him from many rank-and-file Democrats, who thought they had suffered at the polls because their supporters wanted them to fight harder against Bush's Iraq policies, not because they had not been supportive enough.

Long before, Ford had been tagged with a label he hates — "black moderate." He is an obvious example of the post-civil rights generation of

African-American leaders, which is increasingly more pragmatic and centrist than their predecessors. As a member of the "Blue Dog" coalition, a group of conservative House Democrats that often breaks ranks with the party leadership, Ford cannot escape the label — indeed, he based his entire challenge to Pelosi on it — but he does not want to be defined by it.

Ford spent much of the 107th Congress on projects such as cosponsoring a national service bill, promoting collaboration with businesses to improve Memphis schools, and hosting an anti-terrorism summit to make sure Memphis is prepared for an attack. To Ford, issues of racial discrimination still exist; he asked a House panel to investigate Nissan's auto financing practices after a study suggested black customers were charged higher financing fees than white customers. But he said he was just as interested in overhauls of the accounting and pension laws after the Enron and WorldCom scandals, as the damage of corporate scandals cuts across racial lines.

Ford is well-known for his independent streak. Before his 2000 convention speech, he drew national attention for refusing to deliver a version of the address written by Democratic presidential nominee Al Gore's aides that was full of civil rights references Ford considered outdated. And he has been willing to stray from the majority of his party on issues such as trade. For example, although in the 107th he did not back the initial House bill to grant the president fast-track trade negotiating authority, he eventually voted for the version that became law in 2002 because it included assistance for workers whose jobs are lost to liberalized trade.

The elder Harold E. Ford represented Memphis in the House for 22 years. On the day he was sworn into Congress in 1975, family lore holds, his 4-year-old son, who was in the chamber for the ceremony, announced to the other lawmakers, "This is what I want to do when I grow up."

Over the next 20 years, Ford earned a history degree, worked on President Clinton's first transition team, interned at the Senate Budget Committee under Tennessee Democrat James Sasser and served in the Clinton Commerce Department. After working on his father's 1992 and 1994 House campaigns, Ford launched his own 1996 campaign shortly before his graduation from law school. With his father serving as campaign coordinator, he distributed campaign buttons and T-shirts that simply said "Jr."

Memphis Mayor W.W. Herenton, a political rival of the Ford family, openly shopped for a heavy-hitting politician he could back to oppose the younger Ford. But Ford rolled to victory in the three-way Democratic primary with 60 percent of the vote. He defeated GOP candidate Rod DeBerry in the general election and has easily won re-election since.

KEY VOTES

2002

Yes Overhaul campaign finance law; ban "soft money" and restrict advocacy advertising
Yes Back Bush's defense budget increase
No Extend 1996 welfare law
No Adopt Bush's discretionary spending limit
No Pass GOP Medicare prescription drug plan
Yes Create independent Sept. 11 commission
Yes Extend union protections to Homeland Security Department employees
Yes Revive fast-track procedures for trade agreements
Yes Authorize war against Iraq
Yes Advance bankruptcy overhaul opposed by abortion opponents

2001

No Nullify Clinton Labor Department ergonomics rule
No Cut taxes by $1.35 trillion through fiscal 2011
Yes Maintain ban on oil drilling in Arctic National Wildlife Refuge
No Approve Bush proposal to limit managed-care plan liability for coverage decisions
No Divert money from crop subsidy payments to land conservation
Yes Expand law enforcement power to investigate suspected terrorists

CQ VOTE STUDIES

	PARTY UNITY		PRESIDENTIAL SUPPORT	
	Support	Oppose	Support	Oppose
2002	87%	13%	46%	54%
2001	83%	17%	38%	62%
2000	89%	11%	74%	26%
1999	90%	10%	81%	19%
1998	91%	9%	75%	25%

INTEREST GROUPS

	AFL-CIO	ADA	CCUS	ACU
2002	86%	70%	63%	24%
2001	91%	85%	55%	8%
2000	80%	60%	70%	24%
1999	78%	100%	40%	4%
1998	88%	80%	62%	14%

TENNESSEE 9
Memphis

The 9th includes most of Tennessee's largest city, Memphis, which sits atop the bluffs of the Mississippi River. Memphis continues to struggle with racial tension that has hindered its growth since the 1960s, though it grew during the 1990s. The district is almost 60 percent black and gave 72 percent of its vote to Democratic presidential candidate Al Gore in 2000. Much of the white population has moved north and east to the Shelby County suburbs. However, revitalization efforts have paved the way for inner-city economic development and integrated downtown residences such as Harbourtown and South Bluffs.

Memphis is a key distribution center. Federal Express is based at the Memphis International Airport, making it the world's busiest cargo airport and attracting international companies to the area. The economy also depends on St. Jude Children's Research Hospital, one of the nation's top pediatric care centers.

It remains to be seen whether Memphis has fully recovered from the industrial decline that began in the 1970s, but tourism has remained an economic mainstay, with people flocking to honor two American icons — Elvis Presley and Martin Luther King Jr. The hotel where King was assassinated is now a museum.

The area first sent an African-American to Congress in 1974, initiating the reign of Democratic black political power in Memphis. In 1998, more than 40 percent of white voters, who traditionally support Republicans, cast their vote for Rep. Ford, a black Democrat. Republicans have not fielded a challenger since 1998.

MAJOR INDUSTRY
Distribution, health care, government

CITIES
Memphis (pt.), 571,661

NOTABLE
Graceland was the home of Elvis Presley; W.C. Handy developed the blues musical style on Beale Street; Memphis takes its name from the Egyptian city with ports on the banks of another meandering waterway, the Nile; The Peabody hotel in downtown Memphis has ducks that ride the elevator from the rooftop to the ground floor twice each day.

TEXAS

Gov. Rick Perry (R)

First elected: Succeeded George W. Bush, R, on Dec. 21, 2000; elected 2002
Length of term: 4 years
Term expires: 1/07
Salary: $115,345
Phone: (512) 463-2000
Hometown: Austin
Born: March 4, 1950; Paint Creek, Texas
Religion: Methodist
Family: Wife, Anita Perry; two children
Education: Texas A&M U., B.S. 1972 (animal science)
Military Service: Air Force, 1972-77
Career: Farmer; rancher
Political highlights: Texas House, 1984-90; Texas department of Agriculture commissioner, 1990-98; lieutenant governor, 1999-2000
Election results:

2002 GENERAL		
Rick Perry (R)	2,632,541	57.8%
Tony Sanchez (D)	1,819,843	40.0%
Jeff Daiell (LIBERT)	66,717	1.5%

Lt. Gov. David Dewhurst (R)

First elected: 2002
Length of term: 4 years
Term expires: 1/07
Salary: $7,200; $125/day in Senate session
Phone: (512) 463-0001

STATE LEGISLATURE

Legislature: Meets January-May in odd-numbered years
House: 150 members, 2-year terms
2003 breakdown: 88R, 62D; 118 men, 32 women
Salary: $7,200/month; $125/day in session
Phone: (512) 463-0845
Senate: 31 members, 4-year terms
2003 breakdown: 19R, 12D; 27 men, 4 women
Salary: $7,200/month; $125/day in session
Phone: (512) 463-0001

STATE TERM LIMITS

Governor: No
Senate: No
House: No

URBAN STATISTICS

CITY	POPULATION
Houston	1,953,631
Dallas	1,188,580
San Antonio	1,144,646
Austin	656,562
El Paso	563,662

REGISTERED VOTERS

Voters do not register by party.

POPULATION

2002 population (est.)	21,779,893
2000 population	20,851,820
1990 population	16,986,510
Percent change (1990-2000)	+22.8%
Rank among states (2002)	2
Median age	32.3
Born in state	62.2%
Foreign born	13.9%
Violent crime rate	545/100,000
Poverty level	15.4%
Federal workers	173,367
Military	170,659

REDISTRICTING

Texas gained two House seats in reapportionment. The state legislature failed to agree on a plan and a three-judge federal panel implemented a new, 32-district map on Nov. 14, 2001.

MISCELLANEOUS

Web: www.state.tx.us
Capital: Austin

STATE ELECTION OFFICIAL
(512) 463-5650

DEMOCRATIC HEADQUARTERS
(512) 478-9800

REPUBLICAN HEADQUARTERS
(512) 477-9821

District Statistics

	2000 VOTE FOR PRESIDENT															
DIST.	BUSH	GORE	NADER	WHITE	BLACK	ASIAN	HISP	MEDIAN INCOME	WHITE COLLAR	BLUE COLLAR	SERVICE INDUSTRY	OVER 64	UNDER 18	COLLEGE EDUCATION	RURAL	SQ. MILES
1	64%	36%	n/a	75%	16%	0%	7%	$31,894	51%	34%	15%	15%	26%	15%	60%	12,543
2	63	37	n/a	76	14	0	9	$32,986	48	35	17	13	26	11	62	13,710
3	72	28	n/a	70	7	7	14	$65,546	76	15	9	6	29	42	4	462
4	70	30	n/a	77	12	1	9	$38,677	56	29	14	14	27	19	46	6,141
5	62	38	n/a	63	16	2	18	$39,227	58	27	15	11	27	18	23	7,297
6	67	33	n/a	72	10	3	14	$49,763	62	26	12	9	29	23	24	3,837
7	68	32	n/a	50	11	11	26	$48,561	72	16	13	8	26	40	0	194
8	78	22	n/a	77	5	3	13	$60,198	70	19	11	7	29	33	16	1,146
9	55	45	n/a	60	21	3	14	$41,416	60	24	15	11	26	21	10	2,059
10	47	53	n/a	50	11	4	33	$41,374	66	20	14	7	23	35	4	550
11	67	33	n/a	64	15	2	16	$36,378	57	26	17	11	27	19	27	8,993
12	67	33	n/a	71	5	2	20	$44,624	61	26	13	10	27	23	11	1,332
13	75	25	n/a	70	6	1	22	$33,361	53	29	18	14	27	17	27	39,462
14	66	34	n/a	58	8	1	32	$35,966	52	32	16	13	27	15	45	14,458
15	45	55	n/a	19	1	1	78	$27,530	53	28	19	10	33	14	13	6,356

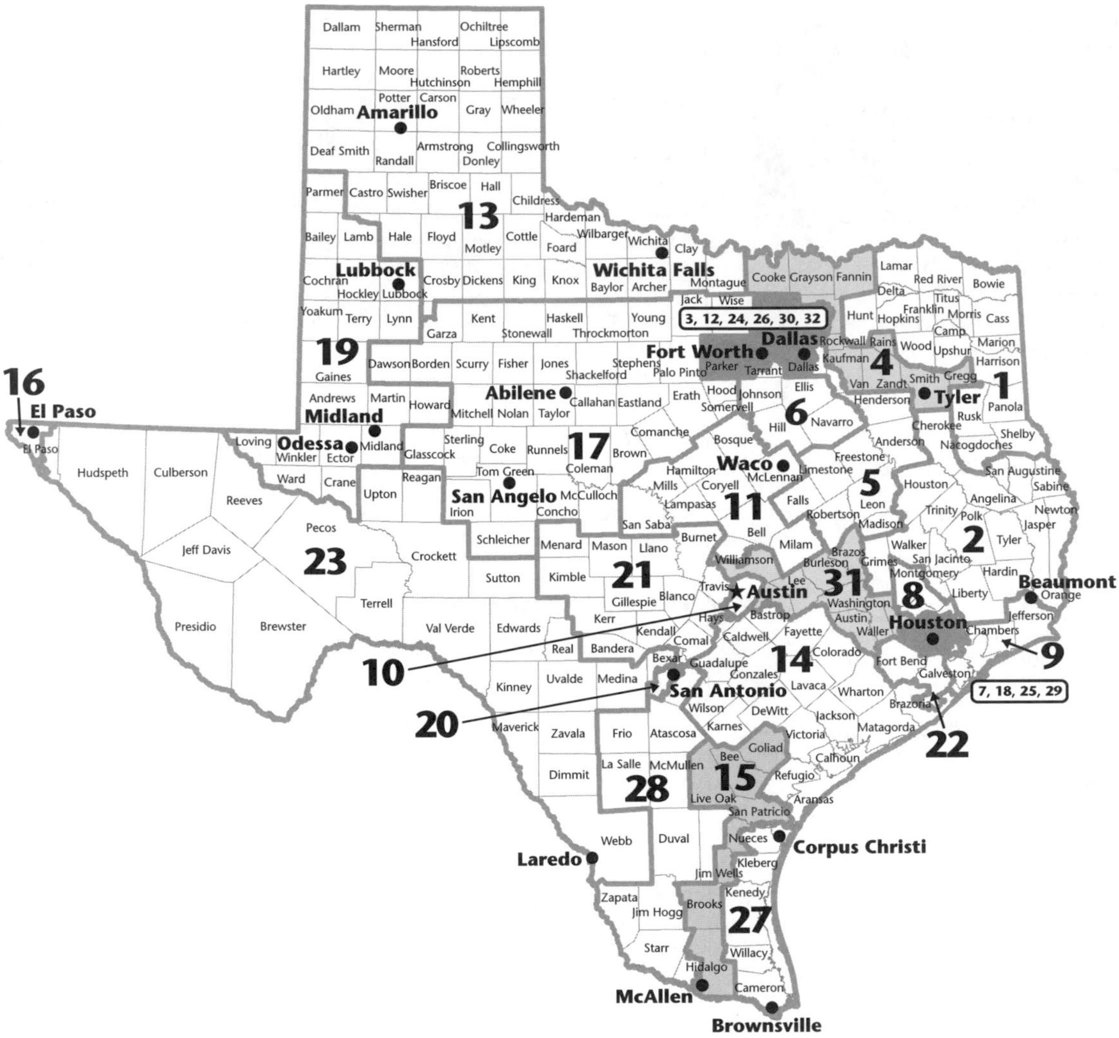

District Statistics

DIST.	2000 VOTE FOR PRESIDENT BUSH	GORE	NADER	WHITE	BLACK	ASIAN	HISP	MEDIAN INCOME	WHITE COLLAR	BLUE COLLAR	SERVICE INDUSTRY	OVER 64	UNDER 18	COLLEGE EDUCATION	RURAL	SQ. MILES
16	41%	59%	n/a	17%	3%	1%	78%	$31,245	58%	25%	17%	10%	32%	17%	2%	581
17	72	28	n/a	75	4	1	20	$32,413	54	28	18	15	26	17	39	33,564
18	26	74	n/a	21	42	3	33	$31,725	55	27	17	10	27	18	0	186
19	76	24	n/a	58	6	1	34	$32,409	58	26	16	12	28	19	19	17,508
20	43	57	n/a	24	5	1	68	$31,801	57	25	19	10	29	16	2	303
21	73	27	n/a	77	2	2	17	$52,751	73	16	11	14	25	39	31	10,979
22	68	32	n/a	60	10	8	20	$62,678	69	20	11	7	30	33	12	1,670
23	59	41	n/a	30	1	1	67	$36,158	61	23	16	9	32	23	20	55,415
24	46	54	n/a	35	22	3	38	$36,962	55	31	14	8	30	18	1	249
25	48	52	n/a	37	23	5	34	$38,048	60	24	16	8	29	28	1	259

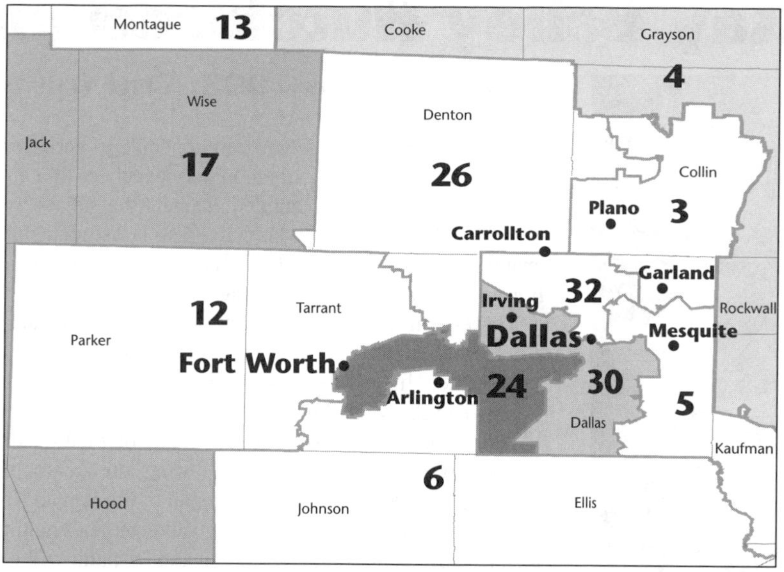

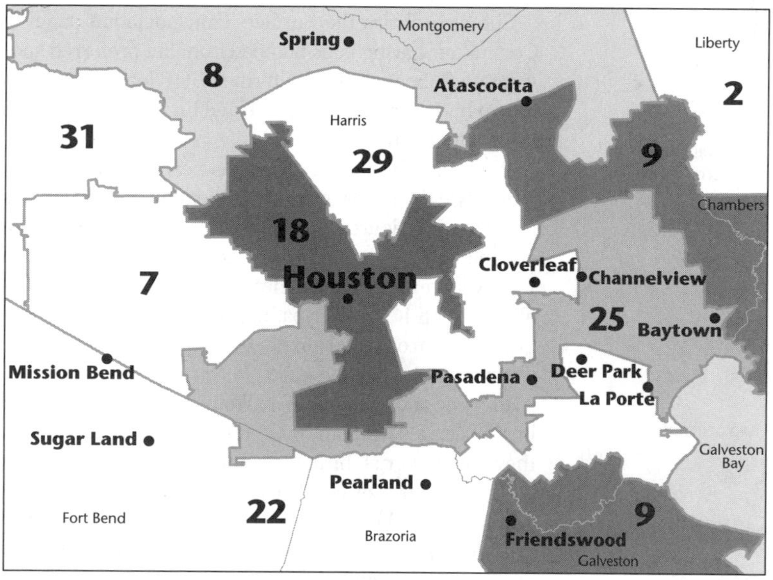

District Statistics

DIST.	2000 VOTE FOR PRESIDENT BUSH	GORE	NADER	WHITE	BLACK	ASIAN	HISP	MEDIAN INCOME	WHITE COLLAR	BLUE COLLAR	SERVICE INDUSTRY	OVER 64	UNDER 18	COLLEGE EDUCATION	RURAL	SQ. MILES
26	73%	27%	n/a	78%	5%	4%	11%	$61,287	73%	16%	11%	5%	28%	39%	8%	1,075
27	49	51	n/a	25	2	1	72	$30,431	55	26	19	11	31	16	10	3,938
28	41	59	n/a	21	7	1	70	$29,127	49	32	19	11	32	10	18	11,805
29	39	61	n/a	20	15	2	62	$32,128	43	41	16	6	33	8	0	239
30	31	69	n/a	25	41	2	31	$35,612	54	30	16	8	29	16	1	289
31	72	28	n/a	69	9	3	17	$50,252	68	20	12	7	28	32	23	5,034
32	65	35	n/a	55	9	6	27	$48,848	71	16	12	8	23	43	0	165
STATE	59	38	2	52	11	3	32	$39,927	61	25	15	10	28	23	17	261,797
U.S.	47.9	48.4	3	69	12	4	13	$41,994	60	25	15	12	26	24	21	3,537,438

Sen. Kay Bailey Hutchison (R)

CAPITOL OFFICE
224-5922
senator@hutchison.senate.gov
hutchison.senate.gov
284 Russell 20510-4304; fax 224-0776

COMMITTEES
Appropriations
(Military Construction - chairwoman)
Commerce, Science & Transportation
(Surface Transportation & Merchant Marine - chairwoman)
Rules & Administration
Veterans' Affairs

HOMETOWN
Dallas

BORN
July 22, 1943, Galveston, Texas

RELIGION
Episcopalian

FAMILY
Husband, Ray Hutchison; two children

EDUCATION
U. of Texas, J.D. 1967, B.A. 1992

CAREER
Broadcast journalist; lawyer; banking executive; candy manufacturer

POLITICAL HIGHLIGHTS
Texas House, 1973-76; National Transportation Safety Board, 1976-78; sought Republican nomination for U.S. House, 1982; Texas treasurer, 1991-93

ELECTION RESULTS

2000 GENERAL		
Kay Bailey Hutchison (R)	4,082,091	65.0%
Gene Kelly (D)	2,030,315	32.4%
Douglas Sandage (GREEN)	91,448	1.5%
Mary Ruwart (LIBERT)	72,798	1.2%
2000 PRIMARY		
Kay Bailey Hutchison (R)		unopposed

PREVIOUS WINNING PERCENTAGES
1994 (61%); 1993 Special Runoff Election (67%)

Elected June 1993; 2nd full term

Hutchison is fond of telling young people to persevere over adversity. "Never give up," she tells them in her speeches. "If a door closes, open a window." Hutchison is grounded in giving that advice by the fact that she has opened some windows herself — as a law student, journalist, state legislator, government official, U.S. senator and parent of two children she and her husband adopted relatively late in life.

Three-term Republican Phil Gramm's decision not to seek re-election in 2002 made Hutchison the senior senator from Texas, President Bush's home state. That will serve naturally to increase her leadership role in the Republican Party and her influence on issues.

Hutchison earlier broke into the ranks of what used to be an all-male Senate GOP leadership team following the death of Georgia's Paul Coverdell in 2000. As vice chairwoman of the Senate Republican Conference, she has reached out to a variety of groups — holding "summits," for instance, on issues affecting women and Hispanics. She also is a member of the Appropriations Committee and chairs its Military Construction Subcommittee.

She also chairs the Surface Transportation panel on the Commerce Committee, having been bumped from her preferred spot at the head of the Aviation Subcommittee by former GOP leader Trent Lott, who, after giving up his leadership post, asserted his seniority on the committee to take the Aviation gavel.

While Hutchison in the past has heard from critics who branded her as more style than substance, her leadership responsibilities solidify her reputation as a key figure in the Republican Party. Her role in the leadership, says one member of her inner circle, is to be a conservative with a friendly face.

As with many women of her generation, Hutchison has had to overcome obstacles on her career path. She initially was unable to get hired after graduating from the University of Texas School of Law in 1967 as one of five women in a class of 500.

In "Nine and Counting: The Women of the Senate," a book Hutchison and her colleagues wrote in 2000, Hutchison said about 30 law firms made clear they could not risk hiring a woman who they assumed would get married and quit or move away. "I had all of the confidence in the world, and suddenly it was meaningless because I couldn't get a job," she said.

The rebuffs led Hutchison into journalism. She worked for a Texas television station until voters sent her to the state legislature from Houston in 1972 at the age of 29. At the time, most women in Texas politics were Democrats. While in Austin, Hutchison teamed up with Democratic legislator Sarah Weddington (the lawyer who filed the abortion rights suit that became *Roe v. Wade*) on bills protecting victims of sex offenses, including a ban on publishing the names of rape victims.

Hutchison arrived on the Washington scene in 1976, when she was appointed to the National Transportation Safety Board by President Ford. She later moved to Dallas and unsuccessfully sought the Republican nomination for an open U.S. House seat in 1982. Hutchison then spent much of the next decade in the business world as a banking executive and candy manufacturer. She returned to elective politics in 1990, winning the post of state treasurer. In 1993 she made the big jump to the Senate by winning a special election called after President Clinton chose longtime Democratic incumbent Lloyd Bentsen to be his first Treasury secretary.

The long way Hutchison had come did not prevent a Texas newspaper from reporting her election with a headline describing her as a "Former University of Texas Longhorn Cheerleader." A Texas native with deep roots in the state, her Lone Star heritage was never more evident than when she preened for the cameras the night before Bush's 2001 inauguration, wearing heavily tooled red cowboy boots under her floor-length gown at the Texas State Society's Black Tie and Boots Ball. Her attire also led Washingtonian magazine to name her as one of the capital's best-dressed lawmakers.

Politically, Hutchison generally sides with conservatives but has expressed some moderate leanings. For instance, she says she supports abortion rights — although, like most Republicans, she opposes a procedure labeled "partial birth" abortion by its opponents.

She has friends on the Democratic side of the aisle, particularly women colleagues such as Barbara A. Mikulski of Maryland and Dianne Feinstein of California. It was Mikulski who invited Hutchison to lunch after Republicans took control of Congress in 1995 to discuss how to maintain civility in the chamber. That same year Hutchison and Mikulski formed a successful alliance to pass Homemaker IRA legislation, which gave stay-at-home mothers the same standing as women working outside the home in establishing tax-deductible individual retirement accounts. Hutchison and Feinstein teamed up in the 108th on legislation to create a nationwide Amber Alert network to help quickly locate abducted children.

Hutchison is no stranger to the national spotlight. She was a leading GOP advocate for repealing the "marriage penalty," a provision in the tax code that resulted in some two-earner married couples paying higher income taxes than if each were single. Congress addressed the issue in major tax cut legislation enacted in 2001.

Hutchison was front and center on the issue of aviation security after Sept. 11, 2001, when terrorists hijacked passenger jets and used them to destroy the World Trade Center and damage the Pentagon. In the 108th Congress, Hutchison is pressing legislation to improve security of aviation cargo. She also is an advocate of making flying as convenient as possible while maintaining security — supporting, for instance, "trusted traveler" programs that allow frequent fliers to submit to background checks and receive identification so they could bypass normal security arrangements.

She has been active on another transportation issue of importance to her home state: trucks from Mexico. She has supported opening the border states of the Southwest to long-haul Mexican trucks, in accordance with the North American Free Trade Agreement, but only as long as they meet the same safety requirements as U.S. trucks.

As a leader of the Military Construction spending subcommittee, she has focused on ensuring that the military gets the most for its money in construction projects. Also on the military front, Hutchison's lobbying helped persuade the Army in 2002 to move its South Command from Puerto Rico to Fort Sam Houston in San Antonio.

Hutchison's legislative agenda is driven by smaller, more personal issues as well as by the bigger, headline-grabbing ones. In 2002, for instance, Bush signed a measure she championed that provided for more research, information and education on blood cancers such as multiple myeloma, a condition that afflicts her brother. Her decades-long problem with a stalker has led her to sponsor legislation making the practice a federal crime.

In August 2001 Hutchison and her husband, Ray, adopted an infant girl, whom they named Kathryn Bailey Hutchison, and in November 2001 an infant boy, whom they named Houston Taylor Hutchison. "We have, for many years, been trying to add to our wonderful family, and this is truly a dream come true," the Hutchisons said after the latter adoption.

KEY VOTES

2002

No Pass farm bill reversing crop subsidy limits
Yes Postpone tougher automobile fuel efficiency standards
No Overhaul campaign finance law; ban "soft money" and restrict advocacy advertising
Yes Set federal election standards
Yes Support oil drilling in Arctic National Wildlife Refuge
Yes Revive fast-track procedures for trade agreements
No Create federal insurance coverage for catastrophic terrorist losses
Yes Tighten federal accounting and corporate governance regulation
No Advance bipartisan Medicare prescription drug plan
Yes Create independent Sept. 11 commission
No Back Democratic Homeland Security Department proposal
Yes Authorize war against Iraq

2001

Yes Confirm John Ashcroft as attorney general
Yes Nullify Clinton Labor Department ergonomics rule
Yes Cut taxes by $1.35 trillion through fiscal 2011
No Pass Democratic bill to bolster rights of patients in managed-care plans
No Permit a new round of military base closings
Yes Expand law enforcement power to investigate suspected terrorists

CQ VOTE STUDIES

	PARTY UNITY		PRESIDENTIAL SUPPORT	
	Support	Oppose	Support	Oppose
2002	92%	8%	96%	4%
2001	90%	10%	96%	4%
2000	96%	4%	45%	55%
1999	90%	10%	29%	71%
1998	92%	8%	37%	63%
1997	95%	5%	63%	37%
1996	98%	2%	34%	66%
1995	96%	4%	29%	71%
1994	94%	6%	38%	62%
1993	88%	12%	46%	54%

INTEREST GROUPS

	AFL-CIO	ADA	CCUS	ACU
2002	23%	5%	95%	100%
2001	19%	10%	85%	96%
2000	0%	0%	93%	96%
1999	0%	0%	94%	88%
1998	0%	0%	100%	88%
1997	0%	5%	100%	92%
1996	0%	5%	92%	100%
1995	8%	0%	100%	87%
1994	0%	10%	100%	96%
1993	0%	13%	100%	94%

Sen. John Cornyn (R)

CAPITOL OFFICE
224-2934
cornyn.senate.gov
517 Hart 20510-4302; fax 228-2856

COMMITTEES
Armed Services
Budget
Environment & Public Works
Judiciary
(Constitution, Civil Rights & Property Rights - chairman)

HOMETOWN
San Antonio

BORN
Feb. 2, 1952, Houston, Texas

RELIGION
Church of Christ

FAMILY
Wife, Sandy Cornyn; two children

EDUCATION
Trinity U., B.A. 1973 (journalism); St. Mary's U., J.D. 1977; U. of Virginia, LL.M. 1995

CAREER
Lawyer

POLITICAL HIGHLIGHTS
Texas District Court judge, 1985-91; Texas Supreme Court, 1991-97; Texas attorney general, 1999-2002

ELECTION RESULTS

2002 GENERAL		
John Cornyn (R)	2,496,243	55.3%
Ron Kirk (D)	1,955,758	43.3%
2002 PRIMARY		
John Cornyn (R)	478,825	77.3%
Bruce Rusty Lang (R)	46,907	7.6%
Douglas G. Deffenbaugh (R)	43,611	7.0%
Dudley F. Mooney (R)	32,202	5.2%
Lawrence Cranberg (R)	17,757	2.9%

Elected 2002; 1st term

Whether or not Cornyn turns out to be the most self-effacing member of the Senate, he provides an easy counterpoint to the stereotype of the larger-than-life Texas politico. His predecessor, Phil Gramm, was one of the Senate's most outspoken, acerbic and confrontational forces. And Cornyn's earnest and dull manner had even his own partisans grumbling during the 2002 campaign that he was not sufficiently animated to win statewide.

During six years as a justice of the state Supreme Court and four more as state attorney general, however, Cornyn (CORE-nin) developed a reputation for dignity and even-handedness that he hopes will serve him well as a senator. Combining his judicial background and his home-state affinity with President Bush, Cornyn was seeking as the 108th Congress began to end an acrimonious partisan impasse over judicial confirmations.

"I hope we don't get so bogged down in recrimination and finger-pointing and tit-for-tat that we forget why it is that we were sent here," said Cornyn, who hoped to use his new Judiciary Committee seat to devise some plan for expediting consideration of Bush's nominees for the federal courts. "We need a clean break and a fresh start."

Cornyn took office in December 2002, when Gramm resigned a month ahead of the conclusion of his third term to give his fellow Republican a head start in setting up his office and getting to know Washington. It was an advantage Cornyn welcomed; of the 10 freshman senators in the 108th, he and Republican Norm Coleman of Minnesota are the only ones who had never before lived in the national capital.

But Cornyn did particularly well in his committee assignments. On Judiciary, his top choice, he landed the chairmanship of the Constitution Subcommittee. On Armed Services, he will be well-situated to shepherd the needs of his state's 19 major military installations. On Environment and Public Works, he was perfectly positioned to advocate for vigorous road-building and airport improvements in Texas as the new highway and aviation laws are written in the 108th. And on Budget, he was expected to stand as a true believer — if not an overly vocal one — in the president's fiscal policies.

Cornyn rose to Republican prominence in Texas in the 1990s a few years ahead of Bush, but the two became somewhat close during their time together in Austin. The former governor telephoned the senator-elect on election night in 2002 to say, "Congratulations, Johnny Boy."

An advocate of indefinitely extending the tax cuts Bush pushed to enactment in 2001, which will otherwise lapse after 2010, Cornyn also backed without reservation Bush's decision to wage war on Iraq, and he favors Bush's effort to deploy a national missile defense system. Like Bush, Cornyn also advocates the concept of allowing people to invest a part of their Social Security taxes in securities. He touted the proposal in his campaign, even though it had fallen out of favor as a Republican campaign issue because of a sharp drop in stock values.

A pet cause of Cornyn's does put him at odds with the White House: As attorney general, he was a strong proponent of the government responsibility to remain accountable to the public. True to form, he opposes Bush's plan to exempt the proposed Department of Homeland Security from federal open records rules. And he was critical of the administration's efforts to keep secret the deliberations of its energy policy task force.

Nor was Cornyn a Republican rubber stamp while in Austin. On the Texas Supreme Court, which handles only civil cases, he wrote the majority opinion upholding the state's so-called Robin Hood school finance law, which requires wealthier school districts to share money with poorer ones. The plan is unpopular with many Republicans.

When he was elected attorney general in 1998, he was the first Republican to hold the post since Reconstruction. He sought to reduce partisanship in the office. And he angered some Republicans by working, unsuccessfully, to scale back a ruling by his Democratic predecessor that had eliminated affirmative action programs in Texas universities.

Like Bush, however, Cornyn's career in state government was characterized by a pro-business, limited government philosophy. On the Supreme Court and as attorney general, Cornyn favored strict restrictions on medical malpractice lawsuits, and on the court he joined a ruling allowing cigarette companies to partially escape blame for smoking-related health claims.

As attorney general, he was criticized by consumer rights groups for not imposing strong enough penalties on corporate offenders. He arranged for multimillion dollar settlements, however: Auto insurance companies paid $5 million to settle undercompensation claims, while nursing home operators paid $4 million to settle claims of negligence. And his office overhauled the state's child support collection system; in 2002, Texas collected 86 percent more than it had four years before.

The son of a B-17 pilot in World War II, Cornyn and his family eventually settled in San Antonio, where his father became an Air Force pathologist. A wrestler in high school and college, Cornyn's college major was journalism. But he was eventually turned off by reporters' low salaries and waited tables at a Steak and Ale restaurant while earning his real estate license. When that career failed to be lucrative (because of a sagging economy), Cornyn headed for law school. He later became a successful lawyer in San Antonio, specializing in defending doctors against medical malpractice lawsuits.

His break into politics was almost unexpected. In 1984, some Republican friends of his — looking to crack the Democrats' longstanding hold on Texas' judicial elections — approached him at a Super Bowl party and asked him to run for a state District Court seat. He did, and he won. Six years later, he was elected to the state Supreme Court. In 1998, he won a bruising attorney general's race against Democrat Jim Mattox, who had held the office for eight years ending in 1991 and had served six years in the House before that.

Cornyn's next big partisan break came at the start of the decade, when as attorney general he was chairman of a commission that proposed new Texas political boundaries for this decade to the state legislature. Cornyn presented a redistricting plan that likely would have resulted in major Republican gains. A less partisan map was eventually imposed by the courts, but Cornyn's efforts raised his standing with presidential political strategist Karl Rove. When Gramm decided to retire, several Republicans expressed interest in running, including Rep. Henry Bonilla. But the field was quickly cleared for Cornyn, and he won a GOP primary against four minimally known opponents with 77 percent of the vote.

After a primary that included Rep. Ken Bentsen of Houston, Democrats nominated Ron Kirk, a charismatic and politically centrist former mayor of Dallas who sought to become the state's first African-American senator. But Cornyn's conservative credentials outweighed Kirk's personality and history-making appeal. Running on his support for a Republican Party that has grown dominant in Texas politics and his allegiance to Bush — an overwhelmingly popular figure in the state he served as governor from 1995 to 2000 — Cornyn won with 55 percent.

Rep. Max Sandlin (D)

CAPITOL OFFICE
225-3035
www.house.gov/sandlin
324 Cannon 20515-4301; fax 225-5866

COMMITTEES
Ways & Means

HOMETOWN
Marshall

BORN
Sept. 29, 1952, Texarkana, Texas

RELIGION
Baptist

FAMILY
Divorced; four children

EDUCATION
Baylor U., B.A. 1975 (journalism & political science), J.D. 1978

CAREER
Lawyer; fuel company executive

POLITICAL HIGHLIGHTS
Harrison County Democratic Party chairman, 1984-86; Harrison County judge, 1986-89; Harrison County Court at law judge, 1989-96

ELECTION RESULTS

2002 GENERAL		
Max Sandlin (D)	86,384	56.5%
John Lawrence (R)	66,654	43.6%
2002 PRIMARY		
Max Sandlin (D)	unopposed	
2000 GENERAL		
Max Sandlin (D)	118,157	55.8%
Noble Willingham (R)	91,912	43.4%

PREVIOUS WINNING PERCENTAGES
1998 (59%); 1996 (52%)

Elected 1996; 4th term

Commerce and government have long been closely intertwined in the Lone Star State, and Sandlin — an energy executive, lawyer and judge — fits the mold of Democratic businessman-politician with the ability to appeal to a range of Texas voters.

After earning his law degree from Baylor, Sandlin set up shop as an attorney. He eventually made a small fortune in the oil, gas and gasoline distribution business and in 1986, moved into the first of two county-level judgeships. He has established himself in the largely rural and politically centrist 1st District by supporting popular conservative causes while staying faithful to Democratic efforts to help senior citizens and lower-income workers.

Sandlin's profile has grown steadily in the House, and in the 108th Congress he won a coveted assignment to the exclusive Ways and Means Committee, where he is the second Texas Democrat along with the far-more-liberal Lloyd Doggett. Sandlin is the only panel Democrat who voted for President Bush's signature 2001 tax cut, a reflection of liberal Minority Leader Nancy Pelosi's efforts to elevate more-moderate lawmakers to positions of power in the caucus. Sandlin also remains one of seven chief deputy whips, a position he also held in the 107th.

A member of the conservative "Blue Dog" and the moderate New Democrat coalitions, Sandlin said he has tried to use his leadership posts "to bring a moderate and centrist position" to his caucus because "I believe that it is important that we govern from the center." His voting record is on the conservative end of the Democratic spectrum; in the 107th Congress he backed Bush more often than all but about three dozen Democrats.

From his early days as a freshman, Sandlin talked of a "spirit of cooperation" with Republicans. "This class has learned from the mistakes and the polarization" of the 104th Congress, he said.

Several Republican initiatives have won Sandlin's endorsement. He is one of the few Democrats to support a constitutional amendment requiring a two-thirds congressional majority to raise federal taxes. He backs a constitutional amendment to outlaw desecration of the U.S. flag, votes to ban a procedure its opponents call "partial birth" abortion, opposes congressional pay raises and often seeks to scale back environmental regulations.

A member of the Congressional Sportsmen's Caucus, Sandlin is an enthusiastic hunter and opposes gun control. He told the Fort Worth Star-Telegram in 1999 that he owned about 15 guns and had already begun to teach his 4-year-old son how to shoot.

But on other issues, Sandlin sides with the more liberal members of his party. He is a staunch supporter of patients' rights legislation that would allow managed-care patients to sue their health care providers. "As we increase access to health care, we must not allow unqualified parties to make critical decisions about patient treatment," he said in the 106th. "Patients need to feel confident that their doctors are giving them all necessary information, without concern of retaliation by a health insurance provider."

Sandlin allies himself with organized labor in its fight against a GOP measure allowing companies to offer their employees compensatory time off instead of pay for overtime work. He also supports such Democratic priorities as increasing the minimum wage and approving funds to hire 100,000 new teachers.

The 2001 collapse of energy giant Enron Corp. reverberated for Sandlin and many of his constituents in the company's home state. During inquiries into Enron's demise, and later into the bankruptcy of WorldCom Inc., Sandlin used his seat on the Financial Services Committee to take top brass to task for mismanagement. When former WorldCom CEO Bernard J. Ebbers delivered an opening statement before the panel and then invoked the Fifth Amendment, Sandlin was the first lawmaker to call for Ebbers to be cited for contempt of Congress.

To take the Ways and Means assignment, Sandlin had to relinquish his posts on the Financial Services and Transportation panels. In two terms on Financial Services, Sandlin pressed for improved access to capital in rural America. In the 106th, he voted for a measure that was designed to provide tax breaks and other incentives for companies that do business in economically distressed areas. "Rural America still lags behind the rest of the country when it comes to earnings, employment, education and other key economic indicators," he said. "We still have a lot of work to do to ensure that places like East Texas are not left on the outside looking in at this strong national economy."

On Transportation, where he had served since he arrived on Capitol Hill, Sandlin sought funding for highway construction projects in his district and advocated funding for Amtrak. The oil-state Democrat also has fought for initiatives aimed at boosting the safety of the nation's 2.2 million miles of oil and gas pipelines.

Sandlin has shown he's not afraid to step into some fiery battles on Capitol Hill. Perhaps the most heated scraps have been over who would win the title of "Zestiest Legislator." In 2002 Sandlin was the only lawmaker to show up for the competition, sponsored by Chili Pepper magazine. He downed eight jalapeños in five minutes, washing them down with swigs of hot sauce. He said his secret was a lifetime of training; he eats peppers daily and splashes hot sauce on almost everything. "I have fire in my belly," he said. In 2003, despite devouring 40 jalapeños, he finished second to Joe Baca of California.

When Democratic Rep. Jim Chapman left the 1st in 1996 for an ultimately unsuccessful Senate bid, Sandlin sought the open seat, stressing his community involvement and promising to be "the chief marketing agent for the district." Aided by Chapman's backing, Sandlin won the nomination with 56 percent of the vote. He won the general election by 5 percentage points, even as GOP presidential candidate Bob Dole narrowly carried the district. In 2000, when Bush carried the district by 28 points, and in 2002, Sandlin posted 12- and 13-point victories, respectively; the 1st District's political makeup was minimally altered by redistricting.

KEY VOTES

2002

- Yes Overhaul campaign finance law; ban "soft money" and restrict advocacy advertising
- Yes Back Bush's defense budget increase
- No Extend 1996 welfare law
- No Adopt Bush's discretionary spending limit
- No Pass GOP Medicare prescription drug plan
- Yes Create independent Sept. 11 commission
- Yes Extend union protections to Homeland Security Department employees
- No Revive fast-track procedures for trade agreements
- Yes Authorize war against Iraq
- No Advance bankruptcy overhaul opposed by abortion opponents

2001

- No Nullify Clinton Labor Department ergonomics rule
- Yes Cut taxes by $1.35 trillion through fiscal 2011
- No Maintain ban on oil drilling in Arctic National Wildlife Refuge
- No Approve Bush proposal to limit managed-care plan liability for coverage decisions
- No Divert money from crop subsidy payments to land conservation
- Yes Expand law enforcement power to investigate suspected terrorists

CQ VOTE STUDIES

	PARTY UNITY		PRESIDENTIAL SUPPORT	
	Support	Oppose	Support	Oppose
2002	83%	17%	50%	50%
2001	79%	21%	40%	60%
2000	75%	25%	57%	43%
1999	74%	26%	68%	32%
1998	72%	28%	63%	37%

INTEREST GROUPS

	AFL-CIO	ADA	CCUS	ACU
2002	78%	70%	60%	40%
2001	83%	80%	52%	32%
2000	80%	60%	71%	33%
1999	78%	70%	60%	24%
1998	80%	80%	61%	40%

TEXAS 1

Northeast – Texarkana, Nacogdoches, Paris

The 1st wraps around Texas' northeast corner along the Oklahoma and Arkansas borders to take in Texarkana, then stretches south along the Louisiana border to take in most of Nacogdoches County. Mostly removed from the Dallas-Fort Worth suburbs, the 1st has a rural Southern feel that is harder to find in other Texas districts.

The economic dominance of natural resources — timber, oil and natural gas — has diminished since the oil bust of the 1980s and the rise of the manufacturing sector, which now drives the economy. The 1st still faces some economic challenges from foreign timber companies and cattle ranchers who can sell their products at lower prices. A small but significant defense industry is centered around Greenville. Slow population growth and miles of forests and agricultural land are hallmarks of the district but do less to improve its economy than the highways that connect the district to the outside world.

Residents of the 1st tend to be conservative, even among Democrats, and the region associates itself with the "Bible Belt" that stretches through much of the South. A bastion of political populism, the district has one of the largest percentages of elderly residents in the state.

Counties in the district's west and south — such as Hunt, Wood, Nacogdoches and Rusk — vote reliably Republican. But conservative Democrats can win in the 1st, especially in the east. In 2002, GOP Gov. Rick Perry lost just Cass, Morris and Marion counties, and GOP Senate nominee John Cornyn lost only Morris and Marion. Morris, home to a big Lone Star Steel plant, was the only county in the 1st — and the only Texas county in a 170-mile radius — not to back George W. Bush in 2000.

MAJOR INDUSTRY

Timber, light manufacturing, agriculture, oil

MILITARY BASES

Red River Army Depot, 4 military, 518 civilian (2002)

CITIES

Texarkana, 34,782; Nacogdoches, 29,914; Paris, 25,898; Greenville, 23,960

NOTABLE

"Uncle Jesse's Memorial Big Bass Classic," inspired by the TV show "Dukes of Hazzard," is an annual event in Paris; Texarkana is split between Texas and Arkansas — it has two mayors, two police forces and two school systems — and is the birthplace of Ross Perot.

Rep. Jim Turner (D)

CAPITOL OFFICE
225-2401
www.house.gov/turner
330 Cannon 20515-4302; fax 225-5955

COMMITTEES
Armed Services
Select Homeland Security - ranking member

HOMETOWN
Crockett

BORN
Feb. 6, 1946, Fort Lewis, Wash.

RELIGION
Baptist

FAMILY
Wife, Ginny Turner; two children

EDUCATION
U. of Texas, B.B.A 1968, M.B.A. 1971, J.D. 1971

MILITARY SERVICE
Army Reserve, 1972-78

CAREER
Lawyer; gubernatorial aide

POLITICAL HIGHLIGHTS
Texas House, 1981-84; mayor of Crockett, 1989-91; Texas Senate, 1991-97

ELECTION RESULTS

2002 GENERAL		
Jim Turner (D)	85,492	60.9%
Van Brookshire (R)	53,656	38.2%
2002 PRIMARY		
Jim Turner (D)		unopposed
2000 GENERAL		
Jim Turner (D)	162,891	91.1%
Gary Lyndon Dye (LIBERT)	15,939	8.9%

PREVIOUS WINNING PERCENTAGES
1998 (58%); 1996 (52%)

Elected 1996; 4th term

Democrats looking to maintain their foothold in Texas politics appear to have found a winning combination in Turner. The straight-laced former Sunday school teacher and military man offers the perfect political platform for his struggling rural East Texas district — fiscal and social conservatism that makes exceptions for the needs of the home folks.

In the 108th Congress, Turner was tapped by Democratic leader Nancy Pelosi for a high-profile task: top-ranking Democrat on the newly formed Committee on Homeland Security — a panel with the daunting task of overseeing the first formative months of the new Homeland Security Department and coordinating Congressional homeland security efforts.

Turner, a Vietnam-era Army veteran, had been the top Democrat on the terrorism task force that the Armed Services Committee created after the Sept. 11, 2001, attacks on the World Trade Center and the Pentagon. He was active in promoting a measure to authorize a memorial to the attacks' victims in Washington, D.C., and he was one of several members who attempted to get to the bottom of the anthrax infestation that followed the attacks. As a member of the Government Reform and Oversight Committee in the 107th, Turner was particularly concerned that "postal workers were exposed, and in some cases infected, with anthrax due to improper communication" within the government.

In the 108th, Turner also is the second-ranking Democrat on the Armed Services panel's new Terrorism and Unconventional Threats Subcommittee.

As a leader of the "Blue Dog" coalition of conservative Democrats, Turner is often the moderate Democrats' voice on fiscal issues, particularly in urging Congress and the president to resist increasing the federal debt. At the same time, he supported the $410 billion farm bill passed in 2002, and he generally advocates increased defense spending, especially if it benefits his district. In the 108th, Turner is one of three Blue Dog co-chairmen.

Despite his conservative leanings, Turner seems to get along well with the party's more liberal leaders, and he is moving quietly up the ranks. He was appointed, along with Martin T. Meehan of Massachusetts, to oversee the party's work on the campaign finance law rewrite. At the behest of the Blue Dogs, Turner filed the discharge petition that eventually forced GOP leaders to bring the measure to the floor. The bill ultimately was passed by Congress and signed by President Bush.

Democrats chose Turner to give their weekly radio address when the House was considering legislation to provide patients certain legal rights when dealing with their health insurers. Turner's history of proposing such legislation in Texas likely won him the radio spot. As a member of the Texas Senate, he had sponsored the first "patient protection" law. Though the legislature passed his bill in 1995, then-Gov. George W. Bush vetoed it. It passed again in 1997 and became law without Bush's signature.

Occasionally, though, Turner is far from the party mainstream. He voted for a measure that overturned President Clinton's workplace ergonomics rules, and he has been a recurrent backer of tax cuts. His support for tax reduction has a limit, however. By 2002, when it had become clear that the government was returning to deficit spending, Turner voted against extending the generous cuts Congress had made the year before.

Despite his efforts to hold down the federal debt and his longstanding advocacy of a bill that would review most government programs every 10 years, Turner is far from anti-government. He backed a bill to allow federal employees to keep frequent flier miles they earned on government travel.

His work on a drug plan for Medicare recipients perhaps best reflects his political style. With many in his party pushing for federal coverage of prescription drugs and many Republicans favoring a less government-oriented approach, Turner and Tom Allen, a Maine Democrat, tried to find a middle ground. They pushed legislation that would require drug companies to lower prices for Medicare beneficiaries, granting them the discounts that other large purchasers receive.

Turner says his ardent support for Medicare and Social Security drive his desire for a balanced federal budget. Many of Turner's constituents in East Texas are dependent on government help or contracts. In addition to supporting the 2002 farm bill, Turner also proposed a measure that would provide immediate and expanded tax incentives for timberland owners who planted trees to replace those cut down.

Turner's policy approach may appear scattershot to onlookers, but the former Army captain does little on the fly. At an early age, Turner realized his interest in politics, serving on student legislative bodies in high school and at the University of Texas, where he earned law and business degrees. While in college, he worked for a state lawmaker and for Democratic Govs. John Connally and Preston Smith. He joined the ROTC and went on active duty briefly following graduate school. After he went on Reserve status, he practiced law, always with the idea of getting involved in politics.

The opportunity came in 1980, when he made a successful run for the Texas House. Turner served four years there, leaving to work for Democratic Gov. Mark White. After a two-year stint as mayor of Crockett, he returned to Austin in 1991 when he won election to the state Senate.

In Turner's many campaigns, he is noted for his unusual campaign literature — a cookbook containing his wife Ginny's favorite recipes. Through the years, the cookbook's offerings have expanded beyond the Turner kitchen, but it remains a popular, and collectible, campaign tool.

Since succeeding his political compatriot but personal opposite — the flamboyant Charlie Wilson — in Congress in 1996, Turner has not lost his common touch. He and his father still frequent a favorite diner, spending hours swapping stories with customers rather than making the rounds to visit with local officials. The practice has paid off — Turner won re-election handily in 1998 and faced no opposition in 2000. He was also spared a significant change in his district lines, although, like most of the state's voters, his constituents are more likely to be Republicans than in the past. In 2002, he won by 23 percentage points.

KEY VOTES

2002

Yes Overhaul campaign finance law; ban "soft money" and restrict advocacy advertising
Yes Back Bush's defense budget increase
No Extend 1996 welfare law
No Adopt Bush's discretionary spending limit
No Pass GOP Medicare prescription drug plan
? Create independent Sept. 11 commission
Yes Extend union protections to Homeland Security Department employees
No Revive fast-track procedures for trade agreements
Yes Authorize war against Iraq
Yes Advance bankruptcy overhaul opposed by abortion opponents

2001

Yes Nullify Clinton Labor Department ergonomics rule
Yes Cut taxes by $1.35 trillion through fiscal 2011
No Maintain ban on oil drilling in Arctic National Wildlife Refuge
No Approve Bush proposal to limit managed-care plan liability for coverage decisions
No Divert money from crop subsidy payments to land conservation
Yes Expand law enforcement power to investigate suspected terrorists

CQ VOTE STUDIES

	PARTY UNITY		PRESIDENTIAL SUPPORT	
	Support	Oppose	Support	Oppose
2002	74%	26%	44%	56%
2001	69%	31%	44%	56%
2000	75%	25%	68%	32%
1999	64%	36%	60%	40%
1998	58%	42%	53%	47%

INTEREST GROUPS

	AFL-CIO	ADA	CCUS	ACU
2002	78%	75%	55%	32%
2001	75%	60%	57%	48%
2000	80%	75%	61%	29%
1999	67%	75%	60%	28%
1998	60%	65%	72%	48%

TEXAS 2

East – Huntsville, Lufkin, Orange

A sprawling mass of east Texas territory, the hardscrabble 2nd borders Louisiana to the east and reaches west to near Bryan. Its southern border skirts the oil city of Beaumont in the 9th and suburbs northeast of Houston. A mostly rural district, the 2nd's most populous cities are Huntsville, just off Interstate 45 in the southwestern part of the district, and Lufkin, located in the north and surrounded by vast timber forests.

The 2nd's economy has been split between the eastern and southern portions, which rely on the chemical and shipping industries based in Orange and nearby Beaumont and Port Arthur, and the northern and western sections, where timber still reigns. Government jobs and contracts became increasingly important to the region as its industrial and manufacturing economies slipped somewhat during the late 1980s and early 1990s. Slow population growth and a high percentage of blue-collar workers have made it difficult to attract higher-paying service jobs. The Texas State Penitentiary at Huntsville, home of the state's death row, is one economic factor in the district.

The southern end of the district is in the orbit of Houston. Liberty and San Jacinto counties experienced robust population growth in the 1990s, and many Liberty residents make a long commute to work in Houston.

A court-drawn redistricting plan following the 2000 census kept the 2nd's shape mostly intact. The plan tweaked the boundaries of the 2nd's share of Nacogdoches and Montgomery counties and moved Shelby County, located on the Louisiana border, to the 1st. The 2nd tends to vote like Texas overall — mostly conservative and Republican, but not overwhelmingly enough to shut out Democrats. In 2002, the 16 counties wholly in the district together voted for Senate and gubernatorial candidates in the same proportion as the state at large (56 percent to 43 percent for John Cornyn and 58 percent to 40 percent for Rick Perry).

MAJOR INDUSTRY
Timber, petrochemicals, shipping

CITIES
Huntsville, 35,078; Lufkin, 32,709; Orange, 18,643; Jacksonville, 13,868

NOTABLE
Cut and Shoot, a town in Montgomery County, is said to be named after a confrontation in 1912; Huntsville's favorite son is Sam Houston, the first president of the Republic of Texas.

Rep. Sam Johnson (R)

CAPITOL OFFICE
225-4201
www.house.gov/samjohnson
1211 Longworth 20515-4303; fax 225-1485

COMMITTEES
Education & Workforce
(Employer-Employee Relations - chairman)
Ways & Means

HOMETOWN
Plano

BORN
Oct. 11, 1930, San Antonio, Texas

RELIGION
Methodist

FAMILY
Wife, Shirley Johnson; three children

EDUCATION
Southern Methodist U., B.B.A. 1951; George Washington U., M.S.I.A. 1974 (international affairs)

MILITARY SERVICE
Air Force, 1951-79

CAREER
Home builder; Air Force pilot

POLITICAL HIGHLIGHTS
Texas House, 1985-91

ELECTION RESULTS

2002 GENERAL		
Sam Johnson (R)	113,974	74.0%
Manny Molera (D)	37,503	24.3%
John Davis (LIBERT)	2,656	1.7%
2002 PRIMARY		
Sam Johnson (R)	17,153	84.3%
Thomas Caiazzo (R)	3,184	15.7%
2000 GENERAL		
Sam Johnson (R)	187,486	71.6%
Billy Wayne Zachary (D)	67,233	25.7%
Lance Flores (LIBERT)	7,178	2.7%

PREVIOUS WINNING PERCENTAGES
1998 (91%); 1996 (73%); 1994 (91%); 1992 (86%); 1991 Special Runoff Election (53%)

Elected May 1991; 6th full term

A career Air Force pilot who spent nearly seven years as a prisoner of war in Vietnam — more than half of that in solitary confinement — Johnson has dedicated much of his work in Congress to improving national security and helping military personnel. But while his priorities reflect a diehard conservatism, his personal demeanor is unassuming and non-combative.

"You can sit there and shoot bullets at the government all day, but unless you get personally involved, you can't get a lot done," he says in a slow Texas drawl.

He says he developed that philosophy during his time as a POW, where he decided to become active in politics as soon as he had gained his freedom and returned to the United States. Since then, he says, he has developed this additional credo: "Sometimes I think you're more effective if you're not in somebody's face. You have to work with everyone in your party and the other party."

As a result, everyone seems to like Johnson, even those with whom he disagrees. Despite his strong conservative beliefs, he has worked with Democrats on issues concerning Social Security and health care. His friendly and easygoing personality has also resulted in a loyal staff. Many of his top aides have worked with him since he first came to Congress in 1991.

But that's not to say Johnson is a shrinking violet: He was particularly outspoken in his criticism of Bill Clinton, dating back to the 1992 presidential campaign, when he characterized the Democratic candidate's post-college trip to Moscow and his avoidance of military service as un-American.

Now in his 70s, Johnson is a dependable anchor for the conservative faction of House Republicans, offering his younger compatriots the lessons of his experience while helping them to remain focused on their goal of limiting federal government. He is one of the four founders of the Republican Study Committee (originally known as the Conservative Action Team, or "CATs"), a group of about 70 of the most conservative House Republicans.

After the terrorist attacks of Sept. 11, 2001, Johnson's focus on national security and the military became even more intense. During a speech on the House floor the next day, Johnson said the devastation in New York and Virginia was worse than the B-52 bombing raids he lived through while a prisoner in Hanoi. Although he supported the resolution authorizing the president to use "all necessary and appropriate force" against those who perpetrated the attacks, Johnson said he would prefer an all-out declaration of war.

When the military campaign began, Johnson encouraged the writing of letters and e-mails to the troops. As an outgrowth of his interest in military morale, he promoted legislation in the 107th Congress to protect the voting rights of overseas military members and their families.

Along with military concerns, Johnson has concentrated on employment and economic issues from seats on both the Ways and Means and Education and the Workforce committees.

As chairman of the latter panel's Subcommittee on Employer-Employee relations, in 2002 he and the full committee chairman, John A. Boehner of Ohio, pushed the legislation to carry out Bush's proposals for altering pension law in the wake of the Enron Corp. bankruptcy, which caused severe financial losses for thousands of employees whose retirement savings were tied up in ultimately worthless corporate stock.

Johnson's staff reports that he is perpetually optimistic, even while pursuing some seemingly endless campaigns. One was waged to eliminate the so-called Social Security earnings test, in which the benefits of some senior citizens were reduced if they continued to earn a salary. He finally saw victory on that front with a law enacted in 2000.

From his Ways and Means seat, long before President Bush took office, Johnson was promoting several of the proposals that ended up in the 2001 law creating the deepest tax cut in two decades: elimination of the inheritance tax and alleviation of the "marriage penalty," a quirk in the tax code that results in some couples paying higher taxes than they would if each person were single. Johnson says he would favor repealing the 16th Amendment, which authorized the collection of federal income tax.

As a Smithsonian Institution regent, Johnson is particularly enthusiastic about the coming National Air and Space Museum annex near Dulles International Airport. He persuaded Speaker Newt Gingrich to name him to the Smithsonian board in 1995 when he and other lawmakers protested an exhibit on the "Enola Gay" — the plane that dropped the first atomic bomb on Japan — because it depicted Japan as a victim. Johnson then helped arrange for a scaled-back exhibit that focused on the mechanics of the plane rather than the morality of its mission.

Johnson did not plan on a military career. He recalls that participation in the ROTC was mandatory when he went to high school toward the end of World War II. He was aiming at a career in business and law when the Korean War intervened, and his entire ROTC class at Southern Methodist University was called to duty. Accepted into flight training school, he soon fell in love with flying and that sold him on a career in the Air Force. In addition to his combat missions over Korea and Vietnam, Johnson was a member of the Thunderbirds precision flying team for two years and served as director of the Air Force's "Top Gun" fighter pilot school.

Johnson's plane was shot down over North Vietnam in 1966. He does not talk much about his days as a POW, but he did write a book about his experience, "Captive Warriors." After his solitary confinement ended, he roomed with John McCain, now the senator from Arizona, at the prison camp.

Upon his release in 1973, he had three operations on his right hand, including a tendon transplant, and was able to resume flying. After retiring from the Air Force in 1979 as a colonel, Johnson went into the home building business in Dallas. He got into local Republican Party affairs and, in 1984, won a seat in the Texas House. When GOP Rep. Steve Bartlett resigned in March 1991 to run for mayor of Dallas, Johnson overcame a tough scramble to win his party's nomination. But in the wealthy, solidly Republican 3rd District, he has had no electoral difficulty since.

KEY VOTES

2002

- No Overhaul campaign finance law; ban "soft money" and restrict advocacy advertising
- Yes Back Bush's defense budget increase
- Yes Extend 1996 welfare law
- Yes Adopt Bush's discretionary spending limit
- Yes Pass GOP Medicare prescription drug plan
- No Create independent Sept. 11 commission
- No Extend union protections to Homeland Security Department employees
- Yes Revive fast-track procedures for trade agreements
- Yes Authorize war against Iraq
- No Advance bankruptcy overhaul opposed by abortion opponents

2001

- Yes Nullify Clinton Labor Department ergonomics rule
- Yes Cut taxes by $1.35 trillion through fiscal 2011
- No Maintain ban on oil drilling in Arctic National Wildlife Refuge
- Yes Approve Bush proposal to limit managed-care plan liability for coverage decisions
- No Divert money from crop subsidy payments to land conservation
- Yes Expand law enforcement power to investigate suspected terrorists

CQ VOTE STUDIES

	Party Unity Support	Party Unity Oppose	Presidential Support Support	Presidential Support Oppose
2002	98%	2%	89%	11%
2001	97%	3%	91%	9%
2000	98%	2%	25%	75%
1999	97%	3%	17%	83%
1998	96%	4%	20%	80%

INTEREST GROUPS

	AFL-CIO	ADA	CCUS	ACU
2002	13%	0%	90%	100%
2001	0%	0%	91%	100%
2000	0%	0%	85%	100%
1999	0%	0%	88%	96%
1998	0%	0%	88%	100%

TEXAS 3

Northeast Dallas suburbs — Plano

The 3rd has moved steadily northward since 1990. It used to be a Dallas-based district, home to some of the city's wealthiest areas, but redistricting in 1996 and 2001 moved the district to the city's northern suburbs, including most of Collin County. Collin — the state's fastest-growing county in the 1990s — includes most of the suburban cities of Plano, Frisco and McKinney. The district still takes in part of northeast Dallas County, including most of the suburbs of Richardson and Garland. Collin has two-thirds and Dallas one-third of the district population.

Despite demographic changes, the district remains economically well-off, white and Republican. Many corporate headquarters have moved into the Plano area, and wealthy executives have built expensive homes in sections such as Deerfield. The concentration of electronic and telecommunications firms along U.S. Highway 75 has earned that area the name "Telecom Corridor." Texas Instruments and Electronic Data Systems are a major presence along the corridor. Just off the Lyndon B. Johnson Freeway along U.S. 75, Richardson has benefited greatly from high-tech firms and is growing at a rapid rate. Frisco also is undergoing a population and development boom. The district has middle-class areas such as Garland, which grew at a steady pace in the 1980s and 1990s. About two-thirds of Garland is in the 3rd. Although downtown Dallas is in the 30th, its white-collar companies rely heavily on the 3rd for their work force.

The district is solidly Republican — Collin County is filled with young, upwardly mobile professionals and is even more Republican than suburbs that are closer to Dallas. In the 2002 Senate race, Republican John Cornyn won 70 percent of the 3rd's share of Collin, capturing all but two precincts in the county, and 68 percent overall. Republican Gov. Rick Perry took 72 percent of the vote in the 3rd.

MAJOR INDUSTRY

Telecommunications, transportation, banking

CITIES

Plano (pt.), 219,890; Garland (pt.), 146,118; Richardson (pt.), 47,347; Dallas (pt.), 45,162; Allen, 43,554

NOTABLE

Southfork Ranch, the fictional home of the Ewing family in the long-running television program "Dallas," is located in Parker.

Rep. Ralph M. Hall (D)

CAPITOL OFFICE
225-6673
rmhall@mail.house.gov
www.house.gov/ralphhall
2405 Rayburn 20515-4304; fax 225-3332

COMMITTEES
Energy & Commerce
Science - ranking member

HOMETOWN
Rockwall

BORN
May 3, 1923, Fate, Texas

RELIGION
Methodist

FAMILY
Wife, Mary Ellen Hall; three children

EDUCATION
Texas Christian U., attended 1943 (pre-law); U. of Texas, attended 1946-47 (pre-law); Southern Methodist U., LL.B. 1951

MILITARY SERVICE
Navy, 1942-45

CAREER
Lawyer; aluminum company president

POLITICAL HIGHLIGHTS
Rockwall County judge, 1951-63; Texas Senate, 1963-73 (president pro tempore, 1968-69); sought Democratic nomination for lieutenant governor, 1972

ELECTION RESULTS

2002 GENERAL		
Ralph M. Hall (D)	97,304	57.8%
John Graves (R)	67,939	40.4%
Barbara Robinson (LIBERT)	3,042	1.8%
2002 PRIMARY		
Ralph M. Hall (D)		unopposed
2000 GENERAL		
Ralph M. Hall (D)	145,887	60.3%
Jon Newton (R)	91,574	37.9%
Joe Turner (LIBERT)	4,417	1.8%

PREVIOUS WINNING PERCENTAGES
1998 (58%); 1996 (64%); 1994 (59%); 1992 (58%); 1990 (100%); 1988 (66%); 1986 (72%); 1984 (58%); 1982 (74%); 1980 (52%)

Elected 1980; 12th term

The oldest House member in the 108th Congress — he turned 80 in 2003 — Hall is well-known at the Capitol for his folksy asides, one of the reminders that he is among the dwindling roster of conservative Southern Democrats in Congress.

That breed has steadily diminished as Republicans have captured more and more ground in the South's traditionally Democratic strongholds. And Hall's voting record could easily be mistaken for one of his younger conservative Republican colleagues. He favors scrapping most of the existing tax code and replacing it with a flat tax or national sales tax. He was chief cosponsor of a constitutional amendment to ban computer-generated child pornography on the Internet. And he was one of only nine House Democrats to support an indefinite extension of the $1.35 trillion tax cut of 2001, which is set to expire in 2010.

Still, Hall insists that he is an "old-time Democrat" intent on pulling his party back to the political center. "I'm a conservative more than I am a Republican or a Democrat, and I'll vote for a conservative thrust," he told the Dallas Morning News in 2001.

Hall's ambivalence with party labels drew attention before the 2002 election, when he told GOP leaders he would consider backing J. Dennis Hastert for Speaker if his vote were the deciding one. Some viewed the commitment as a bid to stave off a strong GOP challenge in his increasingly Republican district. And when the vote for Speaker came as the 108th Congress convened, Hall voted "present" instead of backing Minority Leader Nancy Pelosi of California, saying that his oil-patch district supports the rights of gun owners and is at odds with California on energy policy. Three other conservative Democrats similarly declined to vote for the far-more-liberal Pelosi. "There's got to be room in our party for honest liberals and honest moderates and honest conservatives. I think I cast an honest conservative vote today," Hall said.

It was not the first time Hall had cast such a maverick vote: In 1985 he voted "present" rather than support the re-election of Democrat Thomas P. "Tip" O'Neill Jr. of Massachusetts as Speaker.

In between those votes, Hall compiled a long history of rebuffing his party leaders. In 1998 he was one of only five Democrats to support the impeachment of President Clinton on the critical first charge of lying to a federal grand jury. In 2000 he publicly championed the presidential candidacy of Republican Texas Gov. George W. Bush. He strayed from the party line more often than any other House member in both the 106th and 107th Congresses. He backed President Bush 78 percent of the time in the 107th — more often than any other Democrat who served for the entire two years.

Hall's northeast Texas district was represented for nearly a half-century by Democratic Speaker Sam Rayburn. Today, however, the national Democratic Party has big image problems in that part of the country, which helps explain why Hall so reliably sides with the GOP, even when hardly any other Democrat does so.

Still, Hall has no plans to switch parties. After Democrats became the minority party in 1995, he helped start the "Blue Dog" coalition, a group of about 30 conservative House Democrats that seeks to pull the party to the right. Hall and his colleagues have used the coalition to advocate tax cuts and increased energy production, among other positions.

Stylistically, Hall is anything but a firebrand. An infrequent sponsor of legislation, he prefers to quietly look after the interests of his home state's oil and gas industry as the No. 4 Democrat on the Energy and Commerce Committee. "I don't have any pride of authorship," he says, "and I'll take somebody else's bill if it gives me what I want."

In the 107th, Hall was a key cosponsor of legislation to improve the safety and security of the nation's oil and gas pipelines, which gained new momentum after the terrorist attacks of Sept. 11, 2001.

As the top Democrat on the Science Committee, Hall has worked with Chairman Sherwood Boehlert, a New York Republican, to enhance the often-overlooked panel's prominence. After Sept. 11, he lobbied for designating an undersecretary of science and technology in the new Homeland Security Department. Hall believes cutting-edge research should be an integral part of the government's counterterrorism efforts in order to address vulnerabilities and respond quickly to future attacks.

Hall also is a strong advocate for NASA and has championed the space agency's biomedical and basic science programs. Hall was visibly disappointed when NASA scrapped a planned shuttle mission devoted to microgravity experiments in 2000 so the agency could direct more money to the $60 billion International Space Station. But, characteristically, he declined to publicly chastise agency officials at an oversight hearing. Hall is expected to continue guarding the agency's core science missions as NASA officials try to make cuts to offset cost overruns associated with the space station.

Hall's folksy humor and encyclopedic supply of rural Texas stories can defuse tension, and his political acumen gives him influence when he decides to weigh in. But he generally eschews quick legislative fixes. He was pleased that lawmakers did not move rapidly in drafting legislation to deregulate electric utilities in recent Congresses, saying states were better-positioned to take the lead. He says he places more of a premium on "doing it right, rather than doing it now."

Hall got an early start in politics. He was elected the county judge, or chief executive, of tiny Rockwall County in 1950 while still attending law school nearby in Dallas. Twelve years later, he moved up to the state Senate and spent a decade there, rising to become president pro tempore. After finishing fourth in the Democratic primary for lieutenant governor in 1972, he left public life to concentrate on business. But when 4th District Democrat Ray Roberts announced his retirement in 1980 after 18 years, Hall won the seat by defeating Republican John H. Wright, a Tyler business manager, with 52 percent of the vote. Republicans have not mounted a comparable challenge since.

KEY VOTES

2002

- No Overhaul campaign finance law; ban "soft money" and restrict advocacy advertising
- Yes Back Bush's defense budget increase
- Yes Extend 1996 welfare law
- No Adopt Bush's discretionary spending limit
- Yes Pass GOP Medicare prescription drug plan
- No Create independent Sept. 11 commission
- No Extend union protections to Homeland Security Department employees
- Yes Revive fast-track procedures for trade agreements
- Yes Authorize war against Iraq
- No Advance bankruptcy overhaul opposed by abortion opponents

2001

- Yes Nullify Clinton Labor Department ergonomics rule
- Yes Cut taxes by $1.35 trillion through fiscal 2011
- No Maintain ban on oil drilling in Arctic National Wildlife Refuge
- No Approve Bush proposal to limit managed-care plan liability for coverage decisions
- No Divert money from crop subsidy payments to land conservation
- Yes Expand law enforcement power to investigate suspected terrorists

CQ VOTE STUDIES

	PARTY UNITY		PRESIDENTIAL SUPPORT	
	Support	Oppose	Support	Oppose
2002	40%	60%	70%	30%
2001	25%	75%	86%	14%
2000	35%	65%	22%	78%
1999	30%	70%	31%	69%
1998	23%	77%	30%	70%

INTEREST GROUPS

	AFL-CIO	ADA	CCUS	ACU
2002	22%	15%	85%	88%
2001	25%	25%	83%	96%
2000	10%	20%	80%	88%
1999	22%	20%	71%	84%
1998	20%	15%	76%	96%

TEXAS 4

Northeast — Tyler, Sherman, most of Longview

The 4th covers a wide swath of the Red River Valley area north and east of Dallas, which was once the bailiwick of former Democratic House Speaker Sam Rayburn but now is fertile territory for the GOP. The district extends from the Oklahoma border down to skirt suburban Dallas, and then moves east to take in the oil cities of Tyler and Longview.

East Texas, and the 4th District in particular, has an older, more rural and more blue-collar population than most other areas of the state, and many residents espouse economic conservatism and gun rights. The 4th is mostly white but is one of the few Texas districts where blacks outnumber Hispanics. In Smith and Gregg counties, the two most-populous in the district, nearly one in five residents is black.

Voters in the 4th elect conservatives of both parties to local and national offices, but the GOP has made dramatic inroads since the 1980s. In 2000, George W. Bush garnered 70 percent of the two-party vote in the district, his ninth-highest percentage in Texas, and Republicans John Cornyn and Rick Perry also topped two-thirds of the district vote in their 2002 races for senator and governor, respectively. The district's GOP advantage runs from slight in Fannin County, on the Oklahoma border, to overwhelming in burgeoning Rockwall County, which in the 1990s had the third-fastest population growth rate of Texas' 254 counties.

Many Rockwall residents commute to jobs in Dallas, while those in other counties farm the land for peanuts and other crops that became popular after the cotton industry's decline. The oil bust in the mid-1980s hurt the economy near Tyler and Longview, but other areas have rebounded with the help of several electronics manufacturing plants located in or near the district. Both the agricultural and manufacturing sectors have since posted large gains, offsetting the oil decline.

MAJOR INDUSTRY

Health care, electronics manufacturing, agriculture, oil

CITIES

Tyler, 83,650; Longview (pt.), 71,746; Sherman, 35,082; Denison, 22,773

NOTABLE

Tyler bills itself as the "Rose Capital of the World" and hosts a weeklong festival each October; Former House Speaker Rayburn hailed from Bonham (Fannin County), which is now home to the Sam Rayburn Library and Museum.

Rep. Jeb Hensarling (R)

CAPITOL OFFICE
225-3484
www.house.gov/hensarling
423 Cannon 20515-4305; fax 226-4888

COMMITTEES
Budget
Financial Services

HOMETOWN
Dallas

BORN
May 29, 1957, Stephenville, Texas

RELIGION
Episcopalian

FAMILY
Wife, Melissa Hensarling; one child

EDUCATION
Texas A&M U., B.A. 1979 (economics); U. of Texas, J.D. 1982

CAREER
Child support collection software firm owner; corporate communications executive; congressional and campaign aide; lawyer

POLITICAL HIGHLIGHTS
No previous office

ELECTION RESULTS

2002 GENERAL		
Jeb Hensarling (R)	81,439	58.2%
Ron Chapman (D)	56,330	40.3%
2002 PRIMARY		
Jeb Hensarling (R)	10,475	53.6%
Dan Hagood (R)	3,628	18.6%
Mike Armour (R)	3,247	16.6%
Phil Sudan (R)	1,632	8.4%
Fred A. Wood (R)	574	2.9%

Elected 2002; 1st term

Hensarling's deep roots in Congress go back almost two decades.

Three years out of law school, in 1985 Hensarling (HENN-sur-ling) began a four-year stint overseeing Sen. Phil Gramm's field office network in Texas. He spent two years as executive director of the National Republican Senatorial Committee, which Gramm chaired in the run-up to the 1992 election. In the decade before coming to the House, Hensarling founded a firm that writes child support collection software for local governments and was vice president of an electric power retailer and an investment firm. His origin is rural, though: His father and his grandfather were poultry farmers.

He arrived in Congress as a GOP loyalist, emphasizing tax cuts and individual freedoms. "I believe that faith and family are the genius of America," he says. "The government does a lot in a poor or mediocre fashion."

Hensarling should fit in well with the like-minded Republicans who run the House. He will have the opportunity to pursue his fiscally conservative and pro-business agenda as a member of the Financial Services Committee, a position he requested, and the Budget Committee. He backs an indefinite extension of the 10-year, $1.35 trillion tax cut of 2001 and wants to roll back those taxes that he says hurt small businesses.

Lowering health care costs is also an issue for Hensarling, who said the birth of his daughter, Claire — two weeks before he won the March 2002 primary — brought home to him the potential burden of medical expenses. He endorsed the Medicare prescription drug benefit plan that Republicans pushed through the House in 2002.

Hensarling's opening to Congress came when Texas gained two seats in reapportionment after the 2000 census and the 5th District was reconfigured. Republican Pete Sessions, who had represented the 5th for three terms, decided to run in the new 32nd District instead. Hensarling took a five-way primary with ease and won by 18 percentage points in the fall against Democrat Ron Chapman, a judge in the Dallas area for two decades.

TEXAS 5

East central — part of Dallas, east and south suburbs

The 5th begins in Dallas and its suburbs, then winds more than 150 miles south through all or part of 10 other counties, reaching almost to Bryan and College Station (both of which are in the 31st). Dallas County is home to 63 percent of the 5th's residents.

The district's part of Dallas differs from the glitz and wealth that characterizes the portion in the 32nd. The 5th takes in eastern and northeastern Dallas, which has more of a working-class flavor and is home to many small businesses. Mesquite, a suburb east of the city, also is a major voting base.

Many of the city's suburbs have growing populations and provide easy access to a bustling metropolis while supplying the benefits of small-town life. Prisons are a large employer in rural parts of the district. Cattle, natural gas and coal continue to be big industries as well. Many of the smaller towns previously relied on steel or lumber and were hit hard when those markets declined. Brownfields revitalization efforts are now taking place in the district.

The 5th generally favors Republicans. GOP areas abound in northeastern Dallas, in neighborhoods on both sides of the L.B.J. Freeway, and in Anderson and Henderson counties well southeast of the city. Some heavily minority precincts in the district's northwestern periphery vote solidly Democratic, and Mesquite often is politically competitive. Down south, Falls and Robertson counties have large black populations and vote Democratic, which helps keep the party's candidates competitive in some tight statewide races.

MAJOR INDUSTRY
Technology, prisons, service

CITIES
Dallas (pt.), 188,480; Mesquite (pt.), 123,948; Garland (pt.), 54,729; Balch Springs, 19,375

NOTABLE
The Dallas Arboretum and Botanical Garden; Resistol Arena is home to the Mesquite Championship Rodeo.

Rep. Joe L. Barton (R)

CAPITOL OFFICE
225-2002
www.house.gov/barton
2109 Rayburn 20515-4306; fax 225-3052

COMMITTEES
Energy & Commerce
(Energy & Air Quality - chairman)
Science

HOMETOWN
Ennis

BORN
Sept. 15, 1949, Waco, Texas

RELIGION
Methodist

FAMILY
Wife, Janet Barton; three children

EDUCATION
Texas A&M U., B.S. 1972 (industrial engineering); Purdue U., M.S. 1973 (industrial administration)

CAREER
Engineering consultant

POLITICAL HIGHLIGHTS
Sought Republican nomination for U.S. Senate (special election), 1993

ELECTION RESULTS

2002 GENERAL		
Joe L. Barton (R)	115,396	70.4%
Felix Alvarado (D)	45,404	27.7%
Frank Brady (LIBERT)	1,992	1.2%
2002 PRIMARY		
Joe L. Barton (R)	unopposed	
2000 GENERAL		
Joe L. Barton (R)	222,685	88.1%
Frank Brady (LIBERT)	30,056	11.9%

PREVIOUS WINNING PERCENTAGES
1998 (73%); 1996 (77%); 1994 (76%); 1992 (72%); 1990 (66%); 1988 (68%); 1986 (56%); 1984 (57%)

Elected 1984; 10th term

Barton is arguably the House's most important player on national energy policy. He chairs a key Energy and Commerce subcommittee and, as a former oil industry engineer from a big energy-producing state, he understands the complexities of the issues and the markets.

Two of the Bush administration's top energy initiatives fall under Barton's purview as chairman of the Energy and Air Quality Subcommittee. One is a broad-reaching bill that attempts to reduce U.S. reliance on foreign oil and the other is a revision of the Clean Air Act that tightens federal controls on some harmful plant emissions and loosens others. Both proposals are targets of Democrats and environmentalists.

A House veteran of nearly two decades, Barton has been around long enough to know the political difficulties of passing major legislation in a closely divided Congress. But in the past, he hasn't always been able to close the deal. Barton is staunchly conservative, with an abiding faith in the power of free markets. He's often reluctant to compromise with his liberal opponents if it means creating more government regulation. He is also a tough partisan whose take-it-or-leave-it approach sometimes stymies the bipartisanship necessary to enact major bills.

The president's energy plan stalled in the 107th Congress, in part because Barton insisted that it allow drilling for oil and gas in Alaska's Arctic National Wildlife Refuge, which Senate Democrats and environmental groups avidly opposed. The two sides deadlocked after six months of negotiations, with Barton saying that any bill without Alaska drilling wouldn't be worth doing.

Barton took over the energy subcommittee in 1999 and spent much of the next two years in a futile effort to enact legislation fostering competition in the electric power industry, the last major regulated monopoly. Republicans have wanted to deregulate electricity since they took control of Congress in 1995, but the bills have bogged down in partisan and policy disagreements. Barton resurrected the issue in the 108th Congress, introducing a 600-page draft proposal early in 2003.

The path to final passage is also difficult for another significant issue on Barton's plate, the president's "Clear Skies" proposal on industrial pollutants. The plan restricts emissions of mercury for the first time but does not limit carbon dioxide emissions as environmental groups insist it should. Barton pushed a bill in 2002 that never got through committee; he introduced a revised plan in the 108th.

The congressman is a force behind efforts to build a permanent depository at Yucca Mountain in Nevada for waste from nuclear power plants. In a rare departure from the White House's position, Barton wants to create a special fund for operating the site separate from the government's general revenues. Barton said in 2002: "Nuclear waste is a special commodity. It's in the public good to build this thing and operate it as quickly as possible."

Barton is a balanced-budget crusader whose political mentor is former Texas Republican Sen. Phil Gramm, one of the most well-known budget conservatives of the 1980s and 1990s. Barton took Gramm's seat in the House after Gramm moved to the Senate in 1984. Barton too has had designs on the Senate but without Gramm's same political savvy. In the last decade, Barton had two opportunities to run for open Texas seats, but in both instances he was outflanked by other GOP candidates.

In the House, Barton advocates lower taxes and spending restraint. In the 1990s, he pushed for a constitutional amendment requiring three-fifths majority approval in Congress to raise taxes. In 1996, after Republican budget confrontations with the White House led to two government shutdowns, Barton was one of the last GOP holdouts resisting a compromise with the Clinton administration to resolve the impasse.

Yet high-priced projects for Texas, such as NASA's International Space Station and the superconducting super collider, a giant atom smasher the government eventually scrapped, get Barton's unswerving support.

Barton has crusaded against wasteful spending. When the GOP won control of the House, Barton took the helm of the Oversight panel from Democrat John D. Dingell of Michigan, a merciless investigator who made the subcommittee a power center. Barton's reputation is not as fearsome, but he pursued a busy agenda marked by some high-profile battles.

He led the charge against Clinton-era Energy Secretary Hazel R. O'Leary's controversial travel budget, and he demanded more efficiency at national laboratories. Barton is proudest of the subcommittee's work on the Food and Drug Administration's approval process. In 1997, he and California Democrat Anna G. Eshoo brokered an agreement expediting review of medical devices, from thermometers to pacemakers.

A graduate of Texas A&M University, where Gramm once taught economics, Barton is a former engineering consultant for Atlantic Richfield Co. Inspired by President Reagan to get into politics, his only policy experience before winning election to the House in 1984 was as a White House fellow for the Department of Energy, an opportunity he learned about in Smithsonian magazine.

When Texas Democrat Lloyd Bentsen left the Senate in 1993 to become Clinton's Treasury secretary, Barton jumped into the Republican primary for the special election, emphasizing "family values." But he got only 14 percent of the vote and finished third in a 24-person, all-party primary. When Gramm retired from the Senate in 2001, Barton considered running for that seat but opted out after the White House backed another Republican.

Barton runs strong in his House re-election races, however. In 1998, American Airlines bankrolled a serious challenger after Barton supported a bill making it easier for travelers to use Love Field near downtown Dallas — which brought American more competition at its Dallas-Fort Worth International hub. Barton prevailed in the primary with 73 percent and cruised to re-election in the fall. Post-2000 census remapping put many new voters in Barton's district, but most were conservative Republicans and in 2002 he handily beat Democrat Felix Alvarado, a schoolteacher.

KEY VOTES

2002

- No Overhaul campaign finance law; ban "soft money" and restrict advocacy advertising
- Yes Back Bush's defense budget increase
- Yes Extend 1996 welfare law
- Yes Adopt Bush's discretionary spending limit
- Yes Pass GOP Medicare prescription drug plan
- No Create independent Sept. 11 commission
- No Extend union protections to Homeland Security Department employees
- Yes Revive fast-track procedures for trade agreements
- Yes Authorize war against Iraq
- Yes Advance bankruptcy overhaul opposed by abortion opponents

2001

- Yes Nullify Clinton Labor Department ergonomics rule
- Yes Cut taxes by $1.35 trillion through fiscal 2011
- No Maintain ban on oil drilling in Arctic National Wildlife Refuge
- Yes Approve Bush proposal to limit managed-care plan liability for coverage decisions
- No Divert money from crop subsidy payments to land conservation
- Yes Expand law enforcement power to investigate suspected terrorists

CQ VOTE STUDIES

	PARTY UNITY		PRESIDENTIAL SUPPORT	
	Support	Oppose	Support	Oppose
2002	98%	2%	90%	10%
2001	98%	2%	86%	14%
2000	93%	7%	23%	77%
1999	95%	5%	16%	84%
1998	94%	6%	20%	80%

INTEREST GROUPS

	AFL-CIO	ADA	CCUS	ACU
2002	13%	0%	100%	96%
2001	0%	5%	91%	96%
2000	11%	10%	83%	100%
1999	11%	5%	86%	91%
1998	0%	5%	78%	100%

TEXAS 6

Suburban Dallas – parts of Fort Worth and Arlington; southern suburbs

Once a snaking district that included Republican areas in and outside Fort Worth, the 6th, as redrawn in 2001 redistricting, now is a cohesive block of counties just south of the Dallas-Fort Worth Metroplex. The district takes in southern Tarrant County, including about one-eighth of Fort Worth and most of the suburb of Arlington. While the old district was urban-suburban, the new district is mostly suburban-rural.

More than half of the district population comes out of Tarrant, while most of the rest lives in Johnson and Ellis counties. Rapidly growing Johnson has become a bedroom community for Fort Worth and is home to many of the city's southern suburbs. Ellis County, which includes Waxahachie and Ennis, used to be dependent on cotton farming, but the cement industry has taken hold there. The other two counties in the district — Hill and Navarro — are rural and less-populated, and are sustained by oil, ranching and farming.

Fort Worth's economy has diversified and expanded in recent years, while population growth in Arlington has leveled out after a tremendous boom from the 1950s through the 1990s. There are some black and Hispanic areas in the district, and the Vietnamese and Samoan populations have increased. But the 6th is generally white, financially secure and suburban.

It is also heavily Republican. Most of the Tarrant precincts are aligned with the GOP, though there is some Democratic strength in southern Fort Worth and eastern Arlington. But the overwhelming GOP advantage in Ellis and Johnson, which went for John Cornyn and Rick Perry by better than 2-to-1 ratios in 2002, makes the 6th a safe haven for Republican candidates.

MAJOR INDUSTRY

Transportation, home building, technology, agriculture

CITIES

Arlington (pt.), 191,470; Fort Worth (pt.), 64,649; Mansfield, 28,031

NOTABLE

A superconducting supercollider — or "atom smasher" — was to be located in Waxahachie, but Congress cut all funding for the project in 1993 after some $2 billion had already been spent.

Rep. John Culberson (R)

CAPITOL OFFICE
225-2571
www.culberson.house.gov
1728 Longworth 20515-4307; fax 225-4381

COMMITTEES
Appropriations

HOMETOWN
Houston

BORN
Aug. 24, 1956, Houston, Texas

RELIGION
Methodist

FAMILY
Wife, Belinda Culberson; one child

EDUCATION
Southern Methodist U., B.A. 1981 (history); South Texas College of Law, J.D. 1988

CAREER
Lawyer; political advertising agency employee; oil rig mud logger

POLITICAL HIGHLIGHTS
Texas House, 1987-2001

ELECTION RESULTS

2002 GENERAL		
John Culberson (R)	96,795	89.2%
Drew Parks (LIBERT)	11,674	10.8%
2002 PRIMARY		
John Culberson (R)		unopposed
2000 GENERAL		
John Culberson (R)	183,712	73.9%
Jeff Sell (D)	60,694	24.4%
Drew Parks (LIBERT)	4,182	1.7%

Elected 2000; 2nd term

From a visit to Culberson's Capitol Hill office, it is clear he is an ardent fan of the principal author of the Declaration of Independence and the third president of the United States. Several portraits of Thomas Jefferson are on display, including one hung at precisely Jefferson's 6-foot, 2 1/2-inch height. He has collected other items of Jeffersoniana as well as countless books about the statesman.

Characterized by the Austin American-Statesman as a "self-confessed nerd and bookworm" during his days as a history major in college, it was there Culberson became enamored of Jefferson and his views of government. "Thomas Jefferson's leading principle was pure republicanism," Culberson told the newspaper. He cited Jefferson in court documents he filed in a long-running and quixotic battle to end federal court supervision of the Texas prison system. When it appeared that at least a partial victory was in sight, Culberson said, "We are going to make Thomas Jefferson proud."

He had plenty of experience in state governance when he arrived in Washington, having spent 14 years in the Texas House. He proudly pointed out to his House colleagues that he already had a working relationship with newly elected President George W. Bush, who was governor of Texas from 1995 through 2000.

Culberson's predecessors in his affluent suburban Houston district included the president's father, George Bush, who held the seat for four years, and Bill Archer, the former Ways and Means Committee chairman, who won the seat after Bush and stayed for 30 years.

While the senior Bush and Archer played key roles on the national stage, Culberson is content for the time being to remain behind the scenes. He prefers to sign on as a cosponsor of another lawmaker's bill rather than introduce an identical one with his name on it. He made sure all 27 of his Class of 2000 GOP colleagues were given committee assignments before he sought slots for himself. He says he intends to direct most of his attention to local concerns, including expanding the Interstate 10 freeway and fighting a plan to locate a concrete plant in a small town in west Harris County.

In his first term, Culberson was given a coveted seat on the executive committee of the National Republican Campaign Committee, the campaign arm of the House GOP, and an appointment to the Republican Steering Committee, which makes committee assignments. He won high marks from other lawmakers for his work on the Steering Committee, where he focused on lobbying for good appointments for Republican freshmen. That cost him a chance at his top choice — Transportation and Infrastructure. But 13 other freshmen got slots on the panel, and he told the Houston Chronicle that all 13 had promised to support funding for Culberson's No. 1 legislative priority — expansion of the Katy Freeway, a 22-mile stretch of Interstate 10 heading west from Houston to Katy.

In the 108th Congress, returned to the Steering Committee, Culberson was rewarded for his unselfish work of two years before, getting an assignment to the Appropriations Committee, including a seat on the subcommittee that provides transportation funds.

The Katy Freeway was his top priority in the 107th, and he says it will remain so until the project is completed in 2009. That stretch of Interstate 10 is one of the most congested in the country, carrying as much as five times the designed traffic load. The highway is to be widened to 18 or 20 lanes, with several toll lanes that will help pay for the project and speed up construction. Culberson was involved in the negotiations that led to the project's approval.

Culberson received national attention in the 107th for championing a "trusted traveler" identification card that would help airline passengers get through security checks quicker. After the Sept. 11, 2001, terrorist attacks resulted in tightened airport security, Congress authorized such an identification system. Culberson has pushed for its implementation.

Culberson introduced only one bill in the 107th, but he has had experience writing legislative language. During his tenure in the Texas House, he says he was able to sneak a bill past a host of lobbyists by creative drafting. The bill to keep Houston and other cities from annexing more areas did not include the word "annexation," which lobbyists were looking for in computer word searches. "This flew under radar because I'm a good bill writer," he told the Houston Chronicle.

His desk in his Longworth Building office is a refurbished mahogany rolltop that he bought in an antique store when he discovered that it had once belonged to his great-great uncle Charles Culberson, who was governor of Texas from 1895 to 1899 and a U.S. senator from 1899 to 1923.

Culberson's father owned an advertising agency, where he often produced public relations materials for local candidates. Culberson worked with his father and said he became interested in politics as a result. After high school, he worked on offshore oil rigs before college. He was elected to the Texas House at 29, while in law school.

During his years in the state House, Culberson served as the Republican whip and compiled a staunchly conservative voting record. He was once named one of the 10 "most conservative legislators" in Texas. To make a living, because the Texas Legislature is part-time work, he was a defense lawyer in civil cases.

When Archer announced his retirement in 2000, a passel of Republicans filed to succeed him. Culberson said he was the only candidate with the necessary experience and that, "I won't need any on-the-job training."

He finished first in the seven-way GOP primary and survived an expensive runoff against businessman Peter Wareing. Winning the runoff ensured his election: The 7th is one of the most Republican districts in the nation and he got almost three-quarters of the vote. Democrats did not field a challenger in 2002.

Culberson was able to lend considerable fundraising help to other GOP candidates — an effort that certainly did not hurt his bid to get the Appropriations Committee assignment.

KEY VOTES

2002

- No Overhaul campaign finance law; ban "soft money" and restrict advocacy advertising
- Yes Back Bush's defense budget increase
- Yes Extend 1996 welfare law
- Yes Adopt Bush's discretionary spending limit
- Yes Pass GOP Medicare prescription drug plan
- No Create independent Sept. 11 commission
- No Extend union protections to Homeland Security Department employees
- Yes Revive fast-track procedures for trade agreements
- Yes Authorize war against Iraq
- Yes Advance bankruptcy overhaul opposed by abortion opponents

2001

- Yes Nullify Clinton Labor Department ergonomics rule
- Yes Cut taxes by $1.35 trillion through fiscal 2011
- No Maintain ban on oil drilling in Arctic National Wildlife Refuge
- Yes Approve Bush proposal to limit managed-care plan liability for coverage decisions
- No Divert money from crop subsidy payments to land conservation
- Yes Expand law enforcement power to investigate suspected terrorists

CQ VOTE STUDIES

	PARTY UNITY		PRESIDENTIAL SUPPORT	
	Support	Oppose	Support	Oppose
2002	99%	1%	85%	15%
2001	99%	1%	95%	5%

INTEREST GROUPS

	AFL-CIO	ADA	CCUS	ACU
2002	11%	0%	90%	100%
2001	0%	0%	96%	100%

TEXAS 7

Western Houston; northwestern suburbs

Based in western Houston and split in two by Interstate 10, the 7th is removed from downtown Houston's oil and gas companies but nonetheless has several important corporate residents and The Galleria, a huge shopping and office complex that provides jobs and a major retail presence. Like other areas around Houston, the district rebounded slowly after the oil industry's troubles in the 1980s. But an increasing emphasis on high-tech firms and corporate headquarters enabled the 7th to enjoy sustained economic growth during the 1990s.

The 7th is more racially diverse than it was prior to redistricting in 2001. The new map pushed the 7th farther east, inside the Interstate 610 beltway encircling Houston, to make room for the newly drawn 31st. At its easternmost point, the redrawn 7th nearly touches Compaq Center, the arena where the NBA's Rockets play.

Nearly seven in 10 district residents live in Houston. The 7th's share of the city is mostly middle-class and heavily minority: whites (46 percent) are outnumbered by Hispanics (26 percent), blacks (12 percent) and Asians (12 percent) taken together. Northwest Houston includes a large Hispanic population, particularly between Interstate 10 and the Northwest Freeway, and there are sizable black and Asian populations in southwest Houston. Alief, picked up in redistricting, has a large Vietnamese population.

Much of the district is characterized by white-collar executives, good schools and religious conservatism. The 7th's median income is brought up by wealthy villages like Piney Point, Bunker Hill and Hunters Creek, which are near Interstate 10 and surrounded on all sides by Houston.

Redistricting only marginally lessened the 7th's strong Republican lean. In 2002 statewide races, Republicans John Cornyn and Gov. Rick Perry each took more than two-thirds of the vote in the district.

MAJOR INDUSTRY

Technology, retail, health care

CITIES

Houston (pt.), 449,641; Mission Bend (unincorporated) (pt.), 11,673

NOTABLE

George Bush, who later served as vice president and president, represented the 7th from 1967 to 1971; The Galleria, dubbed "a city within a city," is the fifth-largest mall in the nation.

Rep. Kevin Brady (R)

CAPITOL OFFICE
225-4901
rep.brady@mail.house.gov
www.house.gov/brady
428 Cannon 20515-4308; fax 225-5524

COMMITTEES
Ways & Means

HOMETOWN
The Woodlands

BORN
April 11, 1955, Vermillion, S.D.

RELIGION
Roman Catholic

FAMILY
Wife, Cathy Brady; two children

EDUCATION
U. of South Dakota, B.S. 1990 (mass communication)

CAREER
Chamber of commerce executive

POLITICAL HIGHLIGHTS
Texas House, 1991-96

ELECTION RESULTS

2002 GENERAL		
Kevin Brady (R)	140,575	93.1%
Gil Guillory (LIBERT)	10,351	6.9%
2002 PRIMARY		
Kevin Brady (R)		unopposed
2000 GENERAL		
Kevin Brady (R)	233,848	91.6%
Gil Guillory (LIBERT)	21,368	8.4%

PREVIOUS WINNING PERCENTAGES
1998 (93%); 1996 General Runoff Election (59%)

Elected December 1996; 4th term

The unassuming Brady is keenly aware of — and in fact appears to enjoy — his status as a backbencher in Congress. Although he is perhaps best-known in Washington because of his membership on the Ways and Means Committee, Brady's diverse interests range from health care and education to criminal justice and campaign finance law.

In his first six years on Capitol Hill, many of Brady's bills dealt with obscure issues raised at local "cracker barrel" gatherings in his Houston-area district, and he largely stayed out of the spotlight even when it touched legislation on which he played an active role.

In the 108th Congress, however, he added an appointment as one of about 20 Republican deputy whips to his Ways and Means slot, and he may have difficulty remaining in the background.

Brady is a loyal party man, siding 98 percent of the time with the GOP in the 107th and 88 percent of the time with President Bush, who was governor during Brady's time in the Texas Legislature. But he was born into a family of Democrats. His uncle was a state senator, his father a county party official.

He credits his early experiences with a host of civic groups and his 18 years as a Chamber of Commerce executive with molding his pro-business, staunchly Republican political philosophy. He says he has observed numerous business leaders who are role models for civic involvement and who have shown that private-sector solutions to community problems are often more effective than government programs.

Those who know him say Brady comes across as a regular guy: a dad who sometimes brings his young son to his congressional office, a baseball devotee who relishes the annual charity ballgame against the Democrats.

In the 2002 game, Brady, who was the center fielder on his college baseball team, hit a triple, making an awkward-looking head-first slide into third base. That evoked loud cheers and some razzing from the GOP dugout. "You didn't land, you skipped like a baseball," Tom DeLay told him.

Brady won his seat on Ways and Means — which writes tax, trade health and welfare legislation — at the beginning of the 107th Congress, maintaining a Houston presence on the panel after the retirement of his mentor and Houston neighbor, Bill Archer. Brady supports eliminating the IRS and establishing a 15 percent consumption tax collected by the states.

Transforming government has been a theme for Brady almost since the moment he arrived in Congress. He routinely sponsors legislation, similar to a law in Texas that has eliminated 29 agencies, to set expiration dates for each federal agency, department and program. His "sunset" bill, which he first introduced as a freshman, would create a commission of eight members of Congress and four private citizens who would evaluate each agency and recommend streamlining, privatization or abolishment of those that did not justify their existence.

His interest in reining in government has extended to education, as Brady won inclusion in the 2001 education overhaul of a provision to protect teachers from frivolous lawsuits when they discipline children in school. In the 107th, Brady sponsored successful legislation to permit some political committees to avoid new federal campaign funding disclosure requirements if the information was already required under state law.

While he supports his party most of the time, Brady has bucked the leadership on occasion. In 1999, he voted against Republican-backed gun control legislation — which many Democrats described as having been written by the National Rifle Association — as part of his longstanding advocacy for gun control. When Brady was 12 years old, his father, a lawyer, was shot and killed in a South Dakota courtroom by the deranged spouse of a client, and the incident has shaped his policy position in the politically volatile arena of gun control ever since. As a state representative, Brady also refused to vote for a bill to allow Texans to carry concealed weapons, and he says he still opposes such a measure today.

In 1997, he protested when House GOP leaders manipulated the parliamentary process to make it extremely difficult to stop an automatic cost of living pay adjustment for lawmakers. "Rather than standing on the principle of honest, open government, we hid behind a procedure," he said.

As a member of the International Relations Committee during the 106th, Brady focused his efforts on updating and expanding the scope of extradition treaties to make it more difficult for people indicted in the United States to escape punishment in other countries. After he left the committee in 2001, Brady continued to push for extradition changes, and after the Sept. 11, 2001, terrorist attacks, he renewed his push for such measures, which he said would help catch terrorists.

Brady attended the University of South Dakota. Although he left college in 1978, he did not graduate until 1990 because he had neglected to complete the paperwork for a work-study class. After an opponent in his first Texas House race unearthed Brady's lack of a degree, Brady dug out the old course work to clear up the incomplete grade.

He spent six years as a state representative in Austin, where he says politics did not get in the way of policy nearly as much as it seems to in Washington. When Republican Jack Fields announced he would not seek re-election in the 8th District in 1996, it took Brady an arduous four elections to become his successor. Wealthy Republican physician Gene Fontenot emerged on top in the March GOP primary, but did not win a majority of the vote. Brady had much stronger ties to the district and defeated Fontenot in the April runoff.

Later in the year, however, a panel of three federal judges redrew the 8th as well as 12 other Texas congressional districts in response to a Supreme Court ruling that found illegal "racial gerrymandering" at play in the Texas map. The federal court threw out the primary results from those districts and ordered new elections. In November, Fontenot forced Brady into a December runoff. Brady finally won the seat, taking 59 percent. He has been safely ensconced in Congress ever since. He has had no Democratic challenger since 1996.

KEY VOTES

2002

- ? Overhaul campaign finance law; ban "soft money" and restrict advocacy advertising
- Yes Back Bush's defense budget increase
- Yes Extend 1996 welfare law
- Yes Adopt Bush's discretionary spending limit
- Yes Pass GOP Medicare prescription drug plan
- No Create independent Sept. 11 commission
- No Extend union protections to Homeland Security Department employees
- Yes Revive fast-track procedures for trade agreements
- Yes Authorize war against Iraq
- Yes Advance bankruptcy overhaul opposed by abortion opponents

2001

- Yes Nullify Clinton Labor Department ergonomics rule
- Yes Cut taxes by $1.35 trillion through fiscal 2011
- No Maintain ban on oil drilling in Arctic National Wildlife Refuge
- Yes Approve Bush proposal to limit managed-care plan liability for coverage decisions
- No Divert money from crop subsidy payments to land conservation
- Yes Expand law enforcement power to investigate suspected terrorists

CQ VOTE STUDIES

	PARTY UNITY		PRESIDENTIAL SUPPORT	
	Support	Oppose	Support	Oppose
2002	97%	3%	85%	15%
2001	98%	2%	90%	10%
2000	97%	3%	24%	76%
1999	94%	6%	21%	79%
1998	94%	6%	20%	80%

INTEREST GROUPS

	AFL-CIO	ADA	CCUS	ACU
2002	13%	0%	100%	100%
2001	8%	0%	100%	96%
2000	0%	0%	80%	100%
1999	11%	15%	95%	88%
1998	0%	0%	94%	96%

TEXAS 8

Part of Houston; northern Houston suburbs

Made up of northern Harris County and Houston's rapidly growing northern suburbs in Montgomery County, the 8th is a Republican bastion. In the past three major statewide elections — the 2002 gubernatorial and senatorial races and the 2000 presidential race — the 8th gave the GOP candidate more than 75 percent of the vote, each time topping every other district in the state in its support for the GOP.

Redistricting following the 2000 census chopped the districts' land mass substantially, as a result of strong population growth in the 1990s. Portions removed included rural areas northeast of Houston and Texas A&M University. The district is now much more homogeneous, home to planned communities that house executives from the Houston Advanced Research Center and the region's many medical facilities.

About 60 percent of the district's residents live in Harris County, with the remainder in Montgomery. The Harris County portion of the district contains some of the Houston region's wealthiest areas, including Jersey Village, located just off the Northwest Freeway, and parts of northeastern Houston near Lake Houston.

The 8th's share of Montgomery includes The Woodlands, a large planned community in the county that gets its name from its proximity to Sam Houston National Forest. The Woodlands consists of several villages, each with its own residential neighborhoods and local shops. The area has aggressively courted business, and several petroleum and biotechnology companies make their home here.

The timber industry and some cattle ranches populate the northern part of Montgomery County, though these areas are quickly becoming Houston suburbs. Montgomery County added 112,000 people and grew by 61 percent in the 1990s, a rate that was exceeded by just five of Texas' other 253 counties.

MAJOR INDUSTRY
Health care, education, retail

CITIES
Houston (pt.), 60,058; The Woodlands (unincorporated), 55,649; Conroe, 36,811; Spring (unincorporated), 36,385

NOTABLE
Texas' Lone Star flag was designed in Montgomery County in 1839.

Rep. Nick Lampson (D)

CAPITOL OFFICE
225-6565
www.house.gov/lampson
405 Cannon 20515-4309; fax 225-5547

COMMITTEES
Science
Transportation & Infrastructure

HOMETOWN
Beaumont

BORN
Feb. 14, 1945, Beaumont, Texas

RELIGION
Roman Catholic

FAMILY
Wife, Susan Lampson; two children

EDUCATION
Lamar U., B.S. 1968 (biology), M.Ed. 1971

CAREER
Teacher; home health care business owner

POLITICAL HIGHLIGHTS
Sought Democratic nomination for Texas House, 1970; Jefferson County tax assessor, 1977-95

ELECTION RESULTS

2002 GENERAL		
Nick Lampson (D)	86,710	58.6%
Paul Williams (R)	59,635	40.3%
Dean L. Tucker (LIBERT)	1,613	1.1%
2002 PRIMARY		
Nick Lampson (D)		unopposed
2000 GENERAL		
Nick Lampson (D)	130,143	59.2%
Paul Williams (R)	87,165	39.7%
Chuck Knipp (LIBERT)	2,508	1.1%

PREVIOUS WINNING PERCENTAGES
1998 (64%); 1996 General Runoff Election (53%)

Elected December 1996; 4th term

Lampson has lifelong ties to the 9th District, so without much threat of refutation he can claim firsthand knowledge about the parochial needs in what is termed the Golden Triangle of Southeast Texas.

Born and reared in Beaumont, the area's biggest city, he attended public schools and the local college, then taught high school science and ran a home health care business in the area. He spent the next 18 years in Beaumont as the elected property tax assessor for Jefferson County. Other than trips to Mexico, Lampson had never been outside the United States when he ran for Congress. "Let's just say I had a big learning curve on many issues," he says.

Lampson arrived on Capitol Hill in 1997 with an agenda typical of moderate Democrats. "I wanted to address all of the problems that we face here: education, Social Security and health care," he said. But soon after he was sworn in, he found a new legislative cause based on a rash of child abductions in Texas, including that of a 12-year-old constituent who was later found dead. Lampson co-founded the Missing and Exploited Children's Caucus — now more than 150 members — which presses for legislation to help families protect their children and aid communities and law enforcement agencies in tracking missing children. In recent years, Lampson has paid more attention to the plight of children abducted in the United States and taken overseas.

Lampson's ticket to Congress was a high-profile 1996 victory over Republican Steve Stockman, one of the "giant killers" in the GOP takeover Class of 1994 because he had unseated 42-year incumbent Democrat Jack Brooks.

The reclaiming of the seat was sweet revenge for the Democrats. The party leadership gave Lampson a seat on the Science Committee — a logical assignment for a member whose district includes the Johnson Space Center south of Houston and many energy-related industries.

On the Science panel, Lampson is a strong advocate for the International Space Station, a perennial target of congressional budget-cutters. In the aftermath of the Columbia space shuttle disaster early in 2003, Lampson was quick to focus on the need for alternate means of retrieving three astronauts from the space station while the U.S. shuttle fleet was grounded.

Lampson says he supports the project "because of what America learned about its future in 1969," when Americans first landed on the moon. "I saw firsthand how our progress in space, culminating in the lunar landing, encouraged and inspired students."

As the only lawmaker from southeast Texas on the Transportation and Infrastructure panel, Lampson also has concentrated on parochial needs, pushing to boost funding for the highways in the region and to send more federal dollars to the Port of Houston, which receives more foreign goods than any other port in the nation. He has promoted efforts to establish a high-speed rail corridor on the Gulf Coast and to establish light rail in Houston.

By and large, Democratic leaders are satisfied with Lampson's voting record in the House. Typically, he takes the side of organized labor in its disputes with the GOP over worker-management issues, and he opposes Republican efforts to rein in environmental protections. As a member of the moderate New Democrat Coalition, Lampson describes himself as a bit more liberal than several of his Democratic colleagues in the Texas delegation, who form a core of the conservative "Blue Dog" coalition. "I tell them it's hard to break me out of the moderate mold."

His moderate voting record is a good match for the 9th District, where Lampson is well-known and liked. Lampson's grandparents came to Texas from Sicily. He has five brothers and sisters, and gatherings of the extended family in southeast Texas would often attract 30 or more people. Lampson says he is continually inspired by his older sister, who was stricken with polio when she was 12 and is confined to a wheelchair. She served as her brother's political campaign manager in several of his campaigns.

Lampson was 12 when his father died. He took a janitorial job in the local school to help out the family. Later, he worked his way through college at Lamar University, just three blocks from his high school.

He also earned some money playing the saxophone professionally for six years, which included stints with a number of local bands. He says he gave up professional music when he had to make a choice between a six-week gig in Las Vegas with the Boogie Kings or finishing college. He later played backup sax on a country music CD produced as a fundraising project for the National Center for Missing and Exploited Children.

Lampson interned for Rep. Brooks and was involved in student government throughout college. He wanted to be a dentist but was stymied by organic chemistry, so he earned a biology degree and got a job teaching high school science. He likes to recall a lesson in community activism learned by one of his science classes: In investigating the contents of a stagnant pond near the school, the students found three harmful organisms, and the class then badgered local authorities to clean up the pond.

Lampson was active in local Democratic Party affairs, and after three unsuccessful bids for elective office, he was elected county tax assessor in 1976. Twenty years later, he took on Stockman, who was viewed as one of the most vulnerable House Republicans because of his contacts with militia groups and his conservative voting record. Lampson had little trouble defeating four competitors for the Democratic nomination, and he moved quickly to attack Stockman's record and to label him a right-wing extremist.

But in August, it appeared as if Stockman was getting something of a break when a three-judge federal panel redrew the district's map, along with 12 other Texas districts, in response to a Supreme Court redistricting decision. In the end, Lampson and Stockman faced each other in a December special election, with a team of Justice Department observers monitoring some polling places after charges that white poll watchers linked to Stockman had intimidated minorities in the first round of balloting. Lampson prevailed with 53 percent of the vote and has won three easy re-elections since.

KEY VOTES

2002

- Yes Overhaul campaign finance law; ban "soft money" and restrict advocacy advertising
- Yes Back Bush's defense budget increase
- ? Extend 1996 welfare law
- No Adopt Bush's discretionary spending limit
- No Pass GOP Medicare prescription drug plan
- Yes Create independent Sept. 11 commission
- Yes Extend union protections to Homeland Security Department employees
- No Revive fast-track procedures for trade agreements
- Yes Authorize war against Iraq
- Yes Advance bankruptcy overhaul opposed by abortion opponents

2001

- No Nullify Clinton Labor Department ergonomics rule
- No Cut taxes by $1.35 trillion through fiscal 2011
- Yes Maintain ban on oil drilling in Arctic National Wildlife Refuge
- No Approve Bush proposal to limit managed-care plan liability for coverage decisions
- No Divert money from crop subsidy payments to land conservation
- Yes Expand law enforcement power to investigate suspected terrorists

CQ VOTE STUDIES

	PARTY UNITY		PRESIDENTIAL SUPPORT	
	Support	Oppose	Support	Oppose
2002	87%	13%	36%	64%
2001	83%	17%	34%	66%
2000	82%	18%	69%	31%
1999	84%	16%	77%	23%
1998	86%	14%	81%	19%

INTEREST GROUPS

	AFL-CIO	ADA	CCUS	ACU
2002	89%	75%	55%	21%
2001	100%	85%	48%	21%
2000	90%	75%	57%	24%
1999	78%	90%	32%	16%
1998	100%	90%	33%	16%

TEXAS 9
Southeast – Beaumont, Galveston

From the suburbs east of Houston to the Gulf of Mexico, the 9th is oil country. Its largest cities, Beaumont, Galveston and Port Arthur, are heavily involved in the production and distribution of petroleum products. When the bottom fell out of the industry in the 1980s, unemployment skyrocketed. Many of the district's towns lost population, though they slowly regained people throughout the 1990s.

The 9th's large number of factory jobs makes it one of the few Texas districts where unions wield significant political power. But while the unions underpin the area's economically liberal outlook, residents also tend to be socially conservative. Republicans have attracted votes from Galveston and the "Golden Triangle" — the area bounded by Beaumont, Port Arthur and Orange (in the 2nd District) — by appealing to voters' opposition to gun control. The district is politically competitive: the GOP has a slight edge in Galveston County and dominates the 9th's share of the Houston suburbs, while Democrats run well in Jefferson County, where there are large black populations in Beaumont and Port Arthur.

The sometimes marshy land between Houston and the coast does not yield many crops. Instead, it contains NASA's Lyndon B. Johnson Space Center, refineries and shipbuilding facilities. The 9th also relies on coastal industries, including ship repair and commercial fishing.

Although the 1980s oil bust hurt the 9th's economy, the rapid growth of the petrochemical industry in the 1990s helped the district. Shipbuilders rely on the government, as does the Space Center, located 20 miles southeast of Houston. A growing service sector near Galveston has helped diversify the economy. Galveston, with its nearby beaches, also has emerged as a tourist destination.

MAJOR INDUSTRY

Petrochemicals, shipbuilding, health care

CITIES

Beaumont, 113,866; Port Arthur, 57,755; Galveston, 57,247; League City, 45,444; Texas City, 41,521; Friendswood, 29,037; Houston (pt.), 27,358

NOTABLE

Johnson Space Center serves as the lead NASA center for the International Space Station; Galveston is the site of many Texas firsts, including the first post office (1836) and first law firm west of the Mississippi River (1846); It is also known for the devastating flood of 1900.

Rep. Lloyd Doggett (D)

CAPITOL OFFICE
225-4865
lloyd.doggett@mail.house.gov
www.house.gov/doggett
201 Cannon 20515-4310; fax 225-3073

COMMITTEES
Ways & Means

HOMETOWN
Austin

BORN
Oct. 6, 1946, Austin, Texas

RELIGION
Methodist

FAMILY
Wife, Libby Belk Doggett; two children

EDUCATION
U. of Texas, B.B.A. 1967, J.D. 1970

CAREER
Lawyer

POLITICAL HIGHLIGHTS
Texas Senate, 1973-85; Democratic nominee for U.S. Senate, 1984; Texas Supreme Court, 1989-94

ELECTION RESULTS

2002 GENERAL		
Lloyd Doggett (D)	114,428	84.4%
Michele Messina (LIBERT)	21,196	15.6%
2002 PRIMARY		
Lloyd Doggett (D)	33,083	90.3%
Jennifer Gale (D)	3,554	9.7%
2000 GENERAL		
Lloyd Doggett (D)	203,628	84.6%
Michael Davis (LIBERT)	37,203	15.5%

PREVIOUS WINNING PERCENTAGES
1998 (85%); 1996 (56%); 1994 (56%)

Elected 1994; 5th term

An agile debater, Doggett is one of a handful of rhetorical attack dogs deployed by the Democratic leadership to make life in the majority as miserable as possible for House Republicans. In the 108th Congress, he co-chairs a parliamentary team that uses delaying tactics and organized walkouts against the GOP.

Doggett, the liberal former Texas Supreme Court Justice, once told his hometown newspaper, the Austin American- Statesman: "When the rules of the game are changed, when the voice of the minority is restricted so severely that we can't be heard, then we consider parliamentary tactics."

He frequently can be found on the floor during the period set aside each day for one-minute speeches, which are carried on C-SPAN. He also broadcasts the Democratic message in major floor debates, where his punchy quotes, delivered in a mild twang, sometimes make it on the network news or get picked up by large newspapers.

With a seat on the Ways and Means Committee, Doggett focuses on the party's efforts to raise the federal hourly minimum wage, on doing away with corporate tax shelters and looking for political vulnerabilities in Republican tax cut proposals. He has been on the committee since 1999, when he beat out several competitors for a post on the influential tax-writing panel. In a sense, he takes the place of his predecessor, Democratic Rep. J.J. Pickle, who was on Ways and Means until he retired in 1994.

Doggett railed against President Bush's $1.35 trillion tax cut in 2001, singling out a provision that would reduce taxes for married couples. Doggett, whose constituency is disproportionately single, called the proposal "a single's discrimination tax." He criticized Republicans for including corporate tax breaks in an economic stimulus package after the Sept. 11, 2001, terrorist attacks. "I wouldn't be surprised if they thought tax breaks would be enough for Osama bin Laden to turn himself in," Doggett said.

His single-most influential legislative act in the 107th Congress came three nights after the terrorist attacks, when Doggett raised the lone objection that stopped the House from bypassing normal procedures to expedite a generous bailout package for the airline industry. The bill did not clear Congress for another week, giving lawmakers more time for review and debate. Airlines claimed they needed help immediately because of the steep drop in air travel after terrorists hijacked commercial passenger jets and flew them into the World Trade Center and the Pentagon. When Texas-based Continental Airlines laid off 12,000 employees in spite of the government's help, House GOP Whip Tom DeLay blamed Doggett.

When Republican leaders were pushing for speedy approval of a U.S.-Jordan trade pact in 2001, Doggett objected, opening a floor debate that allowed Democrats to highlight what they called attempts by the Bush administration to weaken the agreement's labor and environmental protections. Doggett's passion for environmental protection extends to his congressional office, where he personally oversees trash recycling.

During the 2002 midterm election campaign, he put Republicans on the defensive by demanding that they advance legislation restricting a company's abilities to move its headquarters offshore to avoid paying some U.S. taxes, a business strategy known as "corporate inversion." Doggett is particularly scornful of drug companies that receive tax deductions for donating outdated or inappropriate drugs overseas. "The dumping of useless drugs is actually worse than no help at all, since such toxic junk must be destroyed by those most in need," Doggett says.

He is also liberal on foreign policy and defense. During House consideration in late 2002 of a resolution authorizing the president to take military action against Iraq, he headed an ad hoc Democratic whip organization to round up votes in opposition. Later, Doggett was a featured speaker at an anti-war rally on the lawn of the Texas state Capitol.

His liberal, pugnacious politics would be politically risky for most Southern Democrats. But Doggett represents a district based in Austin, with its many government workers and left-leaning students and academics affiliated with the University of Texas. Though he once was admonished by the House's presiding officer for calling Speaker Newt Gingrich "a crybaby," many of his constituents felt the same way about Gingrich, a polarizing figure and mastermind behind the 1995 GOP takeover of Congress.

But increasingly, Doggett has had to pay more attention to business issues as Austin has grown as a high technology center. Locals refer to it as "Silicon Hills." Doggett is a co-founder of the congressional Information Technology Working Group, which supports the technology industry's push to ease visa requirements for trained foreigners.

From his hillside apartment back home, Doggett can view all the landmarks of his life. Born and reared in Austin, he went to school there and was student body president at the University of Texas.

Within two years of earning his law degree in 1970, he won election to the state Senate. He served until 1985, compiling a record of support for consumers and civil rights while backing the death penalty and tough criminal sanctions against drug traffickers and violent criminals. In 1984, he ran for the Senate, beating two political veteran House members, Bob Krueger and Kent Hance, in the Democratic primary. It was not to be his year ultimately. In November, he was crushed by GOP Rep. Phil Gramm despite the fact that Gramm had switched to the Republican Party just the year before. Gramm was helped to his 18 percentage point win by President Reagan's immense popularity in Texas and went on to become a U.S. senator.

Four years later, Doggett won a seat on the Texas Supreme Court, which handles only civil cases. He was on the bench when 81-year-old Democratic Rep. Pickle announced his retirement in 1994. Doggett was the first Democrat to announce his candidacy, and his quick start spared him primary competition. Raising $1.2 million, he bucked that year's GOP takeover tide and won with 16 percent over real estate consultant A. Jo Baylor, who was bidding to become the first black Republican woman elected to Congress. Doggett has been re-elected easily ever since.

KEY VOTES

2002

Yes Overhaul campaign finance law; ban "soft money" and restrict advocacy advertising
No Back Bush's defense budget increase
No Extend 1996 welfare law
No Adopt Bush's discretionary spending limit
No Pass GOP Medicare prescription drug plan
Yes Create independent Sept. 11 commission
Yes Extend union protections to Homeland Security Department employees
No Revive fast-track procedures for trade agreements
No Authorize war against Iraq
No Advance bankruptcy overhaul opposed by abortion opponents

2001

No Nullify Clinton Labor Department ergonomics rule
? Cut taxes by $1.35 trillion through fiscal 2011
Yes Maintain ban on oil drilling in Arctic National Wildlife Refuge
No Approve Bush proposal to limit managed-care plan liability for coverage decisions
Yes Divert money from crop subsidy payments to land conservation
Yes Expand law enforcement power to investigate suspected terrorists

CQ VOTE STUDIES

	PARTY UNITY		PRESIDENTIAL SUPPORT	
	Support	Oppose	Support	Oppose
2002	95%	5%	22%	78%
2001	92%	8%	29%	71%
2000	90%	10%	86%	14%
1999	90%	10%	82%	18%
1998	92%	8%	81%	19%

INTEREST GROUPS

	AFL-CIO	ADA	CCUS	ACU
2002	100%	100%	30%	4%
2001	100%	85%	35%	4%
2000	80%	85%	33%	12%
1999	67%	100%	24%	4%
1998	90%	100%	39%	8%

TEXAS 10

Central – Austin

The once expansive rural district that Lyndon B. Johnson represented in the House (1937-49) has been shrinking in size and growing in population ever since he left. Today, the 10th is limited to Austin and eastern Travis County, where the population explosion has brought new inhabitants, many drawn to the area's burgeoning computer industry. The district takes in 80 percent of Travis County's residents (shared with the 21st), and about 85 percent of Austin's population.

Austin is a liberal Democratic island in the vast conservative Republican sea of the Lone Star State. A kind of Seattle for the South, Austin has been attracting music lovers and computer programmers in search of a hip, youthful place in a warm climate. State government workers and the University of Texas at Austin add to the city's liberal political bent, as does the 10th's sizable minority population (Hispanics and blacks, taken together, nearly equal whites).

The troubled oil industry of the mid-1980s did not permanently wound the 10th's economy, which was buoyed by its university and state government employers. In the 1990s, the area became a hub for high-tech startup firms, and its technology sector grew rapidly before hitting a small slump. In 1999, the city opened a new municipal airport on the site of the former Bergstrom Air Force Base — Austin-Bergstrom International Airport. In 2000, Money magazine called Austin one of the nation's 10 best places to live.

The fast-growing 10th was made more Democratic through redistricting following the 2000 census, which excised GOP precincts in western Travis. In 2002, Democrats Ron Kirk and Tony Sanchez won 64 percent and 57 percent of the district's vote in their races for senator and governor.

MAJOR INDUSTRY

Software, technology, service, state government

CITIES

Austin (pt.), 554,906; Pflugerville, 16,335

NOTABLE

Austin's country music scene gets national exposure on the weekly public television show "Austin City Limits"; South by Southwest, a huge pop and rock music festival in Austin, is held each spring; Austin is home to North America's largest urban colony of Mexican free-tailed bats.

Rep. Chet Edwards (D)

CAPITOL OFFICE
225-6105
www.house.gov/edwards
2459 Rayburn 20515-4311; fax 225-0350

COMMITTEES
Appropriations
Budget

HOMETOWN
Waco

BORN
Nov. 24, 1951, Corpus Christi, Texas

RELIGION
Methodist

FAMILY
Wife, Lea Ann Edwards; two children

EDUCATION
Texas A&M U., B.A. 1974 (economics); Harvard U., M.B.A. 1981

CAREER
Radio station executive; congressional aide

POLITICAL HIGHLIGHTS
Sought Democratic nomination for U.S. House, 1978; Texas Senate, 1983-91

ELECTION RESULTS

2002 GENERAL		
Chet Edwards (D)	74,678	51.6%
Ramsey W. Farley (R)	68,236	47.1%
Andrew Paul Farris (LIBERT)	1,943	1.3%
2002 PRIMARY		
Chet Edwards (D)		unopposed
2000 GENERAL		
Chet Edwards (D)	105,782	54.8%
Ramsey W. Farley (R)	85,546	44.3%

PREVIOUS WINNING PERCENTAGES
1998 (82%); 1996 (57%); 1994 (59%); 1992 (67%); 1990 (53%)

Elected 1990; 7th term

After two close elections, Edwards is an endangered incumbent, a rarity in politics these days. As the 108th Congress geared up, he stepped down from his Democratic leadership post, allowing him to focus on his political future, which may include a tough Republican challenger in 2004.

For four terms, the conservative Texan had been chief deputy whip for the House Democrats, making him a vital link between the liberal-leaning leadership and the party's often disgruntled conservatives. He gave that up to focus on his work as the senior Democrat on the Budget Committee and on the Appropriations Military Construction Subcommittee. With the shift, he can distance himself from the liberal wing and emphasize military and business issues important to his district, a place that not only voted heavily for George W. Bush in 2000 but also is home to the president's Crawford ranch.

Edwards usually take pains at home to portray himself as an independent-minded conservative on issues. He supported President Bush 47 percent of the time in the 107th Congress, placing him among the top two dozen Democrats in that category.

Not your typical publicity-hound politician, Edwards favors behind-the-scenes activity. He sponsors few pieces of legislation and wrote just three bills in the 107th Congress. One was a feasibility study on adding the Waco Mammoth Site Area to the National Park System, which became law in 2002. Edwards introduced just five bills from 1997 to 2003. "The reality is, in most cases, bills that become law will be sponsored by the majority party or committee chairmen," Edwards says. "I don't feel a great need to have my name on dozens of bills."

He prides himself on his work on the issue of preserving the separation of church and state. He opposes proposals calling for a national day of prayer, for federal funding for religious groups, and for a constitutional amendment creating a right to religious expression on public property.

It might seem to be a strange choice of issues for someone whose district is based in Waco, home to Baylor University, the largest Baptist-affiliated university in the world. Waco was also the site of the fateful 1993 standoff between federal agents and members of the Branch Davidian religious sect. Edwards finesses the potential conflict between his views and the religious leanings of his district by arguing that religion is too important to be entangled in the corporeal, self-interested realm of politics. He opposes Bush's "charitable choice" initiative because he says it would harm churches by making them dependent on federal money.

Edwards follows his leadership on most votes, supporting affirmative action policies in college admissions and opposing tax-funded vouchers for private school education. But he parts ways on other sensitive social issues. In 2001, he voted to ban all types of human cloning and he offered bills in both the 107th and 108th Congresses to ban most third-trimester abortions. And he often sides with Republicans on the environment, voting in favor of allowing oil drilling in the Arctic National Wildlife Refuge and scaling back federal environmental and land-use regulations.

Edwards is the lone Texas Democrat on the Appropriations Committee, making him the go-to guy for his home-state colleagues. His district includes the massive Army base at Fort Hood, so Edwards also looks out for defense interests, including Texas-based aerospace firms, military retirement benefits and education for the children of military personnel.

Despite the pro-gun rights leanings of his state, Edwards' views on new gun laws have been influenced by two mass killings in his district. While the House in 1991 debated a ban on certain semiautomatic assault-style weapons, news broke that a man with an automatic pistol had killed 22 people and wounded 20 in a Killeen cafeteria. In early 1993, a 51-day standoff between federal agents and the Branch Davidian religious sect just outside Waco resulted in the deaths of four law enforcement officers, Branch Davidian leader David Koresh and nearly all of his followers. These events influenced Edwards 1994 vote in favor of a ban on 19 types of assault-style weapons. His record on gun control is one of the reasons he continues to be a target for the GOP at election time.

Edwards was in high school during the height of the civil rights movement. He says two books — "Black Like Me" and "To Kill a Mockingbird" — convinced him that government should play a vital role in righting social wrongs. At Texas A&M University, he was a leader in the Student Conference on National Affairs, where he got to know the local congressman, Olin E. "Tiger" Teague.

As his college days wound down, Edwards accepted a job on Teague's congressional staff, intending to stay a year and then attend Harvard Business School. One year stretched to two, and in 1976, Teague told Edwards of his plans to retire and urged his protégé to run for his seat. The crowded Democratic primary in 1978 included a young Texas A&M economics professor, Phil Gramm. He edged out Edwards by fewer than 200 votes and went on to win the general election. He later became a U.S. senator.

Edwards went off to Harvard, then returned to Texas thinking about a career in business. But he jumped at a chance to run for the state Senate in 1982, and at 31 became the youngest senator elected to the state legislature. His ambition did not go unnoticed, and he was talked about as a possible candidate for lieutenant governor in 1989. But when Democratic Rep. Marvin Leath announced he would step down in 1990, Edwards moved to the 11th District to run for the House.

The GOP nominee, state Rep. Hugh D. Shine, outspent Edwards and called him a carpetbagger, though Edwards' state Senate district did overlap with the House district. Edwards also secured a pledge from House Speaker Thomas S. Foley to give him Leath's seat on Armed Services. Edwards won with 53 percent of the vote.

He had little re-election difficulty until his last two campaigns, when Republican Ramsey W. Farley held him to 55 percent in 2000 and less than 52 percent in 2002. That leaves Edwards a top GOP target in 2004.

KEY VOTES

2002

- Yes Overhaul campaign finance law; ban "soft money" and restrict advocacy advertising
- Yes Back Bush's defense budget increase
- Yes Extend 1996 welfare law
- No Adopt Bush's discretionary spending limit
- No Pass GOP Medicare prescription drug plan
- Yes Create independent Sept. 11 commission
- Yes Extend union protections to Homeland Security Department employees
- No Revive fast-track procedures for trade agreements
- Yes Authorize war against Iraq
- Yes Advance bankruptcy overhaul opposed by abortion opponents

2001

- No Nullify Clinton Labor Department ergonomics rule
- No Cut taxes by $1.35 trillion through fiscal 2011
- No Maintain ban on oil drilling in Arctic National Wildlife Refuge
- No Approve Bush proposal to limit managed-care plan liability for coverage decisions
- No Divert money from crop subsidy payments to land conservation
- Yes Expand law enforcement power to investigate suspected terrorists

CQ VOTE STUDIES

	PARTY UNITY		PRESIDENTIAL SUPPORT	
	Support	Oppose	Support	Oppose
2002	76%	24%	47%	53%
2001	72%	28%	47%	53%
2000	84%	16%	78%	22%
1999	80%	20%	79%	21%
1998	84%	16%	81%	19%

INTEREST GROUPS

	AFL-CIO	ADA	CCUS	ACU
2002	89%	75%	65%	36%
2001	100%	80%	57%	40%
2000	70%	80%	52%	8%
1999	78%	85%	42%	8%
1998	90%	90%	44%	8%

TEXAS 11

Central – Waco

The 11th is home to President Bush's "Western White House." Located in Crawford, the ranch has given the area a new level of recognition and has contributed to small boosts in the economy when Bush — and his many media followers — travel here.

Bush's attachment to the area and the district's Republican lean make it a GOP target in most every cycle. But Democratic Rep. Edwards has won the seat seven times, as the district is populated with conservative "Yellow Dog" Democrats and ticket splitters. Voters here embrace longevity in their House members — in 66 years, the district has had just three congressmen: Democrats Edwards, Marvin Leath (1979-91) and William Poage (1937-78).

Redistricting following the 2000 census made the 11th slightly more Republican-leaning. The addition of parts of Williamson County, which contains fast-growing suburbs of Austin, probably will quicken the district's GOP trend. Bush received 67 percent of the two-party vote here in 2000, and Republican Gov. Rick Perry took 66 percent in 2002.

About 70 percent of the district population comes out of Bell and McLennan counties. Waco, in McLennan County, is the district's most populous city and is the largest marketing center between Austin and Dallas. Fort Hood, the 11th's massive military base in Bell and Coryell counties, is an economic mainstay that has yet to be substantially affected by defense cutbacks. It has drawn many retired veterans who come to the 11th for its mild climate and three veterans' medical centers.

MAJOR INDUSTRY
Military, agriculture, light manufacturing

MILITARY BASES
Fort Hood (Army), 42,000 military, 6,000 civilian (2002)

CITIES
Waco, 113,726; Killeen, 86,911; Temple, 54,514

NOTABLE
Ranger Museum in Waco includes Billy the Kid's rifle and guns; In 1993, a complex outside Waco known as Ranch Apocalypse was the scene of a deadly standoff between federal agents and members of the Branch Davidian religious group.

Rep. Kay Granger (R)

CAPITOL OFFICE
225-5071
texas.granger@mail.house.gov
www.house.gov/granger
435 Cannon 20515-4312; fax 225-5683

COMMITTEES
Appropriations
Select Homeland Security

HOMETOWN
Fort Worth

BORN
Jan. 18, 1943, Greenville, Texas

RELIGION
Methodist

FAMILY
Divorced; three children

EDUCATION
Texas Wesleyan U., B.S. 1965

CAREER
Insurance agent; teacher

POLITICAL HIGHLIGHTS
Fort Worth Zoning Commission, 1981-1989; Fort Worth City Council, 1989-91; mayor of Fort Worth, 1991-95

ELECTION RESULTS

2002 GENERAL		
Kay Granger (R)	121,208	91.9%
Edward A. Hanson (LIBERT)	10,723	8.1%
2002 PRIMARY		
Kay Granger (R)	20,769	87.1%
Philip Hillery (R)	3,067	12.9%
2000 GENERAL		
Kay Granger (R)	117,739	62.7%
Mark Greene (D)	67,612	36.0%
Rick L. Clay (LIBERT)	2,565	1.4%

PREVIOUS WINNING PERCENTAGES
1998 (62%); 1996 (58%)

Elected 1996; 4th term

Granger's background and temperament are just what GOP leaders need to help translate their legislative agenda into terms that will resonate with voters, particularly women.

A dependable vote for the leadership on most issues and a member of the House GOP's "theme team," Granger often is spotlighted as she explains the party's views. Smart and ambitious, she can speak with authority from the perspective of a businesswoman, a working parent and a local elected official on topics ranging from crime, drugs and military needs to such "Democratic" issues as education and health care.

A divorced mother of three, she was a teacher, then started her own insurance agency and served as mayor of Fort Worth, a nonpartisan post.

Granger was wooed by both parties when she indicated interest in running for the 12th District seat in 1996, and GOP leaders have tried to make sure she is happy about choosing their side. Granger made it clear, even as a freshman, that she had aspirations for a broader role in the party, and she was given a position as an assistant whip. In the 106th Congress, she won assignment to the Appropriations Committee. In the 107th she added a seat on Budget to her duties but gave it up in the 108th for a post on the Homeland Security panel.

She likes to say she wants to "lower voices while raising the sights" of her Republican colleagues, and she still has her own sights set on a role in the House leadership. She considered a bid for a low-rung position on the GOP leadership ladder for the 107th before dropping out at the last moment. As Republicans chose their leaders for the 108th, her name was mentioned as a potential appointee for chief deputy whip, but the newly elected majority whip, Roy Blunt of Missouri, selected Eric Cantor of Virginia instead.

Granger's legislative priorities are shaped by her background. Her interest in championing tax-free education savings accounts for college can be traced to her own experience working her way through school and to the difficulties a favorite niece had in saving enough money to pay for her daughter's education. A former public school teacher, Granger has championed the creation of a National Commission on Youth Crime and School Violence.

As a single parent, she knows the importance of having health insurance, and in the 107th, she wrote legislation to provide a $1,000 tax credit to help uninsured people get health coverage.

Though she supports abortion rights in certain circumstances, Granger says changing the Republican Party's official line against abortion is not a priority. "To some, I think it's the most important issue, but that's not really where I'm coming from," she has said. Annual analyses of her voting record by various interest groups show she backs the abortion rights position about a fourth of the time.

Granger does what she can to keep federal dollars flowing to her district's defense manufacturers, which include Lockheed Martin and Bell Helicopter Textron. She supports continued federal funding of the F-35 Joint Strike Fighter, the F-22 and the V-22 Osprey aircraft.

Late in the 107th Congress, as a year-end deadline loomed for airports to install expensive new explosive detection machines, Granger led the successful push to extend the deadline, noting it would cost the Dallas-Fort Worth Airport $40 million to comply.

Granger noticed the upsurge in the popularity of the American flag in the aftermath of the Sept. 11, 2001, terrorist attacks, and she came up with the idea of offering a U.S. flag, mounted on a mat signed by members of Congress, for auction to raise money for victims of the attacks. Granger and her staff tracked down every member of Congress to sign the mat, and the flag brought in more than $80,000 at an Internet auction.

Granger was born in Greenville, Texas, to two public school teachers who divorced when she was 13. Her mother taught in the Fort Worth area for 45 years. Granger told the Fort Worth Star-Telegram that her mother never told her she could be anything she wanted — rather, she was told she had to be whatever she wanted. "I was not self-made," Granger says. "I was made by my mother."

Granger became a teacher in the same Birdville school district that named an elementary school after her mother. Granger taught literature and journalism for 10 years but then decided to switch careers. She went into the insurance business in 1978, eventually founding her own agency. In 1981, she was appointed to the Fort Worth Zoning Commission, where she served until she was elected to the city council in 1989. Two years later, she was elected mayor.

During her mayoral tenure, citizen patrol initiatives and other anti-gang efforts helped cut city crime by 50 percent. She lured new businesses to the city, and she was able to reduce property taxes for the first time in 11 years. Her pro-business stands endeared her to the Fort Worth business community, which in 1999 made her the first woman chosen as outstanding business executive of the year. Democrats and Republicans alike courted her as a House candidate when Democratic Rep. Pete Geren decided not to seek re-election in 1996.

After choosing to run under the Republican banner and resigning as mayor, Granger heard grumbling from some on the GOP right. She was attacked by two primary opponents as a liberal and was opposed by the Tarrant County Republican chairman. But she won nomination with a whopping 69 percent of the GOP primary vote. That November, she defeated another former Fort Worth mayor, Hugh Parmer, by 17 percentage points, becoming the first Republican woman elected to the House from Texas.

Granger has not seriously been challenged since. In 2002, after defeating a conservative minister in the GOP primary, she easily won in November, as Democrats failed to field a candidate.

Early in 2000, her district office in a Fort Worth office building was destroyed by a tornado, presaging another uncomfortably close brush with disaster: Granger had just left a meeting at the Pentagon on Sept. 11, 2001, when hijacked American Airlines Flight 77 slammed into the building.

KEY VOTES

2002

- No Overhaul campaign finance law; ban "soft money" and restrict advocacy advertising
- Yes Back Bush's defense budget increase
- Yes Extend 1996 welfare law
- Yes Adopt Bush's discretionary spending limit
- Yes Pass GOP Medicare prescription drug plan
- No Create independent Sept. 11 commission
- No Extend union protections to Homeland Security Department employees
- Yes Revive fast-track procedures for trade agreements
- Yes Authorize war against Iraq
- Yes Advance bankruptcy overhaul opposed by abortion opponents

2001

- Yes Nullify Clinton Labor Department ergonomics rule
- Yes Cut taxes by $1.35 trillion through fiscal 2011
- No Maintain ban on oil drilling in Arctic National Wildlife Refuge
- Yes Approve Bush proposal to limit managed-care plan liability for coverage decisions
- No Divert money from crop subsidy payments to land conservation
- Yes Expand law enforcement power to investigate suspected terrorists

CQ VOTE STUDIES

	PARTY UNITY		PRESIDENTIAL SUPPORT	
	Support	Oppose	Support	Oppose
2002	96%	4%	85%	15%
2001	97%	3%	88%	12%
2000	93%	7%	25%	75%
1999	92%	8%	26%	74%
1998	91%	9%	28%	72%

INTEREST GROUPS

	AFL-CIO	ADA	CCUS	ACU
2002	0%	0%	95%	96%
2001	0%	0%	100%	80%
2000	0%	5%	84%	84%
1999	0%	5%	95%	78%
1998	10%	5%	100%	84%

TEXAS 12

Part of Fort Worth and suburbs; Parker County

The Republican-leaning 12th includes much of Tarrant County, including a large segment of Fort Worth, and all of rural Parker County. The mostly white, middle-class district contains downtown Fort Worth but also takes in a mix of suburban and rural areas.

The 12th's solid economy is built around transportation. Three major airports, an Air Force base, three railroad lines and several interstate highways are in or adjacent to the district, supporting myriad businesses. The Union Pacific and now-combined Burlington Northern Santa Fe railroads both are active in the district, but the air industry has far surpassed rail. Large government defense contracts — including those from Lockheed Martin, which has a facility in the district — have helped create jobs and fuel economic growth.

Parker County includes Weatherford, which is becoming more Republican as it undergoes a transition from a rural town into part of Fort Worth's suburbs. Though Parker County covers more than half the district's land mass, it only contains 14 percent of the district's voters.

Redistricting following the 2000 census changed the 12th from a politically competitive district to one dominated by Republicans. Mapmakers gave the neighboring 24th Democratic areas south of downtown Fort Worth. The 12th still includes some Democratic areas downtown, but the parts of Tarrant outside the city are overwhelmingly Republican, as is Parker County. Had the redrawn 12th existed in the 2000 presidential election, George W. Bush would have won two-thirds of the vote.

MAJOR INDUSTRY

Defense technology, transportation, medicine

MILITARY BASES

Naval Air Station Fort Worth, 2,100 military, 2,000 civilian (2002)

CITIES

Fort Worth (pt.), 270,210; North Richland Hills, 55,634; Haltom City (pt.), 39,002; Hurst (pt.), 31,336; Keller (pt.), 23,689

NOTABLE

The National Cowgirl Museum in Fort Worth showcases women rodeo riders and contributors to Western heritage; Cowtown Coliseum, in the historic Stockyards district of Fort Worth, was the site of the world's first indoor rodeo and the world's first live radio broadcast of a rodeo.

Rep. William M. 'Mac' Thornberry (R)

CAPITOL OFFICE
225-3706
www.house.gov/thornberry
2457 Rayburn 20515-4313; fax 225-3486

COMMITTEES
Armed Services
Budget
Select Homeland Security
(Cybersecurity, Science & R&D - chairman)

HOMETOWN
Clarendon

BORN
July 15, 1958, Clarendon, Texas

RELIGION
Presbyterian

FAMILY
Wife, Sally Thornberry; two children

EDUCATION
Texas Tech U., B.A. 1980 (history); U. of Texas, J.D. 1983

CAREER
Lawyer; cattleman; State Department official; congressional aide

POLITICAL HIGHLIGHTS
No previous office

ELECTION RESULTS

2002 GENERAL		
William Thornberry (R)	119,401	79.3%
Zane Reese (D)	31,218	20.7%
2002 PRIMARY		
William Thornberry (R)		unopposed
2000 GENERAL		
William Thornberry (R)	117,995	67.6%
Curtis Clinesmith (D)	54,343	31.2%
Brad Clardy (LIBERT)	2,137	1.2%

PREVIOUS WINNING PERCENTAGES
1998 (68%); 1996 (67%); 1994 (55%)

Elected 1994; 5th term

With an intense interest in national security, Thornberry sponsored a bill calling for a new, executive branch department to oversee homeland security — almost six months before Sept. 11, 2001. After the terrorist attacks on the World Trade Center and the Pentagon, the idea suddenly topped everyone's to-do list, and Thornberry's bill became the foundation for the legislation that passed the House in 2002.

As a relatively junior lawmaker, Thornberry was overshadowed by President Bush and GOP leaders, but his understanding of the government's multifaceted jurisdiction over domestic security made him a valuable adviser to bill drafters. He was rewarded by Republican leaders in 2003 with a seat on the new Homeland Security Committee.

His growing influence on the Armed Services Committee has made him a player on other defense and security issues as well. "Defense is the first priority of the federal government, and we need to take care of that before we address other issues," Thornberry says.

He is a major booster of Bush's plan to develop a controversial U.S. anti-missile defense system, which critics say is technologically infeasible. He is the founder of the new Defense Study Group, made up of 80 House members from both parties to work out solutions to security problems. Thornberry also has taken a lead role in nuclear weapons security, in part because the giant Pantex weapons assembly complex is in his district.

His proposal creating the National Nuclear Security Administration was enacted in 1999. "With the NNSA," he declared, "we are going to make sure that the nation's nuclear weapons facilities are run with a clear, military-like chain of command." In the 107th Congress, Thornberry chaired a special, two-year oversight panel created by the Armed Services Committee to help implement the new law.

The legislation was the fruit of a four-year effort by Thornberry. Almost from the moment he arrived in the House in 1995, he had campaigned to place oversight of nuclear weapons facilities under a single, semi-autonomous federal agency. The idea essentially was ignored until revelations that China allegedly tried to steal highly classified information from Energy Department laboratories.

Thornberry's focus on defense has a parochial side too. The Texan looks out for the interests of Sheppard Air Force Base, near Wichita Falls. He also is a defender of the troubled V-22 Osprey tilt-rotor aircraft, which is made by Bell Helicopter in Amarillo but has crashed in several test flights.

Thornberry will never be mistaken for a moderate — his lifetime score for his votes in the House from the liberal Americans for Democratic Action is 2 — but his style differs from many of the younger conservatives who have pushed the GOP to the right in recent years. He says an effective lawmaker has "energy, patience and persistence." Thornberry tempers his conservatism with pragmatism, much like his former boss, Texas GOP Rep. Larry Combest, for whom he worked in the 1980s.

In the late 1990s, Thornberry went along with several proposals to reduce the estate tax though he continued to push for outright abolition of the tax, which affects many land-owning farmers and ranchers in his district. And he supported the $1.35 trillion tax cut bill in 2001 that phases out the estate tax over several years ending 2010.

Thornberry traces his conservatism to his upbringing on the Texas ranch that has been in his family for more than 70 years. He grew up in a modest house built by his grandfather in the 1930s. "I was taught at a very young age the importance of doing a good job and putting in an honest day's work," he once told a magazine interviewer.

A business-suit-and-boots-wearing member of Capitol Hill's unofficial Boot Caucus, Thornberry often sides with the concerns of ranchers. He is a staunch proponent of property owners' rights and says federal laws and regulations impinge unduly on farmers' land-use decisions. "Property rights become the foundation for quality of life," he says.

Thornberry regularly supports bills to overhaul the Endangered Species Act, which allows the government to block development on private land. In the 106th Congress, he denounced the law as "overzealous regulation."

Agriculture is also important to Thornberry's district, which produces more cotton than any other congressional district. Its farms are among the nation's top producers of wheat and peanuts as well. So Thornberry has a keen interest in federal subsidies for those crops, despite the ideological leanings that prompted him to support the GOP's 1996 "Freedom to Farm" law, which unsuccessfully sought to replace New Deal-era crop subsidies with a system based on the free market. Thornberry bucked House leaders by working with Combest to preserve the federal support system for cotton.

In 2001, he also sided with Combest to push the House to pass legislation that largely undid Freedom to Farm. It maintained or expanded subsidies for row crops and boosted federal payments to ranchers as well.

Much of Thornberry's approach to dealing with colleagues is influenced by the five years he worked as an aide on Capitol Hill after graduating from the University of Texas law school in 1983. He first was a legislative aide to Texas GOP Rep. Tom Loeffler, and then Combest's chief of staff. In 1988, he was deputy assistant secretary of state for legislative affairs in the Reagan administration. He got to know the inner workings of the House and dealt with crises with an unflappable temperament. Now, he is often tapped by Republican leaders to preside over contentious legislative debates.

Thornberry took a break from politics in 1989 and went to work in an Amarillo law firm while helping run his family's cattle ranch. Then in 1994, he challenged Democratic incumbent Bill Sarpalius, who had become vulnerable in the conservative district because of his support for raising taxes as part of President Clinton's 1993 budget plan. Thornberry played up his family's close ties to the land and beat Sarpalius with 55 percent of the vote. He has had no trouble winning re-election since.

KEY VOTES

2002

- No Overhaul campaign finance law; ban "soft money" and restrict advocacy advertising
- Yes Back Bush's defense budget increase
- Yes Extend 1996 welfare law
- Yes Adopt Bush's discretionary spending limit
- Yes Pass GOP Medicare prescription drug plan
- No Create independent Sept. 11 commission
- No Extend union protections to Homeland Security Department employees
- Yes Revive fast-track procedures for trade agreements
- Yes Authorize war against Iraq
- No Advance bankruptcy overhaul opposed by abortion opponents

2001

- Yes Nullify Clinton Labor Department ergonomics rule
- Yes Cut taxes by $1.35 trillion through fiscal 2011
- No Maintain ban on oil drilling in Arctic National Wildlife Refuge
- Yes Approve Bush proposal to limit managed-care plan liability for coverage decisions
- No Divert money from crop subsidy payments to land conservation
- Yes Expand law enforcement power to investigate suspected terrorists

CQ VOTE STUDIES

	PARTY UNITY		PRESIDENTIAL SUPPORT	
	Support	Oppose	Support	Oppose
2002	94%	6%	92%	8%
2001	99%	1%	95%	5%
2000	97%	3%	25%	75%
1999	93%	7%	20%	80%
1998	92%	8%	23%	77%

INTEREST GROUPS

	AFL-CIO	ADA	CCUS	ACU
2002	0%	0%	95%	92%
2001	8%	0%	100%	96%
2000	0%	0%	76%	88%
1999	22%	5%	76%	88%
1998	0%	5%	89%	100%

TEXAS 13
Panhandle — Amarillo; Wichita Falls

The conservative 13th takes in almost all of the Texas Panhandle, including the city of Amarillo, then extends east along the southern Oklahoma border to include the South Plains and much of the Red River Valley. It contains Wichita Falls and reaches as far east as Montague County, about 60 miles northwest of Fort Worth and Dallas. A monstrous and mainly rural district, the 13th takes in all or part of 43 counties, 39 of which have a population of under 25,000.

Oil and cotton dominate the district's economy, and both industries suffered during the 1980s and early 1990s as oil prices dropped and droughts starved the land. Thanks to other industries, the main cities weathered the difficulties. In Amarillo, Pantex is the nation's only nuclear weapons assembly and disassembly plant. The city also has a hand in producing the military's V-22 Osprey, which takes off like a helicopter but flies like a plane. After several crashes during testing, the aircraft's future is uncertain.

In Wichita Falls, factories are numerous, but the jewel of the economy is Sheppard Air Force Base, which so far has escaped downsizing. Many of the district's rural counties depend on the Ogallala Aquifer to grow wheat, sorghum, sugar beets, corn and hay.

The 13th is one of the most Republican districts in Texas. The GOP does especially well in many of the rural small towns that dot the district, particularly around Amarillo. Ochiltree County, a Panhandle county on the Oklahoma border, gave 91 percent to George W. Bush in the 2000 presidential election. Closer to blue-collar Wichita Falls, voters have traditionally favored Democrats at the local level, but even this area votes solidly Republican in state and national elections. In 2002, the 13th gave Republican Gov. Rick Perry 71 percent of the vote.

MAJOR INDUSTRY
Agriculture, oil, defense

MILITARY BASES
Sheppard Air Force Base, 4,953 military, 2,516 civilian (2002)

CITIES
Amarillo, 173,627; Wichita Falls, 104,197; Plainview, 22,336

NOTABLE
A stretch of Route 66, made famous by songs and television, cuts through the 13th; Stanley Marsh's Cadillac Ranch.

Rep. Ron Paul (R)

CAPITOL OFFICE
225-2831
rep.paul@mail.house.gov
www.house.gov/paul
203 Cannon 20515-4314; fax 226-4871

COMMITTEES
Financial Services
International Relations
Joint Economic

HOMETOWN
Surfside

BORN
Aug. 20, 1935, Pittsburgh, Pa.

RELIGION
Protestant

FAMILY
Wife, Carol Wells; five children

EDUCATION
Gettysburg College, B.S. 1957 (pre-med); Duke U., M.D. 1961

MILITARY SERVICE
Air Force, 1963-65; Pa. Air National Guard, 1965-68

CAREER
Physician

POLITICAL HIGHLIGHTS
Republican nominee for U.S. House, 1974; U.S. House, 1976-77; defeated for re-election to U.S. House, 1976; U.S. House, 1979-85; sought Republican nomination for U.S. Senate, 1984; Libertarian nominee for president, 1988

ELECTION RESULTS

2002 GENERAL		
Ron Paul (R)	102,905	68.1%
Corby Windham (D)	48,224	31.9%
2002 PRIMARY		
Ron Paul (R)		unopposed
2000 GENERAL		
Ron Paul (R)	137,370	59.7%
Loy Sneary (D)	92,689	40.3%

PREVIOUS WINNING PERCENTAGES
1998 (55%); 1996 (51%); 1982 (99%); 1980 (51%); 1978 (51%); 1976 Special Runoff Election (56%)

Elected 1996; 7th full term

Also served 1976-77, 1979-85

Paul is not the sort of politician who seeks to succeed by jumping on the bandwagon. In fact, he appears to go out of his way to stay off of it.

During 1999 through 2002, Paul cast the solitary "nay" vote in the House on 51 occasions. In the 107th Congress, for example, he cast the lone dissenting vote against legislation to combat bioterrorism threats and against a bill to enhance the government's bid to curb money-laundering efforts. In the 106th Congress, he was the only House member to vote against giving a congressional gold medal to the Peanuts comic strip creator Charles M. Schulz.

On other occasions, Paul has been in a tiny minority. He was one of three members to vote against the sweeping 2002 law written to crack down on corporate fraud. And he was among just six Republicans who voted later that year against the resolution giving President Bush authority to wage war on Iraq, saying the measure amounted to an unconstitutional transfer of the power to declare war from Congress to the executive branch.

Most often, Paul bolsters his reputation as the House's "Dr. No" by opposing legislation that he views as an unwarranted extension of federal authority. The 1988 Libertarian nominee for president — he won just 432,179 votes — argues that the government has no right to take any action that is not specifically authorized by the Constitution. As a result, he would like to require members of Congress to document the constitutional authority for every bill they introduce. He votes "no" on virtually all appropriations bills that come to the House floor, because they would deliver money to federal programs that in his view have no constitutional justification.

Not only would Paul prefer to return the country to the days when states held most of the power, but he also would like it if the value of the dollar were pegged once again to gold. (Paul has invested much income in gold and silver companies.)

Such absolutist views, and the refusal to compromise that comes with them, mean Paul's effectiveness at the Capitol is limited. But he has nonetheless gained a small but loyal national following that brings him campaign contributions from all corners of the country; the majority of his campaign donations regularly come from outside of Texas.

Marching to a different drummer is not new for Paul. After starting to develop his political theories in medical school and working as an obstetrician, he served two stints in the House in the late 1970s and early 1980s, when there were just a few Republicans in Texas' overwhelmingly Democratic delegation. As the Libertarian presidential candidate, he renounced the Republican Party, spoke out against foreign aid and "corporate welfare" — certain tax breaks and subsidies for big business — and advocated the legalization of drugs.

His Libertarian beliefs make Paul an erratic ally of GOP causes. He opposes legislation that would prohibit same-sex marriage, saying "everyone is an individual and ought to be treated equally." He also opposes a constitutional amendment to ban flag burning and brands federal efforts to combat illegal drugs "an absolute failure." But he parts company with his former Libertarian brethren in advocating an anti-abortion stand. Paul has said that "whether a civilized society treats human life with dignity or contempt will determine the outcome of that civilization."

When he returned to the House in 1996 (defeating the preferred GOP candidate in a hard-fought primary), he received a lukewarm reception from his party. He crossed party lines to vote with Democrats more often than all but four other House Republicans — all of them moderates — in the 107th Congress. And he backed President Bush only half the time — the lowest of any Republican in Congress. Still, top Republicans appear content — or perhaps resigned — to let Paul be Paul.

At times, Paul has shown a bit of flexibility with the GOP leadership. When his party was struggling in 1997 to pass a District of Columbia spending bill, he changed his vote from "no" to "present," allowing the measure to pass by one vote. He votes against farm subsidies, but says the farmers in his district like him "because I protect their right to have a gun and I keep the EPA off their back," as he told the St. Petersburg Times.

Paul takes a dim view of U.S. aid to foreign countries. He has backed efforts to end U.S. support for the International Monetary Fund and to force the United States to pull out of the World Trade Organization. He also opposes "so-called peacekeeping missions" and sponsored legislation that would have required the United States to withdraw from the United Nations.

As a member of the International Relations Committee in the 107th, he decried American foreign policy as "worldwide imperialism" that spurred the Sept. 11, 2001, terrorist attacks. "A growing number of Americans are concluding that the threat we now face comes more as a consequence of our foreign policy than because the bad guys envy our freedoms and prosperity," Paul said nine months afterward.

Although he had in the past voted for trade liberalization, he has opposed the two most recent laws enacted to that end: the 2000 measure granting China permanent normal trade status and the 2002 bill renewing presidential fast-track trade negotiating authority.

Paul first was elected to Congress in an April 1976 special election to replace Democrat Bob Casey, who had resigned to join the Federal Maritime Commission. Paul defeated former state Democratic Rep. Bob Gammage, but in the general election seven months later Gammage felled Paul by 268 votes. In 1978, Paul won back the seat from Gammage by 1,200 votes.

In 1984, Paul left his House seat to run for the Senate but lost the primary to Phil Gramm. Twelve years later, Paul won election in the 14th, which included areas he represented in his earlier House career. In the GOP primary, he ousted Greg Laughlin, who had held the seat since 1989 but had switched to the GOP from the Democrats in 1995. Paul prevailed by pressing his anti-tax and anti-government message; he won the general election by just 3 percentage points, despite criticism that he supported the legalization of drugs. He has since won re-election by comfortable margins.

KEY VOTES

2002

No	Overhaul campaign finance law; ban "soft money" and restrict advocacy advertising
No	Back Bush's defense budget increase
No	Extend 1996 welfare law
Yes	Adopt Bush's discretionary spending limit
?	Pass GOP Medicare prescription drug plan
No	Create independent Sept. 11 commission
No	Extend union protections to Homeland Security Department employees
No	Revive fast-track procedures for trade agreements
No	Authorize war against Iraq
No	Advance bankruptcy overhaul opposed by abortion opponents

2001

Yes	Nullify Clinton Labor Department ergonomics rule
Yes	Cut taxes by $1.35 trillion through fiscal 2011
No	Maintain ban on oil drilling in Arctic National Wildlife Refuge
?	Approve Bush proposal to limit managed-care plan liability for coverage decisions
No	Divert money from crop subsidy payments to land conservation
No	Expand law enforcement power to investigate suspected terrorists

CQ VOTE STUDIES

	PARTY UNITY		PRESIDENTIAL SUPPORT	
	Support	Oppose	Support	Oppose
2002	76%	24%	51%	49%
2001	79%	21%	49%	51%
2000	80%	20%	27%	73%
1999	75%	25%	30%	70%
1998	76%	24%	31%	69%

INTEREST GROUPS

	AFL-CIO	ADA	CCUS	ACU
2002	29%	30%	50%	76%
2001	27%	20%	62%	70%
2000	44%	30%	45%	76%
1999	38%	10%	60%	92%
1998	40%	20%	65%	88%

TEXAS 14

Southeast – Victoria, San Marcos

Spanning a roughly 15,000-square-mile area framed on the outside by San Antonio, Austin, Houston and Corpus Christi, the 14th takes in a stretch of coastal land from near Galveston to Rockport. Inland, it stretches to eastern San Antonio and southern Austin suburbs. Redistricting after the 2000 census moved the district slightly westward, away from Houston and toward San Antonio.

Despite some suburban areas, the district is overwhelmingly coastal and agricultural. Only two cities in the district, Victoria and San Marcos, have more than 25,000 people, and nearly 80 percent of residents are native-born Texans.

Chemical companies, such as Dow, have facilities near the Gulf Coast, where they rode the 1980s oil glut to success by making antifreeze and other products. Victoria is a leading oil and chemical center. Mingled with the chemical producers on the coast are fishermen who haul in boatloads of shrimp.

Farmers in the 14th's interior grow rice, grain and sorghum, while the northwest reaches of the district benefit from Austin's health care and government sectors. The district also holds attraction for nature lovers, who can visit Goose Island State Park, the Aransas National Wildlife Refuge and several bird sanctuaries.

Dominated by farms and petrochemical plants, the 14th leans Republican but has Democratic roots and a sizable minority population. Roughly one-third of residents are of Hispanic origin. The 14th tends to elect Republicans, but not by the overwhelming margins the more solidly Republican suburban Houston districts rack up. Locally, Republicans tend to do very well in the southern portions of the 14th, while the areas around Austin have taken on some of that city's more liberal leanings.

MAJOR INDUSTRY

Petrochemicals, agriculture, shrimping

CITIES

Victoria, 60,603; San Marcos, 34,733; Seguin, 22,011; Bay City, 18,667

NOTABLE

Stephen F. Austin, Texas' founder, was from Jones Creek, near the city of Freeport; West Columbia was chosen by the founders of the Republic of Texas to be the fledgling nation's first capital.

Rep. Rubén Hinojosa (D)

CAPITOL OFFICE
225-2531
rep.hinojosa@mail.house.gov
www.house.gov/hinojosa
2463 Rayburn 20515-4315; fax 225-5688

COMMITTEES
Education & Workforce
Financial Services
Resources

HOMETOWN
Mercedes

BORN
Aug. 20, 1940, Edcouch, Texas

RELIGION
Roman Catholic

FAMILY
Wife, Martha Hinojosa; five children

EDUCATION
U. of Texas, B.B.A. 1962; U. of Texas, Pan American, M.B.A. 1980

CAREER
Food processing executive

POLITICAL HIGHLIGHTS
Texas State Board of Education, 1974-84 (chairman of special populations)

ELECTION RESULTS

2002 GENERAL		
Rubén Hinojosa (D)		unopposed
2002 PRIMARY		
Rubén Hinojosa (D)	46,688	86.7%
Mel Hawkins (D)	7,138	13.3%
2000 GENERAL		
Rubén Hinojosa (D)	106,570	88.5%
Frank L. Jones (LIBERT)	13,167	10.9%

PREVIOUS WINNING PERCENTAGES
1998 (58%); 1996 (62%)

Elected 1996; 4th term

Hinojosa was one of the four Texas Democrats who broke ranks with their party in 2002 and voted to enhance President Bush's trade negotiating power by resurrecting fast-track procedures for congressional consideration of trade agreements. The idea is anathema to labor unions, a bedrock Democratic constituency. But to the congressman representing some of Texas' poorest border towns, enactment of such legislation represents the hope of the highways, commerce and jobs that could help his constituency upgrade its economic standing.

Now a wealthy business owner, Hinojosa (ee-na-HO-suh) rose from modest beginnings in a South Texas farm community where he attended elementary school. There, Mexican-American children were segregated from white students. He grew up speaking Spanish.

Those life experiences have shaped the priorities he brings to Congress, and they inform his positions on issues as far-flung as free trade, student testing and border control. In particular, Hinojosa has promoted initiatives and legislation that he believes will help promote small-business development and educational opportunities for the people of his heavily Hispanic district. He was able to win funding in 2002 for a number of border regional transportation and truck inspection projects.

In the 108th Congress, his new seat on the Resources Committee will enable him to continue to press for a resolution to a water dispute between the United States and Texas. Mexico owes Texas a considerable amount of water that is badly needed by South Texas irrigators, and Hinojosa says the Bush administration "literally sold South Texas down the river" in a 2002 agreement.

In the 107th, he was among a handful of lawmakers who tried to assist residents on both sides of the Rio Grande by seeking an extension of a Justice Department deadline for Mexican workers and other commuters to obtain new border-crossing cards that are laser-printed and tamper-proof.

Hinojosa sits on the Education and the Workforce Committee and became chairman of the Congressional Hispanic Caucus education task force soon after arriving in Washington. In those posts, he has helped direct millions of federal dollars to Hispanic colleges and universities and put more money into efforts to connect schools and libraries to the Internet. In recognition of his lifelong support of education, two Texas school districts in 2002 announced they were naming schools after him.

In the 105th, Hinojosa praised a landmark budget agreement that included funding for scholarships to help middle-class students attend college. However, he maintained that more had to be done. In 1997, he promoted legislation seeking to redirect existing Higher Education Act programs to target resources to the neediest schoolchildren, including Hispanics and American Indians. The following year, he won a substantial increase in federal aid to colleges that serve large numbers of Hispanic students. Funding also was increased for bilingual and migrant education and for Head Start — all Hinojosa priorities.

Hinojosa has broken with Democratic leaders before. During the Clinton administration, he opposed one of its high-profile education proposals: introducing voluntary national tests to track and improve the performance of elementary school students. Recalling his own struggles as a student — Spanish was his first language and English took years to master — Hinojosa argued that a "national test should not be used as a basis for making high-stakes educational decisions" because of "enormous inequalities" between the resources available to schools attended primarily by poor and minority students and schools with more-affluent populations.

The Texan was in the spotlight in the 106th during the debate over granting China permanent normal trade status. With Hinojosa undecided on the issue, the Clinton administration took the extraordinary step of sending him and another lawmaker, New York Democrat Gregory W. Meeks, on a fact-finding tour of China. In the end, Hinojosa backed the administration's plea to open up trade with China — after holding out for funding for an information technology center in South Texas.

Hinojosa has lobbied for a new interstate highway in the 15th District that would serve as a trade route from Mexico and would help relieve local traffic bottlenecks occurring from increased cross-border commercial traffic, a result of the North American Free Trade Agreement. The massive 1998 transportation measure included money to upgrade U.S. 281 from the Mexican border as far north as its intersection with Interstate 37.

Hinojosa's overall voting record is liberal, but he has sided with conservatives on occasion. He supported congressional term limits, backed a constitutional amendment to prohibit flag desecration and voted to ban a procedure its opponents call "partial birth" abortion. He affiliates with the moderate New Democrat Coalition.

The eighth of 11 children born to parents who had immigrated to the United States from Mexico, he eventually became president of a food-processing company with more than 400 employees. He served for a decade on the Texas state board of education and was instrumental in creating the South Texas Community College system in the upper Rio Grande Valley.

The Hinojosa family's prominence and his own community involvement helped Hinojosa win the open 15th District seat in 1996. He succeeded Democrat E. "Kika" de la Garza, who retired after 32 years in the House. Given the 15th's strong one-party voting tradition — it is a Democratic bulwark in the Lone Star State — Hinojosa's biggest challenge in taking the seat was winning his party's nomination. In a hotly contested five-way battle for the Democratic nod, he edged out lawyer Jim Selman.

Against Republican minister Tom Haughey, Hinojosa won by 26 percentage points in 1996 and by 17 points in a 1998 rematch. The GOP did not field a candidate against him in 2000. With the 15th District's boundaries only marginally altered by redistricting in 2002, Republicans again declined to field a candidate.

KEY VOTES

2002

- Yes Overhaul campaign finance law; ban "soft money" and restrict advocacy advertising
- Yes Back Bush's defense budget increase
- No Extend 1996 welfare law
- No Adopt Bush's discretionary spending limit
- No Pass GOP Medicare prescription drug plan
- Yes Create independent Sept. 11 commission
- Yes Extend union protections to Homeland Security Department employees
- Yes Revive fast-track procedures for trade agreements
- No Authorize war against Iraq
- Yes Advance bankruptcy overhaul opposed by abortion opponents

2001

- No Nullify Clinton Labor Department ergonomics rule
- No Cut taxes by $1.35 trillion through fiscal 2011
- Yes Maintain ban on oil drilling in Arctic National Wildlife Refuge
- No Approve Bush proposal to limit managed-care plan liability for coverage decisions
- No Divert money from crop subsidy payments to land conservation
- Yes Expand law enforcement power to investigate suspected terrorists

CQ VOTE STUDIES

	PARTY UNITY		PRESIDENTIAL SUPPORT	
	Support	Oppose	Support	Oppose
2002	89%	11%	41%	59%
2001	85%	15%	33%	67%
2000	92%	8%	88%	12%
1999	89%	11%	78%	22%
1998	91%	9%	79%	21%

INTEREST GROUPS

	AFL-CIO	ADA	CCUS	ACU
2002	71%	80%	61%	20%
2001	75%	85%	52%	13%
2000	90%	80%	50%	8%
1999	78%	100%	40%	4%
1998	89%	95%	59%	16%

TEXAS 15
South – most of Hidalgo County, McAllen

Situated in southern Texas, the convoluted boundaries of the 15th take in the agricultural and cattle areas north of Corpus Christi and then dip down to the Texas-Mexico border. The 15th has a 78.3 percent Hispanic population, making it the most heavily Hispanic district in the nation. The large minority influence contributes to the district's overall Democratic lean.

The 15th also is one of the poorest districts in the nation. Community leaders struggle to bring jobs to the region and to provide job training. Hidalgo County, an agricultural area, is the most populous and fastest-growing in the district. Along the U.S.-Mexico border, *maquiladoras* — assembly or manufacturing plants that use low-cost labor and import many parts from the United States — are the mainstay. The economy is on the rise since the passage of the North American Free Trade Agreement, and trade with Mexican border cities, such as Reynosa, also adds jobs.

Transportation is an issue — the region is said to be the largest populated area that does not have easy access to an interstate highway. Plans are in the works to build a new interstate called I-69 that would connect South Texas to Indianapolis.

The 15th's congressional seat has never been held by a Republican. While Republicans became more competitive in the 1990s, Democrats continue to dominate. George W. Bush took just 45 percent of the two-party vote in the 2000 presidential election, even as he swept the state with 59 percent. Democrats Ron Kirk and Tony Sanchez took more than 60 percent of the two-party vote in their 2002 races for senator and governor.

MAJOR INDUSTRY
Small business, trade, manufacturing

MILITARY BASES
Naval Station Ingleside, 2,443 military, 315 civilian (2002)

CITIES
McAllen, 106,406; Edinburg, 48,465; Pharr, 46,660; Mission (pt.), 32,037

NOTABLE
In 1836, Colonel James Walker Fannin of the Texas independence movement was executed with members of his troop in what was known as the "Goliad Massacre."

Rep. Silvestre Reyes (D)

Elected 1996; 4th term

CAPITOL OFFICE
225-4831
talk2silver@mail.house.gov
www.house.gov/reyes
1527 Longworth 20515-4316; fax 225-2016

COMMITTEES
Armed Services
Veterans' Affairs
Select Intelligence

HOMETOWN
El Paso

BORN
Nov. 10, 1944, Canutillo, Texas

RELIGION
Roman Catholic

FAMILY
Wife, Carolina Reyes; three children

EDUCATION
U. of Texas, attended 1964-65; Texas Western College, attended 1965-66 (criminal justice); El Paso Community College, A.A. 1977 (criminal justice)

MILITARY SERVICE
Army, 1966-68

CAREER
U.S. Border Patrol agent

POLITICAL HIGHLIGHTS
Canutillo School Board, 1968-70

ELECTION RESULTS

2002 GENERAL		
Silvestre Reyes (D)		unopposed
2002 PRIMARY		
Silvestre Reyes (D)		unopposed
2000 GENERAL		
Silvestre Reyes (D)	92,649	68.3%
Daniel Power (R)	40,921	30.2%
Dan Moser (LIBERT)	2,080	1.5%

PREVIOUS WINNING PERCENTAGES
1998 (88%); 1996 (71%)

With the past two years under his belt as chairman of the Congressional Hispanic Caucus, and with more than a quarter-century of service with the U.S. Border Patrol before moving to Washington, Reyes appears uniquely positioned in the 108th Congress to play a role in the ongoing debate over the nation's immigration laws.

Reyes (sil-VES-treh RAY-ess, with rolled r's) is an advocate of broad legalization for many undocumented immigrants, but the terrorist attacks of Sept. 11, 2001, took the wind out of much of his work in the 107th. The month before the attacks, as President Bush signaled support for legalizing 3 million Mexican immigrants, Reyes tried to help Democrats compete by proposing to allow all immigrants to earn legal status, not just Mexicans. A Democratic immigration task force co-chaired by Reyes issued a set of principles that called for legal status for "long-time, hard-working residents of good moral character," as well as speedier approval of legal status for immigrants' family members, an enhanced temporary worker program and more funding for the Border Patrol.

After the attacks, the initiative was shelved as Bush and Congress shifted their focus to tightening border security and making it easier for the government to detain non-citizens. Reyes acknowledged the new environment made it impossible to make much progress on liberalizing the nation's immigration laws, but he said Bush will have to return to the subject before he is up for re-election in 2004 in order to gain credibility with the nation's 35.3 million Latinos. "Politically, talk is cheap," he said. "And they need to walk the walk as well."

Reyes' platform as chairman of the Hispanic Caucus in the 107th became more prominent after the 2000 census, which found that Hispanics had displaced African-Americans as the nation's largest ethnic minority group. Reyes frequently finds himself speaking out on what Congress can do to show more sensitivity to the concerns of this fast-growing demographic group — particularly when the lawmaker finds old insensitivities returning.

During the debate on revamping the campaign finance system, Reyes mostly stayed out of the fray until Mississippi Democratic Rep. Roger Wicker offered an amendment to bar legal permanent residents from contributing to campaigns. To counter what he saw as an immigrant-bashing amendment, Reyes noted that Alfred V. Rascon, the director of the U.S. Selective Service System, had fought in Vietnam and earned the Congressional Medal of Honor while he was a legal permanent resident. The amendment was soundly defeated.

One longtime cause for Reyes had been an overhaul of the Immigration and Naturalization Service, with Reyes arguing that the agency pursued contradictory missions — enforcing the borders and providing services to immigrants — and did not do either well. In the 107th, Reyes cosponsored a Republican bill to split the agency into two bureaus, one for border enforcement, the other for immigration services.

When the INS was absorbed into the new Department of Homeland Security — with the service and enforcement functions separated — Reyes declared himself cautiously optimistic about improvements in both arenas.

Reyes has regularly found himself at odds with colleagues over border issues. Early in his first House term, he objected as the House voted to reverse President Clinton's certification of Mexico as a drug-fighting ally. And he protested as the House also voted to allow the deployment of up to

10,000 U.S. military personnel to help patrol the border. When the House in the 105th weighed in on Mexico's fitness to be certified as a drug-fighting ally, Reyes defended that country's performance, saying, "I have been on the front lines in the so-called war on drugs. . . . I have personally observed Mexico's commitment to stem the tide of drug trafficking."

Called "Silver" by his friends, Reyes is the first Hispanic to represent the 16th District; when the boundaries were drawn for this decade in 2001, Hispanics made up 78 percent of the population. To help what he terms "one of the poorest districts in the country," Reyes seeks federal funding not only for better roads and bridges to handle increased commercial traffic, but also for retraining for those put out of work since many of El Paso's garment industry jobs have shifted to lower-wage Mexico.

Reyes sits on the Armed Services Committee, where he is wary of military downsizing and base closings. He is the top Democrat on the Strategic Forces Subcommittee, which has jurisdiction over anti-missile defenses. He is also on the Veterans' Affairs panel, where he monitors the needs of the 16th District's sizable population of military retirees and is the third-ranking Democrat on the Intelligence Committee.

Reyes, who lost the hearing in his right ear in Vietnam, has objected to "stonewalling" by military officials in addressing various health complaints of Persian Gulf War veterans. He has pressed for an official acknowledgment "that in fact a Gulf War syndrome does exist."

Reyes usually sides with the majority in his party, but he has supported a few measures pushed by conservatives, including a ban on a procedure its opponents call "partial birth" abortion and constitutional amendments limiting congressional terms and outlawing U.S. flag desecration.

In 1969, after returning from Vietnam, Reyes went to work for the INS. Rising to assistant regional commissioner, he oversaw the Border Patrol in McAllen and El Paso. He instituted "Operation Hold the Line" in El Paso, stationing more officers at the border to prevent unauthorized crossings of the Rio Grande — a shift from the previous emphasis on rounding up people already in the country illegally.

When Democrat Ronald D. Coleman announced that he would not seek an eighth term, Reyes retired from the Border Patrol in the fall of 1995 to launch a bid for the House seat representing the district where he was born and reared. In the primary and subsequent runoff, he narrowly defeated a former Coleman aide, Jose Luis Sanchez, before easily dispatching a Republican insurance agent in the general election. In the solidly Democratic district, Reyes has had no difficulty in his three re-election bids.

KEY VOTES

2002

- Yes Overhaul campaign finance law; ban "soft money" and restrict advocacy advertising
- ? Back Bush's defense budget increase
- No Extend 1996 welfare law
- No Adopt Bush's discretionary spending limit
- No Pass GOP Medicare prescription drug plan
- Yes Create independent Sept. 11 commission
- Yes Extend union protections to Homeland Security Department employees
- No Revive fast-track procedures for trade agreements
- No Authorize war against Iraq
- No Advance bankruptcy overhaul opposed by abortion opponents

2001

- No Nullify Clinton Labor Department ergonomics rule
- No Cut taxes by $1.35 trillion through fiscal 2011
- No Maintain ban on oil drilling in Arctic National Wildlife Refuge
- No Approve Bush proposal to limit managed-care plan liability for coverage decisions
- No Divert money from crop subsidy payments to land conservation
- Yes Expand law enforcement power to investigate suspected terrorists

CQ VOTE STUDIES

	PARTY UNITY		PRESIDENTIAL SUPPORT	
	Support	Oppose	Support	Oppose
2002	85%	15%	41%	59%
2001	81%	19%	37%	63%
2000	88%	12%	88%	12%
1999	83%	17%	78%	22%
1998	87%	13%	78%	22%

INTEREST GROUPS

	AFL-CIO	ADA	CCUS	ACU
2002	100%	75%	39%	19%
2001	83%	90%	43%	30%
2000	90%	80%	42%	16%
1999	78%	85%	33%	26%
1998	100%	80%	47%	13%

TEXAS 16

West – El Paso and suburbs

Looking more toward Mexico than Texas, the solidly Democratic 16th includes most of El Paso and some suburbs. Joined to Mexico by the Bridge of the Americas, the 16th has a 77.7 percent Hispanic population, more than any other district in the nation except for South Texas' 15th.

Redistricting following the 2000 census pushed the district north, removing some of the 16th's border with Mexico and taking out a few small towns. Remapping also gave the 16th all of Fort Bliss, removing it entirely from the 23rd. The base, a major employer, gives the area a military flavor.

Mexico has had a long and deep effect on the 16th's economy. El Paso's growth was credited to trade with Mexico long before free-trade zones and global markets flourished. Companies on the U.S. side of the border provide supplies and services to manufacturing plants in Mexico, and residents from El Paso's sister city, Ciudad Juarez, regularly cross the border to spend money in El Paso's stores. In recent years, leaders have been concerned with the effects of NAFTA, which they blame for displacing American workers. The trade agreement has been partially responsible for an explosion of *maquiladoras*, twin plants in which Mexican workers do the bulk of the manufacturing labor and Americans complete the products with final details.

Democrats held the 16th's congressional seat for all but two years in the 20th century, often unchallenged by Republicans since the 1960s. In 2002, Democratic Senate nominee Ron Kirk won 71 percent of the two-party vote in the 16th, his third-best district in the state.

MAJOR INDUSTRY

Manufacturing, apparel, defense

MILITARY BASES

Fort Bliss (Army), 12,000 military, 7,000 civilian (2002)

CITIES

El Paso, 563,662; Socorro, 27,152

NOTABLE

The Border Patrol Museum displays aircraft and vehicles used by the patrol as well as surveillance equipment and confiscated items; Fort Bliss, the largest air defense artillery training center in the world, occupies an area larger than Rhode Island.

Rep. Charles W. Stenholm (D)

CAPITOL OFFICE
225-6605
www.house.gov/stenholm
2409 Rayburn 20515-4317; fax 225-2234

COMMITTEES
Agriculture - ranking member

HOMETOWN
Abilene

BORN
Oct. 26, 1938, Stamford, Texas

RELIGION
Lutheran

FAMILY
Wife, Cindy Stenholm; three children

EDUCATION
Tarleton State Junior College, A.A. 1959; Texas Tech U., B.S. 1961 (agricultural education), M.S. 1962 (agricultural education)

CAREER
Cotton farmer; teacher

POLITICAL HIGHLIGHTS
No previous office

ELECTION RESULTS

2002 GENERAL		
Charles W. Stenholm (D)	84,136	51.4%
Rob Beckham (R)	77,622	47.4%
Fred Jones (LIBERT)	2,046	1.3%
2002 PRIMARY		
Charles W. Stenholm (D)		unopposed
2000 GENERAL		
Charles W. Stenholm (D)	120,670	59.0%
Darrell Clements (R)	72,535	35.5%
Debra Monde (LIBERT)	11,180	5.5%

PREVIOUS WINNING PERCENTAGES
1998 (54%); 1996 (52%); 1994 (54%); 1992 (66%); 1990 (100%); 1988 (100%); 1986 (100%); 1984 (100%); 1982 (97%); 1980 (100%); 1978 (68%)

Elected 1978; 13th term

Stenholm has spent nearly a quarter-century in Congress forging a socially and fiscally conservative path that often meanders far outside the House Democratic mainstream. But rather than undermining his position, his independence has raised Stenholm's stock in both parties, given him a measure of bipartisan respect enjoyed by few on Capitol Hill — and has allowed him to survive politically in West Texas.

Plain-spoken and courteous, Stenholm has attributed his optimistic nature to the fact that farmers like him (cotton was his crop) must weather tough odds to get their jobs done. His style and views have established him as a leader both among House Democrats generally and among centrists specifically; he has served as a deputy whip and as co-chairman of the Democratic Policy Committee.

At the same time, during the disputed presidential election of 2000 his name was mentioned at least as often by Republicans, as a candidate for secretary of agriculture in a Bush administration, as it was by Democrats pondering who might serve in a Gore administration Cabinet.

A Swede by heritage, Stenholm has a generally cool temperament, but he nonetheless is unafraid to shake up his own party when he believes it matters most. After Democrats saw their hopes of retaking the House dashed badly in the 2002 election, Stenholm publicly turned away from the favorite for minority leader, the liberal Nancy Pelosi of California, and led a late charge to elect upstart conservative Harold E. Ford Jr. of Tennessee.

"The Democratic Party needs to find a way to reach out to the center, at the same time that we mobilize our base," he said, noting that he was in the small band of Democrats who won in 2002 by fewer than 10,000 votes — in large part because of their appeal to independents and Republicans.

The Democratic Caucus elected Pelosi in a landslide, but Stenholm registered his opposition by voting "present" when the full House met to choose its Speaker for the 108th Congress. Pelosi and Republican incumbent J. Dennis Hastert, he said, do not "represent the centrist philosophy held by a majority of Americans today."

Stenholm, who wears cowboy boots in the halls of Congress and speaks with a distinct Texas drawl, is constantly challenged to reflect the politics of his increasingly Republican-leaning district. In the 107th he voted with most Democrats against most Republicans only 56 percent of the time, the sixth-lowest party unity score in his caucus. And he backed President Bush 49 percent of the time, more often than all but 20 fellow House Democrats. Still, he says, "I'm a Democrat, period."

Stenholm considers Harry S Truman a role model, and he has been a figure to whom like-minded Democrats gravitate for leadership in their particular brand of activism, especially when it comes to the federal budget. At the start of the 1980s, he was a leader of the "Boll Weevil" Southern Democrats, who joined with Republicans to back the initial budget proposals of President Reagan. In 1995, he co-founded the "Blue Dogs," a coalition of the most conservative House Democrats, and in the 108th he resumed a role as one of the group's three co-chairs.

Over the past eight years, Stenholm has developed a series of budget and tax proposals that were politically viable middle grounds between the right and left. The 2003 Blue Dog budget, for example, stuck to Bush's prescription for holding down federal spending but called for far less ambitious tax cuts. Stenholm said his approach would keep the federal deficit in check and spare his two grandsons from paying "all of Grandad's bills."

Stenholm says leading the centrist charge was his hope from the day he arrived in Washington. "My goal was to become more than one vote on those issues that are important to the 17th District and to the country," he said in 2000. He began playing an important role in the budget debate soon after his arrival in the House in 1979, and he never wavered from his homey fiscal mantra, "Peas before dessert," meaning no tax cuts or spending increases until the budget is balanced.

During the four-year period of surpluses that ended in 2001, Stenholm advocated using the extra money to reduce the national debt and strengthen the Social Security system. He pushed hard for action to overhaul Social Security based on a plan by the National Commission for Retirement Policy; Stenholm was one of the commission's four congressional co-chairmen.

As the top Democrat on the Agriculture Committee, Stenholm's hands-on experience keeps him passionate about helping farmers. He was instrumental in writing the 2002 law that reversed a six-year policy of declining federal crop subsidies; as his work on the new farm bill showed, his support of government assistance for agriculture has been unwavering, despite his general fiscal austerity, and he is respected for his mastery of highly technical legislative matters.

Stenholm enjoyed success early in life. In high school, he earned the highest honor of the Future Farmers of America and played on two state championship football teams. He first experienced the national political scene in 1966, when the Agriculture Department issued a ruling that did not sit well with the cotton communities of the Texas plains. As executive vice president of the Rolling Plains Cotton Growers Association, Stenholm visited Washington to lobby against the ruling and had partial success in changing it.

In 1977, President Carter named Stenholm to a panel that advises the Agricultural and Conservation Service. He resigned the next year to run for the House when Democrat Omar Burleson retired after 16 terms. Winning with 68 percent of the vote, in what was then a solidly Democratic district, Stenholm was re-elected the next six times without a GOP opponent.

As Stenholm's prominence in Washington grew, his political troubles at home intensified, and formidable election competition surfaced in the 1990s as GOP strength increased throughout the South. He has been held to less than 55 percent of the vote in four of his past five elections. And in a district made slightly more Republican through redistricting, he won in 2002 with just 51 percent against investment broker and former Abilene city councilman Rob Beckham.

KEY VOTES

2002

- Yes Overhaul campaign finance law; ban "soft money" and restrict advocacy advertising
- Yes Back Bush's defense budget increase
- No Extend 1996 welfare law
- No Adopt Bush's discretionary spending limit
- No Pass GOP Medicare prescription drug plan
- Yes Create independent Sept. 11 commission
- No Extend union protections to Homeland Security Department employees
- Yes Revive fast-track procedures for trade agreements
- Yes Authorize war against Iraq
- Yes Advance bankruptcy overhaul opposed by abortion opponents

2001

- Yes Nullify Clinton Labor Department ergonomics rule
- No Cut taxes by $1.35 trillion through fiscal 2011
- No Maintain ban on oil drilling in Arctic National Wildlife Refuge
- No Approve Bush proposal to limit managed-care plan liability for coverage decisions
- No Divert money from crop subsidy payments to land conservation
- Yes Expand law enforcement power to investigate suspected terrorists

CQ VOTE STUDIES

	PARTY UNITY		PRESIDENTIAL SUPPORT	
	Support	Oppose	Support	Oppose
2002	59%	41%	45%	55%
2001	53%	47%	53%	47%
2000	59%	41%	52%	48%
1999	49%	51%	53%	47%
1998	50%	50%	49%	51%

INTEREST GROUPS

	AFL-CIO	ADA	CCUS	ACU
2002	50%	40%	70%	50%
2001	50%	50%	74%	64%
2000	50%	45%	70%	52%
1999	67%	55%	68%	54%
1998	60%	40%	76%	48%

TEXAS 17

Central — Abilene, San Angelo

Starting west of Fort Worth, the conservative 17th takes in the central Texas plains and heads through Abilene until reaching the outer edges of Lubbock in western Texas. The culture of the Old West lingers in this part of the Lone Star State with ranches, cotton and cowboys. The district contains all or part of 36 counties.

When the 1980s oil glut hit home in Texas, refineries covered the 17th's prairie. Today, there is only a fraction of the rigs that once blanketed the area, and some of those oil-producing towns have disappeared. Abilene, the district's largest city, has made an effort to revitalize its downtown. Three church-sponsored colleges nurture a powerful evangelical community.

Cattle and cotton are still big in the 17th, but low cattle prices and droughts have jeopardized both. Adding a measure of stability to the economy are Air Force bases near Abilene and San Angelo. The prison industry also has done well, with several state and contract facilities around the district.

The 17th became even more Republican after redistricting following the 2000 census, picking up the city of San Angelo and some of its wealthier suburbs. While the 17th is socially conservative, economic hardships have sent it in search of government assistance in agriculture. At the local level, voters tend to favor Republicans, but conservative Democrats do well in some areas north and west of Abilene. The 17th includes George W. Bush's top-performing county in the nation in 2000 — Glasscock, a lightly populated area east of Midland where he received 92 percent of the vote. Republicans John Cornyn and Rick Perry topped two-thirds of the district vote in the 2002 Senate and gubernatorial races.

MAJOR INDUSTRY

Cattle, cotton, defense, oil

MILITARY BASES

Dyess Air Force Base, 5,160 military, 356 civilian; Goodfellow Air Force Base, 2,000 military, 600 civilian (2002)

CITIES

Abilene, 115,930; San Angelo, 88,439; Brownwood, 18,813

NOTABLE

Abilene is named after the famous cattle shipping center in Abilene, Kan.; The first Hilton hotel was built in Cisco.

Rep. Sheila Jackson-Lee (D)

Elected 1994; 5th term

CAPITOL OFFICE
225-3816
tx18@mail.house.gov
www.house.gov/jacksonlee
2435 Rayburn 20515-4318; fax 225-3317

COMMITTEES
Judiciary
Science
Select Homeland Security

HOMETOWN
Houston

BORN
Jan. 12, 1950, Queens, N.Y.

RELIGION
Seventh-Day Adventist

FAMILY
Husband, Elwyn Lee; two children

EDUCATION
Yale U., B.A. 1972 (political science); U. of Virginia, J.D. 1975

CAREER
Lawyer; congressional aide

POLITICAL HIGHLIGHTS
Democratic nominee for Texas District Court judge, 1984; Democratic nominee for Harris County Probate Court judge, 1986; Houston municipal judge, 1987-89; Democratic nominee for Texas District Court judge, 1988; Houston City Council, 1990-95

ELECTION RESULTS

2002 GENERAL		
Sheila Jackson-Lee (D)	99,161	76.9%
Phillip J. Abbott (R)	27,980	21.7%
Brent Sullivan (LIBERT)	1,785	1.4%
2002 PRIMARY		
Sheila Jackson-Lee (D)	31,563	94.4%
Lenwood Johnson (D)	1,871	5.6%
2000 GENERAL		
Sheila Jackson-Lee (D)	131,857	76.5%
Bob Levy (R)	38,191	22.2%
Colin Nankervis (LIBERT)	2,330	1.4%

PREVIOUS WINNING PERCENTAGES
1998 (90%); 1996 (77%); 1994 (73%)

Whatever the issue, Jackson-Lee seems to have something to say about it, whether she's on the House floor or in front of a television camera. Her outspokenness prompts some of her colleagues to dismiss her as a publicity hound. But it also means her liberal views on everything from affirmative action to immigrant rights don't go ignored in the conservative-run House.

Jackson-Lee wages a ceaseless rhetorical battle with the Republican majority, labeling their ideas "shameless" or "an outrage" to women, minorities and the disadvantaged in society. Her supporters counsel her to be more selective about the battles she picks, but she shuns the advice. Her role model is Democratic Rep. Barbara Jordan, the famed black liberal from Houston who served in the House from 1973 to 1979.

As Jordan did, Jackson-Lee uses her seat on the Judiciary Committee to focus on civil rights, abortion rights and other liberal causes. She has been a ready defender of affirmative action as it has come under increasing criticism as a civil rights-era relic. "We are all familiar with the 'good old boy system,' " Jackson-Lee says. "There still is systemic bias in our society favoring certain groups over others, and many still do not want to accept that fact."

In the 107th Congress, Jackson-Lee won adoption of a proposal making the Environmental Protection Agency's scientific information available to underserved communities such as historically black colleges, minority communities and rural areas. She traveled to South Africa to speak out against racism at a U.N. summit, and she backed sanctions against Sudan. In the 108th, Jackson-Lee became the first-vice chairwoman of the Congressional Black Caucus.

As the top-ranking Democrat on Judiciary's Immigration Subcommittee, she is also quick to defend the rights of immigrants. She was especially critical of the Bush administration's treatment of immigrants after the Sept. 11, 2001, terrorist attacks. The Justice Department secretly arrested and detained hundreds of people, many of them of Arab descent, in an effort to break up terrorist cells operating in the United States.

When it comes to federal help for her Houston-based district, Jackson-Lee is not reluctant to join her ideological nemesis, Majority Leader Tom DeLay, a staunch conservative also from Houston. She sided with DeLay to back President Bush's energy plan because of its potential to boost the area's oil industry. In the 106th Congress, she cosponsored with DeLay a bill strengthening child protective services, an issue the two of them share.

Though she almost always votes with her party (95 percent of the time in the 107th), Jackson-Lee occasionally crosses party lines on trade issues. In 2000, she favored permanent normal trade status for China, arguing that an improved economic picture would aid human rights conditions in China while also helping Houston's economy.

Free trade was a major reason the city's business community, led by energy giant Enron, turned against Jackson-Lee's predecessor, Democrat Craig Washington, who opposed the 1993 North American Free Trade Agreement in addition to failing to back federally financed hometown projects such the space station and the now-scrapped superconducting super collider, an atom smasher. But in the 107th, Jackson-Lee voted against fast-track legislation that gave the president authority to negotiate trade pacts that Congress cannot amend. She said the bill did not contain adequate labor and environmental protection standards.

Jackson-Lee is attentive to parochial needs. From her seat on the Science Committee, she is a stout defender of NASA, whose Houston facility is in an adjoining district. In 2000, she lobbied the Clinton administration to designate parts of Houston as an empowerment zone, making several low-income areas eligible for millions of dollars in aid.

Her constant presence on the House floor to speak on a wide array of topics has raised the bar on political long-windedness. Some colleagues defend their own loquaciousness by declaring, "but I'm no Sheila Jackson-Lee." She also is adept at securing a center aisle seat in the chamber during visits by the president, where she can be in view of TV cameras.

Two topics leave Jackson-Lee with little to say: Her political ties to Enron Chairman Kenneth L. Lay and the high turnover rate of her congressional staff.

Enron's financial collapse in 2001 had a major economic impact on Jackson-Lee's district, but she let other Democrats rail against alleged corporate abuses. Lay was one of her chief fundraisers and backers in 1994 when she beat Washington in the Democratic primary. She also was one of the biggest recipients of campaign donations from the firm.

Regarding her staff, The Weekly Standard magazine reported in February 2002 that Jackson-Lee had overseen 85 full-time staffers since taking office in 1995. The article said Jackson-Lee insists on being chauffeured between her congressional office and nearby apartment and berates staff for minor failures. The same year, Texas Monthly dubbed her "a royal pain" for breaching protocol by arriving 50 minutes late and in business attire at a formal dinner hosted by Queen Sirikit of Thailand.

Born in Queens, N.Y., and educated at Yale and the University of Virginia law school, Jackson-Lee moved to Texas when her husband took a job with the University of Houston. She made two unsuccessful bids for local judgeships before winning appointment as a municipal judge in 1987. In 1990, after another unsuccessful election campaign for a judgeship, she won an at-large seat on the city council, where her initiatives included a gun safety law imposing penalties on parents who failed to keep guns locked up and away from children. She also pushed for expanded summer hours at city parks and recreation centers as a way to reduce gang activity.

In 1994, she challenged Washington, who had lost the support of the Houston business establishment and several other important constituencies by that time. She won with 63 percent of the vote. In the heavily Democratic district, that primary victory was tantamount to election, and she has never faced a serious re-election challenge.

KEY VOTES

2002

- Yes Overhaul campaign finance law; ban "soft money" and restrict advocacy advertising
- No Back Bush's defense budget increase
- No Extend 1996 welfare law
- No Adopt Bush's discretionary spending limit
- No Pass GOP Medicare prescription drug plan
- Yes Create independent Sept. 11 commission
- Yes Extend union protections to Homeland Security Department employees
- No Revive fast-track procedures for trade agreements
- No Authorize war against Iraq
- No Advance bankruptcy overhaul opposed by abortion opponents

2001

- No Nullify Clinton Labor Department ergonomics rule
- No Cut taxes by $1.35 trillion through fiscal 2011
- Yes Maintain ban on oil drilling in Arctic National Wildlife Refuge
- No Approve Bush proposal to limit managed-care plan liability for coverage decisions
- Yes Divert money from crop subsidy payments to land conservation
- No Expand law enforcement power to investigate suspected terrorists

CQ VOTE STUDIES

	PARTY UNITY		PRESIDENTIAL SUPPORT	
	Support	Oppose	Support	Oppose
2002	97%	3%	21%	79%
2001	93%	7%	16%	84%
2000	92%	8%	88%	12%
1999	96%	4%	78%	22%
1998	94%	6%	83%	17%

INTEREST GROUPS

	AFL-CIO	ADA	CCUS	ACU
2002	100%	100%	26%	4%
2001	100%	100%	35%	8%
2000	90%	80%	50%	4%
1999	78%	100%	29%	0%
1998	100%	95%	44%	4%

TEXAS 18
Downtown Houston

Downtown Houston's older black neighborhoods and more-progressive residents make up the 18th, which includes one of the city's poorest areas. Though economically struggling, the district has seen revitalization as downtown experiences a resurgence in construction, with new baseball and basketball stadiums inside its boundaries.

The 18th is diverse: 42 percent of residents are African-American and 33 percent are Hispanic, and a large portion of the city's gay and lesbian residents live in the district. Some of the district's most heavily black areas are just south of downtown, and heavily Hispanic neighborhoods can be found just north of downtown, between Interstate 45 and the Eastex Freeway. Texas Southern University and the University of Houston add to the area's liberal tendencies.

Though the district is overwhelmingly inner-city urban, it does include some areas around downtown, as well as the Heights, a trendier neighborhood populated with some young professionals.

Downtown office buildings are filled with oil and gas employees and other white-collar businesses and service workers, but most commute from outside the district. Downtown also houses some corporate giants and was home to the once-powerful Enron Corp. This area includes the city's Theater District, where the Hobby Center for the Performing Arts opened in 2002, and part of the Museum District (shared with the 25th).

The large black and Hispanic populations make the 18th perhaps the most strongly Democratic district in Texas. In 2002, it gave Democratic Senate nominee Ron Kirk 77 percent of the two-party vote, more than any other district. In the 2000 presidential contest, George W. Bush had his worst showing in Texas (26 percent) in the 18th.

MAJOR INDUSTRY
Energy, government, business services, entertainment

CITIES
Houston (pt.), 577,190

NOTABLE
The district was once represented by the late Rep. Barbara Jordan, D-Texas (1973-79); Minute Maid Park, home of the Houston Astros baseball team, was originally named Enron Field but was renamed in 2002 after the collapse of the energy giant.

Vacant Seat

Rep. Larry Combest, R
Resigned May 31, 2003

Larry Combest, who represented the 19th District for more than 18 years, resigned his seat effective May 31, 2003. He announced the decision soon after winning election in November 2002 to his 10th term, citing personal reasons.

In his resignation letter to Texas Republican Gov. Rick Perry, Combest wrote, "There comes a time in everyone's life when the focus needs to be more on family than other things, and I am at that point in my life."

Perry set a May 3 primary for the special election to fill the remainder of Combest's term. Seventeen candidates filed for the seat, including 11 Republicans, two Democrats, three third-party contenders and one independent. The large field meant that no candidate was likely to receive the majority vote needed for victory on May 3, necessitating a runoff between the top two vote-getters about a month later.

It appeared virtually certain that a Republican would succeed the 58-year-old Combest. The district is one of the nation's premier Republican strongholds — Democrats had not fielded a challenger to Combest since 1998, when their candidate managed only 16 percent.

Leading contenders included state Rep. Carl Isett; land developer Randy Neugebauer; former Lubbock Mayor David Langston; and Mike Conaway, a partner with George W. Bush in the oil business in the 1980s. All are Republicans; the two Democratic hopefuls are political unknowns.

The 19th is situated in Texas' Western panhandle, where cotton, cattle and oil are cornerstones of the economy. Combest was a good fit for the district, serving as chairman of the Agriculture Committee in the 106th and 107th Congresses. A fourth-generation family farmer, Combest was a soft-spoken but stubborn defender of government subsidies.

With Combest due to serve only five months of the 108th, House GOP leaders replaced him as Agriculture chairman at the beginning of 2003.

As chairman in the 107th, Combest was in the midst of the action as Congress wrote a new farm bill. He quietly gave the tug on the thread that unraveled Republican farm doctrine in effect since 1996, pushing through Congress a 10-year farm bill that spurned the free market in favor of big government subsidies for farmers.

He did so in defiance of a popular president from his own party. President Bush had opposed large subsidies to farmers, arguing that they led to overproduction and hindered, not helped, the farm economy. Bush in the end could not overcome a strong bipartisan coalition led by Combest and the powerful farm lobby.

It was not the first time Combest's farm philosophy was at odds with GOP leaders. Combest opposed his party at a pivotal moment in 1996, when free-market conservatives in the new Republican majority were pushing a major rewrite of farm policy called Freedom to Farm. The bill was designed to wean farmers from federal subsidies, giving them declining, fixed payments over time regardless of market conditions. Combest felt that the legislation, which became law, went too far in pulling the safety net out from under agriculture. When world markets pushed commodity prices to historic lows during the late 1990s, farmers found themselves in need of government support as much as ever. "Something is broken," Combest said of the 1996 policy after taking the committee helm.

TEXAS 19
West – Lubbock, Midland

The conservative 19th starts in the Panhandle and extends south through cattle and cotton country until reaching oil field operations near Midland and Odessa. With ranches, cattle and remnants of the cowboy lifestyle, the 19th offers a taste of the Wild West and feels little like the "Old South," which never reached this far west.

While the northern part of the district, which includes Lubbock, is more agricultural, the southern part of the 19th — called the Permian Basin, home to Midland and Odessa — is oil country. The differences set the district up for competing interests, but redistricting following the 2000 census pushed the 19th farther south, giving energy producers more clout.

The district's largest city, Lubbock thrives on the acres upon acres of cotton surrounding it. The city calls itself the world's largest cottonseed-processing center and is home to Texas Tech University. Because the 19th's economy is so dependent on agriculture and oil, it was nearly devastated during the worldwide oil glut of the 1980s and bad weather in the 1990s. Famine and drought have been detrimental to cattle and cotton, and continued low prices have dampened the oil industry. Reese Air Force Base was another major employer, but it was shut down under the 1995 military restructuring.

Conservative Democrats used to dominate the 19th: as recently as 1978, George W. Bush lost a race for this House seat to Democrat Kent Hance. More recently, Republicans have done well at all levels and routinely receive between 60 percent and 70 percent of the vote. The 19th gave Bush 76 percent of the vote in the 2000 presidential contest, his second-highest percentage among the state's congressional districts.

MAJOR INDUSTRY
Cattle, agriculture, oil and gas

CITIES
Lubbock, 199,564; Midland, 94,996; Odessa, 90,943; Big Spring, 25,233

NOTABLE
Singer Buddy Holly was born and raised in Lubbock; Odessa boasts the world's largest barbecue pit.

RECENT ELECTION RESULTS

2002 GENERAL		
Larry Combest (R)	117,092	91.6%
Larry Johnson (LIBERT)	10,684	8.4%
2000 GENERAL		
Larry Combest (R)	170,319	91.6%
John M. Turnbow (LIBERT)	15,579	8.4%
1998 GENERAL		
Larry Combest (R)	108,266	83.6%
Sidney Blankenship (D)	21,162	16.4%
1996 GENERAL		
Larry Combest (R)	156,910	80.4%
John W. Sawyer (D)	38,316	19.6%
1994 GENERAL		
Larry Combest (R)	120,641	100.0%
1992 GENERAL		
Larry Combest (R)	162,057	77.4%
Terry Lee Moser (D)	47,325	22.6%

Rep. Charlie Gonzalez (D)

Elected 1998; 3rd term

CAPITOL OFFICE
225-3236
www.house.gov/gonzalez
327 Cannon 20515-4320; fax 225-1915

COMMITTEES
Financial Services
Small Business
Select Homeland Security

HOMETOWN
San Antonio

BORN
May 5, 1945, San Antonio, Texas

RELIGION
Roman Catholic

FAMILY
Separated; one child

EDUCATION
U. of Texas, B.A. 1969 (government); St. Mary's U. (Texas), J.D. 1972

MILITARY SERVICE
Texas Air National Guard, 1969-75

CAREER
Lawyer; teacher

POLITICAL HIGHLIGHTS
Bexar County judge, 1982-87; Texas District Court judge, 1988-97

ELECTION RESULTS

2002 GENERAL		
Charlie Gonzalez (D)	unopposed	
2002 PRIMARY		
Charlie Gonzalez (D)	unopposed	
2000 GENERAL		
Charlie Gonzalez (D)	107,487	87.7%
Alejandro DePena (LIBERT)	15,087	12.3%

PREVIOUS WINNING PERCENTAGES
1998 (63%)

He is known as *"el hijo"* (the son) by the thousands in San Antonio who still remember Charlie Gonzalez's father — universally known in the city as "Henry B." — who was the first Hispanic Texan in Congress and served there for more than 37 years.

But now that he is in his third term, people are starting to notice that the younger Gonzalez is different in both substance and style from his famously feisty father. The son's pragmatic, New Democrat style contrasts with his father's passionate and often stubborn brand of classic populism.

Since the night of his election in 1998, Gonzalez has indicated he would not hesitate to try to make his mark in Washington by taking positions different from those of his father. Three years later, Gonzalez told the San Antonio Express-News that he had discussed the subject with several of his colleagues whose fathers had also served in the House. "We all share the core values of our parents, but we do not mimic their behavior," he said. The newspaper also quoted a San Antonio Democratic official, Gabe Quintanilla, as saying: "Charlie is not in anybody's shadow. Certainly his father is a legend, but he is his own person."

The younger Gonzalez has developed a public service résumé of his own, including 15 years in elected office as a local and state trial judge. He says that his proudest accomplishments during his days on the bench were to speed the resolution of domestic violence cases and to promote mediation as an alternative to litigation.

On Capitol Hill, Gonzalez has a seat on the Financial Services Committee, the successor to the Banking Committee where his father served during his entire career and which he chaired for six years. In the 107th Congress, Gonzalez worked to expand the role of the North American Development Bank in San Antonio, which had an initial mandate to finance environmental infrastructure projects — water, sewerage, landfill and the like — in communities along the Rio Grande. He warned against proposals to merge the San Antonio bank with its counterpart in Mexico, in which U.S. interests might be subsumed. At the start of the 108th, the House passed a bill Gonzalez sponsored that aims to improve the bank's effectiveness.

He also sits on the Small Business Committee, where he was able to win funding for the establishment of a Women's Business Center to help prospective and current women entrepreneurs.

Although Gonzalez was promoted by Congressional Hispanic Caucus members for a seat on the Energy and Commerce Committee in the 108th Congress, the leadership picked California's Hilda L. Solis instead. But Gonzalez was named to the Homeland Security Committee.

Gonzalez had been a strong supporter of trade liberalization, enthusiastically touting the benefits of the North American Free Trade Agreement of 1993 (which the elder Gonzalez virulently opposed) and voting in his first term to make permanent the normalized trade relationship between the United States and China.

But in the 107th Congress, he reversed course. Siding with labor unions, which had promoted his initial congressional bid, Gonzalez voted against the 2002 law reviving fast-track procedures for congressional action on trade deals; in his view, the bill lacked "meaningful, enforceable provisions to protect the environment and labor."

Gonzalez has also involved himself in the communitywide effort to redevelop Kelly Air Force Base, which was shut in 2001 as a result of the military base-closing process, by offering the base to civilian tenants, such as Lockheed Martin and Boeing.

In his first two terms, Gonzalez also positioned himself as a team player. He is active in fundraising for the Democratic Congressional Campaign Committee, the House Democrats' political arm. He was also elected vice president of his freshman class in 1999. Gonzalez helped co-chair a Democratic task force on the census, which pushed for the use of statistical sampling to augment the 2000 headcount.

Gonzalez's chairmanship of the civil rights task force for the Hispanic Caucus also involved him in census issues. He was a member of the election task force that Democrats formed in the aftermath of the contested 2000 presidential results in Florida.

Gonzalez has sought to have the Hispanic Caucus play a role, admittedly unofficial, in the selection and confirmation of judges, particularly in cases where the prospective nominee is Hispanic or the location of the court is in a substantially Hispanic area. As a consequence, he led the caucus's vocal campaign in 2002 and 2003 against the confirmation of Miguel Estrada as the first Latino on the D.C. Circuit Court of Appeals, considered the most influential federal bench after the Supreme Court.

For the first several years of his congressional tenure, Gonzalez lived in the same Capitol Hill apartment that his father had occupied while a member of the House. He finally moved out — but not too far; he still lives in the same building.

Charlie Gonzalez is the third of eight children and the only one who followed his father into public life. He was a teenager when his father was first elected to Congress. He taught fifth grade for a year on the south side of San Antonio and then worked as a private practice lawyer before being elected to the county bench in 1982. He told a Texas student, in an interview posted on the school district's Web site, that running for Congress "was always in the back of my mind, but I never gave it real consideration since I wanted my dad to serve in Congress forever."

Gonzalez moved up to a state District Court judgeship in 1988, but he resigned in 1997 when his father announced plans to retire. In the campaign the next year, he survived a seven-way Democratic primary, winning the nomination with 62 percent of the vote in a runoff against former San Antonio council member Maria A. Berriozabal. In the general election, he took 63 percent against Republican research scientist James D. Walker.

In both 2000 and 2002, Gonzalez had no major-party opposition, in either the primary or general election.

KEY VOTES

2002

Yes Overhaul campaign finance law; ban "soft money" and restrict advocacy advertising
Yes Back Bush's defense budget increase
No Extend 1996 welfare law
No Adopt Bush's discretionary spending limit
No Pass GOP Medicare prescription drug plan
Yes Create independent Sept. 11 commission
Yes Extend union protections to Homeland Security Department employees
No Revive fast-track procedures for trade agreements
No Authorize war against Iraq
Yes Advance bankruptcy overhaul opposed by abortion opponents

2001

No Nullify Clinton Labor Department ergonomics rule
No Cut taxes by $1.35 trillion through fiscal 2011
Yes Maintain ban on oil drilling in Arctic National Wildlife Refuge
No Approve Bush proposal to limit managed-care plan liability for coverage decisions
No Divert money from crop subsidy payments to land conservation
Yes Expand law enforcement power to investigate suspected terrorists

CQ VOTE STUDIES

	PARTY UNITY		PRESIDENTIAL SUPPORT	
	Support	Oppose	Support	Oppose
2002	94%	6%	28%	72%
2001	86%	14%	32%	68%
2000	93%	7%	88%	12%
1999	94%	6%	84%	16%

INTEREST GROUPS

	AFL-CIO	ADA	CCUS	ACU
2002	100%	100%	45%	0%
2001	78%	95%	43%	4%
2000	90%	80%	50%	8%
1999	78%	100%	36%	0%

TEXAS 20
Downtown San Antonio

A city rich in history, San Antonio witnessed the death of Davy Crockett and the famed fall of the Alamo. Since those rugged days in the early 1800s, San Antonio has grown into one of the nation's largest cities (9th, according to the 2000 census). The strongly Democratic 20th takes in most of the city, including the heavily Hispanic West Side, downtown San Antonio and some surrounding communities.

A huge military presence in San Antonio makes up the biggest chunk of the economy, but mid-1990s downsizing caused the city some economic pains. Kelly Air Force Base, one of the city's largest employers, has closed. Leaders have redeveloped it as a business park, bringing some jobs back to the area. Two other bases are still significant employers.

Although tourism does not make up for the defense industry's losses, it continues to be a reliable moneymaker. The Alamo, site of the 1836 battle with Mexico, is in the heart of downtown. The city's scenic Paseo del Rio, or Riverwalk, also is a popular draw with its shops, restaurants and hotels winding along the San Antonio River. The most urban of San Antonio's four districts, the 20th has felt pressure on its roads, courts and schools as trade has increased because of NAFTA. The city also is working to become a base for cybersecurity efforts.

Democrats dominate most of this Hispanic-majority district. Ron Kirk, the 2002 Democratic Senate nominee, carried the 20th with 60 percent of the vote. The only significant Republican presence in the district is in the largely white, higher-income areas northwest and northeast of San Antonio.

MAJOR INDUSTRY
Military, tourism, trade

MILITARY BASES
Fort Sam Houston (Army), 15,209 military, 8,527 civilian; Lackland Air Force Base, 26,273 military, 9,489 civilian (2002)

CITIES
San Antonio (pt.), 600,760

NOTABLE
Sculptor Gutzon Borglum designed Mt. Rushmore presidential carvings in a studio in San Antonio; St. Anthony Hotel in San Antonio is said to have been the first fully air conditioned hotel in the world, in 1941.

Rep. Lamar Smith (R)

CAPITOL OFFICE
225-4236
www.house.gov/lamarsmith
2231 Rayburn 20515-4321; fax 225-8628

COMMITTEES
Judiciary
(Courts, the Internet & Intellectual Property - chairman)
Science
Select Homeland Security

HOMETOWN
San Antonio

BORN
Nov. 19, 1947, San Antonio, Texas

RELIGION
Christian Scientist

FAMILY
Wife, Elizabeth Smith; two children

EDUCATION
Yale U., B.A. 1969 (American studies); Southern Methodist U., J.D. 1975

CAREER
Lawyer; rancher; reporter

POLITICAL HIGHLIGHTS
Texas House, 1981-82; Bexar County Commissioners Court, 1983-85

ELECTION RESULTS

2002 GENERAL		
Lamar Smith (R)	161,836	72.9%
John Courage (D)	56,206	25.3%
D G Roberts (LIBERT)	4,051	1.8%
2002 PRIMARY		
Lamar Smith (R)		unopposed
2000 GENERAL		
Lamar Smith (R)	251,049	75.9%
Jim Green (D)	73,326	22.2%
C. W. Steinbrecher (LIBERT)	6,503	2.0%

PREVIOUS WINNING PERCENTAGES
1998 (91%); 1996 (76%); 1994 (90%); 1992 (72%); 1990 (75%); 1988 (93%); 1986 (61%)

Elected 1986; 9th term

Smith's soft-spoken demeanor belies his reputation as one of the House's most ardent crusaders against illegal immigration and one of its most zealous defenders of law enforcement powers. In the 108th Congress, he sought to redirect his focus, looking to become a power broker on legislative issues affecting the high-technology sector.

His avenue for doing so is the chairmanship of the Judiciary Committee's Subcommittee on the Courts, the Internet and Intellectual Property. The assignment is a fine forum from which he can address the priorities of his new constituency, which includes the booming tech corridor between San Antonio and Austin, home of Dell Computer Corp.

The new gavel he has chosen is a good example of how a lawmaker's focus can shift as a consequence of redistricting; when Smith first arrived in Congress in 1987, he represented an area of West Texas that was bigger than Ohio, in which thousands of his constituents were separated from the Rio Grande by little more than vast tracts of rangeland. Smith's early legislative concentration was a clear outgrowth of that geography: For six years, until GOP term limits forced him to switch, Smith chaired the Judiciary Subcommittee on Immigration

He took on the chairmanship of the Crime Subcommittee only for the 107th Congress, where he supported the Bush administration's quest to give law enforcement officers more power to pursue suspects. In the process, he became a prominent foe of civil libertarians and privacy advocates, who criticized Smith for being willing to give police and other government agents far too much authority. The criticism did not faze Smith, who has said the nation's desire to combat terrorism more forcefully after the Sept. 11, 2001, attacks requires new ground rules to give law enforcement "all the necessary tools to confront the daunting tasks ahead."

Nine days after the attacks, Smith introduced legislation to broadly expand wiretapping authority by altering the federal eavesdropping law to apply to electronic communications, such as e-mail and instant messaging. The measure became part of the anti-terrorism law enacted later in 2001.

Smith later promoted legislation to stiffen penalties for hacking computer networks by, among other things, boosting the maximum penalty to life in prison for hackers who plot or cause death from an electronic attack. The measure, enacted in the 2002 law establishing the Homeland Security Department, also gave the government new powers to seek information — including financial transactions and the contents of e-mails — from Internet service providers that believe "in good faith" that someone poses a threat. Under Smith's measure, law enforcement officers may conduct emergency surveillance of computers without first obtaining court approval.

Still, Smith bristles at being given a "tough on crime" tag. "That's just too much of a stereotype," he says. "It's trying to provide deterrents so criminals do realize they're going to pay a price if they do commit crimes. . . . It's not always being harder on criminals, it's coming up with solutions that reduce crime."

His hard-line stances are not limited to criminal law; his passion for tighter immigration policies has not waned. Even as his tenure chairing the Immigration Subcommittee was coming to an end, he subpoenaed outgoing Attorney General Janet Reno late in 2000 for records about illegal immigration. In the 106th Congress, Smith coordinated the GOP leadership to block an attempt, promoted by President Clinton, to provide amnesty for illegal immigrants in the United States since 1986. He used the records obtained from Reno to argue that illegal immigration had remained almost the same before and after a previous amnesty program in 1986.

Smith's signature legislative accomplishment is the 1996 law that cracked down on illegal immigration by increasing penalties for document fraud and the smuggling of aliens, and making it easier for illegal immigrants to be detained at the border or deported after arrival. He originally had introduced a much tougher measure that addressed legal as well as illegal immigration, but he narrowed it as specific provisions ran into opposition from Democrats, the Senate and pro-business Republicans.

In 2000, Smith butted heads with business leaders and top Republicans again when he fought a proposal to expand a visa program for highly skilled workers. He drafted several plans to boost the number of visas while requiring employers to demonstrate they had first tried to recruit workers in the United States. House Republican leaders ignored him and pushed into law an expansion of the program without Smith's restrictions.

On the Science Committee, Smith has worked to expand math and science education. An occasional stargazer, in 2002 he joined with a Democratic colleague from Texas, Nick Lampson, to press legislation to lay out clear goals for NASA's human space flight program after completion of the International Space Station. Among the goals is developing, by 2022, a reusable vehicle that could travel to Mars and back.

Smith's genial personality blunts the hard edge of his conservatism and he has enjoyed warm relations with many Democrats. He also occasionally works across party lines. For example, Smith collaborated with Democratic Sen. Joseph I. Lieberman of Connecticut on efforts to increase family-friendly television programming.

A fifth-generation Texan, Smith went to Yale for college and was a business reporter for the Christian Science Monitor in Boston. After earning a law degree in Dallas, he returned home to San Antonio and entered politics. After a year in the state House and two years as a Bexar County commissioner, he won his seat in Congress in 1986 when Republican Tom Loeffler left to run, unsuccessfully it turned out, for governor.

When George W. Bush — then a Midland oilman with one losing congressional race under his belt — did not seek the seat, Smith won a six-way contest for the GOP nod by defeating an even more conservative San Antonio official, Van Archer, in a runoff. With Karl Rove as a strategic consultant, Smith won that fall with 61 percent of the vote over former Democratic state Sen. Pete Snelson in what still stands as by far his closest congressional race.

KEY VOTES

2002

- No Overhaul campaign finance law; ban "soft money" and restrict advocacy advertising
- Yes Back Bush's defense budget increase
- Yes Extend 1996 welfare law
- Yes Adopt Bush's discretionary spending limit
- Yes Pass GOP Medicare prescription drug plan
- No Create independent Sept. 11 commission
- No Extend union protections to Homeland Security Department employees
- Yes Revive fast-track procedures for trade agreements
- Yes Authorize war against Iraq
- Yes Advance bankruptcy overhaul opposed by abortion opponents

2001

- Yes Nullify Clinton Labor Department ergonomics rule
- Yes Cut taxes by $1.35 trillion through fiscal 2011
- No Maintain ban on oil drilling in Arctic National Wildlife Refuge
- Yes Approve Bush proposal to limit managed-care plan liability for coverage decisions
- No Divert money from crop subsidy payments to land conservation
- Yes Expand law enforcement power to investigate suspected terrorists

CQ VOTE STUDIES

	PARTY UNITY		PRESIDENTIAL SUPPORT	
	Support	Oppose	Support	Oppose
2002	97%	3%	89%	11%
2001	99%	1%	95%	5%
2000	99%	1%	25%	75%
1999	96%	4%	19%	81%
1998	95%	5%	23%	77%

INTEREST GROUPS

	AFL-CIO	ADA	CCUS	ACU
2002	13%	0%	100%	96%
2001	8%	0%	100%	96%
2000	0%	5%	85%	96%
1999	13%	0%	88%	84%
1998	0%	0%	100%	92%

TEXAS 21

Central — parts of San Antonio, Austin and suburbs

The 21st is a staunchly Republican, mostly suburban and rural district that connects the cities of San Antonio and Austin via Interstate 35, with the so-called Hill Country and some rural ranching communities in between and to the west.

About 30 percent of the 21st's population comes from San Antonio's Bexar County (pronounced BEAR), with the district taking in the mostly comfortable north and northeast parts of the city and its suburbs, and cupping the airport (located in the 20th). Another 25 percent of the population comes from Austin's Travis County, mostly in suburbs populated with workers in the high-tech industry. Comal County, the only other jurisdiction with at least 50,000 people, is located northeast of San Antonio and takes in almost all of New Braunfels, which was founded by German immigrants in the 1840s. Nearly one in five district residents claims some German ancestry, more than any other Texas district.

Though the 21st has no military bases of its own, nearby installations contribute to the economy. The city of Kerrville has an active veterans hospital. Hill Country is home to many retirees who once lived in Austin or San Antonio. Llano County, in the northern part of the district, has the highest percentage of elderly residents in the state (31 percent). Kerr and Gillespie counties, southwest of Llano, also have large over-65 populations.

The 21st produces a consistent GOP vote at all levels. In 2002, GOP Gov. Rick Perry won 73 percent of the district vote, his third-highest total among Texas' 32 districts.

MAJOR INDUSTRY

Agriculture, techology, government

CITIES

San Antonio (pt.), 162,956; Austin (pt.), 89,846; New Braunfels (pt.), 35,328; Kerrville, 20,425; Canyon Lake (unincorporated), 16,870

NOTABLE

The Admiral Nimitz Museum and Historical Center in Fredericksburg has a major collection of Allied and Japanese aircraft, guns and other artifacts from World War II; Former President Lyndon B. Johnson was born in Blanco County.

Rep. Tom DeLay (R)

CAPITOL OFFICE
225-5951
majorityleader.gov
242 Cannon 20515-4322; fax 225-5241

COMMITTEES
Majority Leader – no committee assignments

HOMETOWN
Sugar Land

BORN
April 8, 1947, Laredo, Texas

RELIGION
Baptist

FAMILY
Wife, Christine DeLay; one child

EDUCATION
Baylor U., attended 1965-67; U. of Houston, B.S. 1970 (biology)

CAREER
Pest control business owner

POLITICAL HIGHLIGHTS
Texas House, 1979-85

ELECTION RESULTS

2002 GENERAL		
Tom DeLay (R)	100,499	63.2%
Tim Riley (D)	55,716	35.0%
Gerald W. LaFleur (LIBERT)	1,612	1.0%
2002 PRIMARY		
Tom DeLay (R)	22,379	79.9%
Michael "Fjet" Fjetland (R)	5,645	20.1%
2000 GENERAL		
Tom DeLay (R)	154,662	60.4%
Jo Ann Matranga (D)	92,645	36.2%
Bob Schneider (REF)	5,577	2.2%
Kent J. Probst (LIBERT)	3,383	1.3%

PREVIOUS WINNING PERCENTAGES
1998 (65%); 1996 (68%); 1994 (74%); 1992 (69%); 1990 (71%); 1988 (67%); 1986 (72%); 1984 (65%)

Elected 1984; 10th term

If it's true, as the political axiom goes, that power is not just what you have but what your enemies think you have, then DeLay is among the most influential people in Washington.

As the new House majority leader, he is second in command in the majority Republican Party, outranked only by Speaker J. Dennis Hastert, with whom he shares a close relationship. Before moving up, DeLay spent eight years as Republican whip, cultivating a reputation for shrewdness and toughness. He rarely picked a floor battle he couldn't win, and he raised millions of dollars in campaign money for fellow Republicans. He also quietly encouraged an image of ruthlessness. When he acquired the nickname "The Hammer" for his habit of pounding political money out of lobbyists and votes out of Republicans, DeLay not only didn't object to the characterization, he told his staff that it helped him do his job.

In the 2002 midterm elections, DeLay was the architect of a massive get-out-the-vote effort aimed at offsetting a well-financed push by labor unions on behalf of Democrats. Republicans defied the usual historical trend by gaining, not losing, seats in a midterm election in which they also held the White House. When Dick Armey of Texas stepped down as majority leader, no one contested DeLay's claim on the job.

DeLay has flourished in part because of his unique, mutually beholden relationship with Hastert. When Republicans took the majority in 1995, Hastert was instrumental in helping DeLay become whip, overcoming the objections of Speaker Newt Gingrich, who preferred his ally, Robert Walker of Pennsylvania, for the job. Four years later, when Gingrich resigned after losing the confidence of the rank and file, DeLay threw his weight behind Hastert's hurried and successful campaign for Speaker. The even-tempered Illinoisan and DeLay have worked together since in a "good cop-bad cop" way, as one top aide described it.

DeLay's popularity with Republicans survived a nasty upheaval in the party in 1997 when he joined a small band of conservatives that tried, unsuccessfully, to oust Gingrich. Afterward, DeLay confessed his role and asked his Republican colleagues to forgive him. Humility paid off, and DeLay's standing with members was restored.

His style is a mixture of high-handedness and persuasiveness, partisan fervor and political practicality. While DeLay can be intense in his pursuit of victory on even minor bills, he lets fellow Republicans know in myriad ways that he has their interests at heart. He makes sure they are not cheated out of their share of pet projects in spending bills. He flies in Texas barbecue for late-night House sessions, and he provides them with deluxe accommodations at the party's conventions every four years.

Another of DeLay's strategies is working with lobbyists to build grassroots support for Republican measures, then using that network to raise large sums for GOP congressional campaigns.

DeLay's relationship with President Bush is not a warm one. When DeLay proposed saving $9 billion in 1999 by postponing payment of a tax credit for low-income workers, candidate Bush warned Congress not to "balance their budget on the backs of the poor." DeLay shot back that the candidate "needs a little education on how Congress works."

DeLay sees himself as a guardian of conservative ideology, even if it means bucking the White House. As majority leader, he is in a better position than ever to defend conservative principles, so any attempts to bridge the partisan divide have to get past him.

A born-again Christian, DeLay's religious views influence his political thinking. In recent years, he has become one of Israel's strongest allies in Congress, believing that Jewish control over the West Bank is a fulfillment of biblical prophecy. As Bush weighed an invasion of Iraq in 2002, DeLay chastised the president's critics, saying, "Every generation must summon the courage to disregard the timid counsel of those who would mortgage our security to the false promises of wishful thinking and appeasement."

DeLay's focus is mainly on issues at home, and particularly on rolling back federal regulations. In 2001, he led the GOP effort to overturn new Labor Department rules on ergonomics, designed to protect workers from repetitive stress injuries. He dislikes most new environmental regulations and once sought repeal of the 1990 Clean Air Act revisions. DeLay wrote parts of the Republican Party's 1994 "Contract With America" that repealed many federal regulations.

Frustration with government rules led DeLay into politics, in fact. He says he encountered too much red tape in the pest exterminating business he ran in Houston. "I was struggling to build a company and the government was getting in my way every time I turned around," he says.

DeLay often is an unvarnished partisan for the GOP. The disputed 2000 presidential contest, he says, was an attempt by Democrats to steal an election — "nothing less than a theft in progress," as he put it at the time. Two years earlier, he attained folk hero status among conservatives for demanding that President Clinton be impeached and removed from office. In 1999, he was admonished by the House ethics committee for threatening to punish a trade association because it had hired a Democrat as its president.

In a fabled altercation on the House floor in 1997, DeLay shoved Wisconsin Democrat David R. Obey after Obey accused him of letting business lobbyists write a deregulation bill in DeLay's office. The two had to be separated by an aide.

In DeLay's tenure as majority whip, Republicans avoided taking contentious bills to the floor until they knew they had the votes or believed they could whip the votes in time for final passage. So DeLay rarely lost a vote. He became a master at counting votes, coddling the troops and then demanding their loyalty on key bills.

DeLay spent much of his childhood in Venezuela with his father, an oil drilling contractor. After six years in the Texas House, he won a GOP-leaning seat in Congress in 1984 with 65 percent of the vote and has since won re-election easily, always garnering at least 60 percent.

KEY VOTES

2002

- No Overhaul campaign finance law; ban "soft money" and restrict advocacy advertising
- Yes Back Bush's defense budget increase
- Yes Extend 1996 welfare law
- Yes Adopt Bush's discretionary spending limit
- Yes Pass GOP Medicare prescription drug plan
- No Create independent Sept. 11 commission
- No Extend union protections to Homeland Security Department employees
- Yes Revive fast-track procedures for trade agreements
- Yes Authorize war against Iraq
- Yes Advance bankruptcy overhaul opposed by abortion opponents

2001

- Yes Nullify Clinton Labor Department ergonomics rule
- Yes Cut taxes by $1.35 trillion through fiscal 2011
- No Maintain ban on oil drilling in Arctic National Wildlife Refuge
- Yes Approve Bush proposal to limit managed-care plan liability for coverage decisions
- No Divert money from crop subsidy payments to land conservation
- Yes Expand law enforcement power to investigate suspected terrorists

CQ VOTE STUDIES

	PARTY UNITY		PRESIDENTIAL SUPPORT	
	Support	Oppose	Support	Oppose
2002	99%	1%	92%	8%
2001	99%	1%	98%	2%
2000	99%	1%	23%	77%
1999	97%	3%	23%	77%
1998	95%	5%	20%	80%

INTEREST GROUPS

	AFL-CIO	ADA	CCUS	ACU
2002	0%	0%	95%	92%
2001	0%	0%	100%	100%
2000	0%	0%	84%	88%
1999	0%	0%	92%	92%
1998	0%	0%	100%	96%

TEXAS 22

Southeast Houston and southern suburbs; most of Fort Bend and Brazoria counties

The solidly Republican 22nd includes nearly all of Brazoria and Fort Bend counties south of Houston, plus a small slice of the city itself. Most residents live in fast-growing Houston suburbs outside Harris County or in more-rural settings. The district contains booming communities such as Sugar Land, as well as upscale homes surrounding the Lyndon B. Johnson Space Center, where many NASA scientists and astronauts live. Numerous residents work at the space center, located in the neighboring 9th District.

About half of the population resides in Fort Bend County, which includes Rep. DeLay's hometown of Sugar Land. Since the 1960s, the area has changed from a sugar-growing center into suburbia. Sugar refiner Imperial Holly still maintains its presence in Sugar Land, but the city has welcomed new planned developments and a range of corporations. It is not uncommon to find six-figure earners living in Sugar Land.

Brazoria County, where more than one-fourth of the population lives, has retained much of its agrarian feel. Many residents grow rice and sorghum and raise cattle. The 22nd's portions of Brazoria are not as upscale as Fort Bend but nonetheless have a median income more than $10,000 above the national mark.

Moving east, the 22nd takes up parts of southeastern Harris County, including a chunk of Houston. This part of Harris tends toward the upscale: Some of the wealthiest areas in the county are in southeast Houston, near Ellington Field, a former Air Force base that now houses the space center's aircraft operations.

MAJOR INDUSTRY

Aerospace, agriculture, retail

CITIES

Sugar Land, 63,328; Missouri City (pt.), 47,419; Houston (pt.), 46,678

NOTABLE

The annual "Texian Market Days" in Fort Bend County include re-enactments of 1830s pioneer life, when the area was settled by some of the "Old 300" families led by Stephen F. Austin; George Observatory in Brazos Bend State Park includes a memorial to the seven astronauts who died aboard the space shuttle Challenger in 1986.

Rep. Henry Bonilla (R)

CAPITOL OFFICE
225-4511
www.house.gov/bonilla
2458 Rayburn 20515-4323; fax 225-2237

COMMITTEES
Appropriations
(Agriculture, Rural Development, FDA & Related Agencies - chairman)

HOMETOWN
San Antonio

BORN
Jan. 2, 1954, San Antonio, Texas

RELIGION
Baptist

FAMILY
Wife, Deborah Knapp Bonilla; two children

EDUCATION
U. of Texas, B.A. 1976 (journalism)

CAREER
Television reporter, producer and executive; gubernatorial aide

POLITICAL HIGHLIGHTS
No previous office

ELECTION RESULTS

2002 GENERAL		
Henry Bonilla (R)	77,573	51.5%
Henry Cuellar (D)	71,067	47.2%
2002 PRIMARY		
Henry Bonilla (R)		unopposed
2000 GENERAL		
Henry Bonilla (R)	119,679	59.3%
Isidro Garza Jr. (D)	78,274	38.8%
Jeffrey C. Blunt (LIBERT)	3,801	1.9%

PREVIOUS WINNING PERCENTAGES
1998 (64%); 1996 (62%); 1994 (63%); 1992 (59%)

Elected 1992; 6th term

Until 2001, Bonilla was known mainly as a frontman in the Republican Party's attempt to appeal to Hispanics. The former TV newsman still plays that role, but he also has held an important legislative responsibility since the 107th Congress — the chairmanship of the Appropriations subcommittee that writes the annual spending bill covering the Agriculture Department and Food and Drug Administration.

In his first two years as chairman, Bonilla (bo-NEE-uh) established himself as a loyal soldier of the Republican leadership, but not a blindly loyal one. He has proven he will use tough tactics when needed to serve their goals, and not in a particularly subtle way. But he also sticks up for his prerogatives as an appropriator.

In 2001, Bonilla and other appropriators warned White House Budget Director Mitchell E. Daniels Jr., who was embarking on a mission to restrain domestic spending, not to try to micromanage their work. And Bonilla was hardly immune from the time-honored temptation to spend money on projects that benefit his interests and those of his colleagues. The first agriculture spending bill on his watch came in at $1.6 billion more than President Bush's request, including a $20 million subsidy for sheep and goat ranchers.

Such subsidies — a relic of the day when a reliable supply of wool and mohair was essential to make military uniforms — had been ended in 1993. But most of the state's 2,000 sheep and goat ranchers live in the vast expanse of West Texas that Bonilla represents, and they argued that federal aid was essential at a time of drought and poor market conditions.

That earmarking left Bonilla with "pork grease on his hands," in the view of the editorial page of the San Antonio Express-News. But for the most part, Bonilla has embraced the administration's goal of spending restraint. His second spending bill was at about the level Bush requested. And agriculture lobbyists say he is not shy about saying no to spending requests.

Bonilla also showed he could play hardball when he wanted to. In 2002, the GOP wanted to avoid using the agriculture spending bill to reopen the contentious issues that had been settled in the rewrite of federal farm policy earlier in the year. When Marcy Kaptur of Ohio, the top Democrat on Bonilla's subcommittee, prepared an amendment to cut farmer subsidies, Bonilla readied an amendment to eliminate 18 projects benefiting Ohio. Kaptur backed off, saying she could not risk the retaliation.

Bonilla is still better-known for the political role he plays in the Republican Party. GOP leaders have made a point of showcasing one of its most prominent Hispanics, who has a compelling political story to tell: He rose from a childhood in a San Antonio housing project to become a potential candidate for statewide office. In some ways, however, Republicans are still waiting for Bonilla to rise to his full potential as a party leader, which would require taking more risks than he has done so far.

Bonilla got his Appropriations seat in his first term. In 2000, he was one of three co-chairmen of the Republican National Convention that nominated George W. Bush for president. He was frequently mentioned as a Bush Cabinet prospect, although the possibility that his Democratic-tilting district might have slipped back into opposition hands worked against his joining the administration. Then Bonilla seriously considered running for the Senate seat of retiring Republican Phil Gramm; he backed out when a poll he commissioned showed that Texas Attorney General John Cornyn, who ultimately won the seat in 2002, had most of the GOP support locked up.

To Bonilla, Hispanics should be natural Republican allies because they speak the same political language — favoring small businesses and a strong military, opposing high taxes and intrusive government. But, he says, the GOP has not done a good job articulating that message to Latino voters.

Until his rise to a subcommittee chairmanship, Bonilla was best-known on Appropriations for fighting often-futile battles against President Clinton's efforts to impose new regulations on businesses. For years, he helped hold up the annual funding bill for the Department of Labor in a bid to block the implementation of workplace standards to minimize repetitive-motion injuries. (After Clinton issued new ergonomics rules in the final days of his administration, GOP lawmakers repealed them early in 2001.) Bonilla also tried unsuccessfully in 1998 to block the House from requiring tougher anti-flammability standards on sleepwear for infants.

On environmental issues, Bonilla is usually friendly to business interests and private property owners. (When a 2000 drought forced water rationing in Texas, his response was hyperbolic: "The plain fact is that the source of all the pain inflicted on this region is the Endangered Species Act.") He was the only member of the Hispanic Caucus to vote for the 1996 law creating work requirements for welfare recipients. He has sought to bar the children of illegal immigrants from attending public schools. And he has criticized the Department of Education's bilingual education requirements, arguing that schools should be able to adopt a more English-centered approach.

He has opposed efforts to designate English as the nation's official language, however, arguing that federal action is unnecessary because "English is already the official language of the world."

Bonilla worked at several TV stations and was press secretary to GOP Gov. Richard Thornburgh of Pennsylvania before returning to San Antonio in 1986 to work as a public affairs executive at the local CBS affiliate. Six years later, he took on four-term Democrat Albert G. Bustamante, whose increasingly luxurious lifestyle had led him to be viewed as out of touch with a district that has some of the poorest neighborhoods in the country. Chatting with voters in Spanish and campaigning beside his wife — anchor of the region's highest-rated TV newscast — Bonilla won by 21 percentage points.

After Bonilla won four relatively easy re-elections, Democrats turned the tables on him in 2002. Henry Cuellar, a former Texas secretary of state, cast himself as a moderate and characterized Bonilla as having lost touch with the district. But the coattails of Tony Sanchez — the unsuccessful Democratic gubernatorial candidate, who like Cuellar was from Laredo — proved insufficient and Bonilla hung on by 4 percentage points.

KEY VOTES

2002

- No — Overhaul campaign finance law; ban "soft money" and restrict advocacy advertising
- Yes — Back Bush's defense budget increase
- Yes — Extend 1996 welfare law
- P — Adopt Bush's discretionary spending limit
- Yes — Pass GOP Medicare prescription drug plan
- No — Create independent Sept. 11 commission
- No — Extend union protections to Homeland Security Department employees
- Yes — Revive fast-track procedures for trade agreements
- Yes — Authorize war against Iraq
- Yes — Advance bankruptcy overhaul opposed by abortion opponents

2001

- Yes — Nullify Clinton Labor Department ergonomics rule
- Yes — Cut taxes by $1.35 trillion through fiscal 2011
- No — Maintain ban on oil drilling in Arctic National Wildlife Refuge
- Yes — Approve Bush proposal to limit managed-care plan liability for coverage decisions
- No — Divert money from crop subsidy payments to land conservation
- Yes — Expand law enforcement power to investigate suspected terrorists

CQ VOTE STUDIES

	PARTY UNITY		PRESIDENTIAL SUPPORT	
	Support	Oppose	Support	Oppose
2002	97%	3%	88%	12%
2001	99%	1%	95%	5%
2000	92%	8%	30%	70%
1999	90%	10%	20%	80%
1998	85%	15%	30%	70%

INTEREST GROUPS

	AFL-CIO	ADA	CCUS	ACU
2002	11%	0%	95%	92%
2001	8%	0%	96%	92%
2000	0%	0%	90%	82%
1999	11%	0%	84%	91%
1998	11%	10%	88%	92%

TEXAS 23

Southwest – Laredo, San Antonio suburbs

The 23rd District is larger than most states east of the Mississippi River — residents like to say the area encompasses two time zones and three climates. Taking up 800 miles of the U.S. border with Mexico along the Rio Grande River, the politically moderate 23rd skims El Paso in the west, and heads over to San Antonio in the east. The largest district in a state that boasts of doing everything bigger and better, the 23rd includes all or part of 24 counties. The district's population is 67 percent Hispanic.

The 23rd includes some of the nation's poorest counties along its southern border. Seasonal employment, the influx of legal and illegal immigrants and an abundance of cheaper Mexican labor contribute to high unemployment. Manufacturing operations along the border known as *maquiladoras* are an integral part of the economy. An increase in trade and manufacturing in the 1990s has benefited the area.

Border communities often seem to have more in common with their Mexican neighbors than with the rest of Texas. Laredo celebrates Mexican Independence Day, and three bridges connect it to its Mexican sister city, Nuevo Laredo.

The 23rd is politically competitive, with Republicans holding a huge advantage in the San Antonio region and Democrats holding an edge in Laredo's Webb County and in some heavily Hispanic counties farther south and in the west. George W. Bush handily won the 23rd in the 2000 presidential election. But the district swung Democratic in 2002, largely because of a strong turnout in Laredo, the hometown of Democratic gubernatorial nominee Tony Sanchez. He won the 23rd with 54 percent of the two-party vote, a bit higher than Democratic Senate nominee Ron Kirk's 53 percent showing.

MAJOR INDUSTRY

Agriculture, trade, tourism, defense

MILITARY BASES

Laughlin Air Force Base, 1,377 military, 945 civilian (2002)

CITIES

Laredo, 176,576; San Antonio (pt.), 133,432; Del Rio, 33,867; Eagle Pass, 22,413

NOTABLE

Texas' largest county, Brewster, is roughly 6,200 square miles, about the size of Connecticut and Rhode Island combined.

Rep. Martin Frost (D)

CAPITOL OFFICE
225-3605
martin.frost@mail.house.gov
www.house.gov/frost
2256 Rayburn 20515-4324; fax 225-4951

COMMITTEES
Rules - ranking member

HOMETOWN
Dallas

BORN
Jan. 1, 1942, Glendale, Calif.

RELIGION
Jewish

FAMILY
Wife, Kathy George Frost; three children

EDUCATION
U. of Missouri, B.A., B.J. 1964 (history & journalism); Georgetown U., J.D. 1970

MILITARY SERVICE
Army Reserve, 1966-72

CAREER
Lawyer; reporter

POLITICAL HIGHLIGHTS
Sought Democratic nomination for U.S. House, 1974

ELECTION RESULTS

2002 GENERAL		
Martin Frost (D)	73,002	64.7%
Mike Rivera Ortega (R)	38,332	34.0%
Ken Ashby (LIBERT)	1,560	1.4%
2002 PRIMARY		
Martin Frost (D)		unopposed
2000 GENERAL		
Martin Frost (D)	103,152	61.8%
Bryndan Wright (R)	61,235	36.7%
Robert Worthington (LIBERT)	2,561	1.5%

PREVIOUS WINNING PERCENTAGES
1998 (57%); 1996 (56%); 1994 (53%); 1992 (60%); 1990 (100%); 1988 (93%); 1986 (67%); 1984 (59%); 1982 (73%); 1980 (61%); 1978 (54%)

Elected 1978; 13th term

Frost entered the 108th Congress with no Democratic leadership position for the first time since 1997, when he resurrected a demoralized Democratic Congressional Campaign Committee and led his party to a historic midterm election gain in 1998. That effort led to four years as Democratic Caucus chairman, a post he was forced to give up because of term limits.

Although Frost had plotted to step up to replace Richard A. Gephardt, who resigned as House minority leader after the 2002 election, he concluded soon after Gephardt's announcement that Nancy Pelosi of California had the votes to win. Ever the tactician, Frost withdrew from the race a week before the balloting. Some Democrats urged Pelosi to draft Frost for another stint at the DCCC, but nothing came of that.

Frost is far from the typical Texas politician. With his familiar frown and his acute attention to organization and detail, he employs focus and intellect where so many others rely on backslapping and cajoling. He follows a centrist path, siding with Republicans on many defense and foreign policy questions, but joining the Democratic mainstream on most domestic and budgetary questions. And he cultivates his status as a leading partisan role-player from his spot as the top Democrat on the House Rules Committee. There, he somberly laments, day after day, the dire consequences of allowing the Republicans to control which legislation gets put to a vote in the House.

But since his fourth marriage, in 1998 — his wife, Kathy, is an Army general — colleagues who know Frost well insist that while he often remains deep in thought, the frown has faded a bit.

His political strengths were evidenced after the 2000 census, when House seats were reapportioned and new maps were drawn for each state's congressional districts — a process that many predicted would favor the GOP. As head of the Democratic effort to minimize the damage, Frost managed what was essentially a draw.

Long after stepping aside as his party's campaign chief, Frost relishes reminding listeners that he was "the only Democrat to beat Tom DeLay twice," taking seats away from the House GOP leadership in 1998 and 2000.

Frost is regarded as an effective pragmatist. "You don't have to be ideological to be partisan," one top aide observes. "He looks at the world from the middle." That view was never more in evidence than during congressional debate on authorizing the use of force against Iraq in 2002. After Gephardt brokered a deal with the White House on some of the specifics, Frost quickly announced his support for the measure, despite the fact that 126 House Democrats objected to the language and voted against it.

In his brief bid to succeed Gephardt, Frost said he would emphasize his party's differences with the GOP on domestic issues, not take on Republicans in the foreign policy arena.

For Frost, the devil — and the key to any task — is always in the details. Gephardt labels Frost "the most focused human being I've ever met." At the DCCC, he set about transforming the organization into a modern political operation: recruiting candidates who themselves were fundraisers, teaching them how to run better races and instituting strict rules that required incumbents to contribute to colleagues and other candidates.

Democrats fell just short of their goal of regaining the majority in 1998, but the party rewarded Frost for the unexpected gains with the caucus post. There, he concentrated on honing the party message and seeking to act as a conduit to other leaders for the concerns of various factions. He also tried to balance Democrats' traditionally strong ties with labor by planning bagel breakfasts with the business community.

As a Jewish Southern white male, Frost represents a variety of constituencies that are important to the party. Coming from a politically competitive district, Frost has learned in his own campaigns — particularly in recent years as aggressive Republican challengers have tried to paint him as a tax-and-spend, left-wing liberal — that a Democrat locked in battle with a GOP foe is wise to stress centrist themes with broad voter appeal. As DCCC chairman, Frost encouraged many candidates to adopt that approach, while carefully recruiting candidates that fit the political makeup of their districts.

Frost also courts his own constituency with work on projects near and dear to them. Having refrained for months from announcing his position on whether to permanently grant China normal trade status — one of President Clinton's final-year priorities — Frost agreed to vote "yes" in a deal with the White House that allowed defense contractor Northrop Grumman Corp. to maintain two plants it had considered moving from Frost's district. He also has lobbied for funds to widen Interstate 30, a crucial Texas traffic artery, and for the Dallas area's light-rail system.

A local tragedy led Frost to take up a cause that led to one of his biggest legislative successes. In 1996, he won enactment of language expanding federal jurisdiction over repeat child molesters and establishing a sentence of life without parole for anyone convicted of a second sex crime against a child. The impetus for the measure was the kidnapping and murder of 9-year-old Amber Hagerman of Arlington, Texas.

Subsequent cases gave Frost and other supporters ammunition in pushing deployment of a nationwide "Amber Alert" program to distribute information about kidnappings. In the 108th, he and Republican Jennifer Dunn of Washington are working to improve the system.

Frost studied journalism in college and then worked for a time at Congressional Quarterly, where he first mastered redistricting and covered agriculture and the environment. Not long after earning a law degree, he made his first foray into politics.

He challenged Rep. Dale Milford for the Democratic nomination in 1974, contending the incumbent was too supportive of President Nixon at the height of Watergate. He lost, but in 1978 he came back and — with the help of organized labor — he defeated Milford and went on to win in November with 54 percent of the vote.

Frost had a number of close races in the 1990s, but his re-elections in 2000 and 2002 were by comfortable margins.

KEY VOTES

2002

Yes Overhaul campaign finance law; ban "soft money" and restrict advocacy advertising
Yes Back Bush's defense budget increase
No Extend 1996 welfare law
No Adopt Bush's discretionary spending limit
No Pass GOP Medicare prescription drug plan
Yes Create independent Sept. 11 commission
Yes Extend union protections to Homeland Security Department employees
No Revive fast-track procedures for trade agreements
Yes Authorize war against Iraq
Yes Advance bankruptcy overhaul opposed by abortion opponents

2001

No Nullify Clinton Labor Department ergonomics rule
No Cut taxes by $1.35 trillion through fiscal 2011
Yes Maintain ban on oil drilling in Arctic National Wildlife Refuge
No Approve Bush proposal to limit managed-care plan liability for coverage decisions
No Divert money from crop subsidy payments to land conservation
Yes Expand law enforcement power to investigate suspected terrorists

CQ VOTE STUDIES

	PARTY UNITY		PRESIDENTIAL SUPPORT	
	Support	Oppose	Support	Oppose
2002	86%	14%	35%	65%
2001	83%	17%	36%	64%
2000	87%	13%	81%	19%
1999	85%	15%	76%	24%
1998	84%	16%	73%	27%

INTEREST GROUPS

	AFL-CIO	ADA	CCUS	ACU
2002	100%	95%	50%	4%
2001	92%	85%	50%	25%
2000	90%	80%	47%	12%
1999	88%	85%	42%	4%
1998	100%	95%	56%	8%

TEXAS 24

Parts of Dallas, Fort Worth and Arlington

The 24th is a swath of working-class neighborhoods that takes in mostly black areas in Fort Worth, Hispanic areas in Dallas and white areas in between. Hispanics make up a plurality of district residents (38 percent), followed by whites (35 percent) and blacks (22 percent).

Nearly 90 percent of district residents live in Arlington, Dallas, Fort Worth or Grand Prairie, all of which the 24th shares with other districts. In Arlington and Grand Prairie, which lie along the Interstate 30 corridor between Fort Worth and Dallas, many residents are unionized workers who work at the General Motors plant in the district or at nearby defense contractors Bell Helicopter, Northrop Grumman and Lockheed Martin. Blue-collar workers in the 24th have borne the brunt of military cutbacks and defense contractor layoffs. The city was dealt a setback in 1998 when Dallas Naval Air Station was shut down.

Arlington's entertainment venues — including the Ballpark at Arlington, home of the Texas Rangers — are large employers in the district, and the University of Texas at Arlington to the southwest benefits the local economy as well. The Fort Worth part of the 24th takes in the city's hospital district, which includes five different medical facilities.

The large urban minority vote propels Democratic candidates to victory in the 24th, even when Republicans win handily statewide. Fort Worth's Tarrant County has a stronger Democratic lean than Dallas County because of the heavily black precincts in southeastern Fort Worth. There is some GOP strength in northeastern Arlington and just southwest of Dallas. But overall, the 24th is solid Democratic territory: In the 2002 Senate race, Democrat Ron Kirk carried the 24th by nearly 20 percentage points, taking 63 percent in Tarrant and 54 percent in Dallas.

MAJOR INDUSTRY

Defense, transportation, entertainment

CITIES

Fort Worth (pt.), 192,305; Arlington (pt.), 140,407; Dallas (pt.), 139,111; Grand Prairie (pt.), 111,637; Duncanville (pt.), 30,665

NOTABLE

Six Flags over Texas amusement park is home to the Texas Giant, often referred to as the No. 1 wooden roller coaster in the world; The Ballpark at Arlington is home to a baseball museum and a children's learning center.

Rep. Chris Bell (D)

Elected 2002; 1st term

A low-key former television and radio reporter who spent four years on the Houston City Council, Bell says his freshman term emphasis will be on bread-and-butter parochial issues such as flood control and a shortage of health clinics that could relieve the burden on emergency rooms.

Bell had wanted to pursue better storm drainage for his city from a seat on the Transportation and Infrastructure Committee. Instead, he was given assignments to the International Relations, Government Reform and Science panels. The latter panel will afford him an opportunity for a voice in the future of NASA after the loss of the space shuttle Columbia in 2003; many of Bell's constituents work at the nearby Johnson Space Center, NASA's flight operations headquarters.

A self-described moderate, Bell advocates full funding of the education overhaul enacted by the 107th Congress.

Bell had to work hard to establish himself as a political candidate. In 1984, when he was a TV reporter in Amarillo, he ran for a state House seat and was defeated. Eleven years later, after he had broken into radio reporting in Houston, Bell narrowly lost a nonpartisan runoff election for the city council. But he came back to win a seat two years later, campaigning on the theme of "customer-driven government."

Bell's most public loss was a distant third-place showing in the 2001 Houston mayoral race, but that campaign nonetheless helped him lay the groundwork for his congressional victory. He spent more than $1 million to advertise his mayoral bid, achieving name recognition that helped him in 2002. When Ken Bentsen gave up his House seat after four terms to seek the Democratic Senate nomination, Bell finished first in a four-way fight for the Democratic nod; he won the runoff by 9 percentage points over Carroll G. Robinson, a Houston City Council member.

Although he was outspent 4-to-1 by Republican industrial insurance executive Tom Reiser, Bell won by 12 points in November in the Democratic-leaning district.

CAPITOL OFFICE
225-7508
www.house.gov/bell
216 Cannon 20515-4325; fax 225-2947

COMMITTEES
Government Reform
International Relations
Science

HOMETOWN
Houston

BORN
Nov. 23, 1959, Abilene, Texas

RELIGION
Episcopalian

FAMILY
Wife, Alison Ayres Bell; two children

EDUCATION
U. of Texas, B.A. 1982 (journalism); South Texas College of Law, J.D. 1992

CAREER
Lawyer; television and radio reporter

POLITICAL HIGHLIGHTS
Democratic nominee for Texas House, 1984; candidate for Houston City Council, 1995; Houston City Council, 1997-2001; candidate for mayor of Houston, 2001

ELECTION RESULTS

2002 GENERAL		
Chris Bell (D)	63,590	54.8%
Tom Reiser (R)	50,041	43.1%
George Reiter (GREEN)	1,399	1.2%
2002 PRIMARY RUNOFF		
Chris Bell (D)	9,572	54.3%
Carroll G. Robinson (D)	8,056	45.7%
2002 PRIMARY		
Chris Bell (D)	7,443	36.1%
Carroll G. Robinson (D)	5,597	27.1%
Paul Colbert (D)	4,307	20.9%
Stephen King (D)	3,274	15.9%

TEXAS 25

Southern Houston and suburbs

The 25th encompasses many of Houston's working-class suburbs as well as some of its toniest estates. It is a semi-circle carved through south and southeast Harris County and a small part of Fort Bend County, stretching from the petrochemical suburbs of Baytown and Pasadena to the multimillion-dollar estates of Bellaire. It contains a mix of blue-collar union supporters, suburban blacks, Reagan Democrats and a sizable portion of Houston's Jewish population.

Redistricting after the 2000 census modified its boundaries, but the 25th still leans Democratic. The redraw reinforced its left-leaning tendencies by removing some more conservative western precincts.

The 25th has been known as a swing district, and often its residents are the quintessential Texas ticket-splitters — they tend to be fiscally conservative but socially progressive, supporting issues such as abortion and gay rights. The 25th's eastern edges have refineries, honky-tonk bars and union Democrats who voted for Ronald Reagan in 1980 and for Al Gore in 2000. Stances on issues, not party affiliation, often decide close elections.

Once mostly agricultural, the district's land was converted long ago to industrial purposes, including refining and plastics production. The 25th also includes most of the Texas Medical Center and the Port of Houston, which are important to Houston's economy. Many residents commute to NASA's nearby Johnson Space Center (located in the 9th). The district also claims Rice University, the Houston Zoo, the Astrodome and Reliant Stadium, home to the Texans football team.

MAJOR INDUSTRY
Energy, shipping, health care, research

CITIES
Houston (pt.), 453,368; Pasadena (pt.), 77,786

NOTABLE
Gilley's, a country and western bar featured in the 1980 movie "Urban Cowboy," was in Pasadena; The club closed and later burned.

Rep. Michael C. Burgess (R)

CAPITOL OFFICE
225-7772
www.house.gov/burgess
1721 Longworth 20515-4326; fax 225-2919

COMMITTEES
Science
Transportation & Infrastructure

HOMETOWN
Highland Village

BORN
Dec. 23, 1950, Rochester, Minn.

RELIGION
Episcopalian

FAMILY
Wife, Laura Lee Burgess; three children

EDUCATION
North Texas State U., B.S. 1972 (biology), M.S. 1976 (physiology); U. of Texas, Houston, M.D. 1977; U. of Texas, Dallas, M.S. 2000 (medical management)

CAREER
Physician

POLITICAL HIGHLIGHTS
No previous office

ELECTION RESULTS

2002 GENERAL		
Michael C. Burgess (R)	123,195	74.8%
Paul William Lebon (D)	37,485	22.8%
David Wallace Croft (LIBERT)	2,367	1.4%
2002 PRIMARY RUNOFF		
Michael C. Burgess (R)	10,522	54.6%
Scott Armey (R)	8,737	45.4%
2002 PRIMARY		
Scott Armey (R)	11,493	45.4%
Michael C. Burgess (R)	5,703	22.5%
Keith A. Self (R)	5,610	22.2%
Roger Sessions (R)	1,630	6.4%
Dave Kovatch (R)	675	2.7%

Elected 2002; 1st term

A second-generation doctor who has delivered more than 3,000 babies, Burgess came to Washington hoping to parlay his expertise into a voice in the health care debate. He favors tax credits to help the poor pay their medical bills, a streamlined approval process for new drugs, a delay in implementing new patient privacy rules — which he views as ineffective and expensive — and a limit on punitive damages in medical malpractice lawsuits.

But as a freshman, Burgess' priorities have been shaped by his standing as a congressman for some of the nation's fastest-growing suburbs. That constituency allowed him to win the only Texas Republican seat on the Transportation Committee as it rewrites federal highway, mass transit and aviation law. He will be seeking to direct more money to roads between Dallas and Fort Worth and will be an advocate for the interests of the Dallas-Fort Worth Airport, one of the nation's biggest, which sprawls into the 26th District.

Burgess' overall tone is conservative. He is a National Rifle Association member and an abortion-rights opponent. He has been an enthusiastic backer of President Bush's fiscal policies but would like to replace the graduated income tax with a flat tax.

In that position he echoes his predecessor, Dick Armey, the majority leader for the final eight of his 18 years in the House. But to get to Congress Burgess had to stop a budding Armey family dynasty in its tracks. The 26th District had been reconfigured for this decade to make an obvious front-runner out of Scott Armey, one of the retiring congressman's five children and the county judge, or executive, of the new district's dominant county.

Armey finished first in a six-way primary, but his 45 percent of the vote was insufficient to prevent a runoff. Burgess played on a nepotism theme, sending out literature that said, "My dad is not Dick Armey," and news reports questioned the younger Armey's ethics. Burgess won the nomination with 55 percent, then cruised through the general election in one of the most solidly Republican districts in the state.

TEXAS 26

Dallas suburbs — Denton County

Tremendous growth in the suburbs north of Dallas pushed the 26th farther from the city in redistricting following the 2000 census. The district now is centered in Denton County, but takes in small parts of Tarrant, Collin and Wise counties. Denton County is home to two-thirds of the district's residents.

As the Dallas-Fort Worth area grew in the 1990s, residents moved north into rural Denton and Collin counties. Denton's population started expanding in the 1970s and continues to grow as upper-middle-class families build large homes. The district takes in northeastern Tarrant County, including the wealthy Fort Worth suburbs of Colleyville and Southlake, as well as the wealthier parts of Hurst, Euless and Bedford (all shared with the 12th). In Collin County, once-rural towns such as Frisco and McKinney (both shared with the 3rd) have caught the overgrowth from the Plano area. However, the north and much of the west edge of the district remains rural and depends on cotton, eggs, cattle and corn.

Transportation is a major economic force here. Part of Dallas-Fort Worth International Airport lies in the 26th, and the airport — one of the three largest in the nation — employs many residents. American Airlines' headquarters is at the airport. A major shipping artery, Interstate 35, which runs from the Mexican border, crosses the district. Alliance Airport, the first airport in the nation to be built specifically to serve the needs of business, also is in the district.

Overall, the 26th is predominantly white, upper class and suburban. Residents voted more than 2-to-1 for George W. Bush in the 2000 presidential election. The area tends to be socially and fiscally conservative, but local issues — such as highway congestion — remain the top priority for many.

MAJOR INDUSTRY
Transportation, telecommunications

CITIES
Denton, 80,537; Lewisville, 77,735; Carrollton (pt.), 59,754; Flower Mound, 50,702

NOTABLE
Texas Motor Speedway, the nation's second-largest sports facility, is in Denton County.

Rep. Solomon P. Ortiz (D)

CAPITOL OFFICE
225-7742
www.house.gov/ortiz
2470 Rayburn 20515-4327; fax 226-1134

COMMITTEES
Armed Services
Resources

HOMETOWN
Corpus Christi

BORN
June 3, 1937, Robstown, Texas

RELIGION
Methodist

FAMILY
Divorced; two children

EDUCATION
Institute of Applied Science, attended 1962; Del Mar College, attended 1965-67

MILITARY SERVICE
Army, 1960-62

CAREER
Law enforcement official

POLITICAL HIGHLIGHTS
Nueces County constable, 1965-69; Nueces County Commission, 1969-77; Nueces County sheriff, 1977-83

ELECTION RESULTS

2002 GENERAL		
Solomon P. Ortiz (D)	68,559	61.1%
Pat Ahumada (R)	41,004	36.5%
Christopher Claytor (LIBERT)	2,646	2.4%
2002 PRIMARY		
Solomon P. Ortiz (D)		unopposed
2000 GENERAL		
Solomon P. Ortiz (D)	102,088	63.4%
Pat Ahumada (R)	54,660	33.9%
William Bunch (LIBERT)	4,324	2.7%

PREVIOUS WINNING PERCENTAGES
1998 (63%); 1996 (65%); 1994 (59%); 1992 (55%); 1990 (100%); 1988 (100%); 1986 (100%); 1984 (64%); 1982 (64%)

Elected 1982; 11th term

Defense issues are Ortiz's major focus. And while he does not have a high-profile personality, his voice is amplified by seniority, which has lifted him to the No. 3 Democratic seat on the Armed Services Committee. There, and as co-chairman of the congressional Depot Caucus, he looks after the interests of South Texas' military bases and troop quality of life.

But in the 107th Congress, circumstances highlighted other aspects of his legislative work. As thousands of farmers in his border district were hard hit by a prolonged drought in the Rio Grande Valley, Ortiz was a leader among Texas politicians demanding that Washington pressure Mexico to deliver billions of gallons of water it owes the United States under a 1944 treaty. Moreover, in dealing with the panoply of homeland defense issues facing Congress after the Sept. 11, 2001, terrorist attacks, Ortiz had to balance three priorities: his conservative instinct on questions of national security, the economic dependence of many of his constituents on easy access for day-trippers crossing the Rio Grande, and his determination to protect Hispanics against discrimination.

The last of those has been a constant theme of Ortiz's two decades in Congress. Befitting a lawmaker whose district borders Mexico, and whose constituency is two-thirds Hispanic, he has been active in such issues as cross-border trade and tourism, immigration, thwarting drug smuggling and what he regards as the entertainment industry's woeful record in presenting positive portrayals of Hispanics. Ortiz's overall voting record is less liberal than those of other Hispanic Democrats in the House; his votes — he backed President Bush half the time in the 107th — would place him comfortably with the centrist New Democrat Coalition of House Democrats, although he has declined to join the group.

Ortiz's legislative agenda is driven more by the economic and social needs of his low-income, relatively poorly educated constituency than by ideology or party. Perhaps for that reason, he was better situated than many Democrats to deal with the shock of the GOP takeover of the House in 1995. And because of his personal relationships with many Republicans, he is able to gain a favorable hearing for many of his proposals. "He worms his way into their hearts," says one longtime aide.

He also has been more willing than more-liberal colleagues to deal on some issues in return for GOP help on others close to home. Ortiz was one of three Democrats who switched from their previous position to help Republicans kill a Democratic-sponsored proposal to federalize airport security workers in the aftermath of the Sept. 11 attacks. While denying that he traded his vote, Ortiz said he asked the Bush administration and the House Republican leadership to pay more attention to border issues and Hispanic members. "I think maybe I'm in a better position to say, 'Hey, I helped you guys in this way, but we've got problems on the border you have not addressed,' " he said. One of those problems was dealt with several months later when the final version of a border security bill included a provision intended to expedite short-term cross-border visits from Mexico. Tightened security had delayed those visits after the attacks.

As the top-ranking Democrat on the Armed Services Military Readiness Subcommittee, Ortiz has warned that defense downsizing and spending cuts have threatened the quality of life of military personnel. And unhappiness over pay, benefits and the overall quality of life, he says, makes it difficult to keep trained and experienced military personnel. This is smart politics in his district, home of two naval air stations and an Army depot. Also, Ortiz's personal experience has led to the conviction that military personnel should be given a chance at upward mobility, as he was.

The military facilities Ortiz represents survived the base closings of the 1990s. Concerned about the installations' future, Ortiz vigorously opposed a new round of base closings in 2005, which Congress enacted in 2001 under threat of a presidential veto. In 2002, he backed a quixotic proposal in Armed Services to cancel the next round, insisting that the country should not be abandoning bases while engaged in a war against terrorism.

Ortiz particularly opposes Pentagon proposals to privatize repair work done at large military maintenance depots, such as the one in Corpus Christi where more than 2,500 civilian federal employees service Army helicopters. He argues that it is dangerous to rely for critical repair work on private companies that might have labor problems or use their monopoly as leverage to boost the cost of the work.

Ortiz supports a South Texas effort to establish a commercial spaceport, focused on unmanned launches. Since the Columbia space shuttle tragedy in 2003, Ortiz noted, "there may be more willingness to consider . . . the possibility of funding unmanned robotic flights."

Ortiz has long been concerned about the treatment of Hispanics in the United States. In 1998, he chafed at a Republican amendment to require Puerto Rico to adopt English as its official language as a condition for being accepted as a state. As chairman of the Congressional Hispanic Caucus in the 102nd Congress, he helped push through legislation increasing access to voting materials in languages other than English.

The child of a migrant family, Ortiz grew up poor near Corpus Christi, working a variety of odd jobs to help out his family. When he was 16, his father died. He dropped out of high school and soon after joined the Army. "It was the one place that would give me free room and board and let me send my check back home to my mother," he recalls.

Ortiz served in the military police, which put him on the path to a trail-blazing career in law enforcement and local government. He mounted his first electoral bid in 1964, defeating the incumbent Nueces County constable. Four years later, he became the first Hispanic elected to the county commission, and then in 1976 he was the first Hispanic to win election as county sheriff, his springboard to the House in 1982. That year, the three-judge federal panel in charge of redistricting created the 27th with a 60 percent Hispanic majority. He won the seat with 64 percent. His district's boundaries have not changed much since, and his recent re-elections have been uneventful.

KEY VOTES

2002

Yes Overhaul campaign finance law; ban "soft money" and restrict advocacy advertising
Yes Back Bush's defense budget increase
No Extend 1996 welfare law
No Adopt Bush's discretionary spending limit
No Pass GOP Medicare prescription drug plan
Yes Create independent Sept. 11 commission
Yes Extend union protections to Homeland Security Department employees
No Revive fast-track procedures for trade agreements
\+ Authorize war against Iraq
No Advance bankruptcy overhaul opposed by abortion opponents

2001

No Nullify Clinton Labor Department ergonomics rule
No Cut taxes by $1.35 trillion through fiscal 2011
No Maintain ban on oil drilling in Arctic National Wildlife Refuge
No Approve Bush proposal to limit managed-care plan liability for coverage decisions
No Divert money from crop subsidy payments to land conservation
Yes Expand law enforcement power to investigate suspected terrorists

CQ VOTE STUDIES

	PARTY UNITY		PRESIDENTIAL SUPPORT	
	Support	Oppose	Support	Oppose
2002	82%	18%	42%	58%
2001	66%	34%	58%	42%
2000	76%	24%	71%	29%
1999	70%	30%	65%	35%
1998	76%	24%	68%	32%

INTEREST GROUPS

	AFL-CIO	ADA	CCUS	ACU
2002	78%	85%	42%	25%
2001	75%	70%	65%	60%
2000	90%	65%	45%	24%
1999	88%	60%	33%	32%
1998	90%	70%	56%	17%

TEXAS 27

Gulf Coast — Corpus Christi, Brownsville

Anchored by Corpus Christi in the north, the 27th runs south to the Rio Grande River, with the Gulf of Mexico on its eastern coast. Ranches are the mainstay between the two largest cities, Corpus Christi and Brownsville, which together contain more than half of the 27th's population. But much of the district is coastal, and the district's two deep-water ports are major economic generators.

Corpus Christi has a solid economy fueled by its reliable tourism industry and a military presence that grew in the 1990s. Oil and gas used to be among the biggest industries in the city in the 1980s, but now petrochemical refining, which is also found up and down the coast, is more common. Farther south, the port city of Brownsville struggles with an influx of illegal immigrants and high poverty, but new manufacturing plants and *maquiladoras* — assembly or manufacturing plants that use low-cost labor and import many parts from the United States — have brightened the area and lowered unemployment rates. Visitors coming from Mexico boost Brownsville's retail industry, and "ecotourism" also adds to the economy by drawing bird and turtle watchers to the area's wetlands. Willacy County is competing to be the location of a new spaceport that would launch satellites and planes into space.

Created after the 1980 census, the 27th has been represented by the same Democrat since its creation. The district's 72 percent Hispanic population gives it a decided Democratic lean, though some affluent areas in Harlingen and Corpus Christi lean Republican. In 2002 statewide races, Democrats Tony Sanchez and Ron Kirk carried the 27th by percentage point margins in the double digits.

MAJOR INDUSTRY
Manufacturing, trade, tourism

MILITARY BASES
Corpus Christi Naval Air Station, 3,137 military, 3,949 civilian; Corpus Christi Army Depot, 11 military, 2,895 civilian; Naval Air Station Kingsville, 664 military, 1,117 civilian (2002)

CITIES
Corpus Christi (pt.), 270,677; Brownsville, 139,722; Harlingen, 57,564

NOTABLE
Padre Island is a popular college spring break location; Port Isabel served as a supply depot during the U.S.-Mexican War (1846-48).

Rep. Ciro D. Rodriguez (D)

CAPITOL OFFICE
225-1640
www.house.gov/rodriguez
1507 Longworth 20515-4328; fax 225-1641

COMMITTEES
Armed Services
Resources
Veterans' Affairs

HOMETOWN
San Antonio

BORN
Dec. 9, 1946, Piedras Negras, Mexico

RELIGION
Roman Catholic

FAMILY
Wife, Carolina Pena Rodriguez; one child

EDUCATION
St. Mary's U. (Texas), B.A. 1973 (political science); Our Lady of the Lake U., M.S.W. 1978

CAREER
Social worker; social work instructor

POLITICAL HIGHLIGHTS
Harlandale School Board, 1975-87; Texas House, 1987-97

ELECTION RESULTS

2002 GENERAL		
Ciro D. Rodriguez (D)	71,393	71.1%
Gabriel Perales Jr. (R)	26,973	26.9%
William Stallknecht (LIBERT)	2,054	2.1%
2002 PRIMARY		
Ciro D. Rodriguez (D)		unopposed
2000 GENERAL		
Ciro D. Rodriguez (D)	123,104	89.0%
William Stallknecht (LIBERT)	15,156	11.0%

PREVIOUS WINNING PERCENTAGES
1998 (91%); 1997 Special Runoff Election (67%)

Elected April 1997; 3rd full term

One of the most liberal Texans in the House, Rodriguez says he won't be limited by his committee assignments, particularly after he has twice been unsuccessful in bids to win an appointment to the Appropriations Committee. While he has settled into seats on the Armed Services, Resources and Veterans' Affairs panels, he describes his focus as social policy, particularly health care and education.

While others on Armed Services debate weapons systems in committee, Rodriguez is just as likely to be discussing school lunches for soldiers' children or evidence of new outbreaks of Persian Gulf War syndrome. He does have one chief military interest — preserving jobs at defense installations and for contractors in the San Antonio area — but he puts much of his attention on other issues facing his constituents.

The 28th District, which is more than two-thirds Hispanic, stretches from the South Side of San Antonio to the Mexican border and includes some of the nation's poorest and least-educated communities. Improving that situation has been one of Rodriguez's prime concerns throughout his career.

Inspired by the civil rights struggle of the 1960s to switch his career from pharmacology to social work, Rodriguez rose from a local school board to the Texas Legislature, where he sat on health and education panels. His voting record places him to the left of the other five Hispanics in the state's delegation. His votes supporting abortion rights and gun control have led his opponents to argue that he is too socially liberal for the district.

In both the 107th and 108th Congresses, he had some regional support for a seat on Appropriations, but to no avail.

In the 108th Congress, Rodriguez became chairman of the Congressional Hispanic Caucus, after serving as vice chairman of the caucus and chairman of its Health Task Force in the 107th. In the 106th, he served on a leadership-appointed education task force, which worked to develop a party agenda on education initiatives for the 107th.

But he has not always walked in lockstep with other Democrats. While the party has given its support for mandatory testing programs, Rodriguez sided with conservative Republicans and liberal Democrats in the 105th and the 107th to oppose standardized testing in reading and math. Referring to his 12 years of experience on the Harlandale School Board in San Antonio, he argued that Texas schoolchildren already are tested enough and that a nationwide exam would be unfair to students with limited English skills who may be learning at a different pace.

But on most education issues, Rodriguez is squarely in the Democratic mainstream. Although in the end he voted to enact the 2001 education overhaul that was one of President Bush's top first-term priorities, Rodriguez generally sided with members of his party during the debate. He voiced strong opposition to a GOP plan to provide some parents with vouchers to help pay their children's tuition at schools of their choice. "Vouchers are not the answer," he said. Rodriguez's wife is an elementary school librarian in San Antonio.

Rodriguez sometimes must pull away from his health and education agendas to attend to military matters of local importance. Brooks and Randolph Air Force bases are located there, and two other military facilities — Fort Sam Houston (the new headquarters of the Army's Southern Command) and Lackland Air Force Base — operate nearby, employing many of Rodriguez's constituents. One of the 28th District's bigger employers is

Kelly U.S.A., a manufacturing and logistics center built on the site of Kelly Air Force Base, which was shuttered during the 1995 round of base closings. Rodriguez has worked on efforts to replace the 10,000-plus military jobs with even better-paying civilian ones for such aerospace firms as Boeing, Lockheed Martin, and Pratt and Whitney.

The 28th's border location sometimes puts Rodriguez in the middle of debates over immigration policy and trade with Mexico. In the 107th, he was one of 11 Hispanic Caucus members to write appropriators urging strong safety requirements for Mexican trucks that would operate in the United States under an agreement in NAFTA. "The issue of safety on our highways is not an 'Hispanic issue,' " Rodriguez and others argued.

Rodriguez was born on the Mexican side of the Rio Grande to a family that often moved back and forth across the border as his father took a series of jobs working on large industrial refrigeration units. The family settled in the San Antonio area when Rodriguez was 3 years old. He became a U.S. citizen when he was 18. Of the six children in the family, he is the only one who attended college.

He entered college intending to be a pharmacist but soon turned to social work. He has held jobs helping heroin addicts and patients in mental health clinics. Rodriguez ran for a local school board because he thought not enough was being done to help schools in poor areas. He served 12 years on the Harlandale board and in 1987 moved to the Texas House, where he continued to work to equalize school funding.

In 1997, when Democratic Rep. Frank Tejeda died early in his third term after a two-year battle with brain cancer, Rodriguez decided to run for the seat. Tejeda's death provoked a scramble among 15 prospective successors, including nine Democrats. Rodriguez dominated the voting in the March special election, but his 46 percent share of the vote fell short of the majority required to win the seat outright.

In the April runoff, Rodriguez faced former San Antonio City Councilman Juan Solis, also a Democrat, who launched an aggressive challenge to Rodriguez, characterizing himself as Tejeda's true heir because he shared the late congressman's anti-abortion position.

But Rodriguez, who attended the same high school and college as Tejeda, attracted most of the support from fellow state legislators and prominent Democrats in city government and won by a 2-to-1 ratio.

In 1998, Rodriguez bested two other Democrats for the nomination for a full term but had no Republican opponent in the fall, and he has cruised to re-election since.

KEY VOTES

2002

- Yes Overhaul campaign finance law; ban "soft money" and restrict advocacy advertising
- Yes Back Bush's defense budget increase
- No Extend 1996 welfare law
- No Adopt Bush's discretionary spending limit
- No Pass GOP Medicare prescription drug plan
- Yes Create independent Sept. 11 commission
- Yes Extend union protections to Homeland Security Department employees
- No Revive fast-track procedures for trade agreements
- No Authorize war against Iraq
- No Advance bankruptcy overhaul opposed by abortion opponents

2001

- No Nullify Clinton Labor Department ergonomics rule
- ? Cut taxes by $1.35 trillion through fiscal 2011
- Yes Maintain ban on oil drilling in Arctic National Wildlife Refuge
- No Approve Bush proposal to limit managed-care plan liability for coverage decisions
- No Divert money from crop subsidy payments to land conservation
- Yes Expand law enforcement power to investigate suspected terrorists

CQ VOTE STUDIES

	PARTY UNITY		PRESIDENTIAL SUPPORT	
	Support	Oppose	Support	Oppose
2002	96%	4%	25%	75%
2001	88%	12%	31%	69%
2000	94%	6%	84%	16%
1999	90%	10%	79%	21%
1998	92%	8%	81%	19%

INTEREST GROUPS

	AFL-CIO	ADA	CCUS	ACU
2002	100%	95%	40%	0%
2001	100%	85%	39%	12%
2000	100%	85%	50%	12%
1999	89%	100%	21%	8%
1998	100%	100%	39%	4%

TEXAS 28
South San Antonio; Alice; Zapata

The 28th starts in southern San Antonio and heads south through brush country to the Mexico border. The district's population center is in the low- and middle-class communities of San Antonio, while the southern part of the district is mostly sparsely populated agricultural land.

Many residents in this Hispanic-majority district face economic struggles. Median household income in the 28th is under $30,000, and less than 10 percent of residents 25 and over have a bachelor's degree. In Starr County, the nation's most heavily Hispanic county (97.5 percent), nearly half of all families live below the poverty line.

San Antonio's five military bases sustain the economy in the northern part of the 28th. The area was dealt a blow by the 2001 closure of Kelly Air Force Base, the largest base in the 20th and a major employer for the 28th's Hispanic residents.

But while other industries help keep San Antonio afloat, there is not as much in the way of enterprise in the south, where the unemployment rate remains high. NAFTA has stimulated the economy somewhat, and towns such as Mission, in Hidalgo County, have lower unemployment rates than they did several years ago. Hidalgo is one of the fastest-growing areas in the state, and the economy is getting better as the number of small businesses has risen. A small technology industry is growing. Citrus growing also is a mainstay here.

Democrats do well in the 28th at every level, though a large Catholic influence gives the district a socially conservative bent. Al Gore received 59 percent of the 28th's vote in the 2000 presidential election.

MAJOR INDUSTRY
Defense, agriculture, tourism

MILITARY BASES
Randolph Air Force Base, 4,900 military, 4,000 civilian (2001); Brooks Air Force Base, 1,198 military, 1,409 civilian (2002)

CITIES
San Antonio (pt.), 247,498; Alice, 19,010; Mission (pt.), 13,371

NOTABLE
San Antonio Missions National Historical Park; Caro Brown, the first woman to win a Pulitzer Prize for journalism, worked at the Alice Daily News during the 1940s and 1950s.

Rep. Gene Green (D)

CAPITOL OFFICE
225-1688
www.house.gov/green
2335 Rayburn 20515-4329; fax 225-9903

COMMITTEES
Energy & Commerce
Standards of Official Conduct

HOMETOWN
Houston

BORN
Oct. 17, 1947, Houston, Texas

RELIGION
Methodist

FAMILY
Wife, Helen Albers Green; two children

EDUCATION
U. of Houston, B.B.A. 1971; Bates College of Law, attended 1971-77

CAREER
Lawyer

POLITICAL HIGHLIGHTS
Texas House, 1973-85; Texas Senate, 1985-92

ELECTION RESULTS

2002 GENERAL		
Gene Green (D)	55,760	95.2%
Paul Hansen (LIBERT)	2,833	4.8%
2002 PRIMARY		
Gene Green (D)		unopposed
2000 GENERAL		
Gene Green (D)	84,665	73.3%
Joe Vu (R)	29,606	25.6%
Ray E. Dittmar (LIBERT)	1,204	1.0%

PREVIOUS WINNING PERCENTAGES
1998 (93%); 1996 (68%); 1994 (73%); 1992 (65%)

Elected 1992; 6th term

Green grew up in a part of the 29th District called "Redneck Alley," home mostly to working-class whites. But the majority of the population in his district now is Hispanic. That demographic reality means Green must focus his attention on constituent services and core Democratic issues such as support for public education, expanded health care, federal programs for minorities, and pocketbook concerns of the working class.

Although the folksy Green often strays from his party when it is time to vote on the environment, gun control, juvenile crime and public housing, he enjoys good relations with Democratic leaders, in part because he doesn't trumpet his disagreements. Since August 2001 he has served on the ethics committee, a generally thankless post, but one that enables members to build up chits from the leadership.

Part of the reason party leaders value Green is that he is one of a dwindling breed on Capitol Hill — the non-Hispanic white Southern Democrat. Their numbers in the House have dropped from 62 in the 103rd Congress to just 35 as the 108th began.

Green won a seat on the Energy and Commerce Committee in the 105th Congress, and he uses that perch to look out for Texas interests in communications, health care and oil and gas development.

Green's committee position also gave him a forum to criticize the treatment of workers hurt by the 2001 bankruptcy of Enron Corp., the giant Houston-based energy trader. Unlike some other Houston-area members of Congress, Green did not have particularly close ties to the company, and he said he would be happy to donate the political contributions he had received from Enron, which totaled less than $10,000 over a decade, to a fund for the company's workers.

Along with Democrat Peter Deutsch of Florida, Green introduced a bill soon after Enron's failure to cap the amount of company securities in a worker's 401(k) retirement fund at 10 percent. Green's focus on the displaced workers is part of a political philosophy developed through decades in public office — a concern for protecting the "little guy," particularly in his working-class district. Although Green has a down-to-earth demeanor, even in congressional hearings, he is nonetheless a practiced politician.

Green is careful to showcase his efforts to increase funding for bilingual education and education for disadvantaged children. In the 106th, he tried unsuccessfully to have the Census Bureau use statistical sampling to ensure that Hispanics and other minorities were not undercounted in the 2000 census. He also has derided efforts of conservatives to have English declared the official language of the United States.

Each year, Green seeks to connect with minority groups by sponsoring events such as Immunization Day, which provides free vaccinations to children, and Citizenship Day, which helps legal residents obtain citizenship.

In his first two terms, he had a seat on the Education Committee, and education issues remain one of his priorities. He strongly defends public education, often noting his wife's career as a public school math teacher. Vouchers to help parents pay private school tuition would do little for his district, Green says, "We need to fix the problems of the millions and not the few." Instead, he favors devoting federal funds to expand Head Start, boost new building construction and train more teachers.

The congressman is a stalwart supporter of expanded health care. Signing on to a measure in the 106th to provide Medicaid and other benefits for pregnant women and children who are legal immigrants, he said, "Investing in the preventive services Medicaid provides saves taxpayers money in the long run." He also backs legislation to give managed-care patients more rights, including the power to sue their health care providers.

Unlike some of the more conservative members of his party, Green stands against GOP tax-cutting efforts. He voted against a popular bill in the 106th to cut taxes on married couples, saying it "only benefits the wealthiest of Americans and does nothing to help the working folks in my district." In the 107th, he opposed President Bush's $1.35 trillion tax cut legislation for much the same reason.

Green has sided with Democratic leaders and their allies on trade issues, which are of particular interest to union workers in his blue-collar district. In the 107th Congress he voted against giving the president fast-track trade negotiating authority, which limits Congress' role in trade agreements. He voted against the North American Free Trade Agreement in the 103rd, despite support for it by Houston's business community.

His support for such Democratic positions notwithstanding, party leaders can never take Green for granted. He voted for Republican-sponsored legislation to toughen criminal penalties for violent juvenile offenders and to overhaul public housing policies. On environmental matters, Green often has joined with Republicans, opposing new Environmental Protection Agency clean air standards that would affect Houston.

He generally favors gun owners' rights, and he has sided with social conservatives in support of a measure that would have allowed the display of the Ten Commandments in public schools and government buildings.

On abortion, Green's current view differs from his earlier position. In February 1992, a month before his first House primary, he dropped his opposition to abortion when he came under attack for having sponsored anti-abortion bills in the state legislature. Green said he had gradually come to alter his views on abortion; critics said he changed his mind to enhance his prospects of winning the congressional seat. In 2002, he opposed GOP-led attempts to ban a procedure opponents call "partial birth" abortion.

Green won a hard-fought five-way primary in 1992, besting Houston City Council member Ben Reyes in two runoffs — the first was voided after election officials found some Republicans had illegally crossed over and cast ballots. Green won the general election with 65 percent of the vote in the largely Democratic 29th District. He continued to strengthen his hold over the next 10 years. In 2002, he easily won re-election in the new 29th when the GOP did not field a candidate.

KEY VOTES

2002

- Yes Overhaul campaign finance law; ban "soft money" and restrict advocacy advertising
- Yes Back Bush's defense budget increase
- No Extend 1996 welfare law
- No Adopt Bush's discretionary spending limit
- No Pass GOP Medicare prescription drug plan
- Yes Create independent Sept. 11 commission
- Yes Extend union protections to Homeland Security Department employees
- No Revive fast-track procedures for trade agreements
- Yes Authorize war against Iraq
- No Advance bankruptcy overhaul opposed by abortion opponents

2001

- No Nullify Clinton Labor Department ergonomics rule
- No Cut taxes by $1.35 trillion through fiscal 2011
- No Maintain ban on oil drilling in Arctic National Wildlife Refuge
- No Approve Bush proposal to limit managed-care plan liability for coverage decisions
- Yes Divert money from crop subsidy payments to land conservation
- Yes Expand law enforcement power to investigate suspected terrorists

CQ VOTE STUDIES

	PARTY UNITY		PRESIDENTIAL SUPPORT	
	Support	Oppose	Support	Oppose
2002	86%	14%	31%	69%
2001	80%	20%	33%	67%
2000	81%	19%	69%	31%
1999	80%	20%	69%	31%
1998	86%	14%	71%	29%

INTEREST GROUPS

	AFL-CIO	ADA	CCUS	ACU
2002	100%	90%	35%	16%
2001	100%	90%	43%	36%
2000	100%	90%	33%	20%
1999	89%	70%	24%	26%
1998	100%	95%	47%	16%

TEXAS 29

Part of Houston and eastern suburbs

Located on the eastern side of Houston's downtown, the 29th is a blue-collar, working-class, Hispanic-majority district near refineries and factories that employ many union members.

The district resembles a backward "C" and arcs from northern to southeastern Houston (slightly more than half of district residents live in the city). In the north the 29th takes in George Bush Intercontinental Airport, a source of employment for many district residents, and part of the comfortable suburb of Humble. It also includes part of the Houston Ship Channel, a major shipping route that has seen increased business since the NAFTA and GATT trade agreements. The district also takes in most of middle-class Channelview, east of Houston. In the bottom half, the 29th includes working-class areas near Interstate 10 such as Jacinto City, Galena Park and South Houston and part of Pasadena.

The 29th was originally drawn in 1992 as a Hispanic-majority district, and Hispanics now comprise 62 percent of the district population. The heaviest concentrations of Hispanics are in South Houston, Jacinto City, Houston and Pasadena. Nearly 60 percent of district residents speak a language other than English at home.

The 29th has the largest blue-collar work force (41 percent), lowest median age (27 years) and smallest percentage of high school graduates (52 percent of the over-25 population) in Texas. It was severely affected in 2001 by one of Houston's worst floods, Tropical Storm Allison.

The district is solidly Democratic, even with the traditionally poor voter turnout in the Hispanic community. In the 2002 senatorial and gubernatorial races, the 29th backed Democrats Ron Kirk and Tony Sanchez by a better than 2-to-1 ratio. Republicans can win only a few precincts up north, near the airport.

MAJOR INDUSTRY

Chemicals, energy, construction, aviation

CITIES

Houston (pt.), 339,295; Pasadena (pt.), 46,643; Cloverleaf (unincorporated), 23,508; Channelview (unincorporated) (pt.), 20,451; South Houston, 15,833

NOTABLE

The district houses much of the city's $15 billion petrochemical complex, which rivals Rotterdam in the Netherlands as the world's largest.

Rep. Eddie Bernice Johnson (D)

CAPITOL OFFICE
225-8885
rep.e.b.johnson@mail.house.gov
www.house.gov/ebjohnson
1511 Longworth 20515-4330; fax 226-1477

COMMITTEES
Science
Transportation & Infrastructure

HOMETOWN
Dallas

BORN
Dec. 3, 1935, Waco, Texas

RELIGION
Baptist

FAMILY
Divorced; one child

EDUCATION
Texas Christian U., B.S. 1967 (nursing); Southern Methodist U., M.P.A. 1976

CAREER
Business relocation company owner; nurse; U.S. Health, Education & Welfare Department official

POLITICAL HIGHLIGHTS
Texas House, 1973-77; Texas Senate, 1987-93

ELECTION RESULTS

2002 GENERAL		
Eddie Bernice Johnson (D)	88,980	74.3%
Ron Bush (R)	28,981	24.2%
Lance Flores (LIBERT)	1,856	1.6%
2002 PRIMARY		
Eddie Bernice Johnson (D)		unopposed
2000 GENERAL		
Eddie Bernice Johnson (D)	109,163	91.8%
Kelly Rush (LIBERT)	9,798	8.2%

PREVIOUS WINNING PERCENTAGES
1998 (72%); 1996 (55%); 1994 (73%); 1992 (72%)

Elected 1992; 6th term

Johnson is liberal, but she is also a true Texan. In politics, she is both gracious and shrewd. She called conservative former senator John Ashcroft to congratulate him on becoming attorney general. And she once took a strong hand in drawing the redistricting map that led to her own election as the first African-American to represent Dallas in the House.

Johnson is a trailblazer for women and blacks who cares passionately about minority rights and advancement opportunities. She is often ready to compromise across the aisle and to reach out to business interests to advance her liberal policy goals. Republican Speaker J. Dennis Hastert says he likes her personally though they have little in common politically.

In 2001, Johnson sponsored a bill to create a biotechnology research grant program to help remedy chronic malnutrition in Africa. At the same time, Republican Nick Smith of Michigan was pushing an unrelated bill, supported by large agribusiness firms, to put more federal money into the development of genetically modified crops. Johnson joined her legislation with Smith's, and the hybrid won easy adoption in the Science Committee.

Johnson hopes part of her legacy in Congress will be to have steered the liberal Congressional Black Caucus, which she chaired in the 107th Congress, to build effective coalitions with business groups rather than relying exclusively on its traditional allies in labor, the clergy and civil rights organizations. It was Johnson's idea for the Black Caucus to hold its first technology and energy summits. Those summits speak directly to Johnson's longstanding vision that bridging the digital divide in poor communities and encouraging minority students to study the hard sciences are two important ways to help black Americans achieve true equality.

A former small-business owner herself, Johnson has cast some pro-business votes in recent years. Breaking ranks with organized labor, she supported legislation in 2000 granting China permanent normal trade status. She said, "Trade with China means jobs for North Texas, growth for Dallas-Fort Worth and the export of American values to the world's most populous nation." But in the 107th, she opposed fast-track legislation, opposed by labor, that called for expedited congressional action — without amendment — on international trade agreements.

Johnson came to the defense of Microsoft Corp. in 2000 as the company was battling a government antitrust plan to split it in two. "Instead of focusing on bringing down [Microsoft founder] Bill Gates, we need to invest in resources to create more Bill Gateses," she said. Microsoft has been a supporter of Johnson's causes. Gates has donated vast sums for minority scholarships and Microsoft has contributed to the Congressional Black Caucus Foundation.

On social policy issues such as abortion rights, welfare and health care, Johnson has both feet planted on the left. After being kissed on the cheek by presidential candidate and fellow Texan George W. Bush at a chance airport encounter, she gave the NAACP this version of the encounter. "You know I can't support you," she said she told Bush. He replied, "I understand. You're a Democrat." Johnson rebutted, "That's not why. It's because of your policies."

Johnson, a nurse by training, has spoken out on shortcomings in Medicare and in the nation's health care system. She joined several women in Congress in sponsoring a bill calling for more research funding for osteoporosis, a bone density deficiency that chiefly affects older women. On the

Science Committee, she has lobbied for a federal grant program to encourage children to study math and science.

Johnson has yet to make it to a top House committee, though she has made known her interest in serving on the Ways and Means Committee. But she uses her assignments on the Transportation and Infrastructure panel and the Science Committee to fight for projects important to her district. On Science, she is the top Democrat on the Research Subcommittee.

In the 107th, she was an outspoken foe of proposals to permit airline pilots to carry guns. She has helped bring federal dollars to the Dallas-Fort Worth Airport. To promote jobs at a Northrop Grumman plant in her district, she supported production of additional B-2 stealth bombers, a stand that put her at odds with fellow liberals in the Black Caucus. The plant employs roughly 6,000 people in the 30th District.

Johnson grew up attending a segregated school in Waco. Her father insisted that she go on to college, and she earned advanced degrees in nursing. Johnson rose to be chief psychiatric nurse at the Veterans Administration Hospital in Dallas.

She won her first state House election in 1972, serving as a legislator until she resigned in 1977 to work as regional director for the Department of Health, Education and Welfare in the Carter administration. She then turned to private business, setting up Eddie Bernice Johnson and Associates, which helped businesses expand or relocate in the Dallas-Fort Worth area. She continued to operate the business after her 1986 election to the state Senate, and she expanded it in 1988 to include airport concessions management. She became so adept at wielding power in the state legislature that she moved up to the U.S. House in 1992 by drawing a district preordained to elect her.

That first House campaign brought some unwanted attention, however. She was fined $44,000 by the Federal Election Commission for failing to file timely and accurate disclosure statements. And her top aide quit, alleging that Johnson required the staff to perform personal errands and engage in campaign activities during office hours.

Johnson generally has won re-election with ease. Initially, her electoral fate was caught up in the judicial and legislative wrangling over minority-majority House districts, including the 30th. After the U.S. Supreme Court threw out certain House districts in Texas as "racial gerrymanders" in 1996, Johnson landed in a substantially redrawn district that was 42 percent new to her. But she captured a 55 percent majority in an eight-person contest and her last three wins have been by huge margins.

KEY VOTES

2002

- Yes Overhaul campaign finance law; ban "soft money" and restrict advocacy advertising
- Yes Back Bush's defense budget increase
- No Extend 1996 welfare law
- No Adopt Bush's discretionary spending limit
- No Pass GOP Medicare prescription drug plan
- Yes Create independent Sept. 11 commission
- Yes Extend union protections to Homeland Security Department employees
- No Revive fast-track procedures for trade agreements
- No Authorize war against Iraq
- Yes Advance bankruptcy overhaul opposed by abortion opponents

2001

- No Nullify Clinton Labor Department ergonomics rule
- No Cut taxes by $1.35 trillion through fiscal 2011
- Yes Maintain ban on oil drilling in Arctic National Wildlife Refuge
- No Approve Bush proposal to limit managed-care plan liability for coverage decisions
- Yes Divert money from crop subsidy payments to land conservation
- No Expand law enforcement power to investigate suspected terrorists

CQ VOTE STUDIES

	PARTY UNITY		PRESIDENTIAL SUPPORT	
	Support	Oppose	Support	Oppose
2002	95%	5%	22%	78%
2001	88%	12%	26%	74%
2000	95%	5%	88%	12%
1999	93%	7%	81%	19%
1998	93%	7%	86%	14%

INTEREST GROUPS

	AFL-CIO	ADA	CCUS	ACU
2002	89%	95%	45%	0%
2001	100%	95%	48%	4%
2000	88%	75%	57%	9%
1999	78%	90%	36%	0%
1998	89%	90%	47%	4%

TEXAS 30

Downtown Dallas; part of Irving

Confined to Dallas County, the 30th stretches from the Dallas-Fort Worth International Airport southeast through Irving and into downtown Dallas. It then dips south to take in some suburbs, such as Lancaster, where many African-American families have relocated after leaving the city.

When the district was drawn after the 1990 census, blacks made up 50 percent of the 30th's constituency. Now they account for just 41 percent, but the district is still largely minority, as 31 percent of residents are Hispanic. There has been a rise in Asian and Indian populations because of corporate expansions. As the population grows, road congestion and air pollution have become concerns. Leaders hope a recent expansion of the city's light rail system into the suburbs will alleviate some of the problems.

Once a quiet suburb, Irving boomed in the 1980s and 1990s. The massive Exxon Mobil Corp. made its corporate home in Irving in late 1999 (in the neighboring 32nd), and the city has been growing fast enough that officials decided in 1999 to overturn Irving's more than 20-year refusal of public housing money, which had been based on concerns over what federal strings would accompany the funds. Many residents make their living in the aviation industry. The district includes Love Field Airport and shares DFW airport, one of the nation's busiest, with the 26th and 32nd.

The 30th is overwhelmingly Democratic. In the 2002 election, it gave 74 percent of its vote to Democratic Senate nominee Ron Kirk, a former Dallas mayor, and 71 percent to Democratic gubernatorial nominee Tony Sanchez. Democrats run strongly in the heavily black precincts just south of Illinois Avenue, and in largely Hispanic precincts near Love Field, giving the party a big edge in a district where the only significant Republican vote is in Irving.

MAJOR INDUSTRY

Banking, technology, transportation

CITIES

Dallas (pt.), 386,837; Irving (pt.), 165,467; DeSoto, 37,646

NOTABLE

Dealey Plaza and the Texas School Book Depository, where President John F. Kennedy was assassinated in 1963; The Texas State Fair attracts 3 million people and features Big Tex — a 52-foot-tall talking cowboy; Texas Stadium in Irving is home to the NFL's Dallas Cowboys.

Rep. John Carter (R)

Elected 2002; 1st term

Carter arrived in Congress at age 61 and after two decades as an elected state district court judge, making him one of the oldest freshmen and one of the more seasoned members of the Republican Class of 2002.

This likely helped Carter get appointments to two groups of GOP insiders: the Policy Committee, which develops GOP legislative policies, and the Steering Committee, which assigns committee seats. As the freshman class representative to that panel, Carter earned political chits with many of his colleagues by helping them obtain their preferred assignments.

His own assignments fit with his background and his district's needs. He can make obvious use of his judicial expertise on the Judiciary Committee. And from a spot on the Education and the Workforce panel, he can address the needs of Texas A & M University, which is seeking to position itself as a key resource for federal homeland security programs. He also took a seat on Government Reform.

Carter holds solidly conservative economic and social views — a virtual requirement for success among his mostly suburban and rural constituents. But he has promised to keep an open mind. "I have spent 20 years listening to both sides of every question, and I think that's really good training for someone who wants to go to Congress," he said.

While he was a trial court judge north of Austin, Carter established the Central Texas Treatment Center for substance abusers. He also helped found the Williamson County Juvenile Academy, which he calls a "quasi-military boot camp and alternative education program."

The 31st District was one of the two new seats that Texas gained in reapportionment following the 2000 census, and it was configured by the GOP-controlled state legislature to guarantee the election of a Republican. Carter finished second in an eight-person field in the GOP primary behind Houston oil executive Peter Wareing, but in their runoff election he prevailed with 57 percent of the vote. Carter won 69 percent in November against Democratic computer consultant David Bagley.

CAPITOL OFFICE
225-3864
www.house.gov/carter
408 Cannon 20515-4331; fax 225-5886

COMMITTEES
Education & Workforce
Government Reform
Judiciary

HOMETOWN
Round Rock

BORN
Nov. 6, 1941, Houston, Texas

RELIGION
Lutheran

FAMILY
Wife, Erika Carter; four children

EDUCATION
Texas Tech U., B.A. 1964 (history); U. of Texas, J.D. 1969

CAREER
Lawyer; state legislative aide

POLITICAL HIGHLIGHTS
Candidate for Texas House, 1980; Texas District Court judge, 1981-2001

ELECTION RESULTS

2002 GENERAL

John Carter (R)	111,556	69.1%
David Bagley (D)	44,183	27.4%
Clark Simmons (LIBERT)	2,037	1.3%
John S. Petersen (GREEN)	1,992	1.2%
R.C. Crawford (I)	1,716	1.1%

2002 PRIMARY RUNOFF

John Carter (R)	13,150	56.8%
Peter Wareing (R)	9,986	43.2%

2002 PRIMARY

Peter Wareing (R)	12,987	36.9%
John Carter (R)	9,144	26.0%
Brad Barton (R)	5,751	16.4%
C. Patrick Meece (R)	3,653	10.4%
Flynn Adcock (R)	1,117	3.2%
Eric Whitfield (R)	1,014	2.9%
Roy Streckfuss (R)	898	2.6%
Terry S. Ward (R)	600	1.7%

TEXAS 31

East central – Houston and Austin suburbs, College Station, Bryan

The 31st is made up of suburbs and rural areas in a large swath of central Texas extending from Austin to Houston and up to College Station.

In the west, the district takes in part of Williamson County, its largest population base. A bedroom enclave north of Austin, the county is home to many who left the city for a more suburban lifestyle. The district's Harris County portion, in its eastern end, features similar Houston suburbs. Ranches and rural areas dominate in between. To the north, the 31st takes in all of Brazos County, including Bryan and College Station, home of Texas A&M University. These areas all strongly favor Republicans.

The district's portions of Williamson and Harris counties are two of the fastest-growing areas of the state. Dell Computer is based in the town of Round Rock (in Williamson), and Motorola and Hewlett-Packard have plants in the 31st. Texas A&M — including the George Bush Presidential Library — also is a major employer. Unlike the more liberal University of Texas at Austin, Texas A&M has a conservative agricultural and military tradition that complements local values such as free-market economics and pro-defense sentiments. As a result, the 31st has given Republicans some of their largest margins in the state at every level.

Two of the district's rural counties, Lee and Burleson, lean Democratic but are sparsely populated.

MAJOR INDUSTRY
Technology, agriculture, education

CITIES
College Station, 67,890; Bryan, 65,660; Round Rock (pt.), 60,060; Cedar Park (pt.), 25,508

NOTABLE
Blue Bell Creameries, maker of Texas' most famous ice cream, is in Brenham; Former baseball pitcher Nolan Ryan owns the Round Rock Express, a minor-league team of the Houston Astros.

Rep. Pete Sessions (R)

CAPITOL OFFICE
225-2231
petes@mail.house.gov
www.house.gov/sessions
1318 Longworth 20515-4332; fax 225-5878

COMMITTEES
Rules
Select Homeland Security

HOMETOWN
Dallas

BORN
March 22, 1955, Waco, Texas

RELIGION
United Methodist

FAMILY
Wife, Nete Sessions; two children

EDUCATION
Southwestern U., B.S. 1978 (political science)

CAREER
Public policy analyst; phone company executive

POLITICAL HIGHLIGHTS
Sought Republican nomination for U.S. House (special election), 1991; Republican nominee for U.S. House, 1994

ELECTION RESULTS

2002 GENERAL		
Pete Sessions (R)	100,226	67.8%
Pauline K. Dixon (D)	44,886	30.4%
Steve Martin (LIBERT)	1,582	1.1%
2002 PRIMARY		
Pete Sessions (R)	19,973	93.5%
Danny Davis (R)	1,391	6.5%
2000 GENERAL		
Pete Sessions (R)	100,487	54.0%
Regina Montoya Coggins (D)	82,629	44.4%
Ken Ashby (LIBERT)	2,842	1.5%

PREVIOUS WINNING PERCENTAGES
1998 (56%); 1996 (53%)

Elected 1996; 4th term

A stalwart conservative who is in tune with his fellow Texan in the White House and the House GOP leadership, Sessions' loyalties have served him well, winning him a coveted assignment to the Rules Committee in his second term and a post on the Homeland Security Committee in his third.

Given Sessions' partisan reliability — his votes in the 107th Congress showed him to be the fourth-most-loyal House Republican — his decision in 2002 to abandon his 5th District seat and run instead in the state's new 32nd District upset party colleagues. Some Republican political strategists complained that the congressman was putting his personal desires ahead of the party's political interests.

The 32nd, in northwest Dallas County, is solidly Republican while the 5th District, which stretches almost 150 miles south of Dallas, only leans in the GOP direction. Republicans were worried that Sessions' move might give Democrats an opening to take the 5th. But Sessions said the 32nd's more compact nature would require less campaign travel, which he viewed as important to his family life. He also said that his decision never really put the 5th in jeopardy.

But many top Republicans leaders, including Sen. Phil Gramm of Texas, urged Sessions to stay put. "When the interests of Pete Sessions and the Republican Party come into conflict, the interests of Pete Sessions win out," complained Danny Davis, a former aide to Texas Republican Sen. Kay Bailey Hutchison. Davis ran against Sessions in the 32nd's GOP primary, but it was no contest: Sessions got more than 93 percent of the vote. In November, he cruised to victory with 68 percent. And, in the 5th District, businessman Jeb Hensarling retained the seat for the GOP with 58 percent.

A son of William F. Sessions, a former federal judge and FBI director, Sessions usually displays partisan tendencies, but he has been known to reach across the aisle to work on such issues as education and health care for disadvantaged and special-needs children and domestic violence.

A vocal supporter of his party's tax-cutting efforts, Sessions in 2000 took over the leadership of the annual House debate over a constitutional amendment to require two-thirds majorities in Congress to raise taxes. "If a tax increase were truly a good idea, certainly two-thirds of the Congress could agree on it," he said.

The proposed constitutional change, which the GOP has brought to the floor every year since the party took control of the House in 1995, is usually championed by Sessions' Texas colleague, Joe L. Barton. But GOP leaders hoped that Sessions, with his seat on the Rules Committee, could somehow steer the debate on the issue and pull in extra votes, and they gave Sessions the lead role. The strategy may have worked, to a very minor degree, but the amendment has never come close to House passage.

Sessions belongs to the Immigration Reform Caucus, a group of about five dozen lawmakers who want to make it more difficult to enter and remain in the country illegally and to impose a temporary moratorium on new immigration. During the 107th, Sessions and his allies linked tighter immigration controls with the nation's war against terrorism after the Sept. 11, 2001, attacks. Sessions backed legislation to increase U.S. border patrols and tighten tracking of foreigners. But he cast one of only nine "no" votes on the aviation security law enacted soon after the terrorist attacks. He said he objected to the federalization of airport security personnel.

Sessions has a prominent role in the House Results Caucus, a group whose motto is: "Give the government the money it needs, but not a penny more." The caucus aims to make the federal government more efficient. Sessions is interested in "outsourcing" some government functions to take advantage of possibly lower costs and private-sector innovation.

On trade matters, Sessions generally backs a free-trade approach, including long support for fast-track authority for the president to negotiate trade agreements that Congress cannot amend. In 2000, he supported permanent normal trade status for China. But Sessions says that his support of expanded trade does not extend to situations in which the United States is at an unfair disadvantage. He has expressed concern that the 1993 North American Free Trade Agreement and the 1994 General Agreement on Tariffs and Trade created an "uneven playing field" for Americans. He has said, however, that "people who are anti-NAFTA are many times isolationists. I am not an isolationist."

As the father of a boy with Down syndrome, Sessions has joined with liberal Democratic Rep. Henry A. Waxman of California in an effort to help families care for children with special needs. They sponsored legislation in both the 106th and 107th Congresses to provide families of disabled children with the opportunity to purchase Medicaid coverage for the child. "I know first-hand why families with disabled children are turning down jobs, turning down overtime and are unable to earn enough money to adequately provide for their family — just so their child can qualify for Medicaid," Sessions said. He dedicated the legislation to one such family in his district.

Born in Waco and educated at Southwestern University in Georgetown, Texas, Sessions went to work after college at Southwestern Bell Telephone Co. and Bell Communications Research.

It took him three tries to get to Congress. His first campaign was in 1991, when he entered the special-election contest to succeed Steve Bartlett, who resigned to run for mayor of Dallas. Sessions finished sixth.

In 1994, after leaving his job at Bell, Sessions ran in the 5th District and took 47 percent against incumbent Democrat John Bryant. After his defeat, he was vice president for public policy at the National Center for Policy Analysis, a Dallas-based conservative think tank.

Redistricting ordered by the federal courts gave the 5th District a slightly more Republican tilt by 1996. With Bryant running for the Senate, Sessions won the seat with 53 percent against John Pouland, a former Dallas County Democratic chairman. Democrats in both 1998 and 2000 thought they had a decent chance to unseat Sessions, but he prevailed by 12 and 10 percentage points.

KEY VOTES

2002

No Overhaul campaign finance law; ban "soft money" and restrict advocacy advertising
Yes Back Bush's defense budget increase
Yes Extend 1996 welfare law
Yes Adopt Bush's discretionary spending limit
Yes Pass GOP Medicare prescription drug plan
No Create independent Sept. 11 commission
No Extend union protections to Homeland Security Department employees
Yes Revive fast-track procedures for trade agreements
Yes Authorize war against Iraq
Yes Advance bankruptcy overhaul opposed by abortion opponents

2001

Yes Nullify Clinton Labor Department ergonomics rule
Yes Cut taxes by $1.35 trillion through fiscal 2011
No Maintain ban on oil drilling in Arctic National Wildlife Refuge
Yes Approve Bush proposal to limit managed-care plan liability for coverage decisions
No Divert money from crop subsidy payments to land conservation
Yes Expand law enforcement power to investigate suspected terrorists

CQ VOTE STUDIES

	PARTY UNITY		PRESIDENTIAL SUPPORT	
	Support	Oppose	Support	Oppose
2002	99%	1%	87%	13%
2001	99%	1%	91%	9%
2000	98%	2%	26%	74%
1999	96%	4%	21%	79%
1998	97%	3%	20%	80%

INTEREST GROUPS

	AFL-CIO	ADA	CCUS	ACU
2002	13%	0%	100%	100%
2001	9%	0%	96%	100%
2000	0%	0%	76%	96%
1999	11%	5%	84%	96%
1998	0%	0%	89%	100%

TEXAS 32
Northwest Dallas County

Though it does not include downtown Dallas, the 32nd is home to much of the Dallas business community. Many who work downtown live here, and several Fortune 500 companies are located off the Lyndon B. Johnson Freeway, which encircles the city.

The 32nd is located in the northwest corner of Dallas County, which contains a northern chunk of the city of Dallas and some of the city's north and west suburbs. The district begins on the edge of downtown, a growing haven for younger workers living in luxury apartments along McKinney Avenue. Nearby is Oak Lawn, home to much of the city's gay community. The district then moves north to take in the exclusive "Park Cities," made up of the cities of Highland Park and University Park. The Park Cities area, which is almost entirely white, has its own school system and local government. The 32nd continues north to the county line, through less exclusive but equally wealthy neighborhoods. Some middle-class neighborhoods exist in the northern part of the district along the L.B.J. Freeway.

The city's "telecom corridor" is in the north part of Dallas, where Texas Instruments is the standard bearer. ExxonMobil is in the 32nd, based in Irving (shared with the 30th), along with other oil companies.

Transportation issues are important to residents, as several highways run through the district, which also takes in a small portion of Dallas-Fort Worth International Airport. Many employees of DFW and Dallas Love Field airport — which borders the district — live here.

The 32nd is solidly Republican. George W. Bush took 65 percent of the district's two-party vote in 2000, and Republicans running statewide routinely garner more than 60 percent here. The GOP is particularly strong in precincts around University Park and Southern Methodist University, while Democrats do well in the far southern reaches of the district near downtown Dallas.

MAJOR INDUSTRY
Telecommunications, oil, retail

CITIES
Dallas (pt.), 406,696; Carrollton (pt.), 49,822; Richardson (pt.), 44,455

NOTABLE
Ross Perot lives in the 32nd; The Dallas Theater Center is located here.

UTAH

Gov. Michael O. Leavitt (R)

First elected: 1992
Length of term: 4 years
Term expires: 1/05
Salary: $100,600
Phone: (801) 538-1000
Hometown: Cedar City
Born: Feb. 11, 1951; Cedar City, Utah
Religion: Mormon
Family: Wife, Jacalyn S. Leavitt; five children
Education: Southern Utah U., B.A. 1978 (business & economics)
Military Service: Utah National Guard, 1969-75
Career: Insurance executive
Political highlights: Utah Board of Regents, 1989-92
Election results:

2000 GENERAL		
Michael O. Leavitt (R)	424,837	55.8%
Bill Orton (D)	321,979	42.3%
Jeremy Friedbaum (IA)	14,990	2.0%

Lt. Gov. Olene S. Walker (R)

First elected: 1992
Length of term: 4 years
Term expires: 1/05
Salary: $75,200
Phone: (801) 538-1040

STATE LEGISLATURE

Legislature: Meets 45 days yearly, January-March
House: 75 members, 2-year terms
2003 breakdown: 56R, 19D; 58 men, 17 women
Salary: $120/day in session
Phone: (801) 538-1029
Senate: 29 members, 4-year terms
2003 breakdown: 22R, 7R; 25 men, 4 women
Salary: $120/day in session
Phone: (801) 538-1035

STATE TERM LIMITS

Governor: 3 consecutive terms (beginning with the 1996 election; Leavitt can run in 2004)
Senate: 3 terms
House: 6 terms

URBAN STATISTICS

CITY	POPULATION
Salt Lake City	181,743
West Valley City	108,896
Provo	105,166
Sandy	88,418
Orem	84,324

REGISTERED VOTERS

Registration by party began in May 1999 but not all voters have declared an affiliation.

POPULATION

2002 population (est.)	2,316,256
2000 population	2,233,169
1990 population	1,722,850
Percent change (1990-2000)	+29.6%
Rank among states (2002)	34
Median age	27.1
Born in state	62.9%
Foreign born	7.1%
Violent crime rate	256/100,000
Poverty level	9.4%
Federal workers	32,961
Military	16,621

REDISTRICTING

Utah retained its three House seats in reapportionment. The state legislature drew a new map, which the governor signed on Oct. 11, 2001.

MISCELLANEOUS

Web: www.state.ut.us
Capital: Salt Lake City
STATE ELECTION OFFICIAL
(801) 538-1041
DEMOCRATIC HEADQUARTERS
(801) 328-1212
REPUBLICAN HEADQUARTERS
(801) 533-9777

District Statistics

	2000 VOTE FOR PRESIDENT															
DIST.	BUSH	GORE	NADER	WHITE	BLACK	ASIAN	HISP	MEDIAN INCOME	WHITE COLLAR	BLUE COLLAR	SERVICE INDUSTRY	OVER 64	UNDER 18	COLLEGE EDUCATION	RURAL	SQ. MILES
1	67%	27%	5%	83%	1%	2%	11%	$45,058	59%	27%	14%	9%	32%	25%	11%	20,768
2	63	29	6	88	1	2	6	$45,583	66	21	14	11	30	31	15	45,624
3	72	23	3	85	0	2	10	$46,568	60	27	14	6	35	22	9	15,751
STATE	67	26	5	85	1	2	9	$45,726	61	25	14	9	32	26	12	82,144
U.S.	47.9	48.4	3	69	12	4	13	$41,994	60	25	15	12	26	24	21	3,537,438

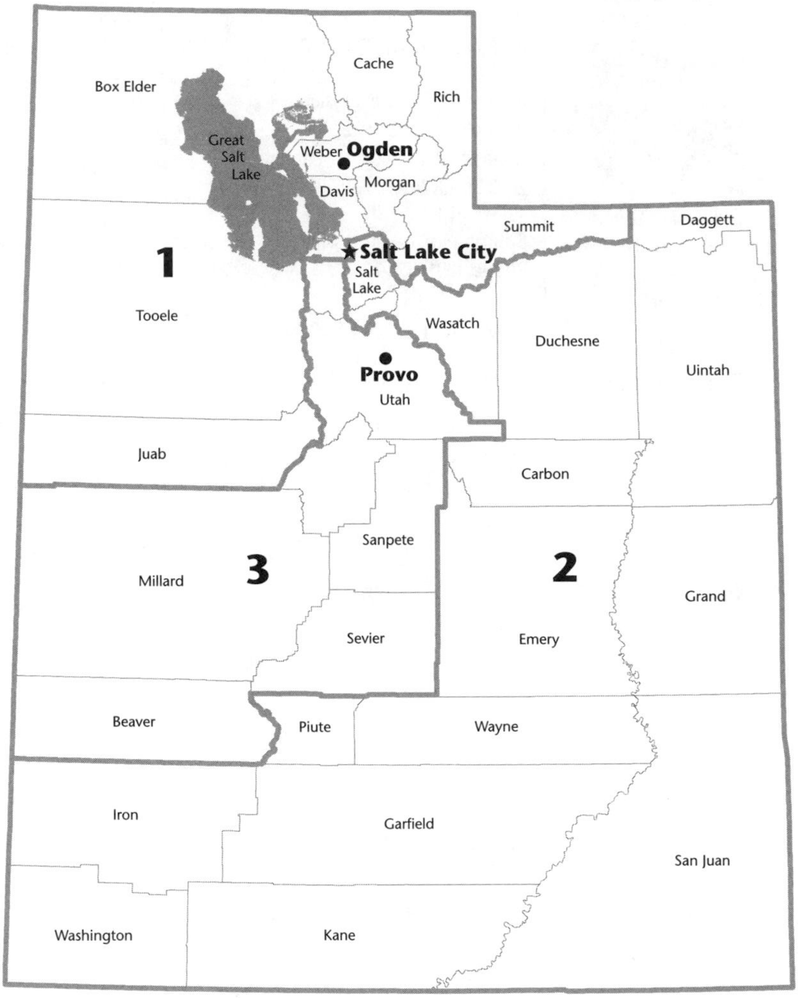
Box Elder
Cache
Rich
Great Salt Lake
Weber
Ogden
Davis
Morgan
Summit
Daggett
Salt Lake City
Salt Lake
1
Tooele
Wasatch
Duchesne
Uintah
Provo
Utah
Juab
Carbon
Sanpete
Millard
3
2
Grand
Sevier
Emery
Beaver
Piute
Wayne
Iron
Garfield
San Juan
Washington
Kane

Sen. Orrin G. Hatch (R)

CAPITOL OFFICE
224-5251
senator_hatch@hatch.senate.gov
hatch.senate.gov
104 Hart 20510-4402; fax 224-6331

COMMITTEES
Finance
Indian Affairs
Judiciary - chairman
Select Intelligence
Special Aging
Joint Taxation

HOMETOWN
Salt Lake City

BORN
March 22, 1934, Pittsburgh, Pa.

RELIGION
Mormon

FAMILY
Wife, Elaine Hatch; six children

EDUCATION
Brigham Young U., B.S. 1959 (history); U. of Pittsburgh, J.D. 1962

CAREER
Lawyer

POLITICAL HIGHLIGHTS
Sought Republican nomination for president, 2000

ELECTION RESULTS

2000 GENERAL		
Orrin G. Hatch (R)	504,803	65.6%
Scott N. Howell (D)	242,569	31.5%
Carlton Edward Bowen (AMI)	11,938	1.6%
Jim Dexter (LIBERT)	10,394	1.4%
2000 PRIMARY		
Orrin G. Hatch (R)		unopposed

PREVIOUS WINNING PERCENTAGES
1994 (69%); 1988 (67%); 1982 (58%); 1976 (54%)

Elected 1976; 5th term

His high-collared shirts and near-perfect voting record on issues tracked by conservative groups give Hatch the outward appearance of a starchy ideologue. But Hatch harbors a soft spot, albeit a small one, for liberals and their causes. He has an unlikely longstanding friendship with the Senate's leading liberal, Edward M. Kennedy of Massachusetts. And he sometimes joins Democrats in support of federal judicial nominees and of social programs that meet his expectations.

Hatch is confounding to many conservatives, who do not like his record on judgeships and do not understand his relationship with Kennedy. The two senators, who often take opposing positions on the Judiciary Committee, regularly exchange heated words on the floor. During a debate in 2003, Kennedy told his friend, "You may bully some, but you're not going to bully me." But the senators also team up on bills, such as one that provided health care to poor children. Kennedy once crossed the Senate aisle to give Hatch a hug. The title of Hatch's autobiography sums up his political nonconformity. It's called "Square Peg."

Hatch's role as chairman of the committee puts him in the middle of some of Congress' most controversial issues, including tort reform, the expansion of law enforcement's powers to fight terrorism and the human cloning debate. He also has the tough task of shepherding President Bush's judicial nominees, a highly partisan undertaking.

Democrats, angry at Hatch and other conservatives for blocking judicial appointments during President Clinton's two terms, are eager to retaliate now that a Republican president is in the White House. Hatch has pushed for confirmation of some of Bush's most controversial picks, just as in the past he supported conservatives Robert Bork and Clarence Thomas for Supreme Court appointments in the face of a torrent of criticism from the left. Hatch himself is sometimes mentioned as a possible candidate for a future opening on the nation's highest court.

Conservatives, similarly, take issue with Hatch on judicial and other matters. During the Clinton administration, Republicans griped that he allowed too many liberals to be confirmed for seats on federal district and appeals courts. Hatch often lectured from the committee dais about the need for an independent judiciary that included both liberal and conservative thinkers. In 1997, Republican hard-liners tried but failed to strip him of his power in judicial nominations.

The party's right wing also finds fault with Hatch's tendency to join with Democrats on issues of intense personal importance to him. After the Sept. 11, 2001, terrorist attacks on New York City and Washington, the Judiciary Committee came under heavy pressure from the administration to rapidly approve a major expansion of law enforcement's investigative powers, raising concerns about possible encroachments on civil liberties. While the White House negotiated with then Chairman Patrick J. Leahy, a liberal Democrat from Vermont, Hatch, worried that the talks would break down, quietly conducted parallel discussions with Leahy. He also courted support among Democrats Joseph R. Biden Jr. of Delaware, Dianne Feinstein of California and Charles E. Schumer of New York.

"This way, if the negotiations with Leahy broke down, we would still have a compromise acceptable to a majority on the committee," Hatch said in his autobiography. The bill, dubbed the USA Patriot Act, passed the Senate overwhelmingly; it became law in 2001.

Hatch is more willing than many GOP conservatives to support government programs for the poor, an outlook rooted in his childhood and in his Mormon faith, which urges members to help the disadvantaged.

He was born in Pittsburgh, the son of a metal lather. The family lost their home during the Depression, so Hatch's father built another one of lumber retrieved from a fire. Hatch remembers that a dairy sign constituted one wall of the house. He worked his way through school, variously toiling as a janitor, an all-night desk clerk in a girls' dormitory and a metal lather like his father. As a lather, he joined the AFL-CIO union.

Hatch has supported federal programs to immunize children, offer job training and give workers time off for family and medical reasons. A 1997 partnership with Kennedy produced a bill to provide insurance to children whose low-income parents do not qualify for Medicaid. It was financed with a 43-cents-a-pack cigarette tax increase.

Conservatives question whether Hatch is too quick to strike deals on their cherished issues. In response, Hatch told the National Review in 1997 that he does not harbor ill will toward people on the opposing side of issues. He said, "One of my biggest failings is that . . . I can't hold a grudge. I can't stay mad."

Hatch's political philosophy is influenced by his membership in the Church of Jesus Christ of Latter-day Saints, the Mormon religion that dominates in Utah and prohibits the consumption of alcohol, tobacco and caffeine. It also encourages large families.

Hatch is a staunch opponent of abortion, though in 2002 he supported a bill allowing human cloning for medical research. Most anti-abortion groups oppose cloning even for research, and Hatch was assailed by leading groups such as the Family Research Council.

In spite of the heat he takes from the right, Hatch is probably still best known for his role in the 1991 hearings into law professor Anita Hill's sexual harassment allegations against conservative Supreme Court nominee Clarence Thomas. Hatch argued against reopening hearings on Thomas even after Hill's accusation against him surfaced. He and Arlen Specter of Pennsylvania led the hard-hitting Republican assault on Hill during the hearings, which were nationally televised.

Few people outside of Capitol Hill would guess that the straight-laced Hatch is also a songwriter whose work has been performed by Gladys Knight, the pop singer who belongs to the Mormon church. He has produced several discs of religious, romantic and patriotic songs. He dedicated a love song to Kennedy and his second wife, Victoria, on their fifth wedding anniversary, and he is often spotted scribbling song lyrics between Senate votes.

In 1999, Hatch launched a quixotic bid for president. Lacking money and broad political support, he finished last in Iowa's GOP caucuses. He dropped out of the race the next week and endorsed Bush, later mending bridges with the new administration by guiding Bush nominee John Ashcroft, a Missouri conservative Republican, through a difficult confirmation as attorney general.

Hatch's first Senate campaign in 1976 was a textbook example of anti-Washington politics. His total lack of government experience was an asset. In his legal practice, he had represented clients fighting federal regulations, and he made Washington's burdensome rulemaking a campaign theme. He won the GOP nomination over Jack W. Carlson, a former assistant secretary of interior, and then defeated incumbent Democrat Frank E. Moss with 54 percent.

He was re-elected in 1982 with 58 percent of the vote in spite of a serious challenge from two-term Salt Lake City Mayor Ted Wilson. In 1988, he defeated Brian Moss, the son of the senator he had ousted, by a 2-to-1 ratio, and his last two re-elections have been by similarly impressive margins.

KEY VOTES

2002

- No Pass farm bill reversing crop subsidy limits
- Yes Postpone tougher automobile fuel efficiency standards
- No Overhaul campaign finance law; ban "soft money" and restrict advocacy advertising
- Yes Set federal election standards
- Yes Support oil drilling in Arctic National Wildlife Refuge
- Yes Revive fast-track procedures for trade agreements
- Yes Create federal insurance coverage for catastrophic terrorist losses
- Yes Tighten federal accounting and corporate governance regulation
- No Advance bipartisan Medicare prescription drug plan
- Yes Create independent Sept. 11 commission
- No Back Democratic Homeland Security Department proposal
- Yes Authorize war against Iraq

2001

- Yes Confirm John Ashcroft as attorney general
- Yes Nullify Clinton Labor Department ergonomics rule
- Yes Cut taxes by $1.35 trillion through fiscal 2011
- No Pass Democratic bill to bolster rights of patients in managed-care plans
- No Permit a new round of military base closings
- Yes Expand law enforcement power to investigate suspected terrorists

CQ VOTE STUDIES

	PARTY UNITY		PRESIDENTIAL SUPPORT	
	Support	Oppose	Support	Oppose
2002	93%	7%	98%	2%
2001	95%	5%	97%	3%
2000	94%	6%	55%	45%
1999	92%	8%	30%	70%
1998	87%	13%	48%	52%
1997	87%	13%	63%	37%
1996	94%	6%	32%	68%
1995	95%	5%	27%	73%
1994	95%	5%	37%	63%
1993	96%	4%	28%	72%

INTEREST GROUPS

	AFL-CIO	ADA	CCUS	ACU
2002	23%	5%	100%	95%
2001	6%	5%	86%	96%
2000	0%	0%	100%	95%
1999	11%	0%	88%	84%
1998	0%	5%	94%	80%
1997	0%	15%	100%	68%
1996	0%	5%	92%	100%
1995	0%	0%	100%	83%
1994	0%	5%	90%	100%
1993	0%	5%	100%	88%

Sen. Robert F. Bennett (R)

CAPITOL OFFICE
224-5444
bennett.senate.gov
431 Dirksen 20510-4403; fax 228-1168

COMMITTEES
Appropriations
(Agriculture, Rural Development & Related Agencies - chairman)
Banking, Housing & Urban Affairs
(Financial Institutions - chairman)
Governmental Affairs
Small Business & Entrepreneurship
Joint Economic - chairman

HOMETOWN
Salt Lake City

BORN
Sept. 18, 1933, Salt Lake City, Utah

RELIGION
Mormon

FAMILY
Wife, Joyce Bennett; six children

EDUCATION
U. of Utah, B.S. 1957 (political science)

MILITARY SERVICE
Utah National Guard, 1957-60

CAREER
Time management company CEO; management consultant; public relations and marketing executive; congressional aide

POLITICAL HIGHLIGHTS
No previous office

ELECTION RESULTS

1998 GENERAL		
Robert F. Bennett (R)	316,652	64.0%
Scott Leckman (D)	163,172	33.0%
Gary R. Van Horn (IA)	15,073	3.0%
1998 PRIMARY		
Robert F. Bennett (R)		unopposed

PREVIOUS WINNING PERCENTAGES
1992 (55%)

Elected 1992; 2nd term

Bennett's ascension in the Senate hierarchy had slowed with the departure of his friend Bob Dole in 1996, but it resumed in the 108th Congress with his appointment as chief deputy Republican whip, a mostly behind-the-scenes job to which a trusted party loyalist is generally assigned.

He is a good fit for the role of adviser to the leadership. Steady and thoughtful, he is a deliberate speaker who measures his words carefully, often using homespun humor to get his point across. And his manner is reserved and quiet, not that of a backslapping politician.

Bennett was particularly close to Dole, who was the GOP floor leader during Bennett's early days in the Senate. When Dole's bid for the Republican presidential nomination was stumbling in early 1996, Bennett was one of the trusted advisers traveling the campaign trail with him. But when Dole left the Senate to devote himself full time to his presidential bid, Bennett failed in the ensuing shuffle to win election by his colleagues to the leadership, as chairman of the Policy Committee.

He remained in the good graces of the two subsequent leaders, however, and they have allowed him to help the party focus on developing its pro-business agenda. Trent Lott named Bennett the founding chairman of the Senate GOP's High Tech Task Force in the 106th Congress; and under Bill Frist in the 108th, Bennett is chairman of the Joint Economic Committee.

Bennett uses the economic panel as a platform to promote pet initiatives, such as a proposal to cut taxes paid by stockholders on corporate dividends. An annual conference in Utah on financial services and technology issues provides another forum for discussing his priorities. "We need to highlight issues," Bennett says. "There's a great ignorance about economics in the country and in Congress as well."

He says a secret to his legislative success is to focus on nonpartisan issues, such as technology and homeland security. "I look for things that are not splashy. If it's something splashy, somebody else will be all over it," he says.

A former time management consultant for business executives, Bennett is a plain-spoken consensus builder who is now the No. 2 Republican on the Banking, Housing and Urban Affairs Committee. Bennett learned about the art of bipartisan compromise from another senator from Utah — his father, Wallace F. Bennett, who served from 1951 through 1974. (The son is taller, but otherwise the two look and act in a remarkably similar manner.)

In the 108th, Bennett is expected to be an occasional rival of Richard C. Shelby of Alabama, Banking's new chairman. With the retirement of Phil Gramm of Texas, Shelby and Bennett will assume higher-profile roles on the committee. Bennett is likely to join GOP leaders in opposing Shelby's consumer-oriented proposals to tighten privacy protection standards and roll back limits on securities fraud lawsuits. Of his battles with Shelby, Bennett says simply, "We agree on lots of things. But he has more of a trial lawyer's perspective than I do."

Bennett employs his soft and measured approach chairing the Legislative Branch Appropriations Subcommittee and as a technology industry champion on the Governmental Affairs Committee. In the 107th, he worked out a compromise on legislation aimed at ensuring the confidentiality of reports that businesses will have to file to the new Department of Homeland Security on the threat of electronic attacks to their computer systems.

Another signature bill of Bennett's was a bipartisan deal he worked out with Connecticut Democrat Christopher J. Dodd on a 1999 law limiting the liability of technology companies for business losses that might have been caused by a computer meltdown at the change of the millennium. Year 2000, or Y2K, computer glitches proved minimal, but the law nonetheless protected companies that made good-faith efforts to warn customers and to fix or replace outdated computers. His chairmanship of a special Senate panel that bird-dogged preparations to deal with potential Y2K problems gave him a leg up on the broader issue of cybersecurity.

Bennett's rangy profile is hard to miss around the Capitol. He often bypasses the elevators to get his exercise on the stairs. His interest in technology is reflected in a penchant for gadgets, such as a gasoline-electric hybrid car that gets more than 60 miles per gallon with low emissions.

Although a solid conservative on regulatory and fiscal issues, Bennett breaks party ranks on occasion. He supports funding for the National Endowment for the Arts, backs efforts to curb tobacco sales to youths and opposes a constitutional amendment to ban desecration of the U.S. flag.

But he is in sync with the GOP line in arguing that too much government regulation would stifle technology companies that are an engine for growth. He joins with other Western Republicans who oppose environmental restrictions on public lands. And he expressed outrage when President Clinton used his executive authority to create national monuments in Utah and other Western states, blocking mining and ranching on those lands.

Although usually amiable, Bennett has engaged in some pointed exchanges with Arizona Republican John McCain. When McCain in 1999 alleged that campaign contributions corrupted the political system, Bennett said McCain had accused him of corruption in seeking federal funds for Utah. "I am unaware of any money given that influenced my action here," he said. "I have been accused of being corrupt. . . . I take personal offense."

On Appropriations, Bennett is adept at looking out for his state. He struck gold in the 105th Congress by winning $640 million for light rail, park-and-ride lots and buses for the 2002 Winter Olympics in Salt Lake City, plus additional funding for security planning. In the 107th, he continued to ensure the flow of federal aid to Utah for the Olympics.

Bennett has a longstanding interest in administrative issues. In 1993, he proposed legislation, which was never acted on, to reorganize congressional committees, adopt a two-year budget cycle and establish congressional task forces to set priorities for legislative action.

Although Bennett's successful 1992 Senate bid at age 59 was his first campaign, he was no political naif. He previously worked in Washington as a White House adviser to President Nixon and worked for his father as an aide and campaign organizer. Bennett was a millionaire businessman — he made his fortune with the Franklin Day Planner, a schedule organizer — when he launched his first electoral bid.

The former student body president at the University of Utah edged past steel company executive Joe Cannon — brother of 3rd District Rep. Christopher B. Cannon — in the GOP primary and faced Democratic Rep. Wayne Owens in the general election. Bennett's connection with the 1972 Watergate break-in became an issue because he had bought a public relations firm that employed E. Howard Hunt, who was indicted in the Watergate burglary. Bennett said he fired Hunt after his actions became known.

Bennett raised $4.5 million and outspent Owens more than 2-to-1 en route to a 15 percentage point victory. Bennett overdid his 1992 fundraising, and in 1996 agreed to pay a $55,000 fine to the Federal Election Commission for what he called "unintentional violations" during the 1992 campaign. In 1998, he raised more than five times as much as the Democrat, surgeon Scott Leckman, and won with 64 percent of the vote.

KEY VOTES

2002

? Pass farm bill reversing crop subsidy limits
Yes Postpone tougher automobile fuel efficiency standards
No Overhaul campaign finance law; ban "soft money" and restrict advocacy advertising
Yes Set federal election standards
Yes Support oil drilling in Arctic National Wildlife Refuge
Yes Revive fast-track procedures for trade agreements
Yes Create federal insurance coverage for catastrophic terrorist losses
Yes Tighten federal accounting and corporate governance regulation
No Advance bipartisan Medicare prescription drug plan
Yes Create independent Sept. 11 commission
No Back Democratic Homeland Security Department proposal
Yes Authorize war against Iraq

2001

Yes Confirm John Ashcroft as attorney general
Yes Nullify Clinton Labor Department ergonomics rule
Yes Cut taxes by $1.35 trillion through fiscal 2011
No Pass Democratic bill to bolster rights of patients in managed-care plans
No Permit a new round of military base closings
Yes Expand law enforcement power to investigate suspected terrorists

CQ VOTE STUDIES

	PARTY UNITY		PRESIDENTIAL SUPPORT	
	Support	Oppose	Support	Oppose
2002	94%	6%	98%	2%
2001	96%	4%	96%	4%
2000	92%	8%	52%	48%
1999	93%	7%	31%	69%
1998	84%	16%	53%	47%
1997	87%	13%	62%	38%
1996	92%	8%	36%	64%
1995	96%	4%	27%	73%
1994	91%	9%	38%	62%
1993	94%	6%	32%	68%

INTEREST GROUPS

	AFL-CIO	ADA	CCUS	ACU
2002	23%	5%	100%	100%
2001	13%	5%	100%	100%
2000	0%	5%	100%	95%
1999	11%	0%	94%	84%
1998	0%	10%	89%	64%
1997	0%	10%	100%	68%
1996	0%	5%	92%	95%
1995	0%	0%	100%	81%
1994	0%	5%	90%	100%
1993	0%	5%	100%	88%

Rep. Rob Bishop (R)

CAPITOL OFFICE
225-0453
www.house.gov/robbishop
124 Cannon 20515-4401; fax 225-5857

COMMITTEES
Armed Services
Resources
Science

HOMETOWN
Kaysville

BORN
July 13, 1951, Salt Lake City, Utah

RELIGION
Mormon

FAMILY
Wife, Jeralynn Bishop; five children

EDUCATION
U. of Utah, B.A. 1974 (political science)

CAREER
High school teacher; lobbyist

POLITICAL HIGHLIGHTS
Utah House, 1979-95 (Speaker, 1993-95); Utah Republican Party chairman, 1997-2001

ELECTION RESULTS

2002 GENERAL		
Rob Bishop (R)	109,265	60.9%
Dave Thomas (D)	66,104	36.9%
Craig Axford (GREEN)	4,027	2.3%
2002 PRIMARY		
Rob Bishop (R)	25,280	59.9%
Kevin S. Garn (R)	16,957	40.2%

Elected 2002; 1st term

A high school teacher for 28 years, Bishop says he will "fight to get the federal government out of the classroom." He says he would have voted against the sweeping education bill that President Bush signed into law, contending that Congress inflated Bush's original package.

He calls himself a "classic conservative," a "fierce" proponent of states' rights and an "ardent" defender of gun owners' rights.

Bishop is low-key and has a dry, self-deprecating sense of humor. When he came to Washington for freshman orientation, he told the Deseret News he didn't want to "pester" leaders by lobbying too hard for committee spots. "I am trying to be a low-maintenance member for them," he said.

Bishop's approach appears to have worked. He received his top choice for a committee assignment, Armed Services, on which he looks out for the interests of Hill Air Force Base — located in Utah's 1st — as well as defense industries that make their home in the district.

He also won sought-after assignments to the Resources panel — which had been chaired by his House predecessor, retired 11-term Republican James V. Hansen — and the Science Committee. He favors "improvement and development of land," saying that "stewardship means respecting and enhancing the land and natural resources; it does not mean locking up the land and throwing away the key."

Bishop's 2002 bid to succeed Hansen was founded on his 16 years of experience in the state legislature, including a stint as speaker during his last two years. He was later the chairman of the Utah Republican Party.

After easily defeating state House Majority Leader Kevin Garn for the Republican nomination, Bishop faced wealthy ad executive Dave Thomas in the general election. Bishop had the advantage in the heavily Republican 1st District and took 61 percent of the vote.

The history teacher says he likes his office in the Cannon Building, noting that Joe Cannon for whom it is named "was a classy and sarcastic Speaker of the House."

UTAH 1

North — part of Salt Lake City, Ogden

In the 1840s, Mormon pioneers journeyed into the mountainous terrain of northern Utah. Today, the 1st retains that Mormon influence. Redistricting following the 2000 census added more than half of Salt Lake City, bringing in most of downtown and Temple Square, which includes the Tabernacle and the headquarters of the Church of Jesus Christ of Latter-day Saints.

Ogden, the 1st's second-largest city, was once a lively railroad town but today looks more toward defense. Hill Air Force Base is one of the state's largest employers. The 1st also contains much of Utah's ski country, including Park City, a wealthy resort town.

Despite the district's overall GOP tilt, many of the added areas in Salt Lake City lean Democratic. George W. Bush received 72 percent of the 2000 vote in the old 1st, but dropped to 67 percent under the new lines. The new 1st combines some of Utah's poorest urban areas with some of its most wealthy, including the heavily populated Davis County, a solidly Republican suburb. Most of the rural areas favor Republicans, though Democrats pick up some votes in Park City and in Weber County — once a center of railroad-related work.

In rural parts of the district, agriculture is king. The aerospace industry also employs many residents. The 2002 Winter Olympics provided an influx of tourism dollars.

MAJOR INDUSTRY
Manufacturing, defense, technology

MILITARY BASES
Hill Air Force Base, 4,800 military, 13,000 civilian; Tooele Army Depot, 300 military, 450 civilian; Deseret Chemical Depot, 318 military, 536 civilian; Dugway Proving Ground, 30 military, 470 civilian (2002)

CITIES
Salt Lake City (pt.), 94,049; Ogden, 77,226; Layton, 58,474; Logan, 42,670

NOTABLE
Great Salt Lake is the world's second-largest saltwater lake; Park City is home to the U.S. Ski and Snowboard Team.

Rep. Jim Matheson (D)

CAPITOL OFFICE
225-3011
www.house.gov/matheson
410 Cannon 20515-4402; fax 225-5638

COMMITTEES
Financial Services
Science
Transportation & Infrastructure

HOMETOWN
Salt Lake City

BORN
March 21, 1960, Salt Lake City, Utah

RELIGION
Mormon

FAMILY
Wife, Amy Matheson; one child

EDUCATION
Harvard U., A.B. 1982 (government); U. of California, Los Angeles, M.B.A. 1987

CAREER
Energy consulting firm owner; energy company project manager; environmental group advocate

POLITICAL HIGHLIGHTS
No previous office

ELECTION RESULTS

2002 GENERAL		
Jim Matheson (D)	110,764	49.4%
John Swallow (R)	109,123	48.7%
Patrick Diehl (GREEN)	2,589	1.2%
2002 PRIMARY		
Jim Matheson (D)		unopposed
2000 GENERAL		
Jim Matheson (D)	145,021	55.9%
Derek W. Smith (R)	107,114	41.3%
Bruce Bangerter (IA)	4,704	1.8%

Elected 2000; 2nd term

The lone Democrat in the congressional delegation of one of the most Republican states in the country, every day of Matheson's tenure comes with the certain knowledge that he is on the short list of electoral targets for GOP political strategists. First elected in 2000 in a district that went for George W. Bush by 23 points, Matheson was re-elected in 2002 by only 1,641 votes after the Republican state legislature redrew his district lines to stack the odds against him even more. It was the fourth-closest House race of 2002.

Matheson says he tries not to dwell on how few Democrats he actually represents, saying he believes his centrist politics and hard work can win over his Republican constituents. During his 2002 campaign, he downplayed his party affiliation, preferring to call himself an "independent voice" and noting that the U.S. Chamber of Commerce endorsed him.

His conservative political views, his personable manner and his well-known name have helped him keep his seat. Matheson is the son of the late Scott M. Matheson, a popular two-term governor from 1977 to 1985.

In the House, Matheson affiliates with the conservative "Blue Dogs," as well as the slightly more centrist New Democrat Coalition. Matheson was named to Blue Dog task forces on both the budget and on energy policy.

Matheson was one of just 28 Democrats who voted in 2001 to enact President Bush's $1.35 trillion tax cut and was also one of only 25 Democrats to back the 2002 law reviving presidential fast-track trade negotiating authority. That same year he was one of just eight Democrats who supported the GOP version of a bill to provide prescription drug coverage for Medicare recipients. He sided with the president 49 percent of the time in the 107th Congress and voted with a majority of his own party 72 percent of the time, ranking him as one of the 25 least-loyal Democrats.

Nevertheless, Matheson has seats on the Financial Services, Science and Transportation committees, all of which are good fits for his district. On Transportation, he has worked to continue funding for Winter Olympics-related highway and transit projects, including a massive overhaul of Interstate 15 and a new light rail commuter line in Salt Lake County. He took the lead in the authorization of a number of pilot projects at airports around the country to test new security technologies that use biometric identifiers, such as retinal scans, photographs, fingerprints, palm prints and voice prints for better identification of travelers.

Matheson won plaudits for his political savvy and pragmatism in his effort to authorize federal money to build a natural history museum at the University of Utah. After his own bill stalled, Matheson recognized that a bill drafted by a Democrat facing a tough re-election battle was unlikely to advance in the GOP-run House. So he approached his Utah colleague, Republican James V. Hansen, chairman of the Resources Committee, and asked Hansen to introduce the measure. The strategy worked, and the museum was authorized.

In another example of bipartisan cooperation, Matheson joined with other Utah lawmakers to win resumption of federal compensation to people who had become ill as a result of exposure to radiation from Cold War-era atomic bomb testing in Nevada, including 185 Utahns. Compensation for those who were called "downwinders" was authorized in 1990, but funding had halted in 2000.

The issue had particular resonance with Matheson, whose father died in 1990 of bone marrow cancer, one of the diseases linked to radiation exposure. Scott Matheson was living in an area of southern Utah affected by the nuclear tests, but he never sought compensation.

Matheson remembered his father when legislation to further the construction of a nuclear waste dump site at Nevada's Yucca Mountain was before the 107th Congress. He voted "no," saying that Westerners had been exposed to enough nuclear dangers.

Although his father was the governor, Matheson says his mother, Norma, who involved herself in all sorts of civic projects, was actually more responsible for his own interest in public service. During his college days as a government major at Harvard, he served a summer internship in the office of Speaker Thomas P. O'Neill Jr. After college, Matheson worked at an environmental policy think tank in Washington for three years. He earned a graduate degree from the University of California at Los Angeles, returned to Utah and worked in a number of private-sector energy jobs. He also started his own energy consulting firm.

Matheson decided to run for Congress in 2000 because of the turmoil surrounding Merrill Cook, the mercurial two-term GOP incumbent in the 2nd District. Cook had received reams of bad publicity over his temperamental outbursts and lost the GOP primary to Internet executive Derek W. Smith. Smith then received his own dose of bad press over his past business practices, and Matheson sailed to victory by 15 percentage points.

In post-2000 census redistricting, the 2nd District may have undergone the most radical transformation of any district in the country. Utah's GOP-controlled legislature set out to draw maps that would favor the election of an all-Republican congressional delegation, and to do that, the mapmakers turned the compact, urban 458-square-mile Salt Lake County 2nd District into a 46,000-square-mile behemoth that stretches from the eastern — and mostly Republican — portion of Salt Lake City far south into rural areas. The new district also includes all five of the state's national parks.

Matheson complained mightily about the reconfiguration of the Salt Lake County district, but to no avail. He then set out to introduce himself to his new southern Utah electorate, reminding them of his family's southern Utah roots. His father was an Iron County deputy attorney and is buried in the southern Utah town of Parowan.

He lost 11 of the 16 counties, but a large margin in the Salt Lake County portion of the district enabled him to edge past Republican state Rep. John Swallow. Swallow had tried to boost his chances with a last-minute blitz of negative advertisements and a visit from Vice President Dick Cheney.

KEY VOTES

2002

Yes Overhaul campaign finance law; ban "soft money" and restrict advocacy advertising
Yes Back Bush's defense budget increase
No Extend 1996 welfare law
No Adopt Bush's discretionary spending limit
Yes Pass GOP Medicare prescription drug plan
Yes Create independent Sept. 11 commission
Yes Extend union protections to Homeland Security Department employees
Yes Revive fast-track procedures for trade agreements
Yes Authorize war against Iraq
Yes Advance bankruptcy overhaul opposed by abortion opponents

2001

No Nullify Clinton Labor Department ergonomics rule
Yes Cut taxes by $1.35 trillion through fiscal 2011
Yes Maintain ban on oil drilling in Arctic National Wildlife Refuge
No Approve Bush proposal to limit managed-care plan liability for coverage decisions
No Divert money from crop subsidy payments to land conservation
Yes Expand law enforcement power to investigate suspected terrorists

CQ VOTE STUDIES

	PARTY UNITY		PRESIDENTIAL SUPPORT	
	Support	Oppose	Support	Oppose
2002	76%	24%	48%	52%
2001	67%	33%	51%	49%

INTEREST GROUPS

	AFL-CIO	ADA	CCUS	ACU
2002	56%	80%	65%	40%
2001	75%	70%	65%	32%

UTAH 2

South and east – part of Salt Lake City, rural Utah

The 2nd was a compact Salt Lake County district for 20 years before redistricting following the 2000 census dramatically altered it to be much more rural. The 2nd now forms a reverse "L" shape, moving south from Salt Lake City to take in the eastern half of the state and moving westward to take in the state's southwest corner, a ranching center and growing retirement hub.

While some of the 2nd's rural eastern communities saw sharp population declines during the 1980s, these areas have begun to rebound. Grand County, once devastated by the collapse of the uranium mining industry, has seen new life since telecommuter and artist communities have sprung up in the town of Moab. However, the area has not yet fully recovered — it is still losing some of its population and unemployment is high.

Democratic areas of Salt Lake City used to make the 2nd a swing district, but the part of Salt Lake County that remains in the redrawn district — and totals about 60 percent of the 2nd's voters — is now more Republican. In the old 2nd, George W. Bush took 56 percent of the vote in the 2000 presidential election, sub-par in a state that gave him a total of 67 percent. But under the new 2nd District lines, Bush received 63 percent. The eastern portion of Salt Lake County provides some Democratic votes, as does Carbon County, a mining center in the middle of the state. Washington and Iron counties, in the southwest, are the district's most Republican.

Land-use issues are important in the district, which includes all five of the state's national parks — Arches, Bryce Canyon, Canyonlands, Capitol Reef and Zion. Much of the district is federal land. President Clinton's designation of the 1.7 million-acre Grand Staircase-Escalante as a national monument in 1996 angered many in the state.

MAJOR INDUSTRY

Financial services, manufacturing, tourism, ranching

CITIES

Sandy, 88,418; Salt Lake City (pt.), 87,694; St. George, 49,663; Murray, 34,024; Millcreek (unincorporated), 30,377

NOTABLE

Zion National Park near Springdale was designated in 1919.

Rep. Chris Cannon (R)

CAPITOL OFFICE
225-7751
cannon.ut03@mail.house.gov
www.house.gov/cannon
118 Cannon 20515-4403; fax 225-5629

COMMITTEES
Government Reform
Judiciary
(Commercial & Administrative Law - chairman)
Resources

HOMETOWN
Mapleton

BORN
Oct. 20, 1950, Salt Lake City, Utah

RELIGION
Mormon

FAMILY
Wife, Claudia Fox Cannon; eight children

EDUCATION
Brigham Young U., B.S. 1974 (economics); Harvard Business School, attended 1975-76; Brigham Young U., J.D. 1980

CAREER
Venture capital executive; steel company executive; Cabinet department lawyer

POLITICAL HIGHLIGHTS
Utah Republican Party finance chairman, 1992-94

ELECTION RESULTS

2002 GENERAL		
Chris Cannon (R)	103,598	67.4%
Nancy Jane Woodside (D)	44,533	29.0%
Kitty K. Burton (LIBERT)	5,511	3.6%
2002 PRIMARY		
Chris Cannon (R)		unopposed
2000 GENERAL		
Chris Cannon (R)	138,943	58.5%
Donald Dunn (D)	88,547	37.3%
Michael J. Lehman (IA)	5,436	2.3%
Kitty K. Burton (LIBERT)	3,570	1.5%

PREVIOUS WINNING PERCENTAGES
1998 (77%); 1996 (51%)

Elected 1996; 4th term

Now in his fourth term in the House, Cannon has become more than simply a reliable Republican vote. He has begun to take on the role of a consensus-seeking, pragmatic legislator. On the Judiciary Committee, historically one of the most partisan House committees, Cannon routinely teams up with committee Democrats to work on a wide range of topics, including high-technology, immigration and anti-terrorism legislation.

In his first four years in Congress, Cannon was best-known for his focus — an obsession according to critics — on the impeachment of President Clinton that continued well beyond his acquittal by the Senate in 1999. At the start of his second term, Cannon was one of the 13 Republican "managers" from the Judiciary panel who presented the House's case for removing Clinton from office in the Senate trial. After the Senate rejected the articles of impeachment, Cannon continued to call for Clinton's resignation and to defend the actions of the managers. He established an Internet-based political action committee — the House Managers PAC — to help ensure his re-election and that of his fellow House prosecutors.

A Salt Lake Tribune profile ventured, "There is no lukewarm setting" on Cannon, whose "rhetoric conveys a sort of Armageddon style of politics: The ultimate showdown between good and evil looms behind every vote." Even ally Howard C. Nielson, a Republican who represented the 3rd District from 1983 to 1991, noted: "He gets a little wild once in a while."

In the 107th Congress, Cannon worked hard on high-technology matters — a topic of considerable importance to his district, which is the birthplace of Word Perfect and home to a significant computer software industry, including Novell and hundreds of other firms.

Cannon and Democrat Rick Boucher of Virginia joined forces on Judiciary on legislation to lift some barriers to the distribution of recorded music via the Internet, focusing on preventing large recording companies from monopolizing the business. Cannon chairs the Commercial and Administrative Law Subcommittee in the 108th. He joined with Judiciary's top-ranking Democrat, John Conyers Jr. of Michigan, to champion an alternative to a bipartisan measure that would have deregulated the telecommunications market for broadband Internet service — one of the high-stakes battles of the 107th Congress.

Cannon also teamed with Conyers on a bill to tighten immigration laws and boost the use of technology at ports of entry. He was the author of legislation, cosponsored by several dozen Democrats, to give some undocumented immigrants a better chance at remaining in the United States to attend college and receive financial aid.

During Judiciary's work on the anti-terrorism package that became law six weeks after the terrorist attacks of Sept. 11, 2001, Cannon was among a coalition of conservative and liberal lawmakers who insisted that some of the sweeping law enforcement powers granted by the measure be phased out after four years.

Like most Western lawmakers, land-use issues are important to Cannon — two-thirds of his district is owned by the federal government. He served as a lawyer in the Interior Department during the Reagan administration. And in 1996, Clinton's designation of the 1.7 million-acre Grand Staircase-Escalante National Monument played a key role in Cannon's election to the House. Local outrage over the president's unilateral step, which largely precluded the development of the area's rich mineral reserves, helped Cannon oust Democrat Bill Orton.

Upon his arrival in Congress, Cannon joined fellow Utah Republican James V. Hansen on the Resources Committee, embarking on a multipronged counterattack on the monument issue. Cannon and Hansen, chairman of the committee through the 107th, tried several times to take away the president's authority to create such monuments unilaterally.

In 2002, Cannon opposed GOP Gov. Michael O. Leavitt's proposal for President Bush to designate a 620,000-acre monument in an area of southeastern Utah known as the San Rafael Swell, insisting that any designation of such a large area be done by Congress. He offered bills in both the 106th and 107th to put in place limited land protections while permitting other uses as well. In the 108th Congress, his chairmanship of the Western Caucus gives him an added platform on public lands issues.

On the Government Reform panel in the 107th, he introduced a bill to require the Census Bureau to come up with a plan to count Americans living abroad in the 2010 census. Had all the Utahns who were living abroad, instead of just military personnel, been counted in 2000, the state's population would have been sufficient to warrant a fourth seat in the House.

Cannon and Merrill Cook, another Utah Republican elected in 1996, never worked well together in Congress. In 2000, Cannon ended up endorsing the man who defeated Cook in the Republican primary, Derek W. Smith, saying Cook's temperamental behavior would cause him to lose in November. Smith lost to Democrat Jim Matheson.

With time out to serve on a church mission in Guatemala, Cannon earned an economics degree from Brigham Young University. He flunked out of Harvard Business School in 1976, then returned to BYU for a law degree. After three years as associate solicitor in the Interior Department and a stint as a Commerce Department lawyer, he returned to Utah to gain success in the business world.

He teamed up with his brother, Joe, to buy and reopen Geneva Steel Co. in 1987. After a falling out with his sibling, Cannon started his own venture capital company, Cannon Industries. He became active in local party politics, and in 1996 he headed up Lamar Alexander's presidential campaign in Utah.

Cannon dipped into his sizable personal fortune — his financial statements put his worth at more than $10 million — to help fund his 8,000-vote victory against Orton. His re-elections since have been comparatively easy. The solid GOP nature of his constituency was not altered in redistricting, and in 2002 he won by 38 percentage points.

KEY VOTES

2002

- No Overhaul campaign finance law; ban "soft money" and restrict advocacy advertising
- ? Back Bush's defense budget increase
- Yes Extend 1996 welfare law
- Yes Adopt Bush's discretionary spending limit
- Yes Pass GOP Medicare prescription drug plan
- No Create independent Sept. 11 commission
- No Extend union protections to Homeland Security Department employees
- Yes Revive fast-track procedures for trade agreements
- Yes Authorize war against Iraq
- Yes Advance bankruptcy overhaul opposed by abortion opponents

2001

- Yes Nullify Clinton Labor Department ergonomics rule
- Yes Cut taxes by $1.35 trillion through fiscal 2011
- No Maintain ban on oil drilling in Arctic National Wildlife Refuge
- Yes Approve Bush proposal to limit managed-care plan liability for coverage decisions
- No Divert money from crop subsidy payments to land conservation
- Yes Expand law enforcement power to investigate suspected terrorists

CQ VOTE STUDIES

	PARTY UNITY		PRESIDENTIAL SUPPORT	
	Support	Oppose	Support	Oppose
2002	96%	4%	87%	13%
2001	99%	1%	95%	5%
2000	99%	1%	24%	76%
1999	96%	4%	15%	85%
1998	94%	6%	19%	81%

INTEREST GROUPS

	AFL-CIO	ADA	CCUS	ACU
2002	0%	0%	94%	95%
2001	8%	0%	100%	100%
2000	0%	0%	95%	100%
1999	22%	10%	92%	92%
1998	0%	5%	100%	95%

UTAH 3

Central — part of Salt Lake County, Provo

Utah's conservative 3rd is located in the central part of the state, taking in some Salt Lake City suburbs and heading south on Interstate 15 to Provo and Orem, the district's economic centers. It also stretches west to pick up rural Millard and Beaver counties on the state's western border. A heavily Mormon-influenced district, the 3rd has one of the highest concentrations of married couples and has the lowest median age (24.5) of any district in the nation.

The Provo-Orem area has a flourishing computer industry. Newly minted graduates from the 3rd's colleges have helped make the area attractive to some of the industry's big-name companies. Brigham Young University, located in Provo, is one of the largest employers in the state. Outside Utah County, cattle ranching, mining and tourism sustain small-town life.

The 3rd included the state's eastern half for 20 years, but redistricting after the 2000 census made the district smaller. The boundary change did not affect the 3rd's GOP lean — George W. Bush received 72 percent of the vote in 2000 under both the old and new lines.

Salt Lake County's residents make up slightly less than half of the 3rd's population. These western suburbs grew rapidly in the 1990s. Many are lower income, socially conservative areas that tend to vote Republican. Most of the state's Asian population is located in this part of the district. The 3rd also takes in some of the city's southern suburbs, which recently have attracted younger married couples.

Ranchers in Millard County and hog farmers in Beaver County also tend to vote Republican. Small Democratic pockets exist in the mining community of Magna, the Salt Lake City suburb of West Valley City and the railroad town of Milford.

MAJOR INDUSTRY
Technology, mining, education, ranching

CITIES
West Valley City, 108,896; Provo, 105,166; Orem, 84,324; West Jordan, 68,336; Taylorsville, 57,439

NOTABLE
Philo T. Farnsworth, credited with inventing TV, lived in Provo; Brigham Young University was founded on an acre of land on Oct. 16, 1875.

VERMONT

Gov. Jim Douglas (R)

First elected: 2002
Length of term: 2 years
Term expires: 1/05
Salary: $125,570
Phone: (802) 828-3333
Hometown: Middlebury
Born: June 21, 1951; East Longmeadow, Mass.
Religion: United Church of Christ
Family: Wife, Dorothy Douglas; two children
Education: Middlebury College, A.B. 1972 (Russian)
Career: Gubernatorial aide
Political highlights: Vt. House, 1973-79 (majority leader, 1977-79); Vt. secretary of state, 1981-93; Republican nominee for U.S. Senate, 1992; Vt. treasurer, 1995-2003
Election results:

2002 GENERAL		
Jim Douglas (R)	103,436	44.9%
Doug Racine (D)	97,565	42.4%
Cornelius "Con" Hogan (I)	22,353	9.7%

Lt. Gov. Brian Dubie (R)

First elected: 2002
Length of term: 2 years
Term expires: 1/05
Salary: $53,303
Phone: (802) 828-2224

STATE LEGISLATURE

General Assembly: Meets January-April
House: 150 members, 2-year terms
2003 breakdown: 74R, 69D, 4PRO, 3I; 104 men, 46 women
Salary: $536/week
Phone: (802) 828-2247
Senate: 30 members, 2-year terms
2003 breakdown: 11R, 19D; 21 men, 9 women
Salary: $536/week
Phone: (802) 828-2241

STATE TERM LIMITS

Governor: No
Senate: No
House: No

URBAN STATISTICS

CITY	POPULATION
Burlington	38,889
Essex	18,626
Rutland	17,292
Colchester	16,986
South Burlington	15,814

REGISTERED VOTERS

Voters do not register by party.

POPULATION

2002 population (est.)	616,592
2000 population	608,827
1990 population	562,758
Percent change (1990-2000)	+8.2%
Rank among states (2002)	49
Median age	37.7
Born in state	54.3%
Foreign born	3.8%
Violent crime rate	114/100,000
Poverty level	9.4%
Federal workers	5,630
Military	4,605

REDISTRICTING

Vermont retained its one House seat in reapportionment.

MISCELLANEOUS

Web: www.state.vt.us
Capital: Montpelier

STATE ELECTION OFFICIAL
(802) 828-2304

DEMOCRATIC HEADQUARTERS
(802) 229-1783

REPUBLICAN HEADQUARTERS
(802) 223-3411

District Statistics

DIST.	2000 VOTE FOR PRESIDENT BUSH	GORE	NADER	WHITE	BLACK	ASIAN	HISP	MEDIAN INCOME	WHITE COLLAR	BLUE COLLAR	SERVICE INDUSTRY	OVER 64	UNDER 18	COLLEGE EDUCATION	RURAL	SQ. MILES
AL	41%	51%	7%	96%	0%	1%	1%	$40,856	61%	25%	15%	13%	24%	29%	62%	9,250
STATE	41	51	7	96	0	1	1	$40,856	61	25	15	13	24	29	62	9,250
U.S.	47.9	48.4	3	69	12	4	13	$41,994	60	25	15	12	26	24	21	3,537,438

Franklin
Grand Isle
Orleans
Essex
Lamoille
Burlington
Caledonia
Chittenden
Montpelier
Washington
Barre
Addison
Orange
At Large
Rutland
Windsor
Rutland
Bennington
Windham
Bennington
Brattleboro

Sen. Patrick J. Leahy (D)

Elected 1974; 5th term

CAPITOL OFFICE
224-4242
senator_leahy@leahy.senate.gov
leahy.senate.gov
433 Russell 20510-4502; fax 224-3479

COMMITTEES
Agriculture, Nutrition & Forestry
Appropriations
Judiciary - ranking member

HOMETOWN
Middlesex

BORN
March 31, 1940, Montpelier, Vt.

RELIGION
Roman Catholic

FAMILY
Wife, Marcelle Leahy; three children

EDUCATION
St. Michael's College, B.A. 1961 (political science); Georgetown U., J.D. 1964

CAREER
Lawyer

POLITICAL HIGHLIGHTS
Chittenden County state's attorney, 1966-75

ELECTION RESULTS

1998 GENERAL		
Patrick J. Leahy (D)	154,567	72.2%
Fred Tuttle (R)	48,051	22.4%
Hugh Douglas (LIBERT)	4,199	2.0%
Barry M. Nelson (I)	2,893	1.4%
Robert Melamede (VG)	2,459	1.1%
1998 PRIMARY		
Patrick J. Leahy (D)	18,643	96.6%
write-ins	647	3.4%

PREVIOUS WINNING PERCENTAGES
1992 (54%); 1986 (63%); 1980 (50%); 1974 (50%)

After nearly three decades in office, Leahy is one of Congress' most prominent liberals, the kind that conservatives love to hate. From his seat on the Judiciary Committee, Leahy has been the Republicans' main antagonist in several high-profile confirmation battles, from that of Supreme Court Justice Clarence Thomas to that of Attorney General John Ashcroft.

His opponents accuse him of blocking some of President Bush's appointments to the federal bench for purely partisan reasons. Leahy responds with his usual sarcasm-tinged humor. "The last election up here [in Vermont], I got 75 percent of the vote. It's really hurting me," he says. Leahy also notes that conservatives at one time were similarly disdainful of fellow Vermonter Jim Jeffords. Jeffords famously got his revenge by abandoning the GOP in 2001 to become an independent, which had the effect of throwing control of the evenly divided Senate to the Democrats.

Leahy's political longevity and his seniority on the busy committee — he is the top-ranking Democrat — allow him to pursue a wide range of legislative interests, from protecting the civil liberties of people suspected of crimes to shielding consumers from privacy invasions over the Internet.

A top goal of his is a bill to make it easier for death row inmates to offer DNA evidence that might exonerate them, an outgrowth of several cases in recent years in which DNA testing revealed that people sentenced to die were innocent. He also wants to establish national standards for defense counsels in death penalty cases. Leahy got the proposals through committee in the 107th Congress, but they never got to the floor for a vote.

Another of his priorities is a worldwide ban on land mines, including U.S. exports. Land mines, easy to plant but difficult to remove after war ends, often maim and kill civilians. Leahy clashed frequently on this issue with the Clinton administration, which opposed a total ban. Since 1989, he has worked to provide medical help for victims of land mines and has pressured the United Nations to eventually bar their use.

First elected in 1974, Leahy is the sixth in seniority among Senate Democrats. On Judiciary, he is a counterweight to the administration's most conservative proposals and nominees for high office, making him a target of the GOP's vocal right wing.

He was the chairman of the panel at the time of the Sept. 11, 2001, attacks on the World Trade Center and the Pentagon. The first major legislation to result was an administration bill greatly expanding law enforcement's powers to investigate terrorists, which critics decried as an overreaching response that trampled civil liberties. Leahy, a former prosecutor, was the leading voice for those concerns as he huddled daily with Utah Sen. Orrin Hatch, the senior Republican on the committee, and Attorney General Ashcroft, whom he previously opposed for appointment.

Ultimately, the legislation, dubbed the USA Patriot Act, gave the Justice Department broad new powers to spy on suspected terrorists and to detain them for questioning. With the country in shock over the attacks, public thinking favored law enforcement over consideration for the accused. Leahy said later that he at least managed to rid the bill of bolder encroachments on civil liberties. "As draconian as it was, the terrorism bill was far more constitutional than it would have been had I not been chairman," Leahy said.

A month after the bill became law, Leahy's office received an anonymous letter laced with deadly anthrax spores, putting him at the center of a weeks-long bioterrorism scare on Capitol Hill.

In the 107th Congress, Leahy pursued a strategy of moving Bush's least controversial judicial candidates first and taking more time with high-profile nominees. Fellow Democrats praised him, but Republicans were livid, especially after he led the opposition to Ashcroft's appointment.

Leahy accused Ashcroft, a conservative one-term senator from Missouri, of previously applying an unfair standard to Clinton's nominees, which Leahy derisively called the "Ashcroft Standard." Leahy turned the tables. Just as Ashcroft had maintained that Clinton's liberal appointees to high postings at Justice would not be able to set aside their views to enforce the law, Leahy said, Ashcroft would be unable to fulfill his pledge to enforce, as attorney general, laws he personally disagreed with. Ashcroft eventually won confirmation, but the battle was bitter and polarizing.

During the 1991 confirmation hearings of Thomas to the highest court, the senator pressed the conservative judge to reveal his position on several issues, including abortion. Leahy elicited Thomas' claim that he had never discussed the landmark *Roe v. Wade* decision legalizing abortion, which Thomas' critics called proof of evasiveness.

Leahy is relatively plugged into pop culture and new technology. He is a fan of both the comic book character Batman and The Grateful Dead, the hippie band with a cult following. In 1996, he was one of the first lawmakers to launch a Web site.

He dives into technology-related issues on Judiciary. He wants to update copyright law to reflect the advent of the Internet, and he supports easing export restrictions on encryption software, which allows digital information to be scrambled during computer transmissions. In 2000, he was tapped to head the Senate Democratic Task Force on Privacy, which focuses on medical records, financial transactions and Internet security. Also that year, he pushed to enactment a law that establishes ways to make electronic signatures legally binding while also protecting consumers.

Like most other liberals, Leahy supports abortion rights. As the senior Democrat on the Appropriations subcommittee on foreign aid, he's been particularly active in supporting international family planning groups that do abortions. But in a rare union with conservatives, Leahy opposes the procedure its critics call "partial birth" abortion. The stand cost him the endorsement of the National Organization for Women in his 1998 re-election race.

Tiny Vermont has just three representatives in Congress, and Leahy is quick to protect the interests of his rural state. A senior member of the Agriculture Committee, he is a defender of Northeastern dairy farmers during the perennial conflicts among dairy-producing regions of the country.

Nearly 30 years ago, a young Leahy went from Chittenden County prosecutor to U.S. senator. He was just 34. The Watergate-inspired backlash in 1974 helped him beat a favored Republican to become Vermont's first Democratic senator since the Republican Party was founded in 1854.

He overcame the GOP landslide of 1980 to win his first re-election by just 2,500 votes. Emphasizing his Vermont roots, he beat New York native Stewart Ledbetter, a former state banking commissioner. That close call lured former GOP Gov. Richard A. Snelling out of retirement six years later, but by then Leahy was well-financed and won with 63 percent.

In 1998, Leahy faced one of the year's most talked-about opponents, 79-year-old dairy farmer Fred Tuttle. The star of a 1996 mock documentary about an unlikely congressional candidate, Tuttle turned fiction into fact by winning the GOP nomination. Spending just $251 — a dollar for each Vermont town — he got national media attention but just 22 percent of the vote.

KEY VOTES

2002

- Yes Pass farm bill reversing crop subsidy limits
- No Postpone tougher automobile fuel efficiency standards
- Yes Overhaul campaign finance law; ban "soft money" and restrict advocacy advertising
- Yes Set federal election standards
- No Support oil drilling in Arctic National Wildlife Refuge
- No Revive fast-track procedures for trade agreements
- Yes Create federal insurance coverage for catastrophic terrorist losses
- Yes Tighten federal accounting and corporate governance regulation
- Yes Advance bipartisan Medicare prescription drug plan
- Yes Create independent Sept. 11 commission
- Yes Back Democratic Homeland Security Department proposal
- No Authorize war against Iraq

2001

- No Confirm John Ashcroft as attorney general
- No Nullify Clinton Labor Department ergonomics rule
- – Cut taxes by $1.35 trillion through fiscal 2011
- Yes Pass Democratic bill to bolster rights of patients in managed-care plans
- Yes Permit a new round of military base closings
- Yes Expand law enforcement power to investigate suspected terrorists

CQ VOTE STUDIES

	PARTY UNITY		PRESIDENTIAL SUPPORT	
	Support	Oppose	Support	Oppose
2002	98%	2%	67%	33%
2001	98%	2%	62%	38%
2000	94%	6%	89%	11%
1999	94%	6%	82%	18%
1998	87%	13%	83%	17%
1997	89%	11%	87%	13%
1996	88%	12%	75%	25%
1995	96%	4%	89%	11%
1994	96%	4%	89%	11%
1993	94%	6%	93%	7%

INTEREST GROUPS

	AFL-CIO	ADA	CCUS	ACU
2002	100%	95%	55%	0%
2001	100%	100%	38%	8%
2000	75%	85%	58%	8%
1999	100%	95%	41%	4%
1998	88%	90%	56%	12%
1997	67%	80%	60%	13%
1996	100%	90%	23%	5%
1995	100%	100%	16%	0%
1994	100%	95%	20%	0%
1993	82%	95%	27%	8%

Sen. James M. Jeffords (I)

CAPITOL OFFICE
224-5141
vermont@jeffords.senate.gov
jeffords.senate.gov
728 Hart 20510-4503; fax 228-0776

COMMITTEES
Environment & Public Works - ranking member
Finance
Health, Education, Labor & Pensions
Veterans' Affairs
Special Aging

HOMETOWN
Shrewsbury

BORN
May 11, 1934, Rutland, Vt.

RELIGION
Congregationalist

FAMILY
Wife, Elizabeth Daley Jeffords; two children

EDUCATION
Yale U., B.S.I.A. 1956; Harvard U., LL.B. 1962

MILITARY SERVICE
Navy, 1956-59; Naval Reserve, 1959-90

CAREER
Lawyer

POLITICAL HIGHLIGHTS
Vt. Senate, 1967-69 (served as a Republican); Vt. attorney general, 1969-73 (served as a Republican); sought Republican nomination for governor, 1972; U.S. House, 1975-89 (served as a Republican)

ELECTION RESULTS

2000 GENERAL		
James M. Jeffords (R)	189,133	65.6%
Ed Flanagan (D)	73,352	25.4%
Charles W. Russell (CNSTP)	10,079	3.5%
Rick Hubbard (I)	5,366	1.9%
2000 PRIMARY		
James M. Jeffords (R)	60,234	77.8%
Rick Hubbard (R)	15,991	20.7%

PREVIOUS WINNING PERCENTAGES
1994 (50%); 1988 (68%); 1986 House Election (89%); 1984 House Election (65%); 1982 House Election (69%); 1980 House Election (79%); 1978 House Election (75%); 1976 House Election (67%); 1974 House Election (53%)
*Elected as a Republican 1974-2000

Elected 1988; 3rd term

Jeffords, the man who single-handedly rearranged the balance of power in the Senate in 2001, is still a force on certain issues but his influence has diminished since the Republicans assumed majority control.

He no longer can push his agenda on education funding the way he could at the height of his power. Jeffords is best-known as the mild-mannered moderate who, fed up with the conservative tilt of the Republican Party, unexpectedly declared himself an independent, throwing the 50-50 Senate to the Democrats by changing the equation to 50-49-1. He voted and caucused with Democrats, and was rewarded with the chairmanship of the Environment and Public Works Committee.

That all changed with the 2002 election, which gave majority control to the Republicans. Jeffords' political treason won't be forgotten easily by newly empowered GOP leaders. Wary of provoking anger from other moderates, they can nonetheless show their disfavor in subtle ways. As one Democrat put it, "All of a sudden your [spending] earmark isn't there in the bill" — a reference to the federal projects that senators try to secure for their states during consideration of the annual appropriations bills.

Still, Jeffords is not entirely without a forum. He is the top-ranking member of the Environment panel, giving him a platform from which to press his goals of substantial increases in funding for clean water projects and safe drinking water systems, and to rally the opposition to Bush administration efforts to weaken air pollution standards.

And as a member of the Health, Education, Labor and Pensions Committee, he will be an ally of the minority Democrats in the reauthorization of the 1975 Individuals with Disabilities Education Act, the special education law he helped write during his House days. Jeffords is one of Congress' strongest advocates of boosting federal spending for special education. He wants the government to pay 40 percent of the costs for the mandates it imposes on local and state governments, something it promised but failed to do in the nearly 30 years since the law as written.

Jeffords allied with Senate Democrats in 2001 to try to add $448 billion over 10 years for special education and debt relief. The proposal ultimately was rebuffed by Republican leaders in final negotiations. Jeffords called the action an "abuse of power," and left the GOP shortly thereafter.

Another significant area where Jeffords still figures is the drive to provide prescription drug coverage for seniors. In 2002, he was one of the cosponsors of a "tri-partisan" prescription drug plan, with Republican Charles E. Grassley of Iowa and Democrat John B. Breaux of Louisiana. Their concept, which won support of Senate Republicans, was to provide seniors with drug coverage either through Medicare or through a stand-alone drug policy to be offered by private insurers.

No matter what his party label, Jeffords' politics long have been liberal to moderate. He votes with the Democrats nearly as often as he votes with the Republicans. He supported President Bush 71 percent of the time on key votes in 2002, a rate only slightly better than the 67 percent for Vermont's other senator, liberal Patrick J. Leahy. Jeffords opposed the president's initial $1.6 trillion tax cut proposal in the 107th Congress, calling it too costly and too tilted toward well-off taxpayers. In 2000, he was one of only 10 Republicans to win an endorsement for re-election by the Sierra Club.

Although his party switch shocked the political establishment, the senator's unhappiness with the GOP had been mounting for some time. In

2000, as chairman of the Health, Education, Labor and Pensions Committee, he should have had center stage in an important redrafting of the government's biggest education bill, which reauthorized federal programs for elementary and secondary schools. Instead, he was usurped by conservative Sen. Judd Gregg of New Hampshire, with the help of the leadership.

Gregg reshaped the bill; for example, he added a demonstration project letting 15 states use federal funds any way they chose for education. The idea was anathema to Jeffords, who believes that without tight federal controls, states tend to use money intended for poor and disadvantaged students for other purposes. Jeffords wound up voting "present" on his own bill in committee, an excruciatingly weak position for a chairman.

Earlier, in 1998, he suffered an embarrassing defeat when he was unable to corral a sufficient number of GOP votes to advance a bill subjecting the tobacco industry to tougher regulation by the Food and Drug Administration. A year before that, conservatives tried to prevent him from ascending to chairman of the Labor and Human Resources Committee after Republican Sen. Nancy Kassebaum of Kansas retired. Majority Leader Trent Lott of Mississippi intervened, allowing Jeffords to take the gavel.

The dispute with fellow Republicans over special education funding in 2001 was the final straw. Jeffords feels passionately about education. He tutors at a public school on Capitol Hill each week, as part of a literacy program he created that gets Washington-area companies involved in supporting schools. At the time, he was chairman of the Senate education panel, and yet he was being stymied from within his own party on one of his central goals in education. He also was disappointed in the level of funding that Bush was proposing for a major new mandate for schools across the board — annual testing to gauge students' academic progress.

Late one Tuesday in the Senate, Jeffords began informing colleagues that he had made up his mind to switch parties. Two days later, he flew home to explain his decision to Vermonters. "It was a unique time in history," Jeffords recalls. "It was the first time you had a situation of a 50-50 Senate. That opened up an opportunity for one individual, myself or any other Republicans that wanted to, within the rules, to change the whole thing. And then I got to thinking. . . . I said, 'If you don't do it, you're going to be to blame for everything that happens from now on, Supreme Court appointments, all of that. Because you had the power to make that change, to stop the abuse of power.' So that's when I decided I had to do it."

Jeffords has deep roots in his state. His family tree dates to 1792, and his father was the chief justice of the Vermont Supreme Court. After serving a term in the state Senate and four years as attorney general, Jeffords lost a GOP gubernatorial primary in 1972, his sole career defeat. The party hierarchy viewed him as too liberal.

He bounced back in 1974, winning a three-way primary for Vermont's lone House seat. He went on to win the general election with 53 percent of the vote over former Burlington Mayor Francis Cain, and held the seat for 14 years. In 1988, he was the heir apparent to the Senate seat held by Republican Robert T. Stafford, who was retiring. Jeffords entered the general election an overwhelming favorite, winning 68 percent of the vote.

In 1994, he faced a tough challenge for a second term from Democratic opponent Jan Backus, an underfunded liberal who had scored an upset victory in the primary. Jeffords eventually won by 10 percentage points.

By 2000, Jeffords faced a new challenge: a politically sensitive run against Democrat Ed Flanagan, the first openly gay Senate candidate ever nominated by a major party. Neither candidate made an issue of Flanagan's sexual orientation, and Jeffords retained the backing of gay rights groups. He won re-election with 66 percent of the vote.

KEY VOTES

2002

Yes Pass farm bill reversing crop subsidy limits
No Postpone tougher automobile fuel efficiency standards
Yes Overhaul campaign finance law; ban "soft money" and restrict advocacy advertising
Yes Set federal election standards
No Support oil drilling in Arctic National Wildlife Refuge
Yes Revive fast-track procedures for trade agreements
Yes Create federal insurance coverage for catastrophic terrorist losses
Yes Tighten federal accounting and corporate governance regulation
No Advance bipartisan Medicare prescription drug plan
Yes Create independent Sept. 11 commission
Yes Back Democratic Homeland Security Department proposal
No Authorize war against Iraq

2001

Yes Confirm John Ashcroft as attorney general
Yes Nullify Clinton Labor Department ergonomics rule
Yes Cut taxes by $1.35 trillion through fiscal 2011
No Pass Democratic bill to bolster rights of patients in managed-care plans
Yes Permit a new round of military base closings
Yes Expand law enforcement power to investigate suspected terrorists

CQ VOTE STUDIES

	PARTY UNITY		PRESIDENTIAL SUPPORT	
	Support	Oppose	Support	Oppose
2002	88%	12%	71%	29%
2001	85%	15%	80%	20%
2000	55%	45%	75%	25%
1999	67%	33%	56%	44%
1998	49%	51%	69%	31%
1997	53%	47%	78%	22%
1996	58%	42%	53%	47%
1995	59%	41%	51%	49%
1994	32%	68%	79%	21%
1993	46%	54%	57%	43%

INTEREST GROUPS

	AFL-CIO	ADA	CCUS	ACU
2002	92%	95%	53%	6%
2001	56%	40%	64%	29%
2000	38%	55%	73%	36%
1999	22%	45%	76%	40%
1998	38%	55%	89%	24%
1997	0%	45%	100%	21%
1996	43%	50%	62%	45%
1995	36%	55%	76%	23%
1994	50%	85%	50%	12%
1993	40%	60%	64%	38%

Rep. Bernard Sanders (I)

CAPITOL OFFICE
225-4115
bernie@mail.house.gov
bernie.house.gov
2233 Rayburn 20515-4501; fax 225-6790

COMMITTEES
Financial Services
Government Reform

HOMETOWN
Burlington

BORN
Sept. 8, 1941, Brooklyn, N.Y.

RELIGION
Jewish

FAMILY
Wife, Jane O'Meara Sanders; one child, three stepchildren

EDUCATION
U. of Chicago, B.A. 1964 (political science)

CAREER
Professor; freelance writer; documentary filmmaker

POLITICAL HIGHLIGHTS
Liberty Union candidate for U.S. Senate, 1972, 1974; Liberty Union candidate for governor, 1972, 1976; mayor of Burlington, 1981-89; independent candidate for governor, 1986; independent candidate for U.S. House, 1988

ELECTION RESULTS

2002 GENERAL		
Bernard Sanders (I)	144,880	64.3%
William Meub (R)	72,813	32.3%
Jane Newton (PRO)	3,185	1.4%
Fawn Skinner (VG)	2,344	1.0%
2000 GENERAL		
Bernard Sanders (I)	196,118	69.2%
Karen Kerin (R)	51,977	18.3%
Peter Diamondstone (D)	14,918	5.3%
Stewart Skrill (I)	11,816	4.2%
Jack "Buck" Rogers (VG)	4,799	1.7%
Daniel Krymkowski (LIBERT)	2,978	1.1%

PREVIOUS WINNING PERCENTAGES
1998 (63%); 1996 (55%); 1994 (50%); 1992 (58%); 1990 (56%)

Elected 1990; 7th term

Sanders is an idealist who has become more pragmatic with each term he spends in Congress. The House's only independent, he pursues a progressive agenda that calls for establishing a national health care system, reducing prescription drug costs, protecting workers' pensions, cracking down on "corporate greed," and cutting defense spending.

Although Sanders calls himself a "Democratic socialist," he often holds the same views as many liberal Democrats. His relations with Democratic leaders have not, however, always been friendly. When he arrived in the House, Sanders was blocked from joining the Democratic Caucus by conservative Democrats and even some liberals, who thought a socialist member would harm the party's image. In a compromise, he stayed out of the caucus but was given committee assignments by the Democrats, rising to the top minority spot on a Banking (now Financial Services) subcommittee in 1998.

He eventually did join the Democratic Caucus. Sanders is also the founder of the Progressive Caucus, the group of the most liberal members of the House; he was chairman for eight years.

His rumpled appearance and informal manner — he calls himself "Bernie" and encourages others to do the same — can give the impression that Sanders is a softie, but under his laid-back surface lurks a passionate activist who often speaks gruffly and never hesitates to make himself heard for a cause he feels is just. He is a frequent guest on television talk shows, offering his blunt assessments about corporate wrongdoing, making his case for workers' rights, and arguing for the protection of civil liberties despite stepped-up efforts to guard against terrorism.

Although he usually votes with the Democrats, Sanders has harsh words for both the Republican and Democratic parties. He told a Washington Post online chat audience, "I am not a Republican or a Democrat, and the reason I am not is because both parties are heavily influenced by big money."

Sanders has earned a lifetime score of 100 percent from the AFL-CIO in its analyses of House votes. He opposes foreign trade agreements that he says put U.S. workers at a disadvantage and favors a substantial increase in the minimum wage. He objects to funding the Export-Import Bank, which helps U.S. firms do business overseas. He tried, unsuccessfully, to bar companies that lay off more domestic workers than foreign workers from receiving Ex-Im financing.

As part of his battle against what he calls "corporate greed," Sanders worked in the 107th Congress to preserve pension plans that workers had been promised despite many companies, including IBM in Vermont, scaling back retirement benefits.

To further his efforts to provide affordable housing, Sanders championed legislation in the 107th to create a national housing trust to provide matching funds to local communities to build, rehabilitate and preserve affordable housing and for rental subsidies.

Sanders says a national health care system would solve the problem of rising health care costs. He was one of the first lawmakers to organize bus trips for senior citizens to go to Canada to fill their prescriptions at a fraction of the U.S. cost. In 2001, he won House approval of his amendment to require pharmaceutical companies that benefit from National Institutes of Health research to sell their drugs for "reasonable" prices.

Sanders hoped to get a seat on Appropriations in the 108th Congress, having extracted a promise from Democratic leader Richard A. Gephardt back in 1999. Sanders declined to run for the Senate in 2000 and for governor in 2002 based, in part, on that promise. But, with the GOP increasing its majority in the 108th, there were few vacancies, and Sanders retained the same two committees — Financial Services and Government Reform — he has had since he arrived on Capitol Hill.

Sanders was born and raised in Brooklyn, where his father, an immigrant from Poland, was a paint salesman. His political philosophy was largely influenced by his older brother and then by his experiences as a student at the University of Chicago. After taking some graduate courses and working for Head Start, he left New York in 1968, part of a wave of liberals abandoning urban life for Vermont's green acres.

While many of his fellow transplants flocked to the Democratic Party, Sanders helped found Vermont's anti-capitalist, anti-Vietnam War Liberty Union Party, from which he ran for statewide office four times in the early 1970s. He never captured more than 6 percent of the vote, but the strong grass-roots base he built paid off in 1981 when he unseated the Democratic incumbent by 10 votes to become Burlington's first socialist mayor. He won three more two-year terms by increasing margins, pursuing populist goals while presiding over the revitalization of the city's downtown. In 1986, he got 14 percent of the vote in a third-party bid for governor.

These days, Sanders pays homage to his progressive roots with a plaque on the wall of his Capitol Hill office honoring Eugene V. Debs, founder of the American Socialist Party. He is the chamber's first identifiable socialist since Victor L. Berger of Wisconsin, who served four terms in the 1910s and 1920s.

Sanders was viewed as a spoiler when he ran in 1988 for Vermont's lone House seat, vacated when GOP Rep. James M. Jeffords, who later became an independent himself, left to run for the Senate. Still, Sanders lost to Republican Peter Smith by only 4 percent. When the two squared off in 1990, Smith's efforts to paint Sanders as an admirer of Communist Cuban dictator Fidel Castro backfired, and Sanders won with 56 percent.

In 1992, he won re-election comfortably against Tim Philbin, a favorite of the state GOP's conservative wing, but he barely held on in 1994, a banner year for Republicans nationwide.

In 1996, he prevailed over two major-party opponents with 55 percent, and his winning tallies rose above 60 percent in 1998 and 2000. In 2002, he defeated Republican lawyer William Meub by a 2-to-1 ratio. The Democrats did not field a candidate.

KEY VOTES

2002

Yes Overhaul campaign finance law; ban "soft money" and restrict advocacy advertising
No Back Bush's defense budget increase
No Extend 1996 welfare law
No Adopt Bush's discretionary spending limit
No Pass GOP Medicare prescription drug plan
Yes Create independent Sept. 11 commission
Yes Extend union protections to Homeland Security Department employees
No Revive fast-track procedures for trade agreements
No Authorize war against Iraq
No Advance bankruptcy overhaul opposed by abortion opponents

2001

No Nullify Clinton Labor Department ergonomics rule
No Cut taxes by $1.35 trillion through fiscal 2011
Yes Maintain ban on oil drilling in Arctic National Wildlife Refuge
No Approve Bush proposal to limit managed-care plan liability for coverage decisions
Yes Divert money from crop subsidy payments to land conservation
No Expand law enforcement power to investigate suspected terrorists

CQ VOTE STUDIES

	PARTY UNITY		PRESIDENTIAL SUPPORT	
	Support	Oppose	Support	Oppose
2002	98%	2%	18%	82%
2001	97%	3%	16%	84%
2000	96%	4%	78%	22%
1999	96%	4%	76%	24%
1998	95%	5%	85%	15%

INTEREST GROUPS

	AFL-CIO	ADA	CCUS	ACU
2002	100%	95%	16%	0%
2001	100%	100%	22%	8%
2000	100%	95%	23%	4%
1999	100%	100%	8%	12%
1998	100%	100%	18%	8%

VERMONT

At large

Resting on the shores of Lake Champlain and rolling through the rustic Green Mountains, the second-least-populous state in the nation feels like a good, small-town neighbor.

Small businesses mix with dairy farms and manufacturing plants, as well as with the electronics companies that arrived in the 1980s. While the technology boom died down in the early 1990s, the state has kept trying to reignite it. Officials also are hoping to convince tourists, so prevalent on the ski slopes in winter, to visit the state year round, though none of Vermont's attractions are advertised on roadside billboards — state law prohibits them.

A growth spurt that began in the early 1960s, when people outnumbered cows for the first time, has altered the state's political profile. Once a bastion of Yankee Republicanism, the state moved solidly to the left with the 1980s and 1990s influx of young liberal urbanites, who joined the remnants of the late-1960s counterculture settlers. In state and federal elections, the strong progressive contingency based in Burlington and surrounding Chittenden County usually outvotes the numerous Yankee libertarian conservatives, based mostly in East Montpelier and some of the Burlington suburbs. Rural areas of the state, especially the northeast corner, also hold a few Republican votes. Democrats dominate the central swath of land along Interstates 89 and 91, as well as the southeast corner. Many small urban centers, such as Montpelier and Rutland, once reliably Republican, now have more Democrats.

Vermont's decision in 2000 to become the first state to recognize same-gender civil unions briefly energized a wave of social conservatism, but the quiet state tired of the controversy and the anticipated backlash quickly fizzled.

MAJOR INDUSTRY
Manufacturing, tourism, dairy farming

CITIES
Burlington, 38,889; Essex, 18,626; Rutland, 17,292; Colchester, 16,986

NOTABLE
In Bristol, the Lord's Prayer Rock stands beside a road — Dr. Joseph Greene had the prayer carved in the rock in 1891, hoping wagon drivers would stop cursing their horses during the muddy season; Ben & Jerry's ice cream was started in Burlington in an old gas station.

VIRGINIA

Gov. Mark Warner (D)

First elected: 2001
Length of term: 4 years
Term expires: 1/06
Salary: $124,855
Phone: (804) 786-2211
Hometown: Alexandria
Born: Dec. 15, 1954; Indianapolis, Ind.
Religion: Presbyterian
Family: Wife, Lisa Collis; three children
Education: George Washington U., B.A. 1977 (political science); Harvard U., J.D. 1980
Career: Technology venture capitalist; campaign manager
Political highlights: Va. Democratic Party chairman, 1993-95; Democratic nominee for U.S. Senate, 1996
Election results:

2001 GENERAL		
Mark Warner (D)	984,177	52.2%
Mark Earley (R)	887,234	47.0%

Lt. Gov. Tim Kaine (D)

First elected: 2001
Length of term: 4 years
Term expires: 1/06
Salary: $36,321
Phone: (804) 786-2078

STATE LEGISLATURE

General Assembly: Meets January-March in even-numbered years; January-February in odd-numbered years
House: 100 members, 2 year terms
2003 breakdown: 64R, 34D, 2I; 85 men, 15 women
Salary: $17,640; $115/day in session
Phone: (804) 698-1527
Senate: 40 members, 4-year terms
2003 breakdown: 23R, 17D; 33 men, 7 women
Salary: $18,000; $115/day in session
Phone: (804) 698-7410

STATE TERM LIMITS

Governor: Cannot serve consecutive terms
Senate: No
House: No

URBAN STATISTICS

CITY	POPULATION
Virginia Beach	425,257
Norfolk	234,403
Chesapeake	199,184
Richmond	197,790
Newport News	180,150

REGISTERED VOTERS

Voters do not register by party.

POPULATION

2002 population (est.)	7,293,542
2000 population	7,078,515
1990 population	6,187,358
Percent change (1990-2000)	+14.4%
Rank among states (2002)	12
Median age	35.7
Born in state	51.9%
Foreign born	8.1%
Violent crime rate	282/100,000
Poverty level	9.6%
Federal workers	156,871
Military	170,046

REDISTRICTING

Virginia retained its 11 House seats in reapportionment. The state legislature drew a new map, which the governor signed on July 19, 2001.

MISCELLANEOUS

Web: www.state.va.us
Capital: Richmond
STATE ELECTION OFFICIAL
(804) 786-6551
DEMOCRATIC HEADQUARTERS
(804) 644-1966
REPUBLICAN HEADQUARTERS
(804) 780-0111

District Statistics

DIST.	2000 VOTE FOR PRESIDENT BUSH	GORE	NADER	WHITE	BLACK	ASIAN	HISP	MEDIAN INCOME	WHITE COLLAR	BLUE COLLAR	SERVICE INDUSTRY	OVER 64	UNDER 18	COLLEGE EDUCATION	RURAL	SQ. MILES
1	58%	40%	n/a	75%	18%	2%	3%	$50,257	63%	23%	14%	11%	26%	27%	36%	3,773
2	55	43	n/a	67	21	4	4	$44,193	63	22	15	9	26	26	8	961
3	32	67	n/a	38	56	1	3	$32,238	55	26	19	12	26	17	8	1,118
4	54	45	n/a	62	33	1	2	$45,249	58	28	14	11	27	20	29	4,489
5	55	42	n/a	72	24	1	2	$35,739	53	33	14	15	23	19	64	8,922
6	60	38	n/a	85	11	1	2	$37,773	56	29	15	15	22	21	35	5,647
7	61	37	n/a	78	16	2	2	$50,990	68	20	12	12	25	33	30	3,514
8	38	58	n/a	57	13	9	16	$63,430	77	11	12	9	20	54	0	123
9	55	43	n/a	93	4	1	1	$29,783	49	36	15	15	21	14	66	8,803
10	56	41	n/a	77	7	7	7	$71,560	72	16	11	7	28	43	17	1,856
11	52	45	n/a	67	10	11	9	$80,397	77	12	12	8	27	49	4	388
STATE	52	44	2	70	19	4	5	$46,677	64	23	14	11	25	30	27	39,594
U.S.	47.9	48.4	3	69	12	4	13	$41,994	60	25	15	12	26	24	21	3,537,438

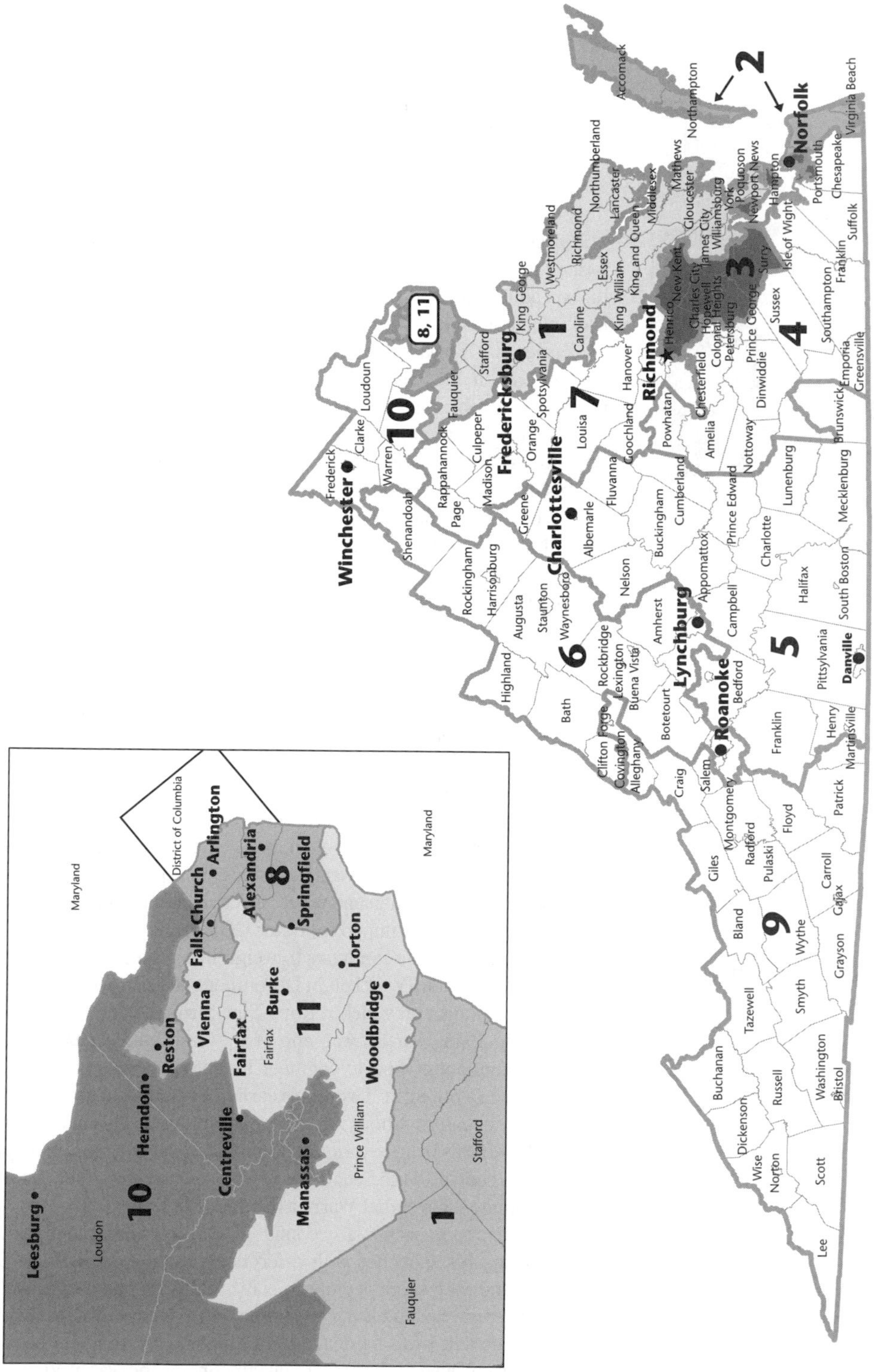

Leesburg
Loudon
10
Herndon
Reston
Centreville
Manassas
Prince William
Vienna
Fairfax
Fairfax
Falls Church
Arlington
District of Columbia
Alexandria
8
Springfield
Burke
11
Lorton
Woodbridge
Maryland
Maryland
Stafford
Fauquier
1
Winchester
Frederick
Clarke
Loudoun
Warren
Shenandoah
10
8, 11
Fauquier
Stafford
Rappahannock
Page
Culpeper
Madison
Fredericksburg
King George
Westmoreland
Northumberland
Richmond
Essex
Lancaster
Middlesex
Mathews
Gloucester
Accomack
Northampton
2
Norfolk
Virginia Beach
Chesapeake
Portsmouth
Suffolk
Hampton
Newport News
Poquoson
York
Williamsburg
James City
Charles City
New Kent
King and Queen
King William
Caroline
Spotsylvania
1
Orange
Greene
Charlottesville
Albemarle
Louisa
7
Hanover
Henrico
Richmond
Goochland
Fluvanna
Powhatan
Chesterfield
Hopewell
Colonial Heights
Petersburg
Prince George
Surry
3
Isle of Wight
Sussex
4
Southampton
Franklin
Emporia
Greensville
Dinwiddie
Amelia
Nottoway
Brunswick
Lunenburg
Mecklenburg
Cumberland
Buckingham
Prince Edward
Charlotte
Appomattox
Halifax
South Boston
Rockingham
Harrisonburg
Augusta
Staunton
Waynesboro
Nelson
Amherst
Lynchburg
Campbell
5
Pittsylvania
Danville
Highland
Bath
6
Rockbridge
Lexington
Buena Vista
Botetourt
Roanoke
Bedford
Franklin
Henry
Martinsville
Clifton Forge
Covington
Alleghany
Craig
Salem
Montgomery
Radford
Floyd
Patrick
Giles
Pulaski
Carroll
Galax
Bland
9
Wythe
Grayson
Tazewell
Smyth
Buchanan
Russell
Washington
Bristol
Dickenson
Wise
Norton
Scott
Lee

Sen. John W. Warner (R)

CAPITOL OFFICE
224-2023
senator@warner.senate.gov
warner.senate.gov
225 Russell 20510-4601; fax 224-6295

COMMITTEES
Armed Services - chairman
Environment & Public Works
Health, Education, Labor & Pensions
Select Intelligence

HOMETOWN
Alexandria

BORN
Feb. 18, 1927, Washington, D.C.

RELIGION
Episcopalian

FAMILY
Divorced; three children

EDUCATION
Washington and Lee U., B.S. 1949 (engineering); U. of Virginia, LL.B. 1953

MILITARY SERVICE
Navy, 1944-46; Marine Corps, 1950-52; Marine Corps Reserve, 1952-64

CAREER
Lawyer; farmer

POLITICAL HIGHLIGHTS
Assistant U.S. attorney, 1956-60; under secretary of the Navy, 1969-72; secretary of the Navy, 1972-74

ELECTION RESULTS

2002 GENERAL

John W. Warner (R)	1,229,894	82.6%
Nancy Spannaus (I)	145,102	9.7%
Jacob G. Hornberger Jr. (I)	106,055	7.1%

2002 PRIMARY

John W. Warner (R)	unopposed

PREVIOUS WINNING PERCENTAGES
1996 (52%); 1990 (81%); 1984 (70%); 1978 (50%)

Elected 1978; 5th term

Warner began his fifth term in the 108th Congress at the peak of his political game. The Republican Senate takeover of 2002 restored him as chairman of the Armed Services Committee, boosting his leverage on the national security issues that always have been his top legislative priority. And his zest for these issues, his instinct for consensus solutions and his aptitude for the political labor needed to hammer them out all appeared undimmed.

Moreover, while many members seem obsessed with writing finely calibrated messages to foster a carefully calculated image, Warner pursues his high-profile policy agenda with the insouciance of an elder statesman who is comfortable in his skin and with what he is doing.

Warner still displays a grandiloquent speaking style that almost defies parody. Early in his Senate career, his stentorian voice, combined with his rugged good looks and marriage to actress Elizabeth Taylor, led some to dismiss him as a wealthy dilettante. But in recent years, Warner is as likely as not to use that florid rhetoric in disarming self-deprecation. Announcing his decision to run for re-election on the day after his 75th birthday in 2002, he declared that senior citizens "deserve our respect, our trust and our admiration — and I'm darn proud to be one of 'em."

His self-confidence may reflect his dominance of Virginia's electoral arena. Though his overall voting record has been in the Senate Republican mainstream, Warner has displayed an independent streak when he viewed the party's position as too confrontational for his state's moderately conservative majority. Over the years, conservatives have complained that his search for compromise has blurred partisan differences that should have been highlighted to mobilize public support for the GOP cause.

In 1996, enraged at such apostasy as Warner's opposition to Supreme Court nominee Robert Bork and GOP Senate candidate Oliver L. North, conservatives had unsuccessfully challenged his renomination and a strong Democratic opponent held him to a victory margin of 5 percentage points. But by 2002, the activists had made their peace with Warner, who faced no serious opposition and was re-elected after a campaign season during which he mostly stumped for other GOP candidates.

For his part, Warner continues to weigh in on the centrist side of intraparty debates. When Trent Lott in December 2002 seemed to laud the segregationist platform on which retiring Sen. Strom Thurmond had run for president in 1948, Warner was one of the first Senate heavyweights to begin working out of view to engineer Lott's replacement as GOP leader by Tennessee's Bill Frist. Two years earlier, he had led a group of centrist Republican senators who tried, unsuccessfully, to dissuade Vermont's James M. Jeffords from leaving the Republican Party — a switch that cost the GOP its control of the Senate for 18 months, and with it the Armed Services Committee gavel that Warner had held since 1999.

Warner has been particularly confident of his own judgment on defense issues, lacing his speeches with references to his experience as undersecretary and then secretary of the Navy in the Nixon administration. In 2002, Warner pressed the Bush administration to be more forthcoming with Congress about its plans for dealing with Iraq and North Korea because he recalled the collapse of congressional support for the war in Vietnam that he witnessed during his Pentagon stint.

But from early on in his Senate career, Warner also backed up his personal experience with an attention to detail and a legislative savvy that now are seen as his forte. Warner informs himself and influences his colleagues through personal observation and face-to-face conversation, rather than through think-tank seminars and academic analyses. Typically, in October 2001, he and Michigan's Carl Levin, the top Democrat on Armed Services, were the first elected officials to visit U.S. troops in Pakistan. He often visits gritty backwaters where U.S. forces are deployed or where U.S. strategic and commercial interests are involved. He also routinely visits the Pentagon to sound out senior officers, some of whom he has dealt with for years.

On pivotal defense issues that divide the two parties, Warner has been a loyal Republican soldier. In 2002, for instance, he led an unprecedented party-line revolt by Armed Services Republicans against the Democratic majority's effort to rein in Bush's anti-missile defense program — an initiative the Democrats dropped in the face of a veto threat.

During the 1980s, however, Warner angered some party colleagues by favoring compromise on issues such as the deployment of anti-satellite weapons and U.S. ships in the Persian Gulf when fellow Republicans wanted a showdown. Moreover, many of his colleagues complained that he failed to do enough to salvage the 1989 nomination of a former Armed Services Committee chairman, John Tower of Texas, to be secretary of defense in the first Bush administration.

In a move widely regarded as payback, Thurmond, who had yielded the senior Republican slot on Armed Services to Warner, reasserted his seniority in 1993. Warner began assiduously shoring up his party standing. When Thurmond became Armed Services chairman in 1995 at the age of 92, Warner took on the delicate task of quietly keeping the panel on course. When Thurmond stepped down as chairman four years later, there was no challenge to Warner's succession. Under GOP term limits, he will be compelled to relinquish the gavel at the end of the 108th Congress.

Some Army officers worried that Warner would shill for the Navy because of his service in the Navy and the Marines, his five years as a top Navy Department official and Virginia's economic stake in the Norfolk Navy base and the Newport News shipbuilding facility. But, while ensuring that the shipyard's future was secure, Warner also emphasized — two years before the Sept. 11, 2001, terrorist attacks — the need to deal with non-traditional threats, such as terrorist attacks with nuclear, chemical or biological weapons. He created a new subcommittee to focus on "emerging threats" and tried to speed the development of robot air and ground combat systems.

Warner has never been the choice of conservatives among Virginia's Republicans. Some saw him as a socialite and fortune hunter. Before his marriage to Taylor, he was married to heiress Catherine Mellon and received a reported $7 million from her in their divorce settlement.

He became the party's Senate nominee in 1978 only after their pick, Richard Obenshain, died in a plane crash two months after defeating Warner at the state GOP convention. Aided by his celebrity marriage to Taylor, whose presence guaranteed large crowds on the campaign trail, Warner won by fewer than 5,000 votes in the closest Senate election in Virginia history.

He won re-election handily in 1984 and 1990, but in 1996, after fending off the intraparty challenge, he was held to 52 percent by Democrat Mark Warner, a cellular telephone entrepreneur (and now governor) who spent more than $10 million of his own money to challenge the incumbent. In 2002, however, Warner drew no Democratic opponent at all. That gave him sufficient political security that he teamed up with his former rival — who had been elected governor in 2001, and to whom he is not related — in an unsuccessful campaign to raise sales taxes to pay for transportation improvements.

KEY VOTES

2002

Yes Pass farm bill reversing crop subsidy limits
Yes Postpone tougher automobile fuel efficiency standards
Yes Overhaul campaign finance law; ban "soft money" and restrict advocacy advertising
Yes Set federal election standards
Yes Support oil drilling in Arctic National Wildlife Refuge
Yes Revive fast-track procedures for trade agreements
Yes Create federal insurance coverage for catastrophic terrorist losses
Yes Tighten federal accounting and corporate governance regulation
No Advance bipartisan Medicare prescription drug plan
Yes Create independent Sept. 11 commission
No Back Democratic Homeland Security Department proposal
Yes Authorize war against Iraq

2001

Yes Confirm John Ashcroft as attorney general
Yes Nullify Clinton Labor Department ergonomics rule
Yes Cut taxes by $1.35 trillion through fiscal 2011
Yes Pass Democratic bill to bolster rights of patients in managed-care plans
Yes Permit a new round of military base closings
Yes Expand law enforcement power to investigate suspected terrorists

CQ VOTE STUDIES

	PARTY UNITY		PRESIDENTIAL SUPPORT	
	Support	Oppose	Support	Oppose
2002	82%	18%	91%	9%
2001	85%	15%	96%	4%
2000	92%	8%	52%	48%
1999	87%	13%	39%	61%
1998	85%	15%	39%	61%
1997	89%	11%	67%	33%
1996	93%	7%	42%	58%
1995	94%	6%	26%	74%
1994	77%	23%	60%	40%
1993	80%	20%	28%	72%

INTEREST GROUPS

	AFL-CIO	ADA	CCUS	ACU
2002	31%	15%	95%	79%
2001	25%	20%	86%	96%
2000	0%	0%	100%	92%
1999	0%	10%	100%	84%
1998	13%	20%	100%	79%
1997	0%	10%	100%	80%
1996	0%	5%	85%	95%
1995	0%	5%	100%	91%
1994	25%	20%	90%	80%
1993	9%	10%	91%	84%

Sen. George Allen (R)

CAPITOL OFFICE
224-4024
allen.senate.gov
204 Russell 20510-4604; fax 224-5432

COMMITTEES
Commerce, Science & Transportation
Foreign Relations
(European Affairs - chairman)
Small Business & Entrepreneurship

HOMETOWN
Midlothian

BORN
March 8, 1952, Whittier, Calif.

RELIGION
Presbyterian

FAMILY
Wife, Susan Allen; three children

EDUCATION
U. of Virginia, B.A. 1974 (history), J.D. 1977

CAREER
Lawyer

POLITICAL HIGHLIGHTS
Republican nominee for Va. House, 1979; Va. House, 1982-91; U.S. House, 1991-93; governor, 1994-98

ELECTION RESULTS

2000 GENERAL		
George Allen (R)	1,420,460	52.3%
Charles S. Robb (D)	1,296,093	47.7%
2000 PRIMARY		
George Allen (R)		unopposed

PREVIOUS WINNING PERCENTAGES
1991 Special House Election (62%)

Elected 2000; 1st term

Ambitious, motivated and hardworking, Allen has nonetheless evinced a laconic style while quickly establishing his legislative credentials and climbing into the Republican inner circle. After only two years in office, he was elected without opposition by his peers to chair the Senate Republicans' political arm in the run-up to the 2004 election, when the GOP will be trying to maintain if not expand its majority of the 108th Congress.

Though others were interested in chairing the National Republican Senatorial Committee, Allen pre-empted their candidacies by winning the tacit blessing of Bill Frist, who had decided to step down from the job weeks before he was catapulted into the majority leader's job.

The Republicans will be defending 15 Senate seats in 2004, compared with 19 for the Democrats, making Allen's goal of bolstering the GOP majority a bit easier to attain. But ultimately, his success as chief recruiter, fundraiser and strategist for the party's Senate candidates will be greatly influenced by the re-election bid of President Bush and by the effectiveness of Frist as the new majority leader.

Allen's new position led him to play a pivotal role in Frist's ascension. He was among the first to approach the Tennessee senator and urge him to challenge Trent Lott for the top Senate GOP job, just days after Lott ignited a political furor in December 2002 with his praise for Strom Thurmond's 1948 segregationist presidential campaign.

Allen had concluded that sticking with Lott as leader would imperil the GOP majority in 2004. When Frist did not dismiss Allen's suggestion, the Virginian, with home-state colleague John W. Warner and a few other senators, began sounding out support for Frist among their colleagues. Days later, it was Allen who telephoned Mississippi to deliver the news to Lott that his survivability in the job was eroding fast; Lott stepped aside as leader two days later, by which point Frist had locked up the race to replace him.

Allen's rise into the leadership ranks is due both to his easygoing style and to his reliable conservatism. He is not afraid to chew tobacco in the Capitol, and his apparently equal comfort whether in jeans and cowboy boots or in a business suit has made him a favorite among colleagues. Even critics who chide Allen for his glibness concede that he is a likeable fellow.

Some compare Allen's persona with that of Ronald Reagan, his political hero. (Allen co-chaired Young Virginians for Reagan during Reagan's 1976 challenge to President Ford.) He also has made an effort to fashion himself as a "common-sense conservative" in the mold of Thomas Jefferson, an intellectual whiz who was the third president as well as founder of the University of Virginia, Allen's alma mater.

A dependable Republican vote on the Senate floor, in the 107th Congress he voted with his party 92 percent of the time when a majority of Republicans were pitted against a majority of Democrats. He voted for the president's position more than 95 percent of the time.

But Allen isn't just a "yes-man" for the president. In fact, his maiden speech in the Senate criticized Bush's reticence to nominate Roger L. Gregory — whose temporary appointment by President Clinton annoyed the GOP — to be the first African-American permanently seated on the 4th U.S. Circuit Court of Appeals, in Richmond. "Let us rise above this procedural aggravation and act in a statesmanlike manner," said Allen. (Ultimately, Gregory was the first Bush appeals court nominee to win confirmation.)

The episode suggests that Allen, who had hung a Confederate flag on the wall of his first house, has left behind his past. As governor during the 1994 state Republican Convention, he said of Democrats, "Let's enjoy knocking their soft teeth down their whiny throats" — a line that brought to mind his victory-driven father, the late George Allen Sr., a Hall of Fame coach in the National Football League. Since joining the Senate, Allen has moderated his tone in order to work with Democrats on high-tech issues and other matters dear to him.

After the Sept. 11, 2001, terrorist attacks, for example, Allen teamed up with Iowa Democrat Tom Harkin to usher through a bill allowing the U.S. government to use the frozen assets of terrorists and states that sponsor terrorism to compensate victims. In addition, Allen ensured that an exception was made to Army policy so that Charles Burlingame, the captain of the United Airlines flight that crashed into the Pentagon, could be buried at Arlington National Cemetery. Allen also worked to secure nearly $20 million to integrate wireless emergency-response systems in the metropolitan Washington area, including suburban Virginia.

Most of Allen's legislative energies are taken up by those types of parochial interests, especially by the concerns of the high-technology sector in Northern Virginia. His seat on the Commerce Committee and his chairmanship of the Senate GOP High Tech Task Force puts him in an excellent position to influence Internet and technology policy. For example, he helped devise the compromise that led to a law enacted in the 107th aimed at creating a child-friendly zone on the Internet.

Allen says he is most proud of helping to secure in the 107th a two-year extension of a ban on Internet access taxes, an effort in which he teamed up with California Democrat Barbara Boxer. The issue resurfaced early in the 108th, with Allen out front in advocating a permanent moratorium on such taxes. He and Boxer also have joined forces on a proposal to sell part of the federally controlled broadcast spectrum to Internet providers that want to supply customers with wireless access.

Along with Commerce, Allen serves on the Foreign Relations Committee. The post is a good match for Virginia, a state with a substantial military presence. Allen's senior colleague, Warner, covers the other half of U.S. global policy as chairman of the Armed Services Committee.

Allen has a gold-plated political résumé. In 1982, he won a seat to the state House, beating the Democratic incumbent who had defeated him in his initial political foray three years earlier. After serving nine years in the General Assembly, Allen easily won a special House election in 1991 to replace Republican D. French Slaughter Jr., who resigned in the face of declining health.

Allen did not seek a full term the next year, however, after a Democratic-drawn redistricting plan put his home in the same district as veteran Republican Thomas J. Bliley Jr. But that left Allen free to run a long campaign for governor, which ended with his easy 1993 victory over Democratic state Attorney General Mary Sue Terry. As governor, he concentrated on abolishing parole and attracting high-tech industry to Virginia. His popularity helped spark a surge that carried the GOP to its current dominance in Virginia politics.

Barred by state law from succeeding himself, Allen left office in 1998. But he quickly geared up for another long campaign to unseat two-term Democrat Charles S. Robb from the Senate. Once a towering political figure in the state, Robb never recovered from a spate of questions about his personal life, and his cold demeanor contrasted poorly with Allen's backslapping fellowship. Allen gained an early advantage in campaign fundraising and moved quickly to secure support in populous Northern Virginia, Robb's home base. He won by 5 percentage points.

KEY VOTES

2002

Yes Pass farm bill reversing crop subsidy limits
Yes Postpone tougher automobile fuel efficiency standards
No Overhaul campaign finance law; ban "soft money" and restrict advocacy advertising
Yes Set federal election standards
Yes Support oil drilling in Arctic National Wildlife Refuge
Yes Revive fast-track procedures for trade agreements
Yes Create federal insurance coverage for catastrophic terrorist losses
Yes Tighten federal accounting and corporate governance regulation
No Advance bipartisan Medicare prescription drug plan
Yes Create independent Sept. 11 commission
No Back Democratic Homeland Security Department proposal
Yes Authorize war against Iraq

2001

Yes Confirm John Ashcroft as attorney general
Yes Nullify Clinton Labor Department ergonomics rule
Yes Cut taxes by $1.35 trillion through fiscal 2011
No Pass Democratic bill to bolster rights of patients in managed-care plans
Yes Permit a new round of military base closings
Yes Expand law enforcement power to investigate suspected terrorists

CQ VOTE STUDIES

	PARTY UNITY		PRESIDENTIAL SUPPORT	
	Support	Oppose	Support	Oppose
2002	90%	10%	93%	7%
2001	93%	7%	97%	3%
House Service:				
1992	95%	5%	78%	22%
1991	86%	14%	69%	31%

INTEREST GROUPS

	AFL-CIO	ADA	CCUS	ACU
2002	23%	10%	95%	84%
2001	13%	15%	100%	96%
House Service:				
1992	25%	15%	75%	88%
1991	33%	—	—	100%

Rep. Jo Ann Davis (R)

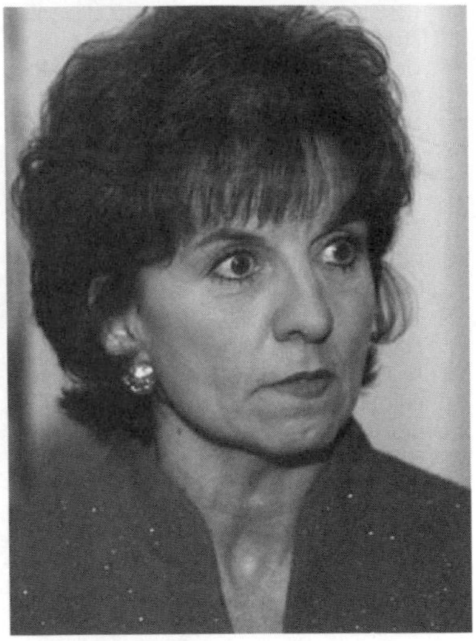

CAPITOL OFFICE
225-4261
www.house.gov/joanndavis
1123 Longworth 20515-4601; fax 225-4382

COMMITTEES
Armed Services
Government Reform
(Civil Service & Agency Organization - chairwoman)
International Relations

HOMETOWN
Gloucester

BORN
June 29, 1950, Rowan, N.C.

RELIGION
Assemblies of God

FAMILY
Husband, Chuck Davis; two children

EDUCATION
Kecouchtan H.S., graduated 1968

CAREER
Realtor; administrative assistant

POLITICAL HIGHLIGHTS
Va. House, 1998-2001

ELECTION RESULTS

2002 GENERAL		
Jo Ann Davis (R)	113,168	95.9%
write-ins	4,829	4.1%
2002 PRIMARY		
Jo Ann Davis (R)		unopposed
2000 GENERAL		
Jo Ann Davis (R)	151,344	57.5%
Lawrence Davies (D)	97,399	37.0%
Sharon Wood (LIBERT)	9,652	3.7%
Josh Billings (I)	4,082	1.6%

Elected 2000; 2nd term

Her humble beginnings and limited education did not keep Davis from becoming a successful businesswoman and conservative activist and, now in Congress, a determined and vocal advocate for the Defense Department, which employs many of her constituents.

Davis, who briefly attended business college before starting in the business world as a secretary and working her way up, also has overcome what she told the Richmond Times-Dispatch was a severe case of shyness to become what a GOP political consultant once termed "an articulate, passionate voice" for traditional values and conservative positions.

Davis is one of three junior GOP lawmakers from the Tidewater area, along with Ed Schrock and J. Randy Forbes, who serve on the Armed Services Committee. Their predecessors — Republicans Herbert H. Bateman and Owen B. Pickett, and Democrat Norman Sisisky — had a combined service record of almost a half-century on the committee and gave the Tidewater extraordinary clout. The lawmakers, however, argued that it was not disproportionate clout, because the area is home to many military installations as well as the shipbuilding cities of Newport News and Hampton. The Norfolk Naval Base, for example, is the world's largest.

The most vocal of the three newcomers, Davis frequently takes to the House floor, often to praise the military and condemn interstate shipments of garbage to Virginia. Virginia is one of the nation's leading recipients of trash from other states — a distinction Davis is not interested in perpetuating. Dating from her service in the state legislature, she has been a leader in the fight to give the state control over how much waste is brought in.

Over the course of eight days in late 2001 and early 2002, Davis stood in the well of the House to read the names of every known victim of the Sept. 11, 2001, terrorist attacks. Several of her colleagues helped, but Davis did the bulk of the reading. She told her colleagues that as the wife of a retired firefighter, the tragedy struck particularly close to home.

That was not the first time Davis paid tribute to what she calls fallen heroes. On several other occasions she has come to the floor to recognize firefighters or servicemen killed in the line of duty.

Diligent and attentive on Armed Services, she led an effort in 2001 to increase funding for a major overhaul of the aircraft carrier *Dwight D. Eisenhower* at the Newport News shipyard. Even though the next round of military base closings is not scheduled until 2005, Davis already has created a task force of community leaders to develop a strategy for keeping the local military installations off the Pentagon's list of candidates for closure.

Davis believes the Navy needs a 375-ship fleet (up from about 314 at the start of 2003) and says that the administration's current plans are inadequate. "Doing five or six ships a year is not going to get it." The administration is "going to have to pony up the money," she said in introducing legislation to increase the fleet's strength.

Davis was in office only a few months when she won approval of legislation to expand the Servicemembers' Group Life Insurance program to include spouses and children of veterans. The changes were retroactive to cover service members killed in the terrorist attack on the *USS Cole* in Yemen in October 2000 and national guardsmen — including 18 from Virginia — who were killed in an airplane crash in March 2001.

Davis affiliates with the Republican Study Committee, a group of several dozen of the most conservative members of the House GOP. She is opposed to abortion, even in cases of rape or incest, and she boasts a grade of "A" from the National Rifle Association.

She will stray from party positions, however. She was one of only 12 Republicans who supported the budget proposal authored by the "Blue Dogs," a coalition of conservative House Democrats. She also was in the Republican minority in votes on drilling for oil in national monuments, cutting sugar subsidies and backing mandatory testing for third- and eighth-graders. In 2002, she was one of only 27 Republicans who voted against enacting the law that gave President Bush fast-track authority to negotiate trade deals that Congress cannot amend.

She is chairwoman of the Government Reform panel's Civil Service Subcommittee in the 108th Congress.

A North Carolina native, Davis and her family moved to the Tidewater area when she was 9. Her father worked at a number of blue-collar jobs, and both he and her mother played in a bluegrass band. She says she lived in trailers for much of her childhood. Religion plays a large role in her life. She told the Times-Dispatch that her model in seeking to overcome her youthful shyness was her father, an outgoing person who made friends easily.

She quit college after just one day because she was homesick. She then became a secretary for a real estate company and stayed for more than a decade. Davis later earned a real estate license at the suggestion of her former boss and opened her own firm. She went on to start two businesses, a management company and a real estate company. She was one of the founding partners of a worldwide network of real estate firms that specialize in helping military families relocate from one base to another.

Active in professional and civic organizations, Davis did not consider politics until a friend suggested it. She won a close election to the Virginia House in 1997, capitalizing on grass-roots support from conservatives.

Early in 2000, Davis was the first Republican to announce her candidacy when Bateman announced his plans to retire after nine terms. (He died that September.) Although she was outspent by almost $1 million in the Republican primary by Paul Jost, a candidate who had the endorsement of GOP Gov. James S. Gilmore III, Davis' strong support from district conservatives propelled her to a narrow victory in the five-way race.

The 1st District's solidly conservative character made it easy for Davis in November, and she won by more than 20 percentage points, becoming the first Republican woman ever to represent Virginia in Congress. Redistricting did not alter the partisan tilt of the 1st, and in 2002 the Democrats did not field a challenger.

KEY VOTES

2002

- No Overhaul campaign finance law; ban "soft money" and restrict advocacy advertising
- Yes Back Bush's defense budget increase
- Yes Extend 1996 welfare law
- Yes Adopt Bush's discretionary spending limit
- Yes Pass GOP Medicare prescription drug plan
- No Create independent Sept. 11 commission
- No Extend union protections to Homeland Security Department employees
- No Revive fast-track procedures for trade agreements
- Yes Authorize war against Iraq
- No Advance bankruptcy overhaul opposed by abortion opponents

2001

- Yes Nullify Clinton Labor Department ergonomics rule
- Yes Cut taxes by $1.35 trillion through fiscal 2011
- No Maintain ban on oil drilling in Arctic National Wildlife Refuge
- Yes Approve Bush proposal to limit managed-care plan liability for coverage decisions
- No Divert money from crop subsidy payments to land conservation
- Yes Expand law enforcement power to investigate suspected terrorists

CQ VOTE STUDIES

	PARTY UNITY		PRESIDENTIAL SUPPORT	
	Support	Oppose	Support	Oppose
2002	96%	4%	82%	18%
2001	92%	8%	86%	14%

INTEREST GROUPS

	AFL-CIO	ADA	CCUS	ACU
2002	25%	5%	75%	96%
2001	17%	5%	83%	100%

VIRGINIA 1

East – parts of Newport News and Hampton, Fredericksburg

The Republican-friendly 1st lies along Virginia's coast, stretching from outer Northern Virginia suburbs and exurbs of Washington, D.C., all the way south to the shipbuilding cities of Hampton and Newport News.

Industry in the 1st revolves around its military installations and NASA sites, which have attracted a growing technology private sector. Colleges and universities also contribute to the district's economic base, as do shipbuilding and tourism. The most popular tourist destinations — Williamsburg, Jamestown and Yorktown — recall Virginia's colonial past. Inland, agriculture and chickens help drive the economy.

Virginia's population expansion is not confined to the Washington suburbs. Spotsylvania County (one-fifth of which is in the neighboring 7th) has experienced rapid growth as a result of its proximity to both Richmond and Washington and its location on the Interstate 95 corridor. Spotsylvania's 58 percent growth in the 1990s was the third-fastest clip in the state. Stafford County, located just north of Fredericksburg, grew by nearly 50 percent in the 1990s, and is now the most populous county in the 1st.

Redistricting following the 2000 census shifted the 1st slightly north toward Washington. The new map removed parts of Newport News and Hampton and added parts of Prince William and Fauquier counties. The changes kept the 1st's solidly GOP orientation intact: George W. Bush took 58 percent in the 2000 presidential election, third-best in the state.

MAJOR INDUSTRY

Defense, technology, agriculture, tourism

MILITARY BASES

Marine Corps Base Quantico, 6,951 military, 3,101 civilian (2002); Naval Surface Warfare Center, Dahlgren Division, 447 military, 3,612 civilian; Yorktown Naval Weapons Station (Naval In-Service Engineering), 1,500; Fort A.P. Hill (Army), 370 military, 283 civilian (2001)

CITIES

Newport News (pt.), 71,800; Hampton (pt.), 31,755; Fredericksburg, 19,279

NOTABLE

Jamestown was the first English settlement in North America; George Washington and Robert E. Lee were born in Westmoreland County.

Rep. Ed Schrock (R)

CAPITOL OFFICE
225-4215
schrock.house.gov
322 Cannon 20515-4602; fax 225-4218

COMMITTEES
Armed Services
Budget
Government Reform
Small Business
(Regulatory Reform & Oversight - chairman)

HOMETOWN
Virginia Beach

BORN
April 6, 1941, Middletown, Ohio

RELIGION
Baptist

FAMILY
Wife, Judy Schrock; one child

EDUCATION
Alderson-Broaddus College, B.A. 1964 (architecture); American U., M.A. 1975 (public relations)

MILITARY SERVICE
Navy, 1964-88

CAREER
Stockbroker; Navy officer

POLITICAL HIGHLIGHTS
Va. Senate, 1996-2001

ELECTION RESULTS

2002 GENERAL		
Ed Schrock (R)	103,807	83.2%
D. C. Amarasinghe (GREEN)	20,589	16.5%
2002 PRIMARY		
Ed Schrock (R)	unopposed	
2000 GENERAL		
Ed Schrock (R)	97,856	52.0%
Jody Wagner (D)	90,328	48.0%

Elected 2000; 2nd term

Schrock spent almost a quarter-century in the Navy, and evidence of that can be seen in his reserved military bearing, his close-clipped hair and his conservative politics.

His background helped him win election in the Republican-leaning 2nd District, where thousands of voters receive their paychecks from the Pentagon. The district takes in the world's largest navy base — Norfolk Naval Base — and a half-dozen other military installations. So it is no surprise that Schrock as a freshman congressman was named to the Armed Services Committee, where his predecessor, Democrat Owen B. Pickett, had been a senior member.

One of three southeast Virginians on the committee, Schrock and those colleagues — Republicans Jo Ann Davis and J. Randy Forbes — have made it a priority to continue the Pentagon's deep involvement in the region. Schrock also was assigned to the Budget, Government Reform and Small Business panels. On the latter, he won a subcommittee chairmanship in the 108th Congress, wielding the gavel of the Regulatory Reform panel.

Schrock weighed in early from his Armed Services perch. In the first few months of the Bush presidency, while Defense Secretary Donald H. Rumsfeld and other administration officials still were assessing defense budget needs, Schrock said the military needed a big increase and he wanted shipbuilding to get among the healthiest boosts.

Noting that the number of lawmakers with military service was much lower than in past decades, Schrock urged his colleagues to educate themselves about military issues. During the summer of 2001, he organized trips for the freshman class to military bases, where he briefed them on the role of the armed services.

After the Sept. 11, 2001, terrorist attacks, Schrock made clear where he felt more government spending should go. Referring to the debate over whether Social Security surpluses should be protected from use for other programs, such as the armed services, Schrock said that when American citizens "watch those towers fall and the Pentagon collapse," they will not hold politicians to their promise to shield the Social Security surplus, he said.

Health care issues, particularly the cost of prescription drugs, are also high on the agenda for Schrock, a 25-year cancer survivor. He beat non-Hodgkins lymphoma after a lengthy struggle in which his weight dropped to 98 pounds — on a 6-foot, 4-inch frame. Although he was exposed to Agent Orange during one of his two tours of duty in Vietnam, Schrock says he does not know if that is what caused his cancer.

Schrock is one of the most dependable team players for the GOP leadership and President Bush, whose positions he backed 95 percent of the time in his first term, seventh-highest among all House Republicans, perhaps explaining why the president dubbed him "Eddie Boy" and invited him twice to ride along on Air Force One. He was elected class president of the 28 Republican members of the House's Class of 2000.

Schrock spent five years in the Virginia Senate, building a reputation as a dependable soldier for party leaders. He was a hard worker who preferred to be in the background. "If you searched the annals of the Virginia Senate over the past five years, one thing you wouldn't find is a memorable speech" by Schrock, the Virginian-Pilot newspaper said after Schrock announced for Congress in 2000. He makes no apologies for his reticence, telling the newspaper, "I don't need to get up and pontificate like some people do."

On Capitol Hill, Schrock also has remained in the background, speaking out only when he has a specific comment about a legislative interest. He refrains from lobbing partisan brickbats, which, he told a reporter in 2000, "make me sick to my stomach." Much of the partisanship on Capitol Hill, Schrock observes, is meant only for home consumption on C-SPAN.

Schrock grew up in Ohio, where his father worked in a steel mill. His family was interested in politics, he said. Schrock remembers watching the 1952 Republican convention at his grandparents' house.

Schrock attended West Virginia's Alderson-Broaddus College, which is affiliated with the Baptist church. He says he didn't consider a military career until a draft notice arrived. Then he joined the Navy and went to Officer Candidate School. While he was stationed in Long Beach, he met his wife, Judy, a teacher.

Schrock retired from the Navy as a captain in 1988, and his last assignment was as a public affairs officer in Norfolk. He then went to work as a stockbroker and was active in community affairs.

Early in 1995 he quit his job to run full time for the Virginia legislature. He said the timing was right, as his son was getting ready to enter college and his career was at a point where he could afford to take a break.

Schrock says his parents knew when he was 15 years old that he would one day become involved in politics. Schrock's retail-style state Senate campaign — he estimates he knocked on more than 18,000 doors — propelled him to a hard-fought GOP primary win and then a victory over a 12-year Democratic incumbent. He told the Virginian-Pilot he was bitten by dogs twice and that his car was shot at, but added that he lowered his cholesterol level with all the walking. In Richmond, Schrock sponsored a measure that created a Cabinet-level technology secretary position in Virginia. He also helped get funding for a technology center in Virginia Beach.

In 1998 local Republican leaders, who had not recruited an official challenger to Pickett, mounted a half-hearted write-in bid on Schrock's behalf. Schrock did not actively pursue the effort, which yielded just a few thousand votes. But a year later, even before Pickett announced his retirement, Schrock entered the 2000 race. He drew no opposition for the GOP nomination. But he faced an unexpectedly strong Democratic opponent — securities lawyer Jody Wagner. A first-time candidate, Wagner had a long record of community involvement and strong fundraising skills. Schrock held on to win with just 52 percent of the vote. But in 2002, the local Democratic organization was unable to recruit a challenger and he took 83 percent against a third-party foe.

KEY VOTES

2002

- No Overhaul campaign finance law; ban "soft money" and restrict advocacy advertising
- Yes Back Bush's defense budget increase
- Yes Extend 1996 welfare law
- Yes Adopt Bush's discretionary spending limit
- Yes Pass GOP Medicare prescription drug plan
- No Create independent Sept. 11 commission
- No Extend union protections to Homeland Security Department employees
- Yes Revive fast-track procedures for trade agreements
- Yes Authorize war against Iraq
- Yes Advance bankruptcy overhaul opposed by abortion opponents

2001

- Yes Nullify Clinton Labor Department ergonomics rule
- Yes Cut taxes by $1.35 trillion through fiscal 2011
- No Maintain ban on oil drilling in Arctic National Wildlife Refuge
- Yes Approve Bush proposal to limit managed-care plan liability for coverage decisions
- No Divert money from crop subsidy payments to land conservation
- Yes Expand law enforcement power to investigate suspected terrorists

CQ VOTE STUDIES

	PARTY UNITY		PRESIDENTIAL SUPPORT	
	Support	Oppose	Support	Oppose
2002	97%	3%	92%	8%
2001	99%	1%	98%	2%

INTEREST GROUPS

	AFL-CIO	ADA	CCUS	ACU
2002	11%	0%	100%	100%
2001	8%	0%	100%	100%

VIRGINIA 2

Southeast – Virginia Beach, parts of Norfolk and Hampton

The 2nd is dominated by Virginia Beach, a center for white-collar, suburban military families and retirees. It also extends north to include parts of Norfolk and Hampton and crosses the Chesapeake Bay inlet to reach Virginia's portion of the Eastern Shore.

Virginia Beach's tourism-driven population boom of the 1980s is over, but the area has held its ground in the face of military base closings. The Norfolk Naval Base continues to dominate the economy, which also is bolstered by shipbuilding and shipping companies. About two-thirds of the district's population lives in Virginia Beach.

The 2nd includes half of the city of Norfolk (shared with the 3rd), a largely blue-collar and Democratic-leaning area that was surpassed by Virginia Beach in the early 1980s as Virginia's most populous city. Norfolk has lost population at about the same rate Virginia Beach has gained residents.

The district is home to Pat Robertson's religious broadcast network. But the 2nd's conservatism derives more from military and economic issues than social questions. Voters here typically side with the GOP: Republicans hold all state legislative seats in Virginia Beach and have made major inroads in Norfolk.

Redistricting following the 2000 census, which added the Eastern Shore and part of Hampton, made the 2nd slightly more Republican-leaning.

MAJOR INDUSTRY

Military, tourism, shipbuilding

MILITARY BASES

Naval Station Norfolk, 82,432 military, 28,125 civilian (2000); Langley Air Force Base, 9,037 military, 1,700 civilian (2002); Naval Air Station Oceana, 9,617 military, 2,273 civilian; Naval Amphibious Base Little Creek, 6,298 military, 2,641 civilian (1999); Atlantic Fleet Combat Training Center, Dam Neck, 2,355 military, 950 civilian (1998); Fort Monroe (Army), 806 military, 1,450 civilian (2001); Fort Story (Army), 1,146 military, 84 civilian (2003)

CITIES

Virginia Beach, 425,257; Norfolk (pt.), 112,102; Hampton (pt.), 54,753

NOTABLE

Cape Henry Lighthouse in Virginia Beach was the first government-built lighthouse in the United States, finished circa 1791.

Rep. Robert C. Scott (D)

Elected 1992; 6th term

The first black person to represent Virginia in Congress since 1891, for the past decade Scott has been an unwavering voice for liberal causes in the House; he is a supporter of abortion rights, an opponent of the death penalty and a staunch critic of Republicans for spending federal funds generously to punish criminals while shortchanging social programs that he views as key elements in crime prevention.

But Scott's unambiguous place on the political spectrum, with his strong civil libertarian strain, can put him in the difficult position of challenging his own party. In 2002, for example, Scott was one of only 12 House Democrats who voted against enacting the revamp of campaign finance law. He viewed one of its core provisions — prohibiting advocacy groups from mentioning specific candidates in their broadcast advertisements close to an election — as an unconstitutional restriction on free speech.

Later, he cast one of only three votes against a resolution that condemned a court ruling against the use of the phrase, "under God," in the pledge of allegiance.

In the 108th Congress, Scott has returned for a third term as the top Democrat on the Judiciary Committee's Crime Subcommittee. From that position, he has been an outspoken and persistent critic of Bush administration proposals to expand law enforcement authority, which he views as a violation of the rights of defendants, consumers and the poor. He often points out that the federal wiretap authority was created as "a tool of last resort" for investigations of organized crime, but that there is now persistent pressure from Republicans — inappropriately so, in his view — to allow wiretapping in probes of a broad array of alleged crimes.

As a consequence, Scott was a vocal opponent of the 2001 law, enacted with overwhelming support by Congress six weeks after the terrorist attacks of Sept. 11, that gave federal law enforcement officers new tools to combat terrorism. Scott said new intelligence-gathering provisions in the statute trample on individual liberties. In December 2001, Scott opposed a border-security measure containing provisions that, he said, "reduce the rights of victims of unconstitutional, unreasonable searches by government officials."

Scott has long argued that the GOP's "tough on crime" approach does not work. He says education and jobs are the answer. "It makes no sense, waiting for the children to mess up and then lock them up, when it is cheaper to invest in crime prevention programs and prevent them from getting in trouble in the first place," he said. Scott says that some, but not all, of his views are based on the racial inequity of the criminal justice system. He points out that the death penalty is disproportionately imposed on black defendants and says racial profiling in police work is a serious problem.

Scott also has been a leading critic of President Bush's proposals for allowing more federal funding to flow to faith-based organizations that provide social services, because under the bill the House passed in 2001 the participating programs would be permitted to use religion as a basis for hiring — which Scott and many Democrats view as discriminatory.

When Republicans try to pass constitutional amendments to protect the flag, promote school prayer, limit taxation or extend rights to crime victims, Scott admonishes members that they took an oath to "support and defend" the Constitution, not "support and amend" it.

From his seat on the Education and the Workforce panel, where he served for five terms, Scott advanced the argument that standardized test

CAPITOL OFFICE
225-8351
www.house.gov/scott
2464 Rayburn 20515-4603; fax 225-8354

COMMITTEES
Budget
Judiciary

HOMETOWN
Newport News

BORN
April 30, 1947, Washington, D.C.

RELIGION
Episcopalian

FAMILY
Divorced

EDUCATION
Harvard U., A.B. 1969; Boston College, J.D. 1973

MILITARY SERVICE
Army Reserve, 1970-74; Mass. National Guard, 1974-76

CAREER
Lawyer

POLITICAL HIGHLIGHTS
Va. House, 1979-83; Va. Senate, 1983-93; Democratic nominee for U.S. House, 1986

ELECTION RESULTS

2002 GENERAL		
Robert C. Scott (D)	87,521	96.1%
write-ins	3,552	3.9%
2002 PRIMARY		
Robert C. Scott (D)		unopposed
2000 GENERAL		
Robert C. Scott (D)	137,527	97.7%
write-ins	3,226	2.3%

PREVIOUS WINNING PERCENTAGES
1998 (76%); 1996 (82%); 1994 (79%); 1992 (79%)

scores — he calls it "high stakes testing" — place low-income school districts and their students at a disadvantage. He left the panel in the 108th to take a seat on the Budget Committee.

Scott leaves behind his liberal mantle when it comes to looking out for southeast Virginia's military and tobacco establishments. A former member of the Army Reserve and the National Guard, Scott is one of the stronger pro-Pentagon voices in the Congressional Black Caucus. He seeks to advance the interests of the military bases and shipbuilders of the 3rd District, where Newport News Shipbuilding and the Army's Fort Eustis are major employers. The district is also home to one of the nation's largest cigarette plants, a south Richmond facility operated by Philip Morris.

Scott was a leading critic of the Republican drive to impeach President Clinton in 1998. He even opposed censuring Clinton for his relationship with Monica Lewinsky, a former White House intern, arguing that the branches of the federal government should not censure one another.

Scott is the son of a surgeon and a teacher. When local white officials resisted court-ordered integration of the public schools, the Scotts, along with other well-to-do black families, sent their son to Groton, the prestigious Massachusetts prep school. He graduated from Harvard University and earned his law degree from Boston College. He returned home to Newport News after law school and became active in local civic groups and political organizations.

Scott won a seat in the state House in 1978 and moved up to the state Senate five years later. In his first run for Congress, in 1986, he failed to unseat Republican Herbert H. Bateman, but he nevertheless captured 44 percent of the vote and broadened his name recognition. Six years later, when redistricting at the start of the 1990s resulted in a 3rd District that was 64 percent black, Scott tried again. With no incumbent running, he took two-thirds of the vote in a three-way Democratic primary and four-fifths of the vote in November. He became the second black Virginian in the House after John Mercer Langston, a Republican elected to the 51st Congress.

Scott won by similarly lopsided margins in 1994 and 1996. When a three-judge federal panel struck down the 3rd's boundaries the next year, Scott's political future seemed in jeopardy, but the new lines drawn by the General Assembly kept the black population at 54 percent, and he won handily two more times. The newest lines, drawn after the 2000 census, created a 56 percent African-American population for the district, and in 2002 the Republicans did not field a candidate against Scott, who won a sixth term.

KEY VOTES

2002

- No Overhaul campaign finance law; ban "soft money" and restrict advocacy advertising
- Yes Back Bush's defense budget increase
- No Extend 1996 welfare law
- No Adopt Bush's discretionary spending limit
- No Pass GOP Medicare prescription drug plan
- Yes Create independent Sept. 11 commission
- Yes Extend union protections to Homeland Security Department employees
- No Revive fast-track procedures for trade agreements
- No Authorize war against Iraq
- No Advance bankruptcy overhaul opposed by abortion opponents

2001

- No Nullify Clinton Labor Department ergonomics rule
- No Cut taxes by $1.35 trillion through fiscal 2011
- Yes Maintain ban on oil drilling in Arctic National Wildlife Refuge
- No Approve Bush proposal to limit managed-care plan liability for coverage decisions
- No Divert money from crop subsidy payments to land conservation
- No Expand law enforcement power to investigate suspected terrorists

CQ VOTE STUDIES

	PARTY UNITY		PRESIDENTIAL SUPPORT	
	Support	Oppose	Support	Oppose
2002	96%	4%	23%	77%
2001	94%	6%	14%	86%
2000	93%	7%	81%	19%
1999	91%	9%	83%	17%
1998	91%	9%	89%	11%

INTEREST GROUPS

	AFL-CIO	ADA	CCUS	ACU
2002	100%	95%	42%	4%
2001	100%	100%	35%	4%
2000	100%	95%	42%	4%
1999	89%	90%	28%	4%
1998	100%	95%	28%	20%

VIRGINIA 3

Southeast – parts of Richmond, Norfolk and Newport News, Portsmouth

The black-majority 3rd begins in historic Richmond and reaches southeast into military and shipbuilding territory, including parts of Newport News, Hampton and Norfolk. Redistricting following the 2000 census added the city of Portsmouth, which had been in the 4th District. The 3rd is the strongest Democratic district in the state.

Originally drawn as a 64 percent black district, the 3rd has been the focal point of Virginia redistricting since 1991. It saw its black population reduced under a court-ordered remap in 1998, then slightly increased under 2001 redistricting. Richmond, Portsmouth and Norfolk, which have substantial black populations, all gave Al Gore more than 60 percent of their vote in the 2000 presidential election. One heavily black precinct in Richmond backed Gore over George W. Bush by 639 to 5.

The 3rd long has benefited from one of the nation's largest ports at Hampton Roads and from growing financial firms in Richmond. State government also drives the economy of Richmond and its vicinity, as does manufacturing. Richmond boasts one of the largest cigarette plants in the nation (Philip Morris).

The Hampton Roads area has a heavy concentration of naval installations as well as shipbuilding and ship repair companies. Among these is the nation's largest privately owned shipyard — Newport News Shipbuilding — which builds Navy carriers and submarines.

MAJOR INDUSTRY

Defense, shipbuilding and repair, shipping, tobacco

MILITARY BASES

Fort Eustis (Army), 5,083 military, 2,526 civilian (2003); Naval Medical Center Portsmouth, 3,362 military, 1,270 civilian; Norfolk Naval Shipyard at Portsmouth, 924 military, 7,695 civilian (2001)

CITIES

Richmond (pt.), 144,520; Norfolk (pt.), 122,301; Newport News (pt.), 108,350; Portsmouth, 100,565; Hampton (pt.), 59,929

NOTABLE

The Edgar Allen Poe Museum is in Richmond, where the author lived and worked.

Rep. J. Randy Forbes (R)

CAPITOL OFFICE
225-6365
www.house.gov/forbes
307 Cannon 20515-4604; fax 226-1170

COMMITTEES
Armed Services
Judiciary
Science

HOMETOWN
Chesapeake

BORN
Feb. 17, 1952, Chesapeake, Va.

RELIGION
Baptist

FAMILY
Wife, Shirley Forbes; four children

EDUCATION
Randolph-Macon College, B.A. 1974 (political science); U. of Virginia, J.D. 1977

CAREER
Lawyer; state legislative aide

POLITICAL HIGHLIGHTS
Va. House, 1990-97 (Republican floor leader, 1994-97); Va. Republican Party chairman, 1996-2000; Va. Senate, 1997-2001 (Republican floor leader, 1998-2000)

ELECTION RESULTS

2002 GENERAL		
J. Randy Forbes (R)	108,733	97.9%
write-ins	2,308	2.1%
2002 PRIMARY		
J. Randy Forbes (R)		unopposed
2001 SPECIAL		
J. Randy Forbes (R)	70,917	52.0%
Louise Lucas (D)	65,190	47.8%

Elected June 2001; 1st full term

Forbes may not have a high-wattage personality — The Economist magazine characterized him as "dour and lugubrious; seemingly incapable of smiling, let alone flirting" — yet his mostly conservative view of the world and his long experience in Virginia politics have made him a favorite of his party leadership.

His 2001 special-election win in the 4th District was a reminder of the GOP's increased dominance in the South and the party's sometimes tense relationship with African-American voters. Forbes won a tightly contested special election against a black woman state senator to succeed longtime 4th District Rep. Norman Sisisky, a conservative Democrat who died March 29, 2001.

Forbes' hold on the competitive swing district improved dramatically following a controversial 2002 reapportionment plan that moved a number of African-American, Democratic-leaning neighborhoods into the neighboring 3rd District, where blacks already constitute the majority of registered voters. Democrats complained the move "packed" minority votes into a single district. The redistricting boosted the population of white voters in the 4th from 57 percent to more than 60 percent.

During his first term, Forbes has focused on local issues such as agriculture and defense while compiling a reliably conservative voting record. His close ties to state and national Republican leaders may prove valuable to a district with a heavy military presence that lost large numbers of federal civilian employees in the 1990s wave of downsizing and could be vulnerable to further cost-cutting. As state GOP chairman from 1996 to 2000, the soft-spoken but intensely competitive Forbes helped boost the political fortunes of former Gov. James S. Gilmore III, who later served as Republican National Committee chairman, and Sen. George F. Allen. Both were classmates of Forbes at the University of Virginia law school.

Forbes served in the Virginia General Assembly while Allen was governor (1994-98) and helped shepherd into law Allen's proposal to abolish parole. A Sunday school teacher at his Baptist church, Forbes opposes abortion and gun control. Those conservative credentials, combined with Forbes' background in business law, persuaded House leaders to appoint Forbes to a seat on the Judiciary Committee.

Forbes has embraced a tough law-and-order agenda, backing a bill that increased prison terms and fines for corporate wrongdoing and another to arm airline pilots with handguns in cockpits for a two-year trial period. He also urged House colleagues to continue to press for a ban on a procedure its opponents call "partial birth" abortion.

Forbes also serves on the Armed Services Committee, with two other Tidewater Virginia Republicans, Jo Ann Davis and Ed Schrock. On Armed Services, he looks out for such facilities as the Army's Fort Lee and the Norfolk Naval Shipyard. Another big federal facility in Forbes' purview is NASA's Langley Research Center in Hampton, a center for aeronautics research that periodically has been mentioned as a potential target if the space agency decides to close one or more of its regional centers.

Forbes also looks out for his rural constituents. He went to bat for peanut farmers, voting against the conference report to the 2002 farm bill because it scrapped the Depression-era peanut quota system — a program in which farmers owned licenses to produce only a certain amount in order to maintain high market prices. The bill provided fixed and counter-cyclical payments and marketing loans and compensated quota holders at 11 cents per pound per year for five years to transition out of the old program.

Forbes and other lawmakers representing peanut-growing areas successfully pressed the Internal Revenue Service to treat any gain from peanut quotas as capital assets instead of regular income, which would be taxed at a higher rate.

A former legislative aide and state representative, Forbes in 1997 won a state Senate seat that Republican Mark Earley had left open to run successfully for state attorney general. He had considered running against Sisisky in 2000, but demurred. He began 2001 as a candidate for lieutenant governor. But when Sisisky died in March, shortly after lung cancer surgery, Forbes switched to the special election to succeed him with encouragement from the Bush administration and the House Republican leadership. Forbes won the nomination in April at a contentious convention and went on to face Democratic state Sen. L. Louise Lucas, who was bidding to become the first black woman elected to Congress from Virginia.

The race captured national attention, quickly turning into the first referendum on the Bush presidency and Republican efforts to boost their slim majority in the House. The candidates and national parties spent more than $7 million during the 32-day campaign — about $52 for every vote cast.

Forbes endorsed a Social Security overhaul that would allow individuals to invest some payroll tax dollars in private accounts. He also pledged to fight for area farmers, citing the difficulties his grandparents faced in farming. At one point, his campaign accused Lucas of race-baiting for distributing a flyer that said Bush's tax cut would not help millions of minority families. Forbes' fortunes were also boosted by Vice President Dick Cheney and Oklahoma Rep. J.C. Watts, then chairman of the House Republican Conference, who each made campaign appearances.

In the end, results broke sharply along racial lines. Lucas won all 28 black-majority voting districts in Chesapeake, Portsmouth and Suffolk and received more than 90 percent of the vote in about half of those precincts. Forbes, however, captured 52 percent of the vote, winning 60 of 69 white-majority voting districts in those three cities and all seven white-majority counties in the district.

Forbes and Lucas were headed for a rematch in the 2002 mid-term elections. Lucas withdrew less than three months before the election, however, citing weak financial support from the Democratic party and a desire to protect jobs in her district at a time when the state was facing a $1.5 billion revenue shortfall. With no opposition, Forbes cruised to his first full term, capturing 98 percent of the vote.

KEY VOTES

2002

- No Overhaul campaign finance law; ban "soft money" and restrict advocacy advertising
- Yes Back Bush's defense budget increase
- Yes Extend 1996 welfare law
- Yes Adopt Bush's discretionary spending limit
- Yes Pass GOP Medicare prescription drug plan
- No Create independent Sept. 11 commission
- No Extend union protections to Homeland Security Department employees
- Yes Revive fast-track procedures for trade agreements
- Yes Authorize war against Iraq
- No Advance bankruptcy overhaul opposed by abortion opponents

2001

- No Maintain ban on oil drilling in Arctic National Wildlife Refuge
- Yes Approve Bush proposal to limit managed-care plan liability for coverage decisions
- No Divert money from crop subsidy payments to land conservation
- Yes Expand law enforcement power to investigate suspected terrorists

CQ VOTE STUDIES

	PARTY UNITY		PRESIDENTIAL SUPPORT	
	Support	Oppose	Support	Oppose
2002	98%	2%	85%	15%
2001	97%	3%	93%	7%

INTEREST GROUPS

	AFL-CIO	ADA	CCUS	ACU
2002	11%	0%	85%	100%
2001	13%	0%	94%	100%

VIRGINIA 4
Southeast – Chesapeake

Located in southeast and south-central Virginia, the 4th includes burgeoning Chesapeake and rural tobacco-growing areas to the west.

Redistricting following the 2000 census transformed the 4th from highly competitive territory to a Republican-leaning district that comfortably — though not overwhelmingly — backed George W. Bush for president in 2000. Mapmakers removed the heavily black, strongly Democratic city of Portsmouth, and reduced the district's black population from 39 percent to 33 percent.

Chesapeake, the 4th's most populous city, grew by nearly one-third in the 1990s. Chesapeake votes dependably Republican, as do the portions of Chesterfield County south of Richmond that are in the northern part of the district.

Democrats fare better in areas with sizable black voting blocks. Petersburg, which is four-fifths black, gave Al Gore his best vote percentage (79 percent) in the state in 2000. Across the Appomattox River from Petersburg is Colonial Heights, which is largely white and gave 71 percent of the vote to Bush.

Although the 4th's military installations lost civilian employees in the 1990s wave of downsizing, the overall effect on the district was negligible, as Chesapeake compensated by attracting new manufacturing businesses. Outside of the 4th's population centers, tobacco and peanut farming play a central role in the economy.

MAJOR INDUSTRY

Military, agriculture, health care, manufacturing

MILITARY BASES

Fort Lee (Army), 3,119 military, 2,388 civilian (2002); Naval Security Group Activity Northwest, 654 military, 231 civilian (1998); U.S. Atlantic Command Joint Warfighting Center, 166 military, 498 civilian (2001)

CITIES

Chesapeake, 199,184; Suffolk, 63,677; Petersburg, 33,740; Hopewell, 22,354

NOTABLE

Suffolk is considered the "peanut capital of the world" — the town has a small museum dedicated to Planters' Mr. Peanut and hosts an annual "peanut fest."

Rep. Virgil H. Goode Jr. (R)

CAPITOL OFFICE
225-4711
www.house.gov/goode
1520 Longworth 20515-4605; fax 225-5681

COMMITTEES
Appropriations

HOMETOWN
Rocky Mount

BORN
Oct. 17, 1946, Richmond, Va.

RELIGION
Baptist

FAMILY
Wife, Lucy D. Goode; one child

EDUCATION
U. of Richmond, B.A. 1969; U. of Virginia, J.D. 1973

MILITARY SERVICE
Va. National Guard, 1969-75

CAREER
Lawyer

POLITICAL HIGHLIGHTS
Va. Senate, 1973-97 (served as a Democrat); sought Democratic nomination for U.S. Senate, 1982, 1994

ELECTION RESULTS

2002 GENERAL		
Virgil H. Goode Jr. (R)	95,360	63.5%
Meredith Richards (D)	54,805	36.5%
2002 PRIMARY		
Virgil H. Goode Jr. (R)		unopposed
2000 GENERAL		
Virgil H. Goode Jr. (I)	143,312	67.4%
John Boyd (D)	65,387	30.7%
Joseph S. Spence (I)	3,936	1.9%

PREVIOUS WINNING PERCENTAGES
1998 (99%); 1996 (60%)
* Elected as a Democrat 1996-1998; Elected as an independent, 2000

Elected 1996; 4th term

It took him years to do it, but Goode officially joined the Republican Party in 2002, aligning himself officially with a party that, based on his voting record, he had joined unofficially long before.

Raised as a conservative Democrat, Goode, through much of his public career, has often said he felt more comfortable voting for Republican policies. As a state senator in 1995, he forced a power-sharing arrangement that gave the GOP four committee chairmanships. When he came to Congress two years later, he promptly joined the "Blue Dog" coalition of conservative Democrats and established a voting record that identified him as a Republican in all but name. Early in 2000, Goode (rhymes with food) resigned from the House Democratic Caucus, declared himself an independent, and began caucusing with the Republican Conference. The GOP leadership rewarded him by giving him a seat on the Appropriations Committee.

Two years later, he announced he would seek re-election as a Republican, and in April 2002, he filed papers seeking the Republican nomination for a fourth term. He was not challenged and became the GOP nominee in June. But on Capitol Hill, he remained an independent in the eyes of the Clerk of the House, who said Goode needed to provide written notice of his affiliation before he officially would be considered a Republican. "I guess I should look into that one of these days," he said, and in August he made his party switch within the House formal.

His languid approach to the matter is a reflection of Goode's go-slow style. His soft, syrupy accent reflects his Southern roots, and his district, which borders North Carolina, is known locally as Southside.

Goode's opposition to gun control, abortion and desecration of the flag match those of most GOP conservatives. He opposes tougher environmental controls on businesses. Even in 1999, when he was still a Democrat, he opposed President Clinton on roll call votes more often than such Republican stalwarts as Tom DeLay of Texas and Henry J. Hyde of Illinois.

He was an active member of the Immigration Reform Caucus, even before the Sept. 11, 2001, terrorist attacks focused more attention on the national security implications of immigration policy and the government's effectiveness at policing its borders. Goode is opposed to the admission of foreign workers under a program that gives visas to foreigners with high-technology job skills. "American citizens need these jobs," he said. Goode also opposes amnesty for those in the United States illegally. In the 107th Congress and again in the 108th, he pursued legislation allowing the military to help the INS or the Customs Service, if requested.

But most of Goode's legislative efforts focus on improving the economy in the relatively poor 5th District. One issue on which he takes a different tack than the majority of Republicans is international trade. Goode says the loss of textile plants in his district is a prime example of the downside of recent trade liberalization. In the 107th, he opposed granting the president fast-track trade negotiating authority.

Also in the 107th, he teamed with Democrat Rick Boucher of the neighboring 9th District to offer legislation to help laid-off workers continue their medical insurance. Their bill called for the government to pay three-quarters of the cost of premiums for as long as 18 months for workers who lost their jobs either as a result of a total company shutdown or downsizing. Goode also pushes a plan to permit taxpayers to donate part of their tax refund to pay for catastrophic health insurance for uninsured people.

Tobacco farming in Virginia is a threatened vocation. Goode joined again with Boucher to propose legislation to end the quota system — providing lump sum payments to farmers who grow a certain quota of tobacco — and replace it with federal licenses. Under their plan, no one would be permitted to raise tobacco without having a license, which unlike the quotas, could not be sold. The idea is to permit the region's generally small tobacco farms to continue without pressure from larger operations to buy their quotas and put them out of business.

During the many years Goode resisted entreaties to switch to the GOP, he would tell people that "Daddy was a Democrat" who had instilled in his son an appreciation for New Deal programs that aided rural areas. Virgil Sr. was in the state legislature and also served as a state prosecutor; a stretch of highway in Rocky Mount is named after him. Virgil Jr. recalls tagging along as his father attended gatherings around the wood stoves at the general stores that were the prime small-town meeting places. "If you could get the country store vote, you had it made," Goode recalls.

After graduation from law school, Goode quickly jumped into politics when an opening developed in the state Senate. He made no secret about his ambitions for higher office, and in 1982 and 1994 he unsuccessfully pursued the Democratic nomination for the U.S. Senate.

His reputation as a political maverick intensified after the 1995 election yielded a state Senate in partisan deadlock. Democrats retained effective control because the Democratic lieutenant governor held a tie-breaking vote. But Goode insisted on an "equitable division" of power in the committee system, and he forced a power-sharing arrangement in which the GOP gained control of four committees. Goode himself surrendered a gavel to a Republican to help grease the deal.

In 1996, the day after Democrat L. F. Payne Jr. announced he would not seek another term, Goode launched his bid for Congress. He campaigned in a down-home style reminiscent of his father's, driving to small-town events where he spoke off the cuff and handed out emery boards and pencils embossed with his name. (His father used to give out small kitchen implements.) He won by 24 percentage points. In 1998, he drew no GOP foe.

Democratic party officials were conflicted by Goode's Republican tilt. While he was likely the only Democrat who could win the seat, his votes in the House rankled. If Goode had not left the party in 2000, he probably would not have gained Democratic backing anyway.

His two victories since, as an independent in 2000 and a Republican in 2002, have been by healthy margins.

KEY VOTES

2002

- No Overhaul campaign finance law; ban "soft money" and restrict advocacy advertising
- Yes Back Bush's defense budget increase
- Yes Extend 1996 welfare law
- Yes Adopt Bush's discretionary spending limit
- Yes Pass GOP Medicare prescription drug plan
- No Create independent Sept. 11 commission
- No Extend union protections to Homeland Security Department employees
- No Revive fast-track procedures for trade agreements
- Yes Authorize war against Iraq
- No Advance bankruptcy overhaul opposed by abortion opponents

2001

- Yes Nullify Clinton Labor Department ergonomics rule
- Yes Cut taxes by $1.35 trillion through fiscal 2011
- No Maintain ban on oil drilling in Arctic National Wildlife Refuge
- Yes Approve Bush proposal to limit managed-care plan liability for coverage decisions
- No Divert money from crop subsidy payments to land conservation
- Yes Expand law enforcement power to investigate suspected terrorists

CQ VOTE STUDIES

	PARTY UNITY		PRESIDENTIAL SUPPORT	
	Support	Oppose	Support	Oppose
2002	93%	7%	74%	26%
2001	92%	8%	79%	21%
2000	94%	6%	14%	86%
1999	22%	78%	16%	84%
1998	28%	72%	26%	74%

INTEREST GROUPS

	AFL-CIO	ADA	CCUS	ACU
2002	11%	5%	75%	96%
2001	25%	10%	83%	96%
2000	10%	10%	66%	100%
1999	44%	25%	84%	92%
1998	30%	30%	72%	83%

VIRGINIA 5

South central – Danville, Charlottesville

Rich in Civil War landmarks, the 5th extends from just north of Charlottesville, in the central part of the state, to the south-central tier bordering North Carolina, an area known as "Southside."

The mostly rural 5th is relatively poor, and the district relies heavily on agriculture and textiles. Known as the heart of tobacco country, the 5th still supports a vast tobacco industry, but in recent years manufacturing has taken a more prominent role. Danville, the district's largest city, is a tobacco and textile center on the North Carolina border. To the west is Martinsville, a textile and furniture town.

The seasonal nature of the economy led to above-average unemployment during some of the 1990s in the district's southwest corner. But the 5th's economy also saw some strong performances during the decade. Bedford County, between Roanoke and Lynchburg (both of which are in the 6th), and Fluvanna County, in the orbit of Charlottesville, have grown by attracting commuters as well as many small businesses. Fluvanna County grew by 61 percent in the 1990s, and Greene County, located north of Charlottesville, grew by 48 percent.

Redistricting following the 2000 census made minor changes to the reliably conservative district, which typically gives GOP candidates vote percentages hovering in the mid-50s. One notable exception to the district's conservative posture is the city of Charlottesville, which is home to the University of Virginia and almost always backs Democrats.

But the conservative rural areas also can support Democratic candidates, provided they express right-of-center views on issues such as gun owners' rights. Democrat Mark Warner employed such a strategy with success in the 5th District during his 2001 gubernatorial bid.

MAJOR INDUSTRY

Agriculture, manufacturing, textiles, service

CITIES

Danville, 48,411; Charlottesville, 45,049; Martinsville, 15,416

NOTABLE

Appomattox Court House is where Gen. Robert E. Lee surrendered to Gen. Ulysses S. Grant, ending the Civil War; Thomas Jefferson's estate, Monticello, and James Monroe's estate, Ash Lawn-Highland, are just south of Charlottesville.

Rep. Robert W. Goodlatte (R)

CAPITOL OFFICE
225-5431
talk2bob@mail.house.gov
www.house.gov/goodlatte
2240 Rayburn 20515-4606; fax 225-9681

COMMITTEES
Agriculture - chairman
Judiciary
Select Homeland Security

HOMETOWN
Roanoke

BORN
Sept. 22, 1952, Holyoke, Mass.

RELIGION
Christian Scientist

FAMILY
Wife, Maryellen Goodlatte; two children

EDUCATION
Bates College, B.A. 1974 (government); Washington and Lee U., J.D. 1977

CAREER
Lawyer; congressional aide

POLITICAL HIGHLIGHTS
Roanoke City Republican Committee chairman, 1980-83; 6th Congressional District Republican Party chairman, 1983-88

ELECTION RESULTS

2002 GENERAL		
Robert W. Goodlatte (R)	105,530	97.1%
write-ins	3,202	3.0%
2002 PRIMARY		
Robert W. Goodlatte (R)		unopposed
2000 GENERAL		
Robert W. Goodlatte (R)		unopposed

PREVIOUS WINNING PERCENTAGES
1998 (69%); 1996 (67%); 1994 (100%); 1992 (60%)

Elected 1992; 6th term

Goodlatte is the new chairman of the Agriculture Committee, but his political philosophy is much the same as that of his predecessor, Texan Larry Combest. Goodlatte is a conservative from a rural district interested in keeping farmers happy.

His ascension probably has the most impact on the food stamp program, which falls under Agriculture's jurisdiction. He has been a steady advocate of cutting costs and reducing waste in the government's main antihunger program for the poor.

Goodlatte (GOOD-lat) also has a strong interest in technology policy, particularly as it affects rural areas. He says rural America will be economically competitive in the future only if it keeps pace in the computer age. He maintains that communications technology today is comparable to the railroad in the 19th century. "If the railroad came through your town and connected you with the rest of the country, you'd boom. If it didn't, you'd go bust," says Goodlatte, co-chairman of the Congressional Internet Caucus.

When Combest announced just after the 2002 election that he planned to leave Congress early in 2003, Goodlatte moved quickly to line up support to replace him as Agriculture chairman. The only potential competitor with more seniority, John A. Boehner of Ohio, was content to remain chairman of the Education and the Workforce Committee, so Goodlatte was the easy choice.

Under Combest, Congress enacted a six-year agriculture bill in 2002. As a result, Goodlatte will not have to contend with the committee's biggest piece of legislation soon — or the ferociously competing interests that the bill typically generates. He is free to pursue other issues.

He has had a longstanding interest in the food stamp program. After Republicans took control of the House in 1995, he helped engineer changes that reduced its mandatory spending levels by more than $10 billion annually. These include a requirement that able-bodied recipients work; a ban on convicted food stamp traffickers and prison inmates receiving food stamps; and improved record-keeping to ensure that dead people are not still listed on the rolls.

A member of the Agriculture Committee since 1993, Goodlatte represents a district with many dairy and poultry farms and forestry operations. The committee also has jurisdiction over national forests, which account for about a third of the land area in Goodlatte's Shenandoah Valley district.

New technologies actually can give bucolic areas such as the 6th District an advantage over big cities, Goodlatte says. The region's natural beauty, relatively low cost of living, low crime and unclogged roads are a powerful draw, particularly if 21st century jobs are available. Goodlatte believes his own experience offers guidance. As a lawyer in Roanoke, he took advantage of the latest communications and information technology to build a competitive practice that included a specialty in immigration law. "Using technology, I was able to compete with lawyers from Washington and New York," he recalls.

Also a member of the Judiciary Committee, Goodlatte long has pursued other technology-related issues. In the past decade, he has been a player in almost every major computer-related bill before Congress, including those aimed at protecting users' privacy, preserving intellectual copyright protections for artists and creators of software, shielding children from indecent material and safeguarding consumers from fraud. He also has been active in efforts to rein in unsolicited e-mail, called "spam."

In the 107th Congress, Goodlatte brokered a deal with social conservatives and casinos on a bill to limit Internet gambling. The bill foundered, but opponents of on-line gambling continue their quest to outlaw it. He also was instrumental in drafting the "eContract," a House Republican high-tech legislative manifesto for the 107th that was aimed at promoting the Internet economy while reducing taxation, regulation and lawsuits. In the 106th, he was the principal House sponsor of legislation providing loan guarantees to help rural satellite and cable television systems deliver local broadcast stations to viewers who would otherwise have no reception.

His positions are driven by the philosophy that government mostly should stay out of the way of innovators and entrepreneurs. That point of view, he argues, is more in tune with the needs of high-tech industries than that of the Democrats. But he also notes that many Internet-related issues lend themselves to bipartisanship. He joined with California Democrat Zoe Lofgren on legislation to permit the export of encryption technology that scrambles digital information during computer transmission.

In the 107th, Goodlatte also sponsored a controversial bill to limit class-action lawsuits against tobacco companies, gun makers and other companies. It passed the House but stalled in the Senate.

Goodlatte had a middle-class upbringing in western Massachusetts. His father managed a Friendly's ice cream store and his mother worked part time in a department store. Though his parents were not politically active, Goodlatte remembers being fascinated early on by current affairs and politics. He was president of the College Republicans at Bates College. After getting a law degree at Washington & Lee in Lexington, Va., Goodlatte entered private practice but also worked for the area's Republican congressman, M. Caldwell Butler.

The GOP long had been competitive in the 6th. Goodlatte thought about running for Congress in 1986, but the arrival of his second child at the start of the campaign season kept him from entering the race. In 1992, however, when Democrat Jim Olin retired after five terms, Goodlatte decided the time was right. He won easily and has not been seriously challenged since. Democrats did not field a challenger in 2002. And three months before winning his sixth term, Goodlatte announced he was renouncing a promise from his original 1992 campaign to stay no more than a dozen years in the House.

KEY VOTES

2002

No Overhaul campaign finance law; ban "soft money" and restrict advocacy advertising
Yes Back Bush's defense budget increase
Yes Extend 1996 welfare law
Yes Adopt Bush's discretionary spending limit
Yes Pass GOP Medicare prescription drug plan
No Create independent Sept. 11 commission
No Extend union protections to Homeland Security Department employees
Yes Revive fast-track procedures for trade agreements
Yes Authorize war against Iraq
No Advance bankruptcy overhaul opposed by abortion opponents

2001

Yes Nullify Clinton Labor Department ergonomics rule
Yes Cut taxes by $1.35 trillion through fiscal 2011
No Maintain ban on oil drilling in Arctic National Wildlife Refuge
Yes Approve Bush proposal to limit managed-care plan liability for coverage decisions
No Divert money from crop subsidy payments to land conservation
Yes Expand law enforcement power to investigate suspected terrorists

CQ VOTE STUDIES

	PARTY UNITY		PRESIDENTIAL SUPPORT	
	Support	Oppose	Support	Oppose
2002	99%	1%	88%	12%
2001	97%	3%	91%	9%
2000	97%	3%	22%	78%
1999	95%	5%	16%	84%
1998	92%	8%	23%	77%

INTEREST GROUPS

	AFL-CIO	ADA	CCUS	ACU
2002	0%	0%	95%	100%
2001	17%	0%	91%	96%
2000	0%	0%	85%	100%
1999	22%	5%	88%	96%
1998	0%	0%	100%	100%

VIRGINIA 6
Northwest – Roanoke, Lynchburg

Running along the Shenandoah Valley, the conservative 6th is a collage of mountainous terrain, small towns, medium-size cities and natural beauty. Beginning in Roanoke, the district's most populous city, one can drive 160 miles northeast along Interstate 81 to Interstate 66, without leaving the 6th District.

The 6th has one of the largest populations of senior citizens in the state, a mostly white-collar work force and a generous dose of Republicans. George W. Bush and George Allen both won 60 percent of the vote in the 2000 presidential and senatorial elections. Augusta and Rockingham counties gave Bush more than 70 percent of their votes.

The brand of Republicanism in the rural valley traditionally has been a moderate one. The 1992 election of GOP Rep. Goodlatte ended the Democrats' decade-long domination of the 6th seat, but Democrats still won in local elections in the 1990s. Roanoke has a strong Democratic base with union ties. But Republicans have done well in Roanoke's suburbs, in Lynchburg and in most rural areas.

Roanoke has a variety of industries, including furniture and electrical products manufacturing. Both Roanoke and Lynchburg saw their populations shrink slightly in the 1990s, but the manufacturing economy was generally solid. Several colleges are in the district as well.

Outside the Roanoke and Lynchburg metropolitan areas, the 6th depends mainly on dairy farming, livestock and poultry. In the north, Rockingham County leads the state in livestock and hay production. Tourists traveling to the district's national parks and caverns also help boost the economy. There are some chemical plants and pulpwood and paper mills in the area north of Roanoke.

MAJOR INDUSTRY

Agriculture, livestock, manufacturing

CITIES

Roanoke, 94,911; Lynchburg, 65,269; Harrisonburg, 40,468; Cave Spring, 24,941; Salem, 24,747; Staunton, 23,853

NOTABLE

Lynchburg is the home of evangelist Jerry Falwell's Liberty University and Thomas Road Baptist Church; President Woodrow Wilson was born in Staunton (pronounced "Stanton").

Rep. Eric Cantor (R)

CAPITOL OFFICE
225-2815
www.house.gov/cantor
329 Cannon 20515-4607; fax 225-0011

COMMITTEES
Ways & Means

HOMETOWN
Glen Allen

BORN
June 6, 1963, Richmond, Va.

RELIGION
Jewish

FAMILY
Wife, Diana Cantor; three children

EDUCATION
George Washington U., B.A. 1985 (political science); College of William & Mary, J.D. 1988; Columbia U., M.S. 1989 (real estate development)

CAREER
Lawyer; real estate developer; campaign aide

POLITICAL HIGHLIGHTS
Va. House, 1992-2001

ELECTION RESULTS

2002 GENERAL		
Eric Cantor (R)	113,658	69.5%
Ben L. "Cooter" Jones (D)	49,854	30.5%
2002 PRIMARY		
Eric Cantor (R)		unopposed
2000 GENERAL		
Eric Cantor (R)	192,652	66.9%
Warren A. Stewart (D)	94,935	33.0%

Elected 2000; 2nd term

A rising star in the House GOP, Cantor's congressional career is on a fast track. Serving in only his second term, he was chosen at the outset of the 108th Congress to be Whip Roy Blunt's chief deputy, a job that in recent years has become a steppingstone to the upper Republican ranks. Cantor also was given a prized seat on the Ways and Means Committee — all before his 40th birthday.

Cantor says he was surprised when Blunt chose him for the GOP leadership's most important appointive job. In one respect, it was not surprising. Cantor is like a younger Blunt. Both are business-oriented conservatives who are temperamentally low-key. Both had solid résumés in state government before coming to Washington, Cantor as a member of the Virginia House and Blunt as Missouri secretary of state.

Blunt also was plucked from relative obscurity in 1999 to be Whip Tom DeLay's chief deputy. DeLay moved up to majority leader in the 108th, and Blunt took his place as whip. Another former chief deputy whip, Republican J. Dennis Hastert, is the House Speaker.

Cantor has been preparing for his career since he was a kid. He talked politics around the dinner table with his father, a longtime Richmond-area GOP official, and stuffed envelopes and knocked on doors at election time. As a teenager, he was a campaign volunteer for the veteran lawmaker whom he eventually replaced, Thomas J. Bliley Jr., a prominent conservative Republican who retired in 1999 after two decades in the House.

With a law degree from William and Mary and a stint in real estate behind him, Cantor arrived in Congress in 2000 not content to confine his pursuits to constituent service and local issues, as many freshmen do. He immediately got on the International Relations Committee, and by the end of his first year in the House, he was a sought-after television news commentator on terrorism and the Middle East conflict.

Early in the 107th Congress, Cantor was named chairman of the Congressional Task Force on Terrorism and Unconventional Warfare, an unofficial caucus that briefs Republicans on issues and makes legislative recommendations. After the Sept. 11, 2001, terrorist attacks, Cantor argued that the eradication of state-sponsored terrorism should be a core objective of U.S. foreign policy. He urged U.S. officials to take a tough stance against Syria, Iran and Iraq.

A strong supporter of Israel, Cantor, who is Jewish, also wants the United States to be aggressive against Yasser Arafat and the Palestinian Authority. He condemned Arafat for permitting excavation work at the Temple Mount in Jerusalem, which was endangering historic artifacts at the site.

With his seat on Ways and Means, Cantor can expand his interests into major tax policy, though he has had to relinquish his seats on the International Relations and Financial Services panels. In the 107th Congress, he introduced a bill to provide a $1,000 per child education tax credit. Parents could use the money for a variety of educational purposes, including books, computers, tutors and private school tuition.

Like his predecessor Bliley, Cantor advocates limited government, lower taxes and a stronger military. Bliley, who chaired the Energy and Commerce Committee for six years, is in fact Cantor's political mentor and an old family friend. Cantor describes himself as a conservative "who likes to work toward consensus." When he was in the state legislature, Cantor was described in the local press as a "calm voice" who, despite a voting record lauded by the National Rifle Association, the Christian Coalition and Family Foundation "does not come across as a firebrand."

His other pursuits in the 107th Congress included rail transportation and proposed new designs for the dollar bill and the nickel. Cantor wants to secure federal funding for the development of the Southeast High Speed Rail Corridor, which would run from Washington to Richmond to Charlotte and eventually to Raleigh, Jacksonville and Atlanta. And, carrying on a Bliley objective, he wants to redesign U.S. currency to place an abbreviated version of the Constitution on the back of each bill. The idea was initiated by middle school and high school students while Bliley was in office. Cantor also wants to retain Monticello on the back of the nickel.

Cantor grew up in a well-to-do, politically active Richmond family and majored in political science at George Washington University. While still a teenager, Cantor worked as a driver in Bliley's first House re-election campaign in 1982. He also worked as an aide to Virginia lawmaker Walter A. Stosch during a legislative session.

After law school and a master's degree in real estate development, he went into the family businesses, which included the law firm founded by his father and uncle, and a real estate development and finance company.

But he remained active in local GOP politics. When his old boss, Stosch, a member of the Virginia House of Delegates, decided to run for the state Senate in 1991, Cantor was well-positioned to make a bid for the open seat. He out-organized and outspent two more-experienced rivals, becoming at 28 the youngest member of the state House. He was one of the founders of the state-financed Virginia Holocaust Museum.

Bliley's campaign machinery stood behind Cantor when needed, and Cantor returned the favor by serving as Bliley's campaign chairman during several of the elder lawmaker's re-election bids. When Bliley announced his retirement, Cantor jumped into the Republican primary to replace him. But despite the backing from Bliley's organization and help with fundraising, Cantor won by a scant 263 votes over state Sen. Stephen H. Martin. The primary win in the heavily Republican district ensured his success in November, however. He swept the general election with two-thirds of the vote.

The district stayed solidly Republican after redistricting. Cantor won re-election in 2002 by 39 percentage points over Democrat Ben Jones, who served two terms in the House from Georgia a decade ago, but who is best-known as Cooter, the hayseed auto mechanic on "The Dukes of Hazard" television series.

KEY VOTES

2002

No Overhaul campaign finance law; ban "soft money" and restrict advocacy advertising
Yes Back Bush's defense budget increase
Yes Extend 1996 welfare law
Yes Adopt Bush's discretionary spending limit
Yes Pass GOP Medicare prescription drug plan
No Create independent Sept. 11 commission
No Extend union protections to Homeland Security Department employees
Yes Revive fast-track procedures for trade agreements
Yes Authorize war against Iraq
Yes Advance bankruptcy overhaul opposed by abortion opponents

2001

Yes Nullify Clinton Labor Department ergonomics rule
Yes Cut taxes by $1.35 trillion through fiscal 2011
No Maintain ban on oil drilling in Arctic National Wildlife Refuge
Yes Approve Bush proposal to limit managed-care plan liability for coverage decisions
No Divert money from crop subsidy payments to land conservation
Yes Expand law enforcement power to investigate suspected terrorists

CQ VOTE STUDIES

	PARTY UNITY		PRESIDENTIAL SUPPORT	
	Support	Oppose	Support	Oppose
2002	99%	1%	90%	10%
2001	98%	2%	95%	5%

INTEREST GROUPS

	AFL-CIO	ADA	CCUS	ACU
2002	11%	0%	100%	100%
2001	8%	0%	100%	100%

VIRGINIA 7

Central — part of Richmond and suburbs

The solidly Republican 7th contains parts of Richmond and its affluent old-money suburbs, and then reaches northwest into farmlands.

Many of the 7th's residents work in Richmond, which grew steadily in the 1990s on the strength of banking and manufacturing. The longtime center of state government and commerce, Richmond also was one of the South's early manufacturing centers, concentrating on tobacco processing. Nearby Philip Morris continues to employ thousands of employees who live in the district.

The largest population block is in Henrico County (shared with the 3rd), which cups Richmond and has a backward C-shape. Henrico generally leans Republican, though it backed Democrat Mark Warner in the 2001 gubernatorial election. Chesterfield County, half of which is in the 4th, borders Richmond to the south and west and also has a strong GOP lean. Richmonders who live in the 7th are generally strong Republican voters who live in the city's western end.

The northern stretch of the 7th is home to traditional farming communities that gradually are being taken over by people who take long commutes to jobs in metropolitan Washington, D.C.

The 7th is a Republican bastion that gave George W. Bush 61 percent of its 2000 presidential vote — his statewide high — and gave 60 percent to George Allen in the 2000 Senate race. Redistricting following the 2000 census made the 7th slightly less Republican by adding some Democratic precincts in Richmond and Henrico County. But the district is still reliably Republican territory.

MAJOR INDUSTRY
Agriculture, government, manufacturing

MILITARY BASES
Defense Supply Center, Richmond, 52 military, 3,015 civilian (2001)

CITIES
Richmond (pt.), 53,270; Tuckahoe, 43,242; Mechanicsville, 30,464

NOTABLE
Luray Caverns is in Page County; The late tennis star Arthur Ashe was born in Richmond in 1943; During a 1960 presidential campaign stop in Culpeper, Lyndon B. Johnson famously asked, "What has Richard Nixon ever done for Culpeper?"

Rep. James P. Moran (D)

CAPITOL OFFICE
225-4376
www.house.gov/moran
2239 Rayburn 20515-4608; fax 225-0017

COMMITTEES
Appropriations
Budget

HOMETOWN
Arlington

BORN
May 16, 1945, Buffalo, N.Y.

RELIGION
Roman Catholic

FAMILY
Divorced; four children

EDUCATION
College of the Holy Cross, B.A. 1967 (economics); City U. of New York, Bernard M. Baruch School of Finance, attended 1967-68; U. of Pittsburgh, M.P.A. 1970

CAREER
Investment broker; congressional aide

POLITICAL HIGHLIGHTS
Alexandria City Council, 1979-84 (vice mayor, 1982-84); mayor of Alexandria, 1985-90

ELECTION RESULTS

2002 GENERAL		
James P. Moran (D)	102,759	59.8%
Scott C. Tate (R)	64,121	37.3%
Ron Crickenberger (I)	4,558	2.7%
2002 PRIMARY		
James P. Moran (D)		unopposed
2000 GENERAL		
James P. Moran (D)	164,178	63.3%
Demaris Miller (R)	88,262	34.1%
Ron Crickenberger (I)	3,483	1.3%
Rick Herron (I)	2,805	1.1%

PREVIOUS WINNING PERCENTAGES
1998 (67%); 1996 (66%); 1994 (59%); 1992 (56%); 1990 (52%)

Elected 1990; 7th term

A former amateur boxer, Moran seems to relish his reputation as one of Congress' premier pugilistic pols. And, while he also has developed the requisite skill set of a senior appropriator — an ability to cut deals across party lines and behind the scenes — Moran's spate of family and financial troubles and his propensity for shoot-from-the-lip comments continue to tarnish his congressional persona.

Early in 2003, after he suggested to a constituent at a public forum that Jewish influence was a major factor in the Bush administration's push to wage war in Iraq, he was roundly repudiated by his Democratic colleagues, many of whom characterized his comments as offensive. He apologized, but House Democratic leader Nancy Pelosi stripped Moran of his post in the party's whip organization and a half-dozen Democratic lawmakers urged Moran not to seek re-election in 2004.

Moran had enhanced his reputation as an able if confrontational negotiator at a meeting with top White House aides in the fall of 2001 when he threatened to push legislation to reopen Reagan National Airport, which the president had ordered closed indefinitely after the Sept. 11 terrorist attacks. Knowing full well the frustration of many lawmakers, who had been denied their most convenient passage out of town, soon after that meeting the administration unveiled an airport reopening plan.

The incident was a prime example of the way Moran can combine a bare-knuckled political style with a capacity to forge coalitions. He often has worked in tandem on parochial issues with Virginia's two GOP senators, John W. Warner and George Allen. Moran also collaborated with a Republican from a neighboring House district, Thomas M. Davis III, to close the District of Columbia's troubled prison in the Virginia suburb of Lorton and to secure federal funds for the replacement of the Woodrow Wilson Bridge.

Except for the first two years of GOP control of the House, Moran has been on the Appropriations Committee since the start of his second term, in 1993. He is the top-ranking Democrat on the Legislative Branch Subcommittee, an ideal post for a lawmaker with constituents who work for Congress. Earlier in his career, Moran spent one term as top Democrat on the other appropriations panel of parochial concern to Virginia's suburbanites — the District of Columbia Subcommittee.

In an effort to position himself as a centrist, Moran in 1997 joined with two House colleagues to found the New Democrat Coalition, which seeks "mainstream, bipartisan solutions" and which now has more than 70 members. While he votes with the majority of his party against most Republicans about four-fifths of the time, he has carved out some areas where he goes against the partisan grain. He has voted, for example, for all four of the major trade liberalization laws of the past decade.

One of Moran's priorities is helping to guarantee a skilled work force for the technology industry. He favors legislation to create business tax credits for training and to launch regional alliances among industry, colleges and the federal government to develop training programs.

Despite Moran's efforts to work with Republicans, his displays of partisan temper are well-remembered. Leaving the House floor in 1995 after a sharp exchange, Moran gave California Republican Randy "Duke" Cunningham a stiff push, initiating a partisan shoving match among other lawmakers. (Cunningham had said that Moran, who voted against committing U.S. forces to the Persian Gulf in 1991, had "turned his back" on Desert Storm.)

The nose is a favorite target in Moran's pugnacious imagination. In 1999 Moran challenged Indiana Republican Dan Burton, who during an International Relations meeting had himself confronted an Agency for International Development official. "You pull that again and I'll break your nose," Moran told his colleague. After President Clinton in 1998 admitted his affair with the former White House intern Monica Lewinsky, Moran told Hillary Rodham Clinton that if he were her older brother, he would have broken her husband's nose.

The son of a professional boxer and Washington Redskins football player, Moran takes pride in his prowess as an amateur heavyweight, including college bouts at Holy Cross and an exhibition match with former heavyweight champion Joe Frazier. Moran emphasizes his fighting spirit as a defender of his constituents. He has championed better pay and benefits for federal workers and more funding for Pentagon programs.

Moran's wife of 11 years, Mary, filed for divorce in 1999, one day after placing an emergency call to police during a domestic argument. No charges were filed, and Moran brought his own divorce complaint three weeks later. Court filings outlined the couple's financial losses: He blamed her for profligate spending; she blamed him for losing $120,000 in stock trading.

First elected to the Alexandria City Council in 1979, Moran saw his career derailed briefly in 1984 when, after pleading no contest to a misdemeanor conflict-of-interest charge, he resigned as vice mayor as part of a plea agreement. Running as an independent the next year, he unseated the incumbent mayor. He was still serving as mayor in 1990 when he first ran for Congress and unseated six-term Republican Stan Parris, himself one of the scrappier street-fighters in Washington-area politics.

Moran and Parris clearly did not like each other. Parris compared Moran to Iraqi leader Saddam Hussein; Moran called Parris a "racist" and a "fatuous jerk" and professed a predictable desire: to "break his nose." The policy difference Moran focused on, however, was his support for abortion rights and the incumbent's anti-abortion views. Moran won with 52 percent.

The 8th District was transformed into a Democratic stronghold by the 1990s redistricting process. After stiff challenges in 1992 and 1994 from Kyle E. McSlarrow, later a top Senate GOP aide and more recently a senior Energy Department official in the Bush administration, Moran won comfortably in the late 1990s. The district was made even more reliably Democratic in the post-2000 census remapping. In the aftermath of Moran's remarks about Jewish influence, a number of Democrats in the district showed interest in mounting a primary challenge in 2004.

KEY VOTES

2002

- Yes Overhaul campaign finance law; ban "soft money" and restrict advocacy advertising
- Yes Back Bush's defense budget increase
- No Extend 1996 welfare law
- No Adopt Bush's discretionary spending limit
- No Pass GOP Medicare prescription drug plan
- Yes Create independent Sept. 11 commission
- Yes Extend union protections to Homeland Security Department employees
- Yes Revive fast-track procedures for trade agreements
- No Authorize war against Iraq
- Yes Advance bankruptcy overhaul opposed by abortion opponents

2001

- No Nullify Clinton Labor Department ergonomics rule
- No Cut taxes by $1.35 trillion through fiscal 2011
- Yes Maintain ban on oil drilling in Arctic National Wildlife Refuge
- No Approve Bush proposal to limit managed-care plan liability for coverage decisions
- Yes Divert money from crop subsidy payments to land conservation
- Yes Expand law enforcement power to investigate suspected terrorists

CQ VOTE STUDIES

	PARTY UNITY		PRESIDENTIAL SUPPORT	
	Support	Oppose	Support	Oppose
2002	84%	16%	42%	58%
2001	79%	21%	40%	60%
2000	83%	17%	77%	23%
1999	79%	21%	75%	25%
1998	79%	21%	81%	19%

INTEREST GROUPS

	AFL-CIO	ADA	CCUS	ACU
2002	67%	70%	68%	21%
2001	83%	85%	57%	8%
2000	60%	70%	66%	12%
1999	67%	90%	64%	12%
1998	70%	75%	61%	8%

VIRGINIA 8

Washington suburbs – Arlington, Alexandria, part of Fairfax County

Taking in the close-in Washington, D.C., suburbs in Northern Virginia, the Democratic 8th is one of the wealthiest districts in the state, though poorer pockets exist along the Route 1 corridor. The area is racially diverse, especially in Arlington County, where nearly one in five residents is Hispanic, and in Alexandria, where nearly one in four is black.

A smattering of landmarks gives the district a colonial flavor, but the area is far from old-fashioned. The 8th bustles with technology businesses and defense contractors, drawn to the district's substantial military presence, including the Pentagon. While government and defense-related employment is important to the economy, technology took off as the hot industry of the 1990s.

The 8th votes heavily Democratic. Alexandria and Arlington give Democrats some of their highest vote percentages in the state and contrast sharply with Virginia's overall Republican lean. In the 2001 gubernatorial election, Democrat Mark Warner won 68 percent of the vote in Arlington and Alexandria, compared with 52 percent statewide.

Half of the 8th's residents live in Fairfax County, where redistricting altered boundaries following the 2000 census. Mapmakers made the 8th's portion of Fairfax more Democratic, and it now stretches west from the county's border with Alexandria past Falls Church and the Tysons Corner area to Reston, instead of south to the Prince William County line.

MAJOR INDUSTRY

Government, technology, defense, service

MILITARY BASES

Pentagon, 23,000 total (2001); Fort Belvoir (Army), 4,500 military, 6,000 civilian (2003); Fort Myer (Army), 1,771 military, 680 civilian; Naval Sea Systems Command, 350 military, 3,750 civilian (includes other naval employees); Henderson Hall, 1,910 military, 200 civilian (2001)

CITIES

Arlington, 189,453; Alexandria, 128,283

NOTABLE

The U.S. Capitol could fit into any one of the Pentagon's five wedge-shaped sections; Despite the Pentagon's 17.5 miles of corridors, it takes only seven minutes to walk between any two points.

Rep. Rick Boucher (D)

CAPITOL OFFICE
225-3861
ninthnet@mail.house.gov
www.house.gov/boucher
2187 Rayburn 20515-4609; fax 225-0442

COMMITTEES
Energy & Commerce
Judiciary

HOMETOWN
Abingdon

BORN
Aug. 1, 1946, Abingdon, Va.

RELIGION
Methodist

FAMILY
Single

EDUCATION
Roanoke College, B.A. 1968 (political science);
U. of Virginia, J.D. 1971

CAREER
Lawyer

POLITICAL HIGHLIGHTS
Va. Senate, 1976-82

ELECTION RESULTS

2002 GENERAL		
Rick Boucher (D)	100,075	65.8%
Jay Katzen (R)	52,076	34.2%
2002 PRIMARY		
Rick Boucher (D)		unopposed
2000 GENERAL		
Rick Boucher (D)	137,488	69.8%
Michael D. "Oz" Osborne (R)	59,335	30.1%

PREVIOUS WINNING PERCENTAGES
1998 (61%); 1996 (65%); 1994 (59%); 1992 (63%); 1990 (97%); 1988 (63%); 1986 (99%); 1984 (52%); 1982 (50%)

Elected 1982; 11th term

Boucher's interest in all things digital might seem to make him a bit of a mismatch with his rural, coal-mining constituency, but he has assiduously tended to the legislative needs of his district's small-town, cattle-raising, tobacco-growing residents. His leadership on Internet issues is not at all inappropriate for the economic hopes of the 9th District.

Precise and wonkish, Boucher (BOUGH-cher) comes naturally to his job. His father was a Republican commonwealth's attorney in Washington County, and both his grandfather and great-grandfather were Democratic state delegates. Boucher has said that, by the time he was 12, he had decided to become a lawyer and be a part of public life.

Though he was drawn to politics at an early age, Boucher shies away from excessive partisanship. His affinity for technology issues, he says, stems in part from the way they do not break along traditional party lines. Indeed, while most of Washington was riveted by the President Clinton impeachment hearings in late 1998, Boucher and fellow Judiciary Committee member Republican Robert W. Goodlatte, from the neighboring 6th District, huddled in the hallway trading thoughts on the future of the Internet.

Boucher's views on Internet issues carry special weight because he is a member of both the Energy and Commerce and Judiciary committees. The two panels share jurisdiction over regulation of the new online economy. On Energy and Commerce, Boucher focuses on technology matters, a subject that has engrossed him since he tried to improve satellite TV service for his constituents in the 1980s.

A co-founder of the Congressional Internet Caucus, Boucher tries to combine his interest in digital technology with his plans for economic development in the 9th. He dreams of electronic classrooms and envisions a linkage of all the high schools and colleges in southwest Virginia via fiber optics.

Boucher has secured grants from the Agriculture Department's Rural Utilities Service and such private concerns as GTE and Sprint to help link up area schools. He believes that electronic communication permits rural areas to be competitive with urban areas in many segments of the economy. "I see telecommunications as a bridge from any rural district to the American economic mainstream," Boucher says.

A key player on satellite, digital copyright and intellectual property issues, Boucher worked in the 106th Congress on legislation to set standards for Internet privacy and bulk commercial e-mail, as well as to require cable TV companies to allow competing firms to use their cable wires for high-speed Internet access. Though none of the efforts produced new laws, they provoked substantial discussion about what role the government should take to regulate the digital economy.

In the 107th, Boucher tried to amend federal copyright laws to ensure that Internet music services could gain access to copyright-protected music at a fair price. He sparred with the music industry over its practice of releasing CDs that cannot be copied or played on computer hard drives. Though the efforts were cheered by independent Internet services and consumer electronics manufacturers, they were resisted by many lawmakers who believe that Congress should strengthen intellectual property protections to address Internet piracy.

Boucher has been trying to foster the growth of the Internet since sponsoring legislation in the 103rd Congress that would have accelerated development of the high-performance computer networks that provide the foundation for the "information superhighway." He won passage of legislative provisions helping to ensure that rural phone customers have access to the latest technologies.

In his own House office, Boucher has eliminated the interoffice memo and decreed that all staff communication be done by e-mail or telephone. He has a grand vision of the future, one in which members carry tiny, wireless "personal digital assistants" with Internet access and e-mail onto the House floor. When legislation is debated, a stream of information literally would be at lawmakers' fingertips.

On Judiciary, Boucher usually takes a bipartisan role. He often is the only Democrat joining with Republicans in supporting tough immigration policies and a prohibition on the recognition of same-sex marriage. And he supports the rights of gun owners.

But in 1998, when the Judiciary Committee engaged in its most high-profile debate of the decade — launching an inquiry into alleged impeachable offenses committed by Clinton — Boucher took a more partisan tack. He was the Democrat who offered the party's resolution to conduct a narrower inquiry, hoping, he said during a rare floor appearance, to avoid a long-running spectacle that could harm the country.

Boucher also backs his party's efforts to raise the minimum wage and opposes many GOP tax-cutting proposals. Organized labor is a strong presence in his district's coal counties, and Boucher has taken its side on trade issues, voting in 2002 against granting the president fast-track authority to negotiate trade agreements that Congress cannot amend.

Boucher has sought to validate his district's musical heritage. He sponsored a 1998 resolution recognizing the twin cities of Bristol, Va., and Bristol, Tenn., as the birthplace of country music. Some historians point to the Bristol area as launching the genre because of the famed "Bristol sessions" of 1927, with country music legends Jimmie Rodgers and the Carter family.

After graduating from the University of Virginia Law School, Boucher joined a Wall Street firm, worked as an advance man for George McGovern's 1972 presidential campaign, and joined the family law firm in 1978.

He won a seat in the state Senate, then took on GOP Rep. William C. Wampler in 1982. With high unemployment plaguing the district's coal fields, Boucher won the hard-fought contest by just 1,123 votes out of more than 150,000 cast. Two years later, he edged to a 4 percentage point victory over state Rep. Jefferson Stafford. He has had little trouble since, only once falling below 60 percent.

KEY VOTES

2002

No Overhaul campaign finance law; ban "soft money" and restrict advocacy advertising
Yes Back Bush's defense budget increase
No Extend 1996 welfare law
No Adopt Bush's discretionary spending limit
No Pass GOP Medicare prescription drug plan
? Create independent Sept. 11 commission
Yes Extend union protections to Homeland Security Department employees
No Revive fast-track procedures for trade agreements
Yes Authorize war against Iraq
Yes Advance bankruptcy overhaul opposed by abortion opponents

2001

No Nullify Clinton Labor Department ergonomics rule
No Cut taxes by $1.35 trillion through fiscal 2011
Yes Maintain ban on oil drilling in Arctic National Wildlife Refuge
No Approve Bush proposal to limit managed-care plan liability for coverage decisions
Yes Divert money from crop subsidy payments to land conservation
No Expand law enforcement power to investigate suspected terrorists

CQ VOTE STUDIES

	PARTY UNITY		PRESIDENTIAL SUPPORT	
	Support	Oppose	Support	Oppose
2002	81%	19%	49%	51%
2001	82%	18%	33%	67%
2000	80%	20%	61%	39%
1999	75%	25%	67%	33%
1998	81%	19%	79%	21%

INTEREST GROUPS

	AFL-CIO	ADA	CCUS	ACU
2002	89%	80%	70%	21%
2001	100%	90%	57%	16%
2000	80%	75%	55%	29%
1999	88%	70%	48%	21%
1998	100%	95%	35%	4%

VIRGINIA 9
Southwest – Blacksburg, Bristol

Covered with forests, mountainous terrain and a slew of small factory and coal towns, the Democratic-leaning 9th is rich in beauty but also is Virginia's poorest district. Located in the southwestern part of the state, the 9th has struggled with high poverty rates and a weak economic base. The median income here is less than $30,000.

Coal mining provides jobs in counties at the western tip of the 9th, which also is the most economically depressed part of the district. Elsewhere, manufacturing is the major industry.

Diversifying the economy and ensuring clean drinking water for the thousands of residents who lack it are priorities in the 9th. Leaders have targeted the Internet as a way to get community exposure and to offer residents new learning opportunities. Although the district's overall population was stagnant in the 1990s, Craig County grew with Salem and Roanoke commuters. Blacksburg remains the largest city and is home to the state's largest university — Virginia Tech. Surrounding Montgomery County is economically atypical of the 9th.

The district is known as the "Fighting 9th," a name that reflects the area's fiercely competitive politics and its ornery isolation from the political establishment in Richmond. In the post-World War II era, when Democrats routinely dominated Virginia politics, the 9th was one of the only areas in which Republicans were consistently strong. Now that the statewide trend has flipped, Rep. Boucher has kept the 9th in Democratic hands since 1983.

Bill Clinton carried the 9th in the 1992 and 1996 presidential elections, but social issues such as gun control compelled many voters to back George W. Bush in 2000. Wise County, which borders Kentucky, narrowly backed Bush after supporting Democratic presidential candidates in 1988, 1992 and 1996. Bush narrowly lost Russell County, which abuts Wise, but he received a higher percentage there than Ronald Reagan did in 1984.

MAJOR INDUSTRY

Manufacturing, coal mining, agriculture

CITIES

Blacksburg, 39,573; Bristol, 17,367; Christiansburg, 16,947; Radford, 15,859

NOTABLE

Brass markers placed through the city of Bristol mark the Virginia-Tennessee state line.

Rep. Frank R. Wolf (R)

Elected 1980; 12th term

CAPITOL OFFICE
225-5136
www.house.gov/wolf
241 Cannon 20515-4610; fax 225-0437

COMMITTEES
Appropriations
(Commerce, Justice, State & Judiciary - chairman)

HOMETOWN
Vienna

BORN
Jan. 30, 1939, Philadelphia, Pa.

RELIGION
Presbyterian

FAMILY
Wife, Carolyn Wolf; five children

EDUCATION
Pennsylvania State U., B.A. 1961 (political science); Georgetown U., LL.B. 1965

MILITARY SERVICE
Army Reserve, 1962-63

CAREER
Lawyer; U.S. Interior Department official; congressional aide; lobbyist

POLITICAL HIGHLIGHTS
Sought Republican nomination for U.S. House, 1976; Republican nominee for U.S. House, 1978

ELECTION RESULTS

2002 GENERAL		
Frank R. Wolf (R)	115,917	71.7%
John B. Stevens Jr. (D)	45,464	28.1%
2002 PRIMARY		
Frank R. Wolf (R)		unopposed
2000 GENERAL		
Frank R. Wolf (R)	238,817	84.2%
Brian M. Brown (LIBERT)	28,107	9.9%
Marc A. Rossi (I)	16,031	5.7%

PREVIOUS WINNING PERCENTAGES
1998 (72%); 1996 (72%); 1994 (87%); 1992 (64%); 1990 (61%); 1988 (68%); 1986 (60%); 1984 (63%); 1982 (53%); 1980 (51%)

A veteran lawmaker whose district has one of the highest numbers of federal workers in the nation, Wolf stands out from some of his conservative colleagues who argue for shrinking the federal government.

Indeed, Wolf, now in his 12th term, is in a position to bring home the federal dollars. He is a House Appropriations subcommittee chairman and his press releases regularly tout the millions of dollars he has helped direct to his Northern Virginia district. One of his key legislative accomplishments during the 107th Congress was enactment of a law creating a new national historic park, the 3,000-acre Cedar Creek and Belle Grove National Historical Park, which preserves a portion of a key Civil War battlefield.

Wolf's passion does not end with his district. He has delivered heartfelt, and at times angry, floor speeches on pet issues, ranging from human rights abuses in Tibet to the menace of large trucks on the highways. Wolf has learned over the years how to pick his fights, make his presence felt, and adopt pragmatism to help the 10th District.

In the 108th, Wolf continues as chairman of the Commerce-Justice-State Appropriations subcommittee, and he also serves on the realigned Transportation and Treasury panel. Wolf also was named to the new subcommittee on Homeland Security Appropriations.

In a display of how his Appropriations assignment can pay off, the 2003 transportation spending bill included almost $50 million for several Northern Virginia transportation improvements and another $5 million to establish in his district a national "first responder" training center, which will prepare firefighters, paramedics and law enforcement officers to handle major emergencies, including acts of terrorism. During consideration of the 2003 spending bill, Wolf joined other Washington, D.C.-area lawmakers to push for a larger pay raise for civilian federal workers than President Bush wanted, arguing that civilian pay raises should be equal to the larger increases the president proposed for military personnel.

Wolf opposed Bush on other matters during the 107th. Although a House-Senate inquiry into the Sept. 11, 2001, terrorist attacks was held, Wolf was one of 25 House Republicans who went against their party to support creation of an independent probe. "Wouldn't you want a second opinion?" he asked. Wolf also was one of eight House Republicans to oppose the administration and House GOP leadership on an aviation security bill because it would have allowed private security companies to continue manning airport screening checkpoints. Wolf voted for a Democratic amendment to make all airport security workers federal employees.

However, on another key homeland security issue affecting federal workers in his district, Wolf sided with party leaders and against federal unions. He voted against an amendment by Republican Constance A. Morella of Maryland, whose district also included many federal employees, that would affirm employees' rights to union representation unless their jobs are materially changed after the transfer to the new department.

Since the GOP takeover of Congress in 1995, Wolf has been an Appropriations subcommittee chairman, one of the House's 13 "cardinals." During his first six years as a chairman, he led the Transportation Subcommittee. House rules forced him to switch to the Commerce, Justice, State and Judiciary panel at the start of the 107th Congress. As the chairman, he now has the ability to protect commerce through the high-technology corridor near Dulles International Airport and to get Justice Department funding to fight methamphetamine production in the Shenandoah Valley.

Wolf presided over a reorganization of the FBI's resources in the wake of the Sept. 11 terrorist attacks. The FBI was blamed for shortcomings that may have made the terrorists' job easier. Sept. 11 also showed Wolf that there was a need for better emergency communications in the D.C. metropolitan area and, with the help of other area representatives, he garnered $48.6 million for communications and other emergency response needs in Northern Virginia.

Wolf's religious faith is a driving force in his work. He has been adamant in his criticism of other countries over the years, including Iraq, China and Sudan, for human rights violations and religious persecution. In an emergency spending bill passed in the summer of 2002, Wolf included millions for overseas media campaigns aimed at fostering religious tolerance and democracy, as well as for international exchange programs and for organizations such as Radio Free Afghanistan.

On the domestic front, he is a firm opponent of legalized gambling and was the chief author of a law to create a national gambling commission to study the impact of gambling on society, maintaining it has led to "human misery" that the industry has ignored. In late 2002, Wolf called on the Bush administration to act to address the issue of Indian gambling, citing reports that some casinos run by American Indians have not benefited their tribes.

On a similar note, Wolf was instrumental in the 107th Congress in forcing NBC to reconsider plans to end a decades-long ban on television commercials for hard liquor. Wolf, who oversees the Federal Communications Commission's budget, worked with fellow appropriator California Democrat Lucille Roybal-Allard to pressure NBC.

Wolf began his quest for a congressional seat barely a year after Democrat Joseph L. Fisher won his House seat in 1974. Wolf's 1976 effort had the backing of the most conservative activists in the local GOP, but he lost the primary. In 1978, with greater name recognition and better financing, Wolf won the Republican nomination but lost to Fisher in November. In 1980, Wolf benefited from a national Republican surge that elected Ronald Reagan president and, capping a five-year effort, he won a narrow victory over Fisher.

Before his election to Congress, Wolf was an aide to Pennsylvania Republican Rep. Edward G. Biester, a deputy assistant secretary of Interior, and a lobbyist for baby food and farm implement manufacturers. He has enjoyed mostly smooth rides to re-election and won in 2002 with 72 percent of the vote.

KEY VOTES

2002

- Yes Overhaul campaign finance law; ban "soft money" and restrict advocacy advertising
- Yes Back Bush's defense budget increase
- Yes Extend 1996 welfare law
- Yes Adopt Bush's discretionary spending limit
- Yes Pass GOP Medicare prescription drug plan
- Yes Create independent Sept. 11 commission
- No Extend union protections to Homeland Security Department employees
- Yes Revive fast-track procedures for trade agreements
- Yes Authorize war against Iraq
- No Advance bankruptcy overhaul opposed by abortion opponents

2001

- Yes Nullify Clinton Labor Department ergonomics rule
- Yes Cut taxes by $1.35 trillion through fiscal 2011
- No Maintain ban on oil drilling in Arctic National Wildlife Refuge
- Yes Approve Bush proposal to limit managed-care plan liability for coverage decisions
- Yes Divert money from crop subsidy payments to land conservation
- Yes Expand law enforcement power to investigate suspected terrorists

CQ VOTE STUDIES

	PARTY UNITY		PRESIDENTIAL SUPPORT	
	Support	Oppose	Support	Oppose
2002	89%	11%	82%	18%
2001	95%	5%	86%	14%
2000	85%	15%	30%	70%
1999	84%	16%	32%	68%
1998	88%	12%	24%	76%

INTEREST GROUPS

	AFL-CIO	ADA	CCUS	ACU
2002	11%	5%	80%	92%
2001	17%	10%	91%	79%
2000	20%	10%	71%	72%
1999	22%	20%	68%	68%
1998	20%	10%	72%	80%

VIRGINIA 10

North — part of Fairfax County, Loudoun County

Located in the northern part of Virginia, the Republican-friendly 10th bridges a dizzying range of economies and lifestyles, with mountains and farmland at one end and congested Washington, D.C., suburbs at the other. A hotbed of economic activity in the 1990s, the 10th is a mostly white-collar area that includes some of the state's wealthiest counties — Loudoun and parts of Fauquier and Fairfax.

Most of the district's population resides in suburban Northern Virginia, and many residents commute to jobs in Washington or the inner suburbs just outside the nation's capital.

Nearly all of the 10th's counties grew substantially in the 1990s. Technology-magnet Loudoun County, which includes Leesburg and Washington Dulles International Airport, is home to more than one-fourth of district residents and nearly doubled in population during the decade. The area is grappling with its expansion, and slow-growth advocates have fared well in recent local elections. About one-third of residents live in Fairfax County (shared with the 8th and 11th), which includes Chantilly.

Beyond suburbia, agriculture and manufacturing fuel the economy. Clarke and Frederick counties produce about half of Virginia's apples and peaches. Winchester (Frederick County), the center of the state's apple-growing industry, is the home base of the Byrd family, which dominated Democratic politics in Virginia for decades. But the district has long since abandoned its Democratic roots.

Robust population growth required mapmakers to shrink the 10th's borders in redistricting following the 2000 census. As redrawn, the district includes a bit more of Fairfax County but decidedly less of Prince William County, which is located south and west of Fairfax. Several northern Shenandoah Valley counties were stripped from the 10th and given to the 6th or 7th districts.

MAJOR INDUSTRY

Federal government, technology, manufacturing, agriculture

CITIES

Chantilly (unincorporated), 41,041; McLean (pt.) (unincorporated), 37,427; Manassas, 35,135; Centreville (pt.) (unincorporated), 33,053

NOTABLE

The CIA headquarters are in Langley; Manassas National Battlefield Park is the site of two Civil War battles.

Rep. Thomas M. Davis III (R)

CAPITOL OFFICE
225-1492
tom.davis@mail.house.gov
www.house.gov/tomdavis
2348 Rayburn 20515-4611; fax 225-3071

COMMITTEES
Government Reform - chairman

HOMETOWN
Falls Church

BORN
Jan. 5, 1949, Minot, N.D.

RELIGION
Christian Scientist

FAMILY
Wife, Margaret "Peggy" Davis; three children

EDUCATION
Amherst College, B.A. 1971 (political science); U. of Virginia, J.D. 1975

MILITARY SERVICE
Army, 1971-72; Va. National Guard, 1972-79; Army Reserve, 1972-79

CAREER
Lawyer; professional services firm executive; state legislative aide

POLITICAL HIGHLIGHTS
Fairfax County Board of Supervisors, 1980-94 (chairman, 1991-94)

ELECTION RESULTS

2002 GENERAL		
Thomas M. Davis III (R)	135,379	82.9%
Frank W. Creel (CNSTP)	26,892	16.5%
2002 PRIMARY		
Thomas M. Davis III (R)		unopposed
2000 GENERAL		
Thomas M. Davis III (R)	150,395	61.9%
Mike Corrigan (D)	83,455	34.4%
Robert McBride (LIBERT)	4,774	2.0%
C.W. "Levi" Levy (I)	4,059	1.7%

PREVIOUS WINNING PERCENTAGES
1998 (82%); 1996 (64%); 1994 (53%)

Elected 1994; 5th term

A political junkie since childhood, Davis cemented his reputation as one of the Republican Party's most adept operatives in 2002 through his chairmanship of the House GOP candidate recruitment, strategy and fundraising arm. The party did not pick up the 10 seats he had initially predicted, but it nonetheless gained a net of six — bucking the historical trend that the president's party loses ground in midterm elections and giving President Bush more breathing room to advance his agenda.

Davis quickly leveraged his success running the National Republican Congressional Committee to win the chairmanship of the Government Reform Committee for the 108th Congress, even though he was sixth in GOP seniority on the panel at the time.

The leadership-driven GOP Steering Committee picked Davis over two others — Christopher Shays of Connecticut, who had the most seniority, and Christopher Cox of California, a member of the leadership — partly as a reward for his NRCC performance but also because Davis promised a new approach for the committee. Under the chairmanship of Indiana's Dan Burton, whose six-year term was up, the panel concentrated on scrutinizing the executive branch. Davis promised to focus the panel on "legislating, not investigating," with an initial emphasis on federal employment and purchasing practices, important issues for the government workers and contractors of Northern Virginia. Davis was actively involved in the 2002 debate over creating the Department of Homeland Security, and his proposals on procurement and contracting policies were included in the law.

Despite Davis' often rumpled appearance, Democrats and Republicans alike expect the committee to be more workman-like under his stewardship. The new chairman decreed that congressional oversight of the District of Columbia and the Postal Service — each of which merited its own committee before the Republicans took over the House in 1995 — would no longer be assigned to a Government Reform subcommittee but would be under the chairman's purview. The affairs of the nation's capital are also of interest to Davis' constituents.

While he has been a friend to the many technology companies, defense contractors and other concerns located near Washington, Davis has come under some criticism from conservative Republicans for being too friendly toward organized labor — and occasionally too collegial with Democrats. In 2002, he declined to campaign against the Democratic incumbent in a neighboring House district, James P. Moran, and he reportedly influenced the state's redistricting that followed the 2000 census in order to strengthen simultaneously Moran's hold on his district and Republican Frank R. Wolf's hold on his.

But he has earned the respect of his colleagues by helping raise record amounts of money for the GOP and by crisscrossing the nation campaigning for candidates during his four-year tenure at the NRCC.

Under his direction, the committee raised a record $160 million for the 2002 election — about $23 million from other House Republicans, who were pressed to donate their extra campaign cash or raise funds especially for battleground races. In 2001, Davis directed the NRCC to spend thousands of dollars on state races in New Jersey and Virginia that would determine which party controlled redistricting in those states. Although Democrats held their advantage in New Jersey, Davis used his Virginia ties to aid the Republican Party's takeover of the General Assembly for the first time since Reconstruction.

Davis was a government contract lawyer before coming to Congress, and his mastery of federal procurement policy is similar to the encyclopedic knowledge of political trends and data that he began aggregating as a child. A Senate page in the mid-1960s, he wrote a college honors paper on "The Political Realignment of the Outer South."

He can readily tap an enormous reservoir of arcana about local political dynamics and regional demographics, much the way an ardent baseball fan can recite from memory the career statistics of favorite players. At the NRCC, he put this knowledge to work finding candidates whose views made them electable at home — even if those same positions strayed from the national party line.

To benefit the local economy, Davis pushed legislation, enacted in the 106th Congress, expanding the number of special, H1-B visas for highly skilled workers; giving legal standing to electronic signatures used in online transactions; and liberalizing trade with China. In the 107th, he was chairman of the Government Reform subcommittee on procurement policy and won a seat on the Energy and Commerce panel. (He had to give up that seat in 2003 upon taking the gavel at Government Reform.)

Davis also uses his growing clout to address more-parochial concerns, such as securing federal funds to replace the aging Woodrow Wilson Bridge, which connects Virginia and Maryland. "In Northern Virginia, safety, quality of life and the overall economy depend largely on maintaining federal funding," he said in 2002.

When Davis has split with the Republican leadership, it often has been to champion the interests of the government workers who are his constituents. He called federal employees "hostages" to the government shutdowns of 1995-96 as he pressured GOP leaders to end their standoff with President Clinton. And he was one of only 11 Republicans in the 104th Congress who opposed a GOP tax cut because it would have been paid for, in part, by requiring federal employees to contribute more to their pension funds.

Unlike so many of his colleagues in the GOP Class of 1994 who came to Congress from the private sector, Davis built a career in government. He had been on the Board of Supervisors in Fairfax County, Washington's fastest-growing suburb, for 15 years when he took on one-term Democratic Rep. Leslie L. Byrne, a member of her leadership's whip organization and an aggressive partisan. He won by 8 percentage points and has bested that margin of victory every time since. Democrats did not even field a challenger in 2002.

KEY VOTES

2002

- No Overhaul campaign finance law; ban "soft money" and restrict advocacy advertising
- Yes Back Bush's defense budget increase
- Yes Extend 1996 welfare law
- Yes Adopt Bush's discretionary spending limit
- Yes Pass GOP Medicare prescription drug plan
- ? Create independent Sept. 11 commission
- No Extend union protections to Homeland Security Department employees
- Yes Revive fast-track procedures for trade agreements
- Yes Authorize war against Iraq
- ? Advance bankruptcy overhaul opposed by abortion opponents

2001

- Yes Nullify Clinton Labor Department ergonomics rule
- Yes Cut taxes by $1.35 trillion through fiscal 2011
- Yes Maintain ban on oil drilling in Arctic National Wildlife Refuge
- Yes Approve Bush proposal to limit managed-care plan liability for coverage decisions
- Yes Divert money from crop subsidy payments to land conservation
- Yes Expand law enforcement power to investigate suspected terrorists

CQ VOTE STUDIES

	PARTY UNITY		PRESIDENTIAL SUPPORT	
	Support	Oppose	Support	Oppose
2002	90%	10%	82%	18%
2001	90%	10%	88%	12%
2000	87%	13%	36%	64%
1999	79%	21%	39%	61%
1998	81%	19%	34%	66%

INTEREST GROUPS

	AFL-CIO	ADA	CCUS	ACU
2002	11%	10%	84%	88%
2001	17%	15%	90%	60%
2000	0%	5%	80%	70%
1999	22%	35%	88%	56%
1998	30%	15%	100%	64%

VIRGINIA 11

Washington suburbs — parts of Fairfax and Prince William counties

Anchored in the suburbs of Washington, D.C., the 11th is home to well-educated, middle- and upper-class suburbanites. It also is racially diverse, with more Asians — 11 percent of residents — than any other Virginia district. Only the inner-suburb 8th has more Hispanic residents.

The district is tailor-made for a moderate Republican, especially one who hews to the center on social issues. The 11th leans to the right on fiscal matters, but traffic congestion is a large problem here, and some residents support tax increases to pay for improvements. Democrat Mark Warner carried the 11th in the 2001 gubernatorial race due in part to his strong support of increased transportation spending for the region.

Fairfax County, including Vienna and Burke, accounts for two-thirds of residents. The rest live in Prince William County, which grew by 30 percent in the 1990s to become Virginia's third-most-populous jurisdiction (after Fairfax County and Virginia Beach), or in Fairfax city.

Many residents work in downtown Washington, either for the federal government or for companies whose business is linked to the government. Despite the public sector influence, technology is the district's fastest-growing industry, and dozens of companies have put down roots in office-park developments in Fairfax County. A growing number of workers telecommute, and the 11th has the highest median income (more than $80,000) of any district in the nation.

The 11th was a quintessential swing district in the 1990s. But a GOP-controlled redistricting plan following the 2000 census turned the district into Republican-leaning territory, mainly by revising the 11th's portions of Fairfax County. Democratic-leaning areas such as Reston and Bailey's Crossroads were removed, and Republican areas were added.

MAJOR INDUSTRY

Federal government, technology, service

CITIES

Burke (unincorporated), 57,737; Dale City (unincorporated), 55,971; Annandale (pt.) (unincorporated), 51,350

NOTABLE

Fairfax Court House is where George and Martha Washington's wills were recorded and still are kept.

WASHINGTON

Gov. Gary Locke (D)

First elected: 1996
Length of term: 4 years
Term expires: 1/05
Salary: $142,286
Phone: (360) 902-4111
Hometown: Seattle
Born: Jan. 21, 1950; Seattle, Wash.
Religion: Chinese Baptist
Family: Wife, Mona Lee Locke; two children
Education: Yale U., B.A. 1972 (political science); Boston U., J.D. 1975
Career: Lawyer; deputy county prosecutor
Political highlights: Wash. House, 1982-93; King County executive, 1993-96
Election results:

2000 GENERAL		
Gary Locke (D)	1,441,973	58.4%
John Carson (R)	980,060	39.7%
Steve LaPage (LIBERT)	47,819	1.9%

Lt. Gov. Brad Owen (D)

First elected: 1996
Length of term: 4 years
Term expires: 1/05
Salary: $74,377
Phone: (360) 786-7700

STATE LEGISLATURE

Legislature: Meets January-May in odd-numbered years; January-March in even-numbered years
House: 98 members, 2-year terms
2003 breakdown: 46R, 52D; 65 men, 33 women
Salary: $33,556
Phone: (360) 786-7750
Senate: 49 members, 4-year terms
2003 breakdown: 25R, 24D; 29 men, 20 women
Salary: $33,556
Phone: (360) 786-7550

STATE TERM LIMITS

Governor: 2 terms
Senate: No
House: No

URBAN STATISTICS

CITY	POPULATION
Seattle	563,374
Spokane	195,629
Tacoma	193,556
Vancouver	143,560
Bellevue	109,569

REGISTERED VOTERS

Voters do not register by party.

POPULATION

2002 population (est.)	6,068,996
2000 population	5,894,121
1990 population	4,866,692
Percent change (1990-2000)	+21.1%
Rank among states (2002)	15
Median age	35.3
Born in state	47.2%
Foreign born	10.4%
Violent crime rate	370/100,000
Poverty level	10.6%
Federal workers	66,061
Military	74,250

REDISTRICTING

Washington retained its nine House seats in reapportionment. The Washington State Redistricting Commission adopted a new map on Jan. 1, 2002.

MISCELLANEOUS

Web: www.state.wa.us
Capital: Olympia

STATE ELECTION OFFICIAL
(360) 902-4151

DEMOCRATIC HEADQUARTERS
(206) 583-0664

REPUBLICAN HEADQUARTERS
(206) 575-2900

District Statistics

DIST.	2000 VOTE FOR PRESIDENT BUSH	GORE	NADER	WHITE	BLACK	ASIAN	HISP	MEDIAN INCOME	WHITE COLLAR	BLUE COLLAR	SERVICE INDUSTRY	OVER 64	UNDER 18	COLLEGE EDUCATION	RURAL	SQ. MILES
1	42%	53%	4%	82%	2%	8%	4%	$58,565	69%	18%	12%	10%	26%	36%	5%	439
2	46	48	5	86	1	3	6	$45,441	55	29	16	12	26	22	31	6,564
3	48	46	5	88	1	3	5	$44,426	57	28	15	11	27	21	29	7,515
4	62	34	2	68	1	1	26	$37,764	53	31	16	11	30	19	29	19,051
5	57	38	4	88	1	2	5	$35,720	60	23	17	13	25	24	28	22,864
6	43	52	4	78	6	4	5	$39,205	55	27	18	14	25	20	21	6,781
7	21	72	7	67	8	13	6	$45,864	71	15	14	12	17	44	2	141
8	47	49	3	82	2	8	4	$63,854	69	20	11	9	28	37	12	2,579
9	43	53	3	73	6	7	7	$46,495	59	25	15	10	26	22	5	608
STATE	45	50	4	79	3	5	7	$45,776	61	24	15	11	26	28	18	66,544
U.S.	47.9	48.4	3	69	12	4	13	$41,994	60	25	15	12	26	24	21	3,537,438

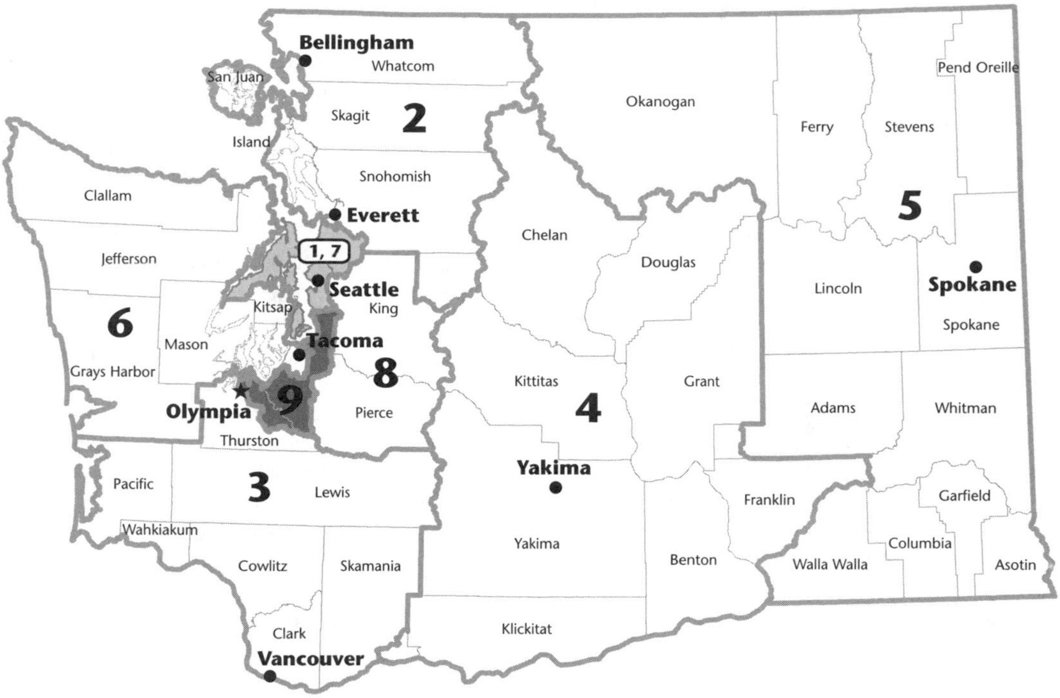
Bellingham
Whatcom
San Juan
Skagit
2
Island
Okanogan
Ferry
Stevens
Pend Oreille
Clallam
Snohomish
Everett
1, 7
Jefferson
Seattle
King
Kitsap
Chelan
Douglas
5
Lincoln
Spokane
Spokane
6
Mason
Tacoma
8
Grays Harbor
Olympia
9
Pierce
Thurston
Kittitas
4
Grant
Adams
Whitman
Yakima
Pacific
3
Lewis
Franklin
Garfield
Wahkiakum
Yakima
Cowlitz
Skamania
Benton
Walla Walla
Columbia
Asotin
Clark
Vancouver
Klickitat

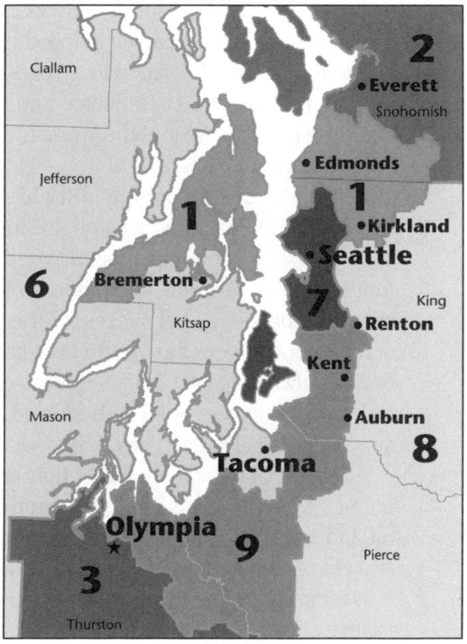
2
Clallam
Everett
Snohomish
Edmonds
Jefferson
1
1
Kirkland
Seattle
6
Bremerton
King
7
Kitsap
Renton
Kent
Mason
Auburn
8
Tacoma
Olympia
9
3
Pierce
Thurston

Sen. Patty Murray (D)

CAPITOL OFFICE
224-2621
senator_murray@murray.senate.gov
murray.senate.gov
173 Russell 20510-4704; fax 224-0238

COMMITTEES
Appropriations
Budget
Health, Education, Labor & Pensions
Veterans' Affairs

HOMETOWN
Seattle

BORN
Oct. 11, 1950, Bothell, Wash.

RELIGION
Roman Catholic

FAMILY
Husband, Rob Murray; two children

EDUCATION
Washington State U., B.A. 1972

CAREER
Parenting class instructor

POLITICAL HIGHLIGHTS
Shoreline School Board, 1983-89; Wash. Senate, 1989-93

ELECTION RESULTS

1998 GENERAL		
Patty Murray (D)	1,103,184	58.4%
Linda Smith (R)	785,377	41.6%
1998 PRIMARY (OPEN)		
Patty Murray (D)	479,009	45.9%
Linda Smith (R)	337,407	32.3%
Chris Bayley (R)	155,864	14.9%
Warren E. Hanson (R)	22,411	2.2%

PREVIOUS WINNING PERCENTAGES
1992 (54%)

Elected 1992; 2nd term

As Murray — the original "soccer mom" in congressional politics — moves toward the end of her second term, she has traded in the storied tennis shoes of her original Senate campaign for a metaphorical pair of business-like pumps. Once considered a legislative lightweight, Murray has steadily provided for both her state and her party, winning a number of important benefactors along the way.

Some observers believe Murray may have rekindled doubts late in 2002 when, in off-the-cuff remarks that Republicans immediately jumped on, she made comments about the popularity in many poor nations of terrorist mastermind Osama bin Laden.

But Democratic leader Tom Daschle early in 2003 named Murray as one of four members of a new executive committee to advise him.

"Because she's so unassuming, she's often underestimated. But she is up-and-coming, one of the Senate's shining stars," Democratic National Committee Chairman Terry McAuliffe told People magazine, which profiled all the women senators in the 107th Congress. In the article on Murray, Daschle said she "never tries to be something she's not."

Her homey affect stems from Murray's political as well as personal history. Her fire for politics was stoked when, in the early 1980s, she packed her two young children in the family car and drove to the state capitol in Olympia to complain about the legislature's plan to discontinue a preschool program. While there, Murray recalls, one of the legislators dismissed her by saying: "You can't make a difference. You're just a mom in tennis shoes."

In the 2001 book "Nine and Counting: The Women of the Senate," Murray explained how that off-hand comment had propelled her into political life: "I figured that I could sit at home and say, 'Oh, well, that's too bad,' or I could get involved and be a part of the decision-making process." The preschool program's cancellation led her to organize a statewide parents' effort to revive it. That led to four years on her local school board, followed by four years in the state Senate and then her election to the Senate in 1992, the political "Year of the Woman" in which 27 women were first elected to Congress.

For the 2002 election cycle, Daschle picked Murray as the first woman head of the Democratic Senatorial Campaign Committee. Although some colleagues privately questioned whether she was too shy for the job's fundraising component, she raised more than $72 million, a record. Some senators chalked up her success to the emotion of the times — loyal Democratic donors were anxious to preserve their party's slim Senate majority as a bulwark against the Republican-dominated White House and House of Representatives — but others said Murray's laid-back but persistent approach had also been key to her success.

After the GOP won control of the Senate in the 2002 elections, Murray noted, "Ultimately, we could not compete with the power of the bully pulpit and a wartime president." The campaign post generally rotates every two years, and Murray stepped down at the end of the year.

Despite spending much of her time with wealthy donors, Murray's legislative agenda has continued to focus on the constituents of modest means with whom she has long associated. In the 107th, her priorities included her long-running battle to cut class size in elementary schools and improve pipeline safety, as well as a newer effort to ban the use of asbestos.

Murray's strong support of most government programs stems from her childhood. She and her six siblings just got by on her father's salary as a dime-store manager. They often fended off childhood ailments without health care because her parents could not afford it. While she was a teenager, Murray's father was diagnosed with multiple sclerosis, and her family briefly went on welfare until her mother could complete a government-funded training program that enabled her to get a job as a bookkeeper. Without that aid, Murray has said, "my family wouldn't have made it."

As a college freshman, she organized a 1968 protest against a school rule requiring women students to wear skirts to dinner.

Throughout her political life, Murray has maintained that women must work harder than men to accomplish the same goals. Although it took Murray some time to learn the ropes in the Senate, she has proven effective at bringing home the bacon. As a member of the Appropriations Committee and top Democrat on the subcommittee that provides transportation funding, she has dedicated much of her energies to helping home-state industries.

In her biggest funding victory of the 107th, Murray led the Washington State delegation's campaign to win a lucrative federal contract for airplane maker Boeing — an Air Force lease of 100 Boeing 767s — even though the company had recently moved its headquarters from Seattle to Chicago. Boeing's aircraft plants still are vitally important to her state's economy.

Murray's penchant for directing tax dollars back home did not go unnoticed. When she attached $3 million for a maritime museum to the transportation spending bill in 2001, she incurred the wrath of Arizona Republican John McCain, who said the money was to be used for transportation projects. As Murray sat stone-faced in the chamber, McCain blasted Murray's project as an example of "pork barrel spending."

McCain and Murray also butted heads on a transportation issue of international importance — whether to severely limit Mexican trucks coming into the United States. The issue was a difficult one for Murray, who supports expanding trade but owes much of her own backing to the labor unions that oppose liberalized international commerce. In the end, Murray compromised with the Bush administration: More trucks were allowed into the United States, but inspections at the busiest border crossings were stepped up. Although many union leaders derided the deal, Murray said it was a way to "ensure our safety and promote commerce at the same time."

In 2002, Murray and McCain overlooked their differences and teamed up on legislation, approved at the end of the session, to increase government oversight of pipelines. Murray's crusade was inspired by a 1999 blast in Bellingham that killed three young people.

Murray also serves on the Health, Education, Labor and Pensions Committee. Much of her effort there has been focused on obtaining federal money to help school districts hire 100,000 additional teachers, with the goal of reducing the size of classes for first-, second-, and third-graders.

Two early breaks gave Murray a decisive boost in her first Senate quest. Her initial goal was to knock off Democratic incumbent Brock Adams; but he dropped out after allegations of sexual impropriety, and the popular Democratic Gov. Booth Gardner decided against seeking the seat. Still, to win the primary and the general election, Murray had to get past two better-known, popular moderates who had years of congressional experience. She did, winning 54 percent of the vote.

Although she was targeted as one of the Senate's most vulnerable incumbents in 1998, Murray ended up taking 58 percent of the vote against Republican Rep. Linda Smith.

Through it all, Murray has used her trademark tennis shoes to remind voters of her humble roots. She passes out "Golden Tennis Shoe" awards to constituents who, like her, have been community activists.

KEY VOTES

2002

- Yes Pass farm bill reversing crop subsidy limits
- No Postpone tougher automobile fuel efficiency standards
- Yes Overhaul campaign finance law; ban "soft money" and restrict advocacy advertising
- Yes Set federal election standards
- No Support oil drilling in Arctic National Wildlife Refuge
- Yes Revive fast-track procedures for trade agreements
- Yes Create federal insurance coverage for catastrophic terrorist losses
- Yes Tighten federal accounting and corporate governance regulation
- Yes Advance bipartisan Medicare prescription drug plan
- Yes Create independent Sept. 11 commission
- Yes Back Democratic Homeland Security Department proposal
- No Authorize war against Iraq

2001

- No Confirm John Ashcroft as attorney general
- No Nullify Clinton Labor Department ergonomics rule
- ? Cut taxes by $1.35 trillion through fiscal 2011
- Yes Pass Democratic bill to bolster rights of patients in managed-care plans
- No Permit a new round of military base closings
- Yes Expand law enforcement power to investigate suspected terrorists

CQ VOTE STUDIES

	PARTY UNITY		PRESIDENTIAL SUPPORT	
	Support	Oppose	Support	Oppose
2002	86%	14%	75%	25%
2001	96%	4%	65%	35%
2000	94%	6%	87%	13%
1999	93%	7%	88%	12%
1998	91%	9%	82%	18%
1997	93%	7%	87%	13%
1996	95%	5%	89%	11%
1995	93%	7%	91%	9%
1994	98%	2%	94%	6%
1993	94%	6%	96%	4%

INTEREST GROUPS

	AFL-CIO	ADA	CCUS	ACU
2002	92%	90%	55%	10%
2001	100%	85%	64%	4%
2000	63%	90%	64%	8%
1999	88%	100%	59%	4%
1998	88%	90%	56%	4%
1997	71%	90%	70%	0%
1996	100%	90%	17%	0%
1995	100%	95%	33%	0%
1994	88%	90%	20%	0%
1993	91%	90%	14%	0%

Sen. Maria Cantwell (D)

Elected 2000; 1st term

Although Cantwell is one of the Senate's youngest members, she is an old hand at politics. A savvy politician who eked out a win in her 2000 campaign to unseat veteran GOP incumbent Slade Gorton, Cantwell leveraged her popularity with the state's left-leaning voters in the Western part of Washington and her own personal fortune to attain a victory that was not declared official until nearly a month after the election.

When all of the state's absentee ballots were counted, Cantwell's hard-fought win by a few thousand votes brought the Senate membership at the start of the 107th Congress to a 50-50 partisan split.

The national interest in the race immediately put the spotlight on the freshman senator. Cantwell used that notice to establish herself by drawing attention to issues that affect her home state, such as energy and technology. As Gorton's replacement on the Energy and Natural Resources Committee, for instance, she championed legislation to update the nation's energy laws.

Cantwell's own private-sector experience as a former software company marketing executive — as well as the computer industry's prominence in her state, which is home to Microsoft — have shaped her political philosophy. She combines a pro-business stance with support for traditional Democratic views on core social issues such as abortion rights.

Cantwell was in the forefront of Democratic efforts late in 2002 and early in 2003 to extend unemployment benefits that ran out Dec. 28, 2002. It was a particularly important matter in Washington, which has one of the highest unemployment rates in the nation. Cantwell, chosen to present the Democrats' response to President Bush's weekly radio address, focused on the unemployment benefits issue, urging Bush to pressure Republicans in Congress to act as soon as the 108th Congress convened.

Cantwell's early voting record was more liberal than some had expected: She voted with party leaders 98 percent of the time during her first year in office. But she moved toward the center during the next year, supporting her party just 82 percent of the time on votes that split the parties.

When she broke with her party it was on matters important to her constituents. She won accolades from major companies in Washington, such as Boeing Co., when she voted to grant the president fast-track authority to negotiate expedited trade agreements that Congress cannot amend. She also voted to give the president the authority to wage war in Iraq, a position that stood to benefit Boeing's military aircraft business.

But in 2002 she backed the Democrats' plan for adding prescription drug coverage to Medicare. And unlike many Western lawmakers, she supports Democratic proposals to require trigger locks for guns and to close the "gun show loophole" that lets people buy guns without background checks. As a House member in 1993, she voted for the Brady bill requiring a waiting period and background check before handgun purchases, and in 1994 she supported a ban on assault-style weapons.

In the Senate, Cantwell is somewhat overshadowed by her Democratic colleague Patty Murray, who has grown in stature through her role as an appropriator and as chairwoman of the Democratic Senatorial Campaign Committee in the 107th Congress. But the junior senator has begun honing her image as a protector of her constituents, citing former Democratic Sen. Henry M. "Scoop" Jackson of Washington as her inspiration.

She burnished her reputation as a defender of her state's consumers by

CAPITOL OFFICE
224-3441
maria@cantwell.senate.gov
cantwell.senate.gov
717 Hart 20510-4705; fax 228-0514

COMMITTEES
Commerce, Science & Transportation
Energy & Natural Resources
Indian Affairs
Small Business & Entrepreneurship

HOMETOWN
Mountlake Terrace

BORN
Oct. 13, 1958, Indianapolis, Ind.

RELIGION
Roman Catholic

FAMILY
Single

EDUCATION
Miami U. (Ohio), B.A. 1980 (public policy)

CAREER
Internet audio company executive; public relations consultant

POLITICAL HIGHLIGHTS
Wash. House, 1987-92; U.S. House, 1993-95; defeated for re-election to U.S. House, 1994

ELECTION RESULTS

2000 GENERAL		
Maria Cantwell (D)	1,199,437	48.7%
Slade Gorton (R)	1,197,208	48.6%
Jeff Jared (LIBERT)	64,734	2.6%
2000 PRIMARY (OPEN)		
Slade Gorton (R)	560,787	43.6%
Maria Cantwell (D)	472,609	36.7%
Deborah Senn (D)	168,110	13.1%
Warren E. Hanson (R)	17,782	1.4%
Jeff Jared (LIBERT)	16,247	1.3%
Barbara Lampert (D)	15,150	1.2%
Robert Tilden Medley (D)	14,009	1.1%

PREVIOUS WINNING PERCENTAGES
1992 House Election (55%)

demanding refunds from energy companies under investigation for allegedly driving up electricity prices during the 2000-01 California electricity crisis, which harmed customers in Washington as well.

During Energy Committee hearings in 2002, Cantwell grilled the chairman of the Federal Energy Regulatory Commission, Patrick Wood III, about his panel's oversight of electricity markets. She called on Wood to allow her state to cancel long-term electricity contracts that had been signed during the crisis.

In the 108th Cantwell got a seat on the Commerce Committee, which she calls "the key committee for Washington state's economy," dealing as it does with telecommunication and other high-tech issues, aviation, fishing and Commerce Department export promotion efforts. It also plays to her high-tech background.

Cantwell opposed Justice Department efforts to break up Microsoft. At the same time, she differed with some in the industry in supporting efforts to require companies that do business on the Internet to divulge how personal data is collected and used.

Cantwell's willingness in 2000 to challenge Gorton, a third-term senator, can be explained in part by her working-class background and family tradition of public service. She is the second of five children and the first person in her family to graduate from college. Her father, Paul, who started his career as a construction worker, served as a county commissioner, city councilman and state legislator in Indiana. He also served as chief of staff for Democratic Rep. Andrew Jacobs of Indiana.

A native of Indiana, Cantwell first came to the Seattle area as a political organizer for Democratic presidential candidate Alan Cranston in the early 1980s. She stayed on in Washington, doing public relations consulting, and was elected to the state legislature at the age of 28.

In the state House, she was noted for her work on balancing environmental concerns and economic growth. Cantwell won election to Congress in 1992 but lost her re-election bid two years later, swept aside by that year's Republican tide, in the person of Rick White.

Between her tenure in the House and her election to the Senate, Cantwell became wealthy as a marketing executive for RealNetworks, a computer software company that sells products designed to send and receive audio and video via the Internet.

In launching her political comeback bid in 2000, Cantwell's ability to sell off nearly $10 million in RealNetworks stock options to finance her Senate campaign allowed her to blow past her once-favored Democratic primary opponent, state Insurance Commissioner Deborah Senn, and gain an even footing with incumbent Gorton.

She may not have the same luxury when she runs for re-election. By 2002, her personal wealth had fallen to an estimated $3.5 million, and despite fundraising help from Democratic senators such as Hillary Rodham Clinton of New York, her campaign accounts continued to carry debt.

Cantwell's image as a high-technology advocate and defender of Democratic ideals was both her political strength and weakness in the 2000 campaign. She won big in the Seattle area. But Gorton's efforts to pigeonhole her as that city's candidate hindered her in the state's more conservative rural areas, and Cantwell carried only five of the state's 39 counties. She defeated Gorton by 2,229 votes, a margin of less than one-tenth of 1 percent.

Cantwell gained some goodwill among other Democrats by campaigning during the 2002 midterm elections. Among the stops she made were trips to promote Massachusetts Sen. John Kerry, Missouri Sen. Jean Carnahan and candidate Erskine Bowles of North Carolina.

KEY VOTES

2002

Yes Pass farm bill reversing crop subsidy limits
No Postpone tougher automobile fuel efficiency standards
Yes Overhaul campaign finance law; ban "soft money" and restrict advocacy advertising
Yes Set federal election standards
No Support oil drilling in Arctic National Wildlife Refuge
Yes Revive fast-track procedures for trade agreements
Yes Create federal insurance coverage for catastrophic terrorist losses
Yes Tighten federal accounting and corporate governance regulation
Yes Advance bipartisan Medicare prescription drug plan
Yes Create independent Sept. 11 commission
Yes Back Democratic Homeland Security Department proposal
Yes Authorize war against Iraq

2001

No Confirm John Ashcroft as attorney general
No Nullify Clinton Labor Department ergonomics rule
No Cut taxes by $1.35 trillion through fiscal 2011
Yes Pass Democratic bill to bolster rights of patients in managed-care plans
Yes Permit a new round of military base closings
Yes Expand law enforcement power to investigate suspected terrorists

CQ VOTE STUDIES

	PARTY UNITY		PRESIDENTIAL SUPPORT	
	Support	Oppose	Support	Oppose
2002	82%	18%	81%	19%
2001	98%	2%	64%	36%
House Service:				
1994	92%	8%	86%	14%
1993	92%	8%	80%	20%

INTEREST GROUPS

	AFL-CIO	ADA	CCUS	ACU
2002	85%	80%	55%	25%
2001	100%	100%	50%	12%
House Service:				
1994	67%	70%	83%	14%
1993	83%	80%	36%	17%

Rep. Jay Inslee (D)

CAPITOL OFFICE
225-6311
jay.inslee@mail.house.gov
www.house.gov/inslee
308 Cannon 20515-4701; fax 226-1606

COMMITTEES
Financial Services
Resources

HOMETOWN
Bainbridge Island

BORN
Feb. 9, 1951, Seattle, Wash.

RELIGION
Protestant

FAMILY
Wife, Trudi Inslee; three children

EDUCATION
Stanford U., attended 1969-70; U. of Washington, B.A. 1973 (economics); Willamette U., J.D. 1976

CAREER
Lawyer

POLITICAL HIGHLIGHTS
Wash. House, 1989-93; U.S. House, 1993-95; defeated for re-election to U.S. House, 1994; sought Democratic nomination for governor, 1996

ELECTION RESULTS

2002 GENERAL		
Jay Inslee (D)	114,087	55.6%
Joe Marine (R)	84,696	41.3%
Mark B. Wilson (LIBERT)	6,251	3.1%
2002 PRIMARY (OPEN)		
Jay Inslee (D)	65,368	56.3%
Joe Marine (R)	42,473	36.6%
Mike the Mover (D)	5,291	4.6%
Mark B. Wilson (LIBERT)	3,025	2.6%
2000 GENERAL		
Jay Inslee (D)	155,820	54.6%
Dan McDonald (R)	121,823	42.7%
Bruce Newman (LIBERT)	7,993	2.8%

PREVIOUS WINNING PERCENTAGES
1998 (50%); 1992 (51%)

Elected 1998; 4th term

Also served 1993-95

Now in his third term representing the Democratic-leaning 1st District, Inslee can rest a little more comfortably than he did in his first congressional incarnation — a one-term stint from 1993-95 in central Washington's more conservative 4th District. The 1st District seems more suited to Inslee, and he can display his partisan stripes more openly than when he first was a congressman a decade ago.

Inslee has increased his victory margin in the 1st from 6 percentage points to 12 points in 2000 to 14 points in 2002, a possible result of his vow to "sharpen those bipartisan skills." He seeks out Republican cosponsors for the bills he introduces and casts himself as a political moderate. He aligned with the New Democrat Coalition, a group of pro-business Democrats.

Inslee has seats on the Resources and Financial Services committees, but much of his legislative agenda is shaped by his constituency. Both Boeing Co. and Microsoft Corp. are major influences in Seattle and employ many of his constituents. As aviation security was tightened in the wake of the Sept. 11, 2001, terrorist attacks, Inslee was adamant that all airline baggage — both carry-on and checked — be screened for explosives. "When you get on a plane, they take your nail clippers and run a wand over your belt, but there is nothing to prevent you from checking 30 pounds of plastique onto the plane," he told the Seattle Post-Intelligencer. "We've put 15 locks on the front door, while the back door remains unlocked."

He won House adoption of an amendment to spend an additional $250 million on passenger and baggage screening, and then he badgered airports and federal agencies to speed up the snail-like pace of getting, installing and using the equipment.

Inslee generally favors increased foreign trade, but in the 107th Congress he voted against the 2002 law giving the president authority to negotiate trade agreements that Congress may not amend. "It takes a lot of political incompetence to get me to vote 'no' on a trade deal," Inslee said. He argued that the Bush administration had not been sufficiently willing to help laid-off American workers with benefits and job training. He was particularly upset that the administration was willing to bail out the airlines after Sept. 11 but did not help the more than 100,000 airline and aviation workers who lost their jobs. "Why," he complained, "do the big dogs always eat first?"

He also supports robust funding for the Export-Import Bank, which helps Boeing compete for international sales against foreign competitors that are subsidized by their governments.

Inslee's record on environmental protection, including his role as the spokesman against a property rights initiative on the 1995 state ballot, has won him kudos from groups such as the Sierra Club and the League of Environmental Voters.

As the top Democrat on Resources' Forests and Forest Health Subcommittee, he objected strenuously when Republicans suggested that a spate of forest fires in 2001 and 2002 were caused by environmentalists who had stalled efforts to thin out forests.

Inslee also worked on legislation to deal with the large increases in electricity prices, particularly on the West Coast. To call attention to the price escalation, he tried to amend a 2001 spending bill to bar the Navy from paying the electric bills for the vice president's mansion, which is Navy property. Dick Armey, majority leader at the time, called the amendment "chicken manure," and it was soundly defeated.

An advocate of consumer privacy, Inslee introduced legislation to require telemarketers to refrain from calling individuals who have placed their names on a "no-call" list. Not worried about his own privacy, Inslee says he has always made his home phone number available to his constituents. Inslee now has a teenager at home, so his staff tells constituents they are more likely to reach the congressman if they call the office.

Inslee grew up in Seattle, where his father was a high school biology teacher and coach. Inslee was a star football and basketball player, and he told the Seattle Post-Intelligencer that he learned valuable lessons of leadership and teamwork through sports that have proven important in politics. Inslee is still athletically active, playing in the annual congressional baseball and basketball games and back home with a group that he co-founded called the Hoopaholics. The group of middle-aged men play basketball games to raise money for children's charities, Inslee says.

After marrying his high school sweetheart and earning a law degree, Inslee moved to the Yakima area in south central Washington, joined a law firm and became involved in civic affairs. His experiences during a debate over a school bond measure inspired him to run for the legislature in 1988. There, he served as vice chairman of the Appropriations Committee and on a panel that helped negotiate a budget deal to reduce the state's deficit.

When 4th District GOP Rep. Sid Morrison declared that he was giving up his seat to run for governor in 1992, Inslee wavered on whether to run, first announcing that he was considering a bid, then saying he wasn't interested. In April 1992, he finally decided to try for the seat. Inslee's folksy style and tireless campaigning lifted him to a narrow primary victory and to an equally narrow win in November over Republican Doc Hastings.

As a member of the 103rd, Inslee was not afraid to buck his party on some high-visibility votes: He voted against President Clinton's deficit-reduction package that raised taxes and a five-day waiting period for handgun purchases. But he also voted to ban some types of assault-style weapons. With the National Rifle Association targeting him for defeat, Inslee lost by almost 7 percentage points in a 1994 rematch with Hastings.

After the loss, Inslee moved back to the Seattle area, settling on Bainbridge Island and returning to legal work. He waged an unsuccessful primary bid for governor in 1996, but in 1998 he unseated two-term Republican Rep. Rick White in the suburban Seattle 1st District. Inslee attacked White's support for Clinton's impeachment. His victory was aided by the third-party candidacy of Bruce Craswell, whose 6 percent tally was regarded as coming largely from White's GOP base.

KEY VOTES

2002

Yes Overhaul campaign finance law; ban "soft money" and restrict advocacy advertising
Yes Back Bush's defense budget increase
No Extend 1996 welfare law
No Adopt Bush's discretionary spending limit
No Pass GOP Medicare prescription drug plan
Yes Create independent Sept. 11 commission
Yes Extend union protections to Homeland Security Department employees
No Revive fast-track procedures for trade agreements
No Authorize war against Iraq
No Advance bankruptcy overhaul opposed by abortion opponents

2001

No Nullify Clinton Labor Department ergonomics rule
No Cut taxes by $1.35 trillion through fiscal 2011
Yes Maintain ban on oil drilling in Arctic National Wildlife Refuge
No Approve Bush proposal to limit managed-care plan liability for coverage decisions
Yes Divert money from crop subsidy payments to land conservation
Yes Expand law enforcement power to investigate suspected terrorists

CQ VOTE STUDIES

	PARTY UNITY		PRESIDENTIAL SUPPORT	
	Support	Oppose	Support	Oppose
2002	96%	4%	28%	72%
2001	91%	9%	33%	67%
2000	80%	20%	67%	33%
1999	88%	12%	78%	22%
1994	83%	17%	78%	22%

INTEREST GROUPS

	AFL-CIO	ADA	CCUS	ACU
2002	89%	95%	45%	4%
2001	92%	90%	41%	4%
2000	70%	70%	71%	28%
1999	78%	100%	32%	8%
1994	56%	70%	n/a%	10%

WASHINGTON 1

Puget Sound (west and east) — north Seattle suburbs

The technology boom, though dulled in recent years, continues to drive growth in the suburban 1st. Microsoft's main Redmond campus, which is just over the district line in the 8th, is the best-known of many technology and biotechnology companies in the region. Suburban areas around Lake Washington and Puget Sound have continued to expand, with many of the "Microsoft Millionaires" moving into the crescent north of Seattle.

Military bases spur the economy on the west side of Puget Sound, but the high-tech companies — especially along Interstate 405 — and home buyers in Seattle's first ring of suburbs are what have attracted newcomers. More than 80 percent of the district's population is on the east side of Puget Sound, in King and Snohomish counties. Redistricting in 2002 gave the 1st a greater share of Snohomish, including a small part of Everett and most of Monroe, and a smaller share of King. The 1st was given a smaller share of Seattle.

Democrats have the edge in the district, with its well-educated, socially liberal professionals. The Snohomish portion is probably the most politically competitive of the three counties; the King and Kitsap County portions are slightly more Democratic.

MAJOR INDUSTRY

Software, military, aviation

MILITARY BASES

Bangor Naval Submarine Base, 5,350 military, 2,150 civilian (2001); Naval Undersea Warfare Engineering Station, 30 military, 1,405 civilian (2002)

CITIES

Kirkland (pt.), 44,406; Edmonds, 39,515; Shoreline (pt.), 35,694; Seattle Hill-Silver Firs (unincorporated), 35,311; Redmond (pt.), 34,759

NOTABLE

Bainbridge Island is a 35-minute ferry ride from downtown Seattle; The city of Lynnwood hosts an annual Trolley Days Festival; Mill Creek is a master-planned community, complete with a new high school, middle school and 18-hole golf course; Poulsbo is home to the annual Scandinavian celebration Viking Fest.

Rep. Rick Larsen (D)

CAPITOL OFFICE
225-2605
rick.larsen@mail.house.gov
www.house.gov/larsen
1529 Longworth 20515-4702; fax 225-4420

COMMITTEES
Agriculture
Armed Services
Transportation & Infrastructure

HOMETOWN
Lake Stevens

BORN
June 15, 1965, Arlington, Wash.

RELIGION
Methodist

FAMILY
Wife, Tiia Karlen; two children

EDUCATION
Pacific Lutheran U., B.A. 1987 (political science); U. of Minnesota, M.P.A. 1990

CAREER
Dental association lobbyist; port economic development official

POLITICAL HIGHLIGHTS
Snohomish County Council, 1998-2000 (chairman, 1999)

ELECTION RESULTS

2002 GENERAL		
Rick Larsen (D)	101,219	50.1%
Norma Smith (R)	92,528	45.8%
Bruce Guthrie (LIBERT)	4,326	2.1%
Bernard Haggerty (GREEN)	4,077	2.0%
2002 PRIMARY (OPEN)		
Rick Larsen (D)	59,238	48.4%
Norma Smith (R)	26,365	21.5%
Herb Meyer (R)	22,168	18.1%
Warren E. Hanson (R)	8,541	7.0%
Bernard Haggerty (GREEN)	3,233	2.6%
Bruce Guthrie (LIBERT)	2,854	2.3%
2000 GENERAL		
Rick Larsen (D)	146,617	50.0%
John Koster (R)	134,660	45.9%
Stuart Andrews (LIBERT)	7,672	2.6%
Glen Johnson (NL)	4,231	1.4%

Elected 2000; 2nd term

A moderate Democrat in a politically competitive district, Larsen is pragmatic and bipartisan. These are good traits to have in his part of northwestern Washington, where the winner in five of the last seven elections has received no more than 52 percent of the vote.

In his first term, Larsen posted a middle-of-the-road voting record in the 107th Congress. He backed President Bush more often than the average Democrat, and he focused many of his legislative efforts on issues of local importance. He affiliates with the moderate New Democrat Coalition.

Washington state is heavily dependent on foreign trade, and Larsen voted for the 2002 law giving the president fast-track authority to negotiate trade agreements that Congress may not amend. He was one of only 25 Democrats to vote with the president. He also strayed from the party line to support permanent repeal of the estate tax.

The Boeing Co. and B.F. Goodrich Aerospace are major employers in the 2nd District. In the aftermath of the Sept. 11, 2001, terrorist attacks, when the airlines were able to win prompt federal assistance, Larsen pointed out that aerospace companies and their workers were just as affected by the decrease in travel as the airlines. He said Boeing laid off 25,000 workers in the Puget Sound area in the year after the terrorist attacks. During the 107th, Larsen sought federal help, including extended unemployment benefits, for displaced workers in the aviation, aerospace and other industries hobbled because of the attacks.

Larsen will be in a better position to help the aerospace companies in the 108th Congress, as he gained a permanent seat on the Armed Services panel. He had been a temporary member since July 2001.

Another parochial concern that resulted from the Sept. 11 attacks is the campaign to stop terrorists from entering the United States. Tightened border security dampened the economies of areas near the Canadian border as routine commerce between the two nations was stalled. Larsen successfully nudged the administration to provide more customs and immigration agents at border crossings. Larsen believes, however, that the federal government should do more by helping local jurisdictions pay for jailing, prosecuting and providing defense lawyers in border-related cases.

Pipeline safety has been an important issue in the district ever since a 1999 pipeline explosion in Bellingham killed three people. Previous efforts had been thwarted, and it looked as if Larsen's initial legislation, introduced soon after he arrived on Capitol Hill, also would founder. But he joined with two members of his state's delegation — Republican Jennifer Dunn in the House and Democrat Patty Murray in the Senate — to offer new legislation. Although not as tough as the original bill, it was able to attract enough support to become law.

Whatcom County, on the Canadian border, is a leading producer of raspberries, and growers have faced serious difficulties in recent years as low-price imports from Chile have flooded the market. From his seat on the Agriculture Committee, Larsen was able to obtain a one-time emergency payment to help raspberry growers. He is working with other Washington lawmakers to deal with the long-range problem of Chilean imports.

Other important issues that carry over from the 107th Congress include Larsen's joint effort with Murray to establish a new, 106,000-acre "Wild Sky" wilderness area along the Skykomish River, and his bid, also with Murray, to significantly increase Medicare payments in Washington. Larsen says a

30 percent lower-than-average payment in the state is causing many doctors to refuse to treat Medicare patients.

High-technology industries remain prominent in Washington, and Larsen is conversant in issues that concern them. He says his top priority is to make sure there are safeguards in place to prevent companies and others from gaining access to and improperly using an individual's medical and financial records.

Larsen was born and raised in Snohomish County, just north of Seattle. One of eight children of a utility company power line worker, he says he was influenced to enter public service by his family. His parents were involved in community activities, and his father served as a city councilman.

In college, Larsen said his career plan was to become a city manager. But after earning a bachelor's degree in political science and a master's in public affairs, Larsen worked for the Port of Everett helping businesses comply with clean water requirements. He then became the director of public affairs for the Washington Dental Association.

His first foray into elective office came in 1997 when he waged a successful door-to-door campaign for the Snohomish County Council. He chaired the council in 1999.

When three-term Republican Rep. Jack Metcalf retired in 2000, local Democratic Party strategists saw enough promise in Larsen to persuade a potential rival, state Rep. Jeff Morris, to stay out of the open-seat 2nd District contest and avoid a divisive primary. Running as the moderate, Larsen scored something of a coup by returning the politically split district to Democratic hands.

Although he supports expanded international trade, Larsen received campaign help from organized labor, as well as other traditional Democratic backers such as abortion rights advocates and environmental groups, all of which mounted ground or mail campaigns on Larsen's behalf in the final weeks of the race. The result was a Democratic takeover, with Larsen prevailing by 12,000 votes against Republican state Rep. John Koster, who had run on a strongly conservative platform.

Redistricting following the 2000 census did little to change the competitive nature of the 2nd District, and the race between Larsen and Norma Smith, a former aide of Metcalf's, was on most observers' watch lists. Larsen was vigorous in bringing in campaign donations throughout his freshman term and so was able to spend $1.8 million, triple what Smith spent. Larsen again won with just 50 percent of the vote, however, and his margin of victory was only 9,000 votes.

KEY VOTES

2002

Yes Overhaul campaign finance law; ban "soft money" and restrict advocacy advertising
Yes Back Bush's defense budget increase
No Extend 1996 welfare law
No Adopt Bush's discretionary spending limit
No Pass GOP Medicare prescription drug plan
Yes Create independent Sept. 11 commission
Yes Extend union protections to Homeland Security Department employees
Yes Revive fast-track procedures for trade agreements
No Authorize war against Iraq
Yes Advance bankruptcy overhaul opposed by abortion opponents

2001

No Nullify Clinton Labor Department ergonomics rule
Yes Cut taxes by $1.35 trillion through fiscal 2011
Yes Maintain ban on oil drilling in Arctic National Wildlife Refuge
No Approve Bush proposal to limit managed-care plan liability for coverage decisions
Yes Divert money from crop subsidy payments to land conservation
Yes Expand law enforcement power to investigate suspected terrorists

CQ VOTE STUDIES

	PARTY UNITY		PRESIDENTIAL SUPPORT	
	Support	Oppose	Support	Oppose
2002	88%	12%	38%	62%
2001	80%	20%	42%	58%

INTEREST GROUPS

	AFL-CIO	ADA	CCUS	ACU
2002	67%	85%	60%	24%
2001	83%	85%	48%	12%

WASHINGTON 2

Puget Sound – Bellingham, most of Everett

West of the Cascade Mountains, in the northwest corner of the state, the 2nd covers an area that is mostly rural in its topography and moderate in its politics. Most of the district's population lives along Interstate 5, a technology corridor that runs up the state's coast, while the rural areas just west of the mountains provide residents with open expanses of land, much of it national forest. Between lies a fertile agricultural plain.

Aspects of the district's economy that were dependent on natural resources — logging, farming and paper production — have continued to decline. But the technology explosion in the 1980s and 1990s helped grow the economy and population. Thousands of Boeing employees work at the company's plant in Everett, but to the east, the district has struggled to find well-paying jobs for those formerly employed in farming and logging. The area seeks to diversify, though technology companies have made inroads as far north as Bellingham.

Traffic congestion into the Seattle area has become such a problem that it is often faster to drive from northern parts of the district into Everett than from Everett south to Seattle. These northwestern areas are home to many retirees who leave Seattle; San Juan County, a collection of islands southwest of Bellingham, has the highest median age in the state (47 years). At the northern border, beefed-up security has slowed trade to Canada.

The 2nd is highly competitive. The western urban centers of Everett in the south and Bellingham in the north are liberal, while the eastern rural sections lean conservative. Al Gore narrowly won the 2nd in 2000.

MAJOR INDUSTRY

Aviation, computer software, shipping

MILITARY BASES

Whidbey Island Naval Air Station, 7,914 military, 1,286 civilian (2001); Everett Naval Station, 5,659 military, 712 civilian (2002)

CITIES

Everett (pt.), 87,329; Bellingham, 67,171; Mount Vernon, 26,232

NOTABLE

Skagit County, home to the world's largest tulip fields, hosts a tulip festival every April; The San Juan Islands are known for their funky, liberal residents, including musician Steve Miller.

Rep. Brian Baird (D)

CAPITOL OFFICE
225-3536
www.house.gov/baird
1421 Longworth 20515-4703; fax 225-3478

COMMITTEES
Budget
Science
Transportation & Infrastructure

HOMETOWN
Vancouver

BORN
March 7, 1956, Chama, N.M.

RELIGION
Protestant

FAMILY
Wife, Rachel Nugent

EDUCATION
U. of Utah, B.S. 1977; U. of Wyoming, M.S. 1980, Ph.D. 1984 (clinical psychology)

CAREER
Professor; psychologist

POLITICAL HIGHLIGHTS
Democratic nominee for U.S. House, 1996

ELECTION RESULTS

2002 GENERAL		
Brian Baird (D)	119,264	61.7%
Joseph Zarelli (R)	74,065	38.3%
2002 PRIMARY (OPEN)		
Brian Baird (D)	77,540	56.8%
Joseph Zarelli (R)	58,939	43.2%
2000 GENERAL		
Brian Baird (D)	159,428	56.4%
Trent Matson (R)	114,861	40.6%
Erne Lewis (LIBERT)	8,375	3.0%

PREVIOUS WINNING PERCENTAGES
1998 (55%)

Elected 1998; 3rd term

In his first three years in Congress, most of Baird's attention was devoted to helping settle local disputes and otherwise attending to the parochial needs of his politically competitive district in southwestern Washington. But on the evening of Sept. 11, 2001, he decided to dedicate himself to an issue of potentially wider import — on Congress itself and on the conduct of the national government in the event of subsequent terrorist attacks.

Amid reports that the Capitol was the intended target of the hijacked airliner that had crashed in Pennsylvania that day, Baird wondered how the House would have continued operating had scores of its members been killed or disabled in an attack. Reminded that vacancies in the House may only be filled by special elections — in contrast to the Senate, where vacancies are filled by gubernatorial appointment — Baird decided to make it his top priority to design a different system for the House.

"We need to make sure there is a mechanism for some quick replacement," he said. "We simply cannot say there will be no House of Representatives for 60 days, or for the period of time needed to hold special elections."

While the constitutional amendment he proposed, which would have allowed temporary replacements for House members pending the outcome of special elections, did not see action, the House did adopt a resolution urging the states to speed up their timetables for holding special elections. And the Working Group on Continuity of Congress — an ad hoc panel appointed by the two party leaders to look into the situation, of which Baird was a member — proposed a number of House rules changes, approved in early 2003, to partially address the problem. Still, Baird said he would spend the 108th Congress advocating additional steps.

A clinical psychologist and psychology professor before coming to Congress, Baird also organized a series of seminars immediately in the wake of the attacks to allow members and their staffs to talk about their fears and to find ways to handle them.

Baird has an earnestness that borders at times on idealism. He drives a Toyota Prius, a hybrid car that runs on both an electric motor and a gasoline engine and boasts gas mileage of about 50 miles per gallon. He co-wrote a proposal for a House rule that would forbid members from dating interns who work for them. Ask him about the issue of campaign financing, and he will tell you that his colleagues are "literally killing" themselves by spending so much time on the phone raising money. Like many would-be reformers, he believes everyday people are losing out because of the need for politicians to raise money. "People they elected to represent them are spending so much time chasing money, they can't work together on the issues," he says.

A classic New Democrat, Baird is a progressive on such issues as education and health care, but he is eager to help businesses — particularly high-tech companies — that provide jobs and make the economy hum. He voted to override President Clinton's vetoes of Republican legislation to ease the tax burden on married couples and to abolish the estate tax. But he opposed President Bush's signature 2001 tax cut. "I don't believe government is the source of all solutions," Baird said, "but I don't think the solution is to blame government for all the problems."

Baird gained his sense of community activism from his parents. His father was a school principal, owned a small business, belonged to a Lion's Club and served on the city council. When no other Democrat opted to run against GOP Rep. Linda Smith in 1996, Baird put together an underfunded, grass-roots campaign that came up 887 votes shy of an upset.

Two years later, when Smith decided to give up her House seat for an ultimately unsuccessful Senate campaign, Baird won the seat by 10 percentage points over GOP state Sen. Don Benton. He improved his victory margin to 16 points in 2000 and 23 points in 2002, when the 3rd District's slight Democratic edge was maintained in redistricting.

As Democratic freshman class president in 1999, Baird strove to help Democrats and Republicans become friends. He and his GOP counterpart, Jim DeMint of South Carolina, organized a wine tasting, a barbecue and other social events. But such efforts quickly went by the board, in part because of the demands of heavy schedules. A larger inhibiting factor was the partisan nature of politics, Baird says, which makes it difficult to socialize with someone whose political party is running attack advertising against you.

Baird himself tries to maintain a bipartisan approach, seeking to secure at least one Republican cosponsor for each bill he introduces. He joined with DeMint, for instance, on a bill designed to promote small businesses.

On national issues, one of Baird's top legislative priorities is education, including smaller class and school sizes and increased aid to college students. Another of his priorities is to increase support for mental health programs, which he views as greatly underfunded.

The 3rd District is home to high-tech workers in Olympia and its suburbs, whose concerns are expanding trade and improving schools, and it also includes rural communities struggling with more basic infrastructure problems. Baird has sought more federal help for these communities to fight illegal production of methamphetamines, a problem in his district and many other rural areas. From his seat on the Transportation and Infrastructure Committee, he has been working to get federal funds for a $196 million project to deepen portions of the Columbia River to increase shipping traffic.

While Baird concedes that following former Speaker Thomas P. "Tip" O'Neill's dictum that all politics is local "makes sense politically," he argues that looking out for his constituents is the job he was elected to do.

Baird is an active outdoorsman. A coffee-table book about the Lewis and Clark expedition is one of the first items to greet visitors to his Capitol Hill office. In 1999, he was able to change the federal designation of the Lewis and Clark National Historic Trail to reflect its ending in Oregon and Washington, not just Oregon. For three years, he housed a Bosnian teenager who had lost a leg at age 14 in a Serbian mortar attack — and taught the teenager how to ski and rock climb.

KEY VOTES

2002

- Yes Overhaul campaign finance law; ban "soft money" and restrict advocacy advertising
- Yes Back Bush's defense budget increase
- No Extend 1996 welfare law
- No Adopt Bush's discretionary spending limit
- No Pass GOP Medicare prescription drug plan
- Yes Create independent Sept. 11 commission
- Yes Extend union protections to Homeland Security Department employees
- No Revive fast-track procedures for trade agreements
- No Authorize war against Iraq
- Yes Advance bankruptcy overhaul opposed by abortion opponents

2001

- No Nullify Clinton Labor Department ergonomics rule
- No Cut taxes by $1.35 trillion through fiscal 2011
- Yes Maintain ban on oil drilling in Arctic National Wildlife Refuge
- No Approve Bush proposal to limit managed-care plan liability for coverage decisions
- Yes Divert money from crop subsidy payments to land conservation
- Yes Expand law enforcement power to investigate suspected terrorists

CQ VOTE STUDIES

	PARTY UNITY		PRESIDENTIAL SUPPORT	
	Support	Oppose	Support	Oppose
2002	92%	8%	32%	68%
2001	87%	13%	30%	70%
2000	89%	11%	75%	25%
1999	89%	11%	77%	23%

INTEREST GROUPS

	AFL-CIO	ADA	CCUS	ACU
2002	100%	90%	58%	12%
2001	83%	85%	41%	12%
2000	80%	70%	75%	12%
1999	88%	95%	33%	4%

WASHINGTON 3

Southwest – Vancouver, most of Olympia

The 3rd is an eclectic, politically competitive district in southwest Washington that scoops up liberals in the state capital of Olympia and suburbanites in Vancouver, which is just across the Columbia River from Portland, Ore. Joining the two cities and bifurcating the district is Interstate 5, west and east of which lies considerable rural territory.

The district's population center is Clark County (Vancouver), where 54 percent of the 3rd's residents live. Clark's population grew 45 percent in the 1990s, as Portland residents flocked across the river to buy cheaper land. Trees and farmland are being cleared to make way for suburban developments, and voters have demanded infrastructure improvements to relieve traffic congestion and school overcrowding.

The 3rd still has vast stretches of woodlands, including the scenic Coastal Range and much of the Cascade Mountains, with Mount Rainier just outside the district's borders in the 8th. Though the timber trade has declined in the Cascade Mountains in the east, the western part of the district still sustains hearty logging. Many former timber workers have transferred to the technology sector.

Clark, like the district at large, is politically competitive. The Democratic vote in Vancouver is offset by Republican strength outside the city, in areas like Battle Ground, Yacolt and La Center. George W. Bush and Sen. Slade Gorton narrowly won Clark in 2000, even as they lost statewide.

Thurston County, which includes Olympia, is more favorable to Democrats. A redistricting commission in 2002 gave about one-sixth of the capital city to the 9th District. Of the other counties in the 3rd, Lewis is strongly Republican and Cowlitz and Pacific vote Democratic, though Bush substantially narrowed the big vote margins Bill Clinton enjoyed.

MAJOR INDUSTRY

Timber, mining, computer hardware

CITIES

Vancouver, 143,560; Olympia (pt.), 35,230; Longview 34,660

NOTABLE

Mount St. Helens erupted May 18, 1980, killing 57 people and destroying enough lumber for 300,000 two-bedroom homes; Lewis and Clark used the Columbia River, the 3rd's southern boundary, to reach the Pacific Ocean in 1805.

Rep. Doc Hastings (R)

CAPITOL OFFICE
225-5816
www.house.gov/hastings
1323 Longworth 20515-4704; fax 225-3251

COMMITTEES
Budget
Rules
Standards of Official Conduct

HOMETOWN
Pasco

BORN
Feb. 7, 1941, Spokane, Wash.

RELIGION
Protestant

FAMILY
Wife, Claire Hastings; three children

EDUCATION
Columbia Basin College, attended 1959-61; Central Washington U., attended 1964

MILITARY SERVICE
Army Reserve, 1964-69

CAREER
Paper supply business owner

POLITICAL HIGHLIGHTS
Wash. House, 1979-87; Republican nominee for U.S. House, 1992

ELECTION RESULTS

2002 GENERAL		
Doc Hastings (R)	108,257	66.9%
Craig Mason (D)	53,572	33.1%
2002 PRIMARY (OPEN)		
Doc Hastings (R)	75,745	69.9%
Craig Mason (D)	18,726	17.3%
Thor Amundson (D)	7,342	6.8%
Gordon Allen Pross (R)	6,500	6.0%
2000 GENERAL		
Doc Hastings (R)	143,259	60.9%
Jim Davis (D)	87,585	37.3%
Fred Krauss (LIBERT)	4,260	1.8%

PREVIOUS WINNING PERCENTAGES
1998 (69%); 1996 (53%); 1994 (53%)

Elected 1994; 5th term

Hastings took a rare turn in the national spotlight during the 107th Congress when it fell to him as a member of the House ethics committee to preside over the inquiry into wrongdoing by Rep. James A. Traficant Jr. Hastings won praise — including from Traficant — for his fairness in building the case to expel the Ohio Democrat, who was convicted on 10 federal charges of bribery, racketeering and tax evasion.

The episode was indicative of Hastings' rise in the Republican ranks since he unseated a one-term Democrat in 1994. Although "Doc" — a family nickname he's had since a child — is not among the party's rhetorical stars, his fierce loyalty to conservative positions has earned him rewards from GOP leaders, including seats on the Rules and Budget panels and — perhaps not so rewarding — a post on the ethics committee.

Hastings also has carefully attended to business at home. As founder and chairman of the House Nuclear Cleanup Caucus, he leads congressional efforts to speed up the pace of environmental restoration of radioactive waste sites. He helps conduct an annual tour of atomic weapons facilities, including the Hanford Nuclear Reservation in his district. The site was once a major district employer and now stands idle as the nation's most toxic relic of the Cold War.

Hastings helped lead an effort to tuck $982 million into the 2003 defense authorization bill for the Department of Energy (DOE) to revamp and accelerate its cleanup efforts. The money included $433 million specifically for Hanford. "This historic agreement will, when fully implemented, result in cost savings of $33 billion and accelerate cleanup by 35 to 40 years," at Hanford alone, Hastings said.

The nuclear cleanup money was a coup — one of several dividends Hastings has sent back to his district as he has risen in the GOP ranks.

Hastings in the 105th Congress got a seat on the Rules Committee, which determines the guidelines for considering legislation on the House floor. He gained another feather in his cap in the 106th Congress when he was appointed an assistant majority whip. Then in the 107th, the leadership gave him a seat on the Budget Committee. As GOP leaders organized for the 108th, Hastings won yet another coveted spot as a member of the Republican Steering Committee, which makes committee assignments.

While Hastings is generally a fiscal conservative, he uses his influential committee posts to win federal funding for local projects and advance the agricultural interests of his district.

In an otherwise tight budget environment during the 107th, Hastings helped push through a bill that scrapped efforts to wean farmers from crop subsidies, at a 10-year cost of at least $73.5 billion. The measure included his top priority, doubling the funding for the Market Access Program, which provides money for promotions, market research and technical assistance to help gain market share overseas. The program's funding increased from $90 million to $200 million by fiscal 2006.

At the urging of Washington state lawmakers, the bill also included $94 million to pay apple producers who suffered losses during the 2000 crop year. The bulk of that funding headed to Hastings' district.

In 2000, Hastings voted for legislation granting China permanent normal trade status, saying that opening trade markets is a priority for his district's producers. "As one of the most trade-dependent states in the nation, the best thing we can do for our farmers and farm communities is to open up new export markets and help level the playing field," he said.

Hastings often portrays himself as a buffer between an overly meddlesome federal government and local officials who know best how to run their own affairs. For example, he advocates giving state and local officials primary authority over management of the Hanford Reach, a 51-mile section of the Columbia River in his district that is one of the largest undisturbed river stretches in the country and a critical spawning ground for salmon. Environmentalists want to designate the Hanford Reach as federally protected and off-limits to development.

In 1997, Hastings took up the fight for the Kennewick Man, a 9,300-year-old skeleton, found in the 4th District, that is one of the oldest sets of human bones discovered in North America. In the midst of the long-running dispute between the Army Corps of Engineers and local tribes over whether the bones should be reburied or kept for scientific study, Hastings proposed a bill to ensure that scientists could study the bones and that their resting place would be preserved.

Beyond local concerns, Hastings has joined with party leaders in advocating a heavy dose of tax cuts, starting with reducing capital gains taxes, repealing the estate tax, and ending the "marriage penalty," a quirk in the tax code that results in some two-earner married couples paying higher taxes than they would if each partner were single.

Before his arrival in Washington, Hastings ran his family's paper supply business in Pasco for years and was active in civic affairs and local Republican politics. He was chairman of the Franklin County GOP central committee and a delegate to two national Republican conventions. He served eight years in the Washington House, winning leadership posts as assistant majority leader and chairman of the GOP caucus.

In 1992, Hastings drew solid backing from GOP religious activists and was considered the most conservative of the four Republicans running to succeed GOP Rep. Sid Morrison, a moderate who ran unsuccessfully for governor that year. Though Hastings won his party's nomination handily, he narrowly lost to Democrat Jay Inslee.

In a 1994 rematch, Hastings cast the campaign as a referendum on Inslee's support for the agenda of President Clinton, whose popularity was then at a low ebb in the GOP-leaning district. Hastings ousted Inslee, and he has held on to the seat easily since then, capturing more than 60 percent of the vote in the last three elections. (Inslee returned to the House in the 106th Congress after moving to the Seattle area and winning election in the 1st District.)

KEY VOTES

2002

- No Overhaul campaign finance law; ban "soft money" and restrict advocacy advertising
- Yes Back Bush's defense budget increase
- Yes Extend 1996 welfare law
- Yes Adopt Bush's discretionary spending limit
- Yes Pass GOP Medicare prescription drug plan
- No Create independent Sept. 11 commission
- No Extend union protections to Homeland Security Department employees
- Yes Revive fast-track procedures for trade agreements
- Yes Authorize war against Iraq
- Yes Advance bankruptcy overhaul opposed by abortion opponents

2001

- Yes Nullify Clinton Labor Department ergonomics rule
- Yes Cut taxes by $1.35 trillion through fiscal 2011
- No Maintain ban on oil drilling in Arctic National Wildlife Refuge
- Yes Approve Bush proposal to limit managed-care plan liability for coverage decisions
- No Divert money from crop subsidy payments to land conservation
- Yes Expand law enforcement power to investigate suspected terrorists

CQ VOTE STUDIES

	PARTY UNITY		PRESIDENTIAL SUPPORT	
	Support	Oppose	Support	Oppose
2002	98%	2%	92%	8%
2001	98%	2%	93%	7%
2000	98%	2%	23%	77%
1999	97%	3%	16%	84%
1998	97%	3%	23%	77%

INTEREST GROUPS

	AFL-CIO	ADA	CCUS	ACU
2002	11%	0%	100%	92%
2001	8%	0%	96%	96%
2000	0%	0%	94%	92%
1999	0%	0%	100%	92%
1998	0%	0%	94%	100%

WASHINGTON 4

Central – Yakima and Tri-Cities

Lying just east of the Cascade Mountains, the 4th comprises a huge swath of central Washington that includes the Yakima Valley, known as the fruit bowl of the Northwest, and the Tri-Cities area, which is home to the Hanford Nuclear Reservation.

Yakima County is the district's largest, both in land area and population. To the east and south is Benton County, which takes in the district's other population center, the Tri-Cities of Pasco, Kennewick and Richland on the Columbia River.

Heavily irrigated agriculture drives the district, which contains an older irrigation area in the Yakima Valley, full of apple orchards and the world's largest producer of hops. It also includes the Columbia Basin project, fed by the Grand Coulee Dam, which has bred hundreds of wineries and potato, corn and fruit farms.

Many of these agricultural areas have attracted large Hispanic populations. Mattawa and Royal City (Grant County) and Mabton, Granger and Toppenish (Yakima) are more than 75 percent Hispanic.

The Hanford reservation and the Pacific Northwest National Laboratory, the district's largest employer, take up a 570-square-mile tract on the Columbia. Hanford's jobs drove the region during the Cold War, but in 1988 the plutonium plant was shut down. Hanford is now the nation's most contaminated nuclear site, with 54 million gallons of deadly material stored in aging underground tanks.

The 4th is the state's most conservative district. George W. Bush won every county in the district in the 2000 presidential election, most by overwhelming margins.

MAJOR INDUSTRY
Scientific research, timber, fruit orchards

CITIES
Yakima, 71,845; Kennewick, 54,693; Richland, 38,708; Pasco, 32,066; Wenatchee, 27,856

NOTABLE
The oldest skeleton ever found in North America was discovered along the banks of the Columbia River in Richland in 1996; Dubbed the "Kennewick Man," he is believed to be more than 9,300 years old.

Rep. George Nethercutt (R)

CAPITOL OFFICE
225-2006
www.house.gov/nethercutt
2443 Rayburn 20515-4705; fax 225-3392

COMMITTEES
Appropriations
Science

HOMETOWN
Spokane

BORN
Oct. 7, 1944, Spokane, Wash.

RELIGION
Presbyterian

FAMILY
Wife, Mary Beth Nethercutt; two children

EDUCATION
Washington State U., B.A. 1967 (English); Gonzaga U., J.D. 1971

CAREER
Lawyer; congressional aide

POLITICAL HIGHLIGHTS
Spokane County Republican Party chairman, 1990-94

ELECTION RESULTS

2002 GENERAL		
George Nethercutt (R)	126,757	62.7%
Bart Haggin (D)	65,146	32.2%
Rob Chase (LIBERT)	10,379	5.1%
2002 PRIMARY (OPEN)		
George Nethercutt (R)	83,972	64.4%
Bart Haggin (D)	38,630	29.7%
Rob Chase (LIBERT)	7,700	5.9%
2000 GENERAL		
George Nethercutt (R)	144,038	57.3%
Tom Keefe (D)	97,703	38.9%
Greg Holmes (LIBERT)	9,473	3.8%

PREVIOUS WINNING PERCENTAGES
1998 (57%); 1996 (56%); 1994 (51%)

Elected 1994; 5th term

Whatever he accomplishes in his congressional career, Nethercutt is likely to be remembered most for how he began it: by defeating Democrat Thomas S. Foley — the first time that a sitting Speaker of the House had been denied re-election since 1862.

Nethercutt's victory was a symbolic high-water mark for the Republican takeover tide of 1994, stunning the political world even as he created what proved to be a nettlesome problem for Nethercutt's long-term political future: a campaign pledge to serve only three terms in Congress.

While getting a good taste of the House and its complexities — as well as a seat on the Appropriations Committee — he publicly agonized and then reneged on that pledge in June 1999. His decision drew ridicule from Doonesbury cartoonist Garry Trudeau, who labeled him the "The Weasel King." U.S. Term Limits and the activists who had poured more than $300,000 into his first campaign went all out to punish him for breaking his vow. The advocacy group hired people in weasel suits to follow him around during his promise-breaking 2000 campaign for a fourth term and peppered the news media with attacks on him.

But Nethercutt dismissed the term-limits activists as "outside agitators" and stressed his work for farmers and other constituents in his increasingly conservative rural district. Praised by Republican leaders for his decision to run again, he cruised to victory with 57 percent of the vote. That discouraged any significant repeat effort by term-limits groups in 2002.

Early in 2003, Nethercutt said he was considering whether to run for higher office in 2004 — for either governor or senator.

While Nethercutt became a symbol for the new Republican order in the House, he was never a "revolutionary" as were so many of his Class of 1994 colleagues. Instead of pressing hard to shrink the size of the government and its budget, Nethercutt in essence emulated Foley in his assiduous efforts to protect the federal dollars that flow back home. Nethercutt was awarded his Appropriations seat on his arrival, a rare reward for a freshman but one that GOP leaders deemed appropriate for toppling Foley — and useful for helping ensure that he could win re-election.

Nethercutt made a long-shot bid for the chairmanship of the Interior Appropriations Subcommittee in the 108th Congress, seeking to leap over Chairman Charles H. Taylor of North Carolina and several more-senior members. He argued that the subcommittee should be headed by a Westerner. But Appropriations Chairman C.W. Bill Young of Florida decided to stick with Taylor.

Nethercutt remained on the Interior Subcommittee, as well as the Agriculture and Defense panels, where he can help to protect Washington's enormous stake in both industries.

Soft-spoken and amiable, Nethercutt comes across as a moderate in person, but his conservative credentials are rarely in doubt. An opponent of abortion rights and gun control, he also has voted with the GOP majority to limit the regulatory authority of the Environmental Protection Agency.

A co-founder of the Congressional Diabetes Caucus and with a personal interest in the issue — his daughter has juvenile diabetes — Nethercutt nonetheless voted, in 2001 and 2003, for legislation to ban human cloning, which holds some promise in medical research.

He has repeatedly tangled with environmentalists by trying to block federal land-use regulations in the Columbia River Basin. And he is a leading opponent of plans to breach four Snake River dams in his district that environmentalists blame for blocking runs of endangered species of salmon. "I don't believe dam removal is the silver-bullet answer, and I won't support a proposal that restores salmon on the backs of those who depend on the system: the agriculture, natural resources, small communities and residents of my Eastern Washington district," he said in 2000.

Though they would never call him a friend, Nethercutt can sometimes be found in the company of liberals on high-profile issues. Breaking with many in his own party, since 2000 he has been a leading advocate of relaxing economic sanctions on Cuba. Citing the potential economic benefits to his farmer constituents, he has taken the lead in pressing for expanded agricultural trade with Cuba and five other rogue countries.

Nethercutt has also fought for his farmers by battling other international sanctions. When it appeared that winter wheat exports might suffer in 1998 because the United States had imposed sanctions against India and Pakistan over their nuclear weapons tests, Nethercutt helped win passage of legislation that exempted agricultural exports from the sanctions.

An ardent death penalty advocate, Nethercutt also bucked his party in the summer of 2002 by signing on to a bill that aimed to make sure those facing the capital punishment in federal cases have access to DNA tests that might prove their innocence. "I support the death penalty, but I want to make sure we're getting the right people," Nethercutt said.

In the 1970s, Nethercutt worked on Capitol Hill for GOP Sen. Ted Stevens of Alaska and then went into private law practice with his father, specializing in estate planning and probate and adoption law. Active in civic affairs, he founded a nursery for victims of child abuse and raised money to combat juvenile diabetes.

Although he was a former Spokane County GOP chairman, he had never held public office before he entered the 1994 House race. With Foley struggling to hold on to the increasingly conservative district, Nethercutt spent more than $1 million, and he was aided by conservative groups making independent expenditures. By campaigning for less government, Nethercutt carried the district's nine rural counties and prevailed by 4,000 votes.

Since then, his margins of victory have been more comfortable, if not overwhelming. Redistricting for this decade did not alter the conservative lean of the 6th and in 2002 — with the term-limits issue behind him — Nethercutt outdistanced radio producer and community activist Bart Haggin by more than 30 points.

KEY VOTES

2002

- No Overhaul campaign finance law; ban "soft money" and restrict advocacy advertising
- \+ Back Bush's defense budget increase
- Yes Extend 1996 welfare law
- P Adopt Bush's discretionary spending limit
- Yes Pass GOP Medicare prescription drug plan
- Yes Create independent Sept. 11 commission
- No Extend union protections to Homeland Security Department employees
- Yes Revive fast-track procedures for trade agreements
- Yes Authorize war against Iraq
- Yes Advance bankruptcy overhaul opposed by abortion opponents

2001

- Yes Nullify Clinton Labor Department ergonomics rule
- Yes Cut taxes by $1.35 trillion through fiscal 2011
- No Maintain ban on oil drilling in Arctic National Wildlife Refuge
- Yes Approve Bush proposal to limit managed-care plan liability for coverage decisions
- No Divert money from crop subsidy payments to land conservation
- Yes Expand law enforcement power to investigate suspected terrorists

CQ VOTE STUDIES

	PARTY UNITY		PRESIDENTIAL SUPPORT	
	Support	Oppose	Support	Oppose
2002	94%	6%	87%	13%
2001	98%	2%	93%	7%
2000	93%	7%	25%	75%
1999	92%	8%	23%	77%
1998	95%	5%	27%	73%

INTEREST GROUPS

	AFL-CIO	ADA	CCUS	ACU
2002	11%	0%	100%	92%
2001	8%	0%	96%	96%
2000	0%	5%	80%	88%
1999	0%	10%	88%	84%
1998	0%	0%	89%	96%

WASHINGTON 5
East – Spokane

The fertile soil of eastern Washington makes the 5th's protein-rich wheat some of the most desired in the world. Politically conservative, the state's largest district has suffered the decline of some of its traditional industries and enjoyed the emergence of others.

Spokane is a trade hub for the inland Northwest. Largely dependent on manufacturing, the area has suffered intermittent layoffs. Increases in electronics manufacturing and the health care industry offered opportunities for workers to retrain. Slightly less than two-thirds of district residents live in Spokane or surrounding Spokane County.

Okanogan County, in the northwest corner of the district, has been particularly hard-hit as the logging and mining industries have slowed and a looming water shortage keeps farmers on edge. But the district remains a top apple producer. Unlike the neighboring Yakima and Columbia irrigation systems, the 5th's agriculture, based in the southern part of the district, is centered mostly on staple crops such as wheat, which receive federal subsidies.

The 5th's politics more closely resemble neighboring Idaho's than western Washington's. Rural communities and the natural resource-dependent economy make for residents who eschew federal interference and support private property rights. Spokane can be politically competitive: George W. Bush won the county by 9 percentage points in 2000 after Bill Clinton narrowly won it in 1996. But the rural areas are heavily Republican. Bush took 74 percent in Garfield County and 72 percent in Columbia County in 2000, his highest percentages in the state.

MAJOR INDUSTRY
Agriculture, electronics manufacturing, health care

MILITARY BASES
Fairchild Air Force Base, 4,000 military, 1,000 civilian (2001)

CITIES
Spokane, 195,629; Walla Walla, 29,686; Opportunity (unincorporated), 25,065; Pullman, 24,675

NOTABLE
Spokane hosts Bloomsday, the largest timed foot race in North America; Sonora Smart Dodd of Spokane thought up the idea for Father's Day while listening to a Mother's Day sermon in 1909; The Grand Coulee Dam created the 130-mile long Lake Roosevelt on the Columbia River.

Rep. Norm Dicks (D)

CAPITOL OFFICE
225-5916
www.house.gov/dicks
2467 Rayburn 20515-4706; fax 226-1176

COMMITTEES
Appropriations
Select Homeland Security

HOMETOWN
Bremerton

BORN
Dec. 16, 1940, Bremerton, Wash.

RELIGION
Lutheran

FAMILY
Wife, Suzanne Dicks; two children

EDUCATION
U. of Washington, B.A. 1963 (political science), J.D. 1968

CAREER
Congressional aide

POLITICAL HIGHLIGHTS
No previous office

ELECTION RESULTS

2002 GENERAL		
Norm Dicks (D)	126,116	64.2%
Bob Lawrence (R)	61,584	31.4%
John Bennett (LIBERT)	8,744	4.5%
2002 PRIMARY (OPEN)		
Norm Dicks (D)	83,455	63.0%
Bob Lawrence (R)	35,639	26.9%
Douglas Milholland (D)	9,758	7.4%
John Bennett (LIBERT)	3,549	2.7%
2000 GENERAL		
Norm Dicks (D)	164,853	64.7%
Bob Lawrence (R)	79,215	31.1%
John Bennett (LIBERT)	10,645	4.2%

PREVIOUS WINNING PERCENTAGES
1998 (68%); 1996 (66%); 1994 (58%); 1992 (64%); 1990 (61%); 1988 (68%); 1986 (71%); 1984 (66%); 1982 (63%); 1980 (54%); 1978 (61%); 1976 (74%)

Elected 1976; 14th term

Like the man himself, a 2002 political fundraiser marking Dicks' 25th year in the House was larger than life. State and local officials queued up to laud the veteran member of the House Appropriations Committee as "the third senator from Washington," a tribute to his knack for bringing federal money not only to his district, but also to the state of Washington.

Dicks is a combination of boisterous bonhomie, irrepressible humor and bullheaded tenacity. He has helped shape some of the major policy debates in the capital, while channeling a steady stream of federal funds back to his home state. A skilled legislative tactician, Dicks learned from a past master, Washington Democrat Warren G. Magnuson, the influential Senate appropriator for whom Dicks worked from 1968, when he finished law school, to 1976, when he began the first of his unbroken string of successful campaigns for his House seat.

The aging Senate baron's gravitas contrasted with his beefy protégé's back-slapping and bear-hugging; Magnuson used to joke that when Dicks was a varsity linebacker at the University of Washington, he was always five yards offside. But with the backing of fellow Washingtonian Tom Foley, then chairman of the House Democratic Caucus, Dicks got a coveted seat on the Appropriations panel in his freshman year.

As an appropriator, he has mirrored Magnuson not only in his finely honed political skills, but also in focusing on defense and natural resources issues crucial to his state, and establishing himself as a serious player in both policy fields.

He also reflects the general policy bent of Magnuson and Henry M. "Scoop" Jackson, another national heavyweight who was the state's other Democratic senator during Dicks' years of apprenticeship. Dicks is liberal on most domestic issues; but on defense, he is a conservative who favors big military budgets and an internationalist who believes in asserting U.S. leadership around the world.

In some cases, he was able to do well for his state while at the same time leaving his mark on national policy. By the late 1980s, he was the leading congressional proponent of the B-2 stealth bomber. The position had a strong parochial dimension: Aerospace giant Boeing, a key element of Washington state's economy, was a major subcontractor. But there also was a serious argument on policy grounds for Dicks' position, and he made the case knowledgeably.

During the 107th Congress, Dicks was deeply frustrated by the Bush administration's refusal to buy additional B-2s. But another initiative with local resonance consumed much of his energy after the Sept. 11, 2001, terrorist attacks. As Boeing's airliner sales dried up because of the sharp drop in air travel, Dicks promoted the acquisition by the Air Force of hundreds of the company's 767 jetliners for use as mid-air refueling tankers and electronic surveillance planes.

One proposal was to lease 100 of the planes as tankers, which critics denounced as a corporate bailout that would cost more in the long run than buying the planes outright. But Dicks contended that the administration's projected defense budgets were so anemic that leasing, which would spread the cost of the planes across many years, was the only way the Pentagon could afford an essential program.

Dicks and other pro-defense Democrats have been unhappy with President Bush's projected budgets, which have not been large enough to pay for modernized weapons and the development of new armaments. Dicks argued that military spending, which approached $400 billion in 2003, should be increased 10 percent. And he says that Bush is pouring too much money into a crash program to deploy anti-missile defenses at the expense of conventional weapons.

On the other hand, Bush's defense budgets were not so tight as to inhibit Dicks' enterprise in steering additional Pentagon funds to his state. Among his additions to the fiscal 2003 defense appropriations bill was $10 million for a University of Washington project to use ultrasound to stop bleeding in battlefield conditions.

GOP control of the House has complicated Dicks' dealings on natural resources issues important to his state, with its significant fishing, timber and tourism interests. As the senior Democrat on the Interior Appropriations Subcommittee since 1997, he has funneled money into the Northwest to preserve national forests, boost recovery of depleted salmon stocks and balance competing environmental and commercial concerns.

Since 1995, however, Republicans from Western states, who take a dim view of federal land-use restrictions, have tried to use the Interior spending bill as a weapon in their war with the federal government. For example, Dicks has had to fend off attacks on a Clinton administration study of endangered salmon populations and other environmental problems in the Columbia River Basin.

Dicks is a staunch defender of federal funding for the arts, and he also falls in line with his party' s liberal wing on other social policy issues. He opposes Republican efforts to offer school vouchers, to repeal a ban on certain semiautomatic assault-style weapons and to prohibit late-term abortions. On the other hand, he supported the bill giving Bush fast-track authority to negotiate foreign trade agreements, reflecting the importance of export sales to such Washington companies as Boeing and Microsoft.

Dicks decided to run for Congress in 1976, when the 6th District seat came open. He tapped into the resources of labor and other interest groups to win the primary and had no trouble against a weak Republican that fall.

In 1980, he was held to 54 percent by Republican James Beaver, a conservative law professor. His challenger in 1982, GOP state Sen. Ted Haley, painted Dicks as a profligate spender too friendly with military contractors. But that charge gave Dicks an excuse to talk about projects he had brought home. Dicks' 63 percent indicated that he was gaining a comfortable margin of political success. Since then, he has dropped below 60 percent only once — in the GOP banner year of 1994.

KEY VOTES

2002

Yes Overhaul campaign finance law; ban "soft money" and restrict advocacy advertising
Yes Back Bush's defense budget increase
No Extend 1996 welfare law
No Adopt Bush's discretionary spending limit
No Pass GOP Medicare prescription drug plan
Yes Create independent Sept. 11 commission
Yes Extend union protections to Homeland Security Department employees
Yes Revive fast-track procedures for trade agreements
Yes Authorize war against Iraq
Yes Advance bankruptcy overhaul opposed by abortion opponents

2001

No Nullify Clinton Labor Department ergonomics rule
No Cut taxes by $1.35 trillion through fiscal 2011
Yes Maintain ban on oil drilling in Arctic National Wildlife Refuge
No Approve Bush proposal to limit managed-care plan liability for coverage decisions
Yes Divert money from crop subsidy payments to land conservation
Yes Expand law enforcement power to investigate suspected terrorists

CQ VOTE STUDIES

	PARTY UNITY		PRESIDENTIAL SUPPORT	
	Support	Oppose	Support	Oppose
2002	85%	15%	36%	64%
2001	82%	18%	36%	64%
2000	89%	11%	88%	12%
1999	90%	10%	84%	16%
1998	85%	15%	85%	15%

INTEREST GROUPS

	AFL-CIO	ADA	CCUS	ACU
2002	88%	80%	60%	13%
2001	82%	90%	50%	8%
2000	80%	80%	45%	8%
1999	67%	90%	28%	0%
1998	90%	95%	39%	0%

WASHINGTON 6

West — Bremerton, Tacoma, Olympic Peninsula

The green, lush habitation of the 6th is part of what gives Washington its nickname, the "Evergreen State." Olympic National Park and Olympic National Forest constitute more than half of the district's land, about 2 million protected acres. Along the coast, the mountains drop to the Pacific Ocean.

Logging and fishing remain major industries in the west, but fights over protection for the spotted owl and other endangered species have forced some companies to cut back their work forces.

Communities are trying to diversify their economies and mostly have had success in attracting high-tech companies. Trade has increased in the port towns of Grays Harbor County. Bremerton, with the Puget Sound Naval Shipyard and Naval Station Bremerton, depends heavily on the military. The 6th also has a substantial Coast Guard presence. The district's representative must balance environmental concerns with labor and defense spending needs.

The 6th includes most of Tacoma and its suburbs. The industrial city's blue-collar, heavily unionized electorate generally gives Democrats the edge in Pierce County, where half of the district population lives. Bremerton, in Kitsap County (19 percent of the 6th's population), leans Democratic, as do Grays Harbor and Jefferson counties. Al Gore won by 52 percent to 43 percent in the 6th, which was marginally redrawn in 2002 by the state's redistricting commission.

MAJOR INDUSTRY

Lumber, fishing, shipping, health care

MILITARY BASES

Puget Sound Naval Shipyard, 29 military, 8,096 civilian; Naval Station Bremerton, 320 military (5,740 military on home-ported ships), 16 civilian (2002)

CITIES

Tacoma (pt.), 176,853; Bremerton, 37,259; University Place, 29,933; Lakewood (pt.), 26,878; Port Angeles, 18,397

NOTABLE

The *USS Missouri*, the battleship on which the Japanese signed their surrender ending World War II, was based in Bremerton from the end of the war until 1998, when it was moved to Hawaii.

Rep. Jim McDermott (D)

CAPITOL OFFICE
225-3106
www.house.gov/mcdermott
1035 Longworth 20515-4707; fax 225-6197

COMMITTEES
Ways & Means

HOMETOWN
Seattle

BORN
Dec. 28, 1936, Chicago, Ill.

RELIGION
Episcopalian

FAMILY
Wife, Therese Hansen; two children

EDUCATION
Wheaton College, B.S. 1958; U. of Illinois, M.D. 1963

MILITARY SERVICE
Navy Medical Corps, 1968-70

CAREER
Psychiatrist

POLITICAL HIGHLIGHTS
Wash. House, 1971-73; sought Democratic nomination for governor, 1972; Wash. Senate, 1975-87; Democratic nominee for governor, 1980; sought Democratic nomination for governor, 1984

ELECTION RESULTS

2002 GENERAL		
Jim McDermott (D)	156,300	74.1%
Carol Thorne Cassady (R)	46,256	21.9%
Stan Lippmann (LIBERT)	8,447	4.0%
2002 PRIMARY (OPEN)		
Jim McDermott (D)	84,876	77.4%
Carol Thorne Cassady (R)	20,688	18.9%
Stan Lippmann (LIBERT)	2,238	2.0%
Brien Bartels (LIBERT)	1,874	1.7%
2000 GENERAL		
Jim McDermott (D)	193,470	72.8%
Joe Szwaja (GREEN)	52,142	19.6%
Joel Grus (LIBERT)	20,197	7.6%

PREVIOUS WINNING PERCENTAGES
1998 (88%); 1996 (81%); 1994 (75%); 1992 (78%); 1990 (72%); 1988 (76%)

Elected 1988; 8th term

McDermott became involved in politics because of his opposition to the Vietnam War, and 30 years later he was voicing the same doubts about another conflict, war with Iraq.

An outgoing man with an instantly recognizable shock of white hair, McDermott can be blunt and confrontational in his effort to promote the Democratic cause. He remains devoted to the historically liberal tilt of his party, even as some insist it must move to the center.

McDermott was elected in June 2002 to a two-year term as president of the liberal Americans for Democratic Action. "I got into politics because I was mad about the Vietnam War, and you and I and people like us were the ones who stopped the war," he told the group's annual convention. "I came out of the military in 1970 during the Vietnam era and said to myself, 'You've got to get involved in politics or the world's course is all going to be decided in Washington, D.C., and we're not going to like what that means.' "

During the Vietnam War, McDermott was stationed in Long Beach, Calif., where as a Navy psychiatrist, his job required him to decide whether to return sailors and Marines to battle. McDermott says one of his heroes is Ernest Gruening, an Alaska Democrat who cast one of only two "no" votes in the Senate for the 1964 Gulf of Tonkin resolution, which led to U.S. involvement in Vietnam.

A third of a century later, McDermott urged a go-slow approach in attacking Afghanistan to root out terrorists and then, a year later, counseled against war with Iraq. "The president can flatten Iraq," he told an anti-war rally in 2003. "There's no question what our power is. But this war is unjust and unjustifiable."

McDermott traveled to Baghdad in 2002 and questioned President Bush's motives in preparing to attack the Mideast nation, just before Congress voted whether to back the president. When Republicans howled about McDermott's Baghdad comments in television interviews, he noted that "those who support a more thorough and cautious debate find their patriotism questioned."

While McDermott's views on war attracted the most attention in the 107th Congress, his top priority remained overhauling the U.S. health care system. Asked by the Seattle Times in 2002 if he could pass just one bill what it would be, McDermott answered "universal health care coverage."

McDermott is the only psychiatrist in Congress, and as such, fellow Democrats have looked to him when developing strategy on health care matters, such as curbing the growing power of managed-care insurers, overhauling the federal Medicare program and providing prescription drug coverage for senior citizens. McDermott has been willing to oblige, and his medical background gives him credibility to do so. But he has never moderated the decidedly independent streak he exercises on the Ways and Means Committee, and on health care he is often to the left of most Democrats.

In 1993, for example, he proposed — and pushed vigorously for — a single-payer health care plan under which all Americans would be guaranteed health insurance benefits through a taxpayer-financed system. He ignored his own leadership's requests that lawmakers delay introducing health care bills until President Clinton had unveiled his health care overhaul plan. He also helped worsen the Clinton plan's dismal prospects, by rallying support among House liberals for his own proposal.

Since then, he has worked on a number of narrower health care bills, including one to establish federal privacy standards for individual medical records. In the 107th Congress, he worked with Republican Ways and Means colleague Jim McCrery of Louisiana to develop a universal health insurance bill that sought to replace employer-based coverage with mandatory individual policies subsidized for low-income families.

McDermott's interest in foreign affairs extends well beyond Afghanistan and Iraq. In the 107th Congress, he co-chaired congressional caucuses on India, which he has visited more than a dozen times, African trade and the problem of international AIDS.

McDermott was born and raised in Illinois, becoming the first member of his family to attend college. After medical school at the University of Illinois, his residency training to become a psychiatrist took him to Seattle. After his two-year stint in the Navy medical corps, he returned to Seattle to begin his medical career.

He quickly entered local politics, winning a seat in the state House in 1970 and starting a lengthy legislative career punctuated by three losing bids for governor — in 1972, 1980 and 1984. He served in the state House for two years and, after a two-year break, won four state Senate elections.

He left the state Senate in 1987 to take a three-year job in the Congo (then known as Zaire) as a Foreign Service medical officer. Less than a year later, when 7th District Democratic Rep. Mike Lowry announced his plans to run for the Senate, McDermott arranged to be released from his Foreign Service commitment and returned stateside to run for Lowry's seat. His name recognition from earlier campaigns gave him a boost, and he captured the four-way Democratic primary against a field that included future Seattle Mayor Norm Rice. In November, McDermott breezed to victory in the strongly Democratic district.

Since then, his re-election races have all been runaways, and McDermott's seat is considered one of the state's safest for the Democratic Party.

At the start of the 108th Congress, McDermott was still embroiled in the long-running lawsuit filed against him by Ohio Republican Rep. John A. Boehner over the release of an illegally taped cellular telephone call in late 1996. After the tape of a conference call among GOP leaders discussing the ethical troubles of Speaker Newt Gingrich worked its way to McDermott, excerpts were cited in newspaper stories. McDermott resigned from the House ethics panel amid allegations that he had leaked the tape to the news media. Boehner, who was one of the participants in the call, sued in 1998, alleging that his privacy had been violated.

KEY VOTES

2002

- Yes Overhaul campaign finance law; ban "soft money" and restrict advocacy advertising
- No Back Bush's defense budget increase
- No Extend 1996 welfare law
- No Adopt Bush's discretionary spending limit
- No Pass GOP Medicare prescription drug plan
- Yes Create independent Sept. 11 commission
- Yes Extend union protections to Homeland Security Department employees
- No Revive fast-track procedures for trade agreements
- No Authorize war against Iraq
- No Advance bankruptcy overhaul opposed by abortion opponents

2001

- No Nullify Clinton Labor Department ergonomics rule
- – Cut taxes by $1.35 trillion through fiscal 2011
- Yes Maintain ban on oil drilling in Arctic National Wildlife Refuge
- No Approve Bush proposal to limit managed-care plan liability for coverage decisions
- Yes Divert money from crop subsidy payments to land conservation
- No Expand law enforcement power to investigate suspected terrorists

CQ VOTE STUDIES

	PARTY UNITY		PRESIDENTIAL SUPPORT	
	Support	Oppose	Support	Oppose
2002	97%	3%	14%	86%
2001	94%	6%	21%	79%
2000	97%	3%	94%	6%
1999	96%	4%	87%	13%
1998	96%	4%	95%	5%

INTEREST GROUPS

	AFL-CIO	ADA	CCUS	ACU
2002	100%	95%	28%	0%
2001	100%	95%	29%	0%
2000	90%	80%	42%	0%
1999	75%	55%	12%	5%
1998	89%	90%	38%	0%

WASHINGTON 7

Seattle and suburbs

Framed by mountains, lakes and Puget Sound, the 7th provides a serene atmosphere for Seattle. Although more rain falls here than almost any other part of the nation, it is considered one of the most desirable places to live. Despite economic downturns that have killed off parts of Seattle's technology boom, the area remains wealthy, diverse, liberal and cosmopolitan.

The district is still home to high-tech startups and industry leaders, including retailer Amazon.com and software manufacturer Adobe. Microsoft's headquarters is in the neighboring 8th. The aviation and biotechnology industries also are big employers.

Economic downturns doomed many technology startups, and Boeing's decision in 2001 to move its corporate headquarters out of the state, along with subsequent layoffs, also hurt. The cost of housing remains high, forcing most low-income residents out of the city. But top-end restaurants and nightlife abound, catering to young singles and empty nesters. In Seattle, one is almost as likely to live alone as with a family.

The 2000 census measured Seattle's population at just more than its 1960 peak. Asians, at 13 percent of the city's population, are roughly equal to Seattle's combined black and Hispanic populations. The percentage of Seattle residents who describe themselves as members of two races is nearly twice the national average. But the city's population growth has not kept pace with the suburbs, especially in the north.

The Port of Seattle is one of the nation's major gateways to Asian markets and makes the 7th's economy dependent on trade.

The 7th's urban setting and large populations of minorities and singles make it a liberal bastion. Democratic candidates regularly dominate the district, and in 2000 the Green Party's Ralph Nader outpolled George W. Bush in some Seattle precincts.

MAJOR INDUSTRY
Aviation, computer software, health care

CITIES
Seattle (pt.), 552,834; White Center (unincorporated), 20,975

NOTABLE
In 1971, the first Starbucks Coffee opened at Pike's Place Market.

Rep. Jennifer Dunn (R)

CAPITOL OFFICE
225-7761
dunnwa08@mail.house.gov
www.house.gov/dunn
1501 Longworth 20515-4708; fax 225-8673

COMMITTEES
Ways & Means
Select Homeland Security
Joint Economic

HOMETOWN
Bellevue

BORN
July 29, 1941, Seattle, Wash.

RELIGION
Episcopalian

FAMILY
Divorced; two children

EDUCATION
Stanford U., attended 1959; U. of Washington, attended 1960-62; Stanford U., A.B. 1963 (English literature)

CAREER
County tax official; computer systems engineer

POLITICAL HIGHLIGHTS
Wash. Republican Party chairwoman, 1980-92

ELECTION RESULTS

2002 GENERAL		
Jennifer Dunn (R)	121,633	59.8%
Heidi Behrens-Benedict (D)	75,931	37.3%
Mark A. Taff (LIBERT)	5,771	2.8%
2002 PRIMARY (OPEN)		
Jennifer Dunn (R)	68,199	64.1%
Heidi Behrens-Benedict (D)	35,681	33.5%
Mark A. Taff (LIBERT)	2,606	2.5%
2000 GENERAL		
Jennifer Dunn (R)	183,255	62.2%
Heidi Behrens-Benedict (D)	104,944	35.6%
Bernard McIlroy (LIBERT)	6,269	2.1%

PREVIOUS WINNING PERCENTAGES
1998 (60%); 1996 (65%); 1994 (76%); 1992 (60%)

Elected 1992; 6th term

Now in her sixth term, Dunn has regained some of the prominence within the Republican majority that she enjoyed earlier in her House career.

She was a rising star in the mid-1990s, winning a Ways and Means Committee seat in her second term and elected in 1997 to an entry-level party leadership post, Republican Conference secretary. Articulate, telegenic and — perhaps most important for a party looking to soften its image and show voters a more diverse face — female, Dunn became a regular presence behind the podium at GOP news conferences.

But after only three terms in the House, Dunn brazenly ran against the party's backroom pick for House majority leader in 1998. Her loss to Dick Armey of Texas was bruising, and Dunn has been much less visible since that setback. Ohio's Deborah Pryce became the most prominent woman in the House GOP.

Dunn has been working quietly to regain star status. She campaigned energetically for George W. Bush in 2000 and was mentioned as a possible secretary of Commerce or Labor. But with the House so narrowly divided, the administration did not want to put GOP seats at risk. Late in 2002, she had interviewed for a $700,000-a- year job as head of the Air Transport Association, the lobbying group for the nation's major airlines, but she announced she would stay in the House.

Shortly thereafter, she won appointment as vice chairman of the Homeland Security Committee, established to oversee the formative days of the new Cabinet department of the same name. The White House and Republican leaders asked her to take on Sen. Patty Murray in 2004, but in April 2003 Dunn announced she wanted to stay in the House.

Dunn's favorite cause during the 107th Congress was repeal of the estate tax. She began pushing that proposal in the 106th Congress. Working with conservative Democrats and associations representing small businesses and farmers, Dunn helped build a broad coalition and saw her bill move through the House and Senate by comfortable margins. But estate tax repeal did not survive President Clinton's veto. In 2001, Dunn took the lead again. A temporary estate tax repeal eventually became part of the $1.35 trillion, 10-year tax cut package President Bush signed into law. Permanent repeal of the estate tax is on the congressional agenda in the 108th Congress.

Dunn's voting record has been consistently conservative, but she usually takes care to couch GOP arguments in non-threatening language. "I have always been a proponent of softening our rhetoric," she has said. "I believe we can pursue the same positions we have been, but we don't need to be as harsh and scary about it."

Dunn helps to put a warm face on Republican efforts to overhaul social programs. During consideration of welfare or labor legislation, she can be heard describing her empathy, "as a single mother who raised two sons," for the difficulties experienced by working parents.

That family-friendly face was evident in the 107th and again early in the 108th, when Dunn and Texas Democrat Martin Frost pushed for legislation to strengthen the AMBER alert system, which quickly publicizes information about abducted children.

Representing the Bellevue-Puget Sound region, Dunn's conservatism comes with a pro-environment twist. She is an enthusiastic mountain trekker at home. In the 107th, she proposed forestry bonds to help nonprofit organizations finance the purchase of logging tracts.

Dunn's voting record on both fiscal and social issues is that of a loyal Republican. As a freshman in 1993, she surprised some of her senior female colleagues by voting against the Family and Medical Leave Act, enacted that year. She supports gun owners' rights, voted to overturn Clinton's ban on discrimination based on sexual orientation, and supported a "religious freedom" constitutional amendment sought by school prayer advocates. Dunn has consistently voted with abortion rights opponents.

Solidly pro-business and a proponent of lowering international trade barriers, Dunn uses her Ways and Means seat to protect the interests of Seattle-area businesses, including aircraft manufacturer Boeing Co., one of the country's largest exporters. Boeing is the biggest beneficiary of a tax break that Dunn helped to preserve in 2002. She was an enthusiastic supporter of granting the president fast-track authority to negotiate trade pacts that Congress cannot amend.

Since she defeated her sixth-grade boyfriend in an election for student body president, Dunn has had a passion for politics. She continued her involvement in student government through high school and at Stanford University. In 1964, she became aware of an upstart Republican politician named Ronald Reagan. He became her political idol, and when she moved back to Washington state, she poured much of her free time into campaigning for him and even named her second son Reagan.

When her marriage to King County's Republican Party chairman dissolved, Dunn worked in the county's tax assessment office before testing her own political ambitions. In 1980, she was elected state party chairman with the help of her contacts in the Reagan campaigns and in county GOP circles. The job allowed her to advance her career while providing enough money to support her two sons and enough flexibility to raise them on her own.

The position, and her fundraising prowess, put Dunn in good standing with both of Reagan's successful presidential campaigns and with his successor, George Bush. She became vice chairman of the Republican National Committee's executive board.

Dunn made her first bid for public office in 1992. She eked out a Republican primary victory in the open 8th District over Pam Roach, a first-term state senator and ardent abortion opponent who cast Dunn as a denizen of the established and more affluent suburbs of King County.

She had an easier time in the general election, taking 60 percent of the vote against Democrat George O. Tamblyn, a Mercer Island businessman. Tamblyn was unable to make a case against Dunn's conservative fiscal views and moderate image on social issues. She has won easily since.

KEY VOTES

2002

- No Overhaul campaign finance law; ban "soft money" and restrict advocacy advertising
- Yes Back Bush's defense budget increase
- Yes Extend 1996 welfare law
- Yes Adopt Bush's discretionary spending limit
- Yes Pass GOP Medicare prescription drug plan
- No Create independent Sept. 11 commission
- No Extend union protections to Homeland Security Department employees
- Yes Revive fast-track procedures for trade agreements
- Yes Authorize war against Iraq
- Yes Advance bankruptcy overhaul opposed by abortion opponents

2001

- Yes Nullify Clinton Labor Department ergonomics rule
- Yes Cut taxes by $1.35 trillion through fiscal 2011
- Yes Maintain ban on oil drilling in Arctic National Wildlife Refuge
- Yes Approve Bush proposal to limit managed-care plan liability for coverage decisions
- No Divert money from crop subsidy payments to land conservation
- Yes Expand law enforcement power to investigate suspected terrorists

CQ VOTE STUDIES

	PARTY UNITY		PRESIDENTIAL SUPPORT	
	Support	Oppose	Support	Oppose
2002	93%	7%	92%	8%
2001	95%	5%	87%	13%
2000	92%	8%	28%	72%
1999	88%	12%	28%	72%
1998	94%	6%	23%	77%

INTEREST GROUPS

	AFL-CIO	ADA	CCUS	ACU
2002	11%	5%	100%	92%
2001	8%	10%	95%	88%
2000	0%	0%	95%	88%
1999	0%	10%	96%	80%
1998	0%	0%	100%	96%

WASHINGTON 8

Eastside Seattle suburbs; Bellevue; eastern Pierce County

Home to some of suburban Seattle's most prosperous areas, the 8th takes in King County's Eastside suburbs east of Lake Washington, where million-dollar homes dot the lakeshore in wealthy hamlets like Hunts Point, Clyde Hill, Yarrow Point and Medina, where Microsoft founder Bill Gates lives. Commuters continue to fill out the exurban land as they are priced out of more-central neighborhoods. The expansion has caused huge traffic problems and ignited debates on smart growth and preservation.

The Eastside suburbs were once farmland but have become fertile ground for the Northwest's technology companies. While attracting residents who work for companies such as Microsoft (whose main campus lies just within the district's boundaries), the 8th also is home to higher-paid, blue-collar workers. Russian and Indian communities also are growing as they take on the area's high-tech jobs. Boeing remains a dominant employer, but its influence on the district waned after the 2001 decision to move its headquarters out of state. Subsequent rounds of layoffs caused some workers to leave the district.

In addition to its near-in Seattle suburbs, the 8th continues east to the border of King County and heads south to take in a mostly rural part of Pierce County, which includes Mt. Rainier National Park.

The 8th's once strongly Republican politics are changing as the first-ring suburbs begin to resemble the urban core. Generally fiscally conservative and socially moderate, the 8th is politically competitive, backing Al Gore narrowly in 2000. Southeast Asian and Middle Eastern immigrants are diversifying the area and will influence future elections.

MAJOR INDUSTRY

Logging, aviation manufacturing, software

CITIES

Bellevue, 109,569; Kent (pt.), 35,620; Sammamish, 34,104; South Hill (unincorporated), 31,623; Renton (pt.), 29,264

NOTABLE

A pontoon bridge made of reinforced concrete was finished July 2, 1940, connecting Mercer Island and Seattle.

Rep. Adam Smith (D)

CAPITOL OFFICE
225-8901
adam.smith@mail.house.gov
www.house.gov/adamsmith
227 Cannon 20515-4709; fax 225-5893

COMMITTEES
Armed Services
International Relations

HOMETOWN
Tacoma

BORN
June 15, 1965, Washington, D.C.

RELIGION
Christian

FAMILY
Wife, Sara Smith; one child

EDUCATION
Fordham U., B.A. 1987 (political science); U. of Washington, J.D. 1990

CAREER
City prosecutor; lawyer

POLITICAL HIGHLIGHTS
Wash. Senate, 1991-97

ELECTION RESULTS

2002 GENERAL		
Adam Smith (D)	95,805	58.5%
Sarah Casada (R)	63,146	38.6%
J. Mills (LIBERT)	4,759	2.9%
2002 PRIMARY (OPEN)		
Adam Smith (D)	57,250	59.5%
Sarah Casada (R)	36,368	37.8%
J. Mills (LIBERT)	2,555	2.7%
2000 GENERAL		
Adam Smith (D)	135,452	61.7%
Chris Vance (R)	76,766	35.0%
Jonathan V. Wright (LIBERT)	7,405	3.4%

PREVIOUS WINNING PERCENTAGES
1998 (65%); 1996 (50%)

Elected 1996; 4th term

Smith has emerged as a leader in the centrist New Democrat wing of his party, a lawmaker who, on the Armed Services panel, is an ally of his home-state technology behemoths and is also an advocate of international trade.

Now in his fourth term, Smith takes a reliably liberal line on most hot-button domestic issues, favoring not only strong environmental protections but also abortion rights and federal arts funding. But Smith, a former municipal prosecutor in Seattle, joins conservatives on measures aimed at strengthening the fight against crime and on some fiscal and pro-business matters. He once portrayed the leadership of his own House Democratic Caucus as "out of touch" with average Americans.

After voting against the legislation in 1998 and 2001, Smith resisted entreaties from party leaders in 2002 and backed the measure to give the president fast-track authority to negotiate trade agreements that Congress cannot amend.

And Smith voted for three Republican bills — to reduce taxes for married couples, phase out the estate tax and boost the tax benefits of retirement savings — that became components of the $1.35 trillion, 10-year tax cut enacted in 2001. He voted against the overall package, however.

When George W. Bush moved into the White House in 2001, Smith said he was willing to "work with him on everything." And in the 107th Congress, in addition to his votes for some tax cuts and the trade measure, Smith backed efforts to cut spending on certain domestic programs. He echoed White House concerns that the fight against terrorism was being used to justify excessive appropriations for a number of non-defense programs. "The federal government cannot continue using the war on terrorism as an excuse to abandon fiscal restraint," Smith said.

Smith's attempt to position himself as a pragmatic centrist has helped him to cement his political standing among the mainly white-collar residents of the district, many of whose livelihoods are connected to Microsoft Corp. and Boeing Co. Smith is the only person ever re-elected to Congress from Washington's 9th District, which was created in 1992 when the state gained an additional seat in that decade's reapportionment. His two predecessors — one a Democrat, one a Republican — each lost after one term.

Smith's record reflects both a desire to increase exports of airplanes and lumber from the Evergreen State and a concern that low-priced imports could hurt labor unions, whose backing was pivotal to his initial election. His father worked as a baggage handler at the Seattle-Tacoma International Airport, and Smith was a member of the Teamsters union while working for the United Parcel Service during college.

As one of three co-chairmen of the pro-business New Democrat Coalition, Smith helped develop a technology "e-genda" in 2002 aimed at increasing funding for worker training and research. It also encouraged industry self-policing efforts over new federal mandates as the preferred way to protect privacy on the Internet and prevent piracy of movies and recorded music.

On Armed Services, Smith has tried to persuade older Cold War veterans to loosen export controls on fast computers and software that have both military and civilian uses. Smith argues that exports should be allowed if similar foreign-made products are widely available. Smith also uses his Armed Services seat to look out for the interests of Boeing, the largest employer in his district, and its two military installations, Fort Lewis and McChord Air Force Base. He has backed eligibility for veterans' college education benefits and defended the F-22 stealth fighter plane.

In the 108th, blocked from getting a seat on the Judiciary Committee when Democrats refused to require a number of senior members to give up their choice second committee slots, Smith instead took a spot on the International Relations panel, giving up his post on the Resources Committee.

In the 107th, as the top Democrat on Resources' Water and Power Subcommittee, Smith championed the environmental regulations advocated by many of his constituents, who are concentrated in the fast-growing suburbs near Puget Sound, including opposing the construction of a third runway at the Sea-Tac airport. He also is a staunch proponent of federal support for renewable energy sources such as solar, wind and geothermal power.

Timber giant Weyerhaeuser Co. is headquartered in the 9th, but Smith usually sided with urban Democrats on Resources in opposing proposals by rural Republicans to relax limits on logging on public lands. In the 107th, he opposed allowing oil and gas drilling in the Arctic National Wildlife Refuge. Smith calls for cutting reliance on fossil fuels, and has backed the idea of requiring federal agencies to buy some of their electricity from ventures that use renewable sources.

Smith likes to point out that he is a lifelong resident of the area he represents in Congress. Technically, though, he is a "Beltway native," having been born in the District of Columbia one week before the Smiths adopted him and took him to the "other Washington." Smith's adoptive father died shortly before Smith headed east for college.

The fall after he earned his law degree in 1990, he won a state Senate seat in an upset and, at 25, became the youngest state senator in the country. Four years later, when many Democratic officeholders in the state were swept away by the 1994 Republican tide, he won a second term.

By 1996, at age 31, Smith was well-known as a tireless campaigner who had made repeat visits to many of the 40,000 homes in his legislative district. So he was considered a rising star among Washington Democrats when he announced he would challenge Tate, a favorite of the social conservative moment who had been swept into office by the GOP tidal wave of 1994. Smith won by 3 percentage points. He has won relatively comfortable re-elections since then. The political makeup of the district was altered minimally by the latest redistricting, and in 2002 he cruised to a 20-point victory over Republican state Rep. Sarah Casada.

KEY VOTES

2002

Yes Overhaul campaign finance law; ban "soft money" and restrict advocacy advertising
Yes Back Bush's defense budget increase
No Extend 1996 welfare law
No Adopt Bush's discretionary spending limit
No Pass GOP Medicare prescription drug plan
? Create independent Sept. 11 commission
Yes Extend union protections to Homeland Security Department employees
Yes Revive fast-track procedures for trade agreements
Yes Authorize war against Iraq
Yes Advance bankruptcy overhaul opposed by abortion opponents

2001

No Nullify Clinton Labor Department ergonomics rule
No Cut taxes by $1.35 trillion through fiscal 2011
Yes Maintain ban on oil drilling in Arctic National Wildlife Refuge
No Approve Bush proposal to limit managed-care plan liability for coverage decisions
Yes Divert money from crop subsidy payments to land conservation
Yes Expand law enforcement power to investigate suspected terrorists

CQ VOTE STUDIES

	PARTY UNITY		PRESIDENTIAL SUPPORT	
	Support	Oppose	Support	Oppose
2002	81%	19%	38%	62%
2001	80%	20%	43%	57%
2000	80%	20%	78%	22%
1999	75%	25%	75%	25%
1998	83%	17%	80%	20%

INTEREST GROUPS

	AFL-CIO	ADA	CCUS	ACU
2002	63%	85%	63%	23%
2001	83%	80%	48%	20%
2000	67%	45%	80%	21%
1999	56%	85%	56%	20%
1998	100%	100%	39%	0%

WASHINGTON 9

South Seattle suburbs; small part of Tacoma

The 9th is a politically competitive, mostly suburban district south of Seattle that runs along Interstate 5, picking up small parts of Tacoma and the capital of Olympia en route to rural areas that afford great views of the 14,410-foot Mount Rainier (in the 8th), the state's highest point.

The district's northern area, just south of the Seattle line, takes in predominantly middle-class King County suburbs, including most of Burien, SeaTac and Tukwila (shared with the 7th) and Renton (shared with the 8th). SeaTac (a partial concatenation of the names of the area's major cities) includes the region's major airport. Boeing has a commercial airplane production facility in Renton. Farther south are slightly more prosperous areas like Kent (shared with the 8th) and Des Moines. Federal Way, in southwest King, includes the headquarters of paper giant Weyerhaeuser.

King County accounts for about half of the 9th's population. The rest live in Pierce County, south of King, or in Thurston County, including northeastern Olympia. In Pierce, the 9th takes in the deep-water Port of Tacoma, which has diversified an economy once dominated by Boeing. The corridor along Interstate 5 has become a magnet for technology companies that provide high-paying jobs for well-educated residents.

Redistricting in 2002 made small changes to the 9th, which during the 1990s was a quintessential swing district that elected a Democratic representative in 1992, a Republican in 1994 and a Democrat in 1996. Democrats fare better in the King and Thurston portions of the district than in Pierce.

MAJOR INDUSTRY

Aviation manufacturing, computer software, hardware

MILITARY BASES

Fort Lewis (Army), 20,484 military, 4,500 civilian (2001); McChord Air Force Base, 3,500 military, 1,100 civilian (2000)

CITIES

Federal Way, 83,259; Kent (pt.), 43,904; Puyallup, 33,011; Lakewood (pt.), 31,333; Des Moines, 29,267; Lacey (pt.), 28,829; Auburn (pt.), 23,271

NOTABLE

Before becoming commander of the American forces in the Persian Gulf, Gen. Norman Schwarzkopf was commander of Fort Lewis; Puyallup Valley claims to be the nation's No. 1 producer of rhubarb.

WEST VIRGINIA

Gov. Bob Wise (D)

First elected: 2000
Length of term: 4 years
Term expires: 1/05
Salary: $90,000
Phone: (304) 558-2000
Hometown: Clendenin
Born: Jan. 6, 1948; Washington, D.C.
Religion: Episcopalian
Family: Wife, Sandra Wise; two children
Education: Duke U., A.B. 1970 (political science); Tulane U., J.D. 1975
Career: Lawyer
Political highlights: W.Va. Senate, 1981-83; U.S. House, 1983-2001
Election results:

2000 GENERAL		
Bob Wise (D)	324,822	50.1%
Cecil H. Underwood (R)	305,926	47.2%
Denise Giardina (MOUNT)	10,416	1.6%

Senate President Earl Ray Tomblin (D)

(no lieutenant governor)
Phone: (304) 357-7801

STATE LEGISLATURE

General Assembly: Meets January-March
House: 100 members, 2-year terms
2003 breakdown: 31R, 69D; 81 men, 19 women
Salary: $15,000; $150/day for extension days
Phone: (304) 340-3200
Senate: 34 members, 4-year terms
2003 breakdown: 10R, 24D; 29 men, 5 women
Salary: $15,000; $150/day for extension days
Phone: (304) 357-7800

STATE TERM LIMITS

Governor: 2 consecutive terms
Senate: No
House: No

URBAN STATISTICS

CITY	POPULATION
Charleston	53,421
Huntington	51,475
Parkersburg	33,099
Wheeling	31,419

REGISTERED VOTERS

Democrat	60%
Republican	29%
Nonpartisan	9%

POPULATION

2002 population (est.)	1,801,873
2000 population	1,808,344
1990 population	1,793,477
Percent change (1990-2000)	+0.8%
Rank among states (2002)	37
Median age	38.9
Born in state	74.2%
Foreign born	1.1%
Violent crime rate	317/100,000
Poverty level	17.9%
Federal workers	21,235
Military	10,203

REDISTRICTING

West Virginia retained its three House seats in reapportionment. The state legislature drew a new map, which the governor signed on Oct. 4, 2001.

MISCELLANEOUS

Web: www.state.wv.us
Capital: Charleston

STATE ELECTION OFFICIAL
(304) 558-6000

DEMOCRATIC HEADQUARTERS
(304) 342-8121

REPUBLICAN HEADQUARTERS
(304) 344-3446

District Statistics

DIST.	2000 VOTE FOR PRESIDENT BUSH	GORE	NADER	WHITE	BLACK	ASIAN	HISP	MEDIAN INCOME	WHITE COLLAR	BLUE COLLAR	SERVICE INDUSTRY	OVER 64	UNDER 18	COLLEGE EDUCATION	RURAL	SQ. MILES
1	54%	43%	2%	96%	2%	1%	1%	$30,303	54%	29%	17%	16%	22%	16%	46%	6,286
2	54	44	2	94	4	1	1	$33,198	55	30	15	15	23	16	54	8,459
3	47	51	1	94	4	0	1	$25,630	53	30	18	16	22	12	62	9,332
STATE	52	46	2	95	3	1	1	$29,696	54	29	17	15	22	15	54	24,078
U.S.	47.9	48.4	3	69	12	4	13	$41,994	60	25	15	12	26	24	21	3,537,438

Hancock
Brooke
Ohio
Wheeling
Marshall
Monongalia
Preston
Wetzel
Morgantown
Marion
Tyler
Parkersburg
Pleasants
Harrison
Taylor
1
Wood
Ritchie
Doddridge
Clarksburg
Barbour
Tucker
Mineral
Grant
Hampshire
Hardy
Morgan
Berkeley
Martinsburg
Jefferson
Wirt
Gilmer
Lewis
Calhoun
Upshur
Randolph
Jackson
Mason
2
Roane
Braxton
Pendleton
Putnam
Huntington
Cabell
Charleston
Clay
Webster
Kanawha
Nicholas
Pocahontas
Wayne
Lincoln
Boone
Fayette
3
Greenbrier
Logan
Beckley
Raleigh
Mingo
Wyoming
Summers
Monroe
McDowell
Mercer
Bluefield

Sen. Robert C. Byrd (D)

Elected 1958; 8th term

CAPITOL OFFICE
224-3954
byrd.senate.gov
311 Hart 20510-4801; fax 228-0002

COMMITTEES
Appropriations - ranking member
Armed Services
Budget
Rules & Administration

HOMETOWN
Sophia

BORN
Nov. 20, 1917, North Wilkesboro, N.C.

RELIGION
Baptist

FAMILY
Wife, Erma Ora Byrd; two children

EDUCATION
American U., J.D. 1963; Marshall U., B.A. 1994 (political science)

CAREER
Butcher

POLITICAL HIGHLIGHTS
W.Va. House, 1947-51; W.Va. Senate, 1951-53; U.S. House, 1953-59

ELECTION RESULTS

2000 GENERAL		
Robert C. Byrd (D)	469,215	77.8%
David T. Gallaher (R)	121,635	20.2%
Joe Whelan (LIBERT)	12,627	2.1%
2000 PRIMARY		
Robert C. Byrd (D)		unopposed

PREVIOUS WINNING PERCENTAGES
1994 (69%); 1988 (65%); 1982 (69%); 1976 (100%); 1970 (78%); 1964 (68%); 1958 (59%); 1956 House Election (57%); 1954 House Election (63%); 1952 House Election (56%)

With his snow-white pompadour and 19th century grandiloquence, Byrd affects the unmistakable air of an aging Senate institution. He happily cultivates that reputation, but by objective measure he *is* one. For almost one-quarter of the time Congress has existed, Byrd has been one of its proudest members; he is now the third-longest-serving lawmaker in history.

As the 108th Congress began, Byrd was beginning a sixth decade at the Capitol and his 45th year as a senator. If he completes his eighth term, he will surpass Strom Thurmond of South Carolina as the longest-serving senator. If he wins re-election in 2006 — a near certainty as long as his health holds up — he would be on course to surpass Arizona's Carl T. Hayden as the longest-serving member of Congress in the fall of 2009, at about the time of Byrd's 92nd birthday.

More important than his longevity, however, is Byrd's continued vigorous pursuit of his self-appointed roles as guardian of the Senate's prerogatives and precedents, its reverential historian and grandmaster of its rules and procedures. He can be prickly and imperious, and he is something of a loner in the institution he so loves. But he literally wrote the book on the Senate — a four-volume history that began as a series of characteristically flowery speeches. His devotion to the Constitution is just as passionate. "This is *my* contract with America," he would say when Republicans in the 1990s trumpeted a legislative manifesto of that name.

Among his favorite passages in the Constitution is Article 1, Section 9, clause 7: "No money shall be drawn from the Treasury, but in consequence of appropriations made by law." The power of the purse has been exercised robustly by Byrd as either the chairman or the top-ranking Democrat on the Appropriations Committee since 1989. In the 108th, he claimed his party's top seat as well on the new Homeland Security Appropriations Subcommittee, positioning him to act on his view that President Bush's budgets provide inadequately for domestic defense. Byrd also opposed the 2002 law creating the Homeland Security Department, saying it cedes too much authority to the executive branch, so the new subcommittee affords him an ideal forum for oversight.

Byrd's zealous pursuit of federal largess for West Virginia has been remarkably effective, and has made him a ready symbol for those who would criticize the congressional spending culture. When he first took the Appropriations gavel in the 101st Congress — after six years as Senate majority leader commingled with six years as minority leader — he promised to steer $1 billion for public works back home; he had exceeded the goal two years later, and the steady stream of earmarks for highways, dams, educational institutions and federal agency offices has continued unabated.

The Charleston Gazette, which has called Byrd a "one-man economic development program," also has compiled a list of more than 30 existing or pending federal projects named for the senator. Byrd, who has hung a lifesize portrait of himself in one of his Capitol offices, makes no pretense of shunning such gestures of gratitude — which mean much to someone whose life story could have been written by Horatio Alger.

He was born Cornelius Calvin Sale Jr. When he was 1, his mother died and his father gave him to an aunt and uncle, Vlurma and Titus Byrd; they reared him in the hardscrabble coal country of southern West Virginia. Byrd graduated first in his high school class and married his high school sweetheart, Erma Ora. But it took him 12 years before he could afford to start college. He worked as a gas station attendant, grocery store clerk, shipyard welder and butcher before his talents as a fiddle player helped him win a seat in the state legislature in 1946. Friends drove Byrd around the hills and hollows, where he brought the voters out by playing "Cripple Creek" and "Rye Whiskey."

Since that first bid for office, Byrd has never lost an election. "There are four things people believe in in West Virginia," he has often said. "God Almighty; Sears, Roebuck; Carter's Little Liver Pills; and Robert C. Byrd."

Byrd has often emerged victorious over more-celebrated lawmakers, and he has bested most of the 11 presidents he has served beside, at least once. But in the 107th Congress, he tasted defeat on a wide range of issues. He was unable to get his way in the homeland security debates. He led the fight against granting President Bush broad authority to wage a pre-emptive military strike on Iraq, but he could not persuade even a majority of his own Senate caucus to vote against the war. He led the opposition to Bush's bid to win back the power to negotiate trade deals that Congress cannot amend, and he lost overwhelmingly.

Perhaps most cutting of all, in 2001 Byrd was unable to prevent the Senate from using the budget law he wrote in 1974 — designed to ease procedural impediments to Congress' trimming of the deficit — to instead give parliamentary protections to the deepest tax cut in two decades.

Byrd is one of the most independent members of his caucus — only 10 Senate Democrats strayed from the party line more often in the 107th — mainly because he puts the prerogatives of the Senate and the needs of his home state before the dictates of political ideology.

But he rallied his party after Republicans swept to power in the 104th. He was a formidable force in blocking GOP proposals he saw as pernicious, notably the line-item veto and a balanced-budget constitutional amendment. And he was a pivotal figure in the 1999 impeachment trial. Although he concluded that President Clinton had lied under oath, Byrd also decided that the lack of public support for removing Clinton from office meant that convicting the president would cause greater damage than allowing him to finish his term. His motion to dismiss the charges against Clinton deflated what was left of the House prosecutors' case.

There are signs that age is beginning to take its toll on Byrd. A tremor causes his hands to shake, sometimes quite noticeably. Yet it is still dangerous to underestimate him, and even worse to ignore him. Perhaps more than with anyone else in his caucus, Democratic leader Tom Daschle tries whenever possible to accommodate Byrd's wishes.

Byrd's political career has featured its share of mistakes, some quite spectacular. As a young man, he joined the Ku Klux Klan — because of his alarm over communism, he says — a decision he came to publicly regret. In 1964, he filibustered the landmark Civil Rights Act, at one point holding the floor with a 14-hour speech that is among the longest on record. He also has lamented that chapter of his career.

Byrd, ever the student of history, has understood its imperatives and has changed with the times. As his party's leader during the Carter and Reagan years, he strove to adapt his old-fashioned style for the television age. Nonetheless, Byrd is becoming increasingly isolated in a Senate made up of younger, more impatient members whose focus is on the next TV interview or the next election.

That does not bother him. On his Senate Web site, he proudly cites a tribute from former Democratic Sen. Sam Nunn of Georgia: "Great men are like eagles. They do not flock together. You find them one at a time, soaring alone, using their skill and their strengths to reach new heights and to seek new horizons. Such a man and such an eagle is Robert Byrd."

KEY VOTES

2002

- Yes Pass farm bill reversing crop subsidy limits
- Yes Postpone tougher automobile fuel efficiency standards
- Yes Overhaul campaign finance law; ban "soft money" and restrict advocacy advertising
- Yes Set federal election standards
- No Support oil drilling in Arctic National Wildlife Refuge
- No Revive fast-track procedures for trade agreements
- Yes Create federal insurance coverage for catastrophic terrorist losses
- Yes Tighten federal accounting and corporate governance regulation
- Yes Advance bipartisan Medicare prescription drug plan
- Yes Create independent Sept. 11 commission
- Yes Back Democratic Homeland Security Department proposal
- No Authorize war against Iraq

2001

- Yes Confirm John Ashcroft as attorney general
- No Nullify Clinton Labor Department ergonomics rule
- No Cut taxes by $1.35 trillion through fiscal 2011
- Yes Pass Democratic bill to bolster rights of patients in managed-care plans
- Yes Permit a new round of military base closings
- Yes Expand law enforcement power to investigate suspected terrorists

CQ VOTE STUDIES

	PARTY UNITY		PRESIDENTIAL SUPPORT	
	Support	Oppose	Support	Oppose
2002	82%	18%	70%	30%
2001	86%	14%	71%	29%
2000	72%	28%	75%	25%
1999	80%	20%	70%	30%
1998	72%	28%	74%	26%
1997	81%	19%	81%	19%
1996	82%	18%	81%	19%
1995	82%	18%	82%	18%
1994	73%	27%	74%	26%
1993	87%	13%	80%	20%

INTEREST GROUPS

	AFL-CIO	ADA	CCUS	ACU
2002	85%	75%	40%	15%
2001	75%	85%	21%	40%
2000	63%	75%	40%	28%
1999	100%	80%	47%	20%
1998	88%	80%	44%	16%
1997	100%	70%	40%	16%
1996	86%	70%	23%	15%
1995	92%	85%	26%	26%
1994	75%	75%	30%	40%
1993	100%	55%	18%	24%

Sen. John D. Rockefeller IV (D)

CAPITOL OFFICE
224-6472
senator@rockefeller.senate.gov
rockefeller.senate.gov
531 Hart 20510-4802; fax 224-7665

COMMITTEES
Commerce, Science & Transportation
Finance
Foreign Relations
Veterans' Affairs
Select Intelligence - vice chairman
Joint Taxation

HOMETOWN
Charleston

BORN
June 18, 1937, Manhattan, N.Y.

RELIGION
Presbyterian

FAMILY
Wife, Sharon Percy; four children

EDUCATION
International Christian U. (Tokyo), attended 1957-60; Harvard U., A.B. 1961 (Asian languages & history)

CAREER
College president; public official

POLITICAL HIGHLIGHTS
W.Va. House, 1967-69; W.Va. secretary of state, 1969-73; Democratic nominee for governor, 1972; governor, 1977-85

ELECTION RESULTS

2002 GENERAL		
John D. Rockefeller IV (D)	275,281	63.1%
Jay Wolfe (R)	160,902	36.9%
2002 PRIMARY		
John D. Rockefeller IV (D)	198,327	89.9%
Bruce Barilla (D)	11,178	5.1%
William "Bill" Galloway (D)	11,173	5.1%

PREVIOUS WINNING PERCENTAGES
1996 (77%); 1990 (68%); 1984 (52%)

Elected 1984; 4th term

It is one of the great ironies of American politics: A state with one of the nation's lowest per capita personal incomes is represented in the Senate by someone whose surname is a synonym for extraordinary wealth.

But Rockefeller relies on self-deprecating humor to convince his constituents to see him as just plain "Jay," an ordinary guy with ordinary tastes. Favorite baseball team, Atlanta Braves; favorite food, lima beans, according to his Senate Web site. Indeed, his low-key personality and bespectacled mien might remind an observer more of Clark Kent than of Superman, but Rockefeller's tireless work on behalf of one of the industrial pillars of his state's long-suffering economy has led some to dub him the "man of steel."

Towering and bookish, Rockefeller cannot hope to match the influence or rococo flair of his senior colleague, Robert C. Byrd, who has used his top position on the Appropriations Committee to funnel billions of dollars back home. But he does rank high on other panels. He chaired Veterans' Affairs during the 107th Congress. On Commerce, he chaired the Aviation Subcommittee after the Sept. 11, 2001, terrorist attacks. On Finance, he leads Democrats on the Health Care Subcommittee. At the start of the 108th, as Rockefeller began his fourth term, he became vice chairman of the Intelligence Committee.

Rockefeller can be among the most partisan of Democrats, arguing that Republicans are out to hurt the little guy. Or he can play the pragmatist, willing to do what it takes to strike a deal. He can work with his party's liberals to push for broader health care coverage, while lining up with the GOP in an effort to overhaul product liability laws.

He has worked hard to gain the confidence of West Virginians from the day he arrived in the state in 1964 as a 27-year-old VISTA anti-poverty volunteer who planned to stay for a year. Working for the Action for Appalachia Youth program seemed a strange choice for Rockefeller, who had spent three years in Tokyo studying Japanese. But the experience was transformational; two years later he had not only found a permanent home, but he had also won election to the state House. And in one way, his family wealth has insulated him from suspicion back home. With no need to curry favor or solicit campaign cash from special interests, Rockefeller can devote all his energies to helping his constituents.

Calling steel a "life or death" issue for his state, Rockefeller has repeatedly waged bare-knuckle legislative battles with administrations of both parties to protect the industry and its workers. As co-chairman of the Senate Steel Caucus, he argues that the U.S. industry is on the verge of collapse as a result of a flood of low-cost imports. Rockefeller sensed an opening after George W. Bush won the presidency, having carried West Virginia on a promise to consider imposing steel tariffs. Bush did so in the spring of 2002, including a 30 percent duty on tin mill steel, which is produced by Weirton Steel, one of West Virginia's largest employers. Rockefeller hailed the move, but by summer he was expressing outrage that Bush had issued exemptions for nearly one-fourth of all foreign steel imports.

Rockefeller also was disillusioned with President Bush over health benefits for retired steelworkers. Many argue that unfunded benefits are a major obstacle to the consolidation of the industry, which is key to its survival. Rockefeller proposed using up to $10 billion from steel import tariffs to pay these "legacy costs." Bush rejected the idea and Rockefeller accused the president of playing "a shell game" with steelworkers.

Another longstanding legislative priority is health care. At the start of the 108th, he renewed his push for legislation that would ease states' responsibility for long-term care costs under Medicaid, increase Medicaid's market power to buy medicines and manage drug benefits, and create incentives for Medicaid outreach and enrollment.

In 1989, Rockefeller chaired the so-called Pepper Commission, a bipartisan panel that recommended long-term care for the elderly and health coverage for the uninsured. However, the package died after the commission failed to agree on how to pay for its proposals.

A decade later, Rockefeller served on another blue-ribbon panel studying the long-term solvency of Medicare. This time, he was one of seven members (of 17) to block a formal recommendation of a plan by Sen. John B. Breaux, the Louisiana Democrat who was the panel's co-chairman. Rockefeller maintained that the proposed Medicare prescription drug benefit was too stingy. As the prescription debate reached an impass in the 107th, Rockefeller fought any plan that would rely on private insurers to hold down costs.

Much of Rockefeller's legislative success in the 107th resulted from his chairmanship of Veterans' Affairs. The list included compensation for female veterans who undergo mastectomies, expanded mortgage assistance, increased annual benefits for Medal of Honor recipients, health care benefit extensions to deceased veterans' spouses who remarry, recruitment incentives for VA nurses, and additional health benefits for veterans living in higher-cost areas.

As Aviation Subcommittee chairman, Rockefeller had a hand in writing the airline industry bailout and aviation security laws enacted soon after Sept. 11; he also pushed to maintain service to small cities, such as those in West Virginia. On Finance, he opposed Bush's $1.35 trillion tax cut of 2001; but he has supported some tax cuts that help West Virginia, such as his proposed tax credit to companies that bring broadband to underserved rural and inner-city areas.

As Congress debated the welfare reauthorization bill in the 107th, Rockefeller and other Democrats called for at least an additional $8 billion for child care services over five years. Rockefeller also wants more information from states to better determine the impact of the legislation.

The great-grandson and namesake of the founder of Standard Oil Co., Rockefeller was reared on Manhattan's Upper East Side and was schooled at Exeter and Harvard. His ascent in West Virginia politics was not all that smooth. After he served in the state House and as secretary of state, he lost a race for governor in 1972. He strengthened his ties to the state by serving as president of West Virginia Wesleyan College and won the governorship on his second try, in 1976.

Barred by state law from a third term, Rockefeller set his eyes on the Senate in 1984, even before Democrat Jennings Randolph decided to retire that year. Rockefeller had become an unpopular governor by then because he had not met the high expectations he had raised for the state's economy. He won with just 52 percent despite spending $12 million against a political neophyte, John Raese. He has won more easily since, claiming his fourth term in 2002 with 63 percent against Jay Wolfe, a former GOP state senator.

Given his name recognition, wealth and political experience, Rockefeller has been mentioned as a potential presidential candidate since he first ran for statewide office in 1968. He seriously considered a race in 1992 but concluded he was not up to a national campaign, and he made the same decision long before the start of the 2004 campaign. "I am sufficiently private to not want to do this," he told the Charleston Daily Mail in 2001. "There's a point where I've decided to say, 'You can't have all of me.' "

KEY VOTES

2002

Yes Pass farm bill reversing crop subsidy limits
No Postpone tougher automobile fuel efficiency standards
Yes Overhaul campaign finance law; ban "soft money" and restrict advocacy advertising
Yes Set federal election standards
No Support oil drilling in Arctic National Wildlife Refuge
No Revive fast-track procedures for trade agreements
Yes Create federal insurance coverage for catastrophic terrorist losses
Yes Tighten federal accounting and corporate governance regulation
Yes Advance bipartisan Medicare prescription drug plan
Yes Create independent Sept. 11 commission
Yes Back Democratic Homeland Security Department proposal
Yes Authorize war against Iraq

2001

No Confirm John Ashcroft as attorney general
No Nullify Clinton Labor Department ergonomics rule
No Cut taxes by $1.35 trillion through fiscal 2011
Yes Pass Democratic bill to bolster rights of patients in managed-care plans
Yes Permit a new round of military base closings
Yes Expand law enforcement power to investigate suspected terrorists

CQ VOTE STUDIES

	PARTY UNITY		PRESIDENTIAL SUPPORT	
	Support	Oppose	Support	Oppose
2002	90%	10%	71%	29%
2001	97%	3%	66%	34%
2000	96%	4%	97%	3%
1999	94%	6%	89%	11%
1998	93%	7%	94%	6%
1997	88%	12%	86%	14%
1996	93%	7%	93%	7%
1995	88%	12%	88%	12%
1994	90%	10%	97%	3%
1993	94%	6%	95%	5%

INTEREST GROUPS

	AFL-CIO	ADA	CCUS	ACU
2002	100%	90%	45%	15%
2001	100%	100%	43%	12%
2000	75%	85%	60%	4%
1999	89%	100%	41%	4%
1998	100%	90%	56%	0%
1997	71%	70%	67%	8%
1996	86%	85%	46%	16%
1995	100%	90%	42%	9%
1994	75%	95%	22%	0%
1993	91%	70%	18%	12%

Rep. Alan B. Mollohan (D)

CAPITOL OFFICE
225-4172
www.house.gov/mollohan
2302 Rayburn 20515-4801; fax 225-7564

COMMITTEES
Appropriations
Standards of Official Conduct - ranking member

HOMETOWN
Fairmont

BORN
May 14, 1943, Fairmont, W.Va.

RELIGION
Baptist

FAMILY
Wife, Barbara Mollohan; five children

EDUCATION
College of William & Mary, A.B. 1966 (political science); West Virginia U., J.D. 1970

MILITARY SERVICE
Army Reserve, 1970-83

CAREER
Lawyer

POLITICAL HIGHLIGHTS
No previous office

ELECTION RESULTS

2002 GENERAL		
Alan B. Mollohan (D)		unopposed
2002 PRIMARY		
Alan B. Mollohan (D)		unopposed
2000 GENERAL		
Alan B. Mollohan (D)	170,974	87.8%
Richard Kerr (LIBERT)	23,797	12.2%

PREVIOUS WINNING PERCENTAGES
1998 (85%); 1996 (100%); 1994 (70%); 1992 (100%); 1990 (67%); 1988 (75%); 1986 (100%); 1984 (54%); 1982 (53%)

Elected 1982; 11th term

Proper, respectful and quietly effective, Mollohan is not a natural politician, but during two decades in the House he has won high marks for hard work. A senior Democrat on the Appropriations Committee, Mollohan has worked steadily to steer federal funding to his state, focusing on ways to promote economic development by expanding the state's industry beyond the historic standbys of coal mining and steel.

In the 108th, he returned for a second tour on the ethics committee when new Minority Leader Nancy Pelosi made him the panel's top Democrat.

Over the years, Mollohan and his Democratic West Virginia colleague on the Senate Appropriations Committee, Chairman Robert C. Byrd, have unabashedly directed federal monies back home. Evidence of their efforts is rife in the 1st District, which includes new prisons, health clinics, federal office and research centers, and road and water projects.

In Mollohan's hometown of Fairmont, just south of Morgantown, is the Alan B. Mollohan Innovation Center, the headquarters of the West Virginia High Technology Consortium, a nonprofit group founded by Mollohan to nurture the area's fledgling high-technology sector. Also in Fairmont is the National White Collar Crime Center, created to lead the nation's fight against Internet fraud.

The son of a congressman, Mollohan worked as a lawyer in Washington, before succeeding his father in the House. He gained a seat on the coveted spending committee in mid-1986, where he was mentored by Democrat John P. Murtha, whose Pennsylvania district borders Mollohan's. With his family background in politics, Mollohan views the legislative process as a give-and-take business, one in which people with opposing opinions work quietly to reach compromise.

When Republicans took control of the House in 1995, Mollohan lost the chairmanship of the Commerce-Justice-State Appropriations Subcommittee, which he had held for just eight months. Since the 106th Congress, he has been the top Democrat on the subcommittee that funds the Veterans Affairs and Housing and Urban Development departments along with NASA, the Environmental Protection Agency and more than a dozen other agencies.

Membership on the panel provides plenty of opportunities to secure funding for home-state projects. NASA may not launch rockets from West Virginia, but it has located small segments of the vast space industry in the state. Even after the Columbia space shuttle disaster, Mollohan remains a strong backer of space exploration.

He works closely with his panel's chairman, Republican James T. Walsh of New York, who also looks for bipartisanship and accommodation. Mollohan can be a dogged partisan fighter, but he generally leaves the shouting to Wisconsin's David R. Obey, senior Democrat on the full committee.

In many ways, Mollohan reflects his blue-collar constituents, with his moderate views on economic policy and his more conservative stance on social issues. In the last decade, Mollohan has strayed from the party line considerably more often than the average Democrat. In the 107th, Mollohan was one of only 12 Democrats to vote in the House against final passage of the 2002 campaign finance law, arguing that it would thwart the right of free speech.

Mollohan takes a strong stand against abortion — he chaired the House Pro-Life Caucus for many years — but his views on that subject do not hamper his ability to work with liberal Democrats in other areas. An outdoorsman and hunter, he has consistently supported gun owners' rights.

Mollohan has sided with conservatives on some issues of environmental regulation, a stance that grows out of his state's dependence on coal mining, steelmaking and other heavy industries. His opposition to what he called "unsound" acid rain legislation that penalized coal-burning plants and factories made him one of only 21 House members in 1990 to vote against the updates to the Clean Air Act.

With steel mills in his district struggling for profitability, Mollohan has backed foreign "anti-dumping" measures. He applauded President Bush's decision in 2002 to impose stiff tariffs on imported steel, though they were not as steep as Mollohan and other steel allies had sought.

Mollohan was 9 years old when his father, Robert H. Mollohan, was elected to Congress. He was on the House floor when his father was sworn into office and, as he told the Charleston Daily Mail, "I remember it like yesterday. I think it was kind of a biological imprinting on my brain. I said, 'This is what I want to do.' That's when I knew."

Robert Mollohan served from 1953 to 1957 and then again from 1969 to 1983. In Alan Mollohan's 1982 campaign to succeed his father, some voters questioned whether the candidate's West Virginia roots ran deep enough. For the previous decade, he had been a Washington lawyer who counted Pittsburgh-based Consolidation Coal Co. as a major client. Rank-and-file miners were leery of a corporate lawyer representing them; many lined up behind Mollohan's pro-labor primary opponent, state Sen. Dan Tonkovich. But the elder Mollohan had close connections with party officials and business and labor leaders; their support proved crucial to his son's narrow primary victory.

That fall, Mollohan took 53 percent, and two years later he was held to 54 percent, but he has not struggled in any general election since. The GOP has not bothered to field a candidate against Mollohan since 1994. In redistricting after the 2000 census, state legislators adhered to the wishes of the three incumbent House members and drew new maps with minimal changes, making each of them slightly more secure.

Ten years earlier, by contrast, the state's loss of one House seat after the 1990 census led Mollohan into a Democratic primary against colleague Harley O. Staggers Jr. Both men had followed their fathers to Congress, but Staggers portrayed himself as the "outsider," criticizing Mollohan for writing overdrafts at the private bank for House members. Mollohan highlighted the importance of his seat on Appropriations. Much more of the reshaped 1st was Mollohan's old territory, and he won the primary by 24 points.

KEY VOTES

2002

- No Overhaul campaign finance law; ban "soft money" and restrict advocacy advertising
- Yes Back Bush's defense budget increase
- No Extend 1996 welfare law
- No Adopt Bush's discretionary spending limit
- No Pass GOP Medicare prescription drug plan
- Yes Create independent Sept. 11 commission
- Yes Extend union protections to Homeland Security Department employees
- No Revive fast-track procedures for trade agreements
- No Authorize war against Iraq
- No Advance bankruptcy overhaul opposed by abortion opponents

2001

- No Nullify Clinton Labor Department ergonomics rule
- No Cut taxes by $1.35 trillion through fiscal 2011
- No Maintain ban on oil drilling in Arctic National Wildlife Refuge
- No Approve Bush proposal to limit managed-care plan liability for coverage decisions
- Yes Divert money from crop subsidy payments to land conservation
- No Expand law enforcement power to investigate suspected terrorists

CQ VOTE STUDIES

	PARTY UNITY		PRESIDENTIAL SUPPORT	
	Support	Oppose	Support	Oppose
2002	78%	22%	34%	66%
2001	65%	35%	45%	55%
2000	70%	30%	69%	31%
1999	64%	36%	58%	42%
1998	74%	26%	69%	31%

INTEREST GROUPS

	AFL-CIO	ADA	CCUS	ACU
2002	89%	75%	40%	24%
2001	92%	65%	48%	48%
2000	90%	60%	52%	28%
1999	88%	60%	36%	31%
1998	100%	70%	27%	32%

WEST VIRGINIA 1

North – Parkersburg, Wheeling, Morgantown

Located in the northernmost part of the state, the Democratic-leaning 1st has a large rural component but is the most urban of West Virginia's three districts. It contains six of the state's 10 largest cities and West Virginia University, the state's largest school. Wheeling, an industrial town and commercial center in the north, and Parkersburg, a regional trade center in the west, are two of the main urban areas.

The district was hit hard by economic depression in the 1980s, losing population as factories shut down and coal mines mechanized. Unemployment remained high in the early 1990s — topping 10 percent in some counties — and 12 of the district's 20 counties lost population during the decade. Coal and steel are still the district's biggest employers, but a budding technology sector has brightened economic prospects. The FBI, Department of Energy and NASA have opened facilities in the district, and Morgantown, home to West Virginia University, is attracting high-tech firms. Located amid the coal fields of Monongalia County (one of the state's leading coal-producing counties), Morgantown also is home to Software Valley, an organization that promotes technology and research activity.

The 1st long has elected Democrats to Congress and has more registered Democrats than Republicans, but Parkersburg and Wheeling have some Republican-leaning state House districts. The 1st gave George W. Bush 54 percent of the vote in the 2000 presidential election, helping him win by a 6-point statewide margin over Democratic nominee Al Gore.

MAJOR INDUSTRY

Coal, steel, technology, chemicals

CITIES

Parkersburg, 33,099; Wheeling, 31,419; Morgantown, 26,809; Weirton, 20,411; Fairmont, 19,097; Clarksburg, 16,743

NOTABLE

Prabhupada's Palace of Gold was built in Moundsville by the International Society for Krishna Consciousness; The Capitol Music Hall in Wheeling hosts Jamboree USA, a country music program that has aired on radio station WWVA since 1933; 1984 Olympic gold medalist Mary Lou Retton is from Marion County.

Rep. Shelley Moore Capito (R)

CAPITOL OFFICE
225-2711
www.house.gov/capito
1431 Longworth 20515-4802; fax 225-7856

COMMITTEES
Financial Services
Small Business
Transportation & Infrastructure

HOMETOWN
Charleston

BORN
Nov. 26, 1953, Glen Dale, W.Va.

RELIGION
Presbyterian

FAMILY
Husband, Charles L. Capito Jr.; three children

EDUCATION
Duke U., B.S. 1975 (zoology); U. of Virginia, M.Ed. 1976 (counselor education)

CAREER
University system information center director; college career counselor

POLITICAL HIGHLIGHTS
W.Va. House, 1997-2001

ELECTION RESULTS

2002 GENERAL		
Shelley Moore Capito (R)	98,276	60.0%
Jim Humphreys (D)	65,400	40.0%
2002 PRIMARY		
Shelley Moore Capito (R)		unopposed
2000 GENERAL		
Shelley Moore Capito (R)	108,769	48.5%
Jim Humphreys (D)	103,003	45.9%
John Brown (LIBERT)	12,543	5.6%

Elected 2000; 2nd term

The only Republican in the West Virginia congressional delegation — and the first one from the Mountaineer State in two decades, Capito's centrist political views and her low-key comfort on the campaign trail have enabled her to survive two of the most expensive House election campaigns of the decade.

She narrowly won in 2000 against wealthy class-action attorney Jim Humphreys, who plowed almost $7 million into the race. In their 2002 rematch, which was the most expensive House campaign that year, Capito won by an impressive 20 percentage points.

An affable and energetic mother of three, Capito (CAP-ih-toe) grew up in a political household — her father, Arch A. Moore Jr., served in the House for 12 years and spent 12 more as West Virginia's governor. She is the second woman to represent the Mountaineer State in Congress.

Capito's Capitol Hill career began with political observers back home wondering if she would ever break ranks with the GOP, reasoning that if she did not she would have difficulty in convincing the 2nd District's Democratic-leaning electorate to back her in 2002. But, before her first term was done, she had gone against the party line on such high-profile issues as campaign finance, trade and family planning.

She voted for the campaign finance overhaul bill that became law in 2002, which included her amendment to increase fundraising limits and to permit additional help from political parties for candidates who face wealthy opponents (like Humphreys), who pour their own money into the race.

Capito, like her Democratic predecessor Rep. Bob Wise, supports gun owners' rights and abortion rights. She says, however, that she wants certain limits on abortion rights, and she opposes a procedure its opponents call "partial birth" abortion. She is also against federal funding for abortions and insists that parents be notified before a minor can obtain an abortion. In the 107th Congress, she came under fire from both sides of the abortion debate when she was one of 33 House Republicans who voted to back international family planning programs but also voted to ban cloning for stem cell research and to provide legal protections for a fetus.

Providing affordable prescription drug coverage for senior citizens was a key issue in Capito's 2000 campaign. She offered two measures in the 107th Congress — one was a comprehensive bill reducing drug prices across the board and the other would authorize a prescription drug discount card program. The Republican leadership gave her a leading role in the effort to sell their prescription drug plan. She was appointed vice chairman of a GOP prescription drug task force and was given a featured role at a press conference on the matter. She kept up a steady drumbeat of press releases to her constituents on the issue and on the first day of the 108th Congress, she reintroduced her comprehensive bill.

GOP leaders named Capito to their Energy Action Team, giving her the chance to offer an amendment to a comprehensive energy policy bill to establish a coal gasification plant, possibly in West Virginia, as part of research efforts to find clean uses for coal, a staple resource of the West Virginia economy.

Proving she would go her own way on certain core Republican issues, Capito also favors an increase in the minimum wage, backs the steel industry against low-cost foreign imports and criticizes the Bush administration's narrow interpretation of protections for whistle blowers who disclose corporate wrongdoing. She is a member of the Republican Main Street Partnership, which includes about 40 moderate House Republicans. In the 108th Congress, she also is the Republican co-chairman of the Congressional Caucus for Women's Issues.

Capito grew up in a political household. She was not quite 3 years old when her father won his first election to the House, and when she went to college her father was the governor. Moore was governor for 12 years before his career ended in scandal when he pled guilty to a five-count federal indictment that included taking illegal campaign contributions for his gubernatorial campaign. He served three years in prison and paid $750,000 to settle a lawsuit brought against him.

Capito says that many people in West Virginia and on Capitol Hill approach her to speak with kindness of her father's deeds. "There's no problem too big or too small that he would not get involved in. . . . Every decision we make in Congress touches people's everyday lives, and I always remember that," she told The Associated Press.

She started college with the thought of becoming a doctor. But as Capito told The Associated Press, "I realized I didn't have the absolute commitment and hunger you need to be a female doctor." She said the 24-hour demands of medicine convinced her "it would be harder to be a female doctor mother than it would be to be a female legislator mother."

She did not enter politics until her youngest child was 11, a deliberate decision on her part. She worked as a college career counselor and for the state Board of Regents.

She won a seat in the West Virginia House of Delegates in 1996, earning notice for her work on children's health issues. After four years in the state House, Capito emerged in 2000 as a highly touted Republican recruit in the race for the 2nd District seat, which opened up when nine-term Democratic Rep. Wise decided to run for governor.

Capito faced Humphreys, a former state senator who spent more than $6 million of his own money on the race. Capito spent $1.3 million and eventually edged Humphreys by 2 1/2 percentage points. She had help from a blizzard of ads by the National Republican Congressional Committee.

Redistricting after the 2000 census made only minor changes in West Virginia district lines, and the new 2nd District map was slightly more favorable to the GOP after the removal of two overwhelmingly Democratic counties. Her rematch with Humphreys drew national attention and the $8 million-plus he spent raised eyebrows, particularly because the 2nd is an inexpensive media market. But Capito again triumphed, beating him by 20 points.

KEY VOTES

2002

- Yes Overhaul campaign finance law; ban "soft money" and restrict advocacy advertising
- Yes Back Bush's defense budget increase
- Yes Extend 1996 welfare law
- Yes Adopt Bush's discretionary spending limit
- Yes Pass GOP Medicare prescription drug plan
- Yes Create independent Sept. 11 commission
- Yes Extend union protections to Homeland Security Department employees
- No Revive fast-track procedures for trade agreements
- Yes Authorize war against Iraq
- Yes Advance bankruptcy overhaul opposed by abortion opponents

2001

- Yes Nullify Clinton Labor Department ergonomics rule
- Yes Cut taxes by $1.35 trillion through fiscal 2011
- No Maintain ban on oil drilling in Arctic National Wildlife Refuge
- Yes Approve Bush proposal to limit managed-care plan liability for coverage decisions
- Yes Divert money from crop subsidy payments to land conservation
- Yes Expand law enforcement power to investigate suspected terrorists

CQ VOTE STUDIES

	PARTY UNITY		PRESIDENTIAL SUPPORT	
	Support	Oppose	Support	Oppose
2002	89%	11%	80%	20%
2001	89%	11%	79%	21%

INTEREST GROUPS

	AFL-CIO	ADA	CCUS	ACU
2002	22%	15%	85%	76%
2001	33%	20%	87%	76%

WEST VIRGINIA 2

Center — Charleston, Eastern Panhandle

The economically diverse 2nd stretches across the mountainous state from the Ohio border to the Eastern Panhandle at Harpers Ferry. The 2nd is home to poor coal mining areas and isolated towns, as well as the more prosperous capital city of Charleston and commuters in the Eastern Panhandle.

Charleston, the district's dominant city, is a center for chemical plants, state employees and retail shopping. But chemical plants cut back in the late 1990s and a tough economy hit manufacturing companies hard. Much of the recent job growth has come from a boom in telemarketing companies moving to the state and from the expansion of retail around Charleston. The mainly Democratic mountain regions north and east of Kanawha County remain heavily dependent on coal. Putnam County, west of Kanawha County, is the site of a Toyota plant in Buffalo.

Economic depression in the 1980s drove residents from the 2nd. But in the 1990s, eastern counties within commuting distance of Washington, D.C., grew rapidly. That growth forced the 2nd to shed two counties — Nicholas and Gilmer — in redistricting following the 2000 census.

The 2nd was loyal to Democrats in congressional elections for 18 years before electing a Republican in 2000. Pockets of Republicans dot the district, particularly in the Panhandle, where GOP voters register in strong numbers and where they can be reached through Washington's media market. The National Republican Campaign Committee's late ads in that market helped Rep. Capito win the seat in 2000.

MAJOR INDUSTRY

Chemicals, lumber, manufacturing

CITIES

Charleston, 53,421; Martinsburg, 14,972; South Charleston, 13,390; Teays Valley (unincorporated), 12,704; St. Albans, 11,567

NOTABLE

Abolitionist John Brown was hanged after attempting to incite a slave revolt in Harpers Ferry in 1859; As of 2002, there were no stoplights in Calhoun County; The U.S. Geological Survey's Leetown Science Center, located near Kearneysville, is the oldest federal fishery research facility.

Rep. Nick J. Rahall II (D)

CAPITOL OFFICE
225-3452
nrahall@mail.house.gov
www.house.gov/rahall
2307 Rayburn 20515-4803; fax 225-9061

COMMITTEES
Resources - ranking member
Transportation & Infrastructure

HOMETOWN
Beckley

BORN
May 20, 1949, Beckley, W.Va.

RELIGION
Presbyterian

FAMILY
Divorced; three children

EDUCATION
Duke U., A.B. 1971 (political science); George Washington U., attended 1972 (graduate studies)

CAREER
Broadcasting executive; travel agent; congressional aide

POLITICAL HIGHLIGHTS
No previous office

ELECTION RESULTS

2002 GENERAL		
Nick J. Rahall II (D)	87,783	70.2%
Paul E. Chapman (R)	37,229	29.8%
2002 PRIMARY		
Nick J. Rahall II (D)	72,655	86.7%
Theodore W. Hamb (D)	11,110	13.3%
2000 GENERAL		
Nick J. Rahall II (D)	146,807	91.3%
Jeff Robinson (LIBERT)	13,979	8.7%

PREVIOUS WINNING PERCENTAGES
1998 (87%); 1996 (100%); 1994 (64%); 1992 (66%); 1990 (52%); 1988 (61%); 1986 (71%); 1984 (67%); 1982 (81%); 1980 (77%); 1978 (100%); 1976 (46%)

Elected 1976; 14th term

Serving his 14th term, Rahall's longevity is his reward for his attentive district-focused politics. He hails from a well-to-do family but his record in the House reflects the blue-collar coal miners of rural southern West Virginia: culturally conservative but also pro-union and welcoming of federal social services and economic development aid.

That puts Rahall (RAY-haul) out of step with the liberal Democratic leadership on issues like abortion and gun control, both of which he opposes. He also goes his own way on one significant foreign policy issue: The grandson of Lebanese immigrants, Rahall is a frequent critic of Israel and an advocate of closer U.S. ties with Arab countries.

Rahall's independence from the party, along with negative reaction to a spate of personal incidents a few years ago, keep the congressman where he is: a solid bet for re-election every two years but not destined for the heights attained by some of his contemporaries. Rahall arrived in the House with the Class of 1976, which included Richard A. Gephardt of Missouri, the future minority leader, and David E. Bonior of Michigan, who became the party whip.

Rahall's most publicized venture in the last Congress was a fact-finding trip to Iraq, and the timing raised eyebrows. He departed on Sept. 11, 2002, the one-year anniversary of the terrorist attacks on the World Trade Center and Pentagon. President Bush had identified Iraq as one of the Arab countries harboring terrorists, and also was threatening a U.S. invasion in retaliation for leader Saddam Hussein's continued weapons buildup in defiance of U.N. accords.

While in Iraq, Rahall met with the foreign minister and with Iraqi citizens. Back in Washington, he pressed for a peaceful resolution that would spare the repressed Iraqis further hardship. He got the cold shoulder from the White House and an upbraiding by his local press, with one newspaper editorial saying: "Nothing substantive can come from Rahall's visit — except from Iraq's perspective."

Rahall opposed the 2002 resolution giving Bush broad authority to use military force against Iraq. He insisted he supported the war on terrorism despite his search for a diplomatic solution to Iraq. "I want to give every middle ground possible a chance to succeed," he said.

A senior member of the Arab-American caucus, Rahall spoke out in 2002 when the Justice Department began detaining people of Arab descent. "There should not be a wholesale roundup of people, or a denial of services based on the way one looks," he said. " . . . No one should be apprehended just because they wear a turban."

Thanks to his long service in the House, Rahall is the top-ranking Democrat on the Resources Committee, and the No. 2 Democrat on the Transportation and Infrastructure Committee. The positions let him pursue his two major concerns: protecting the coal-mining industry and bringing public works and jobs to his economically hard-pressed district.

On the Resources panel, Rahall has waged a long battle to overhaul an 1872 mining law by requiring hard-rock miners to pay royalties for mining on public lands, a policy that would make West Virginia's mostly private mining operations more competitive with mines in the West. He has been unsuccessful but has at least won a year-by-year moratorium on new low-cost mining claims on federal lands.

His staunch defense of mining means his record on the environment is ambiguous for a Democrat. In 1999, Rahall led an effort by the West Virginia delegation to overturn a court decision that some of the state's coal mining operations violated the Clean Water Act in disposing waste from mountaintop mining operations. But in 2002, he opposed efforts by the Pentagon to relax provisions of the Endangered Species Act and the 1918 Migratory Bird Treaty Act. The Defense Department contended that the laws sometimes impeded training programs.

Transportation is one area where Rahall wields substantial influence, especially during the drafting of the huge federal highway bill every six years. He is among a small handful of lawmakers that control what goes in the bill during a redraft in the 108th Congress.

The last time the bill came up, in the 105th Congress, Rahall was one of the "Big Four" lawmakers who hammered out details. They included Chairman Bud Shuster of Pennsylvania, Highways and Transit Subcommittee Chairman Tom Petri of Wisconsin, and the full committee's top Democrat, James L. Oberstar of Minnesota. The 1998 bill had plenty of goodies for West Virginia. When fiscal conservatives, many of them swept into the House by the strong Republican showing in 1994, criticized the legislation, Rahall called them "right-wing wacko kids."

On the panel, Rahall also has focused on truck safety, passenger air service to small communities, and complaints about poor Amtrak and rail freight service in the aftermath of large rail mergers.

Rahall comes from an affluent West Virginia family that owns broadcasting properties. His first job on Capitol Hill was a summer stint delivering mail when he was 20. After graduating from Duke University, he was an aide to Sen. Robert C. Byrd of West Virginia before going home to work in the family businesses.

His chance to run for office came in 1976, when Democratic Rep. Ken Hechler decided to run for governor. Rahall, then 27, spent family money on a media campaign none of his foes could match, and won the nomination with 37 percent of the vote. After the primary, Hechler, who lost for governor, mounted an unsuccessful write-in drive to keep his House seat.

Rahall's only re-election difficulties have come at times his personal behavior was an issue. He racked up gambling debts in the mid-1980s, got divorced, took many trips financed by taxpayers or lobbyists and pleaded guilty to alcohol-related reckless driving charges.

In 2002, Rahall was re-elected in the overwhelmingly Democratic 3rd District by more than 40 percentage points over police officer Paul E. Chapman — the first Republican challenger Rahall had faced since 1994.

KEY VOTES

2002

- No Overhaul campaign finance law; ban "soft money" and restrict advocacy advertising
- Yes Back Bush's defense budget increase
- No Extend 1996 welfare law
- No Adopt Bush's discretionary spending limit
- No Pass GOP Medicare prescription drug plan
- Yes Create independent Sept. 11 commission
- Yes Extend union protections to Homeland Security Department employees
- No Revive fast-track procedures for trade agreements
- No Authorize war against Iraq
- No Advance bankruptcy overhaul opposed by abortion opponents

2001

- No Nullify Clinton Labor Department ergonomics rule
- ? Cut taxes by $1.35 trillion through fiscal 2011
- Yes Maintain ban on oil drilling in Arctic National Wildlife Refuge
- No Approve Bush proposal to limit managed-care plan liability for coverage decisions
- Yes Divert money from crop subsidy payments to land conservation
- No Expand law enforcement power to investigate suspected terrorists

CQ VOTE STUDIES

	PARTY UNITY		PRESIDENTIAL SUPPORT	
	Support	Oppose	Support	Oppose
2002	88%	12%	28%	72%
2001	77%	23%	33%	67%
2000	79%	21%	71%	29%
1999	75%	25%	69%	31%
1998	78%	22%	77%	23%

INTEREST GROUPS

	AFL-CIO	ADA	CCUS	ACU
2002	100%	80%	40%	24%
2001	100%	80%	39%	36%
2000	90%	70%	42%	28%
1999	100%	65%	24%	20%
1998	100%	85%	28%	24%

WEST VIRGINIA 3

South – Huntington, Beckley

The 3rd is a largely rural region taking in the state's southern counties. Known as the "coal district," it is home to six of the state's 10 leading coal-producing counties, including the top two, Boone and Mingo.

In the 1980s, technological advances in coal mining sharply reduced the need for manpower, and the 3rd has struggled to create new jobs. The decline, which also took a toll on the 3rd's population, added misery to a region that always has had pockets of Appalachian poverty. The situation improved in the 1990s and some counties grew slightly, though other counties continued to see residents leave as unemployment rates remained high. In 1999, the district had the third-lowest median income of any congressional district in the nation, at slightly more than $25,600.

The 3rd contributes to the state's tourism industry with its ski resorts, whitewater rafting and The Greenbrier, a luxury resort hotel in White Sulphur Springs that plays host to congressional party retreats. Huntington, the district's largest city, is cushioned by its location on the Ohio River and a diversified economy that includes tobacco growers as well as oil and steel companies.

While Huntington's white-collar sector and tobacco growers help make Cabell County the most Republican part of the 3rd, overall Democrats have held a lock on the district and continue to register in large numbers. Eight of Al Gore's 10 best West Virginia counties in the 2000 presidential race were in the 3rd, topped by McDowell with 66 percent. Still, George W. Bush made major inroads in the 3rd, losing the district by just 4 percentage points after Bill Clinton won handily in 1992 and 1996.

MAJOR INDUSTRY

Coal, wood products, tourism

CITIES

Huntington, 51,475; Beckley, 17,254; Bluefield, 11,451

NOTABLE

There is a now-closed nuclear bomb shelter for Congress under The Greenbrier; Sunshine Farm & Gardens, in Renick, houses one of the nation's most extensive plant collections; Mingo County, site of the West Virginia Mine Wars of the 1920s, is depicted in the movie "Matewan;" "Bloody Mingo" also was the site of part of the feuding between the Hatfields and McCoys.

WISCONSIN

Gov. James E. Doyle (D)

First elected: 2002
Length of term: 4 years
Term expires: 1/07
Salary: $131,768
Phone: (608) 266-1212
Hometown: Madison
Born: Nov. 23, 1945; Washington, D.C.
Religion: Roman Catholic
Family: Wife, Jessica Laird Doyle; two children
Education: Stanford U., attended 1963-66; U. of Wisconsin, B.A. 1967 (history); Harvard U., J.D. 1972
Career: Lawyer; Peace Corps volunteer
Political highlights: Dane County district attorney, 1977-82; Wis. attorney general, 1991-2003
Election results:

2002 GENERAL		
James E. Doyle (D)	800,515	45.1%
Scott McCallum (R)	734,779	41.4%
Ed Thompson (LIBERT)	185,455	10.5%
Jim Young (WG)	44,111	2.5%

Lt. Gov. Barbara Lawton (D)

First elected: 2002
Length of term: 4 years
Term expires: 1/07
Salary: $69,579
Phone: (608) 266-3516

STATE LEGISLATURE

General Assembly: Meets for 10 floor periods of varying lengths over two-year session
House: 99 members, 2-year terms
2003 breakdown: 58R, 40D, 1 vacancy; 72 men, 26 women
Salary: $45,569
Phone: (608) 266-1501
Senate: 33 members, 4-year terms
2003 breakdown: 17R, 14D, 2 vacancies; 23 men, 8 women
Salary: $45,569
Phone: (608) 266-2517

STATE TERM LIMITS

Governor: No
Senate: No
House: No

URBAN STATISTICS

CITY	POPULATION
Milwaukee	596,974
Madison	208,054
Green Bay	102,313
Kenosha	90,352
Racine	81,855

REGISTERED VOTERS

Voters do not register by party.

POPULATION

2002 population (est.)	5,441,196
2000 population	5,363,675
1990 population	4,891,769
Percent change (1990-2000)	+9.6%
Rank among states (2002)	20
Median age	36
Born in state	73.4%
Foreign born	3.6%
Violent crime rate	237/100,000
Poverty level	8.7%
Federal workers	29,286
Military	18,937

REDISTRICTING

Wisconsin lost one House seat in reapportionment. The state legislature drew a new, eight-district map, which the governor signed on March 27, 2002.

MISCELLANEOUS

Web: www.state.wi.us
Capital: Madison

STATE ELECTION OFFICIAL
(608) 266-8005

DEMOCRATIC HEADQUARTERS
(608) 255-5172

REPUBLICAN HEADQUARTERS
(608) 257-4765

District Statistics

	2000 VOTE FOR PRESIDENT															
DIST.	BUSH	GORE	NADER	WHITE	BLACK	ASIAN	HISP	MEDIAN INCOME	WHITE COLLAR	BLUE COLLAR	SERVICE INDUSTRY	OVER 64	UNDER 18	COLLEGE EDUCATION	RURAL	SQ. MILES
1	51%	45%	n/a	87%	5%	1%	6%	$50,372	57%	30%	13%	12%	26%	22%	16%	1,680
2	36	58	n/a	89	4	2	3	$46,979	64	23	14	11	23	32	24	3,511
3	46	49	n/a	96	0	1	1	$40,006	53	31	16	13	25	20	57	13,565
4	30	66	n/a	50	33	3	11	$33,121	54	28	18	11	28	18	0	112
5	62	35	n/a	94	1	2	2	$58,594	68	22	10	14	25	35	15	1,273
6	53	42	n/a	94	1	1	2	$44,242	49	37	14	14	25	17	39	5,641
7	47	48	n/a	95	0	1	1	$39,026	52	34	15	15	25	17	58	18,787
8	52	43	n/a	92	1	1	2	$43,274	54	33	14	13	26	19	44	9,740
STATE	47.6	47.8	4	87	6	2	4	$43,791	57	29	14	13	26	22	32	54,310
U.S.	47.9	48.4	3	69	12	4	13	$41,994	60	25	15	12	26	24	21	3,537,438

Douglas
Bayfield
Iron
Ashland
Vilas
Burnett
Washburn
Sawyer
Price
Oneida
Florence
Forest
Polk
Barron
Rusk
7
Marinette
Lincoln
Langlade
8
St. Croix
Taylor
Chippewa
Dunn
Menominee
Oconto
Marathon
Eau Claire
Shawano
Door
Pierce
Pepin
Eau Claire
Clark
Green Bay
Kewaunee
Buffalo
3
Wood
Portage
Waupaca
Outagamie
Brown
Jackson
Trempealeau
Waushara
Winnebago
Calumet
Manitowic
Lake Winnebago
Oshkosh
Adams
La Crosse
Monroe
Juneau
Marquette
Green Lake
Fond du Lac
Sheboygan
Vernon
6
Ozaukee
Columbia
Dodge
Washington
Sauk
Richland
Crawford
5
4
Madison
Waukesha
Milwaukee
Iowa
Waukesha
2
Dane
Jefferson
Milwaukee
Grant
Racine
1
Racine
Lafayette
Green
Rock
Walworth
Kenosha
Kenosha

Sen. Herb Kohl (D)

CAPITOL OFFICE
224-5653
senator_kohl@kohl.senate.gov
kohl.senate.gov
330 Hart 20510-4903; fax 224-9787

COMMITTEES
Appropriations
Judiciary
Special Aging

HOMETOWN
Milwaukee

BORN
Feb. 7, 1935, Milwaukee, Wis.

RELIGION
Jewish

FAMILY
Single

EDUCATION
U. of Wisconsin, B.A. 1956; Harvard U., M.B.A. 1958

MILITARY SERVICE
Army Reserve, 1958-64

CAREER
Professional basketball team owner; department and grocery store owner

POLITICAL HIGHLIGHTS
Wis. Democratic Party chairman, 1975-77

ELECTION RESULTS

2000 GENERAL		
Herb Kohl (D)	1,563,238	61.5%
John Gillespie (R)	940,744	37.0%
2000 PRIMARY		
Herb Kohl (D)	184,920	89.8%
Jim Sigl (D)	20,858	10.1%

PREVIOUS WINNING PERCENTAGES
1994 (58%); 1988 (52%)

Elected 1988; 3rd term

Through his service on five Appropriations subcommittees — which among them control about two-thirds of all discretionary domestic spending — Kohl has more of a say on the allocation of federal dollars than almost anyone else in Congress. Yet during his first 15 years as a senator, Kohl has been known to be as frugal with public money as he has been lavish with his own personal expenditures.

Kohl is a wealthy man and has been in the public eye for years — as president of the family-owned chain of Kohl's department and food stores in the 1970s and as owner of the Milwaukee Bucks professional basketball team since 1985. But he has never seemed comfortable with the trappings of wealth or power. He prefers to stand in the background as his Senate colleagues go to the microphone, and he drives around Washington in a 1994 Chevy Lumina. When the Senate is in recess, he is often seen eating breakfast at diners near his house in Milwaukee.

Still as shy and unassuming as he was when he arrived on Capitol Hill, Kohl has carved out a niche of influence on dairy, child nutrition and security issues, but he rarely talks about what he is doing.

As chairman of the Agriculture Appropriations Subcommittee in the 107th Congress, he helped develop a compromise on federal milk-pricing policy that he regarded as a major achievement. But after the compromise went through, Kohl was reluctant to discuss how he made it happen. Some call him aloof; others say he is simply a private man who cannot imagine that his thoughts are of great interest to anyone else.

He has won high marks from budget watchdog groups such as the Concord Coalition and Taxpayers for Common Sense. He has not accepted any pay raises since he entered the Senate in 1989, when senators made $89,500. He voted against the giant catch-all spending law enacted at the end of the 105th Congress and against another enacted in 1999, although he voted for the behemoth spending package of 2003, which settled a budgetary standoff that outlasted the 107th.

He has been a solid vote for a constitutional amendment to require a balanced federal budget, and he supported the short-lived presidential line-item veto law. Even when the Treasury had a surplus, he continued to press for fiscal restraint, warning against actions that could plunge the government's books back into the red. In 2001, he was one of only a dozen Democrats to vote for President Bush's $1.35 trillion tax cut, and one of 15 Democrats to back the initial version of the GOP's spending blueprint for the year. Kohl affiliates with the Senate's moderate New Democrats.

Kohl is less tightfisted with his own fortune, estimated in 2002 at more than $100 million. In addition to buying the Bucks in order to keep them in Milwaukee ("I thought it was a stupid investment," he later admitted), Kohl gave the University of Wisconsin, his alma mater, $25 million to build a sports arena. Every year, his Herb Kohl Educational Foundation awards several hundred scholarships of $1,000 to high school graduates, provides fellowships to teachers and gives grants to schools. He also has spent close to $20 million of his own to win his three Senate elections, and he augments the salaries of some of his Senate aides from his own pocket.

Kohl says his wealth gives him great freedom in Congress. "I'm the luckiest guy here because I don't have to ask anybody for money," he told a Harvard Business School newsletter. "That allows me to do what I think is right on every vote."

As the chairman or ranking minority party member of the Agriculture Appropriations panel since 1999, Kohl looks out for Wisconsin's farm interests and champions school breakfast and nutrition programs for low-income children. In the 107th, in addition to his work to resolve the regional fight over federal milk price supports, Kohl played a key role in legislation to give businesses a tax credit if they provide on-site child care for their workers and on a measure to protect children who are part of traveling sales crews.

Kohl hews close to traditional Democratic positions on social issues and generally follows the party line on environmental protection, although he has voted against bills to require increased automobile fuel economy standards. This position has been in support of the remnants of the auto industry in southeast Wisconsin.

Kohl is a strong supporter of gun control. The sniper shootings in the Washington area in the fall of 2002 inspired him to renew his campaign for legislation that would establish a nationwide ballistics database to trace ammunition used in a crime back to the owner of the firearm.

After the Sept. 11, 2001, terrorist attacks, Kohl also took a lead role in insisting on tougher security standards for charter aircraft and tighter controls on the sale, transport or possession of explosives.

Drawing on his business experience, Kohl has been involved in the inquiries that the Judiciary Subcommittee on Antitrust, Business Rights and Competition — where he is the top-ranking Democrat in the 108th — has made into corporate mergers. He has joined with the panel's chairman, Republican Mike DeWine of Ohio, to question whether several proposed mergers, particularly in the telecommunications and aviation industries, offered adequate benefits to consumers.

Kohl's parents immigrated to the United States in the 1920s — his mother from Russia, his father from Poland. They opened a small food store in Milwaukee, where Kohl worked after school and on weekends. He says that experience taught him the value of hard work. One of his childhood friends (and later his college roommate) was Bud Selig, who went on to become a wealthy car dealer, and then owner of the Milwaukee Brewers baseball team and the commissioner of Major League Baseball.

After earning a master's in business from Harvard, Kohl returned home and along with his two brothers set about building a Kohl's chain of stores. There were more than 100 of them when the chain was sold in 1979.

Kohl was involved in the financial side of some political campaigns, but his first public involvement in politics came in 1975 when Democratic Gov. Patrick Lucey asked him to chair the state Democratic Party. He did the job for two years, despite his discomfort with some of its public aspects.

In 1988, when Democrat William Proxmire stepped down after 31 years in the Senate, some Democrats pressed an initially ambivalent Kohl to run. Through retail and basketball he had plenty of name recognition — not that it mattered much, as he spent nearly $7.5 million (most of it his own money) on the campaign. Kohl used his status as one of the state's richest men to stress his independence, based on his ability to self-finance his campaigns. His "Nobody's senator but yours" tag line, which he still uses, reminded voters that he was beholden to no special interest group.

It was a campaign on a scale unlike any the state had seen. Kohl's total outlay was double the previous state record. He won a three-way Democratic primary with 47 percent of the vote and defeated GOP state Sen. Susan Engeleiter by 4 percentage points in the fall.

In subsequent re-election campaigns in 1994 and 2000, Kohl spent $6 million and $4.8 million, respectively, of his own money. He won by 17 points in 1994 and 25 points in 2000.

KEY VOTES

2002

Yes Pass farm bill reversing crop subsidy limits
Yes Postpone tougher automobile fuel efficiency standards
Yes Overhaul campaign finance law; ban "soft money" and restrict advocacy advertising
Yes Set federal election standards
No Support oil drilling in Arctic National Wildlife Refuge
Yes Revive fast-track procedures for trade agreements
Yes Create federal insurance coverage for catastrophic terrorist losses
Yes Tighten federal accounting and corporate governance regulation
Yes Advance bipartisan Medicare prescription drug plan
Yes Create independent Sept. 11 commission
Yes Back Democratic Homeland Security Department proposal
Yes Authorize war against Iraq

2001

No Confirm John Ashcroft as attorney general
No Nullify Clinton Labor Department ergonomics rule
Yes Cut taxes by $1.35 trillion through fiscal 2011
Yes Pass Democratic bill to bolster rights of patients in managed-care plans
Yes Permit a new round of military base closings
Yes Expand law enforcement power to investigate suspected terrorists

CQ VOTE STUDIES

	PARTY UNITY		PRESIDENTIAL SUPPORT	
	Support	Oppose	Support	Oppose
2002	84%	16%	79%	21%
2001	89%	11%	69%	31%
2000	87%	13%	79%	21%
1999	90%	10%	91%	9%
1998	87%	13%	86%	14%
1997	74%	26%	90%	10%
1996	84%	16%	88%	12%
1995	84%	16%	84%	16%
1994	75%	25%	81%	19%
1993	84%	16%	81%	19%

INTEREST GROUPS

	AFL-CIO	ADA	CCUS	ACU
2002	92%	85%	60%	15%
2001	88%	90%	54%	16%
2000	63%	85%	60%	20%
1999	78%	100%	41%	4%
1998	88%	85%	44%	4%
1997	29%	70%	80%	20%
1996	86%	75%	69%	20%
1995	92%	95%	47%	17%
1994	63%	90%	50%	12%
1993	73%	95%	45%	24%

Sen. Russell D. Feingold (D)

Elected 1992; 2nd term

When one senator out of 100 is voting no, odds are good it is Feingold. He doesn't mind being the lone voice of dissent no matter what the issue or the Democratic Party's position. His political quirkiness has appeal among voters who themselves are increasingly independent of the two major political parties, but it also can present dangers at election time. A crusader against the influence of money in politics, he finds himself dangerously outspent by his opponents.

Feingold (FINE-gold) is the co-author of the watershed McCain-Feingold law, the first major revision of campaign laws in nearly three decades, which was enacted by Congress in 2002 after strenuous efforts over the years by party leaders to stop it. The legislation bans unregulated "soft money," which goes to political parties rather than candidates but increasingly is used in novel ways to influence individual campaigns. The law also restricts issue advocacy advertising, which is designed to influence the outcome of an election without specifically endorsing a candidate. Party leaders opposed McCain-Feingold because it cramped fundraising, but the two senators were able to successfully revive it after the bankruptcy of Enron, which led to revelations about the energy giant's political donations and influence.

Long before the bill passed, however, Feingold was willing to put his commitment to changing the system into practice, something even cosponsor John McCain of Arizona and other supporters did not do for fear of being mightily outspent by political foes. In his first re-election campaign in 1998, Feingold refused to accept most forms of political money outside of traditional "hard" donations by individuals and political action committees. Facing a politically sophisticated and well-financed opponent, GOP Rep. Mark W. Neumann, Feingold prevailed by just 2 percentage points.

His iconoclasm often puts Feingold in a minority of one. Six weeks after the Sept. 11, 2001, terrorist attacks, most senators felt compelled to support a proposal giving the Bush administration broad powers to detain and question possible terrorists. Many Democrats felt, as Feingold did, that the USA Patriot Act raised significant concerns about government encroachments on civil liberties. But they voted for it for the sake of national unity and out of a desire to move aggressively to stop terrorists. Democratic Majority Leader Tom Daschle urged Democrats to support what became a bipartisan bill. The final tally was 98-1, with Feingold dissenting. Parts of the bill, he said, were "a grab for powers by the Justice Department," a view shared by many of his colleagues who supported it anyway.

Although he is mostly liberal on issues, Feingold is not always predictable. When many fellow Democrats in 2001 staunchly opposed the nomination of Missouri Sen. John Ashcroft for attorney general because of his ultra-conservative views, Feingold cast the lone Democratic vote in the Judiciary Committee to confirm Ashcroft.

His unwillingness to be part of the crowd can tie up the Senate at times, a source of aggravation to his colleagues. In the final hours before Congress adjourned in 1999, Feingold and a handful of other Midwesterners refused to let their colleagues go home because they opposed provisions in the sole remaining bill, a session-ending appropriations deal, that they claimed were unfair to home-state dairy interests. Feingold stalked the Senate floor with books of cheese recipes, among other potential filibuster reading materials, threatening a several-day delay. He gave up only after overwhelmingly losing a test vote.

CAPITOL OFFICE
224-5323
feingold.senate.gov
506 Hart 20510-4904; fax 224-2725

COMMITTEES
Budget
Foreign Relations
Judiciary
Special Aging

HOMETOWN
Middleton

BORN
March 2, 1953, Janesville, Wis.

RELIGION
Jewish

FAMILY
Wife, Mary Feingold; two children, two stepchildren

EDUCATION
U. of Wisconsin, B.A. 1975 (history & political science); Oxford U., B.A. 1977 (Rhodes scholar); Harvard U., J.D. 1979

CAREER
Lawyer

POLITICAL HIGHLIGHTS
Wis. Senate, 1983-93

ELECTION RESULTS

1998 GENERAL

Russell D. Feingold (D)	890,059	50.5%
Mark W. Neumann (R)	852,272	48.4%

1998 PRIMARY

Russell D. Feingold (D)	unopposed

PREVIOUS WINNING PERCENTAGES
1992 (53%)

Nor does Feingold win popularity contests in the Senate with his crusades to raise Congress' ethical standards. He advocates increasing the waiting period from one year to two before former members can begin earning large sums as lobbyists for private firms. He also wants to repeal automatic pay raises for members of Congress, opposes free trips for lawmakers paid for by lobbyists, and favors a total ban on gifts.

Feingold is among the more socially liberal senators. He favors abolishing the death penalty and supports abortion rights. But unlike many other liberals, Feingold has had a long-running interest in balancing the budget. A member of the Budget Committee, he was calling for reducing the national debt long before the task was made easier by the booming economy and mushrooming tax collections.

Feingold supported the ill-fated line-item veto, and in 1998 he voted to sustain President Clinton's veto of a list of military construction projects even though a $4.2 million training facility in Milwaukee was on the list.

Still, the senator is not a hard-core fiscal conservative. Feingold's deficit reduction efforts often rely on tax increases rather than cuts in spending for social programs. He voted in 1993 for the Clinton deficit-reduction bill, which raised taxes, and opposed the 1997 balanced-budget agreement, which called for both tax cuts and significant spending reductions.

A friend of labor, Feingold voted against a bill granting visas to additional skilled workers to fill high-tech jobs, and against another measure that would have authorized companies to offer their employees compensatory time off instead of pay for overtime work. He also took the unions' side in opposing fast-track authority for the president to negotiate trade agreements that Congress could accept or reject but not amend.

Feingold objects to limiting punitive damages in product liability cases. In the 107th, he opposed GOP-sought revisions to the bankruptcy code that would make it harder for people declaring bankruptcy to walk away from their debts. Credit card companies and other creditors pushed the bill, but Feingold believed that the changes would be too hard on debtors.

His most famous break with his party was in January 1999, when Feingold was the only Democratic senator to vote against a proposal to dismiss the impeachment charges against Clinton. His decision sparked an avalanche of media attention, but Feingold largely shunned the notoriety. In the end, he joined every other Democratic senator in voting to acquit Clinton of perjury and obstruction of justice, saying the charges were insufficient to warrant the president's removal.

Feingold is attentive to home-state concerns, especially those of dairy farmers. He appears to have a genuine affection for campaigning and constituent service. He has kept a pledge from his first Senate campaign to visit all 72 counties in the state every year he is in office. He spends most of his time in Wisconsin and his children attend school there.

In 1992, he burst on the national political scene as a little-known state senator without much campaign money who scored a long-shot primary victory and then knocked off a GOP incumbent. He ran a series of humorous, offbeat television ads. One showed him using the back of his left hand as a map of his travels across Wisconsin, boasting he knew the state like the back of his hand. Another showed him opening an empty closet, assuring viewers, "No skeletons."

Six years later, Feingold's tendency to buck the system nearly cost him his seat. He began his 1998 re-election campaign favored to beat Neumann, a conservative who had been in the House for three years. Feingold declined most forms of outside money, and asked national Democrats not to run ads in his behalf paid for with the kind of fundraising that his bill sought to limit. Feingold barely held on, winning by just 2 percentage points.

KEY VOTES

2002

Yes Pass farm bill reversing crop subsidy limits
Yes Postpone tougher automobile fuel efficiency standards
Yes Overhaul campaign finance law; ban "soft money" and restrict advocacy advertising
Yes Set federal election standards
No Support oil drilling in Arctic National Wildlife Refuge
No Revive fast-track procedures for trade agreements
Yes Create federal insurance coverage for catastrophic terrorist losses
Yes Tighten federal accounting and corporate governance regulation
No Advance bipartisan Medicare prescription drug plan
Yes Create independent Sept. 11 commission
Yes Back Democratic Homeland Security Department proposal
No Authorize war against Iraq

2001

Yes Confirm John Ashcroft as attorney general
No Nullify Clinton Labor Department ergonomics rule
No Cut taxes by $1.35 trillion through fiscal 2011
Yes Pass Democratic bill to bolster rights of patients in managed-care plans
Yes Permit a new round of military base closings
No Expand law enforcement power to investigate suspected terrorists

CQ VOTE STUDIES

	PARTY UNITY		PRESIDENTIAL SUPPORT	
	Support	Oppose	Support	Oppose
2002	84%	16%	67%	33%
2001	89%	11%	61%	39%
2000	92%	8%	90%	10%
1999	88%	12%	82%	18%
1998	86%	14%	83%	17%
1997	86%	14%	86%	14%
1996	87%	13%	86%	14%
1995	90%	10%	79%	21%
1994	84%	16%	65%	35%
1993	94%	6%	85%	15%

INTEREST GROUPS

	AFL-CIO	ADA	CCUS	ACU
2002	92%	90%	20%	5%
2001	94%	95%	29%	20%
2000	88%	100%	20%	8%
1999	100%	100%	24%	8%
1998	100%	90%	28%	12%
1997	86%	95%	20%	8%
1996	86%	95%	31%	10%
1995	100%	100%	42%	13%
1994	100%	100%	10%	4%
1993	91%	100%	0%	12%

Rep. Paul D. Ryan (R)

CAPITOL OFFICE
225-3031
www.house.gov/ryan
1217 Longworth 20515-4901; fax 225-3393

COMMITTEES
Ways & Means
Joint Economic

HOMETOWN
Janesville

BORN
Jan. 29, 1970, Janesville, Wis.

RELIGION
Roman Catholic

FAMILY
Wife, Janna Ryan; one child

EDUCATION
Miami U. (Ohio), B.A. 1992 (political science & economics)

CAREER
Congressional aide; economic policy analyst

POLITICAL HIGHLIGHTS
No previous office

ELECTION RESULTS

2002 GENERAL		
Paul D. Ryan (R)	140,176	67.2%
Jeff Thomas (D)	63,895	30.6%
George Meyers (LIBERT)	4,406	2.1%
2002 PRIMARY		
Paul D. Ryan (R)	unopposed	
2000 GENERAL		
Paul D. Ryan (R)	177,612	66.6%
Jeffrey C. Thomas (D)	88,885	33.3%

PREVIOUS WINNING PERCENTAGES
1998 (57%)

Elected 1998; 3rd term

Ryan is one of the leading congressional proponents of supply-side economics, a theory that assumes the economy will rebound if taxes are cut and federal spending is shrunk. He has the opportunity to promote this theory from his seat on the Ways and Means Committee, which writes tax, trade, welfare, health care, and Social Security legislation. An appointment to the powerful committee was Ryan's reward in the 107th Congress for keeping the 1st District in Republican hands.

Ryan is one of the youngest members of Congress, first elected to the House at age 28. He once worked for Jack F. Kemp and William J. Bennett, former Republican Cabinet secretaries and co-founders of the conservative think tank, Empower America, and he considers them both mentors.

Articulate and partisan, Ryan had been in office about one month in 1999 when he was chosen by GOP leaders to deliver their radio response to President Clinton's weekly radio speech. A few weeks later, the leadership made him the lead sponsor of a measure expressing the congressional commitment to protect the existing level of Social Security benefits. Ryan was chosen, in part, because of his age. During the 2000 debate on the annual congressional spending blueprint, Ryan played an unusually active role for a freshman, performing well in what turned out to be an audition for the Ways and Means seat that he was already eyeing.

Because he is likely to be around in 50 years, Ryan, more than most other lawmakers, has a personal stake in the long-term health of the Social Security program. He is the youngest member of the panel since 26-year-old Massachusetts Democrat James M. Shannon joined in 1979.

Ryan says the federal government is too big. "What was once a system of limited government has insidiously evolved into one with virtually no limits at all," he says. "I want the federal government to do less with less, and I want to see our families do more with more." In the 107th Congress, he was among those conservative Republicans who kept the pressure on President Bush and the Republican leadership to lower taxes and federal spending.

A leader of an emerging group of Republican lawmakers known as "growth hawks," Ryan worries that those who continue to press for deficit reduction are an obstacle to tax cuts needed to stimulate the economy. "The old green eye-shade, Bob Dole-wing of the party is in decline," Ryan says.

He favors tax cuts even greater than the $1.35 trillion that Congress approved in 2001. He pressed for reductions in the capital gains tax rate and was a leader in the effort to make the 2001 tax cuts permanent. "You're talking about my favorite congressman," said Damon Ansell, a leader of Americans for Tax Reform. "This is a guy who really gets it."

Ryan coupled his efforts to reduce taxes with an insistence that government spending also be cut. He wrote several letters to the Republican leadership and the Bush administration demanding that they stand firm against spending increases. "We claim to be the party of fiscal discipline, and we should act like it," he said. He is a member of the Republican Study Committee, a group of the most conservative House Republicans.

Ryan was particularly concerned about congressional spending discipline after the Sept. 11, 2001, terrorist attacks. He joined with two dozen other lawmakers in a letter to Speaker J. Dennis Hastert warning that lawmakers were using the need for increased spending for defense and homeland security as a pretext to engage in a widespread spending spree.

The congressman is also conservative on social issues, arguing that "in many aspects of our society, morality has become relative, ethical behavior is now a mere technicality and God has been pushed from the public realm." He uses his Ways and Means post to protect Wisconsin's groundbreaking welfare system.

Ryan often teams up with fellow Class of 1998 Badger State Republican Mark Green to sponsor legislation. The two offered a measure aimed at lowering the price of gasoline by reducing the number of different blends of reformulated gasoline. Ryan says they got to know each other during freshman orientation. As with Bennett and Kemp, Ryan regards Green, who is 10 years older, as a mentor.

Despite his youth, Ryan is no political novice. After finishing college, he was an aide to Wisconsin GOP Sen. Bob Kasten, both on his personal staff and on the Small Business Committee staff. Then, after a stint at Empower America, Ryan was a top staffer for Kansas Republican Sam Brownback in the House and Senate.

When he first arrived in the House, Ryan bragged about his 120-hour, seven-days-a-week work schedule, saying that he was young and vigorous enough to burn the candle at both ends. Now that he has a wife and baby girl, Ryan says he has slowed down a bit. He says he tries to take most Sundays off to be with his family. But he adds that he's learned to be smarter about using his time effectively. "I'm still pretty energetic," he says.

In college, Ryan intended to become an economist or work in his family's earth-moving and construction business. But his plans changed, he says, because "I just got caught up in it here in Washington." He spent more than five years in Washington before returning home to Wisconsin to work in the family business. When the 1st District's GOP Rep. Mark W. Neumann decided in late 1997 to run for the Senate, Ryan was persuaded to run for the open seat.

Initially, it appeared Ryan would have to fight for the GOP nomination, but his strongest potential rivals dropped out. His opponent in the general election was Democrat Lydia Spottswood, a former Kenosha City Council president who nearly beat Neumann in 1996. Ryan proved to have much stronger campaign skills — he earned the nickname "robocandidate" — and he won by more than 27,000 votes, a surprisingly large margin given that the previous three races in the district had been won by margins of 4,000 votes or less.

In 2000, backed by substantial contributions from the Club for Growth, a group of fiscally conservative Republicans, Ryan breezed to a 33 percentage point victory. In 2002, redistricting gave Ryan a GOP-leaning district, and he won easily, by 36 points.

KEY VOTES

2002

No Overhaul campaign finance law; ban "soft money" and restrict advocacy advertising
Yes Back Bush's defense budget increase
Yes Extend 1996 welfare law
Yes Adopt Bush's discretionary spending limit
Yes Pass GOP Medicare prescription drug plan
No Create independent Sept. 11 commission
No Extend union protections to Homeland Security Department employees
Yes Revive fast-track procedures for trade agreements
Yes Authorize war against Iraq
Yes Advance bankruptcy overhaul opposed by abortion opponents

2001

Yes Nullify Clinton Labor Department ergonomics rule
Yes Cut taxes by $1.35 trillion through fiscal 2011
No Maintain ban on oil drilling in Arctic National Wildlife Refuge
Yes Approve Bush proposal to limit managed-care plan liability for coverage decisions
Yes Divert money from crop subsidy payments to land conservation
Yes Expand law enforcement power to investigate suspected terrorists

CQ VOTE STUDIES

	PARTY UNITY		PRESIDENTIAL SUPPORT	
	Support	Oppose	Support	Oppose
2002	92%	8%	82%	18%
2001	92%	8%	86%	14%
2000	95%	5%	22%	78%
1999	90%	10%	21%	79%

INTEREST GROUPS

	AFL-CIO	ADA	CCUS	ACU
2002	13%	0%	100%	96%
2001	17%	0%	96%	88%
2000	0%	5%	90%	88%
1999	22%	10%	92%	92%

WISCONSIN 1
Southeast – Kenosha, Racine

From the wealthy Milwaukee suburbs on the coast of Lake Michigan to the center of Rock County, the 1st blends rural communities with some of the state's largest industrial areas. The district's two largest cities are sandwiched between Milwaukee and Chicago along the lake: Racine, originally settled by Danish immigrants, and Kenosha, with a large Italian community.

A major manufacturing producer of heavy equipment and other goods, the economy fares best when a weak dollar attracts international buyers. A high foreign exchange rate in the 1990s — compounded by the shutdown of several manufacturing plants — weakened the economy and depressed real estate prices. This attracted commuters, forming large bedroom communities for Milwaukee and Chicago — both less than an hour's drive away. The influx helped the counties along the Illinois border grow almost twice as fast as the state average in the 1990s. On the other side of the district, Janesville has struggled in recent years as demand has softened for trucks from its General Motors plant.

Resorts catering to wealthy vacationers from nearby cities ring Lake Geneva and Lake Delavan (Walworth County), while Kenosha lures gamblers with Dairyland Greyhound Park, a dog-racing track.

Wisconsin lost one seat in the 2000 reapportionment, and redistricting revised the 1st's boundaries to exclude blue-collar, heavily Democratic Beloit (Rock County) and to add more of GOP-leaning Waukesha County and part of Milwaukee County. The district is about evenly split between the two parties: Of the six counties wholly or partly in the 1st, two are strongly Democratic (Kenosha and Rock), two are strongly Republican (Walworth and Waukesha) and two are highly competitive (Racine and Milwaukee). In the 2002 gubernatorial race, Democrat James E. Doyle and Republican Scott McCallum fought to a near-tie in the 1st, with Doyle prevailing by just one-tenth of a percentage point.

MAJOR INDUSTRY

Automotive manufacturing, heavy machine manufacturing, farming

CITIES

Kenosha, 90,352; Racine, 81,855; Janesville (pt.), 59,474; Greenfield, 35,476

NOTABLE

Racine's Salmon-A-Rama fishing match; Orson Welles was born in Kenosha.

Rep. Tammy Baldwin (D)

CAPITOL OFFICE
225-2906
tammy.baldwin@mail.house.gov
tammybaldwin.house.gov
1022 Longworth 20515-4902; fax 225-6942

COMMITTEES
Budget
Judiciary

HOMETOWN
Madison

BORN
Feb. 11, 1962, Madison, Wis.

RELIGION
Unspecified

FAMILY
Partner, Lauren Azar

EDUCATION
Smith College, A.B. 1984 (math & political science); U. of Wisconsin, J.D. 1989

CAREER
Lawyer; public policy analyst

POLITICAL HIGHLIGHTS
Madison City Council, 1986; Dane County Board, 1986-94; Wis. Assembly, 1993-99

ELECTION RESULTS

2002 GENERAL		
Tammy Baldwin (D)	163,313	66.0%
Ron Greer (R)	83,694	33.8%
2002 PRIMARY		
Tammy Baldwin (D)	unopposed	
2000 GENERAL		
Tammy Baldwin (D)	163,534	51.4%
John Sharpless (R)	154,632	48.6%

PREVIOUS WINNING PERCENTAGES
1998 (52%)

Elected 1998; 3rd term

Baldwin is a political trailblazer. She is the first woman elected to Congress from Wisconsin, and she is the first openly gay woman to be elected to Congress. That is not to say she is a political novice. Baldwin was still in law school when she won her first county board election at age 24.

Her challenge is to build a record beyond the distinction of being "first." But the third-termer seems well on her way. She is politically savvy, personally likeable and ambitious; she is close to Minority Leader Nancy Pelosi of California, with whom she shares a lot philosophically. She is outspoken on liberal causes, much like her University of Wisconsin at Madison-based constituency.

She has called for deep federal involvement in health care financing under a single-payer system. She supports same-sex marriage and public financing of political campaigns. She favors abortion rights, and with a seat on the Judiciary Committee, strongly opposes a Republican ban on human cloning even for medical research. The ban would affect promising research at the Madison campus on two embryonic stem cell lines.

Despite her liberal politics, Baldwin has a pragmatic willingness to deal with lawmakers on the other side of the aisle. She says simply, "I can't get legislation passed without Republicans."

During work on the Violence Against Women Act in 2000, Democrats and Republicans found little they could agree on, and most Democratic amendments failed. But Baldwin worked with GOP Crime Subcommittee Chairman Bill McCollum of Florida to win approval of a $10 million grant to help disabled victims of violence. In the 107th Congress, she teamed up with Pennsylvania GOP Rep. Melissa A. Hart on legislation prohibiting hate messages in cereal boxes and other processed food packages.

Baldwin's self-deprecating humor helps her connect on a personal level, especially with conservatives who frown on her lifestyle. She exchanged marriage vows in 1998 with Lauren Azar, a lawyer, though same-sex unions are not legal in Wisconsin.

The two other openly gay House members, Barney Frank of Massachusetts and Jim Kolbe of Arizona, revealed their homosexuality after getting elected.

Baldwin was a hit with her speech in 1999 at the annual Congressional Dinner of the Washington Press Club. "You invited me because I'm one of the first elected officials who represents a group historically discriminated against," she said. "A group that has been kept out of jobs, harassed at the workplace. A group that's been unfairly stereotyped and made the object of rude and base humor. Of course, I'm talking about blondes . . . especially blondes named Tammy."

In her official biography, under the heading, "If at First You Don't Succeed," she recalls: "In 1975, I ran for Student Council President at my middle school . . . AND LOST. In 1980, I competed for a chance to be my high school graduation speaker . . . AND LOST. And in 1983, I ran for class president at my college . . . AND LOST!"

Baldwin keeps a framed favorite quote in her office from anthropologist Margaret Mead: "Never doubt that a small group of thoughtful, committed citizens can change the world. Indeed, it is the only thing that ever has."

A member of the Progressive Caucus, the most liberal faction in the House, Baldwin supports higher unemployment benefits, more social spending and boosts in the minimum wage. She presses for programs such as child nutrition and expansions of both Head Start and the Family and Medical Leave Act. In her first year in Congress, Baldwin won praise from an unlikely source, the conservative National Taxpayers Union. Citing her work on the Budget Committee, the group noted she voted for less spending in 1999 than all but one of her Badger State colleagues.

Health care is a big priority for Baldwin. Raised by her mother, who was still a college student when she gave birth, and her grandmother, she champions Democratic plans to create a prescription drug benefit under Medicare. She has backed proposals allowing patients to sue their HMOs for damages. And, in the wake of Gulf War Syndrome, a mysterious illness striking veterans of the 1991 Persian Gulf War, she has urged creation of a federal agency to look into the health consequences of military service.

Baldwin typically sides with her party in foreign policy disputes with the GOP White House. She was one of the first House Democrats to publicly oppose President Bush's policy on Iraq, nearly 10 months before Congress began consideration of a resolution sanctioning the use of military force. The administration, she said, was preparing to invade Iraq without having shown a clear link between that Arab nation and the Sept. 11, 2001, attacks on the World Trade Center and Pentagon.

She has taken on the parochial cause of more federal funding to fight chronic wasting disease that has ravaged the deer population in her hunting-happy state.

Baldwin got into politics in 1986, when, as a law student at the University of Wisconsin, she won the first of four terms as a Dane County Supervisor. In 1992, she was elected to the Wisconsin Assembly, where she served six years.

Her impressive fundraising, with help from EMILY's List, helped Baldwin win the 1998 primary over two well-known opponents, Dane County Executive Rick Phelps and state Sen. Joe Wineke. Her Republican opponent, former state Insurance Commissioner Josephine Musser, won a six-way primary with just 21 percent of the vote and antagonized conservatives with her support of abortion rights. Baldwin made the most of her television ads and grass-roots organization to win by 6 points.

The district was a battleground again in 2000, with Baldwin eking out a 3-point victory over moderate Republican John Sharpless, a University of Wisconsin history professor. However, in 2002 the GOP could not get a top-tier challenger, eventually going with Ron Greer, a conservative preacher who focused on Baldwin's sexuality. Baldwin raised 16 times more money than Greer and cruised to the first easy victory of her congressional career.

KEY VOTES

2002

Yes Overhaul campaign finance law; ban "soft money" and restrict advocacy advertising
No Back Bush's defense budget increase
No Extend 1996 welfare law
No Adopt Bush's discretionary spending limit
No Pass GOP Medicare prescription drug plan
Yes Create independent Sept. 11 commission
Yes Extend union protections to Homeland Security Department employees
No Revive fast-track procedures for trade agreements
No Authorize war against Iraq
No Advance bankruptcy overhaul opposed by abortion opponents

2001

No Nullify Clinton Labor Department ergonomics rule
No Cut taxes by $1.35 trillion through fiscal 2011
Yes Maintain ban on oil drilling in Arctic National Wildlife Refuge
No Approve Bush proposal to limit managed-care plan liability for coverage decisions
Yes Divert money from crop subsidy payments to land conservation
No Expand law enforcement power to investigate suspected terrorists

CQ VOTE STUDIES

	PARTY UNITY		PRESIDENTIAL SUPPORT	
	Support	Oppose	Support	Oppose
2002	99%	1%	23%	77%
2001	97%	3%	22%	78%
2000	96%	4%	78%	22%
1999	96%	4%	79%	21%

INTEREST GROUPS

	AFL-CIO	ADA	CCUS	ACU
2002	100%	100%	25%	0%
2001	100%	100%	30%	0%
2000	100%	90%	23%	4%
1999	100%	90%	4%	4%

WISCONSIN 2
South – Madison

Once described by former GOP Gov. Lee Dreyfus as "23 square miles surrounded by reality," Madison long has been Wisconsin's liberal centerpiece. But in the suburbs around Wisconsin's university- and government-dominated capital, growing numbers of socially liberal, fiscally conservative young professionals keep Democrats on their toes.

Many magazines have named Madison as one of the nation's most livable cities, citing the bitter winters as the only negative. The state university system's main campus is a major influence on the city. The stable economy is fueled by an educated, white-collar population, while university-associated industries such as biotechnology have been boosted by school resources and expertise. Other large employers include state government, insurance companies and some light-manufacturing firms.

Outside of Madison, the 2nd resembles most of the rest of the state. Dane County's dairy and beef farms have declined, but it is still the second-largest farming region in the state. Tourists are attracted to the district by "Little Switzerland" in Green County, while the Wisconsin Dells — ancient natural limestone formations along the Wisconsin River — attract visitors to the north. Remapping following the 2000 census gave the 2nd Beloit, a struggling blue-collar manufacturing town near the Illinois border.

Only the Milwaukee-based 4th District exceeds the 2nd in its Democratic proclivities. In 2002, Republican Gov. Scott McCallum took just 19 percent of the vote in Madison, where he finished behind the Democratic, Green and Libertarian candidates in some precincts. McCallum captured 24 percent overall in Dane County, his worst showing in the state. The addition of Beloit adds to the 2nd's Democratic heft.

MAJOR INDUSTRY
Higher education, farming, insurance

MILITARY BASES
Truax Field, 75 military, 268 civilian (2000)

CITIES
Madison, 208,054; Beloit, 35,755; Fitchburg, 20,501; Sun Prairie, 20,369

NOTABLE
The Ringling brothers were from Baraboo, where the Circus World Museum is located; Painter Georgia O'Keeffe was raised in Sun Prairie.

Rep. Ron Kind (D)

CAPITOL OFFICE
225-5506
ron.kind@mail.house.gov
www.house.gov/kind
1406 Longworth 20515-4903; fax 225-5739

COMMITTEES
Budget
Education & Workforce
Resources

HOMETOWN
La Crosse

BORN
March 16, 1963, La Crosse, Wis.

RELIGION
Lutheran

FAMILY
Wife, Tawni Kind; two children

EDUCATION
Harvard U., A.B. 1985; London School of Economics, M.A. 1986; U. of Minnesota, J.D. 1990

CAREER
County prosecutor; lawyer

POLITICAL HIGHLIGHTS
No previous office

ELECTION RESULTS

2002 GENERAL		
Ron Kind (D)	131,038	62.8%
Bill Arndt (R)	69,955	33.5%
Jeff Zastrow (LIBERT)	6,674	3.2%
2002 PRIMARY		
Ron Kind (D)		unopposed
2000 GENERAL		
Ron Kind (D)	173,505	63.7%
Susan Tully (R)	97,741	35.9%

PREVIOUS WINNING PERCENTAGES
1998 (71%); 1996 (52%)

Elected 1996; 4th term

A union leader's son who paid his way through Harvard by scrubbing bathrooms, Kind personifies the Wisconsin good-government tradition. He donates his congressional pay raises to charity, and he returns about 10 percent of his office allotment to the federal treasury each year.

Kind's political inspiration is former Wisconsin Democratic Sen. William O. Proxmire, who was famous for showcasing wasteful government spending. As a summer intern for Proxmire in 1984, Kind did research for the senator's annual "Golden Fleece" awards. He says he strives to carry on Proxmire's legacy, and he regularly gets kudos from the budget watchdog group Concord Coalition for his votes on fiscal issues. At the outset of the 108th Congress, Kind was named to the Budget Committee.

Kind is one of three co-chairmen of the New Democrats, a group of House moderates. He is generally more cooperative than combative in his dealings with Republicans. Only the third Democrat to represent his western Wisconsin district in the past 90 years, Kind believes that bipartisanship is essential to legislative success in Washington. Arriving in Washington in 1997, he solicited advice from his moderate Republican predecessor, Steve Gunderson.

Kind and other moderates have been the targets of outreach efforts by new Minority Leader Nancy Pelosi, a liberal Democrat from California who is trying to build bridges among Democratic factions. She appointed Kind as one of seven chief deputy whips.

A member of the Education and the Workforce Committee, Kind is especially active in the New Democrats' efforts to increase funding for education. His amendments to increase professional development for teachers and to help recruit teachers and principals were included in the 2001 education bill President Bush signed into law. Kind also advocates higher spending on special education.

With other New Democrats, Kind was the focus of heavy lobbying pressure when the House voted in 2002 to grant the president expedited trade negotiating authority, known as fast-track. Unions strongly opposed the measure, and Kind already was on the outs with labor for voting in 2000 to normalize trade relations with China. At public appearances in his district, Kind was confronted by placard-wielding constituents. In the end, Kind, the son of union leader who lost his phone company job after a strike, voted with labor and against the bill. He said it did not adequately address environmental concerns or the needs of displaced U.S. workers.

Kind joins with Republicans on a number of issues, including limits on congressional terms and tougher penalties for convicted felons. He has been a key Democratic vote for abortion foes who want to ban a procedure its opponents call "partial birth" abortion. Kind voted to ban the procedure in 2000, 1998 and 1997. But in 2002, he did not support the ban, saying that the Supreme Court's rejection of a Nebraska late-term abortion law caused him to question the ban's constitutionality.

Kind voted with the Republican president on the key foreign policy issue of 2002. He supported a White House-backed resolution sanctioning the use of military force against Iraq. Back home, a group called the La Crosse Coalition for Peace and Justice launched a write-in campaign against Kind, putting up as their candidate Mark Twain, the American folk humorist and writer who once called war "a wanton waste of projectiles."

Though Kind handily won re-election, the long deceased Twain got 500 votes, surprising even members of the peace group.

Federal protection for the dairy industry is the top parochial issue for Kind. His district includes Eau Claire, the historic center of the U.S. dairy industry. In a political advertisement in 2000, Kind and his family sported milk mustaches and the industry's "Got Milk?" message.

Although he left the Agriculture Committee to join Budget, Kind served on the farm panel in the 107th Congress, and had a hand in drafting a six-year farm bill. Wisconsin dairy farmers got some help from that bill, but Kind failed in his main goal — dismantling the Depression-era milk marketing system that pays farmers more for milk the farther they are from Eau Claire.

Kind turned his efforts to increasing reimbursements for farmers who set aside land for conservation, a provision that would benefit small farmers. After a bipartisan amendment he supported was narrowly defeated, Kind voted against the final version of the bill, saying it unfairly favored large commodity growers.

In another local concern, Kind introduced a bill in the 107th Congress creating a research program into the cause of chronic wasting disease, a deadly ailment affecting the state's deer population and hunting industry. And he was among several Northern lawmakers to successfully lobby the U.S. Fish and Wildlife Service against extending duck hunting in Southern states. Kind also is involved in efforts to clean up the upper portion of the Mississippi in this district, especially of harmful farm runoff.

Kind is a local success story. Reared in a blue-collar neighborhood, he was a high school football and basketball star, and won a scholarship to Harvard University, paying his expenses with a campus job cleaning bathrooms. He quarterbacked on the football team before suffering a career-ending shoulder injury.

After earning a law degree and working two years for a Milwaukee law firm, Kind returned home to La Crosse to become a county prosecutor.

Part of his inspiration for entering politics was a backpacking trip through Eastern Europe just as communism was crumbling. Kind joined the thousands of people who dismantled the Berlin Wall with sledgehammers, and shook hands with new Czechoslovakian President Vaclav Havel.

When Gunderson announced his retirement, Kind jumped into the 1996 race. With little money, he waged a grass-roots campaign, defeated Jim Harsdorf, 52 percent to 48 percent, and has had easy re-elections since. He won in 2002 with nearly 63 percent.

KEY VOTES

2002

Yes Overhaul campaign finance law; ban "soft money" and restrict advocacy advertising
No Back Bush's defense budget increase
No Extend 1996 welfare law
No Adopt Bush's discretionary spending limit
No Pass GOP Medicare prescription drug plan
Yes Create independent Sept. 11 commission
Yes Extend union protections to Homeland Security Department employees
No Revive fast-track procedures for trade agreements
Yes Authorize war against Iraq
Yes Advance bankruptcy overhaul opposed by abortion opponents

2001

No Nullify Clinton Labor Department ergonomics rule
No Cut taxes by $1.35 trillion through fiscal 2011
Yes Maintain ban on oil drilling in Arctic National Wildlife Refuge
No Approve Bush proposal to limit managed-care plan liability for coverage decisions
Yes Divert money from crop subsidy payments to land conservation
Yes Expand law enforcement power to investigate suspected terrorists

CQ VOTE STUDIES

	PARTY UNITY		PRESIDENTIAL SUPPORT	
	Support	Oppose	Support	Oppose
2002	86%	14%	29%	71%
2001	87%	13%	28%	72%
2000	86%	14%	81%	19%
1999	82%	18%	76%	24%
1998	86%	14%	77%	23%

INTEREST GROUPS

	AFL-CIO	ADA	CCUS	ACU
2002	78%	90%	47%	8%
2001	92%	90%	39%	12%
2000	80%	80%	50%	8%
1999	56%	90%	44%	4%
1998	90%	85%	56%	20%

WISCONSIN 3

West – Eau Claire, La Crosse

In the 1930s, President Franklin Roosevelt declared Eau Claire the heart of the nation's milk industry, establishing a system that pays dairy producers more for their milk the farther they are from the 3rd's biggest city. Today, the district still has more cows than people, but the Roosevelt system has become outdated and contributed to the shutdown of family farms, forcing the 3rd to look elsewhere to boost its economy.

Despite the flat prairie land and nutrient-rich soil, the rural southwestern part of the district has been hardest hit by the lagging dairy industry. In the north, Eau Claire and La Crosse have seen declines in their manufacturing industries as well. But the five branches of Wisconsin's state university system in the 3rd have placed an emphasis on computer and technology education, and both cities have experienced recent growth in their technology sectors. Meanwhile, bedroom communities in St. Croix County — inhabited by commuters to Minneapolis-St. Paul, just across the Minnesota state line — grew rapidly during the 1990s.

Recreational tourism also contributes to the 3rd's economy. The 200 miles of Mississippi River that the district takes in along the western border with Minnesota and Iowa provide birdwatchers an opportunity to spot bald eagles perched on bluffs. Lakes in the north attract sportsmen and retirees.

The 3rd has a slight Democratic lean and voted narrowly for Democrat James E. Doyle in the 2002 gubernatorial election. But most of the 19 counties wholly or partly in the district are politically competitive; in the 2000 presidential contest, all but four gave the winner a margin of victory of less than 10 percentage points.

MAJOR INDUSTRY

Dairy farming, heavy manufacturing, tourism

MILITARY BASES

Fort McCoy (Army), 398 military, 1,620 civilian (2002)

CITIES

Eau Claire (pt.), 59,794; La Crosse, 51,818; Menomonie, 14,937

NOTABLE

Laura Ingalls Wilder, author of the "Little House" books, was born in Pepin; Taliesin, Frank Lloyd Wright's estate, is in Spring Green.

Rep. Gerald D. Kleczka (D)

CAPITOL OFFICE
225-4572
www.house.gov/kleczka
2217 Rayburn 20515-4904; fax 225-8135

COMMITTEES
Ways & Means

HOMETOWN
Milwaukee

BORN
Nov. 26, 1943, Milwaukee, Wis.

RELIGION
Roman Catholic

FAMILY
Wife, Bonnie Kleczka

EDUCATION
U. of Wisconsin, attended 1961-62, 1967, 1970

MILITARY SERVICE
Wis. Air National Guard, 1963-69

CAREER
Accountant

POLITICAL HIGHLIGHTS
Wis. Assembly, 1969-74; Wis. Senate, 1975-84

ELECTION RESULTS

2002 GENERAL		
Gerald D. Kleczka (D)	122,031	86.3%
Brian Verdin (WG)	18,324	13.0%
2002 PRIMARY		
Gerald D. Kleczka (D)	54,258	71.7%
Nathaniel J. Stampley (D)	21,244	28.1%
2000 GENERAL		
Gerald D. Kleczka (D)	163,622	60.8%
Tim Riener (R)	101,811	37.8%
Nikola Rajnovic (LIBERT)	3,705	1.4%

PREVIOUS WINNING PERCENTAGES
1998 (58%); 1996 (58%); 1994 (54%); 1992 (66%); 1990 (69%); 1988 (100%); 1986 (100%); 1984 (67%); 1984 Special Election (65%)

Elected April 1984; 10th full term

Born and raised in Milwaukee, Kleczka works on issues that matter most in his constituents' workaday lives — affordable health care, taxes, jobs, community development and consumer protection.

Kleczka (KLETCH-kuh) is a pro-union voice for his blue-collar district, where manufacturing is a dwindling but still important factor in the economy. His constituents usually vote Democratic, but they often hold conservative views on such issues as abortion.

Kleczka mirrors that split, crossing party lines from time to time to vote with Republicans on social issues. He has voted to ban a procedure its opponents call "partial birth" abortion. But he supports federal funding for family planning efforts.

Kleczka also backed the GOP-led overhaul of the welfare system, which he criticized as rife with fraud. He took offense when Republicans in 2000 brought up a resolution praising Catholic schools after they passed over a Catholic priest to be the new House chaplain.

He also is not afraid to cast a politically unpopular vote, as he did in 2002 when he was one of just 21 House members to vote against a resolution supporting the Israeli government's assaults on Palestinians.

But Kleczka is a good soldier for the Democrat leadership. His loyalty was key to helping him win a seat on the Ways and Means Committee, although he had to wait nine years for it. He got the choice assignment in 1993, claiming the "Wisconsin seat" that had been held by Democrat Jim Moody, who left the House.

Although he supports limited tax cuts, he says Republican tax cut plans favor the wealthy and endanger the government's budget surplus. He was critical in 2001 of a House Republican proposal to offer businesses billions of dollars in tax breaks and reduce the tax rate on capital gains. "These tax cuts are far more likely to stimulate increased campaign contributions than increased economic activity," Kleczka said.

As the House considered President Bush's budget plan in 2002, Kleczka said Republicans' insistence on tax cuts was hurting the nation's economy. "You folks got your way, and you tax-reliefed this country back into a deficit," he said. As early as 1999, he was warning that an approximately $800 billion tax cut proposal could spawn budget deficits. "Know that the estimated surplus is based on unrealistic economic assumptions," he said. "To think that our unprecedented growth and prosperity will continue forever is pure folly."

Kleczka's stance on fiscal issues earned him a spot on the "honor roll" of fiscally responsible politicians compiled by the Concord Coalition, a moderate fiscal watchdog group. (But the National Taxpayers Union, which encourages low taxes and less spending, slapped Kleczka with an "F" and labeled him a "big spender.")

One of Kleczka's main interests is protecting individual privacy rights. In the 106th and 107th Congresses, he teamed with Ways and Means Republican E. Clay Shaw Jr. of Florida in an attempt to prohibit federal, state and local government agencies from selling Social Security numbers or displaying the numbers on such documents as driver's licenses. His concern is that criminals who obtain Social Security numbers can use them to get credit cards and run up big debts. Bringing the issue home to Kleczka was the fact that two of his aides were victimized by such identity theft.

Health care is another major concern of Kleczka's, whose brother received a lung transplant in 1993. On Ways and Means, he worked on the

Democrats' version of Republican legislation to protect patients' rights in disputes with managed-care firms and to add prescription drug coverage to Medicare. He objected in 2002 when the GOP leadership would not allow a clean up-or-down vote on a Democratic proposal to give Medicare recipients drug coverage. He also has been an outspoken critic of the "Medicare+Choice" program, which was created in 1997 to attract more managed-care insurers to Medicare. Dozens of insurers have pulled out of the program, citing low reimbursement rates and burdensome paperwork. Kleczka called it "the failed experiment to privatize Medicare."

Kleczka has proposed legislation that would prohibit well-to-do Medicare beneficiaries from entering into private contracts with doctors for services currently covered by Medicare. He argued that allowing such arrangements could lead to a two-tiered system of health care for senior citizens and add to the Medicare program's financial woes.

His ties to organized labor have caused Kleczka to break with most Ways and Means members on issues involving expanded trade. In the 107th, he voted against giving President Bush fast-track trade negotiating authority. In 2000, he voted against legislation granting China permanent normal trade status, contending that Congress instead should continue the practice of regularly reviewing trade relations with that country.

A dog lover who sometimes brings his pet to work, Kleczka in 2000 won passage of a bill banning the import of products made with dog or cat fur.

Kleczka launched his political career at the age of 24, winning election to the state Assembly. He later served in the state Senate, rising to become one of the most influential lawmakers on tax and budget matters while retaining his reputation as a down-to-earth deal-maker and a hard-nosed campaigner. When Democratic Rep. Clement J. Zablocki, the Foreign Affairs Committee chairman, died in late 1983, Kleczka was the front-runner to replace him and won an April 1984 special election with a healthy 65 percent.

Kleczka, a Catholic of Polish descent, represented the large Central and Eastern European ethnic population in the city's South Side neighborhoods in his first nine terms, usually winning re-election by comfortable margins.

In 2002, reapportionment cost Wisconsin a House seat and redistricting merged the two Milwaukee districts — Kleczka's South Side 4th and fellow Democrat Thomas M. Barrett's North Side 5th — into one. Barrett's decision to run for governor left Kleczka an easy ride to re-election, with only a Green Party challenger, in a district where he was heavily favored from the start. "Having the entire city of Milwaukee won't change the [job] to any vast degree," he told the Milwaukee Journal-Sentinel.

KEY VOTES

2002

Yes Overhaul campaign finance law; ban "soft money" and restrict advocacy advertising
No Back Bush's defense budget increase
No Extend 1996 welfare law
No Adopt Bush's discretionary spending limit
No Pass GOP Medicare prescription drug plan
Yes Create independent Sept. 11 commission
Yes Extend union protections to Homeland Security Department employees
No Revive fast-track procedures for trade agreements
No Authorize war against Iraq
No Advance bankruptcy overhaul opposed by abortion opponents

2001

No Nullify Clinton Labor Department ergonomics rule
No Cut taxes by $1.35 trillion through fiscal 2011
Yes Maintain ban on oil drilling in Arctic National Wildlife Refuge
No Approve Bush proposal to limit managed-care plan liability for coverage decisions
Yes Divert money from crop subsidy payments to land conservation
Yes Expand law enforcement power to investigate suspected terrorists

CQ VOTE STUDIES

	PARTY UNITY		PRESIDENTIAL SUPPORT	
	Support	Oppose	Support	Oppose
2002	95%	5%	30%	70%
2001	91%	9%	23%	77%
2000	88%	12%	78%	22%
1999	87%	13%	75%	25%
1998	85%	15%	75%	25%

INTEREST GROUPS

	AFL-CIO	ADA	CCUS	ACU
2002	100%	95%	35%	4%
2001	100%	95%	43%	4%
2000	100%	85%	30%	20%
1999	89%	95%	24%	16%
1998	100%	90%	39%	20%

WISCONSIN 4

Milwaukee

As Father James Groppi led civil rights protesters across Milwaukee's 16th Street Bridge over the Menomonee Valley in the 1960s, observers called it the "longest bridge in the world" — quipping that it stretched all the way from Poland to Africa. After redistricting following the 2000 census put all of Milwaukee into a single district for the first time, the 4th must confront the stark racial, cultural and economic differences that divide its northern and southern parts.

Polish immigrants flocked to the southern side of the valley in the early 20th century as Milwaukee grew into one of the nation's larger cities. Then a large black population migrated to the area following World War II, but regulations forced them to the northern side of the valley. As population has declined since the 1960s, the pronounced social and economic differences between the two communities have remained.

Milwaukee today is minority-majority, with blacks (37 percent) and Hispanics (12 percent) together outnumbering whites. Milwaukee was once tagged as "hypersegregated," but city officials say it is becoming more integrated. Still, it is not uncommon to find almost completely black areas in north-central Milwaukee and almost exclusively white areas in the southern part of the city.

As the growing Hispanic population displaces wealthier white-collar workers migrating to suburbs west of Milwaukee, the city's manufacturing industries — especially some of the breweries and tanneries that defined the economy — continue to decline, leaving the city struggling to find a new identity. Milwaukee's large minority population and strong union presence make the 4th staunchly Democratic.

MAJOR INDUSTRY

Machinery manufacturing, service

CITIES

Milwaukee, 596,974; South Milwaukee, 21,256; West Allis (pt.), 20,936

NOTABLE

The world's largest four-sided clock is on the Allen-Bradley building; Milwaukee's Holler House is the nation's oldest sanctioned bowling alley; Socialist Victor L. Berger served in the House (1911-13 and 1923-29); Schlitz, "the beer that made Milwaukee famous," closed its Milwaukee brewery in 1981.

Rep. F. James Sensenbrenner Jr. (R)

CAPITOL OFFICE
225-5101
sensenbrenner@mail.house.gov
www.house.gov/sensenbrenner
2449 Rayburn 20515-4905; fax 225-3190

COMMITTEES
Judiciary - chairman
Select Homeland Security

HOMETOWN
Menomonee Falls

BORN
June 14, 1943, Chicago, Ill.

RELIGION
Episcopalian

FAMILY
Wife, Cheryl Sensenbrenner; two children

EDUCATION
Stanford U., A.B. 1965 (political science);
U. of Wisconsin, J.D. 1968

CAREER
Lawyer

POLITICAL HIGHLIGHTS
Wis. Assembly, 1969-75; Wis. Senate, 1975-79

ELECTION RESULTS

2002 GENERAL		
James Sensenbrenner (R)	191,224	86.1%
Robert R. Raymond (I)	29,567	13.3%
2002 PRIMARY		
James Sensenbrenner (R)		unopposed
2000 GENERAL		
James Sensenbrenner (R)	239,498	74.0%
Mike Clawson (D)	83,720	25.9%

PREVIOUS WINNING PERCENTAGES
1998 (91%); 1996 (74%); 1994 (100%); 1992 (70%); 1990 (100%); 1988 (75%); 1986 (78%); 1984 (73%); 1982 (100%); 1980 (78%); 1978 (61%)

Elected 1978; 13th term

A dogged and irascible conservative, Sensenbrenner does not appear well-suited to the role of conciliator. But in his first term at the helm of the Judiciary Committee, in the 107th Congress, he managed to win grudging praise from Democrats for his efforts to reach across the aisle.

There is no deeper ideological divide in any congressional committee than between Republicans and Democrats on Judiciary. But, in perhaps the panel's best show of bipartisanship in years, Sensenbrenner secured a unanimous vote for sweeping anti-terrorism legislation just three weeks after the terrorist attacks of Sept. 11, 2001.

Sensenbrenner described the moment as a triumph of the committee system over the desires of the Bush administration, which had proposed nearly unfettered powers for law enforcement agents to search, eavesdrop upon, arrest and detain suspects. But his victory was short-lived; Attorney General John Ashcroft persuaded Speaker J. Dennis Hastert to have the House vote instead on a package that was much more akin to what the White House wanted. That was close to what became law, although a version of one pragmatic concession that Sensenbrenner had made to his committee Democrats remained: Most of the expanded surveillance and investigatory powers will expire at the end of 2005 unless Congress extends them.

Sensenbrenner's work on the anti-terrorism law was a window into his emerging style on Judiciary, which has led Democrats to keep an open mind about him. He fiercely guards the panel's jurisdiction and prerogatives, even when that leads to high-profile failure, often at the hands of others in his party. And he keeps the minority party informed along the way.

For instance, Sensenbrenner pushed hard in the 107th for legislation to make it more difficult for people to escape their debts by filing for bankruptcy protection. When the bill almost died because of language to limit the ability of anti-abortion protesters to escape court fines and judgments in bankruptcy court, Sensenbrenner brokered a deal between House abortion foe Henry J. Hyde, an Illinois Republican, and Senate abortion rights advocate Charles E. Schumer, a New York Democrat. But most abortion opponents spurned the deal, and they engineered the rejection of the entire bankruptcy package at the end of 2002.

Sensenbrenner also made repeated offers to negotiate with the administration on legislation to provide insurers a federal backstop for property and casualty losses due to terrorism. But the White House struck a deal with Democratic Sen. Christopher J. Dodd of Connecticut and Republican Rep. Michael G. Oxley of Ohio, leaving Sensenbrenner and other GOP conservatives in the cold. Sensenbrenner was incensed that the plan did not include a ban on punitive damage awards in lawsuits, a top GOP goal.

Brusque and no-nonsense, Sensenbrenner has an obvious distaste for the long-winded rhetoric typical of Judiciary meetings. But he spent his first 16 years in the House as a member of the GOP minority, and he swore that once he wielded power he would not subject Democrats to the same kinds of indignities he believes his party suffered.

Sensenbrenner served four years as chairman of the low-profile Science Committee, where he tried out his approach for wielding a gavel and fostered cooperative relations with the panel's top Democrats. But he almost did not get the Judiciary gavel in the 107th. Republican leaders first considered exempting Hyde from chairmanship term limits so he could stay on. Then Sensenbrenner, who was next in seniority, had to prevail over a challenge from George W. Gekas of Pennsylvania.

His ascent represented a vindication of sorts. During the 104th Congress, he was passed over for a Judiciary subcommittee chairmanship despite being the third-most-senior Republican on the full committee. At the time, it was noted that even some in his own party found Sensenbrenner's personality prickly at best and condescending at worst.

In the 108th Congress, his Judiciary chairmanship resulted in his assignment to the Homeland Security Committee.

A House prosecutor in the 1999 Senate impeachment trial of President Clinton, Sensenbrenner has never shied from partisan behavior. But he nevertheless put the new Bush White House on notice in 2001 that as chairman he would not shrink from executive branch oversight. That became clear a year later, when he joined the top Democrat on Judiciary, John Conyers Jr. of Michigan, in battling the Justice Department for information about the use of its new wiretapping authority. At one point Sensenbrenner said he was prepared to subpoena Ashcroft for the information. Ultimately, the administration released much of what the Judiciary panel sought.

Sensenbrenner is heir to a paper and cellulose manufacturing fortune, most of which stems from his great-grandfather's invention of the sanitary napkin shortly after World War I. Marketing it under the brand name Kotex, Sensenbrenner's ancestor went on to become the chairman of Kimberly-Clark. Sensenbrenner added to his wealth late in 1997, when he won $250,000 in the District of Columbia's lottery. (He purchased the ticket while buying beer for an office Christmas party.) He gave some of the winnings to charity and invested the rest.

Sensenbrenner was elected to Congress in 1978 to fill the 9th District seat of Republican Bob Kasten, who left to run for governor. Sensenbrenner was seen as the obvious successor, having served a decade in the legislature — he was first elected the year he graduated from law school — and risen to become assistant minority leader in the state Senate. His primary opponent was Susan Engeleiter, a fellow state legislator who would later become director of the Small Business Administration in the first Bush administration. Sensenbrenner survived the primary by 589 votes, and went on to defeat Democratic Milwaukee lawyer Matthew J. Flynn with 61 percent of the vote in the fall.

He has won by wider margins in each of his dozen re-elections. Five times the Democrats have not fielded a candidate, most recently in 2002. Because Wisconsin lost a seat in reapportionment, the territory he represents is now the 5th District, but its contours for this decade are largely unchanged.

KEY VOTES

2002

No Overhaul campaign finance law; ban "soft money" and restrict advocacy advertising
Yes Back Bush's defense budget increase
Yes Extend 1996 welfare law
Yes Adopt Bush's discretionary spending limit
Yes Pass GOP Medicare prescription drug plan
No Create independent Sept. 11 commission
No Extend union protections to Homeland Security Department employees
Yes Revive fast-track procedures for trade agreements
Yes Authorize war against Iraq
Yes Advance bankruptcy overhaul opposed by abortion opponents

2001

Yes Nullify Clinton Labor Department ergonomics rule
Yes Cut taxes by $1.35 trillion through fiscal 2011
Yes Maintain ban on oil drilling in Arctic National Wildlife Refuge
Yes Approve Bush proposal to limit managed-care plan liability for coverage decisions
Yes Divert money from crop subsidy payments to land conservation
Yes Expand law enforcement power to investigate suspected terrorists

CQ VOTE STUDIES

	PARTY UNITY		PRESIDENTIAL SUPPORT	
	Support	Oppose	Support	Oppose
2002	94%	6%	85%	15%
2001	91%	9%	77%	23%
2000	91%	9%	20%	80%
1999	92%	8%	21%	79%
1998	86%	14%	22%	78%

INTEREST GROUPS

	AFL-CIO	ADA	CCUS	ACU
2002	13%	0%	95%	92%
2001	8%	10%	74%	96%
2000	22%	20%	70%	88%
1999	11%	10%	80%	96%
1998	0%	5%	78%	92%

WISCONSIN 5
Southeast – Milwaukee suburbs

Residents of Waukesha and Ozaukee counties joke that more people commute from Milwaukee to the suburbs that make up the 5th District than the other way around. Indeed, the affluent counties to the west and north of the city have continued to experience rapid growth as Milwaukee middle managers leave downtown and newly transferred white-collar workers settle in the city's outskirts.

As the suburbs expand, they are becoming increasingly self-sufficient, providing employment in all sectors. Most of the manufacturing jobs outside of the city are located in Waukesha County, west of Milwaukee. Quad Graphics, a major printing company, is headquartered in Pewaukee, while engine manufacturer Briggs and Stratton is located in Wauwatosa. Most residents in Ozaukee County, to the north of the city, hold service and legal-related jobs. Waukesha County's population grew by 18 percent in the 1990s; Washington County, to Waukesha's north, grew by 23 percent, the fourth-fastest in the state.

While the northern and western outskirts of the 5th are still mostly rural and populated with dairy farms and cattle ranches, urban sprawl has started to encroach upon them as well. Most residents of the 5th still proudly celebrate their diverse European heritages — German, Belgian, Dutch and Eastern European folk festivals attract tourists almost every weekend of the summer. Vacationers also travel here for the recreational fishing and boating opportunities along Lake Michigan.

The present-day 5th is descended from the 9th District that existed in the 1990s; the renumbering was required after redistricting following the 2000 census dismantled a Milwaukee-based district (the old 5th). The strong GOP lean in Ozaukee, Washington and Waukesha makes the new 5th the state's most heavily Republican district. It gave 62 percent to George W. Bush in the 2000 presidential election. Democrats are competitive only in Milwaukee County.

MAJOR INDUSTRY
Service, manufacturing, retail

CITIES
Waukesha, 64,825; Wauwatosa, 47,271; Brookfield, 38,649; Menomonee Falls, 32,647; New Berlin (pt.), 31,636

NOTABLE
Harley-Davidson has a product development center in Wauwatosa.

Rep. Tom Petri (R)

CAPITOL OFFICE
225-2476
www.house.gov/petri
2462 Rayburn 20515-4906; fax 225-2356

COMMITTEES
Education & Workforce
Transportation & Infrastructure
(Highways, Transit & Pipelines - chairman)

HOMETOWN
Fond du Lac

BORN
May 28, 1940, Marinette, Wis.

RELIGION
Lutheran

FAMILY
Wife, Anne Neal Petri; one child

EDUCATION
Harvard U., A.B. 1962 (government), J.D. 1965

CAREER
Lawyer; Peace Corps volunteer

POLITICAL HIGHLIGHTS
White House aide, 1969-70; Wis. Senate, 1973-79; Republican nominee for U.S. Senate, 1974

ELECTION RESULTS

2002 GENERAL		
Tom Petri (R)		unopposed
2002 PRIMARY		
Tom Petri (R)		unopposed
2000 GENERAL		
Tom Petri (R)	179,205	65.0%
Daniel Flaherty (D)	96,125	34.9%

PREVIOUS WINNING PERCENTAGES
1998 (93%); 1996 (73%); 1994 (100%); 1992 (53%); 1990 (100%); 1988 (74%); 1986 (97%); 1984 (76%); 1982 (65%); 1980 (59%); 1979 Special Election (50%)

Elected April 1979; 12th full term

Soft-spoken Petri is a friend of conservative tax cut advocates and business lobbyists but also a supporter of big spending on highways and of a campaign spending bill his party leaders hated.

His independent streak sometimes put him on the outs with the conservative GOP leadership. Though he was next in line in seniority, he was denied the chairmanship of the Education and the Workforce Committee in the 107th Congress. The job instead went to John A. Boehner of Ohio, who usually votes with the leadership, is a prolific fundraiser and has extensive contacts as the former chairman of the Republican Conference, the group of all House Republicans. When the Republican Steering Committee held interviews for prospective chairmen, some candidates brought gifts ranging from bags of peanuts to fancy lunch boxes. The professorial Petri (PEA-try) came with a six-point plan.

Another liability in his relations with the leadership resulted from his decision to join a bipartisan band of rebels who got the campaign finance bill to the floor later in the 107th over the objections of Speaker J. Dennis Hastert and other top GOP leaders. Petri signed the so-called discharge petition, which forced the leadership to act once a sufficient number of lawmakers signed. The legislation bans unregulated "soft money," which goes to political parties rather than candidates but increasingly is used in novel ways to influence individual campaigns. Party leaders opposed the bill because it cramped fundraising.

Changes to campaign finance law continues to occupy a prominent place on Petri's agenda. He introduced legislation in the 108th Congress aimed at encouraging more participation in campaigns by low-income constituents. The measure allows 100 percent tax credits for donations of up to $200 per year to federal candidates, or a 100 percent tax deduction for contributions of up to $600 per year.

Losing the chairmanship of the Education panel was a tough break for Petri, who has a longstanding interest in education policy and crosses party lines to get bipartisan legislation. He backs providing parents with taxpayer-financed vouchers to pay private school tuition for students in kindergarten through 12th grade. He worked with Democratic Sen. Christopher J. Dodd of Connecticut on a bill to ensure that sight-impaired students get textbooks in a timely way, and with California Democratic Rep. George Miller to remove the requirement that postsecondary schools be accredited in order to receive federal student aid funds.

Petri continues to hold sway over transportation funding. As a consolation prize for not receiving the Education gavel, he was made chairman of Transportation and Infrastructure's new Highways and Transit subcommittee. The old Ground Transportation Subcommittee was split in two, with Petri getting the newly constituted highway panel. That allowed him to avoid the term limit on chairmanships; he already had spent six years as chairman of the Ground Transportation Subcommittee. On the new panel, he retains authority over highway programs.

He squares his fiscal conservatism with his support for highway spending by arguing that the projects, enormously popular with lawmakers and their constituents, are paid out of the Highway Trust Fund, which is set aside for the purpose of maintaining highways. The fund is financed by gasoline taxes, not by general revenues. Petri has been a key supporter of efforts to keep gasoline taxes walled off from other uses.

Petri worked on the Transportation committee when it crafted the most expensive transportation funding bill in U.S. history — the six-year, $218 billion highway bill enacted in 1998. It prevailed over the bitter objections of Republican House conservatives, who were pushing for a balanced federal budget.

With Petri's help, Wisconsin received a 48 percent boost in road funding, erasing its status as a "donor" state, one that contributes more in gasoline tax receipts than it gets back in federal aid. On a national level, Petri tried to limit some the bill's big-ticket items. He opposed funding for the Auburn Dam in California, which at $950 million would be the most expensive American dam ever built. He also has been a critic of chronic cost overruns on Boston's "Big Dig" highway project. Reauthorization of the highway legislation tops the committee's agenda in the 108th Congress.

In 2002, Petri received a "Hero of the Taxpayer Award" for his 90 percent rating from the Americans for Tax Reform. But even on the GOP's signature issues, Petri sometimes goes his own way. He has been a leading Republican advocate of expanding the earned-income tax credit, a tax break that helps the working poor. Most efforts to increase the credit come from House Democrats.

Petri votes with his party's anti-abortion majority and supports gun owners' rights. He also helps wage the Wisconsin delegation's perennial battle against federal milk price supports. He has called the program "an outdated relic of 1930s agriculture policy" and says it helps milk producers in the Northeast and Southeast while hurting those in the Upper Midwest.

Petri, who was born in northern Wisconsin, earned a law degree from Harvard and later joined the Peace Corps, doing work in Somalia. Once home, he started a law practice in Fond du Lac. He won a state Senate seat in 1972 at age 32.

Petri was chosen to be the GOP Senate nominee against Democrat Gaylord Nelson in 1974, but he lost in the aftermath of the Watergate scandal and what turned out to be a terrible year for Republicans. The exposure and increased name recognition from that race, however, helped him win a close contest for the House in a 1979 special election. He replaced Republican Rep. William A. Steiger, who had died in office.

In his 1992 re-election campaign, Petri was hampered by negative publicity about 77 overdrafts at the private bank for House members. He was returned to Washington with only 53 percent of the vote, his worst re-election total ever. Since then, he has been re-elected easily, and in 2002 he ran uncontested.

KEY VOTES

2002

- Yes Overhaul campaign finance law; ban "soft money" and restrict advocacy advertising
- Yes Back Bush's defense budget increase
- Yes Extend 1996 welfare law
- Yes Adopt Bush's discretionary spending limit
- Yes Pass GOP Medicare prescription drug plan
- No Create independent Sept. 11 commission
- Yes Extend union protections to Homeland Security Department employees
- Yes Revive fast-track procedures for trade agreements
- Yes Authorize war against Iraq
- Yes Advance bankruptcy overhaul opposed by abortion opponents

2001

- No Nullify Clinton Labor Department ergonomics rule
- Yes Cut taxes by $1.35 trillion through fiscal 2011
- Yes Maintain ban on oil drilling in Arctic National Wildlife Refuge
- Yes Approve Bush proposal to limit managed-care plan liability for coverage decisions
- Yes Divert money from crop subsidy payments to land conservation
- Yes Expand law enforcement power to investigate suspected terrorists

CQ VOTE STUDIES

	PARTY UNITY		PRESIDENTIAL SUPPORT	
	Support	Oppose	Support	Oppose
2002	86%	14%	82%	18%
2001	90%	10%	83%	17%
2000	89%	11%	32%	68%
1999	86%	14%	22%	78%
1998	86%	14%	31%	69%

INTEREST GROUPS

	AFL-CIO	ADA	CCUS	ACU
2002	0%	10%	85%	80%
2001	17%	25%	65%	72%
2000	0%	10%	76%	84%
1999	22%	20%	88%	80%
1998	10%	15%	94%	88%

WISCONSIN 6

East central – Oshkosh, Sheboygan, Fond du Lac

In 1854, a group of dissatisfied Whigs, Free Soilers and Democrats met in a Ripon schoolhouse in central Fond du Lac County and created the Republican Party. Today, the rural areas west of Ripon still carry on the GOP tradition of their forefathers, but the blue-collar communities along Lake Michigan's shores, characterized by manufacturing and processing plants, vote Democratic.

On Lake Michigan, Manitowoc County has a longstanding reputation as a shipbuilding center. Sheboygan County is famed for its meat processing — it considers itself the "bratwurst capital of the world" — and also for its manufacturing, including the plumbing company Kohler. Around Lake Winnebago, Oshkosh produces heavy trucks while Neenah and Menasha are major paper-product manufacturers.

The west is farming territory, though family dairy farms have struggled. Some have been assimilated by large corporate farms and others have turned to crops such as beans, peas and corn. Marquette County, located in the southwest, is the least-populous county in the 6th but the fastest-growing in the state (28.5 percent in the 1990s). It is popular among retirees from the Milwaukee and Chicago areas.

Many of the 6th's residents are descendants of German immigrants who settled the area in the 1850s, and the district claims more people of German ancestry (54 percent) than any other in the nation. Although these socially conservative Lutherans combine with a Catholic community to dominate much of the district, some of the state's traditional progressivism remains. The Hmong population — immigrants from East Asia — nearly doubled in the 1990s.

The 6th leans Republican, but not overwhelmingly so. In 2000, George W. Bush won every county here except for Adams, located in the far west. Republican Scott McCallum won the 6th in the 2002 gubernatorial election, narrowly winning Sheboygan and Winnebago.

MAJOR INDUSTRY
Paper, dairy, tourism

CITIES
Oshkosh, 62,916; Sheboygan, 50,972; Fond du Lac, 42,203

NOTABLE
The Wisconsin Maritime Museum is in Manitowoc.

Rep. David R. Obey (D)

CAPITOL OFFICE
225-3365
www.house.gov/obey
2314 Rayburn 20515-4907; fax 225-3240

COMMITTEES
Appropriations - ranking member

HOMETOWN
Wausau

BORN
Oct. 3, 1938, Okmulgee, Okla.

RELIGION
Roman Catholic

FAMILY
Wife, Joan Obey; two children

EDUCATION
U. of Wisconsin, B.S. 1960 (political science), M.A. 1962 (political science)

CAREER
Real estate broker

POLITICAL HIGHLIGHTS
Wis. Assembly, 1963-69

ELECTION RESULTS

2002 GENERAL		
David R. Obey (D)	146,364	64.2%
Joe Rothbauer (R)	81,518	35.8%
2002 PRIMARY		
David R. Obey (D)		unopposed
2000 GENERAL		
David R. Obey (D)	173,007	63.3%
Sean Cronin (R)	100,264	36.7%

PREVIOUS WINNING PERCENTAGES
1998 (61%); 1996 (57%); 1994 (54%); 1992 (64%); 1990 (62%); 1988 (62%); 1986 (62%); 1984 (61%); 1982 (68%); 1980 (65%); 1978 (62%); 1976 (73%); 1974 (71%); 1972 (63%); 1970 (68%); 1969 Special Election (52%)

Elected April 1969; 17th full term

The 108th Congress promises to be a frustrating one for Obey. The entire budget apparatus is in Republican hands, and outgunned Democrats such as Obey — who has been the top Democrat on the Appropriations Committee since 1994 — fear they will be on the outside looking in.

Through countless battles for liberal causes over more than three decades and through seven presidencies, Obey (OH-bee) has gained a reputation as a complex man of indisputable intelligence, occasionally irascible disposition and formidable legislative skill. His combustible manner and brutal honesty on the House floor are matched by his deep understanding of the policy preferences, procedures and politics at work behind the scenes.

During every budget cycle since Republicans took the House, Obey had either President Clinton or majority Senate Democrats to ensure that he did not get trampled in the process. But starting in 2003, he was on his own. The early signs were not encouraging. He derided the first spending bill of the 108th — a behemoth package that wrapped up all the domestic spending bills unfinished at the end of the 107th — as the "biggest backroom deal in terms of spending in the nation's history," loaded with special interest provisions and anti-environmental riders.

Obey considers himself an institutionalist, someone with respect for the House's ideals of civilized debate and collegiality. (He directed a rewrite of the House ethics code after a series of scandals in the 1970s.)

And his dedication to the institution was in evidence in the days after the terrorist attacks of Sept. 11, 2001. Never shy about taking unpopular stands, Obey was a lonely voice insisting that Congress not give President Bush unfettered control over $40 billion in emergency spending to respond to the attacks. "When you give any White House $20 billion with not a single string attached," he said, "you have abdicated Congress' responsibility under the Constitution." Ultimately, his view prevailed.

His pugnacity and partisanship are legendary, and with Republicans running Congress as well as the White House, some of what Obey sees is more than he can bear. Often, he seems close to boiling over, the array of long pencils in his shirt pocket threatening to topple out as he wags his finger in disgust at any number of maneuvers by GOP leaders. Obey generally has good relationships with top Republican appropriators, though.

Obey is, however, sometimes at odds with other senior Democrats on Appropriations, who are sufficiently committed to the accommodating culture of the panel that they end up providing votes for spending packages that violate Democratic principles. (In addition, GOP leaders have made it plain that members who vote against spending bills will find it harder to obtain projects for their districts, which threatens to undercut Obey and erode Democratic unity.)

In the 107th Congress Obey was a constant voice for greater spending for homeland defense programs. In 2001 he made the rounds at various agencies, soliciting and making public the unmet requests they had sent the White House for additional homeland security spending.

But he also shows a genial side, playing the harmonica in a bluegrass band called the Capitol Offenses and occasionally displaying a sense of humor. When asked — during a particularly tense moment in the 2000 budget negotiations — to predict when the 106th Congress would adjourn, Obey began warbling "Silent Night." The session ended Dec. 15.

Obey spent a quarter-century in the House majority, and for the final nine months of 1994 he was Appropriations chairman. For all his liberal passion, he understood that lawmaking involves compromise, and his main objective was to resolve problems with the GOP before they caused delays. As a result, all 13 measures became law by the start of the fiscal year; that has not happened since.

While some long-tenured Democrats have retired rather than endure life in the minority, Obey still seems to relish the fight — framing it in unusually personal terms. Asked in 1998 if he might move on, he said with a grin, "I just wouldn't give the bastards the satisfaction."

Obey takes a hands-on approach to managing each of the 13 annual appropriations bills. During the Clinton administration, he used the annual spending wars to sharpen his party's message to the public, all the while maneuvering to ensure the bills received Clinton's approval. Under Bush, he takes a lead role in opposing the White House's spending priorities.

Like all appropriators, Obey uses his perch to take care of his district. He does not have a reputation as too profligate in this regard, but one item dear to Obey — an $80,000 motorized sled he obtained for a Wisconsin sheriff for rescues on Lake Superior — was singled out in Bush's 2003 budget as an example of wasteful spending.

Although he lists his occupation as real estate broker, Obey has been a legislator almost all his adult life. He was elected to the state House when he was 24 and won election to Congress at age 30, in a 1969 special election to succeed Melvin R. Laird, President Nixon's first defense secretary. Obey was the first Democrat ever to represent the 7th District, and he has won three-fifths of the vote in 15 of 17 re-election races.

His reputation as a liberal stalwart stems from Obey's tussles with Republicans over fiscal policy. But mindful of sentiment in his largely rural and small-town district, he supports gun owners' rights and votes a restrictive line on some abortion issues.

Obey grew up in a staunchly Republican family; he once hitched a wagon to his bicycle and campaigned door to door for GOP Sen. Joseph R. McCarthy and presidential candidate Dwight D. Eisenhower. But he says he reconsidered when McCarthy followers on the local school board tried to have his high school history teacher fired for teaching that the political platform of the Chamber of Commerce and the Constitution were not necessarily the same thing. "When I saw what McCarthyism did to the best teacher I ever had," he said, "it showed me that if you had any dedication to individual liberty and freedom of speech, that at that time in that county, there was no room for you in the local Republican Party."

KEY VOTES

2002

- Yes Overhaul campaign finance law; ban "soft money" and restrict advocacy advertising
- No Back Bush's defense budget increase
- No Extend 1996 welfare law
- No Adopt Bush's discretionary spending limit
- No Pass GOP Medicare prescription drug plan
- Yes Create independent Sept. 11 commission
- Yes Extend union protections to Homeland Security Department employees
- No Revive fast-track procedures for trade agreements
- No Authorize war against Iraq
- No Advance bankruptcy overhaul opposed by abortion opponents

2001

- No Nullify Clinton Labor Department ergonomics rule
- No Cut taxes by $1.35 trillion through fiscal 2011
- Yes Maintain ban on oil drilling in Arctic National Wildlife Refuge
- No Approve Bush proposal to limit managed-care plan liability for coverage decisions
- Yes Divert money from crop subsidy payments to land conservation
- Yes Expand law enforcement power to investigate suspected terrorists

CQ VOTE STUDIES

	PARTY UNITY		PRESIDENTIAL SUPPORT	
	Support	Oppose	Support	Oppose
2002	94%	6%	32%	68%
2001	94%	6%	29%	71%
2000	94%	6%	82%	18%
1999	87%	13%	80%	20%
1998	92%	8%	89%	11%

INTEREST GROUPS

	AFL-CIO	ADA	CCUS	ACU
2002	100%	90%	26%	8%
2001	100%	95%	30%	13%
2000	100%	95%	15%	4%
1999	100%	90%	4%	4%
1998	100%	95%	11%	16%

WISCONSIN 7

Northwest – Wausau, Superior, Stevens Point

Wisconsin's most rural district, the 7th stretches north and west from the state's central counties to the Apostle Islands along the southern coast of Lake Superior. Small towns and family farms checker the district, carrying a populist flavor and still retaining some threads of mid-century LaFollette progressivism.

Farming sustains the district's economy, although cold weather in the north shaves a full month off the growing season. The dairy industry has declined since the 1980s, but small, 60-cow farms still populate the northern half of the 7th. The more nutrient-rich soil in the Central Sands country in the state's midsection produces seed potatoes, cranberries, beans and ginseng. Some small metalworking and paper factories — the industries that attracted immigrants to the 7th in the 19th century — still produce their goods. The insurance industry has waned in recent years.

The tranquil lifestyle in small towns and along hundreds of lakes in the north attracts a particularly large number of senior citizens to the 7th. Young people migrate south to cities, such as Milwaukee and Madison, to find jobs or to take advantage of the University of Wisconsin's main branch, while Hmong immigrants from Asia's eastern coast have settled in the region in large numbers. One fast-growing area is Polk County, on the St. Croix River northeast of the Minneapolis-St. Paul metro area.

Blue-collar regions around Stevens Point and Wausau and along Lake Superior in the north consistently vote Democratic, but the rest of the area is more politically competitive. Descendants of Scandinavian immigrants in north-central Wisconsin and an emerging Christian Right contingent keep the region competitive. Redistricting following the 2000 census did not significantly alter the 7th's political leanings.

MAJOR INDUSTRY

Agriculture, paper, manufacturing

CITIES

Wausau, 38,426; Superior, 27,368; Stevens Point, 24,551

NOTABLE

Marathon County is the nation's largest producer of ginseng; The American Birkebeiner, from Cable to Hayward, is North America's largest cross-country ski marathon; Poniatowski is the center of the northern half of the western hemisphere; Colby cheese is named after a district town; Hayward is home to the National Fresh Water Fishing Hall of Fame.

Rep. Mark Green (R)

CAPITOL OFFICE
225-5665
mark.green@mail.house.gov
www.house.gov/markgreen
1314 Longworth 20515-4908; fax 225-5729

COMMITTEES
Financial Services
International Relations
Judiciary

HOMETOWN
Green Bay

BORN
June 1, 1960, Boston, Mass.

RELIGION
Roman Catholic

FAMILY
Wife, Susan Green; three children

EDUCATION
U. of Wisconsin, Eau Claire, B.A. 1983; U. of Wisconsin, Madison, J.D. 1987

CAREER
Lawyer; teacher

POLITICAL HIGHLIGHTS
Wis. Assembly, 1993-99

ELECTION RESULTS

2002 GENERAL		
Mark Green (R)	152,745	72.6%
Andrew M. Becker (D)	50,284	23.9%
Dick Kaiser (WG)	7,338	3.5%
2002 PRIMARY		
Mark Green (R)		unopposed
2000 GENERAL		
Mark Green (R)	211,388	74.6%
Dean Reich (D)	71,575	25.3%

PREVIOUS WINNING PERCENTAGES
1998 (55%)

Elected 1998; 3rd term

Green says a teaching stint in a remote Kenyan village helped shape his policy views and started him thinking about a career in politics — a career that ended up starting before his immigrant parents had become citizens eligible to vote for their son. The Kenyan experience "sensitized me to the problems of the human condition," he says, but he also came away with the belief that government policies can stifle economic opportunity.

Terming himself a "bleeding-heart conservative," Green says his commitment to improving society is moderated by a belief that government should get out of the way. Yet Green does not subscribe to the anti-government rhetoric of some conservatives. For example, he says U.S. government investment in international education will yield tangible benefits for the United States. "If we can create meaningful educational opportunities in underdeveloped countries, we can prevent radicalization from taking place," he says.

As a freshman in the 106th Congress, Green led some members of the Class of 1998 in developing legislation to make it easier for state governments to win federal approval to try innovative approaches to solving social problems. Wisconsin has been a leader in experimenting with ways to improve programs such as welfare. Green had a front-row seat in those efforts as a three-term member of the state Assembly before coming to Congress.

When he arrived in Washington, Green announced that he intended to focus on taxes, and he did push for the Republican tax agenda from his seat on the Budget Committee. But Green no longer sits on that panel. Instead, he is on the Judiciary, International Relations and Financial Services committees. Those assignments allow him to focus more on social policy, particularly his post as the vice chairman of the Financial Services Housing and Community Opportunity Subcommittee. "I believe that affordable housing is the great untapped issue for conservatives," says Green.

He has used his Judiciary seat to push a "two strikes — they're out" bill, which is similar to legislation he had written in the Wisconsin Legislature. The measure, which the House passed in 2000 and again in 2002, was predicated on studies indicating that sex offenders usually repeat their crime. "This bill is not . . . about deterrence. It is about removing bad people from society," he says. He is trying again in the 108th.

Green also has pushed legislation to give financial assistance to law enforcement officers who purchase homes in high-crime areas and another to help the disabled buy homes. He also backed a post-Sept. 11 bill to allow off-duty and retired police to carry concealed firearms anywhere in the nation to bolster homeland security. But the measure was opposed by fellow Wisconsin Republican F. James Sensenbrenner Jr., Judiciary's chairman, who argued that it would violate states' rights and create a safety hazard.

As the only Republican to knock off an incumbent House Democrat in 1998, Green was treated well by party leaders when he arrived in Washington. He received a spot in the GOP whip organization and a place on the Republican Policy Committee, and is a member of the executive board of the National Republican Campaign Committee. Green's voting record gives the GOP leadership no cause to regret its confidence in him: In the 107th Congress, he backed his party 94 percent of the time.

Green also tends to the home fires. It is politically imperative for lawmakers from Wisconsin to involve themselves in dairy policy, and Green was a member of the conference committee that wrote the final version of the farm bill enacted in 2002, which included a three-and-a-half year, $1.3 billion dairy price-support program. However, Green and other Badger State lawmakers have been less successful in their push for a sweeping rewrite of the Depression-era milk-pricing policy that has given milk producers in other regions a better deal in order to help them compete with producers in the Upper Midwest. Lawmakers from those other parts of the country have repeatedly blocked the efforts, leading Green to declare: "This place is locked in a time warp. This place is using a milk-pricing mechanism that was created in the era of the manual typewriter."

Green also sought to help Wisconsin farmers by pushing to liberalize the income-averaging provisions of the tax code and by supporting better tax treatment for the sale of a family farm to another member of the same family. And he has backed federal funding to fight chronic wasting disease — the deer equivalent of mad cow disease — which has threatened the whitetail herd in Wisconsin and some other states.

Green's family moved to Green Bay when he was 5 years old, ending a long journey for both his parents. His father, a physician, was born in South Africa and grew up in Kenya. His mother, who trained as a nurse, is from England. They became U.S. citizens in 1995.

Green was a champion swimmer in college. After graduation, he went to law school and worked in the office of the state's attorney general. When he finished law school, Green and his wife, Susan, took teaching assignments in Kenya, as Green wanted to visit his father's former home. When they returned, he joined a law firm and became active in Green Bay GOP politics.

In 1992, he won the first of three two-year terms in the Assembly, where he chaired the Judiciary Committee and the Republican Caucus. He declined to run for Congress when longtime GOP Rep. Toby Roth retired in 1996. But he was fast out of the blocks two years later, when Republicans sought to prove that Democrat Jay Johnson's 1996 victory was a fluke in a district that had sent a Democrat to Washington just four times in the 20th century. By keeping pace with Johnson in fundraising and portraying the incumbent as too liberal for the district, Green won by 9 percentage points.

He has comfortably retained his seat since. In a territory made slightly more Republican by redistricting, he took 73 percent in 2002 against Andrew Becker, a Green Bay School Board member.

Green, who endorsed congressional term limits in his initial House campaign, has been mentioned by Wisconsin political observers as a potential statewide candidate — either for Senate in 2004 against Democrat Russell D. Feingold, or for governor in 2006.

KEY VOTES

2002

- No Overhaul campaign finance law; ban "soft money" and restrict advocacy advertising
- Yes Back Bush's defense budget increase
- Yes Extend 1996 welfare law
- Yes Adopt Bush's discretionary spending limit
- Yes Pass GOP Medicare prescription drug plan
- No Create independent Sept. 11 commission
- No Extend union protections to Homeland Security Department employees
- Yes Revive fast-track procedures for trade agreements
- Yes Authorize war against Iraq
- Yes Advance bankruptcy overhaul opposed by abortion opponents

2001

- Yes Nullify Clinton Labor Department ergonomics rule
- Yes Cut taxes by $1.35 trillion through fiscal 2011
- No Maintain ban on oil drilling in Arctic National Wildlife Refuge
- Yes Approve Bush proposal to limit managed-care plan liability for coverage decisions
- Yes Divert money from crop subsidy payments to land conservation
- Yes Expand law enforcement power to investigate suspected terrorists

CQ VOTE STUDIES

	PARTY UNITY		PRESIDENTIAL SUPPORT	
	Support	Oppose	Support	Oppose
2002	94%	6%	82%	18%
2001	94%	6%	91%	9%
2000	93%	7%	22%	78%
1999	90%	10%	21%	79%

INTEREST GROUPS

	AFL-CIO	ADA	CCUS	ACU
2002	11%	0%	95%	88%
2001	17%	0%	96%	88%
2000	10%	5%	85%	84%
1999	0%	5%	92%	87%

WISCONSIN 8

Northeast — Green Bay, Appleton

Each autumn Sunday, all eyes in Wisconsin turn to the 8th's center to watch football's Green Bay Packers. Regardless of the team's fortunes, the Packers represent the emotional heart of the state — and they draw international attention and pull in millions of dollars. But the district's blue-collar feel stems from the paper industry that stretches southwest from Green Bay along the Fox River Valley, an area with more paper mills than anywhere else in the world.

Much of the economy is stable and dependent on natural resources. The sparsely populated north contains the state's largest tracts of forests, supplying the local paper industry. More-fertile land in the southern part of the district supports grain and dairy farming, with some high-skill manufacturing in Green Bay and Appleton. The district is also home to six federally recognized Indian tribes — each of which boasts a reservation-based casino.

The area is famed for its natural beauty and draws large numbers of tourists from Milwaukee and Chicago during the more temperate seasons. Forests and lakes in Vilas County, near the Michigan border, lure outdoorsmen and nature lovers, while Door County, the peninsula jutting into Lake Michigan, attracts wealthier vacationers with upscale second homes, scenic apple orchards and a bustling art community.

The 8th leans slightly Republican. Though blue-collar throughout, the district is largely Catholic, anti-big government and socially conservative. It has been home to some far-right icons such as Joseph R. McCarthy and the John Birch Society in Appleton. Brown County, which includes Green Bay, tends to be politically competitive. Waupaca and Shawano counties, in the district's southwest corner, vote Republican. The GOP runs well in the less-populated northern counties of Vilas and Florence, while Democrats dominate in Menominee County, which is conterminous with an Indian reservation.

MAJOR INDUSTRY

Paper products, casinos, farming

CITIES

Green Bay, 102,313; Appleton (pt.) 69,270; De Pere, 20,559

NOTABLE

About 56,000 people are on the waiting list for Packers season tickets.

WYOMING

Gov. Dave Freudenthal (D)

First elected: 2002
Length of term: 4 years
Term expires: 1/07
Salary: $105,000
Phone: (307) 777-7434
Hometown: Thermopolis
Born: Oct. 12, 1950; Thermopolis, Wyo.
Religion: Episcopalian
Family: Wife, Nancy Freudenthal; four children
Education: Amherst College, B.A. 1973 (economics); U. of Wyoming, J.D. 1980
Career: Lawyer; gubernatorial aide; state economic development official
Political highlights: Wyo. State Planning Coordinator, 1975-77; U.S. attorney, 1994-2001
Election results:

2002 GENERAL		
Dave Freudenthal (D)	92,662	50.0%
Eli Bebout (R)	88,873	47.9%
Dave Dawson (LIBERT)	3,924	2.1%

Secretary of State Joe Meyer (R)

(no lieutenant governor)
First elected: 1998
Length of term: 4 years
Term expires: 1/07
Salary: $92,000
Phone: (307) 777-7378

STATE LEGISLATURE

General Assembly: Meets January-March in odd-numbered years; February-March in even-numbered years
House: 60 members, 2-year terms
2003 breakdown: 45R, 15D; 49 men, 11 women
Salary: $125/day in session
Phone: (307) 777-7852
Senate: 30 members, 4-year terms
2003 breakdown: 20R, 10D; 25 men, 5 women
Salary: $125/day in session
Phone: (307) 777-7711

STATE TERM LIMITS

Governor: 2 terms
Senate: 3 terms
House: 6 terms

URBAN STATISTICS

CITY	POPULATION
Cheyenne	53,011
Casper	49,644
Laramie	27,204
Gillette	19,646

REGISTERED VOTERS

Republican	62%
Democrat	27%
Other	11%

POPULATION

2002 population (est.)	498,703
2000 population	493,782
1990 population	453,588
Percent change (1990-2000)	+8.9%
Rank among states (2002)	50
Median age	36.2
Born in state	42.5%
Foreign born	2.3%
Violent crime rate	267/100,000
Poverty level	11.4%
Federal workers	7,186
Military	6,224

REDISTRICTING

Wyoming retained its one House seat in reapportionment.

MISCELLANEOUS

Web: www.state.wy.us
Capital: Cheyenne

STATE ELECTION OFFICIAL
(307) 777-7186

DEMOCRATIC HEADQUARTERS
(307) 473-1457

REPUBLICAN HEADQUARTERS
(307) 234-9166

District Statistics

DIST.	2000 VOTE FOR PRESIDENT BUSH	GORE	NADER	WHITE	BLACK	ASIAN	HISP	MEDIAN INCOME	WHITE COLLAR	BLUE COLLAR	SERVICE INDUSTRY	OVER 64	UNDER 18	COLLEGE EDUCATION	RURAL	SQ. MILES
AL	68%	28%	0%	89%	1%	1%	6%	$37,892	54%	29%	17%	12%	26%	22%	35%	97,100
STATE	68	28	0	89	1	1	6	$37,892	54	29	17	12	26	22	35	97,100
U.S.	47.9	48.4	3	69	12	4	13	$41,994	60	25	15	12	26	24	21	3,537,438

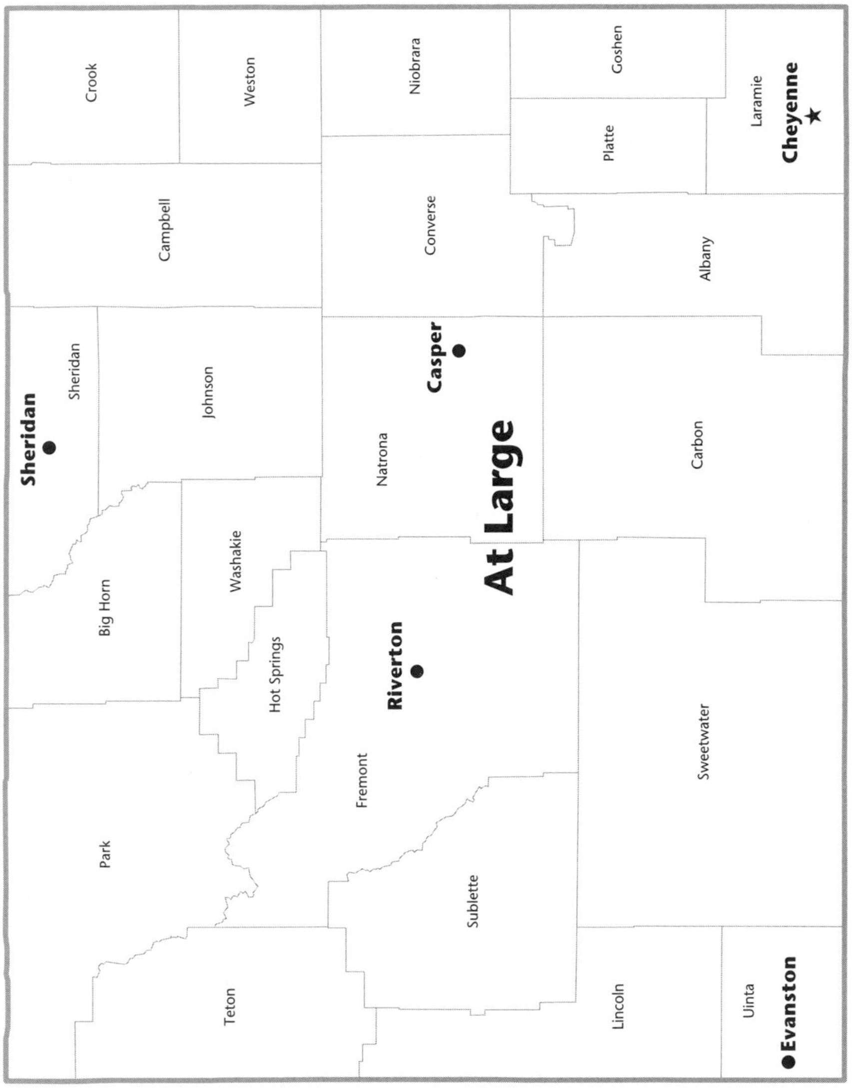

At Large
Crook
Weston
Niobrara
Goshen
Laramie
Cheyenne
Platte
Campbell
Converse
Albany
Sheridan
Sheridan
Johnson
Casper
Natrona
Carbon
Big Horn
Washakie
Hot Springs
Riverton
Fremont
Sweetwater
Park
Sublette
Teton
Lincoln
Uinta
Evanston

Sen. Craig Thomas (R)

CAPITOL OFFICE
224-6441
craig@thomas.senate.gov
thomas.senate.gov
109 Hart 20510-5003; fax 224-1724

COMMITTEES
Energy & Natural Resources
(National Parks - chairman)
Environment & Public Works
Finance
(International Trade - chairman)
Indian Affairs
Select Ethics

HOMETOWN
Casper

BORN
Feb. 17, 1933, Cody, Wyo.

RELIGION
Methodist

FAMILY
Wife, Susan Thomas; four children

EDUCATION
U. of Wyoming, B.A. 1955; La Salle U., LL.B. 1963

MILITARY SERVICE
Marine Corps, 1955-59

CAREER
Power company executive

POLITICAL HIGHLIGHTS
Sought Republican nomination for Wyo. treasurer, 1978, 1982; Wyo. House, 1985-89; U.S. House, 1989-95

ELECTION RESULTS

2000 GENERAL

Craig Thomas (R)	157,622	73.8%
Mel Logan (D)	47,087	22.0%
Margaret Dawson (LIBERT)	8,950	4.2%

2000 PRIMARY

Craig Thomas (R)	unopposed

PREVIOUS WINNING PERCENTAGES
1994 (59%); 1992 House Election (58%); 1990 House Election (55%); 1989 Special House Election (52%)

Elected 1994; 2nd term

Raised on a ranch near Wapiti, just outside Yellowstone Park, Thomas is in many ways a typical Westerner. Affable and laid back, he enjoys nothing more than a horseback ride through the expansive wilderness of his home state, and he goes to great lengths to preserve hunting and fishing grounds.

While Thomas approaches politics with courtesy and diplomacy, he is no pushover. The former Marine Corps captain is a loyal foot soldier for the Senate GOP, keeping other party members in line from his position as a deputy whip and manning what he has termed the "front line" in Republican floor efforts to stymie Democratic plans.

Thomas also is a tireless advocate for the energy, agriculture and private land interests of Wyoming, which is about 50 percent federally owned. The subjects are something Thomas knows a bit about — he was vice president of the Wyoming Farm Bureau and he headed the state's rural electric association before he came to Congress.

Wyoming is one of the most Republican states, supporting President Bush by 41 percentage points over Al Gore in 2000, so Thomas' party and his constituency rarely clash. When they do, Thomas sides with Wyoming.

In the 107th Congress, that meant joining Democrats and other farm-state Republicans in an effort to prevent the nation's increasingly powerful meatpackers from owning and feeding livestock. Thomas was one of 13 Republicans who successfully fought GOP leaders' efforts to kill the proposed ban during debate on the 2002 farm bill.

It also meant questioning the Bush administration's budget for the national parks. At a congressional hearing, Thomas said that Bush's plan to cut some Interior Department programs to pay for park maintenance was "robbing Peter to pay Paul. . . . There's no new money."

And, perhaps most surprisingly, it meant proposing a ban on tour flights over most national parks. Thomas said that helicopter tours would cause too much disruption in Wyoming's Yellowstone and Grand Teton national parks. His proposal won support from the same "green" groups that are used to opposing him. "It's kind of scary," Thomas mused. "I bet they are asking themselves, 'What the hell are we doing?' " Thomas' position was unexpected given his staunch opposition to a Clinton administration ban on snowmobiles in national parks.

Thomas returned to the Environment and Public Works Committee in the 108th, after a two-year hitch on Agriculture, just in time to influence the panel's work to authorize federal highway programs. The panel also has jurisdiction over wildlife refuges and the Clean Water, Clean Air and Endangered Species acts. His appointment was not greeted with enthusiasm by environmentalists, who noted that the League of Conservation Voters had given him a score of 0 for his 2002 votes.

Perhaps Thomas' most notable tiff with environmentalists came in the 104th Congress, when he took the lead on a high-profile measure that would have allowed 12 Western states to take control of 270 million acres of federal land, including wilderness areas that are among the nation's few remaining pristine ecosystems. Thomas said the states could do a better job overseeing the lands than the federal Bureau of Land Management. But the proposal earned a lot of press attention at a time when Republicans were under pressure to prove they cared about protecting the environment. Thomas reluctantly delayed the bill, saying, "This is a concept, a fundamental change that should be talked about in the next few years."

Thomas is a strong advocate of Bush's plan to allow oil drilling in Alaska's Arctic National Wildlife Refuge. And he has proposed revisions to the Endangered Species Act to make it more difficult to get a species included on the list. But Thomas says that he supports multiple uses for lands, including protection of the environment as well as energy and mineral development.

On most topics, Thomas generally sides with the more conservative wing of his party. His allegiance to the party was perhaps most evident in 2002 in his opposition to the farm bill. Despite breaking with party leaders over the meatpacking amendment, Thomas was never considered a vote in play on the farm bill, even though he acknowledged it would help some in his rural state.

He and his state's junior senator, Republican Michael B. Enzi, see eye-to-eye most of the time; in 2002, they agreed 96 percent of the time, making them the pair of senators most in accord.

Thomas' seniority and party loyalty won him a seat on the Finance Committee in 2001 after Sen. James M. Jeffords of Vermont became an independent, thereby freeing up a GOP seat on the panel. From his Finance post, Thomas not only has a hand in tax and trade legislation but also in crafting health care policy, one of his top priorities.

Like many other senators from rural states, Thomas is acutely aware that many of his constituents lack even the most basic medical options. Thomas, who shares the chairmanship of the Senate Rural Health Caucus with Iowa Democrat Tom Harkin, has pressed for legislation that would increase physician recruitment incentives, equalize Medicare payments between rural and urban programs, and help fund "telemedicine" programs.

In the 107th, Thomas had to withstand some sideways glances when he pushed for federal funding to expand the Jackson Hole airport. Although Thomas insisted that the frequent visits of Vice President Dick Cheney, a Wyoming native, had little to do with the need for new facilities, Air Force Two was not capable of landing on one of the old airstrips.

Following in the footsteps of Cheney and strong-willed Wyoming senators Malcolm Wallop and Alan K. Simpson, Thomas' early career was frequently overshadowed. His election performances did not do much to move him from the shadows. He twice sought the GOP nomination for state treasurer, losing both times.

But in 1984, at age 51, he was elected to the Wyoming House, where he was serving four years later when Cheney, then House GOP whip, was nominated to be secretary of defense. Thomas got the nod from the party's state central committee and won the special election to succeed Cheney, with 52 percent.

One of the safest places for a Republican senator is Wyoming, where Democrats have not won a Senate election since 1970. Thomas' 1994 campaign to succeed the retiring Wallop banked on the idea that Wyoming voters would want another senator just as ready and willing to fight the Democratic Clinton administration as Wallop was.

As it turned out, Thomas had read the tea leaves and the voters' mood pretty well. The Democrats nominated popular Gov. Mike Sullivan, but it made no difference. While Sullivan was hardly a liberal, he had a link to President Clinton that dated from their service together in the National Governors Association, and he was the first sitting governor to endorse Clinton for the presidency. Thomas won handily by almost 20 percentage points.

In 2000, he did even better, swamping his Democratic foe, coal miner and Lyndon LaRouche follower, Mel Logan, by a better than 3-to-1 ratio.

KEY VOTES

2002

- No Pass farm bill reversing crop subsidy limits
- Yes Postpone tougher automobile fuel efficiency standards
- No Overhaul campaign finance law; ban "soft money" and restrict advocacy advertising
- Yes Set federal election standards
- Yes Support oil drilling in Arctic National Wildlife Refuge
- Yes Revive fast-track procedures for trade agreements
- No Create federal insurance coverage for catastrophic terrorist losses
- Yes Tighten federal accounting and corporate governance regulation
- No Advance bipartisan Medicare prescription drug plan
- No Create independent Sept. 11 commission
- No Back Democratic Homeland Security Department proposal
- Yes Authorize war against Iraq

2001

- Yes Confirm John Ashcroft as attorney general
- Yes Nullify Clinton Labor Department ergonomics rule
- Yes Cut taxes by $1.35 trillion through fiscal 2011
- No Pass Democratic bill to bolster rights of patients in managed-care plans
- No Permit a new round of military base closings
- Yes Expand law enforcement power to investigate suspected terrorists

CQ VOTE STUDIES

	PARTY UNITY		PRESIDENTIAL SUPPORT	
	Support	Oppose	Support	Oppose
2002	96%	4%	94%	6%
2001	97%	3%	97%	3%
2000	97%	3%	40%	60%
1999	96%	4%	31%	69%
1998	95%	5%	39%	61%
1997	98%	2%	57%	43%
1996	98%	2%	29%	71%
1995	96%	4%	22%	78%
House Service:				
1994	92%	8%	42%	58%
1993	93%	7%	33%	67%

INTEREST GROUPS

	AFL-CIO	ADA	CCUS	ACU
2002	15%	10%	90%	100%
2001	13%	5%	100%	96%
2000	0%	0%	92%	92%
1999	0%	0%	100%	87%
1998	13%	5%	89%	84%
1997	0%	10%	90%	84%
1996	0%	5%	92%	100%
1995	0%	5%	100%	83%
House Service:				
1994	0%	5%	100%	89%
1993	17%	10%	91%	87%

Sen. Michael B. Enzi (R)

CAPITOL OFFICE
224-3424
senator@enzi.senate.gov
enzi.senate.gov
379A Russell 20510-5004; fax 228-0359

COMMITTEES
Banking, Housing & Urban Affairs
(Securities & Investment - chairman)
Budget
Foreign Relations
Health, Education, Labor & Pensions
(Employment, Safety & Training - chairman)
Small Business & Entrepreneurship
Special Aging

HOMETOWN
Gillette

BORN
Feb. 1, 1944, Bremerton, Wash.

RELIGION
Presbyterian

FAMILY
Wife, Diana Enzi; three children

EDUCATION
George Washington U., B.A. 1966 (accounting); U. of Denver, M.S. 1968 (retail marketing)

MILITARY SERVICE
Wyo. Air National Guard, 1967-73

CAREER
Accountant; computer programmer; shoe store owner

POLITICAL HIGHLIGHTS
Mayor of Gillette, 1975-83; Wyo. House, 1987-91; Wyo. Senate, 1991-96

ELECTION RESULTS

2002 GENERAL		
Michael B. Enzi (R)	133,710	73.0%
Joyce Jansa Corcoran (D)	49,570	27.1%
2002 PRIMARY		
Michael B. Enzi (R)	78,612	85.9%
Crosby "Cros" Allen (R)	12,931	14.1%

PREVIOUS WINNING PERCENTAGES
1996 (54%)

Elected 1996; 2nd term

Leveraging a credential that rarely accrues to his benefit — he is the Senate's only accountant — Enzi played a pivotal role in shaping one of the landmark laws of 107th Congress, imposing new federal standards for accounting and corporate governance upon companies that sell stock.

It was a rare moment of prominence at the end of his first term in the Senate, where Enzi (EN-zee) is known as a deliberate and self-effacing voice against expansion of the federal government's reach. And his input into the accounting debate was true to type.

At a point when the legislation seemed stuck at a partisan impasse, Enzi worked undetected by lobbyists' radar to strike a deal with Chairman Paul S. Sarbanes, D-Md., that won the votes of most of Enzi's fellow Republicans on the Banking Committee. The key concession he obtained then — limiting the new accounting regulations to those who audit publicly traded companies — remained, even as the pressure built for an aggressive package in light of a wave of corporate accounting scandals.

In the 108th, Enzi returned to the chairmanship of Banking's Securities and Investment Subcommittee, which he held at the outset of the 107th. He also added a seat on the Budget Committee.

Whether it be on workplace rules for businesses or government limits on the export of high-technology items, Enzi's opposition to government regulation is in keeping with the views of many Westerners — who view Washington more than anything as a hotbed of unwarranted intrusion into their ability to pursue a livelihood.

Enzi particularly opposes regulations that affect public lands, water supply, resource development, and Wyoming's miners and ranchers, although he argued in 2002 that ranchers were in need of generous government help in the form of drought aid.

He opposed the ergonomics regulations imposed in the final days of the Clinton administration and helped to orchestrate the congressional move to repeal them at the outset of the Bush administration. He applauded moves by the Bush White House to develop voluntary guidelines for businesses. He says he first became interested in workplace health and safety regulations when he taught safety courses and collected urine and saliva samples from workers at an oil well-servicing firm, where he was also the accountant and computer programmer.

Enzi says that other lawmakers often have no notion of the problems faced by a small business. While some in Congress refer to companies with 100 to 500 workers as small businesses, he says, "to me, a small business is when the person who writes the checks, also sweeps the front walk, cleans the toilets and waits on the customers." Once, faced with a proposal by the Clinton administration to protect mine workers from noise, Enzi commented, "I seriously question whether those who wrote this rule have ever actually been to a mine."

Enzi also has weighed in on other government regulatory issues, including the Endangered Species Act. He offered a bill to require the federal government to pay all costs relating to implementation of the law. He also introduced legislation to extend Daylight Saving Time for one week in the fall to make Halloween trick-or-treating safer. Enzi has twice introduced this bill at the request of a second-grade teacher and her class in Sheridan. He is following in the tradition established by his predecessor, Republican Alan K. Simpson, who also tried several times to pass the bill.

Since the 106th Congress, Enzi has been a champion of efforts to lessen regulations governing the export of technologies with both military and civilian applications — rules that, in his view, have the effect of blocking U.S. trade in products that are widely available commercially. His bills passed the Senate in 2000 and 2001, but there was never any consensus behind a companion measure in the House.

As a former computer programmer, Enzi understands high technology. He created a stir in his first year in office by announcing his intention to bring his laptop computer onto the Senate floor, where there is a ban on mechanical devices that might prove distracting. The Rules Committee voted to keep computers out of the chamber. In the 108th, Enzi was trying again, pointing out that laptops have become much smaller since 1997 and arguing that portable computers proved essential when the 2001 anthrax mailings kept many lawmakers out of their offices for extended periods.

In the 107th, Enzi also tried unsuccessfully to convince his colleagues to permit states to tax sales made over the Internet, to eliminate Internet vendors' big advantage over retailers in stores, who pay taxes locally.

Enzi generally favors liberalized foreign trade, including agricultural trade with Cuba and expanded ties with China, which could help the farmers and ranchers in his state. In the 107th, he urged the decidedly low-tech export of live sheep to Afghanistan — touting the benefit both to the people of a country raked by the U.S. military and to Western ranchers.

In many respects, Enzi is a man of traditional values. He earned the rank of Eagle Scout, taught Sunday school for 10 years, coached youth soccer and served on his hometown bank's board of directors. He favors congressional initiatives to move power from Washington to the states, increase the role of religion in public schools and promote traditional values through the tax code.

Enzi's father worked in the naval shipyards of Washington State during World War II and moved the family to Wyoming soon after Enzi's birth. Enzi went to college in Washington, D.C., where he initially thought of becoming a diplomat but later switched to accounting. Shortly after he joined the Foreign Relations Committee in 2001, he told his colleagues on the panel, "I quickly discovered I didn't like big cities, and figured out I probably wouldn't like big cities in foreign countries."

He remains close to his roommate from those days, Edward W. "Skip" Gnehm Jr., now ambassador to Jordan, whom he describes as "the closest thing I have to a brother." In the 107th, more than one-third of a century after he gave up the notion of joining the foreign service, he met with Russian legislators to discuss joint efforts against terrorism.

After earning a master's in marketing from the University of Denver, Enzi returned to Wyoming; in addition to his work at the oil well-servicing company, he ran the family shoe-store business (NZ Shoes) with his wife.

Enzi began his political climb in 1974 at age 30, winning the mayoralty of Gillette. During a pair of four-year terms, he was credited with guiding the city through a population explosion. In 1986, he won a seat in the state House; in 1991, he moved up to the state Senate, where he served as chairman of the Revenue Committee.

When he launched his 1996 Senate campaign to replace Simpson, who retired after 18 years, Enzi appeared to face long odds against several high-profile Republican opponents. But by building a network of supporters drawn in part from the Wyoming Christian Coalition and stressing his opposition to abortion, he narrowly won the GOP primary. He took the general election by 12 percentage points over Kathy Karpan, a former two-term Wyoming secretary of state. In 2002, he won 73 percent of the vote over Democrat Joyce Jansa Corcoran, the former mayor of Lander.

KEY VOTES

2002

No Pass farm bill reversing crop subsidy limits
Yes Postpone tougher automobile fuel efficiency standards
No Overhaul campaign finance law; ban "soft money" and restrict advocacy advertising
Yes Set federal election standards
Yes Support oil drilling in Arctic National Wildlife Refuge
Yes Revive fast-track procedures for trade agreements
No Create federal insurance coverage for catastrophic terrorist losses
Yes Tighten federal accounting and corporate governance regulation
No Advance bipartisan Medicare prescription drug plan
Yes Create independent Sept. 11 commission
No Back Democratic Homeland Security Department proposal
Yes Authorize war against Iraq

2001

Yes Confirm John Ashcroft as attorney general
Yes Nullify Clinton Labor Department ergonomics rule
Cut taxes by $1.35 trillion through fiscal 2011
No Pass Democratic bill to bolster rights of patients in managed-care plans
Yes Permit a new round of military base closings
Yes Expand law enforcement power to investigate suspected terrorists

CQ VOTE STUDIES

	PARTY UNITY		PRESIDENTIAL SUPPORT	
	Support	Oppose	Support	Oppose
2002	95%	5%	93%	7%
2001	95%	5%	99%	1%
2000	97%	3%	35%	65%
1999	95%	5%	24%	76%
1998	96%	4%	31%	69%
1997	98%	2%	51%	49%

INTEREST GROUPS

	AFL-CIO	ADA	CCUS	ACU
2002	17%	10%	89%	100%
2001	20%	10%	100%	92%
2000	0%	0%	100%	92%
1999	0%	0%	94%	92%
1998	0%	0%	94%	92%
1997	14%	10%	70%	88%

Rep. Barbara Cubin (R)

CAPITOL OFFICE
225-2311
barbara.cubin@mail.house.gov
www.house.gov/cubin
1114 Longworth 20515-5001; fax 225-3057

COMMITTEES
Energy & Commerce
Resources
(Energy & Mineral Resources - chairwoman)

HOMETOWN
Casper

BORN
Nov. 30, 1946, Salinas, Calif.

RELIGION
Episcopalian

FAMILY
Husband, Frederick William Cubin III; two children

EDUCATION
Creighton U., B.S. 1969 (chemistry); Casper College, attended 1993 (business administration)

CAREER
Medical office manager; realtor; chemist

POLITICAL HIGHLIGHTS
Wyo. House, 1987-93; Wyo. Senate, 1993-95

ELECTION RESULTS

2002 GENERAL		
Barbara Cubin (R)	110,229	60.5%
Ron Akin (D)	65,961	36.2%
Lewis Stock (LIBERT)	5,962	3.3%
2002 PRIMARY		
Barbara Cubin (R)		unopposed
2000 GENERAL		
Barbara Cubin (R)	141,848	66.8%
Michael Allen Green (D)	60,638	28.6%
Lewis Stock (LIBERT)	6,411	3.0%
Victor Raymond (NL)	3,415	1.6%

PREVIOUS WINNING PERCENTAGES
1998 (58%); 1996 (55%); 1994 (53%)

Elected 1994; 5th term

Cubin served as the Republican Conference secretary in the 107th Congress, but she abandoned a bid to move up to vice chairman in the 108th so she could spend more time with her seriously ill husband. But even though she has stepped off the leadership ladder, Cubin remains in position to press her chief legislative goals: domestic energy production and protection of private property rights.

About half of Wyoming's 97,000 square miles are under the federal government's jurisdiction, an important factor in a state whose economy relies heavily on ranching, mining and oil and gas extraction. Cubin (CUE-bin), a descendant of 19th century homesteaders, is convinced that many Easterners do not understand the problems of those who live in the Cowboy State. She regularly battles conservation groups bent on protecting large tracts of land from development — efforts she sees as a potential threat to the livelihood of her constituents.

"Our lands are currently being locked away from public use . . . at an alarming pace," she said in challenging a bill in the 106th Congress that would have provided billions of dollars for land purchases. "The last thing we need in Wyoming is more federal land when the government can't adequately manage the property it has now."

In 2002, she was chosen a "champion" of property rights by the League of Private Property Voters. The League of Conservation Voters gave her a 5 percent rating on environmental issues for the 107th Congress.

Cubin was sufficiently concerned about how the West is treated in Congress that she launched a long-shot bid for the chairmanship of the Resources Committee at the start of the 108th Congress, upon the retirement of Utah's James V. Hansen. Richard W. Pombo of California, a like-minded conservative, won the gavel. But Cubin did manage to secure a waiver from the Republican Steering Committee to remain chairman of the Subcommittee on Energy and Mineral Resources for one term beyond the six-year limit under GOP rules.

Energy development is vital to Wyoming's economy, which makes Cubin's membership on both the Resources and Energy and Commerce committees that much more valuable. A founder of the Congressional Mining Caucus, she has made it a priority to promote two of Wyoming's resource-based industries — the mining of coal and trona, a type of soda ash used in glassware, detergent and baking soda.

Without a place inside the leadership circle in the 108th, Cubin will focus on reviving energy policy legislation that died at the end of the 107th. As before, she will work along the lines of what President Bush wants: to increase the domestic supply of energy and decrease dependency on foreign oil. That includes support for opening Alaska's Arctic National Wildlife Refuge to oil and gas drilling.

Although she is a reliably conservative Republican on most issues, Cubin — like other Westerners — sometimes splits from anti-spending colleagues in her party when the interests of her water-starved, rural state are involved. In 2002, Cubin introduced legislation to provide billions of dollars in emergency drought relief to farmers and ranchers. Congress ultimately put a less generous package in the wrapup spending law enacted early in 2003.

Cubin works with her state's senators, fellow Republicans Craig Thomas and Michael B. Enzi, to increase Wyoming's access to amenities that many Americans take for granted. In the 107th Congress, she asked the

Transportation Department to subsidize air service to the state. She also introduced bills to ease regulations on wireless telecommunications companies operating in rural areas and increase Medicare compensation to rural doctors. And in 2003, Cubin was pushing a bill to require Congress to fully fund the Payments in Lieu of Taxes program, which is intended to compensate counties for federal lands on which local property taxes may not be assessed.

In a 1999 House floor speech, outlining why she is a Republican, Cubin said that the GOP was best at translating the ideals of personal responsibility and individual freedom. "It is time to restore the American precept that each individual is accountable for his actions," she said. Speaking just weeks after the deadly mass shooting of students at Colorado's Columbine High School, Cubin — an ardent gun rights advocate who served three years on the board of the National Rifle Association — said, "As a wife, a woman, a mother of two sons, I believe that only a return to values and personal responsibility will end this sort of violence."

Cubin sought in 1999 to focus attention on a concern of women by taking a lead role in the distribution of cellular telephones to domestic violence prevention groups, in hopes of enhancing the security of victims and potential victims of domestic violence.

Reared in Casper, Cubin earned a degree in chemistry and worked as a teacher, social worker, chemist and real estate agent. She also served as manager of her husband's medical practice. She was active in local party politics and various civic groups, including the Wyoming State Choir, the PTA, a suicide prevention organization and a homeless shelter.

Over the years, her community activities led her to enter elective politics. Cubin served six years in the Wyoming House and two years in the state Senate, specializing in energy-related matters.

Her opening to Congress came in 1994, when Thomas left open the state's one House seat to run for the Senate. Cubin, drawing on her base in Casper and benefiting from the fact that she was the only woman in the race, prevailed in a five-way primary and went on to defeat Democratic lawyer Bob Schuster by 12 percentage points in November. She has won re-election by good margins in recent years, though not without some challenges.

Cubin missed 27 percent of all the roll call votes in the House in the 107th — more than any House member who returned for the 108th — after her husband, Frederick "Fritz" Cubin, was hospitalized several times for non-malignant tumors, pancreatic problems and surgical complications.

KEY VOTES

2002

? Overhaul campaign finance law; ban "soft money" and restrict advocacy advertising
Yes Back Bush's defense budget increase
Yes Extend 1996 welfare law
Yes Adopt Bush's discretionary spending limit
Yes Pass GOP Medicare prescription drug plan
No Create independent Sept. 11 commission
No Extend union protections to Homeland Security Department employees
Yes Revive fast-track procedures for trade agreements
Yes Authorize war against Iraq
No Advance bankruptcy overhaul opposed by abortion opponents

2001

Yes Nullify Clinton Labor Department ergonomics rule
? Cut taxes by $1.35 trillion through fiscal 2011
No Maintain ban on oil drilling in Arctic National Wildlife Refuge
Yes Approve Bush proposal to limit managed-care plan liability for coverage decisions
No Divert money from crop subsidy payments to land conservation
? Expand law enforcement power to investigate suspected terrorists

CQ VOTE STUDIES

	PARTY UNITY		PRESIDENTIAL SUPPORT	
	Support	Oppose	Support	Oppose
2002	97%	3%	85%	15%
2001	98%	2%	89%	11%
2000	97%	3%	24%	76%
1999	94%	6%	18%	82%
1998	96%	4%	21%	79%

INTEREST GROUPS

	AFL-CIO	ADA	CCUS	ACU
2002	0%	0%	88%	100%
2001	0%	5%	93%	100%
2000	10%	5%	80%	100%
1999	22%	5%	91%	88%
1998	0%	5%	94%	100%

WYOMING

At large

Wyoming, the least populated state, basks in its wide open spaces, which define its libertarian politics and natural resource-based economy. Yellowstone National Park is one of the most visited parks in the nation, and tourism is an essential part of Wyoming's economy. The jagged peaks of the Grand Tetons rise more than 5,000 feet from the Jackson Hole Valley floor to their 13,000-foot apex, less than 10 miles from the nation's steepest ski slopes at Jackson Hole Mountain.

The state also relies on mining and commodities sales, so booms and busts coincide with market prices for those goods. After several years of budget shortfalls, the state has experienced surpluses due to rising prices of oil and natural gas, and increased coal bed methane mining. Still, the increased income from natural resources did not equal the income from sales and use taxes and investing activities.

Many of the state's oil and gas jobs are temporary, which contributed to the state's fluctuating population in the 1980s and 1990s — a decline in the 1980s was followed by 9 percent growth in the next decade. Many skilled workers have left the state for better-paying jobs, and college graduates often leave for lack of employment.

Wyoming has not elected a Democrat to Congress since 1976. Residents savor their land and resources and abhor government intrusion of any kind, especially in dictating how land may be used. In most regions, residents are happy with the state's relative seclusion and tranquil lifestyle and are not particularly warm to population growth. The state's lawmakers are loath to raise taxes and dare not entertain a dreaded income tax. Wyoming has no corporate or personal income taxes and has a statewide 4 percent sales tax.

MAJOR INDUSTRY
Mining, tourism, agriculture

MILITARY BASES
Francis E. Warren Air Force Base, 3,514 military, 937 civilian (2001)

CITIES
Cheyenne, 53,011; Casper, 49,644; Laramie, 27,204; Gillette, 19,646

NOTABLE
Yellowstone became the first national park in 1872; Jackson was the first U.S. town ever to elect an all-female slate — mayor, council and marshal — in 1920; Wyoming has more cars per capita than any other state, 1.17.

Del. Eni F.H. Faleomavaega (D)

Elected 1988; 8th term

The longest-serving of the five delegates, Faleomavaega has climbed the seniority ladder on the Resources and International Relations committees — both useful assignments for the eight-term delegate. He has been the top Democrat on a different Resources or International Relations subcommittee in each Congress since the 104th.

His primary focus on Capitol Hill has been to improve American Samoa's economy, which is dominated by tuna fishing and tuna processing. The territory is concerned about competition from South American tuna fleets, and Faleomavaega (FOL-ee-oh-mav-ah-ENG-uh) has fought to exempt tuna from Andean trade pacts. He advocates requiring tuna fishermen to use dolphin-safe techniques, citing the reverence with which Polynesians regard dolphins. He also recalls his own experiences with dolphins during a lengthy 1987 sea voyage on the historic Polynesian sailing canoe, Hokule'a.

Despite the need to attract other industries, Faleomavaega was instrumental in calling attention to working conditions at a Vietnamese-owned garment factory, which eventually was closed. He was arrested in 1995 as he protested French nuclear testing in the South Pacific.

Faleomavaega went to high school in Hawaii when his father was stationed there in the Navy. Though his parents had little formal schooling — neither graduated from high school — they encouraged their children to pursue an education. He earned a bachelor's from Brigham Young University, joined the Army and served in Vietnam, then returned to the mainland for law school.

He worked for eight years in Washington, first as an executive assistant to American Samoa's first elected representative to the Capitol, A.U. Fuimaono, then for California Democratic Rep. Phillip Burton, the Interior Committee chairman, whom he credits for much of his success.

Faleomavaega is a "matai" — a Samoan chief — a title he has held since 1988. Faleomavaega is actually his title; his family name is Hunkin. Faleomavaega returned to Pago Pago in 1981, first as a deputy attorney general and then as lieutenant governor. Since his initial election as a House delegate in 1988 he has had a series of tough re-election battles.

CAPITOL OFFICE
225-8577
faleomavaega@mail.house.gov
www.house.gov/faleomavaega
2422 Rayburn 20515-5201; fax 225-8757

COMMITTEES
International Relations
Resources
Small Business

HOMETOWN
Pago Pago

BORN
Aug. 15, 1943, Vailoatai, Am. Samoa

RELIGION
Mormon

FAMILY
Wife, Hinanui Bambridge Hunkin; five children

EDUCATION
Brigham Young U., A.A. 1964, B.A. 1966 (political science); Texas Southern U., attended 1969 (law); U. of Houston, J.D. 1972; U. of California, Berkeley, LL.M. 1973

MILITARY SERVICE
Army, 1966-69; Army Reserve, 1983-2001

CAREER
Lawyer; territorial prosecutor; congressional aide

POLITICAL HIGHLIGHTS
Democratic candidate for U.S. House, 1984; lieutenant governor, 1985-89

ELECTION RESULTS

2002 GENERAL RUNOFF		
Eni F.H. Faleomavaega (D)	4,959	54.8%
Fagafaga D. Langkilde (I)	4,083	45.2%
2002 GENERAL		
Eni F.H. Faleomavaega (D)	4,294	41.3%
Fagafaga D. Langkilde (I)	3,332	32.1%
Aumua Amata Coleman (R)	2,767	26.6%
2000 GENERAL RUNOFF		
Eni F.H. Faleomavaega (D)	5,500	61.1%
Gus Hannemann (I)	3,505	38.9%

PREVIOUS WINNING PERCENTAGES
1998 (87%); 1996 (57%); 1994 (64%); 1992 (65%); 1990 (55%); 1988 (51%)

AMERICAN SAMOA

The least populated entity represented in the House, and the only one south of the equator, American Samoa is composed of five volcanic islands and two outlying coral atolls (total land area, 76 square miles, slightly more than the District of Columbia) in the south Pacific, about 2,300 miles southwest of Hawaii.

An 1899 treaty gave the United States control over the islands, in the eastern portion of the Samoan archipelago. During World War II, the deep-water harbor at Pago Pago attracted the U.S. Marine Corps, which made the island an advanced training and staging center.

American Samoa is an unincorporated territory of the United States, administered by the Interior Department. Residents are U.S. nationals, not citizens. The territory has had a non-voting delegate since 1981.

Most of the land is communally owned. Per capita income in 2000 was $4,357, and federal aid, including welfare and food stamps, is vital. Economic development, including tourism, is hindered by American Samoa's remote location.

Tuna fishing and tuna-processing plants are the key elements of the private-sector economy, but the islands' tuna processing now is threatened by lower-wage competition from South America. In recent years, there has been a concerted government effort to cope with the islands' limited resources of fresh water.

MAJOR INDUSTRY
Tuna processing, government, handicrafts, tourism

VILLAGES
Tafuna, 8,409; Nu'uuli, 5,154; Pago Pago, 4,278

NOTABLE
Anthropologist Margaret Mead lived and studied on the island of Ta'u; Her findings are in her book, "Coming of Age in Samoa."

Del. Eleanor Holmes Norton (D)

Elected 1990; 7th term

A native Washingtonian, Norton graduated in the last segregated class at Dunbar High School and has spent her life fighting for equal rights. That quest continues in the House, where she wages an uphill battle to give residents of the nation's capital the same political power that is granted every other American in the 50 states.

Her hard work, political skills and straightforward manner have helped Norton make the best of difficult situations, notably in the mid-1990s, when Congress took control of the city's finances. She is well-regarded by many key Republicans, and she has softened some Capitol Hill attitudes toward the city, which has suffered a series of financial and managerial crises.

After more than a decade in the House, Norton would like to hope that she could leave a legacy of statehood for the District of Columbia, but as long as Congress is Republican-controlled, that is unlikely. She is a top Democrat on the Government Reform panel, which has chief jurisdiction over matters involving the district. She works hard to restrain congressional meddling in the city's affairs, which often comes in the form of legislative mandates or prohibitions added to the annual D.C. appropriations bill.

Norton wants to give the District authority to spend locally raised money and to pass city ordinances without congressional review. She was able to win enactment of a law under which D.C. residents may pay in-state tuition at any public university. As security around federal buildings and tourist sites has increased and streets have been closed, Norton has pleaded with federal officials to consider the effect of such actions on traffic and tourism.

Norton's father was a city employee, and her mother was a teacher. After earning a law degree at Yale and working in Mississippi with civil rights groups, she took a job with the American Civil Liberties Union. She ran New York City's Civil Rights Commission in the early 1970s and was chairman of the Equal Employment Opportunity Commission in the Carter administration. She was teaching law at Georgetown University in 1990 when D.C. Delegate Walter E. Fauntroy stepped down to run for mayor. She has typically taken nine out of 10 votes in her general-election victories.

CAPITOL OFFICE
225-8050
www.house.gov/norton
2136 Rayburn 20515-5101; fax 225-3002

COMMITTEES
Government Reform
Transportation & Infrastructure
Select Homeland Security

HOMETOWN
Washington

BORN
June 13, 1937, Washington, D.C.

RELIGION
Episcopalian

FAMILY
Divorced; two children

EDUCATION
Antioch College, B.A. 1960 (history); Yale U., M.A. 1963 (American studies), LL.B. 1964

CAREER
Professor; lawyer

POLITICAL HIGHLIGHTS
New York City Human Rights Commission, 1971-77; Equal Employment Opportunity Commission chairwoman, 1977-81

ELECTION RESULTS

2002 GENERAL		
Eleanor Holmes Norton (D)	119,268	93.0%
Pat Kidd (I)	7,733	6.0%
2002 PRIMARY		
Eleanor Holmes Norton (D)	90,307	98.3%
write-ins (D)	1,590	1.7%
2000 GENERAL		
Eleanor Holmes Norton (D)	158,824	90.4%
Edward Wolterbeek (R)	10,258	5.8%
Robert D. Kampia (LIBERT)	4,594	2.6%

PREVIOUS WINNING PERCENTAGES
1998 (90%); 1996 (90%); 1994 (89%); 1992 (85%); 1990 (62%)

DISTRICT OF COLUMBIA

Residents of the capital city of the world's leading democracy like to point out, often angrily, that they cannot fully participate in democracy themselves: They have no vote in Congress, and the city's budget and laws are subject to review and veto by Congress.

The slogan on the District's license plates sums this up succinctly: "Taxation Without Representation." Efforts to gain full participation in the U.S. government, including bids for statehood, have never come close to success. The 23rd Amendment gave residents a vote for president starting in 1964, and the city elected its first non-voting delegate to the House in 1971 and chose its first elected mayor in 1974.

As the nation's capital, it is no surprise that government is the city's main business. Hundreds of thousands work for the federal and local governments, and thousands of private-sector workers — lobbyists, lawyers, trade association employees, and journalists — have jobs related to government work.

The District has one of the wealthier and most-educated populations in the nation. Per capita income in 1999 was about 33 percent higher than the national average. But the income-earners are not spread evenly throughout the city, and the wealthiest areas are in the northwest quadrant.

The city's population peaked in 1950 at more than 800,000 and has been dropping since then, although the decline slowed in the late 1990s. The 2000 census pegged the population at less than 600,000.

MAJOR INDUSTRY
Government, professional services

MILITARY BASES
Walter Reed Army Medical Center, 2,495 military, 2,914 civilian; Bolling Air Force Base, 1,680 military, 705 civilian; Fort McNair (Army), 459 military, 817 civilian (2001)

NOTABLE
Since residents began casting votes for president in 1964, the Republican candidate's share has ranged from a high of 22 percent in 1972 to 9 percent in 2000.

Del. Madeleine Z. Bordallo (D)

CAPITOL OFFICE
225-1188
madeleine.bordallo@mail.house.gov
www.house.gov/bordallo
427 Cannon 20515-5301; fax 226-0341

COMMITTEES
Armed Services
Resources
Small Business

HOMETOWN
Tumuning

BORN
May 31, 1933, Graceville, Minn.

RELIGION
Roman Catholic

FAMILY
Widowed; one child

EDUCATION
The College of St. Catherine, A.A. 1953 (music & voice)

CAREER
Guam first lady; shoe company founder; radio show host

POLITICAL HIGHLIGHTS
Guam Senate, 1981-83, 1987-95; Democratic nominee for governor, 1990; lieutenant governor, 1995-2003

ELECTION RESULTS

2002 GENERAL		
Madeleine Z. Bordallo (D)	27,081	64.6%
Joseph F. Ada (R)	14,836	35.4%
2002 PRIMARY		
Madeleine Z. Bordallo (D)	17,678	51.9%
Judi Won Pat (D)	12,227	40.9%

Elected 2002; 1st term

The oldest member of the Class of 2002, Bordallo comes to the House with a wealth of political experience and a full dose of enthusiasm to tackle a new job at an age when most members are thinking of retirement.

Like her predecessor, Democrat Robert A. Underwood, Bordallo (bor-DALL-yo) must balance the roles of ambassador, tourism director and House delegate. Her focus on Capitol Hill is a broad one — working to make sure Guam is not overlooked by federal and congressional policymakers. Her seats on the Armed Services and Resources panels are perfect fits for Guam.

"I feel that a delegate goes to Washington not to beg, but to collect," she told Guam's Pacific Daily News. She says her goals are to promote Guam's economic development, make adjustments in the tax code to benefit the territories, regain land no longer used by the Defense Department, and prod the government to provide restitution for islanders who spent 32 months under Japanese occupation during World War II.

Bordallo's political experience includes five terms in the island legislature, two terms as lieutenant governor, an unsuccessful run for governor and eight years as Guam's first lady. A Minnesota native, she moved to Guam in 1948 when her father took a job there as a high school principal. She went to college in Indiana and Minnesota, earning an associate's degree in music. She then returned to Guam, where she married Ricardo J. Bordallo, a local businessman and aspiring politician. She says her husband, who served two terms as governor and died in 1990, kindled her interest in politics.

When Gov. Carl Gutierrez was required by term limits to step down in 2002, Bordallo thought about seeking to succeed him. But the field of candidates was crowded and included Gutierrez's wife, Geri, which could have made for uncomfortable relations between the governor and Bordallo, then lieutenant governor. So when Underwood ran for governor, Bordallo decided to seek the delegate post. The race was a rematch of her 1990 gubernatorial race, which she lost to Republican Joseph F. Ada. This time, however, Bordallo cruised to victory with 65 percent even as Underwood lost.

GUAM

"Where America's Day starts," Guam is the largest and most southerly island in the Marianas archipelago. About 3,500 miles west of Hawaii, it is closer to Tokyo than it is to Honolulu. Guam is only 212 square miles — about three times the size of the District of Columbia. The population was 154,805 in 2000, a 16 percent increase over the decade.

The indigenous people, the Chamorros, first came into contact with Europeans with the visit of Ferdinand Magellan in 1521. Guam was ceded to the United States by Spain in 1898.

The U.S. Navy administered Guam until 1950, when U.S. citizenship was granted and Guamanians elected a local government. Although residents are citizens, they may not vote in presidential elections. Guam has had a non-voting delegate in the House since 1973.

Guam's economy is heavily dependent on U.S. military spending and tourism. The vast majority of visitors are from Japan and the tourism business is subject to the vagaries of the Asian economy. Per capita income in 1999 was $12,722.

Most food and other consumer goods are imported. In recent years, Guam has had to cope with large influxes of illegal immigrants, mostly from China and Burma, who pay smugglers to sneak them onto the island, where they seek asylum in the United States.

Guam has a competitive two-party system: A Republican took the governor's mansion from a Democrat in 2002, while Democrats recaptured control of the Guam Legislature.

MAJOR INDUSTRY
Military, tourism, construction, shipping

MILITARY BASES
Andersen Air Force Base, 2,193 military, 397 civilian; Naval Station Guam, 2,276 military, 339 civilian (2001)

DISTRICTS
Dededo, 42,980; Yigo, 19,474; Tamuning, 18,012

NOTABLE
Guam is the only U.S. territory in the eastern hemisphere.

Res. Cmmsr. Anibal Acevedo-Vilá (D)

Elected 2000; 1st term

CAPITOL OFFICE
225-2615
anibal@mail.house.gov
www.house.gov/acevedo-vila
126 Cannon 20515-5401; fax 225-2154

COMMITTEES
Agriculture
Resources
Small Business

HOMETOWN
San Juan

BORN
Feb. 13, 1962, Hato Rey, P.R.

RELIGION
Roman Catholic

FAMILY
Wife, Luisa Gandara; two children

EDUCATION
U. of Puerto Rico, B.A. 1982 (political science), J.D. 1985; Harvard U., LL.M. 1987

CAREER
Lawyer; gubernatorial aide

POLITICAL HIGHLIGHTS
Puerto Rico House, 1993-2000 (minority leader, 1997-2000)

ELECTION RESULTS

2000 GENERAL		
A. Acevedo-Vilá (POPDEM)	983,488	49.3%
Carlos Romero-Barceló (D)	905,690	45.4%
Manuel Orellana (PRI)	95,067	4.8%
1999 PRIMARY		
A. Acevedo-Vilá (POPDEM)	284,905	56.0%
Jose Mayoral (POPDEM)	215,807	42.4%
write-ins	7,882	1.6%

The only person in the House with a four-year term, Acevedo-Vilá's election as the resident commissioner in 2000 marked a shift in the island commonwealth's priorities in Washington. Along with Puerto Rico's governor, Sila Maria Calderón, Acevedo-Vilá is a member of the Popular Democratic Party (PDP), which favors continued commonwealth status.

That places the push for statehood — championed by Acevedo-Vilá's predecessor, Carlos Romero-Barceló of the New Progressive Party — on the back burner. One thing did not change, however. Acevedo-Vilá affiliates with the Democratic Party on Capitol Hill, as did Romero-Barceló.

And little has changed on the list of top issues for Puerto Rico in Washington, which center on economic development. In the 107th, one of his priorities was to finally bring to an end to the Navy's use of the island of Vieques, about six miles off Puerto Rico's southeastern coast, as a live firing range.

Acevedo-Vilá also works for the island's economic development, including legislation to replace the Section 936 tax incentives for business investment in Puerto Rico, whose 1996-ordered phaseout will be complete in 2006. He also has sought to increase Puerto Rico's share of federal spending for education, nutrition programs, weatherization and children's health insurance.

He was able to get money for Puerto Rican farmers as part of a 2001 supplemental farm aid law as well as $50 million for the Urban Train mass transit project in the San Juan metropolitan area.

Acevedo-Vilá, whose father and sister are lawyers — his father served in the Puerto Rican legislature — earned an advanced law degree from Harvard and clerked for a federal judge in Boston. When he returned to Puerto Rico, he got involved in politics. After a stint as Gov. Rafael Hernandez Colón's legislative affairs adviser, Acevedo-Vilá won a seat in the legislature in 1992. He advanced to a series of leadership posts in the PDP, including the presidency of the party for a two-year term, during which he was the party's point man for the 1998 statehood-or-commonwealth plebiscite. In 2000, Acevedo-Vilá, running on a ticket with Calderón, beat Romero-Barceló by 4 points.

PUERTO RICO

The largest and most populated (3.8 million) of the territories, Puerto Rico has been a self-governing commonwealth of the United States since 1952. The estimated 2.7 million Puerto Ricans living on the U.S. mainland strengthen the island's ties to the United States.

Christopher Columbus visited Puerto Rico in 1493. The Spanish arrived 15 years later and soon brought slaves to work in the sugar cane fields. Slavery was abolished in 1873. Spain ceded Puerto Rico to the United States after the Spanish-American War. Its residents became U.S. citizens in 1917, but they cannot vote for president. Since 1901, Puerto Ricans have been represented in the House by a resident commissioner.

Per capita income in the commonwealth is about $8,000 — high by Caribbean standards, but only about half of that of the poorest state.

The island's political status has been a longstanding issue, with various factions favoring statehood, continued commonwealth status or independence. In recent years, public opinion has been split closely between statehood and commonwealth status. The House in 1998 passed legislation calling for a plebiscite in Puerto Rico — a measure that had been pushed by the then-resident commissioner Carlos Romero-Barceló. The 2000 victories of Acevedo-Vilá and the island's governor, Sila Maria Calderón — both members of the Popular Democratic Party, which favors continued commonwealth status — has placed the statehood issue on the back burner.

MAJOR INDUSTRY
Manufacturing, services, tourism

MILITARY BASES
Fort Buchanan, 392 military, 497 civilian; Roosevelt Roads Naval Station, 2,236 military, 390 civilian (2001)

CITIES
San Juan (unincorporated), 421,958; Bayamón (unincorporated), 203,499; Carolina (unincorporated), 168,164

NOTABLE
Puerto Ricans cannot vote for president, but they take part in the nominating conventions; Puerto Rico Democrats in 2000 had more convention delegates than 24 states.

Del. Donna M.C. Christensen (D)

Elected 1996; 4th term

The daughter of a St. Croix judge, Christensen is a physician by training, and tends to focus on the health and economic well-being of her constituents, and to a lesser extent, issues before the Resources Committee, where she is the top Democrat on the National Parks and Public Lands panel.

Her medical degree made her a natural to head the Congressional Black Caucus's Health Brain Trust, which focuses on health issues of particular importance to minorities, including the worldwide AIDS epidemic and the reluctance of health maintenance organizations to do business in medically underserved areas. On Resources, Christensen devotes much of her legislative effort to obtaining incrementally greater autonomy for the Virgin Islands. She wants to ensure that her constituents get their share of federal dollars from programs such as Medicaid and Supplemental Security Income. She also wants the territory included in homeland security efforts.

To promote economic development, Christensen has worked for favorable tax and tariff laws to help the V.I., as it is known locally, attract business and industry, including tax incentives for the manufacture of watches and jewelry and a continuation of the rum tax rebate. The islands' local treasury receives about $70 million annually from the excise taxes collected by the federal government on the sale of Virgin Islands and Puerto Rican rum.

Inspired by a booklet encouraging African-American students to consider careers in medicine — a pamphlet she had picked up to deliver to someone else — Christensen went to medical school at George Washington University. After postgraduate training in San Francisco and Washington, D.C., she returned to the Virgin Islands where, during the course of a 20-year medical career, she worked in clinics and hospitals on St. Croix. She eventually moved into administrative posts, including acting commissioner of health for the Virgin Islands.

Christensen was also involved in local and national Democratic Party politics. She unsuccessfully sought the Democratic nomination for the delegate post in 1994 but came back in 1996 to edge Del. Victor O. Frazer, running as an independent, and Republican Kenneth Mapp, in a three-way battle.

CAPITOL OFFICE
225-1790
donna.christensen@mail.house.gov
www.house.gov/christian-christensen
1510 Longworth 20515-5501; fax 225-5517

COMMITTEES
Resources
Small Business
Select Homeland Security

HOMETOWN
St. Croix

BORN
Sept. 19, 1945, Teaneck, N.J.

RELIGION
Moravian

FAMILY
Husband, Chris Christensen; two children, four stepchildren

EDUCATION
Saint Mary's College (Ind.), B.S. 1966 (biology); George Washington U., M.D. 1970

CAREER
Physician; health official

POLITICAL HIGHLIGHTS
Virgin Is. Democratic Territorial Committee, 1980-97 (chairwoman, 1980-82); Virgin Is. Board of Education, 1984-86; Virgin Is. acting commissioner of health, 1993-94; sought Democratic nomination for U.S. House, 1994

ELECTION RESULTS

2002 GENERAL		
Donna M.C. Christensen (D)	20,414	67.7%
Virdin C. Brown (ICM)	4,456	14.8%
Lilliana Belardo de O'Neal (R)	4,286	14.2%
Garry A. Sprauve (I)	996	3.3%
2000 GENERAL		
Donna M.C. Christensen (D)	18,625	78.4%
Victor O. Frazer (I)	3,516	14.8%
Jorge J. Estemac (ICM)	1,608	6.8%

PREVIOUS WINNING PERCENTAGES
1998 (80%); 1996 (52%)

VIRGIN ISLANDS

The Virgin Islands, just east of Puerto Rico, are known for their subtropical climate, beautiful beaches, duty-free shopping and — far too often — for being in the path of tropical storms. The first three attributes have helped build a thriving tourism industry, while the latter has made economic development an uneven and difficult process.

Spain asserted its authority over the islands after Christopher Columbus visited them in 1493, and over the next century Spanish settlers killed or drove out the native Indians. Spain showed no real interest in establishing a colony on the Virgin Islands, however.

Denmark established a colony on St. Thomas in the latter half of the 17th century. Sugar plantations drove the islands' economy during the 18th and early 19th centuries, until slavery was abolished in 1848. The U.S. government bought the islands from Denmark for $25 million in 1917.

The Virgin Islands is an unincorporated territory, under the jurisdiction of the Interior Department. Residents are U.S. citizens but may not vote for president. The Virgin Islands has had a non-voting House delegate since 1973.

The U.S. Virgin Islands is actually composed of 68 islands and cays — but only four are inhabited. The territory had a population in 2000 of 108,612, a 7 percent increase over 1990.

Cruise ships make regular stops at the islands, principally at the capital of Charlotte Amalie on St. Thomas, and passengers stream ashore to take advantage of duty-free shopping. Most of the Virgin Islands' tourists arrive on cruise ships and leave without spending a night.

MAJOR INDUSTRY
Tourism, petroleum refining, rum distilling, watch assembly

CITIES
Charlotte Amalie, 11,004; Christiansted, 2,637

NOTABLE
Motorists in the Virgin Islands drive on the left.

Did You Know?

Knowing a lawmaker's political party or what state he or she is from can be helpful in understanding a member of Congress.

But there are many other factors that contribute to members' priorities and interests and to their standing in the congressional universe. Seniority or committee assignments, for example, can provide some insight into a member's clout and areas of expertise. Which informal congressional groups they belong to, how they vote with respect to the wishes of their party or the president, or how various interest groups view their voting records can also be useful in getting a handle on a particular member.

Each member's background contains unique experiences and interests that often provide some insight into his or her behavior as a member of Congress. And sometimes these personal tidbits can offer a fascinating humanizing touch.

For example, did you know that:

Democrat **Anibal Acevedo-Vilá**, the resident commissioner from Puerto Rico, is the only member of Congress with a four-year term.

Neil Abercrombie, D-Hawaii, wrote a novel in which 125 members of the House were killed.

Gary L. Ackerman, D-N.Y., used to live on a houseboat named "Unsinkable." It sank.

The **Arkansas** delegation is well-versed in the medical field: **Marion Berry** is a pharmacist; **John Boozman** is an optometrist; **Mike Ross** owns a pharmacy; **Vic Snyder** is an M.D. — and **Blanche Lincoln** is married to a physician.

Roscoe G. Bartlett, R-Md., holds 20 patents.

When **Evan Bayh**, D-Ind., was a child, one of his babysitters was Lynda Johnson, the president's daughter.

The father of Texas Republican **Kevin Brady** was murdered in a South Dakota courtroom.

Jim Bunning, R-Ky., is a member of the Baseball Hall of Fame.

Ben Nighthorse Campbell, R-Colo., was a member of the 1964 Olympic judo team.

Thomas R. Carper, D-Del., campaigned for Barry Goldwater in 1964 and Eugene McCarthy in 1968.

James E. Clyburn, D-S.C., is the first black elected from South Carolina since 1896. That person was his great uncle, George Washington Murray.

Minnesota GOP Sen. **Norm Coleman** and New York Democratic Sen. **Charles E. Schumer** were high school classmates in Brooklyn.

Elijah E. Cummings, D-Md., was thousands of dollars in debt when he arrived in the House. He spent two winters without heat because he couldn't afford to fix his furnace.

Randy "Duke" Cunningham, R-Calif., was the first air ace of the Vietnam War. Later he was a "top gun" flight instructor.

An aunt of Florida GOP brothers **Lincoln Diaz-Balart** and **Mario Diaz-Balart** was once married to Fidel Castro.

John D. Dingell, D-Mich., succeeded his father. A Dingell has represented Michigan since 1933.

David Dreier, R-Calif., is the youngest-ever chairman of the Rules Committee.

When **Anna G. Eshoo**, D-Calif., was a school girl in Connecticut, President Truman gave her a ride home from school.

American Samoa Democratic Del. **Eni F.H. Faleomavaega's** last name is Hunkin. Faleomavaega is a Samoan title.

Chaka Fattah, D-Pa., was born Arthur Davenport.

Rodney Frelinghuysen, R-N.J., is the sixth member of his family to serve in Congress.

Bill Frist, R-Tenn., didn't register to vote until he was 36.

Bart Gordon, R-Tenn., can run 3 miles in about 17 minutes.

Bob Graham, D-Fla., has saved the more than 4,000 notebooks that he has filled with notes and reminders to himself.

Gil Gutknecht, R-Minn., has a culinary passion for Spam and persuaded the Library of Congress to hold an exhibit on the lunch meat.

A former federal judge, **Alcee L. Hastings**, D-Fla., was impeached and removed from office.

"Doc" Hastings, R-Wash., did not graduate from college.

Orrin G. Hatch, R-Utah, is a songwriter, with a repertoire ranging from bossa nova to rock and rap.

Joel Hefley, R-Colo., won a coin flip with a colleague in the state legislature to determine which of them would run for Congress.

Baron P. Hill, D-Ind., was inducted into the Indiana Basketball Hall of Fame in 2000, along with Larry Bird.

Rush D. Holt, D-N.J., a physicist, is a former champion on the TV quiz show "Jeopardy."

Both **Darlene Hooley**, D-Ore., and **Patty Murray**, D-Wash., got involved in politics because of faulty playground equipment.

Both **Amo Hougton**, R-N.Y., and **Earl Pomeroy,** D-N.D., had plans to move overseas to do humanitarian work until late-breaking political circumstances convinced them to run for the House instead.

Jesse L. Jackson Jr., D-Ill., vacuums his office carpet for relaxation.

James M. Jeffords, I-Vt., holds a black belt in Tae Kwon Do.

Sam Johnson, R-Texas, spent almost seven years in a North Vietnamese prison camp. For a brief stretch, he roomed with **John McCain**, R-Ariz.

Paul E. Kanjorski, D-Pa., a licensed attorney since 1966, never graduated from law school. (He didn't graduate from college, either.)

Dennis J. Kucinich, D-Ohio, was so unpopular as mayor of Cleveland that he wore a bullet-proof vest to throw out the first pitch at an Indians game.

Tom Lantos, D-Calif., fought with the Hungarian resistance against the Nazis. He escaped from a Nazi work camp.

Jim Leach, R-Iowa, quit the Foreign Service to protest the 1973 "Saturday Night Massacre."

John Lewis, D-Ga., was a leader of the famous civil rights march in Selma, Ala., in 1965.

A 24-year-old Yale law student named Bill Clinton campaigned for **Joseph I. Lieberman**, D-Conn., in 1970, as Lieberman ran for the state Senate.

Trent Lott, R-Miss., was an aide to a Democratic member of the House.

Stephen F. Lynch, D-Mass., donated more than half of his liver to his brother.

Carolyn McCarthy, D-N.Y., was propelled into politics by her husband's murder.

Thaddeus McCotter, R-Mich., once played in a band named Sir Funk-a-Lot and the Knights of the Terrestrial Jam.

New Jersey's **Robert Menendez's** 104-103 election as House Democratic Caucus chairman was decided by a vote cast by Mike Feeley, a Colorado Democrat, who was never in Congress.

John L. Mica, of Florida is a longtime Republican; his brother, Dan, served in the House as a Democrat.

Barbara A. Mikulski, D-Md., is the fourth-most-senior woman in congressional history.

Lisa Murkowski, R-Alaska, is the first woman to represent Alaska. She is also the first person ever appointed to the Senate by her father.

Jim Nussle, R-Iowa, once spoke on the House floor with a paper bag over his head.

As a youth, **David R. Obey**, D-Wis., campaigned for Sen. Joseph R. McCarthy.

Major R. Owens, D-N.Y., writes rap lyrics and poetry.

Of the 41 House votes in the 107th Congress on which there was a solitary nay, **Ron Paul**, R-Texas, cast that vote 23 times.

Collin C. Peterson, D-Minn., plays guitar in a country rock band.

Todd R. Platts, R-Pa., commutes to Capitol Hill every day from his home in York, Pa.— 200 miles round trip.

Ralph Regula, R-Ohio, works to preserve the memory of William McKinley.

John D. Rockefeller IV, D-W.Va., says his favorite food is lima beans.

Dana Rohrabacher, R-Calif., says John Wayne taught him how to drink tequila.

Ileana Ros-Lehtinen, R-Fla., is the first Hispanic woman elected to Congress.

Bobby L. Rush, D-Ill., is a former Black Panther. He served six months in prison on a weapons charge.

Jim Ryun, R-Kan., made the cover of Sports Illustrated when he was still in high school.

H. James Saxton, R-N.J., and **Don Sherwood**, R-Pa., were childhood buddies; they grew up three doors apart in the hamlet of Nicholson, Pa.

F. James Sensenbrenner Jr., R-Wis., was one of the wealthiest members of Congress even before he won $250,000 in the D.C. lottery.

José E. Serrano, D-N.Y., learned to speak English by listening to Frank Sinatra records.

As a freshman in the 105th Congress, **John Shimkus**, R-Ill., collected the autographs of every other member of the House.

John M. Spratt Jr., D-S.C., broke his arm when he slipped in some Senate bean soup.

A former teacher, **Tom Tancredo**, R-Colo., first ran for office on a dare from his students.

Lynn Woolsey, D-Calif., went on welfare after a divorce left her on her own with three young children and no job skills.

Peace Corps Volunteers

Members of the 108th Congress who have served in the Peace Corps:

Member	Country	Years
Sen. Christopher J. Dodd, D-Conn.	Dominican Republic	1966-68
Rep. Sam Farr, D-Calif.	Colombia	1964-66
Rep. Michael M. Honda, D-Calif.	El Salvador	1965-67
Rep. Tom Petri, R-Wis.	Somalia	1966-67
Rep. Christopher Shays, R-Conn.	Fiji	1968-70
Rep. James T. Walsh, R-N.Y.	Nepal	1970-72

Rhodes Scholars

Members of Congress who have been Rhodes scholars:

Rep. Tom Allen, D-Maine
Rep. Brad Carson, D-Okla.
Rep. Jim Cooper, D-Tenn.
Sen. Russell D. Feingold, D-Wis.
Sen. Richard G. Lugar, R-Ind.
Sen. Paul S. Sarbanes, D-Md.
Rep. David Vitter, R-La.
Rep. Heather A. Wilson, R-N.M.

Members With Parents Who Served in Congress

Here are the 26 members of the 108th Congress whose mother or father also served in Congress.

Eleven of the people on the list — Chafee, Clay, Dingell, Duncan, Ford, Gonzalez, Meek, Mollohan, Murkowski, Roybal-Allard and Shuster — directly succeeded their parent.

Jones is the only member on the list who belongs to a different political party than his parent.

Member	Parent	Years Parent Served
Rep. Charles Bass, R-N.H.	Rep. Perkins Bass, R-N.H.	1955-63
Sen. Evan Bayh, D-Ind.	Sen. Birch Bayh, D-Ind.	1963-81
Sen. Robert F. Bennett, R-Utah	Sen. Wallace F. Bennett, R-Utah	1951-74
Rep. Shelley Moore Capito, R-W.Va.	Rep. Arch A. Moore Jr.	1957-69
Sen. Lincoln Chafee, R-R.I.	Sen. John H. Chafee, R-R.I.	1976-99
Rep. William Lacy Clay, D-Mo.	Rep. William L. Clay, D-Mo.	1969-2001
Rep. John D. Dingell, D-Mich.	Rep. John D. Dingell Sr., D-Mich.	1933-55
Sen. Christopher J. Dodd, D-Conn.	Rep./Sen. Thomas J. Dodd, D-Conn.	1953-57, 1959-71
Rep. John J. "Jimmy" Duncan Jr., R-Tenn.	Rep. John J. Duncan, R-Tenn.	1965-88
Rep. Harold E. Ford Jr., D-Tenn.	Rep. Harold E. Ford, D-Tenn.	1975-97
Rep. Rodney Frelinghuysen, R-N.J.	Rep. Peter H. Frelinguysen, R-N.J.	1953-75
Rep. Charlie Gonzalez, D-Texas	Rep. Henry B. Gonzalez, D-Texas	1961-99
Rep. Rush D. Holt, D-N.J.	Sen. Rush Dew Holt, D-W.Va.	1935-41
Rep. Walter B. Jones, R-N.C.	Rep. Walter B. Jones Sr., D-N.C.	1966-92
Rep. Patrick J. Kennedy, D-R.I.	Sen. Edward M. Kennedy, D-Mass.	1962-present
Sen. Jon Kyl, R-Ariz.	Rep. John H. Kyl, R-Iowa	1959-65, 1967-73
Rep. Kendrick B. Meek, D-Fla.	Rep. Carrie P. Meek, D-Fla.	1993-2003
Rep. Alan B. Mollohan, D-W.Va.	Rep. Robert H. Mollohan, D-W.Va.	1953-57, 1969-83
Sen. Lisa Murkowski, R-Alaska	Sen. Frank H. Murkowski, R-Alaska	1981-2002
Rep. Nancy Pelosi, D-Calif.	Rep. Thomas D'Alesandro Jr., D-Md.	1939-47
Sen. Mark Pryor, D-Ark.	Rep./Sen. David Pryor, D-Ark.	1966-73, 1979-97
Rep. Lucille Roybal-Allard, D-Calif.	Rep. Edward R. Roybal, D-Calif.	1963-93
Rep. Bill Shuster, R-Pa.	Rep. Bud Shuster, R-Pa.	1973-2001
Rep. Mark Udall, D-Colo.	Rep. Morris K. Udall, D-Ariz.	1961-91
Rep. Tom Udall, D-N.M.	Rep. Stewart L. Udall, D-Ariz.	1955-61
Rep. James T. Walsh, R-N.Y.	Rep. William F. Walsh, R-N.Y.	1973-79

Fastest Members of Congress

Each year a number of members of Congress participate in a three-mile footrace in Washington, D.C. Here are the best times posted by current members of Congress in the 2002 race.

Member	Time	Member	Time
Rep. Bart Gordon, D-Tenn.	17:37	Rep. Peter A. DeFazio, D-Ore.	24:30
Rep. Jim Ryun, R-Kan.	20:11	Rep. Pete Sessions, R-Texas	24:55
Sen. John Ensign, R-Nev.	21:12	Rep. George Nethercutt, R-Wash.	25:47
Rep. Earl Pomeroy, D-N.D.	21:15	Sen. Jeff Bingaman, D-N.M.	26:37
Sen. Lincoln Chafee, R-R.I.	22:36	Rep. James P. Moran, D-Va.	27:01
Sen. Don Nickles, R-Okla.	22:54	Sen. Bill Frist, R-Tenn.	27:18
Rep. Kenny Hulshof, R-Mo.	23:07	Sen. Richard G. Lugar, R-Ind.	28:25
Sen. Jack Reed, D-R.I.	23:28	Rep. Ray LaHood, R-Ill.	30:11
Rep. Earl Blumenauer, D-Ore.	23:43	Sen. Thad Cochran, R-Miss.	33:45
Rep. Mark Udall, D-Colo.	24:04	Sen. Craig Thomas, R-Wyo.	36:28

Senate Presidential Support and Opposition

Support scores represent how often a senator sided with President Bush on roll call votes on which he took a clear position beforehand. During the 107th Congress, there were 135 such votes. Opposition scores represent how often a senator voted against the president's position in 2001 and 2002. Scores are expressed as percentages. Only members of the 108th Congress are listed.

107th Congress: Top Scorers

Support — Republicans

Richard G. Lugar, Ind.	100.0%
Bill Frist, Tenn.	99.2
Judd Gregg, N.H.	98.5
Christopher S. Bond, Mo.	98.4
Sam Brownback, Kan.	98.4
Jon Kyl, Ariz.	97.7
Orrin G. Hatch, Utah	97.7
Trent Lott, Miss.	97.7
Pat Roberts, Kan.	97.7
Charles E. Grassley, Iowa	97.0
Wayne Allard, Colo.	97.0
Chuck Hagel, Neb.	97.0
Don Nickles, Okla.	97.0
Robert F. Bennett, Utah	96.9
John Ensign, Nev.	96.9
Mitch McConnell, Ky.	96.9
Rick Santorum, Pa.	96.9
Ted Stevens, Alaska	96.3
Jim Bunning, Ky.	96.2
Thad Cochran, Miss.	96.2
Mike DeWine, Ohio	96.2
Kay Bailey Hutchison, Texas	96.2

Support — Democrats

Zell Miller, Ga.	85.8%
John B. Breaux, La.	81.7
Ben Nelson, Neb.	81.1
Blanche Lincoln, Ark.	78.8
Max Baucus, Mont.	78.4
Mary L. Landrieu, La.	78.3
James M. Jeffords, Vt. *	76.0
Thomas R. Carper, Del.	75.2
Herb Kohl, Wis.	73.7
Evan Bayh, Ind.	73.3
Dianne Feinstein, Calif.	73.3
Bill Nelson, Fla.	73.3
Jeff Bingaman, N.M.	72.9
Bob Graham, Fla.	72.4
Joseph I. Lieberman, Conn.	72.2
Tom Daschle, S.D.	71.6
Maria Cantwell, Wash.	71.1
Robert C. Byrd, W.Va.	70.9
John Edwards, N.C.	70.9
Daniel K. Inouye, Hawaii	70.5

** An independent, Jeffords cacuses with the Democrats*

Opposition — Republicans

Olympia J. Snowe, Maine	13.3%
Arlen Specter, Pa.	12.3
Susan Collins, Maine	11.9
Lincoln Chafee, R.I.	11.9
John McCain, Ariz.	9.2
Gordon H. Smith, Ore.	7.7
Richard C. Shelby, Ala.	7.0
Jeff Sessions, Ala.	6.3
John W. Warner, Va.	6.1
Ben Nighthorse Campbell, Colo.	6.1

Opposition — Democrats

Mark Dayton, Minn.	36.8%
Hillary Rodham Clinton, N.Y.	36.6
Jon Corzine, N.J.	36.4
Russell D. Feingold, Wis.	36.3
Paul S. Sarbanes, Md.	36.1
Patrick J. Leahy, Vt.	36.1
Richard J. Durbin, Ill.	36.1
Barbara Boxer, Calif.	35.9
Jack Reed, R.I.	35.3
Edward M. Kennedy, Mass.	35.1
Debbie Stabenow, Mich.	35.1

Senate Party Unity and Opposition

Support scores represent how often a senator voted with his or her party's majority against a majority of the other party in the 107th Congress, when there were 325 such "party unity" votes in the Senate. Opposition scores represent how often a senator voted against his or her party's majority on such party unity tests in 2001 and 2002. Scores are expressed as percentages. Only members of the 108th Congress are listed.

107th Congress: Top Scorers

Support — Republicans		Support — Democrats	
Trent Lott, Miss.	97.8%	Paul S. Sarbanes, Md.	98.8%
Mitch McConnell, Ky.	97.2	Jack Reed, R.I.	98.8
Jon Kyl, Ariz.	97.2	Patrick J. Leahy, Vt.	97.8
Don Nickles, Okla.	97.2	Mark Dayton, Minn.	97.8
Jim Bunning, Ky.	97.2	Barbara A. Mikulski, Md.	97.2
Bill Frist, Tenn.	97.2	Edward M. Kennedy, Mass.	97.2
Craig Thomas, Wyo.	96.2	Carl Levin, Mich.	96.9
James M. Inhofe, Okla.	95.8	Barbara Boxer, Calif.	96.5
Wayne Allard, Colo.	95.7	Christopher J. Dodd, Conn.	96.5
Robert F. Bennett, Utah	95.6	Daniel K. Akaka, Hawaii	95.7
Rick Santorum, Pa.	95.3	Debbie Stabenow, Mich.	95.7
Larry E. Craig, Idaho.	95.0	Jon Corzine, N.J.	95.7
Pat Roberts, Kan.	95.0	Richard J. Durbin, Ill.	95.7
Michael B. Enzi, Wyo.	94.6	Hillary Rodham Clinton, N.Y.	95.7
Orrin G. Hatch, Utah	94.3	John Kerry, Mass.	95.6
Sam Brownback, Kan.	94.0	Tom Harkin, Iowa	95.3
Michael D. Crapo, Idaho.	92.9	Daniel K. Inouye, Hawaii	95.1
Chuck Hagel, Neb.	92.9	Harry Reid, Nev.	95.0
Conrad Burns, Mont.	92.7	John D. Rockefeller IV, W.Va.	94.1
Christopher S. Bond, Mo.	92.2	Charles E. Schumer, N.Y.	93.1

Opposition — Republicans		Opposition — Democrats	
Lincoln Chafee, R.I.	48.8%	Zell Miller, Ga.	59.0%
Arlen Specter, Pa.	39.8	Ben Nelson, Neb.	44.6
Olympia J. Snowe, Maine	38.2	John B. Breaux, La.	42.4
Susan Collins, Maine	36.3	Max Baucus, Mont.	32.9
John McCain, Ariz.	28.4	James M. Jeffords, Vt. *	31.2
Gordon H. Smith, Ore.	23.7	Blanche Lincoln, Ark.	27.2
Peter G. Fitzgerald, Ill.	21.9	Mary L. Landrieu, La.	24.8
John W. Warner, Va.	16.0	Thomas R. Carper, Del.	22.0
Thad Cochran, Miss.	15.4	Evan Bayh, Ind.	21.9
Mike DeWine, Ohio	14.8	Robert C. Byrd, W.Va.	15.4

** An independent, Jeffords caucuses with the Democrats*

House Presidential Support and Opposition

Support scores represent how often a House member sided with President Bush on roll call votes on which he took a clear position beforehand. During the 107th Congress, there were 83 such votes in the House. Opposition scores represent how often a House member voted against the president's position. Scores are expressed as percentages. Only members of the 108th Congress who voted more than half the time in 2001 and 2002 are listed.

107th Congress: Top Scorers

Support — Republicans

David Dreier, Calif.	96.3%
Michael G. Oxley, Ohio	96.3
Gary G. Miller, Calif.	95.1
Ed Schrock, Va.	95.1
John A. Boehner, Ohio	95.0
Tom DeLay, Texas	95.0
Joe Knollenberg, Mich.	94.9
E. Clay Shaw Jr., Fla.	94.0
Porter J. Goss, Fla.	93.9
Howard P. "Buck" McKeon, Calif.	93.9
Anne M. Northup, Ky.	93.9
William M. "Mac" Thornberry, Texas	93.9
John E. Sununu, N.H. *	93.8
John Linder, Ga.	93.7
Scott McInnis, Colo.	93.7
Spencer Bachus, Ala.	93.4
Roy Blunt, Mo.	93.2
Richard M. Burr, N.C.	92.8
Eric Cantor, Va.	92.8
Rob Portman, Ohio	92.8
Thomas M. Reynolds, N.Y.	92.8

Opposition — Republicans

Ron Paul, Texas	50.0%
Jim Leach, Iowa	35.4
John J. "Jimmy" Duncan, Jr., Tenn.	30.5
Nancy L. Johnson, Conn.	27.7
Michael N. Castle, Del.	27.7
Wayne T. Gilchrest, Md.	26.9
Christopher Shays, Conn.	26.5
Jim Ramstad, Minn.	26.5
Jeff Flake, Ariz.	26.5
Christopher H. Smith, N.J.	25.3
Jerry Moran, Kan.	25.3
Amo Houghton, N.Y.	25.0
Walter B. Jones, N.C.	24.7
Sherwood Boehlert, N.Y.	24.1
Curt Weldon, Pa.	24.1
Tom Tancredo, Colo.	23.5
Virgil H. Goode Jr., Va.	23.2
Roscoe G. Bartlett, Md.	23.2
Rob Simmons, Conn.	22.9
Timothy V. Johnson, Ill.	22.9

** Sununu is in the Senate in the 108th Congress*

Support — Democrats

Ken Lucas, Ky.	79.3%
Ralph M. Hall, Texas	78.3
Robert E. "Bud" Cramer, Ala.	64.2
Chris John, La.	63.8
Ike Skelton, Mo.	56.8
Bart Gordon, Tenn.	53.8
William O. Lipinski, Ill.	53.4
Mike McIntyre, N.C.	53.1
Cal Dooley, Calif.	52.4
John Tanner, Tenn.	51.9
Brad Carson, Okla.	51.8
Sanford D. Bishop Jr., Ga.	51.2
Solomon P. Ortiz, Texas	50.6
John P. Murtha, Pa.	50.0
Tim Holden, Pa.	49.4
Jim Matheson, Utah	49.4
Charles W. Stenholm, Texas	49.4
Collin C. Peterson, Minn.	47.6
Bob Etheridge, N.C.	47.0
Allen Boyd, Fla.	46.9
Chet Edwards, Texas	46.9

Opposition — Democrats

Barney Frank, Mass.	88.8%
Donald M. Payne, N.J.	86.4
John Conyers Jr., Mich.	86.3
Maxine Waters, Calif.	83.8
Diane Watson, Calif.	83.6
Bernard Sanders, Vt. *	83.1
Bob Filner, Calif.	82.9
Sherrod Brown, Ohio	82.9
Hilda L. Solis, Calif.	82.5
John Lewis, Ga.	82.4
Jim McDermott, Wash.	82.3
Barbara Lee, Calif.	81.9
Melvin Watt, N.C.	81.7
Robert C. Scott, Va.	81.7
Sheila Jackson-Lee, Texas	81.7
Major R. Owens, N.Y.	81.5
Michael E. Capuano, Mass.	81.3
Martin Olav Sabo, Minn.	80.8
Lynn Woolsey, Calif.	80.7
Jim McGovern, Mass.	80.7

** An independent, Sanders caucuses with the Democrats*

House Party Unity and Opposition

Support scores represent how often a House member voted with his or her party's majority against a majority of the other party in the 107th Congress, when there were 413 such "party unity" votes in the House. Opposition scores represent how often a member voted against his or her party's majority on such party unity tests. Scores are expressed as percentages. Only members of the 108th Congress who voted more than half the time in 2001 and 2002 are listed.

107th Congress: Top Scorers

Support — Republicans		Support — Democrats	
Pete Sessions, Texas	98.8%	Jan Schakowsky, Ill.	99.3%
Gary G. Miller, Calif.	98.8	Hilda L. Solis, Calif.	99.3
Philip M. Crane, Ill.	98.7	Bob Filner, Calif.	98.8
Eric Cantor, Va.	98.5	John W. Olver, Mass.	98.5
Roger Wicker, Miss.	98.5	Xavier Becerra, Calif.	98.5
Tom DeLay, Texas	98.5	Lynn Woolsey, Calif.	98.3
John Culberson, Texas	98.5	John F. Tierney, Mass.	98.3
David Vitter, La.	98.5	Pete Stark, Calif.	98.1
John Linder, Ga.	98.4	Sherrod Brown, Ohio	98.1
Henry Bonilla, Texas	98.3	Tammy Baldwin, Wis.	98.0
Ric Keller, Fla.	98.2	Major R. Owens, N.Y.	98.0
Lamar Smith, Texas	98.2	Jim McGovern, Mass.	97.8
Roy Blunt, Mo.	98.2	Nancy Pelosi, Calif.	97.8
Ron Lewis, Ky.	98.1	Donald M. Payne, N.J.	97.7
Jim Ryun, Kan.	98.1	Jerrold Nadler, N.Y.	97.7
Doc Hastings, Wash.	98.0	Martin T. Meehan, Mass.	97.6
Adam H. Putnam, Fla.	98.0	Barbara Lee, Calif.	97.6
John A. Boehner, Ohio	98.0	Lucille Roybal-Allard, Calif.	97.5
Terry Everett, Ala.	98.0	Nydia M. Velázquez, N.Y.	97.5
Jeff Miller, Fla.	98.0	Stephanie Tubbs Jones, Ohio	97.5

Opposition — Republicans		Opposition — Democrats	
Jim Leach, Iowa	27.7%	Ralph M. Hall, Texas	67.0%
Nancy L. Johnson, Conn.	24.3	Ken Lucas, Ky.	55.7
Ron Paul, Texas	22.8	Robert E. "Bud" Cramer, Ala.	44.6
Christopher Shays, Conn.	22.4	Charles W. Stenholm, Texas	43.6
Sherwood Boehlert, N.Y.	21.1	Chris John, La.	42.2
Michael N. Castle, Del.	20.9	Gene Taylor, Miss.	40.0
Jim Ramstad, Minn.	19.6	Collin C. Peterson, Minn.	36.3
Rob Simmons, Conn.	19.5	John Tanner, Tenn.	32.7
Amo Houghton, N.Y.	19.2	Ike Skelton, Mo.	32.6
Frank A. LoBiondo, N.J.	16.9	William O. Lipinski, Ill.	31.1
James C. Greenwood, Pa.	16.3	Tim Holden, Pa.	30.8
Charles Bass, N.H.	15.1	Cal Dooley, Calif.	30.2
Mark Steven Kirk, Ill.	14.9	Bart Gordon, Tenn.	29.9
Timothy V. Johnson, Ill.	14.8	John P. Murtha, Pa.	29.9
Jack Quinn, N.Y.	14.8	Allen Boyd, Fla.	29.3
Sue W. Kelly, N.Y.	14.8	Brad Carson, Okla.	29.2
Wayne T. Gilchrest, Md.	14.0	Mike McIntyre, N.C.	29.2
Rodney Frelinghuysen, N.J.	13.5	Jim Turner, Texas	28.9
Vernon J. Ehlers, Mich.	13.4	Mike Ross, Ark.	28.4
Christopher H. Smith, N.J.	13.2	Alan B. Mollohan, W.Va.	28.4

Former Congressional Staffers

Members of Congress who once worked as congressional aides. Internships are not included.

Member	Employer	Years
Sen. Lamar Alexander, R-Tenn.	Sen. Howard H. Baker Jr., R-Tenn	1967-68
Rep. Tom Allen, D-Maine	Sen. Edmund S. Muskie, D-Maine	1970-71
Rep. Charles Bass, R-N.H.	Rep. William S. Cohen, R-Maine	1974
	Rep. David F. Emery, R-Maine	1975-79
Sen. Robert F. Bennett, R-Utah	Rep. Sherman P. Lloyd, R-Utah	1962
Rep. Sherwood Boehlert, R-N.Y.	Rep. Alexander Pirnie, R-N.Y.	1964-72
	Rep. Donald J. Mitchell, R-N.Y.	1973-79
Rep. Jo Bonner, R-Ala.	Rep. Sonny Callahan, R-Ala.	1985-2002
Sen. Barbara Boxer, D-Calif.	Rep. John L. Burton, D-Calif.	1974-76
Sen. John B. Breaux, D-La.	Rep. Edwin W. Edwards, D-La.	1968-69
Rep. Dave Camp, R-Mich.	Rep. Bill Schuette, R-Mich.	1984-87
Rep. Julia M. Carson, D-Ind.	Rep. Andrew Jacobs Jr., D-Ind.	1965-72
Rep. Ed Case, D-Hawaii	Rep./Sen. Spark M. Matsunaga, D-Hawaii	1975-78
Rep. William Lacy Clay, D-Mo.	House Clerk, House Doorkeeper	1977-83
Rep. Tom Cole, R-Okla.	Rep. Mickey Edwards, R-Okla.	1982-84
Sen. Susan Collins, R-Maine	Rep. William S. Cohen, R-Maine	1975-78
Rep. John Conyers Jr., D-Mich.	Rep. John D. Dingell, D-Mich.	1958-61
Sen. Tom Daschle, D-S.D.	Sen. James Abourezk, D-S.D.	1973-77
Sen. Mark Dayton, D-Minn.	Sen. Walter F. Mondale, D-Minn.	1975-76
Rep. Peter A. DeFazio, D-Ore.	Rep. Jim Weaver, D-Ore.,	1977-82
Rep. Rosa DeLauro, D-Conn.	Sen. Christopher J. Dodd, D-Conn.	1981-87
Rep. Norm Dicks, D-Wash.	Sen. Warren G. Magnuson, D-Wash.	1968-76
Rep. Chet Edwards, D-Texas	Rep. Olin Teague, D-Texas	1975-77
Del. Eni F.H. Faleomavaega, D-Am. Samoa	House Interior and Insular Affairs Committee	1975-81
Rep. Barney Frank, D-Mass.	Rep. Michael J. Harrington, D-Mass.	1971-72
Rep. Robert W. Goodlatte, R-Va.	Rep. M. Caldwell Butler, R-Va.	1977-79
Sen. Chuck Hagel, R-Neb.	Rep. John Y. McCollister, R-Neb.	1971-77
Sen. Tom Harkin, D-Iowa	Rep. Neal Smith, D-Iowa	1969-70
Rep. Jane Harman, D-Calif.	Sen. John V. Tunney, D-Calif.	1972-73
Rep. Jeb Hensarling, R-Texas	Sen. Phil Gramm, R-Texas	1985-89
Rep. Steve Israel, D-N.Y.	Rep. Robert T. Matsui, D-Calif.	1980
	Rep. Richard L. Ottinger, D-N.Y.	1980-83
Rep. Sheila Jackson-Lee, D-Texas	House Select Committee on Assassinations	1977-78
Rep. William J. Jefferson, D-La	Sen. J. Bennett Johnston, D-La.	1973-75
Rep. Mark Steven Kirk, R-Ill.	Rep. John Edward Porter, R-Ill.	1984-89
	House International Relations Committee	1995-2000
Rep. Ray LaHood, R-Ill.	Rep. Thomas F. Railsback, R-Ill.	1977-82
	Rep. Robert H. Michel, R-Ill.	1983-94
Rep. Tom Lantos, D-Calif.	Sen. Joseph R. Biden Jr., D-Del.	1979
Rep. Jim Leach, R-Iowa	Rep. Donald H. Rumsfeld, R-Ill.	1965-66
Rep. Barbara Lee, D-Calif.	Rep. Ronald V. Dellums, D-Calif.	1975-87
Rep. Jerry Lewis, R-Calif.	Rep. Jerry Pettis, R-Calif.	1967
Sen. Blanche Lincoln, D-Ark.	Rep. Bill Alexander, D-Ark.	1982
Rep. Zoe Lofgren, D-Calif.	Rep. Don Edwards, D-Calif.	1970-79
Sen. Trent Lott, R-Miss.	Rep. William M. Colmer, D-Miss.	1968-72
Sen. Mitch McConnell, R-Ky.	Sen. Marlow Cook, R-Ky.	1969-70
Rep. Jim McCrery, R-La.	Rep. Buddy Roemer, R-La.	1981-84
Rep. Jim McGovern, D-Mass.	Sen. George McGovern, D-S.D	1977-80
	Rep. Joe Moakley, D-Mass.	1981-93
Rep. Martin T. Meehan, D-Mass.	Rep. James M. Shannon, D-Mass.	1979-81
Rep. John L. Mica, R-Fla.	Sen. Paula Hawkins, R-Fla.	1981-85

Rep. James P. Moran, D-Va.	Senate Appropriations Committee	1976-79
Rep. George Nethercutt, R-Wash.	Sen. Ted Stevens, R-Alaska	1972-77
Rep. James L. Oberstar, D-Minn.	Rep. John A. Blatnik, D-Minn.	1964-74
Rep. Charles W. "Chip" Pickering Jr., R-Miss.	Sen. Trent Lott, R-Miss.	1991-95
Rep. Nick J. Rahall II, D-W.Va.	Sen. Robert C. Byrd, D-W.Va.	1971-74
Rep. Jim Ramstad, R-Minn.	Rep. Thomas S. Kleppe, R-N.D.	1970
Rep. Denny Rehberg, R-Mont.	Rep. Ron Marlenee, R-Mont.	1979-82
	Sen. Conrad Burns, R-Mont.	1989-91
Sen. Pat Roberts, R-Kan.	Sen. Frank Carlson, R-Kan.	1967-68
	Rep. Keith G. Sebelius, R-Kan.	1968-80
Rep. Paul D. Ryan, R-Wis.	Sen. Bob Kasten, R-Wis.	1991-92
	Rep. Sam Brownback, R-Kan.	1995-97
Rep. Tim Ryan, D-Ohio	Rep. James A. Traficant Jr., D-Ohio	1995-97
Rep. Rob Simmons, R-Conn.	Sen. John H. Chafee, R-R.I.	1979-81
	Senate Intelligence Committee	1981-85
Sen. Olympia J. Snowe, R-Maine	Rep. William S. Cohen, R-Maine	1973
Rep. Mark Souder, R-Ind.	Sen. Dan Coats, R-Ind.	1989-94
Rep. William M. "Mac" Thornberry, R-Texas	Rep. Tom Loeffler, R-Texas	1983-85
	Rep. Larry Combest, R-Texas	1985-88
Rep. Pat Tiberi, R-Ohio	Rep. John R. Kasich, R-Ohio	1983-92
Rep. Fred Upton, R-Mich.	Rep. David A. Stockman, R-Mich.	1976-80
Rep. Chris Van Hollen, D-Md.	Sen. Charles McC. Mathias Jr., R-Md.	1985-87
	Senate Foreign Relations Committee	1987-89
Rep. Nydia N. Velázquez, D-N.Y.	Rep. Edolphus Towns, D-N.Y.	1983
Rep. Peter J. Visclosky, D-Ind.	Rep. Adam Benjamin Jr., D-Ind.	1977-82
Rep. Greg Walden, R-Ore.	Rep. Denny Smith, R-Ore.	1981-86
Rep. Anthony Weiner, D-N.Y.	Rep. Charles E. Schumer, D-N.Y.	1985-91
Rep. Jerry Weller, R-Ill.	Rep. Thomas J. Corcoran, R-Ill.	1980-81
Rep. Roger Wicker, R-Miss.	Rep. Trent Lott, R-Miss.	1980-82
Rep. Frank R. Wolf, R-Va.	Rep. Edward G. Biester, R-Pa.	1968-71

Congressional Half-Life

Current members who have served more than half of their life in Congress. Length of service is as of Jan. 7, 2003.

Member	Age at Swearing-in	Length of Service	Percent of Life In Congress
Rep. John D. Dingell, D-Mich.	29 years, 158 days	47 years, 25 days	62%
Sen. Robert C. Byrd, D-W.Va.	35 years, 44 days	50 years	59
Sen. Edward M. Kennedy, D-Mass.	30 years, 258 days	40 years, 61 days	57
Sen. Daniel K. Inouye, D-Hawaii	34 years, 348 days	43 years, 139 days	55
Rep. David R. Obey, D-Wis.	30 years, 180 days	33 years, 281 days	53
Rep. John Conyers Jr., D-Mich.	35 years, 233 days	38 years	52
Sen. John B. Breaux, D-La.	28 years, 213 days	30 years, 99 days	51

Sen. Joseph R. Biden Jr., D-Del., passed the milestone on Feb. 16, 2003, when he had served exactly half his life in Congress: 30 years, 44 days

Notes:

Sen. Trent Lott, R-Miss., who began serving in the House of Representatives in 1973, is due to join the list March 30, 2004, when he will have served 31 years, 86 days.

Rep. Nick J. Rahall II, D-W.Va., who began serving in the House of Representatives in 1977, is due to join the list Aug. 21, 2004, when he will have served 27 years, 229 days.

Rep. George Miller, D-Calif., who began serving in the House of Representatives in 1975, is due to join the list Nov. 13, 2004, when he will have served 29 years, 303 days.

House 'Blue Dog' Coalition

All members are Democrats

Co-chairmen: Baron P. Hill, Ind., Charles W. Stenholm, Texas, Jim Turner, Texas

Rodney Alexander, La.
Joe Baca, Calif.
Marion Berry, Ark.
Sanford D. Bishop Jr., Ga.
Leonard L. Boswell, Iowa
Allen Boyd, Fla.
Dennis Cardoza, Calif.
Brad Carson, Okla.
Robert E. "Bud" Cramer, Ala.
Lincoln Davis, Tenn.
Harold E. Ford Jr., Tenn.
Ralph M. Hall, Texas
Jane Harman, Calif.
Tim Holden, Pa.
Steve Israel, N.Y.
Chris John, La.
William O. Lipinski, Ill.
Ken Lucas, Ky.
Jim Matheson, Utah
Mike McIntyre, N.C.
Michael H. Michaud, Maine
Dennis Moore, Kan.
Collin C. Peterson, Minn.
Earl Pomeroy, N.D.
Mike Ross, Ark.
Loretta Sanchez, Calif.
Max Sandlin, Texas
Adam B. Schiff, Calif.
David Scott, Ga.
John Tanner, Tenn.
Ellen O. Tauscher, Calif.
Gene Taylor, Miss.
Mike Thompson, Calif.

Progressive Caucus

All members except Sanders are Democrats

Officers

Rep. Dennis J. Kucinich, Ohio – co-chairman
Rep. Barbara Lee, Calif. – co-chairwoman
Rep. Lynn Woolsey, Calif.
Rep. Peter A. DeFazio, Ore.
Rep. Jesse L. Jackson Jr., Ill.
Rep. Major R. Owens, N.Y.
Rep. Bernard Sanders, Vt.
Rep. Hilda L. Solis, Calif.

Members

Rep. Neil Abercrombie, Hawaii
Rep. Tammy Baldwin, Wis.
Rep. Xavier Becerra, Calif.
Rep. Corrine Brown, Fla.
Rep. Sherrod Brown, Ohio
Rep. Michael E. Capuano, Mass.
Rep. Julia Carson, Ind.
Rep. William Lacy Clay, Mo.
Rep. John Conyers Jr., Mich.
Rep. Danny K. Davis, Ill.
Rep. Rosa DeLauro, Conn.
Rep. Lane Evans, Ill.
Del. Eni F.H. Faleomavaega, Am. Samoa
Rep. Sam Farr, Calif.
Rep. Chaka Fattah, Pa.
Rep. Bob Filner, Calif.
Rep. Barney Frank, Mass.
Rep. Raúl M. Grijalva, Ariz.
Rep. Luis V. Gutierrez, Ill.
Rep. Maurice D. Hinchey, N.Y.
Rep. Sheila Jackson-Lee, Texas
Rep. Stephanie Tubbs Jones, Ohio
Rep. Marcy Kaptur, Ohio
Rep. Tom Lantos, Calif.
Rep. John Lewis, Ga.
Rep. Jim McDermott, Wash.
Rep. Jim McGovern, Mass.
Rep. George Miller, Calif.
Rep. Jerrold Nadler, N.Y.
Del. Eleanor Holmes Norton, D.C.
Rep. John W. Olver, Mass.
Rep. Ed Pastor, Ariz.
Rep. Donald M. Payne, N.J.
Rep. Nancy Pelosi, Calif.
Rep. Bobby L. Rush, Ill.
Rep. Jan Schakowsky, Ill.
Rep. José E. Serrano, N.Y.
Rep. Pete Stark, Calif.
Rep. Bennie Thompson, Miss.
Rep. John F. Tierney, Mass.
Rep. Tom Udall, N.M.
Rep. Nydia M. Velázquez, N.Y.
Rep. Maxine Waters, Calif.
Rep. Diane Watson, Calif.
Rep. Melvin Watt, N.C.
Rep. Henry A. Waxman, Calif.

House New Democrat Coalition

All members are Democrats

Co-chairmen: Jim Davis, Fla., Ron Kind, Wis., Adam Smith, Wash.

Tom Allen, Maine
Joe Baca, Calif.
Brian Baird, Wash.
Chris Bell, Texas
Shelley Berkley, Nev.
Marion Berry, Ark.
Earl Blumenauer, Ore.
Lois Capps, Calif.
Dennis Cardoza, Calif.
Brad Carson, Okla.
Ed Case, Hawaii
Jim Cooper, Tenn.
Robert E. "Bud" Cramer, Ala.
Joseph Crowley, N.Y.
Artur Davis, Ala.
Susan A. Davis, Calif.
Peter Deutsch, Fla.
Cal Dooley, Calif.
Rahm Emanuel, Ill.
Anna G. Eshoo, Calif.
Bob Etheridge, N.C.
Harold E. Ford Jr., Tenn.
Charlie Gonzalez, Texas
Jane Harman, Calif.
Baron P. Hill, Ind.
Ruben Hinojosa, Texas
Joseph M. Hoeffel, Pa.
Rush D. Holt, N.J.
Michael M. Honda, Calif.
Darlene Hooley, Ore.
Jay Inslee, Wash.
Steve Israel, N.Y.
Chris John, La.
Nick Lampson, Texas
Jim Langevin, R.I.
Rick Larsen, Wash.
John B. Larson, Conn.
Zoe Lofgren, Calif.
Ken Lucas, Ky.
Denise L. Majette, Ga.
Carolyn B. Maloney, N.Y.
Jim Matheson, Utah
Robert T. Matsui, Calif.
Carolyn McCarthy, N.Y.
Karen McCarthy, Mo.
Mike McIntyre, N.C.
Gregory W. Meeks, N.Y.
Michael H. Michaud, Maine
Juanita Millender-McDonald, Calif.
Brad Miller, N.C.
Dennis Moore, Kan.
James P. Moran, Va.
Grace F. Napolitano, Calif.
David E. Price, N.C.
Silvestre Reyes, Texas
Mike Ross, Ark.
Steven R. Rothman, N.J.
Loretta Sanchez, Calif.
Max Sandlin, Texas
Adam B. Schiff, Calif.
David Scott, Ga.
Brad Sherman, Calif.
Vic Snyder, Ark.
John M. Spratt Jr., S.C.
Charles W. Stenholm, Texas
Bart Stupak, Mich.
John Tanner, Tenn.
Ellen O. Tauscher, Calif.
Mike Thompson, Calif.
Jim Turner, Texas
Tom Udall, N.M.
Robert Wexler, Fla.
David Wu, Ore.

Born Abroad

Members of Congress who were born outside the 50 states and the District of Columbia:

Name	**Country**
Rep. Diana DeGette, D-Colo.	Japan
Rep. Lincoln Diaz-Balart, R-Fla.	Cuba
Rep. Peter Hoekstra, R-Mich.	Netherlands
Rep. Tom Lantos, D-Calif.	Hungary
Sen. John McCain, R-Ariz.	Panama Canal Zone
Rep. Ciro D. Rodriguez, D-Texas	Mexico
Rep. Ileana Ros-Lehtinen, R-Fla.	Cuba
Rep. José E. Serrano, D-N.Y.	Puerto Rico
Rep. Chris Van Hollen, D-Md.	Pakistan
Rep. Nydia M. Velázquez, D-N.Y.	Puerto Rico
Rep. David Wu, D-Ore.	Taiwan

Former Pages

Members of Congress who once served as congressional pages:

Name	**Years**
Rep. Jim Cooper, D-Tenn.	1970
Rep. Ander Crenshaw, R-Fla.	1961
Rep. Thomas M. Davis III, R-Va.	1963-67
Rep. John D. Dingell, D-Mich.	1955
Sen. Christopher J. Dodd, D-Conn.	c. 1960
Rep. Paul E. Kanjorski, D-Pa.	1953-54
Rep. Jim Kolbe, R-Ariz.	1958-60
Sen. Mark Pryor, D-Ark.	1982
Rep. Roger Wicker, R-Miss.	1967

Republican Main Street Partnership

Members of Congress who are members of the partnership, which also includes several governors and former elected officials. All members are Republicans.

Rep. Charles Bass, N.H.
Rep. Doug Bereuter, Neb.
Rep. Judy Biggert, Ill.
Rep. Sherwood Boehlert, N.Y.
Rep. Jeb Bradley, N.H.
Rep. Ginny Brown-Waite, Fla.
Rep. Ken Calvert, Calif.
Rep. Dave Camp, Mich.
Rep. Shelley Moore Capito, W.Va.
Rep. Michael N. Castle, Del., president of the board
Sen. Lincoln Chafee, R.I.
Sen. Norm Coleman, Minn.
Sen. Susan Collins, Maine, board member
Rep. Thomas M. Davis III, Va., board member
Rep. David Dreier, Calif.
Rep. Vernon J. Ehlers, Mich.
Rep. Phil English, Pa.
Rep. Mike Ferguson, N.J.
Rep. Mark Foley, Fla.
Rep. Rodney Frelinghuysen, N.J.
Rep. Wayne T. Gilchrest, Md.
Rep. Paul E. Gillmor, Ohio
Rep. Porter J. Goss, Fla.
Rep. Kay Granger, Texas
Rep. James C. Greenwood, Pa.
Rep. David L. Hobson, Ohio
Rep. Amo Houghton, N.Y., founder and board member
Rep. Johnny Isakson, Ga.
Rep. Nancy L. Johnson, Conn.
Rep. Timothy V. Johnson, Ill.
Rep. Sue W. Kelly, N.Y.
Rep. Mark Steven Kirk, Ill.
Rep. Jim Kolbe, Ariz.
Rep. Ray LaHood, Ill.
Rep. Steven C. LaTourette, Ohio
Rep. Jim Leach, Iowa
Rep. Jerry Lewis, Calif.
Sen. John McCain, Ariz.
Rep. Jim McCrery, La.
Rep. George Nethercutt, Wash.
Rep. Tom Osborne, Neb., board member
Rep. Doug Ose, Calif., board member
Rep. Tom Petri, Wis.
Rep. Jon Porter, Nev.
Rep. Deborah Pryce, Ohio
Rep. Jack Quinn, N.Y.
Rep. Jim Ramstad, Minn.
Rep. Ralph Regula, Ohio
Sen. Pat Roberts, Kan.
Rep. Mike Rogers, Mich.
Rep. E. Clay Shaw Jr., Fla.
Rep. Christopher Shays, Conn.
Rep. Rob Simmons, Conn.
Sen. Gordon H. Smith, Ore.
Sen. Olympia J. Snowe, Maine, board member
Sen. Arlen Specter, Pa.
Sen. Ted Stevens, Alaska
Rep. Fred Upton, Mich., board member
Rep. Greg Walden, Ore.
Rep. James T. Walsh, N.Y.
Rep. Curt Weldon, Pa.
Rep. Jerry Weller, Ill.

Party Switchers

Members of Congress who changed their party affiliations after their election to Congress. A number of other members switched parties before coming to Congress.

Member	Old Party	New Party	Date Switched
Sen. Ben Nighthorse Campbell, Colo.	D	R	March 3, 1995
Rep. Nathan Deal, Ga.	D	R	April 10, 1995
Rep. Virgil H. Goode Jr., Va.	D	I	Jan. 24, 2000
Rep. Virgil H. Goode Jr., Va.	I	R	Aug. 1, 2002
Sen. James M. Jeffords, Vt.	R	I	June 5, 2001
Sen. Richard C. Shelby, Ala.	D	R	Nov. 9, 1994
Rep. Billy Tauzin, La.	D	R	Aug. 6, 1995

Republican Study Committee

Members of the House Republican Study Committee (formerly known as the Conservative Action Team, or CATs). The list is not comprehensive: The RSC organization permits individual members to decide whether to publicize their membership.

Chairman and Founders
Sue Myrick, N.C., chairman
Dan Burton, Ind., founder
John T. Doolittle, Calif., founder
Ernest Istook, Okla., founder
Sam Johnson, Texas, founder

Members
Robert B. Aderholt , Ala.
Todd Akin, Mo.
Spencer Bachus, Ala.
Roscoe G. Bartlett, Md.
Joe L. Barton, Texas
Bob Beauprez, Colo.
John Boozman, Ark.
Kevin Brady, Texas
Dave Camp, Mich.
Chris Cannon, Utah
Eric Cantor, Va.
Christopher Cox, Calif.
Philip M. Crane, Ill.
Barbara Cubin, Wyo.
John Culberson, Texas
Jo Ann Davis, Va.
Jim DeMint, S.C.
Jeff Flake, Ariz.
J. Randy Forbes, Va.
Virgil H. Goode Jr., Va.
Mark Green, Wis.
Gil Gutknecht, Minn.
Melissa A. Hart, Pa.
J.D. Hayworth, Ariz.
Wally Herger, Calif.
Peter Hoekstra, Mich.
John Hostettler, Ind.
Duncan Hunter, Calif.
Walter B. Jones., N.C.
John Kline, Minn.
Ron Lewis, Ky.
Donald Manzullo, Ill.
Gary G. Miller, Calif.
Jeff Miller, Fla.
Jerry Moran, Kan.
C.L. "Butch" Otter, Idaho
Mike Pence, Ind.
Joe Pitts, Pa.
Richard W. Pombo, Calif.
George P. Radanovich, Calif.
Denny Rehberg, Mont.
Thomas M. Reynolds, N.Y.
Jim Ryun, Kan.
Pete Sessions, Texas
John Shadegg, Ariz.
Nick Smith, Mich.
Mark Souder, Ind.
Cliff Stearns, Fla.
John Sullivan, Okla.
Tom Tancredo, Colo.
Billy Tauzin, La.
Charles H. Taylor, N.C.
Lee Terry, Neb.
Todd Tiahrt, Kan.
Patrick J. Toomey, Pa.
David Vitter, La.
Dave Weldon, Fla.
Joe Wilson, S.C.

Senators Up for Election in 2004

15 Republicans, 19 Democrats

Bayh, Evan	D-Ind.
Bennett, Robert F	R-Utah
Bond, Christopher S.	R-Mo.
Boxer, Barbara	D-Calif.
Breaux, John B.	D-La.
Brownback, Sam	R-Kan.
Bunning, Jim	R-Ky.
Campbell, Ben Nighthorse	R-Colo.
Crapo, Michael D.	R-Idaho
Daschle, Tom	D-S.D.
Dodd, Christopher J.	D-Conn.
Dorgan, Byron L.	D-N.D.
Edwards, John	D-N.C.
Feingold, Russell D.	D-Wis.
Fitzgerald, Peter G.	R-Ill.
Graham, Bob	D-Fla.
Grassley, Charles E.	R-Iowa
Gregg, Judd	R-N.H.
Hollings, Ernest F.	D-S.C.
Inouye, Daniel K.	D-Hawaii
Leahy, Patrick J.	D-Vt.
Lincoln, Blanche	D-Ark.
McCain, John	R-Ariz.
Mikulski, Barbara A.	D-Md.
Miller, Zell	D-Ga.
Murkowski, Lisa	R-Alaska
Murray, Patty	D-Wash.
Nickles, Don	R-Okla.
Reid, Harry	D-Nev.
Schumer, Charles E.	D-N.Y.
Shelby, Richard C.	R-Ala.
Specter, Arlen	R-Pa.
Voinovich, George V.	R-Ohio
Wyden, Ron	D-Ore.

Senate New Democrat Coalition

All members are Democrats

Chairman: Bob Graham, Fla.

Evan Bayh, Ind.
John B. Breaux, La.
Thomas R. Carper, Del.
Kent Conrad, N.D.
John Edwards, N.C.
Dianne Feinstein, Calif.
Tim Johnson, S.D.
John Kerry, Mass.
Herb Kohl, Wis.
Mary L. Landrieu, La.
Joseph I. Lieberman, Conn.
Blanche Lincoln, Ark.
Zell Miller, Ga.
Ben Nelson, Neb.
Bill Nelson, Fla.
Mark Pryor, Ark.
Debbie Stabenow, Mich.

Most Bills — House

Current members of the House who introduced the most bills and resolutions in the 107th Congress:

Member	Bills, Resolutions
Robert E. Andrews, D-N.J.	107
Sue Myrick, R-N.C.	66
Christopher H. Smith, R-N.J.	66
Don Young, R-Alaska	65
Ron Paul, R-Texas	64
Carolyn B. Maloney, D-N.Y.	52
Phil English, R-Pa.	50
Charles B. Rangel, D-N.Y.	50
Thomas M. Reynolds, R-N.Y.	46
Frank Pallone Jr., D-N.J.	43

Fewest Bills — House

Current members of the House who introduced the fewest bills and resolutions in the 107th Congress (limited to members who served the entire 107th Congress):

Member	Bills, Resolutions
Allen Boyd, D-Fla.	1
John Culberson, R-Texas	1
Jim Davis, D-Fla.	1
Terry Everett, R-Ala.	1
Ken Lucas, D-Ky.	1
Don Sherwood, R-Pa.	1
Charles W. Stenholm, D-Texas	1
Bart Gordon, D-Tenn.	2
Ruben Hinojosa, D-Texas	2
Jerry Lewis, R-Calif.	2
Alan B. Mollohan, D-W.Va.	2
Solomon P. Ortiz, D-Texas	2
David E. Price, D-N.C.	2
Vic Snyder, D-Ark.	2
Zach Wamp, R-Tenn.	2

Most Bills — Senate

Current members of the Senate who introduced the most bills and resolutions in the 107th Congress:

Member	Bills, Resolutions
Dianne Feinstein, D-Calif.	112
Tom Daschle, D-S.D.	106
Hillary Rodham Clinton, D-N.Y.	90
Jeff Bingaman, D-N.M.	84
John Kerry, D-Mass.	81
Olympia J. Snowe, R-Maine	70
Richard J. Durbin, D-Ill.	66
Christopher J. Dodd, D-Conn.	65
Edward M. Kennedy, D-Mass.	64
Orrin G. Hatch, R-Utah	63
John D. Rockefeller IV, D-W.Va.	63

Fewest Bills — Senate

Current members of the Senate who introduced the fewest bills and resolutions in the 107th Congress:

Member	Bills, Resolutions
Ben Nelson, D-Neb.	2
Robert F. Bennett, R-Utah	10
Robert C. Byrd, D-W.Va.	10
Ted Stevens, R-Alaska	10
Don Nickles, R-Okla.	11
Debbie Stabenow, D-Mich.	11
Lincoln Chafee, R-R.I.	12
Jon Kyl, R-Ariz.	12
Zell Miller, D-Ga.	12
Judd Gregg, R-N.H.	13
Barbara A. Mikulski, D-Md.	13

Former Representatives In Senate

25 Republicans, 23 Democrats, 1 Independent

Member	Party, State	Served in House
Daniel K. Akaka	D-Hawaii	1977-90
Wayne Allard	R-Colo.	1991-97
George Allen	R-Va.	1991-93
Max Baucus	D-Mont.	1975-78
Barbara Boxer	D-Calif.	1983-93
John B. Breaux	D-La.	1972-87
Sam Brownback	R-Kan.	1995-96
Jim Bunning	R-Ky.	1987-99
Robert C. Byrd	D-W.Va.	1953-59
Ben Nighthorse Campbell	R-Colo.	1987-93
Maria Cantwell	D-Wash.	1993-95
Thomas R. Carper	D-Del.	1983-93
Saxby Chambliss	R-Ga.	1995-2003
Thad Cochran	R-Miss.	1973-78
Larry E. Craig	R-Idaho	1981-91
Michael D. Crapo	R-Idaho	1993-99
Tom Daschle	D-S.D.	1979-87
Mike DeWine	R-Ohio	1983-91
Christopher J. Dodd	D-Conn.	1975-81
Byron L. Dorgan	D-N.D.	1981-92
Richard J. Durbin	D-Ill.	1983-97
John Ensign	R-Nev.	1995-99
Lindsey Graham	R-S.C.	1995-2003
Charles E. Grassley	R-Iowa	1975-81
Judd Gregg	R-N.H.	1981-89
Tom Harkin	D-Iowa	1975-85
James M. Inhofe	R-Okla.	1987-94
Daniel K. Inouye	D-Hawaii	1959-63
James M. Jeffords	I-Vt.	1975-89
Tim Johnson	D-S.D.	1987-97
Jon Kyl	R-Ariz.	1987-95
Blanche Lincoln	D-Ark.	1993-97
Trent Lott	R-Miss.	1973-89
John McCain	R-Ariz.	1983-87
Barbara A. Mikulski	D-Md.	1977-87
Bill Nelson	D-Fla.	1979-91
Jack Reed	D-R.I.	1991-97
Harry Reid	D-Nev.	1983-87
Pat Roberts	R-Kan.	1981-97
Rick Santorum	R-Pa.	1991-95
Paul S. Sarbanes	D-Md.	1971-77
Charles E. Schumer	D-N.Y.	1981-99
Richard C. Shelby	R-Ala.	1979-87
Olympia J. Snowe	R-Maine	1979-95
Debbie Stabenow	D-Mich.	1997-2001
John E. Sununu	R-N.H.	1997-2003
Jim Talent	R-Mo.	1993-2001
Craig Thomas	R-Wyo.	1989-95
Ron Wyden	D-Ore.	1981-96

10 Oldest Members of Congress

Member	Birthdate
Sen. Robert C. Byrd, D-W.Va.	Nov. 20, 1917
Sen. Ernest F. Hollings, D-S.C.	Jan. 1, 1922
Rep. Ralph M. Hall, D-Texas	May 3, 1923
Sen. Ted Stevens, R-Alaska	Nov. 18, 1923
Sen. Frank R. Lautenberg, D-N.J.	Jan. 23, 1924
Rep. Henry J. Hyde, R-Ill.	April 18, 1924
Sen. Daniel K. Inouye, D-Hawaii	Sept. 7, 1924
Sen. Daniel K. Akaka, D-Hawaii	Sept. 11, 1924
Rep. Ralph Regula, R-Ohio	Dec. 3, 1924
Rep. Roscoe G. Bartlett, R-Md.	June 3, 1926

10 Youngest Members of Congress

Member	Birthdate
Rep. Adam H. Putnam, R-Fla.	July 31, 1974
Rep. Devin Nunes, R-Calif.	Oct. 1, 1973
Rep. Tim Ryan, D-Ohio	July 16, 1973
Rep. Mike Ferguson, R-N.J.	July 22, 1970
Rep. Harold E. Ford Jr., D-Tenn.	May 11, 1970
Rep. Paul D. Ryan, R-Wis.	Jan. 29, 1970
Rep. Linda T. Sánchez, D-Calif.	Jan. 28, 1969
Rep. Artur Davis, D-Ala.	Oct. 9, 1967
Rep. Patrick J. Kennedy, D-R.I.	July 14, 1967
Rep. Brad Carson, D-Okla.	March 11, 1967

No Blacks or Women

States that have never been represented in Congress by either an African American or a woman:

Delaware **Iowa**
New Hampshire **Vermont**

Closest Elections of 2002

Race	Winner	Votes	Loser	Votes	Margin
Colo. 7	Bob Beauprez, R	81,789	Mike Feeley, D	81,668	121
S.D. Senate	Tim Johnson, D	167,481	John Thune, R	166,957	524
La. 5	Rodney Alexander, D	86,718	Lee Fletcher, R	85,744	974
Ga. 3	Jim Marshall, D	75,394	Calder Clay, R	73,866	1,528
Utah 2	Jim Matheson, D	110,764	John Swallow, R	109,123	1,641
N.Y. 1	Timothy H. Bishop, D	84,276	Felix J. Grucci Jr., R	81,524	2,752
Ala. 3	Mike D. Rogers, R	91,169	Joe Turnham, D	87,351	3,818
Fla. 5	Ginny Brown-Waite, R	121,998	Karen L. Thurman, D	117,758	4,240
Ga. 11	Phil Gingrey, R	69,427	Roger Kahn, D	65,007	4,420
Pa. 6	Jim Gerlach, R	103,648	Dan Wofford, D	98,128	5,520

Fewest Votes Received

House members who won with the fewest votes in 2002:

Member	Votes Received
Loretta Sanchez, D-Calif. (47)	42,501
Ed Pastor, D-Ariz. (4)	44,517
Joe Baca, D-Calif. (43)	45,374
Cal Dooley, D-Calif. (20)	47,627
Nydia M. Velázquez, D-N.Y. (12)	48,408
Lucille Roybal-Allard, D-Calif. (34)	48,734
José E. Serrano, D-N.Y. (16)	50,716
Joseph Crowley, D-N.Y. (7)	50,967
Linda T. Sánchez, D-Calif. (39)	52,256
Xavier Becerra, D-Calif. (31)	54,569

Most Votes Received

House candidates who received the most votes in 2002:

Member	Votes Received
Denny Rehberg, R-Mont (AL)	214,100
Jim Ramstad, R-Minn. (3)	213,334
James L. Oberstar, D-Minn. (8)	194,909
Ray LaHood, R-Ill. (18)	192,567
Wayne T. Gilchrest, R-Md. (1)	192,004
F. James Sensenbrenner Jr., R-Wis. (5)	191,224
Jerry Moran, R-Kan. (1)	189,976
Greg Walden, R-Ore. (2)	181,295
Bill Janklow, R-S.D. (AL)	180,023
Bill Delahunt, D-Mass. (10)	179,238

Most Votes Cast

The 10 congressional districts in which the most votes were cast in 2002:

District	Votes Cast
South Dakota AL	336,807
Montana AL	331,321
Minnesota 3	296,218
Minnesota 6	287,312
Minnesota 2	286,860
Minnesota 8	283,931
Maine 1	270,577
Minnesota 1	265,982
Minnesota 4	264,540
Oregon 4	263,481

Fewest Votes Cast

The 10 congressional districts in which the fewest votes were cast in 2002:

District	Votes Cast
New York 12	50,527
New York 16	55,082
Texas 29	58,593
California 34	65,824
Arizona 4	66,065
Texas 15	66,311
California 31	67,243
California 43	68,340
Texas 20	68,685
New York 7	69,539

Under 50 Percent

Winners of 2002 elections who received less than half the votes cast:

Member	Percent
Bob Beauprez, R-Colo.	47.3%
Ginny Brown-Waite, R-Fla.	47.9
Rick Renzi, R-Ariz.	49.2
Jim Matheson, D-Utah	49.4
Norm Coleman, R-Minn.	49.5
Tim Johnson, D-S.D.	49.6
Jim Talent, R-Mo.	49.8

Ed Case, D-Hawaii, received 43.7 percent in a Jan. 4, 2003, special election.

CAMPAIGN FINANCE

Winners Outspent by Opponents

Winners in 2002 who spent less than their opponents.
Totals cover the period Jan. 1, 2001, through Dec. 31, 2002.

(in order of spending margin)

Senate

Name, Party, State	Expenditures	Opponent	Expenditures
Frank R. Lautenberg, D-N.J.	$2,929,206	Doug Forrester, R	$10,638,966
Jim Talent, R-Mo.	8,777,033	Jean Carnahan, D	12,293,579
John E. Sununu, R-N.H.	3,545,925	Jeanne Shaheen, D	5,821,219
Saxby Chambliss, R-Ga.	7,743,004	Max Cleland, D	9,127,883
Mark Pryor, D-Ark.	4,414,148	Tim Hutchinson, R	5,063,923

House

Name, Party, State	Expenditures	Opponent	Expenditures
Shelley Moore Capito, R-W.Va.	$2,530,078	Jim Humphreys, D	$8,150,237
Chris Bell, D-Texas	1,107,790	Tom Reiser, R	4,542,054
John L. Mica, R-Fla.	1,756,115	Wayne Hogan, D	4,659,352
Jeb Bradley, R-N.H.	1,029,408	Martha Fuller Clark, D	3,511,108
Phil Gingrey, R-Ga.	1,819,423	Roger Kahn, D	4,215,536
Tom Feeney, R-Fla.	1,853,423	Harry Jacobs, D	3,989,408
Ginny Brown-Waite, R-Fla.	922,944	Karen L. Thurman, D	1,944,628
Jim Marshall, D-Ga.	1,006,764	Calder Clay, R	2,014,777
John Kline, R-Minn.	1,534,873	Bill Luther, D	2,263,619
Rodney Alexander, D-La.	831,088	Lee Fletcher, R	1,435,069
Charles Bass, R-N.H.	886,765	Katrina Swett, D	1,457,286
Jim Leach, R-Iowa	780,586	Julie Thomas, D	1,342,801
Baron P. Hill, D-Ind.	1,144,666	Mike Sodrel, R	1,626,646
Timothy H. Bishop, D-N.Y.	972,095	Felix J.Grucci Jr., R	1,399,768
Lois Capps, D-Calif.	1,461,132	Beth Rogers, R	1,844,444
Mark Kennedy, R-Minn.	1,893,753	Janet Robert, D	2,215,961
Joseph M. Hoeffel, D-Pa.	1,554,821	Melissa Brown, R	1,827,440
Scott Garrett, R-N.J.	1,342,264	Anne Sumers, D	1,605,385
Bill Janklow, R-S.D.	1,314,087	Stephanie Herseth, D	1,545,990
Max Burns, R-Ga.	925,706	Charles Walker Jr., D	1,120,201
Susan A. Davis, D-Calif.	582,445	Bill VanDeWeghe, R	742,535
Jim Gerlach, R-Pa.	1,261,590	Dan Wofford, D	1,386,721
Rob Bishop, R-Utah	670,302	David Thomas, D	715,893
Chris Van Hollen, D-Md.	2,985,329	Constance A. Morella, R	3,004,660
Julia Carson, D-Ind.	1,095,367	Brose McVey, R	1,105,370

CAMPAIGN FINANCE

10 Least-Expensive Winning House Campaigns

The chart is based on expenditures from Jan. 1, 2001, through Dec. 31, 2002.

Name	Expenditures	Name	Expenditures
Tom Osborne, R-Neb.	$81,357	Kendrick B. Meek, D-Fla.	$187,507
Porter J. Goss, R-Fla.	90,189	Henry E. Brown Jr., R-S.C.	189,806
Joel Hefley, R-Colo.	100,786	Lloyd Doggett, D-Texas	190,368
Bill Jenkins, R-Tenn.	107,482	Doug Bereuter, R-Neb.	191,344
Nick Smith, R-Mich.	155,157	Robert C. Scott, D-Va.	195,537

CAMPAIGN FINANCE

Top 10 Senate Spenders in 2002

The chart is based on Federal Election Commission reports of expenditures from Jan. 1, 2001, through Dec. 31, 2002.

Name, Party, State	Expenditures	Opponent	Expenditures
Elizabeth Dole, R-N.C.	$13,735,220	Erskine Bowles, D	$13,306,317
Norm Coleman, R-Minn.	10,035,279	Walter F. Mondale, D	1,833,029
		(Paul Wellstone, D)	12,617,876
John Cornyn, R-Texas	9,769,780	Ron Kirk, D	9,426,763
Jim Talent, R-Mo.	8,777,033	Jean Carnahan, D	12,293,579
John Kerry, D-Mass.	8,776,915	Michael Cloud, R	207,684
Saxby Chambliss, R-Ga.	7,743,004	Max Cleland, D	9,116,775
Mary L. Landrieu, D-La.	7,436,554	Suzanne Haik Terrell, R	2,760,276
Tom Harkin, D-Iowa	6,897,168	Greg Ganske, R	5,392,510
Lindsey Graham, R-S.C.	6,213,563	Alex Sanders, D	4,211,812
Max Baucus, D-Mont.	6,189,970	Mike Taylor, R	1,839,020

CAMPAIGN FINANCE

Top 10 House Spenders in 2002

The chart is based on Federal Election Commission reports of expenditures from Jan. 1, 2001, through Dec. 31, 2002.

Name, Party, State	Expenditures	Opponent	Expenditures
Nancy L. Johnson, R-Conn.	$3,752,161	Jim Maloney, D	$2,075,621
John D. Dingell, D-Mich.	3,461,009	Martin Kaltenbach, R, did not file a report	
		Lynn Rivers, D, in primary	1,766,210
Richard A. Gephardt, D-Mo.	3,389,306	Catherine S. Enz, R	114,143
Katherine Harris, R-Fla.	3,298,146	Jan Schneider, D	329,816
Anne M. Northup, R-Ky.	3,215,509	Jack Conway, D	1,539,362
Charles W. "Chip" Pickering Jr., R-Miss.	3,071,060	Ronnie Shows, D	1,439,271
Chris Van Hollen, D-Md.	2,985,329	Constance A. Morella, R	2,996,119
Rahm Emanuel, D-Ill.	2,971,514	Mark A. Augusti, R	217,731
J. Dennis Hastert, R-Ill.	2,970,554	Laurence J. Quick, D	18,136
Patrick J. Kennedy, D-R.I.	2,935,810	David Rogers, R	1,896,428

Campaign Finance

Figures are given for all members of Congress and their general election opponents as reported by the Federal Election Commission (FEC). If only one candidate is listed, either that candidate was unopposed or the second-leading vote-getter did not raise at least $5,000.

For House members, figures are for the 2002 elections. For senators, figures are for their most recent election.

The campaign finance data covers the receipts and expenditures of each candidate during the two-year election cycle. Data for 2002 covers the period Jan. 1, 2001, to Nov. 6, 2002, although subsequent runoffs and special elections are included in the 2002 statistics. Data for 2000 covers the period Jan. 1, 1999, to Dec. 31, 2000. Data for 1998 covers the period Jan. 1, 1997, to Dec. 31, 1998.

The figures for political action committee (PAC) receipts are based on the FEC summary report for each candidate. Amounts designated include contributions from both PACs and candidate committees, but not party committees.

Candidates who ran in special elections in the two-year cycle are marked with †. In these cases, campaign finance figures include money spent on the special elections.

Alabama

	RECEIPTS	FOM PACS	EXPENDITURES
SENIOR SENATOR - 1998			
Shelby (R)	$3,544,147	$1,167,950 (33%)	$1,890,484
Suddith (D)	$16,058	$500 (3%)	$15,723
JUNIOR SENATOR - 2002			
Sessions (R)	$4,635,963	$1,018,184 (22%)	$5,070,766
Parker (D)	$1,191,848	$178,820 (15%)	$1,185,718
DISTRICT 1			
Bonner (R)	$1,605,687	$461,167 (29%)	$1,300,876
Belk (D)	$455,989	$42,770 (9%)	$468,260
DISTRICT 2			
Everett (R)	$1,071,154	$275,139 (26%)	$842,440
DISTRICT 3			
Rogers (R)	$1,641,580	$761,266 (46%)	$1,621,525
Turnham (D)	$993,902	$338,081 (34%)	$985,881
DISTRICT 4			
Aderholt (R)	$706,785	$269,212 (38%)	$644,717
DISTRICT 5			
Cramer (D)	$1,021,353	$481,997 (47%)	$708,244
Engel (R)	$13,659	$0 (0%)	$13,659
DISTRICT 6			
Bachus (R)	$1,101,963	$661,086 (60%)	$709,786
DISTRICT 7			
Davis (D)	$1,573,790	$333,698 (21%)	$1,399,895

Alaska

	RECEIPTS	FOM PACS	EXPENDITURES
SENIOR SENATOR - 2002			
Stevens (R)	$2,718,907	$967,202 (36%)	$2,093,021
Vondersaar (D)	$1,050	$0 (0%)	$1,049
AT LARGE			
Young (R)	$2,151,694	$946,614 (44%)	$1,322,145
Greene (D)	$980	$0 (0%)	$980

Arizona

	RECEIPTS	FOM PACS	EXPENDITURES
SENIOR SENATOR - 1998			
McCain (R)	$4,450,544	$1,146,419 (26%)	$2,461,900
Ranger (D)	$375,463	$25,100 (7%)	$371,439
JUNIOR SENATOR - 2000			
Kyl (R)	$2,985,612	$880,280 (29%)	$2,503,674
Toel (I)	$21,542	$0 (0%)	$21,541
DISTRICT 1			
Renzi (R)	$1,619,052	$451,260 (28%)	$1,534,777
Cordova (D)	$655,697	$245,047 (37%)	$591,142
DISTRICT 2			
Franks (R)	$554,278	$33,149 (6%)	$554,250
Camacho (D)	$45,071	$8,500 (19%)	$38,594
DISTRICT 3			
Shadegg (R)	$625,763	$361,313 (58%)	$789,642
Hill (D)	$11,696	$1,000 (9%)	$11,694
DISTRICT 4			
Pastor (D)	$834,305	$479,555 (57%)	$633,516
Barnert (R)	$5,720	$1,000 (17%)	$3,112
DISTRICT 5			
Hayworth (R)	$1,434,331	$556,057 (39%)	$1,442,398
Columbus (D)	$356,538	$24,500 (7%)	$349,730
DISTRICT 6			
Flake (R)	$373,429	$141,639 (38%)	$258,256
Thomas (D)	$22,309	$11,300 (51%)	$22,076
DISTRICT 7			
Grijalva (D)	$547,498	$244,747 (45%)	$496,662
Hieb (R)	$131,132	$7,150 (5%)	$131,282
DISTRICT 8			
Kolbe (R)	$848,439	$312,860 (37%)	$849,078
Ryan (D)	$279,536	$29,000 (10%)	$290,800

Arkansas

	RECEIPTS	FOM PACS	EXPENDITURES
SENIOR SENATOR - 1998			
Lincoln (D)	$3,056,184	$1,133,856 (37%)	$3,122,776
Boozman (R)	$1,099,108	$162,300 (15%)	$1,093,007
JUNIOR SENATOR - 2002			
Pryor (D)	$4,442,708	$843,572 (19%)	$4,365,349
Hutchinson (R)	$4,858,117	$1,693,422 (35%)	$4,942,828

DISTRICT 1			
Berry (D)	$1,225,992	$539,617 (44%)	$1,279,267
Robinson (R)	$142,785	$4,500 (3%)	$141,779
DISTRICT 2			
Snyder (D)	$425,558	$187,300 (44%)	$440,566
DISTRICT 3			
Boozman (R)†	$694,784	$329,593 (47%)	$642,352
DISTRICT 4			
Ross (D)	$1,988,082	$987,653 (50%)	$2,008,348
Dickey (R)	$1,758,667	$149,056 (8%)	$1,731,752

California

	RECEIPTS	FOM PACS	EXPENDITURES
SENIOR SENATOR - 2000			
Feinstein (D)	$10,464,194	$1,245,727 (12%)	$10,346,170
Campbell (R)	$4,733,507	$11,600 (0%)	$4,378,283
JUNIOR SENATOR - 1998			
Boxer (D)	$12,828,962	$1,214,649 (9%)	$13,737,548
Fong (R)	$10,818,417	$1,510,264 (14%)	$10,764,892
DISTRICT 1			
Thompson (D)	$919,240	$357,113 (39%)	$971,544
Wiesner (R)	$74,447	$2,000 (3%)	$77,151
DISTRICT 2			
Herger (R)	$700,004	$373,047 (53%)	$706,267
Johnson (D)	$10,031	$0 (0%)	$9,022
DISTRICT 3			
Ose (R)	$872,973	$394,942 (45%)	$639,704
Beeman (D)	$73,067	$4,418 (6%)	$54,579
DISTRICT 4			
Doolittle (R)	$1,024,756	$373,955 (36%)	$979,438
Norberg (D)	$8,202	$3,000 (37%)	$7,548
DISTRICT 5			
Matsui (D)	$716,101	$480,599 (67%)	$827,273
Frankhuizen (R)	$6,383	$349 (5%)	$5,692
DISTRICT 6			
Woolsey (D)	$598,228	$260,450 (44%)	$803,235
Erickson (R)	$11,997	$0 (0%)	$10,171
DISTRICT 7			
Miller (D)	$470,622	$339,785 (72%)	$393,995
DISTRICT 8			
Pelosi (D)	$962,928	$534,108 (55%)	$908,123
German (R)	$7,130	$0 (0%)	$7,130
DISTRICT 9			
Lee (D)	$886,751	$216,998 (24%)	$888,133
DISTRICT 10			
Tauscher (D)	$906,663	$544,093 (60%)	$843,416
DISTRICT 11			
Pombo (R)	$956,845	$413,969 (43%)	$1,069,309
Shaw (D)	$600,843	$120,359 (20%)	$587,385
DISTRICT 12			
Lantos (D)	$344,357	$101,008 (29%)	$913,427
Abu-Ghazalah (LIBERT)	$163,718	$1,250 (1%)	$154,663
DISTRICT 13			
Stark (D)	$447,265	$307,977 (69%)	$399,480
Mahmood (R)	$49,951	$0 (0%)	$51,307
DISTRICT 14			
Eshoo (D)	$841,892	$436,423 (52%)	$831,035
Nixon (R)	$53,164	$50 (0%)	$44,823
DISTRICT 15			
Honda (D)	$930,977	$407,328 (44%)	$779,359
Hermann (R)	$30,414	$0 (0%)	$30,450
DISTRICT 16			
Lofgren (D)	$494,737	$208,529 (42%)	$483,391
McNea (R)	$1,965	$0 (0%)	$1,826
DISTRICT 17			
Farr (D)	$555,210	$309,880 (56%)	$554,326
Engler (R)	$1,780	$0 (0%)	$1,532
DISTRICT 18			
Cardoza (D)	$1,591,421	$802,104 (50%)	$1,570,185
Monteith (R)	$1,040,787	$352,371 (34%)	$1,024,285
DISTRICT 19			
Radanovich (R)	$678,730	$304,716 (45%)	$608,815
DISTRICT 20			
Dooley (D)	$946,071	$664,888 (70%)	$622,635
Minuth (R)	$504,106	$57 (0%)	$503,171
DISTRICT 21			
Nunes (R)	$1,216,539	$506,400 (42%)	$1,179,287
LaPere (D)	$18,232	$3,900 (21%)	$19,827
DISTRICT 22			
Thomas (R)	$1,229,987	$926,950 (75%)	$1,589,148
Corvera (D)	$6,159	$3,000 (49%)	$9,158
DISTRICT 23			
Capps (D)	$1,446,250	$529,903 (37%)	$1,436,569
Rogers (R)	$1,725,190	$61,767 (4%)	$1,719,720
DISTRICT 24			
Gallegly (R)	$707,362	$221,048 (31%)	$409,732
DISTRICT 25			
McKeon (R)	$866,906	$288,212 (33%)	$757,816
Conaway (D)	$7,224	$1,583 (22%)	$7,053
DISTRICT 26			
Dreier (R)	$837,200	$320,142 (38%)	$627,105
Mikels (D)	$64,316	$3,600 (6%)	$59,624
DISTRICT 27			
Sherman (D)	$1,204,644	$439,599 (36%)	$696,296
Levy (R)	$20,105	$1,000 (5%)	$20,104
DISTRICT 28			
Berman (D)	$952,662	$234,900 (25%)	$664,844
Hernandez (R)	$6,495	$0 (0%)	$8,953
DISTRICT 29			
Schiff (D)	$1,249,365	$449,999 (36%)	$680,098
DISTRICT 30			
Waxman (D)	$454,072	$362,816 (80%)	$496,130
DISTRICT 31			
Becerra (D)	$638,807	$439,300 (69%)	$421,992
DISTRICT 32			
Solis (D)	$480,641	$249,160 (52%)	$433,245
DISTRICT 33			
Watson (D)†	$1,606,442	$417,823 (26%)	$1,578,226
DISTRICT 34			
Roybal-Allard (D)	$448,923	$232,415 (52%)	$419,702
DISTRICT 35			
Waters (D)	$230,492	$128,875 (56%)	$246,671
Moen (R)	$52,816	$0 (0%)	$51,192

DISTRICT 36			
Harman (D)	$1,358,265	$577,758 (43%)	$1,176,039
Johnson (R)	$159,539	$6,080 (4%)	$150,858
DISTRICT 37			
Millender-McDonald (D)	$260,388	$203,522 (78%)	$236,765
Velasco (R)	$19,817	$0 (0%)	$14,083
DISTRICT 38			
Napolitano (D)	$305,208	$213,400 (70%)	$282,612
DISTRICT 39			
Sanchez (D)	$1,052,506	$422,338 (40%)	$1,043,814
Escobar (R)	$238,169	$45,730 (19%)	$235,373
DISTRICT 40			
Royce (R)	$1,086,255	$304,590 (28%)	$779,088
Avalos (D)	$12,076	$6,500 (54%)	$10,452
DISTRICT 41			
Lewis (R)	$748,852	$354,109 (47%)	$631,475
DISTRICT 42			
Miller (R)	$538,063	$273,098 (51%)	$182,132
DISTRICT 43			
Baca (D)	$487,386	$297,225 (61%)	$500,891
Neighbor (R)	$6,181	$0 (0%)	$4,915
DISTRICT 44			
Calvert (R)	$633,209	$247,765 (39%)	$627,663
DISTRICT 45			
Bono (R)	$521,283	$245,100 (47%)	$554,047
Kurpiewski (D)	$307,618	$104,250 (34%)	$304,105
DISTRICT 46			
Rohrabacher (R)	$390,183	$101,056 (26%)	$371,031
Schipske (D)	$215,195	$24,250 (11%)	$221,397
DISTRICT 47			
Sanchez (D)	$1,432,741	$478,806 (33%)	$1,239,599
Chavez (R)	$47,438	$9,250 (19%)	$46,994
DISTRICT 48			
Cox (R)	$724,875	$271,849 (38%)	$717,625
Graham (D)	$10,289	$750 (7%)	$10,030
DISTRICT 49			
Issa (R)	$554,868	$290,334 (52%)	$320,542
DISTRICT 50			
Cunningham (R)	$788,680	$376,527 (48%)	$751,497
Stewart (D)	$11,393	$3,950 (35%)	$6,385
DISTRICT 51			
Filner (D)	$629,435	$355,271 (56%)	$863,821
Garcia (R)	$131,699	$35,468 (27%)	$113,569
DISTRICT 52			
Hunter (R)	$829,745	$383,929 (46%)	$800,919
DISTRICT 53			
Davis (D)	$985,559	$336,025 (34%)	$560,939
VanDeWeghe (R)	$742,786	$82,693 (11%)	$740,372

Colorado

	RECEIPTS	FOM PACS	EXPENDITURES
SENIOR SENATOR - 1998			
Campbell (R)	$3,224,271	$1,120,303 (35%)	$3,045,982
Lamm (D)	$1,836,621	$187,343 (10%)	$1,818,801
JUNIOR SENATOR - 2002			
Allard (R)	$5,163,810	$1,940,956 (38%)	$5,077,481
Strickland (D)	$5,164,823	$784,890 (15%)	$5,048,097
DISTRICT 1			
DeGette (D)	$853,929	$421,900 (49%)	$765,185
Chlouber (R)	$114,735	$21,450 (19%)	$114,749
DISTRICT 2			
Udall (D)	$1,140,737	$288,421 (25%)	$747,161
Hume (R)	$30,926	$0 (0%)	$35,046
DISTRICT 3			
McInnis (R)	$787,085	$273,850 (35%)	$522,007
DISTRICT 4			
Musgrave (R)	$1,262,103	$426,922 (34%)	$1,249,564
Matsunaka (D)	$960,503	$384,921 (40%)	$950,190
DISTRICT 5			
Hefley (R)	$95,224	$56,583 (59%)	$100,786
Baker (LIBERT)	$34,166	$0 (0%)	$32,333
DISTRICT 6			
Tancredo (R)	$629,952	$225,046 (36%)	$443,895
Wright (D)	$8,466	$200 (2%)	$6,476
DISTRICT 7			
Beauprez (R)	$1,771,680	$439,402 (25%)	$1,664,440
Feeley (D)	$1,158,372	$463,396 (40%)	$1,135,632

Connecticut

	RECEIPTS	FOM PACS	EXPENDITURES
SENIOR SENATOR - 1998			
Dodd (D)	$4,102,172	$1,192,570 (29%)	$4,442,567
Franks (R)	$1,501,937	$71,602 (5%)	$1,478,307
JUNIOR SENATOR - 2000			
Lieberman (D)	$3,666,873	$975,344 (27%)	$3,786,665
Giordano (R)	$1,278,539	$0 (0%)	$1,276,376
DISTRICT 1			
Larson (D)	$670,551	$295,868 (44%)	$558,984
DISTRICT 2			
Simmons (R)	$2,098,656	$809,654 (39%)	$2,078,969
Courtney (D)	$1,232,465	$413,702 (34%)	$1,223,489
DISTRICT 3			
DeLauro (D)	$636,275	$273,025 (43%)	$665,857
Elser (R)	$77,823	$2,500 (3%)	$76,700
DISTRICT 4			
Shays (R)	$972,001	$157,257 (16%)	$896,562
Sanchez (D)	$118,670	$8,900 (7%)	$107,869
DISTRICT 5			
Johnson (R)	$3,373,454	$1,676,167 (50%)	$3,683,586
Maloney (D)	$2,055,976	$1,153,711 (56%)	$2,062,496

Delaware

	RECEIPTS	FOM PACS	EXPENDITURES
SENIOR SENATOR - 2002			
Biden (D)	$2,726,583	$0 (0%)	$2,991,862
Clatworthy (R)	$1,871,163	$13,100 (1%)	$1,804,123
JUNIOR SENATOR - 2000			
Carper (D)	$2,629,812	$599,245 (23%)	$2,608,942
Roth (R)	$4,256,984	$1,727,178 (41%)	$4,366,884
AT LARGE			
Castle (R)	$796,752	$291,941 (37%)	$760,161
Miller (D)	$15,373	$0 (0%)	$13,202

Florida

	RECEIPTS	FOM PACS	EXPENDITURES
SENIOR SENATOR - 1998			
Graham (D)	$4,341,972	$1,164,317 (27%)	$5,094,581
Crist (R)	$1,337,307	$94,841 (7%)	$1,487,498
JUNIOR SENATOR - 2000			
Nelson (D)	$6,639,259	$1,195,617 (18%)	$6,635,832
McCollum (R)	$7,936,639	$1,391,571 (18%)	$8,664,112
DISTRICT 1			
Miller (R)†	$957,698	$336,841 (35%)	$956,353
Oram (D)	$14,149	$0 (0%)	$13,951
DISTRICT 2			
Boyd (D)	$827,715	$446,544 (54%)	$533,952
McGurk (R)	$38,983	$0 (0%)	$34,990
DISTRICT 3			
Brown (D)	$437,160	$300,575 (69%)	$437,188
Carroll (R)	$241,448	$17,750 (7%)	$297,377
DISTRICT 4			
Crenshaw (R)	$529,399	$116,262 (22%)	$301,241
DISTRICT 5			
Brown-Waite (R)	$929,103	$296,908 (32%)	$876,072
Thurman (D)	$1,951,631	$1,299,271 (67%)	$1,866,454
DISTRICT 6			
Stearns (R)	$616,556	$395,411 (64%)	$328,401
Bruderly (D)	$57,417	$1,200 (2%)	$56,712
DISTRICT 7			
Mica (R)	$1,445,716	$649,395 (45%)	$1,738,866
Hogan (D)	$4,667,211	$3,000 (0%)	$4,659,352
DISTRICT 8			
Keller (R)	$1,268,572	$598,565 (47%)	$1,074,597
Diaz (D)	$206,759	$106,104 (51%)	$215,992
DISTRICT 9			
Bilirakis (R)	$690,559	$442,259 (64%)	$816,932
Kalogianis (D)	$349,071	$23,520 (7%)	$306,455
DISTRICT 10			
Young (R)	$569,016	$407,290 (72%)	$469,641
DISTRICT 11			
Davis (D)	$462,126	$317,328 (69%)	$385,272
DISTRICT 12			
Putnam (R)	$602,612	$259,894 (43%)	$361,599
DISTRICT 13			
Harris (R)	$3,320,493	$428,241 (13%)	$3,298,146
Schneider (D)	$387,396	$19,750 (5%)	$327,195
DISTRICT 14			
Goss (R)	$109,702	$25,500 (23%)	$86,006
DISTRICT 15			
Weldon (R)	$731,694	$270,726 (37%)	$703,066
Tso (D)	$54,099	$1,650 (3%)	$51,697
DISTRICT 16			
Foley (R)	$1,584,727	$713,962 (45%)	$812,759
McLain (CNSTP)	$6,767	$0 (0%)	$1,777
DISTRICT 17			
Meek (D)	$291,980	$120,626 (41%)	$165,931
DISTRICT 18			
Ros-Lehtinen (R)	$704,180	$148,331 (21%)	$441,736
DISTRICT 19			
Wexler (D)	$851,437	$272,900 (32%)	$707,607
Merkl (R)	$25,784	$0 (0%)	$25,784
DISTRICT 20			
Deutsch (D)	$824,048	$297,425 (36%)	$667,441
DISTRICT 21			
Diaz-Balart (R)	$498,373	$166,750 (33%)	$398,080
DISTRICT 22			
Shaw (R)	$1,952,396	$860,617 (44%)	$1,923,251
Roberts (D)	$1,154,716	$210,621 (18%)	$1,125,021
DISTRICT 23			
Hastings (D)	$373,902	$32,500 (9%)	$305,632
Laurie (R)	$13,501	$0 (0%)	$13,501
DISTRICT 24			
Feeney (R)	$1,862,890	$651,117 (35%)	$1,829,566
Jacobs (D)	$4,015,167	$267,059 (7%)	$3,946,733
DISTRICT 25			
Diaz-Balart (R)	$1,128,222	$392,824 (35%)	$1,044,351
Betancourt (D)	$174,473	$43,320 (25%)	$148,280

Georgia

	RECEIPTS	FOM PACS	EXPENDITURES
SENIOR SENATOR - 2000			
Miller (D)	$2,684,514	$765,150 (29%)	$2,533,746
Mattingly (R)	$1,114,900	$135,549 (12%)	$1,093,408
JUNIOR SENATOR - 2002			
Chambliss (R)	$7,422,836	$1,282,955 (17%)	$7,475,943
Cleland (D)	$8,146,827	$1,827,709 (22%)	$9,055,254
DISTRICT 1			
Kingston (R)	$784,390	$265,679 (34%)	$786,944
Smart (D)	$21,818	$5,000 (23%)	$21,757
DISTRICT 2			
Bishop (D)	$572,235	$388,422 (68%)	$296,251
DISTRICT 3			
Marshall (D)	$1,035,662	$287,275 (28%)	$979,793
Clay (R)	$1,969,944	$294,335 (15%)	$1,951,093
DISTRICT 4			
Majette (D)	$1,956,518	$315,785 (16%)	$1,920,177
Van Auken (R)	$76,133	$0 (0%)	$88,631
DISTRICT 5			
Lewis (D)	$324,256	$280,500 (87%)	$523,047
DISTRICT 6			
Isakson (R)	$1,027,500	$334,261 (33%)	$515,923
DISTRICT 7			
Linder (R)	$1,647,233	$449,850 (27%)	$2,201,850
DISTRICT 8			
Collins (R)	$743,887	$501,762 (67%)	$766,497
DISTRICT 9			
Norwood (R)	$863,224	$337,796 (39%)	$1,113,074
Irwin (D)	$18,057	$0 (0%)	$17,012
DISTRICT 10			
Deal (R)	$275,056	$169,639 (62%)	$287,508
DISTRICT 11			
Gingrey (R)	$1,863,999	$342,269 (18%)	$1,758,098
Kahn (D)	$3,639,255	$298,350 (8%)	$3,684,359

	RECEIPTS	FOM PACS	EXPENDITURES
DISTRICT 12			
Burns (R)	$886,327	$304,878 (34%)	$760,851
Walker (D)	$1,120,938	$365,643 (33%)	$1,119,951
DISTRICT 13			
Scott (D)	$1,489,182	$447,350 (30%)	$1,484,616
Cox (R)	$646,387	$14,295 (2%)	$642,323

Hawaii

	RECEIPTS	FOM PACS	EXPENDITURES
SENIOR SENATOR - 1998			
Inouye (D)	$1,743,520	$571,755 (33%)	$1,375,601
JUNIOR SENATOR - 2000			
Akaka (D)	$601,881	$316,415 (53%)	$428,516
Carroll (R)	$107,253	$300 (0%)	$97,407
DISTRICT 1			
Abercrombie (D)	$899,235	$473,927 (53%)	$614,700
DISTRICT 2			
Case (D)†	$184,022	$0 (0%)	$204,550
Matsunaga (R)†	$192,131	$88,200 (46%)	$174,388

Idaho

	RECEIPTS	FOM PACS	EXPENDITURES
SENIOR SENATOR - 2002			
Craig (R)	$3,012,333	$1,065,581 (35%)	$2,933,495
Blinken (D)	$2,173,286	$97,000 (4%)	$2,149,333
JUNIOR SENATOR - 1998			
Crapo (R)	$1,803,195	$794,715 (44%)	$1,563,811
Mauk (D)	$243,284	$29,200 (12%)	$241,443
DISTRICT 1			
Otter (R)	$1,015,434	$446,686 (44%)	$897,245
Richardson (D)	$478,245	$132,747 (28%)	$476,354
DISTRICT 2			
Simpson (R)	$342,933	$249,610 (73%)	$317,736
Kinghorn (D)	$12,468	$6,000 (48%)	$12,467

Illinois

	RECEIPTS	FOM PACS	EXPENDITURES
SENIOR SENATOR - 2002			
Durbin (D)	$5,174,051	$1,228,196 (24%)	$4,870,737
Durkin (R)	$795,941	$102,478 (13%)	$770,458
JUNIOR SENATOR - 1998			
Fitzgerald (R)	$17,897,956	$1,003,452 (6%)	$17,677,698
Moseley-Braun (D)	$7,222,013	$1,260,576 (17%)	$7,200,895
DISTRICT 1			
Rush (D)	$253,588	$203,388 (80%)	$277,611
DISTRICT 2			
Jackson (D)	$736,054	$266,862 (36%)	$735,498
Nelson (R)	$9,250	$0 (0%)	$9,249
DISTRICT 3			
Lipinski (D)	$381,441	$250,834 (66%)	$409,087
DISTRICT 4			
Gutierrez (D)	$696,229	$272,625 (39%)	$789,363
DISTRICT 5			
Emanuel (D)	$3,130,200	$420,966 (13%)	$2,929,449
Augusti (R)	$197,678	$13,320 (7%)	$213,766
DISTRICT 6			
Hyde (R)	$586,333	$149,445 (25%)	$839,199
DISTRICT 7			
Davis (D)	$336,879	$211,107 (63%)	$215,233
Tunney (R)	$48,652	$250 (1%)	$47,350
DISTRICT 8			
Crane (R)	$694,677	$499,963 (72%)	$829,528
Bean (D)	$329,027	$106,780 (32%)	$319,128
DISTRICT 9			
Schakowsky (D)	$857,017	$184,625 (22%)	$822,378
DISTRICT 10			
Kirk (R)	$1,703,940	$506,812 (30%)	$1,392,499
Perritt (D)	$476,329	$66,125 (14%)	$458,036
DISTRICT 11			
Weller (R)	$1,952,824	$747,887 (38%)	$2,329,226
Van Duyne (D)	$29,040	$11,100 (38%)	$30,233
DISTRICT 12			
Costello (D)	$778,072	$323,606 (42%)	$450,031
DISTRICT 13			
Biggert (R)	$523,807	$256,736 (49%)	$464,054
DISTRICT 14			
Hastert (R)	$2,988,013	$1,318,855 (44%)	$2,865,888
Quick (D)	$17,997	$3,000 (17%)	$17,638
DISTRICT 15			
Johnson (R)	$500,917	$284,797 (57%)	$393,469
Estabrook (GREEN)	$26,004	$0 (0%)	$25,004
DISTRICT 16			
Manzullo (R)	$1,159,600	$595,580 (51%)	$1,028,317
Kutsch (D)	$71,082	$2,150 (3%)	$45,808
DISTRICT 17			
Evans (D)	$767,451	$365,569 (48%)	$758,653
Calderone (R)	$44,146	$1,000 (2%)	$43,082
DISTRICT 18			
LaHood (R)	$1,121,979	$354,191 (32%)	$1,051,220
DISTRICT 19			
Shimkus (R)	$1,848,115	$1,157,986 (63%)	$2,144,611
Phelps (D)	$1,026,742	$599,313 (58%)	$1,254,459

Indiana

	RECEIPTS	FOM PACS	EXPENDITURES
SENIOR SENATOR - 2000			
Lugar (R)	$3,593,294	$863,899 (24%)	$4,251,603
Johnson (D)	$1,451,828	$138,900 (10%)	$1,451,786
JUNIOR SENATOR - 1998			
Bayh (D)	$4,158,990	$1,078,856 (26%)	$3,914,375
Helmke (R)	$646,906	$34,850 (5%)	$645,999
DISTRICT 1			
Visclosky (D)	$934,581	$412,413 (44%)	$733,318
Leyva (R)	$12,003	$0 (0%)	$11,279
DISTRICT 2			
Chocola (R)	$1,689,148	$617,308 (37%)	$1,645,326
Thompson (D)	$1,439,331	$652,392 (45%)	$1,439,003

	RECEIPTS	FOM PACS	EXPENDITURES
DISTRICT 3			
Souder (R)	$514,178	$194,279 (38%)	$509,932
Rigdon (D)	$133,593	$42,722 (32%)	$131,458
DISTRICT 4			
Buyer (R)	$944,973	$616,694 (65%)	$923,492
Abbott (D)	$27,807	$19,950 (72%)	$21,079
DISTRICT 5			
Burton (R)	$782,040	$242,082 (31%)	$823,363
Carr (D)	$25,793	$5,500 (21%)	$26,102
DISTRICT 6			
Pence (R)	$1,223,216	$435,477 (36%)	$1,199,058
Fox (D)	$341,217	$138,270 (41%)	$334,774
DISTRICT 7			
Carson (D)	$998,492	$464,704 (47%)	$1,070,163
McVey (R)	$1,120,052	$357,329 (32%)	$1,105,370
DISTRICT 8			
Hostettler (R)	$564,189	$5,738 (1%)	$573,220
Hartke (D)	$397,478	$163,280 (41%)	$395,825
DISTRICT 9			
Hill (D)	$1,102,688	$609,734 (55%)	$1,128,530
Sodrel (R)	$1,606,239	$46,570 (3%)	$1,598,881

Iowa

	RECEIPTS	FOM PACS	EXPENDITURES
SENIOR SENATOR - 1998			
Grassley (R)	$3,291,469	$1,339,266 (41%)	$2,781,940
Osterberg (D)	$165,655	$25,200 (15%)	$165,429
JUNIOR SENATOR - 2002			
Harkin (D)	$7,016,840	$1,441,247 (21%)	$6,727,132
Ganske (R)	$5,426,297	$779,685 (14%)	$5,334,084
DISTRICT 1			
Nussle (R)	$1,641,045	$952,523 (58%)	$1,646,744
Hutchinson (D)	$1,020,910	$341,033 (33%)	$1,020,908
DISTRICT 2			
Leach (R)	$748,561	$0 (0%)	$768,502
Thomas (D)	$1,338,851	$394,707 (29%)	$1,329,517
DISTRICT 3			
Boswell (D)	$1,259,938	$829,736 (66%)	$1,247,742
Thompson (R)	$897,811	$248,791 (28%)	$896,676
DISTRICT 4			
Latham (R)	$1,459,091	$988,452 (68%)	$1,507,444
Norris (D)	$1,273,904	$571,234 (45%)	$1,216,317
DISTRICT 5			
King (R)	$701,082	$44,737 (6%)	$696,582
Shomshor (D)	$90,858	$29,025 (32%)	$90,006

Kansas

	RECEIPTS	FOM PACS	EXPENDITURES
SENIOR SENATOR - 1998			
Brownback (R)	$2,147,205	$918,278 (43%)	$1,719,612
Feleciano (D)	$39,450	$12,650 (32%)	$39,500
JUNIOR SENATOR - 2002			
Roberts (R)	$1,408,528	$787,087 (56%)	$1,012,747
Cook (REF)	$3,450	$0 (0%)	$3,473
DISTRICT 1			
Moran (R)	$486,795	$251,461 (52%)	$378,332
DISTRICT 2			
Ryun (R)	$421,716	$229,407 (54%)	$413,490
Lykins (D)	$40,525	$3,000 (7%)	$38,806
DISTRICT 3			
Moore (D)	$1,897,640	$816,507 (43%)	$1,844,236
Taff (R)	$1,203,899	$324,000 (27%)	$1,050,226
DISTRICT 4			
Tiahrt (R)	$976,071	$456,245 (47%)	$1,110,498
Nolla (D)	$681,901	$166,679 (24%)	$686,952

Kentucky

	RECEIPTS	FOM PACS	EXPENDITURES
SENIOR SENATOR - 2002			
McConnell (R)	$4,735,540	$1,192,388 (25%)	$5,241,832
Weinberg (D)	$2,239,125	$198,101 (9%)	$2,189,846
JUNIOR SENATOR - 1998			
Bunning (R)	$3,597,425	$1,363,896 (38%)	$3,746,540
Baesler (D)	$3,855,690	$771,022 (20%)	$3,825,731
DISTRICT 1			
Whitfield (R)	$984,404	$472,815 (48%)	$818,535
Alexander (D)	$540,952	$95,011 (18%)	$563,319
DISTRICT 2			
Lewis (R)	$471,199	$226,510 (48%)	$494,257
DISTRICT 3			
Northup (R)	$3,075,813	$1,037,356 (34%)	$3,147,821
Conway (D)	$1,654,772	$456,281 (28%)	$1,545,549
DISTRICT 4			
Lucas (D)	$1,381,438	$712,767 (52%)	$1,436,907
Davis (R)	$871,195	$192,844 (22%)	$865,946
DISTRICT 5			
Rogers (R)	$720,010	$367,157 (51%)	$452,615
DISTRICT 6			
Fletcher (R)	$1,171,913	$486,556 (42%)	$1,178,065
Galbraith (I)	$18,697	$0 (0%)	$18,697

Louisiana

	RECEIPTS	FOM PACS	EXPENDITURES
SENIOR SENATOR - 1998			
Breaux (D)	$3,992,303	$1,533,040 (38%)	$3,858,472
Donelon (R)	$364,056	$19,845 (5%)	$364,073
JUNIOR SENATOR - 2002			
Landrieu (D)	$6,770,029	$2,614,362 (39%)	$7,326,155
Terrell (R)	$3,387,167	$820,277 (24%)	$2,760,276
Cooksey (R)	$1,899,166	$65,225 (3%)	$1,835,326
Perkins (R)	$639,258	$39,681 (6%)	$634,270
DISTRICT 1			
Vitter (R)	$2,070,339	$253,405 (12%)	$1,689,788
Monica (R)	$188,350	$5,000 (3%)	$10,603
Namer (R)	$78,260	$0 (0%)	$77,947
DISTRICT 2			
Jefferson (D)	$984,454	$592,246 (60%)	$1,023,281
Dixon (D)	$133,428	$16,500 (12%)	$128,954
Hunt (D)	$43,900	$0 (0%)	$43,900
DISTRICT 3			
Tauzin (R)	$1,972,875	$1,462,005 (74%)	$1,507,212
Iwanico (I)	$5,451	$0 (0%)	$2,336

DISTRICT 4			
McCrery (R)	$1,057,908	$517,192 (49%)	$1,085,031
Milkovich (D)	$159,739	$8,750 (5%)	$156,919
DISTRICT 5			
Alexander (D)	$844,896	$506,359 (60%)	$831,088
Fletcher (R)	$1,567,019	$339,190 (22%)	$1,554,778
Barham (R)	$677,872	$43,758 (6%)	$677,871
Holloway (R)	$620,037	$24,350 (4%)	$619,244
Mouser (I)	$111,861	$0 (0%)	$111,695
Wright (R)	$26,105	$0 (0%)	$26,259
DISTRICT 6			
Baker (R)	$842,090	$621,849 (74%)	$790,953
DISTRICT 7			
John (D)	$847,825	$584,338 (69%)	$493,724

Maine

	RECEIPTS	FOM PACS	EXPENDITURES
SENIOR SENATOR - 2000			
Snowe (R)	$2,236,146	$817,009 (37%)	$1,981,504
Lawrence (D)	$739,637	$145,703 (20%)	$727,655
JUNIOR SENATOR - 2002			
Collins (R)	$4,007,560	$1,511,332 (38%)	$3,945,683
Pingree (D)	$3,865,577	$340,306 (9%)	$3,741,905
DISTRICT 1			
Allen (D)	$509,519	$216,298 (42%)	$513,655
Joyce (R)	$171,353	$7,489 (4%)	$168,500
DISTRICT 2			
Michaud (D)	$1,134,983	$589,555 (52%)	$1,119,245
Raye (R)	$1,127,833	$438,980 (39%)	$1,097,673

Maryland

	RECEIPTS	FOM PACS	EXPENDITURES
SENIOR SENATOR - 2000			
Sarbanes (D)	$1,851,731	$748,964 (40%)	$1,837,286
Rappaport (R)	$147,024	$2,510 (2%)	$146,866
JUNIOR SENATOR - 1998			
Mikulski (D)	$2,908,352	$925,021 (32%)	$3,014,312
Pierpont (R)	$297,770	$0 (0%)	$297,768
DISTRICT 1			
Gilchrest (R)	$380,084	$830 (0%)	$435,368
Tamlyn (D)	$26,484	$0 (0%)	$36,528
DISTRICT 2			
Ruppersberger (D)	$1,245,509	$521,028 (42%)	$1,177,302
Bentley (R)	$1,074,396	$366,300 (34%)	$1,071,333
DISTRICT 3			
Cardin (D)	$825,652	$538,990 (65%)	$1,020,680
Conwell (R)	$29,821	$0 (0%)	$27,859
DISTRICT 4			
Wynn (D)	$515,109	$319,546 (62%)	$546,059
DISTRICT 5			
Hoyer (D)	$1,055,858	$770,586 (73%)	$1,162,043
DISTRICT 6			
Bartlett (R)	$188,277	$40,278 (21%)	$237,991
DeArmon (D)	$83,551	$21,250 (25%)	$82,100
DISTRICT 7			
Cummings (D)	$496,075	$232,590 (47%)	$466,157
DISTRICT 8			
Van Hollen (D)	$2,989,215	$515,954 (17%)	$2,985,329
Morella (R)	$2,854,765	$1,187,757 (42%)	$2,910,885

Massachusetts

	RECEIPTS	FOM PACS	EXPENDITURES
SENIOR SENATOR - 2000			
Kennedy (D)	$6,623,179	$864,078 (13%)	$3,662,652
Robinson (R)	$163,929	$0 (0%)	$163,927
Howell (LIBERT)	$1,027,364	$0 (0%)	$1,057,186
JUNIOR SENATOR - 2002			
Kerry (D)	$8,605,482	$16,200 (0%)	$5,971,092
Cloud (LIBERT)	$199,740	$50 (0%)	$199,476
DISTRICT 1			
Olver (D)	$551,915	$204,701 (37%)	$622,719
Kinnaman (R)	$191,238	$13,400 (7%)	$190,368
DISTRICT 2			
Neal (D)	$554,870	$298,717 (54%)	$426,851
DISTRICT 3			
McGovern (D)	$622,483	$239,050 (38%)	$590,334
DISTRICT 4			
Frank (D)	$429,753	$130,725 (30%)	$462,186
DISTRICT 5			
Meehan (D)	$673,740	$0 (0%)	$848,517
McCarthy (R)	$253,877	$19,875 (8%)	$254,715
DISTRICT 6			
Tierney (D)	$740,619	$185,728 (25%)	$499,701
Smith (R)	$51,428	$0 (0%)	$30,078
DISTRICT 7			
Markey (D)	$686,471	$0 (0%)	$680,568
DISTRICT 8			
Capuano (D)	$750,946	$196,625 (26%)	$440,229
DISTRICT 9			
Lynch (D)†	$2,469,979	$372,900 (15%)	$2,368,602
DISTRICT 10			
Delahunt (D)	$588,856	$258,625 (44%)	$255,244
Gonzaga (R)	$57,439	$2,600 (5%)	$54,971

Michigan

	RECEIPTS	FOM PACS	EXPENDITURES
SENIOR SENATOR - 2002			
Levin (D)	$5,090,498	$838,109 (16%)	$4,099,215
Raczkowski (R)	$1,096,368	$0 (0%)	$819,356
JUNIOR SENATOR - 2000			
Stabenow (D)	$8,297,375	$955,856 (12%)	$8,194,394
Abraham (R)	$11,838,542	$2,485,419 (21%)	$13,028,636
DISTRICT 1			
Stupak (D)	$669,103	$485,383 (73%)	$687,151
Hooper (R)	$14,013	$0 (0%)	$12,952
DISTRICT 2			
Hoekstra (R)	$286,423	$5,050 (2%)	$271,132
Wrisley (D)	$23,002	$250 (1%)	$22,897
DISTRICT 3			
Ehlers (R)	$369,082	$113,130 (31%)	$358,693
Lucey (REF)	$1,910	$400 (21%)	$4,117
Lynnes (D)	$10,183	$1,500 (15%)	$8,290

DISTRICT 4			
Camp (R)	$786,625	$394,752 (50%)	$675,824
Hollenbeck (D)	$10,362	$2,060 (20%)	$10,172
DISTRICT 5			
Kildee (D)	$425,161	$222,385 (52%)	$377,831
DISTRICT 6			
Upton (R)	$1,227,976	$599,216 (49%)	$1,544,391
Giguere (D)	$19,880	$2,000 (10%)	$18,028
DISTRICT 7			
Smith (R)	$121,330	$1,030 (1%)	$145,121
Simpson (D)	$46,294	$23,800 (51%)	$48,250
DISTRICT 8			
Rogers (R)	$1,592,498	$623,851 (39%)	$1,389,781
McAlpine (D)	$11,838	$2,000 (17%)	$11,443
DISTRICT 9			
Knollenberg (R)	$2,288,285	$694,686 (30%)	$2,446,119
Fink (D)	$2,467,856	$261,532 (11%)	$2,310,214
DISTRICT 10			
Miller (R)	$1,649,545	$618,591 (38%)	$1,421,613
Marlinga (D)	$988,539	$287,574 (29%)	$970,409
DISTRICT 11			
McCotter (R)	$1,298,841	$505,182 (39%)	$1,239,890
Kelley (D)	$662,571	$340,246 (51%)	$637,683
DISTRICT 12			
Levin (D)	$941,212	$496,935 (53%)	$980,684
Dean (R)	$40,292	$0 (0%)	$27,751
DISTRICT 13			
Kilpatrick (D)	$506,222	$184,250 (36%)	$334,989
DISTRICT 14			
Conyers (D)	$402,130	$300,850 (75%)	$355,779
DISTRICT 15			
Dingell (D)	$3,065,232	$1,735,646 (57%)	$3,387,665

Minnesota

	RECEIPTS	FOM PACS	EXPENDITURES
SENIOR SENATOR - 2000			
Dayton (D)	$12,040,466	$0 (0%)	$11,957,114
Grams (R)	$5,902,543	$1,623,289 (28%)	$6,024,866
JUNIOR SENATOR - 2002			
Coleman (R)	$9,912,726	$1,735,858 (18%)	$9,648,999
Mondale (D)	$2,728,910	$380,004 (14%)	$1,731,176
DISTRICT 1			
Gutknecht (R)	$891,023	$240,281 (27%)	$739,379
Andreasen (D)	$118,646	$30,550 (26%)	$110,980
DISTRICT 2			
Kline (R)	$1,474,153	$576,764 (39%)	$1,475,510
Luther (D)	$2,247,843	$1,072,840 (48%)	$2,257,514
DISTRICT 3			
Ramstad (R)	$1,040,613	$447,764 (43%)	$761,949
DISTRICT 4			
McCollum (D)	$656,667	$343,375 (52%)	$570,458
Billington (R)	$93,252	$550 (1%)	$93,250
DISTRICT 5			
Sabo (D)	$463,827	$260,525 (56%)	$507,205
Mathias (R)	$9,422	$0 (0%)	$9,017
DISTRICT 6			
Kennedy (R)	$1,891,644	$1,000,196 (53%)	$1,862,661
Robert (D)	$2,194,922	$253,280 (12%)	$2,174,114
DISTRICT 7			
Peterson (D)	$412,774	$309,086 (75%)	$509,881
Stevens (R)	$209,099	$16,200 (8%)	$199,575
DISTRICT 8			
Oberstar (D)	$887,237	$594,641 (67%)	$1,022,829
Lemen (R)	$17,048	$0 (0%)	$17,584

Mississippi

	RECEIPTS	FOM PACS	EXPENDITURES
SENIOR SENATOR - 2002			
Cochran (R)	$1,688,273	$824,510 (49%)	$1,432,856
JUNIOR SENATOR - 2000			
Lott (R)	$4,241,819	$791,025 (19%)	$3,663,052
Brown (D)	$51,716	$7,500 (15%)	$40,349
DISTRICT 1			
Wicker (R)	$434,627	$204,700 (47%)	$376,431
DISTRICT 2			
Thompson (D)	$535,397	$296,625 (55%)	$622,345
LeSueur (R)	$95,426	$10,500 (11%)	$100,342
DISTRICT 3			
Pickering (R)	$2,781,336	$1,206,049 (43%)	$2,963,168
Shows (D)	$1,426,732	$746,463 (52%)	$1,434,089
DISTRICT 4			
Taylor (D)	$367,315	$170,000 (46%)	$346,931

Missouri

	RECEIPTS	FOM PACS	EXPENDITURES
SENIOR SENATOR - 1998			
Bond (R)	$5,848,137	$1,919,491 (33%)	$6,229,649
Nixon (D)	$2,573,843	$413,937 (16%)	$2,568,879
JUNIOR SENATOR - 2002			
Talent (R)	$8,547,315	$1,774,818 (21%)	$7,939,585
Carnahan (D)	$12,289,529	$1,618,045 (13%)	$12,164,113
DISTRICT 1			
Clay (D)	$347,168	$206,733 (60%)	$333,446
Schwadron (R)	$12,199	$950 (8%)	$12,198
DISTRICT 2			
Akin (R)	$695,544	$205,964 (30%)	$552,033
DISTRICT 3			
Gephardt (D)	$5,752,567	$1,463,704 (25%)	$3,192,389
Enz (R)	$118,225	$4,700 (4%)	$113,982
DISTRICT 4			
Skelton (D)	$606,114	$344,273 (57%)	$596,705
DISTRICT 5			
McCarthy (D)	$406,004	$272,100 (67%)	$445,602
Gordon (R)	$3,580	$0 (0%)	$4,059
DISTRICT 6			
Graves (R)	$1,223,929	$622,792 (51%)	$1,130,882
Rinehart (D)	$242,836	$3,111 (1%)	$213,356
DISTRICT 7			
Blunt (R)	$1,930,739	$1,249,671 (65%)	$1,273,204

	RECEIPTS	FOM PACS	EXPENDITURES
DISTRICT 8			
Emerson (R)	$974,400	$630,403 (65%)	$744,654
DISTRICT 9			
Hulshof (R)	$890,829	$434,087 (49%)	$849,275

Montana

	RECEIPTS	FOM PACS	EXPENDITURES
SENIOR SENATOR - 2002			
Baucus (D)	$5,945,541	$2,620,108 (44%)	$6,106,052
Taylor (R)	$1,798,533	$77,237 (4%)	$1,793,389
JUNIOR SENATOR - 2000			
Burns (R)	$3,931,267	$1,683,501 (43%)	$4,337,961
Schweitzer (D)	$2,103,712	$354,574 (17%)	$2,033,530
AT LARGE			
Rehberg (R)	$1,093,009	$474,255 (43%)	$908,025
Kelly (D)	$11,967	$250 (2%)	$18,757

Nebraska

	RECEIPTS	FOM PACS	EXPENDITURES
SENIOR SENATOR - 2002			
Hagel (R)	$1,609,967	$883,266 (55%)	$1,350,307
Chase (I)	$24,321	$0 (0%)	$24,293
JUNIOR SENATOR - 2000			
Nelson (D)	$2,782,642	$1,298,059 (47%)	$2,794,887
Stenberg (R)	$1,871,463	$456,076 (24%)	$1,859,252
DISTRICT 1			
Bereuter (R)	$163,640	$130,000 (79%)	$188,151
DISTRICT 2			
Terry (R)	$1,087,706	$504,587 (46%)	$942,666
Simon (D)	$711,014	$73,600 (10%)	$697,127
DISTRICT 3			
Osborne (R)	$124,122	$104 (0%)	$80,424

Nevada

	RECEIPTS	FOM PACS	EXPENDITURES
SENIOR SENATOR - 1998			
Reid (D)	$3,905,324	$1,219,324 (31%)	$4,939,010
Ensign (R)	$3,454,820	$1,295,185 (37%)	$3,490,256
JUNIOR SENATOR - 2000			
Ensign (R)	$4,878,526	$1,715,992 (35%)	$4,872,176
Bernstein (D)	$2,483,512	$333,766 (13%)	$2,449,093
DISTRICT 1			
Berkley (D)	$1,865,692	$709,268 (38%)	$1,665,146
Boggs-McDonald (R)	$984,951	$152,605 (15%)	$983,110
DISTRICT 2			
Gibbons (R)	$495,363	$225,858 (46%)	$602,771
Souza (D)	$15,750	$8,000 (51%)	$13,368
DISTRICT 3			
Porter (R)	$1,926,630	$766,429 (40%)	$1,916,277
Herrera (D)	$1,810,700	$640,189 (35%)	$1,805,792

New Hampshire

	RECEIPTS	FOM PACS	EXPENDITURES
SENIOR SENATOR - 1998			
Gregg (R)	$1,183,131	$685,620 (58%)	$904,448
Condodemetraky (D)	$35,827	$7,350 (21%)	$28,547
JUNIOR SENATOR - 2002			
Sununu (R)	$3,622,980	$1,232,534 (34%)	$3,507,470
Shaheen (D)	$5,823,007	$999,209 (17%)	$5,791,661
DISTRICT 1			
Bradley (R)	$1,057,200	$369,338 (35%)	$1,029,408
Clark (D)	$3,535,600	$531,651 (15%)	$3,491,084
DISTRICT 2			
Bass (R)	$906,580	$425,459 (47%)	$876,632
Swett (D)	$1,485,594	$446,639 (30%)	$1,447,896

New Jersey

	RECEIPTS	FOM PACS	EXPENDITURES
SENIOR SENATOR - 2000			
Corzine (D)	$63,253,520	$235,909 (0%)	$63,209,506
Franks (R)	$6,428,214	$1,221,491 (19%)	$6,394,936
JUNIOR SENATOR - 2002			
Lautenberg (D)	$3,109,237	$413,075 (13%)	$2,844,020
Forrester (R)	$10,604,219	$484,793 (5%)	$10,540,687
DISTRICT 1			
Andrews (D)	$788,336	$386,574 (49%)	$615,531
DISTRICT 2			
LoBiondo (R)	$914,639	$436,964 (48%)	$621,646
DISTRICT 3			
Saxton (R)	$1,172,462	$440,350 (38%)	$683,812
DISTRICT 4			
Smith (R)	$540,831	$229,803 (42%)	$504,280
Brennan (D)	$75,973	$14,928 (20%)	$72,886
DISTRICT 5			
Garrett (R)	$1,401,890	$487,911 (35%)	$1,324,758
Sumers (D)	$1,611,522	$339,582 (21%)	$1,605,412
DISTRICT 6			
Pallone (D)	$998,776	$484,040 (48%)	$825,136
Medrow (R)	$29,192	$4,323 (15%)	$28,970
DISTRICT 7			
Ferguson (R)	$2,159,377	$849,769 (39%)	$2,047,127
Carden (D)	$949,960	$164,387 (17%)	$908,023
DISTRICT 8			
Pascrell (D)	$1,036,506	$377,625 (36%)	$824,593
DISTRICT 9			
Rothman (D)	$791,182	$355,475 (45%)	$567,018
Glass (R)	$13,535	$500 (4%)	$5,457
DISTRICT 10			
Payne (D)	$484,722	$266,878 (55%)	$333,863
DISTRICT 11			
Frelinghuysen (R)	$764,700	$295,071 (39%)	$763,390
Pawar (D)	$19,649	$4,450 (23%)	$15,793
DISTRICT 12			
Holt (D)	$2,013,467	$530,840 (26%)	$1,711,097
Soaries (R)	$637,679	$80,672 (13%)	$624,112

	RECEIPTS	FOM PACS	EXPENDITURES
DISTRICT 13			
Menendez (D)	$2,431,392	$583,028 (24%)	$2,113,182

New Mexico

	RECEIPTS	FOM PACS	EXPENDITURES
SENIOR SENATOR - 2002			
Domenici (R)	$4,195,731	$939,490 (22%)	$4,115,919
Tristani (D)	$732,304	$140,478 (19%)	$834,607
JUNIOR SENATOR - 2000			
Bingaman (D)	$2,730,680	$1,192,335 (44%)	$2,568,649
Redmond (R)	$718,772	$75,409 (10%)	$706,424
DISTRICT 1			
Wilson (R)	$2,723,036	$1,121,151 (41%)	$2,687,255
Romero (D)	$1,252,992	$354,375 (28%)	$1,149,891
DISTRICT 2			
Pearce (R)	$1,577,108	$556,162 (35%)	$1,554,956
Smith (D)	$901,102	$344,927 (38%)	$899,151
DISTRICT 3			
Udall (D)	$430,721	$151,100 (35%)	$290,534

New York

	RECEIPTS	FOM PACS	EXPENDITURES
SENIOR SENATOR - 1998			
Schumer (D)	$16,825,671	$560,446 (3%)	$16,671,877
D'Amato (R)	$17,760,311	$1,926,518 (11%)	$24,195,287
JUNIOR SENATOR - 2000			
Clinton (D)	$41,752,247	$930,192 (2%)	$41,469,898
Lazio (R)	$39,020,511	$2,346,311 (6%)	$40,576,273
DISTRICT 1			
Bishop (D)	$980,164	$191,050 (19%)	$812,503
Grucci (R)	$1,412,106	$699,383 (50%)	$1,360,764
DISTRICT 2			
Israel (D)	$1,470,828	$500,930 (34%)	$1,390,008
Finley (R)	$137,373	$0 (0%)	$106,424
DISTRICT 3			
King (R)	$560,034	$251,550 (45%)	$468,474
Finz (D)	$138,825	$3,450 (2%)	$137,472
DISTRICT 4			
McCarthy (D)	$1,901,695	$490,540 (26%)	$1,769,741
O'Grady (R)	$254,883	$9,140 (4%)	$306,505
DISTRICT 5			
Ackerman (D)	$702,942	$249,175 (35%)	$595,420
DISTRICT 6			
Meeks (D)	$545,560	$239,687 (44%)	$433,575
DISTRICT 7			
Crowley (D)	$905,179	$432,496 (48%)	$920,849
DISTRICT 8			
Nadler (D)	$709,310	$210,125 (30%)	$577,238
Farrin (R)	$75,102	$75 (0%)	$64,595
DISTRICT 9			
Weiner (D)	$910,448	$281,307 (31%)	$269,868
DISTRICT 10			
Towns (D, L)	$764,870	$497,531 (65%)	$684,996
DISTRICT 11			
Owens (D)	$320,489	$180,949 (56%)	$292,614
Cleary (R)	$12,784	$250 (2%)	$10,580
DISTRICT 12			
Velazquez (D)	$435,586	$327,742 (75%)	$519,420
DISTRICT 13			
Fossella (R)	$757,169	$388,322 (51%)	$893,564
Mattsson (D)	$15,898	$0 (0%)	$6,757
DISTRICT 14			
Maloney (D)	$950,972	$370,749 (39%)	$886,233
Srdanovic (R)	$48,021	$0 (0%)	$44,005
DISTRICT 15			
Rangel (D)	$1,664,515	$999,686 (60%)	$1,721,892
Fields (R)	$34,340	$500 (1%)	$33,877
DISTRICT 16			
Serrano (D)	$267,377	$173,750 (65%)	$215,174
DISTRICT 17			
Engel (D)	$1,033,387	$525,525 (51%)	$990,837
Vanderhoef (R)	$207,498	$0 (0%)	$194,064
DISTRICT 18			
Lowey (D)	$1,223,263	$347,100 (28%)	$1,583,489
DISTRICT 19			
Kelly (R)	$981,083	$502,463 (51%)	$906,013
Selendy (D)	$12,775	$0 (0%)	$9,621
DISTRICT 20			
Sweeney (R)	$951,814	$372,412 (39%)	$770,580
Stoppenbach (D)	$18,676	$3,500 (19%)	$18,451
DISTRICT 21			
McNulty (D)	$459,685	$261,525 (57%)	$409,261
Rosenstein (R)	$22,073	$400 (2%)	$20,776
DISTRICT 22			
Hinchey (D)	$647,317	$295,985 (46%)	$645,626
Hall (R)	$36,501	$4,803 (13%)	$39,499
DISTRICT 23			
McHugh (R)	$306,520	$209,144 (68%)	$274,466
DISTRICT 24			
Boehlert (R)	$1,069,135	$567,146 (53%)	$1,025,690
Walrath (C)	$101,949	$6,998 (7%)	$101,944
DISTRICT 25			
Walsh (R)	$773,953	$389,030 (50%)	$924,859
Aldersley (D)	$40,693	$5,198 (13%)	$39,999
DISTRICT 26			
Reynolds (R)	$1,552,380	$662,963 (43%)	$627,935
Nariman (D)	$11,167	$5,000 (45%)	$7,833
DISTRICT 27			
Quinn (R)	$1,038,729	$455,312 (44%)	$745,354
Crotty (D)	$5,896	$0 (0%)	$5,896
DISTRICT 28			
Slaughter (D)	$705,520	$291,145 (41%)	$977,329
Wojtaszek (R)	$214,117	$17,900 (8%)	$213,779
DISTRICT 29			
Houghton (R)	$881,269	$471,583 (54%)	$931,958

North Carolina

	RECEIPTS	FOM PACS	EXPENDITURES
SENIOR SENATOR - 1998			
Edwards (D)	$8,420,983	$0 (0%)	$8,331,382
Faircloth (R)	$9,370,462	$1,963,934 (21%)	$9,375,771
JUNIOR SENATOR - 2002			
Dole (R)	$13,681,111	$1,432,111 (10%)	$13,555,960
Bowles (D)	$13,304,804	$523,128 (4%)	$13,273,188
DISTRICT 1			
Ballance (D)	$760,277	$277,325 (36%)	$669,012
Dority (R)	$18,755	$2,250 (12%)	$12,355
DISTRICT 2			
Etheridge (D)	$903,623	$435,393 (48%)	$631,393
Ellen (R)	$6,472	$0 (0%)	$7,423
DISTRICT 3			
Jones (R)	$747,350	$425,837 (57%)	$448,890
DISTRICT 4			
Price (D)	$760,702	$336,543 (44%)	$656,478
Nguyen (R)	$7,240	$0 (0%)	$6,869
DISTRICT 5			
Burr (R)	$1,205,843	$582,980 (48%)	$401,019
Crawford (D)	$9,104	$600 (7%)	$12,311
DISTRICT 6			
Coble (R)	$454,399	$360,429 (79%)	$310,375
DISTRICT 7			
McIntyre (D)	$774,015	$328,425 (42%)	$555,393
DISTRICT 8			
Hayes (R)	$2,308,903	$1,082,710 (47%)	$2,243,174
Kouri (D)	$672,767	$214,150 (32%)	$666,562
DISTRICT 9			
Myrick (R)	$812,534	$306,816 (38%)	$873,507
DISTRICT 10			
Ballenger (R)	$582,759	$326,035 (56%)	$640,420
Daugherty (D)	$295,332	$1,000 (0%)	$291,932
DISTRICT 11			
Taylor (R)	$1,334,615	$146,482 (11%)	$1,319,171
Neill (D)	$586,501	$2,000 (0%)	$583,492
DISTRICT 12			
Watt (D)	$260,595	$208,020 (80%)	$349,080
Kish (R)	$3,568	$0 (0%)	$3,534
DISTRICT 13			
Miller (D)	$974,687	$393,900 (40%)	$941,014
Grant (R)	$399,943	$100,643 (25%)	$399,153

North Dakota

	RECEIPTS	FOM PACS	EXPENDITURES
SENIOR SENATOR - 2000			
Conrad (D)	$2,256,475	$1,443,306 (64%)	$2,312,543
Sand (R)	$399,590	$49,500 (12%)	$399,584
JUNIOR SENATOR - 1998			
Dorgan (D)	$1,855,934	$1,085,014 (58%)	$1,680,613
Nalewaja (R)	$151,448	$2,750 (2%)	$152,183
AT LARGE			
Pomeroy (D)	$1,770,859	$1,304,926 (74%)	$1,756,768
Clayburgh (R)	$1,085,975	$259,799 (24%)	$1,088,562

Ohio

	RECEIPTS	FOM PACS	EXPENDITURES
SENIOR SENATOR - 2000			
DeWine (R)	$5,583,868	$1,218,826 (22%)	$5,699,889
Celeste (D)	$477,784	$91,402 (19%)	$477,176
JUNIOR SENATOR - 1998			
Voinovich (R)	$6,098,620	$1,311,653 (22%)	$6,756,712
Boyle (D)	$2,233,970	$347,585 (16%)	$2,236,137
DISTRICT 1			
Chabot (R)	$691,847	$329,668 (48%)	$483,049
Harris (D)	$25,971	$14,625 (56%)	$23,384
DISTRICT 2			
Portman (R)	$1,294,391	$8,950 (1%)	$740,779
Sanders (D)	$17,012	$3,000 (18%)	$17,059
DISTRICT 3			
Turner (R)	$1,042,699	$467,726 (45%)	$1,026,328
Carne (D)	$576,018	$260,124 (45%)	$564,974
DISTRICT 4			
Oxley (R)	$1,253,240	$860,564 (69%)	$1,121,999
Clark (D)	$10,500	$10,000 (95%)	$6,847
DISTRICT 5			
Gillmor (R)	$448,404	$349,619 (78%)	$650,588
Anderson (D)	$21,369	$4,600 (22%)	$21,099
DISTRICT 6			
Strickland (D)	$775,007	$533,625 (69%)	$849,326
Halleck (R)	$187,685	$14,620 (8%)	$181,002
DISTRICT 7			
Hobson (R)	$808,980	$358,382 (44%)	$672,273
Anastasio (D)	$15,458	$250 (2%)	$14,496
DISTRICT 8			
Boehner (R)	$1,130,852	$592,680 (52%)	$992,780
Hardenbrook (D)	$18,269	$7,500 (41%)	$17,508
DISTRICT 9			
Kaptur (D)	$415,373	$238,200 (57%)	$329,092
DISTRICT 10			
Kucinich (D)	$511,712	$241,149 (47%)	$465,570
DISTRICT 11			
Jones (D)	$401,633	$274,314 (68%)	$409,722
Pappano (R)	$60,688	$0 (0%)	$95,964
DISTRICT 12			
Tiberi (R)	$1,103,510	$477,823 (43%)	$766,720
Brown (D)	$41,100	$100 (0%)	$41,214
DISTRICT 13			
Brown (D)	$1,149,860	$507,275 (44%)	$578,703
DISTRICT 14			
LaTourette (R)	$555,126	$304,994 (55%)	$513,612
DISTRICT 15			
Pryce (R)	$897,773	$583,522 (65%)	$872,928
DISTRICT 16			
Regula (R)	$282,642	$11,100 (4%)	$245,748
DISTRICT 17			
Ryan (D)	$593,113	$373,088 (63%)	$596,646
Benjamin (R)	$363,309	$160,974 (44%)	$360,919
Traficant (I)	$83,657	$3,400 (4%)	$149,918
DISTRICT 18			
Ney (R)	$654,214	$458,521 (70%)	$713,837

Oklahoma

	RECEIPTS	FOM PACS	EXPENDITURES
SENIOR SENATOR - 1998			
Nickles (R)	$2,718,188	$1,058,146 (39%)	$2,415,565
Carroll (D)	$8,619	$0 (0%)	$8,618
JUNIOR SENATOR - 2002			
Inhofe (R)	$2,992,267	$1,069,350 (36%)	$2,955,965
Walters (D)	$2,085,102	$389,927 (19%)	$2,042,689
DISTRICT 1			
Sullivan (R)†	$1,365,863	$621,955 (46%)	$1,311,010
Dodd (D)†	$551,800	$67,350 (12%)	$542,583
DISTRICT 2			
Carson (D)	$1,032,158	$429,845 (42%)	$1,021,705
Pharaoh (R)	$302,863	$2,500 (1%)	$303,825
DISTRICT 3			
Lucas (R)	$520,868	$256,776 (49%)	$441,804
DISTRICT 4			
Cole (R)	$1,272,284	$534,020 (42%)	$1,191,783
Roberts (D)	$595,689	$229,000 (38%)	$559,683
DISTRICT 5			
Istook (R)	$649,067	$302,586 (47%)	$768,358
Barlow (D)	$232,715	$24,250 (10%)	$230,752

Oregon

	RECEIPTS	FOM PACS	EXPENDITURES
SENIOR SENATOR - 1998			
Wyden (D)	$3,300,468	$1,019,403 (31%)	$2,866,368
Lim (R)	$413,449	$2,000 (0%)	$413,187
JUNIOR SENATOR - 2002			
Smith (R)	$5,250,893	$1,543,784 (29%)	$5,530,479
Bradbury (D)	$2,127,941	$326,694 (15%)	$2,104,194
DISTRICT 1			
Wu (D)	$1,552,039	$324,065 (21%)	$1,014,011
DISTRICT 2			
Walden (R)	$861,674	$371,921 (43%)	$842,862
Buckley (D)	$68,611	$3,550 (5%)	$68,530
DISTRICT 3			
Blumenauer (D)	$478,048	$253,929 (53%)	$353,543
DISTRICT 4			
DeFazio (D)	$375,909	$205,403 (55%)	$279,427
VanLeeuwen (R)	$150,727	$1,950 (1%)	$141,262
DISTRICT 5			
Hooley (D)	$801,683	$439,541 (55%)	$606,884
Boquist (R)	$159,180	$1,854 (1%)	$158,065

Pennsylvania

	RECEIPTS	FOM PACS	EXPENDITURES
SENIOR SENATOR - 1998			
Specter (R)	$6,255,657	$1,399,922 (22%)	$4,535,887
Lloyd (D)	$188,384	$20,594 (11%)	$187,157
JUNIOR SENATOR - 2000			
Santorum (R)	$9,126,046	$1,878,625 (21%)	$10,616,262
Klink (D)	$3,960,955	$923,833 (23%)	$3,941,166
DISTRICT 1			
Brady (D)	$517,460	$211,225 (41%)	$425,936
DISTRICT 2			
Fattah (D)	$224,090	$93,472 (42%)	$185,534
DISTRICT 3			
English (R)	$1,051,672	$589,386 (56%)	$732,941
Benson (GREEN)	$20,708	$100 (0%)	$18,864
DISTRICT 4			
Hart (R)	$1,203,537	$595,331 (49%)	$1,129,739
Drobac (D)	$81,087	$21,000 (26%)	$76,980
DISTRICT 5			
Peterson (R)	$450,110	$224,534 (50%)	$437,756
DISTRICT 6			
Gerlach (R)	$1,137,660	$483,475 (42%)	$1,135,912
Wofford (D)	$1,445,123	$389,750 (27%)	$1,383,927
DISTRICT 7			
Weldon (R)	$535,811	$278,760 (52%)	$589,789
DISTRICT 8			
Greenwood (R)	$899,054	$1,400 (0%)	$695,806
DISTRICT 9			
Shuster (R)†	$1,137,280	$498,563 (44%)	$1,070,912
Henry (D)	$8,424	$4,200 (50%)	$8,714
DISTRICT 10			
Sherwood (R)	$1,212,639	$272,930 (23%)	$1,238,642
DISTRICT 11			
Kanjorski (D)	$996,815	$566,415 (57%)	$1,179,632
Barletta (R)	$528,230	$193,318 (37%)	$524,786
DISTRICT 12			
Murtha (D)	$2,401,968	$738,468 (31%)	$2,332,218
Choby (R)	$17,584	$200 (1%)	$17,584
DISTRICT 13			
Hoeffel (D)	$1,564,535	$624,257 (40%)	$1,549,994
Brown (R)	$1,605,474	$157,736 (10%)	$1,812,174
DISTRICT 14			
Doyle (D)	$690,813	$455,899 (66%)	$631,279
DISTRICT 15			
Toomey (R)	$1,563,022	$685,819 (44%)	$1,014,518
O'Brien (D)	$829,690	$515,383 (62%)	$824,636
DISTRICT 16			
Pitts (R)	$401,355	$168,372 (42%)	$414,345
DISTRICT 17			
Holden (D)	$1,508,207	$788,022 (52%)	$1,714,892
Gekas (R)	$1,350,540	$770,245 (57%)	$1,427,486
DISTRICT 18			
Murphy (R)	$922,968	$457,925 (50%)	$862,255
Machek (D)	$124,620	$55,020 (44%)	$119,764
DISTRICT 19			
Platts (R)	$270,368	$0 (0%)	$224,480

Rhode Island

	RECEIPTS	FOM PACS	EXPENDITURES
SENIOR SENATOR - 2002			
Reed (D)	$2,322,852	$863,064 (37%)	$1,707,655
JUNIOR SENATOR - 2000			
Chafee (R)	$2,531,413	$699,056 (28%)	$2,265,221
Weygand (D)	$2,420,479	$836,823 (35%)	$2,297,885

DISTRICT 1			
Kennedy (D)	$2,558,596	$640,263 (25%)	$2,760,536
Rogers (R)	$1,905,078	$15,750 (1%)	$1,896,428
DISTRICT 2			
Langevin (D)	$786,063	$403,155 (51%)	$774,848
Matson (R)	$7,305	$0 (0%)	$5,964

South Carolina

	RECEIPTS	FOM PACS	EXPENDITURES
SENIOR SENATOR - 1998			
Hollings (D)	$4,547,251	$1,231,069 (27%)	$4,968,456
Inglis (R)	$2,210,434	$17,500 (1%)	$2,143,278
JUNIOR SENATOR - 2002			
Graham (R)	$6,207,367	$1,639,451 (26%)	$6,147,640
Sanders (D)	$4,284,388	$564,259 (13%)	$4,183,141
DISTRICT 1			
Brown (R)	$443,006	$219,373 (50%)	$189,549
DISTRICT 2			
Wilson (R)†	$1,303,327	$366,250 (28%)	$1,270,907
Whittington (UC)	$8,224	$0 (0%)	$8,123
DISTRICT 3			
Barrett (R)	$976,086	$238,250 (24%)	$913,409
Brightharp (D)	$31,810	$400 (1%)	$25,427
DISTRICT 4			
DeMint (R)	$418,419	$0 (0%)	$452,118
DISTRICT 5			
Spratt (D)	$745,649	$505,650 (68%)	$406,711
DISTRICT 6			
Clyburn (D)	$422,958	$233,950 (55%)	$387,983
McLeod (R)	$10,223	$0 (0%)	$10,120

South Dakota

	RECEIPTS	FOM PACS	EXPENDITURES
SENIOR SENATOR - 1998			
Daschle (D)	$5,614,668	$1,901,170 (34%)	$4,861,541
Schmidt (R)	$540,728	$56,201 (10%)	$492,854
JUNIOR SENATOR - 2002			
Johnson (D)	$5,524,580	$2,065,663 (37%)	$6,092,770
Thune (R)	$5,487,625	$1,312,130 (24%)	$5,918,310
AT LARGE			
Janklow (R)	$1,316,515	$389,689 (30%)	$1,295,577
Herseth (D)	$1,543,797	$465,430 (30%)	$1,524,701

Tennessee

	RECEIPTS	FOM PACS	EXPENDITURES
SENIOR SENATOR - 2000			
Frist (R)	$5,825,454	$1,022,063 (18%)	$6,105,303
Clark (D)	$286,469	$85,000 (30%)	$273,406
JUNIOR SENATOR - 2002			
Alexander (R)	$5,841,364	$900,059 (15%)	$3,440,187
Clement (D)	$2,790,653	$660,672 (24%)	$2,791,905
DISTRICT 1			
Jenkins (R)	$145,643	$126,000 (87%)	$104,870
DISTRICT 2			
Duncan (R)	$554,677	$281,533 (51%)	$346,282
DISTRICT 3			
Wamp (R)	$780,619	$1,600 (0%)	$622,912
Wolfe (D)	$35,550	$500 (1%)	$35,550
DISTRICT 4			
Davis (D)	$1,270,628	$543,322 (43%)	$1,224,972
Bowling (R)	$634,340	$216,102 (34%)	$687,666
DISTRICT 5			
Cooper (D)	$1,950,765	$308,816 (16%)	$1,839,424
Duvall (R)	$18,321	$1,000 (5%)	$17,521
DISTRICT 6			
Gordon (D)	$624,604	$420,896 (67%)	$578,991
DISTRICT 7			
Blackburn (R)	$633,824	$21,665 (3%)	$419,835
Barron (D)	$18,971	$5,000 (26%)	$18,969
DISTRICT 8			
Tanner (D)	$621,280	$549,935 (89%)	$532,093
Hart (I)	$31,153	$0 (0%)	$29,715
DISTRICT 9			
Ford (D)	$1,151,531	$487,080 (42%)	$816,896

Texas

	RECEIPTS	FOM PACS	EXPENDITURES
SENIOR SENATOR - 2000			
Hutchison (R)	$3,410,444	$642,467 (19%)	$3,518,862
Kelly (D)	$4,654	$0 (0%)	$4,602
JUNIOR SENATOR - 2002			
Cornyn (R)	$9,615,872	$1,627,531 (17%)	$9,513,548
Kirk (D)	$9,517,001	$931,555 (10%)	$9,315,171
DISTRICT 1			
Sandlin (D)	$995,991	$659,157 (66%)	$1,053,291
Lawrence (R)	$81,433	$3,450 (4%)	$81,432
DISTRICT 2			
Turner (D)	$796,779	$508,000 (64%)	$330,840
Brookshire (R)	$27,902	$0 (0%)	$27,856
DISTRICT 3			
Johnson (R)	$874,572	$427,832 (49%)	$898,884
Molera (D)	$44,701	$297 (1%)	$44,012
DISTRICT 4			
Hall (D)	$635,640	$394,079 (62%)	$488,330
Graves (R)	$152,014	$195 (0%)	$146,984
DISTRICT 5			
Hensarling (R)	$2,060,955	$632,132 (31%)	$2,028,980
Chapman (D)	$945,401	$306,954 (32%)	$910,874
DISTRICT 6			
Barton (R)	$876,013	$544,840 (62%)	$1,279,655
Alvarado (D)	$12,751	$0 (0%)	$12,677
DISTRICT 7			
Culberson (R)	$508,138	$188,900 (37%)	$472,911
DISTRICT 8			
Brady (R)	$367,670	$246,902 (67%)	$216,068
DISTRICT 9			
Lampson (D)	$1,217,656	$473,800 (39%)	$1,044,252
Williams (R)	$48,309	$500 (1%)	$29,261
DISTRICT 10			
Doggett (D)	$542,684	$249,925 (46%)	$187,827
DISTRICT 11			
Edwards (D)	$1,575,492	$959,108 (61%)	$1,528,900
Farley (R)	$617,068	$9,050 (1%)	$614,493

DISTRICT 12			
Granger (R)	$796,819	$318,785 (40%)	$919,865
DISTRICT 13			
Thornberry (R)	$578,848	$153,625 (27%)	$441,738
DISTRICT 14			
Paul (R)	$1,531,303	$27,300 (2%)	$1,261,785
Windham (D)	$39,626	$8,850 (22%)	$40,410
DISTRICT 15			
Hinojosa (D)	$293,466	$167,375 (57%)	$267,561
DISTRICT 16			
Reyes (D)	$459,392	$213,482 (46%)	$391,266
DISTRICT 17			
Stenholm (D)	$1,366,223	$784,175 (57%)	$1,522,455
Beckham (R)	$473,105	$21,000 (4%)	$463,105
DISTRICT 18			
Jackson-Lee (D)	$319,836	$239,764 (75%)	$393,372
Abbott (R)	$23,681	$200 (1%)	$21,455
DISTRICT 19			
Combest (R)	$570,156	$406,936 (71%)	$374,732
DISTRICT 20			
Gonzalez (D)	$615,773	$403,083 (65%)	$614,560
DISTRICT 21			
Smith (R)	$776,495	$226,690 (29%)	$772,915
Courage (D)	$168,569	$40,353 (24%)	$167,000
DISTRICT 22			
DeLay (R)	$1,326,318	$843,191 (64%)	$1,245,873
Riley (D)	$194,760	$17,250 (9%)	$191,787
DISTRICT 23			
Bonilla (R)	$2,237,575	$1,027,187 (46%)	$2,388,909
Cuellar (D)	$1,014,294	$274,965 (27%)	$914,711
DISTRICT 24			
Frost (D)	$1,669,795	$1,005,075 (60%)	$1,542,438
Ortega (R)	$39,941	$3,100 (8%)	$39,910
DISTRICT 25			
Bell (D)	$1,150,506	$469,787 (41%)	$1,054,517
Reiser (R)	$4,563,312	$98,475 (2%)	$4,538,270
DISTRICT 26			
Burgess (R)	$444,823	$187,000 (42%)	$349,599
Lebon (D)	$17,670	$3,800 (22%)	$20,367
DISTRICT 27			
Ortiz (D)	$434,286	$155,300 (36%)	$515,068
Ahumada (R)	$19,803	$300 (2%)	$19,558
DISTRICT 28			
Rodriguez (D)	$401,312	$252,962 (63%)	$399,318
Perales (R)	$17,200	$0 (0%)	$39,786
DISTRICT 29			
Green (D)	$692,741	$513,754 (74%)	$529,578
DISTRICT 30			
Johnson (D)	$399,164	$239,160 (60%)	$453,776
Bush (R)	$5,052	$100 (2%)	$6,547
DISTRICT 31			
Carter (R)	$806,998	$346,266 (43%)	$735,880
Bagley (D)	$24,839	$500 (2%)	$23,763
DISTRICT 32			
Sessions (R)	$727,034	$349,037 (48%)	$507,557
Dixon (D)	$11,371	$0 (0%)	$10,578

Utah

	RECEIPTS	FOM PACS	EXPENDITURES
SENIOR SENATOR - 2000			
Hatch (R)	$3,082,208	$1,220,662 (40%)	$3,130,550
Howell (D)	$299,747	$14,000 (5%)	$299,239
JUNIOR SENATOR - 1998			
Bennett (R)	$1,560,616	$774,405 (50%)	$1,546,219
Leckman (D)	$274,075	$10,750 (4%)	$265,494
DISTRICT 1			
Bishop (R)	$668,377	$271,488 (41%)	$655,144
Thomas (D)	$703,716	$112,250 (16%)	$703,466
DISTRICT 2			
Matheson (D)	$1,458,481	$641,107 (44%)	$1,376,640
Swallow (R)	$1,142,978	$154,238 (13%)	$1,139,372
DISTRICT 3			
Cannon (R)	$358,920	$76,500 (21%)	$364,051
Woodside (D)	$55,013	$4,764 (9%)	$60,834

Vermont

	RECEIPTS	FOM PACS	EXPENDITURES
SENIOR SENATOR - 1998			
Leahy (D)	$1,153,672	$0 (0%)	$1,014,751
JUNIOR SENATOR - 2000			
Jeffords (R)	$2,087,965	$1,112,558 (53%)	$1,889,243
Flanagan (D)	$1,093,161	$67,434 (6%)	$1,054,977
AT LARGE			
Sanders (I)	$651,944	$83,140 (13%)	$616,483
Meub (R)	$196,614	$9,900 (5%)	$184,845

Virginia

	RECEIPTS	FOM PACS	EXPENDITURES
SENIOR SENATOR - 2002			
Warner (R)	$2,617,764	$887,268 (34%)	$1,674,292
Spannaus (I)	$65,529	$500 (1%)	$65,550
JUNIOR SENATOR - 2000			
Allen (R)	$10,073,255	$1,581,172 (16%)	$9,995,980
Robb (D)	$6,737,158	$1,622,753 (24%)	$6,810,252
DISTRICT 1			
Davis (R)	$326,682	$204,865 (63%)	$270,118
DISTRICT 2			
Schrock (R)	$796,813	$353,953 (44%)	$481,981
Amarasinghe (GREEN)	$12,415	$0 (0%)	$12,415
DISTRICT 3			
Scott (D)	$172,015	$120,881 (70%)	$193,203
DISTRICT 4			
Forbes (R)†	$1,859,129	$905,846 (49%)	$1,629,051
DISTRICT 5			
Goode (R)	$733,747	$224,266 (31%)	$701,595
Richards (D)	$215,935	$22,550 (10%)	$198,288
DISTRICT 6			
Goodlatte (R)	$671,602	$297,274 (44%)	$543,450
DISTRICT 7			
Cantor (R)	$1,439,078	$553,795 (38%)	$1,350,682

Jones (D)	$185,450	$1,000 (1%)	$166,332
DISTRICT 8			
Moran (D)	$1,105,379	$485,225 (44%)	$1,568,991
Tate (R)	$90,502	$0 (0%)	$51,221
DISTRICT 9			
Boucher (D)	$1,171,401	$720,359 (61%)	$1,079,870
Katzen (R)	$233,060	$11,876 (5%)	$230,937
DISTRICT 10			
Wolf (R)	$695,984	$268,454 (39%)	$691,008
Stevens (D)	$21,077	$0 (0%)	$20,344
DISTRICT 11			
Davis (R)	$1,386,889	$629,608 (45%)	$1,495,976
Creel (CNSTP)	$9,222	$0 (0%)	$8,777

Washington

	RECEIPTS	FOM PACS	EXPENDITURES
SENIOR SENATOR - 1998			
Murray (D)	$5,341,967	$861,629 (16%)	$5,600,592
Smith (R)	$5,234,596	$687 (0%)	$5,159,527
JUNIOR SENATOR - 2000			
Cantwell (D)	$11,538,665	$0 (0%)	$11,533,295
Gorton (R)	$6,384,256	$1,770,339 (28%)	$6,402,488
DISTRICT 1			
Inslee (D)	$1,428,717	$333,240 (23%)	$591,161
Marine (R)	$190,695	$10,498 (6%)	$190,693
DISTRICT 2			
Larsen (D)	$1,788,063	$706,203 (39%)	$1,766,517
Smith (R)	$560,897	$53,048 (9%)	$549,267
DISTRICT 3			
Baird (D)	$1,266,465	$471,500 (37%)	$771,143
Zarelli (R)	$197,057	$19,004 (10%)	$195,710
DISTRICT 4			
Hastings (R)	$342,449	$167,750 (49%)	$244,124
Mason (D)	$27,818	$2,500 (9%)	$32,008
DISTRICT 5			
Nethercutt (R)	$909,652	$396,056 (44%)	$831,544
Haggin (D)	$38,010	$1,750 (5%)	$35,808
DISTRICT 6			
Dicks (D)	$820,068	$386,325 (47%)	$782,571
Lawrence (R)	$61,294	$0 (0%)	$62,571
DISTRICT 7			
McDermott (D)	$415,537	$233,596 (56%)	$436,384
Cassady (R)	$18,989	$100 (1%)	$18,761
DISTRICT 8			
Dunn (R)	$1,832,279	$714,172 (39%)	$989,914
Behrens-Benedict (D)	$133,307	$10,750 (8%)	$120,333
DISTRICT 9			
Smith (D)	$820,573	$458,457 (56%)	$769,600
Casada (R)	$60,944	$2,500 (4%)	$56,447

West Virginia

	RECEIPTS	FOM PACS	EXPENDITURES
SENIOR SENATOR - 2000			
Byrd (D)	$1,127,278	$509,530 (45%)	$1,045,993
Whelan (LIBERT)	$48,666	$1,140 (2%)	$48,514
JUNIOR SENATOR - 2002			
Rockefeller (D)	$2,466,775	$1,010,101 (41%)	$2,158,227
Wolfe (R)	$136,410	$3,742 (3%)	$136,373
DISTRICT 1			
Mollohan (D)	$361,117	$216,380 (60%)	$326,462
DISTRICT 2			
Capito (R)	$2,579,296	$1,273,171 (49%)	$2,475,697
Humphreys (D)	$8,098,590	$142,500 (2%)	$8,027,019
DISTRICT 3			
Rahall (D)	$571,320	$256,374 (45%)	$366,970

Wisconsin

	RECEIPTS	FOM PACS	EXPENDITURES
SENIOR SENATOR - 2000			
Kohl (D)	$4,986,165	$0 (0%)	$4,991,364
Gillespie (R)	$584,877	$13,500 (2%)	$582,221
JUNIOR SENATOR - 1998			
Feingold (D)	$4,072,878	$398,762 (10%)	$3,846,089
Neumann (R)	$4,409,161	$592,890 (13%)	$4,373,953
DISTRICT 1			
Ryan (R)	$1,241,844	$538,770 (43%)	$948,341
Thomas (D)	$206,393	$0 (0%)	$206,799
DISTRICT 2			
Baldwin (D)	$1,294,044	$376,564 (29%)	$1,214,995
Greer (R)	$167,915	$13,300 (8%)	$165,893
DISTRICT 3			
Kind (D)	$742,633	$343,960 (46%)	$540,314
Arndt (R)	$12,475	$500 (4%)	$12,279
DISTRICT 4			
Kleczka (D)	$576,211	$397,790 (69%)	$478,091
Verdin (WG)	$1,727	$0 (0%)	$1,593
DISTRICT 5			
Sensenbrenner (R)	$567,127	$362,176 (64%)	$493,305
DISTRICT 6			
Petri (R)	$549,962	$310,505 (56%)	$330,600
DISTRICT 7			
Obey (D)	$956,328	$614,264 (64%)	$810,223
Rothbauer (R)	$20,704	$1,000 (5%)	$19,932
DISTRICT 8			
Green (R)	$870,963	$402,718 (46%)	$390,715

Wyoming

	RECEIPTS	FOM PACS	EXPENDITURES
SENIOR SENATOR - 2000			
Thomas (R)	$958,656	$483,343 (50%)	$762,833
Logan (D)	$7,979	$5,700 (71%)	$4,187
JUNIOR SENATOR - 2002			
Enzi (R)	$1,175,276	$791,568 (67%)	$850,095
Corcoran (D)	$8,488	$1,275 (15%)	$8,467
AT LARGE			
Cubin (R)	$592,392	$363,820 (61%)	$596,509
Akin (D)	$10,450	$615 (6%)	$19,154

House Committees

The standing and select committees of the U.S. House are listed below in alphabetical order. Membership is given in order of seniority on the committee. If a non-voting delegate or the resident commissioner is a member of the committee, the party ratio reflects that membership. Non-voting representatives, while they cannot vote on the House floor, enjoy status equal to that of their voting colleagues on committees. Subcommittees membership is listed in order of seniority.

On full commitee rosters, members of the majority party, Republicans, are shown in roman type; members of the minority party, Democrats, are shown in *italic* type. Independents are labeled. The word "vacancy" indicates that a committee or subcommittee seat had not been filled at press time. Subcommittee vacancies do not necessarily indicate vacancies on full committees, or vice versa.

The telephone area code for Washington, D.C., is 202. Abbreviations for House office buildings are: CHOB – Cannon House Office Building, LHOB – Longworth House Office Building, RHOB – Rayburn House Office Building, OHOB – O'Neill House Office Building, and FHOB – Ford House Office Building. The ZIP code is 20515.

AGRICULTURE

225-2171 1301 LHOB
Party Ratio: R 27-D 24
Robert W. Goodlatte, R-Va., chairman

Larry Combest, Texas	*Charles W. Stenholm, Texas*
John A. Boehner, Ohio, vice chairman	*Collin C. Peterson, Minn.*
Richard W. Pombo, Calif.	*Cal Dooley, Calif.*
Nick Smith, Mich.	*Tim Holden, Pa.*
Terry Everett, Ala.	*Bennie Thompson, Miss.*
Frank D. Lucas, Okla.	*Mike McIntyre, N.C.*
Jerry Moran, Kan.	*Bob Etheridge, N.C.*
Bill Jenkins, Tenn.	*Baron P. Hill, Ind.*
Gil Gutknecht, Minn.	*Joe Baca, Calif.*
Doug Ose, Calif.	*Mike Ross, Ark.*
Robin Hayes, N.C.	*Anibal Acevedo-Vilá, P.R.*
Charles W. "Chip" Pickering Jr., Miss.	*Ed Case, Hawaii*
Timothy V. Johnson, Ill.	*Rodney Alexander, La.*
Tom Osborne, Neb.	*Frank W. Ballance Jr., N.C.*
Mike Pence, Ind.	*Dennis Cardoza, Calif.*
Denny Rehberg, Mont.	*David Scott, Ga.*
Sam Graves, Mo.	*Jim Marshall, Ga.*
Adam H. Putnam, Fla.	*Earl Pomeroy, N.D.*
Bill Janklow, S.D.	*Leonard L. Boswell, Iowa*
Max Burns, Ga.	*Ken Lucas, Ky.*
Jo Bonner, Ala.	*Mike Thompson, Calif.*
Mike D. Rogers, Ala.	*Mark Udall, Colo.*
Steve King, Iowa	*Rick Larsen, Wash.*
Chris Chocola, Ind.	*Lincoln Davis, Tenn.*
Marilyn Musgrave, Colo.	
Devin Nunes, Calif.	

CONSERVATION, CREDIT, RURAL DEVELOPMENT & RESEARCH

225-2171 1301 LHOB
Lucas (Okla.), chairman

Republicans: Combest, Moran (Kan.), Osborne, vice chairman, Graves, Putnam, Burns, Bonner, Rogers (Ala.), King (Iowa)
Democrats: Holden, Case, Ballance, Peterson (Minn.), Dooley, Etheridge, Acevedo-Vilá, Marshall, McIntyre

DEPARTMENT OPERATIONS, OVERSIGHT, NUTRITION & FORESTRY

225-4913 1430 LHOB
Gutknecht, chairman

Republicans: Pombo, Smith (Mich.), Ose, Rehberg, vice chairman, Putnam, Janklow, Bonner, King (Iowa), Nunes
Democrats: Dooley, Baca, Acevedo-Vilá, Cardoza, Holden, Hill, Ballance, Thompson (Calif.), Davis (Tenn.)

GENERAL FARM COMMODITIES & RISK MANAGEMENT

225-2171 1301 LHOB
Moran (Kan.), chairman

Republicans: Combest, Boehner, Smith (Mich.), vice chairman, Everett, Lucas (Okla.), Jenkins, Pickering, Johnson (Ill.), Pence, Rehberg, Graves, Burns, Chocola
Democrats: Peterson (Minn.), Thompson (Miss.), Alexander, Ross, Dooley, Pomeroy, Boswell, Etheridge, Hill, Case, Cardoza, Marshall, Larsen, Davis (Tenn.)

LIVESTOCK & HORTICULTURE

225-2171 1432P LHOB
Hayes, chairman

Republicans: Pombo, Ose, vice chairman, Pickering, Osborne, Pence, Putnam, Janklow, Rogers (Ala.), Chocola, Musgrave
Democrats: Ross, Cardoza, Scott (Ga.), Peterson (Minn.), Alexander, Lucas (Ky.), Boswell, Udall (N.M.), Larsen, Baca

SPECIALTY CROPS & FOREIGN AGRICULTURE

225-2171 1301 LHOB
Jenkins, chairman

Republicans: Combest, Everett, vice chairman, Gutknecht, Hayes, Rehberg, Rogers (Ala.), Nunes
Democrats: McIntyre, Etheridge, Hill, Scott (Ga.), Marshall, Thompson (Miss.), Alexander

APPROPRIATIONS

225-2771 H-218 Capitol
Party Ratio: R 36-D 29
C.W. Bill Young, R-Fla., chairman

Ralph Regula, Ohio	*David R. Obey, Wis.*
Jerry Lewis, Calif.	*John P. Murtha, Pa.*
Harold Rogers, Ky.	*Norm Dicks, Wash.*
Frank R. Wolf, Va.	*Martin Olav Sabo, Minn.*
Jim Kolbe, Ariz.	*Steny H. Hoyer, Md.*
James T. Walsh, N.Y.	*Alan B. Mollohan, W.Va.*
Charles H. Taylor, N.C.	*Marcy Kaptur, Ohio*
David L. Hobson, Ohio	*Peter J. Visclosky, Ind.*
Ernest Istook, Okla.	*Nita M. Lowey, N.Y.*
Henry Bonilla, Texas	*José E. Serrano, N.Y.*
Joe Knollenberg, Mich.	*Rosa DeLauro, Conn.*
Jack Kingston, Ga.	*James P. Moran, Va.*
Rodney Frelinghuysen, N.J.	*John W. Olver, Mass.*
Roger Wicker, Miss.	*Ed Pastor, Ariz.*
George Nethercutt, Wash.	*David E. Price, N.C.*
Randy "Duke" Cunningham, Calif.	*Chet Edwards, Texas*
	Robert E. "Bud"

Todd Tiahrt, Kan.
Zach Wamp, Tenn.
Tom Latham, Iowa
Anne M. Northup, Ky.
Robert B. Aderholt, Ala.
Jo Ann Emerson, Mo.
Kay Granger, Texas
John E. Peterson, Pa.
Virgil H. Goode Jr., Va.
John T. Doolittle, Calif.
Ray LaHood, Ill.
John E. Sweeney, N.Y.
David Vitter, La.
Don Sherwood, Pa.
Dave Weldon, Fla.
Mike Simpson, Idaho
John Culberson, Texas
Mark Steven Kirk, Ill.
Ander Crenshaw, Fla.

Cramer, Ala.
Patrick J. Kennedy, R.I.
James E. Clyburn, S.C.
Maurice D. Hinchey, N.Y.
Lucille Roybal-Allard, Calif.
Sam Farr, Calif.
Jesse L. Jackson Jr., Ill.
Carolyn Cheeks Kilpatrick, Mich.
Allen Boyd, Fla.
Chaka Fattah, Pa.
Steven R. Rothman, N.J.
Sanford D. Bishop Jr., Ga.
Marion Berry, Ark.

AGRICULTURE, RURAL DEVELOPMENT, FDA & RELATED AGENCIES
225-2638 2362A RHOB
Bonilla, chairman

Republicans: Walsh, Kingston, Nethercutt, Latham, vice chairman, Emerson, Goode, LaHood
Democrats: Kaptur, DeLauro, Hinchey, Farr, Boyd

COMMERCE, JUSTICE, STATE & JUDICIARY
225-3351 H-309 Capitol
Wolf, chairman

Republicans: Rogers (Ky.), Kolbe, Taylor (N.C.), Regula, Vitter, vice chairman, Sweeney, Kirk
Democrats: Serrano, Mollohan, Cramer, Kennedy (R.I.), Sabo

DEFENSE
225-2847 H-149 Capitol
Lewis (Calif.), chairman

Republicans: Young (Fla.), Hobson, Bonilla, Nethercutt, vice chairman, Cunningham, Frelinghuysen, Tiahrt, Wicker
Democrats: Murtha, Dicks, Sabo, Visclosky, Moran (Va.)

DISTRICT OF COLUMBIA
226-7500 H-147 Capitol
Frelinghuysen, chairman

Republicans: Istook, Cunningham, vice chairman, Doolittle, Weldon (Fla.), Culberson
Democrats: Fattah, Pastor, Cramer

ENERGY & WATER DEVELOPMENT
225-3421 2362 RHOB
Hobson, chairman

Republicans: Frelinghuysen, Latham, Wamp, vice chairman, Emerson, Doolittle, Peterson (Pa.), Simpson
Democrats: Visclosky, Edwards, Pastor, Clyburn, Berry

FOREIGN OPERATIONS & EXPORT FINANCING
225-2041 H-B28 Capitol
Kolbe, chairman

Republicans: Knollenberg, Lewis (Calif.), Wicker, vice chairman, Bonilla, Vitter, Kirk, Crenshaw
Democrats: Lowey, Jackson, Kilpatrick, Rothman, Kaptur

HOMELAND SECURITY
225-5834 B-307 RHOB
Rogers (Ky.), chairman

Republicans: Young (Fla.), vice chairman, Wolf, Wamp, Latham, Emerson, Granger, Sweeney, Sherwood
Democrats: Sabo, Price, Serrano, Roybal-Allard, Berry, Mollohan

INTERIOR
225-3081 B-308 RHOB
Taylor (N.C.), chairman

Republicans: Regula, Kolbe, Nethercutt, Wamp, Peterson (Pa.), vice chairman, Sherwood, Crenshaw
Democrats: Dicks, Murtha, Moran (Va.), Hinchey, Olver

LABOR, HEALTH & HUMAN SERVICES & EDUCATION
225-3508 2358 RHOB
Regula, chairman

Republicans: Istook, Wicker, Northup, vice chairwoman, Cunningham, Granger, Peterson (Pa.), Sherwood, Weldon (Fla.), Simpson
Democrats: Obey, Hoyer, Lowey, DeLauro, Jackson, Kennedy (R.I.), Roybal-Allard

LEGISLATIVE BRANCH
226-7252 H-147 Capitol
Kingston, chairman

Republicans: LaHood, vice chairman, Tiahrt, Culberson, Kirk
Democrats: Moran (Va.), Price, Clyburn

MILITARY CONSTRUCTION
225-3047 B-300 RHOB
Knollenberg, chairman

Republicans: Walsh, Aderholt, vice chairman, Granger, Goode, Vitter, Kingston, Crenshaw
Democrats: Edwards, Farr, Boyd, Bishop (Ga.), Dicks

TRANSPORTATION & TREASURY
225-2141 B-307 RHOB
Istook, chairman

Republicans: Wolf, Lewis (Calif.), Rogers (Ky.), Tiahrt, vice chairman, Northup, Aderholt, Sweeney, Culberson
Democrats: Hoyer, Olver, Pastor, Kilpatrick, Clyburn, Rothman

VA, HUD & INDEPENDENT AGENCIES
225-3241 H-143 Capitol
Walsh, chairman

Republicans: Hobson, Knollenberg, Northup, Goode, vice chairman, Aderholt, LaHood, Weldon (Fla.), Simpson
Democrats: Mollohan, Kaptur, Price, Cramer, Fattah, Bishop (Ga.)

ARMED SERVICES

225-4151 2120 RHOB
Party Ratio: R 33-D 28
Duncan Hunter, R-Calif., chairman

Curt Weldon, Pa.
Joel Hefley, Colo.
H. James Saxton, N.J.
John M. McHugh, N.Y.
Terry Everett, Ala.
Roscoe G. Bartlett, Md.
Howard P. "Buck" McKeon, Calif.
William M. "Mac" Thornberry, Texas
John Hostettler, Ind.
Walter B. Jones, N.C.
Jim Ryun, Kan.
Jim Gibbons, Nev.
Robin Hayes, N.C.
Heather A. Wilson, N.M.
Ken Calvert, Calif.
Rob Simmons, Conn.
Jo Ann Davis, Va.
Ed Schrock, Va.
Todd Akin, Mo.
J. Randy Forbes, Va.
Jeff Miller, Fla.
Joe Wilson, S.C.
Frank A. LoBiondo, N.J.
Tom Cole, Okla.
Jeb Bradley, N.H.
Rob Bishop, Utah
Michael R. Turner, Ohio
John Kline, Minn.
Candice S. Miller, Mich.
Phil Gingrey, Ga.
Mike D. Rogers, Ala.
Trent Franks, Ariz.

Ike Skelton, Mo.
John M. Spratt Jr., S.C.
Solomon P. Ortiz, Texas
Lane Evans, Ill.
Gene Taylor, Miss.
Neil Abercrombie, Hawaii
Martin T. Meehan, Mass.
Silvestre Reyes, Texas
Vic Snyder, Ark.
Jim Turner, Texas
Adam Smith, Wash.
Loretta Sanchez, Calif.
Mike McIntyre, N.C.
Ciro D. Rodriguez, Texas
Ellen O. Tauscher, Calif.
Robert A. Brady, Pa.
Baron P. Hill, Ind.
John B. Larson, Conn.
Susan A. Davis, Calif.
Jim Langevin, R.I.
Steve Israel, N.Y.
Rick Larsen, Wash.
Jim Cooper, Tenn.
Jim Marshall, Ga.
Kendrick B. Meek, Fla.
Madeleine Z. Bordallo, Guam
Rodney Alexander, La.
Tim Ryan, Ohio

PROJECTION FORCES

Bartlett, chairman

Republicans: Simmons, Davis (Va.), Schrock, Saxton, Hostettler, Calvert, Bradley, Kline
Democrats: Taylor (Miss.), Abercrombie, Tauscher, Langevin, Israel, Marshall, Alexander

READINESS

225-6288 2117 RHOB
Hefley, chairman

Republicans: McKeon, Hostettler, Jones (N.C.), Ryun, Hayes, Wilson (N.M.), Calvert, Forbes, Miller (Fla.), Cole, Bishop (Utah), Miller (Mich.), Rogers (Ala.), Franks, McHugh
Democrats: Ortiz, Evans, Taylor (Miss.), Abercrombie, Reyes, Snyder, Rodriguez, Brady (Pa.), Hill, Larson, Davis (Calif.), Larsen, Marshall, Bordallo

STRATEGIC FORCES

Everett, chairman

Republicans: Thornberry, Weldon (Pa.), Wilson (N.M.), Bishop (Utah), Turner (Ohio), Rogers (Ala.), Franks
Democrats: Reyes, Spratt, Sanchez (Calif.), Tauscher, Meek, Ryan (Ohio)

TACTICAL AIR & LAND FORCES

Weldon (Pa.), chairman

Republicans: Gibbons, Akin, Bradley, Turner (Ohio), Gingrey, Everett, McKeon, Jones (N.C.), Ryun, Simmons, Schrock, Forbes, Hefley, Wilson (S.C.), LoBiondo
Democrats: Abercrombie, Skelton, Spratt, Ortiz, Evans, Turner (Texas), Smith (Wash.), McIntyre, Brady (Pa.), Larson, Israel, Cooper, Meek, Alexander

TERRORISM, UNCONVENTIONAL THREATS & CAPABILITIES

Saxton, chairman

Republicans: Wilson (S.C.), LoBiondo, Kline, Miller (Fla.), Bartlett, Thornberry, Gibbons, Hayes, Davis (Va.), Akin, Hefley
Democrats: Meehan, Turner (Texas), Smith (Wash.), McIntyre, Rodriguez, Hill, Davis (Calif.), Langevin, Larsen, Cooper

TOTAL FORCE

McHugh, chairman

Republicans: Cole, Miller (Mich.), Gingrey, Saxton, Ryun, Schrock, Hayes
Democrats: Snyder, Meehan, Sanchez (Calif.), Tauscher, Cooper, Bordallo

BUDGET

226-7270 309 CHOB
Party Ratio: R 24-D 19
Jim Nussle, R-Iowa, chairman

Christopher Shays, Conn., vice chairman
Gil Gutknecht, Minn.
William M. "Mac" Thornberry, Texas
Jim Ryun, Kan.
Patrick J. Toomey, Pa.
Doc Hastings, Wash.
Rob Portman, Ohio
Ed Schrock, Va.
Henry E. Brown Jr., S.C.
Ander Crenshaw, Fla.
Adam H. Putnam, Fla.
Roger Wicker, Miss.
Kenny Hulshof, Mo.
Tom Tancredo, Colo.
David Vitter, La.
Jo Bonner, Ala.
Trent Franks, Ariz.
Scott Garrett, N.J.
J. Gresham Barrett, S.C.
Thaddeus McCotter, Mich.
Mario Diaz-Balart, Fla.
Jeb Hensarling, Texas
Ginny Brown-Waite, Fla.

John M. Spratt Jr., S.C.
James P. Moran, Va.
Darlene Hooley, Ore.
Tammy Baldwin, Wis.
Dennis Moore, Kan.
John Lewis, Ga.
Richard E. Neal, Mass.
Rosa DeLauro, Conn.
Chet Edwards, Texas
Robert C. Scott, Va.
Harold E. Ford Jr., Tenn.
Lois Capps, Calif.
Mike Thompson, Calif.
Brian Baird, Wash.
Jim Cooper, Tenn.
Artur Davis, Ala.
Rahm Emanuel, Ill.
Denise L. Majette, Ga.
Ron Kind, Wis.

EDUCATION & WORKFORCE

225-4527 2181 RHOB
Party Ratio: R 27-D 22
John A. Boehner, R-Ohio, chairman

Tom Petri, Wis., vice chairman	*George Miller, Calif.*
Cass Ballenger, N.C.	*Dale E. Kildee, Mich.*
Peter Hoekstra, Mich.	*Major R. Owens, N.Y.*
Howard P. "Buck" McKeon, Calif.	*Donald M. Payne, N.J.*
Michael N. Castle, Del.	*Robert E. Andrews, N.J.*
Sam Johnson, Texas	*Lynn Woolsey, Calif.*
James C. Greenwood, Pa.	*Ruben Hinojosa, Texas*
Charlie Norwood, Ga.	*Carolyn McCarthy, N.Y.*
Fred Upton, Mich.	*John F. Tierney, Mass.*
Vernon J. Ehlers, Mich.	*Ron Kind, Wis.*
Jim DeMint, S.C.	*Dennis J. Kucinich, Ohio*
Johnny Isakson, Ga.	*David Wu, Ore.*
Judy Biggert, Ill.	*Rush D. Holt, N.J.*
Todd R. Platts, Pa.	*Susan A. Davis, Calif.*
Pat Tiberi, Ohio	*Betty McCollum, Minn.*
Ric Keller, Fla.	*Danny K. Davis, Ill.*
Tom Osborne, Neb.	*Ed Case, Hawaii*
Joe Wilson, S.C.	*Raúl M. Grijalva, Ariz.*
Tom Cole, Okla.	*Denise L. Majette, Ga.*
Jon Porter, Nev.	*Chris Van Hollen, Md.*
John Kline, Minn.	*Tim Ryan, Ohio*
John Carter, Texas	*Timothy H. Bishop, N.Y.*
Marilyn Musgrave, Colo.	
Marsha Blackburn, Tenn.	
Phil Gingrey, Ga.	
Max Burns, Ga.	

21ST CENTURY COMPETITIVENESS

225-4527 2181 RHOB
McKeon, chairman

Republicans: Isakson, vice chairman, Boehner, Petri, Castle, Johnson (Texas), Upton, Ehlers, Tiberi, Keller, Osborne, Cole, Porter, Carter, Gingrey, Burns
Democrats: Kildee, Tierney, Kind, Wu, Holt, McCollum, McCarthy (N.Y.), Van Hollen, Ryan (Ohio), Owens, Payne, Andrews, Hinojosa

EDUCATION REFORM

225-4527 2181 RHOB
Castle, chairman

Republicans: Osborne, vice chairman, Greenwood, Upton, Ehlers, DeMint, Biggert, Platts, Keller, Wilson (S.C.), Musgrave
Democrats: Woolsey, Davis (Calif.), Davis (Ill.), Case, Grijalva, Kind, Kucinich, Van Hollen, Majette

EMPLOYER-EMPLOYEE RELATIONS

225-4527 2181 RHOB
Johnson (Texas), chairman

Republicans: DeMint, vice chairman, Boehner, Ballenger, McKeon, Platts, Tiberi, Wilson (S.C.), Cole, Kline, Carter, Musgrave, Blackburn
Democrats: Andrews, Payne, McCarthy (N.Y.), Kildee, Tierney, Wu, Holt, McCollum, Case, Grijalva

SELECT EDUCATION

225-4527 2181 RHOB
Hoekstra, chairman

Republicans: Porter, vice chairman, Greenwood, Norwood, Gingrey, Burns
Democrats: Hinojosa, Davis (Calif.), Davis (Ill.), Ryan (Ohio)

WORKFORCE PROTECTIONS

225-4527 2181 RHOB
Norwood, chairman

Republicans: Biggert, vice chairwoman, Ballenger, Hoekstra, Isakson, Keller, Kline, Blackburn
Democrats: Owens, Kucinich, Woolsey, Majette, Payne, Bishop (N.Y.)

ENERGY & COMMERCE

225-2927 2125 RHOB
Party Ratio: R 31-D 26
Billy Tauzin, R-La., chairman

Michael Bilirakis, Fla.	*John D. Dingell, Mich.*
Joe L. Barton, Texas	*Henry A. Waxman, Calif.*
Fred Upton, Mich.	*Edward J. Markey, Mass.*
Cliff Stearns, Fla.	*Ralph M. Hall, Texas*
Paul E. Gillmor, Ohio	*Rick Boucher, Va.*
James C. Greenwood, Pa.	*Edolphus Towns, N.Y.*
Christopher Cox, Calif.	*Frank Pallone Jr., N.J.*
Nathan Deal, Ga.	*Sherrod Brown, Ohio*
Richard M. Burr, N.C., vice chairman	*Bart Gordon, Tenn.*
Edward Whitfield, Ky.	*Peter Deutsch, Fla.*
Charlie Norwood, Ga.	*Bobby L. Rush, Ill.*
Barbara Cubin, Wyo.	*Anna G. Eshoo, Calif.*
John Shimkus, Ill.	*Bart Stupak, Mich.*
Heather A. Wilson, N.M.	*Eliot L. Engel, N.Y.*
John Shadegg, Ariz.	*Albert R. Wynn, Md.*
Charles W. "Chip" Pickering Jr., Miss.	*Gene Green, Texas*
Vito J. Fossella, N.Y.	*Karen McCarthy, Mo.*
Roy Blunt, Mo.	*Ted Strickland, Ohio*
Steve Buyer, Ind.	*Diana DeGette, Colo.*
George P. Radanovich, Calif.	*Lois Capps, Calif.*
Charles Bass, N.H.	*Mike Doyle, Pa.*
Joe Pitts, Pa.	*Chris John, La.*
Mary Bono, Calif.	*Tom Allen, Maine*
Greg Walden, Ore.	*Jim Davis, Fla.*
Lee Terry, Neb.	*Jan Schakowsky, Ill.*
Ernie Fletcher, Ky.	*Hilda L. Solis, Calif.*
Mike Ferguson, N.J.	
Mike Rogers, Mich.	
Darrell Issa, Calif.	
C. L. "Butch" Otter, Idaho	

COMMERCE, TRADE & CONSUMER PROTECTION

225-2927 2125 RHOB
Stearns, chairman

Republicans: Upton, Whitfield, Cubin, Shimkus, Shadegg, vice chairman, Radanovich, Bass, Pitts, Bono, Terry, Fletcher, Ferguson, Issa, Otter
Democrats: Schakowsky, Solis, Markey, Towns, Brown (Ohio), Davis (Fla.), Deutsch, Stupak, Green (Texas), McCarthy (Mo.), Strickland, DeGette

ENERGY & AIR QUALITY
225-2927 2125 RHOB
Barton, chairman

Republicans: Cox, Burr, Whitfield, Norwood, Shimkus, vice chairman, Wilson (N.M.), Shadegg, Pickering, Fossella, Buyer, Radanovich, Bono, Walden, Rogers (Mich.), Issa, Otter
Democrats: Boucher, Wynn, Allen, Waxman, Markey, Hall (Texas), Pallone, Brown (Ohio), Rush, McCarthy (Mo.), Strickland, Capps, Doyle, John

ENVIRONMENT & HAZARDOUS MATERIALS
225-2927 2125 RHOB
Gillmor, chairman

Republicans: Greenwood, Shimkus, Wilson (N.M.), Fossella, vice chairman, Buyer, Radanovich, Bass, Pitts, Bono, Terry, Fletcher, Issa, Rogers (Mich.), Otter
Democrats: Solis, Allen, Pallone, Doyle, Davis (Fla.), Schakowsky, Deutsch, Rush, Stupak, Wynn, Green (Texas), DeGette

HEALTH
225-2927 2125 RHOB
Bilirakis, chairman

Republicans: Barton, Upton, Greenwood, Deal, Burr, Whitfield, Norwood, vice chairman, Cubin, Wilson (N.M.), Shadegg, Pickering, Buyer, Pitts, Fletcher, Ferguson, Rogers (Mich.)
Democrats: Brown (Ohio), Waxman, Hall (Texas), Towns, Pallone, Eshoo, Stupak, Engel, Green (Texas), Strickland, Capps, Gordon, DeGette, John

OVERSIGHT & INVESTIGATIONS
225-2927 2125 RHOB
Greenwood, chairman

Republicans: Bilirakis, Stearns, Burr, Bass, Walden, vice chairman, Ferguson, Rogers (Mich.)
Democrats: Deutsch, DeGette, Davis (Fla.), Schakowsky, Waxman, Rush

TELECOMMUNICATIONS AND THE INTERNET
225-2927 2125 RHOB
Upton, chairman

Republicans: Bilirakis, Barton, Stearns, vice chairman, Gillmor, Cox, Deal, Whitfield, Cubin, Shimkus, Wilson (N.M.), Pickering, Fossella, Bass, Bono, Walden, Terry
Democrats: Markey, Rush, McCarthy (Mo.), Doyle, Davis (Fla.), Boucher, Towns, Gordon, Deutsch, Eshoo, Stupak, Engel, Wynn, Green (Texas)

FINANCIAL SERVICES

225-7502 2129 RHOB
Party Ratio: R 37-D 33
Michael G. Oxley, R-Ohio, chairman

Jim Leach, Iowa
Doug Bereuter, Neb.
Richard H. Baker, La.
Spencer Bachus, Ala.
Michael N. Castle, Del.
Peter T. King, N.Y.
Ed Royce, Calif.
Frank D. Lucas, Okla.
Bob Ney, Ohio
Sue W. Kelly, N.Y.
Ron Paul, Texas
Paul E. Gillmor, Ohio
Jim Ryun, Kan.
Steven C. LaTourette, Ohio
Donald Manzullo, Ill.
Walter B. Jones, N.C.
Doug Ose, Calif.
Judy Biggert, Ill.
Mark Green, Wis.
Patrick J. Toomey, Pa.
Christopher Shays, Conn.
John Shadegg, Ariz.
Vito J. Fossella, N.Y.
Gary G. Miller, Calif.
Melissa A. Hart, Pa.
Shelley Moore Capito, W.Va.
Pat Tiberi, Ohio
Mark Kennedy, Minn.
Tom Feeney, Fla.
Jeb Hensarling, Texas
Scott Garrett, N.J.
Tim Murphy, Pa.
Ginny Brown-Waite, Fla.
J. Gresham Barrett, S.C.
Katherine Harris, Fla.
Rick Renzi, Ariz.

Barney Frank, Mass.
Paul E. Kanjorski, Pa.
Maxine Waters, Calif.
Bernard Sanders, I-Vt.
Carolyn B. Maloney, N.Y.
Luis V. Gutierrez, Ill.
Nydia M. Velázquez, N.Y.
Melvin Watt, N.C.
Gary L. Ackerman, N.Y.
Darlene Hooley, Ore.
Julia Carson, Ind.
Brad Sherman, Calif.
Gregory W. Meeks, N.Y.
Barbara Lee, Calif.
Jay Inslee, Wash.
Dennis Moore, Kan.
Charlie Gonzalez, Texas
Michael E. Capuano, Mass.
Harold E. Ford Jr., Tenn.
Ruben Hinojosa, Texas
Ken Lucas, Ky.
Joseph Crowley, N.Y.
William Lacy Clay, Mo.
Steve Israel, N.Y.
Mike Ross, Ark.
Carolyn McCarthy, N.Y.
Joe Baca, Calif.
Jim Matheson, Utah
Stephen F. Lynch, Mass.
Brad Miller, N.C.
Rahm Emanuel, Ill.
David Scott, Ga.
Artur Davis, Ala.

CAPITAL MARKETS, INSURANCE & GSES
225-7502 2129 RHOB
Baker, chairman

Republicans: Ose, vice chairman, Shays, Gillmor, Bachus, Castle, King (N.Y.), Lucas (Okla.), Royce, Manzullo, Kelly, Ney, Shadegg, Ryun, Fossella, Biggert, Green (Wis.), Miller (Calif.), Toomey, Capito, Hart, Kennedy (Minn.), Tiberi, Brown-Waite, Harris, Renzi
Democrats: Kanjorski, Ackerman, Hooley, Sherman, Meeks, Inslee, Moore, Gonzalez, Capuano, Ford, Hinojosa, Lucas (Ky.), Crowley, Israel, Ross, Clay, McCarthy (N.Y.), Baca, Matheson, Lynch, Miller (N.C.), Emanuel, Scott (Ga.)

DOMESTIC & INTERNATIONAL MONETARY POLICY, TRADE & TECHNOLOGY
225-7502 B-304 RHOB
King (N.Y.), chairman

Republicans: Biggert, vice chairwoman, Leach, Castle, Paul, Manzullo, Ose, Shadegg, Kennedy (Minn.), Feeney, Hensarling, Murphy, Barrett, Harris
Democrats: Maloney (N.Y.), Sanders (I), Watt, Waters, Lee, Kanjorski, Sherman, Hooley, Gutierrez, Velázquez, Baca, Emanuel

FINANCIAL INSTITUTIONS & CONSUMER CREDIT
226-3280 2129 RHOB
Bachus, chairman

Republicans: LaTourette, vice chairman, Bereuter, Baker, Castle, Royce, Lucas (Okla.), Kelly, Gillmor, Ryun, Jones (N.C.), Biggert, Toomey, Fossella, Hart, Capito, Tiberi, Kennedy (Minn.), Feeney, Hensarling, Garrett, Murphy, Brown-Waite, Barrett, Renzi
Democrats: Sanders (I), Maloney (N.Y.), Watt, Ackerman, Sherman, Meeks, Gutierrez, Moore, Gonzalez, Kanjorski, Waters, Velázquez, Hooley, Carson (Ind.), Ford, Hinojosa, Lucas (Ky.), Crowley, Israel, Ross, McCarthy (N.Y.), Davis (Ala.)

HOUSING & COMMUNITY OPPORTUNITY
225-6634 B-303 RHOB
Ney, chairman

Republicans: Green (Wis.), vice chairman, Bereuter, Baker, King (N.Y.), Jones (N.C.), Ose, Toomey, Shays, Miller (Calif.), Hart, Tiberi, Harris, Renzi
Democrats: Waters, Velázquez, Carson (Ind.), Lee, Capuano, Sanders (I), Watt, Clay, Lynch, Miller (N.C.), Scott (Ga.), Davis (Ala.)

OVERSIGHT & INVESTIGATIONS
225-7502 139 FHOB
Kelly, chairwoman

Republicans: Paul, vice chairman, LaTourette, Green (Wis.), Shadegg, Fossella, Hensarling, Garrett, Murphy, Brown-Waite, Barrett
Democrats: Gutierrez, Inslee, Moore, Crowley, Maloney (N.Y.), Gonzalez, Hinojosa, Matheson, Lynch

GOVERNMENT REFORM
225-5074 2157 RHOB
Party Ratio: R 24-D 20
Thomas M. Davis III, R-Va., chairman

Dan Burton, Ind.
Christopher Shays, Conn., vice chairman
Ileana Ros-Lehtinen, Fla.
John M. McHugh, N.Y.
John L. Mica, Fla.
Mark Souder, Ind.
Steven C. LaTourette, Ohio
Doug Ose, Calif.
Ron Lewis, Ky.
Jo Ann Davis, Va.
Todd R. Platts, Pa.
Chris Cannon, Utah
Adam H. Putnam, Fla.
Ed Schrock, Va.
John J. "Jimmy" Duncan Jr., Tenn.
John Sullivan, Okla.
Nathan Deal, Ga.
Candice S. Miller, Mich.
Tim Murphy, Pa.
Michael R. Turner, Ohio
John Carter, Texas
Bill Janklow, S.D.
Marsha Blackburn, Tenn.

Henry A. Waxman, Calif.
Tom Lantos, Calif.
Major R. Owens, N.Y.
Edolphus Towns, N.Y.
Paul E. Kanjorski, Pa.
Bernard Sanders, I-Vt.
Carolyn B. Maloney, N.Y.
Elijah E. Cummings, Md.
Dennis J. Kucinich, Ohio
Danny K. Davis, Ill.
John F. Tierney, Mass.
William Lacy Clay, Mo.
Diane Watson, Calif.
Stephen F. Lynch, Mass.
Chris Van Hollen, Md.
Linda T. Sánchez, Calif.
C.A. Dutch Ruppersberger, Md.
Eleanor Holmes Norton, D.C.
Jim Cooper, Tenn.
Chris Bell, Texas

CIVIL SERVICE & AGENCY ORGANIZATION
225-6427 B-371B RHOB
Jo Ann Davis (Va.), chairwoman

Republicans: Murphy, vice chairman, Mica, Souder, Putnam, Deal, Blackburn
Democrats: Davis (Ill.), Owens, Van Hollen, Norton, Cooper

CRIMINAL JUSTICE, DRUG POLICY & HUMAN RESOURCES
225-2577 B- 373 RHOB
Souder, chairman

Republicans: Deal, vice chairman, McHugh, Mica, Ose, Jo Ann Davis (Va.), Schrock, Carter, Blackburn
Democrats: Cummings, Davis (Ill.), Clay, Sánchez (Calif.), Ruppersberger, Norton, Bell

ENERGY POLICY, NATURAL RESOURCES & REGULATORY AFFAIRS
225-4407 B-377 RHOB
Ose, chairman

Republicans: Janklow, vice chairman, Shays, McHugh, Cannon, Sullivan, Deal, Miller (Mich.)
Democrats: Tierney, Lantos, Kanjorski, Kucinich, Van Hollen, Cooper

GOVERNMENT EFFICIENCY & FINANCIAL MANAGEMENT
225-5147 B-373 RHOB
Platts, chairman

Republicans: Blackburn, vice chairwoman, LaTourette, Sullivan, Miller (Mich.), Turner (Ohio)
Democrats: Towns, Kanjorski, Owens, Maloney (N.Y.)

NATIONAL SECURITY, EMERGING THREATS & INTERNATIONAL RELATIONS
225-2548 B-372 RHOB
Shays, chairman

Republicans: Turner (Ohio), vice chairman, Burton, LaTourette, Lewis (Ky.), Platts, Putnam, Schrock, Duncan, Murphy, Janklow
Democrats: Kucinich, Lantos, Sanders (I), Lynch, Maloney (N.Y.), Sánchez (Calif.), Ruppersberger, Bell, Tierney

TECHNOLOGY, INFORMATION POLICY, INTERGOVERNMENTAL RELATIONS & THE CENSUS
225-6751 B-349A RHOB
Putnam, chairman

Republicans: Miller (Mich.), vice chairwoman, Ose, Murphy, Turner (Ohio)
Democrats: Clay, Watson, Lynch

WELLNESS & HUMAN RIGHTS
225-6427 B-371C RHOB
Burton, chairman

Republicans: Cannon, vice chairman, Shays, Ros-Lehtinen
Democrats: Cummings, Sanders (I), Watson

HOUSE ADMINISTRATION
225-8281 1309 LHOB
Party Ratio: R 6-D 3
Bob Ney, R-Ohio, chairman

Vernon J. Ehlers, Mich.
John L. Mica, Fla.
John Linder, Ga.
John T. Doolittle, Calif.
Thomas M. Reynolds, N.Y.

John B. Larson, Conn.
Juanita Millender-McDonald, Calif.
Robert A. Brady, Pa.

INTERNATIONAL RELATIONS

225-5021 2170 RHOB
Party Ratio: R 26-D 23
Henry J. Hyde, R-Ill., chairman

Jim Leach, Iowa
Doug Bereuter, Neb.
Christopher H. Smith, N.J., vice chairman
Dan Burton, Ind.
Elton Gallegly, Calif.
Ileana Ros-Lehtinen, Fla.
Cass Ballenger, N.C.
Dana Rohrabacher, Calif.
Ed Royce, Calif.
Peter T. King, N.Y.
Steve Chabot, Ohio
Amo Houghton, N.Y.
John M. McHugh, N.Y.
Tom Tancredo, Colo.
Ron Paul, Texas
Nick Smith, Mich.
Joe Pitts, Pa.
Jeff Flake, Ariz.
Jo Ann Davis, Va.
Mark Green, Wis.
Jerry Weller, Ill.
Mike Pence, Ind.
Thaddeus McCotter, Mich.
Bill Janklow, S.D.
Katherine Harris, Fla.

Tom Lantos, Calif.
Howard L. Berman, Calif.
Gary L. Ackerman, N.Y.
Eni F.H. Faleomavaega, Am. Samoa
Donald M. Payne, N.J.
Robert Menendez, N.J.
Sherrod Brown, Ohio
Brad Sherman, Calif.
Robert Wexler, Fla.
Eliot L. Engel, N.Y.
Bill Delahunt, Mass.
Gregory W. Meeks, N.Y.
Barbara Lee, Calif.
Joseph Crowley, N.Y.
Joseph M. Hoeffel, Pa.
Earl Blumenauer, Ore.
Shelley Berkley, Nev.
Grace F. Napolitano, Calif.
Adam B. Schiff, Calif.
Diane Watson, Calif.
Adam Smith, Wash.
Betty McCollum, Minn.
Chris Bell, Texas

AFRICA

226-7812 255 FHOB
Royce, chairman

Republicans: Houghton, Tancredo, Flake, Green (Wis.)
Democrats: Payne, Meeks, Lee, McCollum

ASIA & THE PACIFIC

226-7825 B-358 RHOB
Leach, chairman

Republicans: Burton, Bereuter, Smith (N.J.), Rohrabacher, Royce, Chabot, Paul, Flake, Weller, Tancredo
Democrats: Faleomavaega, Brown (Ohio), Blumenauer, Watson, Smith (Wash.), Ackerman, Sherman, Wexler, Meeks

EUROPE

226-7820 2401-A RHOB
Bereuter, chairman

Republicans: Burton, Gallegly, King (N.Y.), Davis (Va.), McCotter, Janklow
Democrats: Wexler, Engel, Delahunt, Lee, Hoeffel, Blumenauer

INTERNATIONAL TERRORISM, NONPROLIFERATION & HUMAN RIGHTS

226-1500 253 FHOB
Gallegly, chairman

Republicans: Smith (N.J.), Rohrabacher, King (N.Y.), Pitts, Green (Wis.), Ballenger, Tancredo, Smith (Mich.), Pence
Democrats: Sherman, Menendez, Crowley, Berkley, Napolitano, Schiff, Watson, Bell

MIDDLE EAST & CENTRAL ASIA

226-9940 B-359 RHOB
Ros-Lehtinen, chairwoman

Republicans: Chabot, McHugh, Smith (Mich.), Davis (Va.), Pence, McCotter, Janklow, Pitts, Harris
Democrats: Ackerman, Berman, Engel, Crowley, Hoeffel, Berkley, Schiff, Bell

WESTERN HEMISPHERE

226-9980 259A FHOB
Ballenger, chairman

Republicans: Paul, Weller, Harris, Leach, Ros-Lehtinen
Democrats: Menendez, Delahunt, Napolitano, Faleomavaega, Payne

JUDICIARY

225-3951 2138 RHOB
Party Ratio: R 21-D 16
F. James Sensenbrenner Jr., R-Wis., chairman

Henry J. Hyde, Ill.
Howard Coble, N.C.
Lamar Smith, Texas
Elton Gallegly, Calif.
Robert W. Goodlatte, Va.
Steve Chabot, Ohio
Bill Jenkins, Tenn.
Chris Cannon, Utah
Spencer Bachus, Ala.
John Hostettler, Ind.
Mark Green, Wis.
Ric Keller, Fla.
Melissa A. Hart, Pa.
Jeff Flake, Ariz.
Mike Pence, Ind.
J. Randy Forbes, Va.
Steve King, Iowa
John Carter, Texas
Tom Feeney, Fla.
Marsha Blackburn, Tenn.

John Conyers Jr., Mich.
Howard L. Berman, Calif.
Rick Boucher, Va.
Jerrold Nadler, N.Y.
Robert C. Scott, Va.
Melvin Watt, N.C.
Zoe Lofgren, Calif.
Sheila Jackson-Lee, Texas
Maxine Waters, Calif.
Martin T. Meehan, Mass.
Bill Delahunt, Mass.
Robert Wexler, Fla.
Tammy Baldwin, Wis.
Anthony Weiner, N.Y.
Adam B. Schiff, Calif.
Linda T. Sánchez, Calif.

COMMERCIAL & ADMINISTRATIVE LAW

225-2825 B-353 RHOB
Cannon, chairman

Republicans: Coble, Flake, Carter, Blackburn, Chabot, Feeney
Democrats: Watt, Nadler, Baldwin, Delahunt, Weiner

CONSTITUTION

226-7680 362 FHOB
Chabot, chairman

Republicans: King (Iowa), Jenkins, Bachus, Hostettler, Hart, Feeney, Forbes
Democrats: Nadler, Conyers, Scott (Va.), Watt, Schiff

COURTS, THE INTERNET & INTELLECTUAL PROPERTY

225-5741 B-351A RHOB
Smith (Texas), chairman

Republicans: Hyde, Gallegly, Goodlatte, Jenkins, Bachus, Green (Wis.), Keller, Hart, Pence, Forbes, Carter
Democrats: Berman, Conyers, Boucher, Lofgren, Waters, Meehan, Delahunt, Wexler, Baldwin, Weiner

CRIME, TERRORISM & HOMELAND SECURITY
225-3926 207 CHOB
Coble, chairman

Republicans: Feeney, Goodlatte, Chabot, Green (Wis.), Keller, Pence, Forbes
Democrats: Scott (Va.), Schiff, Jackson-Lee, Waters, Meehan

IMMIGRATION, BORDER SECURITY & CLAIMS
225-5727 B-370B RHOB
Hostettler, chairman

Republicans: Flake, Blackburn, Smith (Texas), Gallegly, Cannon, King (Iowa), Hart
Democrats: Jackson-Lee, Sánchez (Calif.), Lofgren, Berman, Conyers

RESOURCES
225-2761 1324 LHOB
Party Ratio: R 28-D 24
Richard W. Pombo, R-Calif., chairman

Don Young, Alaska	*Nick J. Rahall II, W.Va.*
Billy Tauzin, La.	*Dale E. Kildee, Mich.*
H. James Saxton, N.J.	*Eni F.H. Faleomavaega, Am. Samoa*
Elton Gallegly, Calif.	*Neil Abercrombie, Hawaii*
John J. "Jimmy" Duncan Jr., Tenn.	*Solomon P. Ortiz, Texas*
Wayne T. Gilchrest, Md.	*Frank Pallone Jr., N.J.*
Ken Calvert, Calif.	*Cal Dooley, Calif.*
Scott McInnis, Colo.	*Donna M.C. Christensen, Virgin Is.*
Barbara Cubin, Wyo.	*Ron Kind, Wis.*
George P. Radanovich, Calif.	*Jay Inslee, Wash.*
Walter B. Jones, N.C.	*Grace F. Napolitano, Calif.*
Chris Cannon, Utah	*Tom Udall, N.M.*
John E. Peterson, Pa.	*Mark Udall, Colo.*
Jim Gibbons, Nev., vice chairman	*Anibal Acevedo-Vilá, P.R.*
Mark Souder, Ind.	*Brad Carson, Okla.*
Greg Walden, Ore.	*Raúl M. Grijalva, Ariz.*
Tom Tancredo, Colo.	*Dennis Cardoza, Calif.*
J.D. Hayworth, Ariz.	*Madeleine Z. Bordallo, Guam*
Tom Osborne, Neb.	*George Miller, Calif.*
Jeff Flake, Ariz.	*Edward J. Markey, Mass.*
Denny Rehberg, Mont.	*Ruben Hinojosa, Texas*
Rick Renzi, Ariz.	*Ciro D. Rodriguez, Texas*
Tom Cole, Okla.	*Joe Baca, Calif.*
Steve Pearce, N.M.	*Betty McCollum, Minn.*
Rob Bishop, Utah	
Devin Nunes, Calif.	
Adam H. Putnam, Fla.	

ENERGY & MINERAL RESOURCES
225-9297 1626 LHOB
Cubin, chairwoman

Republicans: Tauzin, Cannon, Gibbons, Souder, Rehberg, Cole, Pearce, Bishop (Utah), Nunes
Democrats: Kind, Faleomavaega, Ortiz, Napolitano, Udall (N.M.), Carson (Okla.), Two Vacancies

FISHERIES CONSERVATION, WILDLIFE & OCEANS
226-0200 H2-188 FHOB
Gilchrest, chairman

Republicans: Young (Alaska), Tauzin, Saxton, Souder, Bishop (Utah)
Democrats: Pallone, Faleomavaega, Abercrombie, Ortiz, Bordallo

FORESTS & FOREST HEALTH
225-0691 1337 LHOB
McInnis, chairman

Republicans: Duncan, Jones (N.C.), Peterson (Pa.), Tancredo, Hayworth, Flake, Rehberg, Renzi, Pearce
Democrats: Inslee, Kildee, Udall (N.M.), Udall (Colo.), Acevedo-Vilá, Carson (Okla.), Three Vacancies

NATIONAL PARKS, RECREATION & PUBLIC LANDS
226-7736 1333 LHOB
Radanovich, chairman

Republicans: Gallegly, Duncan, Gilchrest, Cubin, Jones (N.C.), Cannon, Peterson (Pa.), Gibbons, Souder, Bishop (Utah)
Democrats: Christensen, Kildee, Kind, Udall (N.M.), Udall (Colo.), Acevedo-Vilá, Grijalva, Cardoza, Bordallo

WATER & POWER
225-8331 1522 LHOB
Calvert, chairman

Republicans: Radanovich, Walden, Tancredo, Hayworth, Osborne, Renzi, Pearce, Nunes
Democrats: Napolitano, Dooley, Inslee, Grijalva, Cardoza, Three Vacancies

RULES
225-9191 H-312 Capitol
Party Ratio: R 9-D 4
David Dreier, R-Calif., chairman

Porter J. Goss, Fla.	*Martin Frost, Texas*
John Linder, Ga.	*Louise M. Slaughter, N.Y.*
Deborah Pryce, Ohio	*Jim McGovern, Mass.*
Lincoln Diaz-Balart, Fla.	*Alcee L. Hastings, Fla.*
Doc Hastings, Wash.	
Sue Myrick, N.C.	
Pete Sessions, Texas	
Thomas M. Reynolds, N.Y.	

LEGISLATIVE & BUDGET PROCESS
225-8925 421 CHOB
Pryce, chairwoman

Republicans: Diaz-Balart (Fla.), vice chairman, Goss, Hastings (Wash.), Dreier
Democrats: Slaughter, Frost

TECHNOLOGY & THE HOUSE
225-4272 421 CHOB
Linder, chairman

Republicans: Myrick, vice chairwoman, Sessions, Reynolds, Dreier
Democrats: McGovern, Hastings (Fla.)

SCIENCE

225-6371 2320 RHOB
Party Ratio: R 25-D 22
Sherwood Boehlert, R-N.Y., chairman

Lamar Smith, Texas	*Ralph M. Hall, Texas*
Curt Weldon, Pa.	*Bart Gordon, Tenn.*
Dana Rohrabacher, Calif.	*Jerry F. Costello, Ill.*
Joe L. Barton, Texas	*Eddie Bernice Johnson, Texas*
Ken Calvert, Calif.	*Lynn Woolsey, Calif.*
Nick Smith, Mich.	*Nick Lampson, Texas*
Roscoe G. Bartlett, Md.	*John B. Larson, Conn.*
Vernon J. Ehlers, Mich.	*Mark Udall, Colo.*
Gil Gutknecht, Minn.	*David Wu, Ore.*
George Nethercutt, Wash.	*Michael M. Honda, Calif.*
Frank D. Lucas, Okla.	*Chris Bell, Texas*
Judy Biggert, Ill.	*Brad Miller, N.C.*
Wayne T. Gilchrest, Md.	*Lincoln Davis, Tenn.*
Todd Akin, Mo.	*Sheila Jackson-Lee, Texas*
Timothy V. Johnson, Ill.	*Zoe Lofgren, Calif.*
Melissa A. Hart, Pa.	*Brad Sherman, Calif.*
John Sullivan, Okla.	*Brian Baird, Wash.*
J. Randy Forbes, Va.	*Dennis Moore, Kan.*
Phil Gingrey, Ga.	*Anthony Weiner, N.Y.*
Rob Bishop, Utah	*Jim Matheson, Utah*
Michael C. Burgess, Texas	*Dennis Cardoza, Calif.*
Jo Bonner, Ala.	*Vacancy*
Tom Feeney, Fla.	
Vacancy	

ENERGY

225-9662 390 FHOB
Biggert, chairwoman

Republicans: Weldon (Pa.), Bartlett, Ehlers, Nethercutt, Akin, Hart, Gingrey, Bonner
Democrats: Lampson, Costello, Woolsey, Wu, Honda, Miller (N.C.), Davis (Tenn.)

ENVIRONMENT, TECHNOLOGY & STANDARDS

225-8844 2319 RHOB
Ehlers, chairman

Republicans: Smith (Mich.), Gutknecht, Biggert, Gilchrest, Johnson (Ill.), Burgess, Vacancy
Democrats: Udall (Colo.), Miller (N.C.), Davis (Tenn.), Baird, Matheson, Lofgren

RESEARCH

225-7858 B-374 RHOB
Smith (Mich.), chairman

Republicans: Smith (Texas), Rohrabacher, Gutknecht, Lucas (Okla.), Akin, Johnson (Ill.), Hart, Sullivan, Gingrey
Democrats: Johnson (Texas), Honda, Lofgren, Cardoza, Sherman, Moore, Matheson, Jackson-Lee

SPACE & AERONAUTICS

225-7858 B-374 RHOB
Rohrabacher, chairman

Republicans: Smith (Texas), Weldon (Pa.), Barton, Calvert, Bartlett, Nethercutt, Lucas (Okla.), Sullivan, Forbes, Bishop (Utah), Burgess, Bonner, Feeney
Democrats: Gordon, Larson, Bell, Lampson, Udall (Colo.), Wu, Jackson-Lee, Sherman, Moore, Weiner, Two Vacancies

SELECT HOMELAND SECURITY

226-8417
Party Ratio: R 27-D 23
Christopher Cox, R-Calif., chairman

Jennifer Dunn, Wash.	*Jim Turner, Texas*
C.W. Bill Young, Fla.	*Bennie Thompson, Miss.*
Don Young, Alaska	*Loretta Sanchez, Calif.*
F. James Sensenbrenner Jr., Wis.	*Edward J. Markey, Mass.*
Billy Tauzin, La.	*Norm Dicks, Wash.*
David Dreier, Calif.	*Barney Frank, Mass.*
Duncan Hunter, Calif.	*Jane Harman, Calif.*
Harold Rogers, Ky.	*Benjamin L. Cardin, Md.*
Sherwood Boehlert, N.Y.	*Louise M. Slaughter, N.Y.*
Christopher Shays, Conn.	*Peter A. DeFazio, Ore.*
Lamar Smith, Texas	*Nita M. Lowey, N.Y.*
Curt Weldon, Pa.	*Robert E. Andrews, N.J.*
Porter J. Goss, Fla.	*Eleanor Holmes Norton, D.C.*
Dave Camp, Mich.	*Zoe Lofgren, Calif.*
Lincoln Diaz-Balart, Fla.	*Karen McCarthy, Mo.*
Robert W. Goodlatte, Va.	*Sheila Jackson-Lee, Texas*
Ernest Istook, Okla.	*Bill Pascrell Jr., N.J.*
Peter T. King, N.Y.	*Donna M.C. Christensen, Virgin Is.*
John Linder, Ga.	*Bob Etheridge, N.C.*
John Shadegg, Ariz.	*Charlie Gonzalez, Texas*
Mark Souder, Ind.	*Ken Lucas, Ky.*
William M. "Mac" Thornberry, Texas	*Jim Langevin, R.I.*
Jim Gibbons, Nev.	*Kendrick B. Meek, Fla.*
Kay Granger, Texas	
Pete Sessions, Texas	
John E. Sweeney, N.Y.	

CYBERSECURITY, SCIENCE & R&D

Thornberry, chairman

Republicans: Sessions, vice chairman, Boehlert, Smith (Texas), Weldon (Pa.), Camp, Goodlatte, King (N.Y.), Linder, Souder, Gibbons, Granger
Democrats: Lofgren, Sanchez (Calif.), Andrews, Jackson-Lee, Christensen, Etheridge, Gonzalez, Lucas (Ky.), Langevin, Meek

EMERGENCY PREPAREDNESS & RESPONSE

Shadegg, chairman

Republicans: Weldon (Pa.), vice chairman, Tauzin, Shays, Camp, Diaz-Balart (Fla.), King (N.Y.), Souder, Thornberry, Gibbons, Granger, Sessions
Democrats: Thompson (Miss.), Harman, Cardin, DeFazio, Lowey, Norton, Pascrell, Christensen, Etheridge, Lucas (Ky.)

INFRASTRUCTURE & BORDER SECURITY

Camp, chairman

Republicans: Granger, vice chairwoman, Dunn, Young (Alaska), Hunter, Smith (Texas), Diaz-Balart (Fla.), Goodlatte, Istook, Shadegg, Souder, Sweeney
Democrats: Sanchez (Calif.), Markey, Dicks, Frank, Cardin, Slaughter, DeFazio, Jackson-Lee, Pascrell, Gonzalez

INTELLIGENCE & COUNTERTERRORISM

Gibbons, chairman

Republicans: Sweeney, vice chairman, Dunn, Young (Fla.), Rogers (Ky.), Smith (Texas), Shays, Goss, King (N.Y.), Linder, Shadegg, Thornberry
Democrats: Langevin, Markey, Dicks, Frank, Harman, Lowey, Andrews, Norton, McCarthy (Mo.), Meek

RULES
Diaz-Balart (Fla.), chairman

Republicans: Dunn, Sensenbrenner, Dreier, Weldon (Pa.), Goss, Linder, Sessions
Democrats: Slaughter, Thompson (Miss.), Sanchez (Calif.), Lofgren, McCarthy (Mo.), Meek

SELECT INTELLIGENCE

225-4121 H-405 Capitol
Party Ratio: R 11-D 9
Porter J. Goss, R-Fla., chairman

Doug Bereuter, Neb., vice chairman
Sherwood Boehlert, N.Y.
Jim Gibbons, Nev.
Ray LaHood, Ill.
Randy "Duke" Cunningham, Calif.
Peter Hoekstra, Mich.
Richard M. Burr, N.C.
Terry Everett, Ala.
Elton Gallegly, Calif.
Mac Collins, Ga.

Jane Harman, Calif.
Alcee L. Hastings, Fla.
Silvestre Reyes, Texas
Leonard L. Boswell, Iowa
Collin C. Peterson, Minn.
Robert E. "Bud" Cramer, Ala.
Anna G. Eshoo, Calif.
Rush D. Holt, N.J.
C.A. Dutch Ruppersberger, Md.

HUMAN INTELLIGENCE, ANALYSIS & COUNTERINTELLIGENCE
225-4121 H-405 Capitol
Gibbons, chairman

Republicans: Boehlert, vice chairman, Cunningham, Hoekstra, Burr, Everett, Collins
Democrats: Boswell, Ruppersberger, Reyes, Peterson (Minn.), Cramer

INTELLIGENCE POLICY & NATIONAL SECURITY
225-4121 H-405 Capitol
Bereuter, chairman

Republicans: LaHood, vice chairman, Cunningham, Hoekstra, Burr, Gallegly
Democrats: Eshoo, Hastings (Fla.), Holt, Ruppersberger

TECHNICAL & TACTICAL INTELLIGENCE
225-4121 H-405 Capitol
Hoekstra, chairman

Republicans: Boehlert, vice chairman, Gibbons, Cunningham, Everett, Gallegly, Collins
Democrats: Cramer, Holt, Eshoo, Peterson (Minn.), Ruppersberger

TERRORISM & HOMELAND SECURITY
225-4121 H-405 Capitol
LaHood, chairman

Republicans: Bereuter, vice chairman, Gibbons, Burr, Everett, Gallegly, Collins
Democrats: Hastings (Fla.), Reyes, Peterson (Minn.), Boswell, Cramer

SMALL BUSINESS

225-5821 2361 RHOB
Party Ratio: R 19-D 17
Donald Manzullo, R-Ill., chairman

Larry Combest, Texas
Roscoe G. Bartlett, Md.
Sue W. Kelly, N.Y.
Steve Chabot, Ohio
Patrick J. Toomey, Pa.
Jim DeMint, S.C.
Sam Graves, Mo.
Ed Schrock, Va.
Todd Akin, Mo.
Shelley Moore Capito, W.Va.
Bill Shuster, Pa.
Marilyn Musgrave, Colo.
Trent Franks, Ariz.
Jim Gerlach, Pa.
Jeb Bradley, N.H.
Bob Beauprez, Colo.
Chris Chocola, Ind.
Steve King, Iowa

Nydia M. Velázquez, N.Y.
Juanita Millender-McDonald, Calif.
Tom Udall, N.M.
Frank W. Ballance Jr., N.C.
Donna M.C. Christensen, Virgin Is.
Danny K. Davis, Ill.
Charlie Gonzalez, Texas
Grace F. Napolitano, Calif.
Anibal Acevedo-Vilá, P.R.
Ed Case, Hawaii
Madeleine Z. Bordallo, Guam
Denise L. Majette, Ga.
Jim Marshall, Ga.
Michael H. Michaud, Maine
Linda T. Sánchez, Calif.
Eni F.H. Faleomavaega, Am. Samoa
Brad Miller, N.C.

REGULATORY REFORM & OVERSIGHT
226-2630 B-363 RHOB
Schrock, chairman

Republicans: Bartlett, Kelly, Franks, Bradley, Two Vacancies
Democrat: Gonzalez, Five Vacancies

RURAL ENTERPRISES, AGRICULTURE & TECHNOLOGY
226-2630 B-363 RHOB
Graves, chairman

Republicans: Shuster, Kelly, Capito, Musgrave, Toomey
Democrat: Ballance, Four Vacancies

TAX, FINANCE & EXPORTS
226-2630 B-363 RHOB
Toomey, chairman

Republicans: Chabot, Musgrave, Gerlach, Beauprez, Franks, DeMint, Chocola
Democrat: Millender-McDonald, Six Vacancies

WORKFORCE, EMPOWERMENT & GOVERNMENT PROGRAMS
226-2630 B-363 RHOB
Akin, chairman

Republicans: Combest, DeMint, Capito, Bradley, Chocola, Vacancy
Democrat: Udall (N.M.), Five Vacancies

STANDARDS OF OFFICIAL CONDUCT

225-7103 HT-2 Capitol
Party Ratio: R 5-D 5
Joel Hefley, R-Colo., chairman

Doc Hastings, Wash.
Judy Biggert, Ill.
Kenny Hulshof, Mo.
Steven C. LaTourette, Ohio

Alan B. Mollohan, W.Va.
Stephanie Tubbs Jones, Ohio
Gene Green, Texas
Lucille Roybal-Allard, Calif.
Mike Doyle, Pa.

TRANSPORTATION & INFRASTRUCTURE

225-9446 2165 RHOB
Party Ratio: R 41-D 34
Don Young, R-Alaska, chairman

Tom Petri, Wis., vice chairman	*James L. Oberstar, Minn.*
Sherwood Boehlert, N.Y.	*Nick J. Rahall II, W.Va.*
Howard Coble, N.C.	*William O. Lipinski, Ill.*
John J. "Jimmy" Duncan Jr., Tenn.	*Peter A. DeFazio, Ore.*
Wayne T. Gilchrest, Md.	*Jerry F. Costello, Ill.*
John L. Mica, Fla.	*Eleanor Holmes Norton, D.C.*
Peter Hoekstra, Mich.	*Jerrold Nadler, N.Y.*
Jack Quinn, N.Y.	*Robert Menendez, N.J.*
Vernon J. Ehlers, Mich.	*Corrine Brown, Fla.*
Spencer Bachus, Ala.	*Bob Filner, Calif.*
Steven C. LaTourette, Ohio	*Eddie Bernice Johnson, Texas*
Sue W. Kelly, N.Y.	*Gene Taylor, Miss.*
Richard H. Baker, La.	*Juanita Millender-McDonald, Calif.*
Bob Ney, Ohio	*Elijah E. Cummings, Md.*
Frank A. LoBiondo, N.J.	*Earl Blumenauer, Ore.*
Jerry Moran, Kan.	*Ellen O. Tauscher, Calif.*
Gary G. Miller, Calif.	*Bill Pascrell Jr., N.J.*
Jim DeMint, S.C.	*Leonard L. Boswell, Iowa*
Doug Bereuter, Neb.	*Tim Holden, Pa.*
Johnny Isakson, Ga.	*Nick Lampson, Texas*
Robin Hayes, N.C.	*Brian Baird, Wash.*
Rob Simmons, Conn.	*Shelley Berkley, Nev.*
Shelley Moore Capito, W.Va.	*Brad Carson, Okla.*
Henry E. Brown Jr., S.C.	*Jim Matheson, Utah*
Timothy V. Johnson, Ill.	*Michael M. Honda, Calif.*
Denny Rehberg, Mont.	*Rick Larsen, Wash.*
Todd R. Platts, Pa.	*Michael E. Capuano, Mass.*
Sam Graves, Mo.	*Anthony Weiner, N.Y.*
Mark Kennedy, Minn.	*Julia Carson, Ind.*
Bill Shuster, Pa.	*Joseph M. Hoeffel, Pa.*
John Boozman, Ark.	*Mike Thompson, Calif.*
John Sullivan, Okla.	*Timothy H. Bishop, N.Y.*
Chris Chocola, Ind.	*Michael H. Michaud, Maine*
Bob Beauprez, Colo.	*Lincoln Davis, Tenn.*
Michael C. Burgess, Texas	
Max Burns, Ga.	
Steve Pearce, N.M.	
Jim Gerlach, Pa.	
Mario Diaz-Balart, Fla.	
Jon Porter, Nev.	

AVIATION

226-3220 2251 RHOB
Mica, chairman

Republicans: Petri, Duncan, Quinn, Ehlers, Bachus, Kelly, Baker, LoBiondo, Moran (Kan.), Isakson, Hayes, Johnson (Ill.), Rehberg, Graves, Kennedy (Minn.), Shuster, Boozman, Sullivan, Chocola, vice chairman, Beauprez, Pearce, Gerlach, Diaz-Balart (Fla.), Porter
Democrats: DeFazio, Boswell, Lipinski, Costello, Norton, Menendez, Brown (Fla.), Johnson (Texas), Millender-McDonald, Tauscher, Pascrell, Holden, Berkley, Carson (Okla.), Matheson, Honda, Larsen, Capuano, Weiner, Rahall, Filner

COAST GUARD & MARITIME TRANSPORTATION

226-3552 507 FHOB
LoBiondo, chairman

Republicans: Coble, Gilchrest, Hoekstra, DeMint, Simmons, Diaz-Balart (Fla.), vice chairman
Democrats: Filner, DeFazio, Brown (Fla.), Millender-McDonald, Lampson, Thompson (Calif.)

ECONOMIC DEVELOPMENT, PUBLIC BUILDINGS & EMERGENCY MGMT.

225-3014 589 FHOB
LaTourette, chairman

Republicans: Capito, Burgess, Burns, vice chairman, Gerlach
Democrats: Norton, Davis (Tenn.), Carson (Okla.), Michaud

HIGHWAYS, TRANSIT & PIPELINES

225-6715 B-370A RHOB
Petri, chairman

Republicans: Boehlert, Coble, Duncan, Mica, Hoekstra, Quinn, LaTourette, Kelly, Baker, Ney, LoBiondo, Moran (Kan.), DeMint, Bereuter, Isakson, Hayes, Simmons, Capito, Brown (S.C.), Johnson (Ill.), Rehberg, Platts, Graves, Kennedy (Minn.), Shuster, Boozman, Beauprez, vice chairman, Burgess, Burns
Democrats: Lipinski, Rahall, Nadler, Johnson (Texas), Taylor (Miss.), Millender-McDonald, Cummings, Tauscher, Pascrell, Holden, Baird, Berkley, Carson (Okla.), Matheson, Honda, Larsen, Capuano, Blumenauer, Lampson, Weiner, Carson (Ind.), Hoeffel, Thompson (Calif.), Bishop (N.Y.), Michaud

RAILROADS

226-0727 589 FHOB
Quinn, chairman

Republicans: Petri, Boehlert, Coble, Mica, Bachus, Moran (Kan.), Miller (Calif.), DeMint, Simmons, Capito, Platts, Graves, Porter, vice chairman
Democrats: Brown (Fla.), Rahall, DeFazio, Nadler, Filner, Cummings, Blumenauer, Boswell, Carson (Ind.), Michaud, Lipinski, Costello

WATER RESOURCES & ENVIRONMENT

225-4360 B-376 RHOB
Duncan, chairman

Republicans: Boehlert, Gilchrest, Ehlers, LaTourette, Kelly, Baker, Ney, Miller (Calif.), Isakson, Hayes, Brown (S.C.), Shuster, Boozman, Sullivan, Chocola, Pearce, vice chairman, Gerlach, Diaz-Balart (Fla.)
Democrats: Costello, Menendez, Taylor (Miss.), Lampson, Baird, Hoeffel, Thompson (Calif.), Bishop (N.Y.), Davis (Tenn.), Norton, Nadler, Johnson (Texas), Blumenauer, Tauscher, Pascrell

VETERANS' AFFAIRS

225-3527 335 CHOB
Party Ratio: R 17-D 14
Christopher H. Smith, R-N.J., chairman

Michael Bilirakis, Fla., vice chairman	*Lane Evans, Ill.*
Terry Everett, Ala.	*Bob Filner, Calif.*
Steve Buyer, Ind.	*Luis V. Gutierrez, Ill.*
Jack Quinn, N.Y.	*Corrine Brown, Fla.*
Cliff Stearns, Fla.	*Vic Snyder, Ark.*
	Ciro D. Rodriguez, Texas

Jerry Moran, Kan.
Richard H. Baker, La.
Rob Simmons, Conn.
Henry E. Brown Jr., S.C.
Jeff Miller, Fla.
John Boozman, Ark.
Jeb Bradley, N.H.
Bob Beauprez, Colo.
Ginny Brown-Waite, Fla.
Rick Renzi, Ariz.
Tim Murphy, Pa.

Michael H. Michaud, Maine
Darlene Hooley, Ore.
Silvestre Reyes, Texas
Ted Strickland, Ohio
Shelley Berkley, Nev.
Tom Udall, N.M.
Susan A. Davis, Calif.
Tim Ryan, Ohio

BENEFITS
225-9164 337 CHOB
Brown (S.C.), chairman

Republicans: Quinn, Miller (Fla.), Bradley, Brown-Waite
Democrats: Michaud, Davis (Calif.), Reyes, Brown (Fla.)

HEALTH
225-9154 338 CHOB
Simmons, chairman

Republicans: Moran (Kan.), Baker, Miller (Fla.), Boozman, Bradley, Beauprez, Brown-Waite, Renzi, Stearns, Murphy
Democrats: Rodriguez, Filner, Snyder, Strickland, Berkley, Ryan (Ohio), Gutierrez, Brown (Fla.), Hooley

OVERSIGHT & INVESTIGATIONS
225-3569 337A CHOB
Buyer, chairman

Republicans: Bilirakis, Everett, Boozman, Vacancy
Democrats: Hooley, Evans, Filner, Rodriguez

WAYS & MEANS

225-3625 1102 LHOB
Party Ratio: R 24-D 17
Bill Thomas, R-Calif., chairman

Philip M. Crane, Ill.
E. Clay Shaw Jr., Fla.
Nancy L. Johnson, Conn.
Amo Houghton, N.Y.
Wally Herger, Calif.
Jim McCrery, La.
Dave Camp, Mich.
Jim Ramstad, Minn.
Jim Nussle, Iowa
Sam Johnson, Texas
Jennifer Dunn, Wash.
Mac Collins, Ga.
Rob Portman, Ohio
Phil English, Pa.
J.D. Hayworth, Ariz.
Jerry Weller, Ill.
Kenny Hulshof, Mo.
Scott McInnis, Colo.
Ron Lewis, Ky.
Mark Foley, Fla.
Kevin Brady, Texas
Paul D. Ryan, Wis.
Eric Cantor, Va.

Charles B. Rangel, N.Y.
Pete Stark, Calif.
Robert T. Matsui, Calif.
Sander M. Levin, Mich.
Benjamin L. Cardin, Md.
Jim McDermott, Wash.
Gerald D. Kleczka, Wis.
John Lewis, Ga.
Richard E. Neal, Mass.
Michael R. McNulty, N.Y.
William J. Jefferson, La.
John Tanner, Tenn.
Xavier Becerra, Calif.
Lloyd Doggett, Texas
Earl Pomeroy, N.D.
Max Sandlin, Texas
Stephanie Tubbs Jones, Ohio

HEALTH
225-3943 1136 LHOB
Johnson (Conn.), chairwoman

Republicans: McCrery, Crane, Johnson (Texas), Camp, Ramstad, English, Dunn
Democrats: Stark, Kleczka, Lewis (Ga.), McDermott, Doggett

HUMAN RESOURCES
225-1025 B-317 RHOB
Herger, chairman

Republicans: Johnson (Conn.), McInnis, McCrery, Camp, English, Lewis (Ky.), Cantor
Democrats: Cardin, Stark, Levin, McDermott, Rangel

OVERSIGHT
225-7601 1136 LHOB
Houghton, chairman

Republicans: Portman, Weller, McInnis, Foley, Johnson (Texas), Ryan (Wis.), Cantor
Democrats: Pomeroy, Kleczka, McNulty, Tanner, Sandlin

SELECT REVENUE MEASURES
226-5911 1135 LHOB
McCrery, chairman

Republicans: Hayworth, Weller, Lewis (Ky.), Foley, Brady (Texas), Ryan (Wis.), Collins
Democrats: McNulty, Jefferson, Sandlin, Doggett, Jones (Ohio)

SOCIAL SECURITY
225-9263 B-316 RHOB
Shaw, chairman

Republicans: Johnson (Texas), Collins, Hayworth, Hulshof, Lewis (Ky.), Brady (Texas), Ryan (Wis.)
Democrats: Matsui, Cardin, Pomeroy, Becerra, Jones (Ohio)

TRADE
225-6649 1104 LHOB
Crane, chairman

Republicans: Shaw, Houghton, Camp, Ramstad, Dunn, Herger, English, Nussle
Democrats: Levin, Rangel, Neal, Jefferson, Becerra, Tanner

Partisan House Committees

REPUBLICAN LEADERS

Speaker . . . . J. Dennis Hastert
Majority Leader . . . . Tom DeLay
Majority Whip . . . . Roy Blunt
Conference Chairwoman . . . . Deborah Pryce
Conference Vice Chairman . . . . Jack Kingston
Conference Secretary . . . . John T. Doolittle
Chief Deputy Whip . . . . Eric Cantor

NATIONAL REPUBLICAN CONGRESIONAL COMMITTEE

479-7070 320 First St. S.E. 20003

Chairman . . . . Thomas M. Reynolds
Executive Committee Chairwoman . . . . Sue Myrick
Candidate Recruitment Chairwoman . . . . Anne M. Northup
Coalitions-Outreach Chairman . . . . John T. Doolittle
Finance Chairman . . . . Jerry Weller
Get out the Vote Chairman . . . . John Culberson
Incumbent Retention Chairman . . . . Jim McCrery
Redistricting Chairman . . . . John Linder

Members: Roy Blunt, John A. Boehner, Henry Bonilla, Ander Crenshaw, David Dreier, Jo Ann Emerson, Phil English, Mark Green, Doc Hastings, David L. Hobson, Johnny Isakson, Jerry Moran, Bob Ney, Rob Portman, Adam H. Putnam, Ed Royce, Pete Sessions, Don Sherwood, John E. Sweeney, Fred Upton, Greg Walden, Roger Wicker

Ex-Officio Members: J. Dennis Hastert, Tom DeLay, Deborah Pryce, Christopher Cox

POLICY COMMITTEE

225-6168 2471 RHOB

Chairman . . . . Christopher Cox

Subcommittee Chairmen: Kenny Hulshof, Mike Pence, Jerry Weller, Lincoln Diaz-Balart, Ernie Fletcher, Heather A. Wilson, David Vitter

Members: J. Dennis Hastert, Tom DeLay, Roy Blunt, Deborah Pryce, David Dreier, Billy Tauzin, Jim Nussle, Bill Thomas, C.W. Bill Young, John T. Doolittle, Eric Cantor, Thomas M. Reynolds, Jack Kingston, John Culberson, John Carter, Adam H. Putnam, Bob Beauprez, Todd R. Platts, Roger Wicker, Joe Knollenberg, John Shadegg, Ron Lewis, Nick Smith, Shelley Moore Capito, Rob Portman, Ander Crenshaw, Michael C. Burgess, Phil Gingrey, Katherine Harris, Melissa A. Hart, Bob Ney, Joe Wilson, Wayne T. Gilchrest, Tom Latham, Jon Porter, Kevin Brady, Robert W. Goodlatte, Patrick J. Toomey, Darrell Issa, Jim DeMint

HOUSE REPUBLICAN STEERING COMMITTEE

225-0600 H-232 Capitol

Chairman . . . . J. Dennis Hastert

Members: Tom DeLay, Roy Blunt, Eric Cantor, Deborah Pryce, Christopher Cox, Jack Kingston, John T. Doolittle, Thomas M. Reynolds, Thomas M. Davis III, C.W. Bill Young, Billy Tauzin, David Dreier, Bill Thomas, Ken Calvert, Adam H. Putnam, Doc Hastings, John Shadegg, Joe L. Barton, Tom Latham, Dave Camp, John M. McHugh, Curt Weldon, Ralph Regula, Harold Rogers, Mac Collins, Don Young, John Culberson, John Carter

DEMOCRATIC LEADERS

Minority Leader . . . . Nancy Pelosi
Minority Whip . . . . Steny H. Hoyer
Caucus Chairman . . . . Robert Menendez
Caucus Vice-Chairman . . . . James E. Clyburn
Assistant to the Leader . . . . John M. Spratt Jr.

Deputy Whips: John Lewis (senior chief), Joseph Crowley (chief), Baron P. Hill (chief), Ron Kind (chief), Ed Pastor (chief), Max Sandlin (chief), Jan Schakowsky (chief), Maxine Waters (chief)

Regional Whips: Joe Baca, Shelley Berkley, Dennis Cardoza, Michael M. Honda, Ron Kind, Betty McCollum, Danny K. Davis, Bobby L. Rush, Vic Snyder, Rick Larsen, Nick Lampson, Sheila Jackson-Lee, Harold E. Ford, Jr., Jim Cooper, Brad Miller, David Scott, Bill Pascrell Jr., Albert R. Wynn, Tim Ryan, Maurice D. Hinchey, Anthony Weiner, Michael E. Capuano, Stephen F. Lynch

DEMOCRATIC CONGRESSIONAL CAMPAIGN COMMITTEE

863-1500 430 S. Capitol St. S.E. 20003

Chairman . . . . Robert T. Matsui
Chairman's Council . . . . John D. Dingell
Executive Board Chairman . . . . Charles B. Rangel
Business Council Chairman . . . . Mike Thompson
Women Lead Chairwoman . . . . Jan Schakowsky
DCCC Vice Chairmen . . . . Edward J. Markey
. . . . Charlie Gonzalez
. . . . Rahm Emanuel
. . . . Lucille Roybal-Allard
. . . . Kendrick B. Meek
DCCC Recruitment Chairman . . . . Bart Gordon

HOUSE DEMOCRATIC STEERING COMMITTEE

225-0100 H-204 Capitol

Chairwoman . . . . Nancy Pelosi
Co-Chairwoman . . . . Rosa DeLauro
Co-Chairman . . . . George Miller
Vice Chairmen . . . . José E. Serrano
. . . . John Tanner
. . . . Maxine Waters

Members: Steny H. Hoyer, Robert Menendez, James E. Clyburn, John M. Spratt Jr., Robert T. Matsui, John Lewis, Baron P. Hill, Ed Pastor, Max Sandlin, Jan Schakowsky, David R. Obey, John D. Dingell, Martin Frost, Charles B. Rangel, Benjamin L. Cardin, C.A. Dutch Ruppersberger, Earl Blumenauer, Michael E. Capuano, Sheila Jackson-Lee, John B. Larson, Zoe Lofgren, Nita M. Lowey, Carolyn McCarthy, Betty McCollum, Alan B. Mollohan, John P. Murtha, Donald M. Payne, Collin C. Peterson, Ciro D. Rodriguez, Mike Ross, Hilda L. Solis, Sherrod Brown, Jerry F. Costello, Joseph Crowley, Jim Davis, Chris John, Carolyn Cheeks Kilpatrick, Earl Pomeroy, Nick J. Rahall II, Mike Thompson, John F. Tierney, Jim Turner, Tom Udall

Senate Committees

The standing and select committees of the U.S. Senate are listed below in alphabetical order. The listings include a telephone number, room number and party ratio for each full committee. Membership is given in order of seniority on the committee. Subcommittee membership is listed in order of seniority.

On full committee rosters, members of the majority party, Republicans, are shown in roman type; members of the minority party, Democrats, are shown in *italic* type.

The word "vacancy" indicates that a committee or subcommittee seat had not been filled at press time. Subcommittee vacancies do not necessarily indicate vacancies on full committees, or vice versa.

Partisan committees are listed on page 1184.

The telephone area code for Washington, D.C., is 202. Abbreviations for Senate office buildings are: SD — Dirksen Building, SH — Hart Building, SR — Russell Building. The ZIP code for all Senate offices is 20510.

AGRICULTURE, NUTRITION & FORESTRY

224-2035 328A SR
Party Ratio: R 11-D 10
Thad Cochran, R-Miss., chairman

Richard G. Lugar, Ind.	*Tom Harkin, Iowa*
Mitch McConnell, Ky.	*Patrick J. Leahy, Vt.*
Pat Roberts, Kan.	*Kent Conrad, N.D.*
Peter G. Fitzgerald, Ill.	*Tom Daschle, S.D.*
Saxby Chambliss, Ga.	*Max Baucus, Mont.*
Norm Coleman, Minn.	*Blanche Lincoln, Ark.*
Michael D. Crapo, Idaho	*Zell Miller, Ga.*
Jim Talent, Mo.	*Debbie Stabenow, Mich.*
Elizabeth Dole, N.C.	*Ben Nelson, Neb.*
Charles E. Grassley, Iowa	*Mark Dayton, Minn.*

FORESTRY, CONSERVATION & RURAL REVITALIZATION

224-2035 328A SR
Crapo, chairman

Republicans: Lugar, Coleman, Talent, McConnell, Roberts
Democrats: Lincoln, Dayton, Leahy, Daschle, Nelson (Neb.)

MARKETING, INSPECTION & PRODUCT PROMOTION

224-2035 328A SR
Talent, chairman

Republicans: Roberts, Fitzgerald, Chambliss, Grassley
Democrats: Baucus, Nelson (Neb.), Conrad, Stabenow

PRODUCTION & PRICE COMPETITIVENESS

224-2035 328A SR
Dole, chairwoman

Republicans: McConnell, Roberts, Chambliss, Coleman, Grassley
Democrats: Conrad, Daschle, Miller, Baucus, Lincoln

RESEARCH, NUTRITION & GENERAL LEGISLATION

224-2035 328A SR
Fitzgerald, chairman

Republicans: Lugar, McConnell, Crapo, Dole
Democrats: Leahy, Stabenow, Miller, Dayton

APPROPRIATIONS

224-7363 S-128 Capitol
Party Ratio: R 15-D 14
Ted Stevens, R-Alaska, chairman

Thad Cochran, Miss.	*Robert C. Byrd, W.Va.*
Arlen Specter, Pa.	*Daniel K. Inouye, Hawaii*
Pete V. Domenici, N.M.	*Ernest F. Hollings, S.C.*
Christopher S. Bond, Mo.	*Patrick J. Leahy, Vt.*
Mitch McConnell, Ky.	*Tom Harkin, Iowa*
Conrad Burns, Mont.	*Barbara A. Mikulski, Md.*
Richard C. Shelby, Ala.	*Harry Reid, Nev.*
Judd Gregg, N.H.	*Herb Kohl, Wis.*
Robert F. Bennett, Utah	*Patty Murray, Wash.*
Ben Nighthorse Campbell, Colo.	*Byron L. Dorgan, N.D.*
	Dianne Feinstein, Calif.
Larry E. Craig, Idaho	*Richard J. Durbin, Ill.*
Kay Bailey Hutchison, Texas	*Tim Johnson, S.D.*
Mike DeWine, Ohio	*Mary L. Landrieu, La.*
Sam Brownback, Kan.	

AGRICULTURE, RURAL DEVELOPMENT & RELATED AGENCIES

224-8090 188 SD
Bennett, chairman

Republicans: Cochran, Specter, Bond, McConnell, Burns, Craig, Brownback
Democrats: Kohl, Harkin, Dorgan, Feinstein, Durbin, Johnson, Landrieu

COMMERCE, JUSTICE, STATE & JUDICIARY

224-7277 S-206 Capitol
Gregg, chairman

Republicans: Stevens, Domenici, McConnell, Hutchison, Campbell, Brownback
Democrats: Hollings, Inouye, Mikulski, Leahy, Kohl, Murray

DEFENSE

224-7255 119 SD
Stevens, chairman

Republicans: Cochran, Specter, Domenici, Bond, McConnell, Shelby, Gregg, Hutchison, Burns
Democrats: Inouye, Hollings, Byrd, Leahy, Harkin, Dorgan, Durbin, Reid, Feinstein

DISTRICT OF COLUMBIA

224-6933 S-128 Capitol
DeWine, chairman

Republicans: Brownback, Hutchison
Democrats: Landrieu, Durbin

ENERGY & WATER DEVELOPMENT
224-8119 129 SD
Domenici, chairman

Republicans: Cochran, McConnell, Bennett, Burns, Craig, Bond
Democrats: Reid, Byrd, Hollings, Murray, Dorgan, Feinstein

FOREIGN OPERATIONS
224-8202 142 SD
McConnell, chairman

Republicans: Specter, Gregg, Shelby, Bennett, Campbell, Bond, DeWine
Democrats: Leahy, Inouye, Harkin, Mikulski, Durbin, Johnson, Landrieu

HOMELAND SECURITY
224-4319 135 SD
Cochran, chairman

Republicans: Stevens, Specter, Domenici, McConnell, Shelby, Gregg, Campbell, Craig
Democrats: Byrd, Inouye, Hollings, Leahy, Harkin, Mikulski, Kohl, Murray

INTERIOR
224-7233 132 SD
Burns, chairman

Republicans: Stevens, Cochran, Domenici, Bennett, Gregg, Campbell, Brownback
Democrats: Dorgan, Byrd, Leahy, Hollings, Reid, Feinstein, Mikulski

LABOR, HEALTH & HUMAN SERVICES & EDUCATION
224-8221 184 SD
Specter, chairman

Republicans: Cochran, Gregg, Hutchison, Craig, Stevens, DeWine, Shelby
Democrats: Harkin, Hollings, Inouye, Reid, Kohl, Murray, Landrieu

LEGISLATIVE BRANCH
224-7238 127 SD
Campbell, chairman

Republicans: Bennett, Stevens
Democrats: Durbin, Johnson

MILITARY CONSTRUCTION
224-8224 127 SD
Hutchison, chairwoman

Republicans: Burns, Craig, DeWine, Brownback
Democrats: Feinstein, Inouye, Johnson, Landrieu

TRANSPORTATION, TREASURY & GENERAL GOVERNMENT
224-8244 196 SD
Shelby, chairman

Republicans: Specter, Bond, Bennett, Campbell, Hutchison, DeWine, Brownback
Democrats: Murray, Byrd, Mikulski, Reid, Kohl, Durbin, Dorgan

VA, HUD & INDEPENDENT AGENCIES
224-8252 130 SD
Bond, chairman

Republicans: Burns, Shelby, Craig, Domenici, DeWine, Hutchison
Democrats: Mikulski, Leahy, Harkin, Byrd, Johnson, Reid

ARMED SERVICES
224-3871 228 SR
Party Ratio: R 13-D 12
John W. Warner, R-Va., chairman

John McCain, Ariz.	*Carl Levin, Mich.*
James M. Inhofe, Okla.	*Edward M. Kennedy, Mass.*
Pat Roberts, Kan.	*Robert C. Byrd, W.Va.*
Wayne Allard, Colo.	*Joseph I. Lieberman, Conn.*
Jeff Sessions, Ala.	*Jack Reed, R.I.*
Susan Collins, Maine	*Daniel K. Akaka, Hawaii*
John Ensign, Nev.	*Bill Nelson, Fla.*
Jim Talent, Mo.	*Ben Nelson, Neb.*
Saxby Chambliss, Ga.	*Mark Dayton, Minn.*
Lindsey Graham, S.C.	*Evan Bayh, Ind.*
Elizabeth Dole, N.C.	*Hillary Rodham Clinton, N.Y.*
John Cornyn, Texas	*Mark Pryor, Ark.*

AIRLAND
224-3871 228 SR
Sessions, chairman

Republicans: McCain, Inhofe, Roberts, Talent, Chambliss, Dole
Democrats: Lieberman, Akaka, Dayton, Bayh, Clinton, Pryor

EMERGING THREATS & CAPABILITIES
224-3871 228 SR
Roberts, chairman

Republicans: Allard, Collins, Ensign, Talent, Chambliss, Graham (S.C.), Dole, Cornyn
Democrats: Reed, Kennedy, Byrd, Lieberman, Akaka, Nelson (Fla.), Bayh, Clinton

PERSONNEL
224-3871 228 SR
Chambliss, chairman

Republicans: Collins, Dole, Cornyn
Democrats: Nelson (Neb.), Kennedy, Pryor

READINESS & MANAGEMENT SUPPORT
224-3871 228 SR
Ensign, chairman

Republicans: McCain, Inhofe, Roberts, Allard, Sessions, Talent, Chambliss, Cornyn
Democrats: Akaka, Byrd, Nelson (Fla.), Nelson (Neb.), Dayton, Bayh, Clinton, Pryor

SEAPOWER
224-3871 228 SR
Talent, chairman

Republicans: McCain, Collins, Graham (S.C.)
Democrats: Kennedy, Lieberman, Reed

STRATEGIC FORCES
224-3871 228 SR
Allard, chairman

Republicans: Inhofe, Sessions, Ensign, Graham (S.C.), Cornyn
Democrats: Nelson (Fla.), Byrd, Reed, Nelson (Neb.), Dayton

BANKING, HOUSING & URBAN AFFAIRS

224-7391 534 SD
Party Ratio: R 11-D 10
Richard C. Shelby, R-Ala., chairman

Robert F. Bennett, Utah	*Paul S. Sarbanes, Md.*
Wayne Allard, Colo.	*Christopher J. Dodd, Conn.*
Michael B. Enzi, Wyo.	*Tim Johnson, S.D.*
Chuck Hagel, Neb.	*Jack Reed, R.I.*
Rick Santorum, Pa.	*Charles E. Schumer, N.Y.*
Jim Bunning, Ky.	*Evan Bayh, Ind.*
Michael D. Crapo, Idaho	*Zell Miller, Ga.*
John E. Sununu, N.H.	*Thomas R. Carper, Del.*
Elizabeth Dole, N.C.	*Debbie Stabenow, Mich.*
Lincoln Chafee, R.I.	*Jon Corzine, N.J.*

ECONOMIC POLICY

224-7391 534 SD
Bunning, chairman

Republicans: Dole, Shelby
Democrats: Schumer, Miller

FINANCIAL INSTITUTIONS

224-7391 534 SD
Bennett, chairman

Republicans: Dole, Chafee, Allard, Santorum, Hagel, Bunning, Crapo
Democrats: Johnson, Miller, Carper, Dodd, Reed, Bayh, Stabenow

HOUSING & TRANSPORTATION

224-7391 534 SD
Allard, chairman

Republicans: Santorum, Bennett, Chafee, Enzi, Sununu, Shelby
Democrats: Reed, Stabenow, Corzine, Dodd, Carper, Schumer

INTERNATIONAL TRADE & FINANCE

224-7391 534 SD
Hagel, chairman

Republicans: Enzi, Crapo, Sununu, Dole, Chafee
Democrats: Bayh, Miller, Johnson, Carper, Corzine

SECURITIES & INVESTMENT

224-7391 534 SD
Enzi, chairman

Republicans: Crapo, Sununu, Hagel, Bunning, Bennett, Allard, Santorum
Democrats: Dodd, Johnson, Reed, Schumer, Bayh, Stabenow, Corzine

BUDGET

224-0642 624 SD
Party Ratio: R 12-D 11
Don Nickles, R-Okla., chairman

Pete V. Domenici, N.M.	*Kent Conrad, N.D.*
Charles E. Grassley, Iowa	*Ernest F. Hollings, S.C.*
Judd Gregg, N.H.	*Paul S. Sarbanes, Md.*
Wayne Allard, Colo.	*Patty Murray, Wash.*
Conrad Burns, Mont.	*Ron Wyden, Ore.*
Michael B. Enzi, Wyo.	*Russell D. Feingold, Wis.*
Jeff Sessions, Ala.	*Tim Johnson, S.D.*
Jim Bunning, Ky.	*Robert C. Byrd, W.Va.*
Michael D. Crapo, Idaho	*Bill Nelson, Fla.*
John Ensign, Nev.	*Debbie Stabenow, Mich.*
John Cornyn, Texas	*Jon Corzine, N.J.*

COMMERCE, SCIENCE & TRANSPORTATION

224-5115 508 SD
Party Ratio: R 12-D 11
John McCain, R-Ariz., chairman

Ted Stevens, Alaska	*Ernest F. Hollings, S.C.*
Conrad Burns, Mont.	*Daniel K. Inouye, Hawaii*
Trent Lott, Miss.	*John D. Rockefeller IV, W.Va.*
Kay Bailey Hutchison, Texas	*John Kerry, Mass.*
Olympia J. Snowe, Maine	*John B. Breaux, La.*
Sam Brownback, Kan.	*Byron L. Dorgan, N.D.*
Gordon H. Smith, Ore.	*Ron Wyden, Ore.*
Peter G. Fitzgerald, Ill.	*Barbara Boxer, Calif.*
John Ensign, Nev.	*Bill Nelson, Fla.*
George Allen, Va.	*Maria Cantwell, Wash.*
John E. Sununu, N.H.	*Frank R. Lautenberg, N.J.*

AVIATION

224-1251 427 SH
Lott, chairman

Republicans: Stevens, Burns, Hutchison, Snowe, Brownback, Smith, Fitzgerald, Ensign, Allen, Sununu
Democrats: Rockefeller, Hollings, Inouye, Breaux, Dorgan, Wyden, Nelson (Fla.), Boxer, Cantwell, Lautenberg

COMMUNICATIONS

224-5184 428 SH
Burns, chairman

Republicans: Stevens, Lott, Hutchison, Snowe, Brownback, Smith, Fitzgerald, Ensign, Allen, Sununu
Democrats: Hollings, Inouye, Rockefeller, Kerry, Breaux, Dorgan, Wyden, Boxer, Nelson (Fla.), Cantwell

COMPETITION, FOREIGN COMMERCE & INFRASTRUCTURE

224-0411 428 SH
Smith, chairman

Republicans: Burns, Brownback, Fitzgerald, Ensign, Sununu
Democrats: Dorgan, Boxer, Nelson (Fla.), Cantwell, Lautenberg

CONSUMER AFFAIRS & PRODUCT SAFETY

224-0411 SR
Fitzgerald, chairman

Republicans: Burns, Smith
Democrats: Wyden, Dorgan

OCEANS, FISHERIES & COAST GUARD
224-4912 425 SH
Snowe, chairwoman

Republicans: Stevens, Lott, Hutchison, Smith, Sununu
Democrats: Kerry, Hollings, Inouye, Breaux, Cantwell

SCIENCE, TECHNOLOGY & SPACE
224-0415 227 SH
Brownback, chairman

Republicans: Stevens, Burns, Lott, Hutchison, Ensign, Allen, Sununu
Democrats: Breaux, Rockefeller, Kerry, Dorgan, Wyden, Nelson (Fla.), Lautenberg

SURFACE TRANSPORTATION & MERCHANT MARINE
224-9000 428 SH
Hutchison, chairwoman

Republicans: Stevens, Burns, Lott, Snowe, Brownback, Smith, Allen
Democrats: Inouye, Rockefeller, Kerry, Breaux, Wyden, Boxer, Lautenberg

ENERGY & NATURAL RESOURCES

224-4971 364 SD
Party Ratio: R 12-D 11
Pete V. Domenici, R-N.M., chairman

Don Nickles, Okla.
Larry E. Craig, Idaho
Ben Nighthorse Campbell, Colo.
Craig Thomas, Wyo.
Lamar Alexander, Tenn.
Lisa Murkowski, Alaska
Jim Talent, Mo.
Conrad Burns, Mont.
Gordon H. Smith, Ore.
Jim Bunning, Ky.
Jon Kyl, Ariz.

Jeff Bingaman, N.M.
Daniel K. Akaka, Hawaii
Byron L. Dorgan, N.D.
Bob Graham, Fla.
Ron Wyden, Ore.
Tim Johnson, S.D.
Mary L. Landrieu, La.
Evan Bayh, Ind.
Dianne Feinstein, Calif.
Charles E. Schumer, N.Y.
Maria Cantwell, Wash.

ENERGY
224-4971 364 SD
Alexander, chairman

Republicans: Nickles, vice chairman, Talent, Bunning, Thomas, Murkowski, Craig, Burns
Democrats: Graham (Fla.), Akaka, Johnson, Landrieu, Bayh, Schumer, Cantwell

NATIONAL PARKS
224-4971 364 SD
Thomas, chairman

Republicans: Nickles, vice chairman, Campbell, Alexander, Burns, Smith, Kyl
Democrats: Akaka, Dorgan, Graham (Fla.), Landrieu, Bayh, Schumer

PUBLIC LANDS & FORESTS
224-4971 364 SD
Craig, chairman

Republicans: Burns, vice chairman, Smith, Kyl, Campbell, Alexander, Murkowski, Talent
Democrats: Wyden, Akaka, Dorgan, Johnson, Landrieu, Bayh, Feinstein

WATER & POWER
224-4971 364 SD
Murkowski, chairwoman

Republicans: Campbell, vice chairman, Smith, Kyl, Craig, Talent, Bunning, Thomas
Democrats: Dorgan, Graham (Fla.), Wyden, Johnson, Feinstein, Schumer, Cantwell

ENVIRONMENT & PUBLIC WORKS

224-6176 410 SD
Party Ratio: R 10-D 9
James M. Inhofe, R-Okla., chairman

John W. Warner, Va.
Christopher S. Bond, Mo.
George V. Voinovich, Ohio
Michael D. Crapo, Idaho
Lincoln Chafee, R.I.
John Cornyn, Texas
Lisa Murkowski, Alaska
Craig Thomas, Wyo.
Wayne Allard, Colo.

James M. Jeffords, I-Vt.
Max Baucus, Mont.
Harry Reid, Nev.
Bob Graham, Fla.
Joseph I. Lieberman, Conn.
Barbara Boxer, Calif.
Ron Wyden, Ore.
Thomas R. Carper, Del.
Hillary Rodham Clinton, N.Y.

CLEAN AIR, CLIMATE CHANGE & NUCLEAR SAFETY
224-8832 410 SD
Voinovich, chairman

Republicans: Crapo, Bond, Cornyn, Thomas
Democrats: Carper, Lieberman, Reid, Clinton

FISHERIES, WILDLIFE & WATER
224-8832 410 SD
Crapo, chairman

Republicans: Warner, Murkowski, Thomas, Allard
Democrats: Graham (Fla.), Baucus, Wyden, Clinton

SUPERFUND & WASTE MANAGEMENT
224-8832 410 SD
Chafee, chairman

Republicans: Warner, Allard, Bond
Democrats: Boxer, Wyden, Carper

TRANSPORTATION & INFRASTRUCTURE
224-8832 410 SD
Bond, chairman

Republicans: Warner, Voinovich, Chafee, Cornyn, Murkowski
Democrats: Reid, Baucus, Graham (Fla.), Lieberman, Boxer

FINANCE

224-4515 219 SD
Party Ratio: R 11-D 10
Charles E. Grassley, R-Iowa, chairman

Republicans	Democrats
Orrin G. Hatch, Utah	*Max Baucus, Mont.*
Don Nickles, Okla.	*John D. Rockefeller IV, W.Va.*
Trent Lott, Miss.	*Tom Daschle, S.D.*
Olympia J. Snowe, Maine	*John B. Breaux, La.*
Jon Kyl, Ariz.	*Kent Conrad, N.D.*
Craig Thomas, Wyo.	*Bob Graham, Fla.*
Rick Santorum, Pa.	*James M. Jeffords, I-Vt.*
Bill Frist, Tenn.	*Jeff Bingaman, N.M.*
Gordon H. Smith, Ore.	*John Kerry, Mass.*
Jim Bunning, Ky.	*Blanche Lincoln, Ark.*

HEALTH CARE

224-4515 219 SD
Kyl, chairman

Republicans: Snowe, Frist, Bunning, Nickles, Thomas, Santorum, Smith, Hatch, Lott
Democrats: Rockefeller, Daschle, Graham (Fla.), Jeffords (I), Bingaman, Kerry, Lincoln, Breaux, Baucus

INTERNATIONAL TRADE

224-4515 219 SD
Thomas, chairman

Republicans: Hatch, Grassley, Smith, Snowe, Frist, Lott, Bunning
Democrats: Baucus, Rockefeller, Conrad, Graham (Fla.), Jeffords (I), Daschle, Kerry

LONG-TERM GROWTH & DEBT REDUCTION

224-4515 219 SD
Smith, chairman

Republicans: Lott, Kyl
Democrats: Graham (Fla.), Conrad

SOCIAL SECURITY & FAMILY POLICY

224-4515 219 SD
Santorum, chairman

Republicans: Grassley, Kyl, Bunning, Nickles, Snowe, Frist
Democrats: Breaux, Daschle, Kerry, Rockefeller, Bingaman, Lincoln

TAXATION & IRS OVERSIGHT

224-4515 219 SD
Nickles, chairman

Republicans: Hatch, Lott, Snowe, Thomas, Santorum, Smith
Democrats: Conrad, Bingaman, Lincoln, Breaux, Baucus, Jeffords (I)

FOREIGN RELATIONS

224-4651 450 SD
Party Ratio: R 10-D 9
Richard G. Lugar, R-Ind., chairman

Republicans	Democrats
Chuck Hagel, Neb.	*Joseph R. Biden Jr., Del.*
Lincoln Chafee, R.I.	*Paul S. Sarbanes, Md.*
George Allen, Va.	*Christopher J. Dodd, Conn.*
Sam Brownback, Kan.	*John Kerry, Mass.*
Michael B. Enzi, Wyo.	*Russell D. Feingold, Wis.*
George V. Voinovich, Ohio	*Barbara Boxer, Calif.*
Lamar Alexander, Tenn.	*Bill Nelson, Fla.*
Norm Coleman, Minn.	*John D. Rockefeller IV, W.Va.*
John E. Sununu, N.H.	*Jon Corzine, N.J.*

AFRICAN AFFAIRS

224-4651 446 SD
Alexander, chairman

Republicans: Brownback, Coleman, Sununu
Democrats: Feingold, Dodd, Nelson (Fla.)

EAST ASIAN & PACIFIC AFFAIRS

224-4651 446 SD
Brownback, chairman

Republicans: Alexander, Hagel, Allen, Voinovich
Democrats: Kerry, Rockefeller, Feingold, Corzine

EUROPEAN AFFAIRS

224-4651 446 SD
Allen, chairman

Republicans: Voinovich, Hagel, Sununu, Chafee
Democrats: Biden, Sarbanes, Dodd, Kerry

INTERNATIONAL ECONOMIC POLICY, EXPORT & TRADE PROMOTION

224-4651 446 SD
Hagel, chairman

Republicans: Chafee, Enzi, Alexander, Coleman
Democrats: Sarbanes, Rockefeller, Corzine, Dodd

INTERNATIONAL OPERATIONS & TERRORISM

224-4651 446 SD
Sununu, chairman

Republicans: Enzi, Allen, Voinovich, Brownback
Democrats: Nelson (Fla.), Biden, Feingold, Boxer

NEAR EASTERN & SOUTH ASIAN AFFAIRS

224-4651 446 SD
Chafee, chairman

Republicans: Hagel, Brownback, Voinovich, Coleman
Democrats: Boxer, Corzine, Rockefeller, Sarbanes

WESTERN HEMISPHERE, PEACE CORPS & NARCOTICS AFFAIRS

224-4651 446 SD
Coleman, chairman

Republicans: Chafee, Allen, Enzi, Sununu
Democrats: Dodd, Boxer, Nelson (Fla.), Biden, Kerry

GOVERNMENTAL AFFAIRS

224-4751 340 SD
Party Ratio: R 9-D 8
Susan Collins, R-Maine, chairwoman

Ted Stevens, Alaska	*Joseph I. Lieberman, Conn.*
George V. Voinovich, Ohio	*Carl Levin, Mich.*
Norm Coleman, Minn.	*Daniel K. Akaka, Hawaii*
Arlen Specter, Pa.	*Richard J. Durbin, Ill.*
Robert F. Bennett, Utah	*Thomas R. Carper, Del.*
Peter G. Fitzgerald, Ill.	*Mark Dayton, Minn.*
John E. Sununu, N.H.	*Frank R. Lautenberg, N.J.*
Richard C. Shelby, Ala.	*Mark Pryor, Ark.*

FINANCIAL MANAGEMENT, BUDGET & INTERNATIONAL SECURITY

224-2254 442 SH
Fitzgerald, chairman

Republicans: Stevens, Voinovich, Specter, Bennett, Sununu, Shelby
Democrats: Akaka, Levin, Carper, Dayton, Lautenberg, Pryor

GOVERNMENT MANAGEMENT, FEDERAL WORKFORCE & THE DISTRICT OF COLUMBIA

224-3682 601 SH
Voinovich, chairman

Republicans: Stevens, Coleman, Bennett, Fitzgerald, Sununu
Democrats: Durbin, Akaka, Carper, Lautenberg, Pryor

PERMANENT INVESTIGATIONS

224-3721 199 SR
Coleman, chairman

Republicans: Stevens, Voinovich, Specter, Bennett, Fitzgerald, Sununu, Shelby
Democrats: Levin, Akaka, Durbin, Carper, Dayton, Lautenberg, Pryor

HEALTH, EDUCATION, LABOR & PENSIONS

224-5375 428 SD
Party Ratio: R 11-D 10
Judd Gregg, R-N.H., chairman

Bill Frist, Tenn.	*Edward M. Kennedy, Mass.*
Michael B. Enzi, Wyo.	*Christopher J. Dodd, Conn.*
Lamar Alexander, Tenn.	*Tom Harkin, Iowa*
Christopher S. Bond, Mo.	*Barbara A. Mikulski, Md.*
Mike DeWine, Ohio	*James M. Jeffords, I-Vt.*
Pat Roberts, Kan.	*Jeff Bingaman, N.M.*
Jeff Sessions, Ala.	*Patty Murray, Wash.*
John Ensign, Nev.	*Jack Reed, R.I.*
Lindsey Graham, S.C.	*John Edwards, N.C.*
John W. Warner, Va.	*Hillary Rodham Clinton, N.Y.*

AGING

224-9243 608 SH
Bond, chairman

Republicans: Alexander, DeWine, Roberts, Ensign, Warner
Democrats: Mikulski, Kennedy, Murray, Edwards, Clinton

CHILDREN & FAMILIES

224-5630 615 SH
Alexander, chairman

Republicans: Enzi, Bond, DeWine, Roberts, Sessions, Ensign, Graham (S.C.), Warner
Democrats: Dodd, Harkin, Jeffords (I), Bingaman, Murray, Reed, Edwards, Clinton

EMPLOYMENT, SAFETY & TRAINING

224-4925 404-A SH
Enzi, chairman

Republicans: Alexander, Bond, Roberts, Sessions
Democrats: Murray, Dodd, Harkin, Jeffords (I)

SUBSTANCE ABUSE & MENTAL HEALTH SERVICES

224-7675 424 SD
DeWine, chairman

Republicans: Enzi, Sessions, Ensign
Democrats: Kennedy, Bingaman, Reed

INDIAN AFFAIRS

224-2251 838 SH
Party Ratio: R 8-D 7
Ben Nighthorse Campbell, R-Colo., chairman

John McCain, Ariz.	*Daniel K. Inouye, Hawaii*
Pete V. Domenici, N.M.	*Kent Conrad, N.D.*
Craig Thomas, Wyo.	*Harry Reid, Nev.*
Orrin G. Hatch, Utah	*Daniel K. Akaka, Hawaii*
James M. Inhofe, Okla.	*Byron L. Dorgan, N.D.*
Gordon H. Smith, Ore.	*Tim Johnson, S.D.*
Lisa Murkowski, Alaska	*Maria Cantwell, Wash.*

JUDICIARY

224-5225 224 SD
Party Ratio: R 10-D 9
Orrin G. Hatch, R-Utah, chairman

Charles E. Grassley, Iowa	*Patrick J. Leahy, Vt.*
Arlen Specter, Pa.	*Edward M. Kennedy, Mass.*
Jon Kyl, Ariz.	*Joseph R. Biden Jr., Del.*
Mike DeWine, Ohio	*Herb Kohl, Wis.*
Jeff Sessions, Ala.	*Dianne Feinstein, Calif.*
Lindsey Graham, S.C.	*Russell D. Feingold, Wis.*
Larry E. Craig, Idaho	*Charles E. Schumer, N.Y.*
Saxby Chambliss, Ga.	*Richard J. Durbin, Ill.*
John Cornyn, Texas	*John Edwards, N.C.*

ADMINISTRATIVE OVERSIGHT & THE COURTS

224-7572 323 SD
Sessions, chairman

Republicans: Grassley, Specter, Craig, Cornyn
Democrats: Schumer, Leahy, Feingold, Durbin

ANTITRUST, COMPETITION POLICY & CONSUMER RIGHTS

224-9494 161 SD
DeWine, chairman

Republicans: Hatch, Specter, Graham (S.C.), Chambliss
Democrats: Kohl, Leahy, Feingold, Edwards

BORDER SECURITY, IMMIGRATION & CITIZENSHIP
224-7878 520 SD
Chambliss, chairman

Republicans: Grassley, Kyl, Sessions, Craig, Cornyn
Democrats: Kennedy, Leahy, Feinstein, Schumer, Durbin, Edwards

CONSTITUTION, CIVIL RIGHTS & PROPERTY RIGHTS
224-4135 524 SD
Cornyn, chairman

Republicans: Kyl, Graham (S.C.), Craig, Chambliss
Democrats: Feingold, Kennedy, Schumer, Durbin

CRIME, CORRECTIONS & VICTIMS' RIGHTS
224-5564 224 SD
Graham (S.C.), chairman

Republicans: Hatch, Grassley, Sessions, Craig, Cornyn
Democrats: Biden, Kohl, Feinstein, Durbin, Edwards

TERRORISM, TECHNOLOGY & HOMELAND SECURITY
224-4933 325 SH
Kyl, chairman

Republicans: Hatch, Specter, DeWine, Sessions, Chambliss
Democrats: Feinstein, Kennedy, Biden, Kohl, Edwards

RULES & ADMINISTRATION

224-6352 305 SR
Party Ratio: R 10-D 9
Trent Lott, R-Miss., chairman

Ted Stevens, Alaska	*Christopher J. Dodd, Conn.*
Mitch McConnell, Ky.	*Robert C. Byrd, W.Va.*
Thad Cochran, Miss.	*Daniel K. Inouye, Hawaii*
Rick Santorum, Pa.	*Dianne Feinstein, Calif.*
Don Nickles, Okla.	*Charles E. Schumer, N.Y.*
Kay Bailey Hutchison, Texas	*John B. Breaux, La.*
Bill Frist, Tenn.	*Tom Daschle, S.D.*
Gordon H. Smith, Ore.	*Mark Dayton, Minn.*
Saxby Chambliss, Ga.	*Richard J. Durbin, Ill.*

SELECT ETHICS

224-2981 220 SH
Party Ratio: R 3-D 3
George V. Voinovich, R-Ohio, chairman

Pat Roberts, Kan.	*Harry Reid, Nev., vice chairman*
Craig Thomas, Wyo.	*Daniel K. Akaka, Hawaii*
	Blanche Lincoln, Ark.

SELECT INTELLIGENCE

224-1700 211 SH
Party Ratio: R 9-D 8
Pat Roberts, R-Kan., chairman

Orrin G. Hatch, Utah	*John D. Rockefeller IV, W.Va., vice chairman*
Mike DeWine, Ohio	*Carl Levin, Mich.*
Christopher S. Bond, Mo.	*Dianne Feinstein, Calif.*
Trent Lott, Miss.	*Ron Wyden, Ore.*
Olympia J. Snowe, Maine	*Richard J. Durbin, Ill.*
Chuck Hagel, Neb.	*Evan Bayh, Ind.*
Saxby Chambliss, Ga.	*John Edwards, N.C.*
John W. Warner, Va.	*Barbara A. Mikulski, Md.*

SMALL BUSINESS & ENTREPRENEURSHIP

224-5175 428A SR
Party Ratio: R 10-D 9
Olympia J. Snowe, R-Maine, chairwoman

Christopher S. Bond, Mo.	*John Kerry, Mass.*
Conrad Burns, Mont.	*Carl Levin, Mich.*
Robert F. Bennett, Utah	*Tom Harkin, Iowa*
Michael B. Enzi, Wyo.	*Joseph I. Lieberman, Conn.*
Peter G. Fitzgerald, Ill.	*Mary L. Landrieu, La.*
Michael D. Crapo, Idaho	*John Edwards, N.C.*
George Allen, Va.	*Maria Cantwell, Wash.*
John Ensign, Nev.	*Evan Bayh, Ind.*
Norm Coleman, Minn.	*Mark Pryor, Ark.*

SPECIAL AGING

224-5364 G31 SD
Party Ratio: R 11-D 10
Larry E. Craig, R-Idaho, chairman

Richard C. Shelby, Ala.	*John B. Breaux, La.*
Michael B. Enzi, Wyo.	*Harry Reid, Nev.*
Susan Collins, Maine	*Herb Kohl, Wis.*
Gordon H. Smith, Ore.	*James M. Jeffords, I-Vt.*
Jim Talent, Mo.	*Russell D. Feingold, Wis.*
Peter G. Fitzgerald, Ill.	*Ron Wyden, Ore.*
Orrin G. Hatch, Utah	*Evan Bayh, Ind.*
Elizabeth Dole, N.C.	*Blanche Lincoln, Ark.*
Ted Stevens, Alaska	*Thomas R. Carper, Del.*
Rick Santorum, Pa.	*Debbie Stabenow, Mich.*

VETERANS' AFFAIRS

224-9126 412 SR
Party Ratio: R 8-D 7
Arlen Specter, R-Pa., chairman

Ben Nighthorse Campbell, Colo.	*Bob Graham, Fla.*
Larry E. Craig, Idaho	*John D. Rockefeller IV, W.Va.*
Kay Bailey Hutchison, Texas	*James M. Jeffords, I-Vt.*
Jim Bunning, Ky.	*Daniel K. Akaka, Hawaii*
Lindsey Graham, S.C.	*Patty Murray, Wash.*
John Ensign, Nev.	*Zell Miller, Ga.*
Lisa Murkowski, Alaska	*Ben Nelson, Neb.*

Partisan Senate Committees

REPUBLICAN LEADERS

President . . . . Vice President Dick Cheney
President Pro Tempore . . . . Ted Stevens
Majority Leader . . . . Bill Frist
Majority Whip . . . . Mitch McConnell
Conference Chairman . . . . Rick Santorum
Conference Vice Chairwoman . . . . Kay Bailey Hutchison
Chief Deputy Whip . . . . Robert F. Bennett
Deputy Whips: Lamar Alexander, Wayne Allard, Conrad Burns, Michael D. Crapo, Ben Nighthorse Campbell, Michael B. Enzi, Lisa Murkowski, Gordon H. Smith, John E. Sununu, Jim Talent

NATIONAL REPUBLICAN SENATORIAL COMMITTEE

675-6000 425 Second St. N.E. 20002

Chairman . . . . George Allen

COMMITTEE ON COMMITTEES

224-2752 SH-730

Chairman . . . . Larry E. Craig

POLICY COMMITTEE

224-2946 SR-347

Chairman . . . . Jon Kyl
Members: Bill Frist, Mitch McConnell, Rick Santorum, Kay Bailey Hutchison, George Allen, Ted Stevens, Thad Cochran, John W. Warner, Richard C. Shelby, Don Nickles, John McCain, Pete V. Domenici, James M. Inhofe, Charles E. Grassley, Richard G. Lugar, Susan Collins, Orrin G. Hatch, Judd Gregg, Trent Lott, Olympia J. Snowe, Arlen Specter

DEMOCRATIC LEADERS

Minority Leader . . . . Tom Daschle
Minority Whip . . . . Harry Reid
Conference Chairman . . . . Tom Daschle
Conference Secretary . . . . Barbara A. Mikulski
Chief Deputy Whip . . . . John B. Breaux
Assistant Floor Leader . . . . Richard J. Durbin
Chief Deputy for Strategic Outreach . . . . Barbara Boxer
Technology and Communications
Committee Chairman . . . . John D. Rockefeller IV
Deputy Whips: Jeff Bingaman, Barbara Boxer, Bill Nelson, Jack Reed

DEMOCRATIC SENATORIAL CAMPAIGN COMMITTEE

224-2447 430 S. Capitol St. S.E. 20003

Chairman . . . . Jon Corzine
Vice Chairwoman . . . . Debbie Stabenow

POLICY COMMITTEE

(202) 224-3232 SH-419

Chairman . . . . Byron L. Dorgan
Regional Chairmen: Patty Murray, Jack Reed, Mary L. Landrieu, Evan Bayh
Members: Tom Daschle, Dianne Feinstein, Joseph I. Lieberman, Daniel K. Akaka, Blanche Lincoln, Russell D. Feingold, Charles E. Schumer, Ron Wyden, Ernest F. Hollings, Tim Johnson, Zell Miller, Bill Nelson, Thomas R. Carper, Jon Corzine, Mark Dayton
Ex-Officio Members: Barbara A. Mikulski, Harry Reid

STEERING AND COORDINATION COMMITTEE

(202) 224-9048 SH-712

Chairwoman . . . . Hillary Rodham Clinton

Joint Committees

JOINT ECONOMIC

224-5171 G-01 SD
Robert F. Bennett, R-Utah, chairman

Senate Members
Republicans: Sam Brownback, Kan., Jeff Sessions, Ala., John E. Sununu, N.H., Lamar Alexander, Tenn., Susan Collins, Maine
Democrats: Jack Reed, R.I., Edward M. Kennedy, Mass., Paul S. Sarbanes, Md., Jeff Bingaman, N.M.
House Members
Republicans: H. James Saxton, N.J., vice chairman, Paul D. Ryan, Wis., Jennifer Dunn, Wash., Phil English, Pa., Adam H. Putnam, Fla., Ron Paul, Texas
Democrats: Pete Stark, Calif., Carolyn B. Maloney, N.Y., Melvin Watt, N.C., Baron P. Hill, Ind.

JOINT LIBRARY

224-3004 522 SH
Ted Stevens, R-Alaska, chairman

Senate Members
Republicans: Trent Lott, Miss., Thad Cochran, Miss.
Democrats: Christopher J. Dodd, Conn., Charles E. Schumer, N.Y.
House Members
Republicans: Vernon J. Ehlers, Mich., vice chairman, Bob Ney, Ohio, Jack Kingston, Ga.
Democrats: John B. Larson, Conn., Juanita Millender-McDonald, Calif.

JOINT TAXATION

225-3621 1015 LHOB
Bill Thomas, R-Calif., chairman

Senate Members
Republicans: Charles E. Grassley, Iowa, vice chairman, Orrin G. Hatch, Utah, Don Nickles, Okla.
Democrats: Max Baucus, Mont., John D. Rockefeller IV, W.Va.
House Members
Republicans: Philip M. Crane, Ill., E. Clay Shaw Jr., Fla.
Democrats: Charles B. Rangel, N.Y., Pete Stark, Calif.

JOINT PRINTING

225-8281 1309 LHOB
Bob Ney, R-Ohio, chairman

Senate Members
Republicans: Saxby Chambliss, Ga., vice chairman, Thad Cochran, Miss., Gordon H. Smith, Ore.
Democrats: Mark Dayton, Minn., Daniel K. Inouye, Hawaii
House Members
Republicans: John T. Doolittle, Calif., John Linder, Ga.
Democrats: John B. Larson, Conn., Robert A. Brady, Pa.

Senate Seniority

Senate rank is first determined by the length of consecutive service in the Senate.

For senators who entered the Senate on the same day, several tie-breaking procedures determine seniority.

In order of precedence, these factors are: previous Senate service, service as the vice president, previous House service; service in the Cabinet, service as a state governor. If a tie still exists, senators are ranked according to the population of their state at the time of swearing in.

Republican Sens. Richard C. Shelby and Ben Nighthorse Campbell began their service as Democrats. The Republican Conference credited their service as Democrats toward their seniority.

REPUBLICANS

1. Ted Stevens, Alaska	Dec. 24, 1968
2. Pete V. Domenici, N.M.	Jan. 3, 1973
3. Richard G. Lugar, Ind.	Jan. 4, 1977
4. Orrin G. Hatch, Utah	Jan. 4, 1977
5. Thad Cochran, Miss.	Dec. 27, 1978
6. John W. Warner, Va.	Jan. 2, 1979
7. Charles E. Grassley, Iowa	Jan. 5, 1981
8. Arlen Specter, Pa.	Jan. 5, 1981
9. Don Nickles, Okla.	Jan. 5, 1981
10. Mitch McConnell, Ky.	Jan. 3, 1985
11. Richard C. Shelby, Ala.	Jan. 6, 1987
12. John McCain, Ariz.	Jan. 6, 1987
13. Christopher S. Bond, Mo.	Jan. 6, 1987
14. Trent Lott, Miss.	Jan. 3, 1989
15. Conrad Burns, Mont.	Jan. 3, 1989
16. Larry E. Craig, Idaho	Jan. 3, 1991
17. Judd Gregg, N.H.	Jan. 5, 1993
18. Ben Nighthorse Campbell, Colo.	Jan. 5, 1993
19. Robert F. Bennett, Utah	Jan. 5, 1993
20. Kay Bailey Hutchison, Texas	June 14, 1993
21. James M. Inhofe, Okla.	Nov. 30, 1994
22. Olympia J. Snowe, Maine	Jan. 4, 1995
23. Mike DeWine, Ohio	Jan. 4, 1995
24. Jon Kyl, Ariz.	Jan. 4, 1995
25. Craig Thomas, Wyo.	Jan. 4, 1995
26. Rick Santorum, Pa.	Jan. 4, 1995
27. Bill Frist, Tenn.	Jan. 4, 1995
28. Sam Brownback, Kan.	Nov. 27, 1996
29. Pat Roberts, Kan.	Jan. 7, 1997
30. Wayne Allard, Colo.	Jan. 7, 1997
31. Jeff Sessions, Ala.	Jan. 7, 1997
32. Gordon H. Smith, Ore.	Jan. 7, 1997
33. Chuck Hagel, Neb.	Jan. 7, 1997
34. Susan Collins, Maine	Jan. 7, 1997
35. Michael B. Enzi, Wyo.	Jan. 7, 1997
36. Jim Bunning, Ky.	Jan. 6, 1999
37. Michael D. Crapo, Idaho	Jan. 6, 1999
38. George V. Voinovich, Ohio	Jan. 6, 1999
39. Peter G. Fitzgerald, Ill.	Jan. 6, 1999
40. Lincoln Chafee, R.I.	Nov. 4, 1999
41. John Ensign, Nev.	Jan. 3, 2001
42. George Allen, Va.	Jan. 3, 2001
43. Jim Talent, Mo.	Nov. 25, 2002
44. Lisa Murkowski, Alaska	Dec. 20, 2002
45. Saxby Chambliss, Ga.	Jan. 7, 2003
46. Lindsey Graham, S.C.	Jan. 7, 2003
47. John E. Sununu, N.H.	Jan. 7, 2003
48. Elizabeth Dole, N.C.	Jan. 7, 2003
49. Lamar Alexander, Tenn.	Jan. 7, 2003
50. John Cornyn, Texas	Jan. 7, 2003
51. Norm Coleman, Minn.	Jan. 7, 2003

DEMOCRATS

1. Robert C. Byrd, W.Va.	Jan. 7, 1959
2. Edward M. Kennedy, Mass.	Nov. 7, 1962
3. Daniel K. Inouye, Hawaii	Jan. 9, 1963
4. Ernest F. Hollings, S.C.	Nov. 9, 1966
5. Joseph R. Biden Jr., Del.	Jan. 3, 1973
6. Patrick J. Leahy, Vt.	Jan. 14, 1975
7. Paul S. Sarbanes, Md.	Jan. 4, 1977
8. Max Baucus, Mont.	Dec. 15, 1978
9. Carl Levin, Mich.	Jan. 15, 1979
10. Christopher J. Dodd, Conn.	Jan. 5, 1981
11. Jeff Bingaman, N.M.	Jan. 3, 1983
12. John Kerry, Mass.	Jan. 2, 1985
13. Tom Harkin, Iowa	Jan. 3, 1985
14. John D. Rockefeller IV, W.Va.	Jan. 15, 1985
15. John B. Breaux, La.	Jan. 6, 1987
16. Barbara A. Mikulski, Md.	Jan. 6, 1987
17. Tom Daschle, S.D.	Jan. 6, 1987
18. Harry Reid, Nev.	Jan. 6, 1987
19. Bob Graham, Fla.	Jan. 6, 1987
20. Kent Conrad, N.D.	Jan. 6, 1987
21. Herb Kohl, Wis.	Jan. 3, 1989
22. Joseph I. Lieberman, Conn.	Jan. 3, 1989
23. Daniel K. Akaka, Hawaii	April 28, 1990
24. Dianne Feinstein, Calif.	Nov. 4, 1992
25. Byron L. Dorgan, N.D.	Dec. 15, 1992
26. Barbara Boxer, Calif.	Jan. 5, 1993
27. Russell D. Feingold, Wis.	Jan. 5, 1993
28. Patty Murray, Wash.	Jan. 5, 1993
29. Ron Wyden, Ore.	Feb. 6, 1996
30. Richard J. Durbin, Ill.	Jan. 7, 1997
31. Tim Johnson, S.D.	Jan. 7, 1997
32. Jack Reed, R.I.	Jan. 7, 1997
33. Mary L. Landrieu, La.	Jan. 7, 1997
34. Charles E. Schumer, N.Y.	Jan. 6, 1999
35. Blanche Lincoln, Ark.	Jan. 6, 1999
36. Evan Bayh, Ind.	Jan. 6, 1999
37. John Edwards, N.C.	Jan. 6, 1999
38. Zell Miller, Ga.	July 27, 2000
39. Bill Nelson, Fla.	Jan. 3, 2001
40. Thomas R. Carper, Del.	Jan. 3, 2001
41. Debbie Stabenow, Mich.	Jan. 3, 2001
42. Maria Cantwell, Wash.	Jan. 3, 2001
43. Ben Nelson, Neb.	Jan. 3, 2001
44. Hillary Rodham Clinton, N.Y.	Jan. 3, 2001
45. Jon Corzine, N.J.	Jan. 3, 2001
46. Mark Dayton, Minn.	Jan. 3, 2001
47. Frank R. Lautenberg, N.J. *Also served 1983-2001*	Jan. 7, 2003
48. Mark Pryor, Ark.	Jan. 7, 2003

INDEPENDENT

1. James M. Jeffords, Vt.	Jan. 3, 1989

House Seniority

REPUBLICANS

House Republicans determine seniority by length of service. Members who previously served in the House are given credit for most of that service.

For members who joined at the beginning of a Congress, service is credited from the first day of the session. Seniority for members who won special elections is credited from the date of the election.

Reps. Virgil H. Goode Jr., Billy Tauzin and Nathan Deal began their service as Democrats. The Republican Conference has credited their service as Democrats toward their seniority. No credit is given for other previous service, such as a senator or governor.

1.	Philip M. Crane, Ill.	Nov. 25, 1969
2.	C.W. Bill Young, Fla.	Jan. 21, 1971
3.	Ralph Regula, Ohio	Jan. 3, 1973
4.	Don Young, Alaska	March 6, 1973
5.	Henry J. Hyde, Ill.	Jan. 14, 1975
6.	Jim Leach, Iowa	Jan. 4, 1977
7.	Doug Bereuter, Neb.	Jan. 15, 1979
8.	Jerry Lewis, Calif.	Jan. 15, 1979
9.	F. James Sensenbrenner Jr., Wis.	Jan. 15, 1979
10.	Bill Thomas, Calif.	Jan. 15, 1979
11.	Tom Petri, Wis.	April 3, 1979
12.	Billy Tauzin, La.	May 17, 1980
13.	David Dreier, Calif.	Jan. 5, 1981
14.	Duncan Hunter, Calif.	Jan. 5, 1981
15.	Harold Rogers, Ky.	Jan. 5, 1981
16.	E. Clay Shaw Jr., Fla.	Jan. 5, 1981
17.	Christopher H. Smith, N.J.	Jan. 5, 1981
18.	Frank R. Wolf, Va.	Jan. 5, 1981
19.	Michael G. Oxley, Ohio	June 25, 1981
20.	Michael Bilirakis, Fla.	Jan. 3, 1983
21.	Sherwood Boehlert, N.Y.	Jan. 3, 1983
22.	Dan Burton, Ind.	Jan. 3, 1983
23.	Nancy L. Johnson, Conn.	Jan. 3, 1983
24.	H. James Saxton, N.J.	Nov. 6, 1984
25.	Joe L. Barton, Texas	Jan. 3, 1985
26.	Howard Coble, N.C.	Jan. 3, 1985
27.	Tom DeLay, Texas	Jan. 3, 1985
28.	Jim Kolbe, Ariz.	Jan. 3, 1985
29.	Cass Ballenger, N.C.	Nov. 4, 1986
30.	Richard H. Baker, La.	Jan. 6, 1987
31.	Elton Gallegly, Calif.	Jan. 6, 1987
32.	J. Dennis Hastert, Ill.	Jan. 6, 1987
33.	Joel Hefley, Colo.	Jan. 6, 1987
34.	Wally Herger, Calif.	Jan. 6, 1987
35.	Amo Houghton, N.Y.	Jan. 6, 1987
36.	Lamar Smith, Texas	Jan. 6, 1987
37.	Fred Upton, Mich.	Jan. 6, 1987
38.	Curt Weldon, Pa.	Jan. 6, 1987
39.	Christopher Shays, Conn.	Aug. 18, 1987
40.	Jim McCrery, La.	April 16, 1988
41.	John J. "Jimmy" Duncan Jr., Tenn.	Nov. 8, 1988
42.	Christopher Cox, Calif.	Jan. 3, 1989
43.	Paul E. Gillmor, Ohio	Jan. 3, 1989
44.	Porter J. Goss, Fla.	Jan. 3, 1989
45.	Dana Rohrabacher, Calif.	Jan. 3, 1989
46.	Cliff Stearns, Fla.	Jan. 3, 1989
47.	James T. Walsh, N.Y.	Jan. 3, 1989
48.	Ileana Ros-Lehtinen, Fla.	Aug. 29, 1989
49.	Ron Paul, Texas *Also served 1976-77, 1979-85*	Jan. 6, 1997
50.	John A. Boehner, Ohio	Jan. 3, 1991
51.	Dave Camp, Mich.	Jan. 3, 1991
52.	Randy "Duke" Cunningham, Calif.	Jan. 3, 1991
53.	John T. Doolittle, Calif.	Jan. 3, 1991
54.	Wayne T. Gilchrest, Md.	Jan. 3, 1991
55.	David L. Hobson, Ohio	Jan. 3, 1991
56.	Jim Nussle, Iowa	Jan. 3, 1991
57.	Jim Ramstad, Minn.	Jan. 3, 1991
58.	Charles H. Taylor, N.C.	Jan. 3, 1991
59.	Sam Johnson, Texas	May 18, 1991
60.	Spencer Bachus, Ala.	Jan. 5, 1993
61.	Roscoe G. Bartlett, Md.	Jan. 5, 1993
62.	Henry Bonilla, Texas	Jan. 5, 1993
63.	Steve Buyer, Ind.	Jan. 5, 1993
64.	Ken Calvert, Calif.	Jan. 5, 1993
65.	Michael N. Castle, Del.	Jan. 5, 1993
66.	Mac Collins, Ga.	Jan. 5, 1993
67.	Nathan Deal, Ga.	Jan. 5, 1993
68.	Lincoln Diaz-Balart, Fla.	Jan. 5, 1993
69.	Jennifer Dunn, Wash.	Jan. 5, 1993
70.	Terry Everett, Ala.	Jan. 5, 1993
71.	Robert W. Goodlatte, Va.	Jan. 5, 1993
72.	James C. Greenwood, Pa.	Jan. 5, 1993
73.	Peter Hoekstra, Mich.	Jan. 5, 1993
74.	Ernest Istook, Okla.	Jan. 5, 1993
75.	Peter T. King, N.Y.	Jan. 5, 1993
76.	Jack Kingston, Ga.	Jan. 5, 1993
77.	Joe Knollenberg, Mich.	Jan. 5, 1993
78.	John Linder, Ga.	Jan. 5, 1993
79.	Donald Manzullo, Ill.	Jan. 5, 1993
80.	John M. McHugh, N.Y.	Jan. 5, 1993
81.	Scott McInnis, Colo.	Jan. 5, 1993
82.	Howard P. "Buck" McKeon, Calif.	Jan. 5, 1993
83.	John L. Mica, Fla.	Jan. 5, 1993
84.	Richard W. Pombo, Calif.	Jan. 5, 1993
85.	Deborah Pryce, Ohio	Jan. 5, 1993
86.	Jack Quinn, N.Y.	Jan. 5, 1993
87.	Ed Royce, Calif.	Jan. 5, 1993
88.	Nick Smith, Mich.	Jan. 5, 1993
89.	Rob Portman, Ohio	May 4, 1993
90.	Vernon J. Ehlers, Mich.	Dec. 7, 1993
91.	Frank D. Lucas, Okla.	May 10, 1994
92.	Ron Lewis, Ky.	May 24, 1994
93.	Charles Bass, N.H.	Jan. 4, 1995
94.	Richard M. Burr, N.C.	Jan. 4, 1995
95.	Steve Chabot, Ohio	Jan. 4, 1995
96.	Barbara Cubin, Wyo.	Jan. 4, 1995
97.	Thomas M. Davis III, Va.	Jan. 4, 1995
98.	Phil English, Pa.	Jan. 4, 1995
99.	Mark Foley, Fla.	Jan. 4, 1995
100.	Rodney Frelinghuysen, N.J.	Jan. 4, 1995
101.	Gil Gutknecht, Minn.	Jan. 4, 1995
102.	Doc Hastings, Wash.	Jan. 4, 1995
103.	J.D. Hayworth, Ariz.	Jan. 4, 1995
104.	John Hostettler, Ind.	Jan. 4, 1995
105.	Walter B. Jones, N.C.	Jan. 4, 1995

106. Sue W. Kelly, N.Y.	Jan. 4, 1995
107. Ray LaHood, Ill.	Jan. 4, 1995
108. Tom Latham, Iowa	Jan. 4, 1995
109. Steven C. LaTourette, Ohio	Jan. 4, 1995
110. Frank A. LoBiondo, N.J.	Jan. 4, 1995
111. Sue Myrick, N.C.	Jan. 4, 1995
112. George Nethercutt, Wash.	Jan. 4, 1995
113. Bob Ney, Ohio	Jan. 4, 1995
114. Charlie Norwood, Ga.	Jan. 4, 1995
115. George P. Radanovich, Calif.	Jan. 4, 1995
116. John Shadegg, Ariz.	Jan. 4, 1995
117. Mark Souder, Ind.	Jan. 4, 1995
118. William M. "Mac" Thornberry, Texas	Jan. 4, 1995
119. Todd Tiahrt, Kan.	Jan. 4, 1995
120. Zach Wamp, Tenn.	Jan. 4, 1995
121. Dave Weldon, Fla.	Jan. 4, 1995
122. Jerry Weller, Ill.	Jan. 4, 1995
123. Edward Whitfield, Ky.	Jan. 4, 1995
124. Roger Wicker, Miss.	Jan. 4, 1995
125. Jo Ann Emerson, Mo.	Nov. 5, 1996
126. Jim Ryun, Kan.	Nov. 27, 1996
127. Robert B. Aderholt, Ala.	Jan. 6, 1997
128. Roy Blunt, Mo.	Jan. 6, 1997
129. Kevin Brady, Texas	Jan. 6, 1997
130. Chris Cannon, Utah	Jan. 6, 1997
131. Jim Gibbons, Nev.	Jan. 6, 1997
132. Virgil H. Goode Jr., Va.	Jan. 6, 1997
133. Kay Granger, Texas	Jan. 6, 1997
134. Kenny Hulshof, Mo.	Jan. 6, 1997
135. Bill Jenkins, Tenn.	Jan. 6, 1997
136. Jerry Moran, Kan.	Jan. 6, 1997
137. Anne M. Northup, Ky.	Jan. 6, 1997
138. John E. Peterson, Pa.	Jan. 6, 1997
139. Charles W. "Chip" Pickering Jr., Miss.	Jan. 6, 1997
140. Joe Pitts, Pa.	Jan. 6, 1997
141. Pete Sessions, Texas	Jan. 6, 1997
142. John Shimkus, Ill.	Jan. 6, 1997
143. Vito J. Fossella, N.Y.	Nov. 4, 1997
144. Mary Bono, Calif.	April 7, 1998
145. Heather A. Wilson, N.M.	June 23, 1998
146. Judy Biggert, Ill.	Jan. 6, 1999
147. Jim DeMint, S.C.	Jan. 6, 1999
148. Ernie Fletcher, Ky.	Jan. 6, 1999
149. Mark Green, Wis.	Jan. 6, 1999
150. Robin Hayes, N.C.	Jan. 6, 1999
151. Gary G. Miller, Calif.	Jan. 6, 1999
152. Doug Ose, Calif.	Jan. 6, 1999
153. Thomas M. Reynolds, N.Y.	Jan. 6, 1999
154. Paul D. Ryan, Wis.	Jan. 6, 1999
155. Don Sherwood, Pa.	Jan. 6, 1999
156. Mike Simpson, Idaho	Jan. 6, 1999
157. John E. Sweeney, N.Y.	Jan. 6, 1999
158. Tom Tancredo, Colo.	Jan. 6, 1999
159. Lee Terry, Neb.	Jan. 6, 1999
160. Patrick J. Toomey, Pa.	Jan. 6, 1999
161. Greg Walden, Ore.	Jan. 6, 1999
162. Johnny Isakson, Ga.	Feb. 23, 1999
163. David Vitter, La.	May 29, 1999
164. Todd Akin, Mo.	Jan. 3, 2001
165. Henry E. Brown Jr., S.C.	Jan. 3, 2001
166. Eric Cantor, Va.	Jan. 3, 2001
167. Shelley Moore Capito, W.Va.	Jan. 3, 2001
168. Ander Crenshaw, Fla.	Jan. 3, 2001
169. John Culberson, Texas	Jan. 3, 2001
170. Jo Ann Davis, Va.	Jan. 3, 2001
171. Mike Ferguson, N.J.	Jan. 3, 2001
172. Jeff Flake, Ariz.	Jan. 3, 2001
173. Sam Graves, Mo.	Jan. 3, 2001
174. Melissa A. Hart, Pa.	Jan. 3, 2001
175. Darrell Issa, Calif.	Jan. 3, 2001
176. Timothy V. Johnson, Ill.	Jan. 3, 2001
177. Ric Keller, Fla.	Jan. 3, 2001
178. Mark Kennedy, Minn.	Jan. 3, 2001
179. Mark Steven Kirk, Ill.	Jan. 3, 2001
180. Tom Osborne, Neb.	Jan. 3, 2001
181. C. L. "Butch" Otter, Idaho	Jan. 3, 2001
182. Mike Pence, Ind.	Jan. 3, 2001
183. Todd R. Platts, Pa.	Jan. 3, 2001
184. Adam H. Putnam, Fla.	Jan. 3, 2001
185. Denny Rehberg, Mont.	Jan. 3, 2001
186. Mike Rogers, Mich.	Jan. 3, 2001
187. Ed Schrock, Va.	Jan. 3, 2001
188. Rob Simmons, Conn.	Jan. 3, 2001
189. Pat Tiberi, Ohio	Jan. 3, 2001
190. Bill Shuster, Pa.	May 15, 2001
191. J. Randy Forbes, Va.	June 19, 2001
192. Jeff Miller, Fla.	Oct. 16, 2001
193. John Boozman, Ark.	Nov. 20, 2001
194. Joe Wilson, S.C.	Dec. 18, 2001
195. John Sullivan, Okla.	Feb. 15, 2002
196. J. Gresham Barrett, S.C.	Jan. 7, 2003
197. Bob Beauprez, Colo.	Jan. 7, 2003
198. Rob Bishop, Utah	Jan. 7, 2003
199. Marsha Blackburn, Tenn.	Jan. 7, 2003
200. Jo Bonner, Ala.	Jan. 7, 2003
201. Jeb Bradley, N.H.	Jan. 7, 2003
202. Ginny Brown-Waite, Fla.	Jan. 7, 2003
203. Michael C. Burgess, Texas	Jan. 7, 2003
204. Max Burns, Ga.	Jan. 7, 2003
205. John Carter, Texas	Jan. 7, 2003
206. Chris Chocola, Ind.	Jan. 7, 2003
207. Tom Cole, Okla.	Jan. 7, 2003
208. Mario Diaz-Balart, Fla.	Jan. 7, 2003
209. Tom Feeney, Fla.	Jan. 7, 2003
210. Trent Franks, Ariz.	Jan. 7, 2003
211. Scott Garrett, N.J.	Jan. 7, 2003
212. Jim Gerlach, Pa.	Jan. 7, 2003
213. Phil Gingrey, Ga.	Jan. 7, 2003
214. Katherine Harris, Fla.	Jan. 7, 2003
215. Jeb Hensarling, Texas	Jan. 7, 2003
216. Bill Janklow, S.D.	Jan. 7, 2003
217. Steve King, Iowa	Jan. 7, 2003
218. John Kline, Minn.	Jan. 7, 2003
219. Thaddeus McCotter, Mich.	Jan. 7, 2003
220. Candice S. Miller, Mich.	Jan. 7, 2003
221. Tim Murphy, Pa.	Jan. 7, 2003
222. Marilyn Musgrave, Colo.	Jan. 7, 2003
223. Devin Nunes, Calif.	Jan. 7, 2003
224. Steve Pearce, N.M.	Jan. 7, 2003
225. Jon Porter, Nev.	Jan. 7, 2003
226. Rick Renzi, Ariz.	Jan. 7, 2003
227. Mike D. Rogers, Ala.	Jan. 7, 2003
228. Michael R. Turner, Ohio	Jan. 7, 2003

DEMOCRATS

House Democrats determine seniority by length of service. Members who previously served in the House are given some credit for that service — when they return, they are ranked above other members of that entering class.

For members who joined at the beginning of a Congress, service is credited from the first day of the session. Seniority for members who won special elections is credited from the date of the election. No credit is given for other previous service, such as a senator or governor.

1.	John D. Dingell, Mich.	Dec. 13, 1955
2.	John Conyers Jr., Mich.	Jan. 4, 1965
3.	David R. Obey, Wis.	April 1, 1969
4.	Charles B. Rangel, N.Y.	Jan. 21, 1971
5.	Pete Stark, Calif.	Jan. 3, 1973
6.	John P. Murtha, Pa.	Feb. 5, 1974
7.	George Miller, Calif.	Jan. 14, 1975
8.	James L. Oberstar, Minn.	Jan. 14, 1975
9.	Henry A. Waxman, Calif.	Jan. 14, 1975
10.	Edward J. Markey, Mass.	Nov. 2, 1976
11.	Norm Dicks, Wash.	Jan. 4, 1977
12.	Richard A. Gephardt, Mo.	Jan. 4, 1977
13.	Dale E. Kildee, Mich.	Jan. 4, 1977
14.	Nick J. Rahall II, W.Va.	Jan. 4, 1977
15.	Ike Skelton, Mo.	Jan. 4, 1977
16.	Martin Frost, Texas	Jan. 15, 1979
17.	Robert T. Matsui, Calif.	Jan. 15, 1979
18.	Martin Olav Sabo, Minn.	Jan. 15, 1979
19.	Charles W. Stenholm, Texas	Jan. 15, 1979
20.	Barney Frank, Mass.	Jan. 5, 1981
21.	Ralph M. Hall, Texas	Jan. 5, 1981
22.	Tom Lantos, Calif.	Jan. 5, 1981
23.	Steny H. Hoyer, Md.	May 19, 1981
24.	Howard L. Berman, Calif.	Jan. 3, 1983
25.	Rick Boucher, Va.	Jan. 3, 1983
26.	Lane Evans, Ill.	Jan. 3, 1983
27.	Marcy Kaptur, Ohio	Jan. 3, 1983
28.	Sander M. Levin, Mich.	Jan. 3, 1983
29.	William O. Lipinski, Ill.	Jan. 3, 1983
30.	Alan B. Mollohan, W.Va.	Jan. 3, 1983
31.	Solomon P. Ortiz, Texas	Jan. 3, 1983
32.	Major R. Owens, N.Y.	Jan. 3, 1983
33.	John M. Spratt Jr., S.C.	Jan. 3, 1983
34.	Edolphus Towns, N.Y.	Jan. 3, 1983
35.	Gary L. Ackerman, N.Y.	March 1, 1983
36.	Gerald D. Kleczka, Wis.	April 3, 1984
37.	Bart Gordon, Tenn.	Jan. 3, 1985
38.	Paul E. Kanjorski, Pa.	Jan. 3, 1985
39.	Peter J. Visclosky, Ind.	Jan. 3, 1985
40.	Benjamin L. Cardin, Md.	Jan. 6, 1987
41.	Peter A. DeFazio, Ore.	Jan. 6, 1987
42.	John Lewis, Ga.	Jan. 6, 1987
43.	Louise M. Slaughter, N.Y.	Jan. 6, 1987
44.	Nancy Pelosi, Calif.	June 2, 1987
45.	Jerry F. Costello, Ill.	Aug. 9, 1988
46.	Frank Pallone Jr., N.J.	Nov. 8, 1988
47.	Eliot L. Engel, N.Y.	Jan. 3, 1989
48.	Nita M. Lowey, N.Y.	Jan. 3, 1989
49.	Jim McDermott, Wash.	Jan. 3, 1989
50.	Michael R. McNulty, N.Y.	Jan. 3, 1989
51.	Richard E. Neal, Mass.	Jan. 3, 1989
52.	Donald M. Payne, N.J.	Jan. 3, 1989
53.	John Tanner, Tenn.	Jan. 3, 1989
54.	Gene Taylor, Miss.	Oct. 17, 1989
55.	Jose E. Serrano, N.Y.	March 20, 1990
56.	Robert E. Andrews, N.J.	Nov. 6, 1990
57.	Neil Abercrombie, Hawaii *Also served Sept. 1986-Jan. 1987*	Jan. 3, 1991
58.	Robert E. "Bud" Cramer, Ala.	Jan. 3, 1991
59.	Rosa DeLauro, Conn.	Jan. 3, 1991
60.	Cal Dooley, Calif.	Jan. 3, 1991
61.	Chet Edwards, Texas	Jan. 3, 1991
62.	William J. Jefferson, La.	Jan. 3, 1991
63.	James P. Moran, Va.	Jan. 3, 1991
64.	Collin C. Peterson, Minn.	Jan. 3, 1991
65.	Maxine Waters, Calif.	Jan. 3, 1991
66.	John W. Olver, Mass.	June 4, 1991
67.	Ed Pastor, Ariz.	Sept. 24, 1991
68.	Jerrold Nadler, N.Y.	Nov. 3, 1992
69.	Xavier Becerra, Calif.	Jan. 5, 1993
70.	Sanford D. Bishop Jr., Ga.	Jan. 5, 1993
71.	Corrine Brown, Fla.	Jan. 5, 1993
72.	Sherrod Brown, Ohio	Jan. 5, 1993
73.	James E. Clyburn, S.C.	Jan. 5, 1993
74.	Peter Deutsch, Fla.	Jan. 5, 1993
75.	Anna G. Eshoo, Calif.	Jan. 5, 1993
76.	Bob Filner, Calif.	Jan. 5, 1993
77.	Gene Green, Texas	Jan. 5, 1993
78.	Luis V. Gutierrez, Ill.	Jan. 5, 1993
79.	Alcee L. Hastings, Fla.	Jan. 5, 1993
80.	Maurice D. Hinchey, N.Y.	Jan. 5, 1993
81.	Tim Holden, Pa.	Jan. 5, 1993
82.	Eddie Bernice Johnson, Texas	Jan. 5, 1993
83.	Carolyn B. Maloney, N.Y.	Jan. 5, 1993
84.	Martin T. Meehan, Mass.	Jan. 5, 1993
85.	Robert Menendez, N.J.	Jan. 5, 1993
86.	Earl Pomeroy, N.D.	Jan. 5, 1993
87.	Lucille Roybal-Allard, Calif.	Jan. 5, 1993
88.	Bobby L. Rush, Ill.	Jan. 5, 1993
89.	Robert C. Scott, Va.	Jan. 5, 1993
90.	Bart Stupak, Mich.	Jan. 5, 1993
91.	Nydia M. Velazquez, N.Y.	Jan. 5, 1993
92.	Melvin Watt, N.C.	Jan. 5, 1993
93.	Lynn Woolsey, Calif.	Jan. 5, 1993
94.	Albert R. Wynn, Md.	Jan. 5, 1993
95.	Bennie Thompson, Miss.	April 13, 1993
96.	Sam Farr, Calif.	June 8, 1993
97.	Lloyd Doggett, Texas	Jan. 4, 1995
98.	Mike Doyle, Pa.	Jan. 4, 1995
99.	Chaka Fattah, Pa.	Jan. 4, 1995
100.	Sheila Jackson-Lee, Texas	Jan. 4, 1995
101.	Patrick J. Kennedy, R.I.	Jan. 4, 1995
102.	Zoe Lofgren, Calif.	Jan. 4, 1995
103.	Karen McCarthy, Mo.	Jan. 4, 1995
104.	Jesse L. Jackson Jr., Ill.	Dec. 12, 1995
105.	Juanita Millender-McDonald, Calif.	March 26, 1996
106.	Elijah E. Cummings, Md.	April 16, 1996
107.	Earl Blumenauer, Ore.	May 21, 1996

108. David E. Price, N.C.	Jan. 6, 1997
Also served 1987-95	
109. Ted Strickland, Ohio	Jan. 6, 1997
Also served 1993-95	
110. Tom Allen, Maine	Jan. 6, 1997
111. Marion Berry, Ark.	Jan. 6, 1997
112. Leonard L. Boswell, Iowa	Jan. 6, 1997
113. Allen Boyd, Fla.	Jan. 6, 1997
114. Julia Carson, Ind.	Jan. 6, 1997
115. Danny K. Davis, Ill.	Jan. 6, 1997
116. Jim Davis, Fla.	Jan. 6, 1997
117. Diana DeGette, Colo.	Jan. 6, 1997
118. Bill Delahunt, Mass.	Jan. 6, 1997
119. Bob Etheridge, N.C.	Jan. 6, 1997
120. Harold E. Ford Jr., Tenn.	Jan. 6, 1997
121. Ruben Hinojosa, Texas	Jan. 6, 1997
122. Darlene Hooley, Ore.	Jan. 6, 1997
123. Chris John, La.	Jan. 6, 1997
124. Carolyn Cheeks Kilpatrick, Mich.	Jan. 6, 1997
125. Ron Kind, Wis.	Jan. 6, 1997
126. Dennis J. Kucinich, Ohio	Jan. 6, 1997
127. Nick Lampson, Texas	Jan. 6, 1997
128. Carolyn McCarthy, N.Y.	Jan. 6, 1997
129. Jim McGovern, Mass.	Jan. 6, 1997
130. Mike McIntyre, N.C.	Jan. 6, 1997
131. Bill Pascrell Jr., N.J.	Jan. 6, 1997
132. Silvestre Reyes, Texas	Jan. 6, 1997
133. Steven R. Rothman, N.J.	Jan. 6, 1997
134. Loretta Sanchez, Calif.	Jan. 6, 1997
135. Max Sandlin, Texas	Jan. 6, 1997
136. Brad Sherman, Calif.	Jan. 6, 1997
137. Adam Smith, Wash.	Jan. 6, 1997
138. Vic Snyder, Ark.	Jan. 6, 1997
139. Ellen O. Tauscher, Calif.	Jan. 6, 1997
140. John F. Tierney, Mass.	Jan. 6, 1997
141. Jim Turner, Texas	Jan. 6, 1997
142. Robert Wexler, Fla.	Jan. 6, 1997
143. Ciro D. Rodriguez, Texas	April 12, 1997
144. Gregory W. Meeks, N.Y.	Feb. 3, 1998
145. Lois Capps, Calif.	March 10, 1998
146. Barbara Lee, Calif.	April 7, 1998
147. Robert A. Brady, Pa.	May 19, 1998
148. Jay Inslee, Wash.	Jan. 6, 1999
Also served 1993-95	
149. Brian Baird, Wash.	Jan. 6, 1999
150. Tammy Baldwin, Wis.	Jan. 6, 1999
151. Shelley Berkley, Nev.	Jan. 6, 1999
152. Michael E. Capuano, Mass.	Jan. 6, 1999
153. Joseph Crowley, N.Y.	Jan. 6, 1999
154. Charlie Gonzalez, Texas	Jan. 6, 1999
155. Baron P. Hill, Ind.	Jan. 6, 1999
156. Joseph M. Hoeffel, Pa.	Jan. 6, 1999
157. Rush D. Holt, N.J.	Jan. 6, 1999
158. Stephanie Tubbs Jones, Ohio	Jan. 6, 1999
159. John B. Larson, Conn.	Jan. 6, 1999
160. Ken Lucas, Ky.	Jan. 6, 1999
161. Dennis Moore, Kan.	Jan. 6, 1999
162. Grace F. Napolitano, Calif.	Jan. 6, 1999
163. Jan Schakowsky, Ill.	Jan. 6, 1999
164. Mike Thompson, Calif.	Jan. 6, 1999
165. Mark Udall, Colo.	Jan. 6, 1999
166. Tom Udall, N.M.	Jan. 6, 1999
167. Anthony Weiner, N.Y.	Jan. 6, 1999
168. David Wu, Ore.	Jan. 6, 1999
169. Joe Baca, Calif.	Nov. 16, 1999
170. Jane Harman, Calif.	Jan. 3, 2001
Also served 1993-99	
171. Brad Carson, Okla.	Jan. 3, 2001
172. William Lacy Clay, Mo.	Jan. 3, 2001
173. Susan A. Davis, Calif.	Jan. 3, 2001
174. Michael M. Honda, Calif.	Jan. 3, 2001
175. Steve Israel, N.Y.	Jan. 3, 2001
176. Jim Langevin, R.I.	Jan. 3, 2001
177. Rick Larsen, Wash.	Jan. 3, 2001
178. Jim Matheson, Utah	Jan. 3, 2001
179. Betty McCollum, Minn.	Jan. 3, 2001
180. Mike Ross, Ark.	Jan. 3, 2001
181. Adam B. Schiff, Calif.	Jan. 3, 2001
182. Hilda L. Solis, Calif.	Jan. 3, 2001
183. Diane Watson, Calif.	June 5, 2001
184. Stephen F. Lynch, Mass.	Oct. 16, 2001
185. Ed Case, Hawaii	Nov. 30, 2002
186. Jim Cooper, Tenn.	Jan. 7, 2003
Also served 1983-95	
187. Rodney Alexander, La.	Jan. 7, 2003
188. Frank W. Ballance Jr., N.C.	Jan. 7, 2003
189. Chris Bell, Texas	Jan. 7, 2003
190. Timothy H. Bishop, N.Y.	Jan. 7, 2003
191. Dennis Cardoza, Calif.	Jan. 7, 2003
192. Artur Davis, Ala.	Jan. 7, 2003
193. Lincoln Davis, Tenn.	Jan. 7, 2003
194. Rahm Emanuel, Ill.	Jan. 7, 2003
195. Raul M. Grijalva, Ariz.	Jan. 7, 2003
196. Denise L. Majette, Ga.	Jan. 7, 2003
197. Jim Marshall, Ga.	Jan. 7, 2003
198. Kendrick B. Meek, Fla.	Jan. 7, 2003
199. Michael H. Michaud, Maine	Jan. 7, 2003
200. Brad Miller, N.C.	Jan. 7, 2003
201. C.A. Dutch Ruppersberger, Md.	Jan. 7, 2003
202. Tim Ryan, Ohio	Jan. 7, 2003
203. Linda T. Sanchez, Calif.	Jan. 7, 2003
204. David Scott, Ga.	Jan. 7, 2003
205. Chris Van Hollen, Md.	Jan. 7, 2003

INDEPENDENT

1. Bernard Sanders, Vt.	Jan. 3, 1991

Index

A

B

C

D

E

F

G

H

I

J

K

L

M

N

O

P, Q

R

S

T

U

V

W,Y

Pronunciation Guide for Congress

The following is an informal pronunciation guide for some members of Congress whose names are frequently mispronounced:

SENATE

Evan Bayh, D-Ind. — BY
John B. Breaux, D-La. — BRO
Lincoln Chafee, R-R.I. — CHAY-fee
Saxby Chambliss, R-Ga. — SAX-bee CHAM-bliss
John Cornyn, R-Texas — CORE-nin
Jon Corzine, D-N.J. — COR-zyne
Michael D. Crapo, R-Idaho — CRAY-poe
Tom Daschle, D-S.D. — DASH-el
Pete V. Domenici, R-N.M. — doe-MEN-ih-chee
Michael B. Enzi, R-Wyo. — EN-zee
Russell D. Feingold, D-Wis. — FINE-gold
Dianne Feinstein, D-Calif. — FINE-stine
James M. Inhofe, R-Okla. — IN-hoff
Daniel K. Inouye, D-Hawaii — in-NO-ay
Mary L. Landrieu, D-La. — LAN-drew
Rick Santorum, R-Pa. — san-TORE-um
Debbie Stabenow, D-Mich. — STAB-uh-now

HOUSE

Anibal Acevedo-Vilá, D-P.R. — AH-nee-baahl Ah-sah-VAY-dough VEE-la
Robert B. Aderholt, R-Ala. — ADD-er-holt
Spencer Bachus, R-Ala. — BACK-us
Bob Beauprez, R-Colo. — bo-PRAY
Xavier Becerra, D-Calif. — HAH-vee-air beh-SEH-ra
Doug Bereuter, R-Neb. — BEE-right-er
Michael Bilirakis, R-Fla. — bil-la-RACK-us
Earl Blumenauer, D-Ore. — BLUE-men-hour
Sherwood Boehlert, R-N.Y. — BO-lert
John A. Boehner, R-Ohio — BAY-ner
Henry Bonilla, R-Texas — bo-NEE-uh
John Boozman, R-Ark. — BOZE-man
Madeleine Z. Bordallo, D-Guam — bore-DAHL-ee-oh
Rick Boucher, D-Va. — BOUGH-cher
Steve Buyer, R-Ind. — BOO-yer
Michael E. Capuano, D-Mass. — KAP-you-AH-no
Steve Chabot, R-Ohio — SHAB-butt
Chris Chocola, R-Ind. — cha-KO-luh
Joseph Crowley, D-N.Y. — KRAU-lee
Barbara Cubin, R-Wyo. — CUE-bin
Peter A. DeFazio, D-Ore. — da-FAH-zee-o
Diana DeGette, D-Colo. — de-GET
Bill Delahunt, D-Mass. — DELL-a-hunt
Rosa DeLauro, D-Conn. — da-LAUR-o
Jim DeMint, R-S.C. — da-MENT
Peter Deutsch, D-Fla. — DOYCH
Mario Diaz-Balart, R-Fla. — DEE-az ba-LART
Lincoln Diaz-Balart, R-Fla. — DEE-az ba-LART
Vernon J. Ehlers, R-Mich. — AY-lurz
Anna G. Eshoo, D-Calif. — EH-shoo
Eni F.H. Faleomavaega, D-Am. Samoa — EN-ee FOL-ee-oh-mav-ah-ENG-uh
Chaka Fattah, D-Pa. — SHOCK-ah fa-TAH
Vito J. Fossella, R-N.Y. — VEE-toe Fuh-SELL-ah
Rodney Frelinghuysen, R-N.J. — FREE-ling-high-zen
Elton Gallegly, R-Calif. — GAL-uh-glee
Jim Gerlach, R-Pa. — GUR-lock
Virgil H. Goode Jr., R-Va. — GOOD (rhymes with "food")
Robert W. Goodlatte, R-Va. — GOOD-lat
Raúl M. Grijalva, D-Ariz. — gree-HAHL-va
Luis V. Gutierrez, D-Ill. — loo-EES goo-tee-AIR-ez
Gil Gutknecht, R-Minn. — GOOT-neck
Jeb Hensarling, R-Texas — HENN-sur-ling
Ruben Hinojosa, D-Texas — ru-BEN ee-na-HO-suh
Joseph M. Hoeffel, D-Pa. — HUFF-ull
Peter Hoekstra, R-Mich. — HOOK-struh
John Hostettler, R-Ind. — HO-stet-lur
Amo Houghton, R-N.Y. — HO-tun
Kenny Hulshof, R-Mo. — HULLZ-hoff
Darrell Issa, R-Calif. — EYE-sah
Ernest Istook, R-Okla. — IZ-took
Gerald D. Kleczka, D-Wis. — KLETCH-kuh
Jim Kolbe, R-Ariz. — COLE-bee
Dennis J. Kucinich, D-Ohio — ku-SIN-itch
Jim Langevin, D-R.I. — LAN-juh-vin
Steven C. LaTourette, R-Ohio — la-tuh-RETT
Frank A. LoBiondo, R-N.J. — lo-bee-ON-dough
Zoe Lofgren, D-Calif. — ZO
Nita M. Lowey, D-N.Y. — LOW-ee
Denise L. Majette, D-Ga. — muh-JET
Donald Manzullo, R-Ill. — man-ZOO-low
Michael H. Michaud, D-Maine — ME-shoo
Jerrold Nadler, D-N.Y. — NAD-ler
Bob Ney, R-Ohio — NAY
David R. Obey, D-Wis. — OH-bee
Doug Ose, R-Calif. — OH-see
Frank Pallone Jr., D-N.J. — puh-LOAN
Bill Pascrell Jr., D-N.J. — pas-KRELL
Ed Pastor, D-Ariz. — pas-TORE
Nancy Pelosi, D-Calif. — pa-LOH-see
Tom Petri, R-Wis. — PEA-try
Richard W. Pombo, R-Calif. — POM-bo
George P. Radanovich, R-Calif. — ruh-DON-o-vitch
Ralph Regula, R-Ohio — REG-you-luh
Denny Rehberg, R-Mont. — REE-berg
Silvestre Reyes, D-Texas — sil-VES-treh RAY-ess (rolled 'R')
Dana Rohrabacher, R-Calif. — ROAR-ah-BAH-ker
Ileana Ros-Lehtinen, R-Fla. — il-ee-AH-na ross-LAY-tin-nen
Jan Schakowsky, D-Ill. — shuh-KOW-ski
José E. Serrano, D-N.Y. — ho-ZAY sa-RAH-no (rolled 'R')
John Shadegg, R-Ariz. — SHAD-egg
John Shimkus, R-Ill. — SHIM-kus
Hilda L. Solis, D-Calif. — soh-LEEZ
Mark Souder, R-Ind. — SOW (rhymes with "now")-dur
Bart Stupak, D-Mich. — STU-pack
Tom Tancredo, R-Colo. — tan-CRAY-doe
Ellen O. Tauscher, D-Calif. — TAU (rhymes with "how")-sher
Billy Tauzin, R-La. — TOE-zan
Todd Tiahrt, R-Kan. — TEE-hart
Pat Tiberi, R-Ohio — TEA-berry
Nydia M. Velázquez, D-N.Y. — NID-ee-uh veh-LASS-kez
Peter J. Visclosky, D-Ind. — vis-KLOSS-key
Anthony Weiner, D-N.Y. — WEE-ner
Lynn Woolsey, D-Calif. — WOOL-zee